SMITHSONIAN INSTITUTION
BUREAU OF AMERICAN ETHNOLOGY
BULLETIN 30

HANDBOOK

OF

AMERICAN INDIANS

NORTH OF MEXICO

EDITED BY

FREDERICK WEBB HODGE

VOLUME IV T to Z

WASHINGTON
GOVERNMENT PRINTING OFFICE
(Fourth impression, September, 1912)

Handbook of North American Indian
North of Mexico

Volume 1 A to G   ISBN 9781582187396
Volume 2 H to M   ISBN 9781582187402
Volume 3 N to S   ISBN 9781582187440
Volume 4 T to Z   ISBN 9781582187426

Volumes 1-4
ISBN 9781582187433

Library of Congress Control Number: 2018953449

The Library of Congress has established a Catalog In Publication for this title.

Republished 2018 by
Digital Scanning Inc.
Scituate Ma 02066

VOLUME IV T to Z

TECUMSEH

Ta (*T!ă*, 'chiton' [?]). A Haida town formerly on the E. coast of North id., Queen Charlotte ids., Brit. Col. It is said to have been occupied by a small family called, after the name of the place, Taahl-lanas.—Swanton, Cont. Haida, 281, 1905.

Ta ('grass'). A clan of the Tewa pueblos of San Juan, Nambe, and Tesuque, N. Mex., and of Hano, Ariz.
Ta,—Fewkes in Am. Anthr., VII, 166, 1894. **Tá-tdóa.**—Hodge, ibid., IX, 351, 1896 (*tdóa*='people'). **Tá-tówa.**—Fewkes, op. cit.

Ta ('deer'). The second Kansa gens.
Ta.—Dorsey in 15th Rep. B. A. E., 230, 1897. **Tä-we-kä-she'-gä.**—Morgan, Anc. Soc., 156, 1877. **Wajaje.**—Dorsey, op. cit.

Taa (*Tá'-a*, 'maize'). A clan of the Zuñi, said to have been formed by the union of a traditional Ataa, or Seed people, with the 6 former Corn clans of the Zuñi.
Ta'a-kwe.—Cushing in Millstone, IX, 2, Jan. 1884; 55, Apr. 1884 (*kwe* = 'people'). **Tâatém'hlanah-kwe.**—Cushing in 13th Rep. B. A. E., 386, 1896 (='people of all seed'). **Tō-wā-que.**—Stevenson in 5th Rep. B. A. E., 541, 1887.

Taahl-lanas ('the people of the town of Ta'). An extinct Haida family which formerly lived on North id., Queen Charlotte ids., Brit. Col. See *Ta*.
T!ā'ał.—Swanton, Cont. Haida, 276, 1905.

Tabagane, Tabaganne. See *Toboggan*.

Tabahtea. A Pomo division, or probably a village, in 1851, w. of the Shanel, in s. Mendocino co., Cal., and speaking the same language.—Gibbs (1851) in Schoolcraft, Ind. Tribes, III, 112, 1853.

Tabeguache (contr. of *Mo-a-wa-ta-ve-wach*, 'people living on the warm side of the mountain.'—Hrdlička). A Ute division formerly living in s. w. Colorado, chiefly about Los Pinos. In 1885 there were 1,252 under the name at Ouray agency, E. Utah. They are now officially designated Uncompahgre Utes, and in 1909 numbered 469 under the Uinta and Ouray agency, Utah.
Mo-a-wa-ta-ve-wach.—A. Hrdlička, inf'n, 1907 (own name). **Pauches.**—Bancroft, Ariz. and N. Mex., 665, 1889 (or Tabuaches). **Pobawotche Utahs.**—Collins (1859) in H. R. Ex. Doc. 69, 36th Cong., 1st sess., 46, 1860. **Sun-hunters.**—Burton, City of Saints, 578, 1861. **Tabaguache.**—Smithson. Misc. Coll., XIV, art. 6, 40, 1878. **Tabahuaches.**—Taylor in Cal. Farmer, May 29, 1863. **Tabechya.**—Burton, op. cit., 578. **Tabeguache Utahs.**—U. S. Stat. at Large, XIV, 275, 1868. **Tabeguachis.**—Mayer, Mexico, II, 38, 1853. **Tabegwaches.**—Morgan, Consang. and Affin., 290, 1871. **Tabehuachis.**—Dominguez and Escalante (1776) in Doc. Hist. Mex., 2a s., I, 401, 1854. **Tabe-naches.**—Graves in Ind. Aff. Rep., 386, 1854. **Tabequache.**—Taylor in

Sen. Ex. Doc. 4, 40th Cong., spec. sess., 11, 1867. **Tabequache Utes.**—Beadle, Undeveloped West, 642, 1873. **Tabewaches.**—ten Kate, Reizen in N. A., 313, 1885. **Tabiachis.**—Domenech, Deserts N. A., I, 444, 1860. **Tabrackis.**—Ibid., II, 66, 1860. **Tavewachi.**—A. Hrdlička, inf'n, 1907 (own name). **Taviachis.**—Escudero, Not. Estad. de Chihuahua, 231, 1834. **Tubuache.**—Taylor in Cal. Farmer, May 29, 1863. **Uncompahgre.**—Ind. Aff. Rep., 327, 1903 (so called from name of reservation). **Yutas Ancapagari.**—Dominguez and Escalante (1776), op. cit., 406. **Yuta Tabehuachi.**—Ibid., 402.

Tabin. A tribe mentioned by Langsdorff (Voy., II, 163, 1814) as inhabiting the coast of California. It seemingly belonged to the Costanoan family.

Tabira (*Ta-bi-ra'*). A former pueblo of the Tompiros, a division of the Piros (q. v.), situated at the southern apex of the Mesa de los Jumanos, N. E. of the present Socorro, central N. Mex. The ruins are commonly known as Gran Quivira, a name erroneously applied in the latter half of the 19th century because of their supposed identification with the Quivira (q. v.) of Coronado and Oñate in the 16th and 17th centuries. A Spanish mission was established at Tabira in 1629 by Fray Francisco de Acevedo, which still existed in 1644, but the two churches and monasteries (one commenced between 1629 and 1644, the other probably between 1660 and 1670) were perhaps never completed. The walls are still standing. The pueblo was permanently abandoned between 1670 and 1675 on account of persistent depredations by the Apache, who were responsible for the depopulation of all the Pueblo villages E. of the Rio Grande in this section. The inhabitants of Tabira fled to Socorro and Alamillo, N. Mex., for safety, finally finding their way to the vicinity of El Paso, Tex. Judging by the extent of the ruins, the former population of Tabira probably did not exceed 1,500. Consult Bandelier in Arch. Inst. Papers, IV, 282 et seq., 1892; Lummis in Scribner's Mag., 466, Apr. 1893; See also *Piros, Pueblos*. 　(F. W. H.)
Grand Quavira.—Marcou in Möllhausen, Pacific, I, 348, 1858. Grand Quivira.—Wallace, Land of Pueblos, 240, 1888. Gran Quivira.—Parke, map N. Mex., 1851. Gran Quivira.—Howe, Hist. Coll., map, 1851. Juan Quivira.—Am. Antiq., X, 255, 1888. La Gran Quivira.—Howe, op. cit., 377. Tabirâ.—Bandelier (1888) in Proc. Cong. Amér., VII, 452, 1890 ("erroneously called Gran-Quivira"). Tabira.—Escalante (1778) quoted by Bandelier in Arch. Inst. Papers, III, 132, 1890. Tavira.—De Fer, carte (1705) cited by Bandelier, ibid., IV, 290, 1892.

Tablets. See *Inscribed tablets, Pierced tablets.*

Tabo. The Rabbit clan of the Hopi.
Tab.—Voth, Oraibi Summer Snake Ceremony, 282, 1903. Tabo wiñwû.—Fewkes in 19th Rep. B. A. E., 583, 1900 (*wiñwû*='clan'). Tab wüñ-wû.—Fewkes in Am. Anthr., VII, 404, 1894. Tap.—Voth, op. cit., 283. Tavo.—Dorsey and Voth, Oraibi Soyal, 12, 1901. Tda'-bo.—Stephen in 8th Rep. B. A. E., 39, 1891.

Tabo. The Rabbit phratry of the Hopi, which comprises the Tabo (Cottontail Rabbit) and Sowi (Jack-rabbit) clans. They claim to have come from the S.

Tab nyû-mû.—Fewkes in Am. Anthr., VII, 404, 1894 (*nyû-mû*= 'phratry'). Ta'-bo.—Ibid., 406.

Tabogimkik. A Micmac village or band in 1760, probably in Nova Scotia.—Frye (1760) in Mass. Hist. Soc. Coll., 1st s., X, 116, 1809.

Tabogine. See *Toboggan.*

Taboo. A Polynesian term (*ta'bu*) applied to an interdiction proper to or laid upon a person, place, day, name, or any conceivable thing, which is thereby rendered sacred and communication with it except to a few people or under certain circumstances forbidden. It was formerly so striking an institution, and was in consequence so frequently mentioned by explorers and travelers, that the word has been adopted into English both as applying to similar customs among other races and in a colloquial sense. Its negative side, being the more conspicuous, became that indicated by the adopted term; but religious prohibitions among primitive peoples being closely bound up with others of a positive character, it is often applied to the latter as well, and writers frequently speak of the taboos connected with the killing of a bear or a bison, or the taking of a salmon, meaning thereby the ceremonies then performed, both positive and negative. In colloquial English usage the term taboo has ceased to have any religious significance.

Whether considered in its negative or in its positive aspect this term may be applied in North America to a number of regulations observed at definite periods of life, in connection with important undertakings, either by individuals or by considerable numbers of persons. Such were the regulations observed by boys and girls at puberty; by parents before the birth of a child; by relatives after the decease of a person; by hunters and fishermen in the pursuit of their occupations; by boys desiring guardian spirits or wishing to become shamans; by shamans and chiefs desiring more power, or when curing the sick, prophesying, endeavoring to procure food by supernatural means, or "showing their power" in any manner; by novitiates into secret societies, and by leaders in society or tribal dances in preparation for them. Among the Lillooet, on the first day of the berry-picking season, only enough berries for that day were gathered, under the impression that gathering more would bring misfortune. Among the Kutchin those who prepared bodies for burial were under certain restriction for some time afterward, and widows and widowers among many tribes suffered similarly. The telling of stories also was tabooed at certain seasons. In tribes divided into totemic clans or gentes each individual was often called on to observe certain regulations in regard to his totem animal. This custom, as among the Yuchi and the Navaho, for example, sometimes took the form of an absolute prohibition against killing the totem animal; but at other times it merely involved an apology to the animal or abstinence from eating certain parts of it. The negative prohibitions, those which may be called the taboos proper, consisted in abstinence from hunting, fishing, war, women, sleep, certain kinds of work, and so forth, but above all in abstinence from eating, while among positive accompaniments may be mentioned washing, sweat-bathing, flagellation, and the taking of emetics and other medicines.

In the majority of American tribes the name of a dead man was not uttered—unless in some altered form—for a considerable period after his demise, and sometimes, as among the Kiowa, the custom was carried so far that names of common animals or other terms in current use were entirely dropped from the language because of the death of a person bearing such a name. Frequently it was considered improper for a man to mention his own name, and the mention of the personal name was avoided by wives and husbands in addressing each other, and sometimes by other relatives as well. But the most common regulation of this kind was that which decreed that a man should not address his mother-in-law directly, or vice versa, and the prohibition of intercourse often applied to fathers-in-law and daughters-in-law also.

The objects of these prohibitions, whether voluntary or otherwise, were as numerous as human desires or human fears. In Polynesia the taboo was largely a method of government, and fear of retribution from both supernatural and mundane sources was the direct cause of the obedience yielded to it. It is not so easy, however, to separate the regulations in America to which this term has been applied, and which were governed by fear of nonfulfilment, from those in which the motive was a desire for additional benefits. Thus omission of the customary puberty, birth, mortuary, war, and hunting regulations no doubt would be considered as inviting certain misfortune, but in most of these there was what may be termed a sliding scale of observance, resulting in a greater or lesser amount of good fortune—or more likelihood of good fortune—in proportion to fuller or more meager observance of such regulations. Then there were other regulations, as those voluntarily adopted by chiefs on the N. Pacific coast who desired more wealth, or those accepted by shamans desiring more power, the omission of which would have occasioned them no loss of the prosperity they were already

enjoying. It will be seen that taboo is one aspect of religious phenomena known by many other names and, at least among the lower races, is almost as broad as religion itself. See *Religion*.   (J. R. S.)

Tabo-Piba ('rabbit [and] tobacco'). A phratral group of the Hopi, consisting of the Rabbit, Jack-rabbit, and Tobacco clans. They claim to have come from a region in S. Arizona called Palatkwabi, and from Little Colorado r.—Fewkes in 19th Rep. B. A. E., 583, 1900. See *Piba, Tabo*.

Tacahlay. One of the Diegueño rancherias represented in the treaty of 1852 at Santa Isabel, S. Cal.—H. R. Ex. Doc. 76, 34th Cong., 3d sess., 132, 1857.

Tacaho. See *Tuckahoe*.

Tacame. A Coahuiltecan tribe living in the 18th century near the lower San Antonio and Nueces rs., Texas. In 1728 Rivera referred to them as living in that neighborhood, and described them, together with the Pampopa, Pastia, and others, as unwarlike wanderers who subsisted on fish and sylvan products (Proyecto, estado 3, ¶ 43). The Tacame entered San Francisco de la Espada mission soon after its foundation, but proved very troublesome by running away. In 1737 they fled to the Colorado r. and established a rancheria which, it was said, consisted of 200 persons. When Governor Sandoval and Father Yzasmendi went after them, they resisted, but 42 were captured and taken back to their mission (Testimony in Archivo Gen., Misiones, XXI, exp. 2, fol. 19). In a short time they again fled, leaving their mission deserted (Lamar Papers, MS. dated 1738); they expressed a desire to go to San Antonio de Valero mission, and were given permission to do so. A few embraced the opportunity, but more of them entered mission Nuestra Señora de la Purísima Concepción, where, after 1741, they lived in considerable numbers (Concepción Marriage Records, passim.). In 1762, 1780, and 1793, respectively, they were reported as still at this mission. In a report of 1780, Governor Cabello gave the habitat of the tribe as near the coast between San Antonio and Nueces rs., the neighborhood where they were first encountered by the Spaniards. The Cacames, said by Solís to have been at San José mission near San Antonio, are evidently the same people.   (H. E. B.)

Arcahamos.—Lamar Papers, Doc. of 1737, MS. **Cacames.**—Solís, Diario (1767) in Mem. de Nueva España, XXVII, 270, MS. (evidently identical). **Tacamanes.**—Description of the Texas missions (1740), ibid., 203. **Tâcames.**—Rivera, Diario, leg. 2602, 1736. **Tacones.**—Revilla Gigedo, Carta, 1793. **Tancames.**—Bonilla (1772) quoted in Texas Hist. Asso. Quar., VIII, 38, 1905. **Tecamenes.**—Barcia, Ensayo, 271, 1723. **Tecamenez.**—Shea, note in Charlevoix, New France, IV, 78, 1870. **Tecamones.**—Barcia, op. cit. **Teheaman.**—Joutel (1687) in Margry, Déc., III, 288, 1878. **Thacame.**—Concepción

Marriage Records, 1759. **Thecamenes.**—Joutel (1687) in French, Hist. Coll. La., I, 137, 1846. **Thecamons.**—Ibid.

Tacanhpisapa ('Black Tomahawk'). A former Mdewakanton band, named from the chief.

Black-Tomahawk.—Neill, Hist. Minn., 144, note, 1858. **Ta-can-rpi-sa-pa.**—Ibid.

Tacatacuru. A river, an island, and probably a village of the Saturiba tribe of N. E. Florida, about 1565. The river is said by Laudonnière to be the one the French called the Seine (Sequana), apparently identical with the St Marys, forming the boundary between Florida and Georgia. The island was evidently what is now Cumberland id. The village is not marked on the De Bry map of 1591 accompanying Le Moyne's Narrative, and may have been either on the N. (Georgia) or S. (Florida) side, but the chief is always mentioned in the French narrative as a kinsman or ally of the "great king Satourioua." Brinton incorrectly locates it on the coast S. of St Augustine, probably confusing it with Tucururu, named by Fray Francisco Pareja in 1612 as one of the Timucuan dialects. (J. M.)

Catacouru.—Laudonnière (1564) in French, Hist. Coll. La., n. s., 351, 1869 (the river; first syllable evidently omitted by mistake). **Tacadocorou.**—Ibid., 315 (chief). **Tacatacouru.**—Ibid., 348 (river). **Tacatacuru.**—Barcia, Ensayo, 121, 1723 (island). **Tecatacourou.**—Laudonnière (1564) in French, Hist. Coll. La., n. s., 349, 1869.

Tachi. One of the larger tribes of the Yokuts (Mariposan) family, living on the plains N. of Tulare lake, S. central Cal. They held the country w. of the Coast range. Powers puts them on Kings r., near Kingston. According to Alexander Taylor, members of this tribe were brought to San Antonio and Dolores (San Francisco) missions as neophytes. Tatché or Telamé is mentioned by Shea (preface to Arroyo de la Cuesta's Vocab. of S. Antonio mission) as the name of the tribe speaking the San Antonio language, a Salinan dialect. These Tatché and Telamé, however, are the Tachi and Telamni who had been taken to the mission, and Taylor may be correct in giving Sextapay as the name of the tribe, or more correctly village site, originally at San Antonio. As is the case with all the Yokuts tribes, only a fragment of the former number remains; but though reduced to a few dozen survivors, the Tachi are today among the half-dozen most numerous tribes left of the original forty or more comprising the Yokuts stock. Most of the survivors occupy a settlement near Lemoore, Kings co. (A. L. K.)

Atach.—Johnston in Sen. Ex. Doc. 61, 32d Cong., 1st sess., 23, 1852. **A-tache.**—Ibid., 22. **Dachi.**—A. L. Kroeber, inf'n, 1907 (a Yokuts form; see *Tadji* below). **La-ches.**—Barbour in Sen. Ex. Doc. 4, 32d Cong., spec. sess., 254, 1853. **Taches.**—Johnston, op. cit., 22. **Tachi.**—Powers in Cont. N. A. Ethnol., III, 370, 1877. **Tadjedjayi.**—A. L. Kroeber, inf'n, 1903 (plural form). **Tadji.**—Ibid. (a Yokuts form; see *Dachi*, above). **Tah'-che.**—Merriam in Science,

XIX, 916, June 15, 1904. **Tal-ches.**—Ind. Aff. Rep., 400, 1857. **Tatché.**—Pimental, Lenguas de Mex., 391, 1865 (or Telamé). **Tatchees.**—Ind. Aff., Rep., 219, 1861.

Tachik (from *těchěk*, 'the bay'). An Unaligmiut Eskimo village on St Michael id., near the Russian redoubt, and now included in the town of St Michael, Alaska.

Tachik.—Petroff in 10th Census, Alaska, 11, 1884. **Tatchek.**—Baker, Geog. Dict, Alaska, 620, 1906 (quoted form). **Techek.**—Ibid. **T'satsúmi.**—Dall, Alaska, 13, 1870. **Tutsógemut.**—Ibid. (name of people).

Tachikhwutme ('village on a plateau'). Mentioned as a former Athapascan village on the coast of California, just N. of the mouth of Klamath r.

Ta-tci'-qwût-me.—Dorsey in Jour. Am. Folk-lore, III, 237, 1890 (Naltunnetunne name). **Ta-tci' te'-ne.**—Dorsey, Smith River MS. vocab., B. A. E., 1884 (Khaamotene name).

Tachikhwutme. A former village of the Chastacosta on Rogue r., Oreg., above the mouth of Illinois r.

Shich-e-quet-to-ny.—Abbott, MS. Coquille census, B. A. E., 1858. **Ta-tci'-qwût.**—Dorsey in Jour. Am. Folk-lore, III, 234, 1890. **Techaquit.**—Ind. Aff. Rep. 1856, 219, 1857. **Te-cheh.quat.**—Gibbs, MS. on coast tribes, B. A. E.

Tachilta. A former village of the Papago in S. Arizona or N. Sonora, Mexico.—Orozco y Berra, Geog., 348, 1864.

Tachis. See *Tawkee*.

Tachukhaslitun. A former village of the Chetco on the S. side of Chetco r., Oreg.

T'a'-tcu-qas-li'-tûn.—Dorsey in Jour. Am. Folk-lore, III, 236, 1890.

Tachuwit. An Alsea village on the N. side of Alsea r., Oreg.

Ta'-tcŭ-wĭt''.—Dorsey in Jour. Am. Folk-lore, III, 229, 1890.

Tachy ('tail of the water'). A village of the Tatshiautin at the mouth of Taché r., Brit. Col. Pop. 32 in 1881; 65 in 1909.

Tachy.—Harmon, Jour., 215, 1820. **Thatce.**—Morice in Trans. Roy. Soc. Can., X, 109, 1893.

Tackapousha. See *Massapequa*.

Tackchandeseechar. A Teton Sioux band belonging to the Saone division.

Tack-chan-de-see-char.—Orig. Jour. Lewis and Clark (1805), VI, 99, 1905. **Tack-chan-de-su-char.**—Am. State Papers, Ind Aff., I, 715, 1832.

Taconnet. An Abnaki village, about the beginning of the 17th century, at the falls of Kennebec r., near Waterville, Kennebec co., Me.

Taconet.—Niles (1761) in Mass. Hist. Soc. Coll., 3d s., VI, 232, 1837. **Taconick.**—Hoyt, Antiq. Res., 212, 1824. **Taconnet.**—French map, 1744, cited by Kendall, Trav., III, 49, 1809. **Taconock.**—Church (1716) quoted by Drake, Ind. Wars, 191, 1825. **Taughtanakagnet.**—Smith (1631) in Mass. Hist. Soc. Coll., 3d s., III, 22, 1833. **Teconet.**—Niles (1761), ibid., VI, 235, 1837. **Teuconick.**—Falmouth conf. (1727) in Me. Hist. Soc. Coll., III, 408, 1853. **Tirionet.**—Record of 1727 in N. H. Hist. Soc. Coll., II, 259, 1827 (misprint). **Tocconnock.**—Church (1690) in Mass. Hist. Soc. Coll., 4th s., V., 276, 1861. **Triconnick.**—Penhallow (1726), in N. H. Hist. Soc. Coll., I, 107, 1824.

Tacquison. A Papago village on the Arizona-Sonora border, with 70 Indian families in 1871.—Wilbur in Ind. Aff. Rep. 1871, 365, 1872.

Tadema. See *Tatemy*.

Tadeovaqui. A rancheria, probably of the Maricopa, on the Rio Gila, Ariz.; visited by Kino and Mange in 1699. Sedelmair (1749) mentions the place as affording a good site for a mission.

San Tadeo Vaqui.—Kino (1699) cited by Bancroft, No. Mex. States, I, 268, 1884. S. Júdas Tadeo.—Sedelmair (1749) cited by Bancroft, Ariz. and N. Mex., 367, 1889. S. Tadeo Batqui.—Kino, map (1701), ibid., 360. S. Thaddæus de Batki.—Kino, map (1702), in Stocklein, Neue Welt-Bott, 74, 1726. Tádes Vaqui.—Mange (1669) cited by Bancroft, Ariz. and N. Mex., 357, 1889.

Tadji-lanas (*Tā'dji lā'nas*, or *Tās lā'nas*, 'sand-town people'). Two important Haida families belonging to the Raven clan. It would probably be truer to say that they were two parts of one family, although they came to be widely separated geographically. According to tradition this family and 4 others once lived together in a town near Sand Spit pt., Queen Charlotte ids., composed of 5 rows of houses. Those in the front row were called Tadji-lanas, because they were close to the beach; those in the next, Kuna-lanas ('Point-town people'), because their row ran out on a point; those in the third, Yaku-lanas ('Middle-town people'), because they occupied the middle row; those in the fourth, Koetas ('Earth-eaters'), because they lived near the trails where it was very muddy; and those in the fifth, Stlenga-lanas ('Rear-town people'), because they lived farthest back. Another tradition relates that this family, together with the Kagials-kegawai of Skedans, sprang from a woman who was on House id. (Atana) when it rose out of the flood. One branch were reckoned among the Gunghet-haidagai, and a subdivision called Kaidju-kegawai owned the southernmost town on the island. By a curious coincidence the northern division, after living for a while on the N. w. coast of Graham id., came to occupy Kasaan in Alaska, the most northerly Haida town. The Gunghet branch is almost extinct.   (J. R. S.)

Tā'dji lā'nas.—Swanton, Cont. Haida, 268, 272, 1905. Tās lā'nas.—Boas in 12th Rep. N. W. Tribes Can., 22, 1898. Tas Lennas.—Harrison in Proc. Roy. Soc. Can., sec. II, 124, 1895.

Tadoiko. A former Maidu village in the neighborhood of Durham, Butte co., Cal.—Dixon in Bull. Am. Mus. Nat. Hist., XVII, map, 1905.

Tadousac ('at the nipples.'—Hewitt). The principal village of the Tadousac on St Lawrence r., at the mouth of Saguenay r. It was formerly an important trading post, founded by Samuel de Champlain, and a Jesuit mission was established there as early as 1616.

Tadeussac.—La Tour map, 1779. Tadoucac.—Dutch map (1621) in N. Y. Doc. Col. Hist., I, 1856. Tadousac.—Champlain (1603), Œuvres, 70, 1870; Harris, Voy. and Trav., II, map, 1705. Tadousae.—Dobbs, Hudson Bay, map, 1744 (misprint). Tadousca.—Harris, op. cit., I, map (misprint). Tadoussac.—Champlain (1604), Œuvres, 216, 1870; map of 1616 in N. Y. Doc. Col. Hist., I, 1856.

Tadoussaciens.—Esnauts and Rapilly map, 1777. Tadusac.—Jefferys, Fr. Doms., pt. 1, map, 1761. Tadussékuk.—Gatschet, Penobscot MS., B. A. E., 1887 (Penobscot name).

Tadousac. A Montagnais tribe or band on Saguenay r., Quebec. In 1863 part of the tribe were on a reservation at Manicouagan, while others were at Peribouka.

Tadush. A Hankutchin village on the upper Yukon, Alaska, at the mouth of Kandik r. Pop. 48 in 1880.

Charleys Village.—Petroff in 10th Census, Alaska, map, 1880. Charley Village.—Baker, Geog. Dict. Alaska, 170, 1906. Tadoosh.—Schwatka, Rep. on Alaska, 88, 1885.

Taenhatentaron. A former Huron village in Ontario, the seat of the mission of Saint Ignace. It was destroyed by the Iroquois in 1649.

Sainct Ignace.—Jes. Rel. 1639, 74, 1858. St. Ignatius.—Shea, Cath. Miss., 179, 1855. Taenhatentaron.—Jes. Rel. 1639, 74, 1858.

Taensa. A tribe related in language and customs to the Natchez, from whom they must have separated shortly before the beginning of the historic period. There is reason to think that part of the Taensa were encountered by De Soto in 1540, but the first mention of them under their proper name is by La Salle and his companions, who visited them in 1682 on their way to the mouth of the Mississippi. They were then living on L. St Joseph, an ox-bow cut-off of the Mississippi in the present Tensas parish, La. Tonti stopped at their villages in 1686 and 1690, and in 1698 they were visited by Davion, La Source, and De Montigny, the last of whom settled among them as missionary the following year. In 1700 Iberville found him there, and the two returned together to the Natchez, De Montigny having decided to devote his attention to that tribe. St Cosme, who soon succeeded De Montigny among the Natchez, considered the Taensa too much reduced for a separate mission, and endeavored, without success, to draw them to the Natchez. In 1706 the fear of an attack from the Yazoo and Chickasaw induced the Taensa to abandon their settlements and take refuge with the Bayogoula, whom they soon after attacked treacherously and almost destroyed. After they had occupied several different positions along the Mississippi southward of the Manchac, Bienville invited them to settle near Mobile and assigned them lands not far from his post. They remained here many years, giving their name to Tensaw r.; but in 1764, rather than pass under the English, they removed to Red r., in company with a number of the other small tribes in their neighborhood. The same year, in company with the Apalachee and Pakana, they applied to the French commandant for permission to settle on Bayou La Fourche; but, though it was granted, neither they nor the Apalachee appear to have taken advantage of it. They remained at first on Red r., but in a few years removed to Bayou Bœuf. About the time when Louisiana passed under control of the United States they sold these lands also and moved to the northern end of Grand lake, where a small bayou bears their name. As an independent tribe they have now disappeared, though some Chitimacha Indians are descended from them. The Taensa were always a comparatively small tribe. In 1698 De Montigny estimated them at 700, and two years later Iberville placed the number of their warriors at 300, while in 1702 he assigned them 150 families, a figure also given by St Cosme the year before. Du Pratz (1718–34) placed the number of their cabins after their removal to Mobile at 100, probably an overestimate. The "Little Taënsas" spoken of by Iberville were evidently the Avoyelles (q. v.). In 1699 a Taensa Indian gave Iberville the following list of villages belonging to his people, but most of the names are evidently in the Mobilian trade language: Taensas, Chaoucoula, Conchayon, Couthaougoula, Nyhougoulas, Ohytoucoulas, and Talaspa.

The Taensa have attained a unique interest in modern times from an attempt of two French seminarists to introduce a product of their own ingenuity as a grammar of the Taensa language. The deception was exposed by Brinton in 1885, but for a while it gave rise to a heated controversy. See *Pseudo-Indian*. Consult Swanton (1) in Am. Anthr., x, 24, 1908, and authors therein cited; (2) in Bull. 43, B. A. E., 1910.　　(J. R. S.)

Caensa.—Neill, Hist. Minn., 173, 1858. Chŏ′sha.—Swanton in Am. Anthr., x, no. 1, 1908 (Chitimacha name). Grands Taensas.—Iberville (1699) in Margry, Déc., iv, 409, 1880. Hastriryini.—Parisot and Adam, Taensa Grammar, 1882 (said to mean 'warriors' and to be their own name). Tabensa.—Coxe, Carolana, map, 1741. Taencas.—Tonti (1682) in French, Hist. Coll. La., i, 62, 1846. Taënsas. — Hennepin, New Discov., 155, 1698. Taensos.—Güssefeld, Map U. S., 1784. Taenzas.—Shea, Cath. Miss., 437, 1855. Tahensa.—Tonti (1684) in Margry, Déc., i, 616, 1876. Takensa.—Joutel (1685) in French, Hist. Coll. La., i, 152, 1846. Talusas.—La Métairie (1682) quoted, ibid., ii, 21, 1875 (miscopied). Tenisaws.—Sibley, Hist. Sketches, 84, 1806. Tensagini.—Parisot and Adam, Taensa Gram., 1882. Tensas.—Pénicaut (1700) in French, Hist. Coll. La., n. s., i, 58, 1869. Tensau.—Drake, Bk. Inds., bk. 4, 55, 1848. Tensaw.—Sibley, Hist. Sketches, 84, 1806. Tenza.—Ibid., 121. Tinjas.—Jefferys, Am. Atlas, map 5, 1776. Tinnsals.—Charlevoix, New France, vi, 39, 1866. Tinsas.—Pénicaut (1700) in Margry, Déc., v, 397, 1883. Tinssas.—Ibid., 508.

Taensa. The chief one of the 7 Taensa villages in 1699.—Iberville in Margry, Déc., iv, 179, 1880.

Tagasoke (*Ta-ga-soke*, 'forked like a spear'). An Oneida village formerly on Fish cr., near Vienna, Oneida co., N. Y.—Morgan, League Iroq., 473, map, 1851.

Tagish. A small tribe living about Tagish and Marsh lakes, Brit. Col. They are classed with the Tlingit stock on the basis of a vocabulary obtained by Dawson (Rep. Geol. Surv. Can., 192B, 1887); but as they resemble the interior Athapascan Indians in every other respect, it is likely that they have adopted their present language from the Chilkat. They are probably part of Dall's "Nehaunee of the Chilkaht river."　　　　　　(J. R. S.)

Stick Indians.—Dawson in Rep. Geol. Surv. Can., 192B, 1887 (coast name for these people and all other interior Indians). Tahk-heesh.—Schwatka in Century Mag., 747, Sept. 1885. Tank-heesh.—Ibid., 743 (may be the Takon of Schwatka).

Taguanate. An unidentified province and town near which Moscoso, after the death of De Soto, built his boats and embarked on the Mississippi in the summer of 1543. According to Lewis (in Span. Explorers, 1528–1543, 252, 1907) the Taguanate province was on White r., and the town was probably in the s. part of Monroe co., Ark., possibly at Indian Bay.

Tagoanate.—Gentl. of Elvas (1557) in Span. Explorers, op. cit., 250. Taguanate.—Ibid., 251.

Tagui. Given as a village near the headwaters of San Luis Rey r., San Diego co., Cal., in 1795 (Grijalva cited by Bancroft, Hist. Cal., i, 563, 1886). Probably the same as Taqui, mentioned by Sanchez in 1821 (ibid., ii, 443) as existing 7 or 8 m. N. of Santa Isabel; and as Tahwie, a Diegueño rancheria represented in the treaty of Santa Isabel, s. Cal., in 1852 (H. R. Doc. 76, 34th Cong., 3d sess., 132, 1857). Kroeber (inf'n, 1907) regards the name as possibly a misprint of Pawi (Spanish Pagui or Pahui), the Luiseño name of Cahuilla valley, the present Cahuilla res. just N. of the headwaters of San Luis Rey r.

Taguta. Given as a Kaiyuhkhotana village on the N. bank of Yukon r., 15 m. below the Kaiyuh mouth, Alaska.

Tagutakaka.—Raymond in Sen. Ex. Doc. 12, 42d Cong., 1st sess., 25, 1871.

Tagwahi (*Tagwâ′hĭ*, 'Catawba place'). The name of several Cherokee settlements. One of them, known to the whites as Toccoa, was situated on Toccoa cr., E. of Clarkesville, Habersham co., Ga.; another was on Toccoa or Ocoee r., about the present Toccoa, in Fannin co., Ga., and a third may have been on Persimmon cr., which is known to the Cherokee as Tagwâ′hĭ, and enters Hiwassee r. some distance below Murphy, in Cherokee co., N. C.—Mooney in 19th Rep. B. A. E., 533, 1900.

Tocoah.—Doc. of 1799 quoted by Royce in 5th Rep. B. A. E., 144, 1887.

Tahagmiut ('people of the shadow,' that is, living toward the sunset). An Eskimo tribe inhabiting the Labrador shore of Hudson str. from Leaf r. w., and the coast of Hudson bay s. to Mosquito bay. They are tall and of fine physique, the men larger on the average than whites, the women equal to the average white

women. Their customs are primitive. Men hold women in little respect, but are jealous of their wives. They are fond of games and athletic sports, and both sexes are passionate gamblers. They trap foxes, wolves, and wolverenes, exchanging the furs for guns, ammunition, cutlery, and hardware at Ft Chimo, distant a whole winter's journey for a dog team. The skirts of their coats are hung with pear-shaped pieces of ivory that rattle when they walk.
Igdlumiut.—Boas in 6th Rep. B. A. E., 462, 1888 ('people of the other side': so called by the Eskimo of Baffin land, on the opposite shore of Hudson str.). Iglu-miut.—Boas in Trans. Anthr. Soc. Wash., III, 95, 1885. Northerners.—Turner in 11th Rep. B. A. E., 177, 1894 (so called by the whites of Labrador). Tahagmyut.—Turner in Trans. Roy. Soc. Can. 1887, sec. II, 101, 1888. Ta hág myut.—Turner in 11th Rep. B. A. E., 177, 1894. Ungavamiut.—Boas in Am. Antiq., 40, 1888.

Tahapit. A Maricopa rancheria on the Rio Gila, Ariz., in 1744.—Sedelmair (1744) cited by Bancroft, Ariz. and N. Mex., 366, 1889.

Tahattawan. See *Nattahattawants*.

Tahchee (*Tătsĭ'*, 'Dutch'). A Western Cherokee chief, one of the earliest emigrants to the Arkansas country to join chief Bowl. After several years in Texas, during which he led war parties against the wilder tribes, he recrossed Red r. and soon made himself so conspicuous in raids on the Osage that a reward of $500 was offered by Gen. Arbuckle for his capture. To show his defiance of the proclamation, he deliberately journeyed to Ft Gibson, attacked a party of Osage at a trading post near by, and scalped one of them within hearing of the drums of the fort. With rifle in one hand and the bleeding scalp in the other, he leaped a precipice and made his escape, although a bullet grazed his cheek. On promise of amnesty and the withdrawal of the reward, he returned and settled with his followers on the Canadian, s. w. of Ft Gibson, establishing a reputation among army officers as a valuable scout and guide. His portrait was painted by Catlin in 1834. See Mooney in 19th Rep. B. A. E., pt. 1, 1900; McKenney and Hall, Ind. Tribes, I, 251–260, 1858; Catlin, North Am. Inds., II, 121, 122, 1844.

Tah-gah-jute. See *Logan*.

Tahiannihouq. An unidentified village or tribe mentioned in 1687 to Joutel (Margry, Déc., III, 409, 1878) while he was staying with the Kadohadacho on Red r. of Louisiana, by the chief of that tribe, as being among his enemies.

Tahijuas. A Chumashan village formerly near Santa Inés mission, Santa Barbara co., Cal.—Taylor in Cal. Farmer, Oct. 18, 1861.

Tahlasi (*Ta'lasĭ'*). A former Cherokee settlement on Little Tennessee r., about Talassee ford, in Blount co., Tenn. The name has lost its meaning. (J. M.)

Ta'lasĭ'.—Mooney in 19th Rep. B. A. E., pt. 1, 533, 1900. Talassee.—Doc. of 1755 quoted by Royce in 5th Rep. B. A. E., 142, 1887. Tallase.—Bartram, Travels, 371, 1792. Telassee.—Doc. of 1799 quoted by Royce, op. cit., 144. Tellassee.—Timberlake, Memoirs, map, 1765.

Tahlequah (*Talikwă'*, meaning lost). The capital of the Cherokee Nation, in N. E. Indian Ter., now incorporated with the state of Oklahoma. The name, corrupted in the E. to Tellico (q. v.), is an old Cherokee town name, and was formally adopted for the new capital in 1839 on the reunion and reorganization of the Old Settler and Emigrant bands of Cherokee in the W. Tahlequah is now an enterprising railroad town of about 4,000 inhabitants, and contains, among other buildings, the former Cherokee capitol and a large Cherokee female seminary. Park Hill, the seat of the old Cherokee mission press, is a few miles distant. Consult Mooney in 19th Rep. B. A. E., pt. 1, 1900.

Tahlkoedi ('people of Tahlko,' where they once camped). A division of the Raven phratry of the Stikine in Alaska.
Dĕtlk·oē'dĕ.—Boas in 5th Rep. N. W. Tribes Can., 25, 1889. Talch-kŭĕdi.—Krause, Tlinkit Ind., 120, 1885. Tāłqoe'dî.—Swanton, field notes, B. A. E., 1904. Tal-qua-tee.—Kane, Wand. in N. A., app., 1859.

Tahltan. The southwesternmost tribal division of the Nahane Indians of the Athapascan family. Their hunting grounds include the drainage basin of Stikine r. and its tributaries as far as the mouth of Iskut r., Dease lake, and the river halfway to McDanes cr. (but according to the old law the head of Dease lake was Kaska territory, and this assumption of rights has never been acknowledged by the Kaska people), the northern sources of the Nass, and some of the southern branches of the Taku, in Alaska and British Columbia. In early days the salmon streams flowing into the Stikine from the N., from 4 m. below Glenora to, but not including, Telegraph cr., were claimed and fished by the Stikine tribe of Tlingit, but this overlapping of the two peoples seems to have produced little friction, possibly because the Tahltan had no living places hereabouts, and in the matter of the exchange of the products of the coast and the interior it was of mutual advantage to keep on friendly terms.

The Tahltan have always lived on the upper reaches of the Stikine and near by on the Tahltan and Tuya rs. In early days their living places were used more as storage depots and were resorted to through the summer months for salmon fishing, which was also the season of ease and feasting, when the pursuit of the fur-bearing animals was without profit—for the Tahltan people have always been hunters and trappers, living in the open throughout the year, meat eaters through necessity and choice, and accepting fish diet only as a change.

The primitive houses were similar to those found in the fishing camps to-day; they were constructed of stout saplings stuck upright in the ground and bound together with bark rope or tree roots and roofed over with slabs of spruce bark. But in camp the typical shelter was a lean-to of bark and brush laid over poles, two being placed opposite each other, with a central fire. To-day, throughout most of the year, they live in the same manner, except that canvas has superseded the bark and brush covering.

After the Cassiar gold excitement in 1874 they built a substantial log village on level space upward of a mile and a half from the junction of the Tahltan with the Stikine, which is generally known as Tahltan, though its native name is Goon-tdar-shaga ('where the spring water stops'). The only other native settlement is at Telegraph Creek, where a number of small log houses have been built to keep pace with the growth of the white settlement.

The social organization of the Tahltan without doubt has developed from association with the coast Tlingit. It is founded on matriarchy and is dependent on the existence of two exogamous parties who intermarry. These parties may be designated, from their totemic emblems, as Cheskea (Raven) and Cheona (Wolf). These are subdivided into families, which assume all the functions of the party and supplement each other at all meetings and on all occasions of ceremony. The family is the unit of social and political life, in which all individuality is merged, succession follows, and inheritance is secured. The families are:

(1) Tuckclarwaydee, of the Wolf party, which, besides having the wolf emblem, is represented by the brown bear, the eagle, and the killer-whale. It originated in the interior about the headwaters of Nass r. This family is credited with having been the first to settle in this country and the founders of the Tahltan tribe.

(2) Nanyiee, of the Wolf party, which, besides having the wolf emblem, is represented by the brown bear, the killer-whale, and the shark. The original home of this people was in the interior, about the headwaters of Taku r., which they descended to salt water and settled among the Stikine Tlingit; in later years they ascended Stikine r. and became a family of the Tahltan, while others crossed the trail in still more recent times and joined their brethren.

(3) Talarkoteen of the Wolf party, represented by the wolf crest. They originated in the interior, about Peace r., and followed down Liard r. to Dease lake and then crossed to the Tuya. They are nearly extinct.

(4) Kartchottee, of the Raven party, represented by both the raven emblem and that of the frog. This family originated in the interior toward the headwaters of the Taku. Some of the family married among the Tahltan in early days. Another branch descended Stikine r. long ago, affiliated with the Kake tribe of the Tlingit people, and generations later their descendents followed up the Stikine and became Tahltan. This is now the most numerous family of the tribe.

The Tahltan live by hunting and trapping. The country is rich in fur-bearing animals and big game. In late years, since hunters have been attracted thither, they have earned considerable as guides, besides working for the trading companies' pack-teams. They are an adaptable people, who are fast giving up the traditions of the past for the luxuries of civilization, with which their earnings supply them, and in the course of a few years there will be little left of their more primitive life. They numbered 229 in 1909, and have reached that stage where they are holding their own. They are of medium stature, spare rather than stout, and have high cheek-bones, full mouth, aquiline nose rather broad at the base, small hands and feet, coarse black hair, and mild and pleasant expression. On the whole they are an honest, agreeable, kindly people, hospitably inclined and dignified in bearing. In many instances their admixture with the Tlingit is expressed in their features, producing a much less pleasing type. In addition to the authors cited below, consult Teit in Boas Anniv. Vol., 337, 1906. (G. T. E.)

Conneuaghs.—Pope, MS. vocab., B. A. E., 1865. Kŭn-ŭn-ăh'.—Dall in Proc. Am. A. A. S., xxxiv, 376, 1886. Nahanies of the Upper Stikine.—Pope, op. cit. Stick.—Smith quoted by Colyer in Ind. Aff. Rep. 1869, 567, 1870. Tahl-tan.—Dawson in Rep. Geol. Surv. Can., 192B, 1889. Talyan.—Smith, op. cit., 568.

Tahluptsi. The almost extinct Yellowwood or Evergreen Oak clan of the pueblo of Zuñi, N. Mex.
Tá'hluptsi-kwe.—Cushing in 13th Rep. B. A. E., 368, 1896 (kwe = 'people').

Tahuagabacahel ('water-hole of the withered pitahaya'). A rancheria, probably of the Cochimi, connected with Purísima mission in s. Lower California in the 18th century.—Doc. Hist. Mex., 4th s., v, 188, 1857.

Tahuglauk. A tribe, evidently mythical, but which, according to Lahontan, lived about the year 1690 in the region of the upper Missouri r., on a river flowing westward into a great salt lake.
Tahuglank.—Harris, Voy. and Trav. II, 920, 1705 (misprint). Tahuglauk.—Lahontan, New Voy., I, 125, 1703. Tahuglucks.—Coxe, Carolana, map, 1741. Tahulauk.—Barcia, Ensayo, 298, 1723.

Tahuunde (Tŭ'hu-ŭn'de, 'mountains-extending-into-river people'). A division of the Mescalero Apache, who claim

as their original habitat the region of
s. w. Texas, N. of the Rio Grande and
extending into s. New Mexico.   (J. M.)

Taiaiagon ('at the crossing or landing.'
—Hewitt). An Iroquois village in 1678
on the N. shore of L. Ontario, near the
present Toronto, Ont.
Taiaiagon.—Hennepin, New Discov., 48, 1698. Te-
gaogen.—Esnauts and Rapilly map, 1777. Teïaïa-
gon.—La Salle (1684) in N. Y. Doc. Col. Hist., IX,
218, 1855. Tejaiagon.—Bellin map, 1755. Tejaja-
gon.—Hennepin, New Discov., 28, 1698. Tejaja-
hon.—Macauley, N. Y., II, 191, 1829. Tezagon.—
French, Hist. Coll. La., I, 59, 1846.

Taikus. A former Maidu settlement
near Cherokee or Pentz's, at the head of
Dry cr., Butte co., Cal.   (R. B. D.)
Tagas.—Schoolcraft, Ind. Tribes, VI, 710, 1857.
Tagus.—Johnston (1850) in Sen. Ex. Doc. 4, 32d
Cong., spec. sess., 45, 1853. Taikû.—Curtin, MS.
vocab., B. A. E., 1885. Taikûshi.—Ibid. Tigres.—
Sen. Ex. Doc. 57, 32d Cong., 2d sess., 15, 1853.

Tailla ('crane.'—Hewitt). An unidentified village on the St Lawrence, near
the present city of Quebec, in 1535.—Cartier (1535), Bref Récit, 32, 1863.

Taimah (also Taiomah, Tama, properly
Taima, 'sudden crash' [of thunder].—
Wm. Jones. The name has been mis-
translated "The bear whose voice makes

TAIMAH

the rocks to tremble"). A subordinate
chief of the Fox tribe, and member of
the Thunder clan, for some years ruler
and law-giver of a Fox village a short
distance above the mouth of Flint cr.,
near the site of Burlington, Ia. He was
also a prominent medicine-man. Always

friendly toward the whites, on one occasion when a vindictive Indian had started
on a long journey for the purpose of killing the Indian agent at Prairie du Chien,
Wis., Taimah hastened to him and by a
timely warning saved his life. He was
one of the signers of the treaty with the
Sauk and Foxes at Washington, Aug. 4,
1824, in which his name appears as
"Fai-mah, the Bear." He died among
his people a few years later. The county
and town of Tama, Ia., preserve his name.

Taimamares. A former tribe of s. Texas,
probably Coahuiltecan, associated with
the Gueiquesales, Manos Prietas, Bocores,
Haeser, Pinanacas, Escabas, Cacastes,
Cocobiptas, Cocomaque, Codame, Con-
totores, Colorados, and Babiamares in
1675 (Fernando del Bosque, 1675, trans.
in Nat. Geog. Mag., XIV, 340, 1903).
They are probably identical with the Teneinamar. Cf. *Tumamamar.*

Taisida (*Tai'-si-da*). A former Maidu
village a few miles s. E. of Marysville,
Yuba co., Cal.—Dixon in Bull. Am. Mus.
Nat. Hist., XVII, map, 1905.
Tai'chida.—Powers in Cont. N. A. Ethnol., III, 282,
1877. Taitcedâwi.—Curtin, MS. vocab., B. A. E.,
1885. Tychedas.—Powers in Overland Mo., XII,
420, 1874.

Tait ('those up river'). A collective
name for the Cowichan tribes on Fraser
r., Brit. Col., above Nicomen and Chilliwack rs.
Haitlin.—Anderson quoted by Gibbs in Hist. Mag.,
1st s., VII, 73, 1863. Sa-chinco.—Ibid. ('strangers':
Shushwap name). Sa-chin-ko.—Mayne, Brit. Col.,
295, 1862. Tait.—Trutch, Map of Brit. Col., 1870.
Tates.—Fitzhugh in Ind. Aff. Rep., 328, 1857.
Teates.—Mayne, op. cit. Teet.—Anderson, op.
cit. Tě'it.—Boas in Rep. 64th Meeting Brit. A.
A. S., 454, 1894.

Taitinapam. A small Shahaptian tribe
speaking the Klikitat language and formerly living between the headwaters of
Lewis and Cowlitz rs. in Skamania co.,
Wash. They were never officially recognized by the Government and if any survive they have probably been merged in
the Klikitat tribe.   (L. F.)
Tai-kie-a-pain.—Stevens in Ind. Aff. Rep., 433,
1854. Tai-tim-pans.—Ford in H. R. Ex. Doc. 37,
34th Cong., 3d sess., 102, 1857. Tai-tin-a-pam.—
Gibbs in Pac. R. R. Rep. I, 403, 1855. Tait-inapum.—
Tolmie quoted by Lord, Nat. in Brit. Col., II, 245,
1866. Taitinipans.—Stevens in H. R. Ex. Doc. 37,
34th Cong., 3d sess., 54, 1857. Tintinapain.—Schoolcraft, Ind. Tribes, V, 490, 1855.

Taiyanyanokhotana. A division of Kaiyuhkhotana living on Kuskokwim r.,
Alaska. Pop. 210 in 1890, 122 males and
88 females. Their chief villages, situated
near the Russian trading post of Kol-
makof, were Napai and Akmiut.
Tai-yā-yăn'-o-khotān'-ā.—Dall in Cont. N. A. Ethnol., I, 26, 1877.

Tajicaringa. A former Tepehuane pueblo in Durango, Mexico, the seat of the
Spanish mission of Magdalena.
Magdalena Tajicaringa.—Orozco y Berra, Geog.,
319, 1864.

Tajique (probably the Hispanized form of the Tewa name (*Tashi'ke͡ʔ*) of the pueblo, the Tigua name being Tûsh-yit-yay, or Tuh-yityay.—Bandelier). A former Tigua pueblo about 30 m. N. E. of Belen, the ruins of which are situated on the N. and W. border of the present settlement of the same name, on the S. bank of the Arroyo de Tajique, in central New Mexico. It was the seat of the mission of San Miguel, established probably in 1629. In 1674 its population, which then numbered about 300, was augmented by the addition of 600 Tigua from Quarai, who were compelled by the Apache to abandon their pueblo. Little peace, however, was found at Tajique, for in the following year this village also was permanently abandoned for the same cause, the inhabitants gradually drifting to El Paso. A remnant of the Tigua now living near the latter place claim to have come originally from Tajique and other pueblos in the N. Consult Bandelier in Arch. Inst. Papers, IV, 257 et seq., 1892; Lummis, Land of Poco Tiempo, 1893. See *Tigua*. (F. W. H.)
Junétre.—Oñate (1598) in Doc. Inéd., XVI, 118, 1871 (believed by Bandelier, Arch. Inst. Papers, IV, 113, 1892, to be probably the same; not to be confounded with the Junetre of the Tewa). San Miguel Taxique.—Vetancurt (1696) in Teatro Mex., III, 324, 1871. Tafique.—Escalante (1778) quoted by Bandelier in Arch. Inst. Papers, III, 132, 1890. Tageque.—Latham, Var. of Man, 395, 1850. Tagique.—Gregg. Comm. Prairies, I, 165, 1844. Ta-jique.—Bandelier in Arch. Inst. Papers, III, 128, 1890. Taxique.—De l'Isle, Carte Mex. et Floride, 1703. Tegique.—Squier in Am. Rev., II, 508, 1848. Tuh-yit-yay.—Lummis quoted by Bandelier in Arch. Inst. Papers, IV, 258, 1892. Tûsh-yit-yay.—Ibid. (this and the last form are given as the Isleta name of the pueblo.)

Takaiak. A Kaiyuhkhotana division and village E. of Yukon r., Alaska, near Nulato. Pop. 81 in 1844.
Letniki-Takaïak.—Zagoskin in Nouv. Ann. Voy., 5th s., XXI, map, 1850. Takaiaksa.—Tikhmenief quoted by Baker, Geog. Dict. Alaska, 396, 1902. Täkäjäksen.—Holmberg quoted by Dall in Cont. N. A. Ethnol., I, 25, 1877.

Takamitka. A former Aleut village on Unalaska id., eastern Aleutians, Alaska.
Tatamitka.—Coxe, Russ. Discov., 164, 1787.

Takapsintonwanna ('village at the shinny ground'). A former band or village of the Wahpeton Sioux.
Takapsiŋtona.—Riggs, letter to Dorsey, 1882. Takapsin-toⁿwaⁿna.—Dorsey (after Ashley) in 15th Rep. B. A. E., 216, 1897. Takapsin-toŋwaŋna.—Ibid.

Takashwangaroras. See *Shikellamy*.

Takasichekhwut (*Tă-χas'-i-tce'-qwût*). A former village of the Chastacosta on the N. side of Rogue r., Oreg.—Dorsey in Jour. Am. Folk-lore, III, 234, 1890.

Takatoka (corrupted from *De'gătă'gă*, a word which conveys the idea of two persons standing together, and so closely united as to form but one human body). A prominent early chief of the Western Cherokee. The name was also applied to Gen. Stand Watie (q. v.).—Mooney in 19th Rep. B. A. E., 515, 1900.

Takchuk. A Kaviagmiut Eskimo village E. of Port Clarence, Alaska.
Klaxermette.—Jackson, Rep. on Reindeer in Alaska, map, 145, 1894. Taksomut.—Nelson in 18th Rep. B. A. E., map, 1899. Taksomute.—Petroff in 10th Census, Alaska, map, 1884. Taksumut.—Dall in Cont. N. A. Ethnol., I, map, 1877.

Takdentan. A Tlingit division at Gaudekan, Alaska, belonging to the Raven phratry.
taktēn-tān.—Krause, Tlinkit Ind., 118, 1885. T!a'qdentān.—Swanton, field notes, B. A. E., 1904.

Takdheskautsiupshe ('path where ticks abound'). An Osage village.
Taⁿȼe'ska utsi' upcĕ'.—Dorsey, Osage MS. vocab., B. A. E., 1883.

Takelma (from the native name *Dãᵃgelmáᵉn*, 'those dwelling along the river'). A tribe which, together with the Upper Takelma (q. v.), or Latᶜgãᵃwáᵉ, forms the Takilman linguistic family of Powell. They occupy the middle portion of the course of Rogue r. in s. w. Oregon from and perhaps including Illinois r. to about Table Rock, the northern tributaries of Rogue r. between these limits, and the upper course of Cow cr. Linguistically they are very sharply distinguished from their neighbors, their language showing little or no resemblance in even general morphologic and phonetic traits to either the Athapascan or the Klamath; it was spoken in at least two dialects. They seem to have been greatly reduced in numbers at the time of the Rogue River war; at the present day the few survivors, a half dozen or so, reside on the Siletz res., Oreg. J. O. Dorsey (Takelma MS. vocab., B. A. E., 1884) gives the following list of village names: Hashkushtun, Hudedut, Kashtata, Kthotaime, Nakila, Salwahka, Seethltun, Sestikustun, Sewaathlchutun, Shkashtun, Skanowethltunne, Talmamiche, Talotunne, Tthowache, Tulsulsun, Yaasitun, and Yushlali. These are nearly all Athapascan in form. The following native Takelma village names were procured by Dr Edward Sapir in 1906: Gelyalk (Gelyãlkᶜ), Dilomi (Dīᵉlōmī), Gwenpunk (Gwenpʼuñkᶜ), Hayaalbalsda (Hayãᵃlbãlsda), Daktgamik (Dakᶜtᶜgamīkᶜ), Didalam (Dīdalăm), Daktsasin (Dakᶜts!asiñ) or Daldanik, Hagwal (Hagwãl), Somouluk (Sᐧōmōᵘlŭkᶜ), and Hatonk (Hat!ōnkᶜ).

Culturally the Takelma were closely allied to the Shasta of N. California, with whom they frequently intermarried. Their main dependence for food was the acorn, which, after shelling, pounding, sifting, and seething, was boiled into a mush. Other vegetable foods, such as the camas root, various seeds, and berries (especially manzanita), were also largely used. Tobacco was the only plant cultivated. Of animal foods the chief was salmon and other river fish caught by line, spear, and net; deer were hunted by running them into an inclosure provided with traps. For winter use roasted salmon and cakes of camas and deer fat were stored away. The main utensils were a great variety of baskets (used for grinding acorns, sifting, cooking, carrying burdens, storage, as food receptacles, and for many other purposes), constructed generally by twining on a hazel warp. Horn, bone, and wood served as material for various implements, as spoons, needles, and root-diggers. Stone was hardly used except in the making of arrowheads and pestles. The house, quadrangular in shape and partly underground, was constructed of hewn timber and was provided with a central fireplace, a smoke-hole in the roof, and a raised door from which entrance was had by means of a notched ladder. The sweat-house, holding about six, was also a plank structure, though smaller in size; it was reserved for the men.

In clothing and personal adornment the Takelma differed but little from the tribes of N. California, red-headed-woodpecker scalps and the basket caps of the women being perhaps the most characteristic articles. Facial painting in red, black, and white was common, the last-named color denoting war. Women tattooed the skin in three stripes; men tattooed the left arm with marks serving to measure various lengths of strings of dentalia.

In their social organization the Takelma were exceedingly simple, the village, small in size, being the only important sociological unit; no sign of totemism or clan groupings has been found. The chieftaincy was only slightly developed, wealth forming the chief claim to social recognition. Feuds were settled through the intervention of a "go-between" hired by the aggrieved party. Marriage was entirely a matter of purchase of the bride and was often contracted for children or even infants by their parents. The bride was escorted with return presents by her relatives to the bridegroom's house; on the birth of a child an additional price was paid to her father. Though no law of exogamy prevailed beyond the prohibition of marriage of near kin, marriage was probably nearly always outside the village. Polygamy, as a matter of wealth, was of course found; the levirate prevailed. Corpses were disposed of by burial in the ground, objects of value being strewn over the grave. .

No great ceremonial or ritual development was attained by the Takelma. The first appearance of salmon and acorns, the coming to maturity of a girl, shamanistic performances, and the war dance were probably the chief occasions for ceremonial activity. Great influence was exercised by the shamans, to whose

malign power death was generally ascribed. Differing from the shamans were the dreamers, who gained their power from an entirely different group of supernatural beings and who were never thought to do harm. Characteristic of the Takelma was the use of a considerable number of charms or medicine formulas addressed to various animal and other spirits and designed to gain their favor toward the fulfilment of some desired event or the warding off of a threatened evil. The most characteristic myths are the deeds of the culture-hero (Daldàl) and the pranks of Coyote. For further information, consult Sapir (1) in Am. Anthr., IX, no. 2, 1907; (2) in Jour. Am. Folk-lore, xx, 33, 1907; (3) Takelma Texts, Anthr. Pub. Univ. Pa. Mus., II, no. 1, 1909.　　　(E. S.)

Dāᵃgelmaᵉn.—Sapir in Am. Anthr., IX, 252, 1907 ('those living alongside the river,' i. e. Rogue r.: own name). Kyu'-kŭtchĭtclûm.—Dorsey, Alsea MS. vocab., B. A. E., 1884 ('people far down the stream [or country]': Alsea name). Na-tcté ʒûnnĕ.—Dorsey, Naltunnetunne MS. vocab., B. A. E., 1884 (Naltunne name). Rogue River.—Dorsey, Takelma MS. vocab., B. A. E., 1884 (name given by people in Oregon). Ta-ɣĕl'-ma.—Dorsey in Jour. Am. Folk-lore, III, 234, 1890. Takilma.—Gatschet in Mag. Am. Hist., VIII, 257, 1882. Upper Rogue River Indians.—Dorsey in Jour. Am. Folk-lore, III, 234, 1890.

Takestina. A Tlingit division at Chilkat, Alaska, belonging to the Wolf phratry. They are said to have lost their way, while migrating northward, in the channel behind Wrangell id. (Taqsī't), whence they came to be called the Taqsī't nation (Taqêstina').　　　(J. R. S.)

takastina.—Krause, Tlinkit Ind., 116, 1885.

Takfwelottine ('people of the living waters'). A tribe or band of the Thlingchadinne dwelling S. E. of Great Bear lake and at the source of Coppermine r., Mackenzie Ter., Canada. Petitot describes them as kindly, jovial, and religious. When he went among them, in 1865, there were 60 shamans for 600 people.

T'akfwel-ottiné.—Petitot, Dict. Dènè-Dindjié, xx, 1876. T'akkwel-ottinè.—Petitot in Bull. Soc. de Géog. Paris, chart, 1875. Tρa-kfwèlè-ρottinè.—Petitot, Autour du lac des Esclaves, 363, 1891. Tρathel-ottiné.—Petitot, MS. vocab., B. A. E., 1865.

Takhaiya. A former Kuitsh village on lower Umpqua r., Oreg.

Ta-qai'-yă.—Dorsey in Jour. Am. Folk-lore, III, 231, 1890.

Takhchapa ('deer head'). A band of the Miniconjou Sioux.

Tahća-pa.—Riggs in The Word Carrier, June-July 1889. Tar-co-eh-parch.—Lewis and Clark (1806) in Am. State Pap., Ind. Aff., I, 715, 1832. Tar-co-eh-parh.—Lewis and Clark, Discov., 34, 1806.

Takhuhayuta ('eat the scrapings of hides'). A band of the Yanktonai Sioux.

Tahuha-yuta.—Dorsey in 15th Rep. B. A. E., 218, 1897. Taquha-yuta.—Ibid.

Takiketak. A Kuskwogmiut Eskimo village on the E. shore of Kuskokwim bay, Alaska. Pop. 21 in 1880.

Takikatagamute.—Nelson quoted by Baker, Geog. Dict. Alaska, 1902. Takiketagamute.—Petroff in 10th Census, Alaska, 17, 1884.

Takimilding. A Hupa village on the E. side of Trinity r., Cal., about 4 m. N. of Tsewenalding. It was formerly the religious center of the Hupa; in it are situated the sacred house and sweat-house. Here are held the acorn feast, the first part of the spring dance, and the fall or jumping dance, and from it the dancers set out in canoes for the beginning of the white deerskin dance. The priest in charge of these ceremonies lives in this village. (P. E. G.)

Hosler.—Powers in Cont. N. A. Ethnol., III, 72, 1877. **Hostler.**—Spalding in Ind. Aff. Rep., 82, 1870 (name used by whites). **Ople-goh.**—Gibbs, MS., B. A. E. (Yurok name). **TakimiLdiñ.**—Goddard, Life and Culture of the Hupa, 12, 1903. **Up-la-goh.**—McKee (1851) in Sen. Ex. Doc. 4, 32d Cong., spec. sess., 194, 1853. **Up-le-goh.**—Gibbs in Schoolcraft, Ind. Tribes, III, 139, 1853.

Takin. An Indian village near Dent's Ferry on Stanislaus r., Calaveras co., Cal. A Yokuts (Mariposan) vocabulary obtained from an Indian of this place is given by Powers in Cont. N. A. Ethnol., III, 571, 1877.

Takini ('improved'). A band of the Upper Yanktonai Sioux.

Takini.—Dorsey in 15th Rep. B. A. E., 218, 1897. Tatkannai.—H. R. Ex. Doc., 96, 42d Cong., 3d sess., 5, 1873 (probably identical).

Takokakaan (*T!āq°q!aqa-ān*, 'town at the mouth of Taku'). A Tlingit town of the Taku people in Alaska. (J. R. S.)

Takon. A subdivision of the Hankutchin, whose village is Nuklako.

Takoongoto (*Ta-ko-ong'-o-to*, 'high bank'). A subclan of the Delawares.—Morgan, Anc. Soc., 172, 1878.

Takoulguehronnon. Mentioned in the middle of the 17th century (Jes. Rel. 1656, 34, 1858) as a tribe defeated by the Iroquois.

Takshak. A Chnagmiut Eskimo village on the N. bank of the Yukon, Alaska, near the delta. Cf. *Chukchagemut.*

Takshagemut.—Dall, Alaska, map, 1870. Taktchag-miout.—Zagoskin in Nouv. Ann. Voy., 5th s., XXI, map, 1850. Taktschagmjut.—Holmberg, Ethnog. Skizz., map, 1855.

Taku. A Tlingit tribe on the river and inlet of the same name, Stevens channel, and Gastineau channel, Alaskan coast. They were said to number 2,000 in 1869, 269 in 1880, and only 223 in 1890. Their winter towns are Sikanasankian and Takokakaan. Social divisions are Ganahadi, Tsatenyedi, and Yenyedi. A tradition, seemingly well founded, places the ancient home of most of these people in the interior, higher up Taku r. An Athapascan tribe was known by the same name. See *Takutine.* (J. R. S.)

Tacos.—Scott in Ind. Aff. Rep., 314, 1868. Tahco.—Anderson quoted by Gibbs in Hist. Mag., 1st s., VII, 75, 1863. Takas.—Halleck in Rep. Sec. War, pt. I, 43, 1868. Tako.—Scouler (1846) in Jour. Ethnol. Soc. Lond., I, 232, 1848. Takon.—Colyer in Ind. Aff. Rep., 575, 1870. Takoos.—Ibid., 574. Taku-kŏn.—Krause, Tlinkit Ind., 116, 1885. Taku-qwan.—Emmons in Mem. Am. Mus. Nat. Hist., III, 233, 1903. Takutsskoe.—Veniaminoff, Zapiski, II, pt. 3, 30, 1840. T!āq°.—Swanton, field notes, B. A. E., 1904. Tarkens.—Colyer in Ind.

Aff. Rep. 1869, 588, 1870. **Tarkoo.**—Dennis in Morris, Treas. Rep., 4, 1879. **Thākhu.**—Holmberg, Ethnog. Skizz., map, 142, 1855.

Takulli ('people who go upon the water'). An ethnic group of Athapascan tribes, under Babine and Upper Skeena agency, inhabiting the upper branches of Fraser r. and as far s. as Alexandria, Brit. Col. They are described (Can. Ind. Aff., 210, 1909) as consisting of 19 bands, all of the Hagwilget or Dené nation. Hale (Ethnol. and Philol., 201, 1846) described them as occupying the country from 52° 30′ N., bordering on the Shuswap to 56°, being separated from the Sekani on the E. by the Rocky mts. and on the w. by the Coast range. Anderson (Hist. Mag., VII, 75, 1863) located them approximately between 52° and 57° N. and 120° and 127° W. Drake (Bk. Inds., viii, 1848) placed them on Stuart lake. Buschmann (Athapask. Sprachst., 152, 1589) located them on the upper Fraser r., Brit. Col. The British Columbia map of 1872 located them s. of Stuart lake, between 54° and 55° N. Dawson (Rep. Geol. Surv. Can., 192B, 1889) states that they, together with the Sekani, inhabit the headwaters of Skeena, Fraser, and Peace rs. Morice (Proc. Can. Inst., 112, 1889) says that they are one of the three western Déné tribes and that their habitat borders that of the Tsilkotin on the s. and extends as far up as 56° N.

The Takulli were first visited by Mackenzie, who, in 1793, traversed their country on his way from L. Athabasca to the Pacific. In 1805 the first trading post was established among them. They are a semisedentary tribe, having fixed homes in regularly organized villages which they leave at regular seasons for purposes of hunting and fishing. They are the most numerous, important, and progressive of all the northern Athapascan tribes. They borrowed many customs from the coast Indians, as the Chimmesyan are in close communication with their northern and the Heiltsuk with their southern septs. The practice of wearing wooden labrets was obtained from the Chimmesyan, while from the coast tribes they adopted the custom of burning the dead. A widow was obliged to remain upon the funeral pyre of her husband till the flames reached her own body; she then collected the ashes of the dead, placed them in a basket, which she was obliged to carry with her during three years of servitude in the family of her deceased husband, at the end of which time a feast was held, when she was released from thralldom and permitted to remarry if she desired. From this custom the tribe came to be called Carriers. No fewer than 8 kinds of snares were employed by the Takulli, and Morice states (Trans. Can. Inst., 137,

1893) that copper and iron implements and ornaments were used by them before the advent of the whites, but that they wrought copper only. He classes them as Upper and Lower Carriers and Babines, although such a distinction is not recognized by the tribe itself. They have a society composed of hereditary "noblemen" or landowners, and a lower class who hunt with or for these; but slavery, as it exists among the neighboring Athapascan tribes, is not practised by them. They have no head chiefs and are exogamous, all title and property rights descending through the mother. Each band or clan has a well-defined hunting ground, which is seldom encroached on by others of the tribe. They are not so numerous now as formerly, a number of their villages having become extinct. An independent band has settled at Ft McLeod, in the Sekani country. Drake (Bk. Inds., viii, 1848) said that in 1820 they numbered 100; Anderson (Hist. Mag., vii, 73, 1863) estimated the population in 1835 as 5,000, and in 1839 as 2,625, of which number 897 were men, 688 women, 578 sons, and 462 daughters. Morice (Proc. Can. Inst., 112, 1889) gave the population as 1,600. The number reported in 1902 was 1,551, and 1,614 in 1909. Hale (Ethnol. and Philol., 201, 1846) and McDonald (Brit. Col., 126, 1862) divided them into 11 clans, as follows: Babine (Nataotin and Hwosotenne), Naskotin, Natliatin, Nikozliautin, Ntshaautin, Nulaautin, Tatshiautin, Tautin, Thetliotin, Tsatsuotin (Tanotenne), and Tsilkotin. The Tsilkotin are a distinct group, as determined by Morice (Trans. Can. Inst., 24, 1893), who gives 9 septs of the Takulli: I, Southern Carriers: 1, Ltautenne (Tautin); 2, Nazkutenne (Naskotin); 3, Tanotenne; 4, Nutcatenna (Ntshaautin); 5, Natlotenne (Natliatin). II, Northern Carriers: 6, Nakraztlitenne (Nikozliautin); 7, Tlaztenne (Tatshiautin). III, Babines: 8, Nitutinni (Nataotin); 9, Hwotsotenne. Dawson (Rep. Progr. Geol. Surv., 30B, 1880) makes the Kustsheotin, whose village is Kezche, distinct from the Tatshiautin, the Tatshikotin from the Nulaautin, and the Stelatin of Stella village from the Natliatin.

Atlāshimih.—Tolmie and Dawson, Vocabs. Brit. Col., 122B, 1884 (Bellacoola name). Canices.—M'Vickar, Hist. Lewis and Clark Exped., ii, 356, note, 1842 (misprint for Carriers). Carrien.—Scouler in Jour. Geog. Soc. Lond., xi, 221, 1841. Carrier-Indians.—Mackenzie, Voy., 257, 1801. Carriers.—Ibid., 284. Chargeurs.—Duflot de Mofras, Expl. de l'Oregon, ii, 337, 1844. Chin.—Dunn, Hist. Oreg. Ter., 101, 1844. Faoullies.—Drake, Bk. Inds., viii, 1848 (misprint). Nagail.—Latham in Jour. Ethnol. Soc. Lond., i, 159, 1848. Nagailas.—Mackenzie, Voy., ii, 175, 1802. Nagailer.—Mackenzie, ibid., 246. Nagalier.—Adelung, Mithridates, iii, 216, 1816 (misprint). Porteurs.—Mayne, Brit. Columbia, 298, 1862. Tacoullie.—Balbi, Atlas Ethnog.,

822, 1826. Taculli.—Latham, Var. of Man, 372, 1850. Tâ-oullies.—Harmon, Jour., 313, 1820. Tacully.—Harmon quoted in Pac. R. R. Rep., iii, pt. 3, 84, 1856. Tahculi.—Gallatin in Trans. Am. Ethnol. Soc., ii, 77, 1848. Tah-cully.—Anderson quoted by Gibbs in Hist. Mag., 1st s., vii, 73, 1883 ('people who navigate deep waters'). Tahekie.—Can. Ind. Rep. for 1872, 7, 1873. Tahelie.—Ibid., 8. Tahkali.—Hale, Ethnol. and Philol., 201, 1846. Tahka-li.—Pope, Sicanny MS. vocab., B. A. E., 1865 ('river people,' from tah-kuh, 'a river'). Tahkallies.—Domenech, Deserts N. Am., i, 444, 1860. Tah-khl.—Dawson in Rep. Geol. Surv. Can. 192B, 1887. Tahkoli.—Buschmann in König. Akad. der Wiss. zu Berlin, iii, 546, 1860. Takahli.—Brit. Columbia map, 1872, Takali.—Wilkes, U. S. Explor. Exped., iv, 451, 1845. Takalli.—McDonald, Brit. Col., 126, 1862. Takelly.—McLean, Hudson's Bay, i, 265, 1849. Ta-Keɪ-ne.—Morice, Notes on W. Déné, 29, 1893 (own name). Tā-kuli.—Richardson, Arct. Exped., ii, 31, 1851. Takulli.—Latham in Trans. Philol. Soc. Lond., 66, 1856. Talkpolis.—Fouquet quoted by Petitot, Dict. Dènè Dindjié, xliv, 1876. Tawcullies.—Richardson in Franklin, 2d Exped. Polar Sea, 197, 1828. Taχelh.—Morice in Proc. Canad. Inst., 112, 1889. Táχköli.—Buschmann, Athapask. Sprachst., 152, 1859. Teheili.—Tolmie and Dawson, Vocabs. Brit. Col., 122B, 1884. Tokali.—Duflot de Mofras, Expl. de l'Oregon, ii, 335, 1844. Tukkola.—Taylor in Cal. Farmer, July 19, 1862.

Takusalgi ('mole people'). One of the Creek clans.

Tákusalgi.—Gatschet, Creek Migr. Leg., i, 155, 1884. Tŭk'-ko.—Morgan, Anc. Soc., 161, 1878.

Takutine. A Nahane tribe living on Teslin r. and lake and upper Taku r., Brit. Col., speaking the same dialect as the Tahltan. Their hunting grounds include the basin of Big Salmon r., extending N. to the Pelly r. and E. to upper Liard r. Dall (Proc. A. A. A. S., 19, 1885) as well as Dawson called them a part of the Tahltan. Dawson (Geol. Surv. Can., 201B, 1889) classes them as distinct from a tribe of similar name in the upper Pelly valley, but they are probably the same, and so also are probably the Nehane of Chilkat r., living on a stream that falls into Lewes r. near L. Labarge. Dall describes the latter as bold and enterprising, great traders, and of great intelligence, while the Takutine, he said (Cont. N. A. Ethnol., i, 33, 1877), are few in number and little known.

Chilkaht-tena.—Dall in Cont. N. A. Ethnol., i, 33, 1877. Nehaunees of the Chilkaht River.—Ibid. Tāh'ko-tin'neh.—Ibid. Ta-koos-oo-ti-na.—Dawson in Rep. Geol. Surv. Can. 1887-88, 200B, 1889. Taku.—Ibid., 193B.

Takuyumam (Ta-ku-yu'-mam). A Chumashan village formerly on the site of Newhall, Los Angeles co., Cal., not far from the Ventura co. line.—Henshaw, Buenaventura MS. vocab., B. A. E., 1884.

Takwanedi (Tā'k!uane'dĭ, 'wintry people'). A division of the Tlingit at Klawak, Alaska, belonging to the Raven phratry.   (J. R. S.)

Takwashnaw. Given as a Lower Cherokee town on Mouzon's map of 1771 (Royce in 5th Rep. B. A. E., 143, 1887). Not identified.

Takya. The Frog or Toad clan of Zuñi pueblo, N. Mex.

Ták'yaɪuna-kwe.—Cushing in 13th Rep. B. A. E., 368, 1896 (kwe = 'people'). Ták'ya-kwe.—Ibid.

Tala ('palmetto town'). One of the Choctaw Six-towns which controlled land, chiefly in Newton co., Miss., lying between Tarlow and Bogue Felamma crs. from the watershed connecting the headwaters of these two streams down to the confluence of each with Pottokchito cr. It was a thickly settled community, nearly all of the people of which went W. in the migration of 1832.—Halbert in Pub. Ala. Hist. Soc., Misc. Coll., I, 381, 1901. **Talla.**—West Florida map, *ca.* 1775. **Tallatown.**—Gatschet, Creek Migr. Leg., I, 109, 1884.

Tala (*tá'la*, 'wolf'). A Yuchi clan. **Dalá.**—Speck, Yuchi Inds., 70, 1909. **Ta'lá tahá.**—Gatschet, Uchee MS., B. A. E., 1885 (= 'wolf gens').

Taladega (*Talatígi*, from *itálua* 'town,' *atígi* 'at the end'). A former Upper Creek town E. of Coosa r., on the site of the present town of the same name, in N. E. Talladega co., Ala. A battle was fought there Nov. 7, 1813.   (A. S. G.) **Taladega.**—Drake, Bk. Inds., bk. 4, 108, 1848. **Talatígi.**—Gatschet, Creek Migr. Leg., I, 144, 1884. **Talladega.**—Flint, Ind. Wars, 187, 1833. **Talledega.**—Hawkins (1814) in Am. State Pap., Ind. Aff., I, 845, 1832.

Taladega. A town of the Creek Nation, on Canadian r., s. w. of Hilabi, Okla. **Taladega.**—Gatschet, Creek Migr. Leg., II, 186, 1888. **Taladigi.**—Ibid.

Talahassee ('old town,' from *tálua* 'town', *hasi* 'old.'—Gatschet). A former Seminole town situated on what in 1775 was the road from the ford of Ocklocknee r. to Mikasuki town, Fla.; now the site of Tallahassee, the capital. According to Bartram (Trav., 225, 1792) it consisted of about 30 houses at that time. **Sim-e-no-le-tal-lau-haf-see.**—Hawkins (1799), Sketch, 25, 1848 (*f=s*). **Spring Gardens.**—H. R. Ex. Doc. 74 (1823), 19th Cong., 1st sess., 27, 1826. **Tahalasochte.**—Bartram, Trav., I, map, 1799. **Talahasochte.**—Ibid., 224, ed. 1792. **Tallahassa.**—H. R. Ex. Doc. 74, op. cit. **Tallahasse.**—Am. State Pap., Ind. Aff. (1802), I, 677, 1832. **Tallehassas.**—Morse, Rep. to Sec. War, 364, 1822.

Talahassudshi ('little Talasse'). A town of the Creek Nation on the N. bank of Canadian r. about 18 m. w. of Eufaula, Okla. See *Talasse.* **Talahássudshi.**—Gatschet, Creek Migr. Leg., II, 186, 1888.

Talahi (*Talá'hĭ*, 'white-oak place,' from *tálŭ'* 'white oak'). A Cherokee settlement about 1776; locality unknown. **Tellowe.**—Bartram, Trav., 371, 1792. **Tetohe.**—Mouzon's map cited by Royce in 5th Rep. B. A. E., 143, 1887 (possibly identical).

Talak (*Ta'lak*). A former Nishinam village in the valley of Bear r., which is the next stream N. of Sacramento, Cal. **Talac.**—Powers in Overland Mo., XII, 22, 1874. **Ta'lak.**—Powers in Cont. N. A. Ethnol., III, 316, 1877.

Talakhacha. A former Seminole town on the w. side of C. Florida, on the Florida coast. Tullishago was chief in 1823.—H. R. Ex. Doc. 74 (1823), 19th Cong., 1st sess., 27, 1826.

Talal. A former village of the Willopah, 6 m. s. of Claquato, Lewis co., Wash. **Chis-le-ráh.**—Gibbs, MS., B. A. E. (Cowlitz name). **Ford's Prairie.**—Ibid. **Tahtl-shin.**—Ibid. (own name). **Tálal.**—Ibid. (Chehalis name). **Tsa-whah-sen.**—Ibid.

Talaniyi ('sumac place,' from *talánĭ* 'red sumac'). A Cherokee settlement in upper Georgia about the period of the removal of the tribe to the W. in 1839; known to the whites as "Shoemake." **Shoemeck.**—Doc. of 1799 quoted by Royce in 5th Rep. B. A. E., 144, 1887.

Talapoosa. A comprehensive name for the Creek towns and tribes formerly on Tallapoosa r., Ala. They belonged to the Upper Creek division, forming its eastern group. There were 13 towns of the Talapoosa in 1715, with 2,343 inhabitants. The most important were Atasi, Fusihatchi, Hillabi, Huhliwahli, Imukfa, Kitchopataki, Kulumi, Talasse, and Tukabatchi.   (A. S. G.) **Talabouches.**—Robin, Voy. à la Louisiane, II, 54, 1807. **Talabouchi.**—De l'Isle, map (1700) in Winsor Hist. Amer., II, 295, 1886. **Talapenches.**—French, Hist. Col. La., II, 70, 1850. **Talapoashas.**—Bossu (1759), Trav. La., I, 229, 1771. **Talapoosas.**—La Harpe in French, Hist. Coll. La., III, 43, 44, 1851. **Talapouche.**—Ibid., 29. **Talapousses.**—Berquin Duvallon, Trav. La., 94, 1806. **Talapüs.**—Hervas, Idea dell' Universo, XVII, 90, 1784. **Talepoosas.**—Keane in Stanford, Compend., 537, 1878. **Talipuçes.**—Barcia, Ensayo, 313, 1723. **Tallabutes.**—German map of Brit. Colonies, *ca.* 1750 (placed on Chatahoochie r.). **Tallapoosa.**—Hawkins (1814) in Am. State Pap., Ind. Aff., I, 860, 1832. **Tallibooses.**—Rivers, Hist. S. C., 94, 1874. **Tallibosuies.**—Coxe, Carolana, 23, 1741. **Tallpoosas.**—McKenney and Hall, Ind. Tribes, III, 80, 1854.

Talaspa. One of the 7 Taensa villages in 1699.—Iberville in Margry, Déc., IV, 179, 1880.

Talasse (*Tá-li-si*, contr. of *itálua-ahássi*, 'old town'). A former Upper Creek town, known also as Big Talasse, on the E. bank of Tallapoosa r., opposite Tukabatchi, in N. w. Macon co., Ala. According to Hawkins (Sketch, 39, 1848) the remains of Old Talasse were 4 m. higher up the river in 1799. On account of its position on the "trader's trail" from Kasihta to the Upper Creek towns it became known also as "Halfway House."   (A. S. G.) **Big Talassee.**—U. S. Ind. Treat. (1797), 69, 1837. **Big Tallasees.**—Ibid. **Big Tallassee.**—Seagrove (1793) in Am. State Pap., Ind. Aff., I, 387, 1832. **Half-way house.**—White (1789), ibid., 22. **Halfway house Indians.**—Jordan (1794), ibid., 485. **Old Tal-e-see**—Hawkins (1799), Sketch, 39, 1848. **Tal-e-see.**—Ibid., 25-27. **Tal-lâ-se.**—Adair, Hist. Am. Inds., 257, 1775. **Tallassee.**—Am. State Pap., op. cit., 552. **Tallisee.**—Ellicott, Journal, 225, 1799. **Taulasse Viejo.**—Alcedo, Dic. Geog., v, 55, 1789 (Spanish form; i. e., "Old Taulasse").

Talasse. A former Upper Creek town on the E. bank of Coosa r., 1 m. below the falls, in Elmore co., Ala. It was generally known to white settlers and traders as Little Talasse, and has been identified as the Italisi, Talise, and Talisse of the chroniclers of the De Soto expedition. According to Benjamin Hawkins (Sketch, 40, 1848) the place mustered 40 gun-men in 1799. It is unlikely that this is the Tali mentioned by Coxe (Carolana, 14, 1741) as on an island in Tennessee r. See *Odshiapofa.*   (A. S. G.) **Acheaubofau.**—Wilkinson and Hawkins (1802) in Am. State Pap., Ind. Aff., I, 670, 1832. **Calés.**—French, Hist. Coll. La., III, 238, 1851 (plural form of

Tali of Coxe). **Hiccory Ground.**—Bartram, Trav., 461, 1792 (traders' name). **Hickory Ground.**—Ibid., ed. 1791. **Hickory Grounds.**—Creek paper (1836) in H. R. Rep. 37, 31st Cong., 2d sess., 122, 1851. **Hicory Ground.**—U. S. Ind. Treat. (1797), 68, 1837. **Italisi.**—Biedma (1544) in French, Hist. Coll. La., II, 102, 1850. **Little Tálisi.**—Gatschet, Creek Migr. Leg., I, 139, 1884. **Little Tallassie.**—McGillivray (1785) in Am. State Pap., op. cit., 17. **Little Tellassee.**—Drake, Bk. of Inds., bk. 4, 46, 1848. **McGillivray's Town.**—Finnelson (1792) in Am. State Pap., op. cit., 289. **O-che-au-po-fau.**—Hawkins (1799), Sketch, 37, 1848. **Ochebofa.**—Pickett, Hist. Ala., II, 267, 1851. **Ocheeaupo-fau.**—Schoolcraft, Ind. Tribes, IV, 380, 1854. **Ocheobofau.**—U. S. Ind. Treat. (1814), 163, 1837. **O-che-ub-e-fau.**—Hawkins, op. cit., 84. **Ocheubo-fau.**—Hawkins (1813) in Am. State Pap., op. cit., 854. **Odshi-apófa.**—Gatschet, Creek Migr. Leg., I, 139, 1884 ('in the hickory grove'). **petit Talessy.**—Milfort, Mémoire, 27, 1802. **Taby.**—Coxe, Carolana, map, 1741 (misprint). **Tahse.**—Jefferys, Am. Atlas, map, 7, 1776 (probably identical). **Talassee.**—Lincoln (1789) in Am. State Pap., op. cit., 79. **Tali.**—Gentl. of Elvas (1539) in Hakluyt Soc. Pub., IX, 67, 1851 (same?; mentioned also as an id. in Tennessee r., by Coxe, Carolana, 14, 1741). **Talicies.**—Barcia, Ensayo, 313, 1723. **Talis.**—Senex, map, 1710. **Talise.**—Garcilasso de la Vega, Fla., 144, 1723. **Talisees.**—Coxe, Carolana, map, 1741. **Talisi.**—Barcia, op. cit., 330. **Talisse.**—Gentl. of Elvas quoted by Shipp, De Soto and Florida, 682, 1881. **Tallahassee.**—Drake, Bk. Inds., bk. 4, 45, 1848 (½ m. from McGillivray's house). **Tallasee.**—Lincoln (1789) in Am. State Pap., op. cit., 72. **Tallassie.**—Robin, Voy., I, map, 1807. **Tallesees.**—Woodward, Reminis., 8, 1859. **Tallessees.**—U. S. Ind. Treat. (1797), 68, 1837. **Tallise.**—Gentl. of Elvas (1557) in French, Hist. Coll. La., II, 154, 1850. **Tallises.**—Coxe, Carolana, 24, 1741. **Taly.**—Morse, N. Am., 254, 1776. **Thase.**—Güssefeld, map U. S., 1784. **Village des Noyers.**—Milfort, Mémoire, 27, 1802 (French form: *noyers* = 'hickory').

Talassehatchi ('Talasse creek'). A settlement of one or more towns of the Upper Creeks on Coosa r., N. E. Ala., perhaps in Calhoun co. Col. Coffee defeated a body of Creek warriors there Nov. 3, 1813. In 1832 it had 79 heads of families. (A. S. G.)

Tallahasse.—Drake, Bk. of Inds., bk. 4, 55, 56, 1848. **Tal-la-se hatch-ee.**—Schoolcraft, Ind. Tribes, IV, 578, 1854. **Tallasschassee.**—Robin, Voy., II, map, 1807. **Tallesee Hatchu.**—U. S. Ind. Treat. (1827), 420, 1837. **Tallushatches.**—Drake, op. cit., 50. **Tallusthatches.**—Drake, Ind. Chron., 198, 1836.

Talatui. An unidentified Miwok division, or probably only a village site, mentioned by Hale, on the authority of Dana, as living on Kassima r., Cal. The Kassima is doubtless the Cosumnes.

Talantui.—Gibbs in Hist. Mag., 1st s., VII, 123, 1863. **Talatui.**—Hale, Ethnol. and Philol., 630, 1846.

Talawipiki. The Lightning clan of the Patki (Cloud, or Water-house) phratry of the Hopi.

Talawipikiwiñwû.—Fewkes in 19th Rep. B. A. E., 583, 1901 (*wiñwû* = 'clan'). **Ta'-la-wi-pi-ki wüñ-wû.**—Fewkes in Am. Anthr., VII, 402, 1894.

Talaxano. A Chumashan village formerly near Santa Inés mission, Santa Barbara co., Cal.—Taylor in Cal. Farmer, Oct. 18, 1861.

Talc. See *Steatite*.

Talhanio. A village of Praying Indians in 1659 on Nantucket id., Mass.—Cotton (1659) in Mass. Hist. Soc. Coll., 1st s., I, 204, 1806.

Taliepataua (perhaps Choctaw: 'cleft in the rock.'—Halbert). A former town in w. Alabama or E. Mississippi, between the territory of the Mauvila and Chickasaw tribes; reached by De Soto Nov. 18, 1540, from the province of Pafallaya, through deserted tracts.

Taliepataua.—Halbert in Trans. Ala. Hist. Soc., III, 70, 1899. **Taliepatava.**—Gentl. of Elvas (1557) in French, Hist. Coll. La., II, 160, 1850.

Talimuchasi ('new town'). A former settlement, probably of the Upper Creeks, on Coosa r., in Talladega or Coosa co., Ala. According to Ranjel (Oviedo, Hist. Gen., I, lib. XVII, 565, 1851) De Soto reached this town the same day he left Coça (Kusa) in 1540. There is a Creek town of the same name in Oklahoma.

Talimachusy.—Oviedo misquoted by Bourne, Narr. De Soto, II, 113, 1904. **Talimuchusy.**—Oviedo, op. cit. **Tallimuchase.**—Gentl. of Elvas (1557) in French, Hist. Coll. La., II, 153, 1850. **Talmotchasi.**—Gatschet, Creek Migr. Leg., II, 186, 1888 (in Oklahoma).

Talimuchasi. A former Upper Creek town and subordinate settlement of Oakfuskee, on the w. side of Tallapoosa r., 4 m. above Niuyaka and 35 or 40 m. above Tukabatchi, probably in Randolph co., Ala. Prior to 1797 it was known as Tukabatchi Tallahassee ('Tukabatchi old town'); from or shortly after that year it was known as Talimuchasi, or Newtown. In 1832 it contained 48 heads of families. Cf. *Telmocresses*.

Tália mutchasi.—Gatschet, Creek Migr. Leg., I, 145, 1884. **Tallmachusse.**—Devereux in H. R. Doc. 274, 25th Cong., 2d sess., 8, 1838. **Tal-lo-wau muchos-see.**—Hawkins (1799), Sketch, 46, 1848. **Talmachuesa.**—Sen. Ex. Doc. 425, 24th Cong., 1st sess., 227, 1836. **Talmachusee.**—Iverson in H. R. Doc. 274, op. cit., 12. **Talmachuson.**—Sen. Ex. Doc. 425, op. cit., 270. **Talmachussa.**—Wyse (1836) in H. R. Doc. 274, op. cit., 63. **Talmachussee.**—Sen. Ex. Doc. 425, op. cit., 218. **Tookaubatche tal-lauhas-see.**—Hawkins, op. cit. **Tuckabatchee Teehassa.**—Swan (1791) quoted by Schoolcraft, Ind. Tribes, v, 262, 1855.

Talinchi. A Yokuts (Mariposan) tribe formerly living in s. central California, between Fresno and San Joaquin rs. They joined in two land cessions to the United States by treaty of April 29, 1851, under the name Tall-in-chee, and by treaty of May 13, 1851, under the name Toeneche. They were then placed on a reserve between Chowchilla and Kaweah rs.

Dalinchi.—A. L. Kroeber, inf'n, 1906 (own name). **Lal Linches.**—Ind. Aff. Rep., 219, 1861. **Sallenches.**—Ind. Aff. Rep. 1856, 252, 1857. **Tai-lin-ches.**—McKee, ibid., 223, 1851. **Talinches.**—Barbour in Sen. Ex. Doc. 4, 32d Cong., spec. sess., 61, 1853. **Tallenches.**—Lewis in Ind. Aff. Rep. 1857, 399, 1858. **Tall-in-che.**—Royce in 18th Rep. B. A. E., 782, 1899. **Tal-lin-ches.**—McKee (1851) in Sen. Ex. Doc. 4, 32d Cong., spec. sess., 75, 1853. **Talluches.**—Henley in Ind. Aff. Rep., 512, 1854. **To-e-ne-che.**—Royce in 18th Rep. B. A. E., 782, 1899. **To-e-ne-ches.**—Barbour (1852) in Sen. Ex. Doc. 4, 32d Cong., spec. sess., 254, 1853. **Tollinches.**—Johnston (1851) in Sen. Ex. Doc. 61, 32d Cong., 1st sess., 22, 1852.

Talio. The name, according to Boas, of 4 Bellacoola towns (Koapk, Nuiku, Aseik, and Talio) at the head of S. Bentinck Arm, Brit. Col. The people of these towns, or the Táliómh, were divided into 4 gentes—Hamtsit, Ialostimot, Spatsatlt, and Tumkoaakyas. In 1909 they were reported as numbering 281 in two towns,

Kinisquit and Bellacoola (or Palamey), under the Northwest Coast agency, the town of Talio apparently having become extinct.

Taléomχ.—Boas in Petermanns Mitteil., pt. 5, 130, 1887. **Talicomish.**—Tolmie and Dawson, Vocabs. Brit. Col., 122B, 1884. **Tā′lio.**—Boas in Mem. Am. Mus. Nat. Hist., II, 49, 1900. **Tālio′mH.**—Boas in 7th Rep. N. W. Tribes Can., 3, 1891. **Tallion.**—Can. Ind. Aff., pt. II, 162, 1901. **Tallium.**—Ibid., 1889, 272, 1890. **Talomey.**—Ibid., pt. II, 70, 1904. **Taluits.**—Brit. Col. map, Ind. Aff., Victoria, 1872.

Talipsehogy. A former Upper Creek town in Alabama, with 19 heads of families in 1832.—Schoolcraft, Ind. Tribes, IV, 578, 1854.

Talirpingmiut ('inhabitants of the right side'). A subdivision of the Okomiut Eskimo, residing on the w. shore of Cumberland sd. Pop. 86 in 1883. Their villages are Umanaktuak, Idjorituaktuin, Nuvajen, and Karusuit. Koukdjuaq was a former village.

Talirpingmiut.—Boas in 6th Rep. B. A. E., 426, 1888. Tellirpingmiut.—Boas in Trans. Anthr. Soc. Wash., III, 96, 1885.

Talisman. See *Fetish, Oyaron, Palladium.*

Talitui. A former Kaiyuhkhotana village on Tlegon r., Alaska.

Tallily.—Zagoskin, Desc. Russ. Poss. Am., map, 1842. Ttalitui.—Zagoskin quoted by Petroff, Rep. on Alaska, 37, 1884.

Talking Rock (trans. of Cherokee *Nûñ′yû′-gûñwani′skĭ*, 'rock that talks'). A former Cherokee settlement or settlements on Talking Rock cr., an affluent of Coosawatee r., N. Ga. The town-house was situated about a mile above the present Talking Rock station on the w. side of the railroad. The name refers, according to one informant, to an echo rock somewhere on the stream below the present railroad station.—Mooney in 19th Rep. B. A. E., 417, 1900.

"Talks and Thoughts." See *Hampton Normal and Agricultural Institute.*

Tallapoolina. A Chumashan village formerly at Rancho Viejo, Ventura co., Cal.—Taylor in Cal. Farmer, May 4, 1860.

Tall Bull (*Hotóa-qa-ihoŏis*). A name hereditary among the Cheyenne and borne at different periods by several distinguished men, of whom the most noted was a prominent leader of the hostile Dog Soldier band, the principals in the outbreak of 1868–69. After nearly a year of savage raiding along the Kansas border, they were completely routed by Gen. E. A. Carr, with part of the Fifth cavalry and a detachment of Pawnee scouts, on July 11, 1869, at Summit Springs cr., N. E. Colorado, Tall Bull being among the slain. See *Cheyenne.* (J. M.)

Tallulah (strictly *Tălulŭ′*). The name of two former Cherokee settlements, one, ancient, situated on the upper part of Tallulah r., in Rabun co., Ga.; the other on Tallulah cr. of Cheowa r., in Graham co., N. C. The word is of uncertain etymology. In documents from the Lower dialect it is spelled with an r. (J. M.)

Taruraw.—Mooney in 19th Rep. B. A. E., pt. I, 533, 1900 (early form). **Toruro.**—Ibid. **Tulloolah.**—Doc. of 1799 quoted by Royce in 5th Rep. B. A. E., 144, 1887. **Turoree.**—Mooney, op. cit. **Turrurar.**—Royce, op. cit., map. **Turruraw.**—Mouzon's map of 1771 quoted by Royce, op. cit.

Talmamiche (*Tal′-ma-mi′-tce*). A Takelma band or village on the s. side of Rogue r., Oreg.—Dorsey in Jour. Am. Folk-lore, III, 235, 1890.

Taloffa Ockhase (*talófa* 'town', *úχ′hasi* 'lake': 'Lake town,' from its situation). A former Seminole town about 30 m. w. s. w. from the upper part of L. George, probably in Marion co., Fla.

TaloffaOckhase.—Romans, Fla., 280, 1775. Tolofa.—Jesup (1837) in H. R. Doc. 78, 25th Cong., 2d sess., 108, 1838.

Talohlafia. The Parrot (Macaw?) clan of Taos pueblo, N. Mex.

Talotlafia tai′na.—M. C. Stevenson, notes, B. A. E., 1910 (*tai′na*= 'people').

Talomeco (Creek: *talua* 'town', *miko* 'chief'). A former town in the vicinity of Savannah r., S. C., visited by De Soto early in 1540, and described by Garcilasso de la Vega (Florida, 130, 1723) as containing 500 well-built but abandoned houses and also a very large "temple," in which were deposited the remains of the caciques, etc. It probably belonged to the Chiaha.

Talon. A division of the Ottawa on Manitoulin id., in L. Huron, that afterward moved to Michilimackinac, Mich., on account of Iroquois hostility.—Lahontan (1703) quoted in N. Y. Doc. Col. Hist., IX, 176, note, 1855.

Talonapin ('fresh meat necklace'). A band of the Hunkpapa Sioux.

Fresh meat necklace people.—Culbertson in Smithson. Rep. 1850, 141, 1851. Ta-lo′-na-pi.—Hayden, Ethnog. and Philol. Mo. Val., 376, 1862. Talo-na p′iⁿ.—Dorsey in 15th Rep. B. A. E., 221, 1897.

Talotunne (*Ta-lo′ ɥûnnĕ*). A Takelma band or village on the s. side of Rogue r., Oreg.—Dorsey in Jour. Am. Folk-lore, III, 235, 1890.

Talpahoka. A former Choctaw town on a western affluent of Chickasawhay r., probably in Jasper co., Miss.—Romans, Florida, 329, 1775.

Talpatqui. An Apalachee town named in a letter from the chief of the tribe to the King of Spain in 1688.—Gatschet, Creek Migr. Leg., I, 76, 1884.

Talsunme ('large acorn'). A former village of the Chastacosta on the N. side of Rogue r., Oreg.

Tăl-sûn′-mĕ.—Dorsey, MS. Chasta Costa vocab., B. A. E., 1884. Ta′-sun-ma′ ɥûnnĕ.—Dorsey in Jour. Am. Folk-lore, III, 234, 1890.

Taltushtuntude. An Athapascan tribe or band that formerly lived on Galice cr., Oreg. They were scattered in the same country as the Takelma, whom they had probably overrun. In 1856 they were removed to Siletz res., where 18 survived in 1877.

Galeese Creek Indians.—Treaty of 1854 in U. S Ind. Treaties, 978, 1873. Galice Creek.—Ind. Aff.

Rep., 300, 1877. **Galleace Creek.**—Palmer in Ind. Aff. Rep. 1856, 214, 1857. **Gleese Cleek.**—Everette, Tutu MS. vocab., B. A. E., 1883. **Grease Creeks.**—Ind. Aff. Rep., 494, 1865. **Kû-lǐs′-kǐtc hǐto′lûm.**—Dorsey, Alsea MS. vocab., B. A. E., 1884. **Tal′-tac ʒûnnĕ.**—Dorsey, Tutu and Chastacosta MS. vocabs., B. A. E., 1884 (Tutu, Chastacosta, and Mishikhwutmetunne name). **Tal′-t′ûc-tûn tû′-de.**—Dorsey, Galice Cr. MS. vocab., B. A. E., 1884 (own name). **Taⁿǫl′-tăc ʒûnnĕ.**—Dorsey, Naltunnetunne MS. vocab., B. A. E., 1884 (Naltunnetunne name).

Taluachapkoapopka ('town where peas are eaten'). A former Seminole town on Pease cr., a short distance w. of lower St Johns r., Fla. Apopka, in w. Orange co., probably occupies its site.

Tal-lau-gue chapco pop-cau.—Hawkins (1799), Sketch, 25, 1848. **Tolocchopka.**—Gaines (1836) in H. R. Doc. 78, 25th Cong., 2d sess., 363, 1838. **Tolopchopko.**—Ibid., map, 768–9.

Taluamikagi. The towns controlled by the peace or white clans, forming one of the two great divisions of the Creek settlements. They were governed by civil officers only, and according to earlier authors were considered as places of refuge for criminals. The following are said to have been the peace towns: Hitchiti, Oakfuski (and 7 branch villages), Kasihta, Abihka, Abikudshi, Talasse, Okchayi, Lutchapoga, Tuskegee, Assilanapi, and Wewoka. Cf. *Kipaya*.   (A. S. G.)

E-tall-wau.—Hawkins (1779), Sketch, 52, 1842. **White towns.**—Ibid.

Taluathlako ('large town'). A town of the Creek Nation, on the North Fork, at the mouth of Alabama cr., Okla.—Gatschet, Creek Migr. Leg., II, 186, 1888.

Tam. The Antelope clan of the Tigua pueblo of Isleta, N. Mex.

T′am-t′aínïn.—Lummis quoted by Hodge in Am. Anthr., IX, 348, 1896 (*t′aínïn*='people').

Tama. The native name of one of the administrative functionaries of the Hasinai. The word was adopted by the Spaniards of Texas and applied quite generally to similar officers among other Indians. The *tamas* were messengers, policemen, and overseers; they prepared materials for ceremonies, ran from house to house calling people together for festivals and meetings, notified them when they must help with communal labor, and stood by to see that each did his part. Speaking of this last function, Jesus María says of them: "These are the ones who hasten affairs; the lazy they whip on the legs with rods" (Jesus María, Relación, MS., 1691; Espinosa, Chrónica Apostólica, 420, 421, 431, 1746).   (H. E. B.)

Tama. See *Taimah*.

Tamaha ('rising moose'). A noted chief of the Mdewakanton Sioux, who lived in the region of Blue Earth and Mille Lacs in Minnesota. He was born on the site of Winona, Minn., about 1775, and in the early part and middle of the last century was one of the chief men of his tribe. He seems to have maintained throughout his long life an excellent reputation for honesty. In childhood, while at play, he sustained the loss of an eye, on which account the French nicknamed him "Le Borgne," or "One Eye," and the English "the One-Eyed Sioux." In 1806–07 he met and formed a great admiration for Lieut. Z. M. Pike, and so constantly did he sing the praises of his white friend that the Indians, with a sense of humor worthy a modern punster, changed the pronunciation of the last syllable of his name from *haw* to *hay*, which made the name signify "pike," the fish. Because of his attachment for Pike, he is said to have been the only Sioux Indian, with one exception, whose sympathies were with the Americans, and who did active service for them during the War of 1812. In this crisis, when Joseph Renville and the old Little Crow led their Sioux followers against the United States forces, Tahama refused to join them. At this period he made his way to St Louis, and at the solicitation of General Clarke, then Indian Commissioner, he entered the service of the United States as a scout and messenger. He returned in 1814 with Manuel Lisa, when the latter was on his way to confer with the Missouri River Indians, and, parting with him at the mouth of James r., carried dispatches to the Americans at Prairie du Chien, Wis. Through many privations and discouragements he remained loyal to the United States and faithfully performed the duties assigned him. While on one of his trips to Prairie du Chien, Tamaha was imprisoned by Col. Robert Dickson, an Indian trader, and at that time an officer in the service of the British, who, under threat of death, attempted to compel him to divulge information relative to the Americans; but Tamaha would not yield. After a term of imprisonment he was released and again visited St Louis in 1816. On this visit he was present at the council held by General Clarke with the forty-six chiefs from the upper Missouri, who had returned with Manuel Lisa. On this occasion General Clarke presented him with a medal of honor and a captain's uniform, and commissioned him chief of the Sioux nation. He is said to have been a man of fine physique and much natural dignity, and an orator of unusual ability. One of his peculiarities was to wear always a stovepipe hat. Until his death, at Wabasha, Minn., in April, 1860, at the age of 85, he was much respected, not only by the whites but by his own people. His name is also written Tahama, Tahamie, Tammahaw. By the French he was called Orignal Levé, the translation of his native designation.   (D. R. C. T.)

Tamakwa (*Ta-mä′-kwa*, 'beaver', lit. 'wood-cutter'). A gens of the Abnaki.—Morgan, Anc. Soc., 174, 1878.

Tamakwapi ('beaver man'). A clan, class, or division, probably of the Delawares, mentioned in the Walam Olum in contradistinction to southerners, wolfmen, hunters, priests, and others.—Brinton, Lenape Leg., 187, 1885.

Beaver-men.—Squier in Beach, Ind. Miscel., 29, 1877. Tamakwapis.—Ibid.

Tamal. A Moquelumnan or Miwok term, signifying 'bay,' used by the division of that family which occupied the coast region immediately N. of San Francisco bay and comprising the greater part of Marin co., Cal. It was applied by them to any bay, but particularly to the largest bay with which they were familiar, what is now known as Tomales bay. Tomales is simply a rendition of the original Indian term in a modified Spanish orthography. The name survives also in Tomales point and the town of Tomales. Mt Tamalpais is an aboriginal name and comes from this term, *tamal* 'bay', and *pais* 'mountain'. The name Tamal and various modifications of it were applied to certain of the neophytes at San Rafael and Sonoma missions. Most of these, it is supposed, came from the vicinity of Tomales bay, or at least from w. of the missions and in the direction of that bay.　　　　　　(s. a. b.)

Tamal.—Chamisso in Kotzebue, Voy., III, 51, 1821. Tamalenos.—Taylor in Cal. Farmer, Mar. 2, 1860. Tamales.—Ibid. Tamallos.—Ibid., Mar. 30. Tamals.—Choris, Voy. Pitt., 6, 1822. Tammalanos.—Taylor, op. cit., Mar. 30. Tomales.—Ibid., Oct. 18, 1861.

Tamali (*Tama'li*). The name of two places, and probably settlements there situated, in the Cherokee country. One was on Valley r., a few miles above Murphy, about the present Tomatola, in Cherokee co., N. C.; the other was on Little Tennessee r., about Tomotley ford, a few miles above Tellico r., in Monroe co., Tenn. The name can not be translated and may be of Creek origin, as that tribe had a town of the same name on lower Chattahoochee r.　　　　(j. m.)

Tamahle.—Bartram, Travels, 372, 1792 (the second or Tennessee town). Tama'li.—Mooney in 19th Rep. B. A. E., 534, 1900. Ta-mé-tah.—Adair, Am. Inds., 257, 1775 (possibly identical). Timotlee.—Royce in 5th Rep. B. A. E., map, 1887. Tomatly.—Doc. of 1755 quoted by Royce, ibid., 142. Tomatola.—Mooney, op. cit. Tommotley.—Timberlake, Memoirs, map, 1765 (on Little Tennessee r.). Tomothle.—Bartram, Travels, 371, 1792 (the N. C. town).

Tamali (*Támá'li*). A former Lower Creek town on Chattahoochee r., 7 m. above Ocheses, probably in Russell co., Ala.

Támá'li.—Gatschet, Creek Migr. Leg., I, 145, 1884. Tamatles.—Morse, Rep. to Sec. War, 364, 1822. Tum-mault-lau.—Hawkins (1799), Sketch, 26, 1848.

Tamanee, Tamanend. See *Tammany.*

Tamanos. A term used to designate shamanistic power, and applied in descriptions of the customs of the tribes of Oregon, Washington, and British Columbia, or of the region in which the Chinook jargon was spoken. The word is derived from Chinook *it!amā'noas*, designating "beings endowed with supernatural power." The Indian word is not equivalent to terms expressing magic power, like *wakanda* of the Siouan tribes, *orenda* of the Iroquois, *naualak* of the Kwakiutl. In the Indian languages of this region, and particularly in Chinook, the term is not applied to designate the shaman, but in literary usage it has come to mean shamanistic acts and all the performances belonging to the secret societies of the N. Pacific coast. Witchcraft is often designated as "black tamanos," while the art of the shaman as a healer is sometimes designated as "white tamanos." In the latter part of the 19th century the word passed out of use among the Lower Chinook, because a person of a name similar to the word *it!amā'noas* died, and in accordance with their custom another word was substituted.　　　　(f. b.)

Tamaque ('beaver'). A famous Delaware chief, of the Unalachtigo tribe, commonly called The Beaver, or King Beaver. He was a brother of the no less famous Shingass, who was one of the most cruel and crafty foes of the settlers in w. Pennsylvania during the years of Indian hostility. The chief place of residence of "King Beaver" was at the mouth of Beaver r., at the place called Shingis Town, and later called "The Beaver's Town" (see *Sawcunk, Tuscarawas*). He also had a place of residence at Kuskuski, and spent part of his time at Kittanning. When the English took possession of Ft Duquesne he moved to Ohio, where his village, near the junction of the Tuscarawas and Big Sandy, was called "The Beaver's Town." He was friendly to the English until after Braddock's defeat (1755), when he allied himself with the French. When Post made his journey in 1758 to the western Indians, "King Beaver," as he calls him, was the chief speaker in all the councils held at Kuskuski. On Post's second mission to the Ohio, in advance of Forbes' expedition (Nov. 1758), he carried letters addressed by General Forbes to "Brethren, Kings Beaver and Shingsa" (Thwaites, Early West. Trav., I, 267, 1904). He at that time spoke of the desire of the Indians to resume their alliance with the English. He was present at the council held at Ft Pitt in the fall of 1759 by Gen. Stanwix, and also at that held by Gen. Moncton in Aug. 1760 (Rupp, Hist. West. Pa., app., 139, 1846). In 1762 Beaver and Shingas sent word to the Governor of Pennsylvania that it was their desire to remain friendly with the English, and in the same year he promised to deliver all the white prisoners with the Indians at Ft Pitt. Col. Burd and Josiah Davenport were appointed commissioners to receive them (Col. Rec. Pa., VIII, 776, 1852). At the beginning of Pontiac's conspiracy he was a leading character in the Indian raids upon the frontier settlements. After Boquet's expedition to the Muskingum in 1764 he entered into a half-hearted peace with the English. In his later years he came under the influence of the Moravian missionaries, and was a zealous convert to Christianity before his death, about 1770.   (G. P. D.)

Tamaroa (Illinois: *Tämaro'wa*, said to mean 'cut tail,' or, lit., 'he has a cut tail,' probably referring to some totemic animal, such as the bear or the wildcat; cognate with Abnaki *tĕmaruwê*.—Gerard). A tribe of the Illinois confederacy. In 1680 they occupied the country on both sides of the Mississippi about the mouths of the Illinois and Missouri rs. They were always friendly to the French, who made their village a stopping place on journeys between Canada and Louisiana. Their enemies were the Chickasaw, who attacked them continually, and the Shawnee. They disappeared as a tribe before the beginning of the 19th century. Hennepin estimated them about 1680 at 200 families.

Camaroua.—Neill, Minn., 173, 1858. Mahoras.—Hennepin, New Discov., 255, 1698. Maroa.—La Salle (1679) in Margry, Déc., I, 479, 1875. Marohans.—Hennepin, op. cit., 186. Marota.—La Salle (1681) in Margry, Déc., II, 134, 1877. Tabaroas.—Barcia, Ensayo, 247, 1723. Tamarais.—Chauvignerie (1736) quoted by Schoolcraft, Ind. Tribes, III, 555, 1853. Tamarcas.—La Tour, map, 1782 (misprint). Tamaroa.—La Salle (1679) in Margry, Déc., I, 479, 1875. Tamarohas.—Tailhan in Perrot, Mém., 221, note, 1869. Tamarois.—Chauvignerie (1736) in N. Y. Doc. Col. Hist., IX, 1057, 1855. Tamarojas.—Iberville (1700) in Margry, Déc., IV, 404, 1880. Tamaronas.—Drake, Bk. Inds., xi, 1848. Tamarones.—Domenech Deserts N. Am., I, 444, 1860. Tamaronos.—Kingsley, Stand. Nat. Hist., pt. 6, 151, 1883. Tamaroras.—La Tour, map, 1779 (misprint). Tamaroua.—Iberville (1702) in Margry, Déc., IV, 601, 1880. Tamarouha.—Gravier (ca. 1700) in Shea, Early Voy., 117, 1861. Tamarous.—Perkins and Peck, Annals of the West, 680, 1850. Tamawas.—McKenney and Hall, Ind. Tribes, III, 79, 1854 (misprint). Tamoria.—Vincennes treaty (1803) in Am. State Pap., Ind. Aff., I, 687, 1832. Tamorois.—Schoolcraft, Ind. Tribes, II, 588, 1852. Tavaroas.—Tonti, Rel. de la Louisiane, 136, 1720. Temorais.—Harrison (1814) quoted by Drake, Tecumseh, 160, 1852. Temorias.—Keane in Stanford, Compend., 538, 1878. Tmarois.—De l'Isle, map (ca. 1705) in Neill, Hist. Minn., 1858. Tomaroas.—Boudinot, Star in the West, 129, 1816.

Tamaroa. The principal village of the Tamaroa, at or near the site of East St Louis, Ill. It was the seat of a French mission about 1700.

Tamarox. A village, presumably Costanoan, formerly connected with San Juan Bautista mission, Cal. — Engelhardt, Franc. in Cal., 398, 1897.

Tamazula (from Nahuatl *tamazulin*, 'toad,' and the termination of abundance, *la*, a corruption of *tla*: 'place where toads abound.'—Buelna). A former settlement of the Guazave on the w. bank of the Rio Sinaloa, 6 m. N. of Chino, about lat. 25° 30′, N. w. Sinaloa, Mex.

Tamachola.—Buelna, Peregrinacion de los Aztecas, 112, 1891 (said to have been the aboriginal name at the time of the conquest). Tamazula.—Orozco y Berra, Geog., 332, 1864. Tamotchala.—Buelna, op. cit.

Tamcan. A tribe named in 1708 in a list of those that had been met or heard of N. of San Juan Bautista mission on the lower Rio Grande (Fr. Isidro Felix de Espinosa, Relación Compendiosa of the Rio Grande missions, MS. in the College of Santa Cruz de Querétaro). The name may perhaps be a form of Tonkawa or of Tacame.   (H. E. B.)

Tamceca. A province or tribe on the Carolina coast, visited by Ayllon in 1521, at which time it was under a chief named Datha.—Barcia, Ensayo, 5, 1723.

Tamelan Kyaiyawan (*Támĕlan K'yai-yawan*, 'where tree boles stand in the midst of the waters'). One of the mythic settling places of the Zuñi tribe after the emergence of its people from the underworld.—Cushing in 13th Rep. B. A. E., 390, 1896.

Tamichopa (so called because of the great quantity of common reed grass which grows in the lowlands along the river.—Rudo Ensayo). A former Opata village on a plateau on the N. side of the upper Rio Yaqui, a few miles from Baserac, N. E. Sonora, Mexico. It was inhabited until 1758, when the Apache compelled its abandonment. It was a visita of Baserac mission. See Bandelier in Arch. Inst. Papers, III, 58, 1890; IV, 522–23, 1892.

Tamitzopa.—Rudo Ensayo (ca. 1762), Guiteras trans., 217, 1894.

Taminy. See *Tammany*.

Tamique. One of the two tribes, the other being the Aranama (Xaraname), for which mission Espíritu Santo de Zúñiga was founded in 1726, on its removal from Lavaca r., near Matagorda bay, Texas. The new site, called by Bustillo y Zevallos, who moved the mission, "the land of the Xaraname," is still marked by the mission ruins at Mission Valley, Victoria co., on Guadalupe r. (not on the San Antonio, as Bancroft and his followers say), about 35 m. from its mouth. From the close association of the Xaraname and the Tamique it is inferred that this was the native home of the latter also (Letters of Bustillo y Zevallos, June 18, 1726, and Pérez de Almazán, July 11, to the Viceroy, MSS. in Archivo General, Prov. Intern., CCXXXVI. The letters just cited settle the hitherto undetermined point as to the date of the removal of the mission. On Apr. 15, 1725, the Viceroy ordered Capt. Bustillo y Zevallos, of the presidio of Loreto, to confer with Governor Pérez de Almazán concerning the removal of Loreto and the adjacent mission to a better site. The conference took place early in Apr. 1726, when the two officers together selected the new location. Before June 18 Bustillo had dug there an acequia for the mission, and the padre from Espíritu Santo had established himself in the new post, planted crops, and begun to attract the Indians. The presidio had not yet been transferred).

The Tamique are quite probably distinct from the Tacame, though it has been surmised that they were identical. The two were given in 1733 as separate tribes by Governor Almazán, who was in a position to know. Nevertheless, according to Bonilla only the Tancame (Tacame) were at Espíritu Santo de Zuñiga mission in 1727, a time when the Tamique are supposed to have been there. This suggests the identity of the two tribes. The Tamique and Xaraname spoke a language different from that of the Karankawan tribes living between themselves and the coast, a fact that was used as an argument for founding mission Nuestra Señora del Rosario as a separate establishment for the latter tribes in 1754 (see Bolton in Tex. Hist. Asso. Quar., x, 1907).

In 1749 Espíritu Santo de Zuñiga mission was again removed, this time to San Antonio r., opposite modern Goliad, the Tamique and the Xaraname going with it. The Xaraname subsequently gave much trouble by deserting, but the Tamique do not figure in the accounts of these difficulties. It can not be because they had become extinct, for a report made by the missionary in 1794 states that they were still at the mission to the number of 25 (Fr. José de Aguilar, quoted in Portillo, Apuntes para la Hist. Antigua de Coahuila y Texas, 308, 1880). The building at Goliad, now popularly designated as "Aranama College," is evidently one of the presidial buildings, and not a part of the mission, as this was across the river.   (H. E. B.)

Tamiquis.—Perez de Almazán, Autos sobre las Providencias, 1733, MS. in Archivo Gen., Prov. Intern., XXXII.

Tamkan. A tribe mentioned by Langsdorff (Voy., II, 163, 1814) as residing inland from the coast of California and as being at enmity with the coast tribes. It possibly belonged to the Costanoan family.

Tammahaw. See *Tamaha.*

Tammany (from *Támanend,* 'the affable.' — Heckewelder). The common form of the name of a noted ancient Delaware chief, written also Tamanee, Tamanen, Tamanend, Tamany, Tamened, Taminy, Temane. In the form of Tamanen his name appears as one of the signers of a deed to William Penn in 1683 for lands not far N. from Philadelphia, within the present Bucks co., Pa.

The missionary Heckewelder, writing in 1817, describes him as the greatest and best chief known to Delaware tribal tradition. "The name of Tamanend is held in the highest veneration among the Indians. Of all the chiefs and great men which the Lenape nation ever had, he stands foremost on the list. But although many fabulous stories are circulated about him among the whites, but little of his real history is known. . . . All we know, therefore, of Tamanend is that he was an ancient Delaware chief, who never had his equal. He was in the highest degree endowed with wisdom, virtue, prudence, charity, affability, meekness, hospitality, in short with every good and noble qualification that a human being may possess. He was supposed to have had an intercourse with the great and good Spirit, for he was a stranger to everything that was bad. . . . The fame of this great man extended even among the whites, who fabricated numerous legends respecting him, which I never heard, however, from the mouth of an Indian, and therefore believe to be fabulous. In the Revolutionary war his enthusiastic admirers dubbed him a saint, and he was established under the name of St. Tammany, the Patron Saint of America. His name was inserted in some calendars, and his festival celebrated on the first day of May in every year." Heckewelder goes on to describe the celebration, which was conducted on Indian lines, including the smoking of the calumet, and Indian dances in the open air, and says that similar "Tammany societies" were afterward organized in other cities. He states also that when Col. George Morgan, of Princeton, N. J., was sent by Congress about the year 1776 upon a special mission to the western tribes, the Delawares conferred upon him the name of Tamanend in remembrance of the ancient chief and as the greatest mark of respect that they could pay to Morgan.

Haines, however (Am. Inds., 658, 1888), in his chapter on the Order of Red Men, quotes a contemporary document from which it appears that the Philadelphia society, which was probably the first bearing the name, and is claimed as the original of the Red Men secret order, was organized May 1, 1772, under the title of "Sons of King Tammany," with strongly Loyalist tendency. It is probable that the "Saint Tammany" society was a later organization of Revolutionary sympathizers opposed to the kingly idea. Saint Tammany parish, La., preserves the memory. The practice of organizing American political and military societies on an Indian basis dates back to the French and Indian war, and was especially in favor among the soldiers of the Revolutionary army, most of whom were frontiersmen more or less familiar with

Indian life and custom. Of several such societies organized about the Revolutionary period the only ones still existing are the secret Improved Order of Red Men (q. v.) and the famous Tammany Society, originally established as a patriotic and charitable organization, but now for many years best known as the dominating factor in the Democratic politics of New York city. It was founded in 1786 by William Mooney, a Revolutionary veteran and former leader of the "Sons of Liberty," and regularly organized with a constitution in 1789 (most of the original members being Revolutionary soldiers), for the purpose of guarding "the independence, the popular liberty, and the federal union of the country," in opposition to the efforts of the aristocratic element, as represented by Hamilton and the Federalists, to make the new government practically a monarchy, with life tenure for President and Senate and a restricted property suffrage. Its two main purposes were declared to be (1) the perpetuity of republican institutions, and (2) the care of Revolutionary soldiers, their widows and orphans, "and of others who might be proper objects of charity." The society—occasionally at first known as the Columbian Order—took an Indian title and formulated for itself a ritual based upon supposedly Indian custom. Thus, the name chosen was that of the traditional Delaware chief; the meeting place was called the "wigwam"; there were 13 "tribes" or branches corresponding to the 13 original states, the New York parent organization being the "Eagle Tribe," New Hampshire the "Otter Tribe," Delaware the "Tiger Tribe," whence the famous "Tammany tiger," etc. The principal officer of each tribe was styled the "sachem," and the head of the whole organization was designated the *kitchi okeemaw*, or grand sachem, which office was held by Mooney himself for more than 20 years. Subordinate officers also were designated by other Indian titles, records were kept according to the Indian system by moons and seasons, and at the regular meetings the members attended in semi-Indian costume.

For the first 30 years of its existence, until the close of the War of 1812, nearly the whole effort of the society was directed to securing and broadening the foundations of the young republic, and it is possible that without Tammany's constant vigilance the National Government could not have survived the open and secret attacks of powerful foes both within and without. In 1790 it was chiefly instrumental in the negotiation of a treaty with the Creek Indians, by which the peace of the southern border was secured.

About the same time it took steps for the establishment of an Indian museum, the germ of the New York Historical Society. In 1808 it collected and gave suitable burial to the bones of the Revolutionary victims of the prison ships at Wallabout bay. In the War of 1812 it furnished three generals to the United States army, and 1,200 men from its own membership for the construction of defenses about New York city. In 1817 it brought back from Canada and interred with fitting ceremony the body of Gen. Richard Montgomery, killed at the siege of Quebec. In 1826, after years of effort, it secured full manhood suffrage in the state of New York, and in 1831 it procured the abolition of imprisonment for debt in New York city. In 1861 it raised from its membership, equipped, and sent to the front, under its own Grand Sachem as colonel, the 42d N. Y. Infantry regiment. The original New York organization still survives, the other branches having long passed out of existence, but of late years it has devoted its energies chiefly to the control of local politics. Its central executive body is known as Tammany Hall. Theoretically the "Society" and the "Hall" are two distinct bodies, the one representing the social and fraternal functions, the other the political "machine"; but as their officership is largely identical, their meetings held in the same "wigwam," and the names similar, the distinction is of minor importance. Consult Heckewelder, Ind. Nations, 1876; Drake, Aboriginal Races of N. Am., 1880; Haines, Am. Ind. (chapter on The Order of Red Men), 1888; Davis, Tammany Hall, in Munsey's Mag., Oct. 1900; Encycl. Americana, art. Tammany, 1904.   (J. M.)

Tammukan. A Cholovone village E. of lower San Joaquin r., Cal.—Pinart, Cholovone MS., 1880.

Tampa. A Calusa village on the s. w. coast of Florida, about 1570, according to Fontaneda (Memoir *ca.* 1575, Smith trans., 19, 1854). He gives it first place in his list of more than 20 Calusa villages and describes it as a large town.

Tamuleko (from *taman*, or *tamalin*, 'north'). A general term, which may be translated "northerners," applied by the Miwok of the southern Sierra Nevada region of California to all the people living to the N. of themselves. The name was applied not only by the Miwok as a whole to a people of another stock living to the N., but the people of any Miwok village employed it in referring to the people of the same stock living in the region perhaps but a few miles N. of themselves. Similarly the people living in the other cardinal directions were called, respectively, Hisotoko, 'easterners,' from *hisum*, 'east'; Chumetoko, 'southerners,' from *chumech*, 'south'; and Olowitok, 'westerners,' from *olowin*, 'west.'　　　　　　　　　　　　(S. A. B.)

Simbalakees.—Bancroft, Nat. Races, I, 363, 1874. **Tamlocklock.**—Ibid., 450. **Tamolécas.**—Powers in Overland Mo., x, 324, 1873. **Ta-mo-le'-ka.**—Powers in Cont. N. A. Ethnol., III, 349, 1877. **Tamuleko.**—S. A. Barrett, inf'n, 1907 (proper form). **Timbalakees.**—Taylor in Cal. Farmer, Mar. 30, 1860. **Yamlocklock.**—Bancroft, op. cit., 450.

Tan (*Tan*). The Sun clans of the Tewa pueblos of San Juan, Santa Clara, San Ildefonso, Tesuque, and Nambe, N. Mex., and Hano, Ariz. That of Nambe is extinct.

Tan-tdóa.—Hodge in Am. Anthr., IX, 352, 1896 (San Juan, Santa Clara, San Ildefonso, and Tesuque form; *tdóa* = 'people'). **Tan-tdóa.**—Ibid. (Nambe form). **Tañ.**—Fewkes, ibid., VII, 166, 1894 (Hano form).

Tanaca. Mentioned by Oviedo (Hist. Gen. Indies, III, 628, 1853) as one of the provinces or villages visited by Ayllon, probably on the South Carolina coast, in 1520.

Tanacharison. See *Half King*.

Tanaha (*Ta'năhă*). The Buffalo clan of the Caddo.

Koho'.—Mooney in 14th Rep. B. A. E., 1093, 1896 (= 'alligator'). **Tánăhă.**—Ibid.

Tanakot. A Kaiyuhkhotana village of 52 inhabitants in 1880 on the right bank of Yukon r., Alaska, near the mouth of Melozi r.

Tahnohkalony.—Baker, Geog. Dict. Alaska, 398, 1901 (cited form). **Tanakhothaiak.**—Petroff in 10th Census, Alaska, map, 1880. **Tanakot.**—Baker, op. cit.

Tanasqui. A Cherokee town visited by Juan Pardo in 1567. The name may be the same as Tănăsī', or Tennessee (q. v.).—Mooney in 19th Rep. B. A. E., 534, 1900.

Tancac. Mentioned by Oviedo (Hist. Gen. Indies, III, 628, 1853) as one of the provinces or villages visited by Ayllon, probably on the South Carolina coast, in 1520.

Tandaquomuc. A Chowanoc (?) village in 1585 at the w. end of Albemarle sd., between the mouths of Chowan and Roanoke rs., in the present Bertie co., N. C.

Tandaquomuc.—Lane's map, 1585, in Hawks, Hist. N. C., I, 1859. **Tantaquomuck.**—Dutch map, 1621, in N. Y. Doc. Col. Hist., I, 1856.

Taneaho. An unidentified village or tribe mentioned to Joutel in 1687 (Margry, Déc., III, 409, 1878) while he was staying with the Kadohadacho on Red r. of Louisiana, by the chief of that tribe, as being among his enemies.

Tanedi (*Tane'dî*, 'people of [the river] Tan'). A division of the Tlingit at Kake, Alaska, belonging to the Raven phratry of that tribe.　　　　　　　　(J. R. S.)

Tanetsukanumanke. One of the Mandan bands.

Good Knife.—Morgan, Anc. Soc., 158, 1877. **Tä-na-tsŭ'-kä.**—Ibid. **Ta-ne-tsu'-ka nu-mañ'-ke.**—Dorsey in 15th Rep. B. A. E., 241, 1897.

Tangdhantangkaenikashika ('those who became human beings by the aid of the large wildcat'). A Quapaw gens.

Panther gens.—Dorsey in 15th Rep. B. A. E., 229, 1897. **Tandꞔan tañ'ꭓa e'nikaci'ꭓa.**—Ibid.

Tangeratsa (*taingees*, 'half,' 'middle;' *atsah*, 'brightish': 'people neither dark nor fair'). One of the castes or classes into which the Kutchakutchin are divided, the others being the Chitsa and the Natesa.—Kirby in Smithson. Rep, 1864, 418, 1865; Hardisty, ibid., 1866. 315, 1872.

A-teet-sa.—Kirby in Hist. Mag., 1st s., VIII, 167, 1864. **Gens de Milieu.**—Whymper, Alaska, map, 1868. **Middle Indians.**—Ross, notes on Tinne, S. I. MS., 474. **Tain-gees-ah-tsah.**—Hardisty, op. cit. **Taitsick-Kutchin.**—Jones in Smithson. Rep. 1866, 323, 1872. **Tanges-at-sa.**—Kirby, ibid., 1864, 418, 1865. **Tchandjœri-Kuttchin.**—Petitot, Dict. Dènè-Dindjié, xx, 1876. **Tenge-rat-sey.**—Jones in Smithson. Rep. 1866, 326, 1872. **Tengratsey.**—Dall, Alaska, 196, 1870. **Teng-rat-si.**—Dall in Cont. N. A. Ethnol., I, 30, 1877. **Tρendjidheyttset-Kouttchin.**—Petitot, Autour du lac des Esclaves, 361, 1891. **Tρion-Kouttchin.**—Ibid. ('people of the water'). **T'tran-jik-kutch-in.**—Ross, MS. notes on Tinne, B. A. E., 474 (trans. 'Big Black river people'). **Zēkā-thaka.**—Richardson, Arct. Exped., I, 398, 1851 (trans. 'people on this side'). **Zi-unka-kutchi.**—Ibid. (trans. 'middle people'). **Ziunka-kutshi.**—Latham, Nat. Races Russ. Emp., 293, 1854.

Tangipahoa (from *tandshi*, 'maize'; *apa*, 'stalk,' 'cob'; *ava*, 'to gather': 'those who gather maize stalks or cobs.'—Wright. Pénicaut explains the river name Tandgepao erroneously as 'white wheat or corn'). An extinct tribe, supposed to be Muskhogean, formerly living on the lower Mississippi and on Tangipahoa r., which flows s. into L. Pontchartrain, s. E. La. Tonti mentions this people as residing, in 1682, on the Mississippi, 12 leagues from the Quinipissa village; but, according to Iberville (Margry, Déc., IV, 168, 1880), the Bayogoula informed him that the Tangipahoa had never lived on the Mississippi; nevertheless both statements agree in making their town one of the 7 villages of the Acolapissa. When La Salle reached their village he found that it had recently been burned, and saw dead bodies lying on one another. According to the information given Iberville by the Bayogoula, the village had been destroyed by the Huma. Nothing definite is known of the language and affinities of the tribe, but their apparent relations with the Acolapissa indicate Muskhogean affinity. Their village was one of those said to belong to the Acolapissa.

Taensapaoa.—Bartram, Trav., 422, 1791. **Tanchipahoe.**—Ellicott (*ca.* 1798), Jour., app., map, 71, 1803 (applied to river). **Tangeboas.**—McKenney and Hall, Ind. Tribes, III, 81, 1854. **Tangibac.**—Hennepin, New Discov., 155, 1698. **Tangibao.**—Iberville (1698) in French, Hist. Coll. La., pt. 2, 23, note, 1875. **Tangibaoas.**—Shea, Cath. Miss., 438, 1855. **Tangibaos.**—Tonti (1682) in French, Hist. Coll. La., I, 63, 1846. **Tan'gipaha'.**—Gatschet quoted by Boyd, Local Names, 46, 1885. **Tangipahos.**—La Harpe (*ca.* 1723) in French, Hist. Coll. La., III, 17, 1851. **Tangipaos.**—Martin, Hist. La., I, 101, 1827. **Tanjibao.**—La Salle in Margry, Déc., II, 198, 1877. **Tansipaho.**—Ellicott (*ca.* 1798), Jour., map, 203, 1803.

Tangouaen. A village where Algonkin and Hurons united for protection against the Iroquois in 1646, perhaps near Georgian bay, Ont.—Jes. Rel. 1646, 76, 1858.

Tangyaka. The Rainbow clan of the Patki (Cloud, or Water-house) phratry of the Hopi.

Tanaka wiñwû.—Fewkes in 19th Rep. B. A. E., 583, 1901 (*wiñwû* = 'clan'). **Ta-ña-ka wün-wû.**—Fewkes in Am. Anthr., VII, 402, 1894.

Tanico. A tribe, or "province," first encountered by the De Soto expedition in 1542, apparently in N. W. Arkansas. They were met also in the same general region by Joutel in 1687. Perhaps identical with the Tunica (q. v.).

Canicons.—La Harpe (1719) in French, Hist. Coll. La., III, 72, 75, 1851. **Tanico.**—Joutel (1687) in Margry, Déc., III, 409, 1878. **Taniquo.**—Joutel, op. cit., 410. **Tanquinno.** — Ibid., 409. **Toniquas.** — Mappa Ind. Occidentalis, Nürnberg, *ca.* 1740.

Tanima (*Tänï′ma*, 'liver-eaters'). A recently extinct division of the Comanche.

Dä-nĕm-mĕ.—Butcher and Leyendecher, Comanche MS. vocab., B. A. E., 1867 (Comanche name). **De-na-vi.**—Comanche and Kiowa treaty, Sen. Ex. Doc., O, 39th Cong., 1st sess., 4, 1866. **De-na-ways.**—Leavenworth (1868) in H. R. Misc. Doc. 139, 41st Cong., 2d sess., 6, 1870 (or Lion [sic] Eaters). **Hai-ne-na-une.**—Schoolcraft, Ind. Tribes, II, 128, 1852 (probably identical; said to mean 'corn eaters'). **Lion Eaters.**—Leavenworth, op. cit. (misprint). **Liver Eater band.**—Comanche and Kiowa treaty, op. cit. **Liver-eaters.**—Neighbors in Schoolcraft, Ind. Tribes, II, 127, 1852. **Tänï′ma.**—Mooney in 14th Rep. B. A. E., 1045, 1896 (correct form). **Tänï′ma.**—Hoffman in Proc. Am. Philos. Soc., XXIII, 300, 1886.

Tanintauei. An Assiniboin band.

Gens des Osayes.—Maximilian, Trav., 194, 1843 ('bone people'). **Tanintauei.**—Ibid.

Tankiteke. A tribe of the Wappinger confederacy formerly living in Westchester co., N. Y., and Fairfield co., Conn., back of the coast. They were sometimes called Pachamis, Pachany, etc., from their chief.

Bachom's country.—Doc. of 1659 in N. Y. Doc. Col. Hist., II, 63, 1858. **Pachany.**—Wassenaar (1632) quoted by Ruttenber, Tribes Hudson R., 80, 1872. **Pachimis.**—Brodhead quoted by Ruttenber, ibid. **Packamins.**—De Laet (1633) in Jones, Ind. Bul., 6, 1867. **Tankitekes.**—Ruttenber, op. cit.

Tanmangile (*Tan′man-gíle*). A Kansa village on Blue r., Kans., and the band that formerly lived there.—J. O. Dorsey, Kansas MS. vocab., B. A. E., 1882.

Tannaouté. An Iroquois village formerly on the N. shore of L. Ontario, Ontario, Canada.

Tannaouté.—Bellin, map, 1755. **Tonnaouté.**—Esnauts and Rapilly map, 1777.

Tannghrishon. See *Half King*.

Tanning. See *Skin and Skin dressing*.

Tano (from *Taháno*, the Tigua form of *T"han-u-ge*, the Tano name for themselves). A former group of Pueblo tribes of New Mexico, whose name has been adopted for the family designation (see *Tanoan Family*). In prehistoric times, according to Bandelier, the Tano formed the southern group of the Tewa, the separation of the two occurring at the ancient village of Tejeuingge Ouiping. In the early historical period the Tano habitat was southward from Santa Fé to the Galisteo basin, a distance of about 20 m.

Coronado passed through the southern part of their territory in 1541, Castañeda describing it as lying between the Quirix (Queres) province and Cicuye (Pecos), and as being almost depopulated on account of depredations by the Teya, a warlike tribe of the plains, 16 years previously. Only 3 pueblos are mentioned by Castañeda as along their route—Ximena (Galisteo), a small, strong village; the Pueblo de los Silos, large, but almost deserted; and another farther eastward, abandoned and in ruins. The last mentioned was probably the one called Coquite by Mota Padilla. In addition to these, however, there were 7 other Tano pueblos in the "snowy mts.," toward Santa Fé.

The Tano were next visited by Espejo, who went eastwardly from the country of the Tigua, in the vicinity of the present Bernalillo, to the province of the Maguas or Magrias (probably a misprint of Tagnos, a form of the Tigua name), in a pine country without running streams, on the borders of the buffalo plains, where he heard news of the death there of Fray Juan de Santa María two years before. As the seat of this friar's missionary labors was Pecos, that pueblo was evidently included by Espejo in his Maguas province, to which he attributed the grossly exaggerated population of 40,000, in 11 pueblos. The accounts of Espejo's journey are unsatisfactory as to directions and distances traveled, and some of the reputed narratives of his expedition are unauthentic. Bandelier regards as the Tano country Espejo's province of Hubates, with 5 pueblos, which he visited, after returning from a western tour, by traveling 12 leagues eastward from the Queres on the Rio Grande. Thence in a day's journey Espejo found the "Tamos" in three large villages, one of which was Pecos. This variance in names is doubtless due to guides speaking different languages. If the number of (Tano) villages given by Castañeda in 1540 is correctly given as 10, and if the number of pueblos mentioned by Espejo in 1583 as contained in his provinces of Hubates and Tamos (7, excluding Pecos) is also correct, then it would seem that the hostility of the Teyas spoken of by Castañeda in 1540 had continued in the interim, and that the Tano had been compelled to abandon three of their settlements. This, however, could not have been the case if the 10 villages (excluding Pecos) in Espejo's province of Maguas is rightly given, as the number agrees with that of Castañeda 40 years before.

In 1630 Benavides estimated the population of the then existing 5 Tano towns at 4,000, all of whom had been baptized. The tribe was almost entirely broken up by the Pueblo revolts of 1680–96, the

Indians removing mainly to the Hopi of Arizona after 1694 and the last tribal remnant in New Mexico dying from smallpox early in the 19th century (Bandelier in Ritch, N. Mex., 201). The Tano language is now spoken only by a few natives settled in the Tewa, Tigua, and Queres pueblos along the Rio Grande, particularly at Santo Domingo.

Following is a list of Tano pueblos so far as known: Ciénega, Dyapige, Galisteo, Guika, Kayepu, Kipana, Kuakaa, Ojana, Paako, Pueblo Blanco, Pueblo Colorado, Pueblo de los Silos, Pueblo Largo, Pueblo Quemado (?), Puerto (?), San Cristóbal, San Lázaro, San Marcos, Sempoapi, Shé, Tuerto, Tungge, Tzemantuo, Tzenatay, Uapige.

Consult Bandelier (1) in Ritch, N. Mex., 201, 1885; (2) Arch. Inst. Papers, III, 125 et seq., 1890; IV, 87 et seq., 1892; (3) Gilded Man, 284, 1893; Bancroft, Ariz. and N. Mex., 1889; Winship, Coronado Exped., 14th Rep. B. A. E., 1896. See *Pueblos, Tewa.*   (F. W. H.)

Gubates.—Mendoza in Hakluyt Soc. Pub., xv, 251, 1854 (after Espejo, 1583). **Habutas.**—Ogilby, America, 295, 1671. **Hubales.**—Sanson, L'Amérique, map, 27, 1657. **Hubates.**—Mendoça, Hist. China (1586), in Hakluyt, Voy., III, 464, 1810. **Hubites.**—Brackinridge, Early Span. Discov., 19, 1857 (misquoting Hakluyt). **Lana.**—Hervas, Idea dell' Universo, XVII, 76, 1784 (name of language; doubtless Tano). **Magrias.**—Espejo (1584) in Doc. Inéd., xv, 156, 1871. **Maguas.**—Ibid., 176 (identified with Tanos by Bandelier in Jour. Am. Eth. and Arch., III, 74, 1892). **Puyatye.**—Bandelier, Delight Makers, 442, 1890; Arch. Inst. Papers, IV, 92, 1892; Gilded Man, 284, 1893 (Queres name). **Tagnos.**—Gregg, Comm. Prairies, I, 124, 1844. **Tahanas.**—Zarate-Salmeron (ca. 1629) quoted by Bancroft, Nat. Races, I, 600, 1882. **Taháno.**—Hodge, field notes, B. A. E., 1895 (Sandia Tigua name). **Tahanos.**—Zarate-Salmeron, op. cit. **Tami.**—Linschoten, Descr. de l'Amérique, map 1, 1638 (probably·identical). **Tanos.**—Benavides, Memorial, 22, 1630. **Thanos.**—Pecos grant (1689) in Arch. Inst. Papers, I, 135, 1881. **T'han-u-ge.**—Bandelier, ibid., IV, 88, 1892 (aboriginal name). **Tubeans.**—Ladd, Story of N. Mex., 92, 1891. **Tubians.**—Davis, Span. Conq. N. Mex., 259, 1869 ("province of the Tubians, otherwise called Hubates"). **Tubirans.**—Davis, misquoted in Bancroft, Ariz. and N. Mex., 88, 1889. **Túven.**—Hodge, field notes, B. A. E., 1895 (Tigua name). **Ubate.**—Mota-Padilla, Hist. de la Conquista, 169, 1742. **Ubates.**—Espejo (1583) in Doc. Inéd., xv, 122, 185, 1871. **Xabotaj.**—Linschoten, Descr. de l'Amérique, map 1, 1638 (probably identical). **Xabotaos.**—Blaeu, Atlas, XII, 62, 1667.

Tanoan Family. A linguistic family consisting of the Tewa, Tano, Tigua, Jemez, and Piro groups of Pueblo Indians, who dwell or dwelt in various substantial villages on and near the Rio Grande in New Mexico. Of the groups mentioned the Tano and the Piro are extinct as tribes, and the Jemez includes the remnant of the former inhabitants of Pecos. Gatschet was of the belief that the Tanoan family is a remote branch of the Shoshonean, but thus far the relationship has not been definitively shown. For information regarding the various divisions, see under their respective names. Consult Powell

in 7th Rep. B. A. E., 121, 1891; Harrington in Am. Anthr., XI, no. 4, 1909.

>**Tay-waugh.**—Lane (1854) in Schoolcraft, Ind. Tribes, v. 689, 1855 (pueblos of San Juan, Santa Clara, Pojuaque, Nambe, "San Il de Conso," and one Moqui [Hopi] pueblo); Keane in Stanford's Compend., Cent. and So. Am., app., 479, 1878. >**Taño.**—Powell in Rocky Mountain Presbyterian, Nov. 1878 (includes Sandia, Téwa, San Ildefonso, San Juan, Santa Clara, Pojoaque, Nambé, Tesuque, Sinecú, Jemez, Taos, Picuri). >**Tegua.**—Keane in Stanford's Compend., Cent. and So. Am., app., 479, 1878 (includes S. Juan, Sta. Clara, Pojuaque, Nambe, Tesugue, S. Ildefonso, Haro [Hano]). =**Téwan.**—Powell in Am. Nat., 605, Aug. 1880 (makes five divisions: 1. Taño (Isleta, Isleta near El Paso, Sandía); 2. Taos (Taos, Picuni [Picuris]); 3. Jemes (Jemes); 4. Tewa or Tehua (San Ildefonso, San Juan, Pojoaque, Nambe, Tesuque, Santa Clara, and one Moki [Hopi] pueblo); 5. Piro). >**E-nagh-magh.**—Lane (1854) in Schoolcraft, Ind. Tribes, v, 689, 1855 (includes Taos, Vicuris, Zesuqua, Sandia, Ystete, and two pueblos near El Paso, Texas). Keane in Stanford's Compend., Cent. and So. Am., app., 479, 1878 (follows Lane, but identifies Texan pueblos with Lentis? and Socorro?). >**Picori.**—Keane in Stanford's Compend., Cent. and So. Am., app., 479, 1878 (or Enaghmagh). =**Stock of Rio Grande Pueblos.**—Gatschet in U. S. Geog. Surv. W. 100th Mer., VII, 415, 1879. =**Rio Grande Pueblo.**—Gatschet in Mag. Am. Hist., 258, 1882.

Tanom. A branch of the Yuki which lived on the E. side of Eel r., about w. of Round valley, central Cal. They were neighbors of the Athapascan Wailaki, and in their most important ceremony resembled these rather than the other Yuki.   (A. L. K.)

Tanotenne ('people a short distance to the north'). A band of the Takulli, apparently officially known as the Ft George band, under Babine and Upper Skeena agency, at the junction of Stuart and Fraser rs., Brit. Col., numbering 130 in 1892, 124 in 1909, in the village of Leitli. Their other village, Chinlak, was destroyed by the Tsilkotin. They have extensive hunting grounds E. of Fraser r. as far as the Rocky and Caribou mts.

Aunghim.—Lennard, Brit. Col., 213, 1862. **Ta-notenne.**—Morice, letter, B. A. E., 1890 ('people a short distance to the north'). **Tsatsnótin.**—Hale, Ethnol. and Philol., 202, 1846. **Tsatsuotin.**—McDonald, Brit. Col., 126, 1862.

Tanpacuazes. A tribe named in 1780 by Cabello, governor of Texas, as one of those living on the coast between the Rio Grande and the Nueces. It was perhaps one of the Coahuiltecan tribes of that region known by some other name (Cabello, Rep. on Coast Tribes, May 28, 1780, MS. in Bexar Archives, cited by H. E. Bolton, inf'n, 1908).

Tanques (Span. *Los Tanques*, 'the tanks,' 'water-holes,' 'pools'). A ruined pueblo, probably of the Tigua, on the Rio Grande, near Albuquerque, N. Mex.—Loew (1875) in Wheeler Surv. Rep., VII, 338, 1879.

Tantucquask. A village of the Powhatan confederacy in 1608 on Rappahannock r., in Richmond co., Va.—Smith (1629), Va., I, map, repr. 1819.

Tanunak. A Nunivagmiut Eskimo village and Jesuit mission near C. Vancouver, Nelson id., Alaska. Pop. 8 in 1880, 48 in 1890.

Dununuk.—11th Census, Alaska, 110, 1893. **Tanunak.**—Petroff, Rep. on Alaska, 54, 1880.—**Tunnuk.**—Nelson in 18th Rep. B. A. E., map, 1899.

Tanwakanwakaghe. An ancient Osage village at the junction of Grand and Osage rs., Mo.

Ṭaⁿ wá-k'aⁿ wa-ɧá-xe.—Dorsey, Osage MS. vocab., B. A. E., 1883.

Tanwanshinka ('small village'). An ancient Osage village situated on Neosho r., Okla. In the year 1850, when De Smet visited the Osage, the village contained 300 persons.

Cawva-Shinka.—De Smet, W. Miss., 365, 1856 ('little town'). **Little Town.**—Ibid. **Taⁿwaⁿ oiñɧa.**—Dorsey, Osage MS. vocab., B. A. E., 1883.

Tanxnitania (from Powhatan *tanx*, 'little'). A tribe of the Manahoac confederacy, living in 1608 in Fauquier co., Va., on the N. side of upper Rappahannock r.

Tanxsnitania.—Smith (1629), Va., I, map, 1819. **Tanxsnitanians.** — Strachey (*ca.* 1612), Va., 104, 1849. **Tauxanias.**—Smith, op. cit., 134. **Tauxilnanians.**—Boudinot, Star in the West, 129, 1816. **Tauxitanians.**—Jefferson, Notes, 179, 1801. **Tauxsintania.**—Simons in Smith (1629), Va., I, 186, 1819. **Tauxuntania.**—Ibid.

Tanyi. The Calabash clans of the Keresan pueblos of Acoma, Sia, San Felipe, and Cochiti, N. Mex. That of Acoma forms a phratry with the Showwiti (Parrot) and Hapanyi (Oak) clans. The dialectal variations in pronunciation of the name are: Acoma, Tányï-hánoqᶜʰ; Sia and San Felipe, Tányï-háno; Cochiti, Tányi-hánuch (Hodge in Am. Anthr., IX, 349, 1896). According to Bandelier (Arch. Inst. Papers, III, 301, 1890) the Calabash clan, since the beginning of the 19th century, seems to represent what might be called the progressive element. Cf. *Shuwimi.*

Táñe.—Stevenson in 11th Rep. B. A. E., 19, 1894 (Sia form). **Tanyi hanutsh.**—Bandelier, Delight Makers, 28, 1890.

Tao. The Beaver gens of the Caddo.—Mooney in 14th Rep. B. A. E., 1093, 1896.

Taoapa. A band of Mdewakanton Sioux formerly living on Minnesota r. in the present Scott co., Minn., and hunting between it and the Mississippi. Their village, generally known as Shakopee's Village, or Little Six's Village, from the chief of the band, was on the left bank of the river and the cemetery on the opposite side in 1835. See *Shakopee.*

Little Six.—Ind. Aff. Rep., 282, 1854. **Sha-kapee's band.**—Blackmore in Jour. Ethnol. Soc. Lond., I, 318, 1869. **Shakopee.**—Minn. Hist. Soc. Coll., III, pt. 1, 132, 1870. **Shăkpá.**—Long, Exped. St Peter's R., I, 385, 1824 ('Six': chief's name). **Shākpay.**—Featherstonhaugh, Canoe Voy., I, 286, 1847. **Shokpay.**—Neill, Hist. Minn., xliv, 1858. **Shokpaydan.**—Ibid., 590 (name of the chief). **Shokpedan.**—Warren in Minn. Hist. Coll., v, 156, note, 1885. **Six.**—Featherstonhaugh, Canoe Voy., I, 286, 1847. **Taoapa.**—Long, Exped. St. Peter's R., I, 385, 1824. **The Six.**—Minn. Hist. Soc. Coll., III, 154, 1874. **Village of Sixes.**—Featherstonhaugh, Canoe Voy., II, 4, 1847. **Xa-kpe-dan.**—Neill, Hist. Minn., 144, note, 1858.

Taol-naas-hadai (*Taol na′as xǎ′da-i*, 'Rainbow-house people'). A subdivision of the Ao-keawai, a Haida family belonging to the Raven clan; named from a house. They belonged to the Alaskan group, or Kaigani.—Swanton, Cont. Haida, 272, 1905.

Taos (Span. pl. adaptation of *Tŏwíh*, its Tewa name). A Tigua pueblo consisting of two house groups, known as North town (Hlauuma) and South town (Hlaukwima), on both sides of Taos r., an E. tributary of the Rio Grande, in Taos co., N. Mex., 52 m. N. E. of Santa Fé. The native name of the pueblo is Tŭatá; of the people, Taínamu. The pueblo is also called *Yahlahaimubahutulba*, 'Red-willow place.' It was first visited in 1540 by Hernando de Alvarado, and in 1541 by Francisco de Barrionuevo, both of Coronado's army, who called it Braba (seemingly a miscopying of Tuata), Yuraba, and Uraba (perhaps intended for the Pecos form Yulata), as well as Valladolid, the last, no doubt, on account of some fancied resemblance to the Spanish city of that name. Taos did not then stand in the spot it occupies to-day, but a few hundred yards to the N. E., and on both sides of the stream as now. One of the narratives of Coronado's expedition (Rel. del Suceso, 14th Rep. B. A. E., 575, 1896) described the town, under the name Yuraba, as having 18 divisions, each with "a situation as if for two ground plots; the houses are very close together, and have five or six stories, three of them with mud walls and two or three with thin wooden walls, which become smaller as they go up, and each one has its little balcony outside of the mud walls, one above the other, all around, of wood. In this village, as it is in the mountains, they do not raise cotton nor breed fowls [turkeys]; they wear the skins of deer and cows [buffalo] entirely. It is the most populous village of all that country; we estimated there were 15,000 persons in it." This estimate is certainly greatly exaggerated.

Taos was visited also in 1598 by Oñate, who applied to it its first saint name—San Miguel. It became the seat of the Spanish mission of San Gerónimo early in the 17th century, and in the middle of the century some families moved to the Jicarillas, at a place called El Quartelejo, in the present Scott co., Kans., but were subsequently brought back by Juan de Archuleta. In the Pueblo revolt of 1680–92 Taos took a conspicuous part. It was the central point from which Popé (q. v.) disseminated his doctrine of independence from Spanish authority, and was one of the first adherents to this cause. On Aug. 10, 1680, the day the outbreak began, the Taos warriors joined those of Picuris and the Tewa in the murder of their priests, as well as of all the colonists on which they could lay hands, and then proceeded to Santa Fé, where they formed part of the 3,000 Pueblos who laid siege to that town for 5 days, when Gov. Otermin succeeded in beating them off and in beginning his retreat to El Paso. All the Pueblos remained independent of the Spaniards until 1692, when Vargas reconquered the province. On his visiting Taos in October the Indians ran away, but were induced to return, professing friendship. After several conflicts with the Tewa in the following year (1693), Vargas again visited Taos on July 3, finding it abandoned, the Indians having taken refuge in a near-by canyon, after placing crosses on their property to command for it respect from the Spaniards. Attempts to negotiate with the natives proving a failure, Vargas sacked their village, taking much corn. Before the close of 1694

revolt of 1680 the population of Taos was about 2,000.

Owing to its situation on the northern frontier, Taos became an important trading rendezvous for the surrounding tribes, and its people also experienced several disastrous conflicts with the Ute, and in 1766 with the Comanche. To these hostilities was doubtless partly due the reduction of the once comparatively large population to 515 in 1910. See *Pueblos*.

In 1847 occurred what is known as the Taos rebellion. Instigated by Mexicans, whose ill feeling for the Americans had been aroused by the Mexican war, the Taos warriors, on Jan. 17, attacked and cruelly killed Gov. Charles Bent and other residents of the near-by Mexican settlement of Fernandez de Taos, and, joined by Mexicans, murdered all but one of nine Americans at Turley's mill, 12

PUEBLO OF TAOS

peace again reigned, many of the pueblos were rebuilt, and new missionaries assigned. But it was not long ere the Pueblos again became restless; on June 4, 1696, another uprising of the northern pueblos, including Taos, took place, in which 5 missionaries and 21 other Spaniards were murdered, the Indians again abandoning their villages, seeking protection in mountain strongholds. In September Vargas attacked the Taos in their fortified canyon, and after a siege they were forced to surrender in the following month. At the beginning of the

m. above. News of the massacre reaching Santa Fé, troops were hastened to the place, which they reached Feb. 3, after several skirmishes on the way. The Indians and Mexicans were fortified in the massive adobe church, which was cannonaded at close range and its walls attacked with axes until its occupants were forced to flee to the near-by pueblo and thence toward the mountains. During the fight 150 of the insurgents were killed, about a third of this number in their attempt to escape from the pueblo. Fifteen others were afterward executed, and one was shot in attempting to escape. The

57009°—Bull. 30, pt 2—12——44

loss of the Americans was 7 killed outright and 45 wounded, some of the latter, including Capt. Burgwin, fatally. Since that time the Taos people were entirely peaceable until May 1910, when a threatened uprising, which had its origin in land encroachment by whites, was speed-

TAOS MAN

ily quelled on the appearance of Territorial troops,

Members of this tribe have probably intermarried extensively with the Ute, some of whose customs they have borrowed. Unlike the other Pueblos (q. v.), the men wear their hair in two long plaits hanging at the sides, and high leggings of deerskin. Their lands are well watered, and their livelihood is gained chiefly by agriculture and by hunting in the adjacent timbered mountains.

Of the mythology of the tribe little has as yet been recorded. The people assert that when their ancestors first came together they spoke a number of languages, but that the tongue of the Feather (Pfia) clan finally prevailed, and this is the language of the tribe to-day.

The following clans have been recorded by Mrs M. C. Stevenson, those with an asterisk being extinct: Tocholimafia (Golden Warbler), Talohlafia (Parrot [Macaw?]), Chiu (Eagle), Toltu (Sun), Ter-taitatana (Day people), Hahl (referring to a small shell), Fialohla (Abalone), Kangtong (Corn), Pachunona (White Shell Bead), Ba (Water), Kang (Corncob), Bachilto (Red Shell), Kahl (Wolf),

Bahur (White Shell), Urhlaina (Green Leaf), Chia (Stone Knife), Bahol (referring to a small animal), Turatu (Elk), Ba taina tongterlana ("Water people far talking"), Nam (Earth), *Towha (Coyote), *Kaki (Raven), *Pachotu (Rattlesnake), *Ton (Tree bole,) *Poyo (Whippoorwill), *Chiyu (Rat), *Towhayu (Fighting Coyote), *Turwillana (referring to a cylindrical fossil marked in rings). In addition the following have been noted by Hodge: Pfia (Feather), Tu (House), Kua (Bear), Pianbotinu (White Mountain), and Ahluhl (of undetermined meaning). Pfiataikwahlaonan, Kwahlaonan, and Hupfokwahlaonan are said to be divisions of a single clan.   (F. W. H.)

YOUNG WOMAN OF TAOS

Braba.—Castañeda (1596) in 14th Rep. B. A. E., 511, 525, 1896. Brada.—Castañeda misquoted by Curtis, Children of the Sun, 121, 1883. ɪ-Tá-i-na-ma.—Miller, Pueblo of Taos, 34, 1898 (='willow people'). Jaos.—Hinton, Handbook to Ariz., map, 1878 (misprint). Kóho'hlté.—Hodge, field notes, B. A. E., 1895 (Jicarilla name). Red Willow Indians.—Army in Ind. Aff. Rep. 1871. 382, 1872. San Gerónimo de los Tahos.—Vetancurt

(1696) in Teatro Mex., III, 318, 1871. **San Gero-nimo de los Taos.**—Benavides, Memorial, 37, 1630. **San Geronimo de Taos.**—Ward in Ind. Aff. Rep. 1867, 213, 1868. **San Geronymo de los Thaos.**—Villa-Señor, Theatro Am., II, 410, 1748. **Sant Miguel.**—Oñate (1598) in Doc. Inéd., XVI, 257, 1871. **S. Gero-nimo de los Thaos.**—Rivera, Diario, leg. 950, 1736. **S. Gerónimo Thaos.**—Alcedo, Dic. Geog., V, 115, 1789. **S. Hieronymo.**—Blaeu, Atlas, XII, 61, 1667. **S. Jérome de los Taos.**—Vaugondy, map Amérique, 1778. **S. Jeronimo de Taos.**—Jefferys, Am. Atlas, map 5, 1776. **S. Jeronimo de Toos.**—Walch, Charte America, 1805. **St Hieronimo.**—De l'Isle, carte Mex. et Floride, 1703. **St Jerome.**—Kitchin, map N. A., 1787. **St Jeronimo.**—Bowles, map Am., 1784. **Tacos.**—Buschmann, Neu-Mexico, 230, 1858 (mis-print). **Tahos.**—Zárate-Salmerón (ca. 1629) quoted by Bancroft, Nat. Races, I, 600, 1882. **Tai-ga-tah.**—Jouvenceau in Cath. Pion., I, no. 9, 12, 1906. **Taíina.**—Hodge, field notes, B. A. E., 1899 (native name of a Taos man). **Taíinamu.**—Ibid. (the tribe). **Takhe.**—Loew (1875) in Wheeler Surv. Rep., VII, 345, 1879 (" Indian name"). **Tao.**—Dis-turnell, map Méjico, 1846. **Taoros.**—Blaeu, Atlas, XII, 61, 1667. **Taos.**—Oñate (1598) in Doc. Inéd., XVI, 109, 306, 1871. **Taosans.**—Foore in Donald-son, Moqui Pueblo Inds., 101, 1893. **Taosas.**—Gregg, Comm. Prairies, I, 124, 1844. **Taoses.**—Rux-ton, Adventures, 199, 1848. **Taosij.**—Sanson, L'Amérique, map, 27, 1657. **Taosis.**—Blaeu, Atlas, XII, 62, 1667. **Taosites.**—Davis, El Gringo, 311, 1857. **Taosy.**—Linschoten, Descr. de l'Amé-rique, map 1, 1638. **Ta-ui.**—Bandelier in Revue d'Ethn., 203, 1886 (the term from which the word Taos was derived). **Ta-uth.**—Gatschet, Laguna MS. vocab., B. A. E., 1879 (Laguna name). **Ta Wolh.**—Curtis, Am. Ind., I, 138, 1907 ('water gurgles': Navaho name). **Taxé.**—Powell in Am. Nat., XIV, 605, Aug. 1880 (Taos name). **Tay-beron.**—Oñate (1598) in Doc. Inéd., XVI, 257, 1871 (province of Taos, or). **Te-gat-há.**—Bandelier, Gilded Man, 233, 1893. **Tejas.**—Garcés (1775–6), Diary, 491, 1900 (probably identical). **Tejos.**—Squier in Am. Rev., 522, Nov. 1848 (identified with Taos). **Te-uat-ha.**—Bandelier in Arch. Inst. Pa-pers, III, 123, 260, 1890 (aboriginal name of the pueblo). **Thaos.**—Freytas, Peñalosa Rel. (1662), 42, 74, 1882. **Toas.**—Gallatin in Nouv. Ann. Voy., 5th s., XXVII, 304, 1851 (misprint). **Tons.**—Pike, Exped., app. to pt. III, 7, 9, 1810 (misprint). **Topoliana-kuin.**—Cushing, inf'n, 1884 ('place of cottonwood trees': Zuñi name; *kuin*, locative). **Tous.**—Arrowsmith, map N. A., 1795, ed. 1814. **Touse.**—Garrard, Wahtoyah, 131, 1850. **Tôwíh.**—Hodge, field notes, B. A. E., 1899 (Tewa name of pueblo). **Tôwirnín.**—Ibid. (Sandia name of pue-blo). **Tuas.**—Mota-Padilla, Hist. Nueva Galicia, 515, 1742 (evidently identical). **Tŭatá.**—Hodge, field notes, B. A. E., 1895 (native name of pue-blo). **Tuopá.**—Ibid. (Picuris name). **Tuwirát.**—Ibid. (Isleta name of pueblo). **Uraba.**—Jara-millo (ca. 1542) in 14th Rep. B. A. E., 587, 1896. **Valladolid.**—Castañeda (1596), ibid., 511, 1896 (so called by Spaniards). **Wee-ka-nahs.**—Joseph in 1st Rep. B. A. E., 101, 1881 (given as their own tribal name). **Yaos.**—Pike, Exped., map, 1810 (mis-print). **Yä'hlâhaimub'âhŭtŭlba.**—Hodge, field notes, B. A. E., 1899 ('red-willow place': another native name). **Yulata.**—Ibid., 1895 (Jemez and Pecos name of pueblo). **Yuraba.**—Relacion del Suceso (ca. 1542) in 14th Rep. B. A. E., 575, 1896.

Tapa ('tortoise'). A Yuchi clan. **Täbᵉä'.**—Speck, Yuchi Inds., 70, 1909. **T'äpä tahá.**—Gatschet, Uchee MS., 71, B. A. E., 1885 (= 'turtle gens').

Tapa ('deer head'). An Omaha gens of the Inshtasanda division. **DeerHead.**—Dorsey in 3d Rep. B. A. E., 245, 1885. **Ṭa-da.**—Ibid. **Ta-pa-taj-je.**—Long, Exped. Rocky Mts., I, 327, 1823.

Tapanash (*Tapänä'sh*). A small Sha-haptian tribe, speaking the Tenino lan-guage, formerly living on the N. bank of Columbia r. in Klickitat co., Wash., a little above Celilo. They are referred to by Lewis and Clark as Eneeshur (q. v.).—Mooney in 14th Rep. B. A. E., 740, 1896.

Tapanissilac. A Chumashan village formerly near Santa Inés mission, Santa Barbara co., Cal.—Taylor in Cal. Farmer, Oct. 18, 1861.

Tapanque. A former Diegueño rancheria near San Diego, s. Cal.—Ortega (1775) quoted by Bancroft, Hist. Cal., I, 254, 1884.

Tapatwa ('alligator'). Given by Gat-schet as a Yuchi clan, but probably no such clan existed among this tribe. **Täpatwä tahá.**—Gatschet, Uchee MS., B. A. E., 70, 1885 (= 'alligator gens').

Tape (*Ta-pe'*). A former village, pos-sibly of the Yokuts (Mariposan), in San Joaquin valley, E. of San Juan Bautista mission, Cal.—Garcia (ca. 1812) cited by Bancroft, Hist. Cal., II, 338, 1886.

Tapeeksin. A band of Indians, prob-ably Salish, mentioned in the treaty of Medicine cr., Wash., 1854. Now either extinct or known under another name. **T'Peeksin.**—Treaty of 1854 in U. S. Ind. Treaties, 561, 1873. **T'Peekskin.**—Ind. Aff. Rep., 265, 1856.

Tapi ('salt'). Given by Gatschet as a Yuchi clan, but probably no such clan existed among this tribe. **Tápi tahá.**—Gatschet, Uchee MS., B. A. E., 71, 1885 (= 'salt gens').

Tapishlecha ('spleen'). An Oglala Sioux band, formerly called Shkopa ('bent'), the name having been changed on account of a member having eaten raw venison. **Škopa.**—Robinson, letter to Dorsey, 1879. **Split Livers.**—Ibid. **Tapicletca.**—Dorsey in 15th Rep. B. A. E., 220, 1897. **Tapišleóa.**—Ibid.

Tapitsiama (*Ta-pit-si'-a-ma*). A pueblo of the Acoma people, which, according to tradition, was inhabited in prehistoric times during the southwestward migra-tion of the tribe from the mythic Shipapu, in the indefinite north. It was the fifth pueblo traditionally occupied by this tribe, and its ruins may still be traced on a mesa 4 or 5 m. N. E. of their present pueblo.　　　　　　　　　　(F. W. H.)

Tapkachmiut. A subdivision of the Malemiut Eskimo whose chief village is Taapkuk. **Tapkachmiut.**—Woolfe in 11th Census, Alaska, 130, 1893. **Tapkhakgmut.**—Zagoskin, Descr. Russ. Poss. Am., I, 73, 1847. **Tup-kug-ameuts.**—Hooper, Cruise of Corwin, 26, 1880.

Tapo. A Chumashan village formerly on the Noriega ranch of Simi, Ventura co., Cal. **Ta-áp'-pu.**—Henshaw, Buenaventura MS. vocab., B. A. E., 1884. **Tapo.**—Taylor in Cal. Farmer, July 24, 1863.

Taposa. A tribe formerly living on Yazoo r., Miss., of which little beyond the name is known. Iberville heard of them in 1699, when they were said to be between the Ofogoula and the Chak-chiuma, on Yazoo r. Baudry des Lozières mentioned them in 1802, under the name Tapouchas, as settled in a village with Chakchiuma and Ibitoupa on upper Yazoo r., and in fact they were really the most northerly Yazoo tribe. They ap-pear to have been one of the tribes confederated with the Chickasaw, and according to Le Page du Pratz spoke the same language. They occupied 25 cabins in 1730.   (A. S. G.)

Tacoposcas.—Williams, Ter. Florida, 175, 1837. Tacusas.—McKenney and Hall, Ind. Tribes, III, 80, 1854. Tapguchas.—Jefferys, Am. Atlas, map 7, 1776. Tapoosas.—Keane in Stanford, Compend., 537, 1878. Taposa.—Iberville (1699) in Margry, Déc., IV, 180, 1880. Tapouchas.—Jefferys, Fr. Dom. Am., 135, map, 1761. Tapousas.—Rafinesque in Marshall, Ky., I, introd., 30, 1824. Tapousoas.—Boudinot, Star in the West, 129, 1816. Tapoussas.—Du Pratz, La., II, 226, 1758. Tapowsas.—Du Pratz misquoted by Schermerhorn (1812) in Mass. Hist. Soc. Coll., 2d s., II, 15, 1814.

Tapouaro. A division of the Illinois confederacy in 1681.—La Salle (1681) in Margry, Déc., II, 201, 1877.

Tappan (of uncertain meaning). A tribe or band of the Unami division of the Delawares, formerly occupying the w. bank of Hudson r. in Rockland co., N. Y., and Bergen co., N. J. They also claimed land on Staten id.

Tapanses.—Schoolcraft, Ind. Tribes, VI, 116, 1857 (from Tappansee, the bay in Hudson r. named by the Dutch from this tribe). Tappaan.—Deed of 1657 in N. Y. Doc. Col. Hist., XIV, 393, 1883. Tappaanes.—De Laet, Nov. Orb., 72, 1633. Tappaen.—De Vries (1639) quoted by Ruttenber, Ind. Geog. Names, 118, 1906. Tappans.—Map of 1614 in N. Y. Doc. Col. Hist., I, 1856. Tappen.—Lovelace (1669) quoted by Ruttenber, Tribes Hudson R., 68, 1872. Tappensees.—Schoolcraft, Ind. Tribes, VI, 147, 1857 (from Tappansee). Tappents.—Wassenaar (1632) quoted by Ruttenber, op. cit., 71.

Taqwayaum. A Ntlakyapamuk village on Fraser r., Brit. Col., below North bend; pop. 73 in 1901, when last reported.

Taqwayaum.—Can. Ind. Aff., pt. II, 164, 1901. Takuyaum.—Ibid., 1893, 301, 1894. Tk·kōēau'm.—Hill-Tout in Rep. Ethnol. Surv. Can., 5, 1899. Tkuayaum.—Can. Ind. Aff. 1892, 312, 1893. Tquayaum.—Ibid., 230, 1886. Tquayum.—Ibid., 277, 1894. Tqwayaum.—Ibid., 1898, 418, 1899.

Taraçones. Mentioned by Barcia (Ensayo, 272, 1723) as a people in the region of Texas where La Salle was killed. Probably Caddo, though Barcia, by the name he gives them, seems to connect them with the Faraon Apache.

Taraha. A tribe or village mentioned by Douay in 1687 as situated N. E. of the Quanoatino, which was really the Caddo name of Red r. of Texas. This section was within the territory of the southern Caddoan group, to which the Taraha may possibly have belonged.

Tarahumare (Hispanized form of the native name *Ralámari*, of obscure meaning, but probably signifying 'foot-runners.'—Lumholtz). A tribe of the Piman family, occupying a territory extending from about lat. 26° to 29°, between lon. 106° and 108° w., embracing the headwaters of the principal streams of southern Sonora and Chihuahua, particularly the Rio Fuerte, in the Sierra Madre. This area is regarded by them as the middle of the world, the belief, similar to that of the Pueblos, having a like origin, no doubt, in their early migrations from the N. and E. They are described as very primitive, for while they readily accepted the teachings of the Spanish missionaries, the number of baptized in 1678 being given as 8,300, they were not permanently affected by them, as the Christianized portion of the tribe are said to be rapidly relapsing into their former aboriginal condition.

The Tarahumare men are vigorous, of medium size, having a dark complexion, a scanty beard, which is plucked as soon as it appears, but long, thick, black hair, which is sometimes twisted into a braid and held in place by a woolen or palm-leaf headband. They are probably the finest runners of all the Indian tribes. They are said to be able to outstrip any horse in a sufficiently long race, having been known to cover more than 100 m. in a day. In their foot races, in which they kick a ball before them, good runners make 40 m. in from 6 to 8 hours. The women also have races in which a wooden ball propelled by a forked stick, or a ring of twisted fiber, kept in motion by a long curved stick, is employed. They formerly tattooed the forehead, lips, and cheeks in various patterns. The principal article of dress of the men is a blanket of native weave, and a shirt belted in, while the women cover the lower part of the body with a woolen skirt only. Sandals, and sometimes straw hats, are worn. Woman holds a comparatively high place in the family life. She is consulted as to bargaining, but on the whole is regarded as inferior to the man. The Tarahumare generally live in hovels in the barren mountains in summer and in caves in winter. Although they are not nomadic, they remove their domestic animals according to the seasons and plant corn in different localities. On the highlands the settlements are more permanent and there the best wooden houses are found, and sometimes ranches containing 5 or 6 families; but even in the highlands a Tarahumare never lives all his life in the same house, for, if an occupant dies, the dwelling is razed. A man sometimes moves his house away because the site is a good one for planting corn, the earth having been enriched by habitation.

They subsist mainly on corn, deer, squirrels, iguanas, mice, and rats, hunting game with the bow and arrow, as firearms are virtually unknown among them. Fish are obtained in large quantities by poisoning the streams, by shooting them with arrows tipped with cactus spines, and by draining pools and capturing the fish in the mud. Maize, beans, chile, tobacco, and potatoes are cultivated in small garden patches formed by rude stone walls constructed along the mountain slopes to retain the soil washed from the heights; they also raise sheep and goats on a small scale, but do not tame the turkey, the eagle, or other birds or animals. Chinaca, a juicy species of thistle, is highly relished, as are also the berries of the madroña, and the secretion of a plant louse, which is gathered, rolled into thick brown sticks, and preserved for winter use. Hunting, arrow making, tillage, and the manufacture of rattles and rasping sticks used as musical instruments are work of the men, while the women prepare the food and are the potters and weavers of the tribe. Among other ceremonials the tribe has planting and harvest dances, and on occasions of thanksgiving they sacrifice meat and an intoxicant prepared from maize. They are said to worship a number of plants, among them being the peyote, from which also is manufactured an intoxicating drink. Mescal also is made and drunk by them. In addition to their celebrated foot races they have games similar to our quoits and shinny; knuckle-bones are used as dice. Their greatest gambling game, known as quinze (Span. 'fifteen'), is played with 4 sticks inscribed with their different values. Their docile character contributed to their reduction by the Spanish missionaries and settlers, notwithstanding their large number, which even now reaches 30,000 and by some is estimated at 40,000. Besides the Tarahumare proper, the tribe includes the Varohio, Guazapar, Pachera, and Tubare. (See Lumholtz, Unknown Mex., 1902.)

The names of the settlements of the Tarahumare proper almost invariably terminate in the locative *chik*, or *chiki*, shortened by the Mexicans to *chi*. They are: Aboreachic, Achyarachki, Akachwa, Akawiruchic, Aoreachic, Ariziochic, Bacaburiachic, Baqueachic, Baquiarichic, Basaseachic, Basigochic, Bawiranachiki, Bichechic, Bocoyna, Cajurachic, Carichic, Chahichic, Chalichiki, Chichiveachic, Chueachiki, Chugita, Chuhuirari, Chuyachic, Cocomorachic, Cusihuiriachic, Coyachic, Cusarare, Galilali, Garabato, Guachochic, Guajochic, Guasigochic, Guazarachic, Gueguachic, Gumisachic, Humarisa, Igualali, Ippo, Isoguichic, Jicamorachic, Kawirasanachic, Kichye, Kuchichic, Kuechic, Makawichic, Mamorachic, Matachic, Mategarele, Nakarori, Napuchic, Nararachic, Naverachic, Nonoava, Norogachic, Ohuivo, Pagaichic, Pahuirachic, Panalachic, Papajichic, Papigochic, Rahasalali, Raiabo, Rararachic, Rasanachic, Reechochic, Rekeachic, Rekorichic, Rekuvirachi, Rekuwichic, Relosoa, Rerawachic, Resochiki, Retawichic, Richuchic, Rocheachic, Saguarichic, Sapechichic, Saweachic, Tehuerichic, Tejolocachic, Temechic, Temosachic, Tepachic, Teporachic, Tomochic, Tonachic, Trusiachic, Turasi, Uruachic,

Vachinapuchic, Vaeachachic, Vahichic, Vakasuachiki, Valebo, Vasoreachic, Vawerachic, Vechaochic, Verachic, Vicharachic, Wiktosachki, Yoquibo.

In addition to these the pueblos of Chinatu and Santa Ana contained both Tarahumare and Tepehuane, while Huexotitlan, Maguina, Tosanachic, Tutuaca, and Yepachic are inhabited by both Tepehuane and Nevome.   (F. W. H.)

Larámari.—Lumholtz, inf'n, 1894 (own name). **Tarahumara.**—Orozco y Berra, Geog., 58, 1864. **Tarahumares.**—Benavides, Memorial, 7, 1630. **Tarahumari.**—Lumholtz in Mem. Int. Cong. Anthr., 101, 1894. **Taraumar.**—Ribas, Hist. Trium., 592, 1645. **Taraumares.**—Zapata (1678) in Doc. Hist. Mex., 4th s., III, 334, 1857. **Tarimari.**—Audubon (1849), Western Jour., 114, 1906. **Taromari.**—Ibid., 113. **Taruararas.**—Hardy, Trav. in Mex., 443, 1829. **Tharahumara.**—Rivera, Diario, leg. 583, 1786.

Taraichi. A Pima settlement in E. Sonora, Mexico, lat. 29° 20′, lon. 108° 30′, not far from the Chihuahua frontier. Pop. 96 in 1730, at which date it appears to have been a sub-mission of Santa Rosalia Onapa.

Angeles Taraichi.—Rivera (1730) cited by Bancroft, No. Mex. States, I, 514, 1884.

Taraichi. A pueblo occupied by the Hizo division of the Varohio, in Chinipas valley, lat. 27° 30′, w. Chihuahua, Mexico. It was the seat of the mission of Nuestra Señora de Guadalupe.

Nuestra Señora de Guadalupe de Voragios.—Orozco y Berra, Geog., 324, 1864. **Taraichi.**—Ibid.

Tarapin. See *Terrapin.*

Tarbogan. See *Toboggan.*

Tarequano. An unidentified tribe represented in considerable numbers at the Camargo mission, on the Rio Grande in Mexico, between 1757 and 1800 (Cuervo, Revista, 1757, MS. in Archivo Gen.; Baptismal records in the church at Camargo, cited by H. E. Bolton, inf'n, 1907).

Tareguano.—Cuervo, op. cit., 1757.

Tareque. A large village of straw houses in 1541, apparently in the Quivira region and probably occupied by the Wichita, at that time living evidently in E. Kansas.

Taracari.—Freytas, Peñalosa, 28, 58, 1882 (given as the chief city of Quivira). **Tareque.**—Coronado (1541) in Doc. Inéd., XIV, 327, 1870. **Tuxeque.**—Coronado (1541) in Smith, Colec. Doc. Fla., I, 153, 1857.

Tares. The "tribe" among whom the mission of Santa Clara, Cal., was founded at a site called Thamien (Engelhardt, Franc. in Cal., 324, 1897). The word is, however, only the term for 'man,' not a tribal name.

Targheliichetunne ('people at the mouth of a small stream'). A former village of the Tututni on the N. side of Rogue r., Oreg.

Ta-rxe′-li i-tce′ ɣûnnĕ′.—Dorsey in Jour. Am. Folklore, III, 233, 1890. **T′a-rxi′-li i-tcĕt′ ɣûnnĕ′.**—Ibid. (Naltunnetunne name).

Targhinaatun. A former village of the Tolowa on the Pacific coast N. of Crescent, Cal.

Ta-rxin′-'a-a′-tûn.—Dorsey in Jour. Am. Folk-lore, III, 236, 1890.

Targhutthotunne ('people on the prairie sloping gently to the river'). A former Tututni village near the coast in Oregon. **T'a′-a-t'ǫo′ ʒûnnĕ.**—Dorsey in Jour. Am. Folk-lore, III, 233, 1890 (Naltunnetunne name). **Ta′-rxût-t'ǫo ʒûnnĕ.**—Ibid.

Tarhe ('crane'). A noted Wyandot chief of the Porcupine clan, born at Detroit in 1742, died at Cranetown, near Upper Sandusky, Wyandot co., Ohio, in Nov. 1818. He was called Le Chef Grue, or Monsieur Grue, by the French; the English knew him as Crane. When in his prime Tarhe was a lithe, wiry man, capable of great endurance. He fought at Point Pleasant on the Kanawha under Cornstalk in 1774, and it is said that, of the thirteen chiefs who participated in the battle of Maumee Rapids, or Fallen Timbers, in 1794, when the Indians met with such disastrous defeat at the hands of Wayne, Tarhe was the only one to escape, and he was badly wounded in the arm. Largely through his influence, and in the face of great opposition, the treaty of Greenville in 1795 was made possible, and he ever after held its provisions inviolate, even to opposing Tecumseh's war policy from 1808 until the War of 1812. He remained faithful to the American cause during this conflict, and, although more than 70 years of age, marched at the head of his warriors through the whole of Gen. Harrison's campaign into Canada, and participated in the battle of the Thames, Oct. 5, 1813, in which Tecumseh was slain. From the close of the war until his death in 1818, Tarhe became well known to the settlers in central Ohio, "many of whom were honored by his friendship and benefited by his influence." Harrison described him in 1814 as a "venerable, intelligent, and upright man," and at another time, while speaking highly of several important chiefs with whom he had been largely in contact, he designated Chief Crane as the noblest of them all. He was chief priest of his tribe, and as such was the keeper of the calumet which bound the tribes N. of the Ohio in a confederation for mutual benefit and protection. After his death a mourning council was held at Upper Sandusky, attended by representatives of all the tribes of Ohio, the Delawares of Indiana, and the Seneca of New York, among the noted chiefs present being Red Jacket. The exact place of his burial is unknown. See Taylor in Ohio Arch. and Hist. Quar., IX, no. 1, 3, 1900.

Tarkepsi (*Tär-kĕp′-si*). One of the Chumashan villages formerly near Santa Inés mission, Santa Barbara co., Cal.—Henshaw, Santa Inés MS. vocab., B. A. E., 1884.

Taronas-hadai (*T″ă′rō nas :had′ă′i*, 'copper house people'). Given by Boas (5th Rep. N. W. Tribes Can., 27, 1889) as the name of a subdivision of the Yakulanas, a Haida family of the Raven clan in Alaska. It in reality refers only to a house name, *tă′go naas*, belonging to that family.

Tarpon. A name, variously spelled, for a game-fish (*Megalops atlanticus*) of the warmer waters of the Atlantic, and which has extended to an East Indian species. The name, which does not belong to any Indian language of the United States, although the contrary has been inferred, appears for the first time in Ligon's History of Barbadoes (1673), and is well known in some of its forms in Guiana and Central America. (w. R. G.)

Tarrypin. See *Terrapin.*

Tarsia. A former settlement of E. Greenland Eskimo of the southern group.—Meddelelser om Grönland, xxv, 28, 1902.

Tarthem. A Salish band formerly under Fraser superintendency, Brit. Col.—Can. Ind. Aff., 79, 1878.

Tasagi's Band. One of the two divisions of the Wahpekute. They had a village of 550 persons on Des Moines r. in 1836. **Tah sau gaa.**—Schoolcraft, Ind. Tribes, III, 612, 1853. **Tasagi's band.**—Flandreau in Minn. Hist. Soc. Coll., III, 387, 1880.

Tasaning. An unidentified tribe, or possibly a band, named after a chief, that sided with the English in the French and Indian war.—Doc. of 1756 quoted by Rupp, Northampton Co., 106, 1845.

Tasawiks (*Tásawiks*). A Paloos village on the N. bank of Snake r., about 15 m. above its mouth, in S. E. Washington.—Mooney in 14th Rep. B. A. E., 735, 1896.

Tascalusa. A powerful chief, apparently of the ancient Alibamu tribe, who commanded the Indians against the Spaniards of De Soto's army in the battle of Mabila, Oct. 18, 1540, described by the historian Bancroft as probably the greatest Indian battle ever fought within the United States. The name signifies 'Black Warrior', from Choctaw and Alibamu *taska* 'warrior,' *lusa* 'black.' It occurs also as Taszaluza, Tascaluça, Tastaluca, and Tuscaluca, and is perpetuated in Black Warrior r. and Tuscaloosa town, Ala. He is described by the historians of the expedition, at his first meeting with De Soto, as very tall and strongly built, symmetrical and handsome in appearance, with an air of haughty dignity, seated upon a raised platform with his son beside him and his principal men around, one of whom held erect a sort of banner of deerskin curiously painted. His head was covered with a turban in the fashion of the Gulf tribes, and over his shoulders was thrown a feather mantle which reached to his feet. He looked on with contempt at the equestrian exercises with which the Spaniards strove to impress him, and gave unwilling ear to their demands for burden carriers and provisions, but when threatened by De Soto replied that he would send messengers ahead to his principal town of Mabila to order all to be prepared. Instead of this, however, he instructed the messengers to call in all the fighting men of his tribe to Mabila, a stockaded town apparently on lower Alabama r., to attack the Spaniards. On the arrival of the advance guard of the Spaniards they unloaded their baggage in the public square, the Indians being apparently friendly and receiving them with a dance of welcome; but while this was going on some of the soldiers noticed them concealing bundles of bows and arrows under branches of trees, and on entering one of the houses the upper platforms near the roof were found filled with armed warriors. De Soto, on being warned, at once made preparations for defense and sent for the chief, who refused to come. An attempt to seize him precipitated the battle, in which the Spaniards were at first driven out of the town, followed by the Indians, who had freed the Indian burden carriers of the Spaniards from their chains and given them bows and arrows to use against the white men. In the open country outside the town the Spaniards were able to use their cavalry, and although the Indians desperately opposed their naked bodies, with bow and arrow, to the swords, long lances, and iron armor of the Spanish horsemen for a whole day, the town was at last set on fire and those who were not cut down outside were driven back into the flames. Men, women, and children fought, and many deliberately committed suicide when they saw that the day was lost. Of about 580 Spaniards engaged some 20 were killed outright, and 150 wounded, despite their horses and protective armor, besides which they lost a number of horses, all their baggage, and some 200 pounds of pearls. De Soto himself was wounded and his nephew was among the killed. The lowest estimate of the Indian loss was 2,500 men, women, and children killed. The fate of Tascalusa was never known, but the body of his son was found thrust through with a lance.

The synonymy following refers to the tribe or district of which Tascalusa was chief. (J. M.)

Tascalifa.—Wytfliet, Descrip. Ptolem. Augmentum, map, 1597. **Tascaluca.**—Gentl. of Elvas (1557) in French, Hist. Coll. La., II, 153, 1850. **Tascalusa.**—Biedma (1544), ibid., 153. **Tasculuza.**—Coxe, Carolana, 24, 1741. **Tastaluça.**—Gentleman of Elvas in Span. Expl. of Southern U. S., 186, 1907. **Taszaluza.**—Biedma in Smith, Colec. Doc. Fla., I, 53, 1857. **Trascaluza.**—Vandera (1579), ibid., 19. **Tusca Loosa.**—Woodward, Reminis., 78, 1859. **Tuscaluca.**—Shipp, De Soto and Fla., 377, 1881.

Tasetsi (*Täsĕ'tsĭ*). A former Cherokee settlement on the extreme head of Hiwassee r., in Towns co., Ga.
Täsĕ'tsĭ.—Mooney in 19th Rep. B. A. E., 531, 1900. Tassetchie.—Doc. quoted by Mooney, ibid.

Tasha. The Wolf clan of the Caddo.—Mooney in 14th Rep. B. A. E., 1093, 1896.

Tashkatze (Keresan: 'place of potsherds'). A former pueblo, probably Keresan, opposite Cochiti, N. central N. Mex. According to Bandelier the village seems to have consisted of 3 rectangular houses and a round tower, and the Tano now of Santo Domingo disclaim its former occupancy by their people.
Tash-gatze.—Ritch, New Mexico, 166, 1885 (mentioned as a Tewa or Tano pueblo). Tash-ka-tze.—Bandelier in Arch. Inst. Papers, IV, 179, 1892.

Tashnahecha ('gopher'). A modern Oglala Sioux band.
Tacnahetca.—Dorsey (after Cleveland) in 15th Rep. B. A. E., 220, 1897. Tašnaheća.—Ibid.

Tashoshgon. A Koyuhkhotana village of 30 people on Koyukuk r., Alaska.—Zagoskin quoted by Petroff in 10th Census, Alaska, 37, 1884.

Tashuanta. A former village on Trinity r., Cal., above the mouth of South fork. Not identified.
Tash-huan-ta.—Gibbs in Schoolcraft, Ind. Tribes, III, 139, 1853. Tash-wau-ta.—McKee in Sen. Ex. Doc. 4, 32d Cong., spec. sess., 194, 1853. Tschawan-ta.—Meyer, Nach dem Sacramento, 282, 1855. Wauch-ta.—Gibbs, MS., B. A. E., 1852.

Tashunkeota ('many horses'). A band of the Sihasapa under Crow Feather (Kanghiwikaya), with 75 lodges in 1862.
Crow, Feather.—Sen. Ex. Doc. 90, 22d Cong., 1st sess., 63, 1832 (given as if the name of two bands). Crow feather band.—Culbertson in Smithson. Rep. 1850, 141, 1851. Tashunkée-o-ta.—Hayden, Ethnog. and Philol. Mo. Val., 375, 1862.

Tasikoyo (*Ta-si'-ko-yo*, from *tasím* 'north,' *kóyo* 'valley,' 'flat'). A former Maidu village at Taylorsville, Plumas co., Cal.
Tasikoyo.—Dixon in Bull. Am. Mus. Nat. Hist., XVII, map, 1905. To-si'-ko-yo.—Powers in Cont. N. A. Ethnol., III, 282, 1877. Tû'sikweyo.—Curtin, MS., B. A. E., 1885.

Tasis. A winter village of the Nootka at the head of Nootka sd., Brit. Col.
Tashees.—Jewitt, Narr., 101, 1815. Tasis.—Galiano, Relacion, 132, 1802.

Tasiusak ('similar to a lake'). A Danish trading post and Eskimo settlement in w. Greenland, lat. 73° 20'.—Meddelelser om Grönland, VIII, map, 1889.
Tassiussak.—Science, XI, 259 1888. Tesseusak.—Kane, Arct. Explor., II, 25, 1856. Tessiusak.—Kane, ibid., I, 426, 1856. Tessi-Usak.—Ibid., II, map. Tessiusak.—Hayes, Arct. Boat Journ., map, 1854.

Tasiusarsik. A village of the Angmagsalingmiut Eskimo at the entrance of the fjord of Angmagsalik, E. Greenland, lat. 65° 40.' Pop. 35 in 1884.—Meddelelser om Grönland, IX, 379, 1889.

Taskigi (*Ta'ski'gi*, abbreviated from *Ta'skigi'yĭ* or *Da'skigi'yĭ*). The name of two former Cherokee towns: (1) on Little Tennessee r., above the junction of the Tellico, in Monroe co., Tenn.; (2) on the N. bank of Tennessee r., just below Chattanooga, Tenn. A third may have been on Tuskegee cr. of Little Tennessee r., near Robbinsville, Graham co., N. C. The name belonged originally to a foreign tribe which was incorporated partly with the Cherokee and partly with the Creeks. It would seem most probable that they were of Muskhogean affinity, but it is impossible to establish the fact, as they have been long extinct, although there is still a "white" or peace town among the Creeks in Oklahoma, bearing their name. In the townhouse of their settlement at the mouth of the Tellico they had an upright pole, from the top of which hung their protecting "medicine," the image of a human figure cut from a cedar log. For this reason the Cherokee sometimes called the place A'tsĭnă'-k'ta'ŭñ, 'Hanging-cedar place.' Before the sale of the land in 1819 they were so nearly extinct that the Cherokee had moved in and occupied the ground. The name is variously written Teeskege, Tuscagee, Tuskegee, etc.—Mooney in 19th Rep. B. A. E., 388, 389, 534, 1900. Cf. *Tuskegee*.

A'tsĭnă'-k'ta'ŭñ.—Mooney op. cit., 511 ('hanging cedar place': a Cherokee name). Toskegee.—Timberlake, Memoirs, map, 1765 (just above the mouth of Tellico). Tuskege.—Bartram, Trav., 372, 1792 (synonym of Taskigi No. 1). Tusskegee.—Doc. of 1799 quoted by Royce in 5th Rep. B. A. E., 144, 1887.

Tasquaringa. A Tepehuane pueblo about 15 leagues from Durango, Mexico. Though a few Mexicans live among them, the inhabitants are little affected by civilization.—Lumholtz, Unknown Mex., I, 469, 1902.

Tasqui.—Mentioned by Juan de la Vandera (Smith, Colec. Doc. Fla., 18, 1859) as a village visited by Juan Pardo in 1557; situated two days' journey from Tasquiqui, identified with Tuskegee, Ala. It was probably inhabited by the Creeks.

Tasqui. A former important village of the Tuscarora of North Carolina, situated in 1711 a day's journey from Cotechna on the way to Ratoway, which was probably Nottoway village. At that time Tasqui was fortified with palisades; its cabins stood in a circle within the line of the palisades, and were neatly constructed of bark. Within the circle was the assembly place; it was here that the delegate of Gov. Spotswood held a conference with the Tuscarora chiefs from Cotechna regarding the freedom of De Graffenried, who was held a prisoner by the Tuscarora. See *Pasqui*. (J. N. B. H.)

Pasqui.—De Graffenried in N. C. Col. Rec., I, 937, 1886.

Tassinong. A former village, probably of the Potawatomi, in Porter co., Ind., near the present town of the same name.—Hough in Indiana Geol. Rep., map, 1883.

Tastaluca. See *Tascalusa*.

Tasunmatunne. A Chastacosta village in the Rogue r. country, w. Oreg.

Ta'-sun-ma' ʒûnnĕ.—Dorsey in Jour. Am. Folklore, III, 234, 1890.

Taszaluza. See *Tascalusa*.

Tatagua. A tribe, numbering 231 in 1862, mentioned by Wentworth as on Ft Tejon res. in s. central California, and also by Taylor in 1863 (Cal. Farmer, May 8, 1863) as of uncertain location. They can not be satisfactorily identified, but were a division either of the Yokuts, the Chumash, or the Shoshoneans.

Laguna.—Wentworth in Ind. Aff. Rep., 325, 1862. Tatagua.—Ibid.

Tatankachesli ('dung of a buffalo bull'). A band of the Sans Arcs Sioux.

Tataŋka ćesli.—Dorsey in 15th Rep. B. A. E., 219, 1897. Tataṅka-tcesli.—Ibid.

Tatapowis. A town of the Wiweakam and Komoyue, gentes of the Lekwiltok, situated on Hoskyn inlet, Brit. Col.

Ta-ta-pow-is.—Dawson in Trans. Roy. Soc. Can., sec. II, 65, 1887.

Tatarrax. A chief mentioned by Gomara (Hist. Gen. Indias, cap. ccxiii, 1553) in connection with Coronado's expedition to Quivira. He is believed to have been the same as the chief of the province of Harahey, identified as the Pawnee country, who, pursuant to a summons from Coronado while at Quivira, evidently on Kansas r., Kans., late in the summer of 1541, visited the Spaniards with 200 warriors armed with bows and "some sort of things on their heads," seemingly referring to the Pawnee mode of hair dressing. If the two are identical, Tatarrax is described as "a big Indian with large body and limbs, and well proportioned (Winship in 14th Rep. B. A. E., 492, 590. 1896). A monument was erected to his memory by the Quivira Historical Society at Manhattan, Kans., in the spring of 1905. Humboldt (New Spain, II, 324, 1811), probably from early maps, erroneously mentions Tatarrax as a kingdom "on the banks of the lake of Teguayo, near the Rio del Aguilar." (F. W. H.)

Tateke (*Tä'teqē*). A Cowichan tribe on Valdes id. (the second of the name), S. E. of Vancouver id. and N. of Galiano id., Brit. Col.; apparently identical with the Lyacksun of the Canadian Indian reports. Pop. 80 in 1909.

Li-icks-sun.—Can. Ind. Aff., 308, 1879. Lyach-sun.—Ibid., 270, 1889. Lyacksum.—Ibid., pt. II, 164, 1901. Lyacksun.—Ibid., 220, 1902. T'ä'teqē.—Boas, MS., B. A. E., 1887.

Tatemy, Moses Fonda (alias Tadema, Tattema, Titami, Totami, Old Moses, Tundy). A famous Delaware chief, interpreter and messenger for the Province of Pennsylvania. He was born on the E. side of the Delaware, somewhere near Cranberry, N. J., in the latter part of the 17th century. He acted as an interpreter for the English at an early date, as in 1737 he was given a tract of about 300 acres on Lehiehtan cr. (now Bushkill cr.), near Stockertown, Northampton co., for his various services to the province. He was living on this tract in 1742. At that date he and several other Delaware Indians presented a petition to the Council of Pennsylvania, in which it was stated that they had embraced the Christian faith, and asked that they be given permission to live under the laws and be granted the rights of the province. Gov. Thomas called them before the Council, and after examining them, decided that they knew "little, if anything," about the Christian religion. He also thought that their reason for making this request was in order that they might evade the Iroquois injunction to remove to Shamokin or to Wyoming. Tatemy then asked that he be permitted to live on the land that had been granted to him by the Proprietors of the province. After much discussion the governor decided to allow him to remain, if the Iroquois would give their consent (Col. Rec. Pa., IV, 624–625, 1851). This action was important, in that it shows the beginning of the Iroquois ascendency in the affairs of the province. This permission was given by the Iroquois, as Tatemy continued to live on his tract for years afterward—if not until his death. His house became one of the landmarks in the region, being situated on the trails leading into the Minisink and near to the Moravian settlements at Nazareth and Bethlehem. Zinzendorf and his party stopped at his house in 1742. He was baptized by David Brainerd, whom he had served as interpreter, on July 21, 1745, at the Indian village of Sakhauwotung (q. v.), when he received the name of Moses Fonda Tatemy (Mem. Moravian Church, 27, 1870). At the conference at Crosswicks, at which Tedyuskung (q. v.) was present, he presented various papers giving him the power of attorney to dispose of various lands in New Jersey (Arch. Pa., III, 344, 1853). From this time he was prominent in all the councils and treaties at Philadelphia and Easton, being associated with Tedyuskung in the attempt to win back the Delawares, chiefly the Minisink, to friendly relations with the province. He served at all these treaties as an interpreter, and was sent on various important missions with Isaac Still and others. (The journal of his mission to Minisink is given in Arch. Pa., II, 504–508, 1852.) In 1757, when Tedyuskung and a party of more than 200 Indians were on their way to the council at Easton (which had been brought about by much trouble), Tatemy's son William, who had strayed from the party, was shot by an Irish lad (Arch. Pa., III, 209, 1853; also Mem. Moravian Church, 334, 1870). This affair threatened to break the peace negotiations. The Delawares were much angered by the outrage and threatened to

avenge the death of the young man. Young Tatemy was taken to the house of a farmer, John Jones, near Bethlehem, where he was attended by Dr Otto, who reported the case to Justice Horsfield and Gov. Denny (Arch. Pa., III, 207, 251, 1853; Mem. Moravian Church, 336–337, 1870). At the treaty at Easton, Tedyuskung spoke of the affair and demanded that, if the young man die, the boy who shot him be tried and punished, according to law, before a deputation of Indians. The governor replied, expressing his sorrow to the father, who was present, and promising that the crime should be punished (Col. Rec. Pa., VII, 674, 1851). After lingering a month young Tatemy died on Aug. 1, being attended in his illness by the Moravian brethren. He was buried at Bethlehem, near "the Crown," in the presence of more than 200 Indians, Rev. Jacob Rogers conducting the services. (The expenses of the funeral and the entertainment of 215 Indians are given in Mem. Moravian Church, 349.) Heckewelder is in error in stating that Tatemy, the Delaware chief, was killed (Ind. Nat., Mem. Hist. Soc. Pa., XII, 302, 337, 1876). The old chief was present at the council at Philadelphia the next fall, where he acted as interpreter. The difficulties were adjusted with the chief and with Tedyuskung. He died some time in 1761, as his name does not appear in any of the records after that year. Heckewelder (op. cit., 337) says that he was loved by all who knew him. A town in Forks township, Northampton co., Pa., perpetuates the name of the old chief. (G. P. D.)

Taterat. An Eskimo village in Aneretok fjord, S. E. coast of Greenland; pop. 20 in 1829.—Graah, Exped. E. Coast Greenland, map, 1837.

Tatesta. A Calusa village on the S. W. coast of Florida, about 1570.
Talesta.—Fontaneda as quoted by Shipp, De Soto and Fla., 586, 1881. Tatesta.—Fontaneda Memoir (ca. 1575), Smith trans., 19, 1854.

Tatitlek. A Chugachigmiut Eskimo village on the N. E. shore of Prince William sd., Alaska; pop. 73 in 1880, 90 in 1890. Formerly it stood at the head of Gladhaugh bay.
Tatikhlek.—Petroff in 10th Census, Alaska, 29, 1884. Tatitlack.—Baker, Geog. Dict. Alaska, 617, 1906 (quoted form). Tatitlak.—11th Census, Alaska, 66, 1893. Tay-tét-lek.—Gerdine quoted by Baker, op. cit. (pronunciation).

Tatlatan. A subtribe of the Ahtena, living above the Tazlina r. on Copper r., Slana r., and Suslota cr., Alaska.
Tatla.—Whymper, Alaska, 55, 1869. Tatlatan.—Allen, Rep., 128, 1887.

Tatlatunne. A village of the Tolowa living on the coast of N. California where Crescent City now stands, or S. of the site.
Kal-wa'-nato-kuc'-te-ne.—Dorsey, Smith R. MS. vocab., B. A. E., 1884 (Khaamotene name). Ta-ah-tèns.—Powers in Overland Mo., VIII, 327, 1872. Tá-ă té-ne.—Dorsey, Smith R. MS. vocab. B. A. E.. 1884.

Tahahteens.—Gatschet in Beach, Ind. Misc., 441, 1877. Tahaten.—Bancroft, Nat. Races, I, 445, 1882. Ta-ta-ten'.—Powers in Cont. N. A. Ethnol., III, 65, 1877. Ta-t'ça'-tûn.—Dorsey in Jour. Am. Folklore, III, 236, 1890 (Naltunnetunne name). Ta-tla' ʒûn-nĕ.—Ibid. (Tututni name). Ta-tqlaq'-tûn-tûn'-nĕ.—Dorsey, Chetco MS. vocab., B. A. E., 1884 (Chetco name). Ta-t'qla'-tûn.—Dorsey, Naltunnetunne MS. vocab., B. A. E., 1884 (Naltunnetunne name).

Tatlitkutchin ('Peel river people'). A Kutchin tribe, closely allied to the Tukkuthkutchin, living on the E. bank of Peel r., Brit. Col., between lat. 66° and 67°. For a part of the season they hunt on the mountains, uniting sometimes with parties of the Tukkuthkutchin. They confine their hunting to the caribou, as they no longer have moose hunters among them. In 1866 they numbered 30 hunters and 60 men.
Fon du Lac Loucheux.—Hooper, Tents of Tuski, 270, 1853. Gens du fond du lac.—Ross, notes on Tinne, S. I. MS., 474. Peel's River Indians.—Kirkby in Hind, Labrador Penin., II, 254, 1863. Peel's River Loucheux.—Anderson, ibid., 260. Sa-to-tin.—Dawson in Rep. Geol. Surv. Can., III, pt. 1, 202B, 1889. Tā-kit kutchin.—Gibbs, MS. notes from Ross, B. A. E. ('people of the bay'). Tā-tlit-Kutchin.—Kirkby in Smithson. Rep. 1864, 417, 1865. T'é-tliet-Kutchin.—Petitot, Dict. Dènè-Dindjié, xx, 1876. Tρétlé-(k)uttchìn.—Petitot, MS. vocab., B. A. E., 1865 ('dwellers at the end of the water'). T'etliet-Kuttchin.—Petitot in Bull. Soc. Géog. Paris, 6th s., X, map, 1875. Tρe-tliet-Kouttchin.—Petitot, Autour du lac des Esclaves, 361, 1891.

Tatooche. A Makah summer village on an island of the same name off C. Flattery, Wash.
Tatooche.—Kelley, Oregon, 68, 1830. Tatouche.—Nicolay, Oregon, 143, 1846 (incorrectly used for the tribe).

Tatpoös (*T'*atpō'os). An extinct Salish tribe formerly occupying the E. part of the larger Valdes id., E. coast of Vancouver id., and speaking the Comox dialect.—Boas, MS., B. A. E., 1887.

Tatquinte. A former village, presumably Costanoan, connected with Dolores mission, San Francisco, Cal.—Taylor in Cal. Farmer, Oct. 18, 1861.

Tatsakutchin ('rampart people') A subdivision of the Kutchakutchin formerly dwelling on both sides of Yukon r., Alaska, at the mouth of Tanana r. They numbered about 50 hunters, who visited Ft Yukon yearly prior to 1863, but in that year they, with the Tennuthkutchin, were destroyed by scarlet fever. At the junction of these streams was a neutral trading point or village, Nuklukayet, originally belonging to the Tenankutchin, where all the tribes inhabiting the banks of the rivers were accustomed to meet in the spring. Besides this village the Tatsakutchin resided in Senati.
Gens de l'abri.—Ross, MS. notes on Tinne, B. A. E. ('people of the shaded country'). Lower Indians.—Ibid. Tatsáh-Kutchin.—Dall, Alaska, 431, 1870. Tåtsäh'-Kŭtchin'.—Dall in Cont. N. A. Ethnol., I, 30, 1877. Tā-tsa Kutchin.—Gibbs, MS., B. A. E. Tā-tsēh kŭtch-in'.—Ross, notes on Tinne, S. I. MS., 474. Teytse-kutchi.—Richardson, Arct. Exped., I, 386, 1851 ('people of the shelter').

Tatsanottine ('people of the scum of water,' scum being a figurative expression for copper). An Athapascan tribe, belonging to the Chipewyan group, inhabiting the northern shores and eastern bays of Great Slave lake, Mackenzie Dist., Canada. They were said by Mackenzie in 1789 to live with other tribes on Mackenzie and Peace rs. Franklin in 1824 (Journ. Polar Sea, I, 76, 1824) said that they had previously lived on the s. side of Great Slave lake. Gallatin in 1836 (Trans. Am. Antiq. Soc., II, 19, 1856) gave their location as N. of Great Slave lake on Yellow Knife r., while Back placed them on the w. shore of Great Slave lake. Drake (Bk. Inds., vii, 1848) located them on Coppermine r.; Richardson (Arct. Exped., II, 4, 1851) gave their habitat as N. of Great Slave lake and from Great Fish r. to Coppermine r. Hind in 1863 (Labrador Penin., II, 261, 1863) placed them N. and N. E. of Great Slave lake, saying that they resorted to Ft Rae and also to Ft Simpson on Mackenzie r. Petitot in 1865 (MS., B. A. E.) said they frequent the steppes E. and N. E. of Great Slave lake; but 10 years later (Dict. Dènè-Dindjié, xx, 1876) he located them about the E. part of the lake. They were more nomadic than their neighbors, which doubtless accounts for the wide area ascribed to them by some of the earlier travelers who met them during their hunting trips in territory belonging to the Etchareottine. Prior to 1850 they were in the habit of visiting the N. end of Great Bear lake to hunt muskoxen and reindeer; but many of their influential men were killed by treachery in a feud with the Thlingchadinne; since then they have kept more to the E. end of Great Slave lake. In their hunting trips northward they came in contact with the Eskimo residing near the mouth of Back r., with whom they were continually at war, but in recent years they seldom traveled farther coastward than the headwaters of Yellow Knife r., leaving a strip of neutral ground between them and their former enemies. According to Father Morice, "they now hunt on the dreary steppes lying to the N. E. of Great Slave lake," and that formerly they were "a bold, unscrupulous and rather licentious tribe, whose members too often took advantage of the gentleness of their neighbors to commit acts of highhandedness which finally brought down on them what we cannot help calling just retribution" (Anthropos, I, 266, 1906). Back, in 1836, stated that the Tatsanottine were once powerful and numerous, but at that time they had been reduced by wars to 70 families. Ross in 1859 (MS., B. A. E.) made the census for the Hudson's Bay Company as follows, but his figures evidently included only one band: At Ft Resolution, 207; at Ft Rae, 12; total, 219, of whom 46 males and 54 females were married, 8 unmarried adult males, 14 widows and unmarried females, 44 boys, and 53 girls, giving 98 males and 121 females of all ages. According to Father Morice they now number about 500, of whom 205 are at Ft Resolution. The Tatsanottine were the Montagnais (see *Chipewyan*) of the Hudson's Bay Company, for whom a special alphabet was designed and books printed in it by the English missionaries (see Pilling, Bibliog. Athapascan Lang., 1892). Petitot found them serious and religiously inclined like the Chipewyan, from whom they differed so slightly in physique and in language that no novice could tell them apart. They formerly manufactured, and sold at fabulous prices, copper knives, axes, and other cutting tools, according to Father Morice. The metal was found on a low mountain in the vicinity of the river called Coppermine r. by the traders on Hudson bay. The diffusion of iron and steel implements at length so depreciated the value of the aboriginal wares that, finding the main source of their revenue cut off through the new order of things, they finally moved to the s.

The Tatsanottine have a myth that one of their women was kidnaped and carried blindfolded off to the country of the Eskimo in Asia and married to one of these, and that she made her escape with her infant in an umiak, reached the shore of America by paddling from isle to isle of the Aleutian archipelago, being protected on the voyage by a white wolf. Reaching the shore of Alaska she abandoned her Eskimo child because it robbed her of pemmican she had made. Seeing a blazing mountain she ascended it, thinking to find a party camping on the summit. She found that the flames were emitted by a molten metal, and when eventually she reached the camp of her own people they accompanied her back by the path she had marked with stones to get some of the metal, which they called bear's dung or beaver's dung, because it was red. They thought she was a woman descended from the skies, but when they had made the journey for the third time some of them laid violent hands on her, whereupon she sat down beside her precious copper, refusing to go home with them. When they came back some time later to seek the volcano of molten copper, she was still there, but sunk to her waist into the earth. She gave them copper, but again refused to go back with them, putting no faith in their promises. She said she would give good metal to those who brought her good meat, iron if the gift were lung, liver, or heart of the caribou, copper for whomsoever gave red flesh, but if anyone brought bad meat they would get

brittle metal in return. Those who came back later for more metal found her buried to the neck in the ground. The last time they came she had disappeared in the bowels of the earth, and from that time no more copper could be found on the bank of Copper r., though there may still be seen the huge stones which the metal woman placed to mark the way. Her tribe have since been called the Copper People, for water scum and beaver dung are both figurative names for this metal.

Base-tlo-tinneh.—Ross, MS., B. A. E. **Birch-rind Indians.**—Franklin, Journ. Polar Sea, I, 76, 1824. **Birch-Rind men.**—Prichard, Phys. Hist., v, 377, 1847. **Birch-rind people.**—Richardson, op. cit. **Copper Indians.**—Hearne, Journ. N. Ocean, 119, 1795. **Copper-Mine.**—Schoolcraft, Trav., 181, 1821. **Couteaux Jaunes.**—Petitot, Dict. Dènè-Dindjié, xx, 1876. **Cuivres.**—Ibid. **Dènè Couteaux-Jaunes.**—Petitot, Autour du lac des Esclaves, 289, 1891. **Gens du Cuivre.**—Ibid., 158. **Indiens Cuivres.**—Balbi, Atlas Ethnog., 821, 1826. **Red Knife.**—Tanner, Narr., 390, 1830. **Red-knife Indians.**—Mackenzie, Voy., 16, 1802. **Red Knives.**—Franklin, Journ. Polar Sea, I, 40, 1824. **T'altsan Ottiné.**—Prichard, Phys. Hist., v, 651, 1847. **Tansawhot-dinneh.**—Schoolcraft, Ind. Tribes, III, 542, 1853. **Täl-sote'-e-nä.**—Morgan, Consang. and Affin., 289, 1871 ('red-knife Indians'). **Tantsanhoot-dinneh.**—Balbi, Atlas Ethnog., 821, 1826. **Tantsa-ut'dtinnè.**—Richardson, Arct. Exped., II, 4, 1851. **Tantsawhoots.**—Keane in Stanford, Compend., 464, 1878. **Tantsawhot-dinneh.**—Franklin, Journ. Polar Sea, 257, 1824 (mistranslated 'birch-rind Indians'). **T'atsan ottiné.**—Petitot, Dict. Dènè Dindjié, xx, 1876 (trans. 'copper people'). **T'attsan-ottinè.**—Petitot in Bull. Soc. Géog. Paris, chart, 1875. **Tautsawot-dinni.**—Latham in Trans. Philol. Soc. Lond., 69, 1856. **Thatsan-o'tinne.**—Morice in Anthropos, I, 265, 1906 (so called by most of their congeners). **Tραltsan Ottinè.**—Petitot, Autour du lac des Esclaves, 158, 1891. **Tρa-'ltsan-Ottinè.**—Ibid., 363. **Tρatsan-Ottinè.**—Ibid., 95. **Tran-tsa ottinè.**—Franklin quoted by Petitot, ibid. **Yellow Knife.**—Dall, Alaska, 429, 1870. **Yellowknife Indians.**—Back, Exped. to Great Fish R., 130, 1836. **Yellow Knife people.**—Ross, MS., B.A.E. **Yellow-knives.**—Can. Ind. Aff., pt. 3, 84, 1902. **Yellow Knives.**—Hind, Lab. Penin., II, 261, 1863.

Tatshiautin ('people of the head of the lake'). A Takulli clan or division, officially known as the "Tatché band," at the head of Stuart lake and on Tachi r. and Thatlah, Tremblay, and Connolly lakes, Brit. Col.; pop. 65 in 1909. Settlements: Kezche, Sasthut, Tachy, Tsisli, Tsisthainli, Yucuche, and probably Saikez.

Tatshiantins.—Domenech, Deserts of N. Am., I, 444, 1860. **Tatshiáutin.**—Hale, Ethnol. and Philol., 202, 1846. **Ta-tshi-ko-tin.**—Tolmie and Dawson, Vocabs. Brit. Col., 123B, 1884. **Ta-tshik-o-tīn.**—Dawson in Geol. Surv. Can. 1879, 30B, 1881. **Tιaz-'tenne.**—Morice, Notes on W. Dénés, 26, 1895 ('people of the end of the lake').

Tatsituk (*Tat'sitŭkᶜ*, 'place of fright'). A Pima village about Cruz's store in s. Arizona.—Russell in 26th Rep. B. A. E., 23, 1908.

Tatsunye. A band or village of the Chastacosta on Rogue r., Oreg.

T'a-ts'ûn'-yĕ.—Dorsey in Jour. Am. Folk-lore, III, 234, 1890.

Tattema. See *Tatemy*.

Tattooing (*tatu* is of Tahitian origin; its equivalent in some of the languages to North America is derived from a roof meaning 'to mark,' 'to write'). The custom of tattooing prevailed to a greater or less extent over the entire country.

When an Eskimo girl reached maturity a line was tattooed from the edge of the lower lip to the point of the chin; later two or more lines were added to mark her as a married woman. With western Eskimo men the tattoo mark meant personal distinction; sometimes successful whalers had the tally of their catches pricked upon the cheek, chest, or arms. Occasionally the wife of such a man had an extra mark put at the corner of her mouth. Along the Pacific coast both men and women were tattooed on the face and body, a custom that recently reached its most ornate development among the Haida

HAIDA TATTOOING (MALLERY)

of Queen Charlotte ids. The designs were of conventionalized "totemic" figures, and seem to have indicated personal or tribal distinction rather than any religious cult. On the middle Atlantic coast geometric designs were tattooed on the person so as to have a decorative effect. The same type of design was incised on the pottery of that region (Holmes in 20th Rep. B. A. E., 151). Tattooing was extensively practised among the tribes of the interior. The Wichita, because of their profuse use of this decoration, were known to the French as "Pani Piqué." Cabeza de Vaca, about 1530, mentions the use of colors, red and blue, in tattooing by the tribes of the Gulf of Mexico, a custom similar to that which still obtains among

the Haida of the N. Pacific coast. Vases have been found in the mounds of the middle Mississippi valley showing the human face with tattoo marks, some of the designs combining geometric and totemic figures. As tattooing gave a permanent line, it served a different purpose from decoration by paint. Among men it marked personal achievement, some special office, symbolized a vision from the supernatural powers, or served some practical purpose, as among the Hupa, where the men have "10 lines tattooed across the inside of the left arm about half way between the wrist and the elbow," for the purpose of measuring strings of "shell money" (Powers in Cont. N. A. Ethnol., III, 76, 1877). Among the Osage a peculiar design was tattooed on the hereditary keepers of the tribal pipes; when one so marked was successful in war and had cut off the head of an enemy, a skull was added to the design, which covered much of his breast and back. Among women the tattooing was more social in its significance. The connection between pottery and basket designs and those tattooed on the face or body of a woman has been noted. Among the Kiowa the tribal mark was a circle on the forehead of the woman. With the Omaha and some of their cognates a small round spot on the forehead of a girl, and a four-pointed star on the back and breast, were marks of honor to signify the achievements of her father or near of kin. In other tribes certain lines on the face indicated the marriageable or married woman.

The Chippewa sometimes resorted to tattooing as a means of curing pain, as the toothache. The process of tattooing was always attended with more or less ceremony; chants or songs frequently accompanied the actual work, and many superstitions were attached to the manner in which the one operated upon bore the pain or made recovery. Most tribes had one or more persons expert in the art who received large fees for their services.

Among the Omaha and cognate tribes the instrument latterly used was a bunch of steel needles fastened tightly in leather, making a kind of stiff brush. The ink was made from charred box-elder wood. The device was first outlined with the ink and the flesh within the outline carefully pricked. The pricking was done twice during the operation to insure a solid figure. Formerly sharp flint points were used for needles. According to Hrdlička, in the S. W. cactus spines served as needles, and charcoal formed the ink. The dyes injected to give color to the design varied in different parts of the country.

Consult Dall in Cont. N. A. Ethnol., I, 1877; Dorsey in 3d Rep. B. A. E., 1884; Goddard in Univ. Cal. Pub., Am. Archæol. and Ethnol., I, no. 1, 1903; Holmes in 20th Rep.

B. A. E., 1903; Mallery in 10th Rep. B. A. E., 1893; Matthews, Ethnog. and Philol. Hidatsa, 1877; Nelson in 18th Rep. B. A. E., 1899; Niblack in Rep. Nat. Mus. 1888, 1890; Powers in Cont. N. A. Ethnol., III, 1877; Sapir in Am. Anthr., IX, no. 2, 1907; Sinclair in Am. Anthr., XI, no. 3, 1909; Swan in Smithson. Cont., XXI, 1874. See also *Adornment, Art.* (A. C. F.)

Tattowhehallys (probably intended for *tálua hallui,* 'upper town'). A town, probably of the Seminole, mentioned by Morse (Rep. to Sec. War, 364, 1822) as "scattered among the other towns," i. e. Lower Creek and Seminole, probably in N. w. Florida or s. Georgia, on Chattahoochee r.

Tatumasket. A Nipmuc village in 1675 in the s. part of Worcester co., Mass., w. of Mendon.—N. H. Hist. Soc. Coll., II, 8, note, 1827.

Tatuppequauog. A village occupied in 1638 by a part of the conquered Pequot, situated on Thames r., below Mohegan, New London co., Conn.—Williams (1638) in Mass. Hist. Soc. Coll., 4th s., VI, 251, 1863.

Tausitu. Given as a Cherokee town in a document of 1799 (Royce in 5th Rep. B. A. E., 144, 1887). Possibly identical with Tlanusiyi or Tasetsi.

Tauskus. A village in 1608 on the E. bank of Patuxent r., in Calvert co., Md.—Smith (1629), Va., I, map, repr. 1819.

Tautaug. See *Tautog.*

Tautin (*Ltau'tenne,* 'sturgeon people'). A sept of the Takulli living on Fraser r. about old Ft Alexander, Brit. Col., once an important post of the Hudson's Bay Co., now abandoned. They were originally some hundreds in number, but died off from the effects of alcohol and loose morals until not 15 were left in 1902 (Morice, Notes on W. Dénés, 24, 1902). Their village, Stella, was contiguous to the fort.

Alexandria Indians.—Brit. Col. map, 1872. Atnalis.—Taylor in Cal. Farmer, July 19, 1862. Calkobins.—Smet, Letters, 157, 1843 (in New Caledonia, w. of the mountains). Enta-otin.—Gibbs, after Anderson, in Hist. Mag., 1st s., VII, 77, 1863 ('the lower people,' as being the lowest Carrier tribe on Fraser r.). Itoaten.—Smet, Oregon Missions, 199, 1847. Ltaoten.—Smet, Missions de l'Oregon, 63, 1848. Ltavten.—Smet, Oregon Missions, 100, 1847. Ţta-uţenne.—Morice, letter, B. A. E., 1890. Ţtha-koh-'tenne.—Morice in Trans. Can. Inst., IV, 24, 1893 ('people of Fraser r.'). Ţthau-'tenne.—Morice in Trans. Can. Inst., IV, 24, 1893 ('sturgeon people'). Talcotin.—Greenhow, Hist. Oregon, 30, 1844. Talkoaten.—Macfie, Vancouver Id., 428, 1865. Talkotin.—Cox, Columbia R., II, 369, 1831. Taltotin.—Keane in Stanford, Compend., 464, 1878. Tantin.—McDonald, Brit. Col., 126, 1862. Taotin.—Gibbs, after Anderson, in Hist. Mag., 1st s., VII, 77, 1863. Taūtin.—Hale, Ethnol. and Philol., 202, 1846. Taw-wa-tin.—Kane, Wanderings in N. A., 242, 1859. Tolkotin.—Cox, Columbia R., II, 369, 1831.

Tautog. The blackfish (*Tautoga americana*) of the New England seacoast; written also *tautaug*. Roger Williams (1643), in his Narraganset vocabulary, has "*tautáuog,* sheepsheads." It is from this plural form of the word in the Algonquian dialect of Rhode Island that *tautog* has been derived. The Indian singular form is *taut,* or *tautau*. Trumbull (Natick Dict., 332, 1903) appears not to confirm the statement of Dr J. V. C. Smith that "*tautog* is a Mohegan word meaning 'black.'" W. R. Gerard (inf'n, 1909) says: "From the fact that Rosier, in an Abnaki vocabulary collected in Maine in 1605, gives *tattaucke* (*tatauk*) as the name for the conner, a closely related fish, it would seem that *tautaug* is not a plural form, and that the name was not confined to the Narraganset." (A. F. C.)

Tauxenent. A tribe of the Powhatan confederacy, with principal village of the same name, estimated by Smith (1608) at 40 warriors, or perhaps 150 souls; situated on the s. bank of the Potomac, in Fairfax co., Va., about the present Mount Vernon.

Tauxenent.—Smith (1606), Va., I, 118, repr. 1819. Tauxinentes.—Boudinot, Star in the West, 129, 1816. Taxenent.—Strachey (ca. 1612), Va., 38, 1849.

Tavaguemue. A Calusa village on the s. w. coast of Florida, about 1570.—Fontaneda, Memoir (*ca.* 1575), Smith trans., 19, 1854.

Tave (*Ta'-ve*). A clan of the Hopi, taking its name from an herb (*Sarcobatus vermiculatus*).—Voth, Hopi Proper Names, 109, 1905.

Tavibo ('white man'). A Paiute chief, born near Walker lake, Esmeralda co., Nev.; died there about 1870. He was famed as a medicine-man, and when the whites crowded the Indians out of the mountain valleys he was interrogated as to the hope of salvation. Having gone up into the mountains to receive a revelation, he prophesied that the earth would swallow the white people and the Indians enjoy their possessions. The people were incredulous about an earthquake that could discriminate between whites and Indians. A second vision revealed to him, therefore, that all would be engulfed, but the Indians would rise again and enjoy forever an abundance of game, fish, and piñon nuts. Shoshoni and Bannock, as well as Paiute, welcomed the pleasant tidings, and devotees flocked to him from Nevada, Idaho, and Oregon. When their faith began to wane he received a third revelation, according to which only believers in his prophecy would be resurrected, while skeptics would remain buried in the earth with the whites.— Capt. J. M. Lee quoted by Mooney in 14th Rep. B. A. E., 700, 1896.

Tawa. The Sun clan of the Hopi.

Ta-jua.—Bourke, Snake Dance, 117, 1884. Tawá-ñamu.—Voth, Traditions of the Hopi, 36, 1905. Tawa win̄wû.—Fewkes in 19th Rep. B. A. E., 584, 1900. Tawa wün̄-wû.—Fewkes in Am. Anthr., VII, 403, 1894. Tda'-wa.—Stephen in 8th Rep. B. A. E., 39, 1891.

Tawakoni (*Ta-wa'-ko-ni* 'river bend among red sand hills(?).'—Gatschet). A

Caddoan tribe of the Wichita group, best known on the middle Brazos and Trinity rs., Texas, in the 18th and 19th centuries. The name "Three Canes," sometimes applied to them, is a translation of the French form "Troiscanne," written evidently not as a translation of the native name, as has been claimed, but to represent its vocal equivalent. Mezières, for example, writing in French, used "Troiscanne" obviously as a vocal equivalent of Tuacana, a usual form of his when writing in Spanish (Letter of July 22, 1774, in Archivo Gen., Prov. Intern., xcix, Expediente, 1). In 1719 La Harpe visited, on the Canadian r., Okla, a settlement of 9 tribes which he collectively called "Touacara," from the name of a leading tribe (Margry, Déc., vi, 278, 282, 289, 1886). That the Tawakoni, later known on the Brazos, were the same people is not perfectly clear, but it seems probable that they were. A fact that helps to establish their identity is that among the 9 tribes visited by La Harpe were the Toayas, Ousitas, and Ascanis, who appear to be the later known Tawehash, Wichita, and Yscani (Waco), close relatives of the Tawakoni and living near them in Texas in the latter part of the 18th century. These tribes all seem to have moved southward into Texas about the middle of the 18th century, being pushed by the hostile Osage from the N. E. and the Comanche from the N. W. (see La Harpe, op. cit., 293). The exact nature and time of the Tawakoni migration, however, are not clear. By 1772 they were settled in two groups on the Brazos and Trinity, about Waco and above Palestine, but there are indications that this settlement was recent and subsequent to considerable wandering. For example, in 1752 De Soto Vermudez (Investigation, 1752, MS.) was informed at the Nasoni village, on the upper Angelina, that the "Tebancanas" were a large nation, recently increased by the Pelones, and living 20 leagues to the northward, with the Tonkawa and Yojuane beyond them. If the direction was correctly given, they must have been somewhere near the upper Sabine. In 1760 and 1761 Fray Calahorra, missionary at Nacogdoches, visited the Tawakoni; they were then living in two neighboring villages, near a stream and five days from the Tawehash, who were then on Red r. below the mouth of the Wichita. These villages seem to have been the same as those mentioned below as found by Mezières on the Trinity in 1772, though they may have been on the Brazos, for the information here is not explicit (Lopez to Parilla, 1760, in Expediente sobre Mision San Saba, Archivo Gen.; Testimonio de Diligencias, Béxar Archives, Province of Texas, 1754–76, MSS.). In

1768 Solís reported the Tawakoni and Yscani as ranging between the Navasota and the Trinity (Diario in Mem. de Nueva España, xxvii, 279); they had evidently settled in the general locality that was to be their permanent home. In 1770 allusion is made to a migration, as a result of peace established with the Spaniards, from the neighborhood of San Antonio and San Sabá, where they had been located for the purpose of molesting the Spanish settlements, to the neighborhood of the Nabedache, who were living on San Pedro cr., in N. E. Houston co. (Mezières, Relación, 1770, MS.). This residence near San Antonio was probably a temporary one of only a portion of the tribe, for the indications are that the country between Waco and Palestine was already their chief range. In 1772 Mezières speaks of the village on the Brazos as though it had been founded recently by a "malevolent chief" hostile to the Spaniards (Informe, July 4, 1772, MS.). Finally, for the migration, it appears that by 1779 the village on the Trinity had also moved to the Brazos, which for a long time thereafter was the principal home of the Tawakoni, who now again became a settled people.

With Mezières' report in 1772 the Tawakoni come into clear light. In that year he visited the tribe for the purpose of cementing a treaty recently made with them by the governors of Texas and Louisiana. One of their villages was then on the w. bank of the Trinity, about 60 m. N. W. of the Nabedache village, on a point of land so situated that in high water it formed a peninsula with only one narrow entry on the w. side. This location corresponds in general with that of the branch of the Trinity now called Tehaucana cr. This village consisted of 36 houses occupied by 120 warriors, "with women in proportion and an infinite number of children." The other village, of 30 families, was 30 leagues away on Brazos r., not far from Waco. Mezières tried to induce the inhabitants of this village to move eastward to the Trinity, farther away from the settlements. This they promised to do after harvest, but the promise was not kept. Mezières recommended the establishment of a presidio on the Tawakoni site when the Indians should be removed (Informe, July 4, 1772, MS.).

In 1778 and 1779 Mezières made two more visits to the Tawakoni. One village, containing 150 warriors, was then on the w. side of the Brazos, in a fertile plain protected from overflow by a high bank or bluff, at the foot of which flowed an abundant spring. Eight leagues above was another village of the same tribe, larger than the first, in a country remarkable for its numerous springs and creeks. It seems that this was the village that in 1772 had been on the Trinity, since for nearly half a century we do not hear of the Trinity village (Mezières, Carta, in Mem. de Nueva España, XXVIII, 274-5). The lower village Mezières called Quiscat (q. v.), or El Quiscat, apparently from its head chief, a name which it kept at least as late as 1795. Morfi (Hist. Tex., ca. 1782, MS.) erroneously (?) says that Quiscat was a village of Kichai and Yscani. The upper village was called Flechazo, and the inhabitants Flechazos, which often appears as a tribal name (Cabello, Informe, 1784, MS; Leal, Noticia, July 10, 1794. See also *Flechazos*).

The Tawakoni and the Waco speak dialects of the Wichita language and sometimes have been considered the same people. Mezières remarked that they lived apart only for convenience in hunting (Informe, July 14, 1772, MS.; Courbière, Relación Clara, 1791, Béxar Archives, MS.). This language, though kindred, is very distinct from that of their relatives, the Hasinai and the Kadohadacho, as was noted in the statement by an official at Nacogdoches in 1765 that two Hasinai chiefs "served as interpreters in their language, which I know, of what it was desired to ask the chief of the Taguais [Tawehash] nation, called Eiasiquiche" (Testimonio de los Diligencias, Béxar Archives, Prov. of Texas, 1754-76). In connection with the ethnological relations of the Tawakoni, the Waco require mention. They were apparently simply one of the Tawakoni villages, perhaps the Quiscat of Mezières' day. The name Waco has not been noted in early Spanish documents, nor does it occur at all, it seems, until the 19th century, when it is first applied by Americans to Indians of the village on the site of modern Waco, who are distinguished from those called Tawakoni living only 2 m. below (Stephen F. Austin, ca. 1822, Austin papers, Class D.; Thos. M. Duke to Austin, June, 1824, ibid., Class P).

The hereditary enemies of the Tawakoni were the Comanche, Osage, and Apache, but toward the end of the 18th century and thereafter the Comanche were frequently counted as allies. The hostility of the Tawakoni toward the Apache was implacable, and Apache captives were frequently sold by them to the French of Louisiana (Macartij, letter, Sept. 23, 1763). With the Hasinai and Caddo, as well as the Tonkawa and Bidai, the Tawakoni were usually at peace. Their villages were market places for the Tonkawa and a refuge for many apostate Jaraname (Aranama) from Bahía del Espíritu Santo.

As in former times, the Tawakoni resemble in methods of agriculture and house-building the other tribes of the Wichita confederacy (q. v.). The Spanish town of Bucareli on the Trinity depended on them in part for food. Austin (op. cit.) reported at the Waco village about 200 acres of corn fenced in with brush fences. According to Mezières (Informe, July 4, 1772) the Tawakoni ate their captives after the cruelest torture and left their own dead unburied in the open prairie.

Until about 1770 the Tawakoni, though friendly toward the French, were hostile to the Spaniards. In 1753, and several times thereafter, they were reported to be plotting with the Hasinai to kill all the Spaniards of E. Texas (De Soto Vermudez, Investigation; Mezières to Fr. Abad, 1758, MS.). The founding of San Sabá mission for the Apache increased this hostility of the Tawakoni, and in 1758 they took part with the Comanche, Tawehash, and others in the destruction of the mission. In 1760 Father Calahorra, of Nacogdoches, made a treaty of peace with the Tawakoni and Waco, but they soon broke it. During the next two years Calahorra made them other visits and got them to promise to enter a mission. Subsequently the mission project was often discussed, but never materialized (Testimonio de Diligencias, Béxar Archives, Prov. of Texas, 1759-76).

The transfer of Louisiana to Spain wrought a revolution in the relations between the Spaniards and the Tawakoni and other tribes. In 1770 Mezières, an expert Indian agent, and now a Spanish officer, met the Tawakoni and other tribes at the Kadohadacho village and effected a treaty of peace in the name of the governors of Louisiana and Texas (Mezières, Relación, Oct. 21, 1770). In 1772 he made a tour among these new allies and conducted the chiefs to Béxar, where, by the Feather dance, they ratified the treaty before Gov. Ripperdá. This friendship was cemented by a more liberal trading policy introduced by Gov. Oreilly of Louisiana (Mezières, Informe, July 4, 1772). The Tawakoni were now relied upon to force the Aranama (Jaraname) back to their mission and to restrain the more barbarous Tonkawa and induce them to settle in a fixed village, which was temporarily accomplished (Mem. de Nueva España, XXVIII, 274). Friendly relations remained relatively permanent to the end of the Spanish regime. In 1778 and 1779 Mezières made two more visits to the Tawakoni villages. In 1796 the Tawakoni sent representatives to the City of Mexico to ask for a mission, and the matter was seriously discussed but decided negatively (Archivo Gen., Prov. Intern., XX, MS.). About

1820 they for some reason became hostile, but on Apr. 23, 1821, Gov. Martinez, through the mediation of the *gran cadó*, or Kadohadacho chief, effected a new treaty with the Tawakoni chiefs Daquiarique and Tacaréhue (Archivo Gen., Prov. Intern., CCLI).

By 1824 the upper Tawakoni village seems to have been moved back toward the Trinity, for in that year Thomas M. Duke, who described the Waco and the small Tawakoni village below them, stated that the principal Tawakoni village was on the waters of the Trinity (Austin Papers, Class P). To the Anglo-Americans the tribe frequently proved troublesome and were sometimes severely punished. They were included in the treaty made with the Republic of Texas in 1843 and also in the treaties between the United States and the Wichita in 1837 and 1856, which established their reservation in the present Oklahoma. In 1855 they were placed on a reservation near Ft Belknap, on the Brazos, and for 3 years they made progress toward civilization; but in 1859 they were forced by the hostility of the whites to move across Red r. (Bancroft, No. Mex. States, II, 406–410, 1889). Since then they have been officially incorporated with the Wichita (q. v.).

If the view that the Waco were only a part of the Tawakoni under a new name is correct, the Tawakoni suffered rather less diminution than other tribes during the half century after 1778. If the view is wrong, they decreased about half their number during that period. (H. E. B.)

Fa-wac-car-ro.—Ind. Aff. Rep., 263, 1851. Iowaulkeno.—Otis, Check List, 135, 1876. Juacanas.—Mezières (1778), Letter in Mem. de Nueva España, XXVIII, 235, MS. Juacano.—Bull. Soc. Geog. Mex., I, 504, 1869 (probably identical). Li-woch-o-nies.—Butler and Lewis in H. R. Doc. 76, 29th Cong., 2d sess., 7, 1847. Macanas.—Mezières (1778) quoted by Bancroft, No. Mex. States, I, 661, 1886 (misprint). Tackankanie.—Maillard, Hist. Texas, 238, 1842. Taguacana.—Croix, Relación Particular (1778), MS. in Archivo Gen. Taguacanas.—Solís (1768), Diary, in Mem. de Nueva España, XXVII, 279, MS. Tahuacana.—Morse, Rep. to Sec. War, 373, 1822. Tahuacane.—Tex. State Archives, 1793. Tahuacano.—Treaty of 1821 with Gov. of Texas, MS., Archivo Gen. Tahuacany.—Bollaert in Jour. Ethnol. Soc. Lond., II, 275, 1850. Tahuacano.—Ibid., 265. Ta-hu'-ka-ni''.—Dorsey, Kwapa MS. vocab., B. A. E., 1891 (Quapa name). Tahwaccaro.—Ind. Aff. Rep., 903, 1847. Tah-wac-car-roes.—Ibid., 1857, 265, 1858. Tahwaccona.—Ibid., 367, 1854. Tah-wae-carras.—Schoolcraft, Ind. Tribes, I, 518, 1851. Tahwah-ca-roo.—Ind. Aff. Rep., 894, 1846. Tah-wah-carro.—Sen. Ex. Conf. Doc. 13, 29th Cong., 2d sess., 1, 1846. Tahwaklero.—Ind. Aff. Rep. 1856, 14, 1857. Takawaro.—Schoolcraft, Ind. Tribes, VI, 489, 1857. Tancaro.—La Harpe (1719) in French, Hist. Coll. La., III, 72, 1851. Taouacacana.—Robin, Voy., III, 5, 1807. Taoucanes.—Mezières (1792), Informe, MS. in Archivo Gen. Tavakavas.—Bruyère (1742) in Margry, Déc., VI, 492, 1886. Tawacairoe.—Ind. Aff. Rep., 372, 1866. Tawacamis.—Sen. Misc. Doc. 53, 45th Cong., 3d sess., 73, 1879. Tawacani.—Latham in Trans. Philol. Soc. Lond., 104, 1856. Tawacanie.—Ind. Aff. Rep. 1849, 30, 1850. Ta-wa-ca-ro.—Ibid., 1859, 310, 1860. Tawacarro.—Schoolcraft, Ind. Tribes, VI, 689, 1857. Tawaccaras.—Ind. Aff. Rep., 397, 1867. Tawaccomo.—Ibid., 369, 1854. Tawaccoroe.—Ibid., 1856, 184, 1857. Tawackanie.—

Maillard, Hist. Texas, 252, 1842. Tawaconie.—Ind. Aff. Rep. 1849, 32, 1850. Tawákal.—Gatschet, Tonkawē MS., B. A. E., 1884 (Tonkawa name). Tawakanas.—Doc. of 1771–2 quoted by Bolton in Tex. Hist. Soc. Quar., IX, 91, 1905. Tawakanay.—Ind. Aff. Rep., 249, 1877. Tawakany.—Austin (*ca.* 1822), MS. in Austin Papers, Class D. Ta-wa-ka-ro.—Ind. Aff. Rep., 527, 1837. Tawakaros.—La Harpe (1719) quoted by Gatschet, Karankawa Inds., 27, 1891. Tawakenoe.—Sibley, Hist. Sketches, 74, 1806. Tawakones.—Davis, Span. Conq. N. Mex., 82, 1869. Tawakoni.—Buschmann (1859) quoted by Gatschet, Karankawa Inds., 33, 1891. Tawaréka.—McCoy, Ann. Reg., no. 4, 27, 1838. Tehuacanas.—Macartij, Letter to Gov. Angel de Navarrete, 1763, MS. in Nacogdoches Archives. Three Canes.—Pénicaut (1714) trans. in French, Hist. Coll. La., n. s., I, 121, 1869. Three Cones.—Schermerhorn in Mass. Hist. Coll., 2d s., II, 25, 1814 (misprint). Tiroacarees.—Arbuckle (1845) in Sen. Ex. Doc. 14, 32d Cong., 2d sess., 134, 1853. To-noc-o-nies.—Butler and Lewis (1846) in H. R. Doc. 76, 29th Cong., 2d sess., 7, 1847. Touacara.—La Harpe (1719) in Margry, Déc., VI, 289, 1886. Touacaro.—Beaurain, note in ibid. Towacanies.—Bonnell, Texas, 139, 1840. Towacanno.—Morse, Rep. to Sec. War, 373, 1822. Towacano.—Trimble, ibid., 259. Towacarro.—Latham in Trans. Philol. Soc. Lond., 103, 1856. Towaccanie.—Falconer in Jour. Roy. Geog. Soc., XIII, 206, 1843. Towaccaras.—Alvord in Sen. Ex. Doc. 18, 40th Cong., 3d sess., 7, 1869. Towackanies.—Marcy, Prairie Trav., 197, 1859. To-wac-ko-nies.—Parker, Texas, 213, 1856. To-wac-o-nies.—Schoolcraft, Ind. Tribes, V, 682, 1855. Towacoro.—Ibid., III, 403, 1853. Towa'kani.—Gatschet, Caddo and Yatassi MS., B. A. E., 82 ('river bend in a sandy place': Wichita name). Tówakarehu.—Dorsey, Wichita MS., B. A. E., 1882 (='three canes'). Towakar-ros.—Sen. Ex. Conf. Doc. 13, 29th Cong., 1st sess., 5, 1846. Towakenos.—Latham in Trans. Philol. Soc. Lond., 102, 1856. Toweca.—Gallatin in Trans. Am. Antiq. Soc., II, 117, 1836. Towiachs.—Latham in Trans. Philol. Soc. Lond., 102, 1856. Towoccaroes.—Alvord in Sen. Ex. Doc. 18, 40th Cong., 3d sess., 6, 1869. Towocconie.—Smithson. Misc. Coll., II, art. 2, 51, 1852. Towockonie.—Marcy in Schoolcraft, Ind. Tribes, V, 712, 1855. To-woo-o-roy Thycoes.—Leavenworth (1867) in H. R. Ex. Doc. 240, 41st Cong., 2d sess., 24, 1870. Towoekonie.—Marcy in Schoolcraft, Ind. Tribes, V, 712, 1855. Tuacana.—Mezières, Relación, 1770, MS. Tuckankanie.—Maillard, Hist. Texas, map, 1842. Tuhuktukis.—Latham in Trans. Philol. Soc. Lond., 103, 1856. Ṭu'-ka-le.—Dorsey, Kansa vocab., B. A. E., 1882 (Kansa name). Tu'-ka-nyi.—Dorsey, Osage vocab., B. A. E., 1883 (Osage name). Tuwakaríwa.—Gatschet, Wichita MS., B. A. E. (Wichita name). Twowakanie.—Yoakum, Hist. Texas, I, 260, 1855. Twowokana.—Ibid., 165. Twowokauaes.—Ibid., 405. Yo-woo-o-nee.—Marcy in Schoolcraft, Ind. Tribes, V, 712, 1855.

Tawamana. The Bird clan of the Hopi. Tawamana winwû.—Fewkes in 19th Rep. B. A. E., 584, 1900 (*winwu*='clan'). Ta-wa-ma-na wün-wü.—Fewkes in Am. Anthr., VII, 404, 1890.

Tawasa (Alibamu: *Tawásha*). A Muskhogean tribe first referred to by the De Soto chroniclers in the middle of the 16th century as Toasi and located in the neighborhood of Tallapoosa r. Subsequently they moved S. E. and constituted one of the tribes to which the name "Apalachicola" was given by the Spaniards. About 1705 attacks by the Alibamu and Creeks compelled them to leave this region also and to seek protection near the French fort at Mobile. In 1707 the Pascagoula declared war against them, but peace was made through the intervention of Bienville. From this time the tribe ceased to be noted by French chroniclers, and at the close of the century it reappears as one of the four Alibamu towns, from which it seems likely that the Tawasa had allied or re-allied themselves with the Alibamu after the disturbance just alluded to. Their subsequent history is probably the same as that of the Alibamu (q. v.). (J. R. S.)

Ooe-Asa.—Adair, Am. Inds., 156, 1775. Tanessee.—Jefferys, Am. Atlas, map 5, 1776. Taouachas.—Pénicaut (1710) in Margry, Déc., v, 486, 1883. Tarwarsa.—Sen. Ex. Doc. 425, 24th Cong., 1st sess., 270, 1836. Tarwassaw.—Woodward, Reminis., 12, 1859. Tavossi.—Alcedo, Dic. Geog., v, 57, 1789. Tawasas.—Swan (1791) in Schoolcraft, Ind. Tribes, v, 262, 1855. Tawássa.—Gatschet, Creek Migr. Leg., I, 88, 1884. Taw warsa.—Schoolcraft, Ind. Tribes, IV, 578, 1854. Taw-wassa.—Pettus in Trans. Ala. Hist. Soc., II, 135, 1898. Toasi.—Gentl. of Elvas (1557) in French, Hist. Coll. La., 154, 1850 (probably identical). Tomasa.—U. S. Ind. Treat. (1827), 421, 1837. Too-wos-sau.—Hawkins, Sketch (1799), 36, 1848. Toüachas.—Pénicaut (1723) in Margry, Déc., v, 457, 1883. Towarsa.—Campbell (1836) in H. R. Doc. 274, 25th Cong., 2d sess., 20, 1838.

Tawash. The extinct Moon clans of Sia and San Felipe pueblos, N. Mex.

Ta-wac.—Stevenson in 11th Rep. B. A. E., 19, 1894 (c=sh). Táwash-háno.—Hodge in Am. Anthr., IX, 351, 1896 (hano='people').

Taweeratt. See Orehaoue.

Tawehash (Ta-we'-hash, commonly known in early Spanish writings as Taovayas.) A principal tribe of the Wichita confederacy, distinct from the Wichita proper, although the terms are now used as synonymous. By the middle of the 18th century they had settled on upper Red r., where they remained relatively fixed for about a hundred years. Rumors of a tribe called the Teguayos, or Aijaos, who may have been the Tawehash, reached New Mexico from the E. early in the 17th century (Bancroft, No. Mex. States, I, 387, 1886). The Toayas found by La Harpe in 1719 on Canadian r. with the Touacara (Tawakoni), Ousitas (Wichita), and Ascanis (Yscanis) were evidently the Tawehash, and his report gives us our first definite knowledge of them (Margry, Déc., VI, 278, 282, 289, 1886). Their southward migration, due to pressure from the Osage, Chickasaw, and Comanche, was probably contemporary with that of their kinsfolk, the Tawakoni (q. v.). That their settlement on Red r. was relatively recent in 1759 is asserted by Antonio Tremiño, a Spanish captive who was released by the tribe in 1765 (Testimony of Tremiño, Aug. 13, 1765, MS. in Béxar Archives).

The Spaniards of New Mexico usually designated the Tawehash as the Jumanos (q. v.); the French frequently called them and the Wichita Pani piqué, or tattooed Pawnee, while to the Spaniards of San Antonio and the officials in Mexico they were uniformly the Taovayas (in varying forms of orthography) and Wichita (see Declaration of Pedro Latren at Santa Fé, Mar. 5, 1750, MS. in Archivo Gen.).

After La Harpe's visit, in 1719, the group of tribes to which the Tawehash belonged became attached, through trade, to the French, while on the other hand they saw little of the Spaniards. But from indifferent strangers the Tawehash and the Spaniards soon became converted into active foes through their differing relations to the Comanche and the Apache. To the Comanche and the Tawehash alike the Apache were a hated enemy, while the founding of San Sabá mission in 1757, for the Lipan Apache, put the Spaniards in the light of Apache allies. The result was the destruction of the mission in Mar. 1758, by a large force of Comanche, Wichita, Tawehash, and other northern Indians. To avenge this injury, Don Diego Ortiz Parrilla, a soldier of renown, was put in command of 500 men—regulars, militia, Tlascaltecan, and mission Indians—and equipped for a four months' campaign. Leaving San Antonio, in Aug. 1759, he marched with Apache allies to the Tawehash settlement, which he found flying a French flag, fortified by ditch and stockade, and so strongly defended that he was repulsed with loss of baggage-train and two cannon. Years afterward Bonilla wrote: "And the memory of this event remains to this day on the Taovayases frontier as a disgrace to the Spaniards" (Breve Compendio, 1772, trans. by West in Tex. Hist. Asso. Quar., VIII, 55, 1905). The cannon were not recovered till 20 years later.

Parrilla's report of the Tawehash fortification was confirmed in 1765 by Tremiño, the released captive mentioned above. According to him it was built especially to resist Parrilla's attack. It consisted of a palisaded embankment about 4 ft high, with deep ditches at the E. and W. ends, to prevent approach on horseback. Inside the enclosure were 4 subterranean houses or cellars for the safety of non-combatants (Tremiño, op. cit.). From the time of Parrilla's campaign forward the Tawehash settlement was referred to in Spanish writings as the "fort of the Taovayas." Of interest in this connection is the record that the Waco, also of the Wichita group, had at their village a similar earthen wall or citadel which was still visible in the latter part of the 19th century (Kenney in Wooten, Comp. Hist. Texas, I, 745, 1898).

In 1760, the year after the famous battle, Fray Calahorra y Saenz, the veteran missionary at Nacogdoches, was sent to the fortaleza to effect a peace, which he accomplished, at least nominally (Fray Joseph Lopez to Parrilla, Exp. sobre San Sabá, MS. in Archivo Gen., 1760). The liberation of Tremiño in 1765 was attended with special marks of friendship. He was escorted to Nacogdoches by head chief Eyasiquiche, who was made a Spanish official and sent home with presents of a cane, a dress-coat, and three horses. He would not consent, however, to Calahorra's proposal of a mission for his people (Calahorra, letter of July 16, 1765, MS. in Béxar Archives). In spite of these signs of amity, the Spaniards still entertained suspicions of the Tawehash, but matters were improved by the efforts of Mezières, a skilful Indian agent. In 1770 he met the Tawehash, Tawakoni, Yscanis, and Kichai chiefs in a conference at the Kadohadacho (Caddo) village. The treaty arranged at this time was ratified at Natchitoches in Oct. 1771, by three Tawehash chiefs, who by proxy represented the Comanche also. Among other things, they promised to give up their Spanish captives and Parrilla's cannon, not to pass San Antonio in pursuit of the Apache without reporting there, and to deliver to the Spanish authorities the head of any violator of the peace. This compact was solemnized by the ceremony of burying the hatchet (Articles of peace, MS. in Archivo Gen., Hist., xx). From this time forward the Tawehash were generally named among the friendly tribes, but they were seldom trusted. They were, however, often turned against the Apache, and in 1813 they aided the revolutionists against the royal arms (Arredondo to the Viceroy, Sept. 13, 1813, MS. in Archivo Gen.). As a tribe they were never subjected to mission influence, which may be said of all the tribes of the Wichita confederacy.

In 1772, and again in 1778, Mezières visited the Tawehash settlement to further cement their friendship, and from his reports we get our fullest knowledge of their relationships and society. They spoke nearly or quite the same language as their kinsmen and allies, the Wichita, Tawakoni, and Yscani. Their settlement was situated on Red r., at the eastern Cross Timbers. At the time of Mezières' second visit it consisted of a population of 800 fighting men and youths, living in two villages on opposite banks of the river. That on the N. side was composed of 37 and the other of 123 grass lodges, each containing 10 or 12 beds. To these two villages Mezières at this time gave the names San Teodoro and San Bernardo, in honor of the commandant general of the interior provinces and of the governor of Louisiana. The Tawehash had extensive agriculture, raising corn, beans, calabashes, watermelons, and tobacco, with which they supplied the Comanche, in exchange for horses and captives. The calabashes they cut up in strips which, when dry, were made into chains or mats for convenience in carrying. Though fish were plentiful in the river, they are said not to have eaten them. Women took part in the government, which was democratic. Chiefs, who prided themselves on owning nothing, did not hold office by hereditary right, but were elected for their valor. Regarding the religion of the people Mezières mentioned "fire worship" and belief in a very material heaven and hell (see also *Wichita*).

There is some ground for thinking that one of the two villages of the Tawehash settlement described by Mezières in 1778 was composed of the Wichita tribe, who six years before had been living on Salt Fork of the Brazos, 60 leagues away. But the Wichita later were still living— a part of the time at least—on the upper Brazos. About 1777 or 1778 the "Panis-Mahas" (Ouvaes, Aguajes, Aguichi [see *Akwech*]) came southward and settled with the Tawehash, but at the time of Mezières' visit in 1778 they had withdrawn temporarily northwestward. Within a few months, however, they returned, and seem to have remained permanently with the Tawehash (Mezières, MS. letters in Mem. de Nueva España, XXVIII, 229, 281–82). They evidently established a separate village, for Fernandez in 1778 and Mares in 1789 each noted in this locality three Jumanes or Tawehash villages a short distance apart (diaries in the Archivo Gen.). Twenty years later Davenport said that on Red r., 100 leagues above Natchitoches, there were still three neighboring villages of these people, which he called the Tahuyás, Huichitas, and Aguichi, respectively (Noticia, 1809, MS. in Archivo Gen.).

Austin's map of 1829 (original in the Department of Fomento, Mexico) and the Karte von Texas of 1839 both show the Tawehash settlement on Wichita r., above the junction of the two main branches. For their treaties with the United States and their removal to reservations, see *Wichita* (confederacy). Consult also *Jumano*. (H. E. B.)

Ahijados.—Freytas, Peñalosa (1662), 35, 66, 1882 (identical?). **Ahijaos.**—Ibid., 34 (identical?). **Ahijitos.**—Morfi, MS. Hist. Texas, bk. 2, ca. 1782 (identical?). **Aijados.**—Bancroft, Ariz. and New Mex., 150, 1889 (identical?). **Aijaos.**—Peñalosa (1662) cited by Bancroft, ibid., 163 (identical?). **Aixaos.**—Benavides, Memorial, 85, 1630 (identical?). **Axtaos.**—Oñate (1606) cited by Prince, Hist. N. Mex., 166, 1883 (identical?). **Ayjados.**—Bandelier in Arch. Inst. Papers, III, 169, 1890 (identical?). **Ayjaos.**—Zarate-Salmeron (ca. 1629), Rel., in Land of Sunshine, 46, Dec. 1899 (identical?). **Jumana.**—Morfi, op. cit. **Jumanes.**—Pedro Latren, op. cit., 1750. **Jumano.**—For other forms of this name see *Jumano*. (Until the recent investigations by Dr H. E. Bolton, the identification of the Jumano was in doubt.—Editor.) **Panipiques.**—Pedro Latren, op. cit. **Panipiquet.**—Form cited in early documents of Texas. **Paniques.**—Latren, op. cit., 1750. **Skin pricks.**—Clark (1804) in Orig. Jour. Lewis and Clark, I, 190, 1904 (referring to their custom of tattooing). **Taaovaiazes.**—Mezières, MS. letter in Mem. de Nueva España, XXVIII, 235, 1778. **Taaovayases.**—Mezières, ibid., 247. 177° **Tabayase.**—Doc. 503 in Tex. State

Archives, 1791–92. **Taboayas.**—Gov. Cabello, Informe, 1784, MS. in Archivo Gen. **Taboayases.**—Mezières, op. cit., 261, 1779. **Taboayazes.**—Gov. Cabello, Rep. on Comanches, 1786, MS. in Béxar Archives. **Tabuayas.**—Rivera to Oconor, 1768, MS. in Béxar Archives. **Taguace.**—Vial, Diary, 1787, MS. in Archivo Gen. **Taguaias.**—Parilla to Viceroy, Nov. 8, 1760, MS. in Archivo Gen. **Taguais.**—Tremiño, op. cit., 1765. **Taguallas.**—Leal, Noticia, 1794, MS. in Béxar Archives. **Taguayares.**—Cabello, Informe, MS., 1784. **Taguayas.**—Lopez to Parilla, Expediente sobre San Sabá, 1760, MS. in Archivo Gen. **Taguayazes.**—Cabello, op. cit. **Taguayces.**—Ibid. **Taguayes.**—Gov. Barrios, Informe, 1771, MS. in Archivo Gen. **Taguayos.**—Courbière, Relación, 1791, MS. in Béxar Archives. **Tahuaias.**—Treaty with the tribe, 1821, MS. in Archivo Gen. **Tahuallaus.**—Arredondo, op. cit., 1813. **Tahuaya.**—Census of 1790 in Texas State Archives, 1792. **Tahuayace.**—Doc. of Sept. 20, 1826, in Texas State Archives. **Tahuayaces**—Vial, Diary, MS., 1787. **Tahuayás.**—Davenport, Noticia, 1809, MS. in Archivo Gen. **Tahuayase.**—Doc. of Aug. 1, 1804, in Texas State Archives. **Tahuayases.**—Treaty with the tribe, 1821, MS. in Archivo Gen. **Tamayaca.**—Bull. Soc. Geog. Mex., 267, 1870. **Taobaianes.**—Mezières, op. cit., 1778. **Taobayace.**—Bull. Soc. Geog. Mex., 267, 1870. **Taobayais.**—Expediente sobre la Dolosa Paz, 1774. **Taobayases.**—Mezières, op. cit., 1778. **Taouayaches.**—Robin, Voy. Louisiane, III, 3, 1807. **Taouayas.**—Exp. sobre la Dolosa Paz, 1774. **Taovayaiaces.**—Mezières, op. cit., 1778. **Taovayases.**—Bonilla (1772), Breve Compendio, in Tex. Hist. Quar., VIII, 57, 1905. **Tauweâsh.**—McCoy, Ann. Reg., no. 4, 27, 1838. **Tavaïases.**—Mezières, Relación, 1770, MS. in Archivo Gen. **Tavaiazes.**—Ibid. **Tavayas.**—Bucareli to Ripperdá, Nov. 18, 1772, MS. in Béxar Archives. **Tavoayases.**—Croix, Relación Particular, 1778, MS. in Archivo Gen. **Tavoyaces.**—Mezières in Mem. de Nueva España, XXVIII, 283. **Ta-wai-hash.**—H. R. Rep. 299, 44th Cong., 1st sess., 1, 1876. **Tawai'-hias.**—(Caddo name). **Tawe'hash.**—Mooney in 14th Rep. B. A. E., 1095, 1896 (Caddo and Kichai name). **Tawweeahs.**—Ind. Aff. Rep., 558, 1837. **Toajas.**—La Harpe (1719) in Margry, Déc., VI, 290, 1886. **Toanyaces.**—Mezières (1778) quoted by Bancroft, No. Mex. States, I, 661, 1886. **Toauyaces.**—Mezières, op. cit., 229, 1778. **Toayas.**—La Harpe, op. cit., 1719. **Tomachas.**—Domenech, Deserts, II, 191, 1860 (misprint). **Too-war-sar.**—Clark (1804) in Orig. Jour. Lewis and Clark, I, 190, 1904. **Toriuash.**—Schoolcraft, Ind. Tribes, II, 126, 1852. **Touashes.**—Bollaert in Jour. Ethnol. Soc. Lond., II, 279, 1850. **Towaahach.**—Lewis and Clark, Journal, 149, 1840. **Towaches.**—Morgan in N. Am. Rev., 55, Jan. 1870. **Towahach.**—Lewis and Clark, Journal, 149, 1840. **Towahhans.**—ten Kate, Synonymie, 10, 1884. **Towash.**—Kenney in Wooten, Comp. Hist. Tex., 753, 1898. **Tow-ash.**—Ind. Aff. Rep. 1849, 33, 1850. **Towcash.**—Trimble quoted by Morse, Rep. to Sec. War, 257, 1822. **Tow-ce-ahge.**—ten Kate, Synonymie, 10, 1884. **Toweache.**—Schermerhorn (1812) in Mass. Hist. Coll., 2d s., II, 26, 1814. **Toweash.**—Thomas (1845) in Sen. Ex. Doc. 14, 32d Cong., 2d sess., 131, 1853. **Toweeahge.**—Catlin, N. A. Inds., II, 73, 1844 (own name). **Tow-eeash.**—Kennedy, Texas, map, 1841. **Towiaches.**—Sibley, Hist. Sketches, 74, 1806. **Towiache-Tawakenoes.**—Balbi, Atlas Ethnogr., 54, 1826 (improperly combined with Tawakoni). **Towiash.**—Latham in Trans. Philol. Soc. Lond., 104, 1856. **Towish.**—Karte von Texas, 1839. **Towoash.**—Drake, Bk. Inds., xii, 1848 (confounded with Tawakoni). **Towoashe.**—Domenech, Deserts, I, 444, 1860. **Towrache.**—Sibley, Hist. Sketches, 108, 1806. **Towzash.**—Butler and Lewis (1846) in H. R. Doc. 76, 29th Cong., 2d sess., 7, 1847. **Toyash.**—Hildreth, Dragoon Campaigns, 160, 1836.

Tawi. A Cholovone village on lower San Joaquin r., Cal.—Pinart, Cholovone MS., B. A. E., 1880.

Tawiskaron (*Tawis'karron'*, *Tawis'kara*, *Thauwiskalau* (Oneida), *Tăwi'-skă-lă* (Cherokee, 'Flint'), Tawiskano for *Tawiskărano'*, and *Saiewiskerat*. The nominal stem, dialectically varied, is in these expressions -*wiskăr*-, -*wisker*-, or -*wiskăl*-, occurring in the lexical terms *owiskără'*, *owiskeră'*, or *owiskălă'*, respectively, and meaning 'ice', 'hail', 'sleet'; these latter are derivatives of the noun *owis'ă'*, 'ice', 'hail', 'sleet', 'frozen snow', 'glare ice', and 'glass goblet' (modern); of this noun the Tuscarora *uwi'çră'* is a dialectic form, whence comes *uwi'sĕkră'* with the specific meaning 'sleet or rain frozen to trees and to the ground'; and the initial *t*- of the first six appellatives is a characteristic prefix of proper names and is in fact an expletive dual sign, originally meaning 'two', 'two-fold', 'complete', 'in a double degree'; and the *a*- for the full *ha*-, affixed to the nominal stem, -*wiskăr*-, is the prefix pronoun of the third person, masculine sex, singular number, and anthropic gender, signifying 'he'; lastly, the verb-stem -*ron'*, suffixed to the nominal stem, is the perfect tense form of the anomalous verb-stem -*rĕn'*, 'affix or add to', or 'be arrayed in'; hence the expression *Tawiskarron'* signifies 'He is arrayed in ice in a double degree.' The expression *Tawiskara*, or rather *Tawis'-kără'*, is the noun modified only by the affixes explained above, and signifies 'He (is) ice in a double degree', the substantive verb being unexpressed but understood. The final vowel and the glottic close of this compound is either modified or dropped when an adjective is suffixed to it, as in the following: The adjective -*ano'* signifies 'cold', 'chilly'; hence *Tawiskarano'* means 'He (is) ice, cold in a double degree.' The substantive verb, as is usual in the present tense of attributive themes, is not here expressed. In the sentence-word *Saiewiskerat*, one of the characteristic functions or activities of the personage designated by this expression is described. The initial syllable *sa*- signifies 'again', 'anew', 'repeatedly', and limits the meaning of the verb in the expression; *ie*- is the pronoun of the third person, indefinite as to sex and number, although usually singular, and commonly signifies 'one', 'one who'; the noun-stem is explained above; lastly, the suffix verb-stem -*at*, being the present tense form of the anomalous verb -*at*, signifies 'present', 'show', 'spread' 'cause to be present'; hence the expression as an appellative means 'Again one causes ice to be present (as is his habit)'. These etymologic derivations of a number of the appellatives applied to a certain personality would seem to connect him directly with the frost-bringing and the ice-forming potency in nature, and that they establish the inference that Tawiskaron is the name of the personification of the winter power transfigured into a man-being, a god of winter, whose functions and activities constitute him the mighty frost king, whose breath and magic power blight the verdure of plants and trees and lock lakes and rivers in bonds of ice. In confirmation of the preceding interpretations, the following expressions are cited from Bruyas' Radices Iroquæorum: *owĭsĕ*, or *gawisa*, 'ice', 'hail', 'glass'; *owiskra*, 'hail', 'sleet'; *gawiskerontion, gawisontion*, 'one is casting or sowing hail, ice, sleet', hence 'one (it) is hailing'; lastly, *watiowiskwentare*, meaning 'it has covered it with frost, with ice'; 'it has spread out ice (like a sheet)'; hence 'it has covered it with glare ice.' In the two sentence-words preceding the last one cited, the final *-ontion* is the perfect tense form of the irregular verb *-otĭ*, 'cast', 'throw', but it has a present meaning, 'is casting, throwing'. The termination of the last citation, *-kwentare*, is a perfect tense form with the meaning of a present tense, viz, 'is lying flat', 'is lying face downward'. The original meaning of the nominal stem *-wiskăr-* of the vocable *owiskără* was apparently 'crystal', 'smooth', 'slippery', 'slick'; hence it came to designate ice on the one hand, and chert or flint on the other. Even among the Cherokee, who are linguistically cognate with the Iroquoian peoples of the E. and N., *Tăwi′skălă* is the name of a mythic anthropic being, called Flint, regarded as the producer of flint rock. They have also preserved in the words *tăwi′ska* or *tăwi′skage*, signifying 'smooth', 'slick', the fundamental meaning the stem had before it came to denote 'flint'. Thus Cherokee usage confirms the suggestion that the basic signification of the stem *-wiskar-*, or *-wiskĕr-*, is 'smooth', 'crystal', 'slippery', 'slick'. A similar connection between terms denotive of 'ice' and 'flint' respectively, exists among some of the Algonquian dialects, and also between these terms and the name for 'wolf', a false connection has been established in some of these same dialects. In Passamaquoddy and Malecite *malsum* and *malsumsis* signify 'wolf' and 'small wolf' respectively, while the first is also a name of this younger brother of Nanabozho (Kuloskap); and in the closely related Micmac, *măls* signifies 'flint' or 'chert'. The last is found in Unami Delaware under the form *máhales*, and in the Unalachtigo Delaware of Campanius Holm under that of *maháres*, with the signification 'flint', 'chert'. But in the Abnaki it appears under the form *monlsem*, with the meaning 'wolf'. In the Chippewa name for 'white flint', *mikwamewabik*, literally 'ice stone' or 'ice rock',

is brought out the reason for the use of the same vocable to denote 'ice', 'frost', 'sleet', on the one hand, and 'chert', 'flint', on the other. The Chippewa term for ice is *mikwam*, and the Cree *miskwamiy*, whence the derivative *miskwamissa*, 'it hails'. *Piponoukhe* (written Kabebonicca by Schoolcraft) signifies freely 'Winter Maker', from *pipon*, 'winter', and the verb-stem *-oke* or *-okhe*, 'make, cause, do'; and *Chakekenapok* means 'the Man of Flint, or the Firestone'. In the foregoing identifications are found the reasons that gave the name 'He is the Flint', 'He Overspreads with Ice', 'He is the Ice', 'He is the Wintermaker', and lastly, 'He is the Wolf', to one and the same personage identified with the production and control of certain phenomena in nature. It has thus become evident that through wrong interpretations of misunderstood homophonic but not cognate terms, various striking appellations, suggested by more or less apparent similarity between the unrelated natural phenomena in question, have been made the name of the imaginary man-being, originally believed to produce and control but one class of phenomena. Brinton (Myths of the New World, 203, 1896) endeavored to show that the name Tawiskara was a cognate or derivative of the Oneida *tetiucalas*, and the Mohawk *tyokaras* or *tewhgarlas*, which he rendered 'dark or darkness' (although they in fact all mean 'at the time it becomes dark, at twilight'), and he purported to quote Bruyas and Cuoq in support of this opinion, although neither of these lexicographers, so far as known, attempted to analyze the name Tawiskaron or Tawiskara).

An imaginary man-being of the cosmogonic philosophy of the Iroquoian and other tribes, to whom was attributed the function of making and controlling the activities and phenomena of winter. He was the Winter God, the Ice King, since his distinctive character is clearly defined in terms of the activities and phenomena of nature peculiar to this season. As an earth power he was one of the great primal man-beings belonging to the second cosmical period of the mythological philosophy of the Iroquoian, Algonquian, and perhaps other Indians. Although his paternity was not beyond question, his parentage was illustrious. In the mythology to which he belonged, his grandmother, *Awĕn‘hāi‘* ('Mature Flower', or probably 'Mature Earth'), called Mesakomikokwi by the Potawatomi, was expelled from the skyland, situated above the visible firmament, because of her husband's jealousy. When in falling she reached the waters of the primal sea that covered the space now occupied by the earth she was received on the carapace of the great primal Turtle who belonged to this second cosmic period, on which his fellows had prepared the nucleus of the earth. Being parthenogenetically pregnant before her expulsion, she in due time gave birth to a daughter, who, on reaching woman's estate, became pregnant while at play, according to one of several differing traditions, by the direct act of the primal man-being called Wind. In due time the young woman gave birth to twins (some traditions say to quadruplets), one being Te'haron'hiawă'k'hon' (q. v.), the other Tawĭ'skaron'. The latter destroyed his mother by refusing to be born in the natural way and in violently emerging through his mother's armpit—some traditions say through her navel. This he was readily fitted to do because his body was composed of chert or flint and his head was in the form of an arrowpoint of flint. According to a variant version, one of the great race of the Turtle, transformed into a handsome young warrior, sought the maiden for his wife. Having refused many other man-beings under the same guise by the advice of her mother, she at last, through the counsel of the same mentor, accepted him. Having come to her lodge on the appointed night, he conversed with her until the time came for retiring, when the young warrior placed two arrows, one plain and the other tipped with flint, horizontally in the bark side of the lodge just above the maiden, and then departed. The next day he returned for a short time, and then taking his arrows withdrew. In due time the twins were born, as related above. It is believed that Tawi'skaron', in the substance of his body and in the shape of his head, was prenatally suggested by the flint-tipped arrow. In concept Tawi'skaron' is so closely identical with the mythic personage called Chakekenapok in Algonquian mythology, a younger brother of Nanabozho, that they may be treated together.

In Iroquoian mythology this being is known under various names indicative of some function or feature attributed to him. Among his Iroquoian names are Tawis'karon (Te'hawis'karron'), Tawis'-kano or Tawiskarano', Saiewiskerat, Tawiskara, O'hā'ä' ('Flint,' Onondaga), Ot'hä'gwĕn'dă' ('Flint,' Seneca), Tehotennhiaron ('He is arrayed in flint,' Mohawk), Atenenhiarhon (a corrupt form of the last), of which the Tuscarora form is Tunĕña'r'hĕn', meaning 'a giant' only, Ro'nikoñrahet'kĕn' ('His Mind is Evil'), and Honon'hi'dăe', ('He is Warty', Seneca).

In Algonquian dialects this personage appears, among others, under the names Malsum, Piponoukhe', Chakekenapok, and Windigo. In one of the earliest accounts of Algonquian cosmical myths it is said that the Montagnais attributed the change of seasons to two brothers—Nipinoukhe ('Summer-maker') and Piponoukhe ('Winter-maker'). Most of these Indians regarded these brothers as human in form, while the rest were not so certain on this point; all, however, were agreed that they were beings who were alive like themselves, for they had been overheard talking and rustling, especially at their return, although no one understood their language. Far in the north dwelt Piponoukhe for a stated time, while his brother lived in the sunny southland. At regular times the two brothers exchanged places, which brought about a change of seasons. The Montagnais called this exchanging of places *Achitescatoueth*. Piponoukhe brought with him cold weather, frost, snow, sleet, and ice, and thereby destroyed everything. This myth has been developed into that of Kulpojut, explained below.

The persistence and the security of life from the destructive powers of the Winter god is metaphorically expressed in the details of the following incident related in one of the longer versions of the common Iroquoian genesis myth. During the creative time Te'haron'hiawă'k'hon' received from his father of the race of the Turtle an ear of corn, with proper instructions as to its care and uses. In time Te'haron'hiawă'k'hon' roasted an ear of corn which he had himself raised, which emitted an appetizing aroma. When Tawis'karon' smelt this odor he informed his grandmother, who ordered him to go to the lodge of his brother to ask him to share this unknown thing with them. On hearing this request Te'haron'hiawă'k'hon' replied that he would consent on condition that Tawis'karon' surrender to him "the flint whereby thou livest." To this Flint replied, "What dost thou mean? Dost thou mean my arrow with the point of flint?" To which the reply came, "No; I mean, indeed, that flint which is in thy body." To this Flint answered, "So be it as thou dost wish it." Then, opening his mouth, he thrust out the flint thing in question. His brother seized it and gently pulled it; he would not break it off, although Flint asked him to do so. "Verily," his brother answered, "thy life belongs to thee, so thou thyself must break it off and give it to me, for on no other condition can our compact be fulfilled." So, reluctantly, Flint performed his part of the agreement, whereupon his brother gave him two grains of the corn, one for the grandmother and one for himself. By this act Tawis'karon' lost his birthright of coequal *orenda* (q. v.), or magic power. This is readily explainable by the phenomena of the beginning of the spring of the year. By the internal heat of the earth, icicles thaw and become detached at their bases and are not broken off within their length; and on clear mornings the face of nature is sometimes covered with heavy hoarfrost which by the internal warmth of things and a slight rise in the temperature of the air becomes detached without melting from the outside, as it were, but falls like flakes of snow. These phenomena show that the power of the Winter god is ending, and that Tawis'karon' surrenders again his flint lance—the piercing, blasting, withering power of frost and winter's cold.

In the cosmical legends of the Iroquoian tribes, Tawis'karon', incited and abetted by his grandmother, makes many attempts to thwart his brother, Te'haron'-hiawǎ'k'ho', in his work of bringing into orderly being the present phenomena and bodies of nature. One of the most exciting of these efforts was the theft of the sun by Tawis'karon', and Awěn'hǎ'i', his grandmother. They carried it far away to the southeast, where they hoped to keep it solely for their own use. But by the potent aid of the magic power of various great man-beings, such as Otter, Beaver, Fox, and Fisher, Te'haron'-hiawǎ'k'ho' was enabled to recapture the sun and to bring it back and then to place it where it now is shining for all people. It is hardly necessary to point out that this incident is the mythologic statement of the fact that in the autumn and winter the sun apparently goes far to the southeast.

Tawis'karon', in emulation of his brother's successful attempts to create various things, made only noxious objects, such as bats, butterflies, owls, frogs, and worms and other creeping things; but his first great labor was to conceal from Te'haron'hiawǎ'k'ho' all the birds and animals in a great cavern in a cliff; this is evidently but a metaphorical statement of the driving of the birds to migration and of the animals to hibernate by the approach of Winter. According to the legend they were in great part freed by Te'haron'hiawǎ'k'ho'. Then Tawis'karon' is discovered by his brother, constructing a bridge of white rocks (i. e., ice) on the surface of the surrounding waters, which he asserted he was gradually extending toward the distant shore of another land wherein dwelt fierce, carnivorous monsters, in order to enable them to come across to feed upon the people and the animals created by Te'-haron'hiawǎ'k'ho'; this was obviously the statement that were all lakes and rivers bridged solidly with ice, the monsters Cold, Want, Famine, and

Death would readily cross and feed on the creatures of his brother, for nothing is killed except for food by the great primal beings. He was stopped in this nefarious work by his brother, who sent the tufted bluebird, with the bloody thigh of a grasshopper in its mouth, to frighten him by its cry. As this bird is one of the first heralds of spring, its cry told Winter that Spring was at hand, and so Tawis'karon' fled with his work only half finished. The bridge of white flint dissolved as fast as he fled to the land. When he became the prisoner of his own brother he attempted to escape on one of the pieces of white flint. It is only a step from a cake of ice to the mythical "white stone canoe," so popular and yet so erroneously attributed to various other beings. Again, he tries to imitate his brother in creating a human being, which was the object of his greatest desire; so having learned from his brother that life was immanent in the substance of the earth, and therefore the products of it, Tawis'karon' decided to outdo him by using the foam of water to form his man-being, as in fact it was; after thus forming the body of the man-being he called his brother to see it, but failing to cause it to show any signs of life, he implored his brother to aid him by giving it life and motion, which was done. As this man-being was pure white it is obvious that this creature was snow, and that without life, which Tawis'karon' could not give it, it could not come and go, as it does, like that which has life and power of motion. Some modern Iroquois who are the adherents of the so-called Handsome Lake reformed Iroquois religion, and others who have become converted to Christianity claim to identify Tawis'-karon' with the devil of Caucasians, and so reasoning from this incident pretend that this devil created the white race. The constant antagonism between Tawis'karon' and his twin brother finally caused the latter to decide upon the destruction of his younger brother. In the details of the fierce combat with unequal weapons to which this resolution led, it is said that the surface of the earth was crumpled into ridges and valleys, that the blood and the fragments from the body of Tawis'karon' became flint stones, and that from his intestines were formed fruitful vines of many kinds—a statement obviously due to the fact that vines growing in the clefts of rocks apparently barren have a peculiar luxuriance.

In the Cherokee story of the Rabbit and Tawiskǎlǎ (Mooney, 19th Rep. B. A. E., 1900) the ceaseless struggle between life, the productive force in nature, represented by the Rabbit, and the destructive powers of nature, represented by Tawiskălă, are quite apparent. The Rabbit in this story is evidently the Algonquian Wabozho ('White Maker') who has been absorbed into the Nanabozho character as explained below. The story relates that Rabbit, while Tawiskălă was in his lodge, drove a sharp stake into the body of his guest, causing it to explode, scattering flint fragments in all directions.

In one of the variants of the common Iroquoian cosmic genesis myth Tawis'-karon' is one of four children, quadruplets, of whom the name of only one, Te'haron'-hiawă'k''ho'', has been recorded. In the Potawatomi version of the Algonquian cycle of genesis myths, however, the Algonquian names of these quadruplets have been preserved by Father De Smet. These latter names are Nanabozho (q. v.), Chipiapoos (?Tcipiapozho), Wabosso (?Wabozho, 'White maker'), and Chakekenapok (Cree Tchakisahigan, 'flint', 'gun-flint', etc.). The infant man-being bearing the last name caused the death of his mother by violently bursting through her side.

In after time some of the functions of Wabozho were evidently absorbed in part by Chakekenapok or attributed to him, either consciously or unconsciously, thus leaving only two great personages or man-beings, for Tcipiapozho while he lived was a rather negative character, largely dominated by Nanabozho, who also appears to have absorbed the name Wabozho and a part of his functions. Thus in the third great cosmic period, the present, a complete parallelism became established between the elemental gods of the Iroquoian and the Algonquian pantheon. For this period the Iroquoian data are more complete and definite. The gods have departed from the earth and have their dwelling in the skyland, the land of disembodied souls. According to the Iroquoian legends descriptive of this skyland, there is far in the rear of the great lodge of Awĕn'hā'i', the grandmother of Tawis'karon', a large compartment in which dwells a man-being of peculiar aspect and functions. His name in the Onondaga dialect is De'hodiătgă'-ewĕn', 'He whose body is divided or split in two parts.' One of these parts, it is said, is crystal ice, and the other is warm flesh and blood. Twice every year this man-being, whose magic power outranks all earth-produced ones, comes to the doorway of his compartment, presenting in each instance a different side of his body. When he presents the side composed of crystalline ice, winter begins on the earth; and when he presents the side constituted of flesh and blood, summer begins. He is evidently composed

of the characters in large measure of Tawis'karon' and Te'haron'hiawă'k''ho'', of the Iroquoian cosmology, and of Piponoukhe and Nipinoukhe, or Nanabozho and Chakekenapok, of the Algonquian cosmical legends; for in them is found a great man-being whose functions are concerned with the change of seasons. His name in Passamaquoddy is Kulpojut (Coolpŭjōt in Micmac by Rand), which signifies 'One rolled over by handspikes.' Each spring and each autumn he is rolled over; he faces the w. for the autumn season, and the E. for the spring. His body, it is said, has no bones. In this lodge of Awĕn'hā'i' and in the skyland Te'haron'hiawă'k''ho'' has become only a shadowy figure, a mere messenger or inspector for the gods. Tawis'karon' has been completely absorbed in the great man-being of ice and flesh, De'hodiă't'-kăewĕn'. Such appears to be the degree of development of the two great dominating figures in the cosmological philosophy of the Iroquoian and the Algonquian peoples. See *Mythology, Nanabozho, Teharonhiawagon.*

For further details consult Sagard, Hist. du Canada, I–IV, 1636, new ed., 1836; Relations des Jesuites, I–III, 1858; De Smet, Oregon Missions, 1847; Blackbird, Hist. Ottawa and Chippewa, 1887; Brinton, Myths of the New World, 1896; Hewitt, Iroquoian Cosmology, in 21st Rep. B. A. E., 1903; Cuoq, Lex. de la Langue Iroq., 1866.   (J. N. B. H.)

Tawkee. (1) The golden-club or floating arum (*Orontium aquaticum*). (2) The Virginia wake-robin (*Arum virginicum*). The word, formerly in use in New Jersey and Pennsylvania, and still surviving locally, was adopted in the 17th century by the Swedish settlers in New Jersey. Rev. A. Hesselius (1725) speaks of "tachis or hopnuts" (Nelson, Inds. of N. J., 78, 1894). Kalm (Trav., I, 389, 1772) cites as Indian names of *Arum virginicum* tawks, tawking, and tuckah, adding that the Swedes of New Jersey call it tawko. Kalm also cites as names of the golden-club tawkim, tuckoim, etc., stating also that the Swedes call it tawkee. The word, which is practically the same as tuckahoe, is derived from *p'tukwi*, or *p'tukqueu*, in the Delaware dialect of Algonquian, signifying 'it is globular,' a term of general application to tuberous roots.   (A. F. C.)

Tawsee. A Cherokee settlement about the period of the Revolution; situated on Tugaloo r., in the present Habersham co., N. E. Ga.
Tahasse.—Bartram Trav., 371, 1792. Torsee.—Doc. of 1755 quoted by Royce in 5th Rep. B. A. E., 143, 1887. Tussee.—Muzon's map (1771) cited by Royce, ibid.

Tawshtye. The extinct Buffalo clan of the former pueblo of Pecos, N. Mex.

Tâshtyë'+.—Hodge in Am. Anthr., IX, 349, 1896 (+ = *ash*='people').

Taxlipu. Given as a Chumashan village formerly near Santa Barbara, Cal. (Bancroft, Nat. Races, I, 459, 1874). Possibly intended for Tashlibunau, the Yokuts name of a place near San Emidio, at the s. extremity of Tulare valley, in Chumash territory.   (A. L. K.)

Tazaaigadika ('salmon eaters'). A Shoshoni division formerly occupying the country about Salmon falls on Snake r., s. Idaho. Their dependence on the salmon which abounded here gave them their name of "Salmon Eaters."

Ag'-gi-tik'-kah.—Stuart, Montana, 81, 1865. **Fish Eaters.**—Ross, Fur Hunters, I, 249, 1855. **Salmon Eaters.**—Stuart, op. cit., 81. **Táza'aigadi'ka.**—Hoffman in Proc. Am. Philos. Soc., XXIII, 298, 1886. **War-are-ree-kas.**—Ross, op. cit.

Taztasagonies. A tribe referred to in 1730 as living northward from San Antonio, Texas, and as being hostile to the tribes of the San Antonio region (Pedro de Rivera, doc. in Arch. Col. Santa Cruz de Querétaro, K, leg. 5, no. 6). About this time the governor of Texas, Mediavilla y Ascona, asked permission to make war on the "Apache, Yita [Yuta, Ute] and Tastasagonia" (ibid., K, leg. 6, no. 15). The tribe is therefore probably one otherwise known under the name of Apache or Comanche.   (H. E. B.)

Tastasagonia.—Mediavilla y Ascona (1746), op. cit.

Tchachagoulas. A name noted on De l'Isle's map of 1707 as that of a town or people on Bayou Lafourche, s. E. La., below Bayougoula. The name contains the Mobilian term *okla*, 'people', but the first part cannot be translated.

Tchachagoulas.—French, Hist. Coll. La., III, 59, note, 1851. **Tchatchagoula.**—De l'Isle map (1707) in Winsor, Hist. Am., II, 294, 1886.

Tchanhié. An unidentified village or tribe mentioned to Joutel in 1687 (Margry, Déc., III, 409, 1878), while he was staying with the Kadohadacho on Red r. of Louisiana, by the chief of that tribe, as being among his enemies.

Tchataksofka ('precipice'). A town of the Creek Nation, 1 m. s. of Eufaula, Okla.—Gatschet, Creek Migr. Leg., II, 186, 1888.

Tchatchiun ('raccoon'). A Yuchi clan.

Djä'tieⁿ.—Speck, Yuchi Inds., 70, 1909. **Tchäto'hiun tahá.**—Gatschet, Uchee MS., B. A. E., 70, 1885 (='raccoon gens').

Tchatikutingi. A former Chitimacha village at the junction of Bayou Tèche with Bayou Atchafalaya, La.

Tcháti Kut.ngi námu.—Gatschet in Trans. Anthr. Soc. Wash., II, 152, 1883.

Tchatkasitunshki. A former Chitimacha village on the site of Charenton, Bayou Tèche, Grand lake, La.

Kawítunshki.—Gatschet in Trans. Anthr. Soc. Wash., II, 151, 1883. **Tchāt Kasítunshki.**—Ibid.

Tcheti (their name for Grand r.). A former Chitimacha village on Grand r., 20 m. E. of Charenton, La.

Tcéti námu.—Swanton, field notes, B. A. E., 1909. **Tchétin námu.**—Gatschet in Trans. Anthr. Soc. Wash., II, 152, 1883 (*námu*='village').

Tchikilli. See *Chekilli*.

Tchikimisi (*Tcikimisi*). A former Maidu village on the s. side of Cosumnes r., not far from the mouth of Camp cr., Eldorado co., Cal.—Dixon in Bull. Am. Mus. Nat. Hist., XVII, map, 1905.

Te (*T!ē*). A Haida town, the principal one owned by the Tas-lanas before they migrated to Alaska. It formerly stood on the w. coast of Graham id., Queen Charlotte ids., Brit. Col., opposite Frederick id.   (J. R. S.)

Tī Ilnigē.—Harrison in Proc. Roy. Soc. Can., sec. II, 124, 1895. **T!ē.**—Swanton, Cont. Haida, 281, 1905.

Te. The Cottonwood clans of the Tewa pueblos of San Juan, Santa Clara, and San Ildefonso, N. Mex.

Te-tdóa.—Hodge in Am. Anthr., IX, 350, 1896 (*tdóa*='people').

Teacuacueitzisti. A dialect of the Cora language, spoken, according to Ortega, by that part of the tribe living in the lower parts of the Sierra Nayarit, toward the w., in Jalisco, Mexico. The name with the termination *isti* or *izti* was for a time applied to a division of the Cora proper, but the dialectal variation being slight, this classification has been abandoned. See *Cora*.

Teacuacitzica.—Orozco y Berra, Geog., 59, 1864. **Teacuacitzisti.**—Ibid. (for the people). **Teacuacueitzisti.**—Ortega, Vocab. Cast. y Cora (1732), 7, reprint, 1888 (pl. form; sing. Teacuaeitzica). **Teakuaeitzizti.**—Pimentel, Leng. de Mex., II, 83, 1865.

Teahinkutchin ('people of the lower country'). A Kutchin tribe or a subdivision of the Natsitkutchin formerly inhabiting the country N. w. of the latter. They hunted the caribou from the Yukon to the coast of the Arctic ocean. They formerly were a strong band, but by 1866 were reduced to only 4 hunters, and now are probably extinct.

Gens de siffleur.—Ross, notes on Tinne, S. I. MS. 474 ('marmot people'). **Tē-ä-hiñ'kūtch'ín.**—Ibid. (trans. 'people of the country below others'). **Te-ha-hin Kutchin.**—Gibbs, MS. notes on Ross, B. A. E. **Teystsekutshi.**—Latham in Trans. Philol. Soc. Lond., 67, 1856.

Teahquois. A Nanticoke village in 1707, probably on the lower Susquehanna r., Pa.—Evans (1707) quoted by Day, Pa., 391, 1843.

Teakata (*te-aka*, a sort of underground cooking pit, hence 'the place where there is the *teaka*' par excellence). The most sacred place of the Huichol, containing a small temple and 7 "god houses," which give it the effect of a little village; situated near Santa Catarina, Jalisco, Mexico. The principal god of the Huichol was the one who cooks the food dearest to the tribe—deer meat and mescal hearts—in a *teaka*, whence the name of the place. Near by is a large shallow cavern called Hainótega, the birthplace and first home of the Huichol God of Fire.—Lumholtz, Unknown Mexico, II, 169, 1902.

Teana. A tribe mentioned in 1708 in a list of those that had been met or heard of N. of San Juan Bautista mission on the lower Rio Grande (Fr. Isidro Felix de Espinosa, Relación Compendiosa of the Rio Grande missions, MS. in the College of Santa Cruz de Querétaro). (H. E. B.)

Teanaustayae. One of the most important Huron villages formerly in Ontario. In 1638 the mission of St Joseph was removed there from Ihontiria. It was destroyed by the Iroquois in 1648.
Ieanausteaiae.—Jes. Rel. 1637, 107, 1858 (misprint). St Joseph.—Shea, Cath. Miss., 178, 1855. Teananstayae.—Ibid., 174. Teansteixé.—Jes. Rel. 1640, 63, 1858 (misprint). Teanaustaiae.—Ibid., 1637, 107, 1858. Teanaostaiaé.—Ibid., 161. Teanosteaé.—Ibid., 70.

Teatontaloga ('two mountains apart'). A Mohawk village existing at different periods in New York. The oldest one known by that name was the principal village of the tribe until destroyed by the French in 1666. It was rebuilt a mile above the former site and was for a time the site of the Jesuit mission of St Mary, but was again destroyed by the French in 1693. Both villages were on the N. side of Mohawk r., close to water, and probably near the mouth of Schoharie cr., in Montgomery co., N. Y. On this spot, on the w. side of the creek, was the last village of that name, better known in' the 18th century as the Lower Mohawk Castle. It was also called Icanderago. Macauley applies this name to the Mohawk band in the vicinity of the village. (J. N. B. H.)
Icanderago.—Macauley, N. Y., II, 96, 1829. I-cander-a-goes.—Ibid., 174-5, 1829 (the band). Lower Mohawk Castle.—Morgan, League Iroq., 474, 1851. Saint Mary.—Shea, Cath. Miss., 258, 1855 (mission name). Ogsadago.—Hansen (1700) in N. Y. Doc. Col. Hist., IV, 802, 1854. Te-ah'-ton-ta-lo'-ga—Morgan, League Iroq., 474, 1851 (Mohawk form). Te-ä-ton-ta-lo'-ga.—Ibid., 18. Te-hon-dä-lo'-ga.—Ibid., 416. Tewauntaurogo.—Edwards (1751) in Mass. Hist. Soc. Coll., 1st s., X, 143, 1809. Tiononderoge.—Ruttenber, Tribes Hudson R., 97, 1872.

Tebi (*Te'-bi*). The Greasewood clan of the Pakab (Reed) phratry of the Hopi.—Stephen in 8th Rep. B. A. E., 39, 1891.

Tebityilat. A former village connected with San Carlos mission, Cal., and said to have been occupied by the Esselen.—Taylor in Cal. Farmer, Apr. 20, 1860.

Tebugkihu ('fire house'). A large oval ruin, the walls of which are still standing 5 to 8 ft high; situated 15 m. N. E. of Keam's cañon and about 25 m. from Walpi, N. E. Ariz. The pueblo was constructed in prehistoric times by the now extinct Firewood clan of the Hopi, ancestors of the inhabitants of the ancient pueblo of Sikyatki.
Fire-house.—Stephen in 8th Rep. B A. E., 20, 1891. Tebugkihu.—Mindeleff, ibid., 57. Tebuñki.—Fewkes in 17th Rep. B. A. E., 633, 1898. Tebvwúki.—Stephen, op. cit.

Tecahanqualahámo.—Mentioned as a pueblo of the province of Atripuy (q. v.), in the region of the lower Rio Grande, N.

Mex., in 1598.—Oñate (1598) in Doc. Inéd., XVI, 115, 1871.

Tecahuistes. A former tribe, probably Coahuiltecan, found on the road from Coahuila to the Texas country in 1690.—Massanet (1690) in Dictamen Fiscal, Nov. 30, 1716, MS.

Tecamamiouen (native name of Rainy lake). A Chippewa band living on Rainy lake, Minn., numbering 500 in 1736. Cf. *Kojejewininewug.*
Tecamamiouen.—Chauvignerie (1736) in N. Y. Doc. Col. Hist., IX, 1054, 1855.

Tecargoni. Mentioned by Orozco y Berra (Geog., 58, 1864) as a division of the Varohio in w. Chihuahua, Mexico, apparently in Chinipas valley.

Tecarnohs ('oozing oil.'—Hewitt). A Seneca settlement, commonly known as Oil Spring village, formerly on Oil cr., near Cuba, Cattaraugus co., N. Y.
Oil Spring.—Morgan, League Iroq., 466, 1851. Tecar'-nohs.—Ibid.

Techicodeguachi. A pueblo, probably of the Opata, in Sonora, Mexico, in 1688. It was a visita of the Spanish mission of Guazavas (q. v.), and was situated in the vicinity thereof, on Rio Batepipo. Pop. 90 at the date named.
Sta Gertrudis Techicodeguachi.—Doc. of 1688 quoted by Bancroft, No. Mex. States, I, 246, 1884. Techico de Guachi.—Mange (ca. 1700), ibid., 233.

Techirogen ('at the fork of the stream.'—Hewitt). An Iroquois village N. of Oneida lake, N. Y., in the middle of the 18th century.—Bellin's map, 1755.

Tecolom. A former village, probably Salinan, connected with San Antonio mission, Monterey co., Cal.—Taylor in Cal. Farmer, Apr. 27, 1860.

Tecolote (from Aztec *tecolotl*, the ground owl). A Papago village in s. w. Pima co., Ariz., near the Mexican border, with 140 families in 1865.
Del Teculote.—Bailey in Ind. Aff. Rep., 208, 1858. Tecolota.—Poston, ibid., 1863, 385, 1864. Tecolote.—Taylor in Cal. Farmer, June 19, 1863.

Tecoripa. A pueblo of the Nevome and formerly the seat of a Spanish mission founded in 1619; situated in central Sonora, Mexico, on the w. branch of lower Rio Yaqui, lat. 29°, lon. 110° 30'. Pop. 269 in 1678; 50 in 1730. Its inhabitants, called by the same name, probably spoke a dialect slightly different from Nevome proper.
Tecorino.—Kino, map (1702) in Stöcklein, Neue Welt-Bott., 74, 1726. Tecoripa.—Rivera (1730) quoted by Bancroft, No. Mex. States, I, 513, 1884. San Francisco de Borja de Tecoripa.—Zapata (1678) in Doc. Hist. Mex., 4th s., III, 358, 1857.

Tecualme. A division of the Cora proper in the Sierra de Nayarit, Jalisco, Mexico. They spoke the same dialect as the Cora. According to Alegre (Hist. Comp. Jesus, III, 205, 1842) they were the last of the three tribes of the Nayarit mts. to yield to the missionaries in the 18th century, when they were placed in pueblos along the Rio San Pedro. One of their former villages was Tonalizco.

Gecualme.—Orozco y Berra, Geog., 280, 1864 (misprint). Jecualme.—Mota Padilla misquoted, ibid., 277. Tecualmes.—Mota Padilla (1742), Conq. Nueva Galicia, 21, 1872.

Tecumigizhik. See *Tikumigizhik*.

Tecumseh (properly *Tikamthi* or *Tecumtha:* 'One who passes across intervening space from one point to another,' i. e. springs (Jones); the name indicates that the owner belongs to the gens of the Great Medicine Panther, or Meteor, hence the interpretations 'Crouching Panther' and 'Shooting Star'). A celebrated Shawnee chief, born in 1768 at the Shawnee village of Piqua on Mad r., about 6 m. s. w. of the present Springfield, Ohio. It was destroyed by the Kentuckians in 1780. His father, who was also a chief, was killed at the battle of Point Pleasant in 1774 (see *Cornstalk*). His mother is said

TECUMSEH

to have been by birth a Creek, but this is doubtful. It must be remembered that a considerable body of Shawnee were domiciliated among the Creeks until long after the Revolution. On the death of his father, Tecumseh was placed under the care of an elder brother, who in turn was killed in battle with the whites on the Tennessee frontier in 1788 or 1789. Still another brother was killed by Tecumseh's side at Wayne's victory in 1794. While still a young man Tecumseh distinguished himself in the border wars of the period, but was noted also for his humane character, evinced by persuading his tribe to discontinue the practice of torturing prisoners. Together with his brother Tenskwatawa the Prophet (q. v.), he was an ardent opponent of the advance

of the white man, and denied the right of the Government to make land purchases from any single tribe, on the ground that the territory, especially in the Ohio valley country, belonged to all the tribes in common. On the refusal of the Government to recognize this principle, he undertook the formation of a great confederacy of all the western and southern tribes for the purpose of holding the Ohio r. as the permanent boundary between the two races. In pursuance of this object he or his agents visited every tribe from Florida to the head of the Missouri r. While Tecumseh was organizing the work in the S. his plans were brought to disastrous overthrow by the premature battle of Tippecanoe under the direction of the Prophet, Nov. 7, 1811. On the breaking out of the War of 1812, Tecumseh at once led his forces to the support of the British, and was rewarded with a regular commission as brigadier-general, having under his command some 2,000 warriors of the allied tribes. He fought at Frenchtown, The Raisin, Ft Meigs, and Ft Stephenson, and covered Proctor's retreat after Perry's decisive victory on L. Erie, until, declining to retreat farther, he compelled Proctor to make a stand on Thames r., near the present Chatam, Ont. In the bloody battle which ensued the allied British and Indians were completely defeated by Harrison, Tecumseh himself falling in the front of his warriors, Oct. 5, 1813, being then in his 45th year. With a presentiment of death he had discarded his general's uniform before the battle and dressed himself in his Indian deerskin. He left one son, the father of Wapameepto, alias Big Jim (q. v.). From all that is said of Tecumseh in contemporary record, there is no reason to doubt the verdict of Trumbull that he was the most extraordinary Indian character in United States history. There is no true portrait of him in existence, the one commonly given as such in Lossing's War of 1812 (1875) and reproduced in Appleton's Cyclopedia of American Biography (1894), and Mooney's Ghost Dance (1896), being a composite result based on a pencil sketch made about 1812, on which were mounted his cap, medal, and uniform. Consult Appleton Cycl. Am. Biog., VI, 1894; Drake, Life of Tecumseh, 1841; Eggleston, Tecumseh and the Shawnee Prophet, 1878; Law, Colonial Hist. Vincennes, 1858; Lossing, War of 1812, 1875; McKenney and Hall, Ind. Tribes, I, 1854; Mooney, Ghost Dance Religion, in 14th Rep. B. A. E., pt. II, 1896; Randall, Tecumseh, in Ohio Archæol. and Hist. Quar., Oct. 1906; Trumbull, Indian Wars, 1851.   (J. M.)

Tedyuskung (possibly a variant of *Kekeuskung*, or *Kikeuskund*, of the Munsee dialect, which signifies 'the healer,' 'one who cures wounds, bruises, etc.'—Hewitt). One of the most famous and crafty of the Delaware chiefs during the period of discussion of the Indian claims following the sale of the lands along the Delaware and Susquehanna to the Proprietors of Pennsylvania by the Iroquois. He was born at Trenton, N. J., about 1705, and died Apr. 16, 1763. Nothing is known of his life before the time he first appears as a historic character, prior to which he was known as "Honest John." When about 50 years of age he was chosen as the chief of the Delawares on the Susquehanna, and from that time until his death he was one of the chief figures in the problem which the authorities of Pennsylvania were trying to solve. He occupied a peculiar position. Sir William Johnson, of New York, was a zealous friend of the Iroquois; Conrad Weiser and George Croghan, of Pennsylvania, were also strongly prejudiced against the Delawares and Shawnee. The question which the government of the province of Pennsylvania had to answer was, How to keep peace with the Iroquois and at the same time prevent the Delawares and the Shawnee, who were becoming more independent of the Iroquois, from going over to the French. The Delawares were beginning to feel that they had been unjustly deprived of their lands by the Pennsylvania authorities aided by the Iroquois. They had been driven from the Delaware to the Susquehanna, and many of them had been forced from that later refuge to the Ohio; and now that France and England had commenced to struggle for the possession of that region they felt that they were being driven from their last resort. They were revolting not only against the English but also against their masters, the Iroquois. At this critical time, when the border settlements in western Pennsylvania were being ravaged by hostile bands of Delawares and Shawnee, and when the English were making preparations for an expedition for the purpose of taking Ft Duquesne, Tedyuskung took his stand as a friend of the English and as a patriot of the Delawares and the Shawnee. The mission of Christian F Post to the Ohio Indians, at Kuskuski, and its success, and the termination of French rule on the Ohio, were in large measure due to the influence and the efforts of this Delaware chief.

Conrad Weiser had told the story of the western Indians at the council at Albany (1754) in order that the Iroquois might know the real situation. The chiefs of the Six Nations realized that something must be done concerning their complaints about the squatters on the Juniata (Col. Rec. Pa., VI, 84, 1851).

At this conference Weiser found that several agents from Connecticut were present, who were seeking to bargain with the Mohawk for land in the Wyoming valley. Before the conference was over these agents went away with deeds for the eastern part of the Wyoming valley and the East branch of the Susquehanna. The Indians went home to the Ohio to find out that the West branch had been sold to Pennsylvania. These facts, and the defeat of Washington at Ft Necessity, followed by Braddock's defeat, led to three years of bloodshed and vengeance. The sale of their lands at Albany, the traffic in rum along the Ohio, and the total neglect by the province of Pennsylvania, caused a complete alienation of these western Indians. Then began the various attempts to win them back, which caused almost endless discussion between the governor, the assembly, and the Proprietors (Col. Rec. Pa., VI, 683; VII, 85, et seq., 1851). The passing of the Scalp Act and the declaration of war against the Delawares caused this tribe to rise in rebellion against the province, and also against longer wearing the hated title of "women" (ibid., VII, 522, 1851). Such was the situation when the council was called at Easton, July, 1756, at which Tedyuskung appeared as the champion of the Delawares. The governor of Pennsylvania opened the council with a speech in which he welcomed the chief. Tedyuskung in his reply said: "The Delawares are no longer the slaves of the Six Nations. I, Tedyuskung, have been appointed king over the Five United Nations. What I do here will be approved by all. This is a good day. I wish the same good that possessed the good old man William Penn, who was the friend of the Indian, may inspire the people of the province at this time" (ibid., 213). A grand reception and feast were given to the Indians present, and "the king and Newcastle" were sent to give the "big peace halloo" to the Indians and invite them to a large conference, which would be held later. Tedyuskung left Easton, but remained at Ft Allen, where his drunken sprees and the actions of Lieut. Miller endangered the whole outcome of the peace negotiations. (For the letters from Ft Allen concerning Tedyuskung and the investigation of affairs by Weiser, see Frontier Forts of Pa., I, 202, 1896, and Archives of Pa., 2d s., II, 745, 1853.)

It was at this time that Tedyuskung was blamed for having dealings with the French. There is no evidence that such was the case. While he was lingering at Ft Allen the governor of Pennsylvania sent Newcastle to New York to find out from the Iroquois if they had deputized Tedyuskung to act for them. This they denied.

War between France and England had been declared and the expedition against Ft Duquesne was being organized. An alliance with the Cherokee and the Catawba was being sought. The Iroquois and the Delawares both said that they would not fight on the same side with these hated foes, hence the whole effect of the Easton council was in danger of becoming dissipated. Then came up the almost endless discussions among the various parties in the councils of the province. Gov. Morris had been succeeded by Gov. Denny, who insisted that the council for which arrangements had been made must be held in Philadelphia and not at Easton. Finally he consented to go to Easton with a heavy guard. Tedyuskung said in his opening speech: "I am sorry for what our people have done. I have gone among our people pleading for peace. If it cost me my life I would do it" (Col. Rec. Pa., VII, 332, 1851).

A general peace was decided upon, and Tedyuskung promised to see that the white prisoners were returned. He went to Ft Allen, where he and his warriors had a drunken frolic. Weiser says of him at this time: "Though he is a drunkard and a very irregular man, yet he is a man that can think well, and I believe him to be sincere in what he said" (Pa. Arch. 2d s., III, 67, 1853). When the council opened at Easton in July (1757), Tedyuskung demanded that he have a clerk of his own. This request caused much discussion, but was finally granted upon Tedyuskung's threat to leave if it was not acceded to (Pa. Arch., 2d s., III, 259 et seq., 1853). Richard Peters was angered at the position taken by the assembly and the commissioners that Tedyuskung's demands for a clerk were right. He was also much provoked by the way the business was carried on, charging Conrad Weiser, George Croghan, and others with trying to unfit "the king" for the transaction of business by getting him drunk every night. But whatever may have been the intentions of the Pennsylvania representatives, the "king" went to the councils each day with a clear head and perfectly able to cope with all of the representatives of the province of Pennsylvania. The principal point at issue concerned the fraud in the land grants (see Walton, Conrad Weiser, 356, 1900). After first refusing to allow Tedyuskung to see the deeds of these sales, as he had requested at the previous council, the governor and the council finally granted his request and permitted him to see the deeds of 1686 and 1737 from the Delawares and that of 1749 from the Iroquois. By request of the chief these deeds were copied

for him by Charles Thompson. After a promise that satisfaction should be made for the fraudulent "Walking Purchase," if any fraud was found, peace with the Delawares seemed assured. In order to make it more complete it was deemed necessary to bring the Indians on the Ohio into friendly relations.

In the spring of 1758 Tedyuskung went to Philadelphia and after a conference with the governor and council he urged them to complete the work of peace by bringing these western Indians into friendly relations at once. This was the first suggestion of an official mission to the Indians on the Ohio, which later resulted in Post's journey to Kuskuski. The council did not take action promptly, so Tedyuskung decided to send two members of his own tribe on the errand of peace; but these messengers did not get beyond Ft Allen. A new difficulty had arisen. Paxinos, the friendly Shawnee chief, had turned against the English, and a general Indian uprising was threatened. When the cause of this was searched for, it was found that both the Iroquois and the Delawares were becoming aroused because of the presence of their hated enemies, the Cherokee and the Catawba, with Gen. Forbes' expedition. Both the general and the governor urged Post and Thompson to go to Wyoming to try to win back the dissatisfied Indians. On their way to Wyoming they met Tedyuskung, who insisted on their going back, as to go on was to endanger their lives. They followed his advice, but on their return to the governor they were immediately sent back to the old chief with offers of peace from the Cherokee deputies. After Tedyuskung had heard this message, and had heard also from the western Indians as to the condition of affairs on the Ohio, he insisted that messengers be sent westward at once. On Post's return and report to the governor he was despatched at once to the Ohio. This mission of the Moravian missionary to the western Indians was one of the most heroic enterprises ever undertaken by any man. The miles of forests were filled with hostile Indians who knew nothing of these peace proposals; the French were doing everything to keep the angered Indians in alliance with them; the winter was fast approaching, and before such a journey could be made the mountains would be covered deep with snow. Post and his work at this critical time have never been justly appreciated. His own unbounded faith and his efforts to win the western Indians prevented defeat similar to that of Braddock.

The fourth council was held at Easton in Oct. 1758. Before it had ended Post had returned from his first mission westward. All the various land disputes came before the council (Walton, Conrad Weiser, 372, 1900).

The one particular dispute with which Tedyuskung had to do was that of the Walking Purchase, and after that the right of the Iroquois to sell the lands of the Delawares. The wily chiefs of the Iroquois realized that the one thing for them to do was to discredit Tedyuskung as to his relation to them, and then break his influence with the council of Pennsylvania. One after another the chiefs asked: "Who made Tedyuskung the great man that he has become?" They denied that he had any authority from them and asked where he had obtained it (Col. Rec. Pa., VIII, 190, 1852.) When Gov. Denny attempted to quiet the anger of these Iroquois by explaining the situation, they listened to him, but when Tedyuskung arose to reply, one by one they left the council room. It was a critical time, but the conference finally ended in a treaty of peace, which was ratified with the western Indians at Pittsburg in 1759.

Post's second mission to Kuskuski and its complete success led to the evacuation of Ft Duquesne by the French and the occupancy of the Ohio by the English.

In 1762 Tedyuskung went to Philadelphia, at which time the governor offered him £400 as a present, if he would withdraw his charge of fraud in the Walking Purchase, which was a source of trouble to the proprietors. The old chief said that he himself had never made such a charge, but that the French had told them that the English had defrauded them of their lands. The governor then told him that if he would make this statement public he would give him the present. This was done.

After all of his dealings with the governor and the council of Pennsylvania the last of the chiefs of the eastern Delawares went to his home in Wyoming, where in the spring of 1763 his house was set on fire, during one of his drunken debauches, and he was burned to death. The perpetrators of this crime were in all probability either of the Seneca or the Mohawk tribe—more likely of the latter.

The chief failing of this wise old Delaware diplomat was his utter subjection to the power of rum. His white allies did little to help him in this regard. His fondness for it was made use of on all occasions. But, however great this failing, he did much to assure success to the English expedition under Gen. Forbes, and to bring the Iroquois to a realization that the Delawares were "no longer women, but men." He was the most virile chief of the Delaware tribe during the years of their subjugation to the Iroquois. His efforts for peace, with Post's heroic

endeavors, did much to win the Ohio from French possession. Without the work of these two men this result could not have been accomplished without the shedding of much blood. A monument to Tedyuskung has been erected in Fairmount Park, Philadelphia.

The name is recorded in various other ways, including Deedjoskon, Detiuscung, Tedeuscung, Tediuscung, Tediuskung, Tedyuscung, Teedyuscung, Tydescung, Tydeuscung.　　　　(G. P. D.)

Teeakhaily Ekutapa. A former Choctaw village on lower Tombigbee r., Choctaw co., Ala.—Romans, Fla., I, 329, 1775.

Teenikashika ('those who became human beings by means of the buffalo'). A Quapaw gens.
Buffalo gens.—Dorsey in 15th Rep. B. A. E., 229, 1897. Te e′nikaci′ʞa.—Ibid.

Teepee. See *Tipi.*

Tees-gitunai (*Tʔē′es gîtᵭnā′i,* 'rocky-coast eagles'). A small branch of the Gituns of Masset, N. coast of the Queen Charlotte ids., Brit. Col.—Swanton, Cont. Haida, 275, 1905.

Teeskun-lnagai (*Tʔē′es kun lnagā′-i,* 'rocky-coast point-town people'). A branch of a Haida family called Kunalanas. They are named from the rocky coast between Masset inlet and Virago sd., Brit. Col., where they used to camp. T′ēs kunîlnagai′.—Boas, 12th Rep. N. W. Tribes Can., 23, 1898. Tʔē′es kun lnagā′-i.—Swanton, Cont. Haida, 270, 1905.

Teesstlan-lnagai (*Tʔē′es sʟʔan lnagā′-i,* 'rocky-coast rear-town people'). A subdivision of the Stlenga-lanas, a great Haida family of the Raven clan, named from the coast between Masset inlet and Virago sd., where they used to camp.— Swanton, Cont. Haida, 271, 1905.

Teeth. See *Anatomy.*

Teeuinge. A large prehistoric pueblo ruin on top of the mesa on the s. side of Rio Chama, about ¼ m. from the river and an equal distance below the mouth of Rio Oso (Bear cr.), in Rio Arriba co., N. Mex. It was built of adobe, with foundation walls strengthened by irregular blocks of heavy black lava. Its ground-plan embraces two large rectangular courts. The remains of ten circular kivas and one shrine are to be seen in and about the pueblo, but the walls are reduced to low mounds. The settlement was undoubtedly of Tewa origin.　　　(E. L. H.)
Teëuinge.—Hewett in Bull. 32, B. A. E., 34, 1906. Te-e-uing-ge.—Bandelier in Arch. Inst. Papers, IV, 58, 1892.

Teeytraan. Mentioned as a pueblo of the province of Atripuy (q. v.) in the region of the lower Rio Grande, N. Mex., in 1598.—Oñate (1598) in Doc. Inéd., XVI, 115, 1871.

Tefaknak. A Magemiut Eskimo village s. of the Yukon delta, Alaska; pop. 195 in 1890.
Tefaknaghamiut.—11th Census, Alaska, 110, 1893.

Tegilque. A former Diegueño village in or near Santa Isabel valley, San Diego co., Cal.—Sanchez, MS. Diario (1821) cited by Bancroft, Hist. Cal., ii, 443, 1886.

Tegninateo. A tribe of the Manahoac confederacy that formerly resided at the head of Rappahannock r. in Culpeper co., Va.

Teganatics.—Boudinot, Star in the W., 129, 1816. Tegninateos.—Tooker, Algong. Ser., v, 66, 1901 (trans.: 'people who climb the mountains'). Tegniniaties.—Jefferson, Notes. table, 139, 1801. Tegoneas.—Strachey (1612), Va., 104, 1849. Tigninateos.—Smith (1629), Va., i, 134, 1819.

Tegotsugn. A clan or band of the Pinal Coyotero at San Carlos agency, Ariz., in 1881.

Doo-goo-son'.—White, Apache Names of Ind. Tribes, MS., B. A. E. (trans.: 'red-ant country'). Tegotsugn.—Bourke in Jour. Am. Folk-lore, iii, 112, 1890.

Teguayo. The name of the country of the Tewa (Tegua) and perhaps of the Tigua, in New Mexico, around which, as in the case of Quivira, considerable mystery arose among the Spanish writers of the 17th century, who, losing sight of the exact application of the term, transplanted the "province" to the then unknown north. Escalante in 1775 regarded it as the country of the Ute, because while traversing it on his journey to Utah lake, Utah, he observed the ruins of many ancient pueblo houses, which he believed to be the original homes of the Tewa and the Tigua. The name is indefinitely located on earlier maps in various places. (F. W. H.)

El Teguayo.—Ritch, New Mexico, 196, 1885. Gran Teguaio.—De l'Isle, Carte Mex. et Floride, 1703 ("habité par les Tiguas"). Great Teguai.—Morse, N. Am., map, 1776 (marked as a town N. of Rio Gila). Great Teguaio.—Senex, map, 1710. Tagago.—Duro, Don Diego de Peñalosa, 53–4, 1882. Taguaio.—Freytas, Peñalosa, Shea ed., 65, 1882. Teguaga.—Güssefeld, Charte Nord Am., 1797. Teguaio.—Delamarche, map Amérique 1792 ("habité par les Teguas"). Teguay.—Peñalosa y Briceño (1661–4) quoted by Bancroft, Ariz. and N. Mex., 168, 1889. Teguayo.—Kino (1694) in Doc. Hist. Mex., 4th s., i, 241, 1856; D'Anville, map Am. Sept., 1746 ("Pays des Teguas"). Teguayo Grande.—Jefferys, Am. Atlas, map 5, 1776 ("or Teguas"). Teguayoqué.—Bandelier in Arch. Inst. Papers, iv, 312, 1892 (Acoma name; apparently identical). Tehuajo.—Rafinesque in Marshall, Ky., i, introd., 27, 1824. Tehuayo.—Freytas (1662), Peñalosa, Shea ed., 90, 1882. Tejago.—Coxe, Carolana, 65, 1741 (probably identical). Theguayo.—Freytas (1662), Peñalosa, Shea ed., 35 et seq., 1882 (also Theguayo). Thoya.—Coxe, Carolana, 65, 1741 (probably identical). Thoyago.—Ibid. Tognayo.—Ward (1864) in Donaldson, Moqui Inds., 82, 1893 (misprint).

Teguepo. A Chumashan village or site in or near Santa Rosa (Santa Inés) valley, N. of Santa Barbara, Cal.—Tapis (1798) cited by Bancroft, Hist. Cal., ii, 28, 1886.

Tegui. Given by Velasco as one of the divisions into which the Opata were divided; it included the pueblos of Alamos, Batuco, Cucurpe, Opodepe, Terapa, and Toape, on the E. bank of Rio San Miguel, between lat. 29° 30′ and 30° 30′, central Sonora, Mexico. As the division was based on neither linguistic nor ethnic characters, Tegui, Teguima, and Coguinachi were soon dropped as classificatory names.

Següí.—Davila, Sonora Hist., 316, 1894. Tegui.—Velasco in Bol. Soc. Mex. Geog. Estad., 1a s., x, 707, 1863.

Teguima. Given by Velasco as one of the divisions of the Opata, inhabiting the valleys of the Moctezuma and upper Sonora rs., between lat. 29° and 31°, Sonora, Mexico. As the division was based on neither linguistic nor ethnic characters, Teguima, Tegui, and Coguinachi were soon dropped as classificatory names. Orozco y Berra (Geog., 338, 344, 1864) uses the term synonymously with Opata, whereas it was only a part of that tribe, apparently speaking a slightly different dialect. The villages pertaining to them, so far as known, are Aconchi, Babiacora, Bacuachi, Banamichi, Chinapa, Cumpus, Cuquiarachi, Huepac, Sinoquipe, and probably also Jitisorichi and Mututicachi.

Ópatas tegüimas.—Orozco y Berra, Geog., 344, 1864. Teguima.—Velasco in Bol. Soc. Mex. Geog. Estad., 1a s., x, 705, 1863. Téhuimas.—Pinart in Bull. Soc. Géog. Paris, 204, Sept. 1880.

Teharonhiawagon (*Te'haronʻhiawă''k-ʻhon'* in Mohawk, usually pronounced *Tʻharonʻhiawă''k-ʻhon'*, and *Tʻhaĕnʻhiawă'-gi'* in Onondaga; these two are typical forms of pronunciation of this expression, and of these there are only dialectic variations in the other Iroquoian tribes. The analysis of the Mohawk form, which represents the component elements of the expression in the least compressed shape, is as follows: *te-*, the prefix of the dual, which becomes in proper names approximately expletive, signifies primarily 'two,' 'double,' 'in a double manner or degree,' indicating aptly the action or presence of two things, especially things double by nature, as the ears, feet, hands, eyes, of the animal body; *ʻha-*, the simple prefix personal pronoun of the third person, singular number, masculine sex, and anthropic gender, means 'he'; were this expression the statement of an act rather than an appellative only, the form *ho-*, 'he-it,' would have been required here; *ronʻhia-*, the nominal stem of the noun *oron' ʻhiă'*, a derivative of *orok*, 'cover,' 'overcast,' 'spread over,' signifies 'sky,' 'firmament,' 'the visible heavens,' or 'blue color'; *wă'k-*, the verb-stem, means 'hold(s),' 'be holding'; and lastly, *ʻhon*,' an adverbial suffix denoting the iteration of the action in time or place denoted by the verb to which it refers; hence, *Teharonhiawagon* signifies literally 'He is holding the sky in two places,' referring to the action of the two hands; but the form of the personal pronoun employed in the expression indicates that this sentence-word is used merely as an appellative and not as the statement of an act, so that

'He, the Sky-holder,' is a close approximation to the accepted signification. Tradition states that this name was given him by his grandmother, *Awĕn'hă'i'*, under the following circumstances: Soon after his birth and the death of his mother, his grandmother asked him and his twin brother, "Do you two know whence you two came, and whither you shall go, when you two depart hence?" This brother replied confidently: "I, myself, do know the place whence you and we have come. Verily, it is from the world on the upper side of the sky. I myself, indeed, will not forget it. I will hold it fast [as if with my hands], the place whence I came." His grandmother said: "Truly, indeed, thou dost know the whole matter. Moreover, I shall call thee, on this account, *T'haĕn'hiawă''gĭ' (De'haĕn'hiawă'k''hon')*, for thy memory has not changed, being as if thou hadst just come thence").

An imaginary anthropic being of the cosmogonic philosophy of the Iroquoian and other American mythologies, who for convenience of expression may be called a man-being. To him, the embodiment or personification of life, was attributed by the wise men of the elder time the formation or creation and preservation of life and the living in the normal and the beneficent bodies and things in terrestrial nature. His peculiar character as one of the great primal earth powers of the second great cosmical period is best defined in terms of the manifestations and activities of the various forms of floral and faunal life—reproduction, germination, budding, and growth—on the earth. His parentage was noble, although his paternity was seemingly not definitely fixed. This interpretation and definition of the mythological concept embodied in the dominating character of Teharonhiawagon are given here as those which most satisfactorily account for the motives and activities manifested in his life, notwithstanding the fact that he has been connected in an indefinite way with the sun or light and the sky by such well-known writers as Lafitau, Charlevoix, Le Jeune, Brinton, and others. These writers have probably been misled by regarding the derivation of the name as conclusive evidence as to the reason for its imposition on him. In the most definite of the cosmic mythical traditions of the Iroquoian peoples Teharonhiawagon was a twin brother of Tawiskaron (q. v.), although other and perhaps earlier and more primitive accounts make him a quadruplet along with his brother mentioned above, the number four however being probably suggested by the well-nigh universal cult of the four quarters.

One of the earliest recorded names applied to Teharonhiawagon is that of the Hurons, written by Sagard. In his Histoire du Canada (1636, repr. 1836) he wrote it *Youskeha*, but in the accompanying Dictionnaire Huronne it appears under the form *Yoscaha*. In the Jesuit Relations it is commonly written *Iouskeha* (*Iŝskeha*), rarely therein *Jouskeha*, although the last is approximately phonetically correct. According to Peter D. Clarke, a native Wyandot (Huron) historian (Traditional Hist. Wyandotts, 150, 1870), this name should be written *Tezhuskahau*, which, he says, is the cognomen of the "God of the Forest, or Nature." His translation is approximately correct, as will appear hereafter. This spelling shows that the *Jouskeha* form of the Jesuit Relations is preferable to that of *Iouskeha;* but *Tezhuskahau* of Clarke may be *Tidjóskă'ă'*, a contracted form of *Tisio'skă'ă'*, the component elements of which are: *ti-*, a demonstrative pronominal prefix referring to size, number, or quantity, 'so,' 'so much,' 'so many'; *s-*, the iterative adverbial prefix, 'again,' 'anew'; *io-*, the prefix personal pronoun of the third person, singular number, zoic gender, meaning 'it'; *skă'-*, the nominal stem of the noun *os'kă'*, 'sprout,' 'shoot'; and *ă'-*, the adjective 'little,' 'small,' sometimes with the caritive sense, 'dear little.' The expression then signifies, 'So it (is) again a dear little sprout.' This is clearly an epithet expressive of the floral side of the character of Teharonhiawagon. This expression is paralleled in signification and composition by the Mohawk *Oteroñtoñni'ă'*, sometimes accompanied by the term *Wă''tă'*, 'maple,' of which the Onondaga *Odĕñ'doñni'ă'* is only a dialectic variant. The analysis of the Mohawk expression is as follows: *o-*, the prefix personal pronoun of the third person, singular number, zoic gender, meaning 'it'; *te-*, a modified form of the reflexive pronoun, signifying 'self'; *roñt-*, the nominal stem of the noun *oroñ'tă'*, 'it-tree'; *oñni'-*, the verbal stem of the perfect tense, signifying 'has made'; *ă'-*, the adjective meaning 'little,' 'small,' and refers to the accompanying noun-stem; the expression then signifies: 'It self a small tree has made,' or 'It has made itself into a small tree,' i. e. 'a sapling.' These derivations of the chief appellatives commonly applied to Teharonhiawagon show that he was never connected in any manner with sun, sky, or dawn.

Teharonhiawagon has been erroneously identified by different authors with Hiawatha (q. v.), with Agreskwe (*Aregwĕns'kwă'*, 'The Reason or Cause for Absence), the Iroquoian War god, and with Agatkonchoria, 'Masked Face,' the name of a society whose members are professed exorcists of disease, deriving their authority from Hadu'i'' (Onondaga) or Shagoᶜᵗ⁺owe''gōwā, the primal being of disease and contemporary of Teharonhiawagon. Megapolensis gives Athzoockuatoriaho as another Mohawk epithet of Teharonhiawagon.

Like most American Indian mythologies, the Iroquoian deals with three great mythic cosmical periods. In the first dwelt a race of gigantic anthropic beings—man-beings, let them be called, because though they were reputed to have been larger, purer, wiser, more ancient, and possessed of more potent *orenda* (q. v.), than man, and having superior ability to perform the great elemental functions characterizing definitely the things represented by them, they nevertheless had the form, mien, and mind of man, their creator; for unconsciously did man create the gods, the great primal beings of cosmic time—the controllers or directors, or impersonations, of the bodies and phenomena of nature—in his own image. To these man-beings, therefore, were imputed the thought, manners, customs, habits, and social organization of their creators; notwithstanding this, man regarded them as uncreated, eternal, and immortal; for by a curious paradox, man, mistaking his own mental fictions, his metaphors, for realities, explained his own existence, wisdom, and activities as the divine product of the creations of his own inchoate mind. The dwelling-place of the first great primal beings, characterized by flora and fauna respectively identical with the plant and animal life appearing later on the earth, was conceived to have been the upper surface of the visible sky, which was regarded as a solid plain. Here lived the first beings in peace and contentment for a very long period of time: no one knows or ever knew the length of this first cosmic period of tranquil existence. But there came a time when an event occurred which resulted in a metamorphosis in the state and aspect of celestial and earthly things; in fact, the seeming had to become or to assume the real, and so came to pass the cataclysmic change of things of the first period into that now seen on the earth and in the sky, and the close of this period was the dawn of the gods of this mythology. Into the sunless and moonless skyland—lighted only by the snowy white flowers of the great tree of light, towering high near the lodge of *Te'haoⁿ-'hweñdjiawă''khoⁿ* ('He the Earth-holder'),—the presiding chief of that realm jealousy crept. This chief, reputed to be invulnerable to sorcery, took a young wife by betrothal in fulfilment of a dream. The name of the young woman was *Awĕn'hā'i'*, 'Mature Flowers,' or 'Mature (i. e. Fertile) Earth.' Through the machinations of Fire-dragon of the White Body, the deadly jealousy of the aged presiding chief was kindled against his young spouse. Unfortunately for her welfare, she, by inhaling the breath of her spouse before the completion of the usual ante-nuptial ordeals, became parthenogenetically pregnant. The betrothed husband, not knowing the cause or source of her condition, questioned her chastity, and with reluctance resolved to rid himself of his suspected but innocent spouse, and at the same time to change the nature of all the man-beings who were his neighbors and associates. To accomplish his purpose, he caused the tree of light which stood over the supposed aperture through which the sun now shines to be uprooted, thus forming an abyss into the empyrean of this world. By stealth he cast his unsuspecting young spouse into this abyss. Some traditions say that this occurred after Awĕn'hā'i' had given birth to a daughter which, by this occurrence, she reconceived and to which she again gave birth on this earth. In like manner the man-beings, Corn, Beans, Sunflower, Tobacco, Deer, Wolf, Bear, Beaver, and all their associates, transformed their kind into the forms and sizes and with the habits by which they are known to-day on earth, and then cast them down into the abyss. Only the ancients, the so-called elder brothers, of these things remained in the skyland. Then the rage of Te'haoⁿ'hwĕñdjiawă'k'-'hoⁿ' subsided. This great cataclysmic change was brought about because none could divine a cure for his illness (jealousy) by "searching his dream-word." Then the tree of light was restored to its place. These events brought about the second cosmical period. The expelled bride, Awĕn'hā'i', while falling through cosmic space, or the upper sky, was seen by the water-fowl and water animals of the primal sea, who at once set themselves the task of providing a habitation for her. Some traditions say that the water-fowl of the larger kinds flew up to meet her and to bring her slowly down as she rested on their united backs. While this was being done, the best divers among the water animals brought up from the depths of the sea some wet earth, which was carefully placed on the carapace of the Great Turtle. This earth at once began to expand in size, and on it Awĕn'hā'i' was gently placed. At once she began to walk about the tiny earth, and it continued to grow in size thereby; she even took handfuls of the earth and scattered it in all directions, which likewise caused it to continue to expand until it had grown so large that she could no longer see its bounds. Then shrubs, red willow, grasses, and other vegetation began to appear. In due time she gave birth to a daughter. After attaining womanhood, this daughter was courted by various animals and beings disguised in the assumed shape of fine-looking young men. But, by her mother's advice, she rejected the suit of all, until a young man of the race of the Great Turtle sought her to wife. He was accepted, and bidden to the lodge of her mother. In the twilight he came bearing two, some say three, arrows, of which one was tipped with a flint point. As the young woman lay down he passed two of the arrows, including the flint-tipped one, over her body; others say that he placed them in the lodge wall just above her body. Then he departed, saying that he would return the next day. At twilight he returned, and, taking his arrows, at once withdrew, saying that he would not return again. In due time the young woman gave birth to twins, one of whom caused her death by violently bursting through her armpit. The name of the culprit was Tawiskaron (q. v.), and that of his brother, the elder, was Teharonhiawagon. Awĕⁿʻhäʹi, the grandmother, being greatly enraged by the death of her daughter, asked the twins which of the twain had committed this act. Tawiskaron quickly replied, accusing his innocent brother. So seizing the supposed culprit, the grandmother cast him far away among the shrubbery. He did not die there, but grew rapidly to manhood; his grandmother hated him bitterly, but was very fond of Tawiskaron.

In time, Teharonhiawagon was taught by his father how to build a lodge, to kindle fire, and to plant and cultivate the ground, his father giving him bean, melon, squash, tobacco, and corn seed. He gave his son likewise the third arrow, by which he must destroy the great water serpent, the Fire-dragon of the White Body, when it should begin to destroy the things he was to create and cause to grow. Teharonhiawagon then toiled at his tasks, forming the animals and birds, and making the useful trees, shrubs, and plants. In all this his grandmother and his twin brother sought to thwart him by all manner of devices, but by the timely counsel of his father he was able to defeat all their efforts. His labor was to prepare the earth for man, whom later he was to create. For ease of transit for man, he had made the rivers and streams with double currents, the one running in one direction and the other in an opposite one; but his brother changed this by putting falls and cascades in the rivers and streams. The grandmother, seeing that Teharonhiawagon had produced great ears of perfect corn, immediately blighted his work, saying, "You desire the people you are about to make to be too happy and too well-provided with necessaries." Notwithstanding the opposition of his brother

and grandmother to his work for the good of man, he thwarted all their schemes. Finally, the grandmother, who had exhausted all her methods of opposition, challenged her grandson, Teharonhiawagon, to play a game of the bowl and plum-pits, the prize of the winner to be the rulership of the world. The grandson willingly accepted the challenge. According to custom ten days were allowed the contestants to prepare for the struggle of *orendas*. At the end of this time the grandmother came to the lodge of her grandson, bringing her bowl and plum-pits. He would use her bowl, but not her pits, as they were something alive and under the control of the mind of the grandmother. His own were the crests of chickadees, who had responded to his call for aid. He took six of these crests, and they magically remained alive. When he and his grandmother were ready, Teharonhiawagon called in a loud voice, "All you whose bodies I have formed, do you now put forth your *orenda* in order that we may conquer in this struggle, so that all of you may live!" Then when it came his turn to shake the bowl, he exclaimed, "Now, verily, shall appear the good or ill fortune of all the things that I have done or made!" The grandmother failed to score, while Teharonhiawagon made the highest score possible at one shake of the bowl, and so won the government of all living things.

Teharonhiawagon, in going from place to place viewing his work, one day found that all the animals he had formed had disappeared. He went at once in many directions seeking them. While thus unsuccessfully engaged, a bird told him that they were shut up in a vast cavern in a rocky cliff, wherein his brother had concealed them. Having discovered the place, he removed the rock that closed the mouth of the cavern and then ordered the animals and the birds to come forth. While the creatures were issuing in obedience to the command of their maker, Tawiskaron and his grandmother, noticing that the animals were again becoming plentiful, and divining the cause, hastened to the mouth of the cavern and at once closed it with the great rock. The few creatures which did not have the opportunity to escape became changed in their natures, which thereafter were evil, uncanny, monstrous, and *otkon* (q. v.). This incident is seemingly a figurative description of the annual forced hibernation of certain animals and reptiles and the migration of certain birds, and shows that Teharonhiawagon had the power to change the seasons by bringing back the summer.

As the animals were intended to serve

57009°—Bull. 30, pt 2—12——46

for the sustenance of human beings about to be formed, Teharonhiawagon enjoined on them the duty of permitting themselves to be taken, provided men in killing them did it with despatch. In furtherance of this contract he questioned some of the animals to learn in what manner their posterity would defend themselves against human beings. The answer of the Bear was that his posterity would flee to escape; thereupon, Teharonhiawagon stuffed the Bear's legs full of fat and meat in order to make him slow and clumsy in running. The Deer answered that his posterity would stand and not flee, and would bite human beings who hunted them; then Teharonhiawagon twisted out the teeth of the Deer's upper jaw, thus rendering his bite harmless. A similar change was made in the buffalo and the elk.

According to the recorded beliefs of the Hurons in the early decades of the 17th century, it was Iouskeha (I8skeha) who provided them with so many fine rivers and lakes and fertile fields. The earth was dry, for a monstrous Frog had gathered all the waters under its arm-pit, so that Iouskeha and his people could obtain no water except through its agency. To free himself and his people from this bondage, Iouskeha made an incision under the arm-pit of the Frog, through which the waters issued in so great abundance that they overflowed the earth, forming rivers, lakes, and seas. Without Iouskeha, they said, their kettles would not boil, for he had learned from the Turtle the art of kindling fire, and this art he had taught them; by his aid alone their hunting was successful: were it not for him they could not so easily have captured game animals, for they had not always enjoyed freedom, having been confined in a vast cavern. In freeing them Iouskeha so charmed them by an arrow stroke in the foot as they came forth that he might easily afterward control and dispose of them at will. The Wolf escaped this stroke, hence it is difficult to take him in the chase. It is from Iouskeha, they said, that they had their verdant fields, corn, beans, tobacco, squashes, and sunflowers; abundant corn harvests and lodges filled with matured ears of corn they owed to no one but Iouskeha. Early in 1636 these Indians were greatly perturbed by the reputed omens of an approaching famine. Iouskeha had been seen in vision, sad, and as lean as a skeleton, holding in his hand a shriveled ear of corn, and some even added that he carried the leg of a human being, which he tore with his teeth. All these were to them infallible signs of a year of great scarcity. Among these same Hurons, Awĕⁿʻhāʹi, the grand-

mother of Iouskeha or Teharonhiawagon, was known by the name Ataentsic or Eataentsic (i. e. Eiǎʹtăgĕⁿʹʹtcĭʻ, 'She Whose Body is Ancient'), which in accordance with the custom of avoiding the utterance of a person's proper name, supplanted her real name. These Hurons believed that their Iouskeha and his grandmother dwelt in a great lodge situated at the eastern (some said western) extremity of the world—that is, not much farther away than the bounds of their hunting grounds; this lodge of Iouskeha was built on the model of their own, and it was reputed to be stocked with an abundance of corn, beans, squashes, sunflower oil, and various dried meats—with all things to support life in great plenty; they believed that he and his grandmother planted and cultivated land, worked, drank, ate, slept, and were lascivious like themselves; that all the animals of the world belonged to them; that Iouskeha was very kind and gave growth to all things, sending fine weather and other good gifts; that he had charge and care of the living, and of the things that concerned life, and so he was judged good. On the contrary, his grandmother had charge of the souls, the manes, and because the Indians believed that she (the Earth) caused men to die, they adjudged her wicked and destructive, and not because she sometimes sent bad weather or at times undid the good things done by her grandson; they believed that Iouskeha grew old like all living things, but that he had the power instantly to rejuvenate himself, and so he never died; that at death the soul of man went directly to the lodge of Iouskeha and Awĕⁿʻhāʹi to dance in the presence of this Woman Ancient of Days for her health. These are substantially the current Iroquois beliefs regarding Teharonhiawagon.

One of the most important and far-reaching of the final labors of Teharonhiawagon on this earth was his great victory in a contest of *orendas* over the hunchback Haduʹʹiʹ, the unborn primal being, Disease and Death, whose forfeiture of life was redeemed by his promise to aid man by curing, on certain conditions, diseases arising from the infection of the earth with the malign potency of the body of **Haduʹʹiʹ** by his having first wandered over it. To this event the important Masked-face Society of exorcists of disease owes its origin. At the New Year ceremony its members essay to exorcise and banish disease and death-causing agencies from the community.

The great and most important New Year ceremony among the Iroquois who still hold to their ancient faith and customs, at which is burned a pure-white dog as a sacrifice, is held in honor of

Teharonhiawagon for his works, blessings, and goodness, which have been enjoyed by the people. See *Mythology, Nanabozho, Tawiskaron*. (J. N. B. H.)

Tehata (probably Cora *teuit* or *teáta*, 'man.'—Brinton). A former settlement of the Nevome of Sonora, Mexico, neighbors of the Basiroa, who lived E. of the Huvaguere and Tehuizo, who in turn resided about 8 leagues E. of Tepahue.—Orozco y Berra, Geog., 58, 1864.

Tehauremet. An unidentified tribe or village of which Joutel (Margry, Déc., III, 288, 1878) learned from the Ebahamo as being N. E. of Maligne (Colorado) r. of Texas.

Tearemetes.—Barcia, Ensayo, 271, 1723. Thearemets.—Joutel in French, Hist. Coll. La., I, 152, 1846. Theauremets.—Ibid.

Tehawut. The Cowlitz name for the Salish on Skukum Chuck, an E. tributary of upper Chehalis r., Thurston co., Wash.

Téhawüten.—Gibbs, MS. no. 248, B. A. E.

Tehoanoughroonaw. An unidentified tribe known to the Iroquois.—McKenney and Hall, Ind. Tribes, III, 80, 1854.

Tehononsadegi ('there his lodge was burned'). A small Seneca village formerly situated in Warren co., Pa., on the right bank of the Allegheny r., 4 m. from the New York state line. It was the residence of the noted Seneca chief Cornplanter. (q. v.)

Chinuchshungutho.—Rosecrantz (1792) in Am. St. Papers, Ind. Aff., I, 337, 1832. Cornplanters.—Brown, West Gaz., 355, 1817. De-o-no-sä-da'-ga.—Morgan, League Iroq., 229, 1851. Jennesedaga.—Alden (1816) in Day, Pa., 656, 1843. Junisadagoe.—Ransom (1794) in Am. St. Papers, Ind. Aff., I, 509, 1832. New Arrow town.—Procter (1791), ibid., 152. Obaletown.—Drake, Bk. Inds., bk. 5, 119, 1848. O'Beel's town.—Procter (1791) in Am. St. Papers, Ind. Aff., I, 151, 1832. Onoghsadago.—Johnson Hall conference (1774) in N. Y. Doc. Col. Hist., VIII, 426, 1857. Seneca Abeal.—Treaty of Fort Stanwix (1784) in Am. St. Papers, Ind. Aff., I, 10, 1832. Tehononsadegi.—Hewitt, inf'n, 1886 (Seneca form). Tenachshegouchtongee.—Procter (1791) in Am. St. Papers, Ind. Aff., I, 152, 1832. Thivengoa.—Pouchot map (1758) in N.Y. Doc. Col. Hist., X, 694, 1858.

Tehoragwanegen ('He has placed two planets together'). An Iroquois warchief of the Caughnawaga Mohawk, Quebec, known also as Thomas Williams; born about 1758–59. His mother was Mary de Roguers, granddaughter of the Rev. John Williams, of Deerfield, Mass., who, with the portion of his family not murdered on the spot, was taken captive by a band of French and Indians on the night of Feb. 29, 1704. Eunice, one of John Williams' daughters, while a captive became strongly attached to the Indians, and afterward, at the instance of the Jesuits, married a Caughnawaga chief known as De Roguers, to whom she bore three children, Catherine, Mary, and John. Mary, the mother of John, the subject of this sketch, died when the latter was only 15 months old, and he was then adopted by his aunt Catherine, the wife of a noted Caughnawaga chief, X. Rice, who had no heirs. Tehoragwanegen, having been born and reared among the Indians, acquired their habits and language. As a boy he was active and sprightly. He was reared by his aunt in the Roman Catholic faith. During the early years of the American Revolution, although then only about 17 years of age, Tehoragwanegen accompanied the war-parties of his tribe on various expeditions against the colonists of the northern frontiers. It appears that his grandmother, Eunice, persistently urged him to follow these hostile bands to prevent, when possible, the massacre of defenceless women and children, and on various occasions he bent every effort to have the American prisoners treated with humanity and kindness. In 1777, at the head of his band, he joined the army of Gen. Burgoyne and took an active part in the campaign around Saratoga that ended in Burgoyne's surrender. Having remonstrated with Burgoyne against the needless cruelty shown toward the colonists by the western Indians, among whom were the Ottawa, Chippewa, Menominee, and Winnebago, Burgoyne rebuked them so severely that they became offended and soon afterward deserted the army. Had Tehoragwanegen's advice been followed, the murder of Miss Jane McCrea near Ft Edward, N. Y., would never have been perpetrated. In 1780 he was attached to the corps of Sir John Johnson during its desolating operations in the Mohawk valley, and expressed so strong disapproval of the conduct of the Tories and some of the allied Indian warriors that he aroused the jealousy and hatred of Johnson, who feared, however, an open rupture with him on account of his high standing with Gov. Carleton of Canada for his valued services to the government. After the peace of 1783, Tehoragwanegen visited his relatives in New England, where he met the Rev. Samuel Kirkland, the celebrated missionary. In 1789, with two others of his tribe, he took steps toward negotiations which resulted in the treaty of New York in 1796, between the state and the Seven Nations of Canada, by which these Indians were compensated for lands of which they had been deprived. The other two delegates were Ohnawiio ('Good Stream') and Atiatoharongwen ('His Body is Taken Down from Hanging'), alias Colonel Lewis Cook.

In 1800 Tehoragwanegen took his two sons to be educated among his relatives. One of these was Eleazer Williams (q. v.), the reputed Dauphin of France. In 1801, Tehoragwanegen, with a party of Caughnawaga, visited, in behalf of the Northwest Bay Company, the Red r. and the Rocky mts. He warmly espoused the American cause during the War of 1812. His death occurred at his native village, Aug. 16, 1849, at the advanced age of 91. See Williams' Life of Te-ho-ra-gwa-neken, 1859.   (J. N. B. H.)

Teh-toot-sah. See *Dohasan.*

Tehueco (according to Buelna the name is from the Cahita term *teeca, tehueca,* 'sky'; or from *teeca* 'sky,' and *tehueli* 'blue'). One of the Cahita tribes living on the Rio Fuerte, about lat. 26° 40′, N. W. Sinaloa, Mexico. It included the settlements of Biara, Charac, Hichucio, Matapan, Sibirijoa, and Tehueco. The dialect spoken was the same as that of the Zuaque.
Tegueco.—Orozco y Berra, Geog., 58, 1864. **The-hueco.**—Ibid. **Zuaque.**—Ibid. (referring to the dialect; strictly a distinct division).

Tehueco. Formerly the principal pueblo of the Tehueco tribe, on the E. bank of Rio Fuerte, N. W. Sinaloa, Mexico.
Teguaco.—Kino, map (1702) in Stöcklein, Neue Welt-Bott, 1726. **Teguéco.**—Hardy, Trav. in Mex., 438, 1829. **Tehueco.**—Orozco y Berra, Geog., map, 1864.

Tehuerichic (referring to a rock in the form of a girl). A small pueblo of the Tarahumare, with a mission church, situated S. E. of Batopilas, S. W. Chihuahua, Mexico.—Lumholtz, inf'n, 1894.
Teguerichic.—Orozco y Berra, Geog., 323, 1894.

Tehuizo. A subdivision or settlement of the Nevome, described as neighbors of the Hios, who were settled 8 leagues E. of Tepahue (Tepachi?), in E. Sonora, Mexico.
Tehuiso.—Orozco y Berra, Geog., 58, 1864. **Te-huizo.**—Ibid., 351.

Teiakhochoe (*Tĕ′iaqɩōtcoē*). A Chinookan tribe formerly residing on the W. bank of Columbia r., in Columbia co., Oreg., about 3 m. above Oak point.—Boas, Kathlamet Texts, 6, 1901.

Teiyughsaragarat. See *Onechsagerat.*

Tejeuingge Ouiping (*Te-je-Uing-ge O-ui-ping*). The ruins of a prehistoric Tewa pueblo on the N. slope of the hill on which stands the pueblo of Pojoaque, near the Rio Grande in New Mexico. According to Bandelier (Arch. Inst. Papers, IV, 84, 1892) the Tewa claim that this pueblo marks the center of the range of their people, and that the division into two branches, of which the Tewa became the northern and the Tano the southern, took place there in very ancient times.

Tejey. A Costanoan village situated in 1819 within 10 m. of Santa Cruz mission, Cal.—Taylor in Cal. Farmer, Apr. 5, 1860.

Tejolocachic. A Tarahumare settlement on the headwaters of Paphigochic r., W. Chihuahua, Mexico, about 8 m. S. of Matachic.—Orozco y Berra, Geog., 323, 1864.

Tejon (Span.: 'raccoon'). A local name often applied to certain groups of Indians at the S. end of San Joaquin valley, Cal. It includes Indians of three linguistic families: Ft Tejon, on Cañada de las Uvas, was held by a division of the Chumash; the upper part of Tejon rancho, including the part of Tejon cr. in the mountains, was held by the Shoshonean Gitanemuk; the lower part of this stream and rancho, including the present ranch settlement (the headquarters of a reservation established in 1853) on Paso cr., belonged either to the same Shoshoneans or to the Yokuts tribe called Yauelmani, or at least was visited by the latter. On the establishment of the Tejon res. in 1853, Indians from a considerable area were assembled thereon. In 1864 most of these were removed to Tule River res., where the Yauelmani are now popularly known as Tejon Indians. On Tejon rancho, at the base of the mountains, there is still a settlement, mainly of Shoshoneans, and these principally of the Gitanemuk.   (H. W. H.)
Tehon.—Ind. Aff. Rep., 246, 1877. **Tejon.**—Williamson in Pac. R. R. Rep., V, 20, 1853. **Tejones.**—Beale (1852) in Sen. Ex. Doc. 4, 32d Cong., spec. sess., 378, 1853. **Tejuneses.**—Galiano, Relacion, cxvii, 1802. **Texon.**—Barbour (1852) in Sen. Ex. Doc. 4, 32d Cong., spec. sess., 256, 1853. **Tin′lin-neh.**—Powers in Cont. N. A. Ethnol., III, 370, 1877. **Tïn′lïu,**—Hoffman in Proc. Am. Philos. Soc., XXIII, 301, 1886.

Tejones (Span.: 'raccoons'). A tribe living at Reynosa, Mexico, on the Rio Grande, at the time of its foundation in the middle of the 18th century. In 1757, when Tienda de Cuervo inspected the new settlement, he reported that this was the native place of the Tejones (Revista, 1757, MS. in Archivo Gen.). Pimentel (Lenguas, II, 409, 1865) uses the name as synonymous with Coahuilteco. If this is correct, it probably settles the question of the linguistic affiliation of their associates, as the Comecrudos, Pintos, Mayapemes, Cueros Quemados, Zalapaguemes, and others. By 1757 the Tejones had entered the missions at both Reynosa and Camargo, but in greater numbers at the former place, where they mingled with the tribes named above (Mission records in the parish churches at Reynosa and Camargo, examined in 1907). According to Ripperdá, governor of Texas, by 1773 most of the tribe had acquired the Spanish language (Complaint about the enslavement of Indians in Nuevo Santander, MS. in Béxar Archives, 1773). The existing mission records at Reynosa and Camargo show that the Tejones remained at these missions well into the 19th century. The remnant of the tribe, together with a few Comecrudos and Pintos, still live (1907) between modern Reynosa and Camargo, at Las Prietas, which is about on the site of Old Reynosa, where Cuervo found the Tejones in 1757. Dr. A. S. Gatschet reported them at the same place in 1887.   (H. E. B.)
Tedexeños.—Orozco y Berra, Geog., 293, 1864 (probably identical). **Texones.**—Ibid., 294.

Tejua. A branch of the Apache who in the 18th century lived in the sierras of Salt r., Ariz. Probably the Tontos.

Fejuas.—Keane in Stanford, Compend., 464, 1878 (misprint). Tehua.—Bancroft, Ariz. and N. Mex., 393, 1889. Tejua.—Front map (1777) in Coues, Garcés Diary, 1900. Yabipais Tejua.—Garcés (1776), Diary, 308, 1900. Yavipaistejua.—Bancroft, loc. cit.

Tekakwitha, Catherine (called also the "Indian Saint," "La Saincte Sauvagesse," and the "Lily of the Mohawks"). The daughter of a Mohawk warrior by a Catholic Christian Algonkin woman who had been captured by the Iroquois at Three Rivers, Quebec; born in 1656 at Caugnahwaga, a palisaded town of the Turtle clan of the Mohawk, on Mohawk r., near the present Auriesville, N. Y. Tekakwitha was about 4 years of age when the village was ravaged by smallpox, among its victims being her mother, who left an infant son that did not long survive. Tekakwitha was about 10 years of age when De Tracy burned the Mohawk villages, an act resulting in the general peace of 1666. After the destruction of their settlement, the Turtle clan removed to the N. side of Mohawk r., where Tekakwitha was reared by her uncle, a bitter opponent of the Christian faith. A couple of years later, Fathers Bruyas, Fremin, and Pierron visited her uncle for three days, during which time she waited on them, thus gaining her first knowledge of Christian faith and practice. On Easter Sunday, 1675, she was baptized by Father Lamberville, and at once became the object of contempt and derision to many of her tribe, the persecution continuing for about two years. By refusing to marry she had already incurred the displeasure and anger of her aunt; for observing the Sabbath she was denied food, and because she would not labor in the corn-fields on that day, she was stoned; a young Mohawk warrior went so far as to raise his tomahawk menacingly over her head, but she awaited the blow with such calmness that her assailant desisted and slunk away.

When still quite young Tekakwitha aided her mother in her domestic duties, and when not thus occupied amused herself, like other Indian children, with her toys. She dressed like other girls of her age, and ornamented her person with necklaces, bracelets, finger-rings, and ear-bobs. As a young woman she was well poised and skilful in doing such work as Indian girls were accustomed to do in elk-hair and porcupine-quills, and from bark and other fibers she made bands for carrying burdens. She also became so adept in the manufacture of wampum belts, such as were used in public affairs, that she was frequently employed in making them. She could also sew well in the Caucasian way, having learned the art from French prisoners among her tribe. She made ribbons or bands of eel-skins, sashes from the fibers of bark, baskets and boxes of willow bark and twigs, and bark buckets for carrying water; she likewise learned how to make pestles for pounding corn; in short, she was ever busy with the multiplicity of duties that fell to the lot of Indian women generally. Although frail, Tekakwitha was the first at work in the morning. The years before her baptism passed in this manner, and she had no other ideals set before her than those current among her pagan relations. It is said she was virtuous in every way, was not attached to beliefs in visions or dreams, had no desire to take part in dances or games, and was not cruel, even to prisoners, like other Indian girls—in short, she was of a disposition unusual among the girls of her time and people.

At this time a number of fervent Catholic Christian Iroquois dwelt at the Sault Saint Louis, some of whom were in the habit of making visits to the villages of the Iroquois in New York for the purpose of proselyting their kindred to the new faith. One of the most successful of these, a former inhabitant and chief of the Oneida village, was Ogenratarihen ('Hot Ashes'), sometimes called Louis Garonhiagué. In 1677, while making a tour of the Indian villages, on learning that Tekakwitha was persecuted on account of her new faith, he, with two companions, placed her in a canoe and started for the Sault, where she arrived in the autumn, bearing letters from Father Lamberville extolling her virtues. Here she grew in Christian knowledge and in the exercises of a holy life, practising great austerities. Visiting Montreal, she saw the nuns of Marguerite Bourgeois at their school work, and aware of the charity of the Hospital Sisters of Ville-Marie shown toward her people, she sought to found a convent on Heron id., among the rapids of Saint Lawrence r. This project was ridiculed by her friends, and even the father was amused; he nevertheless permitted her to make a vow of chastity, and thus she became the first Indian nun among her people. Among the means which Tekakwitha undertook to mortify her body was to engage a friend to flagellate her every Sunday for a year, when she became too weak to bear it longer.

She died Apr. 17, 1680, and was buried s. of La Chine rapids of the St Lawrence, midway between La Prairie and Caughnawaga, Quebec. Six days after her death Father Chauchetière, while at prayer, "had a vision in which Catherine arrayed in glory appeared to him." Her remarkable life so impressed the minds of the faithful, both Indians and whites, that many came to pray at her tomb. It is said that many persons who were ill have been healed through invoking her intercession in their behalf, and that many striking visions and revelations have taken place at her tomb. There is a memorial cross bearing an inscription at Auriesville, N. Y., and at St Joseph's Seminary, Dunwoodie, N. Y., a statue stands in memory of her. Until 1888 a tall mission cross marked her burial place, but in that year the Rev. C. A. Walworth, of Albany, N. Y., erected near it a large granite sarcophagus, bearing the legend in native words, "A beautiful flower, it has blossomed among native men." Consult Chauchetière, Vie de Catherine Tegakouita, 1887, and Ellen H. Walworth in The Indian Sentinel, 1908. (J. N. B. H.)

Tekanitli (pl. of *kanítlĭ*, 'bed,' provincially known as 'cabin,' or 'cabbin,' by early traders and colonists). A Cherokee settlement, commonly known to the whites as Tickanetly, or Cabbins, in upper Georgia, about the period of the removal of the tribe in 1839. (J. M.)
Cabben.—Doc. of 1799 quoted by Royce in 5th Rep. B. A. E., 144, 1887.

Tekep. A Chumashan village formerly near Santa Inés mission, Santa Barbara co., Cal.—Taylor in Cal. Farmer, Oct. 18, 1861.

Tekisedaneyout ('place of the hanging bell.'—Morgan). A Seneca village, commonly known as Red Jacket Village, formerly in Erie co., N. Y.
Red Jacket Village.—Morgan, League Iroq., 466, 1851. Te-kise'-da-ne-yout.—Ibid.

Tekoedi ('people of Tek,' an island near the N. end of Prince of Wales id.). A Tlingit division belonging to the Wolf (or Eagle) phratry and living at Tongas, Sanya, and Killisnoo, Alaska.
tĕkŭĕdi.—Krause, Tlinkit Ind., 120, 1885. tĕkŭĕdĭ.—Ibid., 118. Te'qoedĭ.—Swanton, field notes, B. A. E., 1904.

Tekta. A Yurok village on Klamath r., 3 m. below Klamath P. O., N. w. Cal.

Tekumigizhik. See *Tikumigizhik*.

Tekunratum (*Te-kunr-a-tum*). A former Okinagan band at the mouth of Okinakane r., Wash.—Stevens in Ind. Aff. Rep., 445, 1854.

Telamene. An unidentified tribe or village of which Joutel (Margry, Déc., III, 288, 1878) learned from the Indians (probably Karankawa) near Matagorda bay, Texas, as being N. E. of Maligne (Colorado) r.
Tetamenes.—Joutel (1687) in French, Hist. Coll. La., I, 152, 1846.

Telamni. A Yokuts (Mariposan) tribe formerly living on lower Kaweah r., Cal. Powers (Cont. N. A. Ethnol., III, 370, 1877) placed them 2 m. below Visalia. They are said to have numbered 105 on the Fresno res. in 1861, but are now extinct.
Ta-lum-nes.—Johnston in Sen. Ex. Doc. 61, 32d Cong., 1st sess., 23, 1852. Tedamni.—A. L. Kroeber, inf'n, 1903 (Yaudanchi name; sing. form).

Telám.—Beaumont MS. cited by Coues, Garcés Diary (1775-76), 289, 1900 ("Telám ó Torim"; cf. *Telamoteris* below). Telamé.—Mofras quoted by Shea in Sitjar, Vocab. of San Antonio Mission, preface, 1861. Telamoteris.—Garcés (1775-76), Diary, 289, 1900 (probably identical). Tel-emnies.—Lewis in Ind. Aff. Rep. 1857, 400, 1858. Té-lumni.—Powers in Cont. N. A. Ethnol., III, 370, 1877. Tiedami.—A. L. Kroeber, inf'n, 1903 (Yaudanchi name; pl. form). To-lum-ne.—Royce in 18th Rep. B. A. E., 782, 1899. Torim.—Beaumont MS., op. cit.

Telategmiut. A subdivision of the Chnagmiut Eskimo of Alaska, whose village is Tlatek.—Dall in Cont. N. A. Ethnol., I, 17, 1877.

Tellico (*Tălikwă*, of unknown signification). The name of several Cherokee settlements at different periods, viz: (1) Great Tellico, at Tellico Plains, on Tellico r., in Monroe co., Tenn.; (2) Little Tellico, on Tellico cr. of Little Tennessee r., about 10 m. below Franklin, in Macon co., N. C.; (3) a town on Valley r., about 5 m. above Murphy, in Cherokee co., N. C.; (4) Tahlequah (q. v.), established as the capital of the Cherokee Nation, Okla., in 1839. (J. M.)
Big Tellico.—Doc. of 1779 quoted by Royce in 5th Rep. B. A. E., 144, 1887. Great Tellico.—Doc. of 1755, ibid., 142. Little Tellico.—Doc. of 1799, op. cit. Little Telliquo.—Doc. of 1755, op. cit., 142. Tellico.—Bartram, Travels, 371, 1792.

Telmocresses. A former Lower Creek town described as on the w. bank of Chattahoochee r., 15 m. above the mouth of Flint r., seemingly in Jackson co., Fla. It contained 100 inhabitants about the beginning of the 19th century. Young (Morse, Rep. to Sec. War, 364, 1822) lists it as a Seminole town, while Gatschet (Creek Migr. Leg., I, 71, 1884) regards the name as a corruption of Taluamuchasi (q. v.). See also *Tukabatchi Tallahassee*.

Telua-ateuna (*Te'-lu-a A'-te-u-na* 'those of the easternmost'). A phratry embracing the Tona (Turkey) and Shohoita (Deer) clans of the Zuñi. (F. H. C.)

Temalwahish ('the dry ground'). A Kawia village in Cahuilla desert, s. Cal.
La Mesa.—Barrows, Ethno.-Bot. Coahuilla Ind., 33, 1900. Temal-wa-hish.—Ibid.

Temastian. A former settlement of the Tepecano or of a related tribe, but early in the 18th century it was occupied by Tlaxcaltec, introduced by the Spaniards for defense against the "Chichimecs"; situated about 10 m. E. of Askelton on the Rio de Bolaños, in Jalisco, Mexico.—Hrdlička in Am. Anthr., v, 409, 426, 1903.

Temechic ('bread house.'—Och). A Tarahumare settlement in central Chihuahua, Mexico, on or near the Santa Cruz branch of Rio Conchos.
Temechic.—Orozco y Berra, Geog., 323, 1864. Temeichic.—Och (1756), Journey to the Missions, I, 71, 1809.

Temecula. An important Luiseño village in a valley of the same name in Riverside co., Cal. Pop. in 1865 said to be 388. Compelled to vacate their valley in 1875, its inhabitants moved to Pachanga canyon, 3 m. distant, where they now live under the name of Pichanga Indians. The Temecula res. in 1903 comprised 3,360 acres of almost worthless desert land, with 181 natives under the Pala agency.

Pachanga.—Jackson and Kinney, Rep. Mission Indians, 30, 1883. Pechanga.—Shell in Ind. Aff. Rep. 1904, 165, 1905. Pichanga.—Common form. Temecula.—Gray, So. Pac. R. R. Surv., 69, 1856. Temecule.—Ibid., 71. Temeku.—Kroeber in Univ. Cal. Pub., Am. Archæol. and Ethnol., IV, 147, 1907 (proper Luiseño form).

Temedégua ('valorous people'). A rancheria, probably Cochimi, connected with Purísima (Cadegomo) mission, Lower California, in the 18th century.—Doc. Hist. Mex., 4th s., V, 190, 1857.

Temesathi. A Chumashan village formerly near Santa Inés mission, Santa Barbara co., Cal.—Taylor in Cal. Farmer, Oct. 18, 1861.

Temeteti (*Tĕ-mĕ-tĕ-ti*). A former village of the San Luis Obispo Indians of the Chumashan family near Pt Sal, San Luis Obispo co., Cal.—Schumacher in Smithson. Rep. 1874, 342, 1875.

Temiscaming (from Nipissing *Timikaming*, with intrusive *s* due to Canadian French; sig. 'in the deep water', from *timiw* 'it is deep', *gaming* 'in the water'). A band of Algonkin, closely related to the Abittibi, formerly living about Temiscaming lake, Quebec. They were friendly to the French, and rendered them valuable service during the attack of the English under Peter Schuyler in 1691. There were 205 in 1903 and 245 in 1910, two-thirds of them half-breeds, on a reservation at the head of L. Temiscaming, in Pontiac district, Quebec.

Outemiskamegs.—Bacqueville de la Potherie, Hist., II, 49, 1722. Tamescamengs.—McKenney and Hall, Ind. Tribes, III, 82, 1854. Temiscamings.—Bellin, map, 1755. Temiscamins.—Denonville (1687) in N. Y. Doc. Col. Hist., IX, 361, 1855. Temiskaming.—Can. Ind. Aff. Rep., 55, 1906. Temiskamink.—Lahontan, New Voy., I, 231, 1703. Temiskamnik.—Lahontan (1703) quoted by Richardson, Arct. Exped., II, 39, 1851. Themiscamings.—La Barre (1683) in N. Y. Doc. Col. Hist., IX, 798, 1855. Themiskamingues.—Bacqueville de la Potherie, I, 329, 1722. Themistamens.—Du Chesneau (1681) in Margry, Déc., II, 267, 1877. Timigaming.—Hennepin, Cont. of New Discov., map, 1698. Timiscamiouetz.—Jefferys, Fr. Domins., pt. I, 1761. Timiscimi.—Jes. Rel. 1640, 34, 1858. Timiskaming.—Baraga, Eng.-Otch. Dict., 301, 1878. Timmiscameins.—Keane in Stanford, Compend., 539, 1878. Tomiscamings.—Toussaint, Map of Am., 1839.

Temochichi. See *Tomochichi*.

Temoksee. A small Shoshonean tribe formerly in Reese River valley, N. central Nevada.—Taylor in Cal. Farmer, June 26, 1863.

Temoris. A division of the Guazapar, inhabiting the villages of Santa María Magdalena, Nuestra Señora del Valle Humbroso, and Cerocahui, besides some rancherias in Chinipas valley, on the upper waters of the Rio del Fuerte, w. Chihuahua, Mexico.—Orozco y Berra, Geog., 58, 324, 1864.

Temosachic (corruption of *Remosachic*, 'stone-heap.'—Lumholtz). The most

northerly settlement of the Tarahumare, on the headwaters of the E. branch of the Rio Yaqui, lat. 28° 50, lon. 107° 30′, Chihuahua, Mexico. (Orozco y Berra, Geog., 323, 1864). Its mission church, built about 1720, collapsed in Jan. 1907.

Temtltemtlels (*Tɛ′mltɛmlɛls*, 'those under whom the ground shakes'). A gens of the Nakoaktok and also of the Mamalelekala, Kwakiutl tribes.—Boas in Nat. Mus. Rep. 1895, 330, 1897.

Tenabo (*Ten-a-bo′*). A former pueblo of the Tompiros division of the Piros, probably at the Siete Arroyos, N. E. of Socorro and E. of the Rio Grande, N. Mex. See Bandelier (1) in The Nation, 366, Nov. 7, 1889; (2) in Arch. Inst. Papers, III, 131, 1890; (3) ibid., IV, 272, 1892; (4) Proc. Cong. Int. Amer., VII, 452, 1890.

El Pueblo de los Siete Arroyos.—Bandelier in Arch. Inst. Papers, III, 131, 1890 (probably identical). Siete Arroyos.—Bandelier (1888) in Proc. Cong. Int. Amer., VII, 452, 1890. Tenabó.—Vetancurt (1696), Menologia, 260, 1871.

Tenaktak (*Tɛna′xtax* or *Dɛna′x-daᵋxᵘ*). A Kwakiutl tribe residing on Knight inlet, Brit. Col., with the following gentes, according to Boas: Gamgamtelatl, Gyeksem, Koekoaainok, Yaaikakemae, and Pepatlenok. In 1885 their principal town, which they owned conjointly with the Awaitlala, was Kwatsi. Pop. (probably of these two tribes together) 101 in 1908, 90 in 1910.

Dena′x·daᵋxᵘ.—Boas in Mem. Am. Mus. Nat. Hist., V, pt. I, 94, 1902. Nénachtach.—Boas in Petermanns Mitteil., pt. 5, 130, 1887. Tanahtench.—Can. Ind. Aff. 1904, pt. 2, 71, 1905. Tanak-tench.—Ibid., 362, 1895. Ta-nak-teuch.—Ibid., 279, 1894. Tanakteuk.—Ibid., pt. 2, 76, 1908. Ta-noch-tench.—Sproat, ibid., 145, 1879. Ta-nock-teuch.—Ibid., 189, 1884. Tan-uh-tuh.—Tolmie and Dawson, Vocabs. Brit. Col., 119B, 1884. Tapoctoughs.—Brit. Col. map, 1872. Tawaktenk.—Can. Ind. Aff., pt. 2, 166, 1901. Tenah′tah′.—Boas in Bull. Am. Geog. Soc., 229, 1887. Tena′qtaq.—Boas in 6th Rep. N. W. Tribes Can., 55, 1890. T′Ena′xtax.—Boas in Rep. Nat. Mus. 1895, 331, 1897. Te-nuckt-tau.—Kane, Wand. in N. A., app., 1859. Tē-nuh′-tuh.—Blinkinsap quoted by Dawson in Trans. Roy. Soc. Can., sec. II, 65, 1887.

Tenankutchin ('mountain people'). An Athapascan tribe in Alaska which hunts throughout the basin of Tanana r. and has its villages along the upper stream in lat. 63°, lon. 142°. Dall in 1866 found them almost in a state of nature. Once a year, without their women, they descended the river to the neutral trading post Nuklukayet. They traveled in birch canoes, wore pointed parkees trimmed with beads and feathers, their hair being ochred. Sometimes they journeyed up the Yukon to Ft Yukon for trade. They have more beadwork and are more skilled in its manufacture than any other tribe in Alaska. They use dogs as pack animals and for drawing sleds. They build only temporary shelters, moving from place to place during the year. Deer, moose, and caribou form their chief means of subsistence; these are captured by means of a brush fence extended many miles, in which at intervals snares are set. In many respects the Tenankutchin resemble the Unakhotana, but are reputed to be very fierce and warlike. A peculiar drawling tone characterizes their speech, distinguishing it from the Ahtena. Dentalium nose ornaments were formerly universally worn by the men, but of late they are falling into disuse. These people are much feared by the surrounding tribes. They are supposed to have a totemic system. Their population was given by Richardson in 1851 as 100; by Dall, 1870, 500; Petroff made it from 300 to 700 in 1880; Allen estimated the population in 1885 at 600; the 11th Census (1890) gave it as 373. Divisions of the tribe are Clatchotin, Huntlatin, Nabesnatana, Nukluktana, Nutzotin, Santotin, and Tolwatin. The villages Nandell and Tetling belong to the Nutzotin. In the lower river is Tutlut; at the mouth of the Tanana is Weare, and at the mouth of the Tozi is Tozikakat. Nuklukayet, the mart of other tribes also, is in their territory. Khiltats is one of the winter villages.

Gens de butte.—Whymper, Alaska, 255, 1869. **Gens des Buttes.**—Ross, MS. notes on Tinne, B. A. E. (so called by the Hudson Bay men at Ft Yukon). **Mountain Indians.**—Ibid. **Mountain Men.**—Dall in Proc. A. A. A. S., 270, 1870. **Tananas.**—Whymper, Alaska, 240, 1869. **Tananataná.**—Allen, Rep., 137, 1887. **Tanan-Kuttchin.**—Petitot, Dict. Dènè-Dindjié, xx, 1876. **Tanna-kutchi.**—Richardson, Arct. Exped., i, 398, 1851 (trans. 'people of the bluffs'). **Tā-non Kutchin.**—Ross, quoted by Gibbs, MS., B. A. E. **Tä-nŭn kŭtch-ĭn.**—Ross, MS. notes on Tinne, B. A. E. (trans. 'people of the biggest-river country'). **Tenan kutchin.**—Whymper, Alaska, 239, 1869. **Tenăn'-kŭt-chin'.**—Dall in Cont. N. A. Ethnol., i, 29, 1877. **Tennankutchin.**—Petroff in 10th Census, Alaska, 161, 1884. **Tennan-tnu-kokh-tana.**—Ibid. ('mountain river men': Knaiakhotana, name). **Tρananæ-Kouttchin.**—Petitot, Autour du lac des Esclaves, 361, 1891. **Tρanata-Kuttchin\.**—Petitot, MS. vocab., B. A. E., 1865. **Tschinkaten.**—Wrangell quoted by Dall in Cont. N. A. Ethnol., i, 29, 1877 ('hairy men'). **Zanana.**—Whymper quoted by Wood, Unciv. Races, ii, 1375, 1870.

Tenaskuh (*Ten-as-kuh*). A Koprino Koskimo village in Koprino harbor, N. side of Quatsino sd., Vancouver id., Brit. Col.—Dawson in Can. Geol. Surv., map, 1887.

Tenate (*Tē-nā-ate*, from *tĕn-nē*, 'honestone'). A summer or fall village of the Quatsino on the N. shore of Forward inlet, w. coast of Vancouver id., Brit. Col.—Dawson in Trans. Roy. Soc. Can., v, sec. ii, 68, 1887.

Tenawa (*Tĕna'wa*, from *tĕ'näw'*, 'downstream'). A division of the Comanche, practically exterminated in a battle with the Mexicans about 1845, and now extinct.

Le-nay-wosh.—Butler and Lewis (1846) in H. R. Doc. 76, 29th Cong., 2d sess., 6, 1847. **Ta-nah-wee.**—Smithson. Misc. Coll., ii, 3d art., 54, 1852. **Tanewa-Comanches.**—Alvord (1868) in Sen. Ex. Doc. 18, 40th Cong., 3d sess., 37, 1869. **Tanewahs.**—Ibid., 10. **Te'năhwĭt.**—Mooney, in 14th Rep. B. A. E., 1045, 1896. **Tĕna'wa.**—Ibid. (correct forms). **Tenawa.**—Burnet quoted by Schoolcraft, Ind. Tribes, i, 230, 1853. **Tenéwa.**—ten Kate, Reizen in N. A.,

384, 1885. **Tenewas.**—Hazen (1868) in Sen. Ex. Doc. 18, 40th Cong., 3d sess., 17, 1869. **Tenhuas.**—Bollaert in Jour. Ethnol. Soc. Lond., ii, 265, 1850. **Tennawas.**—Marcy, Army Life, 43, 1866. **Tenuha.**—Bollaert quoted by Latham in Trans. Philol. Soc. Lond., 102, 1856.

Tendoy. Chief of a band of mixed Bannock, Shoshoni, and Tukuarika Indians making their headquarters in the Lemhi valley, Idaho; best known through his friendly attitude toward the whites. About 1869, the attention of the Government having been called to the miserable condition of these Indians, they were found on investigation to be almost destitute, but Tendoy had been able to improve the condition of himself and a few of his followers by his sagacity in trade with the settlers in the mining camps of Montana, which he frequently visited. On the establishment of an Indian agency in Lemhi valley the Indians promised obedience to the agent and friendliness toward the settlers, and owing to the influence of Tendoy these promises were kept inviolate. He rendered valuable service to settlers by protecting them from roving bands of unfriendly Indians, and through his influence no white person in the Lemhi valley was molested during the Nez Percé war. In 1878 the agent reported that some of the Indians would doubtless join the hostiles, "but are held in check by Tendoy, who appears to have proven himself master of the situation." Some of the Indians with whom he associated in the buffalo country advised him to steal horses and kill a few whites, when the authorities at Washington would think more of him and grant his people a larger appropriation. To this he is said to have replied, "I have not the blood of a white man in my camp, nor do I intend such." Tendoy died on the Lemhi reservation May 9, 1907. The settlers, in appreciation of his services, subscribed funds toward the erection of a monument to his memory, and a tract of land containing a number of other Indian graves was set apart for his burial place.　　　　　(F. S. N.)

Teneangopti, Teneangpote. See *Kicking Bird*.

Tenedi (*Tĕ'nedĭ*, 'bark-house people'). A branch of the Tihittan living at Klawak, Alaska.　　　　　(J. R. S.)

Teneinamar. A former tribe in the vicinity of the lower Rio Grande, Texas, spoken of in connection with the Pinanaca and Siaeher. Perhaps identical with the Taimamares, elsewhere referred to.—Fernando del Bosque (1675) in Nat. Geog. Mag., xiv, 344, 1903.

Teneraca. A Tepehuane pueblo situated in a deep gorge of Mezquital r., in s. Durango, Mexico. It is under the missionary jurisdiction of Mezquital.—Lumholtz Unknown Mexico, i, 469, 1902.

Santiago Teneraca.—Orozco y Berra, Geog., 318, 1864.

Tenicapeme. A tribal name appearing in the baptismal records for 1800 at Matamoros, Mexico. It may be the same as Talapagueme, which occurs in the contemporary records for San José mission, Texas; this, in turn, is evidently the same as Salapagueme, the name of a tribe well known at that time at Reynosa and Camargo, on the Rio Grande (Baptismal records at Matamoros, Reynosa, and Camargo, and, for San José mission, at San Antonio, Texas).   (H. E. B.)

Tenino. A Shahaptian tribe formerly occupying the valley of Des Chutes r., Oregon. The Tenino dialect was spoken on both sides of the Columbia from The Dalles to the mouth of the Umatilla. In 1855 they joined in the Wasco treaty and were placed on Warm Spring res., since which time they have usually been called Warm Springs Indians (q. v.), a term embracing a number of tribes of other stocks which were included in the treaty. The present number of Tenino is unknown, but it is probably not more than 30.   (L. F.)

Mĕli'-'lĕma.—Mooney in 14th Rep. B. A. E., 742, 1896 (own name). **Milli-hhláma.**—Gatschet in Mag. Am. Hist., I, 168, 1877 (own name). **Tenino.**—Wasco treaty (1855) in U. S. Ind. Treat., 622, 1873. **Terrino.**—Huntington in Ind. Aff. Rep., 72, 1867 (misprint). **Tishχáni-hhlama.**—Gatschet, loc. cit. (Warm Springs Ind. name for themselves). **Warm Spring Indians.**—Gatschet, ibid. **Warm Springs.**—Common official designation.

Tennessee (*Tă'năsĭ'* or *Tănsĭ'*). The name of two or more Cherokee settlements at an early period. The principal one was on Little Tennessee r., a short distance above its junction with the main stream, in E. Tennessee. Another was on an extreme head branch of Tuckasegee r., above the present Webster, N. C. The name has lost its meaning, all the so-called derivations being fanciful.   (J. M.)

Tennessee.—Timberlake, Memoirs, map, 1765.

Tennuthkutchin ('middle people'). An extinct division of the Kutchakutchin that formerly dwelt between the rapids of the Yukon and the mouth of Porcupine r., Alaska. Gibbs (*ca.* 1857) said they numbered 10 hunters. In 1863 they were swept away, according to Dall, by an epidemic of scarlet fever introduced by the whites.

Birch Indians.—Dall in Cont. N. A. Ethnol., I, 30, 1877 (so called by Hudson's Bay men). **Birch River Indians.**—Whymper, Alaska, 255, 1869. **Gens de bouleau.**—Ibid. **Gens de Bouleaux.**—Dall, Alaska, 431, 1870. **Tennŭth'-kŭt-chin'.**—Dall in Cont. N. A. Ethnol., I, 30, 1877. **Tĕnŭth.**—Ross, notes on Tinne, Smithson. MS. 474. **Ten-uth Kutchin.**—Gibbs, MS., B. A. E. ('shaded people').

Tenskwatawa (*Ten-skwa'-ta-wa skwáte* 'door,' *thénui* 'to be open': 'The Open Door'; called also **Elskwatawa.**—Gatschet). The famous "Shawnee Prophet," twin brother of Tecumseh prominent in Indian and American history immediately before the War of 1812. His original name was Lalawéthika, referring to a rattle or similar instrument. According to one account he was noted in his earlier years for stupidity and intoxication; but one day, while lighting his pipe in his cabin, he fell back apparently lifeless and remained in that condition until his friends had assembled for the funeral, when he revived from his trance, quieted their alarm, and announced that he had been conducted to the spirit world. In Nov. 1805, when hardly more than 30 years of age, he called around him his tribesmen and their allies at their ancient capital of Wapakoneta, within the present limits of Ohio, and announced himself as the bearer of a new revelation from the Master of Life. "He declared that he had been taken up

TENSKWATAWA, THE PROPHET

to the spirit world and had been permitted to lift the veil of the past and the future—had seen the misery of evil doers and learned the happiness that awaited those who followed the precepts of the Indian god. He then began an earnest exhortation, denouncing the witchcraft practices and medicine juggleries of the tribe, and solemnly warning his hearers that none who had part in such things would ever taste of the future happiness. The firewater of the whites was poison and accursed; and those who continued its use would be tormented after death with all the pains of fire, while flames would continually issue from their mouths. This idea may have been derived from some white man's teaching or from the

Indian practice of torture by fire. The young must cherish and respect the aged and infirm. All property must be in common, according to the ancient law of their ancestors. Indian women must cease to intermarry with white men; the two races were distinct and must remain so. The white man's dress, with his flint and steel, must be discarded for the old-time buckskin and the firestick. More than this, every tool and every custom derived from the whites must be put away, and the Indians must return to the methods the Master of Life had taught them. When they should do all this, he promised that they would again be taken into the divine favor, and find the happiness which their fathers had known before the coming of the whites. Finally, in proof of his divine mission, he announced that he had received power to cure all diseases and to arrest the hand of death in sickness or on the battlefield" (Drake, Life of Tecumseh). The movement was therefore a conservative reaction against the breakdown of old customs and modes of life due to white contact, but it had at first no military object, offensive or defensive.

Intense excitement followed the prophet's announcement of his mission, and a crusade commenced against all suspected of dealing in witchcraft. The prophet very cleverly turned the crusade against any who opposed his supernatural claims, but in this he sometimes overreached himself, and lost much of his prestige in consequence.

He now changed his name to Tenskwátawa, significant of the new mode of life which he had come to point out to his people, and fixed his headquarters at Greenville, Ohio, where representatives from the various scattered tribes of the N. W. gathered about him to learn the new doctrines. To establish his sacred character and to dispel the doubts of the unbelievers he continued to dream dreams and announce wonderful revelations from time to time. A miracle which finally silenced all objections was the prediction of an eclipse of the sun which took place in the summer of 1806; this was followed by his enthusiastic acceptance as a true prophet and the messenger of the Master of Life. The enthusiasm now spread rapidly, and emissaries traveled from tribe to tribe as far as the Seminole and the Siksika, inculcating the new doctrines. Although this movement took much the same form everywhere, there were local variations in rituals and beliefs. Prominent among these latter was a notion that some great catastrophe would take place within four years, from which only the adherents of the new prophet would escape. In most places

the excitement subsided almost as rapidly as it had begun, but not before it had given birth among the Northern tribes to the idea of a confederacy for driving back the white people, one which added many recruits to the British forces in the War of 1812. Its influence among Southern tribes was manifested in the bloody Creek war of 1813. The prophet's own influence, however, and the prestige of the new faith were destroyed by Harrison's victory in the vicinity of the town of Tippecanoe, where he had collected 1,000 to 1,200 converts, Nov. 7, 1811. After the War of 1812 Tenskwatawa received a pension from the British government and resided in Canada until 1826, when he rejoined his tribe in Ohio and the following year moved to the w. side of the Mississippi, near Cape Girardeau, Mo. About 1828 he went with his band to Wyandotte co., Kans., where he was interviewed in 1832 by George Catlin, who painted his portrait, and where he died, in Nov. 1837, within the limits of the present Argentine. His grave is unmarked and the spot unknown. Although his personal appearance was marred by blindness in one eye, Tenskwatawa possessed a magnetic and powerful personality, and the religious fervor he created among the Indian tribes, unless we except that during the recent "ghost dance" disturbance, has been equaled at no time since the beginning of white contact. See Mooney in 14th Rep. B. A. E., 1896, and authorities therein cited.   (J. M.)

Ten Tribes of Israel. See *Lost Ten Tribes.*

Tenu. A tribe or subtribe which entered San Antonio de Valero mission, Texas, about 1740, with the numerous group to which the Sana (q. v.) belonged. The affiliation of the Sana seems to have been Tonkawan. Some words of their language have been preserved. (H. E. B.)

Tena.—Valero Baptisms, 1740, partida 509, MS. Tina.—Ibid., 1741, partida 549.

Tenyo. The Pine clan of the Tewa pueblo of Hano, N. E. Ariz., consisting of 29 persons in 1903.

Ten-yo.—Fewkes in Am. Anthr., VII, 166, 1894.

Teopari. A former pueblo of the Jova and seat of a Spanish mission founded in 1676; situated in E. Sonora, Mexico, a few miles S. E. of the Opata village of Nacori. Pop. 369 in 1678; 259 in 1730. Dolores was its visita. The pueblo was abandoned between 1764 and 1800 owing to Apache depredations.

San José de Teopari de Ovas.—Zapata (1678) in Doc. Hist. Mex., 4th s., III, 342, 1857. San José Teopari.—Rivera (1730) quoted by Bancroft, No. Mex. States, I, 514, 1884. Tyopari.—Bandelier in Arch. Inst. Papers, III, 56, 1890; IV, 510, 1892.

Teoskahatay. A Mdewakanton Sioux who accompanied Lesueur to Montreal in 1695 to evidence the good faith of the Sioux tribes in a treaty with the French and Chippewa relating to trade and the passage of the Saint Croix route to the Mississippi. He died at Montreal.

Teotongniaton. A former village of the Neuters in Ontario.

S. Guillaume.—Jes. Rel. 1641, 78, 1858 (mission name). Teotongniaton.—Ibid.

Tepachi (the name of a drink made from fermented aguamas or jocuixtes.—Buelna). A pueblo of the Opata and seat of a Spanish mission founded in 1678; situated on Rio Soyopa, N. E. Sonora, Mexico, about lat. 29° 30′. Pop. 388 in 1678.

S. Joaquin y Sta Ana Tepachi.—Zapata (1678) quoted by Bancroft, No. Mex. States, I, 246, 1884. Tepache.—Rivera, Diario, leg. 1382, 1736. Tepachi.—Escudero, Noticias de Sonora y Sinaloa, 101, 1849.

Tepachic ('stony place.'— Och). A Tarahumare settlement in Chihuahua, Mexico; definite locality unknown.— Orozco y Berra, Geog., 322, 1864.

Tepachuaches. A tribe, probably Coahuiltecan, encountered by Salinas on the road from Coahuila to San Francisco mission, Texas, in 1693.—Salinas (1693) in Dictamen Fiscal, Nov. 30, 1716, MS.

Tepahue. A division of the Mayo and also its principal settlement, situated in the mountains about the upper forks of Mayo r., s. Sonora, Mexico. They spoke a dialect slightly different from the Mayo (Zapata, 1678, in Doc. Hist. Mex., 4th s., III, 385, 1857). The inhabitants of Conicari, a subdivision of this tribe, appear from Zapata's statement to have spoken a dialect somewhat different from the Tepahue proper (Bandelier in Arch. Inst. Papers, III, 53, 1890). According to Ribas (Hist. Trium., 254, 1645), after the reduction of the Mayo the Tepahue established themselves in a pueblo (presumably Tepahue) on upper Mayo r., with "about 600 families, and some 2,000 persons of all ages." The same authority states that Conicari contained about 200 families. According to Orozco y Berra the Tepahue are extinct as a tribe, but there is still a Conicari settlement on or near the ancient site.

Asuncion de Tepave.—Zapata (1678) in Doc. Hist. Mex., 4th s., III, 385, 1857 (the settlement). Asuncion Tepahue.—Orozco y Berra, Geog., 356, 1864. Tepagui.—Croix (1769) in Doc. Hist. Mex., 4th s., II, 22, 1856. Tepaguy.—Rivera, Diario, leg. 1179, 1736. Tepahue.—Orozco y Berra, Geog., 351, 1864. Tepahui.—Croix, op. cit., 100. Tepave.—Zapata (1678) in Doc. Hist. Mex., 4th s., III, 385, 1857. Tepavi.—Writer of 1699, ibid., v, 25, 1857.

Tepecano (Nahuatl: *tepetl* 'mountain', 'hill'; *aco* 'on top of.'—Hrdlička). A small tribe or subtribe of the Tepehuane, living in the sierras of N. Jalisco, Mexico. They are now confined to the pueblo of Askeltan and to a territory not exceeding 150 sq. m. of the valley of the Rio de Bolaños. Their dwellings, where not modified by Spanish influence, consist of one or two small low structures built of unworked stones laid without mortar.

The hair of the men is worn from 3 to 6 in. in length, while that of the women hangs in braids down the back. The present population is estimated at 300. They have as principal officers a gobernador and an alcalde, who are elective. Their pueblos, ancient and modern, are Acapulco, Askeltan, Borego, Huila (Huilacatlan), Mesitas, Nostic, Santa Catarina, Temistian. See Hrdlička in Am. Anthr., v, no. 3, 1903.

Hu-mā-kam.—Hrdlička in Am. Anthr., v, 402, 1903 ('the ones,' 'the people': own name). Hu-māt-kam.—Ibid. (alternative form). Wáculi.—Lumholtz, Unknown Mex., II, 123, 1902 (Huichol name for Tepecano and Tepehuane). Xumátcam.—Ibid. ('the people': own name).

Tepee. See *Tipi*.

Tepehuane (said by Buelna to be from Nahuatl *tepetl* 'mountain', *huan* 'at the junction of'). A Piman tribe formerly

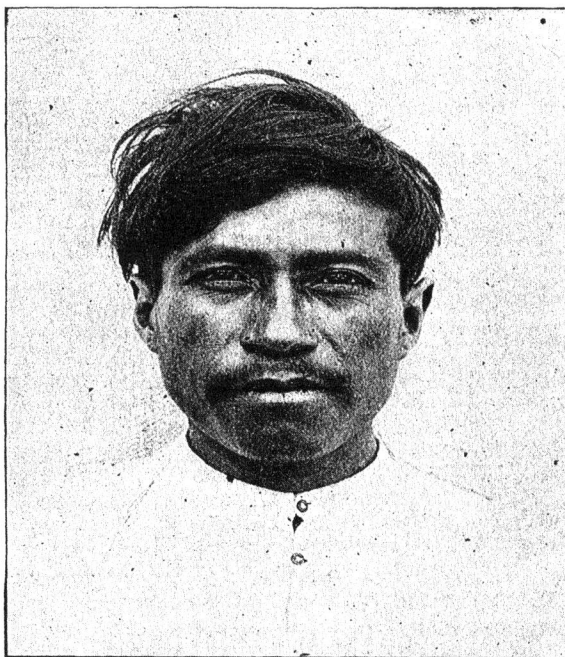

TEPECANO MAN (AM. MUS. NAT. HIST.)

inhabiting mainly the state of Durango, Mexico, but extending also into s. Chihuahua, N. E. and S. E. Sinaloa, N. E. Jalisco, N. Zacatecas, and s. w. Coahuila. They occupied also, with the Nevome and Tarahumare, the village of Tutuaca, about lat. 28° 20′, in w. Chihuahua. Before the advent of the Spanish missionaries among them in 1596 they lived in rancherias among rocks and rugged places, their huts being neatly made of logs, stone, or adobe. They were regarded as brave and warlike, and the Tarahumare and Acaxee suffered greatly from their aggressiveness. They revolted against the Spaniards in 1616, killed all the missionaries, desolated the country, and it is said marched with 25,000 warriors against the city of Durango, but were repulsed by 1,000 Spaniards with a loss of 15,000. The remainder fled to the eastern slope of the Sierra Madre, between lat. 25° and 26°, where most of them, until recent years, led a precarious existence in isolated petty communities without a tribal government. According to the missionaries who labored among them, the Tepehuane were not addicted to lying or theft, and lewdness and drunk-

TEPEHUANE MAN (AM. MUS. NAT. HIST.)

enness were very uncommon among them. Though always ready to defend their settlements against invasion, and notwithstanding their reputation for valor, they have been rather an agricultural than a warlike people. They possessed a number of idols, the principal of which was called Ubamari; their chief settlement was named after it, and formerly offerings of arrows, pottery, bones of animals, flowers, and fruit were made to it. Lumholtz (Unknown Mexico, I, 1902), who visited the tribe during various explorations in 1890–98, says that they are agriculturists, depending almost wholly upon the cultivation of the soil for subsistence. Though maize is their chief reliance other plants are cultivated and cotton is raised to some extent. They always have sufficient corn for their own use, which they store in square upright cribs of canes held in place by withes, on a framework of pine poles. Their houses are commodious log cabins, often with gabled roofs covered with large shingles weighted down. They make of maguey fiber sacks and ropes of excellent quality, as well as girdles and ribbons of wool and cotton for trade, chiefly in Durango. Like most Mexican Indians, they find pleasure in drinking mescal and pulque; their only dance is ceremonial; no games are in use, and gambling or betting is forbidden. Although nominally Christians, they still practise to some extent the rites and ceremonies of their ancient religion. Lumholtz gives 900 as the population of Lajas, or the northern section, and 3,000 as that of the southern section, but according to Hrdlička they number in all between 4,000 and 5,000, about equally divided between the two sections. Their settlements, past and present, so far as recorded, are: Atotonilco, Baborigame, Basonopa, Cacaria, Caiman, Canatlan, Chimaltitlan (?), Cinco Llagas, Coloradas (?), Durango, Galpa, Guerachic, Huaxicori, Ilamatech, Jícara, Joconostla, Lajas, Mezquital, Milpillas, Navogame, Nazas, Ocotan, Papasquiaro, Picachos, Pueblo Nuevo, Quiviquinta, San Antonio, San Bernabé, San Diego del Rio, San José, Santa Catalina, Tasquaringa, Teneraca, Tepehuanes, Tizonazo, Tunal, Tutuaca, Yonora, Zape. See Orozco y Berra, Geog., 318–19, 1864; Pimentel, Lenguas, II, 44–68, 1865; Bandelier in Arch. Inst. Papers, III, 53, 1890; Hrdlička in Am.

TEPEHUANE WOMAN (AM. MUS. NAT. HIST.)

Anthr., V, no. 3, 1903; Lumholtz, Unknown Mexico, 1902.   (F. W. H.)

Lepeguanes.—Miranda (1575) in Doc. Inéd. de Indias, XVI, 566, 1871 (misprint). Ódami.—Lumholtz, Unknown Mex., I, 425, 1902 (own name). O-o-dam.—Hrdlička, inf'n, 1906 (own name; sig. ' people'). Sæló.—Lumholtz, op. cit. ('walking-stick insects'—phasmidæ; Tarahumare name). Tepeguanes.—Miranda (1575), op. cit., 567, Zarate-Salmeron (ca. 1629) in Land of Sunshine, 183, Feb. 1900. Tepehuan.—Orozco y Berra, Geog., 58, 1864. Tepehuane.—Lumholtz in Int. Cong. Anthr., 103–104, 1894. Tepeoanes.—Benavides, Memorial, 7, 1630.

Tepehuanes. A Tepehuane pueblo in s. Chihuahua, Mexico, about lat. 26° 30′, lon. 106° 30′.

Balleza.—Orozco y Berra, Geog., 324, 1864 (apparently the native name). San Pablo de Tepehuanes.—Ibid. Tepehuanes—Ibid., 318.

Tepemaca. One of the tribes living nearest to Dolores, which was not far from Laredo, Texas, in 1757. There is some ground for thinking that they may have been the tribe commonly called by the Spaniards *Cueros Quemados* ('burnt skins'), who lived on both sides of the Rio Grande above and below Reynosa, Mexico (Tienda de Cueros, Revista, 1757, MS. in Archivo Gen.).   (H. E. B.)

Teporachic. A Tarahumare settlement of Chihuahua, Mexico. The total population in 1900 was 261, all regarded as civilized.

Tequassimo. A subtribe of the Choptank, formerly living on Choptank r., Md. In 1749 they were assigned a reservation on the s. bank of the river, in Dorchester co., but by 1837 they had dwindled to a few individuals of mixed Indian and negro blood.—Bozman, Md., I, 115, 1837.

Tequemapo. A Calusa village on the s. w. coast of Florida, about 1570.

Teguemapo.—Fontaneda, as quoted by Shipp, De Soto and Fla., 586, 1881. Tequemapo.—Fontaneda Memoir (*ca.* 1575), Smith trans., 19, 1854.

Tequenondahi ('on the opposite side of the mountain.'—Hewitt). A village in 1534 on lower St Lawrence r., Quebec.—Cartier (1545), Relation, Tross ed., 32½, 1863.

Tequepis. The name, apparently, of two villages, or perhaps of one village claimed by two missions. One was near San Marcos, the other near Santa Inés, both in Santa Barbara co., Cal.

Tequepas.—Taylor in Cal. Farmer, Oct. 18, 1861. Tequepis.—Ibid., Apr. 24, 1863.

Tequesta. A rude and piratical tribe of unknown linguistic affinity, occupying the s. E. Florida coast, within the present Dade and Monroe cos., in the 16th century. They were more or less subject to the Calusa, their neighbors on the w. About all that is known of them is contained in brief references in the Fontaneda Memoir (*ca.* 1575) and in Barcia, Ensayo, 1723, with a short notice in Gatschet, Creek Migr. Leg., I, 1884.   (J. M.)

Tegesta.—French quoted by Shipp, De Soto and Fla., 585, 1881. Tekesta.—Gatschet, Creek Migr. Leg., I, map, 48, 1884. Tequesta.—Barcia, Ensayo, 161, 1723 (the form used by Fontaneda about 1575). Tequeste.—Shea, Cath. Miss., 57, 1855.

Teracosick. A village of the Powhatan confederacy in 1608, on the w. bank of Nansemond r. in Nansemond co., Va.—Smith (1629), Va., I, map, repr. 1819.

Terapa. A former Opata pueblo in the immediate vicinity of Guachinera, E. Sonora, Mexico, lat. 30° 20′, lon. 109°. It was occupied for a period in the 18th century by the inhabitants of Batesopa and Baquigopa.—Bandelier in Arch. Inst. Papers, IV, 520, 1892.

Teras. A former Opata pueblo on the upper waters of the Rio Bavispe, 12 leagues N. of Oputo, in E. Sonora, Mexico. It seems to have been the seat of a missionary establishment and contained a small church, but was abandoned in the 18th century, owing to the hostility of the Apache, Suma, and Jocome.

Tercáo. Mentioned as a pueblo of the province of Atripuy (q. v.), in the region of the lower Rio Grande, N. Mex., in 1598.—Oñate (1598) in Doc. Inéd., XVI, 115, 1871.

Terebin. See *Terrapin.*

Terentief. A Kaiyuhkhotana village on the Yukon below Koyukuk r. Pop. 15 in 1880.

Terentief.—Nelson in 18th Rep. B. A. E., map, 1899. Terentief's Barabara.—Petroff, Rep. on Alaska, 62, 1881. Terentief's station.—Petroff in 10th Census, Alaska, 12, 1884.

Terocodame. A tribe at San Francisco Solano mission, near the Rio Grande, in Coahuila, after 1705. Rivera (Diario, leg. 2763, 1736) mentions it in 1727 as a tribe of Coahuila. Before its removal to San Antonio mission, Texas, Solano was situated "in the Terocodame band" (MS. Baptismal Rec., 1707, partidas 319, 326). The Terocodame seems to have been the most prominent tribe of the locality and to have given its name to the band or confederacy. The baptismal entries mention a certain Manuel, of the Ticmamar nation, who was "captain of the Terocodames" (ibid., 1706, partida 169); a man "of the Oydican nation and of the Terocodame band" (ibid., 1707, partida 271); a man "of the Babor nation, interpreter for the idiom of the Terocodame band" (ibid., partida 248); a woman "of the Terocodame band and of the Juman nation" (ibid., partida 272), etc. The Terocodame were, however, a distinct tribe or subtribe of this band. The records show that they intermarried with the Gabilan, Viddaquimamar, Oydican, Ticmamar, Juman, Mauiga, Maubedan, Tuteneiboica, Matuimi, Jicaragrande, and other tribes or subtribes (Baptismal Rec., passim), the intermarriage occurring in many cases certainly while in the gentile state. On Nov. 21, 1706, 58 gentiles of different divisions were baptized. They apparently had come to the mission in a body, hence it may be inferred that they were more or less closely associated. The divisions represented by those baptized or by their parents are Terocodame, Ticmamar, Gabilan, Viddaquimamar, Bacorame, Cucusa, Macocoma (or Ntacocoma), Juman, Mauiga, Julime (or Juribe), Tepeguan, Quizal, Babor, Mamuqui, Mescal, Colorado, Tuteneiboica, Jicaragrande, Matuimi, and Zenizo. The statements as to the parentage of different individuals baptized show that the intermarriages represented many combinations of these groups—another indication that they were closely associated. According to García the Mescal tribe spoke what is known as the Coahuiltecan language. Apparently there were linguistic differences in the group, for while a Babor was called interpreter for the Terocodame, another individual was called interpreter for the Jumanes (ibid., 1706, partida 169). Some of the Terocodame, as well as other tribes of this group, followed the Solano mission to the San Antonio and were baptized at San Antonio de Valero (Baptismal Rec., 1719). (H. E. B.)

Hieroquodame.—Baptismal Rec., 1712, partida 5, op. cit. Hirequodame.—Ibid. Hyeroquodame.—Ibid., partida 10. Perocodame.—Ibid., 1719, partida 50. Therocodames.—Rivera, op. cit.

Terrapin. Any one of various tortoises of the waters of the s. Atlantic coast of the United States; specifically *Malacoclemmys palustris*. The word is spelled in a variety of ways by the early writers. Whitaker (Good Newes from Va., 42, 1613) speaks of "the torope or little turtle"; Campanius (1645) gives the word for tortoise in the Delaware dialect of New Jersey as *tulpa* or *turpa;* Rasles (1691) gives for turtle in Abnaki, *turebe;* Eliot (Levit., xi, 29) renders tortoises by *tœnuppasog* in the Massachuset dialect; Lawson (Nat. Hist. of Car., 133, 1709) has *terebins;* Beverley (Virginia, 151, 1722) speaks of "a small kind of turtle, or *tarapins* (as we call them)." The "Bre'r Tarrypin" of the "Uncle Remus" stories has become famous. Terrapin is a diminutive from the *torope* or *turŭpe* of the Virginian and Delaware dialects of Algonquian. (A. F. C.)

Terrenate. A Pima rancheria visited by Father Kino in 1697; situated near the headwaters of Rio San Pedro, s. of the Arizona-Sonora boundary. A presidio was established there in 1741, and about 1760–64 the population, including a garrison of about 50 men, numbered 411. The presidio was temporarily transferred to or near Guevavi before 1750. Bartlett (Pers. Narr., I, 419, 1854) described it as a village of 200 or 300 persons in 1851; in 1900 it contained 311 civilized inhabitants and 26 Yaqui.

San Bernardo Gracia Real.—Bancroft, No. Mex. States, I, 528, 1884. Santa Cruz.—Bancroft, Ariz. and N. Mex., 386, 1889 (probably its more recent name). S. Felipe Gracia Real de Terrenate.—Bancroft, ibid., 371. Sn. Felipe.—Venegas, map, 1754, in Bancroft, ibid., 370. St. Philip de JHS.—Venegas, Hist. Cal., I, map, 1759. Teranáte.—Hardy, Trav., 422, 1829. Terrenate.—Bernal (1697) cited by Bancroft, Ariz. and N. Mex., 356, 1889. Terrenati.—Browne, Apache Country, 168, 1869. Texenáte.—Hardy, Trav., 427, 1829.

Tertaitatana. The Day people of Taos pueblo, N. Mex.

Têr taitatána.—M. C. Stevenson, notes, B. A. E., 1910 (*taina*='people').

Terwer. A former Yurok village on Klamath r., Cal., a few miles above its mouth.

Terwar.—Taylor in Cal. Farmer, June 8, 1860.

Tesakayala (*Tésak'a Yäla*, 'place of nude mountains'). One of the mythic settling places of the Zuñi after their emergence from the Underworld.—Cushing in 13th Rep. B. A. E., 390, 1896.

Teshaya. A former Salinan village situated at the site of San Antonio mission, Monterey co., Cal.

Sextapay.—Taylor quoted by Bancroft, Hist. Cal., I, 176, 1886. Teshaya.—Taylor in Cal. Farmer, Apr. 27, 1860. Texhaya.—Bancroft, op. cit. Texja.—Taylor, op. cit.

Teshoa. A discoidal flake or spall knocked from the convex surface of a waterworn stone by a dexterous blow with a hammerstone or by striking a bowlder against another stone. This implement was first noted by Leidy, who found it in use among the Shoshoni of Wyoming. Leidy states that "it was called a 'teshoa,' and is employed as a scraper in dressing buffalo skins." The use of sharp-edged flakes of this type for scrapers and knives was doubtless general among the tribes from the earliest times. Consult Leidy in 6th Rep. Hayden Surv. 1872, 653, 1873; Mercer in Proc. A. A. A. S., xli, 287, 1892; Phillips in Smithson. Rep. 1897, 587, 1898. (W. H. H.)

Teshuhimga. See *White Hair.*

Tesia. A former settlement of the Mayo on the Rio Mayo, above Navajoa, s. w. Sonora, Mexico. The pueblo, now civilized, contained 487 inhabitants in 1900.

San Ignacio de Tesia.—Orozco y Berra, Geog., 356, 1864. Tecia.—Hrdlička in Am. Anthr., vi, 59, 1904. Tésia.—Hardy, Trav. in Mex., 438, 1829. Tessia.—Kino map (1702) in Stöcklein, Neue Welt-Bott, 1726.

Tesik. A village occupied by Chukchi and Aiwan Yuit Eskimo, half and half, on the w. shore of Chechin bay, N. E. Siberia. Pop. 142 in 25 houses about 1895; 94 in 18 houses in 1901.

Öe'čin.—Bogoras, Chukchee, 29, 1904 (Chukchi name). Te'sik.—Ibid. (Eskimo name). Tschetschehn.—Krause in Deutsche Geog. Blätt., v, 80, map, 1882.

Tesinde ('buffalo-tail'). A gens of the Inshtasanda division of the Omaha.

Buffalo.—Morgan, Anc. Soc., 155, 1877. Buffalo-tail.—Dorsey in Bull. Philos. Soc. Wash., 129, 1880. Da-thun'-da.—Morgan, op. cit., 155. Tasin-da.—Long, Exped. Rocky Mts., I, 327, 1823. Ţe-sĭnde.—Dorsey in 15th Rep. B. A. E., 226, 1897.

Tesonachas. Mentioned by Baudry des Lozières (Voy. à la Louisiane, 244, 1802) in a list of tribes with no information concerning it. Unidentified.

Tessamatuck. A village situated in 1608 on Piscataway r., just above the mouth, in Prince George co., Md.—Smith (1629), Va., I, map, repr., 1819.

Tessikdjuak ('big lake'). The chief village of the Ukosiksalirmiut Eskimo at the head of Back r. estuary, Canada.

Tessiqdjuaq.—Boas in 6th Rep. B. A. E., map, 1888.

Tessuntee. A former Cherokee settlement on Cowee r., s. of Franklin, in Macon co., N. C.—Royce in 5th Rep. B. A. E., map, 1887.

Testnigh. A village, probably occupied by the Conestoga, situated in 1608 on the E. bank of Susquehanna r., in Lancaster co., Pa.—Smith (1629), Va., I, map, repr. 1819.

Testthitun ('where [something] reclined'?). A former village of the Tututni on the N. side of Rogue r., Oreg. Tĕ-st'hi'-tûn.—Dorsey in Jour. Am. Folk-lore, III, 233, 1890.

Tesuque (*Tĕt-su'-ge*, 'cottonwood-tree place'). The southernmost of the pueblos occupied by the Tewa; situated 8 m. N. of Santa Fé, N. Mex. It became the seat of a Spanish mission early in the 17th century, but was reduced to a visita of Santa Fé in 1760 and of Pojuaque in 1782. The original pueblo, which bore the same name, occupied a site about 3 m. E. of the present village, and was

TESUQUE MAN

abandoned probably during the Pueblo revolt of 1680–92. The Tesuque people are divided into two organizations, the Winter (Watuyú) and the Summer (Oyíke) people, each with its own caciques. Formerly they adhered strictly to the tribal law which prohibited intermarriage between members of the same clan, but the custom seems no longer to be rigidly followed, and, unlike the Pueblos generally, descent is in the male line. The existing Tesuque clans are: T'ye (Gopher), Tang (*Tan*, Sun), Kongya (*Konya*, Turquoise), Owhát (Cloud). The extinct clans are: Ta (Grass), Nang (*Nan*, Earth), Tse (Eagle), De (Coyote), Kuping (*Kupin*, Coral), Po (Calabash). Pop. 80 in 1906. See *Pueblos, Tewa*. (F. W. H.)

San Diego de Tesuque.—Ward in Ind. Aff. Rep. 1867, 213, 1868. San Lorenzo de Tezuqui.—Vetancurt (1696) in Téatro Mex., IV, 274, 1871. San Lorenzo Tezuqui.—Ibid., III, 316, 1871. Sayaque.—D'Anville, map Am. Sept., 1746 (doubtless identical; not Cicuyé nor Cicuic [Pecos]). S. Diego.—Bancroft, Ariz. and N. Mex., 281, 1889. Tai-tzogai.—Jouvenceau in Cath. Pion., I, no. 9, 12, 1906. Tâ-tsür-ma'.—Hodge, field notes, B. A. E., 1895 (Picuris Tigua name). Tejugne.—Dufouri in Cath. World, 75, Apr. 1884. Temqué.—Domenech, Deserts, II, 63, 1860. Tersuque.—Cooper in Ind. Aff. Rep., 161, 1870. Teseque.—Ind. Aff. Rep., 506, 1889. Tesuke.—Stevenson in 2d Rep. B. A. E., 328, 1883. Tesuki.—Fewkes in 22d Rep. B. A. E., 18, 1904. Tesuque.—Alcedo, Dic. Geog., v, 101, 1789. Tesuqui.—Simpson in Rep Sec. War, 2d map, 1850. Tetsógi.—Stephen in 8th Rep. B. A. E., 37, 1891 (Hano Tigua name). Tĕt-su'-ge.—Hodge, field notes, B. A. E., 1895 ('cottonwood-tree place': Tewa name; the Tewa of San Juan pronounce the name *Tĕt-su-ge'*). Te-tzo-ge.—Bandelier in Ritch, New Mexico, 201, 1885; in Rev. d'Ethnogr., 203, 1886; in Arch. Inst. Pap., III, 260, 1890 (aboriginal name of pueblo). Tezuque.—Villa-Señor, Theatro Am., II, 418, 1748. Thezuque.—Vargas (1704) quoted by Bandelier in Arch. Inst. Pap., III, 144, 1890. Tiótsokoma.—Hodge, field notes, B. A. E., 1895 (Santa Ana Queres name). Tosugui.—Morgan in N. Am. Rev., map, Apr. 1869. Tso'-tâ.—Hodge, field notes, B. A. E., 1895 (Jemez and Pecos name). Tucheaáp.—Ibid. (Isleta Tigua name). Tusuque.—Schoolcraft, Ind. Tribes, III, 406, 1853. Tutsuíba.—Hodge, field notes, B. A. E., 1899 ('small pueblo': Taos name). Tyu'-tso-ku'.—Hodge, field notes, B. A. E., 1895 (Cochiti Queres name). Zesuqua.—Lane (1854) in Schoolcraft, Ind. Tribes, v, 689, 1855.

Tet. A tribe named in 1708 in a list of those that had been met or heard of N. of San Juan Bautista mission on the lower Rio Grande, in Texas (Fr. Isidro Felix de Espinosa, Relación Compendiosa of the Rio Grande missions, MS. in the College of Santa Cruz de Querétaro).

Tetachoya. A former Salinan village near San Antonio mission, Monterey co., Cal.—Taylor in Cal. Farmer, Apr. 27, 1860.

Tetanauoica. The tribal name given in the records for an Indian who was buried in 1707 at San Francisco Solano mission, Texas. The neophytes gathered there belonged mainly to the Coahuiltecan family, which may be true of this band or tribe (Valero Burials, 1707, partida 82, MS.). (H. E. B.)

Tetanetlenok (*T'ē'l'anēlēnóx*). A gens of the Klaskino, a Kwakiutl tribe.—Boas in Rep. Nat. Mus. 1895, 329, 1897.

Tetecores. A former tribe of Coahuila, N. E. Mexico, probably Coahuiltecan, met by Fernando del Bosque in 1675, at which time they and the Babosarigami together numbered 119, including 44 warriors.—Fernando del Bosque (1675) in Nat. Geog. Mag., XIV, 348, 1903.

Têtes de Boule (French: 'round heads'). A rude tribe of wandering hunters formerly roving over an extensive region on the upper branches of St Maurice, Gatineau, and Ottawa rs., Quebec. As described by Henry, about the year 1800, they depended chiefly on rabbits for food and clothing, built mere brush windbreaks for shelter, and placed small piles of firewood near the bark-covered graves of their dead for the use of the spirits. Chauvignerie

(1736) gives them and the Abittibi as totems the pheasant and the eagle. They have been reduced by smallpox and other calamities to 203, living in 1908 on a reservation on St Maurice r., in Champlain co., Quebec. They seem to be closely cognate with their western neighbors, the Nopeming (q. v.), with whom they are often confounded, although apparently a distinct people. See *Michacondibi, Michipicoten.*   (J. M.)

Algonquins à têtes de Boule.—Champigny (1692) in N. Y. Doc. Col. Hist., IX, 535, 1855. **Big-heads.**—Donnelly in Can. Ind. Aff. Rep. 1883, pt. I, 10, 1884. **Bullheads.**—Colden (1727), Five Nations, 134, 1747. **Gens des Terres.**—Jes. Rel. 1671, 25, 1858. **Round Heads.**—Durant (1721) in N. Y. Doc. Col. Hist., V, 589, 1855. **Testes de bœufs.**—La Chesnaye (1697) in Margry, Déc., VI, 6, 1886. **Tetes de Boule.**—Chauvignerie (1736) quoted by Schoolcraft, Ind. Tribes, III, 556, 1853.

Têtes Pelées (French: 'bald heads'). Described by the Nipissing as a people with little or no hair, who came into Hudson bay in large wooden boats to trade. Possibly some white traders.

Testes Pelees.—Sagard (1636), Can., I, 227, 1886.

Tetling. A Tenankutchin village, of 17 inhabitants in 1885, on upper Tanana r., Alaska, where the outlet of Wagner lake joins it in lat. 63° 30'. In 1898 it consisted of 4 log houses.

Tetlings.—Lowe quoted by Baker, Geog. Dict. Alaska, 1902. **Tetling's village.**—Allen, Rep. on Alaska, 137, 1885.

Teton (contr. of *Titonwaⁿ*, 'dwellers on the prairie'). The western and principal division of the Dakota or Sioux, including all the bands formerly ranging w. of Missouri r., and now residing on reservations in South Dakota and North Dakota. The bands officially recognized are: Oglala of Pine Ridge agency; Brulé of Rosebud and Lower Brulé agencies; Blackfoot, Miniconjou, Sans Arc, and Two Kettle of Cheyenne River agency; Hunkpapa, etc., of Standing Rock agency. Their history is interwoven with that of the other Dakota and is little more than a recountal of attacks on other tribes and on border settlers and emigrants. They were first met by Hennepin (1680) 20 or 30 leagues above the falls of St Anthony in Minnesota, probably at Sauk rapids, on Mississippi r., about 70 m. above Minneapolis. He places them in the neighborhood of Mille Lacs, far to the E. of their later home. Lahontan also enumerates them among the tribes on the upper Mississippi, which leads to the conclusion that a part at least of the Teton formerly lived in the prairie region, near the upper Mississippi, though the main body may have been near upper Minnesota r. Le Sueur in 1700 included them in the western Sioux, who lived between the upper Mississippi and the Missouri On a map of De l'Isle (1701) L Traverse is surrounded by villages of wandering Teton. Pachot (Margry, Déc., VI, 518, 1886) located them 80 leagues w. of the Falls of

St Anthony in 1722. Carver (1766) met at least a part of them at the extreme w. point of his journey up Minnesota r., about 200 m. from its mouth. The younger Henry (Coues, New Light, I, 145, 1897) found them in 1800 on the upper Missouri, where Lewis and Clark (Exped., I, 98, 100, 1893) encountered them a few years afterward. These explorers enumerate as divisions: Tetons of the Burnt Woods (Brulés), about 300 men, who rove on both sides of Missouri, White, and Teton rs.; Tetons Okandandas (Oglala), 150 men, who inhabit both sides of the Missouri below Cheyenne r.; Tetons Minnekineazzo, about 250 men, on both sides of the Missouri above Cheyenne r; Tetons Saone, about 300 men, living on both sides of Missouri r. below Beaver cr. Gov. Ramsey said that they lived from Cannonball r. s. to Niobrara r. (Rep. Ind. Aff. 1849, 84, 1850).

The Teton entered into a peace treaty with the United States at Portage des Sioux, Mo., in 1815, which was confirmed by treaty of June 22, 1825, at Ft Lookout, S. Dak. It was warriors of this group who massacred Lieut. Grattan and his party at Ft Laramie, Wyo., in 1854; none, however, took part in the Minnesota massacre of 1862. In 1865 a commission concluded treaties with each of the several divisions of the group, with provision for right of way through their territory. By treaty of 1868 they first agreed to give up their free range and come upon a reservation, including about all of South Dakota w. of the Missouri r. Under their chiefs, Red Cloud, Crazy Horse, and Sitting Bull, they have been the principals in all the Indian wars and outbreaks of the northern plains, notably in 1864, 1876, and 1890.

Gov. Ramsey characterizes the Teton as a large, finely formed, tall, and vigorous people, hardy, indomitable, and restless warriors, daring horsemen, and skilful hunters, possessing in perfection "all the Indian virtues of bravery, cunning, treachery, and hospitality," true to each other and ready foes to all others.

Neill (Minn. Hist. Soc. Coll., I, 258, 1872) says: "They are the plundering Arabs of America, and have of late years been a terror to the emigrants to the Pacific coast." According to Lewis and Clark the interior policing of a village was confided to 2 or 3 officers who were named by the chief for the purpose of preserving order and remained in power some days, till the chief appointed their successors. These were always on the watch to keep tranquillity during the day and guarded the camp at night The short duration of their office was compensated by its authority, their power being supreme, and in the suppression of disturbance no resistance to them was suffered; their persons were sacred, and if in the execution of their duty they even struck a chief of the second class they could not be punished. Riggs mentions as peculiarities of the Teton dialect, compared with those of other divisions of the Dakota group, that *g* hard is used for *h* of the Santee and *k* of the Yanktonai, and that, rejecting *d* altogether, they use *l* in its stead.

The Teton is the most populous and important of the Dakota divisions, constituting four-sevenths of the whole nation. Lewis and Clark (1804) estimated them at 1,000 men, about 4,000 souls, probably much less than the true number. The Indian Bureau in 1842 estimated the total number at 12,000; Ramsey (1849), more than 6,000; Riggs (1851), fewer than 12,500. The Indian Bureau in 1861 gave a total of 8,900. It is probable these estimates were below rather than above the true number, as in 1890 the total Teton population was 16,426, and in 1909 the number, including Yanktonai bands at Standing Rock agency, N. Dak., was 18,098. In addition about 100 of the Sitting Bull refugees are still in Canada.　　　　　　　　　　　　　　(c. t.)

Anthontans.—Coxe, Carolana, 50, 1741. Atintans.—Lahontan (1688) quoted in H. R. Ex. Doc. 96, 42d Cong., 3d sess., 15, 1873. Atintons.—Lahontan (1688), New Voy., I, 231, 1703. Atrutons.—Ramsey in Ind Aff. Rep. 1849, 72, 1850 (misprint). Mascouteins Nadouessi.—Tailhan in Perrot, Mém., 196, 1864. Maskoutens-Nadouessians.—Hennepin, New Discov., 132, 1698 Nadooessis of the Plains.—Jefferys, Am. Atlas, map 8, 1776. Prairie Indians.—Ramsey in Ind. Aff. Rep. 1849, 72, 1850. Scious of the Prairies.—Chauvignerie (1736) quoted by Schoolcraft, Ind. Tribes, III, 557, 1853. Scioux of the Prairies.—Doc. of 1728 in N. Y. Doc. Col. Hist., IX, 1005, 1855. Scioux of the West.—Le Sueur (1700) quoted by Neill, Hist. Minn., 170, 1858 (includes the Yankton and Yanktonai). Sioux des prairies.—Bossu (1756), Trav. La., I, 182, 1771. Sioux nomades.—Tailhan in Perrot, Mém., 232, 1864. Sioux occidentaux.—Ibid. Sioux of the Meadows.—Smith, Bouquet Exped., 76, 1766. Sioux of the Plain.—Seymour, Sketches of Minn., 135, 1850. Sioux of the Savannas.—Jefferys, French Dom. Am., pt. 1, 45, 1761. Sioux-Tentons.—Gass, Voyage, 420, 1810. Sioux Teton.—Lewis and Clark, Discov., 23, 1806. Siton.—Boudinot, Star in the West, 128, 1816 (misprint). Teeton band.—Gass, Jour., 44, 1807. Teetonwan.—Lynd in Minn. Hist. Coll., II, pt. 2, 59, 1864. Teetwans.—Ramsey in Ind. Aff. Rep. 1849, 72, 1850. Teetwaun.—Ramsey in Minn. Hist. Coll., I, 47, 1872. Tee-twawn.—Ramsey in Ind. Aff. Rep. 1849, 69, 1850. Tenton.—Gass, Voy., 56, 1810. Ten-ton-ha.—Ramsey in Ind. Aff. Rep. 1849, 85, 1850. Tentouha.—McKenney and Hall, Ind. Tribes, III, 80, 1854. Tetans.—Ramsey in Ind. Aff. Rep 1849, 85, 1850. Tetaus.—Pike, Exped., app., pt. 1, 59, 1810 (misprint). Tetoan.—Long, Exped. St. Peter's R., I, 380, 1824. Teton.—Gale, Upper Miss., 261, 1867. Tetones.—Lewis and Clark, Discov., 32, 1806. Tetongue.—Clark quoted by Coues, Lewis and Clark Exped., I, 128, note, 1893. Tetons.—De l'Isle, La. map (*ca.* 1701) in Neill, Hist. Minn., 164, 1858. Tetonsarans.—Ind. Aff. Rep., 296, 1846 (misprint for Tetons errans). Teuton-ha.—H. R. Ex. Doc. 96, 42d Cong., 3d sess., 15, 1873 (misprint for Tenton-ha). Thinthonha.—Shea, Discov., 112, 1852. Thinthonna.—Hennepin map (1683) cited by Bandelier in Arch. Inst, Papers, III, pt. 1, 174, 1890. Thintohas.—Barcia, Ensayo, 238, 1723. Thuntotas.—Alcedo, Dic. Geog., III, 213, 1788. Tieton.—Ind. Aff. Rep. 1856, 41, 1857. Tindaw.—Ladd, Story of N. Mex., 67, 1891. Tintangaonghiatons.—Shea, Early Voy., 111, 1861. Tintangaoughiatons.—Le Sueur (1700) in Margry,

Déc., VI, 87, 1886. Tiŋta-toŋwaŋ.—Riggs, Dakota Gram., Texts and Ethnog., 186, 1893 (full name). Tinthenha.—La Potherie, Hist. Am., II, map, 1753 (trans. 'gens des prairies'). Tinthona.—Hennepin, New Discov., map, 1698. Tinthonha.—Shea, Discov. Miss., 113, 1852. Tinthow.—Ladd, Story of N. Mex., 67, 1891. Tintinhos.—Ramsey in Ind. Aff. Rep. 1849, 72, 1850. Tintoner.—Balbi, Atlas Ethnog., 55, 1826. Tintones.—Alcedo, Dic. Geog., V, 137, 1789. Tintonhas.—La Salle Exped. (1679–81) in Margry, Déc., I, 481, 1876. Tintons.—Carver, Trav., 80, 1778. Tintonwans.—Neill, Hist. Minn., 52, 1858. Ti toan.—Keating in Long, Exped. St. Peter's R., I, 378, 1824. Titoba.—Pachot (*ca.* 1722) in Margry, Déc., VI, 518, 1886. Titon.—Schermerhorn (1812) in Mass. Hist. Coll., 2d s., II, 41, 1814. Titones.—Boudinot, Star in the West, 129, 1816. Titongs.—Schoolcraft, Trav., 307, 1821. Titonwan.—Nicollet, Rep. on Upper Miss., map, 1843. Titoŋwaŋs.—Riggs, Dak. Dict., XVI, 1852. Ti-t'wan.—Ramsey in Ind. Aff. Rep. 1849, 85, 1850. Ti-twans.—Ramsey, ibid., 72. Ti-t'-wawn.—Ramsey, ibid., 69. Western Sioux.—Jefferys, French Dom. Am., pt. 1, 45, 1761. West Schious.—Coxe, Carolana, map, 1741. Zeton.—Ruxton, Life in Far West, 201, 1849 (misprint).

Tetzino. A tribe or subtribe, some members of which entered San Antonio de Valero mission, Texas, about 1740, with the group to which the Sana (q. v.) belonged. The affiliation of the Sana seems to have been Tonkawan (Valero Burials, 1742, partida 337; Baptisms, 1742, partida 588, MS.).　　　(h. e. b.)

Teuricachi. A former Opata pueblo and seat of a Spanish mission founded in 1653. Situated in N. E. Sonora, Mexico, on the upper waters of Rio Bavispe, above Oputo. Pop. 224 in 1678, and 52 in 1730. Subsequently abandoned on account of depredations by the Suma and Jano.

Guadalupe Teuricachi.—Zapata (1678) quoted by Bancroft, No. Mex. States, I, 246, 1884. Nuestra Señora de Guadalupe de Teuricatzi.—Zapata (1678) in Doc. Hist. Mex., 4th s., III, 369, 1857. Teuricachi.—Rivera (1730) cited by Bancroft, No. Mex. States, I, 514, 1884. Teuricatzi.—Orozco y Berra, Geog., 343, 1864. Teurizatzi.—Doc. 18th century quoted by Bandelier in Arch. Inst. Papers, IV, 526, 1892. Turi-ca-chi.—Bandelier, ibid., 529.

Tewa ('moccasins,' their Keresan name). A group of Pueblo tribes belonging to the Tanoan linguistic family, now occupying the villages of San Ildefonso, San Juan, Santa Clara, Nambe, Tesuque, and Hano, all except the last lying in the valley of the Rio Grande in N. New Mexico. The pueblo of Hano, in the Hopi country of N. E. Arizona, dates from the time of the Pueblo revolt of 1680–92. Pojoaque was inhabited by Tewa until a few years ago, when intermarriage with Mexicans and the death of the few full-bloods made it practically a Mexican settlement. It had been supposed that the Tano, an offshoot of the Tewa in prehistoric times, spoke a dialect distinct from that of the Tewa, but recent studies by John P. Harrington show that the differences are so slight as to be negligible. In 1598 Juan de Oñate named 11 of the Tewa pueblos and stated that there were others; 30 years later Fray Alonzo Benavides reported the population to be 6,000 in 8 pueblos. The population of the present 6 villages is about 1,200—San Juan, the largest, having 419, and Tesuque, the smallest, 86 inhabitants. Each village of the Tewa is divided into two sections, the Winter people and the Summer people. According to Bandelier, "the dignity of chief penitent or cacique belongs alternately to each of these two groups. Thus the Summer cacique serves from the vernal equinox to the autumnal, and the Winter cacique from the autumnal to the vernal equinox. On very important occasions, however, the Oyiké or Winter cacique is inferior to his colleague." Little is yet known of the social organization and religious institutions of the Tewa people, but there is evidence that at Nambe and Tesuque, at least, descent is reckoned in the male line, and that at the latter pueblo the law prohibiting marriage of persons belonging to the same clan is no longer strictly enforced.

Following are the villages formerly occupied by the Tewa, so far as the names have been recorded or applied: Abechiu, Agawano, Analco, Axol, Camitria, Chipiinuinge, Chipiwi, Chupadero, Cuyamunque, Fejiu, Fesere, Homayo, Houiri, Ihamba, Jacona, Junetre, Kaayu, Keguayo, Kuapooge, Kwengyauinge, Luceros (partially), Navahu, Navawi, Otowi, Perage, Pininicangwi, Pojiuuingge, Pojoaque, Ponyinumba, Ponyipakuen, Poseuingge, Potzuye, Pueblito, Pueblo Quemado (?), Puye, Sajiuwingge, Sakeyu, Sandia (not the Tigua pueblo of that name), Santa Cruz, Sepawi, Shufinne, Teeuinggee, Tejeuingge Ouiping, Tobhipangge, Triapi, Triaque, Troomaxiaquino, Tsankawi, Tsawarii, Tseweige, Tshirege, Yugeuingge.

The following extinct villages were either Tewa or Tano: Chiuma, Guia, Guika, Peñas Negras.

The following were inhabited by either the Tigua or the Tewa: Axoytre, Camitre, Paniete, Piamato, Quioyaco.

See *Pueblos, Tanoan family.* (F. W. H.)

Jehuas.—Bandelier in Rev. d'Ethnog., 203, 1886 (misprint). Tacos.—Siguenza (1691-3), quoted by Buschmann, Neu-Mexico, 264, 1858 (probably identical, although Teguas also is given). Tagna.—Irvine in Ind. Aff. Rep., 160, 1877 (misprint; used for Hano pueblo). Taowa.—Palmer, MS. vocab., B. A. E., title, n. d. Taucos.—Cortez (1799) quoted in Pac. R. R. Rep., III, pt. 3, 121, 1856 (apparently Hano of Arizona). Tawas.—Parke, map of N. Mex., 1851 (=Hano). Tay-wah.—Palmer in Ind. Aff. Rep., 133, 1870 (=Hano). Tay-waugh.—Lane (1854) in Schoolcraft, Ind. Tribes, V, 689, 1855. Tecua.—Garcés (1775) quoted by Orozco y Berra, Geog., 350, 1864. Tegas.—Toussaint, Carte l'Amér., 1839. Teguas.—Oñate (1598) in Doc. Inéd., XVI, 109, 1871. Tégwas.—Petitot, Dic. Dènè-Dindjié, XVII, 1876. Tehaas.—Donaldson, Moqui Pueblo Inds., 106, 1893. Tehuas.—Shea, Cath. Miss., 77, 1855. Tejuas.—Domenech, Deserts N. Am., II, 62, 1860. Tepúas.—Benavides, Memorial, 26, 1630. Tepúas.—Oñate (1598) in Doc. Inéd., XVI, 115, 1871 (identified as the Tewa by Bandelier in Arch. Inst. Pap., I, 19, 1881). Té-quà.—Whipple in Pac. R. R. Rep., III, pt. 3, 13, 1856 (=Hano). Tequas.—Cordova (1619) in Ternaux-Compans, Voy., X, 444, 1838. Tevas.—Benavides (1630) quoted by Bancroft, Ariz. and N. Mex., 164, 1889 ("Toas or Tevas nation"). Téwa.—Ward in Ind. Aff. Rep. 1864, 191, 1865. Theguas.—Escudero, Noticias Nuevo Méx., 82, 1849. Ti'wa.—ten Kate, Synonymie, 8, 1884. Toas.—Benavides (1630) quoted by Bancroft, Ariz. and N. Mex., 164, 1889 (or Tevas nation; misprint). Towas.—Davis, El Gringo, 115, 1857 (=Hano). Tŭ'-ba-na.—Hodge, field notes, B. A. E., 1895 (Taos name). Tu'-věn.—Ibid. (Isleta and Sandia name).

Tewanondadon ('surrounded by mountains.'—Hewitt). A former Mohawk village, situated, according to the Brion de la Tour map of 1781, in the peninsula formed by the outlet of Otsego lake and Shenivas cr., N. Y. In 1753 Rev. Gideon Hawley found in it 3 wigwams and about 30 people.

Tewanondadon.—Esnauts and Rapilly map, 1777. Tewanoudadon.—Lattré map, 1784. Towanoendalough.—Hawley (1794) in Doc. Hist. N. Y., III, 1042, 1850.

Tewetken (*Tě'wɛtqɛn*). A Nanaimo division on the E. coast of Vancouver id., Brit. Col.—Boas in 5th Rep. N. W. Tribes Can., 32, 1889.

Texa. Mentioned as a pueblo of the province of Atripuy (q. v.), in the region of the lower Rio Grande, N. Mex., in 1598.—Oñate (1598) in Doc. Inéd., XVI, 115, 1871.

Texas. A name variously applied by writers, but most commonly used by the Spaniards, from whom French and English writers borrowed it, to designate the Hasinai tribes of Angelina and upper Neches valleys, Texas. There are many variations from this usage in Spanish writings, but nevertheless it is the usual one. As a geographical term the name was first extended from these Hasinai tribes to their immediate country, and then gradually to all the territory included within the present Texas.

Among the tribes of E. Texas the word *texas* (*texias, thecas?, techan, teysas, techas?,* etc., pronounced, there is reason to suspect, as indicated by the last spelling) had wide currency before the coming of the Spaniards. Its usual meaning there was 'friends,' or, more technically, 'allies', and it was used, by the Hasinai at least (to whom the word later became fastened as a name), to designate a large group of tribes, both Caddoan and others, customarily allied against the Apache. The Hasinai seem not to have applied the term to themselves as a local group name at all. On the other hand, they did use it as an everyday form of greeting, like "Hello, friend!" (Testimony given at the Nabedache village, 1692, in the Terán Autos, Archivo Gen., Prov. Intern., CLXXXII). The Spanish narrowing of the term, as a group name, to the Hasinai, is due mainly to the historical circumstance that the Hasinai were the first of the great group of allies, or *texas*, whom they came to know intimately. They were influenced in the first place, however, by an apparent but unexplained partial narrowing of the term by the Indians of w. Texas from whom they first heard it.

Just when and how the name *Texas* first reached the Spaniards is uncertain, but it is known that in the 17th century there grew up in New Spain the notion of a "great kingdom of Texas," coextensive and even associated with that of a "Gran Quivira" (see *Quivira*). Passing by earlier notices, the idea is well illustrated by a report sent in 1683 to the viceroy of New Spain by the governor of New Mexico. Governor Cruzate wrote from El Paso del Norte that a Jumano (Tawehash (?) Indian from the mouth of the Conchos, called Juan Sabeata, had just come and told him of many tribes to the eastward who had sent to ask for missionaries. Among them was the "Gran Reyno de los Texas," situated 15 or 16 days journey from the informant's home. This populous country, which was ruled by a powerful "king," was next-door neighbor to Gran Quivira, so close indeed that the people of the two realms visited back and forth almost daily. Cruzate asked permission to embrace this rare opportunity to send an expedition to the interior, adding that he would be highly gratified if, through his efforts, "another New World" should be discovered, and "two realms with two more crowns" added to the king's dominions (Cruzate to the Viceroy, Oct. 30, 1683, MS.). The desired expedition was sent out in the same year under Domingo de Mendoza, but, although it penetrated far into the interior (reaching the Colorado near Ballinger), it failed to reach the great kingdom of the Texas (Diary of Mendoza, 1683–84, MS.). As conceived of by Juan Sabeata, the Jumano, and by Mendoza, this "kingdom" was apparently localized indefinitely to some place E. of that reached by the expedition, and applied to settled Indians who practised agriculture extensively.

Massanet, the father of the Texas missions, tells us that it was the stories of Gran Quivira and of "the kingdoms of Ticlas, Theas, and Caburcol," handed down from the mouth of the venerable María de Jesus de Ágreda, that attracted him from Spain to the American wilds; and when in 1689 he went with De León to find La Salle's establishment he was preoccupied with these names and fabulous nations. On the way, while still w. of the Hásinai country, they were greeted by Indians who proclaimed themselves *thecas*, 'friends,' as Massanet understood the word, which may or may not be the same as *texas*. E. of the Colorado they were met by the chief of the Nabedache, the westernmost of the Hasinai tribes,

and in the next year they established a mission near this chief's village, w. of Neches r. Judging from the reports of the then recent La Salle expedition, and of most subsequent expeditions, they must have heard while there the native group-name Hasinai; but both Massanet and De León, with preconceived notions, it would seem, of a "great kingdom of the Texas," and thinking they had found it, wrote of this chief as the "governor," and of his people as the very *Texas* who had been visited by the venerable María de Jesus (Massanet, letter, in Tex. Hist. Quar., II, 282–312; De León, Derrotero, 1689, MS. in Mem. de Nueva España, XXVIII; Derrotero, 1690, MS. in Archivo Gen.).

That, from the standpoint of the natives whom Massanet had visited, both of these designations were misleading, was soon shown by a careful observer. Francisco de Jesús María, a missionary left by Massanet among the Nabedache, wrote, after more than a year's residence at his mission, his precious report of Aug. 15, 1691. In it he emphatically asserted that, contrary to prevailing notions, the Indians about him did not constitute a kingdom, that the chief called "governor" by the Spaniards was not the head chief, and that the correct name of the group of tribes was not Texas. *Texias*, he explained, means 'friends,' and is a general name applying to a large group of tribes, some 50 or more in number, who are customarily allied. "The reason why the name is common to all is their long-continued friendship. Hence *Texias* meant friends." The Texias have no king, and not even a common government, he continues, but belong to various "provinces" or confederacies, with 4 or 5 tribes each. Hereupon he enumerates the tribes comprising the Texias, giving a list (obtained, he says, from the Hasinai and the Kadohadacho) of 48 tribes, exclusive of some of the Hasinai. Twenty-one of these were N. and E. of the mission from which he wrote. Five of these 21 composed the "very large province" of "los Caddodachos." Eighteen were to the s. w. and 9 to the s. E. One tribe, the Chuman, we recognize as the Jumano, or Jumane, of the Rio Grande country. It would seem from this that the Jumano and the Hasinai, for quite different reasons, referred to each other as *Texas*, although neither claimed the name for themselves. Continuing, our author tells us that the correct name of the confederacy occupying the valleys of the upper Neches and the Angelina, "which in New Spain they call Texias," is "Aseney" or "Asenay."

This explicit statement by Jesus María concerning the Hasinai usage of the term

Texas or *Texias* seems to be essentially correct, for it is supported by an abundance of both positive and negative testimony and is contradicted by little or none. Only a small portion of this testimony can be included here.

To begin with, it is significant that the several chroniclers of the La Salle expeditions to the tribes in question did not once, so far as is known, use the name *Texas* in their voluminous reports, but called the two main Caddoan groups which they encountered the Cenis (Hasinai) and Cadodaquious. This difference from the reports of Massanet and De Léon is attributed to the fact that the La Salle party were ignorant of the Mexican rumors about the "Gran Reyno de los Texas." Of the French explorers who reported on the Indians of N. E. Texas after La Salle's expeditions and before St Denis went to Mexico (1715), none, it is believed, used the name *Texas* for the Hasinai. The list includes Tonti, the Talons left by Joutel, Iberville, Bienville, and Pénicaut (Tonti in French, Hist. Coll. La., I, 74, 1846; the Talons in Margry, Déc., III, 610–21, 1878; Iberville and Bienville, ibid., IV, 331, 336, 401, 432–34, 1880; Pénicaut, ibid., V, 499–502, 1883).

Returning to positive evidence, Terán, who led the first Spanish expedition after that of De León, set out, as he said, to explore further the "kingdom of Texas," but before he returned he abandoned the name *Texas*, except as an alternative, or as an official designation fixed by his instructions. As he approached the frontier of the Hasinai country he considered it necessary to explain that "this nation is called by the natives Asinay, and Texia, which in their language means friends"; and after reaching the Neches he at least eight times refers to the immediate group of tribes as Asinay, but not once does he call them Texas (Descripción y Diaria Demarcación, in Mem. de Nueva España, XXVII, 21–71, passim). This is enough to show that after he reached the ground his conversion from "Texas" to "Hasinai" was complete. But there is still stronger evidence. All through the voluminous *autos* of the Terán expedition, "Hasinai" is used to the exclusion of *Texas* as a tribal name. Once the usage of *Texas* is explained. Here several of the companions of Terán give, under oath, the opinion that the "Nation Asinay" cannot be the kingdom of Texas told of by the venerable María de Jesús de Ágreda. That kingdom must be sought farther N., beyond the Kadohadacho. As to the name *Texas*, they declare that "the said nation Asinay in their own language call one another, and even us, *Texas*, which means

'friends.' The name of the nation is Asinay. All these nations commonly use the same word to call each other friends. This is so well understood from having seen it and experienced it when, talking with them, they wished to salute" (Autos of the Terán expedition, op. cit.).

One other explanation of what is apparently the same word, *Texas*, deserves especially to be noted, because it makes clearer its more technical usage in the sense of "allies," and also reveals the persistence of its usage in this sense by the natives during a century of contact with French and Spaniards. In 1778 Atanacio de Mezières, in his day and section the dean of Indian agents, wrote that the best way to bring the Comanche to Spanish allegiance would be to attach them, in the honorable position of allies, to a campaign which he was proposing to make against the Apache in company with the principal tribes of N. E. Texas; "because," he explained, "from such a custom comes the name of *Techán* among the natives, which suggests [*alude á*] that of *commilito* [companion in arms], with which the Romans flattered themselves, and which results among the Indians in a close bond of friendship between those who call themselves by it, and in the vulgar opinion that no one may break it without fearing and incurring the penalty which perjurers merit" (Letter to Croix, Feb. 20, 1778, in Mem. de Nueva España, XXVIII, 235). Mezières' customary use of accent marks makes it seem probable that the one he puts in *Techán* is to indicate the quality of the vowel, and not stress of voice.

That the name locally applied to the Neches-Angelina group of tribes was Hasinai, or Asinai, there seems little room for doubt; and the above explanations of the meaning and usages of *Texas*, given by our best qualified witnesses, are, to say the least, probably the most satisfactory we are likely to have. The meanings 'land of flowers', 'paradise', 'tiled roofs', etc., sometimes given for the word, have never been even suggested, so far as known, by first-hand observers. They seem to be fictions of recent date.

Through an erroneous preconception, *Texas* became the official Spanish designation of the Hasinai people and their country. While eyewitnesses continued to insist that Hasinai was the correct name, the authorities in Mexico continued to designate them as the *Texas*, narrowing the name commonly to the Neches-Angelina group, whose most prominent tribes were the Nabedache, Nacogdoche, Neche, Hainai, Nasoni, and Nadaco (q. v.). Owing to the fact that the Hainai were the head tribe of the confederacy, *Texas* was sometimes, in later Spanish days, confined to it. For the same reason the name Hasinai was sometimes restricted to this tribe. In 1822 Morse (Rep. to Sec. War, 373) applied the term *Texas* exclusively to the Nabedache village, which still occupied its primitive site on the "Nechez, at the junction of the Bayou St Pedro." In 1834 Col. Almonte seems to have applied it to all the survivors of the old Hasinai group except the Nacogdoches (Noticia Estadistica, table 3, 1835). (H. E. B.)

Altekas.—La Harpe (1716) in French, Hist. Coll. La., III, 63, 1851. **Laousteque.**—Iberville (1699) in Margry, Déc., IV, 319, 1880. **Lastekas.**—La Harpe (1716) in French, Hist. Coll. La., III, 47, 1851. **Las Tesas.**—St. Denis (1716) in Margry, Déc., VI, 198, 1886. **Las Texas.**—Ibid., 201. **Lastikas.**—La Harpe (1716) in French, Hist. Coll. La., III, 43, 1851. **Tachees.**—Brackenridge, Views of La., 81, 1814. **Tachi.**—Latham in Trans. Philol. Soc. Lond., 101, 1856. **Tachies.**—Sibley, Hist. Sketches, 71, 1806 (given as name of Hainai). **Tackies.**—Sibley (1805) in Am. State Papers, Ind. Aff., I, 721, 1832. **Taigas.**—Bollaert in Jour. Ethnol. Soc. Lond., II, 280, 1850. **Taijas.**—Philippeaux, Map of Engl. Col., 1781. **Taioux.**—French, Hist. Coll. La., III, 60, 1851. **Tayas.**—La Harpe (1719), ibid., 74. **Tecas.**—Linarès (1716) in Margry, Déc., VI, 218, 1886. **Tehas.**—Bollaert in Jour. Ethnol. Soc. Lond., II, 280, 1850. **Teias.**—Coronado (1541) in Smith, Colec. Doc. Fla., 153, 1857. **Teisa.**—Terán (1691) quoted by Bancroft, No. Mex. States, I, 392, 1883. **Teixa.**—Ibid. **Tejanos.**—Kennedy, Texas, I, 217, 1841. **Tejas.**—Manzanet (1689) in Tex. Hist. Asso. Quar., VIII, 213, 1905. **Texas.**—León (1689), ibid. **Texia.**—Charlevoix, New France, IV, 80, 1870 (said to mean 'friends'). **Teyans.**—Eastman, Chicora, 62, 1854 (identified with Apache). **Teyas.**—Coronado (1541) in Doc. Inéd., XIV, 327, 1870; Castañeda (ca. 1565) in 14th Rep. B. A. E., passim, 1896 (identical?). **Teyens.**—Gallatin in Nouv. Ann. Voy., 5th s., XXVII, 266, 274, 1851. **Teyos.**—Ibid., 266. **Yachies.**—Sibley, Hist. Sketches, 67, 1806. **Yatchies.**—Lewis and Clark Jour., 142, 1840.

Texas (the "third story" of a Mississippi steamboat). According to Bartlett (Dict. Americanisms, 700, 1877) "it includes the surroundings of the pilot-house, the whole 'upper story' of the vessel." From the place and ethnic name *Texas*, q. v. (A. F. C.)

Texas Lake. The local name for a body of Salish (probably a part of the Ewawoos) of Fraser River agency, Brit. Col.; pop. 29 in 1910.

Texas Lake.—Can. Ind. Aff., pt. 2, 74, 1902. **Texes Lake.**—Ibid., 195, 1885.

Texja. A former village, probably Salinan, connected with San Antonio mission, Monterey co., Cal.—Taylor in Cal. Farmer, Apr. 27, 1860.

Texmaw. A Chumashan village formerly at La Cañada de las Armas, 12 m. from Santa Barbara mission, Cal.—Taylor in Cal. Farmer, May 4, 1860.

Textiles. See *Weaving*.

Teyaxa. Mentioned as a pueblo of the province of Atripuy (q. v.), in the region of the lower Rio Grande, N. Mex., in the 16th century.—Oñate (1598) in Doc. Inéd., XVI, 115, 1871.

Teypana. A former pueblo of the Piro, situated nearly opposite the present town

of Socorro, on the E. bank of the Rio Grande, in Socorro co., N. Mex. It was visited by Oñate, the colonizer of New Mexico, in 1598, and in all probability was consolidated with Socorro within the next quarter century. (F. W. H.)

Teipana.—Oñate (1598) in Doc. Inéd., XVI, 251, 1871. **Teypamá.**—Ibid., 115. **Teypana.**—Bandelier in Arch. Inst. Papers, IV, 241, 1892.

Tezompa. Formerly a Huichol village, but now a Mexican settlement, situated about 14 m. N. W. of Mezquitic, beyond the present N. E. limit of the Huichol country, in Jalisco, Mexico.—Lumholtz (1) Huichol Inds., 3, 1898; (2) Unknown Mex., II, 112, 1902.

Thadodaho. See *Wathatotarho*.

Thaltelich (from *çaçal* 'back,' because on the 'back' of a slough). An abandoned Chilliwack village on upper Chilliwack r., s. British Columbia.

Çáltelitc.—Hill-Tout in Ethnol. Surv. Can., 4, 1902.

Thamachaychee. See *Tomochichi*.

Thamien. The Costanoan name of the site of Santa Clara mission, Cal., used for a group of Indians connected with it. They lived between Guadalupe and Coyote rs. and the mountains to the w., and from the New Almaden mines on the s. to Alviso on the N., thus including the territory in which the town of San José now stands. The Gergecensens and Socoisukas are mentioned as subdivisions. See Taylor in Cal. Farmer, June 22, 1860.

Tha-o-na-wyuthe. See *Blacksnake*.

Thayendanegea (*Thayĕñdanē'kĕn'*, 'He sets or places together two bets,' referring to the custom of fastening together the articles of approximate value placed as wagers by two phratries in tribal contests. The elements are *t* for *te* 'two'; *ha* 'he-it'; *yenda'* 'a wager'; *-nĕ'kĕn'* 'set side by side iteratively'). A celebrated Mohawk chief, popularly known as Joseph Brant, who took an active part against the white settlers in the border wars during the Revolution, and who first came into official notice as a so-called "Pine-tree chief." He was born on the Ohio in 1742 while his parents were on a hunting expedition to that section. The home of his family was at Canajoharie Castle in the Mohawk valley, N. Y. His father, Tehowaghwengaraghkwin, according to Stone, was a full-blood Mohawk of the Wolf gens, and his mother was also Indian or at least a half-blood. While Joseph was still young his father died, and the mother then married an Indian known among the whites as Brant: hence the name by which Brant is commonly known. His sister Molly, the elder child, became the acknowledged wife, according to the Indian method, of Sir William Johnson. Thayendanegea's career as a warrior began at the age of 13, when he joined the Indians under Sir William Johnson at the battle of L. George in

1755. Johnson sent him to Dr Wheelock's charity school at Lebanon, Conn., where he learned to speak and write English, and acquired some knowledge of general literature and history. He married the daughter of an Oneida chief about 1765, and settled at Canajoharie, where he joined the Episcopal Church and for a time led a peaceful life. His wife died in 1771, leaving a son and a daughter; in the year following he married his first wife's half-sister. He was with Johnson in the Niagara expedition of 1759, and took part in the Pontiac war of 1763, fighting on the English side. Having visited England in 1775, he returned prepared to devote his energies to the British cause in the Revolution, then imminent. He was given a colonel's commission by Gov. Carleton, and sullied

THAYENDANEGEA (JOSEPH BRANT). FROM A PAINTING BY C. W. PEALE IN THE STATE HOUSE AT PHILADELPHIA.

his name by taking an active part in the massacre at Cherry valley and in the raid that desolated Minisink, Orange co., in 1779. He was conspicuous in the battle of Oriskany, Aug. 6, 1777, but was not present at the massacre of Wyoming in 1778, as has been charged. After the treaty of peace between Great Britain and the United States in 1783, still retaining his commission in the British service and drawing half pay, Brant was granted a tract of land, 6 m. wide, on each side of Grand r., Ontario, on which he settled with his Mohawk and other Iroquois followers, and continued to rule over them until his death, Nov. 24, 1807. He was thrice married; his second wife died childless, but by his third wife he had seven children. His youngest son, John (Ahyouwaighs), became chief of the Mohawk

tribe through his mother, who was the eldest daughter of the head chief of the Turtle gens. His daughter Elizabeth married William Johnson Kerr, grandson of Sir William Johnson. The last survivor of the Brant children was Catherine B. Johnson, who died in 1867. Thayendanegea was buried near the little church he had built on Grand r., 3 m. from Brantford, Ontario, and a monument placed over his grave bears the inscription, "This tomb is erected to the memory of Thayendanegea or Capt. Joseph Brant, principal chief and warrior of the Six Nations Indians, by his fellow-subjects, admirers of his fidelity and attachment to the British Crown." In 1879 the grave was desecrated and the bones were stolen by a physician and medical students, but most of them, including the skull, were recently restored to their former resting place. Consult Stone, Life of Brant, 1864. (J. N. B. H.)

Thechuntunne ('people at the foot of the large rock'). A former village of the Tututni on the N. side of Rogue r., Oreg. Abraham Lincoln's village.—Dorsey in Jour. Am. Folk-lore, III, 233, 1890. Çe-tcŭn'ʔŭnnĕ.—Ibid. Se-dj'ûn'-tĭn tĕne'.—Everett, Tutu MS. vocab., B. A. E., 1883 (trans. 'people by the rock land'). Se-tcŭn' ʔŭnnĕ'.—Dorsey, op. cit. (Naltunnetunne name).

Thekkane ('mountain dwellers'). A division of the Sekani living E. of the Rocky mts. about Ft Halkett, Brit. Col., in the region of the Nahane. Thè-kka-'nĕ.—Petitot, Autour du lac des Esclaves, 362, 1891. Tsoⁿ-krône.—Morice, letter, B. A. E., 1890.

Theshtshini ('red streak'). A Navaho clan; apparently coordinate with the Destchin of the Apache. Øestcìni.—Matthews in Jour. Am. Folk-lore, III, 103, 1890. Destsíni.—Matthews, Navaho Legends, 30, 1897.

Thethlkhuttunne ('people at the smooth rock'). A former Chastacosta village on the N. side of Rogue r., Oreg. Çĕçl'-qût tûn'nĕ.—Dorsey in Jour. Am. Folk-lore, III, 233, 1890.

Thetliotin. An unidentified division of the Takulli of British Columbia. Thetliantins.—Domenech, Deserts of N. Am., II, 62, 1860. Thetliótin.—Hale, Ethnog. and Philol., 202, 1846. Tketlcotins.—Domenech, op. cit., I, 444.

Thetsaken. A Squawmish village community on the E. side of Howe sd., Brit. Col. Çĕ'tsākEn.—Hill-Tout in Rep. Brit. A. A. S., 474, 1900.

Thetuksem. A Squawmish village community on the w. side of Howe sd., Brit. Col. Çĕ'tuksEm.—Hill-Tout in Rep. Brit. A. A. S., 474, 1900.

Thetusum. A Squawmish village community on the w. side of Howe sd., Brit. Col. Çĕ'tūsum.—Hill-Tout in Rep. Brit. A. A. S., 474, 1900.

Thilanottine ('dwellers at the foot of the head,' i. e. of the great glacier). An Athapascan tribe of the Chipewyan group who dwell on the shores of Lacrosse lake and in the country between Cold lake and Ft Locha, Athabasca Ter., Canada. Ross (MS., B. A. E.) gives their habitat as extending from Churchill r. to Athabasca and Great Slave lakes. Kennicott (MS., B. A. E.) states that they extend as far N. as Ft Resolution on the s. shore of Great Slave lake. The Thilanottine are of good stature, having well-proportioned bodies, long narrow heads, flat faces, high cheek-bones, and depressed temples, giving the head a marked pear shape. Their hands and feet are unusually small and well formed. They are mildmannered and docile, selfish, and grasping, great liars, but otherwise noted for honesty. Polygamy exists, but is not common. A Roman Catholic mission was established among them in 1856, and their native beliefs and customs have been influenced thereby; otherwise they do not differ materially from the tribes on the N. Their snowshoes are of superior workmanship, the inner part of the frames being straight, the outer edge curved, and both ends pointed, the one in front being turned upward. The lacing is neatly made of deerskin thongs. Their sledges are made of thin strips of red spruce-fir turned up in front and highly polished with a crooked knife to make them run easily. In 1859 the tribe numbered 211, of whom 100 were males and 111 females. In 1902 there were 253—53 adult men, 73 adult women, and 127 children and young people, attached to Onion Lake agency—living in better built houses than the Cree, and engaged in hunting, fishing, and raising cattle, the women doing the farm work, and all enjoying a good reputation for piety, morality, and temperance. Another band of 70—composed of 13 men, 20 women, and 37 children—lived entirely by hunting, trapping, and fishing in the district surrounding Heart lake (Can. Ind. Rep., 169, 1902). The Thilanottine have a legend of the Metal Woman, differing from that of the Taltsanottine. A giant in the time when there were giants encountered another on the shore of the Arctic ocean and a fierce combat resulted, in which he would have succumbed had not a man whom he had befriended cut the tendon of his adversary's leg, causing him to fall so as to form a bridge across Bering strait, over which the reindeer entered America, and later a strange woman came, bringing iron and copper. She repeated her visits until her beneficiaries offered her violence once, whereupon she went underground with her treasure to come back no more.

Chippewayans proprement dits.—Petitot, Dict. Dène-Dindjié, xx, 1876. **Shil-an-ottine.**—Petitot, MS. vocab., B. A. E., 1865 ('those on the other side of the barriers'). **Thi-laɳ-ottiné.**—Petitot, Dict.

Dène-Dindjié, xx, 1876. **Thi-lan-Ottinè.**—Petitot, Autour du lac des Esclaves, 363, 1891.

Thildzhehi. A Navaho clan.
Ǫildjèhi.—Matthews in Jour. Am. Folk-lore, iii, 104, 1890. *Dildzéhi.*—Matthews, Navaho Legends, 30, 1897.

Thithirii. A village, presumably Costanoan, formerly connected with San Juan Bautista mission, Cal.—Engelhardt, Franc. in Cal., 398, 1897.

Thkhaneza ('among the scattered [hills]'). A Navaho clan
Ǫqaʻnezáʻ.—Matthews in Jour. Am. Folk-lore, iii, 103, 1890. Ǫqaʻnezaʻni.—Ibid. *Thaʻnēzáʻ.*—Matthews, Navaho Legends, 30, 1897. *Thaʻnēzáʻni.*—Ibid.

Thkhapaha ('among the waters'). A Navaho clan.
Ǫqáʻpaha.—Matthews in Jour. Am. Folk-lore, iii, 103, 1890. Ǫqáʻpahaȼine.—Ibid. *Thaʻpaha.*—Matthews, Navaho Legends, 30, 1897. *Thaʻpahadĭʻneʻ.*—Ibid. **Topa-an.**—Bourke, Moquis of Ariz., 279, 1884.

Thkhatshini ('among the red [waters or banks]'). A Navaho clan.
Ǫqáʻtcini.—Matthews in Jour. Am. Folk-lore, iii, 103, 1890. *Tháʻtsini.*—Matthews, Navaho Legends, 30, 1897.

Thlachaus. A former Siuslaw village on or near Siuslaw r., Oreg.
Ǫlaʻ-tcaus.—Dorsey in Jour. Am. Folk-lore, iii, 230, 1890.

Thlakalama. A Chinookan tribe formerly residing at the mouth of Kalama r., Cowlitz co., Wash. They spoke the Cathlamet dialect. In 1806 they numbered 200, but are now extinct. (L. F.)
Cathlahaws.—Lewis and Clark Exped., ii, 226, 1814. Klakalama.—Framboise (1805) quoted by Gairdner in Jour. Roy. Geog. Soc., xi, 255, 1841. Thlakalamah.—Franchère Narr., 110, 1854. Tkaláma.—Gibbs, MS. no. 248, B. A. E. (Chinook name.) Tkǃalaʻma.—Boas, infʼn, 1905 (proper name). Wacalamus.—Ross, Adventures, 87, 1849.

Thlalkhaiuntik. A former Yaquina village on the N. side of Yaquina r., Oreg.
Ǫlăĭʻ-kqai-ŭnʻ-tĭk.—Dorsey in Jour. Am. Folk-lore, iii, 229, 1890.

Thlcharghiliitun ('village far from the forks'). A former Chetco village on the upper part of a southern branch of Chetco r., Oreg.
Ǫltoʻa-rxiʻ-li-iʻ-tûn.—Dorsey in Jour. Am. Folklore, iii, 236, 1890.

Thlekakhaik. A former Yaquina village on the N. side of Yaquina r., Oreg., almost opposite the site of the present Elk City.
Ǫlkaʻ-qaik.—Dorsey in Jour. Am. Folk-lore, iii, 229, 1890.

Thlekuaus. A former Siuslaw village on Siuslaw r., Oreg.
Ǫlkûʻ-aus.—Dorsey in Jour. Am. Folk-lore, iii, 230, 1890.

Thlekuhweyuk. An Alsea village on the s. side of Alsea r., Oreg.
Ǫlkuʻ-hwe-yŭkʻ.—Dorsey in Jour. Am. Folk-lore, iii, 230, 1890.

Thlekushauk. An Alsea village on the s. side of Alsea r., Oreg.
Ǫlkuʻ-caʻ-ŭk.—Dorsey in Jour. Am. Folk-lore, iii, 230, 1890.

Thlekwiyauik. A Yaquina village on the s. side of Yaquina r., Oreg.
Ǫlkwi-yauʻ-ĭk.—Dorsey in Jour. Am. Folk-lore, iii, 229, 1890.

Thlelkhus. A Yaquina village on the s. side of Yaquina r., Oreg.

Çlĕl'-qûs.—Dorsey in Jour. Am. Folk-lore, III, 229, 1890.

Thlinaitshtik. A Yaquina village on the s. side of Yaquina r., Oreg.

Çli-nai'-ctĭk.—Dorsey in Jour. Am. Folk-lore, III, 229, 1890.

Thlingchadinne ('dog-flank people'). An Athapascan tribe or group of tribes. Their habitat, according to Dobbs (1744), was on Seal r., in the muskox country. They did not trade with the French because they were afraid to go through the territory of the hostile Maskegon. La Potherie in 1753 located them at the sources of Churchill r. Jefferys in 1761 placed them near Hudson bay N. of their foes, the Maskegon. Franklin in 1824 found them between the Tatsanottine country and Mackenzie r. Back (1835) said that they were in the barren lands about Great Slave lake. Dunn (1844) gave their habitat as Mackenzie r. and Great Bear lake. According to Richardson (1851) they occupied the inland country, E. of the Kawchodinne, from L. La Martre to Coppermine r. Hind in 1863 located them about the N. and N. E. parts of Great Slave lake, resorting to Ft Rae and Ft Simpson. Petitot (Dict. Dènè Dindjié, xx, 1876) gave their habitat as being between Great Slave and Great Bear lakes, E. of Mackenzie r., extending as far as Coppermine r. Expelled from their pristine home by their Cree enemies, they have migrated continuously northward during two centuries. Franklin, Dease, and Simpson found them N. and N. E. of Great Bear lake between 1819 and 1836. Since then they have returned to some of the southern districts. Petitot found Great Slave lake their extreme southern limit.

According to a fable told by the Chipewyan, Tatsanottine, and Kawchodinne, as well as by the Thlingchadinne themselves, the tribe originated from the union of a supernatural dog-man with a Tinne woman. After the discovery of copper by a Tatsanottine woman another woman of the same tribe was dwelling with her two brothers N. of Great Slave lake. One day a strong and handsome stranger arrived, who, on the proposal of the brothers, took her for his wife. Waking in the middle of the wedding night she found her husband gone and heard an animal crunching bones at the fireplace. (There were no dogs then among the Tatsanottine; Franklin found them without these animals in 1820.) The same thing happened the next night. The bride and her brothers lighted torches, but found no animal. On the third night one of the brothers hurled a stone ax into the corner whence the noise of gnawing proceeded. A cry of agony was heard, and when a torch was lighted a great black dog was seen twitching in the death throes. As the human husband did not reappear, the brothers chased forth their sister because she had married a dog-man, a sorcerer, a Tlingit. She wandered into the treeless desert of Coppermine r., where in the course of time she brought forth a litter of puppies, which she kept hidden in a bag of reindeer skin. When they could run alone she was astonished to find on her return from hunting, prints of infants' feet in the ashes. Hiding one day, she saw the little dogs leap from the bag, becoming handsome children as soon as they reached the light. She ran and pulled the string of the bag, but not before three succeeded in jumping back into the dark hole. Two boys and two girls were kept forcibly in the daylight, and these became the progenitors of the Thlingchadinne (Petitot, Autour du Lac des Esclaves, 296, 1891).

Ross (MS., B. A. E.) states that adjoining the Tatsanottine are the Dog-ribs, whose lands extend from Coppermine r. to the s. E. side of Great Bear lake and to about midway between L. La Martre and Mackenzie r. In the latter tract they are much intermingled with the Etchareottine, from whom they can scarcely be distinguished except by their larger stature and their thick, stuttering, and disagreeable manner of enunciation. Petitot describes them as tall and well built, of a bronze or terra-cotta color, nervous of temperament, their hands and feet small and well modeled, the chest wide and deep, with black hair and eyes, heavy eyelids, a sad and reserved look, large mouths, full lips, furnished with slender moustaches on the men, sometimes accompanied by thin beards, their countenances having a peculiar Egyptian cast. The same author (Bull. Soc. Géog. Paris, chart, 1875) divides them into Takfwelottine, Lintchanre, Tseottine, and Tsantieottine. The Thlingchadinne subsist chiefly on the reindeer. They are said to treat their women and dogs with more kindness and consideration than do the Chipewyan tribes. The father loses his name on the birth of a child and is thereafter known as the father of so-and-so, the child. Other tribes of this group have the same custom, but these people change the name after the birth of every child, while an unmarried man is called the father of his favorite dog. Ross in 1858 gave their population as 926, of whom 533 were men and 393 were women; of this number 23 were found at Ft Resolution on Great Slave lake, 150 at Ft Simpson, and 133 at Ft Norman. Father Morice in 1906 gave the total number of Dog-ribs as 1,150.

Attiomospicayes.—La Potherie, Hist. de l'Amér., I, 168, 1753. **Attimospiquaies.**—Ibid., 177 (trans. 'dog-ribs'). **Attimospiquais.** — Dobbs, Hudson Bay, 44, 1744. **Attimospiquay.**—Ibid., 25 (trans. 'coast of dogs'). **Chien-Flancs.**—Petitot, Autour du lac des Esclaves, 301, 1891. **Côtes-de Chien.**—Ibid. **Dog-rib.**—Mackenzie in Mass. Hist. Coll., 2d s., II, 43, 1814. **Dog-ribbed.**—Schoolcraft, Trav., 181, 1821. **Dog Ribs.**—Ross, Advent., 278, 1849. **Dounè Flancs-de-Chien.**—Petitot, Autour du lac des Esclaves, 183, 1891. **Esclaves.**—Balbi, Atlas Ethnog., 821, 1826 (from the Cree name). **Flancs de chien.**—Petitot, Dict. Dènè-Dindjié, xx, 1876. **Flat-side Dogs.**—Smet, Oregon Miss., 164, 1847. **Klay-cha-la-tinneh.**—Ross quoted by Gibbs, MS. B. A. E. ('dog-rib people': Etchareottine name). **Klay-tinneh.**—Ibid. ('dog people': Etchareottine name). **Lintcanre.**—Morice in Anthropos, I, 264, 1906 (the nickname applied by their congeners). **Lowland Dogs.**—Jefferys, French Dom. in Am., I, 44, 1761. **Plascotez de Chiens.**—Dobbs, Hudson Bay, 44, 1744. **Plat côté de Chien.**—Petitot in Bull. Soc. Géog. Paris, chart, 1875. **Plats cotee de Chiens.**—Jeffreys, French Dom. in Am., I, 44, 1761. **Plats-Côtes-de-Chien.**—Petitot, Autour du lac des Esclaves, 301, 1891. **Plats-côtés de Chiens.**—Smet, Miss. de l'Oregon, 109, 1848. **Plats cotez de Chiens.**—Dobbs, Hudson Bay, 19, 1744. **Slave.**—Franklin, Journ. Polar Sea, 259, 1824 (Cree name). **Tête Plat.**—Dobbs, Hudson Bay, 53, 1744. **Thing-è-ha-dtinne.**—Keane in Stanford, Compend., 512, 1878. **Thlingcha.**—Ibid., 538. **Thlingcha-dinneh.**—Franklin, Journ. Polar Sea, 259, 1824. **Thlingcha tinneh.**—Gallatin in Trans. Am. Antiq. Soc., II, 19, 1836. **Thlingeha-dinneh.**—Prichard, Phys. Hist., v, 377, 1847. **Thlingeha-*dinni.*—Latham in Trans. Philol. Soc. Lond., 69, 1856. **Thling-è-ha-'dtinnè.**—Richardson, Arct. Exped., II, 2, 1851.

Thlkwantiyatunne. A band of the Mishikhwutmetunne on Coquille r., Oreg. **Çlkwan'-ti-ya' ṭûnně'.**—Dorsey in Jour. Am. Folk-lore, III, 232, 1890.

Thltsusmetunne ('people on the sand'). A band of the Mishikhwutmetunne who formerly lived near the head of Coquille r., Oreg., but in 1858 (Ind. Aff. Rep., 162, 1861) were at the mouth of Flores cr. **Çlts'ûs-me' ṭûnně'.**—Dorsey in Jour. Am. Folk-lore, III, 232, 1890.—Ind. Aff. Rep., 162, 1861. **Tlsûs-me' ṭûnně.**—Dorsey, Chetco MS. vocab., 183, B. A. E., 1884 (Chetco name).

Thltsusmetunne ('people on the sand'). A village of the Tolowa of N. W. California. **Çlts'us-me'.**—Dorsey in Jour. Am. Folk-lore, III, 237, 1890.

Thlukwiutshthu. A Yaquina village on the s. side of Yaquina r., Oreg. **Çlu'-kwi-u-t'çu'.**—Dorsey in Jour. Am. Folk-lore, III, 229, 1890.

Thlulchikhwutmetunne ('people at the stream called Thlulchi'). A band of the Mishikhwutmetunne on Coquille r., Oreg. **Tçlŭl-tci'-qwŭt-me' ṭûnně'.**—Dorsey in Jour. Am. Folk-lore, III, 232, 1890.

Thobazhnaazhi ('two come together for water'). A Navaho clan. **Ço'bajnaáj.**—Matthews in Jour. Am. Folk-lore, III, 104, 1890. **Co'bajnaàji.**—Ibid. **To'baznaáz.**—Matthews, Navaho Legends, 30, 1897. **To'baznaá-zi.**—Ibid.

Thochalsithaya ('water under the sitting frog'). A Navaho clan, now extinct. **Ço'tcalsiçáya.**—Matthews in Jour. Am. Folk-lore, III, 104, 1890. **To'tsalsitáya.**—Matthews, Navaho Legends, 30, 1897.

Thodhokongzhi ('saline water'). A Navaho clan and the name of one of the traditional stopping places of two of the clans in their early movements. **Ço'ɖokòⁿji.**—Matthews in Jour. Am. Folk-lore, III, 91, 97, 1890. **To'dokónzi.**—Matthews, Navaho Legends, 30, 1897.

Thoditshini ('bitter water'). A Navaho clan, distinct from the Thodhokongzhi. **Ço'ɕitcìni.**—Matthews in Jour. Am. Folk-lore, III, 103, 1890. **Todichini.**—Bourke, Moquis of Ariz., 279, 1884 (trans. 'alkali'). **To'dítsíni.**—Matthews, Navaho Legends, 30, 1897.

Thokhani ('beside the water'). A Navaho clan. **Çò'qani.**—Matthews in Jour. Am. Folk-lore, III, 103, 1890. **To'ḥani.**—Matthews, Navaho Legends, 30, 1897. **Tohanni.**—Bourke, Moquis of Ariz., 279, 1884.

Thomochichi. See *Tomochichi.*

Those Who Camp Next To The Last. A former band of the Sihasapa Teton Sioux under White Thunder.—Culbertson in Smithson. Rep. 1850, 141, 1851.

Those Who Carry. A former band of the Hunkpapa Teton Sioux under Helata, Red Horn. — Culbertson in Smithson. Rep. 1850, 141, 1851.

Those Who Have Water For Themselves Only. A northern Assiniboin band of 35 lodges in 1808.—Henry-Thompson Jour., II, 523, 1897.

Those Who Lodge Close Together. A division of the Crow tribe.—Culbertson in Smithson. Rep. 1850, 144, 1851.

Thotais. A Squawmish village community on the right bank of Squawmisht r., Brit. Col. **Çò'tais.**—Hill-Tout in Rep. Brit. A. A. S., 474, 1900.

Thotsoni ('great water'). A Navaho clan. **Çò'tsoni.**—Matthews in Jour. Am. Folk-lore, III, 104, 1890. **Tó'tsoni.**—Matthews, Navaho Legends, 30, 1897. **Tûtsoni.**—Bourke, Moquis of Ariz., 69, 1884.

Thoucoue. One of the 9 Natchez villages in 1699, perhaps belonging to the Tioux.—Iberville in Margry, Déc., IV, 179, 1880.

Thoyetlini ('junction of the rivers'). A Navaho clan. **Ço'yetlìni.**—Matthews in Jour. Am. Folk-lore, III, 103, 1890. **To'yětlíni.**—Matthews, Navaho Legends, 30, 1897.

Three Fires. A term used to designate the allied Chippewa, Ottawa, and Potawatomi about the period of the American Revolution.—Am. State Papers, Ind. Aff., I, 575, 1832.

Three Legs Town. A former Delaware village, taking its name from a chief, situated on the E. bank of Muskingum r., a few miles s. of the mouth of the Tuscarawas, in Coshocton co., Ohio. The settlement was seemingly abandoned prior to Bouquet's expedition in 1764, although a place on the river was known as Three Legs many years later. **Legs.**—Esnauts and Rapilly map, 1777. **Three Legs.**—Evans, Pedestrious Tour, 160, 1819. **Three Legs Old Town.**—Hutchins, map in Smith, Bouquet Exped., 1766.

Three Rivers. A former trading station and mission village of Montagnais and Algonkin, situated on the site of the present town of Three Rivers, on the N. bank of St Lawrence r., just above the mouth of St Maurice r., Quebec.

Matopelótni.—Gatschet, Penobscot MS., B. A. E., 1887 (Penobscot name). **Three Rivers.**—Jefferys, French Doms., pt. I, 110, 1761. **Tresrevere.**—Williams, Vt., I, 429, 1809. **trois Rivieres.**—Burnet (1727) in N. Y. Doc. Col. Hist., v, 826, 1855. **Trois Rivieres.**—Doc. of 1659, ibid., XIII, 113, 1881. **Troy River.**—Doc. of 1709, ibid., v, 86, 1855.

Three Saints. A Kaniagmiut Eskimo village on Kodiak id., on the site of the earliest Russian settlement in Alaska, founded in 1784 by Shelikof, and named after his ship. Pop. 7 in 1880.

Three Saints Bay.—Petroff in 10th Census, Alaska, 29, 1884. **Ziatitz.**—Coast Surv. charts (corrupted from Russian *sviatoi*, 'saint').

Three Springs. A well-known point, in the middle of the 18th century, on the trail from Frankstown to the Ohio; situated near the borough of the same name in Huntingdon co., Pa. In various contemporary journals it is located 10 m. N. W. of Black Log. See Col. Rec. Pa., v, 750, 762, 1851. (G. P. D.)

Three Springs.—Weiser (1748) in Arch. Pa., II, 13, 1852. **3 Springs.**—Scull map, 1759.

Threse. A band, probably Moquelumnan, formerly frequenting Stanislaus and Tuolumne rs., central Cal.—Wessells (1853) in H. R. Ex. Doc. 76, 34th Cong., 3d sess., 30, 1857.

Throwing stick. This implement, called also throwing board, dart sling, and atlatl, is an apparatus for hurling a lance, spear, or harpoon at birds and aquatic animals. It measures from 16 to 20 in., with extremes from 8 to 30 in. The essential parts are (1) the body; (2) the groove on the upper side for the spear shaft, not always present; (3) the grip, the part held in the hand for throwing; and (4) a hook, hole, or socket to fit the end or the shaft of the projectile. The materials,

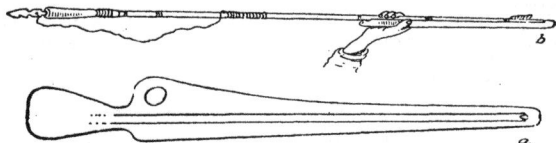

ESKIMO THROWING STICK

forms, and the presence or absence of some of the parts are sure marks by which throwing sticks of different areas can be distinguished. This sling device was widely diffused about the shores of the Pacific. It was used by all the Eskimo tribes, also in S. E. Alaska, the Interior Basin, California, and Florida. The body may be in form a rod, a double cone, or a broad piece of wood. The grip may be the natural form of the stick, or this may be furnished with holes, pockets, pegs, loops, or notches, alone or combined, to insure a firmer grasp, as was especially the case with the throwing sticks of the arctic region. The groove, when present, is either rounded or squared, and it serves as a rest for the shaft between the fingers

and the butt end of the body. The end of the spear is loosely attached to the stick in three ways: (1) by a shallow socket which fits on a spur, (2) by a socket at the end of the stick into which fits a conical projection on the spear shaft, or, (3) as in Greenland, by pegs on the harpoon shaft that fit into holes in the throwing stick. This device attained the highest perfection among the Mexicans and Peruvians, whose atlatl was raised to the dignity of a fighting weapon.

The throwing stick, the varieties of which are endless, added an extra joint to the arm and thus multiplied its efficiency in hurling; it could be used in places where the bow would be impracticable, as in a canoe or where only one hand would be available, also among marshy growth; and it propelled a missile many times heavier than an arrow. The thrower held the grip by his right hand, the thumb turned inward; fitted the butt end of the projectile to the hook, socket, or hole in the outer end of the throwing stick; laid the shaft of the weapon in the groove, holding it down with three fingers, and placed the whole against the right shoulder, point forward, ready to drive the weapon at the game by a propulsive thrust. When the missile struck the animal it held the latter by means of a toggle or barbs, which retarded its progress and helped to bring it in, the whole apparatus being one of the most complicated and ingenious devices of savagery. See *Lance*.

Consult Krause (1) in Internat. Archiv f. Ethnog., xx, 121–153, 1902, and bibliography therein, (2) in Smithson. Rep. 1904, 619, 1905; Mason (1) in Rep. Nat. Mus. 1884, 279, 1885, (2) in Proc. Nat. Mus., xvi, 219, 1894, (3) in Am. Anthr., v, 66, 1892; Culin in Bull. Free Mus. Univ. Pa., I, 183, 1898; Cushing in Proc. Am. Asso. Adv. Sci., XLIV, 1896; Pepper (1) in Internat. Cong. Americanists, 1902, (2) in Putnam Anniv. Vol., 1909; Bushnell in Am. Anthr., VII, no. 2, 1905; Uhle, ibid., XI, no. 4, 1909. (O. T. M.)

Thukhita. A Kuitsh village on lower Umpqua r., Oreg.

Tɔu-qí'-ɹă.—Dorsey in Jour. Am. Folk-lore, III, 231, 1890.

Thunder Bay. A Chippewa or Ottawa band formerly living on Thunder bay, in Alpena co., Mich.—Detroit treaty (1855) in U. S. Ind. Treat., 615, 1873.

Thunderbird. Thunder and lightning were usually supposed to be produced by a being or a number of beings different from all others. On the great plains, where the phenomena of thunderstorms are very striking, and northwestward to the Pacific coast, as well as through the Canadian forest area to the Atlantic, they were supposed to be caused by birds of enormous size, which produced thunder by flapping their wings and the lightning by opening and closing their eyes. The great downpour which generally accompanies thunder was often accounted for by supposing that the bird carries a lake of fresh water on its back. The Mandan supposed that it was because the thunderbird broke through the clouds, the bottom of the skyey reservoir (Maximilian, Trav., 361, 1843). Sometimes only one thunderbird is spoken of, and sometimes a family of them, or else several adults of different colors. Although the species of this bird is often quite indefinite, on the N. Pacific coast it is conceived of as similar to, if not identical with, a large hawk found in the high mountains, while other people likened it to an eagle, and the Ntlakyapamuk of British Columbia thought it resembled a grouse. On the plains a thunderstorm was supposed to be due to a contest between the thunderbird and a huge rattlesnake, or an underground or subaqueous monster—called Únktéhi by the Dakota—and certain writers have unwarrantably deduced a mystic significance from this, such as the war between light and darkness or good and evil. On the N. Pacific coast a thunderbird was supposed to be catching whales during a thunderstorm, and persons profess to have seen whales dropped into trees with the marks of talons on them. According to the Ntlakyapamuk the thunderbird uses its wings as a bow to shoot arrows. "The rebound of his wings in the air, after shooting, makes the thunder. For this reason thunder is heard in different parts of the sky at once, being the noise from each wing. The arrowheads fired by the thunder are found in many parts of the country. They are of black stone and of very large size" (Teit in Mem. Am. Mus. Nat. Hist., II, 338, 1900). The thunderbird was naturally held in awe, and a person who had been struck by lightning and recovered became an efficient shaman.   (J. R. S.)

Thur (*T'hur*). The Sun clan of the Tigua pueblo of Isleta, N. Mex.
T'hur-t'aïnïn.—Lummis quoted by Hodge in Am. Anthr., IX, 352, 1896 (*t'aïnïn* = 'people').

Tiaks (refers to a point in the river). A village of the Upper Fraser band of Ntlakyapamuk at Fosters Bar, E. side of Fraser r., 28 m. above Lytton, Brit. Col.
Fosters Bar.—White man's name. Tia'ks.—Teit in Mem. Am. Mus. Nat. Hist., II, 172, 1900.

Tianto. A former village, possibly of the Quapaw, in Arkansas, s. of Arkansas r., near and apparently under the dominion of Anilco. It was visited by De Soto's expedition in 1542.

Tiatiuk. A Chnagmiut Eskimo village in the Yukon delta, Alaska.
Tée-atee-ógemut.—Dall, Alaska, 264, 1870 (the inhabitants).

Tibahagna. A former Gabrieleño rancheria in Los Angeles co., Cal., at a locality later called Serritos.—Reid (1852) quoted by Taylor in Cal. Farmer, June 8, 1860.

Tibideguachi. A former Opata pueblo in extreme N. E. Sonora, Mexico, containing 214 inhabitants in 1678. Probably abandoned before 1730, as it is not mentioned by Rivera.
Santa Rosa de Tibidequatzi.—Zapata (1678) in Doc. Hist. Mex., 4th s., III, 369, 1857. Sta Rosa Tibideguachi.—Zapata cited by Bancroft, No. Mex. States, I, 246, 1884.

Tidendaye ('strangers'). A clan or band of the Chiricahua (Bourke in Jour. Am. Folk-lore, III, 115, 1890), composed of descendants of Mexicans and Piman Indians, particularly Opata, with whom at different times the Chiricahua lived on terms of peace at Baseraca, Babispe, and Janos, in Sonora and Chihuahua, Mexico. They are coordinate with the Nakaydi of the White Mountain Apache and the Nakai of the Navaho.
Nindáhe.—Bourke in Jour. Am. Folk-lore, III, 115, 1890. Tidendaye.—Ibid.

Tiekwachi. A Siuslaw village on Siuslaw r., Oreg.
T'í-ê'-kwa-tc'í.—Dorsey in Jour. Am. Folk-lore, III, 230, 1890.

Tiengak. A Magemiut Eskimo village on Kvichavak r., Alaska; pop. 60 in 1890.
Tiengaghamiut.—11th Census, Alaska, 111, 1893.

Tientien ('friends'?). A small Wintun tribe said by Powers to have lived in the region from Douglas City or its vicinity to Hay fork of Trinity r., Trinity co., Cal.
Ti-en'-Ti-en'.—Powers in Cont. N. A. Ethnol., III, 230, 1877.

Tietiquaquo. A former settlement, apparently in what is now s. w. Arkansas, near Atiamque, through which the De Soto expedition passed in 1542. Its inhabitants probably belonged to the Caddoan family.

Tigalda. A former Aleut village on Tigalda, one of the E. Aleutian ids., Alaska; pop. 91 in 1833.
Teegaldenskoi.—Elliot, Cond. Aff. Alaska, 225, 1875. Tigaldinskoe.—Veniaminoff, Zapiski, II, 203, 1840.

Tigikpuk ('people living at the base of a volcano': Kaniagmiut name). An unidentified division of the Knaiakhotana of Cook inlet, Alaska.
Ti-gi-qpŭk'.—Hoffman, Kadiak MS., B. A. E., 1882.

Tiglabu ('drums in his own lodge'). A band of the Brulé Teton Sioux.
Ti-glabu.—Cleveland quoted by Dorsey in 15th Rep. B. A. E., 219, 1897.

Tigshelde. A Kaiyuhkhotana village on Innoko r., Alaska.
Tigchelde'.—Zagoskin in Nouv. Ann. Voy., 5th s., XXI, map, 1850. Tizhgelede.—Tikhmenieff (1861) quoted by Baker, Geog. Dict. Alaska, 365, 1901.

Tigua (Spanish form of *Tí'wan*, pl. *Tíwesh'* (Span. *Tiguex*), their own name). A group of Pueblo tribes comprising three geographic divisions, one occupying Taos and Picuris (the most northerly of the New Mexican pueblos) on the upper waters of the Rio Grande; another inhabiting Sandia and Isleta, N. and S. of Albuquerque, respectively; the third division living in the pueblos of Isleta del Sur, Texas, and Senecu del Sur, Chihuahua, on the lower Rio Grande. At the time of Coronado's visit to New Mexico in 1540–42 the Tigua inhabited Taos and Picuris in the N., and, as to-day, were separated from the middle group by the Tano, the Tewa, and the Rio Grande Queres (Keresan). The villages of this middle group in the 16th century extended from a short distance above Bernalillo to the neighborhood of Los Lunas and over an area E. of the Rio Grande near the salt lagoons of the Manzano, in a territory known as the Salinas, from Chilili to Quarai. The pueblos in the S., near El Paso, were not established until late in the 17th century. The Tigua were first made known to history through Coronado's expedition in 1540, whose chroniclers describe their territory, the province of Tiguex, on the Rio Grande, as containing 12 pueblos on both sides of the river, and the people as possessing corn, beans, melons, skins, and long robes of feathers and cotton. The Spaniards were received by them with friendliness, but when it was decided to spend the winter of 1540–41 in Tiguex province, and the Spaniards demanded of the natives "about 300 or more pieces of cloth" with which to clothe the army, even stripping the cloaks and blankets from their backs, the Indians avenged this and other outrages by running off the Spanish horse herd, of which they killed a large number, and fortifying themselves in one of their pueblos. This the Spaniards attacked, and after exchanging signs of peace the Indians put down their arms and were pardoned. Nevertheless, through some misunderstanding the Spaniards proceeded to burn at the stake 200 of the captives, of whom about half were shot down in an attempt to escape the torture to which the others were being subjected. Says Castañeda, the principal chronicler of the expedition: "Not a man of them remained alive, unless it was some who remained hidden in the village and escaped that night to spread throughout the country the news that the strangers did not respect the peace they had made." As a result of this ill-treatment the Tigua abandoned all but two of their villages, one of which was also known to the Spaniards as Tiguex (see *Puaray*), into which they took all their stores and equipped themselves for the inevitable siege. Every overture made by the Spaniards toward peace was now received with derision by the natives, who informed them that they "did not wish to trust themselves to people who

had no regard for friendship or their own word which they had pledged." One of the Tigua villages was surrounded and attacked by means of ladders, but time and again the Spaniards were beaten off, 50 being wounded in the first assault. During the siege, which lasted 50 days, the Indians lost 200 of their number and surrendered 100 women and children. Finally, the water supply of the natives became exhausted, and in an attempt to leave the village at night and cross the river with the remainder of their women, "there were few who escaped being killed or wounded." The other pueblo suffered the same fate, but its inhabitants apparently did not withstand the siege so long. In attempting to escape, the Spaniards pursued "and killed large numbers of them." The soldiers then plundered the town and captured about 100 women and children.

In 1581 Chamuscado, with 8 soldiers and 7 Indian servants, accompanied the Franciscan missionaries, Agustin Rodriguez, Francisco Lopez, and Juan de Santa María, to the country of the Tigua, but all three were killed by the Indians after the departure of the escort. In 1583 Antonio de Espejo with 14 Spanish followers journeyed to New Mexico, and on his approach the Indians of Puaray, where Rodriguez and Lopez had been killed, fled for fear of vengeance. This was the pueblo, Espejo learned, at which Coronado had lost 9 men and 40 horses, thus identifying it with one of the Tigua villages besieged by Coronado 40 years before. In 1591 Castaño de Sosa also visited the Tigua, as did Oñate in 1598, the latter discovering on a wall at Puaray a partially effaced native painting representing the killing of the three missionaries.

In 1629, according to Benavides, the Tigua province extended over 11 or 12 leagues along the Rio Grande and consisted of 8 pueblos, with 6,000 inhabitants. This reduction in the number of villages was doubtless due to the effort of the Spanish missionaries, soon after the beginning of the 17th century, to consolidate the settlements both to insure greater security from the predatory Apache and to facilitate missionary work. Thus, in 1680, the time of the beginning of the Pueblo revolt, the Tigua occupied only the pueblos of Puaray, Sandia, Alameda, and Isleta, all on the Rio Grande. The population of these towns at the date named was estimated by Vetancurt at 200, 3,000, 300, and 2,000, respectively.

The eastern portion of what was the southern area of the Tigua up to about 1674 was limited to a narrow strip along the eastern slope of the Manzano mts., beginning with the pueblo of Chilili in the N., including Tajique and possibly

a pueblo near the present Manzano
(q. v.), and ending with Quarai. In this
area in 1581, according to Chamuscado,
were 11 pueblos. To the E., however,
lay a country bountifully supplied with
game, including the buffalo, while round
about the settlements in every direction
were the saline lagoons from which this
section of country derives its name and
from which salt was obtained for barter
with tribes as far s. as Parral in Chihuahua. Yet the aborigines were beset
with many disadvantages. Their range
was for the greater part an inhospitable
desert, exposed to the depredations of the
ever-wily Apache, whose constant raids
resulted first in the abandonment of Chilili between 1669 and 1674, then Quarai,
about 1674, its inhabitants joining those
of Tajique pueblo, which a year later was
also permanently abandoned. Most of
these villagers of the Salinas fled for
safety to their kindred at Isleta on the
Rio Grande, where they remained until
1680. At this date began the Pueblo revolt against Spanish authority, in which
participated the Tigua of Taos and Picuris,
as well as of Isleta, Sandia, Alameda, and
Puaray. On the appearance of Gov. Otermin in his attempted reconquest of the
country in the following year all these
pueblos except Isleta were abandoned and
were afterward burned by the Spaniards.
Isleta was stormed and about 500 of the
inhabitants were made captives, most of
whom were taken to El Paso and afterward
settled in the pueblo of Isleta del Sur, Texas.
Of the remainder of the population of
Isleta del Norte and Sandia a large portion fled to Tusayan, where they lived with
the Hopi until 1709 or 1718, when the
Isletaños returned and reestablished their
pueblo. The Sandia Indians, however,
who numbered 441, appear to have remained with the Hopi, in a pueblo called
Payupki on the Middle mesa, until 1742,
when they were taken by Padres Delgado
and Pino to the Rio Grande and settled in
a new pueblo at or near the site of their
old one. Alameda and Puaray were never
reestablished as Indian pueblos.

The following are the Tigua pueblos, so
far as known; of these only Isleta, Isleta
del Sur, Picuris, Sandia, Senecu del Sur,
and Taos are now inhabited: Alameda,
Bejuituuy, Carfaray, Chilili, Isleta (N.
Mex.), Isleta del Sur, Kuaua, Lentes,
Manzano, Mojualuna, Nabatutuei, Natch-
urituei, Pahquetooai, Picuris, Puaray,
Puretuay, Quarai, San Antonio, Sandia,
Santiago, Senecu del Sur (includes also
Piro), Shumnac, Tajique, Taos.

The following pueblos, now extinct,
were probably also Tigua: Acacafui, Gua-
yotrí, Henicohio, Leyva, Paniete, Poxen,
Ranchos, Shinana, Tanques, Torreon,
Trimati, Tuchiamas, Vareato.

For pueblos pertaining to either the
Piro or the Tigua, see *Piro*, and for those
inhabited by either the Tigua or the
Tewa, see *Tewa*. See also *Pueblos, Tanoan
Family*.　　　　　(F. W. H.)
Cheguas.—Oñate (1598) in Doc. Inéd., XVI, 306,
1871. **Chiguas.**—Ibid., 102. **E-nagh-magh.**—Lane
(1854) in Schoolcraft, Ind. Tribes, V, 689, 1855 (name
given to the language of "Taos, Vicuris, Zesuqua,
Sandia," etc.). **Ruas.**—Columbus Mem. Vol., 156,
1893 (misprint of Benavides' Tioas). **Tebas.**—
Blaeu, Atlas, XII, 62, 1667 (identified with the
Tigua by Bandelier in Arch. Inst. Papers, I, 20,
1881). **Tebes.**—Sanson, L'Amérique, map, 27, 1657
(=the Tebas of Blaeu). **Tee-wahn.**—Lummis in
St Nicholas, XVIII, 829, Sept. 1891 ("spelled Tiguan
by Spanish authors"). **Téoas.**—Benavides, Memo-
rial, 19, 1630. **Tequa.**—Poore in Donaldson, Moqui
Pueblo Inds., 101, 1893. **Tguas.**—Zaltieri map
(1566) in Winsor, Hist. Am., II, 451, 1886. **Tibex.**—
Doc. of 1540 in 14th Rep. B. A. E., 569, 1896.
Tignes.—Ogilby, America, 300, 1671. **Tignex.**—
Wytfliet, Hist. des Indes, map, 114–15, 1605. **Ti-
goeux.**—Marcy, Army Life, 99, 1866. **Ti-guan.**—
Bandelier in Arch. Inst. Papers, IV, 223, 1892 (own
name; pl. Ti-guesh). **Tiguas.**—Gomara (1554) in
Purchas, Pilgrimes, IV, 1561. **Tiguasi.**—Bracken-
ridge, Early Span. Discov., 18, 1859. **Tigue.**—Abert
in Emory, Recon., 489, 1848. **Tigueans.**—Simpson
in Smithson. Rep. 1869, 320, 1871. **Tiguero.**—
Barcia, Ensayo, 21, 1723. **Tigues.**—Gomara (1554)
cited by Hakluyt, Voy., 455, 1600. **Tigües.**—Mota-
Padilla, Hist. Nueva Galicia, 517, 1742 (or Tiques).
Ti-guesh.—Bandelier in Arch. Inst. Papers, IV, 223,
1892 (pl. of Ti-guan, their own name). **Tiguet.**—
Loew in Wheeler Surv. Rep., app. LL, 175, 1875.
Tiguex.—Coronado (1540) in Hakluyt, Voy., III,
455, 1600; Jaramillo (1540) in Doc. Inéd., XIV, 309,
1871; Castañeda (1596) in Ternaux-Compans, Voy.,
IX, 71, 1838; Coronado Docs. in 14th Rep. B. A. E.,
1896. **Tigüex.**—Coronado (1541) in Doc. Inéd.,
XIII, 261, 1870. **Tiguexa.**—Vaugondy, map Améri-
que, 1778. **Tiguez.**—Gomara, Hist. Gen., 469a, 1606.
Tigüez.—Coronado (1541) in Doc. Inéd., XIII, 267,
1870. **Tiguns.**—Ramusio, Nav. et Viaggi, III, 455,
map, 1565. **Tihuas.**—Barcia, Ensayo, 155, 1723.
Tihueq.—Jaramillo (16th cent.) in Doc. Inéd.,
XIV, 309, 1870. **Tihuex.**—Jaramillo in 14th Rep.
B. A. E., 587, 1896. **Tihuix.**—Torquemada, Monarq.
Ind., III, 359, 1723. **Tiluex.**—Haines, Am. Ind.,
166, 1888. **Tioas.**—Benavides, Memorial, 76, 1630.
Tiquas.—Cordova (1619) in Ternaux-Compans,
Voy., X, 444, 1838. **Tiques.**—Mota-Padilla, Hist.
Nueva Galicia, 516, 1742 (or Tigües). **Tiquex.**—Tay-
lor in Cal. Farmer, Apr. 11, 1862. **Tiquexa.**—Wyt-
fliet, Hist. des Indes, 114, 1605. **Tiuhex.**—Herrera,
Historia, VI, 207, 1728 (misprint). **Tíwa.**—Hodge,
field notes, B. A. E., 1895 (Isleta and Sandia name).
Tizuas—Columbus Mem. Vol., 154, 1893. **Toas.**—
Benavides (1630) misquoted in Am. Ethnol. Soc.
Trans., II, clxix, 1848.

Tihie. Mentioned by Barcia (Ensayo,
4, 1723) as a town or province, under the
chieftainship of Datha, probably on the
coast of South Carolina, visited by Ayllon
in 1520.

Tihilya ('mescal'). Given by Bourke
(Jour. Am. Folk-lore, II, 181, 1889) as a
clan of the Mohave (q. v.).

Tihittan ('bark-house people'). A
Tlingit division at Wrangell, Alaska,
belonging to the Raven phratry. They
are said to have separated from the Kiksadi on account of a quarrel. The Tenedi
of Klawak are a part of the same family.
Ta-ee-tee-tan.—Kane, Wand. in N. A., app., 1859.
Tīgītān.—Krause, Tlinkit Ind., 120, 1885. **Tĭ hĭt
tān.**—Swanton, field notes, B. A. E., 1904. **Tĭr hit
tān.**—Boas, 5th Rep. N. W. Tribes Can., 25, 1889.

Tikaleyasuni (*Tĭkăleyăsŭñĭ*, abbreviated
Tĭkăle'yăsŭñ, 'burning place'). A former
Cherokee settlement, commonly known

as Burningtown, on Burningtown cr., an upper branch of Little Tennessee r., in w. North Carolina.   (J. M.)

Ticoloosa.—Bartram, Travels, 371, 1792.

Tikchik. A Nushigagmiut Eskimo village on L. Tikchik, on the Kuskokwim portage, Alaska; pop. 38 in 1880.—Petroff, Rep. on Alaska, 47, 1880.

Tikera ('the forefinger'). The village of the Tikeramiut Eskimo at Pt Hope, Alaska; pop. 276 in 1880.

Tikera.—Murdoch, MS., B. A. E., 1885. **Tikerana.**—11th Census, Alaska, 162, 1892. **Tikirak.**—Petroff in 10th Census, Alaska, 4, 1884. **Tikirat.**—Nelson in 18th Rep. B. A. E., map, 1899. **Ttikigakg.**—Zagoskin, Descr. Russ. Poss. Am., I, 74, 1847.

Tikerakdjung. (1) A winter settlement of Kingua Eskimo on Imigen id., Cumberland sd., near the entrance to Nettilling fjord, Baffinland. (2) A summer settlement of Talirpia Eskimo on the s. coast of Nettilling lake, Baffinland.

Tikeraqdjung.—Boas in 6th Rep. B. A. E., map, 1888.

Tikeramiut ('inhabitants of the forefinger'). An Eskimo tribe at Pt Hope, Alaska, from which point they receive their name. Pop. 295 in 1900. Their village is Tikera.

Tee-kee-voga-meuts.—Hooper, Cruise of Corwin, 26, 1881. **Tigara Mutes.**—Kelly, Arct. Eskimos, chart, 1890. **Tikera'ñmiun.**—Murdoch in 9th Rep. B. A. E., 44, 1892.

Tikizat. A Nunatogmiut Eskimo village at C. Krusenstern, Alaska; pop. 75 in 1880.

Tee-kee-zaht-meuts.—Hooper, Cruise of Corwin, 26, 1881. **Tikizat.**—Petroff, Rep. on Alaska, 59, 1880.

Tikumigizhik ('He-takes-cross-cuts-in-the-sky,' lit., He is traveling in the sky, and instead of taking the long way round, goes directly across). An influential full-blood chief of a band of about a hundred Chippewa at White Earth, Minn.; born at Gull Lake about 1830, removed to White Earth about 1868, where he became a Christian under the influence of Enmegahbowh. His progressiveness is shown by the fact that he once had 40 acres in wheat and other grains—more than any other full-blood Chippewa. He is a man of keen penetration, undemonstrative, and shrewd. He was a supporter of Hole-in-the-Day in the Minnesota outbreak of 1862, and saw the soldiers placed in a position where they were at the mercy of the Indians; but, as Tikumigizhik expresses it, he and his tribesmen thought of all the widows and orphans that would be made, so they refrained from making an onslaught. Tikumigizhik's sister was the wife of Nebuneshkung.   (J. A. G.)

Tikwalitsi (*Tĭkwăli'tsĭ*, of unknown meaning). A former important Cherokee town on Tuckasegee r., at the present Bryson City, Swain co., N. C. The name appears in old documents as Tuckarechee (lower dialect) and Tuckalegee, and must not be confounded with Tsĭksi'tsĭ or

Tuckasegee.—Mooney in 19th Rep. B. A. E., 534, 1900.

Tucharechee.—Doc. of 1755 quoted by Royce in 5th Rep. B. A. E., 143, 1887.

Tikwalus. A Ntlakyapamuk village on the E. side of Fraser r., 13 m. above Yale, Brit. Col.; pop. 18 in 1897, when the name last appears.

Chapman's bar.—Teit in Mem. Am. Mus. Nat. Hist., II, 169, 1900. **Kekalus.**—Can. Ind. Aff., 230, 1886. **Kequeloose.**—Anderson quoted by Gibbs in Hist. Mag., 1st s., VII, 78, 1863. **Tikolaus.**—Brit. Col. map, Ind. Aff., Victoria, 1872. **Tĭk'ūilūc.**—Hill-Tout in Rep. Ethnol. Surv. Can., 5, 1899. **Ti'kwalus.**—Teit in Mem. Am. Mus. Nat. Hist., II, 169, 1900.

Tilapani. A village or tribe marked on De l'Isle's map of about 1700 (Winsor, Hist. Am., II, 294, 1886), near Atchafalaya bayou, La. Nothing is known of its affiliations, but as the locality given was within the Chitimacha country, it may have belonged to that group.

Tilijaes. One of the Coahuiltecan tribes mentioned by Fray Bartolomé García as speaking the language of his Manual (1760). Orozco y Berra (Geog., 304, 1864) places them on Nueces r., Texas, immediately below the Pampopa, who were 22 leagues from San Juan Bautista mission. He also (p. 302) speaks of them as gathered with other tribes at missions in Coahuila about 1675–77. They were among the original tribes at San Juan Capistrano mission in 1731, and from the time of its founding they were at San Juan Bautista mission. When García wrote they were still in part at San Juan Capistrano.

Filifaes.—Revillagigedo (1793), Carta, quoted by Bancroft, Nat. Races, I, 611, 1886. **Filijayas.**—Taylor in Cal. Farmer, Apr. 17, 1863 (misprint). **Tilijaes.**—Fernando del Bosque (1675) in Nat. Geog. Mag., XIV, 347, 1903. **Tilijais.**—Orozco y Berra, Geog., 302, 1864. **Tilijayas.**—Garcia (1760) quoted by Orozco y Berra, ibid., 306. **Tilofayas.**—Orozco y Berra, ibid., 303. **Tiloja.**—Spanish record cited by H. E. Bolton, inf'n, 1908. **Tilpayai.**—Massault MS. (1690) cited by H. E. Bolton, inf'n, 1908. **Tilyayas.**—Shea, Cath. Miss., 86, 1855. **Tolujaâ.**—Spanish record cited by H. E. Bolton, inf'n, 1908.

Tilkuni (*Tĭ'lqûni*). A Shahaptian tribe mentioned by Mooney as speaking the Tenino language and claiming the territory between Tygh and Warm Springs rs., in Wasco co., Oreg. They are now on Warm Springs res., Oreg., and are probably included under the official term Warm Springs Indians.

Tilhanne.—Lee and Frost, Oregon, 176, 1844. **Tĭ'lqûni.**—Mooney in 14th Rep. B. A. E., 742, 1896.

Tillamook (Chinook: 'people of Nekelim,' or Nehalem.—Boas). A large and prominent Salish tribe on Tillamook bay and the rivers flowing into it, in N. w. Oregon. According to Boas the culture of the Tillamook seems to have differed considerably from that of the N. coast Salish, and has evidently been influenced by the culture of the tribes of N. California. According to Lewis and Clark they occupied 8 villages, of which these explorers name 5: Chishuck, Chucktin, Kilerhurst, Kilherner, and Tower-quotton. The same authorities place the Tillamook population at 2,200. In the reports of the Wilkes Exploring Expedition (1845) their number is given as 400, and by Lane in 1849 as 200. See Boas, Traditions of the Tillamook Indians, Jour. Am. Folk-lore, XI, 23–38, 133–150, 1898.

Cal-a-mex.—Gass, Journal, 189, 1807. **Ca-la-mox.**—Clark (1806) in Orig. Jour. Lewis and Clark, III, 295, 1905. **Cal-la-maks.**—Ibid., VI, 117, 1905. **Cal lá mox.**—Clark (1806), ibid., III, 310, 1905. **Callamucks.**—Lewis (1806), ibid., 308. **Callemax.**—Stuart in Nouv. Annales des Voy., X, 90, 1821. **Callemeux.**—Gass, Voyage, 283, 1810. **Callemex.**—Gass, Journal, 180, 1807. **Callimix.**—Morse, Rep. to Sec. War, 368, 1822. **Clemaks.**—Macdougall in Nouv. Annales des Voy., X, 20, 23, 1821. **Gillamooks.**—Manypenny in H. R. Ex. Doc. 37, 34th Cong., 3d sess., 9, 1857. **Higgaháldshu.**—Nestuka vocab., B. A. E. (Nestucca name). **Hilleamuck.**—Lane (1849) in Schoolcraft, Ind. Tribes, VI, 701, 1857. **Kelamucks.**—Scouler (1846) in Jour. Ethnol. Soc. Lond., I, 237, 1848. **Kilamooks.**—Palmer, Travels, 105, 1847. **Kil á mox.**—Clark (1806) in Orig. Jour. Lewis and Clark, IV, 9, 1905. **Kilamukes.**—Wilkes, U. S. Expl. Exped., V, 116, 1845. **Kilamute.**—Irving, Bonneville's Advent., map, 1850. **Killamook.**—Parker, Journal, 156, 1840. **Killamoucks.**—Lewis and Clark Exped., I, map, 1814 (the river). **Killamouks.**—Farnham, Travels, 111, 1843. **Killamox.**—Clark (1806) in Orig. Jour. Lewis and Clark, VI, 117, 1905. **Killamuck.**—Lewis and Clark Exped., II, 111, 117, 1814. **Killamuks.**—American Pioneer, II, 189, 1843. **Killemooks.**—Townsend, Narr., 175, 1839. **Killernoux.**—Meek in H. R. Ex. Doc. 76, 30th Cong., 1st sess., 10, 1848. **Killimoucks.**—Duflot de Mofras, Oregon, II, 349, 1844. **Killimous.**—Ibid., 357. **Killimux.**—Ross, Advent., 87, 1849. **Killymucks.**—Cox, Columb. Riv., I, 292, 1831. **Klemook.**—Franchère, Narr., 126, 1854. **Kyaukw.**—Dorsey, Alsea MS. vocab., B. A. E., 1884 (Alsea name). **Nsietshawas.**—Latham in Proc. Philol. Soc. Lond., VI, 83, 1854. **Nsietshawus.**—Hale in U. S. Expl. Exped., VI, 211, 1846. **Nsirtshaus.**—Schoolcraft, Ind. Tribes, III, 402, 1853. **Si ni'-tĕ-lĭ.**—Dorsey, Coquille MS. vocab., B. A. E., 1884 ('flatheads': nickname given by the Mishikhwutmetunne to the Alsea, Nestucca, and Tillamook). **Tilamookhs.**—Gibbs, Obs. on Coast tribes of Oregon, MS., B. A. E. **Tillamook.**—Lewis and Clark Exped., II, 117, 1814. **Tillemookhs.**—Gibbs, letter to Hazen, B. A. E., Feb. 26, 1856. **T'íl'-mūk' ʒûnnĕ.**—Dorsey, Coquille MS. vocab., B. A. E., 1884 (Coquille name). **Titamook.**—Ind. Aff. Rep., 74, 1874. **T'ûl-li'-mūks-mé ʒûnnĕ.**—Dorsey, Naltûnnětûnné MS. vocab., B. A. E., 1884 (Naltunnetunne name). **Upper Killamuks.**—Schoolcraft, Ind. Tribes, III, 402, 1853. **Usietshawus.**—Hale in U. S. Expl. Exped., VI, 218, 1846.

Time-keeping. See *Calendar*.

Timethltunne. A band of the Mishikhwutmetunne on Coquille r., Oreg.

Ti-mĕʒl' ʒûnnĕ'.—Dorsey in Jour. Am. Folk-lore, III, 232, 1890.

Timetl (*Tĭ'metl*, 'place where red ocher was obtained'). A village of the Ntlakyapamuk on Fraser r., Brit. Col., just above North bend.—Hill-Tout in Rep. Ethnol. Surv. Can., 5, 1899.

Timigtac. A former village, presumably Costanoan, connected with Dolores mission, San Francisco, Cal.

Timigtac.—Taylor in Cal. Farmer, Oct. 18, 1861. **Timita.**—Ibid. **Titmictac.**—Ibid.

Timpaiavats. A Ute division formerly occupying the valley of Utah lake, the Spanish Forks, and the adjacent mountains in Utah. They were said to number 300 in 1865, but had ceased to exist as a separate body before 1870. In 1873 Powell found 25 on the Uintah res., where they were known under the collective name of Uintah Utes.

Speaking of the Timpanogotzis (Timpaiavats), who derived their name from Timpanogo, by which Utah lake was known to them, Fathers Dominguez and Escalante, in 1776 (Doc. Hist. Mex., 2ª s., I, 467, 1854), say: "On its shores dwell the aforementioned Indians, who live upon the abundant fish supplies of the lake, whence the Yutas Sabuaganas call them fish-eaters. Besides this, they gather on the plains seeds of plants, and make a sort of gruel with them, although they add to this the hunting of hares, rabbits, and sage-hens, of which there is a great abundance; there are also buffaloes not far to the eastward, but the fear of the Comanches prevents them from hunting them. Their dwellings are a sort of small huts of osiers, of which they make also baskets and other necessary utensils. Their dress manifests great poverty; the most decent which they wear is a coat or shirt of deerskin, and legging-moccasins of the same in winter; they have dresses made of hare and rabbit skins. They speak the Yuta language, but with a noticeable variation of accent, and even of some words. They are good featured, and mostly without beard."

Come Pescado.—Dominguez and Escalante (1776) in Doc. Hist. Mex., 2ª s., I, 467, 1854 ('fish-eaters': Spanish form of name given by the Sabuagana, or Akanaquint). **Fish-eaters.**—Harry (1860) in Simpson, Rep. of Expl. Across Utah, 494, 1876. **Lagunas.**—Dominguez and Escalante (1776), op. cit., 411 ("indios de los Timpangotzis ó lagunas"). **Lake Indians.**—Harry, op. cit., 490. **Tem-pan-ah-gos.**—Graves in Ind. Aff. Rep., 386, 1854. **Ten-penny Utahs.**—Wilson (1849) in Cal. Mess. and Corresp., 185, 1850. **Timbabachis.**—Schoolcraft, Ind. Tribes, III, 96, map, 1853. **Timbachis.**—Domenech, Deserts N. A., I, 444, 1860. **Timpachis.**—Mayer, Mexico, II, 38, 1853. **Timpagtsis.**—Dominguez and Escalante (1776), op. cit., 464. **Timpai'-a-vats.**—Powell in Ind. Aff. Rep. 1873, 51, 1874. **Timpana Yuta.**—Burton, City of Saints, 577, 1861. **Timpangotzis.**—Dominguez and Escalante (1776), op. cit., 411. **Timpanigos Yutas.**—Farnham, Travels Californias, 371, 1844. **Timpanocutzis.**—Dominguez and Escalante (1776), op. cit., 464. **Timpancouitzis.**—Escalante (1776) quoted by Whipple in Pac. R. R., Rep., III, pt. 3, 126, 1856. **Timpanoge.**—Tourtellotte in Ind. Aff. Rep., 142, 1870. **Timpanogos.**—Alegre, Hist. Comp. Jesus, I, 336, 1841. **Timpano-gotzis.**—Dominguez and Escalante (1776), op. cit., 469. **Timpanogs.**—Cooley in Ind. Aff. Rep., 17, 1865. **Timpanotzis.**—Escalante, op. cit. **Timpenaguchyă.**—Burton, City of Saints, 475, 1862 (trans. 'water among the stones'). **Tinpay nagoots.**—Gebow, Sho-sho-nay Vocab., 20, 1868 (Shoshoni name). **Tirangapui.**—Dominguez and Escalante (1776) in Doc. Hist. Mex., 2ª s., I, 476, 1854. **Tirangapuy.**—Dominguez and Escalante quoted by Duro, Don Diego de Peñalosa, 142, 1882. **Tiransgapuis.**—Domenech, Deserts N. A., II, 64, 1860. **Tupanogos.**—Collins in Ind. Aff. Rep., 125, 1861.

Timpashauwagotsits (*Tim-pa-shau'-wa-got-sits*). A Paiute band near Providence mts., S. E. Cal.—Powell in Ind. Aff. Rep. 1873, 51, 1874.

Timpoochee Barnard. A Yuchi chief, son of Timothy Barnard, a Scotchman, and a Yuchi woman, who first became generally known when, in 1814, he took part with the American forces against the hostile Creeks. During the battle of General Floyd's troop with the Indians at Camp Defiance, Ala., Jan. 2, 1814 (called the battle of Callabee), Barnard, who had been commissioned as major, distinguished himself, with his band of about 100 Yuchi warriors, especially in rescuing Capt. Broadnix and his company when their retreat was for a time cut off. He signed the Creek treaty of Aug. 9, 1814, at Ft Jackson, Ala., as "Captain of Uchees." (c. t.)

Timsim. A village, presumably Costanoan, formerly connected with Dolores mission, San Francisco, Cal. (Taylor in Cal. Farmer, Oct. 18, 1861). Cf. *Lamsim.*

Timucua. The principal of the Timucuan tribes of Florida. The name is written Timucua or Timuqua by the Spaniards; Thimagoa by the French; Atimaco, Tomoco, etc., by the English. They seem to be identical with the people called Nukfalalgi or Nukfila by the Creeks, described by the latter as having once occupied the upper portion of the peninsula and as having been conquered, together with the Apalachee, Yamasee, and Calusa, by the Creeks. When first known to the French and Spanish, about 1565, the Timucua occupied the territory along middle St John r. and about the present St Augustine. Their chief was known to the French as Olata Ouae Utina, abbreviated to Utina or Outina, which, however, is a title rather than a personal name, *olata* (*hola'ta*) signifying 'chief,' and *utina* 'country.' His residence town on St John r. is believed to have been not far below L. George. He ruled a number of subchiefs or towns, among which are mentioned (Laudonnière) Acuera, Anacharaqua, Cadecha, Calany, Chilili, Eclaou, Enacappe, Mocoso, and Omitiaqua. Of these Acuera is evidently the coast town s. of C. Cañaveral, where the Spaniards afterward established the mission of Santa Lucia de Acuera. The names Acuera, Mocoso, and Utina(ma) are duplicated in the w. part of the peninsula in the De Soto narratives. The Timucua were Christianized by Spanish Franciscans toward the close of the 16th century and brought to a high degree of civilization until the destruction of the missions about the year 1705 (see *Timucuan Family*). The remnant of the tribe at first took refuge at St Augustine, and was afterward established in a new settlement called Pueblo de Atimucas, on Tomoco r., near Mosquito lagoon, in the present Volusia co. A few of them seem to have been in existence as late as the transfer of the territory to the United States in 1821.   (J. M.)

Atimaco.—Roberts, Fla., 89, 1763. **Atimucas.**—Shea, Cath. Miss., 74, 1855. **Atimuqua.**—Smith quoted by Gatschet in Proc. Am. Philos. Soc., XVII, 490, 1878. **Attamasco.**—Williams, Ter. of Fla., 178, 1837. **Núkfalalgi.**—Gatschet, Creek Migr. Leg., II, 66, 1888 (Creek name, perhaps of Catawba origin, for a Florida people, evidently the Timucua and kindred tribes; *algi*=Creek pl. suffix). **Núkfíla.**—Ibid. (another form for Núkfalalgi). **Núk-hótsi.**—Ibid. ('spotted or marked on the neck,' from *inukwa* his neck; a Creek corruption of the Catawba (?) name from which they made Núkfalalgi). **Tamaicas.**—Williams, Ter. Fla., 175, 1837. **Thimagona.**—Gatschet in Proc. Am. Philos. Soc., XVI, 627, 1877 (given as a French form; *n* misprint for *u*). **Thimagoua.**—Gatschet, Creek Migr. Leg., I, 11, 1884. **Thimogoa.**—Laudonnière (1564) quoted by Basanier in French, Hist. Coll. La., 231, 1869. **Timagoa.**—Barcia, Ensayo, 47, 1723. **Timoga.**—De Bry map (1591) in Le Moyne Narr., Appleton trans., 1875. **Timogoa.**—Brackenridge, Views of La., 84, 1815. **Timookas.**—Jefferys, Am. Atlas, map 5, 1776. **Timooquas.**—Lattré, map New Spain, 1784. **Timoqua.**—Gatschet in Proc. Am. Philos. Soc., XVII, 490, 1878 (given as a Spanish form). **Timuaca.**—French, Hist. Coll. La., 2d s., II, 296, 1875. **Timuacana.**—Latham, El. Comp. Philol., 466, 1862. **Timuca.**—Gatschet in Proc. Am. Philos. Soc., XVI, 627, 1877 (given as a Spanish form). **Timucua.**—Ibid. (another Spanish form). **Timuqua.**—Barcia, Ensayo, 287, 1723. **Timuquana.**—Pareja (1612) as quoted by Gatschet in Proc. Am. Philos. Soc., XVIII, 475, 1880 (Spanish adjective form: "lengua Timuquana"). **Timuquanan.**—Powell in 7th Rep. B. A. E., 123, 1891 (double adjective form coined to designate the family). **Timusquana.**—Palacios quoted by Smith in Hist. Mag., I, 1, 1858 (misprint *s* for *a*). **Tinqua.**—French, Hist. Coll. La., 2d s., II, 296, 1875 (misprint). **Tomachees.**—Coxe, Carolana, map, 1741. **Tommakees.**—Ibid., 22. **Tomocos.**—Bartram, Trav., 378, 1791. **Tomoka.**—Drake, Bk. of Inds., bk. IV, 140–1, 1848 (mentioned as a Florida settlement and as a Seminole chief's name in 1837). **Tumican.**—Hewat, S. C. and Ga., I, 228, 1779. **Tymangoua.**—Anon. author (1565) in Ternaux-Compans, Voy., XX, 237, 1841. **Ustana.**—Palacios (1675) quoted by Smith in Hist. Mag., II, 1, 1858.

Timucuan Family. A group of cognate tribes formerly occupying the greater part of N. Florida, extending along the E. coast from about lat. 28°, below C. Cañaveral, to above the mouth of St John r., and along the w. coast probably from Tampa bay northward to about Ocilla r., where they met the Apalachee, of Muskhogean stock. The Hichiti and Yamasee, also Muskhogean, appear to have occupied their N. frontier nearly on the present state boundary; but the Timucua held both banks of St Marys r. and Cumberland id. S. of lat. 28° the w. coast was held by the Calusa, and the E. coast by the Ais and Tequesta, rude and fierce tribes, of whose language nothing is known, but who seem to have had no relation with the Timucuan tribes. The family designation is derived from the name of one of the principal tribes, the Timucua, Timagoa, Tomoco, or Atimuca, whose territory was about St Augustine and on middle St John r. The name may possibly signify 'lord' or 'ruler.' Other principal tribes were Saturiba on the lower St John; Yustaga, or Hostaqua, about the upper Suwannee; Potano, w. of St John r., between the heads of the Withlacoochee and Suwannee; Tocobaga, between Withlacoochee r. and Tampa bay; Mayaca, on the N. E. coast; Marracou, 40 leagues from the mouth of St John r. Several other tribes can not be so definitely located, and all identification is rendered difficult owing to the confusion existing in the minds of the first explorers between chief names, tribe or village names, and titles. The statement, often repeated, that the chief had the same name as his "province" or tribe was due to misunderstanding. In person the Timucuan people are described as tall and well made. They went almost entirely naked except for the breechcloth, but covered their bodies with an elaborate tattooing. They were agricultural, though apparently not to the same extent as the Muskhogean tribes, depending more on game, fish, oysters, wild fruits, and bread from the nourishing coonti root. Their larger towns were compactly built and stockaded, their houses being circular structures of poles thatched with palmetto leaves, with a large "townhouse" for tribal gatherings in the center of the public square. From misunderstanding of the description, Brinton and others following him have incorrectly described this townhouse as a communal dwelling. Society was based on the clan system, and Pareja (1612) gives an interesting account of the intricate system of kinship relations. The clans were grouped into phratries, usually bearing animal names, and certain chiefships or functions seem to have been hereditary in certain clans. In his time the system was retained even by the mission converts. In military organization and authority of the chiefs they seem to have surpassed the more northern tribes. Scalping and mutilation of the dead were universally practised, and human sacrifice was a regular part of their religious ritual, the victims, as among the Natchez, being sometimes infants belonging to the tribe. There is evidence also of occasional cannibalism. The narrative and descriptive illustrations of Le Moyne, the French Huguenot (1564), shed much light on the home life, war customs, and ceremonies, while from Pareja's confessional a good idea of their beliefs and religious practices is gained. All the dialects of the family seem to have been so closely related as to be mutually intelligible. Pareja names 7, viz: Freshwater District (probably on the interior lakes), Itafi, Mocama (a coast dialect), Potano, Santa Lucia de Acuera (s. from C. Cañaveral), Timacua, and Tucururu (on the Atlantic coast). Besides these there were probably others in the interor and on the w. coast. The language was vocalic and musical, with a very complex grammar.

The history of the Timucuan tribes begins with the landing of Ponce de León near the site of the present St Augustine in 1513. In 1528 Narvaez led his small army from Tampa bay northward to explore the country of the Apalachee and beyond. In 1539 De Soto went over nearly the same route, his historians mentioning some 20 tribal or local names within the region, including Yustaga and Potano. In 1562-64 the French Huguenots under Ribault and Laudonnière attempted settlements at the mouth of St John r., explored the middle course of the stream and the adjacent interior, and became acquainted with the tribes of Saturiba (Satouiroua) and Timucua (Thimagoa), as well as with the Potano (Potanou) and Yustaga (Hostaqua) already visited by De Soto. In 1565 the Spaniards under Menendez destroyed the French posts, killing all their defenders; they then founded St Augustine and began the permanent colonization of the country. Within a few years garrisons were established and missions founded, first under the Jesuits and later under the Franciscans. (See *San Juan, San Mateo, San Pedro.*) The principal center of mission enterprise was in the neighborhood of St Augustine among the Timucua proper. The most noted of these missionaries was Father Francisco Pareja, who arrived in 1594 and after 16 years of successful work retired to the City of Mexico, where he wrote a Timucua grammar, dictionary, and several devotional works, from which, and from the French narrative, is derived practically all that we know of the language, customs, beliefs, and organization of the Timucuan tribes. Pareja died in 1628. In spite of one or two revolts by which several missionaries lost their lives, the Timucuan tribes in general, particularly along the E. coast, accepted Christianity and civilization and became the allies of the Spaniards. In 1699 the Quaker Dickenson visited several of their mission settlements and noted the great contrast between the Christian Indians and the savage tribes of the southern peninsula among whom he had been a captive. A few years later, about 1703, began the series of invasions by the English of Carolina and their savage Indian allies, Creek, Catawba, and Yuchi, by which the missions were destroyed, hundreds of their people killed, and hundreds, possibly thousands, of others, men, women, and children, carried off into slavery, while the remnant took refuge close under the walls of St Augustine. The prosperous Apalachee missions shared the same fate. With the decline of the Spanish power and the incessant inroads of the Creeks and Seminole, the native Indians rapidly dwindled until on the transfer of the territory to the United States in 1821 only a handful remained, and these apparently belonging mostly to the uncivilized tribes of the southern end. It is possible that the remnant of the mission tribes had been later shipped to Cuba by the Spaniards, as had been the case with the Calusa in 1763.

Consult Barcia, Ensayo, 1723; Basanier, Hist. Not. Floride, 1853; Bourne, Narr. De Soto, 1904; Dickenson, Narr. Shipwreck, 1699, repr. 1803; Gatschet in Proc. Am. Philos. Soc., xvi, 1877; xvii, 1878; xviii, 1880; Laudonnière in French, Hist. Coll. La., n. s., 1869; Le Moyne, Narr., 1875; Pareja (1614), Arte de la Lengua Timuquana, 1886.   (J. M.)
For synonyms, see *Timucua*.

Tinachi. A Chumashan village formerly near Santa Inés mission, Santa Barbara co., Cal.—Taylor in Cal. Farmer, Oct. 18, 1861.

Tinajas (Span.: 'water pools,' 'water pockets,' so called because of their fancied resemblance to water jars of earthenware). A former Yuma ranchería, s. E. of the mouth of the Gila, visited and doubtless so named by Father Kino in 1699.
Candelaria.—Font, map (1777), in Bancroft, Ariz. and N. Mex., 393, 1889. La Tinaja.—Venegas, Hist. Cal., I, map, 1759. La Tinaoca.—Kino, map (1701), in Bancroft, op. cit., 360, 1889. Tinajas.—Mange cited by Bancroft, op. cit., 357. Tinajas de Candelaria.—Anza and Font (1776), ibid., 393. Tinaxa.—Kino, map (1702), in Stöcklein, Neue Welt-Bott, 74, 1726.

Tinajas. See *Pottery, Receptacles.*

Tinapihuayas. A former tribe of N. E. Mexico or s. Texas, probably Coahuiltecan, the members of which were gathered into the mission of San Francisco Vizarron de los Pausanes in 1737.—Orozco y Berra, Geog., 303, 1864.

Tinazipeshicha ('bad bows'). A Hunkpapa Sioux band.
Arcs-Brisés.—De Smet, W. Miss., 264, 1848 (trans.: 'broken bows'). Bad Bows.—Culbertson in Smithson. Rep. 1850, 141, 1851. Si-ĉa'-wi-pi.—Hayden, Ethnog. and Philol. Mo. Val., 376, 1862. Tinazipe-oitca.—Dorsey in 15th Rep. B. A. E., 221, 1897. Tinazipe-śiĉa.—Ibid.

Tingmiarmiut. A settlement of Eskimo on the E. coast of Greenland, lat. 62° 40'.—Nansen, First Crossing, I, 323, 1890.

Tinicum (corruption of *Mĕtĭnakunk*, 'at (or on) the edge of the island' (lengthwise); cognate with Long Island, N. Y. (Quiripi?) Matinecoc (for Mĕtĭnakok), and with Abnaki Mĕtĭnakuk (Maine). See *Matinecoc*). A long island in the Delaware r., forming part of Burlington co., N. J., and having on one side high hills, and on the other low lands once inhabited by the Delawares (Lenape). The island became the seat of government of the Swedes, by whom it was called Tennakong.   (W. R. G.)
Tamecongh.—Doc. of 1656 in N. Y. Doc. Col. Hist., I, 596, 1856. Tamicongh.—Ibid. Tenacum.—Van Sweringen (1684), ibid., III, 343, 1853. Tinnecongh.—Doc. of 1656, op. cit.

Tinliu ('at the holes'). The Yokuts (Mariposan) name of the country about Tejon cr., Cal., occupied by the Shoshonean Gitanemuk (i. e., the Serranos of upper Tejon and Paso crs. in the San Joaquin valley drainage) and the Mariposan Yauelmani. Powers (Cont. N. A. Ethnol., III, 370, 1877) gives it, in the form Tinlinneh, as a tribal name. Cf. *Pohallintinleh, Tejon.*

Tinne (*Tin'-ne*, 'people'). The name sometimes given to the northern division of the Athapascan family, comprising the Kaiyuhkhotana, Knaiakhotana, Ahtena, Kuilchana, Unakhotana, Kutchin, Kawchodinne, Thlingchadinne, Etchareottine, Chipewyan, Nahane, Sekani, Takulli, and Tsilkotin. They were divided by Petitot (Dict. Dènè-Dindjié, xx, 1893) into the following groups: I. *Montagnais*, comprising (1) Chipewyan proper, (2) Athabascan, (3) Etheneldeli, (4) Tatsanottine. II. *Montagnards*, comprising (1) Tsattine, (2) Sarsi, (3) Sekani, (4) Nahane, (5) Ettchaottine, (6) Esbataottine. III. *Esclaves*, comprising (1) Etchareottine, (2) Slaves proper, (3) Lintchanre, (4) Kawchodinne, (5) Etagottine. IV. *Dindjié*, comprising (1) Kwitchakutchin, (2) Nakotchokutchin, (3) Tatlitkutchin, (4) Tukkuthkutchin, (5) Vuntakutchin, (6) Hankutchin, (7) Ahtena, (8) Kutchakutchin, (9) Tengeratsekutchin, (10) Tenankutchin, (11) Unakhotana, (12) Knaiakhotana, (13) Koyuhkhotana. He classified them later (Autour du Lac des Esclaves, 361, 1893) as follows: I. *Danè*, vulgo Ingaliks, (1) Koyukukhotana, (2) Unakhotana, (3) Yukonikhotana, (4) Koyuhkhotana. II. *Dindjié*, vulgo Loucheux, (1) Tenankutchin, (2) Natsitkutchin, (3) Kutchakutchin, (4) Tengeratsekutchin, (5) Hankutchin, (6) Vuntakutchin, (7) Tukkuthkutchin, (8) Tatlitkutchin, (9) Nakotchokutchin, (10) Kwitchakutchin. III. *Dounié*, vulgo Montagnais, (1) Etagottine, (2) Klokegottine, (3) Krazlongottine. IV. *Danè*, (1) Nahane, (2) Esbataottine, (3) Sekani, (4) Tsattine, (5) Sarsi. V. *Dènè*, vulgo Hareskins, (1) Nellagottine, (2) Kawchodinne, (3) Thlingchadinne, (4) Kfwetragottine, (5) Etatchogottine, (6) Nigottine. VI. *Dènè Esclaves*, vulgo Slaves, (1) Desnedeyarelottine, (2) Eleidlingottine, (3) Ettcheridieottine, (4) Etchaottine. VII. *Dounè*, vulgo Dogribs, (1) Tseottine, (2) Takfwelottine, (3) Tsantieottine, (4) Lintchanre. VIII. *Dènè Chipewyan*, (1) Tatsanottine, (2) Edjieretrukenade, (3) Desnedekenade, (4) Athabasca, (5) Etheneldeli, (6) Thilanottine. The Takulli and Tsilkotin as well as the Ahtena he classes with the Danè.

Morice divides the Tinne as follows: I. *Western Dénés*, (1) Tsilkotin, (2) Takulli, (3) Nahane. II. *Intermediate Dénés*, (1)

Sekani. III. *Eastern Dénés*, (1) Chipewyan, (2) Etheneldeli, (3) Tsattine, (4) Tatsanottine, (5) Thlingchadinne, (6) Etchareottine, (7) Ettchaottine, (8) Kawchodinne. IV. *Northern Dénés*, (1) Loucheux (Proc. Can. Inst., 113, 1889).

In Anthropos (I, 255–277, 1906) Father Morice makes the following classification, though the names here given are often quoted from other writers and are not always indorsed by him.—I. *Loucheux*, including the 'Kaiyuh-kho-'tenne, Koyūkŭkh-otā'-nā, Yuna-kho-'tenne or Yunukho-'tenne, Tana-kut'qin, Kut'qakut'qin, Natche-kŭtchin' or Nätsit'-kŭt-chin', Vœn-kut'qin, Tŭkkŭth-Kŭtchin, Hankut'qin, Tŭtcone-kut'qin, Artez-kut'qin, Thét'lét-kut'qín, Nakotco-ondjig-kut'qin, and Kwit'qakut'qin. II. *The Subarctic Dénés*, including the Hares, Dog-Ribs, Slaves, and Yellow-Knives. III. *Athabaskans or Eastern Dénés*, including the Cariboo Eaters, Athabaskans, and Chippewayans. IV. *The Intermediate Dénés*, including the Sheep Indians, Mountain Indians, Strong Bows, Nahanais, Beavers, Sarcis, and Sékanais. V. *The Western Dénés*, including the Babines, Carriers, Chilcotins, and the Ts'ets'aut of Boas. See *Athapascan Family*.

Tintaotonwe (*Tinta-otonwe*, 'village on the prairie'). A former Mdewakanton Sioux band. The village was situated on lower Minnesota r. and was once the residence of Wabasha, the Kiyuksa chief, until he removed with most of his warriors, leaving a few families under his son, Takopepeshene, Dauntless, who became a dependent of Shakopee (Shakpe), the neighboring chief of Taoapa.—Long, Exped. St Peters R., I, 585, 1824.

Eagle-Head.—Neill, Hist. Minn., 144, note, 1858 (English for Huyapa, the chief). Eagle head's band.—McKusick in Ind. Aff. Rep., 1863, 16, 1864. Ru-ya-pa.—Neill, op. cit. (the chief). Tetankatane.—Long, Exped. St Peter's R., I, 385, 1824 (trans. 'old village'). Tetarton.—Clark MS. quoted by Coues, Lewis and Clark Exped., I, 101, 1893. Tingtah-to-a.—Catlin, N. Am. Inds., II, 134, 1844. Tingta-to-ah.—Catlin quoted by Donaldson in Nat. Mus. Rep. 1885, 55, 1886. Tin-tah-ton.—Lewis and Clark, Discov., map, 34, 1806. Tiⁿta-otoⁿwe.—Dorsey in 15th Rep. B. A. E., 216, 1897. Tiŋta-otoŋwe.—Ibid. Tintatonwan.—Neill, Hist. Minn., 590, 1858. Tiŋtatoŋwaŋ.—Dorsey, op. cit. Tiⁿta toⁿwaⁿ.—Riggs quoted by Dorsey, ibid. Tinta tonwe.—Hinman in Ind. Aff. Rep., 68, 1860. Tiŋtatoŋwe.—Riggs, Dak. Gram. and Dict., 188, 1852. Village of Prairie.—Clark MS. quoted by Coues, Lewis and Clark Exped., I, 101, 1893.

Tintis. A division or settlement of the Tubare in s. w. Chihuahua, Mexico, on the s. fork of Rio del Fuerte.—Orozco y Berra, Geog., 58, 1864.

Tintlan. A Cowichan settlement on the s. bank of lower Fraser r., Brit. Col., below Sumass lake.—Brit. Col. map, Ind. Aff., Victoria, 1872.

Tiochrungwe (probably 'valley'). A former village of the Tuscarora in New York, situated in 1750 on "the main road" from Oneida to Onondaga.—De Schweinitz, Life and Times of David Zeisberger, 55, 1870.

Tioga (Iroquois: 'where it forks'). A former village situated on the site of Athens, on the right bank of the Susquehanna, near its junction with the Chemung, in Bradford co., Pa. The Iroquois settled here the Saponi, Tutelo, Nanticoke, Munsee, Mahican, and other fragmentary or conquered tribes living under their protection. It was the southern gateway to the country of the Iroquois, all of the great war-paths and hunting trails from the s. and s. w. centering here. Conrad Weiser passed through on his way to Onondaga in 1737. It was abandoned by the Indians in 1778, when they were preparing to retire before the Americans, and the deserted houses were burned by Col. Hartley on Sept. 27. A council was held here by Col. Thomas Pickering in 1790, when Farmer's Brothers (Fish Carrier) and Red Jacket were the chief speakers for the Indians. Col. Thomas Proctor passed through in 1791 when on his way to the council at Buffalo. In addition to the works below, consult Murray, Old Tioga Point, 1908. (J. M. J. P. D.)

Chaamonaqué.—Vaudreuil (1757) in N. Y. Doc. Col. Hist., x, 589, 1858 (Delaware name). Diabago.—Post (1758) quoted by Rupp, West Penn., app., 77, 1846 (misprint). Diahago.—Macauley, N. Y., II, 293, 1829. Diahoga.—Croghan (1757) in N. Y. Doc. Col. Hist., VII, 320, 1856. Ieaogo.—Johnson (1756) in R. I. Col. Rec., V, 529, 1860 (misprint). Iuragen.—Bellin map, 1755. Taaogo.—Ft Johnson conf. (1757) in N. Y. Doc. Col. Hist., VII, 260, 1856. Tä-yo'-ga.—Morgan, League Iroq., 470, 1851 (Cayuga and Seneca form). Teaogon.—James (1757) quoted by Proud, Penn., II, app., 60, 1798. Theaggen.—Pouchot map (1758) in N. Y. Doc. Col. Hist., x, 694, 1858. Théoga.—Vaudreuil (1757), ibid., 588. Théoge.—Ibid. Tiago.—Johnson (1757), ibid., VII, 279, 1856. Tiaoga.—Ft Johnson conf. (1756), ibid., 110. Tiaogos.—Guy Park conf. (1775), ibid., VIII, 560, 1857. Tiego.—Livermore (1779) in N. H. Hist. Soc. Coll., VI, 321, 1850. Tioga.—Jones (1780) in N. Y. Doc. Col. Hist., VIII, 785, 1857. Tioga Point.—Parsons (1756) in Archives of Pa., 2d s., II, 745, 1853. Tiyaoga.—Hawley (1755), ibid., VII, 49, 1856. Tiyaogo.—Johnson (1756), ibid., 149. Tiyoga.—Conf. (ca. 1755) quoted by Ruttenber, Tribes Hudson R., 225, 1872. Tohiccon.—Lewis Evans' map, 1749. Tohicon.—Map of 1768 in N. Y. Doc. Col. Hist., VIII, 1857. Tohikon.—Homann Heirs map, 1756. Toikon.—Esnauts and Rapilly map, 1777. Trijaoga.—Ft Johnson conf. (1756) in N. Y. Doc. Col. Hist., VII, 47, 1856. Trizaoga.—Hawley (1755), ibid., 47. Tyaoga.—Ft Johnson conf. (1756), ibid., 110. Tyoga.—Beatty (1779) quoted by Conover, Kan. and Geneva MS., B. A. E.

Tionontati ('there the mountain stands.'—Hewitt). A tribe formerly living in the mountains s. of Nottawasaga bay, in Grey and Simcoe cos., Ont. They were first visited in 1616 by the French, who called them the Nation du Petun, or Tobacco Nation, from their having large fields of tobacco. In 1640 the Jesuits established a mission among them. The tribe then had 2 clans, the Deer and the Wolf, and 9 villages. On the destruction of the Huron tribes by the Iroquois, in 1648–49, many of the fugitives took refuge with the Tionontati. This drew down upon the latter the anger of the Iroquois, who sent a strong force against them in Dec. 1649. Etarita, one of their principal villages, was surprised during the absence of the warriors, the houses burned, and many of the inhabitants, together with the missionary, massacred. The Tionontati, with the Hurons, who had joined them, now abandoned their country and fled to the region s. w. of L. Superior. In 1658 there were about 500 of the tribe at the Potawatomi mission of St Michel, near Green bay, Wis. Soon afterward they were with the Hurons at Shaugawaumikong (La Pointe), and about 1670 the two tribes were together at Mackinaw, at the entrance to L. Michigan. The Tionontati soon became blended with the Hurons, and the united tribes were henceforth known under the modernized name of Wyandot. As late, however, as 1721 the Tionontati, then living with the Hurons near Detroit, preserved their name and hereditary chieftaincies. They were frequently designated as Tionontati Hurons and have also been confounded with the Amikwa. Their villages, so far as their names are known, were Ehouae (St Pierre et St Paul), Ekarenniondi (St Matthieu), Etarita (St Jean), St Andre, St Barthelemy, St Jacques, St Jacques et St Philippe, St Simon et St Jude, St Thomas. (J. M.)

Chanundadies.—Lindesay (1751) in N. Y. Doc. Col. Hist., VI, 706, 1855. Chenondadees.—Johnson (1747), ibid., 359. Chenundady.—Johnson (1756), ibid., VII, 93, 1856. Chenundies.—Stoddart (1753), ibid., VI, 780, 1855. Chonondedeys.—Johnson (1747), ibid., 387. Denondadies.—Gale, Upper Miss., 164, 1867. Deonondade.—Schuyler (1702) in N. Y. Doc. Col. Hist., IV, 979, 1854. Deonondadies.—Colden (1727), Five Nat., 86, 1747. Dienondades.—Bellomont (1701) in N. Y. Doc. Col. Hist., IV, 834, 1854. Dinondadies.—Jefferys, Fr. Doms., pt. 1, 13, 1761. Dinondodies.—Williams, Vermont, I, 282, 1809. Dionnondadees.—Livingston (1699) in N. Y. Doc. Col. Hist., IV, 571, 1854. Dionondade.—Schuyler (1687), ibid., III, 478, 1853. Dionondadies.—Schoolcraft, Travels, 53, 1821. Dionondadoes.—Livingston (1691) in N. Y. Doc. Col. Hist., III, 781, 1853. Dionondages.—Canada Governor (1695), ibid., IV, 120, 1854. Dionondes.—Schuyler (1702), ibid., 979. Dionoudadie.—McKenney and Hall, Ind. Tribes, III, 79, 1854 (misprint). Donondades.—Canada Governor (1695) in N. Y. Doc. Col. Hist., IV, 122, 1854. Etionnontates.—Jes. Rel. 1670, 6, 1858. Étionnontatehronnons.—Ibid., 86. gens du Petun.—Champlain (1616), Œuvres, IV, 57, 1870. Innondadese.—Hansen (1700) in N. Y. Doc. Col. Hist., IV, 805, 1854. Ionontady-Hagas.—Weiser (1748) in Rupp, West Pa., app., 15, 1846 (made synonymous with Wyandot (q. v.), but apparently another form of Tionontati). Jenondades.—Bellomont (1700) in N. Y. Doc. Col. Hist., IV, 768, 1854. Jenondathese.—Romer, ibid., 799. Jenundadees.—Johnson (1756), ibid., VII, 86, 1856. Jonontady-nago.—Post (1758) in Proud, Pa., II, app., 113, 1798 (made synonymous with Wyandot, but apparently another form of Tionontati). Khionontateh-ronon.—Jes. Rel. 1640, 35, 1858. Khionontaterrhonons.—Jes. Rel. 1635, 33, 1858. Nation de Petun.—Jes. Rel. 1632, 14, 1858. nation du petum.—Champlain (1616), Œuvres, V, 1st pt., 274, 1870. Nation of Tobacco.—Parkman, Pioneers, 384, 1883. Perun.—Shea, Peñalosa, 83, 1882 (misprint). Perúu.—Duro, Don Diego de Peñalosa, 43, 1882. Petuneux.—Sagard (1632), Hist. Can., IV, Huron Dict., 1866. Quicunontateronons.—Sagard (1636), Can., II, 294, 1866 (misprint). Quiemltutz.—Coxe, Carolana, map, 1741 (misprint). Quiennontateronons.—Sagard (1636), Can., II, 325, 1866. Quieunontatéronons.—Sagard (1632), Hist. Can., IV, Huron Dict., 1866 (according to Hewitt, Quieunontati signifies 'where the mountain stands,' while Tionontati signifies 'there the mountain stands'). Shawendadies.—Colden (1727), Five Nat., app., 190, 1747. Tannontatez.—Lamberville (1686) in N. Y. Doc. Col. Hist., III, 489, 1853. Theonontateronons.—Lahontan, New Voy., I, 94, 1703. Thionontatoronons.—Du Chesneau (1681) in Margry, Déc., II, 267, 1877. Tienonadies.—Albany Conference (1726) in N. Y. Doc. Col. Hist., V, 794, 1855. Tienondaideaga.—Albany Conference (1723), ibid., 93. Tinontaté.—La Barre (1683), ibid., IX, 202, 1855. Tiohontatés.—Du Chesneau (1681), ibid., 164 (misprint). Tionnontantes Hurons.—Neill in Minn. Hist. Soc. Coll., V, 401, 1885. Tionnontatehronnons.—Jes. Rel. 1654, 9, 1858. Tionnontatez.—Frontenac (1682) in N. Y. Doc. Col. Hist., IX, 178, 1855. Tionnontatz.—Memoir of 1706, ibid., 802. Tionnonthatez.—La Potherie, III, 143, 1753. Tionnotanté.—Jes. Rel. 1672, 35, 1858. Tionondade.—Livingston (1687) in N. Y. Doc. Col. Hist., III, 443, 1853. Tionontalies.—Domenech, Deserts, I, 444, 1860. Tionontatés.—Du Chesneau (1681) in N. Y. Doc. Col. Hist., IX, 164, 1855. Tobacco Indians.—Schoolcraft, Ind. Tribes, IV, 203, 1854. Tronontes.—Alcedo, Dic. Geog., II, 630, 1787 (possibly identical). Tsomontatez.—Heriot, Travels, 192, 1813 (misprint). T. Son-non-ta-tex.—Macauley, N. Y., II, 174, 1829. Tuinondadeoks.—Ibid. Tuinontatek.—Parkman, Jesuits, xliii, note, 1883. Tyo-non-ta-te'-kā'.—Hewitt, Onondaga MS., B. A. E. (Onondaga name). Younondadys.—Document of 1747 in N. Y. Doc. Col. Hist., VI, 391, 1855.

Tiopane. A tribe, apparently distinct from the Copane, whom the name suggests, living in the 18th century between San Antonio, Texas, and the coast, a habitat close to that of the Copane. In 1733 they were mentioned as one of the tribes that sheltered the Espíritu Santo de Zúñiga mission from the Apache (Gov. Almazan in Autos sobre Providencias, Archivo Gen.). In 1737 they were referred to as the tribe that lived below the crossing of Guadalupe r., probably that between San Antonio and Espíritu Santo de Zúñiga (Complaints of Neophytes, in Archivo Gen., Misiones, XXI). Some of them were taken to the San Antonio missions, and in 1737 they, with the Pastia, fled, and Gov. Sandoval was unable to recover them (ibid.). (H. E. B.)

Sayupanes.—Almazan, Autos sobre Providencias, 1733, MS.

Tiopines. A Coahuiltecan tribe of Texas, identical with the Chayopines of García's Manual (1760). It seems that Tiopines was the earlier form of the name, because in 1754 a missionary at San Antonio asserted that the Tiopines "are now called Chayopines" (Arch. Col. Santa Cruz de Querétaro, K, leg. 4, no. 15, MS.). They may be identical with the Tiopanes (q. v.) or Sayupanes. The Tiopines were one of the "four large nations" which deserted the San José mission at San Antonio early in its career (Petition of Fray Santa Ana, 1750, in Mem. de Nueva España, XXVIII, 140, MS.). Later they became one of the leading tribes at San Juan Capistrano mission. In 1737 they were there with the Tilojá, Orejon, Venado, and other tribes clearly Coahuiltecan. In 1738, 120 runaways of the tribe were recovered from the forest (Lamar Papers, no. 37, MS.). In 1768 they were mentioned as being on Rio Frio, but in 1780 the governor of Texas said their home was near the coast, E. of the Nueces (Cabello, Rep. on Coast Tribes, 1780, MS.). As late as 1780 they were still living at San Juan Capistrano mission (ibid.). (H. E. B.)

Chapopines.—Taylor in Cal. Farmer, Apr. 17, 1863. Chayopines.—García, Manual, title, 1760. Saiopines.—Lamar Papers, no. 37, 10, 1738, MS. Sayopina.—Morfi, Mem. Hist. Tex., MS., bk. II, *ca.* 1782. Sayopines.—Doc. of 1750 in Mem. de Nueva España, XXVIII, 140, MS. Zacopines.—Lamar Papers, no. 37, 1, MS. (miscopy for Zaiopines?).

Tiosahrondion (early Huron form, *Te-ʻoʻchanontian* (1653), probably cognate with Mohawk *Tiioʻsarroñʹnionʹ*, 'There where many (beaver) dams are': from initial prefix *ti-*, the transdirective sign, 'there', 'thither'; *io-*, the compound prefix pronoun of the third person, singular number, zoic gender, 'it-it'; *-ʻsar-*, the nominal stem of *oʻsaʹrǎʹ* or *oʻtceʹrǎʹ* (a dialectic variant) signifying 'a (beaver) dam'; *-roñ*, the verb-stem, '(to) place athwart,' and the adverbial suffix, *-nionʹ*, 'many times', 'many places'). The present Iroquoian name of Detroit, Mich. There seems to be good evidence that the name did not originally belong to this spot. The Huron term, cited above, was first used in the Journal des Jésuites for 1653 (Jesuit Relations, Thwaites ed., XXXVIII, 181, 1899) in conjunction with the place name *Skenʻchioʻe*, 'place of the foxes,' which was there represented to be "toward *Teʻoʻchanontian*," that is to say, "toward the place of the beaver-dams," meaning, evidently vaguely, in the beaver-hunting country. Inland on both sides of the strait connecting L. Huron with L. Erie there were noted beaver grounds, and their importance was so great in the 17th century that Lahontan marked the chief places on his map; there were also well-known beaver grounds lying between the Maumee and Wabash rs. In 1701 the Five Nations gave a deed of trust to the English King of their "beaver-hunting ground" (called Canagariarchio, i. e. *Ganaʹgariaʹ-Kontceriio*, 'it beaver is fine'), a part of which land "runns till it butts upon the Twichtwichs [Miami]," comprising the "country where the bevers, the deers, elks, and such beasts keep and the place called Tieugsachrondie, alias Fort de Tret or Wawyachtenok" (N. Y. Doc. Col. Hist., IV, 908, 1854). At an early period the French realized the great importance of this strait, for it was the key to the three upper lakes and all their dependencies, and gave ready access to the Mississippi by way of Maumee r. and a portage of only 9 m. into the Wabash. So in 1686 Denonville (realizing that if this pass was held by the French, the English would be barred from the Mississippi and the great N. W., but if seized and held by the British, the Canadian fur-trade would be ruined) ordered Greysolon Du Luth to build a small picket fort, giving it the name Gratiot, which he occupied for a short time. In 1688 the Five Nations complained to Gov. Dongan, of New York, asking him to demolish the fort built two years previously. Later Cadillac proposed to establish there a permanent settlement and military post. In this proposal he met with strong opposition by those whose interests would be affected, and also by the Jesuits; finally, however, convincing the proper authorities of the feasibility of his plan and of the immense interests which it would conserve and protect, he began, on July 24, 1701, the picket Fort Pontchartrain, which was about 60 yds square and situated about 120 ft from the river.

In the same year the Five Nations complained that the Hurons had come to dwell at Tiosahrondion and that they had thereby disturbed their beaver and elk hunting; they asserted that they had owned these hunting grounds for 60 (approximately 45) years, and that although the governors of New York and Canada had both admitted that these lands belonged to them, a fort had been built there by the French. To these remonstrances the French governor replied that the fort had been built for their sole benefit, for supplying them with powder and lead and other things needed in their hunting, and to prevent war between them and the Ottawa. At the same time the Hurons complained that the Missisauga (Waganhaes) had taken their beaver-hunting grounds and desired the French governor to remove the Missisauga to their own hunting lands. In 1700 they declared that this was "the only place of beaver hunting." In 1702, 24 "Farr Indians," probably Miami and Wyandot, informed the Five Nations that they had come to dwell at Tiosahrondion, "at one end of your house." The French had previously ordered their Indian allies to make peace with the Five Nations. As early as 1727 many small tribes and parts of tribes, as the Wyandot, Miami, Foxes, Sauk, Ottawa, Missisauga and Potawatomi, had their villages in the vicinity of Tiosahrondion. Ten years later 130 Shawnee warriors asked permission of the Governor of New York and of the Five Nations to go to dwell at Tiosahrondion, because the Seneca and the Cayuga had sold their lands on the Susquehanna from under their feet.

Hennepin (New Discovery, 1697) says that L. Erie was called by the Iroquois *Erigé Tejocharontiong*, which signifies "At the place of the Erie people, there where many (beaver) dams are.'' (J. N. B. H.)

Erigé Tejocharontiong.—Hennepin, Nouvelle Découverte, 49, 1697. **Tahsagrondie.**—Colden (1727), Hist. Five Nations, 22, 1747. **Tahsahgrondie.**—Douglass, Summary, I, 180, 1755. **Te'o'chanontian.**—Jes. Rel. (1653), Thwaites ed., XXXVIII, 181, 1899. **Teughsaghrontey.**—London Doc. (1754) in N. Y. Doc. Col. Hist., VI, 899, 1855. **Tieugsachrondio.**—London Doc. (1701), ibid., IV, 908, 1854. **Tircksarondia.**—London Doc. (1688), ibid., 532. **Tjeughsaghrondie.**—London Doc. (1701), ibid., 909. **Tjeugsaghronde.**—Ibid. **Tjguhsaghrondy.**—Ibid., 892. **Tjughsaghrondie.**—London Doc. (1702), ibid., 979. **Toghsaghrondie.**—London Doc. (1770), ibid., V, 694, 1855. **Tonsagroende.**—Ibid., 543. **Trongsagroende.**—London Doc. (1720), ibid. **Tuchsaghrondie.**—Ibid., VI, 105, 1855. **Tucksagrandie.**—Ibid., 103. **Tuighsaghrondy.**—London Doc. (1701), ibid., IV, 891, 1854. **Tusachrondie.**—London Doc. (1726), ibid., V, 792, 1855. **Tushsaghrendie.**—Ibid., VI, 107, 1855. **Tussaghrondie.**—Ibid., 99. **Tyschsarondia.**—London Doc. (1688), ibid., III, 536, 1853. **Wawiaghtenhook.**—London Doc. (1754), ibid., VI, 899, 1855.

Tiou. A people on lower Mississippi and Yazoo rs., mentioned only during the earlier periods of French colonization in Louisiana. Tradition states that they were once very numerous, but that having been vanquished by the Chickasaw, they fled from their ancient seats, apparently on the upper Yazoo r., to the Natchez, who protected them and allowed them to form a distinct village. It is recorded in Margry (Déc., IV, 429, 1880) that the Bayogoula having prior to Mar. 1700 killed in a conflict all the Mugulasha within their reach, called in families of the Acolapissa and Tiou to occupy their deserted fields and lodges. In 1731, shortly after the Natchez uprising, they are said to have been cut off entirely by the Quapaw, and although this is doubtful, they are not heard of again. Du Pratz informs us that they possessed the *r* sound in their language. If this is true their language was not Muskhogean proper, Natchez, or Siouan, but formed one group with Tunica, Koroa, Yazoo, and perhaps Grigra. (J. R. S.)

Little Tioux.—Dumont in French, Hist. Coll. La., V, 59, 1853. **Sioux.**—Jefferys, Fr. Dom. Am., pt. I, 145, 1761 (misprint). **Teoux.**—McKenney and Hall, Ind. Tribes, III, 81, 1854. **Theoux.**—Boudinot, Star in the West, 129, 1816. **Thioux.**—Jefferys, op. cit., 162. **Thoucoue.**—Iberville (1699) in Margry, Déc., IV, 179, 1880. **Thysia.**—Ibid. **Tiaoux.**—Romans, Florida, I, 101, 1775. **Tihiou.**—Coxe, Carolana, map, 1741. **Tiou.**—La Salle (ca. 1680) in Margry, Déc., II, 198, 1877. **Tioux.**—Dumont, La., I, 135, 1753. **Toaux.**—Baudry des Lozières, Voy. Louisiane, 245, 1802 (misspelled for Teaux).

Tipi (from the Siouan root *ti* 'to dwell', *pi* 'used for'). The ordinary conical skin dwelling of the Plains tribes and of some of those living farther to the N. W. The tipi must be distinguished from the wigwam, wikiup, hogan, and other types of residence structures in use in other sections of the country.

The tipi consisted of a circular framework of poles brought together near the top and covered with dressed buffalo skins sewn to form a single piece, which was kept in place by means of wooden pins and ground pegs. It commonly had about 20 poles, averaging 25 ft in length, each pole being hewn from a stout sapling, usually cedar, trimmed down to the heart wood. The poles were set firmly in the ground so as to make a circle of about 15 ft in diameter, and were held together above by means of a hide rope wound around the whole bunch about 4 ft from the upper ends, leaving these ends projecting above the tipi covering. There were 3 main poles, or with some tribes 4, upon which the weight of the others rested. The cover consisted of from 15

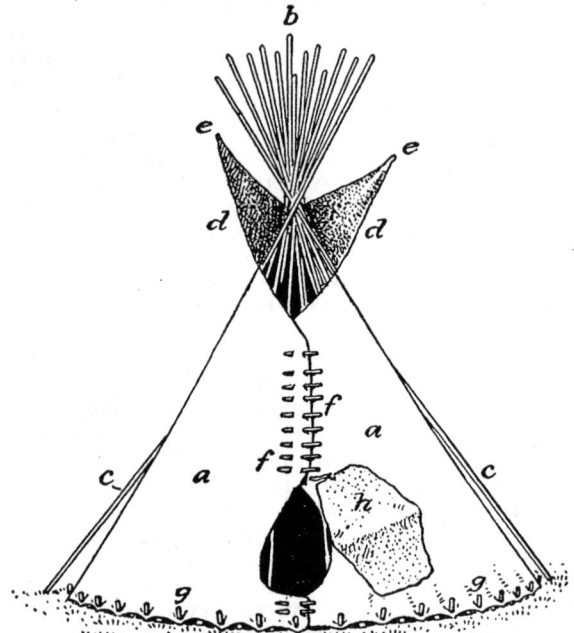

TIPI DIAGRAM (KIOWA STANDARD): *a* Cover (average 18 to 20 buffalo hides). *b* Poles (average 20, besides 2 outside poles). *c* Two outside poles, or flap poles. *d* Flaps (for diverting draft and smoke). *e* "Ears" or pockets at top of flaps for inserting ends of outside poles. *f* Pins for pinning together the two sides of tipi cover (average 8, i. e., 2 below door and 6 above). *g* Pegs for holding edge of tipi cover to ground (average 20). *h* Door, usually a skin kept stretched by means of a transverse stick, or by a hoop frame. Inside, in the middle of the floor, is the fire-pit. There are names for special poles, for ornaments and other attachments, etc.

to 18 dressed buffalo skins cut and fitted in such a way that, when sewn together with sinew thread, they formed a single large sheet of nearly semicircular shape. This was lifted into place against the framework by means of a special pole at the back of the structure, after which the two ends were brought around to the front and there fastened by means of 8 or 10 small wooden pins running upward from the doorway nearly to the crossing of the poles. The lower border was kept in place by means of pegs driven into the ground at a distance of about 2 ft apart around the circle. The doorway faced the E., the usual door being a piece of dressed skin stretched over a rectangular or elliptical frame, frequently decorated with porcupine quills or other ornaments. The dressed skin of a panther, coyote, or buffalo calf, with the hairy side outward, was sometimes used. The fire-pit was directly in the center, and the smoke escaped through the opening in the top, at the crossing of the poles. By means of movable skin flaps on each side of the smoke hole, the course of the smoke could be regulated as the wind shifted, the flaps being kept in place by 2 poles on the outside of the tipi. There were commonly 3 beds or seats, one at each side and one at the back of the tipi, each consisting of a long platform covered with a sort of mat of light willow rods, over which were thrown buffalo robes or blankets. The head end of the mat usually hung from a tripod in hammock fashion. Decorated curtains above the beds kept off the drops of water which came through the smoke hole in rainy weather. The ground was the floor, the part nearest the beds being sometimes cut off from the open space by means of a circular border of interwoven twigs. In warm weather the lower part of the tipi cover was raised to allow the breeze to pass through. In cold weather the open space around the bottom was chinked with grass. The tipi was renewed every one or two years, its completion being the occasion of a dedicatory ceremony, and those of prominent families decorated with heraldic paintings and other ornaments. On account of its exact adaptability to the necessities of prairie life, the tipi was taken by Gen. Sibley as the model for the tent which bears his name. Owing to the smaller number of ponies available for dragging the poles, the tipis of the northern tribes were usually fewer in proportion and larger in size than among the southern tribes. According to Grinnell, the Blackfeet in ancient times had a sort of large triple tipi, with 3 fireplaces. See *Habitations, Skin and Skin-dressing.* (J. M.)

Tipitiwitchet. A former popular name for *Dionæa muscipula*, the Venus's fly-trap, or hog-eye, a North Carolina plant, now nearly extinct, noted for the extraordinary irritability of its leaves, which, when touched by an insect, collapse with a sudden spring and imprison the intruder. The word is from Renape (Virginia Algonquian) *titipiwitshik*, 'they (leaves) which wind around (or involve)'. (W. R. G.)

Tiposies. A hostile tribe, probably Moquelumnan, living N. and E. of San Joaquin r., among the foothills of the Sierra Nevada, on the headwaters of Tuolumne,

Merced, and Mariposa rs., Cal.—Barbour et al. (1851) in Sen. Ex. Doc. 4, 32d Cong., spec. sess., 61, 1853.

Tipoti. Mentioned by Oñate in 1598 (Doc. Inéd., XVI, 102, 1871) as a pueblo of New Mexico, in connection with others, apparently belonging to Keresan Indians.

Tipoy. An unidentified village visited by La Salle in 1686 on his first journey from Ft St Louis, on Matagorda bay, Texas, to search overland for the Mississippi. An Indian from the tribe guided him to the friendly Anami, whom he reached the following day. See Cavelier de la Salle in Shea, Early Voy., 40, 1861.

Tippecanoe (properly *Kitapkwănŭnk* or *Kitapkwănŭnka*, 'buffalo-fish place,' the Miami name for the stream at that point, from *kitápkwan*, 'buffalo-fish.' The corresponding Potawatomi form, according to McCoy, is *Kē-tăp'-ē-kŏn*. Trumbull's interpretation of 'at the great clearing' is probably based on a misconception of the Delaware form, which seems to contain the prefix *kehti*, 'great.'—J. P. Dunn). A noted village site on the w. bank of the Wabash, just below the mouth of Tippecanoe r., in Tippecanoe co., Ind. It was originally occupied by the Miami, the earliest known occupants of the region, and later by the Shawnee, who were in possession when it was attacked and destroyed by the Americans under Wilkinson in 1791, at which time it contained 120 houses. It was soon after rebuilt and occupied by the Potawatomi, and finally on their invitation became in 1808 the headquarters of Tecumseh and his brother, the Prophet, with their followers, whence the name Prophetstown. Their attitude becoming threatening, Gen. William Henry Harrison marched with 900 troops against the town, which was defended by about the same number of warriors recruited from all the neighboring tribes. When near the town, at daybreak of Nov. 7, 1811, his army was attacked by the Indians, under command of the Prophet, Tecumseh himself being then absent in the S. The desperate engagement that followed, known in history as the Battle of Tippecanoe, resulted in the complete defeat and dispersion of the Indians, with a loss on each side of from 50 to 60 killed and a very large proportion of wounded. The site was reoccupied for a short time a few years later. From this victory Harrison was properly and affectionately styled "Old Tippecanoe," and in his presidential campaign in 1848 a song with the refrain of "Tippecanoe and Tyler too" became the rallying cry of his supporters. Consult Mooney, Ghost Dance, 14th Rep. B. A. E., 1896. (J. M.)

Kathtippecamunk.—Brown, West. Gaz., 72, 1817. Ketapekon.—Dunn, True Indian Stories, 307, 1908 ("Ketapekon town, or place": given as meaning of Tippecanoe). Kē-tăp'-ē-kŏn-nŏng.—Ibid. (full name). **Kethepecannank.**—Rupp, W. Penn., 264, 1846. **Kethtipecanunk.**—Scott (1791) in Am. State Papers, Ind. Aff., I, 131, 1832. **Kethtipiconunck.**—Scott, ibid., 133. **Pems-quah-a-wa.**—Hough, map in Indiana Geol. Rep. 1882, 1883 (misprint of Prophet's name). **Prophet's Town.**—Heald (1812) in Am. State Papers, Ind. Aff., I, 806, 1832. **Quitepcomuais.**—Hamtramck (ca. 1790), ibid., 87. **Quitepiconnae.**—Gamelin (1790), ibid., 93. **Tippacanoe.**—Schermerhorn (1812) in Mass. Hist. Soc. Coll., 2d s., II, 5, 1814. **Tippecanoe.**—Wilkinson (1791) in Am. State Papers, Ind. Aff., I, 135, 1832.

Tippecanoe. A Miami village which preceded that of the Shawnee on the same site.
Atihipi-Catouy.—Iberville (ca. 1703) in Margry, Déc., IV, 597, 1880. **Ortithipicatony.**—Iberville as quoted in Minn. Hist. Soc. Coll., I, 341, 1872.

Tipsinah. A name of "the wild prairie turnip, used as food by the northwestern Indians" (Bartlett, Dict. of Americanisms, 707, 1877). This plant is also known as the Dakota turnip, and tipsinah is derived from *tipsiⁿna*, its name in the Sioux language. (A. F. C.)

Tipsistaca. A village, presumably Costanoan, formerly connected with San Juan Bautista mission, Cal.
Tipisastac.—Engelhardt, Franc. in Cal., 398, 1897. **Tipsistaca.**—Taylor in Cal. Farmer, Nov. 23, 1860.

Tirans. A Delaware tribe or band formerly living on the N. shore of Delaware bay, about Cape May or Cumberland co., N. J.
Tiascons.—Evelin (1648) quoted by Proud, Penn., I, 114, 1797. **Tirans.**—Ibid.

Tisattunne. A former Chastacosta village on the N. bank of Rogue r., Oreg.
Ti-sat ̣ûnnĕ.—Dorsey in Jour. Am. Folk-lore, III, 234, 1890.

Tisechu. The principal village of the Choinimni, at the confluence of King's r. and Mill cr., s. central California.
Tis-ē'-chu.—Powers in Cont. N. A. Ethnol., III, 370, 1877. **Tishech.**—A. L. Kroeber, inf'n, 1907 (Yokuts dialectic form). **Tishechu.**—Ibid. (another form).

Tisepan (*tis*='cottonwood'). A Chiricahua clan or band at San Carlos agency, Ariz. They may be identical with the Tizsessinaye and correlated to the Titsessenaye of the Pinal Coyoteros.
Dosapon.—White, MS. Hist. Apaches, B. A. E., 1875. **Sapon.**—Gatschet, Zwölf Sprachen, 65, 1876. **Tisépán.**—ten Kate, Reizen in N. A., 197, 1885. **Tosepón.**—Gatschet, Yuma-Spr., IX, 371, 1877 (trans. 'make bread').

Tishim. The tribal name given for the mother of a child baptized at San Antonio de Valero mission, Texas, in 1753. The only clue to the affiliation of her tribe is that she was married to a Yojuan, whose tribe was Tonkawan (Valero Baptisms, 1753, partida, 874, MS.). (H. E. B.)

Tishrawa. Given as a Karok village just below the junction of Salmon and Klamath rs., N. w. Cal., in 1851.
Tish-rawa.—Gibbs (1851) in Schoolcraft, Ind. Tribes, III, 150, 1853.

Tishum (*Ti'-shum*). A small settlement of the Maidu on the right bank of Feather r., Cal., between the Bear and the Yuba.
Teeshums.—Powers in Overland Mo., XII, 420, 1874. **Ti'-shum.**—Powers in Cont. N. A. Ethnol., III, 282, 1877.

Tisquantum. See *Squanto*.

Tistontaraetonga. An unidentified tribe destroyed by the Iroquois a few years before 1680.—La Salle (1682) in Margry, Déc., II, 237, 1878.

Tiswin. See *Fermentation*.

Titami. See *Tatemy*.

Titicut (*Keh-teih-tuk-qut*, 'on the great river.'—Eliot). A village of Christian Indians in Middleborough town, Plymouth co., Mass., near the present Titicut, probably subject to the Massachuset. In 1698 the inhabitants numbered 40 adults. They sold their last land in 1760. (J. M.)
Cotuhticut.—Drake, Bk. Inds., bk. 3, 10, 1848. **Cotuhtikut.**—Bourne (1674) in Mass. Hist. Soc. Coll., 1st s., I, 198, 1806. **Kehtehticut.**—Rawson and Danforth (1698), ibid., X, 134, 1809. **Kekettiout.**—Writer of 1818, ibid., 2d s., VII, 143, 1818. **Ketchiquut.**—Cotton (1674), ibid., 1st s., I, 200, 1806. **Ketehiquut.**—Backus, ibid., III, 150, 1794. **Ketehtequtt.**—Cotton (1678), ibid., 4th s., VIII, 245, 1868. **Ketticut.**—Writer of 1818, ibid., 2d s., VII, 143, 1818. **Teeticut.**—Winthrop (1636), ibid., 4th s., VI, 514, 1863. **Teightaquid.**—Record of 1644, ibid., 2d s., VII, 137, 1818. **Tetehquet.**—Drake, Bk. Inds., bk. 3, 10, 1848. **Teticut.**—Mass. Hist. Soc. Coll., 2d s., IV, 280, 1816 (the river). **Tihtacutt.**—Eliot (1648), ibid., 3d s., IV, 81, 1834. **Titacutt.**—Winslow (1637), ibid., 4th s., VI, 163, 1863. **Titecute.**—Coddington (1640), ibid., 316. **Titicott.**—Hinckley (1685), ibid., V, 133, 1861. **Titicut.**—Backus, ibid., 1st s., III, 150, 1794.

Titiyu. A village, presumably Costanoan, formerly connected with Dolores mission, San Francisco, Cal.—Taylor in Cal. Farmer, Oct. 18, 1861.

Titlas. An Indian "province," E. of Quivira, which the abbess María de Jesus, of Agreda, Spain, claimed to have miraculously visited in the 17th century.
Tidam.—Zárate-Salmerón (ca. 1629), Relación, in Land of Sunshine, 187, 1900 (apparently identical). **Tulas.**—Vetancurt (1692) in Teatro Mex., III, 303, 1871 (evidently identical).

Titlogat. An Ahtena village, not identified, probably of the Koltshan division.—Wrangell quoted by Dall in Cont. N. A. Ethnol., I, 32, 1877.

Titsessinaye ('little cottonwood jungle'). A clan or band of the Pinal Coyoteros, correlated with the clan of like name among the White Mountain Apache of Arizona (Bourke in Jour. Am. Folk-lore, III, 112, 1890). See *Tisepan*.

Titshotina. A Nahane tribe inhabiting the country between the Cassiar mts. and Liard and Dease rs., Brit. Col. In 1887 they numbered 70 persons.
Achéto-tinneh.—Dall, Alaska, 106, 1870 (= 'people living out of the wind'). **Ti-tsho-tī-na.**—Dawson in Rep. Geol. Surv. Can. 1888, 200B, 1889.

Titskanwatichatak ('real Tonkawa'). A Tonkawa clan.
Titskan wa'titch a'tak.—Gatschet, Tonkawa MS. vocab., B. A. E., 1884.

Titukilsk. A Knaiakhotana village on the E. shore of Cook inlet, Alaska, containing 57 persons in 1880.—Petroff in 10th Census, Alaska, 29, 1884.

Titymagg. A name used by the first English settlers in the Hudson bay country for the whitefish (*Coregonus albus*). Ellis (Voy. to Hudson's Bay, 185, 1748) says it was called by the French whitefish, but by the Indians and English *titymagg*. This word is evidently a corruption of the Chippewa *atikameg*, in Cree *atikkamek*, 'caribou fish,' from *ati'k*, 'deer,' 'caribou,' and *amek*, 'fish.' In Rep. U. S. Fish Com., 1894, *attihawhmeg* is given as a name of the Labrador whitefish (*C. Labrad.*), another species. (A. F. C.)

Tiubta. A village of the Kalendaruk division of the Costanoan family, formerly connected with San Carlos mission, Cal.—Taylor in Cal. Farmer, Apr. 20, 1860.

Tiun (*Tī'ʌn*). A Haida town of the Dostlan-lnagai family, formerly on the w. coast of Graham id., s. of Port Lewis, Queen Charlotte ids., Brit. Col. In the Skidegate dialect this is T!ī'gʌn, which is said to mean 'Slaughter village.' It is probably the settlement referred to in John Work's list (1846) as "Too," with 10 houses and 196 inhabitants. It was one of the first places occurring in his list to be abandoned. (J. R. S.)
Ti'ʌn.—Swanton, Cont. Haida, 280, 281, 1905. Tian Ilnigē.—Harrison in Proc. Roy. Soc. Can., sec. II, 124, 1895. T!ī'gʌn.—Swanton, op. cit. Too.—Work (1846) in Kane, Wand. in N. A., app., 4, 1859 (probably identical).

Tiveçocayo. Mentioned by Oviedo (Hist. Gen. Indies, III, 628, 1853) as one of the provinces or villages visited by Ayllon. The word owes its origin to a false division of two succeeding names which should read "Anicative [or rather Anicatiya], Çocayo." The first is unidentified; the second undoubtedly refers to the Coosa of South Carolina.

Tiyochesli ('dungs in the lodge'). A modern Oglala Sioux band.
Tiyoćesli.—Dorsey (after Cleveland) in 15th Rep. B. A. E., 221, 1897. Tiyotcesli.—Ibid.

Tiyochesli. A band of the Brulé Teton Sioux.
Tiyoćesli.—Dorsey (after Cleveland) in 15th Rep. B. A. E., 219, 1897. Tiyotcesli.—Ibid.

Tiyopaoshannunpa ('smokes at the entrance to the lodge'). A band of the Sans Arcs Sioux.
Tiyopa-oćaⁿnuⁿpa.—Dorsey in 15th Rep. B. A. E., 219, 1897. Tiyopa-otcaⁿnuⁿpa.—Ibid.

Tizaptan ('five lodges'). A Sisseton Sioux band.
Ti-zaptaⁿ.—Dorsey in 15th Rep. B. A. E., 217, 1897. Ti-zaptaŋ.—Ibid. Tizaptaŋna.—S. R. Riggs, letter to Dorsey, 1882.

Tizaptan. A Sihasapa Sioux band; perhaps the same as Glaglahesha.—Swift, letter to J. O. Dorsey, 1884.

Tizhu. A Quapaw gens, now extinct.
Ti'ju.—Dorsey in 15th Rep. B. A. E., 230, 1897.

Tizonazo. A former Tepehuane pueblo in Durango, Mexico, which, according to Orozco y Berra, was occupied by people of the Salineros and Cabezas tribes until they participated in the rebellion of the Toboso, when they were exterminated and the pueblo repeopled with Opata from Ures (q. v.), in Sonora.
S. José del Tizonazo.—Orozco y Berra, Geog., 318, 1864. Tizonazo.—Zapata (1678) in Doc. Hist. Mex., 4th s., III, 310, 1857.

Tizsessinaye ('little cottonwood jungle'). An Apache clan or band at San Carlos and Ft Apache, Ariz., in 1881; corresponding to the Titsessinaye and the Destchetinaye among the Pinal Coyotero.
Chiz-ches-che-nay.—White, Apache names of Ind. Tribes, MS., B. A. E. (trans. 'rocky country and woody country'). Tit-sessinaye.—Bourke in Jour. Am. Folk-lore, III, 112, 1890.

Tkeiktskune (*Tx·ē'ix·tskunē*). A Bellacoola village on the N. side of Bellacoola r., Brit. Col., near its mouth. It was one of the eight villages called Nuhalk.
Nutнē'ıнtskōnē.—Boas in 7th Rep. N. W. Tribes Can., 3, 1891. Tx·ē'ix·tskunē.—Boas in Mem. Am. Mus. Nat. Hist., II, 49, 1900.

Tkhakiyu. A Yaquina village on the N. side of Yaquina r., Oreg., on a small stream E. of Newport.
T'k'qa'-ki-yu.—Dorsey in Jour. Am. Folk-lore, III, 229, 1890.

Tkhlunkhastunne. A band of the Mishikhwutmetunne, who dwelt on Upper Coquille r., Oreg., next to the Kusan and below Coquille City.
Tqlûn-qas' ṭûnně'.—Dorsey in Jour. Am. Folk-lore, III, 232, 1890.

Tkimeye. A Kuitsh village at Winchester bay, near Umpqua r., Oreg.
Tki'-mi-ye'.—Dorsey in Jour. Am. Folk-lore, III, 231, 1890.

Tktakai (*T"k·takai*, 'vine-maple'). A Squawmish village on the right bank of Squawmisht r., Brit. Col.—Hill-Tout in Rep. Brit. A. A. S., 474, 1900.

Tkulmashaauk. A Yaquina village on the s. side of Yaquina r., Oreg.
T'kûl-ma'-ca-auk'.—Dorsey in Jour. Am. Folk-lore, III, 229, 1890.

Tkwakwamish. A former Salish division on Puyallup r. and Vashon id., Wash.; pop. about 50 in 1853.
T'Kawkwamish.—Gibbs in Cont. N. A. Ethnol., I, 178, 1877. T'kwakwamish.—Gibbs quoted by Dall in Cont. N. A. Ethnol., I, 241, 1877. T'Qua-quamish.—Gibbs in Pac. R. R. Rep., I, 435, 1855.

Tkwuratum. Given as an Okinagan band at the mouth of Okinakane r., Wash.
T'Kwuratum.—Gibbs in Pac. R. R. Rep., I, 412, 1855.

Tlaaluis (*Laa'luîs*). One of the five original septs of the Lekwiltok, living on the coast of British Columbia between Bute and Loughborough inlets. After the great war between the Kwakiutl and the Salish they were so reduced in numbers that they joined the Kueha as another gens. (J. R. S.)
Ā-wā-oo.—Dawson in Trans. Roy. Soc. Can., sec. II, 65, 1887. Clal-lu-i-is.—Kane, Wand. in N. A., app., 1859. Laa'luîs.—Boas in Rep. U. S. Nat. Mus. 1895, 332, 1897. Tlaáluis.—Boas in Petermanns Mitteil., pt. 5, 131, 1887.

Tlachtana ('weavers of grass mats'). A Knaiakhotana clan of Cook inlet, Alaska.—Richardson, Arct. Exped., I, 406, 1851.

Tlaiq (*Tlāiq*). A Wikeno village on Rivers inlet, Brit. Col.—Boas in Petermanns Mitteil., pt. 5, 130, 1887.

Tlakatlala (*Lā'qaLala*). A Chinookan tribe formerly living on the N. bank of Columbia r. in Cowlitz co., Wash., about

3 m. above Oak Point.—Boas, Kathlamet Texts, 6, 1901.

Tlakaumoot (*Tl'ak·aumō'ot*). A division of the people of Nuskelst, a Bellacoola town.—Boas in 7th Rep. N. W. Tribes Can., 3, 1891.

Tlakluit (*Ila'xluit*, their own name, of unknown meaning). A Chinookan tribe formerly occupying the N. side of Columbia r. in Klickitat co., Wash., from about 6 m. above The Dalles down to the neighborhood of White Salmon r. They adjoined Shahaptian tribes on the E. and N., while the Chilluckittequaw, known also as White Salmon Indians, were their neighbors in the w. Their farthest point E. was a small island bearing a name meaning 'Atatahlia's roasting place,' in allusion to a mythical incident; proceeding westward their villages were: Wayagwa; Wakemap; Wishram (properly called Nixlúidix·), about 5 m. above The Dalles; Shikeldaptikh, about ½ m. below; Shabanshksh, a mile below Wishram; Skukskhat; Wasnaniks; Niukhtash, at Big Eddy; Hliluseltshlikh; Gawishila, a fishing station; Chalaitgelit; Kwalasints, opposite The Dalles; Gawilapchk, a winter village; Nayakkhachikh, another winter village; Tsapkhadidlit, a wintering place; Shkonana, opposite Crate's Point; Shkagech; Hladakhat, about 10 m. below The Dalles; Shgwaliksh, about 2 m. below (perhaps a Klikitat village); Waginkhak, ½ m. below.

In 1806 Lewis and Clark estimated their number at 1,000. They participated in the Yakima treaty of 1855, but most of them have never gone on the Yakima reservation, although they are nominally under its jurisdiction. They are tribally, but not linguistically, distinct from the Wasco (q. v.). The tribe became notorious for the trouble they caused the early traders and settlers in making the portage at their principal village, Wishram. Their present number is about 150, some of whom live regularly in their fishing village of Wishram on the Columbia. About half this number are mixed bloods. See Sapir, Wishram Texts, Pub. Am. Ethnol. Soc., II, 1909. (L. F. E. S.)

Echebools.—Robertson, Oregon, 129, 1846 (misquoted from Lewis and Clark). E-chee-lute.—Clark (1805) in Orig. Jour. Lewis and Clark, III, 183, 1905. E-che-lute.—Lewis and Clark Exped., II, 142, 1814. E-che-lute.—Clark (1805) in Orig. Jour. Lewis and Clark, III, 164, 1905. Ehelutes.—Lewis (1806), ibid., IV, 73, 1905. Eloot.—Lewis and Clark ·Exped., II, 217, 1814. E-lute.—Clark (1806) in Orig. Jour. Lewis and Clark, IV, 240, 1905. E-skel-lute.—Clark (1806), ibid., VI, 115, 1905. Eskeloot.—Morse, Rep. to Sec. War, 370, 1822. Hellwits.—Ibid., 369. Helwit.—Mooney in 14th Rep. B. A. E., 740, 1896. Iła'xluit.—Sapir in Pub. Am. Ethnol. Soc., II, x, 1909 (own name). Nihaloitih.—Hale in U. S. Expl. Exped., VI, 569, 1846. Nishrams.—Alvord (1853) in Schoolcraft, Ind. Tribes, V, 653, 1855. Ouichram.—Hunt in Nouv. Ann. Voy., X, 81, 1821. Tchelouits.—Stuart, ibid., XII, 26, 1821. Tchilouit.—Mooney in 14th Rep. B. A. E., 740, 1896. Tchiloutts.—Stuart in Nouv. Ann. Voy., X, 112, 1821. Telhuemit.—Schoolcraft Ind. Tribes, VI, 702, 1857. Tilhalluvit.—Lane in Ind. Aff. Rep., 162, 1850. Tilhiellewit.—Lane (1849) in Sen. Ex. Doc. 52, 31st Cong., 1st sess., 174, 1850. Tilhilooit.—Tolmie and Dawson, Comp. Vocab., 121, 1884. Tilhualwits.—Schoolcraft, Ind. Tribes, VI, 689, 1857. Tilhulhwit.—Ibid., I, 521, 1853. Tlaqluit.—Mooney in 14th Rep. B. A. E., 740, 1896 (own name). Wesh-ham.—Noble (1856) in H. R. Ex. Doc. 37, 34th Cong., 3d sess., 109, 1857. Wi'cxam.—Sapir in Pub. Am. Ethnol. Soc., II, x, 1909 (proper form). Wishham.—Lee and Frost, Oregon, 176, 1844. Wish-ram.—Ibid., 38. Wishrans.—Alvord (1853) in H. R. Ex. Doc. 76, 34th Cong., 3d sess., 12, 1857. Wissams.—Shaw (1856) in H. R. Ex. Doc. 37, 34th Cong., 3d sess., 115, 1857. Wisswhams.—Ross, Fur Hunters, I, 186, 1855. Wŭsh qûmă-pûm.—Mooney in 14th Rep. B. A. E., 740, 1896 (Tenino name).

Tlakom (*Tlă'qōm*). A Squawmish village community on Anvil id., in Howe sd., Brit. Col.—Hill-Tout in Rep. Brit. A. A. S., 474, 1900.

Tlakstak (*Lā'qst'ax*). A former Chinookan village on the s. side of Columbia r., Wash. It was occupied by the people who afterward settled Wakanasisi, q. v. (F. B.)

Tlalegak (*Lā'legak*, 'eddy'). A former Chinook (Wahkiakum) town near Pillar Rock, Columbia r., Oreg. (F. B.)
Pillar Rock.—Gibbs in Pac. R. R. Rep., I, 435, 1855.

Tlanak (*Lᴀnᴀxk*). A Tlingit town in the Sitka country, Alaska. (J. R. S.)

Tlanusiyi (*Tlanusi'yĭ*, 'leech place'). An important Cherokee settlement at the junction of Hiwassee and Valley rs., the present site of Murphy, in Cherokee co., N. C. (J. M.)
Clennuse.—Bartram, Travels, 371, 1792. Klausuna.—Mooney in 19th Rep. B. A. E., 535, 1900. Quanuse.—Bartram, op. cit. (perhaps synonymous, although in the same list as the above). Quoneashee.—Mooney, op. cit. (quoted). Tlanusi'yt.—Mooney, op. cit. (correct Cherokee form).

Tlascopsel. According to the royal cédula of Apr. 16, 1748 (Archivo Gen. de Méx., R. Céd., LXVIII, MS.), providing for the establishment of three missions on San Xavier (San Gabriel) r., Texas, this was one of the tribes which previously asked for a mission there. They have not been identified and probably are known in history by some other name. In discussing the cédula referred to, a contemporary who evidently had lived in Texas wrote: "The Lacopseles, which later are called Tlacopseles, besides being very strange (*estraño*) to me, are likewise unknown to the Asinay or Texa language, for it is well known that their alphabet does not contain *l*, which occurs twice in each name." He concludes, therefore, that the name must have been reported in the Yadocxa (Deadose, which was that of the Bidai and Arkokisa) language (MS., *ca.* 1748, in the archives of the College of Guadalupe de Zacatecas, Mexico). (H. E. B.)
Lacopseles.—Bonilla, Breve Comp. (1772), trans. by West in Tex. Hist. Quar., VIII, 46, 1904. Tlascopsel.—Morfi. Mem. Hist. Tex., bk. II, *ca.* 1782, MS.

Tlasenuesath (*Tla'sᴇnūesath*). A sept of the Seshart, a Nootka tribe.—Boas in 6th Rep. N. W. Tribes Can., 32, 1890.

Tlashgenemaki. A Chinookan family living on the N. bank of Columbia r., in Wahkiakum co., Wash., below Skamokawa.

Lā'ogᴇnᴇmaxîx̣.—Boas, Kathlamet Texts, 6, 1901.

Tlastlemauk (*Tlästlᴇmuuq*, 'Saltwater creek'). A Squawmish village community in Burrard inlet, Brit. Col.—Hill-Tout in Rep. Brit. A. A. S., 475, 1900.

Tlastshini ('red flat'). A Navaho clan.

Tlastcìni.—Matthews in Jour. Am. Folk-lore, III, 103, 1890. Tlastsíni.—Matthews, Navaho Legends, 30, 1897

Tlatek. A Chnagmiut Eskimo village on the N. bank of Yukon r., Alaska, 35 m. above Andreafski.

Tlatek.—Baker, Geog. Dict. Alaska, 1902. Tlatekamat.—Post-route map, 1903. Tlatekamute.—Raymond in Sen. Ex. Doc. 12, 42d Cong., 1st sess., 25, 1871 (referring to the inhabitants)

Tlathenkotin ('people of the river that trails through the grass'). A division of the Tsilkotin living in Tlothenka village on Chilkotin r., near Fraser r., Brit. Col. Pop. 190 in 1892, besides 35 in the independent village of Stella.

T'ɩ̂â-theñ-ᴋoh'-tin.—Morice in Trans. Can. Inst., IV, 23, 1893.

Tlatlasikoala (*Lā'Lasiqoala*, 'those on the ocean'). A Kwakiutl tribe which formerly lived at the N. E. end of Vancouver id., but later moved to Hope id. Its gentes, according to Boas, are Gyigyilkam, Lalauilela, and Gyeksem. This tribe and the Nakomgilisala are known to the whites collectively as the Nawiti (q. v.). Within recent years they have always lived together. In 1906 their combined population was 69. (J. R. S.)

Klatolseaquilla.—Brit. Col. map, 1872. La'Lasiqoala.—Boas in Rep. U. S. Nat. Mus. 1895, 329, 1897. La'Lasiqwala.—Boas in Mem. Am. Mus. Nat. Hist., V, pt. II, 350, 1905. Tlátlashekwillo.—Tolmie and Dawson, Vocabs. Brit. Col., 118B, 1884. Tlatla-Shequilla.—Scouler (1846) in Jour. Ethnol. Soc. Lond., I, 233, 1848. Tlatlasik·oa'la.—Boas in 6th Rep. N. W. Tribes Can., 53, 1890. Tlátlasiqoala.—Boas in Petermanns Mitteil., pt. 5, 131, 1887. Tla-tli-sikwila.—Dawson in Trans. Roy. Soc. Can., sec. II, 65, 1887. Tsatsaquits.—Brit. Col. map, 1872.

Tlatlelamin (*LaLᴇlā'min*, 'the supporters'). A gens of the Nimkish, a Kwakiutl tribe.—Boas in Rep. U. S. Nat. Mus. 1895, 331, 1897.

Tlatskanai. An Athapascan tribe that formerly owned the prairies bordering Chehalis r., Wash., at the mouth of Skookumchuck r., but, on the failure of game, left the country, crossed the Columbia, and occupied the mountains on Clatskanie r., Columbia co., Oreg. (Gibbs in Cont. N. A. Ethnol., I, 171, 1877). "This tribe was, at the first settlement of the Hudson's Bay Company in Oregon, so warlike and formidable that the company's men dared not pass their possessions along the river in less numbers than 60 armed men, and then often at considerable loss of life and always at great hazard. The Indians were in the habit of exacting tribute from all the neighboring tribes who passed in the river, and disputed the right of any

persons to pass them except upon these conditions" (Dart in Ex. Doc. 39, 32d Cong., 1st sess., 6, 1852). In 1851 the tribe was reduced to 3 men and 5 women, and since then has become extinct.

A·látskné-i.—Gatschet, Kalapuya MS,, B. A. E., 72. Athlaχsni.—Ibid. (Kalapuya name). Clacksstar.—Lewis (1806) in Orig. Jour. Lewis and Clark, IV, 213, 1905. Clack-star.—Lewis and Clark Exped., II, 226, 1814. Clackster.—Clark (1806) in Orig. Jour. Lewis and Clark, IV, 217, 1905. Clakstar.—Am. Pioneer, I, 408, 1842. Claskanio.—Lee and Frost, Oregon, 99, 1844. Class-can-eye-ah.—Ross, Fur Hunters, I, 198, 1855. Clatacamin.—Schoolcraft, Ind. Tribes, VI, 686, 1857. Clat-sacanin.—Ind. Aff. Rep., 161, 1850. Clatsaconin.—Schoolcraft, Ind. Tribes, VI, 701, 1857. Clatstoni.—Wyman in Boston Soc. Nat. Hist., IV, 84, 1854. Claxtar.—Lewis and Clark Exped., II, 212, 1814. Clax-ter.—Clark (1805) in Orig. Jour. Lewis and Clark, III, 295, 1905. Clockstar.—Morse, Rep. to Sec. War, 371, 1822. Klatscanai.—Thwaites in Orig. Jour. Lewis and Clark, IV, 218, 1905. Klatskanai.—Gibbs quoted by Dall in Cont. N. A. Ethnol., I, 241, 1877. Klatskania.—Pres. Mess., Ex. Doc. 39, 32d Cong., 1st sess., 2, 1852. Klats-kanuise.—Ind. Aff. Rep. 1857, 354, 1858. Klatstonis.—Townsend, Nar., 175, 1839. Tlascani.—Gallatin in Schoolcraft, Ind. Tribes, III, 401, 1853. Tlaskanai.—Keane in Stanford, Compend., 539, 1878. Tlatscanai.—Thwaites in Orig. Jour. Lewis and Clark, IV, 218, 1905. Tlatskanai.—Hale, Ethnog. and Philol., 204, 1846. Tlatskanie—Ibid., 198.

Tlauitsis (*Lau'itsîs*, 'angry people'). A Kwakiutl tribe on Cracroft id., Brit. Col., but which formerly lived on Hardy bay. Their gentes, according to Boas, are Sisintlae, Nunemasekalis, Tletlket, and Gyigyilkam. In 1885 their town was Kalokwis, on the w. end of Turnour id. Pop. 67 in 1901, 102 in 1908.

Claw-et-sus.—Kane, Wand. in N. A., app., 1859. Clowetoos.—Brit. Col. map, 1872. Clow et sus.—Schoolcraft, Ind. Tribes, V, 488, 1855. Kea-witsis.—Can. Ind. Aff., 362, 1895. Klah-wit-sis.—Ibid., 143, 1879. Klâ-wit-sis.—Dawson in Trans. Roy. Soc. Can., sec. II, 65, 1887. Kla-wi-tsush.—Tolmie and Dawson, Vocabs. Brit. Col., 118B, 1884. Klowitshis.—Ibid. Lau'itsîs.—Boas in Rep. U. S. Nat. Mus. 1895, 330, 1897. Tlau'itsis.—Boas in 6th Rep. N. W. Tribes Can., 54, 1890. Tlauitsis.—Boas in Bull. Am. Geog. Soc, 229, 1887 (misprint).

Tlayacma.—A former village connected with San Francisco Solano mission, Cal.—Bancroft, Hist. Cal., II, 506, 1886.

Tlduldjitamai (*LdᴀΙdjï tāmā'-i*, 'Mountain-woman's children'). A subdivision of the Djiguaahl-lanas, a great Haida family of the Eagle clan. It has long been extinct.—Swanton, Cont. Haida, 273, 1905.

Tleatlum (*Tle'atlum*). A Squawmish village community on Burrard inlet, Brit. Col.—Hill-Tout in Rep. Brit. A. A. S., 475, 1900.

Tlegonkhotana. A division of the Kaiyuhkhotana living on Tlegon r., Alaska, consisting of the villages Innoka, Tlegoshitno, and Talitui.

Thljegonchotana.—Zagoskin, Reise, 324, 1849. Tlegon Khotana.—Petroff, Alaska, 37, 1884.

Tlegoshitno. A Kaiyuhkhotana village on Shageluk r., Alaska.

Tlégogitno.—Zagoskin in Nouv. Ann. Voy., 5th s., XXI, map, 1850. Tlegoshitno.—Petroff, Rep. on Alaska, 37, 1884. Tlegozhitno.—Zagoskin, Descr. Russ. Poss. Am., map, 1842.

Tlegulak ('buoys.'—Boas). A former

Chinookan village 2 m. below Rainier, on the s. side of Columbia r., Oreg.

Lgu'laq.—Boas, Kathlamet Texts, 182, 1901.

Tlekem (*Ḻē'q'ᴇm*). A gens of the Walas Kwakiutl, a sept of the true Kwakiutl.—Boas in Rep. U. S. Nat. Mus. 1895, 330, 1897.

Tlelding. A former Athapascan village on Trinity r., just below the mouth of South fork, Cal. Its inhabitants spoke the language of the Hupa, from whom they differed in no respect except slightly in religion and in their political relations. Just above this village, which is now deserted, are the pits of many houses marking the site of a settlement which the natives believe to have been occupied by the Kihunai before the coming of Indians. The largest pit is pointed out as the location of Yimantuwingyai's house when he was chief of the immortal Kihunai at Tlelding. The Southfork Indians, as they are commonly called, came into violent conflict with military forces in the fifties and were removed to Hupa valley at the establishment of the reservation. The few surviving families now live near their old home. (P. E. G.)

A-hel-tah.—Gibbs in Schoolcraft, Ind. Tribes, III, 139, 1853. Kailtas.—Powers in Overland Mo., IX, 162, 1872. Kēl'-ta.—Powers in Cont. N. A. Ethnol., III, 89, 1877. Khlēl'-ta.—Ibid. Leldiñ.—Goddard, Life and Culture of the Hupa, 7, 1903. Ta-hail-la.—McKee in Sen. Ex. Doc. 4, 32d Cong., spec. sess., 194, 1853. Ta-hail-ta.—Meyer, Nach dem Sacramento, 282, 1855.

Tlenedi. The principal social group among the Auk tribe of Alaska. It belongs to the Raven phratry.

Ḻ!ēnē'dî.—Swanton, field notes, B. A. E., 1904. tlēnédi.—Krause, Tlinkit Ind., 116, 1885.

Tlesko. A Tleskotin village on Chilcotin r. near its junction with Fraser r., Brit Col.—Morice in Trans. Roy. Soc. Can., sec. II, 109, map, 1892.

Tleskotin ('people of the Splint river'). A division of the Tsilkotin living in the village of Tlesko (q. v.); pop. 75 in 1892.

Tḽəs-Koh'-tin.—Morice, Notes on W. Dénés, 23, 1893.

Tletlket (*Ḻē'Lqĕt*, 'having a great name'). A gens of the Walas Kwakiutl and another of the Tlauitsis.

Ḻē'Lqĕt.—Boas in Rep. U. S. Nat. Mus. 1895, 330, 1897. Ḻē'Lqētē.—Ibid. Tléqēti.—Boas in Petermanns Mitteil., pt. 5, 131, 1887.

Tlgunghung (*Lɢᴀ'ñxᴀñ*, 'face of the ground' [?]). A Haida town of the Djiguaahl-lanas family, formerly on the N. side of Lyell id., Queen Charlotte ids., Brit. Col.—Swanton, Cont. Haida, 278, 1905.

Tlhingus (*Ḻ!xíñᴀs*, 'flat slope'). A Haida town of the Kagials-kegawai family, formerly on Louise id., Queen Charlotte ids., Brit. Col.—Swanton, Cont. Haida, 279, 1905.

Tlialil. A former Koyukukhotana village on Koyukuk r., Alaska; it contained 27 people and 3 houses in 1844.

Tlialil-kakat.—Zagoskin quoted by Petroff in 10th Census, Alaska, 37, 1884.

Tliktlaketin (*ḺíɢḺa'qᴇtín*, 'ferry,' 'crossing place'). A Ntlakyapamuk village on the E. side of Fraser r., 3 m. below Cisco, Brit. Col.; so named because the Indians were accustomed to cross the river in their canoes here.—Teit in Mem. Am. Mus. Nat. Hist., II, 169, 1900.

Tlikutath (*Tl'i'kutath*). A sept of the Opitchesaht, a Nootka tribe.—Boas in 6th Rep. N. W. Tribes Can., 32, 1890.

Tlingit (*Ḻingí't*, 'people'). The usual name for those peoples constituting the Koluschan linguistic family. They inhabit the islands and coast of N. w. America from about lat. 54° 40′ to 60°, or from the mouth of Portland canal on the s. (except the E. and s. part of Prince of Wales id., occupied by the Kaigani, or Alaskan Haida) to Chilkat on Controller bay, their last permanent settlement, just beyond which they meet the Eskimo as well as the Ahtena, an Athapascan tribe.

Anthropometric investigations seem to indicate that, from a physical point of

TLINGIT, TAKU TRIBE

view, the Tlingit (Koluschan), Tsimshian (Chimmesyan), and Haida (Skittagetan) should be grouped together, and by the similarity of their social organization and languages the Haida and the Tlingit are associated still more closely.

Tlingit tradition points to the Tsimshian coast as their original home. In 1741 Chirikoff and Bering reached the Tlingit coast, and during the next half century Russian, Spanish, English, French, and American explorers and traders were frequent visitors. In 1799 a fort was built near where Sitka now stands, but in 1802 the Sitka Indians rose, killed part of the inmates, and drove away the remainder. In 1804 Baranoff attacked the natives in their fort, finally driving them out, and then established a post there which grew into Sitka, the capital of Russian America. Russian rule, especially under Baranoff, was of the harshest character (see *Russian influence*), and there was constant trouble between the warlike Tlingit and their masters. In 1867 the tribes were transferred, with Alaska, to the jurisdiction of the United States.

The Indians of this group looked to the sea for their main livelihood, and depended on land hunting to a less extent, though for natural reasons more than did the Haida. Shellfish and various roots also constituted not a small part of their diet. Seals, otters, and porpoises were important objects of pursuit. The Tagish of Lewis r., who are supposed to be Tlingit, live like the Athapascan tribes, which they resemble in all respects except language. The Tlingit display much mechanical skill, especially in canoe-building, carving, the working of stone and copper, blanket and basket making, etc. The practice of slavery, so common on the N. W. coast, was much in vogue among them, and formerly they made distant expeditions for the purpose of obtaining slaves.

Though dialectic differences exist in the Tlingit language, they are comparatively slight, and the active intercourse maintained by the several divisions under the incentive of trade has doubtless been instrumental to some extent in producing the marked homogeneity in character and customs that everywhere prevail. At the same time the speech of Yakutat diverges somewhat from that of the towns farther s., and between the northern and the southern towns in the remaining territory there is a certain amount of variation.

According to Veniaminoff these Indians in 1835 numbered about 5,850. In 1839 an enumeration of the Tlingit and Kaigani was made under the direction of Sir James Douglas and showed, exclusive of the Yakutat, Sitka, and Tagish, 5,455 Tlingit. A census compiled in 1861 by Lieut. Wehrman, of the Russian navy, gave 8,597 Tlingit, including 828 slaves. The figures given by Petroff (10th Census, Alaska, 31–32, 1884) are 6,763, and those of the Eleventh Census, excluding the Ugalakmiut, which are improperly counted with them, 4,583. It would appear that the Tlingit population has been declining steadily during the last 70 years, but there is evidence that this decline has ceased.

Most of the Tlingit tribes deserve to be called rather geographical groups. They are the following: Auk, Chilkat, Henya, Huna, Hutsnuwu, Kake, Kuiu, Sanyakoan, Sitka, Stikine, Sumdum, Tagish, Taku, Tongas, and Yakutat or Hlahayik. Emmons adds two others, the Gunaho (see *Gonaho*) and Guthleuh of Controller bay. The Kajechadi is a Tlingit division that has not been identified.

Socially they are divided, like the Haida, into 2 phratries, Yehl (Raven), and Goch (Wolf) or Chak (Eagle), each of which (again like the Haida) is subdivided into consanguineal bands or clans. These are:

Yehl.—Ankakehittan, Deshuhittan, Ganahadi, Hlukahadi, Kahlchanedi, Kashkekoan, Kaskakoedi, Kachadi, Katkaayi, Kiksadi, Koskedi, Kuhinedi, Kuyedi, Nushekaayi, Sakutenedi, Tahlkoedi, Takdentan, Takwanedi, Tanedi, Tenedi, Tihittan, Tlenedi, Tluknahadi.

Goch or *Chak.*—Chukanedi, Daktlawedi, Hehlqoan, Hlkoayedi, Hokedi, Kagwantan, Kakos-hittan, Katagwadi, Kayashkidetan, Kokhittan, Nanyaayi, Nastedi, Nesadi, Shunkukedi, Siknahadi, Sitkoedi, Takestina, Tekoedi, Tlukoedi, Tsaguedi, Tsatenyedi, Was-hinedi, Wushketan, Yenyedi.

Outside of either clan.—Nehadi.

The Tlingit towns, both occupied and abandoned, are: Akvetskoe, Angun, Anchguhlsu, Chilkat, Chilkoot, Chitklin's Village, Dahet, Deshu, Dyea, Gash, Gaudekan, Gonaho, Gutheni, Hlahayik, Hlukkukoan, Hukanuwu, Kahlchatlan, Kake, Katchanaak, Katkwaahltu, Katlany's Village, Keshkunuwu, Klawak, Klughuggue, Klukwan, Kona, Kuiu, Kukanuwu, Kustahekdaan, Ledyanoprolivskoe(?), Nahltushkan, Shakan, Sikanasankian, Sitka, Skagway, Sumdum, Takokakaan, Tlistee, Tluhashaiyikan, Tlushashakian, Tongas, Tsantikihin, Tuxican, Yakutat, and Yendestake.

For the synonymy of the stock, see *Koluschan Family.* (H. W. H. J. R. S.)

Clingats.—Macfie, Vancouver Island, 452, 1865. G-tinkit.—Langsdorff, Voy., II, 128, 1814. G'tinkit.—Ibid., 116. Kaljuschen.—Holmberg, Ethnog. Skizz., 9, 1855 (Russian or Aleut, referring to their labrets). Kaloshes.—Beardslee in Sen. Ex. Doc. 105, 46th Cong., 2d sess., 31, 1880. Kaloshians.—Fast, Antiq. of Alaska, 18, 1869. Kaluschians.—Langsdorff, Voy., II, 82, 1814. Klinget.—Willard, Life in Alaska, 63, 1884. Koliugi.—Humboldt, New Spain, II, 394, 1811. Koljuches.—Campbell in Quebec Lit. and Hist. Soc. Trans., 61, 1881. Koljuschen.—Holmberg, Ethnog. Skizz., 9, 1855. Koljush.—Campbell in Canadian Naturalist, 2d s., IX, 203, 1881. Kolloshians.—Sen. Misc. Doc. 136, 41st Cong., 2d sess., 20, 1870. Koloches.—Pinart in Revue d'Anthropologie, no. 4, 1, 1873. Koloshi.—Veniaminoff, Zapiski, II, pt. III, 28, 1840. Kolyuzhi.—Ibid. Ll'inkit.—Pinart, Notes sur les Koloches, 2, 1873. S-chinkit.—Langsdorff, Voy., II, 128, 1814. S'khinkit.—Ibid., 116. Street natives.—Holmberg, Ethnog. Skizz., I, 1855. Thlinkiten.—Ibid. Tlingit.—Emmons in Mem. Am. Mus. Nat. Hist., III, 229, 1903. Tlinkit.—Krause, Tlinkit Indianer, 96, 1885. Tlinkit-antu-kwan.—Veniaminoff, Zapiski, II, pt. III, 28, 1840 (= 'people in the Tlingit country'). Tshingits.—Fast, Antiq. Alaska, 18, 1869. Tshinkitani.—Gallatin in Trans. Am. Antiq. Soc., II, 14, 1836 (=Lingît-â'ni, 'Tlingit country'). Wooden-lips.—Jewitt, Narrative, 161, 1815.

Tliqalis (*Tli'qalis*). The name of an ancestor of a Quatsino gens, by which the gens was sometimes known.—Boas in Petermanns Mitteil., pt. 5, 131, 1887.

Tlistee (*Ll'isti'*). A former town in the N. part of the Tlingit territory, Alaska; definite locality unknown. (J. R. S.)

Tlitlalas (Tl'ĭ′tlalas). An ancestor of a Quatsino gens, by whose name the gens itself was sometimes called.—Boas in Petermanns Mitteil., pt. 5, 131, 1887.

Tlizihlani ('many goats'). A Navaho clan, evidently of modern origin.
Tlizilàni.—Matthews in Jour. Am. Folk-lore, III, 104, 1890. Tlĭzĭláni.—Matthews, Navaho Leg., 30, 1897.

Tlkamcheen (Lkamtci′n, 'confluence [of rivers]'). A village of the Lytton band of Ntlakyapamuk, on the s. side of Thompson r. at its junction with the Fraser, Brit. Col. Pop. 137 in 1901; in 1908, evidently including other bands, 467.
Klech-ah′-mech.—Gibbs in Cont. N. A. Ethnol., I, 248, 1877. Klick-um-cheen.—Can. Ind. Aff., pt. II, 164, 1901. Klickunacheen.—Ibid., 1898, 418, 1899. Lkamtci′n.—Teit in Mem. Am. Mus. Nat. Hist., II, 171, 1900. Lytton.—Ibid. (white man's name). Ti-chom-chin.—Can. Ind. Aff. 1883, 189, 1884. Tikumcheen.—Ibid., 1891, 249, 1892. Tlkamcheen.-Ibid., 301, 1893. Tl-kam-sheen.—Dawson in Trans. Roy. Soc. Can., sec. II, 44, 1891. Tlkumcheen.—Can. Ind. Aff. 1896, 434, 1897. Tlk·umtoĭ′n.—Hill-Tout in Rep. Ethnol. Surv. Can., 4, 1899.

Tluhashaiyikan (L!uxd′caiyĭk-ān, 'town straight opposite Mt Edgecombe'). A former Tlingit town in the Sitka country, Alaska. (J. R. S.)

Tluknahadi ('king-salmon people'). A Tlingit division living at Sitka, Alaska, and belonging to the Raven phratry. Their former home is said to have been at the mouth of Alsek r.
klŭk-nachádi.—Krause, Tlinkit Ind., 118, 1885. Lŭknᴀxā′dĭ.—Swanton, field notes, B. A. E., 1904.

Tlukoedi (L!ū′q!oedĭ, 'white people'). Said to be the name of an old Tlingit family belonging to the Wolf phratry, now almost extinct. They were named from the white color of water. (J. R. S.)

Tlushashakian (L!ucā′cak!i-ān, 'town on top of a sand hill'). An old town on the N. side of the w. entrance to Cross sd., Alaska. It is in the Huna country, but is said to have been occupied anciently by many families of the Wolf phratry, since scattered all over the Alaskan coast. It is perhaps identical with Klughuggue. (J. R. S.)

Tluskez (the name refers to a carp-like fish). A Ntshaautin village on a small lake tributary to Blackwater r., Brit. Col. It is probably the village where Mackenzie (Voy., 299, 1801) was hospitably received on his journey to the Pacific, whose inhabitants he found more cleanly, healthy, and agreeable in appearance than any that he had passed.
Klusklus.—Fleming in Can. Pac. R. R. Surv., 120, 1877. Kuzlakes.—Macfie, Vancouver Isl., 428, 1865. Tus'kez.—Morice in Trans. Can. Inst., 25, 1893. Rothfisch-Manner.—Vater, Mith., III, pt. 3, 421, 1816. Slaoucud-dennie.—Latham quoted by Bancroft, Nat. Races, I, 145, 1874. Sla-ū′-ah-kustinneh.—Dall, MS., B. A. E. Slouacous dinneh.—Balbi, Atlas Ethnog., 821, 1826. Slouacus Dennie.—Gallatin in Trans. Am. Antiq. Soc., II, 20, 1836. Sloua-cuss Dinais.—Mackenzie, Voy., 284, 1802. Slouacuss Tinneh.—Bancroft, Nat. Races, I, 145, 1874. Slowacuss.—Ibid., III, 585, 1882. Slowercuss.—Cox, Columbia R., II, 374, 1831. Slowercuss-Dinai.—

Ibid. Slua-cuss-dinais.—Vater, Mith., III, pt. 3, 421, 1816. Sluacus-tinneh.—Cox, op cit.

To ('sweet-potato'). Given by Gatschet as a Yuchi clan, but probably no such clan exists in this tribe.
Tó tahá.—Gatschet, Uchee MS., B. A. E., VIII, 71, 1885 (tahá='clan').

Toa. A Maricopa rancheria on the Rio Gila, Ariz., in 1744.—Sedelmair (1744) cited by Bancroft, Ariz. and N. Mex., 366, 1889.

Toaedut. A Maricopa rancheria on the Rio Gila, Ariz., in 1744.—Sedelmair (1744) cited by Bancroft, Ariz. and N. Mex., 366, 1889.

Toag. See Togue.

Toalli. A district, probably in s. w. Georgia, visited by DeSoto, Mar. 23, 1540. The houses are described by the Gentleman of Elvas (Bourne, Narr. of De Soto, I, 52, 1904) as having been roofed with cane after the fashion of tile; some with the sides of clay (plastered?), and kept very clean.
Otoa.—Biedma (1544) in French, Hist. Coll. La., II, 100, 1850. Toalli.—Gentl. of Elvas, op. cit.

Toanche (Teandeouïata, 'one enters by it'). A Huron village situated at different times at several points on and adjoining Thunder bay, Ontario, and bearing several names. It was a port of entry of the Huron Bear tribe, hence its name. Before 1635 it had been twice destroyed by fire. Through fear of French revenge for the killing of Brulé at this place, it was abandoned in 1633, and a new village, Ihonatiria, was established by a part of its inhabitants, while the remainder went to Ouenrio. (J. N. B. H.)
Otoüacha.—Champlain (1632), Œuvres, v, pt. I, 249, 1870. Saint Nicolas.—Sagard (1626), Hist. Can., II, 296, 1866. Teandeouïata.—Jes. Rel. 1635, 28, 1858. Teandeouïhata.—Ibid., 29. Teandewiata.—Ibid., III, index, 1858. Thouenchin.—Memoir of 1637 in Margry, Déc., I, 4, 1875. Toanché.—Jes. Rel. 1635, 28, 1858. Toenchain.—Sagard (1636), Can., I, 215, 1866. Toenchen.—Ibid., 233. Touanchain.—Champlain, Œuvres, v, pt. I, 249, note, 1870. Touenchain.—Sagard, Hist. Can., II, 296, 1866.

Toanimbuttuk. A former Nishinam village in the valley of Bear r., which is the next stream N. of Sacramento, Cal.—Powers in Overland Mo., XII, 22, 1874.

Toapara. A former Opata pueblo N. of Oputo, in E. Sonora, Mexico, abandoned in the 18th century owing to the hostility of the Apache, Suma, and Jocome.
San Juan del Rio.—Doc. of 18th cent. quoted by Bandelier in Arch. Inst. Papers, IV, 525, 1892. Toapara.—Ibid.

Toape. A Eudeve pueblo and seat of a Spanish mission founded in 1647; situated at the head of Rio San Miguel, lat. 30° 20′, lon. 110° 30′, Sonora, Mexico. Pop. 240 in 1678, 187 in 1730.
S. Miguel Toape.—Zapata (1678) cited by Bancroft, No. Mex. States, I, 245, 1884. Terapa.—Orozco y Berra, Geog., 343, 1864. Toape.—Rivera (1730) cited by Bancroft, op. cit., 513. Tuape.—Modern map form.

Toapkuk. An Eskimo village of the Malemiut at C. Espenberg, Alaska. Pop. 42 in 1880.

Ta-apkuk.—Petroff in 10th Census, Alaska, 4, 1884.
Tapkhak.—Zagoskin in Nouv. Ann. Voy., 5th s.,
XXI, map, 1850.　Tarpkarzoomete.—Jackson, Reindeer in Alaska, map, 145, 1894.　Toapkuk.—Nelson
in 18th Rep. B. A. E., map, 1899.

Tobacco. On the arrival of the first
Europeans in North America the natives
were observed to make offerings of the
smoke of some plant, generally believed
to be tobacco, to their many deities and
spirits; by it disease was treated, and the
smoke ascending from the pipe was regarded as an evidence of such an act as the
sealing of an agreement or the binding of a
treaty. Tobacco was likewise offered in
propitiation of angry waters, to allay destructive winds, and to protect the traveler. Oviedo (Hist. de las Indias, I, 130,
1851) says that the Indians of Hayti in
the 16th century "had the custom of
taking fumigations for the purpose of getting intoxicated (which they call *tabaco*)
with the smoke of a certain herb." Ernst
(Am. Anthr., II, 133, 1889) states that
Oviedo is certainly right in giving the
name (strictly *taboca*, a word of Guarani
origin) to a Y-shaped inhaler still used by
several South American tribes for the
absorption of certain powders (*niopo*,
parica). Columbus, on Oct. 15, 1492,
met a man in a canoe going from Santa
Maria to Fernandina, the second and third
of the Bahama ids. that he touched, who
was carrying dry leaves which he thought
must be appreciated among the Indians
because they had brought him some at
San Salvador. Las Casas (Hist. Gen. de
las Indias, cap. 46, 1875–76) says that
messengers whom Columbus sent ashore
in Cuba found "men with half-burned
wood in their hands and certain herbs to
take their smokes, which are some dry
herbs put in a certain leaf, also dry, like
those the boys make on the day of the
Passover of the Holy Ghost; and having
lighted one part of it, by the other they
suck, absorb, or receive that smoke inside with the breath, by which they become benumbed and almost drunk, and so
it is said they do not feel fatigue. These,
muskets as we will call them, they call
tabacos. I knew Spaniards on this island
of Española who were accustomed to take
it, and being reprimanded for it, by telling them it was a vice, they replied they
were unable to cease using it. I do not
know what relish or benefit they found in
it." Navarrete says: "Such is the origin
of our cigars" (Thatcher, Columbus, I,
561, 1903). These authors are among the
first to refer to tobacco, the use of which
spread rapidly over the world. Benzoni
(Hist. New World, Hakluyt. Soc. Pub.,
80, 1857) in 1541–56 tells how slaves
brought to America from Ethiopia by
the Spaniards preserved the leaves of a
plant that grows in these new countries,
which was picked in its season, tied up in
bundles, and suspended by them near

their fireplaces until dry; to use them
they take a leaf of their grain (maize),
and one of the other plant being put in
it, they roll them tight together. So
much, he says, "do they fill themselves
with this cruel smoke that they lose their
reason" and "fall down as if they were
dead, and remain the greater part of the
day or night stupefied," though others
"are content with imbibing only enough
of this smoke to make them giddy, and
no more." This author says that in
Mexico the name of the herb itself was
tobacco.

There is some question as to the uses
to which tobacco was put in the West
Indies, in South America, and in parts of
southern Central America. In all of these
sections there were names for the plant
itself, and in most of these regions cigars
or cigarettes were in common use, but the
tobacco pipe appears to have been unknown until recent times. In 1540 Hernando Alarcon (Ternaux-Compans, Voy.,
IX, 322, 1838) described the natives on
the lower Rio Colorado as carrying "small
reed tubes for making perfumes, as do the
Indian *tabagos* of New Spain."

Nicolas Monardes (De Simplicibus
Medicamentis, 1574) called the plant
"tobacco," as did other authors of the
period. It was credited with wonderful
properties, curing not only disease but
wounds. It was extolled as an intoxicant and as a preventive of hunger and
thirst, and was said to invigorate the
weary and to ward off disease. The
Mexicans called the plant *yetl*, the Peruvians *sayri*. Hariot (Narr. of Va., repr.
1893) said in 1585: "There is an herbe
which is sowed a part by it selfe, & is
called by the inhabitants *Vppówoc:* In
the West Indies it hath diuers names, according to the seuerall places & countries
where it groweth and is vsed. The Span-
iardes generally call it Tobacco. The
leaues thereof being dried and brought
into powder: they vse to take the fume
or smoke thereof by sucking it through
pipes made of claie into their stomacke
and heade; from whence in purgeth su-
perfluous fleame & other grosse humors,
openeth all the pores & passages of the
body: by which meanes the vse thereof
not only preserueth the body from obstructions; but also if any be, so that they
haue not beene of too long continuance,
in short time breaketh them: wherby
their bodies are notably preserued in
health, know not many greeuous diseases wherewithall wee in England are
oftentimes afflicted."

The word tobacco is of American origin,
and has been adopted, with slight variation, into most foreign languages to
designate the plant now smoked throughout the world, although there is evidence that the early Spanish settlers

employed the word to designate the instrument in which the plant was smoked, rather than the plant itself. In early French narratives of Canada the word *petun* is almost always used. This term is of Tupi origin and is still found among the dialects of that language in Brazil under the forms *pety*, *petim*, *petun*, *petin*, *pitima*, *petume*, *petemma*, etc., whereas the word "tobacco" appears to be traceable to the Carib word *taue*, *tawe*, *touica*, *tamoui*, etc., and the Chibcha *dua*, *duva*, *dawa*, etc., the differences being merely dialectic. The word *sic*, *sii'c*, *zig*, *sic'al*, etc., is often employed by the Maya of Yucatan to designate the cigar, although this people has other words for tobacco, as *mai* and *kutz*. In all the Indian languages of North and South America words are found to designate the tobacco plant, and in the languages of the northern tribes especially there are commonly two words for tobacco, probably referring to different varieties of *Nicotiana*.

Nadaillac says that the tobacco plant was introduced into Europe by the Spaniards as early as 1518. Diego Columbus, in his will dated May 2, 1523, made a legacy to a tobacco merchant of Lisbon, showing how rapidly traffic in the new panacea sprang up. Jean Nicot, French ambassador to the King of Portugal, sent seeds of the plant to Catherine de Medici about 1559, a service commemorated by the name *Nicotiana* given to the plant. As many as 40 varieties of the tobacco plant have been noted by botanists. It was called by the French "herbe de la reine" and "herbe sainte"; by the Dutch "the ambassador's plant"; the Spaniards called it "yerba sancta" because of its wonderful virtue in treating disease, which Oviedo (Purchas, Pilgrimage, v, 957, 1626) said "was not only for sanity but for sanctity also." The Portuguese called it "erba santa croce." Sir Francis Drake referred to *tobah* as early as 1578, and was the first to take Virginia tobacco (*Nicotiana tabacum*) to Europe, according to Fairholt. The cigarette has been smoked in the S. W. from time immemorial, and the sacred cigarette deposited by priests in caves as a votive offering, thousands being found in cave shrines in Arizona.

The practice of making cane cigarettes survived up to a recent period among the Pima of Arizona, who, before going to war against the Apache, made from a reed growing along the Rio Gila a smoking tube the length of the first two joints of the index finger. around the middle of which was tied a miniature belt woven from cotton and agave fiber, with fringed ends, and called a blanket, this clothed reed being regarded as male or female

according to certain marks upon it. Before the departure of a war party these tubes were charged with tobacco and smoked toward the cardinal points, to the fetishes, and to all the objects that were to be used in the campaign, each warrior smoking his own tube. At the close of the ceremony the tubes were deposited as offerings in shrines dedicated to the War god, which were generally in caves. Fewkes in 1907 found in one of six ceremonial rooms excavated by him at Casa Grande, Ariz., hundreds of these tubes in the fireplaces. Their surfaces were charred, but they were still distinguishable. Large numbers of similar tubes were found by Cushing in ceremonial caves in the Gila and Salt r. valleys.

In South America tobacco appears to have been used chiefly in the form of snuff. There is some evidence that the plant was chewed in Central America. The Indians of North America generally are said to have cultivated tobacco from a very early period, several varieties of which were known to them. The Tionontati, because they grew the plant in commercial quantities, were called by the French Nation de Petun.

Tobacco was cultivated in most tribes by the men alone, and was usually smoked by them only; among the Iroquois and some of the Pueblos trade tobacco was not smoked in solemn ceremonies. At times both priests and laymen smoked plants or compounds that were strongly narcotic, those using them becoming ecstatic and seeing visions. To the Indian the tobacco plant had a sacred character; it was almost invariably used on solemn occasions, accompanied by suitable invocations to their deities. It was ceremonially used to aid in disease or distress, to ward off danger, to bring good fortune, to generally assist one in need, and to allay fear. The planting of medicine tobacco is one of the oldest ceremonies of the Crows, consisting, among other observances, of a solemn march, a foot race among the young men, the planting of seed, the building of a hedge of green branches around the seed bed, a visit to the sweat house, followed by a bath and a solemn smoke, all ending with a feast; when ripe, the plant was stored away, and seeds were put in a deerskin pouch and kept for another planting (Simms in Am. Anthr., vi, 331, 1904). The Mandan and Arikara, among others, are known to have cultivated tobacco from very early time, while the Siksika, essentially a hunting tribe, cultivated tobacco, according to Grinnell, as their only crop. The tobacco plant was carefully dried by the Indians and kept as free from moisture as possible; that intended for immediate use was kept in bags of deerskin or birch bark, skins of small animals, or baskets neatly woven of roots and grasses. The bags were often elaborately decorated by the women.

Of the family *Solanaceæ* few species were used as narcotics. *Cornus sericea* and *C. stolonifera* grow over the greater part of North America and are used for smoking nearly as extensively as *Nicotiana*. Matthews thinks that red willow has been mistaken for these by several authors. Kinnikinnick, an Algonquian word signifying '(what is) mixed by hand,' is used to designate a mixture of tobacco with some other plant, either for the purpose of imparting a more pleasant odor or to reduce its strength, as the trade tobacco alone is commonly too strong to suit the fancy of the Indian. Among the western tribes tobacco was ordinarily used by mixing with it gum, sumac, and bearberry, the bark, leaves, and roots of two kinds of willow, manzanita leaves, Jamestown weed, touchwood, dogwood bark, arrowwood, and a variety of other woods, barks, leaves, twigs, and even insects. The plant was commonly used throughout Europe as an antidote against the plague and other diseases. Its cultivation, to the exclusion of other vegetal products, brought the colonies of Virginia and Maryland on more than one occasion to the verge of starvation. Statistics show that in 1908 the product of tobacco in the United States amounted to 718,061,380 pounds. The value of manufactured tobacco for the year 1900 was $283,076,546.

Consult Bragge, Bibliotheca Nicotiana, 1880; Neander, Tobaccologia, 1644; Fairholt, Tobacco, its History and Associations, 1859; Grinnell, Blackfoot Lodge Tales, 1892; Jacobstein, Tobacco Industry in U. S., 1907; Monardes, Hist. Medicinal, 1574; Nadaillac, Les Pipes et le Tabac (Materiaux pour l'Histoire Primitive de l'Homme, 1885); Curtis, Am. Ind., I–V, 1907–09; McGuire in Rep. Nat. Mus., 1897. See *Pipes, Smoking*. (J. D. M.)

Tobagan. See *Toboggan*.

Tobhipangge (*T"o̅ B'hi-päng-ge*). A former Tewa village 8 m. N. E. of the present Nambe pueblo, N. Mex. The Nambe people assert that it was reared, occupied, and abandoned by their ancestors prior to the Spanish advent in the 16th century.—Bandelier in Arch. Inst. Papers, IV, 84, 1892.

Tobique. A band of Malecite living on a reserve consisting of 14,800 acres of forest and farming lands at the junction of Tobique and St John rs., Victoria co., New Brunswick. They numbered 157 in 1910, and are Roman Catholics. They gain a livelihood by hunting, by serving as guides and lumbermen, and as laborers for the residents of Perth and And-

over; they also sell their native wares, such as snowshoes, axe-handles, baskets, and barrel-staves, and farm to some extent.

Tobic.—Vetromile, Abnakis, 122, 1866. Tobique.—Shea, Cath. Miss., 157, 1855.

Toboggan. A sort of sledge in use among the Algonquian Indians of N. E. North America, and adopted from them, with the name, by the whites. The toboggan is made of thin, narrow boards, 10 or 12 ft long, bent over and lashed at the end and covered with rawhide. Those intended to be drawn by dogs are much larger than those now used for sliding down hills in sport. The word, which has been spelled in English in a variety of ways, as *tarbogan, tobogan,* and *toboggan,* which is the usual form in English Canada, came into the language from Canadian French, in which the word is old, occurring as *tabaganne* in Leclercq (Nouv. Rel. de la Gaspésie, 70, 1691). In French Canadian the word appears in divers forms, as *tabagane, tabogine, tobagan, tobogan,* etc., some of them influenced by English spellings. According to Gerard (inf'n, 1908) "the word is from Abnaki *udăbă'găn,* meaning '(what is) used for dragging,' from *udăbă'ge,* 'he uses for dragging,' from *udă'be,* 'he drags, or hauls, with a cord.' The name was that of an Indian drag made of the skin of a deer. A sleigh or drag made of wood or branches was designated as *udăbăuäsk,* a name which, after the introduction of wheeled vehicles, was applied to a wagon or a carriage." See *Sleds*.

A probable variant of toboggan is *Tom Pung,* which has been also reduced to *pung* (q. v). The adoption of the use of the toboggan by the whites of parts of Canada and the United States as a winter sport has given rise to derivative words, as the verb *toboggan, tobogganer, tobogganist*. A sport known as "water tobogganing" was introduced by Paul Boynton. (A. F. C.)

Toby. See *Winema*.

Tocane. A Chumashan village between Goleta and Pt Concepcion, Cal., in 1542.

Tocane.—Cabrillo, Narr. (1542), in Smith, Colec. Doc. Fla., 183, 1857. Tolane.—Taylor in Cal. Farmer, Apr. 17, 1863.

Tocas. A former tribe of N. E. Mexico or S. Texas, probably Coahuiltecan, who were gathered into mission San Buenaventura de las Cuatro Ciénegas, in Coahuila.—Orozco y Berra, Geog., 302, 1864.

Tocaste. A village entered by De Soto in 1539, shortly before reaching Cale (Olagale), and probably about the upper Withlacoochee r., S. from the present Ocala, Fla. (J. M.)

Tocaste.—Gentl. of Elvas (1557) in Bourne, De Soto Narr., I, 36, 1904; Ranjel (ca. 1546), ibid., II, 65, 1904.

Tocax. A place, apparently in the Cherokee country, visited by Juan Pardo in 1566. It may possibly have some connection with Toxaway, or Tagwahi (q. v.).—Mooney in 19th Rep. B. A. E., 535, 1900.

Tocholimafia. The Golden Warbler clan of Taos pueblo, N. Mex.

Tócholimaña tai'na.—M. C. Stevenson, notes, B. A. E., 1910.

Tochotno. A former Kuilchana village on Kuskokwim r., Alaska; pop. 9 in 1844.—Zagoskin quoted by Petroff in 10th Census, Alaska, 37, 1884.

Tocia. A Chumashan tribe, one of several formerly occupying the country from Buena Vista and Carises lakes and Kern r to the Sierra Nevada and Coast range, Cal. By treaty of June 10, 1851, these tribes, which had been reduced through conflict with the Spaniards and with neighboring Indians, reserved a tract between Tejon pass and Kern r., and ceded the remainder of their lands to the United States. See Barbour in Sen. Ex. Doc. 4, 32d Cong., spec. sess., 256, 1853.

Tockaawgh, Tockahow, Tockwock, Tockwogh. See *Tuckahoe.*

Tocobaga. A tribe, apparently of Timucuan affinity, holding in the 16th century a considerable territory along the w. coast of Florida northward from Tampa bay and perhaps including the region of Withlacoochee r. The Paracoxi, Hurripacuxi, etc., of the De Soto narratives, mentioned as the name of the chief or province, seem to be properly the title of the chief, signifying, respectively, 'chief' and 'war chief' in the Timucua language (Gatschet). Later in the century, when the Spaniards began to establish posts and missions, the tribe was uniformly called Tocobaga. They were at war with their southern neighbors, the Calusa, until peace was made through the efforts of Menendez about 1570. Like the other ancient tribes of Florida, they probably dwindled to final extinction from the inroads of invading Seminole.   (J. M.)

Hurripacuxi.—Biedma (1544) in Bourne, De Soto Narr., II, 5, 1904. Orriparacogi.—Ranjel (*ca.* 1546), ibid., 60. Orriparagi.—Ibid. Orriygua.—Ibid., 58. Paracoxi.—Gentl. of Elvas (1557), ibid., I, 32, 1904. Tocobaga.—Fontaneda (*ca.* 1575) in French, Hist. Coll. La., 2d s., 263, 1875. Tocobaja.—Fontaneda Mem., Smith trans., 18, 1854. Toco-baja-Chile.— Fontaneda in Doc. Inéd., V, 537, 1866 (cacique's name): Tocobajo.—Fontaneda in French, op. cit., 254. Tocobayo.—Fairbanks, Hist. Fla., 92, 1901. Tocobogas.—Jefferys, Topog. of N. Am., chart 67, 1762. Tocopata.—De l'Isle, map (1707) in Winsor, Hist. Am., II, 294, 1886. Tocovaga.—Fontaneda in Ternaux-Compans, Voy., XX, 36, 1841. Togabaja.—Ibid., 20. Tojobaco.—Ibid., 21. Tocovajachile.—Fontaneda, Mem., Smith trans., 18, 1854 (name of the chief of Tocobaga). Topocapas.—Barcia, Ensayo, 344, 1723 (identical?). Urribaracuxi.—Garcilaso de la Vega (1591) quoted by Shipp, De Soto, 271, 1881. Urripacoxit.—De Soto letter (1539), Smith trans., 8, 1854. Urriparacoxi.—Ranjel (*ca.* 1546) in Bourne, De Soto Narr., II, 65, 1904.

Toctoethla. A former Seminole town, settled by 40 or 50 warriors from Kanchati; situated w. of Chattahoochee r., 10 m. above Flint r. junction, in Jackson co., Fla.—Bell in Morse, Rep. to Sec. War, 307, 1822.

Tocwogh (corruption of *P'tukweu,* contracted to *tukweu* and pronounced *tuk'-wo.* See *Tuckahoe.*—Gerard). A former tribe on Chester r. on the E. shore of Maryland. In 1608 Smith estimated them at 100 warriors; they were then allies of the Conestoga. Their principal village, of the same name, was on the s. bank of the river, about 7 m. from its mouth, in Queen Anne co. Brinton identifies them with the Nanticoke, although Smith mentions the two as distinct tribes.

Tockwaghs.—Schoolcraft, Ind. Tribes, VI, 131, 1857. Tockwhoghs.—Smith (1629), Va., I, 74, repr. 1819. Tockwocks.—Bozman, Md., I, 114, 1837. Tockwogh.—Smith, op. cit., map. Tockwoghes.— Ibid., 120. Tockwoughes.—Ibid., 135. Tocwoys.— Rafinesque in Marshall, Ky., I, introd., 37, 1824 (misprint). Toghwocks.—Shea, Cath. Miss., 486, 1855.

Tododaho. See *Wathatotarho.*

Toggle. See *Fishing, Hunting.*

Togiagamiut. An Eskimo tribe inhabiting the country about Togiak bay and adjacent lakes, Alaska. They are primitive in their habits, but excellent hunters. Women dress in the feathered skins of swans, geese, and cranes. The villages are Ekilik, Imiak, Kashaiak, Kassianak, Kulukak, Togiak, Tuniakpuk, Ualik.

Togiagamut.—Nelson in 18th Rep. B. A. E., map, 1899.

Togiak. A Togiagamiut village at the mouth of Togiak r., Alaska; pop. 276 in 1880, 94 in 1890.

Togiagamiut.—11th Census, Alaska, 164, 1893 (the people). Togiagamute.—Petroff, Rep. on Alaska, 48, 1881. Tugiak.—Tebenkof (1849) quoted by Baker, Geog. Dict. Alaska, 1902. Tugiatak.—Sarichef (1826) quoted by Baker, ibid.

Togiak. A trading station on the E. shore of Togiak bay, Alaska; pop. 28 in 1880, 14 in 1890.

Togiak Station.—Petroff in 10th Census, Alaska, 17, 1884.

Togiaratsorik. A Kuskwogmiut Eskimo village on the left bank of Kuskokwim r., Alaska; pop. 52 in 1880.

Taghiaratzoriamute.—Petroff, Rep. on Alaska, 53, 1880. Togiarhazoriamute.—Hallock in Nat. Geog. Mag., IX, 88, 1898.

Togue. A name applied in Maine to the species of lake-trout known in some other parts of the country as namaycush. The form *toag* is also in use, and the spelling *togue* would indicate a derivation through Canadian French from Micmac or Passamaquoddy. According to Livingston Stone (Rep. U. S. Comm. Fish, 1872–73, 220), the togue is the great graytrout (*Salmo toma*) found in New Brunswick and Maine, and called in L. Temiscouata, *tuladi.* The precise origin of the word seems not to be known.   (A. F. C.)

Togwingani (*To-gwing'-a-ni*). A Paviotso tribe living about Malheur lake, E. Oreg., in 1881. "Captain Egan" was its chief, and the tribe has usually been called Snakes.—Powell, Paviotso MS., B. A. E., 1881.

Tohaha. A subtribe, apparently Tonkawan, living in the latter part of the 17th century near the Colorado r., on the line of travel from San Antonio to E. Texas. They were closely associated with but distinct from the Toho, and also closely allied with the Emet and Cavas. What seems to be the first mention of them was made in 1683 by Juan Sabeata, Mendoza's guide to central Texas. He included them and the Emet (Emati) in the list of tribes said by him to live 3 days E. of the lower Rio Grande. La Salle heard of the Tohaha in 1687 before crossing the Colorado. They were probably identical with the Teao, through whose village La Salle passed a short distance E. of the same river. This conclusion is based on the fact, aside from the similarity of names and associates, that in 1689 and 1690 Massanet, from personal knowledge, three times reported the Tohaha (whom he called Toaa, or Toao) as living in the very vicinity where La Salle had so shortly before visited the Teao.

By a process of elimination, supplemented by some positive data, it may be inferred that the Tohaha were probably Tonkawan. In 1691 Massanet enumerated the Toaa, Tojo, Emet, Cavas, and Sana in a list of tribes living E. of Arroyo del Cibolo and speaking a non-Coahuiltecan language. According to Joutel the Teao spoke a language different from that of the Cenis (Hasinai). If the Toyal mentioned by Belleisle (1719–21) were the Tohaha, as seems not unlikely, his account would indicate that they were not allied with the coast tribes, and therefore were probably not Karankawan. Moreover, there is some positive evidence that the Sana (q. v.), at least, were of Tonkawan affiliation. While the Tohaha seem not to be mentioned after Belle Isle's account, assuming their identity with the Toyal, the Toho and their other associates continue to be mentioned for some time. (H. E. B.)

Teâo.—Joutel (1637) in Margry, Déc., III, 298, 1878. Toaa.—Massanet (1689) in Tex. Hist. Asso. Quar., II, 286, 1899. Toao.—Massanet (1689), ibid., 213. Tohaha.—Joutel (1687), op. cit., 288. Tohahe.—Shea, note in Charlevoix, New France, IV, 78, 1870. Tohaka.—Joutel, Jour., Eng. trans., 90, 1719. Toyals.—Belleisle (1719–21) in Margry, Déc., VI, 339, 1886 (identical?). Tuxaxa.—Juan Sabeata (1683) in Mendoza, Viaje, MS.

Tohaktivi (To-hak-ti-vi). A Paviotso tribe formerly about the White mts., near the head of Owens r., E. Cal.—Powell, Paviotso MS., B. A. E., 1881.

Tohlka (T!ō′ĭk!a). A Haida town of the Tohlka-gitunai family, formerly on the N. coast of Graham id., just w. of the entrance to Masset inlet, Brit. Col.—Swanton, Cont. Haida, 281, 1905.

Tohlka-gitunai (T!ō′ĭk!a gĭtΛnā′-i, 'the Gituns of Tohlka'). A Haida family of the Eagle clan, named from its town, Tohlka (q. v.). They formed one family

with the Widja-gitunai, Chets-gitunai, and Djus-hade.   (J. R. S.)

T!ō′ĭk!a gĭtΛnā′-ī.—Swanton, Cont. Haida, 275, 1905. Tōtlgya gyit'inai'.—Boas, 12th Rep. N. W. Tribes Can., 23, 1898.

Tohnokalong. A Yukonikhotana village on the N. bank of Yukon r., lon. 54° 25′.

Toho. A subtribe, apparently Tonkawan, closely associated with but distinct from the Tohaha. In the latter part of the 17th century they lived on Colorado r., Texas. For their location, probable linguistic affiliation, and early mention, see Tohaha. While the Tohaha disappear after 1721, at the latest, the Toho, in later times more commonly called Tou or Tuu, and their associates, the Emet and Cavas (Caguas), continue to be known. About 1740 and thereafter they entered San Antonio de Valero mission in considerable numbers, and were there as late as 1765. In addition to the authorities cited below, consult the manuscript mission records of San Antonio de Valero. The names Tuu and Tou suggest Tups and Tops (q. v.), names of a tribe apparently Karankawan.   (H. E. B.)

Atayos.—Cabeza de Vaca (1534), Smith trans., 121, 1871. Atoyos.—Davis, Span. Conq. N. Mex., 82, 1869 (misprint). Tayos.—Cabeza de Vaca as quoted by Barcia, Ensayo, 13, 1723 (these three forms probably refer to the Toho rather than to the Adai). Thoo.—Massanet (1690) in Dictamen Fiscal, Nov. 30, 1716, MS. Tohan.—Joutel, Jour., Eng. ed., 90, 1719. Tohau.—Joutel in Margry, Déc., III, 288, 1878. Toho.—Talon (1698), ibid., 612. Tokau.—Joutel, Jour., Eng. ed., 115, 1719. Too.—Massanet (1689), MS. Toxo.—Joutel quoted in Tex. Hist. Asso. Quar., VIII, 213, 1905.

Tohol. Mentioned as a pueblo of the province of Atripuy (q. v.) in the region of the lower Rio Grande, N. Mex., in 1598.—Oñate (1598) in Doc. Inéd., XVI, 115, 1871.

Tohome. A former Muskhogean tribe of the Gulf coast, speaking a dialect of Choctaw (Margry, Déc., IV, 427, 514–31, 1880). Their cabins stood 8 leagues N. of the French settlement at Mobile, on the w. side of Mobile r. The number of warriors was estimated in 1702 at 350. They were allies of the French and had been baptized in the Roman Catholic faith.

Aomé.—French, Hist. Coll. La., III, 235, 1851. Chohomes.—Iberville (1702) in Minn. Hist. Coll., I, 340, 1872. Thomé.—Pénicaut (1709) in French, Hist. Coll. La., n. s., I, 103, 1869. Thomez.—Pénicaut (1702), ibid., 78. Tohome's.—Iberville (1700) in Margry, Déc., IV, 427, 1880. Tomeas.—McKenney and Hall, Ind. Tribes, III, 79, 1854. Tomes.—Iberville (1700) in Margry, Déc., IV, 514, 1880. Tomez.—Pénicaut (1710), ibid., V, 427, 1883. Tommakees.—French, Hist. Coll. La., II, 234, 1850 (perhaps identical). Toomes.—Iberville (1700) in Margry, Déc., IV, 372, 1880.

Tohontaenrat ('they are white-eared.'—Hewitt). A Huron tribe formerly living in Ontario and a member of the Huron confederation. Scanonaenrat, where the Jesuits established the mission of St Michel, was their only recorded village. In 1649, on the overthrow of the Hurons by the Iroquois, the Tohontaenrat abandoned their village and were adopted by the Seneca. See *Kanagaro*. (J. M.)

Tahontaenrat.—Jes. Rel. 1644, 93, 1858. **Tohontaenras.**—Jes. Rel. 1637, 113, 1858. **Tohontaenrat.**—Jes. Rel. 1639, 50, 1858. **Tohotaenrat.**—Parkman, Jesuits, map, 1883.

Tohookatokie. Mentioned together with Wichita, Caddo, Biloxi, Alabama, Delawares, Shawnee, Creeks, Choctaw, Chickasaw, Quapaw, and a number of others as troublesome intruders in Texas in 1849. The list as given contains several duplications and other errors. This name can not be identified with any regular tribe name, and may possibly be intended for a band of Cherokee under the leadership of the chief Degatâga, known to the whites as Tokatoka. (J. M.)

Tahookatuke.—Latham, Var. of Man, 350, 1850. **Tohookatokies.**—Catlett (1849) in Ind. Aff. Rep., 1849, 33, 1850. **Tuhuktukis.**—Latham, op. cit.

Tohopeka (Creek: *Tuhúpki*, from *ituhúpki*, 'wooden fence,' and, by extension, 'fort'). The Horseshoe, or Great Bend of Tallapoosa r., Ala., the site of a temporary fort where the warlike remnants of the Creeks, numbering 1,000, experienced their last and decisive defeat from the American army under Gen. Jackson, with its Cherokee allies, Mar. 27, 1814, leaving 557 dead on the field. See Drake, Bk. Inds., bk. 4, 60, 1848. (A. S. G.)

Tohopekaliga (Creek: 'fence or fort placed there'). A former Seminole village, probably on the shore of a lake of the same name in s. w. Orange co., Fla. Philip was their chief in 1837.

Tohopíkaliga.—H. R. Ex. Doc. 74 (1823), 19th Cong., 1st sess., 27, 1826. **Tohopkolikies.**—Drake, Bk. Inds., bk. 4, 140, 1848. **Topochalinky.**—H. R. Doc. 78, 25th Cong., 2d sess., map, 768–9, 1838 (probably identical). **Topekaliga.**—Jesup (1837), ibid., 65.

To-ho-sa. See *Dohasan*.

Tohou. The Puma clan of the Chua (Rattlesnake) phratry of the Hopi.

To'-ho-üh wuñ-wü.—Fewkes in Am. Anthr., VII, 402, 1894 (*wuñ-wü*=clan). **Tohoû-wiñwû.**—Fewkes in 19th Rep. B. A. E., 582, 1900.

Toikhichi. A former Yokuts (Mariposan) tribe on Kings r., Cal.—A. L. Kroeber, inf'n, 1906.

Toikiming. A village of Praying Indians in 1659, on Nantucket id., Mass.—Cotton (1659) in Mass. Hist. Soc. Coll., 1st s., I, 204, 1806.

Toisa. A Potawatomi village, named from the chief, which formerly occupied the w. bank of Tippecanoe r., nearly opposite Bloomingsburg, Fulton co., Ind. The reservation was sold in 1836.—Tippecanoe treaty (1832) in U. S. Ind. Treat., 702, 1873.

Toiwait (*To-i-wait*). A Paviotso tribe formerly about the lower sink of the Carson, w. Nevada (Powell, Paviotso MS., B. A. E., 1881). They were said to number about 400 in 1870, most of them having been removed to the E. part of the territory.

Toy Pah-Utes.—Campbell in Ind. Aff. Rep., 111, 1870. **Toy Pi-Utes.**—Ind. Aff. Rep., 119, 1866. **Toy'-yu-wi-ti-kut'-teh.**—Powers, Inds. W. Nevada, MS., B. A. E., 1876 (formerly at the upper sink of the Carson; sig. 'tule eaters'; said to have been applied also to the Paviotso at the lower sink).

Tojagua. Mentioned by Oñate (Doc. Inéd., XVI, 115, 1871) as a pueblo of New Mexico in 1598. It was possibly Keresan.

Toajgua.—Bancroft, Ariz. and N. Mex., 136, 1889 (misquoting Oñate). **Toyagua.**—Columbus Mem. Vol., 155, 1893 (misprint).

Tok. A Koyukukhotana village on an island at the junction of Koyukuk r. with the Yukon, Alaska, having 6 inhabitants in 1844.

Tok.—Baker, Geog. Dict. Alaska, 1902. **Tokhakate.**—Zagoskin in Nouv. Ann. Voy., 5th s., XXI, map, 1850. **Tok-kakat.**—Tikhmenief quoted by Baker, ibid. **Tok-khakat.**—Zagoskin quoted by Petroff in 10th Census, Alaska, 37, 1884.

Tokaunee's Village. A former mixed Winnebago and Menominee village, named after a chief, situated on the site of Mauston, Juneau co., Wis., in 1837. It contained only five or six wigwams.—De la Ronde in Wis. Hist. Soc. Coll., VII, 359, 1876.

Tokeatl's Village. A summer camp of a Taku chief in Alaska; pop. 26 in 1880.—Petroff in 10th Census, Alaska, 32, 1884.

Tokoaath (*Tok'oā'ath*, 'Toquat proper'). A sept of the Toquart, a Nootka tribe.—Boas in 6th Rep. N. W. Tribes Can., 32, 1890.

Tokoais (*Tok'oā'is*, 'looking down on his family'—the name of an ancestor). A division of the Nuhalk, a subdivision of the Bellacoola of the coast of British Columbia.—Boas in 7th Rep. N. W. Tribes Can., 3, 1891.

Tokoanu. The Black-ant clan of the Ala (Horn) phratry of the Hopi.

To-ko'-a-nü wüñ-wü.—Fewkes in Am. Anthr., VII, 401, 1894 (*wüñ-wü*=clan).

Tokochi. The Wildcat clan of the Hopi.

Tokotci wiñwû.—Fewkes in 19th Rep. B. A. E., 584, 1900. **To-ko-tci wüñ-wü.**—Fewkes in Am. Anthr., VII, 404, 1894.

Tokogalgi (Creek: 'tadpole people'). A small Yuchi town on Kichofuni cr., an affluent of Flint r., s. w. Georgia.

Toc-so-gul-egau.—Hawkins (1799), Sketch, 63, 1848. **Tohogalias.**—Moll map in Humphreys, Acct., 1730. **Tokogalgi.**—Gatschet, Creek Migr. Leg., I, 146, 1884.

Tokonabi (Hopi: 'place of the running water in the canyon.'—Fewkes). A ruined pueblo in s. Utah, in the neighborhood of the junction of the Little Colorado with the Colorado, known by tradition as the place whence came the Ala (Horn) and the Chua (Snake) clans of the Hopi.

Tokonabi.—Fewkes in 19th Rep. B. A. E., 587, 1900. **Tokóonavi.**—Voth, Traditions of the Hopi, 30, 1905.

Toktakamai ('place of thimble-berries'). A Squawmish village on the right bank of Squawmisht r., w. Brit. Col.

Tawkamee.—Brit. Adm. chart, no. 1917. **Tōktā'-kamai.**—Hill-Tout in Rep. Brit. A. A. S., 474, 1900. **Tqt'a'qumai.**—Boas, MS., B. A. E., 1887.

Tolemato. A Yamasee village and mission station about 1595 on the coast of

Georgia. In 1597, in anger at the reproofs of Father Corpa, the missionary, the son and heir of the chief of Guale organized a revolt against the missions, resulting in the murder of Father Corpa and 3 other missionaries, the destruction of much property at the different mission villages, and the abandonment of all the missions of that region for several years. See *Topiqui*. (J. M.)

Tolemaro.—Barcia, Ensayo, 170, 1723. Tolemato.—Ibid. Tolomato.—Fairbanks, Fla., 111, 1901.

Toloawathla. A former Seminole town on the w. side of Chattahoochee r., Fla., 10 m. above the forks. Eheconhataunco was its chief in 1823. (H. R. Ex. Doc. 74 (1823), 19th Cong., 1st sess., 27, 1826.)

Tolocabit ('place of the big head'). A former village, occupied by either the Cahuilla (Kawia) or the Serranos, on the site of Redlands, s. Cal.

San Timéteo.—Burton (1853) in H. R. Ex. Doc. 76, 34th Cong., 3d sess., 117, 1857. San Timoteo.—Caballeria, Hist. San Bernardino Val., 39, 1902. Tolocabit.—Ibid.

Tolowa. An Athapascan tribe of extreme N. w. California. When first known they occupied the coast from the mouth of

TOLOWA MAN AND WIFE

Klamath r. nearly to the Oregon line, including Smith r. valley and the following villages: Echulit, Khoonkhwuttunne, and Khosatunne of the Khaamotene branch; Chesthltishtunne, Tatlatunne,

Ataakut, Meetkeni, Stuntusunwhott, Targhinaatun, Thltsusmetunne, and Turghestltsatun. They were gathered on a reservation in 1862, which was established on leased land, but it was abandoned in 1868, since which time the Tolowa have shifted for themselves. They are much demoralized and greatly reduced in numbers. Their language is unintelligible to the Hupa. In culture they resemble the Hupa and the Yurok, the chief difference being in their folklore and religion. They have been greatly influenced by the sea.

Áqüstă.—Dorsey, Naltunnetunne MS. vocab., B. A. E., 1884 ('southern language': Naltunnetunne name). A'-qu-stă.—Dorsey, Chetco MS. vocab., B A. E., 1884. Au'-kwŭ-ctă.—Dorsey, Alsea MS. vocab., B. A. E., 1884. Lagoons.—Heintzleman in Ind. Aff. Rep. 1857, 392, 1858. Lopas.—Ibid. Tahle-wah.—Schoolcraft, Ind. Tribes, III, 422, 1853. Talawa.—Heintzleman in Ind. Aff. Rep., 391, 1858. Talu-wa.—Crook, MS., B. A. E. Tolana.—Heintzleman in Ind. Aff. Rep., 286, 1858. Tolawa.—Bancroft, Nat. Races, I, 445, 1874. To-le-wah.—Gibbs in Schoolcraft, Ind. Tribes, III, 139, 1853. Tolowa.—Taylor in Cal. Farmer, June 8, 1860 (Yurok name of Echulit, applied by whites to the whole tribe).

Toltichi. A divergent northern dialect of the Yokuts, formerly spoken farthest up San Joaquin r., Cal. The last person actually using this dialect (a woman) is said to have died about 30 years prior to 1907. See Kroeber in Univ. Cal. Pub., Am. Arch. and Eth., II, 311, 354, 1907.

Toltsasding. A former Hupa village on Trinity r., Cal., at the mouth of Supply cr.

Tŏʟtsasdiñ.—Goddard, Life and Culture of the Hupa, 12, 1903.

Toltu.—The Sun clan of Taos pueblo, N. Mex.

Toltu tai'na.—M. C. Stevenson, notes, B. A. E., 1910 (*tai'na*='people').

Tolungowon. An Oneida settlement near Green Bay, Wis., in 1836.

Tolungowon.—Crawford (1836) in H. R. Doc. 178, 26th Cong. 1st sess., 17, 1840.

Tolwatin. A division of the Tenankutchin on Tanana r., Alaska.—Allen, Rep. on Alaska, 137, 1887.

Tomachichi. See *Tomochichi*.

Tomahawk. The name applied to a weapon or a group of weapons in common use among the Algonquian tribes of E. United States. The early writers on Virginia cite the word from the dialects of that region as *tommahick*, *tomahack*, *tamahake*, *tamahaac* (Strachey, 1612), etc.; other early forms are *tommyhawk* and *tomhog* (Church, Philip's War, 24, 1716). The Delaware dialect has *tomahikan*; the Mahican, *tumnahecan*; the Massachuset, *tomhegan*; the Abnaki, *tamahigan*. The word has come into English probably from the Virginian dialect. That this word is common to widely scattered Algonquian peoples is indicated by the fact that *ootommoheggun* is the Cree word for hammer. A common conception of the tomahawk is that it was the nearest aboriginal representative of the European hatchet, although the term was early applied to various forms of the club, as indicated in the following citations.

Describing a clandestine visit to one of the houses of worship of the Virginia Indians, Beverley says: "We found large Shelves, and upon these Shelves three Mats, each of which was roll'd up, and sow'd fast. These we handed down to the light, and to save time in unlacing the Seams, we made use of a Knife, and ripp'd them, without doing any damage to the Mats. In one of these we found some vast Bones, which we judg'd to be the Bones of Men, particularly we measur'd one Thigh-bone, and found it two foot nine inches long: In another Mat, we found some *Indian Tomahawks* finely

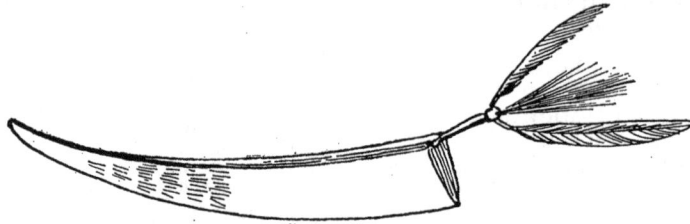

TOMAHAWK DESCRIBED AND ILLUSTRATED BY BEVERLEY

GLOBE-HEADED CLUB, SOMETIMES REFERRED TO AS A TOMAHAWK

grav'd and painted. These resembl'd the wooden Faulchion us'd by the Prize-fighters in England, except that they have no guard to save the Fingers. They were made of a rough heavy Wood, and the

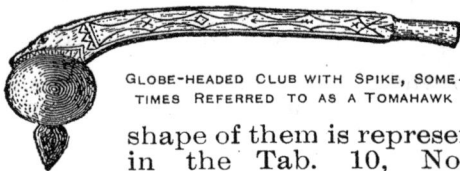

GLOBE-HEADED CLUB WITH SPIKE, SOME-TIMES REFERRED TO AS A TOMAHAWK

shape of them is represented in the Tab. 10, No. 3. Among these Tomahawks was the largest that ever I saw; there was fasten'd to it a Wild Turky's Beard painted red, and two of the longest Feathers of his Wings hung dangling at it, by a string of about 6 Inches long, ty'd to the end of the Tomahawk." (Beverley, Virginia, 29, 1705.)

CLUB WITH SPIKE, OFTEN DESCRIBED AS A TOMAHAWK

The tomahawk was very generally employed in ceremony, and the matter of its use and embellishment are well set forth by Rogers: "Another instrument of great esteem and importance among them is the tomahawk. This is an ancient weapon universally used by them in war, before they were taught the use of iron and steel; since which hatchets have been substituted in lieu of them. But this instrument still retains its use and importance in public transactions; and, like the pipe, is often very significant. This weapon is formed much like a hatchet, having a long stem or handle; the head is a round ball or knob of solid wood, well enough calculated to knock men's brains out, which on the other side of the stem terminates in a point where the edge would be, if made a hatchet, which point is set a little hooking or coming toward the stem; and near the center, where the stem or handle pierces the

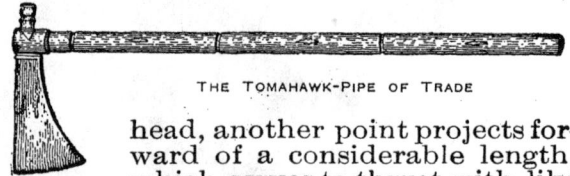

THE TOMAHAWK-PIPE OF TRADE

head, another point projects forward of a considerable length, which serves to thrust with like a spear or pike pole.

"The tomahawk likewise is ornamented with feathers and paintings, disposed and variegated in many significant forms, according to the occasion and end for which it is used, and on it they keep journals of their marches and most important and noted occurrences in a kind of hieroglyphics. When the council is called to deliberate war, the tomahawk is painted all over red, and when the council sits it is

CELT-HATCHET, COMMONLY REGARDED AS THE TYPICAL TOMAHAWK

laid down by the chief, and if war is concluded upon, the captain of the young warriors takes it up and with it in his hands dances and sings the war-song, as before mentioned. When the council is over, this hatchet, or some other of the kind, is sent by the hands of some warrior to every tribe concerned, and with it he presents a belt of wampum and delivers his message, throwing the hatchet on the ground, which is taken up by one of their most expert warriors, if they chuse to join; if not, they return it, and with a belt of their wampum suitable to the occasion." (Knox, Voy. and Trav., II, 165-6, 1767.)

The following from McCulloh's Researches (134, 1829) is of much later date than the preceding, and indicates the conception of the tomahawk at that time: "The tomahawk, which is sometimes considered a weapon peculiar to the American Indians, was originally a club carved into some convenient shape. It was most commonly a stout stick about three feet in length, terminating in a large knob, wherein a projecting bone or flint was often inserted. The hatchets of the Indians that are now called tomahawks are of European device, and the stone hatchets so often found in our fields and called by the same term were not military weapons, but mechanical tools." See *Axes, Calumet, Celts, Hatchets.*

In addition to the works cited above, consult Gerard in Am. Anthr., IX, no. 1, 1907; X, no. 2, 1908; Gookin (1674) in Mass. Hist. Soc. Coll., I, 152, 1792; Josselyn (1675), ibid., 3d s., III, 309, 1833; Holmes in Am. Anthr., X, no. 2, 1908 (and authorities therein cited); Smith, Hist. Virginia, Arber ed., 1884; Strachey, Virginia, 106, 1849; Tooker, Algonquian Ser., III, 40, 1901; Wood, New England's Prospect, 66, 1634.   (W. H. H.)

Tomás (Span. *Thomas*). The most noted Bidai chief of the 18th century, frequently mentioned in Spanish documents after 1755. Within or before this year he was officially named *capitan* by the Spanish authorities. His village was w. of Trinity r., Texas, near modern Bidais cr., which appears on a Spanish map of the latter part of the 18th century as Rio Santo Tomás (Mapa Geográfica de las Provincias Septentrionales, n. d., Béxar Archives).   (H. E. B.)

Tomassee. The name of two or more former Cherokee settlements, viz: (1) On Tomassee cr. of Keowee r., in Oconee co., S. C.; (2) on Little Tennessee r. near the entrance of Burningtown cr., in Macon co., S. C. The correct form and interpretation of the name are unknown.
Timossy.—Mooney in 19th Rep. B. A. E., 535, 1900 (quoted form). **Tomassee.**—Doc. of 1755 quoted by Royce in 5th Rep. B. A. E., 143, 1887. **Tymahse.**—Mooney, op. cit. (quoted form).

Tomau. A noted Menominee chief, properly called Thomas Carron. He was born, according to Grignon (Wis. Hist. Soc. Coll., III, 267, 1857), about 1752, though the inscription on the monument erected over his grave by John Law, of Green Bay, makes him but 56 years of age at his death, July 8, 1818 (Morse, Rep. Sec. War, 53, 1822; Draper in Wis. Hist. Soc. Coll., I, 58, 1855). He was the second son of Old Carron, a

half-blood French and Menominee, acting head chief. His mother was probably an Abnaki. Though not the official chief of the tribe by inheritance, he was regarded as chief in authority, since the hereditary title was held by one incapable of ruling. He was met by Zebulon Pike in 1805, who employed him as guide and speaks of his friendship for Americans, though subsequent acts did not serve to confirm this opinion. It is, however, true that, notwithstanding Tecumseh's eloquent appeal to the Menominee to join in the war on the United States settlements, Tomau stood firmly for peace, yielding only so far as to consent that such of his young men as wished to join as individuals might do so. He advised against so doing, however, and only a few availed themselves of the privilege. Later, on the other hand, Tomau allied himself with the British, and with probably 100 of his warriors accompanied Col. Dickson in 1812 in the capture from the Americans of Ft Mackinaw, though there was no fighting. It was during this expedition that Oshkosh was placed under Tomau's special care. He was also with Proctor and Dickson in the attack on Ft Sandusky, and in 1814, with about 80 Menominee, accompanied Dickson to Mackinaw, where they took part in the battle in which the American commander Maj. Holmes fell. In 1816 Tomau gave permission to the United States troops to build a fort in Menominee territory. Two years later he died at Mackinaw from excessive intoxication, and was buried there. Tomau was of the Prairie-chicken clan, and was thrice married; his first wife, Kiwakomuqkiu ('Wandering Around') was a Menominee woman, by whom he had two sons. Separating from this wife he married two sisters, with both of whom he lived until they died and by one of whom he had four children. Consult Hoffman in 14th Rep. B. A. E., pt. 1, 54, 1896.

Tombigbee (*Itúmbi-bíkpi*, 'coffin maker.'—Gatschet). A former Choctaw town on or near Tombigbee r., w. Alabama.
Tambeché.—Lattré, map of U. S., 1784. **Tombecbé.**—Alcedo, Dic. Geog., V, 169, 1789. **Tombechbé.**—Romans, Fla., 326, 1775. **Tombeche.**—Jefferys, Am. Atlas, map 5, 1776. **Tombeechy.**—Jefferys, French Dom. Am., 135, map, 1761.

Tomcha (*Tom'-cha*). A former Maidu settlement on the left bank of Feather r., E. of Lomo, Sutter co., Cal.   (R. B. D.)
Toam'-cha.—Powers in Cont. N. A. Ethnol., III., 282, 1877.

Tomé (contr. of the name of Abbé Santo Tomás.—Lummis). A former pueblo of Genizaros (q. v.), situated on the Rio Grande 2 leagues s. of Isleta, N. Mex., on the site of a prehistoric pueblo, probably of the Tigua. The inhabitants of the settlement consisted of neophytes who had been captured by the Apache and Comanche, sold by them to the Spaniards, and released from servitude by the governor of New Mexico to form this settlement as a mission visita of Isleta pueblo. This seems to have been in 1740, although in the previous year a grant of 121,593 acres in and about Tomé was made to J. Valera and others, representing 30 families, evidently Spanish (Bancroft, N. Mex. and Ariz., 243, 253, 758–9, 1889). In 1748 Villa-Señor (Theatro Am., 416) reported the population to be 40 families; in 1766 there were 70 families. According to Lummis (New Mex. David, 95, 100, 1891) Tomé was settled by Ignacio Baca with 50 Spanish families in 1769, and it seems to have lost its character as an Indian settlement about this time. From 1852 to 1872 and from 1874 to 1876 Tomé was the county seat of Valencia co. In the spring of 1905 it was destroyed by a sudden rise of the Rio Grande.　　　(F. W. H.)

Concepcion.—Bancroft, Ariz. and N. Mex., 281, 1889 (visita name). Genizaros.—Villa-Señor, Theatro Am., II, 416, 1748. S. Thomas.—Pike, Exped., map, 1810. Tomé Dominguez.—Bancroft, N. Mex. and Ariz., 243, 1889. Town of the Broken Promise.—Lummis, N. Mex. David, 100, 1891 (transl. of Indian [Tigua?] name). Valencia.—Bancroft, Ariz. and N. Mex., 253, 1889 (Tomé or; not the present town of Valencia).

Tomeychee. See *Tomochichi*.

Tomhog, Tommyhawk. See *Tomahawk*.

Tomo. A Calusa village on the s. w. coast of Florida about 1570.—Fontaneda Memoir (*ca.* 1575), Smith trans., 19, 1854.

Tomochachi. See *Tomochichi*.

Tomochic ('winter house.'—Och). A Tarahumare settlement in w. Chihuahua, Mexico, near the head of Mayo r., lat. 28° 30′, lon. 107° 40′.—Orozco y Berra, Geog., 323, 1864.

Tomochichi (spelled also Bocachee, Temochichi, Thamachaychee, Thomochichi, Tomachachi, Tomeychee, etc., and said by Gatschet to mean 'the one who causes to fly up' [?]). A Creek chief, noted in the early history of Georgia. He was originally of Apalachukla, a Lower Creek town on Chattahoochee r. in Alabama, and his name appears in behalf of this settlement in a treaty between the Creeks and the Carolina government in 1721. Shortly afterward, for some unknown reason, he was outlawed from his people and withdrew with a few followers to Savannah r., where, by permission of South Carolina, he established himself in a new town called Yamacraw (q. v.), at the present Savannah, Ga. On the foundation of the Georgia colony by Oglethorpe in 1733, Tomochichi assumed a friendly attitude toward the newcomers and was instrumental in bringing about a treaty of alliance between that colony and the Lower Creeks in that year. At the same time a reconciliation was effected between himself and his tribe, and he was

given permission to collect his friends from the various Lower Creek towns to take up their residence with him at Yamacraw. In the next year, 1734, with his wife, nephew, and several others, he accompanied Oglethorpe to England, where his well-known portrait was painted. He continued to be helpful to the colonists after his return until his death, which occurred in his own town, Oct. 5, 1739, he being then perhaps 75 years of age. He was given a public funeral at Savannah, where a monument to his memory was erected in 1899 by the Colonial Dames of America. Consult Gatschet, Creek Migr. Leg., I, II, 1884, 1888; Jones, Hist. Sketch of Tomochichi, 1868.

The portrait here reproduced, representing the chief and his nephew Toonahowi, is from an engraving by Klein-

TOMOCHICHI AND HIS NEPHEW

schmidt, of Augsburg, Germany, of the original painting by Verelst in 1734, which for some years hung in the room of the Georgia Office in London. This engraving appeared as the frontispiece in Urlsperger, Ausfuehrliche Nachricht von den Salzburgischen Emigranten, Halle, 1735, and has since been reproduced in Jones, Hist. of Ga., I, 1883; Winsor, Narr. and Crit. Hist. Am., v, 1887, and elsewhere.　　　(J. M.)

Tomoy. A Costanoan village formerly within 2 m. of Santa Cruz mission, Cal.—Taylor in Cal. Farmer, Apr. 5, 1860.

Tompiro. A name used by some Spanish writers of the 17th century for that division of the Piro which occupied, until about 1675, the Salinas region E. of the Rio Grande in central New Mexico. Their pueblos included Abo, Tabira, and Tenabo. See *Jumano*, *Piro*, *Salineros*, and the pueblos named.

Tompiras.—Benavides, Memorial, 21, 1630. **Tompires.**—Blaeu, Atlas, XII, 62, 1667. **Tompiros.**—Benavides cited by Bancroft, Ariz. and N. Mex., 164, 1889. **Tōpira.**—Benavides, Memorial, 21, 1630. **Topires.**—D'Anville, map Am. Sept., 1746. **Tōpiros.**—Perea, Verdadera Rel., 2, 1632. **Tumpiros.**—Vetancurt (1696) in Teatro Mex., III, 300, 1871.

Tom Pung. An old name for a cutter; a pung. According to Trumbull (Trans. Am. Philol. Asso., 26, 1872), "a hundred years ago a one-horse sleigh, whether a jumper or a cutter, was called in Massachusetts a '*Tom Pung*'—written and pronounced as if the syllables were two independent words." In Dennie's Farmers' Museum (243, 1798) a writer represents the town of Roxbury, Mass., as sending to Boston "the gliding *Tom Pung* and the rattling cart." *Tom Pung* is the older word of which *pung* is a reduction. Trumbull, with apparent justification, derives *Tom Pung* from toboggan (q. v.) through folk-etymology. (A. F. C.)

Tomsobe. A Calusa village on the s. w. coast of Florida, about 1570.

Lonsobe.—Fontaneda (*ca.* 1575) in Ternaux-Compans, Voy., XX, 40, 1841 (misprint). **Sonsobe.**—Fontaneda, Memoir, B. Smith trans., 27, 1854. **Tomsobe.**—Ibid., 19. **Tonsobe.**—Shipp, De Soto and Fla., 586, 1881 (misprint).

Tom's Town. A former settlement of the Delawares on Scioto r., a short distance below the present Chillicothe, and not far from the mouth of Paint cr., Ohio. In 1750 it contained five or six families. (G. P. D.)

Harrickintoms.—Darlington, Gist's Jour. (1750), 42, 1893. **Hurricane Toms.**—Archives of Pa., 2d s., maps, app, I–X. **Toms Town.**—Hutchins map in Smith, Bouquet Exped., 1766.

Tomwhiksen (*Tom-whik-sen*). A former winter village of the Lummi, situated on Hale passage, Wash.—Gibbs, Clallam and Lummi, 37, 1863.

Ton ('tree bole'). An extinct clan of Taos pueblo, N. Mex.

Ton tai'na.—M. C. Stevenson, notes, B. A. E., 1910 (*tai'na*='people').

Tona. The Turkey clan of the Zuñi of New Mexico.

Tóna-kwe.—Cushing in 13th Rep. B. A. E., 368, 1896 (*kwe*='people').

Tonachic ('where there are pillars'). A Tarahumare pueblo, containing a total of 604 inhabitants in 1900; situated in the district of San Andrés del Rio, Chihuahua, Mexico. Lumholtz states that when he visited the place in 1890 it contained about 2,700 inhabitants, and that the Indians had been more or less driven off by the whites. In mission times Tonachic was a place of some importance. It still has a fine church with some rich furnishings, though many of them have been stolen. See Lumholtz, Unknown Mex., I, 204, 1902.

Tonalizco. A former pueblo of the Tecualme in the Sierra de Nayarit, Jalisco, Mexico.—Orozco y Berra, Geog., 280, 1864.

Tonanulgar. A former Creek town on Uchee cr., Russell co., Ala.

Tonanulga.—Seale (1837) in H. R. Doc. 452, 25th Cong., 2d sess., 54, 1838. **Tonanulgar.**—Ibid., 48.

Tonanulla. A former Creek town not far from Tonanulgar, probably in Russell co., Ala.

Tonanulla.—Seale (1837) in H. R. Doc. 452, 25th Cong., 2d sess., 54, 1838. **Wartoolaharka.**—Ibid.

Tonapa. A native (Diegueño?) village formerly situated not far from the headwaters of San Dieguito r., San Diego co., Cal., in a little valley called Eschá.—Grijalva (1795), cited by Bancroft, Hist. Cal., I, 563, 1886.

Tonarooka. A former town of the Tuscarora of North Carolina, situated in 1711 on a branch of Neuse r., between "Fort Narhante's" and Catechna.—S. C. Hist. and Geneal. Mag., IX, 36, 1908.

Tonashi. The Badger clan of the Zuñi of New Mexico.

Tónashi-kwe.—Cushing in 13th Rep. B. A. E., 368, 1896 (*kwe*='people').

Tonati. A pueblo of the Cora and seat of a mission, probably on the Rio San Pedro, in Jalisco, Mexico.

Santísima Trinidad de la Mesa del Tonati.—Orozco y Berra, Geog., 280, 1864.

Tonawanda ('confluent stream'). A Seneca settlement on Tonawanda cr., in Niagara co., N. Y. In 1890 there were 517 Seneca and a few other Iroquois on the reservation.

Tä'-nä-wun-da.—Morgan, League Iroq., 467, 1851 (Seneca form). **Tonawanda.**—Ibid. **Tonawando.**—Ogden deed (1838) in U. S. Ind. Treat., 557, 1873. **Tonawanta.**—Day, Penn., 654, 1843. **Tonnewanta.**—Iroquois complaint (1821) in Drake, Bk. Inds., bk. 5, 102, 1848. **Tonnoraunto.**—Writer of 1792 in Mass. Hist. Soc. Coll., 1st s., I, 286, 1806 (misprint). **Tyo'-nä-wĕⁿ'-dĕ'ᶐ.**—J. N. B. Hewitt, inf'n, 1887.

Tonawitsowa (*To-na-wits'-o-wa*). A Shoshoni tribe of 6 bands formerly in N. Nevada, in the vicinity of Battle mtn. and Unionville.—Powell in Ind. Aff. Rep. 1873, 52, 1874.

Tonchuun (*Ton-ch-un'*). A pueblo ruin, probably prehistoric, situated 5 m. S. E. of Pecos pueblo, N. Mex. The building was 400 ft long and contained more than 300 rooms in its ground plan. According to tradition it was occupied by a colony from Jemez and was the last of the outlying villages to become concentrated in the great pueblo of Pecos. See Hewett in Am. Anthr., VI, 433, fig. 9, 1904.

Tondakhra ('beaver'). A Huron village in Ontario in 1637. It was situated on the w. side of the N. peninsula of Tiny twp., 4 m. N. W. of Lafontaine and about 1 m. S. E. of Clover pt. See Jes. Rel., Thwaites ed., XIII, 270, 1898; XXXIV, 254, 1898.

Tonebao ('turtle'). A phratry and a gens of the Mahican.

Tone-bä'-o.—Morgan, Anc. Soc., 174, 1877 (the phratry). **Toon-pa-ooh.**—Barton, New Views, XXXIX, 1798 (the gens).

Tong. The Antelope clan of the Tewa pueblo of San Ildefonso, N. Mex.

Toⁿ-tdóa.—Hodge in Am. Anthr., IX, 348, 1896 (*tdóa*='people').

Tongas (*Tᴬngā'sh*, named from an island on which they formerly camped). A Tlingit tribe at the mouth of Portland canal, Alaska, numbering 273 in 1880 and 255 in 1890, probably including the Sanya. Their town on Tongass id., Alexander archipelago, bearing the same name, is being abandoned for Ketchikan. Its social divisions are Daktlawedi, Ganahadi, and Tekoedi.   (J. R. S.)
Kee-tah-hon-neet.—Kane, Wand. N. A., app., 1859. TᴀNgā'ᴄ.—Swanton, field notes, B. A. E., 1904. Tangasskoe. — Veniaminoff, Zapiski, II, pt. III, 30, 1840. Ta'nta hade.—Swanton, field notes, 1900–01 (Kaigani name). Tongass.—Kane, op. cit. Tont-a-quans.—Colyer in Ind. Aff. Rep. 1869, 537, 1870. Tungāss.—Krause, Tlinkit Ind., 111, 1885. Tungāss-kŏn.—Ibid., 120. Tungrass.—Peirce in H. R. Rep. 830, 27th Cong., 2d sess., 62, 1842.

Tongigua ('little village'). One of the early Quapaw villages which Joutel (1687) says was situated on the border of Mississippi r. on the right in ascending (Margry, Déc., III, 457, 1878), probably in N. W. Mississippi. De Soto in 1541 found the village of Quizquiz, which seems to have been Quapaw, on the E. bank.
Dogenga.—McKenney and Hall, Ind. Tribes, III, 81, 1854. Doginga.—Douay cited by Shea, Discov., 170, 1852. Taⁿwaⁿ-jiɧa.—Dorsey, Kwapa MS. vocab., B.A.E., 1883. Taⁿwaⁿzhika.—Gatschet, Creek Migr. Leg., I, 30, 1884. Thonges.—Hamilton in Trans. Neb. Hist. Soc., I, 48, 1885. Thons.—Du Lac, Voy. Louisianes, 262, 1805. Togenga.—Shea, Early Voy., 76, 1861. Togunguas.—Barcia, Ensayo, 288, 1723. Tongenga.—Tonti (1688) in French, Hist. Coll. La., I, 71, 1846. Tongigua.—Joutel (1687) in Margry, Déc., III, 457, 1878. Tonginga.—Joutel (1687) in French, Hist. Coll. La., I, 176, 1846. Tonguinga.—Ibid., III, 444, 1878. Tonningua.—Joutel in French, Hist. Coll. La., I, 179, 1846. Topingas.—Charlevoix, Voy., II, 246, 1761. Touginga.—La Harpe (1722) in Margry, Déc., VI, 365, 1886. Toyengan.—Shea, Discov., 170, 1852.

Tongonaoto (*Tong-o-nä'-o-to*, 'drift log'). A subclan of the Delawares.—Morgan, Anc. Soc., 172, 1877.

Tongs. See *Pincers.*

Tonguish's Village. A former Potawatomi settlement, taking its name from its chief, otherwise called Toga, near Rouge r., in the s. part of Oakland co. or the N. part of Wayne co., Mich., about 20 m. N. W. of Detroit. By treaty of 1807 a tract of two sections of land was reserved for the use of this band, but by treaty of 1827 it was ceded to the United States "in order to consolidate some of the dispersed bands . . . at a point removed from the road leading from Detroit to Chicago, as far as practicable from the settlements of the whites." For the life of Tonguish, see Mich. Pion. and Hist. Coll., VIII, 161, 1886.
Tonguish Village.—Pottawotomi treaty (1827) in U. S. Ind. Treat., 674, 1873. Tonquish's village.—Detroit treaty (1807), ibid., 194.

Tonicahaw (perhaps from *Tonik-hikia*, 'standing post'). A former Choctaw town noted by Romans as having been near the line between Neshoba and Kemper cos., Miss. See Halbert in Pub. Miss. Hist. Soc., VI, 427, 1902.

Tonichi. A pueblo of the Nevome (containing also some Eudeve and Opata) and seat of a Spanish mission founded in 1628. Situated in E. Sonora, Mexico, on the Rio Yaqui below its junction with the Papigochi, lat. 29°, lon. 109°. Pop. 510 in 1678, 379 in 1730. The Rudo Ensayo (*ca.* 1762) mentions it as a visita of Onavas. It is now a civilized community, with 372 inhabitants in 1900.
Sta María del Pópulo Tonichi.—Zapata (1678) cited by Bancroft, No. Mex. States, I, 246, 1884. Toniche.—Escudero, Noticias Son. y Sin., 101, 1849. Tonichi.—Rivera, Diario, leg. 1382, 1736. Tonici.—Kino, map (1702), in Stöcklein, Neue Welt-Bott, 74, 1726. Tonitsi.—Orozco y Berra, Geog., 351, 1864. Tonitza.—Rudo Ensayo (*ca.* 1762), 124, 1863.

Tonihata. An island in the St Lawrence, upon which was a mixed Iroquois village in 1671 and later. It is supposed to have been the modern Grenadier id., between Ogdenburgh and L. Ontario, in Leeds co., Ontario.
Koniata.—Esnauts and Rapilly map, 1777. Otondiata.—De Courcelles (1671) in N. Y. Doc. Col. Hist., IX, 77, 1855. Otoniata.—Denonville (1687), ibid., 361. Otoniato.—Ibid. Toniata.—Chauvignerie (1736), ibid., 1056. Tonihata.—Jefferys, Fr. Doms., pt. 1, 15, 1761. Tonniata.—Frontenac (1692) in N. Y. Doc. Col. Hist., IX, 531, 1855.

Tonikan Family. A linguistic family established by Powell (7th Rep. B. A. E., 125, 1891) to include the language of the Tunica (q. v.) tribe in the lower Mississippi region.
=Tunicas.—Gallatin in Trans. and Coll. Am. Antiq. Soc., II, 115, 116, 1836 (quotes Sibley, who states they speak a distinct language); Latham, Nat. Hist. Man, 341, 1850 (opposite mouth of Red r.; quotes Sibley as to distinctness of language). =Tonica.—Gatschet, Creek Migr. Leg., I, 39, 1884 (brief account of tribe). =Tonika.—Gatschet in Science, 412, Apr. 29, 1887 (distinctness as a family asserted). =Tonikan.—Powell, op. cit.

Tonkawa. A prominent tribe, forming the Tonkawan linguistic family, which, during most of the 18th and 19th centuries, lived in central Texas. According to Gatschet (Karankawa Inds., 37, 1891) they call themselves *Titskan wátitch*, while the name Tonkawa is a Waco word, *Tonkawéya* meaning 'they all stay together.'

Ethnology.—The ethnological relations of the tribe are still obscure. It has been surmised that it was a composite of the remnants of other tribes, and this is apparently true of their later organization at least; yet the fact that their language and culture were so different from those of the great neighboring groups indicates that fundamentally they were a distinct people. Closely associated with them, and of similar culture, were lesser tribes or subtribes, notably the Yojuane, Mayeye, and Ervipiame. It has recently been established by a study of the records of the San Xavier missions that these tribes spoke the Tonkawa language, but that the Deadoses (Agdocas, Yadocxas), who were often associated with the Tonkawa, spoke the language of the Bidai and Arkokisa (see *San Francisco Xavier de Horcasitas,*

Mayeye, Yakwal). The Yojuane and Mayeye were apparently in part absorbed by the Tonkawa in the latter part of the 18th century. The Yakwal (Yakawana), re-

TONKAWA MAN

membered in Tonkawa tradition (Gatschet, op. cit.), were very probably the Yojuane. There was, besides these, a large group of lesser tribes on the border between the Tonkawan and Coahuiltecan territories, notably the Sana, Emet, Cavas, Toho, and Tohaha, who, we are told in positive terms by competent early witnesses, did not speak the Coahuiltecan language. There is strong probability that a study of the surviving fragments of their language will prove them also to have been Tonkawan (see *Sana*). Some of the traditions of the Tonkawa point to an early residence on the Gulf coast, but their language does not bear the marks of such a birthplace.

Until the 19th century the Tonkawa were almost always hostile to the Lipan and other Apache tribes, and this fact kept them generally at peace with the Comanche, Wichita, and Hasinai, whom they often joined in Apache wars. They were usually friendly also with the Bidai, Arkokisa, and Xaraname (Aranama) to the s., and with the numerous Coahuiltecan tribes to the s. w. Relations with the Comanche and Wichita were frequently strained, however, even during this period. In the 19th century relations with these groups were reversed, the Tonkawa then being usually friendly with the Lipan and hostile toward the

Comanche and Wichita. When, about 1790, the Apache effected an alliance with the Bidai, Arkokisa, and Attacapa, the Tonkawa were brought into hostile relations with these tribes (Gil Ybarbo to Gov. Muñoz, Mar. 22 and Apr. 26, 1791, MS. in Béxar Archives).

Relations with French and Spanish.—In 1691 Francisco de Jesus María unmistakably included this tribe and their associates, the Yojuane, in his list of enemies of the Hasinai, writing the names "Tanquaay" and "Diujuan" (Relación, Aug. 15, 1691, MS.). The Tonkawa seem not to be mentioned again until 1719, but the Yojuane appear in the interim, when, about 1714 (the chronology is not clear), they destroyed the main fire temple of the Hasinai (Espinosa, Chrónica Apostólica, 424, 1746; see also Dictamen Fiscal, 1716, in Mem. de Nueva España, XXVII, 193). To the French the Tonkawa became definitely known through La Harpe's expedition of 1719. His lieutenant, Du Rivage, reported that 70 leagues up Red r. from the Kadohadacho he met several tribes, which he called respectively the Tancaoye, Joyvan (Yojuan), Quidehais (Kichai?), Naouydiches (Nabedache?), Huanchané, and Huane. They were wanderers, following the buffalo for a living. Famous warriors all, the "Tancaoye" were the most renowned, and their chiefs

TONKAWA WOMAN

bore many battle scars. They were just returning from a war with the Apache, which fact, together with the tribal names given, makes it seem probable that the party was a composite one of Caddoan and Tonkawan tribes, such as in later times frequently went against the Apache. From this time forth the Tonkawa were generally friendly with the French (La Harpe in Margry, Déc., VI, 277–78, 1886).

With the Spaniards the Tonkawa first came into intimate contact through the establishment of the missions on San Xavier (San Gabriel) r., Texas. As early as 1740 the missionaries had thought of taking them to San Antonio, but considered them too remote (Descripción, 1740, MS. in Mem. de Nueva España, XXVIII, 203). Between 1746 and 1749 three missions were planted on the San Xavier, and among the tribes there were the Mayeye, Yojuane, and Tonkawa (see *San Francisco Xavier de Horcasitas*). While there they suffered from a terrible epidemic of smallpox and from Apache raids. On the other hand, they deserted the missions to go with the Hasinai against the Apache, and got the Spaniards into trouble by selling Apache captives to the Hasinai. By 1756 these missions were abandoned and the protecting garrison was transferred to the new Lipan mission of San Sabá. In common with the other foes of the Apache, the Tonkawa were converted into enemies of the Spaniards by the establishment of this mission for the Lipan, and they took part in its destruction in 1758.

Habitat.—It has not been possible to determine with confidence the range and headquarters of the Tonkawa before the decade between 1770 and 1780, when the reports become full and satisfactory. At this time their customary range was between the middle and upper Trinity on the N. E., and the San Gabriel and the Colorado on the s. w., rather above than below the San Antonio road. Their favorite headquarters were about halfway between Waco and the Trinity crossing of the San Antonio road, near an eminence known to the natives as the Turtle (Mezières, Informe, July 4, 1772; Letter to Croix, May 28, 1778; Gil Ybarbo to Cabello, Dec. 5, 1778; Croix, Relación Particular, 1778, MSS. See *Tortugas*). Since they first became known, the Tonkawa had perhaps drifted gradually southward, though this is not certain. It was true of the Wichita tribes for the same period, and would be a logical consequence of pressure by the Comanche and the Osage. Yet the testimony before 1770 is not conclusive. Du Rivage saw the Tonkawa near Red r., but this may have been a temporary location. In 1740 they and the Yojuane were reported to be "not far from [the] Texas," but whether w. or N. we are not told. When in 1752 De Soto Vermudez inquired of the Nasoni, on the

upper Angelina, what tribes lived to the northward, he was told that 20 leagues away (northward by the implication of the question) were the Tebancanas (Tawakoni), and that beyond them followed the Tancaguies and Yujuanes. If the direction was correctly given as northward, the Tonkawa were then clearly farther N. than their central rendezvous of a later date. Similarly a copy of the La Fora map (*ca.* 1767), but not the original, shows the Yojuane village to have been near the upper Sabine, but the source and the date of this annotation are not known. On the other hand, as has been shown, after 1746 the Tonkawa and Yojuane frequented the missions on the San Gabriel, associating there with related tribes native of the locality, which would indicate that it was within the usual Tonkawa range. Moreover, when 'in 1768 Solís crossed Texas from Béxar to Nacogdoches, he noted in his diary after passing the Brazos that in this neighborhood lived Tancagues, Yojuanes, and Mayeyes. It would seem, therefore, that when Mezières wrote, the country of the Turtle had for some time been for the Tonkawa the middle of a long range from N. E. to s. w. After this time, as the Apache receded, there was apparently considerable southwestward extension of their range, though for some years they had headquarters E. of the Brazos. It is to be noted that writers have usually erred by calling the Tonkawa a southwestern Texas tribe, which was not true for a century after they came into history. On the other hand, the location assigned them on Powell's linguistic map applies only to the latter part of the 19th century (see Descripción, 1740, op. cit.; De Soto Vermudez, Investigation, MS. in Archivo Gen., 1752; La Fora map in Dpto. de Fomento, Mexico; Solís, Diario, MS. in Mem. de Nueva España, XXVII, 277; Davenport, Noticia, 1809, MS. in Archivo Gen.; Terán, Noticia, 1828, in Bol. Soc. Geog. Mex., 1890; Powell's map in 7th Rep. B. A. E.).

Customs.—The Tonkawa always bore a bad reputation among both Indians and whites, although toward the Americans they were uniformly at peace The characteristics assigned to them by Du Rivage in 1719 are those most frequently mentioned in later times, when they became better known. They were warlike wanderers, planting few or no crops, living on game, and following the buffalo long distances. When hard pressed they could eat food usually considered revolting. Their general reputation as cannibals is borne out by concurrent tradition and history, by their designation in the sign language, and by the names applied to them by other tribes. Mezières said of them that they were despised by other tribes as vagabonds, ill-natured, and disposed to thievery, a character frequently given them in later times. They lived in scattered villages of skin tipis, which they moved according to the caprice of the chiefs or the demands of the chase. In the 18th century they were fine horsemen and had good animals. Their offensive weapons then were firearms, bows and arrows, and the spear; their defensive arms were the leather jacket (*cuera*), shield, and cap or helmet, on which they often wore horns and gaudy plumage.

Once, when in their midst, Mezières wrote a statement of their dependence on the buffalo that deserves to be recorded. "Besides their meat," he said, "it furnishes them liberally what they desire for conveniences. The brains are used to soften skins, the horns for spoons and drinking cups, the shoulder-blades to dig up (*cavar*) and clear off the ground, the tendons for thread and bowstrings, the hoof to glue the arrow-feathering. From the tail-hair they make ropes and girths; from the wool, belts and various ornaments. The hide furnishes saddle and bridle, tether ropes, shields, tents, shirts, footwear, and blankets to protect them from the cold." They were great deer as well as buffalo hunters, and when their buffalo range was partly cut off by the Comanche, their dependence on this animal increased. A trader informed Sibley in 1805 that he had obtained from the Tonkawa as many as 5,000 deerskins in one year, besides tallow, robes, and tongues. Their market for hides in earlier times had usually been the Tawakoni villages (Mezières, op. cit.; Sibley, Hist. Sketches, 1806).

Spanish Relations after 1770.—For about 15 years after the failure of the San Xavier missions, the Tonkawa were regarded by the Spaniards as open enemies; but in 1770 an equal period of nominal peace began, during which the Spanish policy toward the tribe was marked by three main features: (1) to win their good-will by friendly visits and by sending them authorized traders with supplies; (2) to force them to keep peace with the Tawakoni, Yscani, and Kichai, who were relied on to restrain the Tonkawa by good example or coercion; (3) to induce them, by persuasion and by threats of withdrawing the traders, to abandon their vagabond life and settle in a fixed village. The principal agents in this work were De Mezières, Gil Ybarbo, Nicolás de la Mathe, and Andrés de Courbière—all but one Frenchmen from Natchitoches, it will be noted. Their efforts at coercion through trade were evidently made nugatory by clandestine French traffic that could not be stopped.

Failure to successfully effect these policies was charged to the bad influence of the noted Tonkawa chief of the day, Tosque, or El Mocho. He was an Apache by birth, who had been captured and adopted by the Tonkawa. During one of his exploits against the Osage he had lost his right ear, whence his nickname, *El Mocho*, "the maimed" or "cropped." By his prowess in war and his eloquence in council he raised himself to a position of influence. Chance, in the form of an epidemic, occurring in 1777–78, removed his rivals and left him head chief. His baneful influence before this had won him the enmity of the Spaniards, and Mezières, under official orders, had bribed his rivals to assassinate him, but he was saved by the epidemic mentioned. Now resort was had to flattery and gifts. In 1779 Mezières held a long and loving conference with El Mocho at the lower Tawakoni village, and the result was that they went together to Béxar to see the governor. There, on Oct. 8, 1779, in the presence of more than 400 Tonkawa people, Governor Cabello with great ceremony appointed El Mocho "capitan grande" of his tribe, decorating him with a medal of honor, and presenting him a commission, a uniform, a baston, and a flag bearing the cross of Burgundy. In return, of course, El Mocho made grave promises to obey and to form the desired pueblo (Cabello, Informe, 1784, ¶ 61, MS.).

The promise to settle down, however, remained unfulfilled, while El Mocho's insincerity was still further proved by events of 1782. In that year the Lipan, Mescaleros, and Apache, as the records give the names, desirous of better means of acquiring arms, made overtures of peace to the Tonkawa, who easily obtained weapons from the French. El Mocho consented to a meeting. The place appointed was the bank of Guadalupe r.; the time, the moons of November and December. Cabello, unable to prevent the gathering, sent a spy in Indian disguise—probably the great Indian linguist and interpreter, Andrés de Courbière—who reported the proceedings in detail. According to him, more than 4,000 Indians attended, and the barter of firearms for stolen horses was lively. But the alliance was defeated by El Mocho's ambitions. He tried to induce the Apache tribes to make him their head chief, in return for which he would rid the country of Spaniards. This self-seeking aroused the jealousy of the Apache chiefs, quarrels ensued, and on Christmas day the meeting broke up without the alliance being effected (Cabello, op. cit., ¶ 63).

This event, combined with personal jealousies within the Tonkawa tribe, was the undoing of El Mocho, for return was now made by the Spaniards to the policy of assassination. After much intriguing and waiting, El Mocho was taken unawares on July 12, 1784, and murdered in the plaza at Bahía (Goliad), a place fated to be in later days the scene of other equally atrocious deeds. It is to be remarked that for the story of these dark dealings of both the Spanish authorities and their enemy we have only the reports, entirely candid, of the former (Cazorla, Capt. of Bahía, to Cabello, July 12, 1784, Archivo General, Hist., vol. c; Cabello to Neve, July 15, ibid.).

The removal of El Mocho was justified by subsequent events. By June, 1785, Courbière was able to report that the new Tonkawa chief had established a permanent village on Navasota r.; and during the next 10 years "the village of the Tancagues" was referred to as though it were a fixed and definite entity. But thereafter the tribe was usually described as wanderers; thereafter, likewise, they were alternately at peace and at war with the Spaniards (Cabello to Rengel, June 7, 1785, Béxar Archives; Gil Ybarbo to Governor Muñoz, Mar. 22 and Apr. 26, 1791, Béxar Archives; Leal, Noticia, July 10, 1794, Béxar Archives).

Population; Recent History.—A junta held at Béxar, Jan. 5, 1778, estimated the Tonkawa at 300 warriors. In April of that year Mezières, when on his second visit to the tribe, gave the same figure, including some apostate Xaraname (Aranama). In Sept., 1779, when again at their settlement, he reported that since the recent epidemic of smallpox there remained 150 warriors. Three years later a spy who spent several days at a gathering of Apache and Tonkawa on Guadalupe r. reported that only 600 Tonkawa were present, the rest having remained at home. If he told the truth, he could hardly have meant that these were all warriors. Sibley in 1805 gave their strength at 200 men; Davenport, about 1809, placed it at 250 families, and Terán, 1828, at 80 families. In 1847 the official estimate was 150 men (see Cabello, Informe, 1784, 12, 63; Mezières, Letters to Croix, Apr. 5, 1778, and Sept. 13, 1779, in Mem. de Nueva España, XXVIII, 272, 246; Sibley, op. cit.; Davenport, Noticia, *ca.* 1809, MS. in Archivo Gen.; Terán, Noticia, 1828, in Bol. Soc. Geog. Mex., 266, 1870). In the fall of 1855 the Government settled them, together with the Caddo, Kichai, Waco, Tawakoni, and Penateka Comanche, upon two small reservations on the Clear Fork of Brazos r., Texas. In consequence of the violent opposition of the Texans, culminating in an attack upon the agency, the Indians were removed in 1857 to Washita r., Okla., the Tonkawa being temporarily camped about the mouth of Tonkawa cr., just above the present Anadarko. In the confusion brought about by the civil war the other tribes saw an opportunity to pay off old scores against the Tonkawa, who were generally hated for their cannibalistic practices as well as for serving as government scouts against the more western tribes. On the excuse that the Tonkawa and their agent were in alliance with the Confederacy, a body of Delawares, Shawnee, and Caddo attacked the Anadarko agency and the Tonkawa camp on the night of Oct. 25, 1862, killing two of the agency employees and massacring 137 men, women, and children out of a total of about 300 of the Tonkawa tribe. The survivors, after some years of miserable wandering, were finally gathered in at Ft Griffin, Texas, to save them from complete extermination by their enemies. In 1884 all that were left—92, including a number of Lipan—were removed to Oklahoma, being assigned the next year to their present location at Oakland agency, near Ponca. In 1908 they numbered but 48, including several intermarried Lipan.

The Tonkawa remember a number of subdivisions, which seem to have been subtribes rather than gentes, as follows: Awash, Choyopan, Haiwal, Hatchukuni, Kwesh, Nilhawai, Ninchopan, Pakani, Pakhalatch (see *Pajalat*), Sanukh, Talpkweyu, Titskanwatichatak. (H. E. B.)

Fou-ka-was.—Ind. Aff. Rep., 263, 1851. Jancas.—Baptismal rec. San Antonio de Valero mission, 18th cent. Kádiko.—Gatschet, MS., B. A. E., 1884 (Kiowa name; probably corruption of *Kú-ikogo*, 'man-eating men'). Kankaways.—Maillard, Hist. Tex., 238, 1842. Kariko.—Gatschet, MS., B. A. E., 1884 (Comanche name: sig. 'cannibals,' from Kiowa *Kádiko*). K'iñähi-píako.—Mooney in 17th Rep. B. A. E., I, 411, 1898 ('man-eaters': Kiowa name). Komkomé.—Joutel (1687) in Margry, Déc., III, 288, 1878. Konkoné.—Shea, note in Charlevoix, New Fr., IV, 78, 1870. Konkone.—Joutel (1687) in French, Hist. Coll. La., I, 152, 1846. Korkone.—Ibid., 137. Long-wha.—Sen. Ex. Conf. Doc. 13, 29th Cong., 1st sess., I, 1846. Macanas.—Bancroft, No. Mex. States, I, 661, 1886 (misprint). Man-eaters.—Bollaert in Jour. Ethnol. Soc. Lond., II, 275, 1850 (trans. of Lipan name). Miúχsĕn.—Gatschet, Tonkawa MS., B. A. E., 1884 (Cheyenne name). Némĕréχka.—Gatschet, Comanche MS., B. A. E. ('men-eaters': Comanche name). Nimĕtéka.—ten Kate, Reizen in N. Am., 383, 1885 ('man-eaters': Comanche name). Sonkawas.—Parker, Am. Ind. Womanhood, 7, 1892. Tancaguas.—Morfi, Mem. Hist. Texas, bk. II, *ca.* 1782. Tancagueis.—Barrios: Informe, 1772, MS. in Archivo Gen. Tancagues.—Mezières (1778) quoted by Bancroft, No. Mex. States, I, 661, 1886. Tancaguez.—Courbière, Relación, 1791, MS. in Béxar Archives. Tancaguies.—De Soto Vermudez, Investigation, 1752, MS. in Archivo Gen. Tancahuas.—Whiting in Rep. Sec. War, 242, 1850. Tancahues.—Doc. 155 (1792) in Tex. State Arch. Tancahuos.—Davenport, Noticia, *ca.* 1809, MS. in Archivo Gen. Tancamas.—MS. of 1740 in Mem. de Nueva España, XXVIII, 203. Tancanes.—Ybarbo to Cabello, Dec. 7, 1778, MS. in Archivo Gen. Tancaouay.—Robin, Voy. La., III, 5, 1807. Tancaoves.—Ripperdá, letter of Apr. 27, 1777, MS. in Mem. de Nueva España, XXVIII, 225. Tancaoye.—La Harpe (1719) in Margry, Déc., VI, 277, 1886. Tancards.—Pike, Trav., 319, 1811. Tancases.—Fr. Ganzabal, letter, 1748, MS. in Mem. de Nueva España, XXVIII, 71. Tancavëys.—Mezières, Rel., 1770, MS. in Archivo Gen. Tancoways.—Whipple, Pac. R. R. Rep., III, pt. 3, 76, 1856,

Tañ'-ka-wă.—Dorsey Kwapa MS. vocab., B. A. E., 1891 (Quapaw name). Tankaway.—Pénicaut(1719) in French, Hist Coll. La., n. s., VI, 155, 1869. Tanko.—Froebel, Seven Yrs. Trav. 453, 1859. Tanks.—Sibley, Hist. Sketches, 74, 1806. Tanquaay.—Francisco de Jesus María, Rel., 1691, MS. Taukaways.—Drake, Bk. Inds., XI, 1848. Tchankáya.—Gatschet, Tonkawe MS., B. A. E., 69 (Karankawa name). Tenkahuas.—Neighbors in H. R. Doc. 100, 29th Cong., 2d sess., 3, 1847. Tenkanas.—Sen. Misc. Doc. 53, 45th Cong., 3d sess., 80, 1879. Thancahues.—Menchana to Oconor, Mar. 9, 1774, MS. in Archivo Gen. Tineyizháne.—Gatschet, Naisha Apache vocab., B. A. E., 69 (Kiowa Apache name). Titskan watitch.—Gatschet, Tonkawe MS., B. A. E., 1884 (own name: sig. 'indigenous people'). Toncahiras.—Schoolcraft, Ind. Tribes, VI, 689, 1857. Toncahuas.—Bollaert in Jour. Ethnol. Soc. Lond., II, 275, 1850. Toncawes.—H. R. Rep. 299, 44th Cong., 1st sess., 1, 1876. Tongues.—Michler, Recon., 64, 1850. Tonkahans.—Drake, Bk. Inds., XI, 1848. Tonkahaws.—Domenech, Deserts N. Am., I, 444, 1860. Tonkahiras.—Schoolcraft, Ind. Tribes, I, 518, 1851. Tonkahuas.—Bonnell, Tex., 137, 1840. Ton-ka-hues.—Ind. Aff. Rep., 257, 1853. Ton-kah-ways.—Parker, Tex., 221, 1856. Tonkawas.—Doc. of 1771-2 quoted by Bolton in Tex. Hist. Asso. Quar., IX, 91, 1905. Tonkaways.—Latham in Trans. Philol. Soc. Lond., 103, 1856. Tonkawē.—Dewees (1854) quoted by Gatschet, Karankawa Inds., 30, 1891. Tonkawéya.—Buschmann (1859) quoted by Gatschet, ibid., 33. Tonkeways.—Bollaert in Jour. Ethnol. Soc. Lond., II, 265, 1850. Tonkhuas.—Coombs in Ind. Aff. Rep. 1859, 233, 1860. Tonkowas.—Marcy, Prairie Trav., 197, 1861. Tonks.—So-called by Texans. Ton-quewas.—Butler in H. R. Doc. 76, 29th Cong., 2d sess., 7, 1847. Tonqueways.—Battey, Advent., 58, 1875. Tonquoways.—Webber, Gold Mines of the Gila, 194, 1849. Tonqus.—Ibid. Toukaways.—Parker in Schoolcraft, Ind. Tribes, V, 683, 1855. Yánehe.—Gatschet, MS., B. A. E. (Lipan name). Zancagues.—Doc. (1790) in Tex. State Archives.

Tonkawan Family. A linguistic stock established by Powell (7th Rep. B. A. E., 125, 1891) to include the Tonkawa tribe, but subsequently determined by Bolton to embrace also a number of small tribes, including the Ervipiame, Mayeye, and Yojuane. See *Tonkawa*.

=Tonkawa.—Gatschet, Zwölf Sprachen aus dem Südwesten Nordamerikas, 76, 1876 (vocabulary of about 300 words and some sentences); Gatschet, Die Sprache der Tonkawas, in Zeitschrift für Ethnologie, 64, 1877; Gatschet (1876) in Proc. Am. Philos. Soc., XVI, 318, 1877. =Tonkawan.—Powell, op. cit.

Tonkaway-root. A name among herbalists and "herb doctors" for the root of *Gonolobus publifloras*.

Tonoyiet's Band. A Paviotso band, named from its chief (Woman Helper), formerly below Big Meadows, Truckee r., w. Nevada. Pop. 280 in 1859.

To-no-yiet.—Dodge in Ind. Aff. Rep. 1859, 374, 1860. Tonoziet.—Burton, City of Saints, 576, 1861. Woman helper band.—Ibid.

Tontos (Span.: 'fools,' so called on account of their supposed imbecility; the designation, however, is a misnomer). A name so indiscriminately applied as to be almost meaningless. (1) To a mixture of Yavapai, Yuma, and Mohave, with some Piñaleno Apache, placed on the Rio Verde res., Ariz., in 1873, and transferred to San Carlos res. in 1875; best designated as the Tulkepaia, q. v. (2) To a tribe of the Athapascan family well known as Coyotero Apache. (3) To the Piñalenos of the same family. (4) According to Corbusier, to a body of Indians descended

mostly from Yavapai men and Pinal Coyotero (Pinaleño) women who have intermarried. The term Tontos was therefore applied by writers of the 19th century to practically all the Indians roaming between the White mts. of Arizona and the Rio Colorado, comprising parts of two linguistic families, but especially to the Yavapai, commonly known as Apache Mohave. The synonymy following, therefore, does not always represent true equivalents of any tribal name. The Tonto Apache transferred to San Carlos in 1875 numbered 629, while the Yavapai sent to that reserve numbered 618 and the Tulkepaia 352. The Tontos officially designated as such numbered 772 in 1908,

TONTO APACHE

of whom 551 were under the San Carlos agency, 160 under the Camp Verde school superintendency, and 11 at Camp McDowell. See *Apache, Tejua*.

Ahwa-paia-kwanwa.—Corbusier in Am. Antiq., VIII, 277, 1886 (= 'enemy,' 'all,' and 'speak,' referring to their mongrel tongue). Apache Tonto.—Bonnycastle, Span. Am., 70, 1819. Apache Tontoes.—White, Hist. Apaches, MS., B. A. E., 1875. Del-dje'.—ten Kate, Synonymie, 5, 1884 ('red ant': Apache name). Deldzjé.—ten Kate, Reizen in N. Am., 199, 1885. Dilzhăn.—Curtis, Am. Ind., I, 134, 1907 ('spatter talkers': Apache name). Dil-zhay.—White, Apache Names of Indian Tribes, MS., B. A. E. ('red soil with red-ants'; also applied to the Mohave). Four Peak Indians.—Curtis in Ind. Aff. Rep. 1871, 62, 1872. Gohun.—Bandelier in Arch. Inst. Papers, III, pt. 1, 110, 1890. Guhunes.—Ibid., 113. Har-dil-zhays.—White, Hist. Apaches, MS., B. A. E., 1875 ('red country Indians' or 'Indians living where there were red-ants': Apache name). Ko-un.—Bandelier in Arch. Inst. Papers, III, pt. 1, 110, 1890. Koun.—Curtis, Am. Ind., I, 134, 1907 ('rough': Apache name). Kuhns.—White, Hist. Apache Inds., MS., B. A. E., 1875 (so called by Mexicans "on account of their 'foolishness'"). Lo-co.—White, op. cit. (Apache name: trans. 'fools'). **Santo.**—Ind. Aff. Rep., 122, 1861 (misprint). **Tantos.**—Lane (1854) in School-craft, Ind. Tribes, v, 689, 1855. **Tci-çe-kwe.**—ten Kate, Synonymie, 7, 1884 ('marauders': Zuñi name). **Tinto.**—Ind. Aff. Rep., 506, 1865 (misprint). **Tondo.**—Ibid., 139 (misprint). **Tontears.**—Emory, Recon., 96, 1848 (misprint). **Tonto.**—Ind. Aff. Rep. 1854, 380, 1855. **Tonto-Apaches.**—Mowry in Ind. Aff. Rep. 1857, 302, 1858. **Tontoes.**—White, Hist. Apaches, MS., B. A. E., 1875. **Tonto-Tinné.**—ten Kate, Reizen in N. Am., 199, 1885. **Tontu.**—Ind. Aff. Rep., 153, 1868. **Touto Apaches.**—Stratton, Captivity, 123, 1857 (misprint). **Tsji'she-kwe.**—ten Kate, Reizen in N. Am., 291, 1885 (Zuñi name). **Viniettinen-né.**—Escudero, Notic. Estad. de Chihuahua, 212, 1834. **Vinni ettinenne.**—Orozco y Berra, Geog., 59, 1864.

Tonzaumacagua. A small tribe represented at San Antonio de Valero mission, Texas, in the 18th century.

Too. A Haida town given in John Work's list (Schoolcraft, Ind. Tribes, v, 489, 1855) as containing 10 houses and 196 inhabitants in 1836–41. This was probably Tiun.

Tooahk. Said to be a band of Salish on Muckleshoot res., Wash., in 1857.
Tooahk.—Gosnell in Ind. Aff. Rep. 1857, 338, 1858. **Upper Puyallup.**—Ibid.

Tooantuh (properly *Dústú*, a species of frog; known also as Spring Frog). A noted Cherokee of highly respected character, born near the mouth of Chucka-

TOOANTUH

mogga cr., near Lookout mtn, Tenn., about 1754. He was noted for his skill in trapping and hunting, and for his success in the athletic sports of his people, ball-playing in particular. Kind and amiable in disposition, Tooantuh always advo-

cated peace, and frequently exercised a restraining influence on the more warlike of his people, but was quick to avenge an injury to the members of his tribe. In 1818, when Tooantuh was about 64 years of age, a party of Osage wantonly murdered several Cherokee. Tooantuh, with a band of followers, went in pursuit, and by the time the Osage had reached their village they were surprised by an attack, their village burned, 80 of them killed or captured, and their band completely broken. He served under Gen. Jackson in the campaign against the Creeks in 1813–14, and was conspicuous for his coolness and discipline shown in battle. On the removal of the Cherokee to Indian Ter., Tooantuh was among the first to settle on a farm, devoting himself the remainder of his days to agriculture.

Tooelicans (*Too-el-icans*). Mentioned by Irving (Bonneville's Adventures, 388, 1850) as a tribe dwelling about the headwaters of Wallowa r., in N. E. Oregon, in connection with the Shoshoko. They are spoken of as shy and avoiding intercourse with the whites; possibly a Shoshoni band, otherwise unidentified.

Tookseat (*Took'-seat*, from *ptuk-sīt*, 'wolf,' lit. 'round foot'). A phratry of the Delawares.—Morgan, Anc. Soc., 171, 1877.

Tooksetuk ('wolf'). A phratry of the Mahican.
Mech-cha-ooh.—Barton, New Views, xxxix, 1798. **Took-se-tuk'.**—Morgan, Anc. Soc., 174, 1877.

Tools. See *Implements*.

Toopik. A tent or house; a word in local use in Alaska; from *tupik* in certain western Eskimo dialects, signifying tent. (A. F. C.)

Tooptatmeer. One of the two Woccon towns, supposed to have been in Greene co., N. C., in 1709, the towns together having 120 warriors.—Lawson (1714), Hist. Car., 383, 1860.

Toosey. A band of Tsilkotin, seemingly named from a chief, under Williams Lake agency, Brit. Col. Pop. 62 in 1908, 50 in 1910.
Taasey.—Can. Ind. Aff. Rep. 1895, 359, 1896. **Tassey.**—Ibid., 1894, 279, 1895. **Toosey.**—Ibid., pt. II, 162, 1901. **Toosey's tribe.**—Ibid., 1884, 190, 1885.

Tooshkipakwisi (*Toosh-ki-pa-kwis-si*, 'green leaves'). A subclan of the Delawares.—Morgan, Anc. Soc., 172, 1877.

Tooshwarkama (*Toosh-war-ka'-ma*, 'across the river'). A subclan of the Delawares.—Morgan, Anc. Soc., 172, 1878.

Toowed. One of the Diegueño rancherias represented in the treaty of 1852 at Santa Isabel, s. Cal.—H. R. Ex. Doc. 76, 34th Cong., 3d sess., 132, 1857.

Topaidisel. A Patwin tribe formerly living at Knight's Landing, Yolo co., Cal.—Powers in Cont. N. A. Ethnol., III, 219, 1877.

Topame. A former Luiseño village in upper San Luis Rey valley, San Diego co., Cal.—Grijalva (1795) cited by Bancroft, Hist. Cal., I, 563, 1886.

Topanika (*To-pan'-i-kwa*). An Unaligmiut Eskimo village on the E. coast of Norton sd., Alaska; pop. 10 in 1880.
Tapkhamikhuagmut.—Zagoskin, Descr. Russ. Poss. Am., I, 72, 1847. Taupanica.—Whymper, Alaska, 158, 1869. Topanica.—W. U. Tel. Exped., map, 1867. Topánika.—Dall, Alaska, 20, 1870. Tuphamikva.—Petroff in 10th Census, Alaska, map, 1884. Tup-hamikwa.—Petroff, Rep. on Alaska, 59, 1880. Tup-hanikwa.—Nelson in 18th Rep., B. A. E., map, 1899.

Topayto. A former village connected with San Francisco Solano mission, Cal.—Bancroft, Hist. Cal., II, 506, 1886.

Topeent. A Massachuset village in 1614 on the N. coast of Plymouth co., Mass.
Topeent.—Smith (1616) in Mass. Hist. Soc. Coll., 3d s., VI, 108, 1837. Topent.—Smith (1629), Va., II, 183, repr. 1819.

Topenebee (according to J. P. Dunn the name indicates 'a quiet sitting bear', the 'bear' part being probably understood from the "totem" reference). A noted Potawatomi, chief of his tribe in s. Michigan for 40 years. He first appears in history as a signer, in behalf of the "Pattawatimas of the river St Joseph," of the celebrated treaty of Aug. 3, 1795, negotiated by Anthony Wayne with numerous tribes at Greenville, Ohio; from that time until 1833 he signed eleven other treaties between the United States and the Potawatomi, and in another (Sept. 30, 1809) his mark was made by his brother, Shissahecon. By the treaty of Oct. 27, 1832, under the provisions of which the Potawatomi ceded their territory in Michigan s. of Grand r., Topenebee was granted a section of land by patent. When Tecumseh visited the Potawatomi in 1810 for the purpose of enlisting their aid in the uprising against the whites, Topenebee became an adherent of the new doctrine and led his warriors to join the union. The Potawatomi readily fell prey to the encroachment of the whites, and suffered the usual effect of the introduction of liquor; to this Topenebee was no exception. On one occasion Lewis Cass, serving as treaty commissioner, on advising him to keep sober and care for his people, was characteristically answered, "Father, we do not care for the land, nor the money, nor the goods: what we want is whiskey; give us whiskey!" He was present at the Ft Dearborn massacre, Chicago, Aug. 15, 1812, and aided in saving the lives of the Kinzies, Mrs Heald, Mrs Helm, and Sergeant Griffith. Subordinate to Topenebee were the subchiefs Pokagon, Weesaw, and Shavehead. The wife of Pokagon was a niece of Topenebee, and Weesaw married Topenebee's daughter. On the removal of the tribe to the W. in 1838, under the provisions of the treaty of 1833,

Topenebee, Pokagon, and others remained behind and took up lands in Silver Creek twp., where Topenebee died in Aug. 1840.

Topenebee's Village. A Potawatomi village, taking its name from the chief, which formerly existed on St Joseph r., opposite Niles, Berrien co., Mich. The reservation was sold in 1833.
To-pe-ne-bee.—Chicago treaty (1833) in U. S. Ind. Treat., 176, 1873. Topenibe.—Mississinewa treaty (1826), ibid., 673. To-pen-ne-bee.—Tippecanoe treaty (1832), ibid., 702. Topinibe.—St Marys treaty (1819), ibid., 670. Top-ni-be.—Chicago treaty (1832), ibid., 153.

Topinish (from *Qápnĭsh-'lĕma*, 'people of the trail coming from the foot of the hill'). A small Shahaptian tribe, speaking the Klikitat language, on Topinish r., Yakima res., Wash.
Qápnĭsh-'lĕma.—Mooney in 14th Rep. B. A. E., 739, 1896 (proper name). Topinish.—Ibid. Topnish.—Ind. Aff. Rep., 352, 1885.

Topiqui. A Yamasee (?) village and Spanish mission station in the province of Guale about 1595. In the revolt of 1597 it was attacked and the priest in charge, Father Rodriguez, was murdered. In consequence the mission was abandoned for several years. See *Tolemato*. (J. M.)
Topiqui.—Barcia, Ensayo, 171, 1723. Topoqui.—Shea, Cath. Miss., 68, 1855.

Topkok. A Kaviagmiut Eskimo village w. of Golofnin bay, Alaska; pop. 15 in 1880.
Tap-hok.—11th Census, Alaska, 162, 1893. Tup-ka-ak.—Petroff in 10th Census, Alaska, 11, 1884.

Toponanaulka. A former Seminole town 3 m. w. of New Mikasuky, probably in Lafayette co., Fla. Obiakee was the chief in 1823 (H. R. Ex. Doc. 74 (1823), 19th Cong., 1st sess., 27, 1826).

Topotopow. A Chumashan village formerly on Hernando Ticos' rancho, near San Buenaventura mission, Cal.—Taylor in Cal. Farmer, May 4, 1860.

Tops. A small tribe in Texas, formerly connected with San Francisco Xavier de Horcasitas mission (Documents in the College of Santa Cruz de Querétaro, K., leg. 6, nos. 12 and 18). See *Tups*.

Tops. See *Games, Toys*.

Toquart. A Nootka tribe on the N. shore of Barclay sd., s. w. coast of Vancouver id. Their septs, according to Boas, are Tokoaath, Maakoath, Wastsanek, Totakamayaath, Tsaktsakoath, Mukchiath, Tushkisath, Kohatsoath, Chenachaath, Metstoasath, and Chomaath. Their village is Mahcoah. Pop. 24 in 1910.
Tŏk'oā'ath.—Boas in 6th Rep. N. W. Tribes Can., 31, 1890. Tokwaht.—Swan in Smithson. Cont., XVI, 3, 1870. Too-qu-aht.—Can. Ind. Aff. 1883, 188, 1884. Toquaht.—Sproat, Savage Life, 308, 1868. Toquart.—Mayne, Brit. Col., 251, 1862. Toquatux.—Grant in Jour. Roy. Geog. Soc., 293, 1857. To-quh-aht.—Can. Ind. Aff. 1880, 315, 1881. Touquaht.—Can. Ind. Aff., pt. 2, 88, 1910. Toyn-aht.—Brit. Col. map, 1872.

Toquimas ('black backs'). A Mono band formerly living in lower Reese r. valley, N. central Nevada.—Taylor in Cal. Farmer, June 26, 1863.

Toquo (*Dăkwă'ĭ*, 'place of the Dăkwă'', referring to a great mythic fish). A former Cherokee settlement on Little Tennessee r., about the mouth of Toco cr., in Monroe co., Tenn.   (J. M.)

Joco.—Bartram, Travels, 371, 1792 (misprint for Toco). Toco.—Mooney in 19th Rep. B. A. E., 514, 1900 (traders' name). Toqua.—Timberlake, Memoirs, map, 1765. Toquah.—Doc. of 1799 quoted by Royce in 5th Rep. B. A. E., 144, 1887. Toquo.—Mooney, op. cit.

Toral. An Ahtena village on Copper r., Alaska, at the mouth of Chitina r.
Tarál.—Allen, Rep., 48, 1887. Toral.—Post route map, Alaska, 1903.

Torches. See *Illumination*.

Torepe's Band. A Paviotso band, named from its chief, otherwise called Lean Man, formerly living near the lower crossing of Truckee r., w. Nev. They were under the head chieftaincy of Winnemucca. Pop. 360 in 1859.
Torape.—Burton, City of Saints, 576, 1861. To-Repe's band.—Dodge in Ind. Aff. Rep. 1859, 374, 1860.

Torhunte. A Tuscarora village, about 1711, on a N. affluent of Neuse r., in North Carolina.—War map, 1711–15, in Winsor, Hist. Am., v, 346, 1887.

Torin. A former populous Yaqui settlement on the N. bank of the lower Rio Yaqui, lat. 28°, lon. 109° 30′, Sonora, Mexico.
San Ignacio Torin.—Orozco y Berra, Geog., 355, 1864. Torim.—Hrdlička in Am. Anthr., VI, 62, 1904. Torin.—Velasco (1850) cited by Bancroft, Nat. Races, I, 608, 1882.

Tornait. An Eskimo village on the s. w. coast of Greenland.—Nansen, First Crossing of Greenland, II, 287, 1890.

Tornait. A winter village of the Nugumiut Eskimo above Bear sd., in Frobisher bay, Baffin land.—Boas in 6th Rep. B. A. E., 422, 1888.

Tornit. A fabulous race which the Central Eskimo believe to be akin to themselves, but much taller and stronger, having very long arms and legs and being able to toss huge bowlders as though they were pebbles. The Akudnirmiut call them Tuniqdjuait. They lived with the Eskimo in stone houses larger than theirs, as shown by the ruins that are still pointed out. Under their long deerskin coats they carried lamps with which to cook the meat of seals as soon as they were killed. They could make stone implements only, no bows nor kaiaks, but these they stole from the Eskimo, who were afraid to defend their property until a young Eskimo drilled a hole in the skull of one of them who had ruined his kaiak, while the giant was asleep. The Tornit then feared that they would all be killed, and secretly stole away, cutting off the skirts of their coats and tying up their hair so that they should not be recognized if pursued. The Greenland Eskimo believed the Tornit to be a mythical race of giants who lived on the ice cap and were seen rarely hunting at the heads of the fiords. The Labrador Eskimo, like those of Hudson bay and Baffin land, imagine them to be more like themselves.—Boas in 6th

Rep. B. A. E., 634, 640, 1888; Trans. Roy. Soc. Can., v, sec. 2, 38, 1888.

Toro (a contraction of *torote*, a kind of tree.—Buelna). A settlement of the Mayo on the E. bank of Rio del Fuerte, about lat. 26° 45′, in extreme N. Sinaloa, Mexico. Pop. 558 in 1900.
Tóro.—Hardy, Trav. in Mex., 438, 1829.

Torope. See *Terrapin*.

Torose. A village, presumably Costanoan, formerly connected with Dolores mission, San Francisco, Cal.—Taylor in Cal. Farmer, Oct. 18, 1861.

Torountogoats (*To-ro-un to-go-ats*). One of the tribes known under the collective term Gosiute; formerly in Egan canyon, E. Nevada; pop. 204 in 1873.—Powell and Ingalls in Ind. Aff. Rep. 1873, 51, 1874.

Torreon (Span.: 'round tower'). A small ruined pueblo, probably of the Tigua, at the modern town of the same name, about 28 m. E. of Belen, N. Mex. The aboriginal name of the settlement is unknown. According to Bandelier (Arch. Inst. Papers, IV, 259, 1892) the pueblo was asserted to have been of the "small-house" type.
Toreon.—Loew (1875) in Wheeler Surv. Rep., VII, 340, 1879 (misprint). Toreuna.—Bandelier cited in Arch. Inst. Rep., v, 58, 1884. Torreon.—Abert in Sen. Ex. Doc. 23, 30th Cong., 1st sess., 68, 1848.

Tŏrres. A Kawia village in Cahuilla valley, s. Cal. The name is now applied to a reservation covering the territory where live the Kawia of Torres, Lawilvan, Tova, and Sokut Menyil. It consists of 19,200 acres of unpatented desert land 75 m. from Mission Tule River agency, in Riverside co. The reservation contained a population of 271 Indians in 1904.

Torsalla. Given as one of the "Keowee towns" among the Cherokee in a document of 1755 (Royce in 5th Rep., B. A. E., 143, 1887). Not identified.

Tortugas (Span.: 'turtles'). An unidentified tribe mentioned by Uhde as formerly living on the Texas coast between the Rio Grande and the Nueces. The name was also applied to a prairie in the tidewater section of Texas where there was a turtle-shaped hill and several remarkable springs of water. At certain seasons of the year this prairie was frequented by the Tonkawa, q. v. (See Uhde, Die Länder, 121, 1861; Sibley, Hist. Sketches, 74, 1806; Gatschet, Karankawa Inds., 36, 1891.)

Torture. See *Ordeals*.

Toryohne ('wolf'). A clan of the Iroquois.
Cahenhisenhonon.—French writer (1663) in N. Y. Doc. Col. Hist., IX, 47, 1855. Çkwă-ri′-nää.—Hewitt, inf'n, 1886 (Tuscarora name). Enanthayonni.—French writer (1666) in N. Y. Doc. Col. Hist., IX, 47, 1855. Okuaho.—Megapolensis (1644), ibid., III, 250, 1853. Tor-yoh-ne.—Morgan, League Iroq., 80, 1851 (Seneca form).

Tosanachic (Spanish corruption of Tarahumare *Rosanachic*, 'where there is white,' referring to the white cliffs in the vicinity.—Lumholtz). A pueblo in w.

Chihuahua, Mexico, between lat. 28° and 29°, with a mixed population of Nevome and Tarahumare, chiefly the latter.
San Juan Evangelista Tosonachic.—Orozco y Berra, Geog., 324, 1864. **Tosanachic.**—Lumholtz, Unknown Mexico, I, 120, 1902.

Tosarke's Band. A Paviotso band, named from its chief (Gray Head), formerly near Carson and Walker lakes, Nev.
To-sarke.—Dodge in Ind. Aff. Rep. 1859, 374, 1860.

Toshence. The last of anything: a term local in Massachusetts. Gerard (*Sun*, N. Y., July 30, 1895) states that the word consists of the two last syllables of *mattasons*, the Massachuset name for the last child of the family. Trumbull (Natick Dict., 73, 1903) gives the Massachuset term as *muttásons*, 'youngest son,' with the suggested etymology *mat-asu*, 'not after,' of which *muttásons* would appear to be a diminutive. Gerard (inf'n, 1908) gives as the true meaning 'the little after which naught,' i. e., 'the last little one,' hence, by extension, the very last of anything.   (A. F. C.)

Toshittan (*Tos-hit-tan*, 'shark house people'). Given as the name of a social division among the Nanyaayi at Wrangell, Alaska, but really only a name for the inhabitants of a certain house, Ketgohit, belonging to them.
Tos hit tan.—Boas in 5th Rep. N. W. Tribes Can., 25, 1889.

Tosneoc. A Tuscarora village in N. E. North Carolina in 1701.—Lawson (1709), Hist. Car., 383, 1860.

Tota. A rancheria, probably Maricopa, on Gila r., Ariz., visited by Father Kino in 1700–01.
La Tota.—Kino map (1702) in Stöcklein, Neue Welt-Bott, 74, 1726. **Tota.**—Kino map (1701) in Bancroft, Ariz. and N. Mex., 360, 1889.

Totakamayaath (*Tó'tak·amayaath*). A sept of the Toquart, a Nootka tribe.—Boas in 6th Rep. N. W. Tribes Can., 32, 1890.

Totam. See *Totem.*

Totami. See *Tatemy.*

Totant. A Massachuset village in 1614 on the coast of Massachusetts, probably on or near the site of Boston.—Smith (1616) in Mass. Hist. Soc. Coll., 3d s., VI, 108, 1837.

Totapoag. An Indian rendezvous in 1682 in Nipmuc territory, described as being half way between Hadley and Lancaster, in the central part of Worcester co., Mass.—Russell (1682) in Mass. Hist. Soc. Coll., 4th s., VIII, 85, 1868.

Totatkenne (*To-ta-t'qenne*, 'people a little down the river'). A Sekani tribe inhabiting the E. slope of the Rocky mts. and adjacent plains s. of Peace r., Brit. Col.—Morice in Trans. Can. Inst., 29, 1895.

Totchikala. A former Aleut village on Unalaska, Aleutian ids.
Totchikala.—Coxe, Russian Discov., 161, 1787. **Totzikala.**—Ibid., 163.

Totem (irregularly derived from the term *ototeman* of the Chippewa and other cognate Algonquian dialects, signifying generically 'his brother-sister kin,' of which *ote* is the grammatic stem signifying (1) the consanguine kinship existing between a propositus and a uterine elder sister or elder brother; and (2) the consanguine kinship existing between uterine brothers and sisters, inclusive of alien persons naturalized into such kinship group by the rite of adoption (q. v.); that is, the uterine brother-sister group of persons, thus delimited by blood ties or legal fictions, who in each generation are severally and collectively related as uterine brothers and sisters, among whom intermarriage is strictly forbidden, and who therefore constitute an incest group in so far as its members are severally concerned. The stem *ote* is never employed in discourse without a prefixed personal pronoun denotive of the grammatic relation of person, or without the nominal suffix -*m*, indicative of exclusive possessive relation, approximately equivalent to English 'own,' or without the objective third person ending -*an* in Chippewa and -*a* in Cree. In the following irregular manner has the word *totem* been produced from the first cited expression *ototeman* (*ototema* in the Cree): by dropping the initial *o*-, 'his,' by unwarrantedly retaining as a proclitic the epenthetic -*t*- whose use in this and similar combinations is for the purpose of avoiding the coalescence of the two adjunct *o*-vowels, and by dropping the objective third person suffix -*an*, and by erroneously retaining the exclusive possessive suffix -*m*, thus producing *totem* from *ototeman* instead of the grammatic stem *ote*. Thus the word *totem* in form is not in any sense a grammatic derivative of its primary. And so *ote*, the conceptual element of the factitious word *totem*, has no demonstrable relation to the notion "clay," or "mark," as hitherto assumed.

The Abbé Thavenet, a missionary to the Algonkin at Lake of the Two Mountains, Canada, in the early part of the 19th century, wrote an explanation of the use and meaning of the stem *ote*, in part as follows: "It is to be presumed that in uniting into a tribe, each clan preserved its *manitou*, the animal which in the country whence the clan came was the most beautiful or the most friendly to man, or the most feared, or the most common; the animal which was ordinarily hunted there and which was the ordinary subsistence of the clan, etc.; that this animal became the symbol of each family and that each family transmitted it to its posterity to be the perpetual symbol of each tribe [clan]. One then must when speaking of a clan designate it by the animal which is its symbol. *Makwa nindotem* then signifies 'the Bear is my clan, I am of the clan of the Bear,' and not at all, as is commonly said, 'the Bear is my mark.' When an Indian says to another *pindiken nindotem*, can one believe that he says to him, 'enter then, my mark?' Is it not more reasonable to believe that he says to him, 'enter then, my clansman,' as we say, 'enter then, my countryman?' But since the traders, and the Indians in imitation of them, attach to the word *otem*, the idea of mark, I know that I must not offend too much against this prejudice" (cited by Cuoq, Lex. de la Lang. Algonq., 313, 1886). Here Thavenet gives the correct native Algonkin usage of the term, and also the traditional native explanation of the origin of the clan patron spirits. As a translation of 'family-mark,' Bishop Baraga (Otchipwe Dict. and Gram., 1878–82) wrote *odem;* but, being evidently aware that this rendering does not express the true sense of the term, he added parenthetically, "*odem* or *otem*, means only his parents, relations. In Cree, *ototema*, his relations"— thus clearly indicating that 'family-mark' is a definition of *ote-m*, which is not an element of the native concept of the stem. Under *ototema*, in his list of terms of kinship, Lacombe (Dict. de la Langue des Cris, 1874) wrote "kinsman, relation," without any reference to 'family-mark.' Constructively confirmative of the definition of the stem *ote*, given above, is the evidence found in the analysis of the common Algonquian term *otenā* or *otenaw*, signifying 'village, town, or settlement.' Its component lexical elements are *ote*, 'brother-sister kin,' 'clan,' and the nominal adformative *-nā*, signifying 'a dwelling-place'; whence it is seen that *otenā* or *otenaw* originally meant 'the dwelling-place of the clan.' or 'dwelling-place of the brother-sister kin.'

In specifying the name of a particular clan or gens it is necessary commonly to employ the name, usually a cognomen only, of the object or animal by which that clan or gens is distinguished from all others and by which it is protected, where such a cult is in vogue. There are other methods of distinguishing related or confederated groups one from another. The purely philosophical term "totemism" is of course a Caucasian derivative of the word *totem*, and has a wide and varied application. The term *totem* has been rather indiscriminately applied to any one of several classes of imaginary beings which are believed by a large number of the Indian tribes and peoples of North America to be the tutelary, the guardian, or the patron spirit or being of a person, or of an organization of persons, where such a cult or practice prevails.

The native American Indian, holding peculiar self-centered views as to the unity and continuity of all life and the consequent inevitable interrelations of the several bodies and beings in nature, especially of man to the beings and bodies of his experience and environment, to whom were imputed by him various anthropomorphic attributes and functions in addition to those naturally inherent in them, has developed certain fundamentally important cults, based on those views, that deeply affect his social, religious, and civil institutions. One of these doctrines is that persons and organizations of persons are one and all under the protecting and fostering tutelage of some imaginary being or spirit. These tutelary or patron beings may be grouped, by the mode and the motive of their acquirement and their functions, into two fairly well defined groups or classes: (1) those which protect individuals only, and (2) those which protect organizations of persons. But with these two classes of tutelary beings is not infrequently confounded another class of protective imaginary beings, commonly called fetishes (see *Fetish*), which are regarded as powerful spiritual allies of their possessors. Each of these several classes of guardian beings has its own peculiar traditions, beliefs, and appropriate cult. The modes of the acquirement and the motives for the acquisition of these several classes of guardian beings differ in some fundamental and essential respects. The exact method of acquiring the clan or gentile group patrons or tutelaries is still an unsolved problem, although several plausible theories have been advanced by astute students to explain the probable mode of obtaining them. With respect to the personal tutelary and the fetish, the data are sufficiently clear and full to permit a satisfactory description and definition of these two classes of tutelary and auxiliary beings. From the available data bearing on this subject, it would seem that much confusion regarding the use and acquirement of personal and communal tutelaries or patron beings has arisen by regarding certain social, political, and religious activities as due primarily to the influence of these guardian deities, when in fact those features were factors in the social organization on which has been later imposed the cult of the patron or guardian spirit. Exogamy, names and class names, and various taboos exist where "totems" and "totemism," the cults of the guardian spirits, do not exist.

Some profess to regard the clan or gentile group patron or tutelary as a mere development of the personal guardian, but from the available but insufficient data bearing on the question, it appears to be, in some of its aspects, more closely connected in origin, or rather in the method of its acquisition, with the fetish, the Iroquois *otchină'kĕn'/dă'*, 'an effective agency of sorcery,' than with any form of the personal tutelary. This patron spirit of course concerns the group regarded as a body, for with regard to each person of the group, the clan or gentile guardian is inherited, or rather acquired, by birth, and it may not be changed at will. On the other hand, the personal tutelary is obtained through the rite of vision in a dream or a trance, and it must be preserved at all hazards as one of the most precious possessions. The fetish is acquired by personal choice, by purchase, or by inheritance, or from some chance circumstance or emergency, and it can be sold or discarded at the will of the possessor, in most cases; the exception is where a person has entered into a compact with some evil spirit or being that, in consideration of human or other sacrifices in its honor at stated periods, the said spirit undertakes to perform certain obligations to this man or woman, and in default of which the person forfeits his right to live.

"Totemism" is a purely philosophical term which modern anthropologic literature has burdened with a great mass of needless controversial speculation and opinion. The doctrine and use of tutelary or patron guardian spirits by individuals and by organized bodies of persons were defined by Powell as "a method of naming," and as "the doctrine and system of naming." But the motive underlying the acquisition and use of guardian or tutelary spirits, whether by an individual or by an organized body of persons, is always the same, namely, to obtain welfare and to avoid ill-fare. So it appears to be erroneous to define this cult as "the doctrine and system of naming." It is rather the recognition, exploitation, and adjustment of the imaginary mystic relations of the individual or of the body of organized persons to the postulated *orendas* (q. v.), mystic powers, surrounding each of these units of native society. With but few exceptions, the recognized relation between the clan or gens and its patron deity is not one of descent or source, but rather that of protection, guardianship, and support. The relationship as to source between these two classes of superior beings is not yet determined; so to avoid confusion in concepts, it is better to use distinctive names for them, until their connection, if any, has been definitely ascertained: this question must not be prejudged. The hypothetic inclusion of these several classes in a general one, branded with the rubric "totem" or its equivalent, has led to needless confusion. The native tongues have separate names for these objects, and until the native classification can be truthfully shown to be erroneous, it would seem to be advisable to designate them by distinctive names.

Notwithstanding the great amount of study of the literature of the social features of aboriginal American society, there are many data relative to this subject that have been overlooked or disregarded.

Long (Voy. and Trav., 86–87, 1791), a trader among the Chippewa in the latter half of the 18th century, wrote: "One part of the religious superstition of the Savages, consists in each of them having his *totam*, or favourite spirit, which he believes watches over him. This *totam* they conceive assumes the shape of some beast or other, and therefore they never kill, hunt, or eat the animal whose form they think this *totam* bears." He adds: "This idea of destiny, or, if I may be allowed the phrase, '*totamism*,' however strange, is not confined to the Savages." From this misleading and confused statement have the words *totam* and its derivative *totamism*, slightly changed in spelling, been introduced into literature. In this crude statement Long described the personal tutelary, but gave it the name signifying 'clan kinship.' He or his interpreter was evidently led into this error by the custom of distinguishing a particular clan from others, when speaking of them, by the class name or cognomen of its patron or tutelary; it was due to faulty diction, for it is not probable that the Chippewa and their related tribes would have an object, believed to shape the course of human life, which had no distinctive name. Such a name is recorded by the eminent German traveler, Kohl, who was among the Chippewa and neighboring tribes in 1855. He said (Kitchi-Gami, 58, 1860) that these Indians deify natural strength and terrestrial objects; that nearly every Indian had discovered such an object, in which special confidence is placed by him, and to which he more frequently directs his thoughts and to which he more zealously sacrifices, than to any other being; that the Chippewa proper name for these objects is *nigouimes*, which signifies 'my hope,' approximately; that one calls a tree, another a stone or rock, 'his hope.' The rendering 'my hope' is probably only an approximate expression of the native concept embodied in the term, the derivation of which is not definitely known. It may possibly be related to the Chippewa *nagamón*, 'song, chant,' and to the Cree *nigamohew*, 'to teach the knowledge of medicines by chanting.' But *nigouimes* is the Chippewa name of the personal tutelary, whatever may be its etymologic derivation.

Owing to misapprehension of externals and therefore to misinterpretation of them in the vast body of literature on the significance of imaginary patrons or tutelaries of persons and of organizations of persons, *totem* has come to signify the patron or guardian, the tutelary or protector, of a person, of a clan or a gens, or of a society or tribe, hence to denote the name, crest, brand, or symbol of a clan, a man, a society, or a tribe, and, finally, to the fetish or familiar of a person. Its primary native use, with certain important limitations, makes it approximately equivalent to the English term 'one's kinship.'

The fact that the Indians themselves distinguished the fetish, the personal tutelary or guardian, and the clan, gentile, or society patron, one from another, by the use of appropriate appellations, rites, and observances, indicates, it would seem, a consciousness on their part that the differences in function, character, and mode of acquirement of these several classes of objects were sufficiently great to warrant them in doing so.

Among the Omaha and their congeners, according to Miss Fletcher, a youth at his initiation obtains his personal tutelary—his so-called totem—directly through the assumed efficacy of a definite rite performed by the young person himself: he does not inherit it from an ancestor, and he does not receive it as a gift from any living person. This ceremony of initiation into manhood rests on the assumption that man's powers and activities can be supplemented by the elements and the animals only through the grace of *wakonda* (q. v.), obtained by the rite of vision consisting of ritualistic acts and a fervent prayer of humility, expressing a longing for something not possessed, a consciousness of insufficiency of self, and an abiding desire for something capable of bringing welfare and prosperity to the suppliant. On reaching the age of puberty, the youth, under the instructions of his parents or other patrons, begins his initiation by having moistened earth placed on his head and face, by having a small bow and arrows given him, with directions to seek a secluded spot among the hills. Having reached such a place, he must chant the prescribed prayer, uplifting his hands, wet with his tears, to the heavens, and then he must place his hands on the earth; and he must fast until he falls asleep or into a trance. Whatsoever he sees or hears while in this state is the being that will become the special medium through which he can receive superhuman aid and comfort. Then, returning home, he rests and partakes of food. For four days he must speak but little, and he must not in that time reveal his vision under penalty of losing its producer. Later he may confide it to some old man, known to have had a similar vision or dream. Then it is his duty to seek until he finds the animal or bird seen in his revelation, when he must slay

it, selecting and retaining a small part of it (in cases where no concrete form was seen, symbols of it are made to represent it). This token or memento is ever after the sign of his vision or dream, the most sacred thing he can ever possess. This symbol may consist of the feather of a bird, a tuft of hair or other part of an animal or a bird, a black stone, or a translucent pebble. This token or memento, his personal tutelary, is never the object of worship. It is the tie, the fragment, connecting its possessor with the potentiality and power of the entire species represented by the being or form seen in his vision or dream. Belonging to various objects and beings, all tutelaries are not equally potent in the view of the natives, for they can not exceed the power of the particular species to which they severally belong. Nevertheless, when the novice is being instructed for the rite of the vision, he is forbidden to ask in his prayer for the sight of any particular object. It is an opinion held among the natives that although no one may consciously choose his personal tutelary, natural gifts of mind and character are apt to attract powerful animals and agencies. Usually, the tutelary referred to members of the surrounding fauna— the deer, the buffalo, the bear, the turtle, the birds, and the reptiles; and to representatives of the flora—the corn; and to the elements—the thunder, the earth, the water, and the winds. Nothing in any manner connoted man himself. There is, moreover, no indication of ancestor-worship, and no suggestion of a natural blood kinship subsisting between the man and his tutelary. These statements embody very briefly the chief characteristics of the personal tutelary among the Omaha and the tribes linguistically related to them.

The influence of these guardian spirits on the social, religious, and political institutions of the natives differs greatly from tribe to tribe. Among the Omaha, those who have received visions of the same being or object usually unite into a cult or religious society. The Bear Society is composed of persons from every gentile kinship group who have seen a bear in the rite of the vision. The bond of union here was not blood kinship, but a communal right in a common apparition. These societies possess prescribed rites, rituals, and suitable officers. Miss Fletcher suggests that in the past the experience gained in the conduct of these cult or religious societies was later made useful in the formative period of the artificial social structure of the *toñ-woñ-gdhoñ*, or gens, of the Omaha. The native term signifies 'a place of dwellings where kindred dwell together,' which is not essentially different in meaning from the Algonquian *otenaw* noted above. In this tribe there are ten ruling gentes, which are exogamous; they trace the descent of blood through the father only; they possess a particular name which refers directly or symbolically to the patron or tutelary of the gens; they have a gentile patron being, whose cult is marked by a taboo; they possess a gentile list of personal names peculiar to itself, of which one is given when the hair of a child is first cut, the form of which symbolizes the tutelary until he reaches the age of 7 years. This "cut" and the taboo are enforced under the threatened penalties of blindness, bodily deformity, and disease for any failure to observe faithfully these obligations. Each gens has obligatory cultural rites, in which its members offer respectful homage to the gentile patron spirit. These observances, however, do not imply ancestor-worship. The symbol of the gentile guardian spirit is borne through life and is placed on the dead for identification by the kindred. The gentile patron being, however, gives no immediate hold on the superhuman, as does the personal tutelary. It may be questioned whether the suggested development of a social organization by the establishment of distinct groups of persons who should be bound together by the ties of blood kinship, based on the pattern and experience of existing religious cults, is not a rather too conscious working-out of such ideas of a semi-barbaric, people. It would seem to be a reversal of the usual course of social development.

According to Boas, the social organization of the Salish tribes of the interior of British Columbia is very loose, there being no recognized tribal unit. Village population among them undergoes frequent and considerable fluctuation, and there were no exogamic groups, no hereditary nobility, and no ritualistic societies. Nevertheless, the acquisition of guardian spirits at the age of puberty is an essential feature of their religious beliefs, and these tutelaries are obtained through prescribed ceremonials. However, only a few shamans are believed to have inherited their guardian spirits from their parents.

Hill-Tout says that the most characteristic feature of the social side of the religious activity of the Salish tribes of the coast and of the lower Fraser delta is "their totem or kin-group crests," and that these kin-groups are not commonly called by animal or plant names as among the Haida and the Tlingit. They are, however, distinguished one from another by crests, "each family of standing possessing its own crest or crests." These are plastic or pictographic emblems of the supposed ancestral "totems of the family or kin-group," and are regarded as the guardian spirits of the household.

Among the Vancouver id. tribes, these inherited crests largely replace the personal tutelary of the interior Salish which is there acquired by means of dreams and visions—not the ordinary dream or vision, but one superinduced by long and special ceremonial preparation. As the tutelary usually has only specific or specialized functions or spheres of action, the initiate may not be satisfied with the first one thus received, and so enters upon a second, a third, and even a fourth ceremonial preparation for a dream or a vision; and so he may be years in seeking what is satisfactory to him (Ontario Arch. Rep., XVIII, 229, 230, 1905). Hill-Tout adds that between the tutelary and the person a very mystic relationship is supposed to exist. Prayer in the usual sense was not offered to the tutelary, but its aid and protection were rather expected as its duty in warning the obsessed person by dreams and visions of approaching danger in all the issues of life.

Teit (Mem. Am. Mus. Nat. Hist., Anthr., I, 354, 1898–1900), writing of the Thompson River Indians (Ntlakyapamuk), says that every person had his own guardian spirit which was obtained during the puberty ceremonies, and that none except a few shamans inherited without these rites their parental tutelary spirits which had been regarded as particularly powerful. He also states that "there were no totems, except at Spuzzum, where two families, who were descendants of members of the coast tribes, claimed the totems of their ancestors," but that "blood relationship was considered a tie which extended over generations, both in the male and the female lines," a statement which clearly indicates that blood kinship with what it implies is above all others the great cohesive force in savage life.

Father Morice says that among the western Déné there were several kinds of tutelary or patron spirits or beings— the clan patron, the fetish (his honorific), and the personal tutelary, to which may be added those local deities which preside over some rock, cave, or consecrated spot. Father Morice believes that the cult of the clan patron and the fetish (his honorific) came to the Déné from the natives of the Pacific coast. He states that the honorific was assumed with appropriate rites by any person desirous of gaining social rank, to which they could not otherwise aspire owing to certain restrictions of the laws of heredity. This authority does not relate how the clan tutelary is acquired among these people, but he says that the "personal totems" are those primary spirits which occasionally manifest themselves to man, are personified in the earthly individuals of the faunal and the floral worlds, and give evidence of a beneficent disposition by adopting a person as a ward and protecting him through life in return for some kindness shown their incarnate and terrestrial representatives—the animals and the plants and other objects of human environment. They reveal themselves in dreams and visions. Father Morice is of the opinion that "totemism" among the Déné is not a social institution, but that it is exclusively a religious cult; he is inclined to regard the clan patron spirit as a mere extension of the cult of the personal tutelary, but assigns no satisfactory reason for this belief. The owner of a tutelary must circumspectly bear about his person and openly exhibit in his lodge the spoils of the animal denoted by it—its entire skin, or only a part of it, or a carved emblem of it; and under no circumstances would anything induce him wilfully to kill it, or at least to eat the flesh of the being, the prototype of which had become, as it were, sacred to him. Its aid and protection are asked on all important occasions and emergencies. It would appear that this writer, in his attempt to explain the clan patron, has confused the fetish (honorific) with the personal tutelary. The hidden power with which the devotee believes he has thus become possessed he calls *coen* in the Carrier tongue, which signifies 'at the same time magic and song,' thus closely approximating the Iroquois *orenda*. Morice (Ontario Arch. Rep., XVIII, 206, 1905) relates that, in preparing himself for practice, the shaman divests himself of all his raiment and dons the spoils (a bearskin, the claws of a grizzly bear, the feathers of an owl, etc.) or the mask of his fetish or tutelary. He states that each of the Déné clans has a patron spirit, an animal or other being, traditionally connected with the establishment of these political and social units in pristine times, and to which the members of the clans paid great respect and even veneration. On ceremonial occasions the entire clan is impersonated by it, for it becomes the symbol or crest of the clan. He adds that the personal tutelary, common to both the eastern and the western Déné, "being as indigenous to them as most of the institutions in vogue among all the northern American Indians," is an essential element of their religious system and does not affect "society as such."

Spinden (Mem. Am. Anthr. Asso., II, 241, 1908) writes that among the Nez Percé Indians there is "a lack of anything like a gens grouping," adding that the social organization of the Shahaptian stock furnishes excellent material for the study of the simple development of a tribe, and that "the tribes arose from the natural division of the stock according to the geographical areas." The Nez Percés sent their children, both boys and girls, at about 10 years of age, to the mountains to fast and keep vigil, for the purpose of acquiring, if possible, a guardian spirit. But it is not everyone who succeeds in obtaining such a tutelary. The name or description of the thing seen is adopted as a sacred name, which sometimes denoted some trophy of the hunt borne by the imaginary animal seen in vision. The imaginary being, thus obtained as a tutelary, is believed to protect its possessor and to endow him with "certain physical or mental qualities and pronounced skill in certain things," especially those properties or qualities most characteristic of the animal or object seen. The Sun imparted wisdom and mystic insight. There are certain restrictions in regard to the killing of the guardian animal; and "the names and the sacred songs obtained by vigil descended through the family," some persons inheriting as many as 10 or 15 songs (p. 249). But it does not appear that the guardian spirit itself was thus inherited. The tutelary animal was not usually named by its ordinary title, but by a special name, and some have several such cognomens (p. 263). In the case of shamans, men and women, the guardian beings were regarded as of a higher class or order, as they commonly represented objects from the heavens—the sun, the moon, the clouds, the eagle, the fishhawk, and the crane.

Speck (Ethn. Yuchi Indians, Anthr. Pub. Univ. Pa., I, 70 et seq., 1909) says that the Yuchi trace descent through the female line and that therefore these people have clans; that "the members of each clan believe that they are relatives and, in some vague way, the descendants of certain preëxisting animals whose names and identity they now bear. The animal ancestors are accordingly totemic. In regard to the living animals, they, too, are the earthly types and descendants of the preëxisting ones, hence, since they trace their descent from the same sources as the human clans, the two are consanguinely related," so that the members of a clan feel obliged not to do violence to the wild animal having the form and name of their tutelaries. The flesh or fur of such animals may be obtained from the members of other clans, who are under no obligation not to kill these animals. The idea of clan is expressed by the word *yū'ta*, 'on the house.' Our authority adds that the different individuals of the clans inherited the protection of their clan totems when they passed the initiation rites, thenceforth retaining these as protectors through life. As the members of clans are considered to be the descendants of their totemic animals, they are in a sense the cousins, so to speak, of the earthly animals which are also descendants of the supernatural animals. The clan taboos and incidental beliefs need not be repeated here, as they have been mentioned in dealing with customs and the clans. But the animals of the earth, in general, are considered as thinking beings, with interests in life, customs, and feelings not unlike those of men. Even to-day these mutual elements in the lives of men and animals are felt to exist. The animals are all believed to have their protecting supernatural kinsmen, as well as men; for that reason in hunting them their protecting spirits have to be overcome before one can hope to bring them down. It is the same with human beings. If one's guardian spirit is all right, no harm can come. So in warfare, the idea is to strengthen one's own guardian spirit and to weaken the enemy's. In this respect hunting and fishing are much like warfare. The magic songs and formulas engage in the supernatural struggle and open the way, while the actual weapons do the work when the spiritual barriers are removed.

According to Boas (Kwakiutl Indians, Rep. U. S. Nat. Mus., 1895, 1897) the Tlingit, Haida, Tsimshian, Bellabella, and Kitamat have "animal totems in the proper sense of this term," but these tutelary guardians are not found among the Kwakiutl, who belong to the same linguistic stock as the Kitamat. This author states that the natives do not regard themselves as descendants of the "totem" or tutelary, and that the northern tribes of the coast Salish have no "animal totem in the restricted sense of this term." Boas was unable to obtain any information regarding the conjectured origin of the clan or gentile patron or tutelary, except the dubious light drawn from the native traditions, but states that these legends correspond in character "almost exactly to the tales of the acquisition of manitows among the eastern Indians, and they are evidence that the 'totem' of this group of tribes is, in the main, the hereditary manitow of a family." He also states that "each man among these tribes acquires a guardian spirit," but is restricted to only such as belongs to his clan. Native tradition can shed no satisfactory light on the question of the source and origin of the clan or gentile patron spirit.

Writing of the California Indians in general, Merriam (Am. Anthr., x, no. 4, 1908) says that these Indians believe that they "came from" certain animals, trees, or rocks. This belief, while agreeing in the main with that of the modern more or less accultured Yuchi, is in strong contrast with the evidence on this

point from E. and N. W. America, where apparently the peoples do not regard themselves as descendants of their clan or gentile patron spirits. Merriam remarks that "of the several degrees and phases of totemism, at least three occur in California, namely, (1) the non-hereditary individual totem; (2) the hereditary patriarchal totem; and (3) the hereditary matriarchal clan totem." He is also averse to the proposed restriction of the term "totemism" to "cases ordinarily known as clan totemism," for the reason that "clan totemism is so obviously only a higher development of personal totemism," deeming such restriction purposeless. But there is no proof that such a development of the personal tutelary rests on a basis of fact.

In the acquirement of the personal tutelary the Iroquois ritual does not contemplate the killing of the object seen in a vision or in a dream for the purpose of obtaining a part of it as a token, symbol, or a memento of it. So adversative to this practice of the Omaha and other tribes is the Iroquois procedure that some persons, who have seen a particular animal, regarded their own fate and destiny so closely connected with that of the tutelary animal that they measured the length of their own lives by that of their tutelary, believing that its death not only portended but also hastened their own. More fortunate did those regard themselves whose tutelary was some material object, embued with life by the creative breath of myth, whose destruction was not so certain or so common as that of an animal or a bird. Thus it is seen how diverse are the dogmas and beliefs connected with the personal tutelary. Moreover, in the rites designed to obtain a personal tutelary for a youth, it was the duty of the father's clan, or phratry of clans, at the New Year ceremony of the Iroquois, to receive and to interpret the dream or vision, and to make of wood, bark, stone, or other material a symbol, token, or representation of the object divined from the dream or vision to be the tutelary of the youth, which is given the youth to keep and carefully preserve.

Kroeber (Ethnol. Gros Ventre, 147, 1908) writes that the Gros Ventres (Atsina) are organized into gentes similar to those of the Siksika (Blackfeet) and the Sioux, bearing nicknames which are in no way totemic; that descent is traced through the paternal line; that there is prohibition of marriage within each gens; and that the prohibition of marriage extends to members of the mother's gens, for the members of both the father's and the mother's gentes are regarded as related within the prohibited degrees of kinship. He also states that only some of the Gros Ventres seek to acquire a personal guardian spirit, that this is undertaken only after reaching manhood, and that not all those who make the attempt succeed. The attempt is made in the usual manner, by fasting and retreating to some secluded spot. The man killed the animal thus found, apparently for the purpose of obtaining parts of it for an emblem; afterward he would not kill or eat that kind of animal. A few women acquired guardian spirits, not while in retreat to some mountain, but only during absence from the camp.

Like that of the Yuchi, one of the cardi-nal doctrines of the Iroquoian and Algon-quian mythic philosophy is that every kind of animal being has an elder brother, a primal being, wonderfully large and potent, which is, so to speak, the source of all the individuals of its own kind. These primal beings are the younger brothers of Teharonhiawagon of the Iro-quois and of Nanabozho of the Algonquian tribes, respectively the impersonations of all the thousand forms of faunal and floral life on earth. He who sees one of these elder brothers of any kind of animal being will be successful in the succeeding hunt of that animal; for it is by the favor of these elder brothers of the game animals that the hunter obtains any measure of success in killing the younger brothers of the primal beings (Hewitt, Iroq. Cosmol., 21st Rep. B. A. E., 1903). For in fulfil-ment of engagements with Teharonhia-wagon and Nanabozho in the second cos-mic period, these elder brothers are in duty bound to provide man not only with protection but also with animal food by means of the sacrifice of their younger brothers who are enjoined to permit them-selves to be taken by man, so long as the hunter makes himself ritualistically pure for the purpose and is solicitous not to kill his victims except with the least pos-sible cruelty. For this reason prayers for successful hunting and fishing were ad-dressed to the game it is desired to kill, a procedure naturally assumed to be pleasing to the ruling elder brother.

Long has declared that the favorite spirit must not be killed or eaten, but the Omaha must kill his personal tutelary before its tutelaryship is established. Conversely, there were some Iroquois who feared the death of the animal or bird which he regarded as his personal tutelary, lest he himself should also die. The ground that is common in these two methods is the manner of ascertaining or discovering the tutelary (through the rite of dreaming or seeing in vision) and in the motive for acquiring it, namely, the effort to obtain the favor of the imaginary bodies on which it was supposed human welfare largely depended. In the last analysis human welfare is the motive for acquiring a guardian or tutelary power or

being. There are, of course, many ways of providing the means of entering into close relation with these supposed control-ling powers of the sources of human well-being, and consequently there are many methods of establishing this interrelation between a person and some assumed pro-tecting power, or between an organized body of persons and a guardian or patron being or power, for a specific or a general aid and auxiliary to the promotion and preservation of the well-being of the per-son or persons guarded. (J. N. B. H.)

Totem Poles. Carved cedar poles erected by Indians along the N. Pacific coast from Vancouver id. to Alaska. Among the Haida they are of three principal varieties: the outside and inside house poles, and memorial columns. Besides the house poles the four main supporting posts and the two outside front corner posts were sometimes carved. The outside house pole, standing in front of the house mid-way between the corners, was 3 ft or more

MODEL OF
TOTEM POLE

wide at the base and some-times more than 50 ft high, being hollowed along the back for easier handling. Close to the base it was pierced with a round aper-ture which served as a door, though some of the later poles were left solid, a door of European pattern being made at one side. Inside house poles were erected only by the very wealthy. They stood in the middle of the house, directly behind the fire, and marked the seat of honor. Grave posts were of many different shapes. Sometimes they consisted of a very thick post surmount-ed by a large carved box, which contained smaller boxes holding the bones of the deceased; sometimes the box was longer and was supported by two posts. Oftentimes, how-ever, the body of the deceased was placed in a mortuary house, and the pole, usually a tall, slender shaft, was erected elsewhere. The carvings on grave posts and grave boxes were almost always crests owned by the family of the deceased, while those on house poles might be crests or they might illustrate stories, and occasionally a figure of the house-owner himself was added, or the figure of some one whom he wished to ridicule. These posts were erected during the great feasts commonly known as pot-latches, when an immense amount of prop-erty was given away and quantities of food were consumed. The trunks out of which they were to be carved were cut down, rolled into the water, and towed to the vil-lage amid songs and dancing. One or more regular carvers were employed to put on the designs and they were paid handsomely. (For specific descriptions see works cited below.) In comparatively modern times numbers of models of these poles have been made by native carvers to sell to white visitors. These are sometimes of wood, sometimes of a peculiar black slate found at one place not far from Skidegate, Queen Charlotte ids. According to native Haida accounts carved designs were originally made directly on the front slabs of the house, afterward on a broad, thick plank, and finally on poles. This comparatively modern evolution is corroborated by the Tlingit, who have only the grave post, upon which they carve representations of stories as well as crests. Tsimshian posts were more slender than those put up by the Haida, but the ones erected in front of Kwakiutl houses are usually much more slender still, and all are heraldic, referring to the tradition of the house-owner. The main supporting posts bear crests or record an episode connected with the building of the house. The main posts which support the houses of the Nootka and the coast Salish, when carved at all, represented an event that happened to the owner, such as the acquiring of a guardian spirit, or an event in the history of his sept. Some eastern tribes, such as the Creeks, Delawares, Shawnee, and Iroquois, set up small poles that are analogous to these totem poles, although the outward resemblance is slight. Those of the Delawares and Shawnee were erected in the four corners of their medicine-lodges, while those of the Iroquois were similarly placed in the houses of shamans and were adorned with representations of the shamans' tutelary spirits.

Consult Boas in Rep. Nat. Mus. 1895, 1897, and in recent reports of the Brit. A. A. S.; Niblack in Nat. Mus. Rep. 1888, 1890; Swan in Smithson. Cont., XXI, 1874; Swanton, (1) Cont. Haida, 1905, (2) in 26th Rep. B. A. E., 1908. (J. R. S.)

Totero. The settlement of the Tutelo (q. v.), in the middle of the 18th century, on Meherrin r., Va. According to Catesby (Nat. Hist. Car., II, xi, 1743) "the houses were built with strong posts or trees drove into the ground close to one another, the interstices being stopped up with moss, and covered with the bark of the sweet-gum tree."

Totheet. A Massachuset village in 1614, on the N. shore of Plymouth co., Mass.
Totheet.—Smith (1616) in Mass. Hist. Soc. Coll., 3d s., VI, 108, 1837 (misprint). Totheet.—Smith (1629), Va., II, 183, repr. 1819.

Totiakton ('it is a bend of the stream'). The large palisaded western "castle" of the Seneca tribe, situated in the 17th century on the Honeoye outlet, not far from Honeoye Falls, in Monroe co., N. Y. This castle was the residence of the noted Seneca federal chief Shadekaronhies, representing the fourth and last brotherhood of Seneca federal chiefs. The castle was sometimes known by his name. In 1687 it was, with the three others, destroyed by Denonville and was not rebuilt, as the Seneca thereafter retired eastward, westward, and southward, establishing their villages in the Genessee valley and in the vicinity of Canandaigua lake. (J. N. B. H.)
Danoncaritaoui.—Lahontan, New Voy., I, 77, 1703. Da-yo-de-hok'-to.—Morgan, League Iroq., 19, 1851. Deyudehaakdoh.—Charlevoix, New Fr., III, 289, 1868. Father Fremin's village.—Gallinée map, ca. 1670. Kanonʹkeïʹꞩáhwï'.—J. N. B. Hewitt, inf'n (correct Seneca form). La Conception.—Greenhalgh (1677) in N. Y. Doc. Col. Hist., III, 252, 1853. Sha'tekarónꞩyes.—Hewitt, inf'n (correct Mohawk form; the Seneca form omits the r). Sonnontouan.—Jes. Rel. 1657, 45, 1858. Tegarondies.—Hennepin, New Discov., 53, 1698. Tegaronhies.—Lahontan (1703), New Voy., I, 77, 1735. Thegaronhies.—Ibid., 1703. Theodehacto.—Cortland (1687) in N. Y. Doc. Col. Hist., III, 435, 1853. Tiotehatton.—Greenhalgh (1677), ibid., 251. Tiotohatton.—Greenhalgh (1677) quoted by Morgan, League Iroq., 316, 1851. Tohaiton. — Belmont (1687) quoted by Conover, MS., B. A. E. Totiakto.—Denonville (1687) in N. Y. Doc. Col. Hist., IX, 367, 1855. Totiakton.—Denonville (1687) quoted by Morgan, op. cit., 316.

Totola. A village, presumably Costanoan, formerly connected with Dolores mission, San Francisco, Cal.—Taylor in Cal. Farmer, Oct. 18, 1861.

Totoma (from t!ōʹt!ō, 'thin'). A former Maidu village on the E. side of the N. branch of Feather r., about midway between Yankee and Hengy, Butte co., Cal.
Tó-to.—Powers in Cont. N. A. Ethnol., III, 282, 1877. Totoma.—Dixon in Bull. Am. Mus. Nat. Hist., XVII, map, 1905. Totû.—Curtin, MS. vocab., B. A. E., 1885.

Totontaratonhronon ('otter people': Huron name). A small Algonquian tribe living on St Lawrence r., probably near the mouth of Ottawa r., Canada. In 1641 they removed to the Huron mission of St Jean Baptiste (q. v.) and had 15 houses, having been driven out of their own country. (J. N. B. H.)
Atonthratarhonon.—Jes. Rel., III, index, 1858. Atontrataronnons.—Jes. Rel. 1644, 100, 1858. Atontratas.—Shea, Cath. Miss., 356, 1855. Atontratoronons.—Ragueneau (1653) quoted by Shea in Charlevoix, Hist. New Fr., II, 256, note, 1866. Tonthratarhonon. — Jes. Rel., III, index, 1858. Tontthrataronons.—Jes. Rel. 1641, 83, 1858. Totontaratonhronon.—Jes. Rel. 1640, 35, 1858.

Totopotomoi. Principal chief of the Pamunkey Indians (q. v.) of Virginia about 1650. He seems to have been the second in succession from Opechancanough (q. v.), the last chief of the confederated Powhatan tribes, slain by the English in 1644. In 1656 he joined the Virginia forces with nearly 100 warriors to repel an invasion by the inland tribes, but in a bloody engagement on James r., near the present Richmond, the Virginians were defeated, and Totopotomoi, with nearly all of his warriors, was killed. So bitter was the feeling against the commander, Col. Edward Hill, for the disastrous result, that he was deprived of all official position and his property confiscated to pay the expenses of the expedition.

Totopotomoi was survived by his widow, Queen Anne (q. v.), who held a prominent place in Virginia Indian history for 40 years. He figures also in Butler's satire Hudibras. Totopotomoy cr., Va., takes its name from him.   (J. M.)

Totstalahoeetska. A former Seminole town on the w. side of Tampa bay, Fla. Its population was made up chiefly of Upper Creeks who fled there after the war of 1813–14.
Totstalahoeetska.—Bell in Morse, Rep. to Sec. War, 306, 1822. Watermelon Town.—Ibid.

Totuskey. A division of the Powhatan confederacy, comprising the Moraughtacund and Secacawoni tribes, in Virginia. In 1608 the two tribes numbered 180 warriors, while 60 years later they were reduced to 70 warriors.
Totuskeys.—Jefferson, Notes, 138, 1801.

Touaguainchain. A Huron village in Ontario in 1615 (Champlain, 1615, Œuvres, IV, 28, 1870). A note by the editor of Champlain suggests that it may have been the Sainte Madeleine of the Jesuit Relation of 1640.

Touchouasintons ('village of the pole'). A band of western Dakota, perhaps the Wazikute of the Yanktonai.
Touchouaesintons.—Shea, Early Voy., 111, 1861.
Touchouasintons.—Le Sueur (1700) quoted by Neill, Hist. Minn., 170, 1858.

Touenho. A former Onondaga hamlet, situated in 1688 s. of Brewerton, which is at the w. end of L. Oneida, N. Y.
Goienho.—Jes. Rel. 1656, 12, 1858 (given as the name of L. Oneida, but "it has been mentioned and probably belonged to Brewerton."—Beauchamp). Tou-en'-ho.—Beauchamp, Aborig. Place Names, 153, 1907.

Tougoulas (interpreted by Gatschet as from Choctaw *iti*, 'forest'; *ókla*, 'people': 'forest people', but more likely 'Tioux people'). One of the 9 Natchez villages at the close of the 17th century.—Iberville in Margry, Déc., IV, 179, 1880.

Touladi. The great lake-trout (*Salvelinus namaycush*), called by the French Canadians queue-fourchue; a word written also *tuladi*, in use among the fishermen and settlers, French and English, of E. Quebec. According to Chambers (The Ouananiche, 270, 1896) *touladi* is the name of this fish in the Micmac and Abnaki dialects of Algonquian.   (A. F. C.)

Toulibi. See *Tulibee*.

Toupa. A chief or tribe in alliance with the chief of Audusta (Edisto), S. C., and in friendly relations with the French in 1562. The name is indicated as that of a village, inland from Port Royal, on the De Bry map of 1591 (Le Moyne Narr., Appleton trans., 1875).
Touppa—Laudonnière (1562) in French, Hist. Coll. La., n. s., 201, 1869.

Touraxouslins. Mentioned by Tonti (French, Hist. Coll. La., I, 82, 1846), in connection with the Kickapoo, as a tribe living apparently in Illinois, about the head of Illinois r., in 1690. Possibly the Mascoutens.

Tourima. One of the early Quapaw villages, situated on the w. bank of the Mississippi, probably near the mouth of the Arkansas. It is stated by more than one authority that the people of this village and of Tongigua were at least for a time united in one village. Father Poisson (1720) places all the villages on Arkansas r. When the Quapaw migrated they applied the old names to their new settlements, even when they finally settled on their reservation in the present Oklahoma.
Thoriman.—Joutel (1687) in Margry, Déc., III, 444, 1878. Ti'-u-a'-dọi-maⁿ.—Dorsey in 15th Rep. B. A. E., 229, 1897. Tiwadimaⁿ.—Gatschet, Creek Migr. Leg., I, 30, 1884. Toreman.—Charlevoix quoted by Shea, Discov., 170, 1852. Torima.—Pénicaut (1700) in Margry, Déc., V, 402, 1888. Toriman.—Hennepin, New Discov., pt. 2, 45, 1698. Torimanes.—Barcia, Ensayo, 288, 1723. Torinan.—Crépy, Carte de l'Am., n. d. Torremans.—Tonti (1687) in French, Hist. Coll. La., I, 71, 1846. Tourima.—Gravier (1701) in Shea, Early Voy., 131, 1861. Tourimans.—Pénicaut (1700) in French, Hist. Coll. La., n. s., I, 62, 1869.

Tova. A Kawia village in Cahuilla valley, s. Cal.
Agua Dulce.—Barrows, Ethno-Bot. Coahuilla Ind., 34, 1900. Toro.—Burton (1856) in H. R. Ex. Doc. 76, 34th Cong., 3d sess., 117, 1857 (probably identical). To-va.—Barrows, op. cit.

Toviscanga. A former Gabrieleño rancheria at or near San Gabriel mission, Los Angeles co., Cal. According to Taylor this was the name of the site of the mission, and near by was a large rancheria. See *Sibagna*.
Tobiscanga.—Taylor in Cal. Farmer, Feb. 22, 1860. Toviscanga.—Ibid., May 11, 1860. Tuvasak.—A. L. Kroeber, inf'n, 1905 (Luiseño name).

Tovu (*Tö'vu*). The Fire clan of the Hopi. Cf. *Tuvou*.

Towahhah. A Salish division formerly in extreme N. w. Washington, now on Lummi res.; pop. 90 in 1867.
No-ah-ha.—Mallet in Ind. Aff. Rep., 198, 1877. Noo-wha-ha.—U. S. Stat. at Large, XII, 927, 1863. No-wha-ah.—Finkbower in Ind. Aff. Rep. 1867, 59, 1868. Tow-ah-ha.—Gibbs in Cont. N. A. Ethnol., I, 180, 1877.

Towahnahiooks. The name said by Lewis and Clark to have been applied by the Eneeshur and the Skilloot to Des Chutes r., Oreg., and also to a Shoshoni band which lived on the upper waters thereof in spring and summer but spent the fall and winter months on the Willamette. The name of the stream is spelled by Lewis and Clark in various ways, as Chahwahnahiooks, Towahnahiooks, Towanahiooks, Towannahiooks, Towarnaheooks, Towarnahiooks, etc.
Towahnahiook.—Lewis and Clark Exped., Coues ed., III, 913, 1893. Towanahioohs.—Ibid., 949. Zwan-hi-ooks.—Lee and Frost, Oregon, 177, 1844.

Towakwa. A former pueblo of the Jemez of New Mexico; definite location unknown.
To-ua-qua.—Bandelier in Arch. Inst. Papers, IV, 207, 1892. To-wa-kwá.—Hodge, field-notes, B. A. E., 1895.

Towalt. A local name of a species of salmon (*Salmo confluentus*) found in the waters of Puget sd. and elsewhere on the N. w. Pacific coast; from *towatlin*, the name of this fish in the Nisqually dialect of the Salish language.   (A. F. C.)

Towayat's Village. A summer camp of a Stikine chief named Toyä′t, on Etolin id., Alaska; pop. 82 in 1880.—Petroff in Tenth Census, Alaska, 32, 1884.

Towerquotton. One of the southernmost Tillamook villages in 1805, on a creek emptying into Tillamook bay, Oreg. The name was really that of the chief (Lewis and Clark Exped., II, 117, 1814).

Towha ('coyote'). An extinct clan of Taos pueblo, N. Mex.
Tówha tai′na.—M. C. Stevenson, notes, B. A. E., 1910 (*tai′na*='people').

Towhayu ('fighting coyote'). An extinct clan of Taos pueblo, N. Mex.
Tówhayu tai′na.—M. C. Stevenson, notes, B. A. E., 1910 (*tai′na*='people').

Town-band Indians. A former Dakota band, probably of the Mdewakanton.—McLeod (1852) in Sen. Ex. Doc. 29, 32d Cong., 2d sess., 11, 1853.

Toxaway (*Dúksa′ĭ*, or *Dúkw′sa′ĭ*, of unknown meaning). A former Cherokee settlement in South Carolina, on a creek of the same name, a head-stream of Keowee r., having its source in Jackson co., N. C. The name has been wrongly interpreted to mean 'place of shedding tears.'   (J. M.)
Taxawaw.—Royce in 5th Rep., B. A. E., map, 1887. Tosawa.—Doc. of 1755 cited by Royce, ibid., 143. Toxaway.—Mooney in 19th Rep. B. A. E., 516, 1900 (common name).

Toybipet. A Gabrieleño rancheria formerly in Los Angeles co., Cal., at a locality later called San José.
Sibapot.—Latham in Proc. Philol. Soc. Lond., VI, 76, 1854 (probably identical). Toibi.—Kroeber in Univ. Cal. Pub., Am. Arch. and Eth., VIII, 39, 1908 (native name). Toybipet.—Ried quoted by Taylor in Cal. Farmer, June 8, 1860.

Toys. Indian children do not differ from the children of other races in their fondness for toys, and it is found that among them toys adapted to all the periods from infancy to adolescence were in common use. The psychology of toys involves reactions between the child mind and the adult mind in great variety, and sex, age, social stage, and environment are factors for differentiation. Three classes of toys may be distinguished: (1) Those for attracting, soothing, and amusing infants; (2) those invented or appropriated by children for their own use; (3) those supplied by adults from educational, religious, or esthetic motives. Examples of the first class are the infant's rattle and attractive objects hung on the cradle bow; of the second, clay figures, bits of wood or stone or rags, or the like, treasured by children and idealized in their imagination. Dolls and their appurtenances, cradles, and miniature implements are educative for future occupations, and representations of spiritual beings, such as the *tihus* or dolls of the Hopi and Zuñi, and other cult objects and fetishes, impress religious ideas. Purely esthetic toys are extremely rare. In many cases children's toys are cult objects that were once sacred and esoteric, surviving for play, e. g., the bull-roarer (q. v.).

A greater variety of toys is observed among the Eskimo than among any other of the American aborigines. Nelson enumerates sleds, boats, hunting outfits, bows and arrows, dolls, models of dishes and other things, tops, ingenious mechanical toys simulating the movements of animals, and carved figures of ducks, seals, etc. Murdoch names dolls, kaiaks, imitation implements, whirligigs, teetotums, buzzes, whizzing-sticks, and pebble-snappers. Turner figures various dolls from Labrador. The doll is a favorite toy of Eskimo children, and great numbers of them are carved from ivory, wood, and stone. They are often provided with fur clothing, bedding, lamps, etc. In ethnographic collections there are few toys from the tribes of the United States, probably because collectors thought them unimportant, though from the Pueblos there is a good representation. Plains children, however, possessed dolls, sleds, clay figures of animals, clay blocks for building, tops, balls for bowling and for games like those of their elders, and a multitude of small utensils which imitate those used by adults. Zuñi and Hopi children have toy cradles, drums, bows, rattles, dishes, house-models, dolls, tops, pea-shooters, mechanical birds, grotesques in pottery, etc. The Mohave make bizarre dolls of pottery or willow bast. Rude dishes, figures of animals, etc., formed evidently by children, are frequently encountered in the Pueblo ruins of the S. W. See *Child life, Games, Dolls.*

Consult Chamberlain, Child in Folkthought, 206–11, 1896; Culin in 24th Rep. B. A. E., 1907; Murdoch in 9th Rep. B. A. E., 1891; Nelson in 18th Rep. B. A. E., 1899; J. Stevenson in 3d Rep. B. A. E., 1884; M. C. Stevenson in 11th Rep. B. A. E., 1894; Turner, ibid.   (W. H.)

Tozikakat ('mouth of Tozi river'). A Tenankutchin village on the N. bank of the Yukon, at the mouth of Tozi r., Alaska.—Petroff in 10th Census, Alaska, map, 1884.

Trachite. An eruptive rock, usually of light grayish hues and of medium hardness, used to a limited extent by the aborigines in the manufacture of implements.   (W. H. H.)

Track Rock. A name, which should properly be in the plural, applied to a group of about half a dozen micaceous sandstone rocks, covered with petroglyphs presumably of Indian origin, on both sides of the trail crossing over Track Rock gap, about 5 m. E. of Blairsville, Union co., Ga. It is in the old country of the Cherokee, who call the locality by names which mean "Where there are tracks," or "Branded place." The carvings are of various patterns, some of them resembling human or animal footprints, "turkey tracks," circles, etc., disposed without any apparent order or purpose. The Cherokee have no definite idea of their origin or meaning, and it is probable that they were made at various times by wandering hunters for their own amusement while resting in the gap. The wonderful description given by Stevenson in 1834 and copied without investigation by White (Hist. Coll. Ga., 1855) and Jones (Antiq. Southern Inds., 1873) is greatly exaggerated. For description, illustration, and Indian myths, consult Mooney, Myths of the Cherokee, 19th Rep. B. A. E. See also *Footprint sculptures, Pictographs.*   (J. M.)

Trade language. See *Chinook jargon, Comanche, Mobilian, Sign language.*

Trading posts. The earliest trade between Europeans and the Indians N. of Mexico was through the Basque people. These daring sailors by following the whale reached the fishing banks of Newfoundland at an early period. In 1497 Cabot touched upon that island and noted its "bigge fysshe." He was told by the natives that they were called *baccalaos,* the Basque for 'codfish,' and he gave that name to Canada. The word still lingers in Newfoundland as the designation of an island north of Conception bay. When Bretons, Normans, Portuguese, Spaniards, and Englishmen made their way to these fisheries, the Basques, who preceded them, had to a degree familiarized the natives with their tongue, and Basque words became a part of the trade jargon that came into use. Cartier, in 1534–35, found the natives of the gulf and river of St Lawrence familiar with the European fur trade, and certain places on that stream were known to both races as points for the drying of fish and the trading of furs. The traffic spread to the southward, and from a letter of Pedro Menendez to Philip II it is learned that in 1565 and for some years earlier "bison skins were brought down the Potomac and thence carried along shore in canoes to the French about the Gulf of St Lawrence. During two years 6,000 skins were thus obtained." The first trading post in 1603 was at Tadousac, on the St Lawrence at the mouth of the Saguenay; five years later Quebec was founded, and in 1611 Montreal was made the trading post for all the region westward. The earliest English post was with the colony on James r., Va., where pelts and corn were traded, and in 1614, when some needy tribes came to purchase maize, Sir Thomas Dale took, in repayment thereof, "a mortgage of their whole countries." In 1615, six years after the navigation by Hudson of the river

which bears his name, the Dutch built a large post at Albany. For the next 50 years the eastern colonies made no special attempt to penetrate the interior of the continent, but in 1673 Canada authorized the movement by which the priest Marquette and the trader Joliet discovered the Mississippi. Meanwhile individual traders had traveled beyond the Great Lakes, and Groseilliers and Radisson, French traders, had found that Hudson bay could be reached overland. The failure of the French Government to award to these men the right to trade and to establish a post on the bay caused them to apply to England, in which they were successful, and in 1668 Ft Charles was built at the southeastern extremity of Hudson bay. The success of this post led to the formation of the monopoly called "The Governor and Company of Adventurers of England trading into Hudson's Bay." Their successors, a hundred years later, in 1670, were incorporated by royal charter as The Hudson's Bay Company, with "absolute proprietorship, supreme jurisdiction in civil and military affairs, to make laws, and to declare war against pagan peoples." For more than half a century the posts of this company controlled the trade and administered whatever of law there existed in the vast regions N. and W. of the Lakes to the Pacific. In 1685 La Salle landed on the coast of Texas, opening the way for French trading enterprises on the lower Mississippi and its tributaries, and for the establishment of colonies in that region under the control of commanders of the posts. French trade during the 17th and 18th centuries developed a class of men known as *courreurs des bois,* who made themselves at home with the natives. These were the advance guard of civilization, and later served as interpreters, clerks, etc., to the Hudson's Bay, Northwest, American Fur, and other less important companies engaged in Indian trade up to the middle of the 19th century.

The trading post was generally a large square inclosed by a stockade; diagonally at two corners were turrets, with openings for small cannon and rifles in each turret so as to defend two sides of the wall. Within the stockade were the storehouses, quarters for the men, and a room for general trade.

In Virginia beads early became the "current coin" in trade with the Indians, and in 1621 Capt. Norton was sent over with some Italian workmen to establish a glass furnace for the manufacture of these articles. In 1640 and 1643 wampum (q. v.) was made legal tender in New England and was extensively used in trading with the Indians. During the next century trade was mostly by barter or in the currency of the colonies or the Government. The employment of liquor to stimulate trade began with the earliest venture and was more and more used as trade increased. The earnest protests of Indian chiefs and leaders and of philanthropic persons of the white race were of no avail, and not until the United States Government prohibited the sale of intoxicants was there any stay to the demoralizing custom. Smuggling of alcohol was resorted to, for the companies declared that "without liquor we can not compete in trade." To protect the Indians from the evil effects of intoxicants and to insure them a fair return for their pelts, at the suggestion of President Washington, the act of Apr. 18, 1796, authorized the establishment of trading houses under the immediate direction of the President. In 1806 the office of Superintendent of Indian Trade was created, with headquarters at Georgetown, D. C. In 1810 the following list of trading houses was furnished the chairman of the Senate committee on Indian Affairs: "At Coleraine, on the river St Marys, Ga.; at Tellico blockhouse, Southwestern territory; at Ft St Stevens, on the Mobile, Mississippi T.; at Chickasaw Bluffs, on the Mississippi, Mississippi T.; at Ft Wayne, on the Miami of the Lakes, Indiana T.; at Detroit, Michigan T.; at Akansas, on the river Akansas, Louisiana T.; at Nachitoches, on the Red r., Orleans T.; at Belle Fontaine, mouth of the Missouri, Louisiana T.; at Chicago, on L. Michigan, Indiana T.; at Sandusky, L. Erie, Ohio; at the island of Michilimackinac, L. Huron, Michigan T.; at Ft Osage, on the Missouri, Louisiana T.; at Ft Madison, on the upper Mississippi, Louisiana T." At that time there were few factories in the country where goods required for the Indian trade could be made, and as the Government houses were restricted to articles of domestic manufacture their trade was at a disadvantage, notwithstanding their goods were offered at about cost price, for the Indian preferred the better quality of English cloth and the surreptitiously supplied liquor. Finally the opposition of private traders secured the passage of the act of May 6, 1822, abolishing the Government trading houses, and thus "a system fraught with possibilities of great good to the Indian" came to an end. The official records show that until near the close of its career, in spite of the obstacles it had to contend with and the losses growing out of the War of 1812, the Government trade was self-sustaining. From colonial days and until the decline of the fur trade, near the middle of the 19th century, wars, in which both Indians and the white race were implicated, were fomented by the rivalry of competing traders. Posts were scattered along the rivers from the Great Lakes to the Pacific. Montreal and St

Louis were the two great outfitting centers, as well as the distributing markets for the furs. Where Kansas City now stands the traders bound up the Missouri by boat and those who were going overland parted company. Here the great Oregon trail started and stretched, a brown ribbon, across hundreds of miles of prairie. Forty-one m. to the westward, near the present town of Gardner, Kans., this trail branched to Santa Fé, where trade was maintained with the Pueblos and other Indians of the S. W. A sign-board set up at the parting of the trail indicated the long western branch as the "Road to Oregon." Along this historic trail trading posts were located, to which white and Indian trappers and hunters from the surrounding region brought their pelts. Fts Laramie, Bridger, Hall, Boisé, Wallawalla, Vancouver, and Astoria have now become cities. So also have the principal posts along the lakes and rivers, Detroit, Prairie du Chien, Council Bluffs, Pierre, Mandan, Spokane, Winnipeg, and many others, all of which are now centers of rich agricultural regions. In recent years steps have been taken to mark some of the old routes with suitable monuments. See also *Commerce, Fur trade, Trails and Trade routes.*

Consult Adair, Am. Inds., 1775; H. H. Bancroft, Works, I–XXXIX, 1886–90; Bartram, Travels, 1792; Bryce, Hist. of Great Company, 1900; Charlevoix, New France, Shea trans., 1866–72; Chittenden, Fur Trade, 1902; Colden, Five Nations, 1755; Coues, (1) Henry-Thompson Jour., 1897, (2) Jour. Jacob Fowler, 1898, (3) Larpenteur's Pers. Narr., 1898; Dunn, Oregon Terr., 1845; Farrand, Basis Am. Hist., 1904; Fletcher, Ind. Ed. and Civ., 1888; Fry and Jefferson, Map, 1777; Gregg, Commerce of the Prairies, 1844; Hulbert, Red Men's Roads, 1900; Irving, Astoria, 1897; Jefferson, Notes, 1825; Jesuit Relations, Thwaites ed., 1898–1901; Lawson, Hist. Carolina, repr. 1860; Lescarbot, Hist. Nouv. France, 1866; Lewis and Clark, Orig. Jour., 1904–05; Mackenzie, Voy., 1801; Marcy, Explor. Red River, 1854; Margry, Découvertes, 1875–86; Mooney in 17th Rep. B. A. E., 1898; Morgan, League of Iroquois, ed. 1904; Parkman, (1) Oregon Trail, 1883, (2) Pioneers, 1883; Roosevelt, Winning of the West, 1889; Sagard, Voy., 1865; John Smith's Works, Arber ed., 1884; Speed, Wilderness Road, 1886; Ternaux-Compans, Voy., VII, 1837; Thwaites, Early Western Trav., I–XXXII, 1904–07, and the publications of the various State historical societies.   (A. C. F.)

Trails and Trade routes. All early accounts indicate that from a period long prior to the coming of the whites the Indian was familiar with places often hundreds of miles distant one from another, and that they traveled over the same route in coming and going. The trader was inclined to follow the water courses, unloading his boat to pass obstructions and transporting the canoe and its cargo over short distances, called portages or carries, between different waters. Supplemental, however, to these open and in time of war obviously dangerous routes, were paths or trails, many of them originally made by the tracks of deer or buffalo in their seasonal migrations between feeding grounds or in search of water or salt licks. The constant passing over the same path year after year and generation after generation often so packed the soil that in places, especially on hillsides, the paths are still traceable by depressions in the ground or by the absence of or the difference in vegetation. Many of them have been obliterated by the roads and railways of modern times. The Jesuit Relations (1658) indicate the several routes followed from the St Lawrence and the Great Lakes to Hudson bay for trade, hunting, or fishing; one of these is mentioned as having extended a distance of 250 leagues. Many maps of the colonial period, supplemented by other records, indicate that these ways of communication extended with few breaks practically the entire length and breadth of the continent. While the streams answered in certain instances as suitable routes of travel, at times they had their drawbacks, owing to snags, freshets, or when the channel approached close to the shore, thus exposing persons in boats or on rafts to attack from enemies concealed in the vegetation along the banks. In many instances distant points were connected by trails, or traces, the latter word adopted from early French maps. Owing to the Indian habit of marching in single file, the Eastern trails seldom exceeded 18 in. in width, yet these were the ordinary roads of the country traveled by hunters, migrating bands, traders, embassies, and war parties. So long as the trails led through friendly territory, they followed the lines of least natural resistance. War parties after leaving friendly territory passed into the wilderness over routes selected by scouts, which routes they followed by significant marks, natural or artificial. In some places the paths of wild beasts were followed, in others the beds of streams were chosen, so that the footprints of the party would be obliterated. Other things being equal, the trail was not laid out along rough, stony ground, because of the rapid wearing away of footgear; nor through greenbrier, nor dense brush, nor laurel or other thickets, because of the difficulty of making rapid progress. These trails were generally along high ground, where the soil dried quickly, where the underbrush

was least dense, where the fewest and shallowest streams were to be crossed; and on journeys where mountains were encountered, the paths, with few exceptions, followed the lowest points, or gaps, in many of which stone piles are found. In the extreme S. W. these stone heaps have resulted from the Indians casting a stone when approaching a steep ascent, in order, they say, to prevent them from becoming fatigued. The numerous and wide watercourses and the dense forest growth along the coast of New England made progress on foot almost impossible; consequently the birchbark canoe was almost the only means of conveying the natives and their goods from point to point. Farther s. the dugout canoe was of such weight as to make any but the shortest carries most difficult. In the Middle states the country is more open and freer from underbrush, and the use of paths became a matter of necessity. Along the N. W. coast travel was along the beach or off shore in canoes. In the E. trails consisted of footpaths, whereas those of the plains in later times were wide roads beaten down by large parties passing with horses, dragging tipi poles and travois. These trails were well marked, often being depressed 2 ft below the surface, the difference in vegetable growth along them showing distinctly for many years where the path had been. In the S. W. there were long trails by which the Hopi and other Pueblo Indians traveled to and from the sources of supply of salt from the Colorado r. and elsewhere; long journeys were also made to obtain supplies of shells or turquoise for ornaments, clay for pottery, or stone to answer the requirements of trade or domestic use. The Iroquois of central New York were familiar with the country as far w. as the Black hills of Dakota, whence they returned with prisoners; the same Indians went from New York to South Carolina to attack the Catawba and into Florida against the Creeks. Western Indians traveled hundreds of miles to obtain blankets from the Pueblos, and some Plains Indians are known to have traveled 2,000 m. on raids. The Santa Fé trail and the Oregon trail were well-known routes whose beginning was Independence, Mo., one ending in New Mexico, the other at the Willamette. On early maps many Indian trails and trade routes are indicated, some along the streams and others across country. The route from Montreal up the Ottawa to L. Huron and Green bay may readily be traced; or from Montreal down to the Richelieu, up the latter, through L. Champlain into L. George, and by a portage to the Hudson. Another route went across country from Albany, on the Hudson, to Rochester and Buffalo on the lakes. Farther s. was the "trading" path from Richmond to the Cherokee country. Two roads led to the W., one down the Ohio, the other through the Wilderness by way of Cumberland gap. The great highway leading from Cumberland gap to the mouth of the Scioto was known as the Warriors' Path. The road from Philadelphia to Kentucky by Cumberland gap was nearly 800 m. in length. Daniel Boone crossed the mountains by following up the Yadkin to its headwaters, thence down the mountains by easy grade to the W. The Indian road, by the treaty of Lancaster, ran from the Yadkin, crossed the headwaters of the James, thence down the Shenandoah, across the Potomac, thence to Philadelphia by way of York and Lancaster, a distance of 435 m. No wagon passed by the Wilderness road, which extended westward through Kentucky, Indiana, and Illinois, before 1795. The white man, whether hunter, trader, or settler, blazed the trees along the Indian trails in order that seasonal changes might not mislead him should he return. The winter trails of the N. were over the frozen rivers or lakes or along paths made by snowshoes and sleds, which packed the snow solidly. These trails of the Indians, first followed by the trapper and trader, were later used by the missionary, the hunter, the soldier, and the colonist in their conquest of the wilderness. See *Commerce, Fur trade, Trading posts, Travel,* and the authorities thereunder cited. (J. D. M.)

Tramasqueac (contr. of Renape *Tĕramaskekok,* 'people of the white-cedar swamps.' The white cedar (Renape, *tĕarar*) referred to is *Chamæcyparis sphæroidea,* which grows in swamps from Maine to Florida.—Gerard). A Secotan village in 1585 on Alligator r., Tyrrell co., N. C.
Tamasqueac.—Smith (1629), Va., I, map, repr. 1819. Tramasquecook.—Dutch map (1621) in N. Y. Doc. Col. Hist., I, 1856.

Transportation. See *Boats, Commerce, Trails and Trade Routes, Travel.*

Traps. Although devices for inducing animals to effect self-imprisonment, self-arrest, or suicide differ from hunting weapons in that the victim is the active agent, the two classes merge into each other. The Indians had land, water, and air traps, and these acted by tension, ratchet, gravity, spring, point, or blade. They were self-set, ever-set, victim-set, or man-set, and were released, when necessary, either by the hunter out of sight or by the victim. The following list embraces all varieties of traps used by Indians N. of Mexico, and they were very clever in making them effective without the use of metal: *A.* Inclosing

traps: (*a*) pen, (*b*) cage, (*c*) pit, (*d*) door; *B.* Arresting traps: (*e*) meshes, (*f*) hooks, (*g*) nooses, (*h*) clutches; *C.* Killing traps: (*i*) weights, (*k*) piercers, (*l*) knives. Pen traps were of the simplest kinds—dams placed in the water or stockades on land. Some of these were immense, covering many square miles. The cage was merely a pen for flying creatures. Doors or gates for this whole class were vertical shutters sliding between stakes and set free by some kind of latch or trigger. Arresting traps were all designed to take the place of the human hand. Meshes were the opened fingers; hooks, the bent forefinger; nooses, the encircling closed fingers; the clutch, the grasping hand. Killing traps were weapons acting automatically. They were complex, consisting of the working part and the mechanism of setting and release. The Eskimo and Indian devices were of the simplest character, but very effective with unwary game. The victim was caught in a pound, deadfall, cage, hole, box, toil, noose, or jaw; or upon a hook, gorge, pale, knife, or the like.

ESKIMO WOLF TRAP. (NELSON)

The Indian placed an unstable prop, catch, or fastening, to be released in passing, curiously prying, gnawing, rubbing, or even in digesting, as when the Eskimo doubled up a skewer of baleen, inclosed in frozen fat, and threw it in the snow for the bear to swallow. Inclosing traps were common on land and in waters abounding in fish. Parry describes traps of ice with doors of the same material. The tribes of California and of the plains dug pits and covered them with brush on which a dead rabbit was tied, and the hunter concealed beneath grasped the bird by the feet, dragged it below, and crushed it between his knees. Arresting traps were most common, working by meshes, barbs, nooses, or by means of manual seizure. The aborigines were familiar with the gill net, trawl lines, gorge hook, snares, springs, trawl snares, and birdlime. Killing traps included ice, stone, and log deadfalls for crushing, impaling devices, and set knives for braining or for inciting mutual slaughter, the object of perhaps the most ingenious and efficient of Indian traps, consisting of a sharp blade inclosed in frozen fat, which was set up in the path of wolves. When a wolf in licking the fat cut its tongue the smell of blood infuriated the whole pack and drove them to destroy one another. See *Fishing, Hunting.*

Consult Mason in Smithson. Rep. 1901, 461–73, 1902, and authorities cited; Stites, Economics of the Iroquois, 1905; Boas, Murdoch, Nelson, Turner, and others in the Reports of the Bureau of American Ethnology; Niblack in Nat. Mus. Rep. 1888, 294, 1890. (O. T. M.)

Travel. The North American Indian had poor facilities for getting about on land. The Arctic peoples, however, with their sleds and dogs, may be said to have been pioneers of fast travel. Of such great and universal use was this method of locomotion among them that before their language became differentiated into dialects that rendered them unintelligible one to another they had covered the entire Arctic coast from E. Greenland to Siberia. The Algonquian tribes of northern Canada, together with the Athapascans in the Mackenzie r. country, also used the dog and sled for transportation and travel. South of this region the tribes had everywhere to walk until the Spaniard introduced the horse. The Indians were not discouraged by the lack of beasts of burden. They had covered the entire continent with a network of trails, over which they ran long distances with phenomenal speed and endurance; the Tarahumare mail carrier from Chihuahua to Batopilas, Mexico, runs regularly more than 500 m. a week; a Hopi messenger has been known to run 120 m. in 15 hours; and there are many instances of journeys extending over months or years, involving great hardship. It is most probable that the narrow highways alluded to were first laid down in the food quest. The animals that were wanted knew where were the best feeding grounds and supplies of water, and the Indians had only to follow the paths already made by the game to establish the earliest roads. Hulbert in his "Historic Highways of America" traces the trails followed by the Indians in their migrations and their ordinary trade routes, especially those of the mound-builders, and he gives lists, especially of the trails in the Ohio valley, where these mounds were most abundant. The range of the buffalo afforded especially favorable routes. The portages across country between the watersheds of the different rivers became beaten paths. The Athapascan Indians were noted travelers; so also were the Siouan and other tribes of the Great Plains, and to a smaller degree the Muskhogean, while the Algonquian tribes journeyed from the extreme E. of the United States to Montana in the w., and from the headwaters of the Saskatchewan to the Gulf of Mexico. Evidences of such

movements are found in the ancient graves, as copper from L. Michigan, shells from the Atlantic ocean and the Gulf of Mexico, and stone implements from various quarters. Pipes of catlinite (q. v.) are widely distributed in the graves and mounds. These articles show that active trade was going on over a wide region. There is good evidence that the men engaged in this trade had certain immunities and privileges, in so far as the pipestone quarry was on once neutral ground. They were free from attack, and were allowed to go from one tribe to another unimpeded. See *Boats, Commerce, Fur trade, Sledges, Snow-shoes, Trails and Trade Routes, Travois.*

Consult Friederici, Die Schiffahrt der Indianer, 1907; Mason in Rep. Nat. Mus. 1894, 1896, and the authorities cited under the above captions. (O. T. M.)

Traverse de Sioux. The local designation of a part of the Sisseton Sioux formerly living on Minnesota r., Minn., and taking their name from a trading post on that stream, above St Peter.

Travertin. See *Gypsum, Marble.*

Travois. A sort of sledge or litter, drawn by a single dog or horse, formerly in common use among the Plains tribes. The name, usually pronounced *trav-oy*, is the

DAKOTA TRAVOIS

French Canadian term for the shafts of a vehicle, and is a derivation from the older Latin word signifying a brake or shackle. The travois was sometimes specially constructed for the purpose, particularly in the case of the smaller ones intended to be drawn by dogs, but was more frequently a temporary combination of tipi poles and tipi cover while moving camp. When it had been decided to move, and the tipis had been taken down, the poles of each tipi were tied into 2 bunches of about 10 poles each by means of rawhide ropes passed through holes already bored for the purpose through their upper ends. These were then bound on each side of the horse with a rope passing in front of the saddle in such a way that the upper ends of the poles rested about the animal's shoulders while the lower ends trailed on the ground behind. The tipi cover was folded into a compact bundle and tied over the poles behind the horse, thus forming a litter upon which other household belongings, including sometimes the old people and children, were placed, to the limit of the animal's capacity. When the party reached its destination, the load was unpacked and the tipi again set up.

For special occasions a drag litter was constructed in the same fashion, with two poles for side pieces, supporting the central rest, which was either a piece of rawhide suspended between the poles by means of a rope passed through holes along the edge, or sometimes a netting of rawhide ropes stretched within a circular hoop or frame. By reason of its springiness this contrivance was more comfortable for riding than the other, and was therefore used for transporting sick or aged people, children, and even young puppies. A rounded top to keep off sun or rain was sometimes woven from willow rods, and when used for transporting small children this top was made to form a complete dome-shaped cage, with a doorway which was securely closed after the children had been put inside. The cage travois for carrying puppies was of similar pattern, but smaller, and was usually drawn by the mother of the puppies herself. The travois, drawn by dogs, is mentioned as early as the narratives of Coronado's expedition in 1540–42 (14th Rep. B. A. E., 1896). In modified form it has been proposed for army field use in transporting wounded.   (J. M.)

Trays. See *Receptacles*.

Trea. Mentioned by Oñate in 1598 (Doc. Inéd., XVI, 114, 1871) as a pueblo of the Jemez (q. v.) in New Mexico. It can not be identified with the present native name of any of the ruined settlements in the vicinity of Jemez. In Oñate's second list (ibid., 102) Fiapuzi is mentioned. A comparison of the lists shows the latter name to be a misprinted combination of "Trea" and "guati," the latter being the first part of the name of the next pueblo mentioned (Guatitruti). A similar error occurs in the name Mecastría in the same list.   (F. W. H.)

Treaties. The political status of the Indians residing within the territorial limits of the United States has been changed in one important respect by official action. From the formation of the Government to Mar. 3, 1871, the relations with the Indians were determined by treaties made with their tribal authorities; but by act of Congress of the date named the legal fiction of recognizing the tribes as independent nations with which the United States could enter into solemn treaties was finally set aside after it had continued for nearly a century. The effect of this act was to bring under the immediate control of Congress the relations of the Government with the Indians and to reduce to simple agreements what had before been accomplished by treaties as with a foreign power. Why the Government, although claiming complete sovereignty over the territory and inhabitants within its domain, adopted the method of dealing with the Indians through treaties, which in the true legal sense of the term can only be entered into by independent sovereignties, may be briefly stated:

The first step of the Government in determining its policy toward the Indians, whether expressed or implied, was to decide as to the nature of their territorial rights, this being the chief factor in their relations with the whites. This decision is distinctly stated by the United States Supreme Court in the case of Johnson and Graham's lessee *v.* McIntosh (8 Wheaton, 453), as follows: "It has never been contended that the Indian title amounted to nothing. Their right of possession has never been questioned. The claim of the Government extends to the complete, ultimate title, charged with the right of possession, and to the exclusive power of acquiring this right," which has been subsequently confirmed by repeated decisions of the court. The next step was to determine the branch of the Government to carry out this policy. By the 9th article of the Articles of Confederation it was declared that "the United States in Congress assembled have the sole and exclusive right and power of regulating the trade and managing all affairs with the Indians not members of any of the states." It is clear, therefore, that while acting under the Articles of Confederation the right of managing relations with the Indians was vested in Congress alone. In the formation of the Constitution this is briefly expressed under the powers of the legislative department, as follows: "To regulate commerce with foreign nations and among the several states, and with the Indian tribes."

It is apparent, from the use of the term "tribes," that the framers of the Constitution had in contemplation the method of dealing with the Indians as tribes through treaties. This is clearly shown by the act of Mar. 1, 1793, in which it is stated that no purchase or grant of lands shall be of any validity "unless the same be made by a treaty or convention entered into pursuant to the Constitution." This action of Congress necessarily placed the initiatory steps in dealing with the Indians under the jurisdiction of the President as the treaty-making power, subject to confirmation by the Senate.

The colonies and also the mother country had treated with the Indians as "nations," their chiefs or sachems often being designated "kings," and this idea, being retained by the founders of our Government, was ingrafted into their policy. Notwithstanding the evident anomaly of such course, this implied equality was recognized in the dealings between the two until the act of Mar. 3, 1871. During all this time Indian titles to lands were extinguished only under the treaty-making clause of the Constitution; and these treaties, though the tribe may have been reduced to a small band, were usually clothed in the same stately verbiage as the most important treaty with a great European power. From the execution of the first treaty between the United

arising from the sale of the land vacated. The right of Congress to abrogate a treaty made with the Indians when public necessity or their own welfare required it, has been asserted by the United States Supreme Court, and this right has been exercised in one or two instances, as in the case of the treaties with the Sisseton and Wahpeton Sioux by act of Feb. 16, 1863, and that of Lone Wolf *v.* Hitchcock, Sec. Int., in 1903. It was stated by the Indian Office as early as 1890 that the Indian title to all the public domain had then been extinguished, except in Alaska, the portion included in 162 reservations, and the lands acquired by the Indians through purchase. As the title to reservations is derived in most cases from the United

PENN TREATING WITH THE INDIANS AT SHACKAMAXON, PA., IN 1682. (FROM A PAINTING BY BENJAMIN WEST OWNED BY THE HISTORICAL SOCIETY OF PENNSYLVANIA)

States and the Indian tribes residing within its limits (Sept. 17, 1778, with the Delawares) to the act of Mar. 3, 1871, the Government pursued a uniform course of extinguishing the Indian title only with the consent of those tribes which were recognized as having claim to the soil by virtue of occupancy, and of settling other affairs with the Indians by means of treaties signed by both parties. Excepting in the case of the Creeks at the close of the Creek war, in 1814, and in that of the Sioux in Minnesota after the outbreak of 1862, the Government has never extinguished an Indian title by right of conquest; and in those cases the Indians were provided with other reservations and were subsequently paid the net proceeds

States, and title by purchase directly or indirectly from the same source, it may be stated that title to all the public domain except in Alaska had practically been extinguished by treaties previous to Mar. 3, 1871, and by agreements between that date and 1890.

As the dealings with Indians regarding lands constitute the most important transactions with which the Government has been concerned, and those to which most of the treaties relate, the Indian policy of the United States is most clearly shown thereby. By some of the European governments having American colonies—as, for example, Spain—the Indian claim was recognized only to so much land as was occupied or in use, but it has been usual for the United States to allow it to extend to the territory claimed, where the boundaries were recognized and acknowledged by the surrounding tribes. It would seem, in fact, that the United States proceeded on the theory that all the lands within their territorial bounds were held by the natives, and hence that the possessory right of the Indians thereto must be extinguished. The only variation from this rule was in the case of the Uinta Ute, where an omitted portion of their claimed territory was taken possession of (18th Rep. B. A. E., pt. II, 824, 1900). From the formation of the Goverment to Mar. 3, 1871, there were entered into 371 treaties with the Indians, including the Ft Laramie treaty of Sept. 17, 1851, with the Sioux, Assiniboin, Blackfeet, et al., which never appeared in the statutes, although acted on and subsequently recognized. This treaty, however, was printed in the Laws and Treaties of 1883 and 1903. The treaty of Sept. 23, 1805 (at the mouth of St Peters or Minnesota r.), with the Sioux, was also not printed in the statutes, though ratified by the Senate, and was never proclaimed by the President (see Compilation of Treaties, 1903, p. 793). The following list of the 370 treaties (that of Ft Laramie in 1851 being omitted) was published by the Indian Office in 1903:

List of all Indian treaties and agreements made with the several tribes of Indians in the United States which have been ratified (alphabetically arranged), with the date of each treaty and where the same appears in the Statutes at Large.

Statutes at Large		Date of treaty	Name of Indian tribe
Vol.	Page		
17	159	*May 23, 1872	Absentee Shawnee and Potawatomi.
10	979	July 1, 1852	Apache.
10	1013	July 27, 1853	Apache, Kiowa, and Comanche.
14	713	Oct. 17, 1865	Apache, Cheyenne, and Arapaho.
15	589	Oct. 21, 1867	Apache, Kiowa, and Comanche.
7	377	Oct. 11, 1832	Appalachicola.
7	427	June 18, 1833	do.
12	1163	Feb. 18, 1861	Arapaho and Cheyenne.
14	703	Oct. 14, 1865	do.
14	713	Oct. 17, 1865	Arapaho, Cheyenne, and Apache.
15	593	Oct. 28, 1867	Arapaho and Cheyenne.
15	655	May 10, 1868	Arapaho and Cheyenne (Northern).
19	254	Sept. 23 to Oct. 27, 1876	Arapaho, Cheyenne (Northern), and Sioux.
7	259	July 18, 1825	Arikara (" Rikara ").
......	......	July 27, 1866	Arikara, Grosventre (Hidatsa), and Mandan, unratified agreement, Fort Berthold (see page 322, "Indian Laws").
15	673	July 3, 1868	Bannock and Shoshoni, Eastern band.
......	......	May 14, 1880	Bannock, Shoshoni, and Sheepeater (see page 339, "Indian Laws").
11	657	Oct. 17, 1855	Blackfoot (Piegan, Blood, and Grosventre), Flathead, and Nez Percé.
14	727	Oct. 19, 1865	Blackfoot band of Sioux.
7	409	Oct. 27, 1832	Brothertown and other tribes.
11	657	Oct. 17, 1855	Blood (Blackfoot, Piegan, and Grosventre), Flathead, and Nez Percé.
14	765	Apr. 7, 1866	Bois Forte band of Chippewa.
7	470	July 1, 1835	Caddo.
7	472	.....do.......	do.
7	181	Sept. 25, 1818	Cahokia, Peoria, Kaskaskia, and other tribes.
10	1125	Nov. 29, 1854	Calapooia (Kalapuya) and Umpqua.
10	1143	Jan. 22, 1855	Calapooia (Kalapuya) and confederated bands of Willamette valley.
12	945	June 9, 1855	Cayuse, Umatilla, and Wallawalla.
10	1122	Nov. 18, 1854	Chasta, Umpqua, and other tribes.
7	18	Nov. 28, 1785	Cherokee.
7	39	July 2, 1791	do.
7	42	Feb. 17, 1792	do.
7	43	June 26, 1794	do.
7	62	Oct. 2, 1798	do.
7	228	Oct. 24, 1804	do.
7	93	Oct. 25, 1805	do.
7	95	Oct. 27, 1805	do.
7	101	Jan. 7, 1806	do.
7	103	Sept. 11, 1807	do.
7	138	Mar. 22, 1816	do.
7	139	.....do.......	do.
7	148	Sept. 14, 1816	do.
7	156	July 8, 1817	do.
7	195	Feb. 27, 1819	do.
7	311	May 6, 1828	do.
7	414	Feb. 14, 1833	do.
7	478	Dec. 29, 1835	do.
7	488	Mar. 1, 1836	do.
9	871	Aug. 6, 1846	do.
14	799	July 19, 1866	do.
16	727	Apr. 27, 1868	do.
7	255	July 6, 1825	Cheyenne.

* Act of Congress.

List of all Indian treaties and agreements, etc.—Continued.

Statutes at Large		Date of treaty	Name of Indian tribe
Vol.	Page		
12	1163	Feb. 18, 1861	Cheyenne and Arapaho.
14	703	Oct. 14, 1865	do.
14	713	Oct. 17, 1865	Cheyenne, Arapaho, and Apache.
15	593	Oct. 28, 1867	Cheyenne and Arapaho.
15	655	May 10, 1868	Cheyenne and Arapaho (Northern).
19	254	Sept. 23 to Oct. 27, 1876	Cheyenne, Arapaho (Northern), and Sioux.
7	24	Jan. 10, 1786	Chickasaw
7	65	Oct. 24, 1801	do.
7	89	July 23, 1805	do.
7	150	Sept. 20, 1816	do.
7	192	Oct. 19, 1818	do.
7	381	Oct. 20, 1832	do.
7	388	Oct. 22, 1832	do.
7	450	May 24, 1834	do.
10	974	June 22, 1852	do.
11	573	Jan. 17, 1837	Chickasaw and Choctaw.
10	1116	Nov. 4, 1854	do.
11	611	June 22, 1855	do.
14	769	Apr. 28, 1866	do.
7	16	Jan. 21, 1785	Chippewa and other tribes.
7	28	Jan. 9, 1789	do.
7	49	Aug. 3, 1795	do.
7	87	July 4, 1805	do.
7	105	Nov. 17, 1807	do.
7	112	Nov. 25, 1808	do.
7	131	Sept. 8, 1815	do.
7	146	Aug. 24, 1816	do.
7	160	Sept. 29, 1817	do.
7	178	Sept. 17, 1818	do.
7	203	Sept. 24, 1819	Chippewa.
7	206	June 16, 1820	do.
7	207	July 6, 1820	Chippewa and Ottawa.
7	218	Aug. 29, 1821	Chippewa and other tribes.
7	272	Aug. 19, 1825	do.
7	290	Aug. 5, 1826	Chippewa.
7	303	Aug. 11, 1827	Chippewa and other tribes.
7	315	Aug. 25, 1828	Chippewa, Ottawa, and Potawatomi.
7	320	July 29, 1829	do.
7	431	Sept. 26, 1833	do.
7	442	Sept. 27, 1833	do.
7	491	Mar. 28, 1836	Chippewa and Ottawa.
7	503	May 9, 1836	Chippewa (Swan Creek and Black River bands).
7	528	Jan. 14, 1837	Chippewa (Saginaw band).
7	536	July 29, 1837	Chippewa.
7	547	Dec. 20, 1837	Chippewa (Saginaw band).
7	565	Jan. 23, 1838	do.
7	578	Feb. 7, 1839	do.
7	579	.....do.......	do.
7	591	Oct. 4, 1842	Chippewa of Mississippi and Lake Superior.
9	853	June 5 and 17, 1846	Chippewa and other tribes.
11	621	July 31, 1855	Chippewa and Ottawa.
11	631	Aug. 2, 1855	Chippewa of Sault Ste Marie.
11	633	.....do.......	Chippewa of Saginaw and Swan Creek and Black River.
14	657	Oct. 18, 1864	do.
9	904	Aug. 2, 1847	Chippewa of Mississippi and Lake Superior.
9	908	Aug. 21, 1847	Chippewa (Pillager band).
10	1109	Sept. 30, 1854	Chippewa of Lake Superior (L'Anse and Vieux Desert, La Pointe, Lac de Flambeau, Fond du Lac, Ontonagon, and Grand Portage or Pigeon River bands).
10	1165	Feb. 22, 1855	Chippewa (Mississippi, Pillager, Lake Winnibigoshish, Mille Lac, Gull Lake, Rabbit Lake, and Sandy Lake bands).
12	1105	July 16, 1859	Chippewa of Swan Creek and Black River, and Munsee.
12	1249	Mar. 11, 1863	Chippewa (Mississippi, Pillager, Lake Winnibigoshish, Mille Lac, etc., bands).
13	667	Oct. 2, 1863	Chippewa (Red Lake and Pembina bands).
13	689	Apr. 12, 1864	do.
13	693	May 7, 1864	Chippewa (Mississippi, Pillager, and Lake Winnibigoshish bands).
14	657	Oct. 18, 1864	Chippewa of Saginaw, Swan Creek, and Black River.
14	765	Apr. 7, 1866	Chippewa of Bois Forte.
16	719	Mar. 19, 1867	Chippewa of Mississippi.
7	21	Jan. 3, 1786	Choctaw.
7	66	Dec. 17, 1801	do.
7	73	Oct. 17, 1802	do.
7	80	Aug. 31, 1803	do.
7	98	Nov. 16, 1805	do.
7	152	Oct. 24, 1816	do.
7	210	Oct. 18, 1820	do.
7	234	Jan. 20, 1825	do.
7	333	Sept. 27, 1830	do.

List of all Indian treaties and agreements, etc.—Continued.

Statutes at Large		Date of treaty	Name of Indian tribe
Vol.	Page		
7	340	Sept. 28, 1830	Choctaw.
11	573	Jan. 17, 1837	Choctaw and Chickasaw.
. 10	1116	Nov. 4, 1854	do.
11	611	June 22, 1855	do.
14	769	Apr. 28, 1866	do.
10	1048	May 6, 1854	Christian, cession from Delawares to.
7	474	Aug. 24, 1835	Comanche and Wichita.
9	844	May 15, 1846	Comanche and other tribes.
10	1013	July 27, 1853	Comanche, Kiowa, and Apache.
14	717	Oct. 18, 1865	Comanche and Kiowa.
15	581	Oct. 21, 1867	do.
15	589	.....do	Comanche, Kiowa, and Apache.
12	963	June 25, 1855	Confederated bands of middle Oregon.
14	751	Nov. 15, 1865	do.
10	1027	Sept. 19, 1853	Crow Creek or Umpqua.
7	35	Aug. 7, 1790	Creek.
7	56	June 29, 1796	do.
7	68	June 16, 1802	do.
7	96	Nov. 14, 1805	do.
7	120	Aug. 9, 1814	do.
7	171	Jan. 22, 1818	do.
7	215	Jan. 8, 1821	do.
7	217	.....do	do.
7	237	Feb. 12, 1825	do.
7	286	Jan. 24, 1826	do.
7	289	Mar. 31, 1826	do.
7	307	Nov. 15, 1827	do.
7	366	Mar. 24, 1832	do.
7	417	Feb. 14, 1833	do.
7	574	Nov. 23, 1838	do.
9	821	Jan. 4, 1845	Creek and Seminole.
11	599	June 13, 1854	Creek.
11	699	Aug. 7, 1856	Creek and Seminole.
14	785	June 14, 1866	Creek.
7	266	Aug. 4, 1825	Crow.
15	649	May 7, 1868	do.
......	......	May 14, 1880	Crow unratified (see p. 337, "Indian Laws").
22	42	June 12, 1880	do.
22	157	Aug. 22, 1881	do.
7	13	Sept. 17, 1778	Delaware.
7	16	Jan. 21, 1785	Delaware, Wyandot, Chippewa, and Ottawa.
7	28	Jan. 9, 1789	Delaware and other tribes.
7	49	Aug. 3, 1795	do.
7	74	June 7, 1803	do.
7	81	Aug. 18, 1804	Delaware.
7	87	July 4, 1805	Delaware and other tribes.
7	91	Aug. 21, 1805	do.
7	113	Sept. 30, 1809	do.
7	115	.....do	do.
7	118	July 22, 1814	do.
7	131	Sept. 8, 1815	do.
7	160	Sept. 29, 1817	do.
7	178	Sept. 17, 1818	do.
7	188	Oct. 3, 1818	Delaware.
7	326	Aug. 3, 1829	do.
7	327	Sept. 24, 1829	do.
7	397	Oct. 26, 1832	Delaware and Shawnee.
9	337	Dec. 14, 1843	Delaware and Wyandot.
10	1048	May 6, 1854	Delaware.
12	1129	May 30, 1860	do.
12	1177	July 2, 1861	do.
14	793	July 4, 1866	do.
12	927	Jan. 22, 1855	Dwamish, Suquamish, and other tribes.
7	49	Aug. 3, 1795	Eel River and other tribes.
7	74	June 7, 1803	do.
7	77	Aug. 7, 1803	do.
7	91	Aug. 21, 1805	do.
7	113	Sept. 30, 1809	do.
7	115	.....do	do.
7	118	July 22, 1814	do.
7	309	Feb. 11, 1828	Eel River or Thorntown party of Miami.
12	975	July 16, 1855	Flathead, Kutenai, and Upper Pend d'Oreille.
11	657	Oct. 17, 1855	Flathead, Kutenai, Upper Pend d'Oreille, and Nez Percé.
7	224	Sept. 18, 1823	Florida, tribes in.
......	......	July 27, 1866	Fort Berthold unratified agreement with Arikara, Grosventre (Hidatsa), and Mandan (see p. 322, "Indian Laws").
......	......	Sept. 17, 1851	"Fort Laramie" treaty (see p. 317, "Indian Laws"; also p. 1047, Revised Treaties).
7	135	Sept. 14, 1815	Fox.
7	328	July 15, 1830	Fox and other tribes.
15	467	Oct. 1, 1859	Fox and Sauk of Mississippi.

List of all Indian treaties and agreements, etc.—Continued.

Statutes at Large		Date of treaty	Name of Indian tribe
Vol.	Page		
15	495	Feb. 18, 1867	Fox and Sauk of Mississippi.
10	1074	May 18, 1854	Fox and Sauk of Missouri.
12	1171	Mar. 6, 1861	Fox and Sauk of Missouri, and the Iowa.
11	657	Oct. 17, 1855	Grosventre (Atsina), Piegan, Blackfoot, and Blood.
......	......	July 27, 1866	Grosventre (Hidatsa), Arikara, and Mandan, Fort Berthold agreement (see p. 322, "Indian Laws").
14	789	Oct. 20, 1865	Hunkpapa ("Onkpahpah").
7	136	Sept. 16, 1815	Iowa.
7	231	Aug. 4, 1824	do.
7	272	Aug. 19, 1825	Iowa and other tribes.
7	328	July 15, 1830	do.
7	511	Sept. 17, 1836	Iowa, and Sauk and Fox.
7	547	Nov. 23, 1837	Iowa.
7	568	Oct. 19, 1838	do.
10	1069	May 17, 1854	do.
12	1171	Mar. 6, 1861	Iowa, and Sauk and Fox of Missouri.
7	137	Oct. 28, 1815	Kansa (Kaw).
7	244	June 3, 1825	do.
7	270	Aug. 16, 1825	do.
9	842	Jan. 14, 1846	do.
12	1111	Oct. 5, 1859	do.
12	1221	Mar. 13, 1862	do.
7	49	Aug. 3, 1795	Kaskaskia and other tribes.
7	74	June 7, 1803	do.
7	77	Aug. 7, 1803	do.
7	78	Aug. 13, 1803	Kaskaskia.
7	181	Sept. 25, 1818	Kaskaskia, Peoria, Cahokia, and other tribes.
7	403	Oct. 27, 1832	do.
10	1082	May 30, 1854	do.
15	513	Feb. 23, 1867	Kaskaskia and Peoria, "omnibus treaty."
7	533	May 26, 1837	Kataka (Kiowa Apache), Kiowa, and Tawakoni.
7	49	Aug. 3, 1795	Kickapoo and other tribes.
7	74	June 7, 1803	do.
7	77	Aug. 7, 1803	do.
7	117	Dec. 9, 1809	Kickapoo.
7	130	Sept. 2, 1815	do.
7	145	June 4, 1816	Kickapoo and Wea.
7	200	July 30, 1819	Kickapoo.
7	202	Aug. 30, 1819	do.
7	208	July 19, 1820	do.
7	210	Sept. 5, 1820	do.
7	391	Oct. 24, 1832	do.
7	393	Nov. 26, 1832	do.
10	1078	May 18, 1854	do.
13	623	June 28, 1862	do.
7	533	May 26, 1837	Kiowa and other tribes.
10	1013	July 27, 1853	Kiowa, Comanche, and Apache.
14	717	Oct. 18, 1865	Kiowa and Comanche.
15	581	Oct. 21, 1867	do.
15	589	......do......	Kiowa, Comanche, and Apache.
16	707	Oct. 14, 1864	Klamath and Modoc, and Yahooskin band of Snakes.
12	975	July 16, 1855	Kootenay, Flathead, and Upper Pend d'Oreille.
11	657	Oct. 17, 1855	Kootenay, Blackfeet, Flathead, Upper Pend d'Oreille, and Nez Percé.
14	699	Oct. 14, 1865	Lower Brulé Sioux.
12	939	Jan. 31, 1855	Makah.
7	264	July 30, 1825	Mandan.
......	......	July 27, 1866	Mandan, Arikara, and Grosventre (Hidatsa), Fort Berthold agreement (see p. 322, "Indian Laws").
7	328	July 15, 1830	Mdewakanton band of Sioux and other tribes.
7	153	Mar. 30, 1817	Menominee.
7	272	Aug. 19, 1825	Menominee and other tribes.
7	303	Aug. 11, 1827	Menominee, Chippewa, and Winnebago.
7	342	Feb. 8, 1831	Menominee.
7	346	Feb. 17, 1831	do.
7	405	Oct. 27, 1832	do.
7	409	......do......	do.
7	506	Sept. 3, 1836	do.
9	952	Oct. 18, 1848	do.
10	1064	May 12, 1854	do.
11	679	Feb. 11, 1856	do.
7	49	Aug. 3, 1795	Miami and other tribes.
7	74	June 7, 1803	do.
7	91	Aug. 21, 1805	do.
7	113	Sept. 30, 1809	do.
7	115	......do......	do.
7	118	July 22, 1814	do.
7	131	Sept. 8, 1815	do.
7	189	Oct. 6, 1818	Miami.
7	300	Oct. 23, 1826	do.
7	309	Feb. 11, 1828	Miami, Eel River band.
7	458	Oct. 23, 1834	Miami.

List of all Indian treaties and agreements, etc.—Continued.

Statutes at Large		Date of treaty	Name of Indian tribe
Vol.	Page		
7	463	Oct. 23, 1834	Miami.
7	462	July 31, 1837	do.
7	569	Nov. 6, 1838	do.
7	582	Nov. 28, 1840	do.
10	1093	June 5, 1854	do.
15	513	Feb. 23, 1867	Miami and other tribes.
7	78	Aug. 13, 1803	Michigamia and other tribes.
7	181	Sept. 25, 1818	do.
7	403	Oct. 27, 1832	do.
12	963	June 25, 1855	Middle Oregon, Confederated bands of.
14	751	Nov. 15, 1865	do.
14	695	Oct. 10, 1865	Miniconjou band of Sioux.
12	1042	*June 27, 1860	Minnesota reservation Sioux.
7	261	July 30, 1825	Minnitaree or Belantse-etoa (Hidatsa).
7	328	July 15, 1830	Missouri and other tribes.
7	429	Sept. 21, 1833	Missouri and Oto.
7	524	Oct. 15, 1836	Missouri and other tribes.
10	1038	Mar. 15, 1854	Missouri and Oto.
10	1130†	Dec. 9, 1854	do.
11	605†	.....do	do.
16	707	Oct. 14, 1864	Modoc and Klamath, and Yakooskin band of Snakes.
7	61	Mar. 29, 1797	Mohawk.
10	1143	Jan. 22, 1855	Molala and Willamette Valley tribes.
12	981	Dec. 21, 1855	Molala.
7	87	July 4, 1805	Munsee and other tribes.
7	409	Oct. 27, 1832	do.
7	550	Jan. 15, 1838	do.
7	580	Sept. 3, 1839	Munsee and Stockbridge.
11	577	.....do	do.
11	663	Feb. 5, 1856	do.
12	1105	July 16, 1859	Munsee and Chippewa of Swan creek and Black river.
9	974	Sept. 9, 1849	Navaho.
15	667	June 1, 1868	do.
7	409	Oct. 27, 1832	New York tribes.
7	550	Jan. 15, 1838	do.
7	561	Feb. 13, 1838	do.
12	957	June 11, 1855	Nez Percé.
11	657	Oct. 17, 1855	Nez Percé and other tribes.
14	647	June 9, 1863	Nez Percé.
15	693	Aug. 13, 1868	do.
10	1132	Dec. 26, 1854	Nisqualli, Puyallup, and Shomamish and other tribes.
7	252	July 5, 1825	Ogalala and Sioune (Teton Saone).
14	747	Oct. 28, 1865	Oglala Sioux.
7	328	July 15, 1830	Omaha and other tribes.
7	524	Oct. 15, 1836	do.
7	129	July 20, 1815	Omaha.
7	282	Oct. 6, 1825	do.
10	1043	Mar. 16, 1854	do.
14	667	Mar. 6, 1865	do.
15	513	Feb. 23, 1867	"Omnibus treaty" (see Kaskaskia, Peoria, and other tribes).
7	47	Dec. 2, 1794	Oneida, Tuscarora, and Stockbridge.
7	566	Feb. 3, 1838	Oneida (First Christian and Orchard parties).
12	963	June 25, 1855	Oregon (Middle), Confederated bands of.
14	751	Nov. 15, 1865	do.
7	107	Nov. 10, 1808	Osage, Great and Little.
7	133	Sept. 12, 1815	do.
7	183	Sept. 25, 1818	do.
7	222	Aug. 31, 1822	do.
7	240	June 2, 1825	do.
7	268	Aug. 10, 1825	do.
7	576	Jan. 11, 1839	do.
14	687	Sept. 29, 1865	do.
17	228	*June 5, 1872	do.
7	154	June 24, 1817	Oto.
7	328	July 15, 1830	Oto and other tribes.
7	429	Sept. 21, 1833	Oto and Missouri.
7	524	Oct. 15, 1836	Oto and other tribes.
10	1038	Mar. 15, 1854	Oto and Missouri.
10	1130†	Dec. 9, 1854	do.
11	605†	.....do	do.
7	16	Jan. 21, 1785	Ottawa and other tribes.
7	28	Jan. 9, 1789	do.
7	49	Aug. 3, 1795	do.
7	87	July 4, 1805	do.
7	105	Nov. 17, 1807	do.
7	112	Nov. 25, 1808	do.
7	131	Sept. 8, 1815	do.
7	146	Aug. 24, 1816	do.
7	160	Sept. 29, 1817	do.

      *Act of Congress.   †The same treaty published in different volumes.

List of all Indian treaties and agreements, etc.—Continued.

Statutes at Large		Date of treaty	Name of Indian tribe
Vol.	Page		
7	178	Sept. 17, 1818	Ottawa and other tribes.
7	207	July 6, 1820	Ottawa and Chippewa.
7	218	Aug. 29, 1821	Ottawa and other tribes.
7	272	Aug. 19, 1825	do.
7	315	Aug. 25, 1828	do.
7	320	July 29, 1829	do.
7	359	Aug. 30, 1831	Ottawa.
7	420	Feb. 18, 1833	do.
7	431	Sept. 26, 1833	Ottawa, Chippewa, and Potawatomi.
7	442	Sept. 27, 1833	do.
7	491	Mar. 28, 1836	Ottawa and Chippewa.
9	853	June 5 and 17, 1846.	Ottawa and other tribes.
11	621	July 31, 1855	Ottawa and Chippewa.
12	1237	June 24, 1862	Ottawa of Blanchard's Fork and Roche de Bœuf.
15	513	Feb. 23, 1867	Ottawa of Blanchard's Fork and Roche de Bœuf, and other tribes.
7	172	June 18, 1818	Pawnee, Grand.
7	173	June 19, 1818	Pawnee, Pitavirate Noisy.
7	174	June 20, 1818	Pawnee, Republican.
7	175	June 22, 1818	Pawnee, Marhar (Omaha).
7	279	Sept. 30, 1825	Pawnee.
7	448	Oct. 9, 1833	do.
9	949	Aug. 6, 1848	do.
11	729	Sept. 24, 1857	do.
19	28	*Apr. 10, 1876	do.
7	181	Sept. 25, 1818	Peoria, Kaskaskia, Cahokia, and other tribes.
7	403	Oct. 27, 1832	do.
10	1082	May 30, 1854	do.
15	513	Feb. 23, 1867	Peoria and Kaskaskia, "omnibus treaty."
7	49	Aug. 3, 1795	Piankashaw and other tribes.
7	74	June 7, 1803	do.
7	77	Aug. 7, 1803	do.
7	83	Aug. 27, 1804	Piankashaw.
7	100	Dec. 30, 1805	do.
7	124	July 18, 1815	do.
7	410	Oct. 29, 1832	Piankashaw and Wea.
10	1082	May 30, 1854	Piankashaw, Wea, and other tribes.
15	513	Feb. 23, 1867	Piankashaw and Wea, "omnibus treaty."
11	657	Oct. 17, 1855	Piegan, Blackfoot, Blood, and Grosventre, Flathead, and Nez Percé.
7	155	June 25, 1817	Ponca.
7	247	June 9, 1825	do.
12	997	Mar. 12, 1858	do.
14	675	Mar. 10, 1865	do.
7	28	Jan. 9, 1789	Potawatomi and other tribes.
7	49	Aug. 3, 1795	do.
7	74	June 7, 1803	do.
7	87	July 4, 1804	do.
7	91	Aug. 21, 1805	do.
7	105	Nov. 17, 1807	do.
7	112	Nov. 25, 1808	do.
7	113	Sept. 30, 1809	do.
7	123	July 18, 1815	Potawatomi.
7	131	Sept. 8, 1815	Potawatomi and other tribes.
7	146	Aug. 24, 1816	do.
7	160	Sept. 29, 1817	do.
7	178	Sept. 17, 1818	do.
7	185	Oct. 2, 1818	Potawatomi.
7	218	Aug. 29, 1821	Potawatomi and other tribes.
7	272	Aug. 19, 1825	do.
7	295	Oct. 16, 1826	Potawatomi.
7	305	Sept. 19, 1827	do.
7	315	Aug. 25, 1828	Potawatomi and other tribes.
7	317	Sept. 20, 1828	Potawatomi.
7	603	.....do......	do.
7	320	July 29, 1829	Potawatomi, Chippewa, and Ottawa.
7	604	.....do......	do.
7	378	Oct. 20, 1832	Potawatomi.
7	394	Oct. 26, 1832	do.
7	399	Oct. 27, 1832	do.
7	431	Sept. 26, 1833	Potawatomi and other tribes.
7	442	Sept. 27, 1833	do.
7	467	Dec. 4, 1834	Potawatomi.
7	467	Dec. 10, 1834	do.
7	468	Dec. 16, 1834	do.
7	469	Dec. 17, 1834	do.
7	490	Mar. 26, 1836	do.
7	498	Mar. 29, 1836	do.
7	499	Apr. 11, 1836	do.
7	500	Apr. 22, 1836	do.

* Act of Congress.

List of all Indian treaties and agreements, etc.—Continued.

Statutes at Large		Date of treaty	Name of Indian tribe
Vol.	Page		
7	501	Apr. 22, 1836	Potawatomi.
7	505	Aug. 5, 1836	do.
7	513	Sept. 20, 1836	do.
7	514	Sept. 22, 1836	do.
7	515	Sept. 23, 1836	do.
7	532	Feb. 11, 1837	do.
9	853	June 5 and 17, 1846.	do.
12	1191	Nov. 15, 1861	do.
14	763	Mar. 29, 1866	do.
15	531	Feb. 27, 1867	do.
17	159	*May 23, 1872	Potawatomi and Absentee Shawnee.
10	1132	Dec. 26, 1854	Puyallup, Nisqually, and Shomamish, and other tribes.
7	176	Aug. 24, 1818	Quapaw.
7	232	Nov. 15, 1824	do.
7	424	May 13, 1833	do.
15	513	Feb. 23, 1867	Quapaw, "omnibus treaty."
12	971	{July 1, 1855} {Jan. 25, 1856}	Quinaielt and Quileute.
10	1018	Sept. 10, 1853	Rogue River.
10	1119	Nov. 15, 1854	do.
7	28	Jan. 9, 1789	Sauk and other tribes.
7	84	Nov. 3, 1804	Sauk and Fox.
7	134	Sept. 13, 1815	Sauk.
7	135	Sept. 14, 1815	Sauk and Fox.
7	141	May 13, 1816	Sauk.
7	223	Sept. 3, 1822	Sauk and Fox.
7	229	Aug. 4, 1824	do.
7	272	Aug. 19, 1825	Sauk and other tribes.
7	328	July 15, 1830	do.
7	374	Sept. 21, 1832	Sauk and Fox.
7	511	Sept. 17, 1836	Sauk and Fox, and Iowa.
7	516	Sept. 27, 1836	Sauk and Fox.
7	517	Sept. 28, 1836	do.
7	540	Oct. 21, 1837	do.
7	543	.....do.......	do.
7	596	Oct. 11, 1842	do.
15	467	Oct. 1, 1859	Sauk and Fox of the Mississippi.
15	495	Feb. 18, 1867	do.
10	1074	May 18, 1854	Sauk and Fox of Missouri.
12	1171	Mar. 6, 1861	Sauk and Fox of Missouri, and the Iowa.
14	731	Oct. 20, 1865	Sans Arcs band of Sioux.
7	368	May 9, 1832	Seminole.
7	423	Mar. 28, 1833	do.
9	821	Jan. 4, 1845	Seminole and Creek.
11	699	Aug. 7, 1856	do.
14	755	Mar. 21, 1866	Seminole.
7	15	Oct. 22, 1784	Seneca and other tribes.
7	33	Jan. 9, 1789	do.
7	44	Nov. 11, 1794	do.
7	601	Sept. 15, 1797	Seneca.
7	70	June 30, 1802	do.
7	72	.....do.......	do.
7	118	July 22, 1814	Seneca and other tribes.
7	131	Sept. 8, 1815	do.
7	160	Sept. 29, 1817	do.
7	178	Sept. 17, 1818	do.
7	348	Feb. 28, 1831	Seneca.
7	351	July 20, 1831	Seneca and Shawnee.
7	411	Dec. 29, 1832	do.
7	550	Jan. 15, 1838	Seneca and other tribes.
7	586	May 20, 1842	Seneca.
11	735	†Nov. 5, 1857	Seneca, Tonawanda band.
11	738	†....do......	do.
12	991	†....do.......	do.
15	513	Feb. 23, 1867	Seneca, "omnibus treaty."
7	55	May 31, 1796	Seven Nations in Canada.
7	26	Jan. 31, 1786	Shawnee.
7	49	Aug. 3, 1795	Shawnee and other tribes.
7	74	June 7, 1803	do.
7	87	July 4, 1805	do.
7	112	Nov. 25, 1808	do.
7	118	July 22, 1814	do.
7	131	Sept. 8, 1815	do.
7	160	Sept. 29, 1817	do.
7	178	Sept. 17, 1818	do.
7	284	Nov. 7, 1825	Shawnee.
7	351	July 20, 1831	Shawnee and Seneca.
7	355	Aug. 8, 1831	Shawnee.
7	397	Oct. 26, 1832	Shawnee and Delaware.

*Act of Congress.   † The same treaty published in different volumes.

List of all Indian treaties and agreements, etc.—Continued.

Statutes at Large		Date of treaty	Name of Indian tribe
Vol.	Page		
7	411	Dec. 29, 1832	Shawnee and Seneca.
10	1053	May 10, 1854	Shawnee.
15	513	Feb. 23, 1867	Shawnee, "omnibus treaty."
......	......	May 14, 1880	Sheepeater, Shoshoni, and Bannock (see page 339, "Indian Laws").
10	1132	Dec. 26, 1854	Shomamish, Nisqualli, and Puyallup, and other tribes.
18	685	July 2, 1863	Shoshoni, Eastern band.
18	291	Sept. 26, 1872	do.
13	663	July 30, 1863	Shoshoni, Northwestern band.
18	689	Oct. 1, 1863	Shoshoni, Western band.
13	681	Oct. 12, 1863	Shoshoni, Goship band.
15	673	July 3, 1868	Shoshoni and Bannock, Eastern band.
......	......	May 14, 1880	Shoshoni, Bannock, and Sheepeater (see page 339, "Indian Laws").
22	148	July 18, 1881	Shoshoni and Bannock.
......	......	Sept. 23, 1805	Sioux (see page 316, "Indian Laws").
7	126	July 19, 1815	Sioux of the Lakes.
7	127	.....do.......	Sioux of the River Saint Peter.
7	143	June 1, 1816	Sioux.
7	250	June 22, 1825	Sioux of several bands.
7	252	July 5, 1825	Sioux, Sioune (Teton Saone), and Ogalala.
7	257	July 16, 1825	Sioux, Hunkpapa band.
7	272	Aug. 19, 1825	Sioux and other tribes.
7	328	July 15, 1830	do.
7	510	Sept. 10, 1836	Sioux of Wabashaw's (the Kiyuksa) tribe.
7	524	Oct. 15, 1836	Sioux and other tribes.
7	527	Nov. 30, 1836	Sioux of several tribes.
7	538	Sept. 29, 1837	Sioux.
7	542	Oct. 21, 1837	Sioux of the Yankton tribe.
10	949	July 23, 1851	Sioux.
10	954	Aug. 5, 1851	do.
11	749	†Sept. 17, 1851	Sioux, "treaty at Fort Laramie" (see page 1047, Revised Treaties; also page 317, "Indian Laws").
11	743	Apr. 19, 1858	Sioux of the Yankton tribe.
12	1031	June 19, 1858	Sioux.
12	1037	.....do.......	Sioux, Sisseton, and Wahpeton.
12	1042	*June 27, 1860	Sioux (Minnesota Reservation Sioux).
14	695	Oct. 10, 1865	Sioux, Miniconjou band.
14	699	Oct. 14, 1865	Sioux, Lower Brulé band.
14	727	Oct. 19, 1865	Sioux, Blackfeet band.
14	731	Oct. 20, 1865	Sioux, Sans Arcs band.
14	735	.....do.......	Sioux, Yanktonai band.
14	739	.....do.......	Sioux, Hunkpapa (Onkpahpah) band.
14	743	Oct. 28, 1865	Sioux, Upper Yanktonai band.
14	747	.....do.......	Sioux, Oglala band.
14	723	Oct. 19, 1865	Sioux, Two Kettles band.
15	505	Feb. 19, 1867	Sioux, Sisseton and Wahpeton bands.
15	635	Apr. 29, 1868	Sioux, the different tribes.
18	167	{Sept. 20, 1872} {*May 2, 1873}	Sioux, Sisseton, and Wahpeton (page 1051, Revised Treaties; see page 328, "Indian Laws").
19	254	Sept. 23 to Oct. 27, 1876.	Sioux, the different tribes, and Northern Cheyenne and Northern Arapaho.
7	328	July 15, 1830	Sisseton and other tribes of Sioux, Iowa, Omaha, etc.
7	527	Nov. 30, 1836	Sisseton and other tribes of Sioux.
12	1037	June 19, 1858	Sisseton and Wahpeton Sioux.
15	505	Feb. 19, 1867	do.
18	167	{Sept. 20, 1872} {*May 2, 1873}	Sisseton and Wahpeton Sioux (page 1051, Revised Treaties; see page 328, "Indian Laws").
7	15	Oct. 22, 1784	Six Nations.
7	33	Jan. 9, 1789	do.
7	44	Nov. 11, 1794	do.
7	409	Oct. 27, 1832	do.
7	550	Jan. 15, 1838	do.
7	561	Feb. 13, 1838	do.
12	933	Jan. 26, 1855	Sklallam (Skokomish).
16	707	Oct. 14, 1864	Snake (Klamath, Modoc, and Yahooskin band).
14	683	Aug. 12, 1865	Snake, Walpapi tribe.
7	409	Oct. 27, 1832	St Regis and other tribes.
7	561	Feb. 13, 1838	do.
7	47	Dec. 2, 1794	Stockbridge, Oneida, and Tuscarora.
7	342	Feb. 8, 1831	Stockbridge and other tribes.
7	405	Oct. 27, 1832	do.
7	409	.....do.......	do.
7	580	Sept. 3, 1839	Stockbridge and Munsee.
11	577	.....do.......	do.
9	955	Nov. 24, 1848	Stockbridge.
9	964	.....do.......	do.
11	663	Feb. 5, 1856	Stockbridge and Munsee.
12	927	Jan. 22, 1855	Suquamish, Dwamish, and other tribes.
18	673	Oct. 7, 1863	Tabeguache band of Ute.
7	181	Sept. 25, 1818	Tamaroa and other tribes.
7	533	May 26, 1837	Tawakoni, Kiowa, and Kataka (Kiowa Apache).

* Act of Congress.   † Unratified, but appropriations are made under it.

List of all Indian treaties and agreements, etc.—Continued.

Statutes at Large		Date of treaty	Name of Indian tribe
Vol.	Page		
7	125	July 19, 1815	Teton.
7	250	June 22, 1825	Teton, Yankton, and Yanktonai Sioux.
7	47	Dec. 2, 1794	Tuscarora, Oneida, and Stockbridge.
14	723	Oct. 19, 1865	Two Kettles band of Sioux.
12	945	June 9, 1855	Umatilla, Wallawalla, and Cayuse.
10	1027	Sept. 19, 1853	Umpqua, Cow Creek band.
10	1122	Nov. 18, 1854	Umpqua, Chasta (Chastacosta), and other tribes.
10	1125	Nov. 29, 1854	Umpqua and Kalapuya.
12	975	July 16, 1855	Upper Pend d'Oreille, Flathead, and Kutenai.
11	657	Oct. 17, 1855	do.
14	743	Oct. 28, 1865	Upper Yanktonai Sioux.
9	984	Dec. 30, 1849	Ute.
13	673	Oct. 7, 1863	Ute, Tabeguache band.
15	619	Mar. 2, 1868	Ute, Confederated bands.
18	36	Sept. 13, 1873	Ute.
21	199	Mar. 6, 1880	do.
7	328	July 15, 1830	Wahpekute Sioux and other tribes.
7	527	Nov. 30, 1836	do.
7	328	July 15, 1830	Wahpeton and Sisseton bands of Sioux.
12	1037	June 19, 1858	do.
15	505	Feb. 19, 1867	do.
18	167	{Sept. 20, 1872 *May 2, 1873	{Wahpeton and Sisseton bands of Sioux (p. 1051, Revised Treaties; see page 328, "Indian Laws").
12	945	June 9, 1855	Wallawalla, Cayuse, and Umatilla.
12	963	June 25, 1855	Wallawalla and other middle Oregon tribes.
14	683	Aug. 12, 1865	Walpapi tribe of Snake.
12	963	June 25, 1855	Wasco, Wallawalla, and other tribes in middle Oregon.
7	49	Aug. 3, 1795	Wea and other tribes.
7	74	June 7, 1803	do.
7	91	Aug. 21, 1805	do.
7	116	Oct. 26, 1809	do.
7	145	June 4, 1816	Wea and Kickapoo.
7	186	Oct. 2, 1818	Wea.
7	209	Aug. 11, 1820	do.
7	410	Oct. 29, 1832	Wea and Piankashaw.
10	1082	May 30, 1854	do.
15	513	Feb. 23, 1867	Wea and Piankashaw, "omnibus treaty."
7	474	Aug. 24, 1835	Wichita and Comanche.
10	1143	Jan. 22, 1855	Willamette Valley.
7	144	June 3, 1816	Winnebago.
7	272	Aug. 19, 1825	Winnebago and other tribes.
7	303	Aug. 11, 1827	Winnebago, Chippewa, and Menominee.
7	315	Aug. 25, 1828	Winnebago and other tribes.
7	323	Aug. 1, 1829	Winnebago.
7	370	Sept. 15, 1832	do.
7	544	Nov. 1, 1837	do.
9	878	Oct. 13, 1846	do.
10	1172	Feb. 27, 1855	do.
12	1101	Apr. 15, 1859	do.
12	658	*Feb. 21, 1863	do.
14	671	Mar. 8, 1865	do.
16	361	*July 15, 1870	do.
17	185	*May 29, 1872	do.
7	16	Jan. 21, 1785	Wyandot and other tribes.
7	28	Jan. 9, 1789	do.
7	49	Aug. 3, 1795	do.
7	77	Aug. 7, 1803	do.
7	87	July 4, 1805	do.
7	105	Nov. 17, 1807	do.
7	112	Nov. 25, 1808	do.
7	118	July 22, 1814	do.
7	131	Sept. 8, 1815	do.
7	160	Sept. 29, 1817	do.
7	178	Sept. 17, 1818	do.
7	180	Sept. 20, 1818	Wyandot.
7	364	Jan. 19, 1832	do.
7	502	Apr. 23, 1836	do.
11	581	Mar. 17, 1842	do.
9	337	Dec. 14, 1843	do.
9	987	Apr. 1, 1850	do.
10	1159	Jan. 31, 1855	do.
15	513	Feb. 23, 1867	Wyandot, "omnibus treaty."
12	951	June 9, 1855	Yakima.
7	128	July 19, 1815	Yankton.
7	250	June 22, 1825	Yankton and other tribes.
7	524	Oct. 15, 1836	do.
7	542	Oct. 21, 1837	Yankton Sioux.
11	743	Apr. 19, 1858	do.
14	735	Oct. 20, 1865	Yanktonai Sioux.

* Act of Congress.

Since the act of Mar. 3, 1871, the dealings with the Indians, except in cases in which the President has been empowered to act, have been by agreements. To Mar. 21, 1902, these have numbered 74. Previous to the Declaration of Independence treaties were made with the Indians by the individual colonies and also by Great Britain. The New England colonies, and Pennsylvania, New Jersey, Maryland, and Virginia seem to have treated directly and independently of the mother country; while treaties with the Indians of New York, the Carolinas, and Georgia were made partly by the colonies and partly by the agents of the British government. Under the Articles of Confederation the right of treating with the Indians was clearly reserved to the respective states in which the Indians resided, but under the Constitution the party with whom this right remained has been a subject of dispute, although theoretically the right seems to have remained with the 13 original states until transferred by them to the United States.

For additional information consult the various official compilations of Indian Treaties up to 1837 and those of 1873 and 1904; also Reports of the Commissioner of Indian Affairs, especially those for 1890 and 1903. For treaties relating to land cessions, see 18th Rep. B. A. E., pt. II, 1900. See also *Governmental Policy, Land Tenure, Reservations.* (C. T.)

Treaty Party. A name applied to the Cherokee removed w. of the Mississippi under the New Echota treaty of 1835, to distinguish them from those previously in the W. and known as Western Cherokee, or Old Settlers.
Eastern Cherokees.—Washington treaty proc. (1846) in U. S. Ind. Treaties, 82, 1873. Treaty Party.—Ibid.

Trelagú. Mentioned as a pueblo of the province of Atripuy (q. v.), in the region of the lower Rio Grande, N. Mex., in 1598.—Oñate (1598) in Doc. Inéd., xvi, 115, 1871.

Trelaquepú. Mentioned as a pueblo of the province of Atripuy (q. v.), in the region of the lower Rio Grande, N. Mex., in 1598.—Oñate (1598) in Doc. Inéd., xvi, 115, 1871.

Tremblers. An unidentified branch of the Apache of Arizona, "who acquired their name from their emotions at meeting the whites."
Tremblers.—Canadian guide quoted by Emory, Recon., 70, 1848. Trementinas.—Villa-Señor, Theatro Am., pt. 2, 412, 1748.

Trenaquel. Formerly the most southerly of the Piro pueblos on the w. bank of the Rio Grande, probably on the site of the present town of San Marcial, Socorro co., N. Mex. It was visited by Oñate in 1598 and mentioned by him as one of the pueblos of the province of

Atripuy (q. v.). Qualacú was the most southerly of the Piro villages on the opposite bank of the river. See Oñate (1598) in Doc. Inéd., xvi, 115, 1871; Bandelier in Arch. Inst. Papers, iv, 252, 1892.

Trephining. See *Medicine and Medicine-men.*

Treyéy. Mentioned as a pueblo of the province of Atripuy (q. v.), in the region of the lower Rio Grande, N. Mex., in 1598.—Oñate (1598) in Doc. Inéd., xvi, 115, 1871.

Treypual. Mentioned as a pueblo of the province of Atripuy (q. v.), in the region of the lower Rio Grande, N. Mex., in 1598.—Oñate (1598) in Doc. Inéd., xvi, 115, 1871.

Triapí. A Tewa pueblo in New Mexico in 1598.
Triapé.—Bandelier in Arch. Inst. Papers, i, 19, 1881 (misprint). Triapí—Oñate (1598) in Doc. Inéd., xvi, 115, 1871.

Triáque. A Tewa pueblo in New Mexico in 1598.—Oñate (1598) in Doc. Inéd., xvi, 116, 1871.

Triati. An unidentified pueblo in New Mexico in 1598.—Oñate (1598) in Doc. Ind., xvi, 103, 1871.

Tribe. Among the North American Indians a tribe is a body of persons who are bound together by ties of consanguinity and affinity and by certain esoteric ideas or concepts derived from their philosophy concerning the genesis and preservation of the environing cosmos, and who by means of these kinship ties are thus socially, politically, and religiously organized through a variety of ritualistic, governmental, and other institutions, and who dwell together occupying a definite territorial area, and who speak a common language or dialect. From a great variety of circumstances—climatic, topographic, and alimental—the social, political, and religious institutions of the tribes of North American Indians differed in both kind and degree, and were not characterized by a like complexity of structure; but they did agree in the one fundamental principle that the organic units of the social fabric were based on kinship and its interrelations, and not on territorial districts or geographical areas.

In order to constitute a more or less permanent body politic or tribe, a people must be in more or less continuous and close contact, and possess a more or less common mental content—a definite sum of knowledge, beliefs, and sentiments—which largely supplies the motives for their rites and for the establishment and development of their institutions, and must also exhibit mental endowments and characteristics, that are likewise felt to be common, whose functioning results in unity of purpose, in patriotism, and in what is called common sense.

The tribe formed a political and territorial unit which, as has been indicated, was more or less permanently cohesive: its habitations were fixed, its dwellings were relatively permanent, its territorial boundaries were well established, and within this geographical district the people of the tribe represented by their chiefs and headmen assembled at stated times at a fixed place within their habitation and constituted a court of law and justice. At the time the North American Indians were first brought within the view of history, they were segregated into organized bodies of persons, and wherever they assembled they constituted a state, for they united the personal and the geographical ideas in fact, if not in theory.

Various terms have been employed by discoverers, travelers, and historians to designate this political and territorial unity. French writers employed "canton," "tribu," and "nation"; English writers used "tribe," "canton," and "kingdom"; while others have used "pagus," "shire," and "gau," the territorial meaning of which is that of a section or division of a country, whereas the concept to be expressed is that of a country, an entire territorial unit. Because the word "tribe" in its European denotation signifies a political unit only, its use without a definition is also inaccurate. The jejune and colorless terms "band" and "local group" are often employed as adequately descriptive of an organized body of Indian people; but neither of these expressions in the majority of cases should be used except when, from the lack of definite ethnologic information regarding the institutions of the people so designated, the employment of a more precise and descriptive term is precluded.

The effective power of the tribe for offense and defense was composed not only of the accumulated wealth of its members and the muscular strength, stamina, and experience of its quota of warriors, but also of the *orenda* (q. v.), or magic power, with which, it was assumed, its people, their weapons and implements, and their arts and institutions, were endowed.

Some tribes constituted independent states, while others through confederation with other tribes became organic units of a higher organization, retaining governmental control of purely local affairs only. Sometimes alliances between tribes were made to meet a passing emergency, but there was no attempt to coordinate structures of the social fabric in such manner as to secure permanency. Nevertheless in North America a number of complex, powerful, and well-planned confederations were established on uni-

versal principles of good government. Of this kind the League of the Five Tribes of the Iroquois in the closing decades of the 16th century was especially typical. This League was founded on the recognition and practice of six fundamentals: (1) the establishment and maintenance of public peace; (2) the security and health or welfare of the body; (3) the doing of justice or equity; (4) the advocacy and defense of the doing of justice; (5) the recognition of the authority of law, supported as it was by the body of warriors; and (6) the use and preservation of the *orenda* or magic power. The sum of the activities of these six principles in the public, foreign, and private life of these tribes so confederated resulted in the establishment and preservation of what in their tongue is called the Great Commonwealth.

In the history of the American Indian tribes, differences in culture are as frequent as coincidences. Different peoples have different ideas, different ideals, different methods of doing things, different modes of life, and of course different institutions in greatly different degrees and kinds. The course of the history of a people is not predetermined, and it is divergent from varying and variable conditions. Different results are consequent upon different departures. In some places tribal organizations are established on a clan or a gentile basis; in other regions a system of village communities was developed; and in still others pueblos or village communities were founded. From these different modes of life, influenced by varying environment and experiences, many new departures, resulting in unlike issues, were made. For the reason that the elementary group, the family, whence the other units are directly or mediately derived, is always preserved, coincidences are not infrequent. The term "family" here is taken in its broad sociologic sense, which is quite different from the modern use of it as equivalent to fireside (see *Family*). In gentile and clan tribal organizations a family consists of the union of two persons, each from a different gens or clan, as the case might be, and their offspring, who therefore have certain rights in, and owe certain obligations to, the two clans or gentes thus united in marriage by the two parents.

In historical times, in the group of Iroquois peoples, the tribes consisted of from 3 to 12 or 14 clans, irrespective of population. For social, political, and religious purposes the clans of a tribe were invariably organized into two tribal portions or organic units, commonly denominated phratries, each of which units in council, in games, in ceremonial assemblies, or in any tribal gathering occupied around the actual or assumed fire a place opposite to that held by the other phratry. In the placing of these clan groups the cult of the quarters is merely vestigial, having long ago lost its influence. In the great tribal gambling games between the units of the tribe (for phratry must at all times contend against phratry), the eastern side of the "plot" was regarded as insuring success; but at the present day the phratries alternate annually in occupying this auspicious quarter, although the phratry occupying this side is not at all times successful.

This dualism in the organization of the social, religious, and political units, next in importance to that of the tribe itself, is seemingly based on a concept derived from the primitive philosophy of the tribe regarding the procreation, reproduction, and maintenance of life on earth. The clans of a phratry, or association of clans, called one another "brothers," and the clans of the opposite phratry "cousins" or "offspring." In the elder period the phratry—the organic unit next to the tribe—was an incest group to the members of it, and consequently marriage was prohibited within it, hence the phratry was exogamous. But owing to the many displacements of the tribes by the advance of Caucasians this regulation in regard to the phratry has fallen into disuse, so that at the present time the clan alone is the exogamous group, just as the gens is the only exogamous group in those tribes in which gentile organizations prevail and gentile brotherhoods were formerly in vogue. There were, however, never any phratriarchs as such. The chiefs and other officers of the several clans acted as the directors and rulers of the two phratries, whose acts, to have tribal force and authority, must have had the approval of both phratries acting conjointly through their recognized representatives. Neither phratry could act for the tribe as a whole. The members of a phratry owed certain duties and obligations to the members of the opposite one; and these obligations were based not only on considerations of consanguinity and affinity but also on esoteric concepts as well. The reason for the last expression will be found to be cosmical and will be emphasized later.

Selecting the Iroquois tribes as fairly typical of those in which the clan organization had reached its highest development, it is found that in such a tribe citizenship consisted in being by birth or adoption (q. v.) a member of a clan, and membership by birth in a clan was traced only through the mother and her female ancestors; hence it was solely through the mother that the clan was preserved and kept distinct from every other. But although the child acquired his birth-rights only through his mother, singularly enough it was through the father that his or her kinship was extended beyond his own into that of his father's clan, which owed to the offspring of its sons certain important obligations, which bound these two clans together not only by marriage but by the stronger tie of a recognized kinship. By this process the clans of the tribe were bound together into a tribal unity. By the organization of the clans of the tribe into two exogamic groups, the possible number of clans between which the said mutual rights, privileges, and duties of fatherhood might subsist were in most cases reduced by about half; but this reduction was not the object of this dualism in tribal structure. The wise men of the early Iroquois, having endowed the bodies and elements of their environment and the fictions of their brains with human attributes, regarded these bodies and phenomena as anthropic beings, and so they imputed to them even social relations, such as kinship and affinity, and not the least of these imputed endowments was that of sex—the principles of fatherhood and motherhood. These beings were therefore apportioned in relative numbers to the two sexes. Even the Upper and the Lower and the Four Quarters were regarded as anthropic beings. They, too, were male and female; the Sky was male and a father; and the Earth was female and a mother; the Sun, their elder brother, was male, and the Moon, their grandmother, was female. And as this dual principle precedent to procreation was apparently everywhere present, it was deemed the part of wisdom, it would seem, to incorporate this dual principle by symbolism into the tribal structure, which was of course devised to secure not only welfare to its members living and those yet unborn, but also to effect the perpetuation of the tribe by fostering the begetting of offspring. If then a clan or a gens or a phratry of clans or gentes came to represent symbolically a single sex, it would consequently be regarded as unnatural or abnormal to permit marriage between members of such a symbolic group, and so prohibition of such marriage would naturally follow as a taboo, the breaking of which was sacrilegious. This would in time develop into the inhibition of marriage commonly called exogamy as a protest against unnatural and incestuous sex relations. The union of man and woman in marriage for the perpetuation of the race was but a combination in the concrete of the two great reproductive principles pervading all nature, the male and the female—the father and the mother. It would seem, then, that exogamy is not an inhibition arising from any influence of the clan or gentile tutelary, as some hold, but is rather the result of the expression or the typifying of the male and the female principles in nature—the dualism of the fatherhood and the motherhood of nature expressed in the social fabric.

In pursuing the study of this dualism in organic tribal structure it is important to note the appellations applied by the Iroquois to these two esoteric divisions.

When the Five Tribes, or the Five Nations as they were sometimes called, united in the formation of their famous League of the Iroquois, this dualistic concept was carefully incorporated into the structure of the organic federal law. The Mohawk, the Onondaga, and the Seneca were organized into a phratry of three tribes, ceremonially called the "Father's Brothers," while the Oneida and the Cayuga were organized into a phratry of two tribes, ceremonially called "My Offspring," or the phratry of the "Mother's Sisters." These esoteric designations are echoed and reëchoed in the long and interesting chants of the Condolence Council, whose functions are constructive and preservative of the unity of the League, and of course adversative to the destructive activity of death in its myriad forms.

It is equally important and interesting to note the fact that the name for "father" in the tongues of the Iroquois is the term which in the cognate Tuscarora dialect signifies 'male,' but not 'father,' without a characteristic dialectic change. It is thus shown that fundamentally the concepts "father" and "male" are identical.

In the autumn at the Green Corn Dance, and in the second month after the winter solstice at the extensive New Year ceremonies, the chiefs and the elders in each phratry receive from those of the other the enigmatic details of dreams dreamed by fasting children, to be interpreted by them in order to ascertain the personal tutelary (? totem, q. v.) of the dreamer. And in the earlier time, because the procreation of life and the preservation of it must originate with the paternal clan or association of clans, the members of such a clan should in a reasonable time replace a person killed or captured by enemies in the clan of their offspring. The paternal clan and the phratry to which it belonged was called, with reference to a third person, *hoñdoñnis' 'hěnʼ*, i. e. 'his father's brothers (and kindred).' Since the clan, and therefore the tribe of which it is a component part, is supported by the numbers of those who compose it, whether men or women (for its power and wealth lie chiefly in the numbers of its constitu-

ents), it followed that the loss of a single person was a great one and one that it was necessary to restore by replacing the lacking person by one or many according to the esteem and the standing in which he was held. This peculiar duty and obligation of the members of the paternal clans to their offspring in the other clans is still typified among the modern Tuscarora and other Iroquois tribes on the first day of the new year. On this day it is customary to make calls of congratulation and for the purpose of receiving a present, usually some article of food, such as small cakes, doughnuts, apples, pieces of pie, etc. But every person on entering the house of a clansman of his or her father may demand, in addition to the ordinary presents provided, "a baby," using for this purpose the ordinary term for a baby, *owiʼrǎʼǎʼ*. To comply with these apprehended demands, the thrifty housewife, to aid her good man in fulfilling his obligations, usually has prepared in advance a goodly number of small mummy-like figures of pastry, 8 or 10 inches in length, to represent symbolically the "babies" demanded.

So it would seem that marriage, to be fruitful, must be contracted between members of the male and the female parts of the tribal unity. In primitive thought, kinship, expressed in terms of agnatic and enatic kinship, of consanguinity and affinity, was the one basis recognized in the structure of the social organization. At first all social relations and political and religious affiliations were founded on ties of blood kinship of varying degrees of closeness; but later, where such actual blood kinship was wanting, it was assumed by legal fictions (see *Adoption*). Within the family as well as outside of it the individual was governed by obligations based primarily on kinship of blood and on certain fundamental cosmical concepts consonant therewith.

The Omaha tribe is constituted of ten gentes organized into two divisions of five gentes each, and this dualism in the organization of the tribal gentes into two constituent exogamous bodies is apparently prevalent in all the tribes cognate with the Omaha, with perhaps the exception of the Ponca. When on the great annual tribal hunt, the Omaha tribe camped ceremonially in the form of an open or broken circle. When the tribe performed its religious rites this circle was always circumspectly oriented. But when the tribe was moving, the opening of the camp-circle always faced the direction in which the tribe was marching, although the opening was symbolically toward the E. This symbolic fiction was accomplished by turning the circle in such manner that if the actual opening faced the w. the five tribal gentes whose invariable place was on the N. side of the circle when actually oriented would still be found on the N. side of the camp-circle and the other five gentes on the s. But it seems that this order was not always punctiliously observed at home. This persistent adjustment of the order in which the gentes were placed in regard to the real orient was a reflex of the cult of the quarters and apparently rested on a concept concerning the origin of life and of the bodies of the environing world. Like the Iroquois, and perhaps all the other Indian peoples of North America, the Omaha imputed life and human attributes and qualities to the various bodies and elements in nature. So regarding them as anthropomorphic beings, even social relations such as kinships and affinities were attributed to them, and not the least among these imputed properties was sex. Like all living things these bodies must need be apportioned to the two sexes. And as the various regions and quarters were regarded as beings, they also were male or female by nature. The Sky is male and a father, and the Earth is female and a mother; the Above is masculine, and the Below is feminine; the Sun is male, the Moon female. Since these two principles are necessary to the propagation of the races of men and animals, they were also made factors in the propagation and conservation of the necessaries of life. And as this dualism appeared seemingly in all living things, it was deemed needful to embody these two so necessary principles symbolically in the organic units of the tribal organization; and so it would appear that the one side as the representative of the Sky was made male and the other as representing the Earth was made female. Therefore it would seem that marriage to be fruitful must be between the male and the female parts of the tribal unity. Descent being traced solely through the father, it was he who sustained the gens and kept it distinct from every other. By birth the child derived his name, his place, his taboo, and his share in the rites of his gens solely from his father; but, on the other hand, it was through his mother's gens that his kinship was projected beyond the gens of his birth. So it is clear that it is the tie of maternal kinship—the bond of affinity—that actually binds together the gentes and that impresses every individual with the cohesive sentiment that he is a member of an inter-related kinship body of persons.

According to Miss Fletcher (Nat. Mus. Rep., 1897), from whom the data characterizing the Omaha tribal organization has been largely derived, the distinctive features of the Omaha gens and those of its close cognates are, in general, that descent is traced only through the father, that the chieftainship is apparently not hereditary, that its members do not derive their lineage from a common ancestor, that it possesses a set of personal names, that it practises a common rite, that it is not named after any individual, and that it is exogamous. So that the Omaha tribe, having ten such gentes organized in two exogamous associations, to each of which belongs a tribal pipe and a phratriarch who is one of the governing council of seven chieftains, has, among other things, ten religious rites, ten taboos, ten sets of personal names, and a governing council of seven chieftains. Formerly marriage was permitted only between members of the two exogamous associations, but not between the members of either among themselves.

According to Boas there are remarkable differences in the complex social organizations of the tribes of the N. W. coast. Of these the Haida and the Tlingit, both having maternal descent, are each composed of two exogamous organic and organized halves or units, which among the Tlingit are called the Raven and the Wolf, respectively, while among the Haida they are known by the names Eagle and Raven. The sociology of these two tribes, while approximating in general structure that of the Tsimshian, having likewise a definite maternal organization, is less complex, for among the latter there are apparently four exogamous associations with subdivisions or subclans. Before any satisfactory knowledge of the tribal structure and its functions can be obtained, it is necessary to possess in addition to the foregoing general statements a detailed and systemized knowledge of the technique by which these several organic units, singly and jointly, transact the affairs of the tribe. This kind of information is still in large measure lacking for a great proportion of the North American Indian tribes. Among the Kwakiutl, Boas found a peculiar social organization which closer study may satisfactorily explain. Among the northern Kwakiutl tribes there are a number of exogamic clans in which descent is traced preferably in the maternal line, but in certain cases a child may be counted as a member of his father's clan. Yet, Boas adds, "By a peculiar arrangement, however, descent is so regulated that it proceeds in the maternal line."

In speaking of the widely prevalent dualism in the highest organic units of the tribal structure, especially with reference to these tribes of the N. W., Boas remarks: "Since the two-fold division of a whole tribe into exogamic groups is a phenomenon of very wide occurrence, it is fruitless to speculate on its origin in this special case, but it is worth while to point out that Dr Swanton in his investigations among the Haida was led to the conclusion that possibly the Eagle group may represent a foreign element in the tribe," and states what but few others appear to see: that the crest system ("totemism") on the Pacific coast is not necessarily connected with this peculiar division of the tribe. But it has already been herein indicated in what manner this dualism has been made a feature in the social structure of at least two linguistic stocks, and that the reasons there advanced may be tentatively accepted as at least a probable explanation of such divisions in other tribes having analogous social institutions, unless it can be shown with greater reason to be due to some other equally potent cause.

Among the Salish, the clan and the gentile forms of social structure do not occur. In this respect the littoral Salish differ materially from those of the interior. Among the latter, according to Hill-Tout, the social fabric is so simple and loose that it "borders closely upon anarchy," while among the former it is comparatively complex, and the commune is divided into "a number of hard and fast classes or castes," three in number, exclusive of the slave class. Boas, writing in 1905 of the Salish tribes of the interior of British Columbia, says that in the "very loose" social organization of these people, if such it may be called, no tribal unit is recognized; that there are no exogamic groups; and no hereditary nobility was found, personal distinction being acquired chiefly by wealth and wisdom. While the exigencies of the food quest compelled these Indians to change their habitations from season to season, their permanent villages were situated in the river valleys. There are according to this author frequent and considerable fluctuations in the population of the villages, but it does not appear that these changes result in a diminution of the tribal population. It appears that deer-fences and fishing places were the property of certain persons and families, and moreover that the hunting territory was regarded as the common property of the whole tribe. From the prominence given to the "family" in marriage observances, in burial customs, and in property rights, it is possible that further investigation will reveal a much more complex and cohesive organization than is now known to exist.

According to Chamberlain the social structure of the Kutenai is remarkably simple, being in strong contrast to the social systems of great complexity found in British Columbia and on the N. W. coast. There is no evidence that the Kutenai have or ever had clan or gentile institutions or secret societies. Each tribal or local community had a chief whose office was hereditary, although the people always had the right to select some other member of the family when for any cause it was needful so to do. The power and authority of the chief was limited by the advice and action of the council. Formerly, a chief was elected to direct the great hunting expeditions. The population of the tribe was supported by the adoption of aliens by residence and by marriage. Descent was probably traced through the mother, and marriage of first cousins was strictly forbidden. These apparently tentative statements of Chamberlain indicate that the tribe was held together by the ties of consanguinity and affinity.

See *Adoption; Clan and Gens; Confederation; Family; Government; Kinship; Sociology.* (J. N. B. H.)

Tricentee. Given as one of the "Keowee towns" among the Cherokee in a document of 1755 (Royce in 5th Rep. B. A. E., 143, 1887). Possibly Tessuntee (q. v.).

Trimatí. Mentioned, in connection with Puaray, apparently as a pueblo of the Tigua of New Mexico in 1598.—Oñate (1598) in Doc. Inéd., XVI, 115, 1871.

Trinachak. An Eskimo village in the Nushagak district, Alaska; pop. 20 in 1890.

Trinachamiut.—11th Census, Alaska, 164, 1893.

Tripanick. A tribe of Algonquian or possibly of Siouan stock formerly living in the vicinity of Albemarle sd., N. C.

Tripanicks.—Hakluyt (1600), Voy., III, 312, 1810. Tripanieks.—Lane (1585) quoted by Hawks, N. C., I, 111, 1859. Trypaniks.—Lane (1585) in Smith, Va., I, 87, repr. 1819.

Tripas Blancas (Span.: 'white bellies'). A tribe living mainly in Coahuila, Mexico, and probably of Coahuiltecan stock, which in the 17th and 18th centuries was found at Nadadores, San Francisco Solano, and San Buenaventura missions, Coahuila. In 1688 they revolted and destroyed both the Nadadores and San Buenaventura missions (Portillo, Apuntes para la Hist. Antigua de Coahuila y Texas, 253, 1888; Valero Baptisms, 1705, 1707; Valero Burials, 1708, MS.). (H. E. B.)

Triwta. A former village connected with San Carlos mission, Cal., and said to have been Esselen.—Taylor in Cal. Farmer, Apr. 20, 1860.

Troomaxiaquino. A Tewa pueblo in N. Mex. in 1598. The ruins have been located by Bandelier in Rio Arriba co.

Pajaritos.—Bandelier in Ritch, N. Mex., 201, 1885 (Span. 'birds'). Troomaxiaquino.—Oñate (1598) in Doc. Inéd., XVI, 116, 1871. Troo-maxia-qui-no.—Bandelier, op. cit. Trovmaxiaquino.—Bancroft, Ariz. and N. Mex., 136, 1889 (misprint).

Trophies. The North American Indians preserved and frequently wore as an adjunct of costume the tails, claws, paws, teeth, horns, feathers, pelts, and other parts of the animals that they killed. Somewhat less frequently scalps, skulls, fingers, hands, arms, skins, hearts, teeth, and other parts of the human body, nearly always taken from the enemies belonging to alien tribes, were preserved in a similar manner.

As for the signification of such trophies, whose use is not peculiar to any single people or time, the explanation is not simple. The purposes of trophies may be arranged in the order of their complexity as follows: (1) ornaments; (2) proofs of skill and prowess; (3) records of events in chase or war; (4) tokens of blood revenge; (5) fetishes, which may be the property of special persons, as sorcerers and medicine-men, or of societies, fraternities, or tribes. In no case does the trophy rise higher in the scale than fetishism.

Among the ancient Pueblo Indians trophies made of the jaws of animals were used. These were frequently sections cut from the jaw of the mountain lion and pierced for suspension, or the whole lower jaw of a deer decorated with bands of red paint. In one grave was found the skull of a dog, polished from long use.

Bear-claw necklaces were frequently worn as trophies by the Indians of the United States. The Cree of the Hudson bay region wore as a trophy the lip of the black bear, which was preserved, dressed, and ornamented with beads and strips of cloth. The Hopi of Arizona wore the paws of the porcupine. There were innumerable other kinds of trophies.

The western Eskimo introduced the trophy into art, engraving representations of skins, heads, or tails of animals killed in the chase on ivory drill-bows, bag handles, etc. Necklaces of human fingers and trophies of hands and limbs have been found among the Cheyenne, Apache, Navaho (?), Ute, Shoshoni, Chippewa, Sioux, some California tribes, the Virginia Indians, Mohawk, Caddo, Florida tribes, and others. A necklace composed of 8 left-hand middle fingers, 5 pouches made of human scrota, arrowheads, glass and wampum beads, and fetishes cut from stone, captured by Gen. Crook in 1876 from the Cheyenne medicine-man Tall Wolf, are in the U. S. National Museum, as are also two necklaces consisting of the nails and first joints of human fingers, fastened to a beaded band of leather, from the Apache and the Ute. The medicine-men possessed a majority of the trophies preserved among the Indians and employed them for their supposed magic power. Some trophies, however, such as scalps, were tribal medicine. See Bourke in 9th Rep. B. A. E., 480–89, 1892; Hrdlička in Am. Anthr., x, 288, 1908; Friederici, (1) Skalpieren, 1906, (2) in Smithson. Rep. 1906, 423, 1907. (w. h.)

Trotsikkutchin ('people of the fork of the river'). A Kutchin tribe on Yukon and Stewart rs., Yukon territory, extending up the latter stream to the mouth of Beaver r., where they meet the Esbataottine, to whom they are hostile. They are said to spear salmon in the shoals of the Yukon. Ross described their songs as more musical than those of any other northern Indians.
Rampart Indians.—Ross, notes on Tinne, B. A. E. **Tathzey-kutchi.**—Richardson, Arct. Exped., I, 398, 1851 ('rampart people'). **Tathzey-kutshi.**—Latham, Nat. Races Russ. Emp., 293, 1854 (includes Kutchakutchin, Hankutchin, and Tutchonekutchin). **Tatzei-kutshi.**—Latham in Trans. Philol. Soc. Lond., 67, 1856. **Tĭn'-zĭt Kŭtch'-ĭn.**—Ross, notes on Tinne, B. A. E. ('people of the ramparts'). **T'kitskĕ.**—Whymper, Travels in Alaska, map, 1869. **Tlagga-silla.**—Richardson, Arct. Exped., I, 399, 1851 ('little dogs'). **To-tshik-o-tin.**—Dawson in Rep. Geol. Surv. Can. 1887, 202B, 1889. **Tran-jik-koo-chin.**—Hardisty in Smithson. Rep. for 1866, 311, 1872. **Tratsè-kutshi.**—Latham, Nat. Races Russ. Emp., 293, 1854. **Trŏ'-tsĭk kŭtch'-ĭn.**—Ross, notes on Tinne, B. A. E. **Tsœs-tsieg-Kutchin.**—Petitot, Dict. Dènè-Dindjié, xx, 1876. **Upper Gens du fou.**—Ross, notes on Tinne, MS., B. A. E.

Tructa. A village, presumably Costanoan, formerly connected with San Juan Bautista mission, Cal.—Engelhardt, Franciscans in Cal., 398, 1897.

Trula. Mentioned as a pueblo of the province of Atripuy (q. v.), in the region of the lower Rio Grande, N. Mex., in 1598.—Oñate (1598) in Doc. Inéd., xvi, 115, 1871.

Trusiachic (*trusi*, a kind of herb; *chik*, 'place of'). A small Tarahumare rancheria not far from Norogachic, Chihuahua, Mexico.—Lumholtz, inf'n, 1894.

Tsaeqalalis (*Tsāēqálalis*). The name of an ancestor of a Koskimo gens; also applied to the gens itself.—Boas in Petermanns Mitteil., pt. 5, 131, 1887.

Tsaganha. An Iroquoian term, having here the phonetics of the Onondaga dialect, and freely rendered, 'One utters unintelligible speech,' and so approximately synonymous with 'alien,' 'foreigner.' Its literal meaning is 'one rolls (or purls) one's mouth (speech).' This term was applied to the several Algonquian tribes dwelling E. and s. of the Iroquois in widely separated localities; the Hurons applied the name to the "Canadiens" of 1626, i. e. the Algonquians dwelling on the Lower St Lawrence. It was applied indiscriminately to the Abnaki, Mohegan, Mahican, Delawares, Munsee, Stockbridges, Brothertons, and generally to all the New England and contiguous southern Algonquian tribes. (J. N. B. H.)

Agotsaganens.—Jogues (1643) in Jes. Rel., Thwaites ed., XXVIII, 113, 1898. **Agotsaganes.**—Clark quoted by Brinton, Lenape, 255, 1885. **Agotsakann.**—Cuoq, Lexique Iroquoise, 155, 1882 (name of "Les Abenaquis de St François"). **Agozhàgauta.**—Ettwein quoted by Brinton, op. cit., 14. **Anasaquanan.**—Sagard, Huron Dictionnaire (1632) in Hist. Can., IV, s. v. *Nations*, repr. 1836. **Aosaannen.**—Potier, Radices Huronnes, MS., 1751. **Atsagannen.**—Bruyas, Radices, 42, 1863. **Tsa ga ha.**—Hewitt, inf'n, 1907 (Seneca form). **Tsaganha.**—Hewitt, inf'n, 1907 (Onondaga, Mohawk, Oneida, and Tuscarora common form).

Tsaguedi (*Tságuedî*, 'people of Tsagua,' or 'seal people'). A Tlingit division at Kake, Alaska, said to have once constituted a part of the Daktlawedi. (J. R. S.)

Tsahais (*Tsă-hais'*). A former Siuslaw village on Siuslaw r., Oreg.—Dorsey in Jour. Am. Folk-lore, III, 230, 1890.

Tsahis (*Tsáh'is*). The principal town of the true Kwakiutl, surrounding Ft Rupert, Brit. Col.
Fort Rupert Village.—Dawson in Trans. Roy. Soc. Can., sec. II, 65, 1887. **Sā-kish.**—Ibid. **Tsáh'lis.**—Boas in Jour. Am. Geog. Soc., XIX, 227, 1887.

Tsahkoolintin (*Tsáh-koo-lin-t'n*). The Chehalis name for an ancient village on the s. side of Gray's harbor, Wash.—Gibbs, MS. no. 248, B. A. E.

Tsahpekw (*Tsah'pekw*). A Yurok village on the N. w. coast of California, at Stone lagoon, about 15 or 20 m. N. of Trinidad. (A. L. K.)

Tsahwitook (*Tsah-wit-ook*). A body of Salish of Victoria superintendency, Brit. Col.; pop. 71 in 1882, the last time the name appears.

Tsaiiyeuk (*Tsai'-î-ye-uk*). A village of the Kueha sept of the Lekwiltok at the entrance of Bute inlet, Brit. Col.—Dawson in Trans. Roy. Soc. Can. 1887, sec. II, 65, 1888.

Tsaite (*Tsai-tē*). An ancient village on the w. end of Harbledown id., Brit. Col.—Dawson in Can. Geol. Surv., map, 1887.

Tsakhtsinshup. A former Chitimacha village on Grand r., near Plaquemine bayou, La.
Tsáχtsinshup námu.—Gatschet in Trans. Anthr. Soc. Wash., II, 152, 1883 (*námu*='village').

Tsako (from *sta-a-ke*, 'mud'). A Clallam village on Dungeness r., N. w. Wash.
Tsa-ko.—Eells in letter, B. A. E., May 21, 1886. **Tsohkw.**—Treaty of 1855 in U. S. Ind. Treaties, 800, 1873.

Tsaktono. A (former?) Maidu division living beyond Bidwell's bar, Butte co., Cal.
Tsaqtono.—Curtin, MS. vocab., B. A. E., 1885.

Tsaktsakoath (*Tsa'k·tsak·oath*). A sept of the Toquart, a Nootka tribe.—Boas in 6th Rep. N. W. Tribes Can., 32, 1890.

Tsakuam (*Ts'ăkuä'm*). A Cowichan tribe living in the town of Shilekuatl, at Yale, on Fraser r., Brit. Col. (Boas in Rep. Brit. A. A. S., 454, 1894). The Indian population of Yale in 1910 was 76.

Tsakwalooin. A village of the Wiwekae, near C. Mudge, Brit. Col.
Euclitus.—Downie in Jour. Roy. Geog. Soc., XXXI, 249, 1861. **Tsa-kwa-loo'-in.**—Dawson in Trans. Roy. Soc. Can., sec, II, 65, 1887. **Uculta.**—Ibid.

Tsalakmiut. A Lakmiut band that resided on Lakmiut r., Oreg., until they became extinct in 1877.—Gatschet, Atfalati MS., B. A. E., 1877.

Tsamak. A former Maidu group which in 1840 lived on or near Feather r., Sutter co., Cal.
Chamak.—Hale, Ethnog. and Philol., 632, 1846. **Tsamak.**—Ibid.

Tsamala (*Tsa-ma'-la*). One of the Chumashan villages formerly near Santa Inés mission, Santa Barbara co., Cal.—Gould, Santa Inez MS. vocab., B. A. E., 1887.

Tsam Bahenom. A former Maidu village situated a short distance N. E. of Mooretown, Butte co., Cal.—Dixon in Bull. Am. Mus. Nat. Hist., XVII, map, 1905.

Tsampiak (*Tsampiák*). A Lakmiut band formerly residing near Lakmiut r., a w. tributary of the Willamette, in Oregon.—Gatschet, Atfalati MS., B. A. E., 1877.

Tsanchifin. The Lakmiut name of a band of Calapooya proper, formerly living on the site of Eugene City, Oreg.
Chafan.—Dayton treaty (1855) in U. S. Ind. Treat., 19, 1873. **Tsan tchiffin ami'm.**—Gatschet, Atfalati MS., B. A. E., 1877.

Tsankawi ('place of the round cactus'). A prehistoric Tewa ruin on a lofty mesa between the Rito de los Frijoles on the s. and Los Alamos canyon on the N., about 5 m. w. of the Rio Grande, N. Mex. The ruins cover approximately 275 by 360 ft, and consist of the remains of four virtually independent blocks of community houses, built of dressed stones, surrounding a court with openings at the N. w. and s. E. corners. There are about 200 rooms in the ground-plan; when occupied the houses were probably of three stories at the highest points and accommodated 300 to 400 people. On the s. face of the mesa are numerous cliff houses of the character usually designated cavate lodges. See Hewett (1) in Am. Anthr., VI, 644, 1904, (2) in Bull. 32, B. A. E., 1906.
Sankawee.—Hewett, Syllabus of Lectures, 1900. **Tsankawi.**—Hewett, op. cit.

Tsanklightemifa. A band of the Calapooya proper which formerly lived at Eugene City, Oreg.
Tsän kliχ temifa ami'm.—Gatschet, Atfalati MS., B. A. E., 1877.

Tsankupi. A band of the Calapooya proper, formerly residing at Brownsville, Linn co., Oreg.
Coupé.—Ross, Adventures, 236, 1849. **Tekopa.**—Dayton treaty (1855) in U. S. Ind. Treat., 19, 1873. **Tsän tkûpi' ami'm.**—Gatschet, Lakmiut MS., B. A. E., 1877.

Tsano. The Yurok name of a Karok village of three houses near Orleans Bar on Klamath r., N. w. Cal., in 1852. Probably identical with Katipiara. (A. L. K.)
Chee-nah.—McKee (1851) in Sen. Ex. Doc. 4, 32d Cong., spec. sess., 161, 1853. **Chee-nas.**—Ibid., 215 (given as a Hupa division). **Cheina.**—Ibid., 194. **Skeina.**—Gibbs (1851) in Schoolcraft, Ind. Tribes, III, 150, 1853. **Tchai-noh.**—Ibid. **Tschih-nahs.**—Meyer, Nach dem Sacramento, 282, 1855. **T'shah-nee.**—Gibbs, MS. Misc., B. A. E., 1852.

Tsantatawa. A Lakmiut band that resided s. of Lukamiute r., a w. affluent of Willamette r., in Oregon.—Gatschet, Lakmiut MS., B. A. E., 1877.

Tsantieottine ('people of the excrement lake'). A clan or division of the Thlingchadinne dwelling on La Martre lake and r., Mackenzie Ter., Can.
Tsan-t'iè-ottinè.—Petitot in Bull. Soc. Géog. Paris, chart, 1875. **Tsan-tρié-ρottinè.**—Petitot, Autour du Lac des Esclaves, 363, 1891. **Tson-tρié-ρottinè.**—Ibid., 303. **Western Dog-ribbed Indians.**—Hearne, Jour. to N. Ocean, 262, 1795.

Tsantikihin (*Tsantĭk!ĭhīn*, 'small flounder creek'). A former Tlingit town in the Auk country, Alaska, now known as Juneau. (J. R. S.)

Tsantokayu (*Tsan-tókayu*). One of the two Yonkalla tribes or bands of Oregon.—Gatschet, Atfalati MS., B. A. E., 1877.

Tsantuisha. A Lakmiut band on Lukamiute r., a w. tributary of the Willamette in Oregon.
Tsantuisha ami'm.—Gatschet, Atfalati MS., B. A. E., 1877.

Tsanusdi. See *Ross, John.*

Tsapakah (*Tsa'-pa-kah*, 'red bank'). A Paviotso band formerly in Smith valley, w. Nev.—Powers, Inds. W. Nevada, MS., B. A. E., 1876.

Tsapkhadidlit (*Tsapxádidlit*, 'creek bordered by alders'). A Tlakluit wintering place on Columbia r., Wash. (E. S.)

Tsartlip. A body of Sanetch on the s. E. end of Vancouver id.; pop. 72 in 1910.
Tsartlip.—Can. Ind. Aff. 1904, pt. ii, 69, 1905.

Tsatarghekhetunne ('people among the ash trees'). A band of the Mishikhwutmetunne on Coquille r., Oreg.
Ts'a'-ta-rxĕ-qe'ɋûnnĕ'.—Dorsey in Jour. Am. Folklore, III, 232, 1890.

Tsatauwis. A Siuslaw village on Siuslaw r., Oreg.
Ts'ă'-ɋau-wĭs.—Dorsey in Jour. Am. Folk-lore, III, 230, 1890.

Tsatenyedi ('people of Tsate river'). A Tlingit division in Taku inlet, Alaska, belonging to the Wolf phratry.
tsata-hēni(?).—Krause, Tlinkit Ind., 116, 1885. **Tsat!ēnyĕ'dî.**—Swanton, field notes, B. A. E., 1904.

Tsattine ('dwellers among the beavers'). An Athapascan tribe, belonging to the Sekani group, who roam over the wide prairies s. of Peace r. and E. of the Rocky mts. Mackenzie spoke of them as one of the small tribes of Rocky Mountain Indians living in the Chipewyan country and speaking their language (Mass. Hist. Soc. Coll., 2d s., II, 42, 1814). On his map he locates them between Peace r. and Liard r., and says their name is derived from that of an affluent of the latter. It was, however, Peace r. that they called *Tsades*, 'the river of beavers' (Petitot, La Mer Glaciale, 292, 1887), and was the source of the supply of beaver furs early in the 19th century. Ross (MS., B. A. E.) said in 1858 that they resided in the country along Peace r.

from below Ft Vermilion to the Rocky mts., roaming as far as the upper Hay r. on one side and a little Slave lake on the other. Gibbs (MS., B. A. E.) located them w. of L. Athabasca, on Peace r. Hind (Labrador Penin., II, 261, 1863) said that they resorted to Fts Vermillion and Dunvegan. Petitot (Dict. Dènè Dindjié, xx, 1876) said that they hunted along Peace r. and that they formerly included the Sarsi. Dawson (Rep. Geol. Surv. Can., 1879–80, 51, 1881) gave their territory as along Peace r. N. to Battle r., E. to Simonelle r. to the fork of Smoky r., and w. to the portage of the Mountain of Rocks on Peace r., where they mingled with the Sekani. Morice (Trans. Can. Inst., 113, 1889) placed them in his Eastern Déné division of the Athapascan, following the classification of Ross and Gibbs, and gave their habitat as along Peace r., trading at Hudson's Hope and Ft St John. In 1890 he stated that they inhabited both sides of Peace r. from Hudson's Hope to Ft Dunvegan. They are bolder and braver than their neighbors on the N. and superior in most ways to the Chipewyan, whom they much resemble in features, customs, and moral character. Their dialect is softer than that of the other Tinne tribes, it having been modified by their intercourse with the Cree. Possessing horses and subsisting principally on the products of the chase, they are more nomadic than the other mountain tribes. They are good workers in iron and make neat spurs and crooked knives out of worn-out files. In 1858 Ross found 35 of the tribe at Ft Resolution, on Great Slave lake. In 1889 Morice gave their supposed population for the entire tribe as 800, in 1906 as 700.
Beaver.—Mackenzie, Voy., II, 81, 1802. **Beaver Hunters.**—Smet, Oregon Miss., 164, 1847. **Beavers.**—Morice in Anthropos, I, 272, 1906. **Castors.**—Petitot, Dict. Dènè-Dindjié, xx, 1876. **Copper.**—Keane in Stanford, Compend., 464, 1878 (mistake). **Danè.**—Petitot, Kutchin, MS. vocab., B. A. E., 1869. **Gens de Castor.**—Smet, Missions de l'Oregon, 109, 1844. **Isa-ttiné.**—Ibid. (misprint). **Tsāh'-tyuh.**—Ross, MS. notes on Tinne, B. A. E. **Tsa-ottiné.**—Petitot, MS. vocab., B. A. E., 1865. **Tsaten.**—Morice in Proc. Can. Inst., 112, 1889. **Tsa-'tenne.**—Morice in Anthropos, I, 272, 1906. **Tsa-tinneh.**—Ross quoted by Gibbs, MS., B. A. E. **Tsa-tqenne.**—Morice, letter, B. A. E., 1890. **Tsa-ttiné.**—Petitot, Dict. Dènè-Dindjié, xx, 1876. **Tsa-tinnè.**—Petitot quoted by Hale in Rep. Brit. A. A. S. on N. W. Tribes, 21, 1888. **Tzah-dinneh.**—Balbi, Atlas Ethnog., 821, 1826.

Tsawarii (*Tsa-wa'-ri-i*). The Tewa name of a pueblo that once stood at or near the present hamlet of La Puebla, or Pueblito, a few miles above the town of Santa Cruz, in s. E. Rio Arriba co., N. Mex. According to Tewa informants it was once occupied by some of their people who went to live with the Hopi (see *Hano*). The place seems to be identical with the Tcewadi or Tceewadigi of Hano Tewa tradition as recorded by Fewkes and Stephen. It would seem that the inhabitants of San Cristóbal (q. v.) occupied Tsawarii, or the site after its abandonment, on removing from their own home. (F. W. H.)

Chawári.—Hodge, field notes, B. A. E., 1895 (Nambe information). Tceewádigi.—Stephen in 8th Rep. B. A. E., 35, 1891. Tceewáge.—Ibid. Tcewadi.—Fewkes in 19th Rep. B. A. E., 614, 1900. Tsawárii.—Hodge, op. cit. (Santa Clara information).

Tsawatenok (*Ts'ā'watEēnôx*, or *Dzā'-wadEēnoxᵘ*, 'people of the eulachon country'). A Kwakiutl tribe on Kingcombe inlet, Brit. Col. Their gentes (according to Boas) are Lelewagyila, Gyigyekemae, Wiwokemae, Gyagygyilakya, and Kakawatilikya. In winter they occupy the town of Kwaustums conjointly with the Hahuamis and Guauaenok; in summer they go to Hata and Kwae. Pop. in 1910 (probably including the Guauaenok), 226, all of whom are members of the Anglican church.

Dzā'wadEēnoxᵘ.—Boas in Mem. Am. Mus. Nat. Hist., V, pt. I, 7, 1902. Soi-il-enu.—Kane, Wand. in N. A., app., 1859. Soi it inu.—Schoolcraft, Ind. Tribes, V, 488, 1855. Toah-waw-lay-neuch.—Sproat in Can. Ind. Aff., 145, 1879. Toa-waw-ti-e-neuh.—Can. Ind. Aff. 1896, 435, 1897. Tsah-waw-tay-neuch.—Ibid.,148,1879. Tsah-waw-ti-neuch.—Ibid.,1884,189, 1885. Tsah-waw-ty-neuchs.—Ibid., 1880, 119, 1881. Tsaūat'ēnoq.—Boas in Petermanns Mitteil., pt. 5, 130, 1887. Tsawadainoh.—Tolmie and Dawson, Vocabs. Brit. Col., 118B, 1884. Tsawahtee.—Brit. Col. map, 1872. Tsawalinough.—Ibid. Tsawantiano.—Can. Ind. Aff., pt. 2, 76, 1908. Tsa-wan-ti-e-neuh.—Can. Ind. Aff. 1895, 362, 1896. Tsawantieneuk.—Ibid., 1904, pt. II, 71, 1905. Tsawataineuk.—Ibid., pt. 2, 86, 1910. Tsā'watEēnoq.—Boas in 6th Rep. N. W. Tribes Can., 55, 1890. Ts'ā'watEēnôx.—Boas in Rep. Nat. Mus. 1895, 331, 1897. Tsawat'enoq.—Boas in Bull. Am. Geog. Soc., 228, 1887. Tsawatli.—Tolmie and Dawson, op. cit. (name given by white people). Tsa-waw-ti-e-neuk.—Can. Ind. Aff., 364, 1897. Tsā'-wut-ai-nuk.—Dawson in Trans. Roy. Soc. Can., sec. II, 65, 1887. Tsa-wutti-ē-nuh.—Tolmie and Dawson, op. cit., 119B.

Tsawokot (*Tsa wo'-okot amim*). The Lakmiut name of a Calapooya band formerly residing N. of Eugene City, Oreg.—Gatschet, Lakmiut MS., B. A. E., 1877.

Tsawout. A body of Sanetch near the s. E. end of Vancouver id., Brit. Col.; pop. 103 in 1902, 94 in 1910.

Tsanout.—Can. Ind. Aff., pt. 2, 164, 1901. Tsarout.—Ibid., 1883, 190, 1884. Tsawout.—Ibid., 417, 1898.

Tsayiskithni ('sage-brush hill'). A Navaho clan.

Tsa'yiskígni.—Matthews in Jour. Am. Folk-lore, III, 103, 1890. Tsa'yiskí'dni.—Matthews, Navaho Legends, 30, 1897.

Tschantoga ('people of the woods', from *chan*, 'tree'). A division of the Assiniboin, which Dobbs (Hudson's Bay, 35, map, 1744) placed a considerable distance N. W. of L. Winnipeg, Canada. Smet (Oregon Miss., 150, 1847) said that they did not number more than 50 lodges, divided into several bands, and were seldom seen on the plains, but "travel over the mountains and through the woods, over the different forks and branches of

the sources of the Sascatshawin and Athabaska." Jefferys in 1741 placed them N. W. of L. Winnipeg, and in 1776 in lat. 55°. Their usual habitat at that time was not far from Saskatchewan r. They are probably the same as the Strongwood Assiniboin, who in 1808 were on Battle r. and between it and the s. branch of the Saskatchewan, according to Henry (Coues, Henry-Thompson Jour., II, 522, 1897). They ranged as far s. as Little Missouri r., if identical with the Oseegah of Lewis and Clark (Discov., 43, 1806) and the Waziah that Hayden found in United States territory, though they traded at the Hudson's Bay Co.'s posts on Assiniboin r. Denig said that the Waziah whom he met in Dakota, 60 lodges under chief Le Robe de Vent, came from the N. in 1839. According to Hayden they numbered 120 to 200 persons in 1862. Lewis (Statist. View, 1817) said there were between Little Missouri and Assiniboin rs. 100 lodges, 250 warriors, and a total population of 880. Under the official designation "Stonies" they now occupy a reserve of 69,720 acres, divided by Bow r., in the foothills of the Rocky mts., about 40 m. w. of Calgary, Alberta. They are described as of pleasant visage, active and fleet of foot, and the most energetic of all the tribes of the Canadian N. W. They gain a livelihood by stockraising, by selling timber, furs, and beadwork, and by laboring for ranchmen. A mission was established among them in 1873, and in 1904 the McDougall boarding school at Morley accommodated 48 children. Pop. 667 in 1910. Cf. *Chabin*, or Gens des Montagnes, of Maximilian.

Assiniboels of the North.—Jefferys, Am. Atlas, map. 8, 1776. Assiniboins des Forêts.—Smet, Miss. de l'Oregon, 100, 1848. Assiniboins of the forest.—Smet, Oregon, Miss., 150, 1847. Assiniboins of the North.—Jefferys, French Dom., pt. 1, map, 1741. Assiniboins of the Rocky Mountains.—Keane in Stanford, Compend., 536, 1878. Assiniboins of the Woods,—Dobbs, Hudson's Bay, 35, 1744. Gens de Feuillees.—Lewis and Clark Exped., I, 184, 1817. Gens de Feuilles.—Ibid., I, 146, 1814. Gens des Bois.—Maximilian, Trav., 194, 1843. Gens de Tee.—Lewis, Statistical View (1806), quoted by Coues, Lewis and Clark Exped., I, 193, 1893 (said to be a misprint for Gens des Feuilles). Gens du Nord.—Hayden, Ethnog. and Philol. Mo. Val., 387, 1862. Mountain Assinaboins. — Brown in Beach, Ind. Miscel., 76, 1877. Mountain Stoneys.—Maclean, Can. Savage Folk, 21, 1896. O-see'-gāh.—Lewis quoted by Coues, Lewis and Clark Exped., I, 193, note, 1893. Osegah.—Schermerhorn (1812) in Mass. Hist. Soc. Coll., 2d s., II, 42, 1814. Oseegahs.—Keane in Stanford, Compend., 470, 1878. Stonies.—Can. Ind. Aff. Reps. (official name). Strong Wood Assiniboines. — Henry in Coues, Henry-Thompson Jour., II, 523, 1897. Strongwood Assinniboines.—Hind, Red River Exped., II, 152, 1860. To-kum'-pi.—Hayden, Ethnog. and Philol. Mo. Val., 387, 1862. Tschunguscetoner.—Balbi, Atlas, Ethnog., 55, 1826. Wah-ze-ah we-chas-ta.—Denig in 15th Rep. B. A. E., 223, 1897. Waĥ-zi-ah.—Hayden, Ethnog. and Philol. Mo. Val., 387, 1862. Waziya witcacta.—Dorsey in 15th Rep. B. A. E., 223, 1897. Waziya wicasta.—Ibid. Wood Assiniboines.—Maclean, Can. Savage Folk, 21, 1896. Wood Stoneys.—Ibid.

Tschichgi (refers to a color). A Knaiakhotana clan on Cook inlet, Alaska.—Richardson, Arct. Exped., 407, 1851.

Tschigin. Given by Humboldt (New Spain, II, 344, 1822) as a Yuit Eskimo village between St Lawrence bay and East cape, Siberia. It is in reality a Chukchi settlement.

Tscholban. A tribe mentioned by Langsdorff (Voy., II, 163, 1814) as residing inland from the coast of California and as being at enmity with the coast tribes. Cf. *Cholovone.*

Tse. The Spruce (?) clan of the Tewa pueblo of San Ildefonso, N. Mex.
Tse-tdóa.—Hodge in Am. Anthr., IX, 352, 1896 (*tdóa*='people').

Tse (*Tsĕ*). The Eagle clans of the Tewa pueblos of Santa Clara, Tesuque, San Ildefonso, and Nambe, N. Mex. That of Tesuque is extinct. See *Seping.*
Tsĕ-tdóa.—Hodge in Am. Anthr., IX, 350, 1896 (*tdóa*='people'). Tzedoa.—Bandelier, Delight Makers, 181, 1890. Tze-ojua.—Bandelier in Arch. Inst. Papers, III, 312, 1890.

Tsechah ('down against the rocks'). A Hwotsotenne village on Bulkley r., Brit. Col.
Tsétcah.—Morice in Trans. Roy. Soc. Can., X, 109, 1893.

Tsedtuka ('buffalo bull'). The 6th Tsishu gens of the Osage.
Tse ꭲuꭓa.—Dorsey in 15th Rep. B. A. E., 234, 1897.

Tsedtukaindtse (*Tse ꭲu'ꭓa inꭲse'*, 'buffalo-bull face'). The 2d gens on the left, or Tsishu, side of the Osage tribal circle.—Dorsey in 15th Rep. B. A. E., 233, 1897.

Tsehchic (*Tseh-chic*). The Chehalis name of an ancient village on the s. side of Gray's harbor, Wash.—Gibbs, MS. no. 248, B. A. E.

Tsehlakaiia ('white standing rock'). Mentioned in the genesis myth of the Navaho as a place occupied for 13 years by the progenitors of the Tsezhinkini (Dark Cliff House) clan of that tribe.
Tse'lakaiiá.—Matthews in Jour. Am. Folk-lore, III, 90, 1890.

Tsehump. A band of Sanetch on the S. E. end of Vancouver id., Brit. Col.; pop. 21 in 1910.
Tsehum.—Can. Ind. Aff., pt. 2, 69, 1904. Tsekum.—Ibid., 190, 1883. Tse-kun.—Ibid., 1892, 313, 1893. Tsi-klum.—Ibid., 308, 1879.

Tsekankan. A former Maidu village a few miles S. E. of Nevada City, Nevada co., Cal.—Dixon in Bull. Am. Mus. Nat. Hist., XVII, map, 1905.

Tsekehneaz ('little people on the rocks'). A tribe of the Sekani whose range lies between McLeod lake and the summit of the Rocky mts., Brit. Col.
Tse'-kéh-na.—Morice, letter, B. A. E., 1890. Tsé-kéh-ne-az.—Morice in Trans. Can. Inst., 1893, 28, 1895.

Tseklten (*Tsęxltē'n*). A division of the Squawmish on Howe sd., w. coast of Brit. Col. (F. B.)

Tselkazkwo ('axe-edge river'). A Hwotsotenne village on Bulkley r., Brit. Col.

Tseꭲ-'kaz-Kwoh.—Morice, Notes on W. Dénés, 27, 1895.

Tselone ('people of the end of the rocks'). A Sekani division trading at Bear lake outpost on Finlay r., lat. 57°, Brit. Col. They inhabit a plain that intersects the Rocky mts., believed by the tribes in the s. to be at the end of the range.
Tse'-loh-ne.—Morice, letter, B. A. E., 1890. Tseloné.—Morice in Proc. Can. Inst. 1889, 112, 1890 ('people of the end of the rocks').

Tsenacommacoh. A group of bands or villages of the Powhatan confederacy, comprising all those on James r., Va.—Strachey (1612), Va., 29, 1849.

Tsenahapihlni ('overhanging rocks'). A Navaho clan.
Tse'nahapi'lni.—Matthews, Navaho Legends, 30, 1897. Tse'nahapîlni.—Matthews in Jour. Am. Folk-lore, III, 104, 1890.

Tsenkam (*Ts'ᴇ'nꭓ'am*). A subdivision of the Tsentsenkaio, a gens of the Walas Kwakiutl.—Boas in Rep. Nat. Mus. 1895, 332, 1897.

Tsentsenkaio (*Ts'ᴇ'nts'ᴇnx·qaiō*, 'the Ts'ᴇ'nx·qaiōs'). A gens of the Walas Kwakiutl, subdivided into the Tsenkam and the Haimaaksto.
Ts'ᴇ'ntsᴇnHk'aiō.—Boas in 6th Rep. N. W. Tribes Can., 54, 1890. Ts'ᴇ'nts'ᴇnx-qaiō.—Boas in Rep. Nat. Mus. 1895, 332, 1897. Tsénꭓq'aió.—Boas in Petermanns Mitteil., pt. 5, 131, 1887.

Tseokuimik (*Ts'ē'okuimiX*). A clan of the Somehulitk, a Kwakiutl tribe.
Ts'ē'okuimiX.—Boas in Rep. Nat. Mus. 1895, 328, 1897. Ts'ē'uîtx.—Ibid.

Tseoomkas. The principal village of the Klaskino, on Klaskino inlet, N. w. coast of Vancouver id., Brit. Col.
Tsē-oom'-kas.—Dawson in Trans. Roy. Soc. Can. 1887, sec. II, 65, 1888.

Tseottine ('people of the bark canoes'). A clan or division of the Thlingchadinne living along the s. shore of Great Bear lake, Mackenzie Ter., Canada. The dog is their totem.
Ttsé-ottiné.—Petitot, Dict. Dènè-Dindjié, xx, 1876. Ttsè-pottinè.—Petitot, Autour du Lac des Esclaves, 363, 1891.

Tsera. The name of a village as given to Joutel in 1687 by an Ebahamo Indian and described as being N. or N. w. of Maligne (Colorado) r., Texas. The region designated was at that time occupied by Tonkawan tribes. The village can not be definitely classified. See Gatschet, Karankawa Inds., 46, 1891. (A. C. F.)
Thesera Bocretes.—Barcia, Ensayo, 271, 1723. Tsera.—Joutel (1687) in French, Hist. Coll. La., I, 138, 1846. Tserabocherete.—Joutel (1687) in Margry, Déc., III, 289, 1878 (= Tsera and Bocherete). Teserabocretes.—Joutel (1687) in French, Hist. Coll. La., I, 152, 1846.

Tseshaath (*Ts'ēcā'ath*, 'Seshart proper'). A sept of the Seshart, a Nootka tribe.—Boas in 6th Rep. N. W. Tribes Can., 32, 1890.

Tseskadin ('fallen cottonwood'). An Apache clan or band at San Carlos agency and Ft Apache, Ariz., in 1881 (Bourke in Jour. Am. Folk-lore, III, 111, 1890); corresponding to the Navaho Tsinsakathni.

Diskáděn.—Gatschet, Apache MS., B. A. E., 1883 (trans. 'group of cottonwood trees').

Tsetaame (*Tse-ta′-a-mĕ*). A former village of the Chastacosta on the N. side of Rogue r., E. of its junction with Applegate r., Oreg.—Dorsey in Jour. Am. Folk-lore, III, 234, 1890.

Tsetautkenne ('people against the rocks'). A division of the Sekani, residing about the E. base of the Rocky mts., N. of Peace r., chiefly around Ft St John, Brit. Col.

Cheta-ut-tinné.—Richardson, Arct. Exped., I, 180, 1851. **'Dtcheta-ta-ut-tunne.**—Ibid. **Tse-ta-hwo-tqenne.**—Morice, letter, B. A. E., 1890. **Tsé′-ta-ut′qenne.**—Morice in Trans. Can. Inst. 1893, 29, 1895.

Tsetheshkizhni ('rocky pass'). A Navaho clan.

Tse′ɼeckíjni.—Matthews in Jour. Am. Folk-lore, III, 104, 1890. **Tse′dĕskï′zni.**—Matthews, Navaho Legends, 31, 1897.

Tsethkhani ('among the rocks'). A Navaho clan.

Tse′ɋqáni.—Matthews in Jour. Am. Folk-lore, III, 104, 1890. **Tse′tháni.**—Matthews, Navaho Legends, 30, 1897.

Tsetintunne (*Ts′e-tĭn′ ɼûn′ne*). The highest of 4 former villages of the Tututni on a stream emptying into Rogue r. near its mouth, in Oregon.—Dorsey in Jour. Am. Folk-lore, III, 236, 1890.

Tsetlani (*Tse′tláni*, 'bend in a canyon'). A Navaho clan.—Matthews, Navaho Legends, 29, 1897.

Tsetsaa (*Tsē′tsaa*). A gens of the Koskimo, a Kwakiutl tribe.—Boas in Rep. U. S. Nat. Mus. 1895, 329, 1897.

Tsetsabus (a Twana name said to signify 'ancient capital'). A place near Port Townsend, Wash., where nearly all the Puget Sound Indians were said to have occasionally met. (A. S. G.)

Tsetsaut (*Ts′Ets′ā′ut*, 'people of the interior': Niska name). An Athapascan band long settled among the Niska on Portland canal, Alaska, reduced in 1895 to 12 individuals. They are a branch of the western Nahane, speaking a dialect similar to the Tahltan. This territory extended from Chunah r. to Observatory inlet and northward to the watershed of Iskoot r. About 1830 they numbered 500, but were practically exterminated by continued attacks of their kinsmen, the Lakweip, and of the Tlingit. They once lived on Behm channel, and were friendly with the Sanya until these determined to kill them and enslave their women and children, whereupon they migrated to Portland channel and, when reduced in numbers, fell under the control of the Niska. See Boas in 10th Rep. N. W. Tribes Can., 34, 1895, and in Jour. Am. Folk-lore, IX, no. 4, 1896; X, no. 1, 1897.

Tsetsetloalakemae (*TsētsēLoă′laqEmaē*, 'the famous ones'). A gens of the Nimkish, a Kwakiutl tribe.—Boas in Rep. U. S. Nat. Mus. 1895, 331, 1897.

Tsetthim (*Ts′e-t′çĭm*). A Kuitsh village

on lower Umpqua r., Oreg.—Dorsey in Jour. Am. Folk-lore, III, 231, 1890.

Tsetutkhlalenitun (*Tse-tût′-qla-le-ni′-tûn*). A former village of the Chastacosta on the N. side of Rogue r., Oreg. —Dorsey in Jour. Am. Folk-lore, III, 234, 1890.

Tsetuttunne (*Ts′etût′ ɼûnnĕ*, 'people where the road is on the beach'). A former village of the Tututni on the coast of Oregon, s. of Rogue r.—Dorsey in Jour. Am. Folk-lore, III, 236, 1890.

Tsewenalding. A former Hupa village on the E. side of Trinity r., near the middle of Hupa valley, N. Cal. Its inhabitants were driven from their homes in 1864 by the warriors of Takimilding village, who obtained the aid of the military then stationed at Ft Gaston. (P. E. G.)

Cernalton.—Ind. Aff. Rep. 1871, 682, 1872. **Olle-pot′l.**—Gibbs, MS., B. A. E., 1852 (Yurok name). **Sermalton.**—Ind. Aff., Rep. 246, 1877. **Tsewenal-diñ.**—Goddard, Life and Culture of the Hupa, 12, 1903. **We-la-poth.**—McKee (1851) in Sen. Ex. Doc. 4, 32d Cong., spec. sess., 194, 1853. **Wi-la-pusch.**—Meyer, Nach dem Sacramento, 282, 1855.

Tsewhitzen. A Clallam village formerly on Port Angeles Spit, 2 or 3 m. w. of Yinnis, Wash. In 1887 Eells stated that about 35 Indians lived here.

Tse-hwit-zen.—Eells, letter, B. A. E., May 21, 1886. **Tse-whit-zen.**—Gibbs in Pac. R. R. Rep., I, 429, 1855.

Tseyanathoni ('horizontal water under cliffs'). A Navaho clan, now extinct.

Tse′yanaɋò′ni.—Matthews in Jour. Am. Folk-lore, III, 104, 1890. **Tse′yanató′ni.**—Matthews, Navaho Legends, 30, 1897.

Tseyikehe ('rocks standing near one another'). A Navaho clan.

Tse′yikèhe.—Matthews in Jour. Am. Folk-lore, III, 104, 1890. **Tse′yikèheɋine.**—Ibid. **Tse′yikéhedïne′.**—Matthews, Navaho Legends, 30, 1897.

Tsezhinkini ('house of the black cliffs'). A Navaho clan.

Tse′dzĭnkï′ni.—Matthews, Navaho Legends, 29, 1897. **Tse′jinkíni.**—Matthews in Jour. Am. Folk-lore, III, 103, 1890.

Tsezhinthiai ('trap dyke'). A Navaho clan.

Tse′jinɋiài.—Matthews in Jour. Am. Folk-lore, III, 103, 1890. **Tse′jinɋiàɋine.**—Ibid. **Tse′zĭn-diaí.**—Matthews, Navaho Legends, 30, 1897.

Tshirege (Tewa: 'bird'). A large prehistoric pueblo of the Tewa, built of pumice and volcanic tufa, situated on the N. edge of the great Mesa del Pajarito, about 6 m. w. of the Rio Grande and 7 m. s. of San Ildefonso pueblo, N. N. Mex. From this ruin the Pajarito ('Little Bird') park receives its name. See Hewett in Bull. 32, B. A. E., 1907.

Pajaro Pinto.—Bandelier in Arch. Inst. Papers, IV, 79, 1892. **Pueblo of the Bird.**—Bandelier, Delight Makers, 378, 1890. **Tchrega.**—Hewett in Am. Anthr., VI, 645, 1904. **Tshirege.**—Hewett in Bull. 32, B. A. E., 23, 1906. **Tzi-re-ge.**—Bandelier in Arch. Inst. Papers, op. cit., 16.

Tsiakhaus (*Tsi′-a-qaus′*). A Kuitsh village on lower Umpqua r., Oreg.—Dorsey in Jour. Am. Folk-lore, III. 231, 1890.

Tsiama. A prehistoric pueblo of the Acoma tribe, which, according to tradition, was inhabited during their migration from the mystic Shipapu in the indefinite N. The ruins are situated at the mouth of Cañada de la Cruz, at or near the present Laguna village of Tsiama, N. Mex.   (F. W. H.)

Tsiama (Keresan: *Tsi'-a-ma*, 'place of the Sia people'). Formerly a summer village of the Laguna tribe of New Mexico, now a permanently inhabited pueblo of that people, situated 10 m. w. of Laguna pueblo. So called because, it is said, some Sia people once lived there. See *Keresan Family, Laguna.* (F. W. H.)
Seama.—Segura in Ind. Aff. Rep., 173, 1890. **Tsía-ma.**—Hodge, field notes, B. A. E., 1895. **Zi-am-ma.**—Pradt quoted by Hodge in Am. Anthr., IV, 346, 1891.

Tsiekhaweyathl (*Tsi-ĕ'-qă we-yaçl'*, 'dry land where there are small stones'). A Siuslaw village on Siuslaw r., Oreg.—Dorsey in Jour. Am. Folk-lore, III, 230, 1890.

Tsihlinainde ('mountain-standing-across people'). A division of the Mescalero Apache who claim as their former home the region of the San Andrés mts., N. Mex., hence their name. (J. M.)
Chilpaines.—Orozco y Berra, Geog., 59, 1864 (probably identical). **Tsĭ'l-īná-inde.**—Mooney, field notes, B. A. E., 1897.

Tsilacomap. A former village, probably Salinan, connected with San Antonio mission, Monterey co., Cal.—Taylor in Cal. Farmer, Apr. 27, 1860.

Tsilaluhi (*Tsilalú'hĭ*, 'sweet-gum place'). A former Cherokee settlement on a small branch of Brasstown cr. of Hiwassee r., just within the line of Towns co., Ga.—Mooney in 19th Rep. B. A. E., 537, 1900.

Tsilkotin ('people of young-man's river'). An Athapascan tribe of British Columbia, occupying a territory lying chiefly in the valley of Chilcotin r. at about lat. 52°. Their nearest relatives are the Takulli, or Carriers, whose territory is adjacent on the N., and who are the only Athapascan people with whom they come in contact. Toward the w. a pass leads through the Coast range to Bellacoola, and intercourse with the tribe of that name, which was formerly frequent (see *Nakuntlun*), is still kept up to some extent. In early days there was also some communication with the Kwakiutl of Knights inlet on the s. w. On the E. the Tsilkotin are separated from the Shuswap by Fraser r., and do not hold very intimate relations with that people. In earlier times the two tribes were constantly at war, the Tsilkotin invading their country and penetrating as far as Similkameen valley, whose inhabitants are descended from the invaders, who compelled the Salish to make peace and permit intermarriage. Even to-day there is a decided undercurrent of suspicion between the Tsilkotin and the Shuswap. Toward the s. their nearest neighbors are the Lillooet, but contact between the two tribes is slight.

In former times, and down to within about 40 years, the center of territory and population of the Tsilkotin was Anahem lake; and from here they covered a considerable extent of country, the principal points of gathering being Tatlah, Puntze, and Chizŭikut lakes. They ranged as far s. as Chilco lake, and at the time of salmon fishing were accustomed to move in large numbers down to Chilcotin r., to a point near the present Anahem res., always returning to their homes as soon as the season was past. More recently they have been brought to the eastward, and to-day the chief centers of the tribe are three reservations in the valley of the Chilcotin—Anahem, Stone, Risky Creek—and the Carrier res. at Alexandria, on Fraser r., where a few Tsilkotin families reside (see *Stella*). Besides these there are a number of families leading a seminomadic life in the old tribal territory, in the woods and mountains to the westward. These latter Indians, considerably less influenced by civilization than their reservation relatives, are known by the whites as "Stone Chilcotin," or "Stonies." Although subjected to intercourse with the whites for a comparatively short period, the Tsilkotin have assimilated the customs and ideas of their civilized neighbors to such an extent that their own have largely disappeared, except among the families still living in the mountains. The sedentary Tsilkotin, who have abandoned semisubterranean huts and live like their white neighbors in log houses covered with mud, now cultivate cereals, peas, and potatoes, and are reported to be moral, temperate, and religious. These Morice divides into the Tleskotin, Tlathenkotin, and Toosey. Their population was estimated at 450 in 1906. For their mythology, see Farrand in Mem. Am. Mus. Nat. Hist., Anthr. III, no. 1, 1900. (L. F.)
Chilcotin.—Cox, Columbia R., II, 368, 1831. **Chileatin.**—Taylor in Cal. Farmer, July 19, 1862. **Chilhχotin.**—Morice in Proc Can Inst. 1889, 110, 1890. **Chilicootens.**—Macfie. Vancouver Id., 428, 1865. **Chilicootens.**—Whymper, Alaska, 48, 1869. **Chilicotin.**—Fleming in Can. Pac. R. R. Rep., 121, 1877. **Chiιkho'tenne.**—Morice in Trans. Roy. Soc. Can., X, map, 1892. **Chi-ι-χohten.**—Morice, letter, B. A. E., 1890 (Takulli name). **Chilko-tin.**—Latham in Trans. Philol. Soc. Lond., 66, 1856. **Chillcoatens.**—Wilkes, U. S. Expl. Exped., IV, 450, 1845. **Chiltokin.**—McDonald, Brit. Col., 126, 1862. **Tchilkoten.**—Smet, Oregon Miss., 100, 1847. **Tshilkotin.**—Tolmie and Dawson, Vocabs. Brit. Col., 122B, 1884. **Tsiιkoh'tin.**—Morice in Trans. Can. Inst. 1893, IV, 22, 1895. **Tsilkótin.**—Hale, Ethnog. and Philol., 202, 1846. **T'silkotinneh.**—Dall in Proc. A. A. A. S., XXXIV, 1886.

Tsillane (*Tsill-ane*). An unidentified Okinagan tribe.—Ross, Advent., 290, 1847.

Tsiltaden ('mountain side'). A clan or band of the Chiricahua Apache, associated with and hence taken to be a part of the Pinaleños; correlated with the Tziltadin clan of the Pinal Coyoteros, the Tziseketzillan of the White Mountain Apache, and the Tsayiskithni of the Navaho. They are now under San Carlos agency, Ariz.

Chileons.—Ind. Aff. Rep., 82, 1871. Chilian.—Boudinot, Star in the West, 126, 1816. Chilion.—Ind. Aff. Rep., 246, 1877. Chillons.—Gatschet, Zwölf Sprachen, 65, 1876. Chilon.—Ind. Aff. Rep. 1902, 594, 1903. Oil-tar-den.—White, Hist. Apaches, MS., B. A. E., 1875. Hahel-topa-ipa.—Ibid. (Yavapai name). Hútashi. — Gatschet, Comanche MS. vocab., B. A. E. (Comanche name). Siltáden.—Gatschet, Yuma-Spr., I, 371, 1883 (trans. 'dwell without on the mountains'). Tsilhtáden.—Gatschet, MS., B. A. E., 1883. Tsiltáden.—Ibid. (trans. 'live on the mountain'). Tsiltarden.—Gatschet, Zwölf Sprachen, 65, 1876 (includes Coyoteros). Zill-tar'-dens.—White, Apache Names of Ind. Tribes, MS., B. A. E. (trans. 'live outside in the mountains'). Zill-tar-dins. — White, Hist. Apaches, MS., B. A. E., 1875 (=Coyoteros).

Tsimshian ('people of Skeena r.'). The most important of the three main divisions of the Chimmesyan linguistic family, and that which gives it its name. In the strictest sense it designates the following closely related tribes or divisions living between Nass and Skeena rs., N. Brit. Col.: Kilutsai, Kinagingeeg, Kinuhtoiah, Kishpachlaots, Kitlani, Kitsalthlal, Kitunto, Kitwilgioks, Kitwilksheba, and Kitzeesh. To these are sometimes added the Kitzilas and Kitzimgaylum, who live farther up Skeena r., near the canyon, but speak the same dialect. The appellation has also been extended to cover all other tribes speaking this dialect, viz, the Kitkahta, Kitkatla, and Kittizoo, who live on the islands southward. The divisional names given are also names of the ancient towns. To these may be added the following modern towns: New Kitzilas, Metlakatla (New and Old), Port Essington, and Port Simpson. Pop. in 1908 (including 465 enumerated in Duncan's colony, Alaska, in 1900), 1,840.

The name for this division has been so often extended to include other branches of it that some of the synonyms may have a similar extension. (J. R. S.)

Chimpsain.—Halleck in Ind. Aff. Rep. 1869, 563, 1870. Chimseyans.—Kingsley, Stand. Nat. Hist., VI, 136, 1883. Chymshean Nation.—W. A. Howard, Notes on Northern Tribes, MS., B. A. E., 1860. Elqī'miE.—Boas in 5th Rep. N. W. Tribes Can., 9, 1889 (Bellacoola name). Fort Simpson Indians.—Scott (1859) in H. R. Ex. Doc. 65, 36th Cong., 1st sess., 115, 1860 (portion in that town). Isimpshean.—Can. Ind. Aff., 7, 8, 1872 (misprint). Kilat.—Swanton, field notes, 1900–01 (Masset Haida name). Kilgat.—Ibid. (Skidegate Haida name). Kil-kat.—Gibbs in Cont. N. A. Ethnol., I, 136, 1877 (Haida name). Kwē'tEla.—Boas, op. cit. (Heiltsuk name). Milbauks-chim-zi-ans.—Crosbie in H. R. Ex. Doc. 77, 36th Cong., 1st sess., 7, 1860 (Tsimshian on Milbank sd.). Nishmumta.—Tolmie and Dawson, Vocabs. Brit. Col., 115B, 1884. Shimshyans.—Pinart, Notes sur les Koloches, 2, 1873. Shineshean.—Phelps quoted by Bancroft, Hist. Wash., 135, 1890. Simpsian.—Mahoney in Ind. Aff. Rep. 1869, 576, 1870. Simpsians.—Mahoney (1869) in Sen. Ex. Doc. 68, 41st Cong., 2d sess., 21, 1870. Simseans.—Taylor in Cal. Farmer, July 25, 1862. Skeena Indians.—Collective name of many authors for the Tsimshian; also extended to the Kitksan. Ts'ɛmɐ̂ia'n.—Boas in Zeitschr. für Ethnol., 231, 1888. Tsimchian.—Ibid. T'simpheeans.—Can. Ind. Aff., 122, 1880. Tsimpsean.— Wright, Among the Alaskans, 1882. T'simpshean.—Can. Ind. Aff., 125, 1879. T'simpsheean.—Ibid., 123, 1879. Tsimpsians.—Ibid., 193, 1906. Tsimsean.—Swan in Morris Treas. Rep., 144, 1879, Tsimseyans.—Gibbs in Cont. N. A. Ethnol., I, 268, 1877. Tsimsheeans.—Mayne, Brit. Col., 287, 1862, Tsimshian.—Boas in 5th Rep. N. W. Tribes Can., 8, 1889. T'sim-si-an'.—Gibbs in Cont. N. A. Ethnol., I, 143, 1877. Ts'ōtsQE'n.—Boas in 5th Rep. N. W. Tribes Can., 9, 1889 (Tlingit name). Tuhakwilh.—Tolmie and Dawson, op. cit., 122B, 1884 (Bellacoola name). Zimshian-Indianer.—Von Schulenberg, Sprache der Zimshian Ind., 1894.

Tsina. The Turkey clans of the Keresan pueblos of Laguna, Acoma, Santa Ana, Sia, San Felipe, and Cochiti, N. Mex. Members of the Tsina clan of Laguna claim that their ancestors came originally from Acoma. The Turkey clan of Cochiti is extinct. (F. W. H.)

Tsï-háno.—Hodge in Am. Anthr., IX, 352, 1896 (Sia form; háno='people'). Tsína-háno.—Ibid. (San Felipe form). Tsï'na-hánoᶜʰ.—Ibid. (Laguna form). Tsína-hánoqᶜʰ. — Ibid. (Acoma form). Tsínha-háno.—Ibid. (Santa Ana form). Tsï'n-háno.—Ibid. (Cochti form; should be hánuch). Tzina hanutsh.—Bandelier, Delight Makers, 255, 1890 (Cochiti form).

Tsinazhini ('black horizontal forest'). A Navaho clan.

Tsinadzï'ni.—Matthews, Navaho Legends, 30, 1897. Tsinajini.—Matthews in Jour. Am. Folk-lore, III, 103, 1890. Tzinachini.—Bourke, Snake Dance, 279, 1884 (trans. 'wooded mountain gens').

Tsiniksistsoyiks (*Tsin-ik-sis'-tso-yiks*, 'early finished eating'). A band of the Piegan tribe of the Siksika, as well as of the Siksika proper.

Early Finished Eating.—Grinnell, Blackfoot Lodge Tales, 225, 1892. Tsin-ik-sis-tso-yiks.—Ibid., 209.

Tsinsakathni ('lone tree'). A Navaho clan.

Tsinsaká∅ni.—Matthews in Jour. Am. Folk-lore, III, 103, 1890. Tsïnsaká∂ni.—Matthews, Navaho Legends, 30, 1897.

Tsinthobetlo (*Tsinçòbetlo*, 'tree sweeping the water,' referring probably to a birch). Mentioned in the Navaho genesis myth as one of the stopping places of that tribe on the Rio San Juan, N. W. N. Mex., where the then existing clans were joined by the Tsinazhini clan.—Matthews in Jour. Am. Folk-lore, III, 92, 1890.

Tsiomhau (*Ts'iomxau*). A Wikeno village on Rivers inlet, Brit. Col.—Boas in Petermanns Mitteil., pt. 5, 130, 1887.

Tsipiakwe (Zuñi: 'straight-down-hair people.' — Cushing). An unidentified tribe whose habitat, according to Cushing, is said by the Zuñi to have been on the headwaters of Salt r. in E. Arizona or W. New Mexico, while the Hopi asserted to Fewkes that they lived midway between Zuñi and the Hopi country of N. E. Arizona. They are known to history solely through the attempt of Fray Martin de Arvide, in Feb. 1632, to visit them from Zuñi in company with 2 soldiers, 5 Zuñi, and a mestizo. The missionary and the soldiers were murdered by their companions five days out from Zuñi. According also to Cushing the Zuñi say that the tribe was exterminated by the

Apache soon after the attempted visit of the friar. (F. W. H.)

Cipias.—Barcia, Ensayo, 199, 1723. **Tcipiya.**—Fewkes in 22d Rep. B. A. E., 23, 1904 (Hopi name). **Tsípiakwe.**—Cushing in 13th Rep. B. A. E., 328, 1896 (*kwe* = 'people'). **Tzip-ia Kue.**—Bandelier in Arch. Inst. Papers, IV, 381, 1892. **Zipias.**—Vetancurt (1696), Menologia, 53, 1871. **Zippia-Kue.**—Bandelier in Jour. Am. Eth. and Arch., III, 97, 1892.

Tsishusindtsakdhe ('Tsishu wearing a tail of hair on the head'). The first gens on the Tsishu, or left, side of the Osage tribal circle.

Lock-wearer.—Dorsey in Am. Nat., XVIII, 115, 1884. **Sníꜩsaƞǧĕ.**—Dorsey, Osage MS. vocab., B. A. E., 1883. **Tsiou Sínꜩsaƞǧĕ.**—Dorsey in 15th Rep. B. A. E., 233, 1897. **Tsiou Wanŭⁿ′.**—Ibid. (= 'elder Tshishu,' another name).

Tsishuutsepedhungpa. One of the three divisions of the Osage.

Chee′-zhoo.—Dorsey in Am. Nat., XVIII, 113, 1884 (pronunciation). **Tsi′ou uꜩse peǧúⁿda.**—Dorsey in 15th Rep. B. A. E., 233, 1897.

Tsishuwashtake ('Tsishu peacemakers'). The leading gens on the left, or Tsishu, side of the Osage tribal circle.

Chee-zhoo peace-makers.—Dorsey in Am. Nat., XVIII, 113, 1884. **Ni′waǧĕ.**—Dorsey in 15th Rep. B. A. E., 233, 1897 ('giver of life'). **Red eagle.**—Dorsey in Am. Nat., XVIII, 113, 1884. **Taⁿ′waⁿ ꜧa′xe.**—Dorsey in 15th Rep. B. A. E., 233, 1897 ('village maker'). **Tsi′ou Waota′ꜧe.**—Ibid.

Tsiskwahi (*Tsiskwā′hĭ*, 'bird place,' from *Anǐ′-Tsi′skwa*, 'Bird people,' a Cherokee clan). One of the 5 districts or "towns" which William H. Thomas, in his capacity of agent for the Eastern Cherokee, laid off on the East Cherokee res., in Swain co., N. C., after the removal of the rest of the tribe to Indian Ter. in 1838. The name is still retained. (J. M.)

Bird town.—Mooney in 19th Rep. B. A. E., 161, 509, 1900 (common name). **Tsiskwâ′hǐ.**—Ibid. (Cherokee name).

Tsisli. A village of the Tatshiautin at the mouth of Tatlah r., Brit. Col., connected with Tsisthainli.—Can. Ind. Aff., 213, 1902.

Tsistetsiyi (*Tsistetsi′yǐ*, 'mouse place'). A former Cherokee settlement on South Mouse cr., a branch of Hiwassee r., in Bradley co., Tenn. The present town of Cleveland, on the same creek, is known to the Cherokee by the same name.—Mooney in 19th Rep. B. A. E., 537, 1900.

Tsisthainli. A Tatshiautin village on Lac Trembleur, Brit. Col.; pop. 13 in 1902, 22 in 1910.

Tsistiks (*Tsĭ-stĭks′*, 'little birds'). A society of the Ikunuhkahtsi, or All Comrades, in the Piegan tribe of the Siksika. It includes boys from 15 to 20 years of age.—Grinnell, Blackfoot Lodge Tales, 221, 1892.

Tsistuyi (*Tsistu′yǐ*, 'rabbit place'). A former Cherokee settlement on the N. bank of Hiwassee r., at the entrance of Chestua cr., in Polk co., Tenn. In the Proceedings of the Board of Commissioners dealing with the Indian Trade in South Carolina (87, 92–93, MS. in the State Archives at Columbia) a Yuchi town called Chestowee, or Chestoowa, is said to have been cut off by the Cherokee in 1714 either in revenge for the murder of a Cherokee or at the instigation of some English traders.

Cheestooyee.—McKenney and Hall, Ind. Tribes, II, 80, 1858. **Chestoowa.**—MS., op. cit., 1714. **Chestowa.**—Ibid. **Chestuee.**—Doc. of 1799 quoted by Royce in 5th Rep. B. A. E., 144, 1887. **Tsistu′yǐ.**—Mooney in 19th Rep. B. A. E., 538, 1900.

Tsitoklinotin. A part of the Hankutchin living near the mouth of Forty-mile cr., on Yukon r., Brit. Col.

Tcu-Kutchi.—Richardson, Arctic Exped., I, 397, 1851 ('people of the water'). **Tshu-*Kutshi*.**—Latham in Trans. Philol. Soc. Lond., 67, 1856. **Tsit-o-klin-otin.**—Dawson in Rep. Geol. Surv. Can. 1888, 202B, 1889.

Tsits. The Water clans of the Keresan pueblos of Laguna, Acoma, Sia, San Felipe, and Cochiti, N. Mex. The Water clan of Laguna, which claims to have come originally from Acoma, forms a phratry with the Kurtsi (Antelope) clan. The corresponding clan of Acoma also forms a phratry with the Antelope clan of that village. The Cochiti Water clan was almost extinct in 1895. (F. W. H.)

Síts-hano^ch.—Hodge in Am. Anthr., IX, 352, 1896 (Laguna form). **Tsits-háno.**—Ibid. (San Felipe form; *háno* = 'people'). **Tsï′ts-hano.**—Ibid. (Sia form). **Tsíts-hanoq^ch.**—Hodge, field notes, B. A. E., 1895. **Tsíts-hánuch.**—Ibid. (Cochiti form). **Tzitz hanutch.**—Bandelier, Delight Makers, 28, 1890 (Cochiti form).

Tsitsakwich. A modern Clallam village on Dungeness Spit, Wash., 2 or 3 m. w. of the old town of Stehtlum. This probably contains the 100 people said by Eells to have lived about Jamestown in 1886.

Tsi-tsa-kwĭtc.—Eells, letter, B. A. E., May 21, 1886.

Tsitsi. A former village of the Ntshaautin of British Columbia.—Morice in Trans. Can. Inst., IV, 25, 1895.

Tsitsimelekala (*Tsītsĭmē′lEqala*, 'the TsîmēˈlEqalas'). A gens of the Nakoaktok, a Kwakiutl tribe.—Boas in Rep. Nat. Mus. 1895, 329, 1897.

Tsitualaqumae (*Tsitualaqúmāe*). The name of an ancestor of a Tlauitsis gens; also sometimes given to the gens itself.—Boas in Petermanns Mitteil., pt. 5, 130, 1887.

Tsiyahi (*Tsiyā′hǐ*, 'otter place'). The name of several Cherokee settlements: (1) a former village on a branch of Keowee r., near the present Cheohee, Oconee co., S. C.; (2) a still existing settlement of the Eastern Cherokee on Cheowa r., about Robbinsville, Graham co., N. C.; (3) a former settlement in Cades cove, on Cove cr., Blount co., Tenn. (J. M.)

Cheeowhee.—Mooney in 19th Rep. B. A. E., 538, 1900. **Cheowa.**—Ibid. **Chewe.**—Bartram, Travels, 371, 1792. **Chewohe.**—Mooney, op. cit.

Tskoakkane (*Tsxoaxqā′nē*). A Bellacoola village on Bellacoola r., Brit. Col., above Nukaakmats.

TsQoaQk·ā′nē.—Boas in 7th Rep. N. W. Tribes Can., 3, 1891. **Tsxoaxqā′nē.**—Boas in Mem. Am. Mus. Nat. Hist., II, 49, 1898.

Tsofkara. A Karok village of 9 houses in 1852; situated on the E. bank of Klamath r., N. w. Cal., nearly half way between Orleans Bar and Salmon r.
Soof-curra.—Taylor in Cal. Farmer, Mar. 23, 1860. T'sof-ka'-ra.—Gibbs, MS. Misc., B. A. E., 1852. Tuck-a-soof-curra.—Taylor in Cal. Farmer, Mar. 23, 1860. Witsogo.—A. L. Kroeber, inf'n, 1903 (Yurok name probably of Tsofkara).

Tsomootl (*Tsomō'ol*). A Bellacoola village on Bellacoola r., Brit. Col., above Senktl.—Boas in Mem. Am. Mus. Nat. Hist., II, 49, 1898.

Tsomosath (*Tsō'mōs'ath*). A sept of the Opitchesaht, a Nootka tribe.
Somass.—Mayne, Brit. Col., 167, 1862. Tsomass.—Ibid., 251. Tsō'mōs'ath.—Boas in 6th Rep. N. W. Tribes Can., 32, 1890.

Tsonai (*Tsō'nai*). A Seechelt sept which formerly lived at Deserted bay, the junction of Queens reach and Princess Royal reach, Jervis inlet, Brit. Col. The founder is said to have come from Ft Rupert.—Hill-Tout in Jour. Anthr. Inst., 21, 1904.

Tsooquahna. A Nitinat village on the s. w. coast of Vancouver id., about 1 m. w. of the outlet of Nitinat lagoon; pop. 20 in 1902.
Tsuquanah.—Can. Ind. Aff., suppl., 81, 1902.

Tsoowahlie. A Chilliwack town on Sagwalie res., near Fraser r., Brit. Col.; pop. 49 in 1910.
Soowahlie.—Can. Ind. Aff., pt. II, 75, 1904. Sowhylie.—Ibid., 78, 1878. Sūwä'lē.—Hill-Tout in Rep. N. W. Tribes Can., 4, 1902. To-y-lee.—Can. Ind. Aff., 317, 1880. To-ylee.—Ibid., 188, 1884. Tsoowahlie.—Ibid., pt. II, 160, 1901. Ts'uwä'lē.—Boas in Rep. 64th Meeting Brit. A. A. S., 454, 1894.

Tsotaee (*Tso-tä'-ee*, 'stick-cutter,' i. e. 'beaver'). A clan of the Hurons or Wyandot.—Morgan, Anc. Soc., 153, 1878.

Tsotsena (*Ts'ō'ts'ēna*, 'thunder-birds'). A gens of the Awaitlala, a Kwakiutl tribe.—Boas in Rep. Nat. Mus. 1895, 331, 1897.

Tsudinuntiyi (*Tsu'dinûñti'yĭ*, 'throwing-down place'). A former Cherokee settlement on lower Nantahala r., in Macon co., N. C.—Mooney in 19th Rep. B. A. E., 538, 1900.

Tsuka. A former Maidu village in the neighborhood of Forbestown, Butte co., Cal.—Dixon in Bull. Am. Mus. Nat. Hist., XVII, pt. III, map, 1905.

Tsulalgi ('fox people'). A clan of the Creeks.
Chŭ'-lä.—Morgan, Anc. Soc., 161, 1877. Djúlạlgi.—Speck, Creek Inds., 115, 1907. Tsúlalgi.—Gatschet, Creek Migr. Leg., I, 155, 1884.

Tsulamsewi (prob. 'red river'). The Maidu name of Chico cr., Butte Co., Cal., and, according to Curtin, applied also to the Maidu living at its head. (R. B. D.)
Palanshan.—Bancroft, Nat. Races, I, 450, 1882. Palanshawl.—Ibid. Tsulam Sewi.—Curtin, MS. vocab., B. A. E., 1885.

Tsulus ('open' or 'open flat'). A village of the Nicola band of Ntlakyapamuk near Nicola r., about 40 m. above Spences Bridge, Brit. Col.
Cūlū'c.—Hill-Tout in Rep. Ethnol. Surv. Can., 4, 1899. Sulu's.—Teit in Mem. Am. Mus. Nat. Hist.,

II, 174, 1900. Tshoo-loos'.—Dawson in Trans. Roy. Soc. Can., sec. II, 44, 1891. Tsulu's.—Teit, op. cit.

Tsunakthiamittha (*Tsûn'-na-kçi'-ă-mĭt'-çă*). A Kuitsh village on lower Umpqua r., Oreg.—Dorsey in Jour. Am. Folk-lore, III, 231, 1890.

Tsurau. The southernmost Yurok village of N. w. California, on the coast at Trinidad.
Chori.—Gibbs (1851) in Schoolcraft, Ind. Tribes, III, 133, 1853. Tschura.—Meyer, Nach dem Sacramento, 236, 1855. Tschura-Allequas.—Ibid. Tsurau.—A. L. Kroeber, inf'n, 1907. Zoreisch.—Loeffelholtz (1857) quoted by Brinton in Science, 105, Feb. 23, 1894.

Tsutsiola (*Tsoo-tsī-ola*). A Quatsino village on the E. side of the mouth of Forward inlet, w. coast of Vancouver id.—Dawson in Can. Geol. Surv., map, 1887.

Tsuwaraits. A Paiute band formerly in Meadow valley, S. E. Nev.; pop. 155 in 1873.
Tsauwárits.—Gatschet in Wheeler Surv. Rep., VII, 410, 1879. Tsou-wa'-ra-its.—Powell in Ind. Aff. Rep. 1873, 50, 1874.

Tsuzel (*TsuzEl*, 'palisaded inclosure containing houses'). A Ntlakyapamuk village on Fraser r., Brit. Col., above Lytton.—Hill-Tout in Rep. Ethnol. Surv. Can., 4, 1899.

Tthilkitik (*Tçĭl-ki'-tĭk*). A Yaquina village on the N. side of Yaquina r., Oreg.—Dorsey in Jour. Am. Folk-lore, III, 229, 1890.

Tthinatlitunne (*Tçi'nat-li' ṛúnnĕ'*, 'people at the forks'). A band of the Mishikhwutmetunne formerly residing on Coquille r., Oreg., at the site of Coquille.—Dorsey in Jour. Am. Folk-lore, III, 232, 1890.

Tthowache (*Tço-wa'-tcĕ*). A Takelma band or village on the s. side of Rogue r., Oreg., near "Deep Rock."—Dorsey in Jour. Am. Folk-lore, III, 235, 1890.

Tu. Given by a native as the name of the House clan of the pueblo at Taos, N. Mex.
Tu-taĭina.—Hodge, field notes, B. A. E., 1899 (*taĭina* = 'people').

Tuakay ('salt springs'). An Apache clan at San Carlos agency and Ft Apache, Ariz., in 1881 (Bourke in Jour. Am. Folk-lore, III, 111, 1890); correlated with the Thodhokongzhi of the Navaho.

Tuakdjuak. An Okomiut Eskimo summer settlement of the Saumingmiut subtribe on Cumberland penin., Baffinland.
Touaqdjuaq.—Boas in 6th Rep. B. A. E., map, 1888.

Tuancas. A former tribe of N. E. Mexico or S. Texas, probably Coahuiltecan, who were gathered into San Bernardo mission after 1732.—Orozco y Berra, Geog., 303, 1864.

Tuapait. An Eskimo village in s. w. Greenland, lat. 60° 7'.—Meddelelser om Grönland, XVI, map, 1896.

Tuarpukdjuak. A winter village of the Nugumiut Eskimo in Countess of Warwick sd., Baffin land.
Tuarpukdjuaq.—Boas in 6th Rep. B. A. E., 422, 1888. Twerpukjua.—Hall, Arct. Researches, 268, 1865.

Tubac. A former Spanish presidio and mission, established in 1752 among the Papago, on the w. bank of Rio Santa Cruz, s. of Tucson, Ariz. The population in 1754–57 was 411, including the garrison of 50; by 1762 the natives had moved to Tumacacori, and in 1776 the presidio was moved to Tucson; after this transfer, but prior to 1784, a company of Pima allies was stationed at Tubac, and in 1824 a garrison was again established there. In 1842–43 it was occupied by friendly Apache. It was again a garrison in 1851, consisting of a collection of dilapidated buildings and huts, about half of which were tenantless, and also a church partly in ruins; its population was then about 100. In 1858–60, besides a mixed population of Mexicans and Americans, Tubac contained a temporary camp of 100 Papago. (F. W. H.)

San Ignacio.—Bancroft, Ariz. and N. Mex., 383, 1889. S. Ignacio de Tubac.—Ibid., 371. Tubác.—Garcés (1775), Diary, 63, 1900. Tubaca.—Rudo Ensayo (ca. 1762), 193, 1863. Tubáe.—Hardy, Travels, 421, 1829 (misprint).

Tubare (*Tu-ba'-re*). A Piman tribe of s. w. Chihuahua, Mexico, which formerly inhabited the territory drained by the extreme headwaters of the Rio Fuerte from San Andrés, 3 m. from Morelos, to Baborigame, but their rancherias are now scattered only between San Andrés and the village of Tubares, most of them living at San Miguel. They are chiefly of mixed Mexican blood, only about two dozen pure bloods remaining, and of these only 5 or 6 speak their native tongue. They are said to have been formerly very warlike, fighting the Tarahumare, whom they resembled in their general customs, as the remnant now do in physical appearance (Lumholtz, Unknown Mexico, I, 441–444, 1902). They are described as having been industrious. Articles of clothing of their own manufacture formed their chief objects of barter. The unoccupied cave houses on the headwaters of the Fuerte are attributed to them. They spoke a dialect closely related to the Guazapare and Varohio, although their intercourse with others was carried on in Nahuatl. Their villages are or were Concepción, San Andrés, San Ignacio, San Miguel, and possibly Loreto. Bandelier (Arch. Inst. Papers, III, 53, 1890) says they also included the Tintis.

Tovares.—Orozco y Berra, Geog., 324, 1864. Tubar.—Ibid., 58. Tubare.—Lumholtz in Scribner's Mag., XVI, 33, 1894. Tubaris.—Rivera, Diario, leg. 1514, 1736. Tuvalím.—Lumholtz, Unknown Mex., I, 443, 1902 (own name).

Tubasa. A Papago rancheria in 1770, probably on the Rio Santa Cruz, between San Xavier del Bac and the Rio Gila, s. Ariz.—Arricivita, Crónica Seráfica, II, 416, 1792.

Tubatulabal ('pine-nut eaters.'—Merriam). A small tribe which formerly inhabited the valley of Kern r., s. Cal., above the falls, extending probably to the river's source, but centering especially about the junction of the main and s. forks. With the Bankalachi (q. v.) they constitute one of the four principal coordinate branches of the Shoshonean family. See Kroeber in Univ. Cal. Pub., Am. Arch. and Eth., IV, 122, 1907.

Bakhkanapül.—Kroeber in Univ. Cal. Pub., Am. Arch. and Eth., IV, 124, 1907 (own name; said to mean or refer to all those who speak their language). Kern River.—Henley in Ind. Aff. Rep., 511, 1854. Ku-chi-bich-i-wa-nap' Pal-up'.—Powers in Cont. N. A. Ethnol., III, 393, 1877 (trans. 'little stream'). Pa-kan'-e-pul.—Merriam in Science, XIX, 916, June 15, 1904. Pallegawonáp.—Gatschet in Geog. Surv. W. 100th Merid., 411, 1879. Pal-li-ga-wo-nap'.—Powers in Cont. N. A. Ethnol., III, 393, 1877. P'hallatillie.—Gatschet, op. cit. (perhaps identical). Pitanisha.—Kroeber in Univ. Cal. Pub., Am. Arch. and Eth., IV, 124, 1907 (the usual Yokuts name, from *Pitani-u*, the place-name of the forks of Kern r.). Pi-tan'-ni-suh.—Powers, op. cit. Po-la-ga-mis.—Wessells (1853) in H. R. Ex. Doc. 76, 34th Cong., 3d sess., 32, 1857 (s. E. of L. Tulare, and doubtfully identified with above; they may be the Yokuts Paleuyami). Polokawynahs.—Maltby quoted by Bancroft, Nat. Races, I, 456, 1874. Te-bot-e-lob'-e-lay.—Merriam, op. cit. Tillie.—Gatschet, op. cit. (probably identical). Ti-pa-to-la'-pa.—Powers, op. cit. Tomo'la.—Powers, op. cit. (given as a distinct tribe at Kern r. falls, but there was no other there). Tübatulabal.—Kroeber in Univ. Cal. Pub., Am. Arch. and Eth., IV, 122, 1907. Wah-lik-nas'-se.—Merriam, op. cit. (Yokuts equivalent of tribal name; sig. 'pine-nut eaters'; Wateknasi.—Kroeber in Univ. Cal. Pub., Am. Arch. and Eth., IV, 124, 1907 (said to mean 'pine-nut eaters,' sometimes so called by Yokuts).

Tubes. Objects of problematic use obtained from burial places and inhabited sites over a large part of the country. They range in length from less than 1 in. to 14 in. or more, and the cross-section is in general circular or elliptical, though some have a side ground flat. The outline is approximately cylindrical, conical, or like an elongated hourglass. The last frequently has a narrow ridge around the smallest part, which is not always midway between the ends. In cylindrical specimens the bore is usually of uniform diameter the entire length, but sometimes there is an offset or a sudden tapering near one end, giving a much smaller opening. Some of the longer specimens have two wing-like projections opposite each other at this end; others are beveled, like a blunt wedge. In conical tubes the bore increases nearly uniformly from the smaller end. In the hourglass form it tapers more rapidly than the exterior from each end and to the constriction, being sometimes very small at this point. Various materials were used in their manufacture, includ-

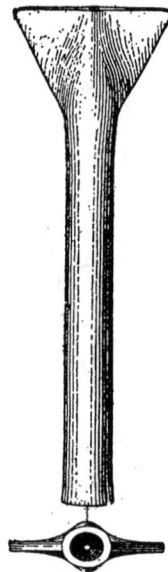
TUBE OF BANDED SLATE; OHIO

ing sandstone in many sections, slate in the Northern Central states and on the N. W. coast, and chlorite and steatite farther s. and in California. From West Virginia, and to a less extent from the adjoining states, some large cylinders are made of soft mottled stone resembling steatite. Tubes of pottery are found in many sections, while those of horn, bone, wood, and joints of reed were observed by early explorers in all parts of the country. The hourglass form seems to belong to the southward of the Ohio r. The smaller tubes were probably used as beads, and it is possible that some were used as tobacco pipes, the tubular tobacco pipe of the Pacific Coast states presenting nearly identical conformation. See *Pipes, Smoking*.　　　　　　　　　　　(G. F.)

Tubianwapu (*Tu-bi'-an-wa-pu*). A Paviotso tribe formerly about Virginia City, Nev.—Powell, Paviotso MS., B. A. E., 1881.

Tubish. The extinct Sorrow-making clan of the Hopi.
Tubic wiñwû.—Fewkes in 19th Rep. B. A. E., 583, 1901 (*wiñwû*=' clan'). Tü-bic wuñ-wü.—Fewkes in Am. Anthr., VII, 402, 1894.

Tubisuste. A village, presumably Costanoan, formerly connected with Dolores mission, San Francisco, Cal.—Taylor in Cal. Farmer, Oct. 18, 1861.

Tubo. A former rancheria, probably of the Sobaipuri, visited by Kino about 1697; situated apparently on Arivaipa cr., a tributary of San Pedro r., E. of old Camp Grant, s. Ariz. Bernal (Bancroft, Ariz. and N. Mex., 356, 1889) in 1697 stated that the settlement was on a creek flowing E.

Tubuktulik. A large Kaviagmiut Eskimo village formerly on the N. shore of Norton sd., Alaska.
Tubukhtuligmut.—Zagoskin, Descr. Russ. Poss. Am., pt. I, 73, 1847. Tubuktuligmiut.—Tikhmenief (1861) quoted by Baker, Geog. Dict. Alaska, 1902.

Tuburch. A Maricopa rancheria on the Rio Gila, Ariz., in 1744.
Tuburch.—Sedelmair (1744) cited by Bancroft, Ariz. and N. Mex., 366, 1889. Tuburh.—Ibid.

Tubuscabors. A former Pima rancheria on or near the Rio Gila, s. Ariz., visited by Anza and Font in 1775.—Bancroft, Ariz. and N. Mex., 392, 1889.

Tubutama. A Papago village and a former mission on the E. bank of the N. branch of the Rio Altar, in N. w. Sonora, Mexico. The mission was founded evidently in 1689, Fr. Antonio Arras being its first missionary. At the beginning of 1691 it contained 500 neophytes. It was subsequently destroyed by the natives and reestablished in 1720. In 1730 it contained 131 inhabitants, and there were connected with it 9 minor villages; but the mission was again laid waste during the Pima insurrection of 1751. The four Franciscans, including Fray Francisco Garcés, who were murdered by the natives at the mission of Concepción, near Yuma, Ariz.,

July 17, 1781, were buried in a single coffin in the Tubutama church. Tubutama is now a civilized pueblo and contained 300 inhabitants in 1900.　　　(F. W. H.)
San Pablo Tubutama.—Rivera (1730) quoted by Bancroft, No. Mex. States, I, 514, 1884 (doubtless intended for San Pedro). San Pedro Tubutama.—Kino (*ca.* 1694) in Doc. Hist. Mex., 4th s., I, 244, 1856. Tbutama.—Venegas, Hist. Cal., II, 179, 1759 (misprint). Tibutama.—Ibid., I, 303. Tubutama.—Kino map (1702) in Stöcklein, Neue Welt-Bott., 74, 1726. Tuhutama.—Venegas, op. cit., II, 176.

Tubutavia. A Maricopa rancheria on the Rio Gila, Ariz., in 1744.—Sedelmair (1744) cited by Bancroft, Ariz. and N. Mex., 366, 1889.

Tuca. A village, presumably Costanoan, formerly connected with Dolores mission, San Francisco, Cal.—Taylor in Cal. Farmer, Oct. 18, 1861.

Tucara. A tribe, apparently Tonkawan, represented in 1722 among the Indians destined for San Xavier de Náxera mission, whose establishment at San Antonio, Texas, was projected in that year (Valero Baptisms, 1722, partida 121, MS.). Later some of the tribe were at San Antonio de Valero mission (ibid., 1728, partida 211).　　　(H. E. B.)
Tiucara.—Valero Burials, 1722, partida 121, MS. Tucane.—Valero Baptisms, 1728, partida 211, MS.

Tucavi. A Maricopa rancheria in the 18th century; possibly identical with Tucsani.
Rancheria de la Pasion de Tucavi.—Garcés (1776), Diary, 436, 1900.

Tuchi. A Calusa village on the s. w. coast of Florida, about 1570.—Fontaneda Memoir (*ca.* 1575), Smith trans., 19, 1854.

Tuchiamas. A pueblo of New Mexico, probably of the Tigua, in 1598.
Tuchiamas.—Oñate (1598) in Doc. Inéd., XVI, 115, 1871. Tuchimas.—Columbus Mem. Vol., 155, 1893 (misprint).

Tuckagulga. A former Seminole town on the E. bank of Ochlocknee r., near L. Imonia, Leon co., Fla.—H. R. Ex. Doc, 74 (1823), 19th Cong., 1st sess., 27, 1826.

Tuckahaw. One of the former 7 Chickasaw villages of N. Mississippi.—Romans, Fla., 63, 1775.

Tuckahoe. Any one of several vegetable substances used for food by the Indians of the Middle and some of the S. Atlantic states, particularly the goldenclub, or floating arum (*Orontium aquaticum*), and the Virginia wake-robin (*Arum virginicum*); also *Pachyma*, *Lycoperdon*, or other fungi eaten by the Indians, known variously as Virginia truffle, Indian bread, Indian loaf, etc. (Gore in Smithson. Rep. 1881, 687–701, 1883). The word is variously spelled by the early writers. Capt. John Smith (in Purchas) has *tockawhoughe;* Strachey (Hist. of Trav. into Va., 1618) has in his vocabulary "bread made of a root called *taccaho*, appoans," and elsewhere (p. 121) *tockowhough;* Beverley (Hist. Va., bk. III, 153, 1707) has *tuckahoe*. Other early forms are *tockahow, tockwogh, tockwock,* and *tockaawgh*. The Virginian *tocka-whonghe*, as the cognate Delaware *p'tuck-queu* and the Cree *pittikwow* indicate, signifies 'it is globular,' and was a general term applied to bulbous roots used by the Indians of this region for food purposes. According to Bartlett (Dict. Americanisms, 722, 1877), "the term *tuckahoe* is often applied to an inhabitant of Lower Virginia, and to the poor land in that portion of the state." In some parts of the South *tuckahoe* means 'poor white.'   (A. F. C.)

Tuckaseegee (*Tsiksi′tsĭ*, or, in dialectic form, *Tŭksi′tsĭ*, of unknown meaning). The name of two former Cherokee settlements: (1) about the junction of the two forks of Tuckasegee r., above Webster, Jackson co., N. C. (not to be confounded with Tikwalitsi, q. v.); (2) on a branch of Brasstown cr. of Hiwassee r., in Towns co., Ga.   (J. M.)
Tsĭksi′tsĭ.—Mooney in 19th Rep. B. A. E., 537, 1900 (correct Cherokee form). Tuckasegee.—Doc. of 1755 quoted by Royce in 5th Rep. B. A. E., 143, 1887. Tŭksi′tsĭ.—Mooney, op. cit. (dialectic form).

Tuckernuck. A word used in some parts of s. E. Massachusetts in the sense of picnic: from the name of an island off Nantucket, probably from *petukwinak*, 'round island' (Gerard). The name seems to have been given the island in reference to its shape.

Tucsani. A rancheria, probably of the Maricopa, on the Rio Gila, Ariz., visited by Kino and Mange in 1699. Not to be confounded with Tucson or Tusonimo. See *Upasoitac*.
S. Limon Tucsani.—Kino (1699) as quoted by Bancroft, No. Mex. States, I, 268, 1884. S. Simeon de Tucsani.—Kino, map (1702) in Stöcklein, Neue Welt-Bott, 74, 1726. S. Simon Tucsani.—Mange (1699) quoted by Bancroft, Ariz. and N. Mex., 357, 1889. S. Simon Tuesani.—Kino, map (1701) in Bancroft, ibid., 360. Tucsares.—Sedelmair (1744), ibid., 366.

Tucsasic. A former Maricopa rancheria, on Gila r., s. Ariz.—Rudo Ensayo (*ca.* 1763), 22, 1863.

Tucson (Papago: *Tu-uk-so-on′*, 'black base,' in allusion to a dark volcanic stratum in an adjacent mountain). A former rancheria, probably of mixed Papago, Sobaipuri, and Pima, on the site of the present city of the same name in Arizona. Much misunderstanding has arisen respecting the establishment of the settlement, which, as an Indian town, was doubtless prehistoric. It was first mentioned by the Jesuit Father Kino, in 1699, under the name San Agustin, a name transferred to the Spanish presidio (Presidio de San Agustin del Tuquison) established there in 1776 on its removal from Tubac; and, to distinguish the near-by Indian village, the latter was called San Agustin del Pueblito de Tucson. The native population in 1760–67 was 331, and 200 families were settled there in 1772; but two years later, when visited by Anza, it contained only 80 families of so-called

"Pimas." Tucson remained a military outpost of Mexico until 1853, when it was taken possession of by the United States as a part of the Gadsden purchase. In 1848 its population was 760, increased in December of that year by refugees from Tubac and Tumacacori on account of Apache troubles. Tucson was the capital of Arizona from 1867 to 1877. See Bancroft, Ariz. and N. Mex., 1889; Bartlett, Pers. Narr., II, 1854; Coues, Garcés Diary, 1900; McGee in Coville and Macdougal, Des. Bot. Lab., 1903.   (F. W. H.)
Fruson.—Cooke in Emory, Recon., 554, 1848 (misprint). Fucson.—ten Kate in Bull. Soc. d'Anthr. de Paris, 374, 1883 (misprint). Lucson.—Johnston in Emory, Recon., 591, 1848 (misprint). S. Agustin del Pueblito de Tucson.—Writer in Dos Repúblicas, Sept. 16, 1877, quoted by Bancroft, Ariz. and N. Mex., 379, 1889 (the rancheria). S. Agustin de Tuson.—Yuma Sentinel, Apr. 13, 1878, quoted by Bancroft, ibid. (presidio name in 1777). San José de Tucson.—Reyes (1772), ibid., 381 (the rancheria). Sa-*sits-go-lon-a*.—White, Apache Names of Indian Tribes, MS., B. A. E. ('many chimneys': Apache name). Stjoekson.—ten Kate, Reizen in N. A., 159, 1885 (native name). Styucson.—Bandelier in Rev. d'Ethnog., 203, 1886 (native name). Teusón.—Hughes, Doniphan's Exped., 247, 1848. Toison.—Hardy, Travels, 421, 1829 (trans.: 'golden fleece'). Tubso.—Folsom, Mexico, map, 1842. Tubson.—Pike, Exped., 3d map, 1810. Tucsson.—Rudo Ensayo (*ca.* 1763), 103, 1863. Tuczon.—Pope, Explor., map, 1854. Tueson.—Cooke in Emory, Recon., 555, 1848. Tugson.—Anza (1775) quoted by Bancroft, Ariz. and N. Mex., 382, 1889. Tuguison.—Ibid. Tuison.—Anza (1780) quoted, ibid., 392. Tuozon.—Marcy, Prairie Trav., map, 1861. Tuquison.—Anza (1780) quoted by Bancroft, Ariz. and N. Mex., 392, 1889. Tuqulson.—Font, map (1777), ibid., 393. Tuuksoon.—McGee in Coville and Macdougal, Des. Bot. Lab., 15, 1903 (aboriginal name).

Tucubavia. A former Pima rancheria on the headwaters of Rio Altar, N. Sonora, Mexico, visited by Father Kino in 1694 and 1700. It afterward formed one of the visitas of the mission of Guevavi.
Tacubavia.—Bancroft, No. Mex. States, I, 258, 1884. Tucubavi.—Rudo Ensayo (*ca.* 1763), 193, 1863. Tucubavia.—Kino (1694) in Doc. Hist. Mex., 4th s., I, 252, 1856. Tucuvavi.—Rudo Ensayo, op. cit., 161.

Tucumu. A Chumashan village formerly situated at Arroyo Hondo, near Santa Barbara, Cal.
Tucremu.—Taylor in Cal. Farmer, Apr. 17, 1863. Tucumu.—Cabrillo (1542) in Smith, Colec. Doc. Fla., 181, 1857. Túh'-mu.—Henshaw, Buenaventura MS. vocab., B. A. E., 1884.

Tucururu. A former Timucuan dialect, and probable subtribe, on the Atlantic coast of Florida or Georgia, apparently on Cumberland id., within the territory claimed by Saturiba (q. v.).—Gatschet (quoting Pareja, *ca.* 1612), Timucua Lang., in Proc. Am. Philos. Soc., XVIII, 479, 1880.

Tudisishn ('black water'). An Apache band or clan at San Carlos agency and Ft Apache, Ariz., in 1881.—Bourke in Jour. Am. Folk-lore, III, 111, 1890.

Tueadasso (*Tiio′eädă″so*, 'tails [of rushes or other plants] floating there.'—Hewitt). A former Onondaga village near the present Jamesville, Onondaga co., N. Y.
Cachiadachse.—Weiser (1743) in Min. Prov. Council Pa., IV, 660, 1851. Cajadachse.—Weiser

quoted by Beauchamp in Bull. N. Y. State Mus. no. 108, 154, 1907. **Tiachton.**—Beauchamp, ibid. **Tiatáchtont.**—Spangenberg (1745) in Pa. Mag., III, 61, 1879. **Tiojachso.**—Beauchamp, op cit. **Tu-e-a-das'-so.**—Morgan, League Iroquois, II, 87, 1904.

Tuerto. A former pueblo of the Tano, near the present Golden City, Santa Fé co., N. Mex., which, according to Bandelier (Arch. Inst. Papers, IV, 124, 1892), was probably abandoned in 1591 on account of a raid by other Indians. Zárate-Salmerón, about 1629 (Bancroft, Native Races, I, 600, 1882), states that it was one of the two pueblos of the Pecos tribe. Possibly identical with the Puerto (q. v.) of Oñate.
El Tuerto.—Bandelier in Arch. Inst. Papers, IV, 108, 1892. **Kaapô.**—Bandelier, Gilded Man, 221, 1893. **Ka-po.**—Bandelier in Arch. Inst. Papers, IV, 108, 1892 (Tano name). **Tuerto.**—Bandelier in Ritch, N. Mex., 201, 1885.

Tuesapit. A Maricopa rancheria on the Rio Gila, Ariz., in 1744.—Sedelmair (1744) cited by Bancroft, Ariz. and N. Mex., 366, 1889.

Tuetinini ('no-water people'). A division of the Mescalero Apache who claim the region about Marathon, Texas, as their former home.
Tuĕ'tĭnĭ'ni.—Mooney, field-notes, B. A. E., 1897. **Twĕ'tĭnĭ'nde.**—Ibid.

Tugaloo (*Dugilu'yĭ*, abbreviated as *Dugilu'*, and seeming to refer to a place at the forks of a stream). A former Cherokee settlement on the river of the same name, at the junction of Toccoa cr., in Habersham co., Ga. The name is sometimes written Toogelah and Toogoola. (J. M.)
Dugilu'yĭ.—Mooney in 19th Rep. B. A. E., 516, 1900 (proper Cherokee name). **Toogelah.**—Mooney, ibid. (a form sometimes used). **Toogoola.**—Ibid. (a form sometimes used). **Tugilo.**—Bartram, Travels, 372, 1792.

Tugulan. Given by Humboldt (New Spain, II, 344, 1822) as a Yuit Eskimo village in N. E. Siberia, but more likely a Chukchi settlement.

Tuhaushuwitthe (*Tu'-hau-cu-wi'-t'çe*). A Yaquina village on the s. side of Yaquina r., Oreg.—Dorsey in Jour. Am. Folk-lore, III, 229, 1890.

Tuhezep (*Tûxezē'p*, shortened form of *xûzē'ĕp*, 'sharp ground or place for pitching lodges,' so called from small sharp stones around there.—Teit). A Ntlakyapamuk village on the E. side of Fraser r., about a mile above Lytton, Brit. Col.
Tayosap.—Can. Ind. Aff., 79, 1878. **Tûxezē'p.**—Teit in Mem. Am. Mus. Nat. Hist., II, 172, 1900.

Tuhitspiyet (*Tu-hi'ts-pi-yet*, from *tu*, 'village', 'camp', 'band', and *hits-pi-yu*, 'a point': 'village on a point or peninsula'). A band of the Skidi Pawnee.—Grinnell, Pawnee Hero Stories, 239, 1889.

Tuhkpahhukstaht (*Tuhk-pah-huks-taht*, 'pumpkin-vine village'). A band of the Skidi Pawnee, so named, it is said, from the fact that once, after planting time, this band went off on the summer hunt, and while they were away the pumpkin vines grew so luxuriantly that they climbed

over their lodges, covering and hiding them.—Grinnell, Pawnee Hero Stories, 237, 1889.

Tuhukmache. A Yokuts (Mariposan) tribe that probably resided on Kings r., but perhaps on the Kaweah. They were one of a group of tribes of central California that joined in ceding their lands to the United States by treaty of May 13, 1851. (A. L. K.)
To-ke-ma-che.—Wessells (1853) in H. R. Ex. Doc. 76, 34th Cong., 3d sess., 31, 1857. **Tu-huc-mach.**—Royce in 18th Rep. B A. E., 782, 1899. **Tu-hue-ma-ches.**—Barbour in Sen. Ex. Doc. 4, 32d Cong., spec. sess., 254, 1853. **Tu-huk-nahs.**—Johnston in Sen. Ex. Doc. 61, 32d Cong., 1st sess., 22, 1852.

Tui (*Tu'i*). The Yurok name of a Karok village on the w. side of Klamath r., N. W. Cal., between Orleans Bar and Redcap cr. (A. L. K.)

Tuiban. A tribe mentioned by Langsdorff (Voy., II, 163, 1814) as inhabiting the coast of California. It seemingly belonged to the Costanoan family.

Tuim. The Wolf clan of the Tigua Pueblo of Isleta, N. Mex.
Túim-t'aínïn.—Lummis quoted by Hodge in Am. Anthr., IX, 352, 1896 (*t'aínïn* = 'people').

Tuiskistiks (*Tŭis-kĭs'-tĭks*, 'mosquitos'). A society of the Ikunuhkahtsi, or All Comrades, in the Piegan tribe of the Siksika. It is composed of men who were constantly going to war.—Grinnell, Blackfoot Lodge Tales, 221, 1892.

Tuiunuk ('marsh people'). The Kaniagmiut Eskimo name for a division of the Knaiakhotana of Cook inlet, Alaska.—Hoffman, Kadiak MS., B. A. E., 1882.

Tujanisuissilac. A Chumashan village formerly near Santa Inés mission, Santa Barbara co., Cal.—Taylor in Cal. Farmer, Oct. 18, 1861.

Tukabatchi. A former Upper Creek town on the w. bank of Tallapoosa r., opposite Talasse, in Elmore co., Ala. A trader's trail crossed the river at this point. In later times the place became a tribal center, though it suffered much in the wars with the Chickasaw. It was here that Tecumseh (q. v.) met the Upper Creeks when he tried to incite them to war against the United States. The people of the town had several traditions in regard to their origin, one of which claimed that they came from the N. It is probable they were in part Shawnee. They had in possession certain metal plates which they had preserved from time immemorial. Adair (Hist. Ind., 178, 1775) says that in his time they consisted of 5 copper and 2 brass plates which were produced only at the busk (q. v.). In 1799 the place could muster 116 warriors, and in 1832 it contained 386 houses. See Gatschet, Creek Migr. Leg., I, 147–8, 1884.
Adgebaches.—Coxe, Carolana, 23, 1741 (perhaps identical). **Is-po-co-gee.**—Hawkins (1799), Sketch, 27, 1848 (ancient name). **Ispokógi.**—Gatschet, Creek Migr. Leg., I, 148, 1884 (= 'town of

survivors': ancient name). **Itálua fátcha-sígo.**— Ibid. (= 'town deviating from strictness': ancient name). **Itálua ispokógi.**—Ibid. (='town of survivors': ancient name). **Tauchebatchee.**— Schermerhorn (1812) in Mass. Hist. Soc. Coll., 2d s., II, 18, 1814. **Teickibatiks.** — McGillivray (1877) in Am. State Papers, Ind. Aff., I, 18, 1832. **Tocabatché.**—Anville, map N. Am., 1746. **Togobatche.** — Lattré, map U. S., 1784. **Tokaubatchee.**—U. S. Ind. Treaties, 324, 1837. **Tookabatcha.**—Woodward, Reminis., 31, 1859. **Tookabatchee.**—Brown, West. Gaz., 11, 1817. **Took-au-batche.**—Hawkins (1799), Sketch, 27, 52, 1848. **Tookaubatchians.**—Jackson (1813) in Drake, Bk. Inds., bk. 4, 51, 1848. **Topacas.**—Barcia, Ensayo (1693), 313, 1723. **Toukaubatchee.**—U. S. Ind. Treat. (1814), 162, 1837. **Tuccabatche.**—Bartram, Travels, 461, 1791. **Tuchabatchees.**—U. S. Ind. Treat. (1797), 70, 1837. **Tuckaabatchees.**—Drake, Bk. Inds., bk. 4, 48, 1848. **Tuckabatcha.**—Ind. Aff. Rep., 149, 1858. **Tuckabatche.**—Bartram, Trav., 445, 1791. **Tuckabatches.**—Knox (1791) in Am. State Papers, Ind. Aff., I, 127, 1832. **Tuckabatchie.**—Knox, ibid., 260. **Tuckabatchy.**—Woodward, op. cit. **Tuckabathees.**—U. S. Ind. Treat. (1797), 68, 1837. **Tuckafaches.**—Ker, Travels, 300, 1816. **Tuckapaus.**—Ibid. (probably identical). **Tuckaubatchees.** — Finnelson (1792) in Am. State Papers, op. cit., 289. **Tuckhabatchees.**—McKenney, Mem. and Trav., I, 164, 1846. **Tugibáχtchi.**—Gatschet, Creek Migr. Leg., I, 147, 1884 (ancient form). **Tukabaches.**—Drake, Ind. Chron., 201, 1836. **Tukabatchey.**—Adair, Am. Inds., 178, 179, 1775. **Tukabatchies.**—Drake, Bk. Inds., bk. 4, 57, 1848. **Tukawbatchie.**—Gallatin in Trans. Am. Antiq. Soc., II, 95, 1836. **Tukipá'htchi.**— Gatschet, op. cit. (ancient form). **Tukipáχtchi.**— Ibid. **Tukkebatche.**—Adair, Am. Inds., 257, 1775.

Tukabatchi. A town of the Creek Nation, on the N. side of Wewoka cr., Okla. The people formerly lived between Eufaula and Hillabi towns, Ala.—Gatschet, Creek Migr. Leg., II, 186, 1888. **Tukabáχtchi.**—Ibid.

Tukachkach. A Chumashan village formerly at El Esterito, near San Buenaventura, Ventura co., Cal. **Tu'-katc-katc.**—Henshaw, Buenaventura MS. vocab., B. A. E., 1884.

Tukhenikashika (*Tuqe'-nikaci'qa*, 'reddish-yellow-buffalo people'). A Quapaw gens.—Dorsey in 15th Rep. B. A. E., 229, 1897.

Tukhtukagi (*Tuχtu-kági*, 'corn-cribs set up'). A former Creek village, subordinate to Oakfuskee, on the w. bank of Tallapoosa r., 20 m. above Niuyaka, probably in Randolph co., Ala. **Corn House.**—Schoolcraft, Ind. Tribes, IV, 578, 1854. **Thu-le-oc-who-cat-lau.**—Hawkins (1779), Sketch, 46, 1848 (probably identical). **Tooh-to-cau-gee.**— Ibid. ('corn house standing'). **Totacaga.**—Swan (1791) in Schoolcraft, op. cit., V, 262, 1855. **Toutacaugee.**—Treaty of 1814 in U. S. Ind. Treat., 162, 1837. **Tuχtu kági.**—Gatschet, Creek Migr. Leg., I, 148, 1884.

Tukinobi. A former pueblo of the Hopi, traces of the ruins of which are discernible on a large hill on the summit of East Mesa, Tusayan, N. E. Arizona.— Fewkes in 17th Rep. B. A. E., 589, 1898.

Tukkuthkutchin ('squint-eyed people'). A Kutchin tribe at the head of Porcupine r., occupying the territory between the headwaters of the Porcupine r. and Ft McPherson, in the northern Yukon Ter., Canada. Their eyes are frequently small and oblique, hence their name. Although barbarous they are more intelligent than other tribes. They are a commercial people, living by barter.

Though good hunters, rarely lacking food, they do not hunt furs, but exchange their beads, which form the circulating medium, for the peltry of the neighboring tribes. They are fond of oratorical display, and in their harangues the voice of the speaker gradually rises, becoming a screech at the climax. They subsist at all seasons almost exclusively on caribou, which they hunt on the mountains. Formerly they were numerous, but by 1866 they had become reduced to 15 hunters or 40 men. Dawson (Rep. Geol. Surv. Can. 1888, 206B, 1889) gave the number of inhabitants of Peel r. and La Pierres House, the Tatlitkutchin and Tukkuthkutchin together, as 337, consisting of 185 males and 152 females. Morice estimated their number at 150 in 1906.

Dakaz.—Morice in Anthropos, I, 261, 1906. **Dakkadhæ.**—Petitot, Autour du lac des Esclaves, 361, 1891. **Dakkadhè.**—Petitot, Dict. Dènè-Dindjie, xx, 1876 ('squinters'). **Deagothee Loochoo.**— Schoolcraft, Ind. Tribes, II, 28, 1852. **Deegothee.**— Gallatin in Trans. Am. Antiq. Soc., II, 19, 1836. **Degathee Dinees.**—Keane in Stanford, Compend., 511, 1878. **Degothees.**—Schoolcraft, Ind. Tribes, III, 542, 1853. **Degothi-Kutchin.**—Bancroft, Nat. Races, I, 146, 1874. **Degutbee Dinees.**—Mackenzie, Voy., 49, 1802. **Deguthee Dennee.**—Franklin, Sec. Exped., 40, 1828 ('the people who avoid the arrows of their enemies by keeping a lookout on both sides'). **Deguthee Dine.**—Mackenzie, Voy., II, 213, 1802. **Deguthee Dinees.**—Mackenzie, Voy., 51, 1801. **Digothi.**—Latham, Nat. Races Russ. Emp., 292, 1854. **Digothi-Kutchin.**—Simpson, Nar. of Discov., 103, 1843. **Gens-de-ralt.**—Colyer in Ind. Aff. Rep. 1869, 593, 1870. **Gens de rats.**—Whymper, Alaska, 255, 1869. **Klô-ven-Kouttchin.**—Petitot, Autour, 361, 1891 (gens du bord des Prairies). **Klovén-Kuttchin.**—Petitot, Dict. Dènè-Dindjié, xx, 1876 ('people at the end of the prairie'). **Kukuthkutchin.**—Bancroft, Nat. Races, I, 147, 1874 (misprint). **Lapiene's House Indians.**—Kirkby in Hind, Labrador Penin., II, 254, 1863. **Louches.**—Petitot, Autour du lac des Esclaves, 361, 1891. **Louchioux Proper.**—Ross, notes on Tinne, S. I. MS. 474. **Nattsæ-Kouttchin.**—Petitot, Autour du lac des Esclaves, 361, 1891 (marmot people). **Njïth.**—Ibid. ('between others'). **Porcupine.**—Colyer in Ind. Aff. Rep. 1869, 593, 1870. **Porcupine River Indians.**— Whymper, Alaska, 255, 1869. **Quarrelers.**—Mackenzie, Voy., 51, 1801. **Quarrellers.**—Franklin, Nar. Journ. Polar Sea, 261, 1824. **Querelleurs.**— Balbi, Atlas Ethnog., 821, 1826. **Rat Indians.**— Hardesty in Smithson. Rep. 1866, 311, 1872. **Rat River Indians.**—Whymper, Alaska, 255, 1869. **Squinters.**—Latham in Trans. Philol. Soc. Lond., 67, 1856. **Squint-Eyes.**—Franklin, Nar. Journ. Polar Sea, 261, 1824. **Takadhé.**—Petitot, MS. vocab., 1865, S. I. 6613. **Takaz.**—Morice in Anthropos, I, 261, 1906 (Dakaz, or). **Ta'-kŭ'rth.**—Ross, notes on Tinne, S. I. MS. 474 ('twisted'). **Ta-kuth Kutchin.**—Gibbs, MS. notes from Ross, B.A.E. ('wry-necked people'). **Tä-Küth-Kutchin.**—Hind, Labrador Penin., II, 254, 1863. **Tdha-kkè-Kuttchin.**— Petitot, Dict. Dènè-Dindjié, xx, 1876 ('mountain race'). **Tdha-Kouttchin.**—Petitot, Autour du lac des Esclaves, 361, 1891 ('mountain people'). **Tdhakuttchin.**—Petitot in Bull. Soc. Géog. Paris, chart, 1875. **Thyoothe.**—Latham in Trans. Philol. Soc. Lond., 67, 1856. **Tuk-kuth.**—Hardisty in Smithson. Rep. 1866, 311, 1872. **Tukúkth-Kutchin.**—Dall, Alaska, 430, 1870. **Tŭkkŭth'-kŭtchin'.**—Dall in Cont. N. A. Ethnol., I, 31, 1877. **Tukudh.**—Keane in Stanford, Compend., 540, 1878. **Tykothee.**— Balbi, Atlas Ethnog., no. 821, 1826. **Tykotheedinneh.**—Franklin, Nar. Journ. Polar Sea, 261, 1824. **Yukuth.**—Keane in Stanford, Compend., 545, 1878 (misprint). **Yukuth Kutchin.**—Bancroft, Nat. Races, I, 115, 1882 (misprint).

Tuklak. A Kuskwogmiut Eskimo village on Kuskokwim r. below the Yukon portage, Alaska; pop. 92 in 1880.

Tookhlagamute.—Petroff in 10th Census, Alaska, 17, 1884. Touckagnokmiut.—Zagoskin in Nouv. Ann. Voy., 5th s., xxi, map, 1850.

Tuklukyet. A Yukonikhotana village, on the N. bank of Yukon r., 15 m. below the mouth of Tozi r., Alaska.—Baker, Geog. Dict. Alaska, 1902.

Tukpafka ('punk-wood,' 'tinder'). An upper Creek village, from which Niuyaka was settled in 1777. According to Hawkins it was on Chattahoochee r., probably in w. Georgia, in 1777. It contained 126 families in 1832. Whipple (Pac. R. R. Rep., iii, pt. 3, 8, 1856) speaks of a remnant of the people as living with the Kichai and Kickapoo on Canadian r., Ind. T. (Oklahoma), in 1853.

Punknot.—Weatherford (1793) in Am. State Papers, Ind. Aff., i, 385, 1832. Toak paf car.—Census of 1832 in Schoolcraft, Ind. Tribes, iv, 578, 1854. Topofkies.—Domenech, Deserts N. A., i, 444, 1860. Toprofkies.—Jacob, Life of P. Gass, 121, 1859. Totepauf-cau.—Hawkins (1799), Sketch, 45, 1848. Tucpauska.—Bartram, Trav., 462, 1773.

Tukpafka. A town of the Creek Nation, on Canadian r., about 8 m. below the mouth of Little r., Okla.

Topofkees.—Whipple in Pac. R. R. Rep., iii, pt. 3, 8, 1856. Tukpafka.—Gatschet, Creek Migr. Leg., ii, 186, 1888.

Tukuarika ('sheep-eaters,' referring to the mountain sheep). A division of Shoshoni said to have lived in Yellowstone park, subsequently in w. central Idaho on the Lemhi fork of Salmon r., and on the Malade. They were subsequently on the Lemhi res., Idaho, but in 1907 they were removed to the Ft Hall res. They numbered 90 in 1904, but are no longer separately enumerated.

Great Kammas Indians.—Valkenburgh in Ind. Aff. Rep., 235, 1865. Kammas Prairie tribe.—Cooley, ibid., 30. Loo-coo-rekah.—Mann, ibid., 1864, 172, 1865. Mountain-Sheep-Eaters.—Hoffman in Proc. Am. Philos. Soc., xxiii, 297, 1886. Salmon River Snakes.—Stuart, Montana, 81, 1865. Sheep-Eaters.—Doty in Ind. Aff. Rep. 1864, 175, 1865. Toocoo recah.—Gebow, Sho-sho-nay Vocab., 19, 1868 (Shoshoni name). Took'-a-rik-kah.—Stuart, op. cit. Tucaricas.—U. S. Stat. at Large, xvi, 346, 1878. Tuka-rika.—Gatschet in Geog. Surv. W. 100th Mer., vii, 410, 1879. Tu'kuari'ka.—Hoffman, op. cit.

Tukulitlatun. A former village of the Chastacosta on the N. side of Rogue r., Oreg.

Tu'-xŭ-lĭt-la'-tûn.—Dorsey in Jour. Am. Folk-lore, iii, 234, 1890.

Tukutnut. A former village of the Rumsen division of the Costanoan family near Monterey, Cal.

Santa Teresea.—Taylor in Cal. Farmer, Apr. 20, 1860 (misprint for Santa Teresa). Tucutnut.—Ibid.

Tukwilisitunne. A former village of the Chastacosta on the N. side of Rogue r., Oreg.

Tu'-kwi-li-si' ɋûnnĕ'.—Dorsey in Jour. Am. Folklore, iii, 234, 1890.

Tula. A province, probably in w. Arkansas, on Arkansas r., visited by De Soto's army in 1542. As the language differed from that of the Quapaw to the

E., the people were possibly of the Caddoan stock.

Tula.—Biedma (1544) in French, Hist. Coll. La., ii, 106, 1850. Tulla.—Gentl. of Elvas (1557), ibid., 179.

Tuladi. See *Touladi*.

Tulalip. One of three divisions of the Twana, a Salish tribe on the w. side of Hood canal, Wash. This branch, according to Eells, lives on a small stream, near the head of the canal, called Dulaylip. The name has also been given to a reservation on the w. side of Puget sd.

Do'hleli'p.—Eells, MS., B. A. E. (Twana name). Du-hle-lips.—Eells in Smithson. Rep. 1887, 605, 1889. Nuhiyup.—Eells, MS., op. cit. (Clallam name). Teelalup.—Hill in H. R. Ex. Doc. 37, 34th Cong., 3d sess., 81, 1857. Thwlé-lûp.—McCaw, Puyallup MS. vocab., B. A. E., 1885 (Puyallup name). Tulalip.—Ind. Aff. Rep. 1901, 704, 1902 (name of res. and agency).

Tulareños (Span.: 'those of the *tulares*,' or tracts of land containing *tules* or reeds). A term applied loosely to the tribes of the great valley of San Joaquin r. and Tulare lake, and even of lower Sacramento valley, Cal. As this territory included Moquelumnan, Yokuts (Mariposan), and Shoshonean tribes, the word is without ethnic significance. Until July 20, 1903, there was a "Mission-Tule River Consolidated Agency" in California, when, by order of the Secretary of the Interior, it was subdivided, part becoming the Mission res. (with 2,897 Indians in 1908), the other the Tule River res. (with 151 Indians).

Talarénos.—Mayer, Mexico, ii, 38, 1853. Tooleerayos.—Beechey, Voy., i, 381, 1831. Tula.—Emmons in Schoolcraft, Ind. Tribes, iii, 201, 1853. Tulara.—Ibid. Tulare Lake Indians.—Johnston in Sen. Ex. Doc. 61, 32d Cong., 1st sess., 23, 1852. Tulareños.—Duflot de Mofras, Expl., ii, 335, 1844. Tulare River Indians.—Henley in Ind. Aff. Rep., 511, 1854. Tularesin.—Capron, Hist. Cal., 20, 1854. Tule River.—Ind. Aff. Rep. 1901, 686, 1902. Tuluraios.—Beechey, op. cit., ii, 401, 1831. Yutas Talareños.—Mühlenpfordt, Mejico, ii, 538, 1844 (the Paiute living on the streams s. of Tulare lake; misprint).

Tulares. A band, probably of the Olamentke, formerly living on the N. coast of San Francisco bay, Cal., but nearly extinct in 1853.—Gibbs in Schoolcraft, Ind. Tribes, iii, 421, 1853.

Tule River Reservation. A reservation of 48,551 acres of partly arable land occupied by 151 Mission Indians of various tribes under the Tule River school superintendent, s. Cal.

Tulibee. A species of whitefish (*Coregonus tullibee*) of the Great Lakes and the waters of the Canadian N. W., the mongrel whitefish. The Canadian-French form of the word, which came into English as *tulibee*, or *tullibee*, from N. w. Canada, is *toulibi*, representing the *otonabi* of the Cree-Chippewa dialects of Algonquian, with the well-known interchange of *n* and *l* and the dropping of the first syllable. The word signifies literally 'mouth water,' from *oton*, 'its mouth,' and *abi*, 'water,' 'liquid,' referring to the watery flesh of this fish. (A. F. C.)

Tulik (Aleut: 'fissure'). An Aleut village formerly on Umnak, Aleutian ids., Alaska, situated near a volcano of the same name. Pop. 26 in 1834.
Tooleekskoi.—Elliott, Cond. Aff. Alaska, 225, 1875. Tulik.—Holmberg, Ethnol. Skizz., 142, 1855. Tulinskoe.—Veniaminof, Zapiski, II, 202, 1840.

Tulkepaia (Yuman: *Tulkepáia venuna tche'hwale*, probably meaning 'spotted-belly sparrows.'—Corbusier). A body of Yuman Indians, popularly known as Apache Yumas, said by Corbusier (1886) to have recently sprung from a mixture of Yuma, Mohave, and Yavapai. They claimed as their home the desert stretch of w. Arizona between the Colorado r. and the country of the Yavapai, over which they roamed until placed on the Rio Verde res., Ariz., in May, 1873. In 1875 most of these, numbering in all about 500, were removed to the San Carlos res., where they numbered 352 in the following year. They speak the Yavapai dialect with a few lexical differences. See *Tontos*. (A. S. G.)
Apache Yuma.—White, MS. Hist. Apaches, B. A. E., 1875. Dil-zhays.—Ibid. Go'hun.—Ibid. Har-dilzhays.—Ibid. ('Red country Indians'; 'Indians living where there are red ants': Apache name). Hatilshé.—White in Zeitschr. f. Ethnol., 370, 1877 (the Tonto, Yuma, and Mohave, so-called by the Apache). Ko-páya.—White quoted by Gatschet Yuma-Sprachstamm, 370, 1877 (own name, abbreviation of Tulke-páya). Ko-uávi.—Gatschet, ibid. (own name). Ko'un.—White, MS. Hist. Apaches, op. cit. Kowávi.—Gatschet, op. cit. Kuhn.—White, MS. Hist., op. cit. (so-called by Mexicans). Kūn.—Ibid. Natchon.—Corbusier misquoted by Shufeldt, Ind. Types of Beauty, 17, 1891. Natchous.—Corbusier in Am. Antiq., VIII, 276, 1886 ('lizard': Apache name). Quejuen.—Froebel, Seven Years' Travel, 511, 1859. Tolekopáya.—White quoted by Gatschet, op. cit., 411. Tolgopeya.—Ibid. Tolkepayá.—ten Kate, Reizen in N. A., 199, 1885. Tolkipeya.—White quoted by Gatschet, op. cit., 371. Tolkopáya.—Ibid. Tsilgopáya.—Ibid. Tsilgopeya.—Ibid. Tulkepaia venuna tchehwale.—Corbusier, op. cit. (=spotted belly T.). Túlykapáya.—Harrington in Jour. Am. Folk-lore, XXI, 324, 1908 ('lizard folk': given as Tonto name for themselves). Ya-vę-pe'-Ku-tcăn'.—ten Kate, Synonymie, 5, 1884 (given as their own name).

Tullibee. See *Tulibee*.

Tullihas. A village situated in 1755 on the w. branch of Muskingum r., Ohio, about 20 m. above the forks, and occupied by Delawares, Mahican, and Caughnawaga.—Smith (1799) quoted by Drake, Trag. Wild., 185, 1841.

Tulomos. Mentioned as a tribe or division of the Costanoan Indians, probably inhabiting the peninsula of San Francisco, Cal., and connected with the mission of Dolores. Together with the Olhones, Ahwastes, Altahmos, and Romonans they have been called Costanos. (A. L. K.)
Tu-lo-mos.—Schoolcraft, Ind. Tribes, II, 506, 1852. Tulumonos.—Latham in Proc. Philol. Soc. Lond., 79, 1852–53. Tuolomos.—Taylor in Cal. Farmer, Jan. 11, 1861.

Tulpkweyu (contr. from *tarapkwéye-u*, a

species of snake). A Tonkawa gens.—Gatschet, Tonkawe vocab., B. A. E., 1884.

Tulsa (properly *Tálsi*, contracted from *Tallahassee*). A Creek town on the left bank of Arkansas r., in tp. 19 N., R. 12 E., Okla. See Gatschet, Creek Migr. Leg., II, 186, 1888. See *Talasse*.

Tulsa. A Creek town at the old Creek council-ground, at Council Hill, near the head of Grave cr., in the S. E. part of the Creek Nation, Okla.—Gatschet, Creek Migr. Leg., II, 186, 1888. See *Talasse*.
Lutchapóga.—Gatschet, ibid., 185.

Tulshk. A Yaquina village on the s. side of Yaquina r., Oreg.
T'ulck.—Dorsey in Jour. Am. Folk-lore, III, 229, 1890 (c=sh).

Tulsulsun (*Túl-sŭl'-sŭn*). Given by Dorsey (Jour. Am. Folk-lore, III, 235, 1890) as a Takelma band or village in Oregon, but identified by Sapir (Am. Anthr., IX, 254, 1907) as merely the Takelma name (*Dalsalsân*) of Illinois r.

Tultschina ('bathers in cold water'). A Knaiakhotana clan of Cook inlet, Alaska.—Richardson, Arct. Expd., I, 407, 1851.

Tuluka. A former Patwin village in Pope valley, Napa co., Cal. According to Powers the Spaniards carried away most of the tribe in 1838 to Sonoma mission, where the larger portion soon died from smallpox. There were only 3 survivors in 1842.
Re'-ho.—Powers in Cont. N. A. Ethnol., III, 228, 1877 (named from a chief). Tulkays.—Taylor in Cal. Farmer, Mar. 30, 1860. Tu-lo-kai'-di-sel.—Powers, op. cit. Tuluka.—S. A. Barrett, inf'n, 1905.

Tuluka. A Kuskwogmiut Eskimo village on the right bank of Kuskokwim r., Alaska; pop. 59 in 1880, 17 in 1890.
Toolooka-anahamute.—Petroff in 10th Census, Alaska, 16, 1884. Tooluka-anahamute.—Ibid., map. Tulukagnagamiut.—11th Census, Alaska, 164, 1893.

Tuluksak. A Kuskwogmiut Eskimo village on the left bank of Kuskokwim r., Alaska, 40 m. above Bethel; pop. 150 in 1880, 62 in 1890.
Iululiak.—Hallock in Nat. Geog. Mag., IX, 90, 1898 (misprint). Toulakságamut.—Spurr (1898) quoted by Baker, Geog. Dict. Alaska, 1902. Tuluksagmiut.—11th Census, Alaska, 164, 1893.

Tulwutmetunne ('people in the open prairie'). A band of the Mishikhwutmetunne formerly residing on Coquille r., Oreg.
Lûl-wût'-me.—Dorsey in Jour. Am. Folk-lore, III, 232, 1890. Lûl'-wût-me' ʒûnně'.—Ibid.

Tumac. Said to be the westernmost settlement of the Maricopa on Gila r., s. w. Ariz., in the 18th century.—Orozco y Berra, Geog., 348, 1864.

Tumacacori (from Pima *Tsü-ma-ka'-kork*, 'curved peak.'—ten Kate). A former rancheria of one of the Piman tribes, probably Sobaipuri, on Rio Santa Cruz, s. of Tubac and 8 leagues N. N. w. of Guevavi, s. Arizona. It was visited by Father Kino in 1697–1701, and afterward became a visita of Guevavi, with 199 natives in 1764–67, and 39 in 1772, at which date it was almost in ruins from Apache depredations in 1769. In 1784 or earlier it had become the mission of San José, and was occupied as such until 1820, when the church, erected by the Jesuits in 1752, was destroyed by the Apache. The ruins are still visible.

Jumagacori.—Mange quoted by Bancroft, Ariz. and N. Mex., 358, 1889. San José.—Bancroft, ibid., 385. S. Cayetano.—Bernal (1697) quoted by Bancroft, ibid., 356 (Tumacacori, or). S. Cayetano Tumapacori.—Kino (1697) in Doc. Hist. Mex., 4th s., I, 288, 1856. S. Cayetano Tumagacori.—Mange quoted by Bancroft, Ariz. and N. Mex., 358, 1889. St Cayetano.—Venegas, Hist. Cala., I, map, 1759. Sumacacori.—Croix (1769) in Doc. Hist. Mex., 4th s., II, 15, 1856. Termacácori.—Hardy, Travels, 422, 1829. Tsjoemakákork.—ten Kate, Reizen in N. A., 160, 1885 (Pima name). Tumacacori.—Garcés (1769) in Doc. Hist. Mex., 4th s., II, 374, 1856.

Tumalenia (*Tu-ma-leh-nia*). A tribe, probably Moquelumnan, formerly living at Bodega bay, Cal., and speaking a language different from the Gallinomero, the next tribe to the N.—Gibbs in Schoolcraft, Ind. Tribes, III, 102, 1853.

Tumamar. A tribe or subtribe, evidently Coahuiltecan, encountered N. of the Rio Grande as early as 1675, when Fernando del Bosque crossed into Texas (Nat. Geog. Mag., XIV, 340–45, 1903). Early in the 18th century they became well known at San Francisco Solano mission on the Rio Grande in Mexico, and after this mission became San Antonio de Valero, on the Rio San Antonio in Texas, some members of the tribe followed it (Baptismal Rec. of San Antonio de Valero, MS.). At the first mission named they mingled freely with the Terocodame, a Tumamar being at one time chief of the latter band. The tribe ranged far to the E., sometimes being met on the Brazos (Espinosa, Diario, entry for June 10, 1716, MS.). The tribal name, which was most commonly written Tumamar and Ticmamar, seems to have disappeared before the middle of the 18th century.   (H. E. B.)

Taimamares.—Fernando del Bosque (1675), op. cit. Tasmamares.—Orozco y Berra, Geog., 306, 1864. Ticmanares.—Espinosa (1716), op. cit. Tumamar.—Fernando del Bosque (1675), op. cit. (given as chief's name).

Tumidok. According to Powers, a division of the Miwok formerly living in the region of Mokelumne r., in Calaveras and Amador cos., Cal. In reality the name has the same significance as Tamuleko, q. v.

Toomedocs.—Powers in Overland Mo., X, 324, 1873. Tu'-mi-dok.—Powers in Cont. N. A. Ethnol., III, 349, 1877.

Tumkoaakyas (*Tumqoā'akyas*). A Bellacoola gens at Talio, Brit. Col.—Boas in 7th Rep. N. W. Tribes Can., 3, 1891.

Tummeli (*Tum'-meli*). A Maidu division living along the S. fork of American r., from a little above Coloma to Riverton, Eldorado co., Cal.   (R. B. D.)

Tumna (properly *Dumna*). A former Yokuts (Mariposan) tribe that lived on upper San Joaquin r. and N. to Kings r., Cal. They were one of the tribes that ceded their lands to the United States by treaty of Apr. 29, 1851, and were then placed on a reserve between Chowchilla and Kaweah rs.   (A. L. K.)

Dumna.—Kroeber in Univ. Cal. Pub., Am. Arch. and Eth., II, 311, 1907 (proper name). Loomnears.—Henley in Ind. Aff. Rep., 512, 1854. Toom-na.—Ind. Aff. Rep., 223, 1851; Royce in 18th Rep. B. A. E., 782, 1899. Toom-nas.—Ind. Aff. Rep., 223, 1851.

Tump. According to Bartlett (Dict. of Americanisms, 723, 1877), "to tump" signifies "to draw a deer or other animal home through the woods after he has been killed": a word in use in the hunting regions of Maine, from the Abnaki dialect of Algonquian.   (A. F. C.)

Tumpataguo. One of 36 tribes reported in 1683 to Domingo de Mendoza (Viaje, MS. in Archivo Gen. de Méx.) as being friendly to the Jumano (Tawehash) and living three days' journey eastward from the junction of the Rio Grande and the Conchos. This would place them in s. w. Texas.   (H. E. B.)

Tump-line. A pack strap or portage strap. Bartlett (Dict. of Americanisms, 723, 1877) says: "A strap placed across the forehead to assist a man in carrying a pack on his back. Used in Maine, where the custom was borrowed from the Indians." The first part of this word is derived, according to De Cost Smith, from *mádûmbî*, which in the Abnaki dialect of Algonquian signifies 'pack strap,' 'burden strap'; *line* is English. According to Prince (Am. Anthr., IX,

TUMP-LINE IN USE

no. 3, 1907) the modern Abnaki form is *madomba*, and the present-day Mashpee *tà'mpàm*.   (A. F. C.)

Tumpzi. A tribe or subtribe, of unknown affinity, represented in 1728 at San Antonio de Valero mission, Texas (Valero Burials, 1728, partida 154, MS.).

Tumtls ('paint'). A Squawmish village on the E. side of Howe sd., Brit. Col.—Hill-Tout in Rep. Brit. A. A. S., 474, 1900.

Tumun. A name said by Powers (Cont. N. A. Ethnol., III, 349, 1877) to be applied by the Miwok N. of Stanislaus r., Stanislaus co., Cal., to their northern congeners. Powers derives the name from *tu'mun*, 'north.' It is, however, very probably another rendition of *chumetoko*, a term derived from the Miwok *chumech*, 'south,' and itself signifying 'southerners.' Cf. *Tamuleko*.   (S. A. B.)

Tunagak. An Eskimo village in the Kuskokwim district, Alaska; pop. 71 in 1890.

Tunaghamiut.—11th Census, Alaska, 164, 1893.

Tunal. A former pueblo of the Tepehuane, in Durango, Mexico; definite locality unknown.

el Tunal.—Orozco y Berra, Geog., 318, 1864.

Tunanpin (*Tu'-nan-p'in*, 'black bear').

A gens of the Iowa, consisting of the Tapothka, Punghathka, Munchinye, and Kirokokhoche subgentes.

Too-num'-pe.—Morgan, Anc. Soc., 156, 1877. Tu'-nan-p'in.—Dorsey in 15th Rep. B. A. E., 238, 1897.

Tunanpin. A gens of the Missouri (q. v.).

Moon'-cha.—Morgan, Anc. Soc., 156, 1877. Tu-nan'-p'in.—Dorsey in 15th Rep. B. A. E., 240, 1897.

Tunanpin. A gens of the Oto (q. v.).

Me-je'-rä-ja.—Morgan, Anc. Soc., 156, 1877 (='Wolf'; given as distinct from Bear gens). Moon'-cha.—Ibid. ('Bear'). Mün-tci'-ra-tce.—Dorsey in 15th Rep. B. A. E., 240, 1897 ('Wolf'). Tunan'-p'in.—Ibid. ('Black bear').

Tundastusa (Apache: 'water spread out,' from the many springs forming marshy areas). A large prehistoric pueblo ruin on a low elevation between two washes entering Forestdale cr. from the N., on the White Mtn. Apache res., 10 m. S. E. of Showlow, Ariz. It was partially excavated in 1901 by Dr Walter Hough, of the National Museum, who is inclined to the belief that it was a settlement of a Zuñi clan or clans on its northward migration. See Nat. Mus. Rep. 1901, 289, 1903.

Forestdale ruin.—Ibid.

Tundy. See *Tatemy*.

Tunessassah ('where there is fine sand.'—Hewitt). An Iroquois village formerly on upper Allegheny r., perhaps in Warren co., Pa., and occupied by Seneca, Cayuga, and Onondaga.—Macauley, N. Y., II, 200, 299, 300, 1829.

Tung. The Sun clan of the Tewa pueblo of Hano, N. E. Ariz., only one individual (a man) of which survived in 1893.

Tañ'.—Fewkes in Am. Anthr., VII, 166, 1894. Tda'-wu.—Stephen in 8th Rep. B. A. E., 39, 1891 (Hopi name). Tjon-a-ai'.—Ibid. (Navaho name). Tuñ.—Ibid.

Tungge (Tewa: 'village of the basket'). A former pueblo of the Tano on a bare slope near the banks of a stream (which in the mountains farther s. is called Rio de San Pedro, lower down Uña de Gato, and in the vicinity of the ruins Arroyo del Tunque), at the N. E. extremity of the Sandia mts., in Sandoval co., N. Mex. It was the westernmost of the Tano villages in prehistoric times, and was evidently in ruins in 1541, the date of Coronado's expedition, having been abandoned a few years prior to that date in consequence of an attack by nomadic Indians from the plains. The pueblo was extensive, forming a number of irregular squares, and the houses were constructed of adobe with rubble foundations. See Bandelier in Arch. Inst. Papers, IV, 109, 121, et seq., 1892.

El Tunque.—Bandelier, op. cit., 109. Pueblo de Tunque.—Doc. of 1770 cited by Bandelier, ibid., 112. Tung-ge.—Ibid., 109 (aboriginal name). Tung-ke.—Bandelier in Ritch, N. Mex., 201, 1885; in Arch. Inst. Papers, III, 129, 1890. Tunque.—Bandelier in Ritch, op. cit. Village of the Basket.—Bandelier in Arch. Inst. Papers, IV, op. cit.

Tungulungsi (*Tung-ul-ung'-si*, 'smallest turtle'). A subclan of the Delawares.—Morgan, Anc. Soc., 172, 1877.

Tungyaa. According to tradition of the Santa Clara Indians, an ancient Tewa pueblo on a black mesa near the w. bank of the Rio Grande, above the San Ildefonso ford, N. Mex.   (F. W. H.)

Tuniakpuk. A Togiagmiut Eskimo village on lower Togiak r., Alaska; pop. 137 in 1880.

Tuniakhpuk.—Petroff in 10th Census Alaska, map, 1884. Tuniakpuk.—Baker, Geog. Dict. Alaska, 641, 1906. Tunniakhpuk.—Petroff, op. cit., 17.

Tunica (*ta*, an article; *uni*, 'people'; *ka*, nominal suffix.—Gatschet). A tribe, forming a distinct linguistic family known as Tonikan, formerly dwelling on the lower Mississippi. The Tunica are prominent in the early history of the lower Mississippi region because of their attachment to the French and the faithful service rendered them as allies in contests with neighboring tribes. When first visited they lived in Mississippi on lower Yazoo r. In 1699 La Source (Shea, Early Voy., 80, 1861) estimated the number of their cabins at about 260, scattered over 4 leagues of country. He states that they lived entirely on Indian corn and did no hunting. Gravier, who visited the tribe in 1700, states that they occupied 7 hamlets containing 50 or 60 small cabins. In 1706, according to La Harpe, the Tunica were driven from their villages by the Chickasaw and Alibamu and joined the Huma; and it is said that subsequently they killed more than half that tribe and occupied its territory. In 1730 they met with a reverse at the hands of those Natchez who had taken refuge among the Chickasaw; their village was burned and a large number of them killed. In 1760 they occupied 3 villages, the largest of which was on a lake at Tunica bayou. Baudry des Lozières in 1802 ascribed to them a population of 120 men, a total of about 450.

Hutchins (Imlay, West. Ter., 419, 1797) notes a Tunica village on the E. bank of the river opposite the upper plantations of Pte Coupée, containing in 1784 about 20 warriors. Later the Tunica moved up to Marksville prairie in Avoyelles parish, on the s. side of lower Red r. Still later they appear under the local name of Avoyelles Indians (not to be confounded with an older tribe of that name), a name applied also to the Biloxi, who settled here in 1762 after leaving their coast seats. The remnant of the Tunica, consisting of about 30 people, are now E. and S. E. of Marksville, the parish seat, on what is called Marksville prairie. They speak Tunica, Creole, and English.

Gravier's description of the Tunica in 1700 indicates that their women made an excellent fabric of mulberry cloth; there was a fair division of labor between the sexes; the men cultivated the soil, planted and harvested the crops, cut the wood and brought it to the cabin, and dressed the deer and buffalo skins; the women performed the indoor work and made pottery and clothing; polygyny was rare among them (Shea, Early Voy., 134). The Tunica language, hitherto unknown or unpublished, was studied in 1886 by Gatschet. It is vocalic and harmonious, rich in verbal forms and possessing also a declension of the noun, and, what is more remarkable, nominal and pronominal gender. It appears to have no genetic connection with any other family of languages.

Counica.—Neill, Hist. Minn., 173, 1858 (misprint). Otonnica.—Tonti (1687) in Shea, Discov., 226, 1852. Runicas.—Sibley (1805) in Am. State Papers, Ind. Aff., I, 724, 1832. Tanico.—Gentl. of Elvas (1542) in French, Hist. Coll. La., II,-178, 1850 (probably identical). Tanik8a.—Marquette map (ca. 1673) in Shea, Discov., 1852. Tanikwa.—Marquette quoted by Shea, Early Voy., 80, 1861. Tonicas.—Pénicaut (1700) in French, Hist. Coll. La., I, 61, 1869. Tonicaus.—La Harpe (1719) in Margry, Déc., VI, 302, 1886. Tonikas.—Bossu, Travels La., I, 35, 1771. Toumachas.—Berquin-Duvallon, Travels in La., 94, 1806. Toumika.—Gravier (1700) in Shea, Early Voy., 133, 1861. Tounica.—Coxe, Carolana, map, 1741. Tounika.—Gravier (1701) in French, Hist. Coll. La., II, 80, 1875. Tourika.—Métairie (1682) in French, ibid., 22. Tuncas.—Latham, Essays, 408, 1860. Tunicas.—Jefferys, French Dom. Am., I, 145, 1761. Tu-ni′-cka aⁿ-ya-di′.—Dorsey, Biloxi MS. dict., B. A. E., 1892 (one of the Biloxi names). Tu-ni′-cka haⁿ-ya′.—Ibid. (another Biloxi name). Tunscas.—Sibley misquoted by Schermerhorn (1812) in Mass. Hist. Soc. Coll., 2d s., II, 27, 1814.

Tunicha. Mentioned as a Navaho settlement, but actually intended to designate that part of the tribe in and about the Tunicha mts., N. Mex., in contradistinction to the western portion of the tribe.

Tumecha.—Domenech, Deserts of N. A., II, 7, 1860. Tumicha.—Cortez (1799) in Pac. R. R. Rep., III, pt. 3, 119, 1856. Tunicha Indians.—Shepherd (1859) in H. R. Ex. Doc. 69, 36th Cong., 1st sess., 16, 1860.

Tunuliarbik. A former Eskimo settlement and Dutch trading station in s. w. Greenland.—Crantz, Hist. Greenland, I, 18, 1767.

Tununirmiut ('people of the back country'). One of the two subdivisions of the Agomiut Eskimo, living at Pond inlet, opening into Eclipse sd., N. E. coast of Baffinland.

Toonoonek.—Parry, Second Voy., 359, 1824. Tudnunirmiut.—Boas in Trans. Anthr. Soc. Wash., III, 96, 1885. Tununirmiut.—Boas in 6th Rep. B. A. E., 442, 1888.

Tununirusirmiut ('people of the smaller back country'). A subtribe of Agomiut Eskimo living at Admiralty inlet, the N. shore of Cockburn id., and the s. shore of North Devon.

Toonoonee-roochiuh.—Parry, Second Voy., 370, 1824. Tudnunirossirmiut.—Boas in Trans. Anthr. Soc. Wash., III, 96, 1885. Tununirusirmiut.—Boas in 6th Rep. B. A. E., 442, 1888.

Tunxis (from Wuttunkshau, 'the point where the river bends.'—Trumbull). An important tribe that lived on middle Farmington r. near the great bend, about where Farmington and Southington, Hartford co., Conn., are now. They were subject at an early period to Sequassen, the sachem who sold Hart-

ford to the English. Ruttenber includes them in the Wappinger. They sold the greater part of their territory in 1640. About 1700 they still had a village of 20 wigwams at Farmington, but in 1761 there were only 4 or 5 families left.

Juncks'es.—Wadungum, a Mohegan chief (1700), in N. Y. Doc. Col. Hist., IV, 614, 1854 (misprint). Sepos.—Stiles (1761) in Mass. Hist. Soc. Coll., 1st s., X, 104, 1809. Sépous.—Ibid. Sopus.—Jones, Ind. Bull., 13, 1867 (also used for the Esopus). Tuncksis.—Trumbull, Ind. Names Conn., 74, 1881 (early form). Tunxis.—Stiles (1761) in Mass. Hist. Soc. Coll., 1st s., X, 104, 1809. Unxus.—R. I. Col. Rec. cited by Trumbull, Ind. Names Conn., 74, 1881.

Tuolumne (Tu-ol′-um-ne). A collective term for the tribes on Tuolumne r., Cal., all or most of whom were probably of Moquelumnan stock. Merriam (Am. Anthr., IX, 341, 348, 1907) distinguishes the Tuolumne tribe of this family.

Fawalomnes.—Bancroft, Nat. Races, I, 450, 1874. Sololumnes.—Hale, Ethnol. and Philol., 630, 1846. Solumnees.—Taylor in Cal. Farmer, June 8, 1860. Tawalemnes.—Bancroft, Nat. Races, I, 450, 1874. Touserlemnies.—Taylor, op. cit. To-wal-um-ne.—Fremont, Geog. Memoir, 16, 1848. Tuolumne.—Schoolcraft, Ind. Tribes, IV, 407, 1854. Tu-ol′-um-ne.—Merriam in Am. Anthr., IX, 348, 1907. Tuolumnes.—Taylor, op. cit. Turealemnes.—Hale, Ethnol. and Philol., 630, 1846. Yolumne.—Barbour in Sen. Ex. Doc. 4, 32d Cong., spec. sess., 251, 1853. Yo-lum-ne.—Royce in 18th Rep. B. A. E., 782, 1899.

Tupichihasao. A mission village, probably on the lower Georgia coast, the inhabitants of which were among those revolting against the Spaniards in 1687.—Barcia, Ensayo, 287, 1723.

Tupirbikdjuin. A summer settlement of the Kingnait Okomiut Eskimo near the coast of Cumberland sd.—Boas in 6th Rep. B. A. E., map, 1888.

Tupo. A former rancheria, probably Papago or Sobaipuri, 12 to 16 leagues w. of San Xavier del Bac.; visited by Father Kino in 1696.

Cops.—Mange (1701) quoted by Bancroft, Ariz. and N. Mex., I, 358, 1889. Tupo.—Kino (1696) in Doc. Hist. Mex., 4th s., I, 266, 1856. Tups.—Mange quoted by Bancroft, Ariz. and N. Mex., 358, 1889.

Tupo. A former rancheria, apparently Papago, visited by Kino and Mange in 1701. Situated in a volcanic desert about 10 m. from the Gulf of California, N. w. Sonora, Mexico.

Aibacusi.—Kino (1701) quoted by Bancroft, No. Mex. States, I, 495, 1884. Tupo.—Ibid.

Tups. A tribe of Karankawan affiliation that entered Nuestra Señora de la Candelaria mission (q. v.) on San Gabriel r., Texas, in 1750. In the same locality there were three missions, one avowedly assigned to Tonkawan tribes, the second to the Bidai-Arkokisa group, and the third, La Candelaria, to the Karankawan group. The tribes represented there were the Coco, Karankawa, Tups, Cujane, Estepisas, and Esquein (Testimonio de Diligencias, doc. 12, leg. 6, letter K, Arch. Col. Santa Cruz de Querétaro; Letter of Fray María Ano de los Dolores, 1750, ibid., doc. 18). After Candelaria mission was abandoned, a part of the tribe went with the Cocos to San Antonio de Valero. See *Tops*. (H. E. B.)

Thops.—Pedro Ramon in doc. 10, leg. 6, letter K, Arch. Col. Santa Cruz, *ca.* 1756. Tup.—Morfi, Mem. Hist. Tex., bk. II, *ca.* 1782, MS.

Tupuic. A village, presumably Costanoan, formerly connected with Dolores mission, San Francisco, Cal.—Taylor in Cal. Farmer, Oct. 18, 1861.

Tupuinte. A village, presumably Costanoan, formerly connected with Dolores mission, San Francisco, Cal.—Taylor in Cal. Farmer, Oct. 18, 1861.

Tupustikutteh (*Tu-pūs'-ti-kut'-teh,* 'grass-nut eaters'). A Paviotso band formerly on Carson r., w. Nevada.—Powers, Inds. W. Nevada, MS., B. A. E., 1876.

Tuquisan. A Maricopa settlement on Gila r., s. Ariz., in the 18th century.—Orozco y Berra, Geog., 348, 1864.

Turami. A Costanoan village formerly within 10 m. of Santa Cruz mission, Cal.—Taylor in Cal. Farmer, Apr. 5, 1860.

Turasi ('where there are peaches'). A small pueblo of the Tarahumare, near Norogachic, Chihuahua, Mexico.—Lumholtz, inf'n, 1894.

Turatu. The Elk clan of Taos pueblo, N. Mex.

Tura'tu tai'na.—M. C. Stevenson, notes, B. A. E., 1910 (*tai'na*='people').

Turco. See *Turk*.

Turghestltsatun. A Tolowa village on the Pacific coast N. of the mouth of Klamath r., Cal.

Ta-kĕçl'-tûn ʒûn'-nĕ.—Dorsey, Chetco MS. vocab., B. A. E., 1884. Ta-kĕsçl'-tsa te'-ne.—Dorsey, Smith River MS. vocab., B.A.E., 1884. Tû-rxĕstl' tsa'-tûn.—Dorsey, Naltunnetunne MS. vocab., B. A. E., 183, 1884.

Turip. A Yurok village on Klamath r., about 8 m. above the mouth, in N. W. California. (A. L. K.)

Turisai. A former rancheria, probably of the Sobaipuri, and a visita of the Jesuit mission of Suamca. Probably situated on or near the Rio Santa Cruz in s. Arizona or N. Sonora.

S. Pedro Turisai.—Bancroft, Ariz. and N. Mex., 371, 1889 (after early docs.).

Turk. A nickname (*El Turco*) given by the members of Coronado's expedition in 1540–42 to a native of the province of Harahey (identified with the Pawnee country), because of his peculiar headdress. The Turk, who was a "slave" at Pecos pueblo (Cicuyé), N. Mex., probably first because of a desire to return to his people, later at the instigation of the Pueblos who had suffered atrocities at the hands of the Spaniards, represented to Coronado that in Quivira, and especially in Harahey and "the Guaes," there was much gold, which he called *acochis* (q. v.). Fired with enthusiasm at what the Indian had told him, Coronado started with his army from Tiguex on the Rio Grande the following spring (1541), guided by the Turk and accompanied by a Quivira Indian named Ysopete. After

wandering for some time on the Staked plains of E. New Mexico and w. Texas, Coronado became convinced that the Turk was trying to lead the army astray, whereon he put him in irons, sent back to the Rio Grande the main body of his force, placed himself under the guidance of Ysopete, and in 42 days of northward journeying reached the country of Quivira, in the present Kansas. Traversing the length of this province, Coronado, after the middle of August, reached Kansas r., whence he summoned Tatarrax, chief of Harahey, which lay next beyond. Regardless of the presence of Tatarrax with 200 warriors of the tribe to which the Turk belonged, and whom the latter endeavored to set against the Spanish force of 30 men, the treacherous guide was strangled to death, and Coronado prepared for his return journey. (F. W. H.)

Turkey Hill. A small village near Derby, New Haven co., Conn., subject to the Paugusset. In 1761 there were only a dozen Indians there.—Birdsey (1761) in Mass. Hist. Soc. Coll., 1st s., x, 111, 1809.

Turkeytown (translation of the native term *Gûñ'-dǐ'gadu-hûñ'yǐ,* and derived from the name of a chief, Turkey or Little Turkey). A former Cherokee settlement on the w. bank of Coosa r., opposite the present Center, Cherokee co., Ala. (J. M.)

Gûñ'-dǐ'gaduhûñ'yǐ.—Mooney in 19th Rep. B. A. E., 521, 1900 (Cherokee name). Turkey Town.—Doc. of 1799 quoted by Royce in 5th Rep. B. A. E., 144, 1887.

Turniptown (from the native term *U'lûñ'yǐ,* 'tuber place'). A former Cherokee settlement on Turniptown cr., above Ellijay, Gilmer co., Ga. (J. M.)

Turnip Mountain.—Doc. of 1799 quoted by Royce in 5th Rep. B. A. E., 144, 1887. U'lûñ'yǐ.—Mooney in 19th Rep. B. A. E., 542, 1900.

Turquoise. Stones of greenish hue were especially valued by the American aborigines, and this was due, apparently, to the association of certain religious notions with the color. Turquoise is one of the most beautiful of the green gem stones, and, according to Clark and Diller, is a hydrous aluminum sulphate colored by a copper phosphate, containing also a little iron and magnesia. It displays a wide range of pale bluish and greenish tints, and occurs in thin seams or in pockets associated with eruptive rocks, or as grains and pebbles in the sands and gravels of the valleys. It is found in various localities, notably in Colorado, New Mexico, Utah, Nevada, and California, and was mined by the natives in pre-Spanish times at Cerrillos mt., near Santa Fé, N. Mex. (Blake), and on Turquoise mt. in Cochise co., Ariz.

The first Spanish explorers found this stone in use for personal ornaments by the native tribes, and it appears that they had been conducting mining operations on quite an extensive scale, especially at Los Cerrillos, N. Mex., where many of their rude stone mining hammers and sledges have been found (see *Mines and Quarries*). It is even surmised that the more highly civilized tribes of Mexico found and utilized this source of the much-valued gem. The turquoise is highly prized by the present tribes of the arid region, and is ground into beads and pendants, which are pierced by the aid of primitive drills, and is made into settings for mosaic work (see *Mosaic*). Kunz states that "the selling price is now [1886] very low, the Indians disposing of their specimens at the rate of 25 cents for the contents of a mouth, where they usually carry them. A string made of many hundreds of stones they value at the price of a pony." See *Utahlite*.

Consult Blake in Am. Jour. Sci., 2d s., xxv, 1858; Silliman in Eng. and Min. Jour., xxxii, 1881; Fewkes (1) in Am. Anthr., ix, no. 11, 1896; (2) in 17th Rep. B. A. E., pt. 1, 1898; (3) in 22d Rep. B. A. E., 1904; Kunz, Gems and Precious Stones, 1890; Clark and Diller in Am. Jour. Sci., 3d s., xxxii, 1886; Pepper (1) in Am. Anthr., vii, no. 2, 1905, (2) in Putnam Anniv. Vol., 1909. (w. h. h.)

Turtleback. See *Stonework*.

Turtle Mountain Sioux. An Assiniboin band occupying a reserve of 640 acres at the base of Turtle mt., 12 m. s. e. of Deloraine, Manitoba. They numbered 45 until the autumn of 1908, when 30 of their number joined the Oak Lake band on its reservation 5 m. N. of Pipestone, Manitoba.

Turtle Portage. A Chippewa station in Wisconsin, occupied by the tribe for a long time before settling at Flambeau lake.—Warren (1852) in Minn. Hist. Soc. Coll., v, 192, 1885.

Turtletown (trans. of *Săligŭgĭ*, 'turtle'). A Cherokee settlement in upper Georgia about the period of the removal of the tribe in 1839. (j. m.)

Turwillana (referring to a cylindrical fossil marked in rings). An extinct clan of Taos pueblo, N. Mex.
Turwil'lana tai'na.—M. C. Stevenson, notes, B. A E., 1910 (*tai'na* = 'people').

Tusanes. A former tribe of N. E. Mexico or s. Texas, probably Coahuiltecan. According to Portillo (Apuntes para la Hist. Antig. de Coahuila y Tex., 285, 1888), who calls them "Tusan or Carrizo," 213 of their number were at San Juan Bautista mission in 1761.—Orozco y Berra, Geog., 303, 1864.

Tuscaluca. See *Tascalusa*.

Tuscarawas. A former settlement of Delawares and Wyandot on Tuscarawas r., Ohio, near the mouth of Big Sandy r. It was near the great trail leading from Muskingum on the s. and Sandusky on the N. to the Indian settlements in w. Pennsylvania, being situated almost due w. from Shingas Town at the mouth of Beaver r. The early traders gave the name Muskingum, or Elk's Eye, to the three streams now known as the Muskingum, Tuscarawas, and Big Sandy. On account of its location near the intersection of the three trails, this settlement, which was made some time before 1750, was well known to traders. Gist passed through it in the year named on his way to Muskingum, when it was composed of a few wigwams. After 1758, when Tamaque (q. v.), or King Beaver, the leading chief of the Delawares on the Ohio, left w. Pennsylvania on account of the fall of Ft Duquesne, he made this his headquarters, and from this time the place was frequently spoken of as "The Beavers Town." After Zeisberger and his Delaware converts deserted the Moravian settlement on Beaver r., Pa., they moved to the Tuscarawas valley, which at once became the center of missionary effort among the western Indians. Tamaque became one of the converts. The Moravian missionary Heckewelder labored for many years in this field, during which time he had many narrow escapes from death at the hands of hostile Indians led by the white renegade Simon Girty. Heckewelder says: "In the year 1762, while I lived at Tuscarawas on the Muskingum, they [the Delawares] were settled on that river and its branches." Bouquet's force encamped near the place in Oct. 1764, at which time it was entirely deserted by its inhabitants, who had fled in terror before the advancing army, leaving about 100 wigwams, an evidence of their numbers. At this time the village had been occupied by a mixed population of about 150 families of Delawares, Shawnee, Wyandot, Miami, and Mingos. McCullough speaks of the settlement at this time where a "number of traders resided" (McCullough, Narr., in Border Life, 104, 1839; see also the Journal of Bouquet Expedition, 13, 1765; Parkman, Conspiracy of Pontiac, ii, 227, 1901, and letter of General Gage, ibid., app. F). A number of Indians met Bouquet at Tuscarawas, making overtures for peace. The army moved on to Muskingum, where a council was held, after which a number of white prisoners were given up and hostages given for the return of all prisoners at Ft Pitt in the coming spring. Many of the Indian warriors followed their former captives, whom they had learned to hold in high regard, back to Ft Pitt, but many of these captives returned not long afterward to their Indian homes on the Tuscarawas. (g. p. d.)
Beaver's Town.—Croghan (1761) in Mass. Hist. Soc. Coll., 4th s., ix, 379, 1871. **Beaver Town.**—Hutchins map in Smith, Bouquet Exped., 1766. **King Beaver's Town.**—Smith, Bouquet Exped., 67, 1766.

Tuscalaways.—McCullough (1764), Narr., 104, 1839. Tuscarawa.—Croghan (1765) in Rupp, West. Penn., app., 166, 1846. Tuscarawas.—Lewis Evans' map, 1755. Tuscarawi—Loskiel, Hist. Miss. Unit. Breth., pt. 3, 74, 1794. Tuscarorans.—Güssefeld map, 1784. Tuscaroras.—La Tour map, 1779 (error). Tuscarowas.—Bouquet (1764) in Rupp, West. Penn., app., 148, 1846. Tuscavoroas.—Esnauts and Rapilly map, 1777 (misprint). Tuscorawas.—Heckewelder in Trans. Am. Philos. Soc., IV, 396, 1834. Tuskarawas.—Hutchins map in Smith, Bouquet Exped., 1766.

Tuscarora (*Skarū'rĕⁿ*', 'hemp gatherers,' the *Apocynum cannabinum*, or Indian hemp, being a plant of many uses among the Carolina Tuscarora; the native form of this appellative is impersonal, there being no expressed pronominal affix to indicate person, number, or gender). Formerly an important confederation of tribes, speaking languages cognate with

ELIAS JOHNSON—TUSCARORA

those of the Iroquoian linguistic group, and dwelling, when first encountered, on the Roanoke, Neuse, Taw (Torhunta or Narhontes), and Pamlico rs., N. C. The evidence drawn from the testimony of writers contemporary with them, confirmed in part by tradition, makes it appear that while occupying this primitive habitat the Tuscarora league was composed of at least three tribal constituent members, each bearing an independent and exclusive appellation. The names of these component members still survive in the traditions of the Tuscarora now dwelling in w. New York and s. Ontario, Canada. The first of these tribal names is *Kă'tĕ'nu'ā'kā'*, i. e. 'People of the Submerged Pine-tree'; the second *Akawĕñ-tc'ākā'* (meaning doubtful); and the third, *Skarū'rĕⁿ*', 'Hemp Gatherers.' Cusick

(Hist. Six Nations, 34, 1828) wrote these tribal appellations "Kautanohakau," "Kauwetseka," and "Tuscarora" respectively, and (p. 31) refers also to the "Esaurora, or Tuscarora," from which it may be inferred that Esaurora is a synonym of Skarū'rĕⁿ'. According to the same authority (p. 36), the Tuscarora, on traditionary evidence, possessed in early times the "country lying between the sea shores and the mountains, which divide the Atlantic states," in which they had 24 large towns and could muster 6,000 warriors, probably meaning persons. Lawson, a better authority, wrote that in 1708 the Tuscarora had 15 towns and about 1,200 warriors—perhaps a minimum estimate of the true number of their fighting-men; and Johnson (Legends, etc., of the Iroquois, 1881) says that the Tuscarora in North Carolina had 6 towns and 1,200 warriors, which was probably approximately true of the Tuscarora proper. Col. Barnwell, the commander of the South Carolina forces in the war of 1711–12, said that the Tuscarora or "the enemy can't be less than 1,200 or 1,400 [warriors], which may be easily judged by their large settlements;" but Gov. Spotswood of Virginia placed their fighting strength at 2,000 men in 1711. According to Barnwell the Tuscarora had 3 towns on Pamlico r., of which one was Ucouhnerunt, but that most of their towns were on Neuse r. and its many affluents. Some indication of the extent of the territory claimed by the Tuscarora may be obtained from the terms of the truce declared between the Tuscarora and Col. Barnwell in 1712. It was agreed therein that the Tuscarora were "to plant only on Neuse river, the creek the fort is on, quitting all claims to other lands. . . . To quit all pretensions to planting, fishing, hunting or ranging to all lands lying between Neuse river and Cape Feare, that entirely to be left to the So. Carolina Indians, and to be treated as enemies if found in those ranges without breach of peace, and the enemy's line shall be between Neuse and Pamblico . . . fishing on both sides Bear river." This would indicate that Cape Fear r. was the southern boundary of the Tuscarora territory.

History.—The data for the history of the Tuscarora are meager and fragmentary, hence while they were at first an important people of North Carolina, little is definitely known regarding them, and that little usually applies to only a part of the people. The first authentic information concerning the Tuscarora is that recorded by Lawson, the Surveyor-General of North Carolina, who knew them well, having lived in close contact with them for many years. His History of Carolina, having been written about

1709 and published in 1718, contains nothing in regard to the Tuscarora during the most eventful period of their history, namely, that covering the years 1711 to 1713. During this time they fought two wars with the colonists of North Carolina, who were effectively aided by those of South Carolina and Virginia, reenforced by their tributary Indian allies. The first war began with the capture of Lawson and the Baron De Graffenried by about 60 Tuscarora and the condemnation to death of the former in Sept. 1711. Immediately following, a portion of the Tuscarora under Hencock, the Coree, Pamlico, Matamuskeet, Bear Rivers, and Machapungo, conspired to cut off the whites, each one of the tribes agreeing to operate in its own district whence they were being driven by the steady encroachment of the colonists. This compact resulted in the massacre of about 130 of the colonists on Sept. 22, 1711, on Trent and Pamlico rs., by the tribes mentioned. Col. Barnwell was sent by South Carolina to aid the hard-pressed colonists of North Carolina, and succeeded in driving the Tuscarora into one of their palisaded towns about 20 m. above Newbern, N. C., where he defeated them and later induced them to accept terms of peace; but Barnwell violated this treaty by seizing some of the Indians and sending them away into slavery. This was the beginning of the second war between the Tuscarora and their allies and the people of North Carolina. Again an appeal was made to South Carolina for aid, which responded by sending Col. James Moore with a small militia force and about 900 tributary Indians.

Of the Tuscarora, Lawson said that they possessed many amiable qualities; that, in fact, they were "really better to us than we have been to them, as they always freely give us of their victuals at their quarters, while we let them walk by our doors hungry, and do not often relieve them. We look upon them with disdain and scorn, and think them little better than beasts in human form; while with all our religion and education, we possess more moral deformities and vices than these people do." This attitude of the whites toward the Indians naturally led to the troubles later, which ended in much bloodshed and cruelty on both sides. Although the Tuscarora were regarded as mild, kind, peaceable, ingenious, and industrious, they were speedily brutalized by the vices of the colonists with whom they came in contact; their women were debauched by the whites, and both men and women were kidnapped to be sold into slavery. The colonists of North Carolina, like their Puritan brethren of New England, did not recognize in the Indian any right to the soil, hence the lands of the Tuscarora and of their Indian neighbors and allies were appropriated without thought of purchase. It is not strange, therefore, that such conduct on the part of the whites should eventually have awakened distrust and jealousy in the minds of the erstwhile amiable Tuscarora, which, fomented by these and other grievances, finally ripened into a hatred which led to resistance and reprisal.

Perhaps the most lucid and condensed statement of the wrongs suffered by the Tuscarora before vainly attempting to right them is contained in a petition made to the Provincial Government of Pennsylvania in 1710. More than a year before the massacre of 1711 the Tuscarora had officially formulated a number of proposals embodying their grievances and their desire to have these adjusted or removed by the conclusion of peace, and to this end they sent, through the Conestoga (Susquehanna), an embassy with these pacific overtures to the people and government of Pennsylvania. The governor and provincial council dispatched two commissioners to meet this embassy at Conestoga on June 8, 1710, where, in addition to the Tuscarora emissaries, they found Civility and four other Conestoga chiefs, and Opessa, the head chief of the Shawnee. In the presence of these officials the Tuscarora ambassadors delivered their proposals, attested by eight wampum belts, at the same time informing the Pennsylvania commissioners that these were sent as an overture for the purpose of asking for a cessation of hostilities until the following spring, when their chiefs and headmen would come in person "to sue for the peace they so much desired." By the first belt, the elder women and the mothers besought the friendship of the Christian people, the Indians and the government of Pennsylvania, so they might fetch wood and water without risk or danger. By the second, the children born and those about to be born, implored for room to sport and play without the fear of death or slavery. By the third, the young men asked for the privilege to leave their towns without the fear of death or slavery to hunt for meat for their mothers, their children, and the aged ones. By the fourth, the old men, the elders of the people, asked for the consummation of a lasting peace, so that the forest (the paths to other tribes) be as safe for them as their palisaded towns. By the fifth, the entire tribe asked for a firm peace. By the sixth, the chiefs asked for the establishment of a lasting peace with the government, people, and Indians of Pennsylvania, whereby they would be relieved from "those fearful apprehensions they have these several years felt." By the seventh, the Tuscarora begged for a "cessation from mur dering and taking them," so that thereafter they would not fear "a mouse, or anything that ruffles the leaves." By the eighth, the tribe, being strangers to the people and government of Pennsylvania, asked for an official path or means of communication between them.

Stripped of metaphor and the language of diplomacy, the purport of this message is plain; it was the statement of a tribe at bay, that in view of the large numbers of their people who were being kidnapped to be sold into slavery or who were being killed while seeking to defend their offspring and their friends and kindred, they desired to remove to a more just and friendly government than that whence they came. At this time there was no war between them and the white people; there had as yet been no massacre by the Tuscarora, no threat of hostility on the part of the Indians, yet to maintain peace and to avoid the impending shedding of blood, they were even then willing to forsake their homes. The commissioners of Pennsylvania, however, informed the delegates, among other things, that "to confirm the sincerity of their past carriage toward the English, and to raise in us a good opinion of them, it would be very necessary to procure a certificate from the government they leave, to this, of their good behaviour, and then they might be assured of a favourable reception" (Min. Prov. Coun. Pa., II, 511, 1852). The Conestoga ("Seneques") chiefs present at this conference stated that by the advice of their council it had been determined to send these belts, brought by the Tuscarora, to the Five Nations. It was the reception of the belts with their pitiful messages by these Five Nations that moved the latter to take steps to shield and protect the Tuscarora, which gave so much apprehension to the northern colonies.

The rapid encroachment of the whites on the lands of the Tuscarora and their Indian neighbors for a period of sixty years after the first settlements, although there was an air of peace and harmony between the two races, were wrongs which dwarfed in comparison with the continued practice of kidnapping their young to be sold into slavery. This was the true cause of the so-called Tuscarora war in 1711-13. This phase of the question is overlooked or quite disregarded by most historians; but years before the massacre of 1711, Tuscarora Indians were brought into Pennsylvania and sold as slaves, a transaction that excited grave apprehension in the minds of the resident Indian tribes. To allay as much as possible this growing terror among them, the provincial council of Pennsylvania enacted in 1705 that, "Whereas the importation of Indian slaves from Carolina, or other places, hath been observed to give the Indians of this province some umbrage for suspicion and dissatisfaction," such importation be prohibited after Mar. 25, 1706. This enactment was based solely on expediency and self-interest, since it was evident that the Indians to the southward were in a general commotion. During the Tuscarora war an act was passed, June 7, 1712, forbidding the importation of Indians, but providing for their sale as slaves to the highest bidder in case any should be imported for that purpose. It is known that the prisoners of Col. Barnwell and Col. Moore were all sold as slaves, even the northern colonies being canvassed for a market for them; indeed, the *Boston News Letter* of 1713 contained an advertisement offering these very Indians for purchase.

According to De Graffenried, Surveyor-General Lawson in 1709-10 settled his people, the Swiss and Palatines, on the s. bank of Trent r., on a tongue of land called Chattawka, formed by the Trent and the Neuse in North Carolina, in a hot and unhealthful situation. De Graffenried bitterly complained that the Surveyor-General was dishonest for having charged him a "heavy price" for it, and for the consequences of his not knowing that Lawson had no title to the land and that the place was still inhabited by the Indians, although the Surveyor-General had attested that the land was free of encumbrance and unoccupied. This encroachment on the Indian lands was one of the fundamental causes of the so-called Tuscarora war. It is well known that the Coree, together with their close allies, the hostile Tuscarora, in 1711 took vengeance on the Swiss and Palatines settled on Trent r., killing about 70 of them, wounding many others, and destroying much of their property. De Graffenried says that one of the several causes of the war was the "rough treatment of some turbulent Carolinians, who cheated those Indians in trading, and would not allow them to hunt near their plantations, and under that pretense took away from them their game, arms, and ammunition," and that the despised Indians being "insulted in many ways by a few rough Carolinians, more barbarous and inhuman than the savages themselves, could not stand such treatment any longer, and began to think of their safety and of vengeance. What they did they did very secretly."

In a letter of Maj. Christopher Gale to his brother, Nov. 2, 1711, he describes a condition, fairly representative of the times, as to the relations between the whites and the Indians around them. During an attack on one of the many small garrisons maintained for the protection of the settlements, "a number of Indian prisoners of a certain nation, which we did not know, whether they were friends or enemies, rose in the garrison, but were soon cut to pieces, as those on the outside repelled. In the garrison were killed 9 men, and soon after 39 women and children sent off for slaves." This shows that for the purposes of slavery little distinction, if any, was made between one tribe and another.

De Graffenried, while a captive among the hostile Tuscarora, negotiated, subsequent to the execution of the unfortunate Lawson, a private treaty with them by offering to every one of the chiefs of the 10 villages of the hostiles a cloth jerkin, 2 bottles of powder, 500 grains of small shot, 2 bottles of rum, and something more to the head chief for his own ransom. Among other things he agreed to remain neutral during the continuance of the war, and that he, the "said Governor of the German colony promises to remain within his limits and to take no more lands from them without due warning to the king [head chief] and his nation." Thus De Graffenried admitted taking Indian lands without consulting the Indians, although he says elsewhere, "It must be observed that it was neither I, nor my colony, who were the cause of that terrible slaughter or Indian war," apparently overlooking the fact that the greatest massacre was among his own Swiss and Palatines, indicating that the Indians thus resented the wrongs committed by him and his people.

In order to secure the aid of the Catawba ("Flatheads") against the hostile Tuscarora, the Carolina authorities promised them that in the event of success in the war the Indians were to obtain goods "cheaper than formerly." But after faithfully aiding the Carolinians in 1711–13 in dispersing the hostile Tuscarora, the Catawba were deceived as to the promised reduction in the price of goods sold to them, and from this misunderstanding arose the troubles leading later to the Catawba war in 1714–15 (N. Y. Doc. Col. Hist., v, 444, 1855).

The chiefs of the Five Nations, in conference with Gov. Hunter at Albany, Sept. 25, 1714, acquainted him with the fact that the "Tuscarora Indians are come to shelter themselves among the Five Nations; they were of us and went from us long ago, and now are returned and promise to live peaceably among us. And since there is peace now everywhere, we have received them. Do give a belt of wampum. We desire you to look upon the Tuscaroras that are come to live among us as our children, who shall obey our commands and live peace-

ably and orderly" (N. Y. Doc. Col. Hist., v, 387, 1855). This proposal, for it was practically such, was not yet accepted by the New York Government in 1715 (ibid., 413).

On June 23, 1712, Gov. Hunter, of New York, wrote to the Lords of Trade that "the war betwixt the people of North Carolina and the Tuscarora Indians is like to embroil us all," and expressed the fear that under French instigation the Five Nations would fulfill their threat to join the Tuscarora (ibid., 343). Again, on Sept. 10, 1713, Hunter wrote to Secretary Popple that "the Five Nations are hardly to be diswaded from sheltering the Tuscaruro Indians, which would embroil us all," and expressed regret that he had no funds with which to buy presents to be employed in dissuading them from forming an alliance with the Tuscarora.

On Sept. 10, 1713, an Onondaga chief, in conference with commissioners from Gov. Hunter at Onondaga, said: "Brother Corlaer says the Queen's subjects towards the South are now at war with the tus-Carorase Indians. These Indians went out heretofore from us, and have settled themselves there; now they have got into war and are dispersed. . . . They have abandoned their Castles and are scattered hither and thither; let that suffice; and we request our Brother Corlaer to act as mediator between the English of Carrelyna and the tuskaroras that they may no longer be hunted down, and we assure that we will oblige them not to do the English any more harm, for they are no longer a Nation with a name, being once dispersed" (N. Y. Doc. Col. Hist., v, 376, 1855).

In 1717 Gov. Hunter, of New York, informed the Five Nations that there were Virginia traders who still bartered with the Tuscarora, thus showing that, contrary to the common opinion, there were still a part of these Indians in Carolina and s. Virginia.

In a letter dated at Narhantes Fort, Feb. 4, 1712, Col. Barnwell gives a list of the various tribes of Southern Indians who composed his motley army. In his own spelling these were: the Yamasses, Hog Logees, Apalatchees, Corsaboy, Watterees, Sagarees, Catawbas, Suterees, Waxams, Congarees, Sattees, Pedees, Weneaws, Cape Feare, Hoopengs, Wareperes, Saraws, and Saxapahaws. Ft Narhantes, according to Barnwell, was the largest and most warlike town of the Tuscarora. It was situated about 27 m. below a former settlement of the Saxapahaw or "Shacioe Indians," which these Indians had been forced to abandon along with others at the beginning of Feb. 1712, by the Narhantes Tuscarora who had fallen upon them and had killed 16 persons, owing to the refusal of the Saxapahaw to join the Tuscarora against the English. The Saxapahaw had just reached the Wattomas when Barnwell arrived there. After reaching Neuse r. Barnwell numbered his men before crossing, and found that he had 498 Indians and 33 white men. He complained that there was a great desertion of the Indians; that only 67 remained of Capt. Bull's 200. On taking Ft Narhantes, "head Town of ye Tuscaruros," on Jan. 30, 1712, he and his men were greatly surprised and puzzled to find within two log houses much stronger than the outer fort. After gaining an entrance, he says, while "we were putting the men to the sword, our Indians got all the slaves and the plunder, only one girl we gott." This was the strongest fort in that part of the country. His loss was 7 white men killed and at least 32 wounded; the Indian loss was 6 killed and 28 wounded; the Tuscarora loss was 52 men killed and at least 10 women, and 30 prisoners. Barnwell was much chagrined at his great loss, "with no greater execution of ye enemy." De Graffenried, in speaking of this encounter, says he "marched against a great Indian village, called Core, about 30 miles distant from Newbern, drove out the King and his forces, and carried the day with such fury, that, after they had killed a great many, in order to stimulate themselves still more, they cooked the flesh of an Indian 'in good condition' and ate it." So it appears that Narhantes was a Coree village, whose King was called Cor Tom. Barnwell then advanced on Catechna, or King Hencock's town, in which had taken refuge a medley of Indians from the Weetock, Bay, Neuse, Cor, Pamlico, and a portion of the Tuscarora tribe. After two assaults, which the Indians successfully repulsed, Barnwell, in order to save from massacre the white prisoners within the fort, induced the Indians to enter into a truce with him on condition that the white prisoners be liberated; and he returned to Newbern with his small army for refreshment. Barnwell had hoped for great honors and gifts from North Carolina, but being disappointed in this hope, and wishing to return home with his forces with some profit, he lured, under pretence of peace, a large number of the Indians to the neighborhood of Cor village and then broke the truce by capturing them and carrying them away to be sold into slavery. This naturally incensed the Tuscarora and other Carolina Indians, and caused them to lose all confidence in the word of a white man. This change of affairs resulted in repeated raids by the Indians along Neuse and

Pamlico rs., and "the last troubles were worse than the first."

Solicitations by the North Carolina authorities were made to the Government of South Carolina for new aid, which was granted, under Colonel Moore, with a body of 33 white men and more than 900 Indian allies, who were probably reenforced by North Carolina recruits. His objective point was the palisaded town of Catechna, or Hencock's village. In a letter dated Mar. 27, 1713, to President Pollock of North Carolina, just after he had taken the palisaded town of "Neoheroka" in Greene co., N. C., which lay on his route to Catechna, he reported that the attack was begun on the 20th and that on the morning of the 23d "wee had gott ye fort to ye ground." He states that the prisoners taken were 392, that the scalps taken in the fort numbered 192, that there were 200 killed and burned in the fort, and 166 persons killed and taken "out of ye fort on ye Scout," a total of 950. His own loss was 22 white men killed and 36 wounded; the loss of his Indians was 35 killed and 58 wounded. This severe loss so awed the Tuscarora that they abandoned fort "Cohunche," situated at Hencock's town, and migrated northward toward the territory of the Five Nations.

Prior to the arrival of Col. Moore, President Pollock had entered into an arrangement with Tom Blunt, the leading chief of the "Northern Tuscarora," to seize chief Hencock, who was the reputed head of the hostile Tuscarora, and to bring him alive to the President for the purpose of adjusting their mutual difficulties and to negotiate peace. Blunt's Tuscarora were to destroy the hostiles who had taken part in the massacre and to deliver hostages for their own good behavior—this arrangement was to continue only until the new year. After the defeat of the Tuscarora by Moore, another treaty was made with Tom Blunt and his Tuscarora, thus leaving as hostile only the small tribes of the Coree, Matamuskeet, and Catechna. All of Moore's Indians except about 180 returned to South Carolina to sell their captives into slavery. With the remaining forces Moore soon reduced and drove away the few remaining hostiles.

The date of the adoption of the Tuscarora into the council board of the League of the Iroquois, through the Oneida, their political sponsors, is indefinite, judging from the differing dates, ranging from 1712 to 1715, given by various well-informed writers. In their forced migration northward the Tuscarora did not all decamp at once. The hostiles and their most apprehensive sympathizers were most probably the first to leave their ancient homes in North Carolina. On the total defeat and dispersion of the hostile Tuscarora and their allies in 1713, the scattered fragments of tribes fled and sought an asylum with other tribes, among whom their identity was not always maintained. Although the Five Nations gave asylum to the fugitive Tuscarora, there is also abundant evidence that, for political reasons perhaps, the Tuscarora were not for many years after their flight from North Carolina formally admitted into the Council Board of the League of the Five Nations as a constitutive member. The fact is that the Tuscarora were 90 years in removing from their North Carolina home to more friendly dwelling-places in the N., and there is no evidence that they were formally incorporated into the confederation of the Five Nations, as a coequal member, before Sept. 1722. On Sept. 6, 1722, Gov. Burnet held a conference with the Five Nations at Albany, at which Governor Spotswood of Virginia was present. For the purpose of preventing forays between the Five Nations and their allies on the one hand, and the Southern Indians on the other, Spotswood induced the Five Nations to consent to the running of a dividing line along the Potomac and the high ridge of the Allegany mtns. This agreement was made in the name of the Five Nations and the Tuscarora, indicating that the latter had become a factor in the councils of the League of the Iroquois. In closing the conference, it is stated that the Indians "gave six shouts—five for the Five Nations and one for the castle of Tuscaroras, lately seated between the Oneidas and Onondagas." The record continues that at the conclusion of this conference, on Sept. 13, the Five Nations sought a special interview with the Governor of Pennsylvania, and that on Sept. 14 the governor received "the ten chiefs of the Five Nations, being two from each, together with two others, said to be of the Tuscororoes." This appears to be the first official mention of the Tuscarora as taking part in the management of the public affairs of the League. The Tuscarora mentioned here, however, did not include those who dwelt on the Juniata and on the Susquehanna at Oquaga and its environs, nor those still in North Carolina.

In a petition of John Armstrong for land lying in Tuscarora valley on Juniata r., Pa., about 6 m. from the mouth of Tuscarora cr., the Indians living there at that time are called Lakens; this land was taken up by Armstrong on Feb. 3, 1755. On the same day, George Armstrong obtained a warrant for land situated on the s. side of Tuscarora cr., "opposite to the settlement of the Indians called Lackens." It would thus appear

that at this date this band of Tuscarora were known, at least locally, as Lakens or Lackens.

Elias Johnson, in his Legends, says that it was the Seneca who first adopted the Tuscarora as a constituent member of the League. This, however, is at variance with the common but authentic traditions of all the tribes and with the official statement of Col. (afterward Sir) William Johnson to the Oneida, made at Mt Johnson, Sept. 8, 1753. He said, "Brethren of Oneida. . . . My best advice is to have your castles as near together as you conveniently can with the Tuscaroras, who belong to you as children, and the Scanihaderadighroones lately come into your alliance or families, which makes it necessary for me to fix a new string to the cradle which was hung up by your forefathers when they received the Tuscaroras, . . . to feed and protect."

After the close of the war of 1711–13 in North Carolina, the neutral Tuscarora, with remnants of allied tribes still remaining in that country, were placed under the rule of chief Tom Blunt, or Blount, by treaty with the provincial government of North Carolina. From an act of the general assembly of North Carolina, in 1778, it is learned that Withmell Tuffdick was then the ruling chief; but the last ruling chief of the North Carolina Tuscarora was Samuel Smith, who died in 1802.

In 1767, the renown of the Moravian mission station at Friedenshuetten (q. v.) in Pennsylvania was so great that many Indians from various tribes, including the Tuscarora, probably from Oquaga, Ingaren, and vicinity, were constantly stopping there. Many passed through it merely to see a place so famous for its hospitality. In May, 1766, 75 Tuscarora, according to Loskiel, on their way from North Carolina, halted here and remained for some weeks. They are described as lazy and "refuse to hear religion." During their stay the Tuscarora were so alarmed at the sight of the first snow that they left their huts down by the river and took refuge with the missionaries. A number of Tuscarora arrived at the mission to remain there; these had planted their crops during 1766 at the mouth of Tuscarora cr., Wyoming co., Pa.

On Dec. 16, 1766, Sir William Johnson received at Mt Johnson, N. Y., 160 Tuscarora who had just arrived from North Carolina. They complained to him that on their way thither they had been robbed at Paxtang, in Pennsylvania, of their horses and other property to the value of about $300.

Later the Tuscarora on the Susquehanna, dwelling at Oquaga and in its vicinity, had lands assigned them by the

Oneida, their political sponsors. These lands were bounded on the E. by Unadilla r., on the w. by the Chenango, and on the s. by the Susquehanna. In the northern part of this allotment were situated the towns of Ganasaraga, on the site of Sullivan, Madison co., N. Y., and Kaunehsuntahkeh. A number of the Tuscarora lived with the Oneida in their chief village. On these lands a large portion of the Tuscarora remained until the events of the Revolution displaced them. By the terms of the treaty of Ft Herkimer in 1785 with the state of New York, to which the Tuscarora were nominal parties, the Oneida, the original proprietors of the lands then occupied by the Tuscarora, conveyed to New York the lands of the Tuscarora and retained the proceeds of the sale; thus the Tuscarora were again without a home. Thereafter they became dispersed. Later they had a village, called Junastriyo (Tcunästri′io') in the Genessee valley, below Avon, N. Y.; another, called Jutaneaga (Tcutänĕñ′′kiä'), at the fork of Chittenango cr.; and another called Kanhato (Kă′n-'ha′′nŭ').

According to Johnson (Legends, etc.) a part of the fugitive Tuscarora settled at a point about 2 m. w. of Tamaqua, Schuylkill co., Pa., where they planted apple trees and lived for a number of years. It is probable that it was these Tuscarora who later removed to Oquaga, in the vicinity of which they had three other towns in 1778. Another band of fugitives settled in Tuscarora valley (as it was called later from them), on Juniata r., Pa. They remained here at least as late as 1762. In a minute of a conference held at Lancaster, Pa., Aug. 11, 1762, between Lieut. Gov. Hamilton of Pennsylvania and delegates from the Ohio Delawares, the Tuscarora of Oquaga and Lower Tuscarora, the Shawnee, the Kickapoo, the Wea, and the Miami, it is stated that six Tuscarora were present, of whom three were chiefs, who brought from their people a letter in which they asked the Governor to furnish them with a pass, saying, "We should be glad to be informed of the state and behavior of our brethren in Tuscarora valley, and to have some directions about the way, as we propose to make them a visit, and also should be glad of a pass or recommendation in writing, that we may be friendly received on our way to and at the valley."

Major portions of the Oneida and the Tuscarora, in accordance with standing agreements with the United Colonies, remained faithful to the American cause during the Revolution. When the Indian allies of the British, even some of their brethren of the Six Nations, learned that a majority of the Tuscarora had cast their lot with the Colonies, they invaded the Tuscarora country, burned their lodges, and destroyed their crops and other property. Thus again by the fortunes of war the Tuscarora were scattered and homeless. A large party of these settled at a place called Oyonwayea, or Johnson's Landing, in Niagara co., N. Y., about 4 m. E. of the outlet of Niagara r., at the mouth of Four Mile cr., in order not to be directly among the many Indians friendly to the British cause camped around Ft Niagara. At the close of the war, two families, probably clans, of Tuscarora from Oyonwayea made their way to the N. E. limits of their present reservation, where they found many walnuts and butternuts, and a fine stream. Here they decided to winter. Being missed from Oyonwayea, scouts were sent out, who found them in their newly chosen settlement, a situation so favorable that, after the gratuitous cession of their former home among the Oneida, Oyonwayea was abandoned and all the families removed to the new site. Although the Tuscarora had only a tacit permission from the Seneca to reside at this place, the last settlement became the foundation of the present Tuscarora reservation in New York. At the treaty held at Genessee, Sept. 15, 1797, between Robert Morris and the Seneca tribe, the Tuscarora chiefs complained, for the first time since their admission to the councils of the League, that the Five Nations had from time to time allotted lands to their people, but that each time these lands had been included in a subsequent cession to the whites, and that the Tuscarora had received nothing in return for their right of occupancy or for their improvements. The justice and merits of their complaint having been acknowledged by the Five Nations, Morris reserved to the Tuscarora, by grant, two square miles, covering their settlement on the ridge mentioned above, and the Seneca thereupon granted them an adjoining square mile. About 1800–02 a deputation was sent to North Carolina to learn whether they could obtain funds in payment for the lands they formerly occupied there, with the result that, by aid of the North Carolina legislature, they were able to lease the Carolina lands, which yielded a fund of $13,722. This sum enabled the Secretary of War in 1804, under authority of Congress, to purchase 4,329 acres for the Tuscarora from the Holland Land Co., adjoining the three square miles already occupied by them. Such is the origin of the land holdings of the New York Tuscarora.

It was while the Tuscarora deputation was in North Carolina that the remnant of the tribe still residing there was brought to the N. and joined their brethren in New York state.

The Tuscarora in sympathy with those of the Six Nations that adhered to the cause of Great Britain in the Revolution were granted lands in severalty on Grand River res., Ontario.

The evangelizing work of Christian missionaries began among the Tuscarora in w. New York as early as 1805 under the patronage of the New York Missionary Society. At first there were only six persons among the Tuscarora willing to abjure their ancient faith and customs, at least in name and appearance, and join in the missionary work; the remainder were generally strongly averse to the work of the missionaries. So violent were the struggles between the two unequal parties that in the spring of 1820 the "pagans" succeeded in inducing about 70 persons to emigrate to Canada, where they settled among the pagans of the Six Nations on the Grand River res., Ontario. The church membership at this time was 16 persons. Little progress was apparent in the education of the Tuscarora, although the New York Society had maintained a school among them.

Ethnology.—The Tuscarora in New York are governed by a council of irresponsible chiefs, for the Indians have forgotten and so neglect the means to be employed in enforcing the will of the clan in case a chief fails in his plain duty; the criminal law of New York at this point nullifies the early sovereignty of the clan over its members. In common with the other tribes of the Iroquoian linguistic stock, the Tuscarora traced the descent of blood through the line of the mother, and made the civil and official military chieftainships hereditary in the *ohwatcira* of certain clans (see *Clans*) over which the woman chiefs and the elder women presided. The simplest political unit was the *ohwatcira*, of which one or more constituted a clan, which was the simplest organized political unit. The Tuscarora were constituted of at least eight clans, which primitively were organized into phratries. There are no data, other than those furnished by tradition and analogy, as to the organization of the Tuscarora confederation. The clans were exogamic as to their own members, as were also the phratries in primitive times. The Tuscarora of New York being completely isolated from any of their own people who still profess their ancient dogmas and beliefs and who still practise their ancient rites and ceremonies, have preserved only a hazy recollection of their early customs, ceremonies, and rites; even less do they comprehend the meaning of the ceremonies still practised by the so-called pagan members of cognate tribes. They are all professed Christians, and so turn away from the old forms of thought and practice of their ancestors.

The exact number of clans still existing among the Tuscarora is not definitely known, for the native authorities themselves do not agree on the number and the names of those still recognized—some informants give seven, while others with equal credibility give eight. There is likewise some diversity in regard to the correct names of certain clans. One list has Bear, Wolf, Turtle, Beaver, Deer, Eel, and Snipe; another has Bear, Eel, Large Turtle, Small Turtle, Beaver, Deer, Wolf, and Snipe; still another list has Bear, Eel, Deer, Turtle, Gray Wolf, Yellow Wolf, Beaver, and Snipe; and yet another is like the last, except that the Turtle clan is replaced by the clans Small Turtle and Large Turtle. Like differences appear in the lists of clans of the other Iroquois tribes.

The names of the civil chiefs still in use among the present two divisions of the Tuscarora (that in Ontario and the other in w. New York) are: (A) *Säkwari′çrä′* (Sacharissa), 'The spear trailer'; Ni‘hawĕñnä′′ă‘, 'His voice is small'; *Hotio‘kwawă′′kĕn‘*, 'He holds or grasps the multitude,' or possibly, 'He holds or grasps his own loins'; these three belong to the Turtle clan. (B) *Näkäiĕñ′tĕn* (signification not clear); *Utäkwă‘tĕn′ă‘*, 'The Bear cub'; *Ionĕñtchänĕñ′′năkĕn‘*, 'Its fore-paw pressed against its breast'; these three belong to the Bear clan. (C) *Näio‘käwe′′ă‘* (signification not known); *Neiotchă′k′doñ‘*, 'It is bent'; these two belong to the Wolf clan. (D) *Karoñdawă′′kĕn‘*, 'One is holding the tree'; *Thanädăk′hwă′* (signification not clear); these two belong to the Snipe clan. (E) *Kari‘hĕñ′tiä′*, 'It goes along teaching'; *Ni‘hno‘kä′wä′*, 'He annoints the hide'; *Näkă‘hĕñwă′′ç‘hĕñ*, 'It is twenty canoes'; these three belong to the Beaver clan. Among the Canadian Tuscarora on Grand River res., Ontario, the first and last names of the Turtle clan, the first title of the Wolf clan, and the first title of the Snipe clan appear to be the only ones now in use, although these four titles are questionably also in use among the New York Tuscarora.

There is no definite information available as to the former and more complete organization into clan phratries. Some of the translations of the chieftain titles above would seem to indicate that they were originally designations of some habit, attitude, or other characteristic feature of the clan tutelary or patron, questionably called "totem". The clan name, with one or two exceptions, is not the ordinary name of the clan guardian or patron, but is rather descriptive of some feature or attitude, or is the name of the usual habitat, of the tutelary; for example, the name of the Bear clan signifies literally, 'Broken-off tail'; that of the Plover or Killdee (Snipe), 'Clean-sand people'; that of the Beaver, 'People of the stream'; that of the Turtle clan, 'Climbing-the-mountain people,' named from the position of the turtle basking; etc. It is probable that plover or killdee should be substituted in the foregoing lists of clans, for the name clearly refers to the killdee's habit of running along the clean sand at the water's edge.

De Graffenried gives (N. C. Col. Rec., I, 905 et seq.) an interesting account of the preparations made for the execution of Lawson and himself by the hostile Tuscarora. In the open space or public square mentioned there was a large fire, near which was the shaman or high priest, a grizzled sorcerer, who made two white rings on the ground, whether of flour or white sand was not stated. In front of the two victims was placed a wolf skin, and a short distance farther there stood an Indian in a terrifying posture, holding in one hand a knife and in the other a tomahawk; he was apparently the executioner. He did not move from the spot. On the farther side of the fire were assembled young men, women, and children, who danced with weird and frightful contortions and attitudes. In the center of the circle of dancers were seated two singers who intoned a dismal song, "rather fit to provoke tears and anger than joy." Within the circle of dancers the shaman stood unterrified, uttering his threatenings and adjurations and performing his exorcisms, against the foes of his people and their *orenda* or "medicine," when there would come a pause in the dancing. Finally, with shouts and howls the dancers ran into the neighboring forest. In a short time they returned with their faces painted black, white, and red, in bands, and with their hair loose and flying, oiled and sprinkled with fine down or cotton from the cattail flag and with small white feathers, and some returned arrayed in all kinds of furs. After their return, the dance was renewed. Back of the two victims stood a double line of armed warriors who kept their posts until everything was over; back of this guard was the council of war, whose members were seated on the ground in a circle, gravely deliberating on the fate of the two noted prisoners. Finally, they acted on the advice of "King" Tom Blunt, the head-chief of their neighbors, "the villages of the Tuscaroros," properly so called, that King Hencock should liberate De Graffenried, and could deal with Lawson as

he and his council pleased. The manner of Lawson's death, as learned from Indian information, is found in a letter of Maj. Christopher Gale to his brother, Nov. 2, 1711, wherein it is said that the Indians stuck the unfortunate prisoner "full of fine small splinters of torchwood, like hogs' bristles, and so set them gradually on fire." De Graffenried was not permitted to know how Lawson was executed.

To this account of the Tuscarora method of preparing for the execution of captives may be added their triumphal ceremonies which De Graffenried says they performed after their defeat of a relief party of Swiss and Palatines. He reports that they built bonfires at night, and especially a large one in the place of executions, where they raised "three wolf's hides, figuring as many protectors or gods," to which offerings, consisting of their jewels, were made by the women. In the middle of the circle, the chief shaman performed all manner of contortions, conjurations, and imprecations against the enemies of his country, while the populace danced in a circle around the wolf-hides.

The council of "King" Hencock, which consisted of 40 elders, was called by the Tuscarora, according to De Graffenried, the "Assembly of the Great," a translation of the Tuscarora terms for the council of chiefs, the general word for chief signifying 'one is great,' either in size or position. At the council before which Lawson and De Graffenried were tried the "forty elders" were seated around a great fire kindled in a large open space devoted to important festivals and public executions. On this occasion these chiefs and the accused were seated on rush mats, which were customarily provided for the comfort of guests as a mark of deference and honor. Although the two captives were acquitted by the first council, they were again tried before a second council, after Lawson incautiously had had a bitter quarrel with Cor Tom, the chief of Cor town, who was not at the first council. The two captives were not given mats upon which to sit, and Lawson was condemned to death and De Graffenried was acquitted.

Lawson asserts that the most powerful tribe "scorns to treat or trade with any others, of fewer numbers and less power in any other tongue but their own, which serves for the lingua of the country; with which we travel and deal." As an example of this, the Tuscarora are cited. Being the most numerous tribe in North Carolina, their language was necessarily understood by some persons in every town of all the neighboring tribes.

The Tuscarora carried on a pernicious trade in rum with the Indians dwelling to their westward. In 1708 rum had been but recently introduced among the latter, chiefly by the Tuscarora, who transported it in rundlets several hundred miles, amongst other Indians. They sold it at " so many mouthfuls for a buckskin, they never using any other measure," the buyer always choosing a man having the largest mouth possible to accompany him to the market, and the mouthful was scrupulously emptied into a bowl brought for the purpose. The Tuscarora also traded with the Shakori and Occaneechi, selling them wooden bowls and ladles for rawhides.

Their lodges, usually round in form, were constructed of poles, covered with the bark of cypress, red or white cedar, or sometimes pine. At one place Lawson met more than 500 Tuscarora in one body in a hunting camp. They had constructed their lodges with bark, "not with round tops, as they commonly use, but ridge fashion, after the manner of most Indians." Among them he found much corn, while meat and venison were scarce, because of the great number of people, for although they were expert hunters, they were too populous for one range.

According to Lawson, the native Tuscarora of North Carolina had rather flat bodies, due probably to the fact that in early infancy the children were swathed to cradle-boards. He adds: "They are not of so robust and strong bodies as to lift great burdens, and endure labor and slavish work, as Europeans are; yet some that are slaves prove very good and laborious." They were dextrous and steady, and collected in the use of their hands and feet; their bearing was sedate and majestic; their eyes were commonly full and manly, being black or dark hazel in color, and the white of the eye was usually marbled with red lines; their skin was tawny, and somewhat darkened by the habit of anointing it with bear's oil and a pigment resembling burnt cork. When they wished to be very fine they mixed with the oil a certain red powder made from a scarlet root growing in the hilly country. This root was held in great esteem among them, selling it one to another at a very high price, on account of the distance from which it came and the danger to which they were exposed in obtaining it. The Tuscarora and other Indians attempted to cultivate this plant, but it would not grow in their land. As a substitute they sometimes used puccoon root, which also has a crimson color, but this dyed the hair an ugly hue. The heads even of the aged were scarcely ever bald; their teeth were tinged yellow from smoking tobacco, to which habit both men and women were much addicted; they however did not snuff or chew tobacco. They plucked the hair from their faces and bodies. There were but few deformed or crippled persons among them.

The Tuscarora had many dances suitable to various occasions; these as a rule were accompanied with public feasts prepared under the direction of the women chiefs. Every dance had its peculiar song, but probably was not changed for every occasion on which the dance was performed, although Lawson states that "all these songs are made new for every feast; nor is one and the same song sung at two several festivals. Some one of the nation, which has the best gift of expressing their designs, is appointed by their king and war captains to make these songs." To these festivals the people came from all the towns within 50 or 60 m., "where they buy and sell several commodities."

The Tuscarora, in like measure with the northern Iroquois, were passionately given to gaming, frequently stripping one another of every piece of property available. Sometimes they went even so far as to bet themselves away to the winner, readily becoming his slave until he or his relatives could pay the redemption price; nevertheless they bore their losses with great equanimity, no matter how ruinous they were. Among their games was that of a bundle of 51 split reeds about 7 in. in length and neatly made. The game consisted in throwing a part of the bundle before an opponent, who must on sight guess the number thrown. It is said that experts were able to tell the number correctly ten times in ten throws. A set of these reeds was valued at a dressed doe skin. The Tuscarora also had the well-known bowl and plum-seed game, which is such an important adjunct to the thanksgiving festivals of the northern Iroquois. They also had a number of other games, but some of their neighbors had games which they did not have.

There were feasts among the Tuscarora when several villages united to celebrate some event or when two or more tribes assembled to negotiate peace. There were feasts and dances of thanksgiving, and invocations to the gods that watched over their harvests, when their crops were garnered and when the first fruits of the year were gathered.

Population.—No trustworthy estimates of the Tuscarora population at any given date, exclusive of those of Lawson and Barnwell, previous to 1830, are available for the entire Tuscarora people. The earliest and perhaps most authoritative estimate of the total Tuscarora population at a given time was that of Lawson in 1708. His estimate of 15 towns and 1,200 fighting men would indicate a population of about 4,800 at that date; Colonel Barnwell's figures are somewhat larger than Lawson's, though they appear to be conservative; his estimate was 1,200 to 1,400 warriors, or a maximum population of about 5,600 persons. The estimate of Chauvignerie in 1736 was 250 warriors, or about 1,000 persons. His estimate was restricted to the Tuscarora living near Oneida, N. Y., hence did not include those living in North Carolina or on the Susquehanna and Juniata rs. Other estimates of this group give them 1,000 (1765), 2,000 (1778), 1,000 (1783), 400 (1796) in the United States; 414 (1885) in New York and an equal number in Canada, or a total of 828; 364 (1909) in New York, and 416 (1910) in Canada, a total of 780.

Settlements.—The following Tuscarora towns have been mentioned in writings pertaining to this people: Annaooka, Chunaneets, Coerntha, Cohunche, Conauhkare, Contahnah, Cotechney, Coram, Corutra, Eno, Ganasaraga, Ganatisgowa, Harooka, Harutawaqui, Ingaren, Junastriyo, Jutaneaga, Kanhato, Kaunehsuntahkeh, Kenta, Kentanuska, Naurheghne, Nonawharitse; Nursoorooka, Nyuchirhaan, Ohagi, Oonossora, Oneida (in part), Oquaga, Shawhiangto, Tasqui, Tiochcrungwe, Tonarooka, Torhunte, Tosneoc, Tuscarora, Unanauhan, Ucouhnerunt. Some of these towns were in North Carolina, others on Juniata r. in Pennsylvania, others on the Susquehanna in Pennsylvania, others on the Susquehanna in New York, while others were s. of Oneida lake in New York, and one in Genessee valley. The exact situation of the majority of these towns is not definitely known. In some instances the Tuscarora shared a town with other tribes, as was the case at Anajot (Oneida, or Ganowarohare) and Onohoquaga.

Treaties.—The Tuscarora have taken part in the following treaties between the United States and the Six Nations: Ft Stanwix, N. Y., Oct. 22, 1784; Ft Harmar, Ohio, Jan. 9, 1789; Canandaigua (Konondaigua), N. Y., Nov. 11, 1794; Oneida, N. Y., Dec. 2, 1794; Buffalo Creek, N. Y., Jan. 15, 1838.

For further information consult Elias Johnson (native Tuscarora), Legends, Traditions and Laws of the Iroquois, or Six Nations, and History of the Tuscarora Indians, 1881; Documents Relating to the Colonial History of New York, I–XI, 1855–61; Documentary History of New York, I–IV, 1849–51; Pennsylvania Archives, I–XII, 1852–56; Minutes of the Provincial Council of Pennsylvania (Colonial Records), I–XVI, 1852–53; South Carolina Historical and Genealogical Magazine, I–X, especially IX and X; Virginia Magazine, I–XV, 1893–1908; Lawson, History of Carolina, 1714, repr. 1860;

Publications of the Buffalo Hist. Soc., especially vol. VI. (J. N. B. H.)
Ă-ko-t'ăs-kă-ro'-rĕⁿ'.—Hewitt, Mohawk MS. vocab., B. A. E., 1884 (Mohawk name). **Ani'-Skălă'-lĭ.**—Mooney in 19th Rep. B. A. E., 509, 1900 (Cherokee name). **A-Skălă'lĭ.**—Ibid. (or Skălă'lĭ; sing. form). **Ă-t'ăs-kă-lo'-lĕⁿ'.**—Hewitt, Oneida MS. vocab., B. A. E., 1882 (an Oneida name). **Caskarorins.**—Document *ca.* 1758 in N. Y. Doc. Col. Hist., X, 675, 1858. **Caskarouns.**—Mackenzie, Voy., app., 315, 1802. **Dus-ga-o'-weh'.**—Morgan, League Iroq., 53, 1851. **Kaskarorens.**—Montreal Conference (1754) in N. Y. Doc. Col. Hist., X, 267, 1858. **Keew-ahomomy.**—Irvine (1728) in Col. Rec. N. C., II, 812, 1886 (given as the Saponi name; the correct form is probably Tewohomomy, as given by the Va. boundary commissioners; cf. *Dus-gaoweh* ante). **Skălă'lĭ-.**—Mooney in 19th Rep. B. A. E., 509, 1900 (Cherokee name, sing. form; see *A-Skălă'lĭ*, ante). **Skă-ru'-rĕⁿ.**—Hewitt, Tuscarora MS. vocab., B. A. E., 1880 (name used by the tribe). **Tachekaroreins.**—Document of 1741 in N. Y. Doc. Col. Hist., IX, 1081, 1855. **Tascorins.**—Quebec Conference (1748), ibid., X, 186, 1858. **Tascororins.**—Quebec Conference (1748), ibid., 187. **Tascuroreus.**—Chauvignerie (1736) in Schoolcraft, Ind. Tribes, III, 555, 1853. **Taska'ho.**—Gatschet, Wyandot MS., B. A. E., 1881 (Wyandot name). **T'ăs-kă-lo'-lĕⁿ'.**—Hewitt, Oneida MS. vocab., B. A. E., 1882 (an Oneida name). **Taskalo'nugi.**—Gatschet, Shawnee MS., 1879 (Shawnee name). **Taskarorens.**—Duquesne (1754) in N. Y. Doc. Col. Hist., X, 266, 1858. **Taskarosins.**—Writer of 1756, ibid., 487 (misprint). **Taskiroras.**—Lederer (1670) quoted by Hawks, N. C., II, 51, 1858. **Taskororins.**—Letter of 1756 in N. Y. Doc. Col. Hist., X, 480, 1858. **Tasks.**—Spotswood (1717) in Va. Hist. Soc. Coll., n. s., II, 236, 1885. **Tescarorins.**—Document of 1747 in N. Y. Doc. Col. Hist., X, 97, 1858. **Tewohomomy.**—Va. Boundary Comrs. (1728) in Col. Rec. N. C., II, 786, 1886 (?Saponi name; Irvine gives the word as Keew-aho, probably a misprint). **Tharhkarorin.**—Vaudreuil (1755) in N. Y. Doc. Col. Hist., X, 322, 1858. **Theskaroriens.**—Vaudreuil (1755), ibid., 377. **Toscororas.**—Trader (1778) in Schoolcraft, Ind. Tribes, III, 561, 1853. **Toskiroros.**—Lederer map (1670) in Hawks, N. C., II, 1858. **Touscaroros.**—Homann Heirs' map, 1756. **Turcaroras.**—Macauley, N. Y., II, 178–9, 1829 (misprint). **tuscarara.**—Hunter (1712) in N. Y. Doc. Col. Hist., V, 343, 1855. **Tuscararo.**—Humphreys, Acct., X, 1730. **Tuscareras.**—Memoir of 1727 in N. Y. Doc. Col. Hist., IX, 998, 1855. **Tuscarooroes.**—Document of 1726 in Col. Rec. N. C., II, 644, 1886. **Tuscarora.**—Lords of Trade (1712) in N. Y. Doc. Col. Hist., V, 346, 1855. **Tuscaroras.**—Albany Conference (1714) quoted by Ruttenber, Tribes Hudson R., 190, 1872. **tusCarorase.**—Hansen (1713) in N. Y. Doc. Col. Hist., V, 376, 1855. **Tuscaroraw.**—La Tour map, 1782. **Tuscarore haga.**—Pyrlaeus map (*ca.* 1750) quoted in Am. Antiq., IV, 75, 1882. **Tuscarorens.**—Chauvignerie (1736) in N. Y. Doc. Col. Hist., IX, 1057, 1855. **Tuscarories.**—Carver, Travels, 173, 1778. **Tuscaroroes.**—Ffrench & Worley (1710) in Day, Penn., 391, 1843. **Tuscarow.**—Humphreys, Acct., 26, 1730. **Tuscarura.**—Lords of Trade (1712) in N. Y. Doc. Col. Hist., V, 346, 1855. **Tuscaruro.**—Spotswood (1711) in Col. Rec. N. C., I, 796, 1886. **Tuscoraras.**—Turkish Spy quoted by Malcolme, Collection of Letters, 1739. **Tuscorora.**—Writer, *ca.* 1795, in Drake, Bk. Inds., bk. 5, 94, 1848. **Tuscorooroes.**—Pollock (1712) in Col. Rec. N. C., I, 893, 1886. **Tuscoroura.**—Spotswood (1713), ibid., II, 79, 1886. **Tuscorure.**—Spotswood (1711), ibid., I, 782, 1886. **Tuscouroro.**—Spotswood (1713), ibid., II, 15, 1886. **T'us-kai'-y'ĕⁿ'.**—Hewitt, Onondaga MS. vocab., B. A. E., 1882 (Onondaga name). **T'us-kă-o-wäⁿ'.**—Hewitt, Cayuga MS. vocab., B. A. E., 1884 (Cayuga name). **Tuskararo.**—Assembly (1722) in Col. Rec. N. C., II, 456, 1886. **Tuskaroes.**—Document of 1733 in N. Y. Doc. Col. Hist., V, 963, 1855. **Tuskarooroe.**—Assembly (1721) in Col. Rec. N. C., II, 428, 1886. **tuskarora.**—Document of 1711, ibid., I, 819, 1886. **Tuskarorahs.**—Penhallow (1726) in N. H. Hist. Soc. Coll., I, 79, 1824. **Tuskarorers.**—Albany Conference (1746) in N. Y. Doc. Col. Hist., VI, 317, 1855. **Tuskarores.**—Albany Conference (1722)

ibid., v, 660, 1855. **Tuskarorins.** — Montreal Conference (1756), ibid., x, 500, 1858. **Tuskaroro.**—Assembly of 1723 in Col. Rec. N. C., II, 485, 1886. **Tuskawres.**—Albany Conference (1744) in N. Y. Doc. Col. Hist., VI, 264, 1855. **T'us-ke-o'wän'.**—Hewitt, Seneca MS. vocab., B. A. E., 1880 (Seneca name). **Tuskeroode.**—Irvine (1728) in Col. Rec. N. C., II, 812, 1886 (a creek). **Tuskeruda.**—Va. Boundary Comrs. (1728), ibid., 786. **Tuskeruros.**—Lawson (1700), Hist. Car., 103, 1860. **Tuskierores.**—Albany Conference (1737) in N. Y. Doc. Col. Hist., VI, 107, 1855. **Tuskoraries.**—Goldthwait (1766) in Mass. Hist. Soc. Coll., 1st s., x, 121, 1809. **Tuskorore.**—Albany Conference (1715) in N. Y. Doc. Col. Hist., v, 444, 1855. **Tuskroroes.** — Assembly of 1723 in Col. Rec. N. C., II, 485, 1886. **Tusks.**—Spotswood (1713), ibid., 26. **Tuskurora.** — Assembly of 1714, ibid., 140. **Tusquarores.** — Albany Conference (1724) in N. Y. Doc. Col. Hist., v, 713, 1855. **Tusqueroro.**—Document of 1711 in Col. Rec. N. C., I, 818, 1886.

Tuscarora. The name°of three former villages of the Tuscarora in the 18th century: One is placed by the Brion de la Tour map of 1781 a short distance E. of "Anatsagane" (probably the present Stockbridge, Madison co., N.Y); another was situated about 3 m. below Oquaga, Broome co., N. Y., on the w. side of the Susquehanna, approximately on the site of Windsor, and at the time it was destroyed by Col. Butler, in 1778, it contained 7 or 8 houses; the last was situated 12 m. by land and 20 by water below Oquaga, in the vicinity of Great Bend, Susquehanna co., Pa., and was destroyed by Gen. Clinton, Aug. 17, 1779. The last may possibly be identical with Ingaren, but as there were three other Tuscarora villages in this vicinity, the identification is uncertain.   (J. N. B. H.)

Tushepaw. A term used by Lewis and Clark to designate the Indians "residing on a N. fork of Clark r., in the Rocky mts. in spring and summer, and on the Missouri in winter." They have not been positively identified, but the evidence (Gibbs et al.) makes it probable that they were Kutenai. According to Gatschet the term (Túshipa) is a Shoshoni designation for the tribes living to the N. of them and including the Nez Percés as well as the Kutenai. It is probable that the term as employed by Lewis and Clark included both the tribes named as well as bands of the Wallawalla and possibly other Shahaptian divisions. Lewis and Clark mention the Ootlashoot, Micksucksealton, and Hohilpo as Tushepaw tribes. None of these has been identified. The Tushepaw proper numbered 430, in 35 houses, in 1805.   (L. F.)
Flatheads.—Lewis and Clark, Discov., 59, 1806. **Tah-se-pah.**—Gebow, Sho-sho-nay Vocab., 11, 1868 (Shoshoni name). **Tåsh-è-på.**—Long, Exped. Rocky Mts., II, lxxix, 1823 (sig. 'pierced noses'). **Tate Platt.**—Orig. Jour. Lewis and Clark, VI, 111, 1905. **Tátsepa.**—Gebow, op. cit. **Toustchipas.**—Hunt in Nouv. Ann. Voy., x, 74, 1821. **Tuchapacs.**—Gass, Voyage, 203, 1807. **Tuchapaks.**—Lewis, Travels, 22, 1809. **Tuckapacks.**—Clark (1806) quoted by Janson, Stranger in Am., 233, 1807. **Tucknapax.**—Gass, Journal, 132, 1810. **Tus-che-pas.**—Irving, Astoria, 315, 1849. **Tushapaws.**—Orig. Jour. Lewis and Clark, III, 27, 1905. **Tus-he-pah.**—Lewis and Clark Exped., I, map, 1817. **Tushepahas.**—Drake, Bk. Inds., xii, 1848. **Tushepau.**—Orig. Jour. Lewis and Clark, III, 52, 1905. **Tushepaw Flatheads.**—Lewis and Clark Exped., I, 445, 1814. **Tushepaws.**—Ibid., 440. **Tushshepah.**—Ibid., II, 471, 1814. **Tussapa.**—Gass, Journal, 132, 1810. **Tut-see'-wâs.**—Lewis and Clark Discov., 59, 1806 (native name).

Tushguesta. A former village connected with San Carlos mission, Cal., and said to have been Esselen.—Taylor in Cal. Farmer, Apr. 20, 1860.

Tushkisath (*Tuckis'a'th*). A sept of the Toquart, a Nootka tribe.—Boas in 6th Rep. N. W. Tribes Can., 32, 1890.

Tushquegan. An Ottawa village, taking its name from the chief, who was also known as McCarty, that former y existed on the s. bank of Maumee r opposite Toledo, Ohio. The reservat a was sold in 1833.
M'Carty's village.—Maumee treaty (1819) in U. S. Ind. Treat., 205, 1873. **Tushquegan.**—Ibid.

Tushtun ('dragon-fly'). An Apache clan or band at San Carlos agency and Ft Apache, Ariz., in 1881.—Bourke in Jour. Am. Folk-lore, III, 112, 1890.

Tuskawillao. One of the 5 former Chickasaw towns in N. w. Mississippi.
Tuskawillao.—Adair, Am. Inds., 353, 1775. **Tuskowellow.**—West Fla. map, ca. 1775.

Tuskegee (perhaps from Creek *task'ya* or *tastanági*, 'warrior'). A former sm 'l Upper Creek town in the fork of Coo ι and Tallapoosa rs., Elmore co., Al According to Hawkins (Sketch, 38, 39, 1848) it contained 30 buildings and 35 gunmen in 1799; they had lost their own language and spoke that of the Creeks, whose customs and manners they also had adopted. It was the residence of the noted Alexander MacGillivray, his lands lying along Coosa r. See Gatschet, Creek Migr. Leg., I, 145–6, 1884. Cf. *Taskigi*.
Jascag.—Jefferys, French Dom., map, 134, 1761 (wrongly on E. bank of Chattahoochee r.). **Jascage.**—Ibid. **Jaskegis.**—Roberts, Fla., 13, 1763. **Jaskigis.**—Alcedo, Dic. Geog., II, 498, 1787. **Jasquijis.**—Bartram, Voy., I, map, 1799. **Joskage.**—Jefferys, Am. Atlas, map 5, 1776. **Tae-keo-ge.**—Adair, Am. Inds., 257, 1775. **Taskegee.**—Drake, Ind. Chron., 211, 1836. **Taskígi.**—Gatschet, Creek Migr. Leg., I, 145, 1884 (as pronounced by Creeks). **Taskikis.**—Bossu (1759), Travels La., I, 229, 1771. **Tasquiqui.**—Vandera (1569) in Smith, Colec. Doc. Fla., 18, 1859. **Tiscugas.**—McCall, Hist. Ga., I, 367, 1811. **Tooses.**—Robin, Voy., I, map, 1807. **Touzas.**—Dumont, La., I, 135, 1753 (identical?). **Tuskeegies.**—Romans, Fla., I, 280, 1775. **Tuskeego.**—Sen. Ex. Doc. 425, 24th Cong., 1st sess., 282, 1836. **Tus-ke-gee.**—Hawkins (1799), Sketch, 37, 1848. **Tuskegees.**—Weatherford (1793) in Am. State Papers, Ind. Aff., I, 386, 1832. **Tuskíki.**—Gatschet, Creek Migr. Leg., I, 145, 1884 (alternative of Taskigi). **Tuskogee.**—Hawkins (1799), Sketch, 39, 1848. **Tuskugu.**—Treaty of 1827 in U. S. Ind. Treat., 420, 1837.

Tuskegee. The name of two towns of the Creek Nation, Okla.: one on Deep fork of Canadian r., w. of Ocmulgee, the other 10 m. w. of Eufaula. For the ethnology of the Creeks of Taskigi, consult Speck in Mem. Am. Anthr. Asso., II, pt. 2, 1907.
Taskígi.—Gatschet, Creek Migr. Leg., II, 186, 1888. **Tuskega.**—Ind. Aff. Rep., 149, 1858 ("in the Canadian dist.").

Tuskhlustunne. A former village of the

Mishikhwutmetunne on Coquille r., Oreg.
Tûs-qlûs' ᴧûnnĕ'.—Dorsey in Jour. Am. Folk-lore, III, 232, 1890.

Tuskokogie. A former Iroquois village, apparently under Oneida jurisdiction, situated, according to the Brion de la Tour map, 1781, just above Schoherage, on the w. bank of the E. branch of Susquehanna r. This is probably an error for Chenango r., N. Y. (J. N. B. H.)

Tuslalahockaka. A former Seminole town 10 m. w. of Walacooche, Fla. Alac Hajo was its chief in 1823.—H. R. Ex. Doc. 74 (1823), 19th Cong., 1st sess., 27, 1826.

Tuslatunne. A former Chastacosta village on the N. bank of upper Rogue r., Oreg.
Tus-la ᴧûnnĕ.—Dorsey in Jour. Am. Folk-lore, III, 234, 1890.

Tusolivi. A tribe or subtribe living in 1709 on Colorado r., Texas, in a rancheria with Simaomo and Yojuan. This rancheria was visited in the year named by Fr. San Buenaventura y Olivares and Fr. Espinosa, of the Rio Grande missions, who estimated the population of the settlement at 2,500. The presence of the Yᴧjuan in the rancheria would indicate Tᴧnkawan affiliation (Diary of San ᴧuenaventura y Olivares, 1709, MS. in ᴧollege of Santa Cruz de Querétaro). See *Simaomo,* and cf. *Tusonid.* (H. E. B.)

Tusonid. One of the tribes represented at San Juan Bautista mission, on the Rio Grande, Texas, in 1772 (MS. in College of Santa Cruz de Querétaro, K, leg. 15, doc. 10). Cf. *Tusolivi.*

Tusonimon. A former Sobaipuri rancheria about 4 leagues w. of Casa Grande, near the Rio Gila, s. Arizona, visited by Father Kino about 1697.
Sta Isabel.—Bernal (1697) in Bancroft, Ariz. and N. Mex., 356, 1889. **Tusonimó.**—Ibid. **Tusonimon.**—Mange (1697) in Schoolcraft, Indian Tribes, III, 303, 1853; Bernal (1697) in Bancroft, Ariz. and N. Mex., 356, 1889. **Tussoninio.**—Orozco y Berra, Geog., 348, 1864.

Tusquittah (*Da'skwĭtûñ'yĭ* 'rafters place,' from *daskwĭtûñ'ĭ* 'rafters,' *yĭ,* the locative). A former Cherokee settlement on Tusquittee cr., near Hayesville, Clay co., N. C. The creek was named after the settlement. (J. M.)
Da'skwĭtûñ'yĭ.—Mooney in 19th Rep. B. A. E., 514, 1900 (native name). **Tusquittah.**—Present map form. **Tusquittee.**—Doc. of 1799 quoted by Royce in 5th Rep. B. A. E., 144, 1887.

Tussawehe ('white knives'). Probably a Shoshoni tribe, although their country, in the mountains along Humboldt r. and Goose cr., N. Nevada, adjoined that of the Paiute. The name White Knives was sometimes applied to the tribe because of the beautiful flint found in their territory from which they made knives. (H. W. H.)
Goose Creek Diggers.—Stuart, Mont., 81, 1865. **To'-sa wee.**—Ibid. **Tosawitches.**—Davies in Ind. Aff. Rep., 129, 1861. **To-si-witches.**—Simpson (1859), Rep. of Expl. Across Utah, 34, 1876. **To-si-**

withes.—Ibid., 510. **To-so-ees.**—Taylor in Cal. Farmer, June 26, 1863. **To-so-wates.**—Powell in H. R. Misc. Doc. 86, 43d Cong., 1st sess., 1, 1874. **Tosowes.**—Dole in Ind. Aff. Rep. 1864, 14, 1865. **To-sow-witches.**—Hurt, ibid., 1856, 228, 1857. **Tussá-wehe.**—Gatschet in Geog. Surv. W. 100th Mer., VII, 410, 1879. **White Knives.**—Holeman in Ind. Aff. Rep., 152, 1852.

Tustatunkhuushi. A band of the Mishikhwutmetunne formerly residing on Coquille r., Oreg.
Tûs'-ta-tûn qu'-u-cĭ.—Dorsey in Jour. Am. Folk-lore, III, 232, 1890.

Tustur. An unidentified tribe allied with the Iroquois and the tribes of the Ohio valley, possibly the Miami.
Tustans.—Stone, Life of Brant, I, 295, 1864. **Tusturs.**—Lord Dorchester (1791) quoted by Lincoln in Mass. Hist. Soc. Coll., 3d s., V, 159, 1886.

Tutachro. A Chumashan village formerly near Purísima mission, Santa Barbara co., Cal.—Taylor in Cal. Farmer, Oct. 18, 1861.

Tutago. A Kaiyuhkhotana village on Yukon r. at the mouth of Auto r., Alaska; pop. 32 in 1848.
Tchouchago.—Zagoskin in Nouv. Ann. Voy., 5th s., XXI, map, 1850. **Ttutaho.**—Tikhmenief (1861) quoted by Baker, Geog. Dict. Alaska, 82, 1901. **Tuttago.**—Zagoskin, Descr. Russ. Poss. Am., map, 1848. **Yakutskalitnik.**—Raymond in Sen. Ex. Doc. 12, 42d Cong., 1st sess., 26, 1871. **Yakutzkelignik.**—Whymper, Alaska, 264, 1869.

Tutahaco. A name of somewhat indefinite application. It is recorded by Castañeda (14th Rep. B. A. E., 492, 519, 525, 544, 1896) as that of a province of 8 Pueblo villages, apparently on the Rio Grande in New Mexico, 4 leagues s. E. of Tiguex, visited by members of Coronado's expedition in 1540–41. The place last mentioned was undoubtedly in the vicinity of the present Bernalillo, consequently the Tigua villages about the present Isleta are generally regarded as having formed Tutahaco province; on the other hand, if the distance (4 leagues) is an error, the former Piro and Tigua villages E. of the Rio Grande, in the Salinas, may have been meant, otherwise they were the only pueblos in New Mexico or Arizona that were not visited by members of Coronado's force. Jaramillo (14th Rep. op. cit., 545) confounded Tutahaco with Acoma, possibly on account of the resemblance of the last syllable to the Acoma name of their pueblo (*Ako*). The Tigua (Isleta) name of Acoma is *Tuthlauay;* and of the Pueblo people who formerly lived s. of them (evidently the Piro), *Tükahun.* See Bandelier in Arch. Inst. Papers, IV, 234 et seq., 1892. (F. W. H.)
Cutahaco.—Domenech, Deserts, I, 88, 1853 (misprint). **Tutahaco.**—Castañeda and Jaramillo in 14th Rep. B. A. E., op. cit. **Tutahuco.**—Davis, Span. Conq. N. Mex., 189, 1869 (misprint). **Tutaliaco.**—Castañeda (1596) in Ternaux-Compans, Voy., IX, 57, 1838 (evidently identical, although used for Acoma). **Tutchaco.**—Gallatin in Nouv. Ann. Voy., 5th s., XXVII, 264, 1851 (misprint). **Tutuhaco.**—Castañeda (1596) in Ternaux-Compans, Voy., IX, 139, 1838.

Tutalosi (Creek: *tutalósi,* 'chicken,' 'fowl'). A former Hitchiti town on Tutalosi cr., a branch of Kinchafoonee cr., probably in Lee or Terrell co., Ga. In later years its people moved w. of Chattahoochee r. and were known thereafter as Hitchiti.

Fowl Town.—Of several authors. **Tatayáhukli.**—Gatschet, Creek Migr. Leg., I, 149, 1884 (Hitchiti name of its people). **Tuttallasee.**—Hawkins (1814) in Am. State Papers, Ind. Aff., I, 845, 1832. **Tut-tal-leo-see.**—Ibid., 859. **Tut-tal-lo-see.**—Hawkins (1779), Sketch, 65, 1848.

Tutchonekutchin ('crow people'). A Kutchin tribe on Yukon r. from Deer r. to Ft Selkirk, Yukon Ter., Canada. They number about 1,100 and differ but little from their Kutchin neighbors below.

Caribou Indians.—Dall in Cont. N. A. Ethnol., I, 32, 1877 (so called by Hudson's Bay Co. people). **Carribou Indians.**—Ross, MS. notes on Tinne, B. A. E. **Crow People.**—Dall in Cont. N.A. Ethnol., I, 32, 1877. **Gens de bois.**—Whymper, Alaska, 255, 1869. **Gens des Foux.**—Dall, Alaska, 429, 1870. **Gens-de-wiz.**—Raymond in Ind. Aff. Rep. 1869, 593, 1870 (misprint). **Klo-a-tsul-tshik'.**—Dawson in Rep. Geol. Surv. Can. 1888, 202B, 1889. **Mountain Indians.**—Hardisty in Smithson. Rep. 1866, 311, 1872. **Nehaunee.**—Dall in Cont. N. A. Ethnol., I, 32, 1877 (so called by Hudson's Bay Co. men). **Tatanchaks.**—Colyer in Ind. Aff. Rep. 1869, 593, 1870. **Tatanchakutchin.**—Raymond, in Jour. Am. Geog. Soc., III, 178, 1873. **Tatanchok-Kutchin.**—Whymper in Jour. Roy. Geog. Soc., 233, 1868. **Tatchone Kutchin.**—Keane in Stanford, Compend., 464, 1878. **Touchon-ta-Kutchin.**—Kirkby in Smithson. Rep. 1864, 418, 1865. **Touchon-tay Kutchin.**—Kirby (1862) quoted by Hind, Lab. Penin., II, 254, 1863. **Tŭt-chohn'-kŭt-ohin.**—Dall in Proc. Am. A. A. S., 379, 1886. **Tutchóne-Kutchin.**— Dall, Alaska, 429, 1870. **Tutchonekut'qin.**— Morice in Anthropos, I, 506, 1906. **Tutchon Kutchin.**—Whymper, Alaska, 271, 1869. **Tŭtch-ŭn-tāh' kŭtchin.**—Ross, Notes on Tinne, S. I. MS. 474. **Tŭtcone-kut'qin.**— Morice in Anthropos, I, 261, 1906 (='crow people'). **Wood Indians.**—Dawson in Rep. Geol. Surv. Can., 202B, 1889 (so called by fur traders).

Tutelary. See *Oyaron, Totem.*

Tutelo. One of the eastern Siouan tribes, formerly living in Virginia and North Carolina, but now extinct. Hale (Proc. Am. Philos. Soc., Mar. 2, 1883) first made it known that the Tutelo language pertained to the Siouan stock, a discovery which, followed by the investigations of Gatschet, Mooney, and J. O. Dorsey, brought to light the fact that a considerable group of Siouan tribes formerly inhabited the piedmont region of Virginia and the Carolinas. The relation of the Tutelo appears to have been most intimate with the Saponi, the language of the two tribes being substantially the same. Their intimate association with the Occaneechi and their allied tribes indicates ethnic relationship. The history of the Tutelo is virtually the same as that of the Saponi. The name Tutelo, although by the English commonly used to designate a particular tribe, was by the Iroquois applied as a generic term for all the Siouan tribes of Virginia and Carolina, being applied more particularly to the allied tribes gathered at Ft Christanna (see *Christanna Indians*). They are first mentioned by Capt. John Smith in 1609 under the names of Monacan and Mannahoac, with many subtribes, occupying the upper waters of James and Rappahannock rs., Va., and described by him as very barbarous, subsisting chiefly on the products of the chase and wild fruits. They were at constant war with the Powhatan Indians and in mortal dread of the Iroquois. Lederer, in his exploration from Virginia into North Carolina in 1670, passed through their territory and mentions the names of Nahyssan (Monahassanough) and Sapon (Saponi). In their frontier position at the base of the mountains the Saponi and Tutelo were directly in the path of the Iroquois.

Unable to withstand the constant attacks of these northern enemies, they abandoned this location some time between 1671 and 1701, and removed to the junction of Staunton and Dan rs., where they established themselves near their friends and kinsmen, the Occaneechi, occupying two of the islands in the Roanoke immediately below the forks, the Tutelo settling on the upper one. How long they remained here is unknown; it is certain, however, that in 1701 Lawson found the Saponi on Yadkin r., N. C., and says that the Tutelo were living in the neighboring mountains toward the w., probably about the headwaters of the Yadkin. At this time, according to Lawson, the 5 Siouan tribes, the Tutelo, Saponi, Keyauwee, Occaneechi, and Shakori, numbered together only about 750 souls. Soon after Lawson's visit they all moved in toward the white settlements, and, crossing the Roanoke, occupied a village called Sapona town, a short distance E. of the river, about 15 m. w. of the present Windsor, Bertie co., N. C. Soon after this they removed and settled near Ft Christanna (see *Christanna Indians, Totero*). In 1722, through the efforts of the Colonial governments, peace was finally made between the Iroquois and the Virginia tribes. In consequence the Saponi and Tutelo some years later moved to the N. and settled on the Susquehanna at Shamokin (q. v.), Pa., under Iroquois protection, later moving up the river to Skogari. Their chiefs were allowed to sit in the great council of the Six Nations. In 1763 the two tribes, together with the Nanticoke and Conoy, numbered, according to Sir Wm. Johnson, 200 men, possibly 1,000 souls. In 1771 the Tutelo were settled on the E. side of Cayuga inlet, about 3 m. from the s. end of the lake, in a town called Coreorgonel, which was destroyed in 1779 by Gen. Sullivan. The last surviving full-blood Tutelo known was Nikonha, from whom Hale obtained the linguistic material by which he determined the relation of the tribe to the Siouan stock. He died in 1871. It is believed there are still a few mixed-bloods in Canada, but the last one who could speak the language was John Key, or Gostango ('Below the Rock'), whose Tutelo name was Nastabon ('One Step'), and who died in 1898, aged about 80 years (Chadwick, People of the Longhouse, 19, 1897; Boyle in Ann. Archæol. Rep. Ontario, 55, pl. xviii, b, 1898). Lawson describes the Tutelo as "tall, likely men, having great plenty of buffaloes, elks, and bears, with every sort of deer amongst them, which strong food makes large, robust bodies." Nevertheless the evidence is clear that they were cultivators of the soil and relied thereon to a large extent for subsistence. The photograph of Nikonha, given by Hale, shows a face full oval in outline and large features of an almost European cast, "evidently," says Hale, "not individual or family traits, as they reappear in the Tutelo half-breeds on the Reserve, who do not claim a near relationship to Nikonha." On the other hand Zeisberger, who visited the remnant of the tribe while settled at Shamokin, speaks of the village as "the only town on the continent inhabited by Tuteloes, a degenerate remnant of thieves and drunkards." Lederer describes the Nahyssan chief as an absolute monarch, and the people as tall, warlike, and rich. In their temples, or medicine lodges, they had large quantities of pearls, which they had taken in war from more southern tribes. Their tribal ensign consisted of three arrows.

Consult Hale in Proc. Am. Philos. Soc., XXI, no. 114, 1883; Mooney, Siouan Tribes of the East, 1894.   (J. M.)

Kattera.—De l'Isle, map 41, in Kitchin, New Atlas, 1800. Nahyssan.—Lederer, Discov., 9, 1672 (Mooney regards this as a form of Yesan). Shateras.—Bellomont (1699) in N. Y. Doc. Col. Hist., IV, 488, 1854. Taderighrones.—Ibid., index, 312, 1861. Tadirighrone.—Albany conf. (1722), ibid., V, 660, 1855. Tateras.—Boudinot, Star in the West, 100, 1816. Tedarighroones.—Lond. doc. 31 (1753) in N. Y. Doc. Col. Hist., VI, 811, 1855. Tedarrighroones.—Doc. of 1753, ibid., 812. Tedderighroones.—N. Y. Doc. Col. Hist., index, 312, 1861. Tedirighroonas.—Doc. of 1756, ibid., VII, 55, 1856. Tehotirigh.—Hale in Proc. Am. Philos. Soc., XXI, no. 114, A, 11, 1883. Tehutili.—Ibid. Tentilves.—Boudinot, Star in the West, 129, 1816. Tetarighroones.—Doc. of 1753 in N. Y. Doc. Col. Hist., VI, 814, 1855. Teuteloe.—Macauley, Hist. N. Y., II, 180, 1829. Thedirighroonas.—N. Y. Doc. Col. Hist., index, 312, 1861. Thoderighroonas.—Doc. of 1756, ibid., VII, 136, 1856. Tiederighroenes.—Doc. of 1759, ibid., 380. Tiederighroonas.—Doc. of 1755, ibid., VI, 982, 1855. Tiederighroones.—N. Y. Doc. Col. Hist., index, 312, 1861. Tiederigoene.—Stone, Life Sir William Johnson, I, 485, note, 1865. Tiederigroenes.—Doc. of 1755 in N. Y. Doc. Col. Hist., VI, 964, 1855. Tiutei.—Hale in Proc. Am. Philos. Soc., XXI, no. 114, A, 11, 1884. Tiuterih.—Ibid. Toalaghreghroonees.—Doc. of 1748 in N. Y. Doc. Col. Hist., VI, 447, 1855. Toalaghreghsoonees.—Doc. of 1748, ibid., 441. Toataghreghroones.—Ibid., note. Toderechrones.—Ibid., V, 671, 1855. Toderichroone.—Ibid., 491. Todericks.—Boudinot, Star in the West, 100, 1816. Todevighrono.—Johnson, map (1771) quoted by Hale in Proc. Am. Philos. Soc., XXI, no. 114, A, 8, 1884 (misprint). Todirichrones.—Hale, ibid., 5. Todirichroones.—Doc. 1722 in N. Y. Doc. Col. Hist., V, 673, 1855. Tolera.—Batts (1671), ibid., III, 194, 1853.

Tolere.—Lambreville (1686), ibid., 489. Toleri.—N. Y. Doc. Col. Hist., index, 313, 1861. Tortero.—Logan, Hist. So. Car., I, 33, 1859. Totaly.—Macauley, Hist. N. Y., II, 166, 1829. Totaro.—Harrison, letter to Dorsey, May 25, 1886 (present name of a district in Brunswick co., Va., between Lawrenceville and Belfield). Toteloes.—Schoolcraft, Ind. Tribes, III, 196, 1853. Totera.—Clayton (1671) in Fernow, Ohio Valley, 223, 1890. Toteras.—Brickell, Nat. Hist. N. Car., 343, 1737. Toteri.—N. Y. Doc. Col. Hist., index, 313, 1861. Toteroes.—Doc. of 1722, ibid., V, 673, 1855. Toteros.—Gallatin in Trans. Am. Antiq. Soc., II, 85, 1836. Totierono.—Paris doc. 12 (1756) in N. Y. Doc. Col. Hist., X, 500, 1858. Totiri.—Paris doc. 8 (1736), ibid., IX, 1057, 1855. Totora.—Clayton (1671) quoted by Fernow, Ohio Val., 221, 1890. Tottero.—Spotswood (1711) quoted by Burk, Va., III, 89, 1805. Totteroy.—Anville (1746), map 50, in Kitchin, New Atlas, 1800. Tutaloes.—Chadwick, People of the Longhouse, 19, 1897. Tutecoes.—Stone, Life of Sir Wm. Johnson, If, 487, 1865. Tuteeves.—Doc. of 1764 in N. Y. Doc. Col. Hist., VII, 641, 1856. Tutelas.—Brainerd (1745) quoted by Day, Penn., 525, 1843. Tútele.—Gatschet, MS., B. A. E. (Shawnee name). Tutelo.—Shea, Cath. Miss., 24, 1855. Tuteloes.—Doc. of 1700 in N. Y. Doc. Col. Hist., VIII, 229, 1857. Tūtie.—Hale in Proc. Am. Philos. Soc., XXI, no. 114, 11, 1884. Tutiloes.—Davies, Mod. Geog., 532, 1805. Tutloe.—Macauley, Hist. N. Y., II, 169, 1829. Tuttelars.—Doc. of 1756 in Rupp, Northampton Co., Pa., 106, 1845. Tuttelee.—Jones, Ojibway Inds., 21, 1861. Tutulor.—Peters (1761) in Mass. Hist. Soc. Coll., 4th s., IX, 440, 1870. Yesáh.—Hale in Proc. Am. Philos. Soc., XXI, no. 114, A, 11, 1884. Ye-san.—Hale, letter to Powell, B. A. E., 1877 (own name). Yesáng.—Hale, op. cit., 11.

Tutelpinco. A town, possibly of one of the Caddoan tribes, w. of the Mississippi, through which De Soto's army passed early in 1542. Described as being one or two days' journey from the Ayays (Eyeish) and in the vicinity of a great lake. See Gentl. of Elvas (1557) in French, Hist. Coll. La., II, 184, 1850.

Tuteneiboica. A tribe, perhaps Coahuiltecan, represented at San Francisco Solano mission, Texas, in 1706. It was associated with the Terocodame tribe (Valero Baptisms, 1706, partida 220, MS.).

Tutlut. A Tenankutchin village at the junction of Tanana and Tutlut rs., Alaska.

Too-clok band.—Schwatka, Rep. on Alaska, 95, 1885. Tutlut.—Petroff in 10th Census, Alaska, map, 1884.

Tutoida. A former Sobaipuri rancheria on the Rio San Pedro, Ariz., probably between Arivaipa cr. and the Gila. It was visited by Father Kino in 1697.

Tutoida.—Kino (1697) in Doc. Hist. Mex., 4th s., I, 280, 1856. Zutoida.—Bernal (1697) quoted by Bancroft, Ariz. and N. Mex., 356, 1889.

Tutoimana (*Tŭtóimanah'*, 'backward or shy clan'). A modern nickname for a band of the Northern Cheyenne.—Grinnell, Social Org. Cheyennes, 136, 1905.

Tutomagoidag. A former Maricopa rancheria on the Rio Gila, Ariz.

S. Mathias de Tutomagoidag.—Kino, map (1701), in Stöcklein, Neue Welt-Bott, 75, 1726. St Mathias de Tuto Magoidag.—Venegas, Hist. Cala., I, map, 1759. Tutomagoidag.—Kino, map (1701), in Bancroft, Ariz. and N. Mex., 360, 1889.

Tutonaguy. A village in 1535 on the N. bank of St Lawrence r., 25 leagues above the site of Quebec.—Cartier (1534) quoted in Hakluyt, Prin. Navigations, 235, 1598.

Tutonashikisd ('water tanks'). An Apache clan or band at San Carlos agency and Ft Apache, Ariz., in 1881.—Bourke in Jour. Am. Folk-lore, III, 112, 1890.

Tutsoshin. A band or clan of the Pinal Coyoteros living at San Carlos agency, Ariz., in 1881.—Bourke in Jour. Am. Folk-lore, III, 112, 1890.

Tutuaca. A former settlement of the Tepehuane (containing also some Tarahumare and Nevome) about lat. 28° 20′, lon. 107° 50′, w. Chihuahua, Mexico. It was the seat of a mission in the 17th century.
Jesus del Monte de Tutuaca.—Orozco y Berra, Geog., 324, 1864 (mission name). Tutuaca.—Zapata (1678) cited by Bandelier in Arch. Inst. Papers, III, 79, 1890.

Tutuetac. A Piman rancheria in the 18th century, situated about 16 m. N. W. of Tucson and w. of Rio Santa Cruz, in s. Arizona, visited by Anza and Font in 1775.—Bancroft, Ariz. and N. Mex., 392, 1889.

Tutum. A former Yuma rancheria, visited in 1699 by Kino and Mange, who applied the saint name.
S. Matias Tutum.—Mange in Bancroft, Ariz. and N. Mex., 357, 1889.

Tututni. An Athapascan tribe or group of small tribes formerly occupying villages along lower Rogue r., Oreg., and on the

GEORGE HARVEY—TUTUTNI

coast N. and s. of its mouth. Parrish in 1854 (Ind. Aff. Rep. 1854, 495, 1855) located 8 bands on the coast and 3 on Rogue r. The gentile system prevailed among them, men marrying outside of their own villages, and a child belonging to the village of its father; yet they can not be considered as one tribe, as villages warred one upon another without violation of national unity or tribal sentiment (Dorsey in Jour. Am. Folk-lore, III, 232, 1890). The Tututni were removed to Siletz res. as prisoners of war in 1856. They formerly practised polygyny, widows being buried alive in the graves of their deceased husbands (Everette, Tutu MS. vocab., B. A. E., 1883). In 1854 (Ind. Aff. Rep. 1854, 495, 1855) the total population was 1,311, consisting of 448 men, 490 women, 205 boys, and 168 girls. According to Parrish (op. cit.) the bands were: Nasohmah (Nasumi, a Kusan village), Chocreletan (Chocrelatan), Quahtomah (Kwatami), Cosuttheutun (Kwusatthlkhuntunne), Euquachee (Yukichetunne), Yahshute (Chemetunne), Chetlessentun (Chetlesiyetunne), Wishtenatin (Khwaishtunnetunne), Cheattee (Chetco), Tototin (Tututunne), Mackanotin (Mikonotunne), and Shistakoostee (Chastacosta). Dorsey (op. cit., 233) gave the following list of former bands or villages on the coast N. of Rogue r.: Chemetunne, Kaltsergheatunne, Kosotshe, Kwatami, Kthukhwuttunne, Kwusathlkhuntunne, Natutshltunne, Niletunne, and Yukichetunne. The following were on both banks: Chetlesiyetunne, Etaatthatunne, Kunechuta, Kushetunne, Mikonotunne, Targheliichetunne, Targhutthotunne, Testthitun, Thethlkhuttunne, and Thechuntunne. On or near the coast s. of Rogue r. were the following: Aanetun, Chetleschantunne, Enitunne, Khainanaitetunne, Kheerghia, Khwaishtunnetunne, Nakatkhaitunne, Natthutunne, Nuchumatuntunne, Sentethltun, Skumeme, Tsetintunne, and Tsetuttunne. Kthutetmetseetuttun was on the coast just N. of Rogue r.　　　　　　　　　(J. O. D.)

Coquins.—Duflot de Mofras, Expl., II, 335, 1844. H'lilush.—Gatschet, Nestucca vocab., B. A. E. (Nestucca name). Lototen.—Hubbard (1856) in Cal. Farmer, June 8, 1860. Lower Rogue River.—Dorsey, Tutu MS. vocab., B. A. E., 1884. Potámeos Indians.—Townsend, Nar., 228, 1839. Rascal Indians.—Hale, Ethnol. and Philol., 221, 1846. Roger's River.—Farnham, Trav., 112, 1843 (error). Rogue Indians.—Hale, Ethnol. and Philol., 221, 1846. Rogue River.—Gatschet in Beach, Ind. Misc., 441, 1877. Rogue River Indians.—Gatschet, Umpqua MS. vocab., B. A. E., 1877. Rogue's River.—Nicolay, Oregon, 143, 1846. Tálĕmaya.—Gatschet, Umpqua MS. vocab., B. A. E., 1877. Ta-qu'-qûc-oĕ.—Dorsey, Chetco MS. vocab., B. A. E., 1884 ('northern language': Chetco name). Tatatna.—Armstrong, Oregon, 117, 1857. T'ĕ-ta' ʇûnnĕ.—Dorsey, Naltûnnetûnnĕ MS. vocab., B. A. E., 1884 (Naltunnetunne name). Too-too-ten.—Gibbs, MS. on coast tribes, Oregon, B. A. E. Too-too-te-ny.—Ind. Aff. Rep. 1856, 199, 1857. Too-toot-nie.—Gibbs, MS. on coast tribes, Oregon, B. A. E. Too-too-ton.—Palmer in Ind. Aff. Rep., 467, 1854. Tootootone.—Ibid., 1856, 219, 1857. Totones.—Schoolcraft, Ind. Tribes, VI, 702, 1857. Totonic tribes.—Ibid., 702. Tototan.—Ibid., III, 96, map, 1853. To-to-taws.—Domenech, Deserts N. Am., I, map, 1860. To-to-tut-na.—Parrish in Ind. Aff. Rep. 1854, 494, 1855. Totutime.—Bancroft, Nat. Races, I, 327, 1882. Totutúne.—Hale, Ethnol. and Philol., 221, 1846. T'û'-qwe-t'a' ʇûnnĕ'.—Dorsey in Jour. Am. Folk-lore, III, 232, 1890 (='all the people'). Tutatamys.—Hubbard (1856) in Cal. Farmer, June 8, 1860. **Tutoten.**—Schoolcraft, Ind. Tribes, VI, 702, 1857. **Tutunah.**—Taylor quoted by Bancroft, Nat. Races, I, 443, 1874. **Tututamys.**—Gatschet in Beach, Ind. Misc., 441, 1877. **Tū-tüten.**—Gibbs (1854) in Cont. N. A. Ethnol., I, 165, 1877.

Tututunne ('people close to the water'). A gens of the Tututni, located by Gairdner in 1835 (Jour. Geog. Soc. Lond., XI, 256, 1841) about 10 m. above the mouth of Rogue r., Oreg. In 1884 Dorsey found 97 on the Siletz res., Oreg.

Stotonia.—Framboise quoted by Gairdner, op. cit. **Tootootana.**—Dole in Ind. Aff. Rep., 221, 1861. **Tootoo-te-nay.**—Palmer in Ind. Aff. Rep. 1856, 199, 1857. **Toot-oot-en-ays.**—Victor in Overland Mo., VII, 347, 1871. **Too-toot-e-ways.**—Ind. Aff. Rep., 470, 1865. **Too-toot-na.**—Newcomb in Ind. Aff. Rep., 162, 1861. **Too-toot-nay.**—Ind. Aff. Rep., 300, 1877. **Too-tootne.**—Palmer in Ind. Aff. Rep. 1856, 219, 1857. **Too-too-to-neys.**—Ind. Aff. Rep. 1857, 321, 1858. **Too-too-to-nies.**—Dunbar in Ind. Aff. Rep. 1856, 201, 1857. **Too-too-to-ny.**—Abbott, Coquille MS. census, B. A. E., 1858. **Toot-toot-en-ay.**—Ind. Aff. Rep. 1867, 62, 1868. **Tototen.**—Schoolcraft, Ind. Tribes, VI, 702, 1857. **Tototin.**—Metcalfe in Ind. Aff. Rep. 1857, 357, 1858. **Tototune.**—Latham in Trans. Philol. Soc. Lond., 76, 1856. **Toutounis.**—Duflot de Mofras, Explor., II, 335, 1844. **Tou-touten.**—Kautz, MS. census, B. A. E., 1855. **Ḷu'-tu.**—Dorsey in Jour. Am. Folk-lore, III, 233, 1890. **Tutu' těn'e.**—Everette, Tutu MS. vocab., B. A. E., 1883 (trans.: 'people by the river shore'). **Tu-tŭ-to-ni.**—Schumacher in Bull. U. S. G. and G. Surv., III, 28, 1877. **Ḷu-tu ḷunně.**—Ibid. ('people close to the water': own name) **Two-took-e-way.**—Taylor in Sen. Ex. Doc. 4, 40th Cong., spec. sess., 27, 1867. **Yo-to-tan.**—Pres. Mess., Ex. Doc. 39, 32d Cong., 1st sess., 2, 1852 (misprint).

Tutuwalha ('the guardians,' in allusion to three high columns of sandstone near by). Two former pueblos of the Hopi of Arizona, one of which was situated on the Middle mesa, the other being the Squash village on the terrace below.— Stephen in 8th Rep. B. A. E., 26, 1891.

Tutzone ('plenty of water'). An Apache band or clan at San Carlos agency and Ft Apache, Ariz., in 1881 (Bourke in Jour. Am. Folk-lore, III, 112, 1890), corresponding to the Tutzose of the Pinal Coyoteros and the Thotsoni of the Navaho.

Tutzose.—Bourke, op. cit.

Tutzose. A band or clan of the Pinal Coyoteros.—Bourke in Jour. Am. Folk-lore, III, 112, 1890. Cf. *Tutzone.*

Tuvachi. One of the Bird clans of the Kokop (Wood) phratry of the Hopi.

Tüvatci wiñwû.—Fewkes in 19th Rep. B. A. E., 584, 1900 (*wiñwû* = 'clan'). **Tü-vü-tci wüñ-wû.**— Fewkes in Am. Anthr., VII, 404, 1894.

Tuvak. A Tahagmiut Eskimo village on the N. coast of Labrador, lon. 70°.— Hind, Lab. Penin., II, map, 1863.

Tuvou. The Piñon clan of the Hopi; apparently the same as the Tovu (Fire) clan (q. v.).

Tuvoû wiñwû.—Fewkes in 19th Rep. B. A. E., 584, 1900 (*wiñwû* = 'clan'). **Tü-vo'-ü wüñ-wû.**—Fewkes in Am. Anthr., VII, 404, 1894.

Tuwa. The Sand phratry of the Hopi, which comprises the Kukuch, Bachipkwasi, Nananawi, Momobi (varieties of the Lizard), Pisa (White Sand), Tuwa (Red Sand), Chukai (Mud), Sihu (Flower or Bush), and Nanahu (Small Striped

Squirrel) clans. They claim to have come from a region in s. Arizona called Palatkwabi, and from Little Colorado r. The Earth or Sand phratry of Fewkes is identical with the Lizard phratry of Stephen.

Tü-wa' nyû-mû.—Fewkes in Am. Anthr., VII, 404, 1894 (*nyû-mû* = 'phratry').

Tuwa. The Sand clan of the Hopi.

Tdu'-wa.—Stephen in 8th Rep. B, A. E., 39, 1891 (= 'Red Sand'). **Tûwá.**—Voth, Oraibi Summer Snake Ceremony, 284, 1903. **Tüwa wiñwû.**— Fewkes in 19th Rep. B. A. E., 583, 1900 (*wiñwû* = 'clan'). **Tü-wa wüñ-wü.**—Fewkes in Am. Anthr., VII, 404, 1894.

Tuwahokasha (*Tu-wa-hok'-a-sha*, from *tuh* 'village', *wa* the characteristic roach on the head of a man who has been shaved on both sides, *hok'-a-sha* 'curving over': 'village on a ridge'). A band of the Skidi Pawnee.—Grinnell, Pawnee Hero Stories, 238, 1889.

Tuwa-Kukuch ('Sand [and] Lizard'). A phratral group of the Hopi of Arizona, consisting of the Sand, Lizard, and Flower or Bush clans. They claim that their ancestors came from a region in s. Arizona called Palatkwabi, and from Little Colorado r. (J. W. F.)

Tüwa-Kükütc.—Fewkes in 19th Rep. B. A. E., 583, 1900.

Tuwanek (*Tūwắnᴇkǫ*). A Seechelt sept which formerly lived at the head of Narrow's Arm, Seechelt inlet, Brit. Col.— Hill-Tout in Jour. Anthr. Inst., 25, 1904.

Tuwurints (*Tu-wur-ints*). One of the tribes known under the collective term Gosiute, formerly living on Snake cr., s. w. Utah.—Powell and Ingalls in Ind. Aff. Rep. 1873, 51, 1874.

Tuxedo. A dinner jacket, so called from *Tuxedo*, the name of a summer resort in Passaic co., N. J., on the lake of the same name. The word is derived from the Delaware dialect of Algonquian, in which the Wolf subtribe was called *P'tuksit*, spelled by Morgan Took-seat. This name is a socio-esoteric term for wolf and signifies literally, 'he has a round foot,' from *p'tuksiteu* (*eu* = *o*). (A. F. C.)

Tuxican. An old Tlingit town belonging to the Henya, situated on a narrow strait on the N. w. coast of Prince of Wales id., Alaska. Formerly it was the chief Henya town, but the Henya have now moved to Klawak.

Ták-ssi-kān.—Krause, Tlinkit Ind., 120, 1885 (given as the name of a family). **Ta'qdjîk-ān.**—Swanton, field notes, B. A. E., 1904.

Tuyunga. A former Gabrieleño village in Encino or San Fernando valley, Los Angeles co., Cal.—Padre Santa María (1796) quoted by Bancroft, Hist. Cal., I, 553, 1886.

Tuzahe. Mentioned as a pueblo of the province of Atripuy (q. v.), in the region of the lower Rio Grande, N. Mex., in 1598.—Oñate (1598) in Doc. Inéd., XVI, 115, 1871.

Tuziyammos. A Paviotso tribe formerly

about Warner lake, s. Oreg. Hótcu, or Ochoho as he was commonly known, was its chief, and by the latter name the tribe was usually called. They were moved to the Yainax agency, Oreg., but subsequently left it and ranged to the s., especially about Camp Bidwell, N. E. Cal., where the remnants of the tribe are now supposed to be. (H. W. H.)
Ocheo's band.—Dyar in Ind. Aff. Rep. 1873, 324, 1874. Tu-zi′ yam-mos.—Powell, Paviotso MS., B. A. E., 1881.

Tuzsint. A village, presumably Costanoan, formerly connected with Dolores mission, San Francisco, Cal.—Taylor in Cal. Farmer, Oct. 18, 1861.

Twana. A Salish division living along both sides of Hoods canal, w. Wash. The name is said to signify 'a portage,' the portage referred to being that between the head of Hoods canal and the headwaters of Puget sd. According to Eells there are three bands—the Colcine, Skokomish, and Tulalip. From the name of one of these bands all of them are sometimes called Skokomish. Pop. about 265 in 1853. They are probably the Skokomish of the Indian Office reports, numbering 203 in 1909.
Deewano.—Simmons in Ind. Aff. Rep., 224, 1858. Duwano.—Simmons, ibid., 192, 1860. Skokomish.—Mooney in 14th Rep. B. A. E., pl. lxxxviii, 1896. Toanda.—Stevens in Ind. Aff. Rep., 459, 1854. Toando.—Farnham, Travels, 111, 1843. To-an-hooch.—Gibbs in Pac. R. R. Rep., I, 435, 1855. Toanhoock.—Ibid., 431. Toan-hŭch.—Gibbs in Cont. N. A. Ethnol., I, 177, 1877. To-an-kooch.—Stevens, op. cit., 452. Too-an-hooch.—Treaty of 1859 in U. S. Ind. Treaties, 800, 1873. Too-au-hoosh.—Ross in Ind. Aff. Rep. 1869, 135, 1870. Towanda.—King, ibid., 104, 1868. Tu-ad-hu.—Eells in Smithson. Rep. 1887, 605, 1889 (own name). Tu-ád-hu.—Eells, Nisqualli vocab., B. A. E., 1878 (Nisqualli name). Tu-an′-hu.—Eells in Smithson. Rep. 1887, 605, 1889 (Clallam name). Tu-a-nooch.—Starling in Ind. Aff. Rep., 170, 1852. Tu-a-noock.—Ibid., 172. Tucanoh.—Schoolcraft, Ind. Tribes, VI, 689, 1857 (misprint). Twana.—Eells in Smithson. Rep. 1887, 605, 1889. Twanoh.—Lane in Sen. Ex. Doc. 52, 31st Cong., 1st sess., 173, 1850. Twanug.—6th Rep. N. W. Tribes Can., map, 1890. Wilfa Ampáfa amím.—Gatschet, Lakmiut MS., B. A. E., 105 (Lakmiut-Kalapuya name).

Tweeg. A large North American batrachian (*Menopoma alleghanensis*), called also hell-bender, mud-devil, groundpuppy, spring-keeper, man-eater, etc. The name is from Lenape (Delaware) *twe'kw*, a radical word. (W. R. G.)

Tweezers. See *Pincers*.

Twenty-nine Palms. A reservation of 160.21 acres of patented desert land, near the 116th meridian, in the Mohave desert, Cal., nearly half way between Indio on the Southern Pac. R. R. and Bagdad on the Santa Fé Pac. R. R. The settlement formerly belonged to the Serranos, but in 1867 the Chemehuevi, after fighting the Mohave, by whom they were defeated, fled to this place; meanwhile the Serranos have died out or moved away. In 1908 the entire population, with the exception of a single Serrano, was Chemehuevi. Within the last few years several Cheme-

huevi removed from Twenty-nine Palms, on account of lack of subsistence, to the Cabezon res. of the Cahuillas (Kawia), near Coachella, 3 m. s. E. of Indio. (See Kroeber in Univ. Cal. Pub., Am. Arch. and Eth., VIII, 33, 37, 1908.)
Mara.—Kroeber in Univ. Cal. Pub., Am. Arch. and Eth., VIII, 33, 1908 (native name). Twentymile Palms.—Ind. Aff. Rep. 1902, 175, 1903.

Two Runs. A former Cherokee village on Etowah r., at the crossing of the old Indian trail between Coosa and Tugaloo rs., in the present Bartow co., N. W. Ga.—Royce in 5th Rep. B. A. E., map, 1887.

Twostars, Solomon. An hereditary chief of the Sisseton Sioux; born at Lacquiparle, Minn., in 1827. He early became a convert to Christianity under the ministry of Riggs and Williamson, and was a federal scout in the Sioux outbreak of 1862. He was still living at Sisseton agency, S. Dak., in 1907. (D. R.)

Tyacappan. A village formerly in the vicinity of Trinity r., Texas, visited by La Salle in 1687 while on the way from Ft St Louis on Matagorda bay to the Mississippi. Douay says that the village was large and that its people possessed horses. La Salle relates that the houses were of interlaced canes, covered with fine white plaster. Here was found a boy who could speak Spanish. The village was in the Caddoan country, and the people may have belonged to that family. (A. C. F.)
Ticapanas.—Cavelier (1687) quoted by Shea, Early Voy., 37, 1861. Tyakappa.—Coxe, Carolana, map, 1741. Tyakappan.—Douay (1687) in Shea, Discov. Miss. Val., 212, 1852. Tycappans.—Coxe (1741) in French, Hist. Coll. La., II, 241, 1850.

Tyaia. The extinct Piñon clan of Sia pueblo, N. Mex.
Tyaía-háno.—Hodge in Am. Anthr., IX, 351, 1896 (*háno*='people').

Tyajuindena (*Tya-juin-den-a*). A former pueblo of the Jemez (q. v.) in New Mexico, the exact site of which is not known.—Bandelier in Arch. Inst. Papers, IV, 207, 1892.

Tyasoliwa. A former pueblo of the Jemez of New Mexico; definite location undetermined. (F. W. H.)

Tyee. 1. A man of importance; a chief; somebody. 2. Important; superior; great. The word is used in parts of the Pacific coast: from *tyee* 'chief,' in the Chinook jargon, a term ultimately derived from the Nootka dialect of the Wakashan family. (A. F. C.)

Tyendinaga (probably named in honor of *Thayendanegea*, q. v.). A Mohawk reservation of about 17,000 acres of tillable land, occupied in 1910 by 1,323 Indians, on Quinté bay near the E. end of L. Ontario, in Hastings co., Ontario. The Indians are known officially as "Mohawks of the Bay of Quinté."—Can. Ind. Aff. Reps.

Tyigh. A Shahaptian tribe speaking the Tenino language and formerly occupying the country about Tygh and White rs. in

Wasco co., Oreg. They took part in the Wasco treaty of 1855 and are now on Warm Springs res., Oreg. Their number is not reported, as they are classed under the indiscriminate term "Warm Springs Indians," but in 1854 they were said to number 500, and in 1859, 450.   (L. F.)

Attayes.—De Smet, Letters, 220, 1843 (probably identical). Iyich.—Taylor in Cal. Farmer, June 12, 1863. Tai'-ăq.—Mooney in 14th Rep. B. A. E., 742, 1896. Taighs.—Shea, Lib. Am. Ling., VI, vii, 1862. Ta-ih.—Wasco treaty (1855) in U. S. Ind. Treaties, 622, 1873. Tairtla.—Pandosy in Shea, Lib., Am. Ling., VI, 9, 1862. Téaχtkni.—Gatschet in Cont. N. A. Ethnol., II, pt. 2, 395, 1890 (Klamath name). Teaχtkni máklaks.—Ibid. Télknikni.—Ibid. Thy.—Stevens in H. R. Ex. Doc. 37, 34th Cong., 3d sess., 42, 1857. Tiach.—Thompson in H. R. Ex. Doc. 93, 34th Cong., 1st sess., 74, 1856. Tigh.—Shaw (1856) in H. R. Ex. Doc. 37, 34th Cong., 3d sess., 113, 1857. Traht.—Shaw in H. R. Ex. Doc. 76, 34th Cong., 3d sess., 177, 1857. Tsĕ Amínĕma.—Gatschet, Lakmiut MS. vocab., B. A. E., 105 (Lakmiut name). Tye of Deshute.—Stevens in Sen. Ex. Doc. 66, 34th Cong., 1st sess., 9, 1856. Tygh.—Logan in Ind. Aff. Rep. 1864, 97, 1865. Tyh.—Stevens in Ind. Aff. Rep. 1856, 185, 1857. Ty-ich.—Thompson, ibid., 493, 1854. Tyicks.—Dennison, ibid., 1859, 435, 1860. Tyigh.—Curtin quoted by Powell in 6th Rep. B. A. E., xxxvii, 1888. Upper De Chutes.—Treaty of 1855 in U. S. Ind. Treat., 622, 1873.

Tyonek ('little chief'). A trading station and Knaiakhotana settlement on the w. side of Cook inlet, Alaska. The station in 1881 consisted of 2 whites, 6 creoles, and 109 natives (Petroff, Rep. on Alaska, 29, 1884). In 1890 (11th Census, Alaska, 169, 1893) there were 115 inhabitants and 21 houses. The total number of natives in the district is 150 to 200. Besides hunting and trapping they catch king salmon to sell to the canneries. All are members of the Russian church. Formerly they acted as middlemen in the trade with the Knaikhotana on Sushitna r., who now come down to the station with their furs.

Tyonek.—Baker, Geog. Dict. Alaska, 416, 1902. Toyonok.—Petroff in 10th Census, Alaska, map, 1884. Tu-i-u'-nŭk.—Hoffman, MS., B. A. E. (said to be Kaniagmiut name; trans. 'marsh people'). Tyoonok.—Post-route map, 1903.

Tyuga. An unidentifiable Pomo division or village, said to have been near the Makoma, in Sonoma co., Cal., in 1858.—Bancroft, Nat. Races, I, 451, 1874.

Tyuonyi (Keres: 'treaty', 'compact'). A gorge about 20 m. w. of Santa Fé, N. Mex., otherwise known as the Rito de los Frijoles, in which are the remains of numerous cave dwellings and extensive pueblo ruins, the former habitations probably of Keresan tribes. See Bandelier cited below; Hewett in Am. Anthr., VI, 638, 1904; IX, nos. 3, 4, 1909.

Rito de los Frijoles.—Powell in 4th Rep. B. A. E., xxxvi, 1886 (Spanish name). Tyuonyi.—Bandelier, Delight Makers, 3, et seq., 1890. Tyuo-nyi.—Bandelier in Arch. Inst. Papers, IV, 145, 1892. Yu-ñu-ye.—Powell, op. cit., 1886 (given as Cochiti name).

Tyupi. The Badger clans of the pueblos of Laguna and Sia, N. Mex. That of the former claims to have come originally from Zuñi.

Chópï-hánoᶜʰ.—Hodge in Am. Anthr., IX, 349, 1896 (Laguna form; hánoch = 'people'). Tyúpï-háno.—Ibid. (Sia form).

Tzaedelkay ('white sand'). An Apache band or clan at San Carlos agency and Ft Apache, Ariz., in 1881.

Tza-é-delkay.—Bourke in Jour. Am. Folk-lore, III, 112, 1890.

Tzahavak. A Chingigmiut Eskimo village near C. Newenham, Alaska; pop. 48 in 1880.

Tzaharagamut.—Post-route map, 1903. Tzahava-gamut.—Nelson in 18th Rep. B. A. E., map, 1899. Tzahavagamute.—Petroff, Rep. on Alaska, 53, 1881.

Tzauamuk (refers to the noise of rolling stones in the bed of a stream). A Ntlakyapamuk village 6 or 7 m. above Boston Bar, Frazer r., Brit. Col.; pop. 5 in 1897, when last separately enumerated.

Chomok.—Can. Ind. Aff., 230, 1884. Chomok-Spayam.—Ibid., 418, 1898 (names of two towns combined). Tay-ab-Muck.—Can. Ind. Aff., 79, 1878. Tsa'umâk.—Teit in Mem. Am. Mus. Nat. Hist., II, 169, 1900. Tzau'āmuk.—Hill-Tout in Rep. Ethnol. Surv. Can., 5, 1899.

Tzebinaste ('round rock'). An Apache band or clan at San Carlos agency and Ft Apache, Ariz., in 1881.

Tze-binaste.—Bourke in Jour. Am. Folk-lore, III, 112, 1890.

Tzecheschinne ('black rock'). An Apache band or clan at San Carlos agency and Ft Apache, Ariz., in 1881; apparently corresponding to the Tsinazhini, or perhaps the Tsezhinthiai or the Tsetheshkizhni of the Navaho.

Chez-ye-na.—White, Apache Names of Ind. Tribes, MS., B. A. E. ('black rocks'). Tze-ches-chinne.—Bourke in Jour. Am. Folk-lore, III, 112, 1890. Tzĕj-in-né.—ten Kate, Synonymie, 5, 1884.

Tzekinne ('people of the rocks'). A mixed people, partly Apache and partly Piman, descendants of the cliff-dwelling Sobaipuri, whom the Apache drove out of Aravaipa canyon, s. E. Ariz., and forced to flee to the Pima at the beginning of the 19th century. A few descendants are said to dwell among the White Mountain Apache.

Tsiχ'-χaⁿ'-ä.—Gatschet, Apache MS., B. A. E., 1883 ('living on the mountain top'). Tze-kinne.—Bourke in Jour. Am. Folk-lore, III, 114, 1890 (= 'stone house people').

Tzekupama. A band formerly inhabiting the lower Colorado valley, in the present Arizona or California, and who were conquered, absorbed, or driven out by the Mohave.—Bourke in Jour. Am. Folk-lore, II, 185, 1889.

Tzemantuo. A prehistoric ruined pueblo of the compact, communal type, situated about 5 m. s. of Galisteo, Santa Fé co., N. Mex. The Tano now living at Santo Domingo claim that it was a village of their ancestors.

Pueblo Colorado.—Bandelier in Ritch, New Mex., 201, 1885. Tze-man Tu-o.—Bandelier in Arch. Inst. Papers, IV, 106, 1892.

Tzenatay. A former Tano pueblo opposite the little settlement of La Bajada, on the declivity sloping from the w. toward the bed of Santa Fé cr., 6 m. E. of the Rio Grande and 20 m. s. w. of Santa Fé, N. Mex. The village was constructed of volcanic rock and rubble, and probably sheltered 500 people. It had evidently been destroyed by fire, and, with a number of other pueblos in this region that appear to have met a similar fate, is commonly known by the Spanish name Pueblo Quemado, 'burnt village.' According to Bandelier (Arch. Inst. Papers, IV, 95 et seq., 1892) it is not known whether this village was abandoned prior to the 16th century; it may have been the Pueblo Quemado mentioned by Oñate in 1598, but as the remains of a prehistoric Tano or Tewa village 6 m. s. w. of Santa Fé were known by the same name, possibly the latter was the village referred to.

El Pueblo Quemado.—Bandelier, op. cit., 96. Popolo Bruciato.—Columbus Mem. Vol., 155, 1893 (Italian form). Pueblo quemado.—Oñate (1598) in Doc. Inéd., XVI, 114, 1871 (possibly identical).

Tzetseskadn ('top-of-hill people'). An Apache band or clan at San Carlos agency and Ft Apache, Ariz., in 1881 (Bourke in Jour. Am. Folk-lore, III, 112, 1890); corresponding to the Bithani of the Navaho.
Sid-is-kíne.—White, Apache Names of Ind. Tribes, MS., B. A. E. (trans. 'red dirt' or 'red rocks'). Tze-tzes-kadn.—Bourke, op. cit.

Tziltadin ('mountain slope'). A band or clan of the Pinal Coyoteros at San Carlos agency, Ariz., in 1881 (Bourke in Jour. Am. Folk-lore, III, 114, 1890). It corresponds to the Tsiltaden (q. v.) of the Chiricahua Apache.

Tzintzilchutzikadn ('acorn'). An Apache band or clan at San Carlos agency and Ft Apache, Ariz., in 1881.—Bourke in Jour. Am. Folk-lore, III, 111, 1890.

Tziseketzillan ('twin peaks'). An Apache band or clan at San Carlos agency and Ft Apache, Ariz., in 1881.
Tzis-eque-tzillan.—Bourke in Jour. Am. Folk-lore, III, 112, 1890.

Tzlanapah ('plenty of water'). An Apache band or clan at San Carlos and Ft Apache agency, Ariz., in 1881. According to Bourke (Jour. Am. Folk-lore, III, 111, 1890) the name is one of the arbitrary variants of "Tusayan," the native name adopted by the Spaniards for the Hopi country, and still used; but Bourke is probably in error.
Clin'-ar-par.—White, Apache Names of Ind. Tribes, MS., B. A. E. Sla-na-pa.—Bourke in Jour. Am. Folk-lore, III, 126, 1890. Tu-sahn.—Ibid. Tusayan.—Ibid. Tu-sla.—Ibid. Tu-sla-na-pa.—Ibid. Tu-slan-go.—Ibid.

Tzolgan ('white mountain'). An Apache band or clan at San Carlos agency and Ft Apache, Ariz., in 1881.—Bourke in Jour. Am. Folk-lore, III, 111, 1890.

Tzues. A Makah village 4 m. s. of Waatch, N. w. Washington; pop. 99 in 1863.
Tsoo-Yess.—U. S. Ind. Treat., 461, 1873. Tsuess.—Swan in Smithson. Cont., XVI, 6, 1870. Tsū-yess.—Gibbs in Cont. N. A. Ethnol., I, 173, 1877.

Uacazil ('sandy cave'). A rancheria, probably Cochimi, under Purísima (Cadegomo) mission, s. Lower California,

in the 18th century.—Doc. Hist. Mex., 4th s., V, 188, 1857.

Uahatzae (*Uä-hä-tza-e*). A former pueblo of the Jemez (q. v.), in New Mexico, the exact site of which is not known.—Bandelier in Arch. Inst. Papers, IV, 207, 1892.

Uainuints ('digger people'). A Paiute band formerly living about St George, s. w. Utah, numbering 80 in 1873. The significance of the name arises from the fact that this was the only Paiute band in this region which practised agriculture. The English translation of the name, "Diggers," subsequently was applied to all root-digging Indians, and, as according to the general idea this practice implied a low type of culture, the term became synonymous with all that is low and degraded.   (H. W. H.)
U'-ai-Nu-ints.—Powell in Ind. Aff. Rep. 1873, 50, 1874. Urai-Nuints.—Ingalls in H. R. Ex. Doc. 66, 42d Cong., 3d sess., 2, 1873.

Ualik. A Togiagamiut Eskimo village on Kulukak bay, Alaska; pop. 68 in 1880.
Ooailik.—Post-route map, 1903. Ooallikh.—Petroff in 10th Census, Alaska, 17, 1884.

Uames. Given by Ker (Travels, 93, 1816), as the name of a tribe in the Caddo country, apparently in extreme N. w. Louisiana. Not identifiable, and probably an invented name.

Uapige (Tewa: *Uap-i-ge*, or *Wap-i-ge*). A prehistoric Tano pueblo E. of Lamy station, on the A. T. & S. F. R. R., some distance in the mountains, in N. central New Mexico.—Bandelier in Arch. Inst. Papers, IV, 100, 1892.

Ubakhea. A Pomo division, or probably a village, near the Shanel, in s. Mendocino co., Cal., and speaking the same language.—Gibbs (1851) in Schoolcraft, Ind. Tribes, III, 112, 1853.

Uchak. A Kuskwogmiut Eskimo village on the right bank of Kuskokwim r., Alaska.
Uchagmjut.—Holmberg, Ethnog. Skizz., map, 1855. Ugokhamiut.—11th Census, Alaska, 164, 1893.

Uchapa. Given as a Karok village on Klamath r., N. w. Cal.
Ut-cha-pah.—McKee (1851) in Sen. Ex. Doc. 4, 32d Cong., spec. sess., 194, 1853. Ut-cha-pas.—Ibid., 215 (given as a Hupa division). Ut-chap-pah.—Ibid., 161. Ut-scha-pahs.—Meyer, Nach dem Sacramento, 282, 1855.

Uchean Family. A linguistic family limited, so far as is positively known, to a single tribe, the Yuchi (q. v.).
=Uchees.—Gallatin in Trans. and Coll. Am. Antiq. Soc., II, 95, 1836 (based on the Yuchi alone); Bancroft, Hist. U. S., III, 247, 1840; Gallatin in Trans. Am. Ethnol. Soc., II, pt. 1, cxix, 77, 1848; Keane in Stanford, Compend., Cent. and So. Am., app., 472, 1878 (suggests that the language may have been akin to Natchez). =Utchees.—Gallatin in Trans. and Coll. Am. Antiq. Soc., II, 306, 1836; Gallatin in Schoolcraft, Ind. Tribes, III, 401, 1853; Keane in Stanford, Compend., Cent. and So. Am., app., 472, 1878. =Utschies.—Berghaus (1845), Physik. Atlas, map 17, 1848; ibid., 1852. =Uché.—Latham, Nat. Hist. Man., 338, 1850 (Coosa river); Latham in Trans. Philol. Soc. Lond., II,

31–50, 1846; Latham, Opuscula, 293, 1860.
=**Yuchi.**—Gatschet, Creek Migr. Leg., I, 17, 1884;
Gatschet in Science, 413, Apr. 29, 1887.
=**Uchean.**—Powell in 7th Rep. B. A. E., 126, 1891.

Uchitak. An Unaligmiut Eskimo village near Tolstoi pt., Norton sd., Alaska.
Outchitak-Mioute.—Zagoskin in Nouv. Ann. Voy., 5th s., XXI, map, 1850.

Uchium. A division of the Olamentke, and according to Chamisso one of the most numerous connected with Dolores mission, Cal., in 1816.
Aguasajuchium.—Taylor in Cal. Farmer, Oct. 18, 1861 (Aguasto and Juchium (Uchium) combined). **Huchun.**—Ibid. **Juchium.**—Ibid. **Outchioung.**—Bancroft, Nat. Races, I, 453, 1874 (misquoted from Choris.) **Outchiouns.**—Choris (1816), Voy. Pitt., 6, 1822. **Uchium.**—Taylor, op. cit. **Utschim.**—Bancroft, op. cit. (misquoted from Chamisso). **Utschium.**—Taylor in Cal. Farmer, June 8, 1860 (misquoted from Chamisso). **Utschiun.**—Chamisso (1816) in Kotzebue, Voy., III, 51, 1821.

Uchiyingich. A settlement of the Yaudanchi, a Yokuts (Mariposan) tribe, on Tule r., Cal., at the large painted rocks on the present Tule River res. The word has some reference to these paintings. It is the name of a village site, not of a tribe, as given by Powers.	(A. L. K.)
O-ching'-i-ta.—Powers in Cont. N. A. Ethnol., III, 370, 1877.

Uchucklesit. A Nootka tribe on Uchucklesit harbor, Barclay sd., w. coast of Vancouver id., Brit. Col. Pop. 34 in 1910. Their principal village is Elhlateese.
Cojuklesatuch.—Grant in Jour. Roy. Geog. Soc., 293, 1857. **Hāutcu'k·tlěs'ath.**—Boas, 6th Rep. N.W. Tribes Can., 31, 1890. **How-chuck-les-aht.**—Can. Ind. Aff., 308, 1879. **Howchucklus-aht.**—Brit. Col. map, 1872. **Howchuk-lis-aht.**—Can. Ind. Aff. 1897, 357, 1898. **Howchuklisat.**—Can. Ind. Aff., pt. II, 158, 1901. **Howschueselet.**—Kelley, Oreg., 68, 1830. **Ouchuchlisit.**—Mayne, Brit. Col., 251, 1861. **Ouchuk-lis-aht.**—Can. Ind. Aff., 51, 1875.

Ucita. The first village in Florida entered by De Soto in 1539. It was situated on the shore of Tampa bay, the town house being upon a high artificial mound, and was deserted by the Indians on the approach of the Spaniards.	(J. M.)
Eçita.—Ranjel (ca. 1546) in Bourne, De Soto Narr., II, 58, 1904. **Oçita.**—Ibid., 52. **Ucista.**—Drake, Tragedies of Wilderness, 18, 1841 (misprint). **Ucita.**—Gentl. of Elvas (1557) in Bourne, op. cit., I, 22, 1904.

Uclenu. Mentioned by Kane (Wand. in N. A., app., 1859) as the name of a tribe occupying Scotts id., N. w. of Vancouver id., Brit. Col. According to Boas it is the name of the island "Yutl," belonging to the Nakomgilisala, compounded with -ēnoq, 'inhabitants of.'

Ucluelet. A Nootka tribe at the N. entrance of Barclay sd., w. coast of Vancouver id., Brit. Col. Not to be confounded with the Lekwiltok. Their principal town is Ittatso; pop. 150 in 1904, 132 in 1910.
Emlh-wilh-laht.—Can. Ind. Aff., 310, 1892. **Ewlbwiehaht.**—Ibid., pt. 2, 158, 1901. **Ewlhwiehaht.**—Ibid., pt. 2, 74, 1902. **Ewl-hwilh-aht.**—Ibid., 357, 1897. **Ucle-tah.**—Mayne, Brit. Col., 251, 1862. **Uclúlet.**—Swan, MS., B. A. E. **Ugluxlatuch.**—Grant in Jour. Roy. Geog. Soc., 293, 1857. **W-ltoo-ilth-aht.**—Can. Ind. Aff., 308, 1879. **Yongletats.**—Domenech, Deserts, 445, 1860. **Youchehtaht.**—Brit. Col. map, 1872. **You-clul-aht.**—Sproat, Savage Life, 308, 1868.

Yutlū'lath.—Boas, 6th Rep. N. W. Tribes Can., 31, 1890.

Ucouhnerunt. A former hut town of the Tuscarora of North Carolina, situated in 1711 on Pamlico r., probably in the vicinity of the present Greenville, Pitt co.—S. C. Hist. and Geneal. Mag., IX, 39, 1908.

Udekumaig (adĭ'kamäg, 'caribou fish,' meaning whitefish.—W. J.). A gens of the Chippewa.
Ad-dik-kun-maig.—Tanner, Narr., 314, 1830. **Adi-'kamäg.**—Wm. Jones, inf'n, 1907. **Ude-kumaig.**—Warren (1852) in Minn. Hist. Soc. Coll., V, 44, 1885.

Udluhsen ('skin-scraping place'). An Ita Eskimo settlement on Herbert id., Whale sd., N. Greenland.
Oomiak-soak.—Kane, Arct. Explor., II, 212, 1856. **Udluhsen.**—Stein in Petermanns Mitteil., no. 9, map, 1902.

Uedle. A Yuit Eskimo village in the N. part of East cape, Siberia.
Ouedle.—Petroff in Tenth Census, Alaska, map, 1884. **Uedle.**—Krause in Deutsche Geog. Blätter, V, 80, map, 1882.

Ugagogmiut. A subdivision of the Aglemiut Eskimo dwelling on the banks of Ugaguk r., Alaska.
Ugāgŏg'-mūt.—Dall in Cont. N. A. Ethnol., I, 19, 1877.

Ugalakmiut ('far people'). A tribe of Alaskan Eskimo living on the coast at the mouth of Copper r. and on Kayak id. According to the latest writers they have been so far metamorphosed by contact with the Tlingit as to be more properly Tlingit than Eskimo. They live mainly by fishing. Between them and the Chugachigmiut the Copper River Indians have intruded (Dall, Alaska, 401, 1870). They have been classed by some as Tlingit, by others as Athapascan, confusion having arisen from Indian vocabularies taken from visitors in the Ugalakmiut villages. A distinction was made between the Ugalakmiut, who were regarded as a small division of the Chingachimiut, and a supposed Indian tribe, by some considered Tlingit, by some as Athapascan, called Ugalentsi. When it was found that the natives of Kayak and the opposite mainland have an Innuit vocabulary, they were classed as a separate Eskimo tribe, to which the name Ugalentsi was transferred, which is merely their own name with a Russian termination (Dall in Cont. N. A. Ethnol., I, 21, 1877). Their principal village is Eyak.
Guth-le-uk-qwan.—Emmons in Mem. Am. Mus. Nat. Hist., III, 231, 1903 (Tlingit name of natives from C. Yaktag, through Controller bay, and on Kayak id.). **Lakhamute.**—Petroff in 10th Census, Alaska, 146, 1884. **Oogahlensie.**—Veniaminof quoted by Elliott, Cond. Aff., Alaska, 227, 1875. **Oogalenskie.**—Ibid., 30. **Ougalachmioutsy.**—Gallatin in Trans. Am. Antiq. Soc., II, 14, 1836. **Ougalentze.**—Petroff in 10th Census, Alaska, 146, 1884. **Oughalakmute.**—Petroff in Am. Nat., XVI, 568, 1882. **Oughalentze.**—Ibid. **Ugalachmiuti.**—Humboldt, Essai Polit., I, 347, 1811. **Ugalakmutes.**—Dall in Proc. Am. A. A. S., XVIII, 267, 1870. **Ugalakmutsi.**—Richardson, Arct. Exped., I, 402, 1851. **Ugalenschen.**—Erman, Archiv, VII, 128, 1849. **Ugalensé.**—Dall in

Proc. Am. A. A. S., XVIII, 269, 1870. **Ugalents.—**
Latham in Jour. Ethnol. Soc. Lond., 189, 1848.
Ugalentses. — Latham, Essays, 270, 1860. **Uga-**
léntsi.—Dall, Alaska, 430, 1870. **Ugalentzes.—**
Scouler in Jour. Geog. Soc. Lond., I, 219, 1841.
Ugalenz.—Latham, Essays, 275, 1860. **Ugalenzes.—**
Keane in Stanford, Compend., 541, 1878. **Uga-**
lenzi.—Scouler in Jour. Ethnol. Soc. Lond., I, 232,
1848. **Ugaljachmjuten.—**Bancroft, Nat. Races, I, 96,
1882. **Ugaljachmutzi.—**Adelung, Mithrid., III, 3d
abth., 228, 1816. **Ugalukmute.—**Bancroft, Nat.
Races, I, 96, 1882. **Ugalyachmutsi.—**Latham in
Jour. Ethnol. Soc. Lond., 187, 1848. **Ugalyach-**
mutzi.—Bancroft,Nat.Races, I, 96,1882. **Ugalyackh-**
mutsi.—Latham in Trans. Philol. Soc. Lond., 68,
1856. **Wallamute.—**Petroff in 10th Census, Alaska,
146, 1884.

Ugamitzi. A former Aleut village on
Unalaska, Aleutian ids., Alaska.—Coxe,
Russ. Discov., 163, 1787.

Uganik. A Kaniagmiut Eskimo village
on the N. coast of Kodiak id., Alaska;
pop. 73 in 1880, 31 in 1890.
Ooganok.—Petroff in 10th Census, Alaska, 29, 1884.
Oohanick.—Lisianski (1805) quoted by Baker,
Geog. Dict. Alaska, 1902. **Uganak.—**11th Census,
Alaska, 79, 1893.

Ugashigmiut. A local subdivision of
the Aglemiut Eskimo of Alaska.
Ugas'hig-mūt.—Dall in Cont. N. A. Ethnol., I, 19,
1877.

Ugashik. An Aglemiut Eskimo village
at the mouth of Ugashik r., Alaska; pop.
177 in 1880, 154 in 1890.
Oogashik.—Elliott, Our Arct. Prov., map, 1886.

Ugiatok. A former Aleut village on
Agattu id., Alaska, one of the Near id.
group of the Aleutians, now uninhabited.

Ugjuktung ('abounding in seal'). An
Okomiut Eskimo winter village of the
Saumingmiut subtribe in Baffinland.—
Boas in Deutsche Geog. Blätt., VIII, 32,
1885.

Ugjulirmiut ('people possessing seal').
A tribe of Eskimo occupying King Wil-
liam id. and Adelaide penin., lat. 68°.
These are the Eskimo who fell heir to
the wrecked ship of Franklin. The
Netchilirmiut, who in recent times regu-
larly visited King William land, became
mixed with the Ugjulirmiut. Their vil-
lage is Kingmiktuk.
Kρikeρtaloρméut.—Petitot in Bib. Ling. et Ethn.
Am., III, xi, 1876 (sig. 'islanders': Kopagmiut
name). **Oo-geoo-lik.—**Ross, Second Voy., 308, 1835.
Ook-joo-lik.—Gilder, Schwatka's Search, 85, 1881.
Ookwolik.—Ibid., 199. **Ugjulik.—**Boas in Zeitschr.
Ges. Erdk., 226, 1883. **Ugjulirmiut.—**Boas in Trans.
Anthr. Soc. Wash., III, 101, 1885. **Ukdschulik.—**
Schwatka quoted in Ausland, 653, 1885. **Ukdshú-**
lik.—Schwatka in Century Mag., XXII, 76, 1881.

Uglariak. A winter settlement of the
Aivilirmiut Eskimo at the entrance of
Repulse bay, N. end of Hudson bay, Can.
Uglariaq.—Boas in 6th Rep. B. A. E., 447, 1888.

Uglirn. A winter settlement of Iglu-
lirmiut Eskimo on an island in N. w. Fox
basin, lat. 68°.
Ooglit.—Parry, Second Voy., 359, 1824. **Ooglitt.—**
Lyons, Priv. Jour., 406, 1825. **Uglirn.—**Boas in 6th
Rep. B. A. E., map, 1888.

Uglovaia. A Chnagmiut Eskimo village on the right bank of the lower Yukon, Alaska; pop. 102 in 1880.
Ooglovia.—Petroff, Rep. on Alaska, 57, 1880. **Sa-**
botnisky.—Nelson in 18th Rep. B. A. E., map, 1899.

Uglivia.—Ibid. **Ugloyaia.—**Baker, Geog. Dict.
Alaska, 648, 1906.

Ugovik. A Kuskwogmiut Eskimo vil-
lage on the right bank of Kuskokwim r.,
Alaska; pop. 206 in 1880, 57 in 1890.
Odgavigamut.—Post route map, 1903. **Ogavima-**
mute.—Bruce, Alaska, map, 1895. **Oogovigamute.—**
Petroff in 10th Census, Alaska, map, 1884. **Oogo-**
wigamute.—Petroff, Rep. on Alaska, 53, 1881.
Ugavigamiut.—11th Census, Alaska, 164, 1893.
Ugavik.—Hallock in Nat. Geog. Mag., IX, 90,
1898.

Ugtikun. A former Aleut village on
Agattu id., Alaska, one of the Near id.
group of the Aleutians, now uninhabited.

Ugtumuk. A former Aleut village on
Agattu id., Alaska, one of the Near id.
group of the Aleutians, now uninhabited.

Uhaskek. A Kaniagmiut Eskimo vil-
lage on the S. E. coast of Kodiak id.,
Alaska.
Oohaskeck.—Lisianski quoted by Baker, Geog.
Dict. Alaska, 1902. **Uhaskek.—**Baker, ibid.

Uinkarets (*U-in-ka'-rets*, 'where the
piñe grows'). A Paiute band in the
mountains of the same name, N. Arizona.—Powell in Ind. Aff. Rep. 1873, 50,
1874.

Uinta (contr. of *Uintats*). A division
of Ute formerly living in N. E. Utah, of
which° the so-called Elk Mountain Ute
were probably a subdivision. Powell
found 194 on the Uinta res. in 1873. The
name was subsequently applied to the reservation in N. E. Utah and to various bands
assembled there, which thus included the
Cumumbah, Kosunats, Pikakwanarats,
Pahvants, Sanpet, Seuvarits, Timpaiavats,
and Yampa, as well as the original Uinta.
The name Uinta is still applied to some
of these bands, while the remainder,
including the Yampa and some others,
are called White River Utes. The Indians now officially regarded as Uinta
numbered 443 in 1909, under the
Uintah and Ouray school superintendent, Utah.   (H. W. H.)
Ewinte.—Wilson in Ind. Aff. Rep. 1849, 67, 1850.
Pag-wa-nu-chi.—Hrdlička, inf'n, 1907 (given as one
of their own names, sig. 'people with a little different language and dress'). **Uintah Valley In-**
dians.—Cooley in Ind. Aff. Rep., 17, 1865. **U'-in-**
tats.—Powell in Ind. Aff. Rep. 1873, 51, 1874.
Uinta Utes.—Forney in Ind. Aff. Rep. 1859, 366,
1860. **Uinta Yuta.—**Burton, City of Saints, 577,
1861. **Uwinty-Utahs.** — Schoolcraft, Ind. Tribes,
V, 199, 498, 1855. **Yoov'té.—**Hrdlička, inf'n, 1907
(own name).

Uintahite. A certain mineral: from
the place name *Uintah* and the English
suffix *-ite*. The word Uintah, or Uinta,
applied to a tribe and a mountain range
in Utah, is derived from the Ute dialect
of the Shoshonean stock.   (A. F. C.)

Uintatherium. A fossil mammal from
the Eocene period of North America: so
named from *Uintah* (see *Uinta*) and the
Greek *therion*, beast.   (A. F. C.)

Uinuk. A Kaviagmiut Eskimo village
at the mouth of Nome r., Alaska; pop.
10 in 1880.
Oo-innakhtagowik.—Petroff in 10th Census, Alaska,
11, 1884. **Ooinukhlagowik.—**Jackson in Rep. Bur.

Ed.,map,145,1894. **Ooinuktagowik.**—Petroff in 10th Census, Alaska, map, 1884. **Uinakhtagewik.**—Nelson in 18th Rep. B. A. E., map, 1899. **Uinuk.**—Baker, Geog. Dict. Alaska, 1902.

Uissuit. Dwarfs which the Central Eskimo believe to inhabit the depths of the sea. They fish for them with hook and line, but none is ever caught, because, it is believed, when one is hooked and drawn up, as soon as he comes near the surface he flashes his legs above water and dives below. — Boas in 6th Rep. B. A. E., 621, 1888.

Uitorrum. A group of Maricopa rancherias visited by Anza, Garcés, and Font in 1775. Situated on the s. bank of Gila r., s. w. Ariz., not far w. of Gila bend. **San Diego.**—Garcés (1775), Diary, 117, 1900. **San Diego de Uitorrum.**—Ibid. (1776), 455.

Ujuiap. A tribe, apparently Tonkawan, which entered San Antonio de Valero mission, Texas, in 1741, with the group to which belonged the Sana (q. v.) tribe. Baptisms of members of the tribe there continued at least until 1755 (Valero Baptisms, 1741–55, passim, MS.). A number of words of their language have been preserved. (H. E. B.) **Ajuyap.**—Valero Baptisms, 1755, partida 883, MS. **Aujuiap.**—Valero Baptisms, 1741, partida 569, MS. **Ujuiapa.**—Ibid., partida 524.

Ukadlik. A winter village of Nugumiut Eskimo on the coast between Frobisher bay and Cumberland sd., Baffin land. **Ukadliq.**—Boas in 6th Rep. B. A. E., 422, 1888. **Ukadliκ.**—Boas in Petermanns Mitteil., XVII, suppl., no. 80, 67, 1885.

Ukagemiut. A subdivision of the Chnagmiut Eskimo, whose village is Ukak. **Ukāg′emūt.**—Dall in Cont. N. A. Ethnol., I, 17, 1877.

Ukak. A Kaialigmiut Eskimo village on Hazen bay, Alaska; pop. 25 in 1880. **Ookagamiut.**—Nelson in 18th Rep. B. A. E., map, 1899. **Ookagamute.**—Petroff in 10th Census, Alaska, 11, 1884.

Ukak. A Chnagmiut Eskimo village on the N. bank of the lower Yukon in Alaska. **Ookagamute**—Petroff in 10th Census, Alaska, map, 1884. **Ukagamut**—Nelson in 18th Rep. B A. E. map, 1899. **Yukagamut.**—Post route map, 1903. **Yukagamute.**—Raymond in Sen. Ex. Doc. 12 42d Cong., 1st sess., 25 1871.

Ukakhpakhti (etymologically the same as the tribal name, and Capaha and Pacaha, village names given by De Soto's chroniclers). One of the 5 Quapaw villages known to the French in the 17th and early part of the 18th centuries. The village visited by Marquette in 1683 was probably in Phillips co., Ark., lower on the Mississippi than the one seen by De Soto in 1541. When Gravier arrived, 27 years later, he found the people still lower down. Of the village at which Marquette stopped nothing was left save the old "outworks," doubtless mounds, walls, etc. La Harpe (1722) said that the people of this village were originally from the Kansa nation, evidently an echo of the tradition relating to the former unity of the "Dhegiha" group. Pénicaut (1700)

speaks of the "Arkansas nation," living on Arkansas r., as distinct from "the Torimas and the Kappas," who lived with them. Jefferys (1761) located them above the "Sothouis" (Uzutiuhi). Poisson (1727) gives the relative position of the four villages as follows: "Entering the Arkansas by the lower branch, from the mouth of this branch to where the river separates into two streams it is 7 leagues, and from thence to the first village, which contains two nations, the Tourimas and the Tougingas; from this first village to the second there are 2 leagues by water and 1 league by land; the latter they call the village of the Sauthouis; the third village is a little higher up, on the bank of the same river; this is the village of the Kappas." Shea supposed that this band existed no longer except in name, but J. O. Dorsey in 1883 found some of the Quapaw who claimed to belong to it. **Cappa.**—Joutel (1687) in French, Hist. Coll. La., I, 176, 1846. **Uӽa′qpa-qti.**—Dorsey in 15th Rep. B. A. E., 229, 1897.

Ukashik. A former Aleut village on Agattu id., Alaska, one of the Near id. group of the Aleutians, now uninhabited.

Ukhwaiksh. A Yaquina village on the N. side of Yaquina r., Oreg. **Ŭ-qwaikc′.**—Dorsey in Jour. Am. Folk-lore, III, 229, 1890.

Ukiadliving ('autumn settlement'). A winter settlement of Okomiut Eskimo of Saumia on N. Cumberland sd.; pop. 17 in 1883. **Okkiadliving.**—Boas in Trans. Anthr. Soc. Wash., III, 98, 1885. **Ukiadliving.**—Boas in 6th Rep. B. A. E., map, 1888; Boas in Petermanns Mitteil., no. 80, 70, 1885. **Ukiolik.**—Rink, Eskimo Tribes, 33, 1887.

Ukivogmiut. A division of Kaviagmiut Eskimo, occupying King id., Bering str.; pop. 200 in 1890. Their village is Ukivok. **Okuvagamute.**—Petroff, Rep. on Alaska, 59, 1881. **Ukivŏg′-mūt.**—Dall in Cont. N. A. Ethnol., I, 15, 1877. **Ukivokgmut.**—Zagoskin, Descr. Russ. Poss. Am., pt. I, 73, 1847. **Ukivokmiut.**—11th Census, Alaska, 130. 1893.

Ukivok. A Kaviagmiut Eskimo village on King id., Bering str., Alaska. It is said to consist of about 40 dwellings partly excavated in the side of a ravine and built up with stone walls. The summer houses are made of walrus skin. **Ookevok.**—Kelly, Arctic Eskimo, chart, 1890. **Ookivok.**—Petroff in 10th Census Alaska, map, 1884. **Oukivak.**—Jackson, Reindeer in Alaska, map, 145, 1894. **Oukwak.**—Hooper Cruise of Corwin, 15, 1881. **Ovkévok.**—Baker, Geog. Dict. Alaska, 649, 1906 (cited form). **Ukivak**—Ibid. (cited form). **Ukivŏk.**—Dall in Cont. N. A. Ethnol., I, 15, 1877; Baker, op. cit. **Ukivuk.**—Baker, ibid. (cited form). **Ukiwuk.**—Ibid. (cited form).

Uknavik ('on the other side'). A Kuskwogmiut Eskimo village and mission station on Kuskokwim r., 10 m. below the Yukon portage, Alaska. **Gavimamut.**—Post-route map, 1903. **Oknavigamut.**—Spurr and Post (1898) quoted by Baker, Geog. Dict. Alaska, 1902.

Uknodok. A former Aleut village on

Hog id., Captains bay, Unalaska, Aleutian ids., Alaska.
Ouknadok.—Lutke quoted by Baker, Geog. Dict. Alaska, 205, 1902. Uknadak.—Veniaminof quoted by Baker, ibid. Uknodok.—Sarichef (1792) quoted by Baker, ibid. Ukunadok.—Coxe, Russian Discov., 167, 1787.

Ukodlint. A Kaviagmiut Eskimo village on Golofnin bay, Alaska.—11th Census, Alaska, 162, 1893.

Ukohtontilka ('ocean people,' their own name). The Coast Yuki, a branch of the Yuki of N. California detached from the main body and inhabiting the coast from Tenmile r. to Rockport or Usal in N. W. Mendocino co., and extending inland as far as Jackson Valley cr. (A. L. K.)
Uk-hóat-nom.—Powers in Cont. N. A. Ethnol., III, 126, 1877 (stated to be the Yuki name for the Coast Yuki, and incorrectly to mean 'on the ocean'). Uk'hotnom.—A. L. Kroeber, inf'n, 1903 (another form).

Ukomnom. The branch of the Yuki of N. California inhabiting Round valley and the surrounding country. (A. L. K.)
Ūk-um-nom.—Powers in Cont. N. A. Ethnol., III, 126, 1877.

Ukshivikak. A Kaniagmiut Eskimo village on the s. w. coast of Kodiak id., Alaska.
Ukshivkag-miut.—Russ.-Am. Co. map cited by Baker, Geog. Dict. Alaska, 1902 (miut='people'). Ukshivikak.—Baker, ibid.

Uktahasasi (óktaha, 'sand'). A branch colony of the Upper Creek town of Hillabi, formerly on a branch of Hillabi cr., Clay co., Ala., near the present town of Ashland. It had 34 heads of families in 1832. See Sand Town. (H. W. H.)
Oak-li-sarcy.—Sen. Ex. Doc. 425, 24th Cong., 1st sess., 215, 1836. Oaktarsarsey.—Ibid., 279. Oak Tarsarsey.—H. R. Ex. Doc. 276, 24th Cong., 1st sess., 250, 1836. Oak-taw sar-seg.—Census of 1832 in Schoolcraft, Ind. Tribes, IV, 578, 1854. Ook-tau-hau-zau-see.—Hawkins (1799), Sketch, 43, 1848. Sand Town.—U. S. Ind. Treat. (1825), 326, 1837. Ûktaha sàsi.—Gatschet, Creek Migr. Leg., I, 149, 1884.

Ukuk. A village of the Kaialigmiut Eskimo on Nelson id., Alaska; pop. 68 in 1890.—11th Census, Alaska, 111, 1893.

Ukusiksalik. A winter village of the Aivilirmiut Eskimo on Wager r., N. end of Hudson bay.—Boas in 6th Rep. B. A. E., 449, 1888.

Ukusiksalirmiut ('people possessing potstone kettles'). A tribe of the Central Eskimo living on Back r., Can., and formerly on the shores of Boothia land. According to Schwatka they are nearly extinct, the few survivors living at Dangerous rapids. They live on musk ox and fish, do not hunt seal, and have no fuel.
Oogueesik Salik.—Schwatka in Science, 543, 1884. Ooguensik-salik-Innuits.—Ausland, 653, 1885. Ooqueesiksillik.—Schwatka in Century, XXII, map, 1881. Ootkooseek-kalingmœoot.—Franklin, Journ. to Polar Sea, II, 42, 1824. Stone Kettle Esquimaux.—Ibid. Thleweechodezeth.—Back, Narr., map, 1836. Ukusiksalik.—Boas in 6th Rep. B. A. E., 458, 1888. Ukusiksalingmiut.—Boas in Trans. Anthr. Soc. Wash., III, 101, 1885. Ukusiksalirmiut.—Boas in 6th Rep. B. A. E., 458, 1888. Ukusiksillik.—Klutschak, Als Eskimo unter den Eskimo, map, 64, 1881. Utku-hikalik.—Richardson,

Polar Regions, 170, 1861. Ut-ku-hikaling-mëut.—Ibid., 300. Ut-ku-sik-kaling-me' ut.—Richardson, Arct. Exped., I, 362, 1851. Utkusiksalik.—Boas in Zeitsch. Ges. f. Erdk., 226, 1883. Utkutọiki-aliñ-méut.—Petitot in Bib. Ling. et Ethn. Am., III, xi, 1876. Uvkusigsalik.—Rink, Eskimo Tribes, 33, 1887.

Ukviktulik. A Kaviagmiut Eskimo village on the N. side of Norton sd., Alaska.
Ukvikhtuligmut.—Zagoskin, Descr. Russ. Poss. Am., pt. I, 73, 1847.

Ulak (úlak, 'carving knife'). A village inhabited about equally by Chukchi and Yuit Eskimo, just N. of East cape, N. E. Siberia. They numbered 231, in 38 houses, about 1895.
Uwe'len.—Bogoras, Chukchee, 30, 1904 (Chukchi name).

Ulezara. A Kevalingamiut Eskimo village near C. Kruzenstern, Alaska.
Ulezaramiut.—11th Census, Alaska, 162, 1893 (miut= 'people').

Ulksin (U'lk·s'n, 'point'). A Squawmish village community on Burrard inlet, Brit. Col.—Hill-Tout in Rep. Brit. A. A. S., 475, 1900.

Ullibahali. A palisaded village visited in 1540 by De Soto and mentioned in the account of the expedition of Tristan de Luna in 1560. In all probability it is identical with Huhliwahli (q. v.).
Allibamous.—Coxe, Carolana, 24, 1741 (probably identical). Olibahali.—Barcia (1693), Ensayo, 34, 1723. Olibahalies.—Coxe, op. cit. Ulibahali.—Harris, Voy. and Trav., I, 807, 1705. Ullibahali.—Gentl. of Elvas (1557) in French, Hist. Coll. La., II, 153, 1850. Ullibalies.—Coxe, op. cit. Ullibalys.—Ibid., 26. Vlibahalj.—Map of 1597 in 5th Rep. B. A. E., 128, 1887.

Ulokak. An Eskimo village in the Kuskokwim district, Alaska; pop. 27 in 1890.
Ulokagmiut.—11th Census, Alaska, 164, 1893 (miut= 'people').

Ulu. The woman's knife of the Eskimo. The modern kitchen chopping knife and the saddler's knife are derived from ancient similar tools plied by women. The Eskimo knives were made in great variety, ranging from a chipped stone wrapped with a splint on one edge for a grip, to knives having exquisite carved handles of ivory, shaped to the hand and furnished with steel blades. As the women were the only workers on skins of animals, these were their peculiar tools, for which they found a great number of uses in skinning the game, preparing skins, and cutting out garments of many parts. See Mason in Rep. U. S. Nat. Mus. 1890, 411–16, 1891.

Ulukakhotana. A division of Kaiyuhkhotana living on Unalaklik r., Alaska; pop. 25 in 1890. The natives have been expelled by Eskimo intruders and have settled on Yukon r. The chief village is Iktigalik.
Oolukak.—Zagoskin (1842) quoted by Petroff in 10th Census, Alaska, 37, 1884. Ulukagmuts.—Holmberg quoted by Dall, Alaska, 432, 1870. Ulū'-kākhotän'-ā.—Dall in Cont. N. A. Ethnol., I, 25, 1877. Ulukuk.—Whymper, Alaska, 180, 1869.

Ulukuk. A Malemiut Eskimo village on Ulukuk r., E. of Norton sd., Alaska.

Ulukak.—Jackson, Reindeer in Alaska, map, 145, 1894. **Ulukuk.**—Dall, Alaska, map, 1870.

Umana ('the heart'). A winter village of Ita Eskimo on Wolstenholme sd., N. Greenland.
Omenak.—Inglefield in Jour. Roy. Geog. Soc., 138, 1853. **Oomenak.**—Kane, Arct. Explor., I, 45, 1856. **Ū′mana.**—Stein in Petermanns Mitteil., 198, 1902.

Umanak. A village of the southern group of East Greenland Eskimo, lat. 63°.—Rink in Deutsche Geog. Blätt., VIII, 345, 1886.

Umanak. A Moravian mission station and Eskimo settlement in w. Greenland, near Godthaab.—Nansen, First Crossing, II, 204, 1890.

Umanak. An Eskimo settlement in Umanak fjord, N. of Nugsuak penin., w. Greenland, about lat. 71°.

Umanaktuak. A winter settlement of Talirpia Okomiut Eskimo on an island near the s. w. coast of Cumberland sd., not far from the entrance.
Annanactook.—Kumlien in Bull. 15, U. S. Nat. Mus., 15, 1879. **Umanaqtuaq.**—Boas in 6th Rep. B. A. E., 426, 1888. **Umanaĸtuaĸ.**—Boas in Petermanns Mitteil., XVII, no. 80, p. 70, 1885.

Umatilla. A Shahaptian tribe formerly living on Umatilla r. and the adjacent banks of the Columbia in Oregon. They were included under the Wallawalla by Lewis and Clark in 1805, though their language is distinct. In 1855 they joined in a treaty with the United States and settled on Umatilla res. in E. Oregon. They are said to number 250, but this figure is doubtful, owing to the mixture of tribes on the reservation. (L. F.)
Umatila.—Nesmith in Ind. Aff. Rep. 1857, 323, 1858. **Umatillas.**—U. S. Stat., XII, 945, 1863. **Utella.**—Raymond in H. R. Ex. Doc. 93, 34th Cong., 1st sess., 106, 1856. **Utillas.**—Schoolcraft, Ind. Tribes, V, 493, 1855. **You-ma-talla.**—Ross, Fur Hunters, I, 186, 1855. **Yumatilla.**—Gatschet in Am. Antiq., II, 216, 1880.

Umiak. See *Oomiak*.

Umivik. A village of the southern group of East Greenland Eskimo on Gyldenlöve fjord, lat. 64° 24′.

Umivik. A village of the Angmagsalingmiut Eskimo on an island in Angmagsalik fjord, Greenland; pop. 19 in 1884.
Umerik.—Rink in Deutsche Geog. Blätt., VIII, 348, 1886. **Umivik.**—Meddelelser om Grönland, IX, 379, 1889.

Umnokalukta. A Kowagmiut Eskimo fishing village on Black r., a s. branch of Kobuk r., Alaska.

Um-nok-a-luk-ta.—Healy, Cruise of Corwin, 28, 1887.

Umpqua. An Athapascan tribe formerly settled on upper Umpqua r., Oreg., E. of the Kuitsh. Hale (Ethnol. and Philol., 204, 1846) said they were supposed to number not more than 400, having been greatly reduced by disease. They lived in houses of boards and mats, and derived their sustenance mainly from the river. In 1902 there were 84 on Grande Ronde res., Oregon. Their chief village was Hewut. A part of them, the Nahankhuotana, lived along Cow cr. All the Athapascan tribes of s. Oregon were once considered divisions of the Umpqua. Parker (Jour., 262, 1842) named as divisions the unidentified Palakahu, the uncertain Skoton and Chasta, and the Chilula and Kwatami.
A-ampkua amim.—Gatschet, Kalapuya MS., B. A. E. (Atfalati name). **Amgútsuish.**—Gatschet, MS., B. A. E. (Shasta name). **Ámpkokñi máklaks.**—Gatschet in Cont. N. A. Ethnol., II. pt. 2, 20, 1890 (Klamath name). **Ámpkua.**—Gatschet, Nestucca MS. vocab., B. A. E. (Nestucca name). **Aⁿkwa.**—Sapir in Am. Anthr., IX, 253, 1907 (own name). **Cactaⁿ′-qwût-me′ ꝫûnnĕ.**—Dorsey, Naltûnnetûnnĕ MS. vocab., B. A. E., 1884. **Cicta′-qwŭt-me′ ꝫûnnĕ.**—Dorsey, Tutu MS. vocab., B. A. E., 1884 ('Umpqua r. people'). **Ci-sta′-qwŭt.**—Dorsey, Chasta Costa MS. vocab., B. A. E., 1884. **Etnémitane.**—Gatschet, Umpqua MS. vocab., B. A. E., 1877 (own name). **Etnémi-tenéyu.**—Ibid. **Ömkwa.**—Buschmann, Athapask. Sprachstamm, 153, 1854. **Tsan Ámpkua amím.**—Gatschet, Lakmiut MS., B. A. E., ('people on the Umpqua': Lakmiut name). **Umbaquâ.**—Parker, Jour., 257, 1840. **Umbiqua.**—Ibid., map, 1888. **Umguas.**—Hale, Ethnol. and Philol., 198, 1846. **Umkwa.**—Ibid., 204. **Ûm′-kwa-me′ ꝫûnnĕ.**—Dorsey, Chetco MS. vocab., B. A. E., 1884. **Umpaquah.**—Ind. Aff. Rep., 218, 1856. **Umpqua.**—Hale, Ethn. and Philol., 204, 1846. **Umpquahs proper.**—Gibbs, Obs. on coast tribes, MS., B. A. E. **Umpqua Irins.**—Dole in Ind. Aff. Rep., 220, 1861. **Umqua.**—Framboise quoted by Gairdner (1835) in Jour. Geog. Soc. Lond., XI, 256, 1841. **Umque.**—Duflot de Mofras, Expl., II, 103, 1844. **Unikwa.**—Schoolcraft, Ind. Tribes, I, 437, 1851 (misprint). **Upper Umpqua.**—Milhau, Hewūt MS. vocab., B. A. E. **Yāⁿgalăᶜ.**—Sapir in Am. Anthr., IX, 253, 1907 (Takelma name). **Yampequaws.**—Meek in H. R. Ex. Doc. 76, 30th Cong., 1st sess., 10, 1848.

Unaduti (*Ună′dŭtĭ*, 'woolly, or bushy, head,' from *unădéna*, 'woolly,' *dŭtĭ*, referring to the head). A distinguished mixed-blood Cherokee chief, commonly known to the whites as Dennis W. Bushyhead; born Mar. 18, 1826, at a small Cherokee settlement then on Mouse cr., about

UMATILLA WOMEN

3 m. N. of the present Cleveland, Tenn.; died in the Cherokee Nation, Ind. T., Feb. 4, 1898. He was the eldest son of Rev. Jesse Bushyhead (Unâdûtĭ), a prominent native Baptist minister who was associated with Rev. Evan Jones, the missionary, in his Scripture translations, and was also several times a tribal delegate to Washington. The chief's mother was a half-blood Cherokee, formerly a Miss Wilkinson. As a boy he attended a Presbyterian mission school on Candy cr., w. of Cleveland, Tenn., and also the mission under Rev. Evan Jones at Valleytown, N. C. On the removal of the tribe to Indian Ter., in 1838, he went w. with his father, who was in charge of one detachment of the emigrants numbering 1,200 persons. The start was made in October, the journey occupying 6 months. He afterward for some time attended school in New Jersey. In 1849 he joined the gold rush to California, where he remained until 1868, when he returned to Indian Ter., making his residence at Tahlequah, and entered actively into Cherokee politics. He served two terms as principal chief (1879–86), was subsequently twice appointed tribal delegate to Washington, and in 1890 served as one of the commissioners to treat with the United States for the sale of the Cherokee strip.   (J. M.)

Unakagak. A Kaialigmiut Eskimo village at the head of Hazen bay, Alaska; pop. 20 in 1880.
Oonakagamute.—Petroff in 10th Census, Alaska, 11, 1884. Unakagamut.—Nelson in 18th Rep. B. A E., map, 1899.

Unakhotana ('far-off people'). An Athapascan tribe living along the Yukon from Tanana r. down to the Koyukuk and on the latter stream. It is divided into the Koyukukhotana and the Yukonikhotana. Allen (Rep., 143, 1887) estimated the whole tribe at 550.
Hattchenae.—Petitot, MS., B. A. E., 1865. Junachotana.—Zagoskin, Reise, I, 324, 1849. Junakachotana.—Ibid. Jünnäkächotäna.—Holmberg, Ethnog. Skizz., 6, 1855 (see also Koyukhotana). Kahvichpaks.—Elliot, Cond. Aff. Alaska, 29, 1875. Ketlitk-Kutchín.—Dall, Alaska, 431, 1870 ('valley people'). Mnakho-tana.—Allen, Rep., 143, 1887 (misprint). Ounhann-Kouttànæ.—Petitot, Autour du lac des Esclaves, 361, 1891. T'éttohié-Dhidié.—Petitot, Dict. Dènè-Dindjié, xx, 1876 ('people sitting in the water'). Unakatana.—Bancroft, Nat. Races, I, 133, 1874. Unakatana Yunakakhotana.—Ibid., 147. Unakho-tána.—Dall, Alaska, 431, 1870.

Unakite. A species of igneous rock, "an irregular crystallization of old-rose feldspar and green epidote" (Phalen in Smithson. Misc. Coll., Quar. Iss., I, 312, 1904). The name was applied first in 1874 by F. H. Bradley (Am. Jour. Sci., 3d s., VII, 519–520, 1874), from its occurrence in the Unaka mts. between North Carolina and Tennessee. It has also been found near Luray, Va. The -ite is the English suffix of Greek origin, and unaka is de-

rived from one of the Indian languages of the country.   (A. F. C.)

Unalachtigo (properly W'nalàchtko, 'people who live near the ocean,' because of their proximity to Delaware bay.—Brinton). The southernmost of the three main divisions of the Delawares, occupying the w. bank of Delaware r., in Delaware, and probably also the E. bank, in New Jersey, since many of the Delawares were forced to cross the river to escape the inroads of the Conestoga. Their totem was the turkey, whence they have been known as the Turkey tribe of the Delawares. According to Brinton the totem has no reference to gentes, but was merely the emblem of a geographic division. Their principal seat was Chikohoki, on the site of Burlington, N. J.   (J. M.)
Chihohockies.—Drake, Bk. Inds., bk. v, 31, 1848. Chihokokis.—McKenney and Hall, Ind. Tribes, III, 80, 1854. Chiholacki.—Proud, Penn., II, 297, note, 1798. Chikimini.—Brinton, Lenape Leg., 214, 1885. Chikini.—Ibid., 215. Pullaeu.—Ibid., 39 ('he does not chew,' referring to the turkey). Pul-la'-ook.—Morgan, Anc. Soc., 172, 1878 (trans. 'turkey'). Unalàchtgo.—Heckewelder (1819) quoted by Brinton, Lenape Leg., 143, 1885. Unalàchtigo.—Barton, New Views, xxvii, 1797. Unalachtin.—Ruttenber, Tribes Hudson R., 336, 1872. W'nalàchtko.—Brinton, op. cit., 36. Wonalatoko.—Tobias (1884) quoted by Brinton, ibid., 89. Wunalàchtigo.—Barton, New Views, xxvii, 1797.

Unalakligemiut (Unälăklig'emūt). A subdivision of the Unaligmiut Eskimo of Alaska, inhabiting the banks of Unalaklik r.—Dall in Cont. N. A. Ethnol., I, 17, 1877.

Unalaklik. An Unaligmiut Eskimo village at the mouth of Unalaklik r., Norton sd., Alaska. Pop. 100 in 1880, 175 in 1890. It being the terminus of the winter route from Anvik on the Yukon, the inhabitants are a mixed race of Eskimo and Athapascan.
Oonalakleet.—Petroff, Rep. on Alaska, 59, 1880. Ounalaklik.—Zagoskin in Nouv. Ann. Voy., 5th s., xxi, map, 1850. Unalachleet.—W. U. Tel. Exped. map, 1867, cited by Baker, Geog. Dict. Alaska, 1902. Unalaklit.—Nelson in 18th Rep. B. A. E., map, 1899.

Unalaska. The larger of the dialectic divisions of the Aleut, occupying the Aleutian ids. w. of Ataka and the extremity and N. coast of Alaska penin. Whereas the Atka show some resemblance to Asiatics, probably owing to a mixture of blood since the Russian conquest, these are more akin in appearance, customs, and language to the Kaniagmiut.
Fuchs-Aleuten.—Holmberg, Ethnog. Skizz., 7, 1855. Kihigòuns.—Pinart in Mém. Soc. Ethnog. Paris, xi, 157, 1872. Kogholaghi.—Coxe, Russian Discov., 219, 1787 (applied to inhabitants of Unalaska id.; probably their own name). Nieskakh-itina.—Petroff in 10th Census, Alaska, 164, 1884 (Kenai name for Aleuts of Alaska penin.). Unalaschkaer.—Holmberg, Ethnog. Skizz., 7, 1855. Unalashkans.—Dall in Proc. Am. A. A. S., xviii, 268, 1869. Unaliskans.—Keane in Stanford, Compend., 541, 1878.

Unalga. A former Aleut village on Unalga, Adreanof group, Aleutian ids., Alaska, with 23 inhabitants in 1831.
Oonalga.—Petroff in 10th Census, Alaska, 35, 1884. Oonalgenskoi.—Elliott, Cond. Aff. Alaska, 225, 1875. Unalginskoe.—Veniaminof, Zapiski, II, 203, 1840.

Unaligmiut. A tribe of Alaskan Eskimo inhabiting the E. shore of Norton sd. back to the coast range. They are the northernmost of the fishing tribes of Eskimo, and their racial characteristics have been modified by intermarriage with the stronger western Eskimo, whose raids from the N. decimated the population on Norton sd. until there were only 150 Unaligmiut left by Dall's reckoning in 1875; at the census of 1890, only 110. He distinguished the following subtribes: Kegiktowregmiut, Pastoligmiut, Pikmiktaligmiut, and Unalakligemut. Their villages are: Anemuk, Iguik, Kiktaguk, Pikmiktalik, Tachik, Topanika, Unalaklik.
Aziagmūt.—Worman cited by Dall in Cont. N. A. Ethnol., I, 17, 1877 (see *Aziagmut*). **Oonaligmute.**—Petroff in 10th Census, Alaska, 126, 1884. **Tachĭgmyut.**—Turner, Unalit MS. vocab., B. A. E., 1877 (sig. 'bay people'). **Tatschigmut.**—Wrangell quoted by Dall, op. cit. **Tatschigmüten.**—Wrangell in Ethnog. Nach., 122, 1839. **Unāleet.**—Dall, op. cit. (so called by other natives). **Unaligmut.**—Nelson in 18th Rep. B. A. E., map, 1899. **Unaligmutes.**—Dall in Proc. Am. A. A. S., XVIII, 266, 1869.

Unami. One of the principal divisions of the Delawares (q. v.), formerly occupying the Pennsylvania side of Delaware r., from the junction of the Lehigh southward about to the Delaware line. According to Brinton, many of the New Jersey Delawares were Unami who had crossed the Delaware to escape the inroads of the Conestoga, and Ruttenber classes with this division the Navasink, Raritan, Hackensack, Aquackanonk, Tappan, and Haverstraw, of northern New Jersey. The Unami held precedence over the other Delawares. Their totem was the turtle (*pakoango*). According to Morgan, they were one of the three gentes of the Delawares, while Brinton says the turtle was merely the symbol of a geographic division. The Unami have sometimes been called the Turtle tribe of the Delawares. (J. M.)
Pakoango.—Brinton, Lenape Leg., 39, 1885 ('the crawler,' a term descriptive of the turtle). **Pokekoo-un'-go.**—Morgan, Anc. Soc., 172, 1877 (trans. 'turtle'). **Unami.**—Post (1758) quoted by Rupp, West Penn., app., 121, 1846. **Unamines.**—Doc. (1759) quoted by Rupp, Northampton Co., 50, 1845. **Unamini.**—Brinton, Lenape Leg., 214, 1885. **Urawis.**—Niles (*ca.* 1761) in Mass. Hist. Soc. Coll., 4th s., v, 541, 1861 (misprint). **Wanàmi.**—Barton, New Views, xxvii, 1798. **Wenaumeew.**—Aupaumut (1791) quoted by Brinton, Lenape Leg., 20, 1885 (Mahican name). **W'nāmiu.**—Brinton, ibid., 36. **Wonami.**—Tobias (1884) quoted by Brinton, ibid., 89. **Wunaumeeh.**—Barton, New Views, app., 10, 1798.

Unanauhan. A Tuscarora village in N. E. North Carolina in 1701.—Lawson (1709), Hist. Car., 383, 1860.

Unangashik. An Aglemiut Eskimo village at Heiden bay, Alaska penin., Alaska; pop. 37 in 1880, 190 in 1890.
Oonangashik.—Petroff, Map of Alaska, 1880. **Oonongashik.**—Petroff, Rep. on Alaska, 45, 1880.

Unatak. A Kowagmiut Eskimo village on Kobuk r., Alaska.
Un-nah-tak.—Healy, Cruise of Corwin, 27, 1887.

Una Vida. An important ancient ruin in Chaco canyon, N. W. N. Mex., about 4 m. above Pueblo Bonito. It is situated on uneven ground on the N. side of the arroyo at the base of the canyon wall. The main building is L-shaped, the extremities of the wings being connected by a semicircular wall. The wings are 274 and 253 ft in length. The remains of a partly subterranean circular kiva, 60 ft in diameter, are situated within the court; another is in the inclosure at the angle of the two wings; 3 more are built within the walls of one wing, and another large kiva is outside of the E. wall. The material of which the pueblo was built is grayish yellow sandstone in rather large blocks; the style of masonry is plain, no attempt at ornamentation being found as in other buildings of the group. This building is in a very ruinous condition. Two hundred ft N. W. of the main building, on a point of the bluff about 50 ft above, is another ruin, the principal feature of which is a kiva, 54 ft in diameter, surrounded by 15 to 20 rooms. The ruin is called Saydegil ('house on the side of the rocks') by the Navaho. See Simpson, Exped. to Navajo Country, 78, 1850; Jackson in 10th Rep. Hayden Surv., 1878; Hardacre in Scribner's Mo., 278, Dec. 1878.   (E. L. H.)

Uncas (corruption of *Wonkus*, 'fox,' lit. 'the circler.'—Gerard). A Mohegan chief, son of Owenoco, who in 1626 married a daughter of Sassacus, chief of the Pequot, and became one of their leaders (De Forest, Inds. of Conn., 86, 1852). He was known also as Poquim or Poquoiam. A rebellion against Sassacus led to his defeat and banishment, whereupon he fled to the Narraganset, but soon made his peace and returned. This conduct was repeated several times. He warred against the Pequot, Narraganset, and other tribes. After taking prisoner Miantonomo he executed him at command of the English. He sided with the English in King Philip's war in 1675. His death occurred in 1682 or 1683. The family line became extinct early in the 19th century. De Forest (op. cit., 86) says: "His nature was selfish, jealous, and tyrannical; his ambition was grasping and unrelieved by a single trait of magnanimity." Stratagem and trickery were native to his mind. His personal habits were bad and he was addicted to more than one vice of the whites. He protested against the introduction of Christianity among his people. A monument to his memory was erected by the citizens of Norwich, Conn., in July, 1847, the cornerstone of which was laid by President Jackson in 1833. Another memorial, consisting of a bronze statue surmounting a large bowlder, was erected by Mrs Edward Clark, afterward the wife of Bishop H. C. Potter, on the site of the home of James Fenimore Cooper, at Cooperstown, N. Y. (A. F. C.)

Uncowa (from *ongkoue*, 'beyond,' with reference to Pequannoc r.). A small band formerly living about Fairfield, Fairfield co., Conn. Their village, of the same name, was near the site of Fairfield. They are placed by Ruttenber in the Mattabesec division of the Wappinger group.

Onckeway.—Doc. of 1655 in N. Y. Doc. Col. Hist., XIII, 58, 1881. Uncaway.—Bradford (*ca.* 1650) in Mass. Hist. Soc. Coll., 4th s., III, 427, 1856. Uncoway.—Hubbard (1680), ibid., 2d s., v, 455, 1815. Unkowas.—De Forest, Inds. Conn., 49, 1851. Unkwas.—Macauley, N. Y., II, 164, 1829.

Undl-skadjins-gitunai (ᵋAɴᴛ *squadjǐ'ns gǐᴛᴀɴā'-i*, 'Gituns on the river Skadjins'). A subdivision of the Gituns, a Haida family of the Eagle clan living at Masset, Brit. Col. The name was derived from that of a small stream which flows into the upper expansion of Masset inlet, and upon which they used to camp.—Swanton, Cont. Haida, 275, 1905.

Unga. An Aleut village on Unga id., Shumagin group, Alaska; pop. 116 in 1833, 185 in 1880, 159 in 1890.

Delarof.—Veniaminof quoted by Petroff in 10th Census, Alaska, 35, 1884. Delarov.—Petroff, Rep. on Alaska, 24, 1880. Oongenskoi.—Elliott, Cond. Aff. Alaska, 225, 1875. Ougnagok.—Lutke quoted by Baker, Geog. Dict. Alaska, 148, 1902. Ounga.—Petroff in 10th Census, Alaska, 23, 1884. Ugnasik.—Holmberg, Ethnog. Skizz., map, 1855.

Ungalik. A Malemiut Eskimo village at the mouth of Ungalik r., E. end of Norton sd., Alaska; pop. 15 in 1880.

Oonakhtolik.—Petroff in 10th Census, Alaska, 11, 1884. Ounag-touli.—Zagoskin in Nouv. Ann. Voy., 5th s., XXI, map, 1850. Unagtuligmut.—Zagoskin, Descr. Russ. Poss. Am., pt. I, 72, 1847. Unaktolik.—Elliott, Our Arct. Prov., 145, 1886. Unatolik.—Elliott, op. cit. Ungalik.—Baker, Geog. Dict. Alaska, 1902. Unoktolik.—Coast Surv. chart quoted by Baker, ibid.

Ungquaterughiate. See *Shikellamy.*

Unharik. Given in 1852 as a Karok village on Klamath r., N. w. Cal.

Oon-hárik.—Gibbs, MS. Misc., B. A. E., 1852.

Unisak. A Yuit Eskimo village of the Aiwan division on Indian pt., N. E. Siberia. Pop. 500 in 51 houses about 1895; 442 in 61 houses in 1901.

Nukamok.—Petroff in 10th Census, Alaska, map, 1884. Uñi'in.—Bogoras, Chukchee, 29, 1904 (Chukchi name). Uñi'sak.—Ibid. (Eskimo name).

United States Board of Indian Commissioners. A Board of ten men appointed and directly commissioned by the President of the United States "from men eminent for their intelligence and philanthropy to serve without pecuniary compensation," to use the language of the law which in 1869 created the Board at the suggestion of President Grant, that by its advice and suggestions it might cooperate with the Government in securing a sound and progressive administration of Indian affairs and in promoting the education and civilization of the native American tribes.

The especial significance of the 40 years' history of the Commission lies in the fact that upon an important branch of the Government's administrative work there has been brought to bear enlightened public opinion, through a slowly changing body of men of high character, especially interested in the reforms to be secured, uninfluenced by partisan considerations and free from danger of removal for party advantage when impelled to criticism of administrative faults or defects.

Determined to put an end to needless wars with Indian tribes, President Grant, referring to his "Peace Policy" and to this newly created Commission, in his annual message of December, 1869, said: "I have adopted a new policy toward these wards of the nation (they can not be regarded in any other light than as wards), with fair results, so far as tried, and which I hope will be attended ultimately with great success."

Commissioned under the law of April 10, 1869, the Board began its work under regulations issued by President Grant, which authorized it to inspect the records of the Indian Office and to obtain full information as to the conduct of all parts of the affairs thereof; gave to its members full power to inspect Indian agencies, to be present at payments of annuities, at consultations or councils with Indians; to advise agents respecting their duties; to be present at purchases of goods for Indian purposes; to inspect said purchases, advising with the Commissioner of Indian Affairs in regard thereto; and to advise respecting instructions to agents and changes in the methods of purchasing goods or of conducting the affairs of the Indian Bureau proper.

Among the members of the Commission have been such prominent business men as Felix R. Brunot, of Pittsburg (first chairman of the Board); William Welsh and George H. Stuart, of Philadelphia; William E. Dodge, Gen. Clinton B. Fisk, Darwin R. James, and William H. Lyon, of New York, and John V. Farwell, of Chicago.

Abuses in connection with the purchase of Indian supplies and the business of Indian traders demanded and received immediate attention and drastic reform. The Board advised a change in the methods of purchase, securing strict impartiality in the reception of bids and the allotment of contracts, and a system of rigid inspection after goods have been delivered at a Government warehouse, thus insuring goods in quality and grade equal to the samples offered, preventing fraud, and saving large sums to the Government each year. The system planned and inaugurated by the business men of the Board, after a few years of practical direction by the Commission, was adopted substantially by the Department and is still in use by the Indian Bureau, to the great advantage of the Indians as well as of the Government.

In their first annual report to the President the Board indicated, besides these reforms in business methods, certain lines of work which they proposed to undertake and certain reforms which seemed desirable. They urged that the Indians should be taught as soon as possible the advantages of individual ownership of property; that land in severalty should be given them as soon as it was desired by any; that tribal ownership and tribal relations should be discouraged; that individual titles to land should be made inalienable from the family of the holder for at least two or three generations, and that the Five Civilized Tribes of Indian Ter. should be taxed and made citizens of the United States as soon as possible. They advised that the system of treaties with Indian tribes should be discontinued; and that as soon as a just method to accomplish it could be devised, there should be in the interest of the Indians themselves an abrogation of existing treaties with tribes. They declared it to be the immediate duty of the Government to establish schools and employ teachers, to introduce the English language in every tribe, and especially to educate the Indians in the dignity of work, in the industries and arts of civilization and the principles of Christianity, that Indians might be fitted for citizenship and be made citizens. From the first, the object held in view by the Commission has been the absorption of all Indians as soon as practicable into the body politic as American citizens. Their first report also commended the President for his avowed purpose to select Indian agents with a view to their moral as well as their business qualifications for their work, and aside from political and partisan considerations.

As early as 1878 the Commission made a draft of a bill to allot land and secure homesteads to Indians; and they steadfastly and earnestly advocated that reform, against strong opposition, until its triumph in Congress under the wise and effective leadership of Senator Dawes in the general severalty act of 1887 which justly bears his name. Now that more than 70,000 Indians (besides the 65,000 in Indian Ter., citizens by virtue of the Curtis act, which followed the Dawes act) have become American citizens under the provisions of the Dawes bill, it excites wonder to recall the fact that until this tardy act of justice to Indians in 1887 the only people from any quarter of the globe who could not become American citizens by birth, residence, or naturalization were our own American Indians, the only strictly native-born Americans by race.

To assist in the Christian education of the Indians was urged upon all denominations of Christians as a patriotic duty by President Grant in 1869; and for many years the Board of Indian Commissioners cooperated in this work by holding twice in each year (at the annual meeting of the Board at Washington in January, and at the Lake Mohonk Indian Conference — see *Mohonk Indian Conference,*— called and entertained by Hon. Albert K. Smiley, a member of the Commission), a conference with the secretaries and workers of the various religious organizations which carried on missions and schools among Indians. After appropriations for Government schools had steadily grown from $20,000 in 1877 to $3,757,909 in 1910 (a growth which the Board has earnestly recommended and steadily favored), and after direct Government aid had been withdrawn from all denominational schools, annual conferences at Washington with representatives of mission societies were for a time discontinued. When the Board was created, fewer than 5,000 Indian children had any kind of school facilities. Now the Government provides school facilities for the children of all Indian tribes except the Navaho; and in 1910 more than 30,000 Indian children were enrolled in schools.

In their first annual report the Board, in speaking of the proposed policy of education, said: "To expect the Christianization and civilization of any barbarous people within the term of a few short years would be to ignore all the facts of history, all the experiences of human nature." Now that for a full generation this independent, nonpartisan Board has continued to act as assistants to the Government, often as interpreters to the public of the policy of the administration, often by criticism and suggestion as exponents to the Government of the thought and sentiment of the most intelligent friends of the Indians, so much of progress is evident that the Commission with great hope and confidence continue their work which looks to the speedy abolition of all tribal relations, and to the discontinuance at the earliest practicable date of all special supervision of Indians by the Government.

For the last 10 years the Board has warmly advocated breaking up into individual holdings the immense tribal funds now held in trust by the Government. They advocate the fixing of an early date after which no child born to Indians shall have any right to a share in tribal funds save as he may inherit from others their divided interest under the laws of the state or territory where he may reside, and the division of tribal funds into individual holdings, each Indian entitled to a share to be recognized on the books of the Treasury of the United States; payments of interest to be made directly to the individual Indian by name, the principal to be paid to individual Indians whenever in the opinion of the President they may be fit to receive and use it. So only, in the opinion of the Board, can Indians be trained to use their property. The keeping of permanent family records at each agency, with this purpose in view; the strengthening of family life among the Indians by requiring a license for marriage and by active measures to prevent polygamy, are regulations adopted recently by the Government at the urgent request of the Board.

The chairmen of the Board have been Felix R. Brunot (1869–73), Clinton B. Fisk (1874–77, and 1880–89), A. C. Barstow (1878–79), Merrill E. Gates, (1890–99), Darwin R. James (1899–1909). Francis E. Leupp, former Commissioner of Indian Affairs; Charles J. Bonaparte, Attorney-General of the United States, and Maurice F. Egan, present minister to Denmark, are among recent members of the Board. Gen. Eliphalet Whittlesey was its secretary from 1882 to 1899. Its present (1910) officers and members are: Andrew S. Draper, chairman; Merrill E. Gates, secretary; and Commissioners Albert K. Smiley, William D. Walker, Joseph T. Jacobs, Patrick J. Ryan, Andrew S. Draper, George Vaux, jr., Warren K. Moorehead, and Samuel A. Eliot. The office of the Board is Corcoran Building, Washington, D. C.   (M. E. G.)

Unkagarits (*Un'-ka-gar-its*). One of the tribes known under the collective term Gosiutes, formerly in Skull valley, s. w. Utah; pop. 149 in 1873.—Powell and Ingalls in Ind. Aff. Rep. 1873, 51, 1874.

Unkakaniguts (*Un-ka-ka'-ni-guts*, 'red land people'). A Paiute band formerly in Long valley, s. w. Utah; pop. 36 in 1873.
Un-ka-ka'-ni-guts.— Powell in Ind. Aff. Rep. 1873, 50, 1874. Unkar kauagats-Ta-Nouts.—Ingalls in H. R. Ex. Doc. 66, 42d Cong., 3d sess., 2, 1873.

Unkapanukuints (*Unkápa nu-kwints*, 'redwater river people'). A Paiute band near Cedar City, s. w. Utah. Pop. 97 in 1873. In 1904 there were 30 Paiute near Cedar City, probably the remnant of this band.
Nulkwints.—Powell misquoted in Sen. Ex. Doc. 42, 43d Cong., 1st sess., 15, 1874 (separated from Unka-pa by comma). Un-ka-pa.—Ibid. Unka-'-pa-Nu-kuints'.—Powell in Ind. Aff. Rep. 1873, 50, 1874. Unka-toma.—Ingalls in H. R. Ex. Doc. 66, 42d Cong., 3d sess., 2, 1873 (probably identical).

Unkcheyuta ('eat dung'). A Miniconjou Sioux band.
Uŋkée-yuta.—Dorsey, after Swift, in 15th Rep. B. A. E., 220, 1897. Uñktce-yuta.—Ibid.

Unkoahs. Given by Doty (Ind. Aff. Rep. 1864, 175, 1865) as one of the two chief bands of the western Shoshoni, but they may have been Paiute.

Unktoka ('our enemies'). A tribe which, according to the Iowa, formerly lived in N. Wisconsin and was destroyed by them about the beginning of the 19th century.—Lynd in Minn. Hist. Soc. Coll., II, pt. 2, 59, 1864.

Unojita. One of 36 tribes reported in 1683 to Domingo de Mendoza as being friendly to the Jumano and living three days' journey eastward from the junction of the Rio Grande and Conchos rs., in Texas.—Mendoza, Viaje, 1683–84, MS. in Archivo Gen. de México.

Unshagii (*Un'-shä-gi-i'*). A former pueblo of the Jemez of New Mexico; definite location unknown.—Hodge, field notes, B. A. E., 1895.

Unuwat. A "castle" of the Mahican, taking its name from the chief, situated on the E. bank of Hudson r. in Rensselaer co., N. Y.—Ruttenber, Tribes Hudson R., 85, 1872.

Unyijaima. Mentioned as a village, presumably Costanoan, formerly connected with San Juan Bautista mission, Cal.
Uñijaima.—Engelhardt, Franc. in Cal., 398, 1897.

Unyjaware (Iroquois name). One of the 5 Abnaki villages in 1700.—Bellomont (1700) in N. Y. Doc. Col. Hist., IV, 758, 1854.

Upan ('elk'). A gens of the Kansa.
O'-pä.—Morgan, Anc. Soc., 156, 1877. O-pûhⁿ nika-shing-ga.—Stubbs, Kaw MS. vocab., B. A. E., 25, 1877. Upaⁿ.—Dorsey in 15th Rep. B. A. E., 231, 1897.

Uparch. A Maricopa rancheria on the Rio Gila, Arizona, in the 18th century.
S. Felipe Uparch.—Sedelmair (1744) cited by Bancroft, Ariz. and N. Mex., 366, 1889. Uparch.—Rudo Ensayo (ca. 1763), 22, 1863.

Upasoitac. A Maricopa rancheria near the great bend of the Rio Gila, Ariz., visited by Anza in 1744, and by Anza, Font, Garcés, and others, in 1775.
Oparsoitac.—Arricivita (1791) cited by Bancroft, Ariz. and N. Mex., 390, 1889. Posociom.—Anza and Font (1780), ibid., 392. Pueblo de los Santos Apostoles San Simon y Judas.—Garcés (1775), Diary, 113, 1900. San Simon y Judas de Vpasoitac.—Garcés (1776), ibid., 455. S. Simon.—Arricivita, op. cit. S. Simon y Judás de Opasoitac.—Anza and Font (1780) cited by Bancroft, op. cit., 392. Uparsoitac.—Ibid. Vparsoytac.—Garcés (1775), Diary, 138, 1900.

Upernivik. A Danish post in w. Greenland, lat. 74°. It contains 4 frame houses, occupied by Danish officers and their families, a wooden church, and a number of Eskimo huts made of turf.—Bessels, Am. Nordpol-Exped., 85, 1878.

Upeshipow. A tribe, related to the Cree, living near the E. coast of James bay, Canada, between Rupert and Great Whale rs., bordering on the Eskimo of Labrador. One band, the Winnepeskowuk, lived on East Main r., another was said to live on Moose r., probably the Monsoni, who were doubtless a cognate if not the same tribe.

Upe-shi-pow.—Hutchins (1770) quoted by Richardson, Arct. Exped., II, 38, 1851.

Upkhan ('elk'). A gens of the Hanka division of the Osage.

U′pqaⁿ.—Dorsey in 15th Rep. B. A. E., 234, 1897.

Upop (*U-póp*). A Chumashan village formerly near Pt Concepcion, Cal.—Henshaw, Buenaventura MS. vocab., B. A. E., 1884.

Upper Chinook. A general term for the Chinookan tribes of Columbia r., above (E. of) the Lower Chinook. As commonly used it refers to the tribes between the mouth of Willamette r. and The Dalles, Oreg.

Guithlia′-kjshatchk.—Gatschet, MS., B. A. E., 1877. ('Indians above the falls': Lower Chinook name). **Hauts-Tchinouks.**—Mofras, Expl. dans l'Oregon, II, 335, 1844. **Tchaꭓlátꭓksh.**—Gatschet, op. cit. (Clackama name). **Upper Chinook.**—Hale in U. S. Expl. Exped., VI, 214, 1846.

Upper Cowlitz. A division of the Cowlitz on the upper waters of Cowlitz r., Wash.

Upper Creeks. A term applied to that division of the Creeks formerly living about Coosa and Tallapoosa rs., N. E. Ala., and for a short distance below their junction. Lincoln in 1798 (Am. State Papers, Ind. Aff., I, 79, 1832) stated that there were about 45 Upper Creek towns. See *Creeks*.

Maskō′ki Hatchapála.—Gatschet, Creek Migr. Leg., I, 237, 1884 (Creek name). **Overhill Creeks.**—Lee quoted by Drake, Bk. Inds., bk. IV, 68, 1848. **The Nation.**—Bartram, Trav., 208, 1791. **Upper Creeks.**—Ibid., 378.

Upper Fraser Band. One of 4 subdivisions of the Upper Ntlakyapamuk of the interior of British Columbia.

SLaxa′yux.—Teit in Mem. Am. Mus. Nat. Hist., II, 170, 1900. **Upper Fraser band.**—Ibid.

Upper Kutenai. The larger of the 2 divisions of the Kutenai, speaking a different dialect and more amenable to civilizing influences than the Lower Kutenai. They live in the region inclosed between Selkirk and the Rocky mts., on the lakes at the head of Columbia r., and on Upper Kootenai r. and L. Pend d' Oreille, Brit. Col. Their subdivisions are Akiskenukenik, Akamnik, Akanekunik, and Akiyenik.

Ki′tōnā′Qa.—Chamberlain in 8th Rep. N. W. Tribes Can., 6, 1892. **Upper Kootanais.**—Mayne, Brit. Col., 298, 1862. **Upper Kootanie.**—Tolmie and Dawson, Comp. Vocabs., 124B, 1884. **Upper Kootenay.**—Boas in 5th Rep. N. W. Tribes Can., 10, 1889. **Upper Kootenuha.**—Tolmie and Dawson, op. cit.

Upper Mdewakanton. The northern bands of the Mdewakanton Sioux in Minnesota.

Upper Me-dé-wakan-t'wan.—Ramsey in Ind. Aff. Rep. 1849, 81, 1850.

Upper St. Croix Lake Band. A band of the Munominikasheenhug.

Upper Sioux. The Sisseton and Wahpeton Sioux, on upper Minnesota r., as distinguished from the Lower Sioux (Mdewakanton and Wahpekute).—Ind. Aff. Rep., 1859, 101, 1860.

Upper Takelma. A Takelman tribe that dwelt eastward of the Takelma proper, occupying the poorer land of the upper Rogue, eastward from about Table Rock toward the Cascades and in the neighborhood of the present town of Jacksonville, Oreg. These eastern Takelma seem to have been on the whole less advanced than their down-river kinsmen. They are said to have been shorter in stature than these, to have used log rafts instead of canoes, and, because of greater economic distress, to have used for food crows, ants' eggs, and the like, much to the disgust of the Takelma proper, who, however, do not seem to have been particularly averse to the eating of lice and grasshoppers themselves. The Upper Takelma were much more warlike than their western neighbors, and were accustomed to make raids on the latter in order to procure supplies of food and other valuables. The slaves they captured they often sold to the Klamath of the Lakes, directly to the E. The few words obtained of their language show it to have been very nearly the same as that of the Takelma proper, but with distinct phonetic and lexicographic dialectic differences. (E. S.)

Lat′gāᵃwáˢ.—Sapir in Am. Anthr., IX, 252, 1907 ('those living in the uplands': Takelma name). **Wùlx.**—Sapir, ibid. ('enemies': also sometimes so called by the Takelma, although applied specifically to the Shasta).

Upper Thompson Indians. The Ntlakyapamuk on Fraser r. and its tributaries above Cisco, Brit. Col. They embody 4 minor divisions: the Lytton, Upper Fraser, Spences Bridge, and Nicola bands.

Nku′kûmamux.—Teit in Mem. Am. Mus. Nat. Hist., II, 168, 1900 (= 'people above'). **Upper Thompsons.**—Ibid.

Upper Yanktonai. One of the two principal local divisions of the Yanktonai Sioux, so named because their habitat was farther up Missouri r. than that of the Hunkpatina (U. S. Ind. Treat., II, 905, 1904). They include the Wazikute, Takini, Shikshichena, Kiyuksa, and Pabaksa.

North Yanktons.—Prescott in Schoolcraft, Ind. Tribes, II, 169, note, 1852. **Upper Yanctonais.**—Stanley in Poole, Among the Sioux, app., 231, 1881. **Yank-ton of the north or plains.**—Lewis and Clark Discov., table, 34, 1806. **Yanktons of the North.**—Ibid., 24. **Yanktons of the Plains.**—Lewis and Clark Exped., I, 61, 1814.

Upputuppet. Mentioned by Kane (Wand. in N. Am., 274, 1859) as a band numbering 70 or 80 warriors at the mouth of Palouse r., Wash. The term is not met with elsewhere and probably refers to a division or a settlement of the Paloos.

Uracas. Mentioned in connection with some mythical as well as existent tribes of the plains in the 17th century.—Vetancurt (1693) in Teatro Am., III, 303, 1871.

Uracha. A tribe or band represented by one individual at San Antonio de Valero mission, Texas, in 1764 (Valero Baptisms, 1764, partida 1500, MS.). There is no indication of the tribe's affiliation.

Urchaoztac. A Maricopa rancheria on the Rio Gila, Ariz., in 1744.—Sedelmair (1744) cited by Bancroft, Ariz. and N. Mex., 366, 1889.

Urebure. A village, presumably Costanoan, formerly connected with Dolores mission, San Francisco, Cal.—Taylor in Cal. Farmer, Oct. 18, 1861.

Ures (Opata: *uri*, 'man'). A former pueblo of the Opata, containing also Nevome, and the seat of a Spanish mission founded in 1636; situated on the E. bank of the E. branch of Rio Sonora, central Sonora, Mex. Pop. 904 in 1678, 592 in 1730. The name was applied also to the inhabitants, and Ure and Ore were sometimes used synonymously with Opata. Orozco y Berra (Geog., 58, 351, 1864) classes Ures both as a Nevome pueblo and as an Opata division. Bandelier (Arch. Inst. Papers, III, 58, 1890) says the Ures were Opata. After the extermination of the Salineros and Cabezas of Tizonezo, in Durango, that pueblo was repeopled by some of the Ures inhabitants. Ures is now a Mexicanized town of 2,350 inhabitants, including descendants of the former Opata population and a number of Yaqui. See *Corazones*.
Hures.—Ribas (1645) quoted in Arch. Inst. Papers, III, pt. 1, 58, 1890. San Miguel Ures.—Zapata (1678) quoted by Bancroft, No. Mex. States, 245, 1884. Ures.—Kino, map (1702) in Stöcklein, Neue Welt-Bott, 74, 1726.

Urhlaina (a variety of trees). A clan of Taos pueblo, N. Mex.
Ur'thlaina tai'na.—M. C. Stevenson, notes, B. A. E., 1910 (*tai'na* = 'people').

Urihesahe. Mentioned as a Choctaw clan (Wright in Ind. Aff. Rep., 348, 1843). Not identified.

Urn-burial. This method of disposing of the dead, which consisted of the burial of cremated or noncremated human remains in vessels that were covered, uncovered, or inverted over the remains, was practised in places by the Indians, from ocean to ocean, in the territory now forming the United States, principally in the S., but nowhere has it been found to be exclusive and apart from other forms of burial. The custom continued into the historical period (Yarrow, Moore). Noncremated human remains were buried in vessels of stone, covered in various ways, in S. California (Yarrow), the only locality in the United States where stone vessels are known to have been used for burial purposes. Similar remains have been found in a covered receptacle of earthenware in Tennessee (Holmes). In Alabama, where alone plural burials of noncremated remains in a single vessel are sometimes met with, unburned

human bones have been found in vessels with and without covers, as is also the case in Georgia. In N. Florida two bowls containing noncremated remains were found with vessels inverted above them (Moore). Cremated human remains in covered vessels have been unearthed in Arizona (Hough, Cushing, Fewkes, Hrdlička); in large seashells and in shells of turtles in Illinois (McAdams); in an urn in Michigan (Gillman), and in vessels, variously covered or uncovered, in Georgia (Moore). In Georgia, also, human remains, sometimes cremated and sometimes not, were placed on the sand with vessels of earthenware inverted above them (Moore). In S. California entire skeletons having the skulls covered with inverted stone mortars, and in one case with an inverted metal pan, are said to have been found (Yarrow); and earthenware bowls were similarly turned over skulls belonging to entire skeletons in Arizona (Fewkes; Hodge, inf'n, 1904), in New Mexico (Duff; Hewett, inf'n, 1904), and in two instances in lower Alabama (Moore). In Utah burials of noncremated remains have been found covered with baskets (Pepper). Urn-burial was not practised by the tribes occupying peninsular Florida, but in the N. W. part of that state, urn-burial consisting, with but few exceptions, of lone skulls sometimes accompanied with fragments of other bones placed on the sand and covered by inverted bowls have been found (Moore). In South Carolina urn-burial probably was practised, but authentic details are wanting. Published reports of the discovery of urn-burials in Missouri, Indiana, and Kentucky have been shown to be incorrect.

Consult Cushing in Internat. Cong. Americanists, 7th sess., 1889, Berlin, 1890; Du Bois in Am. Anthr., IX, no. 3, 1907; Duff in Am. Antiq., XXIV, Sept.–Oct., 1902; Fewkes in 22d Rep. B. A. E., 1904; Gillman in Proc. Am. A. A. S., 1876, XXV, 1877; Holmes in 4th Rep. B. A. E., 1886; Hough in Nat. Mus. Rep. 1901, 1903; Hrdlička in Am. Anthr., VII, 480, 1905; Moore (1) in Am. Anthr., VI, no. 5, 1904, (2) ibid., VII, no. 1, 1905, (3) various memoirs in Jour. Acad. Nat. Sci. Phila., XI, XII, XIII, 1897–1905; McAdams in Proc. Am. A. A. S., 1880, XXIX, 1881; Pepper in Jour. Am. Mus. Nat. Hist., II, no. 4, Guide leaflet 6, 1902; Yarrow in Rep. U. S. Geog. Surv. W. 100th Merid., VII, 1877.   (C. B. M.)

Urns. See *Receptacles*.

Urraca. Mentioned by Castaño de Sosa (Doc. Inéd., XV, 191, 1871) as a pueblo S. of the Queres (Keres), on the Rio Grande, N. Mex., in 1590. It seemingly belonged to the Tigua.

Uruachic. A Tarahumare settlement in

Chihuahua, Mex.; definite locality unknown.—Orozco y Berra, Geog., 323, 1864.

Usal. A part of the Sinkyone living on the California coast from Usal northward.

Camel-el-poma.—Ind. Aff. Rep. 1857, 404, 1858. Cam-el-lel-Pomas.—Ind. Aff. Rep. 1864, 119, 1865. Kam′-a-lel Pó-mo.—Powers in Cont. N. A. Ethnol., III, 155, 1877. Kush-Kish.—Tobin in Ind. Aff. Rep. 1857, 405, 1858. Usal.—A. L. Kroeber, inf'n, 1903. Utinom.—A. L. Kroeber, inf'n, 1903 ('reed people': Yuki name). Yon-sal-pomas.—Ind. Aff. Rep. 1857, 405, 1858. Yoshol.—A. L. Kroeber, inf'n, 1903 (Pomo name). Yo-sol Pomas.—Ind. Aff. Rep. 1864, 119, 1865. Yú-sâl Pómo.—Powers in Cont. N. A. Ethnol., III, 155, 1877.

Uscamacu. A tribe or village mentioned by La Vandera (B. Smith, Colec. Doc. Fla., I, 16, 1857) as a day's journey from St Helena, which was visited by Juan Pardo in 1567. Not identified, but possibly the Yamasee of N. Florida or S. South Carolina.

Escamacu.—Barcia, Ensayo, 141, 1723.

Ushu. The Columnar Cactus clan of the Chua (Snake) phratry of the Hopi.

Ucü wiñwû.—Fewkes in 19th Rep. B. A. E., 582, 1900. U′-cü wuñ-wü.—Fewkes in Am. Anthr., VII, 402, 1894 (wuñ-wii = clan). U′-se.—Stephen in 8th Rep. B. A. E., 38, 1891.

Usi. A village, probably on the coast of South Carolina, in 1569; distant about 60 leagues "by salt water" from Santa Elena, about the present Beaufort.—Juan de la Vandera (1569) in Smith, Colec. Doc. Fla., I, 17, 1857.

Uskwaliguta. See *Hanging-maw*.

Ussa Yoholo. See *Osceola*.

Ussete. A village, presumably Costanoan, formerly connected with Dolores mission, San Francisco, Cal.—Taylor in Cal. Farmer, Oct. 18, 1861.

Ustanali (*U'stăna'lĭ*, denoting a natural barrier of rocks across a stream). The name of several former Cherokee settlements. One was on Keowee r., below the present Ft George, in Oconee co., S. C.; another seems to have been somewhere on the waters of Tuckasegee r., in w. North Carolina; a third, prominent during and after the Revolutionary period, was just above the junction of Coosawatee and Conasauga rs. to form the Oostanaula, in Gordon co., Ga., and adjoining New Echota. Other settlements of the same name may have been on Eastanollee cr. of Tugaloo r., in Franklin co., Ga., and on Eastaunaula cr., flowing into Hiwassee r., in McMinn co., Tenn. In addition to the forms cited below, the name is variously spelled Eastinaulee, Eastanora, Estanaula, Eustenaree, Istanare, Oostanaula, Ustenary, etc.—Mooney in 19th Rep. B. A. E., 543, 1900.

Oos-te-nau-lah.—Royce in 5th Rep. B. A. E., map, 1887. Oostinawley.—Doc. of 1799 quoted by Royce, ibid., 144. Ostonoos.—Barcia, Ensayo, 261, 1723 (identical?). Oustanale.—Doc. of 1755 quoted by Royce, op. cit., 143. Oustanalle.—Ibid.

Ustisti. Mentioned in a document of 1755 as one of the Cherokee lower towns. It is also said to have been the name of an ancient Cherokee clan, the Holly.

Oustestee.—Royce in 5th Rep. B. A. E., 143, 1887. Ustisti.—Ibid.

Ustoma (*Us'-to-ma*). A Maidu village near Nevada City, Nevada co., Cal.

Oostomas.—Powers in Overland Mo., XII, 420, 1874. Us-tó-ma.—Powers in Cont. N. A. Ethnol., III, 282, 1877. Ustu.—Bancroft, Nat. Races, I, 450, 1874.

Utaca. One of 36 tribes reported in 1683 to Domingo de Mendoza as being friendly to the Jumano and living three days' journey eastward from the junction of the Rio Grande and the Conchos, in Texas.—Mendoza, Viaje, 1683–84, MS. in Archivo Gen. de México.

Utagami ('middle of the river'). An extinct band of the Peoria.

Utahlite. A hydrous phosphate of aluminum somewhat similar to turquoise and capable of being highly polished. Although rare, its occurrence has been noted in certain prehistoric ruins in Utah, having been employed by the ancient Pueblo inhabitants evidently for ornaments. From *Utah*, the state name, which in turn is derived from that of the *Ute* or *Uta* tribe.

Utalliam. A Costanoan village situated in 1819 within 10 m. of Santa Cruz mission, Cal.—Taylor in Cal. Farmer, Apr. 5, 1860.

Utchowig. A village, probably belonging to the Erie, situated in 1608 on a w. tributary of the Susquehanna, in Pennsylvania.—Smith (1629), Va., I, map, repr. 1819.

Utchuchu. A village, presumably Costanoan, formerly connected with San Juan Bautista mission, Cal.—Taylor in Cal. Farmer, Nov. 25, 1860.

Ute. An important Shoshonean division, related linguistically to the Paiute, Chemehuevi, Kawaiisu, and Bannock. They formerly occupied the entire central and w. portions of Colorado and the E. portion of Utah, including the E. part of Salt Lake valley and Utah valley. On the S. they extended into New Mexico, occupying much of the upper drainage area of the San Juan. They appear to have always been a warlike people, and early came into possession of horses, which intensified their aggressive character. None of the tribes practised agriculture. Very little is known of their social and political organization, although the seven Ute tribes of Utah were at one time organized into a confederacy under chief Tabby (Taíwi). Dialectic differences exist in the language, but these do not appear to be great and probably presented little difficulty to intercourse between the several bands or geographical bodies. In the N. part of their range, in Utah, they appear to have become considerably intermixed by marriage with their Shoshoni, Bannock, and Paiute kindred, and on the s. with the Jicarilla Apache.

The first treaty with the Ute, one of peace and amity, was concluded Dec. 30, 1849. By Executive order of Oct. 3, 1861, Uintah valley was set apart for the Uinta tribe and the remainder of the land claimed by them was taken without formal purchase. By treaty of Oct. 7, 1863, the Tabeguache were assigned a reservation and the remainder of their land was ceded to the United States. On May 5, 1864, various reserves, established in 1856 and 1859 by Indian agents, were ordered vacated and sold. By treaty of Mar. 2, 1868, a reservation for the Tabeguache, Moache, Capote, Wiminuche, Yampa, Grand River, Uinta, and other bands was created in Colorado and the remainder of their lands relinquished; but by agreement of Sept. 13, 1873, a part of this reservation was ceded to the United States. When it was found that a portion of this last cession was included in the Uncompahgre valley, the part so included was retroceded to the Ute by Executive order of Aug. 17, 1876. By Executive order of Nov. 22, 1875, the Ute res. was enlarged, but this additional tract was restored to the public domain by order of Aug. 4, 1882. By act of June 18, 1878, a portion of the act of May 5, 1864, was repealed and several tracts included in the reservations thereunder established were restored to the public domain. Under agreement of Nov. 9, 1878, the Moache, Capote, and Wiminuche ceded their right to the confederated Ute res. established by the 1868 treaty, the United States agreeing to establish a reservation for them on San Juan r., which was done by Executive order of Feb. 7, 1879. On Mar. 6, 1880, the Southern Ute and the Uncompahgre acknowledged an agreement to settle respectively on La Plata r. and on the Grand near the mouth of the Gunnison, while the White River Ute agreed to move to the Uinta res. in Utah. Sufficient agricultural land not being found at the point designated as the future home of the Uncompahgre, the President, by Executive order of Jan. 5, 1882, established a reserve for them in Utah, the boundaries of which were defined by Executive order of Jan. 5, 1882. By act of May 24, 1888, a part of the Uinta reservation was restored to the public domain.

The Southern Ute lands in Colorado were in part subsequently allotted in severalty, and on Apr. 13, 1899, 523,079 acres were opened to settlement, the remainder (483,750 acres) being retained as a reservation for the Wiminuche. A large part of the Uinta valley res. in Utah has also been allotted in severalty, more than a million acres set aside as forest and other reserves, and more than a million acres more opened to homestead entry; the residue (179,194 acres under reclamation) is unallotted and unreserved. Of the Uncompahgre res. in Utah, 12,540 acres have been allotted and the remainder restored to the public domain by act of June 7, 1897.

Various numerical estimates of the Ute have been made from time to time, but they are generally unreliable. The restless character of these Indians and their unfriendly spirit have rendered a correct census or even a fair estimate impossible. Some estimates have included many Paiute, while others have included only a portion of the Ute proper, so that the figures have varied from 3,000 to 10,000. An estimate of 4,000 for the year 1870 would probably be within safe bounds. It is not likely that the combined numbers of the several Ute bands ever exceeded 10,000. The official reports give 3,391 as on the several reservations in 1885, and 2,014 in 1909. They have

GROUP OF UTE MEN (OURAY, SEATED, IN MIDDLE)

been classed as follows: Capote, Cumumbah, Kosunats, Moache, Pahvant, Pikakwanarats, Sanpet, Seuvarits, Tabeguache, Timpaiavats, Uinta, Wiminuche, Yampa. According to Hrdlička the three divisions now recognized by the Ute are Tabeguache or Uncompahgre, Kaviawach or White River Ute, and Yoovte or Uinta. Sogup and Yubuincariri are given as the names of former bands. Most of the divisional names have become obsolete, at least in official reports, and the Ute on the several reservations are now classed under collective terms. These, with their numbers in 1909, were as follows: Wiminuche under the Ft Lewis school, Colo., 454; Capote and Moache under the Southern Ute school, Colo., 352; Uinta (443), Uncompahgre (469), and White River Ute (296) under the Uintah and Ouray agency, Utah.

In July, 1879, about 100 men of the

White River agency, Colo., roamed from their reservation into s. Wyoming to hunt. During this time some forests were fired by railway tiemen, resulting in great loss of timber, and calling forth complaint against the Indians, who were ordered to remain henceforth on their reservation. In Sept. the agent, Meeker, was assaulted after a quarrel with a petty chief, and requested military aid, which was granted. Orders were later issued for the arrest of the Indians charged with the recent forest fires, and Maj. Thornburgh was sent with a force of 190 men. Suspecting the outcome, the Indians procured ammunition from neighboring traders and informed the agent that the appearance of the troops would be regarded as an act of war. On Sept. 20 Thornburgh's detachment was ambushed, and their leader and 13 men were killed. The command fell back. On Oct. 2 a company of cavalry arrived, and 3 days later Col. Merritt with 600 troops reached the scene. At or near the agency the bodies of Meeker and 7 employees were found; all but one of the agency buildings had been rifled and burned. The conflict was soon ended, mainly through the peaceful attitude and influence of chief Ouray.

In the summer of 1906 about 400 Ute, chiefly of the White River band, left their allotments and the Uintah res. in Utah to go to the Pine Ridge res., S. Dak., there to enjoy an unrestricted communal life. They made the journey leisurely, and although no depredations were committed on the way, settlers became alarmed. Every peaceful effort was made to induce the absentees to return to Utah, but all excepting 45, who returned home, remained obdurate, and after having been charged with petty thefts while in Wyoming, the matter was placed under the jurisdiction of the War Department, troops were sent to the scene in October, and the Indians accompanied them peacefully to Ft Meade, S. Dak., in November. In the following spring (1907) arrangements were made whereby the absentee Ute were assigned 4 townships of the Cheyenne River res., S. Dak., which was leased by the Government, at the expense of the Ute annuity fund, for 5 years. The Indians were removed in June to their new lands, where they remained until the following June (1908), when, at their own request, they were returned to their old home in Utah, arriving there in October. Cf. *Yuta.*

Digger Ute.—Marcy, Army Life, 229, 1866 (apparently a general name for the Ute). Eutahs.—Schoolcraft, Ind. Tribes, v, 498, 1855. Eutaw.—Irving, Rocky Mts., II, 213, 1837. Grasshopper Indians.—Pattie, Pers. Narr., 101, 1833. Gutahs.—Domenech, Deserts, II, 4, 1860. Iätä-go.—Mooney in 14th Rep. B. A. E., 1043, 1896 (Kiowa name). Ietan.—See under that name. Inta.—Escudero, Not. de Son. y Sin., 67, 1849 (= Iuta). Jut-

joat.—Orozco y Berra, Geog., 59, 1864. Mactciñgeha wai[n].—Dorsey. Çegiha MS. Dict., B. A. E., 1878 (= 'rabbit-skin robes': Omaha and Ponca name). Möh-tau-hai'-ta-ni-o.—Hayden, Ethnog. and Philol. Mo. Val., 290, 1862 (= 'the black men': Cheyenne name). Muxtawátan.—ten Kate, Reizen, 8, 1885 ('black people': Cheyenne name). Násuia kwe.—ten Kate, ibid., 7 ('deer-hunting men': Zuñi name). No-o-chi.—A. Hrdlička, inf'n, 1907. No-o-chi-uh.—Ibid. No-ónch.—Ibid. (own name). Nota-á.—ten Kate, op. cit., 6 (Navaho name). Notch.—Ibid., 8 (own name). Nuts.—Ibid. (alternative of Notch). Quazula.—Zárate-Salmerón (ca. 1629) in Land of Sunshine, 183, Jan., 1900 (a province; name in Jemez language: seemingly the Ute). Qusutas.—Ibid. Sápa wicaśa.—Cook, Yankton MS. vocab., B. A. E., 184, 1882 (Dakota name). Sarpa-wee-cha-cha.—Corliss, Lacotah MS. vocab., B. A. E., 106, 1874 (Teton name; intended for Sapa wicaśa, 'Black people'). Spanish Yutes.—Fremont, Exped. to Rocky Mts., 141, 1854. Tâ'hana.—Hodge, field-notes, B. A. E., 1895 (Taos name). Tcingawúptuh.—Stephen in 8th Rep. B. A. E., 30, 1891 (former Hopi name). Utahs.—Vargas (1694) quoted by Davis, Span. Conq. N. Mex., 404, 1869. Utas.—Prichard, Phys. Hist. Man., v, 415, 1847. Utaws.—Parker, Journal, 79, 1840. Ute.—Bent (1846) in Cal. Mess. and Corresp., 193, 1850. Útsiā.—Voth, Traditions of the Hopi, 267, 1905 (Hopi name). Wáateniïts.—Curtis, N. Am. Ind., v, 154, 1909 ('black': Atsina name). Yita.—Mediavilla y Ascona (1746), doc. in Colegio de Santa Cruz de Querétaro, Mex., K, leg. 5, no. 6. Yiuhta.—Pimentel, Lenguas, II, 347, 1865 (confounded with Comanche). Yóta.—Curtis, N. Am. Ind., I, 135, 1907 (Jicarilla Apache form). Youtah.—Gebow, Shosho-nay Vocab., 21, 1868 (Shoshoni name). Youtas.—Duflot de Mofras, Expl., II, 335, 1844. Youts.—Smet, Letters, 36, 1843. Yú'hta.—Gatschet, Comanche MS., B. A. E. (Comanche name). Yulas.—Escudero, Not. Nuevo-Méx., 83, 1849. Yumyum.—Writer (ca. 1702) in Doc. Hist. Mex., 4th s., v, 150, 1857 (Orozco y Berra, p. 59, says Maricopa name). Yútā.—Dorsey, Kansa MS. vocab., B. A. E., 1882 (Kansas name). Yutama.—Bourke, Moquis of Ariz., 118, 1884 (Hopi name). Yutamo.—Stephen in 8th Rep. B. A. E., 35, 1891 (Hopi name). Yutas.—Gregg, Comm. Prairies, I, 285, 1844. Yútawáts.—Mooney in 17th Rep. B. A. E., 167, 1898 (so called by Plains tribes). Yute.—Garrard, Wah-to-yah, 185, 1850. Yutta.—Doc. of 1720 quoted by Bandelier in Arch. Inst. Papers, v, 183, 1890.

Utensils. See *Implements, Receptacles.*

Utenstank. A village of the Powhatan confederacy in 1608, situated on the N. bank of Mattapony r. in Caroline co., Va.—Smith (1629), Va., I, map, repr. 1819.

Uthlecan. See *Oolichan.*

Utikimitung. A village of the Talirpingmiut Okomiut Eskimo, on the s. shore of Cumberland sd.

Utiqimitung.—Boas in 6th Rep. B. A. E., map, 1888.

Utina (Timucua: *uti,* land; *na,* my: 'my country'). In the narrative of the French Huguenot colony in Florida, 1564, Utina, Ouae Utina, or Olata Ouae Utina, is given as the name of the head chief of the Timucua, and on the De Bry map of 1591 (Le Moyne, Narr., 1885) we find Utina as a town within the same territory. It appears, however, to be a title rather than a geographic or personal name, and does not occur in subsequent Spanish history. *Olata,* or *holata,* is one of the Timucua titles for "chief," and it has been adopted into the Creek language. (J. M.)

Olata Ouae Utina.—Laudonnière in French, Hist. Coll. La., 243, 1869. Otina.—Barcia, Ensayo, 50, 1723. Ouae Utina.—Laudonnière, op. cit., 256.

Outina.—Brackenridge, Views of La., 84, 1814. Utina.—Laudonnière (1564) quoted by Basanier in French, Hist.Coll. La., 261, 1869. Utinama.—Gentl. of Elvas (1557) in Bourne, De Soto Narr., I, 39, 1904 (in N. w. Florida, 1539).

Utina. In the narrative of De Soto's expedition it is stated that the Spaniards passed a town, apparently about Suwannee r., called Utinama (Gentl. of Elvas, 1557) or Utinamocharra (Ranjel, ca. 1546), probably a confusion between a title and a proper name. The *ma* is a locative suffix; the *mocharra* remains unexplained. The town probably belonged to the Potano tribe.   (J. M.)
Utinamocharra.—Ranjel (ca. 1546), in Bourne, De Soto Narr., II, 70, 1904 (N. w. Florida, 1539).

Utinomanoc. Mentioned as one of the tribes from which neophytes were drawn by San Francisco Solano mission, Cal. It was probably Moquelumnan. See Bancroft, Hist. Cal., II, 506, 1886; Engelhardt, Franc. in Cal., 451, 1897; Barrett in Univ. Cal. Pub., VI, no. 1, 44, 1908.

Utitnom. The branch of the Yuki of N. California that inhabited the angle between the confluence of Middle and South Eel rs. and extended westward across South Eel r.

Utkiavi ('high place'). The village of the Utkiavinmiut Eskimo at C. Smyth, Alaska, lat. 71° 23′; pop. 225 in 1880. A Government station was established there in 1881.
Ooglaamie.—Murdoch in 9th Rep. B. A. E., 26, 1892 (given as incorrect form). Ooglamie.—U. S. Signal Serv. map, 1885. Ootivakh.—Baker, Geog. Dict. Alaska, 1902. Ootiwakh.—Petroff in 10th Census, Alaska, 4, 1884. Ootkaiowik.—Ibid. Otke-a-vik.—Simpson, Observations, map, 1855. Otkiawik.—Baker, op. cit. Ot-ki-a-wing.—Maguire in Parl. Rep., XLII, 186, 1854. Otkiovik.—British Admiralty chart cited by Murdoch in 9th Rep. B. A. E., 26, 1892. Otkiwik.—Brit. Admiralty chart. Uglaamie.—Murdoch, op. cit. (given as incorrect form). Utkeavic.—11th Census, Alaska, 162, 1893. Utkeagvik.—Zagoskin, Descr. Russ. Poss. Am., pt. I, 74, 1847. Utkiavi.—Baker, op. cit. Utkiaving.—Ibid. Utkiavwĭñ.—Murdoch, op. cit.

Utkiavinmiut. An Eskimo tribe w. of Pt Barrow, Alaska; pop. about 140 in 1883, 246 in 1890. They flourished about 1870, but have since declined and keep up their numbers by accessions from the Nunatogmiut. Their villages are Pengnok and Utkiavi; summer camps are Ernivwin, Imekpung, Ipersua, Kuosugru, Nakeduxo, Nunaktuau, Sakamna, Sinyu. Walakpa.
Ootkeaviemutes.—Kelly, Arct. Eskimos, chart, 1890. Ootkeavies.—Ibid., 14. Utkiavwĭñmiun.—Murdoch in 9th Rep. B. A. E., 43, 1892.

Utlaksuk. An Eskimo settlement near the N. end of Baffin bay, w. Greenland.
Utlak-soak.—Kane, Arct. Explor., II, 55, 1856.

Utlums. An abandoned Salishan village on the s. side of Galiano id., Brit. Col.
Ut-lums.—Dawson, Can. Geol. Surv., map, 1887.

Utoca. An ancient village in N. Florida, probably Timucuan.—Robin, Voy., II, map, 1807.

Utorkarmiut. A ruined Eskimo village on the E. shore of Sermiligak fjord, E.

Greenland.—Meddelelser om Grönland, XXVII, 22, 1902.

Utsehta ('lowlanders'). One of the three principal divisions of the Osage tribe.
Lesser Osage.—Fisher, New Trav., 250, 1812. Little Osage.—Treaty of 1865 in U. S. Indian Treat., II, 878, 1904. Little Ossage.—Schermerhorn (1812) in Mass. Hist. Soc. Coll., 2d s., II, 31, 1814. Oo′-zâ-tâu.—Lewis and Clark Discov., 13, 1806. Petit Osage.—Bradbury, Trav. in Am., 36, 1817. Petits Os.—Du Lac, Voy. dans les Louisianes, map, 1805. Petit Zo.—Lewis and Clark Discov., 13, 1806. Teat Saws.—Featherstonhaugh, Slave States, 71, 1844. Uꞩseꞩ′ta.—McGee in 15th Rep. B. A. E., 162, 1897 (own name).

Uttamussac. A village of the Powhatan confederacy in 1608, situated on the N. bank of Pamunkey r. in King William co., Va. The principal temple of the confederacy was here.
Uttamussack.—Smith (1629), Va., I, 138, repr. 1819. Vtamussack.—Strachey (1612), Va., 90, 1849. Vttamussak.—Smith, op. cit., map.

Uttamussamacoma. A village of the Powhatan confederacy in 1608, situated on the s. bank of Potomac r. in Westmoreland co., Va.
Vttamussamacoma.—Smith (1629), Va., I, map, repr. 1819.

Utuka ('the old place'). The chief village of the Utukamiut Eskimo at Icy cape, Alaska; pop. 50 in 1880, 48 in 1890.
Otok-kok.—Petroff, Rep. on Alaska, 59, 1880. Otukah.—Baker, Geog. Dict. Alaska, 1902. Ō′-tu-kâh.—Murdoch quoted by Baker, Geog. Dict. Alaska, 1902. Utuka.—11th Census, Alaska, 152, 1893.

Utukamiut. A nomadic tribe of Eskimo which originated at Icy cape and now range along the Arctic coast from Pt Hope to Wainright inlet and inland to Colville r. Through intermarriage with the Nunatogmiut, Kowagmiut, and Kopagmiut they have developed physically and mentally beyond the sedentary tribes of N. w. Alaska. Their villages are Kaiaksekawik, Kelemanturuk, and Utuka.
Ootooka Mutes.—Kelly, Arct. Eskimos, chart, 1890. Ootookas.—Ibid., 14. Oto-kog-ameuts.—Hooper, Cruise of Corwin, 26, 1880. Utukakgmut.—Zagoskin, Descr. Russ. Poss. Am., pt. I, 74, 1847. Utukamiut.—Woolfe in 11th Census, Alaska, 130, 1893.

Utumpaiats (*U-tum′-pai-ats*, 'people of arrowhead lands'). A Paiute band formerly in or near Moapa valley, s. E. Nevada; pop. 46 in 1873.—Powell in Ind. Aff. Rep. 1873, 50, 1874.

Uturituc (Pima: 'the corner,' because it was situated at the angle of the new and the old stream beds of the Gila). A former Pima village on the Rio Gila, probably on the site of the present Sacaton, about 3 Spanish leagues N. w. of Casa Grande ruin, s. Ariz. It was visited by Garcés and Anza in 1775, at which time it contained 300 inhabitants. See Anza in Bancroft, Ariz. and N. Mex., 389, 1889; Anza and Font, ibid., 392; Garcés (1775–76), Diary, 65, 1900; Bartlett, Pers. Narr., II, 268, 1854.
San Juan Capistrano.—Garcés (1775), Diary, 109, 1900. San Juan Capistrans de Virtud.—Font (1775)

quoted by Schoolcraft, Ind. Tribes, III, 301, 1853. **S. Juan Capistrano.**—Anza quoted by Bancroft, Ariz. and N. Mex., 389, 1889. **S. Juan Capistrano de Ulurituc.**—Anza and Font, ibid., 392. **San Juan de Capistrano.**—Garcés (1776), Diary, 455, 1900. **Tutirituçar.**—Anza quoted by Bancroft, Ariz. and N. Mex., 389, 1889. **Tutunitucan.**—Anza and Font, ibid., 392. **Utilltuc.**—Ibid. **Uturicut.**—Humboldt, New Spain, II, 303, 1811. **Uturituc.**—Font (1775) in Ternaux-Compans, Voy., IX, 383, 1838. **Vturituc.**—Garcés (1775), Diary, 65, 1900.

Uulgo. Mentioned by Rivera (Diario, leg. 1514, 1736) with the Pima, Opata, Jova, Eudeve, Yaqui, Seri, and Tepoca, apparently as a tribe of N. w. Mexico. Not identified, and seemingly a misprint of some other name.

Uupon. See *Black drink, Yopon.*

Uva. A Chumashan tribe of the Tulare basin, Cal., reduced in 1851 to 20 individuals through conflict with the Spaniards and neighboring tribes. They joined with other small tribes in the treaty of June 10, 1851, by which they reserved a tract between Tejon pass and Kern r., and ceded the remainder of their lands to the United States. **Uras.**—Barbour in Sen. Ex. Doc. 4, 32d Cong., spec. sess., 124, 1853. **Uvas.**—Barbour in Ind. Aff. Rep., 233, 1851.

Uvingasok. An Eskimo village in w. Greenland, lat. 73° 17'.—Science, XI, 259, 1888.

Uwarosuk ('big stone'). An Ita Eskimo settlement on Murchison sd., lat. 77° 7', N. Greenland. **Uwarrow Suk-suk.**—Kane, Arct. Explor., II, 235, 1856.

Uyak. A Kaniagmiut Eskimo village near the Salmon canneries, on Uyak bay, Kodiak id., Alaska. Pop. 76 in 1880; fewer than 20 in 1890. **Bobrowskoje.**—Holmberg, Ethnog. Skizz., map, 1855. **Ooiak.**—Petroff in 10th Census, Alaska, 29, 1884. **Ooiatsk.**—Lisianski (1805) quoted by Baker, Geog. Dict. Alaska, 1902. **Ugujuk.**—Holmberg, op. cit. **Uyak.**—11th Census, Alaska, 79, 1893.

Uzela. An Apalachee(?) village visited by De Soto in 1539, just before reaching the principal town of the tribe, and probably not far from the present Tallahassee, Fla. **Uzela.**—Gentl. of Elvas (1557) in French, Hist. Coll. La., II, 134, 1850.

Uzinki (Russian: 'narrow'). A village of Kaniagmiut creoles on Spruce id., Kodiak group, Alaska. Pop. 45 in 1880; 74 in 1890. **Oozinkie.**—Petroff in 10th Census, Alaska, 28, 1884. **Uzinkee.**—11th Census, Alaska, 74, 1893.

Uzutiuhi. A Quapaw band and ancient village. There still survived in 1891 certain gentes belonging to it. The first mention of the village, unless found in some of the names of De Soto's chroniclers, is probably the Atotchasi of Marquette's map (1673). Ototchassi of Thevenot is greatly out of place, as are most of the names on his map. In 1727 Poisson located it near the French fort on Arkansas r., near its mouth. **Aesetooue.**—Iberville (1702) in Margry, Déc., IV, 601, 1880. **Assotoué.**—Tonti (1687) in French, Hist. Coll. La., I, 71, 1846. **Atotchasi.**—Marquette quoted by Shea, Discov., 268, 1852. **Erabacha.**—

Coxe, Carolana, 11, 1741. **Louchetchouis.**—Baudry des Lozières, Voy. à la Louisiane, 243, 1802 (probably identical). **Osatoves.**—Barcia, Ensayo Cron., 288, 1723. **Osotonoy.**—Tonty (1687) in French, Hist. Coll. La., I, 60, 1846. **Osotteoez.**—Douay (1687) quoted by Shea, Discov., 170, 1852. **Ossoteoez.**—Hennepin, New Discov., pt. 2, 44, 1698. **Ossotéoué.**—Margry, Déc., III, 595, 1878. **Ossotonoy.**—Shea, Discov., 170, 1852. **Ossotoues.**—McKenney and Hall, Ind. Tribes, III, 81, 1854. **Ossotteoez.**—Charlevoix, New France, IV, 108, note, 1870. **Ossoztoues.**—Tonti in French, Hist. Coll. La., I, 83, 1846. **Ototchassi.**—Thevenot in Shea, Discov., 268, 1852. **Otsotchaué.**—Joutel (1687) in Margry, Déc., III, 463, 1878. **Otsotchoué.**—Charlevoix, New France, IV, 108, note, 1866. **Otsotchove.**—Joutel (1687) in French, Hist. Coll. La., I, 176, 1846. **Otsoté.**—Joutel (1687) in Margry, Déc., III, 444, 1878. **Oues-peries.**—Coxe, Carolana, 11, 13, 1741. **Oufotu.**—Sibley (1805) in Lewis and Clark, Discov., 85, 1806. **Ousolu.**—Sibley (1805) in Am. St. Papers, Ind. Aff., I, 725, 1832. **Ousontiwi.**—Coxe, Carolana, map, 1741. **Ousoutiwy.**—Ibid., 11. **Ozotheoa.**—McKenney and Hall, Ind. Tribes, III, 81, 1854. **Ozotoues.**—Tonti (1687) in French, Hist. Coll. La., I, 82, 1846. **Satos.**—Schoolcraft, Ind. Tribes, III, 557, 1853 (identical?). **Sauthouis.**—Shea, Discov., 170, note, 1852. **Sittëoüi.**—Gale, Upper Miss., 202, 1867. **Sothoues.**—McKenney and Hall, Ind. Tribes, III, 82, 1854. **Sothouis.**—Jefferys, French Dom. Am., 144, 1761. **Sotos.**—Doc. of 1736 in N. Y. Doc. Col. Hist., IX, 1057, 1855 (identical?). **Sotonis.**—De la Tour map, 1779 (misprint). **Sotouis.**—Jefferys, French Dom. Am., pt. 1, 134, 1761. **Souchitiony.**—Iberville (1700) in Margry, Déc., IV, 429, 1880. **Southois.**—Charlevoix, Hist. Jour., 307, 1763. **Southouis.**—Shea, Discov., 268, 1852. **Soutouis.**—Carte des Poss. Angl., 1777. **Uzutiúhe.**—Gatschet, Creek Migr. Leg., I, 30, 1884. **U-zu'-ti-u'-hi.**—Dorsey, Kwapa MS. vocab., B. A. E., 1883. **U-zu'-ti-u'-wĕ.**—Dorsey in 15th Rep. B. A. E., 229, 1897. **Zautoouys.**—La Harpe (1721) in Margry, Déc., VI, 357, 1886. **Zautooys.**—Ibid., 365.

Vaaf (*Va'-af*). Apparently a gentile organization among the Pima, belonging to the Suwuki Ohimal, or Red Ants, phratral group.—Russell in 26th Rep. B. A. E., 197, 1908.

Vaba. A rancheria, probably Cochimi, under Purísima (Cadegomo) mission, on the Pacific coast of Lower California in the 18th century.—Doc. Hist. Mex., 4th s., v, 189, 1857.

Vabacahel ('water of the rancheria'). A rancheria, probably Cochimi, connected with Purísima (Cadegomo) mission, Lower California, in the 18th century.—Doc. Hist. Mex., 4th s., v, 189, 1857.

Vachinápuchic ('the pass straight ahead'). A Tarahumare rancheria about 25 m. N. E. of Norogachic, Chihuahua, Mexico.—Lumholtz, inf'n, 1894.

Vacoregue (Nahuatl: *atl,* 'water'; *core,* 'the turning'; *hui,* 'place of': 'place of the turn of the river.'—Buelna). A division of the Cahita on the lower Rio Fuerte and the coast between that river and the Rio Sinaloa, in Sinaloa, Mexico. Besides the Vacoregue proper this division embraced the Ahome, Batucari, Comopori, and Guazave—all named from their settlements and speaking the same dialect of the Cahita. They eked out a livelihood by fishing, and after being converted to Christianity founded a town on the Rio Fuerte, not far from Ahome. **Bacoregues.**—Bancroft, No. Mex. States, I, 214, 1886. **Bacorehui.**—Ribas quoted by Brinton, Am.

Race, 127, 1891. **Guasave.**—Ibid., map (Vacoregue, or). **Guazave.**—Orozco y Berra, Geog., 58, 1864. **Vacoregue.**—Ibid.

Vaeachachic (*vae*, 'pasture'; *chic*, 'place of'). A small rancheria of the Tarahumare near Norogachic, Chihuahua, Mexico.—Lumholtz, inf'n, 1904.

Vagerpe. A village, presumably Costanoan, formerly connected with Dolores mission, San Francisco, Cal.—Taylor in Cal. Farmer, Oct. 18, 1861.

Vagitchitchate. A Kaiyukhotana village near the mouth of Innoko r., w. Alaska.—Zagoskin in Nouv. Ann. Voy., 5th ser., xxi, map, 1850. **Kushichagat.**—Tikhmenief quoted by Baker, Geog. Dict. Alaska, 365, 1901. **Vashichagat.**—Zagoskin quoted by Petroff in 10th Census, Alaska, 37, 1884.

Vahadha ('tobacco'). Given by Bourke (Jour. Am. Folk-lore, ii, 181, 1889) as a clan of the Mohave (q. v.).

Vahia. The name of the site of San Miguel mission, Cal., established in Salinan territory. **Vahiá.**—Engelhardt, Franc. in Cal., 404, 1897. **Vaticá.**—Ibid.

Vahichi ('swamp'). A small rancheria of the Tarahumare near Norogachic, Chihuahua, Mexico.—Lumholtz, inf'n, 1894.

Vajademin. A rancheria, probably Cochimi, under Purísima (Cadegomo) mission, Lower California, in the 18th century.—Doc. Hist. Mex., 4th s., v, 188, 1857.

Vakasuachiki ('plenty of reeds,' or 'place where reeds shoot up'). A Tarahumare rancheria in Chihuahua, Mexico.—Lumholtz, inf'n, 1894.

Valebo ('large mesa'). A small rancheria of the Tarahumare near Norogachic, Chihuahua, Mexico.—Lumholtz, inf'n, 1894.

Valle (Span.: 'valley'). A former village of the central Papago, probably in Pima co., Ariz., with 97 families in 1865.—Davidson in Ind. Aff. Rep., 135, 1865.

Vallecillo (Span.: 'little valley'). An Opata pueblo visited by Coronado in 1540; situated in the valley of the Rio Sonora, N. w. Mexico, in the vicinity of Arizpe. Probably identical with a village later known by another name. **El Vallecillo.**—Castañeda, Relación (1596), in Ternaux-Compans, Voy., ix, 158, 1838. **Little Valley.**—Winship in 14th Rep. B. A. E., 515, 1896.

Valle de las Viejas (Span.: 'valley of the old ones'). A former Diegueño village in San Diego co., Cal.—Hayes (1850) quoted by Bancroft, Nat. Races, i, 458, 1882.

Valleytown (native name *Gŭ′năhitŭñ′yĭ*, 'long place'). A former Cherokee settlement where now is the town of the same name, on Valley r., in Cherokee co., N. C. The various settlements on Valley r. and the adjacent part of Hiwassee were known collectively as the "Valley towns." 　　　　　(J. M.)

Vánca. A tribe, evidently Coahuiltecan, met by Massanet (Diary, in Mem. de Nueva España, xxvii, 94, MS.) in 1691 w. of Rio Hondo, Texas, together with the Patchal, Papañaca, and others.

Vareato. Mentioned, in connection with Puaray, apparently as a pueblo of the Tigua of New Mexico in 1598.—Oñate (1598) in Doc. Inéd., xvi, 115, 1871.

Varohio. A division of the Tarahumare in w. Chihuahua and s. e. Sonora, Mexico, mainly on the Rio Chinipas, but extending N. to the town of Loreto and w. to the Rio Mayo. It includes the Chinipa, Guailopo, Maguiaqui, Hizo, Husoron, Cuteco, and Tecargoni. The Varohio proper occupied Loreto and Santa Ana pueblos. **Chinipa.**—Orozco y Berra, Geog., 58, 1864 (used synonymously with Varohio, but strictly only a division thereof.) **Huarogio.**—Lumholtz in Scribner's Mag., xvi, 31, 32, July, 1894; Lumholtz in Proc. Int. Cong. of Anthr., 103, 1894. **Varogio.**—Orozco y Berra, Geog., 58, 1864. **Varohio.**—Ibid. **Voragio.**—Ibid.

Vases. See *Pottery, Receptacles.*

Vasisa. One of the 7 Apalachee towns named in a letter from the chiefs of the tribe to the King of Spain in 1688; situated probably on Wacissa r., Jefferson co., Fla., and evidently destroyed by the English and their Indian allies under Gov. Moore in 1704. In 1822 Creek (i. e. Seminole) immigrants from Chattahoochee r. occupied a town called Wacissatalofa, 'Wacissa town,' about the head of St Marks r. in the same neighborhood. 　　　　　(J. M.)
Vasisa.—Doc. of 1688 quoted by Gatschet, Creek Migr. Leg., i, 76, 1884 (Apalachee town). **Wa-cissatalofa.**—Bell in Morse, Rep. to Sec. War, 306, 1822 (Creek town).

Vasoreachic (*vasoli*, an herb; *chic*, 'place of'). A Tarahumare rancheria near Norogachic, Chihuahua, Mexico.—Lumholtz, inf'n, 1894.

Vawerachi (*Va-we′-ra-chi*, 'place of much water'). A small rancheria of the Tarahumare near Norogachic, Chihuahua, Mexico.—Lumholtz, inf'n, 1894.

Vaynorpa. A village of the Opata on the E. bank of Rio San Miguel, about lat. 30°, Sonora, Mexico.—Bandelier in Arch. Inst. Papers, iii, 71, 1890; iv, 487, 1892.

Vayuavabi. A ruined village of the Opata E. of Nacori, about lat. 29° 30′, E. Sonora, Mexico. **Va-yua-va-bi.**—Bandelier in Arch. Inst. Papers, iii, 62, 1890. **Vay-ua-va-vi.**—Ibid., iv, 508, 1892.

Vazacahel ('mesquite water'). A rancheria, probably Cochimi, connected with Purísima (Cadegomo) mission, Lower California, in the 18th century. **Vaxacahel.**—Doc. Hist. Mex., 4th s., v, 190, 1857. **Vazacahel.**—Ibid.

Vechaochi (*Ve-cha′-o-chi*, 'place of the prickly herb,' possibly referring to a cactus). A small rancheria of the Tarahumare near Norogachic, Chihuahua, Mexico.—Lumholtz, inf'n, 1894.

Vectaca. A village, presumably Costanoan, formerly connected with Dolores mission, San Francisco, Cal.—Taylor in Cal. Farmer, Oct. 18, 1861.

Velasco, Luis de. The brother of a chief of a Virginia district known to the Spaniards as Axacan (q. v.), on a stream flowing into Chesapeake bay. Spanish navigators, in company, perhaps, with some Dominican monks, had visited the country in 1559-60 and carried the boy to Mexico, where the viceroy, Don Luis de Velasco, caused him to be baptized and gave him his name. In 1566, while in Havana, Don Luis accompanied a party of 30 Spanish soldiers under a captain, and two Dominicans, to his home country, where it was planned to establish a mission; but the venture proving a failure, the monks and the Indian sailed for Spain. At court he so ingratiated himself into the good will of King Philip II that he lived at the royal expense during all his stay, when he returned to Havana with some Dominican missionaries who had embarked for Florida. The Florida mission having been abandoned, Don Luis, in his apparent zeal to convert his countrymen, joined the Jesuits under Father Segura on their departure for Florida in 1570. On August 5 Father Segura and 8 other Jesuits, together with the Indian, sailed for Chesapeake bay, reaching on Sept. 10 the province of Axacan, where they entered a river and landed. So impoverished was the country that the vessel was sent back with a message appealing for the relief of the destitution of the Indians in the following spring. On the departure of the vessel the fathers moved to another stream, 2 leagues distant, near a settlement governed by a younger brother of Don Luis, where a hut and a chapel were erected and where the Indian served as interpreter for some time, when he abandoned the missionaries under pretense of preparing for their reception at another village. Early in Feb. 1571, a messenger was sent by the missionaries to induce Don Luis to return. He received them with a great show of friendship and promised to return on the following day, but the same night the Indians, led by Luis, overtook the little party and murdered them. On Feb. 8, the remainder of the missionary band at their settlement were disarmed of their hatchets by a ruse, when the Indians fell upon and killed all except a little boy, Alonso, who was rescued by Menendez later in the year when he visited Axacan to wreak vengeance on the natives for the murders they had committed. Consult Lowery, Spanish Settlements—Florida, 1562-1574, 1905, and authorities therein cited; Murray, Lives Cath. Heroes, 1896; French, Hist. Coll. La., n. s., II, 230, 1875; Shea (1) in Beach, Ind. Miscel., 1877, (2) in Cath. World, Mar. 1875, (3) Cath. Missions, 1855, (4) Cath. Church in Col. Days, 1886; Brown, (1) First Republic in Amer., 1898; (2) Genesis of U. S., 1890. (J. M.)

Venaambakaia. A band or division of the Pomo, formerly living near the Russian settlement of Ross, in Sonoma co., Cal.—Powell in Cont. N. A. Ethnol., III, 493, 1877.

Venados (Span. pl. 'deer'). One of the tribes mentioned by Fray Bartolomé García as speaking the language of his Manual (1760). This tribe was either quite widely distributed or else the name was applied to several distinct bands, all evidently Coahuiltecan. In 1731 San Juan Capistrano mission was founded in Texas for the "Benados" and Toloujaá (Tiloja), and the Benado chief was made first "governor" of the mission (Test. de Asiento de Misiones, MS., 1731, in Gen. Land Off., Austin, Texas). In 1737 they deserted the mission (doc. in Lamar Papers, 1737, MS.). After 1757 large numbers of them were gathered at the Camargo mission, on the Rio Grande, and they were still living there as late as 1809 (Baptismal records in the parish church of Camargo, examined in 1907). Some time in the 18th century some of the tribe were at the Vizarron mission in northern Mexico (Portillo, Apuntes, 323, 1888). (H. E. B.)
Benados.—Test. de Asiento, 1731, op. cit.

Venango. A former Seneca settlement at the mouth of French cr., in Venango co., Pa., at the site of the present Franklin. According to the deposition of Stephen Coffen (1754) it was "called by the Indians Ganagarah'hare, on the Banks of Belle Rivière, where the River o Boeff empties into it" (Arch. Pa., 2d s., VI, 184, 1877). The place was later occupied by a mixed population of Seneca, Delawares, Shawnee, Wyandot, Ottawa, and other tribes allied with the French. The place first came into notice when the French agent Joncaire visited the Indians in 1753, in advance of the French expedition. He distributed presents to the Indians about the region, and expelled the English traders. John Fraser, who had been at the place for several years, selling goods and acting as a gunsmith, wrote to the Pennsylvania Council explaining that the French were building a fort "at Caseoago up French creek," the reference being to the French fort at Le Bœuf, now Waterford, Pa. No French fort was built at Cussewago. Many writers are in error in locating the French fort at this place, and in calling the locality where the French fort was built Cussewago. Shippen, in a letter concerning the matter, says: "Weningo is the name of an Indian Town on Ohio, where Mr. Freser has had a Gunsmith Shop for many years; it is situate eighty Miles up the same River beyond the Log's Town Casewago is Twenty miles above Weningo" (Col. Rec. Pa., v, 660, 1851). The entrance of the French expedition in 1753 caused great excitement among the Iroquois, who regarded it as an invasion of their lands; and also among the Delawares, Shawnee, and other Indians at Logstown for the same reason (see letter of Lieut. Holland, Col. Rec. Pa., v, 623; Letter of Gov. Dinwiddie, 630; Letter from Council of Onondaga, 637; Letter of Half King, 635; Weiser's Journal of his mission to Onondaga, 642–647). This expedition followed a different course from that of Céloron de Bienville (1749), which reached Allegheny r. by way of L. Chautauqua and Conewango r. It made the portage from Presqu' Isle (Erie, Pa.) to the headwaters of River au Bœuf (French cr.) and then down this stream to its mouth (Venango). Forts were built at the two former locations in 1753. It was the intention to build a third fort at Venango, but owing to the opposition of the Indians and the lateness of the season, this project was temporarily abandoned (Letter of M. Duquesne to M. de Rouille, Aug. 1753, in Arch. Pa., 2d s., vi, 161, 1877). Possession was taken of the place by Capt. Chalbert de Joncaire, who expelled the traders from John Fraser's house, and erected a French flag on the building, which he made his headquarters. He spent his time trying to win the Indians on the Ohio to the French interest. The presence of the French force within the region claimed by the English led to the mission of Washington and Gist, who were sent by the Governor of Virginia to warn the French invaders to depart (Washington's Jour., 1753; Gist's Jour., 1753; Frontier Forts, ii, 1 et seq., 1895). The French fort at Venango was finished in the spring of 1754; it was called Ft Machault by the French, but was always called "the French fort at Venango" by the English. During the French occupancy of the Ohio this fort became a center of Indian influence on the upper Allegheny (Frontier Forts, ii, 585, 1896). After the fall of Ft Duquesne in 1758, the fort at Venango was strengthened and a larger garrison placed at it; it then became a rendezvous for all the Indians hostile to the English. In the summer of 1759 there were about 1,000 Indians of various tribes gathered in the vicinity. Col. Hugh Mercer, the commander of Ft Pitt, wrote to Gov. Denny, telling him of the gathering of the French and Indians at Venango for the purpose of taking Ft Pitt (Col. Rec. Pa., viii, 292, 1852). In the summer of 1759 the French force deserted all their posts in N. W. Pennsylvania, leaving the entire region in possession of the English (Col. Rec. Pa., viii, 394–396, 1852). After the abandon-

ment of Venango by the French a new fort was built by the English in the summer of 1760, which was called Ft Venango, but only a small garrison, under Lieut. Gordon, was stationed at the place. During the Pontiac war the little garrison and fort at Venango was blotted out by the hostile Seneca, not a soul escaping. Lieut. Gordon was slowly burned to death (Bouquet's letter, Col. Rec. Pa., ix, 35, 1852). All the frontier forts of w. Pennsylvania were besieged by the Indians at the same time, and all except Ft Ligonier and Ft Pitt fell under the fury of the Indians. After the destruction of Ft Venango the entire region in N. W. Pennsylvania was in full possession of the Indians (Parkman, Conspiracy of Pontiac, ii, 18–25, 1901; Frontier Forts, ii, 592, 1896; Arch. of Pa., 2d s., vi, 579 et seq., 1877). At the treaty of Ft Pitt in 1765 many Indian deputies were present from the upper Allegheny region (Col. Rec. Pa., ix, 250 et seq., 1852). The close of the Revolution brought fears of another Indian uprising in Pennsylvania. Settlements had been made at various points on the Allegheny N. of Kittanning, to protect which Ft Franklin was built, about half a mile up French cr. (Arch. of Pa., xi, 270, 1855). During the Indian troubles in 1794 this fort was strengthened. A garrison was kept at this point until 1796, when a new location was selected nearer the mouth of French cr. This building, called the "Old Garrison," was occupied until 1803, when, all danger of Indian invasion having passed away, the military post was abandoned.   (G. P. D.)

Fort Franklin.—Howell map, 1792. Fort Machault.—Duquesne (1756) in Arch. Pa., 2d s., vi, 253, 1877. Fort Mackhault.—Vaudreuil (1757), ibid., 406. Fort of Venango.—Pa. Council (1789) in Col. Rec. Pa., xvi, 1853. Ganagarahhare.—Coffen (1754), ibid., vi, 9, 1851. Ganagarah'hare.—Arch. of Pa., 2d s., vi, 184, 1877. Machaull.—Fevre (1758), ibid., iii, 363, 1853. Oninge.—Homann Heirs map, 1756. Oningo.—Esnauts and Rapilly map, 1777. P. Machault.—Pouchot map, 1758. Quingo.—La Tour map, 1784 (misprint). Venanga.—Lattre map, 1784. Venango.—Washington (1753) in Proud, Penn., ii, app., 43, 1798. Venango Fort.—Scull map, 1770. Venango.—Morse, Hist. Am., map, 1798 (misprint). Veneango.—Easton conf. (1757) in N. Y. Doc. Col. Hist., vii, 287, 1856. Veningo.—Shirley (1755), ibid., vi, 957, 1855. Village du Loups.—Bonnecamp map, 1749. Vinango.—Homann Heirs map, 1756. Viningo.—Gist map, 1753. Wenango.—Lewis Evans map, 1755. Weningo.—Shippen (1753) in Col. Rec. Pa., v, 660, 1851. Weningo Town.—Peters (1754), ibid., 759.

Vende Flechas (Span.: 'arrow sellers'). A band represented in 1794 by six members at Espíritu Santo de Zúñiga mission, Texas. They were called by the missionary there a branch of the Xaraname (Aranama) tribe (Portillo, Apuntes, 308, 1888).

Veráchi ('where corn grows'). A small rancheria of the Tarahumare near Norogachic, Chihuahua, Mexico.—Lumholtz, inf'n, 1894.

Vermilion. A division of the Kickapoo that formerly lived on Wabash r., Ind., about the mouth of Vermilion r.
Kickapoos of the Vermilion.—Treaty of 1820 in U. S. Ind. Treat., 454, 1873. Vermilions.—Trader (1778) quoted by Schoolcraft, Ind. Tribes, III, 561, 1853. Vermillion Kickapoos.—Harrison (1811) in Am. St. Papers, Ind. Aff., I, 780, 1832. Vermillions.—Dodge (1779) quoted by Jefferson, Notes, 145, 1825.

Vescuachi. A pueblo of the Opata on Rio Sonora, Sonora, Mexico, in 1678–88 (Zapata, 1678, quoted by Bancroft, No. Mex. States, I, 246, 1884). See Chinapa.

Veselofski (Russian: 'cheerful'). A former Aleut village at C. Cheerful, Unalaska, Aleutian ids., Alaska; pop. 15 in 1831.
Vaysaylovskoi.—Elliott, Cond. Aff. Alaska, 225, 1875. Veselofski.—Sarichef (1792) quoted by Baker, Geog. Dict. Alaska, 122, 1902. Veselóvskoe.—Veniaminof, Zapiski, II, 202, 1840. Vesselovsky.—Petroff in 10th Census, Alaska, 34, 1884. Wesselowskoje.—Holmberg, Ethnog. Skizz., map, 1855.

Vesnak. A former Nishinam division near the mouth of American r., on the s. side, in Sacramento co., Cal.
Veshanacks.—Taylor in Cal. Farmer, June 8, 1860. Vesnacks.—Bancroft, Nat. Races, I, 450, 1874.

Vesperic Indians. A term proposed by Schoolcraft (Ind. Tribes, II, 28, 1852; V, 104, 1855; VI, 35, 1857) to designate the entire group of tribes geographically limited to the exact area of the United States.

Vessels. See Pottery, Receptacles.

Viayan. A Coahuiltecan band mentioned in 1754, with the Piguiques, as a subtribe of the Pamaques, q. v. (Informe, in Mem. de Nueva España, XXVII, 307, MS.). They are listed by Morfi as a Texas tribe (Mem. Hist. Tex., bk. II, ca. 1782).

Vichárachi ('where there are needles,' referring to cactus spines). A small rancheria of the Tarahumare near Norogachic, Chihuahua, Mexico.—Lumholtz, inf'n, 1894.

Viddaquimamar. A tribe or band, perhaps Coahuiltecan, which lived during the first decade of the 18th century at San Francisco Solano mission, s. of the Rio Grande and below the site of Eagle Pass, Texas. They were closely associated with the Terocodame and Tunamar (Ticmamar) bands (Baptismal records of the mission, MS.).
Biddaquimamar.—Baptismal rec., 1707, op. cit.

Viger. A Malecite settlement in Viger township, Temiscouata co., Quebec, containing 106 inhabitants in 1910.

Vihiyo (Víhiyo, 'chiefs,' sing. viy'). The name used to designate the tribal council of 44 chiefs of the Cheyenne (q. v.); sometimes regarded, but improperly, as constituting a regular warrior society of the tribe.   (J. M.)

Vikhit ('knowing people': Kaniagmiut name). An Ahtena division next below the Koltshan on Copper r., Alaska.
Vi-qit.—Hoffman, MS., B. A. E., 1882.

Village, Village site. See Mounds, Pueblos, Shell-heaps.

Village du Puant. A former village, probably of the Winnebago, on Wild Cat cr., about a mile above its junction with the Wabash, above Lafayette, in Tippecanoe co., Ind. It was abandoned before 1819. The site was included in the "Langlois reserve." See St Mary's Treaty (1819) in U. S. Ind. Treat., 493, 1873.

Vinasale. A trading post on Kuskokwim r., Alaska; pop. 140 in 1890.
Venizali.—Hallock in Nat. Geog. Mag., IX, 91, 1898. Vinisahle.—11th Census, Alaska, 164, 1893.

Vinatacot. The site and probably the local tribe at Santo Rosario mission, lat. 30° 3′, Lower California.
Vinatacot.—Taylor in Cal. Farmer, Jan. 24, 1862. Vintacottas.—Taylor in Browne, Res. Pac. Slope, app., 53, 54, 1869 (wrongly identified with the Uchities).

Viní. Mentioned as a New Mexico mission in 1742.—Mendoza et al. (1742–3) quoted by Bancroft, Ariz. and N. Mex., 244, 1889.

Visions. See Dreams, Oyaron.

Vossnessenski. An Aleut village and trading post on the island of that name in the Shumagin group, Alaska. Pop. 22 in 1880; 43 in 1890.
Vosnessensky.—Petroff in 10th Census, Alaska, 23, 1884. Voznesensky.—11th Census, Alaska, 86, 1893.

Vuikhtulik. A Nushagagmiut Eskimo village on the N. shore of L. Alaknakik, Alaska; pop. 51 in 1880.
Vuikhtuligmute.—Petroff, Rep. on Alaska, 50, 1880 (miut= 'people').

Vumahein. Mentioned as a pueblo of the province of Atriquy (q. v.), in the region of the lower Rio Grande, New Mexico, in 1598.—Oñate (1598) in Doc. Inéd., XVI, 115, 1871.

Vuntakutchin (Vun-tta-kwi-chin, 'people of Willow creek,' referring to Charlie's cr., where willows abound.—Schmitter). A Kutchin tribe, now greatly modified by contact with whites, occupying the country N. of Porcupine r., Alaska, as far as the Eskimo territory on the Arctic coast. They trade at Ft Yukon and at Ft Egbert in common with the western Kutchin. They formerly traded at Ft Selkirk, Pelly Banks, and Francis lake, but abandoned their trips on the destruction of the trading-posts at these points.

The Vuntakutchin subsist entirely by hunting and fishing, agriculture being unknown to them, although their territory is fertile. During the winter they move about wherever game is plentiful; in the spring they go to the river, where they make canoes and nets in preparation for salmon fishing, and during the summer dry and cache large quantities of fish; in the fall the entire family goes hunting, and when a good supply of game is accumulated it is cached on the spot; later, in October, they return to the river for about two months, when they make snowshoes, toboggans, and other articles for winter use. Wolfish dogs, their only domestic animals, are employed in winter for drawing toboggans and sleds, and in summer for hauling boats up the river banks. For inland travel, when there ·is no snow, the dogs are used as pack-animals. Each man owns a team of about five dogs.

The habitations formerly consisted of tents of caribou skin, supported by poles which were left behind when the occupants moved. Most of the people now live in rude, ill-ventilated cabins of a single room, built of logs chinked with moss, and with roofs of saplings covered with turf.

The native costume consisted of a parka of caribou skin—a hooded coat reaching to the knees, put on over the head. Sometimes sealskin parkas were obtained in trade from the natives of the lower river. Trousers, or a combination of trousers and stockings, of dressed mooseskin were also worn, as likewise were mittens and moccasins of the same material, cut in generous size in order that they could be lined with grass during cold weather. The coat of a chief was ornamented with quillwork, front and back, and had a special collar of moose-skin, fringed and quilled, which was significant of his office. A special hunting belt of caribou skin, quillworked, was provided; from it hung an ornamented moose-skin knife-sheath. Most of the native clothing has been supplanted by the cast-off clothing of the whites, or by cheap fabrics introduced by traders. Garments were decorated with porcupine quills dyed red by boiling in cranberry juice, or blue by boiling in huckleberry juice; pure white quills were not dyed; various colored flowers were also boiled and their coloring matter used for dyeing quills. Small geometrical figures were made by sewing the flattened-out quills to a backing of skin, and long stripes were made by rolling the quills into narrow spirals and sewing them side by side. The hair was formerly allowed to grow long, tied in a bunch behind, with a small knot over each temple. Swan feathers were chopped fine and applied with grease to the rear bunch daily until it became a large mass. Rings of small bird bones were worn in the nasal septum, especially on gala occasions. The older people still have their noses pierced.

Skin-dressing is the work of women. The hide is soaked in water to soften it, and the hair is scraped off with the end of a sharp bone spatula. All sewing is still done with bone awls. The women also make beadwork for sale to whites.

Moose-skin mittens are likewise made for the white trade.

Formerly a healthy people, the Vuntakutchin, like the other Kutchin tribes, have suffered greatly by the inroads of disease since their contact with whites and the adoption of some of the habits and devices of frontier civilization, and especially the change in their dwellings. Tuberculosis is the most deadly enemy with which they have to cope, very few of them being free from it. Tonsilitis, respiratory diseases and digestive diseases, and myalgia are ever present. Diphtheria carries off many in occasional epidemics.

The diet of the Vuntakutchin consists chiefly of fish, game, and berries. Their principal game animals are caribou, moose, bear, and mountain sheep. The fish is chiefly salmon. Various berries and a large tuber form their chief vegetal food. Ravens, hawks, eagles, dogs, and wolves are not eaten. They seldom eat wolverene, though lynx and one kind of owl are consumed. Salmon (they prefer the dog salmon) are caught in handnets, but fish-wheels are gradually replacing the primitive method. Whitefish and grayling are regarded as luxuries. Fish are dressed by the women, and dried on racks until ready for caching. Caribou are run between two long rail fences converging into a corral, snares are placed at intervals, and the caribou that try to escape are shot with arrows. Moose are stalked and shot with arrows; sometimes, in spring, they are snared in creeks, into which they are driven with the aid of dogs and are then dispatched with pikes. Bears are deceived by the natives who imitate the cry of a raven when it has discovered a dead moose; the Indian, armed with a spear, then kills the bear at close range. Birds and other small game are killed with blunt-pointed arrows.

Baskets for cooking are made of spruce roots; these are watertight when soaked, and water is boiled in them by means of hot stones. Birchbark utensils are also made, but chiefly for use on the hunt. Fire was made with flint and iron pyrites, a fungus furnishing the tinder; the fire-drill was also used. Stone hammers fastened to wooden handles with strips of caribou skin are still employed for breaking bones. Stone hatchets were used until recent years. Hunting knives are of bone, ground flat and sharpened on both edges, and sometimes copper knives are obtained in trade from White r. The spear was made by binding a hunting knife of caribou-horn to the end of a pole 6 ft long. Bows and arrowshafts, as well as fish-net, snowshoe, toboggan, and canoe frames, are made of birch; their wooden objects are nearly always painted with red ocher, which is used also as a face paint. Babiche of walrus-hide, obtained in trade with down-stream natives, is used for netting snowshoes, fish-nets, and the like.

The tribe was governed by a chief whose authority is said to have been despotic; he detailed hunting parties and dictated their duties, and had sole power to apportion the product of the hunt. During the absence or incapacity of a chief, a patriarchal form of government exists, important matters being decided by the elders in council. Public opinion has great weight in controlling the chief's personal actions. Sometimes the Vunta-kutchin intermarry with other tribes, and sometimes outside children are adopted into a family. Couples were often betrothed in marriage while children, the arrangement of course being made by their parents, although the engaged couple had a voice in the question of the final marriage. When between 10 and 15 years the boy went to live with the parents of the girl, but they were not married until the boy was able to support a wife. On the death of a wife or a husband it was not customary for the survivor to remarry for several years.

Ceremonial tribal feasts are given on various occasions, such as at the birth of a child, when the eldest son kills his first game, or when a girl reaches puberty. In the last instance the girl, after the feast, goes about a mile from home, where she lives in isolation for a year under the care of a relative of her betrothed. During this period fresh meat is tabooed, otherwise game would become scarce during the ensuing year. The body of a deceased chief was burned by men employed for the purpose; the burned bones and ashes were then placed in a wooden receptacle and hung in a tree. The men who burned the body ate no fresh meat for a year, else, it was believed, they too would die. It is said that a belief is current among them to the effect that when a person dies his spirit returns to a woman and is reborn. Property is not inherited by relatives on the death of a chief, but is distributed to visitors at a potlatch which lasts several days, or until the supplies are exhausted, and to which members of related tribes are invited.

As among many tribes the medicine-men perform their functions by dreams, incantation, and magic, whether it is desired to heal the sick, to overcome the enemy, or to make a hunt successful. The power supposed to be possessed by a medicine-man to promote the tribal welfare is believed also to be employed sometimes in the malevolent practice of sorcery.

Richardson (Arct. Exped., 397, 1851) gave their population in 1817 as 80 men; in 1866 they numbered 60 men, of whom about 25 were hunters. Their present population is not known.

Consult Schmitter in Smithson. Misc. Coll., LVI, no. 4, 1910.

Gens des Rats.—Dall in Cont. N. A. Ethnol., I, 31, 1876 (so called by voyageurs). Gens du Rat.—Ross, MS. Notes on Tinne, B. A. E. Rat Indians.—Ibid. Rat People.—Dall in Proc. Am. A. A. S. 1869, 271, 1870. Vánæ-ta-Kouttchin.—Petitot, Autour du lac des Esclaves, 361, 1891 ('people of the lakes'). Van-tah-koo-chin.—Hardisty in Smithson. Rep. 1866, 311, 1872. Vanta-Kutchi.—Richardson, Arct. Exped., I, 399, 1851. Vanta-Kutchin.—Bancroft, Nat. Races, I, 115, 1882. Vanta kutshi.—Latham, Nat. Races Russ. Emp., 294, 1854. Von'-ta-Kuttchin'.—Petitot, MS. vocab., B. A. E., 1865. Vœn Kuttchin.—Petitot, Dict. Dènè-Dindjié, xx, 1876. Vondt-way-Kutchin.—Jones in Smithson. Rep. 1866, 320, 1872. Vǔn'-täh kū'tch'-ĭn.—Ross, MS. notes on Tinne, B. A. E. Vunta-Kutchin.—Dall in Proc. Am. A. A. S. 1869, 271, 1870. Zjen Kuttchin.—Petitot, Dict. Dènè-Dindjié, xx, 1876 ('rat people'). Zjén-ta-Kouttchin.—Petitot, Autour du lac des Esclaves, 361, 1891 ('muskrat people').

Waahoo. See *Waahoo*.

Waaih (*Wa-ai'h*, 'maggot'). An extinct division of the Comanche.—Mooney in 14th Rep. B. A. E., 1045, 1896.

Waatch. A Makah village at the mouth of a creek of the same name, 4 m. from Neeah, Wash.; pop. 126 in 1863.

Wāatch.—Swan in Smithson. Cont., XVI, 6, 1870.

Wabakwa (*Wâ-ba-kwa'*). A former pueblo of the Jemez tribe, situated on a mesa N. of their present village in New Mexico. (F. W. H.)

Waban ('east'). A "Praying Indian" of the Nipmuc tribe, born at Musketaquid, the site of Concord, Mass., about 1604; died late in 1676 or early in 1677. His later home was 4 or 5 m. from Roxbury, on the S. side of Charles r., near Watertown mill, now in Newton township, at a place where John Eliot in 1646 established his first mission and which he named Nonantum, signifying 'I rejoice.' When John Eliot first visited the place in 1646 he was welcomed by Waban, who ever after encouraged the missionary in his labors and manifested sincere friendship toward the whites. He is said to have been the first Massachusetts chief to profess Christianity. In 1651 the mission of Natick was established, and Waban and his people removed thereto. In 1674 he was the chief man of the latter place, which then contained 29 families, and is described by Gookin as "a person of great prudence and piety: I do not know of any Indian that excels him." When in 1676 a civil community was established there Waban was made a "ruler of fifty," and subsequently a justice of the peace. While serving in this capacity, it is said that he was asked by a young justice what he would do when Indians got drunk and quarreled. Waban replied, "Tie um all up, and whip um plaintiff, and whip um 'fendent, and whip um witness." He married the eldest daughter of Tahattawan, or Attawan, sachem of Musketaquid. In Apr. 1675, about two months before King Philip's war, Waban visited one of the magistrates for the purpose of informing him of the impending outbreak of the Indians, and in the following month he repeated the warning, stating that Philip's men "were only waiting for the trees to get leaved out that they might prosecute their designs with more effect." He appears to have been sent to Deer island with other prisoners in Oct. 1675, many of whom had been falsely accused, and was one of the ill who were returned in May of the following year. Waban's name is conspicuous on the Eliot memorial, erected about 1879 at the head of the valley between the hills Nonantum and Waban, at Newton.

Wabanaquot ('White Cloud'). A Chippewa chief, son of Wabojeeg, born at Gull Lake, Minn., 11 m. from the present Brainerd, about 1830. He was not of an old hereditary line, his father having been appointed chief by the United States agent solely on account of his amiability. On his father's death he succeeded to the office, and was generally considered principal chief of the Mississippi bands of Chippewa. In 1868 he removed with his band and many others to White Earth res., where he lived until his death in 1898. He was considered a fine speaker by his tribesmen, but was not a man of sterling principle, having come under the influence of a malicious half-breed trader who kept him supplied with whisky, and in return induced Wabanaquot to further his nefarious designs, to the detriment of his people (see *Wendjimadub*). In particular the trader led Wabanaquot to bitterly fight three excellent agents who were doing much good for the Indians. This hostility covered about 10 years. White Cloud became a Christian about 1871; but his drinking and other vices prevented him from doing honor to his professed belief. A monument was erected over his grave by the state, the only Indian in Minnesota thus honored, but this is regarded as having been due to political machinations rather than to Wabanaquot's worth. (J. A. G.)

Wabaquasset. A tribe or band, subject to the Mohegan, formerly living w. of Quinebaug r., in Windham co., Conn.

Man-hum-squeeg.—Trumbull (1818) in Mass. Hist. Soc. Coll., 1st s., IX, 80, 1804 ('Whetstone country,' the territory of the Wabaquasset). Wabaquasset.—Doc. of 1700 in N. Y. Doc. Col. Hist., IV, 615, 1854. Wabaquassuck.—Caulkins, Norwich, 137, 1866. Wabaquisit.—Gookin (1677) in Trans. Am. Antiq. Soc., II, 465, 1836. Wabbequasset.—Trumbull in Mass. Hist. Soc. Coll., 1st s., IX, 80, 1804. Wabequassets.—Doc. of 1700 in N. Y. Doc. Col. Hist., IV, 615, 1854. Wabequisset.—Caulkins, Norwich, 117, 1866. Wabquissit.—Gookin (1674) in Mass. Hist. Soc. Coll., 1st s., I, 190, 1806. Wapaquassett.—Owaneco's rep. (1700) in N. Y. Doc. Col. Hist., IV, 614, 1854. Whetstone country.—Trumbull in Mass. Hist. Soc. Coll., 1st s., IX, 80–81, 1804 (the territory).

Wabaquasset. The village of the Wabaquasset, situated about 6 m. from Quinebaug r., a short distance s. of the present Woodstock, Conn.

Wabasemowenenewak ('white dog tribe'). An unidentified Chippewa band living near a white rock, perhaps in Minnesota.

Wåbåsêmô Wenenewak.—Long, Exped. St Peter's R., II, 153, 1824. Wâbąsimōwininiwąg.—Wm. Jones, inf'n, 1905.

Wabash. In 1682 La Salle mentioned the Ouabachi as one of the tribes defeated by the Iroquois a few years previously. It is impossible to determine whether it was really the name of a tribe or only a collective term for the Indians living on Wabash r. in Indiana and Illinois. In the 18th century the Wea, Piankashaw, Eel River Miami, and perhaps also the Kickapoo, were commonly known as the Wabash confederates. The name, according to J. P. Dunn, is an abbreviation of the Miami name for the stream, *Wa-ba-shǐ'-kǐ*, or *Wa-pa-shǐ'-kǐ*, meaning 'bright white,' or 'gleaming white,' and referring to the limestone bed of the stream in its upper course.

Ouabachi.—La Salle (1682) in Margry, Déc., II, 237, 1877. Ouabash Nations.—Doc. of 1748 in N. Y. Doc. Col. Hist., X, 156, 1858. Wabash Indians.—Knox (1789) in Am. State Papers, Ind. Aff., I, 13, 1832. Wabash confederacy.—McKee (1774) in Rupp, W. Pa., app., 203, 1846. Wabash confederates.—Detroit council (1786) in Am. State Papers, Ind. Aff., I, 8, 1832. Waubash Indians.—Johnson (1772) in N. Y. Doc. Col. Hist., VIII, 314, 1857.

Wabash. To cheat. Schele de Vere (Americanisms, 18, 1872) says that the phrase "he has been *wabashed*," was known to the people of Indiana and the W. generally. Derived from the name of the Wabash r. in Indiana.

Wabasha. See *Wapasha*.

Wabashiu (*Wabä'shiu*, 'marten'). A subphratry or gens of the Menominee (Hoffman in 14th Rep. B. A. E., pt. 1, 42, 1896). Cf. *Wabezhaze*.

Wabey. A band of Sisseton and Wahpeton Sioux at Sisseton agency, S. Dak.—Ind. Aff. Rep. 1873, 226, 1874.

Wabezhaze ('marten'). A gens of the Chippewa. Cf. *Wabashiu*.

Wa-be-zhaze'.—Morgan, Anc. Soc., 166, 1877. Wábishesh.—Gatschet, Ojibwa MS., B. A. E. Waub-ish-ash-e.—Warren in Minn. Hist. Soc. Coll., V, 44, 1885.

Wabigganus. A village connected in 1614 with the Abnaki, probably situated near the mouth of Penobscot r., Me.

Wabigganus.—Smith (1631) in Mass. Hist. Soc. Coll., 3d s., III, 22, 1833. Warbigganus.—Smith (1616), ibid., VI, 94, 1837.

Wablenicha ('orphans'). A modern Oglala Sioux band, or a society of descendants of chiefs who had visited Washington.

Wablenića.—Dorsey (after Cleveland) in 15th Rep. B. A. E., 220, 1897. Wablenitca.—Ibid. Wam-bili'-ne-óa.—Hayden, Ethnog. and Philol. Mo. Val., 376, 1862.

Wabokieshiek ('The Light,' or 'White Cloud'). A medicine-man, also known as The Prophet, the friend and adviser of Black Hawk. He was born about 1794, and presided over a village known as "Prophet's Village," on Rock r., about 35 m. above its mouth, on the site of the present Prophetstown, Ill. Half Winnebago and half Sauk, he had great influence with both tribes, and was noted for cruelty and his hostility toward Americans. When Black Hawk's lieutenant, Neapope, went to Malden, Canada, to consult with the British authorities in regard to the right of the Indians to retain their lands on Rock r., he stopped on his return at the Prophet's village, where he remained during the winter, and told Wabokieshiek of his mission. The Prophet, always ready for mischief and delighted at this opportunity to make

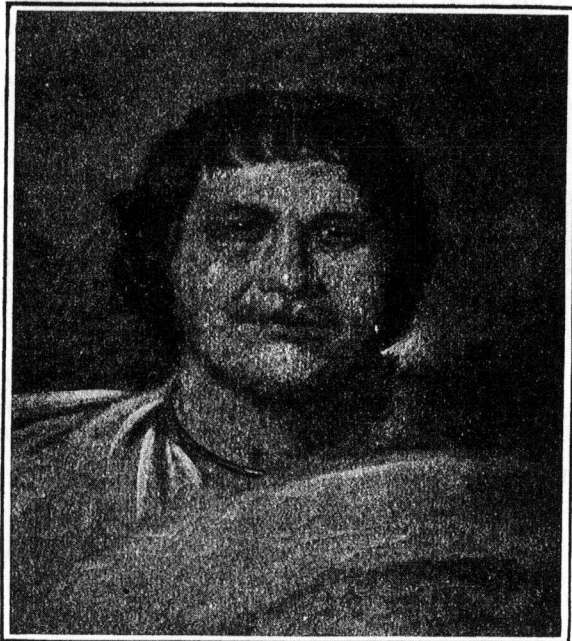

WABOKIESHIEK (WHITE CLOUD). AFTER A PAINTING BY R. M. SULLY IN THE WISCONSIN HISTORICAL SOCIETY

trouble for the whites, is said to have performed some incantations, had several visions, and prophesied that if Black Hawk would move against the whites he would be joined by the "Great Spirit" and a large army which would enable him to overcome the whites and regain possession of his old village. These predictions, added to Neapope's false reports from the British, induced Black Hawk to continue the war which bears his name. Keokuk is said to have blamed the Prophet for all the trouble. After the defeat of the Indians at Bad Axe in 1832, Black Hawk and the Prophet made their escape, but were captured by Chaetar and One-Eyed Dekaury, two Winnebago Indians, in an attempt to reach Prairie La Crosse, where they expected

to cross the Mississippi and be safe. They were delivered to Gen. Street on Aug. 27, 1832. Arriving at Jefferson Barracks, 10 m. below St Louis, they were put in irons, to their extreme mortification and of which they complained bitterly. In April of the following year they were taken to Washington, where they were permitted to see President Jackson, to whom Wabokieshiek appealed for their freedom; instead, they were sent to Fortress Monroe, Va., where they remained until June 4, when they were released. Having lost his prestige as a prophet, Wabokieshiek lived in obscurity among the Sauk in Iowa until their removal to Kansas, and died among the Winnebago about 1841. He is described as being six ft tall, stout and athletic of figure, with a countenance in keeping with his militant disposition. At variance with accounts of his depravity is a statement by Maj. Thomas Forsythe, for years the agent of the Sauk and Foxes, in which he says of Wabokieshiek: "Many a good meal has the Prophet given to the people traveling past his village, and very many stray horses has he recovered from the Indians and restored them to their rightful owners, without asking any recompense whatever." It is also said that during the progress of the Black Hawk war, Col. Gratiot, agent for the Winnebago, who on account of his humane and honorable treatment of the Indians was considered most likely to influence them, was selected to visit the hostile camp and induce the Prophet to turn the British band back to its Iowa reservation. On reaching the Prophet's village, Gratiot and his party were surrounded by the hostiles and made prisoners, despite their flag of truce, and he would have lost his life had not the Prophet come to his rescue. He was taken to Wabokieshiek's house and allowed to explain the object of his mission, but could not dissuade the Indians from their purpose. Although the warriors clamored for Gratiot's life, Wabokieshiek was determined to save him, and after keeping him for several days found an opportunity to allow him to escape.

While in Jefferson Barracks Wabokieshiek's portrait was painted by Catlin, and is now in the National Museum; another portrait, by R. M. Sully, made while the Prophet was a prisoner at Fortress Monroe, is here reproduced.

Consult Fulton, Red Men of Iowa, 1882; Stevens, Black Hawk War, 1903; Wis. Hist. Soc. Coll., x, 1888.   (F. S. N.)

Wabozo (Wä-bo'-zo, 'rabbit'). A gens of the Potawatomi.—Morgan, Anc. Soc., 167, 1877.

Wacahoota. A former Seminole settlement in Florida.—Worth in H. R. Doc. 262, 27th Cong., 2d sess., 30, 1842.

Wacamuc. The chief village of the Cathlacumup of the Chinookan family in Oregon in 1835.—Framboise quoted by Gairdner in Jour. Geog. Soc. Lond., XI, 255, 1841.

Waccamaw. One of the small tribes formerly dwelling on the Lower Pedee and its branches in South Carolina and the adjacent border of North Carolina. Nothing is known of their language, and very little else concerning them, as they were never prominent in history. Their associations indicate that they were Siouan. Their habitat was along Waccamaw r., which enters the Pedee from the N. almost at its mouth. They were mentioned first in 1715 as living near the Winyaw, both tribes receiving ammunition from the Cheraw, who attempted to gain them as allies of the Yamasee and other tribes against the English. At this time they were living in 6 villages with a population of 610 (Rivers, Hist. S. Car., 94, 1874). In 1755 the Cherokee and Notchee were reported to have killed some Pedee and Waccamaw in the white settlements (Gregg, Hist. of Old Cheraws, 15, 1867). Like the Pedee, Cheraw, and other tribes of that region (Mooney, Siouan Tribes of the East, 76, 1894), the remnant was probably finally incorporated with the Catawba.

Waccamaus.—Letter of 1715 in N. C. Col. Rec., II, 252, 1886. **Waccamaw.**—Christian (*ca.* 1771) in Hawkins, Miss., 88, 1845. **Waccamawe.**—Letter of 1715 in N. C. Col. Rec., II, 252, 1886. **Waccomassees.**—Rivers, Hist. S. Car., 94, 1874. **Wacemaus.**—Letter of 1715 in N. C. Col. Rec., II, 251, 1886. **Waggamaw.**—Map of S. C., 1760. **Waggoman.**—War map of 1715 in Winsor, Hist. Am., V, 346, 1887 (misprint). **Wicomaw.**—Bowen map, 1760. **Wigomaw.**—Moll, map Car., 1720.

Waccogo. A village connected in 1614 with the Abnaki, probably situated on or near the s. coast of Maine; possibly identical with Wachuset.

Waccogo.—Smith (1631) in Mass. Hist. Soc. Coll., 3d s., III, 22, 1833. **Wakcogo.**—Smith (1616), ibid., VI, 94, 1837.

Wachamshwash. A former Modoc village on Lost r., near Tule or Rhett lake, in Klamath co., s. w. Oreg.

Wátchamshwash.—Gatschet in Cont. N. A. Ethnol., II, pt. I, XXXII, 1890.

Wachanaruka. A former Costanoan village of the Rumsen division, on the site of the Salinas rancho of Cooper, Monterey co., Cal.—Taylor in Cal. Farmer, Apr. 20, 1860.

Wachapalaschuk (*Wachap'álaschuk*). The name of an ancestor of a gens of the Kwakiutl proper; also applied to the gens itself (Boas in Petermanns Mitteil., pt. 5, 131, 1887).

Wachape ('stabber'). A modern band of the Oglala Sioux.

Waćape.—Dorsey (after Cleveland) in 15th Rep. B. A. E., 221, 1897. **Watcape.**—Ibid.

Wacharones. A Costanoan group for-

merly connected with Soledad and San Juan Bautista missions, Cal.

Goatcharones.—Taylor in Cal. Farmer, Apr. 20, 1860 (at Soledad). **Guachurrones.**—Engelhardt, Franciscans in Cal., 398, 1897 (at San Juan Bautista). **Huachirrones.**—Arroyo de la Cuesta, Idiomas Californias, 1821, MS. trans., B. A. E. (at San Juan Bautista).

Wachaskesouek. A tribe mentioned in 1648, in connection with bands of the Ottawa, as allies of the Hurons, living s. of L. Huron.

Ouachaskesouek.—Jes. Rel. 1648, 62, 1858. **Wachaskesouek.**—Jes. Rel., III, index, 1858.

Wachbit. A former Shoshonean settlement on the site of San Bernardino, Cal., or perhaps only the native name of that locality.

Wach-bit.—Kroeber in Univ. Cal. Pub., Am. Arch. and Eth., VIII, 39, 1908.

Wachegami (prob. 'beaver-dam lake,' or possibly 'shining lake.'—Hewitt). An unidentified tribe or band living in Canada N. of L. Nipissing; probably named from a lake on which they resided.

Ouachegami.—Jes. Rel. 1640, 34, 1858. **Wachegami.**—Jes. Rel., III, index.

Wacheonpa ('roasters'). A modern band of the Oglala Sioux.

Waćeoŋpa.—Dorsey (after Cleveland) in 15th Rep. B. A. E., 220, 1897. **Watceoⁿpa.**—Ibid.

Wacheunpa ('roasters'). A band of the Brulé Teton Sioux.

Broiled meat people.—Culbertson in Smithson. Rep. 1850, 141, 1851. **Waćeoŋpa.**—Cleveland, letter to Dorsey, 1884. **Waće-uŋpa.**—Dorsey in 15th Rep. B. A. E., 218, 1897. **Wa-ói'-ōm-pa.**—Hayden, Ethnog. and Philol. Mo. Val., 376, 1862. **Watceuⁿpa.**—Dorsey in 15th Rep. B. A. E., 218, 1897.

Wacheunpa ('roasters'). A band of the Yankton Sioux.

Waćeuŋpa.—Dorsey in 15th Rep. B. A. E., 217, 1897. **Watceuⁿpa.**—Ibid.

Wachuset ('at the small mountain.'—Gerard). A tribe formerly living on upper Nashua r. in Worcester co., Mass. They are commonly classed as Nipmuc, but seem to have been connected with the Pennacook confederacy.

Watchusets.—Hubbard (1680) in Mass. Hist. Soc. Coll., 2d s., V, 408, 1815.

Wachuset. The principal village of the Wachuset, situated in the vicinity of Mt Wachusett, about where Princeton, Mass., now stands.

Wachusett.—Winthrop (*ca.* 1644) quoted by Drake, Bk. Inds., bk. II, 46, 1848. **Wadchuset.**—Eliot (1648) in Mass. Hist. Soc. Coll., 3d s., IV, 82, 1834. **Wadjusset.**—Writer of 1676 quoted by Drake, Ind. Chron., 135, 1836.

Waco. One of the divisions of the Tawakoni, whose village stood until after 1830 on the site of the present city of Waco, Texas. The name does not seem unmistakably to appear until after 1820, occurring first in Anglo-American accounts. As the Tawakoni evidently are the Touacara, whom La Harpe visited in 1719 on Canadian r., it is not impossible (and it has been assumed) that the Honecha, or Houecha, given by La Harpe and Beaurain as one of the Touacara group, are identical with the Waco.

Yet, if the later Waco had kept this name throughout the 18th century, it is strange that it should not appear in some of the many Spanish reports and descriptions of them under the name Tawakoni, after 1770. It has been thought that the Quainco of De l'Isle's map are the same as the Waco.

That the Waco village of the 19th century was identical with one or the other of the two neighboring Tawakoni villages on the Brazos, known in the later 18th century respectively as the village of El Quiscat and that of the Flechazos, is clear, though it is not easy to determine which one, since both were in the immediate neighborhood of Waco. As the ethnology, customs, and early history of these two villages are quite fully given

LONG SOLDIER—A WACO

under *Tawakoni*, they need not be described here.

About 1824, according to Stephen F. Austin, the main Waco village consisted of 33 grass houses, occupying about 40 acres, and inhabited by about 100 men. Half a mile below was another village of 15 houses, built close together. The Waco were then cultivating about 200 acres of corn, enclosed with brush fences ("Description of Waco Villages," n. d., in Austin Papers, Class D). At the site of the Waco village a native earthwork, like that of their kindred, the Taovayas (Tawehash), and known to have been used for military purposes as late as 1829, is said to have been until very recently still visible at the city of Waco (Kenney in Wooten, Comp. His. Tex., I, 745,

1898). For the relations of the tribe with the Anglo-American Texans, see Kenney, op. cit.

The Waco were included in the treaties made between the United States and the Wichita in 1835 and 1846, and also in 1872, when their reservation in the present Oklahoma was established. In 1902 they received allotments of land and became citizens.   (H. E. B.)

Gentlemen Indians.—Bollaert in Jour. Ethnol. Soc. Lond., II, 275, 1850 (sometimes so called). Honechas.—La Harpe (1719) in Margry, Déc., VI, 289, 1886. Houechas.—Beaurain (1719), ibid. Huanchané.—La Harpe, ibid., 277. Huanches.—La Harpe in French, Hist. Coll. La., III, 72, 1851. Huané.—La Harpe in Margry, Déc., VI, 277, 1886. Hueco.—Tex. State Arch., Sept. 20, 1826. Ouainco.—La Tour, map of N. Am., 1782. Quaineo.—De l'Isle, map (*ca.* 1700), in Winsor, Hist. Am., II, 294, 1884. Tal'-le-wit-sus.—Whipple, Pac. R. R. Rep., III, 68, 1856 (given as their own name). Wacco.—Maillard, Hist. Texas, 232, 1842. Wacha.—Brown, West. Gaz., 152, 1817. Wachos.—Gallatin in Trans. Am. Antiq. Soc., II, 117, 1836. Waco.—Drake, Bk. Inds., xii, 1848. Wacoah.—Hildreth, Dragoon Campaigns, 166, 1836. Wacoes.—Bonnell, Texas, 140, 1840. Waecoe.—Schoolcraft, Ind. Tribes, I, 518, 1851. Waeko.—Möllhausen, Tagebuch, 73, 1858. Wàkò.—M'Coy, Ann. Reg., no. 4, 27, 1838. Wakoe.—Falconer in Jour. Roy. Geog. Soc., XIII, 209, 1843. Wakos.—Hazen (1868) in Sen. Ex. Doc. 18, 40th Cong., 3d sess., 13, 1869. Weeco's.—Bollaert in Jour. Ethnol. Soc. Lond., II, 265, 1850. Wecos.—Domenech, Deserts N. A., II, 25, 1860. Weeco.—Bollaert, op. cit., 275. Wéko.—Gatschet, Tonkawe MS., B. A. E., 1884 (Tonkawa name). We'ku.—Gatschet, Caddo and Yatassi MS., B. A. E. Wékush.—Gatschet, Wichita MS., B. A. E., 1884 (Wichita name). Whacoe.—Burnet (1847) in Schoolcraft, Ind. Tribes, I, 239, 1851. Wico.—Hildreth, Dragoon Campaigns, 177, 1836. Wi'ko.—Gatschet, Caddo and Yatassi MS., B. A. E. Wi'-ku.—Dorsey, Kwapa MS. vocab., B. A. E., 1891 (Quapaw name).

Waconiask. A village of the Powhatan confederacy in 1608, on the N. bank of Rappahannock r. in King George co., Va.—Smith (1629), Va., I, map, repr. 1819.

Wacuntug. A village of Praying Indians in the Nipmuc country in 1674, situated on the w. side of Blackstone r., near the present Uxbridge, Worcester co., Mass. It seems at one time to have been subject to the Narraganset.

Wacantuck.—Barber, Hist. Coll., 612, 1839. Wacumtung.—Hoyt, Antiq. Res., 95, 1824. Waeuntug.—Gookin (1674) in Mass. Hist. Soc. Coll., 1st s., I, 194, 1806. Wayunckeke.—Williams (1660) in R. I. Col. Rec., I, 39, 1856.

Waddapawjestin (probably from *watpa chistina*, 'small stream'). A Dakota band, probably a part of the Wahpeton.

Waddapadschestiner.—Balbi, Atlas Ethnog., 55, 1826. Waddapaw-jestin.—Carver, Trav., 80, 1778.

Wadington Harbor Indians. A body of Salish of Fraser River agency, Brit. Col., numbering 37 in 1895, the last time the name appears.

Waddington Harbour.—Can. Ind. Aff., 277, 1894. Wadington Harbor.—Ibid., 189, 1883.

Wadjahonak ('those who seek a living'). The name given by the Algonkin of Oka (q. v.) to the Iroquois women of the same settlement on account of their custom of peddling their manufactures to the neighboring whites, a thing which the

Algonkin women of Oka never do.—Cuoq, Lexique Algonquine, 416, 1886.

Wafford, James D. (*Tsuskwănŭñ'nă-wa'tă*, 'Worn-out blanket'). A Western Cherokee mixed-blood, speaking and writing both languages, born in the old Cherokee Nation near the site of the present Clarkesville, Ga., in 1806, and dying when about 90 years of age at his home in the E. part of the Cherokee Nation, adjoining the Seneca res., in the present Oklahoma. The name figures prominently in the early history of North Carolina and Georgia. His grandfather, Colonel Wafford, was an officer in the American Revolutionary army, and shortly after the treaty of Hopewell, in 1785, established a colony known as "Wafford settlement," in upper Georgia, on territory which was afterward found to be within the Indian boundary and was acquired by special treaty purchase in 1804. His name is appended, as witness for the State of Georgia, to the treaty of Holston, in 1794. On his mother's side Wafford was of mixed Cherokee, Natchez, and white blood, she being a cousin of Sequoya (q. v.). He was also remotely connected with Cornelius Dougherty, the first trader established among the Cherokee. In the course of his long life he filled many positions of trust and honor among his people. In his youth he attended the mission school at Valleytown under Rev. Evan Jones, and just before the adoption of the Cherokee alphabet he finished the translation into phonetic Cherokee spelling of a Sunday-school speller. In 1824 he was the census enumerator for that district of the Cherokee Nation embracing upper Hiwassee r., in North Carolina, with Nottely and Toccoa in the adjoining portion of Georgia. His fund of Cherokee geographic information thus acquired was found to be invaluable. He was one of the two commanders of the largest detachment of emigrants at the time of the removal, and his name appears as a councilor for the Western Cherokee in the Cherokee Almanac for 1846. When employed for the Bureau of American Ethnology by Mr Mooney, at Tahlequah, in 1891, his mind was still clear and his memory keen. Being of practical bent, he was concerned chiefly with tribal history, geography, linguistics, and every-day life and customs, on all of which subjects his knowledge was exact and detailed, but there were few myths for which he was not able to furnish confirmatory testimony. Despite his education he was a firm believer in the *Nŭñně'hĭ*, or fairies, and several of the best legends connected with them were obtained from him. His death took from the Cherokee one of the last connecting links between the present and the past.   (J. M.)

Waganakisi ('bent tree,' from a tree on a neighboring hill). A former Ottawa village on the site of Harbor Springs, Emmet co., Mich. It was one of the oldest and most important Ottawa settlements in Michigan, having been established about 1743, after the expulsion of the Mascoutens from the district. In 1825 the Catholic mission of St Vincent de Paul was established there.

Abercrosh.—Harrison (1814) quoted by Drake, Tecumseh, 162, 1852. **Abre Croche.**—Dunham (1807) in Am. State Papers, Ind. Aff., I, 798, 1832. **Arbre croche.**—Beauharnois (1741) in N. Y. Doc. Col. Hist., IX, 1072, 1855. **Forked tree.**—Tanner, Narr., 515, 1830 (given as a totem among "Ottawwaws and Ojibbeways"). **L'Arbrech-roche.**—Detroit treaty (1855) in U. S. Ind. Treat., 614, 1873. **L'Arbre Croche.**—Kendall, Trav., II, 287, 1809 (French trans. of Indian name). **L'Arbre Cruche.**—Brown, W. Gaz., 165, 1817. **Middletown.**—Shea, Cath. Miss., 390, 1855. **Middle Village.**—Detroit treaty (1855) in U. S. Ind. Treat., 614, 1873. **Wâganakisi.**—Baraga, Eng.-Otch. Dict., 154, 1878 (Chippewa form). **War-gun-uk-ke-zee.**—Tanner, Narr., 40, note, 1830. **Waw-gun-nuk-kiz-ze.**—Ibid., 256. **Waw-gun-uk-ke-zie.**—Ibid., 380. **Wawkwunkizze.**—Ibid., 315.

Waginkhak (*Waginxak.*) A former village of the Tlakluit, ½ m. below the Dalles of Columbia r., Wash.   (E. S.)

Ǥáuamuitk.—Edward Sapir, inf'n, 1908 (sig. 'mud place').

Waglezaoin ('water-snake earring'). A Miniconjou Sioux band.

Wagleza-oiⁿ.—Dorsey in 15th Rep. B. A. E., 220, 1897. **Wa-ha-le'-zo-wen.**—Hayden, Ethnog. and Philol. Mo. Val., 376, 1862 (trans. 'striped snake earring band').

Waglukhe ('followers'). An Oglala Sioux division, including two bands composed largely of mixed-bloods.

In-breeders.—Robinson, letter to Dorsey, 1879. **Loafers.**—Ibid. **Wagluge.**—Ibid. **Wag-luñe.**—Dorsey in 15th Rep. B. A. E., 220, 1897. **Waglukhe.**—McGee, ibid., 161. **Wagluqe.**—Dorsey, ibid., 220.

Waglukhe. A band of the Brulé Teton Sioux.

Wagluñe.—Dorsey (after Cleveland) in 15th Rep. B. A. E., 219, 1897. **Wagluqe.**—Ibid.

Wagmezayuha ('has corn'). A band of the Brulé Teton Sioux.—Dorsey (after Cleveland) in 15th Rep. B. A. E., 219, 1897.

Waha. The Cloud clan of Jemez pueblo, N. Mex. A corresponding clan existed also at the related pueblo of Pecos.

Wâ'häh.—Hodge in Am. Anthr., IX, 349, 1896 (Pecos form). **Wâhätsa-ásh.**—Ibid. (Jemez form; *tsaash*='people'). **Wâ-käh.**—Hewett, ibid., n. s., VI, 431, 1904 (Pecos form).

Wahaka (*Wa-ha'-ka*). A former Awani village at the base of the rock known as "Three Brothers," in Yosemite valley, Mariposa co., Cal.; also the name of the rock itself.—Powers in Cont. N. A. Ethnol., III, 365, 1877.

Wahe. A Chinookan village formerly at the head of the Cascades of Columbia r., Oreg.

Wah-he.—Lee and Frost, Oregon, 176, 1844.

Wahi's Band. A Paviotso band under Wahi (Fox), formerly at the big bend of Carson r., w. Nev.; said to number 130 in

1859.—Dodge in Ind. Aff. Rep. 1859, 374, 1860.

Wahkiakum. A Chinookan tribe formerly living on the N. bank of Columbia r. near its mouth. Their territory adjoined that of the Chinook and extended upstream toward Oak point. According to Stuart (1821) they were an offshoot of the Chinook who had separated from the main body about two generations before under chief Wahkiacum and were afterward known by his name. In 1805 Lewis and Clark estimated their number at 200. They have been lost sight of as a tribe since about 1850, when Gibbs referred to their chief as almost the last survivor of the tribe. Their principal village seems to have been near Pillar rock, a short distance above Grays bay. According to Boas they had two villages near Pillar rock—Tlalegak, a little below the rock, and Chakwayalham farther down the river. (L. F.)

Ouakicoms.—Stuart in Nouv. Annales d. Voy., X, 111, 1821. Ouakikours.—Ibid., 23. Waakiacums.—Dunn, Hist. Oreg., 114, 1844. Waakicum.—Drake, Bk. Inds., xii, 1841. Wâch-kí-a-cum.—Orig. Jour. Lewis and Clark, IV, 45, 1905. Wackiacums.—Ibid., 155. Wâc-ki-a-cums.—Ibid., 183. Wackki-acums.—Ibid., 206. Wâck-ki-a-cums.—Ibid., 31. Wahkaykum.—Franchère, Narr., 105, 1854. Wahkenkumes.—Robertson, Oreg., 129, 1846. Wahkiacum.—Lewis and Clark Exped., ii, 69, 1814. Wahkiahkums.—Lyman, Hist. Oreg., i, 62, 1903. Wahkia-kum.—Stevens in Ind. Aff. Rep., 239, 1854. Wahkiakume.—Lewis and Clark Exped., i, map, 1814. Wahkiakums.—Ibid., ii, 89, 1817. Wahkyeoums.—Hale in U. S. Expl. Exped., vi, 569, 1846. Wahkyekum.—Ibid., 215. Wahkyskum.—Medill in H. R. Ex. Doc. 76, 30th Cong., 1st sess., 7, 1848. Waikaikum.—Wilkes, U. S. Expl. Exped., v, 120, 1845. Wa-kái-a-kum.—Gibbs, Chinook Vocab., iv, 1863. Wakaíkam.—Hale in U. S. Expl. Exped., vi, 215, 569, 1846. Wakaikum.—Gairdner quoting Framboise (1835) in Jour. Geog. Soc. Lond., xi, 255, 1841. Wakiakums.—Keane in Stanford, Compend., 542, 1878. Wakicums.—Ross, Adventures, 87, 1847. Waqa-iqam.—Boas, Kathlamet Texts, 6, 1901. Warciacoms.—Orig. Jour. Lewis and Clark, iii, 300, 1905. War. ci a cum.—Ibid., 252. War-ci-â-cum.—Ibid., 208. Warkiacom.—Ibid., iv, 200, 1905. Warkiacum.—Lewis and Clark Exped., 700, 1893. Waukiacum.—Orig. Jour. Lewis and Clark, iv, 25, 1905. Wau-ki-á-cums.—Ibid., 35. Waukiecums.—Ibid., 156. Waukikam.—Ex. Doc. 39, 32d Cong., 1st sess., 6, 1852. Wau-ki-kum.—Ibid., 2.

Wahkila (probably from Miwok *wakalu*, 'river'). Mentioned as the name of a so-called band, probably Moquelumnan, formerly frequenting Stanislaus and Tuolumne rs., central Cal. They were on the reserve between Stanislaus and Tuolumne rs. in 1851.

Wah-ki-la.—Wessells (1853) in H. R. Ex. Doc. 76, 34th Cong., 3d sess., 30, 1857. We-chil-la.—Johnston in Sen. Ex. Doc. 61, 32d Cong., 1st sess., 20, 1852.

Wahlakalgi. One of the extinct Creek gentes, which, to judge from the term *wa'hlita*, 'to distribute', probably had reference to warfare.

Wä-hläk-kŭl'-kee.—Morgan, Anc. Soc., 161, 1877. Wá'hlakalgi.—Gatschet, Creek Migr. Leg., i, 156, 1884.

Wahnaataa. See *Waneta*.

Wahnacsoutah. A former band and village of the Wahpeton Sioux, numbering 332, on Minnesota r., about 50 m. from the mouth.—Schoolcraft, Ind. Tribes, iii, 612, 1853.

Wahoma. A former Luiseño village in San Diego co., s. Cal.—Hayes (1850) quoted by Bancroft, Nat. Races, i, 460, 1886.

Wahoo. A Georgia and South Carolina name for *Ulmus alata*, the cork or winged elm, but for many years applied to the species of elm indiscriminately. The bark of the cork elm, which is pliable, has been used for making ropes and cord, hence the name Lynn wahoo, where "Lynn" is miswritten for *lin* or *lind* (*Tilia*). (2) *Tilia heterophylla*, from the resemblance of its wood to that of the cork elm. A variant of the name is *whahoo*. The name is from *úhawhu*, in the Creek language. (W. R. G.)

Wahoo. A name for *Euonymus purpureus*, the spindle-bush, burning bush, or Indian arrowwood; spelled also *whahoo*, *waahoo*, and *wahoon*. The word is from Dakota *waⁿhu*, 'arrowwood' (fide the late Rev. J. O. Dorsey). (W. R. G.)

Wahowah. See *Hopehood*.

Wahowpum (from *hăháu*, a species of willow; *pŭm*, 'people': 'willow people'). A small Shahaptian tribe, speaking the Tenino language, formerly living on the N. side of Columbia r., near the mouth of Olive cr., in Klickitat co., Wash. They are mentioned by Lewis and Clark, who evidently used the term to include a large number of Klickitat bands.

Hăhau'pŭm.—Mooney in 14th Rep. B. A. E., 739, 1896 ('willow people': native name). Wah-howpum.—Schoolcraft, Ind. Tribes, v, 706, 1855. Wahowpum.—Lewis and Clark Exped., ii, 472, 1814. Wahupums.—Wilkes, Hist. Oregon, 44, 1845.

Wahpekute (*wakhpe*, leaf; *kute*, to shoot: 'shooters in the leaves'). One of the 7 primary divisions of the Dakota. Although the name Santee was originally applied only to the Mdewakanton, it was early extended to the Wahpekute, so closely were the two tribes connected, and eventually by the Teton also to the two other tribes of the eastern Dakota. Historic and linguistic evidence proves the close affinity of the tribes of this group. The Wahpekute were doubtless living in the vicinity of the Mdewakanton of Mille Lac, Minn., when first visited by the French (1678–1680), and were still so closely combined with them as to be included under the one term. In 1766 Carver met the Wahpekute somewhere on Minnesota r. They were in 1804, according to Lewis and Clark, on both sides of that stream below Redwood r., and numbered about 150 men. Pike (1806) spoke of them as the smallest band of the Sioux, residing generally between Mississippi and Missouri rs., and hunting commonly at the head of Des Moines r. He characterizes them as "the most stupid and inactive of all the Sioux." Long (Exped. St. Peter's R., I, 386, 1824) says: "This tribe has a very bad name, being considered to be a lawless set of men. They have a regular hereditary chief, Wiahuga ('the raven'), who is acknowledged as such by the Indian agent, but who, disgusted by their misbehaviour, withdrew from them and resides at Wapasha's. . . . They have no fixed villages, they inhabit skin lodges, and rove at the head of Cannon and Blue Earth rs. Their hunting grounds are in that vicinity and west of it." He estimated them at 100 lodges, 200 warriors, and 800 souls. According to Sibley (Minn. Hist. Coll., III, 250, 1880) they were in 1834 in villages on Cannon r., a short distance from the present city of Faribault, Minn., and at a few other points. They numbered then about 150 warriors. Between 1842 and 1857 they were under two chiefs named Wamdisapa (Black Eagle) and Tasagi. The lawless and predatory habits of Wamdisapa and his band prolonged the war with the Sauk and Foxes in which they had been engaged, and created difficulties between them and the rest of the Wahpekute which caused a separation. Wamdisapa and his band went w. and occupied lands about Vermillion r., S. Dak. So thoroughly were they separated from the rest of the Wahpekute that when the latter, together with the Mdewakanton, made a treaty at Mendota in 1851 ceding their lands in Minnesota, the remnant of Wamdisapa's band was not regarded as being a part of the tribe and did not participate in the treaty. In 1857 all that remained of this straggling band were some 10 or 15 lodges under Inkpaduta (q. v.). It was this remnant that committed the massacre in 1857 about Spirit lake and Springfield, Minn. (Flandreau in Minn. Hist. Coll., III, 387, 1880). In 1856, according to the Report on Indian Affairs for that year, the Mdewakanton and Wahpekute together numbered 2,379. A part at least of the tribe participated in the massacre of 1862. They are now with the Mdewakanton on the Santee res., Nebr.

Afrahcootans.—Carver, Trav., 80, 1778. **Anibishiw ininiwak.**—Gatschet, MS., B. A. E. (Chippewa name). **Gens de Feuilles-tirées.**—Burton, City of Sts., 117, 1866. **Gens des Feuilles tirees.**—Schoolcraft, Ind. Tribes, III, 563, 1853 (French for Wahpekute). **Hu-sha-sha band.**—Gale, Upper Miss., 252, 1867. **Leaf Bed.**—Coyner, Lost Trappers, 70, 1847. **People of the Leaves detached.**—Pike (1806), quoted by Schoolcraft, Ind. Tribes, III, 563, 1853. **People of the Shot Leaf.**—Minn. Hist, Coll., III, 250, 1880. **Sioux of the Broad Leaf.**—Brown, W. Gaz., 209, 1817. **Sioux Wahpacoota.**—Lewis and Clark Discov., 28, 1806. **Waakpacootas.**—Domenech, Deserts N. Am., II, 26, 1860. **Wachpecoutes.**—Pike, Exped., pt. 1, app., 25, 1810. **Wahch-Pe-Kutch.**—Maximilian, Trav., 149, 1843. **Wahch-Pekuté.**—Ibid., 134. **Wah-hay-koo-tay.**—Hatch in H. R. Misc. Doc. 167, 44th Cong., 1st sess., 424, 1876. **Wahkpacoota.**—Schoolcraft, Ind. Tribes, II, 168, 1852. **Wahkpacootays.**—Minn. Hist. Coll., II, pt.

2, 5, 1865. **Wahkpakoota.**—Ind. Aff. Rep., 856, 1848. **Wahkpakota.**—Long, Exped. St. Peters R., I, 386, 1824. **Wahkpako toan.**—Ibid.,378. **Wahpaakootas.**—Ind. Aff. Rep., 495, 1839. **Wahpaakootah.**—Treaty of 1837 in U. S. Stat. at Large, VII, 527, 1846. **Wah-pa-coo-la.**—Brackenridge, Views of La., 78, 1814. **Wâh'-pa-coo-ta.**—Lewis and Clark Discov., 30, 1806. **Wahpacoota Sioux.**—Marshall (1852) in Sen. Ex. Doc. 29, pt. 2, 32d Cong., 2d sess., 8, 1853. **Wahpacootay Sioux.**—Ind. Aff. Rep. 1849, 114, 1850. **Wah-pa-costa.**—Cor. on Emig. of Inds., doc. 512 (1830), v, 22, 1835, **Wah-pa-koo-ta.**—U. S. Stat. at Large, XII, 237, 1863. **Wahpakootah Sioux.**—Ind. Aff. Rep. 1856, 37, 1857. **Wahpakooty.**—Sen. Ex. Doc. 29, pt. 2, 32d Cong., 2d sess., 4, 1853. **Wahpakutas.**—Ind. Aff. Rep. 1856, 53, 1857. **Wahpatoota.**—Lewis and Clark Exped., I, 61, 1814. **Wah-pay-hoo-tays.**—Ramsey (1853) in Sen. Ex. Doc. 61, 33d Cong., 1st sess., 327, 1854. **Wahpaykootay.**—Ind. Aff. Rep., 18, 1851. **Wahpaykootays.**—Minn. Hist. Coll., II, pt. 2, 35, 1865. **Wahpeconte.**—Burton, City of Sts., 117, 1861. **Wahpekootays.**—Parker, Minn. Handbk., 141, 1857. **Wahpekute.**—Riggs, Dakota Gram. and Dict., vii, 1852. **Wahpekutes.**—Warren, Dacota Country, 15, 1855. **Wahpekute's band.**—Ind. Aff. Rep., 68, 1860. **Wahpekutey.**—Williamson in Minn. Geol. Rep. 1884, 111, 1885. **Wahpekuti.**—Ind. Aff. Rep. 1855, 68, 1856. **Wahpe-kwtes.**—Spencer in H. R. Ex. Doc. 68, 37th Cong., 3d sess., 8, 1863. **Wakhpekute.**—Williamson in Minn. Geol. Rep., 111, 1884. **Wakpakootas.**—Minn. Hist. Coll., III, 250, 1880. **Wak-pe-ka-te.**—Smithson. Misc. Coll., 14, art. 6, 8, 1878. **Wak-pe-ku-te.**—Flandrau in Minn. Hist. Coll., III, 387, 1880. **Walipekutes.**—Keane in Stanford, Compend., 542, 1878 (misprint). **Wapakotah.**—Schoolcraft, Ind. Tribes, VI, 707, 1857. **Wa-pa-too-ta.**—Lewis and Clark Exped., I, map, 1814. **Wapaykoota.**—Sen. Ex. Doc. 29, 32d Cong., 2d sess., 25, 1853. **Wappacoota.**—Treaty of 1825 in U.S.Ind. Treat.,367,1826. **Wark-pay-ku-tay.**—Ramsey in Ind. Aff. Rep. 1849, 82, 1850. **War-pe-kintes.**—Ramsey, ibid., 74. **Warpekute.**—Nicollet, Rep. on Upper Miss. R., 13, 1843. **Warpekutey.**—Ibid., map. **Washpcoute.**—Boudinot, Star in the W., 129, 1816. **Washpecoate.**—Schermerhorn in Mass. Hist. Coll., 2d s., II, 41, 1814. **Washpeconte.**—Pike, Trav., 128, 1811. **Washpecoutongs.**—Schoolcraft, Trav., 307, 1821. **Waupacootar.**—Clark, MS., quoted by Coues, Lewis and Clark Exped., I, 101, note, 1893. **Wha-pa-ku-tahs.**—Cullen in Ind. Aff. Rep. 1857, 79, 1858.

Wahpeton (*wakhpé*, 'leaf'; *tonwan* (French nasal *n*), 'a village'; hence probably 'dwellers among leaves'). One of the 7 primary divisions of the Dakota. Historic and linguistic evidence proves the affinity of this tribe with the Sisseton, Wahpekute, and Mdewakanton. Hennepin (1680) mentions them as living in the vicinity of Mille Lac, Minn., near the Mdewakanton, Sisseton, and Teton. On his map they are placed a little to the N. E. of the lake. Le Sueur (1700) places the Oudebatons, or "river village," among the eastern Sioux, and the Ouapetons, "village of the leaf," among the Sioux of the west. As both these names seem to be forms of Wahpeton, it is probable that they are applied to different villages of the tribe, which was subsequently found most of the time in two bands. It was not until Lewis and Clark and Pike visited the N. W. that the name appeared again in history. According to the former (1804) they resided on Minnesota r., just above its mouth, and claimed the country to the mouth of Chippeway r., thence N. E. to Crow Wing r. Pike (1806) says: "They hunt on the St. Peter's [Minnesota r.], also on the Mississippi, up Rum r., and sometimes follow the buffalo on the plains.''

They gradually moved up Minnesota r., so that in 1849 they lived N. and w. of the Wahpekute, their villages extending far upstream toward its source. They had one of their most important villages in the vicinity of Lac qui Parle. Here missionaries established themselves as early as 1835, at which date the tribe numbered about 1,500 persons. According to Sibley (Minn. Hist. Coll., III, 250, 1880) the lower Wahpeton were found on Minnesota r., not far from Belleplaine; the upper Wahpeton villages were on the shores of Lac qui Parle. They were ultimately gathered with the Sisseton on L. Traverse res. The esti-

OTHER DAY—WAHPETON

mates of population vary from 900 to 1,500. In 1909 the Sisseton and Wahpeton together, under the Sisseton agency, S. Dak., were reported as numbering 1,936. They were participants in the Minnesota outbreak and massacre of 1862.

According to Long (Exped. St. Peter's R., I, 367, 1824) these Indians were good-looking and straight; none were large, nor were any remarkable for the symmetry of their forms. They were, for the greater part, destitute of clothing, except the breechcloth, though some of the young men were dressed with care and ostentation. ''They wore looking-glasses suspended from their garments. Others had papers of pins, purchased from the traders, as ornaments. We observed that one, who

appeared to be a man of some note among them, had a live sparrow hawk on his head, by way of distinction; this man wore also a buffalo robe, on which 8 bear tracks were painted. . . . The squaws we saw had no ornament, nor did they seem to value themselves upon their personal appearance. . . . Both males and females have small feet and hands. . . . The dress of the women consisted of a long wrapper, with short sleeves, of dark calico; this covered them from the shoulders to the waist; a piece of blue broadcloth, wound two or three times round the waist, its end tucked in, extended to the knee. They also wore leggings of blue or scarlet cloth. Their forms were rather clumsy; their waists not very delicate; they exhibited a great breadth of hips, and their motions were not graceful.'' The village consisted of skin lodges, yet they cultivated maize to some extent. According to Pike the tribe devoted a considerable portion of the year to pursuit of the buffalo.

Lewis and Clark mention two divisions, the Wakpaatonwan and Otekhiatonwan. Parker (Minn. Handbk., 140, 1857), adds the Inyancheyakaatonwan and Inkpa. Ashley (15th Rep. B. A. E., 216, 1897, and letters) enumerates the following bands: Inyancheyakaatonwan, Takapsintonwanna, Wiyakaotina, Otechiatonwanna, Witaotina, Wakpaatonwan, Chankaghaotina, Inkpa, Mdeiyedan, and Inyangmani. Waddapawjestin and the village of Wahnacsoutah can not be identified with any of these.

Gens de Feuille.—Pike, Trav., 110, 1811. Gens de la Feuille.—Badin (1830) in Ann. de la Prop. de la Foi, IV, 536, 1843. Gens des Feuilles.—Pike, Exped., 93, 1810. Houebaton.—Crepy, Carte de l'Am. Sept., n. d. Houetbatons.—Du Lhut (1678) in Margry, Déc., VI, 22, 1886. Leaf.—Drake, Bk. Inds., viii, 1848. Leaf Nation.—Clark, MS. quoted by Coues, Lewis and Clark Exped., I, 101, note, 1893. Leaf Villagers.—Mazekootemane in Minn. Hist. Soc. Coll., III, 83, 1880. Men of the River.—Hennepin, New Discov., 184, 1698. Oetbatons.—La Chesnaye (1697) in Margry, Déc., VI, 6, 1886. Ouadbatons.—La Hontan (1700), New Voy., I, 231, 1703. Ouadebathons.—Hennepin, New Discov., 184, 1698. Ouadebatons.—La Salle, Exped. (1679–81), in Margry, Déc., I, 481, 1875. Oua de Battons.—Hennepin, New Discov., map, 1698. Ouaepetons.—Le Sueur (1700) in Margry, Déc., VI, 87, 1886 (trans. 'Gens de la Feuille'). Ouapetons.—Le Sueur (1700) quoted by Neill, Hist. Minn., 170, 1858. Ouatabatonha.—Pachot (1722) in Margry, Déc., VI, 518, 1886. Oudebaetons.—Raudot (1710), ibid., 15. Ouyopetons.—Pénicaut (1700), ibid., V, 414, 1883. Ovadebathons.—Coxe, Carolana, map, 1741. People of the Leaf.—Minn. Hist. Coll., III, 172, 1880. People of the Leaves.—Pike (1806) quoted by Schoolcraft, Ind. Tribes, III, 563, 1853. People of the River.—Minn. Hist. Coll., I (1850–56), 336, 1872. Quioepetons.—Le Sueur (1700) in Margry, Déc., VI, 86, 1886. Quiopetons.—Le Sueur (1700) quoted by Neill, Hist. Minn., 170, 1858. Sioux of the Leaf.—Treaty of 1816 in U. S. Ind. Treat., 191, 1837. Sioux Wahpatone.—Lewis and Clark Discov., 28, 1806. Wabipetons.—Keane in Stanford, Compend., 542, 1878 (misprint). Wahkpa toan.—Long, Exped. St. Peter's R., I, 378, 1824. Wahk-patons.—Prescott (1847) in Schoolcraft, Ind. Tribes, II, 171, 1852. Wahpatoan Sioux.—Ind. Aff. Rep. 1856, 38, 1857.

Wahpaton.—U. S. Stat. at Large, XII, 1037, 1863. **Wâh′-pa-tone.**—Lewis and Clark Discov.. 30, 1806. **Wah-pay-toan.**—U. S. Stat. at Large, X, 51, 1853. **Wah-pay-toan-wan Dakotahs.**—Sen. Ex. Doc. 61, 33d Cong., 1st sess., 333, 1854. **Wah-pay-to-wan.**—Ramsey (1853) in Sen. Ex. Doc. 61, 33d Cong., 1st sess., 324, 1854. **Wahpeeton.**—Schoolcraft, Ind. Tribes, III, 612, 1853. **Wah-pee-ton Sioux.**—Ind. Aff. Rep., 431, 1839. **Wahpehtonwan.**—Minn. Hist. Coll., III, 190, 1880. **Wahpeton.**—Treaty of 1830 in U. S. Ind. Treat., 635, 1826. **Wahpetongs.**—Schoolcraft, Trav., 307, 1821. **Waĥpetoŋwaŋ.**—Riggs, Dakota Gram. and Dict., vi, 1852 (trans. 'village in the leaves'). **Wahpe-tonwans.**—Warren, Dacota Country, 15, 1856. **Wakhpetonwan.**—Williamson in Minn. Geol. Rep. 1884, 111, 1885. **Wakpaton Dakota.**—Sibley in Minn. Hist. Coll., III, 99, 1880. **Wakpayton.**—Minn. Hist. Coll., III, 172, 1880. **Wakpe-ton Dakota.**—Stanley in Smithson. Misc. Coll., XIV, no. 216, 7, 1867. **Wapatone.**—Lewis and Clark Jour., 132, 1840. **Wa-pa-toone.**—Arrowsmith, map N. Am. (1795), 1814. **Wapintowaher.**—Balbi, Atlas Ethnog., 55, 1826. **Wappitong.**—Treaty of 1825 in U. S. Ind. Treat., 367, 1826. **Wa-qpe′-toⁿ-waⁿ.**—Powell in 7th Rep. B. A. E., 115, 1891. **Wark-pey-t′wawn.**—Ramsey in Ind. Aff. Rep. 1849, 83, 1850 (given as pronunciation). **Warpaton.**—Cooper in Sen. Ex. Doc. 61, 33d Cong., 1st sess., 378, 1854. **Warpeton.**—Nicollet, Rep. on Upper Miss. R., 13, 1843. **War-pe-ton-wan.**—Ramsey in Ind. Aff. Rep. 1849, 83, 1850. **War-pe-t′wans.**—Ramsey, ibid., 74. **Washpelong.**—Boudinot, Star in the W., 129, 1816 (misprint). **Washpetong.**—Pike quoted by Schermerhorn in Mass. Hist. Coll., 2d s., II, 40, 1814. **Washpotang.**—Schermerhorn, ibid., 41. **Waupatone.**—Clark, MS. quoted by Coues, Lewis and Clark Exped., I, 101, note, 1893. **Wawpeentowahs.**—Carver, Trav., 80, 1778. **Whapetons.**—Corliss, Lacotah MS. vocab., B. A. E., 107, 1874.

Wahsuahgunewininewug (*Waswagŭniwininiwŭg*, 'people who fish by torchlight.'—W. J.). A division of the Chippewa.
Wah-suah-gun-e-win-in-e-wug.—Warren in Minn. Hist. Soc. Coll., V, 39, 1885 (trans.: 'men of the torches'). **Wāswāgạnīwininiwạg.**—Wm. Jones, inf'n, 1905.

Wahtatkin. An unidentified Paviotso tribe living E. of the Cascade mts., and s. of the Blue mts. in Oregon.
Wah-tat-kin.—Huntington in Ind. Aff. Rep., 466, 1865. **Wa-tat-kah.**—U. S. Ind. Treat., 806, 1873.

Wahti. One of the Diegueño rancherias represented in the treaty of 1852 at Santa Isabel, s. Cal.—H. R. Ex. Doc. 76, 34th Cong., 3d sess., 133, 1857.

Wahyahi (*Wa'yā′hĭ*, 'wolf place,' i. e. place of the Wolf clan). Wolftown settlement on upper Soco cr., on the East Cherokee res., in Jackson co., N. C.—Mooney in 19th Rep. B. A. E., 546, 1900. **Wolftown.**—Mooney, ibid.

Waiilatpuan Family (from *Wayíletpu*, pl. of *Wa-ílet*, '[one] Cayuse man.'—Gatschet). A linguistic family composed of two divisions: the Cayuse and the Molala, the former occupying the territory from Des Chutes r. to the Blue mts., including the headwaters of Wallawalla, Grande Ronde, and Umatilla rs., in Oregon and Washington. The territory of the Molala is not so certain, but was probably for the greater part in the Cascade range between Mts Hood and Scott, and on Molala cr. in w. Oregon. The Waiilatpuan language has not yet been thoroughly studied, and, while classed as independent, may prove to be related to the Shahaptian, with the tribes of which family the Cayuse have always been closely associated. According to Gatschet the two dialects of the language are very distinct, which would indicate a geographical separation of the two tribes of long standing. There is, however, a tradition among the Cayuse of the western migration of the Molala which would support a contrary view. The tribes of the family have probably always been weak in numbers, and, although constantly decreasing in historic times, have been noted for warlike qualities. Both branches are now nearly extinct. (L. F.)
=**Waiilatpu.**—Hale in U. S. Expl. Exped., VI, 199, 214, 569, 1846 (includes Cailloux or Cayuse or Willetpoos, and Molele); Gallatin, after Hale, in Trans. Am. Ethnol. Soc., II, pt. 1, c, 14, 56, 77, 1848; Berghaus (1851), Physik. Atlas, map 17, 1852; Buschmann, Spuren der aztek. Sprache, 628, 1859; Bancroft, Nat. Races, III, 565, 1882 (Cayuse and Mollale). =**Wailatpu.**—Gallatin in Schoolcraft, Ind. Tribes, III, 402, 1853 (Cayuse and Molele). ×**Sahaptin.**—Latham, Nat. Hist. Man., 323, 1850 (cited as including Cayús?). ×**Sahaptins.** — Keane in Stanford, Compend., Cent. and So. Am., app., 474, 1878 (cited because it includes Cayuse and Mollale). =**Molele.**—Latham, Nat. Hist. Man., 324, 1850 (includes Molele, Cayús?). >**Cayús?.**—Latham, ibid. =**Cayuse.**—Gatschet in Mag. Am. Hist., 166, 1877 (Cayuse and Moléle); Gatschet in Beach, Ind. Miscel., 442, 1877. =**Waiilatpuan.**—Powell in 7th Rep. B. A. E., 127, 1891.

Waikenmuk (said to mean 'people up north,' or 'what is down north'). A Wintun tribe formerly living on upper Trinity r., Trinity co., Cal., their territory extending to Scott mtn.
Wai′-kēn-mok.—Powers in Cont. N. A. Ethnol., III, 230, 1877. **Wi Kain Mocs.**—Powers in Overland Mo., XII, 531, 1874.

Waikosel (interpreted 'in the north,' and 'on the plains'). A Wintun or Patwin village formerly in Cortina valley, Colusa co., Cal.
Wai′-ko-sel.—Powers in Cont. N. A. Ethnol., III, 219, 1877. **Wicosels.**—Powers in Overland Mo., XIII, 543, 1874.

Wailaki (Wintun: 'northern language'). An Athapascan tribe or group of many villages formerly on the main Eel r. and its N. fork from Kekawaka cr. to within a few miles of Round valley, Cal. After some fighting with the whites they were placed on Round valley res., where a few of them still reside. Their houses were circular. They had no canoes, but crossed streams by weighting themselves down with stones while they waded. They lived by the river during the wet months of the year, when their chief occupation was fishing, done at especially favorable places by means of nets and spears. The summer and fall months were spent on the sides and tops of the ridges, where the women were able to gather the bulbs, seeds, and nuts, and the men could unite in deer drives and other methods of hunting. They usually buried their dead, but burned those who fell in battle. They took the whole heads of their enemies as trophies, with which they were accustomed to dance. Like the Yuki the women have their noses and cheeks as well as their chins tattooed. Coyote holds the principal place in their mythology, where he is represented as acting under the direction of his father. He secured for men daylight and the heavenly bodies, and fire which he succeeded in stealing from their guardians. He established the fishing places, and ordained social and other customs. An adolescent ceremony was held for the girls, and most of the boys were trained with the candidates for medicine-men, who were restricted as to their food, drink, and sleep for many days. This training took place in the fall under the direction of two or more old shamans. Public exhibitions, consisting in part of dancing, were given by the candidates. Large conical dance houses were erected occasionally, and dedicated with ceremonies of dancing and singing; such were important occasions of mingled social and religious character.   (P. E. G.)

Kak'-wits.—Powers in Cont. N. A. Ethnol., III, 124, 1877 ('northern people': Yuki name). Kas'-tel-Po-mo.—Ibid., 147. Tlackees.—Taylor in Cal. Farmer, Sept. 5, 1862. Uye-Lackes.—Stevenson in Ind. Aff. Rep. 1856, 251, 1857. Wailakki.—Powers in Cont. N. A. Ethnol., III, 114, 1877. Wi Lackees.—Powers in Overland Mo., IX, 499, 1872. Wilacki.—Keane in Stanford, Compend., 465, 1878. Wi Tackees.—Powers in Overland Mo., IX, 306, 1872. Wi Tackee-Yukas.—Ibid. Wrylackers.—Maltby in Ind. Aff. Rep., 91, 1866. Wye-Lackees.—Geiger in Ind. Aff. Rep. 1859, 438, 1860. Wylachies.—Maltby in Ind. Aff. Rep., 112, 1865. Wylackies.—Hanson in Ind. Aff. Rep. 1863, 93, 1864. Wylaks.—Taylor in Cal. Farmer, June 8, 1860. Ylackas.—Taylor, ibid., June 22, 1860.

Wailaksel ('in the north'). A Patwin tribe that formerly lived on Middle Cache cr., Colusa co., Cal.
Weelacksels.—Powers in Overland Mo., XIII, 543, 1874. Wi'-lak-sel.—Powers in Cont. N. A. Ethnol., III, 219, 1877.

Waisha (*Wa'-isha*). A former Modoc camping place on Lost r., 3 or 4 m. N. W. of Tule lake, and near the hills that culminate in Laki peak, s. w. Oreg.—Gatschet in Cont. N. A. Ethnol., II, pt. I, xxxii, 1890.

Waisuskuck. A Potawatomi village, named from a chief, in N. E. Illinois in 1832.—Tippecanoe treaty (1832) in U. S. Ind. Treat., 698, 1873.

Waitlas. A village of the Goasila at the mouth of Samo r., Smith inlet, Brit. Col.
Oi-cle-la.—Kane, Wand. in N. A., app., 1859. Wycless.—Boas in Bull. Am. Geog. Soc., 226, 1887.

Waitus. A Siuslaw village on Siuslaw r., Oreg.
Wai'-ʇūs.—Dorsey in Jour. Am. Folk-lore, III, 230, 1890.

Waiushr. The Duck clan of San Felipe pueblo, N. Mex.
Waiushr-háno.—Hodge in Am. Anthr., IX, 350, 1896 (*háno*='people').

Wakan (cf. *Wakonda*). An Iowa gens or band, now extinct.
Wa-kaⁿ'.—Dorsey in 15th Rep. B. A. E., 239, 1897. Wä-keeh'.—Morgan, Anc. Soc., 156, 1877.

Wakan. An Oglala Sioux band.
Wakaŋ.—Dorsey (after Cleveland) in 15th Rep. B. A. E., 220, 1897. Wakaⁿ.—Ibid.

Wakan. A Hunkpapa Sioux band.
Devil's medicine man band.—Culbertson in Smithson. Rep. 1850, 141, 1851. Wakaⁿ.—Dorsey in 15th Rep. B. A. E., 221, 1897. Wakaŋ.—Ibid.

Wakan. An Oto gens or band.
Wä'-kä.—Morgan, Anc. Soc., 156, 1877. Wa-kaⁿ'.—Dorsey in 15th Rep. B. A. E., 240, 1897.

Wakanasisi (*Wä'k!anasi'si*). A locality on the N. side of Columbia r., Wash., nearly opposite the mouth of the Willamette; also the name of the Chinookan tribe, strictly called Galakanasisi (Gä'L!ak!anasisi, 'those of the woodpecker'), formerly living at that point and in its vicinity. Before moving to this place they lived at Lakstak, on the s. side of the Columbia, a little below Nakoaik, and were then called Gatqstax (Boas). About 1840 their chief was Kiesno, whose name is sometimes given to their main village. After the epidemic of 1829 the Wakanasisi were greatly reduced in numbers and included the remnants of several neighboring tribes. In 1849 they numbered fewer than 100, and are now extinct.   (L. F.)

Awakanáshish.—Gatschet, Kalapuya MS., B. A. E., 31, 1877 (Kalapuya name). Gä'L!ak!anasisi.—Boas, inf'n, 1905 ('those of the woodpecker'). Gatqstax.—Boas, inf'n, 1905. Guáthlakanashishi.—Gatschet, Kalapuya MS., B. A. E., 1877. Kiesno's village.—Tolmie in Trans. Oreg. Pion. Ass'n, 32, 1884. Lamχeíχat.—Ibid. (Kalapuya name). Waccanessisí.—Gatschet in Mag. Am. Hist., I, 167, 1877. Wakanascoces.—Lane in Senate Ex. Doc. 52, 31st Cong., 1st sess., 174, 1850. Wa-kan-a-shee-shee.—Lyman in Oreg. Hist. Soc. Quar., I, 323, 1900. Wákänäshishi.—Gatschet, MS., B. A. E., 1877 (Clackama name). Wakanasisse.—Gibbs, MS. no. 248, B. A. E. Wakanasissi.—Tolmie in Trans. Oreg. Pion. Ass'n, 32, 1884.

Wakanda. See *Wakonda*.

Wakanikikarachada ('they call themselves after a snake'). A Winnebago gens.
Wa-kaⁿ' i-ki'-ka-ra'-tca-da.—Dorsey in 15th Rep. B. A. E., 240, 1897. Wä-kon'-nä.—Morgan, Anc. Soc., 157, 1877.

Wakantaenikashika ('those who became human beings by the aid of a thunder-being'). A Quapaw gens.
Thunder-being gens.—Dorsey in 15th Rep. B. A. E., 229, 1897. Wakan'ʇä e'nikaci'ʇa.—Ibid.

Wakasassa ('where there are many cattle'). A former Seminole town located by Bell on the E. side of the mouth of Suwannee r., Levy co., Fla., but more probably on the stream of the same name. The people came originally from Coosa r., Ala., under the "prophets" McQueen and Francis. A small stream and bay s. of Suwannee r. retain the name.
Waw-ka-sau-su.—Bell in Morse, Rep. to Sec. War, 306, 1822.

Wakashan Family. A linguistic family occupying the w. coast of British Colum-

bia between lat. 54° and 50° 30′, the N. and
W. parts of Vancouver id., and the extreme
N. W. corner of Washington, nearly to
lat. 48° N. The name is derived from
waukash, 'good,' which Cook heard at
Friendly cove, Nootka sd., and supposed
to be the name of a tribe. The culture
of these people is almost identical with
that of the coast Salish to the s. and
E. of them, and with that of the Tsimshian, Haida, and Tlingit in the N.
In physical characteristics they rather
approach the coast Salish, and their
language conforms in type most closely
with that of the Salish and Chimakuan.
Juan de Fuca probably reached the
coast of British Columbia and was the
first white man to see the lands of the
Wakashan. If Fuentes be not an imaginary person, nor his voyage a fable, he
sailed in 1640 through the archipelago
where the Wakashan live. Ensign Juan
Perez is believed to have anchored in
Nootka sd. in 1774. In the following year
Bodega and Maurelle passed along the
Wakashan coast on their way s. In 1786
English vessels under Capts. Hanna, Port-
lock, and Dixon called at this coast, and
from that time visits of British and American trading vessels were constant, Nootka
in particular being much frequented.
Between 1792 and 1794 Capt. George Vancouver visited the country. In 1803 the
Boston, of Boston Mass., was destroyed
by the people of Nootka, and all on board
except two persons were killed. From
the account of one of these, John R. Jewitt, we have important information regarding the tribes of the w. coast of Vancouver id. The Hudson's Bay Co. established a post at Victoria in 1843, and
from that time relations with the natives
became more intimate. Since then the
native population has pretty steadily declined. Mission stations have been established at many points with considerable
success in the N., but half of the southern
Kwakiutl still hold to their ancient customs and beliefs. Most of the Nootka
have been converted by Roman Catholic
missionaries. Wakashan dwellings were
large structures of huge cedar beams and
planks, and stood in a row fronting the
sea. Each accommodated several families which had separate fires. The canoe
was one of the essentials of existence on
these shores, where there were no better
seamen than the tribes of the w. coast of
Vancouver id. These and a few of the
neighboring tribes in Washington were
the only people who pursued and killed
the whale, others being content to wait
until the animals drifted ashore dead.
For the rest of their diet they depended
mainly upon fish, but they also hunted
land and sea animals and collected shellfish, roots, and berries, each family owning

its own fishing grounds and salmon creeks,
which it guarded jealously. Although
good carvers of wood, they were excelled
in this respect by the Haida and Tlingit.
The northern tribes, the Heiltsuk Kwakiutl, reckoned descent in the female line;
but the southern tribes, though in a tran-
sitional state, are rather to be reckoned
in the paternal stage. Intertribal warfare
was constant and slavery an institution.
Head flattening was practised considerably by the tribes of Vancouver id. The
potlatch was one of the cardinal institutions, and around it centered a large part
of the social and religious interests of the
people. Owing mainly to smallpox and
vices, the number of Wakashan has fallen
off steadily since their first contact with
whites. In 1909 there were enumerated
in the Dominion of Canada 4,150, to which
are to be added 434 Makah in Washington;
total, 4,584. Of these 2,090 were Kwakiutl
and 2,494 Nootka.   (J. R. S.)

>**Wakash.**—Gallatin in Trans. Am. Antiq. Soc.,
II, 15, 306, 1836 (of Nootka Sound; gives Jewitt's vocab.); Gallatin in Trans. Am. Ethnol. Soc., II, pt.
1, 77, 1848 (based on Newittee); Berghaus (1851),
Physik. Atlas, map 17, 1852; Gallatin in School-
craft, Ind. Tribes, III, 402, 1853 (includes Newit-
tee and Nootka Sound); Latham in Trans. Philol.
Soc. Lond., 73, 1856 (of Quadra and Vancouver's
id.); Latham, Opuscula, 340, 1860; Latham, El.
Comp. Philol., 403, 1862 (Tlaoquatsh and Wakash
proper; Nútka and congeners also referred here).
✕**Wakash.**—Latham, Nat. Hist. Man., 301, 1850
(includes Naspatle, proper Nutkans, Tlaoquatsh,
Nittenat, Klasset, Klallems; the last named is
Salishan). ═**Wakashan.**—Powell in 7th Rep. B.
A. E., 128, 1891. ✕**Nootka-Columbian.**—Scouler in
Jour. Roy. Geog. Soc., XI, 221, 1841 (includes Qua-
dra and Vancouver id., Haeeltzuk, Billechoola,
Tlaoquatch, Kawitchen, Noosdalum, Squallya-
mish, Cheenooks); Prichard, Phys. Hist. Man-
kind, V, 435, 1847 (follows Scouler); Latham in
Jour. Ethnol. Soc. Lond., I, 162, 1848 (remarks on
Scouler's group of this name); Latham, Opuscula,
257, 1860 (the same). <**Nootka.**—Hale in U. S.
Expl. Exped., VI, 220, 569, 1846 (proposes family
to include tribes of Vancouver id. and tribes on
south side of Fuca str.). >**Nutka.**—Buschmann,
Neu-Mexico, 329, 1858. >**Nootka.**—Gatschet in
Mag. Am. Hist., 170, 1877 (mentions only Makah,
and Classet tribes of Cape Flattery); Gatschet
in Beach, Ind. Misc., 446, 1877. ✕**Nootkahs.**—
Keane in Stanford, Compend., Cent. and So.
Am., 473, 1878 (includes Muchlahts, Nitinahts,
Ohyahts, Manosahts, and Quoquoulths of present
family, together with a number of Salishan tribes).
✕**Nootka.**—Bancroft, Nat. Races, III, 564, 608, 1882
(a heterogeneous group, largely Salishan, with
Wakashan, Skittagetan, and other families represented). >**Straits of Fuca.**—Gallatin in Trans.
Am. Antiq. Soc., II, 134, 306, 1836 (vocabulary of,
referred here with doubt; considered distinct by
Gallatin). ✕**Southern.**—Scouler in Jour. Roy.
Geog. Soc., XI, 224, 1841 (same as his Nootka-Columbian above). ✕**Insular.**—Scouler, ibid. (same
as his Nootka-Columbian above). ✕**Haeltzuk.**—
Latham in Jour. Ethnol. Soc. Lond., I, 155, 1848
(cites Tolmie's vocab.; spoken from 50° 30′ to 53°
30′); Latham, Opuscula, 251, 1860 (the same).
>**Haeeltsuk and Hailtsa.**—Latham, Nat. Hist. Man.,
300, 1850 (includes Hyshalla, Hyhysh, Esleytuk,
Weekenoch, Nalatsenoch, Quagheuil, Tlatla-Shequilla, Lequeeltoch). >**Hailtsa.**— Latham in
Trans. Philol. Soc. Lond., 72, 1856; Buschmann,
Neu-Mexico, 322, 1858; Latham, Opuscula, 339, 1860;
Latham, El. Comp. Philol., 401, 1862 (includes coast
dialects between Hawkesbury id., Broughton's
archipelago, and northern part of Vancouver id.).
>**Ha eelb zuk.**—Schoolcraft, Ind. Tribes, V, 487,

1855; Kane, Wand. in N. A., app., 1859 (or Balla-bola; a census of N.W. tribes classified by language). >**Ha-ilt'-zŭkh.**—Dall, after Gibbs, in Cont. N. A. Ethnol., I, 144, 1877 (vocabularies of Bel-bella of Milbank sd. and of Kwákiŭtl'). <**Nass.**—Gallatin in Trans. Am. Ethnol. Soc., II, pt. 1, c, 1848. <**Naass.**—Gallatin, ibid., 77 (includes Hailstla, Haceltzuk, Billechola, Chimeysan); Gallatin in Schoolcraft, Ind. Tribes, III, 402, 1853 (includes Huitsla). ×**Nass.**—Bancroft, Nat. Races, III, 564, 606, 1882 (includes Hailtza of present family). >**Aht.**—Sproat, Savage Life, app., 312, 1868 (name suggested for family instead of Nootka-Columbian); Tolmie and Dawson, Comp. Vocabs., 50, 1884 (vocab. of Kaiookwäht). ×**Puget Sound Group.**—Keane in Stanford, Compend., Cent. and So. Am., 460, 474, 1878. ×**Hydahs.**—Keane, ibid., 473 (includes Hailtzas of the present family). >**Kwakiool.**—Tolmie and Dawson, Comp. Vocabs., 27–48, 1884 (vocabs. of Haishilla, Hailtzuk, Kwiha, Likwiltoh septs: also map showing family domain). >**Kwá'kiutl.**—Boas in Petermanns Mitteil., 130, 1887 (general account of family, with list of tribes).

Wakatomica. The name of two Shawnee towns in Ohio about the Revolutionary period, one being possibly the successor and continuation of the other. (1) One, apparently the earlier, was one of a group of two or more towns, occupied chiefly by Shawnee, situated on the Muskingum, below the junction of the Walhonding and below the present Coshocton, Coshocton co. It was visited by the missionary Zeisberger in 1772 and with another of the group was destroyed by the Americans under Col. McDonald in 1774 and not thereafter rebuilt, the Shawnee removing to the Scioto and the Miami. (2) The other of the same name, possibly built by refugees from the first, was situated, according to former agent Johnston, on the headwaters of Mad r., just below the present Zanesfield in Logan co., within the Greenville treaty cession of 1795. It was sometimes known also as the Upper Shawnee village, because it was the highest of those on the waters of the Miami. (J. M.)

Waccotomica.—Connelley in Heckewelder, Narr. (1820), Connelley repr., 241, note, 1907. **Wachatawmaha.**—Bouquet (1764) in Rupp, W. Penn., app., 155, 1846. **Wachatomakak.**—Connelley in Heckewelder, op. cit., 241, note. **Wagetomica.**—Ibid. **Waghatamagy.**—Bouquet (1764) in Rupp, op. cit., 157. **Waghhatawmaky.**—Ibid., 155. **Wakatamike.**—Smith, Bouquet Exped., 16, 1766. **Wakatameki.**—Heckewelder, op. cit., 245. **Wakatomaca.**—Connelley in Heckewelder, op. cit., 253, note. **Wakatomica.**—Butterfield, Washington-Irvine Corr., 5, 1882. **Wakautamike.**—Smith, op. cit., 18. **Waketameki.**—Heckewelder, op. cit., 241. **Waketummakie.**—McKee (1774) in Rupp, W. Penn., app., 211, 1846. **Wakitamiki.**—Connelley in Heckewelder, op. cit., 241, note. **Wankatamikee.**—La Tour map, 1784 (misprint). **Wapatomaca.**—Connelley in Heckewelder, op. cit., 253, note. **Wapatomica.**—Butterfield, op. cit., 332. **Wappatomica.**—Howe, Hist. Coll. Ohio, 150, 1851. **Waughcotomoco.**—Connelley in Heckewelder, op. cit., 241. **Waukatamike.**—Smith, Bouquet Exped., 67, 1766. **Waukataumikee.**—Hutchins, map, ibid. **Waukatomike.**—Ibid.

Wakchekhiikikarachada ('they call themselves after a water monster'). A Winnebago gens.

Wahk-chá-he-dä.—Morgan, Anc. Soc., 157, 1877. **Wa-ktce'-qi i-ki'-ka-ra'-tca-da.**—Dorsey in 15th Rep. B. A. E., 241, 1897.

Wakemap (*Wa'q!Emap*). A former village of the Tlakluit on Columbia r., Wash. (E. S.)

Wakeshi (*Wake-shĭ'*, 'fox'). A gens of the Potawatomi.—Morgan, Anc. Soc., 167, 1877.

Wakhakukdhin ('those among the cacti'). A band of Pahatsi Osage mentioned by De Smet as forming a village with a population of 500 on Neosho r., Ind. T., in 1850.

Waqdąnkǫiⁿ.—Dorsey, Osage MS. vocab., B. A. E., 1883. **Weichaka-Ougrin.**—Smet, West. Miss., 255, 1856.

Wakhkel. A Yurok village on Klamath r., N. w. Cal., about 4 m. above its mouth.

Wakhker. A Yurok village on Klamath r. just below Wakhtek and adjacent to it, at Klamath P. O., N. w. Cal.

Wakhna ('snorts'). A band of the Brulé Teton Sioux.

Walina.—Dorsey, after Cleveland, in 15th Rep. B. A. E., 219, 1897. **Waqna.**—Ibid.

Wakhshek. A Yurok village on lower Klamath r., 3 m. below Weitchpec, N. w. Cal. Not to be confounded with a place called Wa'shoi, 7 or 8 m. downstream.

Wah-sherr.—Gibbs (1851) in Schoolcraft, Ind. Tribes, III, 138, 1853. **Wah-si.**—McKee (1851) in Sen. Ex. Doc. 4, 32d Cong., spec. sess., 194, 1853. **Wakhshek.**—A. L. Kroeber, inf'n, 1907. **Wichsis.**—McKee, op. cit., 215. **Wi-uh-sis.**—Meyer, Nach dem Sacramento, 282, 1855.

Wakhtek. A Yurok village on lower Klamath r., at Klamath P. O., N. w. Cal.

Wakhtek.—A. L. Kroeber, inf'n, 1907. **Wauhtecq.**—Gibbs (1851) in Schoolcraft, Ind. Tribes, III, 138, 1853.

Wakichi. A former Mariposan (Yokuts) tribe of California which spoke a dialect that indicates closest relationship with the valley half of the northern group of Yokuts.—Kroeber in Univ. Cal. Pub., Am. Arch. and Eth., II, 260, 1907.

Wakmuhaoin ('pumpkin-rind earring'). A Yankton Sioux band.

Wakmuha oiⁿ.—Dorsey in 15th Rep. B. A. E., 217, 1897. **Wakmuha-oiⁿ.**—Ibid.

Wakoawissojik (*Wăkoshäwisochigi*, 'they of the fox name.'—W. J.). The Fox gens of the Sauk and Foxes.

Ouagoussak.—Jes. Rel. 1672, lviii, 40, 1899. **Wăgushagi.**—Wm. Jones, inf'n, 1906. **Wä-ko-a-wis'-so-jik.**—Morgan, Anc. Soc., 170, 1877. **Wâkoshäwisotcigi.**—Wm. Jones, inf'n, 1907.

Wakokayi ('blue-heron breeding place'). Two former Upper Creek towns: one on Hatchet cr., Coosa co., Ala., the other on lower Coosa r., below Wetumpka, Elmore co., Ala.

Blow-horn Nest.—Gatschet, Creek Migr. Leg., I, 149, 1884. **Vaccay.**—Vaugondy, map Amérique, 1778 (on upper Coosa r., Ala.). **Wacacoys.**—Swan (1791) in Schoolcraft, Ind. Tribes, V, 262, 1855. **Waccay.**—Jefferys, French Dom., I, 134, map, 1761. **Waccocoie.**—Schoolcraft, Ind. Tribes, IV, 380, 1854. **Wackakoy.**—Finnelson (1792) in Am. State Papers, Ind. Aff., I, 289, 1832. **Wiccakaw.**—Bartram, Trav., 462, 1791. **Woc-co-coie.**—Hawkins (1799), Sketch, 43, 1848. **Wocke Coys.**—Weatherford (1793) in Am. State Papers, op. cit., 385. **Wokukay.**—Alcedo, Dic. Geog., V, 344, 1789. **Wolkukay.**—Bartram, Voy., I, map, 1799.

Wakokayi. A town of the Creek Nation, Okla.

Wakoká-i.—Gatschet, Creek Migr. Leg., II, 186, 1888. **Wakokáyi.**—Ibid.

Wakonda (*Wa-koɲ'-da*). A term employed by the Omaha, Ponca, Osage, Quapaw, Kansa, Oto, Missouri, and Iowa tribes of the Siouan family when the power believed to animate all natural forms is spoken to or spoken of in supplications or rituals. The dialects of the first five tribes are closely related; the Omaha and Ponca speak practically alike; the Osage, Quapaw, and Kansa differ somewhat from the former in pronunciation, while the Oto, Missouri, and Iowa have so far changed their speech as to be unintelligible to the others. The word *wakoɲda*, spelled *wakaɲda* by Riggs in his Dakota Dictionary, is given by him as a verb signifying 'to reckon as holy or sacred, to worship'; the noun is *wakaɲ*, and is defined as 'a spirit, something consecrated.' The same authority gives the meaning of *wakaɲ*, as an adjective, as 'spiritual, sacred, consecrated, wonderful, incomprehensible, mysterious.' The same general meaning that runs through the Dakota words *wakoɲda* and *wakaɲ* inheres in the word *wakoɲda* as used by the Omaha and their cognates; with the latter the word may be regarded as an appellative, for while it is the name given to the mysterious all-pervading and life-giving power to which certain anthropomorphic aspects are attributed, the word is also applied to objects or phenomena regarded as sacred or mysterious. These two uses of the word are never confused in the minds of the thoughtful. When during his fast the Omaha sings, "*Wakoɲda*, here needy he stands, and I am he!" his address is to "the power that moves," "causes to move," that is, gives life; for the ability to move is to the Omaha mind synonymous with life. In this prayer the Omaha is not crying to those forces or forms spoken of as *wakoɲda* in songs that relate to objects seen in dreams or to symbols of magic. This distinction is sometimes difficult for one of another race to follow, but that there is a distinction to the native mind is not to be doubted. The *wakaɲ taɲka*, the great *wakaɲ* or spirit of the Dakota, is not quite the same as that which the Omaha means by *wakoɲda*. The term 'great' in *wakaɲ taɲka* implies a comparison, and such an idea does not seem to belong to *wakoɲda*, for *wakoɲda* stands by itself, unlike any other, and represents a concept that seems to be born of the Indian's point of view toward nature and natural phenomena, including man himself. To the Omaha nothing is without life: the rock lives, so do the cloud, the tree, the animal. He projects his own consciousness upon all things, and ascribes to them experiences and characteristics with which he is familiar; there is to him something in common between all creatures and all natural forms, a something which brings them into existence and holds them intact; this something he conceives of as akin to his own conscious being. The power which thus brings to pass and holds all things in their living form he designates as *wakoɲda*. That he anthropomorphizes this power is evident from his supplication, made with fasting and symbols of humility, by which he seeks to awaken pity or compassion, human attributes, as "here needy he stands," and thus expects to win some kind of recognition. He is taught that when he fasts and prays he must not ask for any special favor or gift; that which he is able to receive will be given him. This teaching throws a side-light on his concept of *wakoɲda*, showing that it implies intelligence as well as power; but the concept seems to be vague, and ideas dissolve into indefiniteness in the "mysterious," the "incomprehensible" atmosphere that surrounds the unseen power denominated *wakoɲda*.

That there is a creative aspect to *wakoɲda* is made clear from the use of the word *wakoɲdagi: gi* is the sign of possession, therefore the phenomena termed *wakoɲdagi* evince something belonging to or of the power denominated *wakoɲda*. For example, when a child is first able to walk, this new manifestation of ability to move about is called *wakoɲdagi;* but should a person, from sickness or other disability, lose the power to walk, but recover it, the act of resumption would not be called *wakoɲdagi*. The first speech of the child is the manifestation of a new power, and is *wakoɲdagi*. *Wakoɲda* is invisible, and therefore allied to the idea of spirit. Objects seen in dreams or visions partake of the idea or nature of spirit, and when these objects speak to man in answer to his entreaty, the act is possible because of the power of *wakoɲda*, and the object, be it thunder-cloud, animal, or bird, seen and heard by the dreamer, may be spoken of by him as a *wakoɲda*, but he does not mean that they are *wakoɲda*. The association in which the term *wakoɲda* is used determines the character of its meaning. *Wakoɲda*, the power addressed during the fast as having power to help the one standing "in need," is not the same *wakoɲda* as the thunder that speaks to a man in a dream is sometimes called; yet there is a relation between the two, not unlike that signified by the term *wakoɲdagi* when applied to the first manifestation of an ability; for all power, whether shown in the thunderstorm, the hurricane, the animals, or man, is of *wakoɲda*. Whatever is mysterious and beyond ordinary experience or effort approaches the realm of the concept which the word *wakoɲda* signifies to the Omaha and his cognates.

Wakoɲda is difficult to define, for exact terms change it from its native uncrystallized condition to something foreign to aboriginal thought. Vague as the concept seems to be to one of another race, to the Indian it is as real and as mysterious as the starry night or the flush of the coming day. See *Totem*.   (A. C. F.)

Wakouingouechiwek. An Algonquian tribe or band living on a river about 60 leagues s. of Hudson bay and 150 leagues N. w. of Three Rivers, Quebec. They were probably a part of the Mistassin living on Marten r.

к8aк8aк8chiouets.—Jes. Rel., LX, 244, 1900. K8a-к8chi8ets.—Jes. Rel., LXIII, 248, 1900. Koüakoüi-koüesioüek.—Jes. Rel. 1672, 54, 1858. Kouakouikoue-siwek.—Jes. Rel., LXXIII, 60, 1901. Kwakwakou-chiouets.—Ibid., LX, 245. Ouakouingouechiouek.—Jes. Rel. 1658, 20, 1858. Oukouingouechiouek.—Ibid.

Wakpaatonwan ('village on the river'). A Wahpeton Sioux band.

Waȟpetoɲwaɲ-ȟća.—S. R. Riggs, letter to Dorsey, 1882 (trans. 'real Wahpeton'). Wakpa-atoɲwaɲ.—Ashley quoted by Dorsey in 15th Rep. B. A. E., 216, 1897. Wakpa-atoⁿwaⁿ.—Ibid. Wakpaton.—Ashley, letter to Dorsey, 1886. Watpaton.—Ibid.

Wakpaatonwedan ('those who dwell on the creek'). One of the two early divisions of the Mdewakanton Sioux. They had their village on Rice cr., Minn. (Neill, Hist. Minn., 144, note, 1858). The Mdewakanton as described by Le Sueur (1689) seem to have been composed of this division alone. In 1858 it comprised the following bands: Kiyuksa, Ohanhanska, Tacanhpisapa, Anoginajin, Tintaotonwe, and Oyateshicha.

Wakpokinyan ('flies along the creek'). A Miniconjou Sioux band.

River that flies.—Culbertson in Smithson. Rep. 1850, 142, 1851. Wak-po′-ki-an.—Hayden, Ethnog. and Philol. Mo. Val., 875, 1862. Wakpokinya.—Swift, letter to Dorsey, 1884. Wakpokiɲaɲ.—Dorsey in 15th Rep. B. A. E., 220, 1897. Wakpo-kiⁿyaⁿ.—Ibid.

Waksachi. A Shoshonean tribe on the Kaweah r. drainage, extending into the mountains, in s. central California. They lived above the Wikchamni and below the Badwisha. Merriam (Science, XIX, 916, 1904) classes them as a "Paiute" tribe in Eshom valley, N. of Kaweah r., where the remnant of the tribe appears now to reside.

Wack-sa-che.—Barbour (1852) in Sen. Ex. Doc. 4, 32d Cong., spec. sess., 255, 1853. Wakesdachi.—Kroeber in Univ. Cal. Pub., Am. Archæol. and Ethnol., IV, 121, 1907 (Yokuts pl. of Waksachi). Waksachi.—Ibid. Wasakshes.—Taylor in Cal. Farmer, June 8, 1860. Wik′-sach-i.—Powers in Cont. N. A. Ethnol., III, 370, 1877. Wock-soche.—Johnston in Sen. Ex. Doc. 61, 32d Cong., 1st sess., 23, 1852. Wok-sach-e.—Wessells (1853) in H. R. Ex. Doc. 76, 34th Cong., 3d sess., 32, 1857. Wuk-să′-che.—Merriam in Science, XIX, 916, June 17, 1904.

Waḳtonila ('the band that kills no people'). An unidentified Sioux band.

Wak-to-ni-la.—Hayden, Ethnog. and Philol. Mo. Val., 376, 1862.

Walakpa (*Wă′lăkpa*). A summer village of the Utkiavinmiut Eskimo in N. Alaska.—Murdoch in 9th Rep. B. A. E., 83, 1892.

Walakumni. A division of the Miwok between the Cosumne and Mokelumne rs., Cal. This name was probably Wakalumni, another form of Mokelumne.

Walacumnies.—Bancroft, Nat. Races, I, 450, 1874. Walagumnes.—Hale, Ethnog. and Philol., VI, 630, 1846.

Walalsimni. A band formerly frequenting the Stanislaus and Tuolumne rs. in central California. It probably belonged to the Moquelumnan family.

Walalshimni.—A. L. Kroeber, inf'n, 1907 (so called by people to the s. of the territory mentioned). Walalsimni.—Ibid. Wal-lal-sim-ne.—Wessells (1853) in H. R. Ex. Doc. 76, 34th Cong., 3d sess., 30, 1857.

Walam Olum. The sacred tribal chronicle of the Lenape or Delawares. The name signifies 'painted tally' or 'red score,' from *walam*, 'painted,' particularly 'red painted,' and *olum*, 'a score or tally.' The Walam Olum was first published in 1836 in a work entitled "The American Nations," by Constantine Samuel Rafinesque, an erratic French scholar, who spent a number of years in this country, dying in Philadelphia in 1840. He asserted that it was a translation of a manuscript in the Delaware language, which was an interpretation of an ancient sacred metrical legend of the tribe, recorded in pictographs cut upon wood, which had been obtained in 1820 by a Dr Ward from the Delawares then living in Indiana. He claimed that the original pictograph record had first been obtained, but without explanation, until two years later, when the accompanying songs were procured in the Lenape language from another individual, these being then translated by himself with the aid of various dictionaries. Although considerable doubt was cast at the time upon the alleged Indian record, Brinton, after a critical investigation, arrived at the conclusion that it was a genuine native production, and it is now known that similar ritual records upon wood or birchbark are common to several cognate tribes, notably the Chippewa.

After the death of Rafinesque his manuscripts were scattered, those of the Walam Olum finally coming into the hands of Squier, who again brought the legend to public attention in a paper read before the New York Historical Society in 1848, which was published in the American Review of Feb. 1849, reprinted by Beach in his Indian Miscellany in 1877, and again in a later (15th) edition of Drake's Aboriginal Races of North America. All of these reprints were more or less inaccurate and incomplete, and it remained for Brinton to publish the complete pictography, text, and tradition, with notes and critical investigation of the whole subject, with the aid of native Lenape scholars, in "The Lenâpé and their Legends, with the complete text and symbols of the Walam Olum," as No. 5 of his library of Aboriginal American Literature, Phila., 1885.

After sifting the evidence as to its authenticity, Brinton concludes (p. 158): "It is a genuine native production, which was repeated orally to some one indifferently conversant with the Delaware language, who wrote it down to the best of his ability. In its present form it can, as a whole, lay no claim either to antiquity or to purity of linguistic form. Yet, as an authentic modern version, slightly colored by European teachings, of the ancient tribal traditions, it is well worth preservation and will repay more study in the future than is given it in this volume. The narrator was probably one of the native chiefs or priests, who had spent his life in the Ohio and Indiana towns of the Lenape, and who, though with some knowledge of Christian instruction, preferred the pagan rites, legends, and myths of his ancestors. Probably certain lines and passages were repeated in the archaic form in which they had been handed down for generations." (J. M.)

Walapai (*Xawálapáiy*ᵃ, 'pine tree folk.'—Harrington). A Yuman tribe

WALAPAI MAN

originally living on middle Colorado r., above the Mohave tribe, from the great bend eastward, well into the interior of Arizona, occupying Hualapai, Yavapai, and Sacramento valleys, the Cerbat and Aquarius mts. forming the southern part of their range. They lived

WALAPAI WOMAN

chiefly by the chase and on roots and seeds. They are said to have been brave and enterprising, but physically inferior to the Mohave. The Havasupai, who are an offshoot, speak a closely-related language. The Walapai numbered 728 in 1889, 631 in 1897, and 498 in 1910. They are under the administration of a school superintendent on the Walapai res. of 730,880 acres in N. W. Arizona, and are making little progress in civilization. They cultivated only 57 acres during 1904, but owned 2,000 horses. The name Santa Margarita was applied by the Spaniards to one of their rancherias.

E-pa.—A. Hrdlička, inf'n, 1906 (given as their own name). Gualliba.—Garcés (1776), Diary, 404, 1900 (Yavapai name). Gualliva.—Ibid., 444 (mentioned distinctly from "Jaguallepai," but evidently the same). Hawálapai.—Curtis, N. Am. Ind., II, 116, 1908 ('pinery people': Yuma name; *Hawalpái* is the Mohave form, ibid., p. 114). Hah-wál-coes.—Whipple, Exp. San Diego to Colorado R., 17, 1851. Haulapais.—White, MS. Hist. Apaches, B. A. E., 1875. Hawalpai.—Curtis, N. Am. Ind., II, 118, 1908 ('pinery people': Maricopa name). Hä-wol-lä Pai.—Ewing in Great Divide, 203, Dec. 1892 (trans. 'mountain people'). Hoallo-pi.—Thomas, MS., B. A. E., 1868. Huaepais.—Ind. Aff. Rep. 1863, 387, 1864. Hualapais.—Ind. Aff. Rep.,128,1865. Hualipais.—Ibid.,1867,395,1868. Huallapais.—Terry in Rep. Sec. War, pt. I, 46, 1868–69. Huallopi.—Thomas, MS., B. A. E., 1868. Hualopais.—Ind. Aff. Rep., 1864, 156, 1865. Hualpáich.—Whipple, Pac. R. R. Rep., III, pt. 3 16,

1856 (Yuma name). **Hualpais.**—Ind. Aff. Rep 1863, 390, 1864. **Hualpas.**—U.S Stat., XXIII, 377, 1885. **Hulapais.**—Ind. Aff. Rep. 1867, 381, 1868. **Hwalapai.**—Ibid., 246, 1877. **Jaguallapai.**—Garcés (1776), Diary, 308, 1900. **Jagullapai.**—Garcés (1775–76), misquoted by Orozco y Berra, Geog., 41, 1864. **Jaguyapay.**—Escudero, Not. Estad. de Chihuahua, 228, 1834. **Jallaguapais.**—Garcés, op cit., 309. **Jaqualapai.**—Font, map (1777), in Bancroft, Ariz. and N. Mex., 393, 1889. **Jaquallapai.**—Garcés (1775–76), quoted by Bancroft, ibid., 394. **Matávĕkĕ-Páya.**—Corbusier, MS., B. A. E., 27, 1873–75 ('people to the north' [?]: Yavapai name). **Oohp.**—ten Kate, Reizen, 160, 1885 (Pima name). **Oop.**—Ibid. (alternative form). **Pá χuádo ámĕti.**—Gatschet in Zeitschr. f. Ethnol., 86, 1886 ('people far down river': Yavapai name). **Setá Kóχnináme.**—ten Kate, Synonymie, 7, 1884 (Hopi name). **Täbkĕpáya.**—Gatschet, Yuma-Sprachstamm, II, 124, 1877 (Yavapai name; abbr. from Matávĕkĕ páya). **Tiqui-Llapais.**—Domenech, Deserts N. A., I, 444, 1860. **Wálapai kwe.**—ten Kate, Synonymie, 7, 1884 (Zuñi name; kwe='people'). **Walapais.**—Bell in Jour Ethnol. Soc. Lond., I, 243, 1869. **Wal-la-pais.**—Powell in Scribner's Mag., 213, Dec. 1875. **Walyepai.**—Kroeber in Univ. Cal. Pub., IV, 107, 1907 (Chemehuevi name). **Xawályapáy.**—Harrington in Jour. Am. Folk-lore, XXI, 324, 1908 ('pine-tree folk': own name).

Walas (Wă′las, 'the great ones'). A gens of the Nakoaktok and of the Mamalelekala Kwakiutl tribes.—Boas in Rep. U. S. Nat. Mus. 1895, 329, 1897.

Walas Kwakiutl ('the great Kwakiutl'). A sept of the true Kwakiutl, comprising the Tsentsenkaio, Gyekem, Waulipoe, Tlekem, and Tletlkete gentes. Pop. 30 in 1889, the last time they were enumerated separately.
Lâ′kuilila.—Boas in Rep. U. S. Nat. Mus. 1895, 330, 1897 ('the tramps': a nickname). **Lock-qualillas.**—Lord, Natur. in Brit. Col., I, 165, 1866. **Wa′las Kwa-kiutl.**—Boas, op. cit., 330. **Wālis-kwāki-ool.**—Dawson in Trans. Roy. Soc. Can., sec. II, 65, 1887. **Waw-lis-knahkewlth.**—Can. Ind. Aff., 189, 1884. **Waw-lis-knahk-newith.**—Ibid., 1889, 270, 1890.

Walasnomoqois. An ancestor of a Kwakiutl gens whose name was sometimes given to the gens itself.—Boas in Petermanns Mitteil., pt. 5, 131, 1887.

Waleghaunwohan ('boil food with the paunch skin'). A band of the Brulé Teton Sioux.
Those that boil their dishes.—Culbertson in Smithson. Rep. 1850, 141, 1851. **Walega-oŋ-wohaŋ.**—Dorsey (after Cleveland) in 15th Rep. B. A. E., 219, 1897. **Walexa-oⁿ-wohaⁿ.**—Ibid.

Walekhe (Wă-lĕ-khe). The site of an old village probably occupied by San Luis Obispo Indians, on Santa Maria cr., San Luis Obispo co., Cal.—Schumacher in Smithson. Rep. 1874, 343, 1875.

Wallaneg. See Woolyneag.

Wallanmi. A Costanoan village formerly within 10 m. of Santa Cruz mission, Cal.—Taylor in Cal. Farmer, Apr. 5, 1860.

Wallawalla ('little river'). A Shahaptian tribe formerly living on lower Wallawalla r. and along the E. bank of the Columbia from Snake r. nearly to the Umatilla in Washington and Oregon. While a distinct dialect, their language is closely related to the Nez Percé. Their number was estimated by Lewis and Clark as 1,600 in 1805, but it is certain this figure included other bands now recognized as independent. By treaty of 1855 they were removed to the Umatilla res. in Oregon, where they are now (1910) said to number 461, but are much mixed with Nez Percés, Umatilla, and Cayuse. In the Wasco treaty of 1855, by which the Warm Springs res. was established, a number of Shahaptian tribes or bands are mentioned as divisions of the Wallawalla which had no real connection with that tribe.   (L. F.)
Oualla-Oualla.—Dufiot de Mofras, Oreg., II, 335, 1844. **Ouallas-Ouallas.**—Stuart in Nouv. Ann Voy., XII, 36, 1821. **Wahlahwahlah.**—Domenech, Deserts N. Am., II, 188, 1860. **Walawala.**—Gallatin in Trans. Am. Ethnol. Soc., II, 73, 1848. **Wal-a-Waltz.**—Gass, Jour., 203, 1807. **Wallah Wallah.**—Stevens in Ind. Aff. Rep., 426, 1852. **Wal-la-walla.**—Gass, Jour., 205, 1807. **Walla-Wallahs.**—Wyeth (1848) in Schoolcraft, Ind. Tribes, I, 221, 1851. **Walla-Walla-pum.**—Lord, Nat. in Brit. Col., 245,

WOMAN'S SHIRT—WALLAWALLA

1866. **Wal-la-waltz.**—Gass, Jour., 203, 1807. **Wallawollah.**—Cass (1834) quoted by Schoolcraft, Ind. Tribes, III, 609, 1853. **Wallewahos.**—Gallatin in Trans. Am. Antiq. Soc., II, map, 1836. **Wallow Wallow.**—Lewis and Clark Exped., Coues ed., 969, 1893. **Wollahwollah.**—Ind. Aff. Rep., 252, 1854. **Wollaolla.**—Morse, Rep. to Sec. War, 370, 1822. **Wollawalla.**—Ibid., 369. **Wollawollahs.**—Lewis and Clark Exped., II, 253, 1814. **Wollawwallah.**—Ibid., I, map, 1817. **Wol-law-wol-lah.**—Ibid., I, map, 1814.

Wallets. See Receptacles.

Wallie (from wallim, 'down below'). A name said to have been applied by Yosemite Indians to all tribes living below them, as on the Stanislaus and Tuolumne rs., Cal. Probably only the country, not its inhabitants, were actually so called. Most or all of them belonged to the Moquelumnan family.
Wallas.—Patrick in Ind. Aff. Rep. 1856, 240, 1857 (applied to Indians of Tuolumne co., Cal.). **Wal′-

li.—Powers in Cont. N. A. Ethnol., III, 349, 1877. **Wallies.**—Powers in Overland Mo., x, 325, 1874.

Walpapi. A Shoshonean division, belonging to the Mono-Paviotso branch of the family, closely affiliated with the Yahuskin, with whom they have been officially associated for nearly half a century. By treaty of Aug. 12, 1865, they ceded their territory about the shores of Goose, Silver, Warner, and Harney lakes, Oregon, and were assigned lands in the s. part of Klamath res., established the previous year. The Walpapi and the Yahuskin together have numbered 135 to 166 persons between 1877 and 1891. In 1906 the combined bands (officially designated as "Paiute") on the Klamath res. numbered 113; in 1909, 103. Two of their settlements or camping places are Chakeletsiwish and Kostuets, occupied also by Yahuskin. Their great war chief Pauline, also called Panaine, Paulihe, Pau-le-nee, and Pah-ni-nees, was killed in 1867.

Noll-pah-pe Snakes.—Applegate in Ind. Aff. Rep., 89, 1866. **Pauline's band.** — Huntington, ibid., 103, 1865. **Wall-Pah-Pe.**—U. S. Stat. at Large, xv, 218, 1869. **Walpahpe Snakes.**—Ind. Aff. Rep., 74, 1874. **Wal-pah-pee Snakes.**—Ibid., 62, 1872. **Walpalla.**—Ibid., 171, 1877. **Walpapi.**—Gatschet, Klamath Inds., II, xxxv, 1890. **Wohlpahpe Snakes.**—Ind. Aff. Rep., 110, 1874. **Woll-pah-pe.**—Huntington in Ind. Aff. Rep., 466, 1865.

Walpi (from *wala*, 'gap', 'notch'; *opi*, locative: 'Place of the notch,' in allusion to a gap in the mesa on which it is situated). One of the 6 villages of the Hopi (q. v.) in N. E. Arizona, situated on the summit of East mesa, at its s. end (for an illustration, see *Pueblos*). The ancestral clans which founded Walpi built their first village below the present site, on the N. W. side of the mesa point among the foot-hills on the lowest terrace; this site is now marked by a ruin called Kuchaptuvela, 'Ash-hill terrace'. About 1629 the village was moved to a higher terrace, on the W. point of the mesa, at a site covered with ruins known as Kisakobi (q. v.), 'Place of the ladder house,' where was built a mission chapel the remains of walls of which may still be traced. During a large part of the 17th century Spanish missionaries labored here, but with slight success, and in 1680, as a result of the Pueblo rebellion (see *Pueblos*), the mission was destroyed and the missionary killed, putting an end to efforts to Christianize the Hopi until after Arizona passed into possession of the United States. A short time after the destruction of the mission, impelled by fear of vengeance on the part of the Spaniards, as well as by the increasing attacks of Apache, Navaho, and Ute, the village was removed to the top of the rocky mesa where it now stands. Walpi has three rows of houses separated by courts. The middle or largest row is four stories high, long and narrow, and presents a broken sky-line. This row of buildings is the oldest, having been originally built by the Bear and Snake clans. The main plaza or court lies E. of this row, and communication with the rear court of the village is by means of an alley, roofed by buildings. There is a similar covered entrance at the s. end.

The secret ceremonies of the Hopi are performed in rooms called kivas and kihus, the former isolated from the house groups and used by fraternities of priests composed of different clans, while the kihus are generally limited in use to certain clans. The kivas are rectangular subterranean rooms oriented to the Hopi cardinal points, and are entered by ladders from the roofs. Each kiva has an elevated floor, for the use of spectators, at the N. end, a firehole in the middle of

KOPELI, NATIVE OF WALPI

the floor, and a symbolic opening, called the sipapu, in the floor. There are five kivas in Walpi, four of which are built in recesses and walled up on the outside; the fifth is constructed in a depression in the mesa. These are known as the Mungkiva ('Chief kiva'), Wikiwaliobikiva ('Watch-place kiva'), Alkiva ('Horn kiva'), Chivatokiva ('Goat kiva'), and Nacabkiva ('Half-way kiva'). The kihus are known as the Flute kihu, the Sun kihu, and the Warrior kihu. The western row of houses, separated by a court from the Bear-Snake row, was built by Flute and related clans; the short row on the eastern rim of the mesa, once populous, has now fallen into disuse. In early days it was occupied by the Asa clan, whose descendants now inhabit Sichomovi.

A mushroom-shaped rock, the result of subaerial erosion, stands in the open area on the s. E. side of the village, and near this rock the public portion of the Snake Dance (q. v.) and of other ceremonies is held.

The direct trails to Walpi are steep and in some places difficult. Many years ago part of the ascent was made at the s. E. side by a ladder drawn up at night. The N. E. trail into Walpi is the most accessible, having been greatly improved in recent years. The population of Walpi is mixed with Tewa and other progressive Pueblo peoples, and has been in closer contact with the whites than any other Hopi pueblo. The progressive character of the Walpi people is shown by the number of modern houses built in recent years at the foot of the mesa near the springs and fields.

The following groups of clans, among others, are represented at Walpi: Chua (Snake), Honau (Bear), Kachina (Sacred Dancer), Patki (Cloud), Pakab (Reed or Arrow), Kokop (Firewood), Asa (Tansy Mustard), Tuwa-Kukuch (Sand-Lizard), Lengya (Flute), Ala (Horn), and Piba-Tabo (Tobacco-Rabbit). The ancestors of these clans lived in pueblo or cliff houses, now ruins, situated in various directions and in some cases remote from Walpi. The original settlers were the Bear people, who are reputed to have come from Jemez (q. v.). These colonists were later joined by the Snake and Horn peoples, whose ancestors lived in extreme N. Arizona. The Kachina clan came from the E.; the Reed people are descendants of women captured at a Hopi town, now a ruin, called Awatobi. The Kokop clan came from Jemez, and made Walpi their home after the fall of their own pueblo, Sikyatki, in prehistoric times. The Patki, Kukuch, and Piba-Tabo originally came from the s., where ruins of their pueblos are still visible at Winslow and near Hardy, Ariz., on Little Colorado r. The Flute people came from N. Arizona, where they once lived with the Horn and Snake clans. The Asa migrated from Zuñi. The sociologic history and growth of Walpi are as follows: (1) Formed by Bear clans; (2) increased by the accession of Snake clans; (3) enlarged by clans after the overthrow of Sikyatki; (4) destruction of Awatobi and assimilation of many clans therefrom; (5) advent of Asa clans from Zuñi; (6) advent of clans from the Little Colorado; (7) advent of the Tewa clans, some of whose descendants now live in Hano.

The population now numbers about 200, but according to Vetancurt it had about 1,200 inhabitants in 1680. This estimate is evidently exaggerated.

Consult Bourke, Snake Dance of the Moquis, 1884; Donaldson, Moqui Indians of Arizona, 1893; Fewkes, various writings in Reps. B. A. E., Am. Anthr., and Jour. Am. Folk-lore; Hough, Moki Snake Dance, 1898; V. Mindeleff in 8th Rep. B. A. E., 1891; C. Mindeleff in 19th Rep. B. A. E., 1900, and the writings cited below.   (J. W. F.)

Alaki.—Fewkes in 19th Rep. B. A. E., 611, 1900 ('Horn house,' on account of the many Horn (Ala) people there: traditional name). Cuelpe.—Parke, map of N. Mex., 1851; Davis, El Gringo, 115, 1857. Et-tah-kín-nee.—Eaton in Schoolcraft, Ind. Tribes, IV, 220, 1854 (Navaho name). Gualpa.—Garcés (1776), Diary, 394, 1900. Gualpes.—Ibid., 360. Gualpi.—Porras (ca. 1630) quoted by Vetancurt, Menolog. Fran., 211, 212, 1871. Gualpimas.—Vetancurt (1693) in Téatro Mex., III, 322, 1871. Guelpee.—Taylor in Cal. Farmer, Apr. 10, 1863 (or Hualpee). Hoepeekee.—Eastman, map (1853) in Schoolcraft, Ind. Tribes, IV, 24–25, 1854. Horn Pueblo.—Fewkes in 19th Rep. B. A. E., 611, 1900 (or Alaki). Huallpi.—Alcedo, Dicc Geog., II, 379, 1787. Huál-pé.—ten Kate, Reizen in N. A., 242, 1885. Hualpee.—Beadle, Undeveloped West, 576, 1873. Hual-pee.—Ives, Colo. R., map, 1861. Hualpi.—Villa-Señor, Theatro Am., II, 425, 1748. Hualpy.—Loew in Pop. Sci. Mo., V, 352, July 1874. Hualvi.—Loew (1875) in Wheeler, Surv. Rep., VII, 345, 1879. Huatl-vi.—Loew in Ann. Rep. Wheeler Surv., 178, 1875. I-ya'-kin.—A. M. Stephen, inf'n, 1887 ('high house': Navaho name). Janogualpa.—Garcés (1776) quoted by Bancroft, Ariz. and N. Mex., 137, 395, 1889 (apparently a mistaken combination of Hano and Walpi). Jual-pi.—Palmer in Ind. Aff. Rep., 133, 1870. Mo'-qui.—Barber in Am. Nat., 730, Dec. 1877 (or Gual'-pi). Obiki.—Loew in Pop. Sci. Mo., V, 352, July 1874 ("erroneously called Hualpy"). O-pe'-ki.—Jackson cited by Barber in Am. Nat., 730, Dec. 1877 (or Gual'-pi). O-pi-ji-que.—Ward (1861) quoted by Donaldson, Moqui Pueblo Inds., 14, 1893. Opijiqui.—Taylor in Cal. Farmer, June 19, 1863. Opquive.—Schoolcraft, Ind. Tribes, I, 519, 1851. Opquivi.—Calhoun quoted by Donaldson, Moqui Pueblo Inds., 14, 1893. Quái-l-pi.—Donaldson, ibid. (misprint of Whipple's Guál-pi). S. Bernardino Gualpi.—Vargas (1692) quoted by Bancroft, Ariz. and N. Mex., 201, 1889. Talvoi.—Escudero, Not. Estad. de Chihuahua, 231, 1834 (probably identical). Wa-ci-pi.—Shipley in Ind. Aff. Rep., 310, 1891. Wall-a-pi.—Irvine in Ind. Aff. Rep., 160, 1877. Wál-pé.—ten Kate, Reizen in N. A., 454, 1885 (or Huál-pé). Walpi.—Common form. Walpians.—Fewkes in Am. Anthr., VII, 396, 1894 (the people). Washpi.—Hodge, field notes, B. A. E., 1895 (Acoma form). Wathl-pi-è.—Whipple in Pac. R. R. Rep., III, pt. 3, 13, 1856 (Zuñi name). Wolapi.—Shufeldt, Indian Types of Beauty, 10, 1891. Wol-pi.—Powell in Scribner's Mag., 202, Dec. 1875.

Wamdisapa's Band. One of the two divisions of the Wahpekute Sioux, of which Wamdisapa (Black Eagle) was chief between 1842 and 1851. Their predatory habits led to and prolonged a war with the Sauk and Foxes, in consequence of which they separated from the main body of Wahpekute before 1851, going to Vermilion r., S. Dak. Subsequently Inkpaduta (Scarlet Point) was chief of the band, which, after becoming reduced to 10 or 15 lodges, was known by his name. They returned to Spirit lake and Des Moines r., and, their lands having been ceded by the treaty of Mendota, Minn., in 1851, they came into conflict with the Government. Their right to a part of the purchase money being refused, they murdered the settlers and were hunted down by soldiers.

Black Eagle['s band].—Flandrau in Minn. Hist. Coll., III, 387, 1880. **Ink-pa-du-ta**['s band].—Ibid. **Ink-pah-doo-ta** band.—Hatch in H. R. Misc. Doc. 167, 44th Cong., 1st sess., 424, 1876. **Wam-di-sapa's** people.—Flandrau, op. cit.

Wamditanka ('Great war eagle'). A chief of one of the bands of Mdewakanton Sioux at the time of the Sioux uprising in 1862; commonly called Big Eagle, and sometimes known as Jerome Big Eagle. According to his personal narrative, recorded by R. L. Holcombe (Minn. Hist. Soc. Coll., VI, pt. 3, 382–400, 1894), he was born in 1827 at the Indian village near the site of Mendota, Dakota co., Minn., and on the death of his father, Gray Iron, succeeded him as chief. In his youth he often went with war parties against the Chippewa and other enemies of his tribe, and on occasion wore a head-dress with six feathers representing as many Chippewa scalps taken by him. Although Wamditanka took part with the Sioux in the uprising of 1862, he claims that he did not participate in the massacres of the settlers, but even used his influence, in some instances, to save from death both whites and converted mixed-bloods. The evidence shows this claim to be substantially correct, and that he was perhaps pressed into the war by his people. At this time his village was on Crow cr., in McLeod co., Minn. His band consisted of about 150 to 200 persons, including about 40 warriors. Soon after the battle of Birch Coolie, Minn., in 1862, Wamditanka and his band, with others, surrendered to Gen. Sibley. He was tried, convicted, and sentenced to three years imprisonment, part of the time at Davenport, Iowa, the remainder at Rock Island, Ill. After his discharge he was converted to Christianity. He was twice married; his second wife was still alive in 1894, at which time his home was at Granite Falls, Yellow Medicine co., Minn. He visited Washington with a delegation of his tribe in 1858, and was one of the signers of the treaty with the Sioux negotiated June 19 of that year.　　　　(C. T.)

Wamesit. An important tribe of the Pennacook confederacy, occupying the s. bank of Merrimac r. below the mouth of Concord r., Mass. In King Philip's war of 1675 they suffered severely and decreased so greatly that in 1686 they sold their territory and probably joined the other Pennacook at St Francis in Canada.
Pacotucketts.—Sanford, U. S., cxxxix, 1819. **Paw-tucketts.**—Farmer in N. H. Hist. Soc. Coll., I, 219, 1824. **Wambesitts.**—Kidder in Me. Hist. Soc. Coll., VI, 236, 1859.

Wamesit. The village of the Wamesit, situated near the present Lowell, Mass. It was the gathering place of the confederacy during the fishing season; hence the name. It was one of the Praying towns before the outbreak of King Philip's war in 1675.
Pautuket.—Eliot (1651) in Mass. Hist. Soc. Coll., 3d s., IV, 123, 1834 (from *pautuk*, 'falls'). **Pawtucket.**—Eliot (1651), ibid., 168. **Pawtukett.**—Gookin (*ca.* 1674) quoted by Vater, Mith., pt. 3, sec. 3, 377, 1816. **Wagmesset.**—Writer of 1676 quoted by Drake, Ind. Chron., 126, 1836. **Wamasit.**—Salisbury (1678) in N. Y. Doc. Col. Hist., XIII, 526, 1881. **Wameset.**—Record of 1676 in N. H. Hist. Soc. Coll., III, 99, 1832. **Wamesit.**—Gookin (1674) in Mass. Hist. Soc. Coll., 1st s., I, 163, 1806. **Wammeset.**—Hubbard (1680), ibid., 2d s., V, 32, 1815. **Wamesut.**—Tooker in Am. Anthr., X, 285, 1897. **Waymessick.**—Deed of 1686 in Mass. Hist. Soc. Coll., 1st s., VI, 278, 1800.

Wammikan. A raft of hewed logs, upon which is constructed a shanty, provided with cooking and sleeping arrangements. See *Wanigan*, of which the word is a corruption.　　　　(W. R. G.)

Wamnughaoin ('shell ear pendant'). A band of the Sihasapa or Blackfoot Sioux.
Wamnuga-oiŋ.—Dorsey in 15th Rep. B. A. E., 219, 1897. **Wamnuxa-oiⁿ.**—Ibid.

Wampampeag. See *Wampum*.

Wampanoag ('eastern people'). One of the principal tribes of New England. Their proper territory appears to have been the peninsula on the E. shore of Narragansett bay now included in Bristol co., R. I., and the adjacent parts in Bristol co., Mass. The Wampanoag chiefs ruled all the country extending E. from Narragansett bay and Pawtucket r. to the Atlantic coast, including the islands of Nantucket and Martha's Vineyard. Rhode Island in the bay was also at one time the property of this tribe, but was conquered from them by the Narraganset, who occupied the w. shore of the bay. On the N. their territory bordered that of the tribes of the Massachuset confederacy. The Nauset of Cape Cod and the Saconnet near Compton, R. I., although belonging to the group, seem to have been in a measure independent. Gosnold visited Martha's Vineyard in 1602 and "trafficked amicably with the natives." Other explorers, before the landing of the Pilgrims, visited the region and provoked the natives by ill treatment. Champlain found those of C. Cod unfriendly, probably on account of previous ill treatment, and had an encounter with them. When the English settled at Plymouth in 1620 the Wampanoag were said to have about 30 villages, and must have been much stronger before the great pestilence of 1617 nearly depopulated the southern New England coast. Their chief was Massasoit, who made a treaty of friendship with the colonists, which he faithfully observed until his death, when he was succeeded by his son, known to the English as King Philip. The bad treatment of the whites and their encroachment upon the lands of the Indians led this chief, then at the head of 500 warriors of his own tribe, to form a combination of all the Indians from Merrimac r. to the Thames for the purpose of driving out or exterminating the whites. The war, which began in 1675 and lasted 2 years, was the most destructive in the history of New England and was most disastrous to the Indians. Philip and the leading chiefs were killed, the Wampanoag and Narraganset were practically exterminated, and the survivors fled to the interior tribes. Many of those who surrendered were sold into slavery, and others joined the various Praying villages in s. Massachusetts. The greater part of the Wampanoag who remained in the country joined the Saconnet. The Indians of C. Cod and Martha's Vineyard generally remained faithful to the whites, the latter persistently refusing to comply with Philip's solicitations to join him in the contest.

The principal village of the Wampanoag, where the head chief resided, was Pokanoket. Other villages probably belonging to the tribe were Acushnet, Agawam, Assameekg, Assawompset, Assonet, Betty's Neck, Chaubaqueduck, Coaxet, Cohannet, Cooxissett, Cowsumpsit, Gayhead, Herring Pond, Jones River, Kitteaumut, Loquasquscit, Mattakeset, Mattapoiset, Miacomit, Munponset, Namasket, Nashamoiess, Nashanekammuck, Nukkehkummees, Nunnepoag, Ohkonkemme, Pachade, Pocasset, Quittaub, Saconnet, Saltwater Pond, Sanchecantacket, Seconchqut, Shawomet, Shimmoah, Talhanio, Toikiming, Wauchimoqut, Wawayontat. (J. M.)

Massasoits.—Dee in Smith (1629), Va., II, 229, repr. 1819. Massasowat. — Ibid. Massasoyts. — Mourt (1622) in Mass. Hist. Soc. Coll., 1st s., VIII, 226, 1802. Pawkunnawkutts.—Chase in Smithson. Rep. for 1883, 881, 1885. Philip's Indians.—Trumbull, Conn., I, 221, 1818. Wampangs.—Writer of 1676, quoted by Drake, Ind. Chron., 125, 1836. Wampano.—McKenney and Hall, Ind. Tribes, III, 80, 1854. Wampanoags.—Niles (ca. 1761) in Mass. Hist. Soc. Coll., 3d s., VI, 190, 1837. Wam-pa-no-gas.—Macauley, N. Y., II, 162, 1829. Wampanooucks.—Writer of 1675 in Mass. Hist. Soc. Coll., 3d s., I, 67, 1825. Wampeage. — Record (1653) quoted by Macauley, N. Y., II, 353, 1829. Wamponoags.—Writer of 1807 in Mass. Hist. Soc. Coll., 2d s., III, 83, 1815. Wapenocks.—Le Laet (1640) in N. Y. Hist. Soc. Coll., 2d s., I, 294, 1841. Whampinages.—Brinley (1658) in Mass. Hist. Soc. Coll., 1st s., V, 217, 1816. Wompanaoges.—Ibid., X, 15-20, 1809. Wompanoag.—Oliver (ca. 1675) quoted by Drake, Bk. Inds., bk. III, 35, 1848. Womponoags.—Hoyt, Antiq. Res., 112, 1824.

Wampapin. A name for the water chinquapin, *Nelumbo lutea*, corrupted from *wankipin*, 'crooked root,' the Chippewa name for the long, nodose rootstock of the plant, which after being boiled to destroy its acidity is used as food. It is called *tarawa* and *taluwa*, 'hollow root,' by the Oto and Quapaw. The name is still further corrupted in the West to *yankapin*. (W. R. G.)

Wampatuck ('goose'). A Massachuset chief of the country s. of Boston, Mass., a son of Chickataubut (q. v.), from whom the English purchased much land. He was killed in 1669 in a battle with the Mohawk. (A. F. C.)

Wampeag. See *Peag*, *Wampum*.

Wampee. A name used in parts of the Southern states for the pickerel-weed (*Pontederia caudata*). Gerard (Garden and Forest, July 26, 1896) says that the term *wampee* was applied by Drayton in 1802 to the Indian turnip (*Arisæma triphyllum*), and by Rafinesque in 1830 to *Peltandra alba*. (A. F. C.)

Wamping. A former village, Mohican or Wappinger, on the lower Hudson r., N. Y., under Iroquois protection.—Albany treaty (1664) in N. Y. Doc. Col. Hist., III, 68, 1853.

Wampoose. The American elk, *Cervus americana*, called also gray moose and wapiti; an animal about the size of a horse and strikingly similar to the stag of Europe. It was formerly extensively distributed throughout the present limits of the United States, but is now confined mostly to the N. and N. w. portions. The name is of Abnaki origin, from *wanbus* or *wanpus*, 'white moose'; the Algonquians making no distinction between white and gray. (W. R. G.)

Wampum (the contracted form of New England Algonquian *wampŭmpeak*, *wampŭmpeage*, or *wampŏmpeag*, expressed phonetically as *wanpanpiak* or *wanbanbiag*, the component lexical elements of which are *wamp*, for *wanb*, a derivative of *wab*, '(being) white'; *umpe* or *ompe*, for *anbi* or *anpi*, 'a string (of shell-beads)'; *ak* or *ag*, the grammatic sign of the animate plural. As the native expression was too cumbersome for ready utterance by the New England colonists, the sentence-word was divided by them into *wampum*, and *peak* or *peage*, regardless of the exact line of phonetic division between the component lexical elements of the expression). The shell beads in use among the North American Indians, wrought out of several kinds of shells found along both the western and the eastern littorals of the continent, including various species of Veneridæ, as the *poquaûhaug* (Venus mercenaria), usually contracted to *quahaug* or *quahog*, formerly sometimes called *hens*, the common round or hard-shell clam, which in the S. sometimes attains a weight of 4 pounds; the periwinkle (Pyrula carica and P. canaliculata), or winkle, the *meteaûhock* of Roger Williams; the whelk (Buccinum undatum); fresh-water shells of the genus Unio; and, on the Pacific coast, the Dentalium (D. entalis, and D. indianorum), the abalone or haliotis (H. rufescens, H. splendens, and H. cracherodii), the scallop shells or pectens, and the olivella (O.

biplicata); and a number of other sea-shells.

In the manufacture of these shell beads much patient labor and a marked degree of skill and careful manipulation were required. Their manufacture was apparently not confined to any class of persons among the natives, for Roger Williams (Key, 128, 1827) remarks that in general those who live along the seashore manufacture the beads, and that "as many make as will." In New England and along the Atlantic seaboard wampum was chiefly of two colors: the white, and the violet or purple, which latter varied in shade from pale or pink violet to dark rich purple. The value of these shell beads was determined by their color and degree of finish. In form they were cylindrical, being from about $\frac{1}{8}$ to $\frac{3}{16}$ in. in diameter, and from $\frac{1}{8}$ to $\frac{7}{16}$ in. in length. Notwithstanding the abundant literature concerning the multifarious uses of these shell beads in trade, in the embroidering of articles of dress, the making of objects for personal adornment and badges of rank and official dignity, and in the fiducial transactions of private and public life, no technical statement of the exact methods employed by the natives in their manufacture is available.

According to Barber and Howe (Hist. Coll. N. J., 1844) the method of manufacture after contact with the whites was as follows: The wampum was wrought, largely by the women,

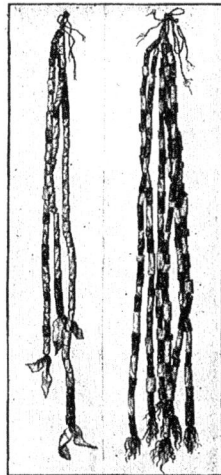

STRINGS OF WAMPUM

from the thick blue portions of the shell, and the process, though simple, required a skill acquired only by long practice. The intense hardness and brittleness of the materials made it impossible to wear, grind, and bore the shell by machinery alone. First the thin portions were removed with a light sharp hammer, and the remainder was clamped in a scissure sawed in a slender stick, and was then ground into an octagonal figure, an inch in length and half an inch in diameter. This piece being ready for boring was inserted into another piece of wood, sawed like the first stick, which was firmly fastened to a bench, a weight being so adjusted that it caused the scissure to grip the shell and to hold it securely. The drill was made from an untempered handsaw, ground into proper shape and tempered in the flame of a candle. Braced against a steel plate on the operator's chest and nicely adjusted to the center of the shell, the drill was rotated by means of the common hand-bow. To clean the aperture, the drill was dextrously withdrawn while in motion, and was cleared by the thumb and finger of the particles of shell. From a vessel hanging over the closely clamped shell drops of water fell on the drill to cool it, for particular care was exercised lest the shell break from the heat caused by friction. When the drilling reached halfway through the shell, the shell was reversed and the boring was completed from the opposite side. To finish the surface and to shape the edges were the next processes. A wire about a foot long was fastened at one end to a bench; beneath and parallel with the wire was a grindstone with a grooved face, which was worked by a foot-treadle. The beads were strung on the wire and the free end grasped in the left hand and the wire of beads was drawn into the groove of the fast-revolving grindstone. By means of a flat piece of wood, held in the right hand, the beads were continually turned. By this process the beads soon became round, smooth, and polished, and were then strung on hempen strings about a foot in length. Five to ten such strings could be made in a day, and were sold to country merchants at the rate of $12\frac{1}{2}$ cents apiece.

Wampum very early in the intercourse between the whites and the Indians, as it already was among themselves, became a medium of exchange at fixed values, not only in merchandise but also in dollars and cents. So important was this use of it that Weeden (Johns Hopkins Univ. Stud., 2d s., VIII–IX, 1884) wrote a monograph on wampum with the suggestive title, "Indian Money as a Factor in New England Civilization," in which this phase of the subject is fully discussed. Powers, Stearns, Goddard, and others mention facts showing that shell money at an early time on the Pacific coast became a medium of exchange, not only among the Indians but also among the whites. Goddard (Life and Culture of the Hupa, 48–49, 1903) says that a single shell of the decorated dentalium is measured and its value determined by the creases on the left hand; that strings of these shells reaching from the thumbnail to the point of the shoulder contain 11 of the largest and 14 of the smallest of these shells; that some of the natives have a set of lines tattooed on the inner side of the left forearm, which indicate the length of 5 shells of the several standards of length. Rosendale (Wampum Currency, 1896) shows by ample citations from the ordinances of New Netherland that the period from 1641 to 1662 "marked the decadence of wampum as currency." His article is valuable and interesting for giving the value of the different kinds and grades of wampum in stivers and guilders at the periods mentioned.

Williams (op. cit.), speaking of the *poquaûhock* or *quahaug*, called *hens* by the English, or the hard round clam, says that the Indians "break out of the shell about half an inch of a black part of it, of which they make their *suckaûhock*, or black money," and that they manufacture from the stem or stock of the *meteaûhock*, or periwinkle, their "wómpam or white money," of half the value of the *suckáwhock* or black money or shell beads. In his lexicon Williams gives the words *sawhóog* and *sawhósachick* as the native terms for 'loose beads,' *enomphósachick* as that for 'strung ones,' and *máchequoce* as 'a girdle, or belt,' curiously made from one to five or more inches in width of these shell beads. Such a belt, he tells us, was worth sometimes more than £10 sterling, and was worn either as a girdle or as a scarf or sash around the shoulders or breasts, hence the common name of belt for this article. Strings were also worn as ornaments around the necks of women and children. Williams quaintly adds: "Princes make rich caps and aprons (or small breeches) of these beads, thus curiously strung into many forms and figures: their black and white finely mixed together." As to their means of manufacture he says also that before the Indians obtained awl blades from Europeans they "made shift to bore this their shell money with stone," and that the work of smoothing the beads "they doe on stones" and other things.

Lawson (Hist. Car., 315–316, 1714) writes that the Indians of Carolina had two different kinds of shell money, called *peak* and *ronoak*, chiefly the former kind, which at New York went by the name of *wampum*, and was used as current money. He believed that *peak* was used on the continent "as far as the bay of Mexico." The *peak*, he says, was called "porcelan" by many writers, and was made in great quantities in New York and "with us in some measure." It was made from shells found on the coast, very large and hard, so that it was difficult to cut them; that

some English smiths attempted "to drill this sort of shell money" for profit, but found the task too hard, and saw that nothing could be gained, for the "drilling was the most difficult part of the work to the Englishmen, which the Indians manage with a nail stuck in a cane or reed, which was rolled by them on their thighs with the right hand and the bit of shell was held in the left, so in time they drill a hole quite through it, which is a tedious work; but especially in making their *ronoak*, four of which will scarce make one length of their wampum." He does not say how the drilling was done before the Indians had nails. For this shell money "skins, furs, slaves, and whatever the Indians possessed might be bought; by it they might be enticed to do anything—to part with anything except their children for slaves; by its means murders and other crimes were adjusted and settled." Beverley (Hist. Va., bk. III, 58, 1705) says that the Indians of the Virginia and Carolina littoral had *peak* and *roenoke;* that the *peak* was of two colors, dark purple and white; that they (presumably the purple and the white) were alike in size and figure, being made of different portions of the same shell (evidently the *poquaûhock*); they were polished as smooth as glass, and were strung through holes drilled through their centers; the purple or dark-colored beads were more valuable than the white, bringing among the Indian traders 18 pence per yard, while the white brought only 9 pence; and that these Indians made of these shell beads pipes (probably tubular objects), 2 or 3 in. long and "thicker than ordinary, which are much more valuable;" that they also made *runtees* of the same shell, grinding them smooth as the beads of the *peak*, "the strung beads," and that these *runtees* were either large like an oval bead, drilled through the length of the oval, or they were flat and circular, nearly an inch in width and ⅛ in. thick, and were drilled edgewise. The *peak*, the *runtees*, and the "pipes," he continues, were used for coronets, bracelets, belts, or else the shell beads were made into long strings to hang down before the breast, to lace up their garments, or to adorn their tomahawks

USE OF WAMPUM BELTS IN INDIAN COUNCIL. (AFTER LAFITAU)

and other weapons and implements; lastly, he adds, that these Indians made another kind of beads, of less value than the other, from the cockle shell, which was broken into small fragments, which were left with rough edges, and drilled through in the same manner as the other shell beads forming the *peak*; these rough-edged "beads" were called *roenoke* (the *ronoak* of Lawson), and they were used in the same manner as the *peak* or strung beads.

To the Iroquois and to many other Indians white as a color was auspicious, and its use in ritual and ceremony therefore indicated peace, health, welfare, and prosperity—ideas expressed by white wampum when ceremonially employed; on the contrary, black as a color was inauspicious, and its use therefore indicated hostility, sorrow, death, condolence, and mourning—ideas expressed by dark or purple wampum when ceremonially employed; nevertheless the dark or purple variety of wampum was commercially much more valuable than the white kind, and the darker its shade the more valuable it was. Commonly the ratio was as one to two. In commercial transactions wampum was used strung or unstrung. In trade it was usually exchanged by count when loose, by the string, or by the fathom. The fathom was a count. Williams (Key, chap. xiv) says that *piúckquat* was the native name for 10 sixpence, or 60 pence, and that this was called *nquittómpeg*, that is, 'one fathom,' 5 shillings. So a fathom was a count of beads, the number of which was determined by the number legally current for a penny. Williams said that 6 white and 3 black beads were current for a penny; therefore at this ratio 360 white and 180 black beads constituted a fathom. A large portion of the white shell beads was consumed in the manufacture of various articles of personal adornment and in the embroidery of various articles of raiment for both men and women. For use in public affairs and in official communications, in ritualistic and fiducial transactions, wampum was wrought into two well-known products—strings, often tied into bundles or sheaves of strings, and belts or scarfs or sashes. The first variety was made originally by stringing the wampum beads on small strands of skin or sinew, and later on a strong thread or on several threads twisted together; these strings of shell beads were called "branches" by French writers generally, probably including the bunches or sheaves. In making these strings of beads it was possible, by using all white, all purple, or by a combination of the two colors in definite proportions, regulated by the color symbolism of the people, to

convey mnemonically a variety or a difference of ideas, indicated by the proportion, the sequence of the two colors, and the figures or outlines portrayed by them on the strand or string; for example, there might be one white bead and then one purple bead alternately on the strand, or a white bead and then two purple beads alternately, or there might be two or more white beads followed by two or more purple beads alternately on the strand; or the strand might be composed one half of white and the other half of purple beads; or one half of the string of beads might be arranged in one way and the other half in another. Thus it was possible by these simple devices to indicate by means of the two available colors a number of combinations, differing one from another sufficiently to convey a number of ideas without much chance for confusion. The white strings tinged red by vermilion or some other red color were used as a challenge or declaration of war, or as an invitation to friends to join in a war. For these reasons some strings of beads consisted wholly of white beads, while others were composed entirely of purple or dark beads. A string composed entirely of dark beads is the official string

THE PENN TREATY BELT

of beads by which one of the Iroquois tribes notifies its brother and cousin tribes of the death of one or more of its chiefs. White strings were commonly employed in matters of ordinary routine, requiring only some degree of formality, or merely as preliminary exhibits to others of more and deeper import. The second kind of shell-bead product was the more or less broad sash, scarf, or belt, on which the white and the purple beads, first suitably proportioned on strings, were fastened together by small strands of sinew or skin in such manner as to form a neat and durable fabric. By suitable combinations of the two colors dominant in the beads various symbolic figures and devices were neatly and deftly wrought into the body of the belt or scarf. Sometimes the fabric took the form of a symbolic sun. But the breadth and length of the belt or sash, and the proportions of the white and the purple beads composing it, were naturally determined by the nature and importance of the occasion for its use. According to Lafitau (1724), a very good authority, the usual size of a belt in his time was 11 strands of 180 beads each, or about 1,980 wampum beads. There are references to belts composed of 6,000 and 7,000 beads, and proportionately long. Some belts were employed to convey a double message—that is, one half to one person and the other half to another, or two messages to one person or people.

The chiefs and the elders of the people were accustomed to assemble to rehearse the matters mnemonically connected with the several wampum strings, sheaves of strings, and belts in their keeping. In complex and important affairs, certain of these annalists were charged with remembering only a particular portion of the record, while to others were entrusted other portions, thereby rendering it the more easy to remember the details of the entire matter without forgetting any material circumstance. To aid these annalists and others they devised the complex and varied forms of wampum strands, sheaves, and belts already noted. Belts were used for various purposes, as the ratification of treaties, the confirmation of alliances, and the authentication of proposals made by one people to another.

In addition to packs of skins and furs, the public treasure of a people, such as the tribes of the Iroquois league, consisted largely of wampum, together with the strands, bunches, or sheaves of strings or strands, and the belts, scarfs, or sashes made from it, as above described. Not having the use of writing of any kind, the Indians, naturally apt to forget events and occurrences happening among them, devised the variety of uses for wampum and its products.

In addition to the descriptive names or merely denotive designations of wampum and the things made from it, a number of terms of political import were applied to these wampum strings and belts by the Iroquoian tribes, which indicate the importance attached to these several objects. By all these tribes the term *kană''să'*, 'a braid or plaited object,' was applied to strings of wampum of whatever nature. The Mohawk applied the term *găioñ'nï'* to the belt of wampum, while the Onondaga and the Seneca use *kăs'hwĕn''tă'*. Figuratively, and perhaps ceremonially, these people apply the following names to wampum employed officially and formally: *kari''hwă'* (*găi'-'hwă'*, dialectic variant), 'the business, the affair, or the authentic credential'; *gawĕñ'nă'*, 'the voice, the word, or the proposition,' because every proposal of a public nature, as an edict, required for its authentication a belt or a string of wampum according to its importance and to the exigency of the case; and *kăian-erĕn''seră'* (*găianĕñ''să'*, a dialectic variant), 'welfare,' 'the commonwealth,' 'justice,' here 'the law.' For wampum the Mohawk have the name *oneko'r'hă'*,

which by strict dialectic changes of sounds (*n*=*t*, and the dropping of *r*) becomes *otko''ä'*, which is the Onondaga and the Seneca name for it.

The Dutch about New York (Manhattan) applied the Algonquian term *sewan* (also written *sewant, sewared, zeewand,* etc.), 'scattered or loose (beads),' to all shell beads, in the same manner that the English called all *peage*, or strung beads, wampum, 'white.' The Dutch applied the name *Sewan hacky*, 'Wampum land,' to Long Island, perhaps in imitation of the natives, for it was noted for its abundance of shells suited to shell-bead making. In New England *mowhackees*, 'black beads,' was used.

As early as 1640, in New England and especially in New Netherland, there was much trouble and discontent owing to the manufacture of counterfeit and unfinished wampum. It was complained that payments were made in nothing but rough, unpolished stuff, while the good, polished beads, commonly called "Manhattan wampum," was exported, concealed, or at least not to be had at all. Many ordinances of the Director and Council of New Netherland were passed in more or less successful attempts to remedy this growing evil. The following citation from such an ordinance, passed May 30, 1650, shows to what an alarming extent wampum was counterfeited: "Whereas, we have by experience, and for a long time seen the decline and daily depreciation of the loose wampum among which are circulating many with holes and half finished; also some of stone, bone, glass, muscle-shells, horn, yea, even of wood and broken beads, together with the manifold complaints of the inhabitants that they cannot go to market with such wampum, nor obtain any commodities, not even a small loaf of white bread or pot of beer from the traders, bakers, or tapsters for loose wampum. . . . in order hereby to prevent the further importation of all lump and unperforated wampum, so as in future to obviate all misunderstanding, the Hon'ble Director and Council aforesaid, do ordain that the commercial shall pass and be good pay as heretofore, to wit, six white or three black for one stiver; on the contrary, poor strung wampum shall pass eight white and four black for one stiver [stiver=one penny]."

On the Pacific coast, according to Powers, Gibbs, and other writers, immense quantities of shell money or beads were in circulation, the value of which fluctuated greatly from tribe to tribe. Much of it was made from the so-called tusk-shell, a species of dentalium, which was obtained in the following manner: To the end of a suitable pole a strip of wood was secured, being placed transversely to the line of the pole, and first studded with bone or wooden teeth. From the bow of a canoe or boat, propelled usually by a woman, the tusk-shell fisher stood and carefully prodded the sands at the bottom of the water a number of times with his comblike instrument, and then drew it up to see whether any of the shells had become impaled on the teeth of the instrument. Sometimes four or five of the shells were brought up, and sometimes none at all. This was a practical method of obtaining these shells, as they are not found between tide marks. The form of this shell, which gave it its name of tusk-shell, is tooth- or fang-shaped, having an orifice at both ends. A fine specimen is about 3 in. in length, but usually they are much shorter. With the small end invariably downward, it is found burrowed in the sand in from 4 to 8 fathoms of water in sheltered harbors or inlets. The women string these shells neatly on bits of dried sinew; they are afterward ornamented with fragments of haliotis shell and with tufts of mountain-goat's wool. A string of 25 of these shells, which, placed end to end, reached one fathom or 6 ft, was called a *hiaqua* (q. v.) and was the standard of value. The short or broken shells were strung in like manner, and these inferior strings were called *kopkops*, of which 40 were equal in value to one *hiaqua*. Bands or belts were also made of dentalium shells, and these also served as currency and for ornament. But according to Gibbs "forty to the fathom" was the standard, or one *hiaqua*, which would purchase as a rule one male and two female slaves: this was approximately £50 sterling. According to Powers and others *álli-co-chick* was the name of this tusk-money in California. In the central and southern part of the state there was a staple currency known as *hawock*, or *hawok*, made from the shells of "a bivalve, a ponderous clam when adult." The shell was cut into small disks, of which the larger were worth about 25 cents and the smaller about 4 cents. Some of the disks, 2 in. in diameter and ½ in. in thickness, were worth a dollar apiece. Powers mentions a necklace of *hawok*, worn by a young woman, which was 10 yds long, consisting of 1,160 pieces, and was worth about $225. The olivella shell money was known as *kol-kol*, or *col-col*. The shell was prepared by simply grinding off the apex and stringing it mouth-to-mouth with others. This money, it is said, was "slightly esteemed," perhaps owing to the great abundance of the species. The abalone or haliotis shell money was known as *uhl-lo* or *ül-lo;* this was made from a very beautiful shell, rather too large and cum-

bersome to be used as money. The shell was prepared for use by cutting it into oblong strips from 1 in. to 2 in. long and about ⅓ in. in width. Holes were drilled near one end of the strip, and the strips were then strung edge to edge. Ten pieces constituted a string. The larger pieces were worth $1 apiece, thus making the value of a string about $10.

The literature pertaining to shell money and to shell objects is extensive. The more important writings on the subject are: Barber and Howe, Hist. Coll. N. J., 1844; Beach, Indian Miscel., 295, 1877; Beauchamp (1) in Am. Antiq., Mar. 1889; (2) in Bull. N. Y. State Mus., VIII, no. 41, 1901, with bibliog.; Beverley, Hist. Va., bk. III, 58, 1705; Boas, (1) in Rep. Brit. A. A. S., 36, 1889; (2) in Rep. on N. W. Tribes Can., 85, 1890; Bradford in Mass. Hist. Soc. Coll., 4th s., 3, 234–35, 335–36, 1856; Brinton, Myths of the New World, 1903; Burnaby, Travels in N. Am., 60, 1775; Bushnell in Jour. Anthr. Inst. Gt. Brit., XXXVI, 172, 1906; Cartier in Hakluyt, Voy., III, 272, 1600, repr. 1810; Carver, Travels, 235, 1796; Cox, Adventures, 332–33, 1831; Eells in Smithson. Rep. 1887, 647, 1889; Forsyth, Acct. Man. and Cust. of the Sauk, 3, 1826; Goddard in Univ. Cal. Pub., I, 49, 1903; Gookin (1674) in Mass. Hist. Soc. Coll., 1st s., I, 152, 1792; Hale in Am. Nat., XVIII, 1884; Holm (1646) in Mem. Hist. Soc. Pa., III, 1834; Holmes in 2d Rep. B. A. E., 179, 1883; Ingersoll in Am. Nat., XVII, no. 5, 1883; Jewitt, Narr., 76, 1815; Jones, Antiq. So. Ind., 1873; Josselyn, Acct. Two Voy. to New Eng., 1865; Kane, Wanderings in N. Am., 238, 1859; Lawson (1714), Hist. Car., 1860; Lord, Naturalist in Brit. Col., II, 22, 1866; Morgan, (1) League of the Iroq., 1904; (2) in Rep. N. Y. State Mus., 5, 71, 73, 1852; Norton in Am. Mag., Mar. 1888; Penn in Harvey, Hist. Shawnee Inds., 20, 1855; Powers in Cont. N. A. Ethnol., III, 1877; Pratt in Proc. Davenport Acad. Sci., II, 1876; Proud, Hist. Pa., I, 133–34, 1797–98; Ross, Adventures in Oregon, 95, 1849; Ruttenber, Ind. Tribes Hudson R., 26, 1872; Smith, Hist. N. Y., II, 42, 1829; Stearns, (1) in Rep. U. S. Nat. Mus., 1887, 297–334, 1889, with bibliography; (2) in Proc. Cal. Acad. Sci., July, 1873; (3) in Am. Nat., XI, 1877; Stites, Economics of the Iroq., 1905; Thompson, Hist. Long Island, I, 84–88, 1843; Timberlake, Memoir, 50, 62, 1765; Townshend, Quinnipiack Inds., 33, 1900; Trumbull, Hist. Conn., 52, 1818, repr. 1898; Van der Donck, Descrip. New Netherlands, 206, 1841; Weeden, Indian Money, 1884; Whipple, Pac. R. R. Rep., III, 115, 1856; Williams (1643), Key into Lang. of Amer., 1827 and 1866; Woodward, Wampum, 1878.　　(J. N. B. H.)

Wampum, The. See *Waumegesako.*

Wamsutta. Cotton cloth manufactured at the Wamsutta mills at New Bedford, Mass., named after a Massachuset sachem, the eldest son of Massasoit. The name is apparently a contraction of Womosutta, 'Loving-heart'. (W. R. G.)

Wanaghe (*Wanaxe*, 'ghost'). A division of the Kansa.—Dorsey in 15th Rep. B. A. E., 231, 1897.

Wanamakewajenenik ('people eating meat out of skin bags'—that is, 'pemmican-eaters'). A Chippewa band formerly living near Lake of the Woods, on the N. border of Minnesota.
Tecomimoni.—Chauvignerie (1736) quoted by Schoolcraft, Ind. Tribes, III, 556, 1853. **Wǎnǎ-mǎkė̇-wǎjěněnǐk.**—Long, Exped. St. Peter's R., II, 153, 1824. **Wanama'kēwǎjink.**—Wm. Jones, inf'n, 1905.

Wananish. See *Ouananiche.*

Wanashquompskqut. See *Squam.*

Wanatah. A Potawatomi village formerly in La Porte co., Ind., a short distance E. of the present Wanatah.—Hough, map in Indiana Geol. Rep. 1882, 1883.

Waneta ('The Charger'). A Yanktonai Sioux of the Pabaksa or Cuthead band, son of Shappa or Red Thunder; born on Elm r., in the present Brown co., S. Dak., about 1795. He enlisted with his father in the English service in the War of 1812, and fought valiantly at Ft Meigs and Sandusky, winning his name by his bravery in charging the Americans in the open, and being seriously wounded in the battle at the latter place. After the war he was given a captain's commission by the British, and visited England. He continued to sympathize with the British until 1820, when he attempted to destroy Ft Snelling by stealth, but being thwarted in his enterprise by Col. Snelling, he afterward heartily supported American interests. Waneta was a dominant chief of the Sioux and exceedingly active in his operations. He signed the treaty of trade and intercourse at Ft Pierre, July 5, 1825, and on Aug. 17 of the same year signed the treaty of Prairie du Chien which fixed the boundaries of the Sioux territory. He died in 1848 at the mouth of the War-reconne, the present Beaver cr., Emmons co., N. Dak. His name is variously spelled, as Wahnaataa, Wanotan, and Wawnahton. (D. R.)

Wanigan. A receptacle in which small supplies or a reserve stock of goods are kept; also a large chest in which the lumbermen of Maine and Minnesota keep their spare clothing, pipes, tobacco, etc. Called also *wongan*-box, and spelled *wangun* and *wangan*. (2) A boat used on the rivers of Maine for the transportation of the entire personnel of a logging camp, along with the tools of the camp and provisions for the trip. See *Wammikan.* (3) A place in a lumber camp where accounts are kept and the men paid.

"Running the *wangan*" is the act of taking a loaded boat down a river, from station to station, particularly in swiftly flowing water. The word is from Abnaki *waniigan*, 'trap'; literally, that into which any object strays, wanders, or gets lost; a receptacle for catching and holding stray objects; from *wan*, 'to wander', 'go astray', 'get lost', -*igan*, often used in Abnaki in the sense of 'trap'. Similarly, a locker in a hunting phaëton is called a 'trap', and this eventually gave its name to the vehicle itself. (W. R. G.)

Wanineath (*WaninEa'th*). A sept of the Seshart, a Nootka tribe.—Boas in 6th Rep. N. W. Tribes Can., 32, 1890.

Waninkikikarachada ('they call themselves after a bird'). A Winnebago gens.
Thunder.—Morgan, Anc. Soc., 157, 1877. **Wa-kon'-chä-rä.**—Ibid. **Wa-niñk' i-ki'-ka-ra'-tca-da.**—Dorsey in 15th Rep. B. A. E., 240, 1897.

Wankapin. See *Wampapin.*

Wanlish. A division of the true Kwakiutl, probably named mistakenly from its chief.—Lord, Nat. in Brit. Col., I, 165, 1866.

Wannalancet. A son of Passaconaway, who succeeded his father as sachem of Penacook on the Merrimac. He was a life-long friend of the English and signed the treaty of Dover. In 1659 Wannalancet was imprisoned for debt. (A. F. C.)

Wannawegha ('broken arrow'). A former band of the Miniconjou Sioux, possibly identical with the Wanneewack-ataonelar band of Lewis and Clark.
Wannawega.—Dorsey in 15th Rep. B. A. E., 220, 1897. **Waⁿ-nawexa.**—Ibid. **Wan-nee-wack-a-ta-o-ne-lar.**—Lewis and Clark Discov., 34, 1806.

Wannigan. See *Wanigan.*

Wanotan. See *Waneta.*

Wanupiapayum. A division of the Shoshonean Kawia (Cahuilla) formerly living about Banning and San Timoteo, Cal.
Akavat.—Kroeber in Univ. Cal. Pub., VIII, 35, 1908 (Serrano name of their country). **Wanupi-apayum.**—Ibid.

Waokuitem (*Waō'kuitEm*). A clan of the Wikeno, a Kwakiutl tribe.—Boas in Rep. Nat. Mus. 1895, 328, 1897.

Waoranec. A tribe of the Esopus which resided on the w. bank of the Hudson, near Esopus cr., in Ulster co., N. Y.
Murderer's kill Indians.—Dongan deed (1685) in Ruttenber, Tribes Hudson R., 93, 1872. **Waoran-ecks.**—De Laet (1633) quoted by Ruttenber, ibid., 72. **Waoraneky.**—De Laet, Nov. Orb., 72, 1633. **Warenecker.**—Wassenaar (1632) quoted by Ruttenber, op. cit., 71. **Warenocker.** — Ibid., 93. **Waroanekins.**—De Laet (1633) quoted in Jones, Ind. Bull., 6, 1867. **Warranoke.** — Addam (1653) quoted by Drake, Bk. Inds., bk. II, 79, 1848. **Wor-anecks.**—Map of 1614 in N. Y. Doc. Col. Hist., I, 1856.

Wapacut. A dictionary name for the great white owl, or snowy owl (*Nyctea scandiaca*): probably from one of the northern dialects of Algonquian, Wood Cree or Labrador, in which *wapacuthu* would correspond to the Cree *wâpaskisiw* and the

Chippewa *wâbakosi*, 'it is white,' from the radical *wâp* or *wâb*, 'white.' (A. F. C.)

Wapakoneta (*Wa-pa-ko-nĕ'-ta*, 'white jacket'). A Shawnee village, named from a chief, on Auglaize r., on the site of the present Wapakoneta, Auglaize co., Ohio. The Shawnee settled there by consent of the Miami, after losing their country on the Scioto by the treaty of Greenville in 1795. They occupied it as their principal village until 1831, when they sold their reservation and removed to the W. It was the residence of Logan. (J. M.)

Logan's village.—Drake, Bk. Inds., bk. v, 134, 1848. **Wapaghkanetta.** — Johnston quoted by Brown, W. Gaz., 287, 1817. **Wapaghkonetta.**—Johnston, ibid., 326. **Wapahkonetta.**—Sen. Doc. 137, 29th Cong., 1st sess., 1, 1846. **Wapakanotta.**—Drake, Tecumseh, 17, 1852. **Wapakonákunge.**—Gatschet inf'n, 1903 ('where Wapakoneta lived': Miami name). **Wapauckanata.**—Harrison (1814) quoted by Drake, Tecumseh, 159, 1852. **Wapaughkonetta.**—St Marys treaty (1817) in U. S. Ind. Treat., 1034, 1873. **Wapaughkonnetta.**—W. H Shawnee in Gulf States Hist. Mag., I, 415, 1903. **Wapoghoognata.**—Drake, Bk. Inds., bk. v, 134, 1848. **Wappaukenata.**—Brown, W. Gaz., 272, 1817. **Warpicanata.**—Woodward, Reminisc., 36, 1859. **Wauphauthawonaukee.**—McKenney and Hall, Ind. Tribes, III, 111, 1854.

Wapakwe (*Wä-pa-kwe'*) The Opossum gens of the Mahican.

Wapasha ('Red Leaf'). A succession of chiefs of the Mdewakanton Sioux, extending through tradition to a time immemorial. The first Wapasha of which there is historical knowledge was born at the head of Rum r., Minn., in 1718. His father was a chief of the same name, and his mother a Chippewa captive. In 1747, through relatives of his mother, he negotiated peace between the Chippewa and his own people. About 1763 an English trader, known to the Indians as Mallard Duck, was killed at his store at St Anthony's falls by a Sioux named Ixatape, in retaliation of which the English withdrew trade from the Sioux. By this time they had become so dependent on the traffic that destitution and suffering ensued, and Wapasha determined to take the murderer to Quebec and deliver him to the English. In company with a hundred of his tribesmen he started with Ixatape, but one by one the members of the party returned to the Mississippi, so that by the time Green Bay was reached but few remained, and there Ixatape escaped; but, undaunted, Wapasha with five others kept on, and, reaching Quebec, offered himself as a vicarious sacrifice for the sins of his people. His unselfish action made a deep impression upon the English, and he was afterward accorded much honor. He led the Sioux in a well-planned campaign in 1778 to drive back the Chippewa and recover the ancestral lands of the Sioux about Spirit lake, Minn., but after some notable victories his party fell into ambush at the mouth of Elk r. and many of his warriors were

slain. Two years later he was able to avenge this loss upon the Chippewa in a notable battle near Elk r. He served the English in the Revolution, and upon his visit to Mackinaw, Col. DePeyster, the commandant, dedicated to him a poem and made him the subject of a great ovation. He served in the West with Langlade, but his service was not of great importance. Before his death, which occurred about 1799, he established his band at the site of Winona, Minn., at a village called Kiyuksa (q. v.).

WAPASHA II succeeded his father and inherited the latter's mild temperament and benevolent disposition. He came into notice when he met Lieut. Z. M. Pike, in April, 1806, at Prairie du Chien, and advised the latter to make Little Crow the American chief of the Sioux. He conceived a liking for Americans which proved to be lasting. Although he was in nominal alliance with the English in the War of 1812, he was constantly under suspicion of disloyalty to them, and Rollette, his son-in-law, was court-martialed on the charge that he was in collusion with Wapasha against English interests. After the war he was very prominent in all the relations between the whites and the Sioux, and died about 1855.

WAPASHA III, known as Joseph Wapasha, succeeded his father as chief of the old Red Leaf band, and went with his people to the reservation on upper Minnesota r. He was opposed to the outbreak of 1862, but when it was forced by Little Crow he mildly assisted in it. After the war he was removed to the Missouri with his people and finally located at Santee, Nebr. He signed the treaty of 1868, which ended the Red Cloud war, and died Apr. 23, 1876.

WAPASHA IV (Napoleon), the son of Joseph, is (1909) nominal chief of the Santee at Santee agency, Nebr. He is civilized and a citizen. (D. R.)

Wapato. See *Wappatoo*.

Wapello ('chief'). Head chief of the Fox tribe, born at Prairie du Chien, Wis., in 1787. His village was on the E. side of the Mississippi, near the foot of Rock id., and not far from Black Hawk's village. In 1816 it was one of the three principal settlements in the vicinity of Ft Armstrong, Iowa, opposite the present Rock Island, Ill. Although stout and short of stature, Wapello was of attractive appearance, owing partly to his kindly expression; he was peaceful and intelligent, and entertained friendly regard for the whites. Like Keokuk, and unlike Black Hawk, he was willing to abide by the terms of the treaty of 1804 which provided for the removal of the Indians to the w. of the Mississippi, and in 1829 he quietly removed to Muscatine slough with his people, and later settled near the present Wapello, Louisa co., Iowa, in which state a county was afterward named in his honor. Wapello was next in rank to Keokuk, whom he accompanied with others to the E. in 1837, in charge of their agent, Gen. Joseph M. Street. While in Boston, and in reply to an address by Gov. Everett, Wapello made a speech expressing sentiments favorable to the whites, which was received with great applause. He died while on a hunting trip near the present Ottumwa, Iowa, Mar. 15, 1842. In accordance with his request he was buried near Gen. Street, to whom he had been deeply attached. A monument has been erected to his memory at Agency City, Iowa. Wapello was one of the signers of the following treaties between the United States and the Sauk and Foxes: Ft Armstrong, Sept. 3, 1822; Prairie du Chien, July 15, 1830; Ft Armstrong, Sept. 21, 1832; Dubuque co., Iowa, Sept. 28, 1836; Washington, Oct. 21, 1837. See Fulton, Red Men of Iowa, 1882; Stevens, Black Hawk War, 1903; McKenney and Hall, Ind. Tribes, 1854. (F. S. N.)

Wapeminskink (*Wah - pĭ - mĭns'- kĭnk*, 'chestnut-tree place'). A former Delaware town on the w. fork of White r., at the site of Anderson, Madison co., Ind. From being the residence of Anderson (*Kŏk-tō'-wha-nŭnd*, 'making a cracking noise'), the principal chief, about 1800–1818, it was commonly known as Anderson's Town. The land was sold in 1818. (J. P. D.)
Anderson's Town.—Hough, map, in Indiana Geol. Rep. 1882, 1883. Kik-the-swe-mud.—Hough, ibid. (=Koktowhanund, the chief). Wah-pi-mĭns'-kink.—Dunn, True Ind. Stories, 253, 1909. Wapeminskink.—Brinton, Lenape Leg., 124, 1885 (incorrectly identified with Wapicomekoke).

Wapicomekoke (*Wah-pi-ko-me-kunk*, 'White-river town', from *Wah-pi-ko-me'-kah*, 'white waters,' the Miami and old Delaware name of White r., Ind.). A former town of the Munsee branch of the Delawares, on the site of the present Muncie, Delaware co., Ind. It was the easternmost town of the Delawares in Indiana, and the first reached by the trails from the E., N., and s. It was formed by removal from an older town a short distance up the river, commonly known as Outainink (*Utenink*, 'at the place of the town'), or Old Town. It has been confounded with a neighboring Delaware village, Wapeminskink, better known as Anderson's Town. The land was sold in 1818. (J. P. D.)
Munsey Town.—Treaty of 1818 in U. S. Ind. Treat., 493, 1873. Wah-pi-ko-me-kunk.—J. P. Dunn, inf'n, 1907. Wapicomekoke.—Ibid. Woapikamikunk.—Brinton, Lenape Leg., 124, 1885.

Wapisiwisibiwininiwak ('Swan creek men,' from *wapisi*, 'swan'; *sibi*, 'river'; *ininiwak*, 'men'). A band of Chippewa that formerly resided on Swan cr., near L. St Clair, Mich. They sold the greater part of their lands in 1836 and part of them removed to Kansas, where they were joined by the rest in 1864. Their descendants now form part of the mixed band of "Munsee and Chippewa" in Kansas, numbering together about 90 individuals. (J. M.)
Swan-Creek band.—Washington treaty (1836) in U. S. Ind. Treat., 227, 1873. Wâbisíbiwininiwag.—Wm. Jones, inf'n, 1905 (correct name). Wapisiwi-sibi-wininiwak.—Gatschet, Ojibwa MS., B. A. E., 1882.

Wapiti (*wapĭtĭ*, 'white rump'). The Shawnee name of *Cervus canadensis*, the American elk, called also gray moose, the *mos* or *mus* of the Lenape, the *maⁿrus* of the Kenebec, the *waⁿboz* of the Penobscot, the *mishewe* of the Chippewa, the *shewea* of the Miami, the *makyase* of the Pequot, etc.; a deer about the size of the horse and so strikingly similar in appearance to the stag of Europe that it was supposed by the early settlers to be the same species and was called by the same name. Its horns, which are round and not flat, like those of the moose and caribou, are 5 to 6 ft long and much branched, and its color in summer is light chestnut-red with white rump, in winter grayish, and to the latter fact the Penobscot name (meaning 'white moose') alludes. The animal was formerly extensively distributed throughout the present limits of the United States, but is now confined mostly to the N. and N. w. portions. In Minnesota it is found in large herds, and, on the upper Missouri, Yellowstone, and other streams, in still larger ones. Of the vast numbers in these regions, some idea may be formed from the piles of shed horns which the Indians were in the habit of heaping up in the prairies. One of these, in Elkhorn prairie, was, before its destruction in 1850, about 15 ft high, and was for many years a conspicuous landmark. Others, still larger, are found on the upper Yellowstone. (W. R. G.)

Wapon. The extinct White Shell-bead clan of Sia pueblo, New Mexico.
Wa'pon.—Stevenson in 11th Rep. B. A. E., 19, 1894. Wápon-háno.=Hodge in Am. Anthr., IX, 352, 1896 (*hano*='people').

Wapoo. A small tribe of the Cusabo group, formerly living on Wapoo cr. and the immediately adjacent coast of South Carolina. They have long been extinct. Bartram (Trav., 54, 1792) mentions them among the tribes in the vicinity of Charleston, which he says "cramped the English plantations." Nothing further has been recorded in regard to them. The tribe is designated on De l'Isle's map (Winsor, Hist. Am., II, 1886), about the year 1700, under the name Ouapamo, as situated on Wingau r., S. C.

Wappatoo. A bulbous root (*Sagittaria variabilis*) used for food by the Indians of the W. and N. W.: from the Cree *wâpatow* or the Chippewa *wâpato* or *wâbado*, 'white fungus.' This word, spelled also *wapato*, has passed into the Chinook jargon of the Columbia r. region, in which *wappatoo* means 'potato,' but its origin is very uncertain. The Chippewa name *wâpato* has been applied to some plant called rhubarb. As a place name it occurs in *Wapatoo*, an island off the coast of Washington, and in *Wapato*, a village in Washington co., Oreg.　　　　　　(A. F. C.　W. R. G.)

Wappatoo. The tribes on and around Sauvies id. at the mouth of Willamette r., Oreg. Under this name Lewis and Clark (Exped., II, 472–473, 1814) included Nechacokee (Nechacoke), Shoto, Multnomah, Clannahqueh (Clahnaquah), Nemalquinner, Cathlacommatups (Cathlacomatup), Cathlanaquiahs, Clackstar (Tlatskanai), Claninnatas, Cathlacumups, Clannarminnamuns (Kathlaminimim), Quathlahpohtle (Cathlapotle), Cathlamahs (Cathlamet). The name (Wapato Lake) is now officially used to designate a small remnant of 4 Indians on Grande Ronde res., Oreg., probably the survivors of those mentioned by Lewis and Clark.　　　　　　(L. F.)

Wappinger ('easterners,' from the same root as *Abnaki*, q. v.). A confederacy of Algonquian tribes, formerly occupying the E. bank of Hudson r. from Poughkeepsie to Manhattan id. and the country extending E. beyond Connecticut r., Conn. They were closely related to the Mahican on the N. and the Delawares on the S. According to Ruttenber their totem was the wolf. They were divided into 9 tribes: Wappinger proper, Manhattan, Wecquaesgeek, Sintsink, Kitchawank, Tankiteke, Nochpeem, Siwanoy, and Mattabesec. Some of these were again divided into subtribes. The eastern bands never came into collision with the Connecticut settlers. Gradually selling their lands as they dwindled away before the whites, they finally joined the Indians at Scaticook and Stockbridge; a few of them also emigrated to Canada. The western bands became involved in war with the Dutch in 1640, which lasted five years, and is said to have cost the lives of 1,600 Indians, of whom the Wappinger proper were the principal sufferers. Notwithstanding this, they kept up their regular succession of chiefs and continued to occupy a tract along the shore in Westchester co., N. Y., until 1756, when most of those then remaining, together with some Mahican from the same region, joined the Nanticoke, then living under Iroquois protection at Chenango, near the present Binghamton, N. Y., and, with them, were finally merged into the Dela-

wares. Their last public appearance was at the Easton conference in 1758. Some of them also joined the Moravian and Stockbridge Indians, while a few were still in Dutchess co. in 1774.

They had the following villages: Alipconk, Canopus, Cupheag, Keskistkonk, Kestaubuinck, Kitchawank, Mattabesec, Menunkatuc, Nappeckamak, Naugatuck, Nipinichsen, Nochpeem, Ossingsing, Pasquasheck, Paugusset, Pauquaunuch, Pomperaug, Poningo, Poodatook, Poquannoc, Pyquaug, Quinnipiac, Rechtauck. Roatan, Sackhoes, Sapohanikan, Senasqua, Tunxis, Turkey Hill, Uncowa, Wecquaesgeek, Wongunk, Woronock.　　　(J. M.)

Abingas.—Schoolcraft in N. Y. Hist. Soc. Proc., 101, 1844. **Apineus.**—McKenney and Hall, Ind. Tribes, III, 81, 1854 (probably the Wappinger). **Wabigna.**—Am. Pioneer, II, 192, 1843 (misprint). **Wabinga.**—Schermerhorn (1812) in Mass. Hist. Soc. Coll., 2d s., II, 6, 1814. **Wabingies.**—Boudinot, Star in the West, 129, 1816. **Wam-pa-nos.**—Macauley, N. Y., II, 174, 1829. **Wamponas.**—Doc. of 1755 quoted by Rupp, Northampton Co., 88, 1845. **Wapanoos.**—Map of 1616 in N. Y. Doc. Col. Hist., I, 1856. **Wapingeis.**—McKenney and Hall, Ind. Tribes, III, 80, 1854. **Wapinger.**—Doc. of 1766 in N. Y. Doc. Col. Hist., VII, 868, 1856. **Wapingoes.**—Lovelace (1668), ibid., XIII, 420, 1881. **Wapings.**—Boudinot, Star in the West, 129, 1816. **Wappanoos.**—Van der Donck (1656) quoted by Ruttenber, Tribes Hudson R., 51, 1872. **Wappenger.**—Courtland (1688) in N. Y. Doc. Col. Hist., III, 562, 1853. **Wappenos.**—De Rasières (1626) quoted by Ruttenber, Tribes Hudson R., 51, 1872. **Wappinges.**—Winfield, Hudson Co., 8, 1874. **Wappinx.**—Treaty (1645) quoted by Winfield, ibid., 45.

Wappinger. The leading tribe of the Wappinger confederacy, occupying the territory about Poughkeepsie, in Dutchess co., N. Y.

Highland Indians.—Lovelace (1669) in N. Y. Doc. Col. Hist., XIII, 440, 1881. **Indians of the Long Reach.**—Doc. of 1690 quoted by Ruttenber, Tribes Hudson R., 178, 1872. **Wappinck.**—Treaty of 1644 in N. Y. Doc. Col. Hist., XIII, 17, 1881. **Wappinex.**—Treaty of 1645 quoted by Ruttenber, Tribes Hudson R., 118, 1872. **Wappingers.**—Writer of 1643 in N. Y. Doc. Col. Hist., I, 185, 1856. **Wappingh.**—Doc. of 1663, ibid., XIII, 282, 1881. **Wappingos.**—Lovelace (1669), ibid., 427. **Wappings.**—Doc. of 1650, ibid., XIII, 27, 1881. **Wappinoes.**—Nimham (1730) quoted by Ruttenber, Tribes Hudson R., 51, 1872. **Wappinoo.**—Van der Donck (1656) quoted by Ruttenber, ibid., 77. **Wequehachke.**—Loskiel (1794) quoted by Ruttenber, ibid., 369 (Loskiel gives it as the Indian name of the Highlands, meaning 'the hill country'; Ruttenber says it may have been the real name of the Wappinger proper).

Wappo (from Span. *guapo*, 'brave'). A small detached portion of the Yukian family of N. California, separated from the Huchnom, the nearest Yuki division, by 30 or 40 m. of Pomo territory. They lived chiefly in the mountains separating Sonoma from Lake and Napa cos., between Geysers and Calistoga. A portion of them, called Rincons by Powers, occupied Russian River valley in the vicinity of Healdsburg.

Ashochemies.—Powers in Overland Mo., XIII, 542, 1874. **Ash-o-chi-mi.**—Powers in Cont. N. A. Ethnol., III, 196, 1877. **Guapos.**—Bancroft, Hist. Cal., IV, 71, 1886. **Satiyomes.**—Ibid., III, 360, 1886. **Satiyomis.**—Ibid., IV, 71, 1886. **Seteomellos.**—Taylor in Cal. Farmer, Mar. 30, 1860. **Soteomellos.**—Taylor misquoted by Bancroft, Nat. Races, I, 448, 1874. **Sotomieyos.**—Taylor in Cal. Farmer, Mar. 30, 1860. **Sotoyomes.**—Bancroft, Hist. Cal., IV, 72, 1886. **Wapo.**—Ind. Aff. Rep. 1856, 257, 1857. **Wappo.**—Powers in Cont. N. A. Ethnol., III, 196, 1877 (given as Spanish name). **Wattos.**—Stearns in Am. Nat., VI, 206, 1882.

Waptailmin ('people of the narrow river'). The principal band of the Yakima (q. v.), formerly living on Yakima r. just below Union Gap, near the present town of North Yakima, Wash.

Wapumne. A former Nishinam settlement near Michigan bar, on the middle fork of American r., Cal. (R. B. D.)
Wajuomne.—Bancroft, Nat. Races, I, 450, 1874. **Wapoomney.**—Ibid. **Wapumney.**—Sutter (1862) quoted by Powers in Cont. N. A. Ethnol., III, 323, 1877. **Wapümnies.**—Powers in Overland Mo., XII, 22, 1874.

Waputyutsiama (Keres: 'little doorway leading west'). A former summer village of the Laguna Indians of New Mexico, now a permanently occupied pueblo of that tribe; situated 6 m. w. of Laguna.
Puertecito.—Pradt quoted by Hodge in Am. Anthr., IV, 346, 1891 (Span.: 'little door'). **Wapu-chu-se-amma.**—Ibid. **Waputyutsiáma.**—Hodge, field-notes, B. A. E., 1895.

Waquithi (*Wa'-qui-thi*, 'bad faces'). A band of the Arapaho (q. v.).

Waquoit. A village of Praying Indians in 1674 about the site of the present Waquoit, Barnstable co., Mass. It was probably subject to either the Wampanoag or the Nauset.
Wakoquet.—Bourne (1674) in Mass. Hist. Soc. Coll., 1st s., I, 197, 1806. **Wawquoit.**—Freeman (1792), ibid., 230. **Weequakut.**—Bourne (1674), ibid., 197.

Waradika. A band of the Bannock.
Rye-Grass-Seed-Eaters.—Hoffman in Proc. Am. Philos. Soc., XXIII, 299, 1886. **Wara'dika.**—Ibid. **Warraricas**—Lander in Sen. Ex. Doc. 42, 36th Cong., 1st sess., 138, 1860 (trans. 'sunflower seed eaters').

Waranawonkong. An important tribe of the Munsee, formerly living on the w. bank of Hudson r., in the country watered by Esopus, Wallkill, and Shawangunk crs., mainly in Ulster co., N. Y. Their principal village was on the Shawangunk, and they had another one, probably of the same name as the tribe, on Esopus cr. They were the leading tribe of the Esopus Indians, but were nearly exterminated by the Dutch in the war of 1663, though they still had a chief in 1684. (J. M.)
Waerinnewangh.—Doc. of 1655 in N. Y. Doc. Col. Hist., XIII, 47, 1881. **Waranancongyns.**—Gallatin in Trans. Am. Antiq. Soc., II, 34, 1836. **Waranawancougy.**—De Laet, Nov. Orb., 72, 1633. **Warana-wankongs.**—Schoolcraft, Ind. Tribes, III, 75, 1853. **Waranowankings.**—Schoolcraft in N. Y. Hist. Soc. Proc., 108, 1844. **Waranwankongs.**—Van der Donck (1656) quoted by Ruttenber, Tribes Hudson R., 72, 1872. **Waronawanka.**—Map of 1614 in N. Y. Doc. Col. Hist., I, 1856. **Warrana-wankongs.**—De Laet (1633) quoted by Ruttenber, op. cit. **Warranawonkongs.**—De Laet (1633), ibid., 95. **Warrawannankonoks.**—Wassenaar (1632), ibid., 71. **Warynawoncks.**—Doc. (ca. 1663) in N. Y. Doc. Col. Hist., XIII, 259, 1881.

War and War discipline. The Indians recognized two kinds of warfare, to which they gave distinctive names: defensive warfare, or fighting for the protection of women and children, the home and the village, and aggressive war, or the going forth of expeditions to avenge injuries or to take spoils. The aim of warfare was to destroy, and as every person, old or young, was a part of the present or future strength of the enemy, neither age nor sex was spared and no noncombatants were recognized. Mutilation of the dead was neither universal nor constant among the tribes, but the cutting off of the head or taking of the scalp was generally practised. The fundamental reason for scalping (q. v.) has not yet been fully explained, but there is evidence to indicate that it was connected with the rites observed when a boy was recognized as a member of the band and his life was dedicated to the God of War. The ordinary physical training of young men fitted them to endure the discipline and hardships of war. From the time he determined to join a war party the man was obliged to abstain from all personal indulgence, and to accept whatever duty might be prescribed by the leader until the disbanding of the party on its return home.

There were grades and ranks among warriors, each having its peculiar insignia. All rank was gained by personal achievement, but before a man could count his war honors, wear their appropriate insignia, or assume the grade or rank to which they entitled him, he had to be given the right to do so publicly and generally in connection with more or less elaborate religious ceremonies, conducted by societies or by tribal officials. Among some tribes honors won in defensive warfare ranked higher than those gained in aggressive ventures. As war honors were public tokens of a man's courage and ability, they were regarded as his credentials; therefore when a man was called to any position or service, either social or tribal, custom required that before he entered on his duties he should give his public record by counting his honors in order to show his fitness to receive the distinction offered him. Among some tribes, at the telling of each honor a blow was struck on a post or some other object, and this form of recital has become known by the composite term "counting coup" (see *Coup*).

The treatment of captives (q. v.) varied among the different tribes. Adoption (q. v.) was common to nearly all, particularly in the disposal of women and children. Although the life of a captive was generally regarded as forfeit, yet among many tribes there were ways by which either a captive could save his own life or it could be saved by members of the tribe.

Among some tribes there was a particular village or clan that had the right to shelter or protect a fugitive; among others the chief's tent afforded asylum, or if food was offered and taken the captive was spared; others subjected captives to ordeals (q. v.) which if the captive survived he was saved. In most cases the survivors were finally adopted by their captors. Exchange of captives between tribes was of rare occurrence. Some tribes had a war chief whose duties pertained exclusively to war. When an attack, either offensive or defensive, was made which involved the entire tribe, the war chief led the warriors. War parties, however, were composed wholly of volunteers, and were organized solely for aggressive warfare. They varied in size from half a dozen men to a hundred or more. Large parties which intended going a considerable distance from home were attended by hunters, whose duty it was to keep the warriors supplied with game. Occasionally a few women were of the party: they were not under orders, but acted as servers, and when the spoils were divided they were given a share. The initiation and organization of a war party for offensive warfare differed among the tribes, as did the religious rites which preceded its departure. Among the Pueblos these rites were in charge of a war priesthood; in all tribes the rites were more or less directly under the men to whom were confided the keeping of rituals and the direction of ceremonies related to war. In general, a man had to prepare for the office of leader by fasting and continence, and as upon him rested the responsibility of the failure or success of the party, he must be careful to observe all the rites by which he could personally appeal to the supernatural. He assigned the men to their various duties, and to him each man had to render implicit obedience: any refusal to carry out the orders of the leader was punished by flogging. He appointed two lieutenants, or "little leaders," who, in case of his death, should act in his place. Frequently, however, a war party had two leaders, equal in authority. In battle the warriors were not required to keep close together except when making a charge, but while each man fought more or less independently, friend stood by friend to death, and only under great stress was the body of a companion left to the knife of the victor. Frequently the severest fighting took place about the body of a fallen comrade. The leader exercised no control over the men in regard to taking honors, such as touching, striking, or scalping an enemy: each man was free to take all the honors he could, but only the leader had the right to divide

the spoils, and no one could question his apportionment. Not infrequently a war party carried some article sacred to the band, and rites connected with it had to be observed. In such cases the responsibility of the outcome of the expedition was believed to rest with this emblem. The warrior societies of several of the Plains tribes possessed a particular object similar in use to the ceremonial lance of the Kiowa. This was attached by an elk-skin sash to the neck of the leader, who under certain circumstances took his place in front of his line of warriors, and thrusting the lance into the ground through a hole in the end of the sash, there fought or awaited death: he could not retreat unless one of his own party should pull up the lance to which he was in honor fixed (Mooney). Dreams (q. v.) sometimes influenced the acts of a war party. Instances have been known where, because of a dream, the entire party has disbanded and returned home. There were grades or ranks among warriors, each having its peculiar insignia, and all rank was gained by personal achievement. In defensive warfare the warriors sprang to the alarm and aimed to engage the enemy beyond the limits of the village, while the women hastily threw up breastworks or dug pits in which to thrust the children out of reach of flying arrows. Women fought only at close range, using their knives or any available objects as weapons; but in rare cases women went to war and fought on equal terms with the men of the party. Prisoners, particularly if women or children, were frequently adopted, otherwise they were killed. The club, knife, spear, javelin, and bow and arrows were the Indian's principal weapons; the throwing-stick had only a limited range. Poisoned arrows are reported as having been used by a number of the tribes, and while the poison itself was sometimes effective, the main reliance was on the theurgical potency of the substances used.

Consult Chamberlain in Jour. Am. Folk-lore, xx, 1–16, 1907; Matthews, Hidatsa, 1877; Curtis, N. Am. Ind., i–v, 1907–1909; Dorsey in 3d and 15th Reps. B. A. E.; Mooney, Winship, and Hoffman in 14th Rep.; Mooney in 17th Rep.; Mindeleff in 19th Rep.; Murdoch in 9th Rep.; Powell in 1st Rep.; McGee in Am. Anthr., xi, 1898; Dixon in Bull. Am. Mus. Nat. Hist., xvii, pt. 3, 1905; Grinnell, (1) Pawnee Hero Stories, 1889; (2) Blackfoot Lodge Tales, 1892; (3) in Am. Anthr., xii, no. 2, 1910; Holm, Descr. New Sweden, 1834; Sapir in Am. Anthr., ix, no. 2, 1907. See also *Captives, Coup, Fortifications, Military societies, Ordeals, Scalping, Slavery.*   (A. C. F.)

Waranoke. An Algonquian band or village about the site of Westfield, Hampden co., Mass.

Waranoco.—Trumbull, Ind. Names Conn., 91, 1881. **Waranoke.**—Trumbull, Conn., I, 159, 1818. **Warronco.**—Barber, Hist. Coll., 299, 1839. **Warronooke.**—Trumbull, Ind. Names Conn., op. cit.

Warartika (*War-ar′-ti-ka*). A Paviotso tribe formerly about Honey lake, N. E. Cal.—Powell, Paviotso MS., B. A. E., 1881.

Warchinktarhe. An unidentified band of the Brulé Teton Sioux.—Lewis and Clark, Discov., 341, 1806.

Ward, Nancy. A noted Cherokee half-breed woman, the date and place of whose birth and death are alike unknown. It is said that her father was a British officer named Ward and her mother a sister of Atakullakulla, principal chief of the Nation at the time of the first Cherokee war. She was probably related to Brian Ward, an oldtime trader among the Cherokee. During the Revolutionary period she resided at Echota, the national capital, where she held the office of "Beloved Woman," or "Pretty Woman," by virtue of which she was entitled to speak in councils and to decide the fate of captives. She distinguished herself by her constant friendship for the Americans, always using her best effort to bring about peace between them and her own people, and frequently giving timely warning of projected Indian raids, notably on the occasion of the great invasion of the Watauga and Holston settlements in 1776. A Mrs Bean, captured during this incursion, was saved by her interposition after having been condemned to death and already bound to the stake. In 1780, on occasion of another Cherokee outbreak, she assisted a number of traders to escape, and the next year was sent by the chiefs to make peace with Sevier and Campbell, who were advancing against the Cherokee towns. Campbell speaks of her in his report as "the famous Indian woman, Nancy Ward." Although peace was not then granted, her relatives, when brought in later with other prisoners, were treated with the consideration due in return for her good offices. She is described by Robertson, who visited her about this time, as "queenly and commanding" in appearance and manner, and her house as furnished in accordance with her high dignity. When among the Arkansas Cherokee in 1819, Nuttall was told that she had introduced the first cows into the Nation, and that by her own and her children's influence the condition of the Cherokee had been greatly elevated. He was told also that her advice and counsel bordered on the supreme, and that her interference was allowed to be decisive even in affairs of life and death. Although he speaks in the present tense,

it is hardly probable that she was then still alive, and he does not claim to have met her. Her descendants are still found in the Nation. Consult Haywood, Nat. and Aborig. Hist. Tenn., 1823; Ramsey, Tenn., 1853; Nuttall, Trav., 130, 1821; Campbell letter, 1781, and Springstone deposition, 1781, in Virginia State Papers, I, 435, 436, 447, 1875; Appleton's Cyclop. Am. Biog.; Mooney in 19th Rep. B. A. E., pt. 1, 1900.   (J. M.)

Warm Spring Apache. So called from their former residence at the Ojo Caliente, or Warm Spring, in s. w. N. Mex., near the extreme headwaters of Gila r. They were evidently Chiricahua Apache in the main, and were probably the Apaches de Xila (Gileños) of Benavides in 1630. Victorio and Nana were among their noteworthy leaders in recent times. Some of them are on the Mescalero res., N. Mex.

Hot Spring Apaches.—Bancroft, Ariz. and N. Mex., 563, 1889. **Oji Caliente.**—Bell in Jour. Ethnol. Soc. Lond., I, 262, 1869. **Ojo Caliente Apaches.**—Common name. **Warm Spring Indians.**—U. S. Stat. at Large, XVII, 438, 1878. **Warm Springs.**—Hinton, Handbook of Arizona, 359, 1878.

Warm Springs Indians. A term used to denote the different tribes resident on Warm Springs res., Oreg., most of whom were placed there under the Wasco treaty of 1855. The chief tribes of the reservation are Wasco, Paiute, Tenino, and Tyigh. The number on the reservation was 780 in 1910, while about 80 others are reported to be permanently absent from the reservation.   (L. F.)

Lókuashtkni.—Gatschet in Cont. N. A. Ethnol., II, pt. II, 195, 1890 (Klamath name). **Túmmaí mámpka wé-i peyaktchímmem.**—Gatschet, Kalapuya MS., B. A. E., 30, 1877 (Atfalati name). **Waitá′nknî.**—Gatschet in Cont. N. A. Ethnol., II, pt. II, 467, 1890 (Klamath name). **Wétänkni.**—Ibid. **Yámakni.**—Ibid., 195.

Warrasqueoc (from *wáraskik*, 'swamp in a depression' of land.—Gerard). A tribe of the former Powhatan confederacy, living on the s. bank of James r. in Isle of Wight co., Va. Their principal village was situated in 1608 at the mouth of Warrasqueoc cr.

Wamasqueaks.—Boudinot, Star in West, 129, 1816 (misprint). **Waraskoyack.**—Simons in Smith (1629), Va., I, 180, repr. 1819. **Waraskweag.**—Gerard in Am. Anthr., VI, 319, 1904. **Warraskorack.**—Smith (1629), Va., I, map, repr. 1819. **Warraskoyack.**—Strachey (1612), Va., 35, 1849. **Warrasqueaks.**—Jefferson, Notes, 179, 1801. **War-rassqueaks.**—Macauley, N. Y., II, 168, 1829. **Warriscoyake.**—Doc. of 1624 in Mass. Hist. Soc. Coll., 4th s., IX, 65, note, 1871.

Warrennuncock. An unidentified tribe, mentioned in 1672 (Lederer, Discov., 2, 1672); probably one of the small tribes of the Carolinas known under another name.

Wasabe (*Wä-sa′-ba*, 'bear'). A subgens of the Dhatada gens of the Omaha.

Wasabaetage.—Balbi, Atlas Ethnog., 56, 1826. **Wa-sa-ba-eta-je.**—Long, Exped. Rocky Mts., I, 326, 1823. **Wasabe-hit'aji.**—Dorsey in 3d Rep. B. A. E., 220, 1885 ('touches no skin of a black bear').

Wasabe ('black bear'). A Kansa gens, the 5th on the right side of the tribal circle.

Sin'-ja-ye-ga.—Morgan, Anc. Soc., 156, 1877. **Wasabe.**—Dorsey in 15th Rep. B. A. E., 231, 1897. **Wasŏb-be nika-shing-ga.**—Stubbs, Kaw MS. vocab., B. A. E., 25, 1877.

Wasabehitazhi ('touch not the skin of a black bear'). A subgens of the Omaha.

Wasabe-hit'aji.—Dorsey in 15th Rep. B. A. E., 228, 1897.

Wasaenikashika ('those who became human beings by means of the black bear'). A Quapaw gens.

Black-bear gens.—Dorsey in 15th Rep. B. A. E., 229, 1897. Wasa' e'nikaci'ȼa.—Ibid.

Wasamegin. See *Massasoit.*

Wasapetun ('having four locks of hair'). The 12th Osage gens, the 5th on the right side of the tribal circle, being composed of two of the original Hangka fireplaces, Sindtsakdhe and Wasapetun.

Black bear.—Dorsey in Am. Nat., 114, 1884. Wasa'de tŭⁿ.—Dorsey in 15th Rep. B. A. E., 234, 1897.

Wasapokent. A village situated in 1608 on the w. bank of Patuxent r., in St Marys co., Md.

Wasapekent.—Bozman, Md., I, 141, 1837. Wasapokent.—Smith (1629), Va., I, map, repr. 1819.

Wasasa's Village. A former Cherokee settlement, named from a chief, situated on Browns cr., a southern affluent of the Tennessee r. in N. Alabama.—Royce in 5th Rep. B. A. E., map, 1887.

Wascacug. A village on the E. bank of Patuxent r. in Calvert co., Md., in 1608.—Smith (1629), Va., I, map, repr. 1819.

Wasco (from the Wasco word *wacq!ó,* 'cup or small bowl of horn,' the reference being to a cup-shaped rock a short distance from the main village of the tribe; from the tribal name *Ğałasq!ó,* 'Those that belong to Wasco,' or 'Those that have the cup,' are derived many of the forms of the name that follow in the synonymy. The derivation of the name from the Shahaptian *wask!ú,* 'grass,' lacks probability). A Chinookan tribe formerly living on the s. side of Columbia r., in the neighborhood of The Dalles, in Wasco co., Oreg. This tribe, with the Wishram (also known as Tlakluit and Echeloot), on the N. side of the river, were the easternmost branches of the Chinookan family. These two tribes were practically identical in language and culture, though they have been removed to different reservations. On the N., E., and S. they bordered on Shahaptian tribes, on the w. on closely related Chinookan tribes (White Salmon and Hood River Indians, Mooney's Chiluktkwa and Kwikwulit). Morse, in 1822, estimated the number of the Wasco at 900. They joined in the treaty of 1855, and removed to the Warm Springs res., Oreg., where about 200 now reside. The Wasco occupied a number of villages, some of these being used only for camping during the salmon runs. The names of these villages and fishing stations from E. to W. are: Hlgahacha, Igiskhis, Wasko (a few miles above the present town of The Dalles), Wogupan, Natlalalaik, Gawobumat, Hliekala-imadik, Wikatk, Watsokus, Winkwot (at The Dalles), Hlilwaihldik, Hliapkenun, Kabala, Gayahisitik, Itkumahlemkt, Hlgaktahlk, Tgahu, Hliluktik, Gahlentlich, Gechgechak, Skhlalis.

The Wasco were a sedentary people, depending for their subsistence mainly upon fish (several varieties of salmon, suckers, sturgeon, eels), to a less extent upon edible roots, berries, and, least important

WASCO MAN

of all, game. Salmon were caught in the spring and fall, partly with dip-nets, partly by spearing; smaller fish were obtained with hook and line or by means of basket traps. Definitely located fishing stations were a well-recognized form of personal property; the capture of the first salmon of the season was accompanied with a ceremony intended to give that particular fishing station a good season's catch. Pounded salmon flesh was often stored away for winter use; it also formed an important article of trade with neighboring tribes, the chief rendezvous for barter being the falls a few miles above The Dalles. Also berries were dried and preserved for winter use. The most notable of their industries were work in wood (bowls, spoons), horn (spoons, cups), and twined basketry (bags, various forms of stiff baskets). Coiled basketry has been learned since closer contact with the Klikitat; the chief materials used in twining are cedar roots and various grasses, of late also trader's cord and yarn. Realistic figures are carved in wood and horn; while the basket designs are partly geometrical, recalling the basketry art of N. California, and, as in that area, bearing conventional pattern names, partly realistic, though crudely so (angular figures of men, eagles, and deer are characteristic of the basketry art of the lower Columbia). The latter designs may be plausibly explained as an adaptation of forms familiar from wood-carving to twined basketry with its straight line and angular patterns. The original Wasco costume consisted of blanket robes (the pelts of bear, deer, wolf, coyote, raccoon, and mountain goat in summer), sleeveless shirts of raccoon or coyote skin, breechcloths of raccoon skin, and moccasins of deerskin; hats and gloves were made of coyote skin. Two types of house were in use—the partly underground winter house, roofed with cedar bark and having board platforms about the walls for beds, and the summer house with frame of fir poles and covering of tules or cedar bark; the latter type might have several fireplaces, accommodating three or four families. Sweat-houses were frequently used and were of quasi-supernatural significance.

In childhood the head was flattened by pressure on the forehead, and the ears were punctured with five holes in each ear; adults whose heads were not flattened were derided as no better than slaves. As regards naming, the most interesting fact is perhaps the absolute impossibility of translating a single Wasco name, the Chinookan dialects differing in this respect from the vast majority of American languages. Puberty ceremonies were observed in the case of both girls and boys; the former were subject to the usual taboos, after the fulfilment of which a menstrual dance was held, while the latter "trained" for the acquirement of strength and one or several guardian spirits. Burial was on boards put away in "dead people's houses"; slaves were sometimes buried alive to accompany a chief to the next world. Three classes of society were recognized: chiefs (the chieftainship was hereditary), common folk, and slaves (obtained by capture). There was no clan or totem organization, the guardian spirits referred to being strictly personal in character; the village was the main social unit. Religious ideas centered in the acquirement and manifestation of supernatural power obtained from one or more guardian spirits. The main social dances were the menstrual dance, the guardian spirit dance, in which each participant sang the song revealed to him by his protector, and the scalp dance. The most striking fact in the mythology of the tribe is the great rôle that Coyote plays as culture-hero and transformer. See Sapir, Wishram Texts, Pub. Amer. Ethnol. Soc., II, 1909. (E. S.)

Afúlakin.—Gatschet, Kalapuya MS., B. A. E. (Calapooya name). **Ámpχänkni.**—Gatschet in Cont. N. A. Ethnol., II, pt. II, 21, 1890 ('where the water is': Klamath name). **Awásko ammim.**—Gatschet, Kalapuya MS., B. A. E. (Kalapuya name). **Caclasco.**—Lee and Frost, Oregon, 186, 1844. **Cathlas.**—Stuart in Nouv. Annales d. Voy., XII, 27, 1821. **Cathlascans.**—Scouler in Jour. Ethnol. Soc. Lond., I, 237, 1848. **Cathlasco.**—Gatschet in Mag. Am. Hist., I, 167, 1877. **Cathlascons.**—Scouler in Jour. Geog. Soc. Lond., XI, 224, 1841. **Cathlaskos.**—Morse, Rep. to Sec. War, 368, 1822. **Cathlassis.**—Stuart, op. cit., 26. **Cathlatscos.**—Scouler in Jour. Geog. Soc. Lond., XI, 224, 1841. **Catlascon.**—Ibid., 243. **Guithlasko.**—Gatschet in Cont. N. A. Ethnol., II, pt. I, 93, 1890 (Klakama name). **Ka-clas-ko.**—Lee and Frost, Oregon, 176, 1844 (Chinook name). **Sáχlatks.**—Gatschet, Molale MS., B. A. E., 27, 1877 (Molale name). **Uncoes.**—H. R. Rep. 98, 42d Cong., 3d sess., 457, 1873. **Wacoes.**—Palmer in Ind. Aff. Rep. 1855, 194, 1856. **Wasco.**—Hines, Oregon, 30, 159, 1851. **Was-co-pam.**—Lee and Frost, Oregon, 167, 1844. **Wascoparns.**—Dart in Ind. Aff. Rep., 215, 1851. **Wascopaw.**—Lane (1849) in Sen. Ex. Doc. 52, 31st Cong., 1st sess., 171, 1850. **Wascopens.**—Meek in H. R. Ex. Doc. 76, 30th Cong., 1st sess., 10, 1848. **Wascopums.**—White, Ten Years in Oregon, 259, 1850. **Wasko.**—Mooney in 14th Rep. B. A. E., 741, 1896. **Waskopam.**—Gatschet in Cont. N. A. Ethnol., II, pt. I, 93, 1890 (Tenino name). **Waskosin.**—Shea, Cath. Miss., 478, 1855. **Waskows.**—Alvord (1853) in Schoolcraft, Ind. Tribes, V, 652, 1855. **Wiss-co-pam.**—Ross, Fur Hunters, I, 1855. **Woscopom.**—Trans. Oreg. Pion. Asso., 85, 1887.

Wascoo. Given by Ker (Trav., 104, 1816) as the chief village of the "Ilisees" (q. v.).

Wasechun-tashunka. See *American Horse*.

Washa. A small tribe, probably of Muskhogean stock, which, when first known to Europeans, inhabited the lower part of Bayou Lafourche, La., and hunted through the country between that river and the Mississippi. In 1699 Bienville made an unsuccessful attempt to open relations with them, but in 1718, after the close of the Chitimacha war, they were induced to settle on the Mississippi 3 leagues above New Orleans, and they appear to have remained near that place to the time of their extinction or their absorption by other tribes. They were always closely associated with another small tribe called Chaouacha, with which they finally became united. In 1805 Sibley stated that there were only four individuals of this tribe living scattered among various French families. The name Ouacha is perpetuated in that of a lake near the Louisiana coast, and it also appears as an alternative name for L. Salvador.   (J. R. S.)

Chacha.—Lattre, map U. S., 1784. **Onachas.**—Jefferys, French Dom. Am., I, 163, 1761 (misprint). **Ouacha.**—Iberville (1699) in Margry, Déc., IV, 155, 1880. **Ouanchas.**—McKenney and Hall, Ind. Tribes, III, 79, 1854. **Wachas.**—Brown, West. Gaz., 152, 1817. **Wanchas.**—Bossu (1759), Trav. La., I, 281, 1771. **Warshas.**—Martin, Hist. La., I, 143, 1827. **Washas.**—Sibley (1805), Hist. Sketches, 84, 1806. **Washaws.**—Drake, Bk. Ind., xii, 1848.

Washabe ('dark buffalo'). The 6th Ponca gens, the 2d on the Wazhazhe side of the tribal circle.

Wacabe.—Dorsey in 15th Rep. B. A. E., 228, 1897. **Wä-shä'-ba.**—Morgan, Anc. Soc., 155, 1877.

Washakie ('shoots [the buffalo] running.'—Corbusier. It is also said that the name means 'gambler's gourd,' and that its bearer was originally known as Pinaquana, meaning 'smell of sugar'). A Shoshoni chief, of mixed Shoshoni and

WASHAKIE

Umatilla blood (according to some authorities he was half white), born about 1804. Before reaching maturity he left the Umatilla and joined his mother's people, the Shoshoni. Washakie was noted chiefly for his friendship toward the whites and as a warrior against his tribal enemies. He early became the chief of the Eastern Band of Shoshoni of Wyoming, known also as Washakie's Band, by reason of his prowess and leadership, but when about 70 years of age some of the younger men aspiring to the chiefship, took steps to depose him. Washakie disappeared from the camp, and two months later, on the night when the council met to take action, he suddenly appeared with six scalps which he

had taken alone on the war-path, thus setting at rest all further opposition to his chieftaincy on the ground of age. Washakie is described as having been light in color, of commanding figure, very tall, powerfully built, and of dignified carriage, and had a reputation for great endurance. He realized the importance of his position, and was fond of form and ceremony in his dealings with white people. When in the 50's emigrants passed in large numbers through the Shoshoni country in Wyoming, Washakie and his people exercised great forbearance, following the injunctions of the Government agents to aid overland travelers in recovering strayed or lost stock, helping the emigrants across dangerous fords, and refraining from all acts of reprisal when animals of the white men destroyed the Indian root and herding grounds. So friendly and helpful were Washakie and the members of his band that 9,000 emigrants signed a paper commending their kind treatment. Washakie owed his great popularity among his people to his exploits on the war-path, especially against the Siksika (Blackfeet) and the Crows, and also, it is asserted, because in his younger days he brooked no opposition in the tribe and allowed no asylum to a horse thief or a vagabond. Another war-chief of the Shoshoni, named Pushican, or Purchican, bore on his forehead the scar of a blow from Washakie's tomahawk received during an altercation. He was for many years in the employ of the American and Hudson's Bay fur companies, and was long the valued companion of white hunters and trappers. Before the battle of Bear r. in 1863, in which Gen. Connor defeated the Bannock and hostile Shoshoni who refused to heed Washakie's warning, he fled with the greater portion of his tribe to Ft Bridger, Wyo., thus saving many of his people from destruction. When Ft Brown was established on the site of Lander, Wyo., in 1869, Washakie met the soldiers and avowed his friendship for the whites, and frequently served as a scout in campaigns against the Cheyenne, Sioux, Arapaho, Ute, and other hostile tribes. Members of his band also performed valiant service against the Cheyenne following the Custer defeat in 1876. At the time of his death, Feb. 20, 1900, Washakie was a devout member of the Protestant Episcopal church and a firm friend of the missionaries. He was buried, with military honors, in the cemetery at Ft Washakie, Wyo., where a monument has been erected over his grave. He was succeeded by his son, known as Dick Washakie.

Washakie's Band. The easternmost division of the Shoshoni proper, so called from their chief. They formerly ranged from Wind r. in lat. 43° 30′ on the N., in Wyoming, and from South pass to the headwaters of the North Platte on the E., and to Bear r. near the mouth of Smith fork, in Idaho, on the W. On the S. they extended as far as Brown's Hole, on Green r., Wyo. They are known officially as Shoshoni in distinction from the Bannock, Sheepeaters, etc., and were placed upon the Shoshoni res. in W. Wyoming by treaty of 1868. They numbered 870 in 1885, while the Shoshoni under the Shoshoni agency numbered 816 in 1909.

Eastern Snakes.—Lander in Sen. Ex. Doc. 42, 36th Cong., 1st sess., 121, 1860. **Green River Snakes.**—Stuart, Montana, 80, 1865. **Po-hah.**—Lewis and Clark, Exped., I, map, 1814. **Po'hoi.**—Gatschet, Comanche MS., B. A. E. (Comanche name of Eastern Shoshoni of Wyoming). **Pokahs.**—Morse, Rep. to Sec. War, map, 1822. **Washai'ki.**—Gatschet in Geog. Surv. W. 100th Mer., VII, 409, 1879. **Wash'-a-keeks band.**—Stuart, Montana, 81, 1865. **Washano.**—Schoolcraft, Ind. Tribes, V, 199, 1855. **Washikeek.**—Lander in Sen. Ex. Doc. 42, 36th Cong., 1st sess., 121, 1860. **Waushakee's band.**—Doty in Ind. Aff. Rep. 1864, 175, 1865.

Washashewanun. The first gens on the right, or Hangka, side of the Osage circle. **Elder Osage.**—Dorsey in 15th Rep. B. A. E., 234, 1897. **Waoa′oe Wanŭⁿ′.**—Dorsey, ibid.

Washatnagunashka. A Montagnais village on a bay on the N. shore of the gulf of St Lawrence, Quebec.—Stearns, Labrador, 271, 1884.

Washetan (*Wacetaⁿ*, 'reptile people'). A division of the Inshtasanda gens of the Omaha.—Dorsey in 15th Rep. B. A. E., 228, 1897.

Washichunchincha ('sons of white men'). A modern band or division of the Yankton Sioux. **Half-blood band.**—Dorsey in 15th Rep. B. A. E., 217, 1897. **Wacitcuⁿ-tciⁿtca.**—Ibid. **Wašićuⁿ-ćiⁿća.**—Ibid.

Was-hinedi (*Wạs!hĭ′nedĭ*, 'lousy creek people'). A Tlingit division at Kake, Alaska, belonging to the Wolf phratry. Tradition says a man from Lousy cr. was so infested with vermin that he died, in consequence of which they applied the name to his people. (J. R. S.)

Washo (from *washiu*, 'person,' in their own language.—Kroeber). A small tribe, forming a distinct linguistic family, the Washoan, which, when first known to Americans, occupied Truckee r., Nev., as far down as the Meadows, though their right to the latter was disputed by the Mono. The Washo also held Carson r. down to the first large canyon below Carson City, the borders of L. Tahoe, and Sierra and other valleys as far as the first range S. of Honey lake, Cal., the mountains being resorted to only in summer. There are some evidences that they once were established in the valleys farther to the E. than where found by the whites, whence they had been driven by the Paiute, between whom and themselves existed a state of chronic ill feeling, breaking out occasionally into open hostility. About 1860–62 the Paiute conquered the Washo in a contest over the site of Carson and forbade them thenceforth to own horses (Mooney). Of late years they have been confined to the country from Reno, on the railroad, to a short distance S. of Carson City, and have adopted a parasitic mode of life, being almost entirely dependent upon the towns and ranches. Recent study of their language indicates no linguistic relationship with any other people. In physique and general appearance they correspond more closely with the California Indians than with the tribes to their eastward. In 1859 the Washo numbered about 900, but are now reduced to about a third of that number. On the language of the Washo, consult Kroeber in Univ. Cal. Pub., Am. Arch. and Eth., IV, no. 5, 1907. (H. W. H.)

Tsaisuma.—A. L. Kroeber, inf'n, 1904 (name given by the northeastern Maidu). **Wah-shoes.**—Simpson, Rep. of Expl. Across Utah in 1859, 460, 1876. **Washaws.**—Holeman in Ind. Aff. Rep., 444, 1853. **Wa-sho.**—Dodge in Ind. Aff. Rep. 1859, 374, 1860. **Washoe.**—Kroeber in Univ. Cal. Pub., Am. Arch. and Eth., IV, 252, 1907. **Wásiu.**—Mooney, inf'n, 1900 (Paiute name). **Was-saws.**—Hurt in Ind. Aff. Rep. 1856, 228, 1857.

Washoan Family. The linguistic family represented by the Washo tribe (q. v.). =**Washo.**—Gatschet in Mag. Am. Hist., 255, Apr. 1882. <**Shoshone.**—Keane in Stanford, Compend., Cent. and So. Am., 477, 1878 (contains Washoes). <**Snake.**—Keane, ibid. (same as Shoshone, above). =**Washoan.**—Powell in 7th Rep. B. A. E., 131, 1891.

Washpa. The Dance-kilt clan of Sia and Cochiti pueblos, New Mexico. In the former the clan is extinct. **Huashpa hanutsh.**—Bandelier, Delight Makers, 256, 1890. **Wash'pa.**—Stevenson in 11th Rep. B. A. E., 19, 1894 (given as name of Cactus clan). **Wáshpa-háno.**—Hodge in Am. Anthr., IX, 350, 1896 (Sia name; *hano* = 'people'). **Wáshpa-hánuch.**—Ibid. (Cochiti form).

Washpashuka (*Wash-pa′-shu-ka*). A pueblo of the Acoma tribe, which, according to tradition, was inhabited in prehistoric times during their migration from the mythic Shipapu in the indefinite north. It is said to have been the second pueblo traditionally occupied by this people.—Hodge in Century Mag., LVI, 15, May 1898.

Wasmacus. A village on the W. bank of Patuxent r., in St Marys co., Md., in 1608.—Smith (1629), Va., I, map, repr. 1819.

Wasnaniks (*Was-na′-niks*). A former village of the Tlakluit below The Dalles of Columbia r., Wash. (E. S.)

Wastsanek (*Wä′stsanⱸk*). A sept of the Toquart, a Nootka tribe.—Boas in 6th Rep. N. W. Tribes Can., 32, 1890.

Wasupa. A former Seminole town 2 m. E. of Sumulgahatchee, 18 m. from St Marks, probably in Wakulla or Jefferson co., Fla.—H. R. Ex. Doc. 74 (1823), 19 Cong., 1st sess., 27, 1826.

Watakihulata ('beloved people'). One of the two Choctaw phratries, consisting of the Chufaniksa, Iskulani, Chito, and Shakchukla clans.

Hattak-i-hol-lihtah.—Reed in Sturm's Statehood Mag., I, 85, Nov. 1905. Okoelaïhoeláhta.—ten Kate, Reizen in N. A., 403, 1885. Wă-tăk-i-Hŭ-lä′-tä.—Morgan, Anc. Soc., 162, 1877.

Watap. Roots of the pine, spruce, tamarack, etc., used to sew birch-bark for canoes and other purposes: from *watap*, in the Chippewa and closely related Algonquian dialects, signifying root of the tamarack. The word has come into English through Canadian French. Cuoq (Lex. Alg., 426, 1886) says the word is known from one end of Canada to the other and deserves adoption by the French Academy.   (A. F. C.)

Watauga (*Watá′gï*, of unknown meaning). A name occurring as that of two or more towns in the old Cherokee country; one was an important settlement on Watauga cr., a branch of Little Tennessee r., a few miles below Franklin, in Macon co., N. C.; another was traditionally located at Watauga Old Fields, about the present Elizabethton, on Watauga r., in Carter co., Tenn. The name is also written Watoga, Wattoogee, Whatoga, etc.—Mooney in 19th Rep. B. A. E., 546, 1900.

Wataga.—Royce in 5th Rep. B. A. E., map, 1887. Watoga.—Doc. of 1799 quoted by Royce, ibid., 144. Watoge.—Doc. of 1755, quoted by Royce, ibid., 142. Whatoga.—Bartram, Travels, 371, 1792 (in N. C.).

Watcheeshoo. A Montagnais village near Manicouagan bay, on the N. shore of the gulf of St Lawrence, Quebec.—Stearns, Labrador, 271, 1884.

Watchful Fox. See *Keokuk*.

Wateree (perhaps from Catawba *wateran*, 'to float on the water.'—Gatschet). One of the early tribes of the Carolinas, probably Siouan. As described by Juan de la Vandera in his account of the expedition of Juan de Pardo in 1567, they then lived at a great distance from the coast, near the Cherokee frontier. In 1670 Lederer, whose statement is doubtful, places them apparently in North Carolina, on the extreme upper Yadkin, far to the N. W. of their later habitat, with the Shoccore and Eno on the N. E. and the Cheraw on the W. In 1700 they lived on Wateree r., below the present Camden, S. C. On a map of 1715 their village is placed on the W. bank of Wateree r., perhaps in Fairfield co. Moll's map of 1730 locates their village on the E. bank of the river. When Lawson met them, in 1700, they were a much larger body than the Congaree, and spoke an entirely different language, which was unintelligible to the latter people. The Yamasee war broke the power of the Wateree, and according to Adair (1743) they became confederates of the Catawba, though still retaining their own village and language. Vandera says they were ruled by two female chiefs, who held dignified court, with a retinue of young men and women. He also describes them as being rather the slaves than the subjects of their chiefs, which agrees with what Lawson says of the Santee. Lederer, who speaks from hearsay only, mentions the killing of women of a hostile tribe, by a chief, in order that their spirits might serve his dying son in the other world. Lawson says that their houses were as poor as their industry; that the men were tall and well-built, friendly, but great pilferers, and very lazy, even for Indians. See Mooney, Siouan Tribes of the East, 80, 1894.

Chichanee.—Rivers, Hist. So. Car., 36, 1856. Chickanee.—Lawson (1714), Hist. Car., 59, 1860. Chickaree.—Howe quoted by Schoolcraft, Ind. Tribes, IV, 158, 1854. Guatari.—Vandera (1569) in Smith, Colec. Doc. Fla., I, 17, 1857. Watarees.—Jefferys, French Dom. Am., pt. 1, 134, map, 1761. Watary.—Lederer, Discov., 16, 1672. Wateree.—Lawson (1714), Hist. Car., 56, 1860. Wateree Chickanee.—Ibid., 59. Waterrees.—Ibid., 99. Watterree.—Moll, map Car., 1720.

Water-monsters. See *Mythology*.

Wathatotarho ('he obstinately refused to acquiesce'; also *Thadodaho, Tododaho, Atotarho*). The official name and title of a chiefship hereditary in the Bear clan of the Onondaga, and heading the roll of federal chiefs. The first known chieftain to bear the name flourished about the year 1570. He was one of the great men of his time and people, who reso-

IROQUOIS CONCEPTION OF WATHATOTARHO

lutely deferred to the last his assent to the adherence of his tribe to the confederation of peoples then forming, which afterward became famous under the name of the League of the Iroquois, or Five Nations. According to native tradition Wathatotarho possessed great force of character, being haughty, ambitious, crafty, and remorseless, brooking no equal. He was reputed to be a dreaded sorcerer and was even charged with being a cannibal. By taking too literally the figures of speech by which were designated the qualities that made him feared and dreaded by his opponents, tradition assigns to him a preterhuman nature, even representing his head as having been clothed, in lieu of hair, with living vipers, his hands and feet as having the shape of huge turtle-claws, and whose other organs were similarly monstrous in form, in keeping with his demoniacal mind. Hence he is said to have had "seven crooks in his body," referring figuratively to his unnatural hair, hands and feet, eyes, throat, hearing, sexual parts, and mind, but now erroneously taken literally. After the Mohawk, Oneida, and Cayuga had united in a tentative league, they were enabled to gain his assent to the adhesion of the Onondaga to the proposed confederation. By his defiance, however, he obtained for the Onondaga certain concessions, among them being that the league council-fire should be kept at their chief town; that they should have 14 chiefs, while no other tribe should have more than 10; that the federal council should be summoned only by Wathatotarho; that no act of the council would be valid unless sanctioned by the Onondaga speaker as being in accordance with the rules and principles of the league; that Wathatotarho, being the leading chief of the Onondaga tribe, should have four peers assigned to him as special aids; and that the Onondaga, represented by their chiefs, should have confirmatory, arbitrative, and advisory functions in the deliberations of the league council. His great antagonists were Dekanawida and Hiawatha, who by wise statecraft finally overcame his opposition. (J. N. B. H.)

Watlala. A division of the Chinookan family formerly living at the cascades of Columbia r. and, at least in later times, on Dog (now Hood) r. about half way between the cascades and The Dalles, in Wasco co., Oreg. Early writers mention several tribes at or near the cascades, but as the population of that region was very changeable from the fact of its being a much frequented fishing resort, and as many of the so-called tribes were merely villages, often of small size, it is now impossible to identify them with certainty. After the epidemic of 1829, the Watlala seem to have been the only remaining tribe, the remnants of the others having probably united under that name, though they were commonly called Cascade Indians by the whites. In 1854 they were reported to number 80. In 1855 they joined in the Wasco treaty under the name of the "Ki-gal-twal-la band of the Wascoes" and the "Dog River band of the Wascoes," and were removed to the Warm Springs res. in Oregon, where a few still survive.

The term Watlala is also used by some writers, following Hale, to include all the Upper Chinook. The names given by different writers to the tribes living at or near the cascades, which may have been the Watlala or later have been included under them, are Cathlakaheckit, Cathlathlala, Cathlayackty, Clahclellah, Katlagakya, Yehuh. (L. F.)
Al-e-is.—Gass, Journal, 197, 1811. Carcader.—De Smet, Letters, 232, 1843. Cascade Indians.—Nicolet, Oregon, 143, 1846. Dog River.—Taylor in Cal.

Farmer, June 12, 1863. GiIā′xicatck.—Boas, Chinook Texts, 276, 1894 (Chinook name). Ki-gal-twalla.—U. S. Stat. at Large, XII, 963, 1863. Ki-gal-twal-la.—Wasco treaty, 1855, in U. S. Ind. Treat., 622, 1873. Kwikwû′lĭt.—Mooney in 14th Rep. B. A. E., 741, 1896. Wahclellah.—Lewis and Clark Exped., II, 231, 1814. Wah-lal-la.—Dayton treaty, 1855, in U. S. Ind. Treat., 18, 1873. Wah-ral-lah.—Lyman in Oreg. Hist. Soc. Quar., I, 323, 1900. Watlala.—Hale in U. S. Expl. Exped., VI, 214, 1846. Watlalla.—Medill in H. R. Ex. Doc. 76, 30th Cong., 1st sess., 7, 1848.

Watok. Mentioned as a Yokuts (Mariposan) or a Shoshonean tribe in s. central California, probably on or near Kings r. The Wat-tokes are mentioned in 1857 as high up on Kings r., and in 1861 as on Fresno res.
Wartokes.—Ind. Aff. Rep., 219, 1861. Watooga.—Gatschet in Mag. Am. Hist., 158, 1877. Wat-tokes.—Lewis in Ind. Aff. Rep. 1857, 399, 1858.

Watopachnato. A division of the Assiniboin which in 1804, according to Lewis and Clark, roved the plains between the Missouri and the Saskatchewan, above the Yellowstone and the heads of Assiniboine r. They numbered 1,600, including 450 warriors, in 200 tipis, and resembled their congeners, the Watopapinah and the Itscheabine, in their habits and alliances. Hayden estimated them at 100 lodges, averaging 4 persons, in 1862.
Big Devils.—Orig. Jour. Lewis and Clark, VI, 104, 1905 (traders' nickname). Gens de l'age.—Maximilian, Travels, 194, 1843. Gens des grand diable.—Orig. Jour., op. cit. Gens du Gauché.—Hayden, Ethnog. and Philol. Mo. Val., 387, 1862. Gens du large.—Maximilian, Travels, 194, 1843. Mahtopanato.—Orig. Jour., op. cit., 105. Na-co′-ta Mah-to-pâ-nar-to.—Ibid., 104. Old Gauché's gens.—Denig quoted by Dorsey in 15th Rep. B. A. E., 223, 1897. Otopachgnato.—Maximilian, op. cit. (apparently a duplication). Waĥ-to′-paĥ-an-da-to.—Hayden, op. cit. Wah-to-pah-han-da-toh.—Denig quoted by Dorsey, op. cit. Watópachnato.—Maximilian, Travels, 194, 1843.

Watopapinah ('canoe people'). A band of the Assiniboin which, according to Lewis and Clark in 1804, roved on Mouse (Souris) r. and the branches of the Assiniboine N. of the Mandan tribe, in the United States and Canada. At this period they numbered 450 warriors, in 200 tipis. In 1806 Henry (Coues, New Light, II, 522, 1897) said they had 160 lodges, while Hayden (Ethnog. and Philol. Mo. Val., 387, 1862) in 1856 said that they ranged from White Earth r. to the sources of the Souris and Pembina rs. and occupied 220 lodges, averaging 4 persons.
Assiniboin Menatopa.—Lewis and Clark Exped., I, 146, 1814. Band lar Gru (crain) or canoe.—Orig. Jour. Lewis and Clark, VI, 104, 1905. Canoe and Paddling Assiniboines.—Henry quoted by Coues, New Light, 522, 1897. Canoe Assiniboines.—Ibid. Canoe band.—Culbertson in Smithson. Rep. 1850, 143, 1851. Canoe Indians.—Ind. Aff. Rep., 289, 1854. Gens de Canot.—Brackenridge, Views of La., 79, 1814 (=Manelopec, ibid., ed. 1817). Gens des Canoe.—Lewis and Clark Discov., 43, 1806. Gens des canots.—Maximilian, Travels, 194, 1843. Les gens des Caruts.—Ind. Aff. Rep., 289, 1854. Manelopec.—Brackenridge, op. cit., 1814 (='Gens de Canots,' ibid., ed. 1815). Ma-ne-to′-pâ.—Lewis and Clark Discov., 44, 1806. Ma-ne-to-par.—Orig. Jour. Lewis and Clark, VI, 104, 1905. Menatopa.—Lewis and Clark Exped., 184, 1817. Otaopabinè.—

Maximilian, Travels, 194, 1843 (sig. 'les gens des canots'). **Wato-pana.**—Iapi Oaye, XIII, no. 5, p. 17, 1884. **Wah-to-pan-ah.**—Denig quoted by Dorsey in 15th Rep. B. A. E., 222, 1897. **Wah-to'-pap-i-nah.**—Hayden, Ethnog. and Philol. Mo. Val., 387, 1862.

Watsaghika. A former village of the Iruwaitsu Shasta near the head of the canyon and at the extreme w. end of Scott valley, N. Cal.   (R. B. D.) **Watsa-he-wa.**—Gibbs (1851) in Schoolcraft, Ind. Tribes, III, 171, 1853 (given as a band). **Wat-so-ke-wa.**—McKee (1851) in Sen. Ex. Doc. 4, 32d Cong., spec. sess., 171, 1853 (given as a band).

Watsequeorda's Band. A Paviotso band, named from its chief (Four Crows), formerly living on Pyramid lake, w. Nev., and said to number 320 in 1859. **Four Crows band.**—Burton, City of Saints, 576, 1861. **Watsequendo.** — Ibid. **Wat-se-que-order's band.**—Dodge in Ind. Aff. Rep. 1859, 374, 1860.

Wauanouk. A former village near St Francis, Quebec, probably of refugee Wewenoc.—Lattré map, 1784.

Wauban. See *Waban*.

Waubanaquot. See *Wabanaquot*.

Wauchimoqut. A Wampanoag village in 1646, probably near Seekonk, Bristol co., Mass.—R. I. Col. Rec., I, 32, 1856.

Waugau. A former Ottawa village, named from the chief, near the mouth of Maumee r. in Lucas co., Ohio, on a reservation sold in 1833. **Wau-gan.**—Maumee treaty (1833) in U. S. Ind. Treat., 597, 1873 (misprint). **Waugau.**—Detroit treaty (1807), ibid., 194.

Waugullewatl. A former Hupa village on the E. bank of Trinity r., Cal., near the mouth of Willow cr. **Waug-ulle-watl.**—Gibbs, MS., B. A. E., 1852.

Waugullewutlekauh. A former Hupa village on the E. bank of Trinity r., Cal. **Waug-ulle-wutle-kauh.**—Gibbs, MS., B. A. E., 1852.

Waulipoe (*Wa'ulipoë*, 'those who are feared'). A gens of the Kwakiutl proper on the coast of British Columbia.—Boas in Rep. U. S. Nat. Mus. 1895, 330, 1897.

Waumegesako (*Wemigĭsiked*, 'He who makes the *migĭs*, or sacred shell,' i. e. 'Sacred-shell maker.'—J. A. Gilfillan. Also known as The Wampum, and "Mexico"). A leading Chippewa, born about 1789, head chief of a mixed band of Chippewa, Potawatomi, and Ottawa residing at Manitowoc, Wis., where he died in 1844. He took a prominent part in the treaties of Butte des Morts in 1827, Green Bay in 1828, Prairie du Chien in 1829, and Chicago in 1833. At the last treaty, ratified in 1835, the Indian title was extinguished to all the tract of country commencing at Grosse Point, 9 m. N. of Chicago, to the source of Milwaukee r., thence w. to Rock r. A portrait of Waumegesako was painted by Healey, an Irish artist, in 1839, a copy of which is in the collection of the Wisconsin Historical Society. In appreciation of his friendly attitude toward the early settlers, the citizens of Manitowoc have erected a monument to Waumegesako's memory.

Wauregan. A word of frequent occurrence in the earlier literature of New England. Bartlett (Dict. of Americanisms, 741, 1877) states that it was still local in and about Norwich, Conn., in the sense of fine or showy. The word is famous through Dr Elisha Tracy's epitaph on the tombstone of Uncas, the Mohegan sachem:

" For courage bold, for things *wauregan*,
    He was the glory of Moheagon."

Wauregan, according to Gerard, is a corrupt form of *wurĭgĕn*, an inanimate adjective (of which the animate form is *wurĭgu*) belonging to an *R*-dialect of New England, and meaning 'it is good (fine, pretty, etc.)'; cognate with Massachuset *wunĭgĕn*, Lenape (Delaware) *wulĭgĕn*, etc. As a place name the word survives in Wauregan, a village in Windham co., Conn.   (A. F. C.)

Wauswagiming (*Wăswăgaming*, 'at the torchlight fishing lake.'—Gerard). A Chippewa band that lived on the present Lac de Flambeau res. in Wisconsin, on Lac de Flambeau, where they were accustomed to fish by torchlight. **Lac du Flambeau.**—Treaty of 1854 in U. S. Stat. at Large, X, 223, 1855. **Wăswăgaming.**—Wm. Jones, inf'n, 1905 (correct name). **Was-waw-gun-nink.**—James in Tanner, Narr., 361, 1830. **Waus-wag-im-ing.**—Warren (1852) in Minn. Hist. Soc. Coll., v, 192, 1885.

Wautakon. See *Wingatakw*.

Wauteghe (*Wautêghe*). A village about 1750, on the upper Susquehanna, between Teatontaloga and Oquaga.—Hawley (1754) in Mass. Hist. Soc. Coll., 1st s., IV, 63, 1795.

Wavey. A Canadian French corruption of *wehwew*, the Cree (onomatopoetic) name of the snow goose, *Chen hyperboreus*, called by the Chippewa *wewe*. The snow goose is also distinguished as the "common wavey, or wavy", and the "white wavey", while the blue-winged goose (*C. cœrulescens*) is known as the "blue-wavey", and the smallest goose (*C. rossi*) as the "horned wavey". The flying to the south of the wavey in large flocks is regarded by the Indians as a sure sign of approaching winter. (w. r. g.)

Wawarsink (possibly from *wawárăsĭnĭ-keu*, 'many hollow stones,' referring to stones hollowed out by the action of the creek.—Gerard). A former Munsee (?) band on the w. bank of the lower Hudson r., N. Y., having their principal settlement of the same name about the junction of Wawarsing with Rondout cr., in Ulster co. (j. m.)
Wawarasinke.—Doc. of 1685 quoted by Ruttenber, Ind. Geog. Names, 166, 1906. Wawarsing.—Ruttenber, Tribes Hudson R., 392, 1872. Wawarsinks.—Ibid., 95.

Wawayontat. A village of Praying Indians in 1674, situated on Weweantitt r., near Wareham, Plymouth co., Mass.
Wawayontat.—Bourne (1674) in Mass. Hist. Soc. Coll., 1st s., I, 198, 1806. Wawayoutat.—Bourne (1674), quoted by Drake, Bk. Inds., bk. II, 118, 1848.

Wawepex. A Matinecoc village formerly near the present Cold Spring, near Oyster Bay, on the N. shore of Long id., N. Y.—Thompson, Long Id., I, 501, 1843.

Wawikyem (*Wă'wik·em*). A clan of the Wikeno, a Kwakiutl tribe.—Boas in Rep. U. S. Nat. Mus. 1895, 328, 1897.

Wawnahton. See *Waneta*.

Wawyachtonoc ('eddy people', or possibly 'people of the curving channel.' Cf. *Wea*). A tribe or band of the Mahican confederacy formerly occupying a territory in Dutchess and Columbia cos., N. Y., extending to the Housatonic r. in Litchfield co., Conn. Their principal village was Weantinock. Shecomeco, Wechquadnach, Pomperaug, Bantam, Weataug, and Scaticook were villages of this tribe or in alliance with it. Most of these Indians were gathered by the Moravians into the missions at Shecomeco and Scaticook, Conn., and, except some who remained at Scaticook, removed to Pennsylvania and shared the fortunes of the Moravian Indians. (j. m.)
Wawijachtenocks.—Doc. of 1689 quoted by Ruttenber, Tribes Hudson R., 85, 1872. Wawyachteioks.—Doc. of 1689, ibid., 85. Wawyachtonocks.—Ibid. Wayaughtanock.—Caldwell (1702), ibid. Wyeck.—Wassenaar (1632) quoted by Ruttenber, ibid., 71.

Waxhaw. A small tribe that lived in the 17th century in what is now Lancaster co., S. C., and Union and Mecklenburg cos., N. C. They were connected with the neighboring Sugeree, and both were apparently related to the Catawba, and therefore were Siouan. The custom of flattening the head, practised by the Waxhaw, was also mentioned as a custom of the Catawba. Lederer (1672) says they were subject to and might be considered a part of the Catawba. Lawson visited the Waxhaw in 1701 and was hospitably received. He mentions two of their villages situated about 10 m. apart. He describes the people as very tall, and notes particularly their custom of artificially flattening the head during infancy. The dance ceremonies and councils were held in a council house, much larger than the ordinary dwellings. Instead of being covered with bark, like the domiciles, it was neatly thatched with sedge and rushes; the entrance was low, and around the walls on the inside were benches made of cane. Near the Waxhaw were the Catawba, or more likely a band of that tribe. They were probably so reduced by the Yamasee war of 1715 as to have been obliged to incorporate with the Catawba. See Mooney, Siouan Tribes of the East, 1894.
Flatheads.—Mooney, Siouan Tribes of the E., 68, 1894 (general name, applied also to the Catawba). Wachaw.—Vaugondy map, 1775. Wacksaws.—Craven (1712) in N. C. Col. Rec., I, 898, 1886. Wassaws.—Catawba MS. in Schoolcraft, Ind. Tribes, III, 294, 1853. Wastana.—War map (1711–15) in Winsor, Hist. Am., v, 346, 1887 (possibly identical). Waxaus.—Map N. Am. and W. Indies, 1720. Waxaws.—Doc. of 1719 in Rivers, S. Car., 93, 1874. Waxhaws.—Logan, Hist. S. Car., I, 182, 1859. Waxsaws.—Lawson (1714), Hist. Car, 60, 1860. Wisack.—Ibid., 72. Wisacky.—Lederer, Discov., 17, 1672.

Wayagwa (*Wa'-ya-gwa*). A former village of the Tlakluit (q. v.) on Columbia r., Wash. (e. s.)

Wayon. A chief or tribe in alliance with the chief of Audusta (Edisto), S. C., and in friendly relation with the French in 1562. The village was a short distance inland from the French fort near Port Royal.
Mayon.—De Bry map (1591) in Le Moyne, Narr., Appleton trans., 1875 (misprint?). Wayon.—Laudonnière (1564) quoted by French, Hist. Coll. La., n. s., 201, 1869.

Wazhazha ('Osage'). A band of the Brulé Teton Sioux.
Oz-ash.—Lewis and Clark Discov., 34, 1806. Wahzhazas.—Ind. Aff. Rep., 67, 1877. Wajaja.—Dorsey (after Cleveland) in 15th Rep. B. A. E., 219, 1897. Waźaźa.—Ibid. Wazazhas.—Warren, Dacota Country, 16, 1855.

Wazhazha. A band of the Oglala Sioux.
Wahza-zhe.—Ind. Aff. Rep., 296, 1854. Wajaja.—Dorsey in 15th Rep. B. A. E., 220, 1897. Waźaźa.—Ibid. Waz-az-e.—Brackett in Smithson. Rep. 1876, 467, 1877. Wazazies.—Ind. Aff. Rep., 250, 1875. Wazzazies.—Ind. Aff. Rep., 301, 1854.

Wazhazhe. The second Ponca half-tribe, as given by Dorsey, which included four gentes.
Wajaje.—J. O. Dorsey, MS., B. A. E., 1880.

Wazhazhe. A Ponca gens.
Ice.—Morgan, Anc. Soc., 155, 1877. Waḣ'ga.—Ibid. Wa-ja-ja.—Long, Exped. Rocky Mts., I, 328, 1823. Wä-zhä'-zha.—Morgan, op. cit., 155 (trans. 'snake').

Wazhazhe (named from the chief who was originally an Oglala Wazhazha). A band of the Sihasapa Sioux.
Kill Eagle's band.—Dorsey in 15th Rep. B. A. E., 219, 1897. Wajaje.—Ibid. Waźaźe.—Ibid. Wazzazies.—Bordeau in H. R. Doc. 63, 33d Cong., 2d sess., 3, 1855.

Wazhingkaenĭkashika ('those who became human beings by means of a bird'). A Quapaw gens.
Small-bird gens.—Dorsey in 15th Rep. B. A. E., 229, 1897. Wajiñ′ꭓa enikaci′ꭓa.—Ibid.

Wazhush (*wazhash*, 'muskrat'). A gens of the Chippewa. In the beginning of the 19th century they were considered a division of the Kenozhe gens, and resided on the N. shore of L. Superior at Grand Portage and Thunder bay.
Hawoyzask.—Long, Voy. and Trav., 62, 1791. Musquash.—Ibid. Omackāsiwą̆g.—Wm. Jones, inf′n, 1907. Ŏmă̊schkă̊sĕ Wenenewak.—Long, Exped. St. Peter's R., II, 153, 1824. Omush-kas.—Warren (1852) in Minn. Hist. Soc. Coll., V, 84, 1885. O-mush-kas-ug.—Ibid. Rat nation.—Long, Voy. and Trav., 117, 1791.

Wazikute ('shooters among pine trees'). A division of the Upper Yanktonai Sioux. It was an ancient and important division, from which in early times the Assiniboin seceded.
Gens des Pin.—Hayden, Ethnog. and Philol. Mo. Val., 371, 1862. Ouapeontetons.—La Harpe (1700) in Shea, Early Voy., 111, 1861 (trans. 'village of those who shoot in a great pine'). Ouapetontetons.—Le Sueur (1700) quoted by Neill, Hist. Minn., 170, 1858 (trans. 'village of those who shoot at the large pine'). Ouasiconteton.—Le Sueur (1700) in Margry, Déc., VI, 87, 1886 (trans. 'village of those who shoot at the large pine'). Pine-Band.—Hayden, op. cit. Pole people.—Culbertson in Smithson. Rep. 1850, 141, 1851. Shooters in the Pines.—H. R. Ex. Doc. 96, 42d Cong., 3d sess., 5, 1873. Siouxs who Shoot in the Pine Tops.—Treaty of 1816 in U. S. Ind. Treat., 870, 1873. Tᴄaⁿ-ona.—Dorsey in 15th Rep. B. A. E., 218, 1897. Those that Shoot in the pines.—Culbertson in Smithson. Rep. 1850, 141, 1851. Ṭᴄicĭt′aⁿ.—Dorsey in Cont. N. A. Ethnol., VI, 412, 1890 (trans. 'plenty of lodge poles'). Wa-ge′-ku-te.—Hayden, Ethnog. and Philol. Mo. Val., 371, 1862. Wah-zu-cootas.—Schoolcraft, Ind. Tribes, II, 169, 1852.

Wea (probably a contraction of the local name *Wawiaqtenang*, 'place of the round, or curved, channel' (Schoolcraft); possibly contracted from *Wayahtónuki*, 'eddy people,' from *wayaqtonwi*, 'eddy,' both renderings coming from the same root. Wawaqtenang was the common Algonquian name for Detroit. Cf. *Wawyachtonoc*). A subtribe of the Miami. They are first mentioned in the Jesuit Relation for 1673 as living in E. Wisconsin. In the later distribution of the tribes of the confederacy they occupied the most westerly position. Allouez in 1680 found a Wea town on St Joseph r., Ind. Marquette visited a Wea village at Chicago which Courtemanche found still there in 1701. A part of them were for a time with the bands of various tribes gathered about La Salle's fort near Peoria, Ill. La Salle says their band had 35 cabins. In 1719 their chief village, Ouiatenon, was on the Wabash, below the mouth of Wea cr., where, according to Charlevoix, they were living nearly half a century before. This is possibly identical with "Les Gros" village (q. v.) of a document of 1718. Besides this they had two or three villages near by. Ouiatenon was one of the principal headquarters of the French

traders. In 1757 the Wea and Piankashaw endeavored to come into friendly relations with the whites, and an agreement to this end was entered into with Col. George Crogan, but was rejected by the assembly of Virginia. Subsequently various agreements of peace with other tribes and the whites were entered into, chiefly through the efforts of Col. Crogan and Sir Wm. Johnson, to be as often followed by outbreaks. In 1791 their neighboring villages were destroyed by the U. S. troops under Gen. Scott. They participated in the treaty of Greenville, Ohio, Aug. 3, 1795, their deputies signing for them and the Piankashaw. In 1820 they sold their last lands in Indiana, near the mouth of Raccoon cr. in Parke co., and removed with the Piankashaw to Illinois and Missouri. In 1832 the united tribes in turn sold their claims in those states and removed to Kansas, where some had already settled. The few Wea still remaining in Indiana afterward joined them there. In 1854 the Wea and Piankashaw, having rapidly dwindled away, joined the remnants of the cognate Illinois, then known as the Peoria and Kaskaskia. The united body, all that remained of 7 tribes, then numbered but 259, a large proportion of whom were of mixed blood. In 1868 they removed to a tract on Neosho r., in the N. E. corner of the present Oklahoma, where they now are. In 1885 the united tribes numbered 149 souls. In 1909 the number of the confederated Peoria was 204, only about 75 of whom had as much as one-half Indian blood. (J. M.)

Abinones.—Barcia, Ensayo, 236, 1723. Aoiatenon.—La Salle (1682) in Margry, Déc., II, 216, 1877. Aoniatinonis.—La Hontan (1703), New Voy., map, 1735. Aouiatinons.—Gale, Upper Miss., 176, 1867. Aouittanons.—La Hontan (1703), New Voy., map, 1735. Newcalenous.—McKenney and Hall, Ind. Tribes, III, 114, 1854. Ochiatenens.—Allouez (1680) in Margry, Déc., II, 99, 1877. Oiatenon.—La Salle (1680), ibid., 201. Oiatinon.—Hennepin, New Discov., 111, 1698. Ojachtanichroenee.—Livingston (1720) in N. Y. Doc. Col. Hist., V, 567, 1855 (Iroquois name). Ojatinons.—La Hontan, New Voy., I, 231, 1703. Oniactmaws.—Dalton (1783) in Mass. Hist. Soc. Coll., 1st s., X, 123, 1809. Onias.—Stone, Life of Brant, II, 278, 1864 (misprint). Oniatonons.—Imlay, West. Ter., 291, 1797 (misprint). Oniattanon.—Wilkinson (1791) quoted by Rupp, West. Penn., app., 237, 1846 (misprint). Onillas.—Gale, Upper Miss., 75, 1867 (misprint). Oouiatanons.—Beauharnois (1732) in N. Y. Doc. Col. Hist., IX, 1035, 1855. O8iatᴇ8atenon.—MS. Jes. Rel. (1673-79) quoted by Shea in Wis. Hist. Soc. Coll., III, 135, 1857. Otiara8atenon.—Jes. Rel. (1676) quoted, ibid. Oua.—McKenney and Hall, Ind. Tribes, III, 80, 1854. Ouachtanons.—Smith, Bouquet Exped., 64, 1766. Ouachtenons.—Trader quoted by Smith, ibid., 70. Ouachtunon.—Rupp, West. Penn., 149, 1846. 8a8aiation.—Doc. of 1695 in N. Y. Doc. Col. Hist., IX, 619, 1855. Oüaoüiartanons.—Bacqueville de la Potherie, Hist., II, 261, 1753. Ouaouiatanoukak.—Charlevoix (1744) quoted by Tailhan, Perrot Mem., 222, note, 1864. Ouaouiatenonoukak.—Jes. Rel. (1672) quoted by Shea in Wis. Hist. Soc. Coll., III, 135, 1857. Ouaouyartanons.—Bacqueville de la Potherie, Hist., II, 348, 1753. Ouatanons.—Doc. of 1756 in N. Y. Doc. Col. Hist., X, 482, 1858. Ouatenon.—Royce in 1st Rep. B. A. E., map, 1881 (village). Ouatonons.—Hildreth, Pioneer Hist., 307, 1848. **Ouat-tonon.**—Croghan (1765) quoted in Monthly Am. Jour. Geol., 264, 1831. **Oucatonons.**—Boudinot, Star in the W., 128, 1816. **Oüeas.**—Tailhan, Perrot Mém., 222, note, 1864. **Ougatanous.**—Chauvignerie (1736) quoted by Schoolcraft, Ind. Tribes, III, 555, 1853. **Ouias.**—Montreal conf. (1756) in N. Y. Doc. Col. Hist., x, 447, 1858. **Ouiatanon.**—Frontenac (1682), ibid., IX, 178, 1855. **Ouiatenons.**—Perkins and Peck, Annals of the West, 411, 1850. **Ouiatinons.**—Drake, Bk. Inds., xii, 1848. **Ouiato-nons.**—Beauharnois (1736) in N. Y. Doc. Col. Hist., IX, 1050, 1855. **Ouiattanon.**—Harmar (1790) quoted by Rupp, West. Penn., app., 229, 1846. **Ouiattons.**—Harmar, ibid. **Ouicatonans.**—Croghan (1765) in Monthly Am. Jour. Geol., 267, 1831. **Ouil-las.**—De Bougainville (1757) in N. Y. Doc. Col. Hist., x, 608, 1858. **Ouitanans.**—Brown, West. Gaz., 71, 1817. **Ouitanons.**—Vaudreuil (1704) in N. Y. Doc. Col. Hist., IX, 763, 1855. **Ouitatot-nons.**—Jefferson (1785), Notes, 143, 1825. **Ouiti-maus.**—Writer of 1812 quoted by Schoolcraft, Ind. Tribes, III, 555, 1853. **Oujatanons.**—Doc. of 1718 in N. Y. Doc. Col. Hist., IX, 890, 1855. **Ouroctenon.**—Royce in 1st Rep. B. A. E., map, 1881 (village). **Outaganons.**—Doc. of 1756 in N. Y. Doc. Col. Hist., x, 424, 1858 (misprint). **Outias.**—Malartic (1758), ibid., 840 (misprint). **Outinon.**—Schermerhorn (1812) in Mass. Hist. Soc. Coll., 2d s., II, 8, 1814. **Ouyas.**—Vater, Mith., pt. 3, sec. 3, 351, 1816. **8yas.**—Longueuil (1752) in N.Y. Doc. Col. Hist., x, 248, 1858. **8yatanon.**—Longueuil (1752), ibid., 246. **Ouyata-nons.**—La Salle (1679) in Margry, Déc., I, 463, 1875. **Ouyatonons.**—Frontenac (1682) in N. Y. Doc. Col. Hist., IX, 178, note, 1855. **8yatonons.**—Longueuil (1752), ibid., x, 246, 1858. **Ouyattanons.**—Chauvignerie (1736) ibid., IX, 1057, 1855. **Ouyaws.**—Bouquet (1760) in Mass. Hist. Soc. Coll., 4th s., IX, 345, 1871. **Ouyslanous.**—McKenney and Hall, Ind. Tribes, 79, 1854 (misprint). **Oyachtownuk Roanu.**—Dobbs, Hudson's Bay, 28, 1744. **Oyaghtanont.**—Post (1758) quoted by Proud, Penn., II, app., 113, 1798. **Oyatonons.**—Vaudreuil (1711) in N. Y. Doc. Col. Hist., IX, 860, 1855. **Oyyatanous.**—Jefferys, Fr. Doms., pt. 1, 117, 1761. **Pea.**—Brinton, Lenâpe Leg., 11, 1885 (misprint). **Potanons.**—Maximilian, Trav., 82, 1843 (misprint). **Pyato-nons.**—Perkins and Peck, Annals of W., 687, 1850. **Qurachtenons.**—Buchanan, N. Am. Inds., 155, 1824. **Selugrue.**—Frontenac (1682) in N. Y. Doc. Col. Hist., IX, 178, 1855. **Uitanons.**—Maximilian, Reise, I, 186, 1837. **Waas.**—Drake, Bk. Inds., xii, 1848. **Wah-wē-ah'-tung-ong.**—Dunn, True Ind. Stories, 315, 1909 (full name, of which Wea is the abbreviation). **Wah-wee-ah-tenon.**—Hough, map in Ind. Geol. Rep. 1882, 1883. **Wak-we-ot-ta-non.**—Ibid. (village). **Warraghtinooks.**—Canajoharie conf. (1759) in N. Y. Doc. Col. Hist., VII, 384, 1856. **Wash-tenaw.**—Harvey quoted by Day, Penn., 315, 1843. **Watanons.**—Nuttall, Jour., 251, 1821. **Waughwe-oughtennes.**—Croghan (1760) in Mass. Hist. Soc. Coll., 4th s., IX, 260, 1871. **Waugweoughtannes.**—Croghan (1759) quoted by Proud, Penn., II, 296, 1798. **Wauwaughtanees.**—Mitchell map (1755) quoted in N. Y. Doc. Col. Hist., IV, 501, note, 1854. **Wawaightonos.**—German Flats conf. (1770), ibid., VIII, 233, 1857. **Wawcottonans.**—Croghan (1765) quoted in Monthly Am. Jour. Geol., 267, 1831 (misprint). **Wawehattecooks.**—Doc. of 1747 in N. Y. Doc. Col. Hist., VI, 391, 1855. **Waweotonans.**—Hildreth, Pion. Hist., 71, 1848. **Waweoughtannes.**—Croghan (1760) in Mass. Hist. Soc. Coll., 4th s., IX, 372, 1871. **Wawiachtanos.**—Loskiel (1794) quoted by Ruttenber, Tribes Hudson R., 336, 1872. **Wa-wiaghta.**—Johnson (1763) in N. Y. Doc. Col. Hist., VII, 583, 1856. **Wawiaghtanakes.**—German Flats conf. (1770), ibid., VIII, 244, 1857. **Wawiaghtanon.**—Johnson (1765) ibid., VII, 716, 1856. **Wawiaghto-nos.**—Johnson (1763) ibid., 583. **Wawia'hta'nua.**—Gatschet, Shawnee MS., B. A. E., 1880 (Shawnee name; plural, Wawiata'nuagi). **Wawiotonans.**—Croghan (1765) in N. Y. Doc. Col. Hist., VII, 780, 1856. **Wawioughtanes.**—Croghan (1757), ibid., 268. **Wawyachtenoke.**—Livingston (1700), ibid., IV, 651, 1854. **Waya'hto'nuki.**—Gatschet, Miami MS., B. A. E., 1888 (correct Miami form). **Wayough-tanies.**—Croghan (1765) in Monthly Am. Jour. Geol., 272, 1831. **Wea.**—Harmar (1790) in Am. State Papers, Ind. Aff., I, 105, 1832. **Weah.**—Jones, Ojeb-

way Inds., 178, 1861. **Weaus.**—Doc. of 1786 in Mass. Hist. Soc. Coll., 1sts., III, 26, 1794. **Weaws.**—Brown, West. Gaz., 348, 1817. **Weeah.**—Harmar (1790) in Rupp, West.Penn., app., 229, 1846. **Weea's.**—Greenville treaty (1795) in U. S. Ind. Treat., 184, 1873. **Weeaws.**—Brown, West. Gaz., 72, 1817. **Weeds.**—Rupp, West. Penn., app., 253, 1846 (misprint). **Wi-ahtanah.**—Barton, New Views, xxxiii, 1798. **Wi'-ah-tön-oon-gi.**—Dunn, True Indian Stories, 315, 1908 (Miami name of the Wea town). **Wiata-nons.**—Doc. 1756 in N. Y. Doc. Col. Hist., x, 401, 1858. **Wiaut.**—Lattré, map U. S., 1784. **Wyachte-nos.**—Putnam (1792) in Am. State Papers, Ind. Aff., I, 240, 1832. **Wyahtinaws.**—Imlay, W. Ter., 364, 1797. **Wyatanons.**—Duquesne (1754) in N. Y. Doc. Col. Hist., x, 263, 1858. **Wyeacktenacks.**—Lindesay (1749), ibid., VI, 538, 1855. **Wyogtami.**—McKenney and Hall, Ind.Tribes, III, 80, 1854. **Yeahtentanee.**—Drake, Bk. Inds., xii, 1848.

Weakaote (probably from *wiyaka ota*, 'much sand'). A former band or village of the Mdewakanton Sioux.—Long, Exped. St Peters R., I, 385, 1824.

Weanoc. A tribe of the Powhatan confederacy, formerly living in Charles City co., Va., on the N. bank of James r. In 1608 they numbered about 500. They seem to have crossed over to the s. bank of James r. toward the close of the 17th century, perhaps in consequence of a disastrous attack from the Iroquois in 1687. In 1722 Beverley stated that their former settlement in Prince George co., s. of the James, was extinct, and in 1727 it was stated that they had lived at different times on upper Nottoway r. and on a tributary stream, then called Wyanoke cr., near the North Carolina frontier. Nottoway r. was also at one time known by their name.

Chawopoweanock.—Pots in Smith (1629), Va., I, 204, repr. 1819 (incorrect combination of Chawopo and Weanock). **Weanocks.**—Smith, ibid., 116. **Wianocks.**—Boudinot, Star in the W., 129, 1816 (misprint).

Weanoc. The principal village of the Weanoc in 1608, situated below the mouth of Appomattox r., at the present Weyanoke, Prince George co., Va.

Wayanoak.—Colden (1727), Five Nat., 58, 1747. **Wyanoke.**—Beverley, Va., 199, 1722. **Wynoack.**—Moll in Humphreys, Acct., map, 1730. **Wyonoke.**—Doc. of 1727 in Martin, N. C., I, app., xvi, 1829.

Weantinock. The chief village of the Wawyachtonoc, situated on Housatonic r., near the present New Milford, Litchfield co., Conn.

Oweantonoge.—Trumbull, Hist. Conn., II, 82, 1818. **Wean'tinock.**—Trumbull, Ind. Names Conn., 80, 1881. **Wyantenock.**—Doc. of 1702 quoted by Trumbull, Hist. Conn., II, 82, 1818.

Weapemeoc. An Algonquian (?) tribe met by Raleigh's colonists in 1584–89, occupying the territory N. of Albemarle sd., N. C., including probably most of what is now Currituck, Camden, Pasquotank, and Perquimans cos. Their chief town, of the same name, seems to have been in Pasquotank co. Other towns apparently in the same jurisdiction were Pasquenock (Pasquotank?), Chepanoc, and Mascoming. They were said then to have 700 or 800 (warriors), under their chief Okisco. A century later the same territory was occupied by the Yeopim or Jaupim (Weapom-oc?), Pasquotank, Perquiman, and Poteskeet. In 1662 the Yeopim chief sold lands. In 1701, according to Lawson, the other bands still counted 40 warriors, but of the Yeopim only one man survived.   (J. M.)

Jaupin.—Lawson (1714), Hist. Car., 1860. **Weapomeioc.**—Hariot (1585), Narr., map, repr. 1893. **Weapomeiok.**—Layne (1585) in Smith, Va., Arber ed., 312, 1884. **Weepomeokes.**—Haines, Am. Ind., 582, 1888. **Weopomeiok.**—Lane (1586) in Hakluyt, Voy., III, 319, 1810. **Weopomekoes.**—Drake, Inds. N. Am., 345, 1880. **Yaopim.**—Doc. 1693 in Hawks, N. C., II, 137, 1858. **Yeopim.**—Ibid., 450.

Weapons. The offensive weapons of the Indians may be classified by their working parts and hafting, and their use. Striking weapons are of stone, bone, or wood, in the shape of clubs or balls, and into the shapes of the clubs the tribes carved a marvelous amount of their mythology, especially those among whom tractable wood was abundant; cutting weapons, before the introduction of iron, were made of stone or copper; piercing weapons were of any hard substance that would take a point. Many weapons had two or more functions. The Sioux had clubs armed with blades or points; among other tribes cutting or thrusting weapons were weighted. All three classes are subdivided according to the manner of holding or mounting. They were held in the hand, perhaps wrapped with a strip of fur, set in a grip for one hand, mounted on a longer shaft for two hands, or slung to a line. Missile weapons were thrown from a sling, darted from a throwing-stick, hurled from the hand, or shot from a bow. Not all these were equally common. The chisel-edged arrow of Africa was almost unknown in the Western Hemisphere. Piercing implements for hunting were often combined with a device for holding the quarry, and the Mexicans are said to have shot the soldiers of Cortés with harpoon arrows thrown from atlatls; but war arrows had lanceolate, not barbed points. The war arrow also had a single head. The poisoning of arrows is a much mooted question.

The most common defensive weapon of the North Americans was the shield, worn on the left arm by means of thongs fastened on the inside and used both for parrying and for covering the vitals. Shields were usually circular in form and made of the thickest rawhide, though bark, basketry, and rods woven together served the purpose here and there. The making of a shield, for which one or more covers were prepared, was attended with great ceremony. On the surface were painted heraldic devices, and the shield was further adorned with fringes, precious objects, tassels, and the plumes of eagles. A special place was set apart for it in or about the tent.

Armor was not universal and was of two sorts: (1) woven of rods or splints of wood or of plates of ivory; (2) made of thick rawhide. From Bering str. southward all varieties are found. There is historic evidence of skin armor on the Atlantic slope. The fighting of the Indians was chiefly hand to hand, hence there was little need of engineering inventions or coöperative weapons demanding the united effort of a number of men. See *Armor, Arrows, Clubs, Daggers, Knives, Lances, Poisons, Shields, Slings, Spears, Throwing-stick, Tomahawk*, etc.   (O. T. M.)

Weare. A Tenankutchin village at the mouth of Tanana r., Alaska.—Baker, Geog. Dict. Alaska, 1902.

Weataug. A village formerly near the site of the present Salisbury, Litchfield co., Conn., containing 70 wigwams in 1740. Its inhabitants were probably a part of the Mahican.

Weataug.—Trumbull, Ind. Names Conn., 80, 1881. **Weatog.**—Trumbull, Hist. Conn., II, 109, 1818.

Weatherford, William (known also as Lamochattee, or Red Eagle). A halfblood Creek chief, born about 1780; noted for the part he played in the Creek war of 1812–14, in which Gen. Jackson was leader of the American forces. There is some uncertainty as to his parentage. Claiborne (quoted by Drake, Inds. N. Am., 388, 1860) says his "father was an itinerant peddler, sordid, treacherous, and revengeful; his mother a full-blooded savage of the tribe of the Seminoles." Another authority says that a trader, Scotch or English, named Charles Weatherford (believed to have been the father of William), married a half-sister of Alexander McGillivray (q. v.), who was the daughter of an Indian chief of pure blood. In person he was tall, straight, and well proportioned, and nature had bestowed upon him genius, eloquence, and courage, but his moral character was far from commendable. He led the 1,000 Creeks at the massacre of Ft Mimms, Aug. 30, 1813. Gen. Jackson having entered the field, the Creeks were driven from point to point until Weatherford resolved to make a desperate effort to retrieve his waning fortunes by gathering all the force he could command at the Great Horseshoe bend of the Tallapoosa. The signal defeat his forces suffered at this point ended the war, and Weatherford, to save further bloodshed, or perhaps shrewdly judging the result, voluntarily delivered himself to Jackson and was released on his promise to use his influence to maintain peace. He died Mar. 9, 1824, leaving many children, who intermarried with the whites. It is said that after the war his character changed, and he became dignified, industrious, and sober. Consult Red Eagle, by G. C. Eggleston, 1878.   (C. T.)

Weaving. Among the Indians N. of Mexico weaving was done generally by

NAVAHO BELT WEAVER.   (MATTHEWS)

hand; baskets, bags, and mats were made without the aid of apparatus. But in the Atlantic states, the Aleutian ids., and doubtless elsewhere, the warp of wallets was suspended from limbs of trees or some other support, this constituting the first step toward the loom. The Chilkat of S. E. Alaska, in setting up the warp for their elaborate blankets, drove two forked stakes into the ground as far apart as the width of the blanket and laid a stout bar or pole across for a warp beam. From this was suspended a thong or stout cord stretched from side to side, which held the warp of goats' hair and cedar bark. The woman, sitting in front, wrought her intricate patterns with her fingers alone, as does the basket maker, using neither shuttle, heddle,

batten, or other device. The technic in many varieties of twined weaving involved two or more weft strands. The designs were in black, white, yellow, blue, and green, first sketched out in black on a pattern board. Farther s., in the Columbia drainage basin, fine blankets were woven after the same technic, but they were rectangular in form, lacking the elaborate fringes and borders of the Chilkat, and the decorations were geometrical.

In the E. at the time of the discovery and later in the Pacific states the Indians were found weaving into blankets feathers and down of birds as well as rabbit skins cut into narrow strips. The strips of skin were twisted into rolls as thick as a finger, and the shafts of feathers were caught between the strands of twine in twisting. These fluffy rolls constituted a kind of warp, held in place by rows of twined weaving of stout cord or babiche. In the S. W. the Spaniards introduced sheep and probably taught the Indians the use of European hand looms. With these the Pueblo tribes and the Navaho developed a genuine native art, producing narrow garters, belts, girths, and sashes, and, by different processes, larger fabrics, such as dresses and blankets. In these fabrics, as well as in all others produced in this area, the length of the web was that of the article to be produced; no cloth was made in the piece to be afterward cut up. Cotton, yucca, mulberry bark, and other fibers, hair of quadrupeds, and the down of birds formerly furnished the materials for purely native fabrics. A slender rod with a circular block for a fly-wheel served for spindle. Variety in color was given by the native hue of the materials and with dyes. The setting up of the warp was a combination of the Chilkat process and that of the conquerors. The Zuñi even adopted the western European hand heddle. In the S. the woman in weaving also sat on the ground in front of her work, using little

NAVAHO SPINNING AND WEAVING

balls of yarn tied to the warp or a simple bobbin for a shuttle. See *Art, Basketry, Clothing, Dyes and Pigments, Ornament.*

The intricate processes with crude apparatus are discussed and illustrated by Matthews in 3d Rep. B. A. E., 1884. Consult also Mason in Nat. Mus. Rep. 1901, and the bibliography therein; Bushnell in Am. Anthr., XI, no. 3, 1909; Dixon in Bull. Am. Mus. Nat. Hist., XVII, pt. 3, 1905; Niblack in Rep. Nat. Mus. 1888,

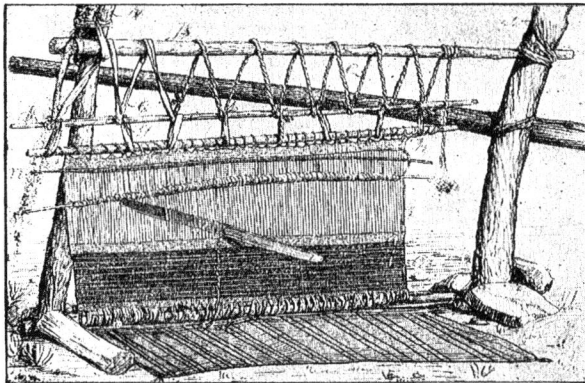

NAVAHO LOOM. (MATTHEWS)

1890; Nordenskiöld, Cliff Dwellers of Mesa Verde, 1893; Speck in Am. Anthr., IX, 293, 1907; Guide to Anthr. Coll. Prov. Mus. Victoria, 1909; Emmons and Boas, Chilkat Blanket, Mem. Am. Mus. Nat. Hist., III, pt. 4, 1907; Stites, Economics of Iroquois, 1905.   (O. T. M.)

Wechikhit. A Yokuts (Mariposan) tribe formerly living on lower Kings r., Cal., in the plains, and one of the group of tribes which ceded their lands to the United States by treaty of Apr. 29, 1851. They were then placed on Fresno res., where they were still represented in 1861. Two or three individuals survive.

Wa-cha-et—Royce in 18th Rep., B. A. E., 782, 1899. Wa-cha-hets.—McKee et al. in Senate Ex. Doc. 4, 32d Cong., spec. sess., 75, 1853. Wa-che-ha-ti.—Wessells (1853) in H. R. Ex. Doc. 76, 34th Cong., 3d sess., 31, 1857. Wa-che-nets.—Ind. Aff. Rep., 223, 1851. Wa-che-ries.—Senate Ex. Doc. 4, 32d Cong., spec. sess., 93, 1853. Waches.—Henley in Ind. Aff. Rep., 511, 1854. Watch-ahets.—Johnston in Sen. Ex. Doc. 61, 32d Cong., 1st sess., 22, 1852. Wat-ches.—Lewis in Ind. Aff. Rep. 1857, 399, 1858. Wechikhit.—Kroeber in Univ. Cal. Pub., Am. Arch. and Eth., II, 360, 1907. Wi'-chi-kik.—Powers in Cont. N. A. Ethnol., III, 370, 1877.

Wechotookme (*We-cho-took-me*). One of the 7 Seminole towns in Florida in 1799; exact locality unknown.—Hawkins (1799), Sketch, 25, 1848.

Wechquadnach (properly *Wequae'adnauke*, 'place at the end of, or extending to, the mountain'; the earlier name was Pachquadnach, 'bare mountain land.'—Trumbull). A Mahican village, probably belonging to the Wawyachtonoc tribe, formerly near Indian pond, N. w. of Sharon, Litchfield co., Conn., adjoining

57009°—Bull. 30, pt 2—12——59

the New York state line. The Moravians had a mission there about 1744. (J. M.)

Pachquadnach.—Ruttenber, Tribes Hudson R., 197, 1872. Wachquadnach.—Ibid., 86. Wechquadnach.—Ibid., 86. Wequadn'ach.—Trumbull, Ind. Names Conn., 83, 1881. Wukhquautenauk.—Ruttenber, Tribes Hudson R., 86, 1872.

Wechquetank (*wechquétank* or *wiquítank*, the Lenape name of a shrub which grew near that vicinity.—Heckewelder). A Delaware village about 8 m. beyond the Blue Ridge, N. w. from Bethlehem, probably near the present Mauch Chunk in Carbon co., Pa. It was settled in 1760 by a colony of Moravian Indians from the mission of Nain. They were driven off by the whites and their village burned in 1763.   (J. M.)

Naquetank.—Flint, Ind. Wars, 41, 1833. Wechquetank.—Loskiel, Hist. Miss. Unit. Breth., pt. 2, 193', 1794. Wequetank.—Loskiel (1794) in Day, Penn., 518, 1843.

Wechurt (*We'tcü(r)t*, 'opposite'). A Pima village at North Blackwater, s. Ariz.—Russell in 26th Rep. B. A. E., 23, 1908.

Wecquaesgeek (from *wikwaskik*, 'end of the marsh, or swamp.'—Gerard). An important tribe of the Wappinger confederacy that formerly occupied s. Fairfield co., Conn., and Westchester co., N. Y., from about Norwalk, Conn., to Hudson r. They were a strong tribe until they had trouble with the Dutch. In 1643 the Dutch massacred more than 100 in a single night, and in the war which ensued two of their three fortified villages were destroyed. In a massacre near Greenwich, Conn., a party led by Underhill killed between 500 and 700 men, women, and children of the Wecquaesgeek and Wappinger, only 8 men escaping. Peace was finally concluded in 1644. In 1663 their single remaining "castle" contained about 400 souls. The tribe still had a chief as late as 1689. Their castles are said to have been very strong, constructed of plank 5 in. thick, 9 ft high, and braced around with thick plank, pierced with portholes. One of their villages was Alipconk, another bore the name of the tribe. See *Rechtauck.*   (J. M.)

Highland Indians.—Lovelace (1669) in N. Y. Doc. Col. Hist., XIII, 440, 1881 (applied also to the Wappinger). Wechquaeskeck.—Doc. of 1644, ibid., I, 150, 1856. Weckquaesgeeks.—Breeden Raedt (ca. 1635) quoted by Ruttenber, Tribes Hudson R., 108, 1872. Weckquesicks.—Hist. Mag., 1st s,., III, 121, 1859. Wecks.—Van der Donck (1656) quoted by Ruttenber, op. cit., 82. Wequa-esgecks.—Schoolcraft, Ind. Tribes, VI, 147, 1857. Weskeskek.—Witt (1689) in N. Y. Doc. Col. Hist., III, 659, 1853. Wesquecqueck.—Doc. of 1644, ibid., I, 211, 1856. Wetquescheck.—Doc. of 1643, ibid., 186. Wioguaesgeck.—Doc. ca. 1643, ibid., 197. Wickerscreek.—Doc. of 1671, ibid., XIII, 460, 1881. Wickersecreeke.—Doc. of 1676, ibid., 496. Wickersheck.—Lovelace (1669), ibid., 440. Wickeskeck.—Lovelace (ca. 1669) quoted by Ruttenber, Tribes Hudson R., 83, 1872. Wickwaskeck.—Doc. of 1650 in N. Y. Doc. Col. Hist., I, 410, 1856. Wicquaesgeckers.—Doc. of 1643, ibid., 199. Wicquaskaka.—Livingston patent quoted in Ruttenber, Tribes Hudson R., 372, 1872.

Wiechquaeskeck.—Treaty of 1660 in N. Y. Doc. Col. Hist., XIII, 148, 1881. **Wiechquaesqueck.**—Doc. of 1663, ibid., 282. **Wiechquaaskeck.**—Treaty of 1664, ibid., 375. **Wieckquaeskecke**—Stuyvesant (1664), ibid., 365. **Wiequaeskeck**—Deed of 1649, ibid., 24. **Wiequaskeck.**—Doc. of 1655, ibid., 52. **Wighquaeskeek.**—Deed quoted in Ruttenber, op. cit., 366. **Wikagÿl.**—Map of 1614 in N. Y. Doc. Col. Hist., I, 1856. **Wiquaeshex.**—Treaty of 1645 quoted by Ruttenber, Tribes Hudson R., 118, 1872. **Wiquaeskeck.**—Treaty of 1644 in N. Y. Doc. Col. Hist., XIII, 17, 1881. **Wiskerscreeke.**—Andros (1680), ibid., 282. **Witqueschack.**—Doc. of 1644, ibid., I, 151, 1856. **Witquescheck.**—Doc. of 1646, ibid., 184. **Witqueschreek.**—Doc. of 1646, ibid., 183. **Wyckerscreeke.**—Doc. of 1671, ibid., XIII, 460, 1881. **Wyquaesquec.**—Doc. of 1641, ibid., I, 415, 1856.

Wecquaesgeek. The principal village of the Wecquaesgeek, situated on the Hudson at Dobbs Ferry, Westchester co , N. Y. Its outlines could be traced in recent times by numerous shell beds.
Weckquaesguk.—Trumbull, Ind. Names Conn., 81, 1881. **Weckquaskeck.**—Ruttenber, Tribes Hudson R., 78, 1872 **Wickquaskeck.**—Van der Donck (1656) quoted by Ruttenber, ibid., 72.

Wecuppom. A village of the Powhatan confederacy, situated in 1608 on the N. bank of the Rappahannock in Richmond co., Va.
Mecuppom.—Simons in Smith (1629), Va., I, 185, repr. 1819 (misprint). **Wecuppom.**—Smith, ibid., map.

Wedges. Wedges were probably in most general use among the woodworking

ANTLER WEDGE; HUPA. (MASON)

tribes of the far N. W. They are made of wood, stone, bone, antler, and copper, but of late years iron and steel have come into favor. These implements are employed in cutting out and splitting lumber for house and boat building, for firewood, and for other purposes. Wedges resemble celts and chisels in general shape, but are not so carefully finished and necessarily show the effect of battering from use under the hammer or maul. The heads of wooden wedges are sometimes protected by a cap of tough withes or spruce roots. Besides the woodworking wedges small wedges of various materials were in common use for tightening fastenings of implement hafts and for like purposes. See *Woodwork.*

For illustrations, see Niblack in Rep. Nat. Mus. 1888, 1890; Nelson in 18th Rep. B. A. E., 1899; Smith in Mem. Am. Mus. Nat. Hist., II, 1900; Teit, ibid.; Mason in Rep. Nat. Mus. 1886, 1889.   (W. H. H.)

Weechitokha. A former Seminole town between Suwannee and Santa Fe rs., in s. w. Columbia co., Fla.—H. R. Ex. Doc. 74 (1823), 19th Cong., 1st sess., 27, 1826.

Weendigo ('cannibal'). A mythical tribe of cannibals said by the Chippewa and Ottawa to inhabit an island in Hudson bay. Some of the Chippewa who dwelt on the N. w. shore of L. Superior were said to practise cannibalism and were

called by this name. The Maskegon on the shores of Hudson bay, though reproached as cannibals by the other tribes, were said to be themselves in constant fear of the Weendigo.
Onaouientagos.—Bacqueville de la Potherie, Hist., II, 49, 1753 (misprint). **Weendegoag**—Tanner, Narr., 316, 1830 (Ottawa form). **Weendigoes.**—Kane, Wanderings of an Artist, 60, 1859. **Windigos.**—Kingsley, Stand. Nat. Hist., pt. 6, 153, 1883.

Weequashing. See *Wigwassing.*

Weesick. A popular name in Connecticut for the fall herring, *Alosa mattowacca.* The meaning is unknown.   (W R G.)

Weesowhetko (*Wee-sow-het'-ko,* 'yellow tree'). A subgens of the Delawares.—Morgan, Anc. Soc., 172, 1877.

Weesquobs. A village of Praying Indians in 1674 near the present Pocasset, Barnstable co., Mass. (Bourne, 1694, in Mass. Hist. Soc. Coll., 1st s., I, 197, 1806), probably subject to the Wampanoag.

Weetamoo. See *Wetamoo.*

Wehatsa. The Calabash clan of Jemez pueblo, N. Mex. A corresponding clan existed also at the related pueblo of Pecos.
Wą-hä.—Hewett in Am. Anthr., n. s., VI, 431, 1904 (Pecos form). **Wa'-ha'-há'.**—Hodge in Am. Anthr., IX, 349, 1896 (Pecos form). **Wĕhätsa-ásh.**—Ibid. (Jemez form; *ash*='people').

Weinshauks. A Pequot village in 1636, the residence of Sassacus, the principal chief. On a map drawn by Williams in 1636 (see Mass. Hist. Soc. Coll., 3d s., I, 161, 1825) it is located between Thames and Mystic rs., near the present Groton, New London co., Conn.

Weitspekan Family. A linguistic family consisting of the Yurok (q. v.) tribe alone, inhabiting the lower Klamath r. valley and the adjacent coast in N. California The name is an adaptation of Weitspus (q. v.).
=**Weits-pek.**—Gibbs in Schoolcraft, Ind. Tribes, III, 422, 1853 (a band and language on Klamath at junction of Trinity); Latham, Elem. Comp. Philol., 410, 1862 (junction of Klamatl and Trinity rs.); Gatschet in Mag. Am. Hist., 163, 1877 (affirmed to be distinct from any neighboring tongue); Gatschet in Beach, Ind. Misc., 438, 1877. < **Weitspek.**—Latham in Trans. Philol. Soc. Lond., 77, 1856 (junction of Klamatl and Trinity rs.; Weyot and Wishosk dialects); Latham, Opuscula, 343, 1860. =**Eurocs.**—Powers in Overland Mo., VIII, 530, June 1872 (of the lower Klamath and coastwise; Weitspek, a village of). =**Eurok.**—Gatschet in Mag. Am. Hist., 163, 1877; Gatschet in Beach, Ind. Misc., 437, 1877. = **Yú-rok.**—Powers in Cont. N. A. Ethnol., III, 45, 1877 (from junction of Trinity to mouth and coastwise); Powell, ibid., 460 (vocabs. of Al-i-kwa, Klamath, Yu'-rok). × **Klamath.**—Keane in Stanford, Compend., Cent. and So. Am., 475, 1878 (Eurocs belong here). =**Weitspekan.**—Powell in 7th Rep. B. A. E., 131, 1891.

Weitspus (from *Weitspekw,* the name of a spring in the village.—Kroeber). A Yurok village on lower Klamath r., opposite the mouth of the Trinity, N. w. Cal. This was one of the most populous Yurok villages, and one of only two or three at which both the Deerskin dance and the Jumping dance were held It is now a post-office under the name of Weitchpec. Including the settlements on the opposite side of the river the Indian population of Weitchpec is now about 100.   (A. L. K.)

Ansafriki.—A. L. Kroeber, inf'n, 1904 (Karok name). **Weitchpec.**—Ibid. (white men's name).

Wejack. A name of the fisher (*Mustela pennanti*) formerly in use among the people of the fur country: from *otchig* or *odjik*, the name of this animal in the Chippewa dialect of Algonquian, which is also the original of *woodchuck* (q. v.). With the confusion of names of fisher and marmot may be compared that of the names of the American glutton and the badger, noted under *Carcajou*.   (A. F. C.)

Wejegi (probably from Navaho, *bitsigi*, 'in its head,' or *bitsé'ge*, 'among its rocks.'—Matthews). The name given by a New Mexican to Gen. J. H. Simpson in 1850 as that of an important ancient pueblo ruin in Chaco canyon, N. W. N. Mex., about 6 m. S. E. of Pueblo Bonito, on the N. side of the arroyo, at the base of the canyon wall. It is a rectangular structure, 225 by 120 ft in exterior dimensions, built around 3 sides of a court, the S. side of which is open, there being no vestige of an inclosing wall as with other Chaco Canyon pueblos. The rooms average about 8 by 14 ft in size, a few being about 8 ft square. Two circular kivas are embraced within the walls, each being 30 ft in diameter. The building was 3 stories high, and considerable portions of wall are still standing, but no timbers remain in place. The plan of the building is remarkably symmetrical, the masonry regular and well finished. The material is grayish yellow sandstone, laid in small tabular pieces with thin mortar. There are small windows in the second story, below which are apertures 2 by 3 ft in size, extending diagonally through the walls. These appear to have been used for loopholes for the defense of the pueblo.   (E. L. H.)

Kĭ'ndotlĭz.—Matthews, Navaho Leg., passim, 1897 ('blue house': Navaho name). **Wegegi.**—Bell in Jour. Ethnol. Soc. Lond., I, 247, 1869. **Weje-gi.**—Simpson, Exped. Navajo Country, 77, 1850. **Weji-gi.**—Hardacre in Scribner's Mo., 275, Dec. 1878.

Wekapaug ('at the end of the pond.'—Trumbull). The principal village of the eastern Niantic, formerly about the site of Charlestown, R. I. Variants of the name are Wecapaug, Wequapaug, Wequapauock, etc.

Wekapaug. A Nipmuc village formerly on the site of West Brookfield, Worcester co., Mass.

Wickabaug.—Chase cited by Kinnicutt, Ind. Names, 95, 1905.

Wekeeponall. A Delaware village in 1758, on the W. bank of the Susquehanna, about the mouth of Loyalsock cr., in the present Lycoming co., Pa. (Post, Jour., 1758, 189, 1904). Probably identical with Queen Esther's Town.

Welagamika ('rich soil'). A Delaware village on the site of Nazareth, Lehigh co., Pa., abandoned about 1748.

Welagamika.—Heckewelder in Trans. Am. Philos. Soc., n. s., IV, 359, 1834. **Welakamika.**—Ibid., 383.

Welika (Creek: *ú-i* 'water', *läíka* 'extending' or 'sitting'). A former Seminole town, 4 m. E. of the Tallahassee towns, probably in Leon co., Fla.—H. R. Ex. Doc. 74 (1823), 19th Cong., 1st sess., 27, 1826.

Welsh Indians. According to a story of the Welsh bards, first printed in Lloyd's History of Cambria in 1584, a certain Prince Madoc of Wales in the year 1170 sailed westward and discovered a new land. Returning to Wales he fitted out a second squadron, which sailed away and was never heard of again. Although the story is lacking in detail or corroborating evidence, its romantic side appealed strongly to Welsh national pride, while on the political side it was eagerly seized to offset in a measure the Spanish claims of priority in American discovery, so that it has been perpetuated and constantly amplified for the last 3 centuries by a succession of writers, who have built up a tribe of "Welsh Indians" on the flimsiest theories until the extension of linguistic investigation has left no resting place on the entire continent for this mythic people. The first discovery of a tribe of Welsh Indians, in this case the Tuscarora of North Carolina, was announced by the Rev. Morgan Jones, who claimed to have been taken prisoner by the Tuscarora, who spared his life when they heard him pray in the Welsh language, which they said was the same as their own. His story was published in the Turkish Spy about 1730 and in the Gentleman's Magazine in 1740, and was widely copied and commented on. In 1768 another Welshman, Rev. Charles Beatty (Journal of a Tour in America), enlarged the story by giving these Indians a Welsh Bible, which they were unable to read, but which their prisoner read and explained to them in the Welsh language to their great edification. About the same time another Welshman, Griffith, who had been captured by the Shawnee in 1764, claimed to have met in his wanderings a tribe of Indians speaking his own language; and in 1774 David Jones, in his Journal, attempted to give examples of Welsh identities for the languages of the Ohio valley. Others have attempted to identify this mythic tribe with the Nottoway, Croatan, Modoc, Moki (Hopi), Padouca (Comanche), Pawnee, Kansa, Oto, and, most of all, with the Mandan, the noted traveler Catlin having devoted a whole chapter to the latter hypothesis, but with as little success as all the others. Some theorists have had the mythic tribe speak "Keltic," and some, notably Custer, have made it Gaelic. It seems hardly necessary to state that there is not a provable trace of Welsh, Gaelic, or any other European language in any native American language, excepting for a few words of recent introduction which have had no effect whatever on the general structure or vocabulary.

Consult Catlin, N. Am. Inds., for Mandan theory; Bowen, Am. Discovered by the Welsh, 1876; Burder, Welsh Inds., 1797; Durrett in Filson Club Pub., no. 23, 1908; Lewis in Trans. Oneida Hist. Soc., 1894; Mooney, Growth of a Myth, in Am. Anthr., Oct. 1891, and numerous authorities noted in Winsor, Narr. Crit. Hist. Am., I, notes 109–111, 1889.

The early stories of a tribe of "White Indians" (q. v.), or "White, Bearded Indians," somewhere in the unknown interior, refer sometimes to this mythic Welsh tribe, but more often appear to arise from misinterpreted Indian accounts of other distant European colonies or visitations, or of some tribe of complexion lighter than usual. See *Lost Ten Tribes of Israel, Popular Fallacies.*   (J. M.)

Madawgwys.—Bowen, Am. Discov. by the Welsh, 93, 1876 (also Madogian and Madogiaint; so called by various authors). **Madocian Inds.**—Ibid., 63 (term used with reference to the Indians of Prince Madoc). **Madogians.**—Janson, Stranger in Am., 270, 1807. **Madogiant.**—Bowen, op. cit., 93. **Mnacedeus.**—Ker quoted by Drake, Bk. Inds., bk. I, 38, 1848. **Welch.**—Drake, ibid., xii. **Welsh Bearded Indians.**—Bowen, op. cit., 129. **Welsh Indianv.**—Croghan (1759) in Rupp, West. Pa., 146, 1846 (misprint).

Welunungsi (*We-lun-ŭng-si*, 'little turtle'). A subclan of the Delawares.—Morgan, Anc. Soc., 172, 1877.

Welwashkeni (*Welwashχē'ni*, 'place of the large spring'). A former Modoc settlement on the s. E. side of Tule lake, at Miller's farm, N. E. Cal.—Gatschet in Cont. N. A. Ethnol., II, pt. I, xxxii, 1890.

Wenameac. See *Winamac.*

Wenatchi (Yakima: *winätshi*, 'river issuing from a canyon,' referring to Wenatchee r.). A Salish division, probably a band of the Pisquows, formerly on Wenatchee r., a tributary of the Columbia in Washington. In 1850 there were said to have been 50 on Yakima res., but 66 were enumerated in the Report on Indian Affairs for 1910 as under the Colville agency. It is uncertain whether these bodies belonged to one original band.

Lower Chehalis.—Common name. **Wanoolchie.**—Ford in Ind. Aff. Rep. 1857, 341, 1858. **Waratcha.**—Ind. Aff. Rep., 219, 1861. **Waratka.**—Ibid., 1864, 499, 1865. **Waratkass.**—Ibid. 1863, 512, 1864. **Wenatcha.**—Lansdale, ibid., 1859, 412, 1860. **Wenatchi.**—Ind. Aff. Rep., 704, 1901. **Wenatshapam.**—U. S. Stat. at Large, XII, 951. **Wenatshapan.**—Ind. Aff. Rep. 1856, 266, 1857. **Wenatshepum.**—Ibid., 110, 1874. **Winä'tshipûm.**—Mooney in 14th Rep. B. A. E., 736, 1896 (given as a synonym of Pisquows). **Wynoochee.**—Gibbs in Pac. R. R. Rep., I, 428, 1855. **Wy-noot-che.**—Ross in Ind. Aff. Rep., 18, 1870.

Wendigo. See *Windigo.*

Wendjimadub ('whence he sits'; that is, supposing he was sitting in one spot, he moves from it and sits in another). A Chippewa chief and orator, with a strain of French blood, born at La Pointe, Wis., about 1838. He married a Mississippi Chippewa, and since 1868 has lived at White Earth, where he is at the head of a band of about 40. Wendjimadub is noted for his independence. When, about 1878, a half-breed trader induced all the other chiefs to join him in opposing a worthy Indian agent, Lewis Stowe, in order that an agent might be appointed who would further his schemes, Wendjimadub was the only one who had the courage to stand up openly in the council before prominent Americans, and take the agent's part, declaring his innocence and showing why the warfare was waged against him. Although uneducated, Wendjimadub is by far the best speaker among the Chippewa. He served in a Minnesota regiment throughout the Civil War. He farms to some extent, but is in sufficiently affluent circumstances to live without working. He has been converted to Christianity.   (J. A. G.)

Wenimesset (*wenomissit*, 'at the grapevine.'—Gerard). A Nipmuc village in 1676, at the present New Braintree, Worcester co., Mass.

Wenimesset.—Rowlandson quoted by Drake, Trag. Wild., 25, 1841. **Wenimisset.**—Kinnicutt, Ind. Names Worcester Co., 56, 1905. **Winnimissett.**—Ibid.

Wenona. A small snake (*Charina bottæ*) found in California and Mexico. From *winona* (q. v.) in the Santee Sioux language, signifying 'first-born child' [if a daughter]. The word is also a place name.   (A. F. C.)

Wenrohronon (*Awĕñro'roñ'noⁿ'*, probably from a combination of the noun *awĕñ'rä'*, the Huron form of the common Iroquoian vocable denoting 'scum,' 'moss,' 'lather,' with the verb stem -*o*', 'to float,' 'to be immersed or contained in liquid or in the earth,' 'to be in solution,' 'to be contained in,' with the tribal appellative suffix -*roñnoⁿ*'. *Awĕñ'ro*' (*ouenro* in the Jesuit Relations), the base of the term, signifies, as a geographic name, 'where scum floats on the water'; hence *Awenrohronon* means 'the people or tribe of the place of floating scum.' The suggested meaning of the name would seem to indicate that the Wenrohronon may have lived in the vicinity of the famous oil spring of the town of Cuba, Allegany co., N. Y., described as a filthy, stagnant pool, about 20 ft in diameter, without an outlet. A yellowish-brown oil collects on its surface, and this was the source of the famous "Seneca oil," formerly a popular local remedy for various ailments. The spring was so highly regarded by the Seneca that they always reserved it in their land-sale treaties). One of the tribes which, according to the Jesuit Relation for 1639, had been associated with the Neutral Nation and which had lived on the eastern borders of the Neutral Nation toward the Iroquois, the common enemy of all these tribes. As the territory of the Neutral Nation on the E. side of Niagara r. extended at this date southward to the "end" of L. Erie and eastward to the watershed of Genesee r., at least, the former habitat of the Wenrohronon must have been s. of this territory. So long as the Wenrohronon kept on good terms with the Neutral Nation they were able to withstand their enemies and to maintain themselves against the latter's raids and incursions. But owing to some dissatisfaction, possibly fear of Iroquois displeasure, the Neutral Nation severed its relations with the devoted Wenrohronon, who were thus left a prey to their enemies. Deciding therefore to seek asylum and protection from some other tribe, they sent an embassy to the Hurons, who received them kindly and accepted their proposal, offering to assist them and to escort them with warriors in their migration. Nevertheless, the fatigue and hardships of the long retreat of more than 80 leagues by a body exceeding 600 persons, largely women and children, caused many to die on the way, and nearly all the remainder arrived at Ossossané and other Huron towns ill from the epidemic which was primarily the occasion of their flight. The Jesuit Relation cited says: "Wherever they were received, the best places in the cabins were assigned them, the granaries or caches of corn were opened, and they were given liberty to make such use of it as their needs required."

It is stated (Jes. Rel. 1647–48, XXXIII, 63, 1898) that the southern shores of L. Erie were formerly inhabited "by certain tribes whom we call the Nation of the Cat (or Panther); they have been compelled to retire far inland to escape their enemies, who are farther to the west," and that this Nation of the Panther has a number of fixed towns, as it cultivates the soil. This shows that the appellation "Nation du Chat" was a generic name for "certain tribes" dwelling s. and s. E. of L. Erie, whose enemies farther westward had forced at least some of them to migrate eastward. From the list of names of tribes cited by Brebeuf in the Jesuit Relation for 1635 (33, 1858) the names of four tribes of the Iroquois tongue dwelling s. of L. Erie and of the domain of the Five Iroquois tribes occur in the order: Andastoerrhonons (Conestoga), Scahentoarrhonons (People of Wyoming valley), Rhiierrhonons (the Erie), and the Ahouenrochrhonons (Wenrohronon). But this last name is omitted from the list of tribal names cited from Father Ragueneau's "Carte Huronne," recorded by Father

LeJeune in his Relation for 1640 (35, 1858), because this tribe, in 1639, becoming too weak to resist the Iroquois, having lost the support of an alliance with the Neutral Nation, and being afflicted with an epidemic, probably smallpox, had taken flight, part seeking refuge among the Hurons and part among the Neutral Nation, with which peoples they became incorporated. The Jesuit Relation for 1641 (80, 1858) says that in the town of Khioetoa, surnamed St Michel, of the Neutral Nation, a certain foreign nation, named A8enrehronon, which formerly dwelt beyond "the Erie or the Nation du Chat (or the Panther Nation)," had for some years past taken refuge. Father Jean de Brebeuf and Father Joseph Marie Chaumonot started from Ste Marie of the Hurons on Nov. 2, 1640, on a mission to the Neutral Nation; but owing to several causes, chiefly false reports spread among them by Huron spies concerning the nature of this mission, they were coldly received by the Neutrals as a whole, and were subjected to much abuse and contumely. But the Wenrohronon dwelling at Khioetoa lent willing ears to the gospel, and an old woman who had lost her hearing was the first adult person among them to be baptized. Bressani's Relation for 1653 (Thwaites ed., XXXIX, 141, 1899), however, says that among the Hurons the Oenronronnons, whether by true or false report, added weight to the charges against the Jesuits of being the cause of the epidemic and other misfortunes of the people. The foregoing quotation definitely declares that this tribe of the Wenrohronon dwelt before their migration "beyond the Erie" or the Panther Nation. It is therefore probable that this tribe lived on the upper waters of the Allegheny, possibly on the w. branch of the Susquehanna, and that it was one of the tribes generically called the Black Minquaas. Writing to his brother on Apr. 27, 1639, Father DuPeron (Jes. Rel. 1639, XV, 159, 1898), in reference to the Wenrohronon, says: "We have a foreign nation which has taken refuge here, both on account of the Iroquois, their enemies, and on account of the epidemic, which is still causing them to die here in large numbers; they are nearly all baptized before death." Of the Wenrohronon, Father Bressani, writing in 1653 (ibid., XXXIX, 141, 1899), says that they had then only recently come into the Huron country, and that they "had formerly traded with the English, Dutch, and other heretical Europeans." Nothing is known of the numbers of the refugee Wenrohronon who fled to the Neutral Nation, but these were in addition to the "more than 600" who arrived in the Huron country in 1639. From Herrman's map of Virginia and Maryland in 1670 (published in 1673) much information is derived in regard to the valley of the Juniata r., the w. branch of the Susquehanna, and the Wyoming or Scahentowanen valley.   As the Wenrohronon were on hostile terms with the Iroquois tribes, and as they were known to have traded with the English, the Dutch, and other Europeans, it would appear that they must have followed the routes to the trading places on the Delaware and the lower Hudson customarily followed by the Black Minquaas, with whom they seem to have been allied. From Herrman's map it is learned also that the Black Minquaas lived w. of the Alleghany mts., on the Ohio or Black Minquaas r., and that these Indians reached Delaware r. by means of the Conemaugh, a branch of the Ohio or Black Minquaas r., and the Juniata, a branch of the Susquehanna, and that prior to 1670 the Black Minquaas came over the Alleghany mts. along these branches as far as the Delaware to trade.   These Wenrohronon were probably closely allied in interests with the Black Minquaas, and so came along the same route to trade on the Delaware. Diverging eastward from the Wyoming valley were three trails—one through Wind gap to Easton, Pa., the second by way of the Lackawanna at Capouse meadows through Cobb's gap and the Lackawaxen to the Delaware and Hudson, and the third, sometimes called the "Warrior's path," by way of Ft Allen and along the Lehigh to the Delaware Watergap at Easton.   From the journal of Rev. Wm. Rogers with Sullivan's expedition against the Iroquois in 1779, it is learned that in the Great Swamp is Locust Hill, where evident marks of a destroyed Indian village were discovered; that the Tobyhanna and Middle crs. flow into Tunkhannock, which flows into the head branch of the Lehigh, which in turn joins the Delaware at Easton; that Moosick mtn., through a gap of which Sullivan passed into the Great Swamp, is on the dividing line or ridge between the Delaware and the Susquehanna.   This indicates the routes by which the Wenrohronon could readily have reached the Delaware r. for trading purposes at a very early date.

LeJeune (Jes. Rel. 1639, XVII, 213, 1898) states that the Wenrohronon, "those strangers who recently arrived in this country," excel in drawing out an arrow from the body and in curing the wound, but that the efficacy of the prescription avails only in the presence of a pregnant woman.   In the same Relation (p. 37) he says that "the number of the faithful who make profession of Christianity in this village amounts to nearly 60, of whom

many are Wenrohronons from among those poor strangers taking refuge in this country."   According to the Jesuit Relation for 1672–73 (LVII, 197, 1899) there were Wenrohronon captives among the Seneca, along with others from the Neutral Nation, the Onnontioga, and the Hurons; the three nations or tribes last-named, according to Father Frémin (1669–70), composed the Seneca town of Kanagaro, the Neutrals and the Onnontioga being described as having seen scarcely any Europeans or having heard of the true God.

The historical references above given indicate that the Wenrohronon, before their wars with the Iroquois and before they were stricken with smallpox, must have been a tribe of considerable importance, numbering at least 1,200 or 1,500, and possibly 2,000 persons.   (J. N. B. H.)

Ahouenroochrhonons.—Jes. Rel. 1635, 34, 1858. **Awenrehronon.**—Jes. Rel., III, index, 1858. **Oenronronnons.**—Jes. Rel. 1653, XXXIX, 141, 1899. **8eanohronons.**—Jes. Rel. 1639, 55, 1858 (misprint, corrected in errata). **Ouenro nation.**—Ibid., 1673, LVII, 197, 1899. **8enrôronons.**—Jes. Rel. 1639, 98, 1858. **Weanohronons.**—Ibid., 1639, XVI, 253, 1898. **Wenro.**—Shea, Cath. Miss., 179, 1855. **Wenrohronons (8enrohronons).**—Jes. Rel. 1639, 55, 1858 (form given in errata).

Weogufka ('muddy water').   A former Upper Creek town on a branch of Ponchishatchee cr., in s. w. Coosa co., Ala., with 103 heads of families in 1832.

Owekofea.—Royce in 18th Rep. B. A. E., Ala. map, 1900. **U-i-ukúfki.**—Gatschet, Creek Migr. Leg., I, 149, 1884. **We-a-guf-ka.**—Sen. Ex. Doc. 425, 24th Cong., 1st sess., 277, 1836. **We guf car.**—Parsons in Schoolcraft, Ind. Tribes, IV, 576, 1854. **Weogufka.**—H. R. Rep. 37, 31st Cong., 2d sess., 122, 1851.

Weogufka.   A town of the Creek Nation, Okla.

U-i-ukúfki.—Gatschet, Creek Migr. Leg., II, 186, 1888.

Wepanawomen.   A village situated in 1608 on the E. bank of Patuxent r. in Anne Arundel co., Md.—Smith (1629), Va., I, map, repr. 1819.

Weperigweia.   An Algonquian tribe living in 1635 N. of St Lawrence r., below Tadoussac, Quebec.

Oueperigoueiaouek.—Jes. Rel. 1643, 38, 1858. **Ouperigoue-ouaouakhi.**—Jes. Rel. 1635, 18, 1858. **Weperigoueiawek.**—Jes. Rel., III, index, 1858.

Wequadong (from *wikuedunk*, 'at the bay').   An ancient Chippewa village where the L'Anse band still live, near L'Anse, at the head of Keweenaw bay, Baraga co., Mich.

Ance.—Shea, Cath. Miss., 390, 1855. **Ance-ke-we-naw.**—Warren (1852) in Minn. Hist. Soc. Coll., V, 38, 1885. **Ause Kenowenou.**—Chauvignerie (1736) quoted by Schoolcraft, Ind. Tribes, III, 556, 1853 (misprint). **Kiouanan.**—Chauvignerie in N. Y. Doc. Col. Hist., IX, 1054, 1855. **Kiouanau.**—Chauvignerie quoted in Minn. Hist. Soc. Coll., V, 427, 1885. **Kiouanous.**—Chauvignerie quoted by Schoolcraft, Ind. Tribes, III, 556, 1853 (misprint). **Kioueouenau.**—Vaudreuil (1719) in N. Y. Doc. Col. Hist., IX, 893, 1855. **Kuk-ke-wa-on-an-ing.**—Warren (1852) in Minn. Hist. Soc. Coll., V, 243, 1885. **L'Anse.**—La Pointe treaty (1854) in U. S. Ind. Treat., 223, 1873. **We-qua-dong.**—Warren (1852) in Minn. Hist. Soc. Coll., V, 38, 1885. **Wikuedo-wininiwak.**—Gatschet, Ojibwa MS., B. A. E., 1882 ('people at the inlet': name of the band). **Wikuedunk.**—Ibid. **Wi'kwädunk.**—Wm. Jones, inf'n, 1905. **Wikwed.**—Baraga, Eng.-Otch. Dict., 154, 1878 (Chippewa form). **Wikwedong.**—Ibid.

Wequashing. See *Wigwassing*.

Werawahon. A village of the Powhatan confederacy, situated in 1608 on the N. bank of Chickahominy r., in New Kent co., Va.—Smith (1629), Va., I, map, repr. 1819.

Werowacomoco ('chief's town'). A town of the Powhatan confederacy, situated in 1608 on the N. bank of York r., in Gloucester co., Va., about opposite the mouth of Queen cr. Although it was the favorite residence of Powhatan, the population did not exceed 200 persons. On account of the encroachments of the whites he subsequently withdrew to Orapaks.

Meronocomoco.—Simons in Smith (1629), Va., I, 162, repr. 1819 (misprint). **Werawocomoco.**—Smith (1629), ibid., 117. **Werowcomoco.**—Ibid., 142. **Wérowocómicos.**—Jefferson, Notes, table, 1801. **Werowocomoco.**—Smith (1629), op. cit., 74.

Werowance. A chief, or head-man, among the former Indians of Maryland and Virginia. Gerard (Am. Anthr., IX, 112, 1907) derives the word from Renape *wirowántĕsu*, 'he is rich,' or 'he exists in affluence,' the chief radical being *wiro*, 'to be rich.' Other forms of the word are weroance, wirowance, wiroans, wyroans, wyraunce, etc.

Wesaenikashika ('snake people'). A Quapaw gens.

Serpent gens.—Dorsey in 15th Rep. B. A. E., 229, 1897. **Wĕs'ă e'nikaci'ɤa.**—Ibid.

Wesawmaun (*We-saw-mä'-un*, 'yellow eel'). A gens of the Mahican.—Morgan, Anc. Soc., 174, 1877.

Weshacum (*wechecum* is given by Roger Williams as the Narraganset name of the sea, to which Trumbull adds: "as the great 'producer' of their staple food, fish"). A Nashua village, apparently the principal one, at Washacum ponds, near Sterling, Worcester co., Mass., in the 17th century.

Washacum.—Willard, Address, 59, 1853. **Wesakam.**—Gookin (1677) in Trans. Am. Antiq. Soc., II, 487, 1836. **Weshacum.**—Doc. ca. 1675 quoted by Drake, Bk. Inds., bk. III, 83, 1848. **Weshakim.**—Gookin (1674) in Mass. Hist. Soc. Coll., 1st s., I, 162, 1806. **Weshakum.**—Gookin (1677) in Trans. Am. Antiq. Soc., II, 512, 1836.

Weskarini. An Algonquian tribe that lived on the N. side of Ottawa r. below Allumette id., Quebec, with the people of which they appear to be closely associated in the Jesuit Relations.

Little Nation of the Algomquins.—Jefferys, Fr. Doms., pt. 1, map, 1761. **Ouaouechkaïrini.**—Jes. Rel. for 1640, 34, 1858. **Ouaouechkairiniouek.**—Jes. Rel. for 1658, 22, 1858. **Ouaouiechkairini.**—Champlain (1613), Œuvres, III, 299, note, 1870. **8a8iechkarini8ek.**—Jes. Rel. for 1646, 34, 1858. **8e8eskariniens.**—Jes. Rel. for 1643, 61, 1858. **Ouescharini.**—Champlain (1613), Œuvres, III, 299, 1870. **Petite Nation.**—Jes. Rel. for 1633, 34, 1858. **Petite nation des Algonquins.**—Jes. Rel. for 1640, 34, 1858. **Petits Algonquins.**—La Tour map, 1784. **Quieunontateronons.**—Sagard, Hist. du Can., III, 738, 1866 (Huron name). **Wawechkaïrini.**—Jes. Rel., III,

index, 1858. **Waweskaïrini.**—Ibid. **Wewechkaïrini.**—Ibid.

Wessagusset. A former Massachuset village near the present Weymouth, Norfolk co., Mass.

Wechagaskas.—Hoyt, Antiq. Res., 89, 1824. **Weechagaskas.**—Gookin (1674) in Mass. Hist. Soc. Coll., 1st s., I, 148, 1806. **Weesagascusett.**—Bradford (ca. 1650), ibid., 4th s., III, 241, 1856. **Wesaguscasit.**—Pratt (1662), ibid., IV, 479, 1858. **Wesaguscus.**—Dudley (1631) in N. H. Hist. Soc. Coll., IV, 227, 1834. **Wesegusquaset.**—Mather (ca. 1680) in Mass. Hist. Soc. Coll., 4th s., IV, 491, 1858. **Wessaguscus.**—Dudley (1630), ibid., 1st s., VIII, 87, 1802. **Wessagusquasset.**—Hubbard (1680), ibid., 2d s., v, 32, 1815. **Wessagussett.**—Ibid., 1st s., I, 125, 1806. **Westaugustus.**—Hubbard (1680), ibid., 2d s., V, 192, 1815. **Wichagashas.**—Schoolcraft, Ind. Tribes, VI, 150, 1857. **Wichaguscusset.**—Mourt (1622) in Mass. Hist. Soc. Coll., 1st s., VIII, 248, 1802. **Wisaguset.**—Josselyn (1675), ibid., 3d s., III, 325, 1833. **Wissaguset.**—Josselyn (1675), ibid., 318.

West Abeika (*Aiabeka*, 'unhealthful place'). A former Choctaw village located by Romans at the head of Chickasawhay r., Miss., probably in the present Neshoba co. It was called West Abeika to distinguish it from another town (see *East Abeika*) of the name at the junction of Sukenatcha and Straight crs.—Halbert in Pub. Miss. Hist. Soc., VI, 425, 427, 1902. See *Abihka*.

Abeka.—Romans, Florida, 323, 1775. **West Abeiko.**—West Florida map, ca. 1775.

West Congeeto. A former Choctaw town on the headwaters of Chickasawhay r., presumably in Kemper co., Miss.

West Congeta.—Romans, Fla., 315, 1775. **West Congeto.**—West Fla. map, ca. 1775.

Westenhuck (corruption of *Hous'atenuc*, Eng. *Housatonic*, 'at the other side of the mountain.'—Trumbull). A former Mahican village near Great Barrington, Berkshire co., Mass. It was the capital of the Mahican confederacy after the removal of the council fire from Schodac. The inhabitants removed to Stockbridge in 1736, soon after the establishment of the mission at that place. A few removed to Pennsylvania, where they joined the Delawares and kindred tribes. Most of the Stockbridges came originally from Westenhuck.   (J. M.)

Waahktoohook.—Hoyt, Antiq. Res., 209, 1824. **Wahktoohook.**—Ibid., 225. **Westenhook.**—Deed of 1679 in N. Y. Doc. Col. Hist., XIII, 545, 1881. **Westenhuck.**—Ruttenber, Tribes Hudson R., 62, 1872 (name used by Moravian missionaries). **W-nahkta-kook.**—Ibid. (name used by English missionaries). **Wnahktukook.**—Barber, Hist. Coll. Mass., 95, 1841. **Wnoghquetookoke.**—Edwards (1788) in Mass. Hist. Soc. Coll., 2d s., X, 95, 1823.

West Greenlanders. A geographic group of Eskimo without recognized subdivisions. They have long been Christianized by German Moravian and Danish missionaries, and live principally about the mission stations. A considerable admixture of white blood is found among them. They are expert in hunting the seal with the large harpoon and bladder, and manage their kaiaks with marvelous skill. They numbered 9,752 in 1880. Their villages, including the Danish trading posts and the mission stations, are as follows: Adjuitsuppa, Agdluitsok, Aglutok, Amerdlok, Angpalartok, Arpik, Arsuk, Atanekerdluk, Blaesedael, Christianshaab, Claushaven, Drynaeskirk, Egedesminde, Episok, Fiskernaes, Frederiksdal, Frederikshaab, Godthaab, Holstenborg, Igdlorpait, Inigsuarsak, Ipik, Itivliarsuk, Ivigtut, Ivikat, Jacobshavn, Julianehaab, Kaersok, Kagsersuak, Kanajormiut, Kangek, Kangiartsoak, Kapisilik, Kariak, Karsok, Karusuk, Kasigianguit, Kekertarsuarak, Kinalik, Kingiktok, Kornok, Lichtenfels, Maklykaut, Merkitsok, Nanortalik, Narsak, Narsarsuk, Nugsoak, Numarsuak, Nunatarsuak, Ny Herrnhut, Okossisak, Pamiadluk, Proven, Ritenbenk, Sagdlet, Saitok, Sardlok, Sarkak, Sermilik, Sukkertoppen, Svartehuk, Tornait, Tuapait, Tunuliarbik, Umanak, Upernivik, Utlaksuk, Uvingasok, Yotlik, Zukkertop.

Westo. A name applied by the coast Indians of southern South Carolina to a tribe dwelling along Savannah r. in the latter part of the 17th century. They were dreaded enemies of the coast people, who declared that they were man-eaters. In 1674 Henry Woodward visited their town, or a town of theirs, situated on a point on the w. bank of Savannah r., two-thirds surrounded by the river and protected by palisades. Their predatory habits made them particularly troublesome in 1669–71, and in 1674 it was necessary to send against them a company of volunteer troops. In 1681 part of the Shawnee drove them from the region about Augusta, Ga., and little is heard of them afterward. It appears, however, that some of the Westo, at least, retired among the Lower Creeks, first to Okmulgee r. and thence to Chattahoochee r., from which circumstance and other evidence it is almost certain that they were identical with the well-known Yuchi (q. v.). This tribe is the "Oustack" of Lederer (1672), and perhaps the Yustaga (q. v.) of the Florida explorers in the 16th century. (J. R. S.)

Oustaca.—De Bry map (1591) in Le Moyne, Narr., Appleton trans., 1875. **Oustack.**—Lederer, Discov., 17, 1672. **Oustacs.**—Gatschet, Creek Migr. Leg., I, 48, 1884. **Westoes.**—Archdale (1707) in Ramsay, Hist. So. Car., I, 34, 1809.

Wetamoo. A female chieftain of a part of the Wampanoag, in the latter part of the 17th century, generally known during Philip's war as the Squaw Sachem of Pocasset. She was the wife of Alexander (Wamsutta), Philip's elder brother, and sister of Wootonekauske, Philip's wife, and until Alexander's death (1662) went under the name of Namumpam. She survived her husband, and after his death was called Wetamoo (Weetamoe, Weetamoo, Wetamoe, Wetamore). She espoused Philip's cause in his war with the English, and aided him with warriors and provisions. After the death of her first husband she married Quinnapin (known also as Petananuet and Peter Nunuit), a son of Ninigret, chief of the Niantic tribe. While fleeing from the English she was drowned, Aug. 6, 1676, in attempting to cross Tehticut r. Her head was cut off and set upon a pole in sight of Indian prisoners who were her adherents. According to Mrs. Rowlandson (Narr., 73, 1828), who was a prisoner of Quinnapin, Wetamoo spent much time in her personal adornment. At a dance "she had a kersey coat covered with girdles of wampum from the loins upward. Her arms from her elbows to her hands were covered with bracelets. There were handfuls of necklaces about her neck, and several sorts of jewels in her ears. She had fine, red, stockings, and white shoes, her hair powdered, and her face painted red." (A. F. C. C. T.)

Wetchon ('panther'). A Yuchi clan.
WētcᵍAn'.—Speck, Yuchi Inds., 71, 1909 (tc=ch). Wetchón tahá.—Gatschet, Uchee MS., B. A. E., 1885 (='panther gens').

Wetlko. A Yurok village on the s. side of the mouth of the Klamath r., N. W. Cal.
Weht'l-qua.—Gibbs (1851) in Schoolcraft, Ind. Tribes, III, 138, 1853.

Wetsagua ('opossum'). A Yuchi clan.
WētsagowAn'.—Speck, Yuchi Inds., 71, 1909. Wetsaguá tahá.—Gatschet, Uchee MS., B. A. E., 1885 (='opossum gens').

Wetsiaus. A Siuslaw village on Siuslaw r., Oreg.
We'-tsi-aus'.—Dorsey in Jour. Am. Folk-lore, III, 230, 1890.

Wetsitsiko. The Yurok name of a Karok village on Klamath r., N. W. Cal., between the mouth of Salmon r. and Orleans Bar.

Wetumpka (Creek: u'-i, or u-i'wa, 'water'; túmkis, 'it is rumbling'). Two former Upper Creek towns, 4 m. apart, on the E. bank of Coosa r., Elmore co., Ala., the falls of the river lying between them. Swan in 1791 called them Big and Little Wetumpkee. The modern town Wetumpka stands on the site of Big Wetumpka, about ½ m. below the falls; and another town, West Wetumpka, has sprung up on the w. side of the river, which flows through a deep canyon at that place. The "Stincard" language spoken by these two towns, which are generally referred to as one settlement, was the Alibamu dialect. (A. S. G.)

Oweatumka.—Woodward, Reminisc., 48, 1859. Wee-tam-ka.—Adair, Am. Inds., 257, 1775. Weetumkus.—Romans, Florida, I, 90, 1775. Weetumpkee.—Adair, op. cit., 330. Wetumpkees (big and little).—Swan (1791) in Schoolcraft, Ind. Tribes, V, 262, 1855. Whittumke.—Bartram, Travels, 461, 1798. Witumki.—Alcedo, Dic. Geog., V, 343, 1789.

Wetumpka. A former Lower Creek town, a branch or colony of Kawita Talahasi (see Kawita), situated 12 m. from it, extending for 3 m. along Wetumpka cr. in N. E. Russell co., Ala.

Weektumkas.—Carroll, Hist. Coll. S. C., I, 190, 1836. **We-tum-cau.**—Hawkins (1799), Sketch, 56, 1848. **Wetumkee.**—Page (1836) in H. R. Doc. 274, 25th Cong., 2d sess., 76, 1838.

Wetumpka. Apparently a former Seminole settlement in central Florida. It was probably near Wetumpka Hammock, in Marion co. Charley Emathla's town and Coe Hadjo's town were near by, and Wetumpka may be the proper name of one of them. (H. W. H.)
Wetumka.—Drake, Bk. Inds., bk. IV, 84, 1848. **Wilamky.**—H. R. Doc. 78, 25th Cong., 2d sess., map, 768-9, 1838. **Witamky.**—McKenney and Hall, Ind. Tribes, II, 160, 1858.

Wevok. A Tikeramiut Eskimo village at C. Lisburne, Alaska.—Hydrogr. chart, 1890, quoted by Baker, Geog. Dict. Alaska, 1902.

Wewamaskem (*Wĕ'wamasqɛm*, 'the noble ones'). A gens of the Mamalelekala, a Kwakiutl tribe.—Boas in Rep. U. S. Nat. Mus. 1895, 330, 1897.

Wewanitowuk. A band of Cree.—Hutchins (1770) quoted by Richardson, Arct. Exped., II, 37, 1851.

Wewasee (*We-wä'-see*, 'buzzard'). A gens of the Shawnee.—Morgan, Anc. Soc., 168, 1877.

Wewenoc. A tribe of the Abnaki confederacy that lived on the coast of Maine about the mouth of the Kennebec r., in Lincoln and Sagadahoc cos. They were closely related to the Arosaguntacook, with whom they combined at an early period when displaced by the English. They figured in the Falmouth treaty of 1749 and other treaties of that period. Before 1727 most of them had removed to St Francis and Bécancour, Quebec, and in 1747 only a few families remained in Maine, who soon afterward removed also to Canada, where a remnant still exists.
8an8inak.—French letter (1721) in Mass. Hist. Soc. Coll., 2d s., VIII, 263, 1819. **8arinakiens.**—Rasle (trans. of 1724) in Mass. Hist. Soc. Coll., 2d s., VIII, 247, 1819. **Sheepscot Indians.**—Williamson in N. Y. Doc. Col. Hist., IX, 475, 1855 (local name). **Sheepscuts.**—Douglass, Summary, I, 184, 1755. **Walinaki.**—Gatschet, Penobscot MS., B. A. E., 1887 (Penobscot name). **Walnonoak.**—Douglass, op. cit., 185. **Wananoak.**—Alcedo, Dic. Geog., V, 331, 1789. **Wanonoaks.**—Jefferys, Fr. Doms., pt. 1, map, 1761. **Waweenock.**—Casco conf. (1727) in N. H. Hist. Soc. Coll., II, 261, 1827. **Wawenech.**—Colman (1727) in Mass. Hist. Soc. Coll., 1st s., VI, 117, 1800. **Wawenock.**—Casco conf. (1727) in N. H. Hist. Soc. Coll., II, 261, 1827. **Weewenooks.**—Falmouth jour. (1749) in Me. Hist. Soc. Coll., IV, 164, 1856. **Weweenooks.**—Falmouth jour. (1749), ibid., 155. **Wewenooks.**—Niles (ca. 1761) in Mass. Hist. Soc. Coll., 4th s., V, 365, 1861. **Wewoonock.**—Falmouth treaty rep. (1726) in Me. Hist. Soc. Coll., III, 390, 1853. **Winnenooks.**—Falmouth treaty rep. (1726) in Me. Hist. Soc. Coll., III, 386, 1853. **Wiscassett.**—Sullivan in Mass. Hist. Soc. Coll., 1st s., IX, 220, 1804 (local name). **Woenoeks.**—Falmouth treaty rep. (1726) in Me. Hist. Soc. Coll., III, 386, 1853. **Womenog.**—Gyles (1726) in Me. Hist. Soc. Coll., III, 357, 1853 (misprint). **Wowenocks.**—Falmouth treaty rep. (1726), ibid., III, 386, 1853.

Wewoka (Creek: *u'-iwa* or *u'-i*, 'water'; *wóχkīs*, 'it is roaring': 'roaring water'). A former Upper Creek town on Wewoka cr., in N. W. Elmore co., Ala., with 40 warriors in 1799 and 100 families in 1832. See *Ouanakina*. (A. S. G.)
Weakis.—Treaty of 1797 in U. S. Ind. Treat., 68, 1837. **Wecoka.**—Robin, Voy., II, map, 1807. **Weeokees.**—Treaty of 1779 in U. S. Ind. Treat., 70, 1837. **Weoka.**—H. R. Ex. Doc. 276, 24th Cong., 1st sess., 325, 1836. **Wewoak-har.**—Sen. Ex. Doc. 425, 24th Cong., 1st sess., 303, 1836. **Wewoakkan.**—Ibid., 279. **We woak kar.**—Schoolcraft, Ind. Tribes, IV, 578. 1854. **Wewoakkar Wockoy.**—Creek paper (1836) in H. R. Rep. 37, 31st Cong., 2d sess., 122, 1851. **We-wo-cau.**—Hawkins (1799), Sketch, 40, 1848. **Wewoko.**—Treaty of 1814 in U. S. Ind. Treat., 162, 1837. **Wiwoka.**—Gatschet, Creek Migr. Leg., I, 150, 1884. **Wiwúχka.**—Ibid. **Wowocau.**—Cornells (1813) in Am. St. Papers, Ind. Aff., I, 846, 1832.

Wewoka. An important town, the former capital of the Seminole Nation, Okla.
Wiwúχka.—Gatschet, Creek Migr. Leg., II, 186, 1888.

Wewutnowhu. A Kawia village in the San Jacinto mts., s. Cal.
Santa Rosa.—Barrows, Ethno-Bot. Coahuilla Ind., 34, 1900. **We-wut-now-hu.**—Ibid.

Weyapiersenwah. See *Bluejacket*.

Weyarnihkato (*We-yar-nih'-kä-to*, 'cave enterer'). A subclan of the Delawares.—Morgan, Anc. Soc., 172, 1877.

Weye. A former town, probably of the Upper Creeks, on middle Coosa r., Ala.—Lattre, map U. S., 1784.

Weyon ('deer'). A Yuchi clan.
Weᵍyᴀⁿ'.—Speck, Yuchi Inds., 70, 1909. **Wéyon tahá.**—Gatschet, Uchee MS., B. A. E., 1885 (= 'deer gens').

Weypulco. A former Upper Creek town on the E. side of Coosa r., Ala.—Jefferys, Am. Atlas, map 5, 1776.

Wezhinshte (freely translated the name signifies 'those by whom the anger or displeasure of the people is made manifest'). The War gens of the Omaha. The skin of the elk is not touched or used by the members of this gens, because the wrappers used to cover the pipes and other sacred articles happened to be the skin of a male elk. It has been erroneously called the Elk gens. (F. L.)
Elk gens.—Dorsey in 3d Rep. B. A. E., 220, 1885 (error). **Wajingaetage.**—Balbi, Atlas Ethnog., 56, 1826. **Wase-ish-ta.**—Long, Exped. Rocky Mts., I, 325, 1823. **Wä'-zhese-ta.**—Morgan, Anc. Soc., 155, 1877. **Wejiⁿcte.**—Dorsey in 3d Rep. B. A. E., 219, 1885.

Whahoo. See *Wahoo*.

Whala. The extinct Bear clan of the former pueblo of Pecos, N. Mex.
Whalatdásh.—Hodge in Am. Anthr., IX, 349, 1896 (*ásh* = 'people'). **Whã-lu.**—Hewett, ibid., n. s., VI, 431, 1904.

Whaleback Shellheap. The extensive oyster-shell heaps of Damariscotta r., Me., lie within the towns of Newcastle and Damariscotta. Besides many small mounds and layers of shell, there are five heaps of large size. Two of these are on the w. shore, the more northerly of which, known as the Peninsular mound, being about 400 ft long. The greatest depth of shells is about 22 ft. A hundred yards downstream is another heap of irregular form, extending along the shore for several hundred feet. On the opposite shore are three principal deposits. The greater part of the largest of these, the Whaleback mound, was removed in 1886, and the shells were ground for commercial purposes. The Peabody Museum of Harvard University purchased the right to all artifacts found. This heap was approximately 300 ft long and 125 ft wide; its greatest depth was 16½ ft. There seem to have been two or three periods of deposition of shells forming the mound, separated by intervals during which thin layers of mold had accumulated.

The mound was composed almost wholly of oyster shells, a few of the larger valves being 11 and 12 in. in length. Occasionally shells of other species of mollusks were found; five or six Indian skeletons were unearthed, and fireplace hearths, ashes, charcoal, and bones of various animals occurred frequently, but artifacts of stone, bone, and antler were extremely rare. A small number of stone adze blades of the nearly straight-edged type were obtained, also a very few rude pestles, hammer-stones, and other common forms. Fragments of a considerable number of earthenware pots were recovered at various depths. The sherds from 10, 12, and 14 ft below the surface have the same characteristics as those from the upper layers, all of them being of the well-known New England Algonquian types. The "roulette" and indented methods of decoration prevailed throughout. The potter's art in this region made little if any advance during the long period necessary for the accumulation of 12 or 14 ft of shells.

Consult Berry in New England Mag., XIX, 1898-9; Putnam in 20th Rep. Peabody Mus., 1887; Wyman in 2d Rep. Peabody Mus., 1869.   (C. C. W.)

Whapi (*Whá-pi'*). The Red-tail Hawk clan of the San Ildefonso Indians of New Mexico; also the name of an ancient pueblo site in the Rio Grande valley about 2 m. N. E. of the Black mesa, traditionally claimed to be a former home of the Whapi clan.   (E. L. H.)

Wharhoots (*Xwaxots*: Chehalis name). A former village of the Chinook tribe on Shoalwater bay, on the site of the present Bruceport, Pacific co., Wash.
Nix̣wā′xōtse.—F. Boas, inf'n, 1905. **Wharhoots.**—Swan, N. W. Coast, 211, 1857. X̣wā′xōts.—Boas, op. cit. (Chehalis name).

Wharnock. A Kwantlen village on Fraser r., a few miles below the mouth of Stave r., Brit. Col.; pop. 29 in 1910.
Hō′nak.—Hill-Tout in Ethnol. Surv. Can., 54, 1902. Stcuwā′oEl.—Boas. MS., B. A. E., 1891 (probably identical). **Wharnock.**—Can. Ind. Aff., pt. II, 160, 1901. **Whonnoch.**—Hill-Tout, op. cit. **Whonock.**—Can. Ind. Aff., 74, 1878.

Whatlminek (*Whatl-min-ēk'*). An Okinagan village 6½ m. N. of Deep cr., Oka-

nagan lake, Brit. Col.—Dawson in Trans. Roy. Soc. Can., sec. II, 44, 1891.

Whetstones. See *Abrading implements*.

Whiggiggin. A written permit to hunt, from local officials or from Indian chiefs. According to Schele de Vere (Americanisms, 21, 1872) this word is in common use in Maine and adjoining parts of Canada: from *awikhigan* in the Abnaki dialect of Algonquian, signifying '(what is) carved (scratched, or engraved),' hence anything written, as a letter, a bill, or a book.   (A. F. C.)

Whilkut. The Hupa name of a small Athapascan division occupying the upper portion of the valley of Redwood cr., N. Cal. Their language differs slightly from that of the Hupa, from whom they were separated by a mountain ridge, and they might be considered a part of that tribe except that they seem to have had no political connection with them and differed in religious practices. The routes of the pack-trains lay through their territory, and the conflicts between the whites and Whilkut were frequent and bloody. The survivors were taken to the reservation at Hupa soon after its establishment, but after 1870 they drifted back to their old homes, where 10 or 12 families are still living. Below them on Redwood cr. are the Chilula.   (P. E. G.)
Hó-al-kut-whuh.—Powers in Cont. N. A. Ethnol., III, 88, 1877 ('givers': Hupa name). **Holtz Indianer.**—Meyer, Nach dem Sacramento, 215, 1855. **Redwood Indians.**—McKee (1851) in Sen. Ex. Doc. 4, 32d Cong., spec. sess., 160, 1853. **Wheelcuttas.**—Bancroft, Nat. Races, I, 446, 1874 ('tributaries': Hupa name). **Whĭl′-kut.**—Powers in Cont. N. A. Ethnol., III, 88, 1877. **Xōi′lkut.**—P. E. Goddard, inf'n, 1903 (Hupa name).

Whipsiwog. A name of the fireweed (*Erechthites hieracifolia*). Gerard (Garden and Forest) July 29, 1896, who cites the word, refers it to *wippisiwok* in the Cree dialect of Algonquian, signifying 'they are hollow,' that is, like a tube, plural of *wippisiw*, 'it is hollow.'   (A. F. C.)

Whirling Bear. See *Mahtoiowa*.

Whirling Thunder. See *Nasheakusk*.

Whiskah. A band of Salish formerly living on a river of the same name, a N. branch of the Chehalis in w. Washington. They are little known to whites except under the comprehensive term "Lower Chehalis."
Whishkah.—Gibbs in Cont. N. A. Ethnol., I, 171, 1877. **Whis-kah.**—Ross in Ind. Aff. Rep., 18, 1870.

Whisky-dick, Whisky-jack. See *Whisky-john*.

Whisky-john. A name in northern Canada and parts of the United States for the Canada jay (*Perisoreus canadensis*). A corruption, by folk-etymology, of *wiskatchán*, the name of this bird in the Cree dialect of Algonquian (Nascapi *us′kachon;* Chippewa *kwingwisht*, the Canada jay or moosebird, according to Dr Wm. Jones), further corrupted into *whisky-jack*, occasionally into *whisky-dick*.   (A. F. C.)

Whistles. See *Music and Musical instruments*.

White Apple. One of the Natchez villages of early writers, which seems to have been situated on the E. side of St Catherines cr., Miss., opposite the Grand village. White Earth has been supposed to be identical with it. For the archeology of this section, see Bull. Free Mus. Univ. Pa., II, 128, 1900.
Apple Village.—Bossu, Travels La., 49, 1771. Great Village.—Dumont in French, Hist. Coll. La., V, 31, 1853. Great White Apple Village.—Ibid., 70, Vpelois.—Iberville (1699) quoted by Brinton in Proc. Am. Philos. Soc., 483, 1873. White Apple Village.—Dumont, op. cit., 49.

White Cap Indians. A band of Sioux from Minnesota, under the chief White Cap (Wapahaska) in 1879, who settled on s. Saskatchewan r. in Assiniboia, Canada.
White Cap Sioux.—Can. Ind. Aff., 95, 1880.

White Cloud. See *Wabanaquot; Wabokieshiek.*

White Dog Sacrifice. The annual immolation of the white dog (or dogs) at the New Year ceremony by the Iroquois is the satisfaction or the fulfilment of a dream of Teharonhiawagon (q. v.), one of their chief gods, who, in the Iroquoian cosmic philosophy, is the impersonation or the embodiment of all faunal and floral life on earth. He is therefore called the Master of Life, or the Life God. As prescribed by the ritual employed, the date for beginning the ceremony, or more properly series of rites, is on the 5th day of the new moon, called *Disgō'nă'* ('long moon'), which is the second coming after the winter solstice, or about the end of January or the early part of February. These New Year rites deal symbolically with very striking phenomena in nature, namely, the weakening or the depression of the power of the Life God by the Monster Forces of the Winter God, exhibited in the seeming demise of nearly all fauna and flora following the departure southward of the Sun, and the dispersion of the Winter God's forces and the renewal of life in all things on earth by his return northward. In the native mind these changes are due largely to enchantments produced by powerful *orendas* (q. v.), or magic powers, struggling for supremacy. So the rites and ceremonies believed to be efficacious in the restoration of health among men are believed to be likewise effective among the gods. Dreams being the recognized means through which tutelaries may reveal the objects or agencies to be employed for the recovery of health when ruined by sorcery, it was assumed that Teharonhiawagon, in view of his weakened power, must have dreamed what would restore his life, the life in nature, to its normal condition;

and the tutelaries of man, his father's clansmen, have revealed, it is thought, the fact that he has dreamed that a sacrificial victim and an offering of tobacco are required to disenchant the life forces in nature and in man. The motive of these New Year rites is therefore (1) to resuscitate all life on earth by supplying to the Master of Life what he has dreamed is imperatively necessary to secure the well-being of his specific incarnations—the normal bodies and beings in nature, and (2) to renew through rite and ceremony all the agencies and means, largely mythic or figmental in character, which are believed to secure and promote man's welfare. Should the blight cast upon the face of nature by the demons of the Winter God, should the migration of birds and fishes, and the hibernation of game and other animals become permanent facts, unchangeable phenomena of the known world, the wise men of the Iroquois taught that all normal life on earth—birds, animals, and men—would perish from the land, and that corn, beans, squashes, and sunflowers, and the precious tobacco, could no longer be planted to sprout and grow to maturity, so that the demon Famine would devour the people. It is this gloomy prospect that impels the tutelary of Teharonhiawagon, the Master of Life, to reveal to his soul, through a dream, what is needed, in the form of an offering by mankind, to thwart the malign purpose of the demons of the Winter God, Tawiskaron (q. v.). He who seeks the fulfilment of his dream must chant his death song, the challenge song of his tutelary, and for this reason Teharonhiawagon, too, sings his death chant in midwinter, for if his dream be disregarded and remain unsatisfied, the complete destruction of all life on earth would take place. The Caucasian custom of drinking the health of a person is a vestigial reflex of a similar concept.

In considering the status, the character, and the dependence on man of Teharonhiawagon as a chief god among others, an important caution is to be kept in mind, namely, that while he is regarded as the Master of Life, it must not be inferred that he is also the god or ruler of all other things; and it must not be overlooked that all gods as such were themselves subject to the inexorable decrees of Fate, of Destiny. In primitive thought the concept or idea of Fate or Destiny is clearly developed out of the countless failures of the gods to bring about results contrary to the established course of nature; every failure of a god to accomplish a certain expected result was at once attributed to one of two things: either to the conjectured inability of the god to change the decree of Fate, i. e. the established order of things, or to an abortive attempt of the people to perform a rite or ceremony in accordance with a prescribed ritual. These considerations exempted Teharonhiawagon and other gods from censure for the nonperformance of the impossible, and they also show that sometimes the gods stood in need of human aid, either directly or ceremonially.

The New Year ceremony is commonly performed in every so-called long-house or assembly-hall in the tribe, for there are sometimes several such structures within the tribal limits, one in each village or small town, although two or more contiguous small villages may unite in holding a joint session. However, the village which is the first to celebrate the festival must begin it on the day prescribed by the ritual, and the other villages consecutively; or the several villages and towns may perform the ceremony simultaneously.

The name given by all the Iroquoian peoples, with perhaps the tentative exception of the Cherokee, to this ceremony is some variant, dialectic or other, of *Onnonhouarori* (Lafitau). In the Jesuit Relations and in other early writings the following forms occur: *Onnonhouaroia, Honnonouaroria, Honnaouaroria, Hononovaroria, Hagnonharioraha, Ononhwaroia, Ononhara, Annonh8aroria* (Huron), *Ganonh8arori* (Mohawk, Bruyas). In the present Onondaga it appears as *Ganon-'hwai'wĭ'*, a form cognate with *iakonon-'hwaiiă''hă'*, signifying 'it drives, urges, or distracts one's brain,' having reference to the supposed promptings of the soul, inspired by the tutelary to seek to acquire something designed to promote and secure the welfare of the body. Hence the song or chant commonly expressed such a desire. In describing such parts of this ceremony as were observed by them, the early Jesuit missionaries among the Hurons and the Iroquois, and the early French writers of Canada, employed expressions like *la folie, ou le renversement de tête ou du cervelle*, i. e. "the madness, or the dizziness or swimming in the head or brain," and *avoir la tête en écharpe*, i. e. "to have the head in a sling," and, taking a part for the whole, "the festival of dreams, or of desires," and confusing the rite of purification by fire with the rite of kindling the new fire, "the fire festivals." Father De Carheil, writing of the Cayuga in 1670, says that they do not worship the dream, as such, as the Master of Life, but a certain *akatkonsoria* ('false-face'), identifying it with Teharonhiawagon. It is only through these expressions that the ceremony may be recognized in these early writings. Among very early writers among the Mohawk, parts of the ceremony have been recorded by Van Curler (1634), and among the Hurons by Sagard (1626) who gave a very incisive account, from which it appears that the participants in some of the rites were more obsessed and maniacal than are those of the present-day Iroquois. Wholly misapprehending the motives underlying the several rites of the ceremony, Brebeuf (1636), like his contemporaries, says that the *Ononhara*, "a certain kind of madness," is for fools (or madcaps).

In early times the number of dogs to be sacrificed was apparently not ritually limited; for in a ceremony held by the Hurons, Feb. 24, 1656, in fulfilment of an order purporting to have been issued by an apparition of Teharonhiawagon himself, 10 dogs, 10 wampum beads from every cabin, a wampum belt 10 strands in breadth, 4 measures of sunflower seed, and as many beans, were sacrificed, for the entire destruction of the country had been threatened in case of a failure to provide the required gifts and offerings. At another, held in 1639, likewise in answer to a direct order of an apparition, 22 presents were asked, among the items of which were 6 dogs of a certain form and color, 50 pieces of tobacco, a large canoe, etc. It is not until late modern times that the dog (or dogs) was not partly eaten after having been partially burned in the sacrificial fire; for as early as 1642 the Jesuit Relations say that the dogs are eaten as "they usually eat their captives." The missionary Kirkland witnessed among the Seneca a ceremony lasting 7 days, in which two white dogs were strangled, painted, decorated, and hung up in the center of the village on the evening preceding the beginning of the rites; and after the performances had lasted several days, the dogs were taken down and placed on a pyre, and when nearly consumed one was removed and placed in a kettle with vegetables and eaten. This shows that as late as 1760 the flesh of the victim was ceremonially eaten among the Iroquois.

According to the ritual, in the performance of this and of all other tribal ceremonies each of the two phratries of clans (see *Tribe*) has essential parts in every act to execute, which the other may not, without at once destroying the assumed mystic effect of the ceremony on the welfare of the people and of the Master of Life.

In the preparations preliminary to the sacrifice of the victim two fire rites are performed, which consume three days; one is for the purpose of rekindling the fires after removing the old from all the cabins of the community. The Directors of the Four Ceremonies appoint two persons, one from each phratry, to do this. Among the Onondaga these two persons are chosen from the Deer and the Wolf clans, respectively, these two being the heads of the phratries to which they belong. In the performance of their sacred duties these two persons, who must have the rank of federal chiefs, must wear the native costume—a feather head-dress made of the webs stripped from the shafts, and a blue sash when available—must be painted with a spot of vermilion on each cheek, and must carry each a wooden paddle, about 4 or 5 ft in length, on which must be delineated the clan tutelary of the bearer. The duty of the Deer herald in every lodge is, while rekindling the fire, to deliver a thanksgiving address with the announcement of the beginning of the *Ganon'hwai'wi*, or New Year ceremony, and to urge the inmates to abandon their labors and amusements in order to attend in person at the long-house or tribal assembly-hall; the duty of the Wolf herald is continuously to chant on the way and in the lodges the *Ganon'hwai'wi*, or the Death chant of Teharonhiawagon. The rites at the assembly-hall do not begin until these two persons return there and make their report.

In making his report of the performance of the sacred commission entrusted to them, the spokesman in behalf of himself and his cousin of the Wolf phratry says, among many other things, that they then place the entire matter on the floor of the assembly-hall and that thereafter the whole responsibility for carrying on the ceremony devolve on the Two Cousins (i. e. the two clan phratries of the tribe) occupying respectively the two sides of the phratral fires; that they two have chanted the Death chant in behalf of Teharonhiawagon; that they have rekindled the fires in his behalf with the paddles; that the session of the *Ganon'hwai'wi*, or New Year ceremony, is now open for all the people, even to the least of the children; and that in the ensuing fire rite they two will pass through the fires in behalf of Teharonhiawagon. Then a speaker chosen from the Deer phratry receives in the name of the people the report with suitable commendations of the two officials, and then in behalf of the assembled people directs his words in a long address to extolling the handiwork of Teharonhiawagon as exhibited in nature. Vividly he addresses the bodies and beings and elements in nature as anthropic persons. Beginning with the lowest in position, he gives thanks to "Our Mother, the Earth," for her blessings; and then in like manner he addresses the Grasses,

the Plants, the Shrubs, and the Trees, severally, feelingly declaring that all these things were made "curative medicine" by Teharonhiawagon to promote the welfare of man; then the Rivers, the Lakes, the Springs, and All Moving Waters, and so too "Our Mothers the Corn, the Beans, and the Squash" receive a like measure of praise and thanksgiving for the blessings supplied by them; then the Game Animals which run or fly or swim likewise receive praise and thanks for the sustenance which they give to man; then, in order, the Fire is thanked for its many blessings to man; in like manner the Sun, "Our Elder Brother," the Moon, "Our Grandmother," and her Assistants, the Morning Star and the Stars, are all thanked for their care and guidance; then the Four Thunderers and Rainmakers, "Our Grandfathers," receive praise and thanks for the many blessings and comforts which they bestow on man and on all living things on earth in watering the earth and all that grows thereon and in keeping the water in springs, rivers, and lakes fresh; lastly, the Air (or the Wind) is thanked for preserving fresh the air that moves on the earth, even as Teharonhiawagon has willed it. The speaker now addresses the people, strongly reminding them that such and so many are the required words of thanksgiving which must be spoken by man to all the things established by Teharonhiawagon and to all those assistant anthropic beings to whom he has assigned a share in the government of the world by entrusting them severally with various duties for the promotion of human welfare and who will aid in protecting man during the New Year ceremony, then just begun, in which it is the solemn duty of man to execute faithfully the decrees of Teharonhiawagon. Finally, apostrophizing the Master of Life, the speaker summarizes all that he has said in behalf of the people and humbly begs of him health, peace, and contentment for all mankind during the period the ceremony will last. Then he announces the beginning of the second fire rite by announcing to the cousin phratry of the Wolf that his phratry has already appointed the official who will take charge of the paddles, and he earnestly enjoins on all persons, both adults and children, the imperative necessity for every one to perform this rite and solemnly cautions every one not to withdraw his hand when a paddle is offered by the chosen official.

This fire rite, called *Aoutaenhrohi* ('to asperge with ashes') by the Hurons, has for its motive the disinfection or rather disenchantment of all persons from the contagion of fevers and hot maladies produced by the Fire-god, the "Demon Aoutaenhrohi," by passing through the breath of fire, and the exorcism and expulsion from the village and country of the malign spirits that caused these evils. The Jesuit Relation for 1637 relates that a woman among the Hurons for whom this fire rite was being performed, passed barefoot through 200 or 300 fires maintained expressly for her in the several cabins, and that she was not thereby burned in the least. At the present time this rite is performed symbolically only. The persons performing the rite each receive a wooden paddle and then repair to each of the two phratral fires in the long-house, where they dip up the ashes and let them fall. For this purpose small parties of men, women, and children are formed from either phratry, acting consecutively or sometimes simultaneously. Every party, however, must have a leader, a chanter, and a speaker who makes an address of praise and of thanksgiving to Teharonhiawagon in behalf of those who accompany him to the two fires. When the people have all passed through the fire, the two persons who acted as heralds perform this fire rite in behalf of Teharonhiawagon himself; and then two men and two women from each phratry with the usual complement of a leader, a chanter, and a speaker, accompanied by all the people, bank the phratral fires lighted in behalf of Teharonhiawagon, and thus the rite closes.

In this rite the parties from the Deer phratry bearing paddles leave the room by the eastern doorway, turn to the lefthand, or sinistrally, and go around the building by the northern side and reënter the room by the western doorway; but the parties from the Wolf phratry bearing paddles leave the room by the western doorway, turn to the lefthand, or sinistrally, and go around the building by the south side and reënter the room by the eastern doorway. Thus half of the circuit is made by one phratry, and the other half by the other; and by turning sinistrally the parties do not at any point in their journey turn their backs to the Sun, their "Elder Brother." This distinctly emphasizes the dual or phratral organization of the tribe (q. v.), whose functions symbolize those of the male and the female principles in nature.

With the close of the two fire rites, the Dream festival or ceremony begins; this usually lasts three days. This rite is the cult of the personal tutelary, and consists (1) in the renewal or rejuvenation of the orenda, or magic power, of the personal tutelary of every person who possesses one, by having its distinctive challenge song or chant resung by the clansmen of the father of the owner, this resinging being done according to ritual by one or more persons with a drum or specific rattles; and (2) in "the divining or seeking to guess the dream-word" of those who have dreamed specific dreams, for the purpose of ascertaining thereby the suggested or revealed tutelary of the dreamer, who is commonly a child, and the bestowal of a small symbolic material representation of this tutelary upon him by his father's clansmen. A challenge song or chant accompanies the bestowal of the symbol referred to, and it is this which is renewed in subsequent years at such a ceremony. Every clan of each phratry appoints a man and a woman to hear these specific dreams from children and diffident persons in their clan, and they afterward relate these dreams to the chiefs or priest-chiefs whose duty it is to divine the tutelary for each. The songs which accompany the tutelaries comprise practically all those belonging to the tribe, with the exception of those employed for condolence and sorcery. The rite begins with the renewal of the two challenge songs of Teharonhiawagon himself; these two are the Great Feather Dance and the Drum Dance. Of course, this consists in singing only one of the scores of songs and chants belonging to each of these rites or dances. In many cases these songs constitute integral parts of the ritual of the Four Ceremonies, which are: (1) the Great Feather Dance, with about 150 songs with dance accompaniment; (2) the Drum Dance, with approximately a like number of songs; (3) the *Adoñ'wă'*, or Clan Personal Chant, every clan having about 100 of these, and (4) the Great Wager or Bet which is laid between the two phratries. This is the game of the plum-pits.

In addition to these songs and dances, some persons may ask to have performed the rite of aspergation with ashes by the *Hoñdu''i'* or False-faces, or that of insufflation by them, or that of the Lament of the Women, or that of the Waving of Evergreen Branches, or that of the *Adă-'goñwi''sĕⁿ* or Dance of the Corn People, or that of the Chant of Death, or any one of many others. It is sometimes necessary that persons from both phratries assist in the performance. There are, too, certain tutelaries whose nature is supposed to be such that their challenge songs need not be renewed at the New Year ceremony, but they may be rejuvenated at any other time at a public or private festival held in their honor. These independent tutelaries are the Sun, whose challenge song is the Skin-drum Dance (*One'hŏ'wĭ'*); the Moon, whose challenge songs are three in number, namely, the *Ă'goñwi''sĕⁿ* or Dance of the Corn Mother, the *Owäsgä′nie′* or Shuffle Dance, the Four Nights Dance; the Thunderers, whose challenge song is the *Wǎ′sa′′sä* or War Dance; and, lastly, those whose challenge songs belong to the *Gǎ′hi′dō′′hwǐ′* or Dance of the Sorcerers. This Dream Rite is closed with the visit of the *Hoñdu′′i′*, or False-face Society, whose reception requires that the dream-word of the eldest of these be divined and the presents required for its satisfaction be provided; thereafter this society disenchants or disinfects the assembly-hall and the village by aspergation with ashes and coals of fire. This rite is the last one preliminary to the sacrifice of the White Dog, which must ritually take place at sunrise of the morning following.

The victim must be of the native variety, white in color, and must be killed by strangulation in order not to break any of its bones. According to the ritual the body must be dressed and adorned, with the face painted in such manner as to represent Teharonhiawagon—the highest type of man; it is profusely marked with red spots about an inch in diameter; white, blue, red, and green ribbons are secured around the neck, body, tail, and legs; the feet are fastened with ribbons to the hips and the neck in such manner that the legs remain at right angles to the body, thus simulating the standing position of the animal; a long loop of ribbon is fastened to the feet for the purpose of carrying it; to the head is attached a small head-dress or crown of feathers, and around the neck is placed a small string of wampum as a credential of the authenticity of its mission; it is borne with the head directed forward, and it is placed on the song-bench in the assembly-hall with its head toward the west. On the bench are placed in order, first a bow and arrows; second, the victim; and, lastly, a parcel of native tobacco: these are the offerings to be made to the representative of Teharonhiawagon. Upon their entering the assembly-hall the priest-chiefs appointed by both phratries must offer these things to the Teharonhiawagon: those of the Wolf, the bow and arrows (which are refused), and the victim; while the Deer priests offer the tobacco. The last two are accepted. Then the Teharonhiawagon leaves the room, followed by the bearers of the offerings and by the people, and repairs to the pyre, which is kindled at a suitable distance to the southeast of the building. The victim and the tobacco are placed on a platform prepared for them on the southwest side of the fire; the sacrificing priest takes his position on the west side of the fire, and, having the victim on his right, faces the east; the chiefs and ceremonial officers gather on the north, west, and south sides of the fire, and back of these the people assemble, and all those who have brought their tutelaries then place them around the sacrificial fire. Thus the sacrificing priest is brought to face the impersonator of Teharonhiawagon, who stands southeastward from the fire. Then thrice in a loud voice the sacrificial chief exclaims "*Ku′′!*" meaning "Here, do thou receive it!" The first two paragraphs and the one in which the sacrifice is made are as follows:

"Now, thou hearest the people who dwell on the earth calling (on thee). Thou dost too plainly see that there where the ceremonial officers have kindled a fire for thee, mankind stand in a body, in a regulated assembly. Moreover, they who stand there are those persons whose lives are still spared on earth and who are indeed thy father's clansmen. Now, moreover, do thou listen, thence, to them when they shall speak. Thou didst ordain it, willing that it should be thus on earth a matter of the greatest moment which should take place in midwinter; that is to say, on the 5th day of the moon Disgō′nǎ′, the matter which thou didst call by the name of the 'Great Sacred Ceremony of the Ganon′hwai′wǐ′.' Thou didst resolve, too, that thou wouldst continue to honor this ceremony, in which mankind should perform the rites of it for thee, and in which they should chant their dream songs, and through which their words should go to thee when giving thee thanksgivings. This is what took place in thy mind, thou who dwellest in the sky.

"Thou didst will, too, that all persons should be equally obligated to perform this ceremony—the *roia′ner* chiefs, the officers, both men and women, of the Four Ceremonies, the public and the children too. Thou didst will, too, that all these persons should pass through the fires kindled for thee by the officers of the Four Ceremonies. Thus did it come to pass in thy mind. And, moreover, nothing obstructs thee, so that thou hast plainly seen that all those whose lives are still spared have now performed this duty: all have fulfilled what thou hast ordained, thou who dwellest in the sky."

Then coming to the paragraph of sacrifice, he continues: "So, then, do thou now know, too, that with due formality mankind make use of what thou didst ordain for us to employ, when thou didst will that this shall be the principal thing, that that shall be their word—this pinioned object [the victim]. Thus it took place in thy mind, thou who dwellest in the sky. So, now, here lies that which shall authenticate the words of man, when thou wilt hear the whole earth speak. Now, moreover, do thou know that that by which thy father's clansmen, mankind, dwelling on the earth, make answer to thy dream-word, goes hence to thee [casts victim on the pyre]. Thou dost plainly see the number of persons who are assembled at the place where those who attend to thy affairs kindled a fire for thee."

The entire invocation would require about 7,400 English words to translate it. At the end of every subsequent paragraph the priest throws a portion of the sacrificial tobacco into the fire, until all is offered. This ends the sacrifice. On the four or five days following, the Rites of the Four Ceremonies are performed in their entirety. These are the rites distinctive of the New Year or Midwinter Ceremony of the Iroquois.   (J. N. B. H.)

White Eagle Band. A former Sioux band, named from its chief.—H. R. Ex. Doc. 96, 42d Cong., 3d sess., 15, 1873.

White Earth. One of the Natchez villages of early writers. It was either on the site of the subsequent concession of White Earth on St Catherines cr., Miss., or else was identical with White Apple.
Terre Blanche.—Dumont in French, Hist. Coll. La., v, 70, 1853 (in a footnote given as the same as the Great White Apple village). Washt Kahápa.—Gatschet, MS., B. A. E. ('town white': Natchez name). White Clay.—Gayarre, La., I, 156, 1851.

White-eyes (*Koquethagechton*). A former chief of the Delawares in Ohio. He was first councilor and in 1776 succeeded to the chieftaincy on the death of Netawatwees pending the minority of the hereditary chief. He encouraged the Moravian missionaries in their efforts to civilize and educate the Indians. In the Revolutionary war, as in the previous conflict between the colonists and the native tribes, he strove to keep the Delawares neutral. When the Iroquois council commanded the Delawares to take up arms for the British, he replied that he was no woman and would do as he pleased. When Captain Pipe almost persuaded his people to take the warpath in the spring of 1778, he told the warriors that he would march at their head if they were determined to go, and would seek to be the first to fall and thus avoid witnessing the utter destruction of the tribe. Compelled to declare himself, he openly espoused the American cause and joined McIntosh's expedition against the British Indians of Sandusky, but died of smallpox at Pittsburg in Nov. 1778, before the force set out. His name is also recorded Koguethagechton, Koquethagechton, and Kuckquetackton.   (F. H.)

White-eyes Village. A Delaware village, named from the chief, that formerly existed at the site of Duncan's Falls, 9 m. below Zanesville, in Muskingum co., Ohio.
Old Indian village.—Royce in 18th Rep. B. A. E., pl. clvi, 1899. Old Town.—Howe, Hist. Coll. Ohio, II, 146, 1896. Old Town village.—Ibid. White-eyes.—Drake, Bk. Inds., bk. v, 28, 1848.

White Hair. An influential Osage chief at the beginning of the 19th century, known also as Teshuhimga, Cahagatonga, and Pahuska or Pawhuska, and by the French as Cheveux Blancs. He was head-man of the Great Osage, whose village, known also as White Hair's Village, was situated in 1806 on the E. side of Little Osage r., in the N. part of the present Vernon co., Mo. (near which Lieut. Z. M. Pike established what he called Camp Independence in 1806), and in 1825 and 1837 on the w. bank of Neosho r. in the present Neosho co., Kan., on land ceded to the United States by treaty of Sept. 29, 1865. The nominal chief of the village, according to Pike, was Cashesegra (Kóshisigré, Big Foot, or Big Track), but Clermont or Clermore (Taⁿwaⁿgahe, Builder of Towns) was the greatest warrior and most influential man, and "more firmly attached to the American interests than any other chief of the nation." He was lawful chief of the Grand Osage, but his hereditary right was usurped by White Hair while Clermont was an infant. Pike asserts that both White Hair and Cashesegra were chiefs of the trader Pierre Chouteau's creating, and neither had the power or disposition to restrain their young men from the perpetration of an improper act, lest they should render themselves unpopular. This was evident during Pike's stay in their country, when White Hair's people left to war against the whites on the Arkansas, the chief being powerless to restrain them. He treated Pike with hospitality, and sent his son, "a discontented young fellow, filled with self-pride," as an embassy with Pike's party, but he soon became tired and returned. Both White Hair and his son were presented by Pike with "grand medals." White Hair seems to be identical with Papuisea (Pahusca?), who was the first Indian signer of the treaty with the Osage at Ft Clark, Nov. 10, 1808. He signed also the treaties of Sept. 22, 1815; Sept. 25, 1818; Aug. 31, 1822; June 2, 1825; and Aug. 10, 1825. He died, probably soon after the date last mentioned, at his village in Vernon co., Mo., and was buried, in a stone tomb, on the summit of Blue Mound. The grave was afterward vandalized by treasure-seekers, and prior to 1850 the chief parts of the skeleton were taken therefrom by Judge Charles H. Allen ("Horse Allen"). About 1871 some Osage went from Kansas to Blue Mound and rebuilt the cairn formerly covering White Hair's remains, but the whites would permit neither the stones nor the few bones of the old chief to remain. The name Pawhuska survives in that of a town in Oklahoma, the present Osage agency.

White Indians. An unidentified or entirely mythic people mentioned by various early writers as existing in some part of the unexplored interior of America, and described sometimes simply as "white," but in other cases as having white skins, with beards, and clothed like Europeans. In some cases the accounts seem to be entirely mythic, based on the supposed existence of a tribe of "Welsh Indians," but in other cases they seem to refer to a settlement or temporary visitation of Europeans in the remote distance, or to the existence of an Indian tribe of somewhat lighter complexion than their neighbors. Thus the white men of whom Coronado heard in w. Texas were De Soto's party advancing from the E.; and the white men N. w. from the St Lawrence, of whom the Jesuits heard from the Indians, were probably whalers coasting along Hudson bay. The Hatteras Indians of Albemarle sd., N. C., were said to show in 1700 traces of white admixture and to claim white descent, which if present may have come from absorption of the lost colony of Roanoke in 1587. The so-called Croatan Indians base their claim on the same theory. Some of the Plains tribes, notably the Cheyenne and the Crows, are lighter in complexion than those of the woods and mountains; some, as the Mandan, are noted for the frequency of light hair and eyes; and in some, especially the Zuñi and the Hopi, albinos are somewhat common. See *Croatan Indians, Popular fallacies, Welsh Indians.*　　　　　　(J. M.)

Barbus.—Imlay, West Ter., 293, 1797 (French: 'bearded'). **Bearded Inds.**—Am. Pioneer, I, 257, 1842. **Blanches.**—Ibid. **Blancs.**—Imlay, op. cit. (French: 'white'). **Blancs Barbus.**—Trader in Smith, Bouquet Exped., 69, 1766 (French: 'white bearded'). **Blanes.**—Boudinot, Star in the West, 126, 1816 (misprint for 'Blancs'). **Blank Barbus.**—Buchanan, N. Am. Inds., 156, 1824. **White Bearded Indians.**—J. J. (1792) in Bowen, Am. Discov. by the Welsh, 87, 1876. **White Indians.**—Dobbs, Hudson Bay, 21, 1744.

White Lodge. A subchief of the Sisseton Sioux whose home camp was at L. Shaokatan, Lincoln co., Minn., until the outbreak of 1862, when he attacked the settlers at L. Shetak and carried away Mrs Wright and Mrs Duly with their children to the Missouri r., where they were later rescued by the "Fool Soldier band" of Teton Sioux. White Lodge escaped into Canada and died at Swift Current about 1870.　　　　　(D. R.)

White Mountain Apache. Formerly the Sierra Blanca Apache, a part of the Coyoteros, so called on account of their mountain home. The name is now applied to all the Apache under Ft Apache agency, Ariz., consisting of Arivaipa, Tsiltaden or Chilion, Chiricahua, Coyotero, Mimbreño, and Mogollon. In 1910 they num-

bered 2,269. Capt. Bourke in 1881–82 obtained at Ft Apache and San Carlos agencies the following names of bands or clans: Satchin, Destchin, Tseskadin, Tzolgan, Tuakay, Klokadakaydn, Tzintzilchutzikadn, Tzlanapah, Tudisishn, Iyaaye, Kiyahani, Akonye, Kaynaguntl, Indelchidnti, Peiltzun, Chilchadilkloge, Natatladiltin, Tzaedelkay, Kaihatin, Mayndeshkish, Tushtun, Tzebinaste, Tutonashkisd, Yachin, Tziseketzillan, Tizsessenaye, Tzecheschinne, Natootzuzn, Tutzone, Chiltneyadnaye, Yagoyekaydn, Tzetseskadn, Inoschuhochen, and Gontiel. There are also the foreign clans Tzekinne and Nakaydi, partly Piman.

Arizonian Apaches.—Bandelier in Arch. Inst. Papers, III, 259, 1890. **Biniette Shedecka.**—White, MS. Hist. Apaches, B. A. E., 1875 (Chiricahua name). **Sierra Blanca Apaches.**—Ind. Aff. Rep.,

WHITE MOUNTAIN APACHE

141, 1868. **Sierra Blancas.**—Bourke in Jour. Am. Folk-lore, III, 119, 1890. **Sierra Blanco Apache.**—Chapin, Sierra Blanca MS. vocab., B. A. E., 1867. **Sierras blancas.**—Villa-Señor, Theatro Am., pt. 2, 413, 1748. **Surra Blancos.**—Ind. Aff. Rep., 506, 1865 (misprint). **White Mountain Apaches.**—Parke, map N. Mex., 1851.

White people. See *Race names.*

White Pigeon (*Wahbememe*). A Potawatomi chief of local prominence in the early years of the 19th century. The little that is known of him is derived chiefly from tradition. It is said that about 1812, while in the neighborhood of Detroit, he learned of an uprising among the Indians and of a threatened attack on the settlement that now bears his name, in St Joseph co., Mich. Far from home and friends, he hastened to the scene of the impending trouble and by a timely warning saved the white settlers from possible massacre. He is described as tall and athletic, an unusually fleet runner, and as having possessed high ideals of truth and honor. According to Indian information he received his name because he was of much lighter complexion than the members of his tribe generally. He died at the age of about 30 years and was buried in a mound on the outskirts of the village of White Pigeon. Here, on Aug. 11, 1909, a monument, suitably inscribed, was erected to his memory under the auspices of the Alba Columba Club of women. White Pigeon signed, in behalf of his band, the Greenville treaty of Aug. 3, 1795, and the treaty of Brownstown, Mich., Nov. 25, 1808. Two of his great-grandsons and a great-granddaughter (the wife of the great-grandson of Simon Pokagon, q. v.) reside near Dorr, Mich. Consult Mich. Pion. Coll., x, 1888; [Cora Cameron,]. White Pigeon, [1909].

White Raccoon's Village. A Miami village, named from the chief (Wahpahsaypon, 'White Raccoon'), near the present Aboite, Allen co., Ind. The site was made an individual grant by treaty of Oct. 23, 1834.   (J. P. D.)

Raccoons village.—Royce, map, in 1st Rep. B. A. E., 1881. Raccoon village.—Treaty of 1834 in U. S. Ind. Treat., 498, 1873. Wah'-pah-say'-pon.—Dunn, True Indian Stories, 313, 1908 (proper name of White Raccoon). Wapasepah.—Ibid. (name of the reservation). White Raccoons village.—Mississinewa treaty (1826) in U. S. Ind. Treat., 498, 1873.

White River Ute. The official collective name for such of the Ute on Uintah res., Utah (to the number of 514 in 1885), as are not classed under Uinta. It comprises the Yampa, and the Green River and Grand River Ute, as well as perhaps other bands. As officially recognized, the White River Ute under the Uinta and Ouray agency, Utah, numbered 356 in 1904 and 298 in 1910. See *Uinta*.

Kaviawach.—A. Hrdlička, inf'n, 1907 (or Ka-wai-ra-chi-u; their own name, having relation to their mountain abode).

White-shield, Harvey. See *Hishkowits; Wopohwats*.

White Swan. A Crow scout, brother of Curly, who served with Reno in the Custer campaign against the Sioux in 1876, which met with such disaster on the Little Bighorn on July 25. He received a severe wound in the retreat out of the valley, which made him a cripple for the remainder of his life. He died in the fall of 1905 and was buried with military honors in the National cemetery on the Custer battlefield in Montana. For a number of years he received a pension from the Government.

White Woman's Town. A former Delaware village near the junction of the Walhonding and the Killbuck, about 7 m. N. W. of the forks of the Muskingum, in the present Coshocton co., Ohio. The settlement was so named because a white girl, Mary Harris, who had been captured by the French Indians about the year 1710 and later became the wife of Eagle Feather, made the place her home at least as early as 1750. The Walhonding r. was known as White Woman's river, or White Woman's creek. Another white wife of Eagle Feather was known as The Newcomer, from whom Newcomerstown (q. v.) received its name.

Femmes blanches.—Esnauts and Rapilly map, 1777. White Womans.—Lattré map, 1784.

Whizzing stick. See *Bullroarer*.

Whonkentia. A tribe of the Manahoac confederacy, formerly living near the head of Rappahannock r. in Fauquier co., Va.

Whonkenteaes.—Smith (1629), Va., I, 134, repr. 1819. Whonkentias.—Strachey (ca. 1612), Va., 104, 1849. Whonkenties.—Jefferson, Notes, 179, 1801.

Whulk. A Nimkish village at the mouth of Nimkish r., E. coast of Vancouver id., Brit. Col.—Dawson in Trans. Roy. Soc. Can., sec. II, 65, 1887.

Whullemooch ('dwellers on Puget sound'). A generic term used by the natives to designate the Salish tribes on the N. w. coast of Washington.—Deans in Am. Antiq., VIII, 41, 1886.

Wiam. A Shahaptian tribe, speaking the Tenino language, formerly living near the mouth of Deschutes r., Oreg. Their chief village was Waiam, on the Columbia r. at the site of the present Celilo. They were included in the Wasco treaty of 1855 as a "band of Walla Wallas," and were removed to the Warm Springs res., where a remnant of the tribe that numbered 130 in 1850 still survives.   (L. F.)

Lower De Chutes.—Treaty of 1855 in U. S. Ind. Treat., 622, 1873. Ouaïoumpoum.—Hunt in Nouv. Ann. Voy., X, 81, 1821. Waiäm.—Mooney in 14th Rep. B. A. E., 741, 1896. Waiäm-'lĕma.—Ibid. (native name). Way-yam-pams.—Ross, Fur Hunters, 186, 1855. Wiam.—Lee and Frost, Oreg., 176, 1844. Wyam.—Wasco treaty (1855) in U. S. Ind. Treat., 622, 1873. Wy-am-pams.—Ross, Advent., 118, 1849. Wyampaw.—Lane in Sen. Ex. Doc. 52, 31st Cong., 1st sess., 174, 1850.

Wiaquahhechegumeeng (*Waiekwákitchigäming*, 'at the end of the great lake,' whence the French *au Fond du Lac*). A Chippewa village at the head of L. Superior, in Douglass co., Wis. The Fond du Lac Chippewa numbered 934 under the La Pointe school superintendent in 1909.

Fond du Lac.—Warren (1852) in Minn. Hist. Soc. Coll., v, 130, 1885. Wi-a-quah-he-che-gume-eng.—Warren (1852), ibid., v, 130, 1885.

Wiatakali ('hanging loft'). A former Choctaw town in the s. part of Neshoba co., Miss., about a mile s. of the De Kalb and Jackson road. It received its name from a brush arbor, called by the Choctaw *wia-takali*, under which they were accustomed to meet for their councils and general amusements.—Halbert in Pub. Ala. Hist. Soc., III, 77, 1899; Gatschet, Creek Migr. Leg., I, 108, 1884.

Wiatiac. A former Mahican village near the present Salisbury, Litchfield co., Conn. The Moravians had some converts there about 1743.

Wehtak.—Ruttenber, Tribes Hudson R., 197, 1872. Wiatiac.—Kendall, Trav., I, 228, 1809. Wiatiacks.—Macauley, N. Y., II, 164, 1829. Wyatiack.—Ruttenber, op. cit.

Wiattachechah. An unidentified Sioux village.

Wi-atta-che-chah.—Prescott in Schoolcraft, Ind. Tribes, II, 171, 1852 (trans. 'bad'; *che-cha* may = *shicha*, 'bad').

Wichita. A confederacy of Caddoan stock, closely related linguistically to the Pawnee, and formerly ranging from about the middle Arkansas r., Kansas, southward to Brazos r., Texas, of which general region they appear to be the aborigines, antedating the Comanche, Kiowa, Mescaleros, and Siouan tribes. They now reside in Caddo co., w. Okla., within the limits of the former Wichita res.

The name *Wi'chita'*, by which they are commonly known, is of uncertain origin and etymology. They call themselves *Kitikiti'sh* (Kirikirish), a name also of uncertain meaning, but probably, like so many proper tribal names, implying pre-eminent men. They are known to the Siouan tribes as *Black Pawnee* (Paniwasaba, whence "Paniouassa," etc.), to the early French traders as *Pani Piqué*, 'Tattooed Pawnee,' to the Kiowa and Comanche by names meaning 'Tattooed Faces,' and are designated in the sign language by a sign conveying the same meaning. They are also identifiable with the people of Quivira met by Coronado in 1541. The Ouachita living in E. Louisiana in 1700 are a different people, although probably of the same stock.

Among the tribes composing the confederacy, each of which probably spoke a slightly different dialect of the common language, we have the names of the Wichita proper (?), Tawehash (Tayovayas), Tawakoni (Tawakarehu), Waco, Yscani, Akwesh, Asidahetsh, Kishkat, Kirishkitsu. A considerable part of the Panimaha, or Skidi Pawnee, also appear to have lived with them about the middle of the 18th century, and in fact the Pawnee and Wichita tribes have almost always been on terms of close intimacy. It is possible that the Yscani of the earlier period may be the later Waco (Bolton). The only divisions now existing are the Wichita proper (possibly synonymous with Tawehash), Tawakoni, and Waco. To these may be added the incorporated Kichai remnant, of cognate but different language. Just previous to the annexation of Texas to the United States, about 1840–5, the Tawakoni and Waco resided chiefly on Brazos r., and were considered as belonging to Texas, while the Wichita proper resided N. of

Red r., in and N. of the Wichita mts., and were considered as belonging to the United States. According to the best estimates for about 1800, the Wichita proper constituted more than two-thirds of the whole body.

The definite history of the Wichita—more particularly of the Wichita proper —begins in 1541, when the Spanish explorer Coronado entered the territory known to his New Mexican Indian guides as the country of Quivira. There is some doubt as to their exact location at the time, probably about the great bend of the Arkansas r. and northeastward, in central Kansas, but the identity of the tribe seems established (consult Mooney in Harper's Mag., June 1899; Hodge in Brower, Harahey, 1899; see *Quivira*).

WICHITA MAN

On the withdrawal of the expedition after about a month's sojourn the Franciscan father Juan de Padilla, with several companions, remained behind to undertake the Christianization of the tribe, this being the earliest missionary work ever undertaken among the Plains Indians. After more than three years of labor with the Wichita he was killed by them through jealousy of his spiritual efforts for another tribe.

In 1719 the French commander La Harpe visited a large camp of the confederated Wichita tribes on South Canadian r., in the eastern Chickasaw Nation, Okla., and was well received by them. He estimated the gathering, including other Indians present, at 6,000 souls. They had been at war with another tribe and had taken a number of prisoners whom they were preparing to eat, having already disposed of several in this way.

They seem to have been gradually forced westward and southward by the inroads of the Osage and the Chickasaw to the positions on upper Red and Brazos rs. where they were first known to the Americans. In 1758 the Spanish mission and presidio of San Sabá, on a tributary of the upper Colorado r., Texas, were attacked and the mission was destroyed by a combined force of Comanche, Tawakoni, Tawehash, Kichai, and others. In the next year the Spanish commander Parilla undertook a retaliatory expedition against the main Wichita town, about the junction of Wichita and Red rs., but was compelled to retreat in disorder, with the loss of his train and field

WICHITA WOMAN

guns, by a superior force of Indians well fortified, and armed with guns and lances and flying the French flag. In 1760 the confederated Wichita tribes. asked for peace and the establishment of a mission, and on being refused the mission, renewed their attacks about San Antonio. In 1765 they captured and held for some time a Spaniard, Tremiño, who has left a valuable record of his experiences at the main Tawehash town on Red r. In 1772 the commander Mezières visited them and other neighboring tribes for the purpose of arranging peace. From his data the Tawakoni, in two towns on Brazos and Trinity rs., may have had 220 warriors, the "Yscanis" (Waco?) 60, and the Wichita proper and "Taovayas" 600, a

total of perhaps 3,500, not including the Kichai. In 1777–8 an epidemic, probably smallpox, swept the whole of Texas, including the Wichita, reducing some tribes by one-half. The Wichita, however, suffered but little on this occasion. In the spring of 1778 Mezières again visited them, and found the Tawakoni (i. e. the Tawakoni and Waco) in two towns on the Brazos with more than 300 men, and the Wichita proper in two other towns on opposite sides of Red r. (below the junction of Wichita r.), these last aggregating 160 houses, in which he estimated more than 800 men, or perhaps 3,200 souls. The whole body probably exceeded 4,000. (H. E. Bolton, inf'n, 1908.)

In 1801 the Texas tribes were again ravaged by smallpox, and this time the Wichita suffered heavily. In 1805 Sibley officially estimated the Tawakoni (probably including the Waco) at 200 men, the "Panis or Towiaches" (Wichita proper) at 400 men, and the Kichai at 60 men, a total of about 2,600 souls, including the incorporated Kichai. An estimate by Davenport in 1809 rated the total about 2,800. A partial estimate in 1824 indicates nearly the same number. At this time the Waco town was on the site of the present Waco, while the Tawakoni town was on the E. side of the Brazos above the San Antonio road. From about this time, with the advent of the Austin colony, until the annexation of Texas by the United States, a period of about 25 years, their numbers constantly diminished in conflicts with the American settlers and with the raiding Osage from the N.

In 1835 the Wichita proper, together with the Comanche, made their first treaty with the Government, by which they agreed to live in peace with the United States and with the Osage and the immigrant tribes lately removed to Indian Ter. In 1837 a similar treaty was negotiated with the Tawakoni, Kiowa, and Kiowa Apache (Ta-wa-ka-ro, Kioway, and Ka-ta-ka, in the treaty). At this time, in consequence of the inroads of the Osage, the Wichita had their main village behind the Wichita mts., on the North fork of Red r., below the junction of Elm fork, W. Okla. In consequence of the peace thus established they soon afterward removed farther to the E. and settled on the present site of Ft Sill, N. of Lawton, Okla.; thence they removed about 1850 still farther E. to Rush Springs. The Tawakoni and Waco all this time were ranging about the Brazos and Trinity rs. in Texas. In 1846, after the annexation of Texas, a general treaty of peace was made at Council Springs on the Brazos with the Wichita proper, Tawakoni, and Waco, together with the Comanche, Lipan, Caddo, and

Kichai, by which all these acknowledged the jurisdiction of the United States. In 1855 the majority of the Tawakoni and Waco, together with a part of the Caddo and Tonkawa, were gathered on a reservation on Brazos r. westward from the present Weatherford. In consequence of the determined hostility of the Texans, the reservation was abandoned in 1859, and the Indians were removed to a temporary location on Washita r., Okla. Just previous to the removal the Tawakoni and Waco were officially reported to number 204 and 171 respectively. In the meantime the Wichita had fled from the village at Rush Springs and taken refuge at Ft Arbuckle to escape the vengeance of the Comanche, who held them responsible for a recent attack upon themselves by United States troops under Major Van Dorn (1858). The Civil War brought about additional demoralization and suffering, most of the refugee Texas tribes, including the Wichita, taking refuge in Kansas until it was over. They returned in 1867, having lost heavily by disease and hardship in the meantime, the Wichita and allied tribes being finally assigned a reservation on the N. side of Washita r. within what is now Caddo co., Okla. In the next year they were officially reported at 572, besides 123 Kichai. In 1902 they were given allotments in severalty and the reservation was thrown open to settlement. The whole Wichita body numbers now only about 310, besides about 30 of the confederated Kichai remnant, being less than one-tenth of their original number.

Like all tribes of Caddoan stock the Wichita were primarily sedentary and agricultural, but owing to their proximity to the buffalo plains they indulged also in hunting to a considerable extent. Their permanent communal habitations were of conical shape, of diameter from 30 to 50 ft, and consisted of a framework of stout poles overlaid with grass thatch so as to present from a short distance the appearance of a haystack. Around the inside were ranged the beds upon elevated platforms, while the fire-hole was sunk in the center. The doorways faced E. and W., and the smoke-hole was on one side of the roof a short distance below the apex. Several such houses are still in occupancy on the former reservation. There were also drying platforms and arbors thatched with grass in the same way. The skin tipi was used when away from home. The Wichita raised large quantities of corn and traded the surplus to the neighboring hunting tribes. Besides corn they had pumpkins and tobacco. Their corn was ground upon stone metates or in wooden mortars. Their women made pottery to a limited degree. In their original con-

dition both sexes went nearly naked, the men wearing only a breech-cloth and the women a short skirt, but from their abundant tattooing they were designated preëminently as the "tattooed people" in the sign language. Men and women generally wore the hair flowing loosely. They buried their dead in the ground, erecting a small framework over the mound.

The Wichita had not the clan system, but were extremely given to ceremonial dances, particularly the picturesque "Horn dance," nearly equivalent to the Green Corn dance of the Eastern tribes. They had also ceremonial races in which the whole tribe joined. Within recent years they have taken up the Ghost dance and Peyote rite. Their head-chief, who at present is of Tawakoni descent, seems to be of more authority than is usual among the Plains tribes. In general character the Wichita are industrious, reliable, and of friendly disposition.   (J. M.)

Black Pani.—Charlevoix, Voy. to Amer., II, 246, 1761. Black Pawnees.—Prichard, Phys. Hist. Man., v, 408, 1847 (confounded with Arikara). Do′gu′at.— Mooney, Ghost Dance, 1095, 1896 ('tattooed people': Kiowa name). Do′kănă.— Mooney, ibid. ('tattooed people': Comanche name). Freckled Panis.—Bouquet (1764) quoted by Jefferson, Notes, 141, 1825. Guichita.—Tex. State Archives, Nov. 15, 1785. Guichittă.—Doc. 503 (1791-2), ibid. Guilach.—Ibid., 1792 (probably identical). Hinás-sau.—Gatschet, Arapaho MS., B. A. E. (Arapaho name). Hinásso.—Ibid. (Arapaho name). Höχ-súwitan.—ten Kate, Synonymie, 9, 1884 ('tattooed people': Cheyenne name). Huichites.—Bull. Soc. Geog. Mex., 267, 1870. Ikarik.—Gatschet, Pawnee MS., B. A. E. (Pawnee name). Ki′-ɸi-ku′-ɸuc.— La Flesche quoted by Dorsey, MS., B. A. E., 1878 (Omaha name). Kiddĕkĕdissĕ.—ten Kate, Synonymie, 10, 1884 (own name). Kidikurús.— Gatschet, Wichita MS., B. A. E., 1884 (own name). Kiri-kur-uks.—Grinnell, Pawnee Hero Stories, 241, 1889 ('bear's eyes': Pawnee name). Kirikurus.— Ibid. (own name). Ki′tikĭti′sh.—Mooney, Ghost Dance, 1095, 1896 (own name). Mítsitá.—Dorsey Kansa MS. vocab., B. A. E., 1882 (Kansa name). Niteheta.—Sibley, Hist. Sketches, 75, 1806 (evident misprint of Witcheta; given as a village). Ochivitas.—Bull. Soc. Geog. Mex., 504, 1869. Onachita.— Ann. de la Propag. de la Foi., I, no. 5, 44, 1853 (misprint). Ositas.—La Harpe (1719) in French, Hist. Coll. La., III, 74, 1851. Ouchitaws.—Bollaert in Jour. Ethnol. Soc. Lond., II, 265, 1850. Ouichi-taws.—Bollaert, ibid., 279. Ouitcitas.—Robin, Voy. a la Louisiane, III, 3, 1807. Ousita.—La Harpe (1719) in Margry, Déc., VI, 289, 1886. Ovagitas.— Barcia, Ensayo, 288, 1723. Ovedsitas.—Doc. of 1771-2 quoted by Bolton in Tex. Hist. Asso. Quar., IX, 91, 1905. ꞩáɸiⁿ wasábĕ.—Dorsey, Çegiha MS. dict., B. A. E., 1878 ('Black bear Pawnees': Ponca and Omaha name). Pamassa.—Vaugondy, Carte Amérique, 1778. Pamasus.—Alcedo, Dic, Geog., II, 630, 1787. Pancasa.—Barcia, Ensayo, 298, 1723. Pancassa.—La Salle (ca. 1680) in Margry, Déc., II, 168, 1877. Paneassa.—La Hontan, New Voy., I, 130, 1703. Paniaisa.—Bowles, Map of America, after 1750. Pania-picque.—Sibley, Hist. Sketches, 19, 1806. Pania Pique.—Jefferson (1806) quoted by Bowen, Am. Discov. by Welsh, 94, 1876. Paniassas.—Carver, Travels, map, 1778. Pani-massas.—Dumont, La., I, 135, 1753. Panionassa.— De l'Isle (1703) cited by Dunbar in Mag. Am. Hist., IV, 249, 1880. Paniouassa.—Beaurain (ca. 1720) in Margry, Déc., VI, 230, 289, 1886. Pani-oussa.—La Harpe (1720), ibid., 290. Paniovasas.— Alcedo, Dic. Geog., IV, 53, 1788. Panis.—Sibley, Hist. Sketches, 74, 1806 (given as French name). Panis noirs.—Bruyère (1742) in Margry, Déc., VI,

474, 1886. **Panis piques.**—Hutchins (1764) in Schoolcraft, Ind. Tribes, III, 557, 1853; Perrin du Lac, Voyages, 368, 1805. **Pani-wasaba.**—A. C. Fletcher, inf'n, 1905 (Omaha name). **Panjassa.**—Bowles, Map of America, after 1750. **Panniassas.**—Jefferys, Am. Atlas, map 5, 1776. **Pányi waçewe.**—Dorsey, Chiwere MS. vocab., B. A. E., 1879 (Iowa, Oto, and Missouri name). **Paunee Piqûé.**—Sibley, Hist. Sketches, 64, 1806 (French name). **Pawnee Pick.**—Irving, Ind. Sketches, II, 74, 1835. **Pawnee Picts.**—Hildreth, Dragoon Campaigns, 160, 1836. **Pawnee Piquas.**—Long, Exped. Rocky Mts., II, 104, 1823. **Pic.**—Sage, Scenes in Rocky Mts., 153, 1846. **Picks.**—Dougherty (1837) in H. R. Doc. 276, 25th Cong., 2d sess., 16, 1838. **Pitchinávo.**—ten Kate, Synonymie, 10, 1884 ('painted breasts': Comanche name). **Prickled Panis.**—Buchanan, N. A. Inds., 155, 1824 (or Freckled Panis). **Quicasquiris.**—La Harpe (1719) in Margry, Déc., VI, 289, 1886. **Quirasquiris.**—Beaurain, ibid., 289. **Quivira.**—For the application of this term to the Wichita and their country, see *Quivira*. **Sónik'ni.**—Gatschet, Comanche MS., B. A. E., 1884 ('grass lodge': Comanche name). **Sóninkanik**—ten Kate, Synonymie, 9, 1884 ('grass lodges': Comanche name). **Speckled Pani.**—Imlay, West. Ter. N. A., 293, 1797. **Thacanhé.**—Iberville (1700) in Margry, Déc., IV, 374, 1880 (cf. *Do'kănă* above). **Tŏēchkanne.**—ten Kate, Reizen in N. A., 373, 1885 ('Donkere Hutten': Comanche name). **Túχguĕt.**—Gatschet, Kiowa MS., B. A. E., 147 ('those who tattoo': Kiowa name). **Túχkanne.**—ten Kate, Synonymie, 9, 1884 ('dusky lodges': Comanche name). **Túχquĕt.**—Gatschet, Kiowa MS., B. A. E. ('those who tattoo': Kiowa name; cf. *Do'gu'at*). **Washita.**—Sibley, Hist. Sketches, 121, 1806. **Washittas.**—Gallatin in Trans. Am. Antiq. Soc., II, 115, 1836. **Wasita.**—Keane in Stanford, Compend., 543, 1878. **Wichetahs.**—Ind. Aff. Rep., 144, 1850. **Wichetas.**—Neighbors in H. R. Doc. 100, 29th Cong., 2d sess., 4, 1847. **Wichita.**—Latham in Trans. Philol. Soc. Lond., 103, 1856. **Wishitaw.**—Otis, Check List, 127, 1880. **Wi'-si-tă.**—Dorsey, Kwapa MS. vocab., B. A. E., 1891 (Quapaw name). **Witch-a-taws.**—Butler and Lewis (1846) in H. R. Doc. 76, 29th Cong., 2d sess., 7, 1847. **Witcheta.**—Stokes (1839) in H. R. Doc. 219, 27th Cong., 3d sess., 202, 1843. **Witchetaw.**—Ind. Aff. Rep., 455, 1845. **Witchitas.**—Schoolcraft, Ind. Tribes, I, 518, 1851. **Witchitaws.**—Arbuckle in H. R. Doc. 311, 25th Cong., 2d sess., 38, 1838. **Wîthchetau.**—McCoy, Ann. Reg., no. 4, 27, 1838. **Witshita.**—Latham, Essays, 399, 1860. **Wîtsită'.**—Dorsey, Osage MS. vocab., B. A. E., 1883 (Osage name).

Wickakee. One of the names of the scarlet painted-cup (*Castilleia coccinea*), called in Massachusetts "Indian paintbrush"; probably derived from one of the Algonquian dialects.

Wickaninnish. Originally the name of a chief, but used by authors to designate several tribes, separately and collectively, between Nootka sd., Vancouver id., and Juan de Fuca str., Brit. Col.

Wickaninnish.—Jewitt, Narr., 37, 1849. **Wick-a-nook.**—Ross, Adventures, 159, 1849 (near Nootka). **Wickinninish.**—Jewitt, op. cit., 76.

Wickiup. The popular name for the brush shelter or mat-covered house, of the Paiute, Apache, and other tribes of Nevada, Arizona, and the adjacent region. The name is of disputed origin, but apparently is from the Sauk, Fox, and Kickapoo *wikíyapi*, 'lodge,' 'dwelling,' 'house.' See *Habitations*.

Wickopy. See *Wicopy*.

Wickup. A New England name, particularly in Massachusetts, of the American linden or basswood (*Tilia americana*), from *wikop*, the name of this tree in Massachuset, Chippewa, and closely related dialects of the Algonquian stock. The willow-herb (*Epilobium angustifolium*) is also known as *wickup* or *Indian wickup*. In this case the name is due to transference. See *Wicopy*. (A. F. C.)

Wicocomoco. A tribe, belonging to the Powhatan confederacy, residing on the s. side of Potomac r., at its mouth, in Northumberland co., Va. Their principal village was at the mouth of Wicomocco r. In 1608 they numbered about 520, but in 1722 had dwindled to a few individuals, who still kept up the name and avoided intercourse with the whites and other Indians. The meaning of the name is unknown, but the last part, *comoco*, is the Powhatan term, in composition, for a stockaded village. (J. M.)

Wicocomocco.—Beverley, Va., 199, 1722. **Wighocomoco.**—Smith (1629), Va., I, map, repr. 1819. **Yoacomoco.**—Herrman, map (1670) in Rep. on the Line between Va. and Md., 1873.

Wicocomoco. A tribe formerly living on Wicomico r., on the E. shore of Maryland, having their principal village, in 1608, on the s. bank of the river in Somerset co. They were of small stature and spoke a language different from that of the Powhatan tribes. They frequently united with the Nanticoke in attacks on the colonists, even crossing to the w. shore for this purpose, but in 1668, as a condition of peace with the English, the Nanticoke "emperor" agreed to deliver the whole Wicocomoco tribe into their hands. A few mongrels still retain the name. (J. M.)

Wecamses.—Sanford, U. S., cxlviii, 1819. **Wiccomisses.**—Md. Archiv., Proc. Counc., 1667–1687, 29, 1887. **Wicomese.**—Map (ca. 1640) in Rep. on the Line between Va. and Md., 1873. **Wicomesse.**—Evelin (1648) in Force, Hist. Tracts, II, 24, 1838. **Wicomick.**—Bozman, Md., II, 310, 1837. **Wicomocos.**—Calvert (ca. 1635) quoted by Schoolcraft, Ind. Tribes, VI, 131, 1857. **Wighcocómicoes.**—Jefferson, Notes, 38, table, 1801. **Wighcocomoco.**—Smith (1629), Va., I, 118, repr. 1819. **Wighcocomocoes.**—Smith, ibid., 129. **Wighcomocos.**—Schoolcraft, Ind. Tribes, VI, 131, 1857. **Wighcomogos.**—Domenech, Deserts, I, 445, 1860. **Wycomes.**—Am. Pioneer, II, 192, 1843. **Wycomeses.**—Evelin (1648) quoted by Proud, Penn., I, 114, 1797.

Wicopy. A New England name of the moosewood (*Dirca palustris*), called also leatherwood on account of the strength and toughness of the bark ropes made from it in Indian fashion. The Indian word from which *wicopy* or *wickopy* is derived applies not to the leatherwood but to the stringy bark of the whitewood or basswood (*Tilia americana*). The origin of the word is seen in Massachuset *wik'pi*, Abnaki *wighebi*, Delaware *wikbi*, Chippewa *wigob*, and Cree *wikupiy*, each signifying 'inner bark,' particularly the bast of the linden. The components of this Algonquian term are: *w*, preformative; *i*, connective; and the radical *kop*, 'inner or second bark.' *Wickup* is the same word. (A. F. C.)

Widja (*Wĭ′dja*). A Haida town of the Widja-gitunai family formerly on the N. coast of Graham id., just w. of the entrance to Masset inlet, Queen Charlotte ids., Brit. Col.   (J. R. S.)
Wĭ′dja.—Swanton, Cont. Haida, 281, 1905. Wĭ′-ts'a.—Boas in 12th Rep. N. W. Tribes Can., 23, 1898.

Widja-gitunai (*Wĭ′dja gitАnā′-i,* 'Gituns of the town of Widja'). A Haida family of the Eagle clan, named from its town on the N. coast of Graham id., Brit. Col., between Masset inlet and Virago sd. This with the Tohlka-gitunai, Chets-gitunai, and Djus-hade formed one larger related group.   (J. R. S.)
Wĭ′dja gītАnā′-i.—Swanton, Cont. Haida, 275, 1905. Wĭ′ts'a gyit'inai′.—Boas in 12th Rep. N. W. Tribes Can., 23, 1898.

Wiekagjoc (apparently a corruption of *wikwajek,* 'head of a creek.'—Gerard). A tribe of the Mahican confederacy dwelling on the E. bank of Hudson r. in the vicinity of Hudson, Columbia co., N. Y.
Wickagjock.—Wassenaar (1632) quoted by Ruttenber, Tribes Hudson R., 71, 1872. Wiekagjocks.—Ruttenber, ibid., 85.

Wieska. See *Nanabozho.*

Wigwam. (1) A name for an Algonquian dwelling, an arbor-like or conical structure in which, from Canada to North Carolina, was employed the same general mode of erection, which varied mainly in the plant materials (saplings, barks, rushes, or flags) used, and which differences in soil and climate changed here and there to a certain extent (see *Habitations*). The word, which appears in English as early as 1634 (Wood, New England's Prospect, 65, 1634) was, like the terms skunk, musquash, etc., borrowed from Abnaki by the colonists of E. Massachusetts, who adopted it as the name for an Indian habitation, in preference to the term *wetu* (*witu*) used by the natives among whom they settled. The Massachuset Indians, like the Narraganset, used also as the name for a house the word *wetuom* (*wituôm*), formed from the same base. Eliot (Indian Grammar Begun, 11, 1666), who was ignorant of the origin of the word under consideration, mentions, we may suppose through an inadvertence, a word *wekuwomut* (for *wetuomut*), which he interprets 'in his house,' and adds: "hence we corrupt this word [to] wigwam." This erroneous etymology, based on a word nonexistent in the Massachuset dialect, and, in fact, impossible in any Algonquian dialect, has unfortunately been copied by nearly every English dictionary.

The Abnaki word *wigwâm,* literally 'dwelling,' is from *wigw,* 'he dwells,' + the formative *-am,* from the Algonquian root *wig, wik* (*ig, ik,* in composition), 'to dwell,' and is cognate with Micmac *wigwâm,* Mohegan *wikwâm,* Lenape (Delaware) *wikwam,* and Chippewa *wigiwam* (from *wigiw,* 'he dwells,' a word obsolete

in Chippewa but preserved in Cree), and Nipissing *wikiwâm,* and, by change, in this dialect, of *w* to *m, mikiwâm.* The Virginia Renape seem not to have employed the word *wikwâm* used by their relatives of the N., but substituted for it the term *kómŭk,* which, like its cognates in other Algonquian dialects (Lenape *gámĭk* or *kámĭk,* Abnaki *gámĭk,* Cree and Chippewa *kámĭk,* Masachuset *kómŭk,* Narraganset *kómŏk,* etc.), was always used in compounds, and never disjunctively. The word *wigwang* used by Beverley (Hist. Virginia, 1705) is merely a corruption of the northern vocable *wigwâm,* with which he was evidently unfamiliar.

(2) A name applied by travelers to the dwellings of Indians other than those of Algonquian stock, or to the habitations of the natives of countries other than North America, as for example: "Their houses or wigwams, which they [the Caribs] call carbets" (Stedman, Exped. against the Revolted Negroes of Surinam, I, 403, 1806); "The Fuegian wigwam resembles, in size . . . a haycock" (Darwin, Jour. of Researches, 212, 1845); "rude jackales, somewhat resembling the wigwams of the Pawnees" (Gregg, Commerce of the Prairies, I, 286, 1851).

(3) A name applied by the founders of the Tammany Society of New York City to their headquarters.

(4) A name sometimes applied to a large structure in which a nominating convention or other political meeting takes place.

Certain summer hospital tents for children are known as "wigwams," and there is also a "wigwam shoe" or "wigwam slipper."   (W. R. G.   A. F. C.)

Wigwassing. A term used on the coast of New England for the operation of taking eels by torch-light; spelled also *wequashing.* In a letter of N. Freeman in 1792 (Mass. Hist. Soc. Coll., 1st s., I, 231, 1806), he says: "The Indians when they go in a canoe with a torch, to catch eels in the night, call it *weequash,* or anglicized, *wequashing.*" The word is a participle of a verb "to *wigwas,*" contracted and anglicized from Massachuset *wikwesweu,* 'he illuminates it (something animate, say a fish) by burning (i. e., torching).'   (W. R. G.)

Wihatset (*Wi-hat′-sĕt*). A populous Chumashan village formerly at Punta Pedregosa, near Point Mugu, Ventura co., Cal.—Henshaw, Buenaventura MS. vocab., B. A. E., 1882.

Wihinasht. A division of Shoshoni, formerly in w. Idaho, N. of Snake r. and in the vicinity of Boise City. The name appears to be obsolete, the surviving Indians having been absorbed by other Shoshoni bands and now being under the Fort Hall school superintendency in

Idaho. They were said to number 1,000 in 1865.

Boisé Shoshonees.—Cooley in Ind. Aff. Rep., 30, 1865. **Wehinnas.**—Wool (1855) in H. R. Ex. Doc. 76, 34th Cong., 3d sess., 150, 1857. **Western Shoshoni.**—Gallatin quoted by Latham in Proc. Philol. Soc. Lond., VI, 73, 1854. **Western Snakes.**—Hale in U. S. Expl. Exped., VI, 218, 1846. **Wihinagūt.**—Powers, Inds. W. Nevada, MS., B. A. E., 1876 (Paiute [Mono?] name). **Wihinasht.**—Hale, op. cit. **Wihinast.**—Latham in Proc. Philol. Soc. Lond., VI, 73, 1854. **Winnas band.**—Kirkpatrick in Ind. Aff. Rep., 268, 1862. **Winnas-ti.**—Russell (1855) in Sen. Ex. Doc. 26, 34th Cong., 1st sess., 13, 1856. **Win-nes-tes.**—Townsend (1855) in H. R. Ex. Doc. 76, 34th Cong., 3d sess., 150, 1857.

Wikaihlako (*Wĭ′-kai-′lăko*, 'large spring'). A former Lower Creek town on the w. side of Chattahoochee r. in Henry co., Ala., 4 m. above Chiskatalofa. It contained 250 inhabitants in 1820.

U-i-káyi-′láko.—A. S. Gatschet, inf°n, 1883 (full Creek name). **Wekisa.**—Drake, Bk. Inds., xii, 1848. **Wekivas.**—Morse, Rep. to Sec. War, 364, 1822. **We-kiwa.**—Treaty of 1827 in U. S. Ind. Treat., 420, 1837. **Wĭ-kai-′láko.**—Gatschet, Creek Migr. Leg., I, 149, 1884.

Wikchamni. A Yokuts (Mariposan) tribe on Kaweah r., near Limekiln or Lemon cove, below the Wiksachi and above the Kawia and Yokol. The present population consists of two or three scattered families and individuals.

Nie-chum-nes.—Barbour in Sen. Ex. Doc. 4, 32d Cong., spec. sess., 254, 1853. **Wachamnis.**—Purcell in Ind. Aff. Rep. 1869, 193, 1870. **Waitshum′ni.**—Hoffman in Proc. Am. Philos. Soc., XXIII, 372, 1886. **We-chummies.**—Lewis in Ind. Aff. Rep. 1857, 185, 399, 1858. **Wic-chum-nee.**—Royce in 18th Rep. B. A. E., 782, 1899. **Wich-a-chim-ne.**—Wessells (1853) in H. R. Ex. Doc. 76, 34th Cong., 3d sess., 32, 1857. **Wichumnies.**—Lewis in Ind. Aff. Rep., 381, 1872. **Wikachumnis.**—Taylor in Cal. Farmer, June 8, 1860. **Wik-chum-ni.**—Powers in Cont. N. A. Ethnol., III, 370, 1877. **Wik-tchum′-ne.**—Merriam in Science, XIX, 915, June 15, 1904. **Wĭktshŏm′ni.**—Hoffman in Proc. Am. Philos. Soc., XXIII, 301, 1886. **Wiscum-nes.**—Johnston in Sen. Ex. Doc. 61, 32d Cong., 1st sess., 22, 1852. **Wükchamni.**—Kroeber in Am. Anthr., VIII, 662, 1906 (correct name).

Wikeno (*Wik′ē′nō*, 'the portage makers'). A Kwakiutl tribe speaking the Heiltsuk dialect and living on Rivers inlet, Brit. Col. Their clans, according to Boas, are: Koikaktenok, Gyigyilkam, Waokuitem, Wawikem, Guetela, and Nalekuitk. Their towns are: Tlaik, Niltala, Wikeno, Nuhitsomk, Somhotnechau, and Tsiomhau. Pop. 131 in 1901, 99 in 1909.

Awī′k·ēnôx.—Boas in Nat. Mus. Rep. 1895, 328, 1897. **Awī′ky′enoq.**—Boas in 6th Rep. N. W. Tribes Can., 52, 1890. **Oweekano.**—Sproat in Can. Ind. Aff., 145, 1879. **O-wee-kay-no.**—Can. Ind. Aff., 304, 1893. **Oweekayo.**—Ibid., 361, 1897. **Wee-kee-moch.**—Kane, Wand. in N. A., app., 1859. **Weekenoch.**—Scouler (1846) in Jour. Ethnol. Soc. Lond., I, 233, 1848. **Wikanee.**—Brit. Col. map, 1872. **Wikeinoh.**—Tolmie and Dawson, Vocabs. Brit. Col., 117B, 1884. **Wik′ēnō.**—Boas in Petermanns Mitteil., pt. 5, 130, 1887. **Wykenas.**—Scott in Ind. Aff. Rep., 316, 1868.

Wikeno. A town of the Wikeno tribe (q. v.) of British Columbia.   (F. B.)

Wikoktenok (*Wĭ′k′ōxtēnôx*, 'eagle'). A clan of the Bellabella, a Kwakiutl tribe.—Boas in Rep. Nat. Mus. 1895, 328, 1897.

Wikorzh (derived from *wihu*, 'fat,' and *koro*, 'cavity,' because it is said the eyes in the cadaver of a certain bear had dis-

appeared and some dried fat still adhered to the orbits; or from *wikuru*, 'netted gourd'). A Hopi clan.

Fat Cavity clan.—Voth, Traditions of the Hopi, 22, 40, 1905. **Wikorzh.**—Ibid., 37. **Wikurzh.**—Ibid.

Wiktosachki ('white-earth place'). A Tarahumare rancheria about 28 m. E. of Chinatu, w. Chihuahua, Mexico.—Lumholtz, inf′n, 1894.

Wikyuwamkamusenaikata ('painted lodge'). A Cree band, taking the name of its chief, living in 1856 about Fort de Prairie, Northwest Ter., Canada.—Hayden, Ethnog. and Philol. Mo. Val., 237, 1862.

WIKENO MAN.   (AM. MUS. NAT. HIST.)

Wilakal. A village of the Agua Caliente Shoshoneans, in the San Jacinto mts., s. Cal. Under the Spanish name of this place (San Ysidro) 2 villages are mentioned in 1865 (Lovett in Ind. Aff. Rep., 125), with populations of 159 and 90, respectively. In 1880 only one is recorded, with between 50 and 75 inhabitants (Jackson and Kinney, Rep. Miss. Ind., 22, 1883). It is now included in Los Coyotes res. See *Pachawal*.

Ho-la-kal.—Barrows, Ethno-Bot. Coahuilla Ind., 34, 1900. **San Isidro.**—Ibid. **San Ysedro.**—Ind. Aff. Rep., 175, 1902. **San Ysidro.**—Jackson and Kinney, Rep. Miss. Ind., 22, 1883. **Wilakal.**—A. L. Kroeber, inf′n, 1905.

Wild rice. The aquatic plant (*Zizania aquatica*) generally known as "wild rice" has been for many generations one of the most important food producers of the Indian country about the Great Lakes and adjacent waters. The comparatively dense population in the wild-rice area and the physical well-being of the Indians there resident have been remarked by many writers. Henry in 1775 and Carver in 1776 record the fact that the great expeditions to the rivers of the W. and the preservation of the "infant colonies" beyond the settled E. would hardly have been possible without this cereal. The nomenclature of the wild-rice area is of importance, since Jenks concludes that in this limited region of North America alone "more geographic names have been derived from wild rice than from any other natural vegetal product throughout the whole continent." The plant itself is multinomial, no fewer than 60 synonyms in English, French, and the Indian tongues being cited by Jenks. The use of wild rice (which is mentioned rather late in the Jesuit Relations) seems to have been stimulated not a little by the pressure of the whites on the Indians, which forced them more and more into closer quarters in this region and cut off some of their resources, especially hunting. Wild rice is remembered in several Indian month-names and some interesting legends are connected with it. The Menominee tribe is so called from the plant. Practically all that is known about the botany of wild rice, its production and food uses, its influence on Indian life and customs, and its use by white settlers, will be found in Dr A. E. Jenks' monograph, "The Wild-Rice Gatherers of the Upper Lakes" (19th Rep. B. A. E., 1900). A list of the tribes using wild rice is there given.   (A. F. C.)

Willanoucha. A former Seminole town near the head of St Marks r., probably in Leon co., Fla.
Willa-noucha-talofa.—Bell in Morse, Rep. to Sec. War, 306, 1822.

Willewah. A band of the Nez Percés (q. v.) mentioned by Lewis and Clark in 1805 and formerly residing in Wallowa valley, Oreg. At that date they numbered about 500. Their descendants afterward formed Joseph's band, and were the leaders in the Nez Percé war of 1877. The majority of this band are now on Colville res., Wash., where they numbered 97 in 1909.
Grand Ronde.—Gibbs in Pac. R. R. Rep., I, 417, 1855. Willa'motki tituχan.—Gatschet, MS., B. A. E., 1878. Willewah.—Lewis and Clark Exped., II, 471, 1814.

Willi. A former Maidu division residing in Sutter co., Cal.
Willem.—Chever in Bull. Essex Inst. 1870, II, 28, 1871. Willie.—Wozencraft (1851) in Sen. Ex. Doc. 4, 32d Cong., spec. sess., 206, 1853.

Williams, Eleazar. The son of Thomas (Tehoragwanegen, q. v.) and Mary Ann Rice Williams (Konwatewenteta), born probably on the shore of L. George, N. Y., in May, 1788, died Aug. 28, 1858, on St Regis res., near Hogansburg, N. Y., neglected and in great destitution. He is said to have been one of 13 children, most of whom were born at Caughnawaga, Quebec, the home of their parents. The childhood of Eleazar passed uneventfully, as usual among children of semi-agricultural Christianized Indians. One of the early playmates of Eleazar related in after life how the latter, wearing a kind of shift as his only garment, sported about the byways of Caughnawaga, exposed to wounds from stones and thorns. Owing to a scrofulous taint in his family, these bruises and injuries left permanent scars, which later in life were increased in size by means of lashes and tartar emetic in such manner as to suggest the scars of the shackles and chains alleged to have been inflicted on him by the jailor Simon of the Tower of the Temple in Paris. In

ELEAZAR WILLIAMS. (FROM A PAINTING IN POSSESSION OF THE WISCONSIN HISTORICAL SOCIETY)

1800, his father (in opposition to the wishes of the mother, on religious grounds, she being a strict member of the Roman Catholic Church) took him and his brother John to Long Meadow, Mass., to be educated among distant relations of the father, but John soon returned home because he made no progress in his studies.

At Long Meadow the boys were left with Mr Nathaniel Ely, who had undertaken to educate them at his own expense, but financial reverses compelled Mr Ely to appeal first to missionary societies for aid, then, in 1804, to the state legislature, each time meeting with success. In 1805 Eleazar visited Montreal; and in the following year, in company with a reputed relation, the Rev. Mr Williams, he went to Boston, where he was questioned by several ministers regarding his studies. While here he met Father Chevreux, to whom he was introduced as an Indian youth studying for the ministry. The Father questioned him, it is said, as to the practice of the Indians in adopting French children, as Williams appeared to him to have French blood. It is possible that at this interview Williams first conceived the idea that he could successfully personate the Dauphin of France. In 1807 he was at Hartford, Mass., where he met President Dwight, who gave him some salutary advice; and in May of the following year a Dr Lyman urged him to become a missionary to the Indians, a suggestion which met with Williams' hearty approval. It was in this year that Mr Ely, his friend and benefactor, died, and with his death closed the first scene of Williams' life among civilized surroundings. He lived at Mansfield and Long Meadow until Dec. 22, 1809, when he was placed under the tuition of Rev. Enoch Hale, of Westhampton, Mass., under whose guidance he remained until Aug. 1812. During this period he was commissioned to make a visit to the St Louis or Caughnawaga Indians to learn what the prospect was of introducing Protestantism among them. In 1810, owing to the condition of his health, Williams abandoned his studies and traveled in the S., where he met his future friend and bishop, Dr Hobart. Again visiting his family at Caughnawaga in the following year, he conversed with their Indian neighbors about the Protestant faith, but the Roman Catholic priests warned them not to listen to his instructions. Nevertheless, the attention shown encouraged him to enter on what was to be his life work.

Early in 1812 Williams went to Canada as an agent of the American Board of Missions, arriving at the Sault St Louis on Jan. 18; but he found it difficult to change the religious beliefs of the people. He continued his missionary tour until March, when the chiefs and counsellors made him a chief of the Iroquois at Caughnawaga, being given the name Onwarenhiiaki, probably meaning 'Tree Cutter.' In July he returned to Westhampton. At the beginning of the War of 1812, Williams, being regarded as a suitable person to aid in preventing the Indians of his tribe from espousing the cause of England, was appointed Superintendent-general of the Northern Indian Department. He was assigned to duty with Gen. Dearborn, but was transferred to service with Gen. Jacob Brown, under whom he acted in a confidential capacity, obtaining through the Canadian Indians valuable information regarding the movements of British troops. At the battle of

Plattsburgh, N. Y., Sept. 14, 1814, he was wounded. At this time he had not completed his theological studies. In Nov. 1820 Gen. A. G. Ellis went to Oneida Castle, N. Y., where Williams had resided for about 3 years as a catechist in the Episcopal Church, in order to aid the latter in teaching school. For this service Williams was to repay Ellis by instructing him in Latin, Greek, and French. Instead of being learned in these languages, however, Ellis found that Williams was ignorant of them, and that he had really been induced to live with Williams in order that the latter might be instructed in the rudiments of English. Ellis lived with Williams about 4 years, during which period the latter made no appreciable progress, not being able then, says Ellis, "to compose five lines of the English decently." Nevertheless, during his residence among the Oneida, Williams, by his persuasive eloquence in the native tongue, had induced the old Pagan party, numbering about three-fourths of the tribe, to abjure paganism. He had further induced them to grant him 100 acres of land for his own use and to sell several hundred acres more to the state to provide a fund to build a church and a schoolhouse. The proceeds of the sale, amounting to about $4,000, were placed by the governor in the hands of Judges Williams and Miller, of Utica, to secure faithful application of the sum to the purpose mentioned. Williams, however, managing to obtain control of the expenditure of the money, erected a church at a cost of $1,200 or $1,400, for which he submitted bills covering the entire sum of $4,000, but in such equivocal shape that they would not bear examination, whereupon the two trustees resigned their trust. For many years the Oneida charged Williams with malfeasance, but the matter was never adjusted or explained. In Oct. 1820 Rev. Jedidiah Morse, who had traveled through the N. W. as far as Green Bay, Wis., presented to Williams a project for removing the New York Indians to the country w. of L. Michigan. Williams was ripe for such a venture, even claiming later that he was the originator of the scheme. In a council with the Oneida, which Morse called to discuss the proposal, Williams acted as interpreter. After the council was over, Morse asked Williams for a copy of the speech of the Oneida chief in reply, which was strongly adverse to Morse's proposal. Several days later Williams completed a fictitious speech, misrepresenting the answer of the Oneida, to which he forged the names of their chiefs. In the following year the chiefs, again in council with Morse, when Williams was not present, repudiated the

Williams interpretation of the speech as "a lie from beginning to end." At this time he was at Green Bay, Wis., with a self-constituted delegation of Oneida, Onondaga, Tuscarora, and Stockbridges, negotiating a project for the removal of all the New York Indians to the country between the Mississippi and Green Bay, Wis., and the establishment among them of an empire with a single supreme head. In the furtherance of this plan in 1821 Williams visited New York and entered into negotiations with the Ogden Land Company, which then held the preemption right to most of the Indian lands in w. New York, looking to the removal of the New York Indians beyond the limits of the state, and received sums of money from time to time for the purpose of advancing the interests of the land company. Williams also busied himself at this time in enlisting the aid of missionary societies in establishing a church among the Indians at Green Bay, and carried on a voluminous correspondence with the War Department (under which the Indian affairs were then administered), in order to obtain recognition of his schemes. Aided by the Ogden Land Company, he finally obtained official permission to lead a delegation of Indians to Green Bay, representing to them that the affair was "under the patronage, protection, and with the assistance of the Government;" but when the proposal was openly made to the New York Indians in council, the Seneca and the other tribes, through the famous Red Jacket, emphatically refused their assent to the project. Nevertheless, through Williams' machinations and the powerful influence behind his schemes, a treaty was finally negotiated in 1832 by which Williams' plan was partly realized. Most of the Oneida removed to Wisconsin, but the Seneca, followed by the Tuscarora and the Onondaga, resolved to hold their lands in New York at all hazard.

When Williams removed to Green Bay in 1823 he married Miss Mary Jourdain. He had promised schools to the Indians and the French traders in consideration of their consent to establish the New York Indians among them; but having failed to redeem these pledges the missionary societies disavowed their confidence in Williams, and in 1827 appointed as missionary the Rev. Richard F. Cadle, who established a school at Menomoneeville, Wis. With the failure of the Green Bay land scheme Williams realized that he was ruined, and withdrew to his home at Kaukalin. He continued to receive aid from some of the missionary boards, since he represented himself as the missionary of the Oneida at Duck Creek, Wis., although he did not perform the duties of

that station. About 1832 the Oneida, becoming wearied with the Williams incubus, held a council, to which they invited Col. George Boyd, U. S. Indian agent, in order to show him that for years Williams had failed to carry out any of his many promises; that, owing "to his want of good faith, his fraud and deceit, they were in the wilderness, utterly abandoned, without schools, churches, or religious privileges of any kind; and worse than all, that the little fund provided by the kindness of the Christian public in the East was anticipated, caught on its way to them by him, and consumed for entirely contrary purposes." At the Indians' request, the agent notified the governor of New York, the United States Government, and the missionary societies, warning the authorities that the Oneida had forever repudiated Williams, and asking that he should not be recognized as acting for them in any capacity. This indictment was so disastrous to Williams that he dropped out of sight until 1853, when he reappeared in a new rôle, that of the Dauphin of France, the Lost Prince, Louis XVII. At once he gained many credulous adherents and apologists, although it had been shown that he was "the most perfect adept at fraud, deceit, and intrigue that the world ever produced." He so far imposed on the credulity of many well-meaning persons that the Rev. John H. Hanson in 1854 published an elaborate work, entitled The Lost Prince, in support of Williams' preposterous claim, based largely on material manufactured by Williams himself. Gen. A. G. Ellis (Wis. Hist. Soc. Coll., VIII, 1879) and William Ward Wight (Eleazar Williams Not the Dauphin of France, 1903) have shown the groundlessness of his claim. For Williams' published translations in the Iroquois language, see Pilling, Bibliography of the Iroquoian Languages, Bull. B. A. E., 167–168, 1888.   (J. N. B. H.)

Williams, Thomas. See *Tehoragwanegen.*

Williams Lake. A Shuswap village or band on Williams lake, which drains westward into Fraser r., Brit. Col., about lat. 52° 10′. Pop. 155 in 1910. The name is applied also to a Canadian Indian agency.

Willopah (*Xwilä′pax,* their name for the river). A Chinookan tribe on the lower course of Willopah r., Wash. They have been so frequently confounded with the Kwalhioqua, an Athapascan tribe living on the upper course of that stream, that the latter have usually been called Willopah. Their villages were Nayakolole, Quelaptonlit, and Talal. Along with the Kwalhioqua they ceded their lands to the United States in 1864. In 1910 there was said to be a single survivor who understood the language. GiLā'x̣wilā'pax.—Boas letter, 1904 (='people of the Willopah'). Gita'x̣wilapax.—Ibid. Ówilapsh — Gatschet, Kalapuya MS., B. A. E., 280 (*Xwilā'pax* and the ending -*pc*, 'people'; = "people of the Willopah": Salish name). Quila'pc.—Boas in 10th Rep. N. W. Tribes Can., 67, 1895. Wheelappa.—Pres. Mess., Ex. Doc. 39, 32d Cong., 1st sess., 2, 1852. Wheelappers.—Ind. Aff. Rep., 158, 1850. Whil'-a-pah.—Swan, N. W. Coast, 211, 1857. Whirlpool.—Domenech, Deserts N. Am., I, 445, 1880. Willapah.—Ind. Aff. Rep., 447, 1854. Willenoh.— Robertson, Oreg., 129, 1846. Willopah.—Ind. Aff. Rep., 448, 1854.

Willstown (named from the half-breed chief known to the whites as Red-headed Will). A former important Cherokee settlement on Wills cr., below Ft Payne, in De Kalb co., Ala. (J. M.) Wili'yĭ.—Mooney in 19th Rep. B. A. E., 546, 1900 (='Will's place': sometimes so called). Willstown.—Doc. of 1799 quoted by Royce in 5th Rep. B. A. E., 144, 1887.

Will's Town. A former settlement of the Shawnee at the site of Cumberland, Md. After this region was deserted by the Shawnee, an Indian named Will lived a short distance from the site of the old Shawnee town at the mouth of Caiuctucuc cr. At the time of the coming of the first white settlers he was living in a cabin on the mountain side. The creek, mountain, and town were afterward named for him. Will's cr. is noted on the maps of Lewis Evans (1755) and Scull (1759, 1770), and on the map in Gist's Journal (1753). (G. P. D.)

Will's Town. A Delaware village on the E. bank of Muskingum r., at the mouth of Wills cr., in Muskingum co., Ohio. It was destroyed by the Americans in 1782. Will's Town.—Hutchins in Smith, Bouquet Exped., map, 1766. Wils T.—La Tour map, 1784.

Wilson, Jack. See *Ghost dance, Wovoka.*

Wiltkun (*Qawi'ĭtkᵘ*). A Klikitat town in S. Washington. (F. B.)

Wiltkwilluk. A former Chinookan village on the S. bank of Columbia r., Oreg., just below Rainier and nearly opposite the mouth of Cowlitz r.—Gibbs, MS. no. 248, B. A. E.

Wiltmeet. The Dutch name of a Waranawonkong village on Esopus cr., probably near Kingston, Ulster co., N. Y. It was destroyed by the Dutch in 1660.— Ruttenber, Tribes Hudson R., 95, 128, 1872.

Wimbee. A village or band of the coast tribes of South Carolina included under the collective term Cusabo (q. v.). The only mention of the name in history seems to be in 1683, when the "chief of Wimbee" sold lands between Combahee and Broad rs. See Mills, Hist. S. C., 106, 1826, and document quoted by Rivers, Hist. S. C., 38, 1856. (J. M.)

Wimego. A Potawatomi village, named from the chief, situated in 1832 on the N. bank of Indian cr., in the N. part of Cass co., Ind.

Wi-me-co's village.—Royce in 18th Rep. B. A. E., pl. cxxvi, 1899. Wi-me-go's village.—Ibid., pl. cxxvĭi.

Wimian (*Wi'mian*). A ruined village pertaining to the Zuñi, situated 11 m. N. of Zuñi pueblo, N. Mex.—ten Kate, Reizen in N. A., 291, 1885.

Wimilchi. A Yokuts (Mariposan) tribe formerly living N. of Kings r., Cal., opposite the Wechikhit. They were gathered on the Fresno res., and with the Tachi (Tadji) numbered 165 in 1861. Ho-mel-ches.—Johnston in Sen. Ex. Doc. 61, 32d Cong., 1st sess., 23, 1852. Mowelches.—Ind. Aff. Rep., 219, 1861. Ne-mil-ches.—Barbour in Sen. Ex. Doc. 4, 32d Cong., spec. sess., 254, 1853. Was-mil-ches.—Ibid., 253. We-mal-che.—McKee in Sen. Ex. Doc. 4, 32d Cong., spec. sess., 75, 1853; Royce in 18th Rep. B. A. E., 782, 1899. We-melches.—Lewis in Ind. Aff. Rep., 1857, 399, 1858. We-mil-che.— Wessells in H. R. Ex. Doc. 76, 34th Cong., 3d sess., 31, 1857. We-mol-ches.—Ind. Aff. Rep., 223 1851.

Wiminuche. A division of Ute formerly ranging in S. W. Colorado, chiefly in the valley of the San Juan and its N. tributaries. There were 463 under the Navajo Springs school, Col., in 1910. Guibisnuches.—Salazar in Ind. Aff. Rep., 141, 1866. Guiguimuches.—Cooley, ibid., 21, 1865. Mamenoche.—Taylor in Sen. Ex. Doc. 4, 40th Cong., spec. sess., 10, 1867. Nomenuches.—Delgado in Ind. Aff. Rep., 163, 1865. Poruches.—Ibid. Wamanus.—McKenney and Hall, Ind. Tribes, III, 80, 1854 (identical?). Wamenuche.—Norton in Ind. Aff. Rep., 145, 1866. Wannemuches.—Cooley, op. cit. Webinoche.—Taylor, op. cit. Webinoche Utahs.—Graves in Ind. Aff. Rep., 135, 1866. Webrinoches.—Ibid., 132. Weeminuche.—Treaty of 1868 in U. S. Ind. Treaties, 981, 1873. Wemenuche.— Nicolay in Ind. Aff. Rep. 1863, 151, 1864. Wemenutche Utahs.—Arny in Ind. Aff. Rep. 1867, 204, 1868. Wibisnuche.—Delgado, ibid., 138, 1866. Wiminanches.—Collins, ibid., 125, 1861. Wimmenuches.—Davis, ibid. 1869, 255, 1870. Woman-o-che Utes.—Marcy, Border Reminis., 335, 1872. Womenunche.—Collins in Ind. Aff. Rep., 238, 1862.

Winamac ('catfish,' from *wēē'nŭd* 'muddy,' *mŭk* 'a fish.'—J. P. Dunn). A principal chief of the Potawatomi in the period of the War of 1812. He was one of the signers of the noted treaty of Greenville in 1795, and of others in 1803 and 1809. In this last treaty, concluded at Ft Wayne, the Miami, Delawares, and Potawatomi sold a large tract of land in central Indiana. This so provoked Tecumseh that he threatened the life of Winamac, but there appears to have been a speedy reconciliation, as we find Winamac leading the warriors of his tribe at the battle of Tippecanoe two years later. In the War of 1812, he, with most of the Indians of the central region, joined the British side. He claimed to have caused the massacre of the surrendered garrison of Ft Dearborn, Chicago, Aug. 15, 1812, but the actual leader in the affair seems to have been Blackbird (Makahta-penashe, not to be confounded with Makatapake, Black Partridge, a friendly Potawatomi of the same period), another Potawatomi chief. Some three months later, Nov. 22, Winamac was killed in an encounter with the Shawnee chief Captain James Logan (Spemicalawba), who had espoused the cause of the Americans in the war. The name appears also as Ouenemek (French form), Wenameac, Wenameck, Winemac, Winnemeg, Wynemac, etc.   (J. M.)

Winamac. Another Potawatomi chief of the same period, the name being a common one in the tribe. Unlike his namesake, he was generally friendly to the Americans and interposed in their behalf at the Ft Dearborn massacre, although he was said to have been among the hostiles at Tippecanoe in 1811. He visited Washington several times and died in the summer of 1821. His village, commonly known by his name, was near the present Winamac, Pulaski co., Ind. See Dunn, True Indian Stories, 1909; Thatcher, Ind. Biog., 1832.   (J. M.)

Winangik (*Wi-nan-gik'*) Given by Powers (Cont. N. A. Ethnol., III, 393, 1877) as a Shoshonean tribe on the N. fork of Kern r., Cal., but there was no tribe in this region except the Tubatulabal (q. v.).

Winanis. See *Ouananiche.*

Winangusconey. See *Moanahonga.*

Windigo. See *Weendigo.*

Winema ('woman chief'). A Modoc woman, better known as Toby Riddle, born in the spring of 1842. She received her name, Kaitchkona Winema (*Kitchkani laki shnawedsh,* 'female subchief'), because, when a child, she guided a canoe safely through the rapids of Link r. She justified her title when, but 15 years of age, she rallied the Modoc warriors as they took to flight when surprised by a band of Achomawi. After she grew up she became the wife of Frank Riddle, a miner from Kentucky. When the Modoc left Klamath res. in 1872 to return to Lost r. he served as interpreter to the various commissions that treated with them. After they had fled to the lava-beds and had defeated a detachment of soldiers, the Government decided to send a commission of men known to be in sympathy with them to arrange a peace. Winema warned Commissioner Meacham of the murderous temper of some of Captain Jack's followers (see *Kintpuash*). Meacham was convinced and told his fellow-commissioners, Gen. Edward R. S. Canby and Rev. E. Thomas, that they were going to their death, but could not swerve them from their purpose. Shonchin (q. v.), the shaman, threatened to kill her unless she confessed who had betrayed the plot, but she declared that she was not afraid to die, and Captain Jack forbade him to shoot a woman. When Gen. Canby refused to withdraw the troops from the lava-beds, the Modoc chief gave the signal, and Canby and Thomas fell instantly. Shonchin then turned his rifle

upon Meacham. Winema, who was present as interpreter, pleaded for the life of the man who, when Indian superintendent, had presented to white men living with Indian women the alternative of legal marriage or criminal prosecution. She seized the chief's wrists and thrust herself between the assassins and the victim, and when he dropped from several bullet wounds and a Modoc seized his hair to take the scalp Winema cried out that the soldiers were coming, whereupon they all fled. When the soldiers came at last, she advanced alone to meet them. Meacham, crippled and invalided, afterward took Winema with her son and Riddle, one of the two whites who escaped from the massacre, to the E. to continue his intercession in behalf of the Indians, especially the Modoc, who had so perfidiously requited his previous benevolence. For her portrait, see *Modoc.* Consult Meacham, Wi-ne-ma, the Woman Chief, 1876.   (F. H.)

Winemac. See *Winamac.*

Wingandacoa. A term which, like "Assamocomoco," was once supposed to be the native name of Virginia. In his report (made in 1584) to Sir Walter Raleigh, Capt. Arthur Barlowe, in narrating what occurred after his landing at the island of Wococon (now Ocracoke), states that on the fourth day he was visited by "diuers boates" with "fortie or fiftie men," among whom was the brother of the ruler of the country, and then proceeds to say: "His name was *Granganimeo,* and the king is called *Wingina,* and the county *Wingandocoa,* and now by her Majestie *Virginia.*" Subsequently, Sir Walter Raleigh, in mentioning the fact that Yucatan, Peru, and Paria are but words in native languages which the Spaniards mistook for place-names, remarks: "The same happened among the English which I sent under Sir Richard Grenville [a slip of the memory for Captains Amidas and Barlowe] to inhabit Virginia. For when some of my people asked the name of the country, one of the savages answered *Wingan-da-coa,* which is as much as to say, 'You wear good clothes' or 'gay clothes.'" From this it would seem that when the English interrogator asked a native, by signs, the name of the country, he accidently embraced in his gestures, intended to include everything in sight, the clothing which he wore. The Indian therefore laconically answered: "Wingatakw," which means simply 'excellent fibrous material.'   (W. R. G.)

Wingatakw. The term for which the impossible "Wingandacoa" is a corruption due to a mishearing; from *wing,* 'good,' 'excellent,' and the nominal termination *-takw* (of which the sound of the *w* can not be expressed by type), 'fibrous stuff.'

It is from the secondary root *tak*, meaning in composition 'fiber,' and, by extension, anything made of fiber, as thread, twine, rope, band, girdle, etc. By a slight dialectic change the termination becomes in Massachuset *-takun*, *-takon*, found in the name *Wautakon* or *Wautakun*, which the Massachuset Indians applied to an Englishman, and which the English colonists supposed to mean 'coat.'   (W. R. G.)

Wingina (abbrev. of *Winginam*, 'he approves,' 'is pleased with,' or 'looks at with complaisance.'—Gerard). The principal chief of the Secotan tribe at the time of Raleigh's first and second expeditions to North Carolina. He was the son of Ensenore and brother of Granganimeo. After the death of the latter, shortly after the arrival of the colonists of 1585, and of the former in the spring of 1586, Wingina, no longer restrained by the influence of these two relatives, who had been friendly to the English, laid plans in secret to destroy the colony. His designs proved abortive, however, and eventually led to his own death. Lane states that Wingina, after the death of his brother, changed his name to Pemisapan.

Winimem (*wini* 'middle,' *měm* 'water': 'middle water', referring to McCloud r.). A Wintun tribe formerly living on McCloud r., Shasta co., Cal.

Cloud River Indians.—Redding in Am. Nat., XIII, 668–9, 1879. Win-ni-mim.—Powers in Cont. N. A. Ethnol., III, 230, 1877.

Wininish. See *Ouananiche*.

Winnebago (*winĭpig*, 'filthy water' [Chippewa]; *winĭpyägohagi*, 'people of the filthy water' [Sauk and Fox].—W. J.) A tribe of the Siouan linguistic family.

Habitat and History.—The Winnebago have been known to the whites since 1634, when the Frenchman Nicollet found them in Wisconsin, on Green bay, at which time they probably extended to L. Winnebago. At this period they were found wedged in by Central Algonquian tribes, particularly by the Sauk and Foxes and the Menominee. To the w. they were in intimate contact with a kindred tribe, the Iowa, who in turn were neighbors of the Oto and Missouri. These four tribes, the Winnebago, Iowa, Oto, and Missouri, speak dialects naturally intelligible to one another, and show many cultural similarities. On the other hand, the Winnebago show many cultural similarities with their Central Algonquian neighbors, particularly in all that pertains to material culture and art, and this double influence, that from their Siouan neighbors and that from their Algonquian neighbors, must be borne in mind in any attempt to understand properly the Winnebago culture.

It is stated in the Jesuit Relation for 1671 (42, 1858) that the Winnebago had always dwelt in the Green Bay region.

Allouez spent the winter of 1669–70 at Green Bay, preaching to the Potawatomi, Menominee, Sauk, Foxes, and Winnebago, whom he found commingled there. The map of 1681 accompanying Marquette's Journal notes a Winnebago village near the N. end of L. Winnebago. At a very early date, it is stated in the Jesuit Relation for 1671, they were almost entirely destroyed by the Illinois, but all captives were at last allowed to return and form a tribe again. Jefferys (1761) refers to them and the Sauk as living toward the head of Green bay. Carver (1778) speaks of "the great town of the Winnebagoes situated on a small island, just as you enter the E. end of L. Winnebago." A "queen," he says, presided

WINNEBAGO CHIEF

then over the tribe. Pike (1806) states that they resided on Wisconsin, Rock, and Fox rs. and Green bay in 7 villages, situated at the entrance and at the end of Green bay, at L. Poygan, and L. Puckway, at the portage of the Wisconsin, and at two places on Rock r. They had a war with the Chippewa in 1827, but this was of short duration. By the treaty of Prairie du Chien in 1825 and another treaty in 1832 they ceded all their lands s. of Wisconsin and Fox rs. in return for a reservation on the w. side of the Mississippi above upper Iowa r. One of their villages in 1832 was at La Crosse, Wis. Smallpox visited the tribe twice before 1836, and in that year more than one-fourth of the people died. In 1837 they relinquished the title to their old country E. of Mississippi r., and in 1840 removed to the Neutral Ground in the territory of Iowa, though a part of the tribe had to be removed by soldiers. They were in 1843 on the Neutral Ground in different bands, the principal one, called the School band, on Turkey r. In 1846 they surrendered their reservation for one N. of Minnesota r. in Minnesota, and in 1848 removed to Long Prairie res., bounded by Crow Wing, Watab, Mississippi, and Long Prairie rs., Minn. Schoolcraft said that the tribe was composed of 21 bands in 1852, having a total population of 2,521 souls. They lost many of their number by disease and were kept on the reservation only by force. In 1853 they were removed to Crow r., and in 1856 to Blue Earth, Minn., where they were just getting a start in civilization when the Sioux war of 1862 broke out, and the people of Minnesota demanded their removal. They were taken to Crow Creek res., S. Dak., on Missouri r., but could not be kept there by the troops. There was much suffering from sickness and other causes. Out of the 2,000 taken to Crow cr. only 1,200 reached the Omaha res., whither they fled for protection. They were then assigned a new reservation on the Omaha lands in N. E. Nebraska, where they have since remained and where their lands have been allotted to them in severalty. When the tribe was removed by force from Minnesota to Crow cr. in 1863, many who had taken up farms remained.

How long the tribe had maintained its position at Green bay previous to the coming of the whites is unknown. As has been seen, it appears they had receded slightly toward the w. before 1766, the time of Carver's visit, who found them on Fox r. The French found them in league with the Menominee, and the 2 tribes gave shelter to the Potawatomi and the Ottawa, who had been driven from their homes by the Iroquois, and also to the Sauk and Fox tribes when these were expelled from s. Michigan. Notwithstanding their friendly relations with the last named, who were the only Algonquian tribes with whom the French had strife, the Winnebago managed to maintain friendship and uninterrupted trade with the French. They generally kept on friendly terms also with their neighbors, the Chippewa, Ottawa, Potawatomi, Kickapoo, and Mascoutens, to do which required great address, as the Sauk and Foxes seem to have been cut loose from their ancient and natural affinities and were perpetually making inroads on Algonquian tribes, particularly, in conjunction with the Sioux, on the Chippewa (Schoolcraft). After the fall of the French power in Canada in 1760 the Winnebago were slow to transfer their allegiance to Great Britain, but when they did they remained firm in their new fealty. When the United States declared their independence in 1776, the Winnebago sided with the Crown, and in all questions of local jurisdiction were arrayed on the side of the British. In the War of 1812 they espoused the cause of England, helped to defeat Col. Crogan at Michilimackinac, Col. Dudley at the rapids of the Miami, and Gen. Winchester at the River Raisin, and were with the tribes that gathered about Detroit. In the years immediately following this war they became insolent. Hoochoop, a chief of the tribe, living at the outlet of L. Winnebago, assumed to be the keeper of Fox r. valley and sometimes levied toll for the privilege of ascent. This people also connected themselves clandestinely with the Sauk and Foxes in the Black Hawk war of 1832. Since that time they have been uniformly peaceable.

Language.—The Siouan dialect spoken by the Winnebago is intimately related to Oto, Iowa, and Missouri, more distantly to Dakota, and still more distantly to Ponca. Its relationship to the northern Siouan dialects (Crow, Hidatsa, and Mandan), to the southern (Biloxi), and eastern (Catawba and Tutelo), is not as yet definitely known. The characteristics of the Winnebago dialect are, grammatically, a strong development of the classifiers of position, and, phonetically, the insertion of vowels between consonantal clusters and the change of the Dakota and Omaha *t*, *d*, and *m*, to *tc*, *dj*, and *w*. (See Handbook of Am. Ind. Languages, Bull. 40, B. A. E., part 1).

Social Organization.—The Winnebago social organization is based on two phratries, known, respectively, as the Upper or Air, and the Lower or Earth, divisions. The Upper division contains four clans, Thunderbird, War People, Eagle, and Pigeon (extinct), and the Lower division eight clans, the Bear, Wolf, Water-spirit, Deer, Elk, Buffalo, Fish, and Snake. An Upper individual must marry a Lower individual, and vice versa. While there is no law restricting marriage between the clans of the two phratries, there is some evidence showing a tendency of certain clans to intermarry. The Thunderbird and Bear clans are regarded as the leading clans of their respective phratries. Both have definite functions. The lodge of the former is the peace lodge, over which the chief of the tribe presides, and in which disputes between Indians are adjudicated. No person could be killed in the lodge, and an offender or prisoner escaping to it was protected as long as he was within its precincts. The lodge of the Bear clan was the war or disciplinary lodge: prisoners were killed, and offenders punished in its precincts. Besides these functions, the Bear clan possessed the right of "soldier killing," and was in charge of both ends of the camping circle during the hunt. Each clan has a large number of individual customs, relating to birth, the naming feast, death, and the funeral wake. The chief item of interest in this connection is the fact that a member of one clan cannot be buried by the members of another clan of the same phratry. (For details of the social organization, see Radin in Am. Anthr., XII, no. 2, 1910.)

Religion.—The Winnebago possess two important tribal ceremonies, the *Mañkáni* or Medicine Dance, and the Winter Feast (*Wagigó*). The Medicine Dance can take place only in summer, and the Winter Feast only in winter. The Medicine Dance is a secret society, ungraded, into which men and women can be initiated on payment of a certain amount of money. Supernatural dreams are not required for initiation at the present day. A new member generally succeeds some deceased relative. There are five ceremonial bands, occupying, respectively, the east, north, west, south, and southeast of the long tent in which the ceremony is performed. The positions of honor, which follow in the manner enumerated above, are dependent on the order of invitation and may differ at each performance. A secret vapor-bath ceremony precedes, and a secret ceremony intervenes between, the first and second parts of the general ceremony. The general ceremony itself is public. The purpose of the society is the prolongation of life and the instilling of certain virtues, none of which, however, relate to war. This instilling is accomplished by means of the "shooting" ceremony, consisting of the simulated shooting of a shell, contained in an otter-skin bag, into the body of the one to be initiated. This ceremony is extremely similar to that in the Algonquian *Midéwiwin*, and to that in the Dakota "Mystery Dance" and the Omaha "Pebble Ceremony." There seems little doubt that the shooting ceremony has been borrowed by the Winnebago from some Central Algonquian tribe, presumably the Sauk and Foxes; also that the teachings have been greatly influenced by those of the *Midéwiwin*. On the other hand, the organization, a large portion of the ritual, and the ritualistic myths are so fundamentally different that it is better to regard the shooting ceremony as a ritual secondarily associated with an old Winnebago ceremony.

The Winter Feast is the only distinctly clan ceremonial among the Winnebago. Each clan has a sacred clan bundle, which is in the hands of some male individual, who hands it down from one generation to another, always taking care, of course, to keep it in the same clan. The Winter Feast is distinctly a war feast, and the purpose in giving it seems to be a desire to increase their war powers by a propitiation of all the supernatural deities known to them. To these they offer food and deerskin. There may be as many as twelve (?) powers propitiated, namely, Earth-maker, Disease-giver, Sun, Moon, Morning Star, the spirits of the Night, Thunderbird, One-horn, the Earth, the Water, the Turtle, and the Rabbit. Of these, food had to be offered to all except the last two, who are really only the culture heroes and probably of recent introduction. The feast is divided into two distinct parts, one for the Disease-giver and one for all the other spirits. The Sauk and Foxes seem to have a similar feast, but its relation to the Winnebago is as yet unknown.

There are a number of important ceremonies besides the above, of which the best known are the Buffalo Dance and the *Herucka*. The former is given in spring, and has for its purpose the magical calling of the buffalo herds. All those who have had supernatural communication with the Buffalo spirit may become members, irrespective of clan. The *Herucka* is the same as the Omaha Grass dance. There are also a number of other dances and feasts, of which little is known as yet, such as the Snake, Scalp, Grizzly-bear, Sore-eye, and Ghost dances.

The religious beliefs of the Winnebago are practically identical with those of the Dakota, Ponca, and Central Algonquian tribes. A figure known as *Man'una* (Earth-maker) corresponds to the *Gitchi Manito* of the Central Algonquian tribes. The mythology consists of large cycles relating to the five personages whom Earth-maker sent out to free the world from giants and evil spirits. They are the Trickster, the Bladder, the Turtle, He-who-wears-heads-as-earrings, and the Hare. Besides these there are numerous myths relating to the Thunderbird and other clan heroes, and likewise numerous miscellaneous myths. Although there are evidences of Central Algonquian influence, the mythology shows a much more intimate relation with that of the other Siouan tribes.

Material Culture.—In their material culture the Winnebago are distinctly timber people, and their houses and dress are practically identical with those of the Sauk and Foxes, Menominee, and others. The same applies to their beadwork, although there is considerable evidence to show that they had a characteristic porcupine-quill industry not very long ago. In their clothing, moccasins, cooking utensils, arms, and in other respects, they show marked individual characteristics which, however, have not been investigated as yet.

The population was estimated by Pike at 1,750 in 1806; by Morse at 5,800 in 1820; in 1837 and again in 1843 their number was given at 4,500. In 1867 there were 1,750 on the Nebraska res. and 700 in Wisconsin. In 1876 there were 1,463 on the Nebraska res. and 860 in Wisconsin; but 204 of the latter removed in 1877 to Nebraska. In 1886 there were 1,222 in Nebraska and 930 in Wisconsin, and in 1910 there were 1,063 in Nebraska and 1,270 in Wisconsin.

The gentes as given by Dorsey are as follows: 1. Shungikikarachada ('Wolf'); 2. Honchikikarachada ('Black Bear'); 3. Huwanikikarachada ('Elk'); 4. Wakanikikarachada ('Snake'); 5. Waninkikikarachada ('Bird'), including: (a) Hichakhshepara ('Eagle'), (b) Ruchke ('Pigeon'), (c) Kerechun ('Hawk'), (d) Wakanchara ('Thunderbird'); 6. Cheikikarachada ('Buffalo'); 7. Chaikikarachada ('Deer'); 8. Wakchekhiikikarachada ('Water-monster').

The Winnebago had a number of villages, those whose names are known being Prairie la Crosse, Sarrochau, Spotted Arm's village, Village du Puant, Wuckan, Yellow Thunder.   (J. O. D. P. R.)

Aoeatsioaenronnon.—Jes. Rel. for 1649, 27, 1858. **Aoueatsiouaen-hronons.**—Vimont, ibid. (1640), 35. **Aoueatsiouaenronnons.**—Ibid. (1646), 81. **A8eatsi-8aenrrhonon.**—Ibid. (1636), 92 (Huron name). **Aouentsiouaeron.**—Sanson, map Can. (1657), in Am. Antiq., I, 233, 1879. **Aweatsiwaenhronon.**—Jes. Rel., III, index, 1858. **Banabeoueks.**—Perrot, Mém., 293, 1864 (misprint for Ouanabeoueks). **Banabeoüik.**—Prise de possession (1671) in N. Y. Doc. Col. Hist., IX, 803, 1855. **Banabeouiks.**—Proces verbal of 1671 in Margry, Déc. I, 97, 1876. **Banaboueks.**—Perrot, Mém., 295, 1864. **Bay Indians.**—Lapham, Blossom, and Dousman, Inds. Wis., 15, 1870. **Fish-eaters.**—Maximilian, Trav., 507, 1843. **Gens de Mer.**—Gale, Upper Miss., 342, 1867. **Hati'hshi' rû'nû.**—Gatschet, MS., B. A. E. ('afraid of sticking in the mire': Wyandot name). **Hoch-uagohrah.**—Gallatin in Trans. Am. Ethnol. Soc., II, cv, 1848 (own name). **Hochungara.**—Dunn, True Ind. Stories, 317, 1909. **Hochungarras.**—Richardson, Arct. Exped., II, 34, 1851. **Hochungohrah.**—Gallatin in Trans. Am. Ethnol. Soc., II, 120, 1836 (trans. 'trout nation'). **Hoh-tchung-grahs.**—Ramsey in Minn. Hist. Coll., I (1850–56), 49, 1872. **Hoochawgenah.**—Tanner, Narr., 313, 1830. **Horoje.**—Gallatin in Trans. Amer. Antiq. Soc., II, 120, 1836 ('fish-eaters'). **Ho-ro-ge.**—Long, Exped. Rocky Mts., I, 339, 1823. **Horoji.**—Dunn, True Ind. Stories, 317, 1909. **Ho-tan-ke.**—Ramsey in Rep. Ind. Aff. for 1849, 88, 1850 (Dakota name). **Hotaŋke.**—Riggs, Dakota Gram. and Dict., 69, 1852. **Hotcañgara.**—Dorsey, MS. Winnebago vocab., B. A. E., 1878 (trans. 'primitive language'). **Ho-tcañ-ga-ra.**—McGee in 15th Rep. B. A. E., 162, 1897 (trans. 'people of the parent speech'). **Hote-shog-garah.**—Investigator, I, 17, 1845. **Hote-shung-garah.**—Ibid. **Hoton-ga.**—Maximilian, Trav., 507, 1843. **Howchungerah.**—Featherstonhaugh, Canoe Voy., I, 168, 1847. **Huŋ'taŋxa.**—Dorsey, Osage MS. vocab., B. A. E., 1883 (Osage name). **Hu'taṅ-xa.**—Dorsey, Kwapa MS. vocab., B. A. E., 1881 (Quapaw name). **Iripegouans.**—Rasles (1723) in Mass. Hist. Coll., 2d s., VIII, 251, 1819. **Mipegoes.**—Boudinot, Star in W., 107, 1816. **Mipegois.**—Ibid., 127. **Nation de Mer.**—Jes. Rel. 1656, 39, 1858. **Nation**

of **Stinkers.**—Neill, Hist. Minn., 100, 1858 (trans. of Nation des Puants, French trans. of the Chippewa name, which is said to have been bestowed in derision of their fondness for bathing in foul water). **Nipegons.**—Carver, Trav., 415, 1778. **Nipegon.**—Long, Exped. Rocky Mts., lxxxvi, 1823. **Ochangras.**—Pike, Trav., 134, 1811. **O-chunga-raw.**—Fletcher in Schoolcraft, Ind. Tribes, IV, 227, 1854 (so called by Oto, Iowa, Omaha, and Missouri). **Ochunkgraw.**—Warren in Minn. Hist. Coll., v, 400, 1885. **O-chunk-o-raw.**—Gale, Upper Miss., 42, 1867. **Octaaros.**—De la Tour, map, 1779 (misprint for Octagros). **Octagros.**—Carte des Poss. Angl., 1777. **Octchagras.**—Jefferys, French Dom. Am., I, 74, 1761. **O. tan. gan.**—Forsyth quoted by Miss E. H. Blair, inf'n, 1909 ('great voice': own name). **Otchagras.**—Jefferys, op. cit., 47. **Otchagros.**—Ibid., map, 134. **O-tchun-gu-rah.**—Ramsey in Ind. Aff. Rep. 1849, 88, 1850. **O-thun-gu-rahs.**—Lapham, Blossom, and Dousman, Inds. Wis., 16, 1870. **Otmagra.**—Adelung, Mithridates, III, 270, note, 1816. **Otonkah.**—Fletcher in Schoolcraft, Ind. Tribes, IV, 227 1854 (Dakota name). **8anabegoueks.**—Perrot, Mém., 295, 1864. **Ouenebegons.**—La Potherie, Hist. Am., II, 49, 1753. **Ouenebigonchelinis.**—Ibid., I, 131 (linis probably intended for Illini). **Ouenibegouc.**—Charlevoix, New France, VI, 225, 1866. **Ouenibigono.**—Perrot, Mém., 293, 1864. **Ouenibigoutz.**—Jes. Rel. 1670, 94, 1858. **Ouinepeag.**—Peet in Am. Antiq., 304, 1886. **Ouinipegong.**—Jes. Rel. 1648, 62, 1858. **Ouinipegou.**—Shea, Discov., xxii, 1852. **Ouinipegouec.**—Coxe, Carolana, map, 1741. **Ouinipégoüek.**—Tailhan in Perrot, Mém., 293, 1864. **Ouinipigou.**—Le Jeune in Jes. Rel. 1640, 35, 1858. **Ounepigous.**—Chauvignerie (1736) quoted by Schoolcraft, Ind. Tribes, III, 556, 1853. **Pauns.**—Le Sueur (1700) in Neill, Hist. Minn., 156, 1858. **Pewins.**—Goldthwait (1766) in Mass. Hist. Soc. Coll., 1st s., X, 122, 1809. **Pouan.**—Doc. of 1736 in N. Y. Doc. Col. Hist., IX, 1055, 1855. **Pouans.**—Chauvignerie, ibid. **Puánag.**—Gatschet in Am. Antiq., II, 78, 1879 (given as Chippewa name). **Puans.**—Hennepin, New Discov., pt. 1, 35, 1698. **Puants.**—Jes. Rel. 1636, 92, 1858. **Puyon.**—Dalton (1783) in Mass. Hist. Soc. Coll., 1st s., X, 123, 1809. **Sea tribes.**—Shea, Cath. Miss., 349, 1855. **Stinkards.**—Jefferys, French Dom. Am., pt. 1, 47, 1761 (trans. of French Puans). **Stinkers.**—Long, Exped. St. Peter's R., II, 216, 1824. **Stinks.**—Lapham, Blossom, and Dousman, Inds. Wis., 8, 1870. **Trout nation.**—Dunn, True Ind. Stories, 315, 1909. **Webings.**—Imlay, W. Terr. N. Am., 294, 1797. **Winbiégûg.**—Gatschet, MS., B. A. E. (Potawatomi name). **Winebago.**—Pike, Exped., I, app., 20, 1810. **Winebagoe.**—Ex. Doc. 90, 22d Cong., 1st sess., 64, 1832. **Winebégók.**—Gatschet, MS., B. A. E. (Chippewa name, from wi'nat, 'dirty'). **Winepegouek.**—Jes. Rel., III, index, 1858. **Winibagos.**—Prichard, Phys. Hist. Mankind, v, 412, 1847. **Winibigong.**—Jes. Rel., III, index, 1858. **Winipegou.**—Ibid. **Winnabagoes.**—Imlay, W. Terr. N. Am., 293, 1797. **Winnebager.**—Adelung, Mithridates, III, 270, 1816. **Winnebages.**—Fletcher in Schoolcraft, Ind. Tribes, IV, 228, 1857 (misprint). **Winnebago.**—Drake, Bk. Inds., 171, 1848. **Winnebagoag.**—Tanner, Narr., 316, 1830 (Ottawa name). **Winnebagoe.**—Charlevoix, New Fr., VI, 225, 1866. **Winnebagoec.**—Gale, Upper Miss., 184, 1867 (Algonkin name). **Winnebagog.**—Atwater, Writings, pt. 2, 167, 1833. **Winnebago Indians.**—Kelton, Ft. Mackinac, 148, 1884. **Winnebagoue.**—Gale, Upper Miss., 342, 1867. **Winnebaygo.**—Treaty of 1829 in U. S. Ind. Treat., 996, 1873. **Winnepans.**—Bluejacket (1807) quoted by Drake, Tecumseh, 94, 1852. **Winnepaus.**—Bluejacket quoted by Brice, Hist. Ft. Wayne, 173, 1868. **Winnepeg.**—Peet in Am. Antiq., VIII, 304, 1886. **Winnibígog.**—Gatschet, MS., B. A. E. (Chippewa name). **Winnipegouek.**—Shea, Discov., xxiii, 1852.

Winnebago. An Indian village on Wildcat cr., Ind., destroyed by the troops under Gen. Hopkins in 1812; named for the Winnebago tribe, which was largely represented among the followers of Tenskwatawa, The Prophet. It contained "about forty houses, many of them from thirty to fifty feet in length, besides many temporary huts in the surrounding prairie. The settlement was situated on what is now known as the Langlois reserve, adjoining the city of Lafayette. It was often called Village du Puant, because the French called the Winnebago *Puans*, i. e. 'fetid.' (J. P. D.)

Winnebegoshishiwininewak ('people on Winnibigashish lake'). A division of the Chippewa formerly living on L. Winnibigashish, Minn.

Lake Winnebagoshish band.—Washington treaty (1864) in U. S. Ind. Treat., 259, 1873. **Wĭnibĭgociciwininiwag.**—Wm. Jones, inf'n, 1905. **Winnebegoshishi-wininewak.**—Gatschet, Chippewa MS., B. A. E., 1882 (own name). **Winnebigoshish.**—Rep. Ind. Aff., 39, 1857.

Winnecowet. A tribe or band, connected with the Pennacook confederacy, formerly living in Rockingham co., N. H.—Potter quoted by Schoolcraft, Ind. Tribes, v, 223, 1855.

Winnefelly. An unidentified Calapooya band that participated in the Dayton treaty of 1855.—U. S. Ind. Treat., 18, 1873.

Winnemeg. See *Winamac*.

Winnemucca, Sarah. A woman of the Paviotso of w. Nevada, commonly called a Paiute, born in 1844 in the vicinity of Humboldt lake, and known after marriage as Sarah Winnemucca Hopkins. Her father, Winnemucca, was chief of the band that lived about Humboldt and Pyramid lakes, sometimes spoken of as Winnemucca's band (q. v.). Her grandfather, who was also a chief, accompanied Gen. Frémont into California and was named by this officer "Captain Truckee," by which designation he was afterward known to the whites until his death, about 1859. In 1860 Sarah and her sister were taken to San José, Cal., and placed in the Sisters' school, where they were allowed to remain but a few weeks; in the same year the band which included her people was confined to lands about Pyramid lake, which, in 1864, were formed into a reservation. In the following year the family lived at Dayton, Nev., and it was at this time, or shortly afterward, that Sarah's mother and sister Mary died. About 1868 Sarah began to act as interpreter for Agent Bateman to the Shoshoni, and later became interpreter and scout for Gen. O. O. Howard's forces during the Paiute and Bannock war of 1877, when no Indian man could be prevailed on to risk the attendant danger, and was instrumental in bringing her father and his immediate band out of the hostile Bannock camp in Oregon. On Jan. 26, 1880, she was appointed interpreter at Malheur agency, Oreg., and in 1881 conducted a school for Indian children at Vancouver barracks, Wash. In the winter of 1879–80 she accompanied her father to Wash-

ington for the purpose of obtaining permission for the return of their people from the Yakima to the Malheur res., which was granted by the Secretary of the Interior, but the plans for carrying it into effect were thwarted by the Yakima agent. In 1881–82 she again visited the East, delivering public lectures in Boston and other cities with the object of making known the story and the trials of her people and of arousing sympathy in their behalf, her complaints being directed principally against the Indian agents. To aid in this effort she wrote a book under the title "Life Among the Piutes, Their Wrongs and Claims," published in 1883. In the meantime, late in 1881 or early in 1882, she married a Lieutenant Hopkins. Although Sarah's attacks on the Indian agents with whom she had to deal brought forth countercharges against her character, these were met and refuted by Gen. Howard and other military officers whom she had aided in the field.

With aid received during one of her visits to Boston lands were purchased for her near the present Lovelock, Nev., and an Indian school was established, which she conducted for 3 years. Here her husband died of tuberculosis and was buried in Lone Mountain cemetery. Sarah thereupon abandoned the school and went to visit her sister in Monida, Mont., where she died Oct. 16, 1891 (inf'n from Miss Jeanne Elizabeth Wier, Reno, Nev., 1905). She was degenerate in her later years.

Winnemucca's Band. A Paviotso band, under chief Winnemucca ('The Giver'), formerly dwelling on Smoke cr., near Honey lake, N. E. Cal., and eastward to Pyramid, Winnemucca, and Humboldt lakes, Nev.; said to number 155 in 1859. In 1877 they were under Malheur agency, Oreg., numbering 150. See *Kuyuidika*.

Wanamuka's band.—Burton, City of Saints, 576, 1861. Winnemucca's Band.—Ind. Aff. Rep., 172, 1877. Wun-a-muc-a's band.—Dodge, ibid., 1859, 374, 1860.

Winnepesauki. A tribe or band of the Pennacook confederacy formerly living around Winnepesaukee lake, N. H.

Winnepesaukies.—Potter quoted by Schoolcraft, Ind. Tribes, v, 222, 1855. Winnepisseockeege.—Treaty (1690) in Mass. Hist. Soc. Coll., 3d s., I, 113, 1825.

Winnepeskowuk. A division of the Upeshipow living in 1770 on East Main r., Canada.—Hutchins (1770) quoted by Richardson, Arctic Exped., II, 38, 1851.

Winnisimmet. A Massachuset village on the site of Chelsea, near Boston, Mass. The chief, Wonohaquaham, with nearly all his people, died of smallpox in 1633.

Winesemet.—Moll, map in Humphreys, Acct., 1730. Winisemit.—Pincheon (1633) in Mass. Hist. Soc. Coll., 2d s., VIII, 231, 1819. Winisimett.—Bradford (ca. 1650), ibid., 4th s., III, 241, 1856. Winisimmit.—Williams (1637), ibid., VI, 218, 1863. Winnesemet.—Prince (1631), ibid., 2d s., VII, 29,

1818. **Winnesimet.**—Hubbard (1680), ibid., v, 194, 1815. **Winnisemit.**—Barber, Hist. Coll., 549, 1839. **Winnisimet.**—Josselyn (1675) in Mass. Hist. Soc. Coll., 3d s., III, 322, 1833.

Winoack. The common name of the single village of the Nottoway in 1701 (Lawson, 1709, N. C., 383, 1860) on Nottaway r. (see *Weanoc*), and on the s. border of Virginia, in Southampton co.

Winona ('first-born child' [if a girl], in the Santee dialect). The chief village of the Kiyuksa band of Mdewakanton Sioux, succeeded by the present town of Winona, Winona co., Minn. The name was introduced to the reading public by Keating, who relates, in his Narrative of Long's expedition to St. Peters r., published in 1823, the story of a Sioux maiden who committed suicide because her relatives sought to make her marry against her will. See *Wenona*.
Weenonah.—Neill, Hist. Minn., xliv, 1858.

Winooskeek. A village occupied by the Scaticook of Hudson r. in 1699. It was in Vermont, on L. Champlain, probably at the mouth of Winooski r., on a spot that had been previously occupied by the same Indians.
Winooskeek.—Schuyler (1699) in N. Y. Doc. Col. Hist., IV, 575, 1854. **Winooskoek.**—Ibid.

Winsack. A village of the Powhatan confederacy, situated in 1608 on the N. bank of Rappahannock r., in Richmond co., Va.—Smith (1629), Va., I, map, repr. 1819.

Wintun ('Indians,' 'people'). One of the 2 divisions of the Copehan family, the other being the Patwin. The Wintun territory was bounded on the N. by Mt Shasta and the domain of the Lutuamian and Shastan families; on the s. by a line running from the E. boundary, about 10 m. E. of Sacramento r., due w. through Jacinto and the headwaters of Stony cr., Colusa co., Cal., to Kulanapan territory. The E. boundary began at the headwaters of Bear cr., bearing s. some miles E. of and parallel to McCloud r. From Pit r. to the neighborhood of Redding they occupied a triangular area E. of the Sacramento. On the w. the Wintun territory was bounded by that of the Kulanapan, Yukian, Chimarikan, and Quoratean families, and the Wailaki tribe.

The Wintun division of the Copehan family is rather homogeneous, the language, customs, and characteristics of the tribes presenting comparatively slight variations. Powers thought the Wintun were originally a sort of metropolitan tribe for the whole of N. California below Mt Shasta. Physically they were inclined to obesity; they were indifferent hunters but good fishermen, and were abundantly supplied with dried salmon. Roots of various kinds, manzanita berries, piñon nuts, and acorns were used as food; and according to Powers clover was eaten in great quantities in the blossoming season.

Dancing was a favorite amusement. Wintun marriage was of the simplest character and the man seldom paid for his bride. The dead were buried in ordinary graves, the bodies being doubled up and wrapped in mats or skins. The Wintun language presents many agreements with that of the Patwin division, vocabularies showing about a third of the words to be common to both. For the Wintun subdivisions, see *Copehan Family*.
Khatukeyu.—A. L. Kroeber, inf'n, 1905 (name given by Shasta of Salmon r.). **Wawáh.**—Powers, Inds. of W. Nevada, MS., 14, 1876 ('strangers': Paiute name for all Sacramento r. tribes). **Wintoon.**—Powers in Overland Mo., XII, 530, 1874. **Wintu.**—Curtin, MS., B. A. E., 1884. **Win-tún.**—Powers in Cont. N. A. Ethnol., III, 229, 1877. **Xátükwiwa.**—R. B. Dixon, inf'n, 1905 (Shasta name for a Wintun Indian).

Winyaw. One of the small tribes living on lower Pedee r. and its tributaries in South Carolina. Of their language nothing is known, and very little else is recorded concerning them, as they were never prominent in history. It is supposed, however, from their associations that they were of Siouan affinity. They dwelt on the w. side of the Pedee near its mouth, about opposite the Waccamaw. The 2 tribes were first mentioned in 1715 as being neighbors and as receiving ammunition from the Cheraw, who attempted to induce them to join in a league against the English. Gov. Johnson in 1715 reported them as having one village, with a population of 106. After this they drop from history, becoming extinct as a tribe.
Weenees.—Rivers, Hist. S. C., 36, 1856. **Weneaw.**—Johnson (1715) in Rivers, Hist. S. C., 94, 1874. **Wineaus.**—Letter of 1715 in N. C. Col. Rec., II, 251, 1886. **Wingah.**—Map of S. C., 1760 (misprint). **Winyaws.**—Mills, Hist. S. C., 108, 1826. **Winyo.**—Bowen, Map of Brit. Am. Plantations, 1760. **Wyniaws.**—Gallatin in Trans. Am. Antiq. Soc., II, 89, 1836.

Wiokemae (*Wĭ'oqEmaē*, 'whom no one dares to look at'). A gens of the Tsawatenok, a Kwakiutl tribe.—Boas in Rep. U. S. Nat. Mus. 1895, 331, 1897.

Wipho (*Wip-ho*). The site of a traditional settlement of early Hopi clans at a spring a few miles N. E. of Walpi pueblo, N. E. Ariz.
Weepo.—Donaldson, Moqui Pueblo Inds., 47, 1893. **Wipho.**—Stephen in 8th Rep. B. A. E., 18, 1891.

Wiroans. See *Werowance*.

Wisakedjak. See *Nanabozho*.

Wisconsins. A name occasionally used to designate the group of tribes living on the banks of Wisconsin r., including the Sauk, Foxes, and others.
Oniscousins.—Boudinot, Star in the W., 128, 1816 (misprint). **Ouesconsins.**—Le Sueur (1695) in Shea, Early Voy., 95, 1861. **Ouisconsins.**—Smith, Bouquet Exped., 69, 1766. **Siskonche.**—French doc. (1689) in N. Y. Col. Doc. Hist., IX, 418, 1855. **Ouiskonches.**—Ibid.

Wishoko. The Turkey-buzzard clan of the Hopi.
Wicoko wiñwü.—Fewkes in 19th Rep. B. A. E., 584, 1900. **Wi-co-ko wün-wü.**—Fewkes in Am. Anthr., VII, 405, 1894. **Wu-so'-ko.**—Stephen in 8th Rep. B. A. E., 39, 1891.

Wishosk. A small tribe, whose name Powell adopted for the Wishoskan linguistic family, on the coast of N. California about Humboldt bay. The word seems to be a misapplication of their own name for their Athapascan neighbors, *Wishashk.* Wiyot (see below), which has sometimes been used as an equivalent, is therefore probably a better term than Wishosk, though not entirely exact. The Wishosk territory extended from the mouth of Mad r., lat. 41°, to a short distance above Blue Lake; thence the boundary followed the watershed, between the streams that flow into Humboldt bay and those that drain into Mad and Eel rs., southward to Eel r., probably slightly below Fortuna (though some accounts make the Wishosk territory extend up Eel r. to the mouth of Van Duzen fork), and across it to the Bear River range, which formed the southern boundary, back to the coast perhaps 5 or 6 m. N. of C. Mendocino. This territory included Lindsey, Jacoby, Freshwater, and Salmon crs., and Elk and Salt rs. The entire stretch of the country of the Wishosk is scarcely 30 m., and the greatest breadth is not more than 12 or 14 m. As this limited territory is heavily timbered with redwood, the people lived almost exclusively along the edge of salt water or on the banks of the two larger rivers flowing into the ocean in their domain. For this reason the Wishosk probably depended less on acorns for food than most of the tribes of California, products of the sea, including the fish that ran up the streams, constituting their chief source of subsistence.

The Wishosk were surrounded on the land side by Athapascan tribes, except at the N., where lower Mad r. formed the boundary between themselves and the coast Yurok. The Wishosk call the Athapascan languages *Wishi'lak,* the Yurok language *Denákwatelak.* For themselves as a body they have, like the other tribes of N. w. California, no geographic or specific name, calling themselves simply 'people.' They call their language, however, as distinct from other languages, *Sulä'telik.* They recognize 3 divisions in their country: the territories about Mad r., Humboldt bay, and Eel r., which they call Batawa't, Wiki', and Wi'yat, respectively. On the addition of *-daredalitl* these terms denote the people of the districts; thus *Wiki-daredalitl* are the people living on Humboldt bay. These, however, are only geographically natural and convenient names, and did not reflect any real political divisions. As was customary in N. w. California the only organization of a political or social nature that they possessed consisted of village settlements. They showed no trace of a totemic or gentile system. They spoke only one dialect; the distinction between the Viard and the Wiyot rests on faulty orthography. The general name for them and their country among the neighboring tribes is some form of the word Wiyot; the Yurok call them *Weyet;* the Karok, *Waiyat;* the Sinkyone, the Athapascans about the lower s. fork of Eel r., call them *Dilwishne* and their country *Weyat.*

The whole Humboldt bay region was rapidly settled by the whites after 1850. The Wishosk suffered considerably at their hands, a large party being massacred on Indian id., near Eureka, on a mistaken suspicion. The numbers of the Wishosk were placed at 800 in 1853, but all figures are only estimates. At present there survive about 70, who live in their original country without recognition by the Government, supporting themselves by civilized labor.

In general culture the Wishosk resembled the tribes of the lower Klamath and Trinity. They had square board houses with gabled roofs built about excavations, redwood canoes, and twined basketry, similar in all essentials to those of the Yurok, Karok, and Hupa. The women also tattooed their chins. They lacked the Deerskin dance and the Jumping or Woodpecker dance of these three tribes. They had a puberty ceremony for girls, that included dancing. According to their mythology the creator was Gudatrigakwitl, 'Above-old-man.' This deity is more distinctly a creator than most of the corresponding mythological characters of other tribes of N. w. California. On the whole but little is known about the religion of the Wishosk. Their language is also very little known. It is complex and obscure, and appears to resemble the adjacent Yurok in general structure, but to be an entirely unrelated and independent family.   (A. L. K.)

Dilwishne.—A. L. Kroeber, inf'n, 1904 (Sinkyone name for the Wishosk and their language). **Humbolt Bay Indians.**—U. S. Stat., XII, 199, 1863. **Koquilth.**—Powers in Cont. N. A. Ethnol., III, 100, 1877 (given as a Wishosk division). **Ko-wilth.**—Powell, ibid., 478. **Ock-co-witth.**—Buchanan (1853) in H. R. Ex. Doc. 76, 34th Cong., 3d sess., 24, 1857. **Solotluck.**—Ibid., 23 (cf. *Sulatelik* following). **Sulatelik.**—A. L. Kroeber, inf'n, 1904 (used by the Wishosk to designate their own language; it comes nearer to being a tribal name for themselves than any other term). **Waiyat.**—Ibid. (Karok name). **Walla-Walloo.**—Gibbs (1851) in Schoolcraft, Ind. Tribes, III, 133, 1853 (said to be so called by the tribes to the N.). **Wee Shotch.**—Buchanan, op. cit., 24. **Weyat.**—A. L. Kroeber, inf'n, 1904 (Sinkyone name for Wishosk country). **Weyet.**—Ibid. (Yurok name). **Wishosk.**—Gibbs, op. cit.

Wishoskan Family. A linguistic family represented by the Wishosk Indians (q. v.).

>**Wish-osk.**—Gibbs in Schoolcraft, Ind. Tribes, III, 422, 1853 (given as the name of a dialect on Mad r. and Humboldt bay). =**Wish-osk.**—Powell in Cont. N. A. Ethnol., III, 478, 1877 (vocabularies of Wish-osk, Wi-yot, and Ko-wilth); Gatschet in

Mag. Am. Hist., 162, 1877 (indicates area occupied by family); Gatschet in Beach, Ind. Misc., 437, 1877. >**Wee-yot.**—Gibbs in Schoolcraft, Ind. Tribes, III, 422, 1853 (given as the name of a dialect on Eel r. and Humboldt bay). X **Weitspek.**—Latham in Trans. Philol. Soc. Lond., 77, 1856 (includes Weyot and Wishosk); Latham, Opuscula, 343, 1860. <**Klamath.**—Keane in Stanford, Compend., Cent. and So. Am., 475, 1878 (cited as including Patawats, Weeyots, Wishosks). =**Wishoskan.**—Powell in 7th Rep. B. A. E., 132, 1891.

Wishram. Formerly the principal village of the Tlakluit, and now their chief fishing settlement; situated on Columbia r., about 5 m. above The Dalles, in Washington. It is said to have contained as many as 400 inhabitants at one time, but now fewer than 150, the total population of the tribe, live there.
Niculuita.—Wilkes in U. S. Expl. Exped., IV, 388, 1845. Niẋlu'idiẋ.—Edward Sapir, inf'n, 1908 (proper name). Wisham.—Wilkes, op. cit. Wŭshqŭm.—Mooney in 14th Rep. B. A. E., 740, 1896. Wushuum.—Dorsey in Am. Anthr., VIII, 475, 1906.

Wishtonwish. A species of prairie-dog, *Cynomys ludovicianus*, of the Missouri region and westward and southward. These animals utter a sharp chirp, which is called barking, and hence their name of "dog." They live in burrows, and large numbers are often found in the same locality, forming communities which hunters call "dog towns." The name under consideration was applied by the Caddoan tribes of Louisiana from the cry uttered by the animals. "As you approach their towns," says Lieut. Pike, "you are saluted on all sides by the cry of '*wishtonwish*' (from which they derive their name with the Indians), uttered in a shrill and piercing manner." J. Fenimore Cooper, in his works "The Wept of Wishtonwish" and "The Last of the Mohicans" erroneously applied the name to the whippoorwill.   (W. R. G.)

Wiskala ('sand.'—Kroeber). A former village of the Awani at the foot of the "Royal Arches"; it was the uppermost village in Yosemite valley, Mariposa co., Cal.
Wiscúlla.—Powers in Overland Mo., x, 333, 1874. Wiskala.—A. L. Kroeber, inf'n, 1905. Wis-kul'-la.—Powers in Cont. N. A. Ethnol., III, 365, 1877.

Wiskinky. One of the officers or governing council of the Tammany Society (q. v.) of the city of New York. William Mooney, the founder of the society, borrowing the general scheme of the organization from the Saint Tammany societies already in existence, called its meeting-place the "wigwam"; its head, the "great father" (afterward the "grand sachem"); its council of twelve, "sachems"; its master of ceremonies, a "sagamore"; and its doorkeeper a "wiskinkie." This last-named word was obtained by Mooney from Capt. Carver's Travels, which had been published shortly previous to the organization of the society, and in which, in an Old Algonkin vocabulary, it ap-

pears, in the form *wiskinkhie*, as a name for 'eyes' (lit. 'his eye').   (W. R. G.)

Wissatinnewag. A village, apparently on Connecticut r., in central Massachusetts in 1663.—Pynchon (1663) in N. Y. Doc. Col. Hist., XIII, 308, 1881.

Wissomanchuh. A former Hupa village on or near Trinity r., Cal.
Wis'-so-man-chuh.—Powers in Cont. N. A. Ethnol., III, 73, 1877.

Wistonwish. See *Wishtonwish*.

Witaotina ('dwellers on the island'). A Wahpeton Sioux band.—Dorsey (after Ashley) in 15th Rep. B. A. E., 216, 1897.

Witawaziyataotina ('village at the north island'). A Sisseton Sioux band.
Witawaziyata.—Ashley, letter to Dorsey, Jan. 18, 1886. Wita-waziyata-otina.—Dorsey in 15th Rep. B. A. E., 216, 1897.

Witchah ('turkey'). A Yuchi clan.
Wĕtᵉá.—Speck, Yuchi Inds., 70, 1909. Witcha'h. tahá.—Gatschet, Uchee MS., B. A. E., 1885 (='turkey gens').

Witchcraft. Witchcraft may be defined as the art of controlling the will and well-being of another person by supernatural or occult means, usually to his detriment. If shamans possessed supernatural powers that could be exerted beneficially, it was naturally supposed that they might also be exerted with injurious results, and therefore where shamanism was most highly developed the majority of supposed witches, or rather wizards, were shamans. At the same time it was believed that anybody might practice witchcraft if he knew the proper formulæ, and, in spite of the fact that a shaman is often represented as causing sickness in order to bring himself practice, the distinction between the legitimate exercise of shamanistic powers and witchcraft seems always to have been recognized.

One mode of bewitching was similar to that employed in Europe and New England. The wizard would possess himself of a lock of the victim's hair, parings from his nails, some of his saliva, a bit of the clothing he had worn, especially such as had absorbed his perspiration, a fragment left after he had eaten, some of his implements, or other personal belongings, and by treating them in certain ways would bring on him local or general sickness or some other misfortune. It was said that the wizard could affect any part if he obtained something taken from it. Thus sore throat might be brought about or a man made to "spit himself to death" by means of a little saliva, and headache might be induced through a few hairs. A Tlingit wizard having obtained one of these articles would make a little image of his victim and torture it in just that part which he desired to harm. A woman envious of another who was a good weaver might try to destroy her skill by torturing the hands of the effigy, and so with other parts. Very much the same custom was recorded by Alexander Henry among the Chippewa, except that the figure was outlined in sand, ashes, or clay. The Kwakiutl wizard stuffed articles obtained from his victim into the mouth, nose and ears of a corpse, or in a more elaborate form of bewitching, called *ē′k·′a*, into human bones and skulls. Dawson's description of this particular form is as follows:

"An endeavor is first made to procure a lock of hair, some saliva, a piece of the sleeve and of the neck of the dress, or of the rim of the hat or headdress which has absorbed the perspiration of the person to be bewitched. These are placed with a small piece of the skin and flesh of a dead man, dried and roasted before the fire, and rubbed and pounded together. The mixture is then tied up in a piece of skin or cloth, which is covered over with spruce gum. The little package is next placed in a human bone, which is broken for the purpose, and afterwards carefully tied together and put within a human skull. This again is placed in a box, which is tied up and gummed over and then buried in the ground in such a way as to be barely covered. A fire is next built nearly, but not exactly, on the top of the box, so as to warm the whole. Then the evilly disposed man, beating his head against a tree, names and denounces his enemy. This is done at night or in the early morning and in secret, and is frequently repeated till the enemy dies. The actor must not smile or laugh, and must talk as little as possible till the spell has worked. If a man has reason to suppose that he is being practiced on in this way, he or his friends must endeavor to find the deposit and carefully unearth it. Rough handling of the box may prove immediately fatal. It is then cautiously unwrapped and the contents are thrown into the sea. If the evilly disposed person was discovered, he was in former years immediately killed. If, after making up the little package of relics as above noted, it is put into a frog, the mouth of which is tied up before it is released, a peculiar sickness is produced, which causes the abdomen of the person against whom the sorcery is directed to swell."

Breaking the spell by separating the articles employed to effect it and throwing them into the sea was common to the Tlingit, and probably other tribes on the N. Pacific coast as well. There was a special set of persons among the Kwakiutl whose business was to undo the wizard's work. These went through the same ceremonies as the wizard himself, but ended by putting everything into the fire. This, therefore, was a sort of purification by fire.

Probably the most common method of bewitching was to inject a spearpoint, arrowpoint, piece of bone, or similar object into the body, either by symbolic propulsion or by exerting mental energy. Thus the Ntlakyapamuk shaman shot the nasal bones of the deer into a person by means of his guardian spirits or his thoughts. A shaman might also draw out the soul from a person and send a spirit of a snake or other animal into him that would prevent him from killing animals. Wizards were often supposed to be able to assume the forms of animals themselves, and other remarkable feats were attributed to them.

Taking the North American peoples as a whole, no crime seems to have been more quickly or more severely punished than witchcraft, mere suspicion being often equivalent to conviction and execution, although bloodshed might follow if the victim's family were strong. The Tsimshian suspected of witchcraft was tied up and starved until he confessed, when he was driven into the sea in order to expel the evil spirit. If he refused to confess, he was starved to death or exposed on the beach at low tide until the water rose over him. The Tlingit wizard was starved for some time, but liberated finally if he refused to confess. In the alternative case all that was done was to force him to take the bundle through which he had operated and scatter it in the ocean. Among the Haida witchcraft was supposed to be due to mice which had got inside of a person's body, and if these could be expelled he might be restored to his right mind. There were said to be as many as ten of these mice sometimes, one of which (the last to leave) was a white one. The charge of witchcraft was not only brought against individuals but entire towns and tribes, and in the S. W. the people of the Hopi pueblo of Awatobi were destroyed on this ground. As an illustration of its influence on religious rites it may be stated that the Powamu ceremony of the Hopi was undertaken to relieve the land from the bewitchment of winter. See *Oyaron.*　　　　　(J. R. S.)

Withlacoochee (*Wi-lak-uchi,* 'little Wi-lako' [Withlako], i. e. 'little great water'). A former Seminole town on Withlacoochee r., probably in Citrus or Sumter co., Fla.
Weecockcogee.—McKenney and Hall, Ind. Tribes, II, 72, 1854.

Withlacoocheetalofa (*talófa* = 'town'). A former Seminole town between St Marks and Ocklocknee rs., probably in Wakulla co., Fla.
Wethoecuchytalofa.—Bell in Morse, Rep. to Sec. War, 307, 1822. Wi-'la-ku-tci talofa.—F. G. Speck, inf'n, 1907 (correct form; *tc=ch*).

Withlako (*wi-lako,* 'great water'). A former Seminole village, 4 m. from

Clinch's battle ground of Dec. 31, 1835, in N. E. Hernando co., Fla. It was destroyed by the Americans in 1836.

Osceola's Town.—Drake, Ind. Chron., 207, 1836. **Ouithloko.**—Ibid. **Powells town.**—Drake, Bk. Inds., bk. IV, 85, 1848.

Witichquaom. A Nanticoke village in 1707, perhaps near Susquehanna r., in s. Pennsylvania.—Evans (1707) quoted by Day, Penn., 391, 1843.

Witukomnom. A division of the Yuki of N. California, living s. of Middle fork of Eel r. in Eden valley and s. to South Eel r. Their dialect differed somewhat from that of the Ukomnom and other divisions of the Yuki proper.

Spanish Yuki.—Powers in Cont. N. A. Ethnol., III, 136, 1877. **Witukomnom.**—A. L. Kroeber, inf'n, 1905.

Wiwash. That part of the Nanticoke who remained in Maryland when the main body moved northward. In 1792 they numbered perhaps 30 or 40 souls, in a village of 7 houses called Locust Necktown, on Choptank r. in Dorchester co.—Gallatin in Trans. Am. Antiq. Soc., II, 53, 1836.

Wiweakam (*Wĭ'wägam,* 'true frog tribe'). Two Lekwiltok gentes, one belonging to the Wiwekae sept, the other to the Kueha. There seems to be considerable confusion between the people bearing this name and those called Wikae. The population of each is enumerated separately in the Canadian Indian Affairs reports, and in 1909 the number of persons in this division was placed at 77. In 1885 their principal town was called Tatapowis. (J. R. S.)

Weewaikun.—Brit. Col. map, 1872. **Weewok.**—Ibid. **We-wai-ai-kum.**—Can. Ind. Aff., 270, 1889. **We-wark-kum.**—Kane, Wand. in N. A., app., 1859. **We-way-a-kum.**—Powell in Can. Ind. Aff., 119, 1880. **Wĭ'wägam.**—Boas in Mem. Am. Mus. Nat. Hist., v, pt. II, 318, 1902. **Wi-wai-ai-kum.**—Can. Ind. Aff., 364, 1897. **Wĭ'wēak·am.**—Boas in 6th Rep. N. W. Tribes Can., 55, 1890. **Wĭ'wēaqam.**—Boas in Petermanns Mitteil., pt. 5, 131, 1887. **Wĭ'-wē-ēkum.**—Dawson in Trans. Roy. Soc. Can., sec. II, 65, 1887. **Wi-wi-kum.**—Tolmie and Dawson, Vocabs. Brit. Col., 119B, 1884.

Wiwekae (*Wĭ'wēq'aē,* 'the Wē'qaēs,' from an ancestor of that name). A sept of the Lekwiltok, living between Bute and Loughborough inlets, Brit. Col. Its gentes, according to Boas, are: Gyigyilkam, Gyeksem, Wiweakam, and a fourth, the name of which is unknown. Their principal town, according to Dawson, is Tsakwalooin, at C. Mudge. Pop. 103 in 1910.

M-Wai-ai-kai.—Can. Ind. Aff., 435, 1896 (misprint). **Waiwaiaikai.**—Ibid., pt. 2, 41, 1909. **We-wai-ai-kai.**—Ibid., 189, 1884. **Wé-wark-ka.**—Kane, Wand. in N. A., app., 1859. **Weway-a-kay.**—Sproat in Can. Ind. Aff., 149, 1879. **We-way-a-ky.**—Powell, ibid., 119, 1880. **Wi-wai-ai-kai.**—Can. Ind. Aff., 362, 1895. **Wiwayiki.**—Brit. Col. map, 1872. **Wi-wē-eke.**—Dawson in Trans. Roy. Soc. Can., sec. II, 65, 1887. **Wĭ'-wēk·aē.**—Boas in 6th Rep. N. W. Tribes Can., 55, 1890. **Wĭ'wēqaē.**—Boas in Rep. U. S. Nat. Mus. 1895, 331, 1897. **Wĭ'wēq'aē.**—Boas in Petermanns Mitteil., XVII, pt. 5, 131, 1887.

Wiyahawir (*Wĭ'-ya-ha-wir*). A former village of the Kikatsik Shasta on the right bank of Shasta r., below Montague, Siskiyou co., Cal. The name (We-o-how) was incorrectly applied by Steele (Ind. Aff. Rep. 1864, 120, 1865) to all the Shasta occupying the E. side of Shasta r., giving it as their own name. (R. B. D.)

We-o-how.—Steele, op. cit. (said to mean 'stone house,' from the large cave in their country).

Wiyakaotina ('dwellers on the sand'). A band of the Wahpeton Sioux.—Dorsey (after Ashley) in 15th Rep. B. A. E., 216, 1897.

Wiyat. The name given by the Wishosk, a small group of the coast of N. California, to that part of their territory about the lower course of Eel r., and applied by several authors to the Wishosk people dwelling in that section or to the family as a whole. Waiyat is the Karok name for the Wishosk (q. v.).

Veeards.—Powers, MS. quoted by Bancroft, Nat. Races, I, 446, 1874. **Viard.**—Powers in Cont. N. A. Ethnol., III, 101, 1877. **Wee-yot.**—Gibbs (1851) in Schoolcraft, Ind. Tribes, III, 434, 1853. **We-yot.**—Ibid., 133. **Wi-yot.**—Powers, op. cit., 478.

Wizikute ('Pine Shooter'). The great chief of the Sioux when Hennepin (who referred to him as Ouasicoude) was among them in 1680. His home was at the head of Rum r., Minn. He seems to have been a wise and good man, who protected the French from the cupidity of some of the other chiefs. When Hennepin and Du Luth were about to return to Canada, Wizikute supplied them with an abundance of wild oats, and " with a pencil, he marked down on a sheet of paper, which I had left, the course that we were to keep for 400 leagues together. In short, this natural geographer described our way so exactly that this chart served us as well as any compass could have done, for by observing it punctually we arrived at the place designed without losing our way in the least." (D. R.)

Woapikamikunk (' at the place where there is much white earth.' — Gerard). The largest of 6 Delaware villages in the valley of White r., Ind., probably settled after 1795. Their Indiana lands were sold in 1818.

Wapeminskink.—Brinton, Lenâpé Leg., 124, 1885. **Woapikamikunk.**—Ibid., 124.

Woccon. A small tribe formerly inhabiting E. North Carolina, related linguistically to the Catawba, hence of Siouan stock. All that is known of them is recorded by Lawson, who states that about 1710 they lived 2 leagues from the Tuscarora on the lower Neuse in 2 villages, Yupwauremau and Tooptatmeer, having 120 warriors. In his map of 1709, reproduced by Hawks (Hist. No. Car., II, 104, 1859), he places them between Neuse r. and one of its affluents, perhaps about the present Goldsboro, Wayne co. They joined the Tuscarora against the whites in the war of 1711–13, as is learned from incidental references in colonial documents, and it is probable that they were extinguished as a tribe by that war. The remnant may have fled N. with the Tuscarora or have joined the Catawba (Mooney, Siouan Tribes of the East, 65, 1894). Lawson preserved a vocabulary of 150 words of their language, which shows that it was closely related to the Catawba, although the two tribes were separated by nearly 200 miles.

Waccoa.—Morse, Rep. to Sec. War, 145, 1822. Waccoam.—Ibid. Waccon.—Doc. of 1712 in N. C. Col. Rec., I, 891, 1886. Wacon.—Lawson, map of 1709, in Hawks, Hist. N. C., II, 104, 1859. Woccon.—Lawson (1714), Hist. Car., 378, 1860. Woccono.—Coues and Kingsley, Standard Nat. Hist., pt. 6, 156, 1883. Wocons.—Rafinesque in Marshall, Ky., I, introd., 23, 1824. Wokkon.—Drake, Bk. Ind., xii, 1848. Woocon.—Schoolcraft, Ind. Tribes, III, 401, 1853. Workons.—Domenech, Deserts N. Am., I, 445, 1860.

Wohawa. See *Hopehood.*

Wohkpotsit (*Wohk′po tsĭt*, obsolete name for 'white wolf'). A family group of Cheyenne, consisting of mixed Sutaio and Heviqsnipahis. They take their name from a chief.

Wohk′ po tsĭt.—Grinnell, Social Org. Cheyennes, 136, 1905. Wóopotsĭ′t.—Mooney in Handbook Am. Inds., I, 256, 1907. Wóqpotsĭt.—Mooney in Mem. Am. Anthr. Asso., I, pt. 6, facing pl. xii, 1907. Young-White-Wolf.—Dorsey in Field Mus. Pub., Anthr. ser., ix, no. 2, 62, 1905.

Wohuamis (*Wŏxuă′mĭs*). A gens of the Koskimo, a Kwakiutl tribe.—Boas in Rep. Nat. Mus. 1895, 329, 1897.

Wokas. A farinaceous food made by the Klamath from the seeds of the great yellow water-lily (*Nymphæa polysepala*): from *wo′-kas*, the Lutuamian name for the plant or its seed.—Coville in Rep. Nat. Mus. 1902, 725–729, 1903.

Woketamosi. A division of the Shawnee (Heckewelder quoted by Brinton, Lenâpé Leg., 30, 1885); not the Piqua, but possibly the Mequachake, Chillicothe, or Kiskopogi.

Wokodot (*Wo-ko′-dot*). A former Maidu village on the site of Nevada City, Nevada co., Cal.—Dixon in Bull. Am. Mus. Nat. Hist., xvii, map, 1905.

Woksihitaniu (*Woksi′hitäniu*, 'kit-fox men,' sing. *Woksi′hitän′*). A warrior society of the Cheyenne (q. v.); sometimes also known as Motsónitäniu, 'Flint men.' They received their name Kit-fox men on account of a ceremonial club, with pendent skin of a kit-fox, carried by their leaders.   (J. M.)

Hoof Rattle.—Dorsey in Field Columb. Mus. Pub. 99, 15, 1905 (probably identical). Woksi′hitäniu—Mooney in Mem. Am. Anthr. Asso., I, 412, 1907.

Woksoyudshi. A former Upper Creek town, probably on lower Coosa r., below Wetumpka, in Elmore co., Ala.

Wacksoyochees.—Swan (1791) in Schoolcraft, Ind. Tribes, v, 262, 1855. Waksoyochees.—Census of 1832 cited by Gatschet, Creek Migr. Leg., I, 150, 1884. Woksoyū′dschi.—Gatschet, ibid.

Wolasatux. A Kaiyuhkhotana village on the E. bank of Yukon r., Alaska, on a small stream N. of Kaiyuk r. Wolasatux was an Indian who alone escaped massacre at Nulato in 1851 and afterward had his barrabora at this spot.

Welasatux.—Dall, Alaska, map, 1870. Wolsatux.—Allen, Rep., map, 1887.

Wolasi (*Wo′lasi*). A Yokuts (Mariposan) tribe which probably resided in or near the Kaweah delta, Cal. They joined in the treaty of May 30, 1851, and were assigned to a reservation between Kaweah and King rs.

No-la-si.—Barbour in Sen. Ex. Doc. 4, 32d Cong., spec. sess., 225, 1853. Wo′lasi.—Kroeber in Univ. Cal. Pub., Am. Arch. and Eth., II, no. 5, 1907. Wo-la-si.—Royce in 18th Rep. B. A. E., 782, 1899. Wo-lass-i.—Johnston in Sen. Ex. Doc. 61, 32d Cong., 1st sess., 23, 1852.

Wolf Lying Down. See *Sleeping Wolf.*

Wolf Rapids. An Ottawa village on Maumee r., Ohio, about the boundary of Wood and Henry cos., on a tract sold in 1831.—Treaty of 1831 in U. S. Ind. Treat., 591, 1873.

Wolf Village. A Sauk and Fox village on the Great Nemaha r., on the Nemaha res., Nebr., in 1861.—Treaty of 1861 in U. S. Ind. Treat., 780, 1873.

Wolutayuta ('eat dried venison from the hind quarter'). A band of the Sans Arcs division of the Teton Sioux.

Those that eat the ham.—Culbertson in Smithson. Rep. 1850, 142, 1851. Woluta-yuta.—Dorsey in 15th Rep. B. A. E., 219, 1897.

Women. One of the most erroneous beliefs relating to the status and condition of the American Indian woman is that she was, both before and after marriage, the abject slave and drudge of the men of her tribe in general. This view, due largely to inaccurate observation and misconception, was correct, perhaps, at times, as to a small percentage of the tribes and peoples whose social organization was of the most elementary kind, politically and ceremonially, and especially of such tribes as were nonagricultural.

Among the other Indian tribes N. of Mexico the status of woman depended on complex conditions having their origin in climate, habitat, mythology, and concepts arising therefrom, and especially in the economic environment and in the character of the social and political organization. It is one of the fundamental deductions of modern mythologic research that the prevailing social, ceremonial, and governmental principles and institutions of a people are closely reflected in the forms, structure, and kind of dominion exercised by the gods of that people. Where numerous goddesses sat on the tribal Olympus, it is safe to say that woman was highly esteemed and exercised some measure of authority. In tribes whose government was based on the clan organization the gods were thought of as related one to another in degrees required by such an institution in which woman is supreme, exercising rights lying at the foundation of tribal society and government. Ethical teaching and observances find their explanation not in the religious views and rites of a people but rather in the rules and principles underlying those institutions which have proved most conducive to the peace, harmony, and prosperity of the community.

In defining the status of woman, a broad distinction must be made between women who are, and women who are not, members of the tribe or community, for among most tribes life, liberty, and the pursuit of well-being are rights belonging only to women who by birth or by the rite of adoption (q. v.) are members or citizens thereof. Other women receive no consideration or respect on account of their sex, although after adoption they were spared, as possible mothers, indiscriminate slaughter in the heat of battle, except while resisting the enemy as valiantly as their brothers and husbands, when they suffered wounds or death for their patriotism.

Among the North American aborigines here dealt with each sex had its own peculiar sphere of duty and responsibility, and it is essential to a proper understanding of the subject that both these spheres of activity should be considered. To protect his family—his wife or wives and their offspring and near kindred—to support them with the products of the chase, to manufacture weapons and wooden utensils, and commonly to provide suitable timbers and bark for the building of the lodge, constituted the duty and obligation which rested on the man. These activities required health, strength, and skill. The warrior was usually absent from his fireside on the chase, on the warpath, or on the fishing trip, weeks, months, and even years, during which he traveled hundreds of miles and was subjected to the hardships and perils of hunting and fighting, and to the inclemency of the weather, often without adequate shelter or food. The labor required in the home and in all that directly affected it fell naturally to the lot of the woman. In addition to the activities which they shared in common with men, and the care of children, women attended to the tanning of skins, the weaving of suitable fibers into fabrics and other articles of necessity, the making of mats and mattresses, baskets, pots of clay, and utensils of bark; sewing, dyeing; gathering and storing of edible roots, seeds, berries, and plants, for future use, and the drying and smoking of meats brought by the hunters. On the march the care of the camp equipage and of the various

family belongings constituted part of the woman's duties, in which she was assisted by the children and by such men as were incapacitated for active fighting or hunting. The essential principle governing this division of labor and responsibility between the sexes lies much deeper than apparently heartless tyranny of the man. It is the best possible adjustment of the available means of the family to secure the largest measure of welfare and to protect and perpetuate the little community. No other division was so well adapted to the conditions of life among the North American Indians. Fortified by the doctrine of signatures and by other superstitious reasons and beliefs, custom emphasized by various rites and observances the division of labor between the sexes. Thus, the sowing of seeds by women was supposed to render such seeds more fertile and the earth more productive than if planted by men, for it was held that woman has and controls the faculty of reproduction and increase. Hence sowing and cultivating the crops became one of the exclusive departments of woman's work.

According to Lewis and Clark (Travels, 307, 1806) the Shoshoni husband was the absolute proprietor of his wives and daughters, and might dispose of them by barter or otherwise at his pleasure; and Harmon (Jour. Voy., 344, 1820) declares that the women of the tribes visited by him were treated no better than the dogs. Writing of the Kutchin, and of the Loucheux Indians in particular, Hardesty (Smithson. Rep. 1866, 312, 1867) says that "the women are literally beasts of burden to their lords and masters. All the heavy work is performed by them." A similar statement is made by Powers (Cont. N. A. Ethnol., III, 23, 1877) in regard to the Karok of California. Schoolcraft (Ind. Tribes, v, 167, 1855) declares that the Cree women are subjected to lives of heavy and exacting toil, and that some mothers among them do not hesitate to kill their female infants to save them from the miseries which they themselves have suffered. Champlain, writing in 1615, states that the Huron and Algonquian women were "expected to attend their husbands from place to place in the fields, filling the office of pack-mule in carrying the baggage and in doing a thousand other things." Yet it would seem that this hard life did not thwart their development, for he adds that among these tribes there were a number of powerful women of extraordinary height, who had almost sole care of the lodge and the work at home, tilling the land, planting the corn, gathering a supply of fuel for winter use, beating and spinning the hemp and the bark fibers, the product of which was utilized in the manufacture of lines and nets for fishing and for other purposes; the women also harvested and stored the corn and prepared it for eating.

The duties of a woman of the Upper Lakes—i. e. of the Ottawa and the Chippewa—were to bring into the lodge, of which she was the mistress, the meat which the husband left at the door; to dry it; to have the care of the cuisine; to get the fish at the landing or harbor and to prepare it for immediate use or for storage; to fetch water; to spin various fibers in order to secure thread for sundry uses; to cut firewood in the surrounding forest; to clear land for planting and to raise and harvest the several kinds of grain and vegetables; to manufacture moccasins for the entire family; to make the sacks to hold grain, and the long or round mats used for covering the lodge or for mattresses; to tan the skins of the animals which her husband or brothers or her own or her sister's sons had killed in the chase; and to make robes of those which were used as furs. She made also bark dishes while her husband or other male members of the household made those of wood; she designed many curious pieces of art work; when her infant, swathed on a cradle-board, cried, she lulled it to sleep with song. When on the move, the woman carried the coverings of the lodge, if not conveyed by a canoe. In all her duties she was aided by her children and by dependents or guests, not rarely by the old men and the crippled who were still able to be of service.

While the tribes of the N. W. coast are distinct in language and in physical features and mental characteristics, they are nevertheless one in culture; their arts, industries, customs, and beliefs differ in so great a degree from those of all other Indian tribes that they constitute a well-defined cultural group. The staple food of these Indians is supplied by the sea, whence the women gather sea-grass, which after being cut, and pressed into square cakes, is dried for winter use; clams and mussels are eaten fresh, or strung on sticks or strands of bark are dried for winter consumption. Considerable quantities of berries and roots are also consumed. The dense forests along the coast furnish wood for building cabins, canoes, implements, and utensils. The red cedar (*Thuya gigantea*) is the most useful as it yields the materials for a large part of their manufactures, its wood being utilized for building and carving, and its bark for the manufacture of clothing and ropes, in which the women perform the greater part of the work. The women have their share also in the preparation and curing of the flesh and furs of

the various game and fur-bearing animals which their husbands and brothers kill. Berries and crab-apples are preserved by them for winter use; the food is stored in spacious boxes made from cedar wood suitably bent, having bottoms sewed to their sides. Women assist in curing and tanning the skins designed for the manufacture of wearing apparel. Dog's hair, mountain-goat's wool, and feathers are woven into fabrics suitable for wear or barter; soft cedar bark is also prepared for use as garments. The women manufacture in great variety baskets of rushes and cedar bark for storage and carrying purposes; mats of cedar bark, and in the South, of rushes, are made for bedding, packing, seats, dishes, and covers for boxes.

Hodge (in article *Pueblos*) is authority for the following statements: That monogamy is the rule among the Pueblos, and that the status of woman is much higher among them than among some other tribes; that among most of the Pueblos the descent of blood, and hence of membership in the clan and so citizenship in the tribe, is traced through the mother, the children belonging to her, or rather to her clan; that the home belongs to her, and that her husband whom she may dismiss upon slight provocation, comes to live with her; that if she have daughters who marry, the sons-in-law reside with her; that it is not unusual to find men and women married dwelling together for life in perfect accord and contentment; that labor is as equitably apportioned between the sexes as is possible under the conditions in which they live; that the small gardens, which are cultivated exclusively by the women, belong to the women; that in addition to performing all domestic duties, the carrying of water and the manufacturing of pottery are tasks devolving strictly on the women; that some of the less irksome agricultural labor, especially at harvest time, is performed by the women; that the men assist the women in the heavier domestic work, such as house-building and fuel-gathering; that the men also weave blankets, make moccasins for their wives, and assist in other tasks usually regarded as pertaining exclusively to women.

According to Mrs Stevenson (23d Rep. B. A. E., 1904), among the Zuñi, who are an agricultural and pastoral people, the little gardens around the villages, which are cultivated exclusively by the women, are inherited by the daughters; a married man carries the products of his fields to the house of his wife's parents, which is then his home. The wife likewise places the produce of the plots of land derived from her father or mother with those of her husband, and while these stored products are designed to be utilized by the entire household, only the wife or the husband may remove them thence. Mrs Stevenson says further that a woman is a member of the Ashiwanni or Rain Priesthood, consisting of nine persons, and constituting one of the four fundamental religious groups in the hierarchical government of the Zuñi; and that while the Zuñi trace descent through the mother and have clans, these clans do not own the fields, as they do among the Iroquois; that by cultivation a man may make use of any unoccupied plot of ground, and thereafter he may dispose of it to anyone within the tribe. It is to be noted that the daughters, and not the sons, inherit the landed property of the married Zuñi man or woman. These few facts show plainly that the Zuñi woman occupies a high status in the social and the political organizations of her tribe.

Among the Iroquois and tribes similarly organized, woman controlled many of the fundamental institutions of society: (a) Descent of blood or citizenship in the clan, and hence in the tribe, was traced through her; (b) the titles, distinguished by unchanging specific names, of the various chieftainships of the tribe belonged exclusively to her; (c) the lodge and all its furnishings and equipment belonged to her; (d) her offspring, if she possessed any, belonged to her; (e) the lands of the clan (including the burial grounds in which her sons and brothers were interred) and so of the tribe, as the source of food, life, and shelter, belonged to her. As a consequence of the possession of these vested rights, the woman exercised the sovereign right to select from her sons the candidates for the chieftainships of her clan, and so of the tribe, and she likewise exercised the concurrent right to initiate the procedure for their deposition for sufficient cause. Being the source of the life of the clan, the woman possessed the sole right to adopt aliens into it, and a man could adopt an alien as a kinsman only with the tacit or expressed consent of the matron of his clan. A mother possessed the important authority to forbid her sons going on the warpath, and frequently the chiefs took advantage of this power of the woman to avoid a rupture with another tribe. The woman had the power of life or death over such alien prisoners as might become her share of the spoils of war to replace some of her kindred who may have been killed; she might demand from the clansmen of her husband or from those of her daughters a captive or a scalp to replace a loss in her family. Thus it is evident that not only the clan and the tribal councils, but also the League council were composed of

her representatives, not those of the men. There were chieftainesses who were the executive officers of the women they represented; these female chiefs provided by public levy or contributions the food required at festivals, ceremonials, and general assemblies, or for public charity. Part of their duty was to keep close watch on the policies and the course of affairs affecting the welfare of the tribe, to guard scrupulously the interests of the public treasury, with power to maintain its resources, consisting of strings and belts of wampum, quill and feather work, furs, corn, meal, fresh and dried or smoked meats, and of any other thing which could serve for defraying the various public expenses and obligations, and they had a voice in the disposal of the contents of the treasury. Every distinct and primordial family or ohwachira (see *Clan*) had at least one of the female chiefs, who together constituted the clan council; and sometimes one of them, by reason of extraordinary merit and wisdom, was made regent in the event of a vacancy in the office of the regular male chief. Hence, in various accounts mention is made of "queens," who ruled their tribes. In view of the foregoing facts it is not surprising to find that among the Iroquoian tribes—the Susquehanna, the Hurons, and the Iroquois—the penalties for killing a woman of the tribe were double those exacted for the killing of a man, because in the death of a woman the Iroquoian lawgivers recognized the probable loss of a long line of prospective offspring. According to Swanton, on the N. W. coast the penalty for the killing of a woman of the tribe was only one-half that for the killing of a man. These instances show the great difference in the value placed on the life of woman by tribes in widely separated areas.

The statement of Powers in regard to the Yokuts of California, that notwithstanding the fact that the husband took up his abode in the lodge of his wife or of his father-in-law, he had the power of life and death over his wife, can not be accepted without qualification. This statement can mean apparently only that this power might be exerted to punish some specific crime, and that it might not be exercised with impunity to satisfy a whim of the husband.

In describing the character of the Muskhogean people, Bartram (1773) says: " I have been weeks and months amongst them, and in their towns, and never observed the least sign of contention or wrangling; never saw an instance of an Indian beating his wife, or even reproving her in anger. . . . for indeed their wives merit their esteem and the most gentle treatment, they being industrious, frugal, careful, loving, and affectionate.''

According to Smith, among the Indians of Virginia, while the men devoted their time and energy to fishing, hunting, warfare, and to other manly exercises out of doors, within the lodge they were often idle, for here the women and children performed the larger share of the work. The women made mats for their own use as well as for trade and exchange, also baskets, mortars, and pestles; planted and gathered the corn and other vegetables; prepared and pounded the corn to obtain meal for their bread, and did all the cooking; cut and brought all the wood used for fuel, and with the help of the children fetched the water used in the lodge. Thus, the women were obliged in performing their duties to bear all kinds of burdens; but they willingly attended to their tasks at their own time and convenience, and were not driven like slaves to do their duty. The descent of blood was traced through the mother. The class of women whom Smith calls ''trading girls'' affected a peculiar tonsure that differed from that of all other women, to prevent mistakes, as the Indians were as solicitous as Caucasians to keep their wives to themselves.

Lawson (Hist. Car., 1866) says that a woman with a large number of children and with no husband to help support her and them, was assisted by the young men in planting, reaping, and in doing whatever she was incapable of performing herself. He says also that they eulogized a great man by citing the fact that he had '' a great many beautiful wives and children, esteemed the greatest blessings amongst these savages.'' It would thus appear that the North Carolina native woman was not the drudge and slave of her husband or men of her tribe. Concerning people of the same general region, Bartram (Trans. Am. Ethnol. Soc., III, pt. 1, 31, 1853) says that among the Cherokee and the Creeks scarcely a third as many women as men were seen at work in their fields. De Soto found in 1540 a woman whom he styled a queen ruling in royal state a tribe on the Savannah r., indicating that woman at that early period was held in high esteem among these people.

From what has been said it is evident that the authority possessed by the Indian husband over his wife or wives was far from being as absolute as represented by careless observers, and there is certainly no ground for saying that the Indians generally kept their women in a condition of absolute subjection. The available data show that while the married woman, because of her status as such, became a member of her husband's household and owed him certain important duties and obligations, she enjoyed a large measure of independence and was treated with great consideration and deference, and had a marked influence over her husband. Of course, various tribes had different conditions to face and possessed different institutions, and so it happens that in some tribes the wife was the equal of her husband, and in others she was his superior in many things, as among the Iroquois and tribes similarly organized.

In most, if not in all, the highly organized tribes, the woman was the sole master of her own body. Her husband or lover, as the case may be, acquired marital control over her person by her own consent or by that of her family or clan elders. This respect for the person of the native woman was equally shared by captive alien women. Mrs Mary Rowlandson, the wife of a clergyman, and a captive in 1676 for 12 weeks among the fierce Narraganset, bears excellent witness to this fact. She wrote: ''I have been in the midst of those roaring lions, and savage bears, that feared neither God, nor man, nor the devil, by day and by night, alone, and in company; sleeping, all sorts together, and not one of them ever offered the least abuse or unchastity to me in word or in action.'' Roger Williams, with reference to another subject, brings this same respect for woman to view; he wrote: ''So did never the Lord Jesus bring any unto his most pure worship, for he abhors, as all men, yea, the very Indians, an unwilling spouse to enter into forced relations'' (R. I. Hist. Tract, 1st ser., 14, p. 15). At a later day, and in the face of circumstances adverse to the Indians, Gen. James Clinton, who commanded the New York division in the Sullivan expedition in 1779 against the hostile Iroquois, paid his enemies the tribute of a soldier by writing in April 1779, to Colonel Van Schaick, then leading the troops against the Onondaga, the following terse compliment: ''Bad as the savages are, they never violate the chastity of any woman, their prisoners.'' However, there were cases in various tribes of violation of women, but the guilty men were regarded with horror and aversion. The culprits, if apprehended, were punished by the kindred of the woman, if single, and by her husband and his friends, if married. Among the Sioux and the Yuchi, men who made a practice of seduction were in grave bodily danger from the aggrieved women and girls, and the resort by the latter to extreme measures was sanctioned by public opinion as properly avenging a gross violation of woman's inalienable right—the control of her own body. The dower or bride price, when such was given, did not confer, it seems, on the husband, absolute right over the life and liberty of the wife: it was rather compensation to her kindred and household for the loss of her services. Among the Navaho the husband possesses in reality but very little authority over his wife, although he has obtained her by the payment of a bride price or present (Westermarck, Human Marriage, 392 et seq.)

Among all the tribes of Indians north of Mexico, woman, during the catamenial period, and, among many of the tribes, during the period of gestation and parturition, was regarded as abnormal, extra-human, sacred, in the belief that her condition revealed the functioning of *orenda* or magic power so potent that if not segregated from the ordinary haunts of men it would disturb the usual course of nature. The proper view point is that while in either condition the woman involuntarily was the seat of processes which marred, if they did not thwart, the normal exercise of human faculties, rather than that she was merely "unclean," and so an object to be tabooed. Yet, it appears that this species of temporary but recurrent taboo did not affect the status of the woman in the social and political organization in any way detrimental to her interests.

It appears also that in many instances woman aspired to excel in some of the vocations which might be regarded as peculiar to the male sex—hunting, fishing, fowling, and fighting beside the man. At times also she was famed, even notorious, as a sorceress. Some of the weirdest tales of sorcery and incantation are connected with the lives and deeds of noted woman sorcerers, who delighted in torture and in destruction of human life.

Some students maintain, on seemingly insufficient grounds, that the institution of maternal descent tends to elevate the social status of woman. Apart from the independence of woman, brought about by purely economic activities arising from the cultivation of the soil, it is doubtful whether woman ever attains any large degree of independence and authority aside from this potent cause. Without a detailed and carefully compiled body of facts concerning the activities and the relations of the sexes, and the relation of each to the various institutions of the community, this question can not be satisfactorily decided. The data concerning the rights of women as compared with those of men to be found in historical accounts of various tribes are so meager and indefinite that it is difficult, if not impossible, to define accurately the effect of either female or male descent on the

status of the woman. It is apparent, however, that among the sedentary and agricultural communities the woman enjoyed a large, if not a preponderating, measure of independence and authority, greater or less in proportion to the extent of the community's dependence for daily sustenance on the product of the woman's activities.

For additional information on the avocations of women among the several tribes, see *Basketry, Dyes and Pigments, Skin and Skin dressing, Weaving.*　　(J. N. B. H.)

Women's National Indian Association. See *National Indian Association.*

Wompam. See *Wampum.*

Wonalancet. See *Wannalancet.*

Wonasquam. A village in 1686 on the seacoast in Essex co., Mass., about the present Annisquam.—Dunton (1705) in Mass. Hist. Soc. Coll., 2d s., II, 122, 1814.

Wongen. See *Wangan.*

Wongunk ('at the bend'). A former village on the E. bank of Connecticut r., about the present Chatham, Middlesex co., Conn., belonging, according to De Forest, to the Mattabesec.
Wangum.—De Forest, Inds. Conn., 54, 1852. Wongonks.—Field, Middlesex Co., 56, 1819. Wongums.—Ibid. Wongunck.—Stiles (1761) in Mass. Hist. Soc. Coll., 1st s., X, 105, 1809. Wongung.—Trumbull, Hist. Conn., I, 40, 1818. Wongunk.—De Forest, op. cit.

Wonongoseak. A former village, probably of the Potawatomi, between the N. and S. branches of Elkhart r., apparently in Noble co., Ind.
Wo-non-go-seak Village.—Hough, map in Indiana Geol. Rep. 1882, 1883.

Woodchuck. One of the names of the ground-hog (*Arctomys monax*), called *moonack* in parts of the S. The present form of the word, as if from "wood" and "chuck," is a corruption by folk-etymology of *woodschock, woodshaw,* or *wejack,* a name applied to this animal by the hunters and traders of the Hudson Bay region. The word is derived from the Cree *otchek* or the Chippewa *otchig* or *odjik,* the name of the fisher (*Mustela pennanti*), this Algonquian term having been transferred by the whites to the ground-hog. In the fur nomenclature of the Hudson's Bay Company the skins of these animals have long been known as *woodschocks.*　　(A. F. C.)

Woodchuck day. Candlemas (February 2d), which is so designated from a rural belief that the appearance of the ground-hog on that day presages a return of cold weather and a late spring.　　(W. R. G.)

Woodwork. Much use is made of wood by the Indians, who, with few exceptions, are skilful workers in that material. Some areas may be classed as favorable for the development of woodworking art, having an abundant supply of straight-grained timber, easily split and worked, and other growths furnishing a variety for all purposes. The richest region is the N. W. coast, where woodworking reached its highest development in historic times. Some densely forested areas, as the Appalachian region, did not seem to foster the art, while in some environments where wood is scarce the Indians have made more extended use of such that is available than tribes better provided with the raw material. Specimens of woodworking survive in ancient deposits of artifacts only where conditions are most favorable, as in the keys of Florida, whose inhabitants worked wood in elaborate designs with shell implements and shark's teeth, or in the dry sands of Arizona, where hard-wood implements, prayersticks of cottonwood, and other objects, have been found.

Fire, the stone ax, and the wedge were the principal tools of the Indian for getting out timber. With these the largest tree could be felled and cut into lengths. Some tribes in the California-Oregon region felled trees by bruising off successive rounds of the wood. Large timber was not demanded, however, except for canoes, house-posts, beams, and totem poles. Boards, when required, were split out with antler wedges, while smaller material was cut with stone or copper tools. The saw, drill, ax, adze, knife, chisel, scraper, rasp, and the smoother, made of suitable stone, shell, copper, or teeth, were used for woodworking, the knife being drawn toward the body. Wood was bent by means of hot water and fire, small rods were straightened with the teeth or with wrenches of bone, horn, or wood, and larger rods or poles in smoke and heat of the fire. In the Pueblo region figurines and other objects of soft wood are modeled entirely by rubbing with coarse sandstone or by attrition upon rock. Canoes were hollowed out with the aid of fire, the charred portions being removed with cutting tools. In every locality each art had its particular tools, varying as to material, hafting, etc., and some arts, as the making of bows and arrows, developed a large number of tools for shaping, finishing, and decorating. Dishes, small boxes, and the like were excavated with great labor by means of scrapers and other cutting tools, as the incisors of the beaver, suitably hafted. The use of curly knots from trees for dishes was widespread, since much of the work in forming the vessel, spoon, or cup had been done by nature. In many cases the interior of the knot had decayed, leaving a shell which became a vessel, with little working. Perforations for lashing, suspending, and fastening were made with the drill. In hard-wood saplings there is often a core of pith which could be pushed out with a cane or grass stem and the hole somewhat enlarged to form a tube. In the Pueblo region roof timbers and the stakes that were used to cover bodies in ancient burials show marks of the stone tools with which they were cut. Firewood was broken from trees by means of large grooved hammers or mauls. Most of the elementary processes known to modern woodworkers were practised by these Indians. Examples of joining, splicing, binding, lashing, pegging, and grooving are found, and in joining birch-bark a process somewhat resembling dovetailing was often employed. The tenon and mortise appear to be absent, their place being taken in Alaskan houses by worked sockets for frame timbers, and in other structures, as the Navaho hogan, by crotched sticks. The N. W. coast tribes had a primitive vise for holding bentwood boxes and dishes. Pegs of bone, ivory, or wood were used instead of nails.

Among the numerous products of woodworking may be mentioned bows, arrows, spears, armor, gaming blocks, trinket boxes, and chests, especially developed by the N. W. coast tribes, boat frames, boats, sleds, bowls, mortars, pestles, fire-drills, pipestems, masks, and figurines. Among these objects are specimens carved with such skill as to entitle them to a place in the class of art productions.

Consult Beverley, Hist. Va., 1722; Boas in Southern Workman, XXXIX, no. 6, 337–343, 1910; Bogoras in Mem. Am. Mus. Nat. Hist., Jesup Exped., VII, 1905; Dixon in Bull. Am. Mus. Nat. Hist., XVII, pt. III, 1905; Kroeber in Pub. Univ. Cal., VIII, no. 2, 1908; Mason (1) in Rep. Nat. Mus. 1894, 1896, (2) in Smithsonian Rep. 1886, 205–239, 1889; Morgan in Cont. N. A. Ethnol., IV, 1881; Nelson in 18th Rep. B. A. E., pt. 1, 1899; Nordenskiöld, Cliff Dwellers of the Mesa Verde, 1893; Powers in Cont. N. A. Ethnol., III, 1877; Swan in Smithson. Cont. Knowl., XXI, 1–18, 1876, (2) ibid., XVI, 1–108, 1870; Swanton in Mem. Am. Mus. Nat. Hist., Jesup Exped., V, pt. 1, 1905; Willoughby in Am. Anthr., n. s., IX, no. 2, 296–306, 1907.   (W. H.)

Woolyneag. A name in the northern parts of New England for the fisher or pekan, *Mustela pennanti*. The name is from Abnaki *wulanikw*, 'handsome squirrel' (from *wul*, 'good,' 'pretty,' etc. + *anikw*, a general name for 'squirrel' in all Algonquian dialects). The name, with variants *woolaneag* and *wooleneag*, is evidently a misapplication.   (W. R. G.)

Woosemequin. See *Massasoit*.

Wootassite. See *Outacity*.

Wooteka. A former village, probably Seminole, E. of Apalachee bay, W. Fla.—Bartram, Voy., I, map, 1799.

Wopohwats (*Wo'poh''wăts*, 'White Shield Owner,' commonly known to the whites as White Shield). A former chief of the Southern Cheyenne, born about 1833 on an upper branch of North Platte r., Wyo.; died in 1883 near the present Kingfisher, Okla. In accordance with Indian custom, he had different names at different periods. As a young man he was known as Mouse Road. His more famous name was bestowed on him in 1862 by his uncle, the noted Black Kettle, killed in the battle of the Washita, who had previously borne the name himself. About the year 1878 he assumed his grandfather's name of Buffalo Beard, which he kept until his death. Having distinguished himself as a warrior, particularly in two engagements with the Pawnee, he became a leader in the Bowstring soldier society, and in 1870 was formally elected to the council of chiefs. In the next year he was one of a delegation sent to Washington to represent the allied Cheyenne and Arapaho tribes then newly established on a reservation in Oklahoma, and with his companions received from President Grant a treaty medal bearing the device of a pipe, a plow, a globe, and a Bible, which were explained to symbolize peace, agriculture, education, and Christianity. White Shield accepted all this literally, and on his return became an earnest advocate of civilization, schools, and mission work. Throughout the outbreak of 1874–75 he held his band quiet at the agency. In 1881 he was again chosen as delegate, but was unable to go by reason of the death of his daughter, tribal custom forbidding participation in public business by anyone in mourning. As was common with the Plains Indians, he had two wives, who were sisters. His son, Harvey White Shield (see *Hishkowits*), is one of the best educated young men in the tribe and an efficient mission helper and interpreter. (J. M.)

Wopum. Mentioned as a Karok village on Klamath r., Cal., inhabited in 1860.
Woo-pum.—Taylor in Cal. Farmer, Mar. 23, 1860.

Woronock. A Wappinger village on the E. bank of lower Housatonic r., in New Haven co., Conn., at the ferry between Milford and Stratford.
Oronoake.—Birdsey (1761) in Mass. Hist. Soc. Coll., 1st s., X, 111, 1809. Oronoke.—Trumbull, Ind. Names Conn., 91, 1881. Oronoque.—Ibid. Woronock.—Ibid.

Worship. See *Orenda*, *Prayer*, *Religion*.

Woruntuck. A village in Massachusetts, apparently on or near Connecticut r., whose inhabitants were driven out by the Mohawk about 1664.—Winthrop (1664) in Mass. Hist. Soc. Coll., 4th s., VI, 531, 1863.

Wosameus. A village in 1608 on the W. bank of Patuxent r. in Prince George co., Md.—Smith (1629), Va., I, map, 1819.

Wotkalgi ('raccoon people'). A clan of the Creeks.
Wótkalgi.—Gatschet, Creek Migr. Leg., I, 155, 1884. Wo'-tko.—Morgan, Anc. Soc., 161, 1878.

Wovoka ('The Cutter'). A Paiute dreamer and medicine-man, and originator of the Ghost dance; born in W. Nevada about 1856. His father, Tavibo, 'White Man,' was also a reputed medicine-man, and the son may have inherited the mystic tendency from him. After his father's death the boy was taken into the family of a white rancher from whom he received the name of Jack Wilson, by which he was commonly known among the whites. He was still alive in 1905, but had lost in large measure his former influence. For an account of his supernatural mission, see *Ghost dance*. Consult Mooney, Ghost Dance Religion, 14th Rep. B. A. E., 1896.

Wowol. A former Yokuts (Mariposan) tribe that lived near the Tachi and Chunut, N. or E. of Tulare lake, Cal. With the Chunut they ceded their lands to the United States by treaty of June 3, 1851, excepting a strip from Tulare to Buena Vista lake. In 1857 they, with the Tachi, numbered 175.
Wah-wol.—Wessells (1853) in H. R. Ex. Doc. 76, 34th Cong., 3d sess., 32, 1857. Woo-wells.—Lewis in Ind. Aff. Rep. 1857, 400, 1858. Wo-wol.—Barbour in Sen. Ex. Doc. 4, 32d Cong., spec. sess., 256, 1853.

Wright, Allen. A Choctaw preacher, born in Mississippi about 1825; he emigrated with most of the tribe to Indian Ter. in 1832, his parents dying soon afterward, leaving him and a sister. He had a strain of white blood, probably one-eighth or one-sixteenth. In his youth he lived some time in the family of the Rev. Cyrus Kingsbury, a Presbyterian missionary, and began his education in a missionary day-school near Doaksville. While here he was converted to the Christian faith, and soon after entered Spencer Academy in the Choctaw Nation. By reason of his studious habits he was sent by the Choctaw authorities to a school in Delaware, but afterward went to Union College, Schenectady, N. Y., where he was graduated in 1852. He then took a full course in Union Theological Seminary, New York City, being graduated in 1855, and in the following year was ordained by the Indian Presbytery. Returning to his people in Indian Ter., he preached to them until his death in 1885. His people appreciating his ability and uprightness, Mr Wright was called to affairs of state, being elected successively a member of the Choctaw House of Representatives and the Senate, and afterward Treasurer. In 1866, after the Civil War, he was sent to Washington as a delegate to negotiate a new treaty with the United States, and during his absence was elected principal chief of the Choctaw Nation, an office which he held until

1870. The Rev. John Edwards characterized Wright as "a man of large intelligence, good mind, an excellent preacher, and a very faithful laborer for the good of his people. No other Choctaw that I ever met could give such a clear explanation of difficult points in the grammar of the Choctaw." About 1873 he translated the Chickasaw constitution, which was published by the Chickasaw Nation, and in 1880 he published a "Chahta Leksikon." Just before his death he completed the translation of the Psalms from Hebrew into Choctaw. Soon after his graduation Mr Wright married Miss Harriet Newell Mitchell, of Dayton, Ohio, to whom were born several children, including Eliphalet Nott Wright, M. D., of Olney, Okla.; Rev. Frank Hall Wright, of Dallas, Texas; Mrs Mary Wallace and Mrs Anna W. Ludlow, of Wapanucka, Okla.; Allen Wright, jr., a lawyer of South McAlester, Okla.; Mrs Clara E. Richards, Miss Kathrine Wright, and James B. Wright, C. E., all of Wapanucka, Okla. For Mr Wright's portrait, see *Choctaw*.

Wrosetasatow. See *Outacity*.

Wuckan. One of the 7 Winnebago villages in 1806, situated on L. Poygan, Winnebago co., Wis.—Pike, Trav., 124, 1811.

Wuia (*Wu-ia*). Given by Ingalls (H. R. Ex. Doc. 66, 42d Cong., 3d sess., 2, 1873) as a Paiute band in Utah. Not identified.

Wuituthlaa. A Kuitsh village on lower Umpqua r., Oreg.
Wu'-i-tû'-çla'-ă.—Dorsey in Jour. Am. Folk-lore, III, 231, 1890.

Wukakeni (*Wukaχē'ni*, 'at the canyon'). A former Modoc settlement on the E. side of Tule lake, N. E. Cal.—Gatschet in Cont. N. A. Ethnol., II, pt. I, xxxii, 1890.

Wukoanu. The Great-ant clan of the Ala (Horn) phratry of the Hopi.
Wu-ko'-a-nü wüñ-wü.—Fewkes in Am. Anthr., VII, 401, 1894 (*wüñ-wü* = 'clan').

Wukoki ('great house or village'). A group of ruined pueblos w. of the Great falls and the Black falls of Little Colorado r., about 40 m. N. E. of Flagstaff, Ariz. Both archeological and traditionary evidence indicate that they were erected in prehistoric times by the Snake clan of the Hopi and formed one of its stopping places in its migration from the N. to its present habitations in N. E. Arizona. See Fewkes in 22d Rep. B. A. E., 56 et seq., 1904.
Black falls ruins.—Fewkes, ibid., 41.

Wukopakabi ('great reed or arrow house'). A ruined pueblo, consisting of a number of mounds very much worn down, covering a rather small site, at Ganado, on the road between Ft Defiance and Keams canyon, Ariz. It is locally known as Pueblo Ganado and Pueblo

Colorado. It was inhabited in ancient times by the Pakab or Reed people of the Hopi, who migrated from Wukopakabi to Awatobi (q. v.). After the destruction of the latter village, in 1700, they went to the Middle mesa of the Hopi and founded a town on the E. side; subsequently they moved to Walpi, on the East mesa, where their descendants now live. These people, as their name signifies, were warriors, and traditionally they are related to the Zuñi. Their descendants hold at the present time, in December, a war celebration. (J. W. F.)
Pueblo Colorado.—A local name. Pueblo Ganado.—Fewkes in 22d Rep. B. A. E., 127, 1904 (Span.; 'sheep village,' another local name).

Wullaneg. See *Woolyneag*.

Wunnashowatuckoog ('people at the fork of the river'). A Nipmuc tribe or band formerly living in the s. part of Worcester co., Mass., probably on Blackstone r. They adjoined the Narraganset, to whom they were said to be subject, although the two tribes are known to have been at war. They sheltered the hostile Pequot in 1637, and for this were attacked by the eastern Nipmuc and, being defeated, retreated toward the Mohawk country. They seem to have returned again, for in 1675 we find the English interfering to protect them from inroads of the Mohegan and Narraganset.
Showatuks.—Williams (1675) in Mass. Hist. Soc. Coll., 4th s., VI, 297, 1863. Wunnashoatuckoogs—Williams (1637), ibid., 3d s., IX, 300, 1846 Wunnashowatuckoogs.—Williams (1636), ibid., I, 161 1825 Wunnashowatuckowogs.—Williams (1675), ibid., 4th s., VI, 297, 1863. Wunnashowatuckqut.—Williams (1637), ibid., 193.

Wushketan ('people having houses on top of one another'). A Tlingit division of the Wolf phratry living at Killisnoo, Gaudekan, and Anchguhlsu, Alaska.
Nuschkē-tān—Krause, Tlinkit Ind., 118, 1885 Uüschkētan.—Ibid. Wū'cketan.—Swanton, field notes, B. A. E., 1904.

Wusquowhananawkit ('at the pigeon country'). A Nipmuc tribe, or, more likely, band, living probably in the central part of Worcester co., Mass., friends of the hostile Pequot in 1636, and neighbors of and possibly related to the Wunnashowatuckoog.
Wusquowhananawkits.—Williams (1636) in Mass. Hist. Soc. Coll., 4th s., VI, 188, 1863. Wusquowhanawkits.—Trumbull, Ind. Names Conn., 91, 1881.

Wutapiu (*Wŭ'tapi'u*, from a Sioux word meaning 'eat' or 'eaters,' sing. *Wŭ'tap*). A principal division of the Cheyenne tribe (q. v.). (J. M.)
Cheyenne Sioux.—Dorsey in Field Columb. Mus. Pub. no. 103, 62, 1905. Wĭ'tapi'u.—Mooney, Ghost Dance, 1025, 1896 (improperly given by misprint from Grinnell MS. as 'haters'). Wŏ'tapío.—Mooney in Mem. Am. Anthr. Asso., I, 406, 1907. Wüñ tä pi u.—Grinnell, Social Org. Cheyenne, 136, 1905.

Wutshik ('fisher'). A subphratry or gens of the Menominee.—Hoffman in 14th Rep. B. A. E., pt. 1, 42, 1896.

Wyah. A Nitinat village on the E. shore of the outlet of Nitinat lagoon, s. w.

coast of Vancouver id.; pop. 63 in 1902.
Whyack.—Whymper, Alaska, 73, 1869. **Wyah.**—
Can. Ind. Aff., 264, 1902.

Wyalusing (*M'chwihillusink*, 'at the dwelling place of the hoary veteran,' so called from an ancient warrior who lived near.—Heckewelder). A former Munsee and Iroquois settlement at the site of the present town of the same name in Bradford co., Pa. It was also the site of an older Indian village, called Gohontoto, which is mentioned by Cammerhoff, who visited the place in 1750. "Here, they tell me," he says, "was in early times an Indian town, traces of which are still noticeable, e. g., corn-pits, etc., inhabited by a distinct nation (neither Aquinoschioni, i. e., Iriquois, nor Delawares), who spoke a peculiar language and were called Tehotitachsae; against these the Five Nations warred, and rooted them out. The Cayugas for a time held a number of them, but the Nation and their language are now exterminated and extinct" (Cammerhoff quoted by Clark in Jour. Mil. Exped. Gen. Sullivan, 124, 1887). In 1752 Papunhank, a Munsee chief, settled at the site with 20 families. He was a frequent visitor to Philadelphia, where he came in contact with the Quakers, and later made great pretensions as a religious teacher. The people of his village became dissatisfied with his instruction, and after a conference decided to take the first religious teacher who came to their village, having been undecided whether they wanted a Quaker or a Moravian. John Woolman, a Quaker evangelist, who had become acquainted with Papunhank during his visits to Philadelphia, set out for Wyalusing in May, 1763, accompanied by Benjamin Parvin. News of the situation reaching David Zeisberger at Bethlehem, he at once started for this promising field, passing Woolman on the mountains below Wilkes-Barré. On the way he met Job Chillaway, a Delaware, the messenger and friend of the English, who was then living in Papunhank's village. Together they entered the settlement and were welcomed by the Indians. In a few days Woolman reached the place; he was informed of the decision of the council, and that as a consequence they had accepted Zeisberger as their teacher. The latter remained until the outbreak of hostilities during the conspiracy of Pontiac, when he removed the Moravian Indians to Bethlehem, thence to Philadelphia (Arch. Pa., IV, 138, 1853). At the urgent invitation of Papunhank, these Indians moved back to Wyalusing, which they reached May 18, 1765. Owing to various causes the mission was abandoned, June 11, 1772, by the Moravians, who removed to Beaver r. (see *Friedenshuetten*). Dur-

ing the Revolution the village became a gathering place for hostile Indians and Tories, many of the raids into the Susquehanna valley being planned here and at Sheshequin. On Sept. 28, 1778, Col. Hartley marched from Sheshequin, which he had destroyed, and camped that night at Wyalusing, which the Indians had deserted just before his arrival. On the 29th his detachment of about 120 was attacked by the Indians a short distance from the village; the Indians were defeated, leaving 10 dead, while Hartley had 4 killed and 10 wounded. From here he marched to Wyoming (Arch. Pa., VII, 5–9, 1853). On Aug. 5–7, 1779, Sullivan's army encamped at the site of the Indian village when on its expedition to the Seneca country. Rev. Mr Rogers, chaplain in this expedition, says in his journal, "No sign of even the smallest hut was left standing" (Jour. Mil. Exped. Gen. Sullivan, 258, 1887). (G. P. D.)

Machachlosung.—Post (1760) in Arch. Pa., III, 743, 1853. **Machelusing.**—Indian letter (1764), ibid., IV, 170, 1853. **Machochlaung.**—Post (1760), op. cit., 744. **Machochloschung.**—Ibid. **Machwihilusing.**—Day, Penn., 138, 1843. **Mahackloosing.**—Proud, Penn., II, 320, 1798. **Makahelousink.**—Tedyuscung (1761) quoted in Col. Rec. Pa., VIII, 636, 1852. **Makehalousing, Papounan's House.**—Ibid., 635. **M'chwihillusink.**—Heckewelder in Trans. Am. Philos. Soc., n. s., IV, 362, 1834. **Michalloasen.**—Pa. Council (1760) in Col. Rec. Pa., VIII, 492, 1852. **Monmuchloosen.**—Pa. Council (1760) in Arch. Pa., III, 743, 1853. **Papounan's Town.**—Hamilton (1761) in Col. Rec. Pa., VIII, 648, 1852. **Waghaloosen.**—Col. Rec. Pa. (1760), ibid., 492. **Wealusing.**—Grant (1779) in Mil. Exped. Gen. Sullivan, 238, 1887. **Wealuskingtown.**—Mach in (1779), ibid., 194. **Wialosing.**—German Flats conf. (1770) in N. Y., Doc. Col. Hist., VIII, 243, 1857. **Wialusing.**—Grant (1779) in Jour. Mil. Exped. Gen. Sullivan, 138, 1887. **Wighaloosen.**—Gov. Penn (1768) in Col. Rec. Pa., IX, 425, 436, 1852. **Wighalosscon.**—Pa. Council (1760), ibid., VIII, 492, 1852. **Wighalousin.**—Gov. Hamilton (1761), ibid., 648. **Wihaloosing.**—Writer of 1784 quoted by Harris, Tour, 211, 1805. **Wildlucit.**—Fellows (1779) in Jour. Mil. Exped. Gen. Sullivan, 86, 1887. **Wyalousing.**—Petition to Gov. Penn (1764) in Col. Rec. Pa., IX, 139, 1852. **Wyalucing.**—Barton (1779) in Jour. Mil. Exped. Gen. Sullivan, 5, 1887. **Wyalusing.**—Hartley (1778) in Arch. Pa., VII, 7, 1853. **Wybusing.**—Campfield (1779) in Jour. Mil. Exped. Gen. Sullivan, 53, 1887. **Wyeluting.**—Livermore (1779) in N. H. Hist. Soc. Coll., VI, 320, 1850. **Wylucing.**—Gookin (1779) in Jour. Mil. Exped. Gen. Sullivan, 104, 1887. **Wylusink.**—Blake (1779), ibid., 39. **Wyolusing.**—Dearborn (1779), ibid., 69.

Wyandot. See *Huron*.

Wyandotte. An American breed of fowls, earlier known as Sebright Cochins, said to have sprung from the mating of a Sebright bantam cock and a Cochin hen. The name was proposed at Worcester, Mass., in 1883, by Mr Houdette, and after some opposition it has been accepted as the name of the fowl (T. F. McGrew, U. S. Dept. of Agr. Bull. 31, 1901). The word is the same as Wyandot, the name of one of the peoples of Iroquoian stock. (A. F. C.)

Wyantenuc. A village in Litchfield co., Conn., where there was a great Indian gathering in 1675; possibly identical with Wiatiac.

Wayattano.—Doc. of 1676 in N. Y. Doc. Col. Hist., XIII, 496, 1881. **Wayattanoc.**—Heading, ibid. **Wyantanuck.**—Leete (1675) in Mass. Hist. Soc. Coll., 4th s., VII, 575, 1865. **Wyantenuck.**—Wadsworth (1694), ibid., I, 108, 1852.

Wynemac. See *Winamac*.

Wyoming (Delaware: *M'cheuwómink*, 'upon the great plain.' The native name, variously corrupted to Chiwaumuc, Wiawamic, Wayomic, Waiomink, etc., finally reached the more euphonious form of *Wyoming*, a word which was long supposed to signify 'field of blood.' The name was made widely known by the poet Campbell in his "Gertrude of Wyoming" (1809), an imaginary tale the scenes and incidents of which are connected with the massacre of the settlers on July 3, 1778, by British soldiers, Tories, and Indians in the above-named picturesque valley. It is not known who suggested the name of the state (which had been proposed as that of a territory as early as 1865), but it was probably some emigrant or emigrants from one of the dozen or more places so called in the different parts of the Union.—Gerard). A settlement, before 1744, of Shawnee and Mahican, after which time and until 1756 it was made up of Shawnee, Mahican, Iroquois, Munsee, and Nanticoke. After the latter date it was a Delaware and Munsee village, the headquarters of Tedyuskung, the leading chief of the Delawares. The principal settlement was at the site of the present Wilkes-Barré, Luzerne co., Pa. The name was applied to the lands in the Wyoming valley, in which there were a number of Indian villages, and then to the chief town of the region. The location is first mentioned in the records of Pennsylvania, at the council of Philadelphia, June, 1728. At the council at Conestoga (May 1728), Tawenna, chief of the Conestoga, said that the attack upon John Burt's house the year before had not been made by the Conestoga, Delawares, Shawnee, or Conoy, but by the Minisink (Col. Rec. Pa., IV, 314, 1851). At the council at Philadelphia in June following, Allumapees stated that the "Menysineks" lived "at the Forks of Sasquehannah above Meehayomy, & that their Kings name is Kindarsowa" (ibid., III, 326, 1852). When the Delaware chiefs signed the famous deed of 1737 (the so-called "Walking Purchase"), they did so with the understanding that those living in the Minisinks would not be obliged to abandon their lands, but would live there in friendship with the English (Walton, Conrad Weiser, 66, 1900; Arch. Pa., I, 541, 1852). At the council at Philadelphia in 1742, when Canassatego ordered the Delawares to leave at once for

Shamokin or Wyoming, he was in ignorance of any such understanding on the part of the Delawares. Weiser, if he had nothing to do with this speech, at least permitted its statements to pass unrebuked. The Delawares went away from this council thoroughly humiliated. Some of them moved to Shamokin, some to Wyoming, but the great majority of them went w. to the Ohio and joined the Shawnee in their effort to throw off the Iroquois yoke. When Zinzendorf and his party of Moravian missionaries visited Wyoming in the fall of 1742, he found it occupied chiefly by the Shawnee, who were in no mood to listen to him, as they feared that he had come to buy their lands (Zinzendorf's Jour. in Mem. Moravian Church, 71, 1870). At this time the flats w. of the Susquehanna were occupied by the Shawnee, while the Mahican had a large village at the N. end of the valley, on the same side of the river. In 1751 the Nanticoke had a settlement at the lower end of the valley on the E. side of the river. At the treaty of Albany, in 1754, when the Iroquois disposed of the lands drained by the Juniata, they reserved these lands at Wyoming as a hunting ground, and as a place of refuge from the French, should they be driven to seek an asylum (Col. Rec. Pa., VI, 119, 1851). They then appointed John Shikellimy, son of Shikellimy, to look after these lands for them. At the council at Easton, 1757, Tedyuskung said: "We intend to settle at Wyoming, and we want to have certain boundaries fixed between you and us, and a certain tract of land fixed, which it shall not be lawful for us or our children ever to sell, or for you or any of your children ever to buy" (ibid., VII, 678, 1851). When it was discovered that this land had been sold by the Mohawk at Albany in 1754 to Lydius, the agent of the Connecticut Company, Conrad Weiser declared that the deed was fraudulent and that unless the settlement was prevented an Indian war would result. Hendrick, the Mohawk chief, summoned to Philadelphia, stated that the deed had been obtained by fraud. The extended discussion between Pennsylvania and Connecticut and the fearful slaughter at Wyoming were the results of this transaction. (For details relating to this subject, consult Arch. Pa., II, 120 et seq., 1852; Walton, Conrad Weiser, 193 et seq., 1900.) In 1755 the Mohawk refused to accept the second instalment of the money for the purchase of the lands, although Hendrick had advised them to do so. In July of that year came Braddock's defeat, and then all the discontented Indians sought vengeance for the many grievances they had against Pennsylvania. In 1756 Wyoming was occupied by a mixed population of Delawares, Shawnee, Iroquois, and Mahican, with a few Chickasaw, the Delawares being in the majority. In the early summer of that year Tedyuskung moved to Tioga with his followers. After the council of 1757 the authorities of Pennsylvania offered to enact a law which would grant the Wyoming lands to Tedyuskung and the Delawares forever, but the project was delayed for various reasons, chiefly because the lands had never been bought from the Iroquois. Tedyuskung insisted that a fort and houses be built at Wyoming for the Delawares, and Weiser was asked to look after this work, but declined to do so on account of his health and because he feared the Iroquois would blame him for doing the work. The council then appointed one of their own number to oversee the work; a force of 50 or 60 carpenters and masons was sent to Wyoming, where 10 wooden houses with stone foundations were erected. In the spring of 1758 Tedyuskung went to Philadelphia from Wyoming, to which place he had removed, and asked that schoolmasters, counsellors, and two ministers be sent to his village, saying, "You must consider that I have a soul as well as another" (Col. Rec. Pa., VIII, 47, 1852). At the treaty at Easton, 1758, he again presented the matter of the fraudulent "Walking Purchase," and charged the Mohawk with selling the lands at Wyoming, which had been promised to the Delawares as a permanent home. The old chief had at last to pay with his life the penalty for what he said at this council. In June, 1758, Charles Thomson and Frederick Post started on their journey to Wyoming, but when they reached a point about 15 m. from their destination they were warned by Tedyuskung, who met them, to advance no farther as the woods about Wyoming were filled with hostile Indians (Jour. Thomson and Post in Arch. Pa., III, 412–422, 1853). In the spring of 1763 a number of families from Connecticut settled at Wyoming (Arch. Pa., IV, 105, 1853). This led to an attack by the Indians in which 20 of the settlers were killed (ibid., 127). No more attempts were made to settle there until 1769, when another company of Connecticut immigrants reached the place, and at once commenced the erection of a fort, called Ft Durkee, situated between Ross and South sts., Wilkes-Barré (Frontier Forts of Pa., I, 425, 1896). Other forts were built in this region about this same time: Ft Wyoming (1771), erected by the Pennsylvania authorities for the reduction of Ft Durkee, was situated at the junction of Northampton and River sts.,

Wilkes-Barré; Mill Creek Fort (1772) on the N. side of the creek of the same name; Forty Fort, in the borough of the same name, built in 1770 by the 40 pioneers of the Connecticut Co. who went to the region in 1769. During the hostilities, which became more threatening in 1778, Forty Fort became the place of refuge to which many of the settlers went. In June of that year, when it was known that the large force of the enemy were approaching Wyoming, under Maj. John Butler, the inhabitants sought refuge in the various forts in the region, but on account of its strength and size the majority gathered in Forty Fort. Butler's force of about 1,100 men, consisting of about 200 British, the same number of Tories, and about 700 Indians, chiefly Seneca and Cayuga, descended the Susquehanna and landed a few miles above Wyoming, whence they marched on the night of July 1 and encamped on the mountain at the head of the valley. The next day demand was made for the surrender of the fort, which was refused. The force gathered in the fort numbered fewer than 400 (chiefly old men and boys, unfitted by reason of their age to be at the front with the American army), commanded by Col. Zebulon Butler. The members of the garrison, no doubt mistaken in their estimates of the number of the enemy, marched out on July 3 to attack them. Then followed the battle, the defeat, the flight, and the awful massacre (Frontier Forts of Pa., I, 438 et seq., 1896; Parkman, Conspiracy of Pontiac, II, 109, 1901 (first massacre 1763); Arch. Pa., VI, 626, 629, 631 et seq., 1853; Egle, Hist. Pa., 898–906, 1883). During the fall and winter of 1778 the entire frontier from Wyoming to Ft Pitt was subject to the raids of the Seneca and Cayuga. Washington decided to send an expedition, under Maj.-Gen. John Sullivan, into the Seneca and Cayuga country to destroy the villages and drive the Indians back to the British lines. Sullivan's army reached Wyoming on June 14, where it remained until July 31, awaiting supplies. At that time the village was filled with the widows and orphans of those who had been slain in the massacre of the year previous.

In addition to the works cited, consult Miner, Hist. Wyoming, 1845; Military Exped. Gen. Sullivan, 1887; Wyoming Commem. Asso., Wyoming: A Record of the One Hundredth Year Commem. Observ., 1882; Wyoming Commem. Asso., 116th Anniv. of Battle and Massacre, 1895; the various publications of this association for each year.   (G. P. D.)

Mahaniahy.—Thomas (1742) in Col. Rec. Pa., IV, 572, 1851. **Maughwawame.**—Day, Penn., 431, 1843, **M'cheuómi.**—Heckewelder in Trans. Am. Philos. Soc., n. s., IV, 361, 1834. **M'cheuw á mi.**—Ibid.

M'chwauwaumi.—Day, op. cit. Mechayomy.—Pa. Council (1732) in Col. Rec. Pa., III, 451, 1852. Meehayomy.—Pa. Council (1728), ibid., 326. Scahandowana.—Ft Johnson conf. (1756) in N. Y. Doc. Col. Hist., VII, 48, 1856. Scahentoarrhonon.—Jes. Rel. 1635, 33, 1858 (Huron name of the people). Scha, han, do, a, na.—Clinton (1750) in N. Y. Doc. Col. Hist., VI, 548, 1855. Schahandowa.—Mt Johnson Council (1755) in Arch. Pa., 2d s., VI, 293, 1877. Schahandowana.—Mt Johnson conf. (1755) in N. Y. Doc. Col. Hist., VI, 984, 1855. Seahautowano.—Weiser (1755) in Arch. Pa., II, 259, 1852. Skehandowa.—Writer of 1737 quoted by Ruttenber, Tribes Hudson R., 194, 1872. Waioming.—Zeisberger (1755) in Arch. Pa., II, 459, 1853. Waiomink.—Day, op. cit., 432. Wajomick.—Loskiel (1794) in Rupp, W. Penn., app., 358, 1846. Wajomik.—Drake, Ind. Chron., 184, 1836. Waughwauwame.—Drake, Tecumseh, 13, 1852. Wawamie.—Day, Penn., 432, 1843. Wayomick.—Horsfield (1755) in Arch. Pa., II, 492, 1853. Wayoming.—Ibid., 491. Weoming.—Machin (1779) in Jour. Mil. Exped. Gen. Sullivan, 194, 1887. Weyoming.—Easton conf. (1757) in N. Y. Doc. Col. Hist., VII, 305, 1856. Wioming.—Evans map, 1749. Wiomink.—Peters (1757) in Arch. Pa., III, 288, 1853. Woyming.—Spangenberg (1756) quoted by Rupp, Northampton Co., 95, 1845. Woyumoth.—Allummapees (1743) in Col. Rec. Pa., IV, 643, 1851. Wyaming.—La Tour map, 1782. Wyomen.—Writer of 1759 quoted by Kendall, Trav., II, 281, 1809. Wyomin.—Canassatego (1742) in Col. Rec. Pa., IV, 580, 1851. Wyoming.—Johnson (1756) in R. I. Col. Rec., V, 529, 1860. Wyomink.—Stanwix (1757) in Arch. Pa., III, 301, 1853. Wyomish.—Hess (1756), ibid., 56.

Wysox. A tribe or band reputed to have lived on a small creek which flows into Susquehanna r. at the present Wysox, Bradford co., Pa. According to Day (Penn., 137, 1843), tradition states that this tribe had two sanguinary battles at the mouth of Towanda cr. with Indians living there, probably the Nanticoke. The Wysox may have been Munsee or Delawares. (J. M.)

Wzokhilain. See *Osunkhirhine.*

Xabaagua. A Chumashan village w. of Pueblo de las Canoas (San Buenaventura), Ventura co., Cal., in 1542.—Cabrillo, Narr. (1542), in Smith, Colec. Doc. Fla., 181, 1857.

Xagua. A Chumashan village w. of Pueblo de las Canoas (San Buenaventura), Ventura co., Cal., in 1542.
Sajay (?).—Taylor in Cal. Farmer Apr. 17, 1863. Xagua.—Cabrillo, Narr. (1542), in Smith, Colec. Doc. Fla., 181, 1857. Xaqua.—Taylor, op. cit.

Xaiméla. Mentioned by Oñate (Doc. Inéd., XVI, 113, 1871) as a pueblo of New Mexico in 1598. Doubtless situated in the Salinas, in the vicinity of Abo, E. of the Rio Grande. It seemingly pertained to the Piro or the Tigua.

Xalanaj. A Chumashan village formerly near Santa Barbara, Cal.—Taylor in Cal. Farmer, Apr. 24, 1863.

Xalou. A Chumashan village formerly near Santa Barbara, Cal.—Taylor in Cal. Farmer, Apr. 24, 1863.

Xamachá. A former Diegueño rancheria near San Diego, s. Cal.—Ortega (1775) quoted by Bancroft, Hist. Cal., I, 253, 1884.

Xamunambe. A province, tribe, or village on the South Carolina coast, visited by Ayllon in 1520 and 1521. Barcia says that it was under a chief called Datha.

Xamunambe.—Documentos Inéditos, XIV, 506, 1870. Xamunanuc.—Oviedo, Hist. Gen. Indies, III, 628, 1853. Xumunaumbe.—Barcia, Ensayo, 4, 1723.

Xana. A former Diegueño rancheria near San Diego, s. Cal.—Ortega (1775) quoted by Bancroft, Hist. Cal., I, 253, 1884.

Xapida. A province or tribe on the Carolina coast, visited by Ayllon in 1521, when it was under the chief Datha.
Xapida.—Barcia, Ensayo 4, 1723. Xapira.—Oviedo, Hist. Gen. Indies, III, 628, 1853.

Xarame (probably pronounced cha-rä′-me). A Coahuiltecan tribe, well known in the 18th century at several Franciscan missions. They seem to have been natives of the region of San Antonio, Tex. In 1699 they were in Coahuila at both San Juan Bautista and San Francisco Solano, below the present Eagle Pass, on the Rio Grande (Portillo, Apuntes, 271, 279, 1888). Soon after this date they were the chief tribe at the latter mission, a Xarame being its "governor" (Paredes, Visita, 1729, par. 7, MS.). Of the 144 Indians baptized there in 1704, 22 were Xarames (Bap. Rec., MS.). When, in 1718, Father Olivares transferred this mission to San Antonio r., Texas, and reestablished it as that of San Antonio de Valero, he took with him the Xarame neophytes to serve as teachers and examples for the Payaya and other new tribes to be gathered (Olivares, Carta, in Mem. de Nueva España, XXVII, 169, MS.). The first baptism at San Antonio de Valero was that of a Xarame child, and the tribe was still represented at that mission late in the 18th century. (H. E. B.)
Charame.—Doc. of May 13, 1752, in Bexár Archives. Chaulamas.—Fr. Isidro Felix de Espinosa, Diary, 1709, MS. Jarame.—Fr. Guerra, 1720, in Valero Baptismal Rec., MS. Jarames.—Morfi (1777) quoted by Bancroft, Nat. Races, I, 612, 1886. Jurame.—Fr. Benito Sanchez, 1727, ibid. Sarame.—Fr. Francisco Ruiz, 1715, ibid. Schiarame.—Residencia of Gov. Bustillo y Zevallos, 1734, MS. in Bexar Archives. Schyarame.—Ibid. Xaram.—Fr. De Soto, 1713, in Solano Baptismal Rec., MS. Xárame.—Fr. Espinosa, Diario, June 10–13, 1716, MS. Xarames.—Revillagigedo (1793) quoted by Bancroft, Nat. Races, 611, 1886. Xharame.—Fr. Prado, 1737, in Valero Baptismal Rec., MS. Zarame.—Fr. Francisco de los Dolores, 1739, ibid.

Xaseum. A former village connected with San Carlos mission, Cal., and said to have been Esselen. It was 10 leagues from Carmelo, in the Sierra, near Pachhepes.—Taylor in Cal. Farmer, Apr. 20, 1860.

Xatóe. Mentioned by Oñate (Doc. Inéd., XVI, 113, 1871) as a pueblo of New Mexico in 1598. Doubtless situated in the Salinas, in the vicinity of Abo, E. of the Rio Grande. It seemingly pertained to the Piro or the Tigua.
Xatol.—Bancroft, Ariz. and N. Mex., 135, 1889 (misprint). Zatoe.—Columbus Mem. Vol., 154, 1893 (misprint).

Xeripam. A tribe named in 1708 in a list of those that had been encountered or heard of to the N. E. of San Juan Bautista mission, on the lower Rio Grande. Although the Yerbipiamos (Ervipiames) are given in the same document as one of the tribes living N. of the mission, the two names probably applied to the same tribe, the Ervipiame (Fr. Isidro Felix de Espinosa, "Relacion Compendiosa" of the Rio Grande missions, MS. in the archives of the College of Santa Cruz de Querétaro).   (H. E. B.)

Xiabu. A village, probably Coahuiltecan, encountered in Coahuila in 1689 by De León (Derrotero, MS.), 5 leagues s. of the Rio Grande, when on his way to Texas.

Xinesi (probably pronounced chē-nä´-sē). The high-priest of the Hasinai confederacy of E. Texas. The bonds of this confederacy, which included about a dozen tribes, seem to have been rather more religious than political. The Hainai was regarded as the head tribe, and what gave it its prestige was the location on its western border, near Angelina r., of the chief temple containing the sacred fire, from which directly or indirectly all the household fires were kindled. For religious purposes there was first a sub-grouping of the confederacy. Thus, for ordinary occasions, the Neche and Hainai tribes held their ceremonies and festivals together, while the Nacogdoche and Nasoni formed another group. But many of their religious and social functions included the whole confederacy. Such were held at the chief fire temple. Presiding over this temple was the head priest called the *xinesi*, or *chenesi*. According to Espinosa, *chenesi* seems to have been a general term meaning priest, yet even he ordinarily restricted the name to this head priest. Terán, Jesus María, and Massanet agree in regarding the *xinesi* as the highest individual authority in the group, but they do not give the same view as to the nature of his position. Massanet regarded him as a high priest; Espinosa regarded him mainly in this light, but testified that his authority was superior to that of any chief; Jesus María calls him not only a priest, but also a "little king," and tells of his great authority as a ruler. The details given as to his functions, however, indicate that he was primarily a priest, but that through his personal dignity and priestly influence he outranked all others, and that his word had great authority in civil as well as in religious affairs.

The *xinesi* lived, as has been indicated, in the center of the confederacy, near Angelina r., w. of Nacogdoches. According to Jesus María, his office was hereditary, and the inference from all circumstances is that it was attached to the Hainai tribe. The most important duty of the *xinesi* was to care for the fire temple near his house, and to consult the Coninisi, or fictitious twin boys, by means of which he talked with the Great Chief Above. The early writers convey the impression that the *xinesi* was a person of great dignity, doing no manual labor, and commanding great personal respect. He was fed and clothed, we are told, by community gifts, to insure which he sometimes preyed upon the superstition of his people. At the house of each *caddi*, or civil chief, and of each of the other dignitaries, a special seat of honor and a bed were scrupulously reserved for the use of the *xinesi* during his visits. (Consult Espinosa, Crónica Apostólica, pt. I, 421, 424, 425, 432, 1746; Jesus María, Relación, 1691, MS.; Massanet, Carta, in Quar. Tex. Hist. Asso., II, 305–312, 1899; Terán, Descripción y Diaria Demarcación, 1691, in Mem. de Nueva España, XXVII, 48, MS.)   (H. E. B.)

Xisca. A village, presumably Costanoan, formerly connected with San Juan Bautista mission, Cal.
Xisca.—Taylor in Cal. Farmer, Nov. 23, 1860. Xiscaca.—Englehardt, Franc. in Cal., 398, 1897.

Xivirca. A village, presumably Costanoan, formerly connected with San Juan Bautista mission, Cal.—Taylor in Cal. Farmer, Nov. 23, 1860.

Xocotoc. A Chumashan village w. of Pueblo de las Canoas (San Buenaventura), Ventura co., Cal., in 1542.
Xocotoc.—Cabrillo, Narr. (1542), in Smith, Colec. Doc. Fla., 181, 1857. Xotococ.—U. S. Geog. and Geol. Surv., VII, 307, 1879.

Xoxi. Mentioned by Oviedo (Hist. Gen. Indies, III, 628, 1853) as one of the provinces or villages visited by Ayllon, probably on the South Carolina coast, in 1520.

Xuacaya. A province or tribe on the Carolina coast, visited by Ayllon in 1521.—Barcia, Ensayo, 5, 1723.

Xugua. A Chumashan village, probably identical with Guacaya (q. v.), formerly on Santa Cruz id. (San Lucas of Cabrillo), Cal.
Ca-wa´.—Henshaw, Buenaventura MS. vocab., B. A. E., 1884 (c=sh). Xugua.—Cabrillo, Narr. (1542), in Smith, Colec. Doc. Fla., 181, 1857. Xuqua.—Taylor in Cal. Farmer, Apr. 17, 1863.

Xumis. A former village connected with San Carlos mission, Cal., and said to have belonged to the Esselen.—Taylor in Cal. Farmer, Apr. 20, 1860.

Xumskhumesilis (*Xúmsχumesīlis*). An ancestor of a Quatsino gens after whom the gens was sometimes named.—Boas in Petermanns Mitteil., pt. 5, 131, 1887.

Xutis. Mentioned by Oñate (Doc. Inéd., XVI, 103, 1871) as a pueblo of New Mexico in 1598. Unidentified.

Yaaga (*Ya´-aga*, 'little willows'). A former large village that formed the center of the Klamath settlements on Williamson r., about a mile from Upper Klamath lake, Oreg., where the Linkville-Ft Klamath road crosses the stream.—Gatschet in Cont. N. A. Ethnol., II, pt. I, xxix, 1890.

Yaaihakemae (*Yaai'x·aqɛmaē*, 'the crabs'). A gens of the Komoyue, a.sept of the true Kwakiutl, and a clan of the Tenaktak.
Yaai'Hak·ɛmaē.—Boas in 6th Rep. N. W. Tribes Can., 54, 1890. Yaai'x·aqɛmaē.—Boas in Rep. U. S. Nat. Mus. 1895, 330, 1897. Yix̣āqɛmāe.—Boas in Petermanns Mitteil., pt. 5, 131, 1887.

Yaasitun (*Ya'-a-si'-tûn*). A Takelma band or village on the s. side of Rogue r., Oreg.—Dorsey in Jour. Am. Folk-lore, III, 235, 1890.

Yacdossa. A former small tribe represented at San Antonio de Valero mission, Texas.

Yacherk. A Nushagagmiut Eskimo village on Igushik r., Alaska.
Yachérgamut.—Spurr quoted by Baker, Geog. Dict. Alaska, 1902 (*mut*=*miut*, 'people'). Yacherk.—Baker, ibid.

Yachikamni. Mentioned by Pinart as the tribe that originally lived on the site of the present city of Stockton, Cal., and hence belonged to the Cholovone tribe of the Mariposan (Yokuts) family. The same is said by Taylor of the Yachimese, the tribes being apparently identical.
Ochecames.—Bancroft, Hist. Cal., IV, 138, 1886. Ochecamnes.—Hale, Ethnog. and Philol., VI, 630, 1846. Ochekamnes.—Gallatin in Trans. Am. Ethnol. Soc., II, 123, 1848. Ochocumnes.—Bancroft, Hist. Cal., IV, 138, 1886. Yachachumnes.—Taylor in Cal. Farmer, June 8, 1860. Yachchumnes.—Ibid., Feb. 22. Yachimese.—Ibid., Dec. 7, 1860. Yatchikamnes.—Pinart, Cholovone MS., B. A. E., 1880. Yatchikumne.—Ibid.

Yachin ('mesquite'). An Apache band or clan at San Carlos agency and Ft Apache, Ariz., in 1881.
Ya-chin.—Bourke in Jour. Am. Folk-lore, III, 112, 1890.

Yacomanshaghking (apparently a corruption of *Yagawanshaking*, 'at the place of small huts.'—Gerard). A Delaware tribe or band that dwelt on the E. bank of Delaware r. in New Jersey, on a small stream about the present Camden.—Herrman, map (1670), in Rep. on Line between Va. and Md., 1873.

Yacomui. A village, presumably Costanoan, formerly connected with Dolores mission, San Francisco, Cal.
Yacomui.—Taylor in Cal. Farmer, Oct. 18, 1861. Yacumi.—Ibid.

Yacum. A warlike Diegueño band, in alliance with the Cocopa, occupying a valley in the mountains between the desert and the Gulf coast, chiefly in Lower California. They were said to number fewer than 200 in 1853. They raised corn, melons, pumpkins, beans, and other crops, by irrigation.
Guaicamaopa.—Kino (*ca.* 1699) in Doc. Hist. Mex., 4th s., I, 349, 1856 (located by Kino at junction of the Gila and the Colorado, but probably the identical tribe; *opa* is a Pima word signifying 'people'). Ha-coom.—Heintzelman (1853) in H. R. Ex. Doc. 76, 34th Cong., 3d sess., 34–53, 1857. Jacum.—Ibid. Yacum.—Ibid.

Yadus (*Yä'dʌs*). An important subdivision of the Stustas, a great Haida family of the Eagle clan. It constituted one of the Kaigani families, and was subdivided like them (in the Tlingit style) into 5 house-groups: Ildjunai-hadai, Naalgus-hadai, Nakons-hadai, Otkialnaashadai, and Otnaas-hadai.—Swanton, Cont. Haida, 276, 1905.

Yagats (*Ya'-gats*). A Paiute band formerly at Amargoza, s. E. Cal.—Powell in Ind. Aff. Rep. 1873, 51, 1874.

Yagenechito (Choctaw: 'large land'). A tribe, probably affiliated with the Chitimacha, located on De l'Isle's map (1703) on Bayou Lafourche, La.
Magenesito.—Iberville (1699) in Margry, Déc., IV, 172, 1880. Yagenechito.—Ibid., 184. Yagnetsito.—De l'Isle, map, 1703. Yaguenechitons.—La Harpe (1706) in French, Hist. Coll. La., III, 35, 1851. Yagueneschito.—Iberville, op. cit., 155.

Yagnashoogawa (possibly for *Yakniachukma*, 'good country'). A former Choctaw town, noted by Romans in 1775 and perhaps identifiable with a traditional town on Indian branch of Running Tiger cr., Kemper co., Miss.—Halbert in Pub. Miss. Hist. Soc., VI, 425, 1902.

Yagua. A Calusa village on the s. w. coast of Florida, about 1570.—Fontaneda Mem. (*ca.* 1575), Smith trans., 19, 1854.

Yagun. An ancient Haida town formerly on the N. coast of Queen Charlotte ids., Brit. Col.
Yā'gʌn.—Swanton, Cont. Haida, 281, 1905.

Yagunkun-lnagai (*Ya'gun-kun-lnagā'-i*, 'Yagun river point-town people'). A branch of the Kuna-lanas, a great Haida family belonging to the Raven clan. The Yagun is the largest stream on the Queen Charlotte ids.   (J. R. S.)
Yāgun kunílnagai'.—Boas, 12th Rep. N. W. Tribes Can., 23, 1898. Ya'gun kun lnagā'-i.—Swanton, Cont. Haida, 271, 1905.

Yagunstlan-lnagai (*Ya'gun sʟ!an lnagā'-i*, 'Yagun river rear-town people'). A local subdivision of the Stlengalanas, a Haida family belonging to the Raven clan.—Swanton, Cont. Haida, 271, 1905.

Yahach. A former Alsea village on the Pacific coast s. of the mouth of the Alsea r., Oreg.
Yahatc.—Dorsey in Jour. Am. Folk-lore, III, 230, 1890. Yahats.—Ibid. Ya'-qai-yŭk.—Ibid. Yawhick.—Ind. Aff. Rep., 107, 1856. Yawhuch.—Ibid., 80, 1863. Youitts.—Lewis and Clark Exped., II, 118, 1814. Youitz.—Drake, Bk. Inds., xi, 1848.

Yahal. A Yaquina village on the N. side of Yaquina r., Oreg.
Ya'-häl.—Dorsey in Jour. Am. Folk-lore, III, 229, 1890.

Yahalgi ('wolf people'). A clan of the Creeks.
Yä'-hä.—Morgan, Anc. Soc., 161, 1878. Yahálgi.—Gatschet, Creek Migr. Leg., I, 155, 1884 (*algi*= 'people').

Yahandika (*Yáhandika*, 'ground-hog eaters'). Given by Hoffman (Proc. Am. Philos. Soc., XXIII, 298, 1886) as one of the former divisions of the Shoshoni.

Yahksis. The principal village of the

Kelsemaht, on Flores id., Clayoquot sd., w. coast of Vancouver id , with 76 inhabitants in 1909.

Yahuskin. A Shoshonean band which prior to 1864 roved and hunted with the Walpapi about the shores of Goose, Silver, Warner, and Harney lakes, Oreg., and temporarily in Surprise valley and Klamath marsh, where they gathered wokas for food. They came specially into notice in 1864, on Oct. 14 of which year they became party to the treaty of Klamath lake by which their territory was ceded to the United States and they were placed on Klamath res., established at that time. With the Walpapi and a few Paiute who had joined them, the Yahuskin were assigned lands in the southern part of the reservation, on Sprague r. about Yainax, where they have since resided, although through intermarriage with other Indians on the reservation their tribal identity became lost by 1898, since which time they have been officially designated as Paiute. Gatschet, who visited them about 1884, says they were then engaged in agriculture, lived in willow lodges and log houses, and were gradually abandoning their roaming proclivities. The Yahuskin have always been officially enumerated with the Walpapi, the aggregate population varying between 1877 and 1891 from 135 to 166 persons. In 1909 they were reported at 103.

Gahooskins.—Applegate in Ind. Aff. Rep., 90, 1866. Yahooshkin.—Gatschet in Cont. N. A. Ethnol., ii, pt. 1, xxxv, 1890. Yahooskin.—Treaty of 1864 in Ind. Laws and Treaties, ii, 663, 1903. Yahooskin Snakes.—H. R. Rep. 98, 42d Cong., 3d sess., 449, 1873. Yahuskin.—Meacham in Ind. Aff. Rep., 52, 1870.

Yaka. The Corn clans of the Keresan pueblos at Laguna, Acoma, Santa Ana, Sia, San Felipe, and Cochiti, N. Mex. The Corn clans of Acoma (Kochinish, Yellow; Kukanish, Red; Kuishkosh, Blue; Kuishtiti, Brown; and Kusesh, White) formed a phratry, as do the Yellow and Red Corn clans of Laguna, who claim to have come originally from Acoma. The Blue, Brown, and White Corn clans of Acoma are now extinct. The varying forms of the clan name among the different Keresan villages are: Laguna, *Yáka-háno ch*; Acoma, *Yáka-hánoq ch*; Santa Ana, *Yak'-háno;* Sia and San Felipe, *Yáka-háno;* Cochiti, *Yák'a-hánuch.* The termination *háno,* etc., signifies 'people.'—Hodge in Am. Anthr., ix, 349, 1896.

Yá-ka.—Stevenson in 11th Rep. B. A. E., 19, 1894. Yakka.—Bandelier, Delight Makers, 257, 1890.

Yakchilak. A Kuskwogmiut Eskimo village near the mouth of Kuskokwim r., Alaska.

Yachtshilágamiut.—Spurr and Post quoted by Baker, Geog. Dict. Alaska, 1902. Yakchilak.—Baker, ibid.

Yakima (*Ya-ki-má*, 'runaway'). An important Shahaptian tribe, formerly living on both sides of the Columbia and on the northerly branches of the Yakima (formerly Tapteal) and the Wenatchee, in Washington. They are mentioned by Lewis and Clark in 1806 under the name Cutsahnim (possibly the name of a chief) and estimated as 1,200 in number, but there is no certainty as to the bands included under that figure. In 1855 the United States made a treaty with the Yakima and 13 other tribes of Shahaptian, Salishan, and Chinookan stocks, by which they ceded the territory from the Cascade mts. to Palouse and Snake rs. and from L. Chelan to the Columbia, and the Yakima res. was established, upon which all the

YAKIMA MAN

participating tribes and bands were to be confederated as the Yakima nation under the leadership of Kamaiakan (q. v.), a distinguished Yakima chief. Before this treaty could be ratified the Yakima war broke out, and it was not until 1859 that the provisions of the treaty were carried into effect. The Paloos and certain other tribes have never recognized the treaty or come on the reservation. Since the establishment of the reservation the term Yakima has been generally used in a comprehensive sense to include all the tribes within its limits, so that it is now impossible to estimate the number of Yakima proper. The total Indian population of the reservation was officially estimated at 1,900 in 1909, but of this number probably comparatively few are true

Yakima. The native name of the Yakima is *Waptailmim*, 'people of the narrow river,' or *Pá'kiut'lĕma*, 'people of the gap,' both names referring to the narrows in Yakima r. at Union Gap, where their chief village was formerly situated. Other bands were the Setaslema, of Setass cr., and the Pisko, of the lower Yakima. Little is known of the particular customs of the Yakima, but there is no reason to suppose that their life differed greatly from that of the Nez Percés (q. v.) and other Shahaptian peoples. Consult Mooney in 14th Rep. B. A. E., pt. 2, 1896.　　　　　(J. M.)

Cat-sa-nim.—Gibbs in Pac. R. R. Rep., I, 417, 1855 (misquoting Lewis and Clark). Cutsahnim.—Lewis and Clark Exped., II, 475, 1814. Cut-sa-nim.—Ind. Aff. Rep., 252, 1854. Cuts-sáh-nem.—Clark (1805) in Orig. Jour. Lewis and Clark, III, 128, 1905. Cuts-sah-nim.—Orig. Jour., ibid., VI, 119, 1905. E'yack-im-ah.—Ross, Fur Hunters, I, 185, 1855. Iaákema.—Hale in U. S. Expl. Exped., VI, 213, 1846. I-ákima.—Gatschet, MS., B. A. E. (Okinagan name). Jaakema.—Hale, op. cit., 569. Pa'kiut-'lĕma.—Mooney in 14th Rep. B. A. E., 737, 1896. Pishwanwapum.—Tolmie quoted by Lord, Nat. in Brit. Col., II, 245, 1866. Pshawanwappam.—Keane in Stanford, Compend., 531, 1878. Shanwappoms.—Lewis and Clark Exped., II, 595, 1817. Shanwappones.—Morse, Rep. to Sec. War, 372, 1822. Stobshaddat.—Lord, Nat. in Brit. Col., II, 246, 1866 ('robbers': so called by Puget Sound tribes). Takama.—Stevens in Sen. Ex. Doc. 34, 33d Cong., 1st sess., 16, 1854. Tobc'-a-dûd.—McCaw, Puyallup MS. vocab., B. A. E., 1885 (Puyallup name). Wa'pamĕtănt.—Mooney in 14th Rep. B. A. E., 744, 1896. Waptai'lmim.—Mooney, ibid., 737. Yāä'kimā.—Chamberlain in Rep. N. W. Tribes Canada, 8, 1892 (Kutenai name; said, by folk-etymology perhaps, to mean 'foot bent toward the instep'). Yacaaws.—Schoolcraft, Ind. Tribes, I, 521, 1853. Yacamaws.—Lane in Sen. Ex. Doc. 52, 31st Cong., 1st sess., 174, 1850. Yackaman.—Cox, Columbia R., II, 14, 1831. Yackamaws.—Lane in Sen. Ex. Doc. 52, 31st Cong., 1st sess., 8, 1850. Yackaws.—Lane in Schoolcraft, Ind. Tribes, III, 632, 1853. Yackimas.—Dart in Ind. Aff. Rep., 216, 1851. Yacomans.—Smet, New Ind. Sketches, 92, 1895. Yakamas.—Stevens in Ind. Aff. Rep., 231, 1854. Yakanias.—Douglas in H. R. Misc. Doc. 98, 30th Cong., 1st sess., 15, 1848. Yakemas.—Hale in U. S. Expl. Exped., VI, 213, 1846. Yakenia.—Medill in H. R. Ex. Doc. 76, 30th Cong., 1st sess., 6, 1848. Yakima.—Gibbs in Pac. R. R. Rep., I, 467, 1855. Yakimaw.—Tolmie quoted by Lord, Nat. in Brit. Col., II, 245, 1866. Yankamas.—Gray, Hist. Oreg., 94, 1870. Yookoomans.—Parker, Jour., 318, 1846.

Yakonan Family. A linguistic family formerly occupying a territory in w. Oregon, on and adjacent to the coast from Yaquina r. s. to Umpqua r. The family was probably never strong in numbers and of late years has declined rapidly. The few survivors are on the Siletz res., in Oregon. The family is of considerable ethnologic interest, since it apparently represents the southern limit of a type of culture exhibited particularly by the Chinookan, Salishan, and other tribes of the coast of Washington and Vancouver id. The Athapascan tribes of s. Oregon and N. California seem to have been more deeply affected by contact with Californian stocks.

The Yakonan conformed physically to the general type of the N. W. coast and are notable as marking the southern limit in that region of the practice of artificial deformation of the head. Their social organization is not fully understood, but there was no totemic clan system, though a tendency to local segregation of groups related by blood was evident in their villages. There was also a preference for marriage outside the tribe, though this did not have the force of an exogamous rule, so far as can be learned. The social orders of nobility and common people, peculiar to the N. W. coast, obtained, and slavery was an institution in full force until the tribes came under the control of the United States. The Yakonan mythology and traditions are distinctly of the type of the coast tribes of Washington, but they show traces of modification by contact with the Californian stocks on the s. The family was composed of 4 tribes occupying adjacent districts, which, from N. to s., were: Yaquina, Alsea, Siuslaw, and Kuitsh. These tribes have played an unimportant rôle in history and little is known of them. On the formation of the Siletz res. in 1855 they were removed thither, and since that time they have declined so rapidly in numbers, principally through the ravages of tuberculosis, that they are now on the verge of extinction.　(L. F.)

>Yakones.—Hale in U. S. Expl. Exped., VI, 198, 218, 1846 (or Iakon, coast of Oregon); Buschmann, Spuren der aztek. Sprache, 612, 1859. >Iakon.—Hale in U. S. Expl. Exped., VI, 218, 569, 1846 (or Lower Killamuks); Buschmann, Spuren der aztek. Sprache, 612, 1859. >Jacon.—Gallatin in Trans. Am. Ethnol. Soc., II, pt. 1, c, 77, 1848. >Jakon.—Gallatin in Trans. Am. Ethnol. Soc., II, pt. 1, 17, 1848; Berghaus (1851), Physik. Atlas, map 17, 1852; Gallatin in Schoolcraft, Ind. Tribes, III, 402, 1853 (language of lower Killamuks); Latham in Trans. Philol. Soc. Lond., 73, 1856; Latham, Opuscula, 340, 1860. >Yakon.—Latham, Nat. Hist. Man, 324, 1850; Gatschet, in Mag. Am. Hist., 166, 1877; Gatschet in Beach, Ind. Misc., 441, 1877; Bancroft, Nat. Races, III, 565, 640, 1882. >Yákona.—Gatschet in Mag. Am. Hist., 256, 1882. =Yakonan.—Powell in 7th Rep., B. A. E., 133, 1891. >Southern Killamuks.—Hale in U. S. Expl. Exped., VI, 218, 569, 1846 (or Yakones); Gallatin in Trans. Am. Ethnol. Soc., II, 17, 1848 (after Hale). >Süd Killamuk.—Berghaus (1851), Physik. Atlas, map 17, 1852. >Sainstskla.—Latham, Nat. Hist. Man, 325, 1850 ("south of the Yakon, between the Umkwa and the sea"). >Sayúskla.—Gatschet in Mag. Am. Hist., 257, 1882 (on Lower Umpqua, Sayúskla, and Smith rivers). >Killiwashat.—Latham, Nat. Hist. Man, 325, 1850 ("mouth of the Umkwa"). ×Klamath.—Keane in Stanford, Compend., Cent. and So. Am., 475, 1878 (cited as including Yacons).

Yaku (*Yak!u*). A Haida town of the Dostlan-lnagai family, that formerly stood on the N. w. coast of Graham id., opposite North id., Queen Charlotte ids., Brit. Col. This town, or it and the neighboring one of Kiusta together, may be that designated Lu-lan-na by John Work, 1836–41, to which he assigned 20 houses and 296 people. Old people remember 4 large houses and 4 small ones in Yaku, and 9 houses in Kiusta. This would seem to indicate a population in Yaku proper of about 100 to 120.　(J. R. S.)

Ia'k'ō.—Boas, 12th Rep. N. W. Tribes Can., 22, 1898. Kakoh.—Dawson, Q. Charlotte Ids., 162B,

1880 (corrupted form). **Yak!ᵘ.**—Swanton, Cont. Haida, 281, 1905. **Yukh.**—Deans, Tales from Hidery, 94, 1899.

Yaku-gitinai (*Yā'ku gitinā'-i*, 'the middle Giti'ns'). A subdivision of the Hlgahet-gitinai, a Haida family of the Eagle clan. They received their name from having lived in the middle of Skidegate village; there they killed a chief and fled to the w. coast.—Swanton, Cont. Haida, 274, 1905.

Yaku-lanas (*Yā'ku lā'nas*, 'middle-town people'). A large and important Haida family belonging to the Raven clan. By the Skidegate people it is said they were so named because they occupied the middle row in a legendary five-row town, where all the Raven side formerly lived (see *Skena*). The Masset people attributed it to the fact that wherever the members of this family settled they occupied the middle of the village. They are said to have come originally from the s. end of Queen Charlotte ids., but the greater part finally moved to Alaska, where they constituted the most important Raven family among the Kaigani. One subdivision, the Aoyaku-lnagai, settled in Masset inlet. Of the Kaigani part of the family there were 4 subdivisions, the Kaad-naas-hadai, Yehl-naas-hadai, Skistlai-nai-hadai, and Nakaduts-hadai. The extinct Ta-ahl-lanas of North id. perhaps belonged to it. Before they left Queen Charlotte ids. their principal town was Dadens. In Alaska it was Klinkwan. The Hlgahet-gu-lanas are said to have once been a part of this family.—Swanton, Cont. Haida, 271, 1905. **Yak' lā'nas.**—Boas, 12th Rep. N. W. Tribes Can., 22, 1898. **Yākwū Lennas.**—Harrison in Proc. Roy. Soc. Can., sec. II, 125, 1895.

Yakutat. A Tlingit tribe centering around the bay of the same name, but extending northward to Copper r. and southward to Dry bay, Alaska. Pop. 826 in 1880, 436 in 1890. Their principal winter town is Yakutat. According to a contributor to *The Alaskan*, the town on Dry bay is called Satah. Emmons considers the Dry bay and Chilkat (Controller bay) Indians as distinct divisions. A summer village near Copper r. is named Chilkat, and Gonaho, Gutheni, and Hlahayik are the names of former towns. Social divisions are Ganahadi, Kashkekoan, Koskedi, and Tekoedi. (J. R. S.)

Chlach-ă-jĕk.—Krause, Tlinkit Ind., 98, 1885. **Jakhuthắth.**—Holmberg, Ethnog. Skizz., map, 142, 1855. **Jakutat.**—Prichard, Phys. Hist. Man., v, 370, 1847. **Jakŭtat-kön.**—Krause, Tlinkit Ind., 116, 1855. **Klahinks.**—Colyer (1869) in Ind. Aff. Rep., 535, 1870. **Łahayĭ'kqoan.**—Swanton, field-notes, B. A. E. (usual name applied by themselves). **Thlar-har-yeek-gwan.**—Emmons in Mem. Am. Mus. Nat. Hist., III, 230, 1903. **Yahkutats.**—Elliott, Cond. Aff. Alaska, 30, 1874. **Yakutats.**—Dall in Proc. Am. A. A. S. 1869, XVIII, 269, 1870. **Yakutatskoe.**—Veniaminoff, Zapiski, II, pt. III, 29, 1840. **Yucatats.**—Mahoney in Ind. Aff. Rep. 1869, 575, 1870.

Yakutat. The principal town of the Yakutat tribe on the bay of the same name in Alaska. Pop. 300 in 1890.
Yākᵘdā't.—Swanton, field notes, B. A. E., 1904.

YAKUTAT PRIEST

Yakwal ('drifted ones,' from *yákwaná*, 'I am carried off by water'). A tribe traditionally found by the Tonkawa on the Gulf coast near Galveston, Texas. They recognized the Yakwal language as a dialect of their own and believed that the separation had been caused by a flood. See *Yojuane*. (A. S. G.)

Yalacasooche. A former Seminole town at the mouth of Ocklawaha r., Putnam co., Fla.—H. R. Ex. Doc. 74 (1823), 19th Cong., 1st sess., 27, 1826.

Yalaka. A former Seminole town 35 m. w. of Volusia or Dexter, in w. Marion co., Fla.—**Amathlas.**—H. R. Doc. 78, 25th Cong., 2d sess., map, 768-9, 1838. **Charles Old Town.**—Drake, Book Inds., bk. IV, 151, 1848 (probably identical). **Charley Emathla's Town.**—Taylor, War map of Fla., 1839. **Yalaka.**—H. R. Ex. Doc. 74 (1823), 19th Cong., 1st sess., 27, 1826.

Yalik. A Kaniagmiut Eskimo village on Nuka bay, E. coast of Kenai penin., Alaska; pop. 32 in 1880.—Petroff in Tenth Census, Alaska, 29, 1884.

Yalisumni. A former Maidu village near Salmon Falls, on the s. side of the South fork of American r., Eldorado co., Cal.—Dixon in Bull. Am. Mus. Nat. Hist., XVII, map, 1905.

Yamacraw. A detached town of the Creek confederacy, formerly on Yamacraw bluff, on the s. bank of Savannah r., in what is now the western suburb of Savannah, Ga. It was settled about 1730 by a small party of outlawed Creeks, with a few Yamasee, numbering in all about 17 or 18 families and 30 or 40 men, under the leadership of Tomochichi (q. v.), who for "some mischief in their own country" had been driven out from among the Lower Creek towns. In 1732 they asked and received from the South Carolina government formal permission to remain in their new settlement, and on the arrival of the Georgia colony under Oglethorpe in the next year Tomochichi made himself instrumental in bringing about a treaty between Georgia and the Lower Creeks, resulting in a reconciliation between himself and his tribe, with permission to bring other friends from the Creek towns to settle at the new location. The site was reserved by the Indians for their own use, but was probably abandoned soon after the death of Tomochichi in 1739.

The Indians of Yamacraw were not a distinct tribe, as has frequently been represented, but simply a refugee band of Creeks, who returned to their original homes after the ban had been removed. At the same time it seems evident that it was composed largely of descendants of those who had lived formerly in this neighborhood and had subsequently retired among the Creeks. The name is of uncertain etymology and seems to be a corrupted form, the Creek language having no r; neither has it any apparent connection with Yamasee. Nevertheless it should be compared with the Yamiscaron

recorded as far back as the expedition of Ayllon in 1520–21. Consult Gatschet, Creek Migr. Leg., I, II, 1884, 1888; Jones, Hist. Sketch of Tomochichi, 1868; Jones, Hist. of Ga., 1883. (J. M. J. R. S.) **Yamacraw.**—Moore (1744) in Ga. Hist. Soc. Coll., I, 103, 1840. **Yammacraw.**—Morse, N. A., 208, 1776.

Yamako. A former Maidu village, about 9 m. E. of Nevada City, Nevada co., Cal.—**Yamagatock.**—Bancroft, Nat. Races, I, 450, 1874 (probably identical). **Yamako.**—Dixon in Bull. Am. Mus. Nat. Hist., XVII, map, 1905. **Yumagatock.**—Bancroft, op. cit.

Yamasee (a name of uncertain etymology, and evidently an abbreviated form). A former noted tribe of Muskhogean stock, best known in connection with early South Carolina history, but apparently occupying originally the coast region and islands of s. Georgia, and extending into Florida. From their residence near Savannah r. they have frequently been confused with the "Savannahs," or Shawano, and the Yuchi. Missions were established in their territory by the Spaniards about 1570, and they lived under the jurisdiction of the Spanish government of Florida until 1687, when, in consequence of an attempt to transport a number of their people as laborers to the West Indies, they revolted, attacked a number of the mission settlements and peaceful Indians, and then fled N. across Savannah r. to the English colony of South Carolina. They were allowed to settle within the present limits of Beaufort co., where at a later period they had several villages, the principal of which was Pocotaligo; others were Tolemato and Topiqui(?). They aided against the Tuscarora in 1712, but in 1715, in consequence of dissatisfaction with the traders, organized a combination against the English which included all, or nearly all, the tribes from C. Fear to the Florida border. The traders were slaughtered in the Indian towns and a general massacre of settlers took place along the Carolina frontier. After several engagements the Yamasee were finally defeated by Gov. Craven at Salkechuh (Saltketchers) on the Combahee and driven across the Savannah. They retired in a body to Florida where they were again received by the Spaniards and settled in villages near St Augustine. From that time they were known as allies of the Spaniards and enemies of the English, against whom they made frequent raids in company with other Florida Indians. A small part of them also appear to have taken refuge with the Catawba, where, according to Adair, they still retained their separate identity in 1743. In 1727 their village near St Augustine was attacked and destroyed by the English, and their Indian allies and most of the inhabitants were killed.   In 1761 the remnant was said to number about 20 men, residing near St Augustine, and they seem also to have had a small settlement near Pensacola. The tradition of their destruction and enslavement by the Seminole is noted by several writers of this and a later period. As late as 1812 a small band retained the name among the Seminole, and some settled among the Hitchiti, but they have now completely disappeared. They were said to be darker than the Creeks, and "flat-footed," and from their proficiency as canoe men gave name to a particular method of rowing known as the "Yamasee stroke."   (J. M.)

Eamuses.—Morse, Rep. to Sec. War, 364, 1822 (extinct; Yamasi probably meant). Iamaços.—Barcia, Ensayo, 287, 1723. Jamasees.—Brinton, op. cit. Tammasees.—Oldmixon in Carroll, Hist. Coll. S. C., II, 413, 1836 (misprint *T* for *Y*). Wimosas.—Woodward, Rem., 25, 1859 (misprint). Yamaçes.—Barcia, op. cit., 348. Yamas.—Schoolcraft, Ind. Tribes, VI, 370, 1857. Yamasees.—McKenney and Hall, Ind. Tribes, III, 82, 1854 (misprint). Yamasees.—Archdale, Carolina, 356, 1707. Yamases.—Bartram, Travels, 378, 1792. Yamassalgi.—Gatschet, Creek Migr. Leg., I, 63, 1884 (Creek name, pl. form). Yamassees.—Rafinesque in Marshall, Ky., introd., 27, 1824. Yámassi.—Gatschet, Creek Migr. Leg., I, 63, 1884. Yamesee.—Moll's map in Humphrey, Acct., 1730. Yammassees.—Brinton, op. cit. Yammonsee.—Thomas (1702) in Hawkins, Missions, 48, 1845. Yammosees.—Humphrey, Acct., x, 1730. Yamoisees.—Drake, Ind. Chron., 173, 1836. Yamossees.—Carroll, Hist. Coll. S. C., II, 549, 1836. Yanioseaves.—Oldmixon (1708) in Carroll, Hist. Coll. S. C., II, 424, 1836 (misprint). Yemasee.—Gatschet, op. cit., I, 63, Yemassees.—Brinton, op. cit. Yemmassaws.—Gatschet, op. cit. Yeomansee.—Rep. (1704) in Hawkins, Missions, 20, 1845.

Yambadika ('yampa-root eaters'). A band of the Bannock.

Root-Eaters.—Hoffman in Proc. Am. Philos. Soc., XXIII, 299, 1886. Yam'badíka.—Ibid. Yumpatick-ara.—Schoolcraft, Ind. Tribes, I, 522, 1853.

Yamel. A Kalapooian tribe formerly living on Yamhill cr., a w. tributary of the Willamette in Oregon. They are now under the Siletz school and numbered only 5 in 1910. The following were their bands as ascertained by Gatschet in 1877: Andshankualth, Andshimmampak, Chamifuamim, Chamiwi, Champikle, Chinchal.

Tchă-yamel-amim.—Gatschet, Atfalati MS., B.A.E., 1877 (Atfalati name). Yámĕl.—Gatschet in Jour. Am. Folk-lore, XII, 213, 1899. Yamhelas.—Coues, Henry-Thompson Jour., 812, 1897. Yam Hill.—Lee and Frost, Oregon, 90, 1844. Yamstills.—Slocum in Sen. Doc. 24, 25th Cong., 2d sess., 15, 1838.

Yammostuwiwagaiya (*Yäm-mos tu-wi-wa-gai-ya*). A Mono band formerly living in Paradise valley, w. Nev.

Yäm-mos tu-wi-wa-gai-ya.—Powell, Paviotso MS., B.A.E., 1881. Yam-mū's.—Powers, Inds. W. Nev., MS., B.A.E., 1876 (trans. 'big plains').

Yampa. A plant (*Carum gairdneri*) whose roots are much used for food by the Indians of the Oregon region, the Klamath, Umatilla, Ute, and others: from *yámpä*, the name of this plant in the Ute dialect of Shoshonean.   (A. F. C.)

Yampa. A division of Ute formerly living in E. Utah on and about Green and Grand rs. In 1849 they occupied 500 lodges. The name does not appear in recent official reports, and the original Yampa are included under the term White River Ute. The Akanaquint and Grand River Ute were bands of this division.

Tamp-Pah-Utes.—Simpson (1859), Rep. of Expl. Across Utah, 35, 1876. Wampa.—Cummings in Ind. Aff. Rep., 153, 1866. Yampa.—U. S. Stat. at Large, xv, 619, 1869. Yam Pah-Utes.—Tourtellotte in Ind. Aff. Rep., 142, 1870. Yampatick-ara.—Schoolcraft, Ind. Tribes, I, 198, 1853. Yampi-Utes.—Gatschet, Comanche MS. vocab., B. A. E. (said to have originated from union of Kwahari Comanche women with Ute men). Yamp-Pah-Utahs.—Simpson, op. cit., 459. Yan-pa-pa Utahs.—Wilson in Ind. Aff. Rep. 1849, 67, 1850. Yep-pe.—Lewis and Clark Exped., I, map, 1814 (possibly identical). Yom-pa-pa Utahs.—Wilson (1849) in Cal. Mess. and Corresp., 185, 1850.

Yampas. A former village connected with San Carlos mission, Cal., and said to have been Esselen.—Taylor in Cal. Farmer, Apr. 20, 1860.

Yan ('directly opposite' a ledge). A former Haida town on the w. side of the mouth of Masset inlet, Queen Charlotte ids., Brit. Col. It was built in comparatively recent times after troubles between two Masset families. One family stayed in Masset, while the other, the Aostlan-lnagai, settled at Yan.

Ia'an.—Boas, 12th Rep. N. W. Tribes Can., 23, 1898. Yan.—Dawson, Q. Charlotte Ids., 163, 1880. Yĕn.—Harrison in Proc. Roy. Soc. Can., sec. II, 124, 1895.

Yan. The Willow clan of the Tewa pueblo of Santa Clara, N. Mex.

Yä'n-tdóa.—Hodge in Am. Anthr., IX, 352, 1896 (*tdóa* = 'people').

Yana. A tribe, constituting a distinct linguistic family, formerly occupying the territory from Round mtn. near Pit r., Shasta co., to Deer cr., Tehama co., Cal. The w. boundary was about 10 m. E. of Sacramento r., both banks of that stream being held by the Wintun, with whom the Yana were frequently at war. The E. boundary extended along the spurs running out to the N. and S. from Lassen butte. In Aug. 1864 the neighboring miners organized a massacre of the whole tribe, then numbering about 3,000, of whom all but about 50 were slaughtered in the course of a few days. In 1902 Dixon reported only about half a dozen remaining. A number of their myths have been recorded by Curtin. Consult Powers in Cont. N. A. Ethnol., III, 1877, art. Nosi; Curtin, Creation Myths Prim. America, 1898.   (H. W. H.)

Kom'-bo.—Powers in Cont. N. A. Ethnol., III, 277, 1877 (Maidu name). Noces.—Powers in Overland Mo., XII, 416, 1874. Nosa.—Curtin quoted by Powell in 6th Rep. B. A. E., xxxvII, 1888. Noi-Sas.—Geiger in Ind. Aff. Rep. 1859, 438, 1860. Noser.—Taylor in Cal. Farmer, Nov. 16, 1860. Nó-si.—Powers in Cont. N. A. Ethnol., III, 275, 1877. Noza.—Taylor, op. cit. Nozes.—Powers in Overland Mo., XII, 416, 1874. Nó-zi.—Powers in Cont. N. A. Ethnol., III, 275, 1877. Tisaiqdji.—Curtin, Ilmawi MS. vocab., B. A. E., 1889 (Ilmawi name).

Yanan Family. A linguistic family represented by the Yana tribe (q. v.).

=Nó-zi.—Powers in Cont. N. A. Ethnol., III, 275, 1877 (or Nó-si; mention of tribe; gives numerals and states they are different from any he has found in California). =**Noces.**—Gatschet in Mag. Am. Hist., 160, Mar., 1877 (or Nozes; merely mentioned under Meidoo family). =**Yanan.**—Powell in 7th Rep. B. A. E., 135, 1891.

Yanatoe. A former Choctaw village (Romans, Fla., 311, 1775), probably in s. w. Kemper co., Miss.

Yancomo. Mentioned as a pueblo of the province of Atripuy (q. v.), in the region of the lower Rio Grande, N. Mex., in 1598.—Oñate (1598) in Doc. Inéd., XVI, 115, 1871.

Yanegua (*Yane'gwa*, 'Big-bear'). A Cherokee chief who appears to have been of considerable local prominence in his time, but whose name, even with the oldest of the band, is now but a memory. He was among the signers of the treaties of 1798 and 1805, and by the treaty of 1819 there was confirmed to him a tract of 640 acres as one of those living within the ceded territory who were "believed to be persons of industry and capable of managing their property with discretion," and who had made considerable improvements on the tracts reserved. This reservation, still known as the Big-bear farm, was on the w. bank of the Oconaluftee, a few miles above its mouth, and appears to have been the same afterward occupied by Yonaguska (q. v.).— Mooney in 19th Rep. B. A. E., 547, 1900.

Yaneka. The most southerly "old town" of the Chickasaw, first settled after the Chickasaw, Choctaw, and Chakchiuma separated on the E. side of the Mississippi.—Adair, Am. Inds., 66, 1775.

Yaneka. One of 5 hamlets composing the former Choctaw town of Imongalasha, in Neshoba co., Miss.—Halbert in Pub. Miss. Hist. Soc., VI, 432, 1902.

Yaneks ('at the little butte'). Former settlements of Klamath, Modoc, and Shoshoni along Middle Sprague r., Lake co., Oreg. The name is now applied to the seat of a subagency on Klamath res.— Gatschet in Cont. N. A. Ethnol., II, pt. I, XXXI; pt. II, 100, 1890.
Yaínakshi.—Gatschet, op. cit. **Yaínakskni.**—Ibid., 100 (referring to the people).

Yangna. A Gabrieleño rancheria formerly on the site of Los Angeles, Cal.
Iyakha.—A. L. Kroeber, inf'n, 1905 (Luiseño name; so called from a plant growing abundantly there). **Wenot.**—Kroeber in Univ. Cal. Pub., Am. Eth. and Arch., VIII, 39, 1908 ('stream': so called by native informant "because of a large river there"). **Yanga.**—Ried (1852) quoted by Taylor in Cal. Farmer, June 8, 1860. **Yang-ha.**— Taylor, ibid., May 11, 1860. **Yang-na.**—Ried quoted by Hoffman in Bull. Essex Inst., XVII, 2, 1885.

Yangti (*YAⁿtï'*). The Buzzard clan of the Yuchi.—Speck, Yuchi Inds., 70, 1909.

Yangtsaa. The Coyote clan of Jemez pueblo, N. Mex. A corresponding clan existed also at the former related pueblo of Pecos.
Ya'+.—Hodge in Am. Anthr., IX, 350, 1896 (Pecos name; + = *ash* = 'people'). **Yaⁿtsaá.**—Ibid. (Jemez form).

Yankapin. See *Wampapin*.

Yankton (*ihaⁿke* 'end,' *toⁿ'waⁿ* 'village : 'end village'). One of the 7 primary divisions of the Dakota, constituting, with the closely related Yanktonai, the middle group. J. O. Dorsey arranged the Dakota-Assiniboin in 4 dialectic groups: Santee, Yankton, Teton, and Assiniboin, the Yankton dialect being spoken also by the Yanktonai, for the 2 tribes were the outgrowth of one original stem. Although the name Yankton was known earlier than Yanktonai, it does not follow that the Yankton were the elder tribe. Long (Exped. St. Peter's R., I, 378, 1824) speaks of the Yankton as descendants of the Yanktonai. The Assiniboin, who were an offshoot from the Yanktonai, are mentioned in the Jesuit Relation for 1640 as a tribe;

EAGLE-TRACK — YANKTON

hence the Yanktonai must have been in existence as a tribe before that time. This fact serves as an aid in tracing back the Yankton both historically and geographically. However, the name Yankton and some of its synonyms appear early to have been used to include the 2 tribes, the distinction probably not then being known. The first mention of them is on Hennepin's map (1683), on which they are placed directly N. of Mille Lac, Minn., in the region of Leech lake or Red lake. This position would accord geographically with the withdrawal of the Assiniboin to the Cree. In the account of Hennepin's expedition attributed to Tonti (1697), they are mentioned in connection with the Santee, Teton, and Sioux, located about the headwaters of the Mississippi. Both these references would seem to apply as well to the Yanktonai as to the Yankton; it is probable that both are referred to under one general name. La Chesnaye (1697) included them among the tribes that dwelt N. of Mille Lac, and placed them N. of the Santee and other Sioux. Le Sueur (1700), however, speaks of a village or tribe of the western Sioux (Margry, Déc., VI, 87, 1887), the Hinhanetons, identified by Shea, probably correctly, with the Yankton, which he calls the "village of the quarry of red stone." If this refers, as is maintained by Williamson, to the pipestone quarry in extreme s. w. Minnesota, it would indicate a sudden change of residence, unless the references are in one place to one and in another to the other tribe, or apply to different villages or bands. Williamson (Minn. Hist. Coll., I, 296, 1860) considered the Hinhanetons a part only of the Yankton. There are indications that a westward movement took place about the time Le Sueur visited that region. On De l'Isle's map of 1708 the Yankton are placed on the E. bank of the Missouri, about the site of Sioux City, Iowa. For about a century they dropped almost entirely from history, there being scarcely a notice of them except as included in the general term Sioux. When they were again brought to notice by Lewis and Clark (1804) they had shifted but little from the position they occupied at the beginning of the previous century. According to these explorers they roamed over the regions of the James, Big Sioux, and Des Moines rs. Lewis, in his Statistical View, locates them on James, Big and Little Sioux, Floyd, and Des Moines rs., an area that includes the district of the pipestone quarry, where Le Sueur placed them. From this time they became an important factor in the history of the N. W. Long (1823) says that they are in every respect similar to the Yanktonai and had probably separated from them. They frequented the Missouri and generally trafficked with the traders on that river. Their hunting grounds were E. of the Missouri. Drake (1848) located them in 1836 about the headwaters of Red r. of the North. According to the Report on Indian Affairs for 1842 and a statement by Ramsey in 1849 they lived along Vermillion r., S. Dak. At the time of the Minnesota outbreak in 1862 their head chief, Palaneapape, wisely kept them from joining the hostiles, and sent warning to the white people in Dakota to flee to the forts, thereby saving hundreds of lives. By the treaty of Washington, Apr. 19, 1858, they ceded all their lands in South Dakota, excepting a reservation on the N.

bank of Missouri r., where they have since remained in peace with the whites. Immediately after the allotment act of 1887 the process of allotments in severalty began on this reservation and was completed before the close of 1890.

Lewis, in his Statistical View (1807), says the Yankton are the best disposed Sioux who rove on the banks of the Missouri, but they would not suffer any trader at that date to ascend the river if they could prevent it. Lewis and Clark describe them as being in person stout, well proportioned, and exhibiting a certain air of dignity and boldness. Their dress is described as differing in no respect from that of other bands encountered. They had then only a few guns, being generally armed with bows and arrows, in the use of which they did not appear as expert as the more northerly Indians. Pike describes them and the Yanktonai as never stationary, but, like the Teton, as more erratic than other Sioux. Lewis (1807) estimated their number at 700. Pike (1807) estimated the population of the Yankton and Yanktonai at 4,300. The Report on Indian Affairs for 1842 gives the Yankton a population of 2,500; in 1862 the estimate was 3,000; in 1867, 2,530; in 1886, 1,776. Their present number is not definitely known, the Yankton and the Yanktonai being seemingly confused on the different Sioux reservations. Most of the Indians under the Yankton school, S. Dak., are Yankton, and numbered in all 1,739 in 1909. There were also about 100 under the Fort Totten school, N. Dak., a few under the Crow Creek school, S. Dak., and a few others under the Lower Brulé school, S. Dak. The so-called Yankton on the Fort Peck res., Mont., are really Yanktonai.

The bands as given by J. O. Dorsey (1878) are as follows: Chankute, Chagu, Wakmuhaoin, Ihaisdaye, Wacheunpa, Ikmun, Oyateshicha, and Washichunchincha. Culbertson (Smithson. Rep. 1850, 141, 1851) mentions a "Band who do not cook," and another "Who eat no geese," which can not be identified with any of these divisions; and Schoolcraft (Ind. Tribes, III, 612, 1853) incorrectly makes Wahnaataa, the name of one of the Yankton bands. (c. t.)

Amitons.—La Chesnaye(1697) in Margry, Déc., VI, 6, 1886. E-hawn-k'-t'-wawns.—Ramsey in Ind. Aff. Rep. for 1849, 86, 1850. Hanctons.—Hennepin, New Discov., map, 1698. Hanetones.—Barcia, Ensayo, 238, 1723. Hannetons.—McKenney and Hall, Ind. Tribes, III, 80, 1854. Hinhaneton.—Alcedo, Dic. Geog., II, 362, 1787. Hinhanetons.—Le Sueur (1700) in Margry, Déc., VI, 87, 1886. Hinkaneton.—Morse, Hist. Am., map, 1798. Honctons.—Bacqueville de la Potherie, Hist. Am., II, map, 1753. Ihā'gtawa Kátaꭓka.—Gatschet, MS., B. A. E. (Pawnee name). Ihanketwans.—Ramsey in Ind. Aff. Rep. 1849, 72, 1850. Ihañk'taⁿwiⁿ.—Dorsey, Dhegiha MS. dict., B. A. E., 1878 (Omaha and Ponca name). Ihaŋktoŋwaŋ.—Riggs, Dakota Gram. and Dict., viii, 1852. Ihanktonwans.—Ind. Aff. Rep., 564,

1845. **Ihanktonwe.**—Boyd, Ind. Local Names, 55, 1885 (trans.: 'a town or dwelling at the end'). **Ihank'-t'wans.**—Ramsey in Ind. Aff. Rep. 1849, 85, 1850. **Ihauk-t'wans.**—H. R. Ex. Doc. 96, 42d Cong., 3d sess., 16, 1873. **Janaɟa nikacinga.**—Dorsey in 3d Rep. B. A. E., 212, 1884 ('people who dwelt in the woods': so called anciently by the Omaha). **Jantons.**—De Smet, Miss. de l'Oregon, 264, 1848. **Jantous.**—De Smet, Letters, 23, 1843. **Lower-Yanctons.**—Hayden, Ethnog. and Philol. Mo. Val., 371, 1862. **Shan-ke-t'wans.**—Ramsey in Ind. Aff. Rep. 1849, 74, 1850 (misprint). **Shank' t' wannons.**—Ramsey, ibid., 78. **Shank-t'wans.**—Ramsey, ibid., 75. **South Yanktons.**—Prescott in Schoolcraft, Ind. Tribes, II, 169, note, 1852. **Wichiyela.**—Warren, Dacota Country, 15, 1855 (trans.: 'first nation'). **Wiċiyela.**—Riggs, Dakota Gram. and Dict., viii, 1852 ('they are the people': Teton name, applied also to Yanktonai). **Yanckton.**—Treaty of 1831 in U. S. Ind. Treaties, 783, 1873. **Yancton.**—Long, Exped. Rocky Mts., I, 179, 1823. **Yanctonas.**—Ind. Aff. Rep., 497, 1839. **Yanctongs.**—Pike, Exped., 1810. **Yanctons.**—Ramsey in Ind. Aff. Rep. 1849, 78, 1850. **Yanctonwas.**—Schoolcraft, Ind. Tribes, VI, 689, 1857. **Yanctorinans.**—Ind. Aff. Rep., 295, 1854. **Yanctowah.**—Boller, Among Inds. in Far W., 29, 1868. **Yaneton.**—Martin, Hist. La., 333, 1882. **Yanetong.**—Boudinot, Star in the W., 129, 1816. **Yanka-taus.**—Ruxton, Life in Far W., 111, 1849. **Yanktau-Sioux.**—Sage, Scenes in Rocky Mts., 54, 1846. **Yank toan.**—Long, Exped. St Peter's R., I, 378, 1824 (trans.: 'descended from the fern leaves'). **Yanktons.**—De l'Isle, map of La. (1708) in Neill, Hist. Minn., 164, 1858. **Yanktons of the south.**—Lewis and Clark Exped., I, 184, 1817. **Yanktoons.**—West, Jour., 86, 1824. **Yanktown.**—Culbertson in Smithson. Rep. 1850, 86, 1851. **Yantons.**—Keane in Stanford, Compend., 470, 1878. **Yauktong.**—Tanner, Narr., 324, 1830 (misprint). **Yauktons.**—Parker, Minn. Handbk., 141, 1857. **Yaunktwaun.**—Ramsey in Minn. Hist. Coll., I, (1850–56), 47, 1872. **Yengetongs.**—Schoolcraft, Trav., 308, 1821. **Yonktins.**—Gass, Voy., 407, 1810. **Yonktons.**—Drake, Ind. Chron., 201, 1836.

Yanktonai (*ihanke* 'end,' *tonwan* 'village,' *na* diminutive: 'little-end village.'—Riggs). One of the 7 primary divisions or subtribes of the Dakota, speaking the same dialect as the Yankton and believed to be the elder tribe. Long evidently obtained a tradition from the Indians to this effect. The first apparent reference to one of the tribes in which the other is not included is that to the Yankton by La Sueur in 1700. It is not until noticed by Lewis and Clark in 1804 that they reappear. These explorers state that they roved on the headwaters of the Sioux, James, and Red rs. The migration from their eastern home, N. of Mille Lac, Minn., probably took place at the beginning of the 18th century. It is likely that they followed or accompanied the Teton, while the Yankton turned more and more toward the s. w. Long (1823) speaks of them as one of the most important of the Dakota tribes, their hunting grounds extending from Red r. to the Missouri. Warren (1855) gives as their habitat the country between the James r. and the Missouri, extending as far N. as Devils lake, and states that they fought against the United States in the War of 1812, and that their chief at that time went to England. It does not appear that this tribe took any part in the Minnesota massacre of 1862. In 1865 separate treaties of peace were made with the United States by the Upper and Lower

Yanktonai, binding them to use their influence and power to prevent hostilities not only against citizens, but also between the Indian tribes in the region occupied or frequented by them. Subsequently they were gathered on reservations, the Upper Yanktonai mostly at Standing Rock, partly also at Devils Lake, N. Dak.; the Lower Yanktonai (Hunkpatina) chiefly on Crow Creek res., S. Dak., but part at Standing Rock res., N. Dak., and some at Fort Peck res., Mont.

Their customs and characteristics are those common to the Dakota. Long (1823) states that they had no fixed residence, but dwelt in fine lodges of well-dressed and decorated skins, and frequented, for the purpose of trade, L. Traverse, Big Stone lake, and Cheyenne r. Their chief, Wanotan, wore a splendid cloak of buffalo skins, dressed so as to be a fine white color, which was decorated with tufts of owl feathers and others of various hues. His necklace was formed of about 60 claws of the grizzly bear, and his leggings, jacket, and moccasins were of white skins profusely decorated with human hair, the moccasins being variegated with plumage from several birds. In his hair, secured by a strip of red cloth, he wore 9 sticks, neatly cut and smoothed and painted with vermilion, which designated the number of gunshot wounds he had received. His hair was plaited in two tresses, which hung forward; his face was painted with vermilion, and in his hand he carried a large fan of turkey feathers.

The primary divisions of the tribe are Upper Yanktonai and Hunkpatina. These are really subtribes, each having its organization.

The first notice of subdivisions is that by Lewis and Clark, who mention the Kiyuksa, Wazikute, Hunkpatina, and the unidentified Hahatonwanna, Honetaparteenwaz, and Zaartar. Hayden (1862) mentions the Hunkpatina, Pabaksa, and Wazikute, and speaks of two other bands, one called the Santee, and probably not Yanktonai. J. O. Dorsey gives as subdivisions, which he calls gentes, of the Upper Yanktonai: Wazikute, Takini, Shikshichena, Bakihon, Kiyuksa, Pabaksa, and another whose name was not ascertained. His subdivisions of the Hunkpatina are Putetemini, Shungikcheka, Takhuhayuta, Sanona, Ihasha, Iteghu, and Pteyuteshni. English translations of names of bands of Yanktonai of which little else is known are 'The band that wishes the life' and 'The few that lived.'

The population as given at different dates varies widely. Lewis and Clark (1806) estimate the men at 500, equal to a total of about 1,750; Long (1823), 5,200; Rep. Ind. Aff. for 1842, 6,000; Warren in 1856,

6,400; in 1867, 4,500; Ind. Aff. Rep. for 1874, 2,266; in 1885 returns from the agencies gave 6,618, while in 1886 the reported number was only 5,109. The Lower Yanktonai, or Hunkpatina, are chiefly under the Crow Creek school, S. Dak., where, together with some Lower Brulés, Miniconjou, and Two Kettles, they numbered 1,019 in 1909. There are others under the Standing Rock agency, N. Dak., but their number is not separately enumerated. The Upper Yanktonai are chiefly under the Standing Rock agency, and while their number is not separately reported, there are probably about 3,500 at this place. The Pabaksa branch of the Upper Yanktonai are under the Ft Totten school, N. Dak., but their number is not known. The so-called "Yankton Sioux" under the Ft Peck agency, Mont., are in reality chiefly Yanktonai. These, with several other Sioux tribes, numbered 1,082 in 1909. (c. t.)

Ehanktonwanna.—Lynd in Minn. Hist. Coll., II, pt. 2, 59, 1864. E-hank-to-wana.—Brackett in Smithson. Rep., 471, 1876. E-hawn-k'-t'-wawn-nah.—Ramsey in Ind. Aff. Rep. 1849, 86, 1850 (trans. 'lesser people of the further end'). Eyank-ton-wah.—Schoolcraft, Ind. Tribes, II, 169, 1852. Ihaŋktoŋwaŋna.—Riggs, Dakota Gram. and Dict., VIII, 1852. Ihanktonwanna Dakotas.—Hayden, Ethnog. and Philol. Mo. Val., map, 1862. Ihanktonwannas.—Warren, Dacota Country, 15, 1855. Ihan-k'-tow-wan-nan.—Ramsey in Ind. Aff. Rep. 1849, 86, 1850. Ihank'-t'wan-ahs.—Ramsey, ibid., 85. Ihauk-to-wa-na.—Am. Nat., 829, 1882 (misprint). Ihauk-t'wan-ahs.—H. R. Ex. Doc. 96, 42d Cong., 3d sess., 16, 1873. Jantonnais.—De Smet Miss. de l'Oregon, 264, 1848. Jantonnees.—De Smet, Letters, 37, note, 1843. Jantonnois.—Ibid., 23. Ohantonwanna.—Ind. Aff. Rep., 566, 1845. Yanctannas.—Burton, City of Saints, 118, 1861. Yanctonais.—Harney in Sen. Ex. Doc. 94, 34th Cong., 1st sess., 1, 1856. Yanctonees.—Ind. Aff. Rep., 7, 1856. Yanctonie.—H. R. Ex. Doc. 117, 19th Cong., 1st sess., 6, 1826. Yanctonnais.—Ind. Aff. Rep., 15, 1858. Yangtons Ahnah.—Bradbury, Trav., 83, 1817. Yanktoanan.—Long, Exped. St. Peter's R., I, 378, 1824 (trans. 'Fern leaves'). Yankto-anons.—Maximilian, Trav., 149, 1843. Yanktona.—Ex. Doc. 56, 18th Cong., 1st sess., 9, 1824. Yankton Ahnâ.—Lewis and Clark Discov., 20, 1806. Yankton ahnah.—Ibid., 28. Yanktonai.—Treaty of 1865 in U. S. Ind. Treat., 862, 1873. Yanktonaias.—Corliss, Lacotah MS. vocab., B. A. E., 107, 1874. Yanktonais.—Warren, Dacota Country, 15, 1855. Yanktonans.—Maximilian, Trav., 149, 1843. Yank-ton-ees.—Prescott in Schoolcraft, Ind. Tribes, II, 169, note, 1852. Yanktonians.—Culbertson in Smithson. Rep. 1850, 89, 1851. Yanktonias-Sioux.—Williamson in Minn. Hist. Coll., III, 285, 1880. Yanktonies.—Treaty of 1826 in U. S. Ind. Treat., 871, 1873. Yanktonnan.—Culbertson in Smithson. Rep. 1850, 141, 1851. Yanktonnas.—Warren, Neb. and Ariz., 47, 1875. Yanktons Ahna.—Lewis and Clark Discov., 21, 1806. Yanktons Ahnah.—Lewis, Trav., 171, 1809. Yank-ton-us.—Prescott in Schoolcraft, Ind. Tribes, II, 169, note, 1852. Yonktons Ahnah.—Farnham, Trav., 32, 1843.

Yanostas. A former village connected with San Carlos mission, Cal., and said to have been Esselen.—Taylor in Cal. Farmer, Apr. 20, 1860.

Yaogus (*Yáogʌs*). A Haida town of the Kagials-kegawai family, formerly on the s. w. side of Louise id., Queen Charlotte ids., Brit. Col.—Swanton, Cont. Haida, 279, 1905.

Yapalaga. An ancient town, probably of the Apalachee, on the e. bank of St Marks r., Fla.

Yapalaga.—Jefferys, French Dom., 135, map, 1761. Yapalage.—Roberts, Fla., 14, 1763.

Yapashi. The generic name given by the Keresan tribes to fetishes representing human forms, and hence applied to a prehistoric pueblo, the aboriginal name of which is unknown, on the Potrero de las Vacas, above Cochiti, N. Mex., on account of the presence there of numerous figurines. Not to be confounded with Pueblo Caja del Rio, to which the Cochiti people apply the same name.—Bandelier in Arch. Inst. Papers, IV, 152, 1892.

Tit-yi Hä-nat Kama Tze-shum-a.—Bandelier, op. cit. ('The old houses in the north': Cochiti name). Tit-yi Hä-nat Ka-ma Tze-shum-a Mo-katsh Zaitsh.—Ibid. ('the old houses above in the north where the panthers lie extended': another Cochiti name). Yap-a-shi.—Ibid.

Yapiam. An unidentified Pomo division formerly living on Russian r., Cal.

Japiam.—Wrangell, Ethnog. Nach., 80, 1889.

Yapon, Yapoon. See *Black drink, Yopon.*

Yaqatlenlish (*Yáqatlenl̃isch*). An ancestor of one of the gentes of the Kwakiutl proper, after whom the gens itself was sometimes named.—Boas in Petermanns Mitteil., pt. 5, 131, 1887.

Yaqui (said to mean 'chief river,' referring to the Rio Yaqui). An important division of the Cahita which until re-

YAQUI MAN

cently dwelt along both banks of the lower Rio Yaqui, but is now scattered over the larger part of s. Sonora, Mexico. The first notice of the tribe is probably the narrative of the expedition in 1531 by Nuño de Guzman (Segunda Rel. Anón., in Icazbalceta, Col. Docs., II, 300–02, 1866), in which they are spoken of as related linguistically to the people living on Rio dle Fuerte, a relationship that has since been fully confirmed (see *Cahita*). Capt. Hurdaide made 3 successive attacks on the tribe (1609–10), the last time with 50 mounted Spaniards and 4,000 Indian allies, but was defeated and forced to retreat each time. The Yaqui made overtures of peace, a treaty with the Spaniards was made in 1610, and soon thereafter missionaries began to visit them. Perez de Ribas, a missionary among them between 1624 and 1644, says they were then agriculturists, cultivating not only maize, but also cotton, which they manufactured into cloth, especially mantles. The first serious revolt against the Spaniards occurred in 1740, and was brought on, according to Alegre (Hist. Comp. Jesus, III, 273, 1842), by disputes between Spanish settlers and the missionaries. There was a second outbreak in 1764. The more recent uprisings were in 1825, 1832, 1840, 1867, 1885, and 1901. Hrdlička (Am. Anthr., VI, 61, 1904), who speaks highly of the capabilities of the Yaqui, says: "This is the only tribe on the continent that, surrounded by whites from the beginning of their history, have never been fully subdued." Their native dwellings, in which many of them still live, are quadrilateral structures of poles and reeds, or adobes and reeds or brush, with flat or slightly sloping roofs of grass and mud. These are generally of fair size, with adjoining shelters where the cooking and the other indoor work is done. Their principal industries are agriculture and cattle raising, and the manufacture of cotton and woolen stuffs. They also make hats and fine mats of palm leaf and reed baskets, which they sell at Guaymas. Many of them are employed as laborers in the fields and mines. A few ornaments, as rings, earrings, and beads, are made from silver and other metals. According to Hrdlička (op. cit., 68), there is no organization among the Yaqui, except in that part of the tribe which lives practically free and conducts the revolutions; nor do there appear to be any secret societies. Marriage, natal, and mortuary ceremonies are mainly Roman Catholic; the women marry young; the dead are buried in graves. They had a former custom of exchanging wives. Their principal settlements have been

Bacum, Belen (with others), Bicam, Cocori, Huirivis, Potam, Rahun, and Torin. Estimates of the population of the tribe have varied widely at different dates. The earliest guess, that for 1621, was 30,000; Zapata (1678) reported the population of the 7 principal Yaqui pueblos as 8,116; while in 1760, according to Jesuit accounts, the population of 8 chief settlements was 19,325 (Escudero Not. Estad. Sonora y Sinaloa, 100, 1849). Escudero gives the population in 1849 at 54,000 to 57,000. Stone estimated their number in 1860 at 20,000, which Hrdlička considers approximately correct for 1903. In 1906–7 the Mexican government undertook a plan to overcome permanently the hostile Yaqui by deporting them to Tehuantepec and Yucatan, to which parts several thousand accordingly have been sent.

Consult Ribas, Hist. Trium. Santa Fee, 1645; Zapata (1678) in Doc. Hist. Mex., 4th s., III, 1857; Escudero, op. cit., 1849; Bancroft, No. Mex. States, 1883; Stone, Notes on the State of Sonora, 1861; Hrdlička, op. cit., 1904.　　　(F. W. H.)

Cinaloa.—Hervas, Cat. Leng., I, 322, 1800. Gaqui.—Conklin, Arizona, 341, 1878. Hiaqui.—Orozco y Berra, Geog., 58, 1864. Hyaquez.—Rivera, Diario, leg. 1514, 1736. Hyaquin.—Bandelier, Gilded Man, 124, 1893 (Yaqui or). Hyaquis.—Rivera, op. cit., leg. 1382. Iakïm.—Curtis, Am. Ind., II, 112, 1908 (Papago name). Ibequi.—Latham, El. Comp. Philol., 428, 1862. Yaquima.—Castañeda (1596) in Ternaux-Compans, Voy., IX, 157, 1838. Yaquimis.—Alegre, Hist. Comp. Jesus, II, 32, 1841.

Yaquina. A small tribe, but the most important division of the Yakonan family (q. v.), formerly living about Yaquina r. and bay, w. Oregon. By the early explorers and writers they were classed with the Salishan tribes to the N., but later were shown to be linguistically independent. The tribe is now practically extinct. There are a few survivors, for the greater part of mixed blood, on the Siletz res., Oreg. According to Dorsey (Jour. Am. Folk-lore, III, 229, 1890) the following were villages of the Yaquina: On the N. side of Yaquina r.: Holukhik, Hunkkhwitik, Iwai, Khaishuk, Khilukh, Kunnupiyu, Kwulai, shauik, Kyaukuhu, Kyuwatkal, Mipshuntik, Mittsulstik, Shash, Thlalkhaiuntik, Thlekakhaik, Tkhakiyu, Tshkitshiauk, Tthilkitik, Ukhwaiksh, Yahal, Yikkhaich. On the S. side of the river: Atshuk, Chulithltiyu, Hakkyaiwal, Hathletukhish, Hitshinsuwit, Hiwaitthe, Kaku, Khaiyukkhai, Khitalaitthe, Kholkh, Khulhanshtauk, Kilauutuksh, Kumsuk-

YAQUI WOMEN

wum, Kutshuwitthe, Kwaitshi, Kwilaish-auk, Kwulchichicheshk, Kwullaish, Kwullakhtauik, Kwutichuntthe, Mulsh-intik, Naaish, Paiinkkhwutthu, Pikiiltthe, Pkhulluwaaitthe, Pkuuniukhtauk, Puunt-thiwaun, Shilkhotshi, Shupauk, Thlek-wiyauik Thlelkhus, Thlinaitshtik, Thlukwiutshthu, Tkulmashaauk, Tuhau-shuwitthe, Tulshk.

Iakon.—Hale, Ethnog. and Philol., 218, 1846. **Jacon.**—Gallatin in Trans. Am. Ethnol. Soc., II, 99, 1848. **Jakon.**—Ibid., 17. **Să-ákl.**—Gatschet, Nestucca MS. vocab., B. A. E., 1877 (Nestucca name). **Sĭs'-qûn-me' ʒûnnĕ.**—Dorsey, Chetco MS. vocab., B. A. E., 1884 (Chetco name). **Southern Killamuk.**—Hale, op. cit., 198 (falsely so called). **Tacóón.**—Framboise quoted by Gairdner (1835) in Jour. Geog. Soc. Lond., XI, 255, 1841. **Tcha yákon amím.**—Gatschet, Lakmiut MS., B. A. E., 105 (Lakmiut name). **Yacona Indians.**—Ind. Aff. Rep., 164, 1850. **Yacone.**—Wilkes, West. Am., 88, 1849. **Yacons.**—Domenech. Deserts, I, map, 1860. **Yah-quo-nah.**—Metcalfe in Ind. Aff. Rep., 357, 1857. **Yakon.**—Gatschet in Beach, Ind. Misc., 441, 1877. **Yákona**—Gatschet in Globus, XXXV, no. 11, 168, 1879. **Yakonah.**—Gibbs, Obs. on Coast Tribes of Oreg., MS., B. A. E. **Yakone.**—Hale, op. cit., 218. **Ya-ꭓŭn'-ni-me' ʒûnnĕ.**—Dorsey, Tutu MS. vocab., B. A. E., 1894 (Tutu name). **Ye-k'u'-nă-me'-ʒûnnĕ.**—Dorsey, Naltûnnetûnnĕ MS. vocab., B. A. E., 1884 (Naltunne name). **Youico-mes.**—Domenech, op. cit., I, 445. **Youicone.**—Drake, Bk. Inds., xii, 1848. **Youikcones.**—Lewis and Clark Exped., II, 473, 1814. **Youikkone.**—Amer. Pioneer, II, 192, 1843. **Youkone.**—Lewis and Clark, op. cit., 118. **Yû-kwĭn'-ă.**—Dorsey, Alsea MS. vocab., B. A. E., 1884 (Alsea name). **Yû-kwĭn'-me' ʒûnnĕ.**—Dorsey, Coquille MS. vocab., B. A. E., 1884 (Coquille name).

Yarahatssee (*Ya-ra-hats'-see*, 'tall tree'). A clan of the Hurons (q. v.).—Morgan, Anc. Soc., 153, 1877.

Yascha. The Coral Bead clan of San Felipe pueblo, N. Mex.

Yáscha-háno.—Hodge in Am. Anthr., IX, 349, 1896 (*háno* = 'people').

Yastling (*YasⱢ!ĭ'ñ*). A Haida town of the Koetas family, formerly in Naden harbor, Graham id., Queen Charlotte ids., Brit. Col.—Swanton, Cont. Haida, 281, 1905.

Yatanocas. One of the 9 Natchez villages in 1699.—Iberville in Margry, Déc., IV, 179, 1880.

Yatasi. A tribe of the Caddo confederacy, closely affiliated in language with the Natchitoch. They are first spoken of by Tonti, who states that in 1690 their village was on Red r. of Louisiana, N. w. of the Natchitoch, where they were living in company with the Natasi and Choye. Bienville and St Denys, during their Red r. trip in 1701, made an alliance with the Yatasi and henceforward the tribe seems to have been true to the friendship then sealed. The road frequented by travelers from the Spanish province to the French settlements on Red r. and at New Orleans passed near their village. During the disputes incident to the uncertain boundary line between the Spanish and the French possessions and to the Spanish restrictions on intertrade, they proved their steadfastness to the French interests

by refusing to comply with the Spanish demand to close the road. The Indians maintained that "the road had always been theirs" and that it should remain open. St Denys' invitation to the various tribes dwelling in the vicinity of the post and fort established among the Natchitoch in 1712-14 to settle near by under his protection was opportune, for the Chickasaw were then waging war along Red r. and the Yatasi were among the sufferers. A part of the tribe sought refuge with the Natchitoch, while others fled up the river to the Kadohadacho and to the Nanatsoho and the Nasoni. The wars of the 18th century and the introduction of new diseases, especially smallpox and measles, had such an effect on the Yatasi that by 1805, according to Sibley, they had become reduced to 8 men and 25 women and children. This remnant was then living in a village midway between the Kadohadacho and the Natchitoch, surrounded by French settlements. In 1826 (U. S. Ind. Treat., 465, 1826) they numbered 26 on Red r. Little more than the name of the Yatasi now survives, and those who claim descent from the tribe live with the Caddo on the Wichita res. in Oklahoma.   (A. C. F.)

Yactachés.—Bienville (1700) in Margry, Déc., VI 438, 1880. **Yallashee.**—Warden, Account of U. S., III, 551, 1819. **Yaltasse.**—U. S. Ind. Treat., 465, 1826. **Yatace.**—Pénicaut (1717) in Margry, Déc., V, 547, 1883. **Yatacez.**—Ibid., 504. **Yatache.**—Tonti (1690) in French, Hist. Coll. La., I, 72, 1846. **Yatachez.**—Carte de Taillée des Possess. Anglaises, 1777. **Yatase.**—La Harpe (1719) in French, Hist. Coll. La., III, 18, 1851. **Yatasees.**—Pénicaut (1714), ibid., n. s., I, 122, 1869. **Yatasi.**—Espinosa (1746) quoted by Buschmann, Spuren, 417, 1854. **Yatasie.**—Bull. Soc. Geog. Mex., 504, 1869. **Yatasse.**—Bruyère (1742) in Margry, Déc., VI, 486, 1886. **Yatassee.**—Boudinot, Star in the West, 129, 1816. **Yatassèz.**—Tex. State Arch., Nov. 17, 1763. **Yatassi.**—Gatschet, Creek Migr. Leg., I, 43, 1884. **Yatay.**—La Harpe (1719) in Margry, Déc., VI, 255, 1886. **Yattapo.**—Porter (1829) in Schoolcraft, Ind. Tribes, III, 596, 1853. **Yattasaees.**—Balbi, Atlas Ethnog., 54, 1826. **Yattasces.**—Brackenridge, Views of La., 80, 1815. **Yattasees.**—Pénicaut (1701) in French, Hist. Coll. La., n. s., I, 73, 1869. **Yattasie.**—Schermerhorn (1812) in Mass. Hist. Coll., 2d s., II, 24, 1814. **Yattassees.**—Sibley, Hist. Sketches, 67, 1806.

Yatcheethinyoowuc (Wood Cree: *Ayátchithǐnǐwâk*, 'foreign men,' 'foreigners.'—Lacombe.) A name applied indiscriminately by the Cree to all tribes w. of themselves and the Assiniboin, in Canada. It has no ethnic significance.

Jatche-thin-juwuc.—Egli, Lexicon, 532, 1880. **Yat-cheé-thin-yoowuc.**—Franklin, Narr., 108, 1823.

Yatokya. The Sun clan of the pueblo of Zuñi, N. Mex.

Yä'tok‛ya-kwe.—Cushing in 13th Rep. B. A. E., 368, 1896 (*kwe* = 'people').

Yatza ('knife'). An important camping place on the N. coast of Graham id., between North id. and Virago sd., Brit. Col. A house or two were erected here and potlatches were held for the purpose, which circumstances led Dawson (Q.

Charlotte Ids., 162B, 1880) to suppose it was a new town. (J. R. S.)

Yaudanchi. The Yokuts (Mariposan) tribe on Tule r., s. central Cal., that formerly occupied the region about Porterville, the present Tule River res., and the headwaters of the river. They are now on Tule River res., together with the Yauelmani or "Tejon" Indians and remnants of other Yokuts tribes. (A. L. K.)

Nuchawayi.—A. L. Kroeber, inf'n, 1903 ('mountaineers,' or 'easterners': name given by plains tribes about Tulare lake; plural form; not restricted to Yauelmani). Nutá.—Ibid. (the same; singular form). Olanches.—Taylor in Cal. Farmer, June 8, 1860. Yaudanchi.—Kroeber in Univ. Cal. Pub., II, 171, 1907 (own name, singular). Yaulanchi.—Ibid. (name applied by most of their neighbors). Yawĕdĕn'tshi.—Hoffman in Proc. Am. Philos. Soc., XXIII, 302, 1886. Yáwĕdmŏ'ni.—Ibid., 301 (Wikchumni name). Yoednani.—Kroeber, inf'n, 1903 (pl. form of Yaudimni.) Yolanchas.—Bancroft, Nat. Races, I, 456, 1882. Yowechani.—Kroeber in Univ. Cal. Pub., II, 171, 1907 (own name, plural).

Yauelmani. A Yokuts (Mariposan) division formerly living on Bakersfield plain and removing thence to Kern lake, Cal. The survivors, numbering 50 or more, are now on the Tule River res.

Yauelmani.—Kroeber in Univ. Cal. Pub., II, 279 et seq., 1907. Yow'-el-man'-ne.—Merriam in Science, XIX, 916, June 15, 1904.

Yauko (*Ya'-u-kö*). A former Maidu village about 7 m. N. E. of Chico, in the N. part of Butte co., Cal.—Dixon in Bull. Am. Mus. Nat. Hist., XVII, map, 1905.

Yaunyi. The extinct Granite clan of Sia pueblo, N. Mex.

Yáun-ñi.—Stevenson in 11th Rep. B. A. E., 19, 1894. Yáunyi-háno.—Hodge in Am. Anthr., IX, 352, 1896. (*háno* = 'people').

Yaupon. See *Black drink, Yopon.*

Yavapai (said to be from *enyaéva* 'sun,' *pai* 'people': 'people of the sun'). A Yuman tribe, popularly known as Apache Mohave and Mohave Apache, i. e., 'hostile or warlike Mohave.' According to Corbusier, the tribe, before its removal to the Rio Verde agency in May 1873, claimed as its range the valley of the Rio Verde and the Black mesa from Salt r. as far as Bill Williams mt., w. Ariz. They then numbered about 1,000. Earlier they ranged much farther w., appearing to have had rancherias on the Rio Colorado; but they were chiefly an interior tribe, living s. of Bill Williams fork as far as Castle Dome mts., above the Gila. In the spring of 1875 they were placed under San Carlos Apache agency, where, in the following year, they numbered 618. Dr Corbusier described the Yavapai men as tall and erect, muscular, and well proportioned. The women are stouter and have handsomer faces than the Yuma. Cuercomache was mentioned in 1776 as a Yavapai rancheria or division. In 1900 most of the tribe drifted from the San Carlos res. and settled in part of their old home on the Rio Verde, including the abandoned Camp McDowell

military res., which was assigned to their use Nov. 27, 1901, by the Secretary of the Interior until Congress should take final action. By 1903 these were said to number between 500 and 600 (but probably including Yuma and Apache), scattered in small bands from Camp McDowell to the head of the Rio Verde. By Executive order of Sept. 15, 1903, the old reservation was set aside for their use, the claims of the white settlers being purchased under act of Apr. 21, 1904. Here they are making some progress in civilized pursuits, but in 1905 the ravages of tuberculosis were reported to be largely responsible for a great mortality, the deaths exceeding the births 4 to 1. In 1906 there were officially reported 465 "Mohave Apache" at Camp McDowell and Upper Verde valley, Ariz., and 55 at San Carlos, a total of 520. In 1910 there were 178 Mohave Apache and Yavapai under the Camp McDowell school, 282 under the Camp Verde school, and 89 under the San Carlos school. (H. W. H.)

Apache Mohaves.—Ind. Aff. Rep. 1869, 92, 1870. Apache-Mojaoes.—Bourke, Moquis of Ariz., 80, 1884 (misprint). Apache-Mojaves.—Ind. Aff. Rep. 1864, 21, 1865. Apáches.—Garcés (1775–76), Diary, 446, 1900 (so called by Spaniards). Cruzados.—Oñate (1598) in Doc. Inéd., XVI, 276, 1871 (probably identical; see Bandelier in Arch. Inst. Papers, III, 109, 1890). Dil-zha.—White, MS. Hist. Apaches, 1875 ('Indians living where there are red ants': Apache name). E-nyaé-va Pai.—Ewing in Great Divide, 203, Dec. 1892 (='Sun people,' because they were sun-worshippers). Gohún.—ten Kate, Synonymie, 5, 1884 (Apache name, cf. *Tulkepaia*). Har-dil-zhays.—White, MS. Hist. Apaches, B. A. E., 1875 (Apache name). Inyá-vapé.—Harrington in Jour. Am. Folk-lore, XXI, 324, 1908 (Walapai name). Jum-pys.—Heintzelman (1853) in H. R. Ex. Doc. 76, 34th Cong., 3d sess., 44, 1857. Kohenins.—Corbusier in Am. Antiq., VIII, 276, 1886 (Apache name). Ku-we-vĕ-ka pai-ya.—Corbusier, Yavapai MS., B. A. E., 27, 1873–75 (own (?) name; so called because they live to the south). Nyavapai.—Corbusier in Am. Antiq., VIII, 276, 1886. Nyavi Pais.—Ewing in Great Divide, 203, Dec. 1892. Taros.—Garcés (1775–76), Diary, 446, 1900 (Pima name). Tubessias.—Ruxton misquoted by Ballaert in Jour. Ethnol. Soc. Lond., II, 276, 1850. Yabapais.—Whipple in Pac. R. R. Rep., III, pt. 3, 103, 1856. Yabijoias.—Pike, Exped., 3d map, 1810. Yabipaees.—Humboldt, Pers. Narr., III, 236, 1818. Yabipais.—Garcés (1775–76), Diary, 446, 1900 (Mohave name). Yabipaíye.—ten Kate, Reizen in N. A., 198, 1885. Yabipay.—Hinton, Handbook Ariz., map, 1878. Yabipias.—Humboldt, Atlas Nouvelle-Espagne, carte I, 1811. Yah-bay-päiesh.—Whipple in Pac. R. R. Rep., III, pt. 3, 99, 1856 (given as Maricopa name for Apache). Yalipays.—Hinton, op. cit., 28. Yam-pái ò.—Whipple, Exp'n San Diego to the Colorado, 17, 1851. Yampais.—Eastman map (1853) in Schoolcraft, Ind. Tribes, IV, 24–25, 1854. Yampaos.—Whipple in Pac. R. R. Rep., III, pt. 3, 103, 1856. Yampas.—Bell in Jour. Ethnol. Soc. Lond., I, 243, 1869. Yampay.—Möllhausen, Tagebüch, II, 167, 1858. Yampi.—Thomas, Yuma MS. vocab., B. A. E., 1868. Yampias.—Taylor in Cal. Farmer, Jan. 31, 1862. Ya-pa-pi.—Heintzelman (1853) in H. R. Ex. Doc. 76, 34th Cong., 3d sess., 44, 1857. Yavapaias.—Corbusier in Am. Antiq., VIII, 276, 1886. Yava-pais.—Dunn in Ind. Aff. Rep., 128, 1865. Yavape.—Corbusier in Am. Antiq., VIII, 276, 1886. Yavapies.—Ind. Aff. Rep., 109, 1866. Yavipais.—Arricívita, Cron. Seráfica, 471, 1792. Yavipay.—Escudero, Not. Estad. de Chihuahua, 228, 1834. Yévepáya.—Harrington in Jour. Am. Folk-lore, XXI, 324, 1908 (own name). Yubipias.—

Disturnell, Map Méjico, 1846. **Yubissias.**—Ruxton in Jour. Ethnol. Soc. Lond., II, 95, 1850 (misprint). **Yuni-pis.**—Heintzelman (1853) in H. R. Ex. Doc. 76, 34th Cong., 3d sess., 38, 1857. **Yupapais.**—Ind. Aff. Rep., 156, 1864. **Yurapeis.**—Ibid., 109, 1866.

Yawilchine. A Yokuts (Mariposan) tribe, not further identifiable, probably living formerly between Kaweah and Tule rs., Cal. They joined with other tribes in ceding lands to the United States under the treaty of May 30, 1851, when they were placed on a reserve. In 1882 the Yawitshenni were mentioned as on Tule River res. The word may be only a dialectic synonym of Yaudanchi, plural Yowechani for Yowedchani, which in certain dialects would become Yowelchani. (A. L. K.) **Yah-wil-chin-ne.**—Johnston in Sen. Ex. Doc. 61, 32d Cong., 1st sess., 23, 1852. **Ya-wil-chine.**—Royce in 18th Rep., B. A. E., 782, 1899. **Ya-wil-chuie.**—Barbour in Sen. Ex. Doc. 4, 32d Cong., spec. sess., 255, 1853. **Yawitshénni.**—Hoffman in Proc. Am. Philos. Soc., XXIII, 301, 1886. **Yoelchane.**—Wessells (1853) in H. R. Ex. Doc. 76, 34th Cong., 3d sess., 32, 1857.

Yawpan. See *Black drink, Yopon.*

Yayahaye. A Maricopa rancheria on the Rio Gila, Ariz., in 1744.—Sedelmair (1744) cited by Bancroft, Ariz. and N. Mex., 366, 1889.

Yayaponchatu. A traditional people who once lived in a single village N. of Oraibi, N. E. Ariz. In Hopi story they are said to have been in league with supernatural forces, and by means of fire to have destroyed the villages of Pivanhonkapi and Hushkovi, at the instance of the chief of the former, because his people had become degenerate through gambling.—Voth, Traditions of the Hopi, 241, 1905.

Yayatustenuggee. See *Great Mortar.*

Yazoo (meaning unknown). An extinct tribe and village formerly on lower Yazoo r., Miss. Like all the other tribes on this stream, the Yazoo were small in number. The people were always closely associated with the Koroa, whom they resembled in employing an *r* in speaking, unlike most of the neighboring tribes. The French in 1718 erected a fort 4 leagues from the mouth of Yazoo r. to guard that stream, which formed the waterway to the Chickasaw country. In 1729, in imitation of the Natchez, the Yazoo and Koroa rose against the French and destroyed the fort, but both tribes were finally expelled (Shea, Cath. Miss., 430, 449, 1855) and probably united with the Chickasaw and Choctaw. Whether this tribe had any connection with the West Yazoo and East Yazoo towns among the Choctaw is not known. See Gatschet, Creek Migr. Leg., I, 1884. **Hiazus.**—Rafinesque in Marshall, Ky., I, introd., 28, 1824. **Jakou.**—Gravier (1700) in Shea, Early Voy., 133, 1861. **Jason.**—French, Hist. Coll. La., I, 47, 1846. **Oatsees.**—Martin, Hist. La., I, 249, 1827. **Yachou.**—Iberville (1699) in Margry, Déc., IV, 179, 1880. **Yachoux.**—Charlevoix (1721) in French, Hist. Coll. La., III, 132, 1851. **Yalaas.**—Charlevoix (1774), New France, VI, 39, 1872 (probably identical).

Yasones.—Morse, N. Am., 254, 1776. **Yasons.**—Baudry des Lozières, Voy. La., 242, 1802. **Yasoos.**—Rafinesque, op cit. **Yasou.**—La Métairie (1682) in French, Hist. Coll. La., II, 22, 1875. **Yasoux.**—Pénicaut (1700) in Margry, Déc., V, 401, 1883. **Yasoves.**—Alcedo, Dic. Geog., V, 394, 1789. **Yassa.**—Coxe, Carolana, map, 1741. **Yassaues.**—Ibid. **Yassouees.**—Ibid., 10. **Yasüs.**—Hervas, Idea dell' Universo, XVII, 90, 1784. **Yazoos.**—Dumont in French, Hist. Coll. La., v, 72, 1853. **Yazous.**—Vater, Mithridates, III, sec. 3, 245, 1816. **Yazoux.**—Dumont, La., I, 135, 1753.

Yazoo (or *Yashu*). A former important Choctaw town, belonging to the Uklafalaya, situated in Neshoba co., Miss., near the headwaters of Oktibbeha cr. The site is still called Yazoo Old Town. Tecumseh visited this place in the fall of 1811. It is often mentioned in Government records and was the town where the commissioners appointed to investigate the Choctaw claims under the 14th article of the treaty of Dancing Rabbit cr. held their sessions from Apr. 6 to Aug. 24, 1843. It was sometimes called West Yazoo to distinguish it from another town of the name.—Halbert in Pub. Miss. Hist. Soc., VI, 427, 1902. **Octibea.**—Alcedo, Dic. Geog., III, 365, 1788. **Oktibbeha.**—Romans, Florida, I, 313, 1775. **Old Yazoo Village.**—Claiborne (1843) in Sen. Doc. 168, 28th Cong., 1st sess., 42, 1844. **West Yaso.**—Romans, Florida, map, 1775. **Yahshoo.**—Adair, Am. Inds., 339, 1775. **Yashoo.**—Ibid., 297. **Yazoo Old Village.**—Claiborne, op. cit., 41. **Yazoo Village.**—Bayley, ibid., 42.

Yazoo Skatane (*Yashu Iskitini*, 'little Yazoo'). A former Choctaw town on both banks of Yazoo cr., an affluent of Petickfa cr., on the N. side, in Kemper co., Miss. It extended up Yazoo cr. for about a mile to where there is an important fork. It was called East Yazoo Skatane by Romans to distinguish it from Yazoo (q. v.).—Halbert in Pub. Miss. Hist. Soc., VI, 422–23, 1902. **East Yasoo.**—Romans, Florida, 80, 1775.

Ybdacax. A tribe named in 1708 in a list of those which had been met or heard of N. of San Juan Bautista mission, on the lower Rio Grande (Fr. Isidro Felix de Espinosa, "Relacion Compendiosa" of the Rio Grande missions, MS. in archives of College of Santa Cruz de Querétaro). (H. E. B.)

Ye. The Lizard clan of the Tewa pueblos of San Juan and San Ildefonso, N. Mex. **Yé-tdóa.**—Hodge in Am. Anthr., IX, 351, 1896 (*tdóa* = 'people').

Yecora. A pueblo of the Opata and seat of a Spanish mission founded in 1673, situated in N. E. Sonora, Mexico, probably on Rio Soyopa. Pop. 356 in 1678, 197 in 1730. **Icora.**—Alegre in Bancroft, No. Mex. States, I, 523, 1884 (probably identical). **San Ildefonso Yecora.**—Zapata (1678), ibid., 245. **Yecora.**—Rivera (1730), ibid., 513. **Yecorí.**—Orozco y Berra, Geog., 343, 1864.

Yecora. A pueblo of the Nevome on an upper tributary of Rio Mayo, about lat. 28° 10', lon. 108° 30', Sonora, Mexico.—Orozco y Berra, Geog., 351, 1864,

Yehl ('raven'). One of the two main divisions or phratries of the Tlingit (q. v.) of the Alaskan coast.   (J. R. S.)

Yehlnaas-hadai (*Ye'l na'as xā'da-i,* 'Raven-house people'). A subdivision of the Yaku-lanas, a Haida family of the Raven clan, probably named from one house, although they occupied a large part of the town of Kweundlas.—Swanton, Cont. Haida, 272, 1905.
Yatl nas: had'ā'i.—Boas, Fifth Rep. N. W. Tribes Can., 26, 1889.

Yehuh. According to Lewis and Clark (Exped., II, 472, 1814) a Chinookan tribe living in 1806 just above the Cascades of Columbia r. Nothing more is known of them. See *Watlala.*
Wey-eh-hoo.—Gass, Journal, 1807, p. 199. Yehah.—Bancroft, Nat. Races, I, 317, 1874. Yehhuh.—Lewis and Clark Exped., II, 236, 1814.

Yekolaos. One of the two Cowichan tribes on Thetis id., off the S. E. coast of Vancouver id., Brit. Col. If identical with the Tsussie of the Canadian Reports on Indian Affairs, the population was 53 in 1904.
Tsussie.—Can. Ind. Aff., pt. II 66, 1902. Yéqolaos.—Boas, MS., B. A. E., 1887.

Yellow Lake. A Chippewa village, established about 1740 on Yellow lake, Burnett co., Wis.—Warren (1852) in Minn. Hist. Soc. Coll., v, 171, 1885.

Yellow Liver Band. An unidentified Sioux band, named from its chief, and numbering 60 lodges when brought to Ft Peck agency in Aug. 1872.—H. R. Ex. Doc. 96, 42d Cong., 3d sess., 15, 1873.

Yellow Thunder (*Wa-kun-cha-koo-kah*). A Winnebago chief, said to have been born in 1774, died in 1874. Prior to 1840 the Winnebago occupied the country surrounding L. Winnebago and Green bay, Wis. When it was determined to remove the Indians to a new reservation in N. E. Iowa and S. E. Minnesota, Yellow Thunder, with others of his tribe, was persuaded to visit Washington and "get acquainted with the Great Father." Here, on Nov. 1, 1837, they were induced to sign a treaty ceding to the United States all their lands E. of the Mississippi, and providing for their removal to the W. within eight months. The Indians claimed that they were misled into believing that they had eight years in which to make the change, consequently at the expiration of the stipulated time they were unwilling to go. In 1840 troops were sent to Portage to remove the Indians by force, and Yellow Thunder, through a false report that he intended to revolt, was put in chains; he was soon released, however, and the removal was effected without further trouble. Within a year Yellow Thunder and his wife reappeared at their old home and entered a tract of 40 acres as a homestead on the w. side of Wisconsin r. about 8 m. above Portage. Here he lived quietly until his death in Feb. 1874. Yellow Thunder was greatly respected by his people; he was an able counsellor in their public affairs, industrious, temperate, and a zealous Catholic. His portrait, painted by S. D. Coates, is in the gallery of the Wisconsin Historical Society, and a monument to his memory has been erected a few miles N. of Baraboo, Wis.

YELLOW THUNDER.   (WISCONSIN HISTORICAL SOCIETY)

Yellow Thunder. A former Winnebago village, named after its chief, at Yellow Banks, Green Lake co., Wis.—Whittlesey (1854) in Wis. Hist. Soc. Coll., I, 74, repr. 1903.

Yellow Wolf. A local band of the Cheyenne in 1850.   (J. M.)

Yelmus. A village, presumably Costanoan, whose inhabitants are mentioned as at San Juan Bautista and Dolores missions, Cal.
Yelamu'.—Taylor in Cal. Farmer, Oct. 18, 1861 (at Dolores mission). Yelmus.—Engelhardt, Franciscans in Cal., 398, 1897 (at San Juan Bautista mission).

Yelovoi (Russian: 'spruce'). A Kaniagmiut Eskimo village on Spruce id., Kodiak group, Alaska; pop. 78 in 1880.—Petroff in 10th Census, Alaska, 28, 1884.

Yendestake. A Tlingit village at the mouth of Chilkat r., Alaska, with 171 inhabitants in 1880. According to Emmons it is now occupied only in summer.
Jendestáke.—Krause, Tlinkit Ind., 100, 1885. Tindestak.—Wright, Alaska, 224, 1883. Yêndē'staq!ê.—Swanton, field notes, B. A. E., 1904. Y'hindastachy.—Willard, Life in Alaska, 301, 1884. Yondestuk.—Petroff in 10th Census, Alaska, 31, 1884.

Yennis ('good place'). A Clallam village at Port Angeles or False Dungeness, on Fuca str., N. W. Wash. Eells reported about 35 Indians around Port Angeles in 1887.

Dungeness.—Gibbs in Pac. R. R. Rep., I, 429, 1855 (should be False Dungeness; see Cont. N. A. Ethnol., I, 177, 1877). **I-eh-nus.**—Kane, Wand. in N. A., 229, 1859. **I-e'-nis.**—Eells, letter, B. A. E., May 21, 1886. **Tinnis.**—Gibbs in Pac. R. R. Rep., I, 429, 1855 (misprint). **Yennis.**—Treaty of 1855 in U. S. Ind. Treaties, 800, 1873.

Yenyedi (*Yĕnyē'dĭ*, 'mainland people'). A Tlingit division on Taku inlet, Alaska, belonging to the Wolf phratry.　(J. R. S.)

Yenyoḥol. Mentioned by Oviedo (Hist. Gen. Indies, III, 628, 1853) as a province or village visited by Ayllon, probably on the South Carolina coast, in 1520. In the Documentos Inéditos (XIV, 506, 1870) the name is spelled Yenyochol.

Yepachic. (Tarahumare: *yēpá* 'snow,' *chik* 'place of.') A rancheria on the extreme headwaters of the Rio Aros, a tributary of the Yaqui, in w. Chihuahua, Mexico. It seemingly was originally a Tarahumare settlement, but in 1902 was inhabited by Mexicans and about 20 Nevome, or Southern Pima, with a half-caste Tarahumare as its presidente.— Lumholtz, Unknown Mex., I, 124–128, 1902.

Santiago Yepachic.—Orozco y Berra, Geog., 324, 1864.

Yesheken (*Yĕ'cEqEn*). A division of the Nanaimo on the E. coast of Vancouver id., Brit. Col.—Boas in 5th Rep. N. W. Tribes Can., 32, 1889.

Yesito. A former village, probably Caddoan, near and presumably connected with the Yatasi on Red r. in N. w. Louisiana at the close of the 17th century.— Iberville (1699) in Margry, Déc., IV, 178, 1880.

Yeunaba. A Costanoan village situated in 1819 within 10 m. of Santa Cruz mission, Cal.—Taylor in Cal. Farmer, Apr. 5, 1860.

Yeunata. A Costanoan village situated in 1819 within 10 m. of Santa Cruz mission, Cal.—Taylor in Cal. Farmer, Apr. 5, 1860.

Yeunator. A Costanoan village situated in 1819 within 10 m. of Santa Cruz mission, Cal.—Taylor in Cal. Farmer, Apr. 5, 1860.

Yguases. An unidentified Texas tribe with whom Cabeza de Vaca lived during his stay in Texas in 1527–34. They dwelt inland from the Guaycones and s. E. of the Atayos. The buffalo herds reached their country, but the people used the skins mainly for robes and moccasins. They are spoken of as a well-formed, symmetrical people, good archers, and great runners. They hunted the deer by running the animal down. Cabeza de Vaca speaks of their using "bucklers" of buffalo hide. Their houses were of mats placed upon four hoops. When moving camp the mats were rolled in a bundle and carried on the back. The men perforated the lip and the nipple, and wore a reed thrust through the openings. They planted "nothing from which to profit" and subsisted mainly on roots, frequently suffering long fasts. During these painful periods they bade Cabeza de Vaca "not to be sad, there would soon be prickly-pears," although the season of this fruit of the cactus might be months distant. When the pears were ripe the people feasted and danced and forgot their former privations. They destroyed their female infants to prevent them being taken by their enemies and thus becoming the means of increasing the latter's numbers. They seem to have been more closely related by custom to tribes near the coast, like the Karankawa, than to the agricultural people toward the N. and w. So far as known the tribe is extinct. (A. C. F.)

Iguaces.—Barcia, Historiadores, I, 20, 1749. **Iguases.**—Ibid., 19. **Yeguaces.**—Ibid., 19, 20. **Yeguases.**—Davis, Span. Conq. N. Mex., 82, 1869. **Yeguaz.**—Cabeça de Vaca, Smith trans., 180, 1871. **Yeguazes.**—Ibid., 62, 1851. **Yguaces.**—Barcia, Historiadores, I, 28, 1749. **Yguases.**—Cabeça de Vaca, op. cit., 92, 1871. **Yguazes.**—Ibid., 102, 136.

Yiikulme. A former Maidu village on the w. side of Feather r., just below the village of Hoako, in the present Sutter co., Cal.　(R. B. D.)

Coolmehs.—Powers in Overland, Mo., XII, 420, 1874. **Kūl'-meh.**—Powers in Cont. N. A. Ethnol., III, 282, 1877. **Yiikulme.**—Dixon in Bull. Am. Mus. Nat. Hist., XVII, map, 1905.

Yikkhaich. A Yaquina village on the N. side of Yaquina r., nearly opposite the site of the present Elk City, Oreg.

Lickawis.—Lewis and Clark Exped., II, 118, 1814. **Lukawis.**—Ibid., 473. **Lukawisse.**—Am. Pioneer, II, 189, 1843. **Yi-kq'aio'.**—Dorsey in Jour. Am. Folk-lore, III, 229, 1890.

Yjar. Mentioned by Oñate (Doc. Inéd., XIV, 114, 1871) as a pueblo of the Jemez in New Mexico in 1598. It can not be identified with the native name of any of the ruins in the vicinity of Jemez.

Yxcaguayo.—Oñate, op. cit., 102 (misprint combination of Yjar (Yxar) and the first two syllables of Guayoguia, the name of another pueblo next mentioned).

Ymacachas. One of the 9 Natchez villages in 1699.—Iberville in Margry, Déc., IV, 179, 1880.

Yman. A former small tribe represented at San Antonio de Valero mission, Texas.

Ymic. A tribe given in 1708 in a list of tribes N. E. of San Juan Bautista mission, on the lower Rio Grande (Fr. Isidro Felix de Espinosa, "Relacion Compendiosa" of the Rio Grande missions, in archives of College of Santa Cruz de Querétaro). It may be identical with the Emet (q. v.), or Ymat, frequently met in the district E. of San Antonio.　(H. E. B.)

Ymunakam. A village, presumably Costanoan, formerly connected with San Carlos mission, Cal. It is said to have belonged to the Kalendaruk division.

Ymunacam.—Taylor in Cal. Farmer, Apr. 20, 1860. **Yumanagan.**—Ibid. (connected with Soledad mission.)

Yncaopi. Mentioned by Oñate (Doc. Inéd., xiv, 103, 1871) as a pueblo of New Mexico in 1598.

Yucaopi.—Bancroft, Ariz. and N. Mex., 137, 1889 (misprint).

Yodetabi. A Patwin tribe that formerly lived at Knight's Landing, Yolo co., Cal.

Todetabi.—Powell in 7th Rep. B. A. E., 70, 1891 (misprint). Yo-det′-a-bi.—Powers in Cont. N. A. Ethnol., III, 219, 1877. Yodetabies.—Powers in Overland Mo., XIII, 543, 1874.

Yodok. A former Maidu village on the E. bank of American r., just below the junction of South fork, Sacramento co., Cal.—Dixon in Bull. Am. Mus. Nat. Hist., XVII, map, 1905.

Yogoyekaydn ('juniper'). An Apache band or clan at San Carlos agency and Ft Apache, Ariz., in 1881.—Bourke in Jour. Am. Folk-lore, III, 112, 1890.

Yoholomicco (*yahólo*, 'hallooer,' an initiation title; *miko*, 'chief'). A Creek chief, born on Coosa r., Ga., about 1790; died in Arkansas about 1838. He was headman of

YOHOLOMICCO

Eufaula town, a warrior of prowess, and one of the most persuasive orators in the Creek nation. Of the party of MacIntosh, he fought under Gen. Jackson against the rebel Creeks in 1813–14, and subsequently signed the various treaties ceding Creek lands and agreeing to emigrate beyond the Mississippi. He died of the hardships of the journey when the removal took place, having previously lost his chieftaincy and seat in the council on account of his complaisance to the whites. (F. H.)

Yojuane. A Tonkawan tribe of northern and central Texas, frequently mentioned in 18th century Spanish records. Since their general history, customs, and ethnological relations are outlined under

Tonkawa, only a few characteristic facts concerning them need be given here.

The Yojuane and Tonkawa tribes were unmistakably mentioned in 1691 by Francisco de Jesus María as the "DiuJuan" and the "Tanqua ay," among the enemies of the Hasinai. It is probable that the Ayennis, spoken of in 1698 by Talon, and the Yakwal ('drifted ones') remembered, according to Gatschet, in Tonkawa tradition, were the Yojuane. That the Joyvan met by Du Rivage in 1719 on Red r., 70 leagues above the Kadohadacho, were the same tribe, there is little room for doubt (see Francisco de Jesus María, Relación, 1691, MS.; Interrogations faites à Pierre et Jean Talon, 1698, in Margry, Déc., III, 616, 1878; LaHarpe, ibid., VI, 277, 1886; and cf. *Yakwal*).

Throughout the 18th century the Yojuane shared the common Tonkawan hatred for the Apache. There are indications of an early hostility toward the Hasinai also. For example, about 1714 (the chronology is not clear), according to Espinosa they burned the Neche village and destroyed the main fire temple of the Hasinai confederacy. Ramón in 1716 likewise mentions them among the enemies of the Hasinai (Espinosa, Crónica Apostólica, pt. I, 424, 1746; Dictamen Fiscal, MS., in Mem. de Nueva España, XXVII, 193). Before the middle of the century, however, these relations with the Hasinai seem to have been changed, and in the latter half of the century the tribes frequently went together against the Apache.

The Yojuane tribe comes most prominently into notice between 1746 and 1756, in connection with the San Xavier missions on San Gabriel r., Texas. The four chiefs who went to San Antonio to ask for the missions were of the "Yojuanes, Deadozes, Maieyes, and Rancheria Grande," and Yojuane were among the neophytes gathered at the missions established as a result of that request. With some exceptions the indications are that by the middle of the 18th century the tribe had moved southward with the Tonkawa into central Texas. One of these exceptions is the statement that they had a village on Rio del Fierro, between San Sabá and the Taovayas (the Wichita r., perhaps), but that about 1759 it was destroyed by the Lipan, when the Yojuane fled to the Tonkawa, one of their number becoming a chief of that tribe (Cabello to Loyola, Béxar Archives, Province of Texas, 1786, MS.). The village on the Rio del Fierro could not have been the permanent residence of a large part of the tribe, for several times before this the Yojuane are referred to as living near the Hasinai, who were in E. Texas. In 1772 the Yocovane, apparently the Yojuane, were included by

Mezières among the Tonkawa. This is one of several indications that the Yojuane tribe was absorbed by the Tonkawa in the latter half of the 18th century. In 1819 Juan Antonio de Padilla wrote in his report on the Texas Indians that a tribe of 190 people called "Yuganis," and having customs like the "Cadó," lived "east of Nacodoches on the Nechas river." Terán, in 1828, called what appears to be the same tribe the "Yguanes." These names suggest the Yojuane, whom they may possibly have been, but it seems improbable that they were identical (Padilla, Indios Barbaros de Texas, 1819, MS.; Terán, Noticia, in Bol. Soc. Geog. Mex., 269, Apr. 1870). (H. E. B.)

Ayennis.—Talon (1698) in Margry, Déc., III, 616, 1878 (identical?). DiuJuan.—Francisco de Jesus Maria, Relación, 1691, MS. Iacovane.—Morfi (ca. 1782) in Mem. Hist. Tex., MS. Iojuan.—MS. (ca. 1746) in Archivo Gen. Mexico. Jojuanes.—Solís (1768), Diario, MS. in Mem. de Nueva España, XXVII, 277 (evidently a miscopy for Iojuanes). Joyvan.—LaHarpe (1719), op. cit. Yacavanes.—Bonilla (1772) in Tex. Hist. Asso. Quar., VIII, 66, 1905. Yocovanes.—Mezières, MS. Informe, 29, 1772 (identical?). Yohuane.—Arricivita, Chrónica Apostolica, pt. II, 1792. Yojuanes.—Ramón (1716), Dict. Fiscal, op. cit. Yujuanes.—Gabzabal (1748) letter in Mem. de Nueva España, XXVIII, 71.

Yokaia ('south valley'). An important division of the Pomo, formerly inhabiting the southern part of Ukiah valley, Mendocino co., Cal. The town and valley of Ukiah are named from them. Not to be confused with Yuki.

Ukiahs.—Taylor in Cal. Farmer, June 8, 1860. Ukias.—Ibid., May 18. Ya-ki-as.—McKee (1851) in Sen. Ex. Doc. 4, 32d Cong., spec. sess., 144, 1853. Yaskai.—Schoolcraft, Ind. Tribes, IV, 553, 1854 (probably identical). Yohios.—Taylor in Cal. Farmer, May 18, 1860. Yo-kai-a.—Powers in Cont. N. A. Ethnol., III, 163, 1877. Yo-kai-a-mah.—Ibid. Yukae.—Latham in Proc. Philol. Soc. Lond., VI, 79, 1852-3. Yukai.—Gibbs (1851) in Schoolcraft, Ind. Tribes, III, 112, 1853. Yo-Kei.—Jenkins in Sen. Ex. Doc. 57, 32d Cong., 2d sess., 10, 1853. Yolhios.—Taylor in Cal. Farmer, Mar. 30, 1860.

Yokeag. A corruption of Pequot-Mohegan *yok'hig,* an abbreviation of *yok'higan* '(what is) made soft.' Parched corn reduced to a very fine powder, and sometimes mixed with maple sugar. It is still prepared by the Pequot-Mohegan of the Indian reservation on Thames r., Conn., and is sometimes sold by them to their white neighbors, who eat it with milk and sometimes with ice cream. See *Nocake, Rokeag.* (W. R. G.)

Yokhter. A Yurok village on lower Klamath r., above Pekwan and below Shregegon, but on the opposite side of the river, in N. w. Cal.

Yau-terrh.—Gibbs (1851) in Schoolcraft, Ind. Tribes, III, 138, 1853. Yokhter.—A. L. Kroeber, inf'n, 1905.

Yoki (*Yo'-ki*). The Rain clan of the Patki (Cloud or Water-house) phratry of the Hopi.—Stephen in 8th Rep. B. A. E., 39, 1891.

Yokol (probably a form of *yokuts,* or *yokuch,* 'person,' 'Indian'). A Yokuts (Mariposan) tribe formerly living on Ka-

weah r., Cal., but now extinct. They lived about Kaweah station, near Exeter, Tulare co., on the s. side of the river opposite the Kawia. (A. L. K.)

Yocolles.—Taylor in Cal. Farmer, June 8, 1860. Yoko.—Hoffman in Proc. Am. Philos. Soc., XXIII, 301, 1886. Yokod.—A. L. Kroeber, inf'n, 1905 (name in Yokuts foothill dialects). Yokol.—Ibid. (name in Yokuts valley dialects). Yo-kols.—Johnston in Sen. Ex. Doc. 61, 32d Cong., 1st sess., 23, 1852. Yo-kul.—Wessells (1853) in H. R. Ex. Doc. 76, 34th Cong., sess., 32, 1857. Yowkies.—Purcell in Ind. Aff. Rep., 193, 1870. Yucal.—Hale misquoted by Bancroft, Nat. Races, I, 451, 1874. Yukal.—Hale, Ethnog. and Philol., 631, 1846. Yu'-kol—Powers in Cont. N. A. Ethnol., III, 370, 1877.

Yokolimdu. A former Nishinam village in the valley of Bear r., which is the next stream N. of Sacramento, Cal.

Yokoalimduh.—Powers in Overland Mo., XII, 22, 1874. Yo-ko'-lim-duh.—Powers in Cont. N. A. Ethnol., III, 316, 1877.

Yokulme (*Yū-kul'-mĕ*). A former Maidu village on the w. bank of Feather r., near Starr's Landing, Sutter co., Cal., with 12 inhabitants in 1856. Probably the same as Kulme. (R. B. D.)

Yukulmey.—Taylor in Cal. Farmer, June 8, 1860. Yukutneys.—Bancroft, Nat. Races, I, 450, 1874.

Yokuts. See *Mariposan Family.*

Yolanar. Mentioned as a Creek town (H. R. Ex. Doc. 276, 24th Cong., 300, 1836). It was more likely Seminole and was probably a branch town of Chiaha on Apalachicola r., Fla. Possibly the same as the modern name Iola.

Yolo (said to mean 'region thick with rushes'). A Patwin tribe after which Yolo co., Cal., was named. There were 45 of the tribe living in Yolo co. in 1884.

Tolenos.—Taylor in Cal. Farmer, Mar. 30, 1860 (probable misprint for Yolenos). Yolays.—Bancroft, Nat. Races, I, 362, 1874. Yolos.—Taylor in Cal. Farmer, June 8, 1860. Yoloy.—Bancroft, Nat. Races. I, 450, 1874 (proper form, meaning 'a region thick with rushes'). Yoloytoy.—Bancroft, Hist. Cal., IV, 71, 1886.

Yonaguska (properly *Yǎ'nû-gûñ'skǐ,* 'The bear drowns him,' whence his common name 'Drowning-bear'). The adopted father of Col. Wm. H. Thomas, and the most prominent chief in the history of the East Cherokee, although, singularly enough, his name does not occur in connection with any of the early wars or treaties. This is due partly to the fact that he was a peace chief and counselor rather than a war leader, and in part to the fact that the isolated position of the mountain Cherokee kept them aloof, in a great measure, from the tribal councils of those living to the w. and s. In person he was strikingly handsome, being 6 ft 3 in. in height and strongly built, with a faint tinge of red, due to a slight strain of white blood on his father's side, relieving the brown of his cheeks. In power of oratory he is said to have surpassed any other chief of his day. When the Cherokee lands on Tuckasegee r. were sold by the treaty of 1819, Yonaguska continued to reside on a reservation of 640 acres in a bend of the river a short distance above the present Bryson City, N. Car., on the site of the ancient Kituhwa. He afterward moved over to Oconaluftee, and finally, after the removal, gathered his people about him and settled with them on Soco cr. on lands purchased for them by Thomas. He was a prophet and reformer as well as a chief. When about 60 years of age he had a severe illness, terminating in a trance, during which his people mourned him as dead. At the end of 24 hours, however, he awoke to consciousness and announced that he had been to the spirit world, where he had talked with friends who had gone before, and with God, who had sent him back with a message to the Indians, promising to call him again at a later time. From that day until his death his words were listened to as those of one inspired. He had been somewhat addicted to liquor, but now, on the recommendation of Thomas, not only stopped drinking himself, but organized his tribe into a temperance society. To accomplish this he called his people together in council, and, after clearly pointing out to them the serious effect of intemperance, in an eloquent speech that moved some of his audience to tears, he declared that God had permitted him to return to earth especially that he might thus warn his people and banish whisky from among them. He then had Thomas write out a pledge, which was signed first by the chief and then by each one of the council, and from that time until after his death whisky was unknown among the East Cherokee. Although frequent pressure was brought to bear to induce him and his people to remove to the W., he firmly resisted every persuasion, declaring that the Indians were safer from aggression among their rocks and mountains than they could ever be in a land which the white man could find profitable, and that the Cherokee could be happy only in the country where nature had planted him. While counseling peace and friendship with the white man, he held always to his Indian faith and was extremely suspicious of missionaries. On one occasion, after the first Bible translation into the Cherokee language and alphabet, some one brought a copy of Matthew from New Echota, but Yonaguska would not allow it to be read to his people until it had first been read to himself. After listening to one or two chapters the old chief dryly remarked: "Well, it seems to be a good book— strange that the white people are not better, after having had it so long." He died, aged about 80, in Apr. 1839, within a year after the removal. Shortly before the end he had himself carried into the townhouse on Soco cr., of which he had supervised the building, where, extended on a couch, he made a last talk to his people, commending Thomas to them as their chief and again warning them earnestly against ever leaving their own country. Then wrapping his blanket around him, he quietly lay back and died. He was buried beside Soco, about a mile below the old Macedonia mission, with a rude mound of stones to mark the spot. He left two wives and considerable property, including an old negro slave named Cudjo, who was devotedly attached to him. One of his daughters, Katalsta, still (1909) survives, and is the last conservator of the potter's art among the East Cherokee. (J. M.)

Yonalus. Mentioned by Oñate (Doc. Inéd., XVI, 113, 1871) as a pueblo of New Mexico in 1598. Doubtless situated in the Salinas, in the vicinity of Abo, E. of the Rio Grande. It seemingly pertained to either the Tigua or the Piro.
Xonalús.—Bancroft, Ariz. and N. Mex., 135, 1889 (misprint). Yonalins—Columbus Mem. Vol., 154, 1893 (misprint.)

Yoncopin. See *Wampapin*.

Yonh ('hickory-nut'). A Yuchi clan.
Yónh tahá.—Gatschet, Uchee MS., B. A. E., 71, 1885 (='hickory-nut gens').

Yonkalla. The southernmost Kalapooian tribe, formerly living on Elk and Calapooya crs., tributaries of Umpqua r., Oreg. According to Gatschet there were two bands, called Chayankeld and Tsantokayu by the Lakmiut, but it seems likely that the former name (Tch' Ayankĕ'ld) is merely the native tribal name. The tribe is probably extinct. (L. F.)
Ayankéld.—Gatschet in Jour. Am. Folk-lore, XII, 212, 1899. Jamkallie.—Latham in Jour. Ethnol. Soc. Lond., I, 158, 1848. Tch'Ayankẽ'ld.—Gatschet, Calapooya MS., B. A. E., 1877 ('those living at Ayankeld': own name). Yamkallie.—Scouler in Jour. Roy. Geog. Soc., XI, 225, 1841. Yamkally.—Bancroft, Nat. Races, III, 565, 1882. Yoncolla.—McClane in Ind. Aff. Rep., 184, 1887. Yonkalla.—Gatschet in Jour. Am. Folk-lore, XII, 212, 1899. Youlolla.—Ind. Aff. Rep., 422, 1888.

Yonora. A former Tepehuane pueblo in Durango, Mexico; the seat of the mission of San Miguel.
S. Miguel Yonora.—Orozco y Berra, Geog., 318, 1864.

Yontuh ('acorn'). A Yuchi clan.
Yontu'h tahá.—Gatschet, Uchee MS., B. A. E., 71, 1885 (='acorn gens').

Yoo ('beads'). A Navaho clan.
Yòo.—Matthews in Jour. Am. Folk-lore, III, 104, 1890.

Yopon (*yaupon*). (1) The Southern traders' name of *Ilex cassine*, an elegant species of holly growing to a height of 10 or 15 feet in close proximity to the coast. (2) A beverage prepared from the torrefied leaves, and possessing the properties of an exhilarant and gentle diuretic. This beverage, called by the British traders "black drink" (q. v.), from the color of the strong infusion, was drunk by the Creeks at their "busk" (see *Busk*), and by the elders when assembled in council or when discussing everyday topics. The infusion was used for different purposes, according to its strength. Like the leaves of *Ilex paraguayensis* (maté), guayusa, cacao, guarana, tea, and coffee, the leaves of the holly under consideration owe their property of a nerve excitant to the alkaloid theine which they contain. The inhabitants of the Southern seaboard still annually collect and dry the leaves and use them as tea, which, however, is oppressively sudorific, at least to those who are unaccustomed to the use of it. The name is from Catawba *yopún*, a diminutive of *yop*, 'tree,' 'shrub.' (w. r. g.)

Yoquibo (*yŏkí* 'bluebird', *ívo* 'mesa': 'bluebird on the mesa'). A Tarahumare village between the mining settlements of Batopilas and Zapuri, near the extreme headwaters of the Rio Fuerte, in the Sierra Madre, w. Chihuahua, Mexico.—Lumholtz, Unknown Mex., I, 180, 1902.

Yoricas. A former tribe of s. Texas, perhaps Coahuiltecan, members of which were encountered by Fernando del Bosque, in 1675, in company with some of the Hapes.

Goricas.—Revillagigedo (1793) quoted by Orozco y Berra, Geog., 306, 1864. Goxicas.—Revillagigedo quoted by Bancroft, Nat. Races, I, 611, 1886. Yoricas.—Fernando del Bosque (1675) in Nat. Geog. Mag., XIV, 343, 1903.

Yorkjough. A Seneca village about 12 m. from Anagangaw (Honeoye, q. v.) and about 6 m. from New Genesee, probably in Livingston co., N. Y., destroyed by Gen. Sullivan in 1779.—Livermore (1779) in N. H. Hist. Soc. Coll., VI, 328, 1850.

Yoroonwago. A Seneca village formerly situated on upper Allegheny r., near the present Corydon, Warren co., Pa. It was one of the towns in the Seneca settlement that extended for nearly 8 m. along the Allegheny before 1779, near the later Cornplanter (Seneca) res., N. Y. This village is mentioned by this name by Col. Brodhead, to whom the name was given by John Montour. No such name appears on any of the maps of the period. It was probably situated at or near the village noted on Ellicott's map of 1786 as Tushhanushagota (Arch. Pa., XI, map, 1855); it is also noted on the Historical Map of Pennsylvania (Hist. Soc. Pa., 1875) as Tayunchoneyu, but is wrongly located below Conewango (Warren, Pa.), whereas according to Brodhead's statement it was 20 m. above that place.   (G. P. D.)

Inshaunshagota.—Howells, map, 1792, Tayunchoneyu.—Hist. Map Pa., Hist. Soc. Pa. 1875. Teushanushsong-goghta.—Adlum map, 1790, in Arch. Pa., 3d s., I, 1894. Tushhanushagota.—Ellicott map, 1786, in Arch. Pa., XI, 1855. Yahrungwago.—Brodhead (1779), ibid., XII, 166, 1856. Yoghroonwago.—Ibid., 156. Yoroonwago.—Hist. Map Pa., Hist. Soc. Pa., 1875 (wrongly situated).

Yorotees. Given by Ker (Trav., 139, 1816) as a tribe living 80 m. s. sw. of Red r., apparently in w. Texas, but "on a lake called by the natives Testzapotecas," and numbering 5,000. The so-called tribe is evidently imaginary.

Yotammoto. A former Maidu village near Genesee, Plumas co., Cal.—Dixon in Bull. Am. Mus. Nat. Hist., XVII, map, 1905.

Yotlik. An Eskimo village in w. Greenland, lat. 73° 40'.—Kane, Arct. Explor., II, 52, 1856.

Youahnoe. Given in John Work's list (Schoolcraft, Ind. Tribes, V, 488, 1855) as the name of a Kaigani town having 18 houses and 234 inhabitants in 1836–41. It may possibly have been the summer town of Kaigani.

Youghtanund. A tribe of the Powhatan confederacy living on the s. bank of Pamunkey r., Va., perhaps in Hanover co. Pop. in 1608 estimated at about 240.
Youghtamund.—Strachey (ca. 1612)), Va., 35, 1849. Youghtanund.—Smith (1629), Va., I, 117, repr. 1819. Youthtanundo.—Simons, ibid., 160.

Young Man Afraid of His Horses. A chief of the Oglala Sioux, contemporaneous with Red Cloud and one of the leading lieutenants of the latter in the war of 1866 to defeat the building of the Montana road through the buffalo pastures of Powder r. His Sioux name, Tasunkakokipápi, is not properly interpreted; it really means that the bearer was so potent in battle that the mere sight of his horses inspired fear. After the peace of 1868 he lived at the Oglala agency and died at Pine Ridge, S. Dak.   (D. R.)

Youpon. See *Black drink, Yopon*.

Yowani (probably 'the cutworm,' or 'the caterpillar'). A former important Choctaw town on Chickasawhay r., a mile or two s. of the modern town of Shubuta, Clarke co., Miss. The territory belonging to it extended westward to the eastern dividing ridge of Bogue Homa, northward as far as Pachuta cr., and southward perhaps as far as the confluence of Chickasawhay and Buckatunna rs. Its eastern boundaries are unknown. It is often mentioned by Adair and other contemporary writers. It seems that at one time during the 18th century it was included among the Sixtowns people, and the entire district was then sometimes called Seventowns. It was perhaps in 1764 that a band of Yowani separated from the main clan, emigrated to Louisiana, and united with the Caddo, forming the Yowani band in the Caddo tribe, an organization nearly extinct in 1892. All the remaining Yowani living in their ancient territory removed in 1832, in the second emigration, except two families, whose descendants still live in Mississippi. Some Yowani Choctaw settled about 4 m. N. of Lecompte, Rapides parish, La., but the settlement was probably abandoned before 1850; others went to the Chickasaw Nation, Ind. Ter., where they gained a livelihood as trappers; others settled between Red r. and Bayou Natchitoches, La., while a few passed into Texas. Consult Adair, Am. Inds., 1775; Gatschet, Creek Migr. Leg., I, 79, 1884; Halbert (1) in Pub. Ala. Hist. Soc., Misc. Coll., I, 380, 1901; (2) in Pub. Miss. Hist. Soc., III, 370, 1900; VI, 403–410, 1902.

Ayuwáni.—Gatschet, Caddo and Yatassi MS., B. A. E., 66 (Caddo name). **Aywani.**—Ibid. (another Caddo name). **Ewany.**—Romans, Florida, map, 1775. **Haiowanni.**—Halbert in Pub. Miss. Hist. Soc., 432, 1902. **Hewanee.**—Royce in 18th Rep. B. A. E., Miss. map, 1900. **Hewanny.**—Halbert, op. cit. **Hewhannee.**—Am. State Papers, Ind. Aff., I, 689, 1832. **Heyowani.**—Mooney in 14th Rep. B. A. E., 1093, 1896. **Hiowanni.**—Hamilton in Pub. Miss. Hist. Soc., VI, 405, 1902 (quoting various writers). **Hiyoomannee.**—Am. State Papers, op. cit., 749. **Hiyoowannee.**—Ibid. **Iawani.**—Latham, Varieties of Man, 350, 1850. **Iowanes.**—Ind. Aff. Rep. 1849, 33, 1850. **Iwanies.**—Bollaert in Jour. Ethnol. Soc. Lond., II, 265, 1850. **Tawanis.**—Latham in Trans. Philol. Soc. Lond., 103, 1856. **Yauana.**—Bartram, Voy., I, map, 1799. **Yoani.**—Romans, Florida, 86, 312, 1775. **Yonanny.**—Biog. and Hist. Mem. of N. W. La., 526, 1890. **Youana.**—Alcedo, Dic. Geog., V, 407, 1789. **Youane.**—Jefferys, French Dom. Am., map, 135, 1761. **Youané.**—d'Anville's map in Hamilton, Col. Mobile, 158, 1897. **Youna.**—Lattré, map U. S., 1784. **Yowana.**—Adair, Am. Inds., map, 1775. **Yowáni.**—Gatschet, Creek Migr. Leg., II, 206, 1888. **Yowanne.**—Adair, op. cit., 297.

Ypuc. A Chumashan village formerly in Ventura co., Cal.

Hí'-pŭk.—Henshaw, Buenaventura MS. vocab., B. A. E., 1884. **Ypuc.**—Taylor in Cal. Farmer, July 24, 1863.

Ysbupue. A tribe named in 1708 in a list of those which had been met or heard of N. of San Juan Bautista mission, on the lower Rio Grande (Fr. Isidro Felix de Espinosa, "Relación Compendiosa" of the Rio Grande missions, MS. in archives of College of Santa Cruz de Querétaro, Mexico). (H. E. B.)

Yscanis. A tribe of the Wichita confederacy; they were entirely distinct from the Asinais (Hasinai), though the names of the two tribes have been confused. It is possible that the Ysconis, or Isconis, reported to Domingo de Mendoza in 1684 among the tribes awaiting him somewhere in central or E. Texas, were the Yscanis (Mendoza, Viage, 1683–84, MS.). In 1719 LaHarpe visited them (the "Ascanis") on Canadian r., where they were living a settled life with the Wichita, Taovayas (Tawehash), and Tawakoni. LaHarpe also reported another village of the Ascanis 60 leagues farther to the N. w. (Margry, Déc., VI, 293, 1886). Little more is heard of these tribes till the middle of the 18th century, by which time they had all moved southward into N. Texas, under pressure from their bitter enemies, the Comanche and the Osage. According to an official report made in 1762, the Yscanis had been among the numerous tribes which, about 1746, asked the missionaries at San Antonio for missions in central Texas. If this be true, they were possibly the Hiscas, or Haiscas, mentioned in documents relating to the San Xavier missions (Royal cedulas of Apr. 6, 1748, and Mar. 21, 1752, MSS. in Archivo Gen. de México). In 1760 Fr. Calahorra y Saenz, of Nacogdoches, went among the Yscanis and Tawakoni to establish peace, and soon afterward made an unsuccessful attempt to found a mission for them. These two tribes were at that time living close together on a stream in N. Texas, apparently farther N. than the place where Mezières found them a decade later (contemporary docs. in Béxar Archives). The Yscanis took part in the peace conference held by Mezières in 1770 at the Kadohadacho village, and two years later they sent representatives to Béxar to ratify the convention before the governor of Texas. When, in 1772, Mezières visited the tribe, they were living near the E. bank of the Trinity, somewhere below the present Palestine, 7 leagues E. of one of the Tawakoni villages, and an equal distance W. of the Kichai. The village consisted of 60 warriors and their families. They lived in a scattered agricultural settlement, raised maize, beans, melons, and calabashes, were closely allied with the other Wichita tribes, whose language they spoke, and were said by Mezières to be cannibals. There are indications that after this the Yscanis united with the Tawakoni, with whom they had always been most closely associated, to reappear, perhaps, in the 19th century, as the Waco. In his reports of his expeditions made in 1778 and 1779 to the Wichita tribes Mezières does not mention the Yscanis, but he fully describes the two Tawakoni villages, then both on the Brazos. Morfi, about 1782, on what authority is not known, states that the "Tuacana nation, to which are united some 90 families of the Ixcani, occupies two towns on the banks of the river Brazos de Dios" (Mem. Hist. Tex., bk. II, MS.). This not improbable, for although the Yscanis are sometimes mentioned by name as late as 1794, at least, it is always in connection with the other Wichita tribes, and with no indication as to their location. After 1794, so far as has been learned, the name is not used. But a quarter of a century later, when the Tawakoni villages are again mentioned in the records (now English instead of Spanish), one of them appears as that of the Waco, a name formerly unknown in Texas, and not accounted for by migration. The Waco may have been the Yscanis under a new name. For other information, see *Tawakoni, Tawehash, Waco, Wichita.* (H. E. B.)

Ascanis.—LaHarpe (1719), op. cit. **Haiscas.**—Royal cedula of 1752, op. cit. (identical?). **Hiscas.**—Ibid., 1748. **Hyscanis.**—Kerlérec (1753), Projet de Paix, in Jour. Soc. des Américanistes de Paris, n. s., III, no. 1, 72, 1900. **Isconis.**—Mendoza (1684), op. cit. **Ixcanis.**—Morfi (ca. 1782), op. cit. **Izacanis.**—Cabello, Informe, 1784, MS. **Yscan.**—Gonzalez (1770), MS. letter in the Archivo Gen. Méx. **Yscanes.**—Melchor Afan de Rivera (1768), letter to Hugo O'Conor, MS. in Béxar Archives. **Ysconis.**—Mendoza (1684), op. cit.

Yta. A province or village visited by Ayllon, probably on the South Carolina coast, in 1520. It was then under the chief Datha.
Itha.—Barcia, Ensayo, 4, 1723. **Yta.**—Oviedo, Hist. Gen. Indies, III, 628, 1853. **Ytha.**—Barcia, op. cit.

Ytriza. Mentioned by Oñate (Doc. Inéd., XVI, 103, 1871) as a pueblo of New Mexico in 1598.

Yubuincariri. A tribe or band, probably Shoshonean, living w. of Green r., Utah, in 1776.
Iumbucanis.—Taylor in Cal. Farmer, Jan. 31, 1862. **Jumbuicrariri.**—Mühlenpfordt, Mejico, II, 538, 1842. **Yubuincarini.**—Escalante quoted by Duro, Don Diego de Peñalosa, 142, 1882. **Yubuincariris.**—Dominguez and Escalante (1776) in Doc. Hist. Mex., 2d s., I, 537, 1854.

Yucaipa ('wet lands'). A former village of the Serranos E. of Redlands, s. Cal.
Yucaipa.—Caballeria, Hist. San Bernardino Val., 39, 1902; Kroeber in Univ. Cal. Pub., Am. Arch. and Eth., VIII, 33, 1908. **Yukaipa.**—Kroeber, ibid., 39. **Yukaipat.**—Kroeber, ibid., 34 (Serrano name).

Yucca. The yucca was perhaps the most useful plant known to the Indians of its habitat, which included the Southern states, the Rocky mtn. region, and the Great Plains as far N. as the Dakotas. *Yucca gloriosa* is a native of Virginia, and *Y. filamentosa* ranges southward from that state. It was the "silk grass" so often mentioned by early writers on Virginia. The tribes making most use of this plant are the Comanche, Apache, Navaho, Pueblos, Havasupai, Mohave, Pima, Papago, Maricopa, Walapai, Paiute, Panamint, and Diegueños. There are innumerable specimens of sandals, cordage, etc., from caves and cliff-houses showing the use of yucca by the ancient Southwestern tribes, and that the Southern tribes valued the fiber is indubitable. The fruit of *Y. baccata* and *Y. glauca* is used for food by the Zuñi, Navaho, Apache, and other tribes of New Mexico and Arizona, and the flowers of *Y. filamentosa* and *Y. gloriosa* were eaten by the Virginia Indians and tribes farther s. The roots were the only soap (amole) known to the Southwestern tribes, and the Pueblos especially use it for washing the hair, for which purpose it is a godsend in a territory where the water is generally alkaline. The Kiowa added the roots to a preparation used in tanning skins (see *Skin-dressing*). The Navaho made green dye from the chopped leaves of *Y. baccata* in conjunction with another plant, and the Zuñi used the juice extracted, by boiling, from the fruit of *Y. glauca*, in the manufacture and decoration

of pottery. The dried flower stalk is an excellent material for fire-drills (Apache, Zuñi, cliff-dwellers). The Zuñi shredded the stalk, after boiling, to procure a strong, straight fiber, which they extracted with their teeth. Hairbrushes were made from coarse yucca fibers by many tribes of the extreme S. W., and the Pueblos used thin strips of the leaf as paint brushes in decorating pottery, masks, tablets, dolls, prayer-sticks, etc. In basketry the leaves and slender fibrous roots were extensively used for making trays, plates, bowls, and mats for household use and to shroud the dead. The most useful product of the yucca was its excellent fiber, which was used in straight bunches or twisted into cord for making nets, noose snares, bowstrings, sandals, cloth, and warp for rabbit-skin and feather robes, and for sewing and tying, the leaves or strips of them often being used in the natural state for the latter purpose. For twisting the fiber into cord the Papago had a simple device which was whirled in the hand. The net of the carrying frame (*kihu*) of the Pima and Papago is elaborately worked and resembles lace. Dried flower stalks of the yucca were carried in certain Zuñi ceremonies, and the leaves were used for simulating flagellation in an initiation rite by the Hopi and other Pueblos. (W. H.)

Yuchi ('situated yonder,' probably given by some Indians of the tribe in answer to the inquiry "Who are you?" or "Whence come you?"). A tribe coextensive with the Uchean family (q. v.). Recent investigations point strongly to the conclusion that the Westo referred to by early Carolina explorers and settlers, and from whom Savannah r. was orginally named, were the Yuchi. It is uncertain whether the Stono, whose name is sometimes coupled with the Westo, were related to them, or whether the two tribes have been confused on account of a similarity in designation. The early writers also state that the Westo were driven out of their country in 1681 by the Savannah (Shawnee), but this must mean only a part of them. Another name applied to at least the northernmost Yuchi was Hogologee. These different names have caused much confusion, and standard maps of the 18th century have Westos, Hogologees, and Yuchi (or Uchee) noted independently. It is probable, however, that all of these were Yuchi, representing, instead of separate tribes, a number of successive migrations of Yuchi from Savannah r. to the Chattahoochee—the Westo being those driven out by the Shawnee, the Hogologee those who emigrated with the Apalachicola after the Yamasee war, and the Yuchi those who changed their place of abode between 1729 and 1750, just before and after the settlement of Georgia. Various attempts have been made to find a Yuchi derivation for words and names recorded by ancient chroniclers, but with the possible exception of Yupaha, the name of a country heard of by De Soto but not certainly reached, there is no good evidence in support of them. The name of Cofitachique, which has generally been considered a

YUCHI MAN. (F. G. SPECK, PHOTO.)

Yuchi town, appears to be Muskhogean, and, if the indentification of the Westo with the Yuchi is correct, there is good reason for believing that the people of Cofitachique were something else. Although there is known to have been one settlement of the Yuchi on Tennessee r., the rest of them apparently occupied one continuous area and seem to have constituted a homogeneous people. This area embraced the entire mid-course of Savannah r., and probably included most of the Ogeechee, which was sometimes known as Hughchee (i. e. Yuchi) r. In 1739 a Yuchi town, Mount Pleasant, existed on Savannah r. 25 m. above Ebenezer, hence in Screven co., Ga., probably near the mouth of Brier cr. Tracts on the w. side of that r. extending as far s. as Ebenezer cr., Effingham co., and others above and below Augusta were claimed by the Yuchi as late as 1740. Hawkins in 1799 (Sketch, 61, 1848) stated that Yuchi were formerly settled in small villages at Ponpon, Saltketchers (these two, however, were Yamasee centers), Silver Bluff, and Ogeechee, and were continually at war with the Cherokee, Catawba, and Creeks. This

gives them a wide range on both sides of Savannah r. Filson (Discov. of Ky., 1793) said that the "Uchees occupy four different places of residence, at the head of St. John's, the fork of St. Mary's, the head of Cannouchee (Cannochee), and the head of St. Tilles [Satilla]." The principal Yuchi town among the Lower Creeks had in Hawkins' time (1799) sent out three colonies eastward: Intatchkalgi, Padshilaika, and Tokogalgi (their Creek names). Another Yuchi town is mentioned by Morse (1822) near Miccosukee, Leon co., N. Fla. Some of the Yuchi settled with the Savannah Indians on Tallapoosa r. Hawkins estimated the "gun-men" in Yuchi and these branch villages at 250. Bartram (Trav., 387, 1792) points out their relations to the Creeks as follows: "They are in confederacy with the Creeks, but do not mix with them; and on account of their numbers and strength are of importance enough to excite and draw upon them the jealousy of the whole Muscogulge confederacy, and are usually at variance, yet are wise enough to unite against a common enemy to support the interest and glory of the general Creek confederacy." Their town is described as the largest, most compact, and

YUCHI GIRL. (F. G. SPECK, PHOTO.)

best situated Indian town he ever saw. Their population is stated by him to be from 1,000 to 1,500, and in this estimate he includes 500 warriors. The Creeks claimed to have subjugated the Yuchi and regarded them as slaves (*salafki*), probably only the western or Chattahoochee part, not those who lived among the Seminole and the Yamasee. In recent times this point was mooted even in the Creek legislature, and some members thought the Yuchi should receive no annuities, since they were slaves. The Yuchi were much attached to the ways and customs of their forefathers, and in 1813 they took sides with the Upper Creeks against the Government. Their towns were destroyed in consequence of this by the friendly Creeks. Hawkins (Sketch, 62, 1799) claims a better standard of morality for them than for many of the Creek towns, saying "these people are more civil and orderly than their neighbors, and their women are more chaste and the men better hunters. The men take part in the labors of the women, and are more constant in their attachment to their women than is usual among red people." In 1836 they removed with the Creeks to the present Oklahoma, where fewer than 500 now reside in the N. w. part of the Creek Nation. Part live among the Shawnee on the W.—the so-called Shawano Yuchi. Here they had a separate town body, with representatives in the Creek assembly, until the dissolution of the Creek Nation as such in 1906. They exhibit a tendency toward conservatism and pride. Their loosely-marked settlements were named as follows: Arkansaw River, Big Pond Town, Blackjack Town, Deep Fork Creek, Duck Creek Town, Hogologes, Intatchkalgi, Mount Pleasant, Ogeechee, Padshilaika, Polecat Creek, Red Fork, Silver Bluff, Snake Creek, Spring Garden Town, and Tokogalgi.

In material culture the Yuchi are typical of the agricultural hunting tribes of the s. E. Atlantic and Gulf coast area, living formerly in permanent villages surrounded by cultivated fields and always situated conveniently near some stream where fish abounded. Their houses were grouped about a square plot of ground, which was held as sacred, where religious ceremonies and social gatherings took place. The ordinary houses were of the common coast type, covered with bark or mats, but there was, besides, another more complex and permanent sort with sides plastered with clay. They were good potters, manufacturing various forms by the coiling process, nearly all, however, similar in shape to gourds, from which it is possible the forms were derived. Incised decorations occur only on or near the rim. Decorated effigy pipes of clay are still made, resembling closely some of those found in mounds in Georgia and the Carolinas. Basketry was made of cane and hickory splints, and the art was quite highly developed. Considerable wooden ware was also used. The original style of clothing has been supplanted for several generations by calico and trade goods made into shirts, outside hunting jackets, leggings, turban-like headgear, sashes, neckbands, garters, shoulder straps, and pouches, which are possibly survivals of older forms. Sashes, neckbands, leg-bands, hair pendants, pouches, and shoulder-bands are decorated with geometrical designs in bead embroidery representing animals and natural objects. Some of these designs are said to be worn in imitation of mythic characters and seem to be in a sense symbolical. An influence may have been exerted on Yuchi art by the prairie tribes since the removal to the W. Bows and arrows, clubs, and spears were their chief weapons. The blowgun was much in use in hunting. Dogs, too, were used in the chase, and hunting formulas were believed to affect the movements of the quarry. Fishing was commonly carried on by poisoning the stream with a species of *tephrosia*.

The political organization of the tribe, which has become more pronounced in type since its incorporation into the Creek Nation, is based on the town. This is made up of some 18 or 20 totemic, maternal, exogamic clans, the members of which trace their descent from the totem animal and have certain restrictions in regard to it. At an annual ceremony the clans perform propitiatory and reverential dances in honor of their totems.

The Yuchi clans are as follows, the names in parentheses being the simplified forms of those recorded by Gatschet: Sag$^\varepsilon$ē′ (Sagi), Bear; Dałá (Tala), Wolf; We$^\varepsilon$yA^n′ (Weyon), Deer; Täb$^\varepsilon$ä′ (Tapa), Tortoise; Wētc$^\varepsilon$A^n′ (Wetchon), Panther; Cad$^\varepsilon$ané (Shatane), Wildcat; Catiené (Shathiane), Fox; Godá (Huda), Wind; Cū (Shu), Fish; Cagä^n′(Shakian), Beaver; Cūłané (Shuhlanan), Otter; Djä′tīe^n (Tchatchiun), Raccoon; YūsA^n′(Yussoih), Skunk; WētsagowA^n′ (Wetsagua), Opossum; Cadjwané, Rabbit; Cáya, Squirrel; Wētc$^\varepsilon$á (Witchah), Turkey; Câ′na (Sha), Eagle; YA^{n}tī′, Buzzard; Ca, Snake. Gatschet gives also the Senan (Bird), Tapatwa (Alligator), Tapi (Salt), To Sweet-potato), Yonh (Hickory-nut), and Yontuh (Acorn), but it is doubtful if these clans existed among the Yuchi. There is disagreement among native informants regarding the existence of the Eagle, Buzzard, and Snake clans above given.

The whole male population of the town, and of the tribe as well, is again subdivided into two other social classes, which have certain town offices and functions in the ceremonies inherent in them. These classes are chief and warrior, and inheritance in them is reckoned through the father without regard to clanship of the other sort. Property is handed down partly through father to son and partly from father to sister's children, inheritance being thus an individual and not solely a group matter. The men of different classes are distinguished by facial painting.

The town officials are a town chief and priest, chosen from the chief class of certain leading clans; a master of ceremonies and representative from the warrior class of certain clans, with 3 secondary chiefs and 3 secondary warriors from certain clans. There are, besides, other officials chosen from certain clans and classes, who have charge of different stages of the ceremonies. Unanimous acclamation constitutes appointment to an office. The town itself, represented by its chiefs and lesser officers or warriors, regulates the ceremonies and matters of an internal nature or those dealing with outsiders or other towns.

Each town has a sacred public square, or shrine, where social and religious meetings are held, on the four edges of which stand four ceremonial lodges covered with boughs. In these lodges the different clan groups have assigned places during public occasions. The square ground symbolizes the rainbow, where, in the sky-world, Sun, the mythical culture-hero, underwent the ceremonial ordeals which he handed down to the first Yuchi.

The chief power above that is recognized as the source of life and mystery is the Sun. There seems, as well, to be some unworshiped but acknowledged supernatural source of power from which mechanical magic flows. But the Sun, in his plural concept as chief of the sky-world, the author of the life, the ceremonies, and culture of the people, is by far the most important figure in their religious life. The various animals of the sky-world are important in myth, but in practice the Yuchi do not recognize in them anything more to be feared than in the numerous spirits which dominate other natural objects in their surroundings. Vegetation spirits are closely concerned in their daily and ceremonial life, as is shown in the annual new-fire and harvest ceremony. Besides these, totemic ancestral spirits play a rather important part.

Public religious worship is performed by the whole town in a complex annual ceremony connected with the corn harvest, the different rites of which occupy three days and the intervening nights. The square ground is the scene of action. Ceremonial making of new fire, clan dances mimicking totemic ancestors, dances propitiating evilly-inclined spirits and thanking various beneficent ones as well as inducing them to continue their benefits, scarification of the males for sacrifice and purification, taking an emetic as a purifier, the partaking of the first green corn of the season, and the performance of a characteristic ball game with two sticks, are the main elements of the annual ceremony. Young men are admitted to the ranks of manhood at this time. This important event is carried on in distinct emulation of the Sun to insure a continuance of tribal existence. The sentiment of obedience to the Sun is peculiarly prominent with the Yuchi.

Disease is accredited to the presence of a harmful spirit which has been placed in the system by some offended animal spirit or malevolent conjurer. Herbs, which have names corresponding in some way to the name of the animal causing the trouble, are brewed in a pot and administered internally. By this means of sympathetic healing and by the use of song formulas the disease spirit is driven out by the shaman.

During her catamenial periods, and at childbirth also, the woman secludes herself from her family and house. She lives alone in a temporary hut under a taboo of certain foods. At the birth of the child its navel cord is ceremonially disposed of, and the father is henceforth prohibited from association with his friends, besides having restrictions for a month against the use of certain foods, manual labor, and hunting. The children's cradle is the hammock. On the fourth day after its birth the child is named after a maternal granduncle or grandaunt. Unmarried girls are marked off from others with red paint. The marriage rite is a very simple one, the couple being of different clans, of course, merely agreeing to unite and for a while usually reside in the woman's home. The dead were formerly buried underneath the floor of the house with a supply of food and clothes. Nowadays, however, burial is made in a cemetery, with rites similar to those of former times, and a small log hut is raised over the spot. Here a fire is kept burning for four days, during which time the spirit is on its journey eastward to the land of the dead up above where the Sun is. There are four souls, but only one passes on to the future life, having as a finale to pass an obstacle at the entrance to the sky. If this point is passed in safety the journey is over, otherwise it returns to earth a menace to the happiness of the living.

In mythology there is a sharp contrast between culture-hero and trickster. In the more sacred cosmological myths considerable unity is found, but the trickster tales are loose and often fragmentary. Creations are ascribed mostly to the assembled pre-earthly animals. Earth is brought up from a watery waste by craw-fish. The Sun seems to be connected in some way with the culture-hero. He created the Yuchi, having caused their forebears to spring from a drop of menstrual blood in the sky world, whence they were transferred to this earth. He is likewise the author of the human class and clan system and the religious rites, but he does not appear prominently as a transformer. He is furthermore the giver of all that is materially good and beneficial in their lives. The trickster, on the other hand, is named Rabbit. He effects a few transformations in the course of his mischief-making career, without any particular motive. Other myths are held by the various clans, and repeated generally in praise of their totem. Many myth elements from negro sources may have been embodied by these Indians in their animal tales, probably through contact with the Creek negroes. Other types of widely distributed myths are the race between two animal rivals, the imitation of the host, the magic flight, stealing of fire, tarman story, the legend about an emigration of part of the tribe, the origin of death resulting from someone's mistake, and the explanation of various peculiarities possessed by the present-day animals. See *Westo, Yupaha.*

Consult Speck, Ethnology of the Yuchi Inds., Anthr. Pub. Mus. Univ. Pa., I, no. 1, 1909. (F. G. S.)

Achees.—Prichard, Phys. Hist. Man., v, 401, 1847. Ani'-Yu'tsĭ.—Mooney in 19th Rep. B. A. E., 510, 1900 (Cherokee name; sing. *Yu'tsĭ*). Euchas.— Romans, Florida, I, 280, 1775. Euchees.—Lincoln (1789) in Am. St. Papers, Ind. Aff., I, 79, 1832. Euhchee.—Adair, Hist. Am. Inds., 346, 1775. Eutchees.—Hawkins (1785) in Am. St. Papers, Ind. Aff., I, 39, 1832. Houtchis.—Morse, Rep. to Sec. War, 311, 1822. Ochees.—Drake Bk. Inds., 94, 1848. Ouchee.—Schermerhorn in Mass. Hist. Soc. Coll., 2d s., II, 18, 1812. Round town people.—Swanton in Am. Anthr., XI, no. 3, 497, 1909 (so called by early English). Savannas.—Lattré, map of U. S., 1784. Savanuca.—Bartram, Trav., 461, 1791. Tahogale.—Coxe, Carolana, 13, 1741 (erroneously given as an island in Tennessee r. and the tribe occupying it). Tahogaléwi.—Gatschet, Creek Migr. Leg., I, 19, 1884. (Delaware name.) Tohogaleas.—German map Brit. Col., *ca.* 1750. Tsoyaha.—F. G. Speck, inf'n, 1907 ('offspring of the sun': own name). Uchees.—Barnard (1792) in Am. St. Papers, Ind. Aff., II, 309, 1832. Uches.—Bartram, Trav., 209, 1791. Uchies.—Drake, Bk. Inds., bk. IV, 58, 1848. Uchys.—Woodward, Rem., 25, 1859. Utchees.—Gallatin in Trans. Am. Antiq. Soc., II, 95, 1836. Utchis.—Nuttall, Jour., 236, 1821. Utschies.— Berghaus (1845), Physik. Atlas, map 17, 1848. Yoochee.—Loughridge, in Ind. Aff. Rep., 131, 1851. Yuchi.—Gatschet, Creek Migr. Leg., I, 19, 1884. Yuchiha.—Gatschet, MS., B. A. E. (distributive plural of *Yuchi*).

Yucuche. A Tatshiautin village at the head of Stuart lake, Brit. Col., and the portage between it and Babine lake. Pop. 16 in 1909.

Yə-ĸu-tce.—Morice, Notes on W. Dénés, 26, 1893. Yucutce.—Can. Ind. Aff. Reps.

Yué. The name applied by the Garzas, who were living in 1828 at Mier, on the s. side of the Rio Grande, to the band of Carrizos who lived at Camargo. The band

of Carrizos about Laredo, Texas, they called Yemé. Those at Camargo were at this time still in part unsettled and uncivilized. According to the naturalist Luis Berlandier, who visited these places in the year named, the Garzas were commonly known in the country as Carrizos, yet their languages were entirely distinct, the two tribes being able to understand each other only by signs. He adds that the language of the Yué was limited to the Carrizo tribe only (Berlandier and Chovel, Diario de Viage de Limites, 144, 146, 1850). (H. E. B.)

Yufera. A district (tribe) speaking a distinct dialect of the Timucuan language, mentioned without location or other detail by Pareja (1614), Arte de la Lengua Timuquana, 1886.

Yugeuingge (Tewa: 'village of the ravine'). A former Tewa pueblo on the w. bank of the Rio Grande, opposite the present pueblo of San Juan, near the site of the village of Chamita, N. N. Mex. It was visited in 1542 by Francisco de Barrionuevo, of Coronado's expedition, but little information concerning it was obtained, as the inhabitants at the approach of the Spaniards fled to the mountains, where, it was said, they had four strong villages that could not be reached with horses. The pueblo was voluntarily relinquished to the Spaniards under Oñate in 1598, the inhabitants joining their kindred at San Juan. In the year named the first white settlement in the W. was here made, under the name "San Francisco de los Españoles," and on Sept. 8 the chapel was consecrated. In the following year the name was changed to San Gabriel, which has been retained by the Mexicans as the name of the place to this day. San Gabriel was abandoned in the spring of 1605 and Santa Fé founded as the seat of the New Mexican provincial government. See Bandelier (1) in Arch. Inst. Papers, IV, 58, 1892, (2) Gilded Man, 286, 1893; Winship in 14th Rep. B. A. E., 1896; Hodge in Historic Towns of Western States, 1901. (F. W. H.)

Juke-yunke.—Loew (1875) in Wheeler Surv. Rep., VII, 344, 1879. San Gabriel.—Shea, Cath. Miss., 78, 1870. San Gabriel del Yunque.—Bandelier in Arch. Inst. Papers, III, 107, 1890. Sant Francisco de los Españoles.—Oñate (1598) in Doc. Inéd., XVI, 116, 1871. Sant Gabriel.—Oñate, ibid. Sant Gabriele.— Bandelier, op. cit., I, 19, 1888 (after Oñate). Ynqueyunque.—Davis, Span. Conq. N. Mex., 185, 221, 225, 1869 (misprint). Yuge-uing-ge.—Bandelier in Arch. Inst. Papers, III, 123, 311, 1890 (aboriginal name). Yunque.—Bandelier in Ritch, N. Mex., 201, 1885. Yuqueyunk.—Gallatin in Trans. Am. Ethnol. Soc., II, lxxi, 1848. Yuqueyunque.—Castañeda (1596) in 14th Rep. B. A. E., 525, 1896. Yuqui Yanqui.—Kern in Schoolcraft, Ind. Tribes, IV, map, 38–39, 1854.

Yuit (pl. of *yuk*, 'man': own name.— Bogoras). The Asiatic Eskimo, who emigrated from America probably at no distant period and are settled around East cape, in the neighborhood of Indian pt.

and C. Chukotsky, and on St Lawrence id. Although a few of them have obtained reindeer, in mode of life and general characteristics they resemble the Eskimo of Alaska. Their language, however, varies considerably from that spoken on the American side and is said to be harsher. But few of them have adopted the custom of wearing labrets. They have been frequently confused with their neighbors, the maritime Chukchi. Linguistically they may be distinguished into four groups—the Noökalit of East cape, the Aiwanat of Indian pt., the Wuteëlit of C. Ulakhpen, and the Eiwhuelit of St Lawrence id. Their villages, grouped under these subdivisions, are: *Noökalit:* Enmitahin, Nabukak, Ulak. *Aiwanat:* Avak, Imtuk, Napakutak, Rirak, Tesik, Unisak. (Krause mentions another, at the head of Plover bay, called Nasskatulok, not referred to by Bogoras.) *Wuteëlit:* Chenlin, Cherinak. *Eiwhuelit:* Chibukak, Chitnak, Kialegak, Kukuliak, Puguviliak, Punuk.

Chŭklŭ′k-mut.—Dall in Cont. N. A. Ethnol., I, 13, 1877. Chukohukomute.—Raymond in Sen. Ex. Doc. 12, 42d Cong., 1st sess., 25, 1871. Namollos.—Prichard, Phys. Hist. Mankind, v, 371, 1847. Yu-Ite.—Deniker, Races of Man, 370, 1901. Yu-pi′it.—Bogoras, Chukchee, 11, 1904 (*Yu-pi*=' genuine man ').

Yukhais. An Alsea village on the N. side of Alsea r., Oreg.

Yuk-qais′.—Dorsey in Jour. Am. Folk-lore, III, 230, 1890.

Yukhwustitu. A Siuslaw village on Siuslaw r., Oreg.

Yu′-k′ qwŭ-sti′-ʔû.—Dorsey in Jour. Am. Folk-lore, III, 230, 1890.

Yukian Family (adapted from Wintun *Yuki*, 'enemy'.—Kroeber). A linguistic family in N. California, comprising only the Yuki, divided into several tribes or groups speaking several dialects. Apparently they had no common name of their own. Though the territory of the Yuki was very small, it was divided into three detached areas—one about the present Round Valley res. and s. thereof; another w. of this, along the coast, and a third some distance to the s. in the mountains dividing Sonoma from Napa and Lake cos.

The greater part of the family was comprised within the area first mentioned, which ran along Eel r. from a short distance above the confluence of the North fork, along both sides of the river to the junction of South Eel and Middle fork, extending on the w. to the ridge E. of Long valley. From the junction of the two streams up, the Yuki possessed the entire drainage of Middle fork E. to the watershed of the Coast range, which formed the boundary between them and the Wintun. They appear to have lived also on Hull cr., which drains into the North fork of Eel r. Some of the chief divisions of the Yuki proper were the Ukomnom in and about Round valley, the Sukshultatanom on North fork of Middle fork, the Huititnom on South fork of Middle fork, the Sukanom on Middle fork, the Utinom about the junction of Middle fork and South Eel r., and the Lilshiknom and Tanom on main Eel r. South of this group of tribes, between the Middle fork and the South Eel, in Eden valley and the adjacent country, were the Witukomnom, whose dialect was somewhat different from that of the Yuki proper. South of the Witukomnom again, on both sides of South Eel r., certainly near the mouth of Tomki cr., and probably to the headwaters of the South Eel itself; also on the upper waters of Russian r., at the head of Potter valley, were the Huchnom, who spoke a third dialect, which differed considerably from the Yuki proper. They are known by the Pomo, who are their neighbors on the s., as Tatu, and by the whites as Redwoods.

The second territory held by Yukian tribes extended along the coast from Ten Mile r. to Rockport or Usal, and inland as far as Jackson Valley cr., or more probably the range between this stream and the sea. These people call themselves *Ukohtontilka*, 'Ocean tribe.' They have probably been separated from the main body of the Yuki by Athapascan migration, as the Kato of Cahto and Laytonville occupy a strip of Athapascan territory between the two divisions. The dialect of the coast Yuki does not differ more from that of the Yuki proper than does that of the Huchnom.

The third territory occupied by the Yuki is mainly in the hills between Geysers and Calistoga, but includes a small portion of Russian r. valley, about Healdsburg. These people are called Ashochimi by Powers, and are generally known as Wappo. They are separated from their northern relatives by Pomo tribes, and their language diverges greatly from all other Yuki dialects.

The Yuki are said to have been somewhat more warlike than most of the Californians. The Yuki proper, or portions of them, were at war at times with the Kato and Wailaki, the Wintun, the Huchnom, and certain Pomo tribes. Excepting the Wappo, who fought with the Spaniards in the second quarter of the 19th century, the Yuki were barely beginning to be known at the time when the discovery of gold flooded the state with Americans. They came in conflict with the whites on different occasions, suffering considerably in numbers as a consequence. Round Valley res. was established in the heart of their territory in 1864, and the greater part of the stock, as well as various Athapascan,

Wintun, Pomo, and other tribes, were brought to it, where they still reside. The Yuki proper in 1902 numbered about a hundred, the Huchnom barely a dozen. The coast Yuki amount probably to 15 or 20 individuals, and the number of Wappo, though not accurately known, is undoubtedly also small.

The Yuki much resemble the Pomo in appearance. They are short, broad, and sometimes fat. Measurements give an average height for men of 162 cm., which is a rather low stature. The Yuki show a considerably longer headform than any of their northern, eastern, or southern neighbors, as the Yurok, Hupa, Wintun, Maidu, and Pomo. This deviation is unexplained. The women tattoo their faces, especially across the cheeks and on the chin.

In their mode of life, habits, and beliefs the Yuki generally resemble the better-known Pomo, though the Yuki proper show the closest specific cultural resemblances to the neighboring Athapascan Wailaki. The Huchnom affiliated with the Pomo, and resembled these more nearly in their habits and practices than they did the Yuki proper. They fished and hunted, but most of their food was vegetal. They performed a ceremony conducted by a secret society whose members represented the spirits of the dead. They believed that the world was created by a being, human in shape, called Taikomol, 'He who travels alone,' assisted by the coyote. This deity was represented in a ceremony.   (A. L. K.)

Chu-mai-a.—Powers in Cont. N. A. Ethnol., III, 136, 1877 (Pomo name). Eukas.—Ind. Aff. Rep. 1864, 119, 1865. Noam-kekhl.—Powers in Cont. N. A. Ethnol., III, 230, 1877 ('west dwelling' or 'western tribe': Wintun name). Noam'-kult.—Ibid. Nomee Cults.—Taylor in Cal. Farmer, June 8, 1860. Shumeia.—Powers in Overland Mo., IX, 306, 1872. Uca.—Gibbs in Hist. Mag., 1st s., VII, 123, 1863. Uka.—Taylor in Cal. Farmer, June 22, 1860. Ukies.—Ind. Aff. Rep.,112,1865. Ulkies.—Ind. Aff. Rep., 75,1870. Yuca's.—Russell (1853) in H. R. Ex. Doc. 76, 34th Cong., 3d sess., 74, 1857. Yucas.—Ind. Aff. Rep., 26, 1866. Yuka.—Gibbs, op. cit. Yukeh.—Ibid. Yu-ki.—Powers in Cont. N. A. Ethnol., III, 23, 1877. Yuques.—Gibbs, op. cit.

Yukichetunne ('people at the mouth of the river'). A band of the Tututni formerly living on Euchre cr., N. of Rogue r., Oreg.; now on Siletz res. In 1854 (Ind. Aff. Rep. 1854, 495, 1855) their population consisted of 24 men, 41 women, 18 boys, and 19 girls. In 1863 (ibid., 511, 1864) they numbered 187; two years later (ibid., 470, 1865), their reputed population was 150. They are no longer separately enumerated.

Euchees.—Ind. Aff. Rep. 1863, 511, 1864. Eucher.—Newcomb, ibid., 162, 1861. Euches.—Ind. Aff. Rep., 470, 1865. Euchre.—Victor in Overland Mo., VII, 347, 1871. Euchre Creek.—Reynolds in Ind. Aff. Rep. 1856, 202, 1857. Eu-qua-chee.—Parrish, ibid., 1854, 495, 1855. Eu-quah-chee.—Kautz, MS. Toutouten census, B. A. E., 1855. I-úkä těné.—Everette, Tutu MS vocab., B. A. E., 1883 (trans. 'people by the mossy creek'). Uchres.—Ind. Aff. Rep., 495, 1865.

Uka.—Metcalfe, ibid., 357, 1857. Yoqueechae.—Schoolcraft, Ind. Tribes, III, maps, 1853. Yoquichaes.—Domenech, Deserts of N. Am., I, map, 1860. You-quee-chae.—Ex. Doc. 39, 32d Cong., 1st sess., 2, 1852. Yu'-ɣi.—Dorsey, Alsea MS. vocab., B. A. E., 1884. Yu'-ki-tcĕ' ɹûnnĕ.—Dorsey in Jour. Am. Folk-lore, III, 233, 1890 (Tututni name). Yu-kwā-chi.—Schumacher in Bull. G. and G. Surv., III, 28, 1877. Yu'-kwi-tcê' ɹûnnĕ'.—Dorsey in Jour. Am. Folk-lore, III, 233, 1890 (Naltunnetunne name). Yuquache.—Schoolcraft, Ind. Tribes, VI, 702, 1857.

Yukolumni. Mentioned as a tribe of the Cholovone, who lived E. of the lower San Joaquin r., Cal., and were the northernmost division of the Yokuts (Mariposan) family.

Youcoolumnies.—Bancroft, Nat. Races, I, 450, 1874. Yukolumni.—A. L. Kroeber, inf'n, 1905.

Yukonikhotana. An Athapascan tribe in Alaska whose range is principally N. of the Yukon from the mouth of Tozi r. down to Yukon r. They are few in number and are less nomadic than their eastern neighbors. Beyond the uneventful visits of several explorers, nothing of their history is known. They trade every spring at Nuklukayet with the Kutchin tribes from upper Yukon and Tanana rs. They hunt the moose, reindeer, and fox, the skins of which they either trade or make into clothing, although of late years they are beginning to adopt the clothing of the whites. Their houses are less permanently built than those on the lower part of the Yukon. They have no draft dogs, like their western neighbors, but carry their burdens on their shoulders. There seems to be no system of totems among them, although Petroff (Rep. on Alaska, 161, 1884) states that there is evidence of their division into clans. Intermarriage with their lowland neighbors, to whom they are closely related dialectically, is rare; it is said that they do not purchase their wives, like many Athapascan tribes, but take and divorce their wives at pleasure, there being no marriage ceremony among them. Although the men outnumber the women, polygyny is common among them. They are not copper-colored, but of an ashy olive hue, and are less hairy than the adjacent Eskimo. The dead are frequently buried in an erect position, the sarcophagus being of a rough casklike form. Many of their old customs have been modified or replaced by those of the Eskimo. The population of two villages in 1843 was 56 (Zagoskin quoted by Petroff in 10th Census, Alaska, 37, 1884). Petroff (ibid., 12) gives their total population in villages as 221. The villages are Chentansitzan, Medvednaia, Melozikakat, Noggai, Nowi, Tohnokalony, and Tuklukyet.

Youcan.—Hind, Lab. Penin., I, 54, 1863. Youcon.—Anderson (1858) quoted by Hind, ibid., II, 260, 1863. Youkonikatana.—Dall in Proc. Cal. Acad. Sci., IV, 35, 1873. Youkponi-Kouttànæ.—Petitot, Autour du lac des Esclaves, 361, 1891. Yukonikhotana.—Petroff in 10th Census, Alaska, 161, 1884. Yūkon'-ikhotānā.—Dall in Cont. N. A. Ethnol., I, 28, 1877.

Yukuts. A Squawmish village community on the right bank of Squawmisht r., Brit. Col.

Yik'ts.—Boas, MS., B. A. E., 1887.   Yū′kuts.—Hill-Tout in Rep. Brit. A. A. S., 474, 1900.

Yukweakwioose. A Chilliwack village on lower Chilliwack r., which flows into the lower Fraser, Brit. Col.; pop. 26 in 1909.

Yahweakwioose.—Can. Ind. Aff. Rep., pt. 2, 44 1909. Yakweakwioose.—Can. Ind. Aff. Rep., 277, 1894. Yak-y-you.—Ibid., 309, 1879. Yukkweakwiooose.—Ibid., pt. II, 160, 1901. Yukūkweū′s.—Hill-Tout in Rep. N. W. Tribes of Can., 4, 1902. Yu-kwea-kwi-oose.—Can. Ind. Aff. Rep., 414, 1898. Yuk-yuk-y-yoose.—Brit. Col. map, Ind. Aff., Victoria, 1872.

Yulalona (*Yu-la-lo′-na*). A former settlement of Klamath and Modoc at the site of the present Linkville, Oreg.—Gatschet in Cont. N. A. Ethnol., II, pt. I, xxiv, 1890.

Yuloni (*Yu-lo′-ni*). A division of the Miwok formerly living on Sutter cr., not far from Amador, Amador co., Cal.

Yulonees.—Powers in Overland Mo., x, 322, 1874. Yu-lo′-ni.—Powers in Cont. N. A. Ethnol., III, 349, 1877.

Yuma (*Yahmáyo*, 'son of the captain,' seemingly the title of the son of the hereditary chief, contracted and applied to the tribe through misunderstanding

YUMA MAN

by the early Spanish missionaries.—Hardy. They call themselves *Kwichán*ᵃ). One of the chief divisions, or tribes, of the Yuman family (q. v.), formerly residing on both sides of the Rio Colorado next above the Cocopa, or about 50 or 60 m. from the mouth of the river, and below the junction of the Gila. Ft Yuma is situated about the center of the territory formerly occupied by them. When Oñate visited the locality in 1604–05, he found the 'Coahuanas' (Cuchan) in 9 rancherias on the Colorado, entirely below the mouth of the Gila. Physically the Yuma were a fine people, superior in this respect to most of their congeners. Though brave and not unwarlike they were in no sense nomadic, seldom leaving their own villages where, like the Mohave, they practised a rude agriculture, raising corn, beans, pumpkins, and melons. The Catholic fathers of the 18th century erroneously considered Yuma and Cuchan as separate and distinct groups, the former residing E. of the lower Colorado, and the latter w. of it. They divided the Yuma into several tribes: Alchedomas, Hudcodoadans, etc. Leroux, about 1853, estimated their number at 3,000. In 1910 there were 655 under the Ft Yuma school superintendent, Cal. For the so-called Apache Yuma, see *Tulkepaia*.

The following have been mentioned as Yuma tribes or bands and rancherias: Cerritos, Concepción, Gimiels, Pescadero, Posos, San Dionysio, San Pablo, San Pascual, San Pedro, Santa Isabel, Tinajas, Tutum.

California Indians.—Johnston in Emory, Recon., 612, 1848. Cetguanes.—Venegas, Hist. Cal., I, 308. 1759. Chirumas.—Orozco y Berra, Geog., 59, 353, 1864 (Yumas or). Club Indians.—Emory, Recon., 96, 1848. Cou-chan.—Whipple, Pac. R. R. Rep., III, pt. 3, 99, 1856 (Maricopa name). Cuatganes.—Consag (1746) quoted by Taylor in Cal. Farmer, Dec. 6, 1861. Cuchañ.—Latham in Proc. Philol. Soc. Lond., 75, 1852–53. Cuchana.—Clarke in Jour. Anthr. Inst. G. B., IV, 153, 1875. Cu-cha-no.—Heintzelman (1853) in H. R. Ex. Doc. 76, 34th Cong., 3d sess., 35, 1857. Cuchaus.—Ind. Aff. Rep. 1863, 387, 1864. Cuchian.—Froebel, Seven Years' Travels, 511, 1859. Cueganas.—Venegas, Hist. Cal., I, 57, 1759. Cuichan.—Taylor in Cal. Farmer, Mar. 7, 1862. Cushans.—Whipple in Schoolcraft, Ind. Tribes, v, 214, 1855. Cutcanas.—Rudo Ensayo (1763), 25, 1863. Cutchanas.—Möllhausen, Diary, II, 245, 1858. Cuteanas.—Kino (1701) cited by Coues, Garcés Diary, 551, 1900. Cutganes.—Ibid. Cutganes.—Möllhausen, op. cit., 275. Cutguanes.—Kino quoted by Venegas, Hist. Cal., I, 57, 301, 1759. Dil-zhay′s.—White, Apache names of Ind. tribes, MS., B. A. E. ('red soil with red ants': Apache name; also applied to Tonto and Mohave). Euchas.—Browne, Apache Country, 291, 1869 (misprint of Cuchan). Ganstero.—Taylor in Cal. Farmer, Jan. 31, 1862 (misprint). Garote.—Ibid., Dec. 14, 1860. Garotero.—Schoolcraft, Ind. Tribes, v, 203, 1855. Garretero.—Bigelow in Pac. R. R. Rep., IV, 7, 1856. Garroteros.—Emory, Recon., 96, 1848 ("or club Indians"). Garrotes.—Morgan, Consang. and Affin., 241, 1869 (incorrectly mentioned as part of the Gila Apache). Goyoteros.—Taylor in Cal. Farmer, Mar. 14, 1862 (incidentally mentioned as Indians of the Colorado). Guichyana.—Kroeber in Univ. Cal. Pub., IV, 107, 1907 (Chemehuevi name). Hatilshe′.—White in Zeitschr. f. Ethnologie, 370, 1877 (Yuma, Mohave, and Tonto so called by the Apache). Húkwats.—Ztschr. f. Ethnologie, 370, 1877 ('weavers': Paiute name). Jumas.—Humboldt, Atlas Nouvelle-Espagne, carte 1, 1811. Katchan.—Corbusier in Am. Antiq., 276, Sept. 1886 (Yavapai name). Ke-jawn′.—Ewing in Great Divide, 203, 1892 (so called by neighboring tribes). Kóhun.—ten Kate. Reizen in N. A., 199, 1885. Ko′-utchan.—Zeitschr. f. Ethnologie, 381, 1877. Kuiza′n.—Engelhardt, Kutchan MS., vocab., B. A. E., 184, 1886 (='Indian': own name). Kún.—Ztschr. fur Ethnologie, 370, 1877 (Apache name for Yuma and Tulkepaia). **Kutohán.**—ten Kate, Reizen in N. A., 111, 1885. **Kutzán.**—Ibid. **Kwitcᵛánᵃ.**—Harrington in Jour. Am. Folk-lore, XXI, 324, 1908 (own name). **Octguanes.**—Farnham, Travels, 165, 1844. **Qichŭn.**—Curtis, Am. Ind., II, 116, 1908 ('people': Yuma name). **Tumayas.**—Bollaert in Jour. Ethnol. Soc. Lond., II, 276, 1850 (misprint). **Umahs.**—Schoolcraft, Ind. Tribes, I, 519, 1851. **Umeas.**—Pattie, Pers. Narr, 137, 1833. **Umene.**—Ibid., 91. **Yahmáyo.**—Hardy, Trav. in Mex., 372, 1829 (= 'son of the captain,' evidently the origin of "Yuma"). **Yamas.**—Ibid., 438 (misprint; "so named for the extraordinary length of their hair"). **Yavepé-Kutchán.**—ten Kate, Reizen in N. A., 198, 1885. **Yoem.**—Ibid., 160 (Pima name). **Yum.**—Curtis, Am. Ind., II, 110, 1908 (Pima name). **Yuma.**—Kino (1690) in Doc. Hist. Mex., 4th s., I, 230, 1856. **Yumayas.**—Duflot de Mofras, Expl., I, 355, 1844. **Yump.**—Curtis, Am. Ind., II, 112, 1908 (Papago name). **Yumsa.**—Taylor in Cal. Farmer, June 13, 1862. **Yurmarjars.**—Simpson in Rep. Sec. War, 57, 1850. **Yutcama.**—Sedelmair (1750) quoted by Bancroft, No. Mex. States, I, 541, 1884.

Yumam. A former Maidu village on the site of Oroville, Butte co., Cal.—Dixon in Bull. Am. Mus. Nat. Hist., XVII, map, 1905.

Yuman Family. An important linguistic family whose tribes before being gathered on reservations occupied an extensive territory in the extreme s. w. portion of the United States and N. Lower California, including much of the valley of Colorado r., the lower valley of the Gila, and all of extreme s. California. The family was formerly supposed to include also the Seri of w. Sonora and Tiburon id. in the Gulf of California, but these have been determined to belong to a distinct stock (the Serian) bearing no linguistic relation to any of the tribes within the United States, while the tribes that occupied the s. half of Lower California, so far as can be judged from the meager linguistic evidence, belong to another family yet unnamed. These latter were distinguishable from the Yuman tribes as being probably the lowest in culture of any Indians of North America, for their inhospitable environment, which made them wanderers, was unfavorable to the foundation of government, even of the rude and unstable kind elsewhere found. The names of a large number of rancherias or villages have been preserved, and as many of these antedated mission rule, they indicate that their occupants had at least entered upon a rude social life and lived under some sort of recognized authority, though less definite and binding than among most other tribes. There are also the names of not a few of the divisions usually termed tribes, but the limits of country claimed by these and their interrelations are almost unknown. Father Baegert, who is perhaps the best authority on the Lower California Indians, gave five distinct languages, which represented as many divisions or groups of tribes. These were, from the north southward: Cochimi, Laimon (usually considered a branch of Cochimi), Waicuri, Uchiti

(usually considered a branch of Waicuri), and Pericu. Of these, however, only the Cochimi can be definitely regarded as Yuman. Later authorities usually recognize but three linguistic divisions for Lower California, viz, Pericu, Waicuri (a distinct stock), and Cochimi, the last occupying the peninsula N. of about lat. 26°. This is a very unsatisfactory grouping, as it is improbable that a single language, the Cochimi, extended over 6 degrees of latitude; but it is the best that can be made in our present lack of knowledge, and the linguistic groups may be accepted as divisional names under which to group the numerous rancherias in which these now extinct tribes lived.

Passing from the s. to the N. end of the peninsula a marked change for the better was observed. The social groups appear to have been better defined; the tribes made fine basketry and pottery, and in many other ways were further advanced. They lived in communal huts, very well constructed of cottonwood and well thatched. No better example of the power of environment to better man's condition can be found than that shown as the lower Colorado is reached. Here are tribes of the same family, remarkable not only for their fine physical development, but living in settled villages with well-defined tribal lines, practising a rude but effective agriculture, and well advanced in many primitive Indian arts. The usual Indian staples were raised except tobacco, these tribes preferring a wild tobacco of their region to the cultivated. None of the Colorado r. tribes borrowed the art of irrigation from the Pueblo peoples, consequently their crops often suffered from drought. All of them depended more or less on the chase—the river tribes less, those of the interior more. Mezquite beans, piñon nuts, tornillas, and various seeds and roots were important articles of food. None of them were boatmen; in crossing rivers and transporting their goods they employed rude rafts, or balsas, made of bundles of reeds or twigs. Apparently all the river tribes cremated their dead, and with them all articles of personal property. The climate favored nudity, the men wearing only the breechcloth, and not always that, while women were content with a short petticoat made of strips of bark.

Regarding the character of the tribes of the Rio Colorado in the 18th century, Fray Francisco Garcés (Diary, 1775–76, 435, 1900) says: "The Indian men of its banks are well-formed, and the Indian women fat and healthy; the adornment of the men, as far as the Jamajabs [Mohave], is total nudity; that of the women is reduced to certain short and scanty petticoats of the bark of trees; they bathe at all seasons, and arrange the hair, which they always wear long, in diverse figures, utilizing for this purpose a kind of gum or sticky mud. Always are they painted, some with black, others with red, and many with all colors. All those of the banks of the river are very generous and lovers of their country, in which they do not hunt game because they abound in all provisions."

Important tribes of the northern Yuman area are the Cocopa, Diegueño, Havasupai, Maricopa, Mohave, Tonto, Walapai, Yavapai, and Yuma. These differ considerably, both physically and otherwise, the river tribes being somewhat superior to the others. The Yuma are a fine people, rather superior to the Cocopa, although closely resembling them physically.

The population of the Yuman tribes within the United States numbered about 3,700 in 1909.

In addition to the tribes mentioned, the following were also of Yuman affinity, but so far as known they are either extinct or their tribal identity has been lost: Aguachacha, Bahacecha, Cajuenche, Coanopa, Cocoueahra (?), Gualta, Guamua, Guanabepe, Haglli, Hoabonoma, Iguanes, Japul, Kivezaku, Ojiopas, Quigyuma, Quilmurs, Sakuma, Tzekupama.   (H. W. H.)

>**Yuma.**—Turner in Pac. R. R. Rep., III, pt. 3, 55, 94, 101, 1856 (includes Cuchan, Coco-Maricopa, Mojave, Diegeño); Latham in Trans. Philol. Soc. Lond., 86, 1856; Latham, Opuscula, 351, 1860 (as above); Latham, Opuscula, addenda, 392, 1860 (adds Cuchan to the group); Latham El. Comp. Philol., 420, 1862 (includes Cuchan, Cocomaricopa, Mojave, Dieguno); Gatschet in Mag. Am. Hist., 156, 1877 (mentions only U. S. members of family); Keane in Stanford, Compend., Cent. and So. Am., 460, 479, 1878 (includes Yumas, Maricopas, Cuchans, Mojaves, Yampais, Yavipais, Hualpais); Bancroft, Nat. Races, III, 569, 1882. =**Yuma.**—Gatschet in Beach, Ind Misc., 429, 1877 (habitat and dialects of family); Gatschet in U. S. Geog. Surv. W. 100th Mer., VII, 413, 414, 1879. =**Yuman.**—Powell in 7th Rep. B. A. E. 137, 1891. >**Dieguno.**—Latham (1853) in Proc. Philol. Soc. Lond., VI, 75, 1854 (includes mission of San Diego, Dieguno, Cocomaricopas, Cuchañ, Yumas, Amaquaquas). >**Cochimi.**—Latham in Trans. Philol. Soc. Lond., 87, 1856 (northern part peninsula of California); Buschmann, Spuren der aztek. Sprache, 471, 1859 (center of California peninsula); Latham, Opuscula, 353, 1860; Latham, El. Comp. Philol., 423, 1862; Orozco y Berra, Geog., map, 1864; Keane in Stanford, Compend., Cent. and So. Am., 476, 1878 (head of gulf to near Loreto).

Yumersee (misspelling of *Yamasee*, q. v.). A former Seminole town at the head of Sumulgahatchee r., 20 m. N. of St Marks, Wakulla co., Fla. Alac Hajo was chief in 1823.—H. R. Ex. Doc. 74, 19th Cong., 1st sess., 27, 1826.

Yungyu. The Opuntia Cactus clan of the Chua (Snake) phratry of the Hopi. Yuñû wiñwû.—Fewkes in 19th Rep. B. A. E., 582, 1900. Yü'-ñü wuñ-wü.—Fewkes in Am. Anthr., VII, 402, 1894 (*wuñ-wü*='clan'). Yu'ñ-ya.—Stephen in 8th Rep. B. A. E., 38, 1891.

Yunsawi (*Yûnsä'ï*, 'buffalo place'). A former Cherokee settlement on w. Buf-

falo cr. of Cheowa r., in Graham co., N. C. Buffalo Town.—Doc. of 1799 quoted by Royce in 5th Rep., B. A. E., 144, 1887. Yûnsâ'ï.—Mooney in 10th Rep. B. A. E., 547, 1900.

Yunu. A Maidu division living E. of Chico, Butte co., Cal. Yunû.—Curtin, MS. vocab., B. A. E., 1885.

Yupaha. An ancient province, governed by a woman and said to have much metal, described as lying E. of Apalache, in N. w Florida or s. w. Georgia. It was heard of by De Soto in 1540, and may have been identical with the territory of the Yuchi (q. v.). Yupacha.—Harris, Voy. and Trav., I, 806, 1705. Yupaha.—Gentl. of Elvas (1557) in French, Hist. Coll. La., II, 136, 1850.

Yupon. See *Black drink, Yopon*.

Yupu (*Yü'-pu*). A former Maidu village on the w. bank of Feather r., on the site of the present Yuba City, Sutter co., Cal. In 1850 it contained 180 inhabitants. The name Yuba is a corruption of Yupu.   (R. B. D.) Bubu.—Bancroft, Nat. Races, I, 450, 1874. Nevadas.—Ind. Aff. Rep. 1856, 251, 1857. Ubu.—Bancroft, op. cit. Vubum.—Chever in Bull. Essex Inst. 1870, II, 28, 1871. Yubas.—Day (1850) in Sen. Ex. Doc. 4, 32d Cong., spec. sess., 39, 1853. Yupû.—Curtin, MS. vocab., B. A. E., 1885. Yuvas.—Fremont, Geog. Memoir, 22, 1848.

Yupwauremau. One of the two Woccon towns in Greene co., N. C., in 1700.—Lawson, Hist. Car. (1714), 383, 1860.

Yuquot. The principal town of the Mooachaht, situated in Friendly cove, Nootka sd., w. coast of Vancouver id. In olden times it was a widely known place, continually frequented by trading vessels. Pop. 172 in 1904, 140 in 1910. Moacha.—Can. Ind. Aff., pt. 2, 88, 1910. Nootka.—Jewitt, Narr., passim, 1849. Yucuatl.—Galiano, Relacion, 117, 1802. Yuquot.—Can. Ind. Aff., 264, 1902.

Yurguimes. A former tribe of N. E. Coahuila or s. Texas, perhaps Coahuiltecan.—Doc. quoted by Orozco y Berra, Geog., 306, 1864.

Yurok (from Karok *yuruk*, 'downstream'). A tribe living on lower Klamath r., Cal., and the adjacent coast, constituting the Weitspekan linguistic family. They have no name for themselves other than *Olekwo'l* ('persons'), sometimes written *Alikwa*. The territory of the Yurok extended from Bluff cr., 6 m. above the mouth of the Trinity, down Klamath r. to its mouth, and on the coast from beyond Wilson cr., 6 m. N. of the mouth of the Klamath, to probably Mad r. Their settlements in the valley were confined closely to the river, and those along the coast were close to the beach or on the lagoons. They had no settlements on Redwood cr. except at the mouth. Along Klamath r. the Yurok language was everywhere uniform, but along the coast s. of the mouth of the Klamath there were three slightly varying dialects, one spoken at Gold bluff, one at Redwood cr., and a third at Trinidad, the last differing most from that of the river.

Most of the so-called wars of the Yurok were private feuds, participated in by villages. These took place as frequently between Yurok villages as against alien tribes. In all cases payment for the dead and for all property destroyed was made at the conclusion of peace. Apart from a few vessels that touched at Trinidad in the 18th century, and a few trappers that visited Klamath r., whites did not come into contact with them and were utterly unknown to them before 1850. After the coming of the Americans the Yurok never engaged in war with them as a body, though certain villages became involved in conflicts with the miners and early settlers. The lower 20 m. of Klamath r. were constituted into a reservation as early as 1855. Of recent years this has been discontinued, the few surviving Indians having allotments in severalty. The river above this former reservation, up to the mouth of the Trinity, forms at present a nominal part of the Hupa res. Actually the Government has interfered very little with the Yurok, who have always been entirely self-supporting. They now number 500 or 600 along Klamath r., those on the coast being very few. In 1870 the number on the river was said to be 2,700.

The Yurok are fairly tall for Pacific Coast Indians (168 cm.) and considerably above the average Californian in stature. Their cephalic index is 83, being the highest known from California. It is probable that they do not belong to the Californian type physically, but are a mixture of this with an Athapascan type. Their facial expression is different from that of their neighbors, the Karok and the Hupa, but they do not appear to differ much in their measured proportions from the Hupa. The men are less inclined to be stout than in the interior and in central California. Deformation of the head is not practised, but the women tattoo the chin.

The Yurok, together with several other tribes of N. W. California, especially the Karok and Hupa, formed a distinct ethnographic group, characterized among other things by the considerable influence which ideas of property exerted on social conditions and modes of life. There was no chieftainship, prominence depending altogether on the possession of wealth, to the acquisition of which all efforts were directed. The potlatch of the N. Pacific coast did not exist among them. Marriage was distinctly a property transaction. The medium of exchange consisted chiefly of dentalium shells, though woodpecker scalps and large worked pieces of obsidian were also regarded as valuables. The men wore no regular clothing, using skins as occasion required.

The women wore skirts of dressed skins or sometimes of bark, basketry caps, and, as there was need, cloaks of furs. Along the river acorns were much eaten, but salmon and lampreys made up a very large part of the food. Along the coast products of the sea were more important as food. The Yurok houses were from 18 to 25 ft square, built of split and dressed planks about a square or octagonal pit, with a gabled roof. Their canoes were less than 20 ft in length, square at both ends, made of redwood. They were particularly adapted for use on the rapid river, but were also used for going out to sea. The Yurok and neighboring tribes developed a number of specialized ceremonies, especially the Deerskin and the Jumping or Woodpecker dances. These were held only at certain localities and differed somewhat in each place.

The mythology of the Yurok is characterized by a well-developed conception of the Wage, a race largely responsible for the present condition of the world, who disappeared before the coming of men, and by myths centering about "Widower-across-the-sea" and other creators or culture-heroes. All the myths of the Yurok refer to the country which they now inhabit, most of them being very specifically localized. Historical traditions are lacking except for the most recent generations. Like all the tribes of N. W. California they were essentially unwarlike, engaging in war only for purposes of revenge. The most important contest that they remember took place in the first third of the 19th century between the village of Rekwoi and one of the Hupa villages, in the course of which both settlements were destroyed.

The Yurok were altogether without tribes or political divisions, other than the purely local ones of villages, and lacked totems. Their principal villages on the Klamath, in their order, from Bluff cr. down, were as follows: Atsepar, Loolego, the three villages Pekwuteu, Weitspus, and Ertlerger at the confluence of the Trinity with the Klamath, Wakhshek, Atsep, Kenek, Merip, Kepel, Shaa, Murek, Meta, Nakhtskum, Shregegon, Yokhter, Pekwan, Kootep, Wakhtek, Wakhker, Tekta, Serper, Enipeu, Ayotl, Erner, Turip, Wakhkel, Hoopeu, and Wetlko and Rekwoi on opposite sides of the mouth of the river at Requa. On the coast, 6 m. N. of the mouth, was Amen; to the s. successively were Ashegen, Eshpeu, Arekw, Tsahpekw, Oketo and other villages on Big lagoon, and Tsurau (Trinidad).

Al-i-kwa.—Crooks vocab. in Cont. N. A. Ethnol., III, 461, 1877. Allequas.—Meyer, Nach dem Sacramento, 215, 1855. Eurocs.—Powers in Overland Mo., IX, 157, 1872. Kiruhikwak.—A. L. Kroeber, inf'n, 1904 (name given by the Shasta of Salmon r.).

Klamaths. — Ibid. (a nonsignificant collective name sometimes loosely used, especially locally). Wait'-spek.—Powers in Cont. N. A. Ethnol., III, 44, 1877. Wech-pecs.—McKee in Sen. Ex. Doc. 4, 32d Cong., spec. sess., 193, 1853. Wechpecks.—Ibid., 191. Wech-peks.—Ibid., 215. Weitchpec.—Kroeber, inf'n, 1904 (a name sometimes locally used, especially in Hupa and Karok territory, to which Weichpec is at present the nearest Yurok village). Weithspek.—Loew in Rep. Chief of Eng., III, 546, 1876. Weits-pek.—Gibbs (1851) in Schoolcraft, Ind. Tribes, III, 138, 1853. Wetch-pec.—McKee (1851) in Sen. Ex. Doc. 4, 32d Cong., spec. sess., 194, 1853. Wetch-peck.—Ibid., 161. Wish-pooke.—Ibid., 194 (probably identical). Witsch-piks.—Meyer, Nach dem Sacramento, 282, 1855. Youruk.—Gibbs, op. cit., 151. Yurok.—Powers in Cont. N. A. Ethnol., III, 44, 1877.

Yushlali (*Yuc-la'-li*). A former Takelma village on the s. side of Rogue r., Oreg.—Dorsey in Jour. Am. Folk-lore, III, 235, 1890.

Yussoih ('skunk'). A Yuchi clan. YūsAⁿ.—Speck, Yuchi Inds., 70, 1909. Yusso-i'h tahá.—Gatschet, Uchee MS., B. A. E., 70, 1885 (='skunk gens').

Yustaga. An important tribe in the 16th century, occupying a territory about the head streams of Suwannee r., N. Fla. De Soto passed through their country in 1539, and the French Huguenots, who settled at the mouth of St Johns r. in 1564, also came in contact with them. Cf. *Westo.* Hostaqua.—Laudonnière (1564) in French, Hist. Coll. La., n. s., 288, 1869. Hostaque.—Ibid., 266. Houstaqua.—Ibid., 244. Yustaga.—Biedma (1544) in Bourne, De Soto Narr., II, 7, 1904.

Yusumne (*Yū-sū'm-ne*). A former Maidu village, said by Hale to have been on Feather r., in Sutter co., Cal., but now asserted to have been either on the s. fork of American r., or near Ione, Amador co. (R. B. D.) Yaesumnes.—Hale misquoted by Bancroft, Nat. Races, I, 450, 1874. Yajumui.—Taylor in Cal. Farmer, Oct. 18, 1861. Yalesumnes.—Hale, Ethnog. and Philol., 631, 1846. Yalesumni.—Latham in Proc. Philol. Soc. Lond., VI, 79, 1854. Yasumnes.—Hale, op. cit. Yasumni.—Latham, op. cit. Yosumnis.—Taylor, op. cit., June 8, 1860. Yusumne.—Sutter (1847) quoted by Bancroft, op. cit.

Yuta. A tribe represented at San Antonio de Valero mission, Texas, in the 18th century. Possibly those of this name baptized there were captured Ute (q. v.) from the far N. (H. E. B.)

Yutoyara. A Karok village on the w. bank of Klamath r., a little above Salmon r., N. w. Cal. It was burned in the summer of 1852. Possibly it is identical with Ishipishi. Yutoo'-ye-roop.—Gibbs, MS. Misc., B. A. E., 1852.

Yutsutkenne ('people down there'). A Sekani tribe whose hunting grounds are between McLeod lake and Salmon r., Brit. Col. From time immemorial they have bartered stone axes, arrows, and other implements with the Takulli for beads and articles of metal. Yu-tsú-tqaze.—Morice, letter, B. A. E., 1890. Yutsu-tquenne.—Morice, Notes on W. Dénés, 28, 1893.

Yutum. A Chumashan village between Goleta and Pt Concepcion, Cal., in 1542. Yatum.—Taylor in Cal. Farmer, Apr. 17, 1863. Yutuin.—Ibid. Yutum.—Cabrillo, Narr. (1542), in Smith, Colec. Doc. Fla., 183, 1857.

Yxaulo. A Chumashan village formerly near Santa Barbara, Cal.—Taylor in Cal. Farmer, Apr. 24, 1863.

Zaartar. An unidentified band or division of the Upper Yanktonai Sioux. Waz-za-ar-tar.—Am St. Papers, Ind. Aff. I, 715, 1832. Za-ar-tar.—Lewis and Clark Discov., 34, 1806.

Zaclom. A former village connected with San Francisco Solano mission, Cal.—Bancroft, Hist. Cal., II, 506, 1886.

Zaco. A Chumashan village on San Miguel id., Cal., in 1542. Caco.—Cabrillo, Narr. (1542), in Smith, Colec. Doc. Fla., 189, 1857. Zaco.—Ibid., 186.

Zakatlatan. A Koyukukhotana trading village on the N. bank of Yukon r., lon. 156° 30'. Pop. 25 in 1880; 39 in 1890. Sachertelontin.—Whymper, Trav. Alaska, 226, 1869. Saghadellautin.—Post route map, 1903. Sakadelontin.—Raymond in Sen. Ex. Doc. 12, 42d Cong., 1st sess., 23, 1871. Sakatalan.—Petroff, Rep. on Alaska, 62, 1880. Sakataloden.—11th Census, Alaska, 7, 1893. Zakatlatan.—Petroff, map of Alaska, 1880.

Zakhauzsiken (*Zaxxauzsi'kEn*, 'middle ridge' or 'middle hill'). A village of the Spences Bridge band of Ntlakyapamuk ½ m. back from Thompson r., on the s. side, about 31 m. above Lytton, Brit. Col.—Teit in Mem. Am. Mus. Nat. Hist., II, 173, 1900.

Zaltana ('mountain'). A Knaiakhotana clan of Cook inlet, Alaska.—Richardson, Arct. Exped., I, 407, 1851.

Zandzhulin ('village in a highland grove'). A Kansa settlement at Kaw agency, Ind. T., in 1882. Zandjúliⁿ.—Dorsey, Kansa MS. vocab., B. A. E., 1882. Zŭndjúliⁿ.—Ibid.

Zape. A former Tepehuane pueblo, and seat of the mission of San Ignacio, at the extreme head of Nazas r., lat. 25° 30', lon. 106°, N. w. Durango, Mexico. There are a number of ancient burial caves in the vicinity, and 20 m. s. are the noted ruins usually known by this name (Lumholtz, Unknown Mex., I, 448, 1902). S. Ignacio del Zape.—Orozco y Berra, Geog., 318, 1864.

Zassalete. A former village, probably Salinan, connected with San Antonio mission, Monterey co., Cal.—Taylor in Cal. Farmer, Apr. 27, 1860.

Zdluiat. A Knaiakhotana village of 16 persons in 1880 on the E. side of Knik bay, at the head of Cook inlet, Alaska.—Petroff in 10th Census, Alaska, 29, 1884.

Zeawant. See *Sewan.*

Zhanichi ('wooden house'). A former village on Kansas r., Kan., occupied by that part of the Kansa tribe which followed the chief Nunpewaye, probably before 1820. Jaⁿ-ítci.—Dorsey, Kansa MS. vocab., B. A. E., 1882.

Zhawenikashika. The Beaver gens of the Quapaw. Beaver gens.—Dorsey in 15th Rep. B. A. E., 229, 1897. Jawe'nikaciȟa.—Ibid.

Zillgaw ('many mountains'). A subdivision of Apache in Arizona under the chiefs Eskiltissillaw, Nogenogeys, and

Nardososin, about 1875.—White, Apache Names of Ind. Tribes, MS., B. A. E.

Ziñogaba. Mentioned by the Mohave to Juan de Oñate in 1604 as a tribe of people, with bald heads, living on an island of the same name a day's journey by boat off the California coast. These Indians were said to wear necklaces and ear ornaments of pearl shells, called *xicullo* (*shi-kul-yo*), and to possess "an instrument with which they made the noise when they dance, which is a long stick from which are pendent many pieces of that metal [silver] of which they make dishes in which they eat." The tribe had an old "lady or captainess," called Ciñaca-cohola, "the height of a-man-and-a-half," very broad, with big feet, who had a sister, also a giantess; there was no man of her kind, and she mingled with no one on the island. See Zárate Salmerón (*ca.* 1629) in Land of Sunshine, 106, Jan. 1900. Ziñogova.—Zárate Salmerón, op. cit., 108.

Zoar. A Moravian mission among the Suhinimiut Eskimo on the E. coast of Labrador, established in 1865.

Zoe (*tzoi*, 'wax,' 'pitch tree'. — Buelna). A tribe formerly inhabiting a small territory in lat. 27°, lon. 108°, about the Sinaloa-Chihuahua boundary, Mexico. According to a tradition mentioned by Ribas (Hist. Trium., 145, 1645) they came from the N. together with the Ahome, and although they had a different language and lived somewhat distant from each other, the two tribes preserved constant friendship. The Zoe established themselves on the slopes of the sierra, in a settlement of the same name at the sources of the Rio del Fuerte near the Sinaloa. On their conversion to Christianity the missionaries moved them to the other part of the river, founding a town which comprised the whole tribe. The Zoe and Baimena spoke their particular dialect, although they usually, in communication with others, made use of the Cahita and to some extent also the Nahuatl. They are extinct. (F. W. H.)
Chóis.—Hardy, Trav., 438, 1829 (referred to as a Mayo town). Choiz.—Rivera, Diario, leg. 1514, 1736. Troes.—Orozco y Berra, Geog., 333, 1864. Tzoes.—Ibid. Zoe.—Ibid.

Zogliakten. A Koyukukhotana village of 7 persons in 1844 on the E. bank of Koyukuk r., Alaska.
Tsogliakhten.—Zagoskin quoted by Petroff in 10th Census, Alaska, 37, 1884. Tsogliakten.—Tikhmenief (1861) quoted by Baker, Geog. Dict. Alaska, 1902. Zogliakten.—Zagoskin in Nouv. Ann. Voy., 5th s., XXI, map, 1850.

Zoht. A village of the Nicola band of Ntlakyapamuk living near the w. end of Nicola lake, 50 m. above Spences Bridge, Brit. Col. Pop. 31 in 1901, the last time the name appears.
Nicola.—Brit. Col. map, Ind. Aff., Victoria, 1872 (one of two villages so named on Nicola lake may correspond to this town). Yoht.—Can. Ind. Aff., 277, 1894. Yon-kt.—Ibid., 198, 1885. Zoht.—Ibid.,

232, 1886. Zōqkt.—Hill-Tout in Rep. Ethnol. Surv. Can., 4, 1899.

Zolatungzezhii. A former pueblo of the Jemez in New Mexico, the exact site of which is not known.
Zo-lat-e-se-djii.—Bandelier in Arch. Inst. Papers, IV, 207, 1892. Zo-la'-tuⁿ-ze-zhi-i.—Hodge, field-notes, B. A. E., 1895.

Zomiomi. A village, presumably Costanoan, formerly connected with Dolores mission, San Francisco, Cal.—Taylor in Cal. Farmer, Oct. 18, 1861.

Zonagogliakten. A Koyukukhotana village of 11 persons in 1844 on the E. bank of Koyukuk r., Alaska.
Tsonagogliakten.—Tikhmenief (1861) quoted by Baker, Geog. Dict. Alaska, 1902. Tsonagolyakh-ten.—Zagoskin, Descr. Russ. Poss. Am., map, 1848. Zonagogliakten.—Zagoskin in Nouv. Ann. Voy., 5th s., XXI, map, 1850.

Zorquan. A former small tribe represented at San Antonio de Valero mission, Texas.

Zrohono. A clan of the Hopi which takes its name from a small unidentified mammal.
Zro-ho-na wüñwû.—Fewkes in Am. Anthr., VII, 404, 1894. Zrohono wiñwû.—Fewkes in 19th Rep. B. A. E., 584, 1900.

Zuaque (*suua*, 'interior,' 'middle'; *yaqui*, 'river': 'river of the middle,' referring to the Rio Fuerte, of which Zuaque is the ancient name.—Buelna). A subdivision of the Cahita, speaking both the Tehueco and the Vacoregue dialect and occupying a territory extending 10 leagues along the middle waters of Rio del Fuerte in N. Sinaloa, Mexico. They occupied the pueblos of Mochicaui and San Miguel Zuaque, besides another the name of which is unknown. They did not take kindly to the Jesuit missionaries established in their country at the beginning of the 17th century, exhibiting a "threatening indifference" to their salvation. In 1601 Gov. Hurtaide, with the aid of the Guazave, invaded their country and by a ruse captured and hanged about 40 leading men.
Cuaques.—Ribas, Hist. Triumphos, 171, 1645. Suaque.—Hrdlička in Am. Anthr., VI, 72, 1904. Suaqui.—Bancroft, No. Mex. States, I, 210, 1886. Zuaque.—Orozco y Berra, Geog., 58, 1864.

Zucigin. A village, presumably Costanoan, formerly connected with Dolores mission, San Francisco, Cal.—Taylor in Cal. Farmer, Oct. 18, 1861.

Zukkertop. A Danish trading station in s. w. Greenland.—Crantz, Hist. Greenland, I, 12, 1767.

Zumaque. Mentioned as a pueblo of the province of Atripuy (q. v.), in the region of the lower Rio Grande, N. Mex., in 1598.—Oñate (1598) in Doc. Inéd., XVI, 115, 1871.

Zumblito. A former village, probably Salinan, connected with San Antonio mission, Monterey co., Cal.—Taylor in Cal. Farmer, Apr. 27, 1860.

Zuñi. The popular name of a Pueblo tribe, constituting the Zuñian linguistic family, residing in a single permanent pueblo known by the same name, on the N. bank of upper Zuñi r., Valencia co., N. Mex. (for illustration see *Pueblos*), and, in summer, the three neighboring farming villages of Pescado, Nutria, and Ojo Caliente. Their tribal name is A'shiwi (sing. *Shi'wi*), 'the flesh.' The name of their tribal range is Shi'wona, or Shi'winakwin, which Cushing renders 'the land that produces flesh.' Their common name, Zuñi, is a Spanish adaptation of the Keresan *Süñyitsi*, or *Sü'nyitsa*, of unknown meaning. It has no connection with "people of long finger-nails," as has been erroneously said.

According to Cushing, the Zuñi are descended from two parental stocks, one of

a companion of Alvar Nuñez Cabeza de Vaca on his famous journey from the Gulf of Mexico across Texas and into Mexico), to explore the unknown region to the N. W. Sending the negro and some Indian guides ahead to prepare the tribes for his coming and to report on the prospects of the country, the friar pursued his way through Sonora and into the present Arizona, where he received word from some of the Indians who had accompanied Estevanico that the negro and some of their own people had been killed by the natives of Cibola. After placating his Indian followers, who threatened his life, Fray Marcos again pressed on, viewing the first of the Cibola villages from an adjacent height. He then started

ACROSS THE HOUSE-TOPS OF ZUÑI—TAAIYALONE IN THE DISTANCE

which came originally from the N., the other from the W. or S. W., from the country of the lower Rio Colorado. The latter, who resembled the Yuman and Piman tribes in mode of life, joined the others after their settlement in the Zuñi valley. To this nucleus there were many accretions from other tribes and stocks, as well as many desertions from it, in both prehistoric and historic times.

Although indefinite knowledge of an Indian province containing seven cities in the far N. existed in Mexico soon after the conquest, the first real information regarding the Zuñi tribe and their 7 pueblos was gained by Fray Marcos of Niza, who in 1539 set out, with a Barbary negro named Estevanico (who had been

on his return to Mexico, where he made a report of his discoveries, representing the "Kingdom of Cibola," from what he had heard from the Indians along the route, as a rich and populous province containing 7 cities, of which Ahacus (Hawikuh) was the principal one. His glowing accounts led to the fitting out of an expedition the next year, 1540, under Francisco Vasquez Coronado, the advance guard of which, after crossing the arid region to the S., met the first party of the Zuñi near the mouth of the river of the same name. The first meeting was friendly, but a collision soon occurred, and after a sharp skirmish the Indians retreated to their villages. Continuing their advance, the Spaniards approached the town described by Fray Marcos under the name of Cibola, but which Coronado called Granada. This was Hawikuh. After a contest outside the walls the place was carried by storm, July 7, 1540, when it was found that the warriors had previously removed the greater part of their property, together with their women and children, to their stronghold on Taaiyalone mesa, whither they also fled. The magnificent Kingdom of Cibola, with its 7 cities filled with gold and precious stones, proved to be only a group of ordinary Indian pueblos, and the disappointed Coronado was moved to declare in his official report that the friar had "said the truth in nothing that he reported." Coronado found the 7 towns all within 4 leagues, each having a distinct name, and the largest containing 500 houses, while Cibola (derived from Shiwona, above mentioned), was found to be the name of the whole territory. From Cibola, on the identification of which with the Zuñi country all scientific students agree, expeditions were sent to Tusayan (the Hopi country), the Grand canyon of the Colorado, and to the Rio Grande and beyond, and after the arrival of the main force the Spaniards moved to the latter stream, there to enter winter quarters.

In 1580 the tribe was visited by Francisco Sanchez Chamuscado, in the account of whose journey the name of the province is printed Cami (Cuñi). It was reported to contain 6 villages. In 1583 the province was visited by Antonio de Espejo, who for the first time called the place Zuñi, adding that its other name was Cibola, and who found there some Mexican Indians who had been left by Coronado. Espejo attributed to Zuñi the greatly exaggerated population of 20,000 in 6 villages (one of which was Aquico= Hawikuh = Coronado's Granada), thus indicating that one of their pueblos had been abandoned between 1540 and 1583. Zuñi was again visited by Juan de Oñate, the colonizer of New Mexico, in 1598, when this and several other pueblo provinces were given under the ministerial care of Fray Andrés Corchado, but there was no resident missionary at Zuñi at this time. In 1598 the Zuñi still occupied 6 villages, recorded by Oñate as: Aguicobi or Aguscabi (Hawikuh), Canabi (Kianawe?), Coaqucria (Kiakima), Halonagu (Halona), Macaqui (Matsaki), and Aquinsa (Apinawa?). The ruins of those that are indentified beyond doubt are still plainly to be seen.

The first Zuñi mission was established at Hawikuh by the Franciscans in the summer of 1629. Fray Roque de Figueredo, Fray Agustin de Cuellar, and Fray Francisco de Madre de Dios being its

missionaries, although one or two of these probably were established at Halona. Between this date and 1632 Fray Francisco Letrado was transferred from the Jumano, in E. New Mexico, to the Zuñi, but was murdered by them on Feb. 22 of the latter year, and 5 days later Fray Martin de Arvide, who had passed through Hawikuh on his way to the Zipias, was killed by 5 Zuñi and a mestizo who accompanied him. As in Coronado's time, the Indians again fled to their stronghold on Taaiyalone mesa, where they remained until 1635. From this time until 1670 the history of the Zuñi is almost a blank. On Aug. 7 of

PAHLOWAHTIWA—ZUNI

the year named the Apache or Navaho raided Hawikuh, killed its missionary, Fray Pedro de Avila y Ayala, and burned the church, his remains being recovered the next day by Fray Juan Galdo, priest at Halona. Hawikuh was never reestablished as a mission, and it is even possible that it was not reoccupied at all, Ojo Caliente springing up, a short distance away, as a summer farming settlement.

At the time of the great Pueblo rebellion of 1680 the Zuñi occupied but 3 towns, excluding Hawikuh. These were Halona, Matsaki, and Kiakima; the first at the site of the present Zuñi, on both sides of the river; the other two, which were *visitas* of the Halona mission, at the N. W. and S. W. base of Taaiyalone, respectively. The Zuñi participated in the rebellion, killing their missionary and again fleeing to Taaiyalone, where they remained until New Mexico was reconquered in 1692 by Diego de Vargas.

The people from this time were concentrated on the site of Halona, which meanwhile had fallen to decay, where, chiefly on the N. side of Zuñi r., they built a new pueblo—the present Zuñi. A church was erected here about 1699, but the village was soon again without a resident priest owing to the killing, in 1703, of a few Spanish soldiers who had treated the natives harshly, causing them again

ZUÑI WOMAN

to flee to their stronghold. The Indians remained on Taaiyalone until 1705, when they again settled in the plain and the missionary returned to them. A garrison was kept at the pueblo for some years, and from time to time they were at enmity with the Hopi, but peace was restored in 1713. The subsequent history of Zuñi is not noteworthy. A mission was in existence throughout the 18th and well into the 19th century, but the church gradually fell in ruins and only occasionally was it visited by priests. For some time after the territory came into possession of the United States following the war with Mexico, Zuñi was entirely

abandoned by white people, but in the 70's various attempts were made to missionize the pueblo, with little success. In recent years the Government has built extensive irrigation works and established a large school, and the younger generation are becoming educated in the ways of civilization and have learned the English language.

In character and customs the Zuñi resemble the Pueblo tribes generally. They are quiet, good tempered, and industrious, friendly toward the Americans but jealous and distrustful of the Mexicans, and bitter enemies of the Navaho. They adhere tenaciously to their ancient religion, which is closely interwoven with their social organization. For information concerning their customs and beliefs, see *Pueblos,* and consult Cushing (1) in 2d Rep. B. A. E., 1883, (2) 4th Rep. B. A. E., 1886, (3) 13th Rep. B. A. E., 1896; Stevenson (1) in 5th Rep. B. A. E., 1887, (2) 23d Rep. B. A. E., 1904.

The population of Zuñi at the period of the Pueblo rebellion of 1680 was about 2,500, since which time it has steadily decreased, chiefly by reason of smallpox epidemics. Between 1788 and 1799 the population ranged, according to various estimates, from 1,617 to 2,716; in 1820 it apparently had dwindled to 1,597. In 1880 the population was 1,650; at the present time (1910) it is 1,640, having recovered from an epidemic in 1898–99 which carried away about 250.

According to Cushing the Zuñi have 7 phratral groups, divided into 16 surviving clans, as follows:

(1) Itiwa Áteuna ('those of the midmost all'), embracing Pí-chi-kwe or Mú-la-kwe (Parrot or Macaw folk), Tâ'-a-kwe (Seed or Corn folk), and Yä'-to-k'ya-kwe (Sun folk). (2) Pïshla Áteuna ('those of the northernmost'), embracing Aing'-shi-kwe (Bear folk), Kâ-lok-ta-kwe (Heron or Crane folk), and Tá-thlup-tsi-kwe (Yellow-wood folk). (3) Ky'álishi Áteuna ('those of the westernmost'), embracing Sus'-ki-kwe (Coyote folk) and Pó-yi-kwe (Chaparral cock or Grouse folk). (4) Alaho Áteuna ('those of the southernmost'), embracing Tó-na-shi-kwe (Badger folk) and Aí-ya-ho-kwe (Redtop-shrub folk). (5) Télua Áteuna ('those of the easternmost'), embracing Tó-na-kwe (Turkey folk) and Shó-hoi-ta-kwe (Deer folk). (6) Iyama Áteuna ('those of the uppermost'), embracing K'yá-k'ya-li-kwe (Eagle folk) and An'-a-kwe (Tobacco folk). (7) Mailam Áteuna ('those of the lowermost'), embracing Tá-k'ya-kwe (Toad folk) and Tchí-to-la-kwe (Rattlesnake folk).

Following are the Zuñi pueblos, those marked by an asterisk being now extinct: *Halona, *Hampasawan, *Hawikuh,

*Heshokta, *Heshota Ayathltona, *Heshota Hluptsina, *Heshota Imkoskwin, *Heshotapathltaie, *Heshota Uhla, *Kechipauan, *Kiakima, *Kwakina, *Kwakinawan, *Matsaki, Nutria, Ojo Caliente, Pescado, *Pinawan, *Shopakia, *Wimian, Zuñi.   (F. W. H.)
A'-ci-wi.—ten Kate, Synonymie, 7, 1884 (sing. Ci-wi; own name; c=sh). Ah-shee-wai.—Eaton in Schoolcraft, Ind. Tribes, IV, 220, 1854 (Zuñi name for themselves as a tribe). Ah-shi-wi.—Stevenson in 5th Rep. B. A. E., 541, 1887 (or Zuñi). Amé.—Espejo (1583) in Doc. Inéd., XV, 117, 1871 ('otro nombre Cibola'; misprint of Cuni). Ami.—Ibid., 120, 121. A-she-we.—Fewkes in Jour. Am. Eth. and Arch., I, 98, 1891 (Zuñian name of their tribe). A-shi-ui.—Bandelier in Arch. Inst. Papers, V, 176, 1890 (or Zuñis). Áshiwi.—Cushing in 2d Rep. B. A. E., 9, 1883 (or Zuñis). Asuncion.—Bancroft, Ariz. and N. Mex., 221, 1889 (early mission name of Zuñi pueblo). Buffalo Province.—Davis, El Gringo, 68, 1857. Cabrí.—Chamuscado (1580) in Doc. Inéd., XVI, 203, 1871 (apparently regarded by Bandelier, Jour. Am. Eth. and Arch., III, 63, 1892, as Cami=Zuñi). Camé—Barrundo and Escalante misquoted by Bancroft, Ariz. and N. Mex., 77, 1889. Cami.—Bustamente (1582-83) in Doc. Inéd., XV, 86, 1871 (regarded by Bandelier, Jour. Am. Eth. and Arch., III, 63, 1892, as a misprint of "Zuñi," i. e. Cuni). Cebola.—Loew in Ann. Rep. Wheeler Surv., app. LL, 175, 1875. Cebolla.—Cope, ibid., 173. Cebollians.—Ibid. Cenola.—Hakluyt (1600) misquoted by Cushing in Millstone, IX, 224, Dec. 1884. Ceuala.—Niça (1539) in Ramusio, Nav. et Viaggi, III, 357, 1565 (also Ceuola). Ceuola.—Niça in Hakluyt, Voy., iii, 438, 1600 (or Cibola). Cevola.—Alarcon (1540) in Ternaux-Compans, Voy., IX, 315, 1838. Chí-vo-la.—Niza misquoted by Cushing (1888) in Compte-rendu Internat. Cong. Am., VII, 155, 1890. Cibala.—Emory, Reconnoissance, 128, 1848. Cibola.—Niça (1539) in Hakluyt, Voy., III, 438; Coronado (1540), ibid., 451, 1600. Cibola.—Torquemada, Monarq. Ind., I, 323, 1723. Cibolæ.—Morelli, Fasti Novi Orbis, 23, 1776. Cibolal.—Ten Broeck (1852) quoted by Donaldson, Moqui Pueblo Inds., 27, 1893. Cibolan Indians.—Ogilby, America, 294, 1671. Cibolans.—Cushing in Compte-rendu Internat. Cong. Am., VII, 174, 1890 (the people). Cibolas.—Jefferys, Am. Atlas, map 5, 1776 (Zuni or). Cibola-Zuñi.—Bandelier in Arch. Inst. Papers, III, 64, 1890. Cibole.—Pennant, Arctic Zoology, 3, 1792. Cibolians.—Brackenridge, Early Span. Discov., 28, 1857. Cibolos.—Villa-Señor, Theatro Am., pt. 2, 425, 1748. Cibora.—Humboldt, New Spain, II, 324, 1811. Ciloba.—Ogilby, America, map, 1671 (misprint). Cinola.—Hakluyt (1600) misquoted by Cushing in Millstone, IX, 224, Dec. 1884. Ciuola.—Hakluyt, Voy., 440, note, 1600. Civola.—Mendoza (1540) in Ternaux-Compans, Voy., IX, 292 et seq., 1838. Civoli.—Bandelier in Mag. West. Hist., 666, Sept. 1886 (after Coronado). Civona.—Bandelier, Gilded Man, 142, 1893 (given as a 16th century form). Ci'-wi-na-kwin.—ten Kate, Synonymie, 7, 1884 ('country of Aciwi': Zuñi name for their territory). Ci'-wo-na.—Ibid. Corn Peoples.—Cushing, inf'n, 1891 (or Tâa Ashiwani: sacred name of the tribe). Cuni.—Coronado as quoted by Bandelier in Mag. West. Hist., 668, Sept. 1886. Çuni.—Cordova (1619) in Ternaux-Compans, Voy., X, 444, 1838; Barcia, Ensayo, 170, 1723. Çuñi.—Garcia, Origen de los Inds., index, 1729. Cuñi.—Zárate Salmerón (ca. 1629) in Land of Sunshine, 47, Dec. 1899. Cvñi (1629) quoted by Bandelier in Arch. Inst. Papers, IV, 330, 1892. Gibola.—Mendoza (1599) quoted by Winsor, Hist. Am., II, 489, note, 1886 ("las Bacos de Gibola"). Guadalupe.—Bancroft, Ariz. and N. Mex., 221, 1889 (mission name prior to 1699). Ha-lo-nah.—Jouvenceau in Cath. Pion., I, no. 9, 13, 1906 (see Halona). Juni.—Oñate (1598) in Doc. Inéd., XVI, 269 et seq., 1871. Juñi.—Oñate (1598) as quoted by Bandelier in Arch. Inst. Papers, I, 15, 1881. La Purísima de Zuñi.—Bancroft, Ariz. and N. Mex., 221, 1889 (mission name of Zuñi from July 1699). Luni.—Schoolcraft, Ind. Tribes, III, 393, 1853. Nai-tě'-zi.—ten Kate, Synonymie, 6, 1884 (a Navaho name). Narsh-tiz-a.—White, Apache MS. vocab., B. A. E., 1875 ('dwellers in adobe houses': Apache name). Nashlĭzhě.—Curtis, Am. Ind., I, 134, 1907 ('blackened eyebrows': Apache name). Nashtězhě.—Ibid., 138 (Navaho name). Naž-tě'-zi..—ten Kate, Synonymie, 6, 1884 (a Navaho name; ž=zh). N. S. de Guadalupe de Zuni.—Alencaster (1805) quoted by Prince, N. Mex., 37, 1883. Nuestra Señora de Guadalupe de Zum.—Orozco y Berra in Anales del Minis. de Fom., VI, 255, 1882 (misprint). Nuestra Señora de Guadalupe de Zuñi.—Dominguez and Escalante (1776) in Doc. Hist. Mex., 2ᵃ s., I, 556, 1854. Nuestra Señora Guadalupe de Zuñi.—Ward in Ind. Aff. Rep. 1867, 213, 1868. Saraí.—Hodge, field notes, B. A. E., 1895 (Isleta and Sandia name of the pueblo). Sarán.—Ibid. (Isleta name of the people). Saray.—Bandelier, Gilded Man, 149, 1893 (Tigua name of the pueblo; corrupted into Xalay by the early Spaniards). Septem ciuitatum.—Wytfliet, Hist. des Indes, map, 112-113, 1605 (also Ceuola). Seven Cities of Gold.—Ladd, Story of N. Mex., 71, 1891. Shewena.—Fewkes in Bull. Essex. Inst., XXII, 99, 1890. She-wo-na.—Powell in 2d Rep. B. A. E., XXVII, 1883 (Zuñi name for their country). Shi'-oui.—Whipple, Pac. R. R. Rep., III, pt. 3, 93, 185, 1856 (Zuñi name for one of their tribe). Shi-ua-na.—Bandelier in Rev. d'Ethnog., 203, 1886. Shiuano.—Bandelier, Gilded Man, 149, 1893. Shi-uo-na.—Bandelier in Arch. Inst. Papers, V, 131, 1890. Shí-vo-la.—Cushing in Millstone, V, 225, Dec. 1884 (original pronunciation of Cibola). Shi-wa-na.—Bandelier in Mag. West. Hist., 667, Sept. 1886 (Zuñi name for their tribal range). Shíwi.—Cushing in 13th Rep. B. A. E. 343, 1896 (the tribe). Shiwian.—Cushing in Compte-rendu Internat. Cong. Am., VII, 157, 1890 (adjectival form). Shi-wi-na.—Cushing in Millstone, IX, 3, Jan. 1884. Shi-wi-na-kwin.—Ibid. Shiwinas.—Baxter in Harper's Mag., June 1882. Shíwona.—Cushing in Millstone, IX, 225, Dec. 1884. Sibola.—Gordon, Hist. Mex., II, 235, 1832. Sibolla.—Galvano (1563) in Hakluyt Soc. Pub., XXX, 227, 1862. Siete Cibdades.—Nuño de Guzman (1529) in Icazbalceta, Colec. de Docs., II, 288-306, 1866 (first mention of the seven cities of Cibola). Siñis.—Mota-Padilla, Hist. de la Conq., 515, 1742. Sióki.—Stephen in 8th Rep. B. A. E., 30, 1891 (Hopi name of pueblo). Si-o'-ki-bi.—ten Kate, Synonymie, 7, 1884 (Hopi name for the pueblo). Si-o'-me.—Ibid. (Hopi name for the Zuñi; sing. Si-ó-tăk). Siuola.—Gomara, Hist. Gen., 466A, 1606. Sivola.—Motolinia (1549) quoted by Bandelier in Mag. West. Hist., 669, Sept. 1886. Sivolo.—Ruxton in Jour. Ethnol. Soc. Lond., II, 94, 1850. Sivulo.—Ruxton, Life in Far West, 1849 (after old MS.). Soones.—Emory, Recon., 99, 1848. Sounès.—Gallatin in Nouv. Ann. Voy., 5th s., XXVII, 296, 1851. Sumi.—Oñate (1602) in Doc. Inéd., XVI, 206, 1871 (Zuni or). Suñi.—Mühlenpfordt, Mejico, II, 528, 1844. Sunis.—Freytas, Peñalosa (1662), Shea. ed., 52, 83, 1882; Alcedo, Dic. Geog., II, 549, 1787. Suñis.—Alcedo, Dic. Geog., III, 184, 1788. Sunne.—Hakluyt, Voy., III, 470, note, 1600 (or Zuny). Suny.—Duro, Don Diego de Peñalosa, 75, 1882. Su'nyitsa.—Hodge, field-notes, B. A. E., 1895 (Santa Ana name of pueblo). Sünyítsi.—Ibid (Laguna form; Acoma form, Zunyíts). Tâa Ashiwani.—Cushing, inf'n, 1891 ('Corn peoples': sacred name of the tribe). Tennis.—Sherman in H. R. Rep. 384, 43d Cong., 1st sess., 276, 1874 (misprint.) Truni.—Oñate (1598) in Doc. Inéd., XVI, 115, 1871. Tunis.—Taylor in Cal. Farmer, Feb. 14, 1862. Xalay.—Oñate (1598) in Doc. Inéd., XVI, 115, 1871 (identified by Bandelier, Jour. Am. Eth. and Arch., III, 80, 1892, with Xaray, the Tigua name of Zuñi; see Saray, above). Xaray.—Bandelier in Jour. Am. Eth. and Arch., III, 81, 1892 (Tigua name; cf. Sarai, etc., above). Zani.—Mill, Hist. Mexico, map, 1824. Ze-gar-kin-a.—White, MS. Hist. Apaches, B. A. E., 1875 (Apache name). Zeven steden van Cibola.—ten Kate, Reizen in N. A., 290, 1885 (Dutch form). Zibola.—Villagran, Hist. Nuevo Mexico, 145, 1610. Zivola.—Kino (1699) in Doc. Hist. Mex., 4th s., I, 327, 1856. Zŏënji.—ten Kate, Reizen in N. A., 291, 1885 (Cochiti name). Zouni.—Benavides as quoted by Gallatin in Nouv. Ann. Voy., 5th s., XXVII, 307, 1851. Zugnis.—Borsari, Letteratura degl'

Indig. Americani, II, 1888 (Italian form). **Zumis.**—Blaeu, Atlas, XII, 62, 1667. **Zun.**—Disturnell, map Méjico, 1846. **Zuña.**—Davis, El Gringo, 128, 1857. **Zuñe.**—Ward in Ind. Aff. Rep. 1864, 191, 1865. **Zuni.**—Espejo (1583) in Hakluyt, Voy., III, 471, 1600; Doc. Inéd., XV, 180, 1871. **Zuñi.**—Benavides, Memorial, 34, 1630. **Zunia.**—Calhoun (1849) in Cal. Mess. and Corresp., 205 et seq., 1850. **Zuñians.**—Hughes, Doniphan's Exped., 196, 1848. **Zunias.**—Vetancurt (1693), Téatro Mex., III, 311, 1871. **Zuñi-Cibola.**—Bandelier in Arch. Inst. Papers, III, 153, 1890. **Zuni-Cibola.**—Bandelier in Rev. d' Ethnog., 207, 1886. **Zunie.**—Evans in Ind. Aff. Rep. 1869, 101, 1870. **Zunni.**—Gregg misquoted by Gallatin in Trans. Am. Ethnol. Soc., II, lxxxviii, 1848. **Zuñu.**—Gatschet in Mag. Am. Hist., 260, Apr. 1882 (misprint; also Zuñi). **Zuny.**—Mendoça (1586) in Hakluyt, Voy., 462, 470, 1600 (after Espejo, 1583). **Zura.**—Hervas, Idea dell' Universo, XVII, 76, 1784. **Zuyi.**—Bandelier in Arch. Inst. Papers, III, 154, 1890 (misprint).

Zuñian Family. A distinct linguistic family, comprising only the Zuñi tribe.

=**Zuñi.**—Turner in Pac. R. R. Rep., III, pt. 3, 55, 91–93, 1856 (finds no radical affinity between Zuñi and Keres); Buschmann, Neu-Mexico, 254, 266, 276–278, 280–296, 302, 1858 (vocabs. and general references); Keane in Stanford, Compend., Cent. and So. Am., 479, 1878 ("a stock language"); Powell in Rocky Mtn. Presbyterian, Nov. 1878 (includes Zuñi, Las Nutrias, Ojo de Pescado); Gatschet in Mag. Am. Hist., 260, 1882. =**Zuñian.**—Powell in Am. Nat., 604, Aug. 1880; Powell in 7th Rep. B. A. E., 138, 1891.

Zúñiga. Apparently a Papago rancheria in N. W. Sonora, Mexico; probably named from a Spaniard.—Coues, Garcés Diary, 37, 1900.

Zutsemin ('red ocher,' or 'red earth'). An Okinagan town on upper Similkameen r., Brit. Col.

Vermillion.—Teit in Mem. Am. Mus. Nat. Hist., II, 174, 1900 (white men's name). **Zu'tsamîn.**—Ibid. **Zu'tsEmîn.**—Ibid.

SYNONYMY

Aábahu=Arapaho.
Aacus=Acoma.
A-á-kō-za=Iyakoza.
Aaltu=Ala.
A-ampkua amim=Umpqua.
Aanadako's=Anadarko.
Aä′ninĕna=Atsina.
Aanû′hawa=Hanahawunena.
Aarapahoes=Arapaho.
A-ar-ke=Hopi.
Aas=Eyeish.
Â′-â′tam, Â′-â′tam Â′kimûlt=Pima.
A-auh-wauh=Ahahweh.
Aays=Eyeish.
Ababeves=Ababco.
Abacoes=Abihka.
Abacooche, Abacouchees=Abikudshi
Abacu, Abacus=Hawikuh.
Abagadusets=Bagaduce.
Abalache, Abalachi=Apalachee.
Abanakees, Abanakis, Abanaquis, Abanaquois=Abnaki.
Abarginny=Aberginian.
Abbacoochees=Abikudshi.
Abbāto-tenā′, Abbā-to-tenāh, Abbato-tinneh=Abbatotine.
Abbetikis, Abbitibbes, Abbitibbi=Abittibi.
Abbo=Abo.
Ab-boin-ee Sioux, Ab-boin-ug, Abbwoi-nug=Dakota.
Abchas, Abecaes, Abecas, Abecka=Abihka.
Abecoche, Abecochi, Abecoochee, Abecothee, Abécouéchis=Abikudshi.
Abeeka=East Abeika.
Abeicas, Abeikas, Abekas=Abihka.
Abenaguis, Abenaka, Abena′kes, Abenakias, Abénakis, Abena′kiss, Abenakki, Abenaques, Abenaquioicts, Abenaquiois, Abenaquioue, Abenaquis, Abenati, Abenequas, Abenquois=Abnaki.
Abequin=Abiquiu.
Abercrosh=Waganakisi.
Abergeny, Aberieney=Aberginian.
Abernaquis=Abnaki.
Abicas=Abihka.
Abicu, Abicui, Abiguin=Abiquiu.
Abi′hka=Abihka.
Abi′hkúdshi=Abikudshi.
Abikas, Abikaws=Abihka.
Abimiouec, Abimi8ec=Illinois.
Abinaqui=Abnaki.
Abingas=Wappinger.
Abinohkie=Abnaki.
Abinones=Wea.
Abio=Abo.
Abiquico, Abiquieu, Abiquin, Abiquíri=Abiquiu.
Abitibis, Abittibbes=Abittibi.
Abnakis, Abnaquies, Abnaquiois, Abnaquis, Abnaquois, Abnaquotii, Abnasque, Abnekais=Abnaki.
Ab-oin, Aboinug=Dakota.
Abolachi=Apalachee.
Abonakies=Abnaki.
Abonerhopiheim=Ahouerhopiheim.
Abonnekee=Abnaki.
Aborginny=Aberginian.
Abraham Lincoln's village=Thechuntunne.
Abre Croche=Waganakisi.
Abricu=Abiquiu.
Absaraka, Absarakos, Absaroka, Absarokes, Absároki=Crows.
Absayme=Ansaimes.
Absoroka=Crows.
Abucbochu=Abikudshi.
Abucios=Acoma.
Abuquin=Abiquiu.
Aburcos=Cambujos.

Abuscal=Abascal.
Abwoinug=Dakota.
Acadcan, Acadian Indians=Micmac.
Acansa, Acansea, Acansias=Quapaw.
Acapatos=Atsina.
Acawmuck=Patuxet.
Accahanock=Accohanoc.
Accanceas, Accances=Quapaw.
Accawmacke=Accomac.
Acchusnutt=Acushnet.
Accocesaws, Accockesaws=Arkokisa.
Accohanock=Accohanoc.
Accokesaus, Accokesaws=Arkokisa.
Accomack=Accomac, Patuxet.
Accomentas, Accominticus, Accomintycus, Accomynticus=Accominta.
Acconeechy=Occaneechi.
Ac-cool-le=Akuli.
Accoomeek=Patuxet.
Accopogue=Aquebogue.
Accotronacks=Accohanoc.
Accowmack=Accomac.
Acculee=Akuli.
Acha=Picuris.
Achagué=Outchougai.
Achalaque=Cherokee.
A-cha′-o-tin-ne=Etchareottine.
Achaque=Outchougai.
Achastas, Achastli, Achastlians, Achastliens, Achastlier, Achastlies=Rumsen.
Acheaubofau=Talasse.
Achedomas=Alchedoma.
Achees=Yuchi.
Achelaci, Achelacy, Achelaiy, Achelayy=Hochelayi.
Achena=Atsina.
Acheotenne=Etchareottine.
Aches=Pawnee.
Achese=Chisi.
A-che-to-e-ten-ni, Acheto-e-Tinne, Acheto-tenà=Etchareottine.
Achē′to-tin′neh=Titshotina.
Achiesta=Achasta.
Achiganes=Sooke.
Achiha=Chiaha.
Achilia=Hitchiti.
Achiligoüiane=Achiligouan.
Achiok=Akhiok.
Achipoés, Achipoué=Chippewa.
Achirigouans=Achiligouan.
Achistas=Rumsen.
Achjuch-Aliat=Inguklimiut, Imaklimiut.
Achkingkesaky, Achkinkehacky, Achkinkeshacky=Hackensack.
Achkugmjuten=Aglemiut, Kaniagmiut.
Ach-min-de-cou-may=Kalispel.
Achoic Comihavit=Achois.
Achomáwes=Achomawi.
A-cho-mâ′-wi=Shastan Family.
Achonechy=Occaneechi.
Achoto-e-tenni=Etchareottine.
Achquegenonck, Achquickenough, Achquickenunck, Achquickenunk, Achquikanuncque=Aquackanonk.
Achsisaghecks, Achsissaghecs=Missisauga.
Achulares=Chulare.
Achusse, Achussi=Achusi.
Achwlget=Hagwilget.
Ácihi, Ácihi-ɸine=Ashihi.
Acinay=Caddo.
A′-ci-wi=Zuñi.
Ackiagmute=Akiak.
Ackinckesaky=Hackensack.
Ackoolee=Akuli.

1021

Ackquekenon=Aquackanonk.
Acmaat, A-co, Acogiya=Acoma.
Acohanock=Accohanoc.
Acohee=Ocoee.
Aco-ke-sas=Arkokisa.
Acolocú=Chilili.
Acolta=Lekwiltok.
Acomack, Acomak=Accomac.
Acoman, Acomas, Acome, Acomenses, Acomeses, Acomis, Acomo, Acona=Acoma.
Aconeche, Aconecho, Aconeechy=Occaneechi.
Aconia=Acoma.
Aconichi=Occaneechi.
Aconista=Acomita.
Acoonedy=Occaneechi.
Acossesaws=Arkokisa.
Acosta, Acoste=Coste.
Acota=Acoti.
Acounee=Oconee.
Acpalliut=Akpaliut.
Acquackanonk=Aquackanonk.
Acquaseack, Acquaskack=Acquaskac.
Acquia=Acoma.
Acquicanunck, Acquiggenonck, Acquikanong=Aquackanonk.
Ac-quin-a-nack-su acks=Acquintanacsuak.
Acquinoehionee=Iroquois.
Acquintanacksuah, Acquintanacksuak, Acquintanacsuck, Acquintunachsuah=Acquintanacsuak.
Acquinushionee=Iroquois.
Acquiora=Bagiopa.
Acquitanases=Acquintanacsuak.
Actun=San Rafael.
Acu=Acoma.
Acubadaos=Arbadaos.
Acuca, Acucans, Acuco, Acucu=Acoma.
Acuera=Acquera.
Acuique, A-cu-lah=Pecos.
Acus=Acoma.
Acusy=Achusi.
Acux=Acoma.
Acuyé=Pecos.
Adaes=Adai, San Miguel de Linares.
Adage, Adahi, Adaïces, Adaies, Adaies, Adaihe, Adais, Adaisses, Adaize=Adai.
Ă da ka′ da ho=Arikara.
Á′dal-k′ato′igo=Nez Percés.
Adams Lake Band=South Adrian Band.
Adawadenys=Potawatomi.
Adayes, Adays, Addaise, Addaize, Addees=Adai
Addi=Ati.
Addick=Ahdik.
Addies=Adai.
Ad-dik=Ahdik.
Ad-dik-kun-maig=Udekumaig.
Addle-Heads=Menominee.
Adees=Adai.
Adènè=Athapascan Family.
Adero=Ardeco.
Adeyches=Adai.
Adgebaches=Tukabatchi.
Adgecantehook=Arosaguntacook.
Adiais=Adai.
Adigie, Adigo=Kittanning.
Adi′kamäg=Udekumaig.
Adirondacs, Adirondaks, Adirondax, Adirontak, Adisonkas=Adirondack.
Ad-je-jawk=Ojeejok.
Adla, Adlăhsuin, Adlat=Adlet.
Adnondecks=Adirondack.
Adoena=Athapascan Family.
Adoses=Adai.
Adusta=Edisto.
Adwanuqdji=Atsugewi.
Adyes=Adai.
Adzumáwi=Achomawi.
Aenay=Hainai.
Aequeya=Acquera.
Aes=Eyeish.
Aesetooue=Uzutiuhi.
Aesopus=Esopus.
Affagoula=Ofogoula.
Affats-tena=Abbatotine.
Afrahcootans=Wahpekute.
Afúlakin=Wasco.
A-gai-du-ka, Á-gai-ti-kút-teh=Agaihtikara.
Agaligamute=Aguliak.
Agamenticus=Accominta.
Aganuschioni=Iroquois.

Agaraits, A-gar-it-is=Miskut.
Agawaam=Agawam.
Agáweshkni, Agáweshni=Agawesh.
Agawom, Agawomes=Agawam.
Agerones=Hainai.
Aggawam, Aggawom=Agawam.
Ag-gi-tik′-kah=Tazaaigadika.
Aggoncy, Agguncia=Norumbega.
Aghquessaine, Aghquissasne=Saint Regis.
Aghsiesagichrone=Missisauga.
Âgin=Pecos.
Agissawamg=Agawam.
Agiu=Pecos.
Agiukchugumut=Agiukchuk.
Agivarik=Agivavik.
Aglahmutes, Agläxtana, Aglĕgmiut, Aglegmjuten, Aglĕgmūt=Aglemiut.
Agnascoga=Aquascogoc.
Agnechronons, Agnée, Agneehronon, Agneronons, Agnerronons, Agnic=Mohawk.
Agnié, Agniée, Agniegué=Canienga.
Agniehronnons, Agniehroron, Agnierhonon, Agnieronnons, Agnieronons, Agnierrhonons, Agniers, Agniez, Agnizez=Mohawk.
Âgo=Acoma.
Agolĕgmiut, Agolegmüten, Agolegmutes=Aglemiut.
Agoncy=Norumbega.
Agoneaseah=Iroquois.
Agones=Iowa.
Agonnonsionni, Agonnousioni, Agonnsionni=Iroquois.
Agonwarage=Kagoughsage.
Agoolmutes=Aglemiut.
Agorichi=Aoreachi.
Agotsaganens=Tsaganha.
Agotsaganes=Mahican, Tsaganha.
Agotsagenens=Mahican.
Agotssakann=Tsaganha.
Agouais, Agoual, Âgoues=Iowa.
Agowaun, Agowaywam=Agawam.
Agowik=Iguik.
Agozhaga=Tsaganha.
Agozhagauta=Mahican.
Agua Caliente=Gupa, Sechi.
Aguachaches=Aguachacha.
Agua Dulce=Tova.
Agua Frio=Pueblo Quemado.
Aguanoχgi=Abnaki.
Agua Rias=Agua Fria.
Aguasajuchium=Ahwaste, Uchium.
Aguas Calientes=Hawikuh, Ojo Caliente.
Aguascobi=Hawikuh.
Aguascosack=Aquascogoc.
Aguasto=Ahwastes.
Agua Supais=Havasupai.
Aguato, Aguatobi, Aguatubi, Aguatuby, Aguatuví, Aguatuya, Aguatuybá=Awatobi.
Aguenes=Doguenes.
Aguico, Aguicobi=Hawikuh.
Aguierhonon=Mohawk.
Aguinsa=Kwakina.
Aguitobi=Awatobi.
Aguivira=Quivira.
Aguliagamiut, Aguliagamute=Aguliak.
Aguljmjuten=Aglemiut.
Agulmiut=Chnagmiut.
Agŭlmūt=Kuskwogmiut.
Agulmüten=Aglemiut.
Aguscal=Abascal.
Aguscobi=Hawikuh.
Aguskemaig=Eskimo.
A-gutch-a-ninne, A-gutch-a-ninne-wug=Hidatsa.
Agutit=Kinipetu.
Aguwom=Agawam.
A-gu-yu=Pecos.
Agvan=Avak.
A-ha-chae=Osage.
Ahacus=Hawikuh.
Ah′-ah=Ahalakalgi.
Ahâh-âr-ro′-pir-no-pah=Ahaharopirnopa.
Ahahawa, Ahahaway=Amahami.
Ahahnelins=Atsina.
Ah-ah-wai, Ah-ah-wauk=Ahahweh.
Ahaknañĕlet, A-hak-nan-helet, Ahaknan-helik=Ai vilirmiut.
Ah′alakat=Chemehuevi.
Ahalaχálgi=Ahalakalgi.
Ahálpam=Santiam.

Ahándshiyuk, Ahandshuyuk amim, Ahántchuyuk amim=Ahantchuyuk.
Ahapapka=Ahapopka.
Ah-auh-vauh, Ah-auh-wauh-ug=Ahahweh.
Ahausath=Ahousaht.
Ahawhwauk=Ahahweh.
Ah-bah-to-din-ne=Abbatotine.
Ahcharalar=Atchinahátchi.
Ah-co=Acoma.
Ahehoen, Ahehoenes=Ahehouen.
Ahei'pudin=Lower Chinook.
Ahekouen=Ahehouen.
A'-hel-tah=Tlelding.
Ah-e-o-war=Iowa.
Ahepat Okla=Oypatukla.
Ahgomekhelanaghamiut=Agomekelenanak.
Ah-gote'-sa-ga-näge=Stockbridge.
Ahgulakhpaghamiut=Agulakpak.
Ahguliagamut=Aklut.
Ahgy-tecitteh, Ahgyweit=Agaihtikara.
Ah-hä-chick=Ahachick.
Ah-hì-tä-pe=Siksika.
Ahhousaht=Ahousaht.
Ahiahichi=Eyeish.
Ahialt=Ahealt.
Ah-i'-hi-nin=Pawnee.
Ahijados, Ahijaos, Ahijitos=Tawehash.
Ahinai=Hainai.
Ahipa=Etah.
Ah-knaw-ah-mish, Ah-know-ah-mish=Hahuamis.
Ah-ko=Acoma.
Ahkonapi=Akonapi.
Ahkootskie=Auk.
Ah-kuh'-ne-näk=Akuninak.
Ahkvaystkie=Akvetskoe.
A'hlait'ha=Cochiti.
Áh-lè-là, Ahlelq=Shipaulovi.
Ah-mah-oo=Komoyue.
Ah-mau-dah-kas=Anadarko.
Ah-meek=Ahmik.
Ah-mo-kæ=Hopi.
Ahnahaways=Amahami.
Ah'-nah-ha-nä'-me-te=Ahnahanamete.
Ah-nan-dah-kas, Ahnaudahkas, Ahnaudakas=Anadarko.
Ahnenin, Ahni-ninn=Atsina.
Ahondihronnons=Aondironon.
Ahonerhopiheim=Ahouerhopiheim.
Ahosett=Ahousaht.
Ahouandate=Huron.
Ahouenrochrhonons=Wenrohronon.
Ahousĕt, Ahowartz, Ahowsaht, Ah-owz-arts=Ahousaht.
Ahoya=Hoya.
Ah'-pai-tup-iks=Ahahpitape.
Ah-pe-ki', Ah-pe-ki'-e=Apikaiyiks.
Ah-pen-ope-say=Arikara.
Ahpokagamiut=Apokak.
Ah-qua-sos-ne=Saint Regis.
Ahrenda, Ahrendah-ronons, Ahrendaronons=Arendahronons.
Ah'-ro-whä=Arukhwa (1).
Ah-shee-wai=Zuñi.
Ah-shin'-nä-de'-ah=Ashinadea.
Áh-shi-wi=Zuñi.
Ah-shu-ah-har-peh=Salish.
Ah-Supai=Havasupai.
Aht=Nootka.
Ahtawwah=Ottawa.
Ahtna-Khotana=Ahtena.
Ahuachés=Pawnee.
Ahuátcha=Mescaleros.
Ahuato, Ahuatu, Ahuatuyba=Awatobi.
Ahulqa=Ahulka.
Ahuzto=Awatobi.
Ahwahawas, Ahwahaways, Ah-wâh-hâ-way=Amahami.
Ahwahnachee, Ahwahnechee=Awani.
Ah-wah-sis'-sa=Awausee.
A-hwa-ki-lu=Chimakum.
Ahwāndate=Huron.
Ahwa-paia-kwanwa=Tontos.
Ah-wash-tes=Ahwaste.
Ah-wa-sis-se=Awausee.
Ahwastes=Ahwaste.
Ah-wat-tenna=Awatobi.
Ahwhacknanhelett=Aivilirmiut.
Ah-wha-mish=Hahuamis.
Ahwilgate=Hagwilget.

Ahyak=Ayak.
Ähyäto=Arapaho.
Ahyche=Eyeish.
Ahyoksekawik=Aiachagiuk.
Aiabeka=East Abeika.
Ai-ahá=Chiricahua.
Aiaialgutak=Avatanak.
Aiaichi=Eyeish.
Aiakhatalik=Aiaktalik.
Aianabe=Ayanabi.
Aiano=Kanohatino.
Aiaoua, Aiaouais, Aiaouez=Iowa.
Ai-a-ta=Apache.
Aiauway, Aiavvis=Iowa.
Aibacusi=Tupo.
Aibamos=Alibamu.
Aibeka=West Abeika.
Aibina, Aibino=Aivino.
A'-ic, Aiche, Aiches=Eyeish.
Ai-dĭk'-a-da-hu=Arikara.
Ai'gspalo=Aigspaluma.
Ai'gspaluma=Snakes, Modoc.
Ai-há=Chiricahua.
Aijados, Aijaos=Tawehash.
Aijas=Eyeish.
Aijoues=Iowa.
A'ikoka=Acoma.
Aikspalu=Aigspaluma.
Ailigulsha=Elakulsi.
Ailways=Iowa.
Ainais=Hainai.
Ainones, Ainoves=Iowa.
Aiñ'shi-kwe, Aíŋshi-kwe=Aingshi.
A-i-nun'=Crows.
Aioaez=Iowa.
Aioma, Aiomo=Acoma.
Aiouez, Aiounouea, Aiowais=Iowa.
Ais=Eyeish.
Aisa=Ais.
Aise, A'-ish=Eyeish.
Aisnous=Iowa.
Aitchelich, Aitchelitz=Atselits.
Aiticha=Iticha.
Ai-tiz-zarts, Aitzarts=Ehatisaht.
Aivatanak=Avatanak.
Aivillirmiut=Aivilirmiut.
Aiwahokwe=Aiyaho.
Aix=Eyeish.
Aixacan=Axacan.
Aixai, Aixaj=Eyeish.
Aixaos=Tawehash.
Ai-yah-kín-nee=Hopi.
Aíyaho-kwe=Aiyaho.
Aiyáhokwi=Asa.
Ai-yan, Ai-ya-na=Hankutchin.
Aiyansh=Aiyansh.
Aizes=Eyeish.
Ajaouez, Ajouas=Iowa.
Ajouelles=Avoyelles.
Ajoues, Ajouez=Iowa.
Ajuyap=Ujuiap.
Ák'a íniŭk'ăcin'a=Kanse.
Akama, Akamsca, Akamsea, Akamsians=Quapaw.
Ak'ăn=Anchguhlsu.
Akancas, A Kancea, Akanceas, Akansa, Akansaes, Akansas, Akanscas, Akansea, Akansis, Akanssa, Akanzas=Quapaw.
Akatlak=Akatik.
Aka-ush, Aka'-uskni=Agawesh.
Akavat=Wanupiapayum.
Ăk'-ba-sū'-pai=Havasupai.
Akbat=Akpan.
Akchadak-kochkond=Akchadak.
Ák'eji=Santa Clara.
A'kémorl-Oōhtam=Pima.
Akenatzie, Akenatzy=Occaneechi.
Akensas=Quapaw.
Akfáski=Oakfuskee.
Akharatipikam=Kepel.
Akhonapi=Akonapi.
Akhrakouaehronon, Akhrakvaeronon=Conestoga.
Akiagamiut, Akiágmut, Akiagomute=Akiak.
Akiakchagmiut, Akiatshágamut=Akiachak.
A'kimmash=Clackama.
Akimuri=Aquimuri.
Akinsaws=Quapaw.
Akiskinookaniks=Akiskenukinik.
Akka=Makak.
Akkiagamute, Akkiagmute=Akiak.

Akkolear=Akuliarmiut.
Ak-kŏn=Auk.
Akkoolee=Akuli.
Aklukwagamut=Aklut.
Ak-min'-e-shu'-me=Kalispel.
Akmute=Akmiut.
Aknutl=Honsading.
A-ko=Acoma.
Ako=Abó, Acoma.
Akochakaneñ'=Mahican.
Ákokavi=Acoma.
Akoklako=Lower Kutenai.
Akókovi, Ako-ma=Acoma.
Akonichi=Occaneechi.
Akononsionni=Iroquois.
Akonwarage=Kagoughsage.
Akooligamute=Aklut.
Akoon=Akun.
Akoroa=Koroa.
Á-ko-t'ăs-kă-ro'-rĕⁿ=Tuscarora.
Ă-ko-tcă-kă' nĕⁿ', A-ko-tcă-kă-nhă', A-kots-ha-ka-
  nen=Delaware.
Ak8anake=Abnaki.
Akowetako=Kawita.
Akowini=Akonapi.
Akpani=Akpan.
Akrakwaé=Atrakwaye.
Akuchăklactas=Lower Kutenai.
Akudliarmiut=Akuliarmiut.
Akudnimiut=Akudnirmiut.
Akuesú-pai=Havasupai.
Ákukapi=Acoma.
Akuliak-Eskimos=Akuliarmiut.
Akuliaq=Akuliak.
Akuliukhpak=Akuliukpak.
Akulvikohuk=Akulivikchuk.
Akura-nga=Acuragna.
Akusash-rónu=Saint Regis.
Akutaⁿskoe=Akutan.
Ă-ku-tcă-ka''-nhă=Delaware.
Akûtciny=Aquitun.
Akutskoe=Auk.
A-kwā'-amish=Hahuamis.
Akwanake=Algonkin.
A-kwăn-ke'=Agotsaganha.
Akwesasne=Saint Regis.
Akwetz=Akvetskoe.
Akwilget=Hwotsotenne.
Akwinoshioni=Iroquois.
Ala=Alibamu.
Alabama=Alibamu, Taliepatava.
Ala Bamer=Alibamu.
Alachees, A-lack-a-way-talofa, Alacua=Alachua.
Aládshŭsh=Chinook.
Alaganuk, Alagnak=Alaganik.
Alagonkins=Algonkin.
Alagulsa=Elakulsi.
Alähähó=Kansa.
Alajulapu=Santa Inés.
Alakea=Palaquesson.
Alakĕmáyuk=Lakmiut.
Alaki=Walpi.
Alamada=Alameda.
Alameda la Isleta=Isleta.
Alámmimakt ísh=Klamath.
Alamo=Lawilvan.
Alamo Solo=Cienega.
A-lăn-săr=Atsina.
A'-la-nyû-mû=Ala.
Alapaha-tolafa=Alapaha.
Alatamahas=Altamaha.
A'látskné-i=Tlatskanai.
Alauna=Halona.
Albamas=Alibamu.
Albenaquioue, Albenaquis=Abnaki.
Albikas=Abihka.
Albinones=Wea.
Albiquin=Abiquiu.
Alcea=Alsea.
Alchedomes, Alchedum, Alchedumas, Alchidomas=
  Alchedoma.
Alchones=Olhon.
Alcuco=Acoma.
Alebamah, Alebamons=Alibamu.
Aleche=Eyeish.
Aleegaeening=Shannopin's Town.
Al-e-is=Watlala.
Alemada, Alemeda=Alameda.

Alemousiski=Armouchiquois.
Alena=Halona.
Ale'outeans=Aleut.
Alesar=Atsina.
Aleupkigna=Alympquigna.
Aleut=Esquimauan Family.
Aleuten=Aleut, Esquimauan Family.
Aleutians=Esquimauan Family.
Alexandria=Stella.
Alexandria Indians=Tautin.
Alexandrousk=Alexandrovsk, Nushagak.
Alexeief's Odinotchka=Alexief.
Aleya=Alsea.
Aleytao=Aleta.
Aleyut=Aleut.
Algodomes, Algodones, Algodonnes=Alchedoma.
Algokin, Algomeequin, Algomequins, Algomme-
  quin=Algonkin.
Algommequin de l'Isle=Kichesipirini.
Algomquins, Algoncains, Algongins, Algonguin, Al-
  gonic Indians=Algonkin.
Algonkin Inférieures=Montagnais.
Algonkin-Lenape, Algonkins, Algonkin und Beo-
  thuk=Algonquian.
Algonméquin, Algonquains, Algonquens=Algonkin.
Algonquin=Algonquian.
Algonquins à têtes de Boule=Têtes de Boule.
Algonquins Inférieurs=Montagnais.
Algonquins of Rainy Lake=Kojejewininewug.
Algonquins Superieurs=Ottawa.
Algoomenquini, Algoquins, Algoquois, Algouin-
  quins, Algoumekins, Algoumequini, Algoume-
  quins, Algumenquini=Algonkin.
Aliata, Aliatan, Aliatans of La Playes, Aliatans of
  the West, Aliatons, Aliatons of the west=Ietan.
Alibam, Alibamas, Alibamies, Alibamo, Alibamons,
  Alibamous, Alibanio, Alibanons=Alibamu.
Alioh, Aliche, Alickas=Eyeish.
Alikwa=Yurok.
Alimacany=Alimacani.
Alimamu=Alibamu.
Alimibegoueci=Alimibegouek.
Alimo Bonita, Alimo Bonito=Alamo Bonito.
Alimouek, Alimouk=Illinois.
Alinconguins=Algonkin.
Aliniouek, Alini8ek, Alinouecks=Illinois.
Alipconck, Alipkonck=Alipconk.
Alish, Alishes=Eyeish.
Alitak=Akhiok.
Alitan, Aliton=Ietan.
Aljiman=Eljman.
Al-kă-ao=Alcax.
Alkakalilkes=Alkali Lake.
Alkansas=Quapaw.
Allagae=Ellijay.
Allamutcha Old Town=Alamucha.
Allasis=Atasi.
Allayume=Aleut.
All Chiefs=Motwainaiks.
Allebome=Comanche.
Allegaeniny=Shannopin's Town.
Allegans=Cherokee.
Allegany Indians=Alleghany Indians.
Allegany Village=Deyohnegano.
Allegewe, Allegewi, Allegewy, Alleghans, Alle-
  ghanys=Cherokee.
Allegheny=Alleghany Indians.
Alleguipes=Allaquippa.
Allegwi=Cherokee.
Allemouchicois=Armouchiquois.
Allenemipigons=Chippewa of Lake Nipegon.
Allequas=Yurok.
Allequippe=Allaquippa.
Allianies=Miami.
Alliatan, Alliatans of the west=Ietan.
Allibama, Allibamis, Allibamons, Allibamous=Ali-
  bamu.
Allicamany=Alimacani.
Alligany=Alleghany Indians.
Alligator Hole, Alligator Indians=Alligator.
Alligewi, Allighewis=Cherokee.
Allimacany=Alimacani.
Allinouecks=Illinois.
Allvatalama=Alwathalama.
Almacoac=Anacoat.
Almauchicois, Almonchiguois, Almouchicoisen, Al-
  mouchiquoise=Armouchiquois.
Almpquigna=Alympquigna.
Alnânbaï=Abnaki.

Alomas=Acoma, Halona.
Alona=Halona.
Aloqui=Hopi.
Alpawa=Alpowna.
Al-pĭn-toä=Alpincha.
ALqla′xL=Atlklaktl.
Alquequin=Algonkin.
Alquestan=Azqueltan.
Alsentia=Kaguyak.
Alseya, Al-si=Alsea.
Alsigantĕ′gwi=Arosaguntacook.
Alsigôntegok=St Francis.
Alsiias, Älsi′-meꞇûnnĕ, Alsiya=Alsea.
Altajumi, Altajumo=Áltahmos.
Altamaca, Altapaha=Altamaha.
Altar=Pitic.
Altaraca=Olataraca.
Altasse=Atasi.
Al-ta-tin=Sekani.
Al-tá-tin of Bear Lake=Saschutkenne.
Altatmos=Altahmos.
Altekas=Texas.
Altenkins=Algonkin.
Altignenonghac=Attigneenongnahac.
Altihamaguez, Altikamek, Altikameques=Attika-
    megue.
Alto=Pueblo Alto.
Aluquia=Abiquiu.
A′lva-ye′lɪlɪt=Eskimo.
Alwaththalam=Alwathalama.
Amacabos, Amacava, A-mac-ha′-vès, Amaguaguas=
    Mohave.
Amahim=Anaham.
Amahuayas, Amajabas, Ämajavas=Mohave.
Amakaraongky=Aquackanonk.
Amalecites, Amalicites, Amalingans, Amalistes=
    Malecite.
Amanakoa=Amonokoa.
Amandaicoes=Anadarko.
Amaques, Amaqui=Hopi.
Amarascoggin, Amarascogin, Amarescoggin, Amaris-
    coggins, Amaroscoggen=Arosaguntacook.
Amasaconticook, Amasacontoog, Amasaguanteg=
    Amaseconti.
Amasagunticook=Arosaguntacook.
Amasconly, Amascontie, Amasconty, Amasecontee=
    Amaseconti.
Amasì=Amahami.
Amassacanty, Amassaconty=Amaseconti.
A-ma′-te-wat-se′=Amahami.
Amathlas=Yalaka.
Amatiñami=Amahami.
A ma tinatꞇhi=Amatidatahi.
Amay=Amaye.
Ămăye′l-e′gwa=Big-island.
Ămăye′lĭ-gûnăhi′ta=Long Island.
Amayes=Jemez.
Ambahtawoot, Ambah-tawut-dinni, Amba-ta-ut′tiné,
    Ambatawwoot, Ambawtamoot, Ambawtawhoot-
    dinneh, Ambawtawhoot Tinneh, Ambawtawoot,
    Ambawtowhoot=Abbatotine.
Amdustez=Conestoga.
Amé=Zuñi.
Amediche, Amedichez=Nabedache.
Ameges=Jemez.
Amehouest=Amikwa.
Ameias, Ameies, Amejes=Jemez.
Ameko8es=Amikwa.
Amelestes, Amelicks, Amelingas, Amelistes, Ame-
    listis, Amenecis=Malecite.
Amerascogen, Amerescogin=Arosaguntacook.
Ameries=Jemez.
Ameriscoggins, Amerriscoggin=Arosaguntacook.
A-me-she′=Hidatsa.
Amgútsuish=Umpqua.
Amí=Zuñi.
Amicawaes, Amicois, Amicouës, Amicoures, Ami-
    cours, Amic-ways=Amikwa.
Amies=Jemez.
Amihouis=Amikwa.
Ami′k, Amik=Ahmik.
A-mi-ke-ar-rum=Amaikiara.
Amikois, Amikones, Amikoüai, Amikoüas, Ami-
    kcuek, Amikoües, à Mikouest, Amikouëts, Ami-
    kouis, Amikouys=Amikwa.
A-mĭks′-eks=Inuksiks.
Amilicites=Malecite.
Aminoia=Aminoya.

Amios=Jemez.
Amircankanne, Amireaneau=Arosaguntacook.
Amires=Jemez.
Amirgankaniois=Narraganset.
Amitigoke=Amitok.
Amitioke=Amitormiut.
Amitons=Yankton.
Amitoq, Amittioke, Amityook=Amitok.
Amkepatines=Hunkpatina.
Am-khark-hit-ton=Ankakehittan.
Ammarascoggin, Ammarescoggin, Ammascoggen=
    Arosaguntacook.
Ammisk-watcheéthinyoowuc=Paskwawininiwug.
A-moc-há-ve=Mohave.
A′moekwikwe=Hopi.
Amóhah=Mohave.
Amóhak=Mohawk.
Amojaves=Mohave.
A-mo-kini, A-mo-kwi=Hopi.
Amolélish=Molala.
Amonoscoggan, Amonoscoggin=Arosaguntacook.
Amooklasah Town=Muklassa.
Amoscongen=Arosaguntacook.
Amosequonty=Amaseconti.
Amo-shium-qua=Amushungkwa.
Amoꭓami, Amoꭓawi=Mohave.
Amo-xium-qua, Amoxunqua, Amoxunque=Amu-
    shungkwa.
Ampapa, Ampapes=Hunkpapa.
Ámpkokni máklaks, Ámpkua=Umpqua.
A′mpꭓänkni=Wasco.
Amresscoggin=Arosaguntacook.
Amuchaba=Mohave.
A′muhak=Mohawk.
Á-mu-kwi-kwe=Hopi.
Amutakhwe=New River Indians.
Ana=Cree.
Anabaidaítcho=Nabedache.
Anacarck, Anacbue=Anacbuc.
Anachataqua=Anacharaqua.
Anacoac=Anacoat.
Anacostan=Nacotchtank.
Ana-da-ca, Anadaghcoes, Anadahcoe, An-a-dah-has,
    An-a-dah-kas, Anadahkoes, Anadahkos, Anadakas,
    An-a-dak-has, Anadakkas, Anadáko, Anadaku,
    Anadarcos, Anadarko's, Anadogheos, Anador-
    koes=Anadarko.
Anagados=Anegados.
Anagangaw=Honeoye.
Anagonges, Anáguanoꭓgi=Abnaki.
Anaguas=Mohawk.
Anaha=Inyaha.
Anahanuk=Alaganik.
An-ah-dah-koes, An-ah-dah-kos, Anahdakas=Ana-
    darko.
Anahem, Anahim, Anahim's Tribe=Anaham.
Änähó, Anahons, Anahous=Osage.
Anahuac=Inyaha.
Anaica Apalache=Iniahico.
Anais=Hainai.
Anajot=Oneida (vil.).
Anaknak=Anagnak.
Anakwan‘kĭ=Delawares.
Analac=Analao.
Anames=Aranama.
Ananares=Avavares.
Anandaque=Canandaigua.
Anandarkoes=Anadarko.
Ananis=Biloxi.
Anantooeah=Seneca.
Anapaho=Arapaho.
Anaquago, Anaquaqua=Oquaga.
Anasaguntacooks, Anasaguntakook, Anasagunti-
    cooks=Arosaguntacook.
Anasaquanans=Nascapee.
Anasuguntakook=Arosaguntacook.
Anatoak=Änoatok.
Anatsagane=Stockbridge.
Anaudagas=Onondaga.
Anavares=Avavares.
Anawmanient=Onawmanient.
Anaxis=Biloxi.
Anayachtalik=Aiaktalik.
Anayints=Oneida.
Ance, Ance-ke-we-naw=Wequadong.
Ancestral gens=Hangkaenikashika.
Anchipawah=Chippewa.
Ancienne Lorette=Lorette.

Ancocisco=Aucocisco.
Andagaron=Kanagaro.
Andaicos=Anadarko.
Anda-kρœn=Eskimo.
Andaraqué=Kanagaro.
Andarcos=Anadarko.
Andaslaka, Andastaehronon, Andastaeronnons, Andastaes, Andastagueus, Andastaguez, Andastakas, Andastes, Andastfs, Andastiguez, Andastiquez, Andastoe, Andasto'e'r, Andastoerhonon, Andasto'e'ronnons, Andastoerrhonons, Andastognes, Andastogue, Andastoguehronnons, Andastogueronnons, Andastoguez, Andastohé, Andastonez, Andastoui, Andastracronnons=Conestoga.
Andata honato, Andatahoüat, Andatohats=Ottawa.
Andayes=Adai.
And-dai-coes=Anadarko.
Anderson's River Esquimaux=Kitegareut.
Anderson's Town=Wapeminskink.
Andiatae=Andiata.
Andoouanchronon=Ataronchrono.
Andosagues, Andostaguez, Andostoues=Conestoga.
Andowanchronon=Ataronchronon.
Andreáffsky, Andreievsky, Andreivsky=Andreafski.
Andréjanouschen Aleuten=Atka.
Androscoggins=Arosaguntacook.
Anduico=Anadarko.
Anega=Henya.
Anenatea=Anonatea.
Anendaonactia=Arendaonatia.
Añénépit=Kopagmiut.
Aneretek=Anoritok.
AnExtê't'tîm=Anektettim.
Angalla=Oglala.
Angawom=Agawam.
Angechag'emūt=Ankachagmiut.
Angeles=Los Angeles.
Angeles Taraichi=Taraichi.
An-ghem-ak-ti-koos=Accominta.
Anghet-hada, Angīt Hāadē=Gunghet-haidagai.
Angmagsalink=Angmagsalingmiut.
Angmalortoq=Angmalortuk.
Angnovchamiut=Angnovchak.
Angoon=Angun.
Ang8iens=Angoutenc.
Angoum=Agawam.
Ang8tenc=Angoutenc.
Anguum=Agawam.
Ang-wush-a=Angwusi.
Anhawas=Amahami.
Anhayca, Aniaca Apalache=Iniahico.
Aniáka-háka=Mohawk.
Anibishiw ininiwak=Wahpekute.
Anicoyanque=Anilco.
Anié=Mohawk.
Aniegué=Canienga.
Aniez=Mohawk.
Anigh Kalicken=Amikwa.
Anijue=Anejue.
Ani'-Kawi'tǎ=Kawita.
Anikōëssa=Creeks.
Anileos=Anilco.
Anilukhtakkak=Anilukhtakpak.
Ani'-Na'tsĭ=Natchez.
Ani'-Nûn'dǎwe'gĭ=Seneca.
Ani'pörspi=Nez Percés.
Aní Sě'nika=Seneca.
An-ish-in-aub-ag=Chippewa.
Ani'-Skǎlâ'lĭ=Tuscarora.
Ani'-Suwa'lĭ=Cheraw.
Ani'ta'guǎ=Catawba.
Ani'-Tsa'ta=Choctaw.
Ani'-Tsĭ'ksû=Chickasaw.
Ani'-Wadihĭ'=Paint Town.
Ani' Wasa'sĭ=Osage.
Aniyakh=Aniyak.
Ani'-Yu'tsĭ=Yuchi.
Anjageen=Honeoye.
Anjoues=Iowa.
Ankachagamuk, Ankatchag-miout, Ankatschagmiut, Ankochagamuk=Ankachak.
Ankora=Arikara.
An-Kotchin, An-Kutchin=Hankutchin.
Aⁿkwa—Umpqua.
Anligmut=Kaviagmiut.
ᵋAnꞙ sqadjĭ'ns gîtAnā'-i=Undl-skadjins-gitunai.
Anlygmüten=Kaviagmiut.
Aⁿmesoukkanti, Anmessukkantti, Anmiss8kanti=Amaseconti.

Anmoughcawgen=Arosaguntacook.
Annadahkoes, Anna-darcoes=Anadarko.
Annagaugaw=Honeoye.
Annah=Cree.
Annahawas=Amahami.
Annaho=Osage.
Án-ñamu=Anu.
Annanactook=Umanaktuak.
Annanatook, Annanetoote=Anarnitung.
Anna Ooka=Annaoka.
Annay=Hainai.
Anndggho's=Anadarko.
Anniegué, Anniehronnons=Mohawk.
Anniené=Canienga.
Anniengehronnons, Annienhronnons, Annieronnons, Annieronons, Annierronnons, Anniés, Anniez=Mohawk.
Annirkakan=Arosaguntacook.
Annocchy=Biloxi.
An-no-dar-coes=Anadarko.
Annogonges=Abnaki.
Annovokhamiut=Anovok.
Annugannok, Annuganok=Anugamok.
Annunciation=Sault au Recollet.
Anoeg=Eno.
A-nog-i-na jin=Anoginajin.
Anogogmute, Anogokmute=Anogok.
Anogongaars=Abnaki.
Anonatra=Anonatea.
Anoogamok=Anugamok.
Anoretŏ=Anoatok.
Anós-anyotskans=Arapaho.
Anovala=Nukfalalgi.
Anoy=Avoyelles.
Aⁿpaⁿ e'nikaci'ꞙa=Anpanenikashika.
Anqꞑa'ke hît tān=Ankakehittan.
Ansafriki=Weitspus.
Ansaimas=Ansaimes.
Ansaus=Kansa.
Än-shi-i-que=Aingshi.
Antastoez, Antastogue', Antastosi, Antastouais, Antastouez=Conestoga.
Antogạltsu=Anchguhlsu.
Ante=Aule.
Antelope-eaters, Antelope Skinners=Kwahari.
Ant Hill, Ant Hill of the Middle=Halona.
Anthontans=Teton.
Anthoutantas=Oto.
Än'ti-häⁿ'=Munceytown.
Antouhonorons, Antouoronons, Antovorinos=Seneca
Anunciata=Comaquidam.
Añu-quil-i-gui=Anyukwinu.
A'-nü wüñ-wü=Anu.
Anvic, Anvig=Anvik.
Añwuci wiñwû, Añ-wu'-si wüñ-wü=Angwusi.
Anyayea=Honeoye.
Anygansets=Narraganset.
Aöais=Iowa.
Aoát=Awata.
Aoátovi=Awatobi.
Aoeatsioaenronnon—Winnebago.
Aoechisaeronon=Missisauga.
Aoiatenon=Wea.
Aomé=Tohome.
Aonays=Iowa.
Aondironnons=Aondironon.
Aoniatinonis=Wea.
Aorta band=Heviqsnipahis.
Aosaannen=Tsaganha.
Aouas=Iowa.
Aouasanik=Ouasouarini.
Aouayeilles=Avoyelles.
Aoueatsiouaen-hronons, Aoueatsiouaenronnons, A8eatsi8aenrrhonon, Aouentsiouaeron=Winnebago.
Aouiatinons, Aouittanons=Wea.
Apacci, Apachas=Apache.
Apache Arivapah=Arivaipa.
Apache hordes of Pharaoh=Faraon.
Apache Indians of Nabaju=Navaho.
Apache Mohaves, Apache-Mojaoes, Apache-Mojaves=Yavapai.
Apacherian=Apache.
Apaches=Kiowa Apache.
Apaches Broncos=Chiricahua.
Apaches Calchufines=Calchufines.
Apaches Carlanes=Carlanes.
Apaches-Chiricaguis=Chiricahua.

Apaches de Nabajoa, Apaches de Nabaju, Apaches de Nauajó, Apaches de navaio, Apaches de Navajo, Apaches de Navajox, Apaches de Navayo=Navaho.
Apaches de Peryllo=Apaches del Perrillo.
Apaches des 7 Riviéres=Mescalero.
Apaches Faraones, Apaches Farones=Faraon.
Apaches Gileños, Apaches jileños=Gila Apache.
Apaches Lipanes=Lipan.
Apaches Llaneros, Apaches Mescaleros=Mescaleros.
Apaches Mimbreños=Mimbreños.
Apaches Nabajai=Navaho.
Apaches of Seven Rivers=Mescaleros.
Apaches of the Plains=Kiowa Apache.
Apaches of Xila=Gila Apache.
Apaches orientaux=Querechos.
Apaches Pharaones, Apaches Taraones=Faraon.
Apaches Vaqueros, Apaches Vasqueras=Querechos.
Apaches Xicarillas=Jicarilla.
Apache Tonto, Apache Tontoes=Tontos.
Apache Yuma=Tulkepaia.
Apachis=Apache.
Apachos-Mescaleros=Mescaleros.
Apachu, Apaci=Apache.
Apacus=Hawikuh.
Apades, Apaehe=Apache.
Apáfan=Nestucca.
Apahiachamiut=Apahiachak.
Apahlahche=Apalachee.
A-pa-huache=Apache.
Apalaccium, Apalacha, Apalache=Apalachee.
Apalachecolo=Apalachicola.
Apalachen, Apalaches, Apalachia, Apalachians, Apalachias=Apalachee.
Apalachicoloes, Apalachicoly, Apalachicoulys=Apalachicola.
Apalachinos, Apalachins, Apalachis, Apalachita, Apalachites=Apalachee.
Apalachoocla, Apalachucla=Apalachicola.
Apalans, Apalatchees, Apalatchia=Apalachee.
Apalatchukla=Apalachicola.
Apalatchy=Apalachee.
Apalatchy-Cola=Apalachicola.
Apalatci, Apalchen, Apalehen, Apallachian Indians=Apalachee.
Apalousa, Apalusa=Opelusa.
Apamatica, Apamaticks, Apamatuck, Apamatuk=Appomattoc.
A-pa-năχ'-ke=Abnaki.
Apangape, Apangasse, A-pang-assi=Apangasi.
Apani=Pawnee.
A-pan-tó-pse=Arikara.
Å-på-ó-på=Nez Percés.
Apaptsim=Spatsum.
Ápatc, Apatch, Apatche=Apache.
A'patchu=Navaho.
Apats, Apatschees, Apatsh=Apache.
A'patsjoe=Navaho.
Apaum=Patuxet.
Apayxam=Ebahamo.
Apedes=Apache.
Apelash=Apalachee.
Apeloussas, Apelusas=Opelusa.
Apeolatei=Apalachee.
Apes=Hapes.
Apewaⁿ-tañka=Apewantanka.
Aphoon=Apoon.
Apiches=Eyeish.
Apiches, Apichi=Apache.
Apilaches, Apilashs=Apalachee.
Á-pi-na, A-pinaua=Pinawan.
Apínefu=Chepenafa.
Apineus=Wappinger.
Apinulboines=Assiniboin.
Apis=Hapes.
Apiscas=Abihka.
Apkaw=Chicago.
Apoches Nacion=Apache.
Apoga, Apoge=Kuapooge.
Apokachamute, Apokagmute=Apokak.
Apolacka, Apolashe=Apalachee.
Apomatock=Appomattoc.
Apoung-o-sse=Apangasi.
Appache, Appachees=Apache.
Appah=Etah.
Appalaches, Appalachians=Apalachee.
Appalachicolas=Apalachicola.
Appalachites, Appalachos, Appallatcy, Appallatta=Apalachee.

Appalou=Apalou.
Appalousas=Opelusa.
Appamatox=Appomattoc, Matchotic.
Appamatricx=Matchotic.
Appamattocs, Appamattucks, Appamatucks=Appomattoc.
Appeches=Apache.
Appelathas, Appellachee=Apalachee.
Appelousas=Opelusa.
Appletown=Kendaia.
Apple Village=White Apple.
Appomatocks, Appomattake, Appomatuck, Appomotacks=Appomattoc.
Ap-sah-ro-kee, Äpsárräkă, Apsaruka, Ap-shâ-roo-kee=Crows.
Apuasto=Ahwaste.
A-pū-pe'=Nez Percés.
A-pwá-tci=Apache.
Ap-yang-ape=Apangasi.
Aqbirsiarbing=Akbirsiarbing.
Âqiu=Pecos.
Aqk'amnik=Akamnik.
Aqk'aneqúnik=Akanekunik.
Aqkisk·anŭkᴇnik, Aqkísk·ᴇnŭkinik=Akiskenukinik.
Aqkīyē'nik=Akiyenik.
Aqkōqtlátlqō=Lower Kutenai.
A'-qu-stă=Tolowa.
A-qo=Acoma.
Aqokulo=Chimakum.
Aquaauchuques=Atquanachuke.
Aqua Baiz=Agua Fria.
Aqua Caliente=Gupa.
Aquachacha=Aguachacha.
Aquachonongue, Aquackanonks=Aquackanonk.
Aquahpa, Aquahpah=Quapaw.
Aquamachukes, Aquamachuques=Atquanachuke.
Aquamish=Hahuamis.
Aquanachukes=Atquanachuke.
Aquaninoncke=Aquackanonk.
Aquannaque=Abnaki.
Aquanoschioni, Aquanuschioni, Aquanuschionig=Iroquois.
A-qua-pas=Quapaw.
Aquaquanuncke=Aquackanonk.
Aquarage=Kanagaro.
Aquasasne=Saint Regis.
Aquas-Calientes=Aguas Calientes.
Aquascogoke=Aquascogoc.
Aquas-saw-tee=Koasati.
Aquatasi=Awatobi.
Aquatsagané=Mahican.
Aquatubi=Awatobi.
Aquatzagane=Mahican.
Aqueckenonge, Aqueckkonunque, Aquegnonke=Aquackanonk.
Aqueloa pissas, Aquelon pissas, Aquelou pissas=Acolapissa.
Aqueyquinunke=Aquackanonk.
Aqui=Pecos.
Aquia=Acoma.
Aquicato=Aquicabo.
Aquickanucke, Aquickanunke=Aquackanonk.
Aquico=Hawikuh.
Aquieeronons, Aquiers=Mohawk.
Aquimuricuca, Aquimuricuta=Aquimuri.
Aquinoshioni=Iroquois.
Aquinsa=Kwakina.
Aquinushionee=Iroquois.
Aquira-Otam=Pima.
Aquis=Haqui.
Aquiu=Pecos.
Aquoechononque=Aquackanonk.
Aquohanock=Accohanoc.
Aquoscojos=Aquascogoc.
Aquqenu'kqō, Aquqtlā'tlqō=Lower Kutenai.
Aqusoogock=Aquascogoc.
Aqŭstă=Tolowa.
Aq'weba=Laguna.
Ara=Karok.
Araal=Harahey.
Ara-ara=Karok.
Arabasca=Athapascan Family.
Arabaskaw=Athabasca.
Aracaris=Arikara.
Å-răch-bŏ-oŭ=Mandan.
Arache, Arae, Árahei=Harahey.

Aragaritkas=Neutrals.
Araivapa=Arivaipa.
Ărakádaho=Arikara.
Ara-k'è=Eskimo.
Arambeck, Arampec=Norumbega.
Aranamas, Aranames=Aranama.
Aranbega, Araйmbeg8k=Norumbega.
Arapahas, Arapahays=Arapaho.
Arapahoes=Algonquian Family.
Arapahoos, Ărӓpӑkata, Araphahoe, Araphas, Araphoes, Arapohaes, Arapoho, Arapohose=Arapaho.
Arathapescoas=Athapascan Family.
Arauchi=Aracuchi.
Aravaipa, Aravava, Aravapai, Aravapa Piñals, Aravipais=Arivaipa.
Arbadoes=Arbadaos.
Arbapaoes=Arapaho.
Arbeka=Abihka.
Arbiccoochee=Abikudshi.
Arcahamos=Tacame.
Arcanças, Arcansa=Quapaw.
Archarees=Arikara.
Arche=Harahey.
Ar-che-o-tek-o-pa=Matyata.
Archieco=Chiaha.
Archirigouan=Achiligouan.
Archouguets=Outchougai.
Arc Indians=Quapaw.
Arc Plattes, Arcs-a-plats=Lower Kutenai.
Arcs-Brisés=Tinazipe shicha.
Arcs-Plats, Arcsplattes=Lower Kutenai.
Arctic Highlanders=Ita.
Areibe=Oraibi.
Arenda, Arendacronons, Arendaehronons, Arendaenhronons, Arendarhononons, Arendaronnons, Arendaronons, Arendarrhonons, Arendoronnon=Arendahronons.
Arepahas=Arapaho.
Aresaguntacooks=Arosaguntacook.
À-rė-tĕàr-ò-pǎn-gӑ=Atsina.
Arhan=Arhau.
Arhosett=Ahousaht.
Aribabia=Aribaiba.
Aribac, Aribaca=Arivaca.
Aribaipa=Arivaipa.
Aribaipia=Baipia.
Aribapais—Arivaipa.
Aribaycpia=Baipia.
Aribechi=Arivechi.
Aricara, Aricarees, Aricarie, Aricaris, Aricas, Ariccarees, Aricharaў, Arichard, Arickara, Aricka-ra-one, Arickaraws, Arickare, Arickarees, Arickera=Arikara.
Aridgevoak, Aridgewoak=Norridgewock.
A-rĭk'-a-hŭ, Arikarces, Arĭk'-arĕ, Arikari, Arikera, Arikkaras=Arikara.
Aripa=Arizpe.
Aripahoes, Aripohoes=Arapaho.
Arisaguntacooks=Arosaguntacook.
Arispa=Arizpe.
Ariswánisk=Ariswaniski.
Aritoac=Aritutoc.
Arivac=Baipia.
Arivapa, Arivapa Apaches, Arivapais, Arivaypa Apaches=Arivaipa.
Arivetzi=Arivechi.
Arizo del Aqua=Agua Fria.
Arizonian Apaches=White Mountain Apache.
Arizonian Pimas=Pima.
Arkandada=Oglala.
Arkansa band=Santsukdhi.
Arkansas=Quapaw.
Arkansaw band, Arkansaw Osages=Santsukdhi.
Arkansaws, Arkansea, Arkanses, Arkanzas, Arkensas, Arkensaw, Arkensea=Quapaw.
Armeomeks=Eriwonec.
Ar-me-shay=Hidatsa.
Armewamen, Armewamus=Eriwonec.
Armos=Auk.
Armouchicois, Armucioeses=Armouchiquois.
Arnoniogre=Onondaga (vil.).
Arockamecook=Rocameca.
Aroeck=Arseek.
Aroenemeck=Eriwonec.
Arogisti=Conoy.
Arosagantakŭk, Arouseguntecook = Arosaguntacook.
Arra-Arra=Karok.

Ar-rah-pa-hoo=Arapaho.
Arransoak=Norridgewock.
Arrapahas, Arrapaho, Arrapahoes, Arrapaoes—Arapaho.
Arrapapas=Chantapeta.
Arraphas, Arraphoes, Arrapohoes=Arapaho.
Arrasaguntacook, Arreaguntecooks, Arreguntenooks=Arosaguntacook.
Arrekaras=Arikara.
Arrenamuse=Aranama.
Arrepahas=Arapaho.
Arreraguntecook, Arreruguntenocks, Arresagontacook, Arresaguntacooks, Arresaguntecook, Arreseguntecook, Arreseguntoocook, Arresuguntoocooks=Arosaguntacook.
Arricara, Arricarees, Arrickaraws, Arrickaree, Arrickora, Arriekaris=Arikara.
Arripahoes=Arapaho.
Arrivapis=Arivaipa.
Arrockaumecook=Rocameca.
Arrohateck, Arrohattock, Arrowhatocks, Arrowhatoes=Arrohattoc.
Arrow Men=Moiseyu.
Arroya, Arroyo=Pueblo del Arroyo.
Arroyo del Sonoitac=Sonoita.
Arsahattock=Arrohattoc.
Arseguntecokes=Arosaguntacook.
Arsek=Arseek.
Arselarnaby=Assilanapi.
Arsenipoitis, Arsenipoits=Assiniboin.
Arsikanteg8=Arosaguntacook.
Arsikantekok=St Francis.
Arspahas=Arapaho.
Artaylnovskoi, Arteljnowskoje, Artelnovskoe=Artelnof.
Artez-Kutchi, Artez-kutshi, Artez-Kuttchin=Ahtena.
Artigoniche=Antigonishe.
Artsmilsh=Artsmitl, Lower Chehalis.
Arundacs, Arundax=Adirondack.
Arunseguntekooks=Arosaguntacook.
A-ru'-qwa=Arukhwa.
Aruseguntekooks=Arosaguntacook.
Arwacahwas, Arwachaon=Amahami.
Asaha'ptin=Nez Percés.
As-a-ka-shi=Mandan.
Asanyumu=Asa.
Asaukees=Sauk.
Asay=Hopi.
Ascanis=Yscanis.
Asco=Dooesedoowe.
Aseguang=Gahlinskun.
Asē-ix=Aseik.
Asenys=Caddo.
Ä'sepȁnᵃ, Ä'sepŭnᵃ=Ahseponna.
A'sēq=Aseik.
A-se-quang=Gahlinskun.
Asha-náhm-ka=Shanamkarak.
Ash-bot-chee-ah=Ashbotchiah.
Ashcroft=Stlahl.
A-she-we=Zuñi.
A-shi-ap'-ka-wi=Biktasatetuse.
A-shi-ui, Áshiwi=Zuñi.
Ashley River Indians=Etiwaw.
Ashnuhúmsh=Snohomish.
Ashochemies, Ash-o-chí-mi=Wappo.
Asht-ia-la-qua, Asht-ya-laqua=Astialaqua.
A-shu'-e-ka-pe=Saiish.
Ásihi, Ásihidĭne=Ashihi.
Asila=Axilla.
A-Simaes, Aśimais, Asinaes, Asinai, Asinay=Caddo.
Asinbols, Asiniboels, Asiniboines, Asi'-ni-bwaⁿ, Asinibwanak, A-si-ni-poi'-tuk, Asinipovales=Assiniboin.
Asistagueronon, Asistagueroüon=Potawatomi.
Asivoriches=Seuvarits.
A-Skӑlâ'lĭ=Tuscarora.
Askeenac=Askinuk.
Askeltan=Azqueltan.
Askhomute=Asko.
Askic8aneronons, Askik8anehronons, Askikouaneronons=Nipissing.
Askinac, Askinaghamiut=Askinuk.
Askwálli=Nisqualli.
As-ne-boines=Assiniboin.
Asoni=Caddo.
Asons-aht=Ahousaht.

Asoomaches=Asomoches.
Asopus=Esopus.
Aspalaga=Asapalaga.
Aspasniaga, Aspasniaquan, Aspasniaques=Aspasniagan.
Asperousa=Opelusa.
Asphalashe=Apalachee.
Assagunticook=Arosaguntacook.
Assamacomoe=Secotan.
Assanpinks=Assumpink.
Assawampsit, Assawanupsit=Assawompset.
Asseekales=Hathawekela.
Asseenaboine, Asseeneepoytuck=Assiniboin.
Assegunaigs=Sauk.
Asseinpinks=Assunpink.
Assekelaes=Hathawekela.
Asselibois, Assenepoils=Assiniboin.
Asseni=Caddo.
Asseniboines, Asseniboualak, Assenipoëls, Assenipoils, Assenipoualacs, Assenipoualak, Assenipouals, Assenipouel, Assenipoulacs, Assenipoulaes, Assenipoulaks, Assenipouvals, Assenipovals=Assiniboin.
Assenjigun=Osage.
Assenniboins, Assenpoels=Assiniboin.
Asserué=Caughnawaga.
Assestagueronons=Potawatomi.
As-sif-soof-tish-e-ram=Asisufuunuk.
Assigunaick=Assegun.
Assigunaigs=Assegun, Osage.
Assikánnä=Seneca.
Assilibouels=Assiniboin.
Assilly=Ocilla.
Assiminenkon=Assiminehkon.
Assimpouals, Assinaboes, Assinaboil, Assinaboine, Assinaboins, Assinabwoines=Assiniboin.
Assinais, Assinay, Assine=Caddo.
Assineboes, Assineboin, Assineboine, Assinebwannuk, Assinepoel, Assinepoils, Assinepoins, Assinepotuc, Assinepoualaos, Assiniboelle, Assiniboels=Assiniboin.
Assiniboels of the North=Northern Assiniboin.
Assiniboels of the South=Assiniboin of the Plains.
Assiniboesi, Assiniboile, Assiniboils, Assiniboines=Assiniboin.
Assiniboin Menatopa=Watopapinah.
Assiniboins des Forêts=Tschantoga.
Assiniboins des Plaines=Assiniboin of the Plains.
Assiniboins of the forest=Tschantoga.
Assiniboins of the North=Northern Assiniboin.
Assiniboins of the Rocky Mountains, Assiniboins of the Woods=Tschantoga.
Assinibois, Assiniboleses, Assiniboualas, Assinibouane, Assinibouels=Assiniboin.
Assinibouels of the Meadows=Assiniboin of the Plains.
Assinibouets, Assiniboüles, Assinib'wans=Assiniboin.
Assinipi=Assinapi.
Assinipoals, Assinipoels, Assinipoile, Assinipoileu, Assinipoils, Assiniponiels, Assinipotuc, Assinipoual, Assinipoüalac, Assinipoualaks, Assinipoüars, Assinipoulac, Assinipour, Assinipovals, Assini-poytuk, Assinipwanak, Assinnaboin, Assinnaboines, Assinneboin, Assinnee-Poetuc, Assinnibains, Assinniboan, Assinniboine, Assinniboine Sioux, Assinniboins=Assiniboin.
Assinnis=Caddo.
Assinopoils, Assinpouele, Assinpoulac, Assinpouls=Assiniboin.
Assisagh, Assisagigroone=Missisauga.
Assista Ectaeronnons=Mascoutens.
Assistaeronons, Assistagueronon, Assistaqueronons=Potawatomi.
Assiwikales=Hathawekela.
Assok8ekik=Sokoki.
Assoni, Assony=Caddo.
Assoowamsoo=Assawompset.
Assotoué=Uzutiuhi.
Assowamsett=Assawompset.
Asswekales, Asswikales, Asswikalus=Hathawekela.
Assyletch, Assylitch, Assylitlh=Atselits.
Assynais=Caddo.
Astakaywas, Astakywich, Astaqkéwa=Astakiwi.
Asucsagna=Azucsagna.
Asumpcion=Sandia.
Asuncion=Sia, Zuñi.
Asuncion Álamos=Alamos.

Asuncion Amipas=Cumpus.
Asuncion Arizpe=Arizpe.
Asuncion Batuco=Batuco.
Asuncion de Opodepe=Opodepe.
Asuncion de Raum=Rahun.
Asuncion de Tepave, Asuncion Tepahue=Tepahue.
Aswalthatans=Alwathalama.
As-wüñ-wü=Asa.
At=Ati, Attu.
A'-ta-a-kût'-ti=Ataakut.
Atabi-hogandi=Awatobi.
Atacapas, Atacapaz, Atac-assas=Attacapa.
Atach, A-tache=Tachi.
Ataconchronons=Ataronchronon.
Á-taguí=Lipan.
Ataiwas=Masset.
Ataka=Attu.
Atakapas=Attacapa.
A'-ta-ke-te' tûn'-nĕ=Ataakut.
Atakhtan=Ahtena.
Atako=Attu.
Atakwa=Catawba.
Â'tălĭ da'ndaka'nihă=Lookout Mountain Town.
Ataniek=Atnik.
Ataouabouscatouek=Bouscoutton.
Ataronch=Ataronchronon.
Atases=Atasi.
Á-t'ăs-kă-ló-lĕⁿ'=Tuscarora.
Atassi=Atasi.
Atationoue=Nottoway.
Atawawas=Ottawa.
Atayos=Toho.
Atcansa=Quapaw.
Atchaer=Atka.
Atchalugumiut=Atchaluk.
Atch'ashti amĕumei=Chastacosta.
Atchelity=Atselits.
Atchihwa'=Maricopa.
Atchiligoüan=Achiligouan.
Atchixe'lish=Chehalis.
Atchougek, Atchougue, Atchouguets=Outchougai
A'-tcŭk=Atshuk.
Ateakari, Ateanaca=Ateacari.
A-teet-sa=Tangesatsa.
Atenâ=Ahtena.
Atenas=Shuswap.
Atepíra=Atepua.
Atesalgi, Átesi=Atasi.
Atē'was=Masset.
Ateyala-keokvá=Astialakwa.
Athabasca=Athapascan Family, Chipewyan.
Athabascan=Athapascan Family.
Athabaskans=Athabasca.
Athapacca, Athapaches=Athapascan Family.
Athapacca=Athapascan Family, Chipewyan.
Athapascow=Athabasca.
Athapasque=Athapascan Family.
Athapuscow=Athabasca.
Athistaëronnon=Potawatomi.
Athlámeth=Klamath.
Athlankenetis=Kimsquit.
Athláxsni=Tlatskanai.
Athlets=Paviotso.
Athnaer=Ahtena.
Atí=San Francisco Ati.
Atiaonrek=Neutrals.
Atic=Ati.
Atiga=Kittanning.
Atigagnongueha=Attigneenongnahac.
Atignaoüantan=Attignawantan.
Atignenongach, Atignenonghac=Attigneenongnahac.
Atihipi-Catouy=Tippecanoe.
Ătik'=Ahdik.
Atikamegues=Attikamegue.
Atilamas=Alibamu.
Atimaco, Atimuca, Atimuqua=Timucua.
Atingueennonnihak=Attigneenongnahac.
Atingyahointan, Atingyahoulan=Attignawantan.
Atinikg=Atnik.
Atinjonguin=Neagwaih.
Atinnia8enten, Atinouaentans=Attignawantan.
Atintans, Atintons=Teton.
Atiouandaronks, Atiouendaronk, Atiraguenrek, Atirhagenrenrets, Ati-rhagenrets=Neutrals.
Atison=San Francisco Ati.
Atiwandaronk=Neutrals.
Atkan=Atka.

Atkha=Nazan.
Atkhas=Atka.
Atlachaco=Acoma.
A 'tlã'nuwă=Chattanooga.
Atlāshimih=Takulli.
Atna=Salishan Family.
Atnachtjaner, Atnäer=Ahtena.
Atnahs=Ahtena, Shuswap, Salishan Family.
At-naks=Shuswap.
Atnalis=Tautin.
Atnans, Atnas=Ahtena, Shuswap.
Atnatána, Atnaxthynné=Ahtena.
Atnikmioute, Atnikmut Zagoskin=Atnuk.
A-tó-co, A'-to-ko wuñ-wü=Atoko.
Atokúwe=Apache.
Atonthrataronon, Atontrataronnons, Atontratas, Atontratoronons=Totontaratonhronon.
Å-too-hå-pĕ=Salish.
Atotchasi=Uzutiuhi.
At8agannen=Ontwaganha.
Atowas=Ottawa.
Atowateany=Potawatomi.
Atoyos=Toho.
At-pasha-shliha=Hitchiti.
Atquacke=Aquack.
Atquanachuck, Atquanachuks, Atquanahuckes, Atquinachunks=Atquanachuke.
Atra' K8ae=Atrakwaye.
Atra 'K8ae 'r=Conestoga.
Atra 'kwa 'e=Atrakwaye.
Atra 'kwae 'ronnons, Atrakwer=Conestoga.
Atrutons=Teton.
Atsagannen=Tsaganha.
Atsayongky=Mahican.
Ăt-sĕ'-nā=Atsina.
Atsharoke=Crows.
A-tsho-to-ti-na=Etchareottine.
A'tsĭnă-k'ta'ûñ=Taskigi.
Atsistaehronons=Potawatomi.
Atsistagherronnons=Mascoutens.
Atsistahéroron, Atsistarhonon=Potawatomi.
Atsugei, Atsugĕ'wi=Atsugewi.
Attacapacas, Attacappa—Attacapa.
Attachooka=Ivitachuco.
Attak=Attu.
Attakapas, Attakapo=Attacapa.
Attamasco=Timucua.
Attanak=Atnik.
Attapaha=Altamaha.
Attaquapas=Attacapa.
Attases, Attasis, Attasse=Atasi.
At-tau-gee=Atagi.
Attawas, Attawawas=Ottawa.
Attawits=Kadohadacho.
Attayes=Tyigh.
Attegheny=Alleghany Indians.
Attekamek=Attikamegue.
Attencapas=Attacapa.
Attenkins=Algonkin.
Attenmuk=Atten.
Attenokamiut=Attenok.
Attenonderonk=Neutrals.
At-te-shu-pe-sha-loh-pan-ga=Les Noire Indians.
Attibamegues, Atticameots, Atticameouecs, Atticamiques, Atticamoets=Attikamegue.
Atticmospicayes=Thlingchadinne.
Attignaoouentan, Attigna8antan, Attignaouentan, Attignawantan=Attignawantan.
Attigné=Attique.
Attigneenonguahac=Attigneenongnahac.
Attignouaatitans, Attigouantan, Attigouantines, Attigouautan=Attignawantan.
Attigua=Kittanning.
Attigueenongnahac, Attiguenongha=Attigneenongnahac.
Attihouandaron=Neutrals.
Attikamegouek, Attikamegs, Attikameguekhi, Attikamek, Attikameques, Attikamigues=Attikamegue.
Attik Iriniouetchs=Attikiriniouetch.
Attikouetz=Attikamegue.
Attikou Iriniouetz=Attikiriniouetch.
Attimospiquaies, Attimospiquais, Attimospiquay=Thlingchadinne.
Attingneenongnahac, Attingueenongnahac=Attigneenongnahac.
Attinniaoenten=Attignawantan.
Attinoindarons=Neutrals.
Attinquenongnahac=Attigneenongnahac.

Attionandarons, Attionidarons, Atti8andaron, Atti8andaronk, Attiouendarankhronon, Attiouendaronk=Neutrals.
Atti8endaronk=Huron.
Attiqué=Kittanning.
Attiquenongnah, Attiquenongnahai=Attigneenongnahac.
Attistae, Attistaehronon, Attistaeronons=Potawatomi.
Attiuoindarons, Attiwandaronk, Attiwondaronk=Neutrals.
Attochingochronon=Ojeejok.
Attoo, Attou=Attu.
Attuckapas=Attacapa.
A-tu-a-mih=Atuami.
Átûnĕ=Atnik.
Atŭtá=Cochiti.
Atwagannen=Ontwaganha.
Aua-tu-ui=Awatobi.
Au-ba-coo-che, Au-be-coo-che=Abikudshi.
Au-be-cuh=Abihka.
Aubinaukee=Abnaki.
Aubocoes=Abihka.
Aub-sá-ro-ke=Crows.
Aucasisco=Aucocisco.
Au-che-nau-hat-che=Atchinahatchi.
Au-che-nau-ul-gau=Atchinaalgi.
Auches=Eyeish.
Aucosisco, Aucosiseo=Aucocisco.
Aud-je-jauk=Ojeejok.
Audusta=Edisto.
Augallalla=Oglala.
Augawam, Augawoam=Agawam.
Aughguagey, Aughquaga, Aughquagahs, Aughquagchs, Aughquages, Aughquaghas, Aughwick=Oquaga.
Augoam, Augoan=Agawam.
Augoon=Angun.
Auguan=Agawam.
Au-hai, Aujay=Ojai.
Aujuiap=Ujuiap.
Auke, Auke-qwan=Auk.
Aukpapas=Hunkpapa.
Aúksiwash, Ä'-uksni=Klamath.
Aukwick=Oquaga.
Aú-kwŭ-ctă=Tolowa.
Aulochawan, Au-lot-che-wau=Alachua.
Aumanes=Tawehash.
Aumesoukkantti=Amaseconti.
Aumonssoniks, Aumossomiks=Monsoni.
Aumoughcawgen=Ammoncongan.
Aumoussonnites=Monsoni.
Au-muc-cul-le=Amakalli.
Aumuckcawgen, Aumughcawgen=Ammoncongan.
Aunatok=Anoatok.
Au-net-te chap-oo=Anatichapko.
Aunghim=Tanotenne.
Auniers, Aunies=Mohawk.
Auölasús=Paiute.
Auorobagra=Norumbega.
Au-put-tau-e=Apatai.
Auqardneling=Aukardneling.
Auquaguas=Oquaga.
Auquitsaukon=Delaware.
Aurananeans=Aranama.
Auricara, Aurickarees=Arikara.
Ause Kenowenou=Wequadong.
Ä'-ushkni=Klamath.
Ausinabwaun=Assiniboin.
Ausotunnoog=Stockbridge.
Autallga, Autauga=Atagi.
Autawa=Ottawa.
Authontantas=Oto.
Autia=Aute.
Autiré=Kikatsak.
Autisees=Atasi.
Autobas=Atagi.
Autossee=Atasi.
Autouacks=Ottawa.
Autrechaha=Osage.
Aut-tos-se, Auttotsee=Atasi.
Auuico=Hawikuh.
A'-uyaχ=Kickapoo.
Avaraes, Avares=Avavares.
Ava-Supies=Havasupai.
Avatanakskoi, Avatanovskoe=Avatanak.
Avauwais=Iowa.
Avendahs=Arendahronons.
Avesú-pai=Havasupai.

Avicu=Hawikuh.
Avipa Apache=Arivaipa.
Avnuligmiut=Avnulik.
Avo=Abo.
Avogall, Avovelles=Avoyelles.
Avoy=Iowa.
Avoyall, Avoyellas, Avoyels=Avoyelles.
Avoys=Iowa.
A-vuc-hoo-mar-lish=Casa Montezuma.
Awachawi=Amahami.
A-wac-la'-ŭrk=Arvashlaurk.
Aᵍwaē'ᴸEla=Awaitlala.
A-wa-ha-was, A-wa-ha-ways=Amahami.
Áwahe, Awáhi=Pawnee.
A'wa-i Lala=Awaitlala.
Awakanáshish=Wakanasisi.
Awalache, Awallache=Awani.
Awan=Avak.
Á-wa-na-kwai-k'ya-ko-na=Ánakwaikona.
Awanee=Awani.
A-wā-oo=Tlaaluis.
Awasatciᵘ=Ouasouarini.
Awásko ammin=Wasco.
Awasos=Ahwehsoos.
Á-wås-shė-tån-quå=Cheyenne.
Awassissin=Awausee.
Awata wiñwû=Awata.
Awátch, Awátche=Apache.
A-wa-te-u=Awatobi.
Awatichaï-Echpou, Awatichay=Amatiha.
Awatúbi, Á wat u i, Á wat u ians=Awatobi.
A-wat' wüñ-wü=Awata,
A-waus-e, A-waus-e-wug, A-waus-is-ee=Awausee.
Awcumbucks=Aukumbumsk.
Aweatsiwaenhronon=Winnebago.
Awechisaehronon=Missisauga.
Awegen=Owego.
Awenrehronon=Wenrohronon.
A-wha-whi-lac-mu=Awhawhilashmu.
Awi-adshi=Klikitat.
Awighsaghroene=Awighsaghroone.
Awī'k'ʼēnôx, Awī'ky'ēnoq=Wikeno.
A-wish-in-aub-ay=Chippewa.
Awiz-na=Awigna.
Awks=Auk.
Awó=Pawnee.
Awokànak=Etchareottine.
A'w-o-tum=Pima.
Á'wp=Apache.
Áwp-pa-pa=Maricopa.
Awuci wiñwû=Awushi.
Axa, Axaas=Harahey.
Axanti=Axauti.
Axas=Harahey.
Aχehinén=Pawnee.
Axi=Ati.
Aχihínen=Pawnee.
Axoytre=Axol.
Aχshissayé-rúnu=Chippewa.
Axtaos=Tawehash.
Axua=Comeya.
Ayabasca=Athapascan Family.
Ayabaskau=Athabasca.
Ayabaskawiyiniwag=Sakawithiniwuk.
Ayachaghayuk=Aïachagiuk.
Ayache=Eyeish.
Aȳacheruk=Aiachagiuk.
Ayahwa=Iowa.
Ayakhtalik, Ayaktalik=Aiaktalik.
Ayâ'li'yĭ=Jore.
Ayanabe=Ayanabi.
Ayanais=Hainai.
Ayano=Kanohatino.
Ayans=Hankutchin.
Ayas=Eyeish.
Ayâtchinini, Ayâtchiyiniw=Siksika.
A'-ya-to=Arapaho.
Ayauais, Ayauvai, Ayauwais, Ayauwas, Ayauwaus, Ayauway, Ayauways=Iowa.
Ayavala, Ayaville=Ayavalla.
Ayavois, Ayawai, Ayaways=Iowa.
Ayays=Eyeish.
Aybamos=Alibamu.
Aybino=Aivino.
A-y-charts=Hachaath.
Ayche, Aychis, Ayeche=Eyeish.
Ayenai, Ayenis=Hainai.

Ayennis=Yojuane.
Ayeouais, Aye8ais=Iowa.
Ayes=Eyeish.
Ayetan=Ietan.
Ayhuttisaht=Ehatisaht.
Ayiches, Ayish=Eyeish.
Ayis-iyiniwok=Cree.
Ayjados, Ayjaos=Tawehash.
Aynais, Aynays, Aynics=Hainai.
Ayoa=Iowa.
Ayodsudao=Basotutcan.
Ayoes=Iowa.
Ayona=Kanohatino.
Ayonai=Hainai.
Ayonontouns, Ayonontout=Junundat.
Ayoois, Ayoouais, Ayooúes, Ayo8ois, Ayoua, Ayouahs, Ayoues, Ayouez=Iowa.
Ayououtou=Ayanamon.
Ayouwa, Ayouwais, Ayouwáy, Ayouways, Ayovai, Ayovois, A'yowa, Ayoway=Iowa.
Ayquiyu=Ayqui.
Ays=Ais, Eyeish.
Ayses=Eyeish.
Aytch-arts=Hachaath.
Ayuĭba, Ayuhuwahak=Iowa.
Ayuhwa'sĭ=Hiwassee.
Ayukba=Iowa.
Ayuwáni=Yowani.
Ayuwas=Iowa.
Aywani=Yowani.
Ayzes=Eyeish.
Azachagyagmut=Nokrot.
Azadyze=Adai.
Azäna=Atsina.
Azavay=Sarauahi.
Aziagmüt=Aziagmiut, Unaligmiut.
Aziavigamut, Aziavigamute, Aziavigiokhamiut=Aziavik.

Baachinena, Bääküune'naⁿ=Nakasinena.
Ba-akush'=Dakota.
Baaⁿtcïine'na=Nakasinena.
Babarole=Brulé.
Babayoulas=Bayogoula.
Babesagui=Babasaqui.
Babicori=Babiacora.
Babinas, Babine Indians, Babin Indians, Babinis=Nataotin.
Babor=Pabor.
Baborigami=Baborigame.
Bac=San Xavier del Bac.
Bacabache=Baca.
Bacadeguatzi, Baca de Huachi=Bacadeguachi.
Băcāndēē=Bécancour.
Bacapa=Matape.
Bacaregues=Vacoregue.
Bacatu de Guachi=Bacadeguachi.
Bacatzi=Bacuachi.
Bacayopa=Baquigopa.
Baccaloons, Baccatoons, Baccatous=Buckaloon.
Bacerac=Baserac.
Bachom's country=Tankiteke.
Bacoachi, Bacoaiz, Bacoatzi=Bacuachi.
Bacoregues, Bacorehui=Vacoregue.
Bacouiz=Bacuachi.
Bacuanos=Bacuancos.
Bacun=Bacum.
Bacutia=Bacuvia.
Bad Bows=Tinazipeshicha.
Bad Coup=Esekepkabuk.
Bad Faces=Iteshicha.
Bad Hail=Passing Hail's Band.
Bad Hearts=Kiowa Apache.
Bad Honors=Esekepkabuk.
Badies=Bidai.
Bad Leggins=Esachkabuk.
Bad looking ones=Glaglahecha.
Bad-People=Ettchaottine.
Badwunun=Palwunun.
Badz=Esqugbaag.
Bagopas=Bagiopa.
Bágowits=Navaho.
Báhakosin=Cheyenne.
Bahamos=Ebahamo.
Bahĕ' qúbĕ=Bahekhube.
Bahia=Espíritu Santo de Zúñiga.
Bahium=Bacum.
Bahwetego-weninnewug, Bahwetig=Atsina, Pawating.

Bahyu=Bayu.
Baïagoulas=Bayogoula.
Bailkovskoe=Belkofski.
Baimela=Baimena.
Baiougoula=Bayogoula.
Baisimetes=Bersiamite.
Bai'-yu=Bayu.
Bajio de Aquituno=Aquitun.
Bajiopas=Bagiopa.
Bakab=Pakab.
Bakhkanapul=Tubatulabal.
Bakihoⁿ, Bakihoɥ=Bakihon.
Bald Heads=Comanche.
Bald Hill, Bald Hill Indians=Chilula.
Ballena=Egepam.
Balleza=Tepehuanes.
Bal-loh=Paviotso.
Baluxa, Baluxie=Biloxi.
Balwisha=Badwisha.
Bănabeoueks, Banabeoüik, Banaboueks=Winne-
    bago.
Banac, Ban-acks=Bannock.
Banagiro=Kañagaro.
Banaiti=Bannock.
Banalachic=Panalachic.
Banamichi=Banamitzi.
Banáni, Ban-at-tees, Banax=Bannock.
Band lar Gru (crain) or canoe=Watopapinah.
Band of Kinkash, Band of Kinkrash=Kinkash.
Band of the lights=Chagu.
Band that eats no buffalo=Pteyuteshni.
Bäniatho=Cherokee.
Bannach Snakes, Bannacks, Banneck, Ban-ni-ta=
    Bannock.
Bantom=Bantam.
Banumints=Serranos.
Bapispes=Babispe.
Ba-qa-ŏ=Makah.
Baqueros=Querechos.
Baquioba, Baquiova=Bagiopa.
Ba-ra-shŭp'-gi-o=Dakota.
Barbarole=Chankute.
Barbus=White Indians.
Barchuxem, Barcluxen=Patuxent.
Bar-har-cha=Pahatsi.
Bark Indians=Micmac.
Bark tribe=Ecorce.
Basacora=Bacanora.
Basdećé śni, Basdetce-cni=Basdecheshni.
Baseraca=Baserac.
Base-tlo-tinneh=Tatsanottine.
Bashabas=Abnaki.
Bashonees=Bushamul.
Basisa=Vasisa.
Basket People=Colville.
Basket Village=Tungge.
B(as) Saura=Saura Towns.
Basses Rivières=Lower Creeks.
Bastard Beaver Indians=Etcheridiegottine.
Bas Tchinouks=Lower Chinook.
Batacora, Batacosa=Babiacora.
Batang, Batang-a=Patung.
Bâtard Loucheux, Bâtards-Loucheux=Nellagottine.
Ba-toi'p-kwa-si=Bachipkwasi.
Batemdaikai, Batem-da-kai-ee, Batem-da-kaii=Kato.
Bat House=Chakpahu.
Batin-da-kia=Kato.
Batkiñyamu=Patki.
Batoková=Patoqua.
Bâton Rouge=Mikasuki.
Batosda=San Xavier del Bac.
Battle-le-mule-emauch=Methow.
Batucos=Eudeve.
Batuearis=Batucari.
Batzakákat=Batza.
Baviacora=Babiacora.
Bawateeg, Bawating, Bawitigowininiwag, Bāwi'ti-
    gunk, Bawiting=Pawating.
Bayacchito=Bayou Chicot.
Bayagola, Bayagoubas, Bayagoulas, Baya-Ogoulas=
    Bayogoula.
Bay Indians=Oklahannali, Winnebago.
Bay-ma-pomas=Sinkyone.
Baymoa=Bamoa.
Bayogola, Bayonne Ogoulas, Bayouc Agoulas=
    Bayogoula.
Bayou Chéne=Namukatsup.
Bayou Chico=Bayou Chicot.
Bayouc Ogoulas, Bayuglas=Bayogoula.

Bazhigagat=Bazhi.
Beadeyes=Bidai.
Bean-people, Beansmen=Papago.
Bear=Chonakera, Matonumanke, Tunanpin.
Bearded Indians=White Indians.
Bear Indians=Clatchotin.
Bear Lake Indians=Saschutkenne.
Bear nation=Attignawantan.
Bear's Paw Mountain=Shiptetza.
Beathook=Beothukan Family.
Beauancourt=Bécancour.
Beaux Hommes=Quapaw, Siksika.
Beaver=Etcheridiegottine, Pakhtha, Patha, Taw-
    enikashika, Tsattine.
Beaver band=Zhapeinihkashina.
Beaver Creek=Sawcunk.
Beaver gens=Itchhasualgi, Zhawenikashika.
Beaver Hill Crees=Paskwawininiwug.
Beaver Hunters=Tsattine.
Beaver (Indians)=Amikwa.
Beaver-men=Tamakwapi.
Beavers=Tsattine.
Beaver's Town, Beaver Town=Tuscarawas.
Becaes=Abihka.
Becancourians, Bécancourt, Becquancourt, Becquen-
    court, Becuncourt=Bécancour.
Bedah-marek=Bidamarek.
Bedais, Beddies, Bedees, Bedies=Bidai.
Bedzaqetcha, Bedzietcho=Chippewa.
Be-gá-kŏl-kizju=Mogollon.
Béhathook=Beothukan Family.
Behda=Baada.
Beicas=Abihka.
Be-juij Tu-aij, Be-Jui Tu-ay, Be-juÿ Tu-aÿ=Bejui-
    tuuy.
Bekancourt=Bécancour.
Békiu=Beku.
Belantse-etea, Belautse-etea=Hidatsa.
Belbellahs=Bellabella.
Belem=Belen.
Belhoola=Bellacoola.
Belkovsky=Belkofski.
Bella-Bellas=Bellacoola.
Bellacoola=Salishan Family.
Bellaghchoolas, Bellahoola=Bellacoola.
Bell Bellas=Bellabella.
Bell-houla, Bellichoola=Bellacoola.
Bellkovskoi=Belkofski.
Belochy, Belocsé=Biloxi.
Beloved People=Chufaniksa, Watakihulata.
Beloxi=Biloxi.
Belue=Belen.
Beluxis, Beluxy=Biloxi.
Benados=Venados.
Bénaquis=Abnaki.
Bend Village=Daudehokto.
Benemé, Beñemé, Benyeme=Serranos.
Beothik, Beoths, Beothucs, Beothues, Beothugs,
    Beothuk=Beothukan Family.
Beowawe=Beowawa.
Bergbewohner=Montagnais.
Bersams, Bersiamites, Bersiamits, Bersiamitts=
    Bersiamite.
Berthold Indian Village=Hidatsati.
Bertiamistes, Bertiamites=Bersiamite.
Besançon=Bécancour.
Be-śde'-ke=Foxes.
Bes-he-kwe-guelts=Miseekwigweelis.
Be'shĭltchă=Kiowa.
Bes-tchonhi=Bistchonigottine.
Bethsiamits=Bersiamite.
Bethuck=Beothukan Family.
Bĕtidĕĕ=Arapaho.
Be-ton-auk-an-ub-yig=Betonukeengainubejig.
Betsiamites, Betsiamits=Bersiamite.
Betumki=Mitomkai Pomo.
Bevan-acs, Bewanacs=Dakota.
Bĕ'-χai=Jicarilla.
Biaundo=San Francisco Xavier de Viggé Biaundo.
Bican=Bicam.
Biçá'ni=Bithani.
Biçani=Dsihlthani.
Biccarees=Arikara.
Bi-co-we-tha=Piqua.
Bicuñer=San Pedro y San Pablo.
Bidaises=Bidai.
Bídălpahéⁿko=Pueblos.
Biday, Bidayes=Bidai.
Biddahatsi-Awatiss=Elahsa.

Biddahoochee=Bithahotshi.
Biddaquimamar=Viddaquimamar.
Bidias=Bidai.
Biérai, Biéride=Laguna.
Bierni'n=Keresan Family.
Bif-hill=Pasukdhin.
Big Ankle band=Iyakoza.
Big Bead=Arapaho.
Big Beavers=Moravian.
Big Belley, Big bellied, Big Bellies=Gros Ventres.
Big Chehaus, Big Chehaws=Chiaha.
Big Cove=Kalanuyi.
Big Devils=Watopachnato.
Big Eagle's band=Ohanhanska.
Big Eddy=Niukhtash.
Big-heads=Têtes de Boule.
Big Hills=Pasukdhin.
Big Jim's Band=Kispokotha.
Big-legged horses=Iyakoza.
Big Lick=Ketchewaundaugenink.
Big-lips=Nataotin.
Big Pauch, Big Paunch=Gros Ventres.
Big salt lick=Ketchewaundaugenink.
Big Stone Lake=Inkpa.
Big Talassee, Big Tallasees, Big Tallassees=
    Talasse.
Big Tellico=Tellico.
Big Track=Santsukdhi.
Big Tree=Gaandowanang.
Big Uchee Town=Yuchi town.
Big Ufala=Eufaula.
Bik-ta'-she=Shoshoni.
Bílchula=Salishan Family.
Bilexes=Biloxi.
Bilhoola, Billechoola=Bellacoola, Salishan Family.
Billechula=Salishan Family.
Billikūla=Bellacoola.
Billoxie, Billoxis, Bilocchi, Bilocchy, Bilocci, Bi-
    lochy, Bilocohi, Bilocohy, Biloui, Biloxy=Biloxi.
Bilqula=Bellacoola.
Bilusi, Biluxi=Biloxi.
Bí'lxula=Bellacoola.
Bin-i-ette She-deck-a=San Carlos Apache, White
    Mountain Apache.
Binuxsh, Bínúχshi=Biloxi.
Biquache=Bacuachi.
Birch Bay=Semiahmoo.
Birch Indians=Tennuthkutchin.
Birch-rind Indians, Birch-rind men, Birch-rind
    people=Tatsanottine.
Birch River Indians=Tennuthkutchin.
Bird=Fusualgi.
Bird (gens)=Chorofa.
Bird Pueblo=Pueblo of the Bird.
Bird Town=Tsiskwahi.
Biroros=Piro.
Bisanig=Busanic.
Biscatronges=Coaque.
Bishapa=Bissasha.
Bishkun Tamaha=Bishkon.
Biskatronge=Coaque.
Bisserains, Bisseriniens, Bissiriniens=Nipissing.
Bǐtáhotsi=Bithahotshi.
Bǐtá'ni=Bithani.
Bitomkhai=Mitomkai Pomo.
Bitoupas=Ibitoupa.
Biyous=Bayu.
Bjelkowskoje=Belkofski.
Black=Inkesabe.
Black-arms=Cheyenne.
Black bear=Chonakera, Tunanpin, Wasapetun.
Black-bear gens=Wasaenikashika.
Black Cañon=Snapa.
Black-dog, Black Dog's, Black Dog's band=Ohan-
    hanska.
Black eagle=Hangatanga.
Black Eagle's band=Wamdisapa's Band.
Black Falls ruins=Wukoki.
Blackfeet=Sihasapa, Siksika.
Blackfeet Dakotas, Black-feet Scioux, Blackfeet
    Sioux, Blackfeet Tetons=Sihasapa.
Blackfoot=Siksika.
Blackfoot Dakotas=Sihasapa.
Black-footed ones=Sihasapakhcha.
Blackfoot Sioux=Sihasapa.
Black Hawk Band=Mokohoko.
Black Hook=Backhook.
Black house=Hickerau.
Black Lake of Tears=Shipapulima.

Black Mingo=Winyaws.
Blackmouths=Sukhutit.
Black Panis=Wichita.
Black Pawnee=Arikara, Wichita.
Black-River band=Mekadewagamitigweyawini-
    niwak.
Black Warrior, Black Warriors Town=Tuskalusa.
Black-Water=Nesietsha, Okalusa, Opelousa.
Blanches=White Indians.
Blanco=Pueblo Blanco.
Blancos, Blancs Barbus, Blanes, Blank Barbus=
    White Indians.
Blinde Towne=Ohanoak.
Bloodies, Blood Indians, Blood People, Bloods=
    Kainah.
Blow-horn Nest=Wakokayi.
Blue Earth Indians=Nez Percés.
Blue Earth Village=Mankato.
Blue-lipped people=Blewmouths.
Blue mud Indians, Blue-muds=Nez Percés.
Blue Running Water pueblo=Shakwabaiyaki.
Bluff Indians=Prairie band of Potawatomi.
Blú-kci, B'lúksi=Biloxi.
Blunt Indians=Blount Indians.
Blut (Indianer)=Kainah.
Bobor=Pabor.
Bobrovo, Bobrovskoe, Bobrovskoi=Beaver.
Bobrowskoje=Uyak.
Bocootawwanaukes, Bocootawwonaukes, Bocootaw-
    wonough, Bocootowwonocks=Bocootawwonauke.
Bocrettes=Bocherete.
Bo'dǎlk'iñago=Comanche.
Bodega=Olamentke.
Bŏdĕr'wiǔmi=Paleuyami.
Bœothick, Boeothuk=Beothukan Family.
Bogas=Bauka.
Bcgue Chittos=Boguechito.
Boin-acs, Boines=Dakota.
Bois Brule, Bois brûle Teton=Brulé.
Boise Forte=Sugwaundugahwininewug.
Boise Shoshonees=Wihinasht.
Bois Forts=Sugwaundugahwininewug.
Bois, Nation de=Ottawa.
Bois rûlé Teton, bois Ruley=Brulé.
Bois, Ville de=Logstown.
Bóka=Bauka.
Bokeaí=Hopi.
Bolbon=Bolbone.
Bôli=Buli.
Bolixes, Bolixies=Biloxi.
Bollanos=Bolinas.
Bolshoigor=Big Mountain.
Boluxa, Boluxes, Boluxie=Biloxi.
Bonacks, Bonak=Bannock.
Bonaparte Indians=Newhuhwaittinekin.
Bonarch Diggers, Bonarchs, Bonarks=Bannock.
Bone Indians=Assegun, Osage.
Bon galaatshi=Bankalachi.
Bongees=Sarsi.
Bonifoucas=Bonfouca.
Bonito=Pueblo Bonito.
Bonnacks, Bonnaks, Bonnax=Bannock.
Bonnet=Ekupabeka.
Bonochs=Bannock.
Bonostao=Bonostac.
Bons Irocois=Huron.
Bookû=Bauka.
Boonacks=Bannock.
Booshamool=Bushamul.
Boothians=Netchilirmiut.
Bored Noses=Amikwa.
Borka=Biorka.
Born in the middle=Chegnakeokisela.
Borrados=Tawehash.
Boshgisha=Poskesas.
Boston Bar=Koiaum.
Bot-k'iñ'ago=Atsina.
Botshenins=Occaneechi, Patshenin.
Boucfuca, Boukfuka=Boucfouca.
Bounding-Wind=Kiyuksa.
Bove=San Ildefonso.
Bo-wat-chat, Bowatshat=Mooachaht.
Bow-e-ting=Pawating.
Bow Indians=Quapaw.
Bowpith=Sans Arcs.
Bow-String (Society)=Himoiyoqis.
Bowwetegoweninnewug, Bowwetig=Atsina.
Braba=Taos.
Bracamos=Ebahamo.

Brada=Taos.
Brasstown=Itseyi.
Bread Nation=Pascagoula.
Breakers of the custom=Kiyuksa.
Breed Nation=Pascagoula.
Bridge River=Kanlax.
Broiled meat people=Wacheunpa.
Broken Arrow, Broken Arrow Old Field=Hle-katchka.
Broken Moccasin=Bannock.
Broken Promise, Town of=Tomé.
Bronco=Chiricahua.
Brothertown=Brotherton.
Broulè Sioux, Brucellares, Brulé Dakotas, Brulees, Brule Sioux, Brulies=Brulé.
Brushwood=Chippekawkay.
Brushwood Indians=Etchareottine.
B. Saura (Bas Saura)=Saura Towns.
Buasdabas=Guazavas.
Bubu=Yupu.
Buenaventura=Mishongnovi.
Buenavista=Bacuancos, Quiquiborica.
Buen Llano=Huchiltchik.
Buffalo=Chedunga, Dyosyowan, Tesinde.
Buffalo bull=Chedunga.
Buffalo Dung=Kahmitaiks.
Buffalo-eaters=Kutshundika.
Buffalo Eaters, Buffalo Eaters band=Kotsoteka.
Buffalo gens=Teenikashika.
Buffalo Hunters=Querechos.
Buffalo Indians=Kotsoteka, Lamtama.
Buffaloons=Buckaloon.
Buffalo Province=Zuñi.
Buffalo-tail=Tesinde.
Buffalo Town=Yunsai.
Buffler's Town=Buckaloon.
Buhk'hérk, Búkĭn=Hopi.
Buknatallahassa=Pakan-Tallahasse.
Bulbones=Bolbone.
Buli wiñwû, Bu'-li wüñ-wü=Buli.
Bullheads=Têtes de Boule.
Bulls=Okos.
Bumas=Suma.
Burned=Brulé.
Burningtown=Tikaleyasuni.
Burnt Hip Brulé, Burnt Thighs, Burnt-woods=Brulé.
Busani=Busanic.
Bushones, Bushumnes=Bushamul.
Bus-in-as-see, Bus-in-aus-e, Bus-in-aus-e-wug=Businausee.
Busnio, Busonia, Bussani=Busanic.
Bussenmeus=Bersiamite.
Butchers=Oosabotsee.
Bwan-aos, Bwoinug, Bwoir-nug=Dakota.
Byssiriniens=Nipissing.

Cä=Sa.
Caacac=Caacat.
Caäguas=Cayuse.
Caäki=Cherokee.
Caanʹ, Caanʹqti=Dakota.
Caatri=Catróo.
Cabadilapo=Kato.
Cabaies=Kabaye.
Ca-ba-na-po=Khabenapo.
Cábanckc=Shabanshksh.
Cabazon=Palseta.
Cabbassaguntiac, Cabbassaguntles, Cabbassaguntiquoke=Amaseconti.
Cabben, Cabbins=Tekanitli.
Cabellos realzados=Chippewa.
Cabeson=Palseta.
Cabetas=Kawita.
Cabetka=Caborca.
Cabeugna=Cahuenga.
Cabezon=Palseta.
Cabia=Kabaye.
Cabinoios=Cahinnio.
Cabona, Cabórea=Caborca.
Cabras=Kiabaha.
Cabri=Zuñi.
Cabuenga=Cahuenga.
Cabuitta=Kawita.
Cabujacaamang, Cabujakaamang=Santa Maria Magdalena.
Caburcos=Cambujos.
Cābwāsing=Shabwasing.
Cac=Ke, Shash.

Cacachias=Kaskaskia.
Cacahouanons=Shawnee.
Cacames=Tacame.
Caȼani=Cheyenne.
Cacat=Caacat.
Cacchumas=Chakchiuma.
Cachanuage=Caughnawaga.
Cachapostates=Cachapostales.
Cachecacheki=Kuskuski.
Cachees's band=Cochise Apache.
Cachekacheki=Kuskuski.
Cachenuage=Caughnawaga.
Cachiadachse=Tueadasso.
Cachichi=San Felipe.
Cachies=Kichai.
Cachise Apaches, Cachise Indians=Cochise Apache.
Cachiti=Cochiti.
Cachnawage=Caughnawaga.
Cachnawayes=Conoy.
Cachnewagas, Cachnewago, Cachnuagas=Caughnawaga.
Cachunilla=Cachanila.
Cacknawages=Caughnawaga.
Caclasco=Wasco.
Caonawagees=Caughnawaga.
Caco=Zaco.
Cacopas=Cocopa.
Cacores=Shakori.
Cacouïtas=Kawita.
Cac-tanʹ-qwŭt-meʹ ɉŭnnĕ=Umpqua.
Cacupas=Cocopa.
Cacupas=Cocopa.
Cadadoquis=Kadohadacho.
Cada-kaaman=San Ignacio de Kadakaman.
Cadᵍané=Shatane.
Cadapouces=Catawba.
Cadaquis, Cadaudachos, Cadaux, Caddo-dacho, Caddoe, Caddokies, Caddons, Caddoques, Caddoquies, Caddoquis, Caddow, Cadeaux=Kadohadacho.
Cadeudobet=Cadeudebet.
Cadica=Cadecha.
Cadigomo=Cadegomo.
Cadloes, Cado, Cadodaccho, Cadodache, Cadodachos, Cadodaguios, Cadodakis, Cadodaqui, Cadodaquinons, Cadodaquio, Cadodaquiou, Cadodaquioux, Cadoes, Cadogdachos, Ca-do-ha-da-cho, Cadojodacho=Kadohadacho.
Cadoques=Coaque.
Cados=Peticado.
Cadouca=Comanche.
Cadoux, Cadróns=Kadohadacho.
Caenoestoery=Iroquois.
Caensa=Taensa.
Caeŭjes=Cayuga.
Caeuuquias=Cahokia.
Cafaquj=Cofaqui.
Cafitachyque=Cofitachiqui.
Cafuenchi=Cajuenche.
Caga=Jeaga.
Cagabegux=Coyabegux.
Cagänʹ=Shakian.
Cagatsky=Aleut.
Cāgawāmiʻkāng=Shaugwaumikong.
Caghnawagah, Caghnawagos, Caghnenewaga, Caghnewagos, Caghnuage=Caughnawaga.
Cagnajuet=Cagnaguet.
Cagnawaga, Cagnawage, Cagnawagees, Cagnawauga, Cagnawaugen, Cagnawaugon, Cagnewage, Cagnowages, Cagnuagas=Caughnawaga.
Cagu=Chagu.
Caguillas=Kawia.
Cagüinachi=Coguinachi.
Cagullas=Kawia.
Cahacarague=Kanagaro.
Cahainihoua, Cahainohoua=Cahinnio.
Cahakies=Cahokia.
Cáhan=Dakota.
Cahaniaga=Canienga.
Cahaquonaghe=Kanagaro.
Cahata=Kiowa Apache.
Cahau=Cahokia.
Cahaynohoua=Cahinnio.
Cahelijyu, Cahelixyú=Cahelejyu.
Cahenhisenhonon=Toryohne.
Cahgnawaga=Caughnawaga.
Cahiaguas=Kiowa.
Cáhieʹȼa=Cheyenne.
Cahiguas=Kiowa.
Caʹ-hiks-i-óaʹ-hiks=Pawnee.
Cahinnio=Cachaymon.

Cahinoa, Cahirmois=Cahinnio.
Cahnawaas, Cahnawaga=Caughnawaga.
Cahnilla, Cahnillo=Kawia.
Cahnowas=Conoy.
Cahnowellahella=Ganowarohare.
Cahnuaga=Caughnawaga.
Cahoki, Cahokiams, Cahokies=Cahokia.
Cahoques=Coaque.
Cahoqui, Cahoquias=Cahokia.
Cahouita=Kawita.
Cahrocs, Cahroes=Karok.
Cahto-Pomo=Kato.
Cahuabia=Cahuabi.
Ca-hual-chitz=Paiute.
Cahuavi=Cahuabi.
Căhūgăs=Cayuga.
Cahuilla, Cahuillos=Kawia.
Cahuita=Kawita.
Cahung-Hage=Cahunghage.
Cah-was, Cah-wee-os, Cahwia, Cah-wi-ah, Cah-wil-
    las=Kawia.
Cai-a-was, Caigua, Caiguaras, Caihuas=Kiowa.
Caijougas, Caijouges=Cayuga.
Caileedjee=Kailaidshi.
Cailloux=Cayuse.
Cainameros=Gallinomero.
Caiomulgi=Ocmulgee.
Caiouga=Cayuga.
Caiougo=Goiogouen.
Caiougos, Caiougues=Cayuga.
Caita=Cahita.
Caiuges=Cayuga.
Caiwas=Kiowa.
Caiyougas=Cayuga.
Cai-yu'-clă=Siuslaw.
Cajadachse=Tueadasso.
Cajocka=Cayahoga.
Cajoegers, Cajougas=Cayuga.
Cajouge=Goiogouen.
Cajouges=Cayuga.
Cajouses=Cayuse.
Cajualas, Cajuales=Paiute.
Cajugas, Cajuger, Cajuges, Cajugu=Cayuga.
Cajuhaga=Cayahoga.
Cajukas, Cajyougas, Cajyugas=Cayuga.
Cakainikova=Cahinnio.
Cakanaruk=Kakontaruk.
Cakes=Kake.
Cakinonpas=Kakinonba.
Caknawage=Caughnawaga.
Cakwabaiyaki=Shakwabaiyaki.
Ca-kwa'-len-ya wüñ-wü=Shakwalengya.
Calabaws=Catawba.
Ca'-la-bi=Cheli.
Calaboe=Calaobe.
Calafars=Calcefar.
Calahpoewah=Calapooya.
Calajomanes=Gallinomero.
Cal-a-mex, Ca-la-mox=Tillamook.
Calanay, Calanio, Calany=Sarauahi.
Calapelins=Kalispel.
Calapooa, Calapooah, Calapoogas, Calapooias, Cala-
    poolia, Calapoosas=Calapooya.
Calapooya=Kalapooian Family.
Calapuaya, Calapuyas=Calapooya.
Calasthocle, Calasthorle, Calasthorte=Quinaielt.
Calawa=Shalawa.
Calcharnies=Kulchana.
Cale=Ocali.
Calendaruc=Kalindaruk.
Calés=Talasse.
Calespelin, Calespell, Calespin=Kalispel.
Caliente=Ojo Caliente.
California Indians=Yuma.
Cal-ĭ-ku-we'-witc=Shalikuwewich.
Calipoa=Calapooya, Catawba.
Calipooias, Calipooya, Calipoyas, Calipuyowes=
    Calapooya.
Caliquen=Aquacalecuen.
Calispells=Kalispel.
Calisteo, Calixteo, Calixto=Galisteo.
Calkahaan=Shalkahaan.
Calkobins=Tautin.
Callageheahs=Cherokee.
Cal-lah-po-e-ouah, Callahpoewah=Calapooya.
Cal-la-maks, Cal lá mox, Callamucks=Tillamook.
Callapipas, Callapooahs, Callapoohas, Callapooiales,
    Callapooias, Callapootos, Callapooya, Callapooyahs,
    Callapúyas, Callapuyes=Calapooya.

Calla Wassa=Calahuasa.
Callemax, Callemeux, Callemex, Callimix=Tilla-
    mook.
Call-law-poh-yea-as=Calapooya.
Calloosas, Callos=Colusa.
Caloait, Calooit, Caloort=Skilloot.
Caloosa=Calusa.
Caloosahatche=Calusahatchi.
Calopissas=Acolapissa.
Calos=Calusa.
Caloumas=Kulumi.
Cáltelitc=Thaltelich.
Caltsops=Clatsop.
Caluc, Caluca, Calusas=Calusa.
Camanche, Camanchees=Comanche.
Camaro=Cumaro.
Camaroua=Tamaroa.
Camarsches=Comanche.
Cambas=Norridgewock.
Camé=Zuñi.
Camel-el-poma, Cam-el-lel-Pomas=Usal.
Cami=Zuñi.
Camilya=Comeya.
Camitre=Camitría.
Camocacocke=Pamacocach.
Camoza=Comoza.
Câ'na=Sha.
Canabas=Norridgewock.
Cánabe, Canabi=Kechipauan.
Canadaasago=Canadasaga.
Canadacoa=Canada.
Cañada, La=Santa Cruz.
Canadaqua=Canandaigua.
Cánadáraggo=Ganondasa.
Canadasager, Canadasaggo, Canadasago, Canada-
    seago, Canadasege, Canadasegy=Canadasaga.
Canadauge=Canandaigua.
Canadayager=Canadasaga.
Canadenses=Canada.
Canaderagey=Ganondasa.
Canadesago, Canadesaque=Canadasaga.
Canadese=Canada.
Canadesego=Canadasaga.
Canadia=Kendaia.
Canadiains, Canadiens=Canada.
Canadisega, Canadosago=Canadasaga.
Canadqua=Canandaigua.
Canadsiohare, Canaedsishore=Canajoharie.
Canagacole=Canogacole.
Canagaroh=Kanagaro.
Canagesse=Conoy.
Canaghkonje=Iroquois.
Canaghsadagaes=Oka.
Canagora=Kanagaro.
Canainda=Gannentaha.
Canais=Conoy.
Cänájohä, Cä-nä-jó-hä-e, Cänajohä'ga, Can-ajo'har,
    Canajora, Canajorha=Canajoharie.
Canamoo=Cayamoa.
Canandaqua, Canandarqua, Canandauqua=Canan-
    daigua.
Canandesaga=Canadasaga.
Canandeugue=Canandaigua.
Canaoneuska=Mohawk.
Canaouagon=Connewango.
Canapouces=Catawba.
Canaresse, Canarise, Canarisse=Canarsee.
Canas=Sana.
Canasadagas, Canasadauga, Canasadogh, Canasa-
    dogha=Oka.
Canasagua, Canasauga=Kansaki.
Canasatauga=Oka.
Canaseder=Caneadea.
Canassadaga, Canassategy=Oka.
Canastogues=Conestoga.
Canatino=Kanohatino.
Canaumanos=Gallinomero.
Canavest, Canaways, Canawese=Conoy.
Canars=Lipan.
Canarse, Canarsie=Canarsee.
Canasadauque, Canasadego=Canadasaga.
Canaseraga=Ganasarage.
Canastigione=Canastigaone.
Canatasaga=Canadasaga.
Canaumanos=Gallinomero.
Canawagon=Connewango.
Canawagore=Ganowarohare.
Canawagow=Connewango.
Canawagus=Ganawagus.

Canawahrunas=Caughnawaga.
Canawako=Connewango.
Canawaroghare=Oneida (vil.).
Canawaroghere=Ganowarohare.
Canawest=Conoy.
Canceas=Quapaw.
Canceres, Cancers, Cances, Cancey=Lipan.
Cancey=Kiowa Apache.
Canceze, Cancezs, Canchez=Kansa.
Canchy=Lipan.
Cancons, Can-cow=Konkau.
Cancy=Lipan.
Candadacho=Kadohadacho.
Candaia=Kendaia.
Candelaria=Tinajas, Nuestra Señora de la Candelaria.
Candia=Kendaia.
Çandia=Sandia.
Caneadia=Caneadea.
Canecis=Lipan.
Canedesaga=Canadasaga.
Caneeci=Lipan.
Caneenda=Gannentaha.
Canees=Lipan.
Cañegacola=Cañogacole.
Caneghsadarundax=Oka.
Canél=Shanel.
Canendeshé=Naogeh.
Canesadage=Canadasaga.
Canesraca=Ganasarage.
Canessedage=Oka.
Canessy=Lipan.
Canestio=Kanestio.
Canestogas, Canestogo=Conestoga.
Cangaro=Kanagaro.
Canggaree=Congaree.
Canⁿ'-haⁿ=Dakota.
Çanhaways=Conoy.
Caŋ-ho-ham'-pa=Chankaokhan.
Caniahaga=Cayahoga.
Canibas=Norridgewock.
Canicari=Conicari.
Canices=Takulli.
Canicons=Tanico.
Canide (Indianes)=Canada.
Canidesego, Canidisego=Canadasaga.
Caniengas=Mohawk.
Canijoharie=Canajoharie.
Canimairo, Canimares=Gallinomero.
Caniouis=Kannehouan.
Canips=Kansa.
Canistage, Canistoge=Conestoga.
Canitas=Kawita.
Caŋ kaǧa otina, Caŋka oȟan=Chankaokhan.
Cañȟe' nikaci'ȟa=Shangke.
Çankia=Cahokia.
Caŋ kute=Chankute.
Cannabas=Norridgewock.
Cannadasago, Cannadesago, Cannadisago=Canadasaga.
Cannaha, Cannahios=Kannehouan.
Cannandaquah=Canandaigua.
Cannarse=Canarsee.
Cannassoone=Iroquois.
Cannastion=Kanastunyi.
Cannatchocary=Canajoharie.
Cannecis, Cannecy=Lipan.
Cannehovanes=Kannehouan.
Cannenda=Gannentaha.
Cannensis, Cannessi=Lipan.
Cannibas=Norridgewock.
Cannisdagua, Cannis-daque, Cannisdque=Canadasaga.
Cannissoone=Iroquois.
Canniungaes=Mohawk.
Cannohatinno, Cannohatino=Kanohatino.
Cannojoharys=Canajoharie.
Cannokantimo=Kanohatino.
Cannondesaga=Canadasaga.
Cannongageh-ronnons=Abnaki.
Cannossoene=Iroquois.
Cannostee=Kanastunyi.
Cannusadago=Oka.
Canoatinno, Canoatinos=Kanohatino.
Canodasega, Canodosago=Canadasaga.
Canoe and Paddling Assiniboines, Canoe Assiniboines, Canoe band=Watopapinah.
Canoe Indians=Mahican, Wahtopapinah.
Canoemen=Malecite.

Canoenada=Kanagaro.
Canoga=Gaanoge.
Canohatinno, Canohatino=Kanohatino.
Canoise=Conoy.
Çanojoharrie=Canajoharie.
Caŋona=Wazikute.
Canonchahonronon=Osswehgadagaah.
Cañon du Chelly=Chellé.
Cañon Indians=Lower Thompson Indians.
Canoomakers=Caughnawaga.
Canorise=Canarsee.
Canos=Cofitachiqui.
Canosedagui, Canosedogui=Canadasaga.
Canosi=Cofitachiqui.
Canossadage=Oka.
Canossoené, Canossoone=Iroquois.
Canostogas=Conestoga.
Canouhanans=Kanohatino.
Canowaloa, Canowarighare=Ganowarohare.
Canowaroghere=Ganowarohare, Oneida (vil.)
Canowes, Canoyeas, Canoyias, Canoys=Conoy.
Caⁿsaⁿ'u'niyk'ǎcin'a=Khudhapasan.
Cans, Cansa=Kansa.
Caŋsdaciǩana=Chansdachikana.
Canses, Cansez=Kansa.
Cantajes=Kiowa Apache.
Cantanual=Simaomo.
Cantanyans=Kittanning.
Cantauhaona=Simaomo.
Cantaunkank=Cantaunkack.
Cantey=Lipan.
Cantona, Cantonaes=Simaomo.
Canton Indians=Iroquois.
Çáŋse wáspe=Nanzewaspe.
Cantujuana, Cantuna=Simaomo.
Canundageh=Junundat.
Canundasaga=Canadasaga.
Canungas=Mohawk.
Canwagan=Connewango.
Canzas, Canzés, Canzez=Kansa.
Caodacho=Kadohadacho.
Caoitas=Kawita.
Caokia=Cahokia.
Caonetas, Caonites=Kawita.
Caoques=Coaque.
Caoquias=Cahokia.
Caouikas, Caouitas=Kawita.
Caouquias=Cahokia.
Capa=Quapaw.
Capachiqui=Acapachiqui.
Capaha=Quapaw.
Capahowasick, Capahowosick, Capahowsick=Capahowasic.
Capalino=Homulchison.
Capanay=Kapanai.
Capates=Capote.
Cape Croker=Nawash.
Cape Fears=Cape Fear Indians.
Cape Flattery=Makah.
Cape Fox Indians=Sanyakoan.
Cape Indians=Nauset.
ǫáde íniyk'ǎcin'a=Shapeinihkashina.
Çapel=Kepel.
Cape Sepping=Kechemudluk.
Cape St. James tribe=Gunghet-haidagai.
Capeutoucha=Capoutoucha.
Capichis, Capiga=Capiche.
Capina=Capinans.
Capitan Chiquito=Eskinenar.
Capitano Creek=Homulchison.
Capitinasses=Onondaga.
Ca-po=Santa Clara.
Ca-po-cia band=Kapozha.
Capoo=Santa Clara.
Capoques=Coaque.
Cappa=Ukaqpaqti.
Cappas=Quapaw.
Cap-pel=Kepel.
Captain Pipe's Village=Hopocan.
Capuchies=Capote.
Caquima, Caquimay, Caquineco=Kiakima.
Caracontauon, Caracotanon=Coiracoentanon.
Cara de Montezuma=Casa Grande.
Caraguists=Karigouistes.
Caramanes, Carancaguacas, Carancaguazes, Carancahuas, Carancahuases, Carancahuazes, Carancanay, Carancouas, Caranhouas=Karankawa.
Caranine=Coree.

Carankahuas, Carankawaes, Carankonas, Carankouas, Carankoways=Karankawa.
Carantouanis, Carantouannais, Carantouans=Conestoga.
Carcader=Watlala.
Carcarilica=Kaskaskia.
Cardecha=Cadecha.
Caree, Careés=Kahra.
Cargua=Kiowa.
Cariboo eaters=Etheneldeli.
Caribou=Attikiriniouetch.
Caribou Indians=Tutchonekutchin.
Cariso=Carrizo.
Carizal=Sonoita.
Carjuenche=Cajuenche.
Carlin=Calusa.
Carlook=Karluk.
Carlos=Calusa.
Carmañe Galexá=Santa Rosalia Mulege.
Carmaron=Contarea.
Carmelo=San Carlos.
Carmelo Eslenes=Esselen.
Carme-neh=Siksika.
Carmentaruka=Karmentaruka.
Carp River band=Ommunise.
Carquin=Karkin.
Carragouha=Carhagouha.
Carrahadeer=Caneadea.
Carrechias=Cahokia.
Carrees=Kahra.
Carribas=Norridgewock.
Carribou Indians=Tutchonekutchin.
Carribous=Caribou.
Carrien, Carrier-Indians, Carriers=Takulli.
Carrizalleños=Carrizo.
Carrizo=Klokadakaydn.
Carruco=Chorruco.
Carrying Place Village=Gwaugweh.
Car-soos=Kassovo.
Cartagoua=Carhagouha.
Cartaka=Castake.
Cartoogaja=Catatoga.
Carvillas=Kawia.
Cas=Kaskaskia.
Casa Blanca=Casa Montezuma.
Casa Blanco=Casa Blanca.
Cas-a-do'-ra=Destchin.
Casa Granda=Casa Grande.
Casaliu=Casalic.
Casas Grandas=Casa Grande.
Casawda=Kasihta.
Cascachias, Cascacia=Kaskaskia.
Cascade Indians=Watlala.
Cascade people=Pawating.
Cas, cagh, sa, gey=Kuskuski.
Cascakias, Cascaquias, Cascaschia, Cascaskias, Cascasquia=Kaskaskia.
Cascellis, Cascen=Cascel.
Cascia=Casqui.
Cascil=Cascel.
Cascile=Casalic.
Cascin=Casqui.
Casco=Aucocisco.
Case grandi=Casa Grande.
Caseitas=Kasihta.
Casewago=Cussewago.
Cashaem=Kashong.
Cashchevatebka, Cashchokelka Comanches=Kotsoteka.
Cashhooks=Cushook.
Cashictan=Coshocton.
Cashong=Kashong.
Cashook=Cushook.
Casica=Kasihta.
Casinos=Havasupai.
Casista, Casiste=Kasihta.
Casita=Usseta.
Caskaguias, Caskaquias=Kaskaskia.
Caskarorins, Caskarouns=Tuscarora.
Caskinampo=Kakinonba.
Caskoukia=Cahokia.
Casnino=Havasupai.
Caso=Kotsava.
Casor=Coosa.
Casquasqia=Kaskaskia.
Casque, Casquia=Casqui.
Casquiars, Casquias=Kaskaskia.
Casquin=Casqui.
Casquinampo=Kakinonpa.

Cas-sans=Kassovo.
Cassetash=Kasihta.
Cassia=Kichai.
Cassita=Kasihta.
Cass Lake band=Gamiskwakoka-wininiwak.
Cas-soes, Cas-son, Cassoos=Kassovo.
Casswer=Cumshewa.
Castabanas=Castahana.
Castachas=Cushtusha.
Castahamas=Castahana.
Cäs-tä-k'ó-stä těné=Chastacosta.
Castanoe=Cree.
Castapanas=Castahana.
Castcheteghka-Comanches=Kotsoteka.
Castixes=San Felipe.
Castor=Amikwa.
Castors=Tsattine.
Castors des Prairies=Sarsi.
ɋa'-tä=Choctaw.
Catabans, Catabas, Catabaw=Catawba.
Catacourou, Catacouru=Tacatacuru.
Ɋatada=Dhatada.
Catagos=Castake.
Cataha=Kiowa Apache.
Catahouche=Chattahoochee.
Ca'takâ=Kiowa Apache.
Cä'-tä-na-rä'-qua=Canandaigua.
Catanoneaux=Kutenai.
Cataoulou=Catahoula.
Catapaw=Catawba.
Cataraugos=Cattaraugus.
Catauba, Cataubos, Cataupas=Catawba.
Catawahays=Kutenai.
Catawbas, Catawbai, Catawbaw=Catawba.
Catawese=Catawissa.
Catchne, Catchney=Cotechney.
Catcho=Kadohadacho.
Catechna, Catechne, Catechneys=Cotechney.
Catelamet=Cathlamet.
Ca'-tha=Comanche.
Catharine Town=Catherine's Town.
Cath Camettes, Cathelametts=Cathlamet.
Catherine Town=Catherine's Town.
Cathlacommatups, Cathlacumups, Cath-lah-commah-tup=Cathlacomatup.
Cathlahaws=Thlakalama.
Cathlahcumups, Cath-lah-nah-quiah=Cathlanahquiah.
Cath-lah-poh-tle=Cathlapotle.
Cath-lâk-a-heckits, Cathlakahikits=Cathlakaheckit.
Cathlakamaps=Cathlacumup.
Cathlamah, Cathlamaks, Cath-la-mas, Cathlamats=Cathlamet.
Cathlaminimims=Kathlaminimin.
Cathlamuts, Cathlamux=Cathlamet.
Cathlanamenamons, Cathlanaminim, Cathlanaminimins=Kathlaminimin.
Cathlanaquiah=Cathlanahquiah.
Cathlapootle=Cathlapotle.
Cathlapooya=Calapooya.
Cathlapoutles, Cathlapouttes=Cathlapotle.
Cathlapouyeas=Calapooya.
Cathlas, Cathlascans, Cathlasco, Cathlascons, Cathlascou, Cathlaskos, Cathlassis=Wasco.
Cath-lath-la-las, Cathlathlaly, Cathlathlas=Cathlathlalas.
Cathlatscos=Wasco.
Cathlawah=Cathlamet.
Cathlayackty=Cathlakaheckit.
Cath-le-yach-ē-yachs=Shahala.
Cathlumet=Cathlamet.
Catholic Indians=Pueblos.
Catiené=Shathiane.
Catinakh=Chatinak.
Cat Indians=Erie.
Catiokia=Cahokia.
Catkils=Catskill Indians.
Catlahmas, Catlamas=Cathlamet.
Catlascou=Wasco.
Catlipoh, Catlipoks=Cathlapotle.
Ɋatlō'ltq=Comox.
Cat Nation=Erie.
Catohoche=Chattahoochee.
Catokiah=Cahokia.
Catriti=San Felipe.
Cat-sa-nim=Yakima.
Catsjajock, Catsjeyick=Cutchogue.

Cattabas, Cattabaws=Catawba.
Cattagochee=Chattahoochee.
Cattako=Kiowa Apache.
Cat-tan-a-hâws, Cattanahowes=Kutenai.
Cattanyan=Kittanning.
Cattaraugus=Cattaraugus.
Cattawbas=Catawba.
Catteranga=Cattaraugus.
Cattleputles=Cathlapotle.
Cattoways=Catawba.
Catumghage=Cahunghage.
Cauahogue=Cayahoga.
Cauchi=Naguchee.
Caugh=Kansa.
Caughnawaga=Iroquois.
Caughnawageys, Caughnawanga, Caughnewaga, Caughnewago=Caughnawaga.
Caujuckos=Cayuga.
Cauldrons=Colville.
Caumuches=Comanche.
Caunaujohhaury=Canajoharie.
Caundaisauque, Caundasaque=Canadasaga.
Cauneeyenkees=Mohawk.
Caunouche=Comanche.
Causattuck=Cosattuc.
Cau-ta-noh=Contahnah.
Cautawba=Catawba.
Cautonee, Cautonies=Kutenai.
Cauzes=Kansa.
Cavaianes=Kouyam.
Cavesons=Palseta.
Caveta=Kawita.
Cavezon=Cerro Cabezon.
Cavíos=Kawia.
Caw=Kansa.
Ca-wa=Xugua.
Caw-a-chim=Cowichan.
Cawala=Shawala, Shawnee.
Cawalitz=Cowlitz.
Cawalla=Huhliwahli.
Cawana=Shawnee.
Cawatie=Coyatee.
Cawaupugos=Cumumbah.
Cawa'xamux=Nicola band.
Caw-Caw=Konkau.
Caweos=Kawia.
Cawesitt=Coweset.
Cawgust=Saugus.
Cawidas=Kawita.
Cawina=Cajuenche.
Ca-witchans=Cowichan.
Cawittas, Cawittaws=Kawita.
Caw-mainsh=Comanche.
Cawnees=Koni.
Cawras, Caw-ree=Kahra.
Cawtaskákat=Kautas.
Cawva-Shinka=Tanwanshinka.
Ca'xanîx=Shahanik.
Cayagas, Cayagoes=Cayuga.
Cayahagah=Cayahoga.
Cayaki=Cherokee.
Cayameechee=Kiamisha.
Cayáni=Cheyenne.
Cayantha=Connewango.
Cayanwa=Kiowa.
Cayase=Cayas.
Cayauga=Cayuga.
Cayauge=Goiogouen, Cayuga.
Cayaughkias=Cahokia.
Cay-au-wa, Cay-au-wah=Kiowa.
Cayawah, Cayawash=Kiawaw.
Caycuas=Kiowa.
Cayouges, Cayeuges, Cayeugoes=Cayuga.
Cayguas=Kiowa.
Cayhuga=Cayuga.
Cayingahaugas=Mohawk.
Caymas=Caymus.
Caynawagas=Caughnawaga.
Caynga, Cayogas=Cayuga.
Cayohuas=Kiowa.
Cayomugi=Cayomulgi.
Cayonges, Cayoogoes=Cayuga.
Cayoose=Cayuse.
Cayoques=Coaque.
Cayoquits=Kyuquot.
Cayotes=Coyoteros, Pachawal.
Cayougas, Cayouges, Cayougues, Cayounges=Cayuga.
Cayouses=Cayuse.

Cayoush=Cayoosh Creek.
Cayoux=Cayuse.
Cayowges=Cayuga.
Caypa=Santa Clara.
Cayú=Cayuse.
Cayuaga=Cayuga.
Cayuga=Goiogouen, Gayagaanhe.
Cayuga Castle=Gayagaanhe.
Cayugas=Cayuga, Kiowa.
Cayuges=Cayuga.
Cayuguis=Cayeguas.
Cayukers, Cayungas=Cayuga.
Cayuquets, Cay-u-quits=Kyuquot.
Cayus, Cayuse=Waiilatpuan Family.
Cazaby Pah-Utes=Kotsava.
Cazancanay=Karankawa.
Ca-za-zhee-ta=Cazazhita.
Ceballeta, Cebellikita, Cebellitita=Cebolleta.
Cebola=Zuñi.
Ceboleta=Cebolleta.
Cebolla=Zuñi.
Cebolletta=Cebolleta.
Cebollians=Zuñi.
Ꮯe'ȯin=Tesik.
Ꮯeꞔl'-qût ꝫûn'nĕ=Thethlkhuttunne.
Cecocawanee, Cecocawonee, Cecomocomoco=Secowocomoco.
Cedar Creek=Atchinahatchi.
Ceet-shongos=Brulé.
Ꝥegiha=Dhegiha.
Ꮯegnake-okisela=Chegnakeokisela.
Ꝥe-go'-ni-na=Shungikikarachada.
Ꮯe-ña-na-ká=Chegnakeokisela.
Ꮯeñ-huha-toŋ=Chekhuhaton.
Cehmeque-sabinta=Shivwits.
Ceickasaw=Chickasaw.
Cekacawone=Secacawoni.
Ꝥeꝫaha=Dhegiha.
Cekakawwon=Secacawoni.
Ꮯé-ke yiñ-e=Shekeyine.
'Ce'kiwere=Chiwere.
Cemanlos=Comanche.
Cēmps=Shemps.
Ceneca's=Seneca.
Cenecu=Senecú.
Cenepisa=Acolapissa.
Ceneseans, Cenesians=Caddo.
Câ'ngoqedîna=Shunkukedi.
Cenis=Caddo.
Ꮯe'nlin=Chenlin.
Cenokipe=Sinoquipe.
Cenola=Zuñi.
Cenosio=Geneseo.
Censoo, Censoo=Sinicu.
Cenys=Caddo.
Ꮯe-oħba=Cheokhba.
Ꮯĕ-pa'le-ve'=Shipaulovi.
Ꝥeqemēn=Siccameen.
Ꮯê'qtamux=Ntlakyapamuk.
Ceries Assonys=Caddo.
Ꮯeri'nak=Cherinak.
Cernalton=Tsewenalding.
Cerro-Cavezon=Tze-tses-kadn.
Ꝥestcìni=Theshtshini.
Ꮯe-toûn' ꝫûnnĕ=Thechuntunne.
Cetguanes=Yuma.
Ꝥē'tsākɛñ=Thetsaken.
Ꝥē'tuksɛm=Thetuksem.
Ꝥē'tūsum=Thetusum.
Ceuala, Ceuola=Zuñi
Ceux du Sable=Sable.
Cevola=Zuñi.
Cevolleta, Cevolleto=Cebolleta.
Ꮯgágɛtc=Shkagech.
Ꮯgwáliko=Shgwaliksh.
Chaa=Cheyenne.
Chaamonaqué=Tioga.
Chaas=Ais.
Cha-atl=Chaahl.
Chab-way-way-gun=Shabawywyagun.
Chacacantes, Chacakante=Chacacants.
Chacakengua=Atchatchakangouen.
Chacatos=Choctaw.
Chacchoumas=Chakchiuma.
Chacchoux=Chactoos.
Chacchumas, Chacci Oumas, Chacci Oumas, Chacehoumas=Chakchiuma.
Chacha=Washa.

Chachachouma=Chakchiuma.
Chachakingua=Atchatchakangouen.
Chachamatses=Hahamatses.
Chachelis=Chehalis.
Chachippè=Le Have.
Chachoumas=Chakchiuma.
Chachuā'mis=Hahuamis.
Chachümas, Chackchi-oomas, Chacksihoomas=Chakchiuma.
Chacktaws=Choctaw.
Chaclan, Chaclanes=Saclan.
Chaco cañon=Chacat.
Chacoumas, Chacoume, Chacsihomas, Chacsihoomas=Chakchiuma.
Chactah, Chactanys, Chactas, Chactaws=Choctaw.
Chactchi-Oumas, Chactioumas=Chakchiuma.
Chactots=Chatots.
Chacxoumas=Chakchiuma.
Chadadoquis=Kadohadacho.
Chadeca=Cadecha.
Chaetaw Capitales=Choctaw Capitale.
Chaetoos=Chactoos.
Chafan=Tsanchifin.
Chaganons=Shawnee.
Chagaouamigong=Shaugawaumikong.
Chageluk settlements=Jugelnute.
Chagnet=Chugnut.
Chagoamigon, Chagoimegon, Chag8amigon, Chagouamigong, Chagouemig, Chagouemigon=Shaugawaumikong.
Chaguaguanos=Akanaquint.
Chaguanos=Shawnee.
Chaguyennes=Cheyenne.
Chahâh=Chiaha.
Chahcowahs=Charcowa.
Chahis=Cree.
Chahlolnagai=Lanahilduns.
Chah'-ra-rat=Dakota.
Chah'-shm=Apache.
Chá'hta=Choctaw.
Chahtahs, Chahta-Muskoki, Chahtas=Muskhogean Family.
Chahwahnahiooks=Towahnahiooks.
Chaimut=Chaik.
Chai-nim'-ai-ni=Choinimni.
Chakchuqualk=Chuchchuqualk.
Chakhtogmut=Shaktoligmiut.
Chak-re-le-a-ton=Chockrelatan.
Chaktaws=Choctaw.
Chalaacpauley=Chatukchufaula.
Chalagatsca=Hlekatchka.
Chalakee=Cherokee.
Chalam=Clallam.
Chalaque, Chalaquies=Cherokee.
Chalas=Chala.
Chal-chu-nie=Chatcheeni.
Chalitmiut=Chalit.
Chall-o-wha=Chalowe.
Chaltas=Choctaw.
Chalula=Chilula.
Chamak=Tsamak.
Cha-ma-kia=Kyamakyakwe.
Cha-ma-ko-neo, Cha-ma-ko-nees=Chawakoni.
Chamers=Santsukdhin.
Cham-ma-ko-nec=Chawakoni.
Chämnä'pûm=Chimnapum.
Chamoappans=Shanwappom.
Chamong=Gahato.
Champoicho, Champoicks=Champoeg.
Chanagongum=Chabanakongkomun.
Chan-a-hue=Kechipauan.
Chanahuniege, Chanahunrege=Chananagi.
Chanas=Sana.
Chancers=Santsukhdhin.
Chancrés=Lipan.
Chä'-ne=Chaui.
Chaneers=Santsukdhin.
Chanes=Sana.
Chanetkai=Shanelkeya.
Chang Doa=Kang.
Changuaguanes=Akanaquint.
Chaniers (band)=Santsukdhin.
Chanki=Chunkey.
Chanousanons=Shawnee.
Chan-ta-ko'-da=Cheindekhotding.
Chanundadies=Tionontati.
Chan-wap-pan=Shanwappom.
Chanzes=Lipan.
Chaoenne=Cheyenne.

Chaonanons, Chaoni=Shawnee.
Chaouachas=Chaouacha.
Chaouanaquois, Chaouannons, Chaoüanon, Chaoüanong, Cha8anons, Chaouanos, Chaoüanoüa, Chaouans=Shawnee.
Chaouchas=Chaouacha.
Chaouennons, Chaouenon, Chaouens, Chaounons, Chaouoinons, Chaovanons, Chaovenon, Chaowanons=Shawnee.
Chapanun=Chepanoc.
Cha'parahihu=Hupa.
Chapitoulas=Choupetoulas.
Chapkaku=Chakpahu.
Chapman's Bar=Tikwalus.
Chapopines=Tiopines.
Chap-pah-seins=Chupcan.
Chappaquidgick=Chaubaqueduck.
Chap-po-sans=Chupcan.
Chappunish=Nez Percés.
Chapticons=Chapticon.
Chaquesauma=Chakchiuma.
Chaqueta, Chaquitas=Choctaw.
Cha'-rä=Cheikikarachada.
Chä'-rä=Chaikikarachada.
Characks, Charah=Cheraw.
Charai=Charac.
Charakees, Charakeys=Cherokee.
Charame=Xarame.
Charankoua=Karankawa.
Charanons=Shawnee.
Charay=Charac.
Charcawah=Charcowa.
Char-cheiné=Satchin.
Charcowah=Charcowa.
Chargeurs=Takulli.
Charikees=Cherokee.
Charioquois=Huron.
Chariticas=Arapaho.
Charles=Calusa.
Charles Old Town, Charley Emathla's Town=Yalaka.
Charleys Village=Tadush.
Charokees=Cherokee.
Charraws=Cheraw.
Charretièr's (band)=Chartierstown.
Charrows=Cheraw.
Charrucco=Chorruco.
Chasinskoe=Chatcheeni.
Chasta band of Rogue Rivers=Chasta.
Chasta Scotans, Chasta Scoten, Chasta Scoton=Chasta-Skoton.
Chastay=Chasta.
Chasunous=Shawnee.
Cha-ta=Chetco.
Chatabas=Catawba.
Chatahoochas, Chatahoosie, Chatahouchi=Chattahoochee.
Chata-Muskoki=Muskhogean Family.
Chatas=Chala.
Chata Uche=Chattahoochee.
Chataw=Choctaw.
Chataway=Chetawe.
Chat-chee-nie=Chatcheeni.
Chat-e-cha=Kyatiikya.
Chatinakh=Chatinak.
Chat-Kas, Chatkaws=Choctaw.
Chatoueka=Chattooka.
Chatounio=Chatcheeni.
Chatowe=Chetawe.
Chatsinahs=Chatcheeni.
Chatsops=Clatsop.
Chattaes=Choctaw.
Chattafallai=Chukafalaya.
Chattanqua=Chattooka.
Chattas=Choctaw.
Chattawka=Chattooka.
Chattoes=Choctaw.
Chattoesofkar, Chattofsofker=Chatoksofke.
Chat-to-ho-che=Chattahoochee.
Chattoka=Chattooka.
Chat-tok-sof-ke, Chattoksofker=Chatoksofke.
Chattoocka=Chattooka.
Chattooga=Chatuga.
Chattoos=Chactoos.
Chattossofkins=Chatoksofke.
Chattukchufaule=Chatukchufaula.
Chatugee=Chatuga.
Chauanons=Shawnee.
Chaubunakongkomuk=Chabanakongkomun.
Chau-chil'-la=Chowchilla.

Chaudiere, Chaudieres=Colville.
Chauenese, Chauenous=Shawnee.
Chauhaguéronon=Montagnais.
Chau-kethluc-co=Chukahlako.
Chaulamas=Xarame.
Chaumenes=Tawehash.
Chaunis, Chaunys=Shawnee.
Chauoironon=Montagnais.
Chauwanghungh, Chauwangung=Shawangunk.
Chau-woc-e-lau-hatchee=Sawokli.
Chavanons=Shawnee.
Chavavares=Anavares.
Chaves Pass ruin=Chubkwichalobi.
Chavouanons=Shawnee.
Chawa=Cheyenne.
Chawaccola Hatchu=Sawokli.
Chawachas=Chaouacha.
Chawack=Cheewack.
Cha-wa-na=Kyawana, Tehuatsana.
Chawangon, Chawangong=Shawangunk.
Chawanock=Chowanoc.
Chawanoes, Chawanons=Shawnee.
Chawanook=Chowanoc.
Chawari=Tsawarii.
Chä'-we=Chaui.
Chawenons=Shawnee.
Chawetas=Choctaw.
Chawonacks, Chawonests, Chawonoack, Chawonock, Chawonoks, Chawons, Chawoon=Chowanoc.
Chawopoweanock=Chawopo, Weanock.
Chawraw=Cheraw.
Chawum, Chawun=Pokanoket.
Chawwonoks, Chawwonoke=Chowanoc.
Chaye=Choye.
Chayenne=Cheyenne.
Chayenne Indians=Oglala.
Chaykisaht=Chaicclesaht.
Chayopînes=Tiopines.
Chea=Sia.
Che-ahm=Cheam.
Cheahtoc=Chetco.
Chealis=Chehalis.
Che-anhun=Chiaha.
Cheaptin=Nez Percés.
Chearhan, Che ar haw=Chiaha.
Che-at-tee=Chetco.
Che-au-hau=Chiaha.
Che-au-hoo-che=Chiahudshi.
Che-baah-ah-bish=Chobaabish.
Chebaylis=Chehalis.
Chebegnadose=Bagaduce.
Cheböigan (band)=Cheboygan.
Chebois=Chippewa.
Checagou=Chicago.
Checaldish, Checalish=Chehalis.
Checanadughtwo=Saquidongquee.
Checaws=Chiaha.
Checher Ree=Brulé.
Chechili=Chehalis.
Chechinamiut=Chichinak.
Chechohomynies, Checkahomanies=Chickahominy.
Checklesit=Chaicclesaht.
Checlucca-ninne=Chihlakonini.
Che-com=Shigom.
Checose=Chekase's Village.
Checoutimi, Checoutimiens=Chicoutimi.
Chectaws=Choctaw.
Chedaik=Shediac.
Che-dong-ga=Chedunga.
Cheechawkose=Chechawkose.
Cheechaws=Chiaha.
Cheehales=Chehalis.
Cheehaws=Chiaha.
Cheelake=Cherokee.
Cheelcat, Cheelhaats, Cheelkaats=Chilkat.
Chee-luck-kit-le-quaw=Chilluckittequaw.
Chee-nah=Tsano.
Cheenales=Chehalis.
Chee-nas=Tsano.
Cheenik=Chinik.
Chee-nitch=Chinits.
Cheenook=Chinook, Chinookan Family.
Cheeowhee=Tsiyahi.
Cheerake, Cheerakee, Cheeraque, Cheerokee=Cherokee.
Cheesca=Chisca.
Cheestooyee=Tsistuyi.
Chee'-zhoo=Tsishuutsepedhungpa.
Chee-zhoo peacemakers=Tsishuwashtake.

Chefokhlagamute=Chefoklak.
Chégagou, Chegakou=Chicago.
Chegoimegon=Shaugawaumikong.
Chegoutimis=Chicoutimi.
Cheguas=Tigua.
Chehales=Chehalis.
Chehalim=Chahelim.
Chehau, Chehawah, Chehaws, Chehawuseche=Chiaha.
Chehaylis=Chehalis.
Cheh-chewe-hem=Chuchunayha.
Chehew=Chiaha.
Cheh'-he-tä=Cheghita.
Cheina=Tsano.
Chekahomanies=Chickahominy.
Che'kaihas=Chickasaw.
Chekakou=Chicago.
Chekalis=Chehalis.
Chekasaws=Chickasaw.
Chekasschees=Skaischiltnish.
Chek-e-pā-wha=Kechipauan.
Chekilis=Chehalis.
Che-kiss-chee=Skaischiltnish.
Chekoutimiens, Chekoutimis=Chicoutimi.
Chêl-å-kė, Chelakees=Cherokee.
Che'láko-Nini=Chihlakonini.
Chelaques, Chelekee=Cherokee.
Chelkatskie=Chilkat.
Chellé=Chelly.
Chellicotheé=Chillicothe.
Chellokee, Cheloculgee, Chelokees=Cherokee.
Chelouels=Natchez.
Che-luc-co ne-ne, Chelucconinny=Chihlakonini.
Che-luc-it-te-quaw, Che-luck-kit-ti-quar=Chilluck-ittequaw.
Chelukamanches, Chelukimaukes=Lakmiut.
Che-ma-hua-vas=Chemehuevi.
Chemainis=Chemanis.
Chema-keem, Chemakeum, Chemakum=Chimakuan Family, Chimakum.
Che-ma-wa-was, Chemebet=Chemehuevi.
Chemebet Quajala=Paiute.
Chemegerabas, Chemeguaba=Chemehuevi.
Chemeguabas Sevintas=Shivwits.
Chemeguava, Chemegue=Chemehuevi.
Chemegue cajula, Chemegué Cuajála=Paiute.
Chemegue sevicta, Chemegué Sevínta=Shivwits.
Chemeguet Cajuala=Kawia.
Chemehnevis, Chemehueris, Chemehuevas, Chem-e-hue-vitz, Chemehuewas, Chemeonahas, Cheme-quaba, Chemeque=Chemehuevi.
Chemeque-caprala=Paiute.
Chemicum=Chimakum.
Chemiguabos, Chemiheavis, Chemihua-hua, Chemi-huaras, Chemihuaves, Chemi-huevas, Chemihuevis, Cheminares=Chemehuevi.
Chemmesyan=Chimmesyan Family.
Chemonchovanistes=Chomonchouaniste.
Chemong=Chemung.
Chemovi=Sichomovi.
Chemung=Gahato.
Chenakisses=Chiakanessou.
Chenandoanes=Seneca.
Chenang, Chenango=Shenango.
Chenbosel=Chenposel.
Chenceses=Geneseo.
Chenega=Ingamatsha.
Chenengo=Chenango.
Chenesee Castle, Chenessies, Chenessios=Geneseo.
Cheniers=Santsukdhin.
Cheningo, Cheningué=Shenango.
Chenissios=Geneseo.
Chenkus=Chonque.
Chennesse Castle, Chennussios=Geneseo.
Chenondadees=Tionontati.
Chenondoanah=Gaandowanang.
Chenosio=Geneseo.
Chenoux=Chinook.
Chenoya, Chenoyana=Atsugewi.
Chenukes=Chinook.
Chenunda=Junundat.
Chenundady=Tionontati.
Chenundea=Junundat.
Chenundies=Tionontati.
Chenusies, Chenusios, Chenussio=Geneseo.
Cheokees=Cherokee.
Cheowa=Tsiyahi.
Chepanu, Chepanuu=Chepanoc.
Chepawas=Chippewa.

Chepawy=Chepanoc.
Che-pa-wy-an, Chepayan=Chipewyan.
Chepecho=Pamunkey.
Chep-en-a-pho=Chepenafa.
Chepéouyan, Chepewayan=Chipewyan.
Chepeways=Chippewa.
Chepewyan=Athapascan Family, Chipewyan.
Chepeyan=Chipewyan.
Chepeyans=Athapascan Family.
Cheponssea, Chepontia, Chepousca, Chepoussea=Chepoussa.
Chepowas, Cheppewes=Chippewa.
Cheppewyan, Cheppeyan=Chipewyan.
Cheraguees, Cherahes, Cherakees, Cherakis, Cheraquees, Cheraquis=Cherokee.
Cherecaquis=Chiricahua.
Cherechos=Keresan Family.
Cherermons=Shawnee.
Cheres=Keresan Family.
Chericahui=Chiricahua.
Cherickees, Cherikee=Cherokee.
Chernila, Chernilof=Chinila.
Chernovskoe, Chernovskoi, Chernovsky=Chernofski.
Che-ro-ha-ka=Nottoway.
Cherokis, Cherookees, Cheroquees, Cherrackees=Cherokee.
Cherr'h-quuh=Cherkhu.
Cherrokees, Cherrykees=Cherokee.
Chesapeacks, Chesapeakes, Chesapeians, Chesepians, Chesepioock=Chesapeak.
Che-she-gwa=Kenabig.
Chesheshim=Muaya.
Cheskitalowas=Chiskatalofa.
Chester Valley Indians, Chestes=Shasta.
Chestoowa, Chestowa, Chestuee=Tsistuyi.
Cheta-ut-tinne=Tsetautkenne.
Chetcas, Chetcoe, Chetcoes, Chetcoos=Chetco.
Chetemachas=Chitimacha.
Chethl'=Chak.
Chetho Kette=Chettrokettle.
Cheticnewash=Chititiknewas.
Chetimacha=Chitimacha.
Chetkoe=Chetco.
Chĕtl-ĕ-shĭn, Chetlessentan, Chetlessenten, Chetless-en-tun, Chet-less-in-gen=Chetleschantunne.
Chetocchefaula=Chatukchufaula.
Chetro Ketle, Chetro-Kettle=Chettrokettle.
Cheueux ou poils leué, Cheueux releues=Ottawa.
Cheurkany=Chananagi.
Cheveriches=Seuvarits.
Chevet=Shivwits.
Cheveux Relvés=Ottawa.
Chevlon ruin=Shakwabaiyali.
Chewackala=Sawokli.
Che-wæ-ræ=Oto.
Che-wak-a-to=Sawokli.
Chewe=Tsiyahi.
Chewenee=Choinimni.
Chewohe=Tsiyahi.
Che wok o lee=Sawokli.
Che-won-der-gon-ing=Ketchewaundaugenink.
Cheyenne Sioux=Wutapiu.
Chez-ye-na=Tzecheschinne.
Chia=Chua, Sia.
Chiaas=Ais.
Chiabel-na-poma=Keliopoma.
Chiacantefous=Chiakanessou.
Chiacasas=Chickasaw.
Chiachi-Oumas=Chakchiuma.
Chiaguan=Siaguan.
Chiahnessou=Chiakanessou.
Chĭáian=Pueblos.
Chians=Cheyenne.
Chiappawaws=Chippewa.
Chias=Ais.
Chibenaccadie=Shubenacadie.
Chibois=Chippewa.
Chicaça=Chickasaw, Chicaza.
Chicachas, Chicachos=Chickasaw.
Chicagou, Chicag8, Chicags, Chicagu, Chicagvv=Chicago.
Chicahamanias=Chickahominy.
Chicaksaws=Chickasaw.
Chicalina=Chookheereso.
Chicaqw=Chicago.
Chicaraguis=Chiricahua.
Chicasahay=Chickasawhay.
Chicasan, Chicasas, Chicasauus=Chickasaw.
Chicasawhay=Chickasawhay.

Chicasaws=Chickasaw.
Chicase=Chekase's village.
Chicasou, Chicassas, Chicawchaws, Chicaza, Chichacas=Chickasaw.
Chichagov=Attu.
Chichanee=Wateree.
Chichasau, Chichasaws, Chichashas=Chickasaw.
Chichedec, Chichedek=Chisedec.
Chichequaas=Rancocas.
Chichicticale=Chichilticalli.
Chichigoueks=Chichigoue.
Chichijaya=Cuchiaga.
Chichilli=Chilili.
Chichillicale=Chichilticalli.
Chichilop=Shishalap.
Chichilte Calli, Chichilti, Chichilticah, Chichilti-cal, Chichilticala, Chichilticale, Chichilticalen, Chichilticali, Chichiltic-Calli, Chichiltie, Chichiltie Alli=Chichilticalli.
Chichinagamute=Chichinak.
Chichiti=Chilili.
Chichiticale, Chichitté Calli=Chichilticalli.
Chichiyaga=Cuchiaga.
Chĭchkitonē=Chetsgitunai.
Chichohocki=Chikohoki.
Chichominys=Chickahominy.
Chichuich=Pecos.
Chichula=Chentsithala.
Chickahamanias, Chickahamines=Chickahominy.
Chickahokin=Chikohoki.
Chickahomines, Chickahomones, Chickahomonie=Chickahominy.
Chick-a-lees=Chehalis.
Chickalina=Chucalissa.
Chickanee=Wateree.
Chickanossous=Chiakanessou.
Chickaree=Wateree.
Chickasawka=Chickasawhay.
Chickasaws, Chickassas=Chickasaw.
Chick-atat=Klikitat.
Chickatawbut=Neponset.
Chickeeles, Chickelis=Chehalis.
Chicken-hawk=Khuyeguzhinga.
Chickesaw, Chicketaws=Chickasaw.
Chickiaes=Chiskiac.
Chickisaw=Chickasaw.
Chickitats=Klikitat.
Chickkasah, Chicksas, Chicksaws, Chicksha, Chickshau=Chickasaw.
Chicktaghicks=Illinois.
Chicktaws=Choctaw.
Chickuchatty=Chicuchatti.
Chicocoan=Secacawoni.
Chĭ'-cō-mĭ'-co, Chio'omi'co=Shecomeco.
Chicontami=Chicoutimi.
Chicoria, Chicorie=Chicora.
Chicoutime=Chicoutimi.
Chictaghicks=Illinois.
Chictaws=Choctaw.
Chicuchatty=Chicuchatti.
Chidumas=Alchedoma.
Chien=Cheyenne.
Chien-Flancs=Thlingchadinne.
Chiennes=Cheyenne.
Chifukhlugumut=Chifukluk.
Chigabennakadik=Shubenacadie.
Chigagou=Chicago.
Chigantalgi, Chigantualga=Quigalta.
Chigasaws=Chickasaw.
Chigilousas=Chitimacha.
Chiglit=Kopagmiut.
Chigmut=Chigmiut.
Chignik Bay=Kaluiak.
Chigoula=Chicora.
Chigtaghcicks=Illinois.
Chiguan=Siaguan.
Chiguas=Tigua.
Chigui-cagui=Chiricahua.
Chiha=Chiaha.
Chihales, Chihalis, Chiheelees, Chiheeleesh, Chihelish=Chehalis.
Chih-kah-we-kay=Chippekawkay.
Chihohocki, Chihohockies, Chihokokis, Chiholacki=Chikohoki.
Chihui-cahui=Chiricahua.
Chikachas=Chickasaw.
Chikago, Chikagons, Chikagou, Chikagoüa, Chikagu, Chikagvv=Chicago.
Chikahokin=Chikohoki.

Chikahominy=Chickahominy.
Chikailish=Chehalis.
Chikakas=Chickasaw.
Chikalish=Chehalis.
Chikasahs, Chikasaws, Chíkasha=Chickasaw.
Chikeelis=Chehalis.
Chikelaki=Chikohoki.
Chikelis, Chikilishes=Chehalis.
Chikimini, Chikini=Unalachtigo.
Chikitaws, Chikkasah, Chikkesah=Chickasaw.
Chikohocki=Chikohoki.
Chikoilish=Chehalis.
Chikolacki=Chikohoki.
Chiksah=Chickasaw.
Chiktachiks=Illinois.
Chilacoffee, Chi-lah-cah-tha=Chillicothe.
Chilcahs, Chilcaks, Chilcales, Chilcat, Chilcates=
    Chilkat.
Chilcatin=Tsilkotin.
Chilchadilklogue=Chilchadilkloge.
Chilcoot=Chilkoot.
Chilcoten, Chilcotin=Tsilkotin.
Chilcow Apaches, Chilecago, Chile Cowes=Chiri-
    cahua.
Chileons=Tsiltaden.
Chilhχotin=Tsilkotin.
Chili=Chilili.
Chilian=Tsiltaden.
Chilicagua, Chilicagua Apaches=Chiricahua.
Chilicoatens, Chilicoten=Tsilkotin.
Chilicothe=Chillicothe.
Chilicotin=Tsilkotin.
Chilikoffi=Chillicothe.
Chililé, Chililo, Chilily=Chilili.
Chilion=Tsiltaden.
Chilivik=Selawigmiut.
Chilkāht-Kwān, Chilkahts=Chilkat.
Chilkaht-tena=Takutine.
Chilkasts, Chilkat-qwan, Chilkatskoe, Chilkhat=
    Chilkat.
Chiɾkho'tenne, Chiɾ-χoh-ţen, Chilkotin=Tsilkotin.
Chillacothe=Chillicothe.
Chillates=Chehalis.
Chillcoatens=Tsilkotin.
Chillikoffi=Chillicothe.
Chillili=Chilili.
Chillimiut=Chinik.
Chillokittequaws=Chilluckittequaw.
Chillons=Tsiltaden.
Chilluckkitequaws, Chilluckkittaquaws, Chillukit-
    tequas, Chillukittequaw, Chilluk-Kit-e-quaw, Chil-
    luk-kit-te-quaw=Chilluckittequaw.
Chil-lu-la, Chillulahs=Chilula.
Chillwayhook=Chilliwhack.
Chilocathe=Chillicothe.
Chilon=Tsiltaden.
Chilook=Skilloot.
Chiloweyuk=Chilliwhack.
Chilpaines=Tsihlinainde.
Chilticale=Chichilticalli.
Chiltokin=Tsilkotin.
Chilts, Chiltz=Chehalis.
Chilukki=Cherokee.
Chilû'ktkwa=Chilluckittequaw.
Chilukweyuk=Chilliwhack.
Chim-a-kim=Chimakum.
Chimakum=Chimakuan Family.
Chi-mal'-a-kwe, Chimalaquays, Chimalquays=Chi-
    malakwe.
Chimawava, Chimchinves=Chemehuevi.
Chimedocs=Chumidok.
Chimehuevas, Chimehueve, Chimehwhuebes=Che-
    mehuevi.
Chimekliagamut, Chimekliak=Chimiak.
Chimewawas of Arizona, Chimhueves=Chemehuevi.
Chimiagamute=Chimiak.
Chimicum=Chimakum.
Chim-i-dok=Chumidok.
Chi-mi-hua-hua=Chemehuevi.
Chimingyangamiut=Chimiak.
Chim-nah-pan, Chim-nah-pum, Chim-nah-pun, Chim-
    napoos, Chimnapuns=Chimnapum.
Chimohueois=Chemehuevi.
Chimook=Chinook.
Chimpsain=Chimmesyan Family.
Chimseyans=Tsimshian.
Chimsyans=Chimmesyan Family.
Chimteya=Chumteya.

Chi-mu-a=Cienega.
Chim-ue-hue-vas, Chim-woy-os=Chemehuevi.
Chin=Takulli.
China=Chiaha.
Chin-a Ka-na Tze-shu-ma=Pueblo Caja del Rio.
Chin-a-kum=Chimakum.
Chinango=Shenango.
Chinapi=Chinapa.
Chine-a-kums=Chimakum.
Chinesee, Chinesse=Geneseo
Chingas=Cayuga.
Chingigmut=Chingigmiut.
Chingleclamouche, Chingleolamolik, Chingleolamuk=
    Chinklacamoose.
Chingoteacq, Chingoteagues=Chincoteague.
Chingué=Shenango.
Chin-hook=Chinook.
Chinigmut=Chinik.
Chiningue=Logstown.
Chininoas=Cahinnio.
Chinipa=Varohio.
Chinklacamoose, Chinklacamoose's   Old-town=
    Chinklacamoose.
Chinkoa=Chinko.
Chinloes=Natliatin.
Chinnahpum, Chin-na-pum=Chimnapum.
Chin Nation=Lillooet.
Chinnesee=Geneseo.
Chinnigné=Logstown.
Chinnook, Chinock=Chinook.
Chinokabi=Chinakbi.
Chinook=Chinookan Family.
Chinooks=Chinookan Family, Kalapooian Family.
Chinosia=Geneseo.
Chinouks=Chinook.
Chinouns=Hopi.
Chinquack=Cinquack.
Chinuc, Chinúk=Chinook.
Chinuk=Chinookan Family.
Chinundeda=Junundat.
Chiokuk, Chiookuk=Chiukak.
Chi8=Dakota.
Chiouanons=Shawnee.
Chipaille=Chippoy.
Chipawawas, Chipaways, Chipaweighs=Chippewa.
Chipcoke=Chippekawkay.
Chipeouaian, Chipewan=Chipewyan.
Chipewas=Chippewa.
Chipéway=Chipewyan, Chippewa.
Chipewayan=Chipewyan.
Chipeweghs, Chipeweighs=Chippewa.
Chipewyan Tinney, Chipiouan=Chipewyan.
Chipiwa=Chippewa.
Chip'-kah-kyoon'-gay,   Chipkawkay=Chippekaw-
    kay.
Chipoës=Chippewa.
Chipoussa=Chepoussa.
Chippanum=Chepanoc.
Chippawas, Chippawees=Chippewa.
Chip-pe-coke=Chippekawkay.
Chippeouays, Chippewaes, Chippewais=Chippewa.
Chippewas of Lake Superior=Kitchigumiwinini-
    wug.
Chippewas of Pembina River=Anibiminanisibiwi-
    niniwak.
Chippewaus=Chippewa.
Chippewayan, Chippewayanawok=Chipewyan.
Chippewayans proprement dits=Thilanottine.
Chippewayeen=Chipewyan.
Chippeways=Chippewa.
Chippeways of Leach Lake=Pillagers.
Chippeways of Red Lake=Miskwagamiwisagaigan.
Chippeways of Sand Lake=Kahmetahwungaguma.
Chippeweighs=Chippewa.
Chippeweyan, Chip-pe-wi-yan=Chipewyan.
Chippewyan=Athapascan Family, Chipewyan.
Chippewyse, Chippoways=Chippewa.
Chippowyen=Chipewyan.
Chippuwas=Chippewa.
Chipunish, Chipunnish=Nez Percés.
Chipwaes, Chipwas=Chippewa.
Chipwayan, Chipwayanawok=Chipewyan.
Chipways=Chippewa.
Chipweyan, Chip-wyan=Chipewyan.
Chiquacha=Chickasaw.
Chiquito=Towarnodentiel.
Chiquola=Chicora.
Chirakues=Cherokee.

Chiricagüi, Chiricaguis, Chiricahni, Chir-i-ca-huans, Chiricahues, Chi-ri-ca-hui, Chiricaquis, Chiricuagi, Chiriguais, Chirikahwa=Chiricahua.
Chiripinons=Assiniboin.
Chiriquans, Chirocahue=Chiricahua.
Chirokys=Cherokee.
Chirumas=Yuma.
Chisapeacks, Chisapeans, Chi-sapi-ack=Chesapeake.
Chisca=Quizquiz.
Chisedech=Chisedec.
Chï-shë'=Mescaleros.
Chïshyë'=Apache.
Chiskaot, Chiskiack=Chiskiac.
Chis-le-rah=Talal.
Chismal=Chinatu.
Chisnedinadinaye=Chiltneyadnaye.
Chissenossick=Chiconessex.
Chit-ah-hut=Klikitat.
Chitashuak=Sitnazuak.
Chit-at-hut=Klikitat.
Chitchakos=Chechawkose.
Chit-che-ah=Chitsa.
Chit-co, Chitcoes=Chetco.
Chititi=Chilili.
Chitko=Chetco.
Chit-les-sen-ten=Chetleschantunne.
Chitl-kawt=Chilkat.
Chitnashuak=Sitnazuak.
Chit-o-won-e-augh-gaw=Seneca.
Chitsah, Chit-sangh=Chitsa.
Chitwout Indians=Similkameen.
Chiugas=Cayuga.
Chivano-ki=Casa Grande.
Chí-vo-la=Zuñi.
Chiwalle=Huhliwahli.
Chixaxia=Chickasaw.
Chixoutimi=Chicoutimi.
Chiz-ches-che-nay=Tizsessinaye.
Chkituk=Skittok.
Chlach-ă-jĕk=Yakutat.
Chlă-wäk-kŏn=Klawak.
Chlen-ko-an hade=Klinkwan.
Chlukŏach-adi=Hlukahadi.
Chlul-chagu=Klughuggue.
Chóaenne=Cheyenne.
Choam-Cha di'-la Po'mo=Chomchadila.
Choan, Choanists=Chowanoc.
Cho-bah-áh-bish=Chobaabish.
Chobonakonkon, Chobone-Konhonom, Chobonokono-mum=Chabanakongkomun.
Chocataus=Choctaw.
Chocchuma=Chakchiuma.
Choccolocco=Chukahlako.
Choccomaws=Chakchiuma.
Chochité, Chochiti=Cochiti.
Choch-Katit=Siksika.
Chochocois=Shoshoko.
Chochones=Shoshoni.
Chockalocha, Chockalock=Chukahlako.
Chockechiatte=Chicuchatti.
Chocke-clucca, Chock-olock-o=Chukahlako.
Chockreletan=Chockrelatan.
Chocktaws=Choctaw.
Chocochattee=Chicuchatti.
Cho-co-men-as=Chukaimina.
Choco-nickla=Choconikla.
Cho-co-nish=Nez Percés.
Chocouyem=Chokuyem.
Choc-re-le-a-tan=Chockrelatan.
Chocta=Choctaw.
Choctah, Chocta-Muskhog=Muskhogean Family.
Choctaughs=Choctaw.
Choctaw Muskhogee=Muskhogean Family.
Choctos=Choctaw.
Chocuyem=Chokuyem.
Choemimnees=Choinimni.
Cho-e-nees=Choinok.
Cho-e-nem-nee, Cho-e-nim-ne, Cho-e-nim-nees=Choinimni.
Cho-e-nuco=Choinok.
Choe-wem-nes=Choinimni.
Chohomes=Tohome.
Cho-ho-nuts=Chunut.
Chohoptins=Nez Percés.
Choinóc, Choinook, Choi-nuck=Choinok.
Chóis=Zoe.
Choiska=Chusca.
Choiz=Zoe.
Chokchoomah=Chakchiuma.

Chokechatti=Chicuchatti.
Cho-ke-me-nes, Cho-ke-min-nah, Cho-kem-nies=Chukaimina.
Choke-tar-to-womb=Chokatowela.
Chokfaktoligamute, Chokfoktoleghagamiut=Shokfak.
Chokiamauves, Chokimauves, Chokimena, Cho-ki'-min-ah=Chukaimina.
Chokisgna=Chokishgna.
Chokitapia=Siksika.
Chokonni=Piñalenos.
Choktah, Choktaus, Choktaw=Choctaw.
Cho-ku-yen=Chokuyem.
Chola=Chula.
Cholctaus=Choctaw.
Cholobone=Cholovone.
Chomanes, Chomans, Chomenes=Tawehash.
Chomok, Chomok-Spayam=Tzauamuk.
Chomoncouanistes, Chomonehouanistes=Chomonchouaniste.
Chomontakali=Chomontokali.
Chonanons=Shawnee.
Chonchaes=Chonque.
Chongaskabes=Chongasketon.
Chongas Kabi=Sisseton.
Chongaskabion=Chongasketon.
Chongaskaby=Sisseton.
Chongaskethon, Chongonsceton, Chongousceton=Chongasketon.
Chongue=Chonque.
Chonkasketonwan=Chongasketon.
Chonoghoheere=Canajoharie.
Chonondedeys=Tionontati.
Chonontouaronon=Seneca.
Chonsgaskaby=Chongasketon.
Chonukes=Chinook.
Chonuntoowaunees=Seneca.
Chooochanceys=Chukchansi.
Choogaks=Chugachigmiut.
Chook-chan-cie, Chook-chancy, Chook-cha-nee, Chook-chau-ces, Chook-chaw-ces, Chook-chuncy=Chukchansi.
Chook'heereso=Chucalissa.
Chookka Pharáah=Chukafalaya.
Choomedocs=Chumidok.
Choomteyas=Chumteya.
Choomuch=Chumuch.
Choomwits=Chumwit.
Choo-nemnes=Choinimni.
Choo-noot=Chunut.
Choot-chancers=Chukchansi.
Chopannish=Nez Percés.
Chopees=Chupcan.
Chopemnish, Choponiesh, Choponish, Choponnesh=Nez Percés.
Chópï-hánoch=Tyupi.
Choponsca=Chepoussa.
Choptico, Chopticons=Chapticon.
Chopunish, Chopunmohees, Chopunnish=Nez Percés.
Choquata=Echota.
Choquichoumans=Chakchiuma.
Chora=Cora.
Chorakis=Cherokee.
Chorchake=Corchaug.
Chori=Tsurau.
Choro=Chosro.
Chorouachas=Chaouacha.
Choruico=Chorruco.
Chorzh, Chórzh-ñamu=Chosro.
Chō'sha=Taensa.
Chösh'ka=Soshka.
Cho-shon-nê=Shoshoni.
Chota=Cora, Echota.
Cho-tan-o-man-as=Shutaunomanok.
Chote, Chote great=Echota.
Chotok-saufk=Chatoksofke.
Chouacas, Chouachas=Chaouacha.
Chouacoët=Sokoki.
Chouactas=Choctaw.
Chouala=Cheraw.
Chouanongs, Chouanons, Chouanous=Shawnee.
Chouchillas, Chouchille, Chou-chill-ies=Chowchilla.
Chouchoumas=Chakchiuma.
Chouenons, Chouesnons=Shawnee.
Chougaskabees, Chougasketon=Chongasketon.
Choula=Chula.
Chouman, Choumanes, Choümans, Choumay, Choumenes=Tawehash.

Chouontouaroüon=Seneca.
Chovala=Cheraw.
Chowah, Chowan, Chowane, Chowanoake, Chowa-
nocs, Chowanok, Chowanooke=Chowanoc.
Chow-chi-liers, Chow-chillas, Chow-chille, Chow-
chill-ies, Chowclas=Chowchilla.
Chowees=Chaui.
Chow-e-nim-ne=Choinimni.
Chowockolo, Chowocolo=Sawokli.
Chowou=Chowanoc.
Choya=Coya.
Chrátka-āri=Katkaayi.
Chrēlch-kŏn=Hehlkoan.
Chrelejan=Sulujane.
Chreokees=Cherokee.
Christaneaux, Christenaux, Christeneaux, Chris'-
te-no, Christenois, Christianaux, Christianeaux=
Cree.
Christian Indians=Christanna Indians, Mora-
vians, Pueblos.
Christianux, Christinaux, Christineaux, Christinos,
Christinou=Cree.
Christobal, Christoval=San Cristóbal.
Chritenoes=Cree.
Chualpays=Colville.
Chuanoes=Shawnee.
Chu-cha-cas, Chu-cha-chas=Keresan Family.
Chuchuqualk=Chuckchuqualk.
Chuchuwayha=Chuchunayha.
Chuckehalins=Chukchansi.
Chucklin=Chucktin.
Chucknutts=Chugnut.
Chu'-em-duk=Chuemdu.
Chuga, Chugach, Chugach'ig-mut, Chugachimute,
Chugackimute=Chugachigmiut.
Chugants=Chugnut.
Chugatch=Chugachigmiut.
Chughnot, Chughnuts, Chugnues=Chugnut.
Chuijugers=Cayuga.
Chuka'lako=Chukahlako.
Chukaws=Choctaw.
Chukchagemiut=Chnagmiut.
Chuk-chan'-cy=Chukchansi.
Chukchuk=Chukchagemiut.
Chukchukualk, Chuk-chu-quaeh-u, Chukchuqualk=
Chuckchuqualk.
Chu-ke-chan-se=Chukchansi.
Chukesws=Chickasaw.
Chŭklŭ'k-mut, Chukohukomute=Yuit.
Chuku-chatta=Chicuchatti.
Chŭ'-lä=Tsulalgi.
Chulajam, Chulajame=Sulujame.
Chulpun=Khulpuni.
Chuluaam=Sulujame.
Chulukki=Cherokee.
Chu-mai-a=Yukian Family.
Chumakums=Chimakum.
Chu-mâ'-wa=Chumawi.
Chumeto=Chumteya.
Chu'-mi-dok=Chumuchu.
Chum-te'-ya=Chumteya.
Chūna-kŏn=Huna.
Chunemmes=Choinimni.
Chunky=Chunkey, Chunkey Chitto.
Chunnapuns=Chimnapum.
Chunoiyana=Atsugewi.
Chunute=Chunut.
Chuoanous=Shawnee.
Chupumnes=Chupumni.
Churchers=Praying Indians.
Chuse=Achusi.
Chuskee Tallafau=Chiskatalofa.
Chu-su-te=Chunut.
Chŭts-ta-kŏn=Hutsnuwu.
Chuttusgelis=Nuestra Señora de la Soledad.
Chutukivahia=Poso Verde.
Chutznou=Hutsnuwu.
Chu-ui-chu-pa=Cuchuta.
Chuwon=Chowanoc.
Chwachamaju, Chwachmaja=Khwakhamaiu.
Chyanahue, Chyanaue=Kechipauan.
Chyannes, Chyans, Chyennes=Cheyenne.
Chym-nâh'-pos, Chymnapoms, Chymnapums=Chim-
napum.
Chymseyans=Chimmesyan Family.
Chymshean Nation=Tsimshian.
Chynnes=Cheyenne.
Chyppewan=Chipewyan.
Chyugas=Cayuga.

Ciaguan=Siaguan.
Ciā'mēctix'=Seamysty.
Ciawis=Kiowa.
Cïbaiigạn=Cheboygan.
Cibala=Zuñi.
Cibaleta, Cibaletta=Cebolleta.
Ciba-riches=Seuvarits.
Cibola=Hawikuh, Zuñi.
Cibolæ, Cibolal, Cibolan Indians, Cibolans, Cibo'a
Zuñi, Cibole=Zuñi.
Ciboletta=Cebolleta.
Cibolians=Zuñi.
Cibolleta, Cibolletta=Cebolleta.
Cibolos, Cibora=Zuñi.
Cicaca=Chickasaw.
Cicai'ōQoi=Shishaiokoi.
Ci-câ'-lâp=Shishalap.
Cicauit=Cicacut.
Ci-câwc-ku-i=Sisjulcioy.
Cice=Sia.
Ci-cho-mo-oi, Cichomovi=Sichomovi.
Ci'cïn-xau'=Salmon River Indians.
Cic-lâ-mâ'u=Shishlamaw.
Cicoua=Pecos.
Ci-cta'-qwŭt-me' ɹûnnĕ=Umpqua.
Cicui, Cicuio, Cicuica, Cicuich, Cicuick, Cicuie
Cicuio, Cicuiq, Cicuique, Cicüya, Cicuyan, Cicuyé
Cicuyo=Pecos.
Ci-dá-hetc=Asidahech.
Cieligees=Kailaidshi.
Ciénega de Carabajal=Cienega.
Cienegui=Cieneguilla.
Cieneguilla=Cienega.
Cieneguita=Cashwah.
Cígom=Shigom.
Cijame=Sijame.
Cikaga=Chickasaw.
Cikcitcela=Shikshichela.
Cikcitcena=Shikshichena.
Ɵildjèhi=Thildzhehi.
CilEk'uā'tl=Shilekuatl.
Cileños=Gila Apache.
Cilla=Sia.
Ciloba=Zuñi.
Cilos=Pueblo de los Silos.
Cĭl-qó-ɹoi=Shilkhotshi.
Cil-tar-den=Tsiltaden.
Ci-mi-i=Simi.
Ci-mo-pave, Ci-mó-pa-vi, Ci-motk-pivi=Shongopovi
Cinago=Sinago.
Cinaloa=Cahita, Sinaloa, Yaqui.
Cina-luta-oiⁿ=Shinalutaoin.
Cinco Señores Busanic=Busanic.
Cinecú=Senecu del Sur.
Cinega=Cienega.
Cinelas=Conestoga.
Cingpoils=Sanpoil.
Ciniques, Cinnakee, Cinnigos=Seneca.
Cinola=Zuñi.
Cinoquipe=Sinoquipe.
Cintu-aluka=Comanche.
Cí'-nyu-mûh=Hopi.
Ci-o-hó-pa=Cheokhba.
Ciou, Cioux=Dakota.
Cipaulire, Ci-pau'-lo-vi=Shipaulovi.
Cipias=Tsipiakwe.
Cipoliva, Ci-pow-lovi=Shipaulovi.
Ciq!Eˈldaptix=Shikeldaptikh.
Ciquique=Pecos.
Circe=Sarsi.
Circuic=Pecos.
Cisca=Chisca.
Cisquiouws=Karok.
Cissitons=Sisseton.
Ci'-stă kqwŭs'-tă, Ci'-stă qwûs'-ta ɹûnnĕ=Chasta
costa.
Ci-sta -qwŭt=Umpqua.
Ci-sta'-qwût-mê ɹûnnĕ'=Knitsh.
Ci'-stă-qwût-ni'-li t'ɕat' ɹûnnĕ=Nahankhuotane
Cistocoote=Chastacosta.
Citasees=Atasi.
Citcumave, Ci-tcum-wi=Sichomovi.
Cithinistinees=Cree.
Citico=Sitiku.
Ciuola=Zuñi.
Ci'-u-wá-ŭk=Shiuwauk.
Civano Ki, Ci-vano-Qi=Casa Grande.
Civilized Farmers=Farmers' band.
Civola, Civoli, Civona=Zuñi.

Ci'-wa-nü wüñ-wü=Shiwanu.
Ciwere=Chiwere.
Ci'-wi-na-kwin, Ci'-wo-na=Zuñi.
Ȼixida=Dhighida.
Ciya=Sia.
Ciyo-subula=Shiyosubula.
Ciyo-tañka=Shiyotanka.
Ckac'-tûn=Shkashtun.
Ckíȼi, Ckíyi=Skidi.
C'küet=Shkuet.
Cküö'kEm=Shkuokem.
Ckūtc=Shkutch.
Ȼkwă-rí-rän=Toryohne.
Cla=Sia.
Clackamas, Clackamis, Clackamos, Clackamurs, Clack-a-mus, Clackanurs, Clackarners=Clackama.
Clacks-star, Clackstar, Clackster=Tlatskanai.
Cladsaps=Clatsop.
Clah-in-nata=Claninnatas.
Clahnahquah=Clahnaquah.
Claiakwat=Clayoquot.
Claikahak, Claikahakamut=Chnagmiut.
Claikehakamut=Claikehak.
Clakamus, Clakemas=Clackama.
Clalams=Clallam.
C'lä'lkī=Shlalki.
Ȼlăl'-kqai-ŭn'-tĭk—Thlalkhaiuntik.
Clallems=Clallam.
Clal-lu-i-is=Tlaaluis.
Clal-lums=Clallam.
Clamakum=Chimakum.
Clam-aths=Klamath.
Clamcoets=Karankawa.
Clamets=Klamath, Lutuamian Family.
Clam-nah-min-na-mun=Kathlaminimin.
Clamoctomichs, Cla-moc-to-mick's, Cla-moi-to-micks, Clamoitomish, Clamoitonnish=Klumaitumsh.
Clamore=Santsukdh.
Clamouths, Clamuth, Clamuts=Klamath.
Clanaminamums, Clanaminanums=Kathlaminimin.
Clanimatas=Claninnatas.
Clannahminamun=Kathlaminamin.
Clan-nah-quah, Clan-nah-queh's Tribe of Moltno-mah's=Clahnaquah.
Clan-nar-min-a-mon's, Clannarminimuns, Clan-nar-min-na-mon, Clannarminnamuns=Kathlamini-min.
Clan-utsh-la=Hlauhla.
Clao-qu-aht=Clayoquot.
Clap-sott=Clatsop.
Clarkamees, Clarkames, Clarkamos, Clarkamus=Clackama.
Clasaps=Clatsop.
Claskanio, Class-can-eye-ah=Tlatskanai.
Classet=Makah.
Classops, Clastope=Clatsop.
Clatacamin=Tlatskanai.
Ȼla'-tcaus=Thlachaus.
Clat-sa-canin, Clatsaconin—Tlatskanai.
Clatsaps=Clatsop.
Clatset=Makah.
Clatstoni=Tlatskanai.
Clatstops, Clatsup=Clatsop.
Claucuad=Clayoquot.
Claugh-E-wall-hah=Clowwewalla.
Claushavn=Claushaven.
Claw-et-sus=Tlauitsis.
Claxtar, Clax-ter=Tlatskanai.
Clayhoosh=Clahoose.
Clayoquotoch=Clayoquot.
Cleewallees=Huhliwahli.
Cle-Hure, Cle-Huse=Clahoose.
Ȼlĕl'-qûs=Thlelkhus.
Clemaks=Tillamook.
Clemclemalets, Clem-clem-a-lits=Clemclemalats.
Clennuse=Tlanusiyi.
Clermont's band, Clermo's band=Santsukdhin.
Cleu wathta=Huhliwahli.
Clew=Kloo.
Clewalla, Clewauley, Clewauleys, Clewella, Cle-wulla, Cleyali=Huhliwahli.
Click-a-hut, Clickatat, Clicketats, Clickitats=Kli-kitat.
Clickquamish=Cloquallum.
Clict-ars, Clic-tass=Clickass.
Clikatats=Klikitat.
Climath=Klamath.
Ȼli-nai'-ctĭk=Thlinaitshtik.
Clin'-ar-pan=Tzlanapah.

Clingats=Tlingit.
Clintinos=Cree.
Clinton=Pilteuk.
Clipalines=Shipaulovi.
Clishhooks=Cushook.
Clistenos, Clistinos=Cree.
Ȼlka'qaik=Thlekakhaik.
Ȼlkû'-aus=Thlekuaus.
Ȼlku-ca'-ŭk=Thlekushauk.
Ȼlkū'-hwe-yŭk'=Thlekuhweyuk.
Ȼlkwan'ti-ya'ʒûnnĕ'=Thlkwantiyatunne.
Ȼlkwi-yau'-ĭk=Thlekwiyauik.
Clockstar=Tlatskanai.
Clo-kar-da-ki-ein=Klokadakaydn.
Clokwon=Klukwan.
Cloo=Kloo.
Clossets=Makah.
Clotsops=Clatsop.
Cloud man's band=Makhpiyawichashta.
Cloud River Indians=Winimem.
Clough-e-wal-lah, Clough-e-wall-hah=Clowwe-walla.
Clowetoos, Clow et sus=Tlauitsis.
Clowewallas=Clowwewalla.
Ȼltc'a-rxi-li-i-tun, Ȼltc'a-rxi'-li-i' ʒûnné=Chockrela-tan.
Ȼlti'-ai-äm'-îlȼ kqu-wai'-hu=Khuwaius.
Ȼlts'us-me', Ȼlts'ûs-me' ʒûnnĕ'=Thltsusmetunne.
Ȼluale=Huhliwahli.
Club Indians=Yuma.
Clukemus=Clackama.
Ȼlu-kwi-u-tc'ȼu'=Thlukwiutshthu.
Ȼlulwarp=Shuswap.
Clunsus=Ntlakyapamuk.
Clymclymalats=Clemclemalats.
Clyoquot, Clyquots=Clayoquot.
Cneis=Caddo.
Cnistineaux=Cree.
Cnongasgaba=Chongasketon.
C'npâ'=Snapa.
C'nta'k'tl=Sintaktl.
Coahuanas=Cajuenche.
Coahuilas=Kawia.
Coahuilteco=Coahuiltecan.
Coajata=Cojate.
Coaksett=Coaxet.
Coana=Coama.
Co-a-ni-nis=Havasupai.
Coaqueria=Kiakima.
Coaquis=Coaque.
Coarac=Quarai.
Coashatay, Coashatta, Coassatlis=Koasati.
Coast Crees=Maskegon.
Coast Indians, Coastmen=Costanos.
Coata=San Andrés Coata.
Coatlik=Kotlik.
Cobajais, Cobaji=Kawaiisu.
Ȼo'bajnaàj, Co'bajnaàji=Thobazhnaazhi.
Cobanes=Kohani.
Cobb Indians=Hopahka Choctaw.
Cobboseecontee=Cabbasagunties.
Cobota=Cojate.
Coȼa=Kusa.
Cocamaricopa=Maricopa.
Coȼao=Coosa.
Cocapa=Cocopa.
Coc-co-man=Kokaman.
Cochaly=Cochali.
Cochatties=Koasati.
Cochees=Cochise Apache.
Cocheli=Cochiti.
Cochenawagoes=Caughnawaga.
Co-che-ta-cah, Cochetakers, Co-che-te-ka=Kotsoteka
Cocheti, Cocheto=Cochiti.
Cochiemes=Cochimi.
Cochilis=Cochiti.
Cochimas, Cochime, Cochimíes, Cochimy=Cochimi.
Cochineans=Havasupai.
Cochini=Cochimi.
Cochit, Cochite, Co-chi-te-mi', Cochiteños, Cochitinos, Cochito, Cochitti, Cochity=Cochiti.
Cochnawagah, Cochnewagos, Cocknewakee=Caugh-nawaga.
Cochnewwasroonaw=Conoy.
Cochnichnos=Havasupai.
Cochnowagoes=Caughnawaga.
Cochopas=Cocopa.
Ȼo'ȼïtcìni=Thoditshini.

Cocknawagas, Cocknawagees, Cocknewagos=Caughnawaga.
Cock-o-mans, Coc-ko-nan=Kokaman.
Cocluti=Cochiti.
Coco=Acoma.
Co'ɸokòⁿji=Thodhokongzhi.
Cocomarecopper, Cocomari, Cocomaricopas, Cocomarisepas, Cocomiracopas=Maricopa.
Coco Mongo=Cucomonga.
Co-con-cah-ras=Cocoueahra.
Coçoninos=Havasupai.
Co-co-pah=Cocopa.
Cocorún=Cocori.
Cocospara=Cocospera.
Cocuiarachi=Cuquiarachi.
Coddoque, Codogdachos=Kadohadacho.
Codtanmut=Cataumut.
Coehnawaghas=Caughnawaga.
Goeni=Caddo.
Coenossoeny=Iroquois.
Coespan=Cocospera.
Cœur and Alenes, Cœur d'Aléne, Cœur d'Eleine, Cœur d'Eliene, Cœur d'Eline, Cœur d'Helene, Cœurs d'Aleine, Cœurs d'Alênes, Cœurs-d'aliene, Cœurs d'Helene, Cœurs-pointus=Skitswish.
Cofa=Ocute.
Cofachiqui=Cofitachiqui.
Cofachis=Cofaqui.
Cofaciqui, Cofetaçque=Cofitachiqui.
Cofetalaya, Coffadeliah=Kaffetalaya.
Cofitachyque=Cofitachiqui.
Cofoque=Cofaqui.
Coghnawagees, Coghnawages, Coghnawagoes, Coghnawayees, Coghnewagoes, Cognahwaghan, Cognawagees, Cognawago=Caughnawaga.
Coguifa=Kawia.
Cohainihoua, Cohainotoas=Cahinnio.
Cohakias, Cohakies=Cahokia.
Cohanat=Cohannet.
Cohannies=Kohani.
Cohâssiac=Coosuc.
Cohias=Cohes.
Cohila Apache=Chiricahua.
Cohnana=Cajuenche.
Cohnawaga, Cohnawagey, Cohnawahgans, Cohnewago=Caughnawaga.
Cohoninos=Havasupai.
Cohuana=Cajuenche.
Cohuillas, Cohuilles=Kawia.
Cohunewagus, Cohunnawgoes, Cohunnegagoes, Cohunnewagoes=Caughnawaga.
Cohuntas=Kawita.
Cohu wiñwû, Co-hü wüñ-wû=Shohu.
Coiacohanauke=Quioucohanoc.
Coiaheguxes=Coyabegux.
Coiatee=Coyatee.
Coiegues=Cayuga.
Coiencahes=Karankawa.
Coiras=Koroa.
Coitch=Panamint.
Cojages=Cayuga.
Cojnino=Havasupai.
Cojoges=Cayuga.
Cojonina=Havasupai.
Cojota=Cojate.
Cojuenchis=Cajuenche.
Cojuklesatuch=Uchucklesit.
Coka-towela=Chokatowela.
Co'-ke=Shoke.
Cokes=Coaques.
Cokesit=Coaxet.
Cok-ka-mans=Kokaman.
Cokomaricopas=Maricopa.
Colabazas=Calabazas.
Colapessas, Colapissas=Acolapissa.
Colcharney=Kulchana.
Colchattas=Koasati.
Colching=Kulchana.
Colcins=Colcene.
Cold Spring Village=Deyohnegano.
Coldwater=Ntstlatko.
Colela=Shipapulima.
Colemmys=Kulumi.
Colespelin, Colespells=Kalispel.
Coligua, Colima=Coligoa.
Colimies=Cochimi.
Colipasa=Acolapissa.
Collamee=Kulumi.
Colla-pissas=Acolapissa.

Col-lap-poh-yea-ass=Calapooya.
Colloteros=Coyoteros.
Collville=Colville.
Coloa=Koroa.
Coloclan=Colotlan.
Coloco=Estocoloco.
Colomas=Koloma.
Colomga, Colomiesk=Kulumi.
Coloosas=Calusa.
Colooshatchie=Calusahatchi.
Colorado=Pueblo Colorado, Pueblo Pintado.
Colouse=Korusi.
Colseed=Colcene.
Coltog=Kaltag.
Coltshanie=Kulchana.
Columbia Lakes=Akiskenukinik.
Columbias=Sinkiuse.
Colusa, Colusi Indians=Korusi.
Co-mái-yàh=Comeya.
Comances, Comancha, Comanchees, Comanchero, Comanchos, Comandes, Comandus=Comanche.
Comaniopa=Maricopa.
Comanshima, Comantz=Comanche.
Comaricopas=Maricopa.
Comassakumkanit=Herring Pond.
Comauch=Comanche.
Comea-kin=Comiakin.
Comecrudos=Carrizos.
Comedás=Comeya.
Come Pescado=Timpaiavats.
Cometrudos, Cometudos=Comecrudo.
Comiaken=Comiakin.
Cominas, Cominos=Havasupai.
Comitría=Camitria.
Commagsheak=Comox.
Communipau=Communipaw.
Comondú=San José de Comondu.
Comoripa=Cumuripa.
Co-moux=Comox.
Co-mo-yah, Comoyàtz, Comoyeé, Co-mo-yei=Comeya.
Comshewars=Cumshewa.
Comupas=Cumpus.
Comupaví=Shongopovi.
Comuripa=Cumuripa.
Comuxes=Comox.
Conachitow=Couechitou.
Conadasaga, Conadasego=Canadasaga.
Conaghsadagas=Oka.
Conagohary, Conajoharees, Conajohary, Conajorha=Canajoharie.
Conarie See, Conarise, Conarsie=Canarsee.
Conasadagah, Conasadago, Conasadauga=Oka.
Conastagoe=Conestoga.
Conastee=Kanastuni.
Conastoga, Conastoge, Conastogy=Conestoga.
Conawaghrunas=Caughnawaga.
Conawago=Connewango.
Conaway Crunas=Caughnawaga.
Concabe=Moenkapi.
Concee=Lipan.
Concepcion=Tomé.
Concepcion Babiacora, Concepcion Babicora=Babiacora.
Concepcion Caborca=Caborca.
Concepcion Cuirimpo=Cuirimpo.
Concepcion de Aguico=Hawikuh.
Concepcion de Alona=Halona.
Concepcion de Caborca, Concepcion del Cabetca, Concepcion del Caborca, Concepcion del Cabotea=Caborca.
Concepcion de Quarac=Quarra.
Concepcion Mobas=Movas.
Conception=Ossossane.
Conception del Ukitoa=Oquitoa.
Conchacs, Conchaes, Conchakus=Conshac.
Conchanteti, Conchanti=Kanchati.
Conchaptimicco's town=Conchartimicco's town
Conchaques=Conshac, Koasati.
Conchartree=Kanchati.
Conchas=Conshac.
Conchatas=Koasati.
Conchatez=Conshac, Koasati.
Conchattas=Koasati.
Conchos=Conshac.
Conchttas—Koasati.
Con-Con's, Con-Cous, Con-Cow=Konkau.
Conday=Kendaia.
Conecare=Conicari.
Conejaghera=Conejoholo.

Coneliskes=Cowlitz.
Conerd Helene=Skitswish.
Conessetagoes, Conestauga=Oka.
Conestego, Conestogo, Conestogue=Conestoga.
Coneta, Conetta, Conetuhs=Kawita.
Conewango=Connewango.
Conewaugus=Ganawagus.
Coneyat=Conneaut.
Confederate Indians, Confederate Nations, Confederates=Iroquois.
Congares, Congerees, Congeres=Congaree.
Conge-wee-cha-cha=Congewichacha.
Congree=Congaree.
Conguses=Cayuse.
Conicare=Conicari.
Conijoharre=Canajoharie.
Coninas—Havasupai.
Conissadawga=Oka.
Conistogas=Conestoga.
Conittekooks=Connecticut.
Conkaske-tonwan=Chongasketon.
Connadasaga, Connadasego, Connadesago, Connagasago=Canadasaga.
Connajohary=Canajoharie.
Connamox=Coree.
Connasedagoes=Oka.
Connastago=Conestoga.
Connays=Conoy.
Connecedaga, Connecedegas=Oka.
Connectacuts=Connecticut.
Connefedagoes=Oka.
Connegticuts=Connecticut.
Connejories=Canajoharie.
Conneogie=Connewango.
Conneross=Conoross.
Connesedagoes=Oka.
Connestigunes=Canastigaone.
Conneuaghs=Tahltan.
Connewangoes=Connewango.
Conninggahaughgaugh=Mohawk.
Conninos=Havasupai.
Con-no-harrie-go-harrie=Onoalagona.
Connojohary=Canajoharie.
Connondaguah=Canandaigua.
Connosedagoes, Connosidagoes, Connossedage=Oka.
Connoye, Connoys=Conoy.
Connughhariegughharie=Onoalagona.
Conoatinos=Kanohatino.
Conodosago=Canadasaga.
Conoies, Conois=Conoy.
Conojahary, Conojoharie=Canajoharie.
Conostogas=Conestoga.
Conowaroghere=Ganowarohare.
Conoy-uch-such, Conoyucksuchroona=Conoy.
Conqerees=Congaree.
Conshachs=Conshac.
Conshacs, Conshaes=Koasati.
Conshakis=Conshac.
Conshaques=Concha.
Conshattas=Koasati.
Contah-nah=Cotechney.
Contamis=Kutenai.
Contareia, Contarrea=Contarea.
Contaubas=Catawba.
Contenay=Kutenai.
Contla=Santa Cruz.
Contonnés=Kutenai.
Contznoos=Hutsnuwu.
Conwahago=Caughnawaga.
Conyat=Conneaut.
Cooca=Kusa.
Coochchotellica, Cooch-cho-teth-ca, Coocheetakas=Kotsoteka.
Coochocking=Coshocton.
Coo-er-ee=Kuyuidika.
Coofer, Coofert=Puaray.
Cookchaneys=Chuchansi.
Cookkoooose, Cookkoo-oosee, Cookoose=Coos.
Coolamies=Kulumi.
Coolmehs=Yiikulme.
Coolome, Coolooma, Coo-loo-me, Cooloomee=Kulumi.
Cools-on-tick-ara=Kotsoteka.
Coomine=Kumaini.
Coon=Mikaunikashinga.
Coopanes=Kopano.
Coopspellar=Kalispel.
Coos=Coosuc.
Coosa=Coosha, Kusa.
Coosadas=Koasati.

Coosada Sackla Loosa=Suktaloosa.
Coosada Village=Coosada.
Coosades, Coosadis=Koasati.
Coosah=Coosa.
Coosahatches=Coosahatchi.
Coosahs=Coosha.
Coosak Baloagtaw=Concha.
Coosak hattak=Coosakhattakfalaya.
Coosas=Coos.
Coosatis=Koasati.
Coo-sau=Kusa.
Coosauda, Coo-sau-dee=Koasati.
Coosaw=Coosa, Kusa.
Coosawatee, Coosawaytee=Cusawatee.
Coosawda, Coosawda's, Coosawder=Koasati.
Coos Bay, Co-ose, Coose Bay=Coos.
Coosee=Kusa.
Cooses, Coose Taylors=Coos.
Cooshacking=Coshocton.
Chooshates, Cooshatties, Coosidas=Koasati.
Coosis=Kusa.
Coospellar=Kalispel.
Coosucks=Coosuc.
Coos Village=Melukitz.
Cootanais=Kutenai.
Cootanie=Kitunahan Family.
Cootanies, Cootneys, Cootomies, Cootonaikoon, Cootonais, Cootonay, Cootounies=Kutenai.
Cootstooks pai tah pee=Salish.
Coowarsartdas, Coowertsortda=Koasati.
Cooxet, Cooxitt=Coaxet.
Cooyoko=Shooyoko.
Cooyuweeweit=Kuyuidika.
Copanes=Kopano, Kohani.
Copas=Creeks.
Copatta=Quapaw.
Copiala=Shipapulima.
Copper=Tatsanottine, Tsattine.
Copper Eskimo=Kidnelik.
Copper Indians=Ahtena, Tatsanottine.
Copper-Mine=Tatsanottine.
Coppermine Apaches=Mimbreños.
Coppermine Indians=Gileños.
Copper River Indians=Ahtena.
Cops=Tupo.
Çò'qani=Thokhani.
Co-qua-piet=Koquapilt.
Coquell=Mishikhwutmetunne.
Coquet-lane, Coquetlum, Coquilain=Coquitlam.
Coquill, Coquilla=Mishikhwutmetunne.
Coquille=Mishikhwutmetunne, Mulluk, Nasumi.
Coquilths=Kwakiutl.
Coquimas, Coquimo=Kiakima.
Coquins=Tututni.
Coquitlan, Coquit-lane, Coquitlum=Coquitlam.
Coquitt=Coaxet.
Coquopiet, Coquopilt=Koquapilt.
Coraçones=Corazones.
Coramine=Coree.
Coran-canas=Karankawa.
Coranine=Coree.
Corankoua=Karankawa.
Coras=Nevome.
Cor-a-tem=Kworatem.
Corbeaus, Corbeaux=Crows.
Corcargonell=Coreorgonel.
Corchongs, Corchougs=Corchaug.
Cores=Coree.
Corimpo=Cuirimpo.
Corn Eaters=Arikara.
Corneille=Amahami.
Corn House=Tukhtukagi.
Corn Peoples=Zuñi.
Cornplanter's Town=Connewango.
Cornwalls=Stlaz.
Coroa, Coroha, Corois=Koroa.
Coro Marikopa=Maricopa.
Coronkawa, Coronks=Karankawa.
Corpus Christi de Isleta=Isleta del Sur.
Corroas, Corrois, Corroys=Koroa.
Corsaboys=Cusabo.
Corsas=Kusa.
Corusies=Korusi.
Corvesets=Coweset.
Cor-village=Core.
Cosa=Kusa.
Cosah tribe=Coosa.
Cosatomy=Kushetunne.
Coschotghta=Kotsoteka.

Coscosky=Kuskuski.
Coscospera=Cocospera.
Cosemenes=Cosumni.
Coshattas=Koasati, Muskhogean Family.
Coshattees, Coshatties=Koasati.
Coshockton=Coshocton.
Cosispa=Kasispa.
Cosnina, Cosninos=Havasupai.
Co-soott-hen-ten=Kwusathlkhuntunne.
Cosos=Kassovo.
Cosotoul=Kwusathlkhuntunne.
Cossa=Kusa.
Costa=Coste.
Costanoes=Costanos.
Cos-tche-tegh-kas, Costcheteghta Comanches=Kotsoteka.
Costehe=Coste.
Costeloga=Custaloga's Town.
Costeño=Costanos.
Costrowers=Kassovo.
Cosulhentan, Cosulhenten=Kwusathlkhuntunne.
Cosumnes, Cosumnies=Cosumni.
Cosutheuten, Co-sutt-heu-tun = Kwusathlkhuntunne.
Coswas=Kassovo.
Çō'tais=Thotais.
Cotam=Cotan.
Co-ta-plane-mis=Cotoplanemis.
Cotappos, Cotawpees=Catawba.
Ço'tcalsiçaya=Thochalsithaya.
Cotchita, Cotchiti=Cochiti.
Coteching, Cotechnees=Cotechney.
Côtes-de Chien=Thlingchadinne.
Cotobers=Catawba.
Cotones=Kutenai.
Cotshimi=Cochimi.
Ço̧'tsoni=Thotsoni.
Cottonois=Kutenai.
Cottonwood Banaks=Shohopanaiti.
Cottonwood ruin=Kokopki.
Cottonwoods=Daupom Wintun.
Cottonwood-Salmon-Eaters=Shohoaigakika.
Cotuhticut, Cotuhtikut=Titicut.
Coucha=Concha.
Cou-chan=Yuma.
Couchas=Concha.
Couchates=Koasati.
Cou-cows=Konkau.
Couer d'Alienes=Skitswish.
Couetchiou, Coue-tchitou=Couechitou.
Couetta=Kawita.
Couexi=Coosa.
Coughnawagas=Caughnawaga.
Couirimpo=Cuirimpo.
Couis=Caddo.
Couitias=Kawita.
Coujougas=Cayuga.
Coulapissas=Acolapissa.
Counarrha=Kutenai.
Counica=Tunica.
Coupe=Tsankupi.
Coupe-gorge=Dakota.
Coups de Fleches=Cheyenne.
Cour d'Aleine, Cour d'Alenes, Cour D'Aline, Cour De Lion=Skitswish.
Couroas, Courois=Koroa.
Courterrielles, Courtes Oreilles=Ottawa.
Cousas=Kusa.
Cousatee, Cousoudee=Koasati.
Coussa=Kusa.
Coussac, Coussati, Coussehaté=Koasati.
Coutah-wee-cha-cha=Kutawichasha.
Coutanies=Kitunahan Family, Kutenai.
Coutaria=Kutenai.
Couteaux=Ntlakyapamuk.
Couteaux-Jaunes=Tatsanottine.
Coutenay, Coutnees, Coutonais, Coutonois, Coutouns=Kutenai.
Couuachitóuu=Conchachitou.
Couueta=Kawita.
Covaji=Kawaiisu.
Cove-chances=Chukchansi.
Covera, Covero=Cubero.
Covilles=Colville.
Cowachitow=Couechitou.
Cow-ang-a-chem=Serranos.
Cowanneh=Kawanuyi.
Cowasacks, Cowassuck=Coosuc.
Cow Buffalo=Arukhwa.

Cowchillas=Chowchilla.
Cow-Cow=Konkau.
Cow Creek Indians, Cow Creeks, Cow Creek Umpquas=Nahankhuotane.
Cowe=Cowee.
Coweeta=Kawita.
Cowegans=Cowichan.
Coweitas=Kawita.
Cowela=Kawia.
Cowelits, Cowelitz, Cow-e-na-chino=Cowlitz.
Cowes=Coos.
Coweta, Cowetah, Cowetah Tallahassee, Cowetas, Cowetau, Cowetaw, Cowettas, Cow-e-tugh, Cow-e-tuh, Cow-e-tuh Tal-lau-has-see=Kawita.
Cowe-wa-chin=Cowichan.
Cowhuillas, Cowiahs=Kawia.
Cowichin=Cowichan.
Cowillas, Cow-illers=Kawia.
Cowitchens, Cowitchins=Cowichan.
Cowlitch, Cowlits, Cowlitsick, Cowlitsk=Cowlitz.
Cow Nation=Pueblos.
Cowwesets, Cowweseuck, Cowwesit=Coweset.
Cowwillas=Kawia.
Cow-ye-ka=Kawaiki.
Coxanes=Kohani.
Coxit=Coaxet.
Coyaheros=Coyoteros.
Coyamanque=Cuyamunque.
Coyatero=Coyoteros.
Co-ye-te=Koyeti.
Coyetero=Coyoteros.
Co-ye-tie=Koyeti.
Ço'yetlini=Thoyetlini.
Coyoleno, Coyotaro, Coyote, Coyotens=Coyoteros.
Coyote people=Stoam Ohimal.
Coyotero Apaches=Coyoteros.
Coyoteros=Pinal Coyotero.
Coyotes=Pachawal.
Coyougers, Coyouges=Cayuga.
Coyoukons=Koyukukhotana.
Coyovea=Cayovea.
Coystero=Coyoteros.
Coytee, Coytoy=Coyatee.
Co-Yukon=Koyukukhotana.
Cozao=Coosa.
Cozas=Kusa.
Cpa'ptsEn=Spatsum.
Cpu'zum=Spuzzum.
Cqague'=Skagway.
Çqa'neza',, Çqa'neza'ni=Thkhaneza.
Çqá'paha, Çqá'pahaçine=Thkhapaha.
Çqá'tcini=Thkhatshini.
CQokunQ=Shahanik.
Cq!ô'nana=Shkonana.
Crane gens=Petanenikashika.
Craw-fish band=Chakchiuma.
Craybe=Oraibi.
Cray Fish=Shakchukla.
Cree of the Lowland=Maskegon.
Cree of the Prairie=Paskwawininiwug.
Cree of the Woods=Sakawithiniwuk.
Crees of Moose Factory=Monsoni.
Crevas=Osage.
Cries, Criqs, Criques, Cris, Cristeneaux, Cristinaux, Cristineaux, Cristinos=Cree.
Cristobel=San Cristóbal.
Crists=Cree.
Croatoan=Croatan, Pamlico.
Crooton=Croatan.
Cross Point=Restigouche.
Cross Sound Indians=Huna.
Cross Village=Anamiewatigong.
Crossweeckes=Crossweeksung.
Crosswer=Cumshewa.
Crosweek=Crossweeksung.
Crow Feather, Crow feather band=Tashunkeota.
Crow Mockers Old Place=Crowmocker.
Crow People=Tutchonekutchin.
Crows=Kaka.
Cruel=Dakota.
Crus=Cree.
Cruzados=Yavapai.
Çtlc'a-rxi'-li-i'-tûn=Thlcharghiliitun.
Çū=Shu.
Cuabajai, Cuabajay=Serranos.
Cuâ-câ=Kua-kaa.
Cua-ka=San Marcos.
Cuakyina=Kwakina.
Cuames=Punames.

Cuampes=Cuampis.
Cŭa-pa=Kuapa.
Cuapas=Quapaw.
Cua P'Hoge, Cua-P'ho-o-ge, Cuâ-po-oge, Cua-Po-o-qué=Kuapooge.
Çuaque=Zuaque.
Cuarac, Cuaraí, Cuaray, Cuarrá, Cuarry=Quarai.
Cuartelejo=Quartelejo.
Cuatganes=Yuma.
Cubahatchee, Cube hatcha=Coosahatchi.
Cubic=Cubac.
Cucamungabit=Cucomonga.
Cucapa, Cucapachas, Cucassus=Cocopa.
Cuchañ, Cuchana, Cu-cha-no=Yuma.
Cuchanticas=Kotsoteka.
Cuchaus=Yuma.
Cuchiaga=Cuchiyaga.
Cuchian=Cuchillones, Yuma.
Cuchili=Cochiti.
Cuchillo=Paako.
Cuchimies=Cochimi.
Cuchin=Cochiti.
Cuchinu=Cochimi.
Cuchiyaga=Cuchiaga.
Cucompners=Cucoomphers.
Cucopa=Cocopa.
Cuctachas=Cushtusha.
Cuculutes=Cuculato.
Cu-cu-pahs=Cocopa.
Cucurpo=Cucurpe.
Cu-cu-tci=Shushuchi.
Cucuye=Pecos.
Cudeves=Eudeve.
Cuechunticas=Kotsoteka.
Cueganas=Yuma.
Cuelcajen-né=Guhlkainde.
Cuelóce, Cuelotetrey=Quelotetrey
Cuelpe=Walpi.
Cueres, Cuerez=Keresan Family, San Felipe de Cuerez.
Cuerrò=Quarai.
Cuesninas=Havasupai.
Cuhanas=Cajuenche, Cocopa.
Cuhtzuteca=Kotsoteka.
Cuichan=Yuma.
Cuimnapum=Chimnapum.
Cŭimp=Shuimp.
Cuismer, Cuisnurs=Havasupai.
Cuitoa=Cuitoat.
Cuiukguos=Cayuga.
Cuivira=Quivira.
Cuivres=Tatsanottine.
Cujanes, Cujanos=Kohani.
Cŭk'=Suk.
Cŭłané=Shuhlaŗan.
Culdoah=Kauldaw.
Culisnisna, Culisnurs=Havasupai.
Cull-oo-sau hat-che=Calusahatchi.
Culloumas, Cullowes=Kulumi.
Culsagee=Kulsetsiyi.
Culs-coupés=Kishkakon.
Cultalchulches=Cutalchiches.
Cŭlū'c=Tsulus.
Culul=Kulul.
Cumana=Cajuenche.
Cumanche, Cumancias=Comanche.
Cumanes=Punames.
Cum-ba-twas=Kumbatuash.
Cumeehes=Comanche.
Cumera, Cumero=Cumaro.
Cum-i-um-has, Cum-min-tahs=Cumumbah.
Cummoaquí, Cummooqui=Hopi.
Cumpas=Cumpus.
Cumpes=Cumumbah.
Cum-que-kis=Komkyutis.
Cumshawas, Cumshewes, Cumshuwaw=Cumshewa.
Cum-um-pahs=Cumumbah.
Cumupas=Cumpus.
Cuñai=Cuñeil.
Cunames, Cunanes=Punames.
Cuncaae=Caacat.
Cuneskapi=Nascapee.
Cunhates=Koasati.
Cunhutke=Ikanhatki.
Cuni=Zuñi.
Cŭn-iktceka=Shungikcheka.
Cun-i-um-hahs=Cumumbah.
Cŭñkaha-nap'iⁿ=Shungkahanapin.
Cuñka-yute-cni=Shungkayuteshni.

Cŭñꭗe íniꭒk'aciⁿá=Shunkeinikashina.
Cŭñk i-ki'-ka-ra'-tca-da, Cŭñk-tcañk' i-ki'-ka-ra'-tca-da=Shungikikarachada.
Cŭⁿmikase=Shomakoosa.
Cunnesedago=Canadasaga.
Cunniwagoes=Caughnawaga.
Cuñopavi=Shongopovi.
Cŭn'-taⁿce-we=Shuntanthewe.
Cŭn'-taⁿ-çka=Shuntanthka.
Cuⁿ'-taⁿquo-ꭧce=Shuntankhoche.
Cunyeel=Cuñeil.
Cuoerchitou=Couechitou.
Cuouex=Dakota.
Cûp=Shup.
Cupachas=Cocopa.
Cú-ɗauk=Shupauk.
Cuppunnaugunnit=Cuppunaugunnit.
Øuqe=Dhukhe.
Cuquiaratzi, Cuquiarichi, Cuquiurachi=Cuquiarachi.
Curancahuases=Karankawa.
Curas=Kusa.
Curinghóa=Cuirimpo.
Curois=Koroa.
Curtaka=Castake.
Curtoze-to-gah, Curtz-e-Ticker=Kotsoteka.
Cusabees=Cusabo.
Cusates=Kasihta.
Cusbabi=Cahuabi.
Cuscarawaoke=Cuscarawaoc.
Cuschcushke, Cuscuskie=Kuskuski.
Cuseta, Cusetahs, Cusetas=Kasihta.
Cusha=Coosha.
Cushans=Yuma.
Cushatees, Cushehtah=Koasati.
Cushetaes=Kasihta.
Cushhooks, Cushhouks=Cushook.
Cusihuirachic=Cusihuiriachic.
Cusitas, Cusitash=Kasihta.
Cuskarawaocks=Cuscarawaoc.
Cuskcaskking=Kuskuski.
Cuskœteh-waw-thesseetuck=Siksika.
Cuskuskus=Kuskuski.
Cussabos=Cusabo.
Cussadies=Koasati.
Cusseta, Cussetahs, Cussetas, Cussetau, Cussetaw Cus-se-tuh=Kasihta.
Cusshetaes=Koasati.
Cussitahs, Cussitos, Cussutas=Kasihta.
Custachas=Cushtusha.
Custalaga=Custaloga's Town.
Custasha=Custachas.
Custologa, Custologo=Custaloga's Town.
Custusha=Cushtusha.
Cususkey=Kuskuski.
Cutagamies=Foxes.
Cutahaco=Tutahaco.
Cutalches=Cutalchiches.
Cut Bank=Micacuopsiba.
Cut Beards=Pabaksa.
Cutcanas, Cutchanas=Yuma.
Cutchates=Koasati.
Cuteanas, Cutganas, Cutganes, Cutguanes=Yuma.
Cuthalchuches=Cutalchiches.
Cut heads=Pabaksa.
Cuthi Uskehaca=Cuthi Uckehaca.
Cuthlamuhs, Cuthlamuks=Cathlamet.
Cutifachiqui, Cuti'fiachiqua=Cofitachiqui.
Cutlashoots=Ootlashoot.
Cut Offs=Kiyuksa.
Cutsahnim, Cut-sa-nim, Cuts-sâh-nem, Cuts-sahnim=Yakima.
Cuttako=Kiowa Apache.
Cuttambas, Cuttawa=Catawba.
Cuttawomans=Cuttatawomen.
Cut-throats=Dakota.
Cut Wrists=Cheyenne.
Cuuames=Punames.
Cuunsiora=Gyusiwa.
Cuvarro=Cubero.
Cu-wa-la-cu=Shuwalacu.
Cuwà'lEçEt=Shuwalethet.
Cuwally=Huhliwahli.
Cuyahuga=Cayuga.
Cuyama=Kuyam.
Cuya Mangue, Cuyamanque, Cuyamenque, Cuyammique, Cuyamongo, Cuya-mun-ge, Cuyamungue=Cuyamunque.

Cuyanes=Kohani.
Cuyapipa, Cuyapipe=Cuiapaipa.
Cuybira=Quivira.
Cuyo, Monque=Cuyamunque.
Cuytoa=Cuitoat.
Cuyuse=Cayuse.
Cuzá=Quarai.
Cuzadans=Koasati.
Cuzans=Kusa.
Cuzayá=Quarai.
Cvñi=Zuñi.
Cwahago=Cayahoga.
Cwarenuock=Cawruuoc.
Cycuyo=Pecos.
Cyininook=Cree.
Cynagos=Sinago.
Cyneper, Cynikers=Seneca.
Cyotiero=Coyoteros.
Cypowais plunderers=Pillagers.
Cypoways=Chippewa.
Cyuse=Cayuse.

Dāᵃgelmáᵋn=Takelma.
Däbs'-tenā'=Etagottine.
Dacábimo=Navaho.
Dachi=Tachi.
D'Achiliny=Pawating.
Dacorta, Dacota=Dakota.
Dacota errans=Gens du Large.
Dacotah=Dakota.
Dacotan=Siouan Family.
Dacotas of the St Peter's=Santee.
Da-da'-ze ni'-ka-ciⁿ'-ga=Paiute.
Da-gä-e-ó-gä=Mohawk.
Daha-dinneh, Daha-dinnís, Dahâ-dtinné=Etagottine.
Da-ha-dumies=Etagottine.
Dahcotah, Dahcotas, Dahkota, Dah-ko-tah=Dakota.
Dahodinni, Daho-tena=Etagottine.
Daigano=Diegueño.
Daiyê'=Dyea.
Dakaz, Dakkadhæ, Dakkadhè=Tukkuthkutchin.
Däklá-wēti=Daktlawedi.
Dakoias, Dakotah=Dakota.
Dakotan=Siouan Family.
Dakotha=Dakota.
Dak'ts!āᵃmaláᵋ, Dak'ts!āᵃwanáᵋ=Klamath.
Dăkwâ'ĭ=Toquo.
Dałá=Tala.
Dalinchi=Talinchi.
Dalles, Dalls Indians=Dalles Indians.
Dalsalsàn=Tulsulsun.
Daminoia=Aminoya.
Dancer band=Genega's Band.
Dancers=Kawia.
Danda'gănû=Lookout Mountain Town.
Danè=Athapascan Family, Kaiyuhkhotana, Tsattine.
Danè Esclaves=Etchareottine.
Dā-něm-mě=Tanima.
Danites=Athapascan Family.
Danites Esclaves=Etchareottine.
Danoncaritaoui=Totiakton.
Danoska=Ohanhanska.
Danoχa=Danokha.
Danzarines=Kawia.
Dąq! awe'dî=Daktlawedi.
Darāzhazh=Pawnee.
Darcota, Darcotar, Dareotas=Dakota.
Dark Buffalo=Washabe.
Dasamanquepeio, Dasamanquepeuk, Dasamonpeack, Dasamonquepeio, Dasamoquepeuk, Dasamotiquepero=Dasamonquepeuc.
Dä'sha-i=Kadohadacho.
Dashiton=Deshuhittan.
Dashu=Deshu.
Dä-siɔ'-ja-hă-gä=Hangatanga.
Da'skigi'yĭ=Taskigi.
Da'skwĭtûñyi=Tusquittah.
Dassamonpeack, Dassamopoque=Dasamonquepeuc.
Datcho=Kadohadacho.
Da-thun'da=Tesinde.
Dātse'-aⁿ=Comanche.
Datŭmpa'ta=Kiowa.
Daudehokto=Totiakton.
Dau-pum Wintun=Daupom Wintun.
Dávaχo=Navaho.
David's People=Fetutlin.
Dawamish=Dwamish.

Dawaganhaes, Dawaganhas=Ontwaganha.
Dawhoot-dinneh=Etagottine.
Dawta=Dakota.
Daxē't=Dahet.
Dä-yó-de-hok'-to=Totiakton.
Dɔ̱ɜ-tú=Dhegiha.
Dead Man's Creek=Skichistan.
De-a-g͡hẽ'-ta=Dhighida.
Deagothee Loochoo=Tukkuthkutchin.
Deaguanes=Doguenes.
Decanohoge=Canienga.
De Chentes, De Chute river, De Chutes=Des Chutes.
De Corbeau=Crows.
Decu'=Deshu.
Decū'hĭt tān=Deshuhittan.
de Curbo=Crows.
De-d'á těné=Mishikhwutmetunne.
Deegothee=Tukkuthkutchin.
Deer=Itchualgi.
Deerfield Indians=Pocomtuck.
Deer (gens)=Chaikikarachada.
Deer Head=Tapa.
Deer Horn=Nageuktormiut.
Deerhorn mountaineers=Etechesottine.
Deewano=Twana.
Degathee Dinee, Degothees, Degothi-Kutchin=Tukkuthkutchin.
Deguenes=Doguenes.
Degutbee Dinees, Deguthee Dennee, Deguthee Dine, Deguthee Dinees=Tukkuthkutchin.
Déhkèwi=Kutchin.
De Ho Riss Kanadia=Coreorgonel.
Deis=Sandia.
DeKalb=Olitassa.
Dekanoagah=Conejoholo.
Dekanoge=Canienga.
Delamattanoos, Delamattenoos=Huron.
Delarof, Delarov=Unga.
Delawar, Delawaras, De Lawarrs, Delaways=Delaware.
Del Bajio=Bajio.
Del Caca=Caca Chimir.
Delcalsacat=Kokopki.
Del Charco=Charco.
Del Cojate=Cojate.
Del Cumero=Cumaro.
Deldjé, Deldzjé=Tontos.
Delemattanoes=Huron.
Delewares, Delewars, Deleways=Delaware.
Dellamattanoes=Huron.
Dél Llano=Llano.
Delmash=Mulluk.
Del Orroyo=Pueblo del Arroyo.
Del Pirique=Perigua.
Del Raton=Raton.
Del Teculote=Tecolote.
Dɔluas=Delaware.
Delwashes=Mulluk.
De-na-vi, De-na-ways=Tanima.
DEna'x'daᵋxᵘ=Tenaktak.
Dendjyé=Athapascan Family, Kutchin.
Dènè=Athapascan Family, Kawchodinne.
Dènè Couteaux-Jaunes=Tatsanottine.
Dènè des Montagnes-Rocheuses=Nahane.
Dènè-Dindjié=Athapascan Family.
Dene Etcha-Ottine=Etchaottine.
Deneh-Dindschieh=Athapascan Family.
Dènè of the Rocky Mountains=Montagnard.
Dènè Peaux-de-Lièvre=Kawchodinne.
Dènè Tchippewayans=Chipewyan.
Denighcariages=Amikwa.
Denondadies=Tionontati.
Denver Ute=Grand River Ute.
De-o'-de-sote=Deyodeshot.
Dɔónagäno=Deyohnegano.
Deonondade, Deonondadies=Tionontati.
Deononsadaga=Connewango.
De-o-nun'-dä-gä-a=Deyonongdadagana.
Dě'sa=Kadohadacho.
Děschĭttan=Deshuhittan.
Des Chute's River=Des Chutes.
Des Coupes=Cuts.
Deshoot=Des Chutes.
Deshtchin=Destchin.
Des-nèdhè-kkè-nadè=Desnedekenade.
Des-nèdhè-yaρè-l'Ottinè=Desnedeyarelottine.
Desonontage=Onondaga.
Des Puans=Winnebago.
Dessamonpeake, Dessamopeak=Dasamonquepeuc

Destsini=Theshtshini.
Desumanas=Tawehash.
Detame=Dotame.
Dé-tdóa=De.
Dĕtlk'oē'dē=Tahlkoedi.
Detseka'yaa=Arapaho.
Devil's medicine man band=Wakan.
Devil Town=Skeinah.
Dewagamas, Dewaganas=Ottawa.
Dewaganas=Ontwaganha, Ottawa.
De-wă-kă-nhă'=Chippewa.
Dewamish=Dwamish.
Dewoganna's=Chippewa, Ontwaganha.
Dexter=Chinik.
De-yo-noñ-dă-dä-gän'-ă=Deyonongdadagana.
Dĕys-hne-gă'-no=Deyohnegano.
Deyudehaakdoh=Totiakton.
Diabago=Tioga.
Diagano=Diegueño.
Diahago, Diahoga, Diahogo=Tioga.
Diegana, Diegeenos, Diegenes, Diegino, Diegmons, Dieguenos, Dieguinos, Dieguno=Diegueño.
Dienondades=Tionontati.
Digenes=Diegueño.
Diggers=Bannock, Hohandika, Paiute, Shoshoko, Uainuints.
Digger Ute=Ute.
Digothi, Digothi-kutchin=Tukkuthkutchin.
Di-go-thi-tdinné=Kutchin.
Díhit=Ponca.
Dildzéhi=Thilzhehi.
Dillewars=Delaware.
Dilwishne=Wishosk.
Dil-zha=Yavapai.
Dilzhăn=Tontos.
Dil-zhaý=Mohave, Tontos, Tulkepaia, Yuma.
Dinais=Athapascan Family.
Dindjié=Athapascan Family, Kutchin.
Dindjie Loucheux=Kutchin.
Dindjitch, Dinè=Athapascan Family.
Díné'=Navaho.
Dinnee, Dinneh, Dinni=Athapascan Family.
Dinondadies, Dinondodies=Tionontati.
Diogenes=Diegueño.
Dionnondadees, Dionondade, Dionondadies, Dionondadoes, Dionondages, Dionondes, Dionoudadie=Tionontati.
Dis-cheine'=Destchin.
Discovery Island (Indians)=Skingenes.
Disguino=Diegueño.
Diskádĕn=Tseskadin.
Diskatan=Ixcatan.
Ditt-pax=Oapars.
Diujuan=Yojuane.
Divided People=Kushapokla.
Dj'āaquĭg'it'ena'i=Djahui-gitinai.
Djāaquí'sk·uatl'adagāi=Djahui-skwahladagai.
Djalitason=New River Indians.
Djä'tĭeⁿ=Tchatchiun.
Djémez=Jemez.
Djëné=Navaho.
Djictañadiñ=Djishtangading.
Djimaliko=Chimariko.
Djonontewaka=Seneca.
Djúlalgi=Tsulalgi.
Dl'ia'lɛn k'ēowai'=Hlielung-keawai.
Dl'iā'lɛn kunílnagai'=Hlielungkun-lnagai.
Dnaïnè=Athapascan Family.
Doages=Nanticoke.
Dobimuss=Sannah.
Dock-spus=John Day.
Docota=Dakota.
Do-dah-ho=Dakubetede.
Doegs=Nanticoke.
Dog-drivers=Aglemiut.
Dog-eaters=Arapaho.
Dogenga, Doginga=Tongigua.
Dog Men's=Hotamitanio.
Dog Nation=Cheyenne.
Do-goo-son'=Tegotsugn.
Dog-rib, Dog-ribbed, Dog Ribs=Thlingchadinne.
Dog River=Watlala.
Dogs Naked=Emitahpahksaiyiks.
Dog Soldier=Hotamitaniu.
Dog tribe=Cherokee.
Do'gu'at=Wichita.
Do'-ha-kel'-yă=Kekin
Dohema=Eudeve.
Dohe'ñko=Carrizo.

Do'hleli'p=Tulalip.
Dohme=Eudeve.
Do'kănă=Wichita.
Dolores—Nuestra Señora de los Dolores, Sandia, Santa Maria de los Dolores.
Dolores de los Adaes=Nuestra Señora de los Dolores.
Domingo=Santo Domingo.
Do-no-ha-be=Dahnohabe.
Donondades=Tionontati.
Dononiiote=Oneida (vil.).
Don't Laugh=Kutaiimiks.
Doo-goo-son'=Tegotsugn.
Do-qua-chabsh=Nukwatsamish.
Dosapon=Tisepan.
Dos Pueblos=Miguihui.
Dotlekákat=Dotle.
Douaganhas=Chippewa, Ontwaganha.
Douesdonqua=Doustioni.
Douglas=Kaguyak.
Douglas Lake=Spahamin.
Dounè Flancs-de-Chien=Thlingchadinne.
Dounie' Espa-tpa-Ottinè=Esbataottine.
Doustiany=Doustioni.
Douwaganahs, Dovaganhaes=Ontwaganha, Chippewa.
Dowaganahs=Chippewa.
Dowaganhaas, Dowaganhaes=Ontwaganha.
Dowaganhas=Chippewa, Ontwaganha.
Dowaganhoes=Ontwaganha.
Dowanganhaes=Chippewa, Ontwaganha.
Draguanes=Doguenes.
Drifting Goose band=Putetemini.
Drinkers of the Dew=Keresan Family.
Drynoch=Nokem.
Dshipowē-ha'ga=Chippewa.
Dsilanoçílni=Dsihlnaothihlni.
Dsilçani=Dsihlthani.
Dsilnaoç'ilɸine, Dsilnaoçi'lni, Dsĭ'⁄naoĭ'⁄ni=Dsihlnaothihlni.
Dsi⁄tlá'ni=Dsihltlani.
Dtcha-ta-uttine=Ettchaottine.
Dtcheta-ta-ut-tunne=Tsetautkenne.
'Dtinnè=Athapascan Family.
Du-a+be'=Dwamish.
Duburcopota=Cubo Guasibavia.
Ducktown=Kawanuyi.
Dugh-dwabsh=Dwamish.
Dugilu'yĭ=Tugaloo.
Dū Hāadē=Dostlanlnagai.
Du-hle-lips=Tulalip.
Dûksa'ĭ, Dukw'sa'ĭ=Toxaway.
Dulchanois, Dulchinois=Dulchioni.
Dul-dul'-ça-waí-ă-mĕ=Duldulthawaiame.
Dumna=Tumna.
Dumplin Town=Atagi.
Dunè=Athapascan Family.
Dunewangua=Deyohnegano.
Dungeness=Yennis.
Dununuk=Tanunak.
Dus-ga-ó-weh-o-no=Tuscarora.
Dusty Nose=Iowa.
Dutagamis=Foxes.
Duwano=Twana.
Dwahmish=Dwamish.
Dwă-kă-nĕⁿ, Dwă-kă-nhă'=Chippewa.
Dwi'-wa=Santo Domingo.
Dyudoosot=Deyodeshot.
Dzā'wadEēnoxⁿ=Tsawatenok.
Dzitsĭ'stas=Cheyenne.
Dzos hāedrai'=Djus-hade.

Eagle=Khuya.
Eagle-ey'd Indians=Migichihiliniou.
Eagle Harbor=Orlova.
Eagle head (band)=Tintaotonwe.
Eagle people=Hangkaahutun, Cheghita.
Eambosandata=Khemnichan.
Eamuses=Yamasee.
Eanbosandata=Khemnichan.
Eano=Eno.
E-an-to-ah=Jatonabine.
E-ar'-ke=Hopi.
Ear Rings=Kalispel.
Earth=Manyinka.
Earth Eaters=Hohandika.
Earth-lodge=Mandhinkagaghe.
Eascab=Jatonabine.
East Abecka=East Abeika.

Eastanora=Ustanali.
East Congeata, East Congeeto, East Coongeeto=Co-
uechitou.
Eastern Apache=Querechos.
Eastern Folks=Etheneldeli.
Eastern Sioux=Santee.
Eastern Snakes=Washakie's Band.
Eastinaulee=Ustanali.
Eastlanders=Abnaki.
East Moka-Lassa=Imongalasha Skatane.
Eastward Indians=Eastern Indians.
East Yazoo, East Yazoo Skatane=Yazoo Skatane.
Ea-tau-bau=Catawba.
Eaters=Omisis.
Eat no dogs=Shungkayuteshni.
Eat the ham=Wolutayuta.
Ebahumo=Ebahamo.
Ebeetap-Oocoola=Ebita Poocola Skatane.
Ebicerinys=Nipissing.
Ebikuita, Ebiquita=Mescalero.
Ebitap-oocoolo-cho=Ebita Poocola Chitto.
Ecanchatty=Kanchati.
Ecclemachs=Esselen.
Echay=Itseyi.
Echebools, E-chee-lute=Tlakluit.
Echeetees=Hitchiti.
Echehóa=Echojoa.
Echeles=Hitchiti.
E-che-loot, E-che-lute=Tlakluit.
Echemins=Malecite.
Eche-mo-hua-vas=Chemehuevi.
Echeta, Echetee, Echetes, Echeti, Echetii=Hitchiti.
Echia=Itseyi.
Echi-mo-hua-vas=Chemehuevi.
É-chĭp-è-tȧ=Siksika.
Echitis, Echitos=Hitchiti.
E'-cho=Itchualgi.
Echoe, Echoee=Itseyi.
Echonova=Echojoa.
Echunticas=Kotsoteka.
E-chuse-is-li-gau=Istudshilaika.
Eçita=Ucita.
Eckanachacu, Eckanakaka=Ikanachaka.
Eclemaches=Esselen.
Econachaca=Ikanachaka.
Econautckky, Econautske=Ikanhatki.
Ecoree=Ecorce.
Ecquamish=Hahuamis.
Ecrevisses rouges=Chakchiuma.
Ecselenas, Ecselenes=Esselen.
Ecumohate, E-cun-cha-ta, E-cun-chate=Kanchati.
E-cun-hut-ke, Ecunhutlee=Ikanhatki.
Édawika=Kadohadacho.
Edchautawoot, Edchawtawhoot dinneh, Edchawta-
whoot tinneh, Edchawtawoot=Etchareottine.
Ede-but-say=Kainah.
Edgpüluk=Edgpiiliik.
Edistoes, Edistow=Edisto.
Edjiére-tρou-kkè-nade=Edjieretrukenade.
Edohwe=Kikatsik.
Edshaw-tawoot=Etchareottine.
Eekuk=Ekuk.
Eemitches=Imiche.
Eenò=Eno.
Eefnïvwïn=Ernivwin.
Eert-kai-lee=Kutchakutchin.
Ee-ta-sip-shov=Sans Arcs.
Egeish=Eyeish.
Egowik=Iguik.
Egues=Eudeve.
Egusanna cahel=Eguianna-cahel.
Eh-aht-tis-aht=Ehatisaht.
Ehanktonwanna, E-hank-to-wana=Yanktonai.
Ehateset, É'hatisath, Ehatt-is-aht=Ehatisaht.
Ehawhokales=Sawokli.
E-hawn-k'-t'-wawn-nah=Yanktonai.
E-hawn-k'-t'-wawns=Yankton.
Ehelutes=Tlakluit.
Ehesepiooc=Chesapeake.
Eh-grertsh=Miskut.
Ĕh-hȧ-tzȧ=Ehartsar.
Ehihalis=Chehalis.
Eh-nek=Amaikiara.
Ehonkeronons=Kichesipirini.
Eh8ae=Ehouae.
Eh-qua-nek=Shanamkarak.
Ehriehronnons=Erie.
Ehta-Gottinè=Etagottine.

Ehta-tchô-Gottinè=Etatchogottine.
Ehwae=Ehouae.
Ei-dan-noo=Eidenu.
Eioestures=Eneeshur.
Eiotaro=Coyoteros.
Eirichtih=Arapaho.
Eithinyook, Eithinyoowuc=Cree.
Eityam=Lajas.
Eivesteurs=Eneeshur.
Eivillinmiut=Aivilirmiut.
Eiwili=Aivilik.
Eiwillik=Aivilirmiut.
Ejujuajuin=Idjorituaktuin.
Ekadlŭ'hsuin=Imnongana.
Ekaluktalugumiut=Ekaluktaluk.
Ekeenteeronnon=Huron.
Ekhiondaltsaan=Ekiondatsaan.
Ekilígamut=Ekilik.
Ekklemaches=Esselen.
Ekógmuts=Ikogmiut.
E-ko-to-pis-taxe=Ekatopistaks.
Ekouk=Ekuk.
Ekpimi=Shasta.
Ĕkuiks=Ekuks.
Ekŭ'lath=Ekoolthaht.
E kun duts ke, Ekunhutke=Ikanhatki.
E-kú-pä-be-ka=Ekupabeka.
Ela-a-who=Etleuk.
Elagibucto=Richibucto.
Elah-Sa=Hidatsa.
Elătse'yï=Ellijay.
Elăwâ'diyï=Red Clay.
Elaws=Catawba.
El Cabezon=Cerro Cabezon.
El Corral=Corral.
Elder Brothers=Hathawekila.
Elder Osages=Pahatsi.
Él'é-idlin-Gottine=Eleidlinottine.
Elewalies=Huhliwahli.
El Gusano=Seyupa.
El'-hwa=Elwha.
Elijoy=Ellijay.
Eljiman=Eljman.
El Juez Tarado=Hueso Parado.
Elk=Hotachi, Huwanikikarachada, Khotachi.
Elkatcha=Alkehatchee.
ɥl'katco=Ilkatsho.
Ĕl-ke-ai'=Sia.
Elk gens=Anpanenikashika, Wezhinshte.
Elk'la'sumH=Bellabella.
Elk Mountain Utes, Elk Mountain Yutas=Seuvarits.
Elk river tribe=Eel River Indians.
Elkwah=Elwha.
Ellzu cathlans-coon-hidery=Naikun-kegawai.
Elmian=Eljman.
El Moro=El Morro.
Eloot=Tlakluit.
Elpawawe=Alpowna.
El Pinal Apaches=Pinaleño.
El Pueblo de los Siete Arroyos=Tenabo.
El Pueblo Quemado=Tzenatay.
Elqī'miH=Tsimshian.
El Tunque=Tungge.
E-lute=Tlakluit.
Elwahs=Elwha.
Em-alcom=Homalko.
Emam8eta=Emamoueta.
Emarhe=Ematlochee's Town.
Emat=Emet.
Emeaes, Emeges, Emenes, Emes=Jemez.
Emetgale axá cang=Paya.
Emexes=Jemez.
Emissourita=Missouri.
Emlh-wilh-laht=Uclulet.
Emïnes=Jemez.
Emola=Homolua.
Em-tim'-bitch=Intimbich.
Emucfau, Emuckfau, Emuckfaw, Emukfau=
Imukfa.
Emusas=Emussa.
Enacapen=Enecappe.
E-nagh-magh=Tigua.
E-nam=Inam.
Enansa—Quapaw.
Enanthayonni=Toryohne.
Enarhonon=Arendahronons.
E-năt'-zä=Hidatsa.

Encantada Mesa=Katzimo.
Encarnacion, Encarnacion Sutaquison=Sudacson.
Enchanted Mesa=Katzimo.
Encierro=Pueblo del Encierro.
Enclataws=Lekwiltok.
Endastes=Conestoga.
Enecaq=Enecappe.
E-nee-sher=Eneeshur.
Eneguape=Enecappe.
Enek=Amaikiara.
Enepiahe, Enepiahœ, Enepiahoes=Ervipiames.
Enequaque=Enecappe.
E-ne-show, E-ne-shur, Eneshure, Enesteurs=Enee-shur.
Enfula=Eufaula.
English Bay=Alexandrovsk.
English Indians=Apalachicola.
English town=Inkillis Tamaha.
English Towns=Oklahannali.
Engna=Henaggi.
Enitachopko=Anatichapko.
En-ke-map-o-tricks=Nkamaplix.
En-ke-mip=Nkamip.
Enk-ka-sa-ba=Inkesabe.
Enna-k'è, En-na-k'ie´=Eskimo.
Ennas=Cree.
Ennikaragi=Amikwa.
Enneyuttehage=Oneida (vil.).
Enoe=Eno.
Enook-sha-lig=Inugsulik.
Enotochopco, Enotochopko=Anatichapko.
E-no-tucks=Inotuks.
Enquisacoes=Arkokisa.
Ensanich=Sanetch.
Ensenes=Esselen.
Enta-otin=Tautin.
Entari ronnon=Cherokee.
Entimbich=Intimbich.
Entouhonorons, Entwohonoron=Seneca.
E-nyaé-va Pai=Yavapai.
E-oh=E-eh.
Eokoros=Arikara.
Eoote-lash-Schute=Ootlashoot.
Eototo wiñwû, E-o´-to-to wüñ-wû=Eototo.
E-ow-ick=Chamisso.
E-pa=Walapai.
E–pe-sau-gee=Ipisogi.
Epesengles, Epicerinyens, Epicerinys, Epiciriniens, Episingles, Épissingue=Nipissing.
Epithápa=Popotita.
E-pŏh-si-mĭks=Ipoksimaiks.
Equalett=Ekoolthaht.
Equi=Eudeve.
Equinipichas=Acolapissa.
Equituni=Aquitun.
Erabacha=Uzutiuhi.
Érawika=Kadohadacho.
Ercansaques=Kansa.
Erchipeetay=Siksika.
Èrèttchi-ottinè=Etcheridiegottine.
Erians=Erie.
Erié=Rique.
Erieckronois, Erieehronons, Eriehronon, Erielho-nons, Erieronons, Eriez, Erigas=Erie.
Erige=Rique.
Erige Tejocharontiong=Tiosahrondion.
Erike=Rique.
Eriniouai, Eriniwek=Illinois.
E-rī-o=Erio.
Eriwoneck=Eriwonec.
Erkiléït=Kutchin.
Ermomex=Eriwonec.
Erocoise=Iroquois.
Eromaha=Omaha.
Erqigdlit=Adlet.
Errieronons=Erie.
Ersegontegog=Arosaguntacook.
Erskins=Eskini.
E-rus´-si=Erusi.
Esanapes, Esanopes=Essanape.
Esanties=Santee.
Esau, Esaws=Catawba.
Escabaca-Cascastes=Escaba.
Escamacu=Uscamacu.
Escanjaques, Escansaques, Escanxaques=Kansa
Escelen, Escelenes, Escellens=Esselen.
Escequatas=Mescaleros.
Eschentown=Punxsutawny.

E. Scihous=Santee.
Esclaves=Etchareottine, Thlingchadinne.
Escoumin, Escoumins=Eskimo.
Escurieux=Ecureuil.
Eselenes=Esselen.
Esewonecks=Eriwonec.
Eshkibod=Eskimo.
Esikwíta=Mescaleros, Kiowa Apache.
Eskeemoes=Eskimo.
Eskelen=Esselen.
E-skel-lute, Eskeloot=Tlakluit.
Eskiaeronnon=Chippewa.
Eskima, Eskimantsik, Eskimántzik, Eskimauk, Eskimaux=Eskimo.
Eskimaux=Eskimauan Family.
Eskimeaux, Eskimesi=Eskimo.
Eskimo=Eskimauan Family.
Eś-kin=Eskini.
Es-kin-e-nar=Tzecheschinne.
Es-kin´-ni-zin=Destchin.
Es-kin-os´-pus=Tzetses-adn.
Es-ki´-u-do´-ra=Destchin.
Es-kopiks=Nascapee.
Eskoros=Arikara.
Eslen, Eslenes=Esselen.
Esopes, Esopuz=Esopus.
Espatingh=Hespatingh.
Es-pā-to-ti-na, Espa-tρa-Ottinè=Esbataottine.
Espeleta=Oraibi.
Espicheates=Spichehats.
Espíritu Santo de Cocorin=Cocori.
Esquansaques=Kansa.
Esquiates=Hesquiat.
Esquimantsic, Esquimau, Esquimaux=Eskimo.
Esquimaux=Esquimauan Family.
Esquimeaux, Esquimones=Eskimo.
Es-ree-que-tees=Mescaleros.
Es-sah´-ah-ter=Santee.
Es-san-a-pis, Essannapes=Essanape.
Essapookoon=Mountain Crows.
Essa-queta=Kiowa Apache.
Essekwitta, És-sͅe-kwĭt´-ta=Mescaleros.
Esselenes=Esselen.
Essenapes=Essanape.
Esse-qua-ties=Mescaleros.
Essequeta=Kiowa Apache.
Essi-kuita=Mescaleros.
Essinaboin=Assiniboin.
Esson=Santee.
Estaboga=Istapoga.
Es-ta-ke-wach=Astakiwi.
Estalaoe=Estatoee.
Estanaula=Ustanali.
Estanxaques=Kansa.
E-stä-pa´=Histapenumanke.
Estatoe, Estatoie=Estatoee.
Estechemains, Estecheminès, Estechemins=Male-cite.
Estiaghes, Estiaghicks=Chippewa.
Estilococo=Estocoloco.
Estjage=Chippewa.
Estók pakai peyáp=Comecrudo.
Estók pakawaíla=Pakawa.
Estolococo=Estocoloco.
Estotowe, Estotowe great=Estatoee.
Estward Indians=Eastern Indians.
E-swhedip=Ishwidip.
Eta=Cree.
É-ta-a-tρa ˌɹûn´nĕ, É-ta-a-t´ρût ˌɹûnne=Etaattha-tunne.
E-tach-e-cha=Iteshicha.
Eta-gottiné=Dahotena.
Etah=Ita.
Etak-buoh, Etakmurs=Etakmehu.
E-ta-leh=Arapaho.
E-tall-wau=Taluamikagi.
E-tá-ni-o=Atsina.
E-tans-ke-pa-se-ta-qua=Assiniboin.
Eta-Ottine=Etagottine.
Etchaρé-ottiné=Etchareottine.
Etchemons=Malecite.
Etchian-Kρét=Chitsa.
Etchimins, Etchimis=Malecite.
Etchipoës=Chippewa.
Etchitas=Hitchiti.
Etch-kah-taw-wah=Dakubetede.
Etchmins=Malecite.
Etchoe, Etchowee=Itseyi.
E´-tcu-lĕt ˌɹûn-nĕ, E´-tcu-lĭt´=Echulit.

Etechemies, Etechemin, Etechemines, Etecheminii, Etecheneus, Etemânkiaks, Eteminquois= Malecite.
Etewans= Etiwaw.
Etharita= Etarita.
Ethen-eltèli= Etheneldeli.
Ethinu, Ethinyu= Cree.
Etichimenes= Malecite.
Etichita= Hitchiti.
Etionnontatehronnons, Etionnontates=Tionontati.
E-tish-shóka= Etshoka.
Etiwans= Etiwaw.
Etnémi tane, Etnémi-tenéyu= Umpqua.
Eto-cale= Ocali.
Etohlugamiut= Etoluk.
Eto-husse-wakkes= Itahassiwaki.
Etschimins= Malecite.
Etsh-tawút-dinni= Etchareottine.
Etsī-kin= Etsekin.
Etsitü'biwat= Ditsakana.
Et-tah-kín-nee= Walpi.
Ettchéri-dié-Gottinè= Etcheridiegottine.
Ettine-tinney= Etheneldeli.
Etuck Chukké= Etuk Chukke.
Etzāmish= Songish.
Euchas= Yuchi, Yuma.
Euchees= Yuchi, Yukichetunne.
Eucher, Euches= Yukichetunne.
Euchitaws= Hitchiti.
Euchre, Euchre Creek= Yukichetunne.
Euclataw= Lekwiltok.
Euclitus= Lekwiltok, Tsakwalooin.
Eudebe, Eudeva= Eudeve.
Eufala's, Eufalee, Eufantees= Eufaula.
Euforsee= Hiwassee.
Eufath, Eufaulahatche, Eu-fau-lau, Eu-fau-lau-hat-che, Eufaule, Eufaulies, Eufollahs, Eufowlas= Eufaula.
Euhchee= Yuchi.
Euimes= Jemez.
Eukas= Yukian Family.
É-ukshikni, É-ukskni= Klamath.
Eukwhatsum= Ikwopsum.
Eu'nmun= Avak.
Euphalau, Euphales= Eufaula.
Eu-qua-chee, Eu-quah-chee= Yukichetunne.
Euquatops= Mescaleros.
Eurocs= Yurok.
Eus-á-nich= Sanetch.
E'-ushkni= Klamath.
Eusquemays= Eskimo.
Eustenaree= Ustanali.
Eutahs, Eutaw= Ute.
Eutchees= Yuchi.
Eutempeche's= Intimbich.
Euyrons= Huron.
Eves= Erie.
Evīsts-uní-pahĭs= Heviqsnipahis.
Ewahoos= Ewawoos.
Ewany= Yowani.
Ewā'wus, E-w-aw-was= Ewawoos.
Ewemalas= Alibamu.
Ewinte= Uinta.
Ewlbwiehaht, Ewlhwiehaht, Ewl-hwilh-aht= Ucluelet.
E-wu-ha-wu-si= Shoshoni.
Exaloaping= Ekaloaping.
Exalualuin= Ekalualuin.
Eχaluaqdjuin= Ekaluakdjuin.
Eχaluin= Ekaluin.
Exaluqdjuaq= Ekalukdjuak.
Excanjaque, Excausaquex= Kansa.
Excellemaks= Esselen.
Excomminqui, Excomminquois= Eskimo.
Ex e ni nnth= Cexeninuth.
Exepiahohé= Ervipiames.
Eχoluin= Ekaluin.
E'yack-im-ah= Yakima.
Eyakíni diné= Hopi.
Eyank-ton-wah= Yanktonai.
Eyish= Eyeish.
Eythinyuwuk= Cree.

Factory Indians= Sukinatcha.
Facullie= Takulli.
Fallatahs, Fallatrahs= Atfalati.
Fall Indians= Atsina, Clowwewalla, Des Chutes, Pawating.
Falls Indians= Des Chutes.
Falls Village= Gaskosada.

Falsav(o)ins= Menominee.
False Creek= Snauk.
False Dungeness= Stehtlum, Yennis.
Faraona, Faraon Apaches, Faraones, Fardones, Farreon Apaches= Faraon.
Fat Cavity clan= Wikorzh.
Fatehennyaha= Hotalihuyana.
Father Fremin's village= Totiakton.
Fat Roasters= Ipoksimaiks.
Faux Têtes-Plates= Salish.
Fa-wac-car-ro= Tawakoni.
Fawalomnes= Tuolumne.
Feaga= Jeaga.
Fejuas= Tejua
Fe-jyu= Fejiu.
Felles avoins= Menominee.
Femmes blanches= White Woman's Town.
Ferconteha, Fercouteha= Serecoutcha.
Fetkina= Chnagmiut.
Fetoutlin= Fetutlin.
Fía= Mecastria.
Fiapuzi= Trea, Guatitruti.
Filifaes, Filijayas= Tilihaes.
Fire Heart's band= Chantapeta's Band.
Fire-house= Tebugkihu.
Fire Indians, Fire Nation= Mascoutens.
Fish-eaters= Assiniboin, Mameoya, Tazaaigadika, Timpaiavats, Winnebago.
Fish gens= Huinikashika.
Fish Lake= Komkonatko.
Fishpond, Fish-Pond Town= Hlahlokalka.
Fish Utes= Seuvarits.
Five Canton Nations, Five Indian Cantons, Five Mohawk Nations, Five Nations= Iroquois.
Five Nations of the Sciota Plains= Mingo.
Flachbogen= Kitunahan Family, Lower Kutenai.
Flambeau, Lac du= Wauswagiming.
Flanakaskies= Monahassano.
Flancs de chien= Thlingchadinne.
Flandreau Sioux= Flandreau Indians.
Flat Belly's Village= Papakeecha.
Flatbow= Kitunahan Family.
Flatbows= Lower Kutenai.
Flat Bows= Puhksinahmahyiks.
Flathead Kootanie= Kalispel.
Flatheads= Catawba, Chinook, Choctaw, Histapenumanke, Muskhogean Family, Nez Percés, Salishan Family, Spokan, Tushepaw, Waxhaw.
Flathead-Selish= Salish.
Flats= Choctaw.
Flat-side Dogs= Thlingchadinne.
Flattery= Makah.
Flonk'-o= Lolanko.
Flores= Las Flores.
Flour Village= Corn Village.
Fly gens= Itamalgi.
Foille avoine Chippeways= Munominikasheenhug.
Follaties= Atfalati.
Folleavoine, Folles, Folles Avoines, Fols, Fols Avoin, Fols Avoines, Folsavoins= Menominee.
Fols Avoin Sauteaux, Fols-avoin-Sauters= Munominikasheenhug.
Fols-avoise= Menominee, Munominikasheenhug.
Folsovoins= Menominee.
Fondagame= Roche de Bœuf.
Fond du Lac= Wiaquahhechegumeeng.
Fond du Lac Loucheux= Tatlitkutchin.
Fonechas= Pohoniche.
Foolish Dogs= Hosukhaunu.
Foosce-hat-che, Fooschatchee, Foosee Hatchee, Fooskahatche= Fusihatchi.
Foot Assiniboines= Gens de Pied.
Ford's Prairie= Talal.
Foremost= Hanga.
Forestdale ruin= Tundastusa.
Forked tree= Waganakisi.
Fort Augusta= Shamokin.
Fort Chinnabie= Chinnaby's Fort.
Fort Franklin= Venango.
Fort George= Leitli.
Fort Hamilton= Nunapithlugak.
Fort Hope= Sakahl.
Fort Indians= Kutchakutchin.
Fort Kenai= Kenai.
Fort Machault, Fort Mackhault, fort of Venango= Venango.
Fort Queen= Sequim.
Fort Reliance= Nuklako.
Fort Rupert= Tsahis.

Fort Rupert Indians=Kwakiutl.
Fort Schamockin=Shamokin.
Fort Simpson=Port Simpson.
Fort Simpson Indians=Tsimshian.
Fort Town=Neamathla.
Fosters Bar=Tiaks.
Fou-ka-was=Tonkawa.
Foul Town=Fowl Town.
Fountain=Huhilp.
Four Crows band=Watsequeorda's band.
Four Peak Indians=Pinal Coyotero, Tontos.
Fowl Town=Tutalosi.
Foxers=Foxes.
Foxes=Chula.
Franceses=Pawnee.
Francisco de Necha=San Francisco de los Tejas.
Francisco Xavier=San Francisco Xavier de Viggé Biaundo.
Franckstown=Frankstown.
Fraser's Lake Village=Natleh.
Freckled Panis=Wichita.
Fredericstahl=Frederiksdal.
French Catharinestown, French Catherines town= Catherine's Town.
French Mohawks=Caughnawaga.
French Prairie Indians=Ahantchuyuk.
French Praying Indians=Caughnawaga.
French Town=Ostonwackin.
Frente Negra Mts.=Tutuetac.
Fresh meat necklace people=Talonapin.
Frieden Huetten, Friedenshutten=Friedenshuetten.
Friedensstadt=Languntennenk.
Frijoleros=Papago.
Friyti=Guatitruti.
Frog Indians=Manta.
Fronteras=Corodeguachi.
Fruson=Tucson.
Fuchs-Aleuten=Unalaska.
Fucson=Tucson.
Fuketcheepoonta=Faluktabunnee.
Fulawin=Menominee.
Fulemmy's=Pinder Town.
Fulsowines=Menominee.
Fusahatche=Fusihatchi.
Fushi=Hatakfushi.
Futun=Jutun.
Fwah=Fwaha.

Gă′-än-do-wă-nänñ=Gaandowanang.
Gă-äⁿ-no′-ge′=Gaanoge.
Gä-a-no′-ga, Gä′-a-no-geh, Gä-ä-nóⁿ-ge′=Nyutcirhaaⁿ.
Gabrileños=Gabrieleño.
Gacheos=Cayuga.
Gachimantiagon=Buckaloon.
Gachnawas-haga=Conoy.
Gachoi, Gachoos, Gachpas=Cayuga.
Gä′-dä-gäⁿs′-geoⁿ, Gädä′gesgao=Cattaraugus.
Gä-dä′-o=Gadaho.
Ga-dji′jiñ′ga=Gadjizhinga.
Gaensera=Kanagaro.
Gạgä′n hît tän=Kaganhittan.
Gagara-Shapka=Pogoreshapka.
G·ag·g·ilak‘a=Gyagygyilakya.
Gaghasieanhgwe, Gaghsiungua, Gaghsonghgwa, Gaghsonshwa=Kashong.
Gagnieguez=Mohawk.
Gagsonghwa=Kashong.
Gä′-häⁿyă-yäⁿ′-dă′k=Gahayanduk.
Gahasieanhgwe=Kashong.
Gahéwa=Kiowa.
Gahkwas=Erie.
Gä-′hnă-wă′-ge=Caughnawaga.
Gahooskins=Yahuskin.
Gäh-tau′-go ten′-ni, Gäh-tŏw-gō tin′-nī=Chintagottine.
Gä′-i-gwŭ=Kiowa.
Gaiuckers=Cayuga.
Gai′wa=Kiowa.
Gajuka=Goiogouen.
Gä′ʟ!ak!anasisi=Wakanasisi.
Gaʟä′qstxoqʟ=Killaxthokle.
Galasteo—Galisteo.
Galcäni=Kulchana.
Gal Doe=Kauldaw.
Galeese Creek Indians=Taltushtuntude.
Galiamoix=Katlamoik.

Galice Creek=Taltushtuntude.
Galiste=Galisteo.
Galisteo=Heshota Ayathltona.
Galleace Creek=Taltushtuntude.
Gallisteo=Galisteo.
Galtzanen, Galzanen, Galzani=Kulchana.
ŋ′a′mℨ′amtEʟaʟ=Gamgamtelatl.
Gamoenapa, Gamoenepa, Gamonepa=Communipaw.
Ganachgeritawe=Seneca.
Gä-nä-dä-ä-gwäⁿñ, Gä-na-dä′-gwa, Gä-nä-dä-ló′-quä= Canandaigua.
Gä-nă-dä-sá-ga, Gä-nä-dä-sage, Gă-nă-dă-se′′-ge‘= Canadasaga.
Ganadatsiagon=Gandaseteiagon.
Ganadesaga=Canadasaga.
Ganadoke, Gä-nä′-doque=Ganadogan.
Ganagarahhare, Ganagarah'hare=Venango.
Ganagaro=Kanagaro.
Ganaghsaragey, Ganaghsaragues=Ganasarage.
Ganagsadagas=Oka.
Gä-nă′-dä-on-tweh=Ganedontwan.
Gänäjohälä′-que, Gänäjoha′rla, Ganajohhore, Gä-na-jo-hi′-e=Canajoharie.
Ganaraské=Ganeraske.
Gä-nä-tä-lä′-quä, Ganataqueh=Canandaigua.
Ganatcheskiagon=Gandaseteiagon.
Ganatisgowa=Sganatees.
Ganatoheskiagon=Gandaseteiagon.
Ganaway, Ganawense, Ganawese, Ganawoose, Ganawses=Conoy.
Gānạxte′dî=Ganahadi.
Ganciou, Gancydoes=Ganneious.
Gandachioragon, Gandachiragou=Deyodeshot.
Gandagan, Gandagarae, Gandagaro=Kanagaro.
Gandaoüagué, Gandaouaqué, Gandaougue=Caughnawaga.
Gandaschekiagon=Gandaseteiagon.
Gandastogega, Gandastogués=Conestoga.
Gandatsiagon, Gandatsiagon=Gandaseteiagon.
Gandawagué=Caughnawaga.
Gandougaraé=Kanagaro.
Gandules=Moenkopi.
Ganeagaonhoh, Gä-ne-ä′-ga-o-no=Mohawk.
Ganechsatáge, Ganechstáge=Canadasaga.
Gä-ne-ga-hä′-gä=Mohawk.
Ganeganaga=Caughnawaga.
Ganeidos, Ganeious, Ganejou=Ganneious.
Ganentaa, Ganentaha=Gannentaha.
Ganeousse=Ganneious.
Ganesatague=Oka.
Ganeyont=Ganneious.
Gangascoe=Gangasco.
Gangawese=Conoy.
Ganiegueronons, Gani-inge, Gani-ingehága, Ganingehage=Mohawk.
Gannagaro=Kanagaro.
Gannaouagué=Caughnawaga.
Gannaouens=Conoy.
Gannaraské=Ganeraske.
Gannejouts, Ganneous, Ganneouse=Ganneious.
Ganniag8ari, Ganniagwari=Mohawk.
Ganniataratich-rone=Nanticoke.
Ganniegéhaga, Ganniégeronon, Ganniegez, Ganniegué, Ganniekez=Mohawk.
Ganniessinga=Conoy.
Ganningehage=Mohawk.
Gannogarae=Kanagaro.
Gannondata=Deyodeshot.
Gannongarae, Gannougarae=Kanagaro.
Gannounata=Deyodeshot.
Gano′-a-lo′-hale=Oneida (vil.).
Gä-no-ä-o′-hä, Gä-no′ä-o-hä=Ganowarohare.
Ganochiaragon=Deyodeshot.
Ga-noⁿ-dä′-ä′=Gannentaha.
Gänoⁿwäro′häre‘=Ganowarohare.
Gä-nosé-gă-go, Gä-nos′-gä-goñ=Ganosgagong.
Ganossetage=Conestoga.
Gänowä′lohale, Gä′nowälohar′la=Ganowarohare.
Ga-no′-wau-ga=Caughnawaga.
Gänowaúges=Ganawagus.
Gänowíhä=Ganowarohare.
Gänsâ′gĭ, Gänsâgiyĭ=Kansaki.
Ganstero=Yuma.
Gantsi=Kiowa Apache.
Gä′nundä′gwa=Canandaigua.
Gä-nun′-dä-sa=Ganondaga.
Ga-nun-dä-sa′-gä=Canadasaga.
Gä-nun-ta′-ah=Gannentaha.

Gänus'găgo, Ganuskago=Ganosgagong.
GA'nxet xā-idAga-i=Gunghet-haidagai.
G·anyakoîlnagai=Aoyakulnagai.
Gä-oⁿ-'hia'-di-onⁿ=Caneadea.
Gä-o-no'-geh=Nyuchirhaan.
Ga-o-sa-eh-ga-aah, Gäo'sâgäo=Chinoshahgeh.
Gāot! ā'k-ān=Gaudekan.
Gä-o-ŭs-ă-gé-oⁿ=Chinoshahgeh.
Gä-o-us-geh=Gaousge.
Gäo'yadeo=Caneadea.
G·â'p!ēnoxᵘ=Kopsino.
Gappa=Quapaw.
Gä-quä'-ga-o-no=Erie.
Gaqui=Yaqui.
Gaqúliⁿ=Gakhulin.
Gaqúliⁿuliⁿ'be=Gakhulinulinbe.
Gardeau, Gardow=Gadaho.
Garennajenhaga=Huron.
Garhawquash=Kashong.
Garote, Garotero, Garretero, Garrotero, Garrotes=
   Yuma.
GAsā'n=Kasaan.
Gashowu=Kassovo.
Gä'-sko·'-să-dă=Gaskosada.
Gaspesians, Gaspesies=Gaspesien.
Gataea=Kiowa Apache.
G·'at'aiwas=Masset.
Gataka=Kiowa Apache.
Gąt hī'nî=Gutheni.
Gathsiungua=Kashong.
Gatla'nakoa-iq=Cathlanahquiah.
Gá'tlap'otlh=Cathlapotle.
Gatohuá=Cherokee.
Gatqstax=Wakanasisi.
Gattaçka=Kiowa Apache.
Gattóchwa=Cherokee.
Gatu'gitse', Gatu'gitse'yĭ=Catatoga.
Gatûñ'lti'yĭ=Hemptown.
Gáuamuitk=Waginkhak.
Gaud-ah-kan=Gaudekan.
Gä'-u-gwa=Goiogouen.
Gä-u'-gweh=Cayuga.
Gä-un-do'-wä-na=Gaandowanang.
Gavan=Kodiak.
Gavanskoe, Gavanskoi, Gawanskoje=Iliuliuk.
Gawia=Kawia.
Gáwicila=Kawishila.
Gáwi-laptck=Kawilapchk.
Gayuga=Cayuga.
Gecualme=Tecualme.
Gecuiches=Kawia.
Gediack=Shediac.
Ge-e-way, Ge-e-wē=Santo Domingo.
Geghdageghroano, Geghtigeghroones=Illinois.
G·''ēg·'ō'tē=Gyegyote.
Geliec=Geliac.
Gelinos=Gila Apache.
Gelo=Geliac.
Gemes, Gemex, Gemez=Jemez.
Gemoenepaen, Gemoenepaw=Communipaw.
Genalga=Atchinaalgi.
Ge-nega's band=Genega.
Genesee, Genessees=Geneseo.
Genevavi=Guevavi.
Genicuiches, Genigneihs, Genigueches, Genigueh,
   Geniguichs=Serranos.
Geniocane=Heniocane.
Genizaros=Tomé.
Genneces, Gennesse=Geneseo.
Gens de bois=Hankutchin, Tutchonekutchin.
Gens de bouleau, Gens de Bouleaux=Tennuthkut-
   chin.
Gens de butte=Tenankutclun.
Gens de Canot=Watopapinah.
Gens de Castor=Tsattine.
Gens de faux=Hankutchin.
Gens de Feu=Mascoutens.
Gens de Feuille=Wahpeton.
Gens de Feuillees, Gens de Feuilles=Itscheabine.
Gens de Feuilles-tirées=Wahpekute.
Gens de fine, Gens de Fou, Gens de foux=Hanku-
   tchin.
Gens de la Barbue=Marameg.
Gens de l'abri=Tatsakutchin.
Gens de Lac=Mdewakanton.
Gens de la Feuille=Itscheabine.
Gens de la fourche du Mackenzie=Eleidlinottine.
Gens de l'age=Watopachnato.
Gens de la Grande Rivière=Nakotchokutchin.

Gens De Lai=Mdewakanton.
Gens de la Loutre=Nikikouek.
Gens de la Mer du Nord=Mer, Gens de la.
Gens de la Montagne=Etagottine.
Gens de la Montagne la Corne=Etechesottine.
Gens de Large=Natsitkutchin.
Gens de la rivière au Foin=Klodesseottine.
Gens de l'Outarde=Ouikaliny.
Gens de Marais=Monsoni.
Gens de Mer=Mer, Gens de la; Winnebago.
Gens de Milieu=Tangesatsa.
Gens d'En-haut=Etagottine.
Gens de Orignal=Mousonee.
Gens de Panse=Allakaweah.
Gens de Pitie=Shoshoko.
Gens-de-ralt, Gens de rats=Tukkuthkutchin.
Gens de Roche=Jatonabine.
Gens des Bois=Esbataottine, Hankutchin, Tschan-
   toga.
Gens des Buttes=Tenankutchin.
Gens des Canoe, Gens des canots, Gens des caruts=
   Watopapinah.
Gens des Chaudières=Colville.
Gens des chèvres=Esbataottine.
Gens des Corbeau=Crows.
Gens de Serpent=Shoshoni.
Gens des fees or Girls=Itscheabine.
Gens des Feuilles=Wahpeton.
Gens des Feuilles tirees=Wahpekute.
Gens des filles=Itscheabine.
Gens des Foux=Tutchonekutchin.
Gens des grand diable=Watopachnato.
Gens de siffleur=Teahinkutchin.
Gens des Montagnes=Chabin, Chipewyan.
Gens des Montagnes-Rocheuses=Etagottine.
Gens des Osayes=Fanintauei.
Gens des Pin=Wazikute.
Gens des Rats=Vuntakutchin.
Gens des Roches, Gens des rosches=Jatonabine.
Gens des Serpent=Shoshoni.
Gens des Soulier=Amahami.
Gens des Tee=Itscheabine.
Gens des Terres=Têtes de Boule.
Gens des vach=Arapaho.
Gens de Tee=Oseegah.
Gens de wiz=Tutchonekutchin.
Gens du Caribon, Gens du Caribou=Attikiriniou
   etch.
Gens du Cuivre=Tatsanottine.
Gens du fond du lac=Tatlitkutchin.
Gens du Fort Norman=Desnedeyarelottine.
Gens du Gauche=Watopachnato.
Gens du Lac=Mdewakanton, Minishinakato.
Gens du lac la Truite=Etchaottine.
Gens du Large=Natsitkutchin, Watopachnato.
Gens du Nord=Northern Assiniboin.
Gens du Petun=Tionontati.
Gens du Poil=Chintagottine.
Gens du Rat=Vuntakutchin.
Gens du Sable=Sable.
Gens du Sang=Miskouaha, Kainah.
Gens du Sault=Pawating.
Gens du Serpent=Shoshoni.
Gens en l'air=Etagottine.
Gentagega, Gentaguetehronnons=Gentaienton.
Gentlemen Indians=Waco.
Genuvskoe=Henya.
Georgiefskaia=Kasilof.
G·ēq'ō'lEqoa=Gyekolekoa.
Gerguensens, Gerzuensens=Gergecensens.
Get-an-max=Kitanmaiksh.
Gete'kitigan=Gatagetegauning.
Ge-wa-ga, Ge-waw-ga=Gewauga.
G·ē'xsEm=Gyeksem.
G·ē'xsEms'anaL=Gyeksemsanatl.
Gha'-hi-tä'neo=Khahitan.
Ghecham=Luiseño.
Ghuil-chan=Kulchana.
Ghula'-napo=Kuhlanapo.
Gi-aucth-in-in-e-wug, Gi-aucth-in-ne-wug=Hidatsa
Gibbaways=Chippewa.
Gibola=Zuñi.
Giburi=Quiburi.
Gicarillas=Jicarilla.
Gidanemuk=Serranos.
Gieschgumaníto=Kiskiminetas.
Gíg·abu=Kickapoo.
G·ī'g·EqEmaē=Gyigyekemae.
G·ī'g·îlqam=Gyigyilkam.

Gijames=Sijame.
Gikapu=Kickapoo.
Gikidanum=Serranos.
Gilakhamiut=Gilak.
GiLā′lēlam=Nisal.
Gilands=Coyoteros.
Gilans=Gila Apache.
GiLā′pcō-i=Gitlapshoi.
Gila Pimas=Pima.
GiLā′q!ulawas=Kwalhioqua.
Gilas=Gila Apache.
GiLā′xicatck=Watlala.
GiLā′xwilapax=Willopah.
Gileña, Gileno, Gileños Apaches=Gila Apache.
Gillamooks=Tillamook.
Gi′manoitx=Kitlope.
Gïnä′s=Kiowa Apache.
Ginebigônini=Shoshoni.
Ginetéwi Sawanógi=Absentee.
Gingaskins=Gangasco.
Gingoteque=Chincoteague.
Ginnacee=Geneseo.
Gin-se-ua=Gyusiwa.
Giopas=Ojiopas.
Gi-oshk=Gyaushk.
Giowaka-ā′, Giowatsa-ā′=Santa Clara.
Gipanes=Lipan.
Gi-pu-i=Gipuy.
Girls' band=Itscheabine.
Gis-twe-ah′-na=Hastwiana.
Gitanemok, Gitanemuk, Gitanemum=Serranos.
Git-an-max=Kitanmaiksh.
Gita′q¡ēmas=Clackama.
Gitases=Atasi.
Git-au-max=Kitanmaiksh.
Gitā′xwilapax=Willopah.
Git!ē′ks=Kitaix.
Gitins=Got.
Gitlā′tlpeleks=Palux.
Gitla′wĕwalamt=Clowwewalla.
Gíts' ajĭ=Kichai.
Gittci′s=Kitzeesh.
Gituns=Got.
Glagla-heća, Glagla-hetca=Glaglahecha.
Gleese Cleek=Taltushtuntude.
Gleta=Isleta.
Glisteo=Galisteo.
Gnacsitaries=Gnacsitare.
Gnaden Auetten=Gnadenhuetten.
Gnapaws=Quapaw.
Gnasitares, Gnasitaries=Gnacsitare
Go-about band=Detsanayuka.
Goasavas=Guazavas.
Goatcharones=Wacharones.
Godá=Huda.
Godamyon=Kwatami.
Gogouins=Cayuga.
Gohontoto=Wyalusing.
Gohun=Tontos, Tulkepaia, Yavapai.
Goienho=Touenho.
Goiog8en=Goiogouen.
Goiogoüens=Cayuga.
Goiogouin=Goiogouen.
Goiogouioronons=Cayuga.
Goiogwen=Goiogouen.
Gojogoüen=Cayuga.
Gokapatagans=Kickapoo.
Go-ke-nim-nons=Bokninuwad.
Golden Hill (tribe)=Pauquaunuch.
Gol-doe=Kauldaw.
Gologamiut=Golok.
Goltzane, Golzan, Golzanen=Kulchana.
Gomez=Jemez.
Gonaraske=Ganeraske.
Gonā′xo=Gonaho.
Gō′naxo koan=Gunachonken.
Gonega=Genega.
Gonejou=Ganneious.
Good Knife=Tanetsukanumanke.
Goodnight Indians=Beothukan Family.
Good-Road, Goodroads (band), Goodrod's band=Oyateshicha.
Gooiogouen=Cayuga.
Goose Creek Diggers=Tussawehe.
G-ō′p′ēnôx=Gyopenok.
Goricas=Yoricas.
Gorretas, Gorrettes, Gorrites=Manso.
Goschachguenk, Goschaching, Goschachking=Coshocton.

Goschegoschuenk, Goschgoschuenk=Goshgoshunk.
Goschochking, Goshachking=Coshocton.
Go-sha-utes, Goshee Utes, Goshen Utes=Gosiute.
Goshgoshink=Goshgoshunk.
Goship, Goship Shoshones, Go-ship-Utes, Goshiss=Gosiute.
Goshochking=Coshocton.
Goshoots=Gosiute.
Gosh′-sho-o=Kassovo.
Go-shutes, Gosh Yuta, Gos-ta Utes=Gosiute.
Gos ventures=Gros Ventres.
Gōtc=Goch.
Gothescunqueon, Gothsenquean, Gothseunquean, Gothsinquea=Kashong.
Goulapissas=Acolapissa.
Govero=Cubero.
Goxicas=Yoricas.
Goyagouins, Goyogans, Goyogoans, Goyogoin, Goyogouans, Goyogouens=Cayuga.
Goyogouh=Goiogouen.
Goyogoüin=Cayuga, Goiogouen.
Goyoguans, Goyoguen, Goyoguin, Goyoguoain, Goyo-gwĕⁿ′=Cayuga.
Goyotero=Yuma.
Goyuka=Cayuga.
Gpaughlettes=Kishpachlaots.
Granada, Granade, Granado, Granata=Hawikuh.
Grand Coweta=Kawita.
Grande=Pueblo Pintado.
Grand Eaux, Grandes Eaux=Pahatsi.
Grandes pagnes=Paskwawininiwug.
Grand Osâge=Pahatsi.
Grand Pans, Grand Par, Grand Paunec, Grand Pawnee=Chaui.
Grand Quavira, Grand Quivira=Tabira.
Grand Rapids=Kezche.
Grand Romaine=Romaine.
Grand Ronde=Willewah.
Grands, Grands Panis=Chaui.
Grands Taensas=Taensa.
Grand Tuc, Grand Zo, Grand Zue=Pahatsi.
Gran Quivira=Quivira, Tabira.
Gran Quivra=Tabira.
Gran Teguaio=Teguayo.
Grasshopper Indians=Ute.
Grasshoppers=Masikota.
Grass Sound Indians=Huna.
Grays=Gray Village.
Grease Creek=Taltushtuntude.
Great Belly Indians=Gros Ventres.
Great Kammas=Tukuarika.
Great Miami village=Kekionga.
Great Osage, Great Ossage, Great Ozages=Pahatsi.
Great Pawnee=Chaui.
Great Sáwokli, Great Swaglaw=Sawokli.
Great Teguai=Teguayo.
Great Tellico=Tellico.
Great Village, Great White Apple Village=White Apple.
Greek nation=Creeks.
Green River band=Akanaquint.
Green River Indians=Skopamish.
Green River Snakes=Washakie's Band.
Green River Utahs=Akanaquint.
Greenville=Lakkulzap.
Green Wood Indians=Nez Percés.
Grenada, Grenade=Hawikuh.
Grey Eyes=Inshtasanda.
Grigas=Grigras.
Grizzly Bear gens=Mantuemkashika.
Gros Cap=Michipicoten.
Grosse Ventres, Grossventers, Gross-Ventres, Gross Ventres proper=Gros Ventres.
Gros Ventre=Hidatsa.
Gros Ventre of the Fort Prairie, Gros Ventres, Gros Ventres des Plaines, Gros Ventres des Prairies, Gros Ventres of the Falls=Atsina.
Gros Ventres of the Missouri=Gros Ventres.
Gros Ventres of the Prairie=Atsina.
Gros-Vents=Gros Ventres.
Grosvontres of the Prairie=Atsina.
Ground-Hog-Eaters=Yahandika.
Grouse Men=Sipushkanumanke.
Grovan=Gros Ventres.
G-tinkit, G'tinkit=Tlingit.
Gua=Quanmugua.
Guacane=Guancane.

Guachoia=Guachoya.
Guachoula, Guachoule=Guaxule.
Guachoyanque=Guachoya.
Guachule=Guaxule.
Guachurrones=Wacharones.
Guactum=San Serafin.
Guadalupe=Nuestra Señora de Guadalupe de los Nacogdoches, Nuestra Señora de la Guadalupe, Pojoaque, Zuñi.
Guadalupe de los Nacogdoches=Nuestra Señora de la Guadalupe.
Guadalupe del Paso=El Paso.
Guadalupe Nacori=Nacori.
Guadalupe Ocotan=Ocotan.
Guadalupe-Pa-Pagoe=Guadalupe.
Guadalupe Teuricachi=Teuricachi.
Guadelupe=Guadalupe.
Guaden Huetten=Gnadenhuetten.
Guaes=Kansa.
Guagarispa=Arizpe.
Guagenigronnons=Mohawk.
Guaicamaopa=Yacum.
Gu-ai-hendlas-hade=Kweundlas.
Guak-s'n-a-mish=Squaxon.
Gualciones=Guaycones.
Gualliba, Gualliva=Walapai.
Gualpa, Gualpe, Gualpi, Gualpimas=Walpi.
Guamoa=Guamua.
Guananesses=Conoy.
Guanavepe=Guanabepe.
Guandastogues, Guandostagues=Conestoga.
Guanicarichic=Carichic.
Guapos=Wappo.
Guaquili=Aguaquiri.
Guaragunve, Guardgumve, Guardgunve=Guarungunve.
Guardou=Gadaho.
Guarugumbe, Guarugunve, Guarunguve=Guarungunve.
Guas=Guaes.
Guasabas=Guazavas.
Guasaca=Guacata.
Guasachis=Osage.
Guasámas=Cathlamet.
Guasamota=Guazamota.
Guasarochic=Guazarachic.
Guasavas=Guazavas.
Guasave=San Pedro Guazave, Vacoregue.
Guasers=Guasas.
Gua-shil-la=Goasila.
Guasili, Guasuli=Guaxule.
Guatari=Watereo.
Gua'thlakanashishi=Wakanasisi.
Guathla'payak=Cathlapotle.
Guatitritti=Guatitruti.
Gua'ts'ēnoq, Gua'ts'ēnôx=Quatsino.
Guatzinera=Huachinera.
Guau'aēnoq, Guau'aēnôx=Guauaenok.
Guaxula=Guaxule.
Guayavas=Guazavas.
Guaypipa=Cuiapaipa.
Guazaca=Guazavas.
Guazápare=Guazapar.
Guazarachis=Guazarachic.
Guazas=Guasas, Kiowa.
Guazave=Vacoregue.
Guazavez=Guevavi.
Guazayepo=Guazapares.
Gubates=Tano.
Guchillo=Cuchillo.
Guebavi=Guevavi.
Gueiquizales=Gueiquesales.
Guelpee=Walpi.
Guenocks=Wenok.
Guerechio=Guerachic.
Guerechos=Querechos.
Gueres=Keresan Family.
Guerriers=Dakota.
Guerriers de la Roche, Guerriers de pierre=Assiniboin.
Gué-u-gweh=Goiogouen.
Gueva=Guevu.
Guevaví-Gussudac=Guevavi.
Guhunes=Tontos.
Guibisnuches=Wiminuche.
Guichais=Kichai.
Guichita, Guichitià=Wichita.
Guichyana=Yuma.
Guiguimuches=Wiminuche.

Guilach=Wichita.
Guilistinons=Cree.
Guillicas, Guilucos=Guilitoy.
Guimzique, Guin-se-ua=Gyusiwa.
Guiogouins=Cayuga.
Guipaca=Huepac.
Guipana=Kipana.
Guipaolave, Guipaulavi=Shipaulovi.
Guiperi, Guipui, Gui-pu-y=Gipuy.
Guiricatà=San Juan de Dios.
Guiscat=Quiscat.
Guithl'akimas=Clackama.
Guithlamethl=Cathlamet.
Guithlasko=Wasco.
Guithlia-ishalxi=Ktlaeshatlkik.
Guithli'á-Kishatchk=Upper Chinook.
Guitzeis=Kichai.
Gūi-yūs=Ditsakana.
Gû'lani'yĭ=Guhlaniyi.
Gulf Lake reservation=Gull Lake Band.
Gumshewa=Cumshewa.
Günăchonkon=Gunachonken.
Gû'năhitûñ'yi=Valleytown.
Gunana=Athapascan Family.
Gunaqă'=Gunakhe.
Gûn'-dĭ'gaduhûñyĭ=Turkeytown.
Gun-nah-ho=Gonaho.
Gunter's Landing=Creek Path.
Gu'nwa=Gwinwah.
Gupa-nga-git-om=Gupa.
Gusano=Seyupa.
Gū-shŏ-döj-kā=Kotsoteka.
Gusudac, Gusutaqui=Guevavi.
Gutahs=Ute.
Gû'ta'k=Kiowa Apache.
Guth-le-uk-qwan=Ugalakmiut.
Gū'tskiā'wē=Cree.
Guvoverde=Gubo.
Gu'wisguwĭ'=Cooweescoowee.
Guyandot=Huron.
Guyas=Guaes.
Guylpunes=Khulpuni.
Guymen=Guimen.
Gwahago=Cayahoga.
Gwaugueh=Cayuga.
Gwa-u-gwek=Gayagaanhe.
GwāᵍyasdEmsē=Kwaustums.
Gweugweh=Goiogouen.
Gwe-u-gweh-o-nó=Cayuga.
Gwhunnughshonee=Iroquois.
Gyai'-ko=Comanche.
Gyandottes=Huron.
Gyarzobi, Gya'-zro wüñwü, Gyazru wiñwû=Gyazru.
Gyē'qsEm=Gyeksem.
Gyidesdzó=Kittizoo.
Gyidnadǎ'eks=Kinuhtoiah.
Gyidzaхtlä'tl=Kitsalthlal.
Gyidzī's=Kitzeesh.
Gyi'gyElk'am=Gyigyilkam.
Gyikshan=Kitksan.
Gyilaxstǎ'oks=Gyilaktsaoks.
Gyilōts'ä'ṛ=Kilutsai.
Gyimanoitq=Kitlope.
Gyinaхangyi'ek=Kinagingeeg.
Gyispaqlā'ots=Kishpachlaots.
Gyispayôko=Kishpiyeoux.
Gyiŝpeхlǎ'ots=Kishpachlaots.
GyīspótuwE'da=Gyispawaduweda.
Gyit'amā't=Kitamat.
Gyît'anmā'kys=Kitanmaiksh.
Gyit'Endâ=Kitunto.
Gyitg·ā'ata=Kitkahta.
Gyitingits'ats, Gyit'ĭngyits'ats=Gitin-gidjats.
Gyit'ĭns=Gituns.
Gyitksa'n, Gyitkshan=Kitksan.
Gyitlä'n=Kitlani.
Gyît'laqdā'mĭko=Kitlakdamix.
Gyitlō'p=Kitlope.
Gyitqā'tla=Kitkatla.
Gyits'ala'ser=Kitzilas.
Gyîtsigyu'ktla=Kitzegukla.
Gyits'umrä'lon=Kitzimgaylum.
Gyitwulgyâ'ts=Kitwilgioks.
Gyitwulksęba'=Kitwilksheba.
Gyitwunga'=Kitwingach.
Gyîtwunksē'tlk=Kitwinshilk.
Gyîtwuntlkō'l=Kitwinskole.
Gyitхtsä'хtl=Gyitktsaktl.

Haai'alik·auaē= Haaialikyauae.
Haai'lak·Emaē= Haailakyemae.
Háami= Hami.
Hā'anaLēnôx, Hā'anatlēnoq= Haanatlenok.
Haatse= Haatze.
Háatsü-háno= Hatsi.
Habasopis= Havasupai.
Habasto= Ahwaste.
Habbamalas= Alibamu.
Habe-napo, Ha-bi-na-pa= Khabenapo.
Habitans du Sault= Pawating.
Hab-koo-kee-ah= Acoma.
Habutas= Tano.
Hacā'ath= Hachaath.
Hacansacke, Haccinsack= Hackensack.
Ha-ċe'-pi-ri-i-nu'= Hachepiriinu.
Hachinghsack, Hachkinkeshaky= Hackensack.
Hackhocken= Hockhocken.
Hackinckesaky,   Hackinghesaky,   Hackinghsack,
   Hackinghsackin, Hackinghsakij, Hackingkesacky,
   Hackingkescaky, Hackingsack, Hackinkasacky,
   Hackinkesackinghs, Hackinkesacky, Hackinsack,
   Hackinsagh= Hackensack.
Hackquickanon= Aquackanonk.
Hackquinsack= Hackensack.
Ha'-ckûc-tûn= Hashkushtun.
Haclli= Haglli.
Hæcl'-t'û-qĭo= Hashletukhik.
Ha-coom= Yacum.
Hacquickenunk= Aquackanonk.
Hacquinsack= Hackensack.
Hacu, Hacuqua, Ha-cu-quin, Hacús= Acoma.
Hadaí, Hadaies= Adai.
Haddihaddocks= Powhatan.
Hadovesaves, Hadovessians= Dakota.
Had-sa-poke's band= Hadsapoke.
Haeeltruk, Haeeltsuk, Haeeltz, Haeeltzuk, Haeet-
   suk, Haeltzuk= Bellabella.
Hae-mish= Jemez.
Hagaligis= Hogologes.
Haghquagenonck= Aquackanonk.
Hagulget, Ha-gweïl-kĕt= Hagwilget.
Haha= Assiniboin.
Hāhatona, Haḣatonwan, Haḣatonway= Chippewa.
Hahatouadeba= Hahatonwanna.
Há-hát-tŏng,   Ḣa-há-tu-a,   Ha-ha-twawns= Chip-
   pewa.
Hahauien= Hawikuh.
Hähaúpûm= Wahowpum.
Haha-vasu-pai= Havasupai.
Hahderuka= Crows.
Hahel-topa-ipa= San Carlos Apache.
Hä'hêqolaL= Hahekolatl.
Hah-hah-ton-wah= Chippewa.
Hah-har-tones= Hahatonwanna.
Hah-kóo-kee-ah= Acoma.
Hah8endagerha= Huron.
Haḣtz-nai koon= Atsina.
Ha Huico= Hawikuh.
Ha-hwad'ja, Ha-hwádsha= Pinaleños.
Hah-wál-coes= Walapai.
Hai-ai'nĭma= Sanpoil.
Haialikyā'ūaē= Haailakyemae.
Hai-ankutchin= Hankutchin.
Hai'bata, Hâibâ'yŭ= Santa Clara.
Haicu= Hawikuh.
Haida= Skittagetan Family.
Haidah = Eskimauan Family, Chimmesyan Fam-
   ily, Haida, Koluschan Family, Skittagetan
   Family.
Hai-dai= Haida, Skittagetan Family.
Haideroka= Crows.
Haihaish= China Hat.
Haiish= Eyeish.
Hailtsa, Hailtzuk, Ha-ilt-zukh= Bellabella.
Hai''luntchi= Cayuse.
Hai'mäaxstō= Haimaaksto.
Hai-ne-na-une= Tanima.
Hainpassawan= Hampasawan.
Hains= Cayuse.
Háiokalita= San José.
Haiowanni= Yowani.
Haiphaha'= Santa Clara.
Hair Shirts= Isisokasimiks.
Hairy-Men's band= Hevhaitanio.
Hais= Eyeish.
Haiscas= Yscanis.
Hạ'-ish= Eyeish.

Hai-shi-la, Haishilla= Kitamat.
Haitch Point= Hatch Point.
Haitlin= Tait.
Haits'au, Ha-ju hade= Edjao.
Ha ka= Kiowa Apache.
Háka-hánoqᵒʰ= Hakan.
Hakesians= Haquis.
Hakh kutsor= Ashipak.
Haḳ-koo-kee-ah= Acoma.
Ha-koo-pin= Gupa.
Ha-ku, Hákukue= Acoma.
Hakupin= Gupa.
Ha-kus= Acoma.
Hakwiche= Kawia.
Halaha= Ahulka.
Hal-alt= Hellelt.
Halant= Halaut.
Halbama= Alibamu.
Halchedoma, Halchedumas= Alchedoma.
Halchuchubb= Hatchichapa.
Half breech clout people= Chegnakeokisela.
Half-Cheyenne band= Sutaio.
Half-way Creek= Hatchichapa.
Halfway House, Halfway House Indians= Talasse
Halianacani= Alimacani.
Halibee Inds.= Hillabi.
Halisanes, Halitanes= Ietan.
Halkōmē'lEm= Cowichan.
Hallapootas= Olulato.
Hallebac, Hallibees= Hillabi.
Halliquamaya= Quigyuma.
Hall of Montezuma= Casa Grande.
Halmacanir= Alimacani.
Halonagu= Halona.
Ha-lo-nah= Zuñi.
Hálona-ítiwana, Halona Kuin, Hal-onan, Halona-
   quin, Hal-on-aua, Há-lo-na-wa, Hálonawan=
   Halona.
Haltalt= Hellelt.
Halthum= Haltham.
Halthwypum= Klikitat.
Haltkam, Halt-kum= Haltham.
Háltso, Ḥáltsodĭne'= Khaltso.
Ha'lummi= Lummi.
Ha'lx'aix·tēnôx= Halkaiktenok.
Ha-ma-kaba-mitc kwa-dig= Apache.
Hamalakyauae= Gyigyilkam.
Ham-a-qua= Hanakwa.
Häma'wi= Humahwi.
Hamburg Indians= Kammatwa.
Hamefcutellies, Ha-mef-kut'-tel-li= Atuami.
Hameting-Woleyuh= Hamitin Woliyu.
Hamine-chan= Khemnichan.
Hä-mish= Jemez.
Há-mi-ting-Wo'-li-yuh= Hamitin Woliyu.
Hamockhaves, Hamoekhávé, Hamokába, Hamokavi,
   Ham-oke-avi= Mohave.
Ham-pas-sa-wan= Hampasawan.
Hamtolops= Humptulip.
Hamukahava= Mohave.
Hanaga= Henya.
Hanags= Henaggi.
Hanahaskies= Monahassano.
Hanakwiche= Serranos.
Haname= Cotonam.
Hāⁿanaxawūune'naⁿ= Hanahawunena.
Hānaĺĺinō= Haanatlenok.
Hancock Fort= Cotechney.
Hanctons= Yankton.
Hand Cutters= Dakota.
Handsome Men= Quapaw.
Hanega= Henya.
Hanes= Janos.
Hanetones= Yankton.
Hañgacenu= Hangashenu.
Hañga jiñga= Ibache.
Hañga-qti= Dtesanhadtadhishan.
Hañga utanandji= Hangatanga.
Hanging Ears= Kalispel.
Hanichiná= Isleta.
Hanieas= Henya.
Haⁿ i'niųk'ăciⁿ'a= Hanginihkashina.
Hañχa= Hangka.
Hañ'χa e'nikaci'χa= Hangkaenikashika.
Hañ'χa tañχa= Manshkaenikashika.
Hañχa utaḓanạsi= Hangkautadhantsi.
Hankha aiola= Haanka Ullah.
Hankpapes= Hunkpapa.
Hạn-Ḳutchi, Hạn-kuṭtchin= Hankutchin.

Hannakalals, Hannakallah=Hannakallal.
Hannayaye=Honeoye.
Hannetons=Yankton.
Hanneyaye=Honeoye.
Haⁿnikaciⁿga=Hangnikashinga.
Hanohaskies=Monahassano.
Hánoki, Hánom, Há-no-me, Hánomuh=Hano.
Hano Oshatch=Oshach.
Hanos=Janos.
Han-tē′wa=Hantiwi.
Hanuveche=Serranos.
Hápai, Ha′-pan-ñi=Hapanyi.
Hapapka=Ahapopka.
Ha-pe-ka, Hapitus=Hopi.
Hapsa-ro-kay, Hapsaroke=Crows.
Hapuntíka=Encinal.
Haquā′mis=Hahuamis.
Haquequenunck, Haquicqueenock=Aquackanonk.
Harā′c hit tan=Kayashkidetan.
Harae, Harale, Harall=Harahey.
Har-dil-zhay=Mohave, Tontos, Tulkepaia, Yavapai.
Hardwoods=Sugwaundugahwininewug.
Hare-Eaters=Onavas.
Hare-foot Indians, Hare Indians, Hareskins=Kawchodinne.
Har-har-tones=Hahatonwanna.
Harno, Haro=Hano.
Harones=Huron.
Harrickintoms=Tom's Town.
Harriga=Hirrihigua.
Harrison Mouth=Scowlitz.
Hartley Bay=Kitkahta.
Hasanameset, Hasanamoset, Hasanemesett=Hassanamesit.
Hasátyï=Hasatch.
Hashi=Cora.
Hasínai=Caddo.
Hasinninga=Hassinunga.
Haskánhatso, Haskanhatsódïne‘=Khaskankhatso.
Has-lintah=Haslinding.
Haslī′zdïne‘, Haslī′zni=Khashhlizhni.
Hassanamasasitt, Hassanamaskett, Hassanamesitt, Hassana-misco, Hassanamset, Hassanemesit=Hassanamesit.
Hassaninga=Hassinunga.
Hassannamesit, Hassenemassit, Hassinammisco=Hassanamesit.
Hassiniengas, Hassinugas, Hassinungaes=Hassinunga.
Hass-lin′tung=Haslinding.
Hassunnimesut=Hassanamesit.
Hastriryini=Taensa.
Hăs-twĭ-ă′-nă′=Hastwiana.
Hatarask=Hatteras.
Hatcā′ath=Hachaath.
Hatch-áh-wat=Ahchawat.
Hatcha chubba, Hatchchi chubba, Hatchechubba, Hatche chub-bau, Hatchechubbee, Hatcheechubba=Hatchichapa.
Hatchet-Creek=Potchushatchi.
Hatchita=Hitchiti.
Hatchi tchapa=Hatchichapa.
Hat Creek (Indians)=Atsugewi.
Ha′tĕné=Coos.
Ha-tha-we-ke-lah, Ha-tha-we-ki-lah=Hathawekela.
Hati′hshi′rûnû=Winnebago.
Hatilshé=Mohave, Tulkepaia, Yuma.
Hatindia8ointen=Huron.
Hatiniéye-runu=Mohawk.
Hatiwaⁿta-runh=Neutrals.
Hatorask=Hatteras.
Hatsaganhă′=Ontwaganha.
Hatschi-na-wha=Hatsinawan.
Hattack-falaih-hosh=Oklafalaya.
Hattahappas, Hattakappas=Attacapa.
Hattak-i-hol-lihtah=Watakihulata.
Hattchenae=Unakhotana.
Hatteras Indians=Hatteras.
Ha-ʒu-it‘aji=Hadtuitazhi.
Ha′ʒûnnĕ=Coos.
Hauchelage=Hochelaga.
Haugh-goghnuch-shionee=Iroquois.
Ha-ui-ca, Ha-ui-cu=Hawikuh.
Hau kan hade=Howkan.
Haulapais=Walapai.
Hau-nay-setch=Anasitch.
Haunyauya=Honeoye.
Hăutcu′k‘tlĕs‘ath=Uchucklesit.

Haute=Aute.
Hautlatin=Huntlatin.
H [aut]. Saura=Saura Towns.
Hauts-Tchinouks=Upper Chinook.
Havasopi, ′Havasua Pai, Hava-su-pay=Havasupai.
Haverstroo=Haverstraw.
Havesu-pai=Havasupai.
Havico, Ha-vi-cu, Havicuii=Hawikuh.
Havisua Pai=Havasupai.
Hawalapái, Hawalpai=Walapai.
Ha-waw-wah-lah-too-wah=Jemez.
Ha-wi-k'hu, Há-wi-k'uh-ians=Hawikuh.
Hawitches=Heuchi.
Hawk people=Kretan.
Hă-wol-lå Pai=Walapai.
Haw-on-chee=Heuchi.
Hawoyzask=Wazhush.
Haw-quo-e-hov-took=Chasta.
Haxa=Harahey.
Haxuā′mîs=Hahuamis.
Haya=Harahey.
Hayá-a, Hayáha=Chiricahua.
Haychis=Eyeish.
Haynaggi, Haynargee, Hay-narg-ger=Henaggi.
Haynokes=Eno.
Hay-way-ku, Hay-we-cu=Hawikuh.
Hay-woot=Hewut.
Hazanames=Aranama.
Heabenomas=Hoabonoma.
He′-aӿ∅ĕ taⁿwaⁿ′=Heakdhetanwan.
Hebahamo, Hebohamos=Ebahamo.
Hebonumas=Hoabonoma.
Hecatazi=Hecatari.
Hechapususse=Hitchapuksassi.
Heckwiath=Hesquiat.
He-co-necks=Shanamkarak.
Hedatse=Hidatsa.
Hegue=Eudeve.
He-high-e-nim-mo=Sanpoil.
Héhonqueronon=Kichesipirini.
Heiche=Eyeish.
Hёïltsuk, Hёï′ltsuq=Bellabella.
Heiptint Ampáfa amin=Clatsop.
Hei-to-to-wee=Heitotowa.
Hekịnxtana=Ikogmiut.
Hekwach=Agua Caliente.
Helalt=Hellelt.
Helcen=Helshen.
Helchpuck [Sasy]=Hitchapuksassi.
Helen Island=Red Rock.
Hel-ī-ok=Huililoc.
Hel-lal, Hel-lalt=Hellelt.
Hellwitts=Tlakluit.
Helmacape=Enecappe.
Helowna=Okanagan Lake.
Helto=Holholto.
Helwit=Tlakluit.
Hemeos, Hemes, Hemez=Jemez.
Ħe-mini-ćaŋ, Hemnica, Hemnicaŋ=Khemnichan
Hé-nar-ger=Henaggi.
Hencocks-Towne=Cotechney.
Henex=Jemez.
Henja-kŏn=Henya.
Hĕn′-na-ti=Henuti.
Hennĕ-ga-kŏn, Hennegas=Henya.
Hennĕsh=Choctaw.
Hen-ta-pah-tus, Hen-tee-pah-tees=Hunkpatina.
Henya qoan=Henya.
Hequi=Eudeve.
Herechenes, Hereckenes=Horicon.
Hergerits=Miskut.
Heries=Erie.
Hermes, Hernes=Jemez.
Herringuen=Hormiguero.
Heshohtakwin=Heshoktakwin.
Héshota Ihluctzina=Heshotahluptsina.
Heshota Im-kuosh-kuin, Hesho-ta Im-quosh-quin, Hesh-o-ta-inkos-qua=Heshota Imkoskwin.
Héshota Izina=Pescado.
Heshota Mĭm-kuosh-kuin, Hesho-ta Mimquoshk-kuin=Heshota Imkoskwin.
Heshota O′aquima=Kiakima.
He-sho-ta-pathl-tâîe=Kintyel.
Hesh-o-ta-sop-si-na=Heshotahluptsina.
Hesh-o-ta-thlu-al-la=Heshoktakwin.
Heshota Thluc-tzinan, Heshotathlu′ptsina=Heshotahluptsina.
He-sho-ta-tsi′-na-kwe, He sho ta tsí nan, Hesh-o-ta-tzi-na, Heshota Tzinaⁿ=Pescado.

Heshota Uthia=Heshotauthla.
Hesho-ta Yasht-ok=El Morro.
Hesh-que-aht=Hesquiat.
Hesley=Makhelchel.
Hesquiaht=Hesquiat.
Hessamesit=Hassanamesit.
Hessler=Makhelchel.
He-stands-both-sides=Anoginajin.
Heth-to-ya=Hittoya.
Hetschojoa=Echojoa.
Hĕ′vă tăn i u=Hevhaitanio.
Ḥeve=Eudeve.
Ḥe-wa′-kto-kta, Hewaktokto=Hidatsa.
Hewanee, Hewanny=Yowani.
He-war-tuk-tay=Hidatsa.
Hĕwă-tä-niuw′=Hevhaitanio.
Hewhannee=Yowani.
Hé-wi=Huwi.
Hēχalā′nois=Hekhalanois.
Heyá=Chiricahua.
Heyata-otoŋwe, Ḥeyata tonwan=Kheyataotonwe.
Ḥeyata wićasa=Kheyatawichasha.
Heyowani=Yowani.
H′hana=Khana.
Hiamonce=Hiamonee.
Hiaqui=Yaqui.
Hi-ar′=Chiricahua.
Hiazus=Yazoo.
Hiccory ground=Talasse.
Hich-a-pue-susse=Hitchapuksassi.
Hichetas=Hitchiti.
Hich′hu=Hupa.
Hichipucksassa=Hitchapuksassi.
Hickory=Jicarilla.
Hickory Ground, Hicory Ground=Talasse.
Hidatsa=Elahsa.
Hidatza=Hidatsa.
Hidery=Skittagetan Family.
Hide Strap clan=Piqosha.
Hidhatsa=Hidatsa.
Hieller=Hlielung.
Hiem-ai, Hiémide=Jemez.
Hierbipiames=Ervipiames.
Hieroquodame=Terocodame.
Hietane, Hietans=Ietan.
Hígabu=Kickapoo.
Higgaháldshu=Tillamook.
High Bar=Kwekweakwet.
High-House People=Kinaani.
Highland Brule=Kheyatawichasha.
Highlander=Chipewyan.
Highlanders=Nochpeem.
Highland Indians=Nochpeem, Wappinger, Wec-
    quaesgeek.
Highland Sicangu=Kheyatawichasha.
High Log=Finhalui.
High-minded People=Siksika.
Hightower=Etowah.
High Village=Meteahke.
Highwassee=Hiwassee.
Hihighenimmo, Hihighenimo=Sanpoil.
Hihirrigua=Hirrihigua.
Hiits Hanyi=Itrahani.
Hijames=Sijame.
Hikalia′-kue=Jicarilla.
Hikanagi=Mahican.
Hika′pu=Kickapoo.
Hikihaw, Hikkihaw=Hykehah.
Hî′-la-pi=Hillabi.
Hilchittees=Hitchiti.
Hilend′s Gila Indians=Coyoteros.
Hiletsuck, Hiletsuk=Bellabella.
Hilicopile=Helicopile.
Hilini, Hiliniki=Illinois.
Hillaba, Hillabees, Hilabi, Hillabys, Hill-au-bee=
    Hillabi.
Hilleamuck=Tillamook.
Hillebese=Hillabi.
Hillini-Lléni=Cree.
Himares, Himeris, Himuri=Imuris.
Hinássau, Hinásso=Wichita.
Hinhaⁿ-cŭⁿ-wapa=Hinhanshunwapa.
Hinhaneton=Yankton.
Hiŋhaŋ-s′uŋ-wapa=Hinhanshunwapa.
Hini=Hainai.
Hinkaneton=Yankton.
Hiouacara=Hiocaia.

Hiowanni=Yowani.
Hi′-pūk=Ypuc.
Hirequodame=Terocodame.
Hirocoi=Iroquois.
Hiroons=Huron.
Hiroquais, Hiroquois=Iroquois.
Hirriga=Hirrihigua.
Hiscas=Yscani.
Hishhue=Owaiski.
Hishi=Pueblo Largo.
Hishquayaht=Hesquiat.
His-scarlet-people=Kapozha.
Hĭssí o mé tăn i u=Hisiometaniu.
Histoppa=Histapenumanke.
His-tu-í-ta-ni-o=Atsina.
Hitäniwo′ĭv, Hi-tăn-nẹ-wo′i-e=Arapaho.
Hĭtäsi′na=Cheyenne.
Hi-tca-qce-pa-rặ=Hichakhshepara.
Hitchatees=Hitchiti.
Hitchatooche=Hitchitudshi.
Hitchetaws, Hitchetee=Hitchiti.
Hit-che-too-che=Hitchitudshi.
Hitchi=Kichai.
Hitchies=Hitchiti, Kichai.
Hitchita, Hitchittees, Hitch-ity=Hitchiti.
Hitchopararga=Kitchopataki.
Hi′-tcĭn-sú-wĭt′=Hitshinsuwit.
Hits-tcö′-wön=Hitschowon.
Hitunena, Hitunenina=Atsina.
Hive=Oivimana.
Hi′-wai-i′-t′cĕ=Hiwaithe.
H′iwana=Apache.
Hiwasse=Hiwassee.
Hiyoomannee, Hiyoowannee=Yowani.
Hizantinton=Santee.
Hlakklakatan=Ntlaktlakitin.
Hlgagilda, Hlgai-u=Skidegate.
Hlgun=Hlun.
H′lilush=Tututni.
Hlkenul=Cumshewa.
Hlu-hlu·natan=Ntlaktlakitin.
Hlukak=Hlukahadi.
Hluk-kluk-a-tan=Ntlaktlakitin.
Hmĭsĭs=Omisis.
Hoahonómos=Hoabonoma.
Hŏ′aiath=Oiaht.
Hoak=Hoako.
Hó-al-kut-whuh=Whilkut.
Ho-allo-pi=Walapai.
Hoanantum=Nonantum.
Hoancuts, Hoan′-kut=Honkut.
Hobeckenlopa=Hobeckentopa.
Hobonomas=Hoabonoma.
Hoc′-bo-a, Hoc′-bo-a wüñ-wû=Hosboa.
Hochelagenses=Hochelaga.
Hochelai, Hochelay=Hochelayi.
Ho-chon-chab-ba=Hochonchapa.
Hochuagohrah, Hochungara, Hochungarras, Hó-
    chungohrah=Winnebago.
Hock=Hoako.
Hockanoanos=Hoccanum.
Hockquackanonk, Hockquackonong, Hockqueca-
    nung, Hockquekanung, Hockquickanon=Aquack-
    anonk.
Hocks=Hoako.
Hocktem=Hoitda.
Hococwedoc=Hokokwito.
Hoctatas=Oto.
Hódash=Khotachi.
Ho-dé-no-sau-nee=Iroquois.
Ho-de′-san-no-ge-tä=Onondaga.
Ho-di-hi-dăn′-ne=Pawnee.
Ho-di-noⁿ′-syoⁿ′-ni′, Hodinoχsóni=Iroquois.
Hoe-Buckin-too-pa=Hobeckentopa.
Hoekhocken=Hockhocken.
Hoepeekee=Walpi.
Hoesh=Penateka.
Hŏ′fnowa=Honowa.
Hoganⱡáni=Khoghanhlani.
Hogăpä′goni=Paiute.
Hogelanders=Nochpeem.
Hogohegees, Hogoleeges, Hogoleegis, Hogoligis=
    Hogologes.
Hog Range=Sukaispoka.
Ho-ha, Hohays, Hohe, Hoheh, Ho-he′-i-o, Hoh-hays=
    Assiniboin.
Hohilpo=Salish.
Hóhoka=Hooka.
Ho-ho-qŏm=Casa Montezuma.

Hohtatoga=Huhlitaiga.
Hoh-tchungh-grahs=Winnebago.
Hoh-tin-oah=Hupa.
Hóhu=Hoko.
Hoidxnous=Hutsnuwu.
Hoindeborto=Hunkpatina.
Ho-is=Penateka.
Ho-ith-le-ti-gau=Huhlitaiga.
Hoithlewalee, Ho-ith-le Waule=Huhliwahli.
Ho ĭv ĭ ma nah'=Oivimana.
Hojome=Jocomes.
Hoka=Hoako.
Hokamish=Skokomish.
Ho-kan-dik'-ah, Hokan-tikara=Hohandika.
Ho-ki-um=Hoquiam.
Hok-ok-wi-dok=Hokokwito.
Hoko wiñwû, Ho'-ko wün-wû=Hoko.
Hokwa-imits=Hoquiam.
Ho-la-kal=Wilakal.
Holatlahoanna=Hotalihuyana.
Holbamas=Alibamu.
Hol-cu-ma, Ho-len-mahs, Hol-en-nas=Holkoma.
Holes=Hoh.
Holihtasha=Olitassa.
Holilepas, Holil-le-pas, Ho-lil-li-pah=Ololopa.
Hol'-ko-mah=Holkoma.
Hol-mie-uhs=Holmiuk.
Holoáloopis=Ololopa.
Hol-ó-kom-mah=Holkoma.
Hololipi, Hol-ó-lu-pai=Ololopa.
Holsteinberg=Holstenborg.
Holtz Indianer=Whilkut.
Ho-lŭǫ́-ĭk=Holukhik.
Holy Ghost, Mission of the=Shaugawaumikong.
Holy Ground=Ikanachaka.
Ho-ma=Hotachi.
Homalco=Homalko.
Homamish=Shomamish.
Ho'-mănⁿ-hănⁿ=Omaha.
Homas=Huma.
Homa Susa=Homosassa.
Ho-mel-ches=Wimilchi.
Home-nip-pah=Homnipa.
Home-war-roop=Homuarup.
Homoloa, Homoloua=Homolua.
Honachees=Mono.
Honagá'ni=Khonagani.
Hō'nak=Wharnock.
Honan=Honau.
Honanduk=Adirondack.
Hŏ-nan-ne-hó-ont=Seneca.
Honáni, Ho-na-ni-nyû-mû, Honani wiñwû, Ho-na'-ni wüñwü=Honani.
Ho-nau=Ke.
Honau wiñwû, Honawuu=Honau.
Honcpatela band=Hunkpatina.
Honctons=Yankton.
Honcut=Honkut.
Hone'-cha'-dä=Chonakera.
Honechas=Waco.
Honepapas=Hunkpapa.
Honepatela Yanctonnais, Hone-ta-par-teen=Hunkpatina.
Honey-Eaters=Penateka, Penointikara.
Honeyoye=Honeoye.
Hongashan, Hon-ga-sha-no=Hangashenu.
Hong-Kutchin=Hankutchin.
Honigeters=Penateka.
Ho-ni'-i-ta-ni-o=Pawnee.
Hónin nyumu=Honauuh.
Honkpapa=Hunkpapa.
Hon-mo-yau-cu=Honmoyaushu.
Hon-ñamu=Honau.
Honneyayea=Honeoye.
Honnontages=Onondaga.
Honnonthauans=Seneca.
Honontonchionni=Iroquois.
Honosuguaxtu-wáne=Cayuga.
Honqueronons, Honquerons=Kichesipirini.
Hōⁿtc' i-ki'-ka-ra'-tca-da=Chonakera.
Hontouaganha=Ontwaganha.
Honuχshiníondi=Seneca.
Hon'-wüñ-wü=Honau.
Hooch=Hoh.
Hoochawgenah=Winnebago.
Hoochenoos, Hoochinoo, Hoodchenoo, Hoodsinoo, Hoodsna-hoos=Hutsnuwu.
Hoof Rattle=Woksihitaniu.
Hooh=Hoh.

Hoo-ish=Penateka.
Hookchenoo=Hutsnuwu.
Hookchoie=Okchayi.
Hook-choie-oo-che, Hookchoioocke=Okchayudshi.
Hookluhmic=Lummi.
Hoo-ma=Hotachi.
Hoomi=Ahome.
Hoonah Kow=Huna.
Hoonchenoo=Hutsnuwu.
Hoone-ahs, Hoone-aks=Huna.
Hoo-ne-boo-ly=Hoonebooey.
Hooniahs, Hoonid=Huna.
Hoonselton, Hoonsolton=Honsading.
Hoonyah=Huna.
Hoopa, Hoo-pah=Hupa.
Hoosatunnuk=Stockbridge.
Hooseche, Hoositchi=Osotchi.
Hootchooee=Okchayi.
Hootsinoo, Hootz-ah-tar-qwan=Hutsnuwu.
Hoo-wun'nä=Huwanikikarachada.
Ho-pah=Hupa.
Hope=Sakahl.
Ho-pees=Hopi.
Hope Indians=Sakahls.
Hŏpetacisā'th=Opitchesaht.
Ho-pi'-ci-nu-me=Pueblos.
Hopii=Hopi.
Ho-pil-po=Hohilpos.
Hopíshinome=Pueblos.
Hopíte, Hópitû, Hopituh, Hó-pi-tûh-ci-nu-mûh, Hó-pi-tûh-ci-nyu-mûh, Ho-pi-tuh-lei-nyu-muh=Hopi.
Hopungieasaw, Hopungiesas=Piankashaw.
Hoquium=Hoquiam.
Ho-ra-tá-mŭ-make=Kharatanumanke.
Horcaquisacs, Horconcitos, Horcoquisa, Horcoquisaes=Arkokisa.
Hores=Keresan Family.
Horheton, Horhetton=Hahatonwanna.
Horikans=Horicon.
Hörltchöletchök=Huchiltchik.
Horn House=Kokopki.
Horn Mountain Indians=Etechesottine.
Horn pueblo=Walpi.
Ho-ro-ge, Horoje, Horoji=Winnebago.
Horse-path-town=Hlekatchka.
Horse Trail=Chihlakonini.
Hosboa wiñwû=Hosboa.
Hosett=Ozette.
Hosh-que-aht=Hesquiat.
Hosler=Takimilding.
Hos Ojos Calientes=Ojo Caliente.
Hostaqua, Hostaque=Yustaga.
Hostler=Takimilding.
Hotallehoyarnar=Hotalihuyana.
Ho-tan-ke=Winnebago.
Hotashĭn=Mescaleros.
Ho-ta'-tci=Hotachi.
Ho'tatci=Khotachi.
Hotcañgara=Winnebago.
Hotchon tchápa=Hochonchapa.
Hot Creek Indians=Agawesh.
Ho-te-day=Kikatsik.
Hote-shog-garah, Hote-shung-garah=Winnebago.
Hothleawally=Huhliwahli.
Hothletega, Hothtetoga=Huhlitaiga.
Hoꝗí'nesꝗakonⁿ=Sauk.
Hotinnonchiendi, Hotinnonsionni, Hotinonsionni=Iroquois.
Hotlimamish=Shotlemamish.
Hotoá-nŭtqiu=Mahohivas.
Hoton-ga=Winnebago.
Ho-tor'-lee=Hutalgalgi.
Hotos=Oto.
Hot Spring Apaches=Warm Spring Apache.
Hot Spring Valley Indians=Astakiwi.
Hottimamish, Hottunamish=Shotlemamish.
Hotulgee=Hutalgalgi.
Ho-tum-i-tá-ni-o=Hotamitaniu.
Ho-tum'-mi'-hu-is=Shungkayuteshni.
Houachees=Paiute.
Hou a guan=Howkan.
Houandates=Huron.
Houatoctotas=Oto.
Houattoehronon=Sauk.
Houebaton=Wahpeton.
Houechas=Waco.
Houetbatons=Wahpeton.
Hou-et-chus=Heuchi.

Ho-ui-ri=Howiri.
Houkan Háadē=Howkan.
Houkpapas=Hunkpapa.
Houma=Huma.
Hounena=Crows.
Hounondate, Hourons=Huron.
Housatannuck, Housatonic Indians, Housatonnoc, Houssatonnoc Indians, Houssatunnuck=Stockbridge.
Houstaqua=Yustaga.
Houtchis=Yuchi.
Houtouagaha=Ontwaganha.
How-ach-ees, How-a-chez=Heuchi.
How-a-guan=Howkan.
Ho-wah=Iowa.
Howakan=Howkan.
Howchees=Heuchi.
How-chuck-les-aht, Howchucklus-aht, Howchuk-lis-aht, Howchuklisat=Uchucklesit.
Howchungerah=Winnebago.
How-ech-ee, How-ech-es=Heuchi.
How-ge-chu=Ogeechee.
How-ku-ma=Haukoma.
How-mox-tox-sow-es=Mandan.
How-ru-ma=Haukoma.
Howschueselet=Uchucklesit.
Howtetech, How-te-te'-oh=Hudedut.
Höχsúwitan=Wichita.
Ho-ya=Hoyalas.'
Hrah-hrah-twauns=Chippewa.
Huachirrones=Wacharones.
Huachuca=Huechuca.
Huadíbis=Huirivis.
Huadji lanas=Skedans.
Huaepais=Walapai.
Huajicori=Huaxicori.
Hualapais, Hualipais, Huallapais, Huallopi=Walapai.
Huallpi=Walpi.
Hualopais, Hual-páich=Walapai.
Hualpais=Colville, Walapai.
Hualpas Indians=Walapai.
Huál-pé, Hualpec, Hual-pee, Hualpi, Hualpy, Hualvi=Walpi.
Huanchané, Huanches, Huané=Waco.
Huarogio=Varohio.
Huashashas=Osage.
Huashpa=Washpa.
Huashpa Tzena=Huashpatzena.
Huasiotos=Oto.
Huassavas=Guazavas.
Huatanis=Mandan.
Huatl-vi=Walpi.
Huatoctas=Oto.
Hubales, Hubates, Hubites=Tano.
Huc-aritz-pa=Arizpe.
Hüch=Hoh.
Huch-oo-la-chook-vaché=Casa Montezuma.
Huchun=Uchium.
Huc-klic=Nun.
Hudcoadamas, Hudcoadan, Hudcoadanes=Alchedoma.
Hueco=Waco.
Hue-la-muh=Cowichan.
Hue-lang-uh=Songish.
Huepaca=Huepac.
Huerachic=Guerachic.
Hueso Parrado=Hueso Parado.
Hu-e'-yá=Khuya.
Hue-yang-uh=Clallam.
Hŭ'-hlo=Hlahloalgi.
Huq'tañχa=Winnebago.
Huichites=Wichita.
Huila=Huilacatlan.
Huinihkaciⁿa=Hanginihkashina.
Hu i'niqk'äciⁿ'a=Huinihkashina.
Hú inikacíχa=Huinikashika.
Huiñirren=Huinyirren.
Huiris=Huirivis.
Huis van Montezuma=Casa Grande.
Huitcole=Huichol.
Huixapa=Hunxapa.
Huk=Hoako.
Huk-tyr=Ocotan.
Húkwats=Mohave, Yuma.
Hu-la-napo=Kuhlanapo.
Hulapais=Walapai.
Hú'li Wa'hli=Huhliwahli.

Hull-loo-el-lell, Hullooellell, Hul-loo-et-tell, Hul-lu-et-tell=Hullooetell.
Hulpunes=Khulpuni.
Hultulkakut=Kutul.
Hu-mā-kam=Tepecano.
Hu-má-li-wu=Malahue.
Hum-a-luh=Cowichan, Skagit.
Humanas, Humanas de Tompires, Humanas de Tompiros, Humanos=Tawehash.
Humas=Muskhogean Family, Tawehash.
Humásko=Creeks.
Hu-māt-kam=Tepecano.
Hu-mâ'-whi=Humahwi.
Humbolt Bay Indians=Wishosk.
Humenthí=Munsee.
Humo=Cops.
Hump-tu-lups,=Humptulips.
Humros=Huna.
Humunas de Tompires=Tawehash.
Huna=Gaudekan.
Huna cow, Hūna-kŏn=Huna.
Hu-na-múrp=Hunawurp.
Hunga=Hanga.
Hûng-ga ní-ka-shing-ga=Hangatanga.
Hungo Parie, Hungo Pavia, Hungo Pavie=Hungopavi.
Hun-go-tin'-ga=Hangatanga.
Hun-guh=Hanga.
Hunkappas=Hunkpapa.
Hun-ka-sis-ket=Nsisket.
Hun-koo-chin=Hankutchin.
Hunkpa-te-dans=Hunkpapa.
Hunkpatee, Hunkpati, Hunkpatidan, Hunkplatin=Hunkpatina.
Hŭñ-kqwi'-tĭk=Hunkkhwitik.
Hun-Kutchin=Hankutchin.
Huŋku wanića, Hŭñku-wanitca=Hunkuwanicha.
Hunnas=Huna.
Hun'-sa-tung=Honsading.
Huŋska-ćaŋtoźuha, Hŭⁿska-tcaⁿtojuha=Hunskachantozhuha.
Hunters=Etagottine.
Hunyo Pavie=Hungopavi.
Huokarawacoks=Cuscarawaoc.
Huphale=Eufaula.
Húpi=Hopi.
Húpô=Hupa.
Hurall=Harahey.
Hures=Ures.
Hurones, Huronnes=Huron.
Hurricane Toms=Tom's Town.
Hurripacuxi, Hurriparacussi=Tocobaga.
Hurrons=Huron.
Hŭ'saχa=Hangkaahutun, Husadta.
Hŭ'saχa Wanŭⁿ'=Husadtawanun.
Hu-sha-sha band=Wahpekute.
Huskchanoes=Conestoga.
Huskemaw=Eskimo.
Huskhuskeys=Kaskaskia.
Huskoni=Hushkoni.
Husky=Eskimo.
Huspoa=Hosboa.
Hussanamesit=Hassanamesit.
Hussleakatna=Hussliakatna.
Hu'-tab Pa-dá-niŋ=Pawnee.
Hu-ta'-ci=Lipan.
Huta-Napo=Kuhlanapo.
Hútañga=Kansa.
Hu'-tañ-χa=Winnebago.
Hutáshi=Tsiltaden.
Hutchistanet=Onondaga.
Hutepa=Papago.
Hut-tát-ch'l=Hutatchl.
Hutuk=Hutucgna.
Húuka=Hooka.
Hu-úmûi=Omaha.
Hŭ'-wi wuñ-wü=Huwi.
Húxul=Lipan.
Huzaas=Osage.
Huz-zau, Huz-zaws=Osage.
Hvattoehronon=Sauk.
Hwalapai=Walapai.
Hwat-ĕs'=Hwades.
Hweghkongh=Gweghkongh.
Hwot-es=Hwades.
Hyacks=Eyak.
Hyanaes=Cummaquid.
Hyaquez, Hyaquin, Hyaquis=Yaqui.

Hydahs=Chimmesyan Family, Haida Skitta-
geten Family, Salishan Family.
Hyder=Haida.
Hyem Tu-ay=Puretuay.
Hyeroquodame=Terocodame.
Hyo-hai-ka=Skidegate.
Hyó-qua-hoon=Pecos.
Hyroquoise, Hyroquoyse=Iroquois.
Hyscanis=Yscani.
Hyshalla=Kitamat.

Iaákema=Yakima.
Ia'an=Yan.
Iacona=Jacona.
Iacovane=Yojuane.
I-ă'cu-we tĕne'=Chemetunne.
Iăgᴇn=Hlieḷung.
I-â'-kâr=Ietan.
Íakĭm=Yaqui.
I-ákima=Yakima.
Iä'k'ō=Yaku.
Iakon=Yaquina.
Iamaços=Yamasee.
Iano=Hano.
I'-aŋ-to'-an=Jatonabine.
Iapies=Hapes.
Iaŝića=Farmers' band.
I-at=Mohave.
Iätä-go=Ute.
Iatan=Ietan.
Iawai=Iowa.
Iawani=Yowani.
Iawas, Iaway=Iowa.
Ibatc'ĕ=Ibache.
Ibequi=Yaqui.
Ibetap okla chitto=Ebita Poocola Chitto.
Ibetap okla iskitini=Ebita Poocola Skatane
Ibitachka=Ivitachuco.
Ibitoopas=Ibitoupa.
Ica=Ika.
I-ca=Isha.
Icanderago, Icanderagoes=Teatontaloga.
Icarilla Apaches=Jicarilla.
Icasque=Casqui.
Icbewas=Chippewa.
Icca=Incha.
Iccarilla=Jicarilla.
Iccu-jeune=Mimbreños.
Ice=Nukhe, Wazhazhe.
Icharilla=Jicarilla.
Ic'-hä-she=Kanze.
Ichiaha=Chiaha.
Ichiti=Hitchiti.
I'-chu-ar'-rum-pats=Ichuarumpats.
Iciaha=Chiaha.
Icogmute=Ikogmiut.
Icora=Yecora.
Ictans=Ietan.
Ictáque tci dúba=Ishtakhechiduba.
Ictasanda=Inshtasanda.
Ictŭñga=Ishtunga.
Idahi=Comanche.
Ida-ka-riúke=Idakarawakaha.
Idats'e=Kanse.
Id-do-a=Kikatsik.
Iden-noo=Eidenu.
ᵋI'djao=Edjao.
Idjorituaqtuin, Idjorituaxtiun=Idjorituaktuin.
Idkalloo=Ikalu.
I-do-ka-rai-uke=Idakariuke.
Ieanausteaiae=Teanaustayae.
Ieaogo=Tioga.
I-eh-nus=Yennis.
Iekiɟĕ=Iekidhe.
Ielan=Ietan.
Iᵍen=Rirak.
Ienecu=Senecú del Sur.
I-e'-nis=Yennis.
Ieskaćiŋóa=Ieskachincha.
Ie-ska-pi=Jatonabine.
Ieska-tciⁿtca=Ieskachincha.
Ietam=Ietan.
Ietan=Ute.
Ietanes, Ietans=Ietan.
If-terram=Ift.
Igagmjut=Igak.
Igauik, Igawik=Iguik.
Igdlopait=Igdlerpait.
Igdlulik=Iglulik.

Igdlumiut=Iglulik, Tahagmiut.
Ighelkostlende=Katagkak.
Ighiakchaghamiut=Agiukchuk.
Igiagagamute, Igiagamute=Igiak.
Igihuá-a=Apache.
Igiogagamut=Igiak.
Igita=Etah.
Igivachochamiut=Igivachok.
Iglaka-teqila=Iglakatekhila.
Igloodahominy=Igludahoming.
Igloolik, Igloolip=Iglulik.
Igluduä'hsuin=Igluduasuin.
Iglulingmiut=Iglulirmiut.
Iglu-miut=Tahagmiut.
Ignanine=Imnongana.
Ignerhonons, Ignierhonons=Mohawk.
Ignituk=Iknetuk.
Ignokhatskomute=Ignok.
Igognak, Igonok=Eider.
Igragamiut=Igiak.
Igtigalik=Iktigalik.
Iguaces=Yguases.
Iguanas=Iguanes.
Iguases=Yguases.
Igushel=Igushik.
Iha-ca=Ihasha.
Ihá'gtawa Kátaχka, Ihanketwans, Ihañk'taⁿwiⁿ,
Ihaŋktoŋwaŋ=Yankton.
Ihaŋktoŋwaŋna, Ihanktonwanna Dakotas, Ihank-
tonwannas=Yanktonai.
Ihanktonwans, Ihanktonwe=Yankton.
Ihan-k'-tow-wan-nan, Ihank'-t'wan-ahs=Yank-
tonai.
Ihank'-t'wans=Yankton.
Iha-ŝa=Ihasha.
Ihauk-to-wa-na, Ihauk-t'wan-ahs=Yanktonai.
Ihauk-t'wans=Yankton.
Ïʻhl-dĕné=Navaho.
Ihnek=Amaikiara.
Ihon-a-Does=Juniata.
Ihonattiria=Ihonatiria.
Ihoway=Iowa.
Ih-pó-se-mä=Ipoksimaiks.
Iicarrillas=Jicarilla.
Ika=Aika.
Ikaklagmute=Ikatlek.
Ikaligvigmiut, Ikaligwigmjut=Chinik.
Ikalinkmiut, Ikaliukha, Ikal-ukha=Ekilik.
Ikanafáskalgi=Seminole.
Ikanatcháka=Ikanachaka.
Ikaniúksalgi=Seminole.
Ikan'-tcháti=Kanchati.
I-ka-nuck=Ikaruck.
I'-ka-dŭ'=Kickapoo.
Ikarik=Wichita.
Ikărlo=Ikalu.
Ikatlegomut, Ikatlegomute=Ikatlek.
Ikechipouta=Ikachiocata.
Ikekik=Kiktaguk.
Ikhiak=Eyak.
Ikikiktock=Kiktaguk.
Ik-khagmute=Ikak.
Ik-kil-lin=Kutchakutchin.
Iko-agmiut=Chnagmiut.
Ikoghmiout, Ikogmjut, Ikogmut, Ikogmute=Ikog-
miut.
Ikoklag'mūt=Ikatlek.
Ikouera=Koroa.
Iktigalk=Igtigalik.
Ikuagmiut=Chnagmiut.
Ikuagmjut=Ikogmiut.
Ikuak=Chnagmiut.
Ikutchlok=Kutchlok.
Ikvagmutes=Magemiut.
Ikvogmutes=Ikogmiut.
Ikwanek=Shanamkarak.
Ilamatt=Klamath.
Ilaoquatsh=Clayoquot.
Ilatamaa=Altamaha.
Ita'xluit=Tlakluit.
Ildefonso=San Ildefonso.
Ilesta=Isleta del Sur.
Ilet=Isleta.
Iletsuck=Bellabella.
Ilgát=Chehalis.
Ilghi'mi=Bellacoola.
Ilgonquines=Nipissing.
Ilicos=Anilco.

Ilimouek, Iliné, Ilinese, Ilinesen, Ilinioüek, Ilinois, Ilinoüets, Ilinoüetz, Ilionois=Illinois.
Iliutagamute=Iliutak.
Iljljuljuk=Iliuliuk.
Illenois, Illenonecks, Illicoueck, Illimoüec, Illinese, Illinesen, Il-li-ni, Illiniens, Illiniwek, Illinoias=Illinois.
Illinois Creek=Chasta, Salwahka.
Illinois Valley (band)=Salwahka.
Illinoix, Illinonecks, Illinoneeks, Illinouecks=Illinois.
Illmawees=Ilmawi.
Illonese, Illonois=Illinois.
Illoolook=Iliuliuk.
Illth-cah-get-la=Skidegate.
Illuidlek=Iluilek.
Illuni=Illinois.
Il'séꞓl-ꞓa-wai'-ă-mĕ=Ilsethlthawaiame.
Iltenleiden=Intenleiden.
Iltte-kaï-mamits=Ithkyemamits.
Ilwans=Etiwaw.
Ilyamna=Iliamna.
Ilyamna people=Knaiakhotana.
I'ma=Quapaw.
Imach-leet=Imaklimiut.
Imagnak, Imagninskoe=Imagnee.
Imaham=Imaha.
Imahans=Quapaw.
Imahao, Imahaus=Imaha.
Imakleet, Imaklitgmut=Imaklimiut.
Imangen=Imnongana.
Immaculate Conception=Concepcion, Ihonatiria, Ossossane.
Immaculée Conception de Notre Dame aux Illinois=Immaculate Conception.
Im-mook-fau=Imukfa.
Imnagen=Imnongana.
Imokhtagokhshuk, Imokhtegokhshuk=Imoktegokshuk.
Imoklasha Iskitini=Imongalasha Skatane.
Imoris=Imuris.
Imtelleiden=Intenleiden.
I'mtun=Intuk.
Imuanak=Imnongana.
Imuklásha=Imongalasha.
Imures, Imurez, Imuri, Imuriz=Imuris.
I'-na-cꞓĕ=Nez Percés.
I-na-há-o-win=Inyanḫaoin.
Inajalayehua=Majalayghua.
Inalugmiut=Inguklimiut, Imaklimiut.
Inapaw=Quapaw.
In-as-petsum=Nespelim.
Inatahĭn=Mescaleros.
Inay=Hainai.
In-breeders=Waglukhe.
Inchulukhlaites=Inkalich.
Ĭndá=Comanche.
Indaochaie=Lichtenau.
Inda Tsä'-än=Kiowa Apache.
Inde=Apache.
Indian Oldtown=Oldtown.
Indians of the Long Reach=Wappinger.
Indians of the Lower Kootenay=Lower Kutenai.
Indian Wells=Kavinish.
Indiens Cuivres=Tatsanottine.
Indiens du Sang=Kainah.
Indiens-Loups=Skidi.
Indiens-Pierre=Assiniboin.
Indiens Serpents=Shoshoni.
Indilche-Dentiene=Indelchidnti.
Indio=Paltewat.
Indios Manzos=Pueblos.
Ineja=Inyaha.
In'ĕ-waqube-aꞓiⁿ=Inewakhubeadhin.
Ingahameh, Ingahamiut=Ingahame.
Ingaleek, Ingleet, Ingalete, Ing'aliki=Ingalik.
Ingaliks=Kaiyuhkhotana.
Ingalit=Ingalik.
Iñgꞓe-jide=Ingdhezhide.
Ingechuk=Chnagmiut.
Ingekasagmi=Ignok, Ingalik.
Ingeletes=Ingalik.
Ingeramut=Inger.
Ing-gera-je-da=Ingdhezhide.
Ingichuk=Chnagmiut.
Inglūtāl'igemūt=Inglutaligemiut.
Ingrakaghamiut=Ingrakak.
In-grä'-zhe-da=Ingdhezhide.
Ing-üh-kli-mūt=Inguklimiut.

Ĭng-wë-pi'-raⁿ-di-vi-he-maⁿ=Keresan Family.
Ini=Hainai.
Inicanopa=Pilaklikaha.
Inics, Inies=Hainai.
Ininyu-wë-u=Cree.
Inipoi=Anepo.
Injaya=Inyaha.
Inkalichljuaten=Inkalich.
In-kal-ik=Ingalik, Kaiyuhkhotana.
Inkalite=Ingalik.
Inkaliten=Ingalik, Kaiyuhkhotana, Kuskwogmiut, Magemiut.
Inkasaba=Inkesabe.
Iñꞓøüñ'kaɔiñ'ꞕa=Inkdhunkashinka.
Inkilik, Inkiliken=Ingalik.
Inkilikeu=Kaiyuhkhotana.
Inkilik Ingelnut=Jugelnute.
Ink-ka'-sa-ba=Inkesabe.
Ink-pa-du-ta['s band], Ink-pah-doo-ta band=Wamdisapa's Band.
Inkpatonwan=Inkpa.
Inkülüchlüaten, Inkulukhlaites, Inkuluklaities=Inkalich.
Innatchas=Natchez.
In-neck=Amaikiara.
Innies=Hainai.
In-ninyu-wuk=Cree.
Innoit=Eskimo.
Innondadese=Tionontati.
Innu, Innuees, Innuit=Eskimo.
Innüit=Esquimauan Family.
Inocanopy=Pilaklikaha.
Inoschujöchen=Inoschuochn.
Inparavi=Shipaulovi.
Inpaton=Inkpa.
Inquoi=Iroquois.
Inshaunshagota=Yoroonwago.
In'shin=Konkau.
Insiachamiut=Insiachak.
Inside Fat=Kakapoya.
In-spellum=Nespelim.
Insular=Salishan Family.
Inta=Ute.
Iⁿꞕaꞕpupcĕ'=Intapupshe.
Iⁿ'-tci=Inchi.
In-tem-peach-es, In-tim-peach, In-tim-peches=Intimbich.
Intsi Dindjick=Ahtena.
Intsi-Dindjitch=Koyukukhotana.
In-tuch-cul-gau=Intatchkál̆gi.
Intujen-né=Faraon.
Inugleet=Inguklimiut.
Inuin, Inuit=Eskimo.
I-nuks'-iks=Inuksiks.
Inûna-ina=Arapaho.
Inverted (Society)=Himoiyoqis.
Iꞃyaⁿ-h-oiꞃ=Inyanhaoin.
Iⁿyaⁿ-tceyaka-atoⁿwaⁿ=Inyancheyakaatonwan.
Iⁿyaⁿtoⁿwaⁿ=Jatonabine.
Iⁿyávapé=Yavapai.
Ioewaig=Iowa.
Iogopani, Iogopapi=Shongopovi.
Iohn-a-Does=Juniata.
Iojuan=Yojuane.
Iola=Jore.
Iondes, Ionees, I-on-i, Ionias, Ionies=Hainai.
Ionontady-Hagas=Tionontati.
Iotan=Ietan.
Iottecas=Juniata.
Iowanes=Yowani.
Iowaulkeno=Tawakoni.
Ioway=Iowa.
Ipande, Ipandi=Lipan.
Ipataragüites=Tawehash.
I-pe-re=San Lázaro.
Ipiutelling, Ipnitelling=Idiutelling.
Ipoilq=Sanpoil.
Ipupukhmam=Medilding.
I-qẽr-qa-mūt'=Ikherkhamut.
Iquahsinawmish=Squaxon.
Irans village=Tenankutchin.
Iraqua Indians=Elwha.
Irecoies, Irequois=Iroquois.
Irinions=Illinois.
Iripegouans=Winnebago.
Iriquoi=Iroquois.
Irkρéléït=Athapascan Family, Kutchin.
Irocois, Irocquois, Irognas, Irokesen=Iroquois.
Iron-Cloud=Makhpiyamaza.

Ironeyes, Ironies=Hainai.
Ironois=Iroquois.
Iroondocks=Adirondack.
Iroquaes, Iroque, Iroquese, Iroqueze, Iroquiese, Iroquoi=Iroquois.
Iroquois d'enbas=Mohawk.
Iroquois du Sault=Caughnawaga.
Iroquois inferieurs=Mohawk.
Iroquois of the Sault=Caughnawaga.
Iroquos, Irriquois=Iroquois.
Irrironnons, Irrironons=Erie.
Irrohatock=Arrohattoc.
Irroquois, Irroquoys=Iroquois.
Iruaitsu, I'ruwai=Iruwaitsu.
Is=Ais.
Isaacs=Kwik.
Isallanic race=Cherokee.
Isalleet=Silela.
Isalwalken=Isalwakten.
Isamishs=Samish.
Isammuck=Isamuck.
Isanati=Santee.
Isanisks=Sanetch.
Isanti, Isantie Dakotas, Isanties, I-saŋ'-tis, Isantiton, Isanyate, Isanyati=Santee.
I-sa-pó-a=Crows.
Isaŝhbaĥatsĕ=Sarsi.
Isatis=Santee.
Isa-ttiné=Tsattine.
Isaunties=Santee.
Í-sau-üh wüñ-wû, Isauu wiñwû=Ishauu.
Iscanis=Yscanis.
Ischua=Geneseo.
Isconis=Yscanis.
Iselle=Isleta del Sur.
Iseta=Isleta.
Is-fä-nŭl'-ke=Isfanalgi.
Ísh, I-sha-hue=Ishauu.
Ishango=Brulé.
Ishawu, Íshawuu=Ishauu.
Ish-dä'-sun-da=Inshtasanda.
Ish-e-pish-e=Ishipishi.
Ishguaget=Ishgua.
Ishisageck Roanu=Missisauga.
Ish-poän-ee=Ishpani.
Ish-ta-sun'-da=Inshtasanda.
Ish-te-pit'-e=Siksika.
Ishti semoli=Seminole.
Ĭsh'to-háno=Ishtowa.
Isimpshean=Tsimshian.
Isipopolames=Espopolames.
Ĭ'sium-itä'niuw'=Hisiometaniu.
Is-ksi'-na-tup-i=Esksinaitupiks.
Isla=Isleta del Sur.
Island Innuit=Okiogmiut.
Isle aux Noix=Illinois.
Isle-de-Peins, Isle-de-peiree, Isle-de-Pierre=Sinkiuse.
Isle de Saincte Marie.=Ekaentoton.
Islella=Isleta.
Isle of St. John's=Micmac.
Isle-river Indians=Eel River Indians.
Isletabuh=Isleta.
Isleta del Paso, Isleta del Passo=Isleta del Sur.
Isletans=Isleta.
Isleta of the South=Isleta del Sur.
Isleteños, Isletta=Isleta, Isleta del Sur.
Islinois=Illinois.
Isoletta=Isleta.
Isonisks=Songish.
I-sönsh'-pu-she=Cheyenne.
Isowasson=Sewathen.
Ispa=Arizpe.
Ispáni=Ishpani.
Ispatingh=Hespatingh.
Is-po-co-gee, Ispokógi=Tukabatchi.
Isquahala=Skaialo.
Issa=Catawba.
Issanti=Santee.
Issăppo'=Crows.
Issaqui, Issaquy=Santee.
Issati=Assiniboin, Santee.
Issatie, Issatrians=Santee.
Isshe-pishe-rah=Ishipishi.
Issi-Chupicha, Issi-Schüpischa=Siksika.
Istanare=Ustanali.
Istasunda=Inshtasanda.
Isti simanole=Seminole.
Istudschi läika=Istudshilaika.

Isty-semole=Seminole.
I'sŭ'nigû=Seneca.
I-tach-ee, Itaches=Iticha.
Ita-Eskimos=Ita.
Itahátski=Dakota.
Itah-Ischipahji=Cheyenne.
Itahzipchois=Sans Arcs.
Ita-Iddi=Arapaho.
i-Tá-i-na-ma=Taos.
Italisi=Talasse.
Itálua fátcha-sígo, Itálua ispokógi=Tukabatchi.
Itálua 'láko=Apalachicola.
Itamamiou=Itamameou.
Ĭtămi, Itaner, Itanese=Ita.
Ĭt-ånsĕ-pŏ-pĕ=Cheyenne.
Ĭt-åns-kĕ=Dakota.
I-tá-ŝu-pu-zi=Cheyenne.
I'tăwă'=Etowah.
Itazipchos, Itazipóo, Itazipcoes, Itazipko=Sans Arcs.
Itaziptco-qtca=Itazipcho.
Itchali=Kutchakutchin.
Itchi-mehueves=Chemehuevi.
It-chit-a-bud-ah=Ditsakana.
Itean=Ietan.
I-te-che, I-tech-ees=Iticha.
Ite-citca=Iteshicha.
Ite-citca-etaⁿhaⁿ=Iteshichaetanhan.
Ite ġu=Iteghu.
Iterlĕ'hsoa=Iterlesoa.
Ite-śića=Iteshicha.
Ite śića etaŋhaŋ=Iteshichaaetanhan.
Ite-xu=Iteghu.
Itha=Yta.
Ithalé tĕni=Mishikhwutmetunne.
It-kagh-lie, It-ka-lya-rūin, Ĭt-ka-lyi, Itkpélit, Itkρéléit, Itkû'dlĭñ=Kutchakutchin.
Itoaten=Tautin.
I-to-ches=Iticha.
Itokaĥ tina, Itokaq-tina=Itokakhtina.
Itsă'tĭ=Echota.
I-tsá'-ti=Santee.
Itsisihiŝa, Ĭ tsi ŝí pi ŝa=Siksika.
Ittawans=Etiwaw.
Ĭt-t'hági=Sichomovi.
Ittibloo, Ittiblu, Ittiblu-Netlik=Itibleng.
Ituchas=Iticha.
It-us-shé-na=Cheyenne.
Itynai=Athapascan Family.
Ĭt-zĕ-sŭ-pĕ-shá=Siksika.
I-ŭkä tĕné=Yukichetunne.
I-uke-spi-ule=Aigspaluma.
Iulukiak=Tuluksak.
Iúmanas, Iumanes, Iumanos=Tawehash.
Iumbucanis=Yubuincariri.
Í-um-Ó-otam=Comeya.
I-u'-ni=Calapooya.
Iuragen=Tioga.
Ivan's barrabora=Ivan.
Ivap'i=Karok.
Ĭ vĭsts tsĭ nĭh' pah=Heviqsnipahis.
Ivitachma, Ivitachua, Ivi-ta-chuco, Ivitanoa=Ivitachuco.
Íwanies=Yowani.
Iwikties=Miami.
Iwillichs, Iwillie, Iwillik=Aivilik.
Ixcanis=Yscanis.
Iyakha=Yangna.
Iyakhba, Iyakhwa=Iowa.
I-yá-kĭn=Walpi.
Iyanabi=Ayanabi.
Iyich=Tyigh.
Iyiniwok=Cree.
I-yiss=Iyis.
Iyuĥba=Iowa.
Iyutagjen-né=Navaho.
Izacanis=Yscanis.
Izaty=Santee.

Jaakema=Yakima.
Jaba=Jova.
Jabesua=Havasupai.
Jacarilla Apaches, Jacarrilla Apaches=Jicarilla.
Jacdoas=Judosa.
Jacobs-haven=Jakobshavn.
Jacoma=Gupa.
Jacome, Jacomis=Jocomes.
Jacon=Yaquina.

Jacopin=Gupa.
Jacum=Yacum.
Jaega=Jeaga.
Jaguallapai, Jagullapai, Jaguyapay=Walapai.
Jahuicu=Hawikuh.
Jaibanipitca=Gaibanipitea.
Jakechedunes=Alchedoma.
Jake's people=Niletunne.
Jakhutháth=Yakutat.
Jakis=Sauk.
Jakon=Yaquina.
Jakou=Yazoo.
Jakutat, Jakutat-kŏn=Yakutat.
Jalchedon, Jalchedum, Jalchedunes=Alchedoma.
Jallaguapais=Walapai.
Jallicuamai, Jallicuamay, Jallicumay, Jalliqua-
mai, Jalliquamay=Quigyuma.
Jamaica=Jameco.
Jamajabas, Jamajabs, Jamajas, Jamalas=Mohave.
Jamasees=Yamasee.
Jambujos=Cambujos.
James=Jemez.
James Boy=Hlaphlako.
Jamestown=Huiauultc.
Jamez=Jemez.
Jamos=Janos.
Janaɉa nikaciⁿga=Yankton.
Janaya=Hanaya.
Jancae=Tonkawa.
Janequeile=Serranos.
Janeros=Janos.
Janha-ɉaøicaⁿ=Zhanhadtadhishan.
Janⁱ-i'tci=Zhanichi.
Jano=Hano.
Janogualpa=Hano, Walpi.
Jantonnais, Jantonnees, Jantonnois=Yanktonai.
Jantons, Jantous=Yankton.
Janⁿ-waqube-aøiⁿ=Zhanhadtadhishan.
Jaomeme=Ahome.
Jaos=Taos.
Japiam=Yapiam.
Japiel=Japul.
Japies=Hapes.
Japui=Japul.
Jaqualapai, Jaquallapai=Walapai.
Jarame, Jarames=Xarame.
Jarañames=Aranama.
Jarosoma=Apache.
Jarquin=Karkin.
Jascag, Jascage, Jaskegis, Jaskigis=Tuskegee.
Jason=Yazoo.
Jasquijis=Tuskegee.
Jatapaña=Pima.
Jatche-thin-juwuc=Yatcheethinyoowuc.
Jaupin=Weapemeoc.
Java Supais, Javeusa=Havasupai.
Jawé nikaciɉa=Zhawenikashika.
Jeapes=Hapes.
Jece=Ais.
Jecorilla=Jicarilla.
Jecualme=Tecualme.
Jecuches, Jecuéche, Jecuiches=Kawia.
Jedacne=Jedakne.
Jediuk=Shediac.
Je-gó-sä-saa=Neuter.
Jehuas=Tewa.
Jelish=Salishan Family.
Jemaco=Jameco.
Jemas, Jemes, Jemex, Jemmes, Jemos=Jemez.
Jendestáke=Yendestake.
Jeneckaws=Seneca.
Jenecu=Senecú del Sur.
Jenegueches, Jeneguechi, Jenequiches=Serranos.
Jenies=Jemez.
Jenigueche, Jenigueich, Jenigueih, Jeniguich=Ser-
ranos.
Jennessee=Geneseo.
Jenondades=Tionontati.
Jenondages=Onondaga.
Jenondathese=Tionontati.
Jenontowanos=Seneca.
Jenundadees=Tionontati.
Jequiches=Kawia.
Jerez=Keresan Family.
Jermz=Jemez.
Jernaistes=Caughnawaga.
Jesus Carichic=Carichic.
Jesus del Monte de Tutuaca=Tutuaca.
Jesus María Basani=Bisani.

Jetam, Jetañs=Ietan.
Jettipehika=Chubkwichalobi.
Jeune Lorette=Lorette.
Jeures=Jemez.
Jibewas=Chippewa.
Jicaras, Jicarello Apaches, Jicarila Apache, Jica-
rilla Apaches, Jicarilleros, Jicarillos, Jicarrilla
Apaches, Jiccarilla Apache, Jickorie, Jicorilla,
Jicorilla Apaches=Jicarilla.
Jim Boy's=Hlaphlako.
Jimena=Galisteo.
Jimenez=Jemez.
J. José' Ramos Ayodsudao=Basotutcan.
Jlacus=Jlaacs.
Joara=Cheraw.
Joba, Jobal, Jobales=Jova.
Jobiscauga=Sibagna.
Joco=Toquo.
Jocomeos, Jocomis=Jocomes.
Johnadoes=Juniata.
John Days, John Day's river=John Day.
Jojuanes=Yojuane.
Jollillepas=Ololopa.
Jonatas=Ionata.
Jongoapi, Jongopabi, Jongopai, Jongopavi, Jong-
vapi=Shongopovi.
Jonies=Hainai.
Jon-joncali=Shongopovi.
Jonkta=Chankute.
Jonondese, Jonondeseh=Jonondes.
Jonontadynago=Tionontati.
Joree=Jore.
Joshua, Joshuts=Chemetunne.
Josimnin=Khosimnin.
Joskagi=Tuskegee.
Joso=Hopi.
Jo-so-ge=Abiquiu.
Jotans=Ietan.
Jougopavi=Shumopavi.
Joukiousmé, Jouskiousme=Jukiusme.
Jowai, Jowas, Joways=Iowa.
Joya=La Joya.
Joyl-ra-ua=Opata.
Joyvan=Yojuane.
Jsleta=Isleta.
Juacanas, Juacano=Tawakoni.
Juálati=Atfalati.
Jual-pi=Walpi.
Juan Quivira=Tabira.
Juchium=Uchium.
Jugelnuten, Jugelnuts=Jugelnute.
Jū-ī=Penateka.
Jujubit=Juyubit.
Juke-yunke=Yugeuingge.
Julimeños=Hulimenos.
Jumana=Tawehash.
Jumancas=Pueblo de los Jumanos.
Jumanes, Jumano, Jumanoes, Jumanos=Tawehash.
Jumas=Tawehash, Yuma.
Jumbuicrariri=Yubuincariri.
Jume, Jumees=Hume.
Jumez=Jemez.
Jumpers=Chippewa.
Jum-pys=Yavapai.
Junachotana=Unakhotana.
Juneau=Tsantikihin.
Juneauta=Juniata.
Junétre=Tajique.
Juni=Zuñi.
Juniagacori=Tumacacori.
Juníguis=Serranos.
Jūnnäkächotāna=Koyukhotana, Unakhotana.
Juparivi=Shipaulovi.
Jupes=Ditsakana.
Jupibit=Juyubit
Jurame=Xarame.
Juranames=Aranames.
Juskwaugume=Nipissing.
Jut joat=Ute.
Jyuo-tyu-te Oj-ke=San Juan.

Ka-acks=Kake.
Kaadg ett ee, Kaady-ett-ee=Katcadi.
Ká-ah=Kau.
Ka'-ai=Konglo.
Ka Anjou, Ka Anzou=Kansa.
Kaapô=Tuerto.
Kaas-ka-qua-tee=Kaskakoedi
Kabasa=Kabahseh.

Ká-bi-na-pek=Khabenapo.
Kabu Juacama=Santa Maria Magdalena.
Kach-als-ap=Lakkulzap.
Kachanuage, Kachanuge=Caughnawaga.
Kă-che-kone-a-we'-so-uk=Ketchigumiwisuwugi.
Kachiriodagon=Buckaloon.
Kachkachkia, Kachkaska=Kaskaskia.
Kachnauage, Kachnawarage=Kachnawaacharege.
Kachnuage=Caughnawaga.
Ka-cho-'dtinné=Kawchodinne.
Kachuidagon=Buckaloon.
Kachutok=Kashutuk.
Kacistas=Kasihta.
Kackapoes=Kickapoo.
Kâck!ē qoan=Kashkekoan.
Ka-clas-ko=Wasco.
Kacouchakhi=Piekouagami.
K'ac-ta'-tă=Kashtata.
Kac-tö'k=Kashtok.
Kac-tú=Kashtu.
Kada-Kaaman, Kadakaamang=San Ignacio de Kadakaman.
Kadapau, Kadapaw=Catawba.
K'·'adas k·ē'owai=Kadusgo-kegawai.
Kaddepaw, Kaddipeaw=Catawba.
Kaddo=Kadohadacho.
Kadewabedas=Broken Tooth.
Ka'-di=Kadohadacho.
Kadiagmuts=Kaniagmiut.
Kadiak=Kodiak.
Ka'diko=Tonkawa.
Kadjacken=Kaniagmiut.
Kadjakians=Kangmaligmiut.
Kado, Kadodakio, Kadodakiou, Kadodaquiou=Kado-hadacho.
Kădŭ-wot-kēdi=Hlukahadi.
Kaënna=Kainah.
Kaënsatague=Canadasaga.
Kaéso=Carrizos.
Kaetage, Ka-e-ta-je=Kein.
Kaeyah-Khatana=Kaiyuhkhotana.
Kagagi=Kakake.
Kagataya=Aleut.
Kagerssauk=Kagsersuak.
Kaghenewage', Kaghnawage, Kaghnuwage', Kagna-wage=Caughnawaga.
Kagnewagrage=Kachnawaacharege.
Kagokhakat=Kagokakat.
Kagontān=Kagwantan.
Kagouse=Cayuse.
Kaguiak=Kaguyak.
Kâgûñ'yĭ=Crow Town.
K'agyalskē'owai=Kagials-kegawai.
Kâh=Kansa.
Kah-cho-tinne=Kawchodinne.
Ka-he'-ta-ni-o=Khahitan.
Kahgallegak=Kialegak.
Kah he kwa ke=Kayehkwarageh.
Kahhendohhon=Kahendohon.
Kahinoa=Cahinnio.
Kahk-ah-mah-tsis=Hahamatses.
Kah ken doh hon=Kahendohon.
Kah-Kwah=Erie.
Kahlechtenskoi=Kalekhta.
Kah-lis-pelm=Kalispel.
Kahltog=Kaltag.
Kahlukhtughamiut=Kaluktuk.
Kahmi-atoŋwaŋ=Kakhmiatonwan.
Kahmish=Samish.
Kahna=Kainah.
Ka'hnáwage=Caughnawaga.
Kahnonwolohale, Kahnowolohale=Ganowarohare.
Kahnuages=Caughnawaga.
Kahn-yak=Cooniac.
Ka-h'ō'=Kaughii.
Kahokias=Cahokia.
Kahontáyoⁿ=Kendaia.
Kahoquias=Cahokia.
Ka'hpagi=Quapaw.
Kah-po=Santa Clara.
Kah-po-sia, Kahpozhah, Kahpozhay=Kapozha.
Kahquas=Erie.
Kahruk=Karok.
Kah-tee-pee-rah=Katipiara.
Kahtetl=Medilding.
Ka-hua-i-ko=Laguna.
Kahuilla=Kawia.
Kahuncle, Kahunkle=Kauhŭk.
Kahvichpaks=Unakhotana.

Kahweahs, Kahweaks, Kah-we-as=Kawia.
Kah-we-ŏk'-ki-oong=Kowasikka.
Kahweyahs=Kawia.
Kah-wis'-sah=Kawaiisu.
Kaiaganies=Kaigani.
Kaiaiak=Kaguyak.
Kaialigamut, Kai-ā lig-mūt=Kaialigmiut.
Kaialigumiut=Kaialik.
Kai-a-tee=Coyatee.
K'ai'atl lā'nas=Kaiahl-lanas.
Kaiawas=Kiowa.
Kaiayakak=Kaguyak.
Kai-bab-bit, Kaibabits=Kaibab.
Kài-ɣine, Káidine'=Kai.
Ka'i-e=Kau.
Kaí-e-na=Kainah.
Kaigan=Kaigani.
Kă'igwŭ=Kiowa.
Kä-ih=Kein.
Kai'ïpa=Santa Clara.
Kaí-it-ko-ki-ki-naks=Ahkaiyikokakiniks.
Kaijous=Cayuse.
Kailtas=Tlelding.
Kailwigamiut=Kaialik.
Kaimè, Kai'-na=Kainah.
Kainama, Kai-na-mēah, Kai-na-mé-ro=Gallinomero
Kai'nau=Kainah.
Kainhkhotana=Kaiyuhkhotana.
Kainœ'-koon=Kainah.
Kai-no-méahs=Gallinomero.
Kaiossuit=Karusuit.
Kaioutais=Kawita.
Kaiowan, Kaí-ó-wás, Kaiowé=Kiowa.
Kai'p'a=Santa Clara.
Kai-petl=Kepel.
Kai-Po-mo=Kato.
Kairaikome=Laguna.
Kaishun=Kaisun, Skaito.
Kaispa=Dakota.
Kaiswun Hāadē=Kaisun.
Kăi-tānā=Knaiakhotana.
Ka-itc=Panamint.
Kait-ka=Calapooya.
Kaitlen=Kwantlen.
Kaitze=Katsey.
Kaivavwit=Kaibab.
Kaiviat-am=Serranos.
Kai-vwav-uai Nu-ints=Kaibab.
Kaî-wa=Kiowa.
Kaiwáika=Laguna.
Kai-wane'=Kiowa.
Kai-yo=Koiyo.
Kaiyukatana, Kaiyŭk'ā-kho-tān'ā, Kaiyu-kho-tana=Kaiyuhkhotana.
Kai'-yŭ-wun-ts'ú-nĭtt'ɕaí=Kaiyuwuntsunitthai.
Kajatschim=Kaiachim.
Kăjì=Kichai.
Kajingahaga=Mohawk.
Kaj-kai=San Juan.
Kakagokhakat=Kagokakat.
Ka-kaik=Kakake.
Ka-ka'-i-thi=Salish.
Kă-kaitl=Kaquaith.
Kă-kă-kwis'-so-uk=Kagakwisuwug.
Kakamatsis=Hahamatses.
Ka-kan=Kakhan.
Kakaskígi, Kakasky=Kaskaskia.
Kakeɣa, Kak'exa=Kakegha.
Kakhilgagh-miut=Kaltshak.
Kakhlyakhlyakakat=Kakliaklia.
Kakhonak=Kakonak.
Kakhuana=Cajuenche.
Kakhuiyagamute=Kakuiak.
Kakias=Cahokia.
Kakigue=Kakick.
Kakliakhliakat, Kakliakliakat=Kakliaklia.
Kakmalikg=Kangmaligmiut.
Kăkoh=Yaku.
Ka-ko'-is-tsi'-a-ta'-ni-o=Salish.
Kakoñ'sǎ'-ge=Kagoughsage.
Kakortok=Julianehaab.
Kak8azakhi, Kakouchac, Kakouchakhi, Kakou-chaki=Piekouagami.
Kaksatis=Kiksadi.
Kakus=Kake.
Kakwaika=Chakpahu.
Kakwas=Erie.
Kak'-wits=Wailaki.
Kakwok=Kakuak.

Ka-la´-ci-au-u=Kalashiauu.
Kaladlit=Eskimo.
K'-â´-lâk=Kolok.
Kalaktak=Kalekhta.
Kalalit=Eskimauan Family.
Ka-la-muh=Shuswap.
Kalapooiah=Calapooya, Kalapooian Family.
Kalapooya, Kalapooyahs, Kalapouyas, Kalapuaya=
　　Calapooya.
Kalapuya=Calapooya, Kalapooian Family.
Kal´-´-ă-qu-ni-me´-ne ʒûn´-nĕ=Khwunrghunme.
Kalatekoë=Kilatika.
Ka-la-tih=Medilding.
Ka-la-wa´-cŭk=Kalawashuk.
Kala-Walset, Kalawatshet=Kalawatset.
Kăl´-bŭct'=Kalbusht.
Kal-chaina=Kulchana.
Kal-doe=Kauldaw.
Kalechtinskoje, Kalekhtinskoe=Kalekhta.
Kalespel, Kälespilum=Kalispel.
Kal-hwûn´-ûn-me´-ĕ-ni te´-ne=Khwunrghunme.
Kaliokhlogamute, Kaliookhlogamute=Kaliukluk.
Ka-lis-cha=San Felipe.
Kalispelines, Kalispelms, Kalispelum, Kalispelus-
　　ses=Kalispel.
Kalistcha=San Felipe.
Ka-lis-te-no=Cree.
Kàljukischwigmjut=Igagmjut.
Kaljuschen=Tlingit.
Kalkhagamute=Kaltshak.
Kallapooeas, Kallapooyah, Kallapugas, Kallapūia,
　　Kallapuiah=Calapooya.
Kalmakovsky Redoute=Kolmakovsky.
Kalmaths=Klamath.
Kál-ñamu=Kahl.
Kalo´duosh=Calapooya.
Kā-loo-kwis=Kalokwis.
Kaloosas=Calusa.
Kaloshes=Tlingit.
Kaloshians=Tlingit, Koluschan Family.
Kaloχlátche=Kadohadacho.
Kal-pŭt´-lŭ=Halpadalgi.
Kalthagamute, Kaltkagamiut, Kaltkhagamute=
　　Kaltshak.
Kaltlawewalla=Clowwewalla.
Kalulaā´ʟEx=Kalulaadlek.
Kalulegeet=Kalulek.
Kalusa=Calusa.
Kaluschians=Tlingit.
Kalu-χnádshu=Kadohadacho.
Kal-wa´-natc-kuc´-te-ne=Tatlatunne.
Kam´-a-lel Pó-mo=Usal.
Kam-a-loo´-pa=Kamloops.
Kă-män-tci=Comanche.
Kameglimut=Kamegli.
Kameloups=Kamloops.
Kamia=Diegueños, Kamiah.
Kamia-akhwe=Comeya.
Kāmiạtāw'ngāgamāg=Kahmetahwungaguma.
Kāmiskwāwā'ku'kag=Gamiskwakokawininiwak.
Kamiskwawāngachit=Sillery.
Kamissi=Kiamisha.
Kammack=Kammuck.
Kammas Prairie tribe=Tukuarika.
Kam´-ne=Kainah.
Kamse=Kansa.
Kamŭ´inu=Nez Percés.
Ka-mu-lus=Kamulas.
Kamus=Kimus.
Kă´na=Karnah.
Kanaa, Kanaai=Conoy.
Kanaatino=Kanoatino.
Kanacao'=Kanagaro.
Kanách-ădi, Kanach-tēdi=Ganahadi.
Kanadagago=Canadasaga.
Kanadagerea=Ganadogan.
Kanadaoeaga, Kanadaoegey=Canadasaga.
Kanadaque=Canandaigua.
Kanadaragea=Canadasaga.
Kanadaraygo=Ganondasa.
Kanadasaega, Kanadasagea, Kanadaseagea, Kana-
　　daseago, Kanadaseegy, Kanadasegoa, Kanada-
　　sero=Canadasaga.
Kanadasero=Ganasarage.
Kanadasigea=Canadasaga.
Kanaderagey=Ganondasa.
Kanadesaga, Kanadesego, Kanadesero, Kanades-
　　segy, Kanadessigy=Canadasaga.
Kă-nă-'djo´'-hă-re´=Canajoharie.

Kanadosega, Kanagago=Canadasaga.
Kanagamiut=Kanagak.
Kanagist=Kaniagmiut.
Kanagmiut=Kanak.
Kaneaheăwastsĭk=Cheyenne.
Kanai=Conoy.
Kanajoharry=Canajoharie.
Kanaka Bar, Kanaka Flat=Ntlaktlakitin.
Kanākao', Kanákaro'=Kanagaro.
Kanamara=Gallinomero.
Kanandagua, Kanandaigua, Kanandalangua, Kanan-
　　daque=Canandaigua.
Kanandasagea=Canadasaga.
Ka´-nan-in=Arikara.
Kananouangon (Conewango)=Shenango.
Kanaouagan=Connewango.
Kanasadagea, Kanasedaga=Canadasaga.
Kănăs-nū=Killisnoo.
Kanassarago=Ganasarage.
Kanassatagi lunuak=Oka.
Kăna´sta, Kănastún´yĭ=Kanastuni.
Kä-nä-tä-go´-wä, Kanatakowa=Onondaga (vil.).
Kanatakwenke=Caughnawaga.
Kanatat=Klikitat.
Kă-nă´-tcŭ'-hăre´=Canajoharie.
Kanauagon=Connewango.
Kanawageres=Kanagaro.
Kănăwārkă=Caughnawaga.
Kanawhas=Conoy.
Kan-Ayko=Laguna, Sitsimé.
Kancas, Kancès=Kansa.
Kancho=Kawchodinne.
Kandaia=Kendaia.
K'ăn´-dzi=Lipan.
Kanedasaga, Kanedesago=Canadasaga.
Kaneenda=Gannentaha.
Kaneghsadakeh=Kanesadageh.
Kanentage=Canandaigua.
Kanesadago=Canadasaga.
Kanesadakeh=Canadasaga, Kanesadageh.
Kanesatake, Kanesatarkee=Oka.
Kanesedaga=Canadasaga.
Kaneskies=Knaiakhotana.
K·ang=Kung.
Kangerdlooksoah, Kangerdluhsoa=Kangerdluksoa.
Kangigdlek=Kangidli.
Kang-iq-xlu-q´mūt=Kangikhlukhmut.
Kaŋg´i-śuŋ-pegnaka=Kanghishunpegnaka.
Kang´itoka=Crows.
Kangiugdlit=Kangmaligmiut.
Kangivamiut=Kangidli.
Kaŋ-ġ-i´wi-ca-śa=Crows.
Kaŋgi-yuha=Kanghiyuha.
Kangjulit=Chnagmiut.
Kangmali, Kangmaligmeut, Kangmāli´gmūt, Kang-
　　mali-innuin, Kangmalik, Kangnialis=Kangma-
　　ligmiut.
Kangoot=Kongik.
Kangoot Mutes=Kungugemiut.
Kang-orr-mœoot=Kangormiut.
K·anguatl lä´nai=Kangguatl lanas.
Kan´gûkøluáluksoagmyut=Kangivamiut.
Kanhawas, Kanhaways=Conoy.
Kâ'nhe´ñko=Carrizo.
Kâ´-ni=Koni.
Kaniag-miut, Kaniagmjut=Kaguyak.
Kāniăg´mūt=Kaniagmiut.
Kanibals, Kanibas, Kanibats, Kanibesinnoaks, Kani-
　　bessinnoaks=Norridgewock.
Kanieke-hâka=Mohawk.
Kanienda=Kaneenda.
Kaniénge-onoⁿ=Mohawk.
Kanig-mïout=Kanig.
Kanikgmut=Kungugemiut.
Kanikhluk=Kanikluk.
Kanimares, Kanimarres=Gallinomero.
Kanim Lake=Kenim Lake.
Kaninahoic, Kaninahoich, Kanină´vish, Kanina-
　　wesh=Arapaho.
Kaninim Lake, Kaninis' Tribe=Kenim Lake.
Ka-nip-sum=Kenipsim.
Káni-qa-li-ga-mut=Kanikaligamut.
Kanisky=Knaiakhotana.
Ka-nit=Mandan.
Kaniulit=Chnagmiut.
Kanjagmjut=Kaguyak.
Kañkaⁿ=Ponca.
Kănkau=Konkau.
Kankaways=Tonkawa.

Kankünă, Kankünats kŏgtana=Knaiakhotana.
Kănk·'utlă'atlam=Okinagan.
Kanmali-enyuin=Kangmaligmiut.
Kannadasaga, Kannadesagea, Kannadeseys=Canadasaga.
Kannaogau, Kannawagogh=Caughnawaga.
Kanneastoka=Conestoga.
Kannehonan=Kannehouan.
Kanoagoa=Connewango.
Kanoatina, Kanoatinnos, Kanoatino=Kanohatino.
Kanodosegea=Canadasaga.
Kanonᵏkeï'ta'hwï'=Totiakton.
Kanonskegon=Geneseo.
Kă'nŏqtlă'tlām=Kalispel.
Kanossadage=Oka.
Kanoutinoa=Kanohatino.
Känowanó-häte=Ganowarohare.
Ka-no-zä'-wa=Kanwasowaua.
Kañp-meut=Kangormiut.
Kans, Kansæ, Kansas, Kansé, Kansez=Kansa.
Kansháde, Kanshádi=Kanchati.
Kansies=Kansa.
Kaⁿ-tdóa=Kang.
Kanté=Kente.
Kantha, Kants=Kansa.
Kantsi=Kiowa Apache, Lipan.
Kănu'gû'lâyĭ, Kănu'gû'lûñ'yĭ=Briertown.
Kañûktlualuksoagmyut=Kangidli.
Kanungé-ono=Caughnawaga.
Kanuskago=Ganosgagong.
Kanvagen=Gaandowanang.
Kaⁿxi-cŭⁿ-pegnaka=Kanghishunpegnaka.
Kaⁿxi-yuha=Kanghiyuha.
Kanygmjut=Kanig.
Kanza, Kanzeis, Kanzes=Kansa.
Kaockhia=Cahokia.
Kào-kē'-owai=Aokeawai.
Kaokia, Kaokies=Cahokia.
Kaons=Coos.
Kaoquias=Cahokia.
Kaouaï=Salmon River Indians.
Kaouanoua=Kannehouan.
Kaouechias=Cahokia.
Kaouitas=Kawita.
Kaoükia=Cahokia.
Kaoulis=Cowlitz.
Kaounadeau=Caneadea.
Kaoutyas=Kawita.
Kapaha, Kapas=Quapaw.
Kapatci'tcin, Kapatsitsan=Kapachichin.
K·'á-pätop=Kiowa Apache.
Kap-ho'=Santa Clara.
Kapilano=Homulchison.
Ka-Po=Santa Clara, Tuerto.
Kapoga, Kapo'ja=Kapozha.
Ka-Poo=Santa Clara.
Kaposecooke=Kupkipcock.
Ka-po-sias, Kapota=Kapozha.
Kapoti=Capo'te.
Ka-pou=Santa Clara.
Ka-po'-ża=Kapozha.
Kappa Akansea, Kappas, Kappaws, Kappawson-Arkansas=Quapaw.
Kápung=Santa Clara.
Kąq!anuwŭ'=Kukanuwu.
Kaqmi-atoⁿwaⁿ=Kakhmiatonwan.
Kăq-tcaⁿ-waïc=Kakhtshanwaish.
Ka-quaitl=Kaquaith.
Karaghiyadirha=Caneadea.
Karakenh=Karaken.
Karaler, Karalik, Karalit=Eskimo.
Karankaways, Karankoas, Karan-koo-as=Karankawa.
Kă-rasch-kídetan=Kayashkidetan.
Karathyadirs=Caneadea.
Kareses=Lipan.
Karhatyonni=Karhationni.
Karhawenghradongh=Karhawenradonh.
Karhetyonni=Karhationni.
Ka rho wengh ra don=Karhawenradonh.
Karig8istes=Karigouistes.
Kariko=Tonkawa.
Karkadia=Kaskaskia.
Karkinonpols=Kakinonba.
Karlooch=Karluk.
Kar-luk-wees=Kalokwis.
Karluta=Karluk.
Karmowong=Kaumauang.

Kăro=Gyazru.
Karo-χnádshu=Kadohadacho.
Karquines=Karkin.
Kar-qwan-ton=Kagwantan.
Karro=Gyazru.
Kar'-sa=Kansa.
Karsioot, Karsooit=Karsuit.
Karsuk=Karsok.
Karulik=Kanulik.
K'arussuit=Karusuit.
Kar-wee-wee=Atsmitl.
Kasągaskwątcimä'kăg=Gasakaskuatchimmekak.
Kasahá únûⁿ=Chickasaw.
Kasarsoak=Kagsersuak.
Kasas=Kansa.
Kascakias=Kaskaskia.
Kaschjukwagmjut=Akhiok.
Kaschkaschkung=Kuskuski.
Kăshke-kon=Kashkekoan.
Kasgresquios=Kaskaskia.
Kashanquash=Kashong.
Kashapaokla, Kasháp-úkla=Kushapokla.
Kashaski=Kaskaskia.
Kash-ă-woosh-ah=Kassovo.
Kashega=Kashiga.
Kashigalagamute, Kashigalogumut=Kashigalak.
Kashigin=Kashiga.
Kashonquash=Kashong.
Kashpugowitk=Kespoogwit.
Kashtih asha=Cushtusha.
Kashukvagmiut=Akhiok.
Kashunahmiut, Kashunok=Kashunuk.
Kasil=Casalic.
Kasita=Usseta.
Kaskaias=Kiowa Apache.
Kaskaisas, Kaskaiskas, Kaskakias, Kaskakiés=Kaskaskia.
Kaskanakh, Kaskanek=Kaskanak.
Kaskarorens=Tuscarora.
Kaskascia, Kaskasia, Kaskaskies=Kaskaskia.
Kaskaskunk=Kuskuski.
Kaskasquia=Kaskaskia.
Kaskaya, Kaskia=Kiowa Apache.
Kaskinakh=Kaskanak.
Kaskkasies=Kaskaskia.
Kaskuskies=Kuskuski.
Kas-lin-ta=Haslinding.
Kasoatcha=Kosotshe.
K·'asq'aguē'dē, Kāsq!akue'dî=Kaskakoedɪ
Kasqui, Kasquias=Kaskaskia.
Kasquinanipo=Kakinonba.
Kasquuasquias=Kaskaskia.
Kassan, Kassan Hₐade=Kasaan.
Kássēya, Kasseye'-i=Kadohadacho.
Kassₓachamiut, Kassianmute=Kassiank.
Kassilo, Kassilof=Kasilof.
Kassilúda=Sabdatoto.
Kas-so-teh-nie=Kushetunne.
Kassra-kŭēdi=Kaskakoedi.
Kasta kăgawai, K·astak·ē'raua'i=Daiyuahl-lanas.
Kastaxē'xda-ān=Kustahekdaan.
Kăs'-tel-Po-mo=Wailaki.
Kasua=Cashwah.
Kataba=Catawba.
Kataghayekiki=Aleut.
Kätägi'tigäning=Gatagetegauning.
Katagkag-mioute=Katagkak.
K'a-t'a-gottiné, Kat·'a-gottine=Kawchodinne.
Katahba=Catawba.
Katahooche=Chattahoochee.
Ka-tah-te=Medilding.
Kátai=Kahtai.
Ka-ta-kas=Kiowa Apache.
Kă-'tă-ră'-krăȼ=Cattaraugus.
Kataubahs=Catawba.
Kataχka=Kiowa Apache.
K'atc'a'dē=Katcadi.
Katce=Siksika.
Katchaⁿ=Yuma.
K'a-tchô-gottiné, Katchô-Ottiné=Kawchogottine.
Kat'-chŭ=Katsalgi.
Katcina, Katcina wiñwû=Kachina.
Kates=Kake.
Katezie=Katsey.
Katha'gi=Kansa.
Kathlamak, Kathlamet=Cathlamet.
Kathlaminimim=Kathlaminmin.
Kathlamit, Kathlamut=Cathlamet.
Kathlapootle=Cathlapotle.

Kathlarem=Kathlaram.
Kathlemit=Cathlamet.
Kathlendaruc=Kalindaruk.
Kathtippecamunk=Tippecanoe.
Ka'tihcha, Ka-tish-tya, Katistya, Ka-ti-tya=San
   Felipe.
Kä-tí-ya-ye-mix=Kutaiimiks.
Katkwaltú=Katkwaahltu.
Katlagakya=Shahala.
Katlamak, Katlamat, Katlammets=Cathlamet.
Katlaportl=Cathlapotle.
Katlendarukas=Kalindaruk.
K·'at nas had'ā'i=Kaadnaas-hadai.
Káto-Pomo=Kato.
Katowa=Cherokee.
Kätschadi=Katcadi.
Katskil, Katskill=Catskill Indians.
Kattagmjut=Kattak.
Kattahawkees=Kitkehahki.
Kattanahaws=Kutenai.
Kattaning=Kittanning.
Kattarbe, Kattaupa=Catawba.
Katteka=Kiowa Apache.
Kattera=Tutelo.
Katuku=Chastacosta.
Kaúa=Kawa.
Ka-uay-ko=Laguna.
Kaughnawaugas=Caughnawaga.
Kauia=Kawia.
Ka-uin-a=Kowina.
Kauitchin, K·au'itcin=Cowichan.
Kau'-lĭts=Cowlitz.
Kaumainsh=Comanche.
Kaumanang=Kaumauang.
Kaunaudasage=Canadasaga.
Kau'q-wan=Kaukhwan.
Käüs=Coos.
Kausas=Kansa.
Kau-ta-noh=Contahnah.
Kautika=Kituhwa.
Kauvuyas=Kawia.
Kauwetsaka, Kauwetseka=Akawentchaka.
Ka'-ü wüñ-wû=Kau.
Kau-yai'-chits=Kawia.
Kauzau=Kansa.
Kavagan=Kouyam.
Kavayos=Kawia.
Kavea, Kaveaks, Kaverong Mutes, Kaviacks=
   Kaviagmiut.
Kaviagamute=Kaviazagmiut.
Kaviagmuts, Kaviagmyut, Kaviaks=Kaviagmiut.
Kaviawach=White River Ute.
Kaviazagamute, Kāviāzā' gemut=Kaviazagmiut.
Kavvachias, Kavvchias, Kavvechias, Kavvkias=
   Cahokia.
Kavwaru-maup=Kawia.
Kaw=Kansa.
Kawa=Kiowa.
Kawáhykaka, Kawaíhkaa, Ka-waik', Ka-waikă',
   Káwaikama, Kawáikăme, Ka-waik'-ka-me=
   Laguna.
Kawaiko=Sitsimé.
Kawaikome=Laguna.
Kawaiokuh=Kawaika.
Ka-wai-ra-chi-u=White River Ute.
Kâwanû'ñyĭ=Kawanuyi.
Kăwân'-urá'sûñyĭ=Conoross.
Kāwāpābikạni'kāg=Gawababiganikak.
Kawas=Kiowa.
Kawatskins=Cowichan.
Kawcho-dinneh=Kawchodinne.
Kawelitsk=Cowlitz.
Káwerkewötche=Kawoltukwucha.
Kâ-wi'-a-suh=Kawaiisu.
Kawichen=Cowichan.
Ka-wí-na-han=Siksika.
Kawishm=Kawaiisu.
Kawita Talahássi=Kawita.
Kawitchen=Cowichan.
Kawitshin=Cowichan, Salishan Family.
Kawitskins=Cowichan.
Kawitunshki=Tchatkasitunshki.
Kawi'yĭ=Cowee.
Kawkias=Cahokia.
Kawnjagmjut=Kaguyak.
Kawuytas=Kawita.
Kaw-welth=Chaahl.
Kawytas=Kawita.

Kạw'-ză=Kansa.
Ká-xi=Crows.
Kayā'ckidêtān=Kayashkidetan.
Kayaguas=Kiowa.
Kaya'ha'ge'=Cayahoga.
Kayakshigvikg=Kaiaksekawik.
Kayamishi=Kiamisha.
K·'āya'ng=Kayung.
Kayaways=Kiowa.
Kayayak=Kaguyak.
Kayeghtalagealat=Coreorgonel.
Kayingehaga=Mohawk.
Kayjatin=Kaihatin.
Kaykovskie=Kake.
Kayō'kath, Kayoku-aht=Kyuquot.
Kayouse=Cayuse.
Kayowa, Káyowe'=Kiowa.
Kayowgaws=Cayuga.
Ka-yö-wöc=Cayeguas.
Kayowû=Kiowa.
Kay-tzen-lin=Kaihatin.
Kayuguas=Kiowa.
Kayúgue-ónoⁿ=Cayuga.
Kayul=Cayuse.
Kayuse Creek=Cayoosh Creek.
Kayuses=Cayuse.
Ka'yuwa=Kiowa.
Kayuxes=Cayuse.
Kayyhekwarakeh=Kayehkwarageh.
K'ọá-'ĕ=Kthae.
Kcäl tana=Kulchana.
Kḍạⁿ=Kdhun.
Kçe'-lüt-li'-ᴣûnnĕ'=Kthelutlitunne.
Kchaljkagmjut=Kaltshak.
K'chi-ga-gong'-go=Kchegagonggo.
K'ciwuk'ciwu=Kshiwukshiwu.
K'ọo-ᴣai'-me=Kthotaime.
χọŭⁿ=Kdhun.
K'ọu-na'-ta-a tcûn' ᴣûnnĕ=Kthunataachuntunne.
K'ọu-qwĕs'-ᴣûnnĕ=Kthukhwestunne.
K'ọu-qwĭc' ᴣûnnĕ=Siuslaw.
Kọu-qwût'-tûnnĕ=Kthukhwuttunne.
K'ọu-tĕt'-me-tse'-ĕ-tŭt'-tûn=Kthutetmetseetut-
   tun.
Ke=Kekin.
Kealeegees=Kailaidshi.
Kéa-tdóa=Keya.
Keate, Keati=Kiatang.
Ke-at=Panamint.
Keawahs=Kawia.
Keawas=Kiowa.
Keawaw=Kiawaw.
Keaways=Kiowa.
Keawe, Keawee=Keyauwee.
Kea-wit-sis=Tlauitsis.
Ke-ax-as=Kiyuksa.
Kebiks=Montagnais.
Kecapos=Kickapoo.
Kechies=Kichai.
Kecheel=Kechayi.
Keche-gumme-winine-wug, Kĕchĕkămē¹ Wĕnĕnĕwăk
   =Kitchigumiwininiwug.
Ke-che-se-be-win-in-e-wug, Ke-che-se-be-win-o-wing=
   Kitchisibiwininiwug.
Ke-che-wan-dor-goning, Kech-e-waun-dau-gu-mink=
   Ketchewaundaugenink.
Kechi=Luiseño.
Kechies=Kichai.
Kechis=Kichai, Luiseño.
Kechtawangh=Kitchawank.
Keckkeknepolin=Kickenapawlinǥ
Kecopes=Kickapoo.
Kedi=Huna.
Kee-ark-sar=Kiyuksa.
Keeawawes=Keyauwee.
Keechers=Kichai.
Kee-ches=Kitzeesh.
Keechi, Keechies=Kichai.
Keechik=Kilchik.
Kee-chis=Kitzeesh.
Kee-chum-a-kai-to, Keechum-akarlo=Kitzimgay-
   lum.
Keechy=Kichai.
Keeghik=Nikhkak.
Kee'-hât-sâ, Keeheet-sas=Crows.
Keejik=Nikhkak.
Kee'-kât-sâ=Crows.
Keek heat la=Kitkatla.
Kee-kik-tag-ameuts=Kikiktak.

Keen-ath-toix= Kinuhtoiah.
Kee-nip-saim, Kee-nip-sim= Kenipsim.
Keeowaws, Keeowee= Keyauwee.
Kees= Arikara.
Kee-tah-hon-neet= Tongas.
Keet-heat-la, Keethratlah= Kitkatla.
Keetsas= Kichai.
K·ē′ētsē= Katsey.
Kee-uke-sah= Kiyuksa.
Keew-aho= Tuscarora.
Keewalik= Kugaluk.
Ke-ga-boge= Kickapoo.
Kegaiogue= Kekionga.
Kegarnie= Kaigani.
Kegictowik, Kegictowruk, Kegiktowik= Kiktaguk.
Kegiktowrigemüt= Kegiktowrigemiut.
Kegiktówruk= Kiktaguk.
Kegniogue= Kekionga.
Kegokhtowik= Kiktaguk.
Kehabous= Kickapoo.
Kéh-chen-wilt= Quaitso.
Kehk, Kehons= Kake.
Kehtehticut= Titicut.
Ke′iá-kí-me= Kiakima.
Keiauwees= Keyauwee.
Keilijah= Kailaidshi.
Keimanoeitoh= Kitlope.
Keint-he= Deyodeshot.
Keiscatchewan, Keiskatchewan= Cree.
Kei-u-gues= Cayuga.
Ke-jawn′= Yuma.
Kek= Kake.
Ke-ka-alns= Kikiallu.
Kekalus= Tikwalus.
Kekapos, Kekapou= Kickapoo.
Ke ɤa′tsü= Nanpanta.
Kekaupoag= Kickapoo.
Kёkch-kŏn= Kake.
Ke-ke-on-gay= Kekionga.
Kekerannon-rounons= Nipissing.
Keketticut= Titicut.
Kekies= Kichai.
Ke-ki-on-go= Kekionga.
K·ek·k·′′ēnŏx= Kyekykyenok.
Ke-ko-neck= Shanamkarak.
Kekopos= Kickapoo.
Kekuvskoe= Kake.
Kelamantowruk= Kilimantavie.
Kelamouches= Comanche.
Kё-le′-nyu-mûh= Kele.
Kéles= Karankawa.
Kё-lёv-a-tow-tin= Kilimantavie.
Ke′-le-wuñ-wü= Kele.
Kelistenos= Cree.
Kellamucks= Tillamook.
Kell-aout= Halaut.
Kellespem= Kalispel.
Kel-seem-aht= Kelsemaht.
Kelsey= Makhelchel.
Kёl′ta= Tlelding.
K·eltsmā′ath= Kelsemaht.
Kel-ut-sah= Kilutsai.
Kemahwivi= Chemehuevi.
Kemasuit, Kemesuit= Karusuit.
Kemsquits= Kimsquit.
Ke′na= Kainah.
Kenabeca, Kenabes= Norridgewock.
Kenaghamiut= Kinak.
Kenai, Kenaians, Kenáies= Athapascan Family, Knaiakhotana.
Kenai-tena, Kenaitses, Kenaitze, Kenaiyer, Kenai-yut, Kenaize, Kenaizen= Knaiakhotana.
Kenaizer= Athapascan Family.
Kenajer= Knaiakhotana.
Ke-na-pe-com-a-qua= Kenapacomaqua.
Kenas= Knaiakhotana.
Kenasnow= Killisnoo.
Kenath tui ex= Kinuhtoiah.
Kenay, Kenayern, Kenayzi= Knaiakhotana.
Kenchenkieg= Kinagingeeg.
Kendaes= Kendaia.
Kénébec, Kenebecka= Kennebec.
Kenebecke Indeans, Kenebeke= Norridgewock
Kenebeke= Kennebec.
Ken′-es-ti= Kuneste.
Kengugmiut= Kongik.
Kenhawas= Conoy.
Kenhulká= Ikanhatki.
Kenigayat= Kingiak.

Ke-ni′kaci′ɤa= Kenikashika.
Ke nika-shing-ga= Kekin.
Ke-nish-te′-no-wuk, Ke-nis-te-noag, Kenistenoo, Ke-nistenos= Cree.
Kennachananaghamiut= Kenachananak.
Kennebec, Kennebec Indians, Kennebecks, Kenne-beki= Norridgewock.
Kennedaseage, Kennesedaga= Canadasaga.
Kennuyak= Paugwik.
Ke-noushay= Kenozhe.
Kenowiki= Conoy.
Ke-no-zha= Kenozhe.
Kentaienton= Gentaienton.
Kentsia, Kentsio= Kente.
Ke-nunctioni= Iroquois.
Kēo Hāadē= Aokeawai.
Keomee= Keyauwee.
Keope-e-no= Koprino.
Keowe= Keowee.
Keowewallahs= Clowwewalla.
Keoxa= Kiyuksa.
Kepar= Ishipishi.
Ke-pau-yau= Kipaya towns.
Kёq!= Kake.
Kequeloose= Tikwalus.
Ke-ques-ta= Kikwistok.
Kera= Keresan Family.
Keralite= Eskimo.
Kéran, Keras= Keresan Family.
Kerchi= Kichai.
Kerem-eeos, Keremeoos, Kêremya′uz= Keremeus.
Keres= Keresan Family.
Ke-re-tcŭⁿ= Kerechun.
Kern River= Tubatulabal.
Kerokias= Cahokia.
Keroopinough= Koprino.
Kershaws= Catawba.
Kershong= Kashong.
Kertani= Lower Kutenai.
Kescacons= Kishkakon.
Keshase= Kitzeesh.
Keshpugowitk= Kespoogwit.
Keskeskias= Kaskaskia.
Keskistkonck= Keskistkonk.
Ke-spi-co-tha= Kispokotha.
Kespoogwitunâ′k= Kespoogwit.
Kessler= Makhelchel.
Kesuna= Kashunuk.
Kes-whaw-hay= Keresan Family.
Ket-a-Mats= Kitamat.
Ket-an-dou= Kitunto.
Ketapekon, Kё-tăp′-ē-kŏn-nŏng= Tippecanoe.
Ketawaugas= Cherokee.
Ketchegamins= Kitchigami.
Ketchewaundaguminink= Ketchewaundaugenink.
Ketcheyes, Ketchies= Kichai.
Ketchigamins= Kitchigami.
Kё-tchi-na, Ketchip-a-huan= Kechipauan.
Ketchiquut= Titicut.
Ketciwawiyändaganing= Ketchewaundaugenink.
Ke-tdóa= Ke.
Ketehigamins= Kitchigami.
Ketehiquut, Ketehtequtt= Titicut.
Ketetas= Shanwappom.
k·′ē′tgo hit tan= Ketgohittan.
Kethepecannank= Tippecanoe.
Keth-e-wan-don-gon-ing= Ketchewaundaugenink.
Kethtipecanunk, Kethtipiconunck= Tippecanoe.
Ket-ka-kesh= Kitkehahki.
Ketlakaniak= Cooniac.
Ketlane= Kitlani.
Ketlitk-Kutchín= Unakhotana.
Ke-toon-ok-shelk= Kitwinshilk.
Ketschetnäer= Ahtena.
Ke′tsī= Katsey.
Ketticut= Titicut.
Kettle band, Kettle band Sioux= Oohenonpa.
Kettle Falls, Kettle Indians= Colville.
Kettooah= Kituhwa.
Ket-wilk-ci-pa= Kitwilksheba.
Ketyagoos= Kittizoo.
Kevalinye Mutes, Kevalinyes= Kevalingamiut.
Ke-waught-chen-unaughs= Kewaughtohenemach.
Kewawees= Keyauwee.
Keweah= Kawia.
K′eχerten= Kekerten.
Keyawees= Keyauwee.
Keycchies, Keyche, Keychies= Kichai.
Kéyər-hwotqət= Keyerhwotket.

Keyes, Keyeshees, Keys=Kichai.
Keyuse=Cayuse.
Kezerevsky=Koserefski.
'Keztce=Kezche.
Kfwè-tρa-Gottinè=Kfwetragottine.
Kgallegak=Kialegak.
Kña'-ă=Cheghita.
Khagantayakhun'khin=Aleut.
Khahkhahtons=Chippewa.
K'haibhaí'=Santa Clara.
Khaigamut=Khaik.
Khakhatons, Khakhatonwan=Chippewa.
Khalams=Clallam.
Khaltat's village=Kaltat.
Khanúkh=Goch.
K'ha-po-o=Santa Clara.
Kha-t'a-ottinè=Kawchodinne.
Kha-tcho-gottine=Kawchogottine.
Khatnotoutze=Kagokakat.
Khatukeyu=Wintun.
Kha-tρa-Gottinè=Kawchodinne.
Khecham=Luiseño.
Khēkhu=Kake.
Khenipsim=Kenipsim.
Khīna Hāadē=Haena.
Khiondaësahan=Ekiondatsaan.
Khionontatehronon,   Khionontaterrhonons=Tiono-
    tati.
Khlēl'-ta='Tlelding.
Khogotlinde=Khogoltlinde.
Khootznahoo=Hutsnuwu.
Khoouchtioulik,   Khoouchtioulik-mioute=Koyuk-
    tolik.
Khoso=Hopi.
Khotilkakat, Khotilkakate, Khotylnakat=Kotil.
Khoulpouni=Khulpuni.
Khounanilinde=Khunanilinde.
Khu-a nika-shing-ga=Khra.
Khuilchan, Khuilchana=Kulchana.
Khuingetakhten,   Khuingitatekhten=Kuingshte-
    takten.
Khuligichagat=Khuligichikat.
Khúⁿ-tdóa=Kun.
Kŭn-ŭn-āh'=Tahltan.
Khust-e-nēt,   Khust-e-nēte=Khwaishtunnetunne.
Khutsno, Khutsnu=Hutsnuwu.
Khutulkakat=Kutul.
Ki-a-a=Pueblo Alto.
Kia'anaän=Kechipauan.
Kiaboha=Kiabaha.
Kiaffess=Kuasse.
Kiahoba=Kiabaha.
Kiaíni=Kinaani.
K'iä'-ki-me=Kiakima.
Kiaknukmiut=Kinipetu.
Kialajahs, Kialechies, Kialeegees, Kialega, Kialgie,
    Kialiages=Kailaidshi.
Kialigamiut=Kaialik.
Kialiga's, Kialige, Kialigee, Ki-a-li-jee=Kailaidshi.
Kiallegak=Kialegak.
Kianamaras=Gallinomero.
Kia'-na-wa=Kechipauan.
Ki-a'-ni=Kegi.
Kiānōsili=Kianusili.
Kiapaha=Quapaw.
K'iáp kwai na, K'iap'-kwai-na-kwe, K'iáp kwai na-
    kwin=Ojo Caliente.
Kiasses, Kiasseschaneres=Kuasse.
Kiatagmute=Kiatagmiut.
Kiataro, Kiataw=Coyoteros.
Kiatenes=Kiatagmiut.
Kiatenses=Knaiakhotana.
Kiateros=Coyoteros.
Ki'-â-wâ, Kiaways=Kiowa.
Ki-a-wét-ni=Kiawetnau.
Kiāw-pino=Koprino.
Kiburi=Quiburi.
Kicapoos, Kicapous, Kicapoux, Kicapus=Kickapoo.
Kicaras=Arikara.
Kiccapoos=Kickapoo.
Kichae=Kichai.
Kichaga=Cayahoga.
Kichaoneiak, Kichaoueiak=Kishkakon.
Kichapacs=Kickapoo.
Kiche=Kichai.
Kichesipiiriniouek,   Kichesipiriniwek=Kichesipi-
    rini.
Kichik=Kilchik.
Kichis=Kichai.

Kichkagoneiak, Kichkankoueiak=Kishkakon.
Kichtages=Illinois.
Kichtawan, Kichtawanc, Kichtawanghs, Kichta-
    wons,   Kichtewangh,   Kichtowanghs=Kitcha-
    wank.
Ki'-ǿi-ku'ǿuc=Wichita.
Ki-ǿi-tcac=Kichai.
Kickābāwä=Kishkawbawee.
Kickapoo=Kispokotha.
Kickapoos of the prairies=Prairie Kickapoo.
Kickapoos of the Vermilion=Vermilion.
Kickapos=Kickapoo.
Kick-a-pou-go-wi Town=Kickapougowi.
Kickapous, Kickipoo=Kickapoo.
Kick-sa-tee=Kiksadi.
Kicktages=Illinois.
Kicktawanc=Kitchawank.
Kickuallis=Kikiallu.
Kiclichee=Kailaidshi.
Kicoagoves, Kicoapous, Kicopoux=Kickapoo.
Kictawanc=Kitchawank.
Kī-dagh-ra=Azqueltan.
Kiddan=Skedans.
Kíddĕkĕdissĕ=Wichita.
Kidelik=Kidnelik.
Kidikurús=Wichita.
Kiechee=Kichai.
Kiektaguk=Kiktaguk.
Kienketons=Sisseton.
Kieoux=Cayuse.
Kiesno's village=Wakanasisi.
Kiēteng=Kiatang.
Kiétsash=Kichai.
Ki-e-wah=Kiowa.
Ki-gal-twal-la=Watlala.
Kiganis, Kigarnee, Kigenes=Kaigani.
Kiggĭktagmyut=Kigiktagmiut.
Kighetawkigh Roanu=Illinois.
Kighigufi=Atka.
Kigh-Mioute=Kiktaguk.
Kightages=Illinois.
Kightewangh, Kightowan=Kitchawank.
Kigikhkhun=Atka.
Kigikhtawik, Kigiktauik=Kiktaguk.
Kiglacka, Kiglaška=Kiglashka.
Kignuamiut=Kinguamiut.
Kiguel=Mishikhwutmetunne.
Kigukhtagmyut=Kigiktagmiut.
Ki-gu-ksa Band=Kiyuksa.
Kihâtoak'=Quijotoa.
Ki'hi=Kingegan.
Kihigouns=Unalaska.
Kiñnatsa=Crows.
Kihotoak=Quijotoa.
Ki'-hu=Kegi.
Ki-hua=Santo Domingo.
Kiimilit=Eskimo.
Kij=Gabrieleño.
Kijataigmjuten, Kijataigmüten, Kijaten=Kiatag-
    miut.
Kijik=Nikhkak.
Kikabeux, Kikabons, Kikabou, Kiкaboua, Kikábu=
    Kickapoo.
Kikanonas=Karankawa.
Kikapau, Kikapoes, Kikapoos=Kickapoo.
Kikapouguoi=Kickapougowi.
Kikapous, Kikap8s, Kikapoux, Kikapouz, Kikapu=
    Kickapoo.
Kikastas=Crows.
Kikchtaguk=Kiktaguk.
Kikealans=Kikiallu.
Kikhtaghouk, Kikhtangouk=Kiktaguk.
Kikhtŏg āmūt=Eiwhuelit.
Kikiallis, Kik-i-állus, Ki-kia-loos, Kikialtis=Ki
    kiallu.
Kikikhtagamiut=Kiktak.
Kikikhtagyut, Kikiktagamute, Kikiktagmut=Kı-
    ktak.
Kikiktowruk=Kiktaguk.
Kikkapoos=Kickapoo.
Kikkertarsoak=Kertarsoak.
Kikkerton=Kekerten.
Kikkhlagamute, Kikkhtagamute=Kiktak.
Kik-Khuigamute, Kikkhwigagamute=Kikuikak.
Kikliakliakakate=Kakliaklia.
Kikotan=Kiequotank.
Kikpouz=Kickapoo.
Kiksàn=Kitksan.
Kik-the-swe-mud=Wapeminskink.

Kikwistoq = Kikwistok.
Kik-wüñ-wü = Kik.
Kilametagag = Kilimantavie.
Kilamooks, Kil á mox, Kilamukes, Kilamute = Tilla-
 mook.
Kǐ'lat = Tsimshian.
Kilataks, Kilatica = Kilatika.
Ki-laú'-u-tŭkc = Kilauutuksh.
Kǐlauwitawǐñ = Kilimantavie.
Kilauwitawiñmium = Kusilvak.
Kilawalaks = Kitlakdamix.
Kil-cah-ta = Kitkahta.
Kilchikh = Kilchik.
Kilgat = Tsimshian.
Kilgonwah = Kitwingach.
Kil-hai-oo = Skidegate.
Kil-har-hurst's Town = Kilherhursh.
Kil-har-nar's toun = Kilherner.
Kiliga = Kailaidshi.
Ki lǐn ǐg myut = Kilinigmiut.
Kilisteno, Kilistinaux, Kilistinon = Cree.
Kilistinons of the bay of Ataouabouscatouek = Bou-
 scoutton.
Kilistinos, Kilistinous = Cree.
Kiliwatsal, Kiliwátshat = Kalawatset.
Kil-kait-hade = Hlgahet.
Kilkat = Tsimshian.
Killamook, Killamoucks, Killamouks, Killamox,
 Killamuck, Killamuks = Tillamook.
Killawat = Kalawatset.
Killaxthocles = Killaxthokle.
Kill Buck = Killbuck's Town.
Kill Close By = Nitotsiksisstaniks.
Killeegko = Kailaidshi.
Killemooks, Killernoux = Tillamook.
Killestinoes = Cree.
Killewatsis = Kalawatset.
Killimoucks, Killimous, Killimüx = Tillamook.
Killini = Cree.
Killis-tamaha = Inkillis Tamaha.
Killisteneaux, Killistenoes, Killistinaux, Killis-
 tini, Killistinoer, Killistinoes, Killistinons, Kil-
 listinous, Killistins = Cree.
Killiwashat, Killiwatshat = Kalawatset.
Kill, on, chan, Killoosa, Killowitsa = Kilutsai.
Killsmaht = Kelsemaht.
Killuda = Kiliuda.
Killütsār = Kilutsai.
Killymucks = Tillamook.
Kilootsā = Kilutsai.
Kil-pan-hus = Kilpanlus.
Kilsămāt = Kelsemaht.
Kilyamigtagvik = Kilimantavie.
Kimena = Galisteo.
Ki'mkuitq = Kimsquit.
Kimmocksowick = Karusuit.
Kimmooenim = Kamiah.
Kimnepatoo = Kinipetu.
Ki-mni-can = Khemnichan.
Kimoenims, Kimooenim = Kamiah.
Ki-nä = Kainah.
Kinäbik = Kenabig.
Kinaetzi = Knaiakhotana.
Kinagamute = Kinak.
Kinaghi = Kaniagmiut.
K'iñähi-píäko = Tonkawa.
Kinahungik = Kinagingeeg.
Kinahzin = Casa Morena.
Kinai, Kinaitsa, Kinaitze, Kinaitzi, Kinaizi, Kina-
 jut = Knaiakhotana.
Kinakanes = Okinagan.
Kin-a-roa-lax, Kinawalax = Kitlakdamix.
Kinawas = Kiowa.
Kinckemoeks = Micmac.
Kindais = Kendaia.
Kǐ'nᴅoᴅlǐz = Wejegi.
Kinebikowininiwak = Shoshoni.
Kinegans = Kinugumiut.
Kinegnagamiut = Kinegnagak.
Kinegnagmiut = Kinegnak, Razboinski.
Kine-ne-ai-koon = Kainah.
King-a-ghee, King-a-khi = Kingegan.
Kingawa = Kingua.
King Beaver's Town = Tuscarawas.
Kingee'-ga-mŭt = Kinugumiut.
Kinggigtok = Kingiktok.
King Heijah's = Coe Hadjos Town.
Kinghiak = Kingiak
Kingigamute = Kingegan.

Kingoua = Kingua.
Kiniaak = Kingiak.
Kinibeki = Kennebec.
Kinicklick = Kiniklik.
Kinik = Knik.
K'in'i K'el = Kintyel.
Kinik Mute = Kinugumiut.
Kinipissa = Acolapissa.
Kinishtinak, Kinishtino = Cree.
Kinisquit, Kinisquitt = Kimsquit.
Kinisteneaux, Kinistinaux, Kinistineaux, Kinisti-
 noes, Kinistinons, Kinistinuwok = Cree.
Kiniwas = Kiowa.
Kinkale = Pueblo Pintado.
Kinkhankuk = Kinagingeeg.
Kinkyel = Pueblo Pintado.
Kinlitcì, Kinlitcìni, Kǐnᴌǐtsi', Kǐnlǐtsi'dǐne' = Kinh-
 litshi.
Kǐn-nach-hangīk, Kinnakangeck = Kinagingeeg.
Kǐn-nas-ti = Shongopovi.
Kinnatō-iks = Kinuhtoiah.
Kinnats, Kinnats-Khotana, Kinnatz-kokhtana =
 Knaiakhotana.
Kinnebeck Indians = Norridgewock.
Kinnepatoo, Kinnepatu = Kinipetu.
Kinnick = Kinik.
Kinnipetu = Kinipetu.
Kinnewoolun = Kitlakdamix.
Kinnipiaks = Quinnipiac.
Kinnstoucks = Kinuhtoiah.
Ki'-no = Kainah.
Kinonchepiirinik, Kinonchepirinik = Keinouche.
Kinongeouilini = Sturgeon.
Kinouché, Kinouchebiiriniouek, Kinounchepirini =
 Keinouche.
Kinsaatin = Kwilchana.
Kinse = Cayuse.
Kinstenaux, Kinstinaux = Cree.
Kintail = Kintyel.
Kintcūwhwikût = Kinchuwhikut,
Kintecaw, Kintecoy, Kinte Kaye, Kinticka = Can-
 tico.
Kin-Tiel, Kintyèli = Kintyel.
Kiñugmut, Kinugumut = Kinugumiut.
Kinuiak = Paugwik.
Kinuyak = Kingiak.
Kiñyá-ĭndé = Jicarilla.
Ki'-o-a-me = Santo Domingo.
Kiobobas = Kiabaha.
Kiocsies = Kiyuksa.
Kioetoa = Khioetoa.
Kiohican, Kiohuan, Kiohuhahans = Kiowa.
Kiokakons = Kishkakon.
Kiolege = Kailaidshi.
Kio Michie = Kiamisha.
Kionahaa = Kiowa.
Kioose = Cayuse.
Kioosta = Kiusta.
Kíotsaá = Kio.
Kiouanan, Kiouanau, Kiouanous, Kioueouenau =
 Wequadong.
Kious = Dakota.
Kiovas = Kiowa.
Kiowahs, Kioway = Kiowa.
Ki'-o-wummi = Santo Domingo.
Ki-pan-na = Kipana.
Kipikavvi, Kipikawi, Kipikuskvvi = Pepikokia.
Kip-nai'-ăk, Kipniaguk, Kipnisk = Kipniak.
Ki-Pomas = Kato.
Kiqatsa = Crows.
Kirauash = Querechos.
Kirhawguagh Roanu = Karhagaghrooney.
Ki-ri-kur-uks, Kirikurus = Wichita.
Kiristinon = Cree.
Ki'-ro-ko'-qo-tce = Kirokokhoche.
Kironnonas, Kironomes, Kirononas = Karankawa,
Kiruhikwak = Yurok.
Kisalas = Kitzilas.
Kis'án-dinné, Kisáni = Pueblos.
Kiscacones, Kiscacons, Kiscakons, Kiscakous =
 Kishkakon.
Kiscapocoke = Kispokotha.
Kischigamins = Kitchigami.
Kisch-păch-lă-óts = Kishpachlaots.
Kiscopokes = Kispokotha.
Kis-ge-gas, Kisgegos, Kis-go-gas = Kishgagass.
Kishais = Kichai.
Kishakevira = Hupa.
Kishawin = Kaisun.

Kishequechkela=Kishakoquilla.
Kishey=Kiski.
Kishgahgahs=Kishgagass.
Kishkako=Kishkakon.
Kishke-gas=Kishgagass.
Kishkemanetas, Kishkiminitas=Kiskiminetas.
Kishkuske=Kuskuski.
Kish-pi-youx=Kishpiyeoux.
Kishpochalots, Kishpokalants=Kishpachlaots.
Kisinahis=Kiowa Apache.
Kiskacoueiak=Kishkakon.
Kiskagāhs=Kishgagass.
Kiskakonk, Kiskakons, Kiskakoumac, Kiskakouns=
    Kishkakon.
Kiskaminetas=Kiskiminetas.
Kiskapocoke=Kispokotha.
Kiskemanitas, Kiskemeneco=Kiskiminetas.
Kiskiack, Kiskiak=Chiskiac.
Kis Kies=Kiski.
Kis Kightkonck=Keskistkonk.
Kiskokans=Kishkakon.
Kiskomnitos=Kiskominitoes.
Kiskowanitas=Kiskominitoes.
Kiskuskias=Kaskaskia.
Kisky=Kiski.
Kislistinons=Cree.
Kispachalaidy, Kispachlohts=Kishpachlaots.
Kispaioohs=Kishpiyeoux.
Kispapous=Kickapoo.
Kispiax=Kishpiyeoux.
Kispogógi, Ki-spo-ko-tha=Kispokotha.
Kispyaths, Kispyox=Kishpiyeoux.
Kissah=Coosa.
Kissaiakh=Kashaiak.
Kissgarrase, Kiss-ge-gaas=Kishgagass.
Kissiak, Kissiakh=Kashaiak.
Kisteneaux=Cree.
Kitadah=Kitunto.
Kitaesches, Kitaesechis=Kichai.
Kitaheeta=Hitchiti.
Kitalaska=Kitzilas.
Kitamah, Kitamaht, Kitamatt=Kitamat.
Kit, an, doh=Kitunto.
Ki-tä-ne-mäke=Khitanumanke.
Kitangataa=Kitangata.
Kitanning=Kittanning.
Kitāns=Gituns.
Kitatels=Kitkatla.
Kitawan=Kitahon.
Kitax=Kitaix.
Kit-cathla=Kitkatla.
Kitchaclalth=Kitsalthlal.
Kĭ'tchas=Kichai.
Kitchatlah=Kitkatla.
Kitchawanc, Kitchawonck=Kitchawank.
Kitche, kla, la=Kitsalthlal.
Kitchem-kalem=Kitzimgaylum.
Ki'-tchēsh, Kitchies=Kichai.
Kitchigamich, Kitchigamick=Kitchigami.
Kitchigami-wininiwak=Kitchigumiwininiwug.
Kitchimkale=Kitzimgaylum.
Kitchisibi-wininiwak=Kitchisibiwininiwug.
Kitcho-pataki=Hichopataki.
Kitchtawanghs=Kitchawank.
Kitchu lass=Kitzilas.
Kitchupataki=Kitchopataki.
Kitcigạmīwininiwạg=Kechegummewininewug.
Kitcoonsa=Kitwingach.
Kite=Crows.
Kite Indians, Kites=Staitan.
Kitestues=Kittizoo.
Kitha-ata=Kitkahta.
Kit-hai-uass hādē=Hlgaiu.
Kithannink=Kittanning.
Kithātlă=Kitkatla.
Kithigami=Kitchigami.
Kithkatla=Kitkatla.
Kĭtiga'ru=Kitegareut.
Kit-ih-shian=Kitksan.
Kĭ'tikĭti'sh=Wichita.
Kitimat=Kitamat.
Kitināhs=Kitanmaiksh.
Kitistzoo=Kittizoo.
Kit'-kä=Kitkehahki.
Kitkaata, Kitkāda, Kĭtkaĕt=Kitkahta.
Kitkagas=Kishgagass.
Kitkahā'ki, Kitkahoets=Kitkehahki.
Kitkaht, Kitkathla, Kit-kats=Kitkahta.
Kit'-ke-hak-i=Kitkehahki.

Kit-khall-ah, Kit-khatla=Kitkatla.
Kit-ksum, Kit-ksun=Kitksan.
Kitlacdamax=Kitlakdamix.
Kitlach-damak, Kitlach-damix=Kitlakdamix.
Kitlan, Kitlan Kilwilpeyot=Kitlani.
Kitlatamox=Kitlakdamix.
Kitlax=Kitaix.
Kitloop, Kitlop=Kitlope.
Ki'tōnā'Qa=Kutenai, Upper Kutenai.
Kitoonitza=Kitkatla.
Kĭtsaɔi=Kichai.
Kits-āch-lă-āl'ch=Kitsalthlal.
Kitsagas=Kishgagass.
Kitsagatala=Kitsalthlal.
Kitsaiches=Kichai.
Kitsalas, Kĭtsalass, Kitsallas=Kitzilas.
Kĭtsäsh, Kitsasĭ, Kits de Singes=Kichai.
Kitseesh=Kitzeesh.
Kitseguecla, Kitse-gukla=Kitzegukla.
Kit-se-lai-so, Kĭtselässir, Kitsellase=Kitzilas.
Kitsenelah, Kit-se-quahla, Kit-se-quak-la=Kitze-
    gukla.
Kits-ge-goos, Kits-go-gase=Kishgagass.
Kitsigeuhlé, Kitsiguchs, Kitsiguhli=Kitzegukla.
Kits-iïsch, Kitsis=Kitzeesh.
Kitsoss=Kichai.
Kitspayuchs, Kits-piouse, Kits-pioux, Kits-piox=
    Kishpiyeoux.
Kitspukaloats=Kishpachlaots.
Kits-pyonks=Kishpiyeoux.
Kits-se-quec-la=Kitzegukla.
Kĭ'tsu=Kichai.
Kitsumkalem, Kitsumkalum=Kitzimgaylum.
Kitswingahs=Kitwingach.
Kitswinscolds=Kitwinskole.
Kittak=Kitaix.
Kit ta maat=Kitamat.
Kittamaque-ink, Kittamaqundi=Kittamaquindi.
Kittamarks, Kit-ta-muat=Kitamat.
Kitt-andó=Kitunto.
Kittaning, Kittaones=Kittanning.
Kit-ta-wās=Cumshewa.
Kitté-gá-re-ut, Kitte-garœ-oot, Kit-te-gá-ru=Kitc-
    gareut.
Kit-tek, Kitten, Kit-tex=Kitaix.
Kittimat=Kitamat.
Kit-tistzu=Kittizoo.
Kittlĕān=Kitlani.
Kitt-lope=Kitlope.
Kittoa=Kituhwa.
Kit-too-nuh'-a=Kutenai.
Kittowa=Kituhwa.
Kittrālchlă=Kitkatla.
Kittumarks=Kitamat.
Kittuwa=Cherokee.
Kituanaha=Kitunahan Family, Kutenai.
Kĭtúhwagĭ'=Cherokee.
Kitunaha=Kitunahan Family, Kutenai.
Kitunana, Kitunā'χa=Kutenai.
Kitwancole, Kit-wan-cool=Kitwinskole.
Kit-wang-agh, Kitwangar=Kitwingach.
Kitwanshelt=Kitwinshilk.
Kit-will-coits; Kitwill, quoitz=Kitwilgioks.
Kit, will, su, pat=Kitwilksheba.
Kitwint-shieth, Kitwintshilth=Kitwinshilk.
Kit-wulg-jats=Kitwilgioks.
Kit-wúlkse-lé=Kitwilksheba.
Kitwungā=Kitwingach.
Kitwunkool=Kitwinskole.
Kityagoos=Kittizoo.
Kit-zilass=Kitzilas.
Ki-ua=Santo Domingo.
Kiu-ahs-dée=Shongopovi.
Kiukuswĕskitchimi-ûk=Malecite
Kiuses=Cayuse.
Kivalhioqua=Kwalhioqua.
Kivalinag-miut=Kevalingamiut
Kivalinge=Kechemudluk.
Kivichakh=Kvichak.
Kivome=Santo Domingo.
Kivualinagmut=Kivualinak.
Ki'-wa=Santo Domingo.
Kiwaa=Kiowa.
Kiwaw=Cayuse.
Ki'-wo-mi=Santo Domingo.
Kĭ'xmi=Kinugumiut.
Ki-ya-hanni, Kĭ-ya-jani=Kiyahani.
Kiyataigmeuten, Kiyaten=Kiatagmiut.

Kiyuksan=Kiyuksa.
Kiyuse=Cayuse.
Ki-žăn'-ne̱=Pueblos.
Kizh=Gabrieleño.
K-kaltat=Kaltag.
K'kásăwi=Kowasayee.
K-khaltat=Kaltat.
Kkhaltel=Kaltag.
Kkⁿa-lon-Gottinè=Kraylongottine.
Kkᵨayiᵨa-Gottinè=Krayiragottine.
Kkrayou-Kouttànæ=Kaiyuhkhotana.
Kkᵨayttchare ottiné=Kawchodinne.
Kkᵨay-tᵨèlè-ottine, Kkᵨest' aylé-kkè ottiné=Athabasca.
K'kwā'kum=Kukwakum.
Klaamen=Sliammon.
Klaat-sop=Clatsop.
Klachatah=Klikitat.
Klackamas, Klackamus, Klackamuss=Clackama.
Klackarpun=Ntlakyapamuk.
KLā'ecaLxix=Ktlaeshatlkik.
KLā'gulaq=Katlagulak.
Klahangamut=Klchakuk.
Klahars=Klahosaht.
Klahinks=Yakutat.
Klah-oh-quaht=Clayoquot.
Klahoquaht=Clayoquot.
Klahose, Klahous=Clahoose.
Klah-wit-sis=Tlauitsis.
Klaizarts, Kla-iz-zarts=Makah.
Klakalama=Thlakalama.
Klakamat=Clackama.
Klakatacks=Klikitat.
Klakheluk=Neahkeluk.
Klakimas=Clackama.
Klakwan=Klukwan.
Kla-kwul-lum=Cloquallum.
Klalams, Klalanes, Klallam=Clallam.
Klamacs, Klamaks=Klamath.
Klamaskwaltin=Klamasqualtin.
Klamat=Klamath.
Klamath=Lutuamian Family, Shastan Family.
Klamath Lake Indians=Klamath.
Klamaths=Yurok.
Klamatk=Klamath.
Kla-ma-took=Klamatuk.
Klameth, Klamets=Klamath.
KLā'môîx=Katlamoik.
Klanoh-klatklam=Kalispel.
Klantala=Kwatami.
Kla-oo-qua-ahts, Kla-oo-quates=Clayoquot.
Klapatci'tcin=Kapachichin.
Klarkinos=Klaskino.
Klashoose=Clahoose.
Klās'-kaino=Klaskino.
Klasset=Makah.
Klass-ki-no=Klaskino.
Klatawars=Klatanars.
Klat-la-wash=Klatlawas.
Klat-ol-klin=Katshikotin.
Klatolseaquilla=Tlatlasikoala.
Klatraps, Klatsaps=Clatsop.
Klatscanai, Klatskanai, Klatskania, Klats-ka-nuise=Tlatskanai.
Klatsops=Clatsop.
Klatstonis=Tlatskanai.
Klauoh-klatklam=Kutenai.
Klausuna=Tlanusiyi.
Klā-wit-sis, Kla-wi-tsush=Tlauitsis.
Klawmuts=Klamath.
Klaxermette=Taksomiut.
Klay-cha-la-tinneh=Thlingchadinne.
Klay quoit=Clayoquot.
Klay-tinneh=Thlingchadinne.
Kl-changamute=Klchakuk.
Klech-ah'-mech=Tlkamcheen.
Klegutshégamut=Kleguchek.
Kleketat=Klikitat.
Klemook=Tillamook.
Klen-ee-kate, Klen-e-kate=Koluschan Family.
Kliarakans, Kliavakans=Klinkwan.
Klicatat, Klickataats, Klick-a-tacks, Klickatates, Klickatats, Klickitats=Klikitat.
Klick-um-cheen, Klickunacheen=Tlkamcheen.
Klikalats, Klikatat, Kliketan, Kliketat, Klikitat, Klinget=Tlingit.
Klinquan=Klinkwan.

Klin-tchanᵨe, Klin-tchonᵨèh=Lintchanre.
Kliquital=Klikitat.
Klistinaux, Klistinons, Klistinos=Cree.
Kliuquan=Klinkwan.
Klo-a-tsul-tshik'=Tutchonekutchin.
Klockwaton, Klockwatone=Klochwatone.
K'loᵨtcě'-ɥünně=Klothchetunne.
Klògiɸine, Klógidĭne', Klogni=Klogi.
Kl'o-ke-ottiné, Klo-kke-Gottine, Klo-kke-ottine=Klokegottine.
Klokwan=Klukwan.
Klô-ven-Kouttchin, Klo-vén-Kuttchin=Tukkuthkutchin.
Klowitshis=Tlauitsis.
Kluck-hait-kwee=Kluckhaitkwu.
Kluckwaton, Kluckwatone=Klochwatone.
Klucquan=Klukwan.
Klue, Klue's Village=Kloo.
Klugaducayn=Klokadakaydn.
Klûkätät, Klûk-há-tät=Klikitat.
Klŭk-nachádi=Tluknahadi.
Klukwan=Kake.
Klusklus=Tluskez.
Klutagmiut=Klutak.
Knacsitares=Gnacsitare.
Knaina, Knaiokhotana=Knaiakhotana.
Knakanak=Kanakanak.
Knaut=Kuaut.
Knecktakimut=Chiukak.
Kneestenoag=Cree.
Kngalukmut, Kngalukmute=Kugaluk.
Kniegnagamute=Kinegnak.
Knife Indians=Esbataottine, Ntlakyapamuk.
Knik Station=Knakatnuk.
Kniktag'emūt=Iknetuk.
K'niq'-a-mūt=Knik.
Knisteaux, Knistenaus, Knistenaux, Knisteneau, Knisteneaux, Knisteneux, Knisteno, Knistenoos, Knistinaux, Knistineaux, Knistinos=Cree.
Knives=Ntlakyapamuk.
Koa=Koi.
Koā'antᴇl=Kwantlen.
Koahualla=Kawia.
Koakias=Cahokia.
Koakramiut=Koksoagmiut.
K·'oā'la=Hoya.
Koā'lᴇqt=Koalekt.
K·'oa'pQ=Koapk.
Koaskunā'=Koiskana.
Koassáti=Koasati.
Ko-a-wis-so-jik=Wakoawissojik.
Kocetenays=Kutenai.
Kŏchěchŏ Wěněněwåk=Kojeje-wininewug.
Kochkogamute=Kochkok.
Kochkomut=Koko.
Kochlogtogpagamiut=Kukluktuk.
Kochninakwe, Kochonino=Havasupai.
Ko-cke=Cochiti.
Koco=Hopi.
K'odalpä-K'iñago=Dakota.
Kodenees=Kutenai.
Kodhell-vén-Kouttchin=Kwitchakutchin.
Koechies=Kichai.
Koeracoenetanon=Coiracoentanon.
Koetenais, Koetenay, Koetinays=Kutenai.
Koggiung=Kogiung.
Kogholaghi=Unalaska.
Kogmollik Mutes=Kopagmiut.
Ko-hai, Kohaio=Kuhaia.
Kohátk=Quahatika.
Ko-ha-yo=Kuhaia.
Kohenins=Yavapai.
Kóhꞣkang, Kohꞣñañamu=Kokyan.
Ko'hni'ma, Ko'-hni' na=Havasupai.
Kohó=Tanaha.
Kohoaldje=Paiute, Shivwits.
Kóho'hlté=Taos.
Koho-mats-ka-catch-ka, Ko-ho-mut-ki-garts-kar, Ko-ho-muts ka-catch-ka, Ko-ho-muts-ki-gar, Kohomutskigartokar=Kohamutkikatska.
Kóhonino=Havasupai.
Kohoseraghe=Kanagaro.
Koht-ana=Knaiakhotana.
Kóhun=Yuma.
Koi ai vla=Coila.
Koianglas=Kweundlas.
Koienkahe=Karankawa.
Koikhpagamute, Koikhpagmute=Ikogmiut.

Kó-iks=Laguna.
Kōiltca'na=Kwilchana.
Ko-intchush=Koinchush.
Koiotero=Coyoteros.
Ko'-i-yäk'=Coos.
K·'ō'k·aitq=Kokaitk.
KōkEnū'k·kē=Okinagan.
Kokesailah=Koksilah.
Kokh' lit innuin=Okiogmiut.
Kokhlokhtokpagamute=Kukluktuk.
Kokhuene=Cajuenche.
Kokmalect=Nuwukmiut.
Kokmullit=Nuwuk.
Kókob=Kukuch.
Ko-k·'oc'=Coos.
Kokok=Kochkok.
Kokokiwak=Crows.
Ko-ko-mah village=Kokomo.
Kokomish=Skokomish.
Kokoninos=Havasupai.
Kokopa=Cocopa.
Kokopnyama=Kokopki.
Ko'-kop nyû-mû, Kokop wiñwû, Ko-kop-wüñ-wû=Kokop.
K'ok'-o-ro-t'ŭ'-yu=Pecos.
Koksawopalim=Pueblos.
Koksoagmyut, Koksoak Innuits=Koksoagmiut.
Kokvontan=Kagwagtan.
Kok-wai-y-toch=Kokaitk.
Ko-kyan-a, Kokyan wiñwû, Ko'-kyuñ-üh wüñ-wü=Kokyan.
Kolapissas=Acolapissa.
Kolatica=Kilatika.
Kolchane, Kolchans, Kolchina=Kulchana.
Koliugi=Tlingit.
Koliva=Koroa.
Koljuches, Koljuschen, Koljush, Kolloshians=Tlingit.
Kolmakovsky=Kolmakof.
Kolnit=Skilloot.
Koloches=Tlingit.
Kolok=Coloc.
Kolooch, Koloschen=Koluschan Family.
Koloshi=Tlingit.
Kolshani=Kulchana.
Kolshina=Ahtena.
Kolsids, Kolsins=Colcene.
Koltchanes, Koltschane, Koltschanen, Koltschaner, Koltshan, Koltshanen, Koltshanes, Koltshani, Koltshany=Kulchana.
Kolúch=Koluschan Family.
Kolumakturook, Kolumatourok, Kolumaturok=Kilimantavie.
Koluschen, Koluschians, Kolush=Koluschan Family.
Kol'utush=Calapooya.
Kolwa=Koroa.
Kolyuzhi=Tlingit.
Komantsu=Comanche.
Komarov Odinotchka=Komarof.
Komáts=Comanche.
Kom'-bo=Yanan Family.
K·'ō'm'enoq=Komenok.
Komkiūtis=Komkyutis.
Komkome'=Tonkawa.
K·'ōmkō'tEs=Komkutis.
K·'ō'mkyūtis=Komkyutis.
Kōm Maidüm=Achomawi.
Ko'mpabi'ănta, Kompa'go=Kiowa.
Koms'eka-K'iñahyup=Arapaho.
K·'ō'moks, Ko-mookhs=Comox.
Ko'mpabi'anta=Kiowa.
Ko-mun'-i-tup'-i-o=Nez Percés.
Komux=Comox.
Kōna=Skedans.
Konagens, Konagis=Kaniagmiut.
Konapee=Konope.
Konasadagea=Canadasaga.
Konasgi=Kaniagmiut.
Konasoa, Konassa=Canadasaga.
Konatines=Kanohatino.
Konaz=Kansa.
Ko-ne-a kun=Comiakin.
Kone-Konep=Konekonlp.
Kongigamut, Kongigamute=Kungugemiut.
Kongiganagamute=Kongiganak.
Koniagi, Koniagmutes=Kaniagmiut.
Koniata=Tonihata.
Konick=Cooniac.

Koñigunugumut=Kongiganak.
Kónino=Havasupai.
Konjagen=Esquimauan Family, Kaniagmiut.
Konkhandeenhronon=Conkhandeenrhonon.
Konkoné=Tonkawa.
Ko'nlo=Konglo.
Konnaack=Cooniac.
Konnaudaugua=Canandaigua.
Konoȧtinnos=Kanohatino.
Konondaigua=Canandaigua.
Kononwarohare=Ganowarohare.
Konootená=Kanuti.
Konoshioni, Konossioni=Iroquois.
Konowiki=Conoy.
Konsa, Konses=Kansa.
Konshaws=Coosha.
Kontarea=Contarea.
Konuaga=Caughnawaga.
Konungzi Onîga.=Iroquois.
Ko·nyä-tdo'a=Kungya.
Konza=Kansa.
Kon-za=Kanze.
Kooagamutes=Kowagmiut.
Kooagomutes=Kunmiut.
Koo-a-sah-te=Koasati.
Koo-cha-koo-chin=Kutchakutchin.
Koo-chee-ta-kee, Koo-che-ta-kers=Kotsoteka.
Koochin=Kutchin.
Koo-chi-ta-ker=Kotsoteka.
Koogmute=Kunmiut.
ᵗKo-ōh-lōk-tā-que=Kalokta.
Kooigamute=Kwik.
Kook-a-tee=Hokedi.
Kook-koo-oose=Coos.
Kookpovoros, Kookpowro Mutes=Kukpaurungmiut.
Kook-wai-wai-toh=Kokaitk.
Kool=Kuneste.
Koolsaticara, Koolsatik-ara=Kotsoteka.
Koolvagavigamute=Kulvagavik.
Koomen=Panamenik.
Koona=Skedans.
Koonjeskie=Kunjeskie.
Koo-og-ameuts=Kowagmiut.
Kooq Mutes=Kunmiut.
Kōoqōtlā'nē=Kookotlane.
Koosah=Kusa.
Koo-sām=Husam.
Kooskimo=Koskimo.
Koot=Got.
Kootames, Kootanais, Kootanay, Kootanie=Kutenai.
Kootanies=Kitunahan Family.
Koo-tche-noos=Hutsnuwu.
Koo-tchin'=Kutchin.
Kóo-tdóa=Koo.
Kootenai=Kitunahan Family.
Kootenai, Kootenaies, Kootenais, Kootenay, Kootenia=Kutenai.
Kootenuha=Kitunahan Family.
Kooténuha, Kootones, Kootoonais=Kutenai.
Kootsenoos, Kootsnovskie, Kootznahoo, Kootznoos Kootznov=Hutsnuwu.
Koovuk=Kowak.
Ko-pa=Gupa.
Kópa=Creeks.
Kopachichin=Kapachichin.
Kopagmut, Kopăng-meŭn=Kopagmiut.
Ko-páya=Tulkepaia.
Ko-pe=Copeh.
Kopi·n-tdóa=Kuping.
K·'op-tagúi=Jicarilla.
Koquahpilt=Koquapilt.
Koqueightuk=Kokaitk.
Koquilth=Wishosk.
Koquitan=Coquitlam.
Koracocnitonon, Korakoenitanon=Coiracoentanon.
Korekins=Karkin.
Korenkake=Karankawa.
Korimen=Keremen
Korkone=Tonkawa.
Koronks=Karankawa.
Korovinsky=Korovinski.
Ko-sa-te'haⁿ-ya'=Koasati.
Koschiginskoje=Kashega.
Ko-'se-a-ɹe'-nyoⁿ=Cayuga.
Kose-kemoe=Koskimo.
Koshegenskoi, Koshigin, Koshiginskoe=Kashega.
Kosh-sho'-o=Kassovo.

Kosimo, Koskeemos, K·osk·ē′moq, Koskiemo, Kōs′-kī-mo, Kos-ki-mu=Koskimo.
Koskoquims=Kuskwogmiut.
Koskumos=Koskimo.
Kosmitas, Kosmiti=Hosmite.
Koso=Hopi.
Ko-so-a-cha=Kosotshe.
K′o-so-o=Hopi.
χōs′-o-tcĕ′=Kosotshe.
Ko+s′-tco-te′-ka=Kotsoteka.
Ko-stété=Laguna.
Kŏstshotéka=Kotsoteka.
Ko-sul-te-me=Kwusathlkhuntunne.
Kosumnes=Cosumni.
Kosyrof=Koserefski.
Kotakoutouemi=Otaguottouemin.
Kot-à-Kutchin, Kotch-a-Kutchin=Kutchakutchin.
Kotchitchi-wininiwak=Kojejewininewug.
Ko-té-yi-mĭks=Kutaiimiks.
Ko′tiyti, Kot-ji-ti=Cochiti.
Ko-tŏň′-spi-tup′-i-o=Salish.
K′ótsaä′=Kio.
Kotsokhotana=Kungugemiut.
Ko-tyi-ti=Cochiti.
Kotzebue=Kikiktak.
к8ак8ак8chiouets, к8ак8chi8ets, Koüakoüikoücsi-oüek, Kouakouikouesiwek = Wakouingouechi-wek.
Kouans=Kohani.
K8apahag=Kwapahag.
Kouaras=Quaras.
Kouari=Schoharie.
Kouas=Kawas.
Ko-uávi=Tulkepaia.
Kouayan, Kouayon=Kouyam.
Koudekan=Gaudekan.
Kouera=Koroa.
Kougotis=Komkutis.
Kouivakouintanouas=Coiracoentanon.
Koukhoñtans=Kagwantan.
Kouksoarmiut=Koksoagmiut.
Koulischen=Koluschan Family.
Koumchaouas=Cumshewa.
Ko-un=Tontos, Tulkepaia.
K8na8ons=Kounaouons.
Kourona, Kourovas=Koroa.
Kouschâ Kouttchin=Kutchakutchin.
Kouse=Coos.
Koushnoüs=Hutsnuwu.
Kouskokhantses=Kuskwogmiut.
Koutaines, Koutanis=Kutenai.
Kó-utchan=Yuma.
Koutonais=Kutenai.
Koutzenoos, Koutznous=Hutsnuwu.
Kouyou=Kuiu.
Kowăg′-mut=Kowagmiut.
Kowai=Salmon River Indians.
Kowailchew, Kow-ait-chen=Cowichan.
Kowalitsks=Cowlitz.
Kowăñg-mēun=Kowagmiut.
Kow-a′-sah=Kawaiisu.
Ko-was-ta=Kohashti.
Kowávi=Tulkepaia.
Kowelits, Kowelitsk=Cowlitz.
Kowes, Kowes Bay=Coos.
Kow-hé-tah=Kawita.
Ko-wilth=Wishosk.
Kowitchans, Kowitsin=Cowichan.
Kowlitz=Cowlitz.
Kowmook=Comox.
Kowogoconughariegugharie=Kowogoconnugharie-gugharie.
Kowronas=Koroa.
Kowwasayes, Kowwassaye, Kowwassayee=Kowa-sayee.
Kow welth=Chaahl.
Koχniná kwe, Kóχniname=Havasupai.
Ko-ya-ta, Ko-ya-te, Ko-ya-tes, Ko-ye-to=Koyeti.
Ko-yo-konk-hₐ-ka=Cayuga.
Koyoña wiñwû, Ko-yo′-ño wüñ-wû=Koyonya.
Koyóshtu=Hano.
Koyoukon=Koyukukhotana.
Koyoukouk-Kouttanæ=Koyukukhotana.
Koyu=Kuiu.
Koyŭgmūt=Koyugmiut.
Koyukuk (River), Koyukuk settlements=Koyu-kuk.
Koyükŭń, Koyükŭnskoi=Koyukukhotana.
Ko-za-bi-ti-kut-teh=Kotsava.

Kozyrof=Koserefski.
Kqaí-cŭk=Khaishuk.
K′qaí-kŭ-to′ûm=Khaikuchum.
Kqai-yûk′-kqai=Khaiyukkhai.
K′qai-yú-mi-ɥû=Khaiyumitu.
Kqa-kqaitc′=Khakhaich.
K′qătc-ɥais′=Khachtais.
K′qil′-ŭq=Khilukh.
K′qi-nuq′ ɥûnnĕ=Khinukhtunne.
Kqí′-tä-ḷai′t′çĕ=Khitalaitthe.
Kqlĭm-kwaio′=Khlimkwaish.
K′qloc′-le-qwŭt′-tce=Khloshlekhwutshe.
Kqló-qwai yú-tslu=Khlokhwaiyutslu.
K′qlo-qwec ɥûnnĕ=Coos, Kalawatset, Siuslaw.
K′qōlg=Kholkh.
Kqoptlē′nik=Colville.
Kqûl-hanct′-auk=Khulhanshtauk.
Kqu-waí-hus=Khuwaius.
Kρagmalit, Kρagmalivect, Kρagmaliveit, Kρaməlit, Kramalit, Kρavañaρtat=Kitegareut.
Kreeks=Creeks.
Krees=Cree.
Kreluit=Skilloot.
Krichos=Creeks.
Kricqs, Kries=Cree.
Krihk=Creeks.
Kρikeρtaloρméut=Ugjulirmiut.
Kripniyŭkamiut=Kipniak.
Kriqs, Kris, Kristenaux, Kristeneaux, Kristinaux, Kristino=Cree.
Kroaout=Kuaut.
Kρoteylo eut, Kρoteyoρeut=Kitegareut.
Kshkushking=Kuskuski.
K·″tătäs=Shanwappom.
K·′tcā̄′m=Kicham.
Ktzialtana=Kulchana.
Kū-ăǵ-mut=Kowagmiut.
Kuahadi=Kwahari.
Kuâja=Kwahu.
Kua-kaa=San Marcos.
Kua-kay=Kuakaa.
Kuakumtcen=Kuakumchen.
Kuₐ-kyi-na=Kwakina.
Kualiug-miut=Kugaluk.
Kualt=Kuaut.
Kualyugmut=Kugaluk.
Kuangmiut=Kowagmiut.
Kuant=Kuaut.
Kubakhye=Kawaiisu.
Ku′bəratpat=Penateka.
Kubok=Kowak.
Ku-chi-bich-i-wa-nap′ Pal-up′=Tubatulabal.
Kŭchin=Kutchin.
Kúchnikwe=Havasupai.
Kuc′-le-ta′-ta=Kushletata.
Kud-witcaca=Kutawichasha.
Kueh′a=Komoyue.
Kuenyúgu-háka=Cayuga.
Kuē′qa=Kueha, Komoyue.
Kuē′xa=Komoyue.
Kuē′xâmut=Guetela.
Kugalukmut, Kugalukmute=Kugaluk.
Kugmiut=Kunmiut.
Kuhn=Tulkepaia.
Kuhnauwantheew=Conoy.
Kuhni kwe, Ku′h·nis=Havasupai.
Kuhns=Tontos.
Ku′htche-té′χka=Kotsoteka.
Kuhuáshti=Kohashti.
Kuicha=Komoyue.
Kuik=Atnik.
Kuikawkuk=Hawikuh.
Kuikli=Kwik.
Kúikni=Molala.
Kú-i-litć=Kuilitsh.
Kuilka=Kaskaskia.
Kuilkhlogamute=Kuilkluk.
Kuille-pates=Quileute.
Kui-much-qui-toch=Kimsquit.
Kuin-ae-alts=Quinaielt.
Kuinskanaht=Koiskana.
Kuisaatin=Kwilchana.
Kuitare′-i=Pawnee.
Ku-ítc=Kuitsh.
Kuizán=Yuma.
Kujata=Kiatang.
Kujēēdi=Kuyedi.
Kŭju-kŏn=Kouyou.
Kŭ′kanĭs‘hyáka-hánoq^{ch}=Kukinishyaka.

Kukanuwu=Huna.
Kukapa=Cocopa.
Kŭkettãn=Kokhittan.
Kukhn-yak=Cooniac.
Kukhpagmiut=Kopagmiut.
Kuk-ke-wa-on-an-ing=Wequadong.
Ku-kua=San Marcos.
Kü′-kü-tci, Kü′-kutc wüñ-wü=Kukuchi.
Kukuth-kutchin=Tukkuthkutchin.
Kukuts, Kukutsi=Kukuch.
Ku-kwil′, Ku-kwĭl′ɔûnnĕ, Ku-kwĭl′-tün ɔûnnê=Mishikhwutmetunne.
Kû‘lahĭ=Kuhlahi.
Kulahuasa=Calahuasa.
Kula′ Kai Po′mo=Keliopoma.
Kula-napo, Kulanopo=Kuhlanapo.
Kulà′pten′elt=Quelaptoulilt.
Kuldo, Kuldoe=Kauldaw.
Ku-lees, Ku-leets=Kulleets.
Kul-hŭl-atsĭ=Kadohadacho.
Kû-lĭs′-kitc hĭtc′lûm=Taltushtuntude.
Kulj-khlugamute=Kuilkluk.
Kulkuisála=Koksilah.
Kulkumic=Kulkumish.
Kullas Palus, Kullespelm, Kullespen=Kalispel.
Kulluk=Kulukak.
Kūl′-meh=Yiikulme.
Kulon-tówa=Konglo.
K′ulpa ki′ako=Kretan.
Kulsage=Kulsetsiyi.
Kúlsam-Tgé-us, Kúls-Tgé-ush=Kulshtgeush.
Kulua, Kulwa=Koroa.
Kulwoguwigumut=Kulvagavik.
Kú-man-i-a-kwe=Comanche.
Kumas′ɔûnné=Kimestunne.
Kúmbatkni, Kúmbatuashkni, Kumbatwash=Kumbatuash.
Kum-cutes, Kumkewtis=Komkyutis.
Kumnom=Nuimok.
Kumshahas, Kumshewa, Kumshiwa=Cumshewa.
Ku′-mu=Kunipalgi.
Kumumbar=Cumumbah.
Kūn=Tulkepaia, Yuma.
K·′u′na=Skedans.
Kunali-tdóa=Kungaii.
K·′unakē′owai=Kona-kegawai.
Kunânâ=Nahane.
Kunfetdi-tdóa=Kungfetdi.
Kungeeg-ameuts, Kŭngŭgemūt=Kungugemiut.
Kû-nis′ɔûnné=Alsea.
Kun lā′nas=Kuna-lanas.
Kúñmiun=Kunmiut.
Kûñmûd′lĭñ=Kangmaligmiut.
Kun na-nar-wesh=Arapaho.
K′ûn-nu′-pi-yu′=Kunnupiyu.
Kunoagon=Connewango.
Kunpi-tdóa=Kungpi.
Kunqit=Gunghet-haidagaɪ.
Kunshak bolukta=Concha.
Kunta-witcaca=Kutawichasha.
Kún-tdóa=Kun.
Kuntsä-tdóa=Kungtsa.
Kuntsei-tdóa=Kungtsei.
Kuntsoa-tdóa=Kungtsoa.
Ku′nu-haya′nu=Potawatomi.
Kŭn-ŭn-ah′=Tahltan.
Kunwicása=Kutawichasha.
Kunχit=Gunghet-haidagai.
Kunyä-tdóa, Kunye-tdóa=Kungya.
Kunyï-tdóa=Kungyi.
Kun′-zä=Kanze.
Kuôôlt-e=Kwantlen.
Kuosúgru=Kuosugru.
Ku-dî′-mĭɔl-tǎ′=Kupimithlta.
Kupín-tdóa, Kupi-tóda=Kuping.
Kupûñmiun=Kopagmiut.
Kûrâhi′yĭ=Kulahiyi.
Kuraintu-kwakats=Kwaiantikwokets.
Kurtz=Kurts.
Kuρvik=Kopagmiut.
Kūs=Coos.
Kus=Okuwa.
Kusa=Coos, Creeks.
Ku′să-nûñâ′hi=Creek Path.
Ku′săwet′yĭ=Cusawatee.
Kuscarawaoks, Kuscarawocks=Cuscarawaoc.
Kus-chē-o-tin=Kezche.

Kusch-kē-ti=Koskedi.
Kuschkukchwak-müten=Kuskwogmiut.
ɣus çla′ɔûnnĕ′=Salwahku.
Kūsha=Coosha.
Kushacton=Coshocton.
Kushak=Coosha.
Kushak Chitto=Conchachitou.
Kushak osapa=Conshaconsapa.
Kushak tikpi=Conchatikpi.
Kushang=Kashong.
Kushcushkec=Kuskuski.
Kushichagat=Vagitchitchate.
Kush-Kish=Usal.
Kushkushkee, Kushkushking, Kushkuskies=Kuskuski.
Kushocton=Coshocton.
Kushokwagmut=Kuskwogmiut.
Ku′shpĕlu=Kalispel.
Kushutuk=Kashutuk.
Kusil=Cascil.
Kusilvuk=Kusilvak.
Ku-si-pah=Kosipatuwiwagaiyu.
Kusi-Ûtahs=Gosiute.
Kuskaranaocke, Kuskarawɐck=Cuscarawaoc.
Kusk-ēdi=Koskedi.
Kuskeiskees=Kaskaskia.
Kus-ke-mu=Koskimo.
Kuskogamute, Kuskohkagamiut=Kuskok.
Kusko kûax tana=Kuskwogmiut.
Kuskokvagamute, Kuskokvagmute=Kuskok.
Kuskokvakh=Kuskokvak.
Kuskokwagamute=Kuskok.
Kuskokwigmjuten=Kuskwogmiut.
Kuskokwim=Kulchana, Kuskwogmiut.
Kuskokwimer, Kuskokwimjuts, Kuskokwims, Kuskokwimtsi=Kuskwogmiut.
Kuskoquimers=Kulchana.
Kuskovak, Kuskovakh=Kuskokvak.
Kuskuschki, Kuskuskas=Kuskuski.
Kuskuske=Kaskaskia.
Kuskuskees, Kuskuskies, Kuskuskin, Kuskusko Town, Kuskusky=Kuskuski.
Kuskutchewak, Kuskutschcwak, Kuskwogmut=Kuskwogmiut.
Kūs-me′ɔûnné=Coos.
Ku-so-cha-to-ny=Kosotshe.
Kuspĕlu=Kutenai.
Kussilof=Kasilof.
Kussoe=Coosa.
Kûstä Hãadē=Kiusta.
Kustaloga=Custaloga′s Town.
ɣu′-su-me′ɔûnné=Kosotshe.
Kútanas, Kútani=Kutenai.
Kutani, Kútanis=Kitunahan Family.
Kutchaakuttchin,Kutchak-kutchi=Kutchakutchin
Kūtch′-ä-kūtch′-ĭn=Kwitchakutchin.
Kutchán=Yuma.
Kutchiá Kuttchin=Kutchakutchin.
Kutcitciwininiwag=Kojejewininewug.
Kú-ɔou-wi′-t′çĕ=Kutshuwitthe.
K′u-tdóa=Ku.
Kutenae, Kutenay=Kutenai.
Kutkwutlu=Katkwaahltu.
Kutlik=Kotlik.
Kutnehä′, Kutona, Kutonacha, Kutonaqa, Kutonas=Kutenai.
Ku-tówa=Ku.
Ku-t′qin=Kutchin.
Kŭ′ts=Kurts.
Kutsha-kutshi=Kutchakutchin.
Kutshi, Kutshin=Kutchin.
Kutsnovskoe=Hutsnuwu.
Kuttelspelm=Kalispel.
Kuttoowauw=Cherokee.
Kutzán=Yuma.
Kü-ü-ki=Sacaton.
Ku-û′-sha=Creeks.
Kúuts=Kuts.
Ku-ux-ɐws=Kiyuksa.
Kuvahaivima=Serranos.
Kuwâhi′=Keowee.
Kŭ-wâ′-ku-che=Koakotsalgi.
Ku-we-vĕ-ka pai-ya=Yavapai.
Küwhaía=Kuhaia.
Kuwichpackmüten=Ikogmiut.
Kuwûñmiun=Kowagmiut.
K!û′xînedî=Kuhinedi.
Kuχni-kue=Havasupai.
Kuyakinchi=Koyukukhotana.

Kuyalegees=Kailaidshi.
Ku Ya-mung-ge=Cuyamunque.
Kuyawas=Kiowa.
Kuyukak=Kuiukuk.
Küyükāntsi=Koyukukhotana.
Kuyuktolik=Koyuktolik.
Kuyúku-hága=Cayuga.
Kuyukuks, Kuyukunski=Koyukukhotana.
Kuyutskoe=Kuiu.
Kuzlakes=Tluskez.
Kvieg-miut, Kvieguk-miut=Kviguk.
Kvigathlogamute=Kvigatluk.
Kvigmut=Kwik.
Kvigukmut=Kviguk.
Kvikh=Kwik.
Kvikhagamut=Kvikak.
Kvinghak-mioute, Kvinkhakmut=Kvinkak.
Kviougmioute=Kwik.
Kvishti=Paguate.
Kwa=Kwahu.
Kwa-ai'-tc'ĭ=Kwaitshi.
Kwāāksat=Hoh.
Kwā'g·uł, Kwagutl=Kwakiutl.
Kwaháda, Kwa'hădi=Kwahari.
Kwahadk'=Quahatika.
Kwáhare tetchaχkane=Kwahari.
Kwahkewlth=Kwakiutl.
Kwahnt-len=Kwantlen.
Kwahu wiñwû, Kwa'-hü-wüñ-wû=Kwahu.
Kwaiantl=Quinaielt.
Kwaihāntlas Hāadē=Kweundlas.
Kwaitlens=Kwantlen.
Kwakiool=Kwakiutl.
Kwākiutl=Wakashan Family.
Kwā'kōk·ūʟ=Kwakokutl.
Kwakoom=Kukwakum.
Kwā'kōwēnôx=Kwakowenok.
Kwā-kuhl=Kwakiutl.
KwākūqEmāl 'ênôx=Kwakukemalenok.
Kwakwakouchiouets=Wakouingouechiwek.
K!wálasints=Kwalasints.
Kwa-le-cum=Saamen.
Kwalhiokwas=Kwalhiloqua.
Kwa'lĭ=Qualla.
Kwaliokwa=Kwalhioqua.
Kwalûñ'yĭ=Qualla.
Kwan-le-cum=Saamen.
Kwantlin, Kwantlum, Kwantlun=Kwantlen.
Kwan wüñ-wû=Kwan.
Kwapa, Kwapa-ǵegiha, Kwapa-Dhegiha=Quapaw.
Kwashillas, Kwasila=Goasila.
Kwá-ʒa'-mé ʒûnnĕ'=Kwatami.
Kwat-kewlth=Kwakiutl.
Kwat-seno, Kwats'ēnoq, Kwatsino=Quatsino.
K'wátûmäti'-tĕné=Kwatami.
Kwat-zi-no=Quatsino.
Kwauaenoq, Kwā-wa-ai-nuk, Kwā-wa-a-nuk=Guau-
 aenok.
Kwaw-kewlth=Kwakiutl.
Kwaw-kwaw-apiet, Kwawkwawapilt=Koquapilt.
Kwaw-kwelch=Kwakiutl.
Kwaw-ma-chin=Quamichan.
Kwaw-she-lah=Goasila.
Kwawt-se-no=Quatsino.
Kwayo wiñwû, Kwa'-yo wüñ-wû=Kwayo.
Kwe-ah-kah=Komoyue.
Kwe-ah-kah Saich-kioie-tachs=Kueha.
Kwĕdĕch'=Mohawk.
Kwe-deé-tut=Quileute.
Kweé-ahogemut=Kwiahok.
Kweegamiut=Kwik.
Kweet=Quaitso.
Kwégamut=Kwik.
Kwéhts-hū=Quaitso.
K'wē'k·sōt'ênoq=Koeksotenok.
Kwenaiwitl=Quinaielt.
Kwe-nēt-che-chat, Kwe-nēt-sat'h=Makah.
Kwent-le-ah-mish=Kwehtlmamish.
Kwéres=Keresan Family.
Kwetcap tutwi=Kuchaptuvela.
Kwē'tEla=Tsimshian.
Kwetso=Quaitso.
Kwe'-wû-üh wüñ-wû, Kwewu wiñwû=Kwewu.
Kwi-ah-kah=Komoyue.
Kwichăg-mūt=Kiatagmiut.
Kwichljuagmjuten, Kwichpacker, Kwichpagmju-
 ten, Kwichpak Indians=Ikogmiut.
Kwick-so-ten-o=Koeksotenok.
Kwigalogamut, Kwigalogamute=Kwikak.
Kwigamiut, Kwigamute=Kwik.

Kwigathlogamute, Kwigathlogumut=Kvigatluk.
Kwi-ha=Kueha.
Kwikagamiut, Kwikagamut=Kwikak.
Kwikapa=Cocopa.
Kwikh=Kwik.
Kwikhluágemut=Kwikluagmiut.
Kwikhpag'emūt=Kwikpagmiut.
Kwikhpagmut=Ikogmiut.
Kwī'koaēnôx=Kwikoaenok.
Kwikōtłem=Coquitlam.
Kwiksot'enoq, Kwīk'-so-tino=Koeksotenok.
Kwi'kwitlEm=Coquitlam.
Kwikwû'līt=Watlala.
Kwĭl-aic'-auk=Kwilaishauk.
Kwille-hates, Kwilléhiüt, Kwilleut, Kwilleyhuts,
 Kwilléyute=Quileute.
Kwillu'chinl=Cathlamet.
Kwinaith, Kwinaitl, Kwinaiult, Kwinaiūtl'=Qui-
 naielt.
Kwinishûkûneihäki=Queenashawakee.
Kwi'ñobi, Kwiñ-yap wûñ-wû=Kwingyap.
Kwístyi=Paguate.
ꭗwi sŭt'-qwŭt=Kthutetmetseetuttun.
Kwitara'-a=Pawnee.
Kwitchia-Kutchin=Kwitchakutchin.
Kwi'tctenEm=Kwichtenem.
Kwitcᵞánᵃ=Yuma.
Kwithlūäg'emūt=Kwikluagmiut.
Kwittcha-Kuttchin=Kwitchakutchin.
Kwohatk=Quahatika.
Kwois-kun-a'=Koiskana.
Kwokwöōs=Coos.
Kworatems=Kworatem.
Kwoshonipu=Chimariko.
Kwout=Kuaut.
Kwowahtewug=Mandan.
Kwsí-ʒoi-ʒou'=Kwsichichu.
Kwŭ'da=Kiowa.
Kwŭl-aí-cau-īk=Kwulaishauik.
Kwŭl-haú-ŭn-nītc'=Kwulhauunnitsh.
Kwulkwul=Nayakololay.
Kwŭl-laiċ=Kwullaish.
Kwŭl'-laq-t'au-īk=Kwullakhtauik.
Kwulseet=Colcene.
Kwûl-tci'-tci-tcĕck'=Kwultshitshitseshk.
Kwûl-ʒsaí-yä=Kwultsaiya.
Kwun Hāadē=Skedans.
Kwun Lennas=Kuna-lanas.
Kwûs-atçl'-qûn ʒûn'nĕ=Kwusathlkhuntunne.
Kwûs-se'-ʒûn=Kushetunne.
Kwū-teh-ni=Kwaiailk.
Kwût'-ti-tcun'-t'çĕ=Kwuttitshuntthe.
Kwygyschpainagmiut=Kwinak.
Kχagantaiaĥounĥin=Aleut.
Kyacks=Kake.
Kyahagah=Cayahoga.
Kyahuntgate, Kyahwilgate=Keyerhwotket.
Kyakima, K'yä'-ki-me=Kiakima.
Kya-kuina=Kwakina.
Kyanamara=Gallinomero.
K'ya-na-thlana-kwe=Laguna.
K'yá-na-we=Kechipauan.
Kyä'nusla=Kianusili.
Kyaukw=Tillamook.
Kyaways=Kiowa.
Kȳcŭ-cūt=Kyuquot.
Kye-use=Cayuse.
Kyewaw=Kiawaw.
Kygani=Kaigani.
Kyganie=Skittagetan Family.
Kyganies, Kygany, Kygargey, Kygarney=Kaigani.
Kyiá'hl=Kyialish.
Kyiá'ltkoangas=Kialdagwuns.
Kyiks'adē=Kiksadi.
Kyis=Kichai.
Ky'iü'st'a=Kiusta.
Kyoose=Cayuse.
Kyō'p'ēnoq=Koprino.
Kyristin8ns=Cree.
Kyspyox=Kishpachlaots.
Ky-uk-aht=Kyuquot.
Kyu'-kŭtc hítclûm=Takelma.
Ky-wk-aht, Ky-yoh-quaht=Kyuquot.

Laa'laqsEnt'aiō, Lā'alaxsEnt'aiō=Laalaksentaɩo.
Laáluis=Tlaaluis.
La-ap-tin=Nez Pérces.
La Barrancas=Barrancas.

Laboba=Saboba.
La Boco del Arroyo=Boco del Arroyo.
La Cañada=Santa Cruz.
Lacane=Lacame.
La Canoa=Canoa.
Laccaya=Sakaya.
Lac Court d'Oreille band, Lac Court Oreille Band, Lac Court Orielles, Lac Court Orville, Lac Coutereille=Lac Court Oreilles.
Lac de deux Montagne, Lac de Deux Montagnes=Oka.
Lac du Flambeau=Wauswagiming.
LăcgEnEmaxîχ=Tlashgenemaki.
Lachal-sap=Lakkulzap.
Lachaways=Alachua.
La-ches=Tachi.
La Cienega, La Cienegia, La Cienguilla=Cienega.
Lack-al-sap=Lakkulzap.
Lackaway=Alachua.
Lack-Bows=Sans Arcs.
Lackweips=Lakweip.
La Cloche=Chibaouinani.
Laco=Lagcay.
Lacomnis=Sekumne.
La Concepcion=Purísima Concepción de los Asinais.
La Concepcion Bamoa=Bamoa.
La Concepcion de Quarac=Quarai.
La Conception=Ossossane, Totiakton.
Lacopseles=Tlascopsel.
Lacota, La-cotahs=Dakota.
Lacquesumne=Lakisumne.
Lac qui Parle band, Lacquiparle Indians=Mdeiyedan.
La-Croix=Anamiewatigong.
Lac Shatac=Chetac Lake.
Lac Traverse band=Kahra.
La Dalle Indians, La Dalles Indians=Dalles Indians.
Ládaxat=Hladakhat.
Laek que lib la, Laek-que-lit-ka=Lekwiltok.
La Encarnacion, La Encarnacion del Sutaquison=Sudacson.
La'ēnuχuma=Laenukhuma.
La Estancia=Estancia.
La Fallorine=Munominikasheenhug.
La Feuille's band=Kiyuksa.
La Follovoine=Munominikasheenhug.
La Gallette=Oswegatchie.
Lagana=Laguna.
La Gattell=Oswegatchie.
Łă'gĭ=Hlagi.
Lagoons=Tolowa.
Lagouna=Laguna.
La Gran Quivira=Tabira.
Laguna=Tatagua.
Laguna del Capitan Pablo=San Pablo.
Laguna del Hospital=Camani.
Laguna de San Pablo=San Pablo.
Lagunas=Timpaiavats.
Lagune, Lagunians, La haguna=Laguna.
Lahama=Lahanna.
La Have, La Heve=Le Have.
Łahayĭ'kqoan=Yakutat.
Lahouita=Kawita.
Lahtohs=Methow.
Laich-Kwil-tacks=Lekwiltok.
Laida, Laidennoj=Kasnotchin.
Läitanes=Ietan.
La Jolla=La Joya.
Lak, Lakamellos=Clear Lake Indians.
La Kar=Ietan.
Lake Calhoun band=Kheyataotonwe.
Lake Indians=Dwamish, Lower Kutenai, Senijextee, Timpaiavats.
Lă'k!ēlak, Lă'k!elaq=Clatsop.
Lake of the Two Mountains=Oka.
Lake Winnebagoshish band = Winnebegoshishiwininewak.
Lake Winnipeg band=Nibowisibiwininiwak.
Lakhamute=Ugalakmiut.
Lakmiuk=Lakmiut.
Lakota=Dakota.
Lăkᵘ'-ān=Klukwan.
Lâ'kuilila=Walas Kwakiutl.
Lălachsent'aiō=Laalaksentaio.
La Laguna=Camani.
La'Lasiqoala, La'Lasiqwala=Tlatlasikoala.
Lă'lăuiLEla=Lalauitłela.

Lă'legak=Tlalegak.
LaLElă'min=Tlatlelamin.
Laleshiknom=Kato.
La Litanes=Ietan.
Lal Linches=Talinchi.
'Lá 'lo-algi=Hlahloalgi.
'Lá 'lo-kálka=Hlahlokalka.
La Loup=Skidi.
Lama=Lema.
La-malle=Chelamela.
La Mar=Omaha.
Lamasket=Namasket.
Lamatan=Huron.
La Merced=Merced.
La Mesa=Temalwahish.
Lamikas=Rancocas.
Lamoines=Laimon.
La Montagne=Onondaga.
Lamparacks=Ditsakana.
Lamχei'χat=Wakanasisi.
Lana=Tano.
Lanahltungua, Lā'-na xē'-gAns=Lanahawa.
Lanaxk=Tlanak.
Land Pitches=Sanpet.
Lanecy=Lipan.
Lanegados=Anegados.
Langley=Kwantlen.
L'Anguille=Kenapacomaqua.
Langundowi-Oteey, Languntoutenuenk, Languntoutenünk=Languntennenk.
Lanos=Manso.
L'anse=Wequadong.
'Lánudshi apála=Hlanudshiapala.
Laousteque=Texas.
La Paddo=Comanche.
Lapahógi=Arapaho.
Lapan, Lapanas, Lapane, Lapanne=Lipan.
La-pap-poos, Lapappu=Lapapu.
La Pienés House Indians=Tukkuthkutchin.
La Plais=Comanche.
'Láp-'láko=Hlaphlako.
La Play, La Playes=Comanche.
Lapointe, La Pointe band, Lapointe du S(ain)t. Esprit=Shaugawaumikong.
la Pong=Ponca.
La Ponite Chagauamegou=Shaugawaumikong.
La Porcelaine=Metoac.
Lapototot=Lopotatimni.
La Prairie de la Madelaine, La Prairie de la Magdelaine=La Prairie.
La Présentation=Oswegatchie.
La Purificacion de la Virgen de Alona=Halona.
La Purísima de Zuñi=Zuñi.
La Purissima Conception=Cadegomo.
LăᵋqaLala=Tlakatlala.
Lá'qaui=Lakaui.
Laquaacha=Yukichetunne.
Laq'uyî'p=Lakweip.
Larámari=Tarahumare.
L'Arbrech-roche, L'Arbre Croche, L'Arbre Cruche=Waganakisi.
la Ree=Arikara.
Large Hanga=Hanga.
Large People=Chito.
La'ri'hta=Comanche.
Lar-li-e-lo=Spokan.
La Rochelle=Ossossane.
La Rosario=Santa Rosario.
Lartielo, Lar-ti-e-to's Nation=Spokan.
Las Barancas, Las Barrancas=Barrancas.
La Soledad=Soledad Indians.
La Sone=Sonoita.
L!ā'sq!ēnoxᵘ=Klaskino.
Lastekas, Las Tesas, Las Texas, Lasticas=Texas.
Last Lodge=Kanze.
Lᵊsues=Dakota.
Lă'-tä-dä=Dhatada.
Latchione, Latchivue=Alachua.
Łat'gāᵗᵃwáᵋ=Upper Takelma.
Lătĭlēntāsks=Adirondack.
La Tinaja, La Tinaoca=Tinajas.
Láti-u, Látiwe=Molala.
La Tota=Tota.
Latsop=Clatsop.
Lauanakanuck=Lawunkhannek.
Lau'itsîs=Tlauitsis.
Ława'k=Klawak.
Lawanakanuck, Lawenakanuck, Lawunahhannek, Lawunakhannek=Lawunkhannek.

Łā′xayîk=Hlahayik.
Łaxq!ᵘxo-ān=Hlukkuhoan.
Lâ′xsē=Haailakyemae.
Laχ-skik=Kloo.
Layamon=Laimon.
Laydanoprodevskie=Ledyanoprolivskoe.
Láylekeean=Lelikian.
Layma=Laguna.
Laymon, Laymóna, Laymones=Laimon.
Laysamite=Lesamaiti.
Lazars=Illinois.
La Zoto=Oto.
Lᴄtā′mēctîx=Seamysty.
LdA′ldjî tāmā′-i=Tĭduldji.
Leaf Bed=Wahpekute.
Leaf (Indians), Leaf Nation, Leaf Villagers=Wah-
    peton.
Leapers=Chippewa.
Leather Village=Koserefski.
Lecatuit=Likatuit.
Lecawgoes=Secawgo.
Lecha (Indians)=Gachwechnagechga.
Lechavaksein, Lechawaxen=Lackawaxen.
L'Ecureuil=Ecureuil.
Ledaⁿʹunikaciⁿga=Lunikashinga.
Lee-Biches=Shivwits.
Leeca=Ceca.
Leech River=Pillager.
Lee-ha-taus=Ietan.
Lee Panis, Lee Pawnees=Lipan.
Leequeeltoch=Lekwiltok.
Left hand=Assiniboin.
Legionville=Shenango.
Legs=Three Legs Town.
Lehigh (Indians)=Gachwechnagechga.
Le′-hü wüñ-wü=Lehu.
Leja-ga-dat-cah=Lejagadatkah.
LEk′ä′mEl=Nicomen.
'Lèkátchka=Hlekatchka.
'Le kátska=Hlekatska.
Lekulks=Sokulk.
Łékwiłdaᵍxᵘ, Lē′kwiltoq=Lekwiltok.
Leldiñ=Tlelding.
Lē′lEwag·ila=Lelewagyila.
Lē′Lqēt, Lē′Lqēte=Tletlket.
LEmā′itEmᴄ=Klumaitumsh.
Lᴇmáłłᴄa=Lilmalche.
Lemerlanans=Paouites.
Lemparack=Ditsakana.
Lenais, Lenalenape, Lenalinepies, Lenap, Lenape,
    Lenapegi, Lenappe, Lenappys, Lenawpes=Dela-
    ware.
Le-nay-wosh=Tenawa.
L!ēnē′dî=Tlenedi.
Lenekees=Seneca.
Lenelenape, Lenelenoppes, Lenepee, Leni-Lenape,
    Lenna-lenape, Lennape, Lennapewi, Lenni-lappe,
    Lenni-Lenápe, Lenni-Lennápe, Lenno Lenapees,
    Lenno Lenapi, Lenno-Lennape, Lenopi, Lenoppea=
    Delaware.
Lentis=Lentes.
Leonopi, Leonopy=Delaware.
Leon's Creek=Lions Creek.
Lepan, Le Panis=Lipan.
Lepeguanes=Tepehuane.
Le Plays=Comanche.
Łē′q'Em=Tlekem.
Les Caribou=Attikiriniouetch.
Les Chaudieres=Colville.
Les Cœurs d'Alênes=Skitswish.
Les Folles, Les Fols=Menominee.
Les gens des caruts=Watopapinah.
(les) Honctons, (les) Jantons=Yankton.
Les Mandals=Mandan.
Les Missouris=Missouri.
Lesnoi, Lesnova=Liesnoi.
Les Octata, Les Octotata=Oto.
Lespaía=Encinal.
Les pancaké=Kansa.
Les Pongs=Ponca.
Les Radiqueurs=Shoshoko.
Lesser Osage=Utsehta.
Les Souliers=Amahami.
Letaiyo wiñwû=Letaiyo.
Let-e-nugh-shonee=Iroquois.
Letniki-Takaïak=Takaïak.
Let-tegh-segh-ni-geghtee=Onondaga.
Leunis, Leutis=Lentes.
Lewis River Band=Klikitat.

Lewytos=Liwaito.
Leyza=Leyva.
Lezar=Illinois.
Łgagî′-lda=Skidegate.
Łgā′i=Hlgai.
Lgā-iū′=Skidegate.
LgA′ñxAñ=Tlgunghung.
Łgā′xet gîtînā′-i=Hlgahet-gitinai.
Łgā′xet-gu-lā′nas=Hlgahetgu-lanas.
Lgulaq=Tlegulak.
Lhtaten=Sekani.
Lia=Sia.
Liahtan Band=Ietan.
Liā′icaLxē=Ktlaeshatlkik.
Liards Indians, Liard Slaves=Etcheridiegottine.
L'Iatan=Ietan.
Lichaltchingko=Shilekuatl.
Lichtenau=Agdluitsok.
Lickawis=Yikkhaich.
Lidlepa=Lidlipa.
Li′elAñ=Hlielung.
Lienkwiltak, Liew-kwil-tah=Lekwiltok.
Liguaytoy=Liwaito.
Li-hit′=Ponca.
Li-icks-sun=Tateke.
'Li-i-kátchka=Hlekatchka.
Lí-kwil-tah, Likwiltoh=Lekwiltok.
Lillibique=Lilibeque.
Lilowat=Lillooet.
LílusEltstiχ=Hliluseltshlikh.
Lilχuit=Lillooet.
ŁimA′l na′as xā′da-i=Hlimulnaas-hadai.
Limonies=Laimon.
Linapis, Linapiwi=Delaware.
Liniouek=Illinois.
Linkinse=Sinkiuse.
Linkville Indians=Shuyakeksh.
Linnelinopies=Delaware.
Linneways=Illinois.
Linni linapi, Linnilinopes, Linnope=Delaware.
Linpoilish=Sanpoil.
Linslow=Siuslaw.
Lintcanre=Thlingchadinne.
'Lin-tchanρe=Lintchanre.
Linways=Illinois.
Lion=Hiyaraba.
Lion Eaters=Tanima.
Lipaines=Lipan.
Lipallanes=Lipillanes.
Lipane=Lipan.
Lipanes del Norte=Lipanes de Arriba.
Lipanes del Sur=Lipanes de Abajo.
Lipanes Llaneros, Lipanis=Lipan.
Lipanjen-né=Lipajenne.
Lipanos, Lipau, Lipaw=Lipan.
Lipiyanes=Lipillanes.
Lippans=Lipan.
LîqLa′qEtîn=Tliktlaketin.
Lishu=Sesum.
L!îsti′=Tlistee.
Littafatchee, Littafutchee, Littefutchee=Litte-
    futchi.
Little Alkonkins=Montagnais.
Little Beard's Town=Deyonongdadagana.
Little Chehaus, Little Chiáha=Chiahudshi.
Little Colpissas=Okakapassa.
Little Crow's band=Kapozha.
Little Eufauly=Eufaula.
Little Falls band=Inyancheyakaatonwan.
Little Foolish Dogs=Hosukhaunukarerihu.
Little Girl Assiniboines=Itscheabine.
Little Hit-chetee=Hitchitudshi.
Little Lakes=Mitomkai Poma.
Little Mingoes=Huron.
Little Nation of the Algonquins=Weskarini.
Little Oakchoy, Little Oakjoys=Okchayudshi.
Little Ockfuske=Oakfuskudshi.
Little Osage, Little Ossage=Utsehta.
Little Prairie Indians=Mascoutens.
Little Rapids=Inyancheyaka-atonwan.
Little Robes=Inuksiks.
Little Sáwokli=Sawokliudshi.
Little Shuswap, Little Shuswap Lake=Kuaut.
Little Six's band=Taoapa.
Little Suswap Lake=Kuaut.
Little Swaglaw=Sawokliudshi.
Little Tálisi, Little Tallassie, Little Tellassee=Ta-
    lasse.

Little Tellico, Little Telliquo=Tellico.
Little Tioux=Tiou.
Little Town=Tanwanshinka.
Little Ufala=Eufaula.
Little Valley=Vallecillo.
Livangelva=Livangebra.
Liver Eater band, Liver-eaters=Tanima.
'Liwá'hli=Huhliwahli.
Li-woch-o-nies=Tawakoni.
Lîx·sī'wĕᵃ=Kliksiwi.
Li-yan-to=Siyante.
Lkaᴛamix=Kedlamik.
Ḷkamtcī'n=Tlkamcheen.
Lkamtcī'nEmux=Lytton band.
ᴛ'ka-tco=Ilkatsho.
Lkū'men, Lku'ngEn=Songish.
Llamparicas=Ditsakana.
Llaneros=Gohlkahin, Guhlkainde, Kwahari.
Llano=Huchiltchik.
Llano del Azotado=Tutuetac.
Llégeenos=Diegueño.
Lleni-lenapés=Delaware.
Lleta=Isleta.
Lliamna=Llymna.
Lligunos=Diegueño.
Ll'inkit=Tlingit.
Ll-mache, Ll-mal-che=Lilmalche.
Lo=Lu.
Loafers=Waglukhe.
Locklomnee=Mokelumne.
Locko=Chukalako.
Lockoportay=Lutchapoga.
Lock-qua-lillas=Walas Kwakiutl.
Lockstown=Logstown.
Lock-wearer=Tsishu Sindtsakdhe.
Lo-co=Tontos.
Locollomillos=Clear Lake Indians.
Lodge-in-the-rear=Kanze.
Lodges charged upon=Ahachik.
Lofka's barrabora=Lofka.
Logan's village=Wapakoneta.
Loggs Town=Logstown.
Lóh-whilse=Quaitso.
Lòkaɸine, Lókadĭne'=Loka.
Lókuashtkni=Warm Spring Indians.
Lō'kuīlī'la=Komkyutis.
Lokulk=Sokuɪk.
Loldla=Lolsel.
Loloncooks, Lo-lon'-kūk=Lolanko.
LoLowûq=Klukluuk.
Lomavigamute, Lomawigamute=Lomavik.
Lone Eaters=Nitawyiks.
Lone Fighters=Nitikskiks.
Lo-ne'-kä-she-gä=Lunikashinga.
Long Falls=Skoiyase.
Long Haired Indians=Crows.
Long House Town=Chukafalaya.
Long Island Indians=Metoac.
Long-isle=Eel River Indians.
Longs Cheveux=Nipissing.
Long Swamp=Anatichapko.
Long Swamp Indians=Big Swamp Indians.
Long Swamp Village=Ikatikunahita.
Long Tail Lodge Poles=Inuhksoyistamiks.
Long Tom=Chelamela.
Long-tongue-buff=Laptambif.
Long Town=Chukafalaya.
Long-wha=Tonkawa.
Lonsobe=Tomsobe.
Loo-chau po-gau=Lutchapoga.
Loochoos=Kutchin, Loucheux.
Loo-coo-rekah=Tukuarika.
Lookout Mountain=Lookout Mountain Town.
Lookta-ek=Alaganik.
Loolanko=Lolanko.
Loomnears=Tumna.
Loo nika-shing-ga=Lunikashinga.
Loonsolton=Honsading.
Loo's=Mahican, Skidi.
Lopas=Tolowa.
Lopillamillos=Clear Lake Indians.
Lopotalimnes, Lopotatimnes, Lopstatimnes=Lopotatimni.
Loquilt Indians=Lillooet.
Loqusquscit, Loqusqusitt=Loquasquscit.
Lorett, Loretta=Lorette.
Lorette=Sault au Recollet.
Loretto=Lorette.
Los Adeas=San Miguel de Linares.

Los Angeles=Pecos.
Los Coyotes=Pachawal.
Los Dolores=Dolores, Santa María de los Dolores
Los Leuceuros=Los Luceros.
Los Mecos=Comanche.
Lotchnoay, Lotchway towns=Alachua.
Lō'tlemaq=Lotlemakh.
Lototen=Tututni.
Lou=Skidi.
Louches=Tukkuthkutchin.
Loucheux=Kutchin, Nakatcho.
Loucheux-Batards=Nellagottine.
Louchioux=Kutchin, Loucheux.
Louchioux proper=Tukkuthkutchin.
Louchoux=Loucheux.
Loupelousas=Opelusa.
Loupes=Skidi.
Loupitousas=Opelusa.
Loup Pawnees=Skidi.
Loups=Mahican, Skidi.
Lowaniwi, Lowanuski=Lowako.
Lower Algonkins=Montagnais.
Lower Brulé, Lower Brusle=Kutawichasha.
Lower Coquille=Mulluk, Nasumi.
Lower Chehalis=Wenatchi.
Lower Creeks=Seminole.
Lower De Chutes=Wiam.
Lower Enfalla=Eufaula.
Lower Gens de fou=Hankutchin.
Lower Indians=Tatsakutchin.
Lower Kahltog, Lower Kaltag=Kaltag.
Lower Kootanais, Lower Kootanie, Lower Kootenay=Lower Kutenai.
Lower Kvichpaks=Magemiut.
Lower Mohawk Castle=Caughnawaga, Teatontaloga.
Lower Oakfuske=Oakfuskee.
Lower Pend d'Oreille=Kalispel.
Lower Rogue River=Tututni.
Lower Sauratown=Cheraw.
Lower Shawnee Town=Lowertown.
Lower Sioux=Santee.
Lower Sissetons=Miakechakesa.
Lower Spokan, Lower Spokanes=Skaischiltnish.
Lower Ufale=Eufaula.
Lower Ump-kwa, Lower Umpqua=Kuitsh.
Lower Wahpeton, Lower Wakpatons=Inyancheyakaatonwan.
Lower Yakima=Skaddal.
Lower Yanctonais=Hunkpatina.
Lower Yanctons=Yankton.
Lower Yanktonai, Lower Yanktonnais=Hunkpatina.
Low-him=Lohim.
Lowland Brulé=Kutawichasha.
Lowland Dogs=Thlingchadinne.
Lowlanders=Kaiyuhkhotana.
Lowlanders, Lowland people=Kutchakutchin.
Lowwshkis=Lowako.
L!pē'lEqc=Palux.
Ḻqe'noł lā'nas=Kagials-kegawai.
Ḻqo'ayedî=Hlkoayedi.
Lrak=Ilrak.
Ltaoten=Tautin.
ᴛ'tat-'tennne=Sekani.
ᴛta-utenne, Ltavten=Tautin.
Lthagild=Skidegate.
Lth'ait Lennas=Hlgahetgu-lanas.
ᴛtha-koh-'tenne=Tautin.
Lthyellum Kiiwē=Hlielung-keawai.
Ltsχéals=Nisqualli.
Ltuiskoe=Lituya.
Lu=Lunikashinga.
Lucayasta=Lukaiasta.
Luchepoga=Lutchapoga.
Lu'-chih=Ruche.
Luchi paga, Luchipoga, Luchipogatown=Lutchapoga.
Luck-a-mi-ute, Luckamuke, Luckamutes=Lakmiut.
Luckasos=Kosotshe.
Luckiamut, Luckiamute, Luckimiute, Luckimute=Lakmiut.
Luckkarso=Kosotshe.
Lucson=Tucson.
Lucuyumu=Lacayamu.
Lugh-se-le=Sanyakoan.
Lugua-mish=Suquamish.
Luianeglua=Livangebra.
Luijta=Lintja.

Luiseyove=Quisiyove.
Lukahs=Succcaah.
Lûk'-a-ta-t=Klikitat.
Lükatimü'x=Ntlakyapamuk.
Lukawis, Lukawisse=Yikkhaich.
Lukemáyuk=Lakmiut.
Lukfi=Lukfa.
Lukhselee=Sanyakoan.
Lukkarso=Kotsotshe.
Ļûknax'ā'dî=Tluknahadi.
Luktŏn=Luckton.
Lulak=Lulakiksa.
Lululongtuqui, Lululongturqui=Lululongturkwi.
Lumanos=Tawehash.
Lummas, Lumme, Lummie, Lummi-neuksack=
     Lummi.
Luni=Zuñi.
Lụnikaciⁿga=Lunikashinga.
Lu-pa-yu-ma, Lupilomis, Lu-pi-u-ma=Clear Lake
     Indians.
Ƚuqā'xadî=Hlukahadi.
L!ü'q!oedî=Ylukoedi.
Luq!u'lᴇm=Cloquallum.
Lurcee=Sarsi.
Lusolas=Susolas.
Lusthhapa=Lushapa.
Lutchapóga=Tulsa.
Lute'-ja=Rukhcha.
Lutmáwi, Lutnam=Modoc.
Lutnami, Lutuami=Lutuamian Family, Modoc.
Lutuanis, Lutumani, Luturim=Lutuamian Family.
Lúuptic=Luupsch.
Ļ!uxâ'caiyîk-an=Tluhashaiyikan.
L!xîñᴀs=Tlhingus.
Lχûñgen=Songish.
Lyach-sun=Tateke.
Lyacksum, Lyacksun=Tateke.
Lytton=Tlkamcheen.

Maa'mtag·ila=Maamtagyila.
Maanexit=Manexit.
Maaquas=Mohawk.
Maasets=Masset.
Maastoetsjkwe=Hopi.
Mabile=Mobile.
Mǎ-bǔc-shǒ-rǒch-pǎn-gǎ=Shoshoni.
Macachusetts=Massachuset.
Macadacut=Mecadacut.
Macaiyah=Nkya.
Macanabi=Mishongnovi.
Macanas=Tawakoni, Tonkawa.
Macanoota, Macanootna, Macanootoony's, Macano-
     tens=Mikonotunne.
Macaque, Macaqui, Macaquia=Matsaki.
Macarisqui=Macariz.
M'Carty's village=Tushquegan.
Macau, Ma-caw=Makah.
Macayah=Nkya.
Maccaws=Makah.
Maccou=Maccoa.
Mac-en-noot-e-ways, Mac-en-oot-en-ays, Mac-en-o-
     tin=Mikonotunne.
Macetuchets, Macetusetes=Massachuset.
McGillivray's Town=Talasse.
Machaba=Machawa.
Machachac=Mequachake.
Machachlosung=Wyalusing.
Machaha=Machawa.
Machakandibi=Michacondibi.
Machalla=Machawa.
Machamadoset, Machamoodus=Machemoodus.
Machandibi, Machantiby=Michacondibi.
Machapungas=Machapunga.
Machaull=Venango.
Mac-há-vès, Mac-há-vis=Mohave.
Machayto=Macheto.
Machecous=Creeks.
Machégamea=Michigamea.
Machelusing=Wyalusing.
Machemeton=Mechemeton.
Macheyes=Mayeye.
Machias Tribe=Passamaquoddy.
Machicans=Mahican.
Machichac=Mequachake.
Machies tribe=Passamaquoddy.
Machigama, Machigamea=Michigamea.
Machilimachinack, Machillimakina=Michilimacki-
     nac.

Machilwihilusing, Machilwilusing=Wyalusing.
Machimucket=Massomuck.
Machingans=Mahican.
Machkentiwomi=Mechkentowoon.
Machkoutench, Machkoutenck, Machkouteng=Mas-
     coutens.
Machmadouset=Machemoodus.
Machochlasung, Machochloschung=Wyalusing.
Machoeretini=Conestoga.
Machonce's village, Machonee's village=Macho-
     nee.
Machopeake=Matchopick.
Machopo=Mochopa.
Machua=Machawa.
Ma-chuck-nas, Ma-chuc-na=Michopdo.
Machwihilusing=Wyalusing.
Macjave=Mohave.
Mackacheck=Mequachake.
Mackahs=Makah.
Mackalassy=Muklassa.
Mackanaw=Michilimackinac.
Mackanootenay's Town, Mackanotin=M i k o n o-
     tunne.
Mackasookos=Mikasuki.
Mackatowando=Manckatawangum.
Mackelimakanac=Michilimackinac.
Mack-en-oot-en-ay=Mikonotunne.
MacKenzie River Eskimo=Kopagmiut.
Mackenzie's River Louchioux=Nakotchokutchin.
Mackilemackinac, Mackinac, Mackinaw=Michi-
     limackinac.
Mackóꭕe, Mackúꭕe=Creeks.
Mackwaes, Mackwasii, Mackwes=Mohawk.
McLeod's Lake=Kezonlathut.
Mac-not-na=Mikonotunne.
Maco comaco, Macocanaco=Macocanico.
Macoiya=Mayaca.
Macomilé=Menominee.
Maconabi=Mishongnovi.
Macono=Nasoni.
Mac-o-no-tin=Mikonotunne.
Maconsaw=Seek's Village.
Macoutins=Mascoutens.
Macoya=Mayaca.
Macqs, Macquaas, Macquaaus=Mohawk.
Macquaejeet=Beothukan Family.
Macquas, Macquaus, Macques, Macquess=Mohawk.
Máꞔqui=Matsqui.
Macquis, Macquiss=Mohawk.
Mactciñge-ha waiⁿ=Ute.
Mactotatas=Oto.
Macueques=Hopi.
Madaha=Anadarko.
Madan=Mandan.
Madaouaskairini=Matawachkarini.
Mad-a-wakan-toan, Madawakanton=Mdewakan-
     ton.
Madawamkee=Mattawamkeag.
Madawgwys=Welsh Indians.
Maddy Band=Chemapho.
Madéqsi=Puisu.
Madnǎguk=Lincoln.
Madnussky=Ahtena.
Madoc=Modoc.
Madocian Indians=Welsh Indians.
Madocteg=Medoctec.
Madogiaint, Madogians=Welsh Indians.
Madowesians=Dakota.
Mad river Indians=Batawat.
Maechibaeys=Mohawk.
Ma-ētsi-daka=Mitcheroka.
Mag-a-bo-das=Putetemini.
Magagmjuten=Magemiut.
Magalibô=Maguhleloo.
Magamutes=Magemiut.
Magaugo=Maguaga.
Maꞔa-yute-śni=Magayuteshni.
Magdalena, Magdalena de Buvuibava=Buquibava.
Magdalena Tajicaringa=Tajicaringa.
Mágemutes=Magemiut.
Magenesito=Yagenechito.
Maghai=Mayeye.
Magimūt, Magimüten, Magmiūt, Magmjuten, Mag-
     mutes, Magmutis=Magemiut.
Mago=Mayo.
Magoncog=Magunkaquog.
Magꞷonkkomuk=Magunkaquog.
Magrias=Tano.
Magtate=Mactati.

Maguago, Maguagua=Maguaga.
Maguas=Tąno.
Maguawgo=Maguaga.
Magueck=Mequachake.
Magui=Hopi.
Maguncog, Magunkahquog, Magunkakook, Magun-
    koag, Magunkog=Magunkaquog.
Maha=Omaha.
Ma-ha'-bĭt-tuh=Petenegowats.
Mahackeno=Mahackemo.
Mahackloosing=Wyalusing.
Mahacks, Mahacqs=Mohawk.
Mahaer, Mahági=Omaha.
Mahah=Skidi.
Mahaha=Amahami.
Mahahs=Omaha.
Mahakanders, Mahakans=Mahican.
Mahakas, Mahakes, Mahakinbaas, Mahakinbas,
    Mahakobaas, Mahaks, Mahakuaas, Mahakuase,
    Mahakuasse, Mahakwa=Mohawk.
Mahán=Comanche.
Mahan=Omaha.
Máhana=Comanche.
Máhane=Klikitat.
Mahaniahy=Wyoming.
Ma-há os=Mohave.
Maharha=Omaha.
Maharhar=Amahami.
Maharim=Meherrin.
Mahars=Omaha.
Mahas Maha's=Omaha, Skidi.
Mahatons=Manhattan.
Ma-háu=Mahow.
Mahaukes=Mohawk.
Mahawha=Amahami.
Mahaws=Omaha.
Mahckanders=Mahican.
Mah-een-gun=Myeengun.
Mahegan=Mahican.
Mahehoualaima=Mahewala.
Maheingans, Mahekanders=Mahican.
Maheouala, Maheoula=Mahewala.
Maherin, Maherine, Mahering, Maherrin, Maherring,
    Maherron=Meherrin.
Maheyes=Mayeye.
Mahhekaneew, Mahicanders, Mahicanni, Mahic-
    canni, Mahiccans, Mahiccon, Mahicon, Mahigan,
    Mahiganathicoit, Mahiganaticois, Mahigane, Ma-
    higgins, Mă-hik', Mahíkǝn, Mahikanders, Mahik-
    kanders, Mahillendras, Mahinganak, Mahingani-
    ois, Mahingans, Mahingaus=Mahican.
Mahlemoöt, Mahlemutes, Mahlemuts=Malemiut.
Mah-ma-lil-le-kulla, Mah-ma-lil-le-kullah, Mahma-
    tilleculaats=Mamalelekala.
Mahna-Narra=Mandan.
Mahnesheet=Malecite.
Mahng=Mong.
Mahnomoneeg, Mahnomonie=Menominee.
Mahoc, Mahocks=Manahoac.
Mahogs=Mohawk.
Mahongwis=Iroquois.
Mahónink, Mahony Town=Mahoning.
Mahoras=Tamaroa.
Mañpíyato=Arapaho.
Māhsĭhk'kū ta=Masikota.
Mah-tah-ton=Matantonwan.
Mah-tee-cept, Mahtilpi=Matilpe.
Mahtopanato=Watopachnato.
Mahtulth-pe=Matilpe.
Mahuames=Mariames.
Ma''hwäwⁿ=Mowhawa, Moqwaio.
Ma'hwäwisōwąg=Mowhawissouk.
Mahycander=Mahican.
Mahzahpatah=Mazapeta.
Mai-ai'-u=Muaya.
Maiama=Miami.
Maicanders=Mahican.
Mai¢eckíj, Mai¢eckíjni=Maitheshkizh.
Maiφò', Maiφò'¢ine=Maitho.
Maí-dĕc-kĭž-ne=Jemez.
Mai-deh=Maidu.
Maidĕskĭ'z, Maidĕskĭ'zni=Maitheshkizh.
Maidnorskie=Ahtena.
Maieces=Nayeye.
Maiera=Mayara.
Maieyes=Mayeye.
Maikans, Maikens=Mahican.
Ma'īngan=Mingan.
Mā-ingan, Ma·i·ngan=Myeengun.

Maises=Manso.
Ma'-i-sin-as=Sans Arcs.
Maison Moctecuzoma, Maison Moctecuzuma, Maison
    Moteczuma=Casa Grande.
Maisqui=Matsqui.
Maitiffs=Metis.
Maiφó', Maiφo'¢ĭne=Maitho.
Maiyákma=Makoma.
Maize gens=Atchialgi.
Majabos=Mohave.
Majananí=Mishongnovi.
Majave=Mohave.
Majoa=Mahoa.
Maj-su-ta-ki-as=Musalakun.
Majunkaquog=Magunkaquog.
Ma·kadäwägami'tigwĕyäwininiwąg = Mekadewag-
    amitigweyawininiwak.
Makadewana-ssidok=Siksika.
Makagamute, Makag'mūt=Makak.
Makah=Omaha.
Makahelousink=Wyalusing.
Makaítseek=Klamath.
Makamitek=Makomitek.
Ma'kąndwäwininiwąg, Makandwewininiwag=Pil-
    lagers.
Maχaᴺ=Makan.
Makans, Makas=Makah.
Ma-ka'-tce=Makache.
Makato, Makato's Band=Mankato.
Makaw=Makah.
Makawto=Mankato.
Makehalousing=Wyalusing.
Makeymïut, Makeymut, Makeymute=Makak.
Makha=Makah.
Makicander, Makihander, Makimanes=Mahican.
Makinang=Michilimackinac.
Makingans=Mahican.
Mak-in-o-ten=Mikonotunne.
Makis=Hopi.
Mak-kah=Makah.
Makki=Makak.
Máklaks=Lutuamian Family.
Maklykout=Maklykaut.
Maknootennay, Mäk-nu' tĕne'=Mikonotunne.
Makonee=Machonee.
Makooshenskoi, Makooshin=Makushin.
Makostrake=Mequachake.
Ma-kó-ta=Dakota.
Mä'kotch=Makache, Mankoke.
Maκoucoué=Makoukuwe.
Makoueone=Amikwa.
Makoueoue, Makoukoué, Makoukoueks=Amikwa,
    Makoukuwe.
Makoüten, Makoutensak=Mascoutens.
Makquás=Mohawk.
Makskouteng=Mascoutens.
Makunkokoag=Magunkaquog.
Makuschinskoje, Makushinsk, Makushinskoe, Ma-
    kuski=Makushin.
Makwaes=Mohawk.
Ma-kwis'-so-jik=Makwisuchigi.
Ma'-k'ya-na, Ma-kya-ta=Matyata.
Malaca, Malaccas=Malaka.
Malacite=Malecite.
Mal-a-hut=Malakut.
Ma-lak'-ka=Malaka.
Mā'lakyilatl=Spukpukolemk.
Malala=Molala.
Malamechs, Malamet, Malanas=Marameg.
Malatautes=Oto.
Malchatna=Mulchatna.
Malecetes, Maléchites=Malecite.
Malegmjuti, Maleigmjuten, Maleïmïoute=Malemiut.
Málēlēqala=Mamalelekam.
Malemukes, Malemut, Malemutes=Malemiut.
Máleqatl=Malakut.
Málesít=Malecite.
Mal-hok-ce=Malhokshe.
Malhoming, Malhominis, Mǝlhomins, Malhominy,
    Malhommes, Malhommis=Menominee.
Malicans=Maliacones.
Malicetes, Malicites=Malecite.
Maliconas, Malicones=Maliacones.
Māliegmūt, Malimiüt, Malimüten, Malimyuit=Ma-
    lemiut.
Malinovskie lietnik=Nuniliak.
Malisít=Malecite.
Mallawamkeag=Penobscot.
Malleyes=Mayeye.

Mallica=Malica.
Malmiut=Malemiut.
Malomenis, Malomimis, Malomines, Malominese, Malominis, Malouin, Malouminek, Maloumines= Menominee.
Malowwacks=Metoac.
Malpais=Milpais.
Maltnabah=Multnomah.
Mal-tsho'-qa-mūt=Maltshokamut.
Malukander=Mahican.
Maluksilaq=Maluksilak.
Malzura=San Mateo Malzura.
Mama=Omaha.
Mamakans Apeches=Mescaleros.
Mämakatä′wana-sítä′-ak=Siksika.
Mamaleilakitīsh, Mamaleilakulla=Mamalelekala.
Mämalēlēqala=Mamalelekala, Mamalelekam.
Mama-lil-a-cula, Ma-ma-lil-li-kulla=Mamalelekala.
Mambe, Mambo=Nambe.
Mameag, Mameeag=Nameaug.
Mā′-me-li-li-a-ka=Mamalelekala.
Mamelute=Malemiut.
Mamenoche=Wiminuche.
Mam-il-i-li-a-ka=Mamalelekala.
M'amiwis=Miami.
Mamnit=Namoit.
Má-mo aⁿ-ya-dí, Má-mo haⁿ-yá, Má-mo ha-yaⁿ-dí= Alibamu.
Mamskey=Matsqui.
Manacans=Monacan.
Manaché=Mono.
Managog, Manahoacks, Manahoacs, Manahoaks, Manahocks, Manahokes=Manahoac.
Manakin=Monacan.
Manamet, Manamete=Manomet.
Manamoiak, Manamoick, Manamoyck, Manamoyet= Manamoyik.
Manänexit=Manexit.
Mananiet=Manomet.
Manatee=Minatti.
Manathanes, Manathe, Manathens=Manhattan.
Mancantequuts=Maquantequat.
Manchage, Manchauge=Manchaug.
Manchokatous=Mdewakanton.
Maⱬiñka-gaxe=Mandhinkagaghe.
Maⁿcká e′nikaci′ⱬa=Manshkaenikashika.
Mandals, Mandams, Mandane, Mandanes, Mandani, Mandanne, Mandaus=Mandan.
Mandawakantons, Mandawakanton Sioux=Mdewakanton.
Mandens=Mandan.
Mandeouacantons=Mdewakanton.
Mandes=Manta.
Mandians, Mandin=Mandan.
Mandoages=Nottoway.
Mandon=Mandan.
Mandongs=Nottoway.
Mandˢ=Mandan.
Man Eaters=Attacapa, Tonkawa.
Maneetsuk=Manitsuk.
Manelopec=Watopapinah.
Manessings=Minisink.
Ma-ne-to-pa, Ma-ne-to-par=Watopapinah.
Manetores=Hidatsa.
Maneus=Malecite.
Māng=Mong.
Mangakekias, Mangakekis, Mangakokis, Mangaконкia=Mengakonkia.
Mangeurs de Cariboux=Etheneldeli.
Mangoacks, Mangoags, Mangoako, Mangoangs=Nottoway.
Mangus Colorado's band=Mimbreños.
Manhanset tribe, Manhassett=Manhasset.
Manhates, Manhatesen, Manhattae, Manhattanese, Manhattes, Manhattons=Manhattan.
Manheken, Manhigan-euck=Mohegan.
Manhikani, Manhikans, Manhingans=Mahican.
Maŋḣpíyato=Arapaho.
Maⁿ′ǫuⱬⱻⁱⁿ′taⁿ′waⁿ=Manhukdhintanwan.
Man-hum-squeeg=Wabaquasset.
Maniataris=Hidatsa.
Manikans=Mahican.
Manikwagan=Manicouagan.
Manilla=Mobile.
Manissing=Minisink.
Manitaries=Hidatsa.
Mānk=Mong.
Makato's band=Mankato.

Manki=Makak.
Mankikani=Mahican.
Mannacans=Monacan.
Mannahannocks, Mannahoacks, Mannahoags, Mannahoaks, Mannahocks, Mannahokes=Manahoac.
Mannamett, Mannamit=Manomet.
Mannamoyk=Manamoyik.
Maⁿnaⁿhindje=Tadzhezhinga.
Mannatures=Hidatsa.
Mānnă-wōusŭt=Manosaht.
Mannissing=Manisink.
Man-oh-ah-sahta=Manosaht.
Manōmanee, Manomines, Manominik=Menominee.
Manōminikäcīyag=Munominikasheenhug.
Manook City=Maynook.
Mā′nōosath, Manosit=Manosaht.
Manostamenton=Menostamenton.
Manrhoat, Manrhout=Kiowa.
Mansa=Manso.
Maⁿsaⁿha=Upankhchi.
Mansano=Manzano.
Manses=Manso.
Manskin=Monacan.
Mansoleas, Mansopela, Mansopelea=Mosopelea.
Mansos=Apaches Mansos.
Maⁿⱬa=Modoc.
Mantaas=Manta.
Mantachusets=Massachuset.
Mantacut=Montauk.
Mantaes, Mantaesy=Manta.
Mantanes=Mandan.
Mantantans, Mantantons, Mantanton Scioux, Mantantous=Matantonwan.
Mantaoke=Montauk.
Mantaquak=Nanticoke.
Mantauket=Montauk.
Mantautous=Matantonwan.
Mantaws=Manta.
Mãⁿtĕrâ′ⁿ=Cherokee.
Mantes, Mantees=Manta.
Mantinacocks, Mantinecocks, Mantinicocks=Matinecoc.
Manton=Mandan, Mento.
Mantopanatos=Assiniboin.
Mantos=Manta.
Mantoue, Mantouecks, Mantouek, Mantoueouec= Mundua.
Mantoweeze=Mantowese.
Mantuas=Munsee.
Maⁿtú enikaci′ⱬa=Mantuenikashika.
Mantukes, Mantukett=Nantucket.
Maⁿ′-ⱬu-we=Mento.
Manumit=Manomet.
Manuncatuck=Menunkatuc.
Maŋ-wá-ta-niŋ=Mandan.
Manxo=Manso.
Ma-nyi′-ka-qǫi′=Manyikakhthi.
Maⁿyiñka-gaxe=Manyinka.
Maⁿyiñka jiñga=Manyinkazhinga.
Maⁿyiñka tañga=Manyinkatanga.
Many Medicines=Motahtosiks.
Manzana=Manzano, Mishongnovi.
Manzos=Pueblos.
Maouila=Mobile.
Mapeya=Sandia.
Mapicopas=Maricopa.
Maq=Marhoo.
Maqaise, Maqas=Mohawk.
Maqe-nikaci′ⱬa=Makhenikashika.
Maqpi′ato=Arapaho.
Maquaas=Mohawk.
Maquache Utes=Moache.
Maquaes, Maquaese=Mohawk.
Maquahache=Moache.
Maquais, Maquaise=Mohawk.
Maquamticough=Maquantequat.
Maquarqua=Mayaca.
Maquas, Maquasas, Maquase, Maquash, Maquass, Maquasse=Mohawk.
Máqude=Iowa.
Maquees=Mohawk.
Maquelnoteer, Maquelnoten=Mikonotunne.
Maques, Maquese, Maquess, Maquesyes, Maquez= Mohawk.
Maqui=Hopi.
Maquichees=Mequachake.
Maquin=Maquinanoa.
Maquis, Maquoas=Mohawk.

Maquoche Utahs=Moache.
Maquois=Mohawk.
Maquot=Pequot.
Mara=Twenty-nine Palms.
Marachite=Malecite.
Maracopa=Maricopa.
Maramoick=Manamoyik.
Mår-ån-shŏ-bĭsh-kŏ=Dakota.
Marashites=Malecite.
Marata=Matyata.
Marayam=Serranos.
Marcpeeah Mahzah, Marcpeeah Mazah=Makhpiya-maza.
Marc pee wee Chastah=Makhpiyawichashta.
Marechhawieck=Marychkenwikingh.
Marechites=Malecite.
Marechkawieck, Marechkawink=Marychkenwik-ingh.
Marecopas=Maricopa.
Mareschites=Malecite.
Mar'hoo=Nemah.
Marianes, Marians, Mariarves=Mariames.
Marimiskeet=Mattamuskeet.
Maringayam, Maringints=Serranos.
Marisizis=Malecite.
Maritises=Manta.
Marlain, Marlin=Staitan.
Mar-ma-li-la-cal-la=Mamalelekala.
Maroa, Marohans=Tamaroa.
Marospinc, Marossepinck=Massapequa.
Marota=Tamaroa.
Maroumine=Menominee.
Ma-rpi-ya-ma-za=Makhpiyamaza.
Marraganeet=Narraganset.
Marrarachic=Nararachic.
Marricoke=Merric.
Marsapeag, Marsapeague, Marsapege, Marsape-quas, Marsepain, Marsepeack, Marsepeagues, Marsepeake, Marsepeqau, Marsepin, Marsepinck, Marsepingh, Marsepyn, Marsey=Massapequa.
Marshpaug, Marshpee=Mashpee.
Marsh Village Dakotas, Marsh Villagers=Sisseton.
Marta=Matyata.
Mar-til-par=Matilpe.
Martinez=Sokut Menyil.
Martinne houck=Matinecoc.
Mary River, Mary's River, Marysville=Chepenafa.
Masagnebe, Masagneve=Mishongnovi.
Masaguia, Masaki=Matsaki.
Masalla Magoons=Musalakun.
Masammaskete=Mattamuskeet.
Masanais=Mishongnovi.
Masapequa=Massapequa.
Masaqueve=Mishongnovi.
Masaquia=Matsaki.
Masarquam=Mayaca.
Masathulets=Massachuset.
Másauwuu=Masi.
Masawomekes=Iroquois.
Mascaleros=Mescaleros.
Mascarasi=Macariz.
Mascautins=Mascoutens.
Maschal=Mashcal.
Mascoaties, Mascontans, Mascontenec, Mascontens, Mascontins, Mascontires, Mascordins, Mascotens, Mascotins, Mascouetechs=Mascoutens.
Mascouteins Nadouessi=Teton.
Mascoutens=Saint Francis Xavier.
Mascoutins, Mascoutins=Mascoutens.
Masep'=Kadohadacho.
Masepeage=Massapequa.
Ma-se-sau-gee=Missisauga.
Masetusets=Massachuset.
Mashamoquet, Mashamugget, Mashamugket=Mas-somuck.
Mashantucket=Maushantuxet.
Mashapauge, Mashapawog=Maushapogue.
Mashapeag, Masha-Peage=Massapequa.
Mashikh=Mashik.
Mashkegonhyrinis, Mashkegons, Mashkégous=Mas-kegon.
Mashkoutens=Mascoutens.
Ma-shong'-ni-vi, Mashóniniptuovi=Mishongnovi.
Mashpah=Mashpee.
Mashpeage=Massapequa.
Mashpege, Mashpey=Mashpee.
Mashquaro=Musquarro.
Mashukhara=Shasta.
Masiassuck=Missiassik.

Masichewsetts=Massachuset.
Ma síh kuh ta=Masikota.
Masi wiñwú, Ma-si' wüñ-wû=Masi.
Mas-ka-gau=Maskegon.
Maskasinik=Mascoutens.
Maskego, Maskegonehirinis, Maskégous, Maskégo-wuk, Maskigoes, Maskigonehirinis=Maskegon.
Mas-ko-ki=Creeks, Muskhogean Family.
Maskō'ki Hatchapála=Upper Creeks.
Maskóki Hatch'-áta=Lower Creeks.
Maskokúlki=Creeks.
Maskouaro=Musquarro.
Maskoutechs, Maskoutecks, Maskouteins, Maskou-tenek, Mask8tens, Maskoutens=Mascoutens.
Maskoutins, Maskuticks=Mascoutens.
Masonah Band=Nasumi.
Masphis=Mashpee.
Masquachki=Creeks.
Masquarro=Musquarro.
Masquikoukiaks, Masquikoukiocks=Maskegon.
Massachewset, Massachisans, Massachuselts, Mas-sachuseuks, Massachusiack, Massachussets, Mas-sachusuks, Massadzosek, Massajosets=Massa-chuset.
Massakiga=Arosaguntacook.
Massamugget=Massomuck.
Mas-sang-na-vay=Mishongnovi.
Massapeags=Massapequa.
Massapee=Mashpee.
Massapegs=Massapequa.
Massasagues, Massasaugas=Missisauga.
Massasinaway=Missisinewa.
Massasoiga=Missisauga.
Massasoits, Massasowat, Massasoyts=Wampanoag.
Massassuk=Missiassik.
Massathusets, Massatuchets, Massatusitts=Massa-chuset.
Massauwu=Masi.
Massawamacs, Massawomacs, Massawomecks, Mas-sawomees, Massawomekes, Massawonacks, Mas-sawonaes=Iroquois.
Massawteck=Massawoteck.
Massechuset=Massachuset.
Masseets=Masset.
Masselans=Mosilian.
Massepeake=Massapequa.
Massesagues=Missisauga.
Massetta, Massettes=Masset.
Massetusets=Massachuset.
Mass hade=Masset.
Massicapanoes=Monasiccapano.
Massillimacinac=Michilimackinac.
Massinacack=Massinacac.
Massinagues=Missisauga.
Massinnacacks=Massinacac.
Massorites, Massorittes, Massourites=Missouri.
Massowomeks=Iroquois.
Masstachusit=Massachuset.
Mas-tcal=Mashcal.
Mas-tutc'-kwe=Hopi.
Ma-su-ta-kaya, Ma-su-ta-kéa=Masut Pomo.
Matabantowaher=Matantonwan.
Matabesec, Matabezeke=Mattabesec.
Matachuses, Matachuyes=Massachuset.
Matages=Kiowa Apache.
Matahuay, Matajuiai=Mataguay.
Matakees, Matakeeset, Matakeesit=Mattakeset.
Mataki'la=Maamtagyila.
Matalans=Mitline.
Matale de Maño=Saboba.
Matamaskite=Mattamuskeet.
Matampken=Matomkin.
Matamuskeet=Mattamuskeet.
Mataouchkariniens, Mataoûakirinoüek, Mataouch-kairini, Mataouchkairinik, Mataouchkairiniouek, Mataouchkairiniwek, Mataouchkarini=Mata-wachkarini.
Mataoüiriou, Mataovan=Mattawan.
Matapa=Matape.
Matapaman=Mattapanient.
Matapoisett=Mattapoiset.
Matassins=Mistassin.
Matathusetts=Massachuset.
Matauwakes=Metoac.
Matavĕkĕ-Páya=Walapai.
Matawachkairini, Matawachwarini=Matawachka-rini.
Mātawāng, Matawin Indians=Mattawan.

Matchagamia=Michigamea.
Matchapangos, Matchapongos, Matchapungos, Matchapunko=Machapunga.
Match-clats=Muchalat.
Matchedach=Matchedash.
Matchemnes=Machemni.
Matche Moodus=Machemoodus.
Mat-che-naw-to-waig=Iroquois.
Matchepungo=Machapunga.
Matchi Moodus=Machemoodus.
Matchinadoaek=Iroquois.
Matchitashk=Matchedash.
Match-itl-aht=Muchalat.
Matchit Moodus=Machemoodus.
Matchoatickes=Matchotic.
Matchopeak=Matchopick.
Matchopongo=Machapunga.
Matchot=Matchut.
Matebeseck=Mattabesec.
Matechitache=Matchedash.
Matelpa, Matelthpahs=Matilpe.
Mat-hát-e-vatch=Chemehuevi.
Mathatusets, Mathatusitts, Mathesusetes=Massachuset.
Mathiaqua=Mathiaca.
Mathkoutench=Mascoutens.
Mathlanobes, Mathlanobs=Multnomah.
Mathomenis, Mathominis=Menominee.
Maticones=Maliacones.
Má-ti-la-ha=Matillija.
Matilden=Medilding.
Mā-tilh-pī=Matilpe.
Matiliha=Matillija.
Má'tilpis=Matilpe.
Matilton=Medilding.
Matinecocke, Matinecogh, Matinecongh, Matinicock, Matiniconck, Matinnekonck, Matinnicock=Matinecoc.
Mat-jus=Chemehuevi.
Matmork la Puerta=Matamo.
Matninicongh=Matinecoc.
Matokatági=Oto.
Matole=Mattole.
Mato-mihte, Mä-to'-no-mäke=Matonumanke.
Matontenta=Oto.
Mato-Numangkake, Ma-to' nu-mañ'-ke=Matonumanke.
Matoolonha, Matootonha, Ma-too-ton'-ka=Metutahanke.
Matopeló'tni=Three Rivers.
Matora=Mento.
Matotantes=Oto.
Matōtiswaning=Otusson.
Matoua=Mento.
Matou-ouescarini=Matawachkarini.
Matoutenta=Oto.
Matowacks=Metoac.
Matowepesack=Mattabesec.
Matox=Matchotic.
Matpanient=Mattapanient.
Matsigamea=Michigamea.
Matsĭ'shkota=Masikota.
Măts-nik'o'=Matsnikth.
Matsúki=Matsaki.
Mattabeeset, Mattabeseck, Mattabesett, Mattabesicke=Mattabesec.
Mattacheese, Mattacheeset, Mattacheest, Mattachiest, Mattachist=Mattakeset.
Mattachucetts, Mattachusetts, Mattachussetts, Mattacusets=Massachuset.
Mattakeese, Mattakeeset, Mattakesit=Mattakeset.
Mattanawcook=Mattinacook.
Mattapament=Mattapanient, Mattapony.
Mattapanians=Mattapanient.
Mattapanient=Mattapony.
Mattapany=Mattapanient.
Mattapeaset=Mattabesec.
Mattapomens, Mattapoments, Mattaponies=Mattapony.
Mattapuist, Mattapuyst=Mattapoiset.
Mattasoons=Amahami.
Mattassins=Mistassin.
Mattathusetts=Massachuset.
Mattatuck=Mattituck.
Mattatusetts=Massachuset.
Mattaugwessawacks=Dakota.
Mattawankeag=Mattawamkeag.
Mattebeseck=Mattabesec.
Mattecumska, Mattemusket=Mattamuskeet.
Mattetuck=Mattituck

Matthiaqua=Mathiaca.
Mattikongy=Naraticon.
Mattinacock, Mattinnekonck=Matinecoc.
Mattóal=Mattole.
Mattouwacky, Mattowax=Metoac.
Mattpament=Mattapanient.
Mattschotick=Matchotic.
Matu-ĕs'-wi skitchi-nú-ûk=Micmac.
Mat-ul-pai=Matilpe.
Matuwacks=Metoac.
Matza-ki, Matzaqui=Matsaki.
Maubela, Maubila, Maubile, Maubileans, Maubilians=Mobile.
Mauchage, Mauchaug=Manchaug.
Maudaus=Mandan.
Maudowessies=Dakota.
Maugaugon=Maguaga.
Maughwawame=Wyoming.
Mauguawogs, Mauhaukes, Mauhauks, Maukquogges=Mohawk.
Maumée, Maumes, Maumies=Miami.
Mau-os-aht=Manosaht.
Mauquaoy, Mauquas, Mauquauog, Mauquauogs, Mauquaw, Mauquawogs, Mauquawos, Mauques=Mohawk.
Mauraigans, Mauraygans=Mahican.
Mausalea=Mosopelea.
Mausand=Mishongnovi.
Mauscoutens=Mascoutens.
Mauton=Mento.
Mauvais Monde des Pieds-Noirs=Sarsi.
Mauvila, Mauvilians, Mauviliens=Mobile.
Mavaton=Maraton.
Mavila, Mavilians, Mavilla=Mobile.
Mawadaŋǿin=Mandan.
Ma-wahota, Ma-waqota=Mawakhota.
Mawátadan, Mawatani, Mawătaŋna=Mandan.
Mawchiggin=Mohegan.
Maw-dân=Mandan.
Mawhakes, Mawhauogs, Mawhawkes=Mohawk.
Mawhaws=Omaha.
Mawhickon, Mawhiggins=Mohegan.
Mawkey=Hopi.
Mawmee=Miami.
Mawques=Mohawk.
Mawtawbauntowahs=Mdewakanton.
Mawyk=Natick.
Mãx=Nemah.
Maxa-bomdu=Putetemini.
Maxa-yute-cni=Magayuteshni.
Maxe=Kdhun.
Maxul=Mashcal.
Maya=Mayo.
Mayacmas=Makoma.
Mayaco=Mayaca.
Mayacomas=Makoma.
Mayaguaci=Mayajuaca.
Mayaintalap=Serranos.
Mayanexit=Manexit.
Mayarca, Mayarqua=Mayaca.
Maydishkishdi=Mayndeshkish.
Mayeces, Mayees=Mayeye.
Mayekanders=Mahican.
Mayes=Mayeye.
Mayganathicoise=Mahican.
Mayimeuten=Magemiut.
Maykanders=Mahican.
Mayoahc=Kiowa.
Mayon=Wayon.
Mayrra=Mayara.
Mazahuas=Omaha.
Mazames=Mazapes.
Mazaquia=Matsaki.
Ma-za-ro-ta=Magayuteshni.
Maz-peganaŋka=Mazpegnaka.
Mazquia, Mazuqui=Matsaki.
M'cheuómi, M'cheuwámi, M'chwauwaumi=Wyoming.
M'chwihillusínk=Wyalusing.
Mdawakontons, Mdawakontonwans, M'day-wahkaun-twan Dakotas, M'day-wah-kauntwaun Sioux, M'daywawkawntwawns, Mdeiyedan, Mde-wahan-ton-wan, M'dewakanton, M'dewakantonwan, M'de-wakan-towwans, M'de-wakant'wan, Md-Wakans, Mdwakankontonwans=Mdewakanton.
Meadow Indians=Mascoutens.
Me-ä-me-ä-ga, Meames, Meamis=Miami.
Meandans=Mandan.
Meantacut, Meantaukett, Meanticut=Montauk.
Meat-who=Methow.

Mecaddacut=Mecadacut.
Mec-a-no-to-ny=Mikonotunne.
Mecäwä=Pesawa.
Mechayomy=Wyoming.
Mech-cha-ooh=Tooksetuk.
Mechecaukis=Foxes.
Mecheckesiouw=Meggeckessou.
Mechecouakis=Foxes.
Mechemiton=Mechemeton.
Mechias=Machias.
Mechimacks=Micmac.
Mechkentiwoom=Mechkentowoon.
Mechuouakis=Foxes.
Mecita=Hasatch.
Mécontins=Mascoutens.
Mecosukee=Mikasukï.
Mecoutins=Mascoutens.
Mĕc'-tcĕ=Meshtshe.
Mecuppom=Wecuppom.
Me-dama-rec=Bidamarek.
Medaquakantoan, Medawah-Kanton, Med-a-wakan-
　toan, Medawakantons, Medawakanton Sioux,
　Medawakantwan, Medawaykantoans, Me-da-we-
　con-tong, Med-ay-wah-kawn-t'waron, Medaywa-
　kanstoan, Med-ay-wa-kan-toan, Medaywokant'-
　wans=Mdewakanton.
Medchipouria=Mosopelea.
Me-de-wah-kan-toan, Medewakantoans, Medewakan-
　tons, Mede-wakan-t'wans=Mdewakanton.
Medicine=Hanga.
Medildiñ=Medilding.
Mediwanktons=Mdewakanton.
Mednoftsi=Ahtena.
Medocktack, Medocteck, Medoctek, Médocthek, Me-
　doktek, Medostec=Medoctec.
Medsigamea=Michigamea.
Medwakantonwan=Mdewakanton.
Meehayomy=Wyoming.
Me-em-ma=Chimariko.
Meendua=Mundua.
Mee-ne-cow-e-gee=Miniconjou.
Meesee Contee=Amaseconti.
Meeseequaguilch=Miseekwigweelis.
Mee-shom-e-neer=Mishongnovi.
Meesucontu=Amaseconti.
Meethco-thinyoowuc=Kainah.
Meewa, Meewie=Miwok.
Meewoc=Miwok, Moquelumnan Family.
Megancockia=Mengakonkia.
Megesiwisōwᵃ=Mikissioua.
Mégezi=Mgezewa.
Meggeckesjouw=Meggeckessou.
Meghay, Meghey, Meghty=Mayeye.
Me-giz-ze, Me-gizzee=Omegeeze.
Meguak, Megual, Megue=Mohawk.
Megum, Megŭmaawach=Micmac.
Megwe=Mohawk.
Meherine, Meherins, Meheron, Meherries, Meher-
　ring, Meherron=Meherrin.
Mehethawas=Cree.
Mehihammers=Mahican.
Mĕ'h-teh=Meta.
Meidoo=Maidu.
Meihites=Mayeye.
Meipoutsky=Meipontsky.
Me-jé-rä-ja=Michirache, Tunanpin.
Me-kä'=Mikaunikashinga.
Me-ka-nē-ten=Mikonotunne.
Mekasousky=Mikasuki.
Mĕ'-ki-tcûn'-tûn=Mekichuntun.
Melattaw=Amalahta.
Melecites=Malecite.
Melhominys=Menominee.
Melicite=Malecite.
Mĕli'-lĕma=Tenino.
Melisceet=Malecite.
Meliwarik=Milwaukee.
Mellataw=Amalahta.
Melleki, Melleoki, Melloki=Milwaukee.
Melomelinoia, Melominees=Menominee.
Mel'oopa=Nawiti.
Melotaukes=Montauk.
Melwarck, Melwarik=Milwaukee.
Memacanjo=Miniconjou.
Membrenos=Mimbreños.
Memesoon=Comanche.
Memilounioue=Miami.
Meminimisset=Menemesseg.
Memis=Miami.

Mēm-koom-lish=Memkumlis.
Mē'mogg·îns=Memoggyins.
Memonomier=Menominee.
Menaches=Moache.
Menamenies=Menominee.
Menataukett=Montauk.
Menatopa=Watopapinah.
Me-nau-zhe-tau-naung, Me-nau-zhe-taw-naun=Me-
　nawzhetaunaung.
Mencamis - Miami.
Menchærink=Meherrin.
Menchokatouches, Menchokatoux=Mdewakanton.
Menchón=Huron.
Mencouacantons, Mendawahkanton, Men-da-wa-kan-
　ton, Mendeouacanton, Mendeouacantous=Mdewa-
　kanton.
Menderink=Meherrin.
Mendewacantongs, Mende Wahkantoan, Mende-Wa-
　kan-Toann=Mdewakanton.
Mendoerink=Meherrin.
Mendoucaton, Menduwakanton=Mdewakanton.
Mendwrink=Meherrin.
Menekut'thégi—Mequachake.
Me-ne-sharne=Minisala.
Menesinks, Menessinghs=Minisink.
Menetare, Menetarres=Hidatsa.
Mengua, Mengues, Menguy, Mengwe, Mengwee,
　Mengwi=Iroquois.
Menherring, Menheyricks=Meherrin.
Men-i-cou-zha=Miniconjou.
Meniolagamika=Meniolagomeka.
Menisink, Menissinck, Menissing, Menissinges,
　Menissins=Minisink.
Menisupérik=Minesetperi.
Mennisink, Mennissincks=Minisink.
Mennominies=Menominee.
Menoequet=Menoquet.
Men of the Woods=Nopeming.
Menoga=Menoquet.
Menomenes, Me-nó-me-ne-uk, Menomenies, Menom-
　inie, Menominny, Menomoee, Menomones, Me-
　nomonei, Menomones, Menomonies, Menomonys,
　Menonomees, Menonomies=Menominee.
Menowa Kautong, Menowa Kontong=Mdewakan-
　ton.
Menquagon=Maguaga.
Mentakett=Montauk.
Mententons=Matantonwan.
Mentoake=Montauk.
Mentons=Mento.
Mentonton=Matantonwan.
Mentous=Mento.
Menumesse=Menemesseg.
Menuncatuk, Menunkatuck, Menunketuck, Menun-
　ketucke, Menunquatucke=Menunkatuc.
Meontaskett, Meontawket=Montauk.
Meosigamia=Michigamea.
Mequa=Mohawk.
Meracock=Merric.
Meraquaman=Meracouman.
Mercedes=Merced.
Mer-cöm=Mershom.
Merechkawick, Merechkawikingh=Marychkenwi-
　kingh.
Merhuan=Menequen.
Mericock, Mericoke, Merikoke=Merric.
Merimichi=Miramichi.
Merocomecook=Rocameca.
Meroke=Merric.
Meronocomoco=Werowacomoco.
Merrakwick=Marychkenwikingh.
Merriack, Merricocke=Merric.
Merrimacks=Pennacook.
Merrimichi=Miramichi.
Mersapeage, Mersapege=Massapequa.
Mertowacks=Metoac.
Mê'-rxĕt-ke=Meetkeni.
Mesa de Galisteo=Heshota Ayathltona.
Mesa Encantada=Katzimo.
Mesa of Galisteo=Heshota Ayathltona.
Mesasagah=Missisauga.
Mescale=Mescales.
Mescaleres, Mescalers, Mescallaros, Mescaloro Apa-
　ches, Mescalos, Mescaluros=Mescaleros.
Mescate=Mescales.
Mescateras, Mescolero=Mescaleros.
Meshagak=Nushagak.
Mëshäwi8utcig[1]=Mashawauk.

Meshawn=Meeshawn.
Mesh e ne mah ke noong=Michilimackinac.
Meshik=Mashik.
Me-shing-go-me-sia, Me-shin-gi-me-yia=Meshingomesia.
Meshipeshi=Msepase.
Meshkalé kué=Mescaleros.
Meshkwa'kĭhạg[1]=Foxes.
Meshones=Methow.
Me-shong-a-na-we, Meshongnavi, Me-shung-a-na-we, Me-shung-ne-vi=Mishongnovi.
Mesigameas=Michigamea.
Mesilimakinac=Michilimackinac.
Mesita, Mesita Negra=Hasatch.
Meskeman=Meshkemau.
Meskigouk=Maskegon.
Meskwá'kĭ'àg[1]=Foxes.
Mespacht, Mespadt, Mespaetches, Mespat, Mespath, Mespath's Kill, Mespat Kil, Mespats-kil=Maspeth.
Mesquabuck=Mesquawbuck.
Mesquit=Mesquite.
Mesquita, Mesquittes=Mesquites.
Messachusetts, Messachusiack=Massachuset.
Messagnes, Messagues, Messasagas, Messasagies, Messasagoes, Messasagues, Messasaugues, Messassagas, Messassagnes, Messassagues=Missisauga.
Messathusett=Massachuset.
Messawomes=Iroquois.
Messcothins=Mascoutens.
Messenacks=Foxes.
Messen-Apaches=Navaho.
Messenecqz=Foxes.
Messesagas, Messesagnes, Messesago, Messesagues, Messessagues, Messessaques=Missisauga.
Messiasics=Missiassik.
Messinagues, Messisagas, Messisages, Messisagues, Messisaugas, Messisaugers, Messissagas, Messissauga=Missisauga.
Messorites, Messourites=Missouri.
Messthusett=Massachuset.
Mestecke=Mystic.
Měs-těçl-tûn=Mestethltun.
Mestick=Mystic.
Mestigos, Mestizo=Metis.
Metabetshuan=Metabetchouan.
Metackwem=Metocaum.
Metacumbe=Guarungunve.
Metaharta=Hidatsa.
Metapa=Matape.
Metapawnien=Mattapanient.
Metchagamis, Metchigamea, Metchis=Michigamea.
Met-cow-we, Metcowwee=Methow.
Metea's Village=Muskwawasepeotan.
Metehigamis=Michigamea.
Meteowwee=Methow.
Meterries=Meherrin.
Métésigamias=Michigamea.
Methau, Methews, Methoms=Methow.
Metlah Catlah, Metlahkatlah=Metlakatla.
Metocunent=Metocaum.
Me-too'-ta-häk=Mandan. ❀
Metotonta=Oto.
Metousceprinioueks=Miami.
Metouwacks, Metowacks=Metoac.
Metsepe=Maspeth.
Metsigameas=Michigamea.
Mettaꝶakik=Mattawamkeag.
Metutahanke=Mandan.
Meuntacut=Montauk.
Mewahs=Miwok.
Měwě Sagaagan Wěněněwåk=Miskwagamiwisagaigan.
Mexicans=Pueblos.
Méye=Mayeye.
Meyemma=Chimariko.
Meynomenys, Meynomineys=Menominee.
Mezcaleros=Mescaleros.
Mezquites=Mesquites.
Mhíkana=Mahican.
Mi-ah-kee-jack-sah=Miakechakesa.
Mi-ah'-ta-nēs=Mandan.
Mialaquo=Big-island.
Miamee, Miames, Miamiha, Miamiouek=Miami.
Miamis de la Grüe=Atchatchakangouen.
Miami town=Kekionga.
Mianҟkish=Piankashaw.
Miantaquit=Niantic.

Miayŭma=Mahoyum.
Micanopy, Micanopy's town=Pilaklikaha.
Micasukee, Micasukeys, Micasukies, Micasukys=Mikasuki.
Micäwä=Misshawa.
Mi-caws=Makah.
Miccasooky, Miccosaukie, Mic-co-sooc-e=Mikasuki.
Micháelovski Redoubt=Saint Michael.
Michalits=Muchalat.
Michalloasen=Wyalusing.
Michelimakina, Michellimakinac=Michilimackinac.
Michê Michêquipi, Miche-Miche-Quipy=Metsmetskop.
Michesaking=Missisauga.
Michiagamias, Michigamias, Michigamis, Michigania, Michiganians, Michigans, Michigourras=Michigamea.
Michihimaquinac=Michilimackinac.
Michilemackinah, Michilimacquina, Michilimakenac, Michilimakina, Michilimakinac, Michilimakinais, Michilimakinong, Michilimaquina, Michilimicanack, Michilimickinac, Michillemackinack, Michillemakinack, Michillimacinac, Michilimackinacks, Michillimakenac, Michillimakinak, Michillimaquina, Michillmiackinook, Michi Mackina, Michimmakina, Michinimackinac=Michilimackinac.
Michinipicpoet=Etheneldeli.
Michisagnek=Missisauga.
Michiskoui=Missiassik.
Mich-la-its=Muchalat.
Michlimakinak=Michilimackinac.
Michmacs=Micmac.
Michoapdos=Michopdo.
Michonguave=Mishongnovi.
Micibigwadunk=Michipicoten.
Mi-cí-kqwŭt-mé ꝝûnně=Mishikhwutmetunne.
Micilimaquinay, Mīcinimā'kinunk=Michilimackinac.
Mici'qwŭt=Mishikhwutmetunne.
Mickasauky, Micka Sukees, Mickasukians, Mickasukies=Mikasuki.
Mickemac=Micmac.
Mickesawbe=Mickkesawbee.
Mickmacks, Mickmaks=Micmac.
Mick-suck-seal-tom=Micksucksealton.
Mĭ-çlauq'-tcu-wûn'-ti=Klikitat.
Mĭ-çlä'-us-min-t' çai'=Mithlausmintthai.
Micmacks, Micmaks=Micmac.
Micongnivi, Mi-coñ'-în-o-vi=Mishongnovi.
Miconopy=Pilaklikaha.
Mi-con-o-vi=Mishongnovi.
Mic-pâ'p-snâ=Mishpapsna.
Mic-ta-pál-wa=Mishtapalwa.
Mic-ta-pä-wä=Mishtapawa.
Mictawayäng=Mishtawayawininiwak.
Middle Ant Hill=Halona.
Middle Indians=Tangesatsa.
Middle Mohawk Castle=Canajoharie.
Middle Place=Halona.
Middle Spokomish=Sintootoolish.
Middletown=Middle Village.
Midewakantonwans=Mdewakanton.
Miditadi=Hidatsa.
Midnoóskie, Midnóvtsi=Ahtena.
Midu=Maidu.
Miednoffskoi, Miednofskie=Ahtena.
Miembre Apaches, Miembrenos, Miembres=Mimbreños.
Mi-em-ma=Chimariko.
Mienbre=Mimbreños.
Miggaamacks=Micmacs.
Migichihilinious=Migechichiliniou.
Mi'gisi=Omegeeze.
Migiu, Migiugui=Miguihui.
Mĭgizi=Omegeeze.
Miheconders, Mihicanders=Mahican.
Mih-tutta-hang-kusch, Mih-Tutta-Hang-Kush=Metutahanke.
Miká-atí=Shoshoni.
Mikadeshitchishi=Nez Percés.
Mika nika-shing-ga=Mikaunikashinga.
Mikanopy=Pilaklikaha.
Mika' q'e ni' kaci' ꝝa=Mikakhenikashika.
Mika qla jiñga=Mikaunikashinga.
Mikasaukies=Mikasuki.
Mikasi-unikaci[n]ga=Mandhinkagaghe.

Mikasuky=Mikasuki.
Mika unikaciⁿga=Mikaunikashinga.
Mikemak=Micmac.
Mik-iára=Amaikiara.
Mikikoues, Mikikouët, Mikikouet=Nikikouek.
Mikinac=Michilimackinac.
Mĭ'kĭna'k=Mikonoh.
Mĭ'kinā'kiwadciwininiwąg, Mĭ'kĭna'kĭwadshĭwĭnĭ-
    nĭwug, Mi'kinā'kwątciwininiwąg=Mikinakwa-
    dshiwininiwak.
Mikissoua=Mikissioua.
Mikkesoeke=Mikasuki.
Mikmacs, Mikmak=Micmac.
Mikouachakhi=Miskouaha.
Mi'kowa=Mehkoa.
Miksuksealton=Micksucksealton.
Mi'-ku-litc'=Mikulitsh.
Mi'-kwun-nų'ɉûnné'=Mikonotunne.
Mi'kyashĕ=Shoshoni.
Milbauks-chim-zi-ans=Tsimshian.
Mileo-to-nac=Melejo.
Milicetes, Milicite=Malecite.
Milky Hollow Ruin=Milky Wash ruin.
Millbank Indians, Millbank Sound Indians=Bella-
    bella.
Mille Lac band=Misisagaikaniwininiwak.
Milli-hhlama=Tenino.
Milowacks=Metoac.
Miltinoma=Multnomah.
Milwaukie=Milwaukee.
Mimai=Mimal.
Mimbrenas, Mimbrereños, Mimbres, Mimbres
    Apaches=Mimbreños.
Mimetari=Hidatsa.
Miminimisset=Menemesseg.
Mimvre=Mimbreños.
Mina'kwąt=Menoquet's village.
Minataree, Minatares, Minatories=Hidatsa.
Mincees, Minci=Munsee.
Minckquas=Iroquois.
Mińckus=Conestoga.
Mincquaas=Iroquois.
Mić-da,-wâr-câr-ton=Mdewakanton.
Mineamies=Menominee.
Minecogue, Minecosias, Minecougan, Mi-ne-kaɲ'-
    źūs=Miniconjou.
Mineoes=Mingo.
Mĭnĕsupĕ'rik=Minesetperi.
Minetaire, Minetarees, Minetares=Hidatsa.
Minetares of the Prairie=Atsina.
Minetari, Minetaries, Minetarre=Hidatsa.
Minewagi=Milwaukee.
Mingaes=Iroquois.
Míngo=Mingko.
Mingoe, Mingos, Mingwee=Iroquois.
Miniamies=Miami.
Miniamis=Menominee.
Mini-cala=Itazipcho.
Mini-can-gsha=Miniconjou.
Minicau=Piniquu.
Mini-Conjou, Minicoughas, Minicoujons, Mini-kan-
    jous, Minikan oju, Minikanyes, Minikaɲye woźupi,
    Min-i-kaɲ'-źu, Mini-kiniad-za, Minikomjoos, Mini-
    konga, Minikongshas, Minikoóju=Miniconjou.
Miⁿi'niųk'ă ciⁿ'a=Mininihkashina.
Minipătă=Minnepata.
Mini-sala=Itazipcho.
Minishup'sko=Dakota.
Minisincks, Minising=Minisink.
Miniskuya kiçuɲ, Miniskuya kiçun, Miniskuya-
    kitc'uⁿ=Miniskuyakichun.
Minissens=Minisink.
Minissingh, Minissinks=Minisink.
Ministeneaux=Cree.
Minisuk=Minisink.
Minitare, Minitarees=Hidatsa.
Minitares of the Prairie=Atsina.
Minitari=Hidatsa.
Mini'tigunk=Menitegow.
Miⁿ-ke' qaⁿ'-ye=Minkekhanye.
Miⁿ-ke yiñ'-e=Minkeyine.
Minkhotliatno=Mentokakat.
Minnake-nozzo, Min-na-kine-az-zo, Minnecarguis,
    Minne-caushas, Minnecogoux, Minnecojous, Minne-
    congew, Minnecongou, Minneconjon, Minneconjos,
    Minneconjoux, Minnecoujos, Minnecoujou, Minne
    Coujoux Sioux, Minne-Cousha, Minnecowzues=
    Miniconjou.

Minneh-sup-pay-deh=Minesetperi.
Min-ne-kaɲ'-zu, Minnekonjo=Miniconjou.
Minnessinck=Minisink.
Minnetahrees, Minnetahse, Mĭn-nĕ-tă-rĕ, Minne-
    tarees, Minnetarees Metaharta=Hidatsa.
Minnetarees of Fort de Prairie, Minnetarees of the
    Plains, Minnetarees of the Prairie=Atsina.
Minnetarees of the Willows, Minnetaroes, Minnetar
    res=Hidatsa.
Minneways=Illinois.
Minnicongew, Minni-kan-jous, Minnikanye Woz-
    hipu=Miniconjou.
Minnisink, Minnissincks, Minnissinke=Minisink.
Minnitarees, Minnitarees Metaharta=Hidatsa.
Minnitarees of Fort de Prairie=Atsina.
Minnitarees of the Willows, Minnitaris, Minntaree=
    Hidatsa.
Minoia=Aminoia.
Minokantongs=Mdewakanton.
Minominees, Minominies, Minomonees, Minoniones,
    Minoomenee=Menominee.
Minóosky=Ahtena.
Minoquet=Menoquet.
Minowakanton, Minowa Kantong=Mdewakanton.
Minowas=Iowa.
Minoway-Kantong, Minoway Kautong, Minow Kan-
    tong=Mdewakanton.
Minoya=Aminoya.
Minquaas, Minquaes=Conestoga, Iroquois.
Minquaos=Conestoga.
Minquas=Conestoga, Iroquois.
Minquase, Minquays=Conestoga.
Miⁿ'qudje-iⁿts'e=Manhazulintanman.
Minques, Minquinos, Minquosy=Conestoga.
Minseys, Minsimini, Minsis=Munsee.
Miⁿtcíratce=Michirache.
Mintou=Mento.
Minusing=Minisink.
Minúsky=Ahtena.
Miⁿ-xa-saⁿ-ɸatajĭ-ki ɉetaⁿ-ɸataji=Zhanhadtadhis-
    han.
Miⁿxa-saⁿ-wet'agĭ=Minghasanwetazhi.
Miⁿxa'ska=Minghaska.
Miⁿ xa' ska i' niųk'äciⁿ'a=Minghaskainihkashina.
Miook=Miwok.
Mipacmas=Makoma.
Mĭ'-p'cŭn-tĭk=Mipshuntik.
Mipegoes, Mipegois=Winnebago.
Miquesesquelna=Niquesesquelua.
Miqui=Hopi.
Miracopas==Maricopa.
Miramis=Miami.
Mirimichy=Miramichi.
Mirocopas=Maricopa.
Mirrachtauhacky=Montauk.
Mi-sal-la Magun=Musalakun.
Miscaleros=Mescaleros.
Miscelemackena, Misclimakinack=Michilimack-
    inac.
Miscolts=Miskut.
Miscòthins, Miscotins=Mascoutens.
Miscott=Miskut.
Miscouaquis=Foxes.
Misham=Mishawum.
Mi-shan-qu-na-vi=Mishongnovi.
Mishawomet=Shawomet.
Mishinimaki, Mishinimakina, Mishinimakinago,
    Mishini-makinak, Mishinimakinang, Mishinimák-
    inank=Michilimackinac.
Mishiptonga=Kawaika.
Mishkemau=Meshkemau.
Mi-shong-i-niv, Mi-shong'-i-ni-vi, Mi-shong-in-ovi,
    Mishongnavi, Mishongop-avi, Mi-shon-na-vi=
    Mishongnovi.
Mishowomett=Shawomet.
Misiassins (Petits)=Mistassin.
Misilimakenak, Misillimakinac=Michilimackinac.
Misinajua=Misinagua.
Mision de Nacogdoches=Nuestra Señora de Guada-
    lupe de los Nacogdoches.
Mi-sis=Omisis.
Misisagas, Misisagey=Missisauga.
Misiskoui=Missiassik.
Misitagues=Missisauga.
Mis-kai-whu=Miseekwigweelis.
Mis-Keegoes=Maskegon.
Mískígúla=Pascagoula.
Miskogonhirinis=Maskegon.
Miskuakes=Miskouaha.

Miskú-Gami-Saga-igan-anishinábeg = Miskwagami-wisagaigan.
Miskwādäs[i] = Meskwadare.
Mĭskwā̆-kā̆ Mĕwĕ Sā̆gā̆ā̆gā̆n Wĕnĕnĕwā̆k = Miskwagamiwisagaigan.
Miskwiam = Musqueam.
Miskwukeeyuk = Foxes.
Mislimakinac = Michilimackinac.
Misonk = Miemissouks.
Misouris = Missouri.
Misqueam = Musqueam.
Misquito = Mesquite.
Missada, Missages = Missisauga.
Missaquogues = Nesaquake.
Missasagas, Missasago, Missasagué, Missassago, Missassugas, Missaugees = Missisauga.
Misselemachinack, Misselemakinach, Misselemaknach = Michilimackinac.
Missequeks, Missesagas, Missesagoes, Missesagues, Missesaques, Missiagos = Missisauga.
Missilikinac, Missilimachinac, Missilimackinak, Missilimakenak, Missilimakinac, Missilimakinak, Missilimaquina, Missilinaokinak, Missilinianac, Missillimackinac, Missillimakina, Missilmakina = Michilimackinac.
Missinasagues = Missisauga.
Mission de St. Joseph = Goiogouen.
Mission Montezuma = Casa Grande.
Mission of the Holy Ghost = Shaugawaumikong.
Mission Point = Restigouche.
Missiosagaes = Missisauga.
Missiouris = Missouri.
Missiquecks, Missisagaes, Missisages, Missisagis, Missisagos, Missisagues, Missisaguez, Missisaguys, Missisak, Missisakis, Missisaque, Missisaquees, Missisagues = Missisauga.
Missiscoui, Missiskouy = Missiassik.
Mississaga, Mississagets, Mississageyes, Mississagez, Mississagies, Mississaguas, Mississague, Mississaguras, Mississakis, Mississaques, Mississaugers, Mississauges, Mississaugies, Mississaugues, Mississguas = Missisauga.
Mississinaway = Mississinewa.
Mississipone = Misesopano.
Mississippi bands = Kitchisibiwininiwug.
Missitagues = Missisauga.
Missoori = Missouri.
Missopeno = Sopone.
Missounta, Missouria, Missourians, Missourie, Missouriens, Missouries, Missouris, Missourita, Missourite, Missoury = Missouri.
Misstassins = Mistassin.
Missuri, Missurier, Missuris, Missurys = Missouri.
Mistapnis, Mistasiniouek, Mistasireꞑois, Mistasiririns, Mistassini, Mistassinni, Mistassirinins = Mistassin.
Mĭ′stäviĭ′nût = Hotamitanio.
Mistick = Mystic.
Mistigouche = Restigouche.
Mistissinnys = Mistassin.
Mĭ′-sûn = Misun.
Misuris = Missouri.
Mĭ̂ta = Meta.
Mĭtaháwiye = Kitkehahki.
Mitaui = Methow.
Mitchigamas, Mitchigamea, Mitchigamias = Michigamea.
Mitchinimackenucks = Michilimackinac.
Mitchitamou = Mistassin.
Mitc-hi-yu = Michiyu.
Mi-tci′-ra-tce = Michirache.
Mitc-Ka-na-Kau = Miscanaka.
Mithouies = Methow.
Mitiling = Kalopaling.
Mi-til′-ti = Medilding.
Mĭ′tlmetle′ltc = Mitlmetlelch.
Mi-toam′ Kai Pó-mo = Mitomkai Pomo.
Mitshopda = Michopdo.
Mĭtsitá = Wichita.
Mitutahankish, Mitutahañkuc = Metutahanke.
Miúxsĕn = Tonkawa.
Mivira = Quivira.
Mi′-wa, Mi′wi = Miwok.
Mĭ′-wok = Moquelumnan Family.
Miyamis = Miami.
Mĭyi = Mayeye.
Mizamichis = Miramichi.
Mkatewetitéta = Siksika.

Mnacedeus = White Indians.
Mnakho-tana = Unakhotana.
Moacha = Yuquot.
Moachet = Mooachaht.
Moacks = Mohawk.
Moadassa = Muklassa.
Moadoc, Moahtockna = Modoc
Moak = Mohawk.
Möal-kai = Boalkea.
Moan′-au-zi = Mono.
Moan-Kopi = Oraibi.
Moassones, Moassons = Abnaki.
Moatakish = Modoc.
Mō′atcath = Mooachaht.
Moatok-gîsh, Móatokni = Modoc.
Mo-a-wa-ta-ve-wach = Tabeguache.
Moawk = Mohawk.
Mobas = Movas.
Mobeluns, Mobilas, Mobileans = Mobile.
Mobilians = Creeks, Mobile, Muskhogean Family.
Mobiliens = Mobile.
Mocalasa = Muklassa.
Mocas = Hopi.
Moccasin-with-holes = Bannock.
Mochgeyohkonk = Mechgachkamic.
Mochgonnekonck = Shinnecock.
Mochi = Hopi.
Mochicahuy, Mochicohuy = Mochicaui.
Mochies = Hopi.
Mochila = Mochilagua.
Mochomes = Delaware.
Mochop = Mochopa.
Mockhoeken = Hockhocken.
Mo-cko′-ꬻi = Creeks.
Mockways = Mohawk.
Mocoço, Mocosa, Mocoso, Mocosson = Moquoso.
Mocquages, Mocquayes = Mohawk.
Moctesuma = Casa Grande.
Moctezuma = Oposura.
Moctoby = Moctobi.
Modanks, Mo-docks, Modoes, Modok, Mō′dokish, Mō′dokni, Modook = Modoc.
Mo-é-ka-ne-kä′-she-gä = Manyinka.
Mo-é-kwe-ah-hä = Chedunga.
Moelobites = Moctoby.
Moencapi = Moenkapi.
Moenemines Castle, Moeneminnes Castle = Monemius.
Moeng8ena = Moingwena.
Moen-kopi = Moenkapi.
Mœnnitarris = Hidatsa.
Moeroahkongy = Meletecunk.
Mo-e-twas = Palaihnihan Family.
Mogall, Mogallones = Mogollon.
Mogekin = Mohegan.
Mogeris = Hopi.
Mogianeucks = Mohegan.
Mogin = Hopi.
Mogino = Moquino.
Mogkunkakauke = Magunkaquog.
Moglushah town = Mugulasha.
Mogogones, Mogoll, Mogollone = Mogollon.
Mogolushas = Mugulasha.
Mogoso = Moquoso.
Mogoulachas = Mugulasha.
Mogoyones = Mogollon.
Mogozo = Moquoso.
Moguachis = Moache.
Mogui = Hopi.
Moguino = Moquino.
Mohaakx = Mohawk.
Mohacé = Hopi.
Mohacks, Mohaco, Mohacqs, Mohacques, Mohaes, Mohaggs = Mohawk.
Mohagin = Mohegan.
Mohags = Mohawk.
Mohahve = Mohave.
Mohaks, Mohakx = Mohawk.
Mohansick = Manhasset.
Mohaqe, Mohaqs, Mohaques = Mohawk.
Mohaskahod = Mahaskahod.
Mohaucks, Mohaugs, Mohaukes, Mohauks = Mohawk.
Mohavi, Mohawa = Mohave.
Mohawcks = Mohawk.
Mohawe = Mohave.
Mohawkes, Mohawques, Mohaws = Mohawk.
Moheag, Moheagan, Moheaganders, Moheages, Moheagues = Mohegan.

Moheakanneews, Moheakenunks, Moheakounuck, Moheakunnuks, Mohecan, Moheckons, Moheconnock, Mo-hee-gan=Mahican.
Moheegins, Moheegs, Moheek, Moheganicks, Mohegen, Moheges, Mohegin=Mohegan.
Mohego=Mohawk.
Mohegs, Moheken=Mohegan.
Mohekin, Mo-he-kun-e-uk, Mo-he'-kun-ne-uk, Mohekunnuks, Mohekunuh=Mahican.
Mohemenchoes, Mohemenehoes, Mohemonsoes=Mohemencho.
Mohetan=Moheton.
Mohicander, Mohicands=Mahican.
Mohican Johnstown=Mohickon John's Town.
Mohicanrs, Mohicans, Mohiccons, Mohickan, Mohickanders, Mohicken=Mahican.
Mohicken Village=Mohickon John's Town.
Mohickons=Mahican.
Mohigan, Mohiganeucks, Mohiganie, Mohigens, Mohiggans, Mohiggen, Mohiggeners, Mohighens, Mohigin=Mohegan.
Mohigon=Mahican.
Mohigoners=Mohegan.
Mohikan, Mohikander, Mohikonders, Mohikons=Mahican.
Mohineyam=Serranos.
Mohingans, Mohingaus=Mahican.
Móhkach=Mokaich.
Mohk ta hwá tan in=Moqtavhaitaniu.
Moh-kuh'=Makan.
Mohoakk=Mohawk.
Mohocanders=Mahican.
Mohoce=Hopi.
Mohocks, Mohocs=Mohawk.
Mohogans=Mahican.
Mohoges, Mohoggs=Mohawk.
Mohogin=Mohegan.
Mohogs=Mohawk.
Mohokanders=Mahican.
Mohokes, Mohoks=Mohawk.
Mohoning=Mahoning.
Mohontowonga=Manckatawangum.
Mohoqui, Mohotze=Hopi.
Mohoukes, Mohowaugsuck, Mohowawogs, Mohowks, Mohox=Mohawk.
Mōh-tau-hai'-ta-ni-o=Ute.
Móhtawas=Kansa.
Mōh-ta'-wa-ta-ta'-ni-o=Sihasapa.
Mohuache, Mohuache Utahs, Mohuache Utes=Moache.
Mohuccons, Mohuccories=Mahican.
Mohucks=Mohawk.
Mohuhaches=Moache.
Moi-ka-nika-shing-ga=Manyinka.
Moingoana, Moingona, Moins=Moingwena.
Mojaoes, Mojaris, Mojaur, Mojave=Mohave.
Mojual-ua=Mojualuna.
M'okahoki=Okahoki.
Mókai=Calapooya.
Mókaiqch, Mo'-kaitc=Mokaich.
Mokalusha=Imongalasha.
Mo-katsh=Mokaich.
Mokaus, Mokawkes=Mohawk.
Moke=Calapooya.
Mokee=Hopi.
Mokelemnes=Mokelumne.
Móke máklaks=Calapooya.
Mokes=Hopi.
Mokhabas=Mohave.
Moki=Hopi.
Molalalas, Molale, Molalla, Molallah, Molallalas, Molallales, Molalle Indians, Molallie, Mo-layless=Molala.
Molchatna=Mulchatna.
Moleaaleys, Molealleg, Mole Alley, Moleallies=Molala.
Molejé=Santa Rosalina Mulege.
Molel=Molala.
Molele=Molala, Waiilatpuan Family.
Molelie, Molell, Mollalas=Molala.
Molloua, Moloa, Molona=Homolua.
Môlsem=Malssum.
Moltnomas=Multnomah.
Molxaves=Mohave.
Mominimisset=Menemesseg.
Monachans=Monacan.
Monache, Mo-na-chi=Mono.
Monahasanugh, Monahassanughes=Monahassano.
Monahegan, Monahiganeucks, Monahiganick, Mo-

nahiggan, Monahiggannick, Monahigganie, Monahiggens, Monahiggon, Monahigon=Mohegan.
Monahoacs=Manahoac.
Monakin=Monacan.
Monamoy, Monamoyik=Manamoyik.
Monanacah Rahowacah, Monanacans=Monacan.
Monas=Mono.
Monasiccapanoes, Monasiceapanoes, Monasickapanoughs, Monasukapanough=Monasiccapano.
Monatons, Monatuns=Manhattan.
Moncey=Munsee.
Mondaque=Anadarko.
Monecoshe Sioux=Miniconjou.
Mon-eka-goh-ha=Mandhinkagaghe.
Monemiu's castle=Monemius.
Monengwanekan=Shaugawaumikong.
Mongontatchas, Mongoulacha, Mongoulatches=Mugulasha.
Mongsoa Eithynyook, Mongsoa-eythinyoowuc=Monsoni.
Monguagon=Maguaga.
Monhagin=Mohegan.
Monhauset=Manhasset.
Monheagan, Monheags, Monhegans, Monhege, Monhegen, Monhiggin, Monhiggons, Monhiggs=Mohegan.
Monimoy=Manamoyik.
Moningwanekan=Shaugawaumikong.
Monis=Menominee.
Monkey Indians=Hopi.
Monloua=Homolua.
Mon-mish=Samamish.
Monmuchloosen=Wyalusing.
Monnesick=Minisink.
Monocans=Monacan.
Monoes=Mono.
Monohegens=Mohegan.
Monomeni=Menominee.
Monomete=Manomet.
Monomins, Monomonees=Menominee.
Monomoy=Manamoyik.
Monomunies=Menominee.
Mo-no'-ni-o=Mandan.
Mono Pi-Utes=Mono.
Monquoi=Hopi.
Mōns=Mous.
Monsaunis=Monsoni.
Monsays, Monsees, Monseys, Monsi=Munsee.
Monsiemakenack=Michilimackinac.
Monsies=Munsee.
Monsonabi, Monsonavi=Mishongnovi.
Monsone, Monsoni=Mousonee.
Monsonico, Monsonies=Monsoni.
Monsopela=Mosopelea.
Monsounic=Monsoni.
Mons8pelea, Monsoupelea=Mosopelea.
Monsys=Munsee.
Montacut=Montauk.
Montagnais=Chipewyan, Nahane.
Montagnais of Lake St. John=Chicoutimi.
Montagnaits=Montagnais.
Montagnardes=Montagnard.
Montagnards, Montagnars=Montagnais.
Montagnees=Chipewyan.
Montagnes=Chipewyan, Montagnais.
Montagnèse=Mikinakwadshiwininiwak.
Montagnets=Montagnais.
Montagneurs=Onondaga.
Montagnez=Chipewyan, Montagnais.
Montagnois, Montagrets=Montagnais.
Montagués=Montagnais, Onondaga.
Montaignairs, Montaigners, Montaignes, Montaignets, Montainiers=Montagnais.
Montake, Montaks=Montauk.
Montanaro, Montaniak=Montagnais.
Montank, Montauckett, Montaug, Montaukett, Montaukut, Montauque=Montauk.
Montawanskeag=Mattawamkeag.
Montekakat=Mentokakat.
Monterey=San Carlos.
Montezuma=Casa Grande, Casa Montezuma.
Montezuma Pueblo=Pueblo Pintado.
Monthees, Montheys=Munsee.
Montoake, Montocks, Montok=Montauk.
Montotos=Nutunutu.
Montoweses=Mantowese.
Mont-Pelés=Monts Pelés.
Montucks=Montauk.
Mônuhchogok=Manchaug.

Monument, Monumet=Manomet.
Monunkatuck=Menunkatuc.
Monymoyk=Manamoyik.
Monzoni=Monsoni.
Mooacht-aht, Moo-cha-aht=Mooachaht.
Moochas=Motsai.
Moogunkawg=Magunkaquog.
Moohags=Mohawk.
Mooklausa, Mooklausan, Mook-lau-sau=Muklassa.
Moolalle=Molala.
Moolamchapa=Mulamchapa.
Mooleilis=Molala.
Moon'-au-zi=Paiute.
Moon-calves=Menominee.
Moon'-cha=Tunanpin.
Moons=Mous.
Moonyville Saw Mills=Moodyville Saw Mills.
Mooqui=Hopi.
Moor-i-ohs, Moo-ris=Murek.
Moose-deer Indians, Moose Indians, Moose River Indians=Monsoni.
Mooshahneh, Mooshanave, Moo-sha-neh, Mooshongae nay vee, Mooshongeenayvee, Moo-song'-na-ve=Mishongnovi.
Mootaeyuhew=Mataguay.
Mo-o-tzä=Hopi.
Moouchaht=Mooachaht.
Moq, Moqni=Hopi.
Moquaches=Moache.
Moquaes=Mohawk.
Moqua Indians=Hopi.
Moquakues, Moquas, Moquase, Moquauks, Moquawes=Mohawk.
Moquelumne=Moquelumnan Family.
Moquelumnes=Mokelumne.
Moques=Hopi.
Moqui=Hopi, Mohawk, Walpi.
Moquian Pueblos=Hopi.
Moqui concave=Moenkapi.
Moquinas, Moquinos, Moquins, Moquitch, Moquois=Hopi.
Moquopen=Mecopen.
Moquy=Hopi.
Morahicanders=Mahican.
Morahtkans=Mohegan.
Moraigane, Moraiguns, Moraingans=Mahican.
Morai-uh=Murek.
Moranghtaouna=Moraughtacund.
Morargans=Mahican.
Moratico, Moratocks, Moratoks=Moratoc.
Morattico=Moraughtacund.
Morattiggon=Moratiggon.
Moratuck=Moratoc.
Moraughtacud=Moraughtacund.
Morheton=Hahatonwanna.
Morhicans=Mohegan.
Morias=Murek.
Moricetown=Lachalsap.
Mo-ri-ohs=Murek.
Morisons=Monsoni.
Morlal-les=Molala.
Morqui=Hopi.
Morshevoi, Morshewskoje, Morzaivskoi, Morzhevskoe, Morzovoi=Morzhovoi.
Mosack=Masac's Village.
Mosanais, Mosanis, Mosasnabi, Mosasnave=Mishongnovi.
Moscalara=Mescaleros.
Moscama=Mocama.
Moses' Band=Sinkiuse.
Moshamoquett=Massomuck.
Moshanganabi=Mishongnovi.
Moshkos=Foxes, Mascoutens.
Moshome=Navaho.
Moshóngnavé=Mishongnovi.
Mósĭ=Hopi, Kadohadacho.
Mósĭchă=Hopi.
Moskoky=Creeks.
Moskwas=Mooskwasuh.
Mosonique=Mousonee.
Mosopelleas, Mosopolca, Mosopolea=Mosopelea.
Mosquaugsett=Mohawk.
Mosquies=Hopi.
Mosquitans=Mascoutens.
Mosquitos=Mascoutens, Mosquito Indians.
Mossette=Masset.
Mossonganabi, Moszasnavi=Mishongnovi.
Motantees=Oto.

Motarctins=Mascoutens.
Mo-ta-to-sis, Mo-ta'-tōts=Motahtosiks.
Mó'tawâs=Kansa.
Mö'tclath=Muchalat.
Mô'-ts=Hopi.
Motschicahuz=Mochicaui.
Motsónitäniu=Woksihitaniu.
Motssum=Mutsun.
Motútatak=Oto.
Motuticatzi=Mututicachi.
Mouchatha=Mooachaht.
Mougolaches, Mougoulachas=Mugulasha.
Mouguis=Hopi.
Mouhaks=Mohawk.
Mouingoueña=Moingwena.
Mouloubis=Moctobi.
Mountacutt=Montauk.
Mountain=Chipewyan.
Mountaiñ Assinaboins=Tschantoga.
Mountain Comanche=Apache.
Mountaineer=Chipewyan.
Mountaineers=Montagnais, Montagnard, Onondaga.
Mountain Indians=Chipewyan, Etagottine, Koyukukhotana, Montagnais, Tenankutchin, Tutchonekutchin.
Mountain-men=Tenankutchin.
Mountain Sheep-Eaters=Tukuarika.
Mountain Sheep Men=Abbatotine.
Mountain Stoneys, Mountain Stonies=Tschantoga.
Mountaneers, Mountanees=Montagnais.
Mourigan=Mahican.
Mousas=Mouisa.
Mouskouasoaks=Malecite.
Mous-o-neeg=Mousonee.
Mousonis=Monsoni.
Mouuache Utes=Moache.
Mouvill, Mouvilla, Mouville, Movila, Movill=Mobile.
Mowaches=Mooachaht.
Mowacks, Mowakes, Mowaks=Mohawk.
Mówatak=Modoc.
Mo-watch-its, Mowatshat=Mooachaht.
Mowelches=Wimilchi.
Mowhakes, Mowhaks, Mowhakues, Mowhaugs, Mowhauks, Mowhauogs, Mowhawkes, Mowhawks=Mohawk.
Mowheganneak=Mohegan.
Mowhemcho, Mowhememchuges, Mowhemenchouch, Mowhemenchughes, Mowhemincke=Mohemencho.
Mowhoake, Mowhohs=Mohawk.
Mowi'ats=Movwiats.
Mowill=Mobile.
Mo wĭś sĭ yū=Moiseyu.
Mowitchat=Mooachaht.
Mow-mish=Sahmamish.
Mowquakes=Mohawk.
Mow-shai-i-na, Moxainabe, Moxainabi, Moxainavi=Mishongnovi.
Moxi=Hopi.
Moxionavi, Moxonaui, Moxonavi=Mishongnovi.
Moyaoncs, Moyaonees, Moyaones, Moyaons=Moyawance.
Moyave=Mohave.
Moyencopi=Moenkapi.
Moyoones, Moyowahcos, Moyowance=Moyawance.
Mozamleeks=Mozeemlek.
Mozaqui=Matsaki.
Mozeemleck, Mozemleks=Mozeemlek.
Mpaktam=Npiktim.
Mrh=Murek.
Mshawomet=Shawomet.
M'shkudän'nik=Prairie band of Potawatomi.
Muabe=Moenkapi.
Muache=Moache.
Muahuaches, Muares=Moache.
Mû'atokni=Modoc.
Muca=Hopi, Oraibi.
Mu-ca-la-moes=Mescaleros.
Mucclasse=Muklassa.
Muchalaht, Muchlaht=Muchalat.
Muchquauh, Much-quauh=Makwa.
Mû-cĭn'-t'ä ɋŭnnĕ=Coos.
Muckalucs=Klamath.
Muckeleses=Muklassa.
Muckhekanies=Mahican.
Muckkose, Muck-Rose=Maukekose.

Mucoço=Moquoso.
Mucogulgee=Creeks.
Muddy River Indians=Piegan.
Müenkapi=Moenkapi.
Mu-gua=Hopi.
Muhekannew, Muhheakunneuw, Muhheakunnuk, Muhheconnuck=Mahican.
Muhheconnuck=Stockbridge.
Muhheeckanew, Muh-hee-kun-eew, Muhhekaneew, Muhhekaneok=Mahican.
Muhhekaneük=Mohegan.
Muhhekanew=Mahican, Stockbridge.
Muhhekaniew, Muhhekanneuk, Muhhekanok, Muhhekenow, Muhhekunneau, Muhhekunneyuk, Muhkekaneew=Mahican.
Muihibay=Muiva.
Mü-i-nyan wüñ-wü=Muiyawu.
Múkaluk=Klamath.
Mú-ke=Hopi.
Mukeemnes, Mukelemnes=Mokelumne.
Mukickans=Mahican.
Muk-im-dua-win-in-e-wug=Pillagers.
Mukkekaneaw=Mahican.
Mukkudda Ozitunnug=Siksika.
Mukkundwas=Pillagers.
Muk-kwaw=Makwa.
Mukmacks=Micmac.
Muk-me-dua-win-in-e-wug=Pillagers.
Muk-ud-a-shib=Sheshebe.
Mukundua, Muk-un-dua-win-in-e-wing, Muk-un-dua-win-in-e-wug, Mukundwa=Pillagers.
Muk-wah=Makwa.
Mul'-cĭn-tĭk=Mulshintik.
Mulege, Mulexe=Santa Rosalia Mulege.
Muleyes=Mayeye.
Mulknomans=Multnomah.
Mul-lat-te-co=Numaltachi.
Multinoma, Multnomia=Multnomah.
Mumaltachi=Numaltachi.
Mum-i'-o-yiks=Mameoya.
Mumtrahamiut, Mumtrahamut, Mumtrahamute=Mumtrak.
Mumtrekhlagamiut, Mumtrekhlagamute, Mumtrelega=Mumtrelek.
Mûn-an'-nĕ-qu'-ʔûnnĕ=Klikitat.
Munceys=Munsee.
Munchie, Munchies=Hopi.
Muncies, Muncy=Munsee.
Mundaywahkanton, Munday Wawkantons=Mdewakanton.
Mundwa=Mundua.
Mungwas=Iroquois.
Munhegan, Munhicke=Mohegan.
Munina=Ninilchik.
Mün-kqe'-tûn=Kheerghia.
Munnucketucke=Menunkatuc.
Mun-o-min-ik-a-she-ug=Munominikasheenhug.
Munsays=Munsee.
Munsee settlement=Hickorytown.
Mun-see-wuk, Munses, Munsey, Munseyis=Munsee.
Munsey Town=Wapicomekoke.
Munsi, Munsies, Munsy=Munsee.
Muntake, Muntauckett, Muntaukett=Montauk.
Mŭⁿ-tci'-nye=Munchinye.
Mŭⁿ-tci'-ra-tce=Tunanpin.
Mün-ya'u-wu=Muiyawu.
Muoe=Muoc.
Muqui=Hopi.
Muqui concabe=Moenkapi.
Muracumanes=Meracouman.
Muradicos=Shoshoko.
Murderer's kill Indians=Waoranec.
Murdering town=Kuskuski.
Mur-iohs=Murek.
Murphy=Quanusee.
Murthering Town=Kuskuski.
Mur til par=Matilpe.
Muruam=Mariames.
Musaleros=Mescaleros.
Mu-sal-la-kun=Musalakun.
Musaogulge, Muscagee=Creeks.
Muscagoes=Maskegon.
Muscalaroe, Muscaleros, Muscallaros=Mescaleros.
Muscamunge=Mascoming.
Muscogee=Creeks, Muskhogean Family.
Muscogeh, Muscogulges, Muscolgees=Creeks.
Musconogees, Muscononges=Maskegon.
Muscoten, Muscoutans=Mascoutens.

Muscows, Musgogees=Creeks.
Mushá'ch=Moshaich.
Mú-shài-è-nòw-à, Mú-shài-ì-nà, Mushánganevi, Mushangene-vi, Mushangnewy, Mushanguewy, Mushá-ni, Mushaugnevy=Mishongnovi.
Mushkeags, Mushkigos=Maskegon.
Mushkodains, Mush-ko-dains-ug=Mascoutens.
Muskagoes, Mus-ka-go-wuk=Maskegon.
Mus-ka-le-ras, Mus-ka-leros=Mescaleros.
Muskantins=Mascoutens.
Muskeegoo, Muskeg, Muskeggouck=Maskegon.
Muskegoag=Maskegon, Nopeming.
Muskego, Muskegons, Muskegoo, Muskego Ojibways=Maskegon.
Muskegos=Creeks.
Muskeleras, Muskeleros=Mescaleros.
Musketoons=Mascoutens.
Muskhogee, Muskhogies=Muskhogean Family.
Muskigo=Maskegon.
Muskingom, Muskingun, Muskinkum=Muskingum.
Musk-keeg-oes=Maskegon.
Muskogee=Creeks.
Muskoghe=Mascoutens.
Muskogolgees, Muskohge, Muskohogee, Muskokes=Creeks.
Muskoncus=Muscongus.
Mus-koo-gee=Creeks.
Muskotanje=Mascoutens.
Mus-ko-ta-we-ne-wuk=Paskwawininiwug.
Muskoutings, Muskulthe, Muskutáwa=Mascoutens.
Mus-kwä-ka-uk, Muskwake=Foxes.
Musqua=Creeks.
Musquabuck=Mesquawbuck.
Musquacki, Mus-quack-ki-uck=Foxes.
Musquahanos=Musquarro.
Musquakees, Musquakes, Musquakies, Musquakkink=Foxes.
Musquash=Wazhush.
Musquatans, Musquaties=Mascouten.
Musquattamies=Foxes.
Musquattimay=Welegcens.
Musquawkée=Foxes.
Musqueeam, Musqueom=Musqueam
Musquetens=Mascoutens.
Musquiakis=Foxes.
Musquins, Musquint=Oraibi.
Musquitans=Mascoutens.
Musquito=Mesquite.
Musquitoes=Mascoutens, Mosquito Indians.
Musquitons=Mascoutens.
Musscovir=Missouri.
Musshuntucksett=Máushantuxet.
Mussisakies=Missisauga.
Mustac=Mustak.
Müstassins=Mistassin.
Mustees=Metis.
Mustegans=Maskegon.
Musteses=Metis.
Mutawatan=Ute.
Muthelemnes=Mokelumne.
Mutistal=Mutistul.
Mutseen=Mutsun.
Müt-shä=Motsai.
Mûtsíănă-täníu=Kiowa Apache.
Mutsun=Costanoan Family, Moquelumnan Family.
Mutsunes, Mutzun, Mutzunes=Mutsun.
Muutzicat=Muutzizti.
Muwa=Miwok.
Mu-wú=Mugu.
Muχlasalgi=Muklasalgi.
Muχtsuhintan=Apache.
Muχ-tzi'-entăn=Querechos.
Muzaque, Muzaqui=Matsaki.
M-Wai-ai-kai=Wíwekae.
Myacmas, Myacomaps=Makoma.
Myálaname=Pueblos.
Myamicks, Myamis=Miami.
Myanexit=Manexit.
Mynckussar, Myncqueser=Conestoga.
Mynomamies, Mynomanies, Mynonamies=Menominee.
Mystick=Mystic.

Na. For all names beginning with this abbreviation and followed by Sa, Sra, or Señora, see Nuestra.
Na-ai'=Nahane.

Na-aic′=Naaish.
Naa′′iǿine, Naa′ídíne′=Naai.
Na-ai-ik=Naaik.
Naalem=Nehalem.
Na'a'lgạs xā′da-i=Naalgushadai.
Naamhok=Amoskeag, Naumkeag.
Naamkeeks=Amoskeag.
Naamkeke=Naumkeag.
Naamskeket=Namskaket.
Na-ané-ottiné, Na an-nè=Nahane.
Naantucke=Niantic.
Naa-nu-aa-ghu=Nanyaayi.
Naas=Chimmesyan Family.
Naaskaak=Naasumetunne.
Naas River Indians=Niska.
Naass=Chimmesyan Family, Salishan Family.
Naaticokes=Nanticoke.
Naaŭsi=Naasumetunne.
Nababish=Nabobish.
Nabadaches, Nabadachie, Nabádatsu, Nabaducho,
　　Nabaduchoes=Nabedache.
Nabaho, Nabahoes=Navaho.
Nabaidatcho, Na-ba′-i-da′-tŭ=Nabedache.
Nabajó, Nabajoa, Nabajo Apaches, Nabajoe=Na-
　　vaho.
Nabakoa=Nibakoa.
Nabari=Nabiri.
Nabat'hü′tü′ei=Nabatutuei.
Nabato, Nabaydacho=Nabedache.
Nabbehoes=Navaho.
Nabedoches, Nabeidacho, Nabeidatcho, Nabeitdacho,
　　Nabidacho=Nabedache.
Nabijos=Navaho.
Nabiltse=Hupa.
Nabites, Nabiti=Nabiri.
Nabittse=Hupa.
Nabobask, Nabōbic=Nabobish.
Nabojas, Nabojo=Navaho.
Nabojoa=Navojoa.
Nabsquassets=Nobscusset.
Nabuggindebaig=Choctaw, Salish.
Nabu′qak=Nabukak.
Naçacahoz=Natchitoch.
Nacachao, Nacachas=Nacachau.
Nacachez=Nacisi.
Na-cá-ci-kĭn=Hano.
Nacado-cheet=Nacogdoches.
Nacamere=Nacameri.
Nacanes=Detsanayuka.
Nacao=Nacau.
Nacar=Nacori.
Nacassa, Nacassé, Nacatche=Nacisi.
Nacaune=Detsanayuka.
Nacaxes=Nacau.
Na-cé-doc=Natchitoch.
Nacha=Natchez.
Nachee=Natchee, Natchez.
Nachees=Necoes.
Nachés=Natchez.
Naches=Neche.
Nachez=Natchez.
Nachillee=Netchilirmiut.
Nachis=Natchez.
Nachitoches, Nachitock, Nachitooches, Nachitos,
　　Nachittoos, Nachittos=Natchitoch.
Nachodoches=Nacogdoches.
Nacholchavi′gamut=Nakolkavik.
Nacholke, Nachy=Natchez.
Nachtichoukas=Natchitoch.
Nacitos=Natchitoch.
Nacoches=Nacachau.
Nacochtant=Nacotchtank.
Nacocodochy, Nacocqdosez, Nacodissy, Nacod-
　　ocheet=Nacogdoches.
Nacodoches=Nacogdoches, Nuestra Señora de la
　　Guadalupe.
Nacodochitos, Nacogdochet, Nacog-docke=Nacog-
　　doches.
Nacoho=Nacau.
Nacomen=Nicomen.
Naconômes=Detsanayuka.
Nacoochee=Naguchee.
Nacooks=Souhegan.
Nácori Grande=Nacori.
Nacostines=Nacotchtank.
Nacosuras=Nacosari.
Nacota=Assiniboin.
Nacotah=Dakota.
Na-co′-tah O-see-gah=Itscheabine.

Na-co′-ta Mah-to-pâ-nar-to=Watopachnato.
Nacotchtant=Nacotchtank.
Nacpacha=Necpacha.
Nactchitoches, Nactythos=Natchitoch.
Naçume ɹûnnĕ, Náçumĭ=Nasumi.
Nacunes=Detsanayuka.
Nadaco, Nadacoc, Nadacoe=Anadarko.
Nadacogdoches=Nacogdoche.
Nadacogs, Nadaho, Nădä′ko, Nadáku, Nadáku
　　hayánu=Anadarko.
Nadas, Nadassa=Natasi.
Nadatcho=Anadarko, Nabedache.
Nadawessi, Na-da-wessy=Dakota.
Nadchés=Natchez.
Nadchito, Nadchitochés, Nadchitoes=Natchitoch.
Naddouwessioux=Dakota.
Nadeche=Nabedache.
Nadechés=Natchez.
Nadeicha=Kiowa Apache.
Nadesis=Dakota.
Nadezes=Natchez.
Nadiousioux, Nadissioux=Dakota.
Nadíisha-déna′=Kiowa Apache.
Nadocogs=Anadarko.
Nadoeses, Nadoessi, Nadoessians=Dakota.
Nadoessi Mascouteins=Iowa.
Nadoessious, Nadonaisi, Nadonaisioug, Nadonech-
　　iouk, Naonessioux, Nadonessis, Nadooessis
　　=Dakota.
Nadooessis of the Plains=Teton.
Nadouags, Nadouagssioux, Nadouaissious, Nadou-
　　aissioux, Nadouayssioux=Dakota.
Nadouc, Nadouches=Natasi.
Nadoüechio8ec, Nadouechiouec, Nad8echi8ec, Na-
　　douechiouek, Nadoüecious, Nadoüecis, Nad8e8is,
　　Nadouesans, Nadouesciouz, Nadouesiouack, Na-
　　douesiouek, Nadouesioux, Nadouesiouz, Nadoues-
　　sans, Nadouesse=Dakota.
Nad8esseronons sédentaires=Santee.
Nadouessians, Nadouessies=Dakota.
Nadouessi-Maskoutens=Iowa.
Nadouessions, Nadouessiou, Nadoüessioüak, Na-
　　doüessiouek, Nadouessious, Nadouessioux=Da-
　　kota.
Nadouessioux des prairies, Nadouessioux Maskou-
　　tens=Iowa.
Nadouessis, Nadouessons, Nadouessoueronons, Na-
　　doussians, Nadoussieux, Nadoussioux, Nadouwe-
　　sis, Nadovesaves, Nadovessians=Dakota.
Nadowa=Huron.
Nä-do-wagé, Nadowaig, Nadowas=Iroquois.
Nä-do-wa-see-wug, Nadowasis, Nadowassis, Nado-
　　waysioux=Dakota.
Nâdowé=Iroquois.
Nadowesee, Nadowesi, Nadowesioux, Nadowessi,
　　Nadowessiern, Nadowessies, Nado-wessiouex, Na-
　　dowessioux, Nadowesteaus=Dakota.
Na′dshûr′ tü′ei=Nachurituei.
Nadsnessiouck=Dakota.
Nadsonites=Nasoni.
Nadsoos, Nadsous=Nanatsoho.
Na′dû′lĭ′=Natuhli.
Nadussians, Naduwessi, Nadvesiv=Dakota.
Naehiaok=Cree.
Naēkún=Naikun.
Naēkun k′erauä′i=Naikun-kegawai.
Náélim, Na-e′-lûm=Nehalem.
Naembeck, Naemkeck, Naemkeek=Naumkeag.
Naemschatet=Namskaket.
Naê′nasxˑa=Naenshya.
Nae-oche=Naguchee.
Na-fhi-ap, Nafíad, Na-fi-ap, Nafíat, Nafíhuide=
　　Sandia.
Nafoli=Eufaula.
Nagail, Nagailas Indians, Nagailer=Takulli.
Nā′gạs=Nagus.
Nagateux=Naguatex.
Nagçodoche=Nacogdoches.
Na-gè-uk-tor-mè-ut, Naggiuktoρ-meut, Naggœ-ook-
　　tor-mœ-oot=Nageuktormiut.
Naghaikhlavigamute, Naghikhlavigamute=Nakol-
　　kavik.
Nag-mïout=Nak.
Nagodoche, Nagogdoche=Nacogdoches.
Naguadacó, Naguateeres=Natchitoch.
Naguatez=Naguatex.
Năgunābä=Nagonabe.
Nagusi=Nacisi.
Nagu′tsĭ′=Naguchee.
Nahacassi=Nacisi.

Nahajuey=Nahuey.
Nahamcok=Naumkeag.
Nah·ane, Nahanés, Nahanies, Nahanies of the Upper Stikine=Tahltan.
Nahanis=Nahane.
Nahan-'nè, Nahannie=Nahane.
Nahantick, Nahanticut=Niantic.
Nahanχuótăne=Nahankhuotane.
Nahardakha=Nayuharuke.
Nahari=Nabiri.
Naharuke, Nahasuke=Nayuharuke.
Naha-'tdinné=Etagottine.
Nahathaway=Cree.
Nahaunie, Nah-âw'-ny=Nahane.
Nah-bah-tóo-too-ee=Nabatutuei.
Nahchee=Natchez.
Nah-choo-rée-too-ee=Nachurituei.
Nahcoktaws=Nakoahtok.
Nahcotah=Dakota.
Nah-dah-waig=Iroquois.
Nahdawessy=Dakota.
Nahdooways=Iroquois.
Nahdowaseh=Dakota.
Nahdoways=Iroquois.
Na-he-ah-wuk=Sakawithiniwuk.
Naheawak=Cree.
Nahelem=Nehalem.
Naherook=Nayuharuke.
Nahhahwuk, Nahiawah=Cree.
Nahicans, Nahiganiouetch, Nahiganset, Nahigganneucks, Nahiggonset, Nahiggonsick, Nahiggonsycks, Nahigonset, Nahigonsick=Narraganset.
Nahioak=Cree.
Nahiri=Nabiri.
Nahjo=Navaho.
Nah-keoock-to, Nah-keuch-to, Nah-knock-to, Nah-kwoch-to=Nakoaktok.
Nah-ma-bin=Namabin.
Nah-moo-itk=Namoit.
Nahodiche=Nabedache.
Nahopáni=Nakhopani.
Nahordikhe=Nabedache.
Nahotogy=Norwootuc.
Nahoudikhé=Nabedache.
Naḫpahpa=Nakhpakhpa.
Nah-park-lu-lik=Napaklulik.
Nah-poo-itle=Cathlapotle.
Nah-rah-bĕ-gek=Norumbega.
Nah-shah-shai=Hano.
Nahtooessies=Dakota.
Nahto-tin=Nataotin.
Nah-t'singh=Natesa.
Nahucke=Nayuharuke.
Nahuḍiques=Nabedache.
Nahum-keag=Naumkeag.
Nahwahta=Nakoahtok.
Nah-witte, Nahwittis=Nawiti.
Nahy=Natchez.
Nahyssans=Monahassano, Tutelo.
Naiack=Nyack.
Nai-a-gutl=Naagutl.
Nai-a-kook-wie=Nayakaukaue.
Naïantukq-ut=Niantic.
Naicha, Naichas=Neche.
Naichoas=Natchez.
Naieck=Nyack.
N'a'iεk=Naaik.
Naiemkeck=Naumkeag.
Naihantick=Niantic.
Niā'k¡ewanqîX=Niakewankih.
Naikoon=Naikun.
Nā-iku'n qē'gawa-i=Naikun-kegawai.
Na-im-bai, Na-imbe, Na-i-mbi=Nambe.
Naintilic=Niantilik.
Na-isha Apache, Na-i-shañ-dina=Kiowa Apache.
Nais percez=Amikwa.
Nai-tĕ'-zi=Zuñi.
Naitticke=Natick.
Na'izhă'ñ=Lipan.
Naiz Percez=Amikwa.
Najack, Najeck, Najeek=Nyack.
Nakàidine, Nakaídĭne=Nakai.
Na-k' 'āl nas xā' da-i=Nakalnas-hadai.
Nakasas=Nacisi.
Na-ka-si'-nin=Nakasinena.
Na-kas-le-tīn=Nikozliautin.
Na'-kat-qai' ꝗunné'=Nakatkhaitunne.
Nakawawa, Naka-we-wuk=Cree.
Nakazèteo-ten=Nikozliautin.

Na-ḵa-ztli=Nakraztli.
Na-ka-ztli-tenne=Nikozliautin.
Naked Indians=Miami.
Naketoe's, Naketosh, Nakitoches=Natchitoch.
Nā'k·oartok=Nakoaktok.
Nako'dōtch, Nakodō'tche, Nakóhodótse=Nacogdoches.
Nakoktaws=Nakoaktok.
Nak·o'mgyilisila=Nakomgilisala.
Na-ko-nies=Detsanayuka.
Nakonkirhirinous=Nameuilini.
Nakoontloon=Nakuntlun.
Nakoozétenne=Nikozliautin.
Na-ko-poz'-na=Nikapashna.
Nakōshχē'ni=Nakoshkeni.
Nakota=Dakota.
Nakot!ā't=Necotat.
Nakotcho-Kuttchin, Na-kotchρô-ondjig-Kouttchin, Nakotchρo-ondjig-Kuttchin=Nakotchokutchin.
Na-Kotchρô-tschig-Kouttchin=Kutchakutchin.
Nakoukouhirinous=Nakkawinininiwak.
Na-'kra-ztli-'tenne=Nikozliautin.
Na'kraztti=Nakraztli.
Nāks'-at=Mohave.
Naktche=Natchez.
Nakû=Nakankoyo.
Nakúdotche, Nakúhĕdōtch=Nacogdoches.
Ná-kum=Nakankoyo.
Na-kutch-oo-un-jeeh, Nä'-kutch-ū'-ŭn-jūk kū'tchin=Nakotchokutchin.
Na'-kût-qe'=Nakatkhaitunne.
Náꝗût-t'ǫu'-me=Nakwutthume.
Nakwahtoh, Nakwartoq, Nā'k!wax·daεxᵘ, Nā'-kwok-to=Nakoaktok.
Nalal se moch=Natalsemoch.
Na'lani=Comanche.
Na'la'ni=Kiowa.
Nalatchwániak=Norridgewock.
Nalatos=Nulato.
Nalatsenoch=Natalsemoch.
Nā'lekuîtx=Nalekuitk.
Nalo-tin=Nulaantin.
Nal'-te-ne-me' ꝗunnĕ, Nal'tené ꝗunnĕ'=Naltunne-tunne.
Naḷtū'ck-ān=Nahltushkan.
Nalwetog=Norwootuc.
Namaaskeag=Naumkeag.
Namabas=Nanibas.
Namakaus=Navaho.
Namanamin, Namananim=Kathlaminimin.
Namaoskeags=Amoskeag.
Namasakeeset=Mattakeset.
Namascet=Namasket.
Namaschaug=Amoskeag.
Namaschet, Namascheucks=Namasket.
Namaske=Amoskeag.
Namassachusett, Namassakett, Namassekett=Namasket.
Namatakeeset=Mattakeset.
Nă-mă-we'-so-uk=Numawisowagi.
Na̱mäwinini=Nameuilini.
Na̱mäwisōwag̱i=Numawisowagi.
Namba, Nambéhun=Nambe.
Nambeke=Naumkeag.
Nambi=Nambe.
Namcet=Nameaug.
Name'=Nama.
Nameage=Nameaug.
Nameanilieu=Nameuilini.
Nameeag=Nameaug.
Namekeake=Amoskeag.
Nameock, Nameocke, Nameoke=Nameaug.
Name8ilinis=Nameuilini.
Namêug, Nameugg=Nameaug.
Namewilinis=Nameuilini.
Namgauck=Norridgewock.
Nami Te=Nambe.
Namkeake=Amoskeag, Naumkeag.
Namkeg=Naumkeag.
Nammiog=Nameaug.
Namō'itk=Namoit.
Namollos=Yuit.
Namowit=Namoit.
Nampè=Nambe.
Namset=Nauset.
Namskeket=Namskaket.
Nam-tainin=Num.
Namyok=Nameaug.

Nanaā'ri=Nanyaayi.
Nänäbine'naⁿ=Nakasinena.
Nanaçéjiⁿ=Nanashthezhin.
Nanaganset=Narraganset.
Nanaguami=San Rafael.
Nanahas, Nanahaws=Navaho.
Nanaimŭk, Nanainio=Nanaimo.
Nanasłĕ'zin=Nanashthezhin.
Nanatan=Nonotuc.
Nána-tdóa=Nana.
Nâ'nă-tlu'gûñ'=Nanatlugunyi.
Nanatscho=Nanatsoho.
Nâ'nă-tsu'gûñ'=Nanatlugunyi.
Na-na-wá-ni=Nanahuani.
Nancaushy Tine=Nikozliautin.
Nanch-ágetan=Ankakehittan.
Nancokoueten=Nassauaketon.
Nancymond=Nansemond.
Nandacaho, Nandako, Nandakoes, Nandaquees, Nandaquies=Anadarko.
Nandawissees=Dakota.
Nandell's village=Nandell.
Nandoesi, Nandoessies=Dakota.
Nandoquies=Anadarko.
Nand-o-wa-se, Nandowese, Nandowessies=Dakota.
Nandsamunds=Nansemond.
Nandswesseis=Dakota.
Nandtaughtacund=Nantaughtacund.
Nanduye=Nanticoke.
Nanemonds=Nansemond.
Nān-gche-āri=Nanyaayi.
Nanhegans=Mohegan.
Nanheygansett, Nanhigansets, Nanhigganeuck, Nanhigganset, Nanhiggansick, Nanhiggon, Nanhiggonset, Nanhiggonsicks, Nanhiggonticks, Nanhiggs, Nanhigonset, Nanhigonsick, Nanhygansett, Nanhygansit=Narraganset.
Naniabas=Nanibas.
Nanihiggonsicks=Narraganset.
Na'nita=Comanche.
Nanitch=Sanctch.
Nanitomen=Nonantum.
Nānk'hāaⁿsēine'naⁿ=Nakasinena.
Nanne Hamgeh=Abikudshi.
Nanni=Nunni.
Nannogans, Nannogansetts=Narraganset.
Nannortalik=Nanortalik.
Nanoa=Maquinanoa.
Nanohigganeuks, Nanohigganset, Nanohiggunsets=Narraganset.
Nanonĭ'ks-kare'nĭki=Cheyenne.
Nanoos, Nanoose=Snonowas.
Naⁿpaⁿta=Panhkawashtake.
Naⁿpaⁿta énikaci'χa=Nanpantaenikashika.
Naⁿ'paⁿtaqtsi=Panhkawashtake.
Nanrantsoak, Nanrantsouak, Nanrants8ak, Nanrantswacs, Nānrāntswak=Norridgewock.
Nansamond, Nansamund=Nansemond.
Nanscud-dinneh=Naskotin.
Nanseman, Nansemun=Nansemond.
Nansi=Naansi.
Nansoaᴋouatons, Nansouaketon, Nansoüa Kœtons=Nassauaketon.
Nantalee=Natunli.
Nantansoüak=Norridgewock.
Nantaquack, Nantaquaes, Nantaquak=Nanticoke.
Nantautacund=Nantaughtacund.
Naⁿ-tdo'a=Nang.
Nantekokies=Nanticoke.
Nanteqets, Nantequits=Niantic.
Năn-te-wĕ-ki=Seneca.
Nantakokies, Nantico, Nanticock, Nanticoes, Nanticoks, Nanticooks=Nanticoke.
Nantigansick=Narraganset.
Nantihokes, Nantikokies, Nantikokies, Nantiocks, Nantiokes, Nantiquacks, Nantiquaks=Nanticoke.
Nantiyallee=Nantahala.
Nantley Tine=Natliatin.
Nantoue=Mundua.
Náñ-tówa=Nang.
Nantowees, Nantowes=Iroquois.
Năn'χse wáspe=Nanzewaspe.
Nantuckett, Nantucquet=Nantucket.
Nantue=Nanticoke.
Nantukes, Nantukett=Nantucket.
Nantunāgunk=Ontonagon.
Nantycokes=Nanticoke.
Nantygansick, Nantyggansiks=Narraganset.
Na-nua-li-q'mut, Na-nu'-a-lŭk'=Nanualikmut.

Naⁿwuine'naⁿ=Nawunena.
Nanzaticos=Nansattico.
Naodiché, Naonediche=Nabedache.
Naotetains=Nataotin.
Naouadiché, Naoudiché, Naoudishe=Nabedache.
Naouchlágamut=Nauklak.
Naoudoouessis=Dakota.
Naouediche, Naouidiche, Naouydiches, Naovediché=Nabedache.
Napaches=Napochies.
Napachiakáchagamut=Napakiak.
Napahaiagamut, Napahaiagamute, Napahayagamiut, Napahayagamute=Napakiak.
Napaimiut, Napaimute=Napai.
Napaiskágamut=Napaiskak.
Napao=Navaho.
Napaskeagamiut, Napaskiagamute=Napaiskak.
Napetuca=Napetaca.
Napeya, Nâ'pfĕ'ta=Sandia.
Napgitache, Napgitoches=Natchitoch.
Ña-pí-ăp=Sandia.
Napicnoca=Nanipacna.
Na-pi-hah=Sandia.
Napissipi=Nabisippi.
Napituca=Napetaca.
Naponsett=Neponset.
Napossa=Napissa.
Nappa-arktok-towock=Nageuktormiut.
Nappikomack=Nappeckamak.
Napuat=Carrizo.
Napyosa, Napyssas=Napissa.
Na q!ā'las xā'da-i=Nakalas-hadai.
Naqȼeit'a-bajĭ, Naqȼe-it'ajĭ=Nonhdeitazhi.
Naqȼeit'ajĭ=Nonhdeitazhi, Sindeagdhe.
Na q!ē'dᴀts xā'da-i=Nakeduts-hadai.
Na-qi'-tûn tûn'nĕ=Nakhituntunne.
Naqkyina=Lakweip.
Naqoā'ix=Nakoaik.
Nā'q'oaqtôq, Náqoartoq=Nakoaktok.
Naqô'mgilisala, Naqomqilis=Nakomgilisala.
Na qons xā'da-i=Nakons-hadai.
Naqopàni=Nakhopani.
Na'-qo-tcá tûnnĕ=Nakhochatunne.
Naqotodȼa aⁿyadi=Nakhotodhaanyadi.
Naqpaqpa=Nakhpakhpa.
Naquetank=Wechquetank.
Naquitoches=Natchitoch.
Naquizcoza=Nacogdoche.
Naragancetts, Naraganset, Naragansicks, Naraghenses=Narraganset.
Naragooe=Norridgewock.
Narakamig8=Rocameca.
Naráko's=Anadarko.
Naranchouak, Naranchouek, Narangawock, Narangawook=Norridgewock.
Narānkamigdok epitsik arenanbak=Abnaki.
Naransett=Narraganset.
Narantsoak, Narants8ak, Narantsouans, Narants8uk, Narantswouak=Norridgewock.
Nar-a-tah=Comanche.
Naratekons=Naraticon.
Narautsouak, Narauwings=Norridgewock.
Narcotah=Dakota.
Nardichia=Kiowa Apache.
Naregansets=Narraganset.
Narent Chouan, Narentch8an=Norridgewock.
Nar-go'-des-giz'-zen=Akonye.
Narhigansets, Narhiggansetts, Narhiggon=Narraganset.
Napi-an-ottiné=Nahane.
Naricanset=Narraganset.
Naricon=Naraticon.
Naridgewalk, Naridgwalk=Norridgewock.
Narigansets, Narigansette, Nariganssets, Narigenset, Nariggansets, Narighansets=Narihgansets=Narraganset.
Naris=Nariz.
Narises=Narices.
Nar-kock-tau=Nakoaktok.
Nar-ode-só-sin=Natootzuzn.
Narogansetts, Narohigansets=Narraganset.
Narponset=Neponset.
Narrackomagog=Rocameca.
Narrancett, Narragangsett, Narraganses, Narragansett, Narraghansets=Narraganset.
Narrahamegock, Narrakamegock=Rocameca.
Narrangansett=Narraganset.
Narraticongs, Narraticonse, Narratikonck=Naraticon.

Narregansets, Narrhagansitt, Narricanses=Narraganset.
Narridgwalk, Narridgwock=Norridgewock.
Narrigansets, Narrigonset=Narraganset.
Nar-rit-i-congs=Naraticon.
Narrogansets, Narrohigansets, Narrohigganset, Narrohiggenset, Narrohiggin, Narrohiggonsets, Narrowbiggonsets, Narrowgancett, Narrowganneuchs, Narrowganneucks, Narrow Ganset, Narrowganssits, Narrowganzet, Narrow-Higansetts, Narrow Higgansents=Narraganset.
Narsak=Narsuk.
Narsh-tiz-a=Pima, Zuñi.
Nar-wah-ro=Delaware.
Narwootuck=Norwootuc.
Narygansetts=Narraganset.
Na. Sa. (For all references beginning with either of these abbreviations, see *Nuestra Señora*.)
Na s'ā′gas qā′edra=Nasagas-haidagai.
Nas-ah-mah=Nasumi.
Nasahossez=Nacogdoches.
Nasal=Nisal.
Nasamonds=Nansemond.
Nasas=Nazas.
Na s'ā′yas qā′etqa=Nasagas-haidagai.
Nascah, Nascars=Niska.
Nascha=Neche.
Nascopi, Nascopie=Nascapee.
Nascotin, Nascud, Nascud Denee, Nascud Dennies=Naskotin.
Nascupi=Nascapee.
Nª Señora del Socorro=Socorro del Sur.
Nashaue, Nashaway, Nashawog, Nashawogg=Nashua.
Nashédosh, Näshi′tosh=Natchitoch.
Nashkáli dinné=Mescaleros.
Nashkoten=Naskotin.
Nashlĭzhě′=Zuñi.
Nashoba=Nashola.
Nasholah=Nashobah.
Nashoopawaya=Nashwaiya.
Nashope=Nashobah.
Nashouohkamack, Nashouohkamuk=Nashanekammuck.
Nashoway=Nashua.
Nashoweya=Nashwaiya.
Nash tei′se=Pima.
Nashtĕzhě′=Zuñi.
Nashuakemmiuk=Nashanekammuck.
Nashuays, Nashuway, Nashuyas=Nashua.
Na-si-ap=Sandia.
Nasitt=Nauset.
Nasitti=Natchitoch.
Naskantlines=Halaut.
Naskapis, Naskapit=Nascapee.
Naskoaten, Nas-koo-tain=Naskotin.
Naskopie, Naskopis, Naskupis=Nascapee.
Na-sku-tenne=Naskotin.
Nas-o-mah, Nason=Nasumi.
Nasone, Nasony, Nasoris, Nasoui=Nasoni.
Naspapees=Nascapee.
Naspatl, Naspatle, Naspatte=Chaicclesaht.
Nasqá=Niska.
Nasqually=Nisqualli.
Nasquapees, Nasquapicks=Nascapee.
Nasrad-Denee=Naskotin.
Nass=Chimmesyan Family, Niska.
Nassamonds=Nansemond.
Nassaquakes=Nesaquake.
Nassaque=Negusset.
Nassauakuetoun=Nassauaketon.
Nassawach=Nashua.
Nassawaketon=Nassauaketon.
Nasse=Chimmesyan Family.
Nassitoches=Natchitoch.
Nassomtes, Nassoni, Nassonians, Nassonit, Nassonites=Nasoni.
Nas-sou=Nasumi.
Nassoway=Nashua.
Nastic=Nostic.
Nastō′ qē′gawa-i=Nasto-kegawai.
Nas-tû′-kĭn-me′ ʒûnně=Nestucca.
Násuia kwe=Ute.
Nasχa′=Niska.
Na′tăa′=Comanche.
Nataché=Natasi.
Natacooks=Souhegan.

Natafé, Natagees, Natages=Kiowa Apache.
Natahauriz=Nitahauritz.
Nátahě′, Nátahĭ′n=Mescaleros.
Nata-hinde=Nataini.
Natajees, Natajes, Natale=Kiowa Apache.
Na-tal-kuz=Lathakrezla.
Na-ta′ⁿ=Konglo.
Na-ta′-ně=Mescaleros.
Natano=Hupa.
Natao=Adai.
Nataotin Tine=Nataotin.
Na′-ta-rxi′-li-i′ ʒûnně′=Natarghiliitunne.
Nataskouan=Natashquan.
Nátassi=Natasi.
Na-taw-tin=Nataotin.
Na-tcé tûnně=Takelma.
Natche=Natchez.
Natcheek=Nuchek.
Natchees=Natchez.
Natché-Kutchín=Natsitkutchin.
Natches, Natchese=Natchez.
Natchetes=Natchitoch.
Natchets=Natchez.
Natchidosh, Natchiloches, Natchites, Natchitoches, Natchitochis, Natchitotches, Natchittos=Natchitoch.
Natchon=Tulkepaia.
Natchoos=Nanatsoho.
Natchou=Tulkepaia.
Natchû′ri-tü′ei=Nachurituci.
Na′ tci-tce′=Nachiche.
Natcotetains=Ntshaautin.
Na-tcté- ʒûnně=Takelma.
Na-tcûl′-tûn, Na-tcûtçl′ ʒûnně′=Natutshltun.
Na-t′ou ʒûnně′=Natthutunne.
Na-tdo′a=Nang.
Nateekenskoi=Nateekin.
Nate′-l′i′-äte tĕne′=Natarghiliitunne.
Natenéhima, Nat-e-né-hin-a=Dakota.
Nâte-ote-tains=Nataotin.
Nathannas=Nahane.
N a t h e h w y-withinyoowuc, Nathé-wywithin-yu=Cree.
Nathoso, Nathsoos=Nanatsoho.
Naticks=Niantic.
Natics=Natick.
Natieka, Natiekinskoe=Nateekin.
Natik=Natick.
Natilantin=Natliatin.
Natilivik=Netlek.
Natio Euporum, Natio Luporum=Loup.
Nation d′ Atironta=Arendahronons.
Nation de Bois=Missisauga, Ottawa.
Nation de Fourche=Nassauaketon.
Nation de Iroquet=Ononchataronon.
Nation de la Folle Avoine=Menominee.
Nation de la Gruë=Pepicokia.
Nation de la Loutre=Nikikouek.
Nation de la Montagne=Onondaga, Seneca.
Nation de la Roche=Arendahronons.
Nation de l′Isle=Kichesipirini.
Nation de l′Ours=Attignawantan.
Nation de Mer=Winnebago.
Nation de Petum=Tionontati.
Nation des Chats=Erie.
Nation des Loutres=Amikwa.
Nation des Monts pelez=Monts Pelés.
Nation des Ours=Attignawantan.
Nation des Pierres=Avoyelles.
Nation des Porc epics=Kakouchaki.
Nation des Sorciers=Nipissing.
Nation du boeuf=Santee.
Nation du Castor=Amikwa.
Nation du Chat=Erie.
Nation du Chien=Cherokee, Ofogoula.
Nation du Feu=Mascoutens.
Nation du Grand-Rat=Cree.
Nation du petum=Tionontati.
Nation du Porc-Epics=Piekouagami.
Nation du Rocher=Arendahronons.
Nation Neuht=Neutrals.
Nation of Bread=Pascagoula.
Nation of Fire=Mascoutens.
Nation of Stinkers=Winnebago.
Nation of the Beaver=Amikwa.
Nation of the Dog=Ofogoula.
Nation of the great Water=Assiniboin.
Nation of the Marshes=Monsoni.
Nation of the Otter=Nikikouek.

Nation of the Porcupine=Kakouchaki.
Nation of the Rocks=Avoyelles.
Nation of the Snake=Shoshoni.
Nation of the Willows=Havasupai.
Nation of Tobacco=Tiononontati.
Natio perticarum=Conestoga.
Natique=Natick.
Natividad Navajoa=Navojoa.
Natividad Pitiqui=Pitic.
Natle=Natleh.
Natleh-hwo'tenne=Natliatin.
Natlé-tρa-Gottine=Kawchogottine.
Natliäutin, Natlo'tenne=Natliatin.
Natni, Natnihina=Dakota.
Na'-to=Sa.
Natoonata=Nutunutu.
Natorase=Natora.
Natotin Tiné, Na-to-utenne=Nataotin.
Nâ'towéwok=Nottoway.
Ná-to-wo-na=Dakota.
N'atqêlptε'tεnk=Natkelptetenk.
Na-t'qlo' ʒûnné=Natthutunne.
Nat-qwûn'-tcĕ=Natkhwunche.
Natrias=Nutria.
Natságana=Abnaki.
Nat-sah-i=Natesa.
Na'ts-asûñ'tlûñyi=Pine Log.
Natschitos=Natchitoch.
Na-tsik-ku-chin, Nātsik-kûtchin=Natsitkutchin.
Natsilik=Netchilirmiut.
Nat-singh=Natesa.
Natsitoches=Natchitoch.
Natsohocks, Natsohok, Natsohos, Natsoos=Nanatsoho.
Natsshostanno=Natchitoch.
Ná-tsûcl-ta' tûnné'=Natsushltatunne.
Natsytos=Natchitoch.
Nattechez=Natchez.
Nattick=Natick.
Nattsæ-kouttchin=Tukkuthkutchin.
Nattukkog=Souhegan.
Natuági=Iroquois.
Natuck=Natick.
Nátuesse, Natuessuag=Dakota.
Natuikinsk=Nateekin.
Natulaten=Notaloten.
Natykinskoe, Natykinskoje=Nateekin.
Nauajò, Nauajoa=Navaho.
Nau-chee=Natchez.
Naudacho=Anadarko.
Naudawissees, Naudewessioux, Naudoessi=Dakota.
Nau-do-ques=Anadarko.
Naudouescioux, Naudoüessi, Naudouisioux, Naudouisses, Naudouwessies=Dakota.
Naud-o-waig=Iroquois.
Naud-o-wa-se-wug, Naudowasses=Dakota.
Naudoways=Iroquois.
Naudowesies, Naudowesse, Naudowesseeg, Naudowessi, Naudowessies, Naudowissies=Dakota.
Naudtaughtacund=Nantaughtacund.
Naudussi, Nauduwassies=Dakota.
Nauéte=Nawiti.
Naugdoche=Nacogdoches.
Naugvik=Paugwik.
Naumkeak, Naumkeck, Naumkeek, Naumkek, Naumkuk=Naumkeag.
Naumskachett=Namskaket.
Näünë, Na-u-ni=Comanche.
Naurantsoüak, Naurautsoak, Naurautsouak=Norridgewock.
Nausamund=Nansemond.
Nauscud Dennies=Naskotin.
Nauseag=Negusset.
Naushawag=Nashua.
Nausit, Nausites=Nauset.
Na-ussins=Navasink.
Nautaquake=Nanticoke.
Nautaughtacunds=Nantaughtacund.
Nauticokes=Nanticoke.
Nau-tle-a-tin=Natliatin.
Nautowaig, Nautowas, Nautoway=Iroquois.
Nauvogalokhlagamute, Nauwogalokhlagamute = Nanvogaloklagak.
Navadacho=Nabedache.
Navago=Navaho.
Navahóa=Navojoa.
Navahœ, Navajai, Navajhoes, Navajo, Navajoas, Navajoes, Navajoos, Navajoses=Navaho.
Navakwi=Navawi.

Navaoso=Navaho.
Navecinx=Navasink.
Navedacho=Nabedache.
Navejo=Navaho.
Navekwi=Navawi.
Navenacho=Nabedache.
Navesand, Navesinck, Navesinks=Navasink.
Nävĕsú-pai=Havasupai.
Navidacho=Nabedache.
Navidad de Nuestra Señora=Chilili.
Navidgwock=Norridgewock.
Navijoes, Navijos=Navaho.
Navisinks, Navison=Navasink.
Naviti=Nabiri.
Navoasos=Navaho.
Navogame, Navógeri=Nabogame.
Navohoua=Navojoa.
Navóne=Lipan.
Nawadíshe=Nabedache.
Nawas=Nawaas.
Náwathi'nĕha=Nawunena.
Nawdowessie, Nawdowissnees=Dakota.
Na-wee-tee=Nawiti.
Nawes=Nawaas.
Naw-moo-it=Namoit.
Nawsel, Nawsit, Nawsits=Nauset.
Na-wuth-i-ni-han=Nawunena.
Na xawa's xā'da-i=Nahawas-hadai.
Naxnā'xula=Naknahula.
Náχuaíχ=Nakoaik.
Nayack=Nyack.
Nayaerita=Cora.
Nayajuaca=Mayajuaca.
Nayakχálcix=Nayakkhachikh.
Nayantacott, Nayantakick, Nayantakoogs, Nayantaquist, Nayantaquit, Nayantiaquct, Nayanticke, Nayanticks, Nayantiks, Nayantuk, Nayantuquiqt, Nayantuquit=Niantic.
Nayā'qctaowē=Neahkstow.
Nayari, Nayarita, Nayariti=Cora.
Naybé, Naybí=Oraibi.
Nayeck=Nyack.
Nayhantick, Nayhautick=Niantic.
Nayhiggonsiks=Narraganset.
Nayowee=Nayuhi.
Naytasses=Natasi.
Na yū'ans qā'edra, Nā yū'ans qā'etqa=Nayuunshaidagai.
Naywaunaukau-raunuh=Missisauga.
Nazacahoz=Natchitoch.
Nazadachotzi=Nacogdoche.
Nazaganset=Narraganset.
Nazanne=Comanche.
Nazatica=Nussamek.
Nazeteoten=Ntshaautin.
Nazone=Nasoni.
Nazpercies=Nez Percés.
Naz-te'-tci-me' ʒünnĕ=Nestachee.
Naž-tĕ'-zi=Zuñi.
Naz-tük'-e-me' ʒünnĕ=Nestucca.
N'ǫai'tc, N'cal'tc=Nthaich.
N'cék'p't=Nesikeep.
N'cĭckt=Nsisket.
Ndakotahs=Dakota.
Ndakun-dadéhe=Karankawa.
Ndátahĕ'=Mescaleros.
Ndaton8atendi=Potawatomi.
N'day=Apache.
N. D. de Querca=Quarai.
N. D. du Secour=Socorro.
N'De=Apache.
Ndu-tchô-ottinne=Etcheridiegottine.
Ne-ah-coxie=Neacoxy.
Neahkewankih=Neahkowin.
Ne-ah-ko-koi=Nayakaukaue.
Neahkowin=Niakewankih.
Neah Waatch=Neeah.
Neamitch=Dwamish.
Neantick, Neanticot, Neanticutt, Neantucke=Niantic.
Neaquiltough=Lekwiltok.
Neashawanak=Newichawanoc.
Né-a-ya-og'=Chippewa.
Nebadache=Nabedache.
Nebagindibe=Salish.
Nebedache=Nabedache.
Nebicerini=Nipissing.
Nebome=Nevome.
Necait=Niciat.

Necaragee, Necariages=Amikwa.
NE′c′asath=Neshasath.
Necceaquake=Nesaquake.
Neccope=Skopamish.
Necha=Neche.
Nechacohee, Nechacokee=Nechacokee.
Nechao-tin=Ntshaautin.
Nechas=Neche.
Nechecolee=Nechacokee.
Nechegansett=Pennacook.
Nechegansitt=Narraganset.
Nechjilli=Netchilirmiut.
Ne-ci′-he-nen-a=Kiowa.
Necketo, Necketoo=Kutauwa.
Neck Locust=Locust Necktown.
Neckpercie=Nez Percés.
Necomanchee=Nickomin.
Ne-com-ap-oe-lox=Spokan.
Neconbavistes=Nekoubaniste.
Ne-co-ni-ac, Ne Coniacks=Cooniac.
Ne coon=Naikun.
Necosts=Nacotchtank.
Necta=Neshta.
Ne-cul-ta=Lekwiltok.
Ne′dAn xā′da-i=Neden-hadai.
Nedouessaus=Dakota.
Neds-percez=Amikwa, Ottawa.
Neeah=Neah.
Ne-e-ar-gu-ye, Ne-e-ar-guy′-ee=Neagwaih.
Nee-caw-wee-gee=Neecoweegee (band).
Neecelowes, Neecelows=Neeslous.
Needle Hearts=Skitswish.
Ne′ekalɪt, Ne′ekan=Nabukak.
Neekeetoo, Neeketoos=Kutauwa.
Ne-e-no-il-no=Montagnais.
Neepemut=Nipmuc.
Neepercil=Nez Percés.
Neepmucks, Neepnet=Nipmuc.
Ne-er-che-ki-oo, Neerchokioo=Neerchokioon.
Neersaquake=Nesaquake.
Nee-wam-ish=Dwamish.
Negaouich, Negaouichirinouek = Negaouichirini-
　ouek.
Ne-gá-tcĕ=Chippewa.
Negheariages, Neghkareage, Neghkereages=Ami-
　kwa.
Neguadoch=Natchitoch.
Neguascag, Neguaseag, Neguasseag, Neguasset=
　Negusset.
Neguia Dinais=Ntshaautin.
Nehalems, Nehalim, Nehalins=Nehalem.
Nehanes, Nehanies, Nehannees=Nahane.
Nehannes=Ahtena, Nahane.
Nehanni=Nahane.
Nehanticks=Niantic.
Neharontoquoah=Oneida.
Nehaunay=Nahane.
Neháunees=Athtena, Nahane, Tutchonekutchin.
Nehaunees of the Chilkaht River=Takutine.
Ne-haw-re-tah-go-wah=Oneida.
Nehe Marthla's Town=Neamathla.
Ne-heth-a-wa, Nehethe′-wuk, Nehethowuck, Ne-
　hethwa=Cree.
Nehiroirini=Montagnais.
Nehiyaw, Nehiyawok=Cree.
Nehkereages=Amikwa.
Nehogatawonaher=Nehogatawonahs.
Nehum-kek=Naumkeag.
Neideniba, Neidenivas=Naideni.
N′ē′iEk=Naaik.
Ne-î′lĕm=Nehalem.
Neine Katlēne=Ahtena.
Neipnett=Nipmuc.
Neita=Neche.
Neitchilles, Neitschillik=Netchilirmiut.
NEkaā′tʃo=Nukaatko.
NEk·′ā′mEn=Nicomen.
Nekaslay, Nekaslayan, Nekasly=Nikozliautin.
Ne-kat-sap=Nkattsim.
Nekekowannock=Newichawanoc.
Neklakapamuk, Neklakussamuk=Ntlakyapamuk.
Nē-kón hādē=Naikun.
Nekuaiχ=Cathlanahquiah.
Ne-kum′-ke-lis-la=Nakomgilisala.
Nekwun Kūwē=Naikun-kegawai.
Nelcelchumnees=Nelcelchumnee.
Neloubanistes=Nekoubaniste.
Neltū′schk′-ān=Nahltushkan.
Nē′ma=Nemah.

Nē′maʟnōmax=Multnomah.
Nemascut, Nemasket=Namasket.
Nemausin, Néme′nē=Comanche.
Ne′mĕ-re′χka=Tonkawa.
ᵋNE′mgēs=Nimkish.
Ne-mil·-ches=Wimilchi.
Nemiseau=Comanche.
NE′mk·ic=Nimkish.
Nemonsin, Nemosen, Ne-mo-sin, Nemousin=Co-
　manche.
NE′mqic, Némqisch=Nimkish.
Nemshan, Nemshaw, Nemshoos, Nemshous=Nim-
　sewi.
Nénachtach=Tenaktak.
Nenawehks, Nenawewhk, Nena Wewhok=Cree.
Nē′nêlk·′ēnôx=Nenelkyenok.
Neneme′kiwǎgⁱ=Nanamakewuk.
Nenénot=Nascapee.
Nennortalik=Nanortalik.
Nenpersaas=Nez Percés.
NEnstins=Ninstints.
Nentégo=Nanticoke.
Nentegowi, Nentico=Nanticoke.
Nenuswisōwagⁱ=Nanussussouk.
Ne-o-ge-he, Neojehe=Missouri.
Neosho-Senecas=Mingo.
Ne-o-ta-cha=Missouri.
Neotetains=Ntshaautin.
Nepa=Snapa.
Nepahkomuk=Nappeckamak.
Nepeelium=Nespelim.
Nepegigoüit=Nipigiguit.
Nepe′kuten=Napakutak.
Nepercy=Nez Percés.
Neperinks=Nipissing.
Ne persa=Iowa.
Nepesangs, Nepesinks, Nepessins=Nipissing.
Nepgitoches=Natchitoch.
Nepicerinis, Nepicinquis, Nepicirenians, Nepiciri-
　ens, Nepiscenicens, Nepiseriniens, Nepisin, Nepi-
　singuis, Nepisirini, Nepisseniniens, Nepissens,
　Nepisseriens, Nepisseriniens, Nepissings, Nepissin-
　gues, Népissiniens, Nepissiriens, Nepissiriniens=
　Nipissing.
Nepmets, Nep mock, Nepnet=Nipmuc.
Neponcett, Neponsitt=Neponset.
NEqa′umîn=Nikaomin.
Neragonsitt=Narraganset.
Nerdlárin=Navialik.
Neridgewalk, Neridgewok, Neridgiwack, Neridg-
　wock, Neridgwook, Nerigwok=Norridgewock.
Ner-mon-sin-nan-see=Nawunena.
NErôt=Noöt.
Ner Percees=Nez Percés.
Nerridgawock, Nerridgewock=Norridgewock.
Nesaquack, Nesaquak, Nesaquanke=Nesaquake.
Nescope=Skopamish.
Neselitch=Siletz.
Neshamani, Neshaminas, Neshamines, Neshami-
　nies=Neshamini.
Nəsietcah=Nesietsha.
Nes-ī-kip=Nesikeep.
Neskainlith=Halaut.
Neskaupe=Nascapee.
Nesonee=Asahani.
Nespectums, Nes-pee-lum=Nespelim.
Nes Perces=Nez Percés.
Nespilim=Nespelim.
Nespods=Chaicclesaht.
Nəs′qôllək=Neskollek.
Nesquallis, Nesqually=Nisqualli.
Nessawakamighē=Saint Francis.
Nessequack, Nessequauke=Nesaquake.
Nestackee, Nestockies, Nestucalips, Nestucals,
　Nestuces, Nestucka, Nestuckah, Nestuckers,
　Nestuckias=Nestucca.
Nesykep=Nesikeep.
Ne-ta′-ka-ski-tsi-pap′-īks=Nitakoskitsipupiks.
Netches=Natchez.
Netchillik=Netchilik, Netchilirmiut.
Netchillik Eskimo, Netchillirmiut=Netchilirmiut.
Netchiolumi, Netchiolumy=Netlek.
Netcimū′asath=Nechimuasath.
Netelik=Netlek.
Netidlíwi=Netchilirmiut, Netlek.
Netiulūme, Netiulumi, Netlik=Netlek.
Netschilluk Innuit=Netchilirmiut.

Netsepoyé=Siksika.
Netsilley=Etchaottine.
Net-tee-lik=Netchilirmiut.
Nettinat=Nitinat.
Neu-chad-lits, Neuchalits, Neuchallet=Nuchatlitz.
Ne-u-cha-ta=Missouri.
Neuk-sacks=Nooksak.
Neukwers=Nuchwugh.
Ne-u-lub-vig=Neutubvig.
Neum, Ne'-uma, Nē'-ume=Comanche.
Neumkeage=Naumkeag.
Neuses, Neus Indians=Neusiok.
Neustra Senora de Belem=Belen.
Ne-u-tach, Neu-ta-che=Missouri.
Neuter Nation, Neuters, Neutral Nation, Neutre
    Nation=Neutrals.
Neutrias=Nutria.
Neutrios=Neutrals.
Neuusiooc=Neusiok.
Neuwesink=Navasink.
Neu-wit-ties=Nawiti.
Nevachos=Nabedache.
Nevadas=Yupu.
Nevadizoes=Nabedache.
Nevajoes=Navaho.
Neversincks, Neversinghs, Neversink, Nevesin,
    Nevesinck, Nevesings, Nevesinks=Navasink.
Nevichumnes=Newichumni.
Nevisans=Navasink.
Newashe=Nawaas.
Newasol pakawaí=Pakawa.
Newasons=Navasink.
Newatchumne=Newichumni.
Newatees=Nawiti.
Newboyant=Nuvujen.
Newcalenous=Wea.
New Camero Town=Newcomerstown.
Newchawanick=Newichawanoc.
Newchowwe=Nuchawayi.
New civilized band=Farmers' band.
New'-dar-cha=Missouri.
Neweetee, Neweetg=Nawiti.
Newesinghs, Newesink=Navasink.
Newettee=Nawiti.
Newgeawanacke, Newgewanacke=Newichawanoc.
New Gold Harbour Village=Haena.
New Gummi Lurk=Nugumiut.
New-haw-teh-tah-go=Oneida.
New Hernhut=Ny Herrnhut.
Newi-cargut=Nowi.
Newichawanick, Newichawannicke, Newichawan-
    nock, Newichawanocks, Newichewannock, New-
    ichuwenoq, Newichwanicke, Newichwannock,
    Newickawanacks=Newichawanoc.
Newikargut=Nowi.
Newitlies, Newittees, Newitti=Nawiti.
New Keowee=Keowee.
New Kitzilas=Kitzilas.
New Morzhovoi=Morzhovoi.
New-oo'-ah=Kawaiisu.
New River=Chimalakwe.
New River Indians=Comeya.
New Salem=Pequottink.
New Sevilla=Sevilleta.
Newton=Newtown.
New Ulukuk=Igtigalik.
New Westminster=Skaiametl.
New Yamacra=Yamacraw.
New Yarcau, New-Yaucas, New-yau-cau, New Yauco,
    Neu-yau-kau, New York, New Youcka=Niuyaka.
Nexa'dĭ=Nehadi.
Nextucas=Nestucca.
NExumE'ntc=Nickomin.
Neyantick=Niantic.
Neyetsè-kutchi, Neyetse-Kutchin, Neyetse-Kutshi=
    Natsitkutchin.
Neyick=Nyack.
Neyiskat=Nsisket.
Neyūning-Eit-dŭă=Neiuningaitua.
Ne-yu-ta-ca=Missouri.
Nezierces, Nez Percé Flat-Heads=Nez Percés.
Nez Perce Kayuses=Cayuse.
Nez-Perces=Amikwa.
Nez Percez=Amikwa, Nez Percés.
Nezpercies, Nezperees, Nez Perse, Nezpesie, Ne
    Pierces=Nez Percés.
Nez-quales, Nez qually=Nisqualli.
Neztrucca, Neztucca=Nestucca.

Nganudéne=Oldtown.
Nhíkana=Mahican.
N-hla-kapm-uh=Ntlakyapamuk.
N'homi'n=Nehowmean.
N'hothotkō'as=Huthutkawedl.
Nhumeen=Nehowmean.
Niabaha=Kiabaha.
Ni-ack=Naaik.
Ni-a-kow-kow=Nayakaukaue.
Niā'ktiqupeneke=Quelaptoulilt.
Niantaquit, Niantecutt, Nianticut, Niantigs=
    Niantic.
Niantilic=Niantilik.
Niantique, Niantucuts=Niantic.
Niaqonaujang=Niakonaujang.
Niă'rharĭ's-kŭrikiwă'shŭski=Arapaho.
Niā'xaqcē=Neacoxy.
Nibenets=Nipmuc.
Nibissiriniens=Nipissing.
Ni-ca-o-min=Nikaomin.
Nicariages, Nicariagua=Amikwa.
Nicaugna=Nacaugna.
Nic-com-sin=Nkamchin.
Nĭ'chihinĕ'na=Kiowa.
Nichoras=Nixora.
Nĭ'ciatl=Seechelt.
Nickariageys=Amikwa.
Nick-el-palm=Ntlippaem.
Nĭ'-ckitc hĭtclûm=Dakubetede.
Nicoamen, Nicoamin=Nicomen.
Nicochi=Nichochi.
Nicohès=Dooesedoowe.
Nicojack=Nickajack.
Nicola=Nkamchin, Zoht.
Nicola (Upper)=Spahamin.
Nicolai's village=Skolai.
Nicola Mouth=Nkamchin.
Nicomen, Nicomin=Nikaomin.
Nicondiché=Nacaniche.
Nicouta-meens, Nicouta-much=Ntlakyapamuk.
Nicpapa=Hunkpapa.
Nĭ'-ctu-we-ɤûl'-sûc-tûn=Nishtuwekulsushtun.
Nicúdje=Missouri.
Niculuita=Wishram.
Nicute-much=Ntlakyapamuk.
Nie-chum-nes=Wikchamni.
Niĕñtkĕñ=Brotherton.
Niere'rikwats-kûniki=Cheyenne.
Nieskakh-itina=Unalaska.
Nieuesinck, Nieuwesink=Navasink.
Niforas, Nifores=Nixora.
Nig-a-lek=Nigaluk.
Nige-taŋka=Nighetanka.
Nigh tan=Nightasis.
Nigh tasis=Kung.
Nigik=Nikikouek.
Nigiklik-mïout=Nigiklik.
Nigoras=Nixora.
Nigouaouichirinik=Negaouichiriniouek.
Nihaloitih=Tlakluit.
Nihantick=Niantic.
Niĥ'-a-o-ɸiĥ'-a-is=Oohenonpa.
Niharuntaquoa, Nihatiloeñdagowa=Oneida.
Ni-he-ta-te-tup'-i-o=Kalispel.
Ni'ɥka wakan'ɤaχi'=Kdhun.
Nihouhins=Atka.
Nijaos=Nacau.
Nijor, Nijoras, Nijores, Nijotes=Nixora.
Ni'ka=Nekah.
Nikaas=Nestucca.
Ni-kai'-a=Nkya.
Nika-ɖa-ona=Nikapashna.
Nikas=Nestucca.
Nikhak=Nikhkak.
Nikhtagmut=Niktak.
Nikhū-khuin=Atka.
Nikic=Noquet.
Nikicouek=Nikikouek.
Nikie=Noquet.
Nikikoues=Nikikouek.
Nikolai=Skolai.
Nikolaievsky=Nikolaief.
Nikolskoje, Nikolsky=Nikolski.
Nikozliantin=Nikozliautin.
Nikutseg', Nĭkutse'gĭ=Nickajack.
Nĭ'kwăsĭ=Nucassee.
Nikwătse'gĭ=Nickajack.
Nikw'sĭ'=Nucassee.

Nílakskñî má*k*laks=Nilakshi.
Nilaque=Big-island.
Nilco=Anilco.
Niměnim=Comanche.
Nimetapal=Nimitapal.
Nimĕte'ka=Tonkawa.
Nimikh'-hūn'=Atka.
Nimilolo=Nimoyoyo.
Ni-mi-ou-sin=Comanche.
Nimipu=Nez Percés.
Nimkeesh, Nimkis=Nimkish.
Nimollollo=Nimoyoyo.
Nimpkish=Nimkish.
Nim'-shu, Nim-sirs, Nimskews, Nim-sus=Nimsewi.
Ni[n]am=Comanche.
Ninantics=Niantic.
Nindáhe=Tidendaye.
Ninimu=Ninumu.
Ninniwas=Chippewa.
Ninny-pask-ulgees=Ninnipaskulgee.
Ninstance, Ninstence=Ninstints.
Ninstints people=Gunghet-haidagai.
Ninvaug=Ninvok.
Niojoras=Nixora.
Niouetians=Nawiti.
Nipán—Lipan.
Nip-a-qua-ugs=Nesaquake.
Nipeceriniens=Nipissing.
Nipegons=Winnebago.
Nipercineans, Nipicirinien, Nipisierinij=Nipissing.
Nipisiguit=Nipigiguit.
Nipisings, Nipisingues, Nipisinks, Nipisiriniens=Nipissing.
Nipissa=Acolapissa.
Nipissingues, Nipissins, Nipissiriniens, Nipissiriniooek, Nipístingues=Nipissing.
Nipmoog, Nipmucks, Nipmug, Nipmuk, Nipnet, Nipnett=Nipmuc.
Nippegon=Winnebago.
Nippsingues, Nipsang=Nipissing.
Ni-q¢i'-ta[n]-wa[n], Niqdhi ta[n]wa[n]=Nikhdhitanwan.
Nique=Nigas.
Ni'rĭs-hări's-kĭ'riki=Kadohadacho.
Niscotins=Naskotin.
Nishamines=Neshamini.
Nishgar, Nishka=Niska.
Nishmumta=Tsimshian.
Nishrams=Tlakluit.
Nisigas Hāadē=Nasagas-haidagai.
Nisinckqueghacky=Nesaquake.
Nis-ione=Nasoni.
Nis-kah=Niska.
Niskahnuith, Niskainlith=Halaut.
Niskap=Skopamish.
Niskwáli=Nisqualli.
Niskwalli=Nisqualli, Salishan Family.
Nisqualies, Nisqually=Nisqualli.
Nissaquague, Nissaquogue=Nesaquake.
Nis-se-non=Nishinam.
Nissequake, Nissequogue=Nesaquake.
Nissione, Nissohone, Nissoon, Nissoone=Nasoni.
Nistigione=Canastigaone.
Nistoki Ampafa amim=Nestucca.
Nisucap=Nesikeep.
Nitahaurithz=Nitahauritz.
Nitakh=Nitak.
Nitches=Natchez.
Nitcheta=Wichita.
Nitchíhi=Kiowa.
Nitchik Iriniouetchs, Nitchik Iriniouetz, Nitchiks=Nitchequon.
Niten aht=Nitinat.
Ni-the-wuk=Cree.
Nitinaht, Ni'tinath=Nitinat.
Nitlakapamuk=Ntlakyapamuk.
Nitlpam=Ntlippaem.
Ni-to-atz=Lathakrezla.
Nittanat=Nitinat.
Nittauke=Natick.
Nitten-aht, Nittenat, Nittinahts, Nittinat=Nitinat.
Ni-üdje'=Niudzhe.
Niunas=Comanche.
Ni-u'-t'a-tci, Ni-út'ati'=Missouri.
Niuyáχa=Niuyaka.
Nivá-kă'=Chippewa.
Ni'wa¢ĕ=Tsishuwashtake.
Ni'wa[n]-ci'-ke=Niwanshike.
Ni-wittai=Nawiti.
Nixe-tanka=Nighetanka.

Niχlu'idix=Wishram.
Niχwā'xōtsē=Wharhoots.
Ni-yañk'-ta-ke'-te te'-ne=Ataakut.
Nizoræ=Nixora.
Njith=Tukkuthkutchin.
N'kai'ā, Nkaih=Nkya.
Nkaitu'sus=Atchitchiken.
N'-kam-sheen, Nkamtci'n=Nkamchin.
Nkamtci'nEmux=Spences Bridge Band.
Nkatsam, N'ka'tzam=Nkattsim.
N'kau'men=Nikaomin.
N'k·lpan=Ntlippaem.
N'koakoaē'tkō=Nkoeitko.
Nko'atamux=Ntlakyapamuk.
Nkuaikin=Nkóikin.
N'k·u'kapenatc=Nkukapenach.
Nku'kûmamux=Upper Thompson Indians.
Nkumcheen, N'kum'tcīn=Nkamchin.
N-ku-tam-euh, Nkutĕmíχu=Ntlakyapamuk.
NLak·a'pamux, NLak·apamux'ō'ē=Lytton Band.
NLîp'pa'Em=Ntlippaem.
NLki'us=Ntlkius.
Nnéa-gottine=Nigottine.
Nné-la-gottiué, NNè-lla-Gottinè=Nellagottine.
Nni-Gottinè, Nni-ottiné=Nigottine.
Noaches=Yokuts.
Noachis=Nasones.
Noadiche=Nabedache.
No-ah-ha=Towahhah.
Noam-kekhl, Noam-kult=Yukian Family.
Noan'-kakhl=Saia.
Noapeeming=Nopeming.
Noatagamutes=Noatak, Nunatogmiut.
Noatches=Natchez.
Nobows=Sans Arcs.
Nobscussett, Nobsquasitt, Nobsquassit, Nobsqussit=Nobscusset.
Noçà, Noçå¢ine=Notha.
Nocanticks=Niantic.
Nocao=Nacau.
Noccocsee=Naguchee.
Noces=Yanan Family.
Noche=Yokuts.
Noches Colteches=Kawaiisu.
Noches Pagninoas=Bokninuwad.
Nochi=Yokuts.
Nochways=Eskimo.
Nocké=Noquet.
Nocodoch=Nacogdoches.
No-co-me, Noconee, Noconi, Noconi Comanches, Nocoo-nees=Detsanayuka.
Nocotchtanke=Nacotchtank.
No-cum-tzil-e-ta=Nokyuntseleta.
Noddouwessces=Dakota.
Nodehs=Navaho.
Nod-o-waig, Nodoways=Iroquois.
Nod-o-way-se-wug, Nodoweisa, Nodowessies=Dakota.
Nodswaig=Iroquois.
Nodways=Eskimo.
Noghelingamiut=Nogeling.
Noguets=Noquet.
Nohannaies, Nohannie, Nohannís=Nahane.
Nohar-taney=Mandan.
Noh-chamiut=Nochak.
Noń'-ga=Makan.
Noh'hai-è=Etagottine.
Nòh'hané, Noh'hannè, Nohhannies=Nahane.
Nohomeen=Nehowmean.
Nohoolchíntna=Nohulchinta.
No-ho-ro-co=Nayuharuke.
Nohtalohton=Notaloten.
Noh-tin-oah=Hupa.
Noi Mucks=Nuimok.
Noi-Sas=Yanan Family.
Noisy Pawnees=Pitahauerat.
Noi-Yucans=Noyuki.
No-kaig, Nō'ke=Noka.
Nokes, Nokets=Noquet.
Nokhakate, Nok-khakat=Nok.
Noklich=Nuklit.
N'ōkoiē'kEn=Nkoikin.
Nokoni, No-ko-nies=Dtsanayuka.
Nokonmi=Pomo.
Nokrotmiut=Nokrot.
Nokumktesilla=Nakomgilisala.
No-kusé=Nokosalgi.
No-la-si=Wolasi.
Noll-pah-pe Snakes=Walpapi.

Nolongewock=Norridgewock.
Noltanana, Noltnacnah, Nolt-nat-nahs, Noltonatria= Naltunnetunne.
Nolumbeghe, Nolumbeka=Norumbega.
Nōmasénχilis=Nomasenkilis.
Nomee Cults=Yukian Family.
Nomee Lacks, Nome-Lackees=Noamlaki.
Nomenuches=Wiminuche.
Nominies=Onawmanient.
Nommuk=Nummuk.
Non=No.
Nonandom=Nonantum.
Nonapeklowak=Nunapithlugak.
Nonaticks=Nonotuc.
Nonatum=Nonantum.
No-na-um=Nauniem.
Nondacao, Nondaco=Anadarko.
Nondages=Onondaga.
Nondaque=Anadarko.
Nonoaba=Nonoava.
Nonotuck=Nonotuc.
Nontagués, Nontaguez=Onondaga.
Nonto-wă'-kă=Seneca.
Nooatoka Mutes, Nooatoks=Nunatogmiut.
Noobimucks=Normuk.
Noochahlaht, Nooch-aht-aht, Noochahtlaht, Noochalh-laht, Nooch-artl-aht, Noochatlaht=Nuchatlitz.
Noocheek=Nuchek.
No-o-chi, No-o-chi-uh=Ute.
Noocleet=Nuklit.
Noodlook=Nudlung.
Noogsoak=Nugsoak.
Nooherolu=Nayuharuke.
Nooh-lum-mi=Lummi.
Nook-choo=Nukchu.
Nooke=Nuk.
Nooklulmic, Nooklulumu, Nooklummie, Nookluolamic=Lummi.
Nookmete, Nookmut, Nookmute=Nuk.
Nook-sáak, Nook-sac, Nooksack, Nooksáhk=Nooksak.
Nool-ke-o-tin=Nulaantin.
Noo-ná, Noona-agamute=Nuna.
Noonah=Kwahari.
Noonanetum, Noonatomen=Nonantum.
No-ónch=Ute.
Noonitagmioots=Nunatogmiut.
Nooscape=Niskap.
Nooscope=Skopamish.
Noosdalum=Clallam.
Noo-seh-chatl=Nusehtsatl.
Nooselalum, Noostlalums=Clallam.
Noo-taa=Noota.
Noo-tah-ah=Mono.
Nootanana=Naltunnetunne.
Nootapareescar=Noota.
Noothum, Noothummie=Lummi.
Nootka=Skittagetan Family, Chimakuan Family, Chinookan Family, Salishan Family.
Nootka-Columbian=Nootka, Salishan Family.
Nootkahs=Salishan Family.
Nootsak=Nooksak.
Noowoo Mutes=Nuwukmiut.
Noo-we-tee, Noo-we-ti=Nawiti.
Noo-wha-ha=Towahhah.
Noowoo=Nuwuk.
Noowook=Nuvung, Nuwuk.
Noowootsoo=Seamysty.
No Parfleche=Kutaisotsiman.
Nopas=Unharik.
Nopemen d'Achirini, Nopemetus Anineeg, Nopemings, Nopemin of Achirini, Nopemit Azhinneneeg, Nopiming daje inini, Nō'pimingtashineniwag=Nopeming.
Nopnat=Nipmuc.
Nopochinches=Nopthrinthres.
No-pone=Noponne.
No'qEm=Nokem.
Noquai=Noquet.
Noraguas=Nixora.
Norambegue=Norumbega.
Norboss=Norbos.
Nord oüests=Dakota.
Norembega, Norembegua, Norembegue = Norumbega.
Noridgawock, Noridgewalk, Noridgewoc, Noridgewock, Noridgwoag, Noridgwock=Norridgewock.
Norimbegue=Norumbega.

Normok=Normuk.
Norragansett=Narraganset.
Norredgewock=Norridgewock.
Nor-rel-mok=Normuk.
Norridegwock, Norridgawock, Norridgewalk, Norridgowock, Norridgwak, Norridgwocks, Norridgwog, Norridgwogg, Norrigawake, Norrigewack, Norrigewock, Norrigwock, Norrijwok, Norriwook, Norrywok=Norridgewock.
Norteños=Piro.
Northampton Indians=Nonotuc.
North Bend=Kapachichin.
North Dale Indians=Klikitat.
Northern=Chimmesyan, Esquimauan, Koluschan, Skittagetan Family.
Northern Apaches=Jicarilla.
Northern Arapaho=Nakasinena.
Northern Brule=Kheyatawichasha.
Northern Crees=Sakawithiniwuk.
Northerners=Khwakhamaiu, Tahagmiut.
Northern Indians=Etheneldeli.
Northern People=Northern Assiniboin.
Northern Pimas=Pima.
Northern Uttawawa=Cree.
North River=Chuckchuqualk.
North Susseeton=Kahra.
North Thompson=Chuchchuqualk.
North Yanktons=Upper Yanktonai.
Norumbegua, Norumbegue=Norumbega.
Norwidgewalks=Norridgewock.
Norwootuck, Norwottock, Norwuthick=Norwootuc.
Nosa, Noser, Nó-si=Yanan Family.
Nossonis=Nasoni.
Nostlalaim=Clallam.
Notá=Notha.
Nota-á=Ute.
Notádïne'=Notha.
Notaglita=Notaloten.
N'ota-osh, No-taw=Comanche.
Notawasepe, Notawassippi=Natowasepe.
Notch=Ute.
Notchee, Notches=Natchez.
Notchitoches=Natchitoch.
Notinnonchioni=Iroquois.
Notketz=Noquet.
Notley=Natuhli.
No-toan'-ai-ti=Nutunutu.
Notomidoola=Notomidual.
Notonatos, No-ton-no-tos, No-to-no-tos, No-ton-toos, Notoowthas, Notototens=Nutunutu.
Notowegee=Nottoway.
No-tow-too=Nutunutu.
Notre Dame de Betsiamits=Bersiamite.
Notre Dame de Ganentaa=Gannentaha.
Nottawagees=Iroquois, Seneca.
Nottawa Sape, Nottawasippi=Natowasepe.
Nottawayes=Nottoway.
Nottawegas=Iroquois.
Notta-we-sipa=Natowasepe.
Nottawessie=Dakota.
Nottely town=Natuhli.
Notteweges=Iroquois.
Nottoweasses=Dakota.
Nouadiche=Nabedache.
Nouga=Kawchodinne.
Nouïdiche=Nabedache.
Nouitlies=Nawiti.
Noukek=Noquet.
Noulato=Nulato.
Noumpolis=Numpali.
Nouquet=Noquet.
Nousaghauset=Narraganset.
Noutka=Nootka.
Novadiche=Nabedache.
Novajos=Navaho.
Nove Ulukuk=Igtigalik.
Novisans=Navasink.
Novokhtolahamiut=Novoktolak.
Novola=Anouala.
Nov-seh-chatl=Nusehtsatl.
Nowamish=Dwamish.
No-wha-ah=Towahhah.
Nowikakat=Nowi.
Nowodaga=Nowadaga.
Nowonthewog=Norwootuc.
Nowyawger=Niuyaka.
Nō'-xunts'ïtx=Nohuntsitk.
Noya-kakat=Nowi.

Noyatägameuts=Nunatogmiut.
Noyers=Ousagoucoulas.
Noyoee, Noyohee=Nayuhi.
Noyokakat=Nowi.
Noza, Nozes, Nó-zi=Yanan Family.
Nozones=Nasoni.
N'pɛk'tɛm=Npiktim.
N'pochele, N'poch-le, N'pockle=Sanpoil.
Npuitci'n=Npuichin.
Nqa'ia=Nkya.
Nqakin=Nkoikin.
Nqa'ktko=Nkaktko.
Nqau'mîn=Nikaomin.
Nqôe'itko=Nkoeitko.
Nqoï'kîn=Nkoikin.
N'qua-cha-mish=Nukwatsamish.
Nquakin=Nkoikin.
N'Quentl-ma-mish, N'Quentlmaymish=Kwehtlma-
    mish.
Nquipos=Niquipos.
N'quutl-ma-mish=Kwehtlmamish.
Nra del Socorro=Socorro del Sur.
N. S.   See Nuestra Señora.
Nsekaús=Clackama.
Nsɛ'qîp=Nesikeep.
Nsietshawas, Nsietshawus, Nsirtshaus=Tillamook.
Nsqa'qaultɛn=Nskakaulten.
N'squalli=Nisqualli.
Ns tiwat=Clackama.
Ntaauo-tin=Nataotin.
N'täi'kum=Ntekem.
N'tä'-kō=Nkaktko.
Ntcê'kus=Nchekus.
Ntcêqtceqkôkînnk, Ntcê'qtcɛqqôkênk=Nchekchek-
    kokenk.
Ntê'qɛm=Ntekem.
N'tlaka'pamuQ, N-tla-kā-pe-mooh, Ntlakya'pamuQ=
    Ntlakyapamuk.
NtsaLa'tko=Ntstlatko.
Ntshaantin=Ntshaautin.
Ntûl-mûc'-ci=Mulluk.
Nuáka'hn=Missisauga.
Nubenaigooching=Nopeming.
Nücaki=Kisakobi.
Nucasse=Nucassee.
Nucekaá yî=Nushekaayi.
Nuchalkmχ=Nuhalk.
Nuch-a-wan-acks=Newichawanoc.
Nuchawayi=Yaudanchi.
Nüchig'mūt=Nuchek.
Nuchîmases=Newchemass.
Nu-chow-we=Nuchaway.
Nuchusk=Nuchek.
Nuckasee=Nucassee.
Nucleet=Nuklit.
Nuclucayette, Nuclukayette=Nuklukayet.
Nuestra de Señora de los Remedios de Galisteo=
    Galisteo.
Nuestra Señora de Belem, Nuestra Señora de Belen=
    Belen.
N[uestra] S[eñora] de Guadalupe, N. S. de Guad-
    alupe de Alburquerque de los Nacogdoches, N. S.
    de Guadalupe de los Nacodoches, N. S. de Guad-
    alupe de Nacodoches=Nuestra Señora de Guad-
    alupe de los Nacogdoches.
Nuestra Señora de Guadalupe de los Mansos del Paso
    del Norte, Nuestra Señora de Guadalupe del Paso
    del Rio del Norte, Nuestra Señora de Guadalupe
    del Passo=El Paso.
Nuestra Señora de Guadalupe de Pojuaque=Pojoa-
    que.
Nuestra Señora de Guadalupe de Teuricatzi=Teuri-
    cachi.
Nuestra Señora de Guadalupe de Voragios=Taraichi.
Nuestra Señora de Guadalupe de Zum, N[uestra]
    S[eñora] de Guadalupe de Zuni=Zuñi.
Nuestra Señora de Guadelupe del Sur=Nuestra
    Señora de Guadalupe.
N[uestra] S[eñora] de la Assunscion de Zia, N. S.
    de la Asumpscion de Zia=Sia.
Nuestra Señora de la Asuncion Arizpe=Arizpe.
Nuestra Señora de la Belen=Belen.
Nuestra Señora de la Soledad=Soledad.
Nuestra Señora de Loreto de Voragios=Loreto.
Nuestra Señora de los Angeas de Pecos, N[uestra]
    S[eñora] de los Angeles de Pecos, Nuestra Señora
    de los Angeles de Porciúncula, N. S. de los An-
    geles de Tecos=Pecos.

Nuestra Señora de los Dolores=Dolores.
Nuestra Señora de los Dolores del Saric=Saric.
Nuestra Señora de los Dolores de Sandia=Sandia.
Nuestra Señora de los Remedios=Remedios.
Nuestra Señora de los Remedios de Beramitzi=Bana-
    mitzi.
Nuestra Señora del Pilar de Nacogdoches=Nacog-
    doches.
Nuestra Señora del Socorro=Socorro, Socorro del
    Sur.
Nuestra Señora de Pecos, Nuestra Señora de Porti-
    uncula de los Angeles de Pecos=Pecos.
Nuestra Señora Guadalupe de Zuñi=Zuñi.
Nuestra Sonora de Monserrate=Nonoava.
Nuestro Padre San Francisco de los Tejas=San Fran-
    cisco de los Tejas (or Neches).
Nueua Granada, Nueva Granada=Hawikuh.
Nueva Sevilla=Sevilleta.
Nuey-kech-emk=Niueuomokai.
Nugh-Kwetle-babish=Kwehtlmamish.
Nugh-lemmy=Lummi.
Nugh-sahk=Nooksak.
Nugumeute=Nugumiut.
Nugumut=Nuwukmiut.
Nuhiyup=Tulalip.
Nūh-lum-mi=Lummi.
Nū'ik'=Nuiku.
Nu'ixtac=Niukhtash.
Nuk'ā'aqmats=Nukaakmats.
Nukaā'tqo=Nukaatko.
Nukamok=Unisak.
Nukan=Nuokan.
Nŭkătse'gĭ=Nickajack.
Nukeza=Nucassee.
Nukfalalgi, Núkfila=Timucua.
Nū'kHits=Nukits.
Nūkh-lésh=Lummi.
Núk-hótsi=Timucua.
Nu-klac-i-yat, Nuklakyet=Nuklukayet.
Nukluag-mïout=Nukluak.
Nukluhyet, Nuklukáhyet, Nuklukaiet, Nuklukye-
    to=Nuklukayet.
Nūksahk=Nooksak.
Nnktúsĕm=Dakota.
Nu-kuints', Nu-kwints=Unkapanukuints.
Nuk wul tuh=Nakoaktok.
Nulaantins=Nulaautin.
Nulahtuk=Nulatok.
Nulakhtolagamute=Nuloktolok.
Nūlā'to-kho-tān'ā=Nulato.
NuLLē'îx=Nutltleik.
Nult-nort-nas, Nul-to-nat-na, Nûltŏnät'-tĕne=Nal-
    tunnetunne.
Nulukhtulogumut=Nuloktolok.
Nüma=Comanche, Nama, Paiute.
Nŭmä=Nama.
Nŭmäbĭn, Numa-bin=Namabin.
Nu-mah-ka'-kee=Sipushkanumanke.
Numakaki, Numakshi=Mandan.
Nu-mal-tachee=Numaltachi.
Numanas=Pueblo de los Jumanos.
Numangkake=Mandan.
Num-a quag-um=Namakagon.
Nŭmäwĭsowŭg¹=Namawesouk, Namasissouk.
Num-ee-muss=Hupa.
Numepo, Numepoes, Nu-me-poos=Nez Percés.
Númi=Nambe.
Numipu=Nez Percés.
Num-kēs=Nimkish.
Numleki=Noamlaki.
Nummastaquyt=Namasket.
Nummok=Nummuk.
Numpang=Nunnepoag.
Nŭm-taínin=Num.
Nunachanaghamiut, Nŭnachăra gămut, Nunacho-
    gumut=Nunochok.
Nunaikagumute=Nunaikak.
Nunakàchwak=Karluk.
Nunakhtagamute=Nunaktak.
Nunalik=Nuniliak.
Nuna-mish=Dwamish.
Nunatagmut, Nuna-tangmë-un, Nunatañmiun=
    Nunatogmiut.
Nunatochsoak=Nunatarsuak.
Nūnätŏ'gmūt, Nuna-tuńg-mëün=Nunatogmiut.
Nun-da-wä'-o-no', Nundawaronoh=Seneca.
Nuńdawäs=Nundawao.

Nûn'dăwe'gi=Seneca.
Nûñ'dăye'lĭ=Nantahala.
Nundowága=Seneca.
Nŭ'nEmasEqâlis=Nunemasekalis.
Nunivagmut, Nunivagmute, Nunivak people=Nunivagmiut.
Nunjagmjut, Nunochogamute=Nunamiut.
Nunseys=Munsee.
Nuntaly=Nuntaneuck.
Nuntewa, Nuntewes=Iroquois.
Nuntialla=Nantahala.
Nûñyû'-gûñwani'ski=Talking Rock.
Nuo Yaucau=Niuyaka.
Nuptadi=Ruptari.
Nuqā'axmats=Nukaakmats.
Nuqa'lkн, Nuqa'lkmн=Nuhalk.
Nuqe=Nukhe.
Nuqiage=Nuquiage.
Nŭqtú=Dakota.
Nuqueño=Nootka.
Nu'-q'wût-tcu'-tûn=Nukhwuchutun.
Nures=Nuri.
Nurhantsuaks=Norridgewock.
Nŭschĕ-kǟri=Nushekaayi.
Nuschkē-tān=Wushketan.
Nusconcus, Nuscoucus=Muscongus.
Nusdalum=Clallam.
Nushagagmut=Nushagagmiut.
Nushaltχágakni=Nushaltkagakni.
Nushegagmut=Nushagagmiut.
Nushegak=Nushagak.
Nushergagmutes=Nushagagmiut.
Nusiok=Neusiok.
Nusk·'E'lstEmн=Nuskelst.
Nu-sklaim, Nūs-klai'-yūm=Clallam.
Nuskoncus, Nuskoucus=Muscongus.
Nū-so-lupsh=Cowlitz, Kwaiailk.
Nūsq!E'lst=Nuskelst.
Nüss-kā=Niska.
Nustoc=Neusiok.
Nusxē'q!=Nuskek.
Nutá=Yaudanchi.
Nutaa=Mono.
Nu-tca-'tenne=Ntshaautin.
Nutcā'tlath=Nuchatlitz.
Nŭt-chu'=Nuchu.
Nu'-tcu-ma'-tûn ɟûn'nĕ=Kthutetmetseetuttun, Nuchumatuntunne.
Nŭt-él=Sotstl.
Nŭt-ha=Mono.
Nutнē'iнtskōnē=Tkeiktskune.
Nuthesum=Mutsun.
Nutķa=Nootka.
Nū'tl'E'l=Sotstl.
Nŭtltlē'iq=Nutltleik.
Nutonetoos=Nutunutu.
Nuts=Ute.
Nutschek=Nuchek.
Nutuntu=Nutunutu.
Nuvuk, Nuvukdjuaqdjuq=Nuvung.
Núweta=Mandan.
Nuwichawanick=Newichawanoc.
Nu-witti=Nawiti.
Núwúkmùt, Nuwung, Nuwŭñmiun=Nuwukmiut.
Nuxa'lk·!=Nuhalk.
Nuxe=Nukhe.
Nuχitsōmχ=Nukitsomk.
Nûyu'hĭ=Nayuhi.
Nvrvmbega=Norumbega.
N-wa-ih=Nkaih.
Nwă''-ka=Ontwaganha.
N'Wamish=Dwamish.
Nwasabé=Navaho.
Nx'ōmī'n=Nehowmean.
Nχtúsum=Dakota.
Nyakai=Nkya.
Nyantecets, Nyantecutt, Nyanticke=Niantic.
Nyavapai, 'Nyavi Pais=Yavapai.
Nyeck=Nyack.
Nygykligmjut=Nigiklik.
Nyhantick=Niantic.
Nyiskat=Nsisket.
Nypaguɗy=Nipaguay.
Nypissings, Nypsins=Nipissing.
Nyu'-să-ru'-kän=Nursoorooka.
Nzis-kat, Nzyshat=Nsisket.

Oabano=Ouabano.
Oaboponoma=Hoabonoma.
Oacpuaguigua=Saric.
Oadauwaus=Ottawa.
Oajuenches=Cajuenche.
Oaka Loosa=Okalusa.
Oakanagans=Okinagan.
Oakbusky=Oakfuskee.
Oakchog, Oakchoie=Okchayi.
Oakchoieooche=Okchayudshi.
Oakchoys=Okchayi.
Oakfuskies, Oakfusky=Oakfuskee.
Oakgees=Okchayi.
Oakinackene, Oakinagan=Okinagan.
Oakiuskees=Oakfuskee.
Oakjoys=Okchayi.
Oaklafalaya=Oklafalaya
Oak-li-sarcy=Uktahasasi.
Oakmulge, Oakmulgee old fields, Oakmulgee old towns, Oakmulge fields, Oakmulges, Oakmulgis, Oakmulgo=Ocmulgee.
Oak-pa-pas=Hunkpapa.
Oakpuskee=Oakfuskee.
Oak-tar-sar-say, Oak Tarsarsey=Uktahasasi.
Oaktashippas=Octashepas.
Oaktaw sarseg=Uktahasasi.
Oaktchoie=Okchayi.
Oanancock=Onancock.
Oanoska=Ohanhanska.
O'aquima=Kiakima.
Oate-lash-schute=Ootlashoot.
Oathkaqua=Onathaqua.
Oâ-tish-tye=San Felipe.
Oat-la-shoot, Oat-lash-shoots, Oat-lash-shute=Ootlashoot.
Oatsees=Yazoo.
Obekaws=Abihka.
Ŏ-bén-aki, Obenaquiouoit=Abnaki.
Obidgewong=Chippewa.
Obika=Abihka.
Obiki=Walpi.
Obinacks=Abnaki.
Objibways=Chippewa.
Obunegos=Abnaki.
O-bwah-nug=Dakota.
Oçages=Osage.
Ocahumpky=Okehumpkee.
Ocä'ḳamigāwininiwạg=Oschekkamegawenenewak.
Ocala, Ocale, Ocali=Olagale.
Ocameches=Occaneechi.
Ocanes=Lipan.
Ocansa, Ocapa=Quapaw.
Occaanechy=Occaneechi.
Occahanock=Accohanoc.
Occaneches, Occaneeches=Occaneechi.
Occha, Occhoy=Okchayi.
Occone=Oconee.
Occoneachey=Occaneechi.
Occouys=Oconee.
Occuca=Ocuca.
Oćeti Sakowiŋ=Dakota.
Oc-fus-coo-che=Oakfuskudshi.
Oc-fus-kee=Oakfuskee.
Ocha=Hoko.
Ochahannanke=Accohanoc.
Ochanahoen=Ocanahowan.
Ochangras=Winnebago.
Ochasteguin, Ochatagin, Ochataiguin, Ochategin, Ochateguin, Ochatequins=Huron.
O-ché=Odshisalgi.
O-che-au-po-fau, Ochebofa=Talasse.
Ochecames, Ochecamnes=Yachikamni.
Ochecholes=Ochechote.
Ocheeaupofau=Talasse.
Ochees=Yuchi.
Ocheeses=Ocheses.
Ochekamnes=Yachikamni.
Ochekhamni=Okechumne.
Ochelaga=Hochelaga.
Ochelay=Hochelayi.
Ochenang=Chenango, Shenango.
Ochente Shakoan, Ochente Shakons=Dakota, Seven Council Fires.
Ocheobofau=Talasse.
Ocheo's band=Tuziyammos.
Ŏ'chēpě'wạg=Chippewa.
Cchesees=Lower Creeks, Ocheese.
Ochesos=Ocheese.

Ochessigiriniooek, Ochessigiriniouek, Ochestgooetch, Ochestgouetch, Ochestigouecks=Oukesestigouek.
Ocheti Shaowni=Dakota.
O-che-ub-e-fau, Ocheubofau=Talasse.
Ochi=San Juan.
Ochiakenens, Ochiatagonga=Shawnee.
Ochiatenens=Wea.
Ochie'tari-ronnon=Cherokee.
Ochile=Axille.
Ochinakein=Okinagan.
Ochineeches=Occaneechi.
O-ching-i-ta=Uchiyingich.
Ochipawa, Ochipewa, Ochipoy, Ochippewais = Chippewa.
Ochivitas=Wichita.
Ochlewahaw=Oclawaha.
Ocho=Hoko.
Ochocumnes=Yachikamni.
Ochquaqua, Ochtaghquanawicroones, Ochtayhquanawicroons=Oquaga.
O-chuce-ulga=Ochisialgi.
O-chunga-raw, Ochunkgraw, O-chunk-o-raw=Winnebago.
Ochus=Achusi.
Oçita=Ucita.
Ocka=Okchayi.
Ock-co-witth=Wishosk.
Ockfuskee=Oakfuskee.
Ockha, Ockhoys=Okchayi.
Ockinagees=Occaneechi.
Ocki Pah-Utes, Ocki-Pi-Utes=Agaihtikara.
Ockiwere=Chiwere.
Ockmulgo=Ocmulgee.
Oc-la-wa-haw, Oc-le-wau-hau-thluc-co=Oclawaha.
Ocoina=Bocoyna.
Ocon, Oconas, Oconery's, Ocones, Oconis, Oconnee= Oconee.
Ocosaus=Arkokisa.
Ocpack=Okpaak.
Ocquagas=Oquaga.
Ocsachees=Osotchi.
Octaaros=Winnebago.
Octageron=Ostogeron.
Octagouche=Restigouche.
Octagros=Winnebago.
Octata=Oto.
Octchagras=Winnebago.
Octguanes=Yuma.
Octi=Agaihtikara.
Octibea=Yazoo.
Octiyokny=Okitiyakni.
Octoctatas=Oto.
Octogymists=Ottawa.
Octolacto, Octolatas=Oto.
Octonagon Band=Ontonagon.
Octootatas, Octotales, Octotas, Octotata, Octotota= Oto.
Ocumlgi=Ocmulgee.
O-cun-cha-ta=Kanchati.
Ocunnolufte=Oconaluftee.
Ocus=Achusi.
Odagami, Odagumaig=Foxes.
Odahwah, Odahwaug=Ottawa.
Odakeo=Odukeo's band.
Ódami=Tepehuane.
Odawas=Ottawa.
Odchipewa=Chippewa.
O-de-eilah, Ode-i-lah=Kikatsik.
Odgavigamut=Ugovik.
Odgiboweke=Chippewa.
Odiak=Eyak.
O-dish-guag-um-eeg, Odishkwagami, Odishkwa-Gamig, O-dish-quag-um-eeg, O-dish-quag-um-ees, Odishquahgumme=Nipissing.
Odistastagheks=Mascoutens.
Odjibewais, Od-jib-wäg, Odjibwas, Odjibwe, Odjibwek= Chippewa.
Odji'wägĕn'=Gewauga.
Odshi-apófa=Talasse.
Odsinachies=Osotchi.
O-dug-am-eeg, Odugamies, O-dug-aumeeg=Foxes.
O'ēalitq, Ōealitx=Oealitk.
Oekfusaet=Oakfuskee.
Oē'Lîtz=Oetlitk.
Œnné=Eskimo.
Oenock=Eno.
Oenrio=Ouenrio.
Oenronronnons=Wenrohronon
Oetbatons=Wahpeton.

Oē'tlitq=Oetlitk.
Œtsœnhwotenne=Natliatin.
O-e'-tun'-i-o=Crows.
Oeyendehit=Neodakheat.
Ofagoulas, Ofegaulas, Offagoulas, Offegoulas, Offogoula, Ofugulas=Ofogoula.
Ogablallas=Oglala.
Ogährit-tis=Miskut.
Ogalalab Yokpahs, Ogalala Dacotas, O-ga-la'-las, Ogalallahs, Ogalallas, O'Galla, Ogallah, Ogallala, Ogallalahs, Ogallalla, Ogallallah, Ogallallas, Ogallallees=Oglala.
O-ga-pa=Quapaw.
Oga P'Hoge, Og-a-p'o-ge=Kuapooge.
Ogavimamute=Ugovik.
O-ge-chee, Ogechi, Ogeeche=Ogeechee.
Ogeelala=Oglala.
Ogeetches=Ogeechee.
Ogehage=Conestoga.
Ogellahs, Ogellalah, Ogellalas=Oglala.
Oghguagees, Oghguago, Oghkawaga, Oghkwagas, Oghquaga, Oghquago, Oghquajas, Oghquuges= Oquaga.
Oghrekyonny=Ohrekionni.
Ogibois=Chippewa.
Ogillallah=Oglala.
Og-la'-la=Oglalaichichagha.
Oglala-ħća=Oglala.
Oglala-ićićaga, Oglala-itc'itcaxa=Oglalaichichagha
Oglala-qtca=Iteshicha.
Oglallah=Oglala.
Oglemut, Oglemutes=Aglemiut.
Ognitoa=Oquitoa.
Ogoh pæ=Quapaw.
Ogoize=Bannock.
Ogolawla=Oglala.
Ogoleegees=Kailaidshi.
Ogolegees=Hogologes.
Ogowinagak, Ogowinanagak=Kvinkak.
Ogsadago=Teatonaloga.
Oguahpah, O-guah-pas, Oguapas=Quapaw.
Ogue Loussas=Opelousa.
O'Gullalas=Oglala.
Og'ŭlmūt=Aglemiut.
Ohah-hans-hah, O-hah-kas-ka-toh-y-an-te = Ohanhanska.
Ohamiel, Ohamille=Ohamil.
Ohanapa=Oohenonpa.
Ohanock=Ohanoak.
Ohantonwanna=Yanktonai.
Ohavas=Onavas.
Ohdada=Oglala.
O-he-nompa=Ohenonpa.
Ohenonpa Dakotas, Ohenonpas=Oohenonpa.
Ohete-yoe-on-noe=Okitiyakni.
Ohey-aht=Oiaht.
Ohguago=Oquaga.
Oh-hagamiut=Oknagak.
Ohhisheu=Owaiski.
Ohiat=Oiaht.
Ohikkasaw=Chickasaw.
Ohke=San Juan.
Ōhk to ŭnna=Oqtogona.
Ohlones=Olhon.
Oh-nah=Ona.
Ohnowalagantles=Onoalagona, Schenectady.
Ohó-hómo=Dakota.
Ohonoagesu, Ohonoguaga, Ohonoquaugo=Oquaga.
Ohotoma=Pima.
Oh-pah=Opa.
Ohquaga=Oquaga.
Ohquage=Osguage.
Ohque=San Juan.
Ohsarakas=Saratoga.
Ohsháhch=Oshach.
Ohuaqui, Ohuqui=Pojoaque.
Ohyaht, Ohyat=Oiaht.
Oiatenon, Oiatinon=Wea.
Oiatuch=Oiaht.
Oi-cle-la=Waitlas.
Oigoien=Goiogouen.
Oil Spring=Tecarnohs.
Oiogoen=Goiogouen.
Oïogoen, Oiogoenhronnons=Cayuga.
Oiogoien, Oiogouan=Goiogouen.
Oïogouan, Oiogouanronnon=Cayuga.
Oiogouen=Cayuga, Goiogouen.
Oïogouenronnon=Cayuga.
Oiog8en=Goiogouen.

Oiogouin=Cayuga, Goiogouen.
Oioguen, Oiogwen=Goiogouen.
Oiougovenes=Cayuga, Goiogouen.
Oi-ra-uash=Querechos.
Oitapars=Oapars.
Oiudachenaton=Oughetgeodatons.
Oiyotl=Ayotl.
Oiyurpe=Oyukhpe.
Ojachtanichroenee=Wea.
Ojadagochroehne=Catawba.
Ojadagochroene=Cherokee.
O-jang-ge P'ho-quing-ge=Shipapulima.
Ojatinons=Wea.
O-je-bway, Ojeebois, Ojibaway, Ojibbewaig, Ojibbeways, Ojibboai, Ojibeways, Ojibois, Ojibua, Ojibwa, O-jib-wage, Ojibwaig, O-jib-wa-rek, Ojibwas, Ojibways, Ojibway-ugs, Ojibwe=Chippewa.
Oji Caliente=Aguas Calientes, Warm Spring Apache.
Oj-ke=San Juan.
Ojo Benado=Pitchaya.
Ojo Caliente=Aguas Calientes, Hawikuh, Kiapkwainakwin.
Ojo Caliente Apaches=Warm Spring Apache.
Ojo de Pescado=Pescado.
Ojogoüen=Goiogouen.
Ojongoveres=Cayuga.
Ojo Percado, Ojo Pescado, Ojo Pesoado=Pescado.
O-jo-que=San Ildefonso.
Ojos Calientes=Kiapkwainakwin, Ojo Caliente.
Oj-po-re-ge=Abechiu.
Oj-qué=San Juan.
Ojuaque=Pojoaque.
Oka alhtakala, Oka-altakkala, Oka-attakkala=Oka-altakala.
Okadada=Oglala.
O kaġa-wićaśa=Okaghawichasha.
Okähno=Honsading.
Oka Hoola, Oka Hoolah=Okahullo.
Okahumky=Okehumpkee.
Oka Loosa=Okalusa.
Oka Lopassa=Oka Kapassa.
Okames, Okams=Kansa.
Okanagam=Okinagan.
Okanagan=Nkamaplix, Okinagan.
Okanagon, O-kan-ă-kan, Okanakanes, Okanaken=Okinagan.
Okanandans, O-kan-dan-das=Oglala.
O'Kanies-Kanies=Okinagan.
Okanis=Kansa.
Oka-no=Honsading.
Oka talaia, Okatallia=Okatalaya.
Oka-tiokinans=Okitiyakni.
Okatlituk=Oetlitk.
Okaxa-witcaca=Okaghawichasha.
Ok-chai, Okchoys=Okchayi.
Ok-chŭn'wä=Oktchunualgi.
Okdada=Oglala.
Oke-choy-atte=Alibamu, Okchayi.
Okecoussa=Okalusa.
Okee-oġ-mūt, Okeeogmutes=Okiogmiut.
Oke-ho=Hoko.
Oke Lousa, Oké loussa=Okalusa.
Okenaganes, Okenakanes=Okinagan.
Okenechee=Occaneechi.
Okeno=Hoko.
Oke-noke, Okenope=Honsading.
Okesez=Ocheses.
Oketayocenne, Ókete Yocanne, O-ke-teyoc-en-ne=Okitiyakni.
Okfuski=Oakfuskee.
Okfuskū'dshi=Oakfuskudshi.
Okhaganak=Okiogmiut.
Okha Hullo=Okahullo.
Okhata Talaia=Okhatatalaya.
Okhogamute=Oknagak.
Okiakanes, Okinaganes, Okinahane, Okinakain, Okinakan, Okinagane, Okinā'k·ēn, Okinekane, Okin-e-Kanes, O-kin-i-kaines, Okinokans, O-ki-wah-kine=Okinagan.
Ok-kak=Okak.
Okkiadliving=Ukiadliving.
Okkiosorbik=Okiosorbik.
Okkokonimesit=Okommakamesit.
Okkowish=Agawesh.
Oklahaneli, Okla-humali=Oklahannali.
Oklevuaha, Oklewaha=Oclawaha.
Okmulge, Okmulgee, Okmulgi=Ocmulgee.
Oknagamut, Oknagamute=Oknagak.

Oknaka=Oglala.
Oknanagans=Okinagan.
Oknavigamut=Uknavik.
Okoelaihoeláhta=Watakihulata.
Okohoys=Okohayi.
O'kok=Okak.
Okonagan, Okonagon=Okinagan.
Okonee=Oconee.
Okonegan=Okinagan.
Okónhomessit=Okommakamesit.
Okóni=Oconee.
Okoro=Arikara.
Okótsali=Ocota.
Okpiktalik, Okpiktolik=Opiktulik.
Oksak talaya=Osuktalaya.
Okshee=Klamath.
Oktchayi=Okchayi.
Oktchayū'dshi=Okchayudshi.
Oktibbeha=Yazoo.
Okuaho=Toryohne.
Okuvagamute=Okivogmiut.
Oku-wa'-ri=Sia.
Okuwa-tdóa, Ókuwa-tówa=Okuwa.
Okwhûske=Oakfuskee.
Olacatano=Olagatano.
Olacnayake=Oclackonayahe.
O'-lah-ment'-ko=Olamentke.
Olalla=Oraibi.
Olanches=Yaudanchi.
Olashes=Ola.
Olasse=Atasi.
Olata Ouae Utina=Utina.
Olchone=Olhon.
Old Castle=Canadasaga.
Old Chilili=Chilili.
Old Colony Indians=Mashpee.
Old Cusetaw=Kasihta.
Old Estatoee=Estatoee.
Old Field=Gatagetegauning.
Old Fort Hamilton=Nunapithlugak.
Old Gauché's gens=Watopachnato.
Old Harbor=Nunamiut.
Old Indian Village=White-eyes Town.
Old Matacombe=Guarungunve.
Old Merrawnaytown=Chatoksofke.
Oldnass=Niska.
Old Oneida=Ganowarohare.
Old Osonee=Osonee.
Old Peach Orchard Town=Pakan-Tallahassee.
Old Shawness Village=Shawneetown.
Old Showonese Town=Chartierstown.
Old Suwanee town, Old Suwany Town=Suwanee.
Old Tal-e-see=Talasse.
Old Town=Outaunink.
Old Town, Old Town Village=White-eyes Town.
Old Tuni=Heshota Ayathltona.
Old Yazoo Village=Yazoo.
Old Zuñi=Heshota Ayathltona.
Oleachshoot=Ootlashoot.
Oleepas=Ololopa.
Olelachshoot=Ootlashoot.
Olelato=Olulato.
Olgatano=Olagatano.
Olhones=Olhon.
Olibahali=Ullibahali.
Olibahalies=Alibamu, Ullibahali.
Olilefeleia=Oklafalaya.
Olinacks=Abnaki.
O-lip-as, O-lip-pas=Ololopa.
Olitifar=Littefutchi.
Oljon=Olhon.
Ol'-la=Ola.
Olla-jocue=Aiyahokwe.
Ollemon Indians=Olamon.
Olle-pot'l=Tsewenalding.
Olleppauh'l-kah-teht'l=Medilding.
Ollo's=Oto.
Olocatano=Olagatano.
Ololópai=Ololopa.
Olomanosheebo=Romaine.
Olompalis=Olumpali.
Ol-o'-wi-dok, Ol'-o-wit, Ol-o-wi'-ya=Olowitok.
Ol'-po-sel=Olbosel.
Olwere=Chiwere.
Olwiya=Olowitok.
Omá-a=Omowuh.
Omackāsiwag=Omushkasug.
Omaha ħcaka, Omahahs=Omaha.
Omahanes=Okinagan.

Omahaws, Omahuas=Omaha.
Omail=Ohamil.
Omaka, Omalia=Omaha.
Omameeg=Miami.
O-man-ee=Mdewakanton.
O-maη'-ha, O-màη-ha-lica=Omaha.
Omąnisē=Ommunise.
O'manits'ēnôx=Omanitsenok.
Omanomineu, Omanomini=Menominee.
Omans, Omaonhaon=Omaha.
Omåschkåse Wenenewak=Wazhush.
Omashkekok=Maskegon.
Omatchamne=Machemni.
Omate's=Onondaga.
Omato=Huma.
O'-mau=Okuwa, Omowuh
Omau'-hau=Omaha.
O-maum-ee=Mdewakanton.
O-maum-eeg=Miami.
Omawhaw, Omawhawes=Omaha.
Omawuu=Omowuh.
Omeaoffe, Omeaosse, Omeaotes=Omenaosse.
Omee Towns=Maumee Towns.
Omenak=Umana.
O'menē=Nootka.
Omi=Ahome.
Omianicks, Omie=Miami.
Omikoues=Amikwa.
Ōmissis=Omisis.
Omitaqua=Omitiaqua.
Ömkwa=Umpqua.
Ommas=Huma.
Omochumnies=Machemni.
Omoloa=Homolua.
Omouhoa, Omowhows=Omaha.
Ompaām=Patuxet.
Omuhaw=Omaha.
O-mun-o-min-eeg=Menominee.
Omush-kas, O-mush-kas-ug=Wazhush.
Omush-ke-goag, Omushkegoes=Maskegon.
Omutchamne, Omutchumnes=Machemni
Onabas=Onavas.
Onachaquara=Anacharaqua.
Onachas=Washa.
Onachee=Onnahee.
Onachita=Wichita.
Onadago=Onondaga.
Onadahkos, Onadaicas, Onadakoes=Anadarko.
Onaghee=Onnahee.
Onagongues, Onagonque, Onagunga, Onagungees=
     Abnaki.
Onahe, Onahee, Onahie=Onnahee.
Onancoke=Onancock.
Onandaga, Onandages, Onandagos, Onandgo, Onando-
     gas=Onondaga.
Onankok=Onancock.
Onantagues=Onondaga.
Onaouientagos=Weendigo.
Onapien, Onapienes=Onapiem.
Onaucoke=Onancock.
Onaumanients=Onawmanient.
Onawaraghhare=Ganowarohare, Oneida (vil.).
Oncapapas=Hunkpapa.
Onchechaug=Patchoag.
Onch-pa-pah=Hunkpapa.
Oncidas=Oneida.
Onckeway=Uncowa.
Onconntehocks=Abnaki.
Onc-pah-pa, Oncpapa=Hunkpapa.
Ondadeonwas=Cherokee.
Ondages=Onondaga.
Ondataouaouat=Ottawa.
Ondataouatouat=Illinois.
Ondatauauat, Ondatawawat=Ottawa.
Ondatouatandy=Potawatomi.
Ondawagas=Seneca.
Ondiakes=Abnaki.
Ondiondago=Onondaga.
Ondironon=Aondironon.
Ondoutaoüaheronnon=Ondoutaouaka.
Ond8ta8aka=Ottawa.
Oneachquage=Oquaga.
One-capapa=Hunkpapa.
One-daugh-ga-haugh-ga=Onondaga.
Onehohquages=Oquaga.
Oneida Castle=Ganowarohare.
Oneiout=Oneida (vil.).
Onejages=Abnaki.

Onejagese=Sokoki.
Onejoust=Oneida (vil.).
Onendagah=Onondaga (vil.).
Onengioure=Caughnawaga.
Onenhoghkwages,   Onĕⁿ hokwă'ge=Oquaga.
O-nĕⁿ-tă'-kĕ=Onondaga.
Oneout=Oneida (vil.).
Oneugi8re, Onewyiure=Caughnawaga.
Onextaco=Onixayms.
Oneydoes=Oneida.
Oneyoté=Goiogouen, Oneida (vil.).
Onghetgechaton,   Onghetgéodatons=Oughetgeoda-
     tons.
Ongmarahronon, Ongniarahronon, Onguiaahra=Ong-
     niaahra.
Oñ-gwă-noⁿ'-syoⁿ'-ni'=Iroquois.
Oniactmaws, Onias=Wea.
Oniasontke,   Oniasont-Keronons=Honniasontkero-
     non.
Oniatonons, Oniattanon=Wea.
Onie-le-toch=Oealitk.
Onieoute=Oneida (vil.).
Onĭ'hăᵒ, O-ni-'ha-o=Omaha.
Onillas=Wea.
Oninge, Oningo=Venango.
Onioen=Goiogouen.
Onionenhronnons, Oniouenhronon=Cayuga.
Ōnipōwisībīwininiwąg=Onepowesepewenenewak.
Oniscousins=Wisconsin.
Onkapas=Oyukhpe.
Onkdaka=Oglala.
Onkinegans=Okinagan.
Onkoüagannha=Ontwaganha.
Onkpahpah, Onkpapah=Hunkpapa.
Onlogamies=Foxes.
Onnachee=Onnahee.
Onnagonges, Onnagongues, Onnagongwe, Onnagon-
     ques=Abnaki.
Onnandages, Onnatagues=Onondaga.
Onnatucks=Onuatuc.
Onnayayou=Honeoye.
Onneioté=Goiogouen.
Onneiou, Onneioute=Oneida (vil.).
Onnei8theronnon=Oneida.
Onnenatu=Deyodeshot.
Onnentagues=Onondaga.
Onnentissati=Onentisati.
Onneyatte, Onnie8te=Oneida (vil.).
Onnogonges, Onnogongwaes=Abnaki.
Onnoncharonnons=Ononchataronon.
Onnondaga=Onondaga.
Onnondage=Onondaga (vil.).
Onnondages,   Onnondagoes,   Onnondagues=Onon-
     daga.
Onnondague=Onondaga (vil.).
Onnondagues=Onondaga.
Onnondaqué=Onondaga (vil.).
Onnongonges=Abnaki.
Onnoniote=Oneida (vil.).
Onnonlages, Onnontaé=Onondaga.
Onnonta'e, Onnontae, Onnontaghé, Onnontagk, On-
     nontagué=Onondaga (vil.).
Onnontaeheonnons, Onnontaeronnons, Onnontaghé,
     Onnontagheronnons=Onondaga.
Onnontagk,   Onnontagué=Onondaga,   Onondaga
     (vil.).
Onnontaguehronnons, Onnontaguese, Onnnntaguez
     Onnontatae=Onondaga.
Onnontcharonnons=Ononchataronon.
Onnontoeronnons=Onondaga.
Onnosarage Castle=Ganowarohare.
Onnotagues=Onondaga.
Onnutague=Kanagaro.
Ono=Ona.
O-no-ä'-lä-gone-na=Onoalagona, Schenectady.
Onoaughquaga=Oquaga.
Onoconcquehagas=Abnaki.
Onocows=Konkau.
Ono-dauger=Canandaigua.
Onoganges=Abnaki.
Onoghguagy, Onoghquagey=Oquaga.
Onogongoes, Onogonguas, Onogungos=Abnaki.
Onohoghgwáge, Onohoghquaga, Oñohoquaga, Onoh-
     quauga=Oquaga.
Onokonquehaga=Abnaki.
Ononda-agos, Onondades, Onondaëronnons=Onon-
     daga.
Onondaga Castle=Onondaga (vil.).
Onondagaes, Onondagah, Onondagas, Onondagers,
     Onondages, Onondagez=Onondaga.

Onondagharie=Onondaghara.
Onondaghé, Onondagheronons, Onondagos, Ononda-
  gues, Onondajas, Onondakes, Onondawgaws, Onon-
  degas=Onondaga.
Onondowă'=Nundawao.
O-non-é-kä-gä-hä=Mandhinkagaghe.
Onongongues=Abnaki.
Ononhoghquage=Oquaga.
Ononiioté=Oneida (vil.).
O-no'-ni-o=Arikara.
Ononïoté=Oneida (vil.).
Ononjete, Ononjoté=Oneida (vil.).
Onontaé, Onontaehronon, Onontaerhonons, Onontae-
  ronons, Onontaerrhonons, Onontaez, Onontager,
  Onontages, Onontaghés, Onontagué, Onontagueron-
  nons, Onontagueronon, Onontaguese, Onontahé,
  Onontaheronons=Onondaga.
Onontakaës=Ottawa.
Onontake, Onontatacet=Onondaga.
Onontchataranons, Onontchataronons, Onontchatero-
  nons=Ononchataronon.
Ononthagues=Onondaga.
Onontiogas=Onnontioga.
Onoontaugaes=Onondaga.
Onoquagé, Onoquaghe=Oquaga.
Onossky=Ahtena.
Onothaca=Onathaqua.
Onoundages=Onondaga.
Onoyints=Oneida.
Onphŭn enikaciχa=Anpanenikashika.
Onquilouzas=Opelousa.
Ontaanak=Ottawa.
Ontagamies=Foxes.
Ontagués=Onondaga.
Ontaonatz=Ottawa.
Ontaraeronon, Ontarahronon=Kickapoo.
Ontastoes=Conestoga.
Ontationoue=Nottoway.
Ontdwawies=Ottawa.
Ontehibouse=Chippewa.
Ontoagannha, Ontôagaunha=Ontwaganha.
Ontoouaganha=Ontwaganha.
Ontotonta=Oto.
Ontouagannha, Ont8agannha, Ontouagennha=Ont-
  waganha.
Ontponies=Ontponea.
Onttaouactz=Ottawa.
Ontwagannha=Ontwaganha.
Onuatuck=Onuatuc.
Onúg-anúgemut=Onuganuk.
Onughkaurydaaug=Seneca.
O-nun-dä'-ga-o-no, Onundagéga=Onondaga.
Onundawaga=Seneca.
Onundawgoes=Onondaga.
Onuntáte-hä'ge=Juniata.
Onuntewakaa=Seneca.
O-nya-de-a'-kän'-hyät=Neodakheat.
Onyapes=Quapaw.
Onyauyah=Honeoye.
Ooailik, Ooallikh=Ualik.
Oochepayyan=Chipewyan.
Oocooloo-Falaya=Oklafalaya.
Oocuca=Ocuca.
O-o-dam=Tepehuane.
Ood-zâ-tâu=Utsehta.
Ooe-Asa=Tawasa.
Ooe-Asah=Ooeasa.
Oofé-ogoolas=Ofogoula.
Oogahlensie, Oogalenskie=Ugalakmiut.
Ooganok=Uganik.
Oogashik=Ugashik.
Oo-geoo-lik=Ugjulirmiut.
Ooglaamie, Ooglamie=Utkiavi.
Ooglit, Ooglitt=Uglirn.
Ooglovia=Uglovaia.
Oogovigamute, Oogowigamute=Ugovik.
Oogueesik Salik, Ooguensik-salik-Innuits=Ukusik-
  salirmiut.
Oo-gwapes=Quapaw.
Oohaiack=Akhiok.
Oohanick=Uganik.
Oohaskeck=Uhaskek.
Oohenoupa=Oohenonpa
O-ó-ho-mo-i'-o, O-òhomò-yo=Dakota.
Oohp=Navaho, Walapai.
Oohpáp=Maricopa.
Ooiak, Ooiatsk=Uyak.
Oo-innakhtagowïk, Ooinukhlagowik, Ooinuktago-
  wik=Uinuk.

Ookagamiut, Ookagamute=Ukak.
Oo-ka-na-kane=Okinagan.
Ookevok=Ukivokmiut.
Ookhogamute=Oknagak.
Ookivok=Ukivokmiut.
Ook-joo-lik=Ugjulirmiut.
Ook-tau-hau-zau-see=Uklahasasi.
Ookwolik=Ugjulirmiut.
Oolukak=Ulukakhotana.
Oo-ma-ha=Omaha.
Oomenak=Umana.
Oomiak-soak=Udluhsen.
Oómi-nŭ'-tqiu=Himoiyoqis.
Oomnak=Nikolski.
Oomoojek Yutes=Eiwhuelit.
Oonakagamute=Unakagak.
Oonakhtolik=Ungalik.
Oonalakleet=Unalaklik.
Oonalaska=Iliuliuk.
Oonalga, Oonalgenskoi=Unalga
Oonaligmute=Unaligmiut.
Oonancock=Onancock.
Oonángan=Aleut.
Oonangashik=Unangashik.
Ooncows=Konkau.
Oongenskoi=Unga.
Oon-hárik=Unharik.
Oonoghquageys=Oquaga.
Oonongashik=Unangashik.
Oonontaeronnons=Onondaga.
Oop=Apache, Navaho, Walapai.
Oöpáp, Oopas=Maricopa.
Oopungnewing=Operdniving.
Ooqueesiksillik=Ukusiksalirmiut.
Ooscooches, Oosechu=Osotchi.
Oosemite=Awani.
Oo-se-oo-che, Ooseoochee=Osotchi.
Oos-kè-mà=Eskimo.
Oosoomite=Awani.
Oustanale, Oustanalle, Oostanaula, Oos-te-nau-lah,
  Oostinawley=Ustanali.
Oostomas=Ustoma.
Ootagamis=Foxes.
Ootam=Pima.
Oote-lash-shoots=Ootlashoots.
Ootivakh, Ootiwakh, Ootkaiowik=Utkiavi.
Ootkeaviemutes, Ootkeavies=Utkiavinmiut.
Ootkooseek-Kalingmœoot=Ukusiksalirmiut.
Ootooka Mutes, Ootookas=Utukamiut.
Ootslashshoots=Ootlashoot.
Oô-tyi-ti=Cochiti.
Oouiatanons, O8iata8atenon=Wea.
Ooukia=Cahokia.
Oo-yapes=Quapaw.
Oozinkie=Uzinki.
Op=Apache.
O'-pă=Upan.
Opala=Opata.
Opanock=Ohanoak.
Oparsoitac=Upasoitac.
Opas=Maricopa.
Opasura=Oposura.
Opatas cogüinachis=Coguinachi.
Opatas tegüimas=Teguima.
Opate, Opauas=Opata.
Opea=Peoria.
Opechisaht, Opecluset, Ope-eis-aht=Opitchesaht.
O-pe'-ki=Walpi.
Opemens d'Acheliny=Nopeming.
Openadyo, Openagi, Openagos, Openangos=Abnaki.
Opendachiliny=Pawating.
Openoches=Pohoniche.
Opet-ches-aht=Opitchesaht.
Opetsitar=Opitsat.
Opii=Hopi.
O-pi-ji-que, Opijiqui=Walpi.
Opilika, Opilike, Opil'-'lako=Opilhlako.
O-pil-thluc-co=Opilhlako.
O'pimittish Ininiwac=Nopeming.
O'pimmitish Ininiwuc=Cree.
Opings=Pompton.
Opisitar=Opitsat.
Opistopea=Opistopia.
Ople-goh=Takimilding.
Opocoulas=Ofogoula.
O-po-nagh-ke=Abnaki.
O-po-que=San Ildefonso.
Opoteppe=Opodepe.
Opoto=Oputo.

Oppegach, Oppegoeh=Opegoi.
Oppenago=Abnaki.
Op-pe-o=Opegoi.
Oppernowick=Operdniving.
Oppe-yoh=Opegoi.
Opposians=Opossian.
Opquive, Opquivi=Walpi.
O-puh-nar'-ke=Abnaki.
O-pûhⁿ nika-shing-ga=Upan.
Oqomiut=Okomiut.
Oquacho, Oquago=Oquaga.
O-qua-pas, Oquapasos=Quapaw.
Oqué-Loussas=Okalusa.
Oquitod=Oquitoa.
Oquwa, Oquwa-tdóa=Okuwa.
Orabi=Oraibi.
Orages=Osage.
Oraiba, Oraibe, Oraiby, Oraiva, Oraivaz, Oraive, Oraivi=Oraibi.
Orakakes=Orapaks.
Orambe, Orante=Oraibi.
Orapack, Orapakas, Orapakes=Orapaks.
Orarians=Esquimauan Family, Eskimo.
Orawi, Oraybe, Oraybi, Orayve, Orayvee, Orayvi, Orayxa=Oraibi.
Orcamipias, Orcampion, Orcampiou=Orcan.
Orcoquisa=Arkokisa.
Orcoquisac=San Agustin de Ahumada.
Orcoquisacs, Orcoquizas=Arkokisa.
Ore=Opata.
Oregon Jacks=Ntekem.
Orehbe, Oreiba=Oraibi.
Orendakes=Adirondack.
O-rey-be, Oriabe, Oribas, Oribe, Oribi=Oraibi.
Orientales=Penateka.
Original Pueblo=Aridian.
Orisca, Oriska, Oriske=Ganowarohare.
Orista, Oristanum=Edisto.
Oriva=Oraibi.
Orixa=Edisto.
Oᴿke'=San Juan.
Orleans Indians=Karok.
Orondacks, Orondocks, Orondoes=Adirondack.
Orongouens=Cayuga.
Oron-nygh-wurrie-gughre=Onoalagona.
Oronoake, Oronoke=Woronock.
Oroondoks, Oroonducks=Adirondack.
Oropacks, Oropaxe=Orapaks.
Oroyson=Oroysom.
Orp=Apache.
Orquisaco=Arkokisa.
Orribies=Oraibi.
Orroyo=Pueblo del Arroyo.
Ortithipicatony=Tippecanoe.
Oruk=Arekw.
Orundacks=Adirondack.
Orunges=Mahican.
Orville=Lac Court Oreilles.
Oryina=Oraibi.
Osách-háno=Oshach.
Osaga=Osage.
Osage des Chenes, Osages of the Oaks=Santsuk-dhin.
Osagi=Sauk.
Osaginang, Osāgināwᵉ=Saginaw.
Osaji=Hopi.
Osáki, Osankies=Sauk.
Osapa chitto=Sapa Chitto.
Osarge=Osage.
Osark=Ozark.
Osasígi=Osage.
Osatoves=Uzutiuhi.
Osaugeeg, Osaukies=Sauk.
Osault St Louis=Caughnawaga.
O'-saw-kee=Sauk.
O-saw-ses=Osage.
Osay=Hopi.
Osaybe=Oraibi.
Osayes=Osage.
Oscameches=Occaneechi.
Osceola's Town=Withlako.
Oscillee=Ocilla.
Oscoochee=Osotchi.
Osédshi máklaks=Osage.
Oseegah=Itscheabine.
Ose-larneby=Assilanapi.
Oseooche=Osotchi.
Osett, Osette=Ozette.
Osevegatchies=Oswegatchie.

Osewingo=Chenango.
Osh-a-chewan=Osetchiwan.
Óshahak=Dakota.
O'-sharts, Oshatsh=Oshach.
Oshawanoag=Shawnee.
Osheraca=Foxes.
O'shetchiwan=Osetchiwan.
Osheti Shakowin=Dakota.
Oshibwek=Chippewa.
O-sho-na=Oshonawan.
Osht-yal-a=Ostyalakwa.
Osiguevede=Osiquevede.
Osinies=Ozinies.
Osinipoilles=Assiniboin.
Osipees=Ossipee.
Osita=Wichita.
Ositchy=Osotchi.
Oskemanettigons, Oskemanitigous = Oukiskimani-touk.
Oski holba=Escooba.
Ōsmaxmik·ê'lp=Osmakmiketlp.
Osochee=Osotchi.
Osoli=Oraibi.
Osooyoos=Nkamip.
Osotonoy, Osotteoez=Uzutiuhi.
Osoyoos=Nkamip.
Ospa=Ospo.
Osquisakamais=Oskquisaquamai.
Ossachile=Osachile.
Ossage=Osage.
Ossalonida=Assilanapi.
Osseegahs=Itscheabine.
Osse-gon=Ashegen.
Ossepe=Ossipee.
Ossernenon, Osserrïon, Osseruenon=Caughnawaga.
Ossikannä=Seneca.
Ossineboine, Ossiniboine, Ossnobians=Assiniboin.
Ossonane, Ossosandué, Ossosané, Ossossaire=Ossos-sane.
Ossoteoez, Ossotéoué, Ossotonoy, Ossotoues, Ossot-teoez, Ossoztoues=Uzutiuhi.
Ossuchees=Osotchi.
Osswegatche=Oswegatchie.
Ostandousket=Sandusky.
Ostanghaes=Ostonwackin.
Ostiagaghroones, Ostiagahoroones=Chippewa.
Ostonoos=Ustanali.
Ostretchees, Ósudshi, Ósutchi=Osotchi.
Oswagatches, Oswagatic, Osweatchies, Osweegachio, Osweegchie, Oswegachys, Oswegatches, Oswegat-chy, Oswegatsy=Oswegatchie.
Oswichees, Oswichu=Osotchi.
Oswingo=Chenango.
Oswitcha, Oswitche, Oswitchee=Osotchi.
Otagamies=Foxes.
O-ta-har-ton=Otekhiatonwan.
Otahas=Ottawa.
Ŏtăkwanawĕⁿrunĕⁿ=Oquaga.
Otama=Pima.
Otä-nä-sä-ga=Canadasaga.
O.tan.gan=Winnebago.
Otaoas=Ottawa.
Otaopabinè=Watopapinah.
Ota8ais, Otaoüaks, Otaous=Ottawa.
Otasee, Otasse=Atasi.
Otä'tshia widishi'anun=Otachia.
Otauas=Ottawa.
Otaulubis=Outurbi.
Otáwa, Otawas, Otawaus, Otawawas=Ottawa.
Otayáchgo=Nanticoke.
Otchagras, Otchagros=Winnebago.
Otchaqua=Oathaqua.
Otchenti-Chakoang=Dakota.
Otchepóse, Otchipoeses, Otchipois, Otchipoises, Otchipwe=Chippewa.
O-tchun-gu-rah=Winnebago.
Otcitcă`kŏnsag=Outchichagami.
Otee toochinas=Otituchina.
Oteĥiatoŋwaŋ, Oteĥi-atoŋwaŋ=Otekhiatonwan.
O-tel-le-who-yau-nau, Otellewhoyonnee=Hotalihuy-ana.
Ot'el'-nna=Eskimo.
Otenmarhem, Otenmarhen=Ointemarhen.
Otentas=Oto.
Oteqi-atoⁿwaⁿ=Otekhiatonwan.
Ote-toe, Oteuta, Otheues, Othoe, Othonez, Othos, Othoues, Othouez, Othoves=Oto.
O-thun-gu-rahs=Winnebago.

Otiara8atenon=Wea.
Otickwagami=Nipissing.
O-til′-tin=Kutchakutchin.
Otina=Utina.
Otinanchahé=Joasseh.
Otisee=Atasi.
Otissee=Atasi.
Otjibwek=Chippewa.
Otk-e-a-vik=Utkiavi.
8ot k!iál na′as xā′da-i=Otkialnaas-hadai.
Otkiavik, Otkiawik, Ot-ki-a-wing, Otkiwik=Utkiavi.
Otma=Attu.
Otmagra=Winnebago.
8Ot na′as xā′da-i=Otnaas-hadai.
Otno-Khotana, Otnox tana=Ahtena.
Otoa=Toalli.
Otoctatas, Otoctotas, Otoe, Otoetata=Oto.
Otogamies=Foxes.
O-tŏ̄h′-sŏn=Oglala.
Otok-kok=Utuka.
Oto-kog-ameuts=Utukamiut.
Otokotouemi=Otaguottouemin.
Otomie=Omaha.
Otondiata, Otoniata, Otoniato=Tonihata.
Otonkah=Winnebago.
Otonnica=Tunica.
Otontanta=Oto.
Otopachgnato=Watopachnato.
Otopplata, Otoptata=Oto.
Otoseen=Atasi.
Ototantas, Ototatä=Oto.
Ototchassi=Uzutiuhi.
Otoüacha=Toanche.
Otoutanta, Otoutantas Paoté=Oto.
Otowas, Otoways=Ottawa.
Otseningo, Otsiningo, Otsininko=Chenango.
Ots-on-waeken=Ostonwackin.
Otsotchaué, Otsotchoué, Otsotchove, Otsoté=Uzutiuhi.
Otstonwackin=Ostonwackin.
Ottagamies, Ottagaumies=Foxes.
Ottah-wah, Ot-tah-way, Ottaouais, Ottaouets=Ottawa.
Ottapoas=Chippewa.
Ottar-car-me, Ot-târ-gâr-me=Foxes.
Ottasees=Atasi.
Ottauwah, Ottawacks, Ottawacs, Ottawaes, Ottawagas, Ottawaies, Ottawak=Ottawa.
Ottawa lake men=Lac Court Oreilles.
Ottawas of Blanchard's Creek, Ottawas of Blanchard's Fork=Blanchard's Fork.
Ottawawa, Ottawawaas, Ottawawe, Ottawawooes, Ottawaws, Ottaway, Ottawwaws, Ottawwawwag, Ottawwawwug=Ottawa.
Ot-tech-petl=Otshpeth.
Otter, Nation of the=Amikwa.
Ottersea, Ottesa, Ottessa=Atasi.
Ottewas=Ottawa.
Ottigamie, Ottigaumies, Ottiquamies=Foxes.
Ottisse, Ottissee=Atasi.
Otto, Ottoas=Oto.
Ottoawa=Ottawa.
Ottoes=Oto.
Ottogamis=Foxes.
Ottoos, Otto's, Ottotatocs, Ottotatoes=Oto.
Ottova, Ottowaes, Ottowais=Ottawa.
Ottowas=Oto, Ottawa.
Ottowata, Ottowaus, Ottowauways, Ottowawa, Ottowawe, Ottowaws, Ottowayer, Ottoways, Ottowose, Ottwasse=Ottawa.
O′tu′gŭnŭ=Oqtogona.
Ō′-tu-káh=Utuka.
O-tun-nee=Crows.
Oturbe=Atarpe.
Otutaches=Oto.
Oua=Wea.
Ouabaches, Ouabachi=Wabash.
Ouabans=Ouabano.
Ouabash Nations=Wabash.
Ouabenakiouek, 8abenakis, Ouabenaquis, Ouabnaquia=Abnaki.
Ouacé=Ouasouarini.
Ouacha=Washa.
Ouachaskesouek=Wachaskesouek.
Ouachegami=Wachegami.
Ouachibes=Ouachita.
Ouachipuanes=Chipewyan.
Ouachites=Ouachita.
Ouachtanons, Ouachtenons, Ouachtunon=Wea.

Ouadbatons, Ouadebathons, Ouadebatons, Oua de Battons=Wahpeton.
Ouadiche=Nabedache.
Ouaepetons=Wahpeton.
Ouae Utina=Utina.
Ouagoussac=Foxes.
Ouagoussak=Wakoawissojik.
Ouainco=Waco.
Ouaioumpoum=Wiam.
Ouakichs=Nootka.
Ouakicoms, Ouakikours=Wahkiakum.
Ouak8iechiuek=Chisedec.
Ouakouingouechiouek=Wakouingouechiwek.
Ouaḻi=Ouasouarini.
Oualla-Oualla, Ouallas-Ouallas=Wallawalla.
8anabegoueks=Winnebago.
Ouanahinan=Kannehouan.
Ouanchas=Washa.
8an8inak=Wewenoc.
Ouaouackecinatouek=Huron.
8a8aiation=Wea.
Ouaouechkairini, Ouaouechkairiniouek=Weskarini.
Oüaoüiartanons, Ouaouiatanoukak, Ouaouiatenonoukak=Wea.
Ouaouiechkairini, 8a8iechkarini8ek=Weskarini.
Ouaouyartanons=Wea.
Ouapamo=Wapoo.
Ouapeontetons=Wazikute.
Ouapetons=Wahpeton.
Ouapetontetons=Wazikute.
8arasteg8iaks=Malecite.
8arinakiens=Wewenoc.
Ouaroronon=Ongniaahra.
Ouasaouanik=Ouasouarini.
Ouasiconteton=Wazikute.
Ouasitas=Ouachita.
Ouasouarim=Ouasouarini.
Ouasoys=Osage.
Ouassi=Ouasouarini.
Oüassitas=Ouachita.
Ouatabatonha=Wahpeton.
Ouatanons=Wea.
Ouatawais=Ottawa.
Ouatchita=Ouachita.
Ouatemanetons=Ocatameneton.
Ouatenon=Wea.
8atoeronnon, Ouatoieronon=Sauk.
Ouatonons=Wea.
Ouatouáx=Ottawa.
Ouattonon=Wea.
Oubenakis, 8benakis=Abnaki.
Oubestamiouek=Bersiamite.
Oucahipoues=Chippewa.
Oucatonons=Wea.
Ouchage=Osage.
Ouchaouanag, Ouchawanag=Shawnee.
Ouchee=Yuchi.
Ouchessigiriniouek, Ouchestigoüek, Ouchestigouetch, Ouchestigouets=Oukesestigouek.
Ouchibois, Ouchipawah, Ouchipöe, Ouchipoves=Chippewa.
Ouchitaws=Wichita.
Ouchuchlisit, Ou-chuk-lis-aht=Uchucklesit.
Oudebaetons=Wahpeton.
8eanohronons=Wenrohronon.
Oüeas=Wea.
Ouedle=Uedle.
8emess8rit, Ouemessourit=Missouri.
Ouenabegouc=Winnebago.
Ouendat, 8endat=Huron.
Ouenebegonhelinis=Ouinebigonhelini.
Ouenebegons, Ouenebigonchelinis, Ouenibigonc, Ouenibigoutz=Winnebago.
8enrio=Ouenrio.
Ouenro nation, 8enroronons=Wenrohronon.
Ouentouoronons=Seneca.
8e8esḳariniens=Weskarini.
Oueperigoueiaouek=Weperigweia.
Ouescharini=Weskarini.
Oueschekgagamiouilimy = Oschekkamegawenenewak.
Ouesconsins=Wisconsin.
Ouesperies=Uzutiuhi.
Oufe Agoulas, Oufé Ogoulas, Oufe Ogulas, Ouféouglas, Oufi-Ougulas=Ofogoula.
Oufotu=Uzutiuhi.
Ougagliakmuzi-Kinaia=Knaiakhotana.
Ougalachmioutsy, Ougalentze=Ugalakmiut.
Ougapa=Quapaw.

Ougatanous=Wea.
Oughalakhmute, Oughalakmute, Oughalentze=Ugalakmiut.
Oughquaga, Oughquageys, Oughqugoes=Oquaga.
Oughquissasnies=Saint Regis.
Oughtella=Awaitlala.
Ougnagok=Unga.
Ougpauk=Okpaak.
Ouguapas=Quapaw.
Ouh-papas=Hunkpapa.
Ouiagies=Mahican.
Ouias, Ouiatanon, Ouiatenons, Ouiatinons, Ouiatonons, Ouiattanon, Ouiattons, Ouicatonans=Wea.
Ouichaatcha=Osage.
Ouichitaws=Wichita.
Ouichram=Tlakluit.
Ouidachenaton, Ouidaougeouaton, Ouidaougeoumaton, Ouidaougeounaton, Ouidaugeounaton = Oughetgeodatons.
Ouidiches=Nabedache.
Ouileute=Quileute.
Ouillas=Wea.
Ouillequegaws=Kwalhioqua.
Ouimiamies=Miami.
Ouinepeag, Ouinipegong, Ouinipegou, Ouinipegouec, Ouinipégoüek, Ouinipigou=Winnebago.
Ouïoen=Goiogouen.
Oüioenrhonons, Ouiouenronnons=Cayuga.
Ouisconsins, 8iskonche, Ouiskonches=Wisconsin.
Ouispe=Ofogoula.
Ouitanans, Ouitanons, Ouitatotnons=Wea.
Ouitcitas=Wichita.
Ouithloko=Withlako.
Ouitimaus=Wea.
Oujalespious, Oujalespoitons, Oujalespoitous=Oujatespouitons.
Oujatanons=Wea.
Oujatespouetons=Oujatespouitons.
Oukehaee=Okchayi.
Oukinegans=Okinagan.
Oukivak=Ukivok.
Ouknadok=Uknodok.
Oukouingouechiouek=Wakouingouechiwek.
Oukskenah=Klamath.
Oukviktoulia=Opiktulik.
Oukwak=Ukivok.
Oulchionis=Dulchioni.
Ouloulatines=Olulato.
Ouma=Huma.
Oumalominis, Oumaloüminek, Oumaloumines, Oumalouminetz=Menominee.
Oumamens, Oumami, Oumamik=Miami.
Oumamiois=Bersiamite, Oumamiwek.
Oumamioucks=Bersiamite.
8mami8ek, 8mami8ekhi=Oumamiwek.
Oumamiwek=Bersiamite.
Oumanies=Miami.
Oumaniouets, Oumanois=Oumamiwek.
Oumaominiecs=Menominee.
Oumas=Huma.
Oumatachiiriouetz=Oumatachi.
Oumeami, Oumiamies=Miami.
Oumisagai=Missisauga.
Ou-missouri=Missouri.
Ou-Monssonis=Monsoni.
Ounabonims=Menominee.
Ounachkapiouek, Ounadcapis=Nascapee.
Ounagountchaguélioug-iout=Jugelnute.
Ounag-touli=Ungalik.
Ounalaklik=Unalaklik.
Ounángan=Eskimauan Family.
Ounasacoetois=Nassauaketon.
Ounascapis=Nascapee.
8natchatazonons=Ononchataronon.
Ouneiout, Ounejout=Oneida (vil.).
Ounepigous=Winnebago.
Ounescapi=Nascapee.
Ounga=Unga.
Ounhann-Kouttànæ=Unakhotana.
Ounikanes=Amikwa.
Ounneiout=Oneida (vil.).
Ounnenatu=Deyodeshot.
Ounontcharonnous, Ounountchatarounongak=Ononchataronon.
Ounspik=Ofogoula.
Ountchatarounounga=Ononchataronon.
Ouoghquogey=Oquaga.
Ouoguens=Goiogouen.
Oupapa=Quapaw.

Oupapinachiouek, Oupapinachi8ekhi, Oupapinach-i8kü=Papinachois.
Ouperigoue ouaouakhi=Weperigweia.
Oupouteouatamik=Potawatomi.
Ouquagos=Oquaga.
Ourages, Ouragies=Mahican.
Ouramanichek=Oumamiwek.
Ouraouakmikoug=Outaouakamigouk.
Ouristigouche=Restigouche.
Our Lady. See Nuestra Señora.
Our Lady of Sorrows and Saint Anthony of Sandia=Sandia.
Ouroctenon=Wea.
Ous=Osage.
Ousaki, Ousakiouek=Sauk.
Ousasons, Ousasoys=Osage.
Ousatannock Indians, Ousatunnuck=Stockbridge.
Ousauches=Osotchi.
Ousetannuck=Stockbridge.
Ousita=Wichita.
Ousolu=Uzutiuhi.
Ousontiwi, Ousoutiwy=Uzutiuhi.
Ouspie, Oussipes=Ofogoula.
Oustaca, Oustack, Oustacs=Westo.
Oustanale, Oustanalle=Ustanali.
Oustestee=Ustisti.
Oustonnoc=Stockbridge.
Outabitibek, Outabytibis=Abittibi.
Outachepas=Chippewa.
Outagami, Outagamie-ock, Outagamiouek, Outagamy=Foxes.
Outaganons=Wea.
Outagomies=Foxes.
8tak8ami8ek, Outakouamiouek, Outakouamiwek=Attikamegue.
Outantes=Oto.
Outaois, Outaoise, Outaonacs, Outaoüacs=Ottawa.
Outa8acs, 8ta8acs, Outaoüaes, 8ta8aës=Ottawa.
Outaouae Sinagos=Sinago.
Outaouagamis=Foxes.
Outaouagas, Outaouaies, Outaouais, Outa8ais, 8ta8ais=Ottawa.
Outaouak of the Sable=Sable.
Outaouaks=Ottawa.
Outaoüaks Sinagaux=Sinago.
Outaouan, Outaouaos, Outaouas, Outa8as, 8ta8as=Ottawa.
Outaouasinagouk=Sinago.
Outaouas of Talon=Otontagan.
Outaouats, Outaouaus, Outaouax, Outaouays, Outaoues, Outaouis=Ottawa.
8ta8kot8emi8ek=Otaguottouemin.
Outaoüois, Outa8ois=Ottawa.
Outaouoisbouscottous, Outaouois Bouscouttons=Bouscouttou.
Outaoues, Outa8uas, Outaovacs, Outaovas, Outaowaies=Ottawa.
Outapa=Ibitoupa.
Outarwas=Ottawa.
Outatibes=Abittibi.
Outauaes, Outauas, Outauies, Outauois, Outavis, Outavois, Outawacs, Outawais, Outawas, Outawase=Ottawa.
Outawas Sinagos=Sinago.
Outawawas, Outaway, Outawies, Outawois=Ottawa.
Outaypes=Ibitoupa.
Outchibouec, Outchibous=Chippewa.
Outchichagamiouetz=Outchichagami.
Outchioung, Outchiouns=Uchium.
Outchipoue, Outchipwais=Chippewa.
Outchitak-Mioute=Uchtak.
Outchouguets=Outchougai.
Outduaois=Ottawa.
Outehipoues=Chippewa.
Outemiskamegs=Temiscaming.
Outentontes=Oto.
Outeonas=Ottawa.
Outias=Wea.
Outichacouk=Atchatchakangouer.
Outigamis=Foxes.
Outimacs=Ottawa.
Outina=Utina.
Outinon=Wea.
Outiskoüagami, Outisquagamis=Nipissing.
Outitchakouk=Atchatchakangouen.
Outlaw=Pinutgu.
Outoagamis, Outogamis=Foxes.
Outontagans, Outouacks, Outouacs=Ottawa.
Outouagamis=Foxes.
Outouagannha=Shawnee.

Outouais, Outouaouas=Ottawa.
Outougamis=Foxes.
Outouloubys=Outurbi.
Outouvas, Outowacs=Ottawa.
Outpankas, Outponies=Ontponea.
Outsotin=Hwotsotenne.
Outtagamies, Outtagaumie, Outtagomies=Foxes.
Outtamacks, Outtaois, Outtaouacts, Outtaouatz, Outta8es, Outtaouis, Outtauois, Outtawaats, Outtawas, Outtoaets=Ottawa.
Outtongamis, Outtouagamis=Foxes.
Outtouatz=Ottawa.
Outtougamis=Foxes.
Ouxeinacomigo=Sinago.
O-üχtχitan=Osage.
Ou yākū Ilnigē=Aoyakulnagai.
Ouyapes, Ouyapez=Quapaw.
Ouyas, 8yas, 8yatanon, Ouyatanons=Wea.
Ouyatespony=Oujatespouitons.
Ouyatonons, 8yatonons, Ouyattanons, Ouyaws=Wea.
Ouyopetons=Wahpeton.
Ouysianous=Wea.
Ovadebathons=Wahpeton.
Ovagitas=Wichita.
Ovā'gots=Wharhoots.
Ovas=Iowa, Jova.
Ovedsitas=Wichita.
Overhill Creeks=Upper Creeks.
Ovkérok=Ukivok.
Ovvendoes=Owendos.
Owago=Owego.
Owáha, Owahas=Omaha.
Owandats=Huron.
Owaragees=Mahican.
Owassa=Hiwassee.
Owásse wi'dishi'anun=Owasse.
Oways=Kiowa.
Oweantonoge=Weantinock.
Oweatumka=Wetumpka.
Oweckano, O-wee-kay-no, Oweekayo=Wikeno.
Owegé, Owegey, Owegi, Owegy, Oweigey=Owego.
Owekofea=Weogufka.
Owenagungas, Owenagunges, Owenagungies=Abnaki.
Owendaets, Owendats=Huron.
Owendoes=Owendos.
Owendot=Huron.
Owen's River Indians=Kotsava.
Owens Valley Paiutes=Petenegowats.
Owenungas=Abnaki.
Owhát, Owhát-tdóa=Okuwa.
Owhillapsh=Kwalhioqua.
Owhü, Owhü-tdoa=Okuwa.
Owia-lei-toh=Oealitk.
Ówilapsh=Kwalhioqua, Willopah.
Owitchees=Osotchi.
Owīt-lei-toh=Oetlitk.
Owongos=Kowanga.
Owseecheys=Osotchi.
Oxiailles=Okchayi.
Oxitahibuis=Ojiataibues.
Oxmulges=Ocmulgee.
Oxomiut=Okomiut.
Oxquoquiras=Arkokisa.
Oyachtownuk Roanu=Wea.
Oyadackuchraono, Oyadagahroenes, Oyadage'-ono, O-ya-dä'-go-o-no=Cherokee.
Oyágamut=Kuskwogmiut.
Oyaghtanont=Wea.
Oyak=Kuskwogmiut.
Oyanders=Mohawk.
Oyatáge-rónoñ=Cherokee.
O-ya-tay-shee-ka, Oyate-citca, Oyate śića=Oyateshicha.
Oyatonons=Wea.
Oyaudah=Cherokee.
Oydica=Oydican.
Oyelloightuk=Oealitk.
Oyer-lal-lah=Oglala.
Oyique=Oyike.
Oynondage=Onondaga (vil.).
Oyoa=Iowa.
Oyogouins=Cayuga.
Oypatoocoola, Oypat oocooloo=Oypatukla.
Oytapars, Oytapayts=Oapars.
Oyty-aht=Oiaht.
Oyuḣpe, Oyuqpe=Oyukhpe.
Oyyatanous=Wea.

Ozages=Osage.
O-zái=Oraibi.
Ozajes, Ozanges=Osage.
Ozanghe'darankiac=Sagadahoc.
Ozaras, Ozarrar=Maricopa.
Ozas=Osage.
Oz-ash=Wazhazha.
Ozaukie=Sauk.
Ozeailles=Okchayi.
Ozembogus=Ozanbogus.
Ozenick=Ozenic.
Ozenies=Ozinies.
Ozi=Oraibi.
Ozimies=Ozinies
Ozinieke=Ozenic.
Ozotheoas, Ozotoues=Uzutiuhi.

Pa-a'-bi-a=Payabya.
Paachiquis=Pacuaches.
Paaco=Paako.
Paalat=Pajalat.
Paanese=Saponi.
Paante=Panthe.
Pa Bda-ská=Salish.
Pabierni'n=Keresan Family.
Pa-ça'=Patha.
Pacaha=Quapaw.
Pacahuches=Pakawa.
Pacamas=Pacana.
Pacamteho, Pacamtekock, Pacamtekookes=Pocomtuc.
Pacanacot=Pokanoket.
Pacanas=Pacana.
Pacanaukett, Pacanawkite=Pokanoket.
Pácanche=Pakanchi.
Pacanokik=Pokanoket.
Pacaos=Pakawa.
Pacarabo=Cheyenne.
Paccamagannat=Paccamagannant.
Pacer band of Apaches=Kiowa Apache.
Pacha, Pachà, Pachac=Patzau.
Pachagues=Parchaque.
Pachai=Patzau.
Pachajuen=Pataguo.
Pachalaca, Pachalate=Pachalaque.
Pachales=Pachal.
Pachalgagu=Pachalaque.
Pachami, Pachamins=Nochpeem.
Pachanga=Temecula.
Pachany=Tankiteke.
Pachao=Pakawa.
Pacha Oglouas, Pacha-Ogoulas=Pascagoula.
Pachaques=Parchaque.
Pachaug, Pachaxa=Patzau.
Pacheena, Pacheenett, Pachenah=Pacheenaht.
Paches=Apache.
Pachgatgoch=Scaticook.
Pachimis=Tankiteke.
Pachoches=Pakawa, Parchaque.
Pachough=Patchoag.
Pachquadnach=Wechquadnach.
Pachtolik=Pastolik.
Pachules=Pachal.
ᴚaɖin=Pawnee.
ᴚaɖin-mahan=Skidi.
Paɖin-díza=Arikara.
ᴚaɖin wasábĕ=Wichita.
Packachooge=Pakachoog.
Packamins=Tankiteke.
Packanoki, Packanokick=Pokanoket.
Packemitt=Punkapog.
Pack-wans=Pekwan.
Pacoas=Pakawa.
Pacomtuck=Pocomtuc.
Paconekick=Pokanoket.
Pacos=Pakawa.
Pacotucke=Pawcatuck.
Pacotucketts=Wamesit.
Pacpoles=Pacpul.
Pacuaches, Pacuas=Pakawa.
Pacuchianis=Pacuachian.
Padacus=Comanche.
Pa-dai-na, Pa-da'-ni, Padani Maśteta=Pawnee.
Padañka, Padaws, Padducas=Comanche.
Pad-gee-li-gau=Padshilaika.
Pa-dje' ga-dzhiⁿ=Padzhegadzhin.
Padokas, Padoncas, Padonees, Padoo, Padoucahs, Padoucas, Padoucee=Comanche.
Padowagas=Seneca.

Paduca, Paducahs, Paducas, Paduka=Comanche.
Paegan=Piegan.
Paego=Pecos.
Pa-e-guns=Piegan.
Pae-qo, Paequiu, Pae-quiua-la=Pecos.
Pa-erks=Eskimo.
Pae-yoq'ona=Pecos.
Págago=Papago.
Pagampache, Pagampachis=Pahvant.
Págănăvo=Cheyenne.
Pagans=Piegan.
Pagasett=Paugusset.
Paghhuntanuck=Pauhuntanuc.
Pagnati=Paguate.
Pagnines=Paisin.
Pagninoas=Bokninuwad.
Pago=Pecos.
Págonotch=Paiute.
Pagos=Pecos.
Pagosines=Paisin.
Pagouitik=Pawating.
Págowitch, Págowits=Navaho.
Pagsin=Paisin.
Paguaches=Pacuaches.
Paguachis=Pakawa, Pacuaches.
Paguampe=Pahvant.
Pagui=Tagui.
Paguichic, Paguichique=Pagaichi.
Pagu-uits, Pa'-gu-wēts=Navaho.
Pâgwâki=Pequawket.
Pag-wa-nu-chi=Uinta.
Pa-ha-hi'-a=Payabya.
Pa-ha-sa-bé=Mescaleros.
Pa-ha-sca, ȷahatsi=Pahatsi.
Pah Baxa, Pah-bax-ahs=Pabaksa.
Pah-Edes=Paiute.
Pa-hed-ke-teh-a Village=Papakeecha.
ȷaheȷsi=Pahatsi.
Pah-huh-hach-is=Pohoniche.
Pahi Mahas=Skidi.
Pah-kah-nah-vo=Cheyenne.
Pahkee=Siksika.
Pähk-wans=Pekwan.
Pahlachocolo=Apalachicola.
Pa'hlai=Cochiti.
Pah-lo-cho-ko-los=Apalachicola.
Pahmetes=Paiute.
Pahneug=Pawnee.
Pahnutes Utahs=Paiute.
Pa-ho-cha, Pa-ho-dje, Pa-ho-ja=Iowa.
Pahós'-hádsho=Pahosalgi.
Pahouitingdachirini, Pahouiting8ach Irini=Pawating.
Pah8tet=Iowa.
Pah Ranagats, Pah-rán-nè, Pah-Reneg-Utes=Paraniguts.
Pah-rú-sá-páh=Paiute.
Pah-to-cahs=Comanche.
Pah-Touts=Paiute.
Pahuanan=Paguanan.
Pahuata=Paguate.
Pahucae, Pa-hu-cha=Iowa.
Pahui=Tagui.
Pahusitahs, Pah-Utah, Pah-Utes=Paiute.
Pah-Vantes, Pahvants, Pah-Vauts, Pah Vents, Pahvontee=Pahvant.
P'áhwia'hlíap=San Ildefonso.
Pah-witing-dach-irini, Pahwittingdach-irini=Pawating.
Pa'-i=Pawnee.
Paia, Paiaia, Paialla=Payaya.
Pai â'ti=Paiute.
Paiaya=Payaya.
Pä-ifan amím=Alsea.
Pai-Ides=Paiute.
Pai'-in-kqwŭ'-t'ǫu=Paiinkkhwutthu.
Paík=Siksika.
Paikanavos, Paikandoos=Cheyenne.
Paikawa, Paíkawan=Pakawa.
Paiki=Paki.
Pailishs=Copalis.
Paillailles=Payaya.
Paille Coupée=Buckaloon.
Pailsh, Pailsk=Copalis.
Pail-uk-sun=Sailupsun.
Paimȷut, Paimut, Paimute=Paimiut.
Painé=Pawnee.
Pain-pe-tse menay=Dakota.
Paint Creek Town=Chillicothe.

Painted Heart Indians=Skitswish.
Painted Indians=Pintados.
Paisans, Les=Seneca.
Paisau=Patzau.
Paiuches=Paiute.
Paiugan, Paiuguan=Payuguan.
Pai'-u-i-yu'-nĭt t'ǫai=Paiuiyunitthai.
Paiulee, Paiutes, Pai-yu'chimŭ, Pai-yúdshi, Pai-yu'tsĭ=Paiute.
Paiztat=Patzau.
Pajalache=Pachalaque.
Pajalaches, Pajalames=Pajalat.
Pajalaques=Pajalat, Pachalaque.
Pajalat, Pajalatames, Pajalites=Pajalat.
Pajaritos=Troomaxiaquino.
Pajaro Pinto=Tshirege.
Pá-jeh=Patki.
Pajoaque, Pajuagne, Pajuaque=Pojoaque.
Pajuate=Paguate.
Pajuguan=Payuguan.
Pâkábalŭyŭ=San Juan.
Pa'-kab nyû-mû, Pakab wiñwû, Pa'-kab wüñ-wû=Pakab.
Pakachoag=Pakachoog.
Pa'-ka-mal-li=Pakamali.
Pakanas=Pacana.
Pá-ka-na-vo, Pá-ka-na-wa=Cheyenne.
Pakanawkett=Pokanoket.
Pa-kan'-e-pul=Tubatulabal.
Pakanoki, Pakanokick=Pokanoket.
Pákan'-Talahássi=Pakan-Tallahassee.
Pakashoag, Pakaskoag=Pakachoog.
Pakatucke=Pawcatuck.
Pakauds=Pequot.
Pakawaí=Pakawa.
Pake=Paki.
Pa'kēgamāng=Pokegama.
Pakeist=Pekaist.
Pakemitt, Pakenit=Punkapog.
Pa"kiut-'lĕma=Yakima.
Pak-ka-na=Pacana.
Pakoango=Unami.
Pakodch-oog=Pakachoog.
Pakomit=Punkapog.
Pakota=Dakota.
Pá-kua=Pakwa.
Pä-kuh'-thä=Iowa, Pakhtha.
Pakŭ'parai, Pakuqhalai=San Juan.
Pak-wan=Pekwan.
Pa'-kwa wüñ-wû=Pakwa.
Pakwik=Paugwik.
Pákwiti=San Ildefonso.
Pá'l-āb=Cochiti.
Palache, Palachees=Apalachee.
Palachicolas, Palachocalas, Palachoocla, Pā-lā-chooc-la, Pā-lā-chooc-le, Palachuckolas, Palachuola=Apalachicola.
Palagueques, Palaguessons=Palaquesson.
Pá'lahuide=Cochiti.
Palaihnih=Palaihnihan Family, Shastan Family.
Palaihnihan, Palaik=Shastan Family.
Palaiks=Palaihnihan Family.
Palainik=Shastan Family.
Palaña wiñwû=Palanya.
Pa-la'-ni=Pawnee.
Palanshan, Palanshawl=Tsulamsewi.
Palaquechaune, Palaquechauré, Palaquechone, Palaquesones, Palaquessous=Palaquesson.
Palatcy=Apalachee.
Palatka=Pilatka.
Palátkwapi=Palatkwabi.
Pa-la-wä'=Palewa.
Paláwi=Coyoteros.
Palaxy=Apalachee.
Pal-e'-um-mi=Paleuyami.
Palēwa=Palawa.
Pá 'lĭxen ab pónin=Chiricahua.
Pallalat=Pajalat.
Pallalla=Payaya.
Pallalts=Pilalt.
Pallatapalla=Paloos.
Pallaya—Payaya.
Pallegawonáp=Tubatulabal.
Pallet-to Pallas=Paloos.
Pal-li-ga-wo-nap'=Tubatulabal.
Pallotepallers, Pallotepellows=Paloos.
Palma=Pauma.
Palma's rancheria=San Dionysio.
Palm-kech-emk=Pan.
Palm Springs=Sechi.

Paloas, Palloatpallah=Paloos.
Paloguessens=Palaquesson.
Palona, Palonnas=Palomas.
Pallotepallors, Palooche, Paloose, Palouse=Paloos.
Palquesson=Palaquesson.
Paltatro=Paltatre.
Paltocac=Partocac.
Pa'lu=Paviotso.
Pa-lüñ-am wüñ-wû=Palanya.
Pälus=Paloos.
Paluxies, Paluxsies=Biloxi.
Palvas=Paloos.
Pal-wish-a=Badwisha.
Pamacacack, Pamacaeack, Pamacocack=Pamacocac.
Pamanes=Pausanes.
Pamanuk, Pamanuke, Pamaomeck=Pamunkey.
Pamaquid=Pemaquid.
Pamareke=Pamunkey.
Pamassa, Pamasus=Wichita.
Pamauke, Pamaunk, Pamaunkes, Pamaunkie=Pamunkey.
Pamauuaioc=Pomouic.
Pamavukes=Pamunkey.
Pambizimena=Dakota.
Pameik=Pomeioc.
Pames=Pausanes.
Pämisähagi=Pamissouk.
Pamit=Pamet.
Pamitaris' town=Pimitoui.
Pamlicough=Pamlico.
Pammahas=Skidi.
Pamnaouamske, Pamna8amske=Penobscot.
Pamnit=Pamet.
Pamonkies=Pamunkey.
Pamozanes=Pamoranos.
Pampapas=Pamposas.
Pampe Chyimina=Dakota.
Pamphleco, Pampleco=Pamlico.
Pampoas, Pampopas, Pampos=Pamposas.
Pamptaco, Pamptecough, Pamptego, Pamptichoe, Pampticoe, Pampticoke, Pampticough, Pamptucough, Pamtico, Pamticough=Pamlico.
Pamua=Pauma.
Pamunkies=Pamunkey.
Pamunky=Pamacocac.
Pana=Ponca.
Panacas=Pacana.
Panack=Bannock.
Panagamsdé=Penobscot.
Panagues=Pamaques.
Panahamsequit=Penobscot.
Panai Proper=Chaui.
Panaite, Panak=Bannock.
Panaloga=Comanche.
Panampskéwi, Panamské=Penobscot.
Panana=Pawnee.
Pananaioc=Pomouic.
Pánanan=Pawnee.
Pananarocks, Panannojock, Pananuaioc=Pomouic.
Pana-ómpskek, Panaomské, Panaonke, Panaouamské, Panaouamké, Panaouamsde, Pana8amsdé, Panaouamské, Pana8amské, Pana8amsket, Panaouamsquée, Panaouanbskek, Panaouanké, Panaouaske, Panaoumski, Panaounké, Panaouské=Penobscot.
Panaquanike=Quinnipiac.
Panaquid=Pemaquid.
Pana's=Ponca.
Panascan=Pasnacanes.
Panasht=Bannock.
Panawamské, Panawamskik, Panawaniské=Penobscot.
Panawanscot=Oldtown.
Panawanske, Panawanskek=Penobscot.
Panawapskek=Oldtown.
Panawopskéyal=Penobscot.
Pánaχki=Abnaki.
Pançacola=Pensacola.
Pancaké=Kansa.
Pancas=Ponca.
Pancasa, Pancassa=Wichita.
Pancaws=Ponca.
Panches=Tabeguache.
Pandoga, Pandouca=Comanche.
Panea Republicans=Kitkehahki.
Paneas=Pawnee.
Paneassa=Wichita.
Pâ-nee=Chaui.

Panego=Panequo.
Pa-nel-a-kut=Penelakut.
Paneloga, Panelogo, Paneloza=Comanche.
Panemaha=Skidi.
Panes=Pawnee.
Panetoca, Panetonka=Comanche.
Pangkaws, Panᵘka=Ponca.
Panʰ' ka wacta'χe=Panhkawashtake.
Pani=Dakota, Pawnee.
Pania=Ponca.
Paniaisa=Wichita.
Pania Loups=Skidi.
Pania Lousis, Pania Luup=Skidi.
Pania-Picque, Pania Pique=Wichita.
Pania Republican=Kitkehahki.
Panias=Pawnee.
Panias Loups=Skidi.
Panias proper, Panias propres=Chaui.
Panias républicains, Panias Republican=Kitkehahki.
Paniassas=Wichita.
Panies=Pawnee.
Panimachas, Panimaha, Panimaha's, Pani-Mahaws, Pa-nĭ-ma hû, Panimakas, Panimalia, Panimalis=Skidi.
Panimassas=Wichita.
Panimoas, Panimoha=Skidi.
Panⁿ'-iⁿ=Pawnee.
Panionassa, Paniouassa, Panioussa, Paniovasas=Wichita.
Panipiques, Panipiquet, Paniques=Tawehash.
Panis=Pawnee.
Panis Blancs=Pani Blanc, Pawnee.
Panisciowa=Pineshow.
Panislousa, Panismahans, Panis Mahas=Skidi)
Panis noirs, Panis piques=Wichita.
Panis Republican=Kitkehahki.
Panis ricaras=Arikara.
Panivacha=Skidi.
Pani-wasaba, Panjas=Wichita.
Paŋ'-ka, Panka, Pañ'kaⁿ=Ponca.
Pankapog=Punkapog.
Pañk unikaciⁿ ga=Pankunikashinga.
Pannacks, Pannah, Pannakees=Bannock.
Pannamaha=Skidi.
Pannaouamské, Panna8amski, Panna8anskeins, Panna8apské, Pānnawānbskek=Penobscot.
Panneh=Allakaweah.
Panniassas=Wichita.
Pannimalia=Skidi.
Pann8anskeans=Penobscot.
Panoirigoueiouhak=Pawating.
Panomnik=Panamenik.
Panouamké, Panouamsdè, Panoüamské, Pan8amské=Penobscot.
Panoucas=Comanche.
Panoümsqué, Panouske, Pan8umské=Penobscot.
Panpacans=Panpakan.
Panquiaug=Pyquaug.
Pansacolas=Pensacola.
Pantch pinunkansh=Chitimacha.
Päⁿtdóa=Pang.
Pânt-hâm-ba=San Cristóbal.
Panther gens=Tangdhangtankaenikashika.
Pantico, Panticoes, Panticoughs=Pamlico.
Pants Mahas=Skidi.
Panukkog=Pennacook.
Panumits=Serranos.
Pán-wa=Pangwa.
Pánwâpskik=Penobscot.
Pañ'-wa wüñ-wü, Pañwû wiñwû=Pangwa.
Pany, Panyi=Pawnee.
Pányi púca=Arikara.
Pányi waçéwe=Wichita.
Panys=Pawnee.
Panzacola=Pensacola.
Pa O-bde'-ca=Salish.
Paoducas=Comanche.
Paola=Puaray.
Paomet=Pamet.
Paoneneheo, Paoninihiiu, Paonis=Pawnee.
Paonte=Panthe.
Paontetack=Pontetoc.
Paoté=Iowa.
Paouichtigouin, Paouitagoung, Paouitigoueieuhak=Chippewa.
Paouitikoungraentaouak=Pawating.
Paouitingouach-irini=Chippewa.
Paoutées, Paoutés, Paoutez=Iowa.

Papabi-cotam, Papabi-Ootam, Papa'bi-Otawas, Papa-bos, Papabotas=Papago.
Papaconck=Papagonk.
Papaga, Papagi, Papago-cotam, Pa-Pagoe, Papagoes=Papago.
Papagonck=Papagonk.
Papagoose, Papagos=Papago.
Papagos Arenanos=Sand Papago.
Papah-a'atam, Papahi-Ootam, Papah'o, Papahotas=Papago.
Papajichic=Papagichic.
Papajos, Papalotes, Papani, Papa-Otam, Papapootam, Papap Ootan, Papip-Otam=Papago.
Papasquiara=Papasquiaro.
Papavicotam, Papavos, Papawar, Papayos=Papago.
Papechigunach=Restigouche.
Papelotes=Papago.
Papenachois=Papinachois.
Papia Louisis=Skidi.
Papigo=Papago.
Papikaha=Quapaw.
Papillion=Skwailuh.
Papinachaux, Papinaches, Papinachiois, Papinachi-sekhi, Papinakiois, Papinakois, Papinanchois, Papipanachois, Papiragad'ek=Papinachois.
Papitsinima=Dakota.
Papivaches=Papinachois.
Papka, Pápkamiut=Kuskwogmiut.
Pá'pk'um=Popkum.
Paponeches=Papinachois.
Papounan's Town=Wyalusing.
Papshpûn-'lĕma=Kalispel.
PaQā'mali=Pakamali.
Pa'-qọa=Pakhtha.
Paqocte, Pa'ːqo-tce=Iowa.
ꝗaqpü' iniꝙki'ácⁿa=Pakhpuinihkashina.
Pä-qu=Paako.
Paquaanocke=Poquonnac.
Paquakig=Pequawket.
Paquanaug, Paquanick=Poquonnoc.
Paquatauog=Pequot.
Paquatuck, Paquatucke=Pawcatuck.
Paquea=Piqua.
Paquirachic=Pahuirachic.
P'a-qu-lah=Pecos.
Pa'-qu-te, Pa'quꝙsĕ=Iowa.
Para=Puretuay.
Parabuyeis=Tawehash.
Parachoocla, Parachuctaus=Apalachicola.
Paraconos=Pamuncoroy.
Paracossi=Tocobaga.
Paraji=Paraje.
Paranagats=Paraniguts.
Parant Utahs=Pahvant.
Paranükh=Shivwits.
Paravan Yuta=Pahvant.
Parawan Indians, Parawat Yutas=Paruguns.
Paray=Puaray.
Parblos=Pueblos.
Parc aux Vaches=Pokagon.
Parchacas=Parchaque.
Parchiquis=Paachiqui.
Pa-rees-car=Pariscar.
Par-is-câ-ôh-păn-gȧ=Crows.
Parkeeh=Siksika.
Par-lar-nee=Pawnee.
Pár-le-sick=White People.
Parocossi=Tocobaga.
Partocae=Partocac.
Par-too-ku=Comanche.
Parusi=Paiute.
Parvain, Parvan, Par Vans=Pahvant.
Pasagoula=Pascagoula.
Pasaju=Patzau.
Pasamaquoda=Passamaquoddy.
Pascaganlas, Pascagolas, Pascagoulas, Pasca Ogoulas, Pasca Oocolas, Pasca-Oocoolos=Pascagoula.
Pascataquas=Piscataqua.
Pascataway, Pascatawaye, Pascatoe=Piscataway.
Pascatoe, Pascatoways, Pascattawaye=Conoy.
Paschtoligmeuten, Paschtoligmjuten, Paschtoligmüten=Pastoligmiut.
Paschtolik=Pastolik.
Paschtuligmüten=Pastoligmiut.
Pascoboula, Pascogoulas=Pascagoula.
Pascoticons=Conoy.
Pasceg-na=Pascegna.
Pasha=Paska.
Pasheckna=Pascegna.
Pashilqua, Pashilquia=Cayoosh Creek.

Pashingmu=Pascegna.
Pashóhan=Iowa.
Pashtolegmutis, Pashtolits=Pastoligmiut.
Paskagoulas, Paskaguna=Pascagoula.
Pas-ke-sa=Poskesas.
Paskwawiyiniwok=Paskawininiwug.
Paso, Paso del Rio del Norte=El Paso.
Paspagolas=Pascagoula.
Paspahegas, Paspahege, Paspaheghes, Paspaheigh=Paspahegh.
Paspatank=Pasquotank.
Paspatanzie=Pastanza.
Paspihae, Paspihe=Paspahegh.
Pasptanzie=Pastanza.
Pasquasheck=Pasquasheck.
Pasquenan=Pakana.
Pasquenock, Pasquenoke=Pasquenoc.
Pasqui=Tasqui.
Pasquuasheck=Pasquasheck.
Passacolas=Pensacola.
Passadunkee=Passadumkeag.
Passajonck, Passajongh, Passajonk=Passayonk.
Passamacadie, Passamaquoda, Passamaquodda, Passamaquoddies, Passamaquodie, Passamequado, Passammaquoddies=Passamaquoddy.
Passaquenock, Passaquenoke=Pasquenoc.
Passataquack=Piscataqua.
Passayunck=Passayonk.
Passemaquoddy, Passimaquodies=Passamaquoddy.
Passinchan=Iowa.
Passing Hail's band=Ohanhanska.
Passinogna=Pasinogna.
Passo del Norte=El Paso.
Passoi-Ougrin=Pasukdhin.
Passonagesit=Massachuset.
Pass-see-roo=Pasara.
Pastalac, Pastaluc=Pastaloca.
Pastalve=Pasalves.
Pastannownas, Pasta-now-na=Castahana.
Pastias=Pasteal.
Pastol'iak, Pastol'iakh=Pastoliak.
Pastolig'mūt=Pastoligmiut.
Pastoloca=Pastaloca.
Pasuchis=Paiute.
P'asuiáp=Pojoaque.
ꝗasu'ꝗꝗiⁿ, Pasukdhiⁿ=Pasukdhin.
Pasúque=Pojoaque.
Pasxa=Patzau.
Patacales=Pastaloca.
Patagahan, Patagahu, Patagua, Pataguan, Patague, Pataguinta=Pataguo.
Pâ-taína=Paw.
Patamack=Potomac.
Patanou=Potano.
Pataquakes, Pataque=Pataguo.
Patarabueges, Patarabueyes, Patarabuyes, Patarabyes=Tawehash.
Patasce=Pataotrey.
Patas-negras=Siksika.
Patavo=Pataguo.
Pat-a-wat=Batawat.
Patawatamies, Patawatimes, Patawattamies, Patawottomies=Potawatomi.
Patawe=Patwin.
Patawoenicke, Patawomeck, Patawomekes=Potomac.
Patchague=Patchoag.
Patchal=Pachal.
Patchawe=Patwin.
Patcheena=Pacheenaht.
Patchgatgoch=Scaticook.
Patchica=Patica.
Patchisági=Apache.
Patchogue=Patchoag.
Patcinā'ath=Pacheenaht.
Pa-tco'-ka, Pa-tco'-ꝗa-jă=Comanche.
Pa-tdó'a=Pa.
Pä-tdó'a=Pang.
Patesick=Karok.
Pa-tes-oh=Djishtangading.
Paticos=Patica.
Patih-riks=Karok.
Patisch-oh=Djishtangading.
Pat-ki-nyû-mû, Pat'-ki-wûñ-wû=Patki.
Patlapiguas=Potlapigua.
Patomacs=Potomac.
Patonca=Comanche.
Patowamack, Patowmeck, Patowomacks, Patowomeek, Patowomek=Potomac.

Patrantecooke=Pocomtuc.
Patroniting Dach-Irini=Pawating.
Pátsjoe=Navaho.
Patsuikets=Sokoki.
Pattawatamies, Pattawatima, Pattawatimees, Pattawatimy, Pattawatomie, Pattawattamees, Pattawattomies, Pattawattomis=Potawatomi.
Pattawomekes=Potomac.
Pattiwatima=Potawatomi.
Pattsou=Patzau.
Pa-tu-átami=Potawatomi.
Patuckset=Patuxet.
Pa-tŭh-kû, Pa′-tu-kă, Paɹuñke=Comanche.
Pa′-tuñ wuñ-wü=Patuñg.
Patusuc, Patuxite=Patuxet.
Patuxunt=Patuxent.
Patuyet=Patuxet.
Patweens=Patwin.
Pat-wish-a=Badwisha.
Patzar=Patzau.
Pauanas=Pawnee.
Paucatuck, Paucatucke=Pawcatuck.
Pa-uches=Paiute.
Paucomtuck, Paucomtuckqut=Pocomtuc.
Pa-u-da=Paiute.
Paú-e-răts′=Pueblos.
Paugasset=Paugusset.
Pauhoochees=Iowa.
Pauhuntanuck=Pauhuntanuc.
Paukanawket=Pokanoket.
Paukwechin=Panquechin.
Pauline's band=Walpapi.
Paumet=Pamet.
Paunaques=Bannock.
Paunch Indians=Allakaweah.
Paunee=Pawnee.
Paunee Loups=Skidi.
Paunee Piqûé=Wichita.
Paunee Republic=Kitkehahki.
Pauns=Winnebago.
Paüoirigoüeieuhak, Pauoitigoueieuhak, Pauotigoueieuhak=Pawating.
Pauquatuck=Pawcatuck.
Pauquiaug, Pauquog=Pyquaug.
Pauray=Puaray.
Pausanas=Pausanes.
Pautawatimis, Pautawattamies, Pauteauamis=Potawatomi.
Pa-utes=Paiute.
Pautuket=Wamesit.
Pautuxuntes=Patuxent.
Pau-Utahs=Paiute.
Pauvans, Pauvante=Pahvant.
Pauwagta=Pawokti.
Pavant Utahs, Pavant Yuta=Pahvant.
Pau-woc-te=Pawokti.
Pauzanes=Pausanes.
Pavilion, Pavillon=Skwailuh.
Pa-vi-o-tsos=Paviotso.
Pavlooskoi, Pavlovsk=Pavlof.
Pavlovskaia=Kenai.
Pavlovskoe=Pavlof.
Pavlovsky gavan=Kodiak.
Pawactas=Pawokti.
Pawateeg=Pawating.
Pawaustic-eythin-yoowuc=Atsina.
Pawcompt=Pocomtuc.
Pa-weapits=Pawipits.
Pâwhá′hlita=San Ildefonso.
Pâwétĕkŏ Wĕnĕnĕwăk=Pawating.
Pawgassett, Pawgasuck, Pawghkeesuck=Paugusset.
Pawi=Tagui.
Pawichtigou-ek=Pawating.
Pawik=Paugwik.
Pawílkna=Coyoteros.
Pâwhá′hlita=San Ildefonso.
Paw-is-tick I-e-ne-wuck=Atsina.
Pawistucienemuk=Atsina, Pawating.
Pawistuck-Ienewuck=Atsina.
Pawitagou-ek=Pawating.
Pawkanawkuts=Pokanoket.
Pawkeatucket=Pawcatuck.
Pawkees=Siksika.
Pawkunnawkuts=Pokanoket.
Pawkunnawkutts=Pokanoket, Wampanoag.
Pawlowskoje=Pavlof.
Paw-luch=Palus.
Pawmet=Pamet.
Pawnawnees, Pawne=Pawnee.

Pawnee=Lipan.
Pawnee Loup, Pawnee Loupes, Pawnee Maha, Pawnee Mahaw, Pawnee Marhar, Pawnee Mohaw, Pawnee O'Mahaws, Pawneeomawhaw, Pawnee O'Mohaws=Skidi.
Pawnee Pick, Pawnee Picts, Pawnee Piquas=Wichita.
Pawneer=Pawnee.
Pawnee republic, Pawnee Republican=Kitkehahki.
Pawnee-Rikasree=Arikara.
Pawnees republic=Kitkehahki.
Pawnee Tappage, Pawnee Tappahs, Pawnee Tappaye=Pitahauerat.
Pawnemaha=Skidi.
Pawni, Páwnye=Pawnee.
Pawpoesit=Poponesset.
Pawtucket, Pawtucketts, Pawtukett=Wamesit.
Pawtuxunt=Patuxent.
Pawzas=Pawnee.
Paxahitos=Pajarito.
Paχatatch=Pajalat.
Paxchales=Pachal.
Pa′χodshe=Iowa.
Páχuádo ámĕti=Walapai.
ɟaxu′ uɲɟinʹde=Paghuukdhinpe.
Payabyeya=Payabya.
Payaguanes=Payuguan.
Payaguas=Payaya.
Payahan=Payuguan.
Payai=Payaya.
Payairkets=Eskimo.
Payalla=Payaya.
Päyangitchaki=Piankashaw.
Payankatanks, Payankatonks=Piankatank.
Payavan=Payaguan.
Payay, Payayasa, Payayes=Payaga.
Paycines=Paisin.
Paygans=Piegan.
Páyin=Pawnee.
Páyin-manʹhanʹ=Skidi.
Payinʹqtci, Payinqtsi=Chaui.
Paymas=Pima.
Paynutes, Payoche=Paiute.
Pa-yo-go-na, Payoqona=Pecos.
Payories=Peoria.
Payseyas=Payasa.
Paysim=Paisin.
Paystravskoi=Eider.
Payuaque=Pojoaque.
Payuchas, Payuches, Payukue=Paiute.
Payugan, Payuhan, Payuhuan=Payuguan.
Payüpki=Sandia.
Payutas=Paiute.
Payutes=Paviotso.
Payutsín dinné=Paiute.
Paza, Pazac, Pazajo, Pazaju=Patzau.
Pazaticans=Nussamek.
Pazau, Pazaug, Pazhajo=Patzau.
Pazuchis=Paiute.
Pea=Wea.
Peacemaker=Chizhuwashtage.
Peach Orchard Town=Pakan-Tallahassee.
Peacott=Pequot.
Peadea=Pedee.
Peagan, Peagin, Peaginou, Pe-ah-cun-nay=Piegan.
Péahko=Pecos.
Pe-ah's band of Utes=Grand River Ute.
Peahshaws, Peanghichia, Peanguicheas, Peanguichias, Peanguischias, Peanguiseins, Peankshaws, Peanquichas, Peanzichias Miamis=Piankashaw.
Peaouarias=Peoria.
Peaquitt, Peaquods, Peaquots=Pequot.
Pearls-people=Kretan.
Peau de Lièvre=Kawchodinne.
Peauguicheas=Piankashaw.
Peaux de Lièvres=Kawchodinne.
Peaux d'Oreille=Kalispel.
Pecaneaux=Piegan.
Pecankeeshaws=Piankashaw.
Pecan Point=Nanatsoho.
Pecari=Picuris.
Pecas=Pecos.
Pecawa=Piqua.
Peccos=Pecos.
Pecegesiwag=Pashagasawissouk.
Pechanga=Temecula.
Pechir=Piechar.
Peckwalket=Pequawket.
Pe-cla=Peshla.

Pe-cla-ptcetcela=Peshlaptechela.
Peco=Pecos.
Pecoates, Pecoats, Pecods, Pecoites, Pecoits=
  Pequot.
Pecompticks, Pecomptuk=Pocomtuc.
Pecora=Picuris.
Pecotts=Pequot.
Pec-quan=Pekwan.
Pecuarias=Peoria.
Pecucio, Pecucis=Picuris.
Pe-cuil-i-gui=Pekwiligii.
Pecuri, Pecuries=Picuris.
Pecuwési=Piqua.
Pecyou=Peeyou.
Pedadumies=Potawatomi.
Pe-dâhl-lu=Petdelu.
Pedanis=Pawnee.
Pedees=Pedee.
Pedgans=Piegan.
Peducas=Comanche.
Pee-allipaw-mich=Puyallup.
Peegans=Piegan.
Pe'ekit=Nabukak.
Peelig=Pilingmiut.
Peel River Indians, Peel's River Indians, Peel's
  River Loucheux=Tatlitkutchin.
Peenecooks=Pennacook.
Peequots=Pequot.
Pegan, Peganes, Pe-gan-o, Peganœ'-koon, Peganoo-
  eythinyoowuc=Piegan.
Pegans=Chabanakongkomun.
Pe ga'-zan-de=Nez Percés.
Pegóa=Pecos.
Pegods=Pequot.
Peg8akki, Pegouakky=Pequawket.
Pegoucoquias=Pepikokia.
Pegwacket, Pegwackit, Pegwackuk, Pegwaggett,
  Pegwakets=Pequawket.
Pehenguichias=Piankashaw.
Pe-hi'-pte-ci-la=Peshlaptechela.
Pehires=Pehir.
Pehqwoket=Pequawket.
Peht-sau-an=Djishtangading.
Peh-tsik=Karok.
Pehumes=Peinhoum.
Peici, Peicj=Pecos.
Peigans=Piegan.
Peihoum, Peihoun=Peinhoum.
Peíki=Siksika.
Peikuagamiu=Piekouagami.
Peimtegouët=Penobscot.
Peisacho=Peissaquo.
Pe-ji-wo-ke-ya-o-ti=Shoshoni.
Pejodque=Pojoaque.
Pekadasank=Pakadasank.
Pe-kan-ne, Pekanne-koon=Piegan.
Pe xa'-san-xse=Nez Percés.
Pekash=Pequot.
Peki'neni=Potawatomi.
Pekoath, Pekoct, Pekot=Pequot.
Pek8anokets=Pokanoket.
Pek8atsaks=Pequot.
Pékoweu=Piqua.
Péku=Pecos.
Pĕkuégi=Piqua.
Pe"kwilitâ'=Picuris.
Pe-lac-le-ka-ha=Pilaklikaha.
Pelagisía=Piankashaw.
Pelajemôn=White People.
Pelaklekaha, Pelaklikhaha=Pilaklikaha.
Pelátlq=Pilalt.
Pel'catzék=Pelkatchek.
Pelchin=Pelchiu.
Peledquey=Pilidquay.
Pelican Lake band=Sukáauguning.
Pe-ı'ka-tcék=Pelkatchek.
Pel-late-pal-ler, Pelloatpallah, Pelloat pal'ahs, Pel-
  lote-pal-ler=Paloos.
Pelly Bay Eskimo=Sinimiut.
Peloose, Pelouches, Pelouse, Pelouze=Paloos.
Peluches=Apalachee.
Pelus, Peluse=Paloos.
Pema=Pima.
Pematnawi=Lorette.
Pemblicos=Pamlico.
Pem-bul-e-qua=Pebulikwa.
Pemedeniek=Huron.
Pemetegoit=Penobscot.

Pemlico, Pemlicoe=Pamlico.
Pemmaquid, Pemmayquid=Pemaquid.
Pemos=Pima.
Pemplico=Pamlico.
Pempotawuthut, Pempotowwuthut=Schodac.
Pemptagoiett=Penobscot.
Pemptico=Pamlico.
Pems-quah-a-wa=Tippecanoe.
Pemtegoit=Penobscot.
Penacook=Pennacook.
Pe-nă-döj-kā=Penateka.
Penagooge=Pennacook.
Pe-naï'-na=Pawnee.
Penakook=Pennacook.
Penâlahuts=Penelakut.
Penal Apaches=Pinaleños.
Pēnā'leqat, Penalikutson=Penelakut.
Penandé, Penä'nde=Penateka.
Penaquid=Pemaquid.
Penard=Foxes.
Penasco Blanca=Peñasca Blanca.
Penaské=Penobscot.
Pen-a-tacker, Penatakas=Penateka.
Penaubsket, Penboscots, Penboscut=Penobscot.
Pençacola, Pençocolos=Pensacola.
Pend d'Oreilles Lower, Pend d'Oreilles of the Lower
  Lake, Pend d'Oreilles of the Upper Lake=Kalispel.
Pendeña=Pinaleños.
Pends-d'oreille, Pends Oreilles=Kalispel.
Penduhuts=Penelakut.
Penechon=Pineshow.
Penecooke=Pennacook.
Penelakas, Penelethkas, Penetakees, Penetakers,
  Peneteghka, Penetéka, Penetéka-Comanches,
  Pene-teth-ca, Penetethka, Penetoghkos, Penha-
  tethka, Pen-ha-teth-kahs, Pĕn'-ha-tĕth'-kas=Pe-
  nateka.
Penichon=Pineshow.
Penicoock, Penicook=Pennacook.
Pĕn'ikis=Abnaki.
Penikook=Pennacook.
Peniteni=Pimitoui.
Penition=Pineshow.
Penkapog=Punkapog.
Pen loca=Comanche.
Pennacokes, Pennacooke, Pennagog, Pennakooks=
  Pennacook.
Pennatuckets=Pentucket.
Pennecooke, Pennekokes, Pennekook, Pennekooke=
  Pennacook.
Pennelakas, Penne-taha, Pennetekas=Penateka.
Pennicook, Pennikook=Pennacook.
Pennobscot=Penobscot.
Pennokook=Pennacook.
Pennoukady=Passamaquoddy.
Penny Cook, Penny-Cooke, Pennykoke=Pennacook.
Penobcsutt, Penobscotes, Penobscotts, Penobscut,
  Penobskeag, Penobsots=Penobscot.
Peñol, Peñoles=Acoma.
Peñon=El Peñon.
Pensicola=Pensacola.
Pentagoet, Pentagoiett, Pentagonett, Pentagouet,
  Pentag8et, Pentagouetch, Pentagovett, Pente-
  goët=Penobscot.
Penticutt=Pentucket.
P·E'ntlatc=Puntlatsh.
Penttakers=Penateka.
Pentuckett=Pentucket.
Pentug8et=Penobscot.
Peoiras=Peoria.
Peok8agamy=Piekouagami.
Peola, Peonas, Peonies=Peoria.
People in a Circle=Detsanayuka.
People of the Desert=Kwahari.
People-of-the-flat-roof-houses=Querechos.
People of the Fork=Nassauaketon.
People of the Lake=Mdewakanton.
People of the leaf, People of the Leaves=Wahpe-
  ton.
People of the Leaves detached=Wahpekute.
People of the Lowlands=Maskegon.
People of the Pheasants=Sipushkanumanke.
People of the Prairie=Paskwawininiwug.
People of the River=Wahpeton.
People of the Shot Leaf=Wahpekute.
People of the Willows=Havasupai.
People of the Woods=Sakawithiniwuk.
People that don't Laugh=Kutaiimiks.
Peores, Peorians, Peoryas=Peoria.

Peouanguichias=Piankashaw.
Peouarewi, Peouarias, Peouarius, Peoüaroüa, Peoucaria, Peoueria, Peouria, Péouryas=Peoria.
Peoutewaᵗamie=Potawatomi.
P'ē'paLēnôx=Pepatlenok.
Pē'pawiLēnôx=Pepawitlenok.
Pepchalk=Peepchiltk.
Pepepicokia, Pepepoaké=Pepikokia.
Pepht-soh=Djishtangading.
Pepicoquias, Pepicoquis, Pepikokis, Pepikoukia=Pepikokia.
Peptchörl=Peepchiltk.
Pépua-hapítski Sawanógi=Absentee.
Pequa=Pequea.
PE'qaist=Pekaist.
Pequakets=Pequawket.
Pequants=Pequot.
Pequanucke=Poquonnuc.
Pequaquaukes=Pequawket.
Pequatit, Pequatoas, Pequatoos, Pequatt=Pequot.
Pequauket, Pequawett=Pequawket.
Pequea=Piqua.
Pequeag=Pyquaug.
Pequeats=Pequot.
Pequehan=Pequea.
Pequente, Pequents, Pequetans, Pequets, Pequett, Pequid, Pequims, Pequin, Pequite, Pequitóog, Pequitts, Pequoadt, Pequod, Pequoids, Pequoite, Pequoits=Pequot.
Pequot=Nameaug.
Pequote, Pequotoh, Pequoyts=Pequot.
Pequt Nayantaquit=Niantic.
Pequts, Pequtt, Pequttôog, Pequuts, Pequuttoog, Peqvats, Peqwit=Pequot.
Perces=Nez Percés.
Pergniak, Perignak, Perignax=Pernyu.
Periqua=Perigua.
Permavevvi=Pimitoui.
Perocodame=Terocodame.
Perouacca, Perouarca, Peroueria=Peoria.
Perríu, Perun=Tionontati.
Pescagolas=Pascagoula.
Peskadam8kkan, Peskadam-ukotik, Peskadaneeoukkanti, Peskamaquonty=Passamaquoddy.
Pe-śla=Peshla.
Pe-śla-pteéela=Peshlaptechela.
Pesmaquady, Pesmocady, Pesmokanti, Pĕs-ta-mo-kátiŭk=Passamaquoddy.
Pestriakof, Pestriakovo, Pestriakowskoje, Pestryakovskoe=Eider.
Pestumagatick=Passamaquoddy.
Pétâa-kwe=Aiyaho.
Pe-tä-hä'-ne-rat=Pitahauerat.
Petaluma=Chokuyem.
Pêtaⁿ énikaci'ka=Petanenikashika.
Petaro=Petao.
Petawomeek=Potomac.
Petaz, Petçares=Petao.
Petchisági=Apache.
Pë-tdóa=Pë.
Petenegowat Pah-Utes=Petenegowats.
Peterărwi, Peteravak, Peteravik=Pituarvik.
Pethähänerat, Pethowerats=Pitahauerat.
Petikokias=Pepikokia.
Petit Corbeau's band=Kapozha.
Petite Nation, Petite Nation des Algonquins=Weskarini.
Petit Osage=Utsehta.
Petits Algonquins=Weskarini.
Petitscotias=Pepikokia.
Petit-sick=Karok.
Petits Os=Utsehta.
Petit Talessy=Talasse.
Petit Zo=Utsehta.
Petlenum=Chokuyem.
Petonaquats=Petenegowats.
Pe-tou-we-ra=Pitahauerat.
Petowach, Petowack=Pituarvik.
Pe'tqaⁿ i'niųk'äcin'a=Petkhaninihkashina.
Petquottink=Pequottink.
Petsaré=Petao.
Pe' ąse iniųk'äcin'a=Kanse.
Petsikla=Karok.
Pet-tán-i-gwut=Petenegowats.
Pettikokias=Pepikokia.
Pettquotting=Pequottink.
Petuneurs=Cayuga.
Petuneux=Tionontati.
Petząre=Petao.

Peuple de Faisans=Sipushkanumanke.
Pewins=Winnebago.
Pe+χ'-gĕ=Jicarilla.
Peyakwagami=Piekouagami.
Peyaya=Payaya.
Pey metes Utahs=Paiute.
Pey-utes=Paviotso.
Pe-zhew=Besheu.
Pezhi-wokeyotila=Shoshoni.
Pezo=Pissuh.
Pez Perces=Nez Percés.
Phalacheho=Palacheho.
P'hallatillie=Tubatulabal.
Phampleco=Pamlico.
Pharaona, Pharaones=Faraon.
Pheasants=Shiyotanka.
Philip's Indians=Wampanoag.
P'ho, P'ho doa=Po.
P'Ho-juo-ge=San Ildefonso.
Phonecha=Pohoniche.
P'ho-se=Poseuingge.
P'Ho-zuang-ge=Pojoaque.
Pia=Sia.
Piagouagami=Piekouagami.
Piah band=Grand River Ute.
Piakouakamy, Piakuakamits=Piekouagami.
Pialeges=Kailaidshi.
Pianaua=Pinawa.
Piancashaws, Piangeshaw, Pianguichia, Pianguisha, Piankashaws, Piankaskouas, Piankeshas, Piankeshaws, Piankichas, Piànkishas, Piankshaws, Pianquicha, Pianquiches, Pianquishaws=Piankashaw.
Pianrias, Piantias=Peoria.
Piaqui=Pahquetooai.
Pi-auk-e-shaws, Piawkashaws=Piankashaw.
Pi-ba=Sa.
Pi-ba nyû-mû, Piba wiñwû, Pib-wüñ-wü=Piba.
Pic=Wichita.
Pi'-ca=Pisha.
Picaneaux, Picaneux=Piegan.
Picanipalish=Puyallup.
Picaris, Piccuries=Picuris.
Pichar, Pichares=Piechar.
Picheno=Pischenoas.
Pichmichtalik=Pikmiktalik.
Pichons=Pisquows.
Pichouagamis=Piekouagami.
Pi-ci'-kse-ni-tup'-i-o=Shoshoni.
Pickan=Piegan.
Pickar=Piechar.
Pickawa, Pickaway, Pickawee, Pickawes=Piqua.
Pickawillany=Pickawillanee.
Pickovagam=Piekougami.
Pickpocket=Pequawket.
Picks=Wichita.
Pickwacket, Pickwocket=Pequawket.
Piɔl'-kwŭ-tsi-aus'=Pithlkwutsiaus.
Picoris=Picuris.
Picos=Piro.
Pícoweu, Picque=Piqua.
Picqwaket=Pequawket.
Pictoris=Picuris.
Picts=Pickawillanee.
Picuni, Picuri, Picuria, Picuries, Picux=Picuris.
Picwocket=Pequawket.
Pidees=Pedee.
Piecis=Pecos.
Piedes=Paiute.
Piedgans=Piegan.
Pieds-noirs=Siksika.
Pie Edes, Pi-eeds=Paiute.
Piekané, Piekann=Piegan.
Piekouagamiens, Piekovagamiens=Piekouagami.
Pierced-nose=Nez Percés.
Pierced Noses=Iowa, Nez Percés.
Pietmiektaligmiut=Pikmiktalik.
Pieutes=Paiute.
Pigans=Piegan.
Pigeon Roost=Padshilaika.
Piggwacket, Pigocket, Piguachet=Pequawnet.
Piguicanes=Piguiques.
Pigwachet, Pigwacket, Pigwackitt, Pigwocket, Pigwoket, Pigwolket=Pequawket.
Pihir=Pehir.
Pihniques=Piguiques.
Pi'h-tca=Pihcha.
Pihuiques=Piguiques.
Pijiᵘ=Pissuh.
Pijmos=Pima.

Pikani=Piegan.
Pik-cak-ches=Pitkachi.
Pike=Siksika.
Pi'-ke-e-wai-ï-ne=Jicarillas.
Pikhta=Pikta.
Pikierloo=Pikirlu.
Pi-ki-il-t'çe=Pikiiltthe.
Pikiudtlek=Pikiutdlek.
Pikiulaq=Pikiulak.
Pikkawa=Piqua.
Pikmigtalik=Pikmiktalik.
Pikmikta' lig-mut=Pikmiktaligmiut.
Pikogami=Piekouagami.
Pikoweu=Piqua.
Pi-kun-i=Piegan.
Pïkuría=Picuris.
Pilabo, Pilaho=Socorro.
Pilgans=Piegan.
Pillar Rock=Tlalegak.
Pilleurs, Pilliers=Pillagers.
Pilopué=Socorro.
Pimahaitu=Pima.
Pīmâi'nûs=Pemainus.
Pimal=Pinaleños.
Pima-Papabotas=Papago.
Pimas Bajos, Pimas de el Sur=Nevome.
Pimases=Pima.
Pimas frijoleros=Papago.
Pimas Gileños, Pimas Ileños, Pime, Pimera, Pimes,
   Pimese=Pima.
Pimeteois=Pimitoui.
Pimez, Pimi, Pimicas=Pima.
Pímikshi=Pinaleños.
Piminos=Pemainus.
Pimitconis, Pimiteoui, Pimiteouy=Pimitoui.
Pimo, Pimo Galenos, Pimoles, Pimos Illños=Pima.
Pimytesouy=Pimitoui.
Pin-a-au=Pinawan.
Pinal, Pinal Apachen, Pinal Apaches, Pinalino, Pinal
   Leñas, Pinal Leno, Pinal Llanos=Pinaleños.
Pinals Apaches=Pinal Coyotero.
Pinana, Pî-na-ua, Pi'-na-wa=Pinawan.
Pinbiọò', Pinbiọòɹine, Pin bɩ́ó', Pin bɩ́ó'dɹine'=Pin-
   bitho.
Pinchon, Pinchow=Pineshow.
Pinchy=Pintce.
Pinclatchas=Pilaklikaha.
Pincos=Pima.
Pine-Band=Wazikute.
Pinechon=Pineshow.
Pin-e-hoo-te=Pinhoti.
Pineifu=Chepenafa.
Pine Indians=Natchez.
Pinelores, Pinery=Pinaleños.
Pïng-gwí=Picuris.
Pingoshugarun, Pinguishugamiut=Pinguishuk.
Ping-ul-tha=Picuris.
Pinichon=Pineshow.
Pininéos=Pinini.
Pininos=Pima.
Piniocagna=Pimocagna.
Piniscas=Acolapissa.
Pinkeshaws=Piankashaw.
Pinnancas=Pinanacas.
Pinnekooks=Pennacook.
Pinneshaw=Pineshow.
Piñoleno, Pinolero, Pinoles, Piñol-Indianer, Pinols,
   Pinon Lanos, Piñon Llano Apaches=Pinaleños.
Pinoshuragin=Pinguishuk.
Pintadi=Pintados.
Pintado=Pueblo Pintado.
Pintagoné=Penobscot.
Pintahs=Paviotso.
Pintos=Pakawa.
Pinuëltá=Picuris.
Piohum=Peinhoum.
Piorias=Peoria.
Piou=Peinhoum.
Piouanguichias=Piankashaw.
Pioüaroüa=Peoria.
Pip=Piba.
Pí-pás, Pipátsje=Maricopa.
Pipos-altos=Pima.
Piquachet=Pequawket.
Piquag=Pyquaug.
Piqua Town=Pequea.
Piquaug=Pyquaug.
Piqued=Pequea.
Piquiag=Pyquaug.
Piquitin=Pitic.
Pir, Pira, Piri=Piro.

Pirigua=Perigua.
Pirj=Piro.
Pirnas=Pima.
Piruas=Piro.
Pisacack=Pissacoac.
Pisanomo=Perinimo.
Piscahoose=Pisquows.
Piscao=Pescado.
Piscaous=Pisquows.
Piscataquaukes=Piscataqua.
Piscataway, Piscatawese=Conoy.
Piscatchecs=Pitkachi.
Piscatoway, Piscatowayes, Piscattawayes=Conoy.
Piscattoway=Piscataway.
Piscatua=Conoy.
Pischoule, Pischous=Pisquows.
Pisch quit pás=Pishquitpah.
Piscous=Pisquows.
Pisgachtigok=Scaticook.
Píshakulk=Dakota.
Pishekethe=Psakethe.
Pishgachtigok=Scaticook.
Pishiu=Besheu.
Pishquitpaws, Pishquitpows=Pishquitpah.
Pisht, Pishtot, Pishtst=Pistchin.
Pishwanwapum=Yakima.
Pisierinii, Pisirinins=Nipissing.
Piskwas, Piskwaus=Pisquows.
Pispiza-wićaśa=Pispizawichasha.
Pisquitpahs, Pisquitpaks=Pishquitpah.
Pisquous, Pisquouse=Pisquows.
Pissacoack=Pissacoac.
Pissaseck, Pissassack, Pissassees=Pissasec.
Pisscattaways=Conoy.
Piss-cows=Pisquows.
Pist-chins=Pistchin.
Pistol Rivers=Chetleschantunne.
Pi-ta'-da=Pawnee.
Pitagoriciens, Pítagoricos=Pythagoreans.
Pitaháwiratá=Pitahauerat.
Pitanisha, Pi-tan'-ni-suh=Tubatulabal.
Pitanta=Serranos.
Pitavirate Noisy Pawnee tribe, Pitavirate Noisy
   tribe=Pitahauerat.
Pit-cach-es, Pit-cat-chee, Pitcatches, Pitchackies=
   Pitkachi.
Pitchaya-kuin=Pitchaya.
Pitchiboucouni, Pitchiboueouni, Pitchïb8renik=
   Pitchibourenik.
Pitchinávo=Wichita.
Pit-cuch-es=Pitkachi.
Pitehiboutounibuek=Pitchibourenik.
Pitiaches=Pitkachi.
Piticado=Peticado.
Pitit Creek=Koiskana.
Pit-kah'-che, Pit-kah'-te=Pitkachi.
Pi'tōna'kïngkäinạpitcig=Betonukeengainubejig.
Pit River Indians=Shastan Family.
Pitt River Indians=Palaihnihan Family, Shastan
   Family.
Pi-u-chas=Paiute.
Pi-utah=Paviotso.
Piute=Paiute.
Pi-utes=Paviotso.
Piute Snakes=Paiute Snakes.
Piva=Piba.
'P'kâi'st=Pekaist.
Pkíwi-léni=Miami.
Pkqŭl-lu'-wa-ai'-t'çe=Pkhulluwaitthe.
Pku-u'-ni-uqt-auk'=Pkuuniukhtauk.
Plaíkni=Paviotso.
Plai'kni=Klamath, Modoc.
Plain Assineboins=Assiniboin of the Plains.
Plain Crees=Paskwawininiwug.
Plainfield Indians=Quinebaug.
Plañidores=Coaque.
Plankishaws=Piankashaw.
Planwikit=Playwickey.
Plàscotez de Chiens, Plat côté de Chien, Plats cotee
   de Chiens, Plats-côtes-de-Chien=Thlingchadinne.
Plats-côtés-de-chien du fort Raë=Lintchanre.
Plats-côtés de Chiens, Plats cotez de Chiens=Thling-
   chadinne.
Playsanos=Gabrieleño.
Pleasant Point=Sebaik.
Pleureurs=Coaque.
Pluie (Lac la) Indians=Kojejewininewug.
P. Machault=Venango.
Poala=Puaray.
Poam Pomo=Ballokai Pomo.

Póanïn=Apache.
Póbälo=Pueblos.
Pobawotche Utahs=Tabeguache.
Poblaçon=Poblazon.
Po-ca-gan's village, Pocagons Vill.=Pokagon.
Pocan=Ponca.
Pocanakets, Pocanakett, Pocanauket, Pocanawkits, Pocanoket, Pocanokit=Pokanoket.
Pocasicke, Pocassett, Pocassitt=Pocasset.
Pocataligo=Pocotaligo.
Pocatocke, Poccatuck=Pawcatuck.
Pochapuchkung=Pohkopophunk.
Po chis hach cha=Potchushatchi.
Pochoug, Pochoughs=Patchoag.
Po-chuse-hat-che=Potchushatchi.
Pociwû wiñwû=Poshiwu.
Pockaguma=Piekougami.
Pockanockett, Pockanoky=Pokanoket.
Pockentallahassee, Pockentalleehassee=Pakan-Tallahassee.
Pockonockett=Pokanoket.
Pockuschatche=Potchushatchi.
Pocompheake, Pocomptuck, Pocomtakukes, Pocomtock, Pocomtuck=Pocomtuc.
Pocontallahasse=Pakan-Tallahassee.
Pocotaligat=Pocotaligo.
Pocoughtaonack, Pocoughtronack = Bocootawwonauke.
Pocumptucks, Pocumtuck=Pocomtuc.
Pocuntullahases=Pakan-Tallahassee.
Po-da-waud-um-ee, Po-da-waud-um-eeg = Potawatomi.
Podunck=Podunk.
Poenese=Pawnee.
Poeomtucks=Pocomtuc.
Poes=Potawatomi.
Pofuaque=Pojoaque.
Poga, Poge=Kuapooge.
Po-ge-lido-ke=Nez Percés.
Pogodque=Pojoaque.
Pogouaté, Poguaque, Poguaté=Paguate.
Po-hah=Washakie's Band.
Po-ha-ha-chis=Pohoniche.
Pohanti=Paguate.
Pohas=Bannock.
Poh-bantes=Pahvant.
Poh-he-gan=Mahican.
Póhoi=Washakie's Band.
Pohoneche, Po-ho-ne-chees, Pohoneechees, Po-ho-neich-es, Po'-ho-ni-chi=Pohoniche.
Po-hua-gai=San Ildefonso.
Pohuaque=Pojoaque.
Pohuniche=Pohoniche.
Poils leué=Missisauga.
Pointe des Esquimaux=Esquimaux Point.
Pointed Hearted Indians, Pointed Hearts=Skitswish.
Point Pinos=Guayusta.
Point Pleasant=Sebaik.
Poissons blancs=Attikamegue.
Poitoiquis=Poitokwis.
Pojake, Pojanque, Pojanquiti, Pojaugue=Pojoaque.
Pojnati=Pajuate.
Po-jō=Pohoi.
Pojoague, Pojodque, Pojouque, Pojuague=Pojoaque.
Pojuaque=Paguate, Pojoaque.
Pojuate, Pojuato=Paguate.
Po-juo-ge, Po-juo-que=San Ildefonso.
Pokagomin=Pokegama.
Po-ka-guma=Pokegama.
Pokahs=Washakie's Band.
Pokanacket, Pokanocket=Pokanoket.
Pokanoket=Wampanoag.
Pokanokik=Pokanoket.
Po-ke-as=Poskesas.
Pokeesett=Pocasset.
Po-ke-gom-maw, Pokeguma=Pokegama.
Poke-koo-un'-go=Unami.
Po-ken-well, Po-ken-welle=Bokninuwad.
Pokeset, Pokesset=Pocasset.
Poketalico=Pocotaligo.
Pokkenvolk=Hopi.
Pokomtakukes, Pokomtock=Pocomtuc.
Pokonatri=Pohoniche.
Pokoninos, Po-kon-wel-lo=Bokninuwad.
Pokwádi, Po'kwoide=Pojoaque.
Polachucolas=Apalachicola.
Polagamis=Tubatulabal.
Polanches=Paloos.
Pole-Cat band=Hokarutcha.
Pole people=Wazikute.

Pollachuchlæw=Apalachicola.
Pollotepallors=Paloos.
Polokawynahs=Tubatulabal.
Polonches=Paloos.
Polúksalgi=Biloxi.
Polulumas=Pomulumas.
Pol-we-sha=Badwisha.
Poma poma, Poma pomo, Pomas=Ballokai Pomo.
Pomecock, Pomeiock, Pomeioke, Pomejock=Pomeioc.
Pomo=Pima.
Pomonick, Pomouik=Pomouic.
Pomparague=Pomperaug.
Pona=Misesopano, Puna.
Ponacks=Bannock.
Ponacocks, Ponacoks=Pennacook.
Ponanummakut=Potanumaquut.
Ponarak=Dakota.
Ponars=Ponca.
Ponashita, Ponashta=Bannock.
Poncahs, Poncan, Poncar, Poncarars, Poncaras, Poncare, Poncares, Poncaries, Pon'cârs, Poncas, Poncaw, Ponchas=Ponca.
Ponchestanning=Punxsutawny.
Ponch Indians=Allakaweah.
Poncrars, Poncye=Ponca.
Pond D'Oreilles, Pondecas, Pondera, Ponderays, Pond Orrilles, Ponduras=Kalispel.
Pone Pomos=Ballokai Pomo.
Pongkaws, Pongs, Poniars=Ponca.
P'ónin=Apache.
Ponis=Pawnee.
Ponishta Bonacks=Bannock.
Ponka, Ponkahs, Ponkas=Ponca.
Ponkeontamis=Potawatomi.
Ponkipog=Punkapog.
Ponobscot, Ponobscut=Penobscot.
Po-no-í-ta-ni-o=Cheyenne, Southern.
Pononakanit=Punonakanit.
Pons, Ponsars=Ponca.
Ponteatamies, Ponteòtamies, Pontewatamis, Pontowattimies, Poodawahduhme=Potawatomi.
Pooemocs=Puimuk.
Pooesoos=Puisu.
Po-o-ge=Kuapooge.
Poogooviliak, Poogovellyak=Puguviliak.
Poo-joge=San Ildefonso.
Poollachuchlaw=Apalachicola.
Pó-o-mas=Siksika.
Poong-câr=Ponca.
Poonook=Punuk.
Poor=Honowa.
Poo-reh-tú-ai=Puretuay.
Poosoonas=Pusune.
Popaghtunk=Papagonk.
Popcum=Popkum.
Popeloutechom=Popelout.
Popinoshees=Papinachois.
Popolo Bruciato=Tzenatay.
Popponeeste, Popponessit=Poponesset.
Poquannoc, Poquannock=Poquonnoc.
Poquaté=Paguate.
Poquatocke, Poquatucke=Pawcatuck.
Porc-Epic Nation=Piekouagami.
Poquonock=Poquonnoc.
Porcupine=Tukkuthkutchin.
Porcupine People=Piekouagami.
Porcupine River Indians=Tukkuthkutchin.
Porcupine Tribe=Kakouchaki.
Port de la Hève=Le Have.
Port Graham=Alexandrovsk.
Port leue'=Missisauga.
Port Madison=Suquamish.
Portobacco, Porto-Back, Portobacke, Portobaco=Potopaco.
Port Orchard=Dwamish, Suquamish.
Port Orford=Kosotshe.
Port Orford Indians=Kaltsergheatunne, Kwatami.
Port Orfords=Kaltsergheatunne.
Port Stuart Indians=Ähealt.
Port Tabago=Potopaco.
Port Townsend=Chimakum.
Poruches=Wiminuche.
Poscoiac=Pasquayah.
Po-se=Poseuingge.
Po-si'-o, Pósiwuu, Po'-si-wû wüñ-wû=Poshiwu.
Pos-ke-as=Poskesas.
Poskoyac=Pasquayah.
Posociom=Upasoitac.
Posonwû, Posówe=San Ildefonso.

Po-suan-gai=Pojuaque.
Pota-aches=Potoyanti.
Potámeos Indians=Tututni.
Potan=Potam.
Potanons=Wea.
Potanou=Potano.
Potanumccut=Potanumaqjut.
Potapaco, Potapoco=Potopaco.
Potatik=Poodatook.
Potatoe=Ahalakalgi.
Potato Town=Nununyi.
Potatuck=Poodatook.
Potauncak=Potaucao.
Potavalamia=Potawatomi.
Potavou=Potano.
Potawahduhmee, Potawatama=Potawatomi.
Potawatamie tribe of Indians of the Prairie=Prairie band of Potawatomi.
Potawatamis, Potawatimie, Pŏ-tă-wă-tŏ′-mĕ=Potawatomi.
Potawatomies of St. Joseph=St Joseph.
Potawattamies, Potawattimie, Potawattomies, Potawatumies, Po-tă-waw-tŏ′-me, Pŏ-tă′-wĕt me, Potawtumies=Potawatomi.
Po-tdóa, P'o-tdóa=Po.
Potenumacut, Potenummecut=Potanumaquut.
Poteotamis, Potéoüatami, Poteouatamis, Potewatamies, Potewatamik=Potawatomi.
Potick, Potik=Potic.
Potiwattimeeg, Potiwattomies=Potawatomi.
Potoachos, Potoancies, Potoencies=Potoyanti.
Potomack Indians, Potomeack=Potomac.
Pŏ-tŏsh′, Potowatameh, Potowatamies, Potowatomies=Potawatomi.
Potowmack=Potomac.
Potowotamies=Potawatomi.
Potoyantes, Po-to-yan-to, Poto-yau-te=Potoyanti.
Pottawatameh, Pottawataneys, Pottawatimies, Pottawatomies, Pottawattamies, Potta-wat-um-ies, Pottawaudumies, Pottawotamies, Pottawottomies, Pottewatemies, Pottiwattamies, Pottowatamies, Pottowatomy, Pottowattomies, Pottowautomie, Pottowotomees=Potawatomi.
Potzua-ge=Pojoaque.
Pou=Potawatomi.
Poualac, Poualak, Poualakes=Dakota.
Pouan=Winnebago.
Pouanak=Dakota.
Poüankikias=Piankashaw.
Pouarak=Dakota.
Pouderas=Kalispel.
Poueatamis, Pouĕs, Pouhatamies=Potawatomi.
Pouhatan=Powhatan.
Poujuaque=Pojoaque.
Poukas=Ponca.
Poulteattemis, Poulx, Poulx teattemis, Pous, Poutauatemis, Poutawatamies, Poutawottamies, Poutéamis, Poüteaoüatami, Pouteatami, Pouteatimies, Pouteauatamis, Pouteoüatami, Pouteouatamiouec, Pouteatamis, Pouteouatimi, Pouteouetamites, Pouteouitamis, Pouteouotamis, Pouteouatamis, Poutewatamies, Poutoualamis, Poutoüamis, Poutouatamis, Poutouatamittes=Potawatomi.
Poutoucsis=Biloxi.
Poutouotamis, Poutouwatamis, Poutowatomies, Poutuatamis, Poutwatamis, Pouutouatami, Poux, Pouz=Potawatomi.
Povantes=Pahvant.
Povate=Paguate.
Póvoli=Buli.
Povuate=Paguate.
Powakasick=Pocasset.
Powcatuck=Pawcatuck.
Powcomptuck=Pocomtuc.
Powebas=Kawita.
Powells town=Withlako.
Powhatanic confederacy, Powhattans=Powhatan.
Powhawneches=Pohonichi.
Powhoge=San Ildefonso.
Powmet=Pamet.
Powquaniock=Poquonnoc.
Powtawatamis, Powtewatamis, Powtewattimies, Powtowottomies=Potawatomi.
Poχuáki=Pojoaque.
P'ōyắm=Poiam.
Póye-kwe=Poyi.
Poytoquis, Poytoquix=Poitokwis.
Poze=Potre.

Pozos de Enmedio=Posos.
Po-zuan-ge, Pozuang-ge, Pozuaque=Pojoaque.
Prairie Apaches=Kiowa Apache.
Prairie Chicken clan=Seechkaberuhpaka, Sipushkanumanke.
Prairie-Crees=Paskwawininiwug.
Prairie Grossventres=Atsina.
Prairie-hen people=Seechkaberuhpaka, Sipushkanumanke.
Prairie hens=Sipushkanumanke.
Prairie Indians=Paskwawininiwug, Prairie Kickapoo.
Prairie Wolf=Shomakoosa.
Prairie-Wolf People=Mandhinkagaghe.
Premorska, Premorski=Chnagmiut.
Prescado=Pescado.
Prickled Panis=Wichita.
Priest's Rapids=Sokulk.
Primahaitu=Pima.
Primoske, Prinoski=Chnagmiut.
Printed Hearts=Skitswish.
Projoaque=Pojoaque.
Prominent Jaws=Oqtogona.
Pronaria, Pronereas, Pronevoa=Peoria.
Prophet's Town=Tippecanoe.
Protasso, Protassof, Protassov=Morzhovoi.
Prouaria=Peoria.
Provate=Paguate.
Province de Sel, Provincia de la Sal=Coligoa.
Pruara=Puaray.
Psaupsau=Patzau.
Pschwan-wapp-am=Shanwappom.
Pshawanwappam=Yakima.
Pshwa′năpûm=Shanwappom.
Psinontanhinhintons, Psinoutanhhintons=Psinoutanhinhintons.
Pt. Coweta=Kawita.
Pte-yute-cni, Pte-yute-śni=Pteyuteshni.
Ptĭ′tɛk=Petutek.
Ptuksit=Munsee.
Puaguampe=Pahvant.
Puala=Puaray.
Puallip, Puallipamish, Pualli-paw-mish, Pualliss=Puyallup.
Puánag′, Puans=Winnebago.
Puants=Metsmetskop, Winnebago.
Puara, Púarái, Puary=Puaray.
Pucaras=Arikara.
Puc-cun-tal-lau-has-see=Pakan-Tallahassee.
Puckanokick=Pokanoket.
Puckantala, Puckautalla, Puckuntallahasse=Pakan-Tallahassee.
Pudding River Indians=Ahantchuyuk.
Pueble Blanco=Pueblo Blanco.
Pueblo Colorado=Pueblo Pintado, Tzemantuo, Wukopakabi.
Pueblo de Jumanos=Pueblo de los Jumanos.
Pueblo de las Canoas=Shuku.
Pueblo de las Ruedas=Kuuanguala.
Pueblo de las Sardinas=Cicacut.
Pueblo de los Santos Apostoles San Simon y Judas=Upasoitac.
Pueblo de los Siete Arroyos=Tenabo.
Pueblo de Montezuma, Pueblo de Ratones=Pueblo Pintado.
Pueblo de Shé=She.
Pueblo de Tunque=Tungge.
Pueblo Ganado=Wukopakabi.
Pueblo Grande=Kintyel, Pueblo Pintado.
Pueblo of the bird=Tshirege.
Pueblo quemado=Tzenatay.
Pueblos of the Médano=Medano.
Pueblo viejo=Oapars.
Puerito=Puerto.
Puerta de la Purísima Concepcion=Concepción.
Puerta San Felipe=San Felipe.
Puertécito=Waputyutsiama.
Pugallipamish, Pugallup=Puyallup.
Puget Sound Group=Chimakuan Family, Salishan Family.
Pughquonnuck=Pauquaunuch.
Pugupiliak=Puguviliak.
Puíále=Puyallup.
Pui′--mim=Puimem.
Pu′-i-mok=Puimuk.
Pujuaque=Paguate, Pojoaque.
Pujūni=Pusune.
Pukaist′=Pekaist.
Pŭk-tĭs′=Omaha.

Pulacatoo=Pulakatu.
Pulairih=Shastan Family.
Pullaeu, Pul-la'-ook=Unalachtigo.
Pulpenes, Pulpones=Bolbone.
Puma=Pima.
Pumames, Punanes=Punames.
Pü-nañ'-nyu-mû=Puna.
Pŭn-âsh, Punashly=Bannock.
Pü-na'wuñ-wü=Puna.
Punca, Puncah=Ponca.
Puncapaugs, Puncapoag=Punkapog.
Puncas, Puncaw, Punchas, Punchaws=Ponca.
Punckapaug=Punkapog.
Puncksotonay=Punxsutawny.
Pü'n-e=Puna.
Pungelika=Erie.
Punjuni=Pusune.
Punka=Ponca.
Punkapaog, Punkapoge, Punkepaog, Punkipaog, Punkipoag, Punkipog=Punkapog.
Punknot=Tukpafka.
Punkotink=Pungoteque.
Punkqu=Punkapog.
Pun-naks=Bannock.
Punquapoag, Punquapog=Punkapog.
Punta=La Punta.
Punt-ledge=Puntlatsh.
Pun-ye-kia=Encinal.
Punyistyi=Punyeestye.
Punyitsiama=Cubero.
Puotwatemi=Potawatomi.
Pura=Puretuay.
Purames=Punames.
Puray=Puaray.
Purblos, Purbulo=Pueblos.
Purificacion=Halona.
Purisima Concepcion=Cadegomo, Concepción de Nuestra Señora.
Purísima de Babicora=Babiacora.
Purísima de Zuñi=Zuñi.
Pŭr-tyi-tyí-ya=Casa Blanca.
Puruai, Puruay=Puaray.
Pushune=Pusune.
Pu'-shüsh=Puisu.
Pu-sit-yit-cho=Casa Blanca.
Pusuaque=Pojoaque.
Pusuna=Pusune.
Putavatimes, Putawatame, Putawatimes, Putawatomie, Putawawtawmaws=Potawatomi.
Pu'tc-ko-hu=Puchkohu.
Pútewata, Pútewatadaŋ, Putewatimes=Potawatomi.
Putos=Copeh.
Putowatomey's, Puttawattimies, Puttcotungs, Puttewatamies, Puttowatamies, Puttwatimees=Potawatomi.
Püükoñ wiñwû=Puukong.
Pu'-un-t'çi-wa'-ŭn=Puuntthiwaun.
Puyallop, Puyallupahmish, Pu-yallup-a-mish, Puyalûp=Puyallup.
Puyatye=Tano.
Puyon=Winnebago.
Puzhune, Puzlumne=Pusune.
Pwacatuck, Pwoakatuck, Pwocatuck, Pwockatuck, Pwouacatuck=Pawcatuck.
Pχánai=Modoc.
Pyaklékaha=Pilaklikaha.
Pyankashees, Pyankeeshas, Pyankehas, Pyankeshaws, Pyankishaws=Piankashaw.
Pyatonons=Wea.
Py-eeds, Pyentes=Paiute.
Pyquaag, Pyquag=Pyquaug.
Pyros=Piro.
Pytoguis=Poitokwis.
Py-ute=Paviotso.

Qá-am-ó te-ne=Khaamotene.
Qa'aqē=Kaake.
Qackàⁿ qatsò, Qackàⁿ qatsòǥine=Khaskankhatso.
Qaclíj, Qaclíjni=Khashhlizhni.
Qa'gials qē'gawa-i=Kagials-kegawai.
Qā gūtl=Kwakiutl.
Qahatika=Quahatika.
Qá-idju=Kaidju.
Qai'-dju qēgawa-i=Kaidju-kegawai.
Qailertetang=Khailertetang.
Qa-i-ná-na-i-tĕ ʇûnnĕ'=Khainanaitetunne.
Qaiskana'=Koiskana.

Qāisla'=Kitamat.
Q!a'ketan=Ankakehittan.
Qāk·sinē=Kaksine.
Qa-lăk'w'=Khalakw.
Qalā'ltq=Hellelt.
Qaldā'ngasal=Huldanggats.
Q'alē'ts=Kulleets.
Qałguï'ɫgā' xet gîtînā'i=Kahlguihlgahet-gitinai.
Qā'logwis=Kalokwis.
Qā'ɫtcaɫan=Kahltcatlan.
Q!aɫtcaɫe'dî=Kahltcanedi.
Qàlto, Qaltsoǥine=Khaltso.
Qalukwis=Kalokwis.
Q'ānikilaq=Qanikilak.
Qa'pnîsh-ˀlĕma=Topinish.
Qapqapētlp=Kapkapetlp.
Qā'qamātses=Hahamatses.
Qa-qá-toⁿ-waⁿ=Chippewa.
Qā'ʼqawatilik·a=Kakawatilikya.
Qaqiō's=Kekios.
Qaq!ō's hît tān=Kakos-hit-tan.
Qa-quima=Kiakima.
Qa-ra-ta' nu-mañ'-ke=Kharatanumanke.
Qarmang=Karmang.
Qarmaqdjuin=Karmakdjuin.
Qarussuit=Karusuit.
Q'ash-trĕ-tye=San Felipe.
Qassigiaqdjuaq=Kiassigiakdjuag.
Q!ā'sta qē'gawa-i=Daiyuahl-lanas.
Qā'tcadî=Katcadi.
Qātcxʌ'na-āk!=Katchanaak.
Q!a'tgu hît tān=Ketgohittan.
Q!a'tkaayî=Katkaayi.
Qātq!wa'aɫtū=Katkwaahltu.
Qaudjuqdjuaq=Kaudjukdjuak.
Qāüitcin=Cowichan.
Qauitschin=Salishan Family.
Qaumauang=Kaumauang.
Qaupaws=Quapaw.
Qawi'ltkᵘ=Wiltkun.
Qawpaw=Quapaw.
Qǿási úχǿiⁿ, Qdhasi ukdhiⁿ=Khdhasiukdhin.
Q!eckunūwu=Keshkunuwu.
Qeqertaujang=Kekertaujkang.
QEk·wai'akin=Kekwaiakin.
Qê'ɪamix=Kedlamik.
QElā'tl=Kelatl.
Qē'lEs=Keles.
QE'lkEtōs=Kelketos.
Qe-mini-tcaⁿ, Qemnitca=Khemnichan.
Qē'nipsen=Kenipsim.
Qēn-tdóa=Kang.
Qē'qaes=China Hat.
Qeqertaqdjuin=Kekertakdjuin.
Qeqertaujang=Kekertaujang.
Qeqerten=Kekerten.
Qeqertuqdjuag=Kekertukjuag.
Qē'qīōs=Kekios.
Qetlk·oan=Hehlkoan.
Qeuontowanois=Seneca.
Qeyata-otoⁿwe, Qeyata-toⁿwaⁿ=Kheyataotonwe
Qeyata-witcaca=Kheyatawichasha.
Qézoñlathût=Kezonlathut.
Qiassigiaqdjuag=Kiassigiakdjuag.
Qîohûⁿ=Yuma.
Qicinzigua=Gyusiwa.
Qidǿ énikaci'χa=Khidhenikashika.
Qidneliq=Kidnelik.
Qimissing=Kimissing.
Qinaboags, Qineboags=Quinebaug.
Qingaseareang=Kingaseareang.
Qingmiktuq=Kingmiktuk.
Qingua=Kingua.
Qinguamiut=Kinguamiut.
Qinnepioke=Quinnipiac.
Q'i-ra-vash=Querecho.
Qi-ta'nu-mañ'-ke=Khitanumanke.
Qivitung=Kivitung.
Qltlâ'sEn=Kltlasen.
Q'ma'shpăl=Skitswish.
QmE çkoyim, Qmuskī'Em=Musqueam.
Qnicapous=Kickapoo.
Qnivira=Quivira.
Qoaiastems=Kwaustums.
Q'oā'Lna=Koatlna.
Qōā'ltca=Koalcha.
Q'oa'px=Koapk.
Qoasī'la=Goasila.
Qoatse=Kwatsi.

Qodlimarn=Kodlimarn.
Qoĕ′qoaainôx=Koekoaainok.
Qoĕ′qoma*tl*xo=Homalko.
Q′oĕ′tēnôx=Koetenok.
Qoĕ′xsōt′ēnôx=Koeksotenok.
Qo-ganlàni=Khoghanhlani.
Qoiastems=Kwaustums.
Qoĭ′k·axtēnôx=Koikahtenok.
Qoĭqoi=Koikoi.
Qōkĕ′dē=Hokedi.
Qōlē′laqōm=Kolelakom.
Q′ō′ Lēnôx=Kotlenok.
Q′ō′m′ēnôx=Komenok.
Q′ō′mk-ūtis=Komkyutis.
Q′ō′moyuē=Komoyue.
Q′ō′mqŭtîs=Komkutis.
Qona′=Kona.
Qonagá′ni=Khonagani.
Qo-on′-qwŭt-ʒûn′nĕ=Khoonkhwuttunne.
Qō-qai′â=Kokaia.
Q′ō′qa-îtx=Kokaitk.
Qordlubing=Kordlubing.
Q′o′-sa ʒûn′-nĕ=Khosatunne.
Qō′sqēmox, Qósqīmō=Koskimo.
Qo′-ta-tci=Khotachi.
Qotlskaim=Kotlskaim.
Qōtl′-ta-tce′-tcĕ=Khotltacheche.
Qouarra=Quarai.
Qō′utc nas :had′ā′i=Kouchnas-hadai.
Qq′uêres=Keresan Family.
Qra=Khra.
Qra′ hŭñ′-e=Khrahune.
Qra′ ʒre′-ye=Khrakreye.
Qra′ pa çaⁿ=Khrapathan.
Qra′-qtci=Nachiche.
Qsâ′loqul=Ksalokul.
Qsā′psɛm=Ksapsem.
Qset-so-kít-pee-tsée-lee=Shipaulovi.
Qsonnontoans, Qsonnontonans, Qsonontouanes=Seneca.
Qta′-lût-li′ ʒûnnĕ=Khtalutlitunne.
Qtlumi=Lummi.
Quaahda=Kwahari.
Quaasada=Koasati.
Quabaag, Quabaconk, Quabage, Quabagud=Quabaug.
Quabajais, Quabajay=Serranos.
Quabakutt, Quabaog, Quabâquick, Quabauke, Quaboag, Quaboagh, Quabog, Quaboug=Quabaug.
Quachita=Ouachita.
Quach-snah-mish=Squaxon.
Quack=Aucocisco.
Quack-ena-mish=Squaxon.
Quackeweth, Quackewlth, Quackolls=Kwakiutl.
Quacksis=Foxes.
Qua-colth=Kwakiutl.
Quacoratchie, Quacoretche=Quacoshatchee.
Quacós=Kwakiutl.
Quaddies, Quaddy Indians=Passamaquoddy.
Quadodaquees, Quadodaquious=Kadohadacho.
Quadoge, Quadoghe=Huron.
Quádōs=Huados.
Quadroque=Atrakwaye.
Quagheuil=Kwakiutl.
Quaguina=Kiakima.
Quahada Comanches, Quahadas, Quahade-Comanches, Quaha-dede-chatz-Kenna, Qua-ha-de-dechutz-Kenna, Quahades=Kwahari.
Quahkeulth=Kwakiutl.
Qua-ho-dahs=Kwahari.
Quah-tah-mah, Quah-to-mah=Kwatami.
Quaiantl=Quinaielt.
Quaiirnang=Kuaiirnang.
Quai-iunough=Guauaenok.
Quái-l-pi=Walpi.
Quaineo=Waco.
Qua-i-nu=Guauaenok.
Quaitlin=Kwantlen.
Qua-kars=Komoyue.
Quakeweth=Kwakiutl.
Quakoumwahs, Quakouwahs=Kwatami.
Quak-s′n-a-mish=Squaxon.
Quakyina=Kwakina.
Qualatche=Qualatchee.
Quale=Guale.
Qualhioqua=Kwalhioqua.
Qualicum=Saamen.
Qualioguas=Kwalhioqua.
Quallatown=Qualla.

Qualliamish, Quallyamish=Nisqualli.
Qual-quilths=Kwakiutl.
Qualquioqua=Kwalhioqua.
Quâmitchan=Cowichan.
Ouanatusset=Quantisset.
Quandarosque=Ganeraske.
Quanis Savit=San Juan Capistrano.
Quanmu=Quanmugua.
Quannepague=Quinebaug.
Quanoatinno, Quanoatinos, Quanoouatinos, Quanouatins=Kanohatino.
Quans=Kansa.
Quansheto=Conchachitou.
Quantisick=Quantisset.
Quant-lums=Kwantlen.
Quanusee=Tlanusiyi.
Quanutusset=Quantisset.
Quapâs, Quapau, Quapaws-Arkansas, Quapois, Quappas, Quappaws=Quapaw.
Quaquima, Quaquina=Kiakima.
Quaquiolts=Kwakiutl.
Quara, Quarac=Quarai.
Quarlpi=Colville.
Quarra=Quarai.
Quarrelers=Kutchin, Tukkuthkutchin.
Quarrellers=Tukkuthkutchin.
Quarro=Quarai.
Quarrydechocos=Kwahari.
Quartelexo=Quartelejo.
Qua-saw-das=Koasati.
Quash-sua-mish=Squaxon.
Quasmigda=Bidai.
Quasosne=Saint Regis.
Quasquens=Kaskaskia.
Quasson tribe=Manamoyik.
Quataquois, Quataquon=Kiowa Apache.
Quat-china=Kwakina.
Quate=Guale.
Quathlahpohtles, Quathlahpothle, Quathlahpotle, Quathlapohtle=Cathlapotle.
Quathl-met-ha=Comeya.
Quatiske, Quatissik=Quantisset.
Quā′tl=Kwantlen.
Quatoges, Quatoghees, Quatoghies, Quatoghies of Loretto=Huron.
Quatokeronon=Sauk.
Quatomah, Qua-tou-wah=Kwatami.
Quatseeno, Quatsenos=Quatsino.
Quatsinas=Goasila.
Quat-si-nu=Quatsino.
Quattamya=Kwatami.
Quāūaēnoq=Guauaenok.
Quaupuaw=Quapaw.
Quawbaug, Quawbawg=Quabaug.
Quaw-guults=Kwakiutl.
Quawlicum=Saamen.
Quawpa=Quapaw.
Quawpaug=Quabaug.
Quawpaw=Quapaw.
Quaw-she-lah=Goasila.
Quaxule=Guasuli.
Qua-ya-stums=Kwaustums.
Quayneos=Kannehouan.
Quazula=Ute.
Qube=Khube.
Qüǿá pa saⁿ=Khudhapasan.
Qüǿaqtsi i′niʉk′ăciⁿ′a=Hangkautadhantsi.
Qüǿ íniʉk′ăciⁿ′a=Hangkaahutun.
Queackar=Komoyue.
Queakhpaghamiut=Kweakpak.
Quebaug=Quabaug.
Quebec of the Southwest=Acoma.
Quebira=Quivira.
Queeakahs, Quee-ha-ni-cul-ta=Kueha.
Quee ha Qna colt, Quee-ha-qua-coll=Komoyue.
Queékagamut=Kwikak.
Queenapaug=Quinebaug.
Queenapiok, Queenapoick=Quinnipiac.
Queen Charlotte′s Island=Skittagetan Family.
Queen Hester′s Palace or Town=Sheshequin.
Queenhithe, Queen Hythe, Queenioolt=Quinaielt.
Queerchos=Querechos.
Queeschè=Paguate.
Queets, Queet-see=Quaitso.
Quehatsa=Hidatsa.
Quehts=Quaitso.
Quejotoa, Quejoton=Quijotoa.
Quejuen=Tulkepaia.
Que-lai′-ūlt=Quileute.

Quelamoueches, Quĕlancouchis, Quelanhubeches=Karankawa.
Quelelochamiut=Kweleluk.
Quellehutes=Quileute.
Quelotetreny=Quelotetrey.
Quelquimi=Quelqueme.
Quemado=Pueblo Quemado.
Quemalúsi=Santa Teresa.
Quemayá=Comeya.
Quemults=Quinaielt.
Quenait chechat, Que-nait'-sath=Makah.
Quenebage, Quenebaug=Quinebaug.
Quenebec Indians=Norridgewock.
Quenepiage, Quenepiake=Quinnipiac.
Queniauitl=Quinaielt.
Quenibaug=Quinebaug.
Quenipisa=Acolapissa.
Quenishachshachki=Queenashawakee.
Quenistinos=Cree.
Que'-ni-ūlt, Quenoil, Quenoith=Quinaielt.
Quenongebin=Keinouche.
Quenopiage=Quinnipiac.
Quenté=Kente.
Queouës coupées=Kishkakon.
Quepâs, Queppa=Quapaw.
Quera=Keresan Family.
Querchos, Querechaos, Quereches, Querehos=Querechos.
Querepees=Quinnipiac.
Querelleurs=Tukkuthkutchin.
Queres, Quereses=Keresan Family.
Quéres Gibraltar=Acoma.
Querez, Quéris=Keresan Family.
Queristinos=Cree.
Queros=Keresan Family.
Querphas=Quapaw.
Quer'quelin=Nayakololay.
Querra=Quarai.
Quesadas, Queseda=Koasati.
Quesnel, Quesnelle Mouth=Chentsithala
Quetahtore=Carrizo.
Queues coupées=Kishkakon.
Quevenes=Kohani.
Quevindoyan=Ossossane.
que Vira=Quivira.
Quevoil=Quinaielt.
Queyches=Kichai.
Queyugwe, Queyugwehaughga=Cayuga.
Quezedans=Koasati.
Quhlicum=Saämen.
Qui a han less=Kweundlas.
Quiamera=Guayoguia, Mecastria.
Quiaquima, Quia-Quima=Kiakima.
Quiarlpi=Colville.
Quia-shi-dshi=Kiashita.
Quia-tzo-qua=Kiatsukwa.
Quiaviquinta=Quiviquinta.
Quibira=Quivira.
Quiburio=Quiburi.
Quicama, Quicamopa=Quigyuma.
Quicapause, Quicapons, Quicapous=Kickapoo.
Quicasquiris=Wichita.
Quichaais, Quichais, Quicheigno, Quiches=Kichai.
Quichuan=Kiowa.
Quicimas=Quigyuma.
Quicinzigua=Gyusiwa.
Quick-sul-i-nut=Koeksotenok.
Quicoma, Quicona=Quigyuma.
Quicunontateronons=Tionontati.
Quidaho=Kichai.
Qui-dai-elt=Quinaielt.
Quidehaio, Quidehais=Kichai.
Quieetsos=Quaitso.
Quie ha Ne cub ta=Kueha.
Quiemltutz=Tionontati.
Quiennontateronons=Tionontati, Westkarini.
Quiennontateronons=Nipissing.
Quietaroes=Coyoteros.
Quieuindohain, Quieuindohian=Ossossane.
Quigata=Quigaute.
Quigualtanji, Quigualtanqui, Quiguas=Quigalta.
Quiguata, Quiguate=Quigaute.
Quigyamas, Quihuimas=Quigyuma.
Quiilla=Coila.
Quilahutes=Quileute.
Quilaielt=Quinaieltr
Quila'pe=Willopah.
Quilcene=Colcene.
Quilehutes=Quileute.

Quilh-cah=Guhlga.
Quiliapiack, Quilipiacke=Quinnipiac.
Quil-i-utes, Quillahyute, Quillayutes, Quillehetes, Quil-leh-utes=Quileute.
Quilleoueoquas, Quillequaquas, Quillequeognas, Quillequeoqua=Kwalhioqua.
Quilleutes, Quilleyutes, Quillihute=Quileute.
Quillipeage, Quillipiacke, Quillipieck, Quillipiog, Quillipiuk, Quillipyake=Quinnipiac.
Quilliutes, Quilloyaths=Quileute.
Quillypieck=Quinnipiac.
Quilochugamiut=Kwilokuk.
Quil-si-eton=Kwilsieton.
Quimac=Quigyuma.
Quimado=Pueblo Quemado.
Qui'-me=Cochiti.
Quimipeiock=Quinnipiac.
Quimis=Quems.
Quinabaag, Quinaboag=Quinebaug.
Qui-nai-elts, Quin-aik, Qui-nai-lee, Quin-aitle, Quin-aiult, Quinaiutl=Quinaielt.
Quinaoutoua=Quinaouatoua.
Quinapeag, Quinapeake=Quinnipiac.
Quinaquous=Kickapoo.
Quinault, Quinayat=Quinaielt.
Quincapous=Kickapoo.
Quinchaha=Kwinak.
Quinebage, Quineboag=Quinebaug.
Quinechart=Makah.
Quinehaha, Quinehahamute=Kwinak.
Quinepage=Quinebaug.
Quineres, Quinets=Karankawa.
Quinetusset=Quantisset.
Quingas=Keresan Family.
Quingo=Venango.
Quingoes=Cayuga.
Quingoi=Kwingyap.
Quinhaghamiut=Kwinak.
Quinibaug, Quinibauge=Quinebaug.
Quiniilt, Quiniilts, Quinilts, Quiniltz=Quinaielt.
Quinipiac=Quinnipiac.
Quinipisas, Quinipissa=Acolapissa.
Quinipieck, Quinipiuck=Quinnipiac.
Quiniquissa=Acolapissa.
Quinira=Quivira.
Quiniult, Quiniutles=Quinaielt.
Quinnabaug=Quinebaug.
Quin-na-chart, Quinnechant, Quinnechart=Makah.
Quinnepaeg, Quinnepas, Quinnepauge, Quinnepiack, Quinne-py-ooghq, Quinnipauge, Quinnipiak, Quinnipiĕucke, Quinnipiog, Quinnipioke=Quinnipiac.
Quinnipissas=Acolapissa.
Quinnopiage=Quinnipiac.
Quinnuboag=Quinebaug.
Quinnypiag=Quinnipiac.
Quinnypiock, Quinnypiog, Quinopiocke=Quinnipiac.
Quinquimas=Quigyuma.
Quinshaatin=Kwilchana.
Quinskanaht, Quinskanht=Koiskana.
Quinsta=Gyusiwa.
Quintay, Quinte=Kente.
Quinticoock=Connecticut.
Quinults=Quinaielt.
Quinypiock=Quinnipiac.
Quiocohànocs, Quiocohanses=Quioucohanoc.
Quioepetons=Wahpeton.
Quiohohouans=Kiowa.
Quiopetons=Wahpeton.
Quiouaha, Quiouahan=Kiowa.
Quioyaco=Quiotraco.
Quipana=Pawnee, Kipana.
Quipano=Pawnee.
Quiqualtangui, Quiqualthangi=Quigalta.
Quiquimas, Quiquimo, Quiquionas=Quigyuma.
Quiquogas=Cayuga.
Quirasquiris=Wichita.
Quirepeys=Quinnipiac.
Quires, Quirex, Quiria=Keresan Family.
Quiriba=Quivira.
Quiripeys=Quinnipiac.
Quirireches=Querecho.
Quiriribis=Huirivis.
Quirix, Quiros=Keresan Family.
Quirotes=Quirogles.
Quiscate=Quiscat.
Quiseyove=Quisiyove.
Quis-kan-aht=Koiskana.
Quisquate=Quiscat.

Quitcac=Cuitoat.
Quitepcomuais, Quitepiconnae=Tippecanoe.
Quitoa, Quitoac=Cuitoat.
Quitobac=Bacapa.
Quitobaca=Quitovaquita.
Quitoeis=Kichai.
Quitoks=Quitoles.
Quito Vaqueta=Quitovaquita.
Quitres, Quitreys=Kichai.
Quits=Quaitso.
Quitseigus, Quitseings, Quitseis, Quituchiis=Kichai.
Quitways=Miami.
Quitxix, Quitzaene=Kichai.
Quiuira, Quiuiriens=Quivira.
Quiumziqua, Quiumzique, Quiunzique=Gyusiwa.
Quiuquuhs=Cayuga.
Quiusta=Gyusiwa.
Quivera, Quivica, Quivina, Quiviræ, Quivirans, Qui-
   virenses=Quivira.
Quivix=Keresan Family.
Quiyone=Koiaum.
Quiyonghcohanock, Quiyougcohanocks, Quiyough-
   cohanock, Quiyoughqnohanocks=Quioucohanoc.
Quizi=Kichai.
Qujanes=Kohani.
Qumault=Quinaielt.
Qŭndj-alaⁿ=Khundzhalan.
Qunē'tcin=Kunechin.
Qûn-e'-tcu-ʒa'=Khunetchuta.
Q'û'-ni-li-i'-kqwût=Khuniliikhwut.
Qunk-ma-mish=Kwehtlmamish.
Qunnipiĕuk, Qunnipiuck, Qunnipiug, Qunnippiuck=
   Quinnipiac.
Qunnubbágge=Quinebaug.
Qŭnʒsé=Khundtse.
Quoanantino=Kanohatino.
Quoaquis=Coaque.
Quoboag, Quoboge=Quabaug.
Quodadiquio=Kadohadacho.
Quoddies, Quoddy Indians=Passamaquoddy.
Quoisillas=Goasila.
Quoitesos=Quaitso.
Quo-kim=Cajuenche.
Quonahasit, Quonahassit=Conohasset.
Quonantino=Kanohatino.
Quoneashee=Tlanusiyi.
Quonoatinnos=Kanohatino.
Quoquoulth=Kwakiutl.
Quoratem=Kworatem.
Quor-ra-da-chor-koes=Kwahari.
Quotoas=Kwotoa.
Quouan=Kohani.
Quouarra=Quarai.
Quppas=Quapaw.
Quqoā'q=Kukoak.
Ququ'lɛk·=Kukulek.
Qurachtenons=Wea.
Qusisillas=Goasila.
Quss-kan-aht=Koiskana.
Qusutas=Ute.
Qūts hit tan=Kutshittan.
Quunnipieuck=Quinnipiac.
Qû-wûn'-kqwût=Khunkhwuttunne.
Qüya=Khuya.
Qüyegu jiñga=Khuyeguzhinga.
Qüyunikaciⁿga=Husada.
Qvinipiak=Quinnipiac.
Qvivira=Quivira.
Qwai'ctûn-ne' ʒûn'nĕ=Khwaishtunnetunne.
Qwaⁿ-s' a-a'-tûn=Khosatunne.
Qwapaws=Quapaw.
Qwā'qwatl=Hwahwatl.
Qwec' ʒûnnĕ=Khweshtunne.
Qweenylt=Quinaielt.
Q!wē'qolɛn=Nayakololay.
Qwē'qᵘsōt!ēnoxᵘ=Koeksotenok.
Qwikties=Miami.
Qwĭltca'na=Kwilchana.
Qwin'-ctûn-ne'-tûn=Khwaishtunnetunne.
Qwûc-tcu'-mi̥ol-tûn ʒûn'nĕ=Kaltsergheatunne.
Qwû'lh-hwai-pûm=Klikitat.
Qwûn-rxûn'-me=Khwunrghunme.

Rabbitskins=Kawchodinne.
Raccoon=Mikaunikashinga.
Raccoons Village=White Raccoon's Village.
Rackeaway=Rockaway.
Racoon Village=White Raccoon's Village.
Racres=Arikara.

Ra-ŏro-ʒoe=Rathroche.
Radiqueurs=Shoshoko.
Raguapuis=Bagiopa.
Rahum=Rahun.
Raicheshnoe=Riechesni.
Rain Pueblo=Chettrokettle.
Rainy-lake Indians=Kojejewininewug.
Raiz del Mesquite=Mesquite.
Ral-la-wat-sets=Kalawatset.
Ramaya=Santa Ana.
Ramocks=Rancocas.
Rampart=Maynook.
Rampart Indians=Trotsikkutchin.
Ramushouuog=Ramushonoq.
Rancheria de la Pasion de Tucavi=Tucavi.
Rancheria de los Gandules=Moenkapi.
Rancherias de la Pasion=Pasion.
Rancherias de Santa Coleta=Santa Coleta.
Rancho Hediondo=Hediondo.
Rancokas=Rancocas.
Rancokeskill=Ramcock.
Rankokas=Rancocas.
Rankokus Kill=Ramcock.
Rapahanna, Rapahanocks=Rappahannock.
Rapahos=Arapaho.
Rapid Indians=Atsina.
Rappahanoc=Rappahannock.
Rappaho=Arapaho.
Ra-ra-to-oans, Ra-ra-t'wans=Chippewa.
Raretangh, Raritangs, Raritanoos, Raritanus=Rari-
   tan.
Rarondaks=Adirondack.
Rasaoua-koueton=Nassauaketon.
Rasauweak=Rasawek.
Rasbi'nik=Razboinski.
Rascal, Rascal Indians=Tututni.
Rascals' Village=Sotstl.
Rassawck, Rassaweak, Rassawek=Rasawek.
Rat Indians=Tukkuthkutchin, Vuntakutchin.
Ratirúntaks=Adirondack.
Rät-je Kama Tse-shu-ma=Haatze.
Rat nation=Wazhush.
Ratones=Pueblo Raton.
Rat people=Vuntakutchin.
Rat River Indians=Tukkuthkutchin.
Rat tribe=Kake.
Rǎ-tʒa, Rät-ye Ka-ma Tze-shuma=Haatze.
Raún=Rahun.
Raven=Petchalerulipaka.
Raventown=Kalanuyi.
Ravin Indians=Crows.
Ra-we' qaⁿ' ye=Rawekhanye.
Rawe'yapa=Pochotita.
Rayados=Tawehash.
Raychevsnoi=Riechesni.
Raymneecha=Khemnichan.
Rayouse=Cayuse.
Razbinsky, Razboinik=Razboinski.
Rchüch-ē'di=Hokedi.
Real de Bacanuchi=Bacanuchi.
Real de Nacosari=Nacosari.
Rea Ratacks=Klikitat.
Recars=Arikara.
Rechahecrians, Rechehecrians=Cherokee.
Recheshnaia=Nikolski.
Rechgawawanc, Rechkawick, Rechkawyck=Man-
   hattan.
Rechkewick, Rechouwhacky, Rechowacky=Rocka-
   way.
Reckawancks, Reckawawanc, Reckewackes, Reck-
   gawawanc=Manhattan.
Reckheweck=Rechquaakie.
Reckkeweck, Reckkouwhacky, Reckomacki, Reck-
   onhacky, Reckowacky=Rockaway.
Redais=Bidai.
Red Apaches=Apache.
Redcaps=Opegol.
Red crayfish=Chakchiuma.
Red eagle=Tsishuwashtake.
Red Fox=Foxes.
Red Grounds=Kanchati.
Red House=Chichilticalli.
Red Indians=Beothukan Family.
Red Jacket Village=Tekisedaneyout.
Red knife, Red-knife Indians, Red Knives=Tatsa-
   nottine.
Red lobsters=Chakchiuma.
Redoubt St. Michael=St. Michael.
Red people=Suwuki Ohimal.

Red Round Robes=Mokumiks.
Red Shield=Mahohivas.
Red-stick=Mikasuki.
Red Town=Chichilticalli.
Red Water band=Itazipcho, Minisha.
Red Willow Indians=Taos.
Red Wing=Khemnichan,
Redwood Indians=Whilkut.
Redwoods=Huchnom.
Ree=Arikara.
Reed=Kushiksa.
Reese River Indians=Nahalgo.
Refugio=Nuestra Señora del Refugio.
Re'-ho=Tuluka.
Reiners=Foxes.
Re-ka-ras, Re-ke-rahs=Arikara.
Rek-qua=Rekwoi.
Remedios Banamichi=Banamitzi.
Reminica Band=Khemnichan.
Remkokes=Rancocas.
Remnica, Remnichah=Khemnichan.
Renais=Foxes.
Renapi=Delaware.
Renards=Foxes.
Renarhonon=Arendahronons.
Renars, Renarz=Foxes.
Renecuey=Senecu.
Re-nis-te-nos=Cree.
Renni Renape=Delaware.
Republic, Republican, Republican Pawnees, Républiques=Kitkehahki.
Requa=Rekwoi.
Retchechnoi=Nikolski.
Rewechnongh=Haverstraw.
Reweghnoncks=Manhattan.
Reyataotonwe=Kheyataotonwe.
Reyes de Cucurpe=Cucurpe.
Reynards=Foxes.
Rhagenratka=Neutrals.
Rhea=Arikara.
Rhiierrhonons=Erie.
Riana=Kiowa.
Ricapous=Kickapoo.
Ric'-ârâs, Ricaree, Ricaries, Ricaris, Ricars, Ric-caras, Riccaree, Riccarrees=Arikara.
Rice Indians=Menominee.
Rice Makers=Munominikasheenhug.
Richara=Arikara.
Richibouctou=Richibucto.
Rich Prairie Dog=Achepabecha.
Rickapoos=Kickapoo.
Rickaras, Rickarees, Rickerees=Arikara.
Rickohockans=Cherokee.
Rickrees, Ricora=Arikara.
Riechesnoe=Nikolski.
Ri-ga-ta-a-ta-wa=Kheyataotonwe.
Rigibucto=Richibucto.
Rigneronnons, Rigueronnons=Erie.
Rihit=Ponca.
Rikaras, Rikkara=Arikara.
Ri-kwa=Rekwoi.
Rínak=Rirak.
Rinconada=Aritutoc.
Rio Grande de Espeleta=Oraibi.
Riquehronnons=Erie.
Ris=Arikara.
Rishebouctou, Rishebucta=Richibucto.
Rising Sun Folks, Rising Sun men=Etheneldeli.
Ristigouche, Ristigutch=Restigouche.
Rito de los Frijoles=Tyuonyi.
Rittenbenk=Ritenbenk.
River Crows=Minesetperi.
River Indians=Mahican.
River that flies=Wakpokinyan.
Rjätscheschnoje=Nikolski.
Road Indians=Ninnipaskulgees.
Roakeway=Rockaway.
Roasters=Dakota.
Robber Indians=Bannock.
Robbers=Pillagers.
Roccamecco=Rocameca.
Rocher de Bout=Roche de Bœuf.
Ro'ŏ'hɪlɪt=Eskimo.
Rockamagug, Rockamecook=Rocameca.
Rockaway=Rechquaakie.
Rockeway=Rockaway.
Rock Indians=Kumbatuash.
Rock of Katzimo=Katzimo.
Rocks=Jatonabine.

Rockway=Rockaway.
Rocky Mountain Indians=Nahane, Sekani.
Rocomeco=Rocameca.
Rodinunchsiouni=Iroquois.
Roger's river, Rogue Indians=Tututni.
Rogue River=Shasta, Takelma, Tututni.
Rogues=Pillagers.
Rogue's River=Tututni.
Roil-roil-pam=Klikitat.
Roinsac=Kaskaskia.
Rolling Bullet=Huhliwahli.
Romanons=Romonans.
Rondax, Rondaxe=Adirondack.
Roode Huis=Chichilticalli.
Rooktsu=Roktsho.
Rooptahee, Roop-tar-ha, Roop-tar-har=Ruptari.
Rooskoos Tokali=Pooscoostekale.
Root Diggers=Ditsakana, Shoshoko.
Root-Eaters=Ditsakana, Shoshoko, Yambadika.
Rop-tar-ha=Ruptari.
Roquai=Noquet.
Roque-choh=Roktsho.
Rosa Hawicuii=Hawikuh.
Rosario=Jiaspi, Santa Rosario.
Rosario Nacameri=Nacameri.
Roskeemo=Koskimo.
Rothfisch-Manner=Tluskez.
Rouameuo=Rocameca.
Rouinsac=Kaskaskia.
Round Heads=Têtes de Boule.
Round town people=Yuchi.
Roving Dakotas=Gens du Large.
Rowanans=Romonans.
Rrayados=Tawehash.
Rsársavinâ=Sobaipuri.
Ruas=Tigua.
Ruhptare=Ruptari.
Ruibnaia=Ribnaia.
Rumachenanck=Haverstraw.
Rumsenes, Rumsien, Runcienes=Rumsen.
Runicas=Tunica.
Runsenes, Runsienes=Rumsen.
Runsiens=Moquelumnan, Salinan family.
Rúqtca=Rukhcha.
Ruslen=Rumsen.
Ru'-tce=Ruche.
Ru'-tce yiñ-e=Rucheyine.
Ru-tcke=Ruchke.
Ruzany=Busanic.
Rxö'-yi-něs' tûnně'=Rghoeyinestunne.
Ryawas=Kiowa.
Rybnia=Ribnaia.
Rychesnoi=Nikolski.
Rye-Grass-Seed-Eaters=Waradika.
Ryuwas=Kiowa.

Säa-Käalituck=Saukaulutuchs.
Saäkies=Sauk.
Să-ákl=Yaquina.
Sa-ak-tí-kâ-í=Saticoy.
Saalis=Salish.
Saanitch=Sanetch.
Sa-áptin=Nez Percés.
Sa-arcix, Sa arsey=Sarsi.
Saaskies, Saasskies=Sauk.
Sababish=Samamish.
Sabacola=Sawokli.
Sabaguis=Sobaipuri.
Sabanoes=Shawnee.
Sablez=Sable.
Sabsh=Samish.
Sabstnisky=Uglovaia.
Sabuagana Gutas, Sabuaganas=Akanakwint.
Sacalanes=Saclan.
Sacatone=Sacaton.
Saccanesset=Succonesset.
Saccung=Sawcunk.
Sacenong=Saginaw.
Sachap=Satsop.
Sachdagughroonaw, Sachdagughs=Powhatan.
Sachertelontin=Zakatlatan.
Sachet=Skagit.
Sachi=Sauk.
Sachimers=Sakumehu.
Sa-chinco, Sa-chin-ko=Tait.
Sackanoir=Lakmiut.
Sackawee'-thinyoowuc=Sakawithiniwuk.
Sacket=Skagit.
Sacks=Sauk.

Sackung=Sawcunk.
Sacky=Sauk.
Saçl'-rĕq-tûn=Sathlrekhtun.
Sac-me-ugh=Sakumehu.
Sacoes, Saco Indians=Sokoki.
Sacona=Jacona.
Saconet=Saconnet.
Sacramantenos, Sacramento Apaches=Mescaleros.
Sacs=Sauk.
Sacunck=Sawcunk.
Sádalsómte-k'íiàgo=Kiowa Apache.
Sadamon, Sadamons=Sadammo.
Saddals=Skaddal.
Sᵃadjū'gal lā'nas=Sadjugahl-lanas.
Sadujames=Sadammo.
Saeckkill=Sackhoes.
Sae-lies=Salish.
Saelis=Chehalis.
Sœló=Tepehuane.
Sa-essau-dinneh=Etheneldeli.
Sagachiganirini8ek=Sagaiguninini.
Sagadahock=Sagadahoc.
Sagahrganirini, Sagaiganinini=Sagaiguninini.
Sagamore John's Town=Mishawum.
Sag-a-ná-gä=Delaware.
Saganaws=Saginaw.
Sagans=Sugeree.
Sagantwaga - wininiwak = Sugwaundugahwinine-
　wug.
Sᵃagā'ñusîlî=Sagangusili.
Sagaseys=Sauk.
Sagavoq=Sagavok.
Sagayayumnes=Sakaiakumne.
Sagᵃē'=Sagi.
Sagennom=Soyennow.
Sage-nom-nis=Sagenomnas.
Sagetaen-né=Chiricahua.
Saghadellautin=Zakatlatan.
Sagina, Sāgīnāng=Saginaw.
Sāgitawāwininiwạg=Sagewenenewak.
Sagíwa=Sauk.
Sagkonate=Saconnet.
Saguaguana=Akanaquint.
Saguanós=Shawnee.
Saguaripa=Sahuaripa.
Saguina, Saguinam, Saguinan, Saguinau=Saginaw.
Saguna=Laguna.
Sagus, Sagust=Saugus.
S. Agustin=Oiaur.
S. Agustin del Pueblito de Tucson, S. Agustin de
　Tuson=Tucson.
S. Agustin Oiaur=Oiaur.
Sagwandagawinini, Sạgwāndạgāwininiwạg = Sug-
　waundugahwininewug.
Sáhagi=Dakota.
Sahāḡungūsîlî=Sagangusili.
Sahājūgwan alth Lennas=Sadjugahllanas.
Sāhántîlā=Siksika.
Sahapotins, Sahaptain, Sahaptan, Sahaptanian=Nez
　Percés.
Sahaptin=Nez Percés, Waiilatpuan Family.
Sahaptins=Waiilatpuan Family.
Ṣahawahmish=Sahewamish.
Ṣa-hē'=Cree.
Sahehwamish=Sahewamish.
Sah-halah=Shahala.
Ṣah haptinnay=Nez Percés.
Ṣahhihwish=Sahewamish.
Ṣahi'yena=Cheyenne.
Sah-ku-méhu=Sakumehu.
Sahlalah=Silela.
Sahmamish=Samamish.
Sahmish=Samish.
Sahnchecontuckquet=Sanchecantacket.
Sah-nels=Shanel.
Sahnikans=Assumpink.
Sahohes, Sa-hone=Saone.
Sah-o-ne-hont-a-par-par=Saone Hunkpapa.
Sahonies=Saone.
Sah-own=Sangona.
Sahquatucket=Satucket.
Sah-se-sah tinney=Etheneldeli.
Sahuaripas=Jova.
Sah-wah-mish=Sawamish.
Sahwaunoo=Shawnee.
Sai'-a-kwa=Sia.
Sai'-az=Saia.
Saich-kioie-tachs, Saich-kwil-tach=Lekwiltok.
Saiconke=Seekonk.
Saidoka=Modoc.
Sai'-du-ka=Snakes.

Saie'kuŭn=Cree.
Saikiné=Pima.
Saikinné=Papago, Pima,
Sai-lĕtc', Sai-lĕtc'-ĭc-me'-ḷûnne=Siletz.
Sailk-sun=Sailupsun.
Sai-nals=Shanel.
Sainct Gabriel=Ossossane.
Sainct Iacques et sainct Philippe=Saint Jacques et
　Saint Philippe.
Sainct Iean=Etarita.
Sainct Ignace=Taenhatentaron.
Sainct Matthieu=Ekarenniondi.
S[ainct]. Paulus=San Pablo.
S[ainct]. Petrus=San Pedro.
Sainct Pierre et sainct Paul=Ehouae.
Sainct Thomas=Saint Thomas.
Sai-nels-chas-kaw=Shanel.
Sainstkla=Siuslaw.
S[aint]. Antoine de Senecu.
St. Antony=Senecu.
St. Bartholomew=Cochiti.
St. Bigin=Saint Regis.
Saint Coy=Kendaia.
St. Dies=Sandia.
Saint Domingo=Santo Domingo.
Sᵗ.'d'osquet, St. Douskie, St. Dusky=Sandusky.
Sainte Anne de Ristigouche=Restigouche.
S[aint] Edward=Balpia.
Sainte Marie de Sault=Pawating.
St. Estevan, Sᵗ. Estevan Acoma, St. Estevan Queres=
　Acoma.
Saint Estienne=Kiohero.
St. Eulalie=Santa Olalla.
Saint François=Saint Francis.
St. Francais de Sales=Saint Francis.
St. Francis=Nambe.
St. Francis Borgia=Michilimackinac.
St. Francis de Sales=Saint Francis.
Saint Francis Regis=Saint Regis.
St Francis Xavier des Pres=La Prairie.
St. Francoi, St. François=Saint Francis.
Saint François du Lac=La Prairie.
Saint-François-Xavier=Saint Francis Xavier, San
　Francisco Xavier de Vigge Biaundo.
St. François Xavier=Ganowarohare.
St. François Xavier a Laprairie de la Magdeleine=
　La Prairie.
Saint-Francois-Xavier-de-Biaundo=San Francisco
　Xavier de Viggé Biaundo.
Saint-François-Xavier-des-Prés=La Prairie.
St François Xavier du Sault=Caughnawaga.
St. Gregory=Abo.
St.Guillaume=Teotongniaton.
Sᵗ. Hieronimo=Taos.
Saint Iean=Etarita.
S. Iean Baptiste=Saint Jean Baptiste, Cahiague.
St. Ignatius=Taenhatentaron.
St. Isabella=Santa Isabel.
Saint Jacques, St. James=Kanagaro.
Saint Jean=Deyodeshot, San Juan.
Saint Jean Baptiste=Onondaga (vil.).
Saint-Jean des Chevaliers=San Juan.
Sᵗ Jerome, S[aint]. Jerome de los Taos, Sᵗ Jeronimo,
　S[aint]. Jeronimo de Taos=Taos.
S[aint] Joachin=San Joaquin.
S[aint] Joanne=San Juan.
Saint John=Deyodeshot, San Juan.
St. John of God=San Juan de Dios.
St. John's=Etarita, Malecite, San Juan.
Saint John's river Indians, St. John's tribe=Male-
　cite.
Sᵗ Josef=Patoqua.
Saint Joseph=Gayagaanhe, Patoqua, Sillery,
　Teanaustayae.
Sᵗ Laurence=Picuris.
Sᵗ Lazarus=San Lázaro.
St. Lewis, St. Lewisses=San Luis de Apalachi.
S[aint]. Lorent=San Lorenzo.
St. Ludlovic de Vacapa=Bacapa.
S[aint]. Marcellus=Sonoita.
Sᵗ Marco=San Marcos.
Sᵗ Maria=Galisteo.
S[aint]. Mark=San Marcos.
S[aint]. Martin, S[aint]. Martin of the Opas=San
　Martin.
Saint Mary=Teatontaloga.
St. Mary's=Gannentaha, Santa María Magdalena.
Saint Mathias=Ekarenniondi.
St. Mathias de Tuto Magoidag=Tutomagoidag.
S[aint]. Matthaeus de Sicoroidag=Sicoroidag.
St. Michael=San Miguel Zuaque, Scanonaenrat.

Saint Michael's=Kanagaro.
Saint Michel=Saint Michael, Kanagaro, Khioetoa, Scanonaenrat.
St. Nicholas=Kenai.
St. Orloff, St. Orlova=Orlova.
St. Pablo=San Pablo.
St. Paul=Kodiak.
St. Peter=San Pedro.
Saint Peter's=Caughnawaga.
S[aint]. Phelippe, St. Philip=San Felipe.
St. Philip de JHS=Terrenate.
St. Philippe, St. Philips, St. Phillipe, St. Phillippe=San Felipe.
Saint Rene=Onnontare.
Saint Stephen=Kiohero.
St. Yotoc=Sonnioto.
Sai'-o-kwâ=Sia.
Saiopines=Tiopines.
Sa-i-sa-'dtinne=Etheneldeli.
Sai-wash=Shasta.
Sai-yu'-cle-me' ꝗŭnnĕ=Coos.
Sai-yu'-sla-me' ꝗŭnnĕ, Sai-yūs'-t'ꝑû-me' ꝗŭnnĕ=Siuslaw.
Sajay=Xagua.
Så-jĕr-ȯ-pån-gå=Skidi.
Sajirit=San Juan Capistrano.
Sakacawone=Secacawoni.
Sakadelontin=Zakatlatan.
Sakahiganiriouek=Sagaiguninini.
Sa'ka·ȯ·ganing=Sukaauguning.
Sakatalan, Sakataloden=Zakatlatan.
Sakawes, Sakawis=Sauk.
Sakawiyiniwok=Sakawithiniwuk.
Sakâwiyiniw=Sugwaundugahwininewug.
Sakes=Sauk.
Saketon=Sacaton.
Såketûpiks=Siksika.
S'å-kĕ-w'ĕ, Sakewi=Sauk.
Sákhalis=Skatalis.
Sak'hútka=Abihka.
Sakiaqdjung=Sakiakdjung.
Sakiman, Sakinam, Sakinan, Sakinang=Saginaw.
Sa'ki qē'gawa-i=Saki-kegawai.
Sā-kish=Tsahis.
Sakisimme=Lakisumne.
Sa-ki-yû=Sauk.
Sak-ka-ya=Sakaya.
Sak'la'nas=Sagua-lanas.
Saklans=Saclan.
Sakoā'n=Sukkwan.
Sa'kona=Jacona.
Sakonett=Saconnet.
Sa+k'o+t, Säk'o'ta=Cheyenne.
Saks=Sauk.
Såkwi'yï=Soquee.
Saky=Sauk.
Salab wiñwû=Salabi.
SᵉalA'ndas=Salendas.
Salan Pomas=Salan Pomo.
Sāᵍ'ɫdAñ kun=Sahldung.
Salem Indians=Manta.
Sa'lic=Ntlakyapamuk.
Saligugi=Turtletown.
Salinas=Salinan.
Saline=Ketchewaundaugenink.
Saline Apaches=Mescaleros.
Salish=Salishan Family.
Saliütla=Siuslaw.
Sallenches=Talinchi.
Sallicoah=Selikwayi.
Salmeros=Salineros.
Salmon Eaters=Tazaaigadika.
Salmon River Snakes=Tukuarika.
Salsen, Salses=Salsona.
Salsonas=Saclan.
Salst Kamlúps=Kamloops.
Sälst sχästsítlini=Spokan.
Sälsχuyïlp=Colville.
Salt City=Matsaki.
Salteur=Chippewa.
Salt Lake Diggers=Hohandika.
Salt Lick Town=Lick Town.
Salt-water band=Lower Chehalis.
Sal-wă'-qă=Salwahka.
Salzon=Salsona.
Sam-ab-mish=Samamish.
Samackman=Samahquam.

Sam-áhmish=Samamish.
Samalayuca=Ojito de Samalayuca.
Samam-hoo=Semiahmoo.
Samaripa=Sahuaripa.
Samboukas=Samboukia.
S. Ambrosio Busanic=Busanic.
Samdan=Sumdum.
Sā́menos=Somenos.
S'ā́'mic=Samish.
Sa-milk-a-nuigh=Similkameen.
Samipoas=Sanipaos.
Sam-nâ'i, Sam-nán=Picuris.
Samokin=Shamokin.
Samoupavi=Shongopovi.
Samparicka=Ditsakana.
Sampeetches, Sampiches, Sampichya, Sampits, Sampuches=Sanpet.
Sāmtsh=Sanetch.
Sanas=Sana.
San Agustin=Oiaur.
San Agustin del Isleta=Isleta.
San Agustin Oiaur=Oiaur.
Sanakhanskoe=Sanyakoan.
Sanaki'wa=Choctaw.
Sā'nak·oan=Sanyakoan.
San Aldefonso=San Ildefonso.
San Ambrosio de Busanio=Busanic.
San Andres Atotonilco=Atotonilco.
San Andres Chinipas=Chinipa.
San Andres Conicari=Conicari.
San Antonio=Bacuancos, Salinan Family, Senecu.
San Antonio de la Isleta=Isleta, Isleta del Sur.
San Antonio del Pueblo=Pomojoua.
S[an]. Antonio de Senaca, San Antonio de Sencen, San Antonio de Seneci, San Antonio de Senecu=Senecu.
San Antonio de Uquitoa=Oquitoa.
S[an]. Antonio Ilamatech=Ilamatech.
San Antonio of Sinolu=Senecu del Sur.
S[an]. Antonio Oquitoa=Oquitoa.
San Antonio Seneca=Senecu del Sur.
S[an]. Augustin=Oiaur.
San Augustin de Ahumada, San Augustin de Ahumada Rio de la Trinidad=San Agustin de Ahumada.
San Augustin de la Isleta, San Augustin del Isleta=Isleta.
S[an]. Augustinus=Oiaur.
San Bartolomé=Puaray.
San Bartolome Batacosa=Batacosa.
S[an]. Bartolomé Comac=Comac.
San Bartolome de Jongopavi, San Bartolomé de Jougopavi, San Bartolomé de Xongopabi, San Bartolomé de Xongopavi=Shongopovi.
San Bartolomeo=Cochiti.
S[an]. Bernabé Jongopavi=Shongopovi.
San Bernahdino de Ahuatobi, San Bernardino, San Bernardino de Aguatuvi, San Bernardino de Ahuatobi=Awatobi.
San Bernardino del Agua Caliente=San Bernardino.
S[an]. Bernardino Gualpi=Walpi.
S[an]. Bernardo Aquimuri=Aquimuri.
S[an[. Bernardo de Aguatuvi=Awatobi.
San Bernardo de Jongopabi=Shongopovi.
San Bernardo Gracia Real=Terrenate.
San Borja=San Francisco Borja.
S[an]. Buena ventura, San Buena Ventura de Cochita, San Buena Ventura de Cochiti=Cochiti.
S[an]. Buen. de Mossaquavi=Mishongnovi.
S[an]. Cajetanus=Calabazas.
San Capistrano=San Juan Capistrano.
San Carlos de Carmelo, San Carlos del Carmelo, San Carlos de Monterey=San Carlos.
S[an]. Catherina=Cuitciabaqui.
S[an]. Cayetano=Tumacacori.
S[an]. Cayetano de Bac=San Xavier del Bac.
San Cayetano de Calabazas=Calabazas.
S[an]. Cayetano Tumagacori, S[an]. Cayetano Tumapacori=Tumacacori.
San Cázaro=San Lazaro.
San Christóval=San Cristobal.
Sanchu=Sauchu.
San Clemente=Bejuituuy.
S[an]. Cosmas=San Cosme.
San Cristobel, San Cristoforo, San Cristóval=San Cristobal.
Sanctuit=Satuit.
Sandea=Sandia.

Sandedotán=Sandatoton.
Sandesque=Sandusky.
Sand-hill people=Neomaitaneo.
San Diaz=Sandia.
San Diegnito=San Dieguito.
San Diego=Gyusiwa, Tesuque, Uitorrum.
San Diego de Jamez, San Diego de Jemes, San Diego
  de Jemez, San Diego de los Emex, San Diego de los
  Hemes, San Diego de los Temes=Gyusiwa.
San Diego de Tesuque=Tesuque.
San Diego de Uitorrum=Uitorrum.
San Dieguito=San Diego.
San Diepo de Pitquin=Pitic.
San Diepo de Uquitoa=Oquitoa.
Sandilla=Sandia.
San Domingan, San Domingo=Santo Domingo.
S[an]. Doonysio=San Dionysio.
Sandoske, Sandosket, Sandoski, Sandosky, Sandouski,
  Sandousky=Sandusky.
S. Andres Esqugbaag=Esqubaag.
Sand town=Uktahasasi.
Sanduskee, Sanduski, Sanduskians=Sandusky.
Sandusky Senecas=Mingo.
Sandy Lake Indians=Kahmetahwungaguma.
Saneca=Senecu del Sur.
S[an]. Eduard de Baipia, S[an]. Eduardo, S[an].
  Eduardo de Aribacpia, San Edvardo de Baipia=
  Baipia.
Sanels=Shanel.
S[an]. Estanislao Octam, S[an] Estanislao Ooltan=
  Ooltan.
San Estéban de Acoma, San Estéban de Asoma, S[an].
  Estevan de Acoma=Acoma.
San Felepe, S[an]. Felip, S[an]. Felipe de Cueres,
  S[an]. Felipe de Cuerez=San Felipe.
San Felipe de Jesus Guevavi=Guevavi.
San Felipe de Keres, San Felipe de Queres=San
  Felipe.
S[an]. Felipe Gracia Real del Terrenate=Terrenate.
San Felipo, San Felippe, San Fellipe=San Felipe.
San Fernando Villacata=San Fernando Vellicata.
San Filipé=San Felipe.
San Francisco=Caiman, Dolores, Nambe, San
  Francisco de los Tejas (or Neches).
San Francisco de Borja de Tecoripa=Tecoripa.
San Francisco de los Nechas, San Francisco de los
  Neches, San Francisco de los Techas=San Fran-
  cisco de los Tejas (or Neches).
San Francisco de Nambe=Nambe.
San Francisco de Oraibe, San Francisco de Oraybe=
  Oraibi.
San Francisco de Sandia=Sandia.
San Francisco Guazava=Guazavas.
San Francisco Javier=San Francisco Xavier de
  Viggé Biaundo.
San Francisco Javier Arivechi=Arivechi
San Francisco Javier Cuchuta=Cuchuta.
San Francisco Javier de Guazava=Guazavas.
San Francisco Javier Reboyco=Robesco.
San Francisco Lajas=Lajas.
San Francisco Nambe=Nambe.
San Francisco Pajagüe=Pojoaque.
San Francisco Xavier, San Francisco Xavier de
  Vigge=San Francisco Xavier de Viggé Biaundo.
S[an]. Francisco Xavier del Bac=San Xavier del
  Bac.
San Francisquita=Echilat.
San Gabriel, San Gabriel del Yunque=Gabrieleño,
  Yugeuingge.
S[an]. Gaetan=Calabazas.
S. Angel=San Angelo.
San Gerónimo de los Tahos, San Gerónimo de los
  Taos, San Geronimo de Taos=Taos.
San Gerónimo Huexotitlan=Huexotitlan.
San Geronymo=San Geronimo.
San Geronymo de los Thaos=Taos.
Sanghikans, Sangicans=Assumpink.
Sangiestas=Saugiesta.
S[an]. Gioachino=San Joaquin.
San Gregorio=Abo.
San Gregoris Jaumalturgo=Jaumalturgo.
Sangut=Saugus.
Sanhicans, Sanhickans=Assumpink.
San Hieronimo, San Hieronimo de los Corazones=
  Corazones.
S[an]. Hieronymo=Taos.
Sanhikani, Sanhikins=Assumpink.
S[an]. Iacobus de Oiadaibuisc=Ojiataibues.
Sanich=Sanetch.
San Ignacio. See S. Ignacio.

San Ignacio=San Ignacio de Kadakaman, Pa-
  chawal, Tubac.
San Ignacio Cuquiarachi=Corodeguachi.
San Ignacio de Soniquipa, San Ignacio de Soniquipe=
  Sinoquipe.
San Ignacio de Tesia=Tesia.
San Ignacio Guibori=Quiburi.
San Ignacio Onabas=Onavas.
San Ignacio Sinoquipe=Sinoquipe.
San Ignacio Torin=Torin.
San Il de Conso=San Ildefonso.
S[an]. Ildefonso Ostimuri=Ostimuri.
San Ildefonso Yecora=Yecora.
San Ildefonzo, San Ildephonso, San Ilefonso=San
  Ildefonso.
San Imirio=San Emidio.
S[an]. Iosepho=Patoqua.
Sa-nish'=Arikara.
San Isidoro=Pueblo de los Jumanos.
San Isidro=Wilakal.
Sanítika=Arapaho.
San Iuan Baptista=San Juan Bautista.
San Jacinto=Saboba.
S[an]. Javier, S[an]. Javier Bac=San Xavier del
  Bac.
San Javier de Batuco=Batuco.
San Javier del Bac, S[an]. Javier del Bacel=San
  Xavier del Bac.
San Javier de Viggé=San Francisco Xavier de
  Viggé Biaundo.
S[an]. Jldefonso=San Ildefonso.
S[an]. Joaquin. See S. Joaquin.
San Joaquin de Basosuma=Basosuma.
San José=Ichenta, San José de los Nazones, Tu-
  macacori.
San José Charay=Charac.
San José Chinapa=Chinapa.
San José Commondu=San José de Comondu.
S[an]. José de Joconostla=Joconostla.
San José de la Laguna=Laguna.
San José de Matape=Matape.
San José de Pimas=San José de los Pimas.
San José de Teopari de Ovas=Teopari.
S[an]. José de Tizonazo=Tizonazo.
San José de Tucson=Tucson.
S[an]. Josef=Patoqua.
San Josef de La Laguna=Laguna.
S[an]. Josefo=Patoqua.
S[an] José Imuri=Imuris.
S[an] José Matape=Matape.
San Joseph de Commondu, San Joseph de Comondo=
  San José de Comondu.
San Joseph de Jemez=Patoqua.
San Joseph de los Nazones=San José de los Na-
  zones.
San Joseph de los Pimas=San José de los Pimas.
San. Joseph de Soyopa=Soyopa.
San José Teopari=Teopari.
S[an]. Jua, San Juan=San Juan de los Jemez.
San Juan Atotonilco=Atotonilco.
San Juan Baptista=San Juan Bautista.
San Juan B[autista], Maguina=Maguina.
San Juan Capestrano=San Juan Capistrano.
San Juan Capistrano=Juaneños, Uturituc.
S[an]. Juan Capistrano de Ulurituc, San Juan Capis-
  trans de Virtud=Uturituc.
S[an]. Juan Corapa=Corapa.
S[an]Juan de Guachinela=Huachinera.
San Juan de los Caballeros, San Juan de los Cabel-
  leros=San Juan.
San Juan del Rio=Toapara.
S[an]. Juan de Mata=Mata.
San Juaneros, San Juaners=San Juan.
San Juan Evangelista Tosonachic=Tosanachic.
S[an]. Juan Guachinera, San Juan Guachirita=Hua-
  chinera.
S[an]. Juan Peyotan=Peyotan.
S[an]. Juan Quiburi=Quiburi.
San Judas=San Simon y San Judas.
San Júdas Tadeo=Tadeovaqui.
San Juris=San Imiri.
Sankaskitons=Sisseton.
Sankawee=Tsankawi.
Sankewi=Sauk.
Sankhicani=Mohawk, Assumpink.
Sankhicans, Sankhikans, Sankihani, Sankikani, San-
  kikman=Assumpink.
Sänko=Comanche.
Sankonk=Sawcunk.
Sanks=Sauk.

San Laida=Saucita.
San Lasaro=San Lazaro.
S[an]. Limon Tucsani=Tucsani.
San Lodovic=Sevilleta.
San Lorenzo=Azqueltan, Picuris, San Lazaro.
San Lorenzo de la Santa Cruz=Santa Cruz.
San Lorenzo de los Pecuries=Picuris.
San Lorenzo del Real, S[an]. Lorenzo del Realito=
  San Lorenzo.
San Lorenzo de Pecuries, San Lorenzo de Picuries=
  Picuris.
San Lorenzo de Tezuqui=Tesuque.
San Lorenzo el Real Pueblo de Zumas=San Lo-
  renzo.
San Lorenzo Guepaca, San Lorenzo Huepaca=Hue-
  pac.
San Lorenzo Tezuqui=Tesuque.
San Louis de Bacapa=Bacapa.
San Louis Indians=Luiseño.
San Lucas=Galisteo.
S[an]. Lúcas de Galpa=Galpa.
S[an]. Ludlov de Bacapa=Bacapa.
S[an]. Luis=San Luis de Apalache.
San Luis Bacadeguachi=Bacadeguachi.
S[an] Luis Bacapa=Bacapa.
San. Luis Bacuancos=Bacuancos.
San Luis Bacupa, San Luis Beltran de Bacapa, S[an].
  Luis de Bacapa=Bacapa.
San-Luis de Seuilleta=Sevilleta.
San Luisenians, San Luiseños=Luiseño.
San Luis Gonzaga de Bacadeguatzi=Bacadeguachi.
S[an]. Luis Guebavi=Guevari.
San Luisieños=Luiseño.
S[an]. Luis Obispo Sevilleta=Seviletta.
S[an]. Luis Quitobac=Bacapa.
San Luis Rey=Luiseño.
San Luis town=San Luis de Apalache.
San Marcelo, San Marcelo del Sonoita, San Marcelo
  del Xonuida, S[an]. Marcelo Sonoydag=Sonoita.
San Marcial=Trenaquel.
San Marcos=Eljman.
San Marcos de Apalache=San Marcos.
S[an]. Mateo, San Mateo Cant, S[an]. Mateo Caut=
  Cant.
San Mateo de Saguaripa, San Mateo Malzura=San
  Mateo.
S[an]. Mateo Soroydad=Sonoita.
S[an]. Mathias de Tutomagoidag=Tutomogoidag.
S[an]. Mathias Tutum=Tutum.
San Miguel=Guevavi, Haatze, Mactati, San Miguel
  de Linares, San Miguel Zuaque, Taos. See also
  S. Miguel.
San Miguel de Cuellar=San Miguel de Linares.
San Miguel de Guevavi=Guevavi.
San Miguel de los Adeas=San Miguel de Linares.
San Miguel de Oposura=Oposura.
San Miguel de Sonoitac, San Miguel de Ssonoitag=
  Sonoita.
San Miguel Oraybi=Oraibi.
San Miguel Taxique=Tajique.
San Miguel Ures=Ures.
S. Anna=Santa Ana.
Sannagers=Seneca.
Sanona=Sangona.
Sanonawantowane=Cayuga.
San Pablo=Paako. See also S. Pablo.
San Pablo del Pescadero=Pescadero.
San Pablo de Tepehuanes=Tepehuanes.
San Pablo Tubutama=Tubutama.
S[an]. Pantaleon=Aribaiba.
San Pasqual=San Pascual.
San Pedro=Acoma, Paako. See also S. Pedro.
San Pedro Aconchi=Aconchi.
San Pedro and San Pablo=San Pedro y San
  Pablo.
San Pedro del Cuchillo=Paako.
San Pedro de los Jamajabs=San Pedro.
San Pedro Martyr=San Pedro Martire.
San Pedro-Pablo=San Pedro y San Pablo.
San Pedro Tubutama=Tubutama.
San Pedro y San Pablo de Bicuñer=San Pedro y
  San Pablo.
San-Petes=Sanpet.
San Phelipe, San Phelippe, San Philippi, San Phil-
  lippe=San Felipe.
Sanpiche Utahs, San Pitch, San Pitches, Sanpits=
  Sanpet.

San Poels, San Poils=Sanpoil.
San Rafael=Guevavi.
San Rafael Indians=Jukiusme.
Sansarcs Dakotas=Sans Arcs.
San Sebastian Peregrino=San Sebastian.
S[an]. Serafin, S[an]. Serafin Actum, San Serafin de
  Actum, S[an]. Serafino del Napcub=San Serafin.
San Sevastian=San Sebastian.
Sänshkiá-a-rúnû=Miami.
S[an]. Simeon de Tucsani=Tucsani.
S[an] Simon=Upasoitac.
S[an]. Simon Tucsani, S[an]. Simon Tuesani=Tuc-
  sani.
San Simon y Judas de Vpasoitac=Upasoitac.
Sanspoële, Sans Puelles=Sanpoil.
Santa. See also Sta.
Santa Ana=Alamillo, Galisteo, Punyistyi, San-
  tan.
S[an]ta Ana Anamic=Anamic.
Santa Anna=Santa Ana.
Santa Barbara=Salinan Family.
Santa Barbara Indians=Chumashan Family.
Santa Catalina=Cuitciabaqui. See Sta. Catalina.
Santa Catalina Baimena=Baimena.
Santa Catalina Cayamoa=Camoa.
Santa Catalina de Baitrena=Baimena.
Santa Catarina. See also Sta. Catarina.
Santa Cruz=Santa Cruz de Mayo, Terrenate. See
  also Sta. Cruz.
Santa Cruz Bacum=Bacum.
Santa Cruz de Gaibanipitea=Gaibanipitea.
Santa Cruz de Galisteo=Galisteo.
Santa Cruz de Jaibanipitca de Pimas=Gaibani-
  pitea.
Santa Cruz de la Cañada=Santa Cruz.
Santa Cruz del Cuervo=Gaibanipitea.
Santa Cruz de Nanipacna=Nanipacna.
Santa Cruz de Nazas=Nazas.
Santa Cruz Islanders=Mishumash.
S[an]. Tadeo Batqui, San Tadeo Vaqui, S[an]. Thad-
  adeus de Batki=Tadeovaqui.
Santa Dominga, Santa Domingo=Santo Domingo.
Santa Eulalia=Santa Olalla.
Santa Gertrudes=Santa Gertrudis.
Santa Gertrudis. See Sta. Gertrudis.
Santainas=Santiam.
Santa Madaléna, S[anta]. Magdalena, Santa Mag-
  dalena de Buquibava=Buquibava.
Santa Maíta=Mata.
Santa Maria=Jesus María y José, Santa María
  Magdalena. See also Sta. María.
Santa Maria Baceraca=Baserac.
Santa Maria Batuco=Batuco.
Santa Maria de Galisteo=Galisteo.
Santa María de Grado=Santa Cruz.
Santa Maria de Guadelupe=Nuestra Señora de
  Guadalupe.
Santa María del Agua Caliente=Dueztumac.
Santa Maria de los Angeles=Santa Maria Magda-
  lena.
Santa Maria de Ocotan=Ocotan.
S[anta] Maria de Secunca, Santa Maria de Suamca,
  Santa María de Suanca=Suamca.
Santa María Guazamota=Guazamota.
S[anta]. M[aría]. Magdalen=Buquibava.
Santa María Magdalena Soanca=Suamca.
Santa María Milpillas=Milpillas.
Santa María Mobas=Movas.
Santa María Nacameri=Nacameri.
Santa Maria Soamca, Santa Maria Soamnca, Santa
  Maria Soanca=Suamca.
Santa Maria Vaseraca=Baserac.
Santana=Santa Ana.
Santanas=Shawnee.
Sant Antonio de Padua=Puaray.
Sant Antonio de Senecu=Senecu.
Santa Nympha=Santa Nynfa.
Santa Olaya=Santa Olalla.
Santa Rosa=Wewutnowhu. See also Sta. Rosa.
Santa Rosa Corodeguachi=Corodeguachi.
Santa Rosa de Abiquiú=Abiquiu.
Santa Rosa de Coradeguatzi=Corodeguachi.
Santa Rosa de Hauicui=Hawikuh.
Santa Rosa de Santa Maria=Pachera.
Santa Rosalia de Moleje=Santa Rosalia Mulege.
Santa Rosalia de Onopa=Onopa.
S[anta]. Rosalia di Mulegè=Santa Rosalia Mu-
  lege.

Santas=Santee.
Santa Teresa de Guazápares=Guazapares.
Santa Teresea=Tukutnut.
Santa Tulalia=Santa Eulalia.
Santa Ysabel=Santa Isabel.
Sant Buenaventura=Picuris.
Sant Chripstobal=San Cristobal.
Santeaux=Chippewa.
Santee of the East, Santee Sioux—Santee.
Santena, Santeurs=Chippewa.
Sant Francisco de los Españoles, Sant Gabriel, Sant Gabriele=Yugeuingge.
Santiago=Cocospera, Pecos, Ojiataibues.
Santiago Cocóspera=Cocospera.
Santiago de Oiadaibuisc=Santiago.
Santiago Huires=Huite.
Santiago Optuabo=Optuabo.
Santiago Papasquiaro=Papasquiaro.
Santiago Teneraca=Teneraca.
Santiago Yepachic=Yepachic.
Santian=Santiam.
Santie, Santie bands, Santie Sioux=Santee.
San Timétéo, San Timoteo=Tolocabi.
Santisima Nombre de Maria=Jesus María y José.
Santisima Trinidad de la mesa del Tonati=Tonati.
Santísima Trinidad de Potam=Potam.
Santísima Trinidad Vicam=Bicam.
Santísima Virgen de los Dolores=Nuestra Señora de los Dolores de los Aes.
Sant Joan=San Juan.
Sant Joan Baptista=San Juan Bautista.
Sant Joan Batista=San Juan.
Sant Marcos=San Marcos.
Santo=Tontos.
Santo Demingo=Santo Domingo.
Santo Domingo=Quartelejo.
S[anto]. Domingo de Xacoma, S[anto]. Domingo de Xacoms, S[anto]. Domingo de Xacona=Jacona.
S. Antoine de Senecu=Senecu.
San Tomas de Abiquiu=Abiquiu.
S. Antonio=Bacuancos, San Antonio, Senecu.
S. Antonio de Senaca, S. Antonio de Sencen, S. Antonio de Seneci, S. Antonio de Senecu=Senecu.
S. Antonio Ilamatech=Ilamatech.
S. Antonio Oquitoa=Oquitoa.
Santo Rosario de Vinatacot=Vinatacot.
Santos Angeles=Guevavi.
Santos Reyes Cucurpe=Cucurpe.
Santo Tomas=Servas.
Santo Tomás de Abicui, Santo Tomas de Abiquiu=Abiquiu.
Santo Tomas de Sereba, Santo Tomas de Servas=Servas.
Sant8eronons=Seneca.
Sant Pedro y Sant Pablo=Sia.
Sant Phelipe, Sant Philepe=San Felipe.
ɋan-ɋsu'χɸin=Santsukdhin.
Sant Xpoval, Sant Xupal=San Cristobal.
Sant Yldefonso, Sant Ylefonso=San Ildefonso.
Sänuχ=Sanukh.
San Xabier del Bac=San Xavier del Bac.
San Xavier=San Francisco Xavier de Viggé Biaundo.
San Xavier de Báca, S[an]. Xavier del Bac=San Xavier del Bac.
S[an]. Xavier des Praiz, S[an]. Xavier des Prez=La Prairie.
San Xavier de Náxera=San Francisco Javier de Nájera.
San Xavier de Viaundo, San Xavier de Vigge=San Francisco Xavier de Viggé Biaundo.
San Xavier de Zac, S[an]. Xavier du Bac=San Xavier del Bac.
San Ygnacio=San Ignacio.
San Yldefonso, San Yldefonzo=San Ildefonso.
San Ysedro, San Ysidro=Wilakal.
San Zavier de Bac=San Xavier del Bac.
Sanze-Ougrin=Santsukdhin.
S!aodā'n=Sumdum.
Sâ'ok=Sooke.
Saone=Sangona.
Saopi=Farmers' Band.
Saouans=Shawnee.
Saoux=Dakota.
Saoynes=Saone.
Saoyns=Cheyenne.
Sä'pani=Atsina.
Sapa-Pesah=Sapeessa.
Săpa wicaśa=Ute.
Sapenys=Saponi.

Sapes=Esopus.
Sapetan, Sapetens=Nez Percés.
Sa-pi-li=Salpilel.
Sapiny=Saponi.
Sapokanikan=Sapohanikan.
Sapon=Saponi, Tisepan.
Sapona Indians, Saponees, Sapones, Saponeys, Sapongs=Saponi.
Saponickan=Sapohanikan.
Saponies, Saponys, Sapoones, Sapòonies=Saponi.
Sapotans=Nez Percés.
Sapototot=Lopotatimni.
Sappokanican=Sapohanikan.
Sappona, Sapponce, Sapponees, Sapponeys, Sapponi, Sapponie Town, Sappony, Saps=Saponi.
Sap-suckers=Minesetperi.
Saptans, Saptin=Nez Percés.
Sapwell=Sanpoil.
Saqai'dʌgî'lgaña lnagā'-i=Sakaedigialas.
Saqgui' gyit'inai'=Sagui-gitunai.
Sa'qta=Sakta.
Saquaacha=Kwatami.
Saquan=Sequan.
Saquatucket=Satucket.
Saquechuma=Chakchiuma.
Saquenets=Saguenay.
Saques=Sauk.
Saquetuckett=Satucket.
Saquinam, Saquinan=Saginaw.
Saquis=Sauks.
Saqᵘtē'nedî=Sakutenedi.
Saracatzi=Saracachi.
Sarai=Zuñi.
Sarame=Xarame.
Saráni=Sichomovi.
Sarán=Zuñi.
Saranay=Sarauahi.
Sarannah, Sarannas=Shawnee.
Saras=Cheraw.
Saraurahi=Sarauahi.
Saraus, Sarau town=Cheraw.
Saravay=Sarauahi.
Saraw Town, Saraws=Cheraw.
Saray=Zuñi.
Sarcee, Sarcess, Sarcis, Sarcix=Sarsi.
Sarĕtika=Arapaho.
Sargenta rucas=Sargentaruka.
Sarie=Saric.
Sarikvihpak=Starik.
Sário, Sarique=Saric.
Sa-rité-ká-e, Sá-ri-té-ka=Arapaho.
Sar-lis-lo=Spokan.
Sar-lit-hu=Kalispel.
Sa-ron-ra=Sawuara.
Sarpa-wee-cha-cha=Ute.
Sarra Blanco=Sierra Blanca.
Sarrauahi=Sarauahi.
Sarraws=Cheraw.
Sarrii=Saric.
Sarritehca=Arapaho.
Sarsarcs=Sans Arcs.
Sarséwi, Sarxi=Sarsi.
Sasa=Cheraw.
Sasaguel=Sasuagel.
Sas-chu-tqéne, Sas-chut-qenne=Saschutkenne.
Sa-sis-e-tas=Cheyenne.
Sasitka=Siksika.
Sa-sits-go-lons-a=Tucson.
Saskatschawiner=Algonquian Family.
Saskwihanang, Sasquahana, Sasquahannahs, Sasquehannocks, Sasquesahanocks, Sasquesahanoughs, Sasquesahanougs, Sasquisahanoughes = Conestoga.
Sassasouacottons, Sassasouakouetons, Sassassaouacottons=Nassauaketon.
Sassee, Sassis=Sarsi.
Sassory=Nasoni.
Sassquahana=Conestoga.
Sastaghretsy=Huron.
Saste, Sastean=Shastan Family.
Sastharhetsi=Huron.
Sasti=Shastan Family.
Sasuaguel=Sasuagel.
Sä't=Snakes.
Satanas, Satans=Shawnee.
Satarees=Sugeree.
Satauket=Setauket.
Satawomeck, Satawomek, Satawomekes=Potomac.
Satcap=Satsop.

Satchap=Clatsop.
Satchap Indians=Satsop.
Sa-tchô-gottinè=Satchotugottine.
Sä-tdóa=Sa.
Sat-e-loo′-ne=Saschutkenne.
Satiroua=Saturiba.
Satiyomes, Satiyomis=Wappo.
Satoriva=Saturiba.
Satos=Uzutiuhi.
Sä-to-tin=Tatlitkutchin.
Satourlona, Satourioua=Saturiba.
Sà-towa=Sa.
Satrahe=Arikara.
Sat-sa-pish=Satsop.
Sa-tshi-o-tin′=Clatchotin.
Sat-sia-qua, Satsikaa=Siksika.
Satskōmilh, Sätsq=Satsk.
Sattiquo=Sitiku.
Satuket=Satucket.
Saturiora=Saturiba.
Sauaripa=Sahuaripa.
Sauckeys, Saucs=Sauk.
Saudia=Sandia.
Saufpak=Saopuk.
Saugehans=Souhegan.
Sau-ge-nong=Saginaw.
Saughpileel=Salpilel.
Saughtughtett=Satucket.
Saugies=Sauk.
Saugkonnet=Saconnet.
Saugust=Saugus.
S. Augustin, S. Augustinus=Oiaur.
Sau′hto=Comanche.
Saukatucket=Satucket.
Sau-kau-lutuck=Saukaulutuchs.
Saukee=Soquee.
Saukees, Saukeys=Sauk.
Saukhikins=Assumpink.
Saukies=Sauk.
Saukikani=Assumpink.
Sa-ukli=Sawokli.
Sauliers=Amahami.
Saulteaux, Saulteuse, Saulteux=Chippewa.
Sault Indians=Caughnawaga, Chippewa.
Sault Sainte Marie=Pawating.
Sauounons=Shawnee.
Sau′qtitc=Sauktich.
Saura, Saura towns, Sauro=Cheraw.
Saussetons=Sisseton.
Sautains=Santiam.
Sautatho=Sitolo.
Saut au Récollet=Sault au Recollet.
Sauteaux, Sauters, Sauteurs, Sauteus, Sauteux=Chippewa.
Sauthouis=Uzutiuhi.
Saut Indians=Caughnawaga, Pawating.
Sautor, Sautous, Sautoux=Chippewa.
Sautuχ=Comanche.
Sauvages de l'Isle=Kichesipirini.
Sauwanew, Sauwanous=Shawnee.
Sau-woo-ge-lo=Sawokli.
Sau-woog-e-loo-che=Sawokliudshi.
Sau-woo-ge-to=Sawokli.
Saux=Dakota.
Saux of the Wood=Santee.
Sauxpa=Sissipahaw.
Sauyou=Skoiyase.
Savages of the Lake=Senijextee.
Savanahs, Savanaus, Savannahs=Shawnee.
Savannas=Maskegon, Shawnee, Yuchi.
Savannechers, Savannehers, Savanoes=Shawnee.
Savanois=Maskegon.
Savanore, Savanos=Shawnee.
Savansa=Quapaw.
Savanuca=Yuchi.
Savinards=Savinnars.
Savints=Shivwits.
Savonoski=Ikak.
Sa-vour-ras=Sawuara.
Savova, Savovoyam=Sabʊba.
Sa-vow-ra=Sawuara.
Sawaams=Pokanoket.
Sa-wakh′-tu=Shawakhtau.
Sawakola=Sawokli.
Sawala=Shawala, Shawnee.
Sawana, Sawanee, Sä-wan-nä-kee′, Sáwano, Sa-wä-no′-o-no, Sawanoos, Sawanos, Sawánu-háka, Sa-wa-nú-ka, Sä-wan-wä-kee, Sawanwaki=Shawnee.
Sawara=Cheraw.
Sa-wa-rahs=Sawuara.

Sawassaw tinney, Saw-cesaw-tinneh, Saw-cessaw-dinnah=Etheneldeli.
Sawcung=Sawcunk.
Saw-eessaw-dinneh, Sawessaw tinney=Etheneldeli.
Saw-ge-nong=Saginaw.
Sawgus=Saugus.
Sawish=Samish.
Sawkattukett=Satucket.
Sawkee=Sauk.
Sawketakix=Siksika.
Sawkeys, Sawkies, Sawkis=Sauk.
Sawkunck, Sawkung, Sawkunk=Sawcunk.
Saw-meena=Ntlakyapamuk, Siamannas.
Sawocotuck=Sokoki.
Sawonocas=Shawnee.
Sawons=Saone.
Saw-paw=Skinpah.
Sawra, Sawraw, Sawro=Cheraw.
Sawû-no-kĭ, Sawwanew, Sawwannoo, Sawwanoo=Shawnee.
Sa xā′-idΛga-i=Sahaidagai.
Saxapahaw=Sissipahaw.
Saxes=Sauk.
Sáχlatks=Wasco.
Saxœ-kœ-koon=Siksika.
Sayaqúa-kwá=Sia.
Sayaque=Tesuque.
Sä′-yase=Skoiyase.
Saydankooskoi=Biorka.
Say degil=Una Vida.
Say-do-carah=Paviotso.
Sayenagi=Cheyenne.
Say-hah-ma-mish=Sahewamish.
Say-hay=Samamish.
Say-hay-ma-mish, Sayhaywamish=Sahewamish.
Sáyi=Klamath.
Sayokenek=Sayokinck.
Say-ona=Sangona.
Sayonstla=Siuslaw.
Sayopina, Sayopines=Tiopines.
Sayousla, Sayouslaw=Siuslaw.
Sayraidneuskoi=Seredka.
Sayúskla, Sayústkla=Siuslaw.
Saywamines=Sawani.
Sa-zē-oo-ti-na=Sazeutina.
S′Balahco=Smulkamish.
Sba-lush=Swinomish.
S. Bartolomé Comac=Comac.
S. Bernabé Jongopavi=Shongopovi.
S. Bernardino Gualpi=Walpi.
S. Bernardo Aquimuri=Aquimuri.
S. Bernardo de Aguatuvi=Awatobi.
S. Bonifacius=San Bonifacius.
S. Borgia=San Francisco Borja.
S Buenaventura=Cochiti.
S. Buen. de Mossaquavi=Mishongnovi.
Scaacticook, Scaahkook, Scaakticook=Scaticook.
Scabby band=Oivimana.
Scachhook, Scachkoke, Scachkooks, Scachtacook, Scachticooks, Scackhook, Scackkook=Scaticook.
Scad-dals=Scaddal.
Scad-jat=Skagit.
Scaghkooke, Scaghticoke, Scaghtikoke=Scaticook.
Sca-goines=Shregegon.
Scagticokes=Scaticook.
Scahandowana=Wyoming.
Scahcooks=Scaticook.
Scahentoarrhonon=Wyoming.
Scahkooks, Scahook=Scaticook.
S. Cajetanus=Calabazas.
S′calam=Clallam.
Scanehaderadeyghroones, Scaniadaradighroonas, Scanihaderadighroones=Nanticoke.
Scanonaentat, Scanonaerat, Scanonahenrat, Sca-nouaenrat=Scanonaenrat.
Scarred-Arms=Cheyenne.
Scatacook, Scatakook=Scaticook.
Scatchae, Scatchat=Skagit.
S. Catharina=Cuitciabaqui.
Scatoneck=Saconnet.
Scattacook, Scattakooks, Scautacook, Scauticook=Scaticook.
Scauwaga=Skoiyase.
Scawendadeys=Oka.
Scawyase=Skoiyase.
S. Cayetano=Tumacacori.
S. Cayetano de Bac=San Xavier del Bac.
S. Cayetano Tumagacori, S. Cayetano Tumapacori=Tumacacori.
Scenondidies=Oka.

Sceouex, Sceoux=Dakota.
Sceth-tesesay-tinneh=Etcheridiegottine.
Schaachkook, Schaacticook, Schaahkook, Schaa-
    hook, Schaakook=Scaticook.
Schachaméki=Shamokin.
Schachamesink=Shackamaxon.
Schachhenamendi=Shamokin.
Sehachkook, Schachticook, Schackhokes, Schack-
    hook, Schackooke, Schackwock, Schacook, Schact-
    ecoke, Schacthook, Schacticoke, Schactikook,
    Schaggkooke, Schaghkoos, Schaghtacooks,
    Schaghticoke, Schagkook, Schagtihoke = Scat-
    icook.
Schahä'=Arapaho.
Schahamoki=Shamokin.
Schahanapan=Shannopin's Town.
Scha,han,do,a,na, Schahandowa, Schahandowana=
    Wyoming.
Schahi=Cree.
Schahkook, Schahook=Scaticook.
Schahswintowaher=Sisseton.
Schaitl=Shaa.
Schakkook, Schakook=Scaticook.
Schanadarighroenes, Schaniadaradighroonas, Scha,-
    ni,ha,der,adygh,roon,ees=Nanticoke.
Schaouanos=Shawnee.
Scharoyos=Skoiyase.
Schathsooke, Schaticoke, Schaticook, Schauhte-
    cogue=Scaticook.
Schaunactadas=Schenectady.
Schauwunks=Scaticook.
Schavanna, Schaveno, Schawanese, Schawanno,
    Scha,wan,ooes=Shawnee.
Schawendadies=Oka.
Schawenoes, Schawenons, Schawnoah=Shawnee.
Schechschiquanuk=Sheshequin.
Schee-et-st-ish=Schuelstish.
Schenenk=Chenango.
Schengo-kēdi=Shunkukedi.
Sche-perrh=Serper.
Sche-woh=Katimin.
Scheyenne, Schianese, Schiannesse, Schians=Chey-
    enne.
Schiarame=Xarame.
Schilrá=Schira.
S-chinkit=Tlingit.
Schinouks=Chinook.
Schipuwe=Chippewa.
Schischaldinskoje=Sisaguk.
Schissatuch=Seshart.
S-chitcha-chon=Sitka.
Schit-hu-a-ut, Schit-hu-a-ut-uh=Okinagan.
Schitka, Schitka-kŏn, Schitkhakhóān=Sitka.
S'chízui=Skitswish.
Schkagué=Skagway.
S'chkoé, S'chkoéishin=Siksika.
Schoaries=Schoharie.
Schoccories=Shakori.
Schohare, Schoherie, Schohery=Schoharie.
Schonbrun=Schoenbrunn.
Schotack, Schotax=Schodac.
Schouchouaps=Shuswap.
Schoyerre=Skoiyase.
Schre-gon=Shregegon.
S. Christoval=San Cristobal.
Schroo-yel-pi=Colville.
Schuary, Schuye=Schurye.
Schwarzfüssige=Siksika.
Schwo-gel-pi, Schwoyelpi=Colville.
Schyarame=Xarame.
Sciaguan=Siaguan.
Scidi=Skidi.
Scietogas=Shahaptian.
Şcieux=Dakota.
Śćili=Skidi.
Sciller=Sillery.
Scinslaw=Siuslaw.
Scione Sioux=Saone.
Scioto=Sonnioto.
Sciou=Dakota.
Scious of the Prairies=Teton.
Scioux=Dakota.
Scioux de la chasse=Hictoba.
Scioux des Lacs=Menesouhatoba.
Scioux of the East=Santee.
Scioux of the Prairies, Scioux of the West=Teton.
Scioux of the Woods=Santee.
Sciuslau=Siuslaw.
Scial-lum=Clallam.

S. Clara=Santa Clara.
Sclavthamuk=Lillooet.
Scocomish=Skokomish.
Scoffies=Nascapee.
Scohare, Scoharee, Scoharies=Schoharie.
Sconta=Skoton.
Scookuk=Chiukak.
Scootle-mam-ish=Shotlemamish.
Scootuks=Passamaquoddy.
S. Cosmas, S. Cosme=San Cosme.
Scoton=Skoton.
Scotticook=Scaticook.
Scott's Valley Indians, Scott Valley Indians=Iru-
    waitsu.
Scouex=Dakota.
Scowyace=Skoiyase.
S. Crux=Santa Cruz de Mayo.
Scungsicks, Scunksik=Foxes.
Scutskon=Nahltushkan.
Scuzzy=Skuzis.
Sdewaetes=Huhliwahli.
SDiaz=Sandia.
S. Diego=Gyusiwa, San Diego, Tesuque.
S. Diego del Rio=San Diego del Rio.
S Dies=Sandia.
S. Dionysio, S. Dionysius=San Dionysio.
Sdo-hobc', S'do-ho-bish=Snohomish.
Sdok'-al-bǐhw=Snoqualmu.
S. Domingo de Xacomo, S. Domingo de Xacoms, S.
    Domingo de Xacona=Jacona.
S. Doonysio=San Dionysio.
Sdo-qual-bush=Snoqualmu.
Seachkook=Scaticook.
Seaconet, Seaconnet=Saconnet.
Seacos=Shiegho.
Seacotauk=Secatoag.
Seadlermeoo=Sagdlirmiut.
Seahantowana=Wyoming.
Seaketaulke=Secatoag.
Seakonnet=Saconnet.
Seama=Tsiama.
Seanecas=Seneca.
Seapcat, Seapeats=Siapkat.
Seaquatalke, Seaquetalke=Setauket.
Searcie=Sarsi.
Se-ä'-sä-pä=Sihasapa.
Seashelth=Seechelt.
Se-ash-ha-pa=Sihasapa.
Sea-side People=Mohegan.
Seatakot, Seatalcott, Seatalcutt, Seatalkot, Sea-
    Talkott, Seataucok, Seatauk, Seatauke = Se-
    tauket.
Seaticook=Scaticook.
Seatolcotts=Setauket.
Seaton Lake=Seton Lake.
Sea tribe=Winnebago.
Seattle=Suquamish.
Seauex, Seaux=Dakota.
Seawees=Sewee.
Sebaipuris=Sobaipuri.
Sebanoa=Sabino.
Sebassa=Sabassa.
Sebeno, Sebenoa=Sabino.
Seboiak=Sebaik.
Sebollita=Sevilleta.
Seboyeta=Cebolleta.
Se-ca-ca-co-nies, Secacaonies, Secakoonies=Secaca-
    woni.
Sécanais=Sekani.
Se-ćang-ćos=Brulé.
Secassaw=Seccasaw.
Secatague, Secataug, Secatogue, Secatoket, Seca-
    tong=Secatoag.
Secawyace=Skoiyase.
Sechelts=Seechelt.
Se-cho-ma-we=Sichomovi.
Sechs Nationen=Iroquois.
Sechumevay, Se-chum'-e-way=Sichomovi.
Seckoneses=Siconesses.
Secobeck=Secobec.
Secoffee=Nascapee.
Seconett, Seconnett=Saconnet.
Secota=Secotan.
Secoutagh=Secatoag.
Secumnes, Secumni=Sekumne.
Secunnie=Sekani.
Sedankovskoe=Biorka.
Sedard, Sedáro=Sidaru.
Sedentary Nadouesserons=Santee.

Sedentary Village Indians=Pueblos.
Sedge=Sonoita.
Se-dj′ûn′-tĭn tĕne′=Thechuntunne.
S. Eduard de Baipia, S. Eduardo, S. Eduardo Baipia,
　S. Eduardo de Aribacpia, S. Edward=Baipia.
Seé=Seh.
See-char-litch-ar=Secharlecha.
See-cho-mah-wee=Sichomovi.
Se-ĕçl′ ʒûnnĕ=Seethltunne.
See-issaw-dinni=Etheneldeli.
Sĕ-ĕk-pe=Sespe.
Seekta Loosa=Suktaloosa.
Seél=Shanel.
Seelawik Mutes=Selawigmiut.
See-mun-ah=Paraje.
See-oo-nay=Saone.
Seepans=Lipan.
See-pohs-ka-mi-mah-ka-kee, See-poosh-kä=Sipush-
　kanumanke.
Seeseetoan, See-see-ton, Seeseetwaun, See-see-wan,
　Seesetoan, See-se-ton=Sisseton.
Seetauke=Setauket.
Seethenskie=Sitka.
Seewas=Sewee.
Seganiateratickrohne=Nanticoke.
Segantes=Siyante.
Segata-jenne=Chiricahua.
Seginsairn's Village, Seginservin's village, Seginsi-
　win's village=Seginsavin.
Segohquet=Segocket.
Següí=Tegui.
Seguna=Laguna.
Sehalatak=Clackama.
Se-héhwa-mish=Sahewamish.
Sehe-perrh=Serper.
Seheries=Skidi.
Sehtsa-ásh=Seh.
Se-huapm-uh=Shuswap.
Sᴇi′lᴇqamuQ=Stuichamukh.
Seinslaw Eneas=Siuslaw.
Seipa=Seyupa.
Sejen-né=Mescaleros.
Sekacawone, Sekacowones=Secacawoni.
Sékanais, Sékanais toenè, Sékan′-es=Sekani.
Sekioge=Sukiaug.
Sekomne=Sekumne.
Sekonett=Saconnet.
Sekoselar, Sekoselar Innuits=Sikosuilarmiut.
Seksekai=Siksika.
Sekume=Sekumne.
Sekunnet=Saconnet.
Selakampóm=Comanche.
Selawigamute, Selāwig′mut, Selawik=Selawigmiut.
Seldom Lonesome=Miahwahpitsiks.
Selenie=Pavlof.
Sᴇ′Lia=Setlia.
Selish=Salishan Family.
Selloat-pallahs=Paloos.
Selugrue=Wea.
Semãç=Sumass.
Sĕmaccom=Samackman.
Sᴇmā′mila=Ntlakyapamuk, Siamannas.
Semanole=Seminole.
Semät=Kiowa Apache.
Sᴇmᴇxā′u=Semehau.
Semiā′mō=Semiahmoo.
Semillete=Sevilleta.
Seminolas, Seminoleans, Seminolie, Seminol-úlki,
　Seminúniak=Seminole.
Sem-mi-an-mas=Semiahmoo.
Sempiche Utahs=Sanpet.
Sempoils=Sanpoil.
Senaca=Senecu.
Senacaes, Senacars, Senacas=Seneca.
Senachas=Sukinatchi.
Senacu=Senecu.
Senahuow=Lenahuon.
Senakees=Seneca.
Senalton=Tsewenalding.
Senango=Shenango.
Señasca Blanca=Peñasca Blanca.
Sencase=Secmoco.
Sencen=Senecu.
Sendia=Sandia.
Séne, Seneca=Senecu.
Seneca Abeal=Tehononsadegi.
Seneca Castle=Canadasaga.
Senecaes, Senecas=Seneca.

Senecas of Ohio, Senecas of Sandusky, Senecas of
　Sandusky and Stony creek, Senecas of the Glaize=
　Mingo.
Senecca=Seneca.
Seneci=Senecu.
Seneckes=Seneca.
Seneco=Senecu del Sur.
Senecques, Senegars, Senekaas, Senekaes, Senekas,
　Senekées, Senekers, Senekes, Senekies, Senekoes=
　Seneca.
Senekshaw=Chinokabi.
Se-nel′=Shanel.
Senequaes, Senequas, Seneques, Senequois=Seneca.
Sengekontakit=Sanchecantacket.
Senicaes=Seneca.
Seniczo=Sinicu.
Senikers=Seneca.
Senis=Caddo.
Senixzo=Seneca.
Sennagars, Sennakas, Sennakers, Sennecas, Sennec-
　ca, Senneches, Senneckes, Sennecks, Sennekaes,
　Sennekas, Sennekaw, Sennekees, Sennekes, Sen-
　nekies, Senneks, Sennekus, Sennequans, Senne-
　quens, Senneques, Sennickes, Sennicks, Senontou-
　ant=Seneca.
Senor San Francisco=San Francisco de los Tejas.
Senottoway=Seneca.
Sᴇnqtl=Senktl.
Senslaw, Senslaw Eneas=Siuslaw.
Sĕn-têçl′-tûn=Sentethltun.
Sçnłłaē=Sisintlae.
Sᴇ̊nxᴌ=Senktl.
Se-pä-uä, Se-pä-ue=Sepawi.
Se-peh=Seh.
Sepos, Sépous=Tunxis.
Sepponet=Sapponet.
Septem ciuitatum=Zuñi.
Sept Isles=Seven Islands.
Sepunco=Secmoco.
Sepus=Esopus.
Se-qa′-ts′ă ʒûnnĕ=Sekhatsatunne.
SeQuapmuQ=Shuswap.
Sequatake, Sequatogue=Secatoag.
Se-qûc′-tûn ʒûnnĕ′=Sekhushtuntunne.
Sequeen=Mattabesec.
Se-queh-cha=Kwatami.
Sequetauke=Secatoag.
Sequins=Mattabesec.
Sequotan=Secotan.
Seqvins=Mattabesec.
Sê-qwût ʒûnnĕ=Nahankhuotane.
Ser-a-goines, Ser-a-goins=Shregegon.
Serannas=Shawnee.
Seranos=Serranos.
Seraphim=San Serafin.
Seratees=Santee.
Seraticks, Seratics=Arapaho.
Seredkinskoje, Seredninskoe=Seredka.
Seretee=Santee.
Sereva=Servas.
Sermalton=Tsewenalding.
Serpent gens=Wesaenikashika.
Serpents=Shoshoni.
Serragoin=Shregegon.
Serranay=Sarauahi.
Serranos=Comeya.
Serrope=Sarrope.
Servushamnes=Servushamne.
Serwädling=Sarfalik.
Se-see-toans, Se-see-t′wawns=Sisseton.
Sesepaulabá, Sesepaulabe=Shipaulovi.
Sesetons=Sisseton.
Seshaht=Seshart.
Seshal=Seechelt.
Se-shiu-qua=Seshukwa.
Sesiton Sioux=Sisseton.
Sesquehanocks, Sesquihanowes=Conestoga.
Sessatone, Sessatons, Sesseton=Sisseton.
S. Estanislao Octam, S. Estanislao Ooltan=Ooltan.
S. Estevan de Acoma, S. Estevau de Acama=Acoma.
Sést′sethût=Sasthut.
Sesüalik=Sheshalek.
Setaket=Setauket.
Setá kóχnináme=Walapai.
Setalcket Setauck, Setauk, Setawkett=Setauket.
Se-t′ça′-tûn=Setthatun.
Se-tco′-mo-we=Sichomovi.
Se-tcûn′ ʒûnnĕ′=Thechuntunne.
Se-tcuq′-tûn=Sechukhtun.

Se-tdóa=Se.
Seteomellos=Wappo.
SETL=Lillooet.
Setokett=Setauket.
Se-to-qua=Setokwa.
Setorokamiut=Sidarumiut.
Setshómavé, Setshómové=Sichomovi.
Se'-tsû-rxe-a'-ɥé=Setsurgheake.
Settacoo, Sette, Settico=Sitiku.
Setuket=Setauket.
Setusura=Setasura.
Seu-a-rits=Seuvarits.
Seuh-no-keh'te, Seuh-now-ka-ta=Onondaga.
Seuilleta=Sevilleta.
Seven Castles= Seven Nations of Canada.
Seven Cities of Gold=Zuñi.
Seven Fires=Seven Council Fires.
Seven Nations of Indians inhabiting Lower Canada, Seven Nations of Lower Canada Indians, "Seven Tribes" on the River St. Lawrence=Seven Nations of Canada.
Severnik=Sarfalik.
Severnovskia, Severnovze, Severnovzer, Severnovzi= Khwakhamaiu.
Seviches=Shivwits.
Sevillete, Sevilletta=Sevilleta.
Sevinta=Shivwits.
Se'-wa-açl-tcû'-tûn=Sewaathlchutun.
Se-wah=Katimin.
Sewan-akies=Metoac.
Sewanne=Shawnee.
Sewatpalla=Paloos.
Sewernowskije=Aglemiut.
Sewickly's old T., Sewicklys Old Town=Sewickley.
Sewoe=Sewee.
Sewonkeeg=Siwanoy.
Sextapay=Salinan Family, Teshaya.
Seymos=Eskimo.
Seymour Creek=Chechilkok.
Seyuktoon=Siuktun.
Se-yu Pae-la, Se-yu-pä-lo=Seyupa.
Seywamines=Sawani.
Sezaro=Sidaru.
Sezaro Mutes=Sidarumiut.
Sfaganugamute=Sfaganuk.
S. Felip, S. Felipe, S. Felipe de Cueres, S. Felipe de Cuerez=San Felipe.
S. Felipe Gracia Real de Terrenate=Terrenate.
S. Felipe Uparch=Uparch.
Sfoganugamiut=Sfaganuk.
S. Francais de Sales=Saint Francis.
S. Francesco Borgia=San Francisco Borja.
S. Francisco=San Francisco, San Francisco Ati.
S. Francisco Borja Maicoba=Maicoba.
S. Francisco del Caiman=Caiman.
S. Francisco del Mezquital=Mezquital.
S. Francisco Javier Batuco=Batuco.
S. Francisco Ocotan=Ocotan.
S. Francisco Xavier de Bac=San Xavier del Bac.
S. Franciscus=San Francisco Ati.
S. Fran. Javier Cuchuta=Cuchuta.
S. Fran. Javier Reboico=Robesco.
Sfugunugumut=Sfaganuk.
Sg· adzē'guatl lā'nas=Sadjugahl-lanas.
S. Gaetan=Calabazas.
Sg· āga'ngsilai=Sagangusili.
Sg· a'nguai=Ninstints.
S. Gerónimo=San Geronimo.
S. Geronimo de los Thaos, S. Gerénimo Thaos=Taos
S. Gioachino=San Joaquin.
S. Gregoio de Abo S. Gregoria, S. Gregorio de Abo= Abo.
Sguahguaihtl=Kaquaith.
Shaachkook, Shaak-kooke=Scaticook.
Sha-ap-tin=Nez Percés.
Shab-eh-nay=Shobonier.
Shabor, Shacco=Shakori.
Shachkook, Shachook=Scaticook.
Shacioes=Shakori.
Shackakonies=Shackaconia.
Shack-a-po=Kickapoo.
Shackaxons=Shackamaxon.
Shackhook=Scaticook.
Shackory=Shakori.
Shacktaus=Choctaw.
Shacomico=Shecomeco.
Sha-de-ka-ron-ges=Seneca.
Shá-en=Cheyenne.
Shag-a-voke=Sagavok.

Shagawamigong, Shag-a-waum-ik-ong=Shaugawau-mikong.
Shagelook, Shageluk=Jugelnute.
Shagen=Cheyenne.
Shaglook=Jugelnute.
Shāgwau Lennas=Sagua-lanas.
Shāgwikitonē=Sagui-gitunai.
Shahahanih=Shahanik.
Shahalahs=Shahala.
Shahamóki, Shahamokink=Shomokin.
Shahañ=Dakota.
Shahana=Shahala.
Shahaptain=Nez Percés.
Shahaptan=Nez Percés, Salishan Family.
Shahaptanian, Shahaptemish, Shahapts=Nez Percés.
Shah-ha-la=Shahala.
Shahlee=Ootlashoot.
Sha-hō=Cheyenne.
Shahomaking=Shamokin.
Shahray-tick-ah=Arapaho.
Shahshanih=Shahanik.
Shahsweentowahs=Sisseton.
Sha-hue=Ishauu.
Shah-woo-rum=Sawuara.
Sha-i-a-pi, Shai-é-la, Shai-én-a=Cheyenne.
Sha-i-yē=Cree.
Shaiyus=Skoiyase.
Shakahonea=Shackaconia.
Shakamaxon=Shackamaxon.
Shakan=Sukkwan.
Shak-a-pee's band=Taoapa.
Shake-kah-quah=Kickapoo.
Shakhamexunk, Shakhamuxunck=Shackamaxon.
Shakies, Shàkirs=Sauk.
Shaklolik=Shaktolik.
Shakopee=Taoapa.
Shakor̯=Shakori.
Shākpā, Shakpay=Taoapa.
Shaktakook=Scaticook.
Shaktó ligmūt=Shaktoligmiut.
Shaktolit=Shaktolik.
Shākwan Hāadē=Sukkwan.
Sha-la-la=Shahala.
Shalalahs=Silela.
Shalees=Ootlashoot.
Shallalah=Silela.
Shallates=Shallattoo.
Shallees=Ootlashoot.
Shamaken=Shamokin.
Shamanese=Shawnee.
Shamochan, Shamoken, Shamoking=Shamokin.
Shamooinaugh=Nez Percés.
Shánaki=Cherokee.
Shánana=Dakota.
Shanapins, Shanapin's town, Shanappins T.=Shan-nopin's Town.
Shanawageras=Sonojowauga.
Shanaws=Shawnee.
Shanel-kaya=Shnalkeya.
Shaniadaradighroonas, Shanihadaradighroones= Nanticoke.
Shaningo=Shenango.
Shan-ke-t'wans, Shank't'wannons, Shank-t'wans= Yankton.
Shan-nack Shánnakiak=Cherokee.
Shannapins=Shannopin's Town.
Shannoahs=Shawnee.
Shannok=Micmac.
Shannondaque=Canandaigua.
Shannopen T.=Shannopin's Town.
Shanoas=Shawnee.
Shanopens, Shanopins, Shanoppin, Shanoppin's town=Shannopin's Town.
Shanung=Micmac.
Shañwans=Shawnee.
Shanwappoms, Shanwappones=Yakima.
Shan-wap-pums=Shanwappom.
Shaomet=Shawomet.
Shaonois. Shaononons=Shawnee.
Shapalawee, Sha-pan-la-vi, Shapanlobi=Shipaulovi.
Shapashχē'ni=Shapashkeni.
Sha-pau-lah-wee=Shipaulovi.
Sharas=Cheyenne.
Sharetikeh=Arapaho.
Shar'-ha=Cheyenne.
Sharp eyed Indians=Kutchin.
Sharshas=Cheyenne.
Shashones=Shoshoni.
Shásk'-hánoq^{ch}=Soshka.

Shasta, Shasta-Achomawi=Shastan Family.
Shasta Costa=Chastacosta.
Shasta Skoton=Chasta-Skoton.
Shasté=Shahaptian Family.
Shasteecas=Shasta.
Shasti, Shasties=Shahaptian Family.
Shas-ti-ka, Shasty=Shastan Family.
Shā′t=Snakes.
Sha taha=Sha.
Shatasla=Shahaptian Family.
Shatchet=Skagit.
Shatekaróⁿhyes=Totiakton.
Shateras=Tutelo.
Shatetucket=Showtucket.
Sháti=Koasati.
Shatuckett, Shatuskett=Showtucket.
Shauanos=Shawnee.
Shä-u-ee=Shawi.
Shaug-ah - waum - ik - ong, Shaugha-waum-ik-ong=
    Shaugawaumikong.
Shaumeer=Saumingmiut.
Shaumoking=Shamokin.
Shaunas, Shauwaunoes, Shavanos=Shawnee.
Shaved heads=Pawnee.
Shaw=Shawnee.
Shaw-a-gan=Sukkwan.
Shawahahs=Shawnee.
Shawamegin=Shaugawaumikong.
Shawamet=Shawomet.
Shawan=Chowanoc.
Shawana=Shawnee.
Shawana Cabbins=Shawnee Cabins.
Shawanahs, Shawanapi=Shawnee.
Shawanapon, Shawanasson=Shannopin's Town.
Shawanaws, Shawane=Shawnee.
Shawane Cabbins=Shawnee Cabins.
Shawanees=Shawnee.
Shawanee town=Shawneetown.
Shawaneise, Shawanese, Shawanesse, Shawaneu=
    Shawnee.
Shawangung=Shawangunk.
Shawanies, Shawanna, Shawannohs=Shawnee.
Shawannoppan=Shannopin's Town.
Shawannos=Shawnee.
Shawanoe Cabbins=Shawnee Cabins.
Shawanœese, Shawanoes, Shawanœse, Shawànoh,
    Shawanois, Shawanons, Shawano's, Shawanose,
    Shawanous, Shawanowi, Shawans=Shawnee.
Shawash=Achomawi.
Shawatharott=Beothukan Family.
Shaways=Cheyenne.
Shawdtharut=Beothukan Family.
Shawendadies=Tionontati.
Shawenoes=Shawnee.
Shaweygria=Hathawekela.
Shaw-ha-ap-ten, Shaw-Haptens=Nez Percés.
Shawhays=Cheyenne.
Shá-wi-ti=Showwiti.
Shawmokin=Shamokin.
Shawneese, Shawnese, Shawnesse, Shawneys, Shaw-
    no, Shawnoah=Shawnee.
Shawnoah Basse Ville=Lowertown.
Shawnoes=Shawnee.
Shawnuk=Micmac.
Shawomut=Shawomet.
Shawonese=Shawnee.
Shawonese Cabbins=Shawnee Cabins.
Shawoniki, Shawonoes, Shaw-un-oag=Shawnee.
Sháyäge=Cherokee.
Shayén, Sháyenna=Cheyenne.
Shaytee's village=Grand Bois.
Sh-chee-tsoo-ee=Skitswish.
Sheaquaga=Catherine's Town.
Sheastuckle, Sheastukle=Siuslaw.
Sheavwits=Shivwits.
She-bal-ne Pomas=Keliopoma.
She-banlavi=Shipaulovi.
She-ba-retches=Seuvarits.
Shebaula-vi=Shipaulovi.
Sheberetches, She-be-riches, She-be-Ucher=Seuva-
    rits.
She-bo-pav-wee=Shipaulovi.
Shechart=Seshart.
Shecomeka=Shecomeco.
She-dar-haitch=Asidahech.
Shee-ah-whib-bahk, Shee-ah-whíb-bak, Shee-e-huib-
    bac, Shee-eh-whíb-bak=Isleta.
Shee-p'ah-póon=Shipapulima.
Sheep-Eaters=Tukuarika.

Sheep Indians=Abbatotine.
Sheepon-arleeve, Sheepowarleeve=Shipaulovi.
Sheep People=Abbatotine.
Sheepscot, Sheepscuts=Wewenoc.
Sheeshaldenskoi=Sisaguk.
Shegwuu=Katimin.
She-kom=Shigom.
Shekomeko=Shecomeco.
Shell earring band=Inyanhaoin.
She-mo-pá-ve=Shongopovi.
Shenango=Logstown.
Shenawaga=Kashong.
Shenengo=Chenango.
Shennoquankin, Shennoskuankin=Shennosquan-
    kin.
Shē-noma=Hopi.
Sheooke=Suk.
Sheoquaga=Catherine's Town.
Shepálavé, Shepalawa, She-pa-la-wee, She-pau′-la-ve,
    Shepauliva=Shipaulovi.
Shepawees, Shepewas=Chippewa.
Shepeweyan=Chipewyan.
Shepolavi, She-powl-a-we=Shipaulovi.
Shepuway=Chippewa.
Sherwits=Shivwits.
Sheschequon=Sheshequin.
She-sha-aht=Seshart.
Sheshalegamute=Sheshalek.
Sheshatapoosh, Sheshatapooshshoish,   Sheshat-
    poosh=Montagnais.
Sheshebug=Sheshebe.
She-she-gwah, She-she-gwun=Kenabig.
She-shell=Seechelt.
Sheshoalik, She-shore-lik=Sheshalek.
Shetimasha=Chitimacha.
Shetnak=Chitnak.
Shevenagamute=Shevenak.
Shewamett=Shawomet.
Shewena=Zuñi.
Shewhap, Shewhapmuch, Shewhapmuh, Shewhap-
    mukh, She-whaps=Shuswap.
She-wo-na=Zuñi.
She'yen, Sheyennes=Cheyenne.
Sh-ha-ha-nih, Shhahanik=Shahanik.
Shian, Shiä′navo, Shiannes=Cheyenne.
Shi-ap′-a-gi=Santa Clara.
Shiárish=Cheyenne.
Shiáska=Soshka.
Shiastuckle=Siuslaw.
Shi-bal′-ni Po′-mo=Keliopoma.
Shibalta=Nestucca.
Shich-e-quet-to-ny=Tachikhwutme.
Shi-choam-a-vi=Sichomovi.
Shicomiko=Shecomeco.
Shi-da′-hetsh=Asidahech.
Shi-e-á-la=Cree.
Shiĕ′da, Shienne=Cheyenne.
S. Hieronymo=Taos.
Shiewhíbak=Isleta.
Shi-e′-ya=Cree.
Shígapo=Kickapoo.
Shiíni=Lipan.
Shikapu=Kickapoo.
Shikene=Stikine.
Shikχaltini=Avoyelles.
Shil-an-ottine=Thilanottine.
Shillicoffy=Chillicothe.
Shi-ma-co-vi=Shongopovi.
Shimiahmoo=Semiahmoo.
Shimmuo=Shimmoah.
Shimopavi, Shimopova=Shongopovi.
Shimshyans=Tsimshian.
Shinacock, Shinecock=Shinnecock.
Shineshean=Tsimshian.
Shineyagamute=Shiniak.
Shingis's Old Town=Sawcunk.
Shinglemasy=Meshingomesia.
Shingoes=Shenango.
Shiniagmiut=Shiniak.
Shinicoks, Shinicooks=Shinnecock.
Shinikes=Seneca.
Shinikooks=Shinnecock.
Shiningrua=Shinagrua.
Shinnacock=Shinnecock.
Shin-nu-mos=Hopi.
Shínome=Hopi.
Shinuk-kaha=Schekaha.
Shinyagamiut=Shiniak.
Shi′-oui=Zuñi.

Shi′-pàp, Shi-Pap-u, Shi-pa-puyna=Shipapulima.
Shi-pau-a-luv-i, Shi-pau-i-luv-i, Shi-pau′-la-vi, Shi-pav-i-luv-i=Shipaulovi.
Shipi=Kuta.
Shipop=Shipapulima.
Shi-powl-ovi=Shipaulovi.
Ship-tet-sa=Shiptetza.
Shíra-háno=Schira.
Shishaldin, Shishaldinskoe=Sisaguk.
Shishiniwotsítan, Shĭshino′wĭts-Itäniuw′, Shĭ′shĭnó-wŭtz-hitä′neo=Comanche.
Shish-i-nu′-wut-tsit′-a-ni-o=Kiowa.
Shiship=Sheshebe.
Shis-Indy=Apache.
Shis-tah-cos-tahs, Shis-tah-koas-tah, Shis-ta-koos-tee, Shis-tā-kū-sta=Chastacosta.
Shĭtaikt=Snakes.
Shitaimuvi=Shitaimu.
Shitnak=Chitnak.
Shi-ua-na, Shiuano, Shi-uo-na=Zuñi.
Shíu-t′aínïn=Shiu.
Shíuwimi-háno=Shuwimi.
Shiveytown=Sisseton.
Shí-vo-la=Zuñi.
Shiwahpi=Siwapi.
Shi-wa-na=Zuñi.
Shiwanish=Nez Percés.
Shiwi=Zuñi.
Shiwian=Aridian, Zuñi.
Shiwina, Shi-wi-na-kwin, Shiwinas=Zuñi.
Shí-wĭn-è-wà, Shí-wĭn-nà=Sichomovi.
Shi-wo-Kŭg-mut=Eiwhuelit.
Shíwona=Zuñi.
Shiχkaltíni=Tamoucougoula.
Shix river=Kwatami.
Shi-yä ′Shiyans=Cheyenne.
Shkagway=Skagway.
Shkwim, Shkwin=Sequim.
Shlakatats=Klikitat.
Shltuja=Lituya.
Shnégitsuish=Snakes.
Shoalwater Bay Indians=Atsmitl.
Shoccories=Shakori.
Shockays, Shockeys=Sauk.
Shocktaus=Choctaw.
Shodakhai pomo, Sho-do Kai Po′-mo=Shodakhai Pomo.
Shoe Indians=Amahami.
Shoemeck=Talaniyi.
Shoenbrun=Schœnbrunn.
Shoenidies=Oka.
Shogleys, Shogteys=Sawokli.
Shokpay, Shokpaydan, Shokpedan=Taoapa.
Shokumimleppe=Shokumimlepi.
S′Homahmish=Shomamish.
Shomhomokin, Shomoken, Shomokin, Shomoko=Shamokin.
Shomonpavi, Shomoparvee=Shongopovi.
Shomo Takali=Chomontokali.
Shŏnăck=Micmac.
Shoneanawetowah=Cayuga.
Shongalth Lennas=Stustas.
Shongápave′, Shong′a-pa-vi, Shongoba-vi, Shongópavi=Shongopovi.
Shonk-chun′-ga-dă=Shungikikarachada.
Shononowendos=Cayuga.
Shoo-schawp, Shooshaps, Shooswabs=Shuswap.
Shootamool=Shutamul.
Shooter=Khemnichan.
Shooters in the Pines=Wazikute.
Shootk=Shuuk.
Shoouk=Suk.
Shoo-whā′-pa-mooh=Shuswap.
Shopumish=Nez Percés.
Shoquamish=Snoquamish.
Shorbanaxon=Shackamaxon.
Short hair=Peshla.
Short hair band=Peshlaptechela.
Sho-sho-co, Sho-sho-coes, Shoshokoes=Shoshoko.
Shoshon, Sho-sho-nay, Sho-sho-ne, Shoshonee=Shoshoni.
Shó-sho-nee=Snakes.
Shos-shone, Shossoonies, Shothones=Shoshoni.
S′ho-ti-noñ-nă-wäⁿ tŏ′-nă=Cayuga.
S′Hotlmahmish, S′hotlmamish=Shotlemamish.
Shou a gan=Sukkwan.
Shoūdamunk=Nascapee.
Shōudămŭnk=Montagnais.
Shougheys=Sauk.

Shoushwaps, Shouwapemoh, Shouwapemot=Shuswap.
Shouwendadies=Oka.
Shovenagamute=Shevenak.
Show-a-gan=Sukwan.
Showamet=Shawomet.
Showammers=Shawnee.
Showangunck=Showangunk.
Showanhoes, Showannees, Showannoes, Showanoes=Shawnee.
Shô′wati=Showwiti.
Showatuks=Wunnashowatuckoog.
Showays=Cheyenne.
Shô′witi=Showwiti.
Show-mowth-pa=Shongopovi.
Showomut=Shawomet.
Showonese, Showonoes=Shawnee.
Shqúwï=Shruhwi.
Shrótsona=Shrutsuna.
Shua-vit=Suangua.
Shubenakadie, Shubenecadie=Shubenacadie.
Shu-chum-a-vay=Sichomovi.
Shuckers=Shoshoko.
Shuckospoja=Sukaispoka.
Shu-cu=Shuku.
Shuekospaga=Sukaispoka.
Shu Finne=Shufina.
Shuhiaχiä′gish=Shuyakeksh.
Shu-húi-ma=Sowiinwa.
Shuitackle=Sintaktl.
Shuitna=Chuitna.
Shuk-hu-nat-chu=Sukinatchi.
Shukku=Shuku.
Shumeia=Yukian Family.
Shumi=Hopi.
Shu-mo-pa-vay=Shongopovi.
Shumuit=Ashismuit.
Shú-mŭth-pà, Shú-mŭth-pài-ò-wà, Shung-a-pá-vi, Shung-o-pah-wee, Shung-o-pa-we, Shungopawee, Shung-op-ovi=Shongopovi.
Shunkasapa=Ohanhanska.
Shunk′-a-yu-tēsh-ni=Skungkayuteshni.
Shúⁿshuⁿ-wichásha=Shoshoni.
Shu-par-la-vay, Shupaúlavi, Shupowla, Shupowlewy=Shipaulovi.
Shu-qtu′-ta-qlit′=Shukhtutaklit.
Shúren=Churan.
Shurts-ŭn-na=Shrutsuna.
Shu-sho-no-vi=Sichomovi.
Shushwaps=Kitunahan Family, Salishan Family, Shuswap.
Shushwapumsh, Shuswap-much=Shuswap.
Shutsón, Shútsun′, Shutzuna=Shrutsuna.
Shúwhami=Shuwimi.
Shuyakē′kish, Shuyakē′kshni, Shuyakē′kshni máklaks, Shuyakē′-ksi, Shuyéakēks=Shuyakeksh.
Shuyelpees, Shuyelphi, Shuyelpi=Colville.
Shúyikēks=Shuyakeksh.
Shwanoes=Shawnee.
Shw-aw-mish=Squamish.
Shwoi-el-pi=Colville.
Shwufum=Kenek.
Shyatogoes=Shahaptian.
Shyennes=Cheyenne.
Shye-ui-beg=Isleta.
Shyicks=Shyik.
Shyoutémacha=Chitimacha.
Shy-to-gas=Shahaptian Family.
Shyu-amo=Shuwimi.
Siaban=Siaguan.
S. Iacobus de Oiadaibuisc=Ojiataibues.
Siaexer=Haeser.
Siaguane=Siaguan.
Siahs=Saia.
Si′-a-ko=Shiegho.
Siamoeon=Shamokin.
Sianábone, Si′-a-na-vo=Cheyenne.
Sianekees=Seneca.
Sians=Saia.
Siapanes=Lipan.
Sīatlqēlā′aq=Siatlhelaak.
Siaws=Saia.
Siay=Sia.
Siaywas=Liaywas.
Siba-igewi=Sebaik.
Sibapa=Kitkatla.
Sibapot=Toybipet.
Sibillela, Sibilleta=Sevilleta.
Sibola, Sibolla=Zuñi.

Sibolletta=Cebolleta.
Si-cábĕ=Siksika.
Sicacas=Chickasaw.
Sicacha=Chicaça, Chickasaw.
Sicachia=Chickasaw.
Sicanees=Etagottine, Sazeutina.
Sicangu=Kheyatawichasha.
Sićaŋgu=Brulé.
Sicangu-Kutawica'sa=Kutawichasha.
Sicannees=Sazeutina.
Sicanni, Sicanny=Sekani.
Sicaock, Sicaogg=Sukiaug.
Sĭ'cätl=Seechelt.
Si-ca-tugs=Secatoag.
Sicaugu=Brulé.
Sicaunies=Sekani.
Si-ćá-wi-pi=Tinazipeshicha.
Siccane, Siccanie, Siccannie, Siccony=Sekani.
Sichangus, Si-chan-koo=Brulé.
Si-choan-avi, Sichomivi, Si-chum'-a-vi, Sichumnavi, Sichumniva, Sichumovi=Sichomovi.
Sĭ'ciatl=Seechelt.
Sickameen, Sick-a-mun=Siccameen.
Sickanie, Sickannie=Sekani.
Sickenames=Pequot.
Sicketauyhacky, Sicketawach, Sicketawagh, Sicketeuwhacky=Secatoag.
Sickmunari=Sichomovi.
Sick-naa-hulty=Siknahadi.
Sickoneysincks, Siconescinque=Siconesses.
Siconi=Sekani.
Siconysy=Siconesses.
Sicopan=Secotan.
Sicosuilarmiut=Sikosuilarmiut.
Sicouex=Dakota.
Sicumnes=Sekumne.
Sicxacames=Sijame.
Sidanāk, Sidankin=Biorka.
Sidaru, Sida'ruñmiun=Sidarumiut.
Sid-is-kíne=Tzetseskadn.
Sidocaw=Paviotso.
Si'-e=Klamath.
S. Iean=San Juan.
Sienaguilla, Sienega=Cienega.
Sieouex=Dakota.
Sierra=Caruana.
Sierra Blanca Apaches, Sierra Blancas, Sierra Blanco Apache, Sierras blancas=White Mountain Apache.
Sĭē'tcEm=Siechem.
Siete Arroyos=Tenabo.
Siete Cibdades=Zuñi.
Siete Principes Ati=Ati.
Sieux=Dakota.
S. Ignacio=San Ignacio.
S. Ignacio Bacanora=Bacanora.
S. Ignacio del Zape=Zape.
S. Ignacio de Tubac=Tubac.
S. Ignacio Guaynamota=Guaynamota.
S. Ignacio Mochopa=Mochopa.
S. Ignacio Opotu=Oputo.
S. Ignacio Sinoquipe=Sinoquipe.
S. Ignacio Subaque=Suaqui.
S. Ignazio di Kadakaaman=San Ignacio de Kadakaman.
Siguipam=Siupam.
Siguniktāwâk=Sigunikt.
Si-há-sa-pa=Siksika.
Siha-sapa-qtca, Sihasapa-rca=Sihasapakhcha.
Si-he'-bĭ=Suhub.
Si-him-e-na=Siamannas.
Si'-hü wüñ-wü=Sihu.
Sikacha=Chickasaw.
Si-kah-ta-ya, Sikáhtayo=Sikyataiyo.
Si-kā'k-i=Sikyatki.
S!îkąŋxsa'nî=Kake.
Sikani, Sikanie, Sikanni, Sikannie=Sekani.
Sik'-a-pu=Kickapoo.
Sikatsipomaks=Sikutsipumaiks.
Sikcitano=Siksika.
Sí-ke-na=Maricopa, Papago, Pima.
Sikennies=Sekani.
Siketeuhacky=Secatoag.
Siknaq'a'dē, S!îknaxa'dî=Siknahadi.
Sikne=Seneca.
Sikohitsim=Sikokitsimiks.
Sikonesses=Siconesses.
Sikosuilaq=Sikosuilak.
Sikoua=Pecos.

Siksekai=Siksika.
Sik'ses-tĕne'=Kwatami.
Siksićela=Shikshichela.
Sikśióena=Shikshichena.
Siksikai=Siksika.
Siksinokaiiks=Siksinokaks.
Sikskékuanak=Siksika.
Sikuyé=Pecos.
Sikyataiyo wiñwû, Si-kya'-tai-yo wûñ-wû=Sikyataiyo.
Si-kya'-tci, Sikyatci wiñwû=Sikyachi.
Silawĭ'ñmiun=Selawigmiut.
S. Ildefonse, S. Ildefonsia, S. Ildefonso=San Ildefonso.
S. Ildefonso Ostimuri=Ostimuri.
Silem=Sillery.
Silká=Coyoteros.
Silla, Sille=Sia.
Sillerie=Sillery.
Silos=Pueblo de los Silos.
Silpaleels=Salpilel.
Sil'-qke-me'-tce-ta'-tûn=Silkhkemechetatun.
Siltáden=Tsiltaden.
Simamish=Samamish.
Simanō'lalgi, Simanō'la'li=Seminole.
Simas=Pima.
Simbalakees=Tamuleko.
Sim-e-lo-le=Seminole.
Sim-e-no-le-tal-lau-haf-see=Talahassec.
Simenolies=Seminole.
Simiahmoo, Simiamo=Semiahmoo.
Similikameen=Similkameen.
Similoculgee, Siminoles=Seminole.
Sinmagons=Seneca.
Simojueves=Chemehuevi.
Simomo=Simaomo.
Simonde, Simonolays, Simonolays-Crĕcks=Seminole.
Simpsian, Simseans=Tsimshian.
Sím-û-no-lĭ=Seminole.
Simupapa=Sibubapa.
Sinacks=Seneca.
Sinacsops=Smackshop.
Sinacsta=Sinaesta.
Sinagars=Seneca.
Sinagnia=Imagnee.
Sinagoux=Sinago.
Sinahamish, Sinahōmās, Sin-a-ho-mish, Sinahoumez=Snohomish.
Sinakaiáusish=Sinkiuse.
Sinakees, Sinakers=Seneca.
Sinako=Sinago.
Sinaloa=Cahita.
Sina-luta-oiŋ=Shinalutaoin.
Sinamiut=Sinimiut.
Sinapans=Lipan.
Sinapoil, Sinapoiluch=Sanpoil.
Sinarmete=Sinar.
Síñaru=Sinimiut.
Si'-na-rxût-lĭ'-tûn=Sinarghutlitun.
Sinatcheggs=Senijextee.
Sĭ'ndat!aɪs=Sindatahls.
Síndiyúi=Kongtalyui.
Sindjalē=Sindzhale.
Sinecas, Sineckes=Seneca.
Sinecu=Senecu del Sur.
Sin-ee-guo-men-ah=Spokan.
Sinekas, Sinekees, Sinekes, Sinekies, Sineks, Sineques=Seneca.
Sineramish=Snohomish.
Singiok=Sinuk.
Singos=Sinago.
Sing-sings=Sintsink.
Sin-ha-ma-mish=Spokan.
Sinhioto=Sonnioto.
Sin-hu, Sinhumanish=Spokan.
Sinica, Sinicaes, Sinicker=Seneca.
Sinicú=Senecu del Sur.
Sinikers=Seneca.
Sinimijut=Sinimiut.
Siniogamut=Sinuk.
Sinipouals=Sanpoil.
Siniques=Seneca.
Siñis=Zuñi.
Si nĭ'-tĕ-lĭ=Nestucca, Tillamook.
Si ni'-tĕ-lĭ ʇûnnĕ=Alsea.
Sin'-ja-ye-ga=Wasabe.
Sinkáyus=Sinkiuse.

Sinkoman=Spokan.
Sinksink=Sintsink.
Sinkuäíli=Okinagan.
Sinkumaṇa=Spokan.
Sinnacock=Shinnecock.
Sinnagers, Sinnakees, Sinnakers, Sinnakes=Seneca.
Sinnamish=Snohomish.
Sinnaques, Sinnecas, Sinneche, Sinneck, Sinneckes, Sinneco, Sinnecus, Sinnedowane, Sinnek, Sinnekaes, Sinnekas, Sinnekees, Sinnekens=Seneca.
Sinneken's Castle=Oneida (vil.).
Sinnekes, Sinnekies, Sinnekis, Sinnekus, Sinnequaas, Sinnequas, Sinnequens, Sinneques, Sinnequois, Sinnicars, Sinnicas, Sinnichees, Sinnickes, Sinnickins, Sinnicks, Sinnicus, Sinnikaes, Sinnikes, Sinniques, Sinnodowannes, Sinnoḍwannes, Sinnokes, Sinnondewannes=Seneca.
Sinnyu=Sinyu.
Sinodouwas, Sinodowannes=Seneca.
Sinojos=Sinago.
Sinóndowans=Seneca.
Sinoyeca=Loreto.
Sinpaivelish, Sinpauēlish, Sin-poh-ell-ech-ach, Sinpoil, Sin-poil-er-hu, Sin-poil-schne=Sanpoil.
S'inpûktî'm=Npiktim.
Sinselan, Sinselano, Sinselau, Sinselaw=Siuslaw.
Sinsincks, Sinsincqs, Sin-Sing=Sintsink.
Sinsitwans=Sisseton.
Sin-slih-hoo-ish=Sinslikhooish.
Sin-spee-lish=Nespelim.
Sînta'kʟ=Sintaktl.
Siŋ-te'-lĭda wi-ca-śa=Shoshoni.
Sin-too-too, Sintou-tou-oulish=Sintootoolish.
Sĭnꞁsaꭓꬶĕ̆=Tsishusindtsakdhe.
Sintsinck=Manhasset.
Sintsings=Sintsink.
Sinuitskistux=Senijextee.
Sin-who-yelp-pe-took=Colville.
Sinyaupichkara=San Dieguito.
Sioane=Saone.
Sióki, Si-o'-ki-bi, Si-o'-me=Zuñi.
Sionassi=Sconassi.
Sione=Saone.
Sionimone=Sichomovi.
Sionne=Saone.
Siooz, Sios=Dakota.
S. Iosepho=Patoqua.
Siou=Dakota.
Siouan=Siouan Family.
Siou Mendeouacanton=Mdewakanton.
Siounes, Siouones=Saone.
Siouse=Dakota.
Sioushwaps=Shuswap.
Siouslaws=Siuslaw.
Sioust=Dakota.
Sioux=Dakota, Siouan Family, Tiou.
Sioux de l'Est=Santee.
Sioux des prairies=Teton.
Siouxes=Dakota.
Sioux Mindawarcarton=Mdewakanton.
Sioux nomades, Sioux occidentaux=Teton.
Sioux of the Broad Leaf=Wahpekute.
Sioux of the Leaf=Wahpeton.
Sioux of the Meadows, Sioux of the Plain=Teton.
Sioux of the Prairies=Matatoba.
Sioux of the River, Sioux of the River St. Peter's=Santee.
Sioux of the Rocks=Assiniboin.
Sioux of the Savannas=Teton.
Sioux of the Woods, Sioux orientaux=Santee.
Sioux-Osages=Osage.
Siouxs=Dakota.
Sioux sédentaires=Santee.
Siouxs of the Lakes=Mdewakanton.
Siouxs who shoot in the Pine Tops=Wazikute.
Sioux-Tentons, Sioux Teton=Teton.
Sioux Wahpacoota=Wahpekute.
Sioux Wahpatone=Wahpeton.
Siowes=Saone.
Si-oxes=Dakota.
Sipan=Lipan.
Siposka-numakaki=Sipushkanumanke.
Sippahaws=Sissipahaw.
Si-pu'-cka nu-mañ'-ke, Sipuske-Numangkake=Sipushkanumanke.
Siquitchib=Kwatami.
Sira-grins=Shregegon.
Sircie=Sarsi.
Sirinueces, Sirinueses=Shawnee.

Sirkhintaruk=Sargentaruka.
Sirmilling=Sirmiling.
Siros=Piro.
Siroux=Dakota.
Sisaghroano=Missisauga.
Sisapapa=Sihasapa.
Sisatoone, Sisatoons, Siseton, Sisetwans=Sisseton.
Sishat=Seshart.
Sishu=Sesum.
S. Isidoro Numanas=Pueblo de los Jumanos.
Sĭ' sînʟaē=Sisintlae.
Sisin-towanyan, Sisi toan, Sisitons, Sisitoŋwaŋ, Si-sit'wans=Sisseton.
Sisízha-nĭn=Shoshoni.
Sisk=Susk.
Si'ska, Siska Flat=Cisco.
Sis-ky-ou=Karok.
Sisoquichi=Isoguichic.
Sĭs'-qas-li'-tûn=Siskhaslitun.
Sĭs'-qûn-me' ꭧûnnê̂=Yaquina.
Sissatones, Sissatons, Sisseeton, Sissetoans, Sissetong, Sissetonwan=Sisseton.
Sissipahau=Sissipahaw.
Sissisaguez=Missisauga.
Sissispahaws=Sissipahaw.
Sissitoan, Sissiton, Sissitongs, Sissi-t'wan=Sisseton.
Sis-stsi-mé=Sitsime.
Sistasoona, Sistasoone=Sisseton.
Sisticoosta=Chastacosta.
Sistons=Sisseton.
Si-stsi-mé=Sitsime.
Sisumi=Sesum.
Si-tañga=Chedunga.
Sitca=Sitka.
Sītca'nētl=Sichanetl.
Sit-can-xu=Brulé.
Sitcaⁿxu=Sichanghu.
Sitcha=Sitka.
Si-tchom-ovi, Sitcomovi, Si-tcum'-o-vi=Sichomovi.
Sitka-kwan, Sitka-qwan, Sitkas=Sitka.
Sitkeas=Siksika.
Sitkhinskoe=Sitka.
Sitleece=Setlia.
Siton=Teton.
S!itqoe'dî=Sitkoedi.
Síts-hánoᵒʰ=Tsits.
Sitsimé=Laguna.
Sitska binolipaka=Seechkaberuhpaka.
Sittëoüi=Uzutiuhi.
Sittiquo=Sitiku.
Si-'twans=Sisseton.
Siuola=Zuñi.
Siur Poils=Sanpoil.
Siusclau, Siuselaws=Siuslaw.
Si-vel=Lawilvan.
Sivilihoa=Sibirijoa.
Sivilleta=Sevilleta.
Sivinte=Shivwits.
Sivirijoa=Sibirijoa.
Sivits=Shivwits.
Sivola, Sivolo, Sivulo=Zuñi.
Sivux=Dakota.
Si-vwa'-pi, Sivwapi wiñ wû=Siwapi.
Si-wahs=Katimin.
Siwannoki=Casa Grande.
Siwanoos=Siwanoy.
Siwer=Dakota.
Siwhipa=Isleta.
Siwinna=Sichomovi.
Six=Kwatami, Taoapa.
Six Allied Nations=Iroquois.
Sixame=Sijame.
Sixes=Kwatami.
Sixes Old Town=Sutali.
Six-he-kie-koon, Sixikau'a=Siksika.
Six Nations=Iroquois.
Six Nations living at Sandusky=Mingo.
Sixtowns, Six Towns Indians=Oklahannali.
Siya=Sia.
Siyanguayas=Sillanguayas.
Si-yan-ti, Si-yau-te=Siyante.
Siyélpa=Colville.
Siyo-subula=Shiyosubula.
Siyo-taŋka=Shiyotanka.
S. Javier, S. Javier Bac, S. Javier del Bacel=San Xavier del Bac.
S. Jean=San Juan.
S. Jérome de los Taos, S. Jeronimo de Taos, S. Jeronimo de Toos=Taos.

S. Joachin=San Joaquin.
S. Joanne=San Juan.
S. Joaquin=Basosuma.
S. Joaquin y Sta Ana (Nuri)=Nuri.
S. Joaquin y Sta Ana Tepachi=Tepachi.
S. John=San Juan.
S. José=San José.
S. José de Joconostla=Joconostla.
S. José del Tizonazo=Tizonazo.
S. Josef, S. Josefo=Patoqua.
S. José Imuri=Imuris.
S. José Matape=Matape.
S. Joseph de Soyôpa=Soyopa.
S. Jua=San Juan de los Jemez.
S. Juan Bautista=San Juan Bautista.
S. Juan Capistrano, S. Juan Capistrano de Ulurituc=
　Uturituc.
S. Juan Corapa=Corapa.
S. Juan de Guachinela=Huachinera.
S. Juan de Mata=Mata.
S. Juan Guachinera=Huachinera.
S. Juan Peyotan=Peyotan.
S. Juan Quiburi=Quiburi.
S. Júdas Tadeo=Tadeo Vaqui.
Skaachkook, Skaahkook=Scaticook.
Skaap=Khaap.
Skacewanilom=Abnaki.
Skachhooke, Skachkock, Skachkoke, Skachkook,
　Skachticokes, Skackkook, Skackoor, Skacktege=
　Scaticook.
Skad-dat, Skad-datts=Skaddal.
Skadjats, Skadjets, Skagats, Skaget=Skagit.
Skaghhook=Scaticook.
Skaghnanes, Skaghquanoghronos=Nipissing.
Skaguay, Skagwa=Skagway.
Ska-hak-bush=Skahakmehu.
Skaigee=Skoiyase.
Skaikai'eten=Skekaitin.
Skai-na-mish=Skihwamish.
Skaisi=Kutenai.
Skaiwhamish=Skihwamish.
Sk'a'-jub=Skagit.
Skâ-kâ-bĭsh, Ska-ka-mĭsh=Skokomish.
Skakies=Sauk.
Skakobish=Skokomish.
Skălâ'lĭ=Tuscarora.
Skal-lum=Clallam.
Skalza, Skalzi, Skalzy=Kutenai.
Skama=Gulhlgildjing.
Skamoken, Skamokin=Shamokin.
Ska-moy-num-achs=Spokan.
Skanatiarationo, Skaniadaradighroonas, Skaniata-
　rati-háka, Skaniatarationo, Skanigadaradigh-
　roonas, Skaniodaraghroonas=Nanticoke.
Skăocin=Skauishan.
Skao nans=Sulu-stins.
Sk'āpa, Skappah=Skappa.
Sk'a'-qaus=Skakhaus.
Skaquahmish, Skaquamish=Skokomish.
Skă-rú-rĕnʼ=Tuscarora.
Skasquamish=Skokomish.
Skatapushoish=Montagnais.
Skaticook, Skattock=Scaticook.
Sk'au'ēlitsk=Scowlitz.
'Skaui'can=Skauishan.
Skaun-ya-ta-ha-ti-hawk=Nanticoke.
Ska'utăl=Skaddal.
Skawaghkees=Oquaga.
Skawah-looks=Skwawahlooks.
Skawendadys=Oka.
Skawhahmish, Ska-whamish=Skihwamish.
Skäχshurunu=Foxes.
Skä'-yase, Skayes=Skoiyase.
Skea-wa-mish=Skihwamish.
Skecaneronons=Nipissing.
Skec'-e-ree=Skidi.
Ske-chei-a-mouse=Skecheramouse.
Skee-cha-way=Skitswish.
Skeedans=Skedans.
Skee'-de, Skeedee, Skee-e-ree=Skidi.
Skeelsomish=Skitswish.
Skeen=Skinpah.
Skeena Indians=Tsimshian.
Skeeree=Skidi.
Skeetsomish, Skeetsonish=Skitswish.
Skehandowana=Wyoming.
Skeina=Tsano.
Skekaneronons, Skekwanenhronon=Nipissing.
Skelsa'-ulk=Kutenai.

Ske-luh=Okinagan.
Skenappa=Skanapa.
Skenchiohronon=Foxes.
Skensowahneronon=Saint Francis.
Skepah=Skappa.
Skequaneronon=Nipissing.
Skere, Skerreh=Skidi.
Sketapushoish=Montagnais.
S'ke-tehl-mish, S'ketēhmish=Sktehlmish.
Sketigets=Skidegate.
Sket-shiotin=Skichistan.
Sketsomish, Sketsui=Skitswish.
Skeysehamish=Skihwamish.
Ske-yuh=Ntlakyapamuk.
Skey-wah-mish, Skeywhamish=Skihwamish.
S'Khinkit=Tlingit.
Skicoack=Skicoak.
Skid-a-gate=Skidegate.
Skidans, Skidanst=Skedans.
Skî'daoqao=Skidaokao.
Skiddan=Skedans.
Skid-de-gates, Skiddegeet, Skidegat, Skidegate
　Hāade=Skidegate.
Skidegattz=Skidegate, Skittagetan Family.
Skidigate=Skidegate.
Skidoukou=Skidaokao.
Skien=Skinpah.
Skighquan=Nipissing.
Skihoah=Skicoak.
Skilakh=Skilak.
Skillools, Skillute, Skilluts, Skillutts=Skilloot.
Skim-i-ah-moo=Semiahmoo.
Skin=Skinpah.
Skinnacock=Shinnecock.
Skĭ'npä=Skinpah.
Skin pricks=Tawehash.
Skiquamish=Skokomish.
Ski-shis-tin=Skichistan.
Sklĭ' sLa-i na-i xadā'-i=Skistlainai-hadai.
Skit'a-get, Skit-e-gates, Skit-ei-get=Skidegate.
Skit-mish, Skitsaih, Skitsămŭq, Skítsui, Skitsuish=
　Skitswish.
Skittagete=Skidegate.
Skittagets=Skidegate, Skittagetan Family.
Skitt de gates, Skittegas, Skittegats, Skittgetts=
　Skidegate.
Skiuses=Cayuse.
Skiwhamish=Skihwamish.
Sk-Khabish=Sekamish.
Sk'lalc=Stlaz.
S'Klallams, S'Klallan, SKlal-lum=Clallam.
Sklarkum=Sanpoil.
Sk'mūc=Kimus.
Skoa'tl'adas=Skwahladas.
Skoch Hook=Scaticook.
Skoffies=Nascapee.
Skog=Skooke.
Sko-har'-le=Schoharie.
Skohuáshki=Kohashti.
Skoi-el-poi=Colville.
Skois'chint=Mountain Crows.
Skoi-yace=Skoiyase.
Skokale=Shaukel.
Skokamish=Skokomish.
Sko-ki han-ya'=Creeks.
Skŏ-kŏbc'=Skokomish.
Skokomish=Twana.
Skokonish=Skokomish.
Skolale=Shaukel.
Skolsa=Kutenai.
S'Komish=Skokomish.
S'Komook=Comox.
Sko-ne'-ase=Skoiyase.
Skoomic=Squawmish.
Skopa=Tapishlecha.
Sko-pabsh=Skopamish.
Skopah=Skappa.
Skopahmish, Skope-áhmish, Skope-a-mish=Skopa-
　mish.
Sko-sko-mish=Skokomish.
S'Kosle-ma-mish=Shotlemamish.
Skotacook=Scaticook.
Skoton-Shasta=Chasta-Skoton.
Skowall=Skwawahlooks.
Skowliti=Scowlitz.
Skoxwā'k=Skohwak.
Sk'qoā'mic, Sk'qō'mic=Squawmish.
Skraelings, Skrælingav, Skrællings, Skrellings,
　Skroelingues=Eskimo.

Sk-tah-le-gum=Sktahlejum.
Sk-táhl-mish=Sktehlmish.
Skuäĭshĕni=Siksika.
Skuakísagi=Foxes.
Skuck-stan-a-jumps=Sktahlejum.
Sk!ū' das=Skudus.
Skuhuak=Skohwak.
Skuksxat=Skukskhat.
Skukum Chuck=Skookum Chuck.
Skulkayu=Skaukel.
Skunk=Hokarutcha, Kunipalgi.
Skunnemoke=Attacapa.
Skunnepaw=Skanapa.
Skuōūa'k·k=Skohwak.
Skuppah=Skappa.
Sku'-rxût=Skurghut.
Skutani=Atsina.
Skuwha, Skuwka=Skohwak.
Skuyā'm=Skweahm.
Skuyélpi=Colville.
Skuzzy=Skuzis.
Skwahw-sda+bó=Squaxon.
Skwai-aitl=Squaitl.
Skwâk-sin, Skwak-sin-a-mĭsh=Squaxon.
Skwa'-Kwel=Kaquaith.
Skwale, Sk'wa-lé-ûbe, Skwali, Skwalliahmish, Skwalz=
    Nisqualli.
Skw-amish=Squamish, Squawmish.
Skwa'nănă=Squannaroo.
Skwawksen, Skwawksin, Skwawksnamish=Squaxon.
Skwaw-mish=Squamish.
Skyit'au'k·ō=Skidaokao.
Sky-lak-sen=Skaleksum.
Sky-Man=Makhpiyawichashta.
Skynses, Skyuse=Cayuse.
Sky-wa-mish=Skihwamish.
Slā'aqtl, Slā'axʟ=Slaaktl.
S-lab' wûñwü=Salabi.
Slakagulgas=Hlahlokalka.
Sla-na-pa=Tzlanapah.
Slaoucud-dennie, Sla-ū'-ah-kus-tinneh=Tluskez.
Slave=Kawchodinne, Thlingchadinne.
Slave Indians=Etchareottine, Ettchaottine.
Slave Indians of Ft Liard=Etcheridiegottine.
Slaves=Etchareottine.
Slaves proper=Etchaottine.
Slavey=Etchareottine.
SʟaxaˊyuX=Upper Fraser Band.
SʟaZ=Stlaz.
S. Lázaro, S. Lazarus=San Lázaro.
Sleepy Eyes=Chansdachikana.
Sleepy kettle band=Cheokhba.
Sl!e'ña lā' nas=Stlenga-lanas.
SʟêtZ=Stlaz.
S. Limon Tucsani=Tucsani.
Sʟ!í' ndAgwa-i=Stlindagwai.
Slka-tkml-schi=Kalispel.
S. Lorent=San Lorenzo.
S. Lorenzo=Picuris, San Lázaro, San Lorenzo.
S. Lorenzo de los Picuries=Picuris.
S. Lorenzo del Realito=San Lorenzo.
S. Lorenzo de Picuries=Picuris.
Slosh=Schloss.
Slouacous dinneh, Slouacus Dennie, Sloua-cuss
    Dinais, Slouacuss Tinneh, Slowacuss, Slowercuss,
    Slowercuss-Dinai, Slua-cuss-dinais, Sluacus-
    tinneh=Tluskez.
S. Lúcas de Galpa=Galpa.
S. Ludlov de Bacapa=Bacapa.
S. Luis Babi=San Luis Babi.
S. Luis Bacapa=Bacapa.
S. Luis Bacuancos=Bacuancos.
S. Luis de Bacapa=Bacapa.
S. Luis Gonzaga Bacadeguachi=Bacadeguachi.
S. Luis Guebavi=Guevavi.
S. Luis Obispo Sevilleta=Sevilleta.
S. Luis Quitobac=Bacapa.
Sluktla' ktEn=Mtlaktlakitin.
Slumagh=Slumach.
Smacshop, Smacsops=Smackshop.
S. Magdalena=Buquibava.
Sma-hoo-men-a-ish=Spokan.
Smak-shop=Smackshop.
Sma-lèh-hu=Smalihu.
Smalh, Smalhkahmish=Smulkamish.
Sma-lih-hu=Smalihu.
Small-bird gens=Wazhinkaenikashika.
Small Brittle Fat=Inuksikahkopwaiks.
Small People=Iskulani.

Small Robes=Inuksiks.
S. Marcellus, S. Marcelo de Sonoitac, S. Marcelo
    Sonoydag=Sonoita.
S. Maria de Sucunca=Suamca.
S. Mark=San Marcos.
S. Martin, S. Martin of the Opas=San Martin.
Smascops=Smackshop.
S. Mateo=San Mateo.
S. Mateo Caut=Cant.
S. Mateo Soroydad=Sonoita.
S. Mathias de Tutomagoidag=Tutomagoidag.
S. Matias Tutum=Tutum.
S. Matthaeus de Sicoroidag=Sicoroidag.
Smelkameen=Similkameen.
Smel-ka-mish=Smulkamish.
Smess=Sumass.
S. Michael, S. Miguel=San Miguel Zuaque.
S. Miguel Babispe=Babispe.
S. Miguel Bacuachi=Bacuachi.
S. Miguel de Vavispe=Babispe.
S. Miguel Toape=Toape.
S. Miguel Yonora=Yonora.
Smîlê'kamuQ=Stuichamukh.
Smîlê'qamux, Smilkameen, Smilkamīn, Smilkĕmíχ=
    Similkameen.
Smith River Indians=Khaamotene.
Smith Sound Eskimo=Ita.
S[anta]. M[aria]. Magdalen=Buquibava.
Smockshop, Smokshops=Smackshop.
Smulcoe=Smulkamish.
S-na-a-chikst=Senijextee.
S-na-ha-em, Snahaim, Snahain=Snakaim.
Snake Diggers=Paiute, Shoshoni.
Snake Indians=Comanche, Shoshoni.
Snake Root Diggers=Shoshoko.
Snalatine=Atfalati.
Snanaimooh, Snanaimuq=Nanaimo.
Snegs=Shoshoni.
Sn. Felipe=Terrenate.
Sniekes=Seneca.
Snihtlimih=Senktl.
Sn Juan=San Juan.
Snóā=Shoshoni.
Sno-dom-ish=Snohomish.
Sno-kwāl-mi-yūkh, Snokwalmū=Snoqualmu.
Snōnōos, Sno-no-wus=Snonowas.
Snoqualamick, Sno-qual-a-muhe, Sno-qual-a-muke,
    Snoqualimich, Sno-qualimick, Snoqualmie, Sno-
    qualmoo, Sno-qual-mook=Snoqualmu.
Sno-uo-wus=Snonowas.
Sn Phelipe, Sⁿ Philip de queres=San Felipe.
SnpoiliχiX, Snpuélish=Sanpoil.
Snuk=Suk.
Snū'ʟ'ElaʟL=Snutlelatl.
Snχáyus,=Sinkiuse.
Snχúmina=Spokan.
Soacatina=Soacatino.
Soayalpi=Colville.
Soba=Pitic.
Sobahipuris, Sobaihipure, Sobaiporis, Sobaipotis,
    Sobaipures, Sobaipuris Pimas=Sobaipuri.
Sobal-ruck=Smulkamish.
Sobas=Soba.
Sobaypures, Sobaypuris=Sobaipuri.
Soboba=Saboba.
Socatoon=Sacaton.
Soccokis, Soccoquis=Sokoki.
Soccorro=Socorro del Sur.
Soccouky=Sokoki.
Sockacheenum=Shuswap.
Soc-kail-kit=Sokchit.
Sock-a-muke=Sakumehu.
Sockegones, Sockhigones=Sokoki.
Sock Indians=Sooke.
Socklumnes=Mokelumne.
Sock o par toy=Sakapatayi.
Socktish=Sockchit.
Soclan=Saclan.
Socoas=Shokhowa.
Socokis=Sokoki.
Socollomillos=Clear Lake Indians.
Socoquiois, Socoquis, Socoquois=Sokoki.
Socora, Socoro=Socorro, Socorro del Sur.
Socorro=Aymay.
Socorra, Socorre=Socorro.
Socorro=Socorro del Sur.
Socouky=Sokoki.
Soegatzy=Oswegatchie.
Sogahatches=Saugahatchi.

Sogkonate=Saconnet.
Sogo=Soco.
Sogorem=Aperger.
Soguspogus=Sukaispoka.
Sohkon, Sŏh'-koon=Sawcunk.
So'hl=Sonsa.
Sohmish=Samish.
Sohokies=Sokoki.
Soieenos=Somenos.
Soi-il-enu, Soi it inu=Tsawatenok.
Soisehme=Suisun.
Sŏk=Sooke.
Sokakies=Sokoki.
Sokaspoge=Sukaispoka.
So-kéa-keit=Sokchit.
Sokes=Sooke.
Sok-kail-kit=Sokchit.
Sokkie=Sauk.
So-ko'-a=Shokhowa.
Sokokies, Sokokiois=Sokoki.
Sokones, Sokonesset=Succonesset.
Sokoquiois, Sokoquis, Sok8akiak, Sokouakiaks, Sokoueki=Sokoki.
Soktich=Sokchit.
Solackeyu=Solakiyu.
Solameco=Chiaha.
Solano=San Francisco Solano.
Soledad=Nuestra Señora de la Soledad.
Sol-ke-chuh=Saltketchers.
Sololumnes=Tuolumne.
Solotluck=Wishosk.
Solumnees=Tuolumne.
Somass=Tsomosath.
Somena=Ntlakyapamuk, Siamannas.
So-me-nau=Somenos.
Somes=Somo.
Sŏ'mexulîtx=Somehulitk.
Somhótnehan=Somhotnechau.
S'o-mus=Somo.
Sŏmχótnechau=Somhotnechau.
Songars=Songish.
Songasketons, Songaskicons, Songasquitons, Songastikon, Songats, Songatskitons=Sisseton.
Songees=Songish.
Songeskitons, Songeskitoux, Songestikons=Sisseton.
Songhees=Stsanges.
Songhies=Songish.
Songoapt=Shongopovi.
Soni=Sonoita.
Sónikanik, Sóni-k'ni=Wichita.
Sonkaskítons=Sisseton.
Sonkawas=Tonkawa.
Sonnioto=Scioto.
Sonnontoeronnons, Sonnontouaheronnons=Seneca.
Sonnontouan=Totiakton.
Sonnontoüeronnons, Sonnontovans=Seneca.
Sonoaitac, Sonoi, Sonoitac=Sonoita.
Sonoma=San Francisco Solano.
Sonomas, Sonomellos, Sonomos, Sonons=Sonomi.
Sonontoehronnons, Sonontoerrhonons, Sonontouaëronons, Sonontoüanhrronon, Sonontouans, Sonontouehronon, Sonontouons, Sonontrerrhonons=Seneca.
Sonora=Opata.
Sonorita, Sonoytac=Sonoita.
Sonsobe=Tomsobe.
Sontaouans=Ottawa.
Sontouaheronnons, Sontouhoironon, Sontouhouethonons=Seneca.
So-nus'-ho-gwä-to-war=Cayuga.
Sonwuckolo=Sawokli.
Soo=Dakota.
Sooc-he-ah=Sukaispoka.
Soof-Curra=Tsofkara.
Soo-i-soo-nes=Suisun.
Sookee=Soquee.
Sook-e-nock-e=Sukinatchi.
Sook-kamus=Suk, Kimus.
Soones=Zuñi.
Soon-noo-daugh-we-no-wenda=Cayuga.
Soo-pas-ip=Supasip.
Soopis, Soopus=Esopus.
Soo-wän'-a-mooh=Okinagan.
So-päk'-tŭ=Sopaktalgi.
Sopes, Sopez=Esopus.
Sopono=Sopone.
Sopopo=Soyopa.
Sopori=Sepori.

Sopus=Esopus, Tunxis.
Soquachjck, Soquackicks=Sokoki.
Soquagkeeke=Squawkeag.
Soquamish=Suquamish.
Soquatucks, Soquokis, Soquoquioii, Soquoquiss=Sokoki.
Soraphanigh=Sarapinagh.
Sorcerers=Nipissing.
Sore backs=Chankaokhan.
Soricoi, Sorriquois=Micmac.
Sorsi=Sarsi.
Sosemiteiz, S-osemity=Awani.
Soshawnese, Soshonees, Soshones=Shoshoni.
So-so-bâ, So-so'-bu-bar=Shobarboobeer.
So'-so-ì-ha'-ni=Shoshoni.
Sosokos=Shoshoko.
So-so-na, Sosone, Sosonee, Sosones, So'-so-ni=Shoshoni.
Sotaeo=Sutaio.
Sotchaway=Alachua.
Soténnă=Sarsi.
Soteomellos=Wappo.
Sothoues, Sothouis=Uzutiuhi.
Sothuze, Sotoes=Chippewa.
Sotomieyos=Wappo.
Sotonis=Uzutiuhi.
Sotoos=Chippewa.
Sotoriva=Saturiba.
Sotos, Sotouis=Uzutiuhi.
Sotoyomes=Wappo.
SōtsL=Sotstl.
Sotto=Chippewa.
Soturiba=Saturiba.
Souchitiony, Souchitionys=Doustioni, Uzutiuhi.
Souckelas=Sawokli.
Soudayé=Kadohadacho.
Soues, Souex=Dakota.
Sougahatchee=Saugahatchi.
Sougaskicons=Sisseton.
Sou-go-hat-che=Saugahatchi.
Souhane=Suwanee.
Souikilas=Sawokli.
Souissouns=Suisun.
Souix=Dakota.
Soulier Noir, Souliers=Amahami.
Soulikilas=Sawokli.
Soulteaux=Chippewa.
Soundun=Sundum.
Sounès=Zuñi.
Sountouaronons=Seneca.
Souon, Souon-Teton=Saone.
Souquel=Osacalis.
Souricois, Sourikois, Sourikwosiorum, Souriquois, Souriquosii, Sourriquois=Micmac.
Sous=Dakota.
Sou Saida=Saucita.
Soushwaps=Shuswap.
Sousitoon=Sisseton.
Souteus=Chippewa.
Southampton=Saugeen.
Southampton Indians=Shinnecock.
South Bay Indians=Nusehtsatl.
Southern=Chinookan Family, Nootka, Salishan Family.
Southern Apaches=Faraon, Gila Apache.
Southern Arapahoes, Southern Band=Nawunena.
Southern Chiricahua=Chiricahua.
Southern Indians=Cree, Mashpee, Maskegon.
Southern Killamuk=Yaquina.
Southern Minquas=Conestoga.
Southern Pimas=Nevome.
Southois, Southouis=Uzutiuhi.
South Sea Indians=Mashpee.
South Sussetons=Miakechakesa.
South Thompson=Halaut.
Southton=Shinnecock.
South Yanktons=Yankton.
Souties=Chippewa.
Soutouis=Uzutiuhi.
Souwagoolo, Souwogoolo=Sawokli.
Soux=Dakota.
Souyoto=Scioto, Sonnioto.
Sovovo=Saboba.
Sowaams=Pokanoket.
Sowahegen Indians=Souhegan.
Sowam, Sowame, Sowamsett=Pokanoket.
Sowan=Saone.
Sowanakas=Shawnee.
Sówăniă=Southern Cheyenne.

Sowanokas, Sowanokees=Shawnee.
Sowans=Pokanoket.
Sow-a-to=Comanche.
Sowgahatcha, Sow ga hatch cha=Saugahatchi.
Sowhylie=Tsoowahlie.
Sowinû wiñwû, So'-wiñ-wa=Sowiinwa.
Sowi wiñwû=Sowi.
Sowocatuck=Sokoki.
Sowoccolo=Sawokli.
Sowocotuck=Sokoki.
So-wok-ko-los=Sawokli.
Sówoniă=Southern Cheyenne.
Sow-on-no, Sowonokees=Shawnee.
Sowquackick=Sokoki.
Sow-wames, Sowwams=Pokanoket.
Soyennom=Soyennow.
Soyopas=Mohave.
S. Pablo Baibcat=Baibcat.
S. Pablo Comuripa=Cumuripa.
S. Pablo Pescadero=Pescadero.
S. Pablo Quiburi=Quiburi.
Spah-a-man=Spahamin.
Spa-ki-um=Spapium.
Spallumacheen, Spallumcheen=Spallamcheen.
Spanish Indians=Churchcates.
Spanish Yuki=Witukomnom.
Spanish Yutes=Ute.
S. Pantaleon Aribaiba=Aribaiba.
Spapiam=Spapium.
Spa'ptsEn, S-pap-tsin=Spatsum.
Sparrowhawks=Crow.
Spatsim=Spatsum.
S. Paulus=San Pablo.
Spa'xEmîn=Spahamin.
Spayam=Spaim.
Speckled Pani=Wichita.
S. Pedro=Cumuripa.
S. Pedro de Ixtacan=Ixtacan.
S. Pedro Jícara=Jicara.
S. Pedro Turisai=Turisai.
Spē'im=Spaim.
Spelemcheen, Spellamcheen, Spellammachum=Spallamcheen.
Spena=Dakubetede.
Spences Bridge, Spences Bridge Indians=Nskakaulten.
S. Petrus=San Pedro.
Speyam=Spaim.
S. Phelipe, S. Philip=San Felipe.
Spicheats, Spicheets=Spichehat.
S'pi-lil=Salpilel.
Split Livers=Tapishlecha.
Spogans, Spokains, Spokane, Spo-keh-mish, Spokehnish, Spokein, Spokens, Spo-kih-nish, Spokineish, Spokines, Spokomish=Spokan.
Spô'zêm=Spuzzum.
Spring Creeks=Bidai.
Spring Gardens=Talahassee.
Spring Indians=Tyigh.
Spring-people=Nushaltkagakni.
Spuggum=Spuzzum.
Spukä'n=Spokan.
SpuQpuQō'lEmQ=Spukpukolemk.
Spu'zum, Spuzzam=Spuzzum.
Sqahē'ne χā'da-i=Skahene.
Sqa-i=Skae, Skway.
SQaiâ'lō=Skaialo.
SqaiaQōs=Skaiakos.
Sqai'-tāo=Skaito.
Sqā'ma=Sulhlgildjing.
Sq!a'os=Skaos.
SQāqai'Ek=Skakaiek.
Sqa'-qwai yu'-tslu=Skhakhwaiyutslu.
Sqēlo=Skelsh.
SqE'ltEn=Skelten.
Sqē'na=Skena.
Sqnamishes=Squawmish.
Sqoā'tadas=Skwahladas.
Sqohamish=Squawmish.
Sqówi=Shruhwi.
Sǫsắnitc=Sanetch.
Squa-aitl=Squiatl.
Squabage, Squabang, Squabaug, Squabauge, Squaboag, Squabog=Quabaug.
Squ-agh-kie Indians=Squawkihow.
Squaghkies=Foxes.
Squah=Skwah.
Squahalitch Indians=Chilliwack.
Squaheag=Squawkeag.

Squahk-sen, Squah-sin-aw-mish=Squaxon.
Squah-tta=Skwah.
Squai-aitl=Squiatl.
Squakeage, Squakeays, Squakheag, Squakheig=Squawkeag.
Squakie Hill village=Dayoitgao.
Squakies=Squawkihow.
Squakkeag=Squawkeag.
Squakshin, Squakskin, Squaks'na-mish=Squaxon.
Squalli-ah-mish, Squalli-a-mish, Squally-ah-mish, Squallyamish=Nisqualli.
Squam-a-cross=Squannaroo.
Squamish=Suquamish.
Squamisht=Squawmish.
Squan-nan-os, Squan-nun-os=Squannaroo.
SQua'pamuQ=Shuswap.
Squapauke=Quabaug.
Squa-que-hl=Kaquaith.
Squash village=Tutuwalha.
Squa-sua-mish=Squaxon.
Squatchegas=Foxes, Squawkihow.
Squatehokus=Squawkihow.
Squatils, Squatits, Squattets=Squawtits.
Squaw-a-tosh=Colville.
Squawkeague, Squawkheag=Squawkeag.
Squawkey=Squawkihow.
Squawkiehah=Foxes.
Squawkie Hill=Dayoitgao.
Squawkihows=Foxes.
Squawky Hill=Dayoitgao.
Squawlees=Nisqualli.
Squawmish=Suquamish.
Squawskin=Squaxon.
Squawtas=Squawtits.
Squaw Town=Grenadier Squaw's Town.
Squaxins=Squaxon.
Squay, Squay-ya=Skway.
Squeam=Skweahm.
Squeer-yer-pe=Colville.
Squehala=Skaialo.
Squeitletch=Squiatl.
Squekaneronons=Nipissing.
SQuhä'mEn=Skuhamen.
Squ-háno=Shruhwi.
Squiaelps=Colville.
Squiahla=Skaialo.
Squi-aitl=Squiatl.
Squiatl=Nisqualli.
S'qŭïes'-tshi=Arikara.
Squihala=Skaialo.
Squim bay, Squinbay=Sequim.
Squi'ñquñ=Skuingkung.
Squint Eyes=Kutchin, Tukkuthkutchin.
Squohamish=Squawmish.
Squorins, Squoxsin=Squaxon.
S. Rafael, S. Rafael Actun, S. Rafael de los Gentiles, S. Raphaël=San Rafael.
Sri'-gon=Shregegon.
Sroo-tle-mam-ish=Shotlemamish.
S. Rosalia di Mulegè=Santa Rosalia Mulege.
S. Sabas=San Sabas.
S. Salvador=San Salvador.
Ssangha-kŏn=Sanyakoan.
SSaumingmiut=Saumingmiut.
S. Serafin, S. Serafin Actum, S. Serafino del Napcub=San Serafin.
Ssïk-nachădĭ=Siknahadi.
Ssikossuilar-miut=Sikosuilarmiut.
S. Simeon de Tucsani=Tucsani.
S. Simon=Upasoitac.
S. Simon Tucsani, S. Simon Tuesani=Tucsani.
S. Simon y Judás de Opasoitac=Upasoitac.
S'slo-ma-mish=Shomamish.
Ssokŏān hādē=Sukkwan, Koetas.
Sta. See Santa.
Sta-ai'-in=Stryne.
Sta-amus=Stamis.
Sta Ana Anamic=Anamic.
Sta. Bibiana=Bibiana.
Sta. Catalina, Sta. Catalina Cuitciabaqui=Cuitciabaqui.
Sta. Catarina=Cuitciabaqui, Santa Catalina.
Sta. Catarina Caituagaba=Cuitciabaqui.
Stach'ïn, Stackeenes=Stikine.
Sta. Clara=Santa Clara.
Sta Cruz=Nacori.
Sta Cruz Babisi=Babisi.
Sta. Cruz de Gaibauipetea, Sta. Cruz de Jaibanipitca de Pimas=Gaibanipitea.
Stactan=Staitan.

Stadacone=Stadacona.
S. Tadeo Batqui=Tadeovaqui.
Sta-e-tan, Staetons=Staitan.
Sta. Eulalia=Santa Eulalia.
Stagā'ush=Nestucca.
Sta Gertrudis Saric=Saric.
Sta Gertrudis Techicodeguachi=Techicodeguachi.
Sta-he-tah=Staitan.
Stahl, Stahl-lch=Stlaz.
Sta'iEn=Stryne.
Stailakū-mamish=Steilacoomamish.
Stailans=Staitan.
Stain=Stryne.
Sta Isabel=Tusonimon.
Staitan=Cheyenne.
Staked Plain Indians, Staked Plains Omaions, Staked Plains Onawas=Kwahari.
Stakeen, Stakhin, Stak-hīn-kŏn, Stākhin'-kwān, Stakhī nskoe, Stakin=Stikine.
Stak-tabsh=Staktamish.
Stak-ta-le-jabsh=Sktahlejum.
Stak-ta-mish, Staktomish=Kwaiailk.
StAl náas xā'da-i=Stulnaas-hadai.
Sta. María=Galisteo, Suamca.
Sta. Maria de los Angeles de Saguaripa=Sahuaripa.
Sta María del Pópulo Tonichi=Tonichi.
Sta Maria de Uasaraca=Baserac.
Sta. María Nacori=Nacori.
Sta. Maria Sahuaripa=Sahuaripa.
Sta María Tepuspe=Tepuspe.
Sᵗᵃ Mario=Galisteo.
Stámas=Stamis.
Sᵗ Ana=Santa Ana.
Stankckans=Assumpink.
StA'nła-i=Stunhlai.
St. Antonio=Senecu.
Staq-tûbc=Chehalis.
Staraie Selenie=Staria Selenie.
Star gens=Mikakhenikashika.
Starikvikhpak, Starí-Kwikhpak=Starik.⌐
Sta Rosa Abiquiú=Abiquiu.
Sta Rosalía Onapa=Onopa.
Sta Rosa Tibideguachi=Tibideguachi.
Starrahe, Stâr-râh-hé=Arikara.
Starry Kwikhpák=Starik.
Starui gavan=Nunamiut.
Stasa'os qē gawa-i, Stasauskeowai=Stasaos-keg-awai.
Stastas=Stustas.
Statchook=Skatehook.
Statcīa'nī=Stahehani.
Sta. Teresa=Santa Teresa.
Stationary Minetares=Hidatsa.
Stā'-tlum-ooh=Lillooet.
Stauâ'çen=Sewathen.
St!awā's xā'-idaga-i=Stawas-haidagai.
Stawtonik=Statannyik.
Staxēha'ni=Stahehani.
Stcā'tcūHil=Schachuhil.
St. Cayetano=Tumacacori.
Stcê'kus=Nchekus.
Stchitsui=Skitswish.
Stcilks=Schilks.
Stcink=Schink.
Sᵗ Clara=Santa Clara.
St. Croix Indians=Munominikasheenhug, Passamaquoddy.
S'tcukōsh=Nchekus.
St'çu-qwitc=Stthukhwich.
Stcuwā'cEl=Sewathen.
St. Diego de Pitquin=Pitic.
Ste'ămtshi=Crows.
Stecoe, Steecoy=Stikayi.
Steelar=Skidi.
Stegara, Stegarakes, Stegarakies, Stegerakies, Stegora=Stegaraki.
Stéh-cha-sá-mish, Steh-chass, Stehchop=Stehtsasamish.
Stehl-lum=Stehtlum.
Steilacoom, Steilakūmahmish=Steilacoomamish.
Steila-qua-mish, Steil-la-qua-mish=Stillaquamish.
Stekchar=Stehtsasamish.
Stekini Indians=Stikine.
Stékoa, Stekoah=Stikayi.
Stélaoten, Stel-a-tin=Stella.
Stell-cha-sa-mish=Stehtsasamish.
Stèmchi, Stémtchi=Crows.
Stenkenocks=Stegaraki.
Stent-lum=Stehtlum.

Stetch-as=Stehtsasamish.
Stetchtlum, Ste-te-tlûm=Stehtlum.
Stetlum=Lillooet.
St. Eulalia=Santa Eulalia.
Stewarts Lake Indians=Nikozliautin.
S. Thaddæus de Batki=Tadeovaqui.
S Thomas=Tome.
Stiaggeghroano, Stiagigroone=Chippewa.
Sticcoa=Stikayi.
Stichistan=Skichistan.
Stick=Tahltan.
Stickens, Stickienes=Stikine.
Stick Indians=Tagish.
Stickine=Stikine.
Stickoey=Stikayi.
Sticks=Nuchwugh.
Stiel Shoi, Stietshoi=Skitswish.
Stikin=Stikine.
Stili=Skidi.
Stilla=Stella.
Stimk=Crows.
Stincards=Metsmetskop.
Stinkards=Metsmetskop, Winnebago.
Stinkers, Stinks=Winnebago.
Stitchafsamish, Stitcha-saw-mich, Stitcheo-saw-mish=Stehtsasamish.
Stjoekson=Tucson.
St-ka-bish, St-káhmish, St Kalmish, St'kamish=Sekamish.
Stlahl, Stlahl-ilitch=Stlaz.
S'tlaht-tohtlt-hu=Comox.
Stlat-limuh, Stla'tliumH, Stlā'tliumQ, Stlā'tlumQ=Lillooet.
Stl'EngE lā'nas=Aostlanlnagai, Stienga-ιanas.
Stling Lennas=Stlenga-lanas.
Stobshaddat=Yakima.
Sto Dom. de Cochití, Sto. Domingo de Cuevas=Santo Domingo.
Stogaras=Stegaraki.`
Stohenskie=Stikine.
Sto-lo-qua-bish, Stoluchquamish, Sto-luch-wámish, Sto-luck-qua-mish, Stoluckwhamish, Stolutswha-mish=Stillaquamish.
Stone=Assiniboin, Stone Tsilkotin.
Stone Indians=Assiniboin, Jatonabine.
Stone Kettle Esquimaux=Ukusiksalirmiut.
Stone Roasters=Assiniboin.
Stones=Stone Tsilkotin.
Stone Sioux, Stoney=Assiniboin.
Stoney Creek band=Nulaantin.
Stoney Indians=Assiniboin.
Stonies=Assiniboin, Tschantoga.
Stono, Stonoes, Stonoe tribe=Stonos.
Stony Creek Indians=Assunpink.
Stotonia=Tututunne.
Stotonik=Statannyik.
St'óx=Stoktoks.
'St'qē'l=Sutkel.
St-Queen=Sequim.
Straight Mólale=Molala.
Strain=Stryne.
Street natives=Tlingit.
Strongbows=Etcheridiegottine.
Strongwood Assinniboines=Tschantoga.
Strongwood Cree=Sakawithiniwuk.
Stryen=Stryne.
Stryne-Nqakin=Stryne, Nkoikin.
Strynne, Stryune=Stryne.
StsEē'lis=Chehalis.
Stskē'etl, Stsk·ē'iL=Stskeitl.
Stue Cabitic=Stucabitic.
Stū'iH=Stuik.
Stu'ikishχé'ni=Stuikishkeni.
Stū'îx·=Stuik.
Sturgeon Indians=Nameuilini.
Stûwī'HamuQ=Stuichamukh.
Stχuaiχn=Siksika.
Styne Creek=Stryne.
Styucson=Tucson.
Su=Dakota.
Suagna=Suangua.
Suahnee=Suwanne.
Sualatine=Atfalati.
Suali, Sualy=Cheraw.
Suanaimuchs=Nanaimo.
Su-a-na-muh=Okinagan.
Suanee Old Town=Suwanee.
Suaque, Suaqui=Zuaque.
Subaipures, Subaipuris=Sobaipuri.
Suc-co-ah=Succaah.

Succonet, Succonusset=Succonesset.
Suchamier=Lakmiut.
Sucheen=Stikiue.
Suche-poga=Sukaispoka.
Suchni=Suchui.
Suchongnewy=Sichomovi.
Suck-a-mier=Lakmiut.
Suckanessett=Succonesset.
Sūckĕmòs=Eskimo.
Suckiang, Suckiaug, Suckieag=Sukiaug.
Sûcl-ta′-qo-t′ça′ʒûnnĕ′=Sushltakhotthatunne.
Suco=Acoma, Pecos.
Suc-qua-cha-to-ny=Kwatami.
Su′dǫ̆ē=Kadohadacho.
Südpröven=Adjuitsuppa.
Sue=Dakota.
Sufíp=Rekwoi.
Sugans=Sugeree.
Sugar Eater band=Penateka.
Sugar-Eaters=Penointikara.
Sugar or Honey Eaters=Penateka.
Sugartown=Kulsetsiyi.
Sugaus=Sugeree.
Sugg′ān=Sukkwan.
Sug-wau-dug-ah-win-in-e-wug, Sug-wun-dug-ah-win-
　in-e-wug=Sugwaundugahwininewug.
Suhiaχē′gish=Shuyakeksh.
Suhtai=Sutaio.
Sui=Sowi.
Suil=Dakota.
Suipam=Siupam.
Suislaw=Siuslaw.
Suivirits=Seuvarits.
Suka-ishpógi=Sukaispoka.
Sû-kə-tcû-ne′ ʒûnnĕ=Sukechunetunne.
Sukiaugks=Sukiaug.
Sukinatchi=Sukinatcha.
Sûk-kwe′-tcĕ=Kwatami.
Suksanchi=Chukchansi.
Sukwámes, Sukwamish=Suquamish.
Sulajame=Sulujame.
Su-lan-na=Lulanna.
Sulatelik=Wishosk.
Sulawig-meuts=Selawigmiut.
Sulluggoes=Cherokee.
Sulu′s=Tsulus.
Sumacacori=Tumacacori.
Sumanas=Tawehash.
Sumas, Su-mat-se=Sumass.
Sumes=Suma.
Sumi=Zuñi.
Sum-maun=Sumaun.
Summe=Etah.
Sumonpavi, Sumoporvy, Sumopowy, Sumopoy=
　Shongopovi.
Sun=Mienikashika.
Sunahúmes=Snohomish.
Sundia=Sandia.
Sundowns=Sumdum.
Sun-Flower-Seed-Eaters=Shonivikidika.
Sun gens=Mienikashika.
Sun-hunters=Tabeguache.
Suñi=Zuñi.
Suñ ikćeka=Shungikcheka.
Suñis=Zuñi.
Sunk=Suk.
Šuŋkaha napin=Shungkahanapin.
Šuŋka yute-śni=Shungkayuteshni.
Suⁿkísaá=Sungkitsaa.
Sunne=Zuñi.
Sunnekes=Seneca.
Sun-num=Sunum.
Sun-nun′-at=Dakota.
Sunset Indians=Natchez.
Suⁿtí=Suñgitsaa.
Suny=Zuñi.
Sunyendeand=Junundat.
Sŭ′nyitsa, Sünyítsi=Zuñi.
Suoculo=Sawokli.
Suouex=Dakota.
Supais, Supies, Supis=Havasupai.
Suponolevy, Supowolewy=Shipaulovi.
Suppai=Havasupai.
Suqqo-ān=Sukkwan.
Suquahmish=Suquamish.
Su-quah-natch-ah=Sukinatchi.
Sū′Quapmuχ=Shuswap.
Suraminis=Sawani.
Surcee, Surci, Surcie=Sarsi.

Suriquois=Micmac.
Surra Blancos=White Mountain Apache.
Surrenderers=Showtucket.
Surrillos=Castake.
Sû-rxûs′ tĕ-st′hi′-tûn=Surghustesthitun.
Susaguey=Susuquey.
Susanna=Busanic.
Suscahannaes, Suscohannes=Conestoga.
Sushetno=Sushitna.
Sushwap=Kuaut.
Susoles=Susolas.
Susquahanna, Susquahannocks, Susquehanas, Sus-
　quehannagh=Conestoga.
Susquehannah Indians=Oquaga.
Susquehannah Minquays, Susquehanna's, Susque-
　hannocks, Susquehannoes, Susquehannos, Susque-
　hanocks, Susquehanoes, Susquhannok, Susqui-
　hanoughs=Conestoga.
Sussee=Sarsi.
Susseetons=Sisseton.
Sussekoon=Sarsi.
Sussetong, Sussetons, Sussetonwah=Sisseton.
Sussez, Sussi=Sarsi.
Sussitongs=Sisseton.
Sussitongs of Roche Blanche=Kahra.
Su′-su-ne=Shoshoni.
Sūs xā-idAga-i=Sus-haidagai.
Sû′tăgû′=Sitiku.
Sutaguison=Sudacson.
Su′-tai=Sutaio.
Sutaquisan, Sutaquisau, Sutaquison=Sudacson.
Sŭ′tasi′na, Sŭta′ya, Sutayo=Sutaio.
Suth-setts=Seshart.
Sū′-ti=Sutaio.
Sutkhoon=Sutkum.
Sutsets=Seshart.
Sutuami=Lutuamian Family.
Suturees=Sugeree.
Suuk=Suk.
Suuk-kamus=Suk, Kimus.
Suwanee Old Town, Suwa′nĭ=Suwanee.
Suwanoes=Shawnee.
Suwarof=Kingiak.
Suworof=Paugwik.
Suysum=Suisun.
Svernofftsi=Aglemiut.
Swá-dabsh=Siamannas.
Swaggles town, Swaglaws, Swaglers, Swagles=
　Sawokli.
Swa-höl=Sasuagel.
Swa-lash=Swalarh.
Swales=Sawokli.
Swali=Cheraw.
Swampee, Swampies, Swamp Indians, Swampy Creek
　Indians, Swampy Crees, Swampy Krees, Swampys=
　Maskegon.
Swan-Creek band=Wapisiwisibiwininiwak.
Swedebish=Swinomish.
Sweegachie, Sweegassie, Sweegochie=Oswegatchie.
Swees=Sarsi.
Swegaachey, Swĕ-gă′-che, Swegachee, Swegachey,
　Swegachie, Swegachy, Swegatsy=Oswegatchie.
Sweielpa=Colville.
Swetgatchie=Oswegatchie.
Swgahatchies=Sawokliudshi.
Swi-el-pree=Colville.
Swimmish=Sequim.
Swo-Kwabish=Suquamish.
Sχa-nu-χā=Skanuka.
S. Xaver du Bac, S. Xavier, S. Xavier del Bac=
　San Xavier del Bac.
S. Xavier des Praiz, S. Xavier des Prez=La Prairie.
Sxqõmic=Squawmish.
S-yars=Saia.
Sybaik, Sybayks=Sebaik.
Sycuan=Sequan.
Sy-cus=Saikez.
Sydpröven=Adjuitsuppa.
Syllery=Sillery.
Syneck, Synek, Synekees, Synekes, Synicks, Synne-
　kes, Synneks=Seneca.
Syouslaws=Siuslaw.
Sypanes=Lipan.
Syquan=Sequan.
Syuay=Skway.
Sywanois=Siwanoy.

Täa-′ái-yal-a-na-wan=Heshota Ayahltona.
Tâa Áshiwani=Zuñi.

Ta-ah-tèns=Tatlatunne.
Tâaiyá'hltona 'Hlúelawa=Heshota Ayahltona.
T!ā'ał=Taahl-lanas.
Taaogo=Tioga.
Taaovaiazes, Taaoyayases=Tawehash.
Ta-ä'p-pu=Tapo.
Taasey=Toosey.
Tá-ashi=Apache.
Taaš-nēi=Knaiakhotana.
Ta'a-t'co' ɥunnĕ=Targhutthotunne.
Tâatém'hlanah-kwe=Taa.
Tá-ă té-ne=Tatlatunne.
Tab=Tabo.
Täbᵉä'=Tapa.
Tabaguache, Tabahuaches=Tabeguache.
Tabaroas=Tamaroa.
Tabayase=Tawehash.
Tabechya, Tabeguachis, Tabegwaches, Tabehuachis, Tabe-naches=Tabeguache.
Tabensa=Taensa.
Tabequache, Tabequache Utes, Tabewaches, Tabiachis=Tabeguache.
Tabitibis, Tabittibis, Tabittikis=Abittibi.
Täbkĕpáya=Walapai.
Tab nyû-mû=Tabo.
Taboayas, Taboayases, Taboayazes=Tawehash.
Tabo wiñwû=Tabo.
Taboyazes, Tabuayas=Tawehash.
Tabrackis=Tabeguache.
Tab wüñ-wû=Tabo.
Taby=Talasse.
Ta-cáb-cí-nyu-mûh=Navaho.
Tacadocorou=Tacatacuru.
Tacamanes, Tacames=Tacame.
Tacasnanes=Pasnacanes.
Tacatacouru=Tacatacuru.
Ta ɸa'xü=Tadhaghu.
Tacci=Dogi.
Tachees=Texas.
Tachekaroreins=Tuscarora.
Taches=Tachi.
Tachi, Tachies=Texas.
Tachĭgmyut=Unaligmiut.
Tackankanie=Tawakoni.
Tack-chan-de-su-char=Tackchandeseechar.
Tackies=Texas.
Tacnahetca=Tashnahecha.
Tacokoquipesceni=Pineshow.
Tacones=Tacame.
Taconet, Taconick, Taconock=Taconnet.
Tacóón=Yaquina.
Tacopin=Gupa.
Tacoposcas=Taposa.
Tacos=Taos, Tewa, Taku.
Tacoullie=Takulli.
Tacubavia=Tucubavia.
Tacuenga=Cahuenga.
Taculli, Tacullie, Tâ-cullies, Tacully=Takulli.
Tacupin=Gupa.
Tacusas=Taposa.
Tadacone=Stadacona.
Taderighrones=Tutelo.
Tádes Vaqui=Tadeovaqui.
Tadjedjayi=Tadji.
Tadje jiñga=Tadzhezhinga.
Tadje unĭkaciⁿga=Tadzheunikashinga.
Tadji=Tachi.
Tadoosh=Tadush.
Tadoucac, Tadousae, Tadousca, Tadoussac, Tadoussaciens=Tadousac.
Tadpole place=Tokogalgi.
Tä-dum'-ne=Telomni.
Tadusac, Tadussékuk=Tadousac.
Ta-ee-tee-tan=Tihittan.
Tae-keo-ge=Tuskegee.
Taencas=Taensa.
Taensapaoas=Tangibao.
Taensos, Taenzas=Taensa.
Tafique=Tajique.
Tagago=Teguayo.
Tágahosh=Nestucca.
Tagas=Taikus.
Tageque=Tajique.
Ta-ge-uing-ge, Tage-unge=Galisteo.
Taghiaratzoriamute=Togiaratsorik.
Tagique=Tajique.
Tagna=Tewa.
Tagnos=Tano.
Tagoanate=Taguanate.

Tagochsanagechti=Onondaga (vil.).
Taguacana, Taguacanes=Tawakoni.
Taguace, Taguaias=Tawehash.
Taguaio=Teguayo.
Taguais, Taguallas, Taguayares, Taguayas, Taguayazes, Taguayces, Taguayes, Taguayos=Tawehash.
Tagúi=Kiowa Apache.
Tágukerésh=Apache.
Tágukerísh=Kiowa Apache.
Taguna=Laguna.
Tagus=Taikus.
Tagutakaka=Taguta.
Tagwă=Catawba.
Tahagmyut=Tahagmiut.
Tahahteens=Tatlatunne.
Ta-hail-la, Ta-hail-ta=Tlelding.
Tahalasochte=Talahassee.
Tâ'hana=Ute.
Tahanas, Tahanos=Tano.
Tahasse=Tawsee.
Tahaten=Tatlatunne.
Ta'hba=Maricopa, Papago.
Tañća-pa=Takhchapa.
Tah'-che=Tadji.
Tah-chunk wash taa=Oyateshicha.
Tahculi, Tah-cully=Takulli.
Tah-cul-tus=Lekwiltok.
Tahekie, Tahelie=Takulli.
Tahensa=Taensa.
Tahiannihouq=Kannehouan.
Ta-hi-cha-pa-han-na, Ta-hichp'=Kawaiisu.
Tahkali, Tahkallies=Takulli.
Tahk-heesh=Tagish.
Tah-khl, Tahkoli=Takulli.
Tāh'ko-tin'neh=Takutine.
Tah-le-wah=Tolowa.
Ta'hlï'mnïn=Navaho.
Tah-lum-ne=Telomni.
Tahogale, Tahogalewi=Yuchi.
Tahohyahtaydootah=Kapozha.
Tahokias=Cahokia.
Tahontaenrat=Tohontaenrat.
Tahos=Taos.
Tahsagrondie, Tahsahgrondie=Tiosahrondion.
Tah sau gaa=Tasagi's Band.
Tahse=Talasse.
Tah-se-pah=Tushepaw.
Tahtl-shin=Talal.
Tahtoos=Huchnom.
Tahuacana, Tahuacane, Tahuacano, Tahuacany, Tahvaconi=Tawakoni.
Tahuaias, Tahuallaus, Tahuaya, Tahuayace, Tahuayaces, Tahuayas, Tahuayase, Tahuayases=Tawehash.
Tahuglank, Tahuglucks=Tahuglauk.
Tañuha-yuta=Takhuhayuta.
Ta-hu'-ka-ni'=Tawakoni.
Tahulauk=Tahuglauk.
Tahwaccaro, Tah-wac-car-ro, Tahwaccona, Tahwaccorroe, Tah-wae-carras, Tah-wah-ca-roo, Tah-wah-carro, Tahwaklero=Tawakoni.
Tahwei=Tagui.
Tâ'-ia=Nutria.
Taiahounhins=Aleut.
Tâ'-ia-kwe=Nutria.
Tai'-ăq=Tyigh.
Tai'-chi-da=Taisida.
Tá-ide=Pueblos.
Taigas=Texas.
Tai-ga-tah=Taos.
Taighs, Ta-ih=Tyigh.
Taiina, Taíinamu=Taos.
Taijas=Texas.
Tai-kie-a-pain=Taitinapam.
Taikûshi=Taikus.
Tai-lin-ches=Talinchi.
Taímamares=Tumamar.
Tain-gees-ah-tsa=Tengoratsekutchin.
Tain-gees-ah-tsah=Tangesatsa.
Ta i'niɥk'aciⁿ'a=Tadhaghu.
Táinïn=Pueblos.
Tainkoyo=Nishinam.
Tai'ōtl lā'nas=Daiyuahl-lanas.
Taioux=Texas.
Tairtla=Tyigh.
Taitcedâwi=Taisida.

Tai-tim-pans, Tai-tin-a-pam, Tait-inapum, Taitini-pans=Taitinapam.
Taitsick-Kutchin=Tangesatsa.
Tai-tzo-gai=Tesuque.
Taiu-gees-ah-tsah=Tangesatsa.
Taí-wa=Pueblos.
Tâi'ya=Nutria.
Tai-yā-yăn'-o-khotān'ā=Taiyanyanokhotana.
Ta-jua=Tawa.
Takadhé=Tukkuthkutchin.
Takahagane=Ontwaganha.
Takahli=Takulli.
Takaiaksa=Takaiak.
Tăkai'-yakhō-tān'ā=Jugelnute.
Tăkājăksen=Takaiak.
Takali, Takalli=Takulli.
Takama=Yakima.
Tákapo ishak=Attacapa.
Tăkapsiŋtona, Takapsin-toŋwaŋna=Takapsinton-wanna.
Takas=Taku.
Tă-ꭓas'-i-tce'-qwût=Takasichekhwut.
Takástina=Takestina.
Takawaro=Tawakoni.
Takaz=Tukkuthkutchin.
Taꭓꬵéska utsi' upcě'=Takdheskautsiupshe.
Ta-kěꞔl'-tûn ꭓûn'-ně=Turghestltsatun.
Takelly, Ta-Keꭓ-ne=Takulli.
Takensa=Taensa.
Ta-kěsꞔl'-tsa te'-ne=Turghestltsatun.
Takha-yuna=Aleut.
Takhe=Taos.
Takhtam=Serranos.
Takikatagamute, Takiketagamute=Takiketak.
Takilma=Takelma.
TakimiꞭdiñ=Takimilding.
Tā-kit kutchin=Tatlitkutchin.
T'akkwel-ottinè=Takíwelottine.
Takla-uēdi=Daktlawedi.
Tako, Takon=Taku.
Takon Indians=Nuklako.
Takoos=Taku.
Ta-koos-oo-ti-na=Takutine.
Takopepeshene=Pineshow.
Takoulguehronnons=Conestoga.
Takshagemut=Takshak.
Taksomut, Taksomute=Takchuk.
Ták-ssi-kān=Tuxican.
Taksumut=Takchuk.
Taktchag-mïout=Takshak.
Taktēn-tān=Takdentan.
Taktla-uēdi=Daktlawedi.
Taktschagmjut=Takshak.
Taku=Takutine.
Tā'kᵘane'dî=Takwanedi.
Taku-kŏn=Taku.
Ta-kul-i=Takulli.
Taqu-qwan=Taku.
Tā-kŭ'rth=Tukkuthkutchin.
Ta-Kutchi=Eskimo.
Ta-kuth Kutchin=Tukkuthkutchin.
Takutsskoe=Taku.
Ták'yaiuna-kwe=Takya.
Talabouches, Talabouchi=Talapoosa.
Talac=Talak.
Taladígi=Taladega.
Talagans=Cherokee.
Talahaso chte=Talahassee.
Talamatan, Talamatun=Huron.
Talangamanae=Khemnichan.
Talani=Talaniyi.
Talantui=Talatui.
Ta-la-ottine=Chintagottine.
Talapenches, Talapoashas, Talapoosas, Talapouche, Talapousses, Talapüs=Talapoosa.
Talarénos=Tulareños.
Ta'lasĭ', Talassee=Tahlasi.
Talassee=Talasse.
Talatígi=Taladega.
Talawa=Tolowa.
Talchedon, Talchedums=Alchedoma.
Tal-ches=Tachi.
Talch-kŭēdi=Tahlkoedi.
Talcotin=Tautin.
Talegans, Talegawes=Cherokee.
Talehanas, Talehouyana=Hotalihuyana.
Tálěmaya=Tututni.
Taleómꭓ=Talio.
Talepoosas=Talapoosa.

Tal-e-see, Talessy Petit=Talasse.
Talesta=Tatesta.
Tal-hush-to-ny=Mulluk.
Tali, Talicies=Talasse.
Talicomish=Talio.
Taliepatava=Taliepataua.
Talikwa=Tellico.
Talimachusy, Talimuchusy=Tallimuchasi.
Talinches=Talinchi.
Tālio'mн=Talio.
Talipuꞔes=Talapoosa.
Talis, Talise, Talisees, Talisi, Talisse=Talasse.
Talkoaten, Talkotin=Tautin.
Talkρolis=Takulli.
Talla=Tala.
Tallabutes=Talapoosa.
Talladega=Taladega.
Tallagewy=Cherokee.
Tallaháski=Seminole.
Tallahassa=Talahassee.
Tallahasse=Talassehatchi.
Tallahassee=Talahassee, Talasse.
Talla-Hogan, Talla-hogandi=Awatobi.
Tallapoosa=Talapoosa.
Tallase=Tahlasi.
Tallâse=Talasse, Talassehatchi.
Tallasee=Talasse.
Tal la se hatch ee, Tallasschassee=Talassehatchi.
Tallassee, Tallassie=Talasse.
Tallatown=Tala.
Tal-lau-gue chapco pop-cau=Taluachapkoapopka.
Tallawa Thlucco=Apalachicola.
Talledega=Taladega.
Tallegwi=Cherokee.
Tallehassas=Talahassee.
Tallenches=Talinchi.
Tallesee Hatchu=Talassehatchi.
Tallesees, Tallessees=Talasse.
Talle-whe-anas=Hotalihuyana.
Tal'-le-wit-sus=Waco.
Tallibooses, Tallibousies=Talapoosa.
Talligeŭ, Talligewi=Cherokee.
Tallignamay, Talliguämais, Talliguamayque, Talliguamays=Quigyuma.
Talliké=Cherokee.
Tallimuchase=Talimuchasi.
Tall-in-chee, Tal-lin-ches=Talinchi.
Tallion=Talio.
Tallion Nation=Bellacoola.
Tallise, Tallisee, Tallises=Talasse.
Tallium=Talio.
Tallmachusse=Taluamutchasi.
Tal-lo-wau=Apalachicola.
Tal-lo-wau mu-chos-see=Taluamutchasi.
Tal-lo-wau thluc-co=Apalachicola.
Tallpoosas=Talapoosa.
Talltectan=Tahltan.
Talluches=Talinchi.
Tallushatches, Tallushatches=Talassehatchi.
Tally-hogan=Awatobi.
Talmachuesa, Talmachusee, Talmachuson, Talmachussa, Talmachussee=Taluamutchasi.
Tal'-ma-mi'-tce=Talmamiche.
Talmotchasi=Talimuchasi.
Talonapi=Talonapin.
Taloᵗlafia taina=Talohlafia.
Tāłqoe'dî, Tal-qua-tee=Tahlkoedi.
Tálsĭ=Tulsa.
Täl-sote'-e-nä=Tatsanottine.
Tal'-tac ꭓûnně=Taltushtuntude.
Taltotin=Tautin.
T'altsan Ottiné=Tatsanottine.
Tal'-t'ûc-tûn tû'-de=Taltushtuntude
Talu=Talahi.
Tálua'láko=Apalachicola.
Taluits=Talio.
Tălulŭ'=Tallulah.
Ta-lum-nes=Telamni.
Talusas=Taensa.
Ta-lu-wa=Tolowa.
Talvoi=Walpi.
Taly=Talasse.
Talyan=Tahltan.
Tamachola=Tamazula.
Tamahle=Tamali.
Tamaicas=Timucua.
Támaiya=Santa Ana.
Tamajabs=Mohave.
Tamales=Tamal.

Tamalgi=Itamalgi.
Tama'li=Tamahli.
Tamallos, Tamals=Tamal.
Tamankamyam=Serranos.
Tamarais, Tamarcas, Tamarohas, Tamarois, Tama-
  rojas, Tamaronas, Tamarones, Tamaronos, Tama-
  roras, Tamaroua, Tamarouha, Tamarous=Tama-
  roa.
Tamasabes, Tamasabs=Mohave.
Tamasqueac=Tramasqueac.
Tamatles=Tamali.
Tamawas=Tamaroa.
Tamaya, Ta-ma-ya=Santa Ana.
Tamayaca=Tawehash.
Tambeché=Tombigbee.
Tamecongh=Tinicum.
Tames=Jemez.
Tamescamengs=Temiscaming.
Ta-me'-tah=Tamali.
Tami=Tano.
Tamicongh=Tinicum.
Tamiquis=Tamique.
Tamitzopa=Tamichopa.
Tamlocklock=Tamuleko.
Tammalanos=Tamal.
Tammasees=Yamasee.
Tamole'cas, Ta-mo-lé-ka=Tamuleko.
Tamoria, Tamorois=Tamaroa.
Tamos=Pecos.
Tamotchala=Tamazula.
Tamothle=Tamahli.
Tamoucougoula=Avoyelles.
Tampacuases=Karankawa.
Tamp-Pah-Utes=Yampa.
Tä-mul'-kee=Itamalgi.
Tamy, Tamya=Santa Ana.
Ta-nah-wee=Tenawa.
Tanai=Athapascan Family.
Tanakhothaiak, Tanakhotkhaik=Tanakot.
Ta-nak-tench, Ta-nak-teuk=Tenaktak.
Tanana, Tananataná, Tanan-Kuttchin=Tenanku-
  tchin.
Tanasi=Tennessee.
Tä-nä-tju-ne=Kawchodinne.
Tä-na-tsú'-kä=Tanetsukanumanke.
Tä'năwunda=Tonawanda.
Tan-a-ya=Santa Ana.
Tancaguas, Tancagueis, Tancagues, Tancaguez,
  Tancaguies, Tancahua, Tancahues, Tancahuos,
  Tancamas=Tonkawa.
Tancames=Tacame.
Tancanes, Tancaouay, Tancaoves, Tancaoye, Tan-
  cards=Tonkawa.
Tancaro=Tawakoni.
Tancases, Tancavëys=Tonkawa.
Tanchebatchee=Tukabatchi.
Tanchipahoe=Tangibao.
Tanql'-tăc ɉûnné=Taltushtuntude.
Tancoways=Tonkawa.
Tandɉan tañ'ɹa e'nikaci'ɹa=Tangdhangtankae-
  nikashika.
Tä'-ñe=Dyani.
Táñe=Tanyi.
Tanĕks anya=Biloxi.
Tanessee=Tawasa.
Tangā'c, Tangasskoe=Tongas.
Tangeboas, Tangibac, Tangibao, Tangibaoas, Tan-
  gibaos, Tan'gipaha', Tangipahos, Tangipaos=
  Tangipahoa.
Tani'bänĕn, Tani'bänĕnina, Tani'bätha=Kadohada-
  cho.
Tanico=Tunica.
Tanignagmjut=Liesnoi.
Taniguag=Aleksashkina.
Ta nika-shing-ga=Hangatanga.
Tanik8a, Tanikwa=Tunica.
Taniquo=Tanico.
Ta-nish=Arikara.
Taniyumu'h=Paviotso.
Tanjibao=Tangibao.
Tañ'-ka-wă, Tankaway=Tonkawa.
Tank-heesh=Tagish.
Tanko=Nishinam.
Tanko Indian, Tanks=Tonkawa.
Tankum=Tanko.
Tan-nah-shis-en=Jicarilla.
Tannai=Athapascan Family.
Tanna-Kutchi=Tenankutchin.

Tannockes=Bannock.
Tannontatez=Tionontati.
T'anó'=Kloo.
Tano=Hano.
Tanochioragon=Deyodeshot.
Ta-noch-tench, Ta-nock-teuch=Tenaktak.
Tanoi=Hano.
Tä-non Kutchin=Tenankutchin.
Tanoo=Kloo.
Tanoque=Galisteo.
Tanoquevi, Tanoquibi=Hano.
Tanos=Hano, Pecos, Tano.
Tanquaay=Tonkawa.
Tanquinno=Tanico.
Tansawhot-dinneh=Tatsanottine.
Tansi=Tennessee.
Tansipaho=Tangibao.
Tanta hade=Tongas.
Tantawait, Tä'n-táwats=Chemehuevi.
Tan-tdo'a=Tan.
Tantin=Tautin.
Tantos=Tontos.
Tañ-towa=Tan.
Tantsanhoot, Tantsa-ut'dtinné, Tantsawhoot, Tant-
  sawhot-dinneh, Tan-tsawot-dinni=Tatsanottine.
Tanū Hāadē=Kloo.
Tan-uh-tuh=Tenaktak.
Tä-nŭn kūtch-ĭn=Tenankutchin.
Tanus=Hano.
Tan wa'-k'an wa-ɹa'-xe=Tanwakanwakaghe.
Tan wan oiñɹa=Tanwanshinka.
Tanwan-jiɹa=Tongigua.
Tan'wan ɹa'xe=Tsishuwashtake.
Tanwan-zhika=Tongigua.
Tanxnitanians, Tanxsnitania=Tanxnitania.
Tanyi hanutsh=Tanyi.
Tao=Taos.
Taoapa=Tapa.
Taobaianes, Taobayace, Taobayais, Taobayases=
  Tawehash.
Taogarias, Taogria=Ontwaganha.
Taol na'as xä'da-i=Taol-naas-hadai.
Taopi's band=Farmers' Band.
Taoros, Taosans, Taosas, Taoses, Taosij=Taos.
Taos Indians=Moache.
Taosis, Taosites, Taosy=Taos.
Taos Yutas=Moache.
Ta-otin=Tautin.
Taouacacana=Tawakoni.
Taouachas=Tawasa.
Taouayaches, Taouayas=Tawehash.
Taoucanes=Tawakoni,
Taovayaiaces, Taovayases=Tawehash.
Taowa=Tewa.
Ta-o-ya-te-du-ta=Kapozha.
Tao Yutas=Moache.
Tap=Tabo.
Tapage=Pitahauerat.
Tapahanock=Quioucohanoc.
Tapahowerat, Tapaje=Pitahauerat.
Tapakdgi=Klamath.
Tapanses=Tappan.
Ta-pa-taj-je=Tapa.
Tapguchas=Taposa.
Taphulgee=Attapulgas.
Tapicletca=Tapishlecha.
Tapiel=Japul.
Tapisleĉa=Tapishlecha.
Tapkhak=Taapkuk.
Tapkhakgmut=Tapkachmiut.
Tapkhamikhuagmut=Topanika.
Ta'-po-çka=Tapothka.
Tapoctoughs=Tenaktak.
Tapoosas, Tapouchas, Tapousas, Tapousoas, Tapous-
  sas, Tapowsas=Taposa.
Tappa=Pitahauerat.
Tappaan, Tappaanes, Tappaen=Tappan.
Tappage, Tappage Pawnee=Pitahauerat.
Tapparies Comanches=Ditsakana.
Tappaye Pawnee=Pitahauerat.
Tappen, Tappensees, Tappents=Tappan.
T!āq°=Taku.
Ta-qai'-yă=Takhaiya.
T!aqdentān=Takdentan.
Taqdjîk-ān=Tuxican.
Taqêstina'=Takestina.
T!āq°q!aqa-ān=Takokakaan.

Tá·qta=Choctaw.
Taqtci=Takhchi.
ᴌaqti kĭ Aⁿpaⁿ ǥatajī=Dtakhtikianpandhatazhi.
Taquha-yuta='Takhuhayuta.
Taqui=Tagui.
Taquitzata=Ratontita.
Ta-qu'-qûc-cê=Tututni.
Taracari=Tarequê.
Taracone=Faraon.
Taracton, Taractou=Catskill.
Tarahumara, Tarahumari=Tarahumare.
Taraktons=Catskill.
Tarál=Toral.
Tarancahuases=Karankawa.
Taranteens=Abnaki.
Taraones=Faraon.
Tarateens=Abnaki.
Taraumar, Taraumares=Tarahumare.
Tar-co-eh-parch, Tar-co-eh-parh=Takhchapa.
Tareguano=Tarequano.
Tarenteens, Tarentines, Tarentins=Abnaki.
Taρeoρmeut=Kopagmiut.
Tarhetown=Cranetown.
Tarimari=Tarahumare.
Tarkens, Tarkoo=Taku.
Taromari=Tarahumare.
Taros=Yavapai.
Tarpkarzoomete=Taapkuk.
Tarracones=Faraon.
Tarra-Iumanes=Tawehash.
Tarraktons=Catskill.
Tarranteeris, Tarrantens, Tarrantines, Tarrateens, Tarratines, Tarratins, Tarrenteenes, Tarrenteens, Tarrentens, Tarrentines=Abnaki.
Tarreor-meut=Kopagmiut.
Tarruraw=Tallulah.
Tartanee=Dadens.
Taruararas=Tarahumare.
Taruraw=Tallulah.
Tarwarsa, Tarwassaw=Tawasa.
Ta-rxe'-li-i-tce' ʒûnnĕ', T'a-rxi'-li i tcĕt' ʒûnnĕ'=Targhiliitshettunne.
T'a-rxi'-li-i' ʒûnnĕ=Chetlesiyetunne.
Ta-rxiⁿ'-'a-a'-tûn=Targhinaatun.
Ta'-rxût-t'ço ʒûnne=Targhutthotunne.
Tasámewé=Navaho.
Ta-sa-ûn=Hopi.
Tascalifa, Tascaluca=Tascalusa.
Tascorins, Tascororins=Tuscarora.
Tasculuza=Tascalusa.
Tascuroreus=Tuscarora.
Táshash=Kadohadacho.
Ta-shá-va-ma=Navaho.
Tashees=Tasis.
Tåsh-ė̇-på=Tushepaw.
Tash-gatze=Tashkatze.
Tashi=Mescaleros.
Tashin=Apache, Kiowa Apache.
Tashĭ'né=Jicarilla.
Tâshtyë'=Tawshtye.
Tash-Yuta=Moache.
Ta-si'n-da=Tesinde.
Ta sindje qaga=Hangatanga.
Taskáho, T'ás-kă-ló-le'n', Taskalónugi, Taskarorens, Taskarosins=Tuscarora.
Taskegee=Tuskegee.
Taskígi=Tuskegee.
Ta'skigi'yĭ=Taskigi.
Taskikis=Tuskegee.
Taskiroras, Taskororins, Tasks=Tuscarora.
Tās lā'nas, Tas Lennas=Tadji-lanas.
Tasmamares=Tumamare.
Tašnaheća=Tashnahecha.
Tašne=Knaiakhotana.
Tasquiqui=Tuskegee.
Tassautessus=Chickahominy.
Tassenocogoula, Tassenogoula=Avoyelles.
Tassetchie=Tasetsi.
Tassey=Toosey.
Tassiussak=Tasiusak.
Tastaluça=Tascalusa.
Tastasagonia=Taztasagonies.
Ta'-sun-ma' ʒûnnê=Talsunme.
Taszaluza=Tascalusa.
Tatamitka=Takamitka.
Tatanchaks, Tatancha-kutchin, Tatanchoh-Kutchin=Tutchonekutchin.
Tataŋka óesli, Tatañka-tçesli=Tatankachesli.

Tatarabueyes=Tawehash.
Ta-ta-ten=Tatlatunne.
Tatatna=Tututni.
Tatayáhukli=Tutalosi.
Tatayojai=Mataguay.
Ta-t'ça'-tun=Tatlatunne.
Tatché, Tatchees=Tachi.
Tatchek=Tachik.
Ta-tci'-qwût, Ta-tci'-qwût-me, Ta-tci' te'-ne=Tachikhwutme.
T'a'-tcu-qas-li'-tûn=Tatshukhaslitun.
Tá-tcŭ-wĭt''=Tachuwit.
Tá-tdó'a=Ta.
Tāte' Íkia=San Andrés Coamiata.
T'ā't'Entsāit=Ialostimot.
Tate Platt=Tushepaw.
Ta-te-psin=Kiyuksa.
T'ǻ'teçe=Tateke.
Tateras=Tutelo.
Tates=Tait.
Tathzey-Kutchi, Tathzey-Kutshi=Trotsikkutchin.
Tatikhlek, Tatitlack, Tatitlak=Tatitlek.
Tatkannai=Takini.
Tatla=Tatlatan.
Tatliakhtana=Chugachigmiut.
Tatloulgees=Hlahlokalka.
Tatouche=Makah, Tatooche.
Tá-tówa=Ta.
Ta-tqlaq'-tûn ʒûn'-nĕ, Ta-t'qla'-tûn=Tatlatunne.
Tätqu'nma=Soyennow.
Tatsah-Kutchin=Tatsakutchin.
Tatschigmut, Tatschigmüten=Unaligmiut.
Tā-tsēh kŭtch-ĭn'=Tatsakutchin.
Taʒse inihk'ǎciⁿ'a=Kanse.
Tátsepa=Tushepaw.
Ta ts'eyĕ=Tayachazhi.
Tatshiantin, Tatshikotin=Tatshiautin.
T'attsan-ottinè=Tatsanottine.
Ta-tu=Huchnom.
Ta-tze=San Marcos.
Tatzei-Kutshi=Trotsikkutchin.
Tauchebatchee=Tukabatchi.
Taucos=Hano, Tewa.
Taughtanakagnet=Taconnet.
Taugwik=Paugwik.
Ta-ui=Taos.
Taukaways=Tonkawa.
Taukies=Sauk.
Taulasse Viejo=Talasse.
Taupanica=Topanika.
Ta-uth=Taos.
Tauthlacotchcau=Hlekatchka.
Tau-tsawot-dinni=Tatsanottine.
Taúweâsh=Tawehash.
Taux=Nanticoke.
Tauxanias, Tauxilnanians=Tanxnitania.
Tauxinentes=Tauxenent.
Tauxitanians, Tauxsintania, Tauxuntania=Tanxnitania.
Tavaiases, Tavaiazes=Tawehash.
Tavakavas=Tawakoni.
Tavaroas=Tamaroa.
Tavayas=Tawehash.
Tavewachi, Taviachis=Tabeguache.
Tavira=Tabira.
Tavo=Tabo.
Tavoayases=Tawehash.
Tavossi=Tawasa.
Tavoyaces=Tawehash.
Tawaa=Ottawa.
Ta-wac=Tawash.
Tawacairoe, Tawacamis, Tawacani, Tawacanie, Tawa-ca-ro, Tawacarro, Tawaccaras, Tawaccomo, Tawaccoroe=Tawakoni.
Tawachguáno=Nanticoke.
Tawackanie=Tawakoni.
Tawackguáno=Nanticoke.
Tawaconie=Tawakoni.
Ta-wai-hash, Tawai'-hias=Tawehash.
Tawákal, Tawakanas, Tawakanay, Tawakany, Tawa-ka-ro, Tawakaros, Tawakenoe, Tawakones=Tawakoni.
Tawaktenk=Tenaktak.
Tawalemnes=Tuolumne.
Tawanis=Yowani.
Tawaréka=Tawakoni.
Tawas=Ottawa, Tewa.
Tawassa=Tawasa.

Tawatawas, Tawatawee=Miami.
Tawawag, Tawawog=Nameaug.
Ɪawaws, Taways=Ottawa.
Tawcullies=Takulli.
Tawe′nikaci′χa=Tawenikashika.
Ta′-wi-gi=Santo Domingo.
Tă-wis′-tă-wis=Dooesedoowe.
Táwitskash=Kadohadacho.
Tawixtawes, Tawixti=Miami.
Tawixtwi=Miami, Pickawillanee.
Tawkamee=Toktakamai.
Ta Wolh=Taos.
Taw-wassa=Tawasa.
Taw-wa-tin=Tautin.
Taw-weeahs=Tawehash.
Taxawaw=Toxaway.
Taxé=Taos.
Taxejuna=Aleut.
Taχelh=Takulli.
Täxēmna=Aleut.
Taxenent=Tauxenent.
Taxique=Tajique.
Taχkáhe=Apache.
Táχköli=Takulli.
Táxpa=Papago.
Tay-ab-Muck=Tzauamuk.
Tayachquáns=Nanticoke.
Tayas=Texas.
Ta yatcajĭ=Tayachazhi.
Tayberon=Taos.
Taynayan=Santa Barbara.
Täyóga=Tioga.
Tayos=Hainai, Toho.
Tayosap=Tuhezep.
Tay-tĕt-lek=Tatitlek.
Táyude=Isleta.
Tayunchoneyu=Yoroonwago.
Tay-wah, Tay-waugh=Tewa.
Taze-char, Taze-par-war-nee-cha=Sans Arcs.
Tbutama=Tubutama.
Tc!ā′aɫ lā′nas=Chaahl, Chaahl-lanas.
Tca′ i-ki′-ka-ra′-tca-da=Chaikikarachada.
Tcaizra wiñwû, Tcai′-zri-sa wüñ-wü=Chaizra.
Tc!āk!=Chak.
Tcă-kă′-nĕⁿ, Tcă-kă′-nhă′=Delaware.
Tcākqai=Chakkai.
Tca′-kwai-na=Chakwaina.
Tca′-kwai-na nyû-mû=Asa.
Tcakwaina wiñwü=Chakwaina.
Tcakwayā′lxam=Chakwayalham.
Tcâ-lâ-cuc=Chalosas.
Tcalá-itgɛlit=Chalaitgelit.
Tcálke=Cherokee.
Tcā′lkunts=Chalkunts.
Tcami′=Chaui.
Tcañka-oqaⁿ=Chankaokhan.
Tcaⁿ-kaxa-otina=Chankaghaotina.
Tcaⁿ-kute=Chankute.
Tcaⁿ-ona=Wazikute.
Tcānts=Chants.
Tca′ olgáqasdi=Chaolgakhasdi.
Tcapókele=Chapokele.
Tca-qta′ aⁿ-ya-di′, Tca-qta′-haⁿ-ya′, Tca-ta′=Choctaw.
Tcatcī′nî=Chatcheeni.
Tcā′tcōɥil=Schachuhil.
Tcatɛlētc=Chatelech.
Tcāts xā′da-i=Chats-hadai.
Tca′tūā=Chetawe.
Tcawā′gîs stastā′-i=Chawagis-stustae.
Tcawa′xamux=Nicola Band.
Tcawi=Chaui.
Tcaxu=Chagu.
Tc′ɛcā′atq=Nootka.
Tce-d′i′-tĕ-ne′=Chetco.
Tcedŭñga=Chedunga.
Tceewádigi, Tceewáge=Tsawarii.
Tcegnake-okisela=Chegnakeokisela.
Tce′iam=Cheam.
Tce′ i-ki′-ka-ra′-tca-da=Cheikikarachada.
Tce ïndegotdiñ=Cheindekhotding.
Tceχiwere=Chiwere.
Tcekō′altc=Chekoalch.
Tce′-li=Cheli.
Tcê′-mê, Tce-me′ tĕne′, Tcê-me′ ʇûnnĕ=Chemetunne.
Tc′ĕ′nato′aath=Chenachaath.
Tcentsithal′a=Chentsithala.

Tce-oqba=Cheokhba.
Tce p′o-cke yiñ′-e=Cheposhkeyine.
Tceq-huha-toⁿ=Chekhuhaton.
Tcerokiéco=Cherokee.
Tc′ĕs-ǫlt′ĭc′-tûn=Chesthltishtun.
Tc′ĕs-qan′-me=Echulit.
Tcê′tawe=Chetawe.
Tcetcē′lmen=Chetchelmen.
TcētcilQōk=Chechilkok.
Tcê′-ʇi=Chetco.
Tcéti námu=Tcheti.
Tcê′-ʇi ʇûn-nĕ′=Chetco.
Tcĕt-lĕs′-i-ye′ ʇûnnĕ′=Chetlesiyetunne.
Tcĕt-lĕs′-tcan ʇûn′nĕ′=Chetleschantunne.
Tce-ʇo′qaⁿ′-ye=Chedtokhanye.
Tce-ʇo yiñ′-e=Chedtoyine.
Tcēts=Chets.
Tcē′tstlɛs=Skaiametl.
Tcĕt-tan′-nĕ=Chettane.
Tcĕt-tan′ ne′-ne=Chettannene.
Tcê′ ʇûnnĕ=Coos.
Tce-tût′ ʇûnnĕ=Chetuttunne.
Tceuē′q=Cheuek.
Tcewadî=Tsawarii.
Tcē′was=Chewas.
Tce′-xi-ta=Cheghita.
Tcexu′liⁿ=Cheghulin.
Tce yiñ′-ye=Cheyinye.
Tchactas=Choctaw.
Tcha ginduefte-i=ChaginduEftei.
Tchagvagtchatchachat=Chagvagchat.
Tcha helim=Chahelim.
Tcháhiksi-tcáhiks=Pawnee.
Tchaïmuth=Chaik.
Tchai-noh=Tsano.
Tchakänkni=Chakankni.
Tchakáwētch=Chakawech.
Tchä′kĕle Tsíwish=Chakeletsiwish.
Tchakenikni=Chakankni.
Tchakh-toligmiouth=Shaktoligmiut.
Tchaktchán=Chickasaw.
Tcha kutpaliu=Chakutpaliu.
Tchalabones=Cholovone.
Tcha lal=Chalal.
Tcha lawai=Chalawai.
Tcha ma′mpit=Chamampit.
Tcha mifu amim, Tch′ammifu=Chamifu.
Tch′ammiwi=Chamiwi.
Tch′ampiklĕ ami′m=Champikle.
Tchandjoeri-Kuttchin=Tangesatsa.
Tchanka′ya=Tonkawa.
Tcha ntcha′mpĕnau amim=Chanchampenau.
Tchän-tchäntu amim=Chanchantu.
Tchän tkäi′p=Chantkaip.
Tchaouachas=Chaouacha.
Tchaoumas=Chakchiuma.
Tcha panaχtin=Chapanaghtin.
Tcha pu′ngathpi=Chapungathpi.
Tch atági′ɪ=Chatagihl.
Tcha tägshish=Chatagshish.
Tch atakuin=Chatakuin.
Tcha támnei=Chatamnei.
Tchatchakigoa=Atchatchakangouen.
Tchatchakigouas=Kaskaskia.
Tchatchaking=Atchatchakangouen.
Tcha tchambit mantchal=Chachambitmanchal.
Tcha tchannim=Chachanim.
Tcha-tchemewa=Chachemewa.
Tch′atchif=Chachif.
Tcha tchimmahi′yuk=Chachimahiyuk.
Tcha tchmewa=Chachimewa.
Tcha tchokuith=Chachokwith.
Tcha tilkuei=Chatilkuei.
Tchattaouchi=Chattahoochee.
Tcha wayē′d=Chawayed.
Tchă̑-wé=Chaui.
Tcha wúlktit=Chawulktit.
Tcháχki′láko=Chakihlako.
Tchaχla′tχksh=Upper Chinook.
Tchaχsúkush=Nez Percés.
Tcha yákon amim=Yaquina.
Tchă-yamel amim=Yamel.
Tch′ Ayankē′ld=Yonkalla.
Tcha yáχo amím=Alsea.
Tche-a-nook=Cheerno.
Tcheheles=Chehalis.
T′cheh-nits=Chinits.
Tchelouits=Tlakluit.
Tchĕshtalálgi=Potawatomi.

Tchétin námu=Tcheti.
Tche-wassan=Sewathen.
Tchiactas=Choctaw.
Tchiaχsokusň=Ponca.
Tchibaique=Sebaik.
Tchicachae=Chickasawhay.
Tchicachas=Chickasaw.
Tchi-cargut-ko-tan=Nuklako.
Tchidüakoüingoües, Tchiduakouongues=Atchatch-akangouen.
Tchiechrone=Eskimo.
Tchiglit=Kopagmiut.
Tchi-ha-hui-pah=Isleta.
Tchihogásat=Maricopa.
Tchikachaé=Chickasawhay.
Tchikasa=Chickasaw.
Tchikĕmaha=Chitimacha.
Tchikeylis=Chehalis.
Tchĭ-kûn'=Pinaleños.
Tchilcat=Chilkat.
Tchilkoten=Tsilkotin.
Tchilouit=Tlakluit.
Tchinik, Tchinimuth=Chinik.
Tchinooks, Tchi'nouks, Tchinoux=Chinook.
Tchin-t'a-gottinè=Chintagottine.
Tch' intchäl=Chinchal.
Tchin-tρa-Gottine=Chintagottine.
Tchioukakmioute=Chiukak.
Tchipan-Tchick-Tchick=Chippanchickchick.
Tchipwayanawok=Chipewyan.
Tchishe Kwe=Tontos, Tulkepaia.
Tchíshi dinné=Chiricahua.
Tchit-che-ah=Chitsa.
Tchitimachas=Chitimacha.
Tcho-ko-yem=Chokuyem, Moquelumnan Family.
Tcho-lo-lah=Chilula.
Tcholoones, Tcholovones=Cholovone.
Tchoofkwatam=Onavas.
Tchouchago=Tutago.
Tchouchouma=Chakchiuma.
Tchoueragak=Squawkihow.
Tchouktchi=Aglemiut.
Tchoupitoulas=Choupetoulas.
Tchoutymacha=Chitimacha.
Tcho'yopan=Choyopan.
Tch-queen=Sequim.
Tchrega=Tshirege.
Tch ta'githl=Chatagithl.
Tchu'hla=Chuhhla.
Tchúka 'láko=Chukahlako.
Tchukótalgi=Chukotalgi.
Tchúla=Chula.
Tchupukanes=Chupcan.
Tchútpĕlit=Nez Percés.
Tciā'kamic, Tciáqamic=Chiakamish.
Tc'ib-io=Chubiyo.
Tcięck-rúnĕ=Eskimauan Family.
Tciglit=Kopagmiut.
Tcihaciⁿ=Kanze.
Toí haciⁿqtci=Tadzheunikashinga.
ꞇoi'-ink=Chiink.
Tci'-i-ꝫĭ=Chetco.
Tciju Wactage=Chizhuwashtage.
Tci'-ka-sa'=Chickasaw.
Tcik·au'atc=Chikauach.
Tcikimisi=Tchikimisi.
Tc'ilΕQuē'uk=Chilliwhack.
Tçĭl-ki'-tĭk=Tthilkitik.
Tcimai'=Chimai.
Tcim-muk-saitc=Chimuksaich.
Tçi'nat-li' ꝫûnnĕ'=Tthinatlitunne.
Tcingawuptuh=Ute.
Tciⁿju=Chizhu.
Tcinlak=Chinlak.
Tcĭn-tat' tĕne'=Chintagottine.
Tçinúk=Chinook.
Tci-nuña-wuñ-wü=Chinunga.
Tcipiya=Tsipiakwe.
Tcipú=Chippewa.
Tciruen-haka=Nottoway.
Tci'-sro wüñ-wû=Chisro.
Tcitcilē'Εk=Chichilek.
Tci'tlä-tä'mus=Chitlatamus.
TcitQuā'ut=Okinagan.
Tcĭts-hets=Chehalis.
Tciwere=Chiwere.
Tckippewayan=Chipewyan.
Tck'uñgē'n=Chkungen.
Tcö-cö=Choco.

Tcoka-towela=Chokatowela.
Tcō'kō=Sarsi.
Tcō'māath=Chomaath.
Tco'-na-ke-rǎ=Chonakera.
Tcoñ-o, Tcoñ wüñ-wü=Chongyo.
Tco'-ro wüñ-wü, Tcosro wiñwû=Chosro.
Tço-wa'-tce=Tthowache.
Tco'-zir=Chosro.
Tcqe-k'qû=Nestucca.
TctΕmā'x=Nemah.
Tcū, Tcu'-a, Tcû'-a nyû-mu=Chua.
Tcūā'qamuq=Nicola Band.
Tcu'-a-wuñ-wü=Chua.
Tcüb'-i-yo wüñ-wü=Chubiyo.
Tcubkwĭtcalobi=Chubkwichalobi.
Tc'uc'-ta-rxa-sût'-tûn=Chushtarghasuttun.
Tcuin nyumu=Chua.
Tcu'-kai=Chukai, Nung.
Tcū' kanedi=Chukanedi.
Tcuk·tcuk'ts=Chukchukts.
Tc'u-kūkq'=Chukukh.
Tcu-Kutchi=Tsitoklinotin.
Tcŭl-liçl'-ti-yu=Chulithltiyu.
Tçŭl-tci'-qwŭt-me' ꝫûnnĕ'=Thlulchikhwutme-tunne.
Tcumac=Chumash.
Tc'û-na'-rxût ꝫûn'nĕ=Chunarghuttunne.
Tc'unoi'yana=Atsugewi.
Tcûn-se'-tûn-ne'-ta=Chunsetunneta.
Tcûn-se'-tûn-ne'-tûn=Chunsetunnetun.
Tcûn-tca'-tǎ-a' ꝫûnnĕ=Chuntshataatunne.
Tc'û'-pĭtc-n'u'-ckūtc=Chupichnushkuch.
Tçu-qi'-ꝫǎ=Thukhita.
Tc'û-qu'-i-yǎçl'=Chukhuiyathl.
Tc'û-s-tê'-rxut-mûn-ne'-tûn=Chushterghutmunne-tun.
Tcût-lĕs-tcûn tĕne', Tc'ût-lĕs'-tcûn-ꝫûn=Chetle-schantunne.
Tc'ût'-lĕs-ye' ꝫûnnĕ'=Chetlesiyetunne.
Tcût'-tûc-cûn-tcĕ=Chuttushshunche.
Tc!ū'uga=Chuga.
Tc'-wai-yök=Chwaiyok.
Tda'-bo=Tabo.
Tda'-wa=Tawa.
Tda'-wu=Tung.
Tdha-kkè-Kuttchin, Tdha-Kouttchin, Tdha-kut-tchin=Tukkuthkutchin.
Tdu'-wa=Tuwa.
Teachatzkennas=Ditsakana.
Teacuacitzica, Teacuacitzisti, Teacuacueitzisca=Teacuacueitzisti.
Teaga=Jeaga.
Teagans=Piegan.
Teago=Jeago.
Te-ah-ton-ta-lo'ga=Teatontaloga.
Teakawreahogeh=Mohawk.
Teakuaeitzizti=Teacuacueitzisti.
Teanansteixé, Teanaostaiaé, Teanaustaiae=Tea-naustayae.
Teandeoüiata, Teandeoüihata, Teandewiata=To-anche.
Teanosteaé=Teanaustayae.
Teâo=Tohaha.
Teaogon=Tioga.
Tearemetes=Tehauremet.
Teates=Tait.
Teat Saws=Utsehta.
Téaχtkni maklaks=Tyigh.
Tebas, Tebes=Tigua.
Teboaltac=Jeboaltae.
Te-bot-e-lob'-e-lay=Tubatulabal.
Tebuñki, Tebvwúki=Tebugkihu.
Tecamenes, Tecamenez, Tecamones=Tacame.
Tecas=Texas.
Tecatacourou=Tacatacuru.
Te ¢eze ¢atají=Dtedhezedhatazhi, Dtesanhadtad-hisham, Dtesinde.
Techáhet=Sechi.
Techaquit, Te-cheh-quat=Tacshikhwutme.
Techek=Tachik.
Techichas=Chickasaw.
Techico de Guachi=Techicodeguachi.
Techloel=Natchez.
Téchoueguen=Oswego.
Techpamäis=Papago.
Techpás=Pima.
Tecia=Tesia.
Teckat Kenna=Ditsakana.

Tecolota=Tecolote.
Tecomimoni=Wanamakewajenenik.
Teconet=Taconnet.
Tecorichic=Rekorichic.
Tecorino=Tecoripa.
Tecos=Pecos.
Tecua=Tewa.
Tecuiche=Kawia.
Tedamni=Telamni.
Tedarighroones, Tedarrighroones=Tutelo.
Ted-Chath-Kennas, Tedchat-kenna=Ditsakana.
Tedderighroones=Tutelo.
Tede=Athapascan Family.
Tedexeños=Tejones.
Tedirighroonas=Tutelo.
Tee-atee-ogemut=Tiatiuk.
Teegaldenskoi=Tigalda.
Tee-kee-voga-meuts=Tikeramiut.
Tee-kee-zaht-meuts=Tikizat.
Teelalup=Tulalip.
Te énikacíха=Teenikashika.
Te-en-nen-hogh-huut=Seneca.
Teeshums=Tishum.
Teeskege=Taskigi.
Teet=Tait.
Teeticut=Titicut.
Teeton band, Teetonwan, Teetwans, Teetwaun,
    Tee-twawn=Teton.
Tee-wahn=Tigua.
Té-é-wŭn-nà=Hano.
Tefaknaghamiut=Tefaknak.
Teganatics=Tegninateo.
Tegaogen=Taiaiagon.
Tegarondies, Tegaronhies=Totiakton.
Tegas=Tewa.
Tegat-hâ=Taos.
Tegazon=Taiaiagon.
Tegesta=Tequesta.
Tegique=Tajique.
Tegninaties=Tegninateo.
Tegoneas=Tegninateo.
Teguaco=Tehueco.
Teguaga, Teguai, Teguaio=Teguayo.
Teguales=Huhliwahli.
Teguas=Tewa.
Teguay, Teguayo Grande, Teguayoqué=Teguayo.
Tegueco=Tehueco.
Teguemapo=Tequemapo.
Teguerichic=Tehuerichic.
Teguesta=Tequesta.
Tegüima=Opata.
Tégwas, Tehaas=Tewa.
Tehacoachas=Chaouacha.
Te-ha-hin Kutchin=Teahinkutchin.
Tehamas=Noamlaki.
Tehanin-Kutchin=Knaiakhotana.
Tehas=Texas.
Tehawrehogeh=Mohawk.
Téhawüten=Tehawut.
Tĕhayesátlu=Alsea.
Tehdakomit=Kiddekubbut.
Teheaman=Tacame.
Teheili=Takulli.
Tehenooks=Chinook.
Tehon=Tejon.
Te-hon-dä-lo'-ga=Teatontaloga.
Tehoseroron=Dyosyowan.
Tehotirigh=Tutelo.
Tehoua=Puaray.
Tehownea-nyo-hunt=Seneca.
Tehua=Tejua, Tewa.
Tehuacanas=Tawakoni.
Tehuajo=Teguayo.
Tehuas=Tewa.
Tehuayo=Teguayo.
Téhuimas=Teguima.
Tehuiso=Tehuizo.
Tehur-lehogugh=Mohawk.
Tehūtili=Tutelo.
Teh-wa=Hano.
Teïaïagon=Taiaiagon.
Tĕiaqōtcoē=Teiakhochoe.
Teias=Texas.
Teickibatiks=Tukabatchi.
Teightaquid=Titicut.
Teijaondoraghi=Michilimackinac.
Te'o'chanontian=Tiosahrondion.
Teipana=Teypana.
Teisa=Texas.

Tĕit=Tait.
Teixa=Texas.
Tejago=Teguayo.
Tejaiagon, Tejajahon=Taiaiagon.
Tejano=Coahuiltecan.
Tejanos, Tejas, Teji=Texas.
Te-jiñga ɸatajĭ=Dtesinde.
Tejones=Tejon.
Tejos=Taos.
Tejuas=Tewa.
Tejugne=Tesuque.
Tejuneses=Tejon.
Tekan-terigtego-nes=Mohawk.
Tékapu=Kickapoo.
Tĕ'kăpwai=Penateka.
Tekeewaulees=Huhliwahli.
Tekesta=Tequesta.
Tekin=Skinpah.
Tekopa=Tsankupi.
Tĕkŭedi=Tekoedi.
Tĕ'-kwok-stai-e=Kikwistok.
Telám=Telamni.
Telamatenoⁿ=Huron.
Telamé=Telamni.
Telamene=Tehauremet.
Telamoteris=Telamni.
Telassee=Tahlasi.
Telematinos=Huron.
Tel-emnies, Tĕ'-lum-ni=Telamni.
Telhoel=Natchez.
Telhuanas=Hotalihuyana.
Telhuemit=Tlakluit.
Te'liémnim=Navaho.
Télknikni=Tyigh.
Tellassee=Tahlasi.
Tellihuana=Hotalihuyana.
Tellowe=Talahi.
Telluiana=Hotalihuyana.
Telmocresses=Taluamuchasi.
Temecule=Temecula.
Temeichic=Temechic.
Temeku=Temecula.
Temes, Temez=Jemez.
Temiscamins, Temiskaming, Temiskamink, Temis-
    kamnik=Temiscaming.
TE'mltEmlEls=Temtltemtlels.
Temolikita=Guayabas.
Temorais, Temorias=Tamaroa.
Tem-pan-ah-gos=Timpaiavats.
Temqué=Tesuque.
Tena=Tenu.
Tĕ-nā-ate=Tenate.
Tenacum=Tinicum.
Tenahna=Knaiakhotana.
Tenah'tah'=Tenaktak.
Te'nähwĭt=Tenawa.
Tĕnaina=Knaiakhotana.
Tenaoutoua=Nundawao.
TEnáqtaq=Tenaktak.
Ten-a-wish=Tanima.
T'Ena'xtax=Tenaktak.
Tendaganee's village=Roche de Bœuf.
Tene=Athapascan Family.
Teneraca=Santiago Teneraca.
Tenewa=Tenawa.
Tenge-rat-sey, Teng-ratsey, Teng-rat-si=Tangesatsa.
Tenhuas=Tenawa.
Teniqueches=Serranos.
Tenisaws=Taensa.
Tenkahuas, Tenkanas=Tonkawa.
Tennai=Athapascan Family, Navaho.
Tennakong=Tinicum.
Tennan-kutchin, Tennan-tnu-kokhtana=Tenan-
    kutchin.
Tennawas=Tenawa.
Tennis=Zuñi.
Ten-penny Utahs=Timpaiavats.
Tensagini, Tensas, Tensau, Tensaw=Taensa.
Tensawattee=Cusawatee.
Tent=Noöt.
Tented Pueblo=Hampasawan.
Tentilves=Tutelo.
Tenton, Ten-ton-ha, Tentouha=Teton.
Tenúai=Navaho.
Te-nuckt-tau=Tenaktak.
Tenuha=Tenawa.
Tĕ-nuh'-tuh=Tenaktak.
Tenuth, Ten-uth Kutchin=Tennuthkutchin.
Tenyé=Navaho.

Tenza=Taensa.
Téoas, Teoas=Tewa, Tigua.
Teoux=Tiou.
Tepache=Tepachi.
Tepagui, Tepaguy, Tepahui, Tepave, Tepavi=Te-
   pahue.
Te'pdă'=Kiowa.
Tepeguan, Tepeguanes, Tepeoanes=Tepehuane.
Tepicons=Pepikokia.
Tepk'i'ñägo=Kiowa.
Tepúas=Tewa.
Tepuspe=Batuco.
Te'qoedî=Tekoedi.
Té-quà=Tewa.
Tequas=Tewa, Tigua.
Tequenonquiaye=Ossossane.
Tequepas=Tequepis.
Tequeste=Tequesta.
Tequeunoikuaye, Tequeunonkiaye=Ossossane.
Teranáte=Terrenate.
Terapa=Toape.
Terentines, Terentynes=Abnaki.
Termacácori=Tumacacori.
Terre Blanche=White Earth.
Terrenati=Terrenate.
Terre Rouge=Netpinunsh, Foxes.
Terrino=Tenino.
Tersuque=Tesuque.
Ṭesaⁿ haⱡaɟicaⁿ=Dtesanhadtadhishan.
Tesayan=Hopi.
Tescarorins=Tuscarora.
Teseque=Tesuque.
Teserabocretes=Tsera.
Ṭe-sǐnde=Dtesinde.
Ṭe-sǐnde-it'ajǐ=Dtesindeitazhi, Makan.
Ṭ'ĕskunîlnagai'=Teeskun-lnagai.
Tess-cho tinneh=Desnedeyarelottine.
Tesseusak=Tasiusak.
Tessia=Tesia.
Tessieusak=Tasiusak.
Tessiqdjuaq=Tessikdjuak.
Tessi-Usak=Tasiusak.
Testes de bœufs=Têtes de Boule.
Tesuke, Tesuqui=Tesuque.
Tes'-wan=Chilula.
Tetaguichic=Retawichi.
Tetamenes=Telamene.
T'ĕ't'anēLēnôx=Tetanetlenok.
Tetans=Teton.
Tetans of the Burnt Woods=Brulé.
Tetans Saone=Saone.
Tetarighroones=Tutelo.
Tetarton=Tintaotonwe.
T'ə-ⱡa ⱡunnĕ=Kwatami, Tututni.
Tétaus=Ietan, Teton.
Te-tdóa=Te.
Tete Coup, Tête-Coupées=Pabaksa.
Tetehquet=Titicut.
Tête Pelée=Comanche.
Tête Plat=Thlingchadinne.
Tetes Coupes=Pabaksa.
Têtes pelées=Comanche.
Tetes Plates=Chinook, Choctaw, Flathead, Salish.
Teticut=Titicut.
T'etliet-Kuttchin=Tatlitkutchin.
Tetoan=Teton.
Tetohe=Talahi.
Teton Bois brûle=Brulé.
Tetones, Tetongue=Teton.
Teton-Menna-Kanozo, Té-ton min-na-kine-az'-zo=
   Miniconjou.
Té-ton-o-kan-dan-das, Teton Okandandes=Oglala.
Té-ton-sâh-o-ne', Teton Saone=Saone.
Tetons Brulês=Brulé.
Tetons Mennakenozzo, Tetons Minnakenozzo, Tetons
   Minnakineazzo, Tetons Minnekincazzo=Minicon-
   jou.
Tetons of the Boise Brule, Tetons of the Burned
   wood, Tetons of the Burnt-Wood=Brulé.
Te'-ton-sâh-o-ne', Teton Saone=Saone.
Tetonsarans=Teton.
Tetons Okandandas=Oglala.
Tetons Sahone, Tetons Saone=Saone.
Tetsógi=Tesuque.
T'éttchié-Dhidié=Unakhotana.
T'e-ttlel Kuttchin=Tatlitkutchin.
Te-tzo-ge=Tesuque.
Te-uat-ha=Taos.
Teu-a-wish=Tanima.

Teuconick=Taconnet.
Teughsaghrontey=Tiosahrondion.
Teuontowanos=Seneca.
Teuricatzi, Teurizatzi=Teuricachi.
Teushanushsong=Yoroonwago.
Teusón=Tucson.
Teuteloe=Tutelo.
Teu-ton-ha=Teton.
Tevas=Tewa.
Tewa=Hano.
Tewanoudadon=Tewanondadon.
Tewauntausogo=Teatontaloga.
Tewe=Hano.
Tē'wEtqEn=Tewetken.
Tewicktowes=Miami.
Te'-wi-gi=Santo Domingo.
Tewohomony=Tuscarora.
Texenáte=Terrenate.
Texes Lake=Texas Lake.
Texhaya=Teshaya.
Texia=Texas.
Texja=Teshaya.
Texon=Tejon.
Texpamaís=Papago.
Tĕχ-păs'=Pima.
Teyans, Teyas, Teyens=Texas.
Teyoheghscolea=Dyosyowan.
Teyos=Texas.
Teypamá=Teypana.
Teystse-Kutshi=Teahinkutchin.
Teytse-Kutchi=Tatsakutchin.
Te'yuwǐt=Penateka.
Tezuque=Tesuque.
Tgănoⁿe'o'hă'=Ganowarohare.
Tgarihóge=Mohawk.
Tguas=Tigua.
Thabloc-ko=Hlaphlako.
Thacame=Tacame.
Thacanhé=Wichita.
Thœ-canies=Sekani.
Thah-a-i-nin=Apache.
Tha'ká-hinĕ'na, Tha'ká-itän=Kiowa Apache.
Thākhu=Taku.
Thamien=Santa Clara.
Thancahues=Tonkawa.
Tha'nĕzá', Tha'nĕzá'ni=Thkhaneza.
Thanoⁿéohā', Thanoⁿ'waru'hā'r=Oneida (vil.).
Thanos, T'han-u-ge=Tano.
Thaos=Taos.
Thá'paha, Tha'pahadǐ'ine'=Thkhapaha.
Tharahumara=Tarahumare.
Tharhkarorin=Tuscarora.
Thase=Talasse.
Ṭhăsⱡchetcǐ'=Huron.
Thatce=Tachy.
Tha-to-dar-hos=Onondaga.
Thatsan-o'tinne=Tatsanottine.
Thá'tsini=Thkhatshini.
Theacatckkah=Hlekatchka.
Theaggen=Tioga.
Thearemets, Theauremets=Tehauremet.
Thecamenes, Thecamons=Tacame.
Thedirighroonas=Tutelo.
Thegaronhies=Totiakton.
Theguas=Tewa.
Theguayo=Teguayo.
Thehueco=Tehueco.
Thé-ké-né, Thé-kĕn-nēh, Thé-ké-ottiné, Thè-khènè=
   Sekani.
Thè-kka-'nè=Sazeutina, Sekani.
Thé-kké-Ottiné=Sekani.
Theloël, Theloelles=Natchez.
Themiscamings, Themiskamingues, Themistamens=
   Temiscaming.
The Mountain=La Montagne.
The Nation=Upper Creeks.
The Nook=Nuk.
Theodehacto=Totiakton.
Théoga, Théoge=Tioga.
Theonontateronons=Tionontati.
Thé-Ottiné=Etheneldeli.
Theoux=Tiou.
The people that don't laugh=Kutaiimiks.
The Rapid=Sault au Recollet.
The Robes with Hair on the outside=Isisokasimiks
Therocodames=Terocodame.
Thesera Bocretes=Tsera.
The Six=Taoapa.
Theskaroriens=Tuscarora.

Thetliantins=Thetliotin.
The Woman's town=Pasquenoc.
Thé-yé Ottiné=Etheneldeli.
Thezuque=Tesuque.
Thiaha=Chiaha.
Thickcannie=Sekani.
Thickwood=Assiniboin.
Thick Wood Crees=Sakawiyiniwok.
Thick Woodsmen=Sugwaundugahwininewug.
Thihero=Kiohero.
Thikanies=Sazeutina, Sekani.
Thimagona, Thimagoua, Thimogoa=Timucua.
Thing-e-ha-dtinne=Thlingchadinne.
Thinthonha, Thinthonna, Thintohas=Teton.
Thionontatoronons=Tionontati.
Thioux=Tiou.
Thiviment=Itivimiut.
Thlakatchka=Hlekatchka.
Thlakeimas=Clackama.
Thlála'h=Chinook.
Thlamalh=Klamath.
Thla-noo-che au-bau-lau=Hlanudshiapala.
Thlar-har-yeek-qwan=Yakutat.
Thlatlogulgau=Hlahlokalka.
Thlcocotcho=Chukahlako.
Thleacatska=Hlekatchka.
Thlea Walla=Huhliwahli.
Thleweechodezeth=Ukusiksalirmiut.
Thlewhákh=Klawak.
Thlingcha, Thlingcha tinneh, Thlingeha-dinneh, Thlingeha-dinni, Thling-e-ha dtinne=Thlingcha-dinne.
Thlinkeet, Thlinkets, Thlinkit=Koluschan Family.
Thlinkíten=Tlingit.
Thlinkithen=Koluschan Family.
Thljegonchotana=Tlegonkhotana.
Thloblocco-town, Thlobthlocco, Thlob Thlocko=Hlaphlako.
Thlo-ce-chassies=Klokegottine.
Thlopthlocco=Hlaphlako.
Thlot-lo-gul-gau=Hlahlokalka.
Thlowiwalla=Clowwewalla.
Thluëlla'kwe=Pueblos.
Thlu-katch-ka=Hlekatchka.
Thnaina=Athapascan Family, Knaiakhotana.
Thoderighroonas=Tutelo.
Thoig'a-rik-kah=Nez Percés.
Thomé, Thomez=Tohome.
Thompson=Nikaomin.
Thompson River Indians=Ntlakyapamuk, Shuswap.
Thompsons=Ntlakyapamuk.
Thongeith=Songish.
Thonges, Thons=Tongigua.
Thops=Tups.
Thoriman=Tourima.
Thornton Party=Eel River Indians.
Thorntown, Thorntown Miamies=Kowasikka.
Thorntown Party=Eel River Indians.
Those that boil their dishes=Waleghaunwohan.
Those that eat crows=Kanghiyuha.
Those that eat the ham=Wolutayuta.
Those that shoot in the pines=Wazikute.
Thoucoue=Tiou.
Thouenchin=Toanche.
Thoya, Thoyago=Teguayo.
Three Canes, Three Cones=Tawakoni.
Three Kettles=Oohenonpa.
Thu-le-oc-who-cat-lau=Tukhtukagi.
Thunder=Inshtasanda, Lunikashinga, Waninkikikarachada.
Thunder-being gens=Wakantaenikashika.
Thunder-bird=Cheghita, Wakanta.
Thunder people=Hisada, Kdhun.
Thuntotas=Teton.
Thwlé-lûp=Tulalip.
Thwsda'-lub=Clallam.
Thy=Tyigh.
Thycothe=Tukkuthkutchin.
Thy-eye-to-ga=Nez Percés.
Thynné=Athapascan Family.
Thysia=Tiou.
Tiach=Tyigh.
Tiachton=Tueadasso.
Tiago=Tioga.
Tiagotkonniaeston=Amikwa.
Tiã'klēlake=Neahkeluk.
Ti-ä-mi=Dyami.
Ti'ʌn, Tīan Ilnigé=Tiun.

Tiaoga, Tiaogos=Tioga.
Tiaoux=Tiou.
Tiascons=Tirans.
Tiatáchtont=Tueadasso.
Tiawco=Nanticoke.
Tibex=Tigua.
Tibihagna=Tibahagna.
Tibitibis=Abittibi.
Tibutama=Tubutama.
Ticapanas=Tyacappan.
Tichaïchachass=Paltchikatno.
Tichenos=Pischenoas.
Tichero=Kiohero.
Ti-chom-chin=Tlkamcheen.
Tichuico=Pecos.
Tichuna=Acomita.
ʟícicít'aⁿ=Wazikute.
Tickanetly=Tekanitli.
Tickarneens=Siccameen.
Ticmanares=Tumamar.
Ticoleosa=Tikaleyasuni.
Ticori=Picuris.
Ticorillas=Jicarilla.
Ticuic, Ticuique=Pecos.
Tidam=Titlas.
Tiddoes=Caddo.
Tideing Indians=Kiowa.
Tiedami=Telamni.
Tiederighroenes, Tiederighroonas, Tiederighroones, Tiederigoene, Tiederigroenes=Tutelo.
Tiego=Tioga.
T'i-e-kwa-tc'ï=Tiekwachi.
Tiengaghamiut=Tiengak.
Tienique=Pecos.
Tienonadies, Tienondaideaga=Tionontati.
Tieton=Teton.
Tieugsachrondio=Tiosahrondion.
Tigaldinskoe=Tigalda.
T'li'gʌn=Tiun.
Tigara Mutes=Tikeramiut.
Tigchelde'=Tigshelde.
Tigeux=Tigua.
Tigh=Tyigh.
Ti-gi-qpŭk'=Tigikpuk.
Tigĭtan=Tihittan.
Tignes, Tignex=Tigua.
Tigninateos=Tegninateo.
Tigoeux=Tigua.
Tigouex, Tigouex-on-the-rock=Puaray.
Tigres=Taikus.
Ti-guan, Tiguas, Tiguasi, Tigue, Tigueans, Tiguero, Tigues, Ti-guesh, Tiguet=Tigua.
Tiguex=Puaray, Tigua.
Tiguexa, Tiguez, Tiguns=Tigua.
Tihiou=Tiou.
Tihokáhana=Pima.
Tihtacutt=Titicut.
Tihua=Santo Domingo.
Tihuas, Tihueq, Tihuex, Tihuix=Tigua.
Tī Ilnigē=Te.
Ti-ji-só-ri-chi=Jitisorichi.
Tijon, Tijon Indians=Tejon.
Ti'-ju=Tizhu.
Ti-ka'-jä=Chickasaw.
Tĭkăle' yăsûñ=Tikaleyasuni.
Tikerana=Tikera.
Tĭkeráⁿmiun=Tikeramiut.
Tikeraqdjung=Tikerakdjung.
Tikhmenief=Kechemudluk.
Tikirak, Tikirat=Tikera.
Tikolaus, Tĭk'ūilūc=Tikwalus.
Tikumcheen=Tlkamcheen.
Ti'ʹ-kwă=Seneca.
Tilamookhs=Tillamook.
Tï'lawehuíde, Ti'lawéi=Acoma.
Tilhalluvit=Tlakluit.
Tilhalumma=Kwalhioqua.
Tilhanne=Tilkuni.
Tilhiellewit, Tilhilooit, Tilhualwits, Tilhulhwit=Tlakluit.
Tilijais, Tilijayas=Tilijaes.
Tillemookhs=Tillamook.
Tillie=Tubatulabal.
T'ĭl'-mūk' tûnnĕ=Tillamook.
Tilofayas, Tiloja, Tilpayai=Tilijaes.
Tilpā'les=Kilpanlus.
Tĭ'lqûni=Tilkuni.
Tiluex=Tiguex.
Tilyayas=Tilijaes.
Timagoa=Timucua.

Timbabachis, Timbachis=Timpaiavats.
Timbalakees=Tamuleko.
Ti-mĕcl' tûnnĕ'=Timethltunne.
Timigaming, Timiscamiouetz, Timiscimi, Timiskaming=Temiscaming.
Timita=Timigtac.
Timmiscameins=Temiscaming.
Timoga, Timogoa, Timooka, Timooquas, Timoqua=Timucua.
Timossy=Tomassee.
Timotlee=Tamali.
Timpachis, Timpagtsis, Timpana Yuta, Timpangotzis, Timpanigos Yutas, Timpanoautzis, Timpanocuitzis, Timpanoge, Timpanogos, Timpanogotzis, Timpanogs, Timpanotzis, Timpay nagoots, Timpenaguchya=Timpaiavats.
Timuaca, Timuca, Timuqua, Timuquana, Timuquanan, Timusquana=Timucua.
Tina=Tenu.
Tinaï=Athapascan Family.
Tinaina=Knaiakhotana.
Tinajas de Candelaria, Tinajas=Tinajas.
Tinalenos=Pinaleños.
Tinaouatoua=Quinaouatoua.
Tinaxa=Tinajas.
Tinazipe-citca, Tinazipe-śića=Tinazipeshicha.
Tindan=Quivira.
Tindaw=Teton.
Tinde=Apache, Jicarilla.
Tindestak=Yendestake.
Tindi̧ suxtana=Aglemiut.
Tine-yizháne=Tonkawa.
Ting-tah-to-a, Ting-ta-to-ah=Tintaotonwe.
Tiniéma=Tanima.
Tinina=Knaiakhotana.
Tinjas=Taensa.
Tinlinneh, Tĭn'lĭu=Tejon.
Tinnä'-ash=Apache.
Tinnats, Tinnats-Khotana=Knaiakhotana.
Tinnatte=Athapascan Family.
Tinnatz-kokhtana=Knaiakhotana.
'Tinne=Athapascan Family.
Tinnecongh=Tinicum.
Tinneh=Athapascan Family, Esquimauan Family.
Tinney=Athapascan Family.
Tinnis=Yennis.
Tinnsals=Taensa.
Tinontaté=Tionontati.
Tinpay nagoots=Timpaiavats.
Tinqua=Timucua.
Tinsas, Tinssas=Taensa.
Tin-tah-ton=Tintaotonwe.
Tintangaonghiatons, Tintangaoughiatons=Teton.
Tinta tonwan, Tinta tonwe=Tintaotonwe.
Tinthenha, Tinthona, Tinthonha, Tinthow=Teton.
Tintinapain=Taitinapam.
Tintinhos=Teton.
Tinto=Tontos.
Tintoner, Tintones, Tintonhas, Tintons, Tintonwans=Teton.
Tĭn'-zĭt Kūtch'-ĭn=Trotsikkutchin.
Tioas=Tigua.
Tioga Point=Tioga.
Tiohero=Kiohero.
Tiohontatés=Tionontati.
Tiojachso=Tueadasso.
Tionionhoḡarawe=Seneca.
Tionnontantes Hurons, Tionnontatehronnons, Tionnontatez, Tionnontatz, Tionnonthatez, Tionnotanté, Tionondade=Tionontati.
Tiononderoge=Teatantaloga.
Tionontalies, Tionontates=Tionontati.
Tiotehatton, Tiotohatton=Totiakton.
Tioux=Tiou.
Ti-pa-to-la'-pa=Tubatulabal.
Tipisastac=Tipsistaca.
Tippacanoe=Tippecanoe.
Tiquas, Tiques, Tiquexa=Tigua.
Tiqui Llapais=Walapai.
Tiquoz=Tigua.
Tirangapui, Tirangapuy, Tiransgapuis=Timpaiavats.
Tircksarondia=Tiosahrondion.
Ti-ré-wi=Chiwere.
Tir hit tān=Tihittan.
Tirik=Rirak.
Tirionet=Taconnet.
Tirip'ama=Pekwan.
Tiroacarees=Tawakoni.

Tisageohroann=Missisauga.
Tisaiqdji=Yanan Family.
Tiscugas=Tuskegee.
Tishech, Tishechu=Tisechu.
Tishravarahi=Shasta.
Tish-tan'-a-tan, Tish-tang-a-tang=Djishtangading.
Tishχani-hhlama=Tenino.
Tist'shinoie'ka, Tistshnoie'ka=Detsanayuka.
Titacutt=Titicut.
Titamook=Tillamook.
Titecute, Titicott=Titicut.
Ti-tji Hän-at Ka-ma Tze-shu-ma=Pueblo Caja del Rio, Yapashi.
Titkainenom=Noamlaki.
Titmictac=Timigtac.
Ti toan, Titoba, Titon, Titone, Titongs, Titoŋwaŋ, Titonwans=Teton.
Títsakanai=Ditsakana.
Titsiap=Pueblito.
Titskan watitch=Tonkawa.
Titwa=Miami.
Ti-t'wan, Ti-t'-wawn=Teton.
Tit-yi Hä-nat Ka-ma Tze-shum-a, Tit-yi Hä-nat Ka-ma Tze-shum-a Mo-katsh Zaitsh=Yapashi.
Ti'-u-a'-dći-maⁿ, Ti'-u-a-di'-maⁿ=Tourima.
Tiucara=Tucara.
Tiuhex=Tigua.
Tiūtei, Tiūterih=Tutelo.
Ti'vati'ka=Paviotso.
Tiwa=Tewa, Tigua.
Tiwadi'ma=Tourima.
Tiχitíwa hupónun=Mescaleros.
Ti yakh' unin=Aleut.
Tiyaoga, Tiyaogo=Tioga.
Tiyocesli=Tiyochesli.
Tiyoga=Tioga.
Tiyopa-oćaŋnuⁿpa, Tiyopa-otcaⁿnuⁿpa=Tiyopa-ochannunpa.
Tiyotcesli=Tiyochesli.
Tizaptaŋna=Tizaptan.
Tizhgelede=Tigshelde.
Tizuas=Tigua.
Tjeughsaghrondie, Tjeugsaghronde, Tjguhsaghrondy=Tiosahrondion.
Tjon-a-ai'=Tung.
Tjughsaghrondie=Tiosahrondion.
Tjuiccu-jenne, Tjusceujen-né=Gila Apache.
Tjuwā'nχa-îkc=Klikitat.
T-ka=Kammatwa.
Tkaláma=Thlakalama.
Tkanoⁿ'eohā', Tkanoⁿ'warú‘hā'r=Oneida (vil.).
Tkāp-quē-nā=Ojo Caliente.
Tkauyaum=Tagwayaum.
T'Kawkwamish=Tkwakwamish.
tkê'nAl=Cumshewa.
Tketlcotins=Thetliotin.
T'kitskĕ=Trotsikkutchin.
Tk'kōēau'm=Taqwayaum.
tKo-ōh-lōk-tā-que=Kalokta.
T'k'qa'-ki-yu=Tkhakiyu.
Tkuayaum=Taqwayaum.
TkulHiyogoā'ikc=Kwalhioqua.
T'kûl-má-ca-auk'=Tkulmashaauk.
Tkulχiyogoā'îkc=Kwalhioqua.
Tlaámen=Sliammon.
Tlā'asath=Makah.
Tlackees=Wailaki.
Tlagga-silla=Trotsikkutchin.
Tlaglli=Haglli.
Tlahoos=Clahoose.
Tlahosath=Klahosaht.
Tlahús=Clahoose.
Tlaidas=Haida.
Tlāiq=Tlaik.
Tlaiyū Hāadē=Hlgaiu-lanas.
Tlakäi'tat, Tlakatat=Klikitat.
Tlăkĭmĭsh, Tlakĭmĭsh-pûm=Clackama.
Tlalams, Tla'lEm=Clallam.
Tlalliguamayas, Tlalliquamallas=Quigyuma.
Tlalum=Clallam.
Tlamath=Klamath.
Tlamatl=Lutuamian Family, Klamath.
Tlameth=Klamath.
Tlanusi'yĭ=Quanusee.
Tlă'nuwă=Chattanooga.
Tlaō'kwiath, Tlaoquatch, Tlaoquatsh=Clayoquot.
Tlapan=Apalachee.
Tlaqluit=Tlakluit.
Tlā'qōm=Tlakom.

Tlascala=Sia.
Tlascani, Tlaskanai=Tlatskanai.
Tla'skē'noɋ=Klaskino.
Tlastcìni, Tlastsíni=Tlastshini.
Tlatekamut, Tlatekamute=Tlatek.
T'ʆā-theñ-ᴋoh'-tin=Tlathenkotin.
Tlatlashekwillo, Tlatla-Shequilla, Tlátlasiqoala, Tlā-tlī-sī-kwila=Tlatlasikoala.
Tlatsap=Clatsop.
Tlatscanai=Tlatskanai.
Tlats'ēnoɋ=Klaskino.
Tlatskanie=Tlatskanai.
Tlautisis=Tlauitsis.
Tla-we-wul-lo=Clowwewalla.
Tlaxcala=Sia.
Tʆaz-'tenne=Tatshiautin.
Tlégogitno, Tlegozhitno=Tlegoshitno.
Tlᴇmtlᴇ'melᴇts=Clemclemalats.
Tlēɋēti=Tletlket.
Tʆᴇs-ᴋoh'-tin=Tleskotin.
Tlg·aio lā'nas=Hlgaiu-lanas.
Tlg·ā'it=Hlgahet, Skaito.
Tlg·ā'itgu lā'nas=Hlgahetgu-lanas.
Tlg·ā'it gyit'inai=Hlgahet-gitinai.
Tlgaiu lā'nas=Hlgaiu-lanas.
Tlialil-kakat=Tlialil.
Tlickitacks, T'likatat=Klikitat.
T'linkets=Koluschan Family.
Tlinkit=Tlingit, Koluschan Family.
Tlinkit-antu-kwan=Tlingit.
Tlinkwan Hāadē=Klinkwan.
Tlip-pah-lis, Tlip-pat-lis=Kilpanlus.
Tlitk·'atᴇwū'mtlat=Shuswap.
Tlizilàni=Tlizihlani.
Tlk·āgîlt=Skidegate.
Tl-kam-sheen=Tlkamcheen.
Tlkinool=Cumshewa.
Tlk'înōtl lā'nas=Kagials-kegawai.
Tlkumcheen, Tlk-umtcī'n=Tlkamcheen.
Tlokeang=Kato.
Tʆ'o-tœne, Tʆo-toⁿ-na=Klokegottine.
Tʆsûs-me' ʒūnnĕ=Thltsusmetunne.
Tlu=Kloo.
T'lu-ĕl-lá-kwe=Pueblos.
Tluh-ta-us=Newhuhwaittinekin.
Tlū'tlämā'ᴇkā=Assiniboin.
Tmarois=Tamaroa.
Tnac, Tnai, Tnaina, Tnaina Ttynai=Knaiakhotana.
Tnijotobar=Quijotoa.
Toaa=Tohaha.
Toad=Sopaktalgi.
Toaganha, Toagenha=Ontwaganha.
Toags=Nanticoke.
Toah-waw-lay-neuch=Tsawatenok.
Toajas=Tawehash.
Toajgua=Tojagua.
Toak paf car=Tukpafka.
Toalaghreghroonees, Toalaghreghsoonees=Tutelo.
To-alchĭn'di=Chakpahu.
Toam'-cha=Tomcha.
Toanda, Toando, To-an-hooch, Toanhoock, Toan-hūch, To-an-kooch=Twana.
Toanyaces=Tawehash.
Toao=Tohaha.
Tōapúli=Santa Catarina.
Toas=Taos, Tewa, Tigua.
Toasi=Tawasa.
Toataghreghroones=Tutelo.
Toaux=Tiou.
Toauyaces=Tawehash.
Toa-waw-ti-e-neuh=Tsawatenok.
Toayas=Tawehash.
Tobas=Soba.
Tobacco Indians=Tionontati.
Tobacco Plains Kootanie, Tobacco Plains Kootenay=Akanekunik.
To'baznáᴢ, To'baznaázi=Thobazhnaazhi.
Tobó-a-dūd=Yakima.
Tobic=Tobique.
Tobikhars=Gabrieleño.
Tobiscanga=Toviscanga.
Tocabatché=Tukabatchi.
Tocaninambiches=Arapaho.
Toccoa=Tagwahi.
Toc-co-gul-egau=Tokogalgi.
Tocconnock=Taconnet.
To-che-wah-coo=Foxes.
Tockwaghs, Tockwhoghs, Tockwocks, Tockwogh, Tockwoghes, Tockwoughes=Tocwogh.

Toco=Toquo.
Tocoah=Tagwahi.
Toco-baja-Chile, Tocobajo, Tocobayo, Tocobogas, Tocopata, Tocovaga=Tocobaga.
Toctata=Oto.
Tocwoys=Tocwogh.
Toderechrones, Toderichroone, Todericks=Tutelo.
Todetabi=Yodetabi.
Todevigh-rono=Coreorgonel, Tutelo.
Todichini=Thoditshini.
Todirichrones=Tutelo.
Todirichroones=Christanna Indians, Tutelo.
To'ditsíni=Thoditshini.
To'dokónzi=Thodhokongzhi.
Tōēchkanne=Wichita.
To'ē'k'tlisath=Chaicclesaht.
Toenchain, Toenchen=Toanche.
Tœné=Athapascan Family.
To-e-ne-che=Talinchi.
Toenenhoghhunt=Seneca.
Tœni=Athapascan Family.
Togabaja=Tocobaga.
Togenga=Tongigua.
Toghsaghrondie=Tiosahrondion.
Toghwocks=Tocwogh.
Togiagamiut=Togiak.
Togiagamut=Togiagamiut.
Togiagamute, Togiak Station=Togiak.
Togiarhazoriamute=Togiaratsorik.
Tognayo=Teguayo.
Togo=Soco.
Togobatche=Tukabatchi.
Togunguas=Tongigua.
Togyit'inai=Do-gitunai.
Tohaha=Taraha.
Tohahe=Taraha, Tohaha.
Tohaiton=Totiakton.
Tohaka=Tohaha.
Tó'ħani, Tohanni=Thokhani.
Tohiccon, Tohicon, Tohikon=Tioga.
Tohogaleas=Yuchi.
Tohogalias=Tokogalgi.
Tohontaenras=Tohontaenrat.
Tohopikaliga, Tohopkolikies=Tohopekaliga.
Tohotaenrat=Tohontaenrat.
To'-ho-üh=Tohou.
Toibi, Toibi-pet=Toybipet.
Toikon=Tioga.
Toillenny=Heshota Ayahltona.
To-i-nin'-a=Atsina.
Toison=Tucson.
Tojobaco=Tocobaga.
Tokali=Takulli.
Tokatoka=Tohookatokie.
Tokaubatchee=Tukabatchi.
To-ke-ma-che=Tuhukmache.
Tokhakate, Tokio, Tok-kakat, Tok-khakat=Tok.
Tōk'oā'ath=Toquart.
Tokóonavi=Tokonabi.
Tokotci wiñwû, To-ko-tci wüñ-wü=Tokochi.
To-kum'-pi=Northern Assiniboin.
Tokúwe=Apache.
Tokwaht=Toquart.
Tola=Nutria.
Tolana=Tolowa.
Tolane=Tocane.
Tolawa=Tolowa.
Tolekopáya=Tulkepaia.
Tolemaro=Tolemato.
Tolenos=Yolo.
Tolera, Tolere, Toleri=Tutelo.
Tolewah=Tolowa.
Tolgopeya=Tulkepaia.
Tlō'tk!a=Tohlka.
Tolkepayá, Tolkipeya, Tolkopáya=Tulkepaia.
Tolkotin=Tautin.
Tolli Hogandi=Awatobi.
Tollinches=Talinchi.
Tolocchopka=Taluachapkoapopka.
Tolofa=Taloffa Ockhase.
Tolomato=Tolemato.
Tolopchopko=Taluachapkoapopka.
Tolowarch, Tolowar thlocco=Apalachicola.
Tōʟtsasdiñ=Toltsasding.
Tolujaâ=Tilijaes.
To-lum-ne=Telamni.
Tomachas=Tawehash.
Tomachee=Timucua.
Tomales=Tamal.

Tomaroas=Tamaroa.
Tomasa=Tawasa.
Tomatly, Tomatola=Tamali.
Tombecbé,Tombechbé, Tombeche, Tombeechy=Tombigbee.
Tomeas=Tohome.
Tomé Dominguez=Tomé.
Tomés, Tomez=Tohome.
To-Mia=Santa Ana.
Tomiscamings=Temiscaming.
Tom-i-ya=Santa Ana.
Tommakee=Timucua.
Tommotley=Tamali.
Tomocos, Tomoka=Timucua.
Tomo'la=Tubatulabal.
Tomothle=Tamahli.
Tompacuas=Pakawa.
Tompiras, Tompires=Tompiro.
Tóna-kwe=Tona.
Tonanulga=Tonanulgar.
Tonawando, Tonawanta=Tonawanda.
Toncahiras, Toncahuas=Tonkawa.
Ton'cas=Kutawichasha.
Toncawes=Tonkawa.
Ton-ch-un=Tonchuun.
Tondaganie=Roche de Bœuf.
Tondamans=Seneca.
Tondo=Tontos.
Tongarois=Ontwaganha.
Tongass=Tongas.
Tongenga, Tonginga=Tongigua.
Tongorias=Ontwaganha.
Tongues=Tonkawa.
Tonguinga=Tongigua.
Toniata=Tonihata.
Tonica=Tonikan Family.
Tonicas, Tonicaus=Tunica.
Toniche, Tonici=Tonichi.
Tonika=Tonikan Family.
Tonikas=Tunica.
Toniquas=Tanico.
Tonitsi, Tonitza=Tonichi.
Tonjajak=Kukak.
Tonkahans, Tonkahaws, Tonkahiras, Tonkahuas, Ton-ka-hues, Ton-kah-vays, Tonkaways, Tonkawē, Tonkawéya, Tonkeways, Tonkhuas = Tonkawa.
Toñkoñko=Siksika.
Tonkowas, Tonks=Tonkawa.
Tonnaouté=Tannaoute.
Tonnewanta=Tonawanda.
Tonniata=Tonihata.
Tonningua=Tongigua.
Tonnontoins=Seneca.
Tonnoraunto=Tonawanda.
To-noc-o-nies=Tawakoni.
Tóno-Oōhtam=Papago.
Tonoziet=Tonoyiet's Band.
Ton-que-was, Tonqueways=Tonkawa.
Tonquish's village=Tonguish's Village.
Tonquoways, Tonqus=Tonkawa.
Tons=Taos.
Tonsagroende=Tiosahrondion.
Tonsobe=Tomsobe.
Tont-a-quans=Tongas.
Toⁿ-tdóa=Tong.
Tonteac, Tonteaca=Hopi.
Tontears=Tontos.
Tontewaits=Chemehuevi.
Tonthratarhonon=Totontaratonhronon.
Tonto-Apaches=Tontos.
Tonto Cosnino=Havasupai.
Tontoes=Tontos.
Tontonteac=Hopi.
Tontos=Yavapai.
Tonto-Tinné=Tontos.
Tontthrataronons=Totontaratonhronon.
Tontu=Tontos.
Too=Tiun.
Too-an-hooch, Too-au-hoosh=Twana.
Too-clok band=Tutlut.
Too-coo recah=Tukuarika.
Toogelah, Toogoola=Tugaloo.
Tooh-to-cau-gee=Tukhtukagi.
Tookabatcha, Tookabatchee=Tukabatchi.
Took'-a-rik-kah=Tukuarika.
Took-au-bat-che=Tukabatchi.
Took-au-bat-che tal-lau-has-see=Taluamutchasi.
Tookaubatchians=Tukabatchi.
Tookhlagamute=Tuklak.

Tookseat=Munsee.
Tooleekskoi=Tulik.
Tooleerayos=Tulareños.
Toolukaanahamute=Tuluka.
Toomedocs=Tumidok.
Toomes=Tohome.
Toom-na=Tumna.
Toonoonee=Tununirusirmiut.
Toonoonek=Tununirmiut.
Toon-pa-ooh=Tonebao.
Too-num'-pe=Tunanpin.
Too-qu-aht=Toquart.
Toos=Taos.
Tooses=Tuskegee.
Toosey's Tribe=Toosey.
Tootootana=Tututunne.
Too-too-ten=Tututni.
Too-too-te-nay=Tututunne.
Too-too-te-ny=Tututni.
Too-toot-e-ways, Too-toot-na, Too-toot-nay, Too-tootne=Tututunne.
Too-toot-nie, Too-too-ton, Tootootone=Tututni.
Too-too-to-neys, Too-too-to-nies, Too-too-to-ny, Toot-toot-en-ay=Tututunne.
Too-war-sar=Tawehash.
Tooweehtoowees=Miami.
Too-wos-sau=Tawasa.
Topa-an=Thkhapaha.
Topacas=Tukabatchi.
Topana-ulka=Toponanaulka.
Topanica=Topanika.
Topchalinky, Topekaliga=Tohopekaliga.
To-pe-ne-bee, Topenibe, To-pen-ne-bee=Topenebee's Village.
Topent=Topeent.
Top-hulga=Attapulgas.
Topia=Topira.
Topingas=Tongigua.
Topinibe=Topenebee's Village.
Topin-keua, Top-in-te-ua=Hopi.
Tōpira, Topires, Tōpiros=Tompiro.
Topiza=Topira.
Topkegalga, Topkélaké=Attapulgas.
Top-ni-be=Topenebee's Village.
Topnish=Topinish.
Topocapas=Tocobaga.
Topofkees, Topofkies=Tukpafka.
Topoliana-kuin=Taos.
Topony=Sepori.
Topoqui=Topiqui.
Toppahannock=Rappahannock.
Toprofkies=Tukpafka.
Toqua, Toquah=Toquo.
Toquaht, Toquatux, Toquhaht=Toquart.
Torape=Torepe's Band.
Toreman=Tourima.
Toreon, Toreuna=Torreon.
Torim=Telamni.
Torima, Toriman, Torimanes, Torinan=Tourima.
Toriuash=Tawehash.
Toro=Tova.
Torremans=Tourima.
Torreon=Kuaua.
Torsee=Tawsee.
Tortero=Tutelo.
Toruro=Tallulah.
To-sarke=Tosarke's Band.
Tosawa=Toxaway.
To'-sa-wee, To-sa-witches=Tussawehe.
Toscororas=Tuscarora.
Tosepón=Tisepan.
To-si'ko-yo=Tasikayo.
To-si-witches, To-si-withes=Tussawehe.
Toskegee=Taskigi.
Toskiroros=Tuscarora.
Tosoees, To-so-wates, Tosowes, To-sow-witches=Tussawehe.
TöstlEngilnagai'=Dostlan-lnagai.
Tosugui=Tesuque.
Totacaga=Tukhtukagi.
Totaly=Tutelo.
Totanteac=Hopi.
Totaro=Tutelo.
Totatik=Poodatook.
To-ta-t'-qenne=Totatkenne.
Toteloes=Tutelo.
Tote-pauf-cau=Tukpafka.
Totera, Toteri, Toteroes, Toteros=Tutelo.
Tothect=Totheet.

Totiakto=Totiakton.
Totierono, Totiri=Tutelo.
Totiris=Catawba.
Tŏtlgya gyit'inai=Tohlka-gitunai.
Toto=Totoma.
Totonaltam=Azqueltan.
Totonat=Sicobutovabia.
Totones, Totonie tribes=Tututni.
Totonteac, Totonteal, Totontoac=Hopi.
Totora=Tutelo.
Tototan, To-to-taws=Tututni.
Totōteac=Hopi.
Tototen, Tototin, Tototune, To-to-tut-na=Tututni.
To'tsalsitaya=Thochalsithaya.
To-tshik-o-tin=Trotsikkutchin.
Tótsik=Sacaton.
Ţǫ'tsoni=Thotsoni.
Tottero, Totteroy=Tutelo.
Totû=Totoma.
Totutime, Totutúne=Tututni.
Totzikala=Totchikala.
Touacara, Touacaro=Tawakoni.
Touacha=Tawasa.
Toüagannha=Ontwaganha.
Touanchain=Toanche.
Touaqdjuaq=Tuakdjuak.
To-ua-qua=Towakwa.
Touashes=Tawehash.
Touch not the skin of a black bear=Wasabehitazhi.
Touchon-ta-Kutchin, Touchon-tay Kutchin=Tutcho-nekutchin.
Touchouaesintons=Touchouasintons.
Touckagnokmiut=Tuklak.
Toudamans=Seneca.
Touenchain=Toanche.
Touginga=Tongigua.
Touguenhas=Ontwaganha.
Toukaubatchee=Tukabatchi.
Toukaways=Tonkawa.
Toulakságamut=Tuluksak.
Touloucs=Ottawa.
Toumachas, Toumika=Tunica.
Toungletats=Lekwiltok.
Tounica, Tounika=Tunica.
Touppa=Toupa.
Touquaht=Toquart.
Tourika=Tunica.
Tourimans=Tourima.
Tous=Taos.
Touscaroros=Tuscarora.
Touse=Taos.
Touserlemnies=Tuolumne.
Tous les Saints=Kandoucho.
Toustchipas=Tushepaw.
Toutacaugee=Tukhtukagi.
Touto Apaches=Tontos.
Toutounis, Tou-tou-ten=Tututunne.
Toux Enongogoulas=Avoyelles.
Touzas=Tuskegee.
Tovares=Tubare.
Towaahach=Tawehash.
Towacanies, Towacanno, Towacano, Towacarro, Towaccanie, Towaccaras=Tawakoni.
Towaches=Tawehash.
Towackanies, To-wac-ko-nies, To-wac-o-nies, Towacoro=Tawakoni.
Towaganha=Ontwaganha.
Towahach, Towahhans=Tawehash.
To-wă'-kă=Seneca.
Towákani, Tówakárehu, Towakarros, Towakenoe=Tawakoni.
Towako, Towakon=Ottawa.
To-wal-um-ne=Tuolumne.
Towanahiooks=Towahnahiooks.
Towanda=Twana.
Towannahiooks=Towahnahiooks.
Towanoendálough=Teatontaloga.
Towaꝑummuk=Shuswap.
Tō-wáꝑque=Taa.
Towarnaheooks, Towarnahiooks=Towahnahiooks.
Towarsa=Tawasa.
Towas=Hano, Tewa.
Towash=Tawehash.
Towawog=Nameaug.
Towcash, Tow-ce-ahge, Toweache, Toweash=Tawehash.
Toweca=Tawakoni.
Towecenegos=Sinago.

Tow-eeahge, Tow-eeash, Towiaches, Towiache-Tawakenoes=Tawehash.
Towiachs=Tawakoni.
Towiash=Tawehash.
Towigh, Towighroano=Miami.
Tôwíh=Taos.
To-win-ché-bă=Holkomah.
Tôwirnín=Taos.
Towish=Tawehash.
Town Builders, Town-building Indians, Town Indians=Pueblos.
Town of Relief=Aymay.
Town of the Broken Promise=Tomé.
Town of the winds=Pinawan.
Towns-people=Pueblos.
Towoash, Towoashe=Tawehash.
Towoccaroes, Towocconie, To-woc-o-roy Thycoes, Towoekonie=Tawakoni.
Towrache, Towzash=Tawehash.
To-ya=Nutria.
Toyagua=Tojagua.
Toyals=Tohaha.
Toyash=Tawehash.
Toyengan=Tongigua.
To-y-lee=Tsoowahlie.
Toyn-aht=Toquart.
To-yo-a-la-na=Heshota Ayahltona.
Toy Pah-Utes, Toy Pi-Utes, Toy'-yu-wi-ti-kut-teh=Toiwait.
To-žăn'-né=Laguna.
Tozikakat=Nuklukayet.
Tozjanne=Laguna.
T'Peeksin, T'Peekskin=Tapeeksin.
Tpelois=Natchez.
Tqlûn-qas' tûnnĕ'=Tkhlunkhastunne
Tqt'ā'qumai=Toktakamaĭ.
T'Qua-qua-mish=Tkwakwamish.
Tquayaum, Tquayum, Tqwayaum=Taqwayaum.
Traders=Ottawa.
Traht=Tyigh.
Tρa-kfwèlè-ρttinè=Takfwelottine.
Trakouaehronnons=Trak8aehronnons=Conestoga.
Tρaltsan Ottinè=Tatsanottine.
Tramasquecook=Tramasqueac.
Tρananœ-Kouttchin, Tρanata-Kuttchin'=Tenankutchin.
Tran-jik-koo-chin=Trotsikkutchin.
Tρa-pa-Gottinè=Nellagottine.
Trappers=Nanticoke.
Trascaluza=Tascalusa.
Tρathel-ottiné=Takfwelottine.
Tρatsan-Ottinè=Tatsanottine.
Tratsè-kutshi=Trotsikkutchin.
Traveling Hail=Passing Hail's Band.
Treaber Utes=Cumumbah.
Treacherous lodges=Ashbotchiah.
Trementinas=Tremblers.
Tρendjidheyttset-kouttchin=Tangeratsa.
Trēs-qūi-tā=Pohoi.
Tresrevere=Three Rivers.
Tρétlé-(k)uttchín, Tρe-tliet-Kouttchin=Tatlitkutchin.
Tρè-ttchié-dhidié-Kouttchin=Natsitkutchin.
Tria=Sia.
Triapé=Triapi.
Triconnick=Taconnet.
Trijaoga=Tioga.
Tρi-kka-Gottinè=Desnedeyarelottine.
Trile Kalets=Klikitat.
Trinachamiut=Trinachak.
Trinity Indians=Hupa.
Tρion-Kouttchin=Tangeratsa.
Trios=Sia.
Tripaniek=Tripanick.
Trivti, Triyti=Guatitruti.
Trizaoga=Tioga.
Troes=Zoe.
Trois Rivieres=Three Rivers.
Trokesen=Iroquois.
Trongsagroende=Tiosahrondion.
Tronontes=Tionontati.
Troquois=Iroquois.
Trout nation=Winnebago.
Trovmaxiaquino=Troomaxiaquino.
Troy Indians=Pocasset.
Troy River=Three Rivers.
Trudamans=Seneca.
True Thnaina=Knaiakhotana.

Truni=Zuñi.
Trypaniks=Tripanick.
Tsāagwī′ gyit'inai′=Djahui-gitinai.
Tsāagwīsguatl'adegai′=Djahui-skwahladagai.
Tsa-bah-bish, Tsa-bah-bobs=Dwamish.
Tsaba′kosh=Dakota.
Tsága'ha′=Tsaganha.
Tsah-bahbish=Dwamish.
Tsah-tû=Choctaw.
Tsāh′-tyuh=Tsattine.
Tsah-wau-tay-neuch, Tsah-waw-ti-neuch, Tsah-waw-
ty-neuchs=Tsawatenok.
Tsaisuma=Washo.
Tsakaitsetlins, Tsakaitsitlin=Spokan.
Tsă-kă-nhă-o-nän=Delaware.
T'sakbahbish=Dwamish.
Tsálagi, Tsalakies=Cherokee.
Tsalaχgásagi=Chillicothe.
Tsalel, Ts'ä -lil-ä′=Silela.
Tsä-ló-kee=Cherokee.
Tsa mpi′nefa amím=Chepenafa.
Tsan Ámpkua amím=Umpqua.
Tsan á-uta amím=Siuslaw.
Tsänh alokual amín=Calapooya.
Tsan halpam amím=Santiam.
Tsa′nish=Arikara.
Tsan kliχ temifa amim=Tsanklightemifa.
Tsanout=Tsawout.
Tsăn tcha′-ishna amím=Salmon River Indians.
Tsan tchä′lila amím=Silela.
Tsan tchiffin amim=Tsanchiffin.
Tsan tkupi amim=Tsankupi.
Tsan-tρié-ρottinè=Tsantieottine.
Tsanusi′yĭ=Quanusee.
Tsa-ottiné=Tsattine.
Tsapxádidlit=Tsapkhadidlit.
Tsaqtono=Tsaktono.
Tsárăgĭ=Cherokee.
Tsa-re-ar-to-ny=Kaltsergheatunne.
Tsar-out=Tsawout.
Tsashtlas=Siuslaw.
tsata-hēni=Tsatenyedi.
Ts'a′-ta-rxĕ-qe′ ʒŭnnĕ′=Tsatarghekhetunne.
T'saten, Tsa-'tenne, Tsa-tinneh=Tsattine.
Ts'átl lā′nas=Chaahl-lanas.
Tsa-tqenne=Tsattine.
Tsatsaquits=Tlatlasikoala.
Tsatsnotin, Tsatsuotin=Tanotenne.
Tsa-ttinnè=Tsattine.
Tsāūāt'ēnoq=Tsawatenok.
Tsa′-u-i=Chaui.
Tsa′umâk=Tzauamuk.
Tsaumass=Songish.
Tsauwarits=Tsuwaraits.
Tsawadainoh, Tsawahtee, Tsawalinough, Tsawan-
tiano, Tsa-wanti-e-neuh, Tsawataineuk, Tsā′wa-
tE′ēnoq, Ts'ā′watEēnôx, Tsawatli, Tsa-waw-ti-e-
neuk=Tsawatenok.
Tsa-whah-sen=Talal.
Tsáwi=Chaui.
Tsä′-wut-ai-nuk, Tsa-wutt-i-e-nuh, Tsá-wutti-i-nuh=
Tsawatenok.
Tsaxta=Choctaw.
Tsa′yiskíρni, Tsa′yĭskĭ′đni=Tsayiskithni.
Tschah=Hagwilget.
Tschahtas=Muskhogean Family.
Tschaktaer=Choctaw.
Tscharai=Charac.
Tscha-wa-co-nihs=Chawakoni.
Tscha-wan-ta=Tashhuanta.
Tschechschequannink, Tschechschequanüng, Tsch-
echsequannink=Sheshequin.
Tschernowskoje=Chernofski.
Tschetschehn=Tesik.
Tschih-nahs=Tsano.
Tschihri=Pawnee.
Tschilkat, Tschílkāt-kŏn=Chilkat.
Tschilkut=Chilkoot.
Tschinjagmjut=Chingigmiut.
Tschinkaten=Tenankutchin.
Tschinuk=Chinook, Chinookan Family.
Tschipeway, Tschippiweer=Chippewa.
Tschirokesen=Cherokee.
Tschischlkhathkhoan, Tschishlkháth, Tschishlkháth-
khóan=Chilkat.
Tschlahtsoptschs=Clatsop.
Tschnagmeuten, Tschnagmjuten, Tschnägmüten=
Chnagmiut.
Tschuagmuti=Malemiut.

Tschugatschi, Tschugazzes, Tschugazzi=Chuga-
chigmiut.
tschūkanē′di=Chukanedi.
Tschunguscetoner=Tschantoga.
Tschura, Tschura-Allequas=Tsurau.
Tsclallums=Clallam.
Ts′-co=Cheli.
Tsea, Tse-ah=Sia.
Tsĕ Áminĕma=Tyigh.
Ts'ēcā′ath=Seshart, Tseshaath.
Tse′đañka′=Haninihkashina.
Tse′đeckíjni=Tsetheshkizhni.
Tse′çqáni=Tsethkhani.
Tse′dĕskĭ′zni=Tsetheshkizhni.
Tse′dzĭnkĭ′ni=Tsezhinkini.
Tseghi=Chelly.
Tsēgoatl lā′nas=Djiguaahl-lanas.
Tsehalish=Chehalis.
Tse-hwit-zen=Tsewhitzen.
Tse-itso-kit=Mishongnovi.
Tse-itso-kĭt′-bĭt-si′-li=Shipaulovi.
Tse′jinđiài, Tse′jinđiàiđine=Tsezhinthiai.
Tse′jinkíni=Tsezhinkini.
Tsekaníe=Sekani.
Tsé-kéh-na=Tsekehneaz.
Tsé′kéhne, T'sekenné=Sekani.
Tsé-ki-a-tán-yi=Cueva Pintada.
Tsekum, Tse-kun=Tsehump.
Tsĕ 'la′kayat amím=Klikitat.
Tsé-loh-ne=Tselone.
Tsemakum=Chimakum.
Tse-mo-é=Sitsime.
Ts'emŝia′n=Tsimshian.
Tse′nahapĭ′lni=Tsenahapihlni.
Ts'E′nq'am=Tsenkam.
Ts'E′ntsEnHk'aiō, Ts'E′nts'Enx·qaiō, Tsĝnχq'aiō=
Tsentsenkaio.
Ts'ē′okuimîX=Tseokuimik.
Tsepechoen frercuteas=Semonan, Serecoutcha.
Tsepcoen, Tsepehoen, Tsepehouen=Semonan.
Tserabocherete, Tserabocretes=Bocherete, Tsera.
Tse-ρottinè=Tseottine.
Ts'e-rxi′-ä ʒŭnnĕ=Kaltsergheatunne.
Tsé-ŝa do-ħpa-ka, Tsé-sa no-ħpa-ka=Pawnee.
Tsesh-aht=Seshart.
Tsĕ Skuálli amím=Nisqualli.
Tse-ta-hwo-tqenne, Tsé′-ta-ut'qenne = Tsetaut-
kenne.
Tsétcah=Tsechah.
Ts'e-t'çĭm=Tsetthim.
Tse-tdóa=Tse.
Tse′tháni=Tsethkhani.
Tse-tis-tas′=Cheyenne.
TsētsēLoā′laqEmaē=Tsetsetloalakemae.
Tsēts gyit'inai′=Chetsgitunai.
Tset-so-kít=Mishongnovi.
Tse ʒuʹ χa=Tsedtuka.
Tse-tût′-qla-le-ni′tûn=Tsetutkhlalenitun.
Ts'ē′uîtx=Tseokuimik.
Tse-xi′-ä tĕné=Kaltsergheatunne.
Tsǫxltĕn=Tseklten.
Tse′yanaċò′ni, Tse′yanatóni=Tseyanathoni.
Tse′yikéheđine, Tse′yikéhedĭne'=Tseyikehe.
Tse′zĭnđiaí=Tsezhinthiai.
T'shah-nee=Tsano.
T'shanasanákue=Laguna.
T'shashita′-kwe=Isleta.
Tsheheilis=Chehalis.
Tshei-nik-kee=Chainiki.
Tshe-tsi-uetin-euerno=Montagnais.
Tshi-a-uip-a=Isleta.
Tshilkotin=Tsilkotin.
Tshimsian=Chimmesyan Family.
Tshingits, Tshinkitani=Tlingit.
Tshinook=Chinookan Family.
Tshinook, Tshinouk=Chinook.
Tshinuk=Chinookan Family.
Tshi-quit-é=Pecos.
Tshishé=Apache.
Tshithwyook=Chilliwhack.
Tshokfachtolígamut=Shokfak.
Tshokoyem=Chokuyem.
Tshoo-loos′=Tsulus.
Ts-ho-ti-non-do-wă′′-gä′=Seneca.
Tshugazzi=Chugachigmiut.
Tshu-kutshi=Tsitoklinotin.
Tshya-ui-pa=Isleta.
Tsia=Sia.

Tsi′-a-qaus′=Tsiakhaus.
Tsīchoan=Shakan.
Tsiou Sĭnɉsaɧǿě=Tsishusindtsakdhe.
Tsi′ou uɉsé peǿŭⁿᵈda=Tsishuutsepedhungpa.
Tsi′ou Wacta′ɧe=Tsishuwashtake.
Tsiou Wanŭⁿ′=Tsishusindtsakdhe.
Tsi′ou wehaɧįǿe=Haninihkashina.
Tsi-ê′-qă we-yaǫl′=Tsiekhaweyathl.
Tsifeno=Shufina.
Tsi′haciⁿ=Kᵈhun.
Tsihaili=Salishan Family.
Tsihaili-Selish=Chehalis, Salishan Family.
Tsihailish, Tsihalis=Chehalis.
Tsi-háno=Tsina.
Tsi-he-lis=Chehalis.
Tsi′-ka-cě=Chickasaw.
Tsikanni=Sekani.
Tsi-klum=Tsehump.
Tsĭksi′tsĭ=Tuckaseegee.
Tsĭk-û-sû=Chickasaw.
Tsĭkyätitans′=Cueva Pintaᵈa.
Tsilgopáya, Tsilgopeya=Tulkepaia.
Tsilhtáděn=Tsiltaden.
Tsĭ′l-ĭná-inde=Tsihlinainde.
Tsiḳoh′ton, T silkotinneh=Tsilkotin.
Tsilla-ta-ut′ tiné, Tsilla-ta-ut′-tinné, Tsillawadoot, Tsillaw-awdoot, Tsillaw-awdút-dinni, Tsillawdawhoot-dinneh, Tsillawdawhoot Tinneh=Etcheridiegottine.
Tsiltarden=Tsiltaden.
Tsimchian, T′simpheeans, Tsimpsean, T′simpshean, T′simpsheean, Tsimsean, Tsimseyans, Tsimsheeans, T′sim-si-an′=Tsimshian.
Tsimuna=Paraje.
Tsinadₐĭ′ni=Tsinazhini.
Tsinaghse=Shamokin.
Tsinajíni=Tsinazhini.
Tsinǫòbetlo=Tsinthobetlo.
Tsínha=Tsina.
Tsin-ik-tsis′-tso-yiks=Tsiniksistsoyiks.
Tsinsaká¢ni, Tsinsakáᵈni=Tsinsakathni.
Tsinuk=Chinook.
Tsinuk, T′sinuk=Chinookan Family.
Tsinusios=Geneseo.
Ts′iomxau=Tsiomhau.
Tsiphenu=Shufina.
Tsipú=Chippewa.
TsiQuä′gis stastaai′=Chawagis-stustae.
Tsi′-se′=Mescaleros.
Tsistlatho band=Naskotin.
Tsí taka dō ḻipa ka=Seechkaberuhpaka.
Tsitka-ni=Sekani.
Tsītsîmē′lᴇqala=Tsitsimelekala.
Tsitsk=Hagwilget.
Tsi-tská d¢o-qpá-ka=Seechkaberuhpaka.
Tsitsumevi, Tsi-tsumo-vi, Tsitúmovi=Sichomovi.
Tsitz-hanutch=Tsits.
Tsíwiltzha-e=Osage.
Tsiχ′-χaⁿ′-ä=Tzekinne.
Tsji′shekwe=Tontos.
Tsjoemakákork=Tumacacori.
Tskaus=Sakahl.
Tskiri rah′ru=Skidirahru.
Tsnagmyut=Chnagmiut.
Tsnasogh=Shamokin.
Tsniuk=Chinook.
Tsœs-tsieg-Kᵤttchin=Trotsikkutchin.
Tsogliakhten, Tsogliakten=Zogliakten.
Tsohke=Sooke.
Tsohkw=Tsako.
Tsoi-gah=Nez Percés.
Tso-is-kai=Chusca.
Tsomass=Tsomosath.
Tsomontatez=Tionontati.
Tsomō′oʟ=Tsomootl.
Tsonagogliakten, Tsonagolyakhten=Zonagogliakten.
Tsonantonon=Seneca.
Tsonassan=Sewathen.
Tsong=Songish.
Tsoⁿ-krône=Thekkane.
T. Sonnontatex=Tionontati.
Tsonnonthouans, T. Son-non-thu-ans=Seneca.
Tsonnontouan=Nundawao.
T. Sonnontouans, Tsononthouans, Tsonontooas, Tsonontouans, Tsonontowans, Tsonothouans=Seneca.

Tson-tₚié-ₚottinè=Tsantieottine.
Tsoo-ah-gah-rah=Nez Percés.
Tsoolootum=Nakuntlun.
Tsoo-tsī-ola=Tsutsiola.
Tsô-Ottinè=Sarsi.
Tsoo-Yess=Tzues.
Ts′ōtsQᴇⁿN=Tsimshian.
Tsouonthousaas=Seneca.
Tsou-wa′-ra-its=Tsuwaraits.
Tsowassan=Sewathen.
Tsoyaha=Yuchi.
TsQoaQk·ā′nē=Tskoakane.
Tsuess=Tzues.
Tsuhárukats=Nez Percés.
Tsuk-tsuk-kwālk′=Chuckchuqualk.
Tsûlakkĭ=Cherokee.
Tsulula′=Chilula.
Tsûn-′na-kǿi′-ă-mĭt′çă=Tsunakthiamittha.
T′sunük=Chinook.
Tsū′Qōs=Sarsi.
Tsuquanah=Tsooquahna.
Ts′û-qus-li′-qwŭt-me′ ɉŭnně=Dakubetede.
Tsŭshki=Shrutsuna.
Tsuskai=Chusca.
Tsussie=Yekolaos.
Tsútpĕli=Nez Percés.
Ts′uwä′le=Tsoowahlie.
Tsuχódi=Chutotalgi.
Tsúyakē′ks, Tsuyakē′ksni=Shuyakeksh.
Tsū-yess=Tzues.
Tsuyu′gilâ′gĭ=Oothcaloga.
Tsxoaxqá′né=Tskoakane.
Ttikigakg=Tikera.
T′tran-jik kutch-in=Tangesatsa.
Ttsé-ottiné=Tseottine.
Ttutaho=Tutago.
Ttynai, Ttynai-chotana, Ttynnaï=Athapascan Family.
Tuacana=Tawakoni.
Tu-ád-hu=Twana.
Tuagenha=Ontwaganha.
Tualati, Tualatims, Tualatin, Tuality=Atfalati.
Tu-an-hu, Tu-a-nooch, Tu-a-noock=Twana.
Tuape=Toape.
Tuas, Tú′ata=Taos.
Tu-a-wi-hol=Santo Domingo.
Tubaca, Tubáe=Tubac.
Tubar, Tubaris=Tubare.
Tubbies=Choctaw.
Tubeans=Tano.
Tubessias=Yavapai
Tubians=Tano.
Tü-bic wuñ-wü=Tubish.
Tubirans=Tano.
Tubso, Tubson=Tucson.
Tubuache=Tabeguache.
Tubukhtuligmut, Tubuktuligmiut=Tubuktulik.
Tuçan=Hopi.
Tucane=Tucara.
Tucano=Hopi.
Tucanoh=Twana.
Tucaricas=Tukuarika.
Tucayan=Hopi.
Tuccabatche, Tuchabatchees=Tukabatchi.
Tuchano=Hopi.
Tuchapacs, Tuchapaks=Tushepaw.
Tucharechee=Tikwalitsi.
Tuchimas=Tuchiamas.
Tuchsaghrondie=Tiosahrondion.
Tuckaabatchees, Tuckabatcha, Tuckabatche=Tukabatchi.
Tuckabatchee Teehassa=Taluamutchasi.
Tuckabatches, Tuckabatchie, Tuckabatchy, Tuckabathees, Tuckafaches=Tukabatchi.
Tuckalegee=Tikwalitsi.
Tuckankanie=Tawakoni.
Tuckapacks=Tushepaw.
Tuckapas, Tuckapaus=Tukabatchi.
Tuckarechee=Tikwalitsi.
Tuckasegee=Tuckaseegee.
Tuck-a-Soof-Curra=Tsofkara.
Tuckaubatchees, Tuckhabatchee=Tukabatchi.
Tuckis′a′tñ=Tushkisath.
Tucknapax=Tushepaw.
Tucksagrandie=Tiosahrondion.
Tucpauska=Tukpafka.
Tucremu=Tucumu.
Tucsares=Tucsani.
Tucsson=Tucson.

Tucubavi=Tucubavia.
Tucutnut=Tukutnut.
Tucuvavi=Tucubavia.
Tuczon=Tucson.
Tudamanes=Seneca.
Tûde=Athapascan Family.
Tudnunirmiut=Tununirmiut.
Tudnunirossirmiut=Tununirusirmiut.
Tuecuntallauhassee=Pakan-Tallahassee.
Ṭü-ei=Isleta.
Tuenho=Hastwiana.
Tueson=Tucson.
Tugiak, Tugiatak=Togiak.
Tugibáχtchi=Tukabatchi.
Tugilo=Tugaloo.
Tugson, Tuguison=Tucson.
Tuhakwilh=Tsimshian.
Tú-hau-cu-wi'-t'çĕ=Tuhaushuwitthe.
Tu'hlawai=Acoma.
Tuh'-mu=Tucumu.
Tuhoa=Jemez.
Tu-huc-mach, Tu-hue-ma-ches, Tu-huk-nahs=Tu-hukmache.
Tuhuktukis=Tawakoni.
Tuhutama=Tubutama.
Tǔ'hǔ tane=Clackama.
Tuhúvti-ómokat=Siksika.
Tuhwalati=Atfalati.
Tuh-yit-yay=Tajique.
Tu'-iai=Santo Domingo.
Tuighsaghrondy=Tiosahrondion.
Tuihtuihronoons=Miami.
Tuinondadecks, Tuinontatek=Tionontati.
Tuison=Tucson.
Tukabaches, Tukabatchey, Tukabaχtchi=Tukabatchi.
Tukachohas=Piankashaw.
Tükahun=Piros.
Ḷu'-ka-le, Tú-ka-nyi=Tawakoni.
Tuka-ríka=Tukuarika.
Tu'-katc-katc=Tukachkach.
Tukawbatchie, Tukkebatche=Tukabatchi.
Tǔk'-ko=Takusalgi.
Tukkola=Takulli.
Tuk-kuth=Tukkuthkutchin.
Tûk-pa' haⁿ-ya-di'=Attacapa.
Tûkspû'sh, Tûkspûsh-'lĕma=John Day.
Tukudh=Tukkuthkutchin.
Tükuhun=Piros.
Tǔ'-kwǐl-mä'-k'ǐ=Kuitsh.
Tula, Tulara, Tulare Lake Indians, Tulare River Indians, Tularesin=Tulareños.
Tulas=Titlas.
Tülawéi=Acoma.
Tul'bush=Mattole.
T'ulck=Tulshk.
Tule=Tulareños.
Tulinskoe=Tulik.
Tulkays=Tuluka.
Tulkepaia venuna tche'hwhale=Tulkepaia.
Tulla=Tula.
T'ûl-li'-mǔks-mé χûnnĕ=Tillamook.
Tulloolah=Tallulah.
Tu-lo-kai'-di-sel, Tulukagnagamiut=Tuluka.
Tuluksagmiut=Tuluksak.
Tulumono=Tulomos.
Tuluraios=Tulareños.
Ḷûl-wût'-me=Tulwutmetunne.
Túlʸkapáyᵃ=Tulkepaia.
Tuma family=Yuman Family.
Tumangamalum=Gabrieleño.
Tumayas=Yuma.
Tumecha=Tunicha.
Tumeh=Athapascan Family.
Tumewand=Mahican.
Tumican=Timucua.
Tumicha=Tunicha.
Tumitl=Amaikiara.
Túmmai mámpka wé-i peyaktchímmem=Warm Spring Indians.
Tum-mault-lau=Tamali.
Tummewatas=Clowwewalla.
Tumpiros=Tompiro.
TumQoā'akyas=Tumkoaakyas.
Tumwater=Clowwewalla.
Tunaghamiut=Tunagak.
Tu'-na-ji-i'=Santa Ana.
Tu'-naⁿ-p'iⁿ=Tunanpin.

Tŭnavwá=Sia.
Tuncas=Tunica.
Tuncksis=Tunxis.
Tungāss, Tungāss-kŏn=Tongas.
Tung-ke=Tungge.
Tungrass=Tongas.
Tunicas=Tonikan Family.
Tu-ni'-cka aⁿ-ya-di', Tu-ni'-cka haⁿ-yá, Tunik8a=Tunica.
Tuniqdjuait=Tornit.
Tunis=Zuñi.
Tûnnĕ=Athapascan Family.
Tunniakhpuk=Tuniakpuk.
Tunque=Tungge.
Tunscas=Tunica.
Tuntu šuxtana=Algemiut.
Tununuk=Tanunak.
Tuolomo=Tulomos.
Tuolumne Indians, Tuolumnes=Tuolumne.
Tuopá=Taos.
Tuozon=Tucson.
Tupanagos=Timpaiavats.
Tupes=Ditsakana.
Tuphamikhuagmut, Tup-hamikva, Tup-hamikwa, Tup-hanikwa=Topanika.
Tuphulga=Attapulgas.
Tup-ka-ak=Topkok.
Tup-kug-ameuts=Tapkachmiut.
Tups=Tupo.
Tuqe'-nikaci'χa=Tukhenikashika.
Tuqte'umi=Atuami.
Tuquison, Tuqulson=Tuscon.
T'û'-qwe-t'a'χûnnĕ'=Tututni.
Turcaroras=Tuscarora.
Turealemnes=Tuolumne.
Turi-ca-chi=Teuricachi.
Turkey-Home, Turkey Town=Pinhoti.
Turkey tribe of the Delawares=Unalachtigo.
Turlitan=Atfalati.
Turnip Mountain=Turniptown.
Turn water=Stehtsasamish.
Turrurar, Turruraw=Tallulah.
Turtle gens=Kenikashika.
Turtle Mountain band=Mikinakwadshiwininiwak.
Turtle tribe of the Delawares=Unami.
Tû-rxĕstl' tsa'-tûn=Turghestltsatun.
Tusabe=Jicarilla.
Tusachrondie=Tiosahrondion.
Tu-sahn=Tzlanapah.
Tusan=Hopi.
Tusayan=Hopi, Tzlanapah.
Tusayan Moqui=Hopi.
Tuscagee=Taskigi.
Tuscalaways=Tuscarawas.
Tusca Loosa, Tuscaluca=Tascalusa.
Tuscarara, Tuscararo=Tuscarora.
Tuscarawi=Tuscarawas.
Tuscareras, Tuscarooroes=Tuscarora.
Tuscarorans, Tuscaroras=Tuscarawas.
tusCarorase, Tuscaroraw, Tuscarore hága, Tuscarorens, Tuscarores, Tuscarories, Tuscaroroes, Tuscarow=Tuscarora.
Tuscarowas=Tuscarawas.
Tuscarura, Tuscaruro=Tuscarora.
Tuscavoroas=Tuscarawas.
Tus-che-pas=Tushepaw.
Tuscoraras=Tuscarora.
Tuscorawas=Tuscarawas.
Tuscorora, Tuscororoes, Tuscoroura, Tuscorure, Tuscouroro=Tuscarora.
Tu-se-an=Hopi.
Tusehatche.=Fusihatchi.
Tushapaws, Tus-he-pah, Tushepahas, Tushepau, Tushepaw Flatheads=Tushepaw.
Tushhanushagota=Yoroonwago.
Tushsaghrendie=Tiosahrondion.
Tushshepah=Tushepaw.
Tûsh-yit-yay=Tajique.
Tû'sikweo=Tasikoyo.
Tus-kai'-yĕⁿ', Tus-kă-o-wäⁿ', Tuskararo=Tuscarora.
Tuskarawas=Tuscarawas.
Tuskaroes, Tuskarooroe, Tuskarora, Tuskaroraha, Tuskarorers, Tuskarores, Tuskarorins, Tuskaroro, Tuskawres=Tuscarora.
Tuskeegies, Tuskeego=Tuskegee.
Tuskege, Tuskegee=Taskigi.
T'us-ke-ó-wäⁿ', Tuskeroode, Tuskeruda, Tuskeruros, Tuskierores=Tuscarora.

Tuskíki, Tuskogee=Tuskegee.
Tuskoraries, Tuskorore=Tuscarora.
Tuskowellow=Tuskawillao.
Tuskroroes, Tusks=Tuscarora.
Tuskugu=Tuskegee.
Tuskurora=Tuscarora.
Tuskwawgomeeg=Nipissing.
Tu-sla, Tu-sla-na-pa, Tu-slan-go=Tzlanapah.
Tusonimó=Tusonimon.
Tûs-qlûs' ạûnnê'=Tuskhlustunne.
Tusquarores, Tusqueroro=Tuscarora.
Tusquittee=Tusquittah.
Tussaghrondie=Tiosahrondion.
Tussapa, Tussapas=Tushepaw.
Tussee=Tawsee.
Tusskegee=Taskigi.
Tussoninio=Tusonimon.
Tustans=Tustur.
Tûs'-ta-tûn qụ'-u-cĭ=Tustatunkhuushi.
Tusuque=Tesuque.
Tus'-wă=Fusualgi.
Tusyan=Hopi.
Tutahuca=Tutahaco.
Tu-taiina=Tu.
Tutaliaco=Tutahaco.
Tutaloes=Tutelo.
Tutatamys=Tututni.
Tutchaco=Tutahaco.
Tŭt-chohn'-kŭt-chin, Tutchóne-Kutchin, Tutchone-kut'qin, Tutchon Kutchin, Tŭtch-ŭn-tah' kŭtchĭn, Tŭtcone-kut'qin=Tutchonekutchin.
Tutecoes, Tuteeves, Tutelas, Tútele=Tutelo.
Tu Thĭnĭ=Pueblos.
Tuthla-huay, Tuth-la-nay=Acoma.
Tūtie, Tutiloes=Tutelo.
Tutiritucar=Uturituc.
Tutloe=Tutelo.
Tutoi band=Nahaego.
Tutoten=Tututni.
Tu-tsän-nde=Lipan.
Tut-seé-wâs=Tushepaw.
Tutsógemut=Tachik.
Tûtsoni=Thotsoni.
Tuttago=Tutago.
Tuttallasee, Tut-tal-leo-see, Tut-tal-lo-see=Tutalosi.
Tuttelars, Tuttelee=Tutelo.
Ḷu'-tu=Tututunne.
Tutuhaco=Tutahaco.
Tutulor=Tutelo.
Tutunah=Tututni.
Tutunitucan=Uturituc.
Tututamys, Tū-tūten=Tututni.
Tutu' těne', Tu-tū-to-ni=Tututunne.
Tutzose=Tutzone.
Tuuk-soon=Tucson.
Tuvalím=Tubare.
Tuvasak=Toviscanga.
Tuvatci wiñwû=Tuvachi.
Túvën=Tano.
Tuvoû wiñwû=Tuvou.
Tü-vü-tci wün-wû=Tuvachi.
Tuwaẉaríwa=Tawakoni.
Tịuwânxa-îꞣc=Klikitat.
Tü-wa' nyû-mû, Tü-wa wüñ-wü=Tuwa.
Tüwi'-ai, Túwii=Santo Domingo.
Tuwirát=Taos.
Tuwita, Tüwiχuide=Santo Domingo.
Tuxaxa=Tohaha.
Tuxeque=Tareque.
Tûxezê'p=Tuhezep.
Tüχguêt, Túχkanne=Wichita.
Túχtchênóyika=Detsanayuka.
Tuχtu-kági=Tukhtukagi.
Túyětchískě=Dakota.
Tuzan=Hopi.
Tuzhune=Pusune.
Twa''ga'hă'=Ontwaganha.
Twă-kă'-nhă'=Chippewa.
Twakanhahors=Missisauga.
Twalaties, Twalaty, Twalites, Twallalty, Twaltatines=Atfalati.
Twanoh, Twanug=Twana.
Twechtweys, Tweeghtwees=Miami.
Twě'tĭnĭ'nde=Tuetinini.
Twghtwees, Twichtwees, Twichtwichs, Twichtwicks, Twichtwighs, Twichwiches, Twicktwicks, Twicktwigs, Twictwees, Twictwicts, Twight, Twightees, Twighteeys, Twighties, Twightwees, Twightwicks, Twightwies, Twightwighs, Twightwis Roanu, Twigtees, Twigthtwees, Twig-Twee, Twigtwicks, Twig-

twies, Twigtwig, Twiswicks, Twitchwees, Twithuays Ḷwĭ'twĭtheno͞'=Miami.
Two Cauldrons, Two Kettles=Oohenonpa.
Two-Mountain Iroquois=Oka.
Two Rille band=Oohenonpa.
Two-took-e-ways=Tututunne.
Twowakanie, Twowokana, Twowokauaes = Tawakoni.
Tχaiwa'tχsh=Lower Chinook.
Tx·ē'ix·tskune=Theiktskune.
Tyacappa, Tyakappan=Tyacappan.
Tya-me, Tyámi=Dyami.
Tyaoga=Tioga.
Tycappans=Tyacappan.
Tychedas=Taisida.
Tyeachten=Chiaktel.
Tye of Deshute, Tygh, Tyh, Ty-ich, Tyicks=Tyigh.
Tykothee, Tykothee-dinneh=Tukkuthkutchin.
Tymahse=Tomassee.
Tymangoua=Timucua.
Tyndysiukhtana=Aglemiut.
Tyoga=Tioga.
Tyo-na-wen-det=Tonawanda.
Tyo'nesíyo'=Geneseo.
Tyo-non-ta-te-ka=Tionontati.
Tyopari=Teopari.
Typoxies=Siyante.
Tyschsarondia=Tiosahrondion.
Tzaharagamut, Tzahavagamut, Tzahavagamute= Tzahavek.
Tzah-dinneh=Tsattine.
Tzeachten=Chiaktel.
Tzedoa=Tse.
Tzěj-glá=Coyoteros.
Tzěj-in-né=Tzecheschinne.
Tzek-iat-a-tanyi=Cueva Pintada.
Tze-kinne=Pima.
Tzen-o-cué=Senecu.
Tze-ojua=Tse.
Tzia=Sia.
Tzibola=Hawikuh.
Tzi-gu-ma, Tzi-gu-may=Cienega.
t'Zi-i=Sii.
Tzinachini=Tsinazhini.
Tzina hanutch=Tsina.
Tzi-na-ma-a=Mohave.
Tzip-ia Kue=Tsipiakwe.
Tzi-quit-é=Pecos.
Tzi-re-ge=Tshirege.
Tzis-eque-tzillan=Tziseketzillan.
Tzoes=Zoe.
Tzulukis=Cherokee.

Ua-buna-tota=Shipapulima.
U-aha=Omaha.
Ualana=Picuris.
Uala-to-hua, Ual-to-hua=Jemez.
Uash-pa Tze-na=Huashpatzena.
Ubate=Tano.
Ubchacha=Oglala.
Ubu=Yupu.
Uburiqui=Imuris.
Uca=Yukian Family.
Uẹachile=Osachile.
Ucaltas=Lekwiltok.
Uchagmjut=Uchak.
Uché=Uchean Family.
Uchees=Uchean Family, Yuchi.
Uches=Yuchi.
Uchesees=Lower Creeks.
Uchi'chol=Ochechote.
Uchies=Yuchi.
Uchipweys=Chippewa.
Uchres=Yukichetunne.
Uchulta=Lekwiltok.
Uchys=Yuchi.
Ucista=Ucita.
U-cle-ta=Lekwiltok.
Ucle-tah=Lekwiltok, Ucluelet.
Ucletes=Lekwiltok.
Uclúlet=Ucluelet.
Uctetahs=Lekwiltok.
Uculta=Lekwiltok, Tsakwalooin.
Ŭ'-cü wuñ-wü=Ushu.
Udáwak=Ottawa.
Uěch-ē-nēěti=Kuhinedi.
Ueena-caw=Huna.
Ufalees, Ufallahs, Ufallays, Ufallees, Ufaula, Ufauley Ufawlas, Ufewles=Eufaula.

Ugāgŏg′mūt==Ugagogmiut.
Ugaguk==Igagik.
Ugajuk==Uyak.
Ugakhpa==Quapaw.
Ugalachmiuti, Ugalakmutes, Ugalakmutsi, Ugalen-
  schen, Ugalensé, Ugalents, Ugalentse, Ugaléntsi,
  Ugalentze, Ugalenz, Ugalenze, Ugalenzi, Ugaljach-
  mjuten, Ugaljachmutzi==Ugalakmiut.
Ugaijachmutzi == Esquimauan Family, Ugalak-
  miut.
Ugalukmute, Ugalyachmusti, Ugalyachmutsi, Ugal-
  yachmutzi, Ugalyackh-mutsi==Ugalakmiut.
Uganak==Uganik.
Ugaqpa, U-gá-qpa-qti==Quapaw.
Ugas′hig-mūt==Ugashigmiut.
Ugavigamiut, Ugavik==Ugovik.
Ugáχpa, Ugaχpáχti==Quapaw.
Ugiú-ug==Biorka.
Ugjulik==Ugjulirmiut.
Uglaamie==Utkiavi.
Uglariaq==Uglariak.
Uglivia==Uglovaia.
Ugluxlatuch==Ucluelet.
Ugnasik==Unga.
Ugokhamiut==Uchak.
Ugovigamute==Ugovik.
Uguiug==Beaver.
Uhaiak==Akhiok.
Uh-kos-is-co==Aucocisco.
Uhlchako==Ilkatsho.
U-i-kayi ′lako==Wikaithlako.
Uinakhtagewik==Uinuk.
Uintah Valley Indians, U′-in-tats==Uinta.
Uitanons==Wea.
Ui-ukufki==Weogufka.
Ujañge wakixe==Manyinka.
Uj-e-jauk==Ojeejok.
Ujuiapa==Ujuiap.
Uka==Yukian Family, Yukichetunne.
Ukadliq, Ukadlix==Ukadlik.
Ukagamut==Ukak.
Ukāg′emūt==Ukagemiut.
U-kăh-pû==Quapaw.
Ukak==Ikak.
U-ka-nakane==Okinagan.
Uχáqpa==Quapaw.
Uχąa′qpa-qti==Ukakhpakhti.
Uχąqpaqti==Quapaw.
Ŭkasa, Ukasak==Kansa.
U-ka′-she==Mandan.
Ukdschulik, Ukdshúlik==Ugjulirmiut.
Uk-hōat-nom, Uk′hotnom==Ukohtontilka.
Ukiahs, Ukias==Yokaia.
Ukies==Yukian Family.
Ukiolik==Ukiadliving.
Ukivak==Ukivok.
Ukivŏg-mūt, Ukivokgmut, Ukivokmiut==Ukivog-
  miut.
Ukivuk, Ukiwuk==Ukivok.
Ukla falaya==Oklafalaya.
Uknadak==Uknodok.
Ukshivkag-miut==Ukshivikak.
Ukuáyata==Ottawa.
Uk-um-nom==Ukomnom.
Ukunadok==Uknodok.
Ukusiksalik, Ukusiksalingmiut, Ukusiksillik==Uku-
  siksalirmiut.
Ukvikhtuligmut==Ukviktulik.
Ukwû′nĭ, Ukwû′nû==Oconee.
Ulamánusĕk==Olamon.
Ulastĕkwi==Malecite.
U-lè-ò-wà==Oraibi.
Ulezaiamiut==Ulezara.
Ulibahali==Ullibahali.
Ulkies==Yukian Family.
Ullibalies, Ullibalys==Ullibahali.
Ullulatas==Olulato.
Ulnōbah, Ulnŏ mequāegit==Beothukan Family.
Ulokagmiut==Ulokak.
Ulseah==Alsea.
Ultschna==Kulchana.
Ultsehaga, Ultsehua==Eskimo.
Ultz-chna==Kulchana.
Ulucas==Guilitoy.
Ulukagmuts==Ulukakhotana.
Ulukak==Ulukuk.
Ulukuk==Ulukakhotana.
Ululato==Olulato.
U′lûñ′yĭ==Turniptown.

U-ma-"ha"==Omaha.
Umahs==Yuma.
Umanaqluaq, Umanaqtuaq, Umanaqtusq, Umanaχ-
  tuaχ==Umanaktuak.
U-manhan==Omaha.
Umanos==Tawehash.
Ŭmashgohak==Creeks.
Umatila==Umatilla.
Umbaquâ, Umbiqua==Umpqua.
Umeas, Umene==Yuma.
Umerik==Umivik.
Umguas==Umpqua.
Ŭmi′k==Ahmik.
Umkwa, Ŭm′-kwa-me′ ʒûnnĕ==Umpqua.
Umnak==Nikolski.
Um-nok-a-luk-ta==Umnokalukta.
Umpame==Patuxet.
Umpaquah==Umpqua.
Umpkwa, Umpqua==Kuitsh.
Umpquahs proper, Umpqua Irins, Umqua, Umques==
  Umpqua.
Um-too-leaux==Humptulip.
Umudjek==Eiwhuelit.
Unachog==Patchoag.
Unagoungas==Abnaki.
Unagtuligmut==Ungalik.
Unakagamut==Unakagak.
Unakatana, Unakatana Yunakakhotana==Unakho-
  tana.
Unaktolik==Ungalik.
Unalachleet==Unalaklik.
Unalâchtgo, Unalachtin==Unalachtigo.
Unalaklit==Unalaklik.
Unalaschkaer==Unalaska.
Unalaska==Iliuliuk.
Unāleet==Unaligmiut.
Unalginskoe==Unalga.
Unaliskans==Unalaska.
Unamines, Unamini==Unami.
Unangan==Aleut, Esquimauan Family.
Unatagua, Unataguous, Unataquas==Anadarko.
Unatolik==Ungalik.
Unaungna==Chowigna.
Uncachage==Patchoag.
Uncachogue==Poosepatuck.
Uncaway==Uncowa.
Unchagogs, Unchechauge, Uncheckauke==Patchoag.
Uncoes==Wasco.
Uncompahgre==Tabeguache.
Uncoway==Uncowa.
Unc-pah-te==Hunkpatina.
Uncpapa, Uncpappas==Hunkpapa.
Uncpatina==Hunkpatina.
Undatoma′tendi==Potawatomi.
Unéchtgo==Nanticoke.
Unedagoes==Onondaga.
Unescapis, Ungava Indians==Nascapee.
Ungavamiut==Tahagmiut.
Ungiayó-rono==Seminole.
Uñi′in==Unisak.
Unijaima==Unyijaima.
Unikwa==Umpqua.
Un-ka-pa==Unkapanukuints.
Unkar kauagats-Ta-Nouts==Unkakaniguts.
Unka-toma==Unkapanukuints.
Uŋkće-yuta==Unkcheyuta.
Uŋkepatines==Hunkpatina.
Unkowas==Uncowa.
Unkpapa, Unkpapa Dakotas, Unkpapas==Hunkpapa.
Ŭñktce-yuta==Unkcheyuta.
Unkus Indians==Mohegan.
Unkwas==Uncowa.
Un-nah-tak==Unatak.
Unoktolik==Ungalik.
Unov==San Dieguito.
Unquachog, Unquechauge, Unshagogs==Patchoag.
Unuh==Ona.
Ŭnŭğŭn==Esquimauan Family.
Ŭnŭngŭn==Aleut.
Uñ-wu′-si==Angwusi.
Unxus==Tunxis.
Uon-a-gan==Howkan.
Uparsoitac==Upasoitac.
Upatrico==Comupatrico.
Upatsesatuch==Opitchesaht.
Upernavik==Upernivik.
Uphaulie towns==Eufaula.
Upiktalik==Opiktulik.
Up-la-goh==Takimilding.

Uplanders=Plaikni.
Upland Indians=Mohegan.
Up-le-goh=Takimilding.
Upotoi=Apatai.
Up-pa=Hupa.
Up-pa-goines, Up-pah-goines=Opegoi.
Upper Brules=Kheyatawichasha.
Upper Castle=Canajoharie.
Upper Cheehaws=Chiaha.
Upper Chihalis=Kwaiailk.
Upper Coquille=Mishikhwutmetunne.
Upper Cowetas town=Kawita.
Upper Cree=Sakawithiniwuk.
Upper Dakotas=Santee.
Upper De Chutes=Tyigh.
Upper Esquimaux of Begh-ula or Anderson's River=
    Kitegareut.
Upper Eufalla, Upper Euphaules=Eufaula.
Upper Gens du fou=Trotsikkutchin.
Upper Killamuks=Tillamook.
Upper Klamath=Karok.
Upper Kootanais, Upper Kootanie, Upper Kootenay,
    Upper Kootenuha=Upper Kutenai.
Upper Matchodic, Upper Mattschotick=Matchotic.
Upper Medewakantwans=Upper Mdewakanton.
Upper Mohawk Castle=Canienga.
Upper Oakfuske=Oakfuskee.
Upper Pend d'Oreilles=Kalispel.
Upper Platte Indians=Kheyatawichasha.
Upper Puyallup=Tooahk.
Upper Rogue River Indians=Takelma.
Upper Seesetoan=Kahra.
Upper Senecas=Geneseo.
Upper Spokanes=Spokan.
Upper Tsihalis=Kwaiailk.
Upper Ufale=Eufaula.
Upper Umpqua=Umpqua.
Upper Wakpaton=Mdeiyedan.
Up-pup-pay=Nez Percés.
U′pqaⁿ=Upkhan.
Upsáraukas, Upsarocas, Ŭp-så-rŏ-kå, Up-shar-look-
    kar, Upsook, Up-sor-ah-kay=Crows.
Uquiota=Oquitoa.
Ŭ-qwaiké=Ukhwaiksh.
Ura=Uva.
Uraba=Taos.
Uragees=Mahican.
Urai-Nuints=Uainuints.
Urawis=Unami.
Ure=Opata.
Urriba cuxi, Urribarracuxi=Tocobaga.
Ur′thlaina tai′na=Urhlaina.
Usauleys, Usawla, Usawles=Eufaula.
Usaya, Usaya-kue, Usayan=Hopi.
Ŭ′-se=Ushu.
Usechees=Osotchi.
Usheree, Usherie, Ushery=Catawba.
Ush-ke-we-ah=Bannock.
Ushkimani′tigŏg=Oukiskimanitouk.
Ûshpī=Ofogoula.
Usietshawus=Tillamook.
Uskee, Uskeemè, Uskeemi, Uskimay=Eskimo.
Uskŏk=Hiyayulge.
Uskwawgomees=Montagnais.
Usquemows=Eskimo.
Ussagĕnéwi, Ussaghenick=Montagnais.
Usseta=Kasihta.
Ussinebwoinug=Assiniboin.
Ussinnewudj=Sarsi.
Us-suc-car-shay=Mandan.
Ustana=Timucua.
Ustenary=Ustanali.
Ustu=Ustoma.
Usuchees=Osotchi.
Usuoke-haga=Oswegatchie.
Usutchi=Osotchi.
Utagāmīg=Foxes.
Utahs=Ute.
Utaisíta=Kadohadacho.
Utamis=Miami.
Utā′mqtamux=Lower Thompson Indians.
Utaobaes=Ottawa.
Utas=Ute.
Utásĕta=Kadohadacho.
Utawas, Utawawas=Ottawa.
Utaws=Ute.
Utce-ci-nyu-mûh=Apache.
Ut-cha-pah, Ut-cha-pas, Ut-chap-pah=Uchapa.

Utchees=Uchean Family, Yuchi.
Utchis=Yuchi.
Utcitcāk=Ojeejok.
Ute=Moqtavhaitaniu.
Ute Diggers=Paiute.
Utella=Umatilla.
Utiangue, Utianque=Autiamque.
Utillas=Umatilla.
Utilltuc=Uturituc.
Utinama, Utinamocharra=Utina.
Utinom=Usal.
Utiqimitung=Utikimitung.
Utkeagvik, Utkeaire, Utkiaving, Utkiavwïñ=Utki-
    avi.
Utkiavwiñmiun=Utkiavinmiut.
Utku-hikalik, Ut-ku-hikaling-mëut, Ut-ku-sik-kaling-
    mé-ut, Utkusiksalik, Utkutciki-aliñ-méut=Uku-
    siksalirmiut.
Utlak-soak=Utlaksuk.
Utnux tana=Ahtena.
Utovautes=Ottawa.
Útsaamu=Apache.
Utsanango=Chenango.
Ut-scha-pahs=Uchapa.
Utschies=Uchean Family, Yuchi.
Utschim, Utschium, Utschiun=Uchium.
Útsiā=Ute.
Utsúshuat=Quapaw.
Uttawa=Ottawa.
Uttewas=Masset.
Utukakgmut=Utukamiut.
Uturicut=Uturituc.
Uturpe=Atarpe.
Uubum=Yupu.
Uūschkētan=Wushketan.
Uvas=Uva.
Uvkusigsalik=Ukusiksalirmiut.
Uwagâ′hĭ=Ocoee.
Uwáha=Omaha.
Uwarrow Suk-suk=Uwarosuk.
Uwatáyo-rono=Cherokee.
Uwe′len=Ulak.
Uwinty-Utahs=Uinta.
Úxul=Lipan.
Uyāda=Cherokee.
Uye-Lackes=Wailaki.
Uy′gilâ′gĭ=Oothcaloga.
Uzachil=Osachile.
Uzajes=Osage.
Uzela=Osachile.
Uzinkee=Uzinki.
Uzutiuhe, U-zu-ti-u-we=Uzutiuhi.

Va′-aki=Casa Blanca.
Vaca=Baca.
Vacapa=Matape.
Vaccay=Wakokayi.
Vaceraca=Baserac.
Vacupa=Matape.
Vacus=Acoma.
Vagueros=Querechos.
Valachi=Apalachee.
Valencia=Tomé.
Valero=San Antonio de Valero.
Valladolid=Taos.
Vallatoa=Jemez.
Valley Indians=Daupom Wintun.
Valverde=Sempoapi.
Vampe=Nambe.
Vànæ-ta-Kouttchin=Vuntakutchin.
Vancouvers=Klikitat.
Van-tah-koo-chin, Vanta-Kutchi, Vanta-Kutchin,
    Vanta kutshi=Vuntakutchin.
Vanyume=Serranos.
Vaqueros=Querechos.
Varogio=Varohio.
Vashichagat=Vagitchitchate.
Vassconia=Papago.
Vatepito=Batepito.
Vaticá=Vahia.
Văt-qi=Casa Grande.
Va Vak=Casa Blanca.
Vāwúlile=Baborigame.
Vaxacahel=Vazacahel.
Vaysaylovskoi=Veselofski.
Vay-ua-va-vi=Vayuavabi.
Veachile=Axille.

Veeards=Wiyat.
Venanga, Venargo, Veneango, Veningo=Venango.
Venizali=Vinasale.
Ven-ta-Kuttchin=Vuntakutchin.
Vermillion=Zutsemin.
Vermillion Kickapoos, Vermillions=Vermilion.
Veselóvskoe=Veselofski.
Veshanacks, Vesnacks=Vesnak.
Vesselovsky=Veselofski.
Viandots=Huron.
Viard=Wiyat.
Viaundo=San Francisco Xavier de Viggé-Biaundo.
Vicanque=Autiamque.
Victoria, Victoria de Ojio=Ojio.
Vicuris=Picuris.
Vidaes, Vidais, Vidays=Bidai.
Vieux de la Mer=Nellagottine.
Vieux Desert, Vieux De Sert band=Gatagetegauning.
Vigge Biaundo=San Francisco Xavier de Viggé Biaundo.
Villa de los Coraçones=Corazones.
Villa farta=Cholupaha.
Village des Chaouanons=Sewickley.
Village des Noyers=Talasse.
Village du Loups=Venango.
Village Indians=Pueblos.
Village of Odd Waters=Kechipauan.
Village of Prarie=Tintaotonwe.
Village of Sixes=Taoapa.
Village of the Basket=Tungge.
Village of the Rainbow=Bejuituuy.
Village of the Two Mountains=Oka.
Village of the White Flowering Herbs=Hampasawan.
Village of the Winds=Pinawan.
Village of the Worm=Puaray.
Village of the Yellow Rocks=Heshotahluptsina.
Ville de Bois=Logstown.
Ville de Jean=Mohickon John's Town.
Ville des nouveaux venus=Newcomerstown.
Vinango=Venango.
Vineyard Indians=Martha's Vineyard Indians.
Viniettinen-né=Tontos.
Viningo=Venango.
Vinisahle=Vinasale.
Vinni ettinenne=Tontos.
Vintacottas=Vinatacot.
Vĭ-pĭ-sĕt=Casa Montezuma.
Vi-qit=Vikhit.
Viranque=Autiamque.
Vi-ra-rĭ-ka, Virárika=Huichol.
Virgin River Paiutes=Shivwits.
Vĭshálika=Huichol.
Vitachuco=Ivitachúco.
Vi′täpätu′i=Kiowa.
Vites=Huite.
Vivais=Bidai.
Vlibahalj=Ullibahali.
Vnchechange, Vncheckaug=Patchoag
Vnnagoungos=Abnaki.
Vnquechauke=Patchoag.
Voen-Kuttchin=Vuntakutchin.
Vóhopiûm=Santan.
Volvon=Bolbone.
Voragio=Varohio.
Vosnessensky=Vossnessenski.
Voudt-way Kutchin=Vuntakutchin.
Vozesnesky=Vossnessenski.
Vparsoytac=Upasoitac.
Vpelois=White Apple.
Vpland Indianes=River Indians.
Vrribarracuxi=Tocobaga.
Vᵉacus=Acoma.
Vtamussack=Uttamussac.
Vtiangue=Autiamque.
Vttamussak=Uttamussac.
Vttamussamacoma=Uttamussamacoma.
Vttasantasough=Chickáhominy.
Vturituc=Uturituc.
Vuikhtuligmute=Vuikhtulik.
Vule Pugas=Calapooya.
Vulture people=Suwuki Ohimal.

Waahktoohook=Westenhuck.
Waakiacums, Waakicum=Wahkiakum.
Waakpacootas=Wahpekute.
Waas=Wea.
Wáatenĭlits=Ute.
Wabaage=Quabaug.

Wabanackies, Wabanakees, Wabanakis, Wábaníka, Wábaníke, Wabanocky=Abnaki.
Wabaquassuck, Wabaquisit=Wabaquasset.
Wabasca=Athapascan Family.
Wabasha band, Wabashaw band, Wabashaw's band, Wabashaw's sub-band=Kiyuksa.
Wabash confederacy, Wabash confederates, Wabash Indians=Wabash.
Wâbasimōwininiwag=Wabasemowenenewak.
Wabbequasset=Wabaquasset.
Wabenakies, Wabĕnáki senobe, Wabenauki=Abnaki.
Wabequassets, Wabequisset=Wabaquasset.
Wabigna, Wabinga, Wabingies=Wappinger.
Wabipetons=Wahpeton.
Wábishesh=Wabezhaze.
Wâbisĭbiwininiwag=Wapisiwisibiwininiwak.
Wābi′tigwäyāng=Obidgewong.
Wablenica, Wablenitca=Wablenicha.
Wâb-na-ki=Abnaki.
Wabquissit=Wabaquasset.
Wabushaw=Kiyuksa.
Wacabe=Dtesanhadtadhishan.
Waɔaɔe=Osage.
Waɔáɔe skă=Washasheska.
Waɔa′ɔe Wanŭⁿ′=Washashewanun.
Wacacoys=Wakokayi.
Wacalamus=Thlakalama.
Wacamuc=Cathlacumup.
Wacantuck=Wacuntug.
Waćape=Wachape.
Waccamaus, Waccamawe=Waccamaw.
Waccanessisi=Wakanasisi.
Waccay=Wakokayi.
Wacco=Waco.
Waccoa, Waccoam=Woccon.
Waccocoie=Wakokayi.
Waccomassees=Waccamaw.
Waccon=Woccon.
Wacemaus=Waccamaw.
Waɔeoŋpa=Wacheonpa, Wacheunpa.
Waćeuŋpa=Wacheunpa.
Wacha=Waco.
Wa-cha-et, Wa-cha-hets=Wechikhit.
Wachamnis=Wikchamni.
Wachas=Washa.
Wachatawmaha=Wakatomica.
Wachaw=Waxhaw.
Wa-che-ha-ti, Wa-che-nets, Wa-che-ries, Waches=Wechikhit.
Wachipuanes=Chipewyan.
Wâch-kí-a-cum=Wahkiakum.
Wachos=Waco.
Wachpecoutes=Wahpekute.
Wachquadnach=Wechquadnach.
Wachuknas=Michopdo.
Waɸigije=Wadhigizhe.
Wa-ĉi′-ōm-pa=Wacheunpa.
Wa-ci-pi=Walpi.
Wa-cissa-talofa=Vasisa.
Waɸitaⁿ=Wadhitan.
Wacitcuⁿ-tciⁿtca=Washichunchincha.
Wackakoy=Wakokayi.
Wackiacums, Wackkiacums=Wahkiakum.
Wack-sa-che=Waksachi.
Wacksaws=Waxhaw.
Wacksoyochees=Woksoyudshi.
Wacoah, Wacoes=Waco, Wasco.
Wa-come-app=Cathlacumup.
Wacon=Woccon.
Wáculi=Tepecano.
Wacumtung=Wacuntug.
Wacuqɸa=Missouri.
Waɸútada=Oto.
Wadchuset=Wachuset.
Waddapadschestiner=Waddapawjestin.
Waddington Harbour=Wadington Harbor.
Wâd-doké-tâh-tâh=Oto.
Wadjusset=Wachuset.
Wadjüta tañga=Chedunga.
Wadjüta ts′eyĕ=Tayachazhi.
Wa-dook-to-da, Wa-do-tan, Wadótata=Oto.
Wadoüissians=Dakota.
Waecoe, Waeko=Waco.
Waerinnewangh=Waranawonkong.
Waeuntug=Wacuntug.
Waganhaers, Waganhaes=Ontwaganha, Ottawa.
Waganhas, Waganis=Ottawa.
Wagannes=Ontwaganha, Ottawa.

Wa-ge′ku-te=Wazikute.
Wagenhanes=Ottawa.
Waggamaw, Waggoman=Waccamaw.
Waghaloosen=Wyalusing.
Waghatamagy, Waghhatawmaky=Wakatomica.
Wagh-toch-tat-ta=Oto.
Wagínxak=Waginkhak.
Wagluge, Waglulie, Wagluqe=Waglukhe.
Wagmesset=Wamesit.
Wagunha=Ottawa.
Wa′gushag=Foxes.
Wagushagi=Wokoawissojik.
Wä-hä=Wehatsa.
Wâ′häh=Wahat.
Wa′-ha′-há′=Wehatsa.
Wa-ña-lé-zo-wen=Waglezaoin.
Wahannas=Ontwaganha, Ottawa.
Wahashas=Osage.
Wa-ha-shaw′s tribe=Kiyuksa.
Wahasuke=Nayuharuke.
Wâhätsaásh=Waha.
Wahch-Pe-Kutch, Wahch-Pekuté=Wahpekute.
Wahclellah=Watlala.
Wahcoota=Khemnichan.
Waña=Wazhazhe.
Wah-hay-koo-tay=Wahpekute.
Wah-hŏ′-na-hah=Potawatomi.
Wah-how-pum=Wahowpum.
Wáhiúḍaqa, Wáhiúyaha=Potawatomi.
Wah-kah-towah=Chippewa.
Wahkaykum=Wahkiakum.
Wahk-cha′-he-dä=Wakchekhikikarachada.
Wah-kee-on Tun-kah=Wakinyantanka.
Wahkenkumes=Wahkiakum.
Wahki=Casa Grande.
Wahkiacum, Wahkiahkums, Wah-kia-kum, Wahkia-kume, Wahkiakums=Wahkiakum.
Wahkiruxkanumanke=Shoshoni.
Wah-Koo-Tay=Khemnichan.
Wahkpacoota, Wahkpacootay, Wahkpakoota, Wahkpakota, Wahkpako toan=Wahpekute.
Wahkpa toan, Wahk-patons=Wahpeton.
Wahktoohook=Westenhuck.
Wahkuti band=Khemnichan.
Wahkyecums, Wahkyekum, Wahkyskum=Wah-kiakum.
Wahlahwahlah=Wallawalla.
Wä-hläk-kŭl′-kee=Wahlakalgi.
Wah-lal-la=Watlala.
Wah-lik-nas′-se=Tubatulabal.
Wah-ma-dee Tunkah band=Ohanhanska.
Wah muk a-hah′-ve=Mohave.
Wañna=Wakhna.
Wâhnookt=Klikitat.
W′å-h′ó-nå-hå=Potawatomi.
Wahpaakootah, Wahpaakootas, Wah-pa-coo-la, Wâh′-pa-coo-ta, Wahpacoota Sioux, Wahpacootay Sioux, Wah-pa-costa=Wahpekute.
Wah′-pah-say′-pon=White Raccoon's Village.
Wah-pa-koo-ta, Wahpakootah Sioux, Wahpakooty, Wahpakutas=Wahpekute.
Wahpatoan Sioux, Wahpaton, Wah′-pa-tone=Wahpeton.
Wahpatoota, Wahpay-hoo-tays, Wahpaykootays=Wahpekute.
Wah-pay-toan, Wah-pay-toan-wan Dakotas, Wah-pay-to wan=Wahpeton.
Wahpeconte=Wahpekute.
Wahpeeton, Wah-pee-ton Sioux, Wahpehtonwan=Wahpeton.
Wahpekootays, Wahpekutey, Wahpekuti, Wa-hpe-kwtes=Wahpekute.
Wahpetongs, Wañpetoŋwaŋ=Wahpeton.
Wañpetoŋwaŋ-ñca=Wakhpetonwankhcha.
Wahpe-tonwans=Wahpeton.
Wah-pi-mins-kink=Wapeminskink.
Wah-pi-ko-me-kunk=Wapicomekoke.
Wah-ral-lah=Watlala.
Wahsahzhe, Wahsash=Osage.
Wah-sherr=Wakhshek.
Wah-shoes=Washo.
Wah-si=Wakhshek.
Wahtani=Mandan.
Wah-toh-ta-na, Wahtohtanes, Wahtohtata, Wâh-tŏk-tä-tä, Wah-tooh-tah-tah=Oto.
Wañ-to′-pañ-an-da-to, Wah-to-pah-han-da-toh=Watopachnato.
Wah-to-pan-ah, Wah-to′-pap-i-nañ=Watopapinah.

Wahupums=Wahowpum.
Wahute band=Khemnichan.
Wah-wē-ah′-tung-ong, Wah-wee-ah-tenon=Wea.
Wah-wol=Wowol.
Wahza-zhe=Wazhazha.
Wah-ze-ah we-chas-ta=Northern Assiniboin.
Wahzhazas=Wazhazha.
Wañ′-zi-ah=Northern Assiniboin.
Wah-zu-cootas=Wazikute.
Waiäm, Waiäm-′lēma=Wiam.
Waiilatpu=Cayuse, Waiilatpuan Family.
Waikaikum=Wahkiakum.
Waikemi=Daupom Wintun.
Wai′-kēn-mok=Waikenmuk.
Wailakki=Wailaki.
Wailatpu=Cayuse, Waiilatpuan Family.
Waillatpus=Cayuse.
Waiomink=Wyoming.
Wai-ri-ka=Shasta.
Waitä′nknî=Warm Spring Indians.
Wait-lat-pu=Cayuse.
Waitshum′ni=Wikchamni.
Wait-spek=Yurok.
Waiwaiaikai=Wiwekae.
Waiyat=Wishosk.
Wajaja=Wazhazha.
Wajaje=Osage, Ta, Wazhazhe.
Wajingaetage=Wezhinshte.
Wajiñ′ɥa énikaci′ɥa=Wazhinkaenikashika.
Wajomick, Wajomik=Wyoming.
Wajuomne=Wapumne.
Wa-ju′-qdḍä=Missouri.
Wak=Casa Grande.
Wä-kä=Wakan.
Wâ-käh=Waha.
Wa-kái-a-kum, Wakaikam, Wakáikum=Wahkia-kum.
Wakamass, Wakamucks=Cathlacumup.
Wakanasceces, Wa-kan-a-shee-shee, Wăkănăshishi Wakanasisse, Wakanasissi=Wakanasisi.
Wakan′ta=Cheghita.
Wakaⁿtcara=Wakanchara.
Wakash=Nootka, Salishan Family.
Wakatamake, Wakautamike=Wakatomica.
Wakazoo=Mekadewagamitigweyawininiwak.
Wakcogo=Waccogo.
Wä-keeh′=Wakan.
Wakesdachi=Waksachi.
Waketummakie=Wakatomica.
Wakh=Casa Grande.
Wakhpekute=Wahpekute.
Wakhpetonwan=Wahpeton.
Wáki=Shipaulovi.
Wakiakums, Wakicums=Wahkiakum.
Wakidoñka-numak=Shoshoni.
Wakinas=Arikara.
Wàkò, Wakoe=Waco.
Wakoká-i=Wakokayi.
Wa-kon′-chä-rä=Waninkikikarachada.
Wä-kon′-nä=Wakanikikarachada.
Wakootay′s band=Khemnichan.
Wakoquet=Waquoit.
Wakos=Waco.
Wâkoshawisotcigi=Wakoawissojik.
Wakouiechiwek=Chisedec.
Wa-kpa-a-ton-we-dan=Oyateshicha.
Wakpakootas=Wahpekute.
Wakpaton=Wakpaatonwan.
Wakpaton Dakota, Wak-pay ton=Wahpeton.
Wak-pe-ka-te, Wak-pe-ku-te=Wahpekute.
Wak-pe-ton Dakota=Wahpeton.
Wak-po′-ki-an, Wakpokinya=Wakpokinyan.
Waksoyochees=Woksoyudshi.
Wa-ktce′-qi i-ki′-ka-ra′-tca-da=Wakchekhiikika-rachada.
Wakuisaske-óns=Saint Regis.
Wäkushég=Foxes.
Wakuta band, Wa-ku-te, Wakute′s band=Khem-nichan.
Wak-we-ot-ta-non=Wea.
Walacumnies, Walagumnes=Walakumni.
Walalshimni=Walalsimni.
Walamskni, Walamswash=Chastacosta.
Wa-la-nah=Jemez.
Wálapai kwe=Walapai.
Walâsi′yĭ=Frogtown.
Walatoa=Jemez.
Walawala, Wal-a-Waltz=Wallawalla.

Waleǵa oŋ wohaŋ=Waleghaunwohan.
Wales=Eidenu.
Walexa-oⁿ-wohaⁿ=Waleghaunwohan.
Walhalla=Gualala.
Walhominies=Menominee.
Walináki=Wewenoc.
Walipekutes=Wahpekute.
Wālis-kwā-ki-ool=Walas Kwakiutl.
Wā′litsum=Hahamatses.
Walker River Pi-Utes=Agaihtikara.
Walkers=Shoshoko.
Wallah Wallah=Wallawalla.
Wal-lal-sim-ne=Walalsimni.
Wallamettes=Clowwewalla.
Wallamute=Ugalakmiut.
Wal-la-pais=Walapai.
Wall-a-pi=Walpi.
Wallas=Wallie.
Walla-Wallahs, Walla-Wallapum=Wallawalla.
Walla-Walloo=Wishosk.
Wal-la-waltz, Wallawollah, Wallewahos=Wallawalla.
Wal′-li=Wallie.
Wallow Wallow=Wallawalla.
Wall-Pah-Pe=Walapai.
Walnonoak=Wewenoc.
Walnut Village=Ousagoucoulas.
Wal-pah-pee Snakes, Walpahpe Snakes, Walpalla=Walpapi.
Wál-pé, Walpians=Walpi.
Walyepai=Walapai.
Wamakáva=Mohave.
Wamanus=Wiminuche.
Wamasit=Wamesit.
Wamasqueaks=Warrasqueoc.
Wambesitts=Wamesit.
Wam-bi-li′-ne-ća=Wablenicha.
Wamenuche=Wiminuche.
Wameset, Wamesut, Wammeset=Wamesit.
Wamnuǵa-oiŋ, Wamnuxa-oiⁿ=Wamnughaoin.
Wampa=Yampa.
Wampangs, Wampano, Wam-pa-no-gas, Wampa-nooucks=Wampanoag.
Wam-pa-nos=Wappinger.
Wampeage=Wampanoag.
Wamponas=Wappinger.
Wamponoags=Wampanoag.
Wampum-makers=Abnaki.
Wamussonewug=Monsoni.
Wanak=Dakota.
Wanama′kēwajink=Wanamakewajenenik.
Wanàmi=Unami.
Wanamuka's band=Winnemucca's Band.
Wananoak=Wewenoc.
Wánapûm=Sokulk.
Wanats=Huron.
Wanaxe=Wanaghe.
Wānbānaghi, Wānbanaki, Wanbanakkie, Wānbnaghi=Abnaki.
Wanchas=Washa.
Wandats=Huron.
Wanderers=Detsanayuka, Missiassik.
Wan-dor-gon-ing=Ketchewaundaugenink.
Wandots=Huron.
Wané-asûñ′tlûñyĭ=Hickory Log.
Wanexit=Manexit.
Wangadacea=Secotan.
Wang′-kat=Howungkut.
Wangum=Wongunk.
Wa-niñk′-i-ki′-ka-ra′-tca-da = Waninkikikarachada.
Wanjoacks=Nottoway.
Wankatamikee=Wakatomica.
Wannaton=Pabaksa.
Waŋ-naweǵa, Waⁿ-nawexa, Wan-nee-waok-a-ta-o-ne-lar=Wannawegha.
Wannemuches=Wiminuche.
Wanonoaks=Wewenoc.
Wanoolchie=Wenatchi.
Wantats=Huron.
Wa-nuk′e-ye′-na=Hidatsa.
Waoming=Wyoming.
Waoranecks, Waoraneky=Waoranec.
Wa8aiation=Wea.
Wapaghkanetta, Wapaghkonetta, Wapahkonetta, Wapakanotta, Wapakonákunge=Wapakoneta.
Wapakotah=Wahpekute.
Wa′pamĕtănt=Yakima.
Wapanachk=Abnaki.

Wapanachki=Abnaki, Brotherton, Delaware, Stockbridge.
Wapanaki, Wâpanákihak, Wapanaχki há-akon, Wapanends, Wápaniч′kyu=Abnaki.
Wapanoos=Wappinger.
Wapaquassett=Wabaquasset.
Wapasepah=White Raccoon's Village.
Wapasha's band, Wapashaw's village, Wa-pa-shee, Wapatha=Kiyuksa.
Wapato Lake=Atfalati.
Wapatomica=Wakatomica.
Wapatone, Wa-pa-toone=Wahpeton.
Wa-pa-too-ta=Wahpekute.
Wapatu, Wapatu Lake=Atfalati.
Wapauckanata, Wapaughkonetta, Wapaughkonnetta=Wapakoneta.
Wapaykoota=Wahpekute.
Wapeminskink=Woapikamikunk.
Wapenacki=Abnaki.
Wapenocks=Wampanoag.
Wapeto=Atfalati.
Wapingeis, Wapinger, Wapingoes=Wappinger.
Wapings=Pompton, Wappinger.
Wapintowaher=Wahpeton.
Wapo=Wappo.
Wapoghoognata=Wapakoneta.
Wapoomney=Wapumne.
Wapoos=Potawatomi.
Wapoto Lake=Atfalati.
Wappacoota=Wahpekute.
Wappanoos=Wappinger.
Wappato=Atfalati.
Wappatomica=Wakatomica.
Wappatoo=Atfalati.
Wappaukenata=Wapakoneta.
Wappenackie=Abnaki.
Wappenger=Wappinger.
Wappenos=Abnaki, Wappinger.
Wappinck, Wappinex, Wappinges, Wappingh, Wappingos, Wappings, Wappinoes, Wappinoo, Wappinx=Wappinger.
Wappitong=Wahpeton.
Waptai′lmĭm=Yakima.
Wapto=Atfalati.
Wa-pu-chu-se-amma=Waputyutsiama.
Wapumney, Wapumnies=Wapumne.
Wa-pû-nah-kĭ=Abnaki.
Wā′qa-iqam=Wahkiakum.
Waqɸexe-aɸiⁿ=Zhanhadtadhishan.
Waqdʒnχɸin=Wakhakukdhin.
Wa′-q!Emap=Wakemap.
Waqna=Wakhna.
Wa-qotc′=Iowa.
Wa-qpe′-toⁿ-waⁿ=Wahpeton.
Waranakarana=Naywaunaukauraunah.
Waranancongyns, Waranawancougy, Waranawankongs=Waranawonkong.
Waranoco=Waranoke.
Waranowankings, Waranwankongs=Waranawonkong.
War-are-ree-kas=Tazaaigadika.
Waraskoyack, Waraskweag=Warrasqueoc.
Waratcha, Waratka, Waratkass=Wenatchi.
Waraton=Maraton.
Waraye=Osage.
Warbigganus=Wabigganus.
Warchas=Washa.
Warciacoms, War ci a cum, War-ci-â-cum=Wahkiakum.
War eagle people=Hangkautadhantsi.
Warenecker, Warenocker=Waoranec.
War-gun-uk-ke-zee=Waganakisi.
Warkiacom, Warkiacum=Wahkiakum.
Wark-pay-ku-tay=Wahpekute.
Wark-pey-t′wawn=Wahpeton.
Warm Spring Indians=Tenino, Warm Spring Apache.
Warner's Ranch Indians=Agua Caliente.
Waroanekins=Waoranec.
Waronawanka=Waranawonkong.
Warpaton=Wahpeton.
War-pe-kintes, Warpekute, Warpekutey=Wahpekute.
Warpeton, War-pe-ton-wan, War-pe-t′wans=Wahpeton.
Warpicanata=Wapakoneta.
Warraghtinooks=Wea.
Warranawankongs, Warranawonkongs=Waranawonkong.

Warranoke=Waoranec.
Warraricas=Waradika.
Warraskorack, Warraskoyack, Warrasqueaks, War-ras-squeaks=Warrasqueoc.
Warriscoyake=Warrasqueoc.
Warronocke, Warronoco=Waranoke.
Warshas=Washa.
Wartokes=Watok.
Wartoolaharka=Tonanulla.
Warynawoncks=Waranawonkong.
Wasāāzj=Osage.
Wäsä'ba, Wasabaetage, Wa-sa-ba-eta-je=Wasabe.
Wasabe hit'ajĭ=Wasabe, Wasabehitazhi.
Wasá e'nikaci'ɥa=Wasaenikashika.
Wasagahas, Wasagè=Osage.
Wasakshes=Waksachi.
Wasama=Awani.
Wasapekent=Wasapokent.
Wä-sä-sa-o-no, Wä-sä'-seh-o-no=Dakota.
Wasashe, Wa-sa-shis, Wā'sassa=Osage.
Wasawanik=Ouasouarini.
Wa-sa-wi-ca-xta-xni=Ohanhauska.
Wasawsee, Wasbasha=Osage.
Wascoes, Was-co-pam, Wascopan, Wascopaw, Was-copens, Wascopums=Wasco.
Wase-ish-ta=Wezhinshte.
Waseɥu-it'aji=Wasedtuitazhi.
Wä-shä-ba=Washabe.
Washacum=Weshacum.
Washai'ki, Wash'-a-keeks band, Washano=Washakie's Band.
Washas=Osage, Washa.
Wa-sha-she=Osage.
Wash-a-tung=Inshtasanda.
Washaws=Washa, Washo.
Washbashaws=Osage.
Washikeek=Washakie's Band.
Washington Harbor=Sequim.
Washita, Washittas=Wichita.
Washō'χla=Oto.
Washpcoute, Washpecoate, Washpeconte, Wash-pecoutongs=Wahpekute.
Washpelong, Washpetong=Wahpeton.
Washpi=Walpi.
Washpotang=Wahpeton.
Wash-sashe=Osage.
Washtenaw=Wea.
Washt Kahápa=White Earth.
Wā'shŭtse=Sandia.
Waśiéuɥ-ćiɥća=Washichunchincha.
Wasita=Wichita.
Wasiu=Washo.
Wasko, Waskopam, Waskosin, Waskows=Wasco.
Was-mil-ches=Wimilchi.
Wa-sŏb-be nika-shing-ga=Wasabe.
Wássash, Wassashsha=Osage.
Wassawomees=Iroquois.
Was-saws=Washo, Waxhaw.
Wasses=Ouasouarini.
Wastana=Waxhaw.
Wasuihiyayedan, Wasuwicaxtanxi=Passing Hail's Band.
Wāswägaming=Wauswagiming.
Waswaganiwininiwag=Wahsuahgunewininewug.
Waswarini=Ouasouarini.
Was-waw-gun-nink=Wauswagiming.
Wataga, Watâ'gĭ=Watauga.
Watahpahata=Kiowa.
Watanons=Wea.
Watarees, Watary=Wateree.
Watasoons=Amahami.
Wa-tat-kah=Wahtatkin.
Watawawininiwok=Ottawa.
Watcape=Wachape.
Watceoⁿpa, Watceŭⁿpa=Wacheunpa.
Watch-ahets=Wechikhit.
Watchamshwash=Wachamshwash.
Wat-ches=Wechikhit.
Watchusets=Wachuset.
Wateknasi=Tubatulabal.
Wateni'hte=Siksika.
Wate-pana-toes, Watepaneto=Kiowa.
Water=Minnepata.
Wateree Chickanee=Wateree.
Watermelon Town=Totstalahoeetska.
Waterrees=Wateree.
Wathl-pì-è=Walpi.
Watlalla=Watlala.

Watoga, Watoge=Watauga.
Watoĥtata=Oto.
Watooga=Watok.
Watopana=Watopapinah.
Wato'ta=Oto.
Watpaton=Wakpaatonwan.
Watsa-he-wa=Watsaghika.
Watsequendo=Watsequeorda's Band.
Wat-so-ke-wa=Watsaghika.
Wattasoons=Amahami.
Watterree=Wateree.
Wat-tokes=Watok.
Wattoogee=Watauga.
Wattos=Wappo.
Waɥútata=Oto.
Wau-ba-na-kees=Abnaki.
Waubash Indians=Wabash.
Waub-ish-ash-e=Wabezhaze.
Waubose=Maskegon, Sugwaundugahwininewug.
Waub-un-uk-eeg=Abnaki.
Wauch-ta=Tashhuanta.
Waugan=Waugau.
Waughwauwame=Wyoming.
Waughweoughtennes, Waugweoughtannes=Wea.
Wauh-tecq=Wakhtek.
Waukatamike, Waukataumikee, Waukatomike=Wakatomica.
Waukiacum, Wau-ki-a-cums, Waukiecum's, Wauki-kam, Wau-ki-kum=Wahkiakum.
Waukouta band=Khemnichan.
Waulapta, Waulatpas, Waulatpus=Cayuse.
Wau-lit-sah-mosk=Hahamatses.
Waupacootar=Wahpekute.
Waupatone=Wahpeton.
Wauphauthawonaukee=Wapakoneta.
Wausashe=Osage.
Waushakee's band=Washakie's Band.
Wauwaughtanees=Wea.
Wawáh=Maidu, Wintun.
Wawaightonos=Wea.
Wawamie=Wyoming.
Wawarasinke, Wawarsing=Wawarsink.
Wawayoutat=Wawayontat.
Wawbunukkeeg=Abnaki.
Wawcottonans=Wea.
Wawechkaïrini=Weskarini.
Waweenock=Wewenoc.
Wawehattecooks=Wea.
Wawenech, Wawenock=Wewenoc.
Waweotonans, Waweoughtannes=Wea.
Waweskaïrini=Weskarini.
Waw-gun-nuk-kiz-ze, Waw-gun-uk-ke-zie=Waganakisi.
Wa-wha=Osage.
Wawiachtanos, Wawiaghta, Wawiaghtanakes, Wa-wiaghtanon=Wea.
Wawiaghtenkook=Tiosahrondion.
Wawiaghtonos, Wawia'hta'nua=Wea.
Wawijachtenocks=Wawyachtonoc.
Wā'wik·em=Wawikyem.
Wawiotonans, Wawioughtanes=Wea.
Waw-ka-sau-su=Wakasassa.
Wawkwunkizze=Waganakisi.
Waw-lis-knahkewlth, Waw-lis-knahk-newith=Walas Kwakiutl.
Waw-lit-sum=Hahamatses.
Wawpeentowahs=Wahpeton.
Wawquoit=Waquoit.
Wawrigweck, Wawrigwick=Norridgewock.
Wawsash, Waw-sash-e=Osage.
Wawyachteioks=Wawyachtonoc.
Wawyachtenoke=Wea.
Waxaus, Waxaws, Waxsaws=Waxhaw.
Wa·yâ'hĭ=Wahayahi.
Waya'htónuki=Wea.
Wayanaes=Cummaquid.
Wayandotts=Huron.
Wa-yä-tä-nó-ke=Miami.
Wayattano, Wayattanoc=Wyantenuc.
Wayaughtanock=Wawyachtonoc.
Waymessick=Wamesit.
Wayomick, Wayoming=Wyoming.
Wayondots, Wayondotts=Huron.
Wayoughtanies=Wea.
Wayunckeke=Wacuntug.
Wayundatts, Wayundotts=Huron.
Way-yam-pams=Wiam.
Wažaža=Osage, Wazhazha.

Wazaze=Wazhazha, Wazhazhe.
Wazazhas, Wazazies=Wazhazha.
Wä-zhä'-zha=Wazhazhe.
Wa-zha-zhe=Osage.
Wä'-zhese-ta=Wezhinshte.
Wa-zi'-ya-ta Pa-da'-niŋ=Arikara.
Waziya witcacta=Wahziah.
Waziyztz=Wazhazha.
Waz-za-ar-tar=Zaartar.
Wazzazies=Wazhazha, Wazhazhe.
W'Banankee=Abnaki.
Wdowo=Ottawa.
We-a-guf-ka=Weogufka.
Weah=Wea.
Weakaote=Khemnichan.
Weakis=Wewoka.
Wealusing=Wyalusing.
Wealuskingtown=Wyalusing.
Weandots=Huron.
Weanohronons=Wenrohronon.
Weashkimek=Eskimo.
Weatauge=Weataug.
Weathersfield Indians=Pyquaug.
Weatog=Weataug.
Weatsa-he-wa=Watsaghika.
Weaus, Weaws=Wea.
Weber River Yutas, Weber Utes=Cumumbah.
Webings=Winnebago.
Webinoche, Webinoche Utahs, Webrinoches=Wiminuche.
Wecamses=Wicocomoco.
Wecapaug=Wekapaug.
Wecco's=Waco.
Wechagaskas=Wessagusset.
We-che-ap-pe-nah=Itscheabine.
Wechigit=Wichikik.
We-chil-la, We-chill-la=Wahkila.
Wechkentowoons=Mechkentowoon.
Wech-pecs, Wech-pecks, Wech-peks=Yurok.
Wechquaeskeck=Wecquaesgeek.
We-chummies=Wikchamni.
Weckquaesgeek, Weckquaesguk, Weckquaskeck, Weckquesicks, Wecks=Wecquaesgeek.
Wecoka=Wewoka.
Wecos=Waco.
Weeah, Weea's, Weeaws=Wea.
Weechagaskas=Wessagusset.
Weeco=Waco.
Weecockcogee=Withlacoochee.
Weeds=Wea.
Wee-ka-nahs=Taos.
Wee-kee-moch, eekenoch=Wikeno.
We'-e-ko=Waco.
Weektumkas=Wetumpka.
Weelacksels=Wailaksel.
Weelhick Thuppek=Schoenbrunn.
Weeminuche=Wiminuche.
Weendegoag=Weendigo.
Weenees=Winyaw.
Weeokees=Wewoka.
Weepers=Assiniboin, Coaque.
Weepo=Wipho.
Weepomeokes=Weapemeoc.
Weequakut=Waquoit.
Weesagascusett=Wessagusset.
Wee Shotch=Wishosk.
Wee-tam-ka=Wetumpka.
Weetemore=Pocasset.
Weetle-toch=Oetlitk.
Weetumkees, Weetumkus, Weetumpkee=Wetumpka.
Weewaikun=Wiweakam.
Weewenocks=Wewenoc.
Weewok=Wiweakam.
Wee-yot=Wiyat.
Wegegi=Wejegi.
We guf car=Weogufka.
We hee skeu (chien)=Heviqsnipahis.
Wehtak=Wiatiac.
Weh-ta-mich=Klimmim.
Weht'l-qua=Wetlko.
Weichaka-Ougrin=Wakhakukdhin.
Weitchpec=Weitspus, Yurok.
Weithspek=Yurok.
Weitle toch=Oetlitk.
Weits-pek=Yurok.
Weji-gi=Wejegi.
Wejiⁿcte=Wezhinshte.
Wekisa, Wekivas, We-kiwa=Wikaithlako.

Wéko, Wéku, Wékush=Waco.
Welakamika=Welagamika.
We-la-poth=Tsewenalding.
Welasatux=Wolasatux.
We-la-tah=Picuris.
Welch=White Indians.
Welsh Bearded Indians=Welsh Indians.
Welsh Indians=Hopi, White Indians.
Welwashχē'ni=Welwashkeni.
Wemalche, We-melches=Wimilchi.
Wemenuche, Wemenutche Utahs=Wiminuche.
We-messouret=Missouri.
Wemiamik=Miami.
We-mil-che=Wimilchi.
Wemintheew=Munsee.
We-mol-ches=Wimilchi.
Wenango=Venango.
Wenatcha, Wenatshapam, Wenatshapan, Wenatshepum=Wenatchi.
Wenaumeew=Unami.
Wendats=Huron.
Weneaw, Wenee=Winyaw.
We-né-mu=Hueneme.
Wenimisset=Wenimesset.
Weningo, Weningo Town=Venango.
Wenot=Yangna,
Wenrio=Ouenrio.
Wenro=Wenrohronon.
Wenuhtokowuk=Nanticoke.
Weocksockwillacum=Smackshop.
We-o-haw=Wiyahawir.
Weoka=Wewoka.
Weoming=Wyoming.
Weopomeiok, Weopomeokes=Weapemeoc.
Wepawaugs=Paugusset.
Weperigoueiawek=Weperigweia.
Wequadn'ach=Wechquadnach.
Wequa-esgecks=Wecquaesgeek.
Wequapaug, Wequapauock=Wekapaug.
Wequehachke=Wappinger.
Wequetank=Wechquetank.
Werawocomoco, Werowcomoco, Wérowocómicos, Werowacomoco=Werowacomoco.
Wĕs'ă e'nikaci'ŋa=Wesaenikashika.
Wesaguscasit, Wesaguscus=Wessagusset.
Wesakam=Weshacum.
Wĕs'ă nikaciⁿga=Shoshoni.
Wesegusquaset=Wessagusset.
Weshakim, Weshakum=Weshacum.
Wesh-ham=Tlakluit.
Weskeskek, Wesquecqueck=Wecquaesgeek.
Wessaguscus, Wessagusquasset, Wessagussett=Wessagusset.
Wesselowskoje=Veselofski.
Westaugustus=Wessagusset.
West Congeeto, West Congeta, West Congeto, West Cooncheto=Conchachiton.
Westenhook=Westenhuck.
Western Dog ribbed Indians=Tsantieottine.
Western Indians=Creeks.
Western Mackenzie Innuit=Kangmaligmiut.
Western Shoshones=Shoshoko.
Western Sioux=Teton.
Western Snakes=Wihinasht.
West Imongalasha=Imongalasha.
West Yaso, West Yazoo=Yazoo.
We'-suala-kuin=Sandia.
Wetahato=Kiowa.
Wétänkni=Warm Spring Indians.
Wetapahato=Kiowa.
Wetcᵍá=Witchah.
Wetcᵍaⁿ'=Wetchon.
Wetch-pec, Wetch-peck=Yurok.
We-te-pâ-hâ'to=Kiowa.
Wetersoon=Amahami.
Wé-t'hlu-ella-kwin=San Felipe.
Wethoecuchytalofa=Withlacoocheetalofa.
Wetopahata=Kiowa.
Wetquescheck=Wecquaesgeek.
WetsagowAⁿ'=Wetsagua.
Wetshipweyanah=Chipewyan.
Wettaphato=Kiowa.
We-tum-cau, Wetumka, Wetumkee, Wetumpkees=Wetumpka.
We-wai-ai-kai=Wiwekae.
We-wai-ai-kum=Wiweakam.
Wĕ' wamasq·Em=Wewamaskem.
We-wark-ka=Wiwekae.
We-wark-kum=Wiweakam.

Weway-a-kay=Wiwekae.
Weway-a-kum=Wiweakam.
We-way-a-ky=Wiwekae.
Wewechkaïrini=Weskarini.
Weweenocks, Wewenocks=Wewenoc.
Wé-wi-ca-śa=Kainah.
Wewoak-har, Wewoakkan, Wewoakkar, Wewoak-kar Wockoy, We-wo-cau, Wewoko=Wewoka.
Wewoonock=Wewenoc.
We yAⁿ'=Weyon.
Weyandotts=Huron.
Weyat=Wishosk.
Wey-eh-hoo=Yehuh.
Weyet=Wishosk.
Weyoming=Wyoming.
Weyondotts=Huron.
We-yot=Wiyat.
Whacoe=Waco.
Whalatt=Hwotat.
Whampinages=Wampanoag.
Wha-pa-ku-tahs=Wahpekute.
Whapetons=Wahpeton.
Whash-to-na-ton=Khwaishtunnetunne.
Whatatt=Hwotat.
Whatoga=Watauga.
Wheelappa, Wheelappers=Willopah.
Wheelcuttas=Whilkut.
Whe-el-po, Whe-el-poo=Colville.
Whetstone country=Wabaquasset.
Whil-a-pah=Willopah.
Whill Wetz=Cooniac.
Whinega=Huna.
Whippanaps=Abnaki.
Whirlpool=Willopah.
Whishkah=Whiskah.
Whish-ten-eh-ten=Khwaishtunnetunne.
Whisklāleitoh=Kittizoo.
Whistanatin=Khwaishtunnetunne.
White Apple Village=White Apple.
White Bearded Indians=White Indians.
White Bird Nez Percés=Lamtama.
White Cap Sioux=White Cap Indians.
White Clay=White Earth.
White Eagle=Khuya.
White Earth band=Gawababiganikak.
White Fish Indians=Attikamegue.
White-Goose Eskimos=Kangormiut.
White Ground=Ikanhatki.
White Hair's band=Pahatsi.
White Indians=Menominee, Hopi.
White Knives=Tussawehe.
White Pani, White Pania=Pawnee.
White People=Stoam Ohimal.
White Pueblo=Nabatutuei.
White River Indians=Klikitat, Niskap, Skopa-mish, Smulkamish.
White Salmon Indians=Chilluckkittequaw.
White towns=Taluamikagi.
Whittumke=Wetumpka.
Whiwunai=Hopi.
Whonkenteaes, Whonkenties=Whonkentia.
Whonnoch, Whonock=Wharnock.
Whull-e-mooch=Salish.
Whulwhaipum, Whulwhypum=Klikitat.
Whyack=Wyah.
Wiahtanah=Waweatenon.
Wi'-ah-tŏn-oon'-gi=Wea.
Wialetpum=Cayuse.
Wialosing, Wialusing=Wyalusing.
Wiandotts=Huron.
Wiapes=Quapaw.
Wiatanons=Wea.
Wiatiacks=Wiatiac.
Wiaut=Wea.
Wibisnuche=Wiminuche.
Wi bu' ka pa=Mohave.
Wiccakaw=Wakokayi.
Wic-chum-nee=Wikchamni.
Wiccomisses=Wicocomoco.
Wicguaesgeck=Wecquaesgeek.
Wich-a-chim-ne=Wikchamni.
Wichagashas, Wichaguscusset=Wessagusset.
Wichegati=Wichikik.
Wichetahs, Wichetas=Wichita.
Wi'-chi-kik=Wechikhit.
Wichiyela=Yankton.
Wichumnies=Wikchamni.
Wich-sis=Wakhshek.
Wićiyela=Yankton.

Wickabaug=Wekapaug.
Wickagjock=Wiekagjoc.
Wick-a Nook=Wickaninnish.
Wickerscreek, Wickersecreeke, Wickersheck, Wickes-keck=Wecquaesgeek.
Wickinninish=Wickaninnish.
Wickquaskeck, Wickwaskeck=Wecquaesgeek.
Wico=Waco.
Wicoko wiñwû, Wi-co-ko wüñ-wü=Wishoko.
Wicomaw=Waccamaw.
Wicomese, Wicomesse, Wicomick=Wicocomoco.
Wicomocons=Secowocomoco.
Wicomocos=Wicocomoco.
Wicosels=Waikosel.
Wicquaesgeckers, Wicquaskaka=Wecquaesgeek.
Wi'cxam=Tlakluit.
Widshi itíkapá=Maricopa, Papago, Pima.
Wi'dyu=Ditsakana.
Wiechquaeskeck, Wiechquaesqueck, Wiechquas-keck, Wieckquaeskecke=Wecquaesgeek.
Wiekagjocks=Wiekagjoc.
Wiequaeskeck, Wiequaskeck=Wecquaesgeek.
Wighaloosen, Wighalosscon, Wighalousin=Wya-lusing.
Wighcocómicoes, Wighcocomoco, Wighcomocos, Wighcomogos, Wighocomoco=Wicocomoco.
Wighquaeskeek=Wecquaesgeek.
Wigomaw=Waccamaw.
Wihaloosing=Wyalusing.
Wihinagut, Wihinast=Wihinasht.
Wi-ic'-ap-i-nah=Itscheabine.
Wikachumnis=Wikchamni.
Wikagÿl=Wecquaesgeek.
Wi-kai-lako=Wikaithlako.
Wi Kain Mocs=Waikenmuk.
Wikanee=Wikeno.
Wik-chum-ni=Wikchamni.
Wikeinoh=Wikeno.
Wi'ko=Waco.
Wi'k'ŏxtēnŏx=Wikoktenok.
Wik-'sach-i=Waksachi.
Wik-tchum'-ne, Wiktshŏm'ni=Wikchamni.
Wi'-ku=Waco.
Wikuedo-wininiwak, Wikuédunk=Wequadong.
Wikurzh=Wikorzh.
Wi'kwädunk, Wikwed, Wikwedong=Wequadong.
Wi Lackees, Wilacki=Wailaki.
Wi-lak-sel=Wailaksel.
Wilamky=Wetumpka.
Wílana=Picuris.
Wi-la-pusch=Tsewenalding.
Wilatsu'kwe=Coyoteros.
Wild Cat=Koakotsalgi.
Wild Creeks=Seminole.
Wilde Coyotes=Navaho.
Wildlucit=Wyalusing.
Wild Nation=Ettchaottine.
Wild Oats, Nation of the, Wild Rice, Wild Rice Eat-ers, Wild Rice Men=Menominee.
Wílfa Ampáfa amím=Twana.
Wi'-li-gi, Wi'-li-gi-i'=San Felipe.
Wili idshapá=Mohave.
Wili'yi=Willstown.
Willacum=Smackshop.
Willamette Falls Indians=Clowwewalla.
Willamette tribe=Cathlacumup.
Willamette Tumwater band, Willammette Indians=Clowwewalla.
Willámotki tituxan=Willewah.
Willa-noucha-talofa=Willanoucha.
Willapah=Willopah.
Willem=Willi.
Willenoh=Willopah.
Willetpos=Cayuse.
Willhametts=Clowwewalla.
Willie=Willi.
Willinis=Illinois.
Willow Creek Indians=Lowhim.
Wils T.=Will's Town.
Wí-ma=Mimal.
Wimilches=Wimilchi.
Wiminanches, Wiminenuches=Wiminuche.
Wimosas=Yamasee.
Winatshipûm=Wenatchi.
Winbiégûg=Winnebago.
Wind=Hutalgalgi.
Win-de-wer-rean-toon=Mdewakanton.
Wind Family=Hutalgalgi.
Windigos=Weendigo.

Wind people=Kiyuksa.
Winds, Town of the=Pinawan.
Windsor Indians=Podunk.
Wineaus=Winyaw.
Winebago, Winebagoe, Winebégok, Winepegouek=Winnebago.
Winesemet=Winnisimmet.
Winetaries=Hidatsa.
Wingadocea=Secotan.
Wingah=Winyaw.
Wingandacoa, Wingandagoa, Winginans, Wingi-nas=Secotan.
Winibagos=Winnebago.
Wĭnibīgocicīwininiwạg = Winnebegoshishiwinini-wak.
Winibigong, Winipegou=Winnebago.
Winisemit, Winisimett, Winisimmit=Winnisimmet.
Winnabagoes=Winnebago.
Winnakenozzo=Miniconjou.
Winnas band, Winnas-ti=Wihinasht.
Winnebager, Winnebages, Winnebagoag, Winne-bagoe, Winnebagoec, Winnebagog, Winnebagoue, Winnebaygo=Winnebago.
Winnebigoshish=Winnebegoshishiwininewak.
Winnenocks=Wewenoc.
Winnepans, Winnepaus, Winnepeg=Winnebago.
Winnepisseockeege=Winnepesauki.
Winnesemet, Winnesimet=Winnisimmet.
Win-nes-tes=Wihinasht.
Winnibígog=Winnebago.
Winnibigoshish Lake (band)=Winnebegoshishiwi-ninewak.
Win-ni-mim=Winimem.
Winnimĭssett=Wenimesset.
Winnipegouek=Winnebago.
Winnisemit, Winnisimet=Winnisimmet.
Winooskoek=Winooskeek.
Winter Island=Neiuningaitua.
Wintoon, Wintu=Wintun.
Winyo=Winyaw.
Wioming, Wiomink=Wyoming.
Wiondots=Huron.
Wi'oq Emaē=Wiokemae.
Wippanaps=Abnaki.
Wiquashex, Wiquaeskeck=Wecquaesgeek.
Wisack, Wisacky=Waxhaw.
Wisagechroanu=Missisauga.
Wisagusset=Wessagusset.
Wiscassett Indians=Wewenoc.
Wisculla=Wiskala.
Wis-cum-nes=Wikchamni.
Wisham=Wishram.
Wishham=Tlakluit.
Wishitaw=Wichita.
Wish-pooke=Yurok.
Wish-ram, Wishrans=Tlakluit.
Wish-ta-nah-tin, Wishtanatan, Wish-te-na-tin=Khwaishtunnetunne.
Wi'-si-tă=Wichita.
Wiskerscreeke=Wecquaesgeek.
Wis-kul-la=Wiskala.
Wissaguset=Wessagusset.
Wissâkodewinini=Metis.
Wissams=Tlakluit.
Wiss-co-pam=Wasco.
Wissiquack=Nesaquake.
Wiss-whams=Tlakluit.
Wis'-tûm-ä-ti' tĕne'=Khwaishtunnetunne.
Wi Tackees, Wi Tackee-Yukas=Wailaki.
Witaháwiɇatá=Pitahauerat.
Witamky=Wetumpka.
Witanghatal=Serranos.
Wi'-ta-pa-ha, Witapä'hat, Wi'tapähä' tu, Witapätu=Kiowa.
Wĭtapiú=Wutapiu.
Witawaziyata=Witawaziyataotina.
Witch-a-taws, Witcheta, Witchetaw, Witchitas, Witchitaws=Wichita.
Witciⁿyaⁿpina=Itscheabine.
Witetsaán, Wi-tets'-han=Hidatsa.
Wĭthchetau=Wichita.
Without-Bows=Sans Arcs.
Witishaχta'nu=Illinois.
Witoupo, Witowpa, Witowpo=Ibitoupa.
Witqueschack, Wĭtquescheck, Witqueschreek=Wec-quaesgeek.
Wĭ'ts'a=Widja.
Wī'ts'a gyit'inai'=Widja-gitunai.
Witsch-piks=Yurok.

Witshita, Wĭtsită'=Wichita.
Witsogo=Tsofkara.
Witsta=Bellabella.
Witumki=Wetumpka.
Witúne=Kadohadacho.
Wi-tup-a'-tu=Kiowa.
Wi-uh-sis=Wakhshek.
Wiuini'em=Ditsakana.
Wiwagam=Wiweakam.
Wi-wai-ai-kai=Wiwekae.
Wi-wai-ai-kum=Wiweakam.
Wiwas=Quigalta.
Wiwash=Nanticoke.
Wiwayiki=Wiwekae.
Wĭwēaqam=Wiweakam.
Wī-wē-eke=Wiwekae.
Wĭ'-wē-ēkum=Wiweakam.
Wĭwēq'aē=Wiwekae.
Wi-wi-kum=Wiweakam.
Wiwúχka=Wewoka.
Wiyandotts=Huron.
Wi-yot=Wiyat.
W-ltoo-ilth-aht=Ucluelet.
W-nahk-ta-kook, Wnahktukook=Westenhuck.
W'nalāchtko=Unalachtigo.
W'nämiu=Unami.
Wnoghquetookoke=Westenhuck.
Wo-a-pa-nach-kí=Abnaki.
Woapikamikunk=Wapicomekoke.
Woas=Uva.
Wobanaki=Abnaki.
Woc-co-coie, Wocke Coyo=Wakokayi.
Wock-soche=Waksachi.
Wocons=Woccon.
Woenoeks=Wewenoc.
Wo-he-nōm'-pa=Oohenonpa.
Wóhesh=Pawnee.
Wohlpahpe Snakes=Walpapi.
Wokkon=Woccon.
Wok-sach-e=Waksachi.
Wokukay=Wakokayi.
Wolapi=Walpi.
Wo-lass-i=Wowolasi.
Wolf=Mahican, Michirache.
Wolf Eaters=Coyoteros.
Wolf gens=Kharatanumanke.
Wolf Indians, Wolf Pawnee=Skidi.
Wolf People=Mandhinkagaghe.
Wolftown=Wahyahi.
Wolf tribe of the Delawares=Munsee.
Wolkukay=Wakokayi.
Wollah-wollah, Wollaolla, Wollawalla, Wollawollahs, Wollawwallah, Wol-law-wol-lah=Wallawalla.
Woll-pah-pe=Walpapi.
Wol-pi=Walpi.
Wolsatux=Wolasatux.
Wolves=Skidi.
Woman helper band=Tonoyiet's Band.
Woman-o-she Utes=Wiminuche.
Womenog=Wewenoc.
Womenunche=Wiminuche.
Wompanaoges, Wompanoag, Womponoags=Wam-panoag.
Wonalatoko=Unalachtigo.
Wonami=Unami.
Wŏng-ge=Jemez.
Wongonks, Wongums, Wongunck, Wongung=Won-gunk.
Wo-ni-to'-na-his=Brulé.
Woocon=Woccon.
Wood Assiniboines=Tschantoga.
Wood Crees=Sakawithiniwuk.
Wooden-lips=Tlingit.
Wood Indians=Nopeming, Nuchwugh, Tutchone-kutchin.
Wood people=Hankutchin.
Woods Bloods=Istsikainah.
Wood Stoneys=Tschantoga.
Wóopotsĭ't=Wohkpotsit.
Woo-pum=Wopum.
Wooselalim=Clallam.
Woo-wells=Wowol.
Wopowage=Paugusset.
Wóqpotsĭt=Wohkpotsit.
Woranecks=Waoranec.
Woraqa, Wo-rá-qĕ=Potawatomi.
Workons=Woccon.
Worm People=Esksinaitupiks.
Woscopom=Wasco.

Wos-sosh-e=Osage.
Wō'tapío=Wutapiu.
Wo'-tko=Wotkalgi.
Wouachita=Ouachita.
Wowenocks=Wewenoc.
Wowocau=Wewoka.
Wowolasi=Wolasi.
Wōxuā'mîs=Wohuamis.
Woyming, Woyumoth=Wyoming.
Wrangell Bay=Kuiukuk.
Wrole Alley=Molala.
Wrylackers=Wailaki.
W. Schious=Teton.
W'shä'nătu=Shallattoo.
W'tawas=Ottawa.
Wū'cketān=Wushketan.
Wūh'tă pi u=Wutapiu.
Wu'-i-t'û-çla'-ă=Wultuthlaa.
Wuḳaχē'ni=Wukakeni.
Wükchamni=Wikchamni.
Wükhḓuautenauk=Wechquadnach.
Wuk-sä'-che=Waksachi.
Wu'lastûḳ'-wiûḳ=Malecite.
Wulx=Shasta, Upper Takelma.
Wunalàchtigo=Unalachtigo.
Wun-a-muc-a's band=Winnemucca's Band.
Wun-a-muc-a's (the Second) band=Kuyuidika.
Wunaumeeh=Unami.
Wunnashowatuckowogs,   Wunnashowatuckqut=
    Wunnashowatuckoog.
Wû-sa-sĭ=Osage.
Wŭshqûm=Wishram.
Wŭshqûmă-pûm=Tlakluit.
Wushuum=Wishram.
Wu-so'-ko=Wishoko.
Wut-at=Hwotat.
Wute'-elit, Wute'en=Cherinak.
Wutsta'=Bellabella.
Wu'turen=Cherinak.
Wyachtenos, Wyahtinaws=Wea.
Wyalousing, Wyalucing=Wyalusing.
Wyam=Wiam.
Wyaming=Wyoming.
Wy-am-pams, Wyampaw=Wiam.
Wyandote, Wyandotte=Huron.
Wyandot Town=Junundat.
Wyandotts=Huron.
Wyantanuck=Wyantenuc.
Wyantenock=Weantinock.
Wyantenuck=Wyantenuc.
Wyapes=Quapaw.
Wyatanons=Wea.
Wyatiack=Wiatiac.
Wybusing=Wyalusing.
Wyckerscreeke=Wecquaesgeek.
Wycless=Waitlas.
Wycomes, Wycomeses=Wicocomoco.
Wyeacktenacks=Wea.
Wyeck=Wawyachtonoc.
Wy-eilat=Cayuse.
Wye-Lackees=Wailaki.
Wyeluting=Wyalusing.
Wykenas=Wikeno.
Wylachies, Wylackies, Wy-laks=Wailaki.
Wylucing, Wylusink=Wyalusing.
Wyniaws=Winyaw.
Wynoochee=Wenatchi.
Wy-noot-che=Wenatchi.
Wyogtami=Wea.
Wyolusing=Wyalusing.
Wyomen, Wyomin, Wyomink, Wyomish=Wyoming.
Wyondats, Wyondotts=Huron.
Wyquaesquec=Wecquaesgeek.

Xabotaj, Xabotaos=Tano.
Xacatin=Soacatino.
Xacona, Xacono=Jacona.
Xaeser=Haeser.
Xā'exaes=China Hat.
Xagua'tc=Agua Caliente.
Xa-hë-ta'-ño=Apache.
Xai'ma arangua's=Comecrudo.
Xaima'me=Cotonam.
Xa'ina=Haena.
Xa-isla'=Haisla, Kitamat.
Xak nuwū'=Hukanuwu.
Xalay=Zuñi.
Xâmanâô=Hawmanao.
Xamunanuc=Xamunambe.

Xanā'ks'iala=Kitlope.
XanExEwê'ɪ=Hanehewedl.
Xangopany=Shongopovi.
Xapes, Xapies=Hapes.
Xapira=Xapida.
Xaqua=Xagua.
Xaqueuira=Harahey, Quivira.
Xaram=Xarame.
Xaramenes, Xaranames=Aranama.
Xaratenumanke=Pawnee.
Xaray=Zuñi.
Xaslindiñ=Haslinding.
Xatol=Xatoe.
Xátūkwiwa=Wintun.
Xau'-i=Chaui.
Xawályapay=Walapai.
Xā'xamatses=Hahamatses.
Xax'ēqt=Kakekt.
Xĕɫ koan=Hehlkoan.
Xemes, χemes, Xeméz=Jemez.
Xenopué=Genobey.
Xeres=Keresan Family.
Xharame=Xarame.
Xhiahuam, Xhiahuan=Siaguan.
Xiabu=Hiabu.
Xicarillas=Jicarilla.
Xiguan=Siaguan.
Xijames=Sijame.
Xileños, Xilenos=Gila Apache.
Ximena, Ximera=Galisteo.
Xiomato=Piamato.
Xipaolabi=Shipaulovi.
Xiscaca=Xisca.
Xixame=Sijame.
Xocomes=Jocomes.
Xoē'xoē=Koikoi.
Xōi'lkut=Whilkut.
Xommapavi=Shongopovi.
Xōmoks=Comox.
Xonalús=Yonalus.
Xongopabi, Xongopani, Xongopaui, Xongopavi=
    Shongopovi.
Xonoidag=Sonoita.
Xonsadiñ=Honsading.
Xōq!e'dî=Hokedi.
Xougopavi=Shongopovi.
Xoumanes=Tawehash.
Xōwûñkût=Howungkut.
Xō'yalas, Xoyā'les=Hoyalas.
Xptianos Manssos=Manso.
Xuacatino=Soacatino.
Xū'Adji lnagā'-i=Skedans.
Xū'adji-nao=Hutsnuwu.
Xuala, Xualla=Cheraw.
Xuámitsan=Quamichan.
Xuanes=Huanes.
Xuco, Xucu=Shuku.
Xudes=Hwates.
Xuikuáyaxēn=Huikuayaken.
Xumanas, Xumanes, Xumarias, Xumas, Xumáses=
    Tawehash.
Xumátcam=Tepecano.
Xumiéxen=Comiaken.
Xumtáspē=Nawiti.
Xumunaumbe=Xamunambe.
Xumupamí, Xumupani=Shongopovi.
Xuqua=Xugua.
Xūts! hît tān=Kutshittan.
Xuts!nuwū'=Hutsnuwu.
x·û'tx·ûtkawê̄ɪ=Huthutkawedl.
Xwā'xōts=Wharhoots.

Ya'=Yañgtsaa.
Yāᵃgaláᵉ=Umpqua.
Yaai'x·aqEmaē=Yaaihakemae.
Yāä'kimā=Yakima.
Ya-atze=San Marcos.
Yabapais, Yabijoias, Yabipaees, Yabipai=Yavapai.
Yabipai Cajuala=Paiute.
Yabipai Muca=Oraibi.
Yabipais=Yavapai.
Yabipais Cuercomaches=Cuercomache.
Yabipais Jabesua=Havasupai.
Yabipais Lipan=Lipan.
Yabipais Nabajay=Navaho.
Yabipais Natagé=Kiowa Apache.
Yabipais Tejua=Tejua.
Yabipaíye, Yabipay, Yabipias=Yavapai.

Yacaaws, Yacamaws=Yakima.
Yacaws=Makah.
Yacco=Acoma.
Yachachumnes=Yachikamni.
Yachakeenees=Ditsakana.
Yachchumnes=Yachikamni.
Yach'ergamut=Yacherk.
Yachies=Texas.
Yachimese=Yachikamni.
Yachimichas=Chitimacha.
Yachou, Yachoux=Yazoo.
Yachtshil'agamiut=Yakchilak.
Yackaman, Yackamaws, Yackaws, Yackimas=Yak-
     ima.
Yaco=Acoma.
Yacomans=Yakima.
Yacona Indians, Yacone, Yacons=Yaquina.
Yacovanes=Yojuane.
Yactaché=Yatasi.
Yá-cu, Yá-cu-mé ʒůnně=Chemetunne.
Yacumi=Yacomui.
Yä'dᴀs=Yadus.
Yaesumnes=Yusumne.
Yä'gᴀn=Yagun.
Yagnetsito=Yagenechito.
Yagochsanogēchti=Onondaga.
Yaguénéchitons, Yagueneschito=Yagenechito.
Yä'-hä=Yahalgi.
Yahatc, Yahats=Yahach.
Yah-bay-páiesh=Yavapai.
Yahkutats=Yakutat.
Yä'hlâhaimub'âhůtůlba=Taos.
Yahmáyo=Yuma.
Yah-nih-kahs=Ataakut.
Yahooshkin, Yahooskin, Yahooskin Snakes=Yahu-
     skin.
Yahowa=Iowa.
Yah-quo-nah=Yaquina.
Yahrungwago=Yoroonwago.
Yahshoo=Yazoo.
Yah-shoots, Yahshutes=Chemetunne.
Yahweakwioose=Yukweakiwioose.
Yah-wil-chin-ne=Yawilchine.
Yá-idésta=Molala.
Yaínakshi, Yaínakskni=Yaneks.
Yais=Eyeish.
Yajumui=Yusumne.
Yakamas, Yakanias, Yakemas, Yakenia=Yakima.
Yaket-ahno-klatak-makanay, Yä'k'ĕt aqkinūqtlē'ĕt
     aqkts'mä'kinik=Akanekunik.
Ya-ki-as=Yokaia.
Yakimaw=Yakima.
Yakka=Yaka.
Ya'klä'nas=Yaku-lanas.
Ya'kokon ka'pai=Karankawa.
Yakon, Yákona, Yakonah, Yakone=Yaquina.
Yäkᵘ'dä't=Yakutat.
Ya-ʒůn'-ni-me' ʒůnně=Yaquina.
Yakutatskoe=Yakutat.
Yakutskalitnik, Yakutzkelignik=Tutago.
Yakweakwioose=Yukweakwioose.
Yăkwū Lennas=Yaku-lanas.
Yak-y-you=Yukweakwioose.
Yalaas=Yazoo.
Yalchedunes=Alchedoma.
Yale=Shilckuatl.
Yalesumnes, Yalesumni=Yusumne.
Yalipays=Yavapai.
Yallashee, Yaltasse=Yatasi.
Yama=Yuma.
Yamaçes=Yamasee.
Yamágas=Mohave.
Yamagatock=Yamako.
Yamajab=Mohave.
Yámakni=Warm Spring Indians.
Yamas, Yamases, Yamassálgi, Yamassecs, Yamassees,
     Yamassi=Yamasee.
Yamaya=Mohave.
Yamesee=Yamasee.
Yamhareek=Ditsakana.
Yam-Hill=Yamel.
Yamkallie=Yonkalla.
Yamkally=Kalapooian Family, Yonkalla.
Yamlocklock=Tamuleko.
Yammacrans, Yammacraw=Yamacraw.
Yammassees, Yammonsee, Yammosees, Yammossees=
     Yamasee.
Yam-mū's=Yammostuwiwagaiya.
Yamoisees, Yamossees=Yamasee.

Yampah=Comanche.
Yam Pah-Utes=Yampa.
Yä'mpaini=Comanche.
Yam-pái ò=Yavapai.
Yämpai-rĭ'kani=Comanche.
Yampais, Yampaos=Yavapai.
Yamparack, Yamparakas, Yamparecks, Yamparee-
     kas, Yamparîcas, Yam'pari'ka=Ditsakana.
Yampas=Yavapai.
Yam-pa-se-cas, Yampatéka=Ditsakana.
Yampatick-ara=Yampa.
Yampaxicas=Ditsakana.
Yampay=Yavapai.
Yampequaws=Umpqua.
Yamperack, Yamperethka, Yam-per-rikeu, Yam-pe-
     uc-coes=Ditsakana.
Yam-p'-ham-ba=San Cristóbal.
Yampi, Yampias=Yavapai.
Yampirica, Yam-pi-ric-coes=Ditsakana.
Yampi Utes, Yamp-Pah-Utahs=Yampa.
Yanabi=Ayanabi.
Yanckton=Yankton.
Yanctannas=Yanktonai.
Yancton=Yankton.
Yanctonais=Yanktonai.
Yanctonas=Yankton.
Yanctonees=Yanktonai.
Yanctongs=Yankton.
Yanctonie, Yanctonnais=Yanktonai.
Yanctonnais Cutheads=Pabaksa.
Yanctons, Yanctonwas, Yanctorinans, Yanctowah=
     Yankton.
Yánehe=Tonkawa.
Yaneton, Yanetong=Yankton.
Yanga, Yang-ha=Yangna.
Yangtons Ahnah=Yanktonai.
Yanieye-róno=Mohawk.
Yanioseaves=Yamasee.
Yankamas=Yakima.
Yanka-taus, Yanktau-Sioux, Yank toan=Yankton.
Yanktoanan, Yanktoanons=Yanktonai.
Yankton=Brulé.
Yanktona, Yankton Ahnâ, Yankton Ahnah, Yank-
     ton-aias, Yanktonais, Yanktonans, Yank-ton-ees=
     Yanktonai.
Yanktongs=Yankton.
Yanktonians, Yanktonias-Sioux, Yanktonies, Yank-
     tonnan, Yanktonnas=Yanktonai.
Yank-ton (of the north or plains)=Upper Yank-
     tonai.
Yanktons=Yankton.
Yanktons Ahna, Yanktons Ahnah=Yanktonai.
Yanktons of the North, Yanktons of the Plains=
     Upper Yanktonai.
Yanktons of the south=Yankton.
Yank-ton-us=Yanktonai.
Yanktoons, Yanktown=Yankton.
Yänkwă-näⁿ-'syän-ni'=Iroquois.
Yannacock, Yannocock=Corchaug.
Yannubbee Town=Ayanabi.
Yanos=Janos.
Yan-pa-pa Utahs=Yampa.
Yä'n-tdóa=Yan.
Yantons=Yankton.
Yaⁿ tsaá=Yangtsaa.
Yanubbee=Ayanabi.
Yaocomico, Yaocomoco=Secowocomoco.
Yaogᴀs=Yaogus.
Yaomacoes=Secowocomoco.
Yaopim Indians=Weapemeoc.
Yaos=Taos.
Yäpä=Ditsakana.
Yapaches=Apache.
Yapainé=Ditsakana.
Yapalage=Yapalaga.
Ya-pa-pi=Yavapai.
Yaparehca, Yä-pä-rēs-ka, Ya'pa-re'χka, Yapparic-
     koes, Yappariko=Ditsakana.
Ya'-qai-yŭk=Yahach.
Yaquima, Yaquimis=Yaqui.
Ya-seem-ne=Awani.
Yashoo, Yashu=Yazoo.
Yash-ue=Chemetunne.
Yashu Iskitini=Yazoo Skatane.
Yaskai=Yokaia.
YasLĭ'n=Yastling.
Yasones, Yasons, Yasoos, Yasou, Yasoux, Yasoves,
     Yassa, Yassaues, Yassouees=Yazoo.
Ya-su-chah, Yasuchaha, Yasuchan=Chemetunne.

Yasumni=Yusumne.
Yasüs=Yazoo.
Ya-sūt=Chemetunne.
Yatace, Yatache, Yatachez, Yatase, Yatasee, Yatasie, Yatasse, Yatassee, Yatassèz, Yatassi, Yatay=Yatasi.
Yatcheé-thinyoowuc=Siksika.
Yatchies=Texas.
Yatchikamnes, Yatchikumne=Yachikamni.
Yatchitoches=Natchitoch.
Yates=San Marcos.
Yátilatlávi=Navaho.
Yatl nas: had'ā′i=Yehlnaas-hadai.
Yattapo, Yattasaees, Yattasoes, Yattasees, Yattasie, Yattassee=Yatasi.
Yatuckets=Ataakut.
Yatum=Yutum.
Ya-tze=San Marcos.
Yauana=Yowani.
Yauktong, Yauktons=Yankton.
Yaulanchi=Yaudanchi.
Yaunktwaun=Yankton.
Ya′un-ñi=Yaunyi.
Yau-terrh=Yohter.
Yautuckets=Ataakut.
Yavai Suppai=Havasupai.
Yavapaias, Yavape, Yavapies=Yavapai.
Ya-ve̥-pe′-ku-toǎn′=Tulkepaia.
Yavepé-kutchan=Tulkepaia, Yuma.
Yavipai cajuala=Paiute.
Yavipai cuercomache=Cuercomache.
Yavipai-Gileños=Gila Apache.
Yavipai Jabesua, Yavipai javesua=Havasupai.
Yavipai-Lipanes=Lipan.
Yavipai Muca Oraive=Oraibi.
Yavipai-navajoi=Navaho.
Yavipais=Yavapai.
Yavipais-caprala=Paiute.
Yavipais-Nataje=Kiowa Apache.
Yavipais-Navajai=Navaho.
Yavipaistejua=Tejua.
Yavipay=Yavapai.
Yawĕdĕn′tshi, Ya′wĕdmŏni=Yaudanchi.
Yawhick, Yawhuch=Yahach.
Ya-wil-chuie, Yawitchénni=Yawilchine.
Yaχká-a=Crows.
Yayecha=Eyeish.
Yazoo Old Town, Yazoo Old Village, Yazoo Village, Yazous, Yazoux=Yazoo.
Ybitoopas, Ybitoupas=Ibitoupa.
Ycasqui=Casqui.
Ychiaha=Chiaha.
Yeahtentanee=Wea.
Yeannecock=Corchaug.
Yĕ′cEqEn=Yesheken.
Yecorí=Yecora.
Yecujen-ne′=Mimbreños.
Yegaha=Dhegiha.
Yeguaces, Yeguases, Yeguaz, Yeguazes=Yguases.
Yehah, Yehhuh=Yehuh.
Yehl=Hoya.
Yeka=Kikatsik.
Yekuk=Ekuk.
Ye-k′u′-nă-me′ ɟûnnĕ=Yaquina.
Ye-ᴋu-tce=Yucutce.
Yelamu′=Yelmus.
Yeletpo=Cayuse.
Yellowhill=Red Clay.
Yellow Knife, Yellowknife Indians, Yellow Knife people, Yellow Knives=Tatsanottine.
Yellow Medicine's band=Inyangmani.
Yellow Village=Nachurituei.
Yelovoi=Yalik.
Yemassee=Yamasee.
Yemez=Jemez.
Yemmassaws=Yamasee.
Yĕn=Yan.
Yendat=Huron.
Yĕndē′staqlê=Yendestake.
Yendots=Huron.
Yengetongs=Yankton.
Yent=Noöt.
Yeomansee=Yamasee.
Yeopim=Weapemeoc.
YEŏ′t=Noöt.
Yep-pe=Yampa.
Yĕqolaos=Yekolaos.
Yerbipiame=Ervipiames.
Yesáh, Ye-saⁿ, Yesáng=Tutelo.

Yetans=Ietan.
Yéta-ottinè=Etagottine.
Yé-tdóa=Ye.
Yeut=Noöt.
Yévepáyᵃ=Yavapai.
Yguaces, Yguazes=Yguases.
Y′hindastachy=Yendestake.
Yi′atá′teheñko=Carrizo.
Yiᴋɪrga′ulɪt=Eskimo, Imaklimiut, Inguklimiut.
Yik′oa′psan=Ikwopsum.
Yi-kq′aic′=Yikkhaich.
Yik′ts=Yukuts.
Yita=Ute.
Yītℓĕq=Itliok.
Yiuhta=Ute.
Yiχā̆qemāe=Yaaihakemae.
Ylackas=Wailaki.
Y-Mitches=Imiche.
Ymunacam=Ymunakam.
Ymúrez=Imuris.
Yncignavin=Inisiguanin.
Yneci=Nabedache.
Ynqueyunque=Yuqueyunque.
Yoacomoco=Wicocomoco.
Yoamaco, Yoamacoes=Secowocomoco.
Yoamity=Awani.
Yoani=Yowani.
Yocalles=Yokol.
Yocovanes=Yojuane.
Yocut=Mariposan Family.
Yoedmani=Yaudanchi.
Yoelchane=Yawilchine.
Yoem=Yuma.
Yoetahá=Navaho.
Yofale, Yofate=Eufaula.
Yoghroonwago=Yoroonwago.
Yohamite=Awani.
Yohios=Yokaia.
Yoht=Zoht.
Yohuane=Yojuane.
Yohumne=Yandimni.
Yo-kai-a-mah, Yo-Kei=Yokaia.
Yoko=Yokol.
Yokoalimduh=Yokolimdu.
Yokod=Yokol.
Yokpahs=Oyukhpe.
Yo-kul=Yokol.
Yokuts=Mariposan Family.
Yolanchas=Yaudanchi.
Yolays=Yolo.
Yoletta=Isleta.
Yol-hios=Yokaia.
Yoloy, Yoloytoy=Yolo.
Yolumne=Tuolumne.
Yom-pa-pa Utahs=Yampa.
Yonalins=Yonalus.
Yonanny=Yowani.
Yondestuk=Yendestake.
Yongletats=Ucluelet.
Yonkiousme=Jukiusme.
Yon-kt=Zoht.
Yonktins, Yonktons=Yankton.
Yonktons Ahnah=Yanktonai.
Yon-sal-pomas=Usal.
Yoochee=Yuchi.
Yookilta=Lekwiltok.
Yookoomans=Yakima.
Yoov′té=Uinta.
Yoqueechae, Yoquichacs=Yukichetunne.
Yorbipianos=Ervipiames.
Yosahmittis, Yo-sem-a-te, Yosemetos, Yo-semety, Yosemites=Awani.
Yoshol=Usal.
Yoshuway=Chemetunne.
Yosimities=Awani.
Yo-sol Pomas=Usal.
Yosoomite=Awani.
Yostjéemé=Apache.
Yosumnis=Yusumne.
Yóta=Ute.
Yotché-eme=Apache.
Yo-to-tan=Tututunne.
Youana, Youane=Yowani.
Youcan=Yukonikhotana.
Youchehtaht=Ucluelet.
Youcon=Yukonikhotana.
Youcoolumnies=Yukolumni.
Youfalloo=Eufaula.
Youghtamund=Youghtanund.

Youicomes, Youicone, Youikcone, Youikkone=
  Yaquina.
Youitts, Youitz=Yahach.
Youkone=Yaquina.
Youkonikatana=Yukonikhotana.
Youkon Louchioux Indians=Kutchakutchin.
You-ma-talla=Umatilla.
Youna=Yowani.
Young Dogs=Hachepiriinu.
Young-white-wolf=Wohkpotsit.
Younondadys=Tionontati.
You-pel-lay=Santo Domingo.
You-quee-chae=Yukichetunne.
Youρoni-Kouttànæ=Youkonikhotana.
Youruk=Yurok.
Yout=Noöt.
Youtah, Youtas=Ute.
Youthtanunds=Youghtanund.
You-tocketts=Ataakut.
Youts=Ute.
Yowana, Yowanne=Yowani.
Yoways=Iowa.
Yowechani=Yaudanchi.
Yow'-el-man'-ne=Yauelmani.
Yowkies=Yokol.
Yo-woc-o-nee=Tawakoni.
Yrbipias, Yrbipimas=Ervipiames.
Yrekas=Kikatsik.
Yrocois, Yrokoise=Iroquois.
Yroquet=Ononchataronon.
Yroquois=Iroquois.
Ys=Ais.
Yscanes=Yscanis.
Ysleta=Isleta, Isleta del Sur.
Yslete, Ystete=Isleta.
Ytara=Itara.
Ytaua=Etowah.
Ytha=Yta.
Ytimpabichis=Intimbich.
Yuahés=Iowa.
Yuanes=Iguanes.
Yubas=Yupu.
Yubipias, Yubissias=Yavapai.
Yubuincarini=Yubuincariri.
Yucal=Yokol.
Yucaopi=Yncaopi.
Yucas=Palaihnihan Family, Yukian Family.
Yucatat=Yakutat.
Yuchi=Uchean Family.
Yuchiha=Yuchi.
Yuc-la'-li=Yushlali.
Yucuatl=Yuquot.
Yufala, Yufála hupayi, Yufalis=Eufaula.
Yugelnut=Jugelnute.
Yú'hta=Ute.
Yu-i'-ta=Navaho.
Yu-Ite=Yuit.
Yuittcemo=Apache.
Yü'je ma'kaⁿ tce ubu̱'qpayĕ=Yuzhemakanche-
  ubukhpape.
Yujuanes=Yojuane.
Yuka=Yukian family.
Yukae=Yokaia.
Yukagamut=Chnagmiut, Ukak.
Yukagamute=Ukak.
Yukai=Yokaia.
Yukaipa, Yukaipat=Yucaipa.
Yukal=Yokol.
Yukeh=Yukian Family.
Yukh=Yaku.
Yúk'hiti ishak=Attacapa.
Yu-ki=Yukian Family.
Yu-ɥi, Yu'-ki-tcê ɥûnnĕ=Yukichetunne.
Yukkweakwioose=Yukweakwioose.
Yukletas=Lekwiltok.
Yuko-chakat, Yukokakat, Yukokokat=Soonkakat.
Yukol=Yokol.
Yuk-qais'=Yukhais.
Yu'-k'qwŭ-stí-ɥû=Yukhwustitu.
Yukükweü's=Yukweakwioose.
Yukulmey=Yukulme.
Yukuth, Yukuth Kutchin=Tukkuthkutchin.
Yukutneys=Yukulme.
Yu-kwā-chi=Yukichetunne.
Yü'kwilta=Lekwiltok.
Yû-kwĭn'-ă, Yû-kwĭn'-û-me' ɥunnĕ=Yaquina.
Yu'-kwi-tcê' ɥûnnĕ'=Yukitchetunne.
Yuk-yuk-y-yoose=Yukweakwioose.
Yulas=Ute.

Yuláta=Taos.
Yullite=Ahtena.
Yulonees=Yuloni.
Yum=Comeya, Yuma.
Yumanagan=Ymunakan.
Yumagatock=Yamako.
Yumanos=Tawehash.
Yumas=Suma.
Yumatilla=Umatilla.
Yumayas=Yuma.
Yump=Yuma.
Yumpatick-ara=Yambadika.
Yum-pis=Yavapai.
Yumsa=Yuma.
Yumyum=Ute.
Yunnakachotana, Yunnakakhotana =Koyukukho-
  tana.
Yunque, Yunqueyunk=Yugeuingge.
Yunssáha=Dakota.
Yuntaráye-rúnu=Kickapoo.
Yü'-nü wuñ-wü=Yungyu.
Yu-ñu-ye=Tyuonyi.
Yu'ñ-ya=Yungyu.
Yupacha=Yupaha.
Yupapais=Yavapai.
Yu-pi'It=Yuit.
Yuquache=Yukichetunne.
Yuques=Yukian Family.
Yuqui Yanqui=Yugeuingge.
Yuraba=Taos.
Yurapeis=Yavapai.
Yurmarjars=Yuma.
Yú-rok=Weitspekan Family.
Yú-sâl Pómo=Usal.
Yūsʌⁿ'=Yussoih.
Yútă=Ute.
Yutacjen-ne, Yutahá, Yú-tah-kah=Navaho.
Yuta-jenne=Faraon.
Yutajen-ne=Navaho.
Yutama, Yutamo=Ute.
Yu-tar-har'=Navaho.
Yutas=Ute.
Yutas Ancapagari=Tabeguache.
Yutas sabuaganas=Akanaquint.
Yutas Tabehuachis=Tabeguache.
Yutas Talareños=Tulareños.
Yútawáts=Ute.
Yutcama=Yuma.
Yute=Ute.
Yúte-shay=Apache.
Yutíla Pá, Yutilatláwi=Navaho.
Yutlū'lath=Ucluelet.
Yutoo'-ye-roop=Yutoyara.
Yu-tsû-tqaze, Yu-tsu-tquenne=Yutsutkenne.
Yutta=Ute.
Yutuin=Yutum.
Yuvas=Yupu.
Yuva-Supai=Havasupai.
Yvitachua=Tvitachuco.
Yxcaguayo=Guayoguia, Yjar.

Zacatal Duro=Posos.
Zacopines=Tiopines.
Zages=Osage.
Zagnato=Awatobi.
Zagoskin=Ikogmiut.
Zaguaganas, Zaguaguas=Akanaquint.
Zaguate, Zaguato=Awatobi.
Zaivovois=Iowa.
Zá-ke=Sauk.
Zana=Sana.
Zanana=Tenankutchin.
Zancagues=Tonkawa.
Zandia=Sandia.
Zandjé jiñ'ga=Zandzhezhinga.
Zandju'liⁿ=Zandzhulin.
Zanghe'darankiac=Sagadahoc.
Zani=Zuñi.
Zänker-Indianer=Kutchin.
Zantees=Santee.
Za Plasua=Saint Francis.
Zaramari=Tarahumare.
Zarame=Xarame.
Zaravay=Sarauahi.
Zatoe=Xatóe.
Zautoouys, Zautooys=Uzutiuhi.
Zaxxauzsi'kᴇn=Zakhauzsiken.
Zea=Sia.
Ze-gar-kin-a=Pima, Zuñi.

Ze-ka-ka=Kitkehahki.
Zèkā-thaka=Tangesatsa.
Zeke's Village=Seek's Village.
Zemas=Jemez.
Zembogu=Ozanbogus.
Zen-ecú=Senecú.
Zeneschio=Geneseo.
Zeninge=Shenango.
Zennecu=Senecu.
Zesuqua=Tesuque.
Zeton=Teton.
Zi-unka-kutchi, Ziunka-kutshi=Tangesatsa.
Ze-ut=Noöt.
Zeven steden van Cibola=Zuñi.
Zhiaguan=Siaguan.
Zia=Sia.
Ziaban, Ziaguan=Siaguan.
Zi-amma=Tsiama.
Ziatitz=Three Saints.
Zibirgoa=Sibirijoa.
Zibola=Hawikuh, Zuñi.
Ziguma=Cienega.
t'Zi-i=Sii.
Zijame=Sijame.
Zíka hákisiⁿ=Kitkehahki.
Zill-tar'-dens, Zill-tar-dins=Tsiltaden.
Zimshian=Tsimshian.
Zinachson=Shamokin.
Zingomenes=Spokan.
Zïnni jïnnë=Kinnazinde.
Zipias, Zippia-Kue=Tsipiakwe.
Zisagechroann, Zisagechrohne=Missisauga.
Zitos=Pueblo de los Silos.
Ziunka-kutshi=Tangesatsa.
Zivola=Zuñi.
Zizíka áki¢isiⁿ', Zizíka-ákisí=Kitkehahki.
Zjen-Kuttchin, Zjén-ta-Kouttchin=Vuntakutchin.
Zoe=Choiz.

Zoēnji=Zuñi.
Zolajan=Sulujame.
Zo-lat-e-se-djii=Zolatungzezhii.
Zolucans=Cherokee.
Zoneschio, Zoneshio, Zonesschio=Geneseo.
Zoni=Sonoita.
Zonneschio=Geneseo.
Zopex=Soba.
Zopus=Esopus.
ZōQkt=Zoht.
Zoreisch=Tsurau.
Zouni=Zuñi.
Ztolam=Sulujame.
Zuake=Suaqui.
Zuanquiz=Quanquiz.
Zuaque=Tehueco.
Zuaqui=Suaqui.
Zue=Dakota.
Zuelotelrey=Quelotetrey.
Zugnis=Zuñi.
Zuguato=Awatobi.
Zulaja, Zulajan=Sulujame.
Zulocans=Cherokee.
Zumana, Zumanas, Zumas=Suma, Tawehash.
Zumis, Zun, Zuña=Zuñi.
Zŭndju'liⁿ=Zandzhulin.
Zuñe, Zunia, Zuñians, Zuñi-Cibola, Zunie=Zuñi.
Zuñi Vieja=Heshota Ayahltona.
Zunni, Zuñu, Zuny, Zura=Zuñi.
Zures=Keresan Family.
Zutoida=Tutoida.
Zu'tsamîn=Zutsemin.
Zuxt=Zoht.
Zuyi=Zuñi.
Zuzeća kiyaksa=Kiyuksa.
Zuzeća wićása=Shoshoni.
Zuzetca kiyaksa=Kiyuksa.
Zwan-hi-ooks=Towahnahiooks.

BIBLIOGRAPHY

NOTE.—The names of authors and the titles of their papers appearing in magazines and other serial publications are not separately given in this list of works, unless the paper referred to is cited by title in the body of the Handbook. For example, Dr A. L. Kroeber's memoir on The Yokuts Language of South Central California, published as Volume V, part 2, of the University of California Publications in American Archaeology and Ethnology, is referred to by the entry " Kroeber in Univ. Cal. Pub., Am. Arch. and Eth., v, pt. 2, 1907," consequently it is included in this list only under the caption University of California. Many manuscripts in the archives of the Bureau of American Ethnology have been consulted in the preparation of the Handbook, but as they are not readily accessible to students outside of Washington they are not included in this list.

A. A. A. S. *See* AMERICAN ASSOCIATION.

ABBOTT, C. C. Primitive industry. Salem, 1881.

ABERCROMBIE, W. R. Copper river exploring expedition. Washington, 1900.

ABERT, J. W. Report of Lieut. J. W. Abert of his examination of New Mexico, in the years 1846–47. (In Emory, Reconnoissance, 1848.)

ACADEMY OF NATURAL SCIENCES OF PHILADELPHIA. Journal, vols. I–VI, 1817–30. Proceedings, vols. I–LVII, 1841–1905.

—————— *See* MOORE, CLARENCE B.

ADAIR, JAS. The history of the American Indians. London, 1775.

ADAM, LUCIEN. *See* HAUMONT, PARISOT, *and* ADAM.

ADAMS, C. F., *jr.*, *and* ADAMS, HENRY. Chapters of Erie, and other essays. Boston, 1871.

ADELUNG, J. C., *and* VATER, J. S. Mithridates oder allgemeine Sprachenkunde mit dem Vater Unser als Sprachprobe in bey nahe fünfhundert Sprachen und Mundarten. B. I–IV, Berlin, 1806–17.

AIMÉ-MARTIN. *See* LETTRES ÉDIFIANTES.

ALARCON, FERNANDO. Relation. 1540. (In Hakluyt, Voyages, vol. III, 1600, repr. 1810.)

—————— Relation de la navigation et de la découverte . . . 1540. (In Ternaux-Compans, Voyages, tome IX, Paris, 1838.)

ALBACH, JAS. R. Annals of the West. Pittsburg, 1856.

ALBERT, GEORGE DALLAS. History of Westmoreland county, Pennsylvania. Philadelphia, 1882.

ALCALA. *See* GALIANO, D.

ALCEDO, ANTONIO DE. Diccionario geográfico-histórico de las Indias Occidentales ó América. Tomos I–V. Madrid, 1786–89.

ALDRICH, H. L. Arctic Alaska and Siberia, or eight months with Arctic whalemen. Chicago, 1889.

ALEGRE, FRANCISCO JAVIER. Historia de la Compañía de Jesus en Nueva-España. Tomos I–III. Mexico, 1841.

ALEXANDER, JAS. EDWARD. L'Acadie ; or, seven years' explorations in British America. Vols. I–II. London, 1849.

ALLEN, *Miss* A. J. Ten years in Oregon. Travels and adventures of Doctor E. White and Lady, west of the Rocky mountains. Ithaca, 1850.

ALLEN, E. A. Prehistoric world : or, vanished races. Cincinnati, 1885.

ALLEN, HARRISON. Crania from the mounds of the St. John's river, Florida. (Jour. Acad. Nat. Sci. Philadelphia, N. S., vol. X, 1896.)

ALLEN, HENRY T. Report of an expedition to the Copper, Tanana, and Koyukuk rivers, in the territory of Alaska, in the year 1885. Washington, 1887.

ALLEN, J. A. The American bisons, living and extinct. (Memoirs Geol. Surv. Kentucky, vol. I, pt. II, Cambridge, 1876.)

AMERICAN ACADEMY OF ARTS AND SCIENCES. Memoirs, vol. II, pt. II, Charlestown, 1804 ; vol. III, pt. I, Cambridge, 1809.

AMERICAN ANTHROPOLOGICAL ASSOCIATION. Memoirs. Vol. I, pt. 2, Lancaster, Pa., 1906. Vol. I, pt. 6, Lancaster, 1907. Vol. II, pts. 1–4, Lancaster, 1907–08.

AMERICAN ANTHROPOLOGIST. Vols. I–XI, Washington, 1888–98 ; N. S., vols. I–XII, New York and Lancaster, 1899–1910.

AMERICAN ANTIQUARIAN AND ORIENTAL JOURNAL. Vols. I–XXXII, Chicago [and elsewhere], 1878–1910.

AMERICAN ANTIQUARIAN SOCIETY. Transactions and Collections (Archæologia Americana), vols. I–VII, Worcester, 1820–85. Proceedings [various numbers].

AMERICAN ARCHÆOLOGIST. Vol. II, Columbus, 1898. (*Formerly* The Antiquarian, q. v.)

AMERICAN ASSOCIATION FOR THE ADVANCEMENT OF SCIENCE. Proceedings. Vol. I (Philadelphia, 1849) to vol. LVIII (Chicago, 1908).

AMERICAN CATHOLIC QUARTERLY REVIEW. Vol. VI, no. 23, Philadelphia, 1881.

AMERICAN ETHNOLOGICAL SOCIETY. Transactions, vols. I–III, New York, 1845–53. Publications, vols. I–II, Leyden, 1907–09.

AMERICAN GEOGRAPHICAL SOCIETY. Journal, vols. I–XXXII, New York, 1859–1900. Bulletin, vols. XXXIII–XLI, New York, 1901–09. (*Formerly*, 1859–60, American Geographical and Statistical Society.)

AMERICAN GEOLOGIST. Vols. I–XXXIV, Minneapolis, 1888–1904.

AMERICAN HISTORICAL RECORD, and REPERTORY OF NOTES AND QUERIES. Vol. I, Philadelphia, 1872.

AMERICAN JOURNAL OF ARCHÆOLOGY. Vol. I, no. 2, Baltimore, 1885.

AMERICAN JOURNAL OF SCIENCE AND ARTS. Series I–IV, New York and New Haven, 1818–1905.

AMERICAN MAPS. [Miscellaneous collection of early American maps, 1579–1796. Two vols. In the library of the U. S. Geological Survey.]

AMERICAN MUSEUM OF NATURAL HISTORY. Memoirs: Anthropology, vols. I–VI, New York, 1898–1906. Bulletin, nos. 1–22, 1881–1907.

AMERICAN NATURALIST. Vol. I (Salem, 1868) to vol. XXXIX (Boston, 1905).

AMERICAN ORIENTAL SOCIETY. Journal. Vol. IX. New Haven, 1871.

AMERICAN PHILOSOPHICAL SOCIETY. Minutes and proceedings; Digest, vol. I, Philadelphia, 1744–1838. Proceedings, vols. I–XLIV, Philadelphia, 1838–1905. Transactions, vols. I–VI, Philadelphia, 1759–1809. Transactions (new series), vols. I–XIX, Philadelphia, 1818–98.

AMERICAN PIONEER. A monthly periodical devoted to the objects of the Logan Historical Society. vols. I–II, Cincinnati, 1842–1843.

AMERICAN STATE PAPERS. Documents, legislative and executive, of the Congress of the United States. Class II, Indian Affairs. Vols. I–II. Washington, 1832–34.

AMES, JOHN G. Report in regard to the condition of the Mission Indians of California. Washington, 1873 [1874].

ANALES DEL MINISTERIO DE FOMENTO. See MÉXICO, SECRETARÍA DE FOMENTO.

ANDERSON, ALEX. C. Notes on the Indian tribes of British North America and the north west coast. (In Historical Magazine, 1st ser., vol. VII, New York and London, 1863.)

ANDERSON, ALEX. D. The silver country or the great Southwest. New York, 1877.

ANDERSON, J. Nachrichten von Island, Grönland und der Strasse Davis. Hamburg, 1746.

————— Beschryving van Ysland, Groenland en de Straat Davis. Tot 'nut der Wetenschappen en den Koophandel. Amsterdam, 1750.

ANNALES DE LA PROPAGATION DE LA FOI. (Various editions.)

ANNUAL ARCHÆOLOGICAL REPORTS. (In Ann. Rep. Can. Inst. for 1886–94, Toronto, 1888–94, and App. to Rep. Minister of Education, Ontario, 1894–1904, Toronto, 1896–1905.)

ANTHROPOLOGICAL SOCIETY OF WASHINGTON. Transactions, vols. I–III, Washington, 1881–85.

————— See AMERICAN ANTHROPOLOGIST.

ANTHROPOS. Revue Internationale d'Ethnologie et de Linguistique. T. I–V. Salzburg, 1906–10.

ANTIQUARIAN (THE). Vol. I, Columbus, 1897. (Continued as The American Archæologist, q. v.)

ANTIQUITATES AMERICANÆ, sive scriptores septentrionales serum ante-Columbianarum in America. Hafniæ, 1837.

ANTISELL, THOS. Geological report. 1856. (In Pacific Railroad Reps., vol. VIII, Washington, 1857.)

ANVILLE, Le Sieur. See D'ANVILLE.

APPLETONS' CYCLOPÆDIA OF AMERICAN BIOGRAPHY. Vols. I–VII. New York, 1895–1900.

ARBER, EDWARD, ed. The English Scholar's Library. Capt. John Smith, 1608–1631. Birmingham, 1884.

ARCHÆOLOGIA. See SOCIETY OF ANTIQUARIES OF LONDON.

ARCHÆOLOGIA AMERICANA. See AMERICAN ANTIQUARIAN SOCIETY.

ARCHÆOLOGICAL INSTITUTE OF AMERICA. Papers, American series, vol. I, Boston and London, 1881 (reprinted 1883); vol. III, Cambridge, 1890; vol. IV, Cambridge, 1892; vol. V, Cambridge, 1890. Annual Report, First to Eleventh, Cambridge, 1880–90. Bulletin, vol. I, Boston, 1883.

————— See BANDELIER, A. F.

ARCHÆOLOGICAL REPORTS. See ANNUAL ARCHÆOLOGICAL REPORTS.

ARCHÆOLOGIST (THE). Vols. I–II, Waterloo, Ind., 1893–94; vol. III, N. Y., 1895. (Merged with Popular Science News, New York, Oct. 1895.)

ARCHDALE, JNO. A new description of Carolina. London, 1707. (Same, Charleston, 1822.)

ARCHER, WM. See NANSEN, F.

ARCHIV FÜR ANTHROPOLOGIE. B. I–XXX, Braunschweig, 1866–1904.

ARCHIV FÜR WISSENSCHAFTLICHE KUNDE VON RUSSLAND. B. I–XXV, Berlin, 1841–67.

ARMSTRONG, A. Personal narrative of the discovery of the north west passage. London, 1857.

ARMSTRONG, A. N. Oregon: Comprising a brief history and full description of the territories of Oregon and Washington. Chicago, 1857.

ARMSTRONG, P. A. The Piaza or, the devil among the Indians. Morris, Ill., 1887.

ARRICIVITA, JUAN DOMINGO. Crónica seráfica y apostólica del Colegio de Propaganda Fide de la Santa Cruz de Querétaro en la Nueva España. Segunda parte. México, 1792.

————— See ESPINOSA.

ARROWSMITH, A. A map exhibiting all the new discoveries in the interior parts of North America. London, 1795. [Additions to June 1814.]

————— and LEWIS. A new and elegant general atlas. Intended to accompany the new improved edition of Morse's geography. Boston, May 1812.

ASHE, THOMAS. Travels in America performed in 1806. For the purpose of exploring the rivers Alleghany, Monongahela, Ohio and Mississippi, and ascertaining the produce and condition of their banks and vicinity. London, 1808.

ATWATER, CALEB. Description of the antiquities discovered in the state of Ohio and other western states. (In Archæologia Americana, vol. I, 1820.)

————— The writings of. Columbus, 1833.

————— The Indians of the northwest, their manners, customs, &c. &c. Columbus, 1850.

AUDOUARD, OLYMPE. A travers l'Amérique. Le far-west. Paris, 1869.

AUDUBON, JNO. W. Western journal: 1849–1850. Cleveland, 1906.

AUSLAND (DAS). B. I–LXVII, Stuttgart, 1828–94.

B. A. A. S. See BRITISH ASSOCIATION.

BACHE, R. MEADE. Reaction time with reference to race. (Psychological Rev., vol. II, no. 5, New York and London, Sept. 1895.)

BACK, GEO. Narrative of the Arctic land expedition in the years 1833, 1834, and 1835. Philadelphia, 1836. (Same, London, 1836.)

————— Narrative of an expedition in H. M. S. Terror, on the Arctic shores, in the years 1836–7. London, 1838.

BACON, OLMER N. A history of Natick, from its first settlement in 1651 to the present time. Boston, 1856.

BACON, THOS. Laws of Maryland at large, with proper indexes [1637–1763]. Annapolis, 1765.

BACQUEVILLE DE LA POTHERIE, C.-C. LE ROY DE LA. Histoire de l'Amérique Septentrionale, Tomes I–IV. Paris, 1722. (Same, Paris, 1753.)

BAEGERT, JACOB. Nachrichten von der amerikanischen Halbinsel Californien; mit einem zweyfachen Anhang falscher Nachrichten. Mannheim, 1772.

————— An account of the aboriginal inhabitants of the California peninsula. Translated by Charles Rau. (Smithsonian Reps. for 1863 and 1864, reprinted 1865 and 1875.)

BAER, K. E. VON, *and* HELMERSEN, G. VON. Beiträge zur Kentniss des russischen Reiches und der angränzenden Länder Asiens. B. I. St. Petersburg, 1839.

BAFFIN, W. The voyage of W. Baffin, 1620–22. Edited with notes and introduction by C. R. Markham. (Hakluyt Society Pub., vol. LXIII, London, 1881.)

BAKER, C. ALICE. True stories of New England captives. Cambridge, 1897.

BAKER, MARCUS. Geographic dictionary of Alaska. (Bull. U. S. Geological Survey, Washington, 1901. 1902. 1906.)

BAKER, THEODOR. Uber die Musik der nordamerikanischen Wilden. Leipzig, 1882.

BALBI, ADRIEN. Atlas ethnographique du globe, ou classification des peuples anciens et modernes d'après leurs langues. Paris, 1826.

BALFOUR, HENRY. Evolution in decorative art. London, 1893.

BALL, T. H. *See* HALBERT, H. S. *and* BALL.

BALLANTYNE, R. M. Hudson's bay; or everyday life in the wilds of North America. Edinburgh, 1848.

―――― Ungara; a tale of Esquimaux land. London, 1857. London, 1860.

BALLARD, EDWARD. Geographical names on the coast of Maine. (U. S. Coast Survey Rep. for 1868, Washington, 1871.)

BANCROFT, GEO. History of the United States. Vols. I–XI. Boston, 1838–75.

BANCROFT, HUBERT HOWE. The works of. Vols. I–XXXIX. San Francisco, 1886–90. [Vols. I–V, Native races. VI–VII, Central America. IX–XIV, North Mexican States and Texas. XVII, Arizona and New Mexico. XVIII–XXIV, California. XXV, Nevada, Colorado, Wyoming. XXVI, Utah. XXVII–XXVIII, Northwest Coast. XXIX–XXX, Oregon. XXXI, Washington, Idaho, Montana. XXXII, British Columbia. XXXIII, Alaska. XXXIV, California pastoral. XXXV, California inter pocula. XXXVI – XXXVII, Popular tribunals. XXXVIII, Essays and miscellany. XXXIX. Literary industries. Various editions of these works have been used.]

BANDELIER, ADOLF F. Historical introduction to studies among the sedentary Indians of New Mexico. (Papers of the Archæological Institute of America, American ser., vol. I, Boston, 1881.)

―――― [Reports on his investigations in New Mexico during the years 1883–84.] Fifth Ann. Rep. Archæological Institute of America, Cambridge, 1884.)

―――― Alvar Nuñez Cabeza de Vaca. (Magazine of Western History, Cleveland, Ohio, vol. IV, July, 1886.)

―――― La découverte du Nouveau-Mexique par le moine Franciscain Frère Marcos de Nice en 1539. (Revue d'Ethnographie, tome V, Paris, 1886.)

―――― The discovery of New Mexico by Fray Marcos of Nizza. (Magazine of Western History, vol. IV, Cleveland, Sept. 1886.)

―――― Final report of investigations among the Indians of the southwestern United States, carried on mainly in the years from 1880 to 1885. (Papers of the Archæological Institute of America, American series, vol. III, Cambridge, 1890; IV, Cambridge, 1892.)

―――― Historical archives of the Hemenway Southwestern Archaeological Expedition. (Compte-rendu Congrès International des Américanistes, 7me sess., 1888, Berlin, 1890.)

―――― Contributions to the history of the southwestern portion of the United States. (Papers of the Archaeological Institute of America, American series, vol. V, Cambridge, 1890.)

―――― The Delight makers. New York, 1890.

BANDELIER, ADOLF F. Documentary history of the Zuñi tribe. (Jour. Am. Ethnol. and Archæol., vol. III, Boston and New York, 1892.)

―――― The Gilded man (El Dorado) and other pictures of the Spanish occupancy of America. New York, 1893.

BARAGA, FREDERIC. Dictionary of the Otchipwe language, explained in English. Part I, English-Otchipwe, Montreal, 1878. Part II, Otchipwe-English, Montreal, 1880. (In Grammar and Dictionary of the Otchipwe language, new ed., Montreal, 1882.)

―――― A theoretical and practical grammar of the Otchipwe language. Second ed., Montreal, 1878.

BARANTS, WM. *See* DE VEER, G.

BARBER, EDWIN A. Comparative vocabulary of Utah dialects. (Bull. U. S. Geol. and Geog. Survey of the Territories, vol. III, Washington, 1877.)

BARBER, JNO. W. Historical collections, being a general collection of historical facts, traditions, biographical sketches, &c., relating to the history and antiquities of every town in Massachusetts. Worcester, 1839.

―――― The history and antiquities of New England, New York, New Jersey, and Pennsylvania. Hartford, 1844.

―――― *and* HOWE, H. Historical collections of the State of New Jersey. New York, 1844.

BARCIA CARBALLIDO Y ZUÑIGA, ANDRÉS G. Ensayo cronológico para la historia general de la Florida, 1512–1722, por Gabriel de Cardenas Z. Cano [*pseud.*]. Madrid, 1723.

―――― Historiadores primitivos de las Indias Occidentales. Tomes I–III. Madrid, 1749.

BARNUM, FRANCIS. Grammatical fundamentals of the Innuit language as spoken by the Eskimo of the western coast of Alaska. Boston and London, 1901.

BARR, JAS. A correct and authentic narrative of the Indian war in Florida. New York, 1836.

BARRATT, JOS. The Indian of New England and the northeastern provinces; a sketch of the life of an Indian hunter, ancient traditions relating to the Etchemin tribe [etc.]. Middletown, Conn., 1851.

BARREIRO, ANTONIO. Ojeada sobre Nuevo-México. Puebla, 1832.

―――― *See* PINO, PEDRO B.

BARRETT, S. M., ed. Geronimo's story of his life. New York, 1906.

BARRETT - LENNARD, CHAS. E. Travels in British Columbia, with the narrative of a yacht voyage round Vancouver island. London, 1862.

BARROW, J. Chronological history of the voyages into the Arctic regions. London, 1818.

―――― A voyage of discovery in the Arctic regions. London, 1846.

BARROWS, DAVID PRESCOTT. Ethno-botany of the Coahuilla Indians of southern California. (Univ. of Chicago, Dept. Anthropology, Chicago, 1900.)

BARROWS, WM. Oregon. The struggle for possession. Boston, New York, and Cambridge, 1884.

BARSTOW, G. History of New Hampshire from 1614 to 1819. 2d ed. Concord, 1853.

BARTLETT, JNO. R. Personal narrative of explorations and incidents . . . connected with the United States and Mexican Boundary Commission, 1850–53. Vols. I–II. New York, 1854.

―――― Dictionary of Americanisms. A glossary of words and phrases usually regarded as peculiar to the United States. Boston, 1860.

BARTON, BENJ. S. New views of the origin of the tribes and nations of America. Philadelphia, 1797. Same, 1798.

BARTRAM, JNO. Observations on the inhabitants, climate, soil, rivers, productions, animals, and other matters worthy of notice made by Mr. John Bartram, in his travels from Pensilvania to Onondago, Oswego, and the Lake Ontario in Canada, to which is annexed a curious account of the cataracts of Niagara, by Mr. Peter Kalm. London, 1751.

BARTRAM, WM. Travels through North and South Carolina, Georgia, East and West Florida, the Cherokee country, the extensive territories of the Muscogulges or Creek Confederacy, and the country of the Chactaws. Philadelphia, 1791. London, 1792.

———— Voyage dans les parties sud de l'Amérique septentrionale. Traduits de l'anglais par P. V. Benoist. Tomes I–II. Paris, 1799–1801.

BASKIN, FORSTER, & CO. Illustrated historical atlas of Indiana. Chicago, 1876.

BASSANIER, M. Histoire notable de la Floride. Paris, 1586.

BATES, H. W. See STANFORD, EDWARD.

BATTEY, THOS. C. Life and adventures of a Quaker among the Indians. Boston and New York, 1875. (Same, 1876.)

BAUDRY DES LOZIÈRES, LOUIS N. Voyage a la Louisiane et sur le continent de l'Amérique septentrionale, fait dans les années 1794 à 1798. Paris, 1802.

BEACH, WM. W. The Indian miscellany: containing papers on the history, antiquities, arts, languages, religions, traditions and superstitions of the American aboriginies. Albany, 1877.

BEADLE, J. H. The undeveloped west; or, five years in the territories. Philadelphia, Chicago, Cincinnati, St. Louis. [1873.]

———— Western wilds, and the men who redeem them. Detroit, 1877. Cincinnati, 1878.

BEALE, EDWARD F. Letter from the Secretary of the Interior, communicating the report of Edward F. Beale, superintendent of Indian Affairs in California, respecting the condition of Indian affairs in that state. (Senate Ex. Doc. no. 57, 32d Cong., 2d. sess., 1853.)

BEATTY, CHAS. The journal of a two months tour to the westward of the Allegany mountains. 2d ed. Edinburgh, 1798.

BEAUCHAMP, WM. M. The Iroquois trail; or, foot-prints of the Six Nations. Fayetteville, N. Y., 1892.

———— Aboriginal chipped stone implements of New York. (Bull. N. Y. State Mus., no. 16, Albany, 1897.)

———— Polished stone articles used by the New York aborigines. (Ibid., no. 18, Albany, 1897.)

———— Aboriginal occupation of New York. (Ibid., no. 32, Albany, 1900.)

———— Wampum and shell articles used by the New York Indians. (Ibid., no. 41, Albany, 1901.)

———— Horn and bone implements of the New York Indians. (Ibid., no. 50, Albany, 1902.)

———— Metallic ornaments of the New York Indians. (Ibid., no. 73, Albany, 1903.)

———— A history of the New York Iroquois. (Ibid., no. 78, Albany, 1905.)

———— Aboriginal place names of New York. (Ibid., no. 108, Albany, 1907.)

BEAUFOY, M. On the northwest passage. (In Barrington, D., Possibility of approaching the North Pole asserted, London, 1818.)

BECKWITH, E. G. Report. (Pacific Railroad Reports, vol. II, Washington, 1855.)

BECKWITH, HIRAM W. Indian names of water courses in the State of Indiana. (Indiana Department of Geology and Natural History, 12th Ann. Rep., 1882, Indianapolis, 1883.)

———— The Illinois and Indiana Indians. Chicago, 1884.

BECKWOURTH, JAS. P. See BONNER, T. D.

BEECHEY, FREDERIC W. Narrative of a voyage to the Pacific and Beering's strait, to cooperate with the Polar expeditions. Parts I–II. London, 1831. Philadelphia, 1832.

———— Voyages of discovery toward the North Pole. London, 1843.

BELCHER, EDWARD. Narrative of a voyage round the world. Vol. I. London, 1843.

BELCOURT, G. A. Department of Hudson's Bay; translated from the French by Mrs. Letitia May. (Minn. Hist. Soc. Coll., vol. I, St. Paul, 1872.)

BELKOFF, Z. Prayers and hymns of Yukon-Kuskokwim language. New York, 1896.

BELL, A. W. On the native races of New Mexico. (Journal Ethnological Society of London, N. S., vol. I, session 1868–69, London, 1869.)

BELL, C. N. Hudson's bay: our northern waters. Winnipeg, 1884.

BELL, ROBERT. The medicine man, or Indian and Eskimo notions of medicine. (Canada Medical and Surgical Journal, Montreal, Mar.–Apr. 1886.)

BELL, SOLOMON [pseud.]. See SNELLING, W. J.

BELL, WM. A. New tracks in North America. A journal of travel and adventure whilst engaged in the survey for a southern railroad to the Pacific ocean. Vols. I–II. London, 1869.

BELLIN, M. Partie orientale de la Nouvelle France ou de Canada, 1755. (In Homann, J. B., Atlas geographicus major, Norimbergæ, 1759.)

BELTRAMI, GIACOMO C. A pilgrimage in Europe and America, leading to the discovery of the sources of the Mississippi and Bloody river. Vols. I–II. London, 1828.

BENAVIDES, ALONSO DE. Memorial. Madrid, 1630. (Also translation in Land of Sunshine, vol. XIII, Los Angeles, Cal., 1900.)

BENTON, ELBERT JAY. The Wabash trade route in the development of the old Northwest. (John Hopkins Univ. Studies in Hist. and Polit. Sci., ser. XXI, nos. 1–2, Baltimore, 1903.)

BENZONI, GIRALAMO. History of the New World. (Hakluyt Society Pub., vol. XXI, London, 1857.)

BERGHAUS, HEINRICH C. W. Physikalischer Atlas; geographisches Jahrbuch zur Mittheilung aller neuen Erforschungen. 2 vols in 4 pts. Gotha, 1850–52.

———— Allgemeiner ethnographischer Atlas, oder Atlas der Völker-kunde. Gotha, 1852.

BERLANDIER, LUIS, and CHOVELL, RAFAEL. Diario de viage de la Comision de Límites que puso el gobierno de la Republica. Mexico, 1850.

BERQUIN-DUVALLON, M. Vue de la colonie Espagnole du Mississippi, ou des provinces de Louisiane et Floride occidentale, en l'année 1802. Paris, 1803.

———— Travels in Louisiana and the Floridas: From the French, with notes by J. Davis. New York, 1806.

BESSELS, EMIL. Die Amerikanische Nordpol-Expedition. Leipzig, 1878.

BETTS, C. WYLLYS. American colonial history illustrated by contemporary medals. New York, 1894.

BEVERLEY, ROBERT. History of Virginia, by a native and inhabitant of the place. 2d ed. London, 1722.

BIBLIOTHÈQUE de Linguistique et d'Ethnographie Américaines. Vols. I–III. Paris and San Francisco, 1875–76.

BIEDMA, LUIS HERNANDEZ DE. Journal of the expedition of H. de Soto into Florida. (In French, B. F., Historical Collections of Louisiana, pt. 2, 1850.)

———— A relation of what took place during the expedition of Captain Soto. (Hakluyt Soc. Pub., vol. IX, London, 1851.)

———— Relacion de la isla de la Florida. (In Smith, B., Colección de Varios Documentos para la Historia de la Florida y Tierras Adyacentes, tomo I, Londres, 1857.)

———— Relation of the conquest of Florida presented in the year 1544 to the King of Spain in Council. Translated from the original document. (Narratives of the career of Hernando de Soto, translated by B. Smith, New York, 1866.)

———— *See* GENTLEMAN OF ELVAS.

BIGELOW, J. M. General description of the botanical character of the soil and productions along the road traversed. (Pacific Railroad Reports, vol. IV, Washington, 1856.)

BIOGRAPHICAL and historical memoirs of northwest Louisiana, containing a large fund of biography of actual residents, and an historical sketch of thirteen counties. Nashville and Chicago, 1890.

BIRDSALL, W. R. Cliff dwellings of the cañons of the Mesa Verde. (Bull. Am. Geog. Soc., vol. XXIII, New York, 1891.)

BLACK HAWK. *See* PATTERSON, J. B., *ed.*

BLACKMORE, WM. On the North American Indians. (Jour. Ethnol. Soc. London, N. S., vol. I, session 1868–69, London, 1869.)

BLAEU, JEAN. Dovziéme volvme de la geographie blaviane, contenant l'Ameriqve qvi est la V. partie de la terre. Amsterdam, 1667. [Quoted as Blaeu, Atlas, vol. XII.]

BLAKE, E. V. Arctic experiences. New York, 1874.

BLAKE, WM. P. Geological report. (Pacific Railroad Reports, vol. V, Washington, 1856.)

———— The chalchihuitl of the Mexicans ; its locality and association and its identity with turquoise. (Am. Jour. Sci. and Arts, 2d s., vol. XXV, New Haven, 1858.)

BLAKE, WILSON W. The cross, ancient and modern. New York. [1888.]

BLISS, EUGENE F., *ed.* Diary of David Zeisberger, a Moravian missionary among the Indians of Ohio. Vols. I–II. Cincinnati, 1885.

BOAS, FRANZ. Baffin-Land. Geographische Ergebnisse einer in den Jahren 1883 und 1884 ausgeführten Forschungreise. (Ergänzungsheft 80 zu Petermanns Mitteilungen, Gotha, 1885.)

———— Zur Ethnologie Britisch-Kolumbiens. (Petermanns Mitteilungen, Band XXXIII, Heft V, Gotha, 1887.)

———— Census and reservations of the Kwakiutl nation. (Bull. Am. Geog. Soc., vol. XIX, no. 3, New York, 1887.)

———— The central Eskimo. (Sixth Rep. Bur. Am. Ethnology, Washington, 1888.)

———— Songs and dances of the Kwakiutl. (Jour. Am. Folk-lore, vol. I, Boston, 1888.)

———— Die Tsimschian. (Zeitschrift für Ethnologie, B. XX, Berlin, 1888.)

———— The half-blood Indian. An anthropometric study. (Pop. Sci. Mo., vol. XLV, New York, Oct. 1894.)

———— Human faculty as determined by race. (Proc, Am. Asso. Adv. Sci. 1894, vol. XLIII, Salem, 1895.)

———— Zur Anthropologie der nordamerikanischen Indianer. (Verhandl. der Berliner Gesel. für Anthr., Berlin, 1895.)

BOAS, FRANZ. Chinook texts. (Bull. 20, Bur. Am. Ethnology, Washington, 1895.)

———— Anthropometrical observations on the Mission Indians of southern California. (Proc. Am. Asso. Adv. Sci., vol. XLIV, Salem, 1896.)

———— Decorative art of the Indians of the North Pacific coast. (Bull. Am. Mus. Nat. Hist., vol. IX, no. 10, New York, 1897.)

———— The social organization and the secret societies of the Kwakiutl Indians. (Rep. U. S. Nat. Museum for 1895, Washington, 1897.)

———— The mythology of the Bella Coola Indians. (Mem. Am. Mus. Nat. Hist., vol. II, Anthropology I, New York, 1898.)

———— Facial paintings of the Indians of northern British Columbia. (Ibid.)

———— A. J. Stone's measurements of natives of the Northwest Territories. (Bull. Am. Mus. Nat. Hist., vol. XIV, New York, 1901.)

———— The Eskimo of Baffin land and Hudson bay. (Ibid., vol. XV, pt. 1, New York, 1901.)

———— Kathlamet texts. (Bull. 26, Bur. Am. Ethnology, Washington, 1901.)

———— Tsimshian texts. (Bull. 27, Bur. Am. Ethnology, Washington, 1902.)

———— *and* FARRAND, L. Physical characteristics of the tribes of British Columbia. (Rep. Brit. Asso. Adv. Sci. for 1898, London, 1899.)

———— *See* NORTHWESTERN TRIBES OF CANADA ; TEIT, JAMES.

BOAS ANNIVERSARY VOLUME. Anthropological papers written in honor of Franz Boas, Professor of Anthropology in Columbia University, on the twenty-fifth anniversary of his doctorate. New York, 1906.

BOGORAS, WALDEMAR. The Chukchee. I. Material Culture. (Mem. Am. Mus. Nat. Hist., Pub. Jesup N. Pac. Exped., vol. VII, Leiden and New York, 1904.)

BOHUN, EDMUND. *See* HEYLYN, PETER.

BOLLAERT, WM. Observations on the Indian tribes in Texas. (Jour. Ethnol. Soc. London, vol. II, 1850.)

BOLLER, HENRY A. Among the Indians. Eight years in the far west : 1858–1866. Embracing sketches of Montana and Salt Lake. Philadelphia, 1868.

BOLTON, ROBERT. History of the several towns, manors, and patents of the county of Westchester. Vols. I–II. New York, 1881.

BONNELL, GEO. W. Topographical description of Texas. To which is added an account of the Indian tribes. Austin, 1840.

BONNER, T. D. The life and adventures of James P. Beckwourth, mountaineer, scout, and pioneer. New York, 1856.

BONNEVILLE, BENJ. L. E. The Rocky mountains ; or scenes, incidents, and adventures in the far west ; digested from his journal, by Washington Irving. Vols. I–II. Philadelphia, 1837.

———— *See* IRVING, W.

BONNYCASTLE, RICHARD H. Spanish America. Philadelphia, 1819.

———— Newfoundland in 1842. Vols. I–II. London, 1842.

BOSCANA, GERONIMO. Chinigchinich ; a historical account of the origin, customs, and traditions of the Indians at the missionary establishment of St. Juan Capistrano, Alta California ; called the Acagchemem Nation. (In Robinson, Alfred, Life in California, New York, 1846.)

BOSSU, N. Travels through that part of North America formerly called Louisiana. Translated by J. R. Forster. Vols. I–II. London, 1771.

BOSTON SOCIETY OF NATURAL HISTORY. Proceedings. Vols. I–XXXII. Boston, 1844–1905.

BOTELER, W. C. Peculiarities of American Indians from a physiological and pathological standpoint. (Maryland Med. Jour., vol. VII, no. 1, Baltimore, 1880.)

BOUDINOT, ELIAS. A star in the west: or a humble attempt to discover the long lost ten tribes of Israel. Trenton (N. J.), 1816.

BOULET, J. B. Prayer book and catechism in the Snohomish language. Tulalip, Wash., 1879.

BOUQUET, HENRY. See SMITH, WM.

BOURKE, JNO. G. The snake-dance of the Moquis of Arizona, being a narrative of a journey from Santa Fé, New Mexico, to the villages of the Moqui Indians of Arizona. New York, 1884.

———— On the border with Crook. New York, 1891.

———— The medicine-men of the Apache. (Ninth Rep. Bur. Am. Ethnology, Washington, 1892.)

BOURNE, E. G., ed. Narratives of the career of Hernando de Soto. Vols I–II. New York, 1904.

BOVET, FELIX. Le Comte de Zinzendorf. Paris, 1860.

BOWEN, BENJ. F. America discovered by the Welsh in 1170 A. D. Philadelphia, 1876.

BOWEN, EMAN. A map of the British American plantations extending from Boston in New England to Georgia. [n. p., n. d.]

BOWLES, CARINGTON. New one-sheet map of America, divided into its kingdoms, states, governments, and other subdivisions. London, 1784.

BOWLES, JNO. America laid down from the observations of the Royal Academy of Sciences, and compared with the maps of Sanson, Nolin, Du Fer, De l'Isle, and Mitchell. London [after 1750].

———— New pocket map of the United States of America, the British possessions of Canada, Nova Scotia, and New Foundland, with the French and Spanish territories of Louisiana and Florida. 1783.

BOX, MICHAEL J. Adventures and explorations in New and Old Mexico. New York, 1869.

BOYD, STEPHEN G. Indian local names, with their interpretation. York, Pa., 1885.

BOYLE, DAVID. See ANNUAL ARCHÆOLOGICAL REPORTS.

BOZMAN, JNO. L. A sketch of the history of Maryland during the first three years after its settlement. Baltimore, 1811.

———— History of Maryland, from its first settlement in 1633 to the restoration in 1660. Vols. I–II. Baltimore, 1837.

BRACKENRIDGE, H. M. Views of Louisiana; together with a journal of a voyage up the Missouri river, in 1811. Pittsburgh, 1814; Baltimore, 1817.

———— Mexican letters, written during the progress of the late war between the United States and Mexico. Washington, 1850.

———— Early discoveries by Spaniards in New Mexico, containing an account of the castles of Cibola, and the present appearance of their ruins. Pittsburgh, 1857.

———— History of the Whiskey Insurrection, 1794. Pittsburg, 1859.

BRADBURY, JNO. Travels in the interior of America, in the years 1809, 1810, and 1811. Liverpool and London, 1817.

BRADFORD, W. The Arctic regions illustrated with photographs taken on an Arctic expedition to Greenland . . . with descriptive narrative. London, 1873.

BRADLEY, WM. H. Atlas of the world. [n. p.] 1885.

BRAGG, B. Voyage to the North Pole. London, 1817.

BRAGGE, WM. Bibliotheca nicotiana; a catalogue of books about tobacco. Birmingham, 1880.

BRAINERD, DAVID. Memoirs of the Rev. David Brainerd, missionary to the Indians. By Rev. Jonathan Edwards. New Haven, 1822.

BRÄSS, M. Beiträge zur kenntniss der künnstlichen schädelverbildungen. Leipzig, 1887.

BRASSEUR DE BOURBOURG, CHARLES ETIENNE. Quatre lettres sur le Mexique. Paris, 1868.

———— Manuscrit Troano. Études sur le système graphique et la langue des Mayas. Tomes I–II. Paris, 1869–70.

BRENCHLEY, JULIUS. See REMY (JULES) and BRENCHLEY.

BRESSANI, FRANCESCO GIUSEPPE. Relation abrégée de quelques missions de pères de la Compagnie de Jésus, dans la Nouvelle France. Traduit de l'italien et augmenté, par F. Martin. Montréal, 1852.

BREVIS NARRATIO. See BRY, THEODORO DE

BREVOORT, ELIAS. New Mexico. Her natural resources and attractions. Santa Fé, 1875.

BRICE, WALLACE A. History of Fort Wayne, from the earliest known accounts of this point, to the present period. Fort Wayne, 1868.

BRICKELL, JNO. The natural history of North-Carolina. With an account of the trade, manners, and customs of the Christian and Indian inhabitants. Dublin, 1737.

BRINTON, DANIEL G. Notes on the Floridian peninsula, its literary history, Indian tribes and antiquities. Philadelphia, 1859.

———— Myths of the New World. New York, 1868.

———— National legend of the Chahta-Muskokee tribes. Morrisania, N. Y., 1870.

———— American hero-myths. A study in the native religions of the western continent. Philadelphia, 1882.

———— Essays of an Americanist. Philadelphia, 1890.

———— The American race. New York, 1891.

———— ed. Library of aboriginal American literature. Vols. I–VI. Philadelphia, 1882–85. (1, Chronicles of the Mayas. 2, The Iroquois book of rites. 3, The Comedy-ballad of Güegüence. 4, A migration legend of the Creek Indians, vol. I. 5, The Lenâpé and their legends. 6, The annals of the Cakchiquels.)

BRITISH ADMIRALTY CHART. North America west coast and adjacent shores of British Columbia, 1859–64. Surveyed by Capt. G. N. Richards. No. 1,917.

BRITISH AND FOREIGN BIBLE SOCIETY. Historical table of languages and dialects. (Eighty-first report, London, 1885.)

BRITISH ASSOCIATION FOR THE ADVANCEMENT OF SCIENCE. See ETHNOLOGICAL SURVEY OF CANADA; NORTHWESTERN TRIBES OF CANADA.

BRITISH COLUMBIA. Map of British Columbia; being a geographical division of the Indians of the province, according to their nationality or dialect. Victoria, B. C., 1872.

BRITTON, N. L., and BROWN, ADDISON. Illustrated flora of the northern United States, Canada, and the British possessions. Vols. I–III. New York, 1896–98.

BROCA, P. Sur la déformation Toulousaine du crâne. Paris, 1872.

BRODBACK, J. Nach Osten. (East Greenland Expedition.) Niesky, 1882.

BRODHEAD, L. W. The Delaware Water Gap. Philadelphia, 1867. (Same, Philadelphia, 1870.)

BROKE, GEO. With sack and stock in Alaska. London, 1891.

BROOKS, ALFRED H., et al. Reconnoissances in the Cape Nome and Northern Bay regions, Alaska, in 1900. U. S. Geol. Survey, Washington, 1901.

BROOKS, C. W. Jeanette relics. San Francisco, 1884.

BROWER, J. V. Quivira. (Memoirs of Explorations in the Basin of the Mississippi, vol. I, St. Paul, 1898.)

——— Harahey. (Ibid., vol. II, St. Paul, 1899.)

——— Kathio. (Ibid., vol. IV, St. Paul, 1901.)

——— Kakabikansing. (Ibid., vol. V, St. Paul, 1902.)

——— Minnesota. Discovery of its area. (Ibid., vol. VI, St. Paul, 1903.)

——— Kansas. Monumental perpetuation of its earliest history. 1541–1896. Ibid., vol. VII, St. Paul, 1903.)

——— and BUSHNELL, D. I., Jr. Mille Lac. (Ibid., vol. III, St. Paul, 1900.)

BROWN, ALEX. The genesis of the United States. A narrative of the movement in England, 1605–1616, which resulted in the plantation of North America by Englishmen. Vols. I–II. Boston and New York, 1890.

——— The first republic in America. Boston and New York, 1898.

BROWN, JNO. The North West passage. 2d ed. London, 1860.

BROWN, SAMUEL R., ed. The Western Gazetteer. Auburn, 1817.

BROWNE, J. ROSS. Adventures in the Apache country. New York, 1869.

——— Resources of the Pacific slope. With a sketch of the settlement and exploration of Lower California. New York, 1869.

BROWNELL, CHAS. DE W. The Indian races of North and South America. Boston, 1853.

BRUCE, M. W. Alaska, its history and resources. Seattle, 1895.

BRUNER, F. G. Hearing of primitive peoples. (Columbia Univ. Archives of Psychology, no. 11, New York, 1908.)

BRY, THEODORO DE. Brevis narratio eorum qvæ in Florida Americæ Provicia Gallis acciderunt, secunda in illam nauigatione du ce Renato de Laudõniere classis Præfecto anno M.D.LXIIII qvæ est secvnda pars Americæ. Francoforti ad Mœnvm, 1591.

——— et JOANNES, I. DE. Collectiones peregrinationum in Indiam Orientalem et Indiam Occidentalem, XXV partibus comprehensæ. T. I–XXXVII. Francoforti ad Mœnum, 1590–1634.

BRYANT, CHAS. S., and MURCH, ABEL B. History of the great massacre by the Sioux Indians. St. Peter, Minn., 1872.

BRYCE, GEO. Remarkable history of the Hudson's Bay Company. New York, 1900.

BUCHANAN, JAS. Sketches of the history, manners, and customs of the North American Indians, with a plan for their melioration. Vols. I–II. New York, 1824. (Same, 1825.)

BUELNA, EUSTAQUIO. Arte de la lengua Cahita. México, 1891.

——— Peregrinación de los Aztecas y nombres geográficos indígenas de Sinaloa. 2ª ed. México, 1892.

BURDER, GEO. The Welch Indians; or, a collection of papers, respecting a people whose ancestors emigrated to America, in 1170, with Prince Madoc. London [1797].

BUREAU OF AMERICAN ETHNOLOGY. (Smithsonian Institution.) Annual Reports, I–XXVI, Washington, 1881–1908. Bulletins, 1–49, Washington, 1887–1910. Introductions, I–IV, Washington, 1877–1880. Miscellaneous Publications, 1–9, Washington, 1880–1907. Contributions to North American Ethnology (q. v.).

BUREAU OF CATHOLIC INDIAN MISSIONS. Reports. Archdiocese of Baltimore, 1874–1904.

BURK, JNO. D. History of Virginia. Vols. I–III. Petersburg, 1804–05.

——— [The same, continued by S. Jones and L. Hugh Girardin.] Vol. IV. Petersburg, 1816.

BURNABY, ANDREW. Travels through the middle settlements in North America. London, 1775.

BURROUGHS, JNO. Winter sunshine. New York, 1876.

BURTON, RICHARD F. The City of the Saints and across the Rocky mountains to California. London, 1861.

BUSCHMANN, JOHANN CARL ED. Die Völker und Sprachen Neu-Mexiko's und der Westseite des britischen Nordamerika's. Berlin, 1858.

——— Die Spuren der aztekischen Sprache im nördlichen Mexico und höheren amerikanischen Norden. (Abhandlungen der Königlichen Akademie der Wissenschaften zu Berlin, 1854, Berlin, 1859.)

——— Systematische Worttafel des athapaskischen Sprachstamms. Dritte Abtheilung des Apache. (Ibid., 1859, Berlin, 1860.)

BUSHNELL, D. I., Jr. Cahokia and surrounding mound groups. (Papers of the Peabody Mus., vol. III, Cambridge, 1904.)

——— The Choctaw of Bayou Lacomb, St. Tammany parish, Louisiana. (Bull. 48, Bur. Am. Ethnology, Washington, 1909.)

——— See BROWER, J. V., and BUSHNELL.

BUTEL-DUMONT, GEO. M. Mémoires historiques sur la Louisiane, contenant ce qui y est arrivé de plus mémorable depuis l'année 1687 jusqu'à présent. Tomes I–II. Paris, 1753.

——— History of Louisiana. (In French, B. F., Historical Collections of Louisiana, vol. V, New York, 1853.)

BUTLER, W. F. The great lone land; a narrative of travel and adventure in the north-west of America. 5th ed., London, 1873. 7th ed., London, 1875.

——— The wild north land: being the story of a winter journey with dogs across northern North America. London, 1873. 9th ed., London, 1884.

BUTTERFIELD, C. W. Historical account of the expedition against Sandusky. Cincinnati, 1873.

——— History of the Girtys, being a concise account of the Girty brothers. Cincinnati, 1890.

——— Washington-Irvine correspondence. The official letters which passed between Washington and Brigadier General William Irvine and others. Madison, Wis., 1882.

BYINGTON, CYRUS. Chata dictionary: Chata-English and English-Chata. (MS., 5 vols., in the archives of the Bureau of American Ethnology, now (1910) in process of publication.)

BYRD, WM. History of the dividing line and other tracts. Vols. I–II. Richmond, 1866.

CABALLERIA, JUAN. History of San Bernardino valley, 1810–1851. San Bernardino, Cal., 1902.

CABECA DE VACA, ALVAR NUÑEZ. Relation. Translated by Buckingham Smith. New York, 1851. (Same, New York, 1871.)

CABRILLO, JUAN RODRIGUEZ. See FERREL, BARTOLOMÉ.

CALENDAR of Virginia state papers and other manuscripts, 1652–1781. Arranged and edited by William P. Palmer. Vols. I–X. Richmond, 1875–1892.

CALIFORNIA AND NEW MEXICO. Message and correspondence. (Ex. Doc. 17, 31st Cong., 1st sess., Washington, 1850.)

CALIFORNIA FARMER. See TAYLOR, ALEX. S.

CALIFORNIA MISSIONS. Supreme Court of the United States. The United States vs. James R. Bolton. Washington, 1859.

CALLENDER, JNO. An historical discourse on the civil and religious affairs of the Colony of Rhode-Island and Providence Plantations in New-England, in America. Boston, 1739. (Collections R. I. Hist. Soc., vols. I–IV, Providence, 1838.)

CAMBRIDGE ANTHROPOLOGICAL EXPEDITION TO TORRES STRAITS. Reports. Vol. II, pts. I and II, Cambridge, 1901–03.

CAMDEN SOCIETY. Publications. Vols. I–CIX. Westminster, 1838–72.

[CAMERON, Mrs W. C. (CORA).] White Pigeon. [n. p., 1909.]

CAMPBELL, JNO. Origin of the aborigines of Canada. (Trans. Literary and Hist. Soc. Quebec, Sess. 1880–81, Quebec, 1880.)
———— On the origin of some American Indian tribes. (Canadian Naturalist, 2d s., vol. IX, Montreal, 1881.)

CANADA. Journal of the Legislative Assembly of the Province of Canada. Sixth Volume. Session, 1847. Montreal, 1847.
———— See ANNUAL ARCHÆOLOGICAL REPORTS; ETHNOLOGICAL SURVEY OF CANADA; INDIAN AFFAIRS (CANADA).

CANADIAN INSTITUTE. Proceedings: Series 1: The Canadian Journal: a Repertory of Industry, Science and Art; and a Record of the Proceedings of the Canadian Institute. Vols. I–III, Toronto, 1852–55. Series 2: The Canadian Journal of Science, Literature, and History. Vols. I–XV, Toronto, 1856–78. Series 3: Proceedings of the Canadian Institute. Vols. I–VII, Toronto, 1879–90. Annual Reports: 1886–1894 (App. Rep. Min. Education Ont., Toronto, 1888–1894). Transactions: Vols. I–VII. Toronto, 1889–1904.

CANADIAN JOURNAL. See CANADIAN INSTITUTE.

CANADIAN NATURALIST. See NATURAL HISTORY SOCIETY OF MONTREAL.

CANADIAN RECORD OF SCIENCE, including the proceedings of the Natural History Society of Montreal and replacing The Canadian Naturalist. Vols. I–VIII. Montreal, 1885–1902.

CANTWELL, J. C. Report of the operations of the United States Revenue Steamer Nunivak on the Yukon river station, Alaska, 1899–1901. Washington, 1902.

CAPELLINI, GIOVANI. Ricordi di un viaggio scientifico nell' America settentrionale nell 1863. Bologna, 1867.

CAPRON, E. S. History of California; with journal of the voyage from New-York, via Nicaragua, to San Francisco, and back, via Panama. Boston, 1854.

CARDENAS Z. CANO, GABRIEL DE. See BARCIA CARBALLIDO Y ZUÑIGA, A. G.

CARNEGIE MUSEUM. Annals. Vols. I–III. Pittsburg, 1901–06.

CARR, LUCIEN. Observations on the crania from stone graves in Tennessee. (11th Rep. Peabody Mus., Cambridge, Mass., 1878.)
———— Observations on the crania from the Santa Barbara islands, California. (Rep. U. S. Geog. Surveys West of 100th Merid. [Wheeler], vol. VII, Washington, 1879.)
———— Measurements of crania from California. (12th Rep. Peabody Mus., Cambridge, 1880.)
———— Notes on the crania of New England Indians. (Anniv. Mem. Boston Soc. Nat. Hist., Boston, 1880.)
———— Mounds of the Mississippi valley historically considered. (Mem. Geol. Surv. Kentucky, vol. II, Frankfort, 1883.)
———— Food of certain American Indians. (Proc. Am. Antiq. Soc., n. s., vol. X, Worcester, 1895.)
———— Dress and ornaments of certain American Indians. (Ibid., vol. XI, Worcester, 1898.)

CARROLL, B. R. Historical collections of South Carolina; embracing many rare and valuable pamphlets, and other documents, relating to the history of that state, from its first discovery to its independence, in the year 1776. Vols. I–II. New York, 1836.

CARTER, THOS. Medals of the British army, and how they were won. London, 1861.

CARTIER, JACQUES. Brief récit, et succincte narration, de la nauigation faicte es ysles de Canada. Paris, 1545. (Same, Paris, 1863.)

CARVALHO, S. N. Incidents of travel and adventure in the far west; with Col. Fremont's last expedition across the Rocky mountains. New York, 1857.

CARVER, JONATHAN. Travels through the interior parts of North America, in the years 1766, 1767, and 1768. London, 1778.
———— Three years' travels through the interior parts of North America for more than five thousand miles. Philadelphia, 1796.
———— Carver's travels in Wisconsin. New York, 1838.

CASTAÑEDA DE NAGERA, PEDRO DE. Relation du voyage de Cibola, entrepris en 1540. [1596.] (Ternaux-Compans, Voyages, vol. IX, Paris, 1838.)

CATALOGUE des poincoins, coins et médailles du Musée Monetaire. Paris, 1833.

CATESBY, MARK. Natural history of Carolina, Florida, and the Bahama islands. Vols. I–II. London, 1731–43.

CATHOLIC PIONEER. Vol. I, no. 9, Albuquerque, N. M., 1906.

CATLIN, GEORGE. Illustrations of the manners and customs and condition of the North American Indians. Vols. I–II. London, 1841. (Same, London, 1866.)
———— Letters and notes on the manners, customs, and condition of the North American Indians. Vols. I–II. New York and London, 1844.
———— O-kee-pa: a religious ceremony; and other customs of the Mandans. Philadelphia, 1867.

CAULKINS, FRANCES M. History of Norwich, Conn., 1660–1866. New ed. Norwich, 1866.

CÉLORON. See MARSHALL, O. H.

CENSUS. See UNITED STATES CENSUS.

CENTURY ATLAS OF THE WORLD. New York, 1897.

CENTURY CYCLOPEDIA OF NAMES. New York, 1894.

CHADWICK, EDWARD M. The people of the longhouse. Toronto, 1897.

CHAMBERLAIN, A. F. Aryan element in Indian dialects. I. (Canadian Indian, Owen Sound, Ontario, Feb. 1891.)
———— Language of the Mississagas of Skūgog. Philadelphia, 1892.
———— The child and childhood in folkthought. New York, 1896.

CHAMBERS, E. T. D. The ouananiche and its Canadian environment. New York, 1896.

CHAMPLAIN, SAMUEL DE. Voyages; ou journals ès découvertes de la Nouvelle France. Tomes I–II. Paris, 1830.
———— Œuvres de Champlain publiées sous le patronage de l'Université Laval. Par l'Abbé C.-H. Laverdière, M. A. 2e éd. Tomes I–V. Québec, 1870.

CHAPIN, FREDERICK H. Land of the cliff-dwellers. Boston, 1892.

CHAPPELL, EDWARD. Narrative of a voyage to Hudson's bay in his majesty's ship Rosamond. London, 1817.
———— Voyage to Newfoundland and the southern coast of Labrador. London, 1818.

CHARLEVOIX, PIERRE F. X. DE. Histoire et description generale de la Nouvelle France. Tomes I–III. Paris, 1744.
———— Same, translated by John G. Shea. Vols. I–VI. New York, 1866–72.

CHARLEVOIX, PIERRE F. X. DE. Journal of a voyage to North America. Vols. I–II. London, 1761.

—————— Letters to the Dutchess of Lesdiguieres, giving an account of a voyage to Canada and travels through that country and Louisiana to the Gulf of Mexico. London, 1763.

—————— A voyage to North America; undertaken by command of the present King of France. Vols. I–II. Dublin, 1766.

CHERRY, CUMMINGS and JAMES. Maps and reports of the San Juan del Rio ranche, in Sonora, Mexico. Cincinnati, 1866.

CHESNUT, V. K. Principal poisonous plants of the United States. (U. S. Dept. Agric., Div. Bot., Bull. 20, Washington, 1898.)

—————— Plants used by the Indians of Mendocino county, California. (Cont. U. S. National Herbarium, vol. VII, no. 3, Washington, 1902.)

CHITTENDEN, HIRAM MARTIN. American fur trade in the far west. Vols. I–III. New York, 1902.

—————— and RICHARDSON, ALFRED T. Life, letters, and travels of Father Pierre-Jean De Smet, S. J., 1801–1873. Vols. I–IV. New York, 1905.

CHORIS, LOUIS. Voyage pittoresque · autour du Monde, avec des portraits de sauvages d'Amérique, d'Asie, d'Afrique et des isles du Grand Ocean. Accompagné de descriptions par M. le Baron Cuvier, et M. A. de Chamisso, et d'observations sur les crânes humains, par M. le Docteur Gall. Paris, 1822.

CHUDZINSKI, THÉOPHILE. Sur les trois encéphales des Esquimaux morts de la variole du 13 ou 16 Janvier 1881. (Bull. de la Soc. d'Anthr. de Paris, 3ᵉ s., tome IV, 1881.)

CHURCH, THOS. Entertaining passages relating to Philip's war, which began in the month of June, 1675. Boston, 1716.

—————— The history of King Philip's war, and also expeditions against the French and Indians in the eastern parts of New England. To which is added copious notes and corrections by Samuel G. Drake. Boston, 1825.

CLARK, J. V. H. Onondaga; or reminiscences of earlier and later times; being a series of historical sketches relative to Onondaga. Syracuse, 1849.

CLARK, W. P. The Indian sign language. Philadelphia, 1885.

CLARK, WM. See LEWIS (MERIWETHER) and CLARK.

CLARKE, F. W., and DILLER, J. S. Turquoise from New Mexico. (Am. Jour. Science and Arts, 3d s., vol. XXXII, New Haven, 1886.)

CLARKE, HYDE. Researches in prehistoric and protohistoric comparative philology, mythology, and archæology; in connection with the origin of culture in America and its propagation by the Sumerian or Akkad family. (Jour. Anthr. Inst. Great Brit., vol. IV, London, 1875.)

CLARKE, ROBERT. Pre-historic remains which were found on the site of the city of Cincinnati, Ohio. Cincinnati, 1876.

CLAVIGERO, FRANCISCO XAVIER. Storia della California. Vols. I–II. Venice, 1789.

—————— Historia de la antigua ó Baja California. Méjico, 1852.

CLINTON, DE WITT. A memoir of the antiquities of the western parts of the state of New York. Albany, 1820.

COAST AND GEODETIC SURVEY. See UNITED STATES COAST AND GEODETIC SURVEY.

COATS, WM. Geography of Hudson's bay. London, 1852.

COKE, HENRY J. Ride over the Rocky mountains to Oregon and California; with a glance at the West Indies and the Sandwich isles. London, 1852.

COLDEN, CADWALLADER. The history of the Five Indian Nations of Canada, which are dependent on the province of New-York in America. London, 1747. (Same, 1755.)

COLECCIÓN DE DOCUMENTOS INÉDITOS, relativos al descubrimiento, conquista y colonización de las posesiones Españolas en América y Oceanía. Tomos I–XLI. Madrid, 1864–84.

COLLEGE OF WILLIAM AND MARY. History of the College from its foundation, 1693, to 1870. Baltimore, 1870.

COLLINS, C. R. Report on the languages of the different tribes of Indians inhabiting the territory of Utah. (Engineer Dept., U. S. A., Washington, 1876.)

COLONIAL RECORDS OF NORTH CAROLINA. See NORTH CAROLINA.

COLONIAL RECORDS OF PENNSYLVANIA. Vols. I–III, Philadelphia, 1852. Vols. IV–XVI, Harrisburg, 1851–53.

—————— See PENNSYLVANIA, PROVINCIAL COUNCIL.

COLTON, C. Tour of the American lakes, and among the Indians of the North-west territory, in 1830; disclosing the character and prospects of the Indian race. Vols. I–II. London, 1833.

COLUMBIAN HISTORICAL EXPOSITION. Report of the United States Commission to the Columbian Historical Exposition at Madrid, 1892–93. Washington, 1895.

COLUMBUS MEMORIAL VOLUME. Published by the Catholic Club of New York and the United States Catholic Historical Society. New York, Cincinnati, Chicago, 1893.

COMMISSION TO THE FIVE CIVILIZED TRIBES. Reports. (Reports of the U. S. Commissioner of Indian Affairs for 1894–1904, Washington, 1895–1905.)

CONANT, A. J. Foot-prints of vanished races in the Mississippi valley. St. Louis, 1879.

CONANT, LEVI L. The number concept, its origin and development. New York and London, 1896.

CONGRÈS INTERNATIONAL DES AMÉRICANISTES. Compte-rendu. Première session, Nancy, 1875. Paris and Nancy, 1875.

　　Compte-rendu. Seconde session, Luxembourg, 1877. Luxembourg, 1878.

　　Compte-rendu. Troisième session, Bruxelles, 1879. Bruxelles, 1879.

　　Actas. Cuarta reunión, Madrid, 1881. Madrid, 1883.

　　Compte-rendu. Cinquième session, Copenhague, 1883. Copenhague, 1884.

　　Compte-rendu. Sixième session, Turin, 1886. Châlons-sur-Marne, 1886.

　　Compte-rendu. Septième session, Berlin, 1888. Berlin, 1890.

　　Compte-rendu. Huitième session, Paris, 1890. Paris, 1892.

　　Actas. Novena reunión, Huelvas, 1892. Madrid, 1894.

　　Compte-rendu. Dixième session, Stockholm, 1894. Stockholm, 1897.

　　Actas. Undécima reunión, México, 1895. México, 1897.

　　[Compte-rendu.] XIIᵉ session, Paris, 1900. Paris, 1902.

　　Report. Thirteenth session, New York, 1902. Easton, Pa., 1905.

　　Vierzehnte Tagung, Stuttgart, 1904. Stuttgart, 1906.

　　Compte-rendu. Quinzième session, Québec, 1906. Québec, 1907.

CONGRESS. See UNITED STATES CONGRESS.

CONKLIN, E. Picturesque Arizona. Being the result of travels and observations in Arizona during the fall and winter of 1877. New York, 1878.

CONNECTICUT ACADEMY OF ARTS AND SCIENCES. Transactions. Vols I–V. New Haven, 1871–82.

CONOVER, GEO. S. Kanadesaga and Geneva. MS. [n. d.] (In archives of the Bureau of American Ethnology.)
———— Early history of Geneva, formerly called Kanadesaga. (From the Geneva Courier, March, 1879.)
———— Sayerqueraghta, King of the Senecas. Waterloo, 1885.
———— Seneca villages. Principal settlements between Canandaigua and Seneca lake. Geneva, N. Y., 1889.
CONTRIBUTIONS from the U. S. National Herbarium. Vol. v, no. 1, Washington, 1897. Vol. vii, no. 3, Washington, 1902.
CONTRIBUTIONS TO NORTH AMERICAN ETHNOLOGY. Department of the Interior, U. S. Geographical and Geological Survey of the Rocky Mountain Region, J. W. Powell in charge. Vols. I–VII, IX. Washington, 1877–93.
COOK, FREDERICK. Journals of the military expedition of Major General John Sullivan against the Six Nations of Indians in 1779. Auburn, 1887.
COOKE, P. ST. GEORGE. See EMORY, RECONNOISSANCE, pp. 549–563, 1848.
COPWAY, GEO. Life, history and travels of Copway, a young Indian chief of the Ojebwa nation; sketch of the present state of the nation. Albany, 1847.
CÓRDOVA, LUIS CABRERA DE. Découverte du Nouveau-Mexique à la Nouvelle-Espagne. Récit des événements qui s'y sont passés. (In Ternaux-Compans, Voyages, tome X, 429–450, Paris, 1838.)
CORTEZ, JOSÉ. History of the Apache nations and other tribes near the parallel of 35° north latitude. (Pacific Railroad Reports, vol. III, pt. III, chap. 7, Washington, 1856.)
COUES, ELLIOTT, ed. History of the expedition of Lewis and Clark to the sources of the Missouri river, and to the Pacific in 1804–5–6. A new edition. Vols. I–IV. New York, 1893.
———— The expeditions of Zebulon Montgomery Pike. Vols. I–III. New York, 1895.
———— New light on the early history of the greater northwest. The manuscript journals of Alexander Henry and David Thompson, 1799–1814. Vols. I–III. New York, 1897.
———— Journal of Jacob Fowler. New York, 1898.
———— The personal narrative of Charles Larpenteur. Vols. I–II. New York, 1898.
———— On the trail of a Spanish pioneer. The diary and itinerary of Francisco Garcés, 1775–76. Vols. I–II. New York, 1900.
———— and KINGSLEY, JOHN L., eds. The natural history of man. (Standard natural history, vol. VI, Boston, 1883.)
COVILLE, FREDERICK V. Notes on the plants used by the Klamath Indians of Oregon. (Contributions U. S. National Herbarium, vol. V, no. 2, Washington, 1897.)
———— Wokas, a primitive food of the Klamath Indians. (Rep. U. S. Nat. Mus. 1902, Washington, 1904.)
———— and MACDOUGAL, D. T. Desert Botanical Laboratory of the Carnegie Institution. Washington, 1903.
COWPERTHWAITE, THOMAS & CO. A new universal atlas of the world. Philadelphia, 1851.
COX, ROSS. Adventures on the Columbia river. Vols. I–II. London, 1831.
COXE, DANIEL. A description of the English province of Carolana. By the Spaniards call'd Florida, and by the French, La Louisiane. London, 1741. (Same, in FRENCH, B. F., Historical collections of Louisiana, 2d ed., pt. 2, Philadelphia, 1850.)
COXE, WM. An account of the Russian discoveries between Asia and America. London, 1787.

COYNER, DAVID H. The lost trappers: a collection of interesting scenes and events in the Rocky mountains; together with a short description of California. Cincinnati, 1847.
COZZENS, S. W. The marvelous country; or three years in Arizona and New Mexico. London, 1874.
CRAIG, NEVILLE B. See OLDEN TIME.
CRANTZ, DAVID. History of Greenland. Vols. I–II. London, 1767. (Same, London, 1780, 1820.)
———— Forsetzung der Historie von Grönland. Barby, 1770.
———— The ancient and modern history of the Brethren . . . or, Unitas Fratrum; translated by Benjamin Latrobe. London, 1780.
CREMONY, JNO. C. Life among the Apaches. San Francisco, 1868.
CRÉPY. Carte générale de l'Amérique Séptentrionale. Paris, 1783 (?).
———— See NOLIN, J. B.
CREUXIUS, FRANCISCUS. Historiæ Canadensis. Paris, 1664.
———— Map of New France in 1660. (In Jesuit Relations, vol. XLVI, Cleveland, 1899.)
CROGHAN, GEO. The journal of Col. Croghan. (Monthly American Journal of Geology and Natural Science, vol. I, Philadelphia, 1831. Reprinted, Burlington, n. d.)
CUBAS, ANTONIO G. The republic of Mexico in 1876. Translated by George E. Henderson. Mexico [1876].
CUESTA. See ARROYO DE LA CUESTA.
CULIN, STEWART. Games of the North American Indians. (Twenty-fourth Rep. Bur. Am. Ethnology, Washington, 1907.)
CUMING, F. Sketches of a tour to the western country, through the states of Ohio and Kentucky; a voyage down the Ohio and Mississippi rivers. Pittsburgh, 1810.
CUOQ, JEAN A. Lexique de la langue Iroquoise. Montréal, 1882.
———— Lexique de la langue Algonquine. Montréal, 1886.
CURRIER, A. F. A study relative to the functions of the reproductive apparatus in American Indian women. (Medical News, vol. LIX, Philadelphia, 1891; Trans. Amer. Gynec. Soc., Philadelphia, 1891.)
CURTIN, JEREMIAH. Creation myths of primitive America in relation to the religious history and mental development of mankind. Boston, 1898.
CURTIS, EDWARD S. The American Indian. Vols. I–V +. New York, 1907–09.
CURTIS, NATALIE. Songs of ancient America. New York, 1906.
CURTIS, WM. E. Children of the sun. Chicago, 1883.
CUSHING, F. H. Zuñi fetiches. (Second Rep. Bur. Am. Ethnology, Washington, 1883.)
———— A study of Pueblo pottery as illustrative of Zuñi culture growth. (Fourth Rep. Bur. Am. Ethnology, Washington, 1886.)
———— Outlines of Zuñi creation myths. (Thirteenth Rep. Bur. Am. Ethnology, Washington, 1896.)
———— A preliminary report on the exploration of ancient key-dweller remains on the gulf coast of Florida. (Proc. Am. Philos. Soc., vol. XXXV, no. 153, Philadelphia, 1896.)
———— Zuñi folk-tales. New York, 1901.
———— See MILLSTONE.
CUSICK, DAVID. Sketches of ancient history of the Six Nations. 2d ed. Tuscarora, N. Y., 1828.
CUSTER, GEO. A. My life on the plains, and personal experiences with Indians. New York, 1874.
CUVIER, Le Baron. See CHORIS, LOUIS.

DALL, WM. H. On the distribution of the native tribes of Alaska and the adjacent territory. (Proc. Am. Asso. Adv. Sci. 1869, Cambridge, 1870.)
———— Alaska and its resources. Boston, 1870.
———— Tribes of the extreme northwest. (Contributions to North American Ethnology, vol. I, Washington, 1877.)
———— Terms of relationship used by the Innuit. (Ibid.)
———— On succession in the shell-heaps of the Aleutian islands. (Ibid.)
———— On the origin of the Innuit. (Ibid.)
———— On the distribution and nomenclature of the native tribes of Alaska and the adjacent territory. (Ibid.)
———— On the remains of later pre-historic man. (Smithsonian Contributions to Knowledge, vol. XXII, Washington, 1878.)
———— On masks, labrets, and certain aboriginal customs. (Third Rep. Bur. Am. Ethnology, Washington, 1884.)
———— The native tribes of Alaska. (Proc. Am. Asso. Adv. Sci. 1885, vol. XXXIV, Salem, 1886.)
———— Alleged early Chinese voyages to America. (Science, vol. VIII, New York, Nov. 5, 1886.)
———— See GIBBS (GEORGE) and DALL.
DANA, EDWARD S. Text-book of mineralogy. New York and London, 1888. (Same, 1898.)
D'ANVILLE, Le Sieur. Atlas générale, 1727–1780.
———— Amérique Septentrionale. Publiée sous les auspices de Monseigneur le Duc d'Orleans, Prémier Prince du Sang. [Paris,] 1746.
———— North America by the Sieur d'Anville, engraved by R. W. Seale. (In Postlethwayt, Universal Dictionary of Trade and Commerce, translated from the French of M. Savary, London, 1752.)
DARLINGTON, Mrs M. C. (O'HARA). Fort Pitt and letters from the frontier. Pittsburg, 1892.
DARLINGTON, WM. M. Christopher Gist's Journals with historical, geographical, and ethnological notes and biographies of his contemporaries. Pittsburgh, 1893.
———— See MAY, JNO.
DAVENPORT ACADEMY OF NATURAL SCIENCES. Proceedings. Vols. I–IX. Davenport, 1876–1904.
DAVIES, JNO. History of the Carribbee islands. Translated from the French. London, 1666.
DAVILA, F. T. Sonora historico y descriptivo. Nogales, Ariz., 1894.
DAVIS, C. H., ed. Narrative of the North Polar expedition. U. S. ship Polaris, Captain Charles Hall commanding. Washington, 1876.
DAVIS, GEO. L.-L. The day-star of American freedom; or the birth and early growth of toleration, in the province of Maryland. New York, 1855.
DAVIS, JNO. The first voyage of M. John Davis, undertaken in June 1585, for the discoverie of the Northwest passage. Written by M. John Marchant. (Hakluyt, Voyages, vol. III, London, 1600.)
———— See BERQUIN-DUVALLON.
DAVIS, W. W. H. El Gringo; or New Mexico and her people. New York, 1857.
———— The Spanish conquest of New Mexico. Doylestown, Pa., 1869.
DAWSON, GEO. M. Sketches of the past and present condition of the Indians of Canada. Montreal, 1877. (Same, 1879.)
———— Report on the Queen Charlotte islands. (Rep. Geol. Surv. Can. for 1878–79, Montreal, 1880.)

DAWSON, GEO. M. Report on an exploration from Port Simpson on the Pacific coast, to Edmonton on the Saskatchewan, embracing a portion of the northern part of British Columbia and the Peace river country, 1879. (Rep. Geol. Surv. Can., Montreal, 1881.)
———— Note on the occurrence of jade in British Columbia, and its employment by the natives. (Can. Rec. of Sci., vol. II, no. 6, Montreal, Apr. 1887.)
———— Notes and observations of the Kwakiool people of the northern part of Vancouver island and adjacent coasts made during the summer of 1885, with vocabulary of about 700 words. (Proc. and Trans. Roy. Soc. Can. 1887, vol. V, Montreal, 1888.)
———— Report on an exploration in the Yukon district, N. W. T. and adjacent northern portion of British Columbia. (Ann. Rep. Geol. and Nat. Hist. Surv. Can., n. s., vol. III, pt. I, Report B. 1887–88, Montreal, 1889.)
———— Notes on the Shuswap people of British Columbia. (Proc. and Trans. Roy. Soc. Canada 1891, vol. IX, sec. II, Montreal, 1892.)
DAY, SHERMAN. Historical collections of the state of Pennsylvania. Philadelphia, 1843.
DEANS, JAS. Tales from the totems of the Hidery. (Archives Int. Folk-lore Asso., vol. II, Chicago, 1889.)
DE BRY. See BRY.
DE COSTA, B. F. Inventio Fortunata. Arctic exploration with an account of Nicholas of Lynn. (Reprinted from the Bulletin of the American Geographical Society, New York, 1881.)
DE FOREST, JNO. W. History of the Indians of Connecticut from the earliest known period to 1850. Hartford, 1851. (Same, 1852, 1853.)
DE LAET. See LAET.
DELAMARCHE, C. F. Amérique ou Indes Occidentales. Paris, 1792.
DELANO, A. Life on the plains and among the diggings; being scenes and adventures of an overland journey to California. Auburn and Buffalo, 1854.
DE L'ISLE, GUILLAUME. [Carte de] L'Amérique Septentrionale, dressée sur les observations de Mrs. de l'Académie Royale des Sciences. Paris, 1700. (Same, 1703.)
———— Carte du Mexique et de la Floride, des terres Angloises et des isles Antilles, du course et des environs de la rivière de Mississipi. Dressé sur un grand nombre de mémoires, principalmt. sur ceux de mr. d'Iberville et Le Seur. Paris, 1703.
———— Carte de la Louisiane et du cours du Mississipi, dressé sur un grand nombre de mémoires, entre autres sur ceux de mr. le Maire. [n. p., ca. 1718.]
———— Atlas nouveau, des empires, monarchies, royaumes, républiques, etc. Paris, 1733.
DELLENBAUGH, F. S. North-Americans of yesterday. New York and London, 1901.
DE LONG, EMMA. The voyage of the Jeanette. London, 1883.
DENIKER, J. Races of man; an outline of anthropology and ethnography. London and New York, 1900.
DENNETT, DANIEL. Louisiana as it is. New Orleans, 1876.
DENNY, E. Military journal, 1781 to 1795. (Mem. Hist. Soc. Pa., vol. VII, Philadelphia, 1860.)
DE PEYSTER, JNO. W. The Dutch at the North Pole and the Dutch in Maine. New York, 1857.

DERBY, GEO. H. Report of the Secretary of War, communicating, in compliance with a resolution of the Senate, a reconnoissance of the Gulf of California and the Colorado river. 1851. (Senate Ex. Doc. 81, 32d Cong., 1st sess., Washington, 1852.)

DE SCHWEINITZ, EDMUND. The life and times of David Zeisberger. Philadelphia, 1870.

DESCRIPTIVE CATALOGUE, with reproductions of life-size bust portraits of famous Indian chiefs. Exhibited in the Minnesota Pioneer Portrait Galleries, State Fair Grounds, Minneapolis, Sept. 1909.

DE SOTO, HERNANDO. See JONES, C. C.; SHIPP, B.; SMITH, BUCKINGHAM; GARCILASSO DE LA VEGA.

DEUTSCHE GEOGRAPHISCHE BLÄTTER. B. I–XXXII. Bremen, 1877–1909.

DE VEER, G. The three voyages of William Barants to the Arctic regions, 1594–1596. (Hakluyt Society Pub., London, 1876.)

DE VERE, SCHELE. Americanisms; the English of the New World. New York, 1872.

DICKENSON, JONATHAN. Narrative of a shipwreck in the Gulph of Florida. 6th ed. Stanford, N. Y., 1803.

DIEBITSCH–PEARY. See PEARY.

DILLER, J. S. See CLARKE, F. W., and DILLER.

DINWIDDIE, ROBERT. Official records of Robert Dinwiddie, Lieutenant-Governor of the colony of Virginia, 1751–1758. (Coll. Va. Hist. Soc., N. S., vols. III–IV, Richmond, 1883–84.)

DISTURNELL, J. Mapa de los Estados Unidos de Méjico, California, &c. New York, 1846.

DIXON, R. B. Maidu myths. (Bull. Am. Mus. Nat. Hist., vol. XVII, pt. II, New York, 1902.)
———— The northern Maidu. (Ibid., pt. III, New York, 1905.)

DOBBS, ARTHUR. An account of the countries adjoining to Hudson's bay, in the north-west part of America. London, 1744.

DOCUMENTOS INÉDITOS. See COLECCIÓN DE DOCUMENTOS INÉDITOS.

DOCUMENTOS PARA LA HISTORIA DE MÉXICO. Four series. 20 vols. Mexico, 1853–1857.

DODGE, RICHARD I. Our wild Indians. Hartford, 1882.

DOMENECH, EMMANUEL. Missionary adventures in Texas and Mexico. London, 1858.
———— Seven years' residence in the great deserts of North America. Vols. I–II. London, 1860.

DONALDSON, THOS. The Moqui Indians of Arizona and Pueblo Indians of New Mexico. (Eleventh Census, U. S., Extra Census Bulletin, Washington, 1893.)
———— See UNITED STATES CENSUS.

DONIPHAN, A. W. See HUGHES, JNO. T.

DORMAN, RUSHTON M. The origin of primitive superstitions and their development. Philadelphia and London, 1881.

DORSEY, GEO. A. An aboriginal quartzite quarry in eastern Wyoming. (Pub. Field Col. Mus., Anthr. ser., vol. II, no 4, Chicago, 1900.)
———— Arapaho sun dance; the ceremony of the offerings lodge. (Ibid., vol. IV, Chicago, 1903.)
———— Mythology of the Wichita. (Carnegie Institution of Washington, Pub. no. 21, Washington, 1904.)
———— Traditions of the Skidi Pawnee. (Mem. Am. Folk-lore Soc., vol. VIII, Boston and New York, 1904.)
———— Traditions of the Osage. (Pub. Field Col. Mus., Anthr. ser., vol. VII, no. 1, Chicago, 1904.)

DORSEY, GEO. A. The Cheyenne. Pt. 1, Ceremonial organization. Pt. 2, The sun dance. (Ibid., vol. IX, nos. 1 and 2, Chicago, 1905.)
———— The Pawnee—Mythology (pt. I). (Carnegie Institution of Washington, Pub. no. 59, Washington, 1906.)
———— and KROEBER, A. L. Traditions of the Arapaho. (Pub. Field Col. Mus., Anthr. ser., vol. V, Chicago, 1903.)
———— and VOTH, H. R. Oraibi Soyal ceremony. (Ibid., vol. III, no. 1, Chicago, 1901.)
———— Mishongnovi ceremonies of the Snake and Antelope fraternities. (Ibid., no. 3, Chicago, 1902.)

DORSEY, J. OWEN. Omaha sociology. (Third Rep. Bur. Am. Ethnology, Washington, 1884.)
———— Osage traditions. (Sixth Rep. Bur. Am. Ethnology, Washington, 1888.)
———— The Çegiha language. (Contributions to N. A. Ethnol., vol. VI, Washington, 1890.)
———— Omaha and Ponka letters. (Bull. 11, Bur. Am. Ethnology, Washington, 1891.)
———— A study of Siouan cults. (Eleventh Rep. Bur. Am. Ethnology, Washington, 1894.)
———— Omaha dwellings, furniture, and implements. (Thirteenth Rep. Bur. Am. Ethnology, Washington, 1896.)
———— Siouan sociology. (Fifteenth Rep. Bur. Am. Ethnology, Washington, 1897.)

DOTY, JAMES. Reports on the Indian tribes of the Blackfoot nation. 1853. (Pac. R. R. Reps., vol. I, 441–446, Washington, 1855.)

DOUGLAS, JAS. Report of a canoe expedition along the east coast of Vancouver island, 1852. (Jour. Roy. Geog. Soc., London, 1854.)

DOUGLASS, A. E. Table of the geographical distribution of American Indian relics in a collection exhibited in the American Museum of Natural History, New York. (Bull. Am. Mus. Nat. Hist., vol. VIII, art. X, New York, 1896.)

DOUGLASS, W. A summary, historical and political, of the first planting, &c., of the British settlements in North America. Vols. I–II. London, 1755.

DOWNIE, WM. Explorations in Jarvis inlet and Desolation sound, British Columbia. (Jour. Royal Geog. Soc. 1861, XXXI, London, n. d.)

DRAKE, BENJAMIN. Life of Tecumseh, and of his brother, the prophet. Cincinnati, 1841. (Same, 1852.)

DRAKE, DANIEL. Natural and statistical view; or picture of Cincinnati and the Miami country. Cincinnati, 1815.

DRAKE, EDWARD CAVENDISH. A new universal collection of authentic and entertaining voyages and travels. London, 1770.

DRAKE, SAMUEL G. Indian biography, containing the lives of more than two hundred Indian chiefs. Boston, 1832.
———— Book of the Indians of North America. Boston, 1833. (Same, Boston, 1841; Boston [1848].)
———— Biography and history of the Indians of North America; also a history of their wars, their manners and customs, etc. Boston, New York, Philadelphia, 1834. (Same, Boston, 1836, 1837, 1848.)
———— The old Indian chronicle; being a collection of exceeding rare tracts written and published in the time of King Philip's war. Boston, 1836.
———— Tragedies of the wilderness. Boston, 1841.
———— Aboriginal races of North America. Boston, 1848. (Same, Philadelphia, 1860; New York, 1880.)

DRAKE, SAMUEL G. Indian captivities, or life in the wigwam. Auburn, 1851.
—— See CHURCH, THOS. ; HUBBARD, WM.
DUBUQUE, HUGO A. Fall River Indian reservation. Fall River, Mass., 1907.
DUCKWORTH, W. L. H. An acount of some Eskimo from Labrador. (Proc. Cambridge Philos. Soc., vol. IX–X, Cambridge, Eng., 1895–1900.)
—— Contribution to Eskimo craniology. (Jour. Anthr. Inst. Gr. Brit., vol. XXX, London, 1900.)
DU CREUX. See CREUXIUS, F.
DUFLOT DE MOFRAS, EUGÈNE. Exploration du territoire de l'Orégon, des Californies, et de la mer Vermeille, exécutée pendant les années 1840, 1841 et 1842. Tomes I–II. Paris, 1844.
DU LAC. See PERRIN DU LAC.
DUMONT, M. See BUTEL-DUMONT.
DUNBAR, JNO. B. The Pawnee Indians. (Mag. Am. Hist., IV, V, VIII, Morrisania, N. Y., 1880–82.)
DUNN, JACOB P. Massacres of the mountains. New York, 1886.
—— Indiana. A redemption from slavery. Boston and New York, 1905.
—— True Indian stories, with glossary of Indiana Indian names. Indianapolis, 1908. (Same, 1909.)
DUNN, JNO. History of the Oregon territory and British North-American fur trade. London, 1844. (Same, Philadelphia, 1845.)
DU PRATZ. See LE PAGE DU PRATZ.
DURO, CESÁREO F. Don Diego de Peñalosa y su descubrimiento del reino de Quivira. Madrid, 1882.
DURRETT, REUBEN T. Traditions of the earliest visits of foreigners to North America. (Filson Club Pub., no. 23, Louisville, 1908.)
DUVAL, P. Geographicæ universell (1658–1682). [Map.] (In Winsor, Cartier to Frontenac, 1894.)
DUVALLON. See BERQUIN-DUVALLON.

EARLE, ALICE M. Customs and fashions in old New England. New York, 1893.
EARLY WESTERN TRAVELS. See THWAITES, R. G., ed.
EASTBURN, ROBERT. See SPEARS, JOHN R., ed.
EASTMAN, CHAS. Indian boyhood. New York, 1902.
EASTMAN, EDWIN. Seven and nine years among the Camanches and Apaches. Jersey City, 1874.
EASTMAN, MARY H. Chicóra and other regions of the conquerors and the conquered. Philadelphia, 1854.
EDWARD, DAVID B. History of Texas ; emigrant's, farmer's and politician's guide to the character, climate, soil and productions of that country. Cincinnati, 1836.
EDWARDS, JONATHAN. See BRAINERD, DAVID.
EDWARDS, NINIAN W. History of Illinois. Springfield, 1870.
EELLS, MYRON. The Twana Indians of the Skokomish reservation in Washington territory. (Bull. U. S. Geol. and Geog. Surv., vol. III, no. 1, Washington, 1877.)
—— Father Eells or the results of fiftyfive years of missionary labors. A biography of Rev. Cushing Eells, D. D. Boston and Chicago, c. 1894.
—— Ten years of missionary work among the Indians. Boston, 1886.
—— The Twana, Chemakum and Klallam Indians, of Washington territory. (Ann. Report Smithsonian Institution for 1887, pt. I, Washington, 1889.)
EGEDE, HANS. Ausfürliche and warhafte Nachricht vom Anfange und Fortgange der grönländischen Mission. Hamburg, 1740.

EGEDE, HANS. Des alten Grönlands neue Perlustration. Copenhagen, 1742.
—— Description of Greenland. Translated from the Danish. London, 1745.
—— Description et histoire naturelle du Groenland. Copenhague, 1763.
EGGLESTON, EDWARD. Tecumseh and the Shawnee prophet. New York, 1878.
EGGLESTON, GEO. CARY. Red Eagle and the wars with the Creek Indians of Alabama. New York, c. 1878.
EGLE, WM. H. An illustrated history of the commonwealth of Pennsylvania. Harrisburg, 1876. (3d ed., Philadelphia, 1883.)
EGLI, JOHANN J. Nomina geographica. Sprach- und Sacherklärung von 42,000 geographischen Namen aller Erdräume. Leipzig, 1893.
ELDRIDGE, GEO. H. Reconnaissances in the Sushitna basin. (Twentieth Ann. Rep. U. S. Geol. Surv., pt. VII, Washington, 1900.)
ELIOT, JNO. The Holy Bible : containing the Old Testament and the New. Translated into the Indian language, and ordered to be printed by the Commissioners of the United Colonies in New England. Cambridge, 1663.
ELLICOTT, ANDREW. The journal of Andrew Ellicott, late commissioner for determining the boundary between the United States and the possessions of his Catholic Majesty. Philadelphia, 1814.
ELLIOT, D. G. Synopsis of the mammals of North America and the adjacent seas. (Field Columb. Mus. Pub., Zoöl. ser., vol. II, Chicago, 1901.)
ELLIOTT, HENRY W. Report upon the condition of affairs in the territory of Alaska. Washington, 1875.
—— Our Arctic province. New York, 1886.
ELLIS, E. S. Indian wars of the United States. New York, 1892.
ELLIS, FRANKLIN. History of Fayette county, Pennsylvania. Philadelphia, 1882.
ELLIS, HAVELOCK. Mescal : a new artificial paradise. (Contemporary Rev., no. 385, London, Jan. 1898.)
ELLIS, HENRY. Voyage to Hudson's bay. London, 1748. (Same, 1824.)
ELVAS. See GENTLEMAN OF ELVAS.
EMERSON, ELLEN R. Indian myths, or legends, traditions, and symbols of the aborigines of America. Boston, 1884.
EMMONS, G. T. The Chilkat blanket, with notes by Franz Boas. (Mem. Am. Mus. Nat. Hist., vol. III, pt. 4, New York, 1907.)
EMORY, WM. H. Notes of a military reconnoissance, from Fort Leavenworth, in Missouri, to San Diego, in California, including part of the Arkansas, Del Norte, and Gila rivers. Made in 1846–7. Washington, 1848.
ENGELHARDT, ZEPHYRIN. The Franciscans in California. Harbor Springs, Mich., 1897.
ERMAN, A. Ethnographische Wahrnehmungen und Erfahrungen an den Küsten des Berings-Meeres. (Zeitschrift für Ethnologie, B. II–III, Berlin, 1870–71.)
ERMAN, GEO. A., ed. Archiv für wissenschaftliche Kunde von Russland. B. I–XXV. Berlin, 1841–1867.
ESCUDERO, JOSÉ A. DE. Noticias estadísticas del estado de Chihuahua. México, 1834.
—— Noticias estadísticas de Sonora y Sinaloa. México, 1849.
—— See PINO, PEDRO B.
ESNAUTS et RAPILLY. Carte détaillée des possessions angloises dans l'Amérique Septentrionale. Paris, 1777.
—— Carte du théâtre de la guerre entre les Anglais et les Américains, dressée d'après les cartes anglaises les plus modernes. 1782.
—— See LA TOUR, BRION DE.

ESPEJO, ANTONIO DE. Viaje en el año de 1583. (In Hakluyt, Voyages, 1600, reprint 1810.)
——— Relación del viage. (In Colección de Documentos Inéditos, tomo XV, 163–189, 1871.)
ESPINOSA, ISIDRO FELIS DE. Chrónica apostólica, y seráphica de todos los Colegios de Propaganda Fide de esta Nueva-España. Parte primera. México, 1746. [See ARRICIVITA.]
ESSEX INSTITUTE. Historical collections. Vols. I–XLVI. Salem, 1859–1910.
——— Proceedings. Vols. I–VI. Salem, 1848–70.
——— Bulletin. Vols. I–XXX. Salem, 1870–98.
ETHNOGRAPHISCHE NACHRICHTEN. See STATISTISCHE UND ETHNOGRAPHISCHE NACHRICHTEN.
ETHNOLOGICAL SOCIETY OF LONDON. Journal, vols. I–IV, Edinburgh and London, 1848–56. New series, vols. I–II, London, 1869–71.
——— Transactions, vols. I–VIII, London, 1861–69.
ETHNOLOGICAL SURVEY OF CANADA. Reports. (In Reports of the British Association for the Advancement of Science, 1897 to 1902, London, 1898–1903.)
EVANS, JNO. Ancient stone implements, weapons and ornaments, of Great Britain. 2d ed. London, 1897.
EVENTS in Indian history, beginning with an account of the American Indians, and early settlements in North America. Lancaster, 1841.
EVERS, EDWARD. Ancient pottery of southeastern Missouri. (In Contributions to the Archæology of Missouri, St. Louis Acad. of Sci., pt. I, Salem, 1880.)
EWBANK, THOS. North American rock-writing. Morrisania, N. Y., 1866.
——— See WHIPPLE, A. W., EWBANK, and TURNER, W. W.
EXPLORATIONS IN ALASKA. (Annual Rep. U. S. Geol. Surv., vol. XX, pt. 7, Washington, 1900.)

FAIRBANKS, G. R. History of St. Augustine. New York, 1858.
——— History of Florida, 1512–1842. Philadelphia, 1871.
FAIRHOLT, F. W. Tobacco: its history and associations. London, 1859.
FALCONER, THOS. Notes of a journey through Texas and New Mexico in the years 1841 and 1842. (Jour. Roy. Geog. Soc., vol. XIII, London, 1843.)
FARNHAM, THOS. J. Travels in the great western prairies, the Anahuac and Rocky mountains, and in the Oregon territory. New York, 1843. (Same, vols. I–II, London, 1843.)
——— Travels in the Californias and scenes in the Pacific ocean. New York, 1844.
——— Mexico; its geography, its people and its institutions. New York, 1846.
FARRAND, LIVINGSTON. Basis of American history. 1500–1900. (The American Nation: A History, vol. II, New York and London, 1904.)
——— See BOAS, F., and FARRAND.
FAST, EDWARD G. Catalogue of antiquities and curiosities collected in the territory of Alaska, consisting of more than 2,000 specimens. New York, 1869.
FEATHERSTONEHAUGH, G. W. Excursion through the slave states, from Washington on the Potomac to the frontier of Mexico; with sketches of popular manners and geological notices. New York, 1844.
——— A canoe voyage up the Minnay Sotor. Vols. I–II. London, 1847.

FERGUSSON, D. Letter of the Secretary of War, communicating, in answer to a resolution of the Senate, a copy of the report of Major D. Fergusson on the country, its resources, and the route between Tucson and Lobos bay. (Senate Ex. Doc. 1, 37th Cong., spec. sess., Washington, 1863.)
FERLAND, J. B. A. Le foyer Canadien, recueil litteraire et historique. Tome III. Québec, 1865.
FERNOW, BERTHOLD. The Ohio valley in colonial days. Albany, 1890.
FERREL, BARTOLOMÉ. Relation, or diary, of the voyage which Rodriguez Cabrillo made with two ships, from the 27th of June, 1542, until the 14th of April of the following year. (Wheeler Survey Report, vol. VII, pt. I, app., Washington, 1879.)
FEWKES, J. W. Tusayan katcinas. (Fifteenth Rep. Bur. Am. Ethnology, Washington, 1897.)
——— Tusayan snake ceremonies. (Sixteenth Rep. Bur. Am. Ethnology, Washington, 1897.)
——— Archeological expedition to Arizona in 1895. (Seventeenth Rep. Bur. Am. Ethnology, pt. 2, Washington, 1898.)
——— Tusayan Flute and Snake ceremonies. (Nineteenth Rep. Bur. Am. Ethnology, pt. 2, Washington, 1900.)
——— Tusayan migration traditions. (Ibid.)
——— Hopi katcinas. (Twenty-first Rep. Bur. Am. Ethnology, Washington, 1903.)
——— Two summers' work in Pueblo ruins. (Twenty-second Rep. Bur. Am. Ethnology, pt. 1, Washington, 1904.)
FIELD COLUMBIAN MUSEUM. Publications. Anthropological series. Vols. I–IX. Chicago, 1895–1905.
FIELD, DAVID D. Statistical account of the county of Middlesex, Connecticut. Middletown, 1819.
FIELDS, THOS. W. An essay toward an Indian bibliography. New York, 1873.
FILSON CLUB. Publications. Nos. 1–23. Louisville and Cincinnati, 1884–1908.
FILSON, JNO. Discovery, settlement and present state of Kentucke. Wilmington, 1784. (Same, French trans., Paris, 1785.)
——— The discovery, settlement, and present state of Kentucky. Being a supplement to Imlay's Description of the Western Territory, vol. II. New York, 1793.
FINERTY, JNO. F. War-path and bivouac. Chicago, 1890.
FISCHER, JOS. Discoveries of the Norsemen in America. London, 1903.
FISHER, ALEX. Voyage of discovery to the Arctic regions. London, 1821.
FISHER, J. FRANCIS. Description of American medals. (Coll. Mass. Hist. Soc., 3d s., vol. VI, Boston, 1837.)
FISHER, WM. An interesting account of the voyages and travels of Captains Lewis and Clark, in the years 1804–5, & 6. Baltimore, 1812. (Same, 1813.)
——— New travels among the Indians of North America; being a compilation, taken partly from the communications already published, of Captains Lewis and Clark, and partly from other authors who travelled among the various tribes of Indians. Philadelphia, 1812.
FLEMING, SANDFORD. Report on surveys and preliminary operations on the Canadian Pacific railway up to January, 1877. Ottawa, 1877.
FLETCHER, ALICE C. Indian education and civilization. (Spec. Rep. U. S. Bur. Education, Washington, 1888.)
——— Study of Omaha Indian music. (Archæol. and Ethnol. Papers Peabody Mus., vol. I, no. 5, Cambridge, 1893.)

FLETCHER, ALICE C. Indian story and song from North America. Boston, 1900.
———— The Hako, a Pawnee ceremony. (Twenty-second Rep. Bur. Am. Ethnology, pt. 2, Washington, 1904.)

FLETCHER, ROBERT. On prehistoric trephining and cranial amulets. (Contributions to North American Ethnology, vol. v, Washington, 1882.)

FLINT, MARTHA B. Early Long Island, a colonial study. New York and London, 1896.

FLINT, TIMOTHY. Indian wars of the west. Cincinnati, 1833.

FLORIDA MAP. See MACKAY, JOHN, and BLAKE, J. E.; WEST FLORIDA MAP.

FLOWER, WM. H. Catalogue of the specimens illustrating the osteology and dentition of vertebrated animals. Part I. Man. London, 1879.

FOLSOM, GEO. Mexico in 1842; description of the country, its natural and political features, with a sketch of its history. New York, 1842.

FONT, PEDRO. Notice sur la grande maison dite de Moctecuzoma. 1775. (Ternaux-Compans, Voyages, tome IX, 383–386, Paris, 1838.)

FONTANEDA, HERNANDO DE ESCALANTE. Memoria de las cosas y costa y Indios de la Florida. (Documentos Inéditos, tomo v, 532–548, Madrid, 1866. Same, in Smith, B., Letter of Hernando de Soto, and Memoir of Hernando de Escalante Fontaneda, Washington, 1854. Same, French trans., in Ternaux-Compans, Voyages, tome XX, 9–42, Paris, 1841.)

FOOTE, HENRY S. Texas and the Texans. Vols. I–II. Philadelphia, 1841.

FORBES, ALEXANDER. California; a history of upper and lower California from their first discovery to the present time. London, 1839.

FORCE, M. F. Some early notices of the Indians of Ohio. Cincinnati, 1879.

FORCE, PETER. Tracts and other papers, relating principally to the origin, settlement, and progress of the colonies of North America, from the discovery of the country to the year 1776. Vols. I–IV. Washington, 1836.
———— Grinnell Land. Remarks on the English maps of Arctic discoveries in 1850 and 1851. Washington, 1852.

FOSTER, J. R. History of the voyages and discoveries made in the North. London, 1786.
———— See BOSSU, N.

FOSTER, J. W. Pre-historic races of the United States of America. Chicago, 1878.
———— and WHITNEY, J. D. Report on the geology and topography of a portion of the Lake Superior land district, in the state of Michigan. Part I. Copper lands. (H. R. doc. 69, 31st Cong., 1st sess., Washington, 1850.)

FOSTER, THOS. Letter of, relating to the proper management and civilization of the Indian tribes. (Senate Misc. doc. 39, 42d Cong., 3d sess., Washington, 1873.)

FOWKE, GERARD. Archeologic investigations in James and Potomac valleys. (Bull. 23, Bur. Am. Ethnology, Washington, 1895.)
———— Stone art. (Thirteenth Rep. Bur. Am. Ethnology, Washington, 1896.)
———— Archæological history of Ohio. The mound builders and later Indians. Columbus, 1902.
———— See SMITH, HARLAN I., and FOWKE.

FOWLER, JACOB. See COUES, ELLIOTT, ed.

FRANCHÈRE, GABRIEL. Narrative of a voyage to the northwest coast of America in 1811–14. Translated by J. V. Huntington. New York, 1854.

FRANKLIN, JNO. Narrative of a journey to the shores of the Polar sea, in the years 1819, 20, 21, and 22. London, 1823. (Same, London, 1824; Philadelphia, 1824.)
———— Narrative of a second expedition to the Polar sea, 1825–27. London, 1828.

FRAZER, J. G. Totemism. Edinburgh, 1887.

FREE MUSEUM OF SCIENCE AND ART. Dept. of Archæol. and Paleontol., Univ. of Pennsylvania. Bulletins, vols. I–III, Philadelphia, 1897–1902.
———— See UNIVERSITY OF PENNSYLVANIA.

FRÉMONT, JNO. C. Geographical memoir upon upper California. Washington, 1848.
———— The exploring expedition to the Rocky mountains, Oregon and California. To which is added a description of the physical geography of California. Auburn and Buffalo, 1854.

FRENCH, B. F. Historical collections of Louisiana, embracing many rare and valuable documents relating to the natural, civil, and political history of that state. Parts I–V. New York, 1846–53. (Same, New ser., New York, 1869. Same, Second ser., New York, 1875.)

FREYTAS, NICOLAS DE. The expedition of Don Diego Dionisio de Peñalosa, from Santa Fé to the river Mischipi and Quivira in 1662. Translated and edited by John Gilmary Shea. New York, 1882.

FRIEDERICI, GEORG. Indianer und Anglo-Amerikaner. Braunschweig, 1900.
———— Skalpieren und ähnliche Kriegsgebräuche in America. Stuttgart, 1906.
———— Die Schiffahrt der Indianer. Stuttgart, 1907.

FRIENDS. Some account of the conduct of the Religious Society of Friends toward the Indian tribes. Published by the Aborigines Committee of the Meeting for Sufferings. London, 1844. (Publications relative to the Aborigines, no. 9.)

FRIGNET, ERNEST. La Californie, histoire des progrès de l'un des Etats-Unis de l'Amérique et des institutions qui font sa prospérité. 2e ed. Paris, 1867.

FRÖBEL, JULIUS. Seven years' travel in Central America, northern Mexico, and the far west of the United States. London, 1859.

FRONTIER FORTS. Report of the commission to locate the site of the frontier forts of Pennsylvania. Vols. I–II. [Harrisburg,] 1896.

FROST, J. H. See LEE, DANIEL, and FROST.

FROST, JNO. Border wars of the west. Sandusky City, 1854.

FRY and JEFFERSON. [Map of] Virginie, Maryland en 2 feuilles. Paris, 1777.

FULTON, A. R. The Red Men of Iowa. Des Moines, 1882.

FURUHELM, J. Notes on the natives of Alaska. (Contributions to North American Ethnology, vol. I, Washington, 1877.)

GAIRDNER, Dr. Notes on the geography of Columbia river. (Jour. Roy. Geog. Soc. Lond., vol. XI, 1841.)

GALE, GEO. The upper Mississippi; or historical sketches of the mound builders. Chicago, 1867.

GALIANO, DIONISIO ALCALA. Relación del viage hecho por las goletas Sutil y Mexicana en el año de 1792 para reconocer el estrecho de Fuca. Madrid, 1802.

GALL, M. See CHORIS, LOUIS.

GALLATIN, ALBERT. A synopsis of the Indian tribes in North America. (Trans. Am. Antiq. Soc., Archæologia Americana, vol. II, Worcester, Mass., 1836.)

GALVANO, ANTONIO. The discoveries of the world, from their first original unto the year of our Lord 1555. [1563.] (Hakluyt Society Pub., vol. XXX, London, 1862.)

GAMSBY, C. H. Report on winter examination of inlets, British Columbia. (In Fleming, Canadian Pacific Railway Report. Ottawa, 1877.)

GANONG, WM. F. Place nomenclature of the Province of New Brunswick. (Proc. and Trans. Roy. Soc. Can., 2d s., vol. II, Ottawa, 1896.)

GARCÉS, FRANCISCO. See COUES, ELLIOTT, ed.

GARCÍA, BARTHOLOMÉ. Manual para administrar los santos sacramentos de penitencia . . . á los Indios Pajalates, Orejones, Pacaos, [etc.]. n. p., 1760.

GARCÍA, GREGORIO. Origen de los Indios de el nuevo mundo. Madrid, 1729.

GARCILASSO DE LA VEGA. La Florida del Inca. Historia del adelantado, Hernando de Soto. Madrid, 1723.

GARRARD, LEWIS H. Wah-to-yah, and the Taos trail; or prairie travel and scalp dances, with a look at los rancheros from muleback and the Rocky mountain campfire. Cincinnati, 1850.

GARRISON, GEORGE P. · Texas: a contest of civilizations. Boston and New York, 1903.

GARSON, J. G., ed. See NOTES AND QUÉRIES ON ANTHROPOLOGY.

GASS, PATRICK. Journal of the voyages and travels of a corps of discovery, under command of Lewis and Clarke. Pittsburgh, 1807. (Same, Philadelphia, 1810; Dayton, 1847; Welsburg, Va., 1859.)

GASTALDI, JACOMO DI. Map of the world. Venice, 1554.

GATSCHET, ALBERT S. Zwölf Sprachen aus dem südwesten Nord-Amerikas. Weimar, 1876.

—— Der Yuma-Sprachstamm nach den neuesten handschriftlichen Quellen. (Zeitschrift für Ethnologie, B. IX–XXIV, Berlin, 1877–1892.)

—— The Timucua language. (Proc. Am. Philos. Soc., vol. XVII, Philadelphia, 1878.)

—— A migration legend of the Creek Indians. Vol. I, Philadelphia, 1884 [Brinton's Library of Aboriginal American Literature, No. 4]. Vol. II, St. Louis, 1888 [Trans. Acad. Sci. St. Louis, vol. V, nos. 1 and 2].

—— The Beothuk Indians. (Proc. Am. Philos. Soc., Philadelphia, vol. XXII, pt. IV, 408; vol. XXIII, no. 123, July 1886; vol. XXVIII, no. 132, Jan.–June 1890.)

—— The Karankawa Indians, the coast people of Texas. (Archæol. and Ethnol. Papers Peabody Mus., vol. I, no. 2, Cambridge, 1891.)

—— The Klamath Indians of southwestern Oregon. (Contributions to North American Ethnology, vol. II, pt. 1, 2, Washington, 1891.)

GAYARRÉ, CHAS. Louisiana; its colonial history and romance. [Vol. I.] First and second series of lectures. New York, 1851. Louisiana; its history as a French colony. [Vol. II.] Third series of lectures. New York, 1852.

GEBOW, JOS. A. A vocabulary of the Snake, or Sho-sho-nay dialect. 2d ed. Green River City, Wyo., 1868.

GENTLEMAN OF ELVAS. Virginia richly valued by the description of the maine land of Florida; out of the foure yeeres continuall travell and discoverie of Ferdinando de Soto. Written by a Portugall gentleman of Elvas, and translated out of Portuguese by Richard Hakluyt. London, 1609.

—— A narrative of the expedition of Hernando de Soto into Florida. Published at Evora, 1557. Translated from the Portuguese by Richard Hackluyt. London, 1609. (In French, B. F., Hist. Coll. La., pt. II, 2d ed., Philadelphia, 1850.)

GENTLEMAN OF ELVAS. The discovery and conquest of Terra Florida, by Don Ferdinando de Soto, written by a Gentleman of Elvas, and translated out of Portuguese by Richard Hakluyt. Reprinted from the edition of 1611. Edited, with notes and an introduction, and a translation of a narrative of the expedition by Luis Hernandez de Biedma, by Wm. B. Rye. (Hakluyt Soc. Pub., vol. IX, London, 1851.)

—— See BIEDMA, L. H.; SPANISH EXPLORERS.

GEOGRAPHICAL AND GEOLOGICAL SURVEY. See CONTRIBUTIONS TO NORTH AMERICAN ETHNOLOGY.

GEOGRAPHICAL SOCIETY OF PHILADELPHIA. Bulletin, vol. III, no. 4, Philadelphia, 1902.

GEOGRAPHISCHE BLÄTTER. See DEUTSCHE GEOGRAPHISCHE BLÄTTER.

GEOLOGICAL SOCIETY OF AMERICA. Bulletin, vol. II, Rochester, 1891.

GEOLOGICAL SURVEY OF CANADA. Reports of progress, 1843–84, Montreal, 1844–85. Annual Reports, new ser., 1885–1904, Montreal and Ottawa, 1886–1906.

GEORGIA HISTORICAL SOCIETY. Collections. Vols. I–IV. Savannah, 1840–78.

GERARD, W. R. Plant names of Indian origin. (Garden and Forest, vol. IX, New York, 1896.)

GERONIMO. See BARRETT, S. M., ed.

GESELLSCHAFT FÜR ERDKUNDE. Zeitschrift. Berlin, 1883.

GIBBES, R. W. Documentary history of the American Revolution, consisting of letters and papers relating to the contest for liberty, chiefly in South Carolina, in 1781 and 1782. Columbia, S. C., 1853. 1764–1776, New York, 1855. 1776–1782, New York, 1857.

GIBBS, GEO. Report on the Indian tribes of Washington territory, 1854. (Pacific Railroad Reps., vol. I, 402–434, Washington, 1855.)

—— Alphabetical vocabularies of the Clallam and Lummi. (Shea, Library of American Linguistics, vol. XI, New York, 1863.)

—— Alphabetical vocabulary of the Chinook language. (Ibid., vol. XIII, New York, 1863.)

—— Notes on the Tinneh or Chepewyan Indians of British and Russian America. 1, The eastern Tinneh, by Bernard Ross. 2, The Loucheux Indians, by Wm. Hardisty. 3, The Kutchin tribes, by Strachan Jones. (Smithsonian Rep. for 1866, Washington, 1867.)

—— Tribes of western Washington and northwestern Oregon. (Contributions to North American Ethnology, vol. I, Washington, 1877.)

—— Dictionary of the Niskwalli. (Ibid.)

—— Note on the use of numerals among the T'sim si-an'. (Ibid.)

—— and DALL, W. H. Vocabularies of tribes of the extreme northwest. (Ibid.)

GIDDINGS, JOSHUA R. The exiles of Florida: or, the crimes committed by our government against the Maroons, who fled from South Carolina and other slave states, seeking protection under Spanish laws. Columbus, 1858.

GILBERT, BENJ. See SEVERANCE, F. H.

GILDER, W. H. Schwatka's search. New York, 1881.

GILMAN, BENJ. IVES. Hopi songs. (Jour. Am. Ethnol. and Archæol., vol. V, Boston and New York, 1908.)

GIORDA, J. A dictionary of the Kalispel or Flathead Indian language. Pt. I, Kalispel-English. Pt. II, English-Kalispel. St. Ignatius, Mont., 1877–79.

GIST, CHRISTOPHER. See DARLINGTON, WM. M.

GOBINEAU, A. DE. Voyage à Terre-Neuve. Paris, 1861.

GODDARD, PLINY E. Life and culture of the Hupa. (Pub. Univ. Cal., Am. Archæol. and Ethnol., vol. I, no. 1, Berkeley, 1903.)
———— Hupa texts. (Ibid., vol. I, no. 2, Berkeley, 1904.)
GOMARA, FRANÇOIS LOPEZ DE. Histoire generalle des Indes Occidentales, et terres neuues. Paris, 1606.
GOOD, JNO. B. The morning and evening prayer, and the litany, with prayers and thanksgivings, translated into the Neklakapamunk tongue. Victoria, B. C., 1878.
———— Offices for the solemnization of matrimony, the visitation of the sick, the burial of the dead, translated into the Nitlakapamuk, or Thompson River tongue. Victoria, B. C., 1880.
———— A vocabulary and outlines of grammar of the Nitlakapamuk or Thompson tongue (the Indian language spoken between Yale, Lillooet, Cache creek and Nicola lake), together with a phonetic Chinook dictionary. Victoria, 1880.
GOODE, G. B., ed. The Smithsonian Institution, 1846–96. The history of its first half century. Washington, 1897.
GOODMAN, ALFRED T., ed. Journal of Captain William Trent from Logstown to Pickawillany, A. D. 1752. Cincinnati, 1871.
GOOKIN, DANIEL. Historical collections of the Indians in New England, 1792. (Coll. Mass. Hist. Soc., 1st s., vol. I, Boston, 1806.)
———— Historical account of the doings and sufferings of the Christian Indians of New England. (Trans. Am. Antiq. Soc., vol. II, Cambridge, 1836.)
GORDON, JAS. BENTLEY. Historical and geographical memoir of the North-American continent. Dublin, 1820.
GORGES, FERDINANDO. Briefe narration of the plantations into the parts of America, especially that of New England. 1658. (Coll Mass. Hist. Soc., 3d s., vol. VI, Boston, 1837. Same, Coll. Maine Hist. Soc., vol. II, Portland, 1847.)
GOSSE, L. A. Essai sur les déformations artificielles du crâne. Paris, 1855.
GOULD, BENJ. A. Investigations in the military and anthropological statistics of American soldiers. New York, 1869.
GOURGUE, Le Cappitaine. La reprinse de la Floride. (Ternaux-Compans, Voyages, tome XX, Paris, 1841.
———— See LAUDONNIÈRE.
GRAAH, W. A. Narrative of an expedition to the east coast of Greenland. London, 1837.
GRANT, W. C. Description of Vancouver island by its first colonist. (Jour. Roy. Geog. Soc., vol. XXVII, London, 1857.)
———— Remarks on Vancouver island, principally concerning town sites and population. (Ibid., XXXI, London, 1861.)
GRAPHIC sketches from old and authentic works, illustrating the costume, habits, and character, of the aborigines of America. New York, 1841.
GRAVIER, J. See SHEA, JOHN G. (Early Voyages).
GRAY, A. B. Survey of a route for the Southern Pacific railroad, on the 32nd parallel. Cincinnati, 1856.
GRAY, WM. HENRY. A history of Oregon, 1792–1849. Portland, 1870.
GREAT BRITAIN. Parliamentary report, vol. XLII, London, 1854.
GREELY, A. W. Three years of Arctic service. An account of the Lady Franklin Bay expedition of 1881–84. Vols. I–II. New York, 1886.
GREENHOW, ROBERT. History of Oregon and California. London, 1844.
GREGG, ALEXANDER. History of the old Cheraws, containing an account of aborigines of the Pedee, 1730–1810. New York, 1867.

GREGG, JOSIAH. Commerce of the prairies : or the journal of a Santa Fé trader. Vols. I–II. New York, 1844. (Same, Philadelphia, 1850.)
GRIFFITH, ROBERT E. Medical botany. Philadelphia, 1847.
GRINNELL, GEO. BIRD. Pawnee hero stories and folk tales. New York, 1889.
———— Blackfoot lodge tales. New York, 1892.
———— Social organization of the Cheyennes. (Rep. Int. Cong. Amer., 13th sess., 1902, New York, 1905.)
GROOS, KARL. The play of man. New York, 1901.
GROSSE, ERNST. Beginnings of art. New York, 1897.
GÜSSEFELD, F. L. Charte über die XIII. Vereinigte Staaten von Nord-America. [Nuremberg, 1784.]
———— Charte von Nord America. Nürnberg, 1797.
HADDON, A. C. Evolution in art. London, 1895.
———— Study of man. New York, 1898.
HAILMANN, WM. N. Education of the Indian. Albany, 1904.
HAINES, ELIJAH M. The American Indian (Uh-nish-in-na-ba). Chicago, 1888.
HAKLUYT, RICHARD. The principal navigations, voyages, traffiques, and discoveries of the English nation. Vols. I–III. London, 1598–1600.
———— Collection of the early voyages, travels, and discoveries of the English nation. New edition, with additions. Vol. I (–V and Suppl.). London, 1809 [–1812].
———— See GENTLEMAN OF ELVAS.
HAKLUYT SOCIETY. Publications. Vols. I–LXXIX. London, 1847–89.
HALBERT, H. S., and BALL, T. H. The Creek war of 1813 and 1814. Chicago and Montgomery, 1895.
HALDIMAND, FREDERICK. The Haldimand papers, Jan. 1779–Mar. 1783. (Vt. Hist. Soc. Coll., vol. II, Montpelier, 1871.)
HALE, E. M. Ilex cassine, the aboriginal North American tea. (Bull. 14, Div. of Botany, U. S. Dept. Agric., Washington, 1891.)
HALE, HORATIO. Ethnology and philology. (In United States Exploring Expedition during the years 1838–1842, under the command of Charles Wilkes, U. S. N. Vol. VI. Philadelphia, 1846.)
———— Iroquois book of rites. Philadelphia, 1883.
———— The Tutelo tribe and language. (Proc. Am. Philos. Soc., vol. XXI, no. 114, Philadelphia, 1883.)
———— An international idiom. A manual of the Oregon trade language, or " Chinook jargon." London, 1890.
———— See GALLATIN, ALBERT.
HALL, A. J. The gospel according to Saint John. Translated into the Qāgūtl language. London, 1884.
HALL, BENJ. F. The early history of the north western states. Buffalo, 1849.
HALL, C. F. Arctic researches and life among the Esquimaux. New York, 1865.
HALL, G. STANLEY. Adolescence. Its psychology. Vols. I–II. New York, 1904.
HALL, JAS. See MCKENNEY, T. L., and HALL.
HALLECK, WM. H. Report of General Halleck, military division of the Pacific. (Report of the Secretary of War, pt. I; H. R. Ex. Doc. 1, 40th Cong., 3d sess., Washington, 1869.)
HALSEY, F. W. The old New York frontier, its wars with Indians and Tories, its missionary schools, pioneers and land titles. 1614–1800. New York, 1901.
HAMILTON, LEONIDAS LE C. Mexican handbook ; a complete description of the Republic of Mexico. Boston, 1883.

HAMILTON, PATRICK. The resources of Arizona. A description of its mineral, farming and timber lands, &c., with brief sketches of its early history, prehistoric ruins, Indian tribes, Spanish missionaries, past and present. 2d ed. [San Francisco,] 1883.

HAMILTON, PETER J. Colonial Mobile, an historical study largely from original sources, of the Alabama-Tombigbee basin from the discovery of Mobile bay in 1519 until the demolition of Fort Charlotte in 1820. Boston and New York, 1897.

HAMILTON, WM., and IRVIN, S. M. An Ioway grammar, illustrating the principles of the language used by the Ioway, Otoe and Missouri Indians. Ioway and Sac Mission Press, 1848.

HAMY, ERNEST T. See QUATREFAGES, J. L., and HAMY.

HANKS, HENRY G. Deep lying auriferous gravels and table mountains of California. San Francisco, 1901.

HANSON, JNO. H. The lost Prince: facts tending to prove the identity of Louis the Seventeenth, of France, and the Rev. Eleazar Williams, missionary among the Indians of North America. New York, 1854.

HANSON, JNO. W. History of Gardiner, Pittston and West Gardiner, with a sketch of the Kennebec Indians, and New Plymouth Purchase. Gardiner, Me., 1852.

HARDISTY, WM. The Loucheux Indians. (Smithsonian Rep. 1866, Washington, 1867.)

HARDY, R. W. H. Travels in the interior of Mexico, in 1825–28. London, 1829.

HARIOT, THOS. Admiranda narratio fida tamen. de commodis et incolarvm ritibvs Virginiæ. (In Bry, Collectiones, t. I, Francforti, 1590.)
―――― A briefe and true report of the new found land of Virginia. Franckfort, 1590. (Same, New York, 1871.)
―――― Narrative of the first English plantation of Virginia. 1588 and 1590. Reprint, London, 1893.

HARMON, DANIEL W. A journal of voyages and travels in the interiour of North America. Andover, 1820.

HARRIS, GEO. H. Life of Horatio Jones. (Pub. Buffalo Hist. Soc., vol. VI, Buffalo, 1903.)

HARRIS, JOEL CHANDLER. Uncle Remus. His songs and his sayings. New York, 1895.

HARRIS, JNO. Navigantium atque itinerantium bibliotheca, or, a complete collection of voyages and travels. Vols. I–II. London, 1705. (Same, London, 1764.)

HARRIS, THADDEUS M. Journal of a tour into the territory northwest of the Alleghany mountains in 1803. Boston, 1805.

HARRIS, WM. H. Louisiana products, resources and attractions, with a sketch of the parishes. New Orleans, 1881.

HARRIS, W. R. History of the early missions of western Canada. Toronto, 1893.

HARRISSE, HENRY. The discovery of North America. A critical documentary, and historic investigation. London and Paris, 1892.

HARSHBERGER, JNO. WM. Maize: a botanical and economic study. (Cont. Bot. Lab. Univ. Pa., vol. I, no. 2, Philadelphia, 1893.)

HARTWIG, G. The polar world. London, 1869.

HARVEY, HENRY. History of the Shawnee Indians, from the year 1681 to 1854 inclusive. Cincinnati, 1855.

HASSLER, E. W. Old Westmoreland. Pittsburg, 1900.

HASTINGS, LANSFORD W. Emigrant's guide to Oregon and California. Cincinnati, 1845.

HATTON, J., and HARVEY, M. Newfoundland, its history, [etc.] Boston, 1883.

HAUMONTÉ, J. D., PARISOT J., and ADAM, LUCIEN. Grammaire et vocabulaire de la langue Taensa avec textes traduits et commentés. Paris, 1882.

HAWKINS, BENJ. A sketch of the Creek country, in 1798 and 99. (Georgia Hist. Soc. Coll., vol. III, Savannah, 1848.)

HAWKINS, EDWARD. Medallic illustrations of the history of Great Britain and Ireland. Vols. I–II. London, 1885.

HAWKINS, ERNEST. Historical notices of the missions of the Church of England in the North American colonies, previous to the independence of the United States. London, 1845.

HAWKS, FRANCIS L. History of North Carolina. Fayetteville, N. C.: vol. I, 1859; vol. II, 1858.

HAYDEN, FERDINAND V. Contributions to the ethnography and philology of the Indian tribes of the Missouri valley. (Trans. Am. Philos. Soc., N. S., vol. XII, Philadelphia, 1862.)

HAYDEN, H. E. Various silver and copper medals presented to the Indians by the sovereigns of England, France, and Spain, from 1600 to 1800. (Proc. and Coll. Wyoming Hist. and Geol. Soc., vol. II, pt. 2, Wilkes-Barré, Pa., 1886.)

HAYDEN SURVEY. See UNITED STATES GEOLOGICAL AND GEOGRAPHICAL SURVEY OF THE TERRITORIES.

HAYES, I. I. An Arctic boat journey in autumn of 1854. Boston, 1860.

HAYWOOD, JNO. The natural and aboriginal history of Tennessee, up to the first settlements therein by the white people, in the year 1768. Nashville, 1823.

HAZARD, EBENEZER. Historical collections; consisting of state papers, and other authentic documents, intended as materials for an history of the United States of America. Vols. I–II. Philadelphia, 1792–94.

HAZLITT, WM. C. British Columbia and Vancouver island; comprising a historical sketch of the British settlements in the north-west coast of America. London and New York, 1858.

HEALY, M. A. Report of the cruise of the Corwin in 1885. Washington, 1887.

HEARD, ISAAC V. D. History of the Sioux war and massacres of 1862 and 1863. New York, 1863.

HEARNE, SAMUEL. Journey from Prince of Wales's fort in Hudson's bay, to the northern ocean. London, 1795. (Same, Dublin, 1796.)

HECKEWELDER, JNO. G. E. Narrative of the mission of the United Brethren among the Delaware and Mohegan tribes. Philadelphia, 1808. (Same, 1820.)
―――― A narrative of the mission of the United Brethren among the Delaware and Mohegan Indians. Edited by W. E. Connelley. Cleveland, 1907.
―――― An account of the history, manners, and customs of the Indian nations who once inhabited Pennsylvania and the neighboring states. Philadelphia, 1819. (Reprinted, Mem. Hist. Soc. Pa., vol. XII, Philadelphia, 1876.)
―――― Indian names of rivers, streams, and other noted places in the state of Pennsylvania. (Trans. Am. Philos. Soc., N. S., vol. IV, Philadelphia, 1834.)

HEILPRIN, ANGELO. Arctic problem and narrative of the Peary relief expedition of the Academy of Natural Sciences of Philadelphia. Philadelphia, 1893.

HELMERSEN, GREGOR VON. See BAER, KARL E. VON.

HENING, WM. WALLER. Statutes at large; being a collection of all the laws of Virginia. Vol. III. Philadelphia, 1823.

HENNEPIN, LOUIS. Description de la Louisiane nouvellement decouverte au sud oüest de la Nouvelle France. Paris, 1683. (*Same,* trans. by John G. Shea, New York, 1880.)
———— A new discovery of a vast country in America extending above four thousand miles between New France and New Mexico. London, 1698. (*Same,* 2 vols., Chicago, 1903.)
———— A continuation, of the new discovery of a vast country in America, extending above four thousand miles, between New France and New Mexico. London, 1698.
———— Account of M. de la Salle's undertaking to discover the Mississippi by way of the Gulf of Mexico. (In French, B. F., Hist. Coll. La., pt. 1, New York, 1846.)
———— Narrative of a voyage to the upper Mississippi. (In Shea, J. G., Discov. Miss. Val., New York, 1852.)
HENNING, WM. W. *See* HENING.
HENRY, ALEXANDER. Travels and adventures in Canada, and the Indian territories, between 1760 and 1776. New York, 1809.
———— *and* THOMPSON, DAVID. *See* COUES, ELLIOTT, *ed.*
HENSHAW, H. W. [Introductory notes to] the account by the pilot Ferrel of the voyage of Cabrillo along the west coast of North America in 1542. (Wheeler Survey Reports, vol. VII, pt. 1, app., Washington, 1879.)
———— Animal carvings from mounds of the Mississippi valley. (Second Rep. Bur. Am. Ethnology, Washington, 1883.)
———— Perforated stones from California. (Bull. 2, Bur. Am. Ethnology, Washington, 1887.)
———— Indian origin of maple sugar. (Am. Anthropologist, vol. III, Washington, 1890.)
HERIOT, GEO. Travels through the Canadas, containing a description of the picturesque scenery on some of the rivers and lakes. London, 1807. (*Same,* without the second part, Philadelphia, 1813.)
HERMAN'S MAP OF VIRGINIA. *See* REPORT and accompanying documents of Virginia and Maryland Boundary Commissioners, 1873.
HERRERA, ANTONIO DE. Novus orbis, sive descriptio Indiæ Occidentalis, metaphraste C. Barlæo. Amstelodami, 1622.
———— Historia general de los hechos de los Castellanos en las islas i tierra firme del mar oceano. Tomos I–V. Madrid, 1720.
———— General history of the vast continent and islands of America, commonly called the West-Indies, from the first discovery thereof. Translated by John Stevens. Vols. I–VI. London, 1725–26.
HERRICK, EDWARD. Indian narratives; containing a correct and interesting history of the Indian wars. Claremont, N. H., 1854.
HERVAS, LORENZO. Idea dell' universo che contiene la storia della vita dell' uomo, elementi cosmografici, viaggio estatico al mondo planetario, e storia della terra, e delle lingue. Tomo XVII. Cesena, 1784.
———— Catálogo de las lenguas de las naciones conocidas, y numeracion, division, y clases de estas segun la diversidad de sus idiomas y dialectos. Tomos I–VI. Madrid, 1800–05.
HEWAT, ALEX. Historical account of the rise and progress of the colonies of South Carolina and Georgia. Vols. I–II. London, 1779.
HEWETT, EDGAR L. Antiquities of the Jemez plateau. (Bull. 32, Bur. Am. Ethnology, Washington, 1906.)
HEWITT, J. N. B. Legend of the founding of the Iroquois league. (Am. Anthropologist, vol. V, Washington, 1892.)
———— Orenda and a definition of religion. (Ibid., N. S., vol. IV, New York, 1902.)

HEWITT, J. N. B. Iroquoian cosmology. (Twenty-first Rep. Bur. Am. Ethnology, Washington, 1903.)
HEYLYN, PETER. Cosmography, containing the chorography and history of the whole world, and all the principal kingdoms, provinces, seas, and isles thereof. Improved by Edmund Bohun. London, 1703.
HICOCK, W. A. *See* RUPP, I. D.
HIGGINSON, FRANCIS. New England's plantation. London, 1630. (*Same,* in Force, Tracts, vol. I, 1836; Mass. Hist. Soc. Coll., 1st ser., vol. I, 1792; Young, Chronicles of Mass., Boston, 1846.)
HILDRETH, JAS. Dragoon campaigns to the Rocky mountains. New York, 1836.
HILDRETH, SAMUEL P. Pioneer history; account of the first examinations of the Ohio valley and the early settlement of the Northwest Territory. Cincinnati, 1848.
HIND, HENRY Y. Narrative of the Canadian Red River exploring expedition of 1857, and of the Assinniboine and Saskatchewan exploring expedition of 1858. Vols. I–II. London, 1860.
———— Explorations in the interior of the Labrador peninsula, the country of the Montagnais and Nasquapee Indians. Vols. I–II. London, 1863.
HINES, GUSTAVUS. Life on the plains of the Pacific. Oregon, its history, condition and prospects. Buffalo, 1851.
HINMAN, SAMUEL D., *and* WELSH, WM. Journal of the Rev. S. D. Hinman, missionary to the Santee Sioux Indians. And Taopi, by Bishop Whipple. Philadelphia, 1869.
HINTON, RICHARD J. Hand-book to Arizona. San Francisco and New York, 1878.
HISTORICAL MAGAZINE. The Historical Magazine, and Notes and Queries, concerning the antiquities, history, and biography of America. 1st ser., vols. I–X, Boston and London, 1857–66. 2d ser., vols. I–IX, Morrisania, N. Y., 1867–71. 3d ser., vols. I–II, Morrisania, 1872–75.
HISTORICAL SOCIETY OF MICHIGAN. Historical and scientific sketches of Michigan. Detroit, 1834.
———— *See* MICHIGAN PIONEER AND HISTORICAL SOCIETY.
HISTORICAL SOCIETY OF PENNSYLVANIA. Memoirs, vols. I–XIV, Philadelphia, 1826–95.
———— Pennsylvania Magazine of History and Biography, vols. I–XXXII, Philadelphia, 1877–1909.
HITTELL, JNO. S. Yosemite; its wonders and its beauties. San Francisco, 1868.
HITTELL, THEODORE H. History of California. Vols. I–IV. San Francisco, 1885–97.
HODGE, F. W. Coronado's march to Quivira. (In Brower, Harahey, St. Paul, 1899.)
———— *See* SPANISH EXPLORERS.
HODGE, HIRAM C. Arizona as it is; or, the coming country. New York and Boston, 1877.
HODGSON, WM. B. The Creek confederacy. (Coll. Ga. Hist. Soc., vol. III, pt. 1, Savannah, 1848.)
HOFFMAN, C. F. A winter in the far west. Vols. I–II. London, 1835. (*Same,* under the title "A Winter in the West, by a New Yorker.")
HOFFMAN, WALTER J. Miscellaneous ethnographic observations on Indians inhabiting Nevada, California, and Arizona. (Tenth Ann. Rep. Hayden Survey, Washington, 1878.)
———— Hugo Ried's account of the Indians of Los Angeles county, California. (Bull. Essex Institute, vol. XVII, Salem, 1885.)

HOFFMAN, WALTER J. Remarks on Indian tribal names. (Proc. Am. Philos. Soc., vol. XXIII, no. 122, Philadelphia, Apr. 1886.)
———— The Midē'wiwin or "grand medicine society" of the Ojibwa. (Seventh Rep. Bur. Am. Ethnology, Washington, 1891.)
———— The Menomini Indians. (Fourteenth Rep. Bur. Am. Ethnology, pt. 1, Washington, 1896.)

HOLDER, A. B. Age of puberty of Indian girls. (Am. Jour. Obstetrics, vol. XXIII, New York, Oct. 1890.)

HOLM, G. Ethnologisk Skizze af Angmagsalikerne. Kjøbenhavn, 1887.

HOLM, THOS. CAMPANIUS. Short description of the province of New Sweden, now called Pennsylvania. (Mem. Hist. Soc. Pa., vol. III, Philadelphia, 1834.)

HOLMBERG, HEINRICH J. Ethnographische Skizzen über die Völker des russischen Amerika. Helsingfors, 1855.

HOLMES, ABIEL. Annals of America, from 1492 to 1826. Vols. I–II. Cambridge, 1829.

HOLMES, WM. H. Report on the ancient ruins of southwestern Colorado. (10th Ann. Rep. U. S. Geol. and Geog. Surv. Terr., Washington, 1879. Also in Bull. U. S. Geol. and Geog. Surv., vol. II, no. 1, Washington, 1876.)
———— Art in shell of the ancient Americans. (Second Rep. Bur. Am. Ethnology, Washington, 1883.)
———— Illustrated catalogue of a portion of the collections made by the Bureau of Ethnology during the field season of 1881. (Third Rep. Bur. Am. Ethnology, Washington, 1884.)
———— Prehistoric textile fabrics of the United States. (Ibid.)
———— Pottery of the ancient pueblos. (Fourth Rep. Bur. Am. Ethnology, Washington, 1886.)
———— Ancient pottery of the Mississippi valley. (Ibid.)
———— Origin and development of form and ornament. (Ibid.)
———— A study of the textile art in its relation to the development of form and ornament. (Sixth Rep. Bur. Am. Ethnology, Washington, 1888.)
———— An ancient quarry in Indian Territory. (Bull. 21, Bur. Am. Ethnology, Washington, 1894.)
———— Prehistoric textile art of eastern United States. (Thirteenth Rep. Bur. Am. Ethnology, Washington, 1896.)
———— Stone implements of the Potomac-Chesapeake tidewater province. (Fifteenth Rep. Bur. Am. Ethnology, Washington, 1897.)
———— Review of the evidence relating to auriferous gravel man in California. (Smithsonian Rep. for 1899, Washington, 1901.)
———— Order of development of the primal shaping arts. (Ibid., 1901, Washington, 1902.)
———— Flint implements and fossil remains from a sulphur spring at Afton, Indian Territory. (Am. Anthropologist, N. s., vol. IV, New Nork, 1902.)
———— Aboriginal pottery of the eastern United States. (Twentieth Rep. Bur. Am. Ethnology, Washington, 1903.)
———— Fossil human remains found near Lansing, Kans. (Smithsonian Rep. for 1902, Washington, 1903.)
———— Shell ornaments from Kentucky and Mexico. (Smithsonian Misc. Coll., vol. XLV, Quarterly Issue, I, pts. 1 and 2, Washington, July–Sept. 1903.)
———— and MASON, O. T. Instructions to collectors of historical and anthropological specimens. (Bull. 39, U. S. Nat. Mus., pt. Q, Washington, 1902.)

HOMANN HEIRS. America Septentrionalis a domino d'Anville in Galliis edita nunc in Anglia coloniis in interiorem Virginiam deductis nec non fluvii Ohio. Noribergæ, 1756.
———— See GÜSSEFELD; MAPPA.

HOOPER, C. L. Report of the cruise of the U. S. Revenue Steamer Corwin in the Arctic ocean. Washington, 1881.

HOOPER, WM. H. Ten months among the tents of the Tuski. London, 1853.

HOPKINS, SARAH WINNEMUCCA. Life among the Piutes. Edited by Mrs. Horace Mann. Boston, 1883.

HORDEN, JNO. The book of common prayer, and administration of the sacraments. Translated into the language of the Moose Indians of the diocese of Rupert's Land, north-west America. London, 1859.

HORNOT, ANT. Anecdotes Américaines, ou histoire abrégée des principaux événements arrivés dans le Nouveau Monde, depuis sa découverte jusqu'à l'époque présente. Paris, 1776.

HORSFORD, EBEN N. The discovery of the ancient city of Norumbega. Boston and New York, 1890.

HOUGH, DANIEL. Map accompanying Indian names of lakes, etc., by H. W. Beckwith. (In Twelfth Ann. Geol. Rep. of Indiana, Indianapolis, 1883.)

HOUGH, FRANKLIN B. Diary of the siege of Detroit in the war with Pontiac. Albany, 1860.

HOUGH, WALTER. Preservation of museum specimens from insects and the effect of dampness. (Rep. U. S. Nat. Mus. for 1887, Washington, 1889.)
———— Fire-making apparatus in the U. S. National Museum. (Ibid., 1888, Washington, 1890.)
———— Moki snake dance. Chicago, 1898.
———— Lamp of the Eskimo. (Rep. U. S. Nat. Mus. for 1896, Washington, 1898.)
———— Development of illumination. (Smithsonian Rep. for 1901, Washington, 1902.)
———— Archeological field work in northeastern Arizona. The Museum-Gates expedition of 1901. (Report U. S. Nat. Mus. for 1901, Washington, 1903.)
———— Antiquities of the upper Gila and Salt River valleys in Arizona and New Mexico. (Bull. 35, Bur. Am. Ethnology, Washington, 1907.)

HOUSE OF REPRESENTATIVES. See UNITED STATES CONGRESS.

HOWARD, O. O. Nez Perce Joseph. Boston, 1881.

HOWE, HENRY. Historical collections of Ohio, containing a collection of the most interesting facts, traditions, biographical sketches, anecdotes, etc., relating to its general and local history. Cincinnati, 1847. (Same, Cincinnati, 1851; Cincinnati, 1852; Norwalk, Ohio, vol. I, 1898, vol. II, 1896.)
———— See BARBER, J. W., and HOWE.

HOWELLS, W. D. Three villages. Boston, 1884.

HOWGATE, H. W., ed. Cruise of the Florence; or, extracts from the journal of the preliminary Arctic expedition of 1877–78. Washington, 1879.

HOWSE, JOSEPH. A grammar of the Cree language; with which is combined an analysis of the Chippeway dialect. London, 1844.

HOY, P. R. How and by whom were the copper implements made? Racine, 1886.

HOYT, EPAPHRAS. Antiquarian researches; a history of the Indian wars in the country bordering the Connecticut river. Greenfield, 1824.

HRDLIČKA, ALEŠ. Physical and physiological observations on the Navaho. (Am. Anthropologist, N. s., vol. II, New York, 1900.)

HRDLIČKA, ALEŠ. The crania of Trenton, New Jersey, and their bearing upon the antiquity of man in that region. (Bull. Am. Mus. Nat. Hist., vol. XVI, New York, 1902.)
———— The Lansing skeleton. (Am. Anthropologist, N. S., vol. V, Lancaster, Pa., 1903.)
———— Directions for collecting information and specimens for physical anthropology. (Bull. 39, U. S. Nat. Mus., pt. R, Washington, 1904.)
———— Notes on the Indians of Sonora, Mexico. (Am. Anthropologist, N. S., vol. VI, Lancaster, Pa., 1904.)
———— Contribution to the physical anthropology of California. (Pub. Univ. Cal., Am. Archæol. and Ethnol., vol. IV, no. 2, Berkeley, 1906.)
———— Skeletal remains suggesting or attributed to early man in North America. (Bull. 33, Bur. Am. Ethnology, Washington, 1907.)
———— Physiological and medical observations among the Indians of southwestern United States and northern Mexico. (Bull. 34, Bur. Am. Ethnology, Washington, 1908.)
———— Tuberculosis among certain Indian tribes of the United States. (Bull. 42, Bur. Am. Ethnology, Washington, 1909.)
HUBBARD, WM. History of the Indian wars in New England from the first settlement to the termination of the war with King Philip in 1677, with preface and notes by S. G. Drake. Vols. I–II. Roxbury, Mass., 1865.
HUBLEY, ADAM, Jr. See JORDAN, JNO. W.
HUGHES, JNO. T. Doniphan's expedition; containing an account of the conquest of New Mexico. Cincinnati, 1848.
HULBERT, ARCHER B. Red-men's roads. Columbus, 1900.
———— Historical highways of America. Vols. I–XVI. Cleveland, 1902–05.
HUMBOLDT, FRIEDRICH H. ALEX. DE. Essai politique sur le royaume de la Nouvelle-Espagne. Tomes I–V. Paris, 1811. (Same, trans. by John Black, vols. I–IV, London, 1811. Same, vols. I–II, London, 1822.)
———— Atlas géographique et physique du royaume de le Nouvelle-Espagne. Paris, 1811.
———— Personal narrative of travel to the equinoctial regions of the new continent during the years 1799–1804. Translated by H. M. Williams. Vols. I–VII. London, 1814–29.
HUMPHREYS, DAVID. Historical account of the incorporated society for the propagation of the gospel in foreign parts. London, 1730.
HUNTER, JNO. D. Memoirs of a captivity among the Indians of North America. London, 1823.
HUTCHINS, THOS. Topographical description of Virginia, Pennsylvania, Maryland, [etc.] with appendix containing Patrick Kennedy's journal up the Illinois river. London, 1778.
———— Geography of the United States. Philadelphia, 1784.
———— An historical narrative and topographical description of Louisiana, and West-Florida. Philadelphia, 1784. (Same, in Imlay, Topog. Descrip. of the West. Terr. of N. A., London, 1797.)
HYDROGRAPHIC OFFICE. See UNITED STATES.

IAPI OAYE. The Word Carrier. Vols. I–XVI. Greenwood, Dakota; Santee Agency, Nebraska, 1871–87.
ICAZBALCETA, JOAQUIN GARCIA. Coleccion. de documentos para la historia de Mexico. Tomos I–II. Mexico, 1858.
IMLAY, GILBERT. A topographical description of the western territory of North America. London, 1797.

INDIAN AFFAIRS (CANADA). Report of the Deputy Superintendent General of Indian Affairs, 1876–79. Continued as Annual Report of the Department of Indian Affairs for the year 1880[–1910], Ottawa, 1880–1910.
INDIAN AFFAIRS (U. S.). Office of Indian Affairs (War Department). Reports, 1825–1848. Report of the Commissioner (Department of the Interior), 1849–1909.
INDIAN LAWS. See LAWS.
INDIAN TREATIES and laws and regulations relating to Indian affairs. Washington, 1826.
———— Treaties between the United States of America and the several Indian tribes from 1778 to 1837. Washington, 1837.
———— A compilation of all the treaties between the United States and the Indian tribes, now in force as laws. Washington, 1873.
———— Indian affairs. Laws and treaties. Vol. I (Laws). Vol. II (Treaties). Compiled and edited by Charles J. Kappler. Washington, 1904.
INDIANA. Department of Geology and Natural History. Twelfth Annual Report. Indianapolis, 1883.
INGERSOLL, ERNEST. Wampum and its history. (Am. Nat., vol. XVII, no. 5, Philadelphia, 1883.)
INTERNATIONAL CONGRESS OF AMERICANISTS. See CONGRÈS INTERNATIONAL.
INTERNATIONAL CONGRESS OF ANTHROPOLOGY. Memoirs. Chicago, 1894.
INTERNATIONALES ARCHIV FÜR ETHNOGRAPHIE. Band VII. Leiden, Paris, Leipzig, 1894.
INTERNATIONAL FOLK-LORE ASSOCIATION. Archives. Vol. I. Chicago, 1898.
INVESTIGATOR (THE). Religious, moral, scientific, &c. Washington, Jan. 1845–Dec. 1846.
IOWA JOURNAL OF HISTORY AND POLITICS. Vols. I–VII. Iowa City, 1903–09.
IRVING, JNO. T. Indian sketches taken during an expedition to the Pawnee tribes. Vols. I–II. Philadelphia, 1835.
IRVING, WASHINGTON. Astoria or anecdotes of an enterprise beyond the Rocky mountains. New York, 1849. (Same, vols. I–II, New York and London, 1897.)
———— Adventures of Captain Bonneville, U. S. A., in the Rocky mountains and the far west. New York, 1851. (Same, 1868.) See BONNEVILLE.
IRWIN, D. HASTINGS. War medals and decorations issued to the British forces from 1588–1898. 2d ed. London, 1899.
IVES, JOS. C. Report upon the Colorado river of the west, explored in 1857 and 1858. (H. R. Ex. Doc. 90, 36th Cong., 1st sess., Washington, 1861.)

JACKSON, HELEN M. H., and KINNEY, ABBOTT. Report on the condition and needs of the Mission Indians of California to the Commissioner of Indian Affairs. Washington, 1883.
JACKSON, SHELDON. Alaska and missions of the North Pacific coast. New York, 1880.
———— Report on the introduction of reindeer in Alaska. (Rep. U. S. Bur. Education 1894–95, Washington, 1896.)
———— Facts about Alaska. New York, 1903.
———— Our barbarous Eskimos in northern Alaska. (Metropolitan Mag., vol. XXII, no. 3, New York, June, 1905.)
JACKSON, WM. H. Ancient ruins in southwestern Colorado. (Ann. Rep. U. S. Geol. Surv. of Terr. for 1874, Washington, 1876.)
———— Descriptive catalogue of photographs of North American Indians. (Pub. U. S. Geol. Surv. of Terr., no. 9, Washington, 1877.)

JACKSON, WM. H. Report on the ancient ruins examined in 1875 and 1877. (Ann. Rep. U. S. Geol. Surv. of Terr., Washington, 1878.)

JACOBSTEIN, MEYER. The tobacco industry in the United States. (Columbia University Studies in History, Economics and Public Law, vol. XXVI, no. 3, New York, 1907.)

JAMES, EDWIN. Account of an expedition from Pittsburgh to the Rocky mountains, performed in the years 1819 and '20, by order of the Hon. J. C. Calhoun, Sec'y of War: under the command of Major Stephen H. Long. Vols. I–II, and atlas. Philadelphia, 1823. (Same, London, 1823.)

JAMES, GEO. WHARTON. Indians of the Painted Desert region. Boston, 1903.
———— Indian basketry, and how to make Indian and other baskets. New York, 1904.

JAMES, JAS. ALTON. English institutions and the American Indian. (Johns Hopkins Univ. Studies in Hist. and Polit. Sci., 12th ser., vol. X, Baltimore, 1894.)

JANSON, CHAS. W. Stranger in America; observations during a long residence in the United States. London, 1807.

JARAMILLO, JUAN. Relation du voyage fait à la Nouvelle-Terre. (Ternaux-Compans, Voyages, tome IX, Paris, 1838.)
———— Relacion hecha por el Capitan Juan Jaramillo, de la jornada que habia hecho a la tierra nueva en Nueva España y al descubrimiento de Cibola. (Colección de Documentos Inéditos, tomo XIV, 304–17, Paris, 1870. Same, translated by G. P. Winship, in 14th Rep. Bur. Am. Ethnology, 1896.)

JEFFERSON, THOS. Notes on the State of Virginia; with a map of Virginia, Maryland, Delaware, and Pennsylvania. Philadelphia, 1801. (Same, Philadelphia, 1825.)

JEFFERYS, THOS. The natural and civil history of the French dominions in North and South America. Parts I–II. London, 1761.
———— A general topography of North America and the West Indies being a collection of all the maps charts and particular surveys that have been published in that part of the world either in Europe or America. London, 1768.
———— The provinces of New York and New Jersey with part of Pennsylvania and the government of Trois Rivières and Montreal. London, 1768.
———— The American atlas or a geographical description of the whole continent of America. London, 1776.

JENKINS, HOWARD M., ed. Pennsylvania colonial and federal. Vols. I–III. Philadelphia, 1905.

JENKS, ALBERT ERNEST. Childhood of Ji-shib', the Ojibwa. Madison, Wis., 1900.
———— The wild-rice gatherers of the upper lakes. (Nineteenth Rep. Bur. Am. Ethnology, pt. 2, Washington, 1900.)

JESUIT RELATIONS and allied documents. Travels and explorations of the Jesuit missionaries in New France, 1610–1791. Reuben Gold Thwaites, ed. Vols. I–LXXIII. Cleveland, 1896–1901.
———— Relations des Jesuites contenant ce qui s'est passé de plus remarquable dans les missions des pères de la Compagnie de Jesus dans la Nouvelle-France. Embrassant les années 1611–1672. Tomes I–III. Quebec, 1858.

JEWITT, JNO. R. A narrative of the adventures and sufferings, of John R. Jewitt; only survivor of the crew of the ship Boston, during a captivity of nearly three years among the savages of Nootka sound. Middletown, Conn., 1815. (Same, Ithaca, N. Y., 1849.)

JOHNS HOPKINS UNIVERSITY. Circulars, vols. I–XXIV, Baltimore, 1870–1905. Studies in Hist. and Polit. Sci., vols. I–XXVIII, Baltimore, 1883–1910.

JOHNSON, ELIAS. Legends, traditions and laws of the Iroquois, or Six Nations. Lockport, N. Y., 1881.

JOHNSON, OVERTON, and WINTER, WM. H. Route across the Rocky mountains with a description of Oregon and California. Lafayette, Ind., 1846.

JOHNSON, W. FLETCHER. Life of Sitting Bull. [n. p.,] 1891.

JOHNSTON, A. R. Journal of Capt. A. R. Johnston, First Dragoons. 1846. (In Emory, Reconnoissance, 565–614, 1848.)

JOHNSTON, CHAS. Narrative of the incidents attending the capture, detention, and ransom of Charles Johnston. New York, 1827.

JOMARD, EDME FRANÇOIS. Les monuments de la géographie, ou recueil d'anciennes cartes. Paris, 1862, 1866.

JONES, A. D. Illinois and the west. Boston, 1838.

JONES, CHAS. C. Monumental remains of Georgia. Part First. Savannah, 1861.
———— Historical sketch of Tomo-chi-chi. Albany, 1868.
———— Antiquities of the southern Indians, particularly of the Georgia tribes. New York, 1873.
———— Hernando or Fernando de Soto. Adventures and route through Georgia. Savannah, 1880.
———— History of Georgia. Vols. I–II. Boston, 1883.

JONES, DAVID. A journal of two visits made to some nations of Indians on the west side of the river Ohio, in the years 1772 and 1773. Burlington, N. J., 1774.

JONES, JOS. Explorations of the aboriginal remains of Tennessee. (Smithson. Contrib. to Knowledge, vol. XXII, Washington, 1876.)

JONES, N. W. No. I. Indian Bulletin for 1867. Containing a brief account of the North American Indians. New York, 1867.

JONES, PETER. History of the Ojebway Indians; with especial reference to their conversion to Christianity. London [1861].

JONES, STRACHAN. The Kutchin tribes. (Smithson. Rep. 1866, Washington, 1867.)

JONES, U. J. History of Juniata valley. Philadelphia, 1856.

JORDAN, JNO. W., ed. Journal of Lieutenant Colonel Adam Hubley, jr. Philadelphia, 1909.

JOSSELYN, JNO. New England's rarities discovered. London, 1672.
———— An account of two voyages to New-England made during the years 1638, 1663. Boston, 1865.

JOURNAL OF AMERICAN ETHNOLOGY AND ARCHÆOLOGY. J. Walter Fewkes, editor. Vols. I–IV. Boston and New York, 1891–94.
———— See GILMAN, BENJ. I.

JOURNAL OF AMERICAN FOLK-LORE. Vols. I–XXIII. Boston and New York, 1888–1910.

JOURNAL OF GEOLOGY. Vols. I–XIII. Chicago, 1893–1905.

JOUTEL, HENRI. Journal historique du dernier voyage que M. de la Sale fit dans le golfe de Mexique pour trouver l'embouchure de la rivière de Mississippi. Paris, 1713.
———— Mr. Joutel's journal of his voyage to Mexico. London, 1719.
———— Journal of M. de La Salle's last voyage to discover the river Mississippi, 1684. (In French, B. F., Hist. Coll. Louisiana, vol. I, New York, 1846.)

JUKES, J. BEETE. Excursions in and about Newfoundland, during the years 1839 and 1840. Vols. I–II. London, 1842.

KALM, PETER. Travels into North America. 2d ed. Vols. I–II. London, 1772.
——— See BARTRAM, JNO.
KANE, ELISHA K. The U. S. Grinnell expedition in search of Sir John Franklin. New York, 1854.
——— Arctic explorations. Vols. I–II. Philadelphia, 1856.
KANE, PAUL. Wanderings of an artist among the Indians of North America. London, 1859.
KANSAS CITY REVIEW OF SCIENCE AND INDUSTRY. Vol. v, no. 7, Kansas City, 1881.
KAPPLER, CHAS. J., ed. See INDIAN TREATIES.
KAUFFMAN, DANIEL W. See RUPP, I. D.
KEANE, A. H. Ethnography and philology of America. (In Stanford's Compendium of Geography and Travel : Central America, the West Indies, and South America, by H. W. Bates. Appendix.) London, 1878.
——— Ethnology. Cambridge, 1896.
KEATING, WM. H. Narrative of an expedition to the source of St. Peter's river, Lake Winnepeek, Lakes of the Woods, etc. Compiled from the notes of Major Long, Messrs. Say, Keating, and Colhoun. Vols. I–II. Philadelphia, 1824. (Same, London, 1825.)
KELLEY, HALL J. A geographical sketch of that part of North America called Oregon. Boston, 1830.
KELLY, FANNY. Narrative of my captivity among the Sioux Indians. 2d ed. Chicago, 1880.
KELLY, J. W. Memoranda concerning the Arctic Eskimos in Alaska and Siberia. (U. S. Bur. of Education, Circ. of Inf'n no. 2, Washington, 1890.)
——— Ethnographical memoranda concerning Arctic Eskimo in Alaska and Siberia. (Bull. 3, Society of Alaskan Natural History and Ethnology, Sitka, 1890.)
——— See WELLS, ROGER, and KELLY.
KELSEY, C. E. Report of the special agent for California Indians to the Commissioner of Indian Affairs. Carlisle, Pa., 1906.
KELTON, DWIGHT H. Annals of Fort Mackinac. Detroit, 1884.
KENDALL, EDWARD AUGUSTUS. Travels through the northern parts of the United States in the years 1807 and 1808. Vols. I–III. New York, 1809.
KENDALL, GEO. WILKINS. Narrative of the Texan Santa Fé expedition. Vols. I–II. London, 1844. (Same, New York, 1844, 1850.)
KENGLA, L. A. Contribution to the archæology of the District of Columbia. Washington, 1883.
KENNEDY, WM. Texas : the rise, progress, and prospects of the Republic of Texas. Vols. I–II. London, 1841.
KER, HENRY. Travels through the western interior of the United States, from the year 1808 up to the year 1816. Elizabethtown, 1816.
KING, EDWARD (Lord Kingsborough). Antiquities of Mexico. Vol. I. London, 1831.
KING, RICHARD. Narrative of a journey to the shores of the Arctic ocean, in 1833, 1834, and 1835. Vol. I–II. London, 1836.
KINGSLEY, JNO. S., ed. The Standard Natural History. Vols. I–VI. Boston, 1883–85.
KINNEY, ABBOT. See JACKSON, HELEN M. H., and KINNEY.
KINNICUTT, LINCOLN N. Indian names of places in Worcester county, Massachusetts. Worcester, 1905.
KINO, EUSEBIUS. Tabula Californiæ, Anno 1702. (In Stöcklein, Der Neue Welt-Bott, pt. II, facing p. 74, Augspurg und Grätz, 1726.)

KINZIE, Mrs JOHN H. (JULIETTE AUGUSTA). Wau-Bun, the "Early Day" in the North-west. New York, 1856.
KIP, LAWRENCE. Army life on the Pacific. New York, 1859.
KIP, WM. INGRAHAM. The early Jesuit missions in North America ; compiled and translated from the letters of the French Jesuits, with notes. Albany, 1866.
KITCHIN, THOS. [Map of] North America, drawn from the latest and best authorities. London (?) [1787].
KLUTSCHAK, H. W. Als Eskimo unter den Eskimo. Wien und Leipzig, 1881.
KNOX, JNO. New collection of voyages, discoveries, and travels. Vols. I–VII. London, 1767.
KOHL, J. G. Kitchi-gami. Wanderings round Lake Superior. London, 1860.
——— History of the discovery of Maine. (Documentary History of the State of Maine, Coll. Maine Hist. Soc., 2d ser., vol. I, Portland, 1869.)
KOLDEWEY, KARL. The German Arctic expedition of 1869–70. London, 1874.
KOTZEBUE, OTTO VON. Voyage of discovery into the South sea and Behrings straits, for the purpose of exploring a north-east passage, in 1815–1818. Translated by H. E. Lloyd. Vols. I–III. London, 1821.
——— New voyage round the world, in the years 1823–26. Vols. I–II. London, 1830.
KRAUSE, AUREL. Die Tlinkit Indianer, Ergebnisse einer Reise nach der Nordwestkuste von America und der Beringstrasse. (Auftrage der Bremer geographichen Gesellschaft, 1880–81, Jena, 1885.)
KRAUSE, F. Schleudervorrichtungen für Wurfwaffen. (Internat. Archiv f. Ethnog., Band XV, Leiden, Leipzig, Paris, 1902.)
KREHBIEL, H. P. History of the Mennonite general conference. St. Louis, 1898.
KROEBER, A. L. The Arapaho. (Bull. Am. Mus. Nat. Hist., vol. XVIII, New York, 1902.)
——— Ethnology of the Gros Ventre. (Anthr. Papers Am. Mus. Nat. Hist., vol. I, pt. 4, New York, 1908.)
——— See DORSEY, G. A., and KROEBER ; UNIVERSITY OF CALIFORNIA.
KUNZ, GEO. F. Gems and precious stones of North America. New York, 1890.

LACOMBE, ALBERT. Dictionnaire de la langue des Cris. Montréal, 1874.
LADD, HORATIO O. The story of New Mexico. Boston, 1891.
LAET, JOANNE DE. Novvs orbis seu descriptionis. Indiæ occidentalis. Lvgd [uni] Batav[orum], 1633.
——— L'histoire du Nouveau Monde ou description des Indes Occidentales. Leyde, 1640.
LAFITAU, JOS. FRANÇOIS. Mœurs des sauvages ameriquains, comparées aux mœurs des premiers temps. Tomes I–II. Paris, 1724.
LAFLESCHE, FRANCIS. The middle five. Boston, 1901.
LA HARPE, BERNARD DE. Journal historique de l'éstablissement des Français à la Louisiane. Nouvelle Orléans, 1831. (Same, trans. in French, B. F., Hist. Coll. La., vol. III, New York, 1851.)
LAHONTAN, ARMAND L. DE D. Nouveaux voyages de Mr le baron Lahontan, dans l'Amérique Septentrionale. A la Haye, 1703.
——— New voyages to North America. Vols. I–II. London, 1703. (Same, 2d ed., London, 1735.)
LAND OF SUNSHINE. Vols. I–XV. Los Angeles, 1894–1901. (Succeeded by OUT WEST.)
LANG, ANDREW. Custom and myth. London, 1885.

LANG, HERBERT O. History of the Willamette valley, being a description of the valley and resources, with an account of its discovery and settlement by white men. Portland, Oreg., 1885.

LANG, J. D., and TAYLOR, SAMUEL. Report on the Indian tribes west of the Mississippi. Providence, 1843.

LANGDON, F. W. Madisonville pre-historic cemetery; anthropological notes. (Jour. Cincinnati Soc. Nat. Hist., vol. IV, Oct. 1881.)

LANGSDORFF, GEORG H. VON. Voyages and travels in various parts of the world, during the years 1803, 1804, 1805, 1806, and 1807. Parts I-II. London, 1813-14.

LAPHAM, I. A. Antiquities of Wisconsin. (Smithson. Contrib. to Knowledge, vol. VII, Washington, 1855.)

———, BLOSSOM, L., and DOUSMAN, G. D. Number, locality, and times of removal of the Indians of Wisconsin. Milwaukee, 1870.

LA POTHERIE. See BACQUEVILLE DE LA POTHERIE.

LARIMER, SARAH L. Capture and escape; or, life among the Sioux. Philadelphia, 1870.

LARPENTEUR, CHAS. See COUES, ELLIOTT.

LAS CASAS, BARTOLOME. Historia de las Indias. Tomos I-V. Madrid, 1875-76.

LATHAM, ROBERT G. On the languages of the Oregon territory. (Jour. Ethnol. Soc. Lond., vol. I, Edinburgh, 1848.)

——— The natural history of the varieties of man. London, 1850.

——— The native races of the Russian empire. London, New York, Paris, Madrid, 1854.

——— On the languages of New California. (Proc. Philol. Soc. Lond., vol. VI, London, 1854.)

——— On the languages of northern, western and central America. (Ibid., 1856, London, 1857.)

——— Opuscula. Essays chiefly philological and ethnographical. London, 1860.

——— Elements of comparative philology. London, 1862.

LA TOUR, BRION DE. [Carte de] L'Amérique Septentrionale, ou se remarquent les Etats Unis. Paris, 1779.

——— [Carte] Suite du théâtre de la guerre dans l'Amérique Septentrionale, v compris le Golfe du Méxique. Paris, Esnauts et Rapilly, 1782.

——— [Carte] l'Amérique Septentrionale, ou se remarque les Etats Unis. Paris, 1783.

——— Carte des États Unis d'Amérique, et du cours du Missisipi. Paris, 1784.

LATTRÉ. Carte des États-Unis de l'Amérique suivant la traité de paix de 1783, 1784.

LAUDONNIÈRE, RENÉ. Histoire notable de la Floride située ès Indes Occidentales, contenant les trois voyages faits en icelle par certains capitaines et pilotes François; a laquelle a esté adjousté un quatriesme voyage fait par le Capitaine Gourgues, mise en lumière par M. Basnier. Paris, 1586. (Same, Paris, 1853.)

——— History of the first attempt of the French (The Huguenots) to colonize the newly discovered country of Florida. (In French, B. F., Hist. Coll. of La. and Fla., N. S., New York, 1869.)

——— See BRY.

LAUT, AGNES C. Story of the trapper. New York, 1902.

LAVERDIÈRE, C.-H. See CHAMPLAIN.

LAW, JNO. Colonial history of Vincennes, Indiana. Vincennes, 1858.

LAWS AND TREATIES. See INDIAN TREATIES.

LAWS of the Colonial and State governments, relating to Indians and Indian Affairs, from 1633 to 1831. Washington, 1832.

LAWSON, JNO. A new voyage to Carolina; containing the exact description and natural history of that country; together with the present state thereof, and a journal of a thousand miles travel thro' several nations of Indians. London, 1709.

——— History of Carolina, containing the exact description and natural history of that country. London, 1714. (Reprint, Raleigh, 1860.)

LE BEAU, C. Aventures; ou voyage curieux et nouveau parmi les sauvages de l'Amérique Septentrionale. Tomes I-II. Amsterdam, 1738.

LECLERQ, CHRÉTIEN. Nouvelle relation de la Gaspésie. Paris, 1691.

——— First establishment of the faith in New France; now first translated with notes, by J. G. Shea. Vols. I-II. New York, 1881.

LEDERER, JNO. Discoveries in three several marches from Virginia to the west of Carolina, 1669-70. Collected and translated by Sir W. Talbot. London, 1672. (Same, in Harris, Coll. of Voy., vol. II, London, 1705. Same, Rochester, 1902.)

LEE, DANIEL, and FROST, J. H. Ten years in Oregon. New York, 1844.

LEE, NELSON. Three years among the Camanches. Albany, 1859.

LEIBERG, JNO. B. General report on a botanical survey of the Cœur d'Alene mountains in Idaho. (Cont. U. S. Nat. Herbarium, vol. V, no. 1, Washington, 1897.)

LELAND, C. G. Fusang; or, the discovery of America by Chinese Buddhist priests in the 5th century. London, 1875.

——— Algonquin legends of New England. Boston and New York, 1885.

——— See PRINCE, J. D., and LELAND.

LE MOYNE, JACQUES. Narrative of Le Moyne, an artist who accompanied the French expedition to Florida under Laudonnière, 1564. Translated from the Latin of De Bry. Boston, 1875.

——— See BRY, THEODORO DE.

LENHOSSEK, JOS. VON. Die künstlichen schadelverbildungen im algemeinen. Budapest, 1878.

LENNARD, C. E. B. Travels in British Columbia, with narrative of a yacht voyage round Vancouver's island. London, 1862.

LE PAGE DU PRATZ, ANTOINE S. Histoire de la Louisiane. Tomes I-III. Paris, 1758. (Same, English trans., London, 1763, 1774.)

LEROUX, JOS. Le medaillier du Canada. Montréal, 1888.

LESCARBOT, MARC. Histoire de la novvelle-France. Paris, 1612.

LETTRES ÉDIFIANTES et curieuses concernant l'Asie, l'Afrique et l'Amérique. Publiées sous la direction de M. Louis Aimé-Martin. Tomes I-II. Paris, 1838-41.

LEUPP, FRANCIS E. The Indian and his problem. New York, 1910.

LEWIN, L. Ueber Anhalonium Lewinii. (Archiv f. exper. Path. u. Pharmakol., B. XXIV, Leipzig, 1887-88.)

LEWIS, MERIWETHER. The travels of Capts. Lewis and Clarke, from St. Louis, by way of the Missouri and Columbia rivers, to the Pacific ocean; performed in the years 1804, 1805, and 1806. London, 1809. (Same, Philadelphia, 1809.)

——— and CLARK, WM. History of the expedition of Capts. Lewis and Clarke to the sources of the Missouri, across the Rocky mts., 1804-06. Vols. I-II. Philadelphia, 1814. (Same, Dublin, 1817; New York, 1817.)

——— The journal of Lewis and Clarke, to the mouth of the Columbia river beyond the Rocky mountains. Dayton, Ohio, 1840.

LEWIS, MERIWETHER, *and* CLARK, WM. History of the expedition under command of Captains Lewis and Clarke. Revised and abridged with introduction and notes by Archibald McVickar. Vols. I–II. New York, 1842.

—— —— Original journals of the Lewis and Clark expedition, 1804–1806. Reuben Gold Thwaites, ed. Vols. I–VIII. New York, 1904–05.

—— —— *See* COUES, ELLIOTT, *ed.*; FISHER, WM.; GASS, P.; MESSAGE; SIBLEY, JNO.

LEWIS, THEODORE H. *See* SPANISH EXPLORERS.

LEYES DE INDIAS. *See* RECOPILACIÓN.

LIBRARY OF ABORIGINAL AMERICAN LITERATURE. *See* BRINTON, D. G., *ed.*

LIBRARY OF AMERICAN LINGUISTICS. *See* SHEA, JNO. G., *ed.*

LINSCHOTEN, HANS HUGO VAN. Description de l'Amérique & des parties d'icelle, comme de la Nouvelle France, Floride, [etc.]. Amsterdam, 1638.

LISIANSKY, UREY. Voyage round the world in the years 1803–1806. London, 1814.

LLOYD, H. E. *See* KOTZEBUE, OTTO VON.

LLOYD, T. G. B. On the Beothucs. (Jour. Anthr. Inst. Gt. Brit. and Ireland, vol. IV, 21–59, London, 1874.)

—— A further account of the Beothucs of Newfoundland. (Ibid., vol. V, 222–230, London, 1875.)

—— Stone implements of Newfoundland. (Ibid.)

LOEW, OSCAR. Notes upon the ethnology of southern California and adjacent regions. (U. S. War Dept., Ann. Rep. Chief of Engineers for 1876, App. JJ, Washington, 1876.)

LOGAN, JNO. H. A history of the upper country of South Carolina, from the earliest period to the close of the War of Independence. Vol. I. Charleston and Columbia, 1859.

LONG, JNO. Voyages and travels of an Indian interpreter and trader, describing the manners and customs of the North American Indians. London, 1791.

LONG, STEPHEN H. *See* JAMES, EDWIN; KEATING, WM. H.

LORD, JNO. K. The naturalist in Vancouver island and British Columbia. Vols. I–II. London, 1866.

LOSKIEL, GEO. HENRY. History of the mission of the United Brethren among the Indians in North America. London, 1794.

LOSSING, BENSON JNO. Moravian missions. (In Am. Hist. Rec. and Repertory of Notes and Queries concerning Antiq. of Am., Philadelphia, 1872.)

—— American Revolution and the War of 1812. Vols. I–III. New York, 1875.

LOTTER, MATTHIEU ALBERT. Carte nouvelle de l'Amérique Angloise contenant tout ce que les Anglois possedent sur le continant de l'Amérique Septentrionale, savoir le Canada, la Nouvelle Ecosse ou Acadie et les treize provinces unies. Augsbourg [*ca.* 1776].

—— *See* SAUTHIER, C. J.

LOUDON, ARCHIBALD. A collection of some of the most interesting narratives of outrages committed by the Indians in their wars with the white people. Vols. I–II. Carlisle, 1808–11.

LOVE, W. DELOSS. Samson Occom and the Christian Indians of New England. Boston and Chicago, 1899.

LOWDERMILK, W. H. History of Cumberland [Maryland]. Washington, 1878.

LOWERY, WOODBURY. The Spanish settlements within the present limits of the United States. 1513–1561. New York and London, 1901.

—— Spanish settlements within the present limits of the United States: Florida, 1564–1574. New York and London, 1905.

LOZIÈRES. *See* BAUDRY DES LOZIÈRES.

LUDEWIG, HERMANN E. The literature of America. Aboriginal languages, with additions and corrections by William W. Turner. Edited by Nicholas Trübner. London, 1858.

LUMHOLTZ, CARL. Among the Tarahumaris; the American cave dwellers. (Scribner's Mag., vol. XVI, nos. 1–3, New York, July–Sept. 1894.)

—— Tarahumari dances and plant-worship. (Ibid., no. 4.)

—— Cave-dwellers of the Sierra Madre. (Proc. Internat. Cong. Anthropol., Chicago, 1894.)

—— Huichol Indians of Mexico. (Bull. Am. Mus. Nat. Hist., vol. X, New York, 1898.)

—— Symbolism of the Huichol Indians. (Mem. Am. Mus. Nat. Hist., vol. III, Anthr. II, New York, 1900.)

—— Unknown Mexico. Vols. I–II. New York, 1902.

LUMMIS, CHARLES F. A New Mexico David and other stories and sketches of the Southwest. New York, 1891.

—— Some strange corners of our country. New York, 1892.

—— The land of poco tiempo. New York, 1893.

—— The man who married the moon and other Pueblo Indian folk-stories. New York, 1894.

LUNIER, M. Déformations artificielles du crâne. (Dictionnaire de médecine et de chirurgie pratique, tome X, Paris, 1869.)

LUTKE, FEODOR P. Voyage autour du monde. Parts I–III. Translated from Russian [into French] by F. Boyé. Paris, 1835–36.

LYELL, CHAS. Second visit to the United States of North America. Vols. I–II. New York, 1849.

LYON, G. F. Brief narrative of an unsuccessful attempt to reach Repulse bay. London, 1825.

—— Private journal during voyage of discovery under Captain Parry. Boston, 1824. (*Same*, London, 1825.)

MCADAMS, WM. Antiquities of Cahokia, or Monk's mound, in Madison county, Illinois. Edwardsville, Ill., 1883.

—— Records of ancient races in the Mississippi valley. St. Louis, 1887.

MCALEER, GEO. A study in the etymology of the Indian place name Missisquoi. Worcester, Mass., 1906.

MCCALL, GEO. A. Reports in relation to New Mexico. (Senate Ex. Doc. 26, 31st Cong., 2d sess., Washington, 1851.)

M'CALL, HUGH. The history of Georgia, containing brief sketches of the most remarkable events, up to the present day. Vols. I–II. Savannah, 1811–16.

MACAULEY, JAS. The natural, statistical and civil history of the state of New York. Vols. I–III. New York, 1829.

MACCAULEY, CLAY. The Seminole Indians of Florida. (Fifth Rep. Bur. Am. Ethnology, Washington, 1887.)

MCCLELLAN, GEO. B. *See* MARCY, R. B.

MCCLINTOCK, EVA. *See* WILLARD, CAROLINE MCC.

MCCLINTOCK, FRANCIS LEOPOLD. Fate of Sir John Franklin, voyage of the *Fox*. Fifth ed. London, 1881.

MCCOY, ISAAC. The annual register of Indian affairs within the Indian (or western) territory. Washington, 1836–38.

—— History of the Baptist Indian missions, embracing remarks on the former and present condition of the aboriginal tribes; their settlement within the Indian territory, and their future prospects. Washington and New York, 1840.

MCCULLOH, J. H., *Jr.* Researches philosophical and antiquarian, concerning the aboriginal history of America. Baltimore, 1829.

M'DONALD, ALEX. Narrative of some passages in the history of Eenoolooapik: an account of the discovery of Hogarth's sound. Edinburgh, 1841.

MACDONALD, DUNCAN G. F. British Columbia and Vancouver's island. London, 1862.

McDOUGALL, JNO. George Millward McDougall, the pioneer, patriot, and missionary. Toronto, 1888.

MACFIE, MATTHEW. Vancouver island and British Columbia. Their history, resources, and prospects. London, 1865.

McGEE, W J. The Siouan Indians. (Fifteenth Rep. Bur. Am. Ethnology, Washington, 1897.)

———— The Seri Indians. (Seventeenth Rep. Bur. Am. Ethnology, pt. 1, Washington, 1898.)

———— Primitive numbers. (Nineteenth Rep. Bur. Am. Ethnology, pt. 2, Washington, 1900.)

———— See MUÑIZ, M. A., and McGEE.

McGUIRE, JOSEPH D. Study of the primitive methods of drilling. (Rep. U. S. Nat. Mus. for 1894, Washington, 1896.)

———— Pipes and smoking customs of the American aborigines. (Rep. U. S. Nat. Mus. for 1897, Washington, 1899.)

McINTOSH, JNO. The origin of the North American Indians; with a faithful description of their manners and customs. New York, 1853.

MACKAY, JNO., and BLAKE, J. E. Map of the seat of war in Florida compiled by orders of Gen. Z. Taylor principally from the surveys and reconnaisances of the officers of the U. S. Army, 1839. U. S. War Department, Corps of Engineers, Washington, 1839.

M'KEEVOR, THOS. A voyage to Hudson's bay, during the summer of 1812. London, 1819.

McKENNEY, THOS. L. Sketches of a tour to the lakes, of the character and customs of the Chippeway Indians, and of incidents connected with the treaty of Fond du Lac. Baltimore, 1827.

———— Vol. I: Memoirs, official and personal; with sketches of travels among the northern and southern Indians; embracing a war excursion, and descriptions of scenes along the western borders. Vol. II: On the origin, history, character, and the wrongs and rights of the Indians, with a plan for the preservation and happiness of the remnants of that persecuted race. Two volumes in one. New York, 1846.

———— and HALL, JAS. History of the Indian tribes of North America. Vols. I–III. Philadelphia, 1854. (Same, in various editions.)

MACKENZIE, ALEX. Voyages from Montreal, on the river St. Lawrence, through the continent of North America, to the Frozen and Pacific oceans; in the years 1789 and 1793. London, 1801. (Same, Philadelphia, 1802.)

McLACHLIN, R. W. Medals awarded to Canadian Indians. (Canadian Antiq. and Numis. Jour., 3d ser., vol. II, Montreal, 1899.)

McLAUGHLIN, JAS. My friend the Indian. Boston, 1910.

McLEAN, JNO. Notes of a twenty-five years' service in the Hudson's Bay territory. Vols. I–II. London, 1842. (Same, London, 1849.)

McLEAN, Rev. JNO. The Indians, their manners and customs. Toronto, 1889.

———— Canadian savage folk. The native tribes of Canada. Toronto, 1896.

MACLEAN, JNO. P. Mound builders. Cincinnati, 1879.

McVICKAR, ARCHIBALD. See LEWIS and CLARK.

MADRID COMMISSION. See COLUMBIAN HISTORICAL EXPOSITION.

MAGAZINE OF AMERICAN HISTORY. Vols. I–XXIX. New York and Chicago, 1877–93.

MAILLARD, N. DORAN. History of the republic of Texas. London, 1842.

MAINE HISTORICAL SOCIETY. Collections. Vols. I–VI, Portland, 1831–59. Vol. VII, Bath, 1876. Vols. VIII–X, Portland, 1881–91. 2d ser., vols. I–X, Portland, 1890–99.

MALLERY, GARRICK. The former and present number of our Indians. (Proc. Am. Asso. Adv. Sci. 1877, Salem, 1878.)

———— Introduction to the study of sign language among the North American Indians. (Washington, 1880.)

———— A collection of gesture-signs and signals of the North American Indians. (Washington, 1880.)

———— Sign language among North American Indians. (First Rep. Bur. Ethnology, Washington, 1881.)

———— Pictographs of the North American Indians. (Fourth Rep. Bur. Ethnology, Washington, 1886.)

———— Picture-writing of the American Indians. (Tenth Rep. Bur. Ethnology, Washington, 1893.)

MALTE-BRUN, MALTHE KONRAD BRUN, known as. Universal geography, or a description of all parts of the world, on a new plan. Vols. I–V. Boston, 1824–26.

———— Tableau de la distribution ethnographique des nations et les langues au Mexique. (Congrès Internat. des Américanistes, Compte-rendu de la 2e sess., Luxembourg, 1877, tome II, Luxembourg and Paris, 1878.)

MANDRILLON, JOSEPH. Le spectateur Américain, suivi de recherches philosophiques sur la découverte du Nouveau-Monde. Amsterdam, 1785.

———— Le spectateur Américain ou remarques générale sur l'Amérique Septentrionale et sur la république des treizes Etats-Unis. 2e ed. Amsterdam et Bruxelles [n. d.].

MANYPENNY, GEO. W. Our Indian wards. Cincinnati, 1880.

MAPPA geographica complectus. Indiæ occidentalis partem mediam circum Isthmem Panamensem &c. pro presenti statu belli quod est 1740 inter Anglos & Hispanos exortum Homanianis Heredibus 1731. (In Homan, Schule Atlas, 1743.)

MAPS. [As will be seen by reference to the synonymy following the descriptions of tribes and settlements, many maps have been cited in this Handbook, including a number published anonymously. In cases in which the cartographer was known at the time of consultation, the names are given in the citations and will be found in this list; in the case of anonymous maps, however, no attempt has been made to include them herein, owing to their large number and to the difficulty of identifying them.]

MARCY, R. B. Report [on the route from Fort Smith to Santa Fé]. 1849. (Senate Ex. Doc. 64, 31st Cong., 1st sess., Washington, 1850.)

———— The prairie traveller. New York, 1861.

———— Thirty years of army life on the border. New York, 1866.

———— Border reminiscences. New York, 1872.

———— and McCLELLAN, GEO. B. Exploration of the Red river of Louisiana, in the year 1852. (Senate Ex. Doc. 54, 32d Cong., 2d sess., Washington, 1853.)

MARGRY, PIERRE. Découvertes et établissements des Français dans l'ouest et dans le sud de l'Amérique Septentrionale (1614–1754). Mémoires et documents originaux. Pts. I–VI. Paris, 1875–86.

MARIETTI, PIETRO, ed. Oratio Dominica. Romæ, 1870.

MARQUETTE, JACQUES. Discovery of some new countries and nations in northern America. London, 1698.
—— Autograph map of the Mississippi [1673]. (In Shea, J. G., Discov. and Explor. Miss. Val., Redfield, 1852.)
—— See THWAITES, R. G.
MARSHALL, H. The history of Kentucky, containing ancient annals of Kentucky or introduction to the history and antiquities of the State of Kentucky, by C. F. Rafinesque. Vols. I–II. Frankfort, 1824.
MARSHALL, O. H. De Céloron's expedition to the Ohio in 1749. (Mag. Am. Hist., vol. II, New York and Chicago, 1878.)
MARTIN, FRANÇOIS X. History of Louisiana, from the earliest period. Vols. I–II. New Orleans, 1827–29. (Same, 1882.)
—— History of North Carolina from its earliest period. Vols. I–II. New Orleans, 1829.
MARTIN, ROBERT M. Hudson's Bay territories and Vancouver's island, with an exposition of the chartered rights, conduct and policy of the Hudson's Bay corporation. London, 1849.
MARYLAND. Archives of Maryland; published by authority of the State under the direction of the Maryland Historical Society. Vols. I–XXVIII. Baltimore, 1883–1908.
MASON, OTIS T. Ethnological directions relative to the Indian tribes of the United States. Washington, 1875.
—— North American bows, arrows, and quivers. (Smithsonian Rep. 1893. Washington, 1894.)
—— Aboriginal American mechanics. (Mem. Internat. Cong. Anthropol., Chicago, 1894.)
—— Woman's share in primitive culture. New York, 1894.
—— Origins of invention. London and New York, 1895.
—— Primitive travel and transportation. (Rep. U. S. Nat. Mus. 1894, Washington, 1896.)
—— Migration and the food quest; a study in the peopling of America. (Smithsonian Rep. 1894, Washington, 1896.)
—— Directions for collectors of American basketry. (U. S. Nat. Mus., Bull. 39, pt. P, Washington, 1902.)
—— Aboriginal American basketry. (Rep. U. S. Nat. Mus. 1902, Washington, 1904.)
—— et al. Arrows and arrow-makers. (Am. Anthropologist, vol. IV, no. I, Washington, 1891.)
—— See HOLMES, W. H., and MASON.
MASSACHUSETTS. See RECORDS.
MASSACHUSETTS HISTORICAL SOCIETY. Collections. Vols. I–X, Boston, 1792–1809 (vol. I reprinted in 1806 and 1859; vol. V in 1816 and 1835). 2d ser., I–X, Boston, 1814–23 (reprinted 1838–43). 3d ser., I–X, Boston, 1825–49 (vol. I reprinted, 1846). 4th ser., I–X, Boston, 1852–71.
MATIEGKA, J. U. Schädel und Skelette von Santa Rosa (Sta Barbara archipel bei Californien). (Sitzber. d. K. böhm. Ges. d. Wiss., II Classe, Prague, 1904.)
MATSON, N. Memories of Shaubena. 2d ed. Chicago, 1880.
MATTHEW, G. F., and KAIN, S. W. Earthenware pot of the stone age. (Bull. Nat. Hist. Soc. New Brunswick, vol. V, no. XXIII, St. John, 1904.)
MATTHEWS, WASHINGTON. Ethnography and philology of the Hidatsa Indians. (U. S. Geol. and Geog. Surv., Misc. Pub. no. 7, Washington, 1877.)
—— Navajo silversmiths. (Second Rep. Bur. Ethnology, Washington, 1883.)
—— Navajo weavers. (Third Rep. Bur. Ethnology, Washington, 1884.)
—— The mountain chant. (Fifth Rep. Bur. Ethnology, Washington, 1887.)

MATTHEWS, WASHINGTON. The gentile system of the Navaho Indians. (Jour. Am. Folk-lore, III, Boston and New York, April, June, 1890.)
—— Navaho legends. Boston and New York, 1897.
—— Night chant, a Navaho ceremony. (Mem. Am. Mus. Nat. Hist., vol. VI, New York, 1902.)
—— and WORTMAN, J. L. Human bones of the Hemenway collection in the U. S. Army Medical Museum at Washington. (Mem. Nat. Acad. Sci., vol. VI, Washington, 1893.)
MAURAULT, J. A. Histoire des Abenakis depuis 1605 jusqu'a nos jours. Québec, 1866.
MAXIMILIAN, ALEX. P. Reise in das innere Nord-America in den Jahren 1832 bis 1834. B. I–II. Coblenz, 1839–41.
—— Travels in the interior of North America. Translated from the German by H. Evans Lloyd. London, 1843.
MAY, JNO. Journal and letters of Col. John May, of Boston, relative to two journeys to the Ohio country in 1788 and 89. With a biographical sketch by Richard S. Edes, and illustrative notes by Wm. M. Darlington. Cincinnati, 1873.
MAYER, BRANTZ. Mexico, Aztec, Spanish and Republican. Vols. I–II. Hartford, 1853.
—— Tah-gah-jute; or Logan and Cresap, an historical essay. Albany, 1867.
MAYNE, RICHARD C. Four years in British Columbia and Vancouver island. London, 1862.
MAYS, T. J. An experimental inquiry into the chest movements of the Indian female. (Therapeutic Gazette, 3d ser., vol. III, no. 5, Detroit, 1887.)
MAZZEI, P. Recherches sur les Etats-Unis; par un citoyen de Virginie, avec quatres lettres d'un bourgeois de New-Haven. Tomes I–IV. Colle, 1788.
MEACHAM, A. B. Wigwam and warpath; or the royal chief in chains. 2d ed. Boston, 1875.
—— Wi-ne-ma (the woman-chief) and her people. Hartford, 1876.
MEARNS, EDGAR A. Ancient dwellings of the Rio Verde valley. (Pop. Sci. Mo., vol. XXXVII, New York, Oct. 1890.)
MEDDELELSER OM GRØNLAND. Vol. I (1890)– vol. XXXIII (1907). Kjøbenhavn.
MEEK, A. B. Romantic passages in southwestern history, including orations, sketches, and essays. New York, 1857.
MEGAPOLENSIS, JOHANNES. Short sketch of the Mohawk Indians in New Netherland. 1644. (Coll. N. Y. Hist. Soc., 2d ser., vol. III, pt. I, New York, 1857.)
MEGINNES, J. F. Otzinachson; or, a history of the West-branch valley of the Susquehanna. Philadelphia, 1857.
MEIGS, J. A. Observations upon the cranial forms of the American aborigines. Philadelphia, 1866.
—— Description of a human skull. (Smithsonian Rep. 1867, Washington, 1872.)
MELINE, JAS. F. Two thousand miles on horseback. New York, 1867.
MEMORIALS OF THE MORAVIAN CHURCH. See REICHEL, W. C.
MENDIETA, GERÓNIMO DE. Historia eclesiástica Indiana. México, 1870.
MENDOZA, ANTONIO DE. Letter to the Emperor, 1540. (Hakluyt, Voyages, vol. III, 436–438, London, 1600, reprint 1810; Ternaux-Compans, Voyages, tome IX, Paris, 1838; Fourteenth Rep. Bur. Am. Ethnol., Washington, 1896.)
MENDOZA, JUAN GONZALES DE. Histoire du grand royaume de la Chine, sitve aux Indes Orientales divisées en deux parties. Paris, 1588. (Same, trans. in Hakluyt Soc. Pub., vol. XV, London, 1854.)

MENGARINI, GREGORY. A Selish or Flathead grammar. (In Shea, Lib. of Am. Ling., vol. II, New York, 1861.)
———— Indians of Oregon. (Jour. Anthr. Inst. N. Y., vol. I, New York, 1871–72.)
MERCATOR, GÉRARD. Mappemonde de Gérard Mercator. 1569. (In Jomard, Monuments de la Géographie, Paris, 1842–62.)
MERCER, H. C. The Lenape stone or the Indian and the mammoth. New York and London, 1885.
———— Researches upon the antiquity of man. (Pub. Univ. of Pa., series in Philol., Lit., and Archæol., vol. VI, Philadelphia, 1897.)
MEREDITH, H. C. Aboriginal art in obsidian. (Land of Sunshine, vol. XI, no. 5, Los Angeles, 1899.)
MERRIAM, C. HART. Life zones and crop zones of the United States. (U. S. Dept. Agr., Div. Biol. Surv., Bull. 10, Washington, 1898.)
MERRILL, GEO. P. Treatise on rocks, rock-weathering and soils. New York, 1897.
MESSAGE from the President of the United States, communicating discoveries made in exploring the Missouri, Red river and Washita, by Captains Lewis and Clark. February 19, 1806. Washington, 1806.
MEXICAN BORDER COMMISSION. Reports of the committee of investigation sent in 1873 by the Mexican government to the frontier of Texas. Translated from the official edition made in Mexico. New York, 1875.
MEXICO, SECRETARÍA DE FOMENTO. Anales, tome VI, México, 1882.
MEYER, CARL. Nach dem Sacramento. Aarau, 1855.
MICHEL, M. DE. See JOUTEL.
MICHIGAN. See HISTORICAL SOCIETY OF MICHIGAN.
MICHIGAN PIONEER AND HISTORICAL SOCIETY. Historical collections. Vols. I–XXXIV. Lansing, 1877–1906.
MICHLER, N. H., Jr. Reconnoissance. 1849. (In Rep. Sec. War, with reconnoissances of routes from San Antonio to El Paso. Senate Ex. Doc. 64, 31st Cong., 1st sess., Washington, 1850.)
MILES, NELSON A. Personal recollections and observations. Chicago and New York, 1896.
MILFORT, LE CLERC. Mémoire ou coup-d'œil rapide sur mes différens voyages et mon séjour dans la nation Créck. Paris, 1802.
MILL, NICHOLAS. The history of Mexico, from the Spanish conquest to the present æra. London, 1824.
MILLER, GERRIT S., and REHN, JAS. A. G. Systematic results of the study of North American land mammals. (Proc. Boston Soc. Nat. Hist., vol. XXX, no. 1, Boston, 1901.)
MILLER, MERTON L. Preliminary study of the pueblo of Taos, New Mexico. Chicago, 1898.
MILLS, ROBERT. Atlas of the state of South Carolina. Made under the authority of the legislature. 29 maps, folio. Baltimore, 1825.
———— Statistics of South Carolina, including a view of its natural, civil, and military history, general and particular. Charleston, 1826.
MILLS, WM. C. Explorations of the Gartner mound and village site. (Ohio Archæol. and Hist. Quar., vol. XIII, no. 2, Columbus, 1904.)
———— Certain mounds and village sites in Ohio. Vol. I. Columbus, 1907.
MILLSTONE. Vol. IX, no. 1, to vol. X, no. 8, Indianapolis, 1884–85. [Contains a series of articles on Zuñi breadstuff, by F. H. Cushing.]

MILTON, Viscount, and CHEADLE, W. B. North-west passage by land. Being the narrative of an expedition from the Atlantic to the Pacific. London, 1865.
MINDELEFF, COSMOS. Casa Grande ruin. (Thirteenth Rep. Bur. Ethnology, Washington, 1896.)
———— Aboriginal remains in Verde valley, Arizona. (Ibid.)
———— The repair of Casa Grande ruin, Arizona. (Fifteenth Rep. Bur. Am. Ethnology, Washington, 1897.)
———— The cliff ruins of Canyon de Chelly, Arizona. (Sixteenth Rep. Bur. Am. Ethnology, Washington, 1897.)
———— Navaho houses. (Seventeenth Rep. Bur. Am. Ethnology, pt. 2. Washington, 1898.)
———— Localization of Tusayan clans. (Nineteenth Rep. Bur. Am. Ethnology, pt. 2, Washington, 1900.)
MINDELEFF, VICTOR. A study of Pueblo architecture. (Eighth Rep. Bur. Am. Ethnology, Washington, 1891.)
MINER, C. P. History of Wyoming, Pennsylvania. Philadelphia, 1845.
MINNESOTA GEOLOGICAL AND NATURAL HISTORY SURVEY. Geology of Minnesota, Vol. I of the Final Report, Minneapolis, 1884. 13th Report, for 1884, St. Paul, 1885.
MINNESOTA HISTORICAL SOCIETY. Collections. Vols. I–XI. St. Paul, 1872–1905.
MISSISSIPPI STATE HISTORICAL SOCIETY. Publications. Vols. I–VII. Oxford, Miss., 1898–1903.
MITCHELL, JNO. Map of the British and French dominions in North America. London, 1755.
MOFRAS, DUFLOT DE. See DUFLOT.
MOLL, HERMANN. A new map of the north parts of America claimed by France under ye names of Louisiana, Mississipi, Canada, and New France, with ye adjoining territories of England and Spain. (In Moll, World Described, London, 1710–1720.)
———— Map of North America according to ye newist and most exact observations. [1715.]
MÖLLHAUSEN, BALDWIN. Tagebuch einer Reise vom Mississippi nach der Kusten der Sudsee. Leipzig, 1858.
———— Diary of a journey from the Mississippi to the coasts of the Pacific with a United States government expedition. Vols. I–II. London, 1858.
MONARDES, NICOLAS. Historia medicinal de las cosas que se traen de nuestras Indias Occidentales que siruen en medicina. Sevilla, 1574.
———— Histoire des drogues. Lyons, 1602.
MOONEY, JAS. The sacred formulas of the Cherokees. (Seventh Rep. Bur. Am. Ethnology, Washington, 1891.)
———— The Siouan tribes of the east. (Bull. 22, Bur. Am. Ethnology, Washington, 1895.)
———— The Ghost-dance religion and the Sioux outbreak of 1890. (Fourteenth Rep. Bur. Am. Ethnology, pt. 2, Washington, 1896.)
———— Mescal plant and ceremony. (Therapeutic Gazette, 3d ser., vol. XII, Detroit, 1896.)
———— Calendar history of the Kiowa Indians. (Seventeenth Rep. Bur. Am. Ethnology, pt. 1, Washington, 1898.)
———— Myths of the Cherokee. (Nineteenth Rep. Bur. Am. Ethnology, pt. 1, Washington, 1900.)
———— Our last cannibal tribe. (Harper's Monthly, vol. CIII, New York and London, 1901.)
———— The Cheyenne Indians. (Mem. Am. Anthr. Asso., vol. I, pt. 6, Lancaster, Pa., 1907.)

MOORE, CLARENCE B. [See the various important memoirs, by this investigator, on the archeology of the Southern States, published in the Journal of the Academy of Natural Sciences of Philadelphia, from vol. X (1894) to date (1910), and cited throughout this Handbook.]
———— Certain shell heaps of the St. John's river, Florida. (Am. Naturalist, vol. XXVIII, Philadelphia, 1894.)
———— Sheet-copper from the mounds. (Am. Anthropologist, vol. V, no. 1, Lancaster, 1903.)
MOOREHEAD, WARREN K. Fort Ancient, the great prehistoric earthwork of Warren county, Ohio. Cincinnati, 1890.
———— Primitive man in Ohio. New York and London, 1892.
———— Bird - stone ceremonial. Saranac Lake, N. Y., 1899.
———— Prehistoric implements. Cincinnati, 1900.
———— See PEABODY, CHAS., and MOOREHEAD.
MORDACQUE, L. H. History of the names of men, nations, and places. From the French of 'Eusebius Salverte.' Vols. I–II. London, 1864.
MORELLI, D. CYRIACI. Fasti novi orbis et ordinacionum ad Indias pertinentium breviarium cum annotationibus. Venetius, 1776.
MORFI, JUAN A. DE. Documentos para la historia eclesiastica y civil de la provincia de Texas. [1792.] MS.
MORGAN, LEWIS H. Report upon articles furnished the Indian collection. (In 3d Ann. Rep. Regents Univ. of State of New York, 1849, Albany, 1850.)
———— Report on the fabrics, inventions, implements, and utensils of the Iroquois. (In 5th Ann. Rep. Regents Univ. of State of New York, 1851, Albany, 1852.)
———— League of the Ho-dé-no-sau-nee, or Iroquois. Rochester, New York, and Boston, 1851. (Same, New York, 1904.)
———— The seven cities of Cibola. (N. Am. Review, vol. CVIII, Boston, 1869.)
———— Indian migrations. (Ibid., Oct. 1869, Jan. 1870. Reprinted in Beach, Indian Miscellany, Albany, 1877.)
———— Systems of consanguinity and affinity of the human family. (Smithson. Contrib. to Knowledge, vol. XVII, Washington, 1871.)
———— Ancient society or researches in the lines of human progress from savagery through barbarism to civilization. New York, 1877. (Same, 1878.)
———— On the ruins of a stone pueblo on the Animas river in New Mexico; with a ground plan. (In Twelfth Rep. Peabody Museum, Cambridge, 1880.)
———— Houses and house-life of the American aborigines. (Contrib. N. Am. Ethnol., vol. IV, Washington, 1881.)
MORICE, A. G. The Western Dénés. Their manners and customs. (Proc. Can. Inst., 3d ser., vol. VI, no. 2, Toronto, 1889.)
———— The Déné language. (Trans. Canad. Inst., vol I, 1889–90, Toronto, 1891.)
———— Notes, archæological, industrial and sociological, on the Western Dénés. (Ibid., vol. IV, 1892–93, Toronto, 1895.)
———— History of the northern interior of British Columbia, formerly New Caledonia. Toronto, 1904.
MORRIS, WM. GOUVERNEUR. Report upon the customs district, public service, and resources of Alaska territory. (Senate Ex. Doc. 59, 45th Cong., 3d sess., Washington, 1879.)
MORSE, EDWARD S. Worked shells in New England shell-heaps. (Proc. Am. Asso. Adv. Sci., vol. XXX, Salem, 1882.)
———— Ancient and modern methods of arrow-release. (Bull. Essex Inst., vol. XVII, nos. 10–12, Salem, 1885.)

[MORSE, JEDIDIAH.] The History of North America, containing an exact account of their first settlements, with the present state of the different colonies and a large introduction illustrated with a map of North America. London, 1776.
———— The American geography, or a view of the present situation of the United States of America. London, 1792.
———— A map of North America from the latest discoveries. (In An Abridgement of the American Gazetteer, Boston, 1798.)
———— The history of America in two books. 3d ed. (Extracted from the American edition of the Encyclopaedia, Philadelphia, 1798.)
———— A new and elegant general atlas. Comprising all the new discoveries, to the present time. Boston, 1812.
———— A complete system of modern geography, or a view of the present state of the world, being a faithful abridgement of the American Universal Geography (edition 1812) with corrections and additions. Boston, 1814.
———— The American universal geography, or a view of the present state of all the kingdoms, states, and colonies in the known world, 7th ed. Vols. I–II. Charlestown [Boston], 1819.
———— A report to the Secretary of War of the United States, on Indian affairs, comprising a narrative of a tour performed in the summer of 1820. New Haven, 1822.
MORSE, SIDNEY E. A new system of modern geography, or a view of the present state of the world. Accompanied with an atlas. Boston and New Haven, 1822.
MORTON, NATHANIEL. New Englands memorial. 6th ed. Boston, 1855.
MORTON, S. G. Crania Americana; or, a comparative view of the skulls of various aboriginal nations of North and South America. Philadelphia, 1839.
———— An inquiry into the distinctive characteristics of the aboriginal race of America. Philadelphia, 1844.
MOTA PADILLA, MATÍAS DE LA. Historia de la conquista de la provincia de la Nueva-Galicia [1742]. Mexico, 1870.
MOTZ, ALBERT VON. See OWEN, A. R.
MOWRY, SYLVESTER. The geography and resources of Arizona and Sonora. (Jour. Am. Geog. and Statis. Soc., vol. I, New York, 1859.)
———— Arizona and Sonora. New York, 1864.
MOWRY, WM. A. Marcus Whitman and the early days of Oregon. New York, Boston, Chicago, 1901.
MÜHLENPFORDT, EDUARD. Versuch einer getreuen Schilderung der Republik Mejico. B. I–II. Hannover, 1844.
MULLAN, JNO. Report on the Indian tribes in the eastern portion of Washington territory. 1853. (In Pac. R. R. Rep., vol. I, 437–441, Washington, 1855.)
MÜLLER, FRIEDRICH. Grundriss der Sprachwissenschaft. B. I–II. Wien, 1876–82.
MUÑIZ, M. A., and McGEE, W J. Primitive trephining in Peru. (Sixteenth Rep. Bur. Am. Ethnology, Washington, 1897.)
MUNRO, ROBERT. Archæology and false antiquities. London, 1905.
MURCH, ABEL B. See BRYANT, CHAS. S., and MURCH.
MURDOCH, JNO. Study of the Eskimo bows in the U. S. National Museum. (Rep. U. S. Nat. Mus. 1884, Washington, 1885.)
———— Ethnological results of the Point Barrow expedition. (Ninth Rep. Bur. Am. Ethnology, Washington, 1892.)
MURRAY, CHAS. AUGUSTUS. Travels in North America during the years 1834, 1835, and 1836. Vols. I–II. London, 1839.

MURRAY, HUGH. Historical account of discoveries and travels in North America; including the United States, Canada, the shores of the Polar sea, and the voyages in search of a north-west passage; with observations on emigration. Vols. I–II. London, 1829.

MURRAY, JOHN O'KANE. Lives of the Catholic heroes and heroines of America. New York, 1896.

MURRAY, LOUISE WELLES. A history of Old Tioga Point and early Athens, Pennsylvania. Athens, Pa., 1908.

MUSÉE MONETAIRE. *See* CATALOGUE.

NADAILLAC, *Marquis de.* Pre-historic America. Translated by N. D'Anvers. New York and London, 1884.

———— Les pipes et le tabac. (Materiaux pour l'Hist. Prim. et Nat. de l'Homme, 3me sér., tome II, Paris, 1885.)

NANSEN, F. First crossing of Greenland. Vols. I–II. London and New York, 1890.

———— Eskimo life. Translated by William Archer. London, 1893. (*Same*, 2d ed., London, 1894.)

NANTUCKET HISTORICAL ASSOCIATION. Bulletin. Vols. I–II. Nantucket, Mass., 1896–1902.

NATIONAL GEOGRAPHIC MAGAZINE. Vols. I–XXI. Washington, 1889–1910.

NATIONAL MUSEUM. *See* UNITED STATES NATIONAL MUSEUM.

NATURAL HISTORY SOCIETY OF MONTREAL. The Canadian Naturalist and Geologist, and Proceedings of the Natural History Society of Montreal. Vols. I–III. Montreal, 1857–1863.

NATURAL HISTORY SOCIETY OF NEW BRUNSWICK. Bulletin. Nos. I–XXIII. Saint John, 1882–1905.

NEILL, EDWARD D. The history of Minnesota, from the earliest French explorations to the present time. Philadelphia, 1858.

———— History of the Virginia Company of London. Albany, 1869.

NELSON, E. W. The Eskimo about Bering strait. (Eighteenth Rep. Bur. Am. Ethnology, pt. 1, Washington, 1899.)

NELSON, WM. Indians of New Jersey. Paterson, N. J., 1894.

———— Personal names of Indians of New Jersey. Paterson, N. J., 1904.

NEUE WELT-BOTT. *See* STÖCKLEIN, J.

NEW HAMPSHIRE HISTORICAL SOCIETY. Collections. Vols. I–X. Concord, 1824–93.

NEW YORK. University of the State of New York. *See* MORGAN, LEWIS H.

———— Report of special committee to investigate the Indian problem of the State of New York, appointed by the Assembly of 1888. Albany, 1889.

———— The documentary history of the state of New York; arranged under direction of the Hon. Christopher Morgan, Secretary of State, by E. B. O'Callaghan, M. D. Vols. I–IV. Albany, 1849–51.

———— Documents relating to the colonial history of the state of New York. Vols. I–XV. Albany, 1853–87.

NEW YORK HISTORICAL SOCIETY. Collections. Vols. I–V, New York, 1809–30. 2d ser., vols. I–IV, New York, 1841–59.

———— Proceedings. Vols. I–VII. New York, 1843–49.

NEW YORK STATE MUSEUM. Bulletin. Archæology, nos. 16, 18, 22, 32, 41, 50, 55, 73, 78, 87, 89, 108, 113, 117, 125. Albany, 1897–1908.

NIBLACK, A. P. Instructions for taking paper molds of inscriptions in stone, wood, bronze, etc. (Proc. U. S. Nat. Mus. 1883, vol. VI, app., Washington, 1884.)

———— Coast Indians of southern Alaska and northern British Columbia. (Rep. U. S. Nat. Mus. 1888, Washington, 1890.)

NICOLAY, CHAS. G. Oregon territory: a geographical and physical account of that country and its inhabitants, with its history and discovery. London, 1846.

NICOLLET, I. N. Report intended to illustrate a map of the hydrographic basin of the upper Mississippi river. (Senate Doc. 237, 26th Cong., 2d sess., Washington, 1843.)

NILES WEEKLY REGISTER; containing political, historical, [etc.] documents, essays and facts; with notices of the arts. Vols. I–LXXIV. Baltimore (from July 5, 1848, Philadelphia), 1811–48.

NIZA, MARCOS DE. Relation. 1539. (In Hakluyt, Voy., III, 438–446, 1600, reprint 1810; Doc. Inéd. de Indias, III, 325–351, Madrid, 1865; Ramusio, Nav. et Viaggi, III, 356–359, Venice, 1556; Ternaux-Compans, Voy., IX, app., Paris, 1838; Bandelier, Cabeza de Vaca, New York, 1905.)

NOLIN, J. B. [Carte] L'Amérique. Paris, 1755.

NORDENSKIÖLD, G. Cliff dwellers of the Mesa Verde. Translated by D. Lloyd Morgan. Stockholm and Chicago, 1893.

NORRIS, PHILETUS W. The calumet of the coteau. Philadelphia, 1883.

NORTH CAROLINA. The colonial records of North Carolina. Vols. I–X. Raleigh, 1886–90. (*Continued as* State Records of North Carolina.)

———— State records of North Carolina. Vols. XI–XIV, Winston, N. C., 1895–96; vols. XV–XXVI, Goldsboro, 1898–1906.

NORTH DAKOTA. State Historical Society. Collections. Vols. I–II. Bismarck, N. D., 1906–08.

NORTHWESTERN TRIBES OF CANADA. Reports on the physical characters, languages, industrial and social condition of the north-western tribes of the Dominion of Canada. (In Reports of the British Association for the Advancement of Science, 1885 to 1898, London, 1886–99.)

NORTON, CHAS. L. Political Americanisms. New York and London, 1890.

NOTES AND QUERIES ON ANTHROPOLOGY. Edited by J. G. Garson and Chas. H. Read. 3d ed. London, 1899.

NOURSE, J. E. American explorations in ice zones. Boston, 1884.

NOUVELLES ANNALES DES VOYAGES, de la géographie et de l'histoire, ou recueil des relations originales inédites, communiquées par des voyageurs français et étrangers. 208 vols. Paris, 1819–70. First ser., 30 vols., 1819–26. Second ser., 30 vols., 1827–33. Third ser., 24 vols., 1834–39. Fourth ser., 20 vols., 1840–49. Fifth ser., 40 vols., 1845–54. Sixth ser., 44 vols., 1855–65. Seventh ser., 20 vols., 1866–70.

NUTTALL, THOS. A journal of travels into the Arkansa territory, during the year 1819. With occasional observations on the manners of the aborigines. Philadelphia, 1821.

O'CALLAGHAN, E. B. *See* NEW YORK. Documentary History.

OCH, JOS. Nachrichten von verschieden Ländern des spanischen Amerika. Halle, 1809.

OGILBY, JNO. America: being the latest, and most accurate description of the New World; containing the original of the inhabitants, and the remarkable voyages thither. London, 1671.

OHIO CENTENNIAL. *See* OHIO STATE BOARD.

OHIO STATE ARCHÆOLOGICAL AND HISTORICAL SOCIETY. Quarterly. Vols. I–XIX. Columbus, 1887–1910.

OHIO STATE BOARD. Final Report of the Ohio State Board of Centennial Managers. Columbus, 1877.

OLDEN TIME [The]; a monthly publication devoted to the preservation of documents . . . in relation to the early explorations . . . of the country. Edited by Neville B. Craig, esq. Vols I–II. Pittsburgh, 1846–48. *Reprint,* Cincinnati, 1876.

OLDMIXON, JNO. British empire in America. Vols. I–II. London, 1708.

OÑATE, JUAN DE. Memorial sobre el descubrimiento del Nuevo México y sus acontecimientos. Años desde 1595 á 1602. (Colección de Documentos Inéditos, tome XVI, 188–227, Madrid, 1871.)

—— Treslado de la posesion que en nombre de Su Magestad. Año de 1598. (Ibid., 88–141.)

—— Discurso de las jornadas que hizo el campo de Su Magestad desde la Nueva España á la provincia de la Nueva México. Año de 1526 [1598]. (Ibid., 228, 276.)

—— Copia de carta escripta al Virrey Conde de Monterrey, á 2 de Marzo de 1599 años. (Ibid., 302–313.)

OREGON HISTORICAL SOCIETY. Sources of the history of Oregon. Vol. I, pt. 2. Eugene, Oreg., 1897.

—— The Quarterly. Vol. I. Salem, Oreg., 1900.

O'REILLY, BERNARD. Greenland, the adjacent seas, and the northwest passage. New York, 1818. (*Same,* London, 1818.)

OROZCO Y BERRA, MANUEL. Geografía de las lenguas y carta etnográfica de México. México, 1864.

ORTEGA, JOS. DE. Vocabulario en lengua Castellana y Cora. Mexico, 1732. (*Same,* reprint 1888.)

ORTELIUS, ABRAHAM. Theatrum orbis terrarum. Antverpiæ, 1570. (*Same,* 1571.)

OTIS, GEORGE A. List of the specimens in the anatomical section of the U. S. Army Medical Museum. Washington, 1880.

OUT WEST. A magazine of the old Pacific and the new. (*Continuation of* Land of Sunshine.) Vols. XVI–XXXII. Los Angeles, 1902–10.

OVERLAND MONTHLY. Vols. I–LVI. San Francisco, 1868–1910.

OVIEDO Y VALDEZ, GONZALO FERNÁNDEZ DE. Historia general y natural de las Indias. Primera parte. Madrid, 1851.

OWEN, MARY ALICIA. Folk-lore of the Musquakie Indians of North America. (Pub. Folk-lore Soc., vol. LI, London, 1904.)

OWEN, A. K., *and* MOTZ, ALBERT VON. Nuevo mapa estadística y ferrocarillero de México y la frontera del norte. Philadelphia, 1882.

OWENS, J. G. Natal ceremonies' of the Hopi Indians. (Jour. Am. Ethnol. and Archæol., vol. II, Boston and New York, 1892.)

PACHECO, J. F., *and* CÁRDENAS, F. DE. *See* COLECCIÓN DE DOCUMENTOS.

PACIFIC RAILROAD REPORTS. Reports of explorations and surveys to ascertain the most practicable route for a railroad from the Mississippi river to the Pacific ocean. Made under the direction of the Secretary of War. 1853–54. Vols. I–XII, in 13 vols. Washington, 1855–60.

PALFREY, JNO. G. History of New England during the Stuart dynasty. Vols. I–III. Boston, 1858–64.

PALMER, EDWARD. Food products of the North American Indians. (Report of the Commissioner of Agriculture for 1870, Washington, 1871.)

PALMER, FRANK M. The Southwest Museum. (Bull. 2, Southwest Soc., Archæol-Inst. Am., Los Angeles, 1905.)

PALMER, JOEL. Journal of travels over the Rocky mountains, to the mouth of the Columbia river. Cincinnati, 1847. (*Same,* Cincinnati, 1852.)

PALMER, WM. P. *See* CALENDAR.

PALOU, FRANCISCO. Relacion historica de la vida y apostolicas tareas del venerable Padre Fray Junipero Serra. Mexico, 1787. (*Same,* English trans. by Rev. J. Adam, San Francisco, 1884.)

PAREJA, FRANCISCO. Cathecismo, en lengva Castellana, y Timuquana. Mexico, 1612.

—— Arte de la lengva Timvqvana compvesta en 1614. (Bibliothèque Linguistique Américaine, tome XI, Paris, 1886.)

—— *See* GATSCHET, A. S. (Timucua language, 1878.)

PARISOT, J. *See* HAUMONTÉ, PARISOT, *and* ADAM.

PARKE, JNO. G. Map of the Territory of New Mexico. Santa Fé, 1851.

PARKER, NATHAN H. The Minnesota handbook for 1856–57, with map. Boston, 1857.

PARKER, SAMUEL. Journal of an exploring tour beyond the Rocky mountains in the years 1835–37. Ithaca, 1838. (*Same,* 2d ed., 1840; 3d ed., 1842; 5th ed., 1846.)

PARKER, W. B. Notes taken during the expedition commanded by Capt. R. B. Marcy through unexplored Texas, in the summer and fall of 1854. Philadelphia, 1856.

PARKER, W. T. Concerning American Indian womanhood. (Ann. Gynec. and Pædiat., vol. V, Philadelphia, 1891–92.)

PARKMAN, FRANCIS. The Jesuits in North America in the seventeenth century. Boston, 1867.

—— France and England in North America. Vols. I–VIII. Boston, 1867–92.

—— History of the conspiracy of Pontiac. Boston, 1868. (*Same,* Boston, 1883; Boston, 1901.)

—— La Salle and the discovery of the great west. 12th ed. Boston, 1883.

—— The Oregon trail. Sketches of prairie and Rocky Mountain life. 8th ed. Boston, 1883.

—— Pioneers of France in the New World. 20th ed. Boston, 1883.

—— The old régime in Canada. 12th ed. Boston, 1883.

—— Count Frontenac and New France under Louis XIV. 11th ed. Boston, 1883.

—— Montcalm and Wolfe. Vols. I–II. Boston, 1884.

PARLIAMENTARY REPORT. *See* GREAT BRITAIN.

PARRAUD, M. Histoire de Kentucke, nouvelle colonie à l'ouest de la Virginie. Traduit de l'Anglois de M. John Filson. Paris, 1785.

PARRY, W. E. Journal of a second voyage for the discovery of a north-west passage. London, 1824. (*Same,* New York, 1824.)

PARSONS, USHER. Indian names of places in Rhode-Island. Providence, 1861.

PATTERSON, J. B., *ed.* Autobiography of Ma-ka-tai-me-she-kia-kiak, or Black Hawk. Also life, death and burial of the old chief, together with a history of the Black Hawk war. Oquawka, Ill., 1882.

PATTIE, JAS. O. Personal narrative during an expedition from St. Louis, to the Pacific ocean and back through Mexico. Edited by T. Flint. Cincinnati, 1833.

PAUW, CORNELIUS DE. Recherches philosophiques sur les Américains. Tomes I–III. Londres et Berlin, 1770.

PAYNE, EDWARD J. History of the New World called America. Vols. I–II. Oxford and New York, 1892.

PEABODY, CHAS., *and* MOOREHEAD, W. K. Exploration of Jacobs cavern, McDonald county, Missouri. (Phillips Acad., Andover, Mass. Dept. Archæol., Bull. 1, Norwood, Mass., 1904.)

PEABODY, W. B. O. The early Jesuit missionaries of the north western territory. (In Beach, Indian Miscellany, Albany, 1877.)

PEABODY MUSEUM OF AMERICAN ARCHÆOLOGY AND ETHNOLOGY. Cambridge, Mass. Archæological and Ethnological Papers, vols. I–III, 1888–1904. Memoirs, vols. I–III, 1896–1904. Annual Reports, vols. I–XXXVII, 1868–1904.

PEARY, JOSEPHINE D. My Arctic journal. New York and Philadelphia, 1893.

PEARY, ROBERT E. The great white journey. (In Peary, Josephine D., My Arctic Journal, New York and Philadelphia, 1893.)

——— Northward over the "Great Ice." Vols. I–II. New York, 1898.

PECK, J. M. See PERKINS, J. H., and PECK.

PELAEZ, FRANCISCO DE P. G. Memorias para la historia del antiguo reyno de Guatemala. Tomos I–II. Guatemala, 1851–52.

PEÑALOSA, DIEGO D. DE. See FREYTAS, NICOLAS DE; SHEA, JOHN G., ed.

PENHALLOW, SAMUEL. The history of the wars of New-England with the eastern Indians. Boston, 1726. (Coll. N. H. Hist. Soc., vol. I, Concord, 1824; reprint, 1871.)

PÉNICAUT, M. Annals of Louisiana from the establishment of the first colony under d'Iberville, to 1722. (In French, B. F., Hist. Coll. La. and Fla., N. S., New York, 1869.)

——— Relation. (In Margry, Découvertes, tome V, 1883.)

PENNSYLVANIA. See COLONIAL RECORDS OF PENNSYLVANIA; HISTORICAL SOCIETY OF PENNSYLVANIA.

PENNSYLVANIA ARCHIVES. Selected and arranged from original documents, by Samuel Hazard. Vols. I–XII, Philadelphia, 1852–56. 2d ser., vols. I–XIX, Harrisburg, 1875–90.

PENNSYLVANIA, PROVINCIAL COUNCIL. Minutes; published by the State. Vols. I–III, Philadelphia; vols. IV–XVI, Harrisburg, 1852–53.

PEPPER, GEO. H. Native Navajo dyes. (In The Papoose, New York, Feb. 1902.)

——— and Wilson, G. L. An Hidatsa shrine and the beliefs respecting it. (Mem. Am. Anthr. Asso., vol. II, pt. 4, Lancaster, Pa., 1908.)

PEREA, ESTEVAN DE. Verdadera [y Segvnda] relacion, de la grandiosa conversion que ha avido en el Nuevo Mexico. Sevilla, 1632–33.

PEREZ DE RIBAS. See RIBAS.

PERKINS, JAS. H., and PECK, J. M. Annals of the west; accounts of the principal events in the western states and the territories from the discovery of the Mississippi. 2d ed. Enlarged by J. M. Peck. St. Louis, 1850.

PERLEY, CHAS. The history of Newfoundland from the earliest times to the year 1860. London, 1863.

FEROUSE, JEAN F. G. DE LA. Voyage autour du monde. Rédigé par M. L. A. Milet-Moreau. Tomes I–IV. Paris, 1797.

PERRIN DU LAC, F. M. Voyages dans les deux Louisianes, et chez les nations sauvages du Missouri, par les Etats-Unis, en 1801–1803. Paris, 1805. (Same, Lyon, 1805.)

PERROT, NICOLAS. Mémoire sur les mœurs, coustumes et relligion des sauvages de l'Amérique Septentrionale, publié pour la première fois par le R. P. J. Tailhan. Leipzig et Paris, 1864.

PETERMANNS MITTEILUNGEN aus Justus Perthes' geographischer Anstalt. Band 1–56. Gotha, 1855–1910.

PETITOT, EMILE. Géographie de l'Athabaskaw-Mackenzie et des grands lacs du bassin arctique. (Bull. Soc. Géog. Paris, 6e ser., tome X, Paris, 1875.)

PETITOT, EMILE. Dictionnaire de la langue Dènè-Dindjié dialectes Montagnais ou Chippéwayan, Peaux de Lièvre et Loucheux renfermant en outre un grand nombre de termes propres à sept autres dialectes de la même langue précédé d'une monographie des Dènè-Dindjié d'une grammaire et de tableaux synoptiques des conjugaisons. (Bibliothèque de Linguistique et d'Ethnographie Américaines, tome II, Paris, 1876.)

——— Vocabulaire Français - Esquimau. (Ibid., III, Paris, 1876.)

——— On the Athabascan district of the Canadian North West territory. (Proc. Roy. Geog. Soc. and Monthly Record of Geog., vol. V, London, 1883.)

——— On the Athapasca district of the Canadian North-west Territory. (Montreal Nat. Hist. Soc., Record of Nat. Hist. and Geology, Montreal, 1884. Reprinted in Canadian Record of Science, vol. I, Montreal, 1884.)

——— Traditions indiennes du Canada nord-ouest. Alençon, 1887.

——— En route pour la mer glaciale. Paris, 1887.

——— Autour du grand lac des Esclaves. Paris, 1891.

——— Exploration de la region du grand lac des Ours. Paris, 1893.

PETROFF, IVAN. A preliminary report upon the population, industry, and resources of Alaska. (H. R. Ex. Doc. 40, 46th Cong., 3d sess., Washington, 1881.)

——— Report on the population, industries, and resources of Alaska. (U. S. Dept. of the Int., Census Office, 10th Census, vol. VIII, Washington, 1884.)

PEYTON, JNO. L. History of Augusta county, Virginia. Staunton, 1882.

PFEIFFER, IDA. A lady's second journey round the world. New York, 1865.

PHELIPEAU, R. Carte génerale des colonies Angloises dans l'Amérique Septentrionale pour l'intelligence de la guerre présent. D'après des manuscrits Anglais par J. B. Nolin, géographe. Paris, 1783.

PHILOLOGICAL SOCIETY OF LONDON. Transactions. Vols. I–XV. London, 1854–79.

——— See LATHAM, R. G.

PICKERING, JNO. See RASLES, SEBASTIAN.

PICKETT, ALBERT J. Invasion of the territory of Alabama by one thousand Spaniards under Ferdinand De Soto, in 1540. Montgomery, 1849.

——— History of Alabama, and incidentally of Georgia and Mississippi, from the earliest period. 3d ed. Vols. I–II. Charleston, 1851.

PIDGEON, WM. Traditions of De-coo-dah. And antiquarian researches: comprising extensive explorations, surveys, and excavations of the wonderful and mysterious earthen remains of the mound-builders in America. New York, 1858.

PIKE, ZEBULON M. An account of expeditions to the sources of the Mississippi, and through the western parts of Louisiana, and a tour through the interior parts of New Spain. Philadelphia, 1810.

——— Exploratory travels through the western territories of North America. London, 1811.

——— See COUES, ELLIOTT, ed.

PILLING, J. C. Proof-sheets of a bibliography of the languages of the North American Indians. Washington, 1885.

——— Bibliography of the Eskimo language. (Bull. 1, Bur. Am. Ethnology, Washington, 1887.)

——— Bibliography of the Siouan languages. (Bull. 5, Bur. Am. Ethnology, Washington, 1887.)

——— Bibliography of the Iroquoian languages. (Bull. 6, Bur. Am. Ethnology, Washington, 1889.)

PILLING, J. C. Bibliography of the Muskhogean languages. (Bull. 9, Bur. Am. Ethnology, Washington, 1889.)
———— Bibliography of the Algonquian languages. (Bull. 13, Bur. Am. Ethnology, Washington, 1891.)
———— Bibliography of the Athapascan languages. (Bull. 14, Bur. Am. Ethnology, Washington, 1892.)
———— Bibliography of the Chinookan languages. (Bull. 15, Bur. Am. Ethnology, Washington, 1893.)
———— Bibliography of the Salishan languages. (Bull. 16, Bur. Am. Ethnology, Washington, 1893.)
———— Bibliography of the Wakashan languages. (Bull. 19, Bur. Am. Ethnology, Washington, 1894.)
PIMENTEL, FRANCISCO. Cuadro descriptivo y comparativo de las lenguas indígenas de México. Tomos I–II. México, 1862–65. (Same, 1874–75.)
PINART, ALPHONSE L. Eskimaux et Koloches. Idées religieuses et traditions des Kaniagmioutes. (Revue d'Anthropologie, Paris, 1873.)
———— Sur les Atnahs. (Revue de Philologie et d'Ethnographie, no. 2, Paris, 1875.)
PINKERTON, J. Medallic history of England. London, 1790.
———— General collection of voyages and travels, 758–1826. Vols. I–XVII. London, 1808–14.
PINO, PEDRO B. Noticias historicas y estadisticas de la antigua provincia del Nuevo-México, 1812. Adicionadas por A. Barreiro en 1839 ; y ultamente anotadas por J. A. de Escudero. México, 1849.
PITEZEL, JNO. H. Lights and shades of missionary life during nine years spent in the region of Lake Superior. Cincinnati, 1857.
POLLARD, J. G. The Pamunkey Indians of Virginia. (Bull. 17, Bur. Am. Ethnology, Washington, 1894.)
POOLE, DE WITT CLINTON. Among the Sioux of Dakota. Eighteen months experience as an Indian agent. New York, 1881.
POOLE, FRANCIS. Queen Charlotte islands : a narrative of discovery and adventure in the North Pacific. Edited by John W. Lyndon. London, 1872.
POPE, JNO. Tour through the northern and western territories of the United States. Richmond, 1792.
POPE, JNO. Report of explorations of a route for the Pacific railroad near the 32d parallel of north latitude from the Red river to the Rio Grande. 1854. Pac. R. R. Reps., vol. II, Washington, 1855.)
POPULAR SCIENCE MONTHLY. Vols. I–LXXVII. New York, 1872–1910.
PORTER, J. H. Notes on the artificial deformation of children among savage and civilized peoples. (Rep. U. S. Nat. Mus. 1887, Washington, 1889.)
PORTILLO, ESTÉBAN L. Apuntes para la historia antigua de Coahuila y Texas. Saltillo, Mex. [n. d.]
POST, CHRISTIAN FREDERICK. The journal of Christian Frederick Post, from Philadelphia to the Ohio, on a message from the government of Pennsylvania. (In Thomson, Enquiry into the Causes, London, 1759 ; also Thwaites, Early Western Travels, vol. I, Cleveland, 1904.)
POTHERIE. See BACQUEVILLE DE LA POTHERIE.
POTTER, WOODBURN. The war in Florida. Baltimore, 1836.
POWELL, JNO. W. Report of explorations in 1873 of the Colorado of the West and its tributaries. Washington, 1874.

POWELL, JNO. W. Statement made before the committee on Indian affairs as to the condition of the Indian tribes west of the Rocky mountains. (H. R. Misc. Doc. 86, 43d Cong., 1st sess., Washington, 1874.)
———— The ancient province of Tusayan. (Scribner's Monthly Mag., vol. XI, no. 2, New York, Dec. 1875.)
———— On the evolution of language. (First Rep. Bur. Am. Ethnology, Washington, 1881.)
———— Sketch of the mythology of the North American Indians. (Ibid.)
———— Wyandot government. (Ibid.)
———— On limitations to the use of some anthropologic data. (Ibid.)
———— Indian linguistic families of America north of Mexico. (Seventh Rep. Bur. Am. Ethnology, Washington, 1891.)
———— American view of totemism. (Man, vol. II, no. 75, London, 1902.)
———— and INGALLS, G. W. Report of the special commissioners J. W. Powell and G. W. Ingalls on the condition of the Ute Indians of Utah ; the Pai-Utes of Utah, northern Arizona, southern Nevada, and southeastern California ; the Go-si Utes of Utah and Nevada ; the northwestern Shoshones of Idaho and Utah ; and the western Shoshones of Nevada. Washington, 1874.
POWELL, LYMAN P., ed. Historic towns of the western states. New York and London, 1901.
POWERS, STEPHEN. Tribes of California. (Contrib. N. A. Ethnol., vol. III, Washington, 1877.)
POWNALL, THOS. Topographical description of such parts of North America as are contained in the annexed map of the middle British colonies. London, 1776.
PRATZ. See LE PAGE DU PRATZ.
PRENTISS, D. W., and MORGAN, F. P. Therapeutic uses of mescal buttons (Anhalonium Lewinii). (Therapeutic Gazette, 3d ser., vol. XII, no. 1, Detroit, 1896.)
PREUSS, K. TH. Die ethnographische Veränderung der Eskimo des Smith-Sundes. (Ethnologisches Notizblatt, Königlichen Museums für Völkerkunde, Band II, Heft I, Berlin, 1899.)
PRICHARD, JAS. C. Researches into the physical history of mankind. 3d ed. Vols. I–V. London, 1836–47.
———— The natural history of man. Vols. I–II. London, New York, Paris, Madrid, 1855.
PRINCE, J. D., and LELAND, CHAS. G. Kuloskap the master and other Algonkin poems. New York, 1902.
PRINCE, L. BRADFORD. Historical sketches of New Mexico. New York and Kansas City, 1883.
PROUD, ROBERT. The history of Pennsylvania in North America, from the original institution and settlement of that province, under the first proprietor and governor William Penn, in 1681, till after the year 1742. Vols. I–II. Philadelphia, 1797–98.
PROVINCIAL MUSEUM, Victoria, B. C. Guide to anthropological collection in the Provincial Museum. Victoria, B. C., 1909.
PURCHAS, SAMUEL. Pvrchas his pilgrimage. Or relations of the world and the religions observed in all ages and places discovered. Part I [the other three parts were not published]. London, 1613.
———— Haklvytvs posthumus or Pvrchas his pilgrimes. Vols. I–V. London, 1625–26.
PUTNAM, DANIEL. History of middle Tennessee, or, life and times of Gen. James Robertson. Nashville, 1859.

PUTNAM, FREDERIC WARD. On methods of archæological research in America. (Johns Hopkins University Circulars, vol. v, no. 49, 89, Baltimore, 1886.)
———— and WILLOUGHBY, C. C. Symbolism in ancient American art. (Proc. Am. Asso. Adv. Sci., vol. XLIV, Salem, 1896.)
PUTNAM ANNIVERSARY VOLUME. Anthropological essays presented to Frederic Ward Putnam in honor of his seventieth birthday, April 16, 1909. New York, 1909.

QUATREFAGES, JEAN L. A., and HAMY, ERNEST T. Crania ethnica. Paris, 1872–82.

RADLOFF, LEOPOLD. Wörterbuch der Kinai Sprache. (Mém. de l'Acad. Impériale des Sciences de St. Pétersbourg, VII ser., tome XXI, no. 8, St. Pétersbourg, 1874.)
RAFINESQUE, C. S. Introduction [to H. Marshall, History of Kentucky, 1824].
———— The American nations, or outlines of their general history, ancient and modern. Vols. I–II. Philadelphia, 1836.
RÂLE. See RASLES.
RAMSEY, ALEX. Annual report of the superintendent of Indian affairs in Minnesota territory. (Senate Ex. Doc. 1, 31st Cong., 1st sess., Washington, 1849.)
RAMSEY, J. G. M. The annals of Tennessee to the end of the eighteenth century. Philadelphia, 1853.
RAMUSIO, GIOVANNI B. Delle navigationi et viaggi. Terza ed. T. I–III. Venice, 1563–65. (Same, 1606.)
RAND, SILAS T. A first reading book in the Micmac language. Halifax, 1875.
———— Legends of the Micmacs. New York and London, 1894.
RANDALL, E. O. Pontiac's conspiracy. (Ohio Archæol. and Hist. Quar., vol. XII, no. 4, Columbus, 1903.)
———— The Serpent mound, Adams county, Ohio. Columbus [1905].
RASLES, SEBASTIAN. A dictionary of the Abnaki language, in North America. With an introductory memoir and notes by John Pickering. (Mem. Am. Acad. Sci. and Arts, n. s., vol. I, Cambridge, 1833.)
RAU, CHAS. North American stone implements. (Smithsonian Rep. 1872, Washington, 1873.)
———— Ancient aboriginal trade in North America. (Ibid.)
———— Archæological collection of the United States National Museum, in charge of the Smithsonian Institution. (Smithsonian Contrib. to Knowledge, vol. XXII, Washington, 1876.)
———— Observations on cup-shaped and other lapidarian sculptures in the Old World and in America. (Contrib. N. A. Ethnol., vol. V, Washington, 1882.)
———— Prehistoric fishing in Europe and North America. (Smithsonian Contrib. to Knowledge, vol. XXV, Washington, 1884.)
———— See BAEGERT, JACOB.
RAYNAL, GUILLAUME T. F. A philosophical and political history of the East and West Indies. Translated by J. O. Justamond. Vols. I–VIII. London, 1788.
READ, CHAS. H., ed. See NOTES AND QUERIES ON ANTHROPOLOGY.
READ, M. C. Archæology of Ohio. Cleveland [n. d.]
RECOPILACIÓN de leyes de los reynos de las Indias. 3a ed. Tomo I. Madrid, 1774.
RECORD of the great council of the United States Improved Order of Red Men, held at Indianapolis, September, 1898. Vol. X, no. 3.

RECORDS of the Governor and Company of the Massachusetts Bay in New England. Printed by order of the Legislature. Edited by Nathaniel B. Shurtleff, M. D. Vol. II, Boston, 1853. Vols. IV, V, Boston, 1854.
RECORDS OF THE PAST. Vols. I–IX. Washington, 1902–10.
REDDING, B. B. How our ancestors in the stone age made their implements. (Am. Naturalist, vol. XIII, no. 11, Philadelphia, 1879.)
REEVES, A. M. Finding of Wineland the good. London, 1895.
REICHEL, WM. C. Memorials of the Moravian Church. Philadelphia, 1870.
REID, A. P. Religious belief of the Ojibois or Sauteux Indians resident in Manitoba and at Lake Winnepeg. (Jour. Anthr. Inst. Gr. Brit. and Ireland, vol. III, London, 1874.)
RELATIO ITINERIS. See WHITE, ANDREW.
RELATIONS de la Louisiane et du fleuve Mississippi. [Attributed to H. de Tonti.] Amsterdam, 1720.
RELATIONS DES JÉSUITES. See JESUIT RELATIONS.
REMY, JULES, and BRENCHLEY, JULIUS. A journey to Great Salt-Lake City, with a sketch of the history, religion and customs of the Mormons. Vols. I–II. London, 1861.
REPORT and accompanying documents of the Virginia commissioners appointed to ascertain the boundary line between Maryland and Virginia. Richmond, 1873.
RETZIUS, A. A. Om formen af hufvudets benstomme hos olika folleslag. (Forhandl. ved de Skandinaviske Naturforskeres, Christiania, 1847.)
REVERE, JOS. WARREN. A tour of duty in California; including a description of the gold region. Edited by Joseph N. Balestier. New York and Boston, 1849.
RHODE ISLAND. Records of the Colony of Rhode Island. Vols. I–X. Providence, 1856–65.
RHODE ISLAND HISTORICAL SOCIETY. Collections. Vols. I–X. Providence, 1827–97.
RIBAS, ANDRÉS PEREZ DE. Historia de los trivmphos de nvestra santa fee entre gentes las mas barbaras. Madrid, 1645.
RICHARDSON, JNO. Arctic searching expedition: a journal of a boat-voyage through Rupert's land and the Arctic sea. Vols. I–II. London, 1851.
———— The polar regions. Edinburgh, 1861.
RIDER, SIDNEY S. The lands of Rhode Island as they were known to Caunounicus and Miantunnomu. Providence, 1904.
RIGGS, A. L. See IAPI OAYE.
RIGGS, STEPHEN R. Grammar and dictionary of the Dakota language. (Smithsonian Contrib. to Knowledge, vol. IV, Washington, 1852.)
———— Dacota A B C wowapi. New York [1867].
———— Tah-koo wah-kan; or, the gospel among the Dakotas. Boston [1869].
———— Mary and I. Forty years with the Sioux. Chicago [1880].
———— A Dakota-English dictionary. Edited by J. O. Dorsey. (Contrib. N. A. Ethnol., vol. VII, Washington, 1892.)
———— Dakota grammar, texts, and ethnography. (Ibid., vol. IX, Washington, 1894.)
RINK, HENRY. Tales and traditions of the Eskimo. London, 1875.
———— The Eskimo tribes. (Medelelser om Grønland, vol. XI, Copenhagen and London, 1887.)
RITCH, WM. G. Aztlan. The history, resources and attractions of New Mexico. 6th ed. Boston, 1885.
———— Illustrated New Mexico, historical and industrial. 5th ed. Santa Fé, 1885.

RIVERA, PEDRO DE. Diario y derrotero de lo caminado, visto, y obcervado en el discurso de la vistia general de precidios, situados en las provincias ynternas de Nueva España. Guathemala, 1736.

RIVERS, WM. J. Sketch of the history of South Carolina. Charleston, 1856.

———— A chapter in the early history of South Carolina. Charleston, 1874.

ROBERTS, WM. Account of the first discovery and natural history of Florida. London, 1763.

ROBERTSON, WYNDHAM, Jr. Oregon our right and title, with an account of the territory. Washington, 1846.

ROBERTSON, WYNDHAM, and BROCK, R. A. Pocahontas, alias Matoaka, and her descendants. Richmond, 1887.

ROBIN, C. C. Voyages dans l'intérieur de la Louisiane, de la Floride occidentale, et dans les isles de la Martinique et de Saint-Domingue, pendant les années 1802, 1803, 1804, 1805 et 1806. Tomes I–III. Paris, 1807.

ROBINSON, A. Life in California, during a residence of several years in that territory, comprising a description of the country and the missionary establishments. New York, 1846.

ROBINSON, H. The great fur land, or sketches of life in the Hudson's bay territory. London, 1879.

ROGERS, ROBERT. A concise account of North America : containing a description of the several British colonies on that continent, including the islands of Newfoundland, Cape Breton, &c. London, 1765.

ROMANS, BERNARD. A concise natural history of East and West Florida. Vol. I (Vol. II unpublished). New York, 1775.

RONAN, PETER. Historical sketch of the Flathead Indian nation from 1813 to 1890. Helena, Mont., 1890.

ROOSEVELT, THEODORE. The winning of the west. Vols. I–II. New York, 1889.

ROSS, ALEXANDER. Adventures of the first settlers on the Oregon or Columbia river. London, 1849.

———— The fur hunters of the far west ; a narrative of adventures in the Oregon and Rocky mountains. Vols. I–II. London, 1855.

ROSS, BERNARD. The eastern Tinneh. (Smithsonian Rep. 1866, Washington, 1867.)

ROSS, JNO. A voyage of discovery, made under the orders of the admiralty in His Majesty's ships *Isabella* and *Alexander*. London, 1819.

———— Narrative of a second voyage in search of a north west passage, and of a residence in the Arctic regions during the years 1829, 1830, 1831, 1832, 1833. London, 1835.

ROWLANDSON, MARY. Narrative of captivity by the Indians, at the destruction of Lancaster, in 1676. 6th ed. Lancaster, Mass., 1828. (*Same*, Concord, 1824.)

ROY, PIERRE - GEORGES. Les noms géographiques de la Province de Québec. Levis, 1906.

ROYAL ANTHROPOLOGICAL INSTITUTE. *See* ANTHROPOLOGICAL INSTITUTE.

ROYAL GEOGRAPHICAL SOCIETY. Journal. Vols. I–XLIX. London, 1832–79.

ROYAL SOCIETY OF CANADA. Proceedings and Transactions. 1st ser., vols. I–XII, Montreal, 1883–95. 2d ser., vols. I–X, Montreal, 1895–1905.

ROYAL SOCIETY OF LONDON. Philosophical Transactions. Vol. XI. London, 1676.

ROYCE, C. C. Cessions of land by Indian tribes to the United States. (First Rep. Bur. Am. Ethnology, Washington, 1881.)

———— The Cherokee nation of Indians. (Fifth Rep. Bur. Am. Ethnology, Washington, 1887.)

ROYCE, C. C. Indian land cessions in the United States. (Eighteenth Rep. Bur. Am. Ethnology, pt. 2, Washington, 1899.)

RUDO ENSAYO, tentative de una prevencional descripcion geographica de la provincia de Sonora. [Written about 1762.] San Augustin de la Florida, 1863. (English trans. by Eusebio Guitéras, in Records Am. Catholic Hist. Soc., vol. v, 109, 264, Philadelphia, 1894.)

RUPP, ISAAC D. History of Northampton, Lehigh, Monroe, Carbon, and Schuylkill counties, Pennsylvania. Harrisburg, 1845.

———— Early history of western Pennsylvania, and of the West, from 1754 to 1833. Pittsburg and Harrisburg, 1846.

RUSSELL, FRANK. Explorations in the far north. Des Moines, 1898.

———— The Pima Indians. (Twenty-sixth Rep. Bur. Am. Ethnology, Washington, 1908.)

RUTTENBER, EDWARD M. History of the Indian tribes of Hudson's river : their origin, manners, and customs ; tribal and sub-tribal organizations ; wars, treaties, etc. Albany, 1872.

———— Footprints of the Red Men. Indian geographical names. [n. p.] New York State Hist. Asso., 1906.

RUXTON, GEO. A. F. The migration of the ancient Mexicans, and their analogy to the existing Indian tribes of northern Mexico. (Jour. Ethnol. Soc. Lond., vol. II, 90–104, London, 1850.)

———— Adventures in Mexico and the Rocky mountains. New York, 1848. (*Same*, New York, 1849, 1860.)

RYERSON, JNO. Hudson's bay ; or a missionary tour in the territory of the Hon. Hudson's Bay Company. Toronto, 1855.

SAGARD THEODAT, GABRIEL. Dictionnaire de la langue Huronne. Paris, 1632. (*Same*, in his Histoire du Canada, tome IV, Paris, 1866.)

———— Histoire du Canada et voyages que les Frères Mineurs Recollects y ont faicts pour la conversion des infidèles depuis l'an 1615. Tomes I–IV. Paris, 1636 ; reprint, 1866.

———— Le grand voyage du pays des Hurons situé en l'Amérique vers la Mer douce, avec un dictionnaire de la langue Huronne. Tomes I–II. Paris, 1865.

SAGE, RUFUS B. Scenes in the Rocky mountains, and in Oregon, California, New Mexico, Texas, and the grand prairies. Philadelphia, 1846.

ST. COSME. *See* SHEA, JNO. G.

SALMON, THOS. Modern history : or, present state of all nations. 3d ed. Vols. I–III. London, 1744–46.

SALVERTE, ANNE JOSEPH E. B. DE. History of the names of man, nations and places in their connection with the progress of civilization. Vols. I–II. London, 1862–64.

SALVERTE, EUSEBIUS. *See* MORDACQUE, L. H.

SAMMELBÄNDE DER INTERNATIONALEN MUSIKGESELLSCHAFT. Jahrgang IV. Leipzig, 1902–03.

SANFORD, EZEKIEL. History of the United States before the revolution. With some account of the aborigines. Philadelphia, 1819.

SANSON D'ABBEVILLE, N. L'Amerique en plusieurs cartes nouvelles et exactes ; et en divers traittez de geographie & d' histoire. [Paris (?), 1657.]

SANTOSCOY, ALBERTO. Nayarit. Colección de documentos inéditos, historicos y etnográficos, acerca de la sierra de ese nombre. Guadalajara, 1899.

SARGENT, CHAS. SPRAGUE. Report on the forests of North America (exclusive of Mexico). (U. S. Dept. of the Interior, Census Office, 10th Census, Washington, 1884.)

———— Manual of the trees of North America. Boston and New York, 1905.

SARGENT, WINTHROP. History of an expedition against Fort Du Quesne, in 1755, under Major-Gen. Braddock. (Mem. Hist. Soc. Pa., vol. v, Philadelphia, 1856.)

SAUER, MARTIN. Account of a geographical and astronomical expedition to the northern parts of Russia. London, 1802.

SAUTHIER, C. J. A map of the provinces of New York and New Jersey with a part of Pennsylvania and the province of Quebec. Engraved and published by Matthew Albert Lotter. Augsburg, 1777.

SCAIFE, H. LEWIS. History and condition of the Catawba Indians of South Carolina. (Pub. Ind. Rights Asso., Philadelphia, 1896.)

SCHAAFHAUSEN, HERMANN. Anthropologische Studien. Bonn, 1885.

SCHMELTZ, J. D. E. Das Schwirrholtz. (Verhandlungen des Vereins für Naturwissenschaftliche Unterhaltung zu Hamburg, 1894–95, B. IX, Hamburg, 1896.)

SCHOOLCRAFT, HENRY R. Narrative journal of travels from Detroit, north west through the great chain of the American lakes to the sources of the Mississippi river in the year 1820. Albany, 1821.

—— Algic researches. Vols. I–II. New York, 1839.

—— Report of the aboriginal names and geographical terminology of the state of New York. (From Proc. N. Y. Hist. Soc. for 1844.) New York, 1845.

—— Oneóta, or characteristics of the red race of America. From original notes and manuscripts. New York and London, 1845.

—— Notes on the Iroquois. Albany, 1847.

—— Personal memoirs of a residence of thirty years with the Indian tribes on the American frontiers. A. D. 1812–1842. Philadelphia, 1851.

—— Historical and statistical information, respecting the history, condition and prospects of the Indian tribes of the United States. Parts I–VI. Philadelphia, 1851–57.

—— Western scenes and reminiscences. Auburn and Buffalo, 1853.

SCHRADER, F. C. Reconnaissances in Prince William sound. (20th Rep. U. S. Geol. Surv., pt. VII, Washington, 1900.)

SCHULENBERG, A. C. VON. Die Sprache der Zimshian-Indianer in Nordwest-America. Braunschweig, 1894.

SCHULTZ, J. W. My life as an Indian. New York, 1907.

SCHUMACHER, PAUL. Ancient graves and shell heaps in California. (Smithsonian Rep. for 1874, Washington, 1875.)

—— Methods of making stone weapons. (Bull. Geol. and Geog. Surv. Terr., vol. III, no. 3, Washington, 1877.)

—— The method of manufacturing pottery and baskets among the Indians of southern California. (12th Rep. Peabody Mus., Cambridge, 1880.)

SCHWATKA, FREDERICK. Report of a military reconnaissance in Alaska in 1883. Washington, 1885.

SCHWEINITZ, EDMUND DE. Some of the fathers of the American Moravian Church. Bethlehem, 1882.

SCIDMORE, ELIZA R. Alaska, its southern coast and the Sitka archipelago. Boston, 1885.

—— The first district of Alaska from Prince Frederick sound to Yakutat bay. (In Report on Population and Resources of Alaska, 11th Census, Washington, 1893.)

SCIENCE. Vols. I–XXIII, Cambridge, Mass., [from 1885] New York, 1883–94. New ser., Vols. I–XXXII, New York, 1895–1910.

SENEX, JNO. [Map of] North America, 1710.

SERGI, G. Crania esquimesi. (Atti della Società Romana di Antropol., t. VII, fasc. III, Roma, 1901.)

SEVERANCE, FRANK H., ed. Captivity and sufferings of Benjamin Gilbert and his family. Reprinted from the original edition of 1784. Cleveland, 1904.

SEWARD, WM. H. Alaska. Speech of William H. Seward at Sitka, August, 1869. Washington, 1879. (Same, in Old South Leaflets, no. 133, Boston, n. d.)

SEYMOUR, E. S. Sketches of Minnesota, the New England of the west; with incidents of travel in 1849. New York, 1850.

SHAWNEE, W. H. Absentee Shawnee Indians. (Gulf States Hist. Mag., vol. I, 415, Montgomery, 1903.)

SHEA, JNO. GILMARY. Discovery and exploration of the Mississippi valley. New York, 1852. (Same, 2d ed., Albany, 1903.)

—— History of the Catholic missions among the Indian tribes of the United States, 1529–1854. New York, 1855. (Same, New York [1870].)

—— The Indian tribes of Wisconsin. (Coll. Wis. State Hist. Soc., vol. III, Madison, 1857.)

—— Early voyages up and down the Mississippi. Albany, 1861.

—— Relation de la mission du Mississipi du Séminaire de Québec en 1700, par Montigny, St. Cosme, Thaumur de la Source. New York, 1861.

—— The Catholic Church in Colonial days, 1521–1763. New York, 1886.

—— History of the Catholic Church in the United States from the first attempted colonization to the present time. Vols. I–IV. New York, 1886–92.

——, ed. Library of American Linguistics. Vols. I–XIII. New York, 1860–64.
   1. Shea, J. G. French-Onondaga dictionary. 1860.
   2. Mengarini, G. Selish or Flat-head grammar. 1861.
   3. Smith, T. B. A grammatical sketch of the Heve language. 1861.
   4. Arroyo de la Cuesta, F. Grammar of the Mutsun language. 1861.
   5. Smith, T. B. ed. Grammar of the Pima or Nevome. 1862.
   6. Pandosy, M. C. Grammar and dictionary of the Yakama language. 1862.
   7. Sitjar, B. Vocabulary of the language of the San Antonio mission. 1861.
   8. Arroyo de la Cuesta, F. A vocabulary or phrase-book of the Mutsun language of Alta California. 1862.
   9. Maillard, A. S. Grammar of the Mikmaque language of Nova Scotia. 1864.
   10. Bruyas, J. Radices verborum Iroquæorum. 1863.
   11. Gibbs, G. Alphabetical vocabularies of the Clallam and Lummi. 1863.
   12. Gibbs, G. A dictionary of the Chinook jargon. 1863.
   13. Gibbs, G. Alphabetical vocabulary of the Chinook language. 1863.

—— See CHARLEVOIX; FREYTAS; HENNEPIN; LE CLERCQ.

SHELDON, E. M. The early history of Michigan. New York, 1856.

SHEPHERD, HENRY A. Antiquities of the state of Ohio. Cincinnati, 1887.

SHINDLER, A. Z. List of photographic portraits of North American Indians in the gallery of the Smithsonian Institution. (Smithson. Misc. Coll., vol. XIV, no. 216, Washington, 1867.)

SHIPP, BARNARD. The history of Hernando de Soto and Florida; or, record of the events of fifty-six years, from 1512 to 1568. Philadelphia, 1881.

SHORT, JNO. T. North Americans of antiquity. 2d ed. New York, 1880.

SHUFELDT, R. W. Indian types of beauty. (Reprinted from American Field, Washington, 1891.)

S., I. [Map of] America, with those known parts in that unknowne worlde, both people and manner of buildings. Discribed and inlarged by I. S. London, 1626.

SIBLEY, JNO. Historical sketches of the several Indian tribes in Louisiana, south of the Arkansa river, and between the Mississippi and River Grand. (Message from the President communicating discoveries made by Captains Lewis and Clark, Washington, 1806. *Same*, in Am. State Papers, Indian Affairs, vol. I, 1832.)

SILLIMAN, BENJ. Turquois of New Mexico. (Engineering and Mining Jour., vol. XXXII, New York, 1881.)

SILLIMAN'S AMERICAN JOURNAL OF SCIENCE AND ARTS. 1st ser. Vol. I, New York and New Haven, 1818. (*Continued as* American Journal of Science and Arts.)

SIMÉON, RÉMI. Dictionnaire de la langue Nahuatl ou Mexicaine. Paris, 1885.

SIMMONDS, W. The proceedings of the English colonie in Virginia since their first beginning from England in 1606 to 1612. Oxford, 1612. (In John Smith's Works, Arber ed., Birmingham, 1884.)

SIMMS, S. C. Traditions of the Crows. (Pub. Field Col. Mus., Anthr. ser., vol. II, no. 6, Chicago, 1903.)

SIMMS, W. G. History of South Carolina, from its discovery, to its erection into a republic. Charleston, 1840. (*Same*, New York, 1860.)

SIMPSON, JAS. H. Report from the Secretary of War, communicating, in compliance with a resolution of the Senate, the report and map of the route from Fort Smith, Arkansas, to Santa Fe, New Mexico, made by Lieutenant Simpson, 1849. (Ex. Doc. 12, 31st Cong., 1st sess., Washington, 1850.)

———— Report of the Secretary of War, communicating The report of Lieutenant J. H. Simpson of an expedition into the Navajo country in 1849. (Senate Ex. Doc. 64, 31st Cong., 1st sess., Washington, 1850.)

———— Journal of a military reconnaissance, from Santa Fe, New Mexico, to the Navajo country. Philadelphia, 1852.

———— The shortest route to California . . . and some account of the Indian tribes. Philadelphia, 1869.

———— Coronado's march in search of the seven cities of Cibola. (Smithson. Rep. for 1869, Washington, 1871.)

———— Report of explorations across the great basin of the territory of Utah for a direct wagon-route from Camp Floyd to Genoa, in Carson valley, in 1859. (Engineer Dept., U. S. A., Washington, 1876.)

SIMPSON, JNO. Observations on the western Esquimaux. (In Further Papers relative to the Recent Arctic Expeditions, London, 1855.)

SIMPSON, THOS. Narrative of the discoveries on the north coast of America; effected by the officers of the Hudson's Bay Company during the years 1836–39. London, 1843.

SINCLAIR, WM. J. Exploration of the Potter Creek cave. (Pub. Univ. Cal., Am. Archæol. and Ethnol., vol. II, no. 1, Berkeley, 1904.)

SITGREAVES, L. Report of an expedition down the Zuni and Colorado rivers. (Senate Ex. Doc. 59, 32d Cong., 2d sess., Washington, 1853.)

SIX INDIENS ROUGES de la tribu des Grands Osages. Paris, 1827.

SKETCH of the Seminole war by a Lieutenant of the left wing. Charleston, 1836.

SLAFTER, EDMUND F. Pre-historic copper implements. Boston, 1879.

SMET, PIERRE-J. DE. Letters and sketches with a narrative of a year's residence among the Indian tribes of the Rocky mountains. Philadelphia, 1843.

———— Oregon missions and travels over the Rocky mountains, in 1845–46. New York, 1847.

———— Missions de l'Orégon et voyages aux Montagnes Rocheuses aux sources de la Colombie, de l'Athabasca et du Sascatshawin, en 1845–46. Gand [1848].

———— Western missions and missionaries. New York, 1863.

———— New Indian sketches. New York and Montreal [1865].

———— Reisen zu den Felsen-Gebirgen und ein Jahr unter den wilden Indianer-Stämmen des Oregon-Gebietes. St. Louis, Mo., 1865.

———— *See* CHITTENDEN, H. M., *and* RICHARDSON, A. T.

SMITH, BUCKINGHAM. Letter of Hernando de Soto, and memoir of Hernando de Escalante Fontaneda. Washington, 1854.

———— Coleccion de varios documentos para la historia de la Florida y tierras adyacentes. Tomo I. London, 1857.

———— The Timuquana language. (Hist. Mag., 1st ser., vol. II, New York and London, 1858.)

———— *See* CABECA DE VACA.

SMITH, ERMINNIE A. Myths of the Iroquois. (Second Rep. Bur. Am. Ethnology, Washington, 1883.)

SMITH, HARLAN I. Archæology of Lytton, British Columbia. (Mem. Am. Mus. Nat. Hist., vol. II, Anthr. I, New York, 1899.)

———— Archæology of the Thompson river region, British Columbia. (Ibid., 1900.)

———— Shell-heaps of the lower Frazer river, British Columbia. (Ibid., vol. IV, Anthr. III, New York, 1903.)

———— *and* FOWKE, GERARD. Cairns of British Columbia and Washington. (Ibid., 1901.)

SMITH, JNO. The trve travels, adventures and observations of Captaine John Smith, in Europe, Asia, Africke, and America; beginning about the yeere 1593, and continued to this present 1629. Vols. I–II. Richmond, 1819. (Reprint of London ed. of 1629.)

———— The generall historie of Virginia, New-England, and the Summer iles. (Vol. II of The True Travels, Adventures and Observations of Captaine John Smith.) Richmond, 1819.

———— True relation of Virginia, with an introduction and notes by Charles Deane. (Reprint of London ed. of 1608.) Boston, 1866.

———— Works of. 1608. Edited by Edward Arber. English Scholar's Library, no. 16. Birmingham, 1884.

SMITH, JOS. Old Redstone. Philadelphia, 1854.

SMITH, MARCUS. Report on surveying operations in the mountain region during the year 1874. (In Fleming, Canadian Pacific Railway Rep., Ottawa, 1877.)

SMITH, WM. An historical account of the expedition against the Ohio Indians in 1764. Under the command of Henry Bouquet, Philadelphia, 1766.

———— History of the province of New York. Vols. I–II. New York, 1830.

SMITHSONIAN INSTITUTION. Annual Reports, 1846–1908, Washington, 1847–1909. Contributions to Knowledge, vols. I–XXIV, Washington, 1848–1907. Miscellaneous Collections, vols. I–IV, Washington, 1862–1910.

———— *See* BUREAU OF AMERICAN ETHNOLOGY; UNITED STATES NATIONAL MUSEUM.

SMYTH, JNO. F. D. Tour in the United States of America. Vols. I–II. London, 1784.

SNELLING, WM. J. Tales of travels west of the Mississippi. Boston, 1830.

———— Tales of the Northwest: sketches of Indian life and character. Boston, 1830.

SNOWDEN, JNO. ROSS. Description of the medals of Washington, of national and miscellaneous medals, and other objects of interest in the museum of the Mint. Philadelphia, 1861.

SOCIEDAD DE GEOGRAFÍA Y ESTADÍSTICA DE LA REPUBLICA MEXICANA. Boletín. Primera época, I–XII, Mexico, 1839–66. Segunda época, I–IV, Mexico, 1869–72. Tercera época, I–VI, Mexico, 1873–82. Cuarta época, I–IV, Mexico, 1888–97. Quinta época, I–III, Mexico, 1902–10.

SOCIÉTÉ D'ANTHROPOLOGIE DE PARIS. Bulletins. 1st ser., vols. I–VI, 1859–65. 2d ser., vols. I–XII, 1866–77. 3d ser., vols. I–XII, 1878–89. 4th ser., vols. I–X, 1890–99. 5th ser., vols. I–X, 1900–10.

SOCIÉTÉ D'ETHNOGRAPHIE. Mémoires, tome XI, Paris, 1872.

SOCIETY OF ANTIQUARIES OF LONDON. Archæologia; or miscellaneous tracts relating to antiquity. Vol. VIII. London, 1786.

SOCIETY OF FRIENDS. Aborigines Committee of the Meeting for Sufferings. Some Account of the conduct of the Society of Friends towards the Indian tribes in east and west Jersey and Pennsylvania, with a brief narrative of their labors for the civilization and Christian instruction of the Indians. London, 1844.

SOMERS, A. N. Prehistoric cannibalism in America. (Pop. Sci. Mo., vol. XLII, New York, 1893.)

SOSA, GASPAR CASTAÑO DE. Memoria del descubrimiento (27 de Julio de 1590). (Colección de Documentos Inéditos, tome XV, 191–261, Madrid, 1871.)

SOTO, HERNANDO DE. See BIEDMA; GENTLEMAN OF ELVAS; SPANISH EXPLORERS.

SOUTH DAKOTA. State Historical Society. Collections. Vols. I–III. Aberdeen, S. D., 1902–06.

SOUTHWORTH, ALVIN S. The new state of Colorado. (Trans. Am. Geog. Soc. 1874, vol. I, New York, 1876.)

SPANISH EXPLORERS in the Southern United States. 1528–1543. The narrative of Alvar Nuñez Cabeca de Vaca, edited by Frederick W. Hodge. The narrative of the expedition of Hernando de Soto by the Gentleman of Elvas, edited by Theodore H. Lewis. The narrative of the expedition of Coronado, by Pedro de Castañeda, edited by Frederick W. Hodge. New York, 1907.

SPEARS, JNO. R., ed. Dangers and sufferings of Robert Eastburn. Reprinted from the original edition of 1758. Cleveland, 1904.

SPECK, FRANK G. The Creek Indians of Taskigi town. (Mem. Am. Anthr. Asso., vol. II, pt. 2, Lancaster, Pa., 1907.)

———— Ethnology of the Yuchi Indians. (Anthr. Pub. Univ. Mus., Univ. Pa., vol. I, no. 1, Philadelphia, 1909.)

SPEED, THOS. The wilderness road. (Pub. Filson Club, no. 2, Louisville, 1886.)

SPENCER, F. C. Education of the Pueblo child. (Contrib. to Philos., Psychol., and Ed., Columbia Univ., vol. VII, no. 1, New York, 1899.)

SPENCER, O. M. Indian captivity: a true narrative of the capture of the Rev. O. M. Spencer. New York, 1834.

SPINDEN, H. J. The Nez Percé Indians. (Mem. Am. Anthr. Asso., vol. II, pt. 3, Lancaster, Pa., 1908.)

———— See WILL, G. F., and SPINDEN.

SPITZKA, E. A. Contributions to the encephalic anatomy of the races. (Am. Jour. Anat., vol. II, Baltimore, 1902.)

SPOTSWOOD, ALEXANDER. Official letters of. Vols. I–II. Virginia Historical Society, Richmond, 1882–85.

SPROAT, GILBERT M. Scenes and studies of savage life. London, 1868.

SQUIER, E. G. New Mexico and California. (In Am. Rev., vol. II, no. V, New York, Nov. 1848.)

———— Antiquities of the state of New York. With a supplement on the antiquities of the West. Buffalo, 1851.

———— and DAVIS, E. H. Ancient monuments of the Mississippi valley. (Smithsonian Contrib. to Knowledge, vol. I, Washington, 1848.)

STANDARD NATURAL HISTORY. See KINGSLEY, J. S.

STANFORD, EDWARD. Compendium of geography and travel based on Hellwald's "Die Erde und ihre Völker." Translated with ethnographic appendix by A. H. Keane. Vols. I–VI. London, 1878–85.

STANLEY, J. M. Catalogue of portraits of North American Indians painted by J. M. Stanley. (Smithsonian Misc. Coll., no. 53, Washington, 1852.)

STARR, FREDERICK. Some first steps in human progress. Meadville, Pa., and New York, 1895.

———— American Indians. Boston, 1899.

STATISTISCHE UND ETHNOGRAPHISCHE Nachrichten über die russischen Besitzungen. (In Baer and Helmersen, Beiträge zur Kentniss des russischen Reiches, St. Petersburg, 1839.)

STATUTES AT LARGE. See UNITED STATES: STATUTES AT LARGE.

STEARNS, ROBERT E. C. On certain aboriginal implements from Napa, California. (Am. Nat., vol. XVI, Philadelphia, 1882.)

STEARNS, WINFRID A. Labrador: a sketch of its people, its industries and its natural history. Boston, 1884.

STEIN, ROBERT. Geographische Nomenklatur bei den Eskimos des Smith-Sundes. (Petermanns Mitteilungen, B. 48, H. IX, Gotha, 1902.)

STEINMETZ, SEBALD RUDOLF. Ethnologische Studien zur ersten Entwicklung der Strafe. Leiden, 1892.

STEPHEN, ALEXANDER M. The Navajo shoemaker. (Proc. U. S. Nat. Mus. 1888, vol. XI, Washington, 1889.)

STEVENS, EDWARD T. Flint chips. A guide to pre-historic archæology. London, 1870.

STEVENS, HAZARD. Life of Isaac Ingalls Stevens. Vols. I–II. Boston and New York, 1900.

STEVENS, ISAAC I. Narrative and final report of explorations for a route for a Pacific railroad, 1855. (Pacific Railroad Reports, vol. XII, bk. 1, Washington, 1860.)

STEVENS, WM. B. History of Georgia from its first discovery by Europeans to the adoption of the present constitution in 1798. Vols. I–II. New York and Philadelphia, 1847–59.

STEVENSON, JAS. Illustrated catalogue of the collections obtained from the Indians of New Mexico and Arizona. (Second Rep. Bur. Ethnology, Washington, 1883.)

———— Illustrated catalogue of the collections obtained from the Indians of New Mexico in 1880. (Ibid.)

———— Illustrated catalogue of the collections obtained from the pueblos of Zuñi, New Mexico, and Wolpi, Arizona. (Third Rep. Bur. Ethnology, Washington, 1884.)

———— Ceremonial of Hasjelti Dailjis and mythical sand painting of the Navaho Indians. (Eighth Rep. Bur. Ethnology, Washington, 1892.)

STEVENSON, MATILDA C. The religious life of the Zuñi child. (Fifth Rep. Bur. Ethnology, Washington, 1887.)

———— The Sia. (Eleventh Rep. Bur. Ethnology, Washington, 1893.)

STEVENSON, MATIILDA C. The Zuñi Indians; their mythology, esoteric fraternities, and ceremonies. (Twenty-third Rep. Bur. Am. Ethnology, Washington, 1904.)

STEVENSON, T. E. See STEVENSON, MATILDA C.

STITES, SARA HENRY. Economics of the Iroquois. (Bryn Mawr College Monographs, Monograph ser., vol. I, no. 3, Bryn Mawr, Pa., 1905.)

STITH, WM. History of the first discovery and settlement of Virginia. (Sabin's reprint.) New York, 1865.

ST. JOHN, MOLYNEUX. The sea of mountains; an account of Lord Dufferin's tour through British Columbia in 1876. Vols. I–II. London, 1877.

STOBO, ROBERT. Notices of the settlement of the country along the Monongahela, Allegany and upper Ohio rivers. (In Olden Time, vol. I, Pittsburgh, 1846; Cincinnati, 1876.)

STÖCKLEIN, JOS. Der neue Welt-Bott mit allerhand Nachrichten dern Missionariorum Soc. Jesu. Augspurg und Grätz, 1726.

STOLPE, HJALMAR. Studier Amerikansk ornamentik. Stockholm, 1896.

STONE, CHAS. P. Notes on the State of Sonora. (Hist. Mag., vol. v, New York, June 1861.)

STONE, WM. L. Life of Joseph Brant (Thayendanegea), including the border wars of the American revolution and sketches of the Indian campaigns of Generals Harmar, St. Clair, and Wayne. Vols. I–II. Albany, 1864.
———— Life and times of Sir W. Johnson. Vols. I–II. Albany, 1865.

STRACHEY, WM. The historie of travaile into Virginia Britannia, expressing the cosmographie and comodities of the country, together with the manners and customs of the people. (Hakluyt Soc. Pub., vol. VI, London, 1849.)

STRATTON, R. B. Captivity of the Oatman girls. New York, 1857.

STUART, GRANVILLE. Montana as it is. New York, 1865.

STUMPF, CARL. [Various writings in] Vierteljahrsschrift für Musikwissenschaft, vols. I–X, Leipzig, 1885–94.

STURTEVANT, LEWIS. Indian corn and the Indian. (Am. Nat., vol. XIX, Philadelphia, 1885.)

SULLIVAN, J. History of the district of Maine (1604–1795). Boston, 1795.

SULLIVAN, JNO. See COOK, FREDERICK.

SUMNER, WM. G. History of American currency. New York, 1874.

SUTHERLAND, A. A summer in prairieland. Toronto, 1881.

SWAN, JAS. G. The northwest coast, or three years residence in Washington territory. New York, 1857.
———— Indians of Cape Flattery. (Smithsonian Contrib. to Knowledge, vol. XVI, Washington, 1870.)
———— Haidah Indians of Queen Charlotte's islands, British Columbia. (Ibid., vol. XXI, Washington, 1874.)

SWANTON, JNO. R. Contributions to the ethnology of the Haida. (Mem. Am. Mus. Nat. Hist., Jesup N. Pac. Exped., vol. V, pt. 1, Leiden and New York, 1905.) Bur. Am. Ethnology, Washington, 1905.)
———— Tlingit myths and texts. (Bull. 39, Bur. Am. Ethnology, Washington, 1909.)

SYMS, W. G. See SIMMS, W. G.

TAILHAN, J. See PERROT, NICOLAS.

TANNER, JNO. Narrative of captivity and adventures during thirty years' residence among the Indians in North America. Prepared for the press by Edwin James. New York, 1830.

TAYLOR, ALEX. S. The Indianology of California. (In California Farmer and Journal of Useful Sciences, San Francisco, vol. XIII, no. 3 (Feb. 22, 1860) to vol. XX, no. 12 (Oct. 30, 1863).)

TEIT, JAS. The Thompson Indians of British Columbia. (Mem. Am. Mus. Nat. Hist., vol. II, Anthropology I, no. IV, New York, 1900.)

TEN KATE, H. F. C. Indiens des États-Unis du Sud-ouest. (Bull. de la Soc. d'Anthropologie de Paris, IIIe sér., tome VI, Paris, 1883.)
———— Sur la synonymie ethnique et la toponymie chez les Indiens de l'Amérique du Nord. Amsterdam, 1884.
———— Reizen en Onderzoekingen in Noord-Amerika. Leiden, 1885.
———— Somatological observations on Indians of the Southwest. (Jour. Am. Eth. and Arch., vol. III, Boston and New York, 1892.)

TERNAUX-COMPANS, HENRI. Voyages, relations et mémoires originaux pour servir à l'histoire de la découverte de l'Amérique. Tomes I–XX. Paris, 1837–41.

TERRY, JAMES. Sculptured anthropoid ape heads. New York, 1891.

TEXAS STATE HISTORICAL ASSOCIATION. Quarterly. Vols. I–XIII. Austin, 1898–1910.

THACHER, J. B. Christopher Columbus. Vols. I–III. New York, 1903–04.

THATCHER, B. B. Indian biography, or, an historical account of those individuals who have been distinguished among the North American natives. Vols. I–II. New York, 1832.

THEODAT. See SAGARD THEODAT, GABRIEL.

THOMAS, CYRUS. Directions for mound exploration. (Proc. U. S. Nat. Mus. 1884, vol. VII, app., Washington, 1885.)
———— Fort Ancient. (Science, vol. VIII, New York, 1886.)
———— Burial mounds of the northern sections of the United States. (Fifth Rep. Bur. Am. Ethnology, Washington, 1887.)
———— Work in mound exploration of the Bureau of Ethnology. (Bull. 4, Bur. Am. Ethnology, Washington, 1887.)
———— The problem of the Ohio mounds. (Bull. 8, Bur. Am. Ethnology, Washington, 1889.)
———— The circular, square, and octagonal earthworks of Ohio. (Bull. 10, Bur. Am. Ethnology, Washington, 1889.)
———— Catalogue of prehistoric works east of the Rocky mountains. (Bull. 12, Bur. Am. Ethnology, Washington, 1891.)
———— The Maya year. (Bull. 18, Bur. Am. Ethnology, Washington, 1894.)
———— Report on the mound explorations of the Bureau of Ethnology. (Twelfth Rep. Bur. Am. Ethnology, Washington, 1894.)
———— Numeral systems of Mexico and Central America. (Nineteenth Rep. Bur. Am. Ethnology, Washington, 1900.)
———— Introduction to the study of North American archæology. Second impression. Cincinnati, 1903.
———— The Indians of North America in historic times. (In History of North America, Guy Carleton Lee, ed., vol. II, Philadelphia, c. 1903.)

THOMPSON, A. C. Moravian missions. Twelve lectures. New York, 1890. (Same, 1904.)

THOMPSON, BENJ. F. History of Long Island; containing an account of the discovery and settlement. New York, 1839. (Same, 2d ed., vols. I–II, New York, 1843.)

THOMSON, CHAS. An enquiry into the causes of the alienation of the Delaware and Shawnee Indians from the British interest. London, 1759.

THRALL, HOMER S. A pictorial history of Texas, from the earliest visits of European adventurers to A. D. 1879. 5th ed. St. Louis, 1879.

THRUSTON, GATES P. Antiquities of Tennessee. 2d ed. Cincinnati, 1897.

THWAITES, REUBEN GOLD. Father Marquette. New York, 1902.

———, ed. Early western travels 1748–1846. Vols. I–XXXII, Cleveland, 1904–07.

——— See JESUIT RELATIONS.

TIKHMENIEF, P. Historical review of the organization of the Russian American Company and its history to the present time. [In Russian.] Vols. I–II, 1861–63.

TIMBERLAKE, HENRY. Memoirs of Lieut. Henry Timberlake (who accompanied the three Cherokee Indians to England in the year 1762) . . . containing an accurate map of their Over-hill settlement. London, 1765.

TIMS, J. W. Grammar and dictionary of the Blackfoot language in the Dominion of Canada. London, 1889.

TOCHER, J. F. Note on some measurements of Eskimo of Southampton island. (In Man, London, 1902.)

TOLMIE, W. F. Census of various tribes living on or near Puget sound, n. w. America, 1844. (Pac. R. R. Reps., vol. I, 434, Washington, 1855.)

——— Vocabularies of the Kittistzu, Kulleespelm, Shooswaap, and Wakynakaine. (Contrib. N. A. Ethnol., vol. I, Washington, 1877.)

——— and DAWSON, GEO. M. Comparative vocabularies of the Indian tribes of British Columbia. With a map illustrating distribution. (Geol. and Nat. Hist. Surv. of Canada.) Montreal, 1884.

TOLOMEO, CLAVIDIO. La geografia di Clavidio Tolomeo Alessandrino da Girolamo Roscelli. Venetia, 1561.

TONTI, HENRI DE. Account of M. de la Salle's last expedition and discoveries in North America. (In French, B. F., Hist. Coll. Louisiana, vol. I, New York, 1846.)

——— See RELATIONS.

TOOKER, WM. W. Indian place-names in East-Hampton town, with their probable significations. Sag Harbor, N. Y., 1889.

——— John Eliot's first Indian teacher and interpreter, Cockenoe-de-Long Island. New York, 1896.

——— The Algonquian series. Vols. I–X. New York, 1901.

TOPINARD, PAUL. Éléments d'anthropologie générale. Paris, 1885.

TORQUEMADA, JUAN DE. De los viente i un libros rituales i monarchia Indiana. Tomos I–III. Madrid, 1723.

TOUSSAINT, A. Carte de l'Amérique Septentrionale et Méridionale avec cartes particulieres des iles et des cotes environantes. Paris, 1839.

TOWNSEND, JNO. K. Narrative of a journey across the Rocky mountains, to the Columbia river. Philadelphia, 1839.

TOWNSHEND, CHAS. H. The Quinnipiack Indians and their reservation. New Haven, 1900.

TRAILL, CATHARINE P. Canadian Crusoes; a tale of the Rice Lake plains. London, 1854.

TRENT, WM. See GOODMAN, ALFRED T.

TRUMBULL, BENJ. Complete history of Connecticut from 1630 to 1764. Vols. I–II. New Haven, 1818.

TRUMBULL, HENRY. History of Indian wars. Philadelphia, 1851.

TRUMBULL, J. H. On the Algonkin name "manit" (or "manitou"), sometimes translated "great spirit," and "god." (In Old and New, vol. I, Boston, 1870.)

——— On Algonkin names for man. (Trans. Am. Philol. Asso. 1871, Hartford, 1872.)

——— Words derived from Indian languages of North America. (Ibid., 1872, Hartford, 1873.)

TRUMBULL, J. H. Indian languages of America. (Johnson's New Universal Cyclopædia, vol. II, New York, 1877.)

——— Indian names of places, etc., in and on the borders of Connecticut. Hartford, 1881. (See also in Woodward, A., Historical Address, New Haven, 1869.)

——— Natick dictionary. (Bull. 25, Bur. Am. Ethnology, Washington, 1903.)

TUCKER, SARAH. The rainbow in the north; short account of the first establishment of Christianity in Rupert's Land by the Church Missionary Society. New York, 1852.

TURNER, LUCIEN M. Ethnology of the Ungava district. (Eleventh Rep. Bur. Am. Ethnology, Washington, 1894.)

TURNER, W. W. See WHIPPLE, A. W., EWBANK, THOS., and TURNER.

UHDE, ADOLPH. Die Länder am untern Rio Bravo del Norte. Heidelberg, 1861.

UMFREVILLE, EDWARD. The present state of Hudson's bay, containing a full description of that settlement and the adjacent country; and likewise of the fur trade. London, 1790.

UNDERHILL, JNO. News from America; containing the history of the Pequot war. London, 1638. (Mass. Hist. Soc. Coll., 3d ser., vol. VI, Boston, 1837.)

UNITED STATES. The statutes at large and treaties of the United States. Vols. I–XVII, Boston, 1851–75. Vols. XVIII–XXXII, Washington, 1875–1902.

U. S. BUREAU OF EDUCATION. Reports, 1870–1897. Washington, 1875–98.

——— Circulars of Information, Nos. 3 and 4. Washington, 1883.

——— See WELLS, R., and KELLY, J. W.

U. S. CENSUS. Alaska, its population, its industries and resources, by Ivan Petroff. (Vol. VIII of the Reports of the Tenth Census, Washington, 1884.)

——— Report on population and resources of Alaska at the eleventh census, 1890. Washington, 1893.

——— Report on Indians taxed and Indians not taxed in the United States at the eleventh census, 1890. [By Thos. Donaldson.] Washington, 1894.

——— See DONALDSON, THOS.; PETROFF, IVAN.

U. S. COAST AND GEODETIC SURVEY. Report for 1868. Washington, 1871.

——— Maps of Alaska. Washington, 1898–99.

U. S. COMMISSION. Report of the U. S. Commission to the Columbian Historical Exposition at Madrid. Washington, 1895.

U. S. CONGRESS. [Various documents and reports of the Senate and the House of Representatives relating to the Indians.]

U. S. DEPARTMENT OF AGRICULTURE. Biological Survey. North American fauna. Nos. 3 and 16. Washington, 1890, 1899.

——— Bureau of Animal Industry. Bulletin 31. Washington, 1901.

U. S. EXPLORING EXPEDITION. Narrative of the, during the years 1838, 1839, 1840, 1841, 1842. By Charles Wilkes, U. S. N., commander of the expedition. Vols. I–V and atlas. Philadelphia, 1844. (Same, vols. I–V, Philadelphia, 1845. Same, 1850. Continued by the publication of the scientific results of the expedition to vol. XXIV, of which vol. VI is Horatio Hale's Ethnology and Philology, Philadelphia, 1846.)

U. S. GEOGRAPHICAL AND GEOLOGICAL SURVEY OF THE ROCKY MOUNTAIN REGION. See CONTRIBUTIONS TO NORTH AMERICAN ETHNOLOGY.

U. S. GEOGRAPHICAL SURVEYS OF THE TERRITORY OF THE UNITED STATES WEST OF THE 100TH MERIDIAN. Annual Reports. Washington, 1875–78.

——— Volume VII. Archæology. Washington, 1879.

U. S. GEOLOGICAL AND GEOGRAPHICAL SUR-
VEY OF THE TERRITORIES. F. V. Hayden
in charge. Bulletins, vols. I–VI. Wash-
ington, 1874–1882.
———— Annual reports, vols. I–X. Wash-
ington, 1867–78.
U. S. HOUSE OF REPRESENTATIVES. See
U. S. CONGRESS.
U. S. HYDROGRAPHIC OFFICE. [Chart of
the] North Pacific ocean. West coast of
North America; from Juan de Fuca
Strait to Queen - Charlotte islands, in-
cluding Vancouver island; from British
and United States surveys to 1882.
UNITED STATES INDIAN TREATIES. See IN-
DIAN TREATIES.
U. S. INTERIOR DEPARTMENT. Report of
the Secretary of the Interior communicating the correspondence between the
Department of the Interior and the In-
dian agents and commissioners in Cali-
fornia. (Sen. Ex. Doc. 4, 32d Cong.,
spec. sess., Washington, 1853.)
UNITED STATES NATIONAL MUSEUM.
(Smithsonian Institution.) Reports,
1881–1909, Washington, 1883–1909.
Proceedings, vols. I–XXXVI, Washington,
1879–1909. Bulletins, Nos. 1–72, Washington, 1875–1910.
U. S. PATENT OFFICE. Reports, Washington, 1850–51, 1852–53, 1854, 1855, 1856,
1858, 1859, 1860, 1861, 1866.
U. S. SENATE. See U. S. CONGRESS.
U. S. WAR DEPARTMENT. Chief of Engineers. Annual report of the Chief of
Engineers to the Secretary of War for
the year 1876. Pt. III. Washington,
1876. (H. R. Ex. Doc. 1, vol. II, pt. II,
44th Cong., 2d sess.)
UNIVERSITY OF CALIFORNIA. Publications
in American Archæology and Ethnology.
Vols. I–V. Berkeley, 1903–10.
UNIVERSITY OF PENNSYLVANIA. Publications. Series in philology, literature, and
archæology. Vol. II, no. I, Philadelphia,
1892. Vol. VI, Philadelphia, 1897.
———— See FREE MUSEUM OF SCIENCE AND
ART; HARSHBERGER, J. W.; SPECK, F. G.
URBINA, MANUEL. El peyote y el ololiuh-
qui. (Anales del Museo Nacional de
México, tomo VII, México, 1909.)
URLSPERGER, SAMUEL. Ausfürliche Nachricht von den saltzburgischen Emigranten, die sich in America niedergelassen
haben. B. I–III. Halle, 1735–52.

VANCOUVER, GEO. Voyage of discovery to
the North Pacific ocean, and round the
world, 1790–95. Vols. I–VI. London,
1801.
VANDERA, JOAN DE LA. Memoria. En que
se hace relación de los lugares y tierra
de la Florida por donde el Capitan Juan
Pardo entró á descubrir camino para
Nueva España por los años de 1566,
1567. (In French, B. F., Hist. Coll. La.
and Fla., 2d ser., pp. 289–292, New York,
1875.)
VAN DER DONCK, A. Description of New
Netherlands. (New York Hist. Soc. Coll.,
2d ser., vol. I, 1841.)
VANUXEM, LARDNER. Ancient oyster shell
deposits observed near the Atlantic coast
of the United States. (Proc. Amer. Asso.
Geol., 2d sess., 1841, Boston, 1843.)
VATER, JOHANN S. See ADELUNG, J. C., and
VATER.
VAUGONDY, ROBERT DE. [Carte de l'] Amérique ou Indes Occidentales. Paris, 1778.
VELASCO, JOSÉ FRANCISCO. Noticias estadísticas del estado de Sonora. México,
1850.
VENEGAS, MIGUEL. Noticia de la Califor-
nia, y de su conquista temporal y espi-
ritual hasta el tiempo presente. Tomos
I–III. Madrid, 1757.
———— A natural and civil history of Cal-
ifornia. Translated from the original
Spanish, Madrid, 1758. Vols. I–II. Lon-
don, 1759.

VENEGAS, MIGUEL. Histoire naturelle et
civile de la California. Tomes I–III.
Paris, 1767.
VENIAMÍNOFF, IVAN. Zapíski ob ostravax
Unaláshkinskago otdailo. Vols. I–II. St.
Petersburg, 1840. [In Russian.]
———— Ueber die Sprachen des Russischen
Amerika's, nach Wenjaminow. (Archiv
für wissenschaftliche Kunde von Russ-
land, B. VII, Berlin, 1849.)
VERMONT HISTORICAL SOCIETY. Collections.
Vols. I–II. Montpelier, 1870–71.
VERNEAU, R. Le bassin suivant les sexes
et les races. Paris, 1875.
VERRAZANO, HIERONIMO DA. Map of coast
from Florida to the gulf of St. Lawrence,
1529. (Mag. Am. Hist., vol. II, New
York, 1878.)
VERWYST, CHRYSOSTOM. Missionary labors
of Fathers Marquette, Menard and Allouez, in the Lake Superior region. Mil-
waukee and Chicago, 1886.
VETANCURT, AGUSTIN DE. Teatro Mexicano.
Tomos I–IV. México, [reprint] 1870–71.
(Tomo III contains the Crónica de la
provincia del Santo Evangelio de México,
and tomo IV the Menologio Franciscano
de los varones, etc.)
VETROMILE, EUGÈNE. The Abnakis and
their history, or historical notices on the
aborigines of Acadia. New York, 1866.
VICTOR, FRANCES F. The Oregon Indians.
(Overland Monthly, vol. VII, San Fran-
cisco, Oct. 1871.)
———— The early Indian wars of Oregon.
Salem, 1894.
VILLAGRAN, GASPAR DE. Historia de la
Nveva Mexico. Alcala, 1610.
VILLA-SEÑOR Y SANCHEZ, JOS. ANTONIO.
Theatro Americano, descripcion general
de los reynos, y provincias de la Nueva-
España, y sus jurisdicciones. Tomos I–II.
Mexico, 1746–48.
VINING, E. P. An inglorious Columbus.
New York, 1885.
VIRCHOW, RUDOLF. Beiträge zur Craniolo-
gie der Insulaner von der Westküste
Nordamerikas. (Verhandl. der Berliner
Gesell. für Anthr., Berlin, 1889.)
———— Crania ethnica americana. Berlin,
1892.
VIRGINIA COMMISSIONERS. See REPORT.
VIRGINIA HISTORICAL SOCIETY. Collections,
new series. Vols. I–XI. Richmond, 1882–92.
V[ISSIER], P[AUL]. Histoire de la tribu
des Osages. Paris, 1827.
VOLNEY, C. F. A view of the soil and
climate of the United States of America.
Translated, with occasional remarks, by
C. B. Brown. Philadelphia, 1804.
(Same, London, 1804.)
VOTH, H. R. Oraibi Powamu ceremony.
(Pub. Field Col. Mus., Anthr. ser., vol.
III, no. 2, Chicago, 1901.)
———— Oraibi summer Snake ceremony.
(Ibid., no. 4, Chicago, 1903.)
———— The Oraibi Oaqol ceremony. (Ibid.,
vol. VI, no. 1, Chicago, 1903.)
———— Hopi proper names. (Ibid., no. 3,
Chicago, 1905.)
———— See DORSEY, G. A., and VOTH.

WADDELL, JOS. A. Annals of Augusta
county, Virginia. Richmond, 1886.
WAITZ, THEODOR. Anthropologie der Na-
turvölker. B. I–IV. Leipzig, 1859–64.
WALAM OLUM. See BRINTON, D. G. (Lenape
and their Legends).
WALCH, JOHANES. Charte von America.
Augsburg, 1805.
WALKER, JUDSON E. Campaigns of Gen-
eral Custer in the north-west, and the
final surrender of Sitting Bull. New
York, 1881.
WALLACE, SUSAN E. Land of the Pueblos.
New York, 1888.
WALLARD, JOS. Address in commemoration
of the two hundredth anniversary of the
incorporation of Lancaster, Massachu-
setts. Boston, 1853.

WALLASCHEK, RICHARD. Primitive music. London and New York, 1893.

WALTON, JOS. S. Conrad Weiser and the Indian policy of colonial Pennsylvania. Philadelphia, c. 1900.

WARDEN, DAVID B. Statistical, political, and historical account of the United States. Vols. I–III. Edinburgh, 1819.

—————— Recherches sur les antiquités de l'Amérique Septentrionale. Paris, 1827.

WARREN, GOUVENEUR K. Explorations in the Dacota country in the year 1855. (Sen. Ex Doc. 76, 34th Cong., 1st sess., Washington, 1856.)

—————— Preliminary report of explorations in Nebraska and Dakota in the years 1855–56–57. [Reprint.] (Engineer Dept., U. S. Army, Washington, 1875.)

WARREN, JOS. See REVERE, JOS. WARREN.

WARREN, WM. W. History of the Ojibways based upon traditions and oral statements. (Coll. Minn. Hist. Soc., vol. v, St. Paul, 1885.)

WASHINGTON-IRVINE. See BUTTERFIELD, C. W.

WEBB, JAS. W. Altowan; or incidents of life and adventure in the Rocky mountains. Vols I–II. New York, 1846.

WEBBER, CHAS. W. The gold mines of the Gila. Vols. I–II. New York, 1849.

WEEDEN, WM. B. Indian money as a factor in New England civilization. (Johns Hopkins, Univ. Studies in Hist. and Polit. Sci., 2d ser., vols. VIII–IX, Baltimore, 1884.)

WELLCOME, HENRY S. The story of Metlakahtla. New York, 1887.

WELLS, ROGER, and KELLY, J. W. English-Eskimo and Eskimo-English vocabularies. (U. S. Bur. of Education, Circ. of Information no. 2, Washington, 1890.)

WELLS, WM. V. Wild life in Oregon. (Harper's Mag., vol. XIII, New York, June–Nov. 1856.)

WENJAMINOW. See VENIAMÍNOFF, IVAN.

WEST, GEO. A. Aboriginal pipes of Wisconsin. (Wis. Archeologist, vol. IV, nos, 3, 4, Madison, 1905.)

WEST, JNO. The substance of a journal during a residence at the Red River colony, British North America. London, 1824.

WESTERN GAZETTEER. See BROWN, SAMUEL R.

WESTERN RESERVE AND NORTHERN OHIO HISTORICAL SOCIETY. Tracts. Vols. I–II. Cleveland, 1877–88.

WEST FLORIDA. A new map of West Florida, including the Chactaw, Chicasaw, and Upper Creek section. (A manuscript map, ca. 1775, preserved at the U. S. General Land office, Interior Department.)

WHEELER, OLIN D. The trail of Lewis and Clark, 1804–1904. Vol. I–II. New York, 1904.

WHEELER SURVEY. See U. S. GEOGRAPHICAL SURVEYS OF THE TERRITORY of the U. S. West of the 100th Meridian.

WHEELOCK, ELEAZAR. Narrative of the original design, rise, progress, and present state of the Indian charity-school at Lebanon, in Connecticut. Boston, 1763.

WHIPPLE, A. W. Report of Lieutenant Whipple's expedition from San Diego to the Colorado. Washington, 1851. (Exec. Doc. 19, 31st Cong., 2d sess.)

—————— See PACIFIC RAILROAD REPORTS.

WHIPPLE, HENRY B. Lights and shadows of a long episcopate. New York, 1899.

—————— See HINMAN, S. D., and WELSH, WM.

[WHITE, ANDREW] Relatio itineris in Marylandiam. (Maryland Historical Society, Fund Pub. no. 7, Baltimore, 1874.)

WHITE, E. See ALLEN, A. J.

WHITE, FRANCES J. Old-time haunts of the Norwottock and Pocumtuck Indians. Springfield, Mass., 1903.

WHITE, GEO. Statistics of Georgia. Savannah, 1849.

WHITE, GEO. Historical collections of Georgia. 3d ed. New York, 1855.

WHITE, JNO. B. History of Apaches, 1875. (MS. in Bureau of American Ethnology.)

—————— Names of the different tribes in Arizona, and the names by which they are called by the Apaches. [n. d.] (MS. in Bureau of American Ethnology.)

—————— A history of the Indians of Arizona territory, 1873–75. (MS. in Bureau of American Ethnology.)

WHITING, W. H. C. Report of the Secretary of War, enclosing the report of Lieut. W. H. C. Whiting's reconnaissance of the western frontier of Texas. Washington, 1850. (Senate Ex. Doc. 64, 31st Cong., 1st sess.)

WHITNEY, J. D. Auriferous gravels of the Sierra Nevada of California. (Mem. Mus. Comp. Zool., Harvard Univ., vol. VI, no. 1, Cambridge, 1879.)

WHITTLESEY, CHAS. Ancient mining on the shores of Lake Superior. (Smithsonian Contrib. to Knowledge, vol. XIII, Washington, 1863.)

WHYMPER, FREDERICK. A journey from Norton sound, Bering sea, to Fort Youkon (junction of Porcupine and Youkon rivers). (Jour. Roy. Geog. Soc. 1868, vol. XXXVIII, London [n. d.].)

—————— Travel and adventure in the territory of Alaska, formerly Russian America. New York, 1868. (Same, New York, 1869.)

WILKES, CHAS. Western America, including California and Oregon, with maps of those regions and of the Sacramento valley. Philadelphia, 1849.

—————— See UNITED STATES EXPLORING EXPEDITION.

WILKES, GEO. History of Oregon, geographical and political. New York, 1845.

WILL, G. F., and SPINDEN, H. J. The Mandans. A study of their culture, archæology, and language. (Papers Peabody Mus. Am. Archæol. and Ethnol., vol. III, no. 4, Cambridge, Mass., 1906.)

WILLARD, CAROLINE McCOY. Life in Alaska. Letters of Mrs. Eugene S. Willard, edited by her sister Mrs. Eva McClintock. Philadelphia, 1884.

WILLARD, JOS. Address in commemoration of the two hundredth anniversary of the incorporation of Lancaster, Mass. Boston, 1853.

WILLIAMS, JNO. LEE. A view of West Florida, embracing its geography, topography, etc. Philadelphia, 1827.

—————— The territory of Florida; or sketches of the topography, civil and natural history, of the country. New York, 1837.

WILLIAMS, ROGER. A key into the language of America. London, 1643. (Reprinted in Rhode Island Hist. Soc. Coll., vol. I, Providence, 1827; also in Mass. Hist. Soc. Coll., 1st ser., vol. III, Boston, 1794; also in Narragansett Club Pub., 1st ser., vol. I, Providence, 1866.)

WILLIAMS, SAMUEL. Natural and civil history of Vermont. 2d ed. Vols. I–II. Burlington, 1809.

WILLIAMSON, A. W. Minnesota geographical names derived from the Dakota language, with some that are obsolete. Geol. and Nat. Hist. Surv. of Minnesota, 13th Ann Rep., St. Paul, 1885.)

WILLIAMSON, HUGH. History of North Carolina. Vols. I–II. Philadelphia, 1812.

WILLIAMSON, R. S. Report of explorations and surveys in California. (Pac. R. R. Reports, 1853–54, vol. V, Washington, 1856.)

WILLIAMSON, T. S. Who were the first men? (Minn. Hist. Soc. Coll. (1850–56), vol. I, St. Paul, 1872.)

WILLIAMSON, WM. D. History of the state of Maine; from its first discovery, A. D. 1602, to the separation, A. D. 1820. Vols. I–II. Hallowell, 1832.

WILLOUGHBY, CHAS. C. Prehistoric burial places in Maine. (Papers Peabody Mus. Am. Archæol. and Ethnol., vol. I, no. 6, Cambridge, 1898.)
—— See PUTNAM, F. W., and WILLOUGHBY.
WILLSON, BECKLES. The great company (1667–1871) being a history of the honourable company of merchants-adventurers trading into Hudson's bay. Vols. I–II. London, 1900.
WILSON, Captain. Report on the Indian tribes inhabiting the country in the vicinity of the 49th parallel of north latitude. (Trans. Ethnol. Soc. Lond., n. s., IV, London, 1866.)
WILSON, DANIEL. Prehistoric man. Vols. I–II. Cambridge and London, 1862.
WILSON, EDWARD F. Ojebway language : a manual for missionaries and others employed among the Ojebway Indians. Toronto, 1874.
—— Indian tribes. Paper no. 11. The Kootenay Indians. (In Our Forest Children, vol. III, no. 13, Owen Sound, Ontario, Apr. 1890.)
WILSON, G. L. See PEPPER, G. H., and WILSON.
WILSON, THOS. Study of prehistoric anthropology. Hand-book for beginners. (Rep. U. S. Nat. Mus. 1887–88, Washington, 1890.)
—— The swastika, the earliest known symbol and its migrations. (Ibid., 1894, Washington, 1896.)
—— Prehistoric art. (Ibid., 1896, Washington, 1898.)
—— Arrowpoints, spearheads, and knives of prehistoric times. (Ibid., 1897, Washington, 1899.)
WIMER, JAS. Events in Indian history. Lancaster, 1842.
WINFIELD, CHAS. H. History of the county of Hudson, New Jersey, from its earliest settlement. New York, 1874.
WINSHIP, GEO. P. The Coronado expedition. (Fourteenth Rep. Bur. Am. Ethnology, pt. 1, Washington, 1896.)
WINSLOW, EDWARD. Good newes from New-England. London, 1624.
WINSOR, JUSTIN. Narrative and critical history of America. Vols. I–VIII. Boston and New York, 1884–89.
—— Cartier to Frontenac. Geographical discovery in the interior of North America in its historical relations, 1534–1700. Boston and New York, 1894.
WINTER IN THE WEST. See HOFFMAN, C. F.
WISCONSIN ACADEMY OF SCIENCE, ARTS, AND LETTERS. Transactions, vol. IV, 1876–77, Madison, 1878.
WISCONSIN ARCHEOLOGIST (THE). Vols. I–VIII. Milwaukee, 1901–09.
WISCONSIN HISTORICAL SOCIETY. Report and collections of the State Historical Society of Wisconsin. Vols. I–XVI. Madison, 1855–1902.
WISLIZENUS, A. Memoir of a tour to northern Mexico, in 1846 and 1847. (Senate Misc. Doc. 26, 30th Cong., 1st sess., Washington, 1848.)
WISSLER, CLARK. Material culture of the Blackfoot Indians. (Am. Mus. Nat. Hist., Anthr. Papers, vol. V, pt. 1, New York, 1910.)
WITHERS, A. S. Chronicles of border warfare. Cincinnati, 1895.
WOOD, JNO. G. The uncivilized races of men in all countries of the world, being a comprehensive account of their manners and customs and of their physical, mental, moral and religious characteristics. Vols. I–II. Hartford, 1870.
WOOD, SILAS. Sketch of the first settlement of Long Island. (In Macauley, History of New York, New York, 1829.)
WOOD, WM. New Englands prospect. London, 1634.

WOODWARD, ASHBEL. Wampum, a paper presented to the Numismatic and Antiquarian Society of Philadelphia. Albany, 1878.
WOODWARD. THOS. S. Woodward's reminiscences of the Creek, or Muscogee Indians, contained in letters to friends in Georgia and Alabama. Montgomery, 1859.
WOOLFE, HENRY D. Report on population and resources of Alaska at the Eleventh Census, 1890. Washington, 1893.
WORD CARRIER. See IAPI OAYE.
WORSLEY, ISRAEL. View of the American Indians, their general character, customs, language [etc.]. London, 1828.
WORTMAN, J. L. See MATTHEWS, W., and WORTMAN.
WRANGELL, FERDINAND VON. Observations recueillies par l'Amiral Wrangell sur les habitants des côtes nord-ouest de l'Amérique ; extraites du Russe par M. le prince Émanuel Galitzin. (Nouvelles Annales des Voyages, tome I, Paris, 1853.
—— See STATISTISCHE.
WRIGHT, G. FREDERICK. The ice age in North America. New York, 1889.
—— The Nampa image. (Proc. Boston. Soc. Nat. Hist., vol. XXIV, Jan. 1890 ; vol. XXV, Feb. 1891.)
—— Man and the glacial period. New York, 1895.
WRIGHT, JULIA MCNAIR. Among the Alaskans. Philadelphia [1883].
WYETH, NATHANIEL J. Correspondence and journals. (Sources of Hist. of Oregon, vol. I, pts. 3–6, Eugene, Oreg., 1899.)
WYMAN, JEFFRIES. An account of some kjoekkenmoeddings, or shell-heaps in Maine and Massachusetts. (Am. Nat., vol. I, no 11, Salem, 1868.)
—— On the fresh-water shell-heaps of the St. John's river, East Florida. (Am. Nat., vol. II, nos. 8, 9, Salem, 1868 ; also Fourth Memoir Peabody Acad. Sci., Salem, 1875.)
—— Observations on crania and other parts of the skeleton. (4th Ann. Rep. Peabody Mus., Boston, 1871.)
—— Human remains in the shell heaps of the St. John's river, East Florida. Cannibalism. (7th Ann. Rep. Peabody Mus., Cambridge, 1876.)
WYOMING HISTORICAL AND GEOLOGICAL SOCIETY. Proceedings and Collections. Vols. I–VIII. Wilkes-Barré, 1858–1904.
WYTFLIET, CORNELIUS. Descriptionis Ptolemaicæ augmentum, sive Occidentis notitia brevi commentario illustrata. Lovanii, 1597. (Same, 2d ed., Duaci, 1603.)
—— Histoire vniverselle des Indes, orientales et occidentales. Douay, 1605.

YARROW, H. C. Introduction to the study of mortuary customs among the North American Indians. Washington, 1880.
—— A further contribution to the study of the mortuary customs of the North American Indians. (First Rep. Bur. Am. Ethnology, Washington, 1881.)
YATES, LORENZO G. Charm stones. Notes on the so-called " plummets " or sinkers. (Smithsonian Rep. 1886, Washington, 1889.)
YOAKUM, H. History of Texas from its first settlement to its annexation to the United States in 1846. Vols. I–II. New York, 1855–56.

ZAGOSKIN, L. A. Pedestrian exploration of parts of the Russian possessions in America in the years 1842, 1843, and 1844. Vols. I–II. St. Petersburg, 1847–48. [In Russian.]
ZEISBERGER, DAVID. See BLISS, EUGENE F., ed. ; DE SCHWEINITZ, E.
ZEITSCHRIFT FÜR ETHNOLOGIE. B. I–XLII. Berlin, 1869–1910.